COLUMBIAN

STAMP COMPANY INC

BUILDING AND BUYING GREAT STAMP COLLECTIONS

HARRY HAGENDORF

DEALER IN RARE STAMPS

700 WHITE PLAINS ROAD SCARSDALE NY 10583 TELEPHONE 914 725 2290 FAX 914 725 2576
WEBSITE: columbianstamp.com
E-MAIL: Philatlst@aol.com

SCOTT

2001
Specialized Catalogue of United States Stamps & Covers

SEVENTY-NINTH EDITION

CONFEDERATE STATES • CANAL ZONE • DANISH WEST INDIES
GUAM • HAWAII • UNITED NATIONS

UNITED STATES ADMINISTRATION:
Cuba • Puerto Rico • Philippines • Ryukyu Islands

VICE PRESIDENT/PUBLISHER	Stuart J. Morrissey
EDITOR	James E. Kloetzel
ASSOCIATE EDITOR	William W. Cummings
NEW ISSUES MANAGING EDITOR	David C. Akin
ASSISTANT EDITOR/NEW ISSUES & VALUING	Martin J. Frankevicz
VALUING ANALYST	Leonard J. Gellman
ELECTRONIC PRODUCT DEVELOPMENT COORDINATOR	Denise Oder
EDITORIAL ASSISTANTS	Judith E. Bertrand, Beth Brown
CONTRIBUTING EDITOR	Peter Martin
ART/PRODUCTION DIRECTOR	Janine C. S. Apple
PRODUCTION COORDINATOR	Nancy S. Martin
MARKETING/SALES DIRECTOR	William Fay
ADVERTISING	Angela M. Nolte
CIRCULATION/PRODUCT PROMOTION MANAGER	Tim Wagner

Released October 2000
Includes New Stamp Listings through the September, 2000 *Scott Stamp Monthly* Catalogue Update

Copyright© 2000 by

Scott Publishing Co.

911 Vandemark Road, Sidney, OH 45365-0828
A division of AMOS PRESS, INC., publishers of *Linn's Stamp News, Coin World* and *Cars & Parts* magazine.

Scott Publishing Mission Statement

The Scott Publishing Team exists to serve the recreational,
educational and commercial hobby needs of stamp collectors and dealers.

We strive to set the industry standard for philatelic information and products by developing and providing goods that help collectors identify, value, organize and present their collections.

Quality customer service is, and will continue to be, our highest priority.
We aspire toward achieving total customer satisfaction.

Scott Publishing Co.

SCOTT 911 VANDEMARK ROAD, SIDNEY, OHIO 45365 937-498-0802

Dear Scott Catalogue User:

About every 6 weeks or so we hold a meeting called Elders. The group consists of all Scott editorial folks, including the catalogue editorial staff, 2 members of the new issue group, the editor of *Scott Stamp Monthly* and yours truly, the publisher. The objective of these meetings is to leave the day-to-day activities of valuing, editing and writing and think outside the box. We discuss suggestions from outside contributors and ideas from members of the group. Sometimes we get into major stuff (read the next paragraphs) that spells profound changes, and other times we focus on minutiae that would boggle the mind of even the most dedicated collector.

You will find an extraordinary number of changes in the 2001 edition, from items that will affect the structure of the National album to revisions that will be of significant interest to specialists of all stripes.

One noteworthy editorial change creates sixty-nine new major Scott catalogue numbers in the Postage and Air Post sections from stamps that until now have been only lettered minor perforation varieties. Scott has adopted a policy to consistently list as majors all stamps having at least a 1/2 perf gauge difference either horizontally or vertically from otherwise identical varieties.

So what's really the essence of all these changes. Where is the action?

There are changes everywhere. Even some neglected modern issues take a big bounce upward. The market for good quality U.S. stamps continues to roar and the trend has started to branch out into many areas that were previously napping.

Start with the 19th century (always a good place to start). In the classic issues, the demand for very fine unused stamps with original gum continues to push values higher. Scott 1, the 1847 5c red brown, jumps to $5,750 unused from $5,250 unused in both the 2000 *U.S. Specialized* and the 2001 Volume 1 catalogues.

Scott 5A, the 1851 1c blue type 1b, which moved to $13,000 from $12,000 in the 2001 Volume 1, jumps another thousand dollars to $14,000 in the 2001 *U.S. Specialized*. In used condition, it rises to $5,500 from $5,000. Values for 1857-61 perforated issues also rise.

Values of the 1861 issue continue to climb, as do those of the 1867 grilled issues. Unused 1869 Pictorial issues also show much upward movement. The 15c type I, Scott 118, which moved to $6,250 unused from $6,000 in the 2000 *U.S. Specialized*, now leaps forward to $7,000. Similar jumps over new, higher Volume 1 values are made by other 1869 denominations.

The momentum continues into the Banknote issues of 1870 and later, with stamps generally showing increased values in both the unused and used columns. Even lower-value stamps show upward movement. The 1893 1c-$5 Columbians see premiums for the never-hinged condition of unused stamps grow larger.

What about the later issues?

Values for the early Bureau issues and the 1902-03 issues also are on the rise, and premiums for never-hinged condition continue to widen. The 1909 commemoratives see value changes consistent with the increasing demand for never-hinged stamps. Regular issues show value increases through the Washington-Franklins.

Some increases in very modern postage are remarkable. For example, the plate block of the 1994 black "G" stamp, Scott 2881, skyrockets to $75 from $35. The 1995 Flag over Porch self-adhesive booklet with small date, serpentine die cut 8.7, Scott 2920c, shoots to $110 from $42.50.

Is back-of-the-book material just as lively?

There is so much back-of-the-book activity that I can't do it all justice here. In Air Post, the premium for never-hinged condition widens slightly for the early issues. The 1918 24c Inverted Jenny, Scott C3a, jumps to $170,000 unused from $150,000. Early Special Delivery stamps continue their climb in unused condition.

Postage Dues also climb unused, with only the values for mint never-hinged stamps moving after 1917 (Scott J61). The 1879 Special Printings, Scott J8-J14, see some extremely sharp jumps.

Newspaper stamps continue their trend of recent years and rise again unused. Some of the increases are dramatic.

Sales during late 1999 and early 2000 of scarce and important Carrier and Local stamps and covers have led to what can only be termed a revolution in values and listings. Most values in these sections change (1,200 in all), almost universally upward and generally by large percentages.

A great deal of upward movement is seen in the Postal Stationery section, affecting both expensive and not-so-expensive items. More than 1,250 value changes are recorded. In Revenues, more than 2,100 value changes are recorded.

Important sales of Essays, Proofs and Confederate States of America Postmasters' Provisionals also have led to comprehensive revaluings in these areas. Some changes made to seldom-seen items are dramatic.

Where is the substance?

In addition to the article on the sixty-nine new major numbers in the Postage and Air Post sections, written by Catalogue Editor Jim Kloetzel, two other Special Feature articles appear in the 2001 *U.S. Specialized*. The first, by *Scott Stamp Monthly* Editor Peter Martin, deals with the history and printing details of the Fermented Fruit Juice revenue stamps added to the catalogue listings for the first time in the 2001 edition. These stamps, Scott REF1-REF10, follow the listings of the Beer stamps in the revenue section.

The final Special Feature article is by long-time Hawaii collector Fred Gregory of California. The subject is the double overprint varieties of the Hawaii Provisional Government overprints of 1893. These stamps receive a new, more specialized treatment in the 2001 *U.S. Specialized*, which should aid both collectors and dealers. Gregory's article lifts the veil of mystery that surrounds these interesting stamps.

What editorial improvements have been added?

Once again, large numbers of new Earliest Known Uses are recorded in the Postage section of the *U.S. Specialized*. For 2001, more than 125 new dates have been added.

New listings for well-known varieties have been added in 2001 with accompanying illustrations. One is the dramatic "slash on face" variety on the 1903 2c Washington, Scott 319 and 320. In modern postage, the "lipstick on shirt front" variety has been added and illustrated for the 1989 $1 Johns Hopkins Great American stamp, Scott 2194.

In modern postage, a different type of gum has been introduced into the listings to go along with the dull gum and shiny gum previously listed. The low gloss gum recognized by specialists has been added where it exists, bringing the unlettered gum varieties now recognized in the *U.S. Specialized Catalogue* to three.

New methods of listing covers have completely revolutionized the listings in the Carriers and Locals sections. Whereas previously stamps were listed on cover only when they were known to exist tied by a handstamped cancel, it now has been recognized that such a listing system artificially restricts the listings and does not do justice to the normal way many of these stamps were used. The new listings are more sophisticated and more specialized. Further listings will be added in coming years.

The Post Office Seals section also has been completely revamped to bring the listings up to date with current scholarship. This involves the addition of new stamp listings and the reorganization of others.

United Nations sees the addition of the U.N. Interim Administration in Kosovo set of five stamps issued in March 2000.

A tip of the hat.

I would like to praise Jim Kloetzel, the *U.S. Specialized* Editor. I believe that Jim Kloetzel is the best editor that the *U.S. Specialized* has ever had. Under the leadership of Kloetzel the scholarship, breadth, accuracy and comprehensiveness of the *U.S. Specialized* has grown dramatically. Many sections have been completely revised and numerous mysteries of the past have been solved to the satisfaction of dealers and collector experts. I have been at many philatelic banquets where speakers get misty-eyed about famous names of the hobby from the past. Let's take a moment to salute a hero of the present.

Happy collecting,

Stuart Morrissey

Stuart Morrissey/Publisher

Table of contents

EXPANDED COMPREHENSIVE INDEX!

See pages 762-765 for a greatly expanded index — a handy reference so that you can tell if a stamp is listed as a local post, postmasters' provisional, carrier, or telegraph company. Even better for many users, the category index allows a collector or dealer to see quickly that parcel post stamps can be found in three places, semi-postals in two, or post office seals in six.

Acknowledgments

Our appreciation and gratitude go to the following individuals and organizations who have assisted us in preparing information included in this year's edition of the *Scott Specialized Catalogue of U.S. Stamps and Covers*. Some helpers prefer anonymity. Those individuals have generously shared their stamp knowledge with others through the medium of the Scott Catalogue.

Those who follow provided information that is in addition to the hundreds of dealer price lists and advertisements and scores of auction catalogues and realizations which were used in producing the Catalogue Values used herein. It is from those noted here that we have been able to obtain information on items not normally seen in published lists and advertisements. Support from these people of course goes beyond data leading to Catalogue Values, for they also are key to editorial changes.

Karl Agre, M.D., PhD
Michael E. Aldrich
    (Michael E. Aldrich, Inc.)
Arthur L.-F. Askins
Steven R. Belasco
Alan Berkun
John Birkinbine II
Al Boerger
Victor Bove
John D. Bowman
George W. Brett
Roger S. Brody
Lawrence A. Bustillo
    (Suburban Stamp Inc.)
James R. Callis, Jr.
    (Precancel Stamp Society)
A. Bryan Camarda
Alan C. Campbell
Bill J. Castenholz
Richard A. Champagne
Albert F. Chang
Ray L. Coughlin (Coughlin's)
Steven D. Crippe
William T. Crowe
Francis J. Crown, Jr.
Tony L. Crumbley (Carolina
    Coin & Stamp, Inc.)
Kenneth E. Diehl
Bob Dumaine (Sam Houston
    Duck Company)

William S. Dunn
Stephen G. Esrati
J. A. Farrington
Henry Fisher
Robert S. Freeman
Richard Friedberg
Melvin Getlan
Fred F. Gregory
Gary Griffith
Harry Hagendorf
Calvet M. Hahn
Dr. Allan Hauck (International
    Society of Reply Coupon
    Collectors)
Robert R. Hegland
Dale Hendricks
    (Dale Enterprises, Inc.)
Steven Hines
Wilson Hulme
Myron Hyman
Tom Jacks (Mountainside
    Stamps)
Eric Jackson
Michael Jaffe (Michael Jaffe
    Stamps, Inc.)
Clyde Jennings
Henry Karen
    (Michael M. Karen, Inc.)
Allan Katz (Ventura Stamp Co.)
Lewis Kaufman

Patricia A.Kaufmann (Osborne-
    Kaufmann)
Jim Kotanchik
Maurice J. Landry
William Langs
Lester C. Lanphear III
Ken Lawrence
Richard L. Lazorow
    (The Plate Block Stamp Co.)
Ronald E. Lesher, Sr.
Steve Levine
Andrew Levitt
William A. Litle
Larry Lyons
    (Carriers and Locals Society)
George W. MacLellan
Walter J. Mader (Ivy & Mader
    Philatelic Auctions, Inc.)
William K. McDaniel
William E. Mooz
Gary M. Morris
    (Pacific Midwest Co.)
Peter Mosiondz, Jr.
Bruce M. Moyer
    (Valley Stamp & Coin, Inc.)
James Natale
Gerald Nylander
Robert P. Odenweller
Stanley M. Piller
    (Stanley M. Piller & Associates)

Peter W. W. Powell
Bob Prager (Gary Posner, Inc.)
Jon W. Rose
Richard H. Salz
Jacques C. Schiff, Jr.
    (Jacques C. Schiff, Jr., Inc.)
Richard Simchak
Dr. Hubert C. Skinner
Jack Solens
    (Armstong Philatelics)
Merle Spencer
    (The Stamp Gallery)
Richard Stambaugh
Frank J. Stanley, III
Jay B. Stotts
Mark Stucker
Stephen L. Suffet
Alan Thomson (Plate Number
    Coil Collectors' Club)
Henry Tolman II
David R. Torre
Scott R. Trepel
    (Siegel Auction Galleries, Inc.)
W. H. Waggoner
Jerome S. Wagshal
Philip T. Wall
Daniel C. Warren
William R. Weiss, Jr.
    (Weiss Philatelics)
Robert F. Yacano
    (K-Line Philippines)

Expertizing Services

The following organizations will, for a fee, provide expert opinions about stamps submitted to them. Collectors should contact these organizations to find out about their fees and requirements before submitting philatelic material to them. The listing of these groups here is not intended as an endorsement by Scott Publishing Co.

General Expertizing Services

American Philatelic Expertizing
    Service (a service of the
    American Philatelic Society)
PO Box 8000
State College PA 16803
Ph: (814) 237-3808
Fax: (814) 237-6128
www.stamps.org
E-mail: ambristo@stamps.org

Philatelic Foundation
501 Fifth Ave., Rm. 1901
New York NY 10017

Professional Stamp Experts
PO Box 6170
Newport Beach CA 92658
Ph: (877) STAMP-88
Fax: (949) 833-7955
www.collectors.com/pse
E-mail: pseinfo@collectors.com

**Expertizing Services Covering
Specific Fields Or Countries**

American First Day Cover
    Society Expertizing
    Committee
P.O. Box 141379
Columbus, OH 43214

Confederate Stamp Alliance
    Authentication Service
522 Old State Road
Lincoln, DE 19960-9797
Ph: (302) 422-2656
Fax: (302) 424-1990
www.webuystamps.com/csaauth.htm
E-mail: trish@ce.net

Errors, Freaks and Oddities
    Collectors Club Expertizing
    Service
138 East Lakemont Dr.
Kingsland GA 31548
Ph: (912) 729-1573

Hawaiian Philatelic Society
    Expertizing Service
PO Box 10115
Honolulu HI 96816-0115

Ryukyu Philatelic Specialist Society
    Expertizing Service
1710 Buena Vista Ave.
Spring Valley CA 91977-4458
Ph: (619) 697-3205

Addresses, Telephone Numbers & E-Mail Addresses of General & Specialized Philatelic Societies

Collectors can contact the following groups for information about the philately of the areas within the scope of these societies, or inquire about membership in these groups. Many more specialized philatelic societies exist than those listed below. Aside from the general societies, we limit this list to groups which specialize in areas covered by the *Scott U.S. Specialized Catalogue*. These addresses were compiled two months prior to publication, and are, to the best of our knowledge, correct and current. Groups should inform the editors of address changes whenever they occur. The editors also want to hear from other such specialized groups not listed.

American Air Mail Society
Stephen Reinhard
P.O. Box 110
Mineola NY 11501
http://ourworld.compuserve.com/
homepages/aams/
E-mail:sr1501@aol.com

American Ceremony Program
Society
John Olmsted
P.O. Box 1595
Washington D.C. 20013-1595

American First Day Cover
Society
Douglas Kelsey
P.O. Box 65960
Tucson AZ 85728-5960
Ph: (520) 321-9191
E-mail:afdcs@aol.com

American Philatelic Society
P.O. Box 8000
State College PA 16803
Ph: (814) 237-3803
http://www.west.net/~stamps1/aps.
html
E-mail:relamb@stamps.org

American Plate Number Single
Society
Norm J. Wood
777 W. State St., Apt 6H
Trenton NJ 08618
E-mail:stfia@pluto.njcc.com

American Revenue Association
Eric Jackson
P.O. Box 728
Leesport PA 19533-0728

American Society for Philatelic
Pages and Panels
Gerald N. Blankenship
539 North Gum Gully
Crosby TX 77532
Ph: (281) 324-2709
E-mail:gblank1941@aol.com

American Stamp Dealers
Association
Joseph Savarese
3 School St.
Glen Cove NY 11542
Ph: (516) 759-7000
http://www.amerstampdlrs.com
E-mail:asda@erols.com

American Topical Association
Paul E. Tyler
P.O. Box 50820
Albuquerque NM 87181-0820
http://home/prcn.org/~pauld/ata/
E-mail:ATAStamps@aol.com

Canal Zone Study Group
Richard H. Salz
60 27th Ave.
San Francisco CA 94121

Carriers and Locals Society
Steven M. Roth
P.O. Box 57160
Washington D.C. 20036
Ph: (202) 293-6813
E-mail:smroth@wizard.net

Christmas Seal & Charity Stamp
Society
John Denune
234 East Broadway
Granville OH 43023
Ph: (614) 587-0276
http://home.earthlink.net/~rwstuart/
cscss/index.html

Confederate Stamp Alliance
Ronald V. Teffs
19450 Yuma St.
Castro Valley CA 94546
http://www.flash.net/~rhbcsaps/

Errors, Freaks, and Oddities
Collectors Club
Jim McDevitt
138 Lakemont Dr. East
Kingsland GA 31548
Ph: (912) 729-1573
E-mail:cwouscg@aol.com

Hawaiian Philatelic Society
Kay H. Hoke
P.O. Box 10115
Honolulu HI 96816-0115
Ph: (808) 521-5721
http://www.stampshows.com/hps.html
E-mail:bannan@pixi.com

International Philippine
Philatelic Society
Robert F. Yacano
P.O. Box 100
Toast NC 27049
Ph: (336) 783-0768

International Society of Reply
Coupon Collectors
Dr. Allan Hauck
P.O. Box 165
Somers WI 53171-0165

Junior Philatelists of America
Ellie Chapman
P.O. Box 850
Boalsburg PA 16827-0850
http://www.jpastamps.org
E-mail:jpaellie@aol.com

National Duck Stamp
Collectors Society
Anthony J. Monico
P.O. Box 43
Harleysville PA 19438-0043

Official Seal Study Group
Fred Scheuer
P.O. Box1518
Waldport OR 97394
Ph: (541) 563-4442

Perfins Club
Kurt Ottenheimer
462 West Walnut St.
Long Beach NY 11561
E-mail:oak462@juno.com

Plate Number Coil
Collectors Club
Gene C. Trinks
3603 Bellows Court
Troy MI 48083
http://www.geocities.com/Heartland
/Hills/6283
E-mail:gctrinks@tir.com

Post Mark Collectors Club
Dave Proulx
7629 Homestead Dr.
Baldwinsville NY 13207
E-mail:stampdance@baldcom.net

Postal History Society
Kalman V. Illyefalvi
8207 Daren Court
Pikesville MD 21208-2211
Ph: (410) 653-0665

Precancel Stamp Society
Arthur Damm
176 Bent Pine Hill
North Wales PA 19454
Ph: (215) 368-6082

Ryukyu Philatelic Specialist
Society
Carmine J. Di Vincenzo
P.O. Box 381
Clayton CA 94517-0381

Souvenir Card Collectors Society
Dana Marr
P.O. Box 4155
Tulsa OK 74159-0155
Ph: (918) 664-6724
E-mail:dmarr5569@aol.com

State Revenue Society
Scott Troutman
P.O. Box 270184
Oklahoma City OK 73137
http://hillcity-mail.com/SRS

United Nations Philatelists
Blanton Clement, Jr.
292 Springdale Terrace
Yardley PA 19067-3421

United Postal Stationery Society
Joann Thomas
P.O. Box 48
Redlands CA 92373
http://www.uh.edu/~lib19/upss.htm

U.S. Cancellation Club
Roger Rhoads
3 Ruthana Way
Hockessin DE 19707
http://www.geocities.com/
athens/2088/uscchome.html
E-mail:rrrhoads@aol.com

U.S. Philatelic Classics Society
Mark D. Rogers
P.O. Box 80708
Austin TX 78708-0708
http://www.scruz.net/~eho/uspcs
E-mail:mdr3@swbell.net

U.S. Possessions Philatelic
Society
David S. Durbin
1608 S. 22nd St.
Blue Springs MO 64015

United States Stamp Society
(formerly Bureau Issues Association)
Executive Secretary
P.O. Box 722
Westfield NJ 07091-0722
www.usstamps.org

Information on Catalogue Values, Grade and Condition

Catalogue Value

The Scott Catalogue value is a retail value; that is, an amount you could expect to pay for a stamp in the grade of Very Fine with no faults. Any exceptions to the grade valued will be noted in the text. The general introduction on the following pages and the individual section introductions further explain the type of material that is valued. The value listed for any given stamp is a reference that reflects recent actual dealer selling prices for that item.

Dealer retail price lists, public auction results, published prices in advertising and individual solicitation of retail prices from dealers, collectors and specialty organizations have been used in establishing the values found in this catalogue. Scott Publishing Co. values stamps, but Scott is not a company engaged in the business of buying and selling stamps as a dealer.

Use this catalogue as a guide for buying and selling. The actual price you pay for a stamp may be higher or lower than the catalogue value because of many different factors, including the amount of personal service a dealer offers, or increased or decreased interest in the country or topic represented by a stamp or set. An item may occasionally be offered at a lower price as a "loss leader," or as part of a special sale. You also may obtain an item inexpensively at public auction because of little interest at that time or as part of a large lot.

Stamps that are of a lesser grade than Very Fine, or those with condition problems, generally trade at lower prices than those given in this catalogue. Stamps of exceptional quality in both grade and condition often command higher prices than those listed.

Values for pre-1890 unused issues are for stamps with approximately half or more of their original gum. Stamps with most or all of their original gum may be expected to sell for slightly more, and stamps with less than half of their original gum may be expected to sell for somewhat less than the values listed. On rarer stamps, it may be expected that the original gum will be somewhat more disturbed than it will be on more common issues. Beginning with the 1890 issue, unused stamps are assumed to have full original gum. From breakpoints in the listings, stamps are valued as never hinged, due to the wide availability of stamps in that condition. These notations are prominently placed in the listings and in the information preceding the listings. Some sections also feature listings with dual values for hinged and never-hinged stamps.

Values for early and valuable stamps are for examples with certificates of authenticity from acknowledged expert committees, or examples sold with the buyer having the right of certification. This applies to examples with original gum as well as examples without gum. Beware of stamps offered "as is," as the gum on some unused stamps offered with "original gum" may be fraudulent, and stamps offered as unused without gum may in some cases be altered used stamps.

Grade

A stamp's grade and condition are crucial to its value. The accompanying illustrations show examples of Very Fine stamps from different time periods, along with examples of stamps in Fine to Very Fine and Extremely Fine grades as points of reference.

FINE stamps (illustrations not shown) have designs that are severely off center or one side or noticeably off center on two sides. Imperforate stamps may have small margins, and earlier issues may show the design touching one edge of the stamp design. For perforated stamps, perfs may barely clear the design on one side, and very early issues normally will have the perforations slightly cutting into the design. Used stamps may have heavier than usual cancellations.

FINE-VERY FINE stamps may be somewhat off center on one side or slightly off center on two sides. Imperforate stamps will have two margins of at least normal size, and the design will not touch any edge. For perforated stamps, the perfs are well clear of the design, but are still noticeably off center. *However, early issues may be printed in such a way that the design naturally is very close to the edges.* In these cases, the perforations may cut into the design

very slightly. Used stamps will not have a cancellation that detracts from the design.

VERY FINE stamps may be slightly off center on one or two sides, but the design will be well clear of the edge. The stamp will present a nice, balanced appearance. Imperforate stamps will have three normal-sized margins. *However, early perforated issues may be printed in such a way that the perforations may touch the design on one or more sides.* Used stamps will have light or otherwise neat cancellations. This is the grade used to establish Scott Catalogue values.

EXTREMELY FINE stamps are close to being perfectly centered. Imperforate stamps will have even margins that are larger than normal. *Even the earliest perforated issues will have perforations clear of the design on all sides.*

Scott Publishing Co. recognizes that there is no formally enforced grading scheme for postage stamps, and that the final price you pay or obtain for a stamp will be determined by individual agreement at the time of transaction.

Condition

Grade addresses only centering and (for used stamps) cancellation. *Condition* refers to factors other than grade that affect a stamp's desirability.

Factors that can increase the value of a stamp include exceptionally wide margins, particularly fresh color, the presence of selvage, and plate or die varieties. Unusual cancels on used stamps (particularly those of the 19th century) can greatly enhance their value as well.

Factors other than faults that decrease the value of a stamp include loss of original gum, regumming, a hinge remnant or foreign object adhering to the gum, natural inclusions, straight edges, and markings or notations applied by collectors or dealers.

Faults include missing pieces, tears, pin or other holes, surface scuffs, rubbed spots, thin spots, creases, toning, short or pulled perforations, clipped perforations, oxidation or other forms of color changelings, soiling, stains, and such man-made changes as reperforations or the chemical removal or lightening of a cancellation.

On the following page are illustrations of 11 different representative stamps from various time periods, 1847 to the modern era. Beginning with the 1847 10¢ Washington, examples are shown from the 1851-57 imperforates, two examples from the difficult 1857-61 perforated issues, a Black Jack representative of the 1861-67 issues, an 1869 Pictorial definitive, a Bank Note issue from 1888, an 1898 commemorative, a representative 1908-22 Washington-Franklin design, another 20th century definitive from the 1922 issue, and a modern definitive. The examples shown are computer-manipulated images made from single digitized master illustrations.

The editors believe these illustrations will prove useful in showing the margin size and centering that will be seen in the different time periods of U.S. stamp production. Use this Illustated Grading Chart in conjuction with the Illustrated Gum Chart that follows it to better understand the grade and gum condition of stamps valued in the *Scott U.S. Specialized Catalogue.*

For purposes of helping to determine the gum condition and value of an unused stamp, Scott Publishing Co. presents the following chart which details different gum conditions and indicates how the conditions correlate with the Scott values for unused stamps. Used together, the Illustrated Grading Chart on the previous page and this Illustrated Gum Chart should allow catalogue users to better understand the grade and gum condition of stamps valued in the *Scott U.S. Specialized Catalogue.*

Gum Categories:	MINT N.H.	ORIGINAL GUM (O.G.)				NO GUM
	Mint Never Hinged *Free from any disturbance*	**Lightly Hinged** *Faint impression of a removed hinge over a small area*	**Hinge Mark or Remnant** *Prominent hinged spot with part or all of the hinge remaining*	**Large part o.g.** *Approximately half or more of the gum intact*	**Small part o.g.** *Approximately less than half of the gum intact*	**No gum** *Only if issued with gum*
Commonly Used Symbol:	★★	★	★	★	★	(★)
PRE-1890 ISSUES	*Very fine pre-1890 stamps in these categories trade at a premium over Scott value*			Scott Value for "Unused"		Scott "No Gum" Values thru No. 218
1890-1935 ISSUES	Scott "Never Hinged" Values for Nos. 219-771	Scott Value for "Unused" (Actual value will be affected by the degree of hinging of the full o.g.)				
1935 TO DATE	Scott Value for "Unused"					

Never Hinged (NH; ★★): A never-hinged stamp will have full original gum that will have no hinge mark or disturbance. The presence of an expertizer's mark does not disqualify a stamp from this designation.

Original Gum (OG; ★): Pre-1890 stamps should have approximately half or more of their original gum. On rarer stamps, it may be expected that the original gum will be somewhat more disturbed that it will be on more common issues. Stamps issued in 1890 or later should have full original gum. Original gum will show some disturbance caused by a previous hinge(s) which may be present or entirely removed. The actual value of an 1890 or later stamp will be affected by the degree of hinging of the full original gum.

Disturbed Original Gum: Gum showing noticeable effects of humidity, climate or hinging over more than half of the gum. The significance of gum disturbance in valuing a stamp in any of the Original Gum categories depends on the degree of disturbance, the rarity and normal gum condition of the issue and other variables affecting quality.

Regummed (RG; (★)): A regummed stamp is a stamp without gum that has had some type of gum privately applied at a time after it was issued. This normally is done to deceive collectors and/or dealers into thinking that the stamp has original gum and therefore has a higher value. A regummed stamp is considered the same as a stamp with none of its original gum for purposes of grading.

IMPORTANT INFORMATION REGARDING VALUES FOR NEVER-HINGED STAMPS

Collectors should be aware that the values given for never-hinged stamps from No. 219 on are for stamps in the grade of very fine. The never-hinged premiun as a percentage of value will be larger for stamps in extremely fine or superb grades, and the premium will be smaller for fine-very-fine, fine or poor examples. This is particulary true of the issues of the late-19th and early 20th centuries. For example, in the grade of very fine, an unused stamp from this time period may be valued at $100 hinged and $160 never hinged. The never-hinged premium is thus 60%. But in a grade of extremely fine, this same stamp will not only sell for more hinged, but the never-hinged premium will increase, perhaps to 100%-300% or more over the higher extremely fine value. In a grade of superb, a hinged copy will sell for much more than a very fine copy, and additionally the never-hinged premium will be much larger, perhaps as large as 300%-400%. On the other hand, the same stamp in a grade of fine or fine-very fine not only will sell for less than a very fine stamp in hinged condition, but additionally the never-hinged premium will be smaller than the never-hinged premium on a very fine stamp, perhaps as small as 15%-30%.

Please note that the above statements and percentages are NOT a formula for arriving at the values of stamps in hinged or never-hinged condition in the grades of fine, fine to very fine, extremely fine or superb. The percentages given apply only to the size of the premium for never-hinged condition that might be added to the stamp value for hinged condition. The marketplace will determine what this value will be for grades other than very fine. Further, the percentages given are only generalized estimates. Some stamps or grades may have percentages for never-hinged condition that are higher or lower than the ranges given.

Never-Hinged Plate Blocks

Values given for never-hinged plate blocks are for blocks in which all stamps have original gum that has never been hinged and has no disturbances, and all selvage, whether gummed or ungummed, has never been hinged.

Catalogue Listing Policy

It is the intent of Scott Publishing Co. to list all postage stamps of the world in the *Scott Standard Postage Stamp Catalogue*. The only strict criteria for listing is that stamps be decreed legal for postage by the issuing country and that the issuing country actually have an operating postal system. Whether the primary intent of issuing a given stamp or set was for sale to postal patrons or to stamp collectors is not part of our listing criteria. Scott's role is to provide basic comprehensive postage stamp information. It is up to each stamp collector to choose which items to include in a collection.

It is Scott's objective to seek reasons why a stamp should be listed, rather than why it should not. Nevertheless, there are certain types of items that will not be listed. These include the following:

1. Unissued items that are not officially distributed or released by the issuing postal authority. Even if such a stamp is "accidentally" distributed to the philatelic or even postal market, it remains unissued. If such items are officially issued at a later date by the country, they will be listed. Unissued items consist of those that have been printed and then held from sale for reasons such as change in government, errors found on stamps or something deemed objectionable about a stamp subject or design.

2. Stamps "issued" by non-existent postal entities or fantasy countries, such as Nagaland, Occusi-Ambeno, Staffa, Sedang, Torres Straits and others.

3. Semi-official or unofficial items not required for postage. Examples include items issued by private agencies for their own express services. When such items are required for delivery, or are valid as prepayment of postage, they are listed.

4. Local stamps issued for local use only. Postage stamps issued by governments specifically for "domestic" use, such as Haiti Scott 219-228, or the United States non-denominated stamps, are not considered to be locals, since they are valid for postage throughout the country of origin.

5. Items not valid for postal use. For example, a few countries have issued souvenir sheets that are not valid for postage. This area also includes a number of worldwide charity labels (some denominated) that do not pay postage.

6. Intentional varieties, such as imperforate stamps that look like their perforated counterparts and are issued in very small quantities. These are often controlled issues intended for speculation.

7. Items distributed by the issuing government only to a limited group, such as a stamp club, philatelic exhibition or a single stamp dealer, and later brought to market at inflated prices. These items normally will be included in a footnote.

The fact that a stamp has been used successfully as postage, even on international mail, is not in itself sufficient proof that it was legitimately issued. Numerous examples of so-called stamps from non-existent countries are known to have been used to post letters that have successfully passed through the international mail system.

There are certain items that are subject to interpretation. When a stamp falls outside our specifications, it may be listed along with a cautionary footnote.

A number of factors are considered in our approach to analyzing how a stamp is listed. The following list of factors is presented to share with you, the catalogue user, the complexity of the listing process.

Additional printings — "Additional printings" of a previously issued stamp may range from an item that is totally different to cases where it is impossible to differentiate from the original. At least a minor number (a small-letter suffix) is assigned if there is a distinct change in stamp shade, noticeably redrawn design, or a significantly different perforation measurement. A major number (numeral or numeral and capital-letter combination) is assigned if the editors feel the "additional printing" is sufficiently different from the original that it constitutes a different issue.

Commemoratives — Where practical, commemoratives with the same theme are placed in a set. For example, the U.S. Civil War Centenniel set of 1961-65 and the Constitution Bicentennial series of 1989-90 appear as sets. Countries such as Japan and Korea issue such material on a regular basis, with an announced, or at least predictable, number of stamps known in advance. Occasionally, however, stamp sets that were released over a period of years have been separated. Appropriately placed footnotes will guide you to each set's continuation.

Definitive sets — Blocks of numbers generally have been reserved for definitive sets, based on previous experience with any given country. If a few more stamps were issued in a set than originally expected, they often have been inserted into the original set with a capital-letter suffix, such as U.S. Scott 1059A. If it appears that many more stamps than the originally allotted block will be released before the set is completed, a new block of numbers will be reserved, with the original one being closed off. In some cases, such as the British Machin Head series or the U.S. Transportation and Great Americans series, several blocks of numbers exist. Appropriately placed footnotes will guide you to each set's continuation.

New country — Membership in the Universal Postal Union is not a consideration for listing status or order of placement within the catalogue. The index will tell you in what volume or page number the listings begin.

"No release date" items — The amount of information available for any given stamp issue varies greatly from country to country and even from time to time. Extremely comprehensive information about new stamps is available from some countries well before the stamps are released. By contrast some countries do not provide information about stamps or release dates. Most countries, however, fall between these extremes. A country may provide denominations or subjects of stamps from upcoming issues that are not issued as planned. Sometimes, philatelic agencies, those private firms hired to represent countries, add these later-issued items to sets well after the formal release date. This time period can range from weeks to years. If these items were officially released by the country, they will be added to the appropriate spot in the set. In many cases, the specific release date of a stamp or set of stamps may never be known.

Overprints — The color of an overprint is always noted if it is other than black. Where more than one color of ink has been used on overprints of a single set, the color used is noted. Early overprint and surcharge illustrations were altered to prevent their use by forgers.

Se-tenants — Connected stamps of differing features (se-tenants) will be listed in the format most commonly collected. This includes pairs, blocks or larger multiples. Se-tenant units are not always symmetrical. An example is Australia Scott 508, which is a block of seven stamps. If the stamps are primarily collected as a unit, the major number may be assigned to the multiple, with minors going to each component stamp. In cases where continuous-design or other unit se-tenants will receive significant postal use, each stamp is given a major Scott number listing. This includes issues from the United States, Canada, Germany and Great Britain, for example.

Understanding the Listings

On the opposite page is an enlarged "typical" listing from this catalogue. Following are detailed explanations of each of the highlighted parts of the listing.

① **Scott number** — Stamp collectors use Scott numbers to identify specific stamps when buying, selling, or trading stamps, and for ease in organizing their collections. Each stamp issued by a country has a unique number. Therefore, U.S. Scott 219 can only refer to a single stamp. Although the Scott Catalogue usually lists stamps in chronological order by date of issue, when a country issues a set of stamps over a period of time the stamps within that set are kept together without regard to date of issue. This follows the normal collecting approach of keeping stamps in their natural sets.

When a country is known to be issuing a set of stamps over a period of time, a group of consecutive catalogue numbers is reserved for the stamps in that set, as issued. If that group of numbers proves to be too few, capital-letter suffixes are added to numbers to create enough catalogue numbers to cover all items in the set. Scott uses a suffix letter, e.g., "A," "b," etc., only once. If there is a Scott 296B in a set, there will not be a Scott 296b also.

There are times when the block of numbers is too large for the set, leaving some numbers unused. Such gaps in the sequence also occur when the editors move an item elsewhere in the catalogue or remove it from the listings entirely. Scott does not attempt to account for every possible number, but rather it does attempt to assure that each stamp is assigned its own number.

Scott numbers designating regular postage normally are only numerals. Scott numbers for other types of stamps, e.g., air post, special delivery, and so on, will have a prefix of either a capital letter or a combination of numerals and capital letters.

② **Illustration number** — used to identify each illustration. Where more than one stamp in a set uses the same illustration number, that number needs to be used with the description line (noted below) to be certain of the exact variety of the stamp within the set. Illustrations normally are 75, 100, or 150 percent of the original size of the stamp. An effort has been made to note all illustrations not at those percentages. Overprints are shown at 100 percent of the original, unless otherwise noted. Letters *in parentheses* which follow an illustration number refer to illustrations of overprints or surcharges.

③ **Listing styles** — there are two principal types of catalogue listings: major and minor.

Majors may be distinguished by having as their catalogue number a numeral with or without a capital-letter suffix and with or without a prefix.

Minors have a small-letter suffix (or, only have the small letter itself shown if the listing is immediately beneath its major listing). These listings show a variety of the "normal," or major item. Examples include color variation or a different watermark used for that stamp only.

Examples of major numbers are 9X1, 16, 28A, 6LB1, C13, RW1, and TS1. Examples of minor numbers are 22b, 279Bc and C3a.

④ **Denomination** — normally value printed on the stamp (generally known as the *face value*), which is — unless otherwise stated — the cost of the stamp at the time of issue.

⑤ **Basic information on stamp or set** — introducing each stamp issue, this section normally includes the date of issue, method of printing, perforation, watermark, and sometimes additional information. New information on method of printing, water-mark or perforation measurement may appear when that information changes. Dates of issue are as precise as Scott is able to confirm, either year only, month and year, or month, day and year.

In stamp sets issued over more than one date, the year or span of years will be in bold type above the first catalogue number. Individual stamps in the set will have a date-of-issue appearing in italics. Stamps without a year listed appeared during the first year of the span. Dates are not always given for minor varieties.

⑥ **Color or other description** — this line provides information to solidify identification of the stamp. Historically, when stamps normally were printed in a single color, only the color appeared here. With modern printing techniques, which include multicolor presses which mix inks on the paper, earlier methods of color identification are no longer applicable. When space permits, a description of the stamp design will replace the terms "multi" or "multicolored." The color of the paper is noted in italic type when the paper used is not white.

⑦ **Date of issue** — As precisely as Scott is able to confirm, either year only; month and year, or month, day and year. In some cases, the earliest known use (eku) is given. All dates, especially where no official date of issue has been given, are subject to change as new information is obtained. Many cases are known of inadvertent sale and use of stamps prior to dates of issue announced by postal officials. These are not listed here.

⑧ **Value unused** and **Value used** — the catalogue values are in U. S. dollars and are based on stamps that are in a grade of Very Fine. Unused values refer to items that have not seen postal or other duty for which they were intended. For pre-1890 issues, unused stamps must have at least most of their original gum; for later issues, complete gum is expected. Stamps issued without gum are noted. Unused values are for never-hinged stamps beginning at the point immediately following a prominent notice in the actual listing. The same information also appears at the beginning of the section's information. Scott values for used self-adhesive stamps are for examples either on piece or off piece.

Some sections in this book have more than two columns for values. Check section introductions and watch for value column headers. See the sections "Catalogue Values" and "Understanding Valuing Notations" for an explanation of the meaning of these values.

⑨ **Changes in basic set information** — bold or other type is used to show any change in the basic data between stamps within a set of stamps, e.g., perforation from one stamp to the next or a different paper or printing method or watermark.

⑩ **Other varieties** — these include additional shades, plate varieties, multiples, used on cover, plate number blocks, coil line pairs, coil plate number strips of three or five, ZIP blocks, etc.

On early issues, there may be a "Cancellation" section. Values in this section refer to single stamps off cover, unless otherwise noted. Values with a "+" are added to the basic used value. See "Basic Stamp Information" for more details on stamp and cancellation varieties.

⑪ **Footnote** — Where other important details about the stamps can be found.

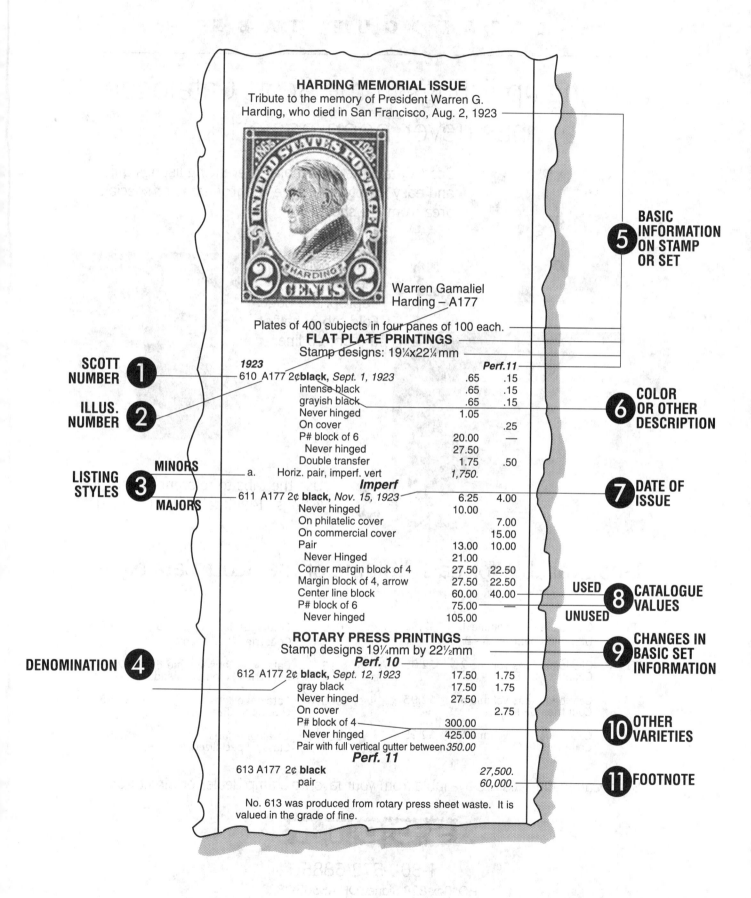

HARDING MEMORIAL ISSUE
Tribute to the memory of President Warren G.
Harding, who died in San Francisco, Aug. 2, 1923

Warren Gamaliel
Harding – A177

Plates of 400 subjects in four panes of 100 each.
FLAT PLATE PRINTINGS
Stamp designs: 19¼x22¼mm

BASIC INFORMATION ON STAMP OR SET — 5

SCOTT NUMBER — 1

ILLUS. NUMBER — 2

LISTING STYLES — 3 MINORS / MAJORS

DENOMINATION — 4

1923 **Perf.11**

610 A177 2¢ **black,** *Sept. 1, 1923*			.65	.15
	intense black		.65	.15
	grayish black		.65	.15
	Never hinged		1.05	
	On cover			.25
	P# block of 6		20.00	—
	Never hinged		27.50	
	Double transfer		1.75	.50
a.	Horiz. pair, imperf. vert		1,750.	

Imperf

611 A177 2¢ black, *Nov. 15, 1923*	6.25	4.00
Never hinged	10.00	
On philatelic cover		7.00
On commercial cover		15.00
Pair	13.00	10.00
Never Hinged	21.00	
Corner margin block of 4	27.50	22.50
Margin block of 4, arrow	27.50	22.50
Center line block	60.00	40.00
P# block of 6	75.00	—
Never hinged	105.00	

ROTARY PRESS PRINTINGS
Stamp designs 19¼mm by 22½mm
Perf. 10

612 A177 2¢ **black,** *Sept. 12, 1923*	17.50	1.75
gray black	17.50	1.75
Never hinged	27.50	
On cover		2.75
P# block of 4	300.00	
Never hinged	425.00	
Pair with full vertical gutter between	350.00	

Perf. 11

613 A177 2¢ **black**		27,500.
pair		60,000.

No. 613 was produced from rotary press sheet waste. It is
valued in the grade of fine.

COLOR OR OTHER DESCRIPTION — 6

DATE OF ISSUE — 7

USED / UNUSED **CATALOGUE VALUES** — 8

CHANGES IN BASIC SET INFORMATION — 9

OTHER VARIETIES — 10

FOOTNOTE — 11

Scott Numbering Practices and Special Notices

Classification of stamps

The *Scott Specialized Catalogue of United States Stamps* lists the stamps of the United States and its possessions and territories and the stamps of the United Nations. The next level is a listing by section on the basis of the function of the stamps or postal stationery. In each case, the items are listed in specialized detail. The principal sections cover regular postage stamps; air post stamps; postage due stamps, special delivery, and so on. Except for regular postage, catalogue numbers for most sections include a prefix letter (or number-letter combination) denoting the class to which the stamp belongs.

The Table of Contents, on page 4A, notes each section and, where pertinent, the prefix used. Some, such as souvenir cards and encased postage, do not have prefixes. Some sections, such as specimens and private perforations, have suffixes only.

New issue listings

Updates to this catalogue appear each month in the *Scott Stamp Monthly*. Included are corrections and updates to the current edition of this catalogue.

From time to time there will be changes in the listings from the *Scott Stamp Monthly* to the next edition of the catalogue, as additional information becomes available.

The catalogue update section of the *Scott Stamp Monthly* is the most timely presentation of this material available. For current subscription rates, see advertisements in this catalogue or write Scott Publishing Co., P.O. Box 828, Sidney, OH 45365-0828.

Additions, deletions & number changes

A list of catalogue additions, deletions, and number changes from the previous edition of the catalogue appears in each volume. See Catalogue Additions, Deletions & Number Changes in the Table of Contents for the location of this list..

Understanding valuing notations

The *absence of a value* does not necessarily suggest that a stamp is scarce or rare. In the U.S. listings, a dash in the value column means that the stamp is known in a stated form or variety, but information is lacking or insufficient for purposes of establishing a usable catalogue value. These could include rarities, such as Scott 3X4 on cover, or items that have a limited market, such as used plate blocks of Scott 1097.

Stamp values in *italics* generally refer to items which are difficult to value accurately. For expensive items, e.g., value at $1,000 or more, a value in italics represents an item which trades very seldom, such as a unique item. For inexpensive items, a value in italics represents a warning.

The Scott Catalogue values for used stamps reflect canceled-to-order material when such are found to predominate in the marketplace for the issue involved. Frequently notes appear in the stamp listings to specify items which are valued as canceled-to-order (Canal Zone Scott O1-O8) or if there is a premium for postally used examples.

Scott values for used stamps are not for precanceled examples, unless so stated. Precanceled copies must not have additional postal cancellations.

An example of a warning to collectors is a stamp that used has a value considerably higher than the unused version. Here, the collector is cautioned to be certain the used version has a readable, contemporaneous cancellation.

The *minimum catalogue value* of a stamp is 20 cents, to cover a dealer's costs of purchase and preparation for resale. The minimum catalogue value of a first day cover is one dollar. As noted, the sum of these values does not properly represent the "value" of a packet of unsorted or unmounted stamps sold in bulk. Such large collections, mixtures or packets generally consist of the lower-valued

stamps. There are examples where the catalogue value of a block of stamps is less than the sum of the values of the individual stamps. This situation is caused by the overhead involved in handling single stamps, and should not be considered a suggestion that all blocks be separated into individual stamps to achieve a higher market value.

Values in the "unused" column are for stamps with original gum, if issued with gum. The stamp is valued as hinged if the listing appears *before* the point at which stamps are valued as never hinged. This point is marked by prominent notes in many sections. A similar note will appear at the beginning of the section's listing, noting exactly where the dividing point between hinged and never hinged is for each section of the listings. Where a value for a used stamp is considerably higher than for the unused stamp, the value applies to a stamp showing a distinct contemporaneous cancellation.

Covers

Prices paid for stamps on original covers vary greatly according to condition, appearance, cancellation or postmark and usage. Values given in this volume are for the commonest form with stamps in a grade of very fine "tied on" by the cancellation. A stamp is said to be "tied" to an envelope or card when the cancellation or postmark falls on both the stamp and envelope or card. Letters addressed to foreign countries showing unusual rates and transit markings normally are much in demand and often command large premiums.

Values are for covers bearing a single copy of the stamp referenced and used during the period when the stamp was on sale at post offices unless stated otherwise. If the postage rate was higher than the denomination of the stamp, then the stamp must represent the highest denomination possible to use in making up this rate. In this case, the value is the on-cover value of the stamp plus the used values of the additional stamps. As a general rule, the stamp must be tied to the cover.

Values for patriotic covers of the Civil War period (bearing pictorial designs of a patriotic nature) are for the commonest designs. Approximately 10,000 varieties of designs are known.

Cancellations

A complete treatment of this subject is impossible in a catalogue of this limited size. Only postal markings of meaning — those which were necessary to the proper function of the postal service — are recorded here, while those of value owing to their fanciness only are disregarded. The latter are the results of the whim of some postal official. Many of these odd designs, however, command high prices, based on their popularity, scarcity and clearness of impression.

Although there are many types of most of the cancellations listed, only one of each is illustrated. The values quoted are for the most common type of each.

Values for cancellation varieties are for stamp specimens off cover. Some cancellation varieties (e.g., pen, precancel, cut) are valued individually. Other varieties on pre-1900 stamps (e.g., less common colors, specific dates, foreign usages) are valued using premiums (denoted by "+") which are added to the stated value for the used stamp. When listed on cover, the distinctive cancellation must be on the stamp in order to merit catalogue valuation. Postal markings that denote origin or a service (as distinguished from canceling a stamp) merit catalogue valuation when on a cover apart from the stamp, provided the stamp is otherwise tied to the cover by a cancellation.

One type of "Paid" cancellation used in Boston, and shown in this introduction under "Postal Markings," is common and values given are for types other than this.

Examination

Scott Publishing Co. will not pass upon the genuineness, grade or condition of stamps, because of the time and responsibility involved. Rather, there are several expertizing groups which undertake this work for both collectors and dealers. Neither will Scott Publishing Co. appraise or identify philatelic material. The Company cannot take responsibility for unsolicited stamps or covers.

How to order from your dealer

It is not necessary to write the full description of a stamp as listed in this catalogue. All that you need is the name of the country or *U.S. Specialized* section, the Scott Catalogue number and whether the item is unused or used. For example, "U.S. Scott 833" is sufficient to identify the stamp of the United States listed as the 2-dollar value of a set of stamps issued between 1938-43. This stamp was issued September 29, 1938. It is yellow green and black in color, has a perforation of 11, and is printed on paper without a watermark by a flat plate press. Sections without a prefix or suffix must be mentioned by name.

Abbreviations

Scott Publishing Co. uses a consistent set of abbreviations throughout this catalogue and the *Standard Postage Stamp Catalogue* to conserve space while still providing necessary information. The first block shown here refers to color names only:

COLOR ABBREVIATIONS

amb	amber	ind	indigo
anil	aniline	int	intense
ap	apple	lav	lavender
aqua	aquamarine	lem	lemon
az	azure	lil	lilac
bis	bister	lt	light
bl	blue	mag	magenta
bld	blood	man	manila
blk	black	mar	maroon
bril	brilliant	mv	mauve
brn	brown	multi	multicolored
brnsh	brownish	mlky	milky
brnz	bronze	myr	myrtle
brt	bright	ol	olive
brnt	burnt	olvn	olivine
car	carmine	org	orange
cer	cerise	pck	peacock
chlky	chalky	pnksh	pinkish
cham	chamois	Prus	Prussian
chnt	chestnut	pur	purple
choc	chocolate	redsh	reddish
chr	chrome	res	reseda
cit	citron	ros	rosine
cl	claret	ryl	royal
cob	cobalt	sal	salmon
cop	copper	saph	sapphire
crim	crimson	scar	scarlet
cr	cream	sep	sepia
dk	dark	sien	sienna
dl	dull	sil	silver
dp	deep	sl	slate
db	drab	stl	steel
emer	emerald	turq	turquoise
gldn	golden	ultra	ultramarine
grysh	grayish	ven	venetian
grn	green	ver	vermilion
grnsh	greenish	vio	violet
hel	heliotrope	yel	yellow
hn	henna	yelsh	yellowish

When no color is given for an overprint or surcharge, black is the color used. Abbreviations for colors used for overprints and surcharges are: "(B)" or "(Blk)," black; "(Bl)," blue; "(R)," red; "(G)," green; etc.

Additional abbreviations used in this catalogue are shown below:

Adm.	Administration
AFL	American Federation of Labor
Anniv.	Anniversary
APU	Arab Postal Union
APS	American Philatelic Society
ASEAN	Association of South East Asian Nations
ASPCA	American Society for the Prevention of Cruelty to Animals
Assoc.	Association
b.	Born
BEP	Bureau of Engraving and Printing
Bicent.	Bicentennial
Bklt.	Booklet
Brit.	British
btwn.	Between
Bur.	Bureau
c. or ca.	Circa
CAR	Central African Republic
Cat.	Catalogue
Cent.	Centennial, century, centenary
CEPT	Conference Europeenne des Administrations des Postes et des Telecommunications
CIO	Congress of Industrial Organizations
Conf.	Conference
Cong.	Congress
Cpl.	Corporal
CTO	Canceled to order
d.	Died
Dbl.	Double
DDR	German Democratic Republic (East Germany)
EC	European Community
ECU	European currency unit
EEC	European Economic Community
EKU	Earliest known use
Engr.	Engraved
Exhib.	Exhibition
Expo.	Exposition
FAO	Food and Agricultural Organization of the United Nations
Fed.	Federation
FIP	Federation International de Philatelie
GB	Great Britain
Gen.	General
GPO	General post office
Horiz.	Horizontal
ICAO	International Civil Aviation Organization
ICY	International Cooperation Year
ILO	International Labor Organization
Imperf.	Imperforate
Impt.	Imprint
Intl.	International
Invtd.	Inverted
IQSY	International Quiet Sun Year
ITU	International Telecommunications Union
ITY	International Tourism Year
IWY	International Women's Year
IYC	International Year of the Child
IYD	International Year of the Disabled
IYSH	International Year of Shelter for the Homeless
IYY	International Youth Year
L	Left
Lieut.	Lieutenant
Litho.	Lithographed

LL...............Lower left	Typo. ....Typographed
LR...............Lower right	
	UAE............United Arab Emirate
mm............Millimeter	UAMPT ......Union of African and Malagasy Posts and
Ms. ....Manuscript	Telecommunications
	UL ....Upper left
NASA.........National Aeronautics and Space Administration	UN ....United Nations
Natl. ....National	UNESCO ....United Nations Educational, Scientific and
NATO........North Atlantic Treaty Organization	Cultural Organization
No. ....Number	UNICEF......United Nations Children's Fund
NY..............New York	Univ ....University
NYC ....New York City	UNPA ....United Nations Postal Administration
	Unwmkd.....Unwatermarked
OAU ....Organization of African Unity	UPU...........Universal Postal Union
OPEC ....Organization of Petroleum Exporting Countries	UR ....Upper Right
Ovpt. ....Overprint	US ....United States
Ovptd. ....Overprinted	USPO.........United States Post Office Department
	USPS..........United States Postal Service (also "U.S. Postage Stamp"
P#..............Plate number	when referring to the watermark)
Perf.............Perforated, perforation	USSR ....Union of Soviet Socialist Republics
Phil.............Philatelic	
Photo..........Photogravure	Vert ....Vertical
PO ....Post office	VP ....Vice president
Pr. ....Pair	
P.R.............Puerto Rico	WCY...........World Communications Year
PRC ....People's Republic of China (Mainland China)	WFUNA......World Federation of United Nations Associations
Prec. ....Precancel, precanceled	WHO ....World Health Organization
Pres. ....President	Wmk ....Watermark
	Wmkd ....Watermarked
R.................Right	WMO ....World Meteorological Organization
Rio..............Rio de Janeiro	WRY ....World Refugee Year
ROC ....Republic of China (Taiwan)	WWF..........World Wildlife Fund
	WWI...........World War I
SEATO........South East Asia Treaty Organization	WWII ....World War II
Sgt. ....Sergeant	
Soc. ....Society	YAR ....Yemen Arab Republic
Souv. ....Souvenir	Yemen PDR.Yemen People's Democratic Republic
SSR ....Soviet Socialist Republic	
St................Saint, street	
Surch..........Surcharge	

Postmasters General of the United States

1775 Benjamin Franklin, July 26.	**1866** Alexander W. Randall, July 25.	**1921** Will H. Hays, Mar. 5.
1776 Richard Bache, Nov. 7.	**1869** John A.J. Creswell, Mar. 6.	**1922** Hubert Work, Mar. 4.
1782 Ebenezer Hazard, Jan. 28.	**1874** Jas. W. Marshall, July 7.	**1923** Harry S. New, Mar. 4.
1789 Samuel Osgood, Sept. 26.	**1874** Marshall Jewell, Sept. 1.	**1929** Walter F. Brown, Mar. 6.
1791 Timothy Pickering, Aug. 12.	**1876** James N. Tyner, July 13.	**1933** James A. Farley, Mar. 4.
1795 Joseph Habersham, Feb. 25.	**1877** David McK. Key, Mar. 13.	**1940** Frank C. Walker, Sept. 11.
1801 Gideon Granger, Nov. 28.	**1880** Horace Maynard, Aug. 25.	**1945** Robert E. Hannegan, July 1.
1814 Return J. Meigs, Jr., Apr. 11.	**1881** Thomas L. James, Mar. 8.	**1947** Jesse M. Donaldson, Dec. 16.
1823 John McLean, July 1.	**1882** Timothy O. Howe, Jan. 5.	**1953** Arthur E. Summerfield, Jan. 21.
1829 William T. Barry, Apr. 6.	**1883** Walter Q. Gresham, Apr. 11.	**1961** J. Edward Day, Jan. 21.
1835 Amos Kendall, May 1.	**1884** Frank Hatton, Oct. 14.	**1963** John A. Gronouski, Sept. 30.
1840 John M. Niles, May 26.	**1885** Wm. F. Vilas, Mar. 7.	**1965** Lawrence F. O'Brien, Nov. 3.
1841 Francis Granger, Mar. 8.	**1888** Don M. Dickinson, Jan. 17.	**1968** W. Marvin Watson, Apr. 26.
1841 Charles A. Wickliffe, Oct. 13.	**1889** John Wanamaker, Mar. 6.	**1969** Winton M. Blount, Jan. 22.
1845 Cave Johnson, Mar. 7.	**1893** Wilson S. Bissell, Mar. 7.	**U.S. POSTAL SERVICE**
1849 Jacob Collamer, Mar. 8.	**1895** William L. Wilson, Apr. 4.	**1971** Elmer T. Klassen, Dec. 7.
1850 Nathan K. Hall, July 23.	**1897** James A. Gary, Mar. 6.	**1975** Benjamin Bailar, Feb. 15.
1852 Samuel D. Hubbard, Sept. 14.	**1898** Charles Emory Smith, Apr. 22.	**1978** William F. Bolger, Mar. 1.
1853 James Campbell, Mar. 8.	**1902** Henry C. Payne, Jan. 15.	**1985** Paul N. Carlin, Jan. 1.
1857 Aaron V. Brown, Mar. 7.	**1904** Robert J. Wynne, Oct. 10.	**1986** Albert V. Casey, Jan. 6.
1859 Joseph Holt, Mar. 14.	**1905** Geo. B. Cortelyou, Mar. 7.	**1986** Preston R. Tisch, Aug. 17.
1861 Horatio King, Feb. 12.	**1907** Geo. von L. Meyer, Mar. 4.	**1988** Anthony M. Frank, Mar. 1.
1861 Montgomery Blair, Mar. 9.	**1909** Frank H. Hitchcock, Mar. 6.	**1992** Marvin T. Runyon, Jr., July 6.
1864 William Dennison, Oct. 1.	**1913** Albert S. Burleson, Mar. 5.	**1998** William J. Henderson, May 16.

Basic Stamp Information

A stamp collector's knowledge of the combined elements that make a given issue of a stamp unique determines his or her ability to identify stamps. These elements include paper, watermark, method of separation, printing, design and gum. On the following pages these important areas are described in detail.

The guide below will direct you to those philatelic terms which are not major headings in the following introductory material. The major headings are:

Plate   Paper   Gum   Postal Markings
Printing   Perforations   Luminescence   General Glossary

Guide to Subjects

Arrows .... See Plate Markings
Bisect .... See General Glossary
Blocks .... See Plate
Booklet Panes .... See Plate
Booklets .... See Plate
Booklets A.E.F. .... See Plate
Bureau Issues .... See General Glossary
Bureau Prints .... See Postal Markings
Cancellations .... See Postal Markings
Carrier Postmark .... See Postal Markings
Center Line Block .... See Plate
Coarse Perforation .... See Perforations
Coils .... See Plate
Coil Waste .... See Plate
Color Registration Markings .... See Plate Markings
Color Trials .... See Printing
Commemorative Stamps .... See General Glossary
Compound Perforation .... See Perforations
Corner Blocks .... See Plate
Cracked Plate .... See Plate
Crystallization Cracks .... See Plate
Curvature Cracks .... See Plate
Cut Square .... See General Glossary
Diagonal Half .... See General Glossary (Bisect)
Die .... See Plate
Double Impression............... See Printing
Double Paper .... See Paper
Double Perforation .... See Perforations
Double Transfer .... See Plate
Dry Printings .... See note after Scott 1029
Electric Eye .... See Perforations
Embossed Printing .... See Printing
End Roller Grills .... See Paper
Engraving .... See Printing
Error .... See General Glossary
Essay .... See Printing
Fine Perforation .... See Perforations
First Day Covers .... See General Glossary
Flat Plate Printing .... See Printing
Flat Press Printing .... See Printing
Foreign Entry .... See Plate
Giori Press .... See Printing
Gridiron Cancellation .... See Postal Markings
Grills .... See Paper
Gripper Cracks .... See Plate
Guide Dots .... See Plate
Guide Lines .... See Plate Markings
Guide line Blocks .... See Plate
Gum Breaker Ridges .... See General Glossary
Gutter .... See Plate Markings
Hidden Plate Number .... See Plate
Horizontal Half .... See General Glossary (Bisect)
Imperforate .... See Perforations

Imprint .... See Plate Markings
Imprint Blocks .... See Plate
India Paper .... See Paper
Intaglio .... See Printing
Inverted Center .... See Printing
Joint Line Pair .... See Plate
Laid Paper .... See Paper
Line Engraved .... See Printing
Line Pair .... See Plate
Lithography .... See Printing
Luminescent Coating .... See Luminescence
Manila Paper .... See Paper
Margin .... See Plate Markings
Margin Blocks .... See Plate
Multicolored Stamps .... See Printing
New York City Foreign
    Mail Cancellations .... See Postal Markings
Offset Printing .... See Printing
Original Gum .... See General Glossary
Overprint .... See Printing
Pair Imperf. Between .... See Perforations
Pane .... See Plate
Part Perforate .... See Perforations
Paste-up .... See Plate
Paste-up Pair .... See Plate
Patent Cancellations .... See Postal Markings
Patriotic Covers .... See General Glossary
Pelure Paper .... See Paper
Phosphor Tagged .... See Luminescence
Plate Arrangement .... See Plate
Plate Flaws .... See Plate
Plate Markings .... See Plate
Postmarks .... See Postal Markings
Precancels .... See Postal Markings
Printed on Both Sides .... See Printing
Proofs .... See Printing
Propaganda Covers .... See General Glossary
Railroad Postmarks .... See Postal Markings
Receiving Mark .... See Postal Markings
Recut .... See Plate
Re-engraved .... See Plate
Re-entry .... See Plate
Re-issue .... See Printing
Relief .... See Plate
Reprints .... See Printing
Retouch .... See Plate
Rosette Crack .... See Printing
Rotary Press Printings .... See Printing
Rotary Press Double Paper .... See Paper
Rough Perforation .... See Perforations
Rouletting .... See Perforations
Se-Tenant .... See General Glossary
Service Indicators .... See Postal Markings
Sheet .... See Plate
Shifted Transfer .... See Plate
Ship Postmarks .... See Postal Markings
Short Transfer .... See Plate
Silk Paper .... See Paper
Specialization .... See General Glossary
Special Printings .... See Printing
Split Grill .... See Paper
Stampless Covers .... See Plate
Stitch Watermark .... See Paper
Strip .... See General Glossary
Surface Printing .... See Printing
Supplementary Mail Cancellations ..... See Postal Markings
Surcharges .... See Printing

Plate

Die   Transfer Roll

Plate

LINE ENGRAVING (INTAGLIO)

Die — Making the die is the initial operation in developing the intaglio plate. The die is a small flat piece of soft steel on which the subject (design) is recess-engraved in reverse. Dies are usually of a single-subject type, but dies exist with multiple subjects of the same design, or even different designs. After the engraving is completed, the die is hardened to withstand the stress of subsequent operations.

Transfer Roll — The next operation is making the transfer roll, which is the medium used to transfer the subject from the die to the plate. A blank roll of soft steel, mounted on a mandrel, is placed under the bearers of a transfer press. The hardened die is placed on the bed of the press and the face of the roll is brought to bear on the die. The bed is then rocked backed and forth under increasing pressure until the soft steel of the roll is forced into every line of the

die. The resulting impression on the roll is known as a "relief" or "relief transfer." Several reliefs usually are rocked in on each roll. After the required reliefs are completed, the roll is hardened.

Relief — A relief is the normal reproduction of the design on the die, in reverse. A defective relief, caused by a minute piece of foreign material lodging on the die, may occur during the rocking-in process, or from other causes. Imperfections in the steel of the transfer roll may also result in a breaking away of parts of the design. If the damaged relief is continued in use, it will transfer a repeating defect to the plate. Also reliefs sometime are deliberately altered. "Broken relief" and "altered relief" are terms used to designate these changed conditions.

Plate — A flat piece of soft steel replaces the die on the bed of the transfer press and one of the reliefs on the transfer roll is brought to bear on this soft steel. The position of the plate is determined by position dots, which have been lightly marked on the plate in advance. After the position of the relief is determined, pressure is brought to bear and, by following the same method used in the making of the transfer roll, a transfer is entered. This transfer reproduces, in reverse, every detail of the design of the relief. As many transfers are entered on the plate as there are to be subjects printed at one time.

After the required transfers have been entered, the positions dots, layouts and lines, scratches, etc., are burnished out. Also, any required guide lines, plate numbers, or other marginal markings are added. A proof impression is then taken and if certified (approved), the plate is machined for fitting to the press, hardened and sent to they plate vault until used.

Rotary press plates, after being certified, require additional machining. They are curved to fit the press cylinder and gripper slots are cut into the back of each plate to receive the grippers, which hold the plate securely to the press. The rotary press plate is not hardened until these additional processes are completed.

Transfer — An impression entered on the plate by the transfer roll. A relief transfer is made when entering the design of the die onto the transfer roll.

Double Transfer — The condition of a transfer on a plate that shows evidences of a duplication of all or a portion of the design. A double transfer usually is the result of the changing of the registration between the relief and the plate during the rolling of the original entry.

Occasionally it is necessary to remove the original transfer from a plate and enter the relief a second time. When the finished re-transfer shows indications of the original transfer, because of incomplete erasure, the result is known as a double transfer.

Triple Transfer — Similar to a double transfer, this situation shows evidences of a third entry or two duplications.

Foreign Entry — When original transfers are erased incompletely from a plate, they can appear with new transfers of a different design which are entered subsequently on the plate.

Re-entry — When executing a re-entry, the transfer roll is reapplied to the plate at some time after the latter has been put to press. Thus, worn-out designs may be resharpened by carefully re-entering the transfer roll. If the transfer roll is not carefully entered, the registration will not be true and a double transfer will result. With the protective qualities of chromium plating, it is no longer necessary to resharpen the plate. In fact, after a plate has been curved for the rotary press, it is impossible to make a re-entry.

Shifted Transfer (Shift) — In transferring, the metal displaced on the plate by the entry of the ridges, constituting the design on the transfer roll, is forced ahead of the roll as well as pressed out at the sides. The amount of displaced metal increases with the depth of the entry. When the depth is increased evenly, the design will be uniformly entered. Most of the displaced metal is pressed ahead of the roll. If too much pressure is exerted on any pass (rocking), the impression on the previous partial entry may be floated (pushed) ahead of the roll and cause a duplication of the final design. The duplication appears as an increased width of frame lines or a doubling of the lines.

The ridges of the displaced metal are flattened out by the hammering or rolling back of the plate along the space occupied by the subject margins.

Short Transfer — Occasionally the transfer roll is not rocked its entire length in the entering of a transfer onto a plate, with the result that the finished transfer fails to show the complete design. This is known as a short transfer.

Short transfers are known to have been made deliberately, as in the Type III of the 1-cent issue of 1851-60 (Scott 8, 21), or accidentally, as in the 10-cent 1847 (Scott 2).

Re-engraved — Either the die that has been used to make a plate or the plate itself may have its temper drawn (softened) and be recut. The resulting impressions for such re-engraved die or plate may differ very slightly from the original issue and are given the label "re-engraved."

Re-cut — A re-cut is the strengthening or altering of a line by use of an engraving tool on unhardened plates.

Retouching — A retouch is the strengthening or altering of a line by means of etching.

PLATE ARRANGEMENT

Arrangement — The first engraved plates used to produce U.S. postage stamps in 1847 contained 200 subjects. The number of subjects to a plate varied between 100 and 300 until the issue of 1890, when the 400-subject plate was first laid down. Since that time, this size of plate has been used for a majority of the regular postal issues (those other than commemoratives). Exceptions to this practice exist, particularly among the more recent issues, and are listed under the headings of the appropriate issues in the catalogue.

Sheet — In single-color printings, the complete impression from a plate is termed a sheet. A sheet of multicolored stamps (two or more colors) may come from a single impression of a plate, i.e., many Giori-type press printings from 1957, or from as many impressions from separate plates as there are inks used for the particular stamp. Combination process printings may use both methods of multicolor production: Giori-type intaglio with offset lithography or with photogravure.

The Huck multicolor press used plates of different format (40, 72 or 80 subjects). The sheet it produced had 200 subjects for normal-sized commemoratives or 400 subjects for regular-issue stamps, similar to the regular products of other presses.

See the note on the Combination Press following the listing for Scott 1703.

In casual usage, a "pane" often is referred to as a "sheet."

Pane — A pane is the part of the original sheet that is issued for sale at post offices. A pane may be the same as an entire sheet, where the plate is small, or it may be a half, quarter, or some other fraction of a sheet where the plate is large.

The illustration shown later under the subtopic "Plate Markings" shows the layout of a 400-subject sheet from a flat plate, which for issuance would have been divided along the intersecting guide lines into four panes of 100.

Panes are classified into normal reading position according to their location on the printed sheet: U.L., upper left; U.R., upper right; L.L., lower left; and L.R., lower right. Where only two panes appear on a sheet, they are designed "R" (right) and "L" (left) or "T" (top) and "B" (bottom), on the basis of the division of the sheet vertically or horizontally.

To fix the location of a particular stamp on any pane, except for those printed on the Combination press, the pane is held with the subjects in the normal position, and a position number is given to each stamp starting with the first stamp in the upper left corner and proceeding horizontally to the right, then staring on the second row at the left and counting across to the right, and so on to the last stamp in the lower right corner.

In describing the location of a stamp on a sheet of stamps issued prior to 1894, the practice is to give the stamp position number first, then the pane position and finally the plate number, i.e., "1R22." Beginning with the 1894 issue and on all later issues the method used is to give the plate number first, then the position of the pane, and finally the position number of the stamp, i.e., "16807LL48" to identify an example of Scott 619 or "2138L2" to refer to an example of Scott 323.

BOOKLET STAMPS

Plates for Stamp Booklets — These are illustrated and described preceding the listing of booklet panes and covers in this catalogue.

Booklet Panes — Panes especially printed and cut to be sold in booklets which are a convenient way to purchase and store stamps. U.S. Booklet panes are straight-edged on three sides, but perforated between the stamps. Die cut, ATM and other panes will vary from this. Except for BK64 and BK65, the A.E.F. booklets, booklets were sold by the Post Office Department for a one-cent premium until 1962. Other sections of this catalogue with listings for booklet panes include Savings, Telegraphs and Canal Zone.

A.E.F. Booklets — These were special booklets prepared principally for use by the U.S. Army Post Office in France during World War I. They were issued in 1-cent and 2-cent denominations with 30 stamps to a pane (10 x 3), bound at right or left. As soon as Gen. John J. Pershing's organization reached France, soldiers' mail was sent free by means of franked envelopes.

Stamps were required during the war for the civilian personnel, as well as for registered mail, parcel post and other types of postal service. See the individual listings for Scott 498f and 499f and booklets BK64 and BK65.

COIL STAMPS

First issued in 1908-09, coils (rolls) originally were produced in two sizes, 500 and 1,000 stamps, with the individual stamps arranged endways or sideways and with and without perforations between.

Rolls of stamps for use in affixing or vending machines were first constructed by private companies and later by the Bureau of Engraving and Printing. Originally, it was customary for the Post Office Department to sell to the private vending companies and others imperforate sheets of stamps printed from the ordinary 400-subject flat plates. These sheets were then pasted together end-to-end or side-to-side by the purchaser and cut into rolls as desired, with the perforations being applied to suit the requirements of the individual machines. Such stamps with private perforations are listed in this catalogue under "Vending and Affixing Machine Perforations."

Later the Bureau produced coils by the same method, also in rolls of 500 and 1,000. These coils were arranged endways or sideways and were issued with or without perforation.

With the introduction of the Stickney rotary press, curved plates made for use on these presses were put into use at the Bureau of Engraving and Printing, and the sale of imperforate sheets was discontinued. This move marked the end of the private perforation. Rotary press coils have been printed on a number of presses over the years and have been made in sizes of 100, 500, 1,000, 3,000 and 10,000 stamps, etc.

Paste-up — the junction of two flat-plate printings joined by pasting the edge of one sheet onto the edge of another sheet to make coils. A two-stamp example of this joining is a "paste-up pair." See Splice.

Guide Line Pair — attached pair of flat-plate-printed coil stamps with printed line between. This line is identical with the guide line (See listing under "Plate Markings") found in sheets.

Joint Line — The edges of two curved plates do not meet exactly on the press and the small space between the plates takes ink and prints a line. A pair of rotary-press-printed stamps with such a line is called a "joint line pair."

Coil stamps printed on the Multicolor Huck Press do not consistently produce such lines. Occasionally accumulated ink will print partial lines in one or more colors, and very occasionally complete lines will be printed. Stamps resulting from such situations are not listed in this Catalogue. The "B" and "C" presses do not print joint lines at all.

Splice — the junction of two rotary-press printings by butting the ends of the web (roll) of paper together and pasting a strip of perforated translucent paper on the back of the junction. The two-stamp specimen to show this situation is a "spliced pair."

Splices occur when a web breaks and is repaired or when one web is finished and another begins.

Plate Number — for U.S. coil stamps prior to Scott 1891, Scott 1947, War Savings Coils and Canal Zone:

On a rotary-press horizontal coil the top or bottom part of a plate number may show. On a vertical coil, the left or right part of a plate number may show. The number was entered on the plate to be cut off when the web was sliced into coils and is found only when the web was sliced off center. Every rotary press coil plate number was adjacent to a joint line, so both features could occur together in one strip.

For U.S. stamps from Scott 1891 onward (excluding Scott 1947) and Official coils:

The plate number is placed in the design area of the stamp, so it will not be trimmed off. Such items are normally collected unused with the stamp containing the plate number in the center of a strip of three or five stamps. They normally are collected used as singles. The line, if any, will be at the right of the plate-number stamp. On the Cottrell press, the number occurs every 24th stamp, on the "B" press every 52nd stamp, on the "C" press every 48th stamp, etc.

Unused plate number strips of three and five are valued in this catalogue.

Hidden Plate Number — A plate number may be found entirely on a coil made from flat plates, but usually is hidden by a part of the next sheet which has been lapped over it.

Coil Waste — an occurrence brought about by stamps issued in perforated sheets from a printing intended for coils. These stamps came from short lengths of paper at the end of the coil run. Sometimes the salvaged sections were those which had been laid aside for mutilation because of some defect. Because the paper had been moistened during printing, it sometimes stretched slightly and provided added printing area. Sheets of 70, 100, and 170 are known. See Scott 538-541, 545-546, 578-579, and 594-595.

"T" — Letter which appears in the lower design area of Scott 2115b, which was printed on a experimental pre-phosphored paper. The stamp with the plate number is inscribed "T1."

SHEET STAMPS

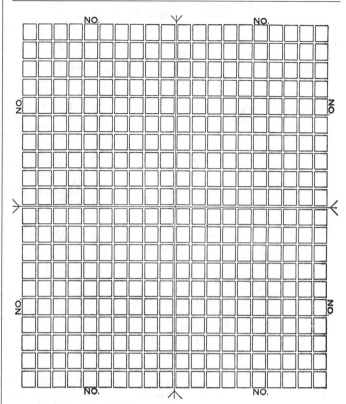

A typical 400-subject plate of 1922

Plate Markings — The illustration above shows a typical 400-subject plate of the 1922 issue with markings as found on this type of plate. Other layouts and markings are found further in the Catalogue text.

Guide Lines — Horizontal or vertical colored lines between the stamps, extending wholly or partially across the sheet. They serve as guides for the operators of perforating machines or to indicate the point of separation of the sheet into panes.

A block of stamps divided by any of the guide lines is known as a "line block" or "guide line block." The block of stamps from the exact center of the sheet, showing the crossed guide lines, is a "center line block."

Gutters — When guide lines are used to mark the division of the sheet into panes, the space between the stamps at the edge of the pane is no different than the space between any other stamps on the sheet. Some plates provide a wide space, or gutter, between the panes. These plates do not produce guide lines.

A pair of stamps with the wide space between is known as a "gutter pair", and blocks with that situation are "gutter blocks." A block of stamps from the exact center of the sheet, showing the two wide spaces crossing, is a "center gutter block" or "cross gutter block."

Gutter pairs or gutter blocks must contain complete stamps on both sides of the gutter, intact including perforation teeth unless imperforate.

Arrows — arrow-shaped markings were used in the margins of stamp sheets, in place of guide lines, on the issues of 1870 through 1894. Since 1894, guide lines with arrows at both ends have been the standard practice on flat-plate printings.

A margin block of at least four stamps, showing the arrow centered at one edge, is known as a "margin block with arrow."

Color Registration Markings — marks of different sizes and shapes used as an aid in properly registering the colors in producing a bicolored or multicolored stamp.

Imprint — design containing the name of the producer of the stamps which appears on the sheet margin usually near the plate number.

A block of stamps with the sheet margin attached, bearing the imprint, is known as the "imprint block." Imprints and plate numbers usually are collected in blocks of six, or of sufficient length to include the entire marking. From 1894 until about 1907, one fashion was to collect the imprints in strips of three, and these have been noted in this Catalogue.

The imprint and plate number combination are found in eight types I-VII, which are illustrated at Scott 245 and Scott E3. Example: "T V" refers to Type V.

Plate Numbers — Serial numbers assigned to plates, appearing on one or more margins of the sheet or pane to identify the plate.

Flat Press Plate Numbers — usually collected in a margin block of six stamps with the plate number centered in the margin.

Rotary Press Plate Numbers — usually collected in a corner margin block large enough to show the plate number(s) and position along the margin and complete selvage on two sides. For issues with a single plate number at the corner of the pane a block of four normally suffices.

During 1933-39, some plates had the number opposite the third stamp (up or down) from the corner of the sheet and for these the number is customarily collected in a corner block of no less than eight stamps. Multicolored stamps may have more than one plate number in the margin and the "plate block" may then be expanded to suit the collector's desire.

The Catalogue listing for plate blocks includes enough stamps to accommodate all numbers on the plate. Plate block listings for se-tenant issues include all the designs as part of the block. When a continuous design is involved, such as Scott 1629-31, the complete design will be included in the plate number block. The entire pane constitutes the plate number block for issues such as the State Birds and Flowers (Scott 1953-2002).

Plate numbers take a further designation from the position on the sheet on which they appear, e.g. U.L. refers to upper left pane, etc.

See note following Scott 1703 for description of combination press markings.

Private Contractor Marks — On rotary plates from Scott 1789 onward: "A" denotes issues produced by private contractor American Bank Note Co., "U" by U.S. Bank Note Co., "K" by KCS Industries, Inc., "S" by Stamp Venturers, Inc., "P" by Ashton-Potter America, "B" by Banknote Corp. of America, "V" by Avery Dennison, "D" by Dittler Brothers, "M" by 3M Corp.

Stars — used on the flat plates to indicate a change from the previous spacing of the stamps. They also were used as a check on the assignment of the printed sheets to a perforating machine of the proper setting. Stars appear on certain rotary plates used for printing stamps for coils, appearing adjacent to the plate joint line and above stamp No. 1 on the 170-subject plates, and to the left of stamp No. 141 on the 150-subject plates.

"A" — On flat plates; used on plates having uniform vertical spacing between rows of subjects, but wider than those with the star marking.

"C.S." and "C" — plate has been chromium plated.

"E.I." — abbreviation for Electrolytic Iron. The designation is for plates made by the electrolytic process.

"F" — used to indicate the plate is ready for hardening. This appears only on flat plates and generally precedes the upper right plate number.

"Top" — marking on the top sheet margin of printings from both plates of some bicolored issues. This marking is used to check printings for "inverts." Beginning with the 6-cent bicolored airpost issue of 1938 (Scott C23), bicolored crosses also were used as an additional check.

"Coil Stamps" — appearing on the side sheet margins, designates plates used in the production of endwise coils.

"S 20," "S 30," "S 40" — marginal markings appearing on certain 150- and 170-subject rotary press plates to designate experimental variations in the depth and character of the frame line to over-come excess inking. "S 30" was adopted as the standard. Blocks showing these markings are listed as "Margin Block with S 20," etc., in this Catalogue.

Initials — used in sheet margins to identify individuals in the Bureau of Engraving and Printing who participated in the production or use of the plates.

Gutter Dashes — on the first 400-subject rotary plates, 3/16-inch horizontal dashes appear in the gutter between the 10th and 11th vertical rows of stamps. This arrangement was superseded by dashes 3/16-inch at the extreme ends of the vertical and horizontal gutters, and a 1/4-inch cross at the central gutter intersection. This latter arrangement continued until replaced by the scanning marks on the Electric Eye plates. See Electric Eye.

Margin — border outside the printed design or perforated area of a stamp, also known as selvage, or the similar border of a sheet of stamps. A block of stamps from the top, side or bottom of a sheet or pane to which is attached the selvage (margin) is known as a "margin block." A block of stamps from the corner of a sheet with full selvage attached to two adjoining sides is known as a "corner block."

NOTE — The descriptions and definitions above indicate that a certain number of stamps make up an arrow or plate number block. Any block of stamps, no matter how large or small, which had an arrow or plate number on its margin would be considered by that name. The usual practice is to collect flat-plate numbers in margin blocks of six and arrow blocks in margin blocks of four. Plate number blocks from rotary press printings generally are collected in blocks of 4 when the plate number appears beside the stamp at any of the four corners of the sheet. Particularly relative to bi-colored stamps, an arrow block is now separated from a plate number block. Thus, in those situations, the two individual types of blocks might form a block of eight or 10, as the situation dictates.

PRINTING

Methods Used — all four basic forms of printing have been used in producing U.S. stamps, engraved, photogravure, lithography, and typography. Holography has been used on some envelopes.

Engraved (Recess or Intaglio) — process where ink is received and held in lines depressed below the surface of the plate. Initially, in printing from such plate damp paper was forced into the depressed lines and therefore picked up ink. Consequently, ink lines on the stamp are slightly raised. This also is noted from the back of the stamp, where depressions mark where ink is placed on the front.

When the ornamental work for a stamp is engraved by a machine, the process is called "engine turned" or lathe-work engraving. An example of such lathe-work background is the 3-cent stamp of 1861 (Scott Illustration No. A25).

Engraved stamps were printed only with flat plates until 1915, when rotary press printing was introduced. "Wet" and "dry" printings are explained in the note in the text of the Catalogue following Scott 1029. The Giori press, used to print some U.S. stamps from 1957 (see Scott 1094, 4-cent Flag issue), applied two or three different colored inks simultaneously.

The Huck Multicolor press, put into service at the Bureau of

Engraving and Printing in 1968, was used first to produce the 1969 Christmas stamp (Scott 1363) and the 6-cent flag coil of 1969 (Scott 1338A). Developed by the Bureau's technical staff and the firm of graphic arts engineers whose name it bears, the Huck press printed, tagged with phosphor ink, gummed and perforated stamps in a continuous operation. Printing was accomplished in as many as nine colors. Fed by paper from a roll, the Huck Multicolor used many recess-engraved plates of smaller size than any used previously for U.S. stamp printing. Its product has certain characteristics which other U.S. stamps do not have. Post office panes of the 1969 Christmas stamp, for example, show seven or eight plate numbers in the margins. Joint lines appear after every two or four stamps. Other presses providing multiple plate numbers are the Andreotti, Champlain, Combination, Miller Offset, A Press, D Press and more.

Photogravure — the design of a stamp to be printed by photogravure usually is photographed through an extremely fine screen, lined in minute quadrille. The screen breaks up the reproduction into tiny dots, which are etched onto the plate and the depressions formed hold the ink. Somewhat similarly to engraved printing, the ink is lifted out of the lines by the paper, which is pressed against the plate. Unlike engraved printing, however, the ink does not appear to be raised relative to the surface of the paper.

Gravure is most often used for multicolored stamps, generally using the three primary colors (red, yellow and blue) and black. By varying the dot matrix pattern and density of these colors, virtually any color can be reproduced. A typical full-color gravure stamp will be created from four printing cylinders (one for each color). The original multicolored image will have been photographically separated into its component colors.

For U.S. stamps, photogravure first appeared in 1967 with the Thomas Eakins issue (Scott 1335). The early photogravure stamps were printed by outside contractors until the Bureau obtained the multicolor Andreotti press in 1971. The earliest stamp printed on that press was the 8-cent Missouri Statehood issue of 1971 (Scott 1426).

Color control bars, dashes or dots are printed in the margin of one pane in each "Andreotti" sheet of 200, 160 or 128 stamps. These markings generally are collected in blocks of 20 or 16 (two full rows of one pane), which include the full complement of plate numbers, Mr. Zip and the Zip and Mail Early slogans.

Details on the Combination Press follow the listing for Scott 1703.

Modern gravure printing may use computer-generated dot-matrix screens, and modern plates may be of various types including metal-coated plastic. The catalogue designation of Photogravure (or "Photo") covers any of these older and more modern gravure methods of printing.

Lithography — this is the most common and least expensive process for printing stamps. In this method, the design is drawn by hand or transferred in greasy ink from an original engraving to the surface of a lithographic stone or metal plate. The stone or plate is wet with an acid fluid, which causes it to repel the printing ink except at the greasy lines of the design. A fine lithographic print closely resembles an engraving, but the lines are not raised on the face or depressed on the back. Thus there usually is a more dull appearance to the lithograph than to the engraving.

Offset Printing or Offset Lithography — a modern development of the lithographic process. Anything that will print — type, woodcuts, photoengravings, plates engraved or etched in intaglio, halftone plates, linoleum blocks, lithographic stones or plates, photogravure plates, rubber stamps, etc. — may be used. Greasy ink is applied to the dampened plate or form and an impression made on a rubber blanket. Paper immediately is pressed against the blanket, which transfers the ink. Because of its greater flexibility, offset printing has largely displaced lithography.

Because the processes and results obtained are similar, stamps printed by either of these two methods normally are considered to be "lithographed."

The first application of lithographic printing for any U.S. items listed in this Catalogue was for Post Office seals, probably using stone printing bases. See also some Confederates States general issues. Offset lithography was used for the 1914 documentary revenues (Scott R195-R216). Postage stamps followed in 1918-20 (Scott 525-536) because of war-time shortages of ink, plates, and manpower relative to the regular intaglio production.

The next use of offset lithography for postage stamps was in 1964 with the Homemakers issue (Scott 1253), in combination with intaglio printing. Many similar issues followed, including the U.S. Bicentennial souvenir sheets of 1976 (Scott 1686-1689), all of which were produced by the combination of the two printing methods. The combination process serves best for soft backgrounds and tonal effects.

Typography — an exact reverse of engraved-plate printing, this process provides for the parts of the design which are to show in color to be left at the original level of the plate and the spaces between cut away. Ink is applied to the raised lines and the pressure of the printing forces these lines, more or less into the paper. The process impresses the lines on the face of the stamp and slightly raises them on the back. Normally, a large number of electrotypes of the original are made and assembled into a plate with the requisite number of designs for printing a sheet of stamps. Stamps printed by this process show greater uniformity, and the stamps are less expensive to print than with intaglio printing.

The first U.S. postal usage of an item printed by typography, or letterpress, under national authority was the 1846 "2" surcharge on the United States City Despatch Post 3-cent carrier stamp (Scott 6LB7). The next usage was the 1865 newspaper and periodical stamp issue, which for security reasons combined the techniques of machine engraving, colorless embossing and typography. This created an unusual first.

Most U.S. stamp typography consists of overprints, such as those for the Canal Zone, the Molly Pitcher and Hawaii Sesquicentennial stamps of 1928 (Scott 646-648), the Kansas-Nebraska control markings (Scott 658-679), Bureau-printed precancels, and "specimen" markings.

Embossed (relief) Printing — method in which the design is sunk in the metal of the die and the printing is done against a platen that is forced into the depression, thus forming the design on the paper in relief. Embossing may be done without ink (blind embossing), totally with ink, or a combination thereof. The U.S. stamped envelopes are an example of this form of printing.

Typeset — made from movable type.

Typeset Stamps — printed from ordinary printer's type. Sometimes electrotype or stereotype plates are made, but because such stamps usually are printed only in small quantities for temporary use, movable type often is used for the purpose. This method of printing is apt to show broken type and lack of uniformity. See Hawaii Scott 1-4 and 12-26.

Holograms — for objects to appear as holograms on stamps, a model exactly the same size as it is too appear on the hologram must be created. Rather than using photographic film to capture the image, holography records an image on a photoresist material. in processing, chemicals eat away at certain exposed areas, leaving a pattern of constructive and destructive interference. When the photoresist is developed, the result is a pattern of uneven ridges that acts as a mold. This mold is then coated with metal, and the resulting form is used to press copies in much the same way phonograph records are produced.

A typical reflective hologram used for stamps consists of a reproduction of the uneven patterns on a plastic film that is applied to a reflective background, ususably a silver or gold foil. Light is reflected off the background through the film, making the pattern present on the film visible. Because of the uneven pattern of the film, the viewer will perceive the objects in their proper three-dimensional relationships with appropriate brightness.

The first hologram on a stamp was produced by Austria in 1988 (Scott 1441).

Foil Application — A modern tecnique of applying color to stamps involves the application of metallic foil to the stamp paper. A pattern of foil is applied to the stamp paper by use of a stamping die. The foil usually is flat, but it may be textured. Canada Scott 1735 has three different foil applications in pearl, bronze, and gold. The gold foil was texured using a chemical-etch copper embossing die. The printing of this stamp also involved two-colored offset lithography plus embossing.

ADDITIONAL TERMS

Multicolored Stamps — until 1957 when the Giori press was introduced, bicolored stamps were printed on a flat-bed press in two runs, one for each color (example: Norse-American Issue of 1925, Scott 620-621). In the flat-press bicolors, if the sheet were fed to the press on the second run in reversed position, the part printed in the second color would be upside down, producing an "invert" such as the famed Scott C3a.

With the Giori press and subsequent presses, stamps could be printed in more than one color at the same time.

Many bicolored and multicolored stamps show varying degrees of poor color registration (alignment). Such varieties are not listed in this Catalogue.

Color Changeling — a stamp which, because of exposure to the environment, has naturally undergone a change of ink colors. Orange U.S. stamps of the early 1900's are notorious for turning brown as the ink reacts with oxygen. Exposure to light can cause some inks to fade. These are not considered color omitted errors. Exposure to other chemicals can cause ink colors to change. These stamps are merely altered stamps, and their value to collectors is greatly diminished.

Color Trials — printings in various colors, made to facilitate selection of color for the issued stamp.

Double Impression — a second impression of a stamp over the original impression.

This is not to be confused with a "double transfer," which is a plate imperfection and does not show a doubling of the entire design. A double impression shows every line clearly doubled. See also "Printed on Both Sides."

Essay — A proposed design, a designer's model or an incomplete engraving. Its design differs in some way — great or small — from the issued item.

Inverted Center — bicolored or multicolored stamp with the center printed upside down relative to the remainder of the design. A stamp may be described as having an inverted center even if the center is printed first. See "Multicolored Stamps."

Flat Plate Printing — stamp printed on a flat-bed press, rather than on a rotary press. See "Plate."

Overprint — any word, inscription or device printed across the face of a stamp to alter its use or locality or otherwise to serve a special purpose. An example is U.S. Scott 646, the "Molly Pitcher" overprint, which is Scott 634 with a black overprinted inscription as a memorial to the Revolutionary War heroine. See "Surcharge."

Printed on Both Sides — Occasionally a sheet of stamps already printed will, through error, be turned over and passed through the press a second time, creating the rare "printed on both sides" variety. On one side the impression is almost always poor or incomplete. This often is confused with an "offset," which occurs when sheets of stamps are stacked while the ink is still wet.

The "printed on both sides" variety will show the design as a positive (all inscriptions reading correctly) and the offset shows a reverse impression. See "Double Impression."

Progressive Proof — a type of essay that is an incomplete engraving of the finished accepted die.

Proofs — trial printings of a stamp made from the original die or the finished plate.

Reprints and Reissues — are impressions of stamps (usually obsolete) made from the original plates or stones. If they are valid for postage and reproduce obsolete issues (such as U.S. Scott 102-111), the stamps are *reissues.* If they are from current issues, they are designated as *second, third,* etc., *printing.* If designated for a particular purpose, they are called *special printings.*

When special printings are not valid for postage, but are made from original dies and plates by authorized persons, they are *official reprints. Private reprints* are made from the original plates and dies by private hands. An example of a private reprint is that of the 1871-1932 reprints made from the original die of the 1845 New Haven, Conn., postmaster's provisional. *Official reproductions* or imitations are made from new dies and plates by government authorization. Scott will list those reissues that are valid for postage if they differ significantly from the original printing.

The U.S. government made special printings of its first postage stamps in 1875. Produced were official imitations of the first two stamps (listed as Scott 3-4), reprints of the demonetized pre-1861 issues (Scott 40-47) and reissues of the 1861 stamps, the 1869 stamps and the then-current 1875 denominations. Even though the official imitations and the reprints were not valid for postage, Scott lists all of these U.S. special printings.

Most reprints or reissues differ slightly from the original stamp in some characteristic, such as gum, paper, perforation, color or watermark. Sometimes the details are followed so meticulously that only a student of that specific stamp is able to distinguish the reprint or reissue from the original.

Rotary Press Printings — stamps which have been printed on a rotary-type press from curved plates. Rotary press-printed stamps are longer or wider than stamps of the same design printed from flat plates. All rotary press printings through 1953, except coil waste (such as Scott 538), exist with horizontal "gum breaker ridges" varying from one to four per stamp. See: "Plate."

Surcharge — overprint which alters or restates the face value or denomination of the stamp to which it was applied. An example is Scott K1, where U.S. stamps were surcharged for use by U.S. Offices in China. Many surcharges are typeset. See: "Overprint" and "Typeset."

COMMON FLAWS

Cracked Plate — A term to describe stamps which show evidences that the plate from which they were printed was cracked.

Plate cracks have various causes, each which may result in a different formation and intensity of the crack. Cracks similar to the above illustration are quite common in older issues and are largely due to the plate being too-quickly immersed in the cooling bath when being tempered. These cracks are known as crystallization cracks. A jagged line running generally in one direction and most often in the gutter between stamps is due to the stress of the steel during the rolling in or transferring process.

In curved (rotary) plates, there are two types of cracks. Once is the bending or curving crack, which is quite marked and always runs in the direction in which the plate is curved.

The accompanying illustration shows the second type, the gripper crack. This type is caused by the cracking of the plate over the slots cut in the underside of the plate, which receive the "grippers" that fasten the plate to the press. These occur only on curved plates and are to be found in the row of stamps adjoining the plate joint. These appear on the printed impression as light irregularly colored lines, usually parallel to the plate joint line.

Rosette Crack — cluster of fine cracks radiating from a central point in irregular lines. These usually are caused by the plate receiving a blow.

Scratched Plate — caused by foreign matter scratching the plate, these usually are too minor to mention. See: "Gouge."

Gouge — exceptionally heavy and usually short scratches, these may be caused by a tool falling onto the plate.

Surface Stains — irregular surface marks resembling the outline of a point on a map. Experts differ on the cause. These are too minor to list.

PAPER

Paper falls broadly into two types: wove and laid. The difference in the appearance is caused by the wire cloth upon which the pulp is first formed.

Paper also is distinguished as thick or thin, hard or soft, and by its color (such as bluish, yellowish, greenish, etc.).

Wove — where the wire cloth is of even and closely woven nature, producing a sheet of uniform texture throughout. This type shows no light or dark figures when held to the light.

Laid — where the wire cloth is formed of closely spaced parallel wires crossed at much wider intervals by cross wires. The resultant paper shows alternate light and dark lines. The distances between the widely spaced lines and the thickness of these lines may vary, but on any one piece of paper they will be the same.

Pelure — type of paper which is very thin and semi-transparent. It may be either wove or laid.

Bluish — The 1909 so-called "bluish" paper was made with 35 percent rag stock instead of all wood pulp. The bluish (actually grayish-blue) color goes through the paper, showing clearly on back and face. See the note with Scott 331.

Manila — a coarse paper formerly made of Manila hemp fiber. Since about 1890, so-called "manila" paper has been manufactured entirely from wood fiber. It is used for cheaper grades of envelopes and newspaper wrappers and normally is a natural light brown. Sometimes color is added, such as in the U.S. "amber manila" envelopes. It may be either wove or laid.

Silk — refers to two kinds of paper found by stamp collectors. One type has one or more threads of silk embedded in the substance of the paper, extending across the stamp. In the catalogues, this type of paper usually is designated as "with silk threads."

The other type, used to print many U.S. revenue stamps, has shortsilk fibers strewn over it and impressed into it during manufacture. This is simply called "silk paper."

Ribbed — paper which shows fine parallel ridges on one or both sides of a stamp.

India — a soft, silky appearing wove paper, usually used for proof impressions.

Double Paper — as patented by Charles F. Steel, this style of paper consists of two layers, a thin surface paper and a thicker backing paper. Double paper was supposed to be an absolute safeguard against cleaning cancellations off stamps to permit reuse, for any attempt to remove the cancellation would result in the destruction of the upper layer. The Continental Bank Note Co. experimented with this paper in the course of printing Scott 156-165. See "Rotary Press Double Paper."

China Clay Paper — See note preceding Scott 331.

Fluorescent or Bright Paper — See "Luminescence."

Rotary Press Double Paper — Rotary press printings occasionally are found on a double sheet of paper. The web (roll) of paper used on these press must be continuous. Therefore, any break in the web during the process of manufacture must be lapped and pasted. The overlapping portion, when printed upon, is known as a "double paper" variety. More recently, the lapped ends are joined with colored or transparent adhesive tape.

Such results of splicing normally are removed from the final printed material, although some slip through quality control efforts.

In one instance known, two splices have been made, thus leaving three thicknesses of paper. All rotary press stamps may exist on double paper.

Watermarks — Closely allied to the study of paper, watermarks normally are formed in the process of paper manufacture. Watermarks used on U.S. items consist of the letters "USPS" (found on postage stamps). "USPOD" (found on postal cards), the Seal of the United States (found on official seals), "USIR" (found on revenue items), and various monograms of letters, numbers, and so on, found on stamped envelopes.

The letters may be single- or double-lined and are formed from dies made of wire or cut from metal and soldered to the frame on which the pulp is caught or to a roll under which it is passed. The action of these dies is similar to the wires causing the prominent lines of laid paper, with the designs making thin places in the paper which show by more easily transmitting light.

The best method of detecting watermarks is to lay the stamp face down on a dark tray and immerse the stamp in a commercial brand of watermark fluid, which brings up the watermark in dark lines against a lighter background.

Note: This method of detecting watermarks may damage certain stamps printed with inks that run when immersed (such a U.S. Scott 1260 and 1832). It is advisable to first test a damaged stamp of the same type, if possible.

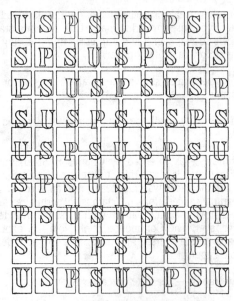

Wmk. 191
PERIOD OF USE
Postage: 1895-1910   Revenue: none

In the 1895-1903 U.S. issues, the paper was fed through the press so that the watermark letter read horizontally on 400 subject sheets and vertically on 200 subject sheets.

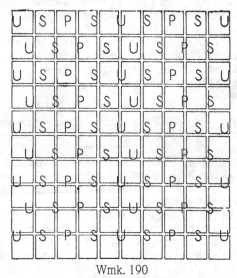

Wmk. 190
PERIOD OF USE
Postage: 1910-1916   Revenue: 1914

USIR
Wmk. 191R
PERIOD OF USE
Postage (unintentionally): 1895   Revenue: 1878-1958
(Scott 271a, 272a), 1951 (832b)

Paper watermarked "USPOD" was used for postal cards from 1873 to 1875. For watermarks used on stamped envelopes, see Envelope Section in the text.

Watermarks may be found normal, reversed, inverted, inverted reversed and sideways, as seen from the back of the stamp.

Stitch Watermark — a type of watermark consisting of a row of short parallel lines. This is caused by the stitches which join the ends of the band on which the paper pulp is first formed. Stitch watermarks have been found on a great many issues, and may exist on all.

GRILLS

The grill consists of small square pyramids in parallel rows, impressed or embossed on the stamp. The object of the process is to break the fibers of the paper so that the ink from the cancellation would soak into the paper and make washing for reuse impossible. Grill impressions, when viewed from the face of the stamp, may be either "points up" or "points down." This process was used on U.S. Scott 79-101, 112-122 and 134-144 as well as some examples of 156-165 and 178-179.

Regular Grill   Continuous Marginal Grill   Split Grill

Continuous Marginal Grill — includes continuous rows of grill points impressed by the untrimmed parts of the ends of the grill rollers, noted as "end roller grill" on the 1870 and 1873 issues, and those grills which came from a continuous band lengthwise of the roller.

Split Grill — situation on a stamp showing portions of two or more grills, caused by a sheet being fed under the grill roller off center.

Double (or Triple) Grill — stamp showing two or more separate grill impressions. This is not to be confused with a split grill, which shows two or four partial impressions from a single grill impression.

Rotary Grills — grilled appearance occasionally found on rotary press printings that was produced unintentionally by a knurled roller during the perforating process.

Similarly, grill-like impressions can be left on stamps dispensed from vending machines.

SEPARATION

"Separation" is the general term used to describe methods used to separate stamps. The standard forms currently in use in the United States are perforating and die-cutting. These methods are done during the stamp production process, after printing. Sometimes these methods are done on-press or sometimes as a separate step. The earliest issues, such as the 1847 5¢ Franklin (Scott 1), did not have any means provided for separation. It was expected the stamps would be cut apart with scissors or folded and torn. These are examples of imperforate stamps. Many stamps were first issued in imperforate formats and were later issued with perforations. Therefore, care must be observed in buying single imperforate stamps to be certain they were issued imperforate and are not perforated copies that have been altered by having the perforations trimmed away. Stamps issued imperforate usually are valued as singles. However, imperforate varieties of normally perforated stamps should be collected in pairs or larger pieces as indisputable evidence of their imperforate character.

PERFORATIONS

The chief style of separation of U.S. stamps has been perforating. This is produced by cutting away the paper between the stamps in a line of holes (usually round) and leaving little bridges of paper between the stamps. These little bridges are the "teeth" of the perforation and, of course, project from the stamp when it is torn from the pane.

As the gauge of the perforation often is the distinguishing difference among stamps, it is necessary to measure and describe them by a gauge number. The standard for this measurement is the number of such teeth within two centimeters. Thus, we say that a stamp is perforated 12 or 10½ to note that there are either 12 or 10½ teeth counted within two centimeters.

Some later U.S. stamps are "stroke" perforated rather than "line" perforated. While it is difficult to tell the difference on a single stamp, with a block of four or more stamps the difference is more easily seen where the horizontal and vertical perforations cross. On the "stroke"-perforated items, the crossing point is clean and no holes are out of line. On the "line"-perforated stamps, the crossing point only rarely is perfect and generally there is a roughness.

Perforation Gauge — tool for measuring perforation, as described above.

Fine Perforation — perforation with small holes and teeth close together.

Coarse Perforation — perforation with large holes and teeth far apart, frequently irregularly spaced.

Rough Perforation — holes not clean cut, but jagged.

Compound Perforation — normally where perforations at the top and bottom differ from the perforations at the sides of the stamp. In describing compound perforations, the gauge of the top is given first, then the sides.

Some stamps are found where one side will differ from the other three, and in this case the reading will be the top first, then the right side, then the bottom, then the left side.

Double Perforations — often found on early U.S. revenue stamps and occasionally on postage issues, double perforations are applied in error. They do not generally command a premium over catalogue values of properly perforated stamps and are not to be confused with a variety found on occasional rotary press printings where stamps adjacent to the center gutters will show the entire width of the gutter and a line of perforations on the far end of the gutter. These are caused by the sheet having been cut off center and are called "gutter snipes." They command a small premium.

Many double perforations were privately made to increase the value of the stamp, and are to be considered damaged stamps.

Electric Eye — an electronically controlled mechanical device acting as a guide in the operation of the perforating machine. Positive identification of stamps perforated by the electric eye process may be made by means of the distinctive marks in the gutters and mar-

gins of the full sheets on the printed web of paper. The original marks consisted of a series of heavy dashes dividing the vertical sheet gutter between the left and right panes (illustration A), together with a single line (margin line, illustration B), in the right sheet margin at the end of the horizontal sheet gutter between the upper and lower panes.

They first were used in 1933 on 400-subject plates for Scott 634, which was distributed to post offices in 1935 (used were plates 21149-50 and 21367-68). On these plates the plate numbers were placed opposite the ends of the third row of stamps from the top or bottom of the full sheet.

In later experiments, the margin line was broken into closely spaced thin vertical lines. Then it was again returned to its original form, but somewhat narrower.

In 1939, the Bureau of Engraving and Printing installed a new perforating machine which required a different layout to operate the centering mechanism. The vertical dashes remained the same, but the margin line was removed from the right sheet margin and a corresponding line ("gutter bar," illustration C) was placed in the left sheet margin at the end of the horizontal sheet gutter. Additional horizontal lines ("frame bars," illustration D) were added in the left sheet margin opposite the top frame line of the adjacent stamp design of all horizontal rows except the upper horizontal row of each left pane, where the frame bar is omitted. The plate numbers were moved back to their normal positions adjoining the corner stamps. Plates for the two types of machines could not be interchanged.

Later in 1939 a "convertible" plate was employed, consisting of a combination of the two previous layouts, the current one with the addition of a margin line (B) in its former position in the right sheet margin, thus making the perforation possible on either machine.

Originally laid out as 400-subject plates, electric eye plates were later used for 200-subject horizontal or vertical format (commemorative, special delivery and airpost issues), 280-subject (Famous Americans and those with similar formats) and 180- and 360-subject plates (booklet panes of definitives, airpost, postal savings and war savings issues).

In laying out the plates for the 400-subject and 200-subject horizontal format issues, the marks retained the same relative position to the stamp designs. This was changed, however, in entering the design for the stamps of the 200-subject vertical format and 280-subject issues because the stamp designs were turned 90 degrees. That is, the designs were entered on the plates with the longer dimension horizontal. Although the electric eye marks were entered on the plates in the usual positions, on the printed sheet they appear as though shifted 90 degrees when the stamps are held in the customary upright position.

Thus a "horizontal" mark on a 400-subject or 200-subject horizontal format sheet would become a "vertical" mark on a 200-subject vertical format or 280-subject sheet. This situation has caused confusion among collectors and dealers in determining a definite description of the various marks. The designation of the position of the plate numbers also has not been uniform for the "turned" designs.

To solve this confusion, the Bureau Issues Association adopted a standard terminology for all the marks appearing on the electric eye sheets. Dashes (A), Margin Line (B), Gutter Bar (C) and Frame Bars (D), whereby each type of mark may be identified readily without referring to its plate number position. The plate number designation of the panes will continue to be established by holding the pane of stamps with the designs in an upright position; the corner of the pane on which the plate number appears will determine the pane is upper left, upper right, lower left, or lower right.

DIE CUTTING

The other major form of U.S. stamp separation is die-cutting. This is a method where a die in the pattern of separation is created that later cuts the stamp paper in a stroke motion. This process is used for self-adhesive postage stamps. Die-cutting can appear in straight lines, such as U.S. Scott 2522; shapes, such as U.S. Scott 1551; or imitating the appearance of perforations, such as U.S. Scott 2920.

On stamps where the die cutting is unintentionally omitted, the terms "die cutting omitted" or "imperforate" may be used interchangeably.

GUM

The Illustrated Gum Chart in the first part of this introduction shows and defines various types of gum condition. Because gum condition has an important impact on the value of unused stamps, we recommend studying this chart and the accompanying text carefully.

The gum on the back of a stamp may be shiny, dull, smooth, rough, dark, white, colored or tinted. Most stamp gumming adhesives use gum arabic or dextrine as a base. Certain polymers such as polyvinyl alcohol (PVA) have been used extensively since World War II.

The *Scott Standard Postage Stamp Catalogue* does not list items by types of gum. The *Scott Specialized Catalogue of United States Stamps* does differentiate among some types of gum for certain issues.

As collectors generally prefer unused stamps with original gum, many unused stamps with no gum have been regummed to make them more desirable (and costly) to collectors who want stamps with full original gum. Some used stamps with faint cancels have had these cancels chemically removed and have been regummed. Skillful regumming can be difficult to detect, particularly on imperforate stamps. Certification of such stamps by competent authorities is suggested.

Reprints of stamps may have gum differing from the original issues. In addition, some countries have used different gum formulas for different seasons. These adhesives have different properties that may become more apparent over time.

Many stamps have been issued without gum, and the catalogue will note this fact. See United States Scott PR33-PR56.

LUMINESCENCE

Kinds of Luminescence — Fluorescence and phosphorescence, two different luminescent qualities, are found in U.S. postage stamps and postal stationery. While all luminescent stamps glow when exposed to short-wave ultraviolet (UV) light, only those with phosphorescent properties display brief afterglow when the UV light source is extinguished.

Fluorescent or "Hi-Bright" Papers — The Bureau of Engraving and Printing, at one point accepting paper for the printing of stamps without regard to fluorescent properties, unknowingly used a mix of paper with infinitely varying amounts of fluorescent optical brighteners added during the papermaking process. In March 1964, to preserve uniformity of product and as a safeguard for an emerging but still incomplete plan for nationwide use of luminescent stamps, BEP purchasing specifications were amended to limit the use of fluorescent paper brighteners. The amended specification permitted paper with some brightener content, but excluded brilliantly glowing papers known in the printing trade as "hi-bright."

Stamps printed on such papers emit a distinctive, intense whitish-violet glow when viewed with either long or short-wave UV. In following years, stamps were produced on papers with lower levels of fluorescence permitted by amended specifications.

Tagged Stamps — The Post Office Department (now the U.S. Postal Service) field-tested automated mail-handling equipment to face, cancel and sort mail at rates up to 30,000 pieces an hour, by sensing UV-light-activated afterglow from phosphorescent substances. For the first tests at Dayton, Ohio, started after August 1, 1963, the 8-cent carmine airpost stamp (Scott C64a) was overprinted (tagged) with a so-called "nearly-invisible" calcium silicate compound which phosphoresces orange-red when exposed to short-wave UV. A facer-canceler, with modifications that included a rapidly cycling on-off UV light, activated the phosphor-tagged airpost stamps and extracted envelopes bearing them from the regular flow of mail.

While the airpost extraction test was still in progress, the entire printing of the City Mail Delivery commemorative (Scott 1238) was ordered tagged with a yellow-green glowing zinc orthosilicate compound intended for use with the automated recognition circuits to be tested with surface transported letter mail.

After the first-day ceremonies October 26, 1963, at Washington, D.C., it was learned the stamps had been tagged to publicize the innovative test by coupling tagging with stamps memorializing "100 years of postal progress" and to provide the first national distribution of tagged stamps for collectors. Between October 28 and November 2, to broaden the scope of the test in the Dayton area, the 4-cent and 5-cent denominations of the regular issue then in use were issued with the same green glowing compound applied in an experimental tagging format (Scott 1036b, 1213b, 1213c, and 1229a).

By June 1964, testing had proven sufficiently effective for the Post Office Department to order all 8-cent airpost adhesive stamps phosphor-tagged for general distribution. By January 1966, all airpost stamps, regardless of denomination, were ordered tagged. Meanwhile, from 1963 through 1965, limited quantities of the Christmas issues were tagged for use in the continuing test in the Dayton area on the use of tagging to automatically position (face) and cancel mail. (Scott 1240a, 1254a-1257a, and 1276a).

On May 19, 1966, the use of phosphor-tagged stamps was expanded to the Cincinnati Postal Region, which then included offices in Ohio, Kentucky and Indiana. During the last half of 1966, primarily to meet postal needs of that region, phosphor-tagged issues were authorized to include additional denominations of regular issues, some postal stationery, and about 12 percent of each commemorative issue starting with the National Park Service 5-cent issue (Scott 1314a) and continuing through the Mary Cassatt 5-cent commemorative (Scott 1322a). After January 1, 1967, most regular values through the 16-cent, all commemoratives, and additional items of postal stationery were ordered tagged.

Adhesive stamps precanceled by the Bureau of Engraving and Printing (Bureau precancels), however, were not tagged, with the exception of Scott 1394, 1596, 1608, and 1610. Because there was no need to cancel mail with these stamps and since precancel permit holders post such mail already faced, postal officials by-passed facer-canceler operations and avoided the cost of tagging.

Overall phosphorescent overprints, when newly issued, are practically invisible in ordinary light. After aging three to five years, the tagging can discolor and become more easily visible. When viewed with UV light, there is little change in the hue of either orange-red or yellow-green emitted light. Even though observable discoloration exists, the presence or absence of tagging is best determined by examination with UV light.

Bar, or block, tagging, instead of the usual overall phosphorescent overprint, was used for some stamps beginning with the Andreotti-printed Mail Order Business commemorative (Scott 1468). These are much easier to identify than the overall overprint, often without need for a UV light.

Band tagging, a bar extending across two or more stamps, was first used with Scott 1489-1498.

Beginning in the 1990s, many stamps are printed on prephosphored paper. Unlike overall tagging, in which the tagging substance is applied to the entire stamp after it is printed, prephosphored paper has the tagging substance added to the surface of the paper during the paper-making process, before printing occurs.

In the late 1990s, some stamps appeared with the tagging formed in the shape of the stamp design elements.

Most of the luminescent issues exist with the luminescent coating unintentionally omitted.

In some postal stationery, such as Scott U551, UC40, UX48a, and UX55, the luminescent element is in the ink with which the stamp design is printed. The luminescent varieties of stamp envelopes Scott U550 and UC37 were made by adding a vertical phosphorescent bar or panel at left of the stamp. On Scott UC42, this "glow-bar" passes through the tri-globe design.

The *Scott Specialized Catalogue of U.S. Stamps and Covers* lists different tagging types when more than one type is known on a stamp. Currently, these types can be large or small block tagging, overall tagging and prephosphored paper. Prephosphored paper is further broken down into two types, each listed separately. It can have a "mottled tagging" appearance, which results from the application of the tagging substance to uncoated paper, or it can have a "solid tagging" appearance, either absolutely uniform or just slightly "grainy." The solid tagging appearance results from the application of the tagging substance to coated paper. Information in the catalogue reflects the most recent findings. Research on tagging is ongoing.

NOTE: Users of UV light should avoid prolonged exposure, which can burn the eyes. Sunglasses (particularly those that feature a "UV block") or prescription eyeglasses, tinted or plain, screen the rays and provide protection.

POSTAL MARKINGS

Postal markings are those marks placed by postal employees of this and other countries on the stamp or cover or both. These marks may indicate the mailing place of a letter, date, rate, route, accounting between post offices, and so on.

In addition to the basis town designations, there are many varieties of supplemental markings. Among these are rate marks, route marks, obliterators, special dating markings usually found on advertised or dead letter covers, transportation markings (rail, steam, ship, airpost, etc.), and service markings (advertised, forwarded, missent, second delivery, mail route, too late, charged, paid box, due, returned for postage, soldier's letter, held for postage, short paid, unpaid, not paid, paid, free, dead letter office, etc.).

These markings originated, for material mailed in what is now the United States, in the Colonial period when manuscript postal markings were first introduced under the Ordinance of December 10, 1672, of New York, which established an inland postal system between the colonies. A "Post Payd" is found on the first letter ever sent under the system, on January 22, 1673. Manuscript postal markings continued in use right through the pre-stamp period and even can be found on some letters today.

The earliest handstamp associated with the American service is a "NEW/YORK" blank handstamp found on letters conveyed via the Bristol Packet line in 1710-12 between New York and England. Following the demise of this operation, the first regular handstamp postal markings were introduced at New York in 1756, when a post office packet service was established between Falmouth, England, and New York. The marking merely was "NEW YORK" on two lines of type. The marking (see illustration), with each word of the city name on a separate line, is represented in presentations such as this as "NEW/YORK." Similar markings were later introduced at other towns, such as ANNA/POLIS, by 1766; CHARLES/TOWN, by 1770; PHILA/DELPHIA, by 1766; HART/FORD, by 1766; while other offices received a single line marking: BOSTON, by 1769; ALBANY, by 1773; PENSACOLA, by 1772; SAVANNA, by 1765, BALTIMORE, by 1772, and WMS-BURG, by 1770.

Some of these early letters also bear a circular date stamp containing the month in abbreviated form, i.e., "IV" for June and "IY" for July, and the date in a 14-17mm circle. Known from at least nine towns, these are called "Franklin marks" after Benjamin Franklin, then deputy postmaster general for the English crown. The marks also are known as "American Bishopmarks" to distinguish them from the Bishopmark used in England, which has a center line.

First U.S. Handstamp   Franklin Mark

During 1774-1775, an American provisional postal system was established in opposition to that of the English crown. Both manuscript and handstamp markings have been attributed to it. This system was taken over by Congress on July 26, 1775, and the same markings were continued in use. The earliest reported

Congressional marks are a manuscript "Camb Au 8" and a blue-green straightline "NEW*YORK*AU*24." Postal markings are known throughout the Revolution, including English occupation markings. Most are manuscript.

In the post-war Confederation period, handstamped circular markings were introduced at Charleston, South Carolina, in 1778-1780, and later at New London, Connecticut. Straightlines and manuscripts continued to dominate until the use of oval markings became widespread about 1800, with circles becoming the predominant markings shortly thereafter.

Handstamp rate markings are known as early as the 1789 penny-weight markings of Albany. Such types of markings became more common in the 1830's and almost the standard by the "5" and "10"-cent rate period which began on July 1, 1845. This period also is when envelopes began to replace folded letter sheets. Before that date, envelopes were charged with an extra rate of postage. These "5," "10," and succeeding "3," "6," "5," and "10" rates of 1851-56 were common on domestic mail until prepayment became compulsory April 1, 1855, on all but drop or local letters domestically. The markings were common on foreign mail through about 1875.

Only 1.3 percent of all letters posted between 1847 and 1852 bore stamps. This proportion increased to 25 percent in 1852, 32 percent in 1853, 34 percent in 1854, 40 percent in 1855, and 64 percent in 1856. Stampless covers are commonplace, although there are some which are highly prized on the basis of their markings. Most are more common than stamped covers of the same period.

While the government began issuing handstamps as early as 1799 and obliterators in 1847, many postmasters were required, or at least permitted, to purchase their own canceling devices or to use pen strokes. Pen cancellations continued to be common in the smaller offices into the 1880's. Because of collector prejudice against pen-canceled stamps, many have ended up being "cleaned" (having the pen cancel removed). These are sold either as unused or with a different, faked cancellation to cover the evidence of cleaning. Ultraviolet light (long-wave) usually will reveal traces of the original pen markings.

From around 1850 until 1900, many postmasters used obliterators cut from wood or cork. Many bear fanciful designs, such as bees, bears, chickens, locks, eagles, Masonic symbols, flags, numerals and so on. Some of the designs symbolized the town of origin. These are not listed in this Catalogue, for they owe their origin to the whim of some individual rather than a requirement of the postal regulations. Many command high prices and are eagerly sought by collectors. This has led to extensive forgery of such markings so that collectors are advised to check them carefully.

Rapid machine cancellations were introduced at Boston in 1880-90 and later spread across the country. Each of the various canceling machine types had identifiable characteristics and collectors form collections based on type. One sub-specialty is that of flag cancellations. While handstamp flag designs are known earlier, the first machine flag cancellation was that of Boston in November-December 1894.

Specialists have noted that different canceling inks are used at different times, depending partly on the type of canceling device used. Rubber handstamps, prohibited in 1893 although used for parcel post and precanceling after that date, require a different type of ink from the boxwood or type-metal cancelers of the classic period, while a still different ink is used for the steel devices of the machine cancels.

Registry of letters was first authorized in this country in the Dutch colony of New Netherland on overseas mail. Records of valuable letters were kept by postmasters throughout the stampless period while an "R" marking was introduced at Philadelphia in 1845 for "recorded" mail. Cincinnati also had such a "recorded" system. The first appearance of the word "registered" appears on mail in November 1847, in manuscript, and in handstamp in May 1850. The official registration for U.S. mail, however, did not begin until July 1, 1855.

In recent years, the handstamped and machine types of cancellations have been standardized by the Post Office Department and its successor and supplied to the various post offices.

Postmarks — markings to indicate the office of origin or manner of postal conveyance. In general terms, the postmark refers to the post office of origin, but sometimes there also are receiving postmarks of the post office of destination or of transit. Other post office markings include: advertised, forwarded, mail route, missent, paid, not paid, second delivery, too late, etc. Postmarks often serve to cancel postage stamps with or without additional obliterating cancels.

Cancellations — postal markings which make further use of the postage stamps impossible. As used in the listings in this Catalogue, cancellations include both postmarks used as cancellations and obliterations intended primarily to cancel (or "kill") the stamp.

Carrier Postmarks — usually show the words "Carrier" "City Delivery," or "U.S.P.O. Dispatch." They were applied to letters to indicate the delivery of mail by U.S. Government carriers. These markings should not be confused with those of local posts or other private mail services which used postmarks of their own. Free delivery of city mail by carriers was begun on July 1, 1863.

Free — handstamp generally used on free, franked mail. The marking occasionally is seen on early adhesives of the United States used as a canceling device.

Railroad Postmarks — usually handstamps, the markings were used to postmark unpouched mail received by route agents of the Post Office Department traveling on trains on railway mail route. The route name in an agent's postmark often was similar to the name of the railroad or included the terminals of the route. The earliest known use of the word "Railroad" as a postmark is 1838. Route agents gradually became R.P.O. clerks and some continued to use their handstamps after the route agent service ceased June 30, 1882. The railroad postmarks of the 1850 period and later usually carried the name of the railroad.

A sub-group of railroad postmarks is made up of those applied in the early days by railroad station agents, using the railroad's ticket dating handstamp as a postmark. Sometimes the station agent was also the postmaster.

In 1864, the Post Office Department equipped cars for the general distribution of mails between Chicago and Clinton, Iowa.

Modern railroad marks, such as "R.P.O." (Railway Mail Service) is a mark indicating transportation by railroad, and includes Railway Post Office, Terminal Railway Post Office, Transfer Office, Closed Mail Service, Air Mail Field, and Highway Post Office.

Effective November 1, 1949, the Railway Mail Service was merged with others of like nature under the consolidated title Postal Transportation Service (PTS). The service was discontinued June 30, 1977.

The modern "railway marks" are quite common and are not the types referred to under cancellations as listed in the Catalogue.

Way Markings — Way letters are those received by a mail carrier on his way between post offices and delivered at the first post office he reached. The postmaster ascertained where the carrier received them and charged, in his postbills, the postage from those places to destination. He wrote "Way" against those charges in his bills and also wrote or stamped "Way" on each letter. If the letter was exempt from postage, it should have been marked "Free."

The term "mail carrier" above refers to any carrier under contract to carry U.S. mail: a stage line, a horseback rider, or a steamboat or railroad that did not have a route agent on board. Only unpouched mail (not previously placed in a post office) was eligible for a Way fee of one cent. The postmaster paid this fee to the carrier, if demanded, for the carrier's extra work of bringing the letter individually to the post office. For a limited time at certain post offices, the Way fee was added to the regular postage. This explains the use of a numeral with the "Way" marking.

Packet Markings — Packet markings listed in this Catalogue are those applied on a boat traveling on inland or coastal waterways. This group does not include mail to foreign countries that contains the words "British Packet," "American Packet," etc, or their abbreviations. These are U.S. foreign-mail exchange-office markings.

Listed packet markings are in two groups: 1) waterways route-agent markings which denote service exactly the same as that of the railroad route-agent markings, except that the route agent traveled on a boat instead of a train; 2) name-of-boat markings placed on the cover to advertise the boat or, as some believe, to expedite payment of Way and Steam fees at the post office where such letters entered the U.S. mails.

Occasionally waterways route-agent markings included the name of a boat, or "S.B.," "STEAMBOAT," or merely a route number. Such supplemental designations do not alter the character of the markings as those of a route-agent.

19th Century U.S. Express Mail Postmarks — In pre-stamp days these represented either an extra-fast mail service or mail under the care of an express-mail messenger who also carried out-of-mail-express packages. The service was permitted as a practical means of competing with package express companies that also carried mail in competition with the U.S. Mail. Several of these early postmarks were later used by U.S. Mail route agents on the New York-Boston and New York-Albany runs, or by U.S. steamboat letter carriers on the coastal run between Boston and St. John, New Brunswick.

Steamboat or **Steam Markings** — Except for the circular markings "Maysville Ky. Steam" and "Terre Haute Stb." and the rectangular "Troy & New York Steam Boat," these markings contain only the word "STEAMBOAT" or "STEAM," with or without a rating numeral. They represent service the same as that of Way markings, except that the carrier was an inland or coastal steamer that had no contract to carry U.S. mails. Such boats, however, were required by law to carry to the nearest post office any mail given them at landings. The boat owner was paid a two-cent fee for each letter so delivered, except on Lake Erie where the fee was one-cent. At some post offices, the Steamboat fee was added to regular postage. In 1861, the two-cent fee was again added to the postage, and in 1863 double postage was charged.

Ship Postmarks — postal markings indicating arrival on a private ship (one not under contract to carry mail). This marking was applied to letters delivered by such ships to the post office at their port of entry as required by law, for which they received a fee and the letter were taxed with a specified fee for the service in place of the ordinary open postage.

The use of U.S. postage stamps on ship letters is unusual, except for letters from Hawaii, because the U.S. inland postage on ship letters from a foreign point did not need to be prepaid. "U.S. SHIP" is a special marking applied to mail posted on naval vessels, especially during the Civil War period.

Steamship Postmarks — akin to Ship postmarks, but they appear to have been used mostly on mail from Caribbean or Pacific ports to New Orleans or Atlantic ports carried on steamships having a U.S. mail contract. An associated numeral usually designates the through rate from where the letter was received by the ship to its inland destination.

Receiving Mark — impression placed on the back of envelopes by the receiving post office to indicate the name of the office and date of arrival. It also is known as a "backstamp." Generally discontinued about 1913, the marking was employed for a time on air mail service until it was found the practice slowed the service. The markings now are used on registry and special delivery mail.

Miscellaneous Route Markings — wordings associated with the previously described markings include Bay Route, River Mail, Steamer, Mail Route, etc. Classification of the marking ordinarily is evident from the usage, or it can be identified from publications on postal markings.

U.S. Foreign-Mail Exchange-Office Markings — These served to meet the accounting requirements of the various mail treaties before the Universal Postal Union was established. The markings usually designate the exchange office or the carrier (British Packet, Bremen Packet, American Packet, etc.). Sometimes these markings are a restatement of the through rate, or a numeral designating the amount credited or debited to the foreign country as a means of allocating the respective parts of the total postage, according to conditions of route, method of transit, weight, etc.

Gridiron Cancellation — commonest types of cancellations on early U.S. stamps. The markings consist of circles enclosing parallel lines. There are, however, many varieties of grid cancellations.

Paid Markings — generally consist of the word "PAID," sometimes within a frame, indicating regular postage prepaid by the sender of a letter. They are found as separate handstamps, within town or city postmarks, and as a part of obliterating cancels. In each case, the "paid" marking may be used with or without an accompany or combined rate numeral indication.

Precancels — stamps having the cancellation applied before the article is presented for mailing. The purpose is to reduce handling and speed up the mails. A permit is required for use by the public, except for special cases, such as the experiments using Scott 1384a, 1414a-1418a, or 1552 for Christmas mail. Normally the precanceling is done with devices not used for ordinary postal service. Most precancellations consist of the city and state names between two lines or bars.

Precancels are divided into two groups: locals and Bureaus. Locals are printed, usually from 100-subject plates, or handstamped, usually by means of a 10- or 25-subject device having a rubber, metal or vinyl surface, at the town using the stamps. Most locals are made with devices furnished by the Postal Service, but a number have been made with devices created in the city using them. Early locals include the printed "PAID" or "paid" on Scott 7 and 9, "CUMBERLAND, ME." on Scott 24-26 and the Glen Allen, Virginia stars.

Many styles of precancellation are known. More than 600,000 different precancels exist from more than 20,000 post offices in the United States.

The Bureaus, or Bureau Prints, are precancels furnished to the post offices by the Post Office Department in Washington. For 75 years these were printed by the Bureau of Engraving and Printing, hence the name "Bureaus." In late 1991, the American Bank Note Co. and J.W. Fergusson and Sons for Stamp Venturers also began producing precanceled stamps under contract with the Postal Service. Other companies have followed. Since the stamps go to the local post office from the same source, the Postal Service, and the method of production is essentially the same as used by the BEP, the term "Bureau precancel" has been retained in this catologue. The cancellations consist of the name of the city and state where the stamps are to be used, lines or the class of mail. They originated in 1916 when postal officials were seeking ways to reduce costs as well as increase the legibility of the overprint. The BEP was low bidder in three cities, which resulted in the "experimentals." These 16 denominations, including two postage dues, were issued for Augusta, Maine (one value); Springfield, Massachusetts (14 values); and New Orleans (six values) in quanities ranging from 4,000,000 down to 10,000. Electrotype plates mounted on a flat bed press were used to print the precancellations.

Regular production of Bureau Prints began on May 2, 1923, with Scott 581 precanceled "New York, N.Y." All regular Bureaus until 1954 were produced by the Stickney rotary press, whereby the stamps, immediately after printing, pass under the precanceling plates. Then the roll is gummed, perforated and cut into sheets or coils. Since 1954, a variety of printing methods have been used.

Precancels are listed in the Catalogue only if the precanceled stamp is different from the nonprecanceled version (untagged stamps such as Scott 1582a); or, if the stamp only exists precanceled (Scott 2265). Classical locals and experimental bureaus are also included as cancellations. See Service Indicators.

Service Indicators — inscription included in the design of the stamp to indicate the category of postal service to be rendered. The first regular postage stamp to include a service indicator was the 7.9-cent Drum stamp of the Americana series, which was for bulk rate mailings. This stamp was issued with Bureau precancels for proper usage from 107 cities. Copies without the Bureau precancellation were for philatelic purposes.

A second category of service indicators came about when the USPS began to include the postal service between the lines of the Bureau precancellation. Examples of this group are "Bulk Rate" and "Nonprofit Organization."

Finally, with the 16.7-cent Transportation coil (Scott 2261), issued July 7, 1988, the USPS went back to including the service indicator in the design with the indicator serving as the cancellation. With the precancellation now part of the design, the USPS stopped offering tagged versions of the stamps for collectors.

In all cases, the "service indicator" stamp does not normally receive an additional cancellation when used for the indicated service. For examples see Postal Markings - Bureau Precancels.

Tied On — when the cancellation (or postmark) extends from the stamp to the envelope.

Postal Markings, Cancellations Examples

Numerals
Values are for rating marks such as those illustrated. Later types of numerals in grids targets, etc., are common.

The common Boston Paid cancellation
(Values are for types other than this)

PAID ALL
PAID

STEAMBOAT

SHIP STEAM

FREE

Steamship

Steamboat
(Route agent marking)

Packet Boat
(Name-of-boat marking)

Packet Boat
(Name-of-boat marking)

Packet Boat
(Name-of-boat marking)

Railroad
(Route agent marking)

U.S. Express Mail
(Route agent marking)

(In red on letter to Germany via Prussian Closed Mail, via British Packet. Credits 7 cent to Prussia.)

Carrier

Canadian

Fort

Vera Cruz, Mexico 1914

Express Company

Army Field Post

Town

Year dated

U.S. Postmark used in China

Exposition Station
Used while exposition is open. Many styles.

Exposition advertising.
Used before exposition opens. Many styles.

U.S. Postmark
used in Japan

New York City Foreign Mail — A group of design cancellations used between 1871 and 1877 in New York City on outgoing foreign mail only. This group of handstamps totals about 200 different fancy stars, geometric designs, wheels conventionalized flowers, etc., the majority within a circle 26-29 mm in diameter.

Patent Defacing Cancellations — When adhesive stamps came into general use, the Post Office Department made constant efforts to find a type of cancellation which would make the re-use of the stamp impossible. Many patents were granted to inventors and some of the cancellations (killers) came into more or less general use. Some of them appear in combination with the town postmarks.

About 125 different types are known on the stamps issues up to about 1887. Their principal use and greatest variety occur on Scott 65, 147, 158, 183 and 184.

Patent cancellations generally fall into three groups:

1) Small pins or punches which pierce the paper or depress it sufficiently to break the fiber.

2) Sharp blades or other devices for cutting the paper.

3) Rotation of a portion of the canceler so that part of the paper is scraped away.

1. Dot punches through paper

2. Blades cut the paper

2. Small circle cuts the paper

3. Scraped in the shaded circle

Supplementary Mail — markings which designate the special post office service of dispatching mail after the regular mail closed. Two kinds of supplementary mail were available:

1. Foreign mail. For New York, the postmaster general established in 1853 a fee of double the regular rate. This paid to get the mail aboard ship after the regular mail closing and before sailing time. The service continued until 1939. Postmark Types A, D, E, F, and G were used.

2. Domestic mail. For Chicago, at no extra fee, supplementary mail entitled a letter to catch the last eastbound train. Postmark Types B and C were used. No foreign destination was implied.

Similar service with "Supplementary" in the postmark apparently available in Philadelphia and possibly elsewhere.

Type A   Type D   Type E

Type F
Combination Handstamp
(Also comes with numeral "1")
(Stamps with numeral cancel alone do not qualify for Supplementary Mail cancel premiums.)

Type G (also with other numerals)

Type B   Type C

World War I Soldiers' Letters — At the time the United States declared war against Germany on April 6, 1917, a postal regulation existed which permitted soldiers, sailors and Marines to send letters without prepayment of postage by endorsing them "Soldier letter" and having them countersigned by an officer. The single postage rate would then be collected from the recipient. Few of the enlisted men, however, took advantage of this privilege in sending letters while in the United States and practically all letters sent by soldiers from some 200 World War I military post offices in the United States bear regular postage stamps.

Fig. A

Soon after the arrival of the first units of the American Expeditionary Force in France, this regulation was modified to include letters which although not endorsed, bore the postmark of the United States Army Postal Service. The War Revenue Act of Congress of October 3, 1917, provided free postage for soldiers, sailors and marines assigned to duty overseas.

Therefore, letters from members of the A.E.F. sent before October 1917 without postage stamps were properly charged with postage due, while those sent after that time went through post free.

This provision for free postage did not ordinarily apply to civilians permitted to accompany the army, such as welfare workers, Post Office Department representatives, war correspondents and others. Neither did it apply to the registration fee on soldiers' letters nor to parcel post matter. It was necessary to pay such postage by means of postage stamps.

Fig. B   Fig. C

The first U.S. Army post office, known as an A.P.O., was established at St. Nazaire, France, on July 10, 1917. The A.P.O.'s were at first operated by the Post Office Department, but in May 1918 the Military Express Service was established and the army took over the operation. Later the name was changed to Postal Express Service.

Fig. D   Fig. E

Army post offices were given code numbers and were at first numbered from No. 1 (St. Nazaire) to No. 18 (Saumur). In December 1917, they were renumbered 701, 702, etc., and some 169 A.P.O.'s were established on the Western Front, including offices in Italy, Belgium, Netherlands, Luxembourg, and Germany after the Armistice. Most of the A.P.O.'s were located at fixed places, but "mobile" post offices were assigned to divisions, army corps and armies and were moved from place to place. Many A.P.O.'s had stations or branches, some of which used postmarks with different code numbers from those assigned to the main office.

Until July 1919, all A.E.F. mail was censored, and letters will be found with "company" censor marks (Fig. E) as well as "regimental" censor marks (Fig. F). Distinctive censor marks were used at the base censor's office in Paris (Fig. G).

Fig. F   Fig. G

An interesting variety of subsidiary markings may be found on soldiers' letters: "ADDRESSEE RETURNED TO U.S.A.," "CANNOT BE FOUND," "DECEASED - VERIFIED," "NO RECORD," "SOLDIER'S MAIL," and "UNIT RETURNED TO U.S."

Many styles of stationery were used, mainly those furnished by welfare organizations. Only a few pictorial envelopes were used, but a considerable variety of patriotic and pictorial postcards may be found in addition to officially printed-form postcards.

Fig. H   Fig. I

A postal agency was in operation in Siberia from 1918 to 1920 and distinctive postmarks and censor marks were used there. A few American soldiers were sent to North Russia, and postmarks used there were those of the British Expeditionary Force's North Russia postal service (Fig. I).

World War I postmarks have been classified by collectors and the "American Classification System" prepared by the War Cover Club is in general use by collectors of these items.

World War II — Beginning in January 1941, U.S. post offices were established in Newfoundland, Bermuda and other naval bases acquired as a result of the exchange of destroyers with Great Britain. The names of the bases were at first included in the postmark. Later A.P.O. code numbers were adopted, in a similar manner to A.P.O. numbers were cut out of the postmark so that nothing appears to indicate the A.P.O. at which a letter was mailed, although the already established practice was continued of the writer giving the A.P.O. number in the return address. Early in 1943, A.P.O. numbers were replaced in the postmarks at many military post offices.

More than 1,000 different A.P.O. numbers were used. At least 90 types of postmarks exist, of which 45 are handstamped and 40 machine struck.

The armed services, both at home and abroad, were given the franking privilege early in April 1942, the frank consisting of the written word "Free" in the upper right corner of the envelope.

A wide variety of censor marks was used, differing radically in design from those used in World War I.

Bureau Precancels

AUGUSTA
MAINE

NEW
ORLEANS
LA.

SPRINGFIELD
MASS.

Experimentals

PERU
IND.

LANSING
MICH.

SAINT LOUIS
MO.

New Orleans
La.

San Francisco
Calif.

PORTLAND
ME.

LAKEWOOD
N.J.

KANSAS
CITY
MO.

POUGHKEEPSIE
N.Y.

LONG ISLAND
CITY, N.Y.

CORPUS
CHRISTI
TEXAS

ATLANTA
GEORGIA

ATLANTA
GA.

PEORIA
IL

CINCINNATI
OH

Service Indicators

Blk. Rt.
CAR-RT
SORT

Bulk Rate

Nonprofit
Org.

Nonprofit
Org.

PRESORTED
FIRST-CLASS

ZIP+4

Local Precancels

QUINCY
ILLINOIS

FITCHBURG
MASS.

LOS ANGELES
CALIF.

Fergus Falls
Minn.

COVINGTON
KY.

REDWOOD CITY
CALIF.

BELMONT
CALIF.

ELGIN
ILLINOIS

Electroplates

Ashland
Wis.

PALMYRA
N. Y.

Northhampton
MASS.

DES PLAINES
ILL.

RICHMOND
VA.

BROOKFIELD
ILLINOIS

PAONIA
COLO.

GOSHEN
IND

TOWER CITY
N. DAK.

NEW BRUNSWICK
N. J.

ORLANDO,
FLA.

RICHTON PARK
ILL.

MULINO,
OREG.

PINE HILL
N.Y.

FARRELL,
PA

SACRAMENTO
CA

Handstamps

General Glossary

Scott Publishing Co. uses the following terms in its Catalogues, as appropriate. Definitions follow each term.

Imperforate — stamps without perforations, rouletting, or other form of separation. Self-adhesive stamps are die cut, though they look imperforate.

Type A   Type B

Part-Perforate — Stamps with perforations on the two opposite sides, the other two sides remaining imperforate. See coils.

Vertical Pair, Imperforate Horizontally — (Type A illustrated) indicating that a pair of stamps is fully perforated vertically, but has no horizontal perforations.

Horizontal Pair, Imperforate Vertically — (Type A) indicating that a pair of stamps is fully perforated horizontally but has no vertical perforations.

Vertical Pair, Imperforate Between — (Type B illustrated) indicating that the vertical pair is fully perforated at the top, side and bottom, but has no perforations between the stamps.

Horizontal Pair, Imperforate Between — (Type B) indicating that the horizontal pair is fully perforated at the top, sides, and bottom, but has no perforations between the stamps.
Note: Of the above two types (A and B), Type A is the more common.

Blind Perforations — the slight impressions left by the perforating pins if they fail to puncture the paper. While multiples of stamps showing blind perforations may command a slight premium over normally perforated stamps, they are not imperforate errors. Fakers have removed gum from stamps to make blind perforations less evident.

Diagonal   *Horizontal*   *Vertical*

Bisect — Stamps cut in half so that each portion prepaid postage. These items were used in emergencies where no stamps of the lower denomination were available. These may be diagonal, horizontal or vertical. Listings are for bisects on full covers with the bisected stamp tied to the cover on the cut side. Those on piece or part of a cover sell for considerably less. "Half-stamps" that receive a surcharge or overprint are not considered bisects.
This catalogue does not list unofficial bisects after the 1880's.

Block of Four, Imperforate Within — Examples exist of blocks of four stamps that are perforated on all four outside edges, but lack both horizontal and vertical perforations within the block. Scott 2096c, the Smokey the Bear commemorative, is an example of an

accidental example of this phenomenon. Scott RS173j and RS174j are examples of a situation where internal perforations were omitted intentionally to create 4-cent "stamps" from four 1-cent stamps.

Rouletting — short consecutive cuts in the paper to facilitate separation of the stamps, made with a toothed wheel or disc.

Booklets — Many countries have issued stamps in booklets for the convenience of users. This idea is becoming increasingly popular today in many countries. Booklets have been issued in all sizes and forms, often with advertising on the covers, on the panes of stamps or on the interleaving.

The panes may be printed from special plates or made from regular sheets. All panes from booklets issued by the United States and many from those of other countries are imperforate on three sides, but perforated between the stamps. Any stamplike unit in the pane, either printed or blank, which is not a postage stamp, is considered a *label* in the Catalogue listings. The part of the pane through which stitches or staples bind the booklet together, or which affixes the pane to the booklet cover, is considered to be a *binding stub* or *tab*.

Scott lists and values booklets in this volume. Except for panes from Canal Zone, handmade booklet panes are not listed when they are fashioned from existing sheet stamps and, therefore, are not distinguishable from the sheet-stamp foreign counterparts.

Panes usually do not have a "used" value because there is little market activity in used panes, even though many exist used.

Cancellations — the marks or obliterations put on a stamp by the authorities to show that it has done service and is no longer valid for use. If made with a pen, it is a "pen cancellation." When the location of the post office appears in the cancellation, it is a "town cancellation." When calling attention to a cause or celebration, it is a "slogan cancellation." Many other types and styles of cancellations exist, such as duplex, numerals, targets, etc.

Coil Stamps — stamps issued in rolls for use in dispensers, affixing and vending machines. Those of the United States, and its territories are perforated horizontally or vertically only, with the outer edges imperforate. Coil stamps of some countries, such as Great Britain, are perforated on all four sides.

Commemorative Stamps — Special issues which commemorate some anniversary or event or person. Usually such stamps are used for a limited period concurrently with the regular issue of stamps. Examples of commemorative issues are Scott 230-245, 620-621, 946, 1266, C68, and U218-U221.

Covers — envelopes, with or without adhesive postage stamps, which have passed through the mail and bear postal or other markings of philatelic interest. Before the introduction of envelopes in about 1840, people folded letters and wrote the address on the outside. Many people covered their letters with an extra sheet of paper on the outside for the address, producing the term "cover." Used air letter sheets and stamped envelopes also are considered covers. Stamps on paper used to cover parcels are said to be "on wrapper." ("Wrapper" also is the term used for postal stationery items which were open at both sides and wrapped around newspapers or pamphlets.) Often stamps with high face values are rare on cover, but more common on wrapper. Some stamps and postal stationery items are difficult to find used in the manner for which they were intended, but quite common when used to make philatelic items such as flight or first day covers. High face-value stamps also may be more common on package address tags. See postal cards.

Error — stamps having some unintentional major deviation from the normal. Errors include, but are not limited to, mistakes in color, paper, or watermark, inverted centers or frames on multicolor printing, missing color or inverted or double surcharges or overprints, imperforates and part-perforates, and double impressions. A factually wrong or misspelled inscription, if it appears on all examples of a stamp, even if corrected late, is not classified as a philatelic error.

First Day Cover — A philatelic term to designate the use of a certain stamp (on cover) or postal stationery item on the first day of sale at a place officially designated for such sale or so postmarked. Current U.S. stamps may have such a postal marking applied considerably after the actual issue date.

Gum Breaker Ridges — Colorless marks across the backs of some rotary press stamps, impressed during manufacture to prevent curling. Many varieties of "gum breaks" exist.

Original Gum — A stamp is described as "O.G." if it has the original gum as applied when printed. Some are issued without gum, such as Scott 730, 731, 735, 752, etc; government reproductions, such as Scott 3 and 4; and official reprints.

Overprinted and Surcharged Stamps — Overprinting is a wording or design placed on stamps to alter the place of use (e.g., "Canal Zone" on U.S. stamps), to adapt them for a special purpose ("I.R." on 1-cent and 2-cent U.S. stamps of the 1897-1903 regular issue for use as revenue stamps. Scott R153-R155A) or for a special occasion (U.S. Scott 646-648).

Surcharge is an overprint which changes or restates the face value of the item.

Surcharges and overprints may be handstamped, typeset or, occasionally, lithographed or engraved. A few hand-written overprints and surcharges are known. The world's first surcharge was a handstamped "2" on the United States City Despatch Post stamps of 1846.

Postal Cards — cards that have postage printed on them. Ones without printed stamps are referred to as "postcards."

Proofs and Essays — Proofs are impressions taken from an approved die, plate or stone in which the design and color are the same as the stamp issued to the public. Trial color proofs are impressions taken from approved dies, plates or stones in varying colors. An essay is the impression of a design that differs in some way from the stamp as issued.

Provisionals — stamps issued on short notice and intended for temporary use pending the arrival of regular (definitive) issues. They usually are issued to meet such contingencies as changes in government or currency, shortage of necessary values, or military occupation.

In the 1840's, postmasters in certain American cities issued stamps that were valid only at specific post offices. Postmasters of the Confederate States also issued stamps with limited validity. These are known as "postmaster's provisionals." See U.S. Scott 9X1-9X3 and Confederate States Scott 51X1.

Se-Tenant — joined, referring to an unsevered pair, strip or block of stamps differing in design, denomination or overprint. See U.S. Scott 2158a.

Tete Beche — A pair of stamps in which one is upside down in relation to the other. Some of these are the result of international sheet arrangements, i.e. Morocco Scott B10-B11. Others occurred when one or more electrotypes accidentally were placed upside down on the plate. See Hawaii Scott 21a and 22a. Separation of the stamps, of course, destroys the tete beche variety.

Specimens — One of the regulations of the Universal Postal Union requires member nations to send samples of all stamps they put into service to the International Bureau in Switzerland. Member nations, of the UPU receive these specimens as samples of what stamps are valid for postage. Many are overprinted, handstamped or initial-perforated "Specimen," "Canceled" or "Muestra." Stamps distributed to government officials or for publicity purposes, and stamps submitted by private security printers for official approval also may receive such defacements.

These markings prevent postal use, and all such items generally are known as "specimens." There is a section in this volume devoted to this type of material. U.S. officials with "specimen" overprints and printings are listed in the Special Printings section.

Territorial and Statehood Dates

	Territorial Date	Statehood Date	
Alabama	Aug. 15, 1817	Dec. 14, 1819	Territory by Act of March 3, 1817, effective Aug. 15, 1817.
Alaska	Oct. 18, 1867	Jan. 3, 1959	A district from Oct. 18, 1867, until it became an organized territory Aug. 24, 1912.
Arizona	Feb. 24, 1863	Feb. 14, 1912	This region was sometimes called Arizona before 1863 though still in the Territory of New Mexico.
Arkansas	July 5, 1819*	June 15, 1836	The territory was larger than the state. After statehood, the left-over area to the west had post offices that continued for some years to use an Arkansas abbreviation in the postmarks although really they were in the "Indian Country."
California		Sept. 9, 1850	Ceded by Mexico by the Treaty of Guadalupe-Hidalgo, concluded Feb. 2, 1848, and proclaimed July 4, 1848. From then until statehood, California had first a military government until Dec. 20, 1849, and then a local civil government. It never had a territorial form of government.
Colorado	Feb. 28, 1861	Aug. 1, 1876	
Connecticut		Jan. 9, 1788	The fifth of the original 13 colonies.
Delaware		Dec. 7, 1787	The first of the original 13 colonies.
Dakota	March 2, 1861	Nov. 2, 1889	Became two states: North and South Dakota.
Deseret	March 5, 1849		Brigham Young created the unofficial territory of Deseret. In spite of the fact that Utah Territory was created Sept. 9, 1850, Deseret continued to exist unofficially, in what is now Utah, at least as late as 1862.
Frankland or Franklin			This unofficial state was formed in Aug. 1784, in the northeast corner of what is now Tennessee, and the government existed until 1788. In reality it was part of North Carolina.
Florida	March 30, 1822	March 3, 1845	
Georgia		Jan. 2, 1788	The fourth of the original 13 colonies.
Hawaii	Aug. 12, 1898	Aug. 21, 1959	The territorial date given is that of the formal transfer to the United States, with Sanford B. Dole as first Governor.
Idaho	March 3, 1863	July 3, 1890	
Illinois	March 2, 1809*	Dec. 3, 1818	
Indiana	July 5, 1800*	Dec. 11, 1816	There was a residue of Indiana Territory which continued to exist under that name from Dec. 11, 1816 until Dec. 3, 1818, when it was attached to Michigan Territory.
Indian Territory		Nov. 16, 1907	In the region first called the "Indian Country," established June 30, 1834. It never had a territorial form of government. Finally, with Oklahoma Territory, it became the State of Oklahoma on Nov. 16, 1907.
Iowa	July 4, 1838	Dec. 28, 1846	
Jefferson	Oct. 24, 1859		An unofficial territory from Oct. 24, 1859, to Feb. 28, 1861. In reality it included parts of Kansas, Nebraska, Utah and New Mexico Territories, about 30% being in each of the first three and 10% in New Mexico. The settled portion was mostly in Kansas Territory until Jan. 29, 1861, when the State of Kansas was formed from the eastern part of Kansas Territory. From this date the heart of "Jefferson" was in unorganized territory until Feb. 28, 1861, when it became the Territory of Colorado.
Kansas	May 30, 1854	Jan. 29, 1861	
Kentucky		June 1, 1792	Never a territory, it was part of Virginia until statehood.
District of Louisiana	Oct. 1, 1804		An enormous region, it encompassed all of the Louisiana Purchase except the Territory of Orleans. Created by Act of March 26, 1804, effective Oct. 1, 1804, and attached for administrative purposes to the Territory of Indiana.
Territory of Louisiana	July 4, 1805		By Act of March 3, 1805, effective July 4, 1805, the District of Louisiana became the Territory of Louisiana.
Louisiana		April 30, 1812	With certain boundary changes, had been the Territory of Orleans.
District of Maine		March 16, 1820	Before statehood, what is now the State of Maine was called the District of Maine and belonged to Massachusetts.
Maryland		April 28, 1788	The seventh of the original 13 colonies.

	Territorial Date	Statehood Date	
Massachusetts		Feb. 6, 1788	The sixth of the original 13 colonies.
Michigan	July 1, 1805	Jan. 26, 1837	
Minnesota	March 3, 1849	May 11, 1858	
Mississippi	May 7, 1798	Dec. 10, 1817	Territory by Act of April 7, 1798, effective May 7, 1798.
Missouri	Dec. 7, 1812	Aug. 10, 1821	The state was much smaller than the territory. The area to the west and northwest of the state, which had been in the territory, was commonly known as the "Missouri Country" until May 30, 1854, and certain of the post offices in this area show a Missouri abbreviation in the postmark.
Montana	May 26, 1864	Nov. 8, 1889	
Nebraska	May 30, 1854	March 1, 1867	
Nevada	March 2, 1861	Oct. 31, 1864	
New Hampshire		June 21, 1788	The ninth of the original 13 colonies.
New Jersey		Dec. 18, 1787	The third of the original 13 colonies.
New Mexico	Dec. 13, 1850	Jan. 6, 1912	
New York		July 26, 1788	The 11th of the original 13 colonies.
North Carolina		Nov. 21, 1789	The 12th of the original 13 colonies.
North Dakota		Nov. 2, 1889	Had been part of the Territory of Dakota.
Northwest Territory	July 13, 1787		Ceased to exist March 1, 1803, when Ohio became a state. The date given is in dispute, Nov. 29, 1802 often being accepted.
Ohio		March 1, 1803	Had been part of Northwest Territory until statehood.
Oklahoma	May 2, 1890	Nov. 16, 1907	The state was formed from Oklahoma Territory and Indian Territory.
Oregon	Aug. 14, 1848	Feb. 14, 1859	
Orleans	Oct. 1, 1804		A territory by Act of March 26, 1804, effective Oct. 1, 1804. With certain boundary changes, it became the State of Louisiana, April 30, 1812.
Pennsylvania		Dec. 12, 1787	The second of the original 13 colonies.
Rhode Island		May 29, 1790	The 13th of the original 13 colonies.
South Carloina		May 23, 1788	The eighth of the original 13 colonies.
South Dakota		Nov. 2, 1889	Had been part of Dakota Territory.
Southwest Territory			Became the State of Tennessee, with minor boundary changes, June 1, 1796.
Tennessee		June 1, 1796	Had been Southwest Territory before statehood.
Texas		Dec. 29, 1845	Had been an independent Republic before statehood.
Utah	Sept. 9, 1850	Jan. 4, 1896	
Vermont		March 4, 1791	Until statehood, had been a region claimed by both New York and New Hampshire.
Virginia		June 25, 1788	The 10th of the original 13 colonies.
Washington	March 2, 1853	Nov. 11, 1889	
West Virginia		June 20, 1863	Had been part of Virginia until statehood.
Wisconsin	July 4, 1836	May 29, 1848	The state was smaller than the territory, and the left-over area continued to be called the Territory of Wisconsin until March 3, 1849.
Wyoming	July 29, 1868	July 10, 1890	

* The dates followed by an asterisk are one day later than those generally accepted. The reason is that the Act states, with Arkansas for example, "from and after July 4." While it was undoubtedly the intention of Congress to create Arkansas as a Territory on July 4, the U.S. Supreme Court decided that "from and after July 4," for instance, meant "July 5."

Territorial and statehood data compiled by Dr. Carroll Chase and Richard McP. Cabeen.

Domestic Letter Rates

Effective Date	Prepaid	Collect

1845, July 1
Reduction from 6¢ to 25¢ range on single-sheet letters

	Prepaid	Collect
Under 300 miles, per ½ oz	5¢	5¢
Over 300 miles, per ½ oz	10¢	10¢
Drop letters	2¢	

1847-1848

	Prepaid	Collect
East, to or from Havana (Cuba) per ½ oz	12½¢	12½¢
East, to or from Chagres (Panama) per ½ oz	20¢	20¢
East, to or from Panama, across Isthmus, per ½ oz.	30¢	30¢
To or from Astoria (Ore.) or Pacific Coast, per ½ oz	40¢	40¢
Along Pacific Coast, per ½ oz	12½¢	12½¢

1847, July 1
Unsealed circulars

	Prepaid	
1 oz. or less	3¢	

1851, July 1
Elimination of rates of 1847-1848 listed above

	Prepaid	Collect
Up to 3,000 miles, per ½ oz.	3¢	5¢
Over 3,000 miles, per ½ oz	6¢	10¢
Drop letters	1¢	

Unsealed circular

	Prepaid	
1 oz. or less up to 500 miles	1¢	
Over 500 miles to 1,500 miles	2¢	
Over 1,500 miles to 2,500 miles	3¢	
Over 2,500 miles to 3,500 miles	4¢	
Over 3,500 miles	5¢	

1852, September 30
Unsealed circulars

	Prepaid	
3 oz. or less anywhere in U.S.	1¢	
Each additional ounce	1¢	
(Double charge if collect)		

1855, April 1
Prepayment made compulsory

	Prepaid	
Not over 3,000 miles, per ½ oz.	3¢	
Over 3,000 miles, per ½ oz.	10¢	
Drop letters	1¢	

1863, July 1
Distance differential eliminated

	Prepaid	
All parts of United States, per ½ oz.	3¢	

1883, October 1
Letter rate reduced one-third

	Prepaid	
All parts of United States, per ½ oz.	2¢	

1885, July 1
Weight increased to 1 oz.

	Prepaid	
All parts of United States, per 1 oz.	2¢	

Effective Date	Prepaid

1896, October 1
Rural Free Delivery started

1917, November 2
War emergency

	Prepaid
All parts of United States, per 1 oz.	3¢

1919, July 1
Restoration of pre-war rate

	Prepaid
All parts of United States, per 1 oz.	2¢

1932, July 6
Rise due to depression

	Prepaid
All parts of United States, per 1 oz.	3¢

1958, August 1

	Prepaid
All parts of United States, per 1 oz.	4¢

1963, January 7

	Prepaid
All parts of United States, per 1 oz.	5¢

1968, January 7

	Prepaid
All parts of United States, per 1 oz.	6¢

1971, May 16

	Prepaid
All parts of United States, per 1 oz.	8¢

1974, March 2

	Prepaid
All parts of United States, per 1 oz.	10¢

1975, December 31

	Prepaid
All parts of United States, 1st oz.	13¢

1978, May 29

	Prepaid
All parts of United States, 1st oz.	15¢

1981, March 22

	Prepaid
All parts of United States, 1st oz.	18¢

1981, November 1

	Prepaid
All parts of United States, 1st oz.	20¢

1985, February 17

	Prepaid
All parts of United States, 1st oz.	22¢

1988, April 3

	Prepaid
All parts of United States, 1st oz.	25¢

1991, February 3

	Prepaid
All parts of United States, 1st oz.	29¢

1995, January 1

	Prepaid
All parts of United States, 1st oz.	32¢

1999, January 10

	Prepaid
All parts of United States, 1st oz.	33¢

Domestic Air Mail Rates

Effective Date	Prepaid
1911-1916 – The Pioneer Period	
Special official Post Office Flights at Fairs, aviation meets, etc., per 1 oz. .... 2¢ (Regulations prohibited an additional charge for air service on Post Office authorized flights.)	

1918, May 15
Service between Washington, DC, New York and
Philadelphia (including 10¢ special delivery fee),
per 1 oz. .... 24¢

1918, July 15
Service between Washington, DC, New York and Philadelphia
(including 10¢ special delivery fee), per 1 oz. .... 16¢
Additional ounces .... 6¢

1918, Dec. 15
Service between selected cities (other cities added later),
per 1 oz. .... 6¢

1919, July 18
No specific airmail rate: mail carried by airplane on
space available basis but airmail service not guaranteed,
per 1 oz. .... 2¢

1924, June 30-July 1
Airmail service per zone (New York-Chicago; Chicago-
Cheyenne, Wyo.; Cheyenne-San Francisco),
per 1 oz. (each zone or portion thereof) .... 8¢

1925, July 1
Special overnight service New York-Chicago (with three
intermediate stops), per 1 oz. .... 10¢

1926, Jan. 19
Contract routes not exceeding 1,000 miles (first flight
Feb. 15) per 1 oz. (each route or portion thereof) .... 10¢
Contract routes between 1,000 and 1,500 miles
(Seattle-Los Angeles, first flight Sept. 15) per 1 oz. .... 15¢
Mail traveling less than entire Seattle-Los Angeles
route per 1 oz. .... 10¢
Contract routes exceeding 1,500 miles (none established
during this rate period) per 1 oz. .... 20¢
Additional service on govt. route, per 1 oz. (each route
or portion thereof) .... 5¢

1927, Feb. 1
All contract routes or govt. zones, or combinations
thereof, per ½ oz. .... 10¢

1928, Aug. 1
All routes, 1st oz. .... 5¢
Each additional ounce or fraction thereof .... 10¢

Effective Date	Prepaid
1932, July 6	
All routes, 1st oz.	8¢
Each additional ounce or fraction thereof	13¢

1934, July 1
All routes, per oz. .... 6¢

1944, Mar. 26
All routes, per oz. .... 8¢

1946, Oct. 1
All routes, per oz. .... 5¢

1949, Jan. 1
All routes, per oz. .... 6¢
Postal cards and postcards, per oz. .... 4¢

1958, Aug. 1
All routes, per oz. .... 7¢
Postal cards and postcards, per oz. .... 5¢

1963, Jan. 7
All routes, per oz. .... 8¢
Postal cards and postcards, per oz. .... 6¢

1968, Jan. 7
All routes, per oz. .... 10¢
Postal cards and postcards, per oz. .... 8¢

1971, May 16
All routes, per oz. .... 11¢
Postal cards and postcards, per oz. .... 9¢

1974, Mar. 2
All routes, per oz. .... 13¢
Postal cards and postcards, per oz. .... 11¢

As of Oct. 11, 1975, separate domestic airmail service was abolished, although at least one more airmail rate was published; effective Dec. 28, 1975, 17¢ per 1st oz., 15¢ each additional oz., 14¢ for postal cards and postcards. It lasted until May 1, 1977.

Many thanks to the American Air Mail Society for sharing information on airmail rates. For further study, we highly recommend the society's book, *Via Airmail, An Aerophilatelic Survey of Events, Routes, and Rates;* Simine Short, editor; James R. Adams, author (available from the American Airmail Society, P.O. Box 110, Mineola, NY 11501. Price: $20, plus $2.50 postage to U.S. addresses; $3.50 to addresses outside the U.S.).

National Album Series

SCOTT NATIONAL SERIES

The National series offers a panoramic view of our country's heritage through postage stamps. It is the most complete and comprehensive U.S. album series you can buy. There are spaces for every major U.S. stamp listed in the Scott Catalogue, including Special Printings, Newspaper stamps and much more.

* Pages printed on one side.
* All spaces identified by Scott numbers.
* All major variety of stamps are either illustrated or described.
* Chemically neutral paper protects stamps.

Item			Retail
100NTL1	1845-1934	97 pgs	$29.95
100NTL2	1935-1976	108 pgs	$29.95
100NTL3	1977-1993	110 pgs	$29.95
100NTL4	1994-1998	76 pgs	$29.95
100S099	1999	24 pgs	$13.95

Supplemented in March.

COMPUTER VENDED POSTAGE

Item			Retail
103CVP0	1989-1994	11 pgs	$3.95

NATIONAL BLANK PAGES (BORDER B)

Item		Retail
ACC120	20 per pack	$6.95

NATIONAL QUAD BLANK PAGES (BORDER B)

Item		Retail
ACC121	20 per pack	$6.95

U.S. BOOKLET PANES

Includes slogan types and tagging varieties.

Item			Retail
101BKP1	1900-1993	103 pgs	$54.95
101BKP2	1994-1998	57 pgs	$34.95
101S099	1999	14 pgs	$11.95

Supplemented in April.

U.S. COMMEMORATIVE AND COMMEMORATIVE AIR PLATE BLOCKS

Divided chronologically into seven parts. Begins with the Pan American issue of 1901.

Item			Retail
120CPB1	1901-1940	80 pgs	$29.95
120CPB2	1940-1959	78 pgs	$29.95
120CPB3	1959-1968	70 pgs	$29.95
120CPB4	1969-1973	47 pgs	$24.95
120CPB5	1973-1979	83 pgs	$29.95
120CPB6	1980-1988	97 pgs	$39.95
120CPB7	1989-1995	97 pgs	$39.95
120CPB8	1996-1998	38 pgs	$19.95
120S099	1999	14 pgs	$11.95

Supplemented in April.

U.S. COMPREHENSIVE PLATE NUMBER COILS

Provides spaces for every coil issue where the plate number is part of the design, and for every existing plate number for each issue. Space provided for strips of 3. Accommodates strips of 5. Includes precancels.

Item			Retail
114PNC1	1981-1988	114 pgs	$49.95
114PNC2	1989-1994	146 pgs	$59.95
114PNC3	1995-1998	108 pgs	$49.95
114S099	1999	42 pgs	$19.95

Supplemented in April.

U.S. COMPREHENSIVE PLATE NUMBER SINGLES

Provides space for every single issue where the plate number is part of the design. Includes spaces for every existing plate number.

Item			Retail
117PNC1	1981-1993	147 pgs	$44.95
117PNC2	1994-1998	107 pgs	$39.95
117S099	1999	28 pgs	$14.95

Supplemented in April. Note: Pages are 3-hole punched to fit Scott 3-ring binder.

U.S. FEDERAL DUCK STAMP PLATE BLOCKS

Contains spaces for all federal migratory bird hunting stamps in plate block form.

Item			Retail
116DKB0	1934-1996	42 pgs	$29.95
116S098	1997-1998	2 pgs	$2.95

Supplemented in April.

National series albums are sold as page-only units. Binders and labels should be purchased separately. Multi-part albums can be combined in larger binders.

Scott National series albums are available from your favorite stamp dealer or direct from :

SCOTT

Box 828 Sidney OH 45365-0828
1-800-572-6855
www.scottonline.com

National Album Series

U.S. FEDERAL AND STATE DUCK SINGLES

Extra space for future issues and blank pages for collateral material.

Item			Retail
115DUK1	1934-1988	83 pgs	$49.95
115DUK2*	1989-1994	189 pgs	$49.95
115DUK3	1995-1998	62 pgs	$36.95

* Part 2 includes many replacement pages which are used to update your album. These are included at no charge. Supplemented in April.

U.S. GUTTER PAIRS AND BLOCKS

An album and series of National supplements that includes spaces for vertical and horizontal gutter pairs and blocks from uncut sheets. Pages for cross-gutter blocks consistent with listings in the *U.S. Specialized.*

Item			Retail
123GPR1	1994-1996	30 pgs	$19.95
123GP97	1997	22 pgs	$14.95
123GP98	1998	22 pgs	$15.95
123GP99	1999	21 pgs	$13.95

U. S. OFFICIAL JOINT ISSUES ALBUM

Features illustrations and descriptive stories for 29 joint issues of the United States and 19 foreign countries. Pages are organized chronologically beginning with the 1959 Canada - U.S. official joint issue commemorating the opening of the St. Lawrence seaway.

Item			Retail
119JNT0	1959-1996	36 pgs	$19.95

Supplemented as needed.

U.S. POSTAL CARD

Includes spaces for all major number postal cards listed in the Scott *U.S. Specialized Catalogue.* Heavyweight paper of the finest quality supports the extra weight of the cards.

Item			Retail
110PCD1	1873-1981	95 pgs	$49.95
110PCD2	1982-1995	126 pgs	$69.95
110PCD3	1996-1998	59 pgs	$29.95
110S099	1999	14 pgs	$11.95

Supplemented in April.

110Z000	Postal Card Blank Pgs (20 per pack)		$6.95

U.S. POSTAL STATIONERY

Provides spaces for cut squares of every major postal stationery item in the Scott *U.S. Specialized Catalogue* and entires of airletter sheets.

Item			Retail
105PST0	1853-1992	104 pgs	$59.95
105S095	1993-1995	6 pgs	$5.95
105S099	1996-1999	4 pgs	$4.95

Supplemented as needed.

U.S. REGULAR AND REGULAR AIR PLATE BLOCKS

Begins with the first airpost issue of 1918 (Scott C1-C3) and the 1922-25 regulars (beginning with Scott 551).

Item			Retail
125RPB0	1918-1991	111 pgs	$49.95
125S095	1992-1995	8 pgs	$7.95
125S098	1996-1998	8 pgs	$7.95

Supplemented as needed.

U.S. REVENUE PAGES

Contains spaces for: Documentary, War Savings, Tobacco Sales Tax, Proprietary, Treasury Savings, Narcotic Tax, Future Delivery, Cordials & Wines, Consular Service Fee, Stock Transfer, Playing Cards, Customs Fee, Postal Note, Silver Tax, Motor Vehicle Use Postal Savings, Cigarette Tubes, Boating Savings, Potato Tax, Firearms Transfer Tax.

Item			Retail
160RVN0		131 pgs.	$49.95

U.S. SIMPLIFIED PLATE NUMBER COILS

Provides space for each stamp design. Lets you mount one plate number example of each issue. Designed for strips of 3. Precancels spaces are included.

Item			Retail
113PNC0	1981-1996	108 pgs	$54.95
113S097	1997	6 pgs	$5.95
113S098	1998	6 pgs	$5.95
113S099	1999	10 pgs	$9.95

Supplemented in April.

U.S. SMALL PANES ALBUM

Features spaces for small panes as listed in the *Scott Specialized Catalogue.* The small pane format for U.S. stamps was introduced in 1987.

Item			Retail
118SMP0	1987-1995	40 pgs	$39.95
118S096	1996	20 pgs	$13.95
118S097	1997	26 pgs	$14.95
118S098	1998	42 pgs	$19.95
118S099	1999	40 pgs	$19.95

Supplemented in April.

U.S. TAGGED VARIETY ALBUM

Includes spaces for the listed varieties of all U.S. stamps that were issued tagged and untagged. A specialized section that belongs in all National albums.

Item			Retail
102TAG0	1963-1987	11 pgs	$7.95
102S093	1988-1993	8 pgs	$5.95

Identifier of Definitive Issues — Arranged by Type Numbers

This section covers only listed postage stamps. See the Proofs section for imperforate items in the stamp colors mentioned which are not listed here and the Trial Color Proofs section for items in other colors.

ISSUES OF 1847-75

A1 Benjamin Franklin   **Reproduction**

5¢ On the originals the left side of the white shirt frill touches the oval on a level with the top of the "F" of "Five." On the reproductions it touches the oval about on a level with the top of the figure "5."

A2 George Washington   **Reproduction**

Original

Reproduction

10¢ On the originals line of coat (A) points to "T" of TEN and (B) it points between "T" and "S" of CENTS.

On the reproductions line of coat (A) points to right tip of "X" and line of coat (B) points to center of "S."

On the reproductions the eyes have a sleepy look, the line of the mouth is straighter, and in the curl of the hair near the left cheek is a strong black dot, while the originals have only a faint one.

Imperforate and Unwatermarked

Design Number		Scott Number
A1	5¢ red brown	1
A1	5¢ blue (reproduction)	948a
A3	5¢ red brown (reproduction, Special Printing)	3
A2	10¢ black	2
A2	10¢ brown orange (reproduction)	948b
A4	10¢ black (reproduction, Special Printing)	4

ISSUE OF 1851-75

A5 Franklin

A5

Type I Has a curved line outside the labels with "U.S. Postage" and "One Cent." The scrolls below the lower label are turned under, forming little balls. The scrolls and outer line at top are complete.

A6

Type Ia Same as I at bottom but top ornaments and outer line at top are partly cut away.

Type Ib Same as I but balls below the bottom label are not so clear. The plume-like scrolls at bottom are not complete.

Type Ic Same as type Ia, but bottom right plume and ball ornament is incomplete. The bottom left plume is complete or almost complete.

A7

Type II The little balls of the bottom scrolls and the bottoms of the lower plume ornaments are missing. The side ornaments are complete.

A8

Type III The top and bottom curved lines outside the labels are broken in the middle. The side ornaments are complete.

Type IIIa Similar to III with the outer line broken at top or bottom but not both. Type IIIa from Plate IV generally shows signs of plate erasure between the horizontal rows. Those from Plate IE show only a slight break in the line at top or bottom.

A9 Type IV

A20 Type V

Type IV Similar to II, but with the curved lines outside the labels recut at top or bottom or both.

The seven types listed account for most of the varieties of recutting.

Type V Similar to type III of 1851-56 but with side ornaments partly cut away.

A5	1¢ blue, type I, imperf.	5
A5	1¢ blue, type Ib, imperf.	5A
A5	1¢ blue, type I, perf. 15½	18
A5	1¢ bright blue, perf. 12 (Special Printing)	40
A6	1¢ blue, type Ia, imperf.	6
A6	1¢ blue, type Ic, imperf.	6b
A6	1¢ blue, type Ia, perf. 15½	19
A6	1¢ blue, type Ic, perf. 15½	19b
A7	1¢ blue, type II, imperf.	7
A7	1¢ blue, type II, perf. 15½	20

A10 Washington, Type I

A10 Type I *There is an outer frame line on all four sides.*

A21 Type II *The outer line has been removed at top and bottom.*

Type IIa The side frame lines extend only to the top and bottom of the stamp design. All type IIa stamps are from plates 10 and 11 (each exists in 3 states), and these plates produced only type IIa. The side frame lines were recut individually for each stamp, thus being broken between the stamps vertically.

Beware of type II stamps with frame lines that stop at the top of the design (from top row of plate) or bottom of the design (from bottom row of plate). These are sometimes offered as No. 26a.

A11 Jefferson, Type I *There are projections on all four sides.*

A22 Type II *The projections at top and bottom are partly cut away. Several minor types could be made according to the extent of cutting of the projections.*

Nos. 40-47 are reprints produced by the Continental Bank Note Co. The stamps are on white paper without gum, perf. 12. They were not good for postal use. They also exist imperforate.

A12 Washington, Type I   **A16** Washington

A12 Type I *The shells at the lower corners are practically complete. The outer line below the label is very nearly complete. The outer lines are broken above the middle of the top label and the "X" in each upper corner.*

A13 Type II *The design is complete at the top. The outer line at the bottom is broken in the middle. The shells are partly cut away.*

A14 Type III *The outer lines are broken above the top label and the "X" numerals. The outer line at the bottom and the shells are partly cut away as in Type II.*

A15 Type IV *The outer lines have been recut at top or bottom or both.*

A23 Type V *The side ornaments are slightly cut away. Usually only one pearl remains at each end of the lower label but some copies show two or three pearls at the right side. At the bottom, the outer line is complete and the shells nearly so. The outer lines at top are complete except over the right "X."*

A17 Washington

A18 Franklin   **A19** Washington

ISSUES OF 1861-75

A24 Franklin

A24 *See the essay section for type A24 in indigo on perf. 12 thin, semi-transparent paper without the dash under the tip of the ornament at the right of the numeral in the upper left corner.*

A24   1¢   blue, perf. 12 .... **63**
A24   1¢   blue, same, laid paper **63c**
A24   1¢   blue, grill 11x14mm **85A**
A24   1¢   blue, grill 11x13mm **86**
A24   1¢   blue, grill 9x13mm **92**
A24   1¢   blue, no grill, hard white paper (Special Printing) **102**

A25 Washington

A25 *See the essay section for type A25 in brown rose on perf. 12 thin, semi-transparent paper with smaller ornaments in the corners which do not end in a small ball.*

A25   3¢   pink, no grill, perf. 12 .... **64**
A25   3¢   pigeon blood pink, same **64a**
A25   3¢   rose pink, same **64b**
A25   3¢   lake, same (Special Printing) **66**
A25   3¢   scarlet, same (Special Printing) **74**
A25   3¢   rose, same **65**
A25   3¢   rose, same, laid paper **65b**
A25   3¢   rose, grilled all over **79**
A25   3¢   rose, grill 18x15mm **82**
A25   3¢   rose, grill 13x16mm **83**
A25   3¢   rose, grill 12x14mm **85**
A25   3¢   rose, grill 11x14mm **85C**
A25   3¢   rose, grill 11x13mm **88**
A25   3¢   red, grill 9x13mm **94**
A25   3¢   brown red, no grill, hard white paper (Special Printing) ... **104**

A26 Jefferson

A26 *See the essay section for type A26 in brown on perf. 12 thin, semi-transparent paper without the leaflet in the foliated ornament at each corner.*

A26   5¢   buff, no grill **67**
A26   5¢   brown yellow, no grill **67a**
A26   5¢   olive yellow, no grill **67b**
A26   5¢   red brown, no grill **75**
A26   5¢   brown, no grill **76**
A26   5¢   dark brown, no grill **76a**
A26   5¢   brown, laid paper **76b**
A26   5¢   brown, grilled all over **80**
A26   5¢   brown, grill 9x13mm **95**
A26   5¢   brown, no grill, hard white paper **105**

A27a

A27 Washington

A27 *A heavy curved line has been cut below the stars and an outer line added to the ornaments above them.*

A27a   10¢   dark green, thin paper **62B**
A27   10¢   yellow green, see illustration A27 .... **68**
A27   10¢   green, grill 11x14mm **85D**
A27   10¢   green, grill 11x13mm **89**
A27   10¢   yellow green, grill 9x13mm **96**
A27   10¢   green, no grill, hard white paper (Special Printing) **106**

A28 Washington

A28 *See the essay section for type A28 in black on perf. 12 thin, semi-transparent paper without corner ornaments.*

A28   12¢   black, no grill **69**
A28   12¢   black, grill 11x14mm **85E**
A28   12¢   black, grill 11x13mm **90**
A28   12¢   black, grill 9x13mm **97**
A28   12¢   black, no grill, hard white paper, (Special Printing) **107**

A29 Washington   **A30** Franklin

See the Trial Color proof section for type A29 in dark violet on perf. 12 thin paper without grill and type A30 in red orange on perf. 12 thin paper without grill.

A29   24¢   red lilac, no grill **70**
A29   24¢   brown lilac, no grill **70a**
A29   24¢   steel blue, no grill **70b**
A29   24¢   violet, no grill, thin, transparent paper **70c**
A29   24¢   grayish lilac, no grill, thin, hard transparent paper **70d**
A29   24¢   lilac, no grill **78**
A29   24¢   grayish lilac, no grill **78a**
A29   24¢   gray, no grill **78b**
A29   24¢   blackish violet, no grill **78c**
A29   24¢   gray lilac, grill 9x13mm **99**
A29   24¢   deep violet, no grill, hard white paper, (Special Printing) **109**
A30   30¢   orange, no grill **71**
A30   30¢   orange, grilled all over **81**
A30   30¢   orange, grill 9x13mm **100**
A30   30¢   brownish orange, no grill, hard white paper, (Special Printing) .. **110**

A31 Washington

A31 *See the essay section for type A31 in dull blue on perf. 12 thin semi-transparent paper without dashes between the parallel lines which form the angle above the ribbon with "U.S. Postage," and without the point of color at the apex of the lower line.*

A31   90¢   blue, no grill **72**
A31   90¢   blue, grill 9x13mm **101**
A31   90¢   blue, no grill, hard white paper, (Special Printing) **111**

ISSUES OF 1861-75

A32 Jackson   **A33** Lincoln

Perf. 12, Unwmkd.

A32	2¢ black, no grill	73
A32	2¢ black, laid paper	73d
A32	2¢ black, grill 12x14mm	84
A32	2¢ black, grill 11x14mm	85B
A32	2¢ black, grill 11x13mm	87
A32	2¢ black, grill 9x13mm	93
A32	2¢ black, no grill, hard white paper, (Special Printing)	103
A33	15¢ black, no grill	77
A33	15¢ black, grill 11x14mm	85F
A33	15¢ black, grill 11x13mm	91
A33	15¢ black, grill 9x13mm	98
A33	15¢ black, no grill, hard white paper, (Special Printing)	108

ISSUES OF 1869-80

A34 Franklin

A34	1¢ buff, grill 9½x9mm	112
A34	1¢ buff, no grill	112b
A34	1¢ buff, no grill, hard white paper (Special Printing)	123
A34	1¢ buff, no grill, soft porous paper (Special Printing)	133
A34	1¢ brown orange, same without gum (Special Printing)	133a

A35 Pony Express   **A36** Baldwin 4-4-0 Locomotive, c. 1857

A35	2¢ brown, grill 9½x9mm	113
A35	2¢ brown, no grill	113b
A35	2¢ brown, no grill, hard white paper (Special Printing)	124
A36	3¢ ultramarine, grill 9½x9mm	114
A36	3¢ ultramarine, no grill	114a
A36	3¢ blue, no grill, hard white paper (Special Printing)	125

A37 Washington   **A38** Shield and Eagle

A39 S.S. Adriatic

A37	6¢ ultramarine, grill 9½x9mm	115
A37	6¢ blue, no grill, hard white paper (Special Printing)	126
A38	10¢ yellow, grill 9½x9mm	116

A38	10¢ yellow, no grill, hard white paper (Special Printing)	127
A39	12¢ green, grill 9½x9mm	117
A39	12¢ green, no grill, hard white paper (Special Printing)	128

A40 Landing of Columbus

A40 Type I *Picture unframed*

A40a Type II *Picture framed*

Type III same as Type I but without the fringe of brown shading lines around central vignette.

A40	15¢ brown & blue, type I, grill 9½x9mm	118
A40	15¢ brown & blue, type I, no grill	118a
A40	15¢ brown & blue, type III, no grill, hard white paper (Special Printing)	129
A40a	15¢ brown & blue, type II, grill 9½x9mm	119

A41 The Declaration of Independence

A42 Shield, Eagle and Flags   **A43** Lincoln

A41	24¢ green & violet, grill 9½x9mm	120
A41	24¢ green & violet, no grill	120a
A41	24¢ green & violet, no grill, hard white paper (Special Printing)	130
A42	30¢ ultramarine & carmine, grill 9½x9mm	121
A42	30¢ ultramarine & carmine, no grill	121a
A42	30¢ ultramarine & carmine, no grill, hard white paper (Special Printing)	131
A43	90¢ carmine & black, grill 9½x9mm	122
A43	90¢ carmine & black, no grill	122a
A43	90¢ carmine & black, no grill, hard white paper (Special Printing)	132
A43	90¢ carmine & black, 28x28mm, imperf., litho. & engraved	2433a
A43	90¢ blue & brown, 28x28mm, imperf., litho. & engraved	2433b
A43	90¢ green & blue, 28x28mm, imperf., litho. & engraved	2433c

A43	90¢ scarlet & blue, 28x28mm, imperf., litho. & engraved	2433d

ISSUES OF 1870-88

The secret mark shown in the detail of A45a is seldom found on the actual stamps. Stamps Nos. 146 and 157 are best identified by color which is red brown for No. 146 and brown for No. 157.

Note I: Special printings of 1880-83 — All denominations of this series were printed on special order from the Post Office Department during the period the stamps were current. The paper being the same as used on current issue, the special printings are extremely difficult to identify. The 2¢ brown, 7¢ scarlet vermilion, 12¢ blackish purple and 24¢ dark violet are easily distinguished by the soft porous paper as these denominations were never previously printed on soft paper. The other denominations can be distinguished by shades only, those of the special printings being slightly deeper and richer than the regular issue. The special printings except No. 211B were issued without gum. The only certain way to identify them is by comparison with stamps previously established as special printings.

A44 Franklin

A44

A44a With secret mark *In the pearl at the left of the numeral "1" there is a small dash.*

A44b Re-engraved *The vertical lines in the upper part of the stamp have been so deepened that the background often appears to be solid. Lines of shading have been added to the upper arabesques.*

A44	1¢ ultramarine, with grill	134
A44	1¢ ultramarine, no grill	145
A44a	1¢ ultramarine, white wove paper no grill	156
A44a	1¢ ultramarine, with grill	156e
A44a	1¢ ultramarine, hard white paper, without gum (Special Printing)	167
A44a	1¢ dark ultra, soft porous paper	182
A44a	1¢ dark ultra, soft porous paper, without gum (Special Printing, see note I)	192
A44b	1¢ gray blue	206

A45 Jackson

A45

45a *Under the scroll at the left of "U.S." there is a small diagonal line.*

A45   2¢ red brown, with grill 135
A45   2¢ red brown, no grill 146
A45a   2¢ brown, white wove paper
               no grill 157
A45a   2¢ brown, with grill 157c
A45a   2¢ dark brown, hard white paper,
               without gum (Special Printing) . 168
A45a   2¢ black brown, soft porous paper,
               without gum (Special Printing) . 193
A45a   2¢ vermilion, yellowish paper 178
A45a   2¢ vermilion, same, with grill 178c
A45a   2¢ vermilion, soft porous paper 183
A45a   2¢ carmine vermilion, hard
               white paper, without gum
               (Special Printing) 180
A45a   2¢ scarlet vermilion, soft porous
               paper, without gum (Special
               Printing, see note I) 203

A46 Washington

A46

A46a With secret mark *The under part of the tail of the left ribbon is heavily shaded.*

A46b Re-engraved *The shading at the sides of the central oval appears only about one half the previous width. A short horizontal dash has been cut about 1mm. below the "TS" of "CENTS."*

A46   3¢ green, with grill 136
A46   3¢ green, no grill 147
A46a   3¢ green, white wove paper,
               no grill 158
A46a   3¢ green, same, with grill 158e
A46a   3¢ blue green, hard white paper,
               without gum (Special Printing) . 169
A46a   3¢ green, soft porous paper 184
A46a   3¢ blue green, soft porous paper,
               without gum (Special Printing
               see note I) 194
A46b   3¢ blue green, re-engraved 207
A46b   3¢ vermilion re-engraved 214

A47 Lincoln

A47

A47a With secret mark *The first four vertical lines of the shading in the lower part of the left ribbon have been strengthened.*

A47b Re-engraved. *6¢ on the original stamps four vertical lines can be counted from the edge of the panel to the outside of the stamp. On the re-engraved stamps there are but three lines in the same place.*

A47   6¢ carmine, with grill 137
A47   6¢ carmine, no grill 148
A47a   6¢ dull pink, no grill,
               white wove paper 159
A47a   6¢ dull pink, with grill 159b
A47a   6¢ dull rose, hard white paper,
               without gum (Special Printing) 170
A47a   6¢ pink, soft porous paper 186
A47a   6¢ dull rose, soft porous paper,
               without gum (Special Printing
               see note I) 195
A47b   6¢ rose, re-engraved 208

A48 Edwin McMasters Stanton

A49 Thomas Jefferson

A48

A48a With secret mark *Two small semi-circles are drawn around the ends of the lines which outline the ball in the lower right hand corner.*

A49

A49a With secret mark *A small semi-circle in the scroll at the right end of the upper label.*

A49b Re-engraved *On the original stamps there are five vertical lines between the left side of the oval and the edge of the shield. There are only four lines on the re-engraved stamps. In the lower part of the re-engraved stamps the horizontal lines of the background have been strengthened.*

A50 Henry Clay

A50

A50a With secret mark *The balls of the figure "2" are crescent shaped.*

A48   7¢ vermilion, with grill 138
A48   7¢ vermilion, no grill 149
A48a   7¢ orange verm., white wove
               paper no grill 160
A48a   7¢ orange verm., same, with
               grill 160a
A48a   7¢ reddish verm., hard white paper,
               without gum (Special Printing) 171
A48a   7¢ scarlet verm., soft porous paper,
               without gum (Special Printing) . 196
A49   10¢ brown, with grill 139
A49   10¢ brown, no grill 150
A49   10¢ brown, soft porous paper 187
A49a   10¢ brown, white wove paper
               no grill 161
A49a   10¢ brown, with grill 161c
A49a   10¢ pale brown, hard white paper,
               without gum (Special Printing) . 172
A49a   10¢ brown, soft porous paper 188
A49a   10¢ deep brown, soft porous paper,
               without gum (Special Printing,
               see note I) 197

A49b 10¢ brown, re-engraved 209
A50 12¢ dull violet, with grill 140
A50 12¢ dull violet, no grill 151
A50a 12¢ blackish violet, white wove
paper, no grill 162
A50a 12¢ blackish violet, with grill 162a
A50a 12¢ dark violet, hard white paper,
without gum (Special Printing) . 173
A50a 12¢ blackish purple, soft porous
paper, without gum
(Special Printing) 198

A51 Webster   A51

A51a With secret mark *In the lower part of the triangle in the upper left corner two lines have been made heavier forming a "V." This mark can be found on some of the Continental and American (1879) printings, but not all stamps show it.*

A51 15¢ orange, with grill 141
A51 15¢ bright orange, no grill 152
A51a 15¢ yellow orange, white wove
paper, no grill 163
A51a 15¢ yellow orange, with grill 163a
A51a 15¢ bright orange, hard white paper,
without gum (Special Printing) . 174
A51a 15¢ red orange, soft porous paper 189
A51a 15¢ orange, soft porous paper,
without gum (Special Printing,
see note I) 199

A52 General Winfield Scott

A53 Hamilton   A54 Perry

Secret marks were added to the dies of the 24¢, 30¢ and 90¢ but new plates were not made from them. The various printings of these stamps can be distinguished only by the shades and paper.

A52 24¢ purple, with grill 142
A52 24¢ purple, no grill 153
A52 24¢ purple, vertically ribbed white
wove paper, no grill 164
A52 24¢ dull purple, hard white paper,
without gum (Special Printing) . 175

A52 24¢ dark violet, soft porous paper,
without gum (Special Printing) . 200
A53 30¢ black, with grill 143
A53 30¢ black, no grill 154
A53 30¢ full black, soft porous paper 190
A53 30¢ gray black, white wove paper,
no grill 165
A53 30¢ greenish black, with grill 165c
A53 30¢ greenish black, hard white paper,
without gum (Special Printing) . 176
A53 30¢ greenish black, soft porous paper,
without gum (Special Printing,
see note I) 201
A53 30¢ orange brown 217
A54 90¢ carmine, with grill 144
A54 90¢ carmine, no grill 155
A54 90¢ carmine, soft porous paper 191
A54 90¢ rose carmine, white wove paper . 166
A54 90¢ violet carmine, hard white paper,
without gum (Special Printing) . 177
A54 90¢ dull carmine, soft porous paper,
without gum (Special Printing,
see note I) 202
A54 90¢ purple 218

ISSUES OF 1875-88

A55 Taylor   A56 Garfield

Perf. 12, Unwmkd.
A55 5¢ blue, yellowish wove paper,
no grill 179
A55 5¢ blue, with grill 179c
A55 5¢ bright blue, hard, white wove
paper, without gum
(Special Printing) 181
A55 5¢ blue, soft porous paper 185
A55 5¢ deep blue, soft porous paper,
without gum (Special Printing,
see note I) 204
A56 5¢ yellow brown 205
A56 5¢ gray brown, soft porous paper,
without gum (Special Printing,
see note I) 205C
A56 5¢ indigo 216

A57 Washington   A58 Jackson

A57 2¢ red brown 210
A57 2¢ pale red brown, soft porous paper
(Special Printing, see note I) ... 211B
A57 2¢ green 213
A58 4¢ blue green 211
A58 4¢ deep blue green, soft porous
paper, without gum (Special
Printing, see note I) 211D
A58 4¢ carmine 215

A59 Franklin
A59 1¢ ultramarine 212

ISSUES OF 1890-93

A60 Franklin   A61 Washington

A62 Jackson   A63 Lincoln

A64 Grant   A65 Garfield

A66 William T.   A67 Daniel
Sherman   Webster

A68 Henry Clay   A69 Jefferson

A70 Perry

A60 1¢ dull blue 219
A61 2¢ lake 219D
A61 2¢ carmine 220
A62 3¢ purple 221
A63 4¢ dark brown 222

A64	5¢ chocolate	223
A65	6¢ brown red	224
A66	8¢ lilac	225
A67	10¢ green	226
A68	15¢ indigo	227
A69	30¢ black	228
A70	90¢ orange	229

ISSUES OF 1894-1903

This series, the first to be printed by the Bureau of Engraving and Printing, closely resembles the 1890 series but is identified by the triangles which have been added to the upper corners of the designs.

The Catalogue divides this group into three separate series, the first of which was issued in 1894 and is unwatermarked. In 1895 the paper used was watermarked with the double line letters USPS (United States Postage Stamp). The stamps show one complete letter of the watermark or parts of two or more letters.

This watermark appears on all United States stamps issued from 1895 until 1910.

In 1898 the colors of some of the denominations were changed, which created the third series noted in the Catalogue.

Other than the watermark, or lack of it, there are three styles of the corner triangles used on the 2 cent stamps and two variations of designs are noted on the 10 cent and $1 denomination. In the following list all of these variations are illustrated and described immediately preceding the denominations on which they appear.

Wmkd. **USPS** (191) Horizontally

or **USPS** Vertically

(Actual size of letter)

A87 Franklin

A88 Washington

A89 Jackson

A90 Lincoln

A91 Grant

A92 Garfield

A93 Sherman

A94 Webster

A95 Clay

A96 Jefferson

A97 Perry

A98 James Madison

A99 John Marshall

A87	1¢ ultramarine, unwmkd.	246
A87	1¢ blue, unwmkd.	247
A87	1¢ blue, wmkd.	264
A87	1¢ deep green, wmkd.	279
A87	1¢ on 1¢ yellow green, "CUBA"	Cuba 221
A87	1¢ deep green, "GUAM"	Guam 1
A87	1¢ yellow green, "PHILIPPINES"	Phil. 213
A87	1¢ yellow green, "PORTO RICO"	P.R. 210
A87	1¢ yellow green, "PUERTO RICO"	P.R. 215

Triangle A (Type I)
The horizontal lines of the ground work run across the triangle and are of the same thickness within it as without.

Triangle B (Type II)
The horizontal lines cross the triangle but are thinner within it than without. Other minor differences exist, but the change to Triangle B is a sufficient determinant.

Triangle C (Types III & IV)
Type III: *The horizontal lines do not cross the double lines of the triangle. The lines within the triangle are thin, as in* Triangle B.

The rest of the design is the same as Type II, except that most of the designs had the dot in the "S" of "CENTS" removed. Stamps with this dot are listed; some specialists refer to them as "Type IIIa" varieties.

Type IV: *Same triangle C as type III, but other design differences including (1) recutting and lengthening of hairline, (2) shaded toga button, (3) strengthening of lines on sleeve, (4) additional dots on ear, (5) "T" of "TWO" straight at right, (6) background lines extend into white oval opposite "U" of "UNITED." Many other differences exist.*

A88	2¢ pink, type I, unwmkd.	248
A88	2¢ carmine lake, type I, unwmkd.	249
A88	2¢ carmine, type I, unwmkd.	250
A88	2¢ rose, type I, unwmkd.	250a
A88	2¢ scarlet, type I, unwmkd.	250b
A88	2¢ carmine, type I, wmkd.	265
A88	2¢ carmine, type II, unwmkd.	251
A88	2¢ carmine, type II, wmkd.	266
A88	2¢ carmine, type III, unwmkd.	252
A88	2¢ carmine, type III, wmkd.	267
A88	2¢ red, type IV, wmkd.	279B
A88	2¢ booklet pane of 6, wmkd., single stamps with 1 or 2 straight edges	279Be
A88	2c on 2¢ reddish carmine, type III "CUBA"	Cuba 222
A88	2c on 2¢ reddish carmine, type IV, "CUBA"	Cuba 222A
A88	2½c on 2¢ reddish carmine, type III, "CUBA"	Cuba 223
A88	2½c on 2¢ vermilion, type III, "CUBA"	Cuba 223b
A88	2½c on 2¢ reddish carmine, type IV, "CUBA"	Cuba 223A
A88	2¢ red, type IV, "GUAM"	Guam 2

A88	2¢	red, type IV, "PHILIPPINES"	**Phil. 214**
A88		Same, booklet pane of 6	**Phil. 214b**
A88	2¢	reddish carmine, type IV, "PORTO RICO"	**P.R. 211**
A88		Same, "PUERTO RICO"	**P.R. 216**
A89	3¢	purple, unwmkd.	**253**
A89	3¢	purple, wmkd.	**268**
A89	3¢	on 3¢ purple, "CUBA"	**Cuba 224**
A89	3¢	purple, "GUAM"	**Guam 3**
A89	3¢	purple "PHILIPPINES"	**Phil. 215**
A90	4¢	dark brown, unwmkd.	**254**
A90	4¢	dark brown, wmkd.	**269**
A90	4¢	rose brown, wmkd.	**280**
A90	4¢	lilac brown, wmkd.	**280a**
A90	4¢	orange brown, wmkd.	**280b**
A90	4¢	lilac brown, "GUAM"	**Guam 4**
A90	4¢	orange brown, "PHILIPPINES"	**Phil. 220**
A91	5¢	chocolate, unwmkd.	**255**
A91	5¢	chocolate, wmkd.	**270**
A91	5¢	dark blue, wmkd.	**281**
A91	5¢	on 5¢ blue, "CUBA"	**Cuba 225**
A91	5¢	blue, "GUAM"	**Guam 5**
A91	5¢	blue, "PHILIPPINES"	**Phil. 216**
A91	5¢	blue, "PORTO RICO"	**P.R. 212**
A92	6¢	dull brown, unwmkd.	**256**
A92	6¢	dull brown, wmkd. USPS	**271**
A92	6¢	dull brown, wmkd. USIR	**271a**
A92	6¢	lake, wmkd.	**282**
A92	6¢	lake, "GUAM"	**Guam 6**
A92	6¢	lake, "PHILIPPINES"	**Phil. 221**
A93	8¢	violet brown, unwmkd.	**257**
A93	8¢	violet brown, wmkd. USPS	**272**
A93	8¢	violet brown, wmkd. USIR	**272a**
A93	8¢	violet brown, "GUAM"	**Guam 7**
A93	8¢	violet brown, "PHILIPPINES"	**Phil. 222**
A93	8¢	violet brown, "PORTO RICO"	**P.R. 213**

Type I *The tips of the foliate ornaments do not impinge on the white curved line below "ten cents."*

Type II *The tips of the ornaments break the curved line below the "e" of "ten" and the "t" of "cents."*

A94	10¢	dark green, unwmkd.	**258**
A94	10¢	dark green, wmkd.	**273**
A94	10¢	brown, type I, wmkd.	**282C**
A94	10¢	orange brown, type II, wmkd.	**283**
A94	10¢	on 10¢ brown, type I, "CUBA"	**Cuba 226**
A94		Same, type II, "CUBA"	**Cuba 226A**
A94	10¢	brown, type I, "GUAM"	**Guam 8**
A94	10¢	brown, type II, "GUAM"	**Guam 9**
A94	10¢	brown, type I, "PHILIPPINES"	**Phil. 217**
A94	10¢	orange brown, type II, "PHILIPPINES"	**Phil. 217A**
A94	10¢	brown, type I, "PORTO RICO"	**P.R. 214**
A95	15¢	dark blue, unwmkd.	**259**
A95	15¢	dark blue, wmkd.	**274**
A95	15¢	olive green, wmkd.	**284**
A95	15¢	olive green, "GUAM"	**Guam 10**
A95	15¢	olive green, "PHILIPPINES"	**Phil. 218**

A95	15¢	light olive green, "PHILIPPINES"	**Phil. 218a**
A96	50¢	orange, unwmkd.	**260**
A96	50¢	orange, wmkd.	**275**
A96	50¢	orange, "GUAM"	**Guam 11**
A96	50¢	red orange, "GUAM"	**Guam 11a**
A96	50¢	orange, unwmkd., "PHILIPPINES"	**Phil. 212**
A96	50¢	orange, wmkd., "PHILIPPINES"	**Phil. 219**

A97 Type I *The circles enclosing "$1" are broken where they meet the curved line below "One Dollar."*

A97 Type II *The circles are complete.*

A97	$1	black, type I, unwmkd.	**261**
A97	$1	black, type I, wmkd.	**276**
A97	$1	black, type II, unwmkd.	**261A**
A97	$1	black, type II, wmkd.	**276A**
A97	$1	black, type I, "GUAM"	**Guam 12**
A97	$1	black, type II, "GUAM"	**Guam 13**
A97	$1	black, type I, "PHILIPPINES"	**Phil. 223**
A97	$1	black, type II, "PHILIPPINES"	**Phil. 223A**
A98	$2	bright blue, unwmkd.	**262**
A98	$2	blue, perf. 11, tagged	**2875a**
A98	$2	bright blue, wmkd.	**277**
A98	$2	dark blue, "PHILIPPINES"	**Phil. 224**
A99	$5	dark green, unwmkd.	**263**
A99	$5	dark green, wmkd.	**278**
A99	$5	dark green, "PHILIPPINES"	**Phil. 225**

ISSUES OF 1902-17

A115 Franklin

A116 Washington

A117 Jackson

A118 Grant

A119 Lincoln

A120 Garfield

A121 Martha Washington

A122 Daniel Webster

A123 Benjamin Harrison

A124 Henry Clay

A125 Jefferson

A126 David G. Farragut

A127 Madison

A128 Marshall

Unless otherwise noted all stamps are Perf. 12 and Wmkd. (191)

Single stamps from booklet panes show 1 or 2 straight edges.

A115	1¢	blue green	**300**
A115	1¢	booklet pane of 6	**300b**
A115	1¢	blue green, imperf.	**314**
A115	1¢	blue green, perf. 12 horiz., pair	**316**
A115	1¢	blue green, perf. 12 vert., pair	**318**
A115	1¢	blue green, "CANAL ZONE PANAMA"	**C.Z. 4**
A115	1¢	blue green, "PHILIPPINES"	**Phil. 226**
A116	2¢	carmine	**301**
A116	2¢	booklet pane of 6	**301c**
A116	2¢	carmine, "PHILIPPINES"	**Phil. 227**
A117	3¢	bright violet	**302**
A117	3¢	bright violet, "PHILIPPINES"	**Phil. 228**
A118	4¢	brown	**303**
A118	4¢	brown, imperf.	**314A**
A118	4¢	brown, "PHILIPPINES"	**Phil. 229**
A119	5¢	blue	**304**
A119	5¢	blue, imperf.	**315**
A119	5¢	blue, perf. 12 horiz. pair	**317**
A119	5¢	blue, "CANAL ZONE PANAMA"	**C.Z. 6**
A119	5¢	blue, "PHILIPPINES"	**Phil. 230**
A120	6¢	claret	**305**
A120	6¢	brownish lake, "PHILIPPINES"	**Phil. 231**
A121	8¢	violet black	**306**
A121	8¢	violet black, "CANAL ZONE PANAMA"	**C.Z. 7**
A121	8¢	violet black, "PHILIPPINES"	**Phil. 232**
A122	10¢	pale red brown	**307**
A122	10¢	pale red brown, "CANAL ZONE PANAMA"	**C.Z. 8**

A122 10¢ pale red brown,
"PHILIPPINES" .... Phil. 233
A123 13¢ purple black 308
A123 13¢ purple black,
"PHILIPPINES" .... Phil. 234
A124 15¢ olive green 309
A124 15¢ olive green,
"PHILIPPINES" .... Phil. 235
A125 50¢ orange 310
A125 50¢ orange, "PHILIPPINES" ... Phil. 236
A126 $1 black 311
A126 $1 black, "PHILIPPINES" ..... Phil. 237
A127 $2 dark blue 312
A127 $2 dark blue, unwmkd., perf. 10 ... 479
A127 $2 dark blue,
"PHILIPPINES" .... Phil. 238
A128 $5 dark green 313
A128 $5 light green, unwmkd., perf. 10 . 480
A128 $5 dark green,
"PHILIPPINES" .... Phil. 239

ISSUES OF 1903

A129 Washington

Type I   Type II

Specialists recognize over a hundred shades of this stamp in various hues of vermilion, red, carmine and lake. The Scott Catalogue lists only the most striking differences.

The Government coil stamp, No. 322 should not be confused with the scarlet vermilion coil of the International Vending Machine Co., which is perforated 12½ to 13.

A129 2¢ carmine, type I, wmkd. 319
A129 2¢ lake, type I 319a
A129 2¢ carmine rose, type I 319b
A129 2¢ scarlet, type I 319c
A129 2¢ lake, type II 319f
A129 2¢ carmine, type I, booklet
pane of 6 .... 319g
A129 Same, type II 319h
A129 2¢ carmine, type II 319i
A129 2¢ carmine rose, type II 319j
A129 2¢ scarlet, type II 319k
A129 2¢ lake, type I, booklet
pane of 6 .... 319m
A129 2¢ carmine rose, type I, booklet
pane of 6 .... 319n
A129 2¢ scarlet, type I, booklet
pane of 6 .... 319p
A129 2¢ lake, type II, booklet
pane of 6 .... 319q
A129 2¢ carmine, type I, imperf. 320
A129 2¢ lake, type II, imperf. 320a
A129 2¢ scarlet, type I, imperf. 320b
A129 2¢ carmine, perf. 12 horiz. pair 321
A129 2¢ carmine, perf. 12 vert. pair 322
A129 2¢ carmine, "CANAL ZONE
PANAMA" .... C.Z. 5
A129 2¢ carmine, "PHILIPPINES" . Phil. 240

A129 2¢ carmine, same, booklet
pane of 6 .... Phil. 240a

ISSUES OF 1908-09

This series introduces for the first time the single line watermark USPS. Only a small portion of several letters is often all that can be seen on a single stamp.

A138 Franklin   **A139** Washington

Wmk. 190

A138 1¢ green, perf. 12,
double line wmk. 331
A138 1¢ green, same, China clay paper 331b
A138 1¢ green, perf. 12,
single line wmk. 374
A138 1¢ green, perf. 12, bluish paper 357
A138 1¢ green, imperf.,
double line wmk. 343
A138 1¢ green, imperf., single line wmk. 383
A138 1¢ green, perf. 12 horiz.,
double line wmk. 348
A138 1¢ green, perf. 12 horiz.,
single line wmk. 385
A138 1¢ green, perf. 12 vert.,
double line wmk. 352
A138 1¢ green, perf. 12 vert.,
single line wmk. 387
A138 1¢ green, perf. 8 ½ horiz.,
single line wmk. 390
A138 1¢ green, perf. 8 ½ vert.,
single line wmk. 392
A139 2¢ carmine, perf. 12,
double line wmk. 332
A139 2¢ carmine, same,
China clay paper 332b
A139 2¢ carmine, perf. 12,
single line wmk. 375
A139 2¢ carmine, perf. 12, bluish paper . 358
A139 2¢ carmine, perf. 11,
double line wmk. 519
A139 2¢ carmine, imperf.,
double line wmk. 344
A139 2¢ carmine, imperf.,
single line wmk. 384
A139 2¢ carmine, perf. 12 horiz.,
double line wmk. 349
A139 2¢ carmine, perf. 12 horiz.,
single line wmk. 386
A139 2¢ carmine, perf. 12 vert.,
double line wmk. 353
A139 2¢ carmine, perf. 12 vert.,
single line wmk. 388
A139 2¢ carmine, perf. 8½ horiz.
single line wmk. 391
A139 2¢ carmine, perf. 8½ vert.,
single line wmk. 393

**Single stamps from booklet panes show
1 or 2 straight edges.**

A138 1¢ green, perf. 12, double line wmk.,
booklet pane of 6 .... 331a
A138 1¢ green, perf. 12, single line wmk.,
booklet pane of 6 .... 374a
A139 2¢ carmine, perf. 12, double line wmk.,
booklet pane of 6 .... 332a
A139 2¢ carmine, perf. 12, single line wmk.,
booklet pane of 6 .... 375a

ISSUES OF 1908-21

FLAT BED AND ROTARY PRESS STAMPS

The Rotary Press Stamps are printed from plates that are curved to fit around a cylinder. This curvature produces stamps that are slightly larger, either horizontally or vertically, than those printed from flat plates. Designs of stamps from flat plates measure about 18½-19mm. wide by 22mm. high. When the impressions are placed sidewise on the curved plates the designs are 19½-20mm. wide; when they are placed vertically the designs are 22½ to 23mm. high. A line of color (not a guide line) shows where the curved plates meet or join on the press.

Rotary Press Coil Stamps were printed from plates of 170 subjects for stamps coiled sidewise, and from plates of 150 subjects for stamps coiled endwise.

A140 Washington

1¢ A138 Portrait of Franklin, value in words.
1¢ A140 Portrait of Washington, value in numerals.
2¢ A139 Portrait of Washington, value in words.
2¢ A140 Portrait of Washington, value in numerals.

A140 1¢ green, perf. 12, single line wmk. . 405
A140 1¢ green, same, booklet pane of 6 . 405b
A140 1¢ green, perf. 11, flat plate,
unwmkd. 498
A140 1¢ green, same, booklet pane of 6 . 498e
A140 1¢ green, same, booklet pane of 30 498f
A140 1¢ green, perf. 11, rotary press
measuring 19mmx22½mm,
unwmkd. 544
A140 1¢ green, same, measuring
19½ to 20mmx22mm 545
A140 1¢ gray green, perf. 11, offset,
unwmkd. 525
A140 1¢ gray green, perf. 12½ 536
A140 1¢ green, perf. 11x10 538
A140 1¢ green, perf. 10x11 542
A140 1¢ green, perf. 10, single line wmk. . 424
A140 1¢ green, same, perf. 12x10 .... 424a
A140 1¢ green, same, perf. 10x12 .... 424b
A140 1¢ green, perf.10, single line wmk.,
booklet pane of 6 .... 424d
A140 1¢ green, perf. 10, flat plate,
unwmkd. 462
A140 1¢ green, same, booklet pane of 6 . 462a
A140 1¢ green, perf. 10, rotary press,
unwmkd. 543
A140 1¢ green, imperf., single line wmk. 408
A140 1¢ green, imperf., unwmkd. 481
A140 1¢ green, imperf., offset 531
A140 1¢ green, perf. 10 horiz., flat plate,
single line wmk. 441
A140 1¢ green, same, rotary press 448

A140 1¢ green, perf. 10 horiz.,
    rotary press, unwmkd. **486**
A140 1¢ green, perf. 10 vert., flat plate,
    single line wmk. **443**
A140 1¢ green, same, rotary press **452**
A140 1¢ green, perf. 10 vert.,
    rotary press, unwmkd. **490**
A140 1¢ green, perf. 8½ horiz.
    single line wmk. **410**
A140 1¢ green, perf. 8½ vert., same **412**

TYPES OF TWO CENTS

TYPE I

TYPE Ia

Type Ia *The design characteristics are similar to type I except that all of the lines of the design are stronger.*

The toga button, toga rope and rope shading lines are heavy.

The latter characteristics are those of type II, which, however, occur only on impressions from rotary plates.

Used only on flat plates 10208 and 10209.

TYPE II

Type II *Shading lines in ribbons as on type I.*

The toga button, rope and rope shading lines are heavy.

The shading lines of the face at the lock of hair end in a strong, vertical curved line.

Used on rotary press printings only.

TYPE III   Type III

Type III *Two lines of shading in the curves of the ribbons.*

Other characteristics similar to type II.

Used on rotary press printings only.

TYPE IV

Type IV *Top line of the toga rope is broken.*

The shading lines in the toga button are so arranged that the curving of the first and last form "ⅭⅠⅮ."

The line of color in the left "2" is very thin and usually broken. Used on offset printings only.

TYPE V

Type V *Top line of the toga is complete.*

There are five vertical shading lines in the toga button.

The line of color in the left "2" is very thin and usually broken.

The shading dots on the nose are as shown on the diagram.

Used on offset printings only.

TYPE Va

Type Va *Characteristics are the same as type V except in the shading dots of the nose. The third row of dots from the bottom has four dots instead of six. The overall height is ⅓ mm shorter than type V.*

Used on offset printings only.

TYPE VI

Type VI *General characteristics the same as type V except that the line of color in the left "2" is very heavy. Used on offset printings only.*

TYPE VII

Type VII *The line of color in the left "2" is invariably continuous, clearly defined and heavier than in type V or Va but not as heavy as type VI.*

An additional vertical row of dots has been added to the upper lip.

Numerous additional dots have been added to the hair on top of the head.

Used on offset printings only.

A140 2¢ carmine, perf. 12, type I,
    single line wmk. **406**
A140 2¢ carmine, same, booklet
    pane of 6 .... **406a**
A140 2¢ pale car. red, perf. 11,
    single line wmk., type I **461**
A140 2¢ rose, perf. 11, flat plate,
    unwmkd., type I **499**
A140 2¢ rose, same, booklet pane of 6 . **499e**
A140 2¢ rose, same, booklet pane of 30 **499f**
A140 2¢ deep rose, perf. 11, unwmkd.,
    type Ia **500**
A140 2¢ carmine rose, perf. 11, rotary
    press, unwmkd., type III **546**
A140 2¢ carmine, perf. 11, offset,
    unwmkd., type IV **526**
A140 2¢ carmine, same, type V **527**
A140 2¢ carmine, same, type Va **528**
A140 2¢ carmine, same, type VI **528A**
A140 2¢ carmine, same, type VII **528B**
A140 2¢ carmine rose, perf. 11x10,
    type II **539**
A140 2¢ carmine rose, same, type III **540**
A140 2¢ rose red, perf. 10, single line
    wmk., type I **425**
A140 2¢ rose red, perf. 10x12,
    single line wmk., type I **425c**
A140 2¢ rose red, perf. 12x10,
    single line wmk., type I **425d**
A140 2¢ rose red, same, perf. 10,
    booklet pane of 6 .... **425e**

A140 2¢ carmine, perf. 10, unwmkd.,
type I **463**
A140 2¢ carmine, same, booklet
pane of 6 .... **463a**
A140 2¢ carmine, imperf., flat plate,
single line wmk., type I **409**
A140 2¢ carmine, imperf., rotary press,
single line wmk., type I **459**
A140 2¢ carmine, imperf., flat plate,
unwmkd., type I **482**
A140 2¢ deep rose, same, type Ia **482A**
A140 2¢ carmine rose, imperf., offset,
unwmkd., type IV **532**
A140 2¢ carmine rose, same, type V **533**
A140 2¢ carmine, same, type Va **534**
A140 2¢ carmine, same, type VI **534A**
A140 2¢ carmine, same, type VII **534B**
A140 2¢ carmine, perf. 10 horiz., flat
plate, single line wmk., type I ... **442**
A140 2¢ red, same, rotary press **449**
A140 2¢ carmine, same, type III **450**
A140 2¢ carmine, perf. 10 horiz.,
rotary press unwmkd., type II ... **487**
A140 2¢ carmine, same, type III **488**
A140 2¢ carmine, perf. 10 vert., flat
plate, single line wmk., type I ... **444**
A140 2¢ carmine rose, same,
rotary press **453**
A140 2¢ red, same, type II **454**
A140 2¢ carmine, same, type III **455**
A140 2¢ carmine, perf. 10 vert.,
rotary press, unwmkd., type II .. **491**
A140 2¢ carmine, same, type III **492**
A140 2¢ carmine, perf. 8½ horiz., type I . **411**
A140 2¢ carmine, perf. 8½ vert., type I ... **413**

TYPES OF THREE CENTS

TYPE I

Type I *The top line of the toga rope is weak and
the rope shading lines are thin. The 5th line
from the left is missing. The line between the
lips is thin.*

TYPE II

Type II *The top line of the toga rope is strong
and the rope shading lines are heavy and complete.*
The line between the lips is heavy.
*Used on both flat plate and rotary press print-
ings.*

TYPE III

Type III *The top line of the toga rope is strong
but the 5th shading line is missing as in type I.*
*Center shading line of the toga button con-
sists of two dashes with a central dot.*
*The "P" and "O" of "POSTAGE" are separat-
ed by a line of color.*
*The frame line at the bottom of the vignette
is complete.*
Used on offset printings only.

TYPE IV

Type IV *The shading lines of the toga rope are
complete.*
*The second and fourth shading lines in the
toga button are broken in the middle and the
third line is continuous with a dot in the center.*
The "P" and "O" of "POSTAGE" are joined.
*The frame line at the bottom of the vignette
is broken.*
Used on offset printings only.

A140 3¢ deep violet, perf. 12,
double line wmk., type I **333**
A140 3¢ deep violet, same,
China clay paper **333a**
A140 3¢ deep violet, perf. 12,
single line wmk., type I **376**
A140 3¢ deep violet, perf. 12,
bluish paper, type I **359**
A140 3¢ light violet, perf. 11,
unwmkd., type I **501**
A140 3¢ light violet, same, booklet
pane of 6 .... **501b**
A140 3¢ dark violet, perf. 11,
unwmkd., type II **502**
A140 3¢ dark violet, same, booklet
pane of 6 .... **502b**
A140 3¢ violet, perf. 11, offset, type III .. **529**
A140 3¢ purple, same, type IV **530**
A140 3¢ violet, perf. 11x10, type II **541**
A140 3¢ deep violet, perf. 10, single
line wmk., type I **426**
A140 3¢ violet, perf. 10, unwmkd.,
type I **464**
A140 3¢ deep violet, imperf.,
double line wmk., type I **345**
A140 3¢ violet, imperf., unwmkd., type I . **483**
A140 3¢ violet, same, type II **484**
A140 3¢ violet, imperf., offset, type IV **535**

A140 3¢ deep violet, perf. 12 vert.,
single line wmk., type I **389**
A140 3¢ violet, perf. 10 vert., flat plate,
single line wmk., type I **445**
A140 3¢ violet, perf. 10 vert., rotary press,
single line wmk., type I **456**
A140 3¢ violet, perf. 10 vert., rotary press,
unwmkd., type I **493**
A140 3¢ violet, same, type II **494**
A140 3¢ violet, perf. 10 horiz., type I **489**
A140 3¢ deep violet, perf. 8½ vert.,
type I **394**
A140 4¢ orange brown, perf. 12,
double line wmk. **334**
A140 4¢ orange brown, same,
China clay paper **334a**
A140 4¢ orange brown, perf. 12,
bluish paper **360**
A140 4¢ brown, perf. 12, single
line wmk. **377**
A140 4¢ brown, perf. 11, unwmkd. **503**
A140 4¢ brown, perf. 10, single
line wmk. **427**
A140 4¢ orange brown, perf. 10,
unwmkd. **465**
A140 4¢ orange brown, imperf. **346**
A140 4¢ orange brown, perf. 12 horiz. ... **350**
A140 4¢ orange brown, perf. 12 vert. **354**
A140 4¢ brown, perf. 10 vert.,
flat plate, single line wmk. **446**
A140 4¢ brown, same, rotary press **457**
A140 4¢ orange brown, perf. 10 vert.,
rotary press, unwmkd. **495**
A140 4¢ brown, perf. 8½ vert.,
single line wmk. **395**
A140 5¢ blue, perf. 12, double
line wmk. **335**
A140 5¢ blue, same China clay paper ... **335a**
A140 5¢ blue, perf. 12 bluish paper **361**
A140 5¢ blue, perf. 12, single line wmk. **378**
A140 5¢ blue, perf. 11, unwmkd. **504**
A140 5¢ rose (error), same **505**
A140 5¢ carmine (error), perf. 10,
unwmkd. **467**
A140 5¢ blue, perf. 10, single line wmk. **428**
A140 5¢ blue, perf. 12x10 .... **428a**
A140 5¢ blue, perf. 10, unwmkd. **466**
A140 5¢ blue, imperf. **347**
A140 5¢ carmine (error), imperf. **485**
A140 5¢ blue, perf. 12 horiz. **351**
A140 5¢ blue, perf. 12 vert. **355**
A140 5¢ blue, perf. 10 vert., flat
plate, single line wmk. **447**
A140 5¢ blue, same, rotary press **458**
A140 5¢ blue, perf. 10 vert., rotary
press, unwmkd. **496**
A140 5¢ blue, perf. 8½ vert. **396**
A140 6¢ red orange, perf. 12, double
line wmk. **336**
A140 6¢ red orange, same,
China clay paper **336a**
A140 6¢ red orange, perf. 12,
bluish paper **362**
A140 6¢ red orange, perf. 12,
single line wmk. **379**
A140 6¢ red orange, perf. 11, unwmkd. . **506**
A140 6¢ red orange, perf. 10,
single line wmk. **429**
A140 6¢ red orange, perf. 10; unwmkd. . **468**
A140 7¢ black, perf. 12, single
line wmk. **407**
A140 7¢ black, perf. 11, unwmkd. **507**
A140 7¢ black, perf. 10, single
line wmk. **430**
A140 7¢ black, perf. 10, unwmkd. **469**
A140 8¢ olive green, perf. 12,
double line wmk. **337**
A140 8¢ olive green, same,
China clay paper **337a**

A140 8¢ olive green, perf. 12,
bluish paper 363
A140 8¢ olive green, perf. 12,
single line wmk. 380
A140 10¢ yellow, perf. 12,
double line wmk. 338
A140 10¢ yellow, same, China
clay paper 338a
A140 10¢ yellow, perf. 12, bluish paper ... 364
A140 10¢ yellow, perf. 12, single
line wmk. 381
A140 10¢ yellow, perf. 12 vert. 356
A140 13¢ blue green, perf. 12,
double line wmk. 339
A140 13¢ blue green, same, China
clay paper 339a
A140 13¢ blue green, perf. 12,
bluish paper 365
A140 15¢ pale ultra, perf. 12,
double line wmk. 340
A140 15¢ pale ultramarine, same,
China clay paper 340a
A140 15¢ pale ultra, perf. 12,
bluish paper 366
A140 15¢ pale ultra, perf. 12,
single line wmk. 382
A140 50¢ violet 341
A140 $1 violet brown 342

ISSUES OF 1912-19

A148   **A149** Franklin

*Designs of 8¢ to $1 denominations differ only
in figures of value.*

A148 8¢ pale olive green, perf. 12,
single line wmk. 414
A148 8¢ olive bister, perf. 11, unwmkd. . 508
A148 8¢ pale olive grn., perf. 10,
single line wmk. 431
A148 8¢ olive green, perf. 10, unwmkd. 470
A148 9¢ salmon red, perf. 12,
single line wmk. 415
A148 9¢ salmon red, perf. 11, unwmkd. 509
A148 9¢ salmon red, perf. 10,
single line wmk. 432
A148 9¢ salmon red, perf. 10, unwmkd. 471
A148 10¢ orange yellow, perf. 12,
single line wmk. 416
A148 10¢ orange yellow, perf. 11,
unwmkd. 510
A148 10¢ orange yellow, perf. 10,
single line wmk. 433
A148 10¢ orange yellow, perf. 10,
unwmkd. 472
A148 10¢ orange yellow, perf. 10 vert.,
same 497
A148 11¢ light green, perf. 11, unwmkd. . 511
A148 11¢ dark green, perf. 10,
single line wmk. 434
A148 11¢ dark green, perf. 10, unwmkd. . 473
A148 12¢ claret brown, perf. 12,
single line wmk. 417
A148 12¢ claret brown, perf. 11, unwmkd. . 512
A148 12¢ claret brown, perf. 10,
single line wmk. 435
A148 12¢ copper red, same 435a
A148 12¢ claret brown, perf. 10, unwmkd. . 474
A148 13¢ apple green, perf. 11, unwmkd. 513
A148 15¢ gray, perf. 12, single line wmk. 418
A148 15¢ gray, perf. 11, unwmkd. 514
A148 15¢ gray, perf. 10, single line wmk. 437

A148 15¢ gray, perf. 10, unwmkd. 475
A148 20¢ ultramarine, perf. 12,
single line wmk. 419
A148 20¢ light ultra., perf. 11, unwmkd. . 515
A148 20¢ ultramarine, perf. 10,
single line wmk. 438
A148 20¢ light ultra, perf. 10, unwmkd. .. 476
A148 30¢ orange red, perf. 12,
single line wmk. 420
A148 30¢ orange red, perf. 11, unwmkd. . 516
A148 30¢ orange red, perf. 10,
single line wmk. 439
A148 30¢ orange red, perf. 10, unwmkd. . 476A
A148 50¢ violet, perf. 12,
single line wmk. 421
A148 50¢ violet, perf. 12, double
line wmk. 422
A148 50¢ red violet, perf. 11, unwmkd. ... 517
A148 50¢ violet, perf. 10, single
line wmk. 440
A148 50¢ light violet, perf. 10, unwmkd. . 477
A148 $1 violet brown, perf. 12,
double line wmk. 423
A148 $1 violet brown, perf. 11, unwmkd. 518
A148 $1 violet black, perf. 10,
double line wmk. 460
A148 $1 violet black, perf. 10, unwmkd. 478

ISSUES OF 1918-20

Perf. 11 Unwmkd.
A149 $2 orange red & black 523
A149 $2 carmine & black 547
A149 $5 deep green & black 524

ISSUES OF 1922-32

A154 Nathan Hale   **A155** Franklin

A156 Warren G. Harding   **A157** Washington

A158 Lincoln   **A159** Martha Washington

A160 Theodore
Roosevelt   **A161** Garfield

A162 McKinley   **A163** Grant

A164 Jefferson   **A165** Monroe

A166 Hayes   **A167** Cleveland

A168 American
Indian   **A169** Statue of
Liberty

A170 Golden Gate   **A171** Niagara Falls

A172 Buffalo   **A173** Arlington
Amphitheater
and Tomb of the
Unknown Soldier

A174 Lincoln
Memorial   **A175** United States
Capitol

A176 "America"

Canal Zone Overprints:
Type A has flat-topped "A's" in "CANAL."
Type B has sharp-pointed "A's" in "CANAL."

Unwmkd.

A154	½¢ olive brown, perf. 11	551
A154	½¢ olive brown, perf. 11x10½	653
A154	½¢ olive brown, "CANAL ZONE"	C.Z. 70
A155	1¢ deep green, perf. 11, flat plate	552
A155	1¢ deep green, booklet pane of 6	552a
A155	1¢ green, perf. 11, rotary press 19¾x22¼mm	594
A155	1¢ green, same, 19¼x22½mm (used)	596
A155	1¢ green, perf. 11x10, rotary press	578
A155	1¢ green, perf. 10	581
A155	1¢ green, perf. 11x10½	632
A155	1¢ green, same, booklet pane of 6	632a
A155	1¢ green, ovpt. Kans.	658
A155	1¢ green, ovpt. Nebr.	669
A155	1¢ green, imperf.	575
A155	1¢ green, perf. 10 vert.	597
A155	1¢ yellow green, perf. 10 horiz.	604
A155	1¢ deep green, "CANAL ZONE" type A, perf. 11	C.Z. 71
A155	1¢ deep green, same, booklet pane of 6	C.Z. 71e
A155	1¢ green, "CANAL ZONE" type B, perf. 11x10½	C.Z. 100
A156	1½¢ yellow brown, perf. 11	553
A156	1½¢ yellow brown, perf. 11x10½	633
A156	1½¢ brown, ovpt. Kans.	659
A156	1½¢ brown, ovpt. Nebr.	670
A156	1½¢ brown, perf. 10	582
A156	1½¢ brown, perf. 10 vert.	598
A156	1½¢ yellow brown, perf. 10 horiz.	605
A156	1½¢ yellow brown, imperf., flat plate	576
A156	1½¢ yellow brown, imperf., rotary press, 19¼x22½mm	631
A156	1½¢ yellow brown "CANAL ZONE"	C.Z. 72

No heavy hair lines at top center of head. Outline of left acanthus scroll generally faint at top and toward base at left side.

Type I

Three heavy hair lines at top center of head; two being outstanding in the white area. Outline of left acanthus scroll very strong and clearly defined at top (under left edge of lettered panel) and at lower curve (above and to left of numeral oval).

Type II

A157	2¢ carmine, perf. 11, flat plate	554
A157	2¢ carmine, same, booklet pane of 6	554c
A157	2¢ carmine, perf. 11, rotary press, 19¾x22¼mm	595
A157	2¢ carmine, perf. 11x10	579
A157	2¢ carmine, perf. 11x10½, type I	634
A157	2¢ carmine, perf. 11x10½, type II	634A
A157	2¢ carmine lake, same, type I	634b
A157	2¢ carmine lake, same, booklet pane of 6	634d
A157	2¢ carmine, overprt. Molly Pitcher	646
A157	2¢ carmine, overprt. Hawaii 1778-1928	647
A157	2¢ carmine, overprt. Kans.	660
A157	2¢ carmine, overprt. Nebr.	671
A157	2¢ carmine, perf. 10	583
A157	2¢ carmine, same, booklet pane of 6	583a
A157	2¢ carmine, imperf.	577
A157	2¢ carmine, perf. 10 vert., type I	599
A157	2¢ carmine, same, type II	599A
A157	2¢ carmine, perf. 10 horiz.	606
A157	2¢ carmine, "CANAL ZONE" type A, perf. 11	C.Z. 73
A157	2¢ carmine, same, booklet pane of 6	C.Z. 73a
A157	2¢ carmine, "CANAL ZONE" type B, perf. 11	C.Z. 84
A157	2¢ carmine, same, booklet pane of 6	C.Z. 84d
A157	2¢ carmine, "CANAL ZONE" type B, perf. 10	C.Z. 97
A157	2¢ carmine, same, booklet pane of 6	C.Z. 97b
A157	2¢ carmine, "CANAL ZONE" type B, perf. 11x10½	C.Z. 101
A157	2¢ carmine, same, booklet pane of 6	C.Z. 101a
A158	3¢ violet, perf. 11	555
A158	3¢ violet, perf. 11x10½	635
A158	3¢ violet, overprt. Kans.	661
A158	3¢ violet, overprt. Nebr.	672
A158	3¢ violet, perf. 10	584
A158	3¢ violet, perf. 10 vert.	600
A158	3¢ violet, "CANAL ZONE" perf. 11	C.Z. 85
A158	3¢ violet, "CANAL ZONE" perf. 10	C.Z. 98
A158	3¢ violet, "CANAL ZONE" perf. 11x10½	C.Z. 102
A159	4¢ yellow brown, perf. 11	556
A159	4¢ yellow brown, perf. 11x10½	636
A159	4¢ yellow brown, ovrpt. Kans.	662
A159	4¢ yellow brown, ovrpt. Nebr.	673
A159	4¢ yellow brown, perf. 10	585
A159	4¢ yellow brown, perf. 10 vert.	601
A160	5¢ dark blue, perf. 11	557
A160	5¢ dark blue, perf. 11x10½	637
A160	5¢ dark blue, ovpt. Hawaii 1778-1928	648
A160	5¢ deep blue, ovpt. Kans.	663
A160	5¢ deep blue, ovpt. Nebr.	674
A160	5¢ blue, perf. 10	586
A160	5¢ dark blue, perf. 10 vert.	602
A160	5¢ dark blue, "CANAL ZONE" type A, perf. 11	C.Z. 74
A160	5¢ dark blue, same, type B	C.Z. 86
A160	5¢ dark blue, same, perf. 11x10½	C.Z. 103
A161	6¢ red orange, perf. 11	558
A161	6¢ red orange, perf. 11x10½	638
A161	6¢ red orange, ovrpt. Kans.	664
A161	6¢ red orange, ovrpt. Nebr.	675
A161	6¢ red orange, perf. 10	587
A161	6¢ deep orange, perf. 10 vert.	723
A162	7¢ black, perf. 11	559
A162	7¢ black, perf. 11x10½	639

A162	7¢ black, ovrpt. Kans.	665
A162	7¢ black, ovrpt. Nebr.	676
A162	7¢ black, perf. 10	588
A163	8¢ olive green, perf. 11	560
A163	8¢ olive green, perf. 11x10½	640
A163	8¢ olive green, ovrpt. Kans.	666
A163	8¢ olive green, ovrpt. Nebr.	677
A163	8¢ olive green, perf. 10	589
A164	9¢ rose, perf. 11	561
A164	9¢ orange red, perf. 11x10½	641
A164	9¢ light rose, ovrpt. Kans.	667
A164	9¢ light rose, ovrpt. Nebr.	678
A164	9¢ rose, perf. 10	590
A165	10¢ orange, perf. 11	562
A165	10¢ orange, perf. 11x10½	642
A165	10¢ orange yellow, ovrpt. Kans.	668
A165	10¢ orange yellow, ovrpt. Nebr.	679
A165	10¢ orange, perf. 10	591
A165	10¢ orange, perf. 10 vert.	603
A165	10¢ orange, "CANAL ZONE" type A, perf. 11	C.Z. 75
A165	10¢ orange, same, type B	C.Z. 87
A165	10¢ orange, same, perf. 10	C.Z. 99
A165	10¢ orange, same, perf. 11x10½	C.Z. 104
A166	11¢ light blue, perf. 11	563
A166	11¢ light blue, perf. 11x10½	692
A167	12¢ brown violet, perf. 11	564
A167	12¢ brown violet, perf. 11x10½	693
A167	12¢ brown violet, "CANAL ZONE" type A	C.Z. 76
A167	12¢ brown violet, same, type B	C.Z. 88
A168	14¢ blue, perf. 11	565
A168	14¢ dark blue, perf. 11x10½	695
A168	14¢ dark blue, "CANAL ZONE" type A, perf. 11	C.Z. 77
A168	14¢ dark blue, same, type B	C.Z. 89
A168	14¢ dark blue, same, perf. 11x10½	C.Z. 116
A169	15¢ gray, perf. 11	566
A169	15¢ gray, perf. 11x10½	696
A169	15¢ gray, "CANAL ZONE" type A	C.Z. 78
A169	15¢ gray, "CANAL ZONE" type B	C.Z. 90
A170	20¢ carmine rose, perf. 11	567
A170	20¢ carmine rose, perf. 10½x11	698
A170	20¢ carmine rose, "CANAL ZONE"	C.Z. 92
A171	25¢ yellow green, perf. 11	568
A171	25¢ blue green, perf. 10½x11	699
A172	30¢ olive brown, perf. 11	569
A172	30¢ brown, perf. 10½x11	700
A172	30¢ olive brown, "CANAL ZONE" type A	C.Z. 79
A172	30¢ olive brown, "CANAL ZONE" type B	C.Z. 93
A173	50¢ lilac, perf. 11	570
A173	50¢ lilac, perf. 10½x11	701
A173	50¢ lilac, "CANAL ZONE" type A	C.Z. 80
A173	50¢ lilac, "CANAL ZONE" type B	C.Z. 94
A174	$1 violet black, perf. 11	571
A174	$1 violet brown, "CANAL ZONE" type A	C.Z. 81
A174	$1 violet brown, "CANAL ZONE" type B	C.Z. 95
A175	$2 deep blue, perf. 11	572
A176	$5 carmine & blue, perf. 11	573

REGULAR ISSUES OF 1925-26, 1930 AND 1932

A186 Harrison

A187 Wilson

A186 13¢ green, perf. 11 622
A186 13¢ yellow green, perf. 11x10½ 694
A187 17¢ black, perf. 11 623
A187 17¢ black, perf. 10½x11 697
A187 17¢ black, "CANAL ZONE" ...... C.Z. 91

A203 Harding

A204 Taft

A203 1½¢ brown, perf. 11x10½ 684
A203 1½¢ brown, perf. 10 vert. 686
A204 4¢ brown, perf. 11x10½ 685
A204 4¢ brown, perf. 10 vert. 687

A226 Washington

A226 3¢ deep violet, perf. 11x10½ 720
A226 3¢ deep violet, same, booklet
pane of 6 .... 720b
A226 3¢ deep violet, perf. 10 vert. 721
A226 3¢ deep violet, perf. 10 horiz. 722
A226 3¢ deep violet,
"CANAL ZONE" .... C.Z. 115

PRESIDENTIAL ISSUE OF 1938

A275 Benjamin Franklin

A276 George Washington

A277 Martha Washington

A278 John Adams

A279 Thomas Jefferson

A280 James Madison

A281 The White House

A282 James Monroe

A283 John Quincy Adams

A284 Andrew Jackson

A285 Martin Van Buren

A286 William H. Harrison

A287 John Tyler

A288 James K. Polk

A289 Zachary Taylor

A290 Millard Fillmore

A291 Franklin Pierce

A292 James Buchanan

A293 Abraham Lincoln

A294 Andrew Johnson

A295 Ulysses S. Grant

A296 Rutherford B. Hayes

A297 James A. Garfield

A298 Chester A. Arthur

A299 Grover Cleveland

A300 Benjamin Harrison

A301 William McKinley

A302 Theodore Roosevelt

A303 William Howard Taft

A304 Woodrow Wilson

A305 Warren G. Harding

A306 Calvin Coolidge

Rotary Press Printing
Unwmkd.

A275 ½¢ deep orange, perf. 11x10½ 803
A275 ½¢ red orange, "CANAL
ZONE" .... C.Z. 118

A276 1¢ green, perf. 11x10½ 804
A276 1¢ green, booklet pane of 6 .... 804b
A276 1¢ green, perf. 10 vert. 839
A276 1¢ green, perf. 10 horiz. 848
A277 1½¢ bister brown, perf. 11x10½ 805
A277 1½¢ bister brown, perf. 10 vert. 840
A277 1½¢ bister brown, perf. 10 horiz. 849
A277 1½¢ bister brown,
         "CANAL ZONE" .... C.Z. 119
A278 2¢ rose carmine, perf. 11x10½ 806
A278 2¢ booklet pane of 6 .... 806b
A278 2¢ rose carmine, perf. 10 vert. 841
A278 2¢ rose carmine, perf. 10 horiz. ... 850
A279 3¢ deep violet, perf. 11x10½ 807
A279 3¢ deep violet, booklet pane of 6 . 807a
A279 3¢ deep violet, perf. 10 vert. 842
A279 3¢ deep violet, perf. 10 horiz. 851
A280 4¢ red violet, perf. 11x10½ 808
A280 4¢ red violet, perf. 10 vert. 843
A281 4½¢ dark gray, perf. 11x10½ 809
A281 4½¢ dark gray, perf. 10 vert. 844
A282 5¢ bright blue, perf. 11x10½ 810
A282 5¢ bright blue, perf. 10 vert. 845
A283 6¢ red orange, perf. 11x10½ 811
A283 6¢ red orange, perf. 10 vert. 846
A284 7¢ sepia, perf. 11x10½ 812
A285 8¢ olive green, perf. 11x10½ 813
A286 9¢ rose pink, perf. 11x10½ 814
A287 10¢ brown red, perf. 11x10½ 815
A287 10¢ brown red, perf. 10 vert. 847
A288 11¢ ultramarine, perf. 11x10½ 816
A289 12¢ bright violet, perf. 11x10½ 817
A290 13¢ blue green, perf. 11x10½ 818
A291 14¢ blue, perf. 11x10½ 819
A292 15¢ blue gray, perf. 11x10½ 820
A293 16¢ black, perf. 11x10½ 821
A294 17¢ rose red, perf. 11x10½ 822
A295 18¢ brn. carmine, perf. 11x10½ 823
A296 19¢ bright violet, perf. 11x10½ 824
A297 20¢ bright blue green, perf. 11x10½ 825
A298 21¢ dull blue, perf. 11x10½ 826
A299 22¢ vermilion, perf. 11x10½ 827
A300 24¢ gray black, perf. 11x10½ 828
A301 25¢ dp. red lilac, perf. 11x10½ 829
A302 30¢ deep ultra, perf. 11x10½ 830
A303 50¢ lt. red violet, perf. 11x10½ 831

Flat Plate Printing
Perf. 11

A304 $1 pur. & blk., unwmkd. 832
A304 $1 pur. & blk., wmkd. USIR 832b
A304 $1 red vio. & blk., thick white paper,
         smooth colorless gum 832c
A305 $2 yellow green & black 833
A306 $5 carmine & black 834

LIBERTY ISSUE 1954-73

A477 Benjamin Franklin

A478 George Washington

A480 Thomas Jefferson

A482 Statue of Liberty

A484 The Hermitage

A486 Theodore Roosevelt

A488 Statue of Liberty (Rotary and flat plate printing)

A489a John J. Pershing

A491 Independence Hall

A490 The Alamo

A481 Bunker Hill Monument and Massachusetts Flag 1776

A483 Abraham Lincoln

A485 James Monroe

A487 Woodrow Wilson

A489 Design slightly altered; see position of torch (Giorgi press printing)

A491a Statue of Liberty

A492 Benjamin Harrison

A493 John Jay

A494 Monticello

A495 Paul Revere

A496 Robert E. Lee

A497 John Marshall

A498 Susan B. Anthony

A499 Patrick Henry

A500 Alexander Hamilton

Unwmkd.

A477 ½¢ red orange, perf. 11x10½ 1030
A478 1¢ dark green, perf. 11x10½........ 1031
A478 1¢ dark green, perf. 10 vert. 1054
A478a 1¼¢ turquoise, perf. 10½x11 ..... 1031A
A478a 1¼¢ turquoise, perf. 10 horiz. 1054A
A479 1½¢ brown carmine, perf. 10½x11 1032
A480 2¢ carmine rose, perf. 11x10 1033
A480 2¢ carmine rose, perf. 10 vert. 1055
A481 2½¢ gray blue, perf. 11x10½ 1034
A481 2½¢ gray blue, perf. 10 vert. 1056
A482 3¢ deep violet, perf. 11x10½ 1035
A482 3¢ deep violet, perf. 10 vert., ... 1057
A482 3¢ deep violet, imperf.,
         size: 24x28mm 1075a
A483 4¢ red violet, perf. 11x10½......... 1036
A483 4¢ red violet, perf. 10 vert. 1058
A484 4½¢ blue green, perf. 10½x11 1037
A484 4½¢ blue green, perf. 10 horiz. 1059
A485 5¢ deep blue, perf. 11x10½ 1038
A486 6¢ carmine, perf. 11x10½, ... 1039
A487 7¢ rose carmine, same 1040
A488 8¢ dark violet blue & carmine,
         flat plate printing, perf. 11,
         approx. 22.7mm high............. 1041
A488 8¢ dark violet blue & carmine,
         rotary press printing, perf. 11,
         appprox. 22.9mm high......... 1041B
A488 8¢ dark violet blue & carmine,
         imperf., size: 24x28mm 1075b
A489 8¢ dark violet blue & carmine,
         perf. 11 1042

A478a Palace of the Governors, Santa Fe

A479 Mount Vernon

A489a 8¢ brown, perf. 11x10½ 1042A
A490 9¢ rose lilac, perf. 10½x11 1043
A491 10¢ rose lake, same 1044
A491a 11¢ carmine & dark violet blue,
         perf. 11 .... 1044A
A492 12¢ red, perf. 11x10½ 1045
A493 15¢ rose lake, perf. 11x10½ 1046
A494 20¢ ultramarine, perf. 10½x11 1047
A495 25¢ green, perf. 11x10½ 1048
A495 25¢ green, perf. 10 vert. 1059A
A496 30¢ black, perf. 11x10½ 1049
A497 40¢ brown red, perf. 11x10½ 1050
A498 50¢ bright purple, perf. 11x10½ .. 1051
A499 $1 purple, perf. 11x10½ 1052
A500 $5 black, perf. 11 1053

ISSUE OF 1962-66

A646 Andrew Jackson   **A650** George
                                    Washington

A646 1¢ green, perf. 11x10½ 1209
A646 1¢ green, perf. 10 vert. 1225
A650 5¢ dk. bl. gray, perf. 11x10½ 1213
A650 5¢ dk. bl. gray, perf. 10 vert......... 1229

PROMINENT AMERICANS
ISSUE 1965-81

A710 Thomas Jefferson

A711 Albert   **A712** Frank Lloyd
Gallatin   Wright and Guggenheim
                        Museum, New York

A713 Francis   **A714** Abraham
Parkman   Lincoln

A715 George   **A715a** Re-engraved
Washington

A716 Franklin D.   **A727a** Franklin D.
Roosevelt   Roosevelt
                        (vertical coil)

A816 Benjamin   **A717** Albert
Franklin and   Einstein
his signature

A718 Andrew   **A718a** Henry Ford
Jackson   and 1909 Model I

A719 John F.   **A817a** Fiorello H.
Kennedy   LaGuardia and
                       New York skyline

A720 Oliver Wendell **A818** Ernest (Ernie)
Holmes   Taylor Pyle

A818a Dr. Elizabeth **A721** George C.
Blackwell   Marshall

A818b Amadeo P.   **A722** Frederick
Giannini   Douglass

A723 John Dewey   **A724** Thomas Paine

A725 Lucy Stone   **A726** Eugene O'Neill

A727 John Bassett Moore

Types of 15¢:

I - Necktie barely touches coat at bottom; cross-hatching of tie strong and complete. Flag of "5" is true horizontal. Crosshatching of "15" is colorless when visible.
II - Necktie does not touch coat at bottom; LL to UR crosshatching lines strong, UL to LR lines very faint. Flag of "5" slants down slightly at right. Crosshatching of "15" is colored and visible when magnified.
A third type, used only for No. 1288B, is smaller in overall size, and "15¢" is ¾mm closer to head.

Unwmkd.
Rotary Press Printing

A710 1¢ green, perf. 11x10½ 1278
A710 1¢ green, perf. 10, vert., tagged . 1299
A711 1¼¢ light green, perf. 11x10½ 1279
A712 2¢ dk. bl. gray, perf. 11x10½ 1280
A713 3¢ violet, perf. 10½x11 1281
A713 3¢ violet, perf. 10 horiz. 1297
A714 4¢ black, perf. 11x10½ 1282
A714 4¢ black, perf. 10, vert. 1303
A715 5¢ blue, perf. 11x10½ 1283
A715 5¢ blue, perf. 10, vert. 1304
A715a 5¢ blue, perf. 11x10½ 1283B
A715a 5¢ blue, perf. 10 vert. 1304C
A716 6¢ gray brown, perf. 10½x11 1284
A716 6¢ gray brown, perf. 10 horiz.,
        tagged 1298
A727a 6¢ gray brown, perf. 10 vert.,
        tagged 1305
A816 7¢ bright blue, perf. 10½x11 ... 1393D
A717 8¢ violet, perf. 11x10½ 1285
A718 10¢ lilac, perf. 11x10½ 1286
A718a 12¢ black, perf. 10½x11 .... 1286A
A719 13¢ brown, perf. 11x10½ 1287
A817a 14¢ gray brown, perf. 11x10½ 1397
A720 15¢ magenta, perf. 11x10½ 1288
A720 15¢ magenta, perf. 10
        (booklet panes only) 1288B
A720 15¢ magenta, perf. 10 vert. 1305E
A818 16¢ brown 1398
A818a 18¢ violet, perf. 11x10½ 1399
A721 20¢ deep olive, perf. 11x10½ 1289
A818b 21¢ green, perf. 11x10½ 1400
A722 25¢ rose lake, perf. 11x10½ 1290
A723 30¢ red lilac, perf. 10½x11 1291
A724 40¢ blue black, perf. 11x10½ 1292
A725 50¢ rose magenta, perf. 11x10½ .. 1293

A726 $1 dull purple, perf. 11x10½ 1294
A726 $1 dull purple, perf. 10 vert.,
    tagged 1305C
A727 $5 gray black, perf. 11x10½ 1295

A815 Dwight D.   **A815a**
Eisenhower

A815 6¢ dark blue gray, perf. 11x10½ .. 1393
A815 6¢ dk. bl. gray, perf. 10, vert. 1401
A815 8¢ deep claret, perf. 11x10½
    (Booklet panes only) 1395
A815 8¢ deep claret, perf. 10 vert. 1402
A815a 8¢ blk., red & bl. gray, perf. 11 1394

FLAG ISSUE 1968-71

A760 Flag and White House

A760 6¢ dark blue, red & green, perf. 11,
    size: 19x22mm **1338**
A760 6¢ dark blue, red & green, perf.
    11x10½, size: 18¼x21mm ... **1338D**
A760 6¢ dark blue, red & green, perf. 10
    vert., size: 18¼x21mm **1338A**
A760 8¢ multicolored, perf. 11x10½ .. **1338F**
A760 8¢ multicolored, perf. 10 vert. .. **1338G**

REGULAR ISSUE 1971-74

A817 U.S. Postal Service Emblem

A923 50-Star and   **A924** Jefferson
13-Star Flags   Memorial and
    quotation from
    Declaration of
    Independence

A925 Mail Transport **A926** Liberty Bell
and "Zip Code"

A817 8¢ multicolored, perf. 11x10½ 1396
A923 10¢ red & blue, perf. 11x10½ 1509
A923 10¢ red & blue, perf. 10 vert. 1519
A924 10¢ blue, perf. 11x10½ 1510
A924 10¢ blue, perf. 10 vert. 1520
A925 10¢ multicolored, perf. 11x10½ 1511
A926 6.3¢ brick red, perf. 10 vert. 1518

AMERICANA ISSUE 1975-81

A984 Inkwell and **A985** Speaker's
Quill   Stand

A987 Early Ballot **A988** Books,
Box   Bookmark, Eyeglasses

A994 Dome of **A995** Contemplation
Capitol   of Justice

A996 Early American **A997** Torch
Printing Press   Statue of Liberty

A998 Liberty Bell **A999** Eagle and Shield

A1001 Ft. McHenry **A1002** Head
Flag   Statue of Liberty

A1003 Old North **A1004** Ft. Nisqually
Church

A1005 Sandy Hook **A1006** Morris
Lighthouse   Township School
    No. 2, Devil's Lake

A1007 Iron "Betty" **A1008** Rush
Lamp Plymouth Colony, Lamp and
17th-18th Centuries   Candle Holder

A1009 Kerosene **A1010** Railroad
Table Lamp   Conductors
    Lantern, c. 1850

COIL STAMPS

A1011 Six-string guitar **A1199** Weaver violins

A1012 Saxhorns **A1013** Drum

A1014 Steinway Grand Piano, 1857

A984 1¢ dark blue, greenish,
perf. 11x10½ 1581
A984 1¢ dark blue, greenish,
perf. 10 vert. 1811
A985 2¢ red brown, greenish,
perf. 11x10½ 1582
A987 3¢ olive, greenish, perf. 11x10½ . 1584
A988 4¢ rose magenta, cream,
perf. 11x10½ 1585
A994 9¢ slate green, gray, perf. 11x10½
(booklet panes only) 1590
A994 9¢ slate green, gray, perf. 11x9¾
(booklet panes only) 1590A
A994 9¢ slate green, gray,
perf. 11x10½ 1591
A994 9¢ slate green, gray,
perf. 10 vert. 1616
A995 10¢ violet, gray, perf. 10 vert. 1617
A995 10¢ violet, gray, perf. 11x10½ 1592
A996 11¢ orange, gray, perf. 11x10½ .. 1593
A997 12¢ red brown, beige,
perf. 11x10½ 1594
A997 12¢ red brown, beige,
perf. 10 vert. 1816
A998 13¢ brown, perf. 11x10½ 1595
A998 13¢ brown, perf. 10 vert. 1618
A999 13¢ multicolored 1596
A1001 15¢ gray, dark blue & red,
perf. 11 1597
A1001 15¢ gray, dark blue & red, perf. 11x
10½ (booklet panes only) 1598
A1001 15¢ gray, dark blue & red,
perf. 10 vert. 1618C
A1002 16¢ blue, perf. 11x10½ 1599
A1002 16¢ blue, perf. 10 vert. 1619
A1003 24¢ red, blue, perf. 11x10½ 1603
A1004 28¢ brown, blue, perf. 11x10½ .. 1604
A1005 29¢ blue, blue, perf. 11x10½ 1605
A1006 30¢ green, perf. 11x10½ 1606
A1007 50¢ black & orange, perf. 11 1608
A1008 $1 brown, orange & yellow, tan,
perf. 11 1610
A1009 $2 dark green & red, tan, perf. 11 1611
A1010 $5 red brown, yellow & orange,
tan, perf. 11 1612
A1011 3.1¢ brown, yellow, perf. 10 vert. 1613
A1199 3.5¢ purple, yellow, perf. 10 vert. . 1813
A1012 7.7¢ brown, bright yellow,
perf. 10 vert. 1614
A1013 7.9¢ carmine, yellow,
perf. 10 vert. 1615
A1014 8.4¢ dark blue, yellow,
perf. 10 vert. 1615C

FLAG ISSUE 1975-77

A1015 13-star
Flag over
Independence Hall

A1016 Flag
over Capitol

A1015 13¢ dark blue & red,
perf. 11x10¾ 1622
A1015 13¢ dark blue & red, perf. 11¼ . 1622C
A1015 13¢ dark blue & red, perf. 10 vert. 1625
A1016 13¢ blue & red, perf. 11x10½
(booklet panes only) 1623
A1016 13¢ blue & red, perf. 10x9¾
(booklet panes only) 1623B

REGULAR ISSUE 1978

A1123 Indian Head
Penny, 1877

A1209 Dolley
Madison

A1126 Red Masterpiece
and Medallion Roses

A1123 13¢ brown & blue, green, bister,
perf. 11 1734
A1126 15¢ multicolored, perf. 10
(booklet panes only) 1737
A1209 15¢ red brown & sepia, perf. 11 ... 1822

REGULAR ISSUE 1978-85

A1124 "A" Eagle

A1207 "B" Eagle

A1332 "C" Eagle

A1333 "C" Eagle
(Booklet)

A1496 "D" Eagle

A1497 "D"
Eagle (Booklet)

A1124 (15¢) orange, Perf. 11 1735
A1124 (15¢) orange, perf. 11x10½
(booklet panes only) 1736
A1124 (15¢) orange, perf. 10 vert. 1743
A1207 (18¢) violet, perf. 11x10½ 1818
A1207 (18¢) violet, perf. 10 (booklet
panes only) 1819
A1207 (18¢) violet, perf. 10 vert. 1820
A1332 (20¢) brown, perf. 11x10½ 1946
A1332 (20¢) brown, perf. 10 vert. 1947
A1333 (20¢) brown, perf. 11x10½ (booklet
panes only) 1948
A1496 (22¢) green, perf. 11 2111
A1496 (22¢) green, perf. 10 vert. 2112
A1497 (22¢) green, perf. 11 (booklet
panes only) 2113

GREAT AMERICANS ISSUE 1980-1999

Dorothea Dix USA 1c A1231	Margaret Mitchell 1 A1551	Igor Stravinsky USA 2c A1232	Mary Lyon USA 2 A1552	Henry Clay USA 3c A1233	Paul Dudley White MD 3 A1553	Carl Schurz 4c USA A1234	Father Flanagan USA 4 A1554
Pearl Buck USA 5c A1235	Hugo L. Black 5 USA A1555	Luis Muñoz Marín Governor Puerto Rico 05 A1556	Walter Lippmann 6 USA A1236	Abraham Baldwin USA 7 A1237	Henry Knox USA 8 A1238	Sylvanus Thayer USA 9 A1239	Richard Russell USA 10c A1240
Red Cloud 10 USA A1557	Alden Partridge USA 11 A1241	USA 13c Crazy Horse A1242	Sinclair Lewis USA 14 A1243	14 USA Julia Ward Howe A1558	Buffalo Bill Cody USA 15 A1559	Rachel Carson USA 17c A1244	Belva Ann Lockwood USA 17 A1560
George Mason USA 18c A1245	USA 19c Sequoyah A1246	Ralph Bunche USA 20c A1247	Thomas H. Gallaudet USA 20c A1248	Harry S Truman USA 20c A1249	Virginia Apgar Physician 1909-1974 20 A1561	Chester Carlson USA 21 A1562	John J. Audubon USA 22 A1250
USA 23 Mary Cassatt A1563	USA 25 Jack London A1564	Sitting Bull USA 28 A1565	Earl Warren Chief Justice of the U.S. USA 29 A1566	Thomas Jefferson USA 29 A1567	Frank C. Laubach USA 30c A1251	Milton S. Hershey PHILANTHROPIST USA 32 A2248	Cal Farley HUMANITARIAN USA 32 A2249
EDITOR Henry R. Luce USA 32 A2250	Lila and DeWitt Wallace PHILANTHROPISTS USA 32 A2251	Charles R Drew MD USA 35c A1252	Dennis Chavez United States Senator USA 35 A1568	Robert Millikan 37c USA A1253	Greville Clark USA 39 A1254	Lillian M. Gilbreth USA 40c A1255	Claire Chennault Flying Tigers 1940s USA 40 A1569
Harvey Cushing MD USA 45 A1570	Ruth Benedict ANTHROPOLOGIST USA 46 A2253	USA 50 Chester W. Nimitz A1256	Hubert H Humphrey Vice President USA 52 A1571	Alice Hamilton, MD SOCIAL REFORMER USA 55 A2255	Justin S. Morrill LAND-GRANT COLLEGES USA 55 A2256	John Harvard USA 56 A1572	H.H.'Hap'Arnold USA 65 A1573

Wendell Willkie 1892-1944 Statesman 75 USA A1574	Mary Breckinridge Nurse-Frontier Nursing Service USA 77 A2257	Alice Paul SUFFRAGIST USA 78 A2258	Bernard Revel USA $1 A1575	Johns Hopkins USA $1 A1576	William Jennings Bryan $2 USA A1577	Bret Harte USA $5 A1578

GREAT AMERICANS ISSUE 1980-99

SEE ILLUSTRATIONS PAGE 62A

WILDLIFE ISSUES 1981-82

A1267 Bighorn

A1268 Puma

A1269 Harbor Seal

A1270 Bison

A1271 Brown bear

A1272 Polar bear

A1273 Elk (wapiti)

A1274 Moose

A1275 White-tailed deer

A1276 Pronghorn

A1334 Rocky Mountain Bighorn

From Booklet Panes

FLAG ISSUES 1981-85

A1277

A1278

A1280

A1279 Field of 1777 flag

A1281

A1498

A1499 Of the People, By the People, For the People

TRANSPORTATION ISSUE 1981-95

SEE ILLUSTRATIONS PAGE 64A

TRANSPORTATION ISSUE 1981-95

Omnibus 1880s USA 1c **A1283**	Omnibus 1880s 1 USA **A1604a**	Locomotive 1870s USA 2c **A1284**	Locomotive 1870s 2 USA **A1604b**	Handcar 1880s USA 3c **A1284a**	Conestoga Wagon 1800s USA 3 **A1622**	School Bus 1920s 3.4 USA **A1506**
Stagecoach 1890s USA 4c **A1285**	Steam Carriage 04 USA 1866 **A1810**	Buckboard 1880s USA 4.9 **A1507**	Motorcycle 1913 USA 5c **A1286**	Milk Wagon 1900s 5 USA **A1623**	Circus Wagon 1900s 05 USA **A1811**	Circus Wagon 1900s USA 5c **A1811a**
Canoe 1800s Additional Nonprofit Postage Paid USA 05 **A1812**	Sleigh 1880s USA 5.2c Auth Nonprofit Org **A1287**	Elevator 1900s 5.3 USA Nonprofit Carrier Route Sort **A1624**	Star Route Truck 5.5 USA 1910s Auth Nonprofit Org **A1508**	Bicycle 1870s USA 5.9c Auth Nonprofit Org **A1288**	Tricycle 1880s 6 USA **A1509**	Tractor 1920s 7.1 USA **A1510**
Baby Buggy 1880s USA 7.4c **A1289**	Carreta 1770s 7.6 USA Nonprofit **A1625**	Ambulance 1860s 8.3 USA **A1511**	Wheel Chair 1920s 8.4 USA Nonprofit **A1626**	Tow Truck 1920s 8.5 USA **A1512**	Mail Wagon 1880s USA 9.3c Bulk Rate **A1290**	Canal Boat 1880s 10 USA **A1627**
Tractor Trailer Additional Presort Postage Paid 1930s USA 10 **A1816**	Oil Wagon 1890s 10.1 USA Bulk Rate **A1513**	Hansom Cab 1890s USA 10.9c Bulk Rate **A1291**	RR Caboose 1890s USA 11c Bulk Rate **A1292**	Stutz Bearcat 1933 11 USA **A1514**	Stanley Steamer 1909 USA 12 **A1515**	Pushcart 1880s 12.5 USA **A1516**
Patrol Wagon 1880s USA 13 Presorted First-Class **A1628**	Coal Car 1870s 13.2 USA Bulk Rate **A1629**	Iceboat 1880s USA 14 **A1517**	Tugboat 1900s USA 15 **A1630**	Popcorn Wagon 16.7 USA 1902 Bulk Rate **A1631**	Electric Auto 1917 USA 17c **A1293**	Dog Sled 1920s 17 USA **A1518**
Racing Car 1911 USA 17.5 ZIP+4 Presort **A1632**	Surrey 1890s USA 18c **A1294**	Fire Pumper 1860s USA 20c **A1295**	Cable Car 1880s USA 20 **A1633**	Cog Railway 1870s 20 USA **A1822**	Fire Engine 1900s 20.5 USA ZIP+4 Presort **A1634**	Railroad Mail Car 1920s Presorted First-Class 21 USA **A1635**
	Lunch Wagon 1890s 23 USA **A1823**	Tandem Bicycle 1890s 24.1 USA ZIP+4 **A1636**	Bread Wagon 1880s 25 USA **A1519**	Ferryboat 1900s 32 USA **A1825**	Seaplane 1914 $1 USA **A1827**	

A1290   9.3¢ carmine rose **1903**
A1627   10¢ sky blue **2257**
A1816   10¢ green, engraved (Bureau
               precanceled) **2457**
A1816   10¢ green, photogravure
               (Bureau precanceled **2458**
A1513 10.1¢ slate blue **2130**
A1291 10.9¢ purple **1904**
A1292   11¢ red **1905**
A1514   11¢ dark green **2131**
A1515   12¢ dark blue **2132**
A1516 12.5¢ olive green **2133**
A1628   13¢ black, (Bureau
               precanceled) **2258**
A1629 13.2¢ slate green,
               (Bureau precanceled) **2259**
A1517   14¢ sky blue **2134**
A1630   15¢ violet **2260**
A1631 16.7¢ rose, (Bureau precanceled) . **2261**
A1293   17¢ ultramarine **1906**
A1518   17¢ sky blue **2135**
A1632 17.5¢ dark violet **2262**
A1294   18¢ dark brown **1907**
A1295   20¢ vermilion **1908**
A1633   20¢ blue violet **2263**
A1822   20¢ green **2463**
A1634 20.5¢ rose, (Bureau precanceled) . **2264**
A1635   21¢ olive green,
               (Bureau precanceled) **2265**
A1823   23¢ dark blue **2464**
A1636 24.1¢ deep ultramarine,
               (Bureau precanceled) **2266**
A1519   25¢ orange brown **2136**
A1825   32¢ blue **2466**
A1827 $1 dark blue & scarlet **2468**

REGULAR ISSUE 1983-99

A1894

A1897

A1898

A2532

A1758

A1296 Eagle and Moon

A1895

A1505 Eagle and Half Moon

A1898a

A2533

A1896

A1894 $2.90 multicolored, perf. 11 ...... **2540**
A1897 $2.90 multicolored, perf. 11x
                10½ **2543**
A1898 $3 multicolored, perf. 11 .... **2544**
A2532 $3.20 multicolored, serpentine
                die cut 11.5......................**3261**
A1758 $8.75 multicolored, perf. 11 ...... **2394**
A1296 $9.35 multicolored, perf. 10 vert.
                (booklet panes only) **1909**
A1296 $9.35 multicolored, booklet
                pane of 3 .... **1909a**
A1895 $9.95 multicolored, perf. 11 ...... **2541**
A1505 $10.75 multicolored, perf. 10 vert.
                (booklet panes only) **2122**
A1898a $10.75 multicolored, perf 11 .... **2544A**
A2533 $11.75 multicolored, serpentine
                die cut 11.5.......................... **3262**
A1896 $14 multicolored, perf 11 .... **2542**

REGULAR ISSUE 1982-85

A1532 George
Washington
Washington Monument

A1390 Consumer
Education

A1533 Sealed Envelopes

A1532   18¢ multicolored, perf. 10 vert. **2149**
A1532   18¢ multicolored, same, untagged
               (Bureau precanceled) **2149a**
A1390   20¢ sky blue, perf. 10 vert. **2005**
A1533 21.1¢ multicolored, perf. 10 vert. **2150**
A1533 21.1¢ multicolored, same, untagged
               (Bureau precanceled) **2150a**

REGULAR ISSUE 1987-88

A1646

A1647

A1648

A1649

A1649a

A1649b

A1649c

A1649d

A1646	22¢ multicolored, perf. 11	2276
A1647	(25¢) multicolored, perf. 11	2277
A1647	(25¢) multicolored, perf. 10	2282
A1647	(25¢) multicolored, perf. 10 vert.	2279
A1648	25¢ multicolored, perf. 11	2278
A1648	25¢ multicolored, perf. 10	2285A
A1649	25¢ multicolored, perf. 10 vert.	2280
A1649a	25¢ multicolored, perf. 11 (booklet panes only)	2283
A1649b	25¢ multicolored, perf. 10 (booklet panes only)	2284
A1649c	25¢ multicolored, perf. 10	2285
A1649d	25¢ multicolored, perf. 10 vert.	2281

REGULAR ISSUE 1989-98

A1793

A1834

A1877

A1884

A1947

A1950

A1951

A1793	25¢ multicolored, die cut, self-adhesive	2431
A1834	25¢ dark red & dark blue, die cut, self-adhesive	2475
A1877	(29¢) black, blue & dark red, die cut, self-adhesive	2522
A1884	29¢ black, gold & green, die cut, self-adhesive	2531A
A1947	29¢ brown & multicolored, die cut, self-adhesive	2595
A1947	29¢ green & multicolored, die cut, self-adhesive	2596
A1947	29¢ red & multicolored, die cut, self-adhesive	2597
A1950	29¢ red, cream & blue, die cut, self-adhesive	2598
A1951	29¢ multicolored, die cut, self-adhesive	2599
A1951	32¢ red, light blue, dark blue & yellow, serpentine die cut 11, self-adhesive	3122
A1951	32¢ red, light blue, dark blue & yellow, serpentine die cut 11.5x11.8, self-adhesive ...	3122E

FLORA & FAUNA ISSUE 1990-2000

A1840

A1841

A2335

A1842

A2336

A1843

A1847

A2350

A1848

A1849

A1852

A1853

A1854

A1844

A1850

A1851

A2351

A2550

A2551

A2552

A2553

A2634

A2635

A2636   A2637

A1845   A2339

A1846

A1840 1¢ multicolored, perf. 11 2476
A1841 1¢ multicolored, perf. 11 2477
A1841 1¢ multicolored, serpentine die cut
        10¾ self-adhesive 3031
A1841 1¢ multicolored, perf. 9.8 vert. ... 3044
A2335 2¢ multicolored, perf. 11.1 3032
A2335 2¢ multicolored, perf. 9¾ vert. 3045
A1842 3¢ multicolored, perf. 11 2478
A2336 3¢ multicolored, perf. 11.1 3033
A1843 19¢ multicolored, perf. 11½ x11 ... 2479
A1847 20¢ multicolored, perf. 11x10
        (booklet panes only) 2483
A1847 20¢ multicolored, serpentine die cut
        10½x11, self-adhesive 3048
A1847 20¢ multicolored, serpentine die cut
        11½ vert, self-adhesive 3053
A2350 20¢ multicolored, serpentine die cut
        11¼, self-adhesive 3050
A2350 20¢ multicolored, serpentine die cut
        10½ x11 on 3 sides, self-adhesive
        (booklet panes only) 3051
A2350 20¢ multicolored, serpentine die cut
        9¾ vert., self-adhesive 3055
A1848 29¢ black & multicolored, perf. 10
        (booklet panes only) 2484
A1848 29¢ red & multicolored, perf. 11
        (booklet panes only) 2485
A1849 29¢ multicolored, perf. 10x11
        (booklet panes only) 2486
A1852 29¢ multicolored, die cut,
        self-adhesive 2489
A1853 29¢ red, green & black, die cut,
        self-adhesive 2490
A1854 29¢ multicolored, die cut,
        self-adhesive 2491
A1844 30¢ multicolored, perf. 11½ x11 ... 2480
A1850 32¢ multicolored, perf. 11x10
        (booklet panes only) 2487
A1850 32¢ multicolored, serpentine die
        cut, self-adhesive.................... 2493
A1850 32¢ multicolored, serpentine
        die cut vert., self-adhesive 2495
A1851 32¢ multicolored, perf. 11x10
        (booklet panes only) 2488
A1851 32¢ multicolored, serpentine die
        cut, self-adhesive.................... 2494
A1851 32¢ multicolored, serpentine die
        cut vert., self-adhesive 2495A
A1853 32¢ pink, green & black, serpentine
        die cut, self-adhesive 2492
A1853 32¢ yellow, orange, green & black, ser-
        pentine die cut 11.3x11.7,
        self-adhesive 3049

A1853 32¢ yellow, orange, green & black,
        serpentine die cut 9.8 vert.,
        self-adhesive 3054
A2351 33¢ multicolored, serpentine die cut
        11½x11¾ on 2, 3, or 4 sides,
        self-adhesive (booklet panes
        only) 3052
A2351 33¢ multicolored, serpentine die cut
        10¾x10½ on 2 or 3 sides,
        self-adhesive (booklet panes
        only) 3052E
A2550 33¢ multicolored, serpentine die cut
        11.2x11.7, self-adhesive
        (booklet panes only).............3294
A2550 33¢ multicolored, serpentine die cut
        9.5x10, self-adhesive
        (booklet panes only).............3298
A2550 33¢ multicolored, serpentine die cut
        8.5 vert., self-adhesive 3302
A2551 33¢ multicolored, serpentine die cut
        11.2x11.7, self-adhesive
        (booklet panes only).............3295
A2551 33¢ multicolored, serpentine die cut
        9.5x10, self-adhesive
        (booklet panes only).............3300
A2551 33¢ multicolored, serpentine die cut
        8.5 vert., self-adhesive 3303
A2552 33¢ multicolored, serpentine die cut
        11.2x11.7, self-adhesive
        (booklet panes only).............3296
A2552 33¢ multicolored, serpentine die cut
        9.5x10, self-adhesive
        (booklet panes only).............3299
A2552 33¢ multicolored, serpentine die cut
        8.5 vert., self-adhesive 3305
A2553 33¢ multicolored, serpentine die cut
        11.2x11.7, self-adhesive
        (booklet panes only).............3297
A2553 33¢ multicolored, serpentine die cut
        9.5x10, self-adhesive
        (booklet panes only).............3301
A2553 33¢ multicolored, serpentine die cut
        8.5 vert., self-adhesive 3304
A2634 33¢ multicolored, serpentine die
        cut 8½ horiz., self-adhesive . 3404
A2635 33¢ multicolored, serpentine die
        cut 8½ horiz., self-adhesive . 3405
A2636 33¢ multicolored, serpentine die
        cut 8½ horiz., self-adhesive . 3406
A2637 33¢ multicolored, serpentine die
        cut 8½ horiz., self-adhesive . 3407
A1845 45¢ multicolored, perf. 11 2481
A2339 $1 multicolored, serpentine die cut
        11½x11¼, self-adhesive.........3036
A1846 $2 multicolored, perf. 11 2482

REGULAR ISSUE 1991-94

A1876

A1881

A1882

A1875

A1878

A1879

A1880   A1883

A1876 (4¢) bister & carmine, perf. 11 2521
A1881 19¢ multicolored, perf. 10 vert. .. 2529
A1881 19¢ multicolored, perf. 10 vert.,
        two rope loops on piling........ 2529
A1881 19¢ multicolored, perf. 10 vert.,
        one rope loop on piling....... 2529C
A1882 19¢ multicolored, perf. 10
        (booklet panes only) 2530
A1875 (29¢) yellow, black, red &
        yellow green, perf. 13 2517
A1875 (29¢) yellow, black, dull red & dark
        yellow green, perf. 10 vert. .. 2518
A1875 (29¢) yellow, black, dull red & dark
        green, bullseye perf. 11.2
        (booklet panes only) 2519
A1875 (29¢) pale yellow, black, red &
        brightgreen, perf. 11
        (booklet panes only) 2520
A1878 29¢ multicolored, engraved,
        perf. 10 vert. 2523
A1878 29¢ multicolored, photogravure,
        perf. 10 vert. 2523A
A1879 29¢ dull yellow, black, red &
        yellow green, perf. 11 2524
A1879 29¢ dull yellow, black, red &
        yellow green, perf. 13x12¾ 2524A
A1879 29¢ pale yellow, black, red & yellow
        green, roulette 10 vert. 2525
A1879 29¢ pale yellow, black, red & yellow
        green, perf. 10 vert. 2526
A1879 29¢ pale yellow, black, red &
        bright green, perf. 11
        (booklet panes only) 2527
A1880 29¢ multicolored, perf. 11
        (booklet panes only) 2528
A1883 29¢ multicolored, perf. 11 2531

REGULAR ISSUE 1991-98

Bulk Rate USA
A1956

USA Bulk Rate
A1957

USA Presorted Std
A2534

Presorted First-Class
A1959

A1960

A1946

A1961

A1939

A1942

A1944

A1956 (10¢) multicolored, perf. 10 vert.
(Bureau precanceled) 2602
A1957 (10¢) orange yellow & multicolored,
perf. 10 vert. (Bureau
precanceled) 2603
A1957 (10¢) gold & multicolored, perf. 10
vert. (Bureau precanceled) .. 2604
A1957 (10¢) gold & multicolored, serpentine
die cut 11.5 vert,
self-adhesive...................... 2907
A2534 (10¢) multicolored, perf. 9.9 vert.
(Bureau precanceled) 3270
A2534 (10¢) multicolored, serpentine die cut
9.9 vert., self-adhesive
(Bureau precanceled) 3271
A1959 (23¢) multicolored, perf. 10 vert.
(Bureau precanceled) 2605
A1960 23¢ multicolored, perf. 10 vert.
(Bureau precanceled) 2606
A1960 23¢ multicolored, perf. 10 vert.,
"23" 7mm long (Bureau
precanceled) 2607
A1960 23¢ violet blue, red & black, perf. 10
vert., "First Class" 8½ mm long
(Bureau precanceled) 2608
A1946 29¢ black & multicolored, perf. 10
(booklet panes only) 2593
A1946 29¢ black & multicolored, perf. 11x10
(booklet panes only).......... 2593B
A1946 29¢ red & multicolored, perf. 11x10
(booklet panes only) 2594
A1961 29¢ blue & red, perf. 10 vert. 2609
A1939 32¢ red brown, perf. 11.2.......... 2587
A1942 $1 blue, perf. 11½ 2590
A1944 $5 slate green, perf. 11½ 2592

G RATE ISSUE 1994-95

A2206

A2210

A2207

A2209

A2208

A2206 (3¢) tan, bright blue & red,
perf. 11x10.8...................... 2877
A2206 (3¢) tan, dark blue & red,
perf. 10.8x10.9................... 2878
A2210 (5¢) green & multicolored, perf. 9.8
vert. (Bureau precanceled) .. 2893
A2207 (20¢) black "G," yellow & multicolored,
perf. 11.2x11.1................... 2879
A2207 (20¢) red "G," yellow & multicolored,
perf. 11x10.9...................... 2880
A2209 (25¢) black "G," blue & multicolored,
perf. 9.8 vert.(Bureau
precanceled) 2888
A2208 (32¢) black "G" & multicolored,
perf. 11.2x11.1................... 2881
A2208 (32¢) black "G" & multicolored, perf.
10x9.9 (booklet panes only) 2883
A2208 (32¢) black "G" & multicolored, die cut,
self-adhesive, small number of
blue shading dots in white stripes
below blue field 2886
A2208 (32¢) black "G" & multicolored,
die cut, self-adhesive, thin
translucent paper, more blue
shading dots in white stripes
below blue field 2887
A2208 (32¢) black "G" & multicolored,
perf. 9.8 vert...................... 2889
A2208 (32¢) red "G" & multicolored, perf.
11x10.9, distance from
bottom of "G" to top of flag
is 13¾ mm.......................... 2882
A2208 (32¢) red "G" & multicolored, perf.
11x10.9 on 2 or 3 sides (booklet
panes only), distance from
bottom of "G" to top of flag
is 13½ mm.......................... 2885
A2208 (32¢) red "G" & multicolored,
perf. 9.8 vert...................... 2891
A2208 (32¢) red "G" & multicolored,
rouletted. 9.8 vert............... 2892
A2208 (32¢) blue "G" & multicolored, perf.
10.9 (booklet panes only).... 2884
A2208 (32¢) blue "G" & multicolored,
perf. 9.8 vert...................... 2890

REGULAR ISSUE 1995-98

A2217

A2218

A2489

A2220

PRESORTED STD
A2509

First-Class Card
A2223

Presorted First-Class
A2225

Presorted First-Class
A2490

A2212

A2230

A2217 (5¢) yellow, red & blue,
perf. 9.8 vert. 2902
A2217 (5¢) yellow, red & blue, serpentine
die cut 11.5 vert.,
self-adhesive...................... 2902B
A2218 (5¢) purple & multicolored,
perf. 9.9 vert. 2903
A2218 (5¢) purple & multicolored,
serpentine die cut 11.2 vert.,
self-adhesive 2904A
A2218 (5¢) purple & multicolored,
serpentine die cut 9.8 vert.,
self-adhesive.....................2904B
A2218 (5¢) blue & multicolored,
perf. 9.9 vert. 2904
A2489 (5¢) multicolored, perf. 10 vert.... 3207
A2489 (5¢) multicolored, serpentine die cut
9.7 vert., self-adhesive
(Bureau precanceled) 3207A
A2220 (10¢) black, red brown & brown,
perf. 9.8 vert. 2905
A2220 (10¢) black, red brown & brown,
serpentine die cut 11.5 vert.,
self-adhesive....................... 2906
A2509 (10¢) multicolored, serpentine die cut
9.8 vert., self-adhesive
(Bureau precanceled)........... 3228
A2509 (10¢) multicolored, perf 9.9 vert.
(Bureau precanceled)........... 3229

A2223(15¢) dark orange, yellow & multicolored (dark, bold colors, heavy shading lines, heavily shaded chrome), perf. 9.8 vert. **2908**

A2223(15¢) buff & multicolored (more subdued colors, finer details, shinier chrome), perf. 9.8 vert. **2909**

A2223(15¢) buff & multicolored, serpentine die cut 11.5 vert., self-adhesive **2910**

A2225(25¢) dark red, dark yellow green & multicolored (dark, saturated colors, dark blue lines in music selection board), perf.9.8 vert. **2911**

A2225(25¢) dark red, yellow green & multicolored, serpentine die cut 9.8 vert, self-adhesive..........**2912B**

A2225(25¢) bright orange red, bright yellow green & multicolored (bright colors, less shading and light blue lines in music selection board), perf. 9.8 vert. **2912**

A2225(25¢) bright orange red, bright yellow green & multicolored, serpentine die cut 11.5 vert., self-adhesive **2912A**

A2225(25¢) bright orange red, bright yellow green & multicolored, imperf, with simulated perforations, self-adhesive **3132**

A2490(25¢) multicolored, perf. 10 vert.... **3208**

A2490(25¢) multicolored, serpentine die cut 9.7 vert., self-adhesive (Bureau precanceled) **3208A**

A2212 32¢ multicolored, perf. 10.4........ **2897**

A2212 32¢ blue, tan, brown, red & light blue, perf. 10.8x9.8 (booklet panes only) **2916**

A2212 32¢ blue, tan, brown, red & light blue (pronounced blue shading in flag and red "1995"), perf. 9.8 vert. **2913**

A2212 32¢ blue, yellow brown, red & gray (gray shading in flag and blue "1995"), perf. 9.8 vert.......... **2914**

A2212 32¢ multicolored, serpentine die cut 8.7 vert., self-adhesive **2915**

A2212 32¢ dark blue, tan, brown, red & light blue, red "1996," serpentine die cut 9.7 vert., straight cut at bottom with 11 teeth above, self-adhesive **2915A**

A2212 32¢ dark blue, tan, brown, red & light blue, red "1997," serpentine die cut 9.8 vert., straight cut at bottom and top with 9 teeth between, self-adhesive **2915D**

A2212 32¢ dark blue, tan, brown, red & light blue (sky shows color graduation at lower right, blue "1996"), serpentine die cut 9.9 vert., self-adhesive **3133**

A2212 32¢ dark blue, tan, brown, red & light blue, serpentine die cut 10.9 vert, self-adhesive **2915C**

A2212 32¢ dark blue, tan, brown, red & light blue, serpentine die cut 11.5 vert, self-adhesive..........................**2915B**

A2212 32¢ multicolored, serpentine die cut 8.8 on 2, 3 or 4 adjacent sides, dated "1995" in blue, self-adhesive (booklet panes only)........**2920**

A2212 32¢ multicolored, serpentine die cut 11.3 on 2, 3 or 4 adjacent sides, dated "1996" in blue, self-adhesive (booklet panes only)............**2920D**

A2212 32¢ dark blue, tan, brown, red & light blue, serpentine die cut 9.8 on 2 or 3 adjacent sides, dated "1996" in red, self-adhesive (booklet panes only) **2921**

A2212 32¢ dark blue, tan, brown, red & light blue, serpentine die cut 9.8 on 2 or 3 adjacent sides, dated "1997" in red, self-adhesive (booklet panes only) **2921b**

A2230 32¢ multicolored, die cut, self-adhesive **2919**

H RATE ISSUE 1999

A2529

A2530

A2531

A2529 (1¢) multicolored, white USA, black "1998," perf. 11.2................ **3257**

A2529 (1¢) multicolored, pale blue USA, blue "1998," perf. 11.2 .... **3258**

A2530 22¢ multicolored, serpentine die cut 10.8, self-adhesive **3259**

A2530 22¢ multicolored, serpentine die cut 9.9 vert, self-adhesive **3263**

A2530 22¢ multicolored, perf. 9¾ vert. ...**3353**

A2531(33¢) multicolored, perf. 11.2........ **3260**

A2531(33¢) multicolored, perf. 9.8 vert... **3264**

A2531(33¢) multicolored, serpentine die cut 9.9 vert., stamp corners at right angles, backing paper same size as stamp, self-adhesive **3265**

A2531(33¢) multicolored, serpentine die cut 9.9 vert., stamp corners rounded, backing paper larger than stamp, self-adhesive.......................... **3266**

A2531(33¢) multicolored, serpentine die cut 9.9, (booklet panes only), self-adhesive **3267**

A2531(33¢) multicolored, serpentine die cut 11.2x11.1 (booklet panes only), self-adhesive **3268**

A2531(33¢) multicolored, die cut 8 (booklet panes only), self-adhesive...... **3269**

REGULAR ISSUE 1999

A2540

A2541

A2540 33¢ multicolored, perf. 11.2 .... **3277**

A2540 33¢ multicolored, serpentine die cut 11.1, self-adhesive **3278**

A2540 33¢ multicolored, serpentine die cut 11½x11¾, self-adhesive **3278F**

A2540 33¢ multicolored, serpentine die cut 9.8 (booklet panes only), self-adhesive **3279**

A2540 33¢ multicolored, perf. 9.9 vert. .. **3280**

A2540 33¢ multicolored, serpentine die cut 9.8 vert., stamp corners at right angles, backing paper same size as stamp, self-adhesive **3281**

A2540 33¢ multicolored, serpentine die cut 9.8 vert., stamp corners rounded, backing paper same larger than stamp, self-adhesive **3282**

A2541 33¢ multicolored, serpentine die cut 7.9 (booklet panes only), self-adhesive **3283**

S C O T T M O U N T S

For stamp presentation unequaled in beauty and clarity, insist on ScottMounts. Made of 100% inert polystyrol foil, ScottMounts protect your stamps from the harmful effects of dust and moisture. Available in your choice of clear or black backs, ScottMounts are center-split across the back for easy insertion of stamps and feature crystal clear mount faces. Double layers of gum assure stay-put bonding on the album page. Discover the quality and value ScottMounts have to offer.

ScottMounts are available from your favorite stamp dealer or direct from:

Discover the quality and value ScottMounts have to offer. For a complete list of ScottMount sizes or a free sample pack call or write Scott Publishing Co.

SCOTTMOUNTS

HOW TO ORDER THE RIGHT SIZE:

Pre-cut ScottMounts come in sizes labeled as stamp width by stamp height, measured in millimeters. Strips of mount material come in three different lengths: 215mm, 240mm and 265mm. The strip you should use is based on the height of the stamp you wish to mount.

ScottMounts are available with clear or black backs. Please indicate color choice when ordering.

Pre-Cut Single Mounts

Size	Description	# Mounts	Item	Price
40 x 25	U.S. Standard Commemorative—Horizontal	40	901	$2.75
25 x 40	U.S. Standard Commemorative—Vertical	40	902	2.75
25 x 22	U.S. Regular Issue—Horizontal	40	903	2.75
22 x 25	U.S. Regular Issue—Vertical	40	904	2.75
41 x 31	U.S. Semi–Jumbo—Horizontal	40	905	2.75
31 x 41	U.S. Semi–Jumbo—Vertical	40	906	2.75
50 x 31	U.S. Jumbo—Horizontal	40	907	2.75
31 x 50	U.S. Jumbo—Vertical	40	908	2.75
25 x 27	U.S. Famous Americans	40	909	2.75
33 x 27	United Nations	40	910	2.75
40 x 27	United Nations	40	911	2.75
67 x 25	PNC, Strips of Three	40	976	4.75
67 x 34	Pacific '97 Triangle	10	984	2.25
111 x 25	PNC, Strips of Five	25	985	4.75
51 x 36	U.S. Hunting Permit/Express Mail	40	986	4.75

Pre-Cut Plate Block, FDC & Postal Card Mounts

Size	Description	# Mounts	Item	Price
57 x 55	Regular Issue Plate Block	25	912	$4.75
73 x 63	Champions of Liberty	25	913	4.75
106 x 55	Rotary Press Standard Commemorative	20	914	4.75
105 x 57	Giori Press Standard Commemorative	20	915	4.75
165 x 94	First Day Cover	10	917	4.75
140 x 90	Postal Card Size	10	918	4.75

Strips 215mm Long

Size	Description	# Mounts	Item	Price
20	U.S. 19th Century/Horizontal Coil	22	919	$5.95
22	U.S. Early Air Mail	22	920	5.95
24	U.S., Canada, Great Britain	22	921	5.95
25	U.S. Comm. and Regular	22	922	5.95
27	U.S. Famous Americans	22	923	5.95
28	U.S. 19th Century	22	924	5.95
30	U.S. 19th Century	22	925	5.95
31	U.S. Jumbo and Semi-Jumbo	22	926	5.95
33	United Nations	22	927	5.95
36	U.S. Hunting Permit, Canada	15	928	5.95
39	U.S. Early 20th Century	15	929	5.95
41	U.S. Semi-Jumbo	15	930	5.95
	Multiple Assortment: one strip of each size 22-41 (Two 25mm strips)	12	931	5.95
44	U.S. Vertical Coil Pair	15	932	5.95
48	U.S. Farley, Gutter Pair	15	933	5.95
50	U.S. Jumbo	15	934	5.95
52	U.S. Standard Commemorative Block	15	935	5.95
55	U.S. Century of Progress	15	936	5.95
57	U.S. Famous Americans Block	15	937	5.95
61	U.S. Blocks, Israel Tab	15	938	5.95

Strips 240mm Long

Size	Description	# Mounts	Item	Price
63	U.S. Jumbo Commemorative—Horizontal Block	10	939	$6.75
66	Israel Tab Block	10	940	6.75
68	U.S. Farley, Gutter Pair & Souvenir Sheets	10	941	6.75
74	U.S. TIPEX Souvenir Sheet	10	942	6.75
80	U.S. Standard Commemorative—Vertical Block	10	943	6.75
82	U.S. Blocks of Four	10	944	6.75
84	Israel Tab Block/Mars Pathfinder	10	945	6.75
89	U.S. Postal Card Size	10	946	6.75

Strips 265mm Long

Size	Description	# Mounts	Item	Price
100	U.N. Margin Inscribed Block	7	947	6.75
120	Various Souvenir Sheets and Blocks	7	948	6.75
40	Standard Commemorative Vertical	10	949	$6.75
55	U.S. Regular Plate Block Strip 20	10	950	6.75
59	U.S. Double Issue Strip	10	951	6.75
70	U.S. Jumbo Com. Plate Block	10	952	9.75
91	Great Britain Souvenir Sheet/Norman Rockwell	10	953	9.75
105	U.S. Standard Plate Number Strip	10	954	9.75
107	Same as above—Wide Margin	10	955	9.75
111	U.S. Gravure-Intaglio Plate Number Strip	10	956	11.25
127	U.S. Jumbo Commemorative Plate Number Strip	10	957	13.75
137	Great Britain Coronation	10	958	14.50
158	U.S. Apollo-Soyuz Plate Number Strip	10	959	15.25
231	U.S. Full Post Office Pane Regular and Commemorative	5	961	14.25

Souvenir Sheets/Small Panes

Size	Description	# Mounts	Item	Price
111 x 25	PNC, Strips of Five	25	985	4.75
204 x 153	U.S. Bicent. White Plains	5	962	$ 6.95
187 x 144	U.N. Flag Sheet	10	963	12.25
160 x 200	New U.N., Israel Sheet	10	964	12.25
120 x 207	AMERIPEX President Sht.	4	965	4.75
229 x 131	World War II Commemorative Sheet	5	968	6.95
111 x 91	Columbian Souvenir Sheet	6	970	2.95
148 x 196	Apollo Moon Landing	4	972	5.95
129 x 122	U.S. Definitive Mini-Sheet	8	989	7.95
189 x 151	Chinese New Year	5	990	7.95
150 x 185	Dr. Davis/World Cup	5	991	7.95
198 x 151	Cherokee	5	992	7.95
198 x 187	Postal Museum	4	994	7.95
156 x 187	Sign Lang., Statehood	5	995	7.95
188 x 197	Country-Western	4	996	7.95
151 x 192	Olympic	5	997	7.95
174 x 185	Buffalo Soldiers	5	998	7.95
130 x 198	Silent Screen Stars	5	999	7.95
190 x 199	Leg. West, Civil, Comic	4	1000	7.95
178 x 181	Cranes	4	1001	7.95
183 x 212	Wonders of the Sea	3	1002	7.95
156 x 264	$14 Eagle	4	1003	7.95
159 x 270	$9.95 Moon Landing	4	1004	7.95
159 x 259	$2.90 Priority/$9.95 Express Mail	4	1005	7.95
223 x 187	Marilyn Monroe	3	1006	7.95
185 x 181	Challenger Shuttle	4	1007	7.95
152 x 228	Indian Dances/Antique Autos	5	1008	7.95
165 x 150	River Boat/Hanukkah	6	1009	7.95
275 x 200	Large Gutter Blocks/Aircraft/Dinosaurs	2	1010	7.95
161 x 160	Pacific '97 Triangle Block of 16	6	1011	7.95
174 x 130	Bugs Bunny	6	1012	7.95
196 x 158	Football Coaches	4	1013	7.95
184 x 184	American Dolls	4	1014	7.95
186 x 230	Classic Movie Monsters	3	1015	7.95
187 x 160	Trans-Mississippi Sheet	4	1016	7.95
192 x 230	Celebrate the Century	3	1017	7.95
156 x 204	Space Discovery	5	1018	7.95
192 x 209	American Ballet	5	1019	7.95
139 x 151	Christmas Wreaths	5	1020	7.95

Available from your favorite stamp dealer or direct from:

P.O. Box 828 Sidney OH 45365-0828

For more information on Scott products visit our web site at:

www.scottonline.com

Subject Index of Regular & Air Post Issues

Using the Scott U.S. Stamp Collector's Database 2000 to collect is as easy as...

Point, click and collect!

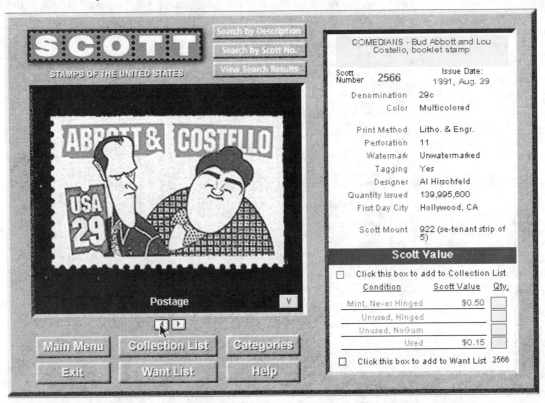

The Scott U.S. Stamp Collector's Database 2000 is compatible with Windows '95 and higher including Windows NT and Macintosh OS7 and higher operating systems. The program requires 16MB of RAM, an 8 bit color display and 15MB of free hard disk space for installation.

Search and find Scott numbers and Scott values for more than 11,000 U.S. stamps at the click of a mouse.

NEW FEATURES:

- Listings for 2,400 plate blocks and more than 4,100 first day covers.

- Includes the 1999 new issues and updated values.

- Improved reporting and tracking features in the want, collection and personal lists.

- Expanded descriptions for better searching and sorting.

- Create your own customized database for items not part of the main program. The Custom database maintains separate totals from the Main Collection list.

- Enhanced print capabilities with print preview.

- Import, export and back-up functions.

- View comprehensive catalogue information and full color stamp illustrations.

Item	Description	Retail
CD2000	CD 2000	$69.95
UP2000	CD 2000 Upgrade*	$34.95

The CD 2000 upgrade is compatible with Scott U.S. Stamp Collector's Database Version 1 and the Ultimate Collector for Stamps.™

To Order Call 1-800-572-6885
or visit your favorite stamp dealer.

www.scottonline.com
Scott Publishing Co., P.O. Box 828, Sidney OH 45365-0828

POSTMASTERS' PROVISIONALS

The Act of Congress of March 3, 1845, effective July 1, 1845, established rates of postage as follows:

"For every single letter in manuscript or paper of any kind by or upon which information shall be asked or communicated in writing or by marks designs, conveyed in the mail, for any distance under 300 miles, five cents; and for any distance over 300 miles, ten cents; and for a double letter there shall be charged double these rates; and for a treble letter, treble these rates; and for a quadruple letter, quadruple these rates; and every letter or parcel not exceeding half an ounce in weight shall be deemed a single letter, and every additional weight of half an ounce, shall be charged with an additional single postage. All drop letters, or letters placed in any post office, not for transmission through the mail but for delivery only, shall be charged with postage at the rate of two cents each."

Circulars were charged 2 cents, magazines and pamphlets 2½ cents; newspapers according to size.

Between the time of the Act of 1845, effecting uniform postage rates, and the Act of Congress of March 3, 1847, authorizing the postmaster-general to issue stamps, postmasters in various cities issued provisional stamps.

Before adhesive stamps were introduced, prepaid mail was marked "Paid" either with pen and ink or handstamps of various designs. Unpaid mail occasionally was marked "Due." Most often, however, unpaid mail did not have a "Due" marking, only the amount of postage to be collected from the recipient, e.g. "5," "10," "18¾," etc. Thus, if a letter was not marked "Paid," it was assumed to be unpaid. These "stampless covers" are found in numerous types and usually carry the town postmark.

New York Postmaster Robert H. Morris issued the first postmaster provisional in July 1845. Other postmasters soon followed. The provisionals served until superseded by the federal government's 5c and 10c stamps issued July 1, 1847.

Postmasters recognized the provisionals as indicating postage prepaid. On several provisionals, the signature of initials of the postmaster vouched for their legitimate use.

On July 12, 1845, Postmaster Morris sent examples of his new stamp to the postmasters of Boston, Philadelphia, Albany and Washington, asking that they be treated as unpaid until they reached the New York office. Starting in that year, the New York stamps were distributed to other offices. Postmaster General Cave Johnson reportedly authorized this practice with the understanding that these stamps were to be sold for letters directed to or passing through New York. This was an experiment to test the practicality of the use of adhesive postage stamps.

ALEXANDRIA, VA

Daniel Bryan, Postmaster

A1

All known copies cut to shape.
Type I - 40 asterisks in circle.
Type II - 39 asterisks in circle.

1846			**Typeset**		*Imperf.*
1X1	A1	5c	**black**, *buff*, type I		
a.		5c	black, *buff*, type II	75,000.	
			On cover (I or II)		135,000.
1X2	A1	5c	**black**, *blue*, type I, on cover		—

Cancellations
Red circular town
Black "PAID"
Black ms. accounting number
("No. 45," "No. 70")

The approximately 6 copies of Nos. 1X1 and 1X1a known on cover or cover front are generally not tied by postmark and some are uncanceled. The value for "on cover" is for a stamp obviously belonging on a cover which bears the proper circular dated town, boxed "5" and straight line "PAID" markings.

No. 1X2 is unique. It is canceled with a black straight line "PAID" marking which is repeated on the cover. The cover also bears a black circular "Alexandria Nov. 25" postmark.

ANNAPOLIS, MD.

Martin F. Revell, Postmaster
ENVELOPE

E1

1846		**Printed in upper right corner of envelope**	
2XU1	E1	5c **carmine red**, *white*	210,000.

No. 2XU1 exists in two sizes of envelope.

Envelopes and letter sheets are known showing the circular design and figure "2" handstamped in blue or red. They were used locally. Value, blue $2,500, red $3,500.

Letter sheets are known showing the circular design and figure "5" handstamped in blue or red. Value, blue $3,500, red $5,000.

Similar circular design in blue without numeral or "PAID" is known to have been used as a postmark.

BALTIMORE, MD.

James Madison Buchanan, Postmaster

Signature of Postmaster A1 — *James M. Buchanan 5 Cents.*

Printed from a plate of 12 (2x6) containing nine 5c stamps (Pos. 1-6, 8, 10, 12) and three 10c (Pos. 7, 9, 11).

1845			**Engr.**		*Imperf.*
3X1	A1	5c	**black**		5,000.
			On cover		10,000.
			Vertical pair on cover		30,000.
3X2	A1	10c	**black**, on cover		50,000.
3X3	A1	5c	**black**, *bluish*	65,000.	5,000.
			On cover		10,000.
3X4	A1	10c	**black**, *bluish*		60,000.

Nos. 3X3-3X4 preceded Nos. 3X1-3X2 in use.
No. 3X3 unused is unique. Value is based on 1997 auction sale.

Cancellations
Blue circular town
Blue straight line "PAID"
Blue "5" in oval
Blue "10" in oval
Black pen

Off cover values are for stamps canceled by either pen or handstamp. Stamps on cover tied by handstamps command premiums.

ENVELOPES

James M. Buchanan.

E1

Three Separate Handstamps

The "PAID" and "5" in oval were handstamped in blue or red, always both in the same color on the same entire. "James M. Buchanan" was handstamped in black, blue or red. Blue town and rate with black signature was issued first and sells for more.

The paper is manila, buff, white, salmon or grayish. Manila is by far the most frequently found 5c envelope. All 10c envelopes are rare, with manila or buff the more frequent. Of the 10c on salmon, only one example is known.

The general attractiveness of the envelope and the clarity of the handstamps primarily determine the value.

The color listed is that of the "PAID" and "5" in oval.

1845			**Various Papers**	Handstamped
3XU1	E1	5c	**blue**	6,000.
3XU2	E1	5c	**red**	10,000.
3XU3	E1	10c	**blue**	20,000.
3XU4	E1	10c	**red**	20,000.

Earliest known use: No. 3XU4, June 12, 1845.

Cancellations
Blue circular town
Blue "5" in oval

The second "5" in oval on the unlisted "5 + 5" envelopes is believed not to be part of the basic prepaid marking, but envelopes bearing this marking merit a premium over the values for Nos. 3XU1-3XU2.

BOSCAWEN, N. H.

Worcester Webster, Postmaster

PAID
5
A1 **CENTS**

1846 (?)   **Typeset**   *Imperf.*
4X1 A1 5c **dull blue,** *yellowish,* on cover   *175,000.*

One copy known, uncanceled on cover with ms. postal markings.

BRATTLEBORO, VT.

Frederick N. Palmer, Postmaster

 Initials of Postmaster — A1

Printed from plate of 10 (5x2) separately engraved subjects with imprint "Eng'd by Thos. Chubbuck, Bratto." below the middle stamp of the lower row (Pos. 8).

1846   *Imperf.*
Thick Softwove Paper Colored Through
5X1 A1 5c **black,** *buff*   *10,000.*
    On cover   *35,000.*
    Two singles on cover   *110,000.*

Cancellations
Red straight line "PAID"
Red pen
Blue "5"

The red pen-marks are small and lightly applied. They were used to invalidate a single sample sheet. One copy of each plate position is known so canceled.

LOCKPORT, N.Y.

Hezekiah W. Scovell, Postmaster

A1

"Lockport, N.Y." oval and "PAID" separately handstamped in red, "5" in black ms.

1846   *Imperf.*
6X1 A1 5c **red,** *buff,* on cover   *150,000.*
Cancellation
Black ms. "X"

One copy of No. 6X1 is known. Small fragments of two other copies adhering to one cover have been found.

MILLBURY, MASS.

Asa H. Waters, Postmaster

George Washington — A1

Printed from a woodcut, singly, on a hand press.

1846   *Imperf.*
7X1 A1 5c **black,** *bluish*   *130,000.* 20,000.
    On cover   90,000.

Earliest known use: Aug. 21, 1846.

Cancellations
Red straight line "PAID"
Red circular "MILBURY, MS.,"
    date in center

NEW HAVEN, CONN.

Edward A. Mitchell, Postmaster
ENVELOPES

E1

Impressed from a brass handstamp at upper right of envelope.
Signed in blue, black, magenta or red ms., as indicated in parenthesis.

1845
8XU1 E1 5c **red** (Bl or M)   *75,000.*
    Cut square   *20,000.*
    Cut to shape   *8,000.*
8XU2 E1 5c **red,** *light bluish* (Bk)   *100,000.*
8XU3 E1 5c **dull blue,** *buff* (Bl)   *100,000.*
    Cut to shape (Bk)   *10,000.*
8XU4 E1 5c **dull blue** (Bl)   *100,000.*

Values of Nos. 8XU1-8XU4 are a guide to value. They are based on auction realizations and take condition into consideration. All New Haven envelopes are of almost equal rarity. An entire of No. 8XU2 is the finest example known. The other envelopes and cut squares are valued according to condition as much as rarity.

REPRINTS

Twenty reprints in dull blue on white paper, signed by E. A. Mitchell in lilac rose ink, were made in 1871 for W. P. Brown and others, value $750. Thirty reprints in carmine on hard white paper, signed in dark blue or red, were made in 1874 for Cyrus B. Peets, Chief Clerk for Mitchell, value $550. Unsigned reprints were made for N. F. Seebeck and others about 1872, value $200.

Edward A. Mitchell, grandson of the Postmaster, in 1923 delivered reprints in lilac on soft white wove paper, dated "1923" in place of the signature, value $200.

In 1932, the New Haven Philatelic Society bought the original handstamp and gave it to the New Haven Colony Historical Society. To make the purchase possible (at the $1000 price) it was decided to print 260 stamps from the original handstamp. Of these, 130 were in red and 130 in dull blue, all on hard, white wove paper, value approximately $125 each.

According to Carroll Alton Means' booklet on the New Haven Provisional Envelope, after this last reprinting the brass handstamp was so treated that further reprints cannot be made. The reprints were sold originally at $5 each. A facsimile signature of the postmaster, "E. A. Mitchell," (blue on the red reprints, black on the blue) was applied with a rubber handstamp. These 260 reprints are all numbered to correspond with the number of the booklet issued then.

NEW YORK, N.Y.

Robert H. Morris, Postmaster

George Washington — A1

Printed by Rawdon, Wright & Hatch from a plate of 40 (5x8). The die for Washington's head on the contemporary bank notes was used for the vignette. It had a small flaw—a line extending from the corner of the mouth down the chin—which is quite visible on the paper money. This was corrected for the stamp.

The stamps were usually initialed "ACM" (Alonzo Castle Monson) in magenta ink as a control before being sold or passed through the mails. There are four or five styles of these initials. The most common is "ACM" without periods. The scarcest is "A.C.M." believed written by Marcena Monson. The rare initials "RHM" (Robert H. Morris, the postmaster) and "MMJr" (Marcena Monson) are listed separately.

The stamps were printed on a variety of wove papers varying in thickness from pelure to thick, and in color from gray to bluish and blue. A thick brown gum was used first, succeeded by a thin whitish transparent gum. Some stamps appear to have a slight ribbing or mesh effect. A few also show letters of a double-line papermaker's watermark, a scarce variety. All used true blue copies carry "ACM" without periods; of the three unused copies, two lack initials.

Nos. 9X1-9X3 and varieties unused are valued without gum. Examples with original gum are extremely scarce and will command higher prices.

Earliest known use: July 15, 1845 (No. 9X1e).

1845-46   **Engr.**   **Bluish Wove Paper**   *Imperf.*
9X1 A1 5c **black,** signed ACM, connected,
    1846   *1,300.*   500.
    On cover   650.
    On cover to France or England   2,250.
    On cover to other European
        countries   5,500.

Pair	5,250.	1,300.
Pair on cover		2,100.
Pair on cover to England		4,500.
Pair on cover to Canada		5,500.
Strip of 3		4,500.
Strip of 3 on cover		9,000.
Strip of 4	11,000.	
Strip of 4 on cover		20,000.
Block of 4		—
Double transfer at bottom (Pos. 2)	1,550.	575.
Double transfer at top (Pos. 7)	1,550.	575.
Bottom frame line double (Pos. 31)	1,550.	575.
Top frame line double (Pos. 36)	1,550.	575.

The only blocks currently known are a used block of 4 off cover (faulty) and a block of 9 on cover.

Cancellations
Blue pen	500.
Black pen	+25.
Magenta pen	+100.
Red square grid (New York)	+50.
Red round grid (Boston)	+350.
Blue numeral (Philadelphia)	+750.
Red "U.S" in octagon frame (carrier)	+1,200.
Red "PAID"	+50.
Red N.Y. circular date stamp	+75.
Large red N.Y. circular date stamp containing "5"	+125.

a.	Signed ACM, AC connected	1,600.	550.
	On cover		725.
	On cover to France or England		2,250.
	On cover to other European countries		6,000.
	Pair	5,250.	1,550.
	Pair, Nos. 9X1, 9X1a	—	3,500.
	Pair on cover		2,100.
	Double transfer at bottom (Pos. 2)	1,700.	675.
	Double transfer at top (Pos. 7)	1,700.	675.
	Bottom frame line double (Pos. 31)	1,700.	675.
	Top frame line double (Pos. 36)	1,700.	675.

Cancellations
Blue pen	550.
Black pen	+25.
Magenta pen	+100.
Red N.Y. circular date stamp	+100.
Large red N.Y. circular date stamp	+150.
Red square grid	+100.
Red "PAID"	+50.

b.	Signed A.C.M.	3,750.	700.
	On cover		850.
	On cover to France or England		2,750.
	On cover to other European countries		6,000.
	Pair		2,400.
	Pair on cover		3,250.
	Double transfer at bottom (Pos. 2)		950.
	Double transfer at top (Pos. 7)	—	950.
	Bottom frame line double (Pos. 31)		950.
	Top frame line double (Pos. 36)		950.

Cancellations
Blue pen	700.
Black pen	+25.
Red square grid	+100.
Red N.Y. circular date stamp	+100.
Large red N.Y. circular date stamp containing "5"	+150.
Red "PAID"	+50.

c.	Signed MMJr		9,000.
	On cover		
	Pair on cover front		26,500.
d.	Signed RHM	13,000.	3,250.
	Pair		12,000.
	On cover		5,000.
	On cover from New Hamburgh, N.Y.		10,000.

Cancellations
Blue pen	3,250.
Black pen	+150.
Red square grid	+250.
Red N.Y. circular date stamp	+400.
Red "PAID"	+300.

Earliest known use: July 17, 1845.

e.	Without signature	3,250.	750.
	On cover		1,100.
	On cover to France or England		2,250.
	On cover to other European countries		6,000.
	On cover, July 15, 1845		30,000.
	Pair		2,400.
	Pair on cover		2,600.
	Double transfer at bottom (Pos. 2)	3,500.	850.
	Double transfer at top (Pos. 7)	3,500.	850.
	Bottom frame line double (Pos. 31)	3,500.	850.
	Top frame line double (Pos. 36)	3,500.	850.
	Ribbed paper	—	

Cancellations
Blue pen	750.
Black pen	+25.
Red square grid	+100.
Red N.Y. circular date stamp	+100.

Large red N.Y. circular date
stamp containing "5" +150.
Red "PAID" +100.

Known used from Albany, Boston, Jersey City, N.J., New Hamburgh, N.Y., Philadelphia, Sing Sing, N.Y., Washington, D.C., and Hamilton, Canada, as well as by route agents on the Baltimore R.R. Covers originating in New Hamburgh are known only with No. 9X1d (one also bearing the U.S. City Despatch Post carrier); one also known used to Holland.

1847	Engr.	Blue Wove Paper	*Imperf.*
9X2 A1	5c	**black**, signed ACM connected	6,500. 3,500.
		On cover	5,750.
		Pair	
		Pair on cover	13,000.
		Double transfer at bottom (Pos. 2)	4,000.
		Double transfer at top (Pos. 7)	4,000.
		Bottom frame line double (Pos. 31)	4,000.
		Top frame line double (Pos. 36)	4,000.
a.		Signed RHM	—
d.		Without signature	11,000. 7,250.

Earliest known use: Mar. 4, 1847.

Cancellations

Red square grid	3,500.
Red "PAID"	+100.
Red N.Y. circular date stamp	+650.

On the only example known of No. 9X2a the 'R' is illegible and does not match those of the other 'RHM' signatures.

1847	Engr.	Gray Wove Paper	*Imperf.*
9X3 A1	5c	**black**, signed ACM connected	5,250. 2,100.
		On cover	5,250.
		On cover to Europe	8,500.
		Pair	7,750.
		Pair on cover	8,750.
		Double transfer at bottom (Pos. 2)	2,500.
		Double transfer at top (Pos. 7)	2,500.
		Bottom frame line double (Pos. 31)	2,500.
		Top frame line double (Pos. 36)	2,500.
a.		Signed RHM	7,000.
b.		Without signature	7,000.

Earliest known use: Feb. 8, 1847.

Cancellations

Red square grid	2,100.
Red N.Y. circular date stamp	2,100.
Red "PAID"	+100.

All used copies of No. 9X3a have red square grid or red "PAID" in arc cancel.

The first plate was of nine subjects (3x3). Each subject differs slightly from the others, with Position 8 showing the white stock shaded by crossed diagonal lines. At some point prints were struck from this plate in black on deep blue and white bond paper, as well as in blue, green, scarlet and brown on white bond paper. These are listed in the Proof and Trial Color Proof sections. Stamps from this plate were not issued.

ENVELOPES

Postmaster Morris, according to newspaper reports of July 2 and 7, 1845, issued envelopes. The design was not stated and no example has been seen.

PROVIDENCE, R. I.

Welcome B. Sayles, Postmaster

A1 A2

Engraved on copper plate containing 12 stamps (3x4). Upper right corner stamp (Pos. 3) "TEN"; all others "FIVE." The stamps were engraved directly on the plate, each differing from the other. The "TEN" and Pos. 4, 5, 6, 9, 11 and 12 have no period after "CENTS."

Yellowish White Handmade Paper
Earliest known use: Aug. 25, 1846 (No. 10X1).

1846, Aug. 24			*Imperf.*
10X1 A1	5c	**gray black**	400. 1,750.
		On cover, tied by postmark	20,000.
		On cover, pen canceled	4,500.
		Two on cover	
		Pair	825.
		Block of four	1,700.
10X2 A2	10c	**gray black**	1,250. 15,000.
		On cover, pen canceled	35,000.
a.		Se-tenant with 5c	2,000.
		Complete sheet	6,300.

Cancellations

Black pen check mark
Red circular town
Red straight line "PAID" (2 types)
Red "5"

All canceled copies of Nos. 10X1-10X2, whether or not bearing an additional handstamped cancellation, are obliterated

with a black pen check mark. There is only one known certified used example off cover of No. 10X2, and it has a minor fault. Value represents a 1997 sale. All genuine covers must bear the red straight line "PAID," the red circular town postmark, and the red numeral "5" or "10" rating mark.

Reprints were made in 1898. In general, each stamp bears one of the following letters on the back: *B. O. G. E. R. T. D. U. R. B. I. N.* However, some reprint sheets received no such printing on the reverse. All reprints are without gum. Value for 5c, $50; for 10c, $125; for sheet, $725. Reprints without the printing on the reverse sell for more.

ST. LOUIS, MO.

John M. Wimer, Postmaster

Missouri Coat of Arms
A1 A2 A3

Printed from a copper plate of 6 (2x3) subjects separately engraved by J. M. Kershaw.

The plate in its first state, referred to as Plate 1, comprised: three 5c stamps in the left vertical row and three 10c in the right vertical row. The stamps vary slightly in size, measuring from 17¾ to 18¼ by 22 to 22½mm.

Later a 20c denomination was believed necessary. So two of the 5c stamps, types I (pos. 1) and II (pos. 3) were changed to 20c by placing the plate face down on a hard surface and hammering on the back of the parts to be altered until the face was driven flush at those points. The new numerals were then engraved. Both 20c stamps show broken frame lines and the paw of the right bear on type II is missing. The 20c type II (pos. 3) also shows retouching in the dashes under "SAINT" and "LOUIS." The characteristics of types I and II of the 5c also serve to distinguish the two types of the 20c. This altered, second state of the plate is referred to as Plate 2. It is the only state to contain the 20c.

The demand for the 20c apparently proved inadequate, and the plate was altered again. The "20" was erased and "5" engraved in its place, resulting in noticeable differences from the 5c stamps from Plate 1. In type I (pos. 1) reengraved the "5" is twice as far from the top frame line as in the original state, and the four dashes under "SAINT" and "LOUIS" have disappeared except for about half of the upper dash under each word. In type II (pos. 3) reengraved, the ornament in the flag of the "5" is a diamond instead of a triangle; the diamond in the bow is much longer than in the first state, and the ball of the "5," originally blank, contains a large dot. At right of the shading of the "5" is a short curved line which is evidently a remnant of the "0" of "20." Type III (pos. 5) of the 5c was slightly retouched. This second alteration of the plate is referred to as Plate 3.

Type characteristics common to Plates 1, 2 and 3:

5 Cent. Type I (pos. 1). Haunches of both bears almost touch frame lines.

Type II (pos. 3). Bear at right almost touches frame line, but left bear is about ¼mm from it.

Type III (pos. 5). Haunches of both bears about ½mm from frame lines. Small spur on "S" of "POST."

10 Cent. Type I (pos. 2). Three dashes below "POST OFFICE."

Type II (pos. 4). Three pairs of dashes.

Type III (pos. 6). Pairs of dashes (with rows of dots between) at left and right. Dash in center with row of dots above it.

20 Cent. Type I. See 5c Type I.

Type II. See 5c Type II.

Nos. 11X1-11X8 unused are valued without gum.

Wove Paper Colored Through

1845, Nov.-1846			*Imperf.*
11X1 A1	5c	**black**, *greenish*	5,500. 3,250.
		On cover	8,000.
		Pair	7,000.
		Two on cover	9,000.
		Strip of 3 on cover	12,000.
11X2 A2	10c	**black**, *greenish*	5,500. 2,750.
		On cover	6,000.
		Pair	6,750.
		Pair on cover	8,000.
		Strip of 3 on cover	12,000.
		On cover, #11X2, 11X6	40,000.
11X3 A3	20c	**black**, *greenish*	22,500.
		On cover	
		On cover, #11X5, two #11X3	150,000.

Printed from Plate 1 (3 varieties each of the 5c and 10c) and Plate 2 (1 variety of the 5c, 3 of the 10c, 2 of the 20c).

1846			
11X4 A1	5c	**black**, *gray lilac*	— 4,250.
		On cover	6,000.
11X5 A2	10c	**black**, *gray lilac*	4,500. 2,200.
		On cover	4,000.
		Pair	5,750.
		Pair, 10c (III), 5c	17,500.
		Strip of 3	9,500.
		Strip of 3 on cover	25,000.
		Pair (10c (II), 10c (III) se-tenant with 5c	20,000.
		Strip of 3 10c (I, II, III) se-tenant with 5c	
11X6 A3	20c	**black**, *gray lilac*	13,500.
		On cover	17,500.
		Pair on cover	37,500.

Pair, 20c + 10c	27,500.
Pair, 20c + 10c, on cover	75,000.
Strip of 3, 20c + 20c + 5c	40,000.

Printed from Plate 2 (1 variety of the 5c, 3 of the 10c, 2 of the 20c).

1846			Pelure Paper
11X7 A1	5c	**black**, *bluish*	— 6,500.
		On cover	8,000.
		Two on cover	22,500.
11X8 A2	10c	**black**, *bluish*	6,500.
		On cover	10,000.
a.		Impression of 5c on back	—

Printed from Plate 3 (3 varieties each of the 5c, 10c).

Cancellations, Nos. 11X1-11X8

Black pen
Ms. initials of postmaster (#11X2, type I)
Red circular town
Red straight line "PAID"
Red grid (#11X7)

Values of Nos. 11X7-11X8, on and off cover, reflect the usual poor condition of these stamps having been printed on fragile pelure paper. Attractive copies with minor defects sell for considerably more.

Values for used off-cover stamps are for pen-canceled copies. Handstamp canceled copies sell for much more. Values for stamps on cover are pen cancels. Covers with the stamps tied by handstamp sell at considerable premiums depending upon the condition of the stamps and the general attractiveness of the cover. In general, covers with multiple frankings (unless separately valued) are valued at the "on cover" value of the highest item, plus the "off cover" value of the other stamps.

For Tuscumbia, Alabama, formerly listed as United States postmasters' provisional No. 12XU1, see the "3c 1861 Postmasters' Provisionals" section before the Confederate States of America Postmasters' Provisionals.

United States Postmaster Provisionals from New York, Providence and St. Louis can be mounted in the Scott National album.

4

POSTAGE

GENERAL ISSUES

Please Note:

Stamps are valued in the grade of very fine unless otherwise indicated.

Values for early and valuable stamps are for examples with certificates of authenticity from acknowledged expert committees, or examples sold with the buyer having the right of certification. This applies to examples with original gum as well as examples without gum. Beware of stamps offered "as is," as the gum on some unused stamps offered with "original gum" may be fraudulent, and stamps offered as unused without gum may in some cases be altered or faintly canceled used stamps.

Issues from 1847 through 1894 are unwatermarked.

Benjamin Franklin A1

George Washington A2

Double transfer of top frame line — 80R1(A)

Double transfer of top and bottom frame lines — 90R1(B)

Double transfer of bottom frame line and lower part of left frame line — (C)

Double transfer of top, bottom and left frame lines, also numerals — (D)

Double transfer of "U," "POST OFFICE" and left numeral — (E)

Double transfer of top frame line, upper part of side frame lines, "U," and "POST OFFICE" — (F)

This issue was authorized by an Act of Congress, approved March 3, 1847, to take effect July 1, 1847, from which date the use of Postmasters' Stamps or any which were not authorized by the Postmaster General became illegal.

This issue was declared invalid as of July 1, 1851.

Produced by Rawdon, Wright, Hatch & Edson.
Plates of 200 subjects in two panes of 100 each.

1847, July 1   **Engr.**   *Imperf.*

Thin Bluish Wove Paper

1	A1	5c **red brown**	5,750.	600.
		pale brown	5,750.	600.
		brown	5,750.	600.
		No gum	2,500.	
		On cover		700.
		On cover to England or France		2,600.
		On cover to other European countries		3,250.
		Pair	14,000.	1,250.
		Pair on cover		1,400.
		Strip of 3	22,000.	2,500.
		Block of 4	37,500.	27,500.
		Block of 4 on cover		80,000.
		Dot in "S" in upper right corner	6,000.	650.
		Cracked plate (69R1)		—
a.		5c **dark brown**	6,000.	625.
		No gum	2,600.	
		grayish brown	6,500.	650.
		blackish brown	6,500.	675.
		No gum	2,800.	
b.		5c **orange brown**	7,000.	850.
		No gum	3,100.	
		brown orange		1,400.
		Block of 4 on cover		—
c.		5c **red orange**	12,500.	5,000.
		No gum	7,000.	
d.		Double impression		—
(A)		Double transfer of top frame line (80R1)		750.
(B)		Double transfer of top and bottom frame lines (90R1)		750.
(C)		Double transfer of bottom frame line and lower part of left frame line		3,000.
(D)		Double transfer of top, bottom and left frame lines, also numerals		3,000.
(E)		Double transfer of "U," "POST OFFICE" and left numeral		1,500.
(F)		Double transfer of top frame line, upper part of side frame lines, "U," and "POST OFFICE"		—

The only known double impression shows part of the design doubled.

Some students believe that the "E double transfer" actually shows plate scratches instead.

Earliest known use: July 7, 1847.

Cancellations

Red	600.
Red town	+400.
Blue	+35.
Blue town	+200.
Black	+100.
Black town	+400.
Magenta	+100.
Orange	+500.
Ultramarine	+400.
Ultramarine, town	+750.
Violet	+450.
Green	+1,500.
"Paid"	+50.
"Paid" in grid (demonetized usage)	+300.
"Free"	+300.
Railroad	+200.
U. S. Express Mail (on the cover)	+100.
U. S. Express Mail (on stamp)	—
"Way"	+250.
"Way" with numeral	—
"Steamboat"	+350.
"Steam"	+200.
"Steamship"	+300.
Philadelphia RR	—
Hotel (on the cover)	+2,000.
Numeral	+100.
Canada	+3,000.
Wheeling, Va., grid	+6,000.
Pen	300.

Double transfer in "X" at lower right — 1R1(A)

Double transfer in "Post Office" — 31R1(B)

Double transfer in "X" at lower right — 2R1(C)

Double transfer of left and bottom frame line — 41R1(D)

2	A2	10c	**black**	27,500.	1,400.
			gray black	27,500.	1,400.
			No gum	13,000.	
			greenish black		1,750.
			On cover		1,750.
			On cover to Canada		2,100.
			On cover to France		5,000.
			On cover with 5c No. 1		30,000.
			Pair	60,000.	3,250.
			Pair on cover		3,750.
			Strip of 3	95,000.	10,000.
			Block of 4	135,000.	75,000.
			Short transfer at top	29,000.	1,500.
			Vertical line through second "F" of "OFFICE" (68R1)	—	1,900.
			With "Stick Pin" in tie (52L1)	—	1,900.
			With "harelip" (57L1)	—	1,900.
	a.		Diagonal half used as 5c on cover		13,000.
	b.		Vertical half used as 5c on cover		35,000.
	c.		Horizontal half used as 5c on cover		—
	(A)		Double transfer in "X" at lower right (1R1)	—	2,000.
	(B)		Double transfer in "Post Office" (31R1)	—	2,500.
	(C)		Double transfer in "X" at lower right (2R1)	—	2,000.
	(D)		Double transfer of left and bottom frame line (41R1)	—	2,000.

Earliest known use: July 2, 1847.
The value for the used block of 4 represents a block with manuscript cancel. One block is recorded with a handstamp cancellation and it is worth significantly more.

Cancellations

Red	1,400.
Blue	+50.

Orange	+500.
Black	+350.
Magenta	+500.
Violet	+650.
Green	+2,000.
Ultramarine	+500.
"Paid"	+100.
"Free"	+500.
Railroad	+1,000.
Philadelphia RR straightline	+500.
U.S. Express Mail (on the cover)	+600.
"Way"	+550.
Numeral	+400.
"Steam"	+350.
"Steamship"	+400.
"Steamboat"	+650.
"Steamer 10"	+1,000.
Canada	+3,000.
Panama	
Wheeling, Va., grid	+5,500.
Pen	750.

REPRODUCTIONS of 1847 ISSUE

Actually, official imitations made from new plates of 50 subjects made by the Bureau of Engraving and Printing by order of the Post Office Department. These were not valid for postal use.

Reproductions. The letters R. W. H. & E. at the bottom of each stamp are less distinct on the reproductions than on the originals.

Original	Reproduction

5c. On the originals the left side of the white shirt frill touches the oval on a level with the top of the "F" of "Five." On the reproductions it touches the oval about on a level with the top of the figure "5."

Original

Reproduction

10c. On the originals line of coat (A) points to "T" of TEN and (B) it points between "T" and "S" of CENTS. On the reproductions line of coat (A) points to right tip of "X" and line of coat (B) points to center of "S."

On the reproductions the eyes have a sleepy look, the line of the mouth is straighter, and in the curl of the hair near the left cheek is a strong black dot, while the originals have only a faint one.

(See Nos. 948a and 948b for 1947 reproductions-5c blue and 10c brown orange in larger size.)

1875			**Bluish paper, without gum**	*Imperf.*
3	A3	5c	red brown (4779)	850.
			brown	850.
			dark brown	850.
			Pair	1,850.
			Block of 4	5,500.
4	A4	10c	**black** (3883)	1,100.
			gray black	1,100.
			Pair	2,300.
			Block of 4	7,250.

Produced by Toppan, Carpenter, Casilear & Co.

Stamps of the 1847, 1851-57 series were printed from plates consisting of 200 subjects and the sheets were divided into panes of 100 each. In order that each stamp in the sheet could be identified easily in regard to its relative position it was devised that the stamps in each pane be numbered from one to one hundred, starting with the top horizontal row and numbering consecutively from left to right. Thus the first stamp at the upper left corner would be No. 1 and the last stamp at the bottom right corner, would be No. 100. The left and right panes are indicated by the letters "L" or "R". The number of the plate is last. As an example, the best-known of the scarce type III, 1c 1851 being the 99th stamp in the right pane of Plate No. 2 is listed as (99R2),*i.e.* 99th stamp, right pane, Plate No. 2.

One plate of the one cent and several plates of the three cents were extensively reentered after they had been in use. The original state of the plate is called "Early" and the reentered state is termed "Late." If the plate was reentered twice, the inbetween state is called "Intermediate." Identification of "Early," "Intermediate" or "Late" state is explained by the addition of the letters "E," "I" or "L" after the plate numbers. The sixth stamp of the right pane of Plate No. 1 from the "Early" state would be 6R1E. The same plate position from the "Late" state would be 6R1L.

One plate of the three cents never had a plate number and is referred to by specialists as "Plate O."

The position of the stamp in the sheet is placed within parentheses, for example: (99R2).

The different values of this issue were intended primarily for the payment of specific rates, though any value might be used in making up a rate. The 1c stamp was to pay the postage on newspapers, drop letters and circulars, and the one cent carrier fee in some cities from 1856. The 3c stamp represented the rate on ordinary letters and two of them made up the rate for distances over 3000 miles prior to Apr. 1, 1855. The 5c stamp was originally for the registration fee but the fee was usually paid in cash. Occasionally two of them were used to pay the rate over 3000 miles, after it was changed in April, 1855. Singles paid the "Shore to ship" rate to certain foreign countries and, from 1857, triples paid the fifteen-cent rate to France. Ten cents was the rate to California and points distant more than 3000 miles. The 12c stamp was for quadruple the ordinary rate. Twenty-four cents represented the single letter rate to Great Britain. Thirty cents was the rate to Germany. The 90c stamp was apparently intended to facilitate the payment of large amounts of postage.

Act of Congress, March 3, 1851. "From and after June 30, 1851, there shall be charged the following rates: Every single letter not exceeding 3000 miles, prepaid postage, 3 cents; not prepaid, 5 cents; for any greater distance, double these rates. Every single letter or paper conveyed wholly or in part by sea, and to or from a foreign country over 2500 miles, 20 cents; under 2500 miles, 10 cents. Drop or local letters, 1 cent each. Letters uncalled for and advertised, to be charged 1 cent in addition to the regular postage."

Act of Congress, March 3, 1855. "For every single letter, in manuscript or paper of any kind, in writing, marks or signs, conveyed in the mail between places in the United States not exceeding 3000 miles, 3 cents; and for any greater distance, 10 cents. Drop or local letters, 1 cent."

The Act of March 3, 1855, made the prepayment of postage on domestic letters compulsory April 1, 1855,

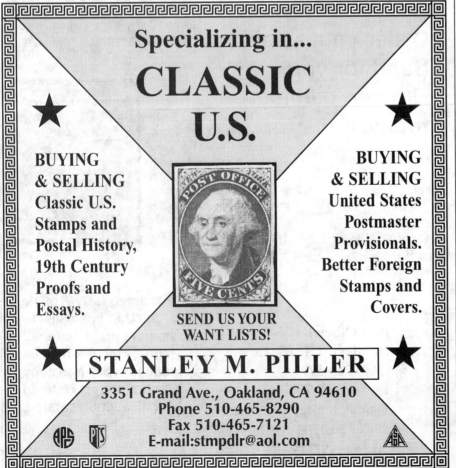

and prepayment of postage on domestic letters compulsory by stamps effective Jan. 1, 1856.

The Act authorized the Postmaster to establish a system for the registration of valuable letters, and to require prepayment of postage on such letters as well as registration fee of 5 cents. Stamps to prepay the registry fee were not required until June 1, 1867.

In Nos. 5-17 the 1c, 3c and 12c have very small margins between the stamps. The 5c and 10c have moderate size margins. The values of these stamps take the margin size into consideration.

Franklin — A5

ONE CENT. Issued July 1, 1851.

Type I. Has complete curved lines outside the labels with "U. S. Postage" and "One Cent." The scrolls below the lower label are turned under, forming little balls. The ornaments at top are substantially complete.

Type Ib. As I, but balls below bottom label are not so clear. Plume-like scrolls at bottom are incomplete.

1851-57   **Imperf.**

5	A5	1c	**blue,** type I (7R1E)	175,000.	40,000.
			Pair, types I, Ib		62,500.
			On cover		47,500.
			On cover, pair, one stamp type I		—
			On cover, strip of 3, one stamp type I		75,000.

Earliest known use: July 5, 1851 (FDC).

Cancellations

Blue	+500.
Blue town	—
Red grid	+2,000.
Red town	—
Red "Paid"	—

Values for No. 5 are for copies with margins touching or cutting slightly into the design, or for copies with four margins and minor faults. Very few sound copies with the design untouched exist, and these sell for much more than the values shown.

Value for No. 5 unused is for copy with no gum.

5A	A5	1c	**blue,** type Ib, *July 1, 1851*		
			(Less distinct examples 3-5, 9R1E)	14,000.	5,500.
			No gum	6,750.	
			Pair	30,000.	11,500.
			On cover		6,000.
			blue, type Ib (Best examples 6, 8R1E)	19,000.	9,000.
			No gum	9,000.	
			On cover		9,500.
			Block of 4, pair type Ib, pair type IIIa (8-9, 18-19R1E)		—

Cancellations

Blue town	+150.
Red town	—
Red Carrier	—
Red "Paid"	+400.
Pen (3, 4, 5 or 9R1E)	3,000.
Pen (6 or 8R1E)	6,000.

A6

Type Ia. Same as I at bottom but top ornaments and outer line at top are partly cut away. Type Ia comes only from the bottom row of both panes of Plate 4. All type Ia stamps have the flaw below "U" of "U.S." But this flaw also appears on some stamps of types Ic, III and IIIa, Plate 4.

Type Ic. Same as Ia, but bottom right plume and ball ornament incomplete. Bottom left plume complete or nearly complete. Best examples are from bottom row, "F" relief, positions 91 and 96R4. Less distinct examples are "E" reliefs from 5th and 9th rows, positions 47L, 49L, 83L, 49R, 81R, 82R, and 89R, Plate 4, and early impressions of 41R4.

6	A6	1c	**blue,** type Ia, *1857*	35,000.	9,500.
			No gum	19,000.	
			On cover		11,000.
			Pair	—	21,000.
			Strip of 3 on cover		72,500.
			Horizontal pair, types Ia, Ic		
			Horizontal strip of 3, types Ia, Ic, Ia		26,000.
			Vertical pair, types Ia, III	50,000.	13,000.
			Vertical pair, types Ia, IIIa	41,000.	11,500.
			Block of 4, types Ia, IIIa	82,500.	
			"Curl on shoulder" (97L4)	37,500.	10,500.
			"Curl in C" (97R4)	37,500.	10,500.

The horizontal strip of 3 represents positions 95-97R4, position 96R4 being type Ic.

Earliest known use: Apr. 19, 1857.

Cancellations

Blue	+100.00
Black Carrier	+350.00
Red Carrier	+350.00
Pen	4,500.

6b	A6	1c	**blue,** type Ic ("E" relief, less distinct examples)	6,000.	1,400.
			No gum	2,750.	
			On cover		2,400.
			Horizontal pair (81-82R4)		—
			Pair, types Ic, III		—
			Pair, types Ic, IIIa		—
			blue, type Ic ("F" relief, best examples, 91, 96R4)	20,000.	6,000.
			No gum	13,000.	
			On cover		6,500.
			Vertical pair (81-91R4)		—

Earliest known use: May 20, 1857 (dated cancel on off-cover stamp); June 6, 1857 (on cover).

Cancellations

Black ("E" relief)	1,400.
Black town ("F" relief)	—
Pen ("E" relief)	700.
Pen ("F" relief)	3,000.

A7

Type II - The little balls of the bottom scrolls and the bottoms of the lower plume ornaments are missing. The side ornaments are complete.

7	A7	1c **blue**, type II, (Plates 1E, 2);			
		July 1, 1851 (Plate 1E)		1,100.	160.00
		No gum		500.00	
		On cover			190.00
		Pair		2,500.	350.00
		Strip of 3		3,750.	550.00
		Block of 4 (Plate 1E)		—	—
		Block of 4 (Plate 2)		5,000.	1,000.
		P# block of 8, Impt. (Plate 2)		35,000.	
		Design complete at top (10R1E only)			2,000.
		Pair, types II, IIIa (Plate 1E)		5,750.	1,150.
		Block of 4, type II and types III, IIIa		—	
		Double transfer (Plate 1E or 2)		1,150.	170.00
		Double transfer (89R2)		1,200.	210.00
		Double transfer, one inverted (71L1E)		1,500.	375.00
		Triple transfer, one inverted (91L1E)		1,500.	375.00
		Cracked Plate (2L, 12L, 13L, 23L and 33L, Plate 2)		1,350.	375.00
		Plate 1L (4R1L only, double transfer), June 1852		1,900.	360.00
		Pair, types II (4R1L), IV		3,750.	650.00
		Plate 3, May, 1856		—	400.00
		On cover			625.00
		Pair		—	900.00
		Block of 4		—	
		Double transfer			450.00
		Plate 4, April, 1857		3,400.	1,100.
		On cover			1,350.
		Pair		—	2,300.
		Pair (vert.), types II, IIIa		—	
		"Curl in hair" (3R, 4R4)		—	1,200.
		Double transfer (10R4)		—	
		Perf. 12½, unofficial		—	5,000.

In addition to the cracked plates listed above (Plate 2) there exist a number of surface cracks coming from the rare Plate 3. See note concerning unofficial perfs following listings for No. 11.

Earliest known use: July 1, 1851 (Plate 1E) (FDC); Dec. 5, 1855 (Plate 2); May 6, 1856 (Plate 3).

Cancellations

Blue	+7.50
Red	+20.00
Magenta	+40.00
Ultramarine	+50.00
Green	+350.00
Orange	—
1855 year date	+10.00
1856 year date	+5.00
1857 year date	+2.50
1858 year date	—
"Paid"	+5.00
"Way"	+35.00
Red "Too Late"	+200.00
Numeral	+15.00
Railroad	+50.00
"Steam"	+50.00
"Steamboat"	+70.00
Red Carrier	+35.00
Black Carrier	+25.00
U. S. Express Mail	+25.00
Printed precancel "PAID"	+750.00
Pen	80.00

A8

Type III - The top and bottom curved lines outside the labels are broken in the middle. The side ornaments are substantially complete.

The most desirable examples of type III are those showing the widest breaks in the top and bottom framelines.

A special example is 99R2. All other stamps come from plate 4 and almost all show the breaks in the lines less clearly defined. Some of these breaks, especially of the bottom line, are very small.

Type IIIa - Similar to III with the outer line broken at top or, rarely, at bottom but not both. The side ornaments are substantially complete.

8	A8	1c **blue,** type III (Plate 4) see below for 99R2		11,500.	2,750.
		No gum		5,500.	
		On cover			3,250.
		Pair		25,000.	5,750.
		Pair, types III, IIIa		18,000.	9,500.
		Strip of 3			8,750.
		Block of 4, types III, IIIa		—	

Cancellations

Blue	+60.00
Red	+125.00
Red Carrier	+200.00
Black Carrier	+250.00
Pen	1,400.

Values for type III are for at least a 2mm break in each outer line. Examples of type III with wider breaks in outer lines command higher prices; those with smaller breaks sell for much less.

(8)	A8	1c **blue**, type III (99R2)		15,000.	4,500.
		No gum		7,500.	
		Pair, types III (99R2), II		—	5,000.
		Pair, types III (99R2), IIIa		20,000.	
		Block of 4, type III (99R2), 3 type II		27,500.	
		On cover (99R2)			10,500.

Cancellations

Blue	+100.00
Green	—
"Paid"	—
Red Carrier	+300.00

8A	A8	1c **blue**, type IIIa (Plate 1E) July 1, 1851		4,250.	975.00
		No gum		2,000.	
		On cover			1,100.
		Pair		9,250.	2,500.
		Double transfer, one inverted (81L1E)		5,000.	1,250.
		Plate 1E (100R)		—	—
		Plate 2 (100R)		—	—
		Plate 4, April, 1857		4,250.	1,050.
		On cover			1,200.
		Pair		9,250.	2,600.
		Block of 4			8,500.

Earliest known use: Apr. 8, 1857 (Plate 4).

Cancellations

Blue	+40.00
Red	+75.00
"Paid"	+90.00
Black Carrier	+150.00
Red Carrier	+135.00
Pen	475.00

Values are for stamps with at least a 2mm break in the top outer line. Examples with a wider break or a break in the lower line command higher prices, those with a smaller break sell for less.

"Paid" Cancellations

Values for "Paid" cancellations are for those OTHER than the common Boston type. See Postal Markings in the Introduction for illustrations.

A9

Type IV. Similar to II, but with the curved lines outside the labels are recut at top or bottom or both.

9	A9	1c **blue**, type IV, 1852		750.00	125.00
		No gum		325.00	
		On cover			150.00
		Pair		1,600.	260.00
		Strip of 3		2,500.	425.00
		Block of 4		3,500.	2,000.
		P# block of 8, Impt. (Plate 1)		—	
		Double transfer		825.00	130.00
		Triple transfer, one inverted (71L1L, 81L1L and 91L1L)		900.00	175.00
		Cracked plate		900.00	175.00
		Bottom frameline broken (89R1L)		—	275.00
		Perf. 12½, unofficial			3,000.
		Strip of 3		—	
		On cover		—	
a.		Printed on both sides, reverse inverted		—	

See note concerning unofficial perfs following listings for No. 11.

VARIETIES OF RECUTTING

Stamps of this type were printed from Plate 1 after it had been reentered and recut in 1852. All but one stamp (4R, see No. 7 for listings) were recut and all varieties of recutting are listed below:

Recut once at top and once at bottom, (113 on plate)		750.00	125.00
Recut once at top, (40 on plate)		775.00	130.00
Recut once at top and twice at bottom, (21 on plate)		800.00	135.00
Recut twice at bottom, (11 on plate)		825.00	145.00
Recut once at bottom, (8 on plate)		850.00	155.00
Recut once at bottom and twice at top, (4 on plate)		875.00	165.00
Recut twice at bottom and twice at top, (2 on plate)		900.00	220.00

Earliest known use: June 8, 1852.

Cancellations

Blue	+5.00
Red	+20.00
Ultramarine	+35.00
Brown	+150.00
Green	+350.00
Violet	+300.00
1853 year date	+250.00
1855 year date	+10.00
1856 year date	+7.50
1857 year date	+10.00
"Paid"	+10.00
"U. S. PAID"	+50.00
"Way"	+50.00
"Free"	+75.00
Railroad	+75.00
"Steam"	+60.00
Numeral	+10.00
"Steamboat"	+90.00
"Steamship"	+60.00
Red Carrier	+15.00
Black Carrier	+25.00
U. S. Express Mail	+60.00
Express Company	—
Packet boat	—
Printed precancel "PAID"	+2,000.
Printed precancel "paid"	+2,000.
Pen	62.50

These 1c stamps were often cut apart carelessly, destroying part or all of the top and bottom lines. This makes it difficult to determine whether a stamp is type II or IV without identifying the position. Such mutilated examples sell for much less.

PLEASE NOTE:
Stamps are valued in the grade of very fine unless otherwise indicated.

Values for early and valuable stamps are for examples with certificates of authenticity from acknowledged expert committees, or examples sold with the buyer having the right of certification. This applies to examples with original gum as well as examples without gum. Beware of stamps offered "as is," as the gum on some unused stamps offered with "original gum" may be fraudulent, and stamps offered as unused without gum may in some cases be altered or faintly canceled used stamps.

VALUES FOR NEVER-HINGED STAMPS PRIOR TO SCOTT No. 219
This catalogue does not value pre-1890 stamps in never-hinged condition. Premiums for never-hinged condition in the classic era invariably are even larger than those premiums listed for the post-1890 issues. Generally speaking, the earlier the stamp is listed in the catalogue, the larger will be the never-hinged premium. On some early classics, the premium will be several multiples of the unused, hinged values given in the catalogue.

Washington — A10

THREE CENTS. Issued July 1, 1851 (Plate 1E).
Type I - There is an outer frame line on all four sides.

10	A10	3c **orange brown**, type I		3,000.	100.00
		No gum		1,400.	
		deep orange brown		3,250.	140.00
		No gum		1,500.	
		copper brown		3,500.	170.00
		No gum		1,600.	
		On cover, orange brown			170.00
		Pair		6,500.	375.00
		Strip of 3		10,500.	850.00
		Block of 4		15,000.	—
		Double transfer			125.00
		Triple transfer			360.00
		Gash on shoulder			110.00
		Dot in lower right diamond block (69L5E)			150.00
		On part-India paper			500.00
a.		Printed on both sides			—

VARIETIES OF RECUTTING

All of these stamps were recut at least to the extent of four outer frame lines and usually much more. Some of the most prominent varieties are listed below (others are described in "The 3c Stamp of U.S. 1851-57 Issue," by Carroll Chase). Basic values for No. 10 are for copies with recut inner frame lines:

No inner frame lines	3,250.	105.00
Left inner line only recut		170.00
Right inner line only recut		115.00
1 line recut in upper left triangle	3,250.	105.00
2 lines recut in upper left triangle		115.00
3 lines recut in upper left triangle		140.00
5 lines recut in upper left triangle (47L0)		450.00
1 line recut in lower left triangle		130.00
1 line recut in lower right triangle		125.00
2 lines recut in lower right triangle (57L0)		450.00
2 lines recut in upper left triangle and 1 line recut in lower right triangle		180.00
1 line recut in upper right triangle		125.00
Upper part of top label and diamond block recut	3,250.	110.00
Top label and right diamond block joined		115.00
Top label and left diamond block joined		115.00
Lower label and right diamond block joined		115.00
2 lines recut at top of upper right diamond block		120.00
1 line recut at bottom of lower left diamond block (34R2E)		475.00

Earliest known use: July 1, 1851 (Plate 1E) (FDC); July 23, 1851 (Plate 2E); July 19, 1851 (Plate 5E); Sept. 8, 1851 (Plate 0).

Cancellations

Blue	+2.00
Red	+5.00
Orange	+35.00
Brown	+40.00
Ultramarine	+25.00
Green	+200.00
Violet	+150.00
1851 year date	+350.00
1852 year date	+350.00
"Paid"	+5.00
"Way"	+40.00
"Way" with numeral	+150.00
"Free"	+50.00
Numeral	+15.00
Railroad	+50.00
U. S. Express Mail	+20.00
"Steam"	+35.00
"Steamship"	+60.00
"Steamboat"	+70.00
Packet Boat	+300.00
Black Carrier (circular)	+400.00
Blue Carrier (circular)	+600.00
Blue Carrier (New Orleans "snowshovel")	+400.00
Green Carrier (New Orleans "snowshovel")	+500.00
Canadian	—
Territorial	+175.00
Pen	55.00

11	A10 3c	**dull red** (1853-54-55), type I	240.00	10.00
		orange red (1855)	240.00	10.00
		rose red (1854-55)	240.00	10.00
		No gum	100.00	
		brownish carmine (1851-52 and 1856)	275.00	12.00
		No gum	115.00	
		claret (1852 and 1857)	290.00	15.00

	No gum	120.00	
	deep claret (1857)	325.00	18.00
	No gum	145.00	
	plum (1857)	750.00	400.00
	No gum	400.00	
	On cover, dull red		12.50
	On cover, orange red		15.00
	On cover, brownish carmine		18.00
	On cover, claret		20.00
	On cover, plum		750.00
	On propaganda cover, dull red		400.00
	Pair	525.00	35.00
	Strip of 3	800.00	95.00
	Block of 4	1,400.	475.00
	P# block of 8, Impt.	3,750.	
	Double transfer in "Three Cents"	275.00	12.00
	Double transfer line through "Three Cents" and rosettes double (92L1L)	390.00	50.00
	Triple transfer (92L2L)	375.00	35.00
	Double transfer, "Gents" instead of "Cents" (66R2L)	375.00	35.00
	Gash on shoulder	265.00	11.00
	Dot on lower right diamond block 69L5L)	325.00	27.50
	Major cracked plate (74L, 84L, 94L, 9R, Plate 5L)	775.00	140.00
	Intermediate cracked plate (80L, 96L, 71R, Plate 5L)	525.00	70.00
	Minor cracked plate (8L, 27L, 31L, 44L, 45L, 51L, 55L, 65L, 78L, 79L, 7R, 71R, and 72R, Plate 5L)	400.00	50.00
	Worn plate	240.00	10.00
	Perf. about 11, unofficial	1,500.	
	Perf. 12½, unofficial		6,000.
	On cover		8,500.
	Pair on cover		—
c.	Vertical half used as 1c on cover		5,000.
d.	Diagonal half used as 1c on cover		5,000.
e.	Double impression		5,000.

The unofficial perf varieties listed represent the first perforated stamps in the U. S. made using a true perforating machine. Known as the "Chicago perfs," both were made by Dr. Elijah W. Hadley, using a machine of his construction. None of the perf 11 stamps are believed to have been used.

VARIETIES OF RECUTTING

All of these stamps were recut at least to the extent of three frame lines and usually much more. Some of the most prominent varieties are listed below (others are described in "The 3c Stamp of U.S. 1851-57 Issue," by Carroll Chase):

Recut inner frame lines	240.00	10.00
No inner frame lines	240.00	10.00
Right inner line only recut	260.00	15.00
1 line recut in upper left triangle	260.00	10.00
2 lines recut in upper left triangle	260.00	10.50
3 lines recut in upper left triangle	275.00	11.00
5 lines recut in upper left triangle (95L1L)	450.00	100.00
1 line recut in lower left triangle	275.00	11.00
1 line recut in lower right triangle	260.00	10.50
1 line recut in upper right triangle	375.00	15.00
Recut button on shoulder (10R2L)	375.00	55.00
Lines on bust and bottom of medallion circle recut (47R6)	775.00	250.00
Upper part of top label and diamond block recut	240.00	10.00
Top label and right diamond block joined	260.00	10.50
Top label and left diamond block joined	275.00	14.00
Lower label and right diamond block joined	275.00	14.00
1 extra vertical line outside of left frame line (29L, 39L, 49L, 59L, 69L, 79L, Plate 3)	265.00	14.00
2 extra vertical lines outside of left frame line (89L, 99L, Plate 3)	325.00	27.50
1 extra vertical line outside of right frame line (58L, 68L, 78L, 88L, 98L, Plate 3)	285.00	15.00
No inner line and frame line close to design at right (9L, 19L, Plate 3)	310.00	18.00
No inner line and frame line close to design at left (70, 80, 90, 100L, Plate 3)	275.00	15.00

Earliest known use: Oct. 4, 1851 (Plate 1L); Jan. 7, 1852 (Plate 2L); Jan. 15, 1852 (Plate 3); Mar. 28, 1855 (Plate 4); Sept. 3, 1855 (Plate 5L); Feb. 18, 1856 (Plate 6); Feb. 13, 1856 (Plate 7); Apr. 25, 1856 (Plate 8).

Cancellations

Blue	+.25
Red	+1.00
Orange	+15.00
Brown	+20.00
Magenta	+15.00
Ultramarine	+15.00
Green	+150.00
Violet	+125.00
Purple	+125.00
Olive	+100.00
Yellow	+5,000.
Yellow, on cover	10,000.
1852 year date	+300.00
1853 year date	+90.00
1854 year date	—
1855 year date	+10.00
1858 year date	+.50
1859 year date	
"Paid"	+1.00
"Way"	+10.00
"Way" with numeral	+60.00
"Free"	+25.00

Numeral	+7.50
Railroad	+20.00
U. S. Express Mail	+5.00
"Steam"	+15.00
"Ship"	+20.00
"New York Ship"	+35.00
"Steamboat"	+45.00
"Steamship"	+45.00
Packet boat	+120.00
Express Company	+120.00
Black Carrier	+60.00
Red Carrier (New York)	+50.00
Green Carrier (New Orleans)	+350.00
Blue Carrier (New Orleans)	+200.00
Canada	—
Territorial	+70.00
Pen	5.00

Thomas Jefferson A11	Washington A12

FIVE CENTS.
Type I - Projections on all four sides.

12	A11 5c	**red brown**, type I, *1856*	17,500.	1,100.
		dark red brown	17,500.	1,100.
		No gum	9,000.	
		On domestic cover		1,500.
		Single on cover to France		1,850.
		Strip of 3 on cover to France		6,000.
		Pair	38,500.	2,400.
		Strip of 3	57,500.	5,250.
		Block of 4	145,000.	45,000.
		Double transfer (40R1)		1,350.
		Defective transfer (23R1)		1,550.

Earliest known use: Mar. 24, 1856.

Cancellations

Red	+75.
Magenta	+125.
Blue	+25.
Green	+750.
1856 year date	+25.
1857 year date	+25.
1858 year date	
"Paid"	+50.
"Steamship"	+200.
U.S. Express Mail	+150.
Express Company	+300.
"Steamboat"	+250.
Railroad	+250.
Numeral	+1,000.
Pen	625.

TEN CENTS
Type I - The "shells" at the lower corners are practically complete. The outer line below the label is very nearly complete. The outer lines are broken above the middle of the top label and the "X" in each upper corner. Beware of type V perforated (No. 35) trimmed to resemble type I imperforate (No. 13).

Types I, II, III and IV have complete ornaments at the sides of the stamps, and three pearls at each outer edge of the bottom panel.

Type I comes only from the bottom row of both panes of Plate 1.

13	A12 10c	**green**, type I, *1855*	14,000.	800.
		dark green	14,000.	800.
		yellowish green	14,000.	800.
		No gum	6,750.	
		On domestic cover		900.
		Pair	28,000.	1,900.
		Strip of 3		2,700.
		Vert. pair, types III, I	18,500.	1,375.
		Vert. pair, types IV, I (86, 96L1)		5,250.
		Vertical strip of 3, types II, III, I		4,250.
		Block of 4, types III, I	42,500.	10,500.
		Block of 4, types III, IV, I		16,000.
		Double transfer (100R1)	14,500.	900.
		"Curl" in left "X" (99R1)	14,500.	900.

Earliest known use: Nov. 14, 1855.

Cancellations

Blue	+40.
Red	+75.
Magenta	+200.
Orange	—
1855 year date	+25.
1856 year date	+25.
1857 year date	+25.
"Paid"	+50.
"Steamship"	+150.
Railroad	+175.
Territorial	+400.
Numeral	+50.
U.S. Express Mail	—
Pen	375.

A13

Type II - The design is complete at the top. The outer line at the bottom is broken in the middle. The shells are partly cut away.

14	A13 10c **green,** type II, *1855*	3,500.	225.
	dark green	3,500.	225.
	yellowish green	3,500.	225.
	No gum	1,600.	
	On domestic cover		290.
	Pair	7,500.	500.
	Strip of 3	12,000.	850.
	Block of 4	16,000.	4,000.
	Pair, types II, III	7,500.	500.
	Pair, types II, IV	31,000.	2,100.
	Vertical strip of 3, types II, III, IV		2,600.
	Block of 4, types II, III	—	3,500.
	Block of 4, types II, IV		
	Block of 4, types II, III, IV		10,000.
	Double transfer (31L, 51L, and 20R, Plate 1)	3,900.	300.
	"Curl" opposite "X" (10R1)	3,900.	325.

Earliest known use: May 12, 1855.

Cancellations

Blue	+10.
Red	+25.
Brown	+25.
Ultramarine	+75.
Magenta	+100.
Green	+200.
Violet	—
1855 year date	—
1856 year date	+50.
1857 year date	+10.
1858 year date	+10.
"Paid"	+25.
"Way"	+50.
"Free"	+75.
Railroad	+75.
Steamship	+75.
Steamboat	+100.
Numeral	+50.
Territorial	+150.
Express Company	+200.
U. S. Express Mail	+75.
Pen	100.

A14

Type III - The outer lines are broken above the top label and the "X" numerals. The outer line at the bottom and the shells are partly cut away similar to Type II.

15	A14 10c **green,** type III, *1855*	3,500.	225.
	dark green	3,500.	225.
	yellowish green	3,500.	225.
	No gum	1,600.	
	On domestic cover		290.
	Pair	7,500.	500.
	Strip of 3	12,000.	850.
	Pair, types III, IV	31,000.	2,100.
	Double transfer at top and at bottom		—
	"Curl" on forehead (85L1)	3,900.	325.
	"Curl" to right of left "X" (87R1)	3,900.	325.

Earliest known use: May 19, 1855.

Cancellations

Blue	+10.
Red	+25.
Magenta	+100.
Violet	—
Brown	+25.
Orange	+35.
Green	+200.
1855 year date	—
1856 year date	+50.
1857 year date	+10.
1858 year date	+10.
"Paid"	+25.
Steamship	+75.
U. S. Express Mail	+75.
Express Company	+200.
Packet boat	

Canada (on cover)		+1000.
Territorial		+150.
Railroad		+75.
Numeral		+50.
Pen		100.

A15

Type IV - The outer lines have been recut at top or bottom or both.

16	A15 10c **green**, type IV, *1855*	25,000.	1,600.
	dark green	25,000.	1,600.
	yellowish green	25,000.	1,600.
	No gum	13,000.	
	On domestic cover		1,900.
	Pair	—	4,250.
	Block of 4 (54-55, 64-65L)	—	—

VARIETIES OF RECUTTING

Eight stamps on Plate 1 were recut. All are listed below.

Outer line recut at top (65L, 74L, 86L, and 3R, Plate 1)	25,000.	1,600.
Outer line recut at bottom (54L, 55L, 76L, Plate 1)	26,000.	1,700.
Outer line recut at top and bottom (64L1)	29,000.	2,000.

Positions 65L1 and 86L1 have both "X" ovals recut at top, as well as the outer line.

Earliest known use: July 10, 1855.

Cancellations

Blue	+75.
Red	+150.
Brown	—
1857 year date	—
1859 year date	—
"Paid"	+150.
Steamship	+300.
Territorial	+500.
Express Company	+750.
Numeral	+150.
Pen	950.

Types I, II, III and IV occur on the same sheet, so it is possible to obtain pairs and blocks showing combinations of types. For listings of type combinations in pairs and blocks, see Nos. 13-15.

Washington — A16

17	A16 12c **black,** *July 1, 1851*	4,500.	325.
	gray black	4,500.	325.
	intense black	4,500.	325.
	No gum	2,100.	
	Single, on cover		1,500.
	Single on cover with No. 11 to France		1,150.
	Pair	9,500.	700.
	Pair, on cover to England		800.
	Block of 4	21,000.	4,500.
	Double transfer	4,750.	350.
	Triple transfer (5R1 & 49R1)	5,000.	425.
	Not recut in lower right corner	4,750.	350.
	Recut in lower left corner (43L, 53L, 63L, 73L and 100L, Plate 1)	4,750.	400.
	Cracked plate (32R1)	—	—
	On part-India paper		850.
a.	Diagonal half used as 6c on cover		2,500.
	Diagonal half used as 6c on "Via Nicaragua" cover		5,750.
b.	Vertical half used as 6c on cover		8,500.
c.	Printed on both sides		10,000.

Earliest known use: Aug. 4, 1851.

Cancellations

Red	+20.
Blue	+5.
Brown	+65.
Magenta	+65.
Orange	+40.
Green	+300.
"Paid"	+25.
"Way"	+75.
Steamship	+100.

Steamboat		+125.
Supplementary Mail Type A		+75.
Railroad		+75.
"Honolulu" in red (on cover)		+400.
U. S. Express Mail		+125.
Pen		160.

Please Note:

Stamps are valued in the grade of very fine unless otherwise indicated.

Values for early and valuable stamps are for examples with certificates of authenticity from acknowledged expert committees, or examples sold with the buyer having the right of certification. This applies to examples with original gum as well as examples without gum. Beware of stamps offered "as is," as the gum on some unused stamps offered with "original gum" may be fraudulent, and stamps offered as unused without gum may in some cases be altered or faintly canceled used stamps.

SAME DESIGNS AS 1851-57 ISSUES
Printed by Toppan, Carpenter & Co.

Nos. 18-39 have small or very small margins. The values take into account the margin size.

1857-61   ***Perf. 15½***

18	A5 1c **blue,** type I (Plate 12),		
	1861	1,750.	550.
	No gum	800.	
	On cover		700.
	On patriotic cover		1,250.
	Pair	3,800.	1,200.
	Strip of 3	5,750.	2,000.
	Block of 4	*10,500.*	
	Pair, types I, II	3,000.	850.
	Pair, types I, IIIa	3,750.	1,050.
	Block of 4, types I, II	7,000.	4,500.
	Block of 4, types I, II, IIIa	7,750.	5,250.
	Double transfer	1,900.	600.
	Cracked plate (91R12)	—	800.

Plate 12 consists of types I & II. A few positions are type IIIa. Late printings of position 46L12 are type III.

Earliest known use: Jan. 25, 1861.

Cancellations

Blue	+10.
Red	+35.
Violet	+100.
Steamboat	—
"Paid"	+25.
"Free"	+750.
Black Carrier	+85.
Red Carrier	+85.
Pen	275.

19	A6 1c **blue,** type Ia (Plate 4)	19,000.	5,500.
	No gum	9,000.	
	On cover		6,500.
	Pair	42,500.	12,000.
	Strip of 3	65,000.	19,000.
	Vertical pair, types Ia, III	33,000.	8,000.
	Vertical pair, types Ia, IIIa	24,000.	6,250.
	Pair, types Ia, Ic	—	—
	Strip of 3, types Ia, Ia, Ic		—
	Block of 4, types Ia, Ic, and IIIa	50,000.	
	Block of 4, pair type Ia and types III or IIIa	—	—
	"Curl on shoulder" (97L4)	20,000.	5,750.

Copies of this stamp exist with perforations not touching the design at any point. Such copies command very high prices.

Type Ia comes only from the bottom row of both panes of Plate 4.

Earliest known use: Nov. 2, 1857 (dated cancel on off-cover stamp).

Cancellations

Red Carrier	+200.
Green	+1,750.
Pen	2,750.

19b	A6 1c **blue,** type Ic ("E" relief, less distinct examples)	2,750.	1,200.
	No gum	1,300.	
	On cover		1,550.
	Horizontal pair (81-82R4)	—	—
	Pair, types Ic, III	—	—
	Pair, types Ic, IIIa	—	—
	blue, type Ic ("F" relief, best examples, 91, 96R4)	10,000.	2,500.
	No gum	5,000.	
	On cover		3,250.

Type Ic - Same as Ia, but bottom right plume and ball ornament incomplete. Bottom left plume complete or nearly complete. Best examples are from bottom row, "F" relief, positions 91 and 96R4. Less distinct examples are "E" reliefs from 5th and 9th rows, positions 47L, 49L, 83L, 49R, 81R, 82R, and 89R, Plate 4, and early impressions of 41R4. Several combination type multiples can be found in the unused complete left pane of 100 from Plate 4.

Copies of the "F" relief type Ic stamps exist with perforations not touching the design at any point. Such copies command a substantial premium.

Cancellations

Pen ("E" relief)	550.
Pen ("F" relief)	1,300.

20	A7 1c **blue,** type II (Plate 2)	1,000.	250.
	No gum	450.	
	On cover		290.

Pair	2,100.	550.
Strip of 3	3,100.	850.
Block of 4	4,750.	2,200.
Double transfer (Plate 2)	1,050.	290.
Cracked plate (2L, 12L, 13L, 23L & 33L, Plate 2)	1,250.	525.
Plate 1L (4R1L only, double transfer), *July 1857*		750.
Pair, types II (4R1L), IV		*1,900.*
Plate 4	3,000.	875.
On cover		*1,050.*
Pair	6,500.	*1,850.*
Strip of 3		—
Double transfer (10R4)	3,250.	*1,450.*
"Curl in hair" (3R, 4R4)		*1,000.*
Plate 11	1,150.	325.
On cover		375.
On patriotic cover		750.
Pair	2,400.	700.
Strip of 3		—
Double transfer	—	—
Plate 12	950.	250.
On cover		290.
On patriotic cover		650.
Pair	2,000.	550.
Strip of 3	3,100.	850.
Block of 4	4,750.	2,200.

Earliest known use: July 25, 1857 (Plate 2), July 26, 1857 (Plate 4), Jan. 12, 1861 (Plate 11), Jan. 22, 1861 (Plate 12).

Cancellations

Blue	+5.
Red	+20.
Green	+200.
1857 year date	+10.
1858 year date	+5.
1861 year date	+5.
"FREE"	—
1863 year date	+200.
"Paid"	+15.
Railroad	+60.
"Way"	+75.
Steamboat	+75.
Red Carrier	+35.
Black Carrier	+50.
Pen	130.

21	A8 1c **blue,** type III (Plate 4), see below for 99R2	12,000.	2,000.
	No gum	5,750.	
	On cover		2,500.
	Pair	27,500.	4,500.
	Strip of 3		6,750.
	Block of 4	—	—
	Pair, types III, IIIa	15,000.	2,650.
	Vertical pair, types III, II	—	—
	Block of 4, types III, IIIa	—	—
	Plate 12 (46L12)	—	—
a.	Horiz. pair, imperf, between		16,000.

Earliest known use: Nov. 20, 1857.

Cancellations

Blue	+35.
Red	+60.
Green	+350.
1858 year date	+35.
"Paid"	+60.
Black Carrier	+175.
Red Carrier	+150.
Pen	1,200.

Values for type III are for at least a 2mm break in each outer line. Examples of type III with wider breaks in outer lines command higher prices; those with smaller breaks sell for less.

No. 21a is unique and is contained in a strip of three. Value reflects auction sale in 1999.

(21)	A8 1c **blue,** type III (99R2)		10,000.
	On cover		—
	Pair, types III (99R2), II		—
	Pair, types III (99R2), IIIa		—
	Strip of 3, types III (99R2), II, IIIa		—
	Block of 9, one type III (99R2), others type II	110,000.	

The only recorded unused copy is the one in the block of 9. Only two covers are recorded bearing No. 21 (99R2).

Earliest known use: Sept. 20, 1857.

22	A8 1c **blue,** type IIIa (Plate 4)	1,800.	450.
	No gum	875.	
	On cover		500.
	On patriotic cover		775.
	Pair	3,900.	950.
	Vertical pair, types IIIa, II		*1,750.*
	Strip of 3	6,000.	1,550.
	Block of 4	8,750.	5,000.
	Block of 4, types IIIa, II	—	—
	Double transfer	1,900.	475.
	Plate 2 (100R)	—	—
	Plate 11 and Plate 12	1,900.	475.
	On cover		525.
	On patriotic cover		950.
	Pair	4,200.	1,050.
	Vert. pair, types IIIa, II (Plate 11)	4,300.	950.
	Strip of 3	6,250.	1,550.
	Strip of 3, types IIIa, II, I (46-48L12)	—	—
	Block of 4	9,250.	
	Block of 4, types IIIa, II (Plate 11)	9,500.	*3,750.*
	Double transfer	2,000.	500.
	Triple transfer (Plate 11)	—	—

Bottom line broken
(46L12) — —
b. Horizontal pair, imperf. between 5,000.

One pair of No. 22b is reported. Beware of numerous pairs that have blind perforations. These are not to be confused with No. 22b.

Earliest known use: July 26, 1857 (Plate 4), Jan. 12, 1861 (Plate 11), Jan. 25, 1861 (Plate 12).

Cancellations

Blue	+5.
Red	+30.
Green	+250.
1857 year date	—
1858 year date	—
1861 year date	—
1863 year date	—
"Paid"	+25.
"Steamboat"	—
Red Carrier	+35.
Black Carrier	+50.
Blue Carrier	+100.
Pen	225.

23	A9 1c **blue,** type IV	7,250.	650.
	No gum	3,500.	
	On cover		850.
	Pair	16,000.	1,450.
	Strip of 3	24,000.	2,250.
	Block of 4		25,000.
	Double transfer	7,500.	700.
	Triple transfer, one inverted (71L1L, 81L1L and 91L1L)	8,000.	850.
	Cracked plate	7,500.	775.
	Bottom line broken (89R1L)	—	1,400.

Two used blocks of No. 23 are presently known: an extremely fine block of five and a poorly centered block of four. Value of used block of four is based on 1998 auction sale of the former.

VARIETIES OF RECUTTING

Recut once at top and once at bottom, (113 on plate)	7,250.	650.
Recut once at top, (40 on plate)	7,350.	660.
Recut once at top and twice at bottom, (21 on plate)	7,500.	675.
Recut twice at bottom, (11 on plate)	7,750.	700.
Recut once at bottom, (8 on plate)	8,000.	725.
Recut once at bottom and twice at top, (4 on plate)	8,250.	750.
Recut once at top and twice at bottom, (2 on plate)	8,500.	800.

Earliest known use: July 25, 1857.

Cancellations

Blue	+5.
Red	+45.
1857 year date	+50.
"Paid"	+25.
Red Carrier	+60.
Black Carrier	+60.
Railroad	+85.
"Way"	+90.
"Steamboat"	+135.
"Steam"	+100.
Pen	325.

A20

Type V - Similar to type III of 1851-57 but with side ornaments partly cut away. Frequently, but not always, with side scratches. Wide breaks in top and bottom framelines.
Type Va - Stamps from Plate 5 with almost complete ornaments at right side and no side scratches. Many, but not all, stamps from Plate 5 are Type Va.

24	A20 1c **blue,** type V (Plates 5, 7, 8, 9, 10) *1857*	175.00	40.00
	No gum	80.00	
	On cover		47.50
	On patriotic cover		300.00
	Pair	375.00	87.50
	Strip of 3	550.00	140.00
	Block of 4	750.00	425.00
	P# strip of 4, Impt.	1,400.	
	P# block of 8, Impt.	3,500.	—
	Double transfer at top (8R and 10R, Plate 8)	240.00	85.00
	Double transfer at bottom (52R9)	300.00	95.00

Curl on shoulder, (57R, 58R, 59R, 98R, 99R, Plate 7)	240.00	67.50
With "Earring" below ear (10L9)	350.00	95.00
"Curl" over "C" of "Cent"	250.00	67.50
"Curl" over "E" of "Cent" (41R and 81R8)	275.00	82.50
"Curl in hair," 23L7; 39, 69L8; 34, 74R9	240.00	57.50
"Curl" in "O" of "ONE" (62L5)	—	—
"Curl" on shoulder (48L5)	—	—
Horizontal dash in hair (24L7)	350.00	85.00
Horizontal dash in hair (36L8)	350.00	85.00
Long double "curl" in hair (52, 92R8)	300.00	80.00
Type Va	425.00	120.00
On cover (Type Va)		175.00
Pair (Type Va)	—	—
Strip of 3 (Type Va)	—	—
Block of 4 (Type Va)	—	—

b. Laid paper —

Earliest known use: Dec. 2, 1857 (Plate 5); Dec. 31, 1857 (Plate 7); Nov. 17, 1857 (Plate 8); Sept. 18, 1859 (Plate 9); June 14, 1860 (Plate 10).

Cancellations

Blue	+2.50
Red	+15.00
Green	+250.00
Brown	+100.00
Magenta	+150.00
Ultramarine	+100.00
1857 year date	+70.00
1858 year date	+2.50
1859 year date	+2.50
1860 year date	+2.50
1861 year date	+2.50
1863 year date	+250.00
Printed Precancel "CUMBER-LAND, ME." (on cover)	—
"Paid"	+5.00
"Free"	+25.00
Railroad	+50.00
Numeral	+7.50
Express Company	+90.00
Steamboat	+55.00
"Steam"	+30.00
Steamship	+40.00
Packet boat	—
Supp. Mail Type A, B, or C	+55.00
"Way"	+30.00
Red Carrier	+7.50
Black Carrier	+12.50
Blue Carrier	+50.00
"Old Stamps-Not Recognized"	+1,500.
Territorial	+80.00
Pen	17.50

25	A10 3c **rose,** type I (no inner frame-lines), (Plates 4, 6, 7, 8)	2,100.	80.00
	rose red	2,100.	80.00
	dull red	2,100.	80.00
	No gum	1,000.	
	claret	2,300.	90.00
	No gum	1,100.	
	On cover		90.00
	On patriotic cover		400.00
	Pair	4,500.	175.00
	Strip of 3	6,750.	290.00
	Block of 4	10,500.	7,000.
	Gash on shoulder	2,200.	85.00
	Double transfer	2,300.	110.00
	Double transfer "Gents" instead of "Cents" (66R2L)	—	625.00
	Triple transfer (92L2L)	—	625.00
	Worn plate	2,100.	80.00
	Major cracked plate (74L, 84L, 94L, 9R, Plate 5L; 47, 48, Plate 7)	3,500.	525.00
	Intermediate cracked plate (80L, 96L, 71R, Plate 5L)	3,350.	310.00
	Minor cracked plate (8L, 27L, 31L, 44L, 45L, 51L, 55L, 65L, 78L, 79L, 7R, 71R, and 72R, Plate 5L)	3,250.	260.00
b.	Vert. pair, imperf. horizontally	10,000.	

All type I stamps were printed from 7 of the plates used for the imperfs., so many varieties exist both imperf. and perf.

VARIETIES OF RECUTTING

Recut inner frame lines (Plates 2L, 3, 5L)	3,100.	200.00
Recut inner frame line only at right		190.00
1 extra vertical line outside of left frame line (29L, 39L, 49L, 59L, 69L, 79L, Plate 3)	—	225.00
2 extra vertical lines outside of left frame line (89L, 99L, Plate 3)	—	275.00
1 extra vertical line outside of right frame line (58L, 68L, 78L, 88L, 98L, Plate 3)	—	225.00
No inner line and frame line close to design at right (9L, 19L, Plate 3)	—	275.00
No inner line and frame line close to design at left (70L, 80L, 90L, 100L, Plate 3)	—	275.00
Lines on bust and bottom of medallion circle recut (47R6)	—	625.00
Recut button (10R2L)		850.00

Other varieties of recutting are described in "The 3c Stamp of U.S. 1851-57 Issue," by Carroll Chase.

Earliest known use: Feb. 28, 1857 (Plate 7).

Cancellations

Blue	+1.00
Red	+5.00
Orange	+150.00
Brown	+100.00
Ultramarine	+100.00
Green	+200.00
1857 year date	+1.00
1858 year date	+1.00
1859 year date	+1.00
"Paid"	+2.50
"Way"	+20.00
Railroad	+25.00
Numeral	+7.50
"Steam"	+20.00
Steamship	+35.00
Steamboat	+45.00
Packet Boat	+50.00
Supplementary Mail Type A	+40.00
U. S. Express Mail	+5.00
Express Company	+65.00
Black Carrier	+30.00
"Old Stamps-Not Recognized"	+1,000.
Territorial	+35.00
Printed precancel "Cumberland, Me." (on cover)	—
Pen	37.50

A21

Type II - The outer frame line has been removed at top and bottom. The side frame lines were recut so as to be continuous from the top to the bottom of the plate. Stamps from the top or bottom rows show the ends of the side frame lines and may be mistaken for Type IIa.

Type IIa - The side frame lines extend only to the top and bottom of the stamp design. All Type IIa stamps are from plates 10 and 11 (each of which exists in three states), and these plates produced only Type IIa. The side frame lines were recut individually for each stamp, thus being broken between the stamp vertically.

Beware of type II stamps with frame lines that stop at the top of the design (from top row of plate) or bottom of the design (from bottom row of plate). These are often offered as No. 26a.

26	A21 3c	**dull red**, type II	75.00	5.00
		red	75.00	5.00
		rose	75.00	5.00
		No gum	30.00	
		brownish carmine	140.00	16.00
		No gum	55.00	
		claret	170.00	21.00
		No gum	75.00	
		orange brown	—	—
		plum	—	—
		On cover, dull red		6.00
		On cover, orange brown		750.00
		On patriotic cover		85.00
		On Confederate patriotic cover		1,200.
		On Pony express cover		
		Pair	160.00	12.50
		Strip of 3	240.00	30.00
		Block of 4	325.00	100.00
		P# block of 8, Impt.	3,000.	
		Double transfer	110.00	16.00
		Double transfer, rosettes double and line through "Postage" (87R15)	—	275.00
		Left frame line double	110.00	15.00
		Right frame line double	110.00	15.00
		Cracked plate (62L, 71L, 72L, Plate 18)	750.00	250.00
		Damaged transfer above lower left rosette	85.00	6.50
		Same, retouched	105.00	7.50
		Same, retouched with 2 vertical lines	120.00	9.00
		Same, both damaged areas retouched	140.00	42.50
		"Quadruple" plate flaw (18L28)	—	600.00
		1 line recut in upper left triangle	—	30.00
		5 lines recut in upper left triangle		100.00
		Inner line recut at right	—	200.00
		Worn plate	85.00	5.50
b.		Horiz. pair, imperf. vertically	4,000.	—
c.		Vert. pair, imperf. horizontally	—	
d.		Horizontal pair, imperf. between	—	
e.		Double impression		2,500.

Frame line double varieties are separate and distinct for virtually the entire length of the stamp. Copies with partly split lines are worth considerably less.

Earliest known use: Sept. 14, 1857.

Cancellations

Blue	+.10
Red	+1.50
Orange	+150.00
Brown	+100.00
Ultramarine	+100.00
Violet	+100.00
Green	+150.00
1857 year date	+3.00
1858-1861 year date	+.25

Printed Circular Precancel "Cumberland, Me." (on cover)	—
"Paid"	+.25
"Paid All"	+15.00
"Free"	+20.00
"Collect"	+40.00
Numeral	+2.50
"Steam"	+12.50
Steamer	
Steamboat	+22.50
Steamship	+22.50
"Way"	+12.50
Railroad	+15.00
U. S. Express Mail	+20.00
Express Company	+65.00
Packet boat	+65.00
Supp. Mail Type A, B or C	+75.00
Black Carrier	+30.00
Red Carrier	+25.00
"Southn. Letter Unpaid"	
Territorial	+20.00
"Old Stamps-Not Recognized"	+500.00
Pen	2.00

26a	A21 3c	**dull red**, type IIa	200.00	45.00
		brownish carmine	200.00	45.00
		rose	200.00	45.00
		No gum	90.00	
		claret	220.00	55.00
		No gum	120.00	
		On cover		70.00
		On patriotic cover		300.00
		Pair	425.00	110.00
		Strip of 3	800.00	225.00
		Block of 4	1,750.	700.00
		P# block of 8, Impt.	10,000.	
		Double transfer	300.00	100.00
		Double transfer of rosettes and lower part of stamp (91R11L)	—	175.00
		Triple transfer	—	350.00
		Damaged transfer above lower left rosette	230.00	70.00
		Same, retouched	220.00	62.50
		Inner line recut at right	—	110.00
		Inner line recut at left	—	225.00
		Left frame line double (70, 80, 90, 100 R 11)	—	140.00
		Worn plate	200.00	45.00
f.		Horiz. strip of 3, imperf. vert., on cover		8,250.

No. 26f is unique.

Earliest known use: June 6, 1857.

Cancellations

Blue	+2.50
Red	+10.00
Orange	+150.00
Brown	+100.00
Ultramarine	+100.00
Violet	+150.00
Green	+175.00
1857 year date	+2.50
1858 or 1859 year date	+1.50
"Paid"	+2.50
"Paid All"	+15.00
"Free"	+20.00
"Collect"	+40.00
Numeral	+2.50
"Steam"	+15.00
Steamer	
Steamboat	+25.00
Steamship	+25.00
"Way"	+15.00
Railroad	+17.50
U. S. Express Mail	+17.50
Express Company	+65.00
Packet boat	+65.00
Black Carrier	+30.00
Red Carrier	+20.00
Territorial	+25.00
Pen	22.50

27	A11 5c	**brick red**, type I, *1858*	22,500.	1,300.
		No gum	11,000.	
		On cover		1,750.
		On patriotic cover		4,750.
		Pair	50,000.	3,000.
		Strip of 3		5,000.
		Block of 4	140,000.	37,500.
		Defective transfer (23R1)	—	—

The unused block of 4 is unique.

Earliest known use: Oct. 6, 1858.

Cancellations

Blue	+65
Red	+100.
Ultramarine	+200.
1859 year date	+50.
1860 year date	+50.
"Paid"	+50.
Supplementary Mail Type A	+150.
"Steamship"	+150.
Pen	750.

28	A11 5c	**red brown**, type I	4,000.	650.
		pale red brown	4,000.	650.
		No gum	1,900.	
		On cover		850.
		Pair	8,750.	1,400.
		Strip of 3		2,250.
		Block of 4	35,000.	5,000.
		Defective transfer (23R1)	—	—
b.		**Bright red brown**	4,250.	850.
		No gum	2,100.	

Earliest known use: Aug. 23, 1857.

Cancellations

Blue	+25.
Red	+45.
1857 year date	+20.
1858 year date	+15.
"Paid"	+35.
Railroad	+75.
"Short Paid"	—
Pen	325.

28A	A11 5c	**Indian red**, type I, *1858*	30,000.	3,000.
		No gum	16,500.	
		On cover		3,750.
		Pair		6,250.
		Strip of 3		9,500.
		Block of 4	—	

Earliest known use: Mar. 31, 1858.

Cancellations

Red	+75.
Blue	+100.
1858 year date	+50.
1859 year date	+25.
Pen	1,750.

29	A11 5c	**brown**, type I, *1859*	2,200.	350.
		pale brown	2,200.	350.
		deep brown	2,200.	350.
		yellowish brown	2,200.	350.
		No gum	1,000.	
		On cover		475.
		Pair	5,000.	750.
		Strip of 3	7,500.	1,200.
		Block of 4	21,000.	4,500.
		Defective transfer (23R1)	—	

Earliest known use: Apr. 4, 1859.

Cancellations

Blue	+10.
Red	+25.
Brown	+30.
Magenta	+125.
Green	+300.
1859 year date	+10.
1860 year date	+10.
"Paid"	+15.
"Steam"	+75.
Steamship	+100.
Numeral	+50.
Pen	175.

Jefferson — A22

FIVE CENTS.

Type II - The projections at top and bottom are partly cut away. Several minor types could be made according to the extent of cutting of the projections.

30	A22 5c	**orange brown**, Type II, *1861*	1,150.	1,100.
		deep orange brown	1,150.	1,100.
		No gum	525.	
		On cover		2,250.
		On patriotic cover		—
		Pair	2,400.	2,750.
		Strip of 3	3,750.	—
		Block of 4	6,000.	

Earliest known use: May 8, 1861.

Cancellations

Blue	+30.
Red	+75.
Green	
"Paid"	+75.
Steamship	+110.
Supplementary Mail Type A	+150.
Railroad	—
Pen	600.

30A	A22 5c	**brown**, type II, *1860*	1,800.	260.
		dark brown	1,800.	260.
		yellowish brown	1,800.	260.
		No gum	850.	
		On cover		325.
		On patriotic cover		—
		Pair	3,900.	550.
		Strip of 3	6,000.	800.
		Block of 4	9,000.	2,750.
		Cracked plate		—
b.		Printed on both sides	4,250.	4,500.

Earliest known use: May 4, 1860.

Cancellations

Blue	+5.
Red	+20.
Magenta	+75.
Green	+350.
"Paid"	+20.
Supplementary Mail Type A	+50.
"Steamship"	+50.
"Steam"	+40.
Express Company	+250.
Railroad	—
Packet boat	—
Pen	130.

31 A12 10c **green**, type I

		16,000.	850.
dark green		16,000.	850.
bluish green		16,000.	850.
yellowish green		16,000.	850.
No gum		7,500.	
On domestic cover			1,200.
On patriotic cover			3,000.
Pair		35,000.	1,850.
Vertical pair, types III, I		21,500.	1,150.
Vertical pair, types IV, I (86, 96 L 1)			—
Strip of 3			—
Vertical strip of 3, types II, III, I			—
Block of 4, types III, I		45,000.	
Block of 4, types III, IV, I			8,000.
Vertical block of 6, 2 each types II, III, I		57,500.	
Double transfer (100R1)		17,500.	950.
"Curl" in left "X" (99R1)		17,500.	950.

Type I comes only from the bottom row of both panes of Plate 1.

Earliest known use: Sept. 21, 1857.

Cancellations

Blue	+15.
Red	+50.
Green	+500.
Supplementary Mail Type A	
"Steamship"	+100.
Canadian	
Pen	425.

Act of February 27, 1861. Ten cent rate of postage to be prepaid on letters conveyed in the mail from any point in the United States east of the Rocky Mountains to any State or Territory on the Pacific Coast and vice versa, for each half-ounce.

32 A13 10c **green,** type II

		4,750.	275.
dark green		4,750.	275.
bluish green		4,750.	275.
yellowish green		4,750.	275.
No gum		2,300.	
On domestic cover			325.
On pony express cover			8,500.
Pair		10,000.	575.
Strip of 3		—	875.
Block of 4		22,500.	4,500.
Pair, types II, III		10,000.	575.
Pair, types II, IV		39,000.	2,650.
Vertical strip of 3, types II, III, IV			—
Block of 4, types II, III		21,000.	2,250.
Block of 4, types II, IV			—
Block of 4, types II, III, IV		77,500.	18,000.
Double transfer (31L, 51L and 20R, Plate 1)		5,000.	300.
"Curl opposite left X" (10R1)			350.

Earliest known use: July 27, 1857 (dated cancel on off-cover stamp).

Cancellations

Blue	+10.
Red	+30.
Brown	+75.
Green	+225.
"Paid"	+20.
1857 year date	+10.
Supplementary Mail Type A	
Steamship	+50.
Packet boat	
Railroad	
Express Company	
Pen	105.

33 A14 10c **green**, type III

		4,750.	275.
dark green		4,750.	275.
bluish green		4,750.	275.
yellowish green		4,750.	275.
No gum		2,300.	
On domestic cover			325.
Pair		10,000.	575.
Strip of 3		—	875.
Pair, types III, IV		2,500.	
"Curl" on forehead (85L1)		—	350.
"Curl" in left X (87R1)			350.

Earliest known use: Oct. 15, 1857.

Cancellations

Blue	+10.
Red	+30.
Brown	+75.
Ultramarine	+45.
1857 year date	+10.
"Paid"	+20.
"Steam"	+45.
Steamboat	
Steamship	+50.
Numeral	+15.
Packet boat	
Pen	105.

34 A15 10c **green,** type IV

		32,500.	2,250.
dark green		32,500.	2,250.
bluish green		32,500.	2,250.
yellowish green		32,500.	2,250.
No gum		17,500.	
On domestic cover			2,650.
Pair			5,750.
Block of 4 (54-55, 64-65L)			—

VARIETIES OF RECUTTING

Eight stamps on Plate I were recut. All are listed below.

Outer line recut at top (65L, 74L, 86L and 3R, Plate I)	32,500.	2,250.

Outer line recut at bottom (54L, 55L, 76L, Plate 1)	33,500.	2,300.
Outer line recut at top and bottom (64L1)	35,000.	2,350.

Earliest known use: Dec. 2, 1858.

Cancellations

Blue	+40.
Red	+75.
Steamship	+200.
Packet boat	
Pen	1,150.

Types I, II, III and IV occur on the same sheet, so it is possible to obtain pairs and blocks showing combinations of types. For listings of type combinations in pairs and blocks, see Nos. 31-33.

(Two typical examples) — A23

Type V - The side ornaments are slightly cut away. Usually only one pearl remains at each end of the lower label, but some copies show two or three pearls at the right side. At the bottom the outer line is complete and the shells nearly so. The outer lines at top are complete except over the right "X."

35 A23 10c **green**, type V, (Plate 2),

1859	275.00	65.00
dark green	275.00	65.00
yellowish green	275.00	65.00
No gum	120.00	
On domestic cover		77.50
On patriotic cover		625.00
On pony express cover		—
On cover to Canada		125.00
Pair	575.00	140.00
Block of 4	1,200.	650.00
P# block of 8, Impt.	17,500.	
Double transfer at bottom (47R2)	350.00	90.00
Small "Curl" on forehead (37, 78L2)	325.00	77.50
Curl in "e" of "cents" (93L2)	350.00	90.00
Curl in "t" of "cents" (73R2)	350.00	90.00
Cracked plate		—

Earliest known use: Apr. 29, 1859.

Cancellations

Red	+7.50
Brown	+100.00
Blue	+5.00
Orange	+150.00
Magenta	+100.00
Green	+250.00
1859 year date	+5.00
"Paid"	+5.00
Red carrier	
Railroad	+40.00
Steamship	+35.00
"Steam"	+30.00
Numerals	+15.00
Supp. Mail Type A or C	+60.00
Express Company	+135.00
"Southn Letter Unpaid"	
Territorial	
Pen	32.50

TWELVE CENTS. Printed from two plates.
Plate I - Outer frame lines complete.
Plate III - Outer frame lines noticeably uneven or broken, sometimes partly missing.

36 A16 12c **black** (Plate 1)

	1,200.	210.
gray black	1,200.	210.
No gum	550.	
Single on cover		550.
Single on cover with No. 26 to France		260.
Pair on cover to England		525.
Pair on patriotic cover		—
Pair	2,750.	475.
Block of 4	7,000.	1,600.
Not recut in lower right corner	1,300.	230.
Recut in lower left corner (43, 53, 63, 73, 100L)	1,350.	220.
Double transfer	1,350.	230.
Triple transfer	1,500.	—
a. Diagonal half used as 6c on cover		17,500.
c. Horizontal pair, imperf. between		12,500.

Earliest known use: July 30, 1857.

Cancellations

Blue	+5.
Red	+10.

Brown	+75.
Magenta	+55.
Green	+250.
1857 year date	+20.
"Paid"	+10.
Supplementary Mail Type A	+60.
Express Company	
Railroad	+60.
Numeral	+20.
"Southn Letter Unpaid"	
Pen	105.

36b A16 12c **black** (Plate 3)

	725.	175.
intense black	725.	175.
No gum	325.	
Single on cover		625.
Single on cover with No. 26 to France		290.
Pair on cover to England		425.
Pair	1,500.	375.
Block of 4	4,250.	2,250.
Double frame line at right	775.	190.
Double frame line at left	775.	190.
Vertical line through rosette (95R3)	900.	250.

Earliest known use: Dec. 3, 1859.

Washington
A17

Franklin
A18

37 A17 24c **gray lilac**, *1860*

	1,500.	350.
a. 24c **gray**	1,500.	350.
No gum	675.	
On cover to England		1,000.
On patriotic cover		4,000.
Pair	3,250.	775.
Block of 4, gray lilac	8,500.	5,750.
P# block of 12, Impt.	30,000.	

The technical configuration of a No. 37 plate block is eight stamps. The unique plate block currently is contained in the listed block of twelve stamps.

Earliest known use: July 7, 1860.

Cancellations

Blue	+10.
Red	+40.
Magenta	+80.
Violet	+110.
Green	+450.
1860 year date	+15.
"Paid"	+25.
"Paid All"	+50.
"Free"	+100.
Supplementary Mail Type A	+150.
Railroad	+150.
Packet Boat	+200.
Red Carrier	
Numeral	+40.
"Southn Letter Unpaid"	
Pen	175.

See Trial Color Proofs for the 24c red lilac.

38 A18 30c **orange**, *1860*

	1,800.	450.
yellow orange	1,800.	425.
reddish orange	1,800.	425.
No gum	825.	
On cover to Germany or France		1,300.
On patriotic cover		9,000.
Pair	4,000.	1,000.
Block of 4	10,500.	6,500.
Double transfer (89L1 and 99L1)	2,000.	525.
Recut at bottom (52L1)	2,100.	575.
Cracked plate		—

Earliest known use: Aug. 8, 1860.

Cancellations

Blue	+20.
Red	+40.
Magenta	+90.
Violet	+90.
Green	+450.
1860 year date	+30.
"Paid"	+35.
"Free"	
Black town	+30.
Supplementary Mail Type A	+125.
Steamship	
Express Company	
Pen	225.

Washington — A19

39	A19	90c **blue**, *1860*	2,600.	6,000.
		deep blue	2,600.	6,000.
		No gum	1,200.	
		On cover		225,000.
		Pair	5,500.	—
		Block of 4	18,000.	45,000.
		Double transfer at bottom	2,750.	
		Double transfer at top	2,750.	—
		Short transfer at bottom right and left (13L1 and 68R1)	2,700.	

The used block of 4 is believed to be unique and has perfs trimmed off at left and bottom clear of design. Value is based on 1993 auction sale.

Earliest known use: Sept. 11, 1860.

Cancellations

Blue	+150.
Red	+500.
Black town	—
1861 year date	—
"Paid"	—
Red Carrier	—
N.Y. Ocean Mail	—
Pen	1,750.

Genuine cancellations on the 90c are very scarce.
All used examples of No. 39 must be accompanied by certificates of authenticity issued by recognized expertizing committees.

See Die and Plate Proofs for imperfs. on stamp paper.

REPRINTS OF 1857-60 ISSUE

These were not valid for postal use, though some values are known with contemporaneous cancels.

Produced by the Continental Bank Note Co.

White paper, without gum.

The 1, 3, 10 and 12c were printed from new plates of 100 subjects each differing from those used for the regular issue.

1875			Perf. 12
40	A5	1c **bright blue** (3846)	650.
		Pair	1,400.
		Block of 4	3,250.
		Cracked plate, pos. 91	800.
		Double transfer, pos. 94	800.
41	A10	3c **scarlet** (479)	2,750.
42	A22	5c **orange brown** (878)	1,100.
		Pair	2,500.
		Vertical margin strip of 4, Impt. & P#	10,000.

43	A12	10c **blue green** (516)	2,250.
		Pair	6,000.
44	A16	12c **greenish black** (489)	3,000.
		Pair	7,250.
45	A17	24c **blackish violet** (479)	3,000.
46	A18	30c **yellow orange** (480)	3,000.
47	A19	90c **deep blue** (454)	4,500.

Nos. 41-46 are valued in the grade of fine.
Nos. 40-47 exist imperforate. Value, set of singles, $25,000.
One set of imperforate pairs is recorded.
Numbers in parentheses are quantities issued.

Produced by the National Bank Note Co.

Franklin
A24   A24

Washington
A25   A25

Jefferson
A26   A26

A27a

Washington
A27

Washington
A28   A28

Washington
A29

Franklin
A30

Washington
A31   A31

1c - There is a dash under the tip of the ornament at right of the numeral in upper left corner.

3c - Ornaments at corners end in a small ball.

5c - There is a leaflet in the foliated ornaments at each corner.

10c (A27) - A heavy curved line has been cut below the stars and an outer line added to the ornaments above them.

12c - There are corner ornaments consisting of ovals and scrolls.

90c - Parallel lines form an angle above the ribbon with "U. S. Postage"; between these lines there is a row of dashes and a point of color at the apex of the lower line.

Patriotic Covers covering a wide range of historical interest were used during the Civil War period, in the North as well as the South, and are collected in State groups as well as generally, both used and unused. There are believed to be as many as 10,000 varieties.

During the war, these stamps were used as small change until Postage Currency was issued.

The Act of Congress of March 3, 1863, effective July 1, 1863, created a rate of three cents for each half ounce, first class domestic mail. This Act was the first law which established uniform rate of postage regardless of the distance. This rate remained in effect until Oct. 1, 1883.

Plates of 200 subjects in two panes of 100 each.

The following items, formerly listed here as Nos. 55-62, are considered to be essays or trial color proofs. They will be found in their respective sections as follows. Previous No. 58 has been combined with No. 62B.

Formerly	Currently	Formerly	Currently
55	63-E11e	59	69-E6e
56	65-E15h	60	70eTC
57	67-E9e	61	71bTC
58	62B	62	72-E7h

The paper of Nos. 62B-72 is thicker and more opaque than the essays and trial color proofs, except Nos. 62B, 70c, and 70d.

1861   *Perf. 12*

62B	A27a	10c **dark green**	6,500.	900.
		dark yellow green	6,500.	900.
		No gum	3,250.	
		On cover		1,250.
		On patriotic cover		2,500.
		Pair	14,500.	2,000.
		Block of 4	30,000.	11,000.
		Foreign entry 94R4	7,750.	—
		Block of 4, one stamp 94R4	—	

The foreign entry is of the 90c 1861.

Earliest known use: Sept. 17, 1861.

Cancellations

Red	+80.
Blue	+50.
"Paid"	+60.
Steamship	+100.
Express Company	+200.
Supplementary Mail Type A	+125.

1861-62   *Perf. 12*

63	A24	1c **blue,** *Aug. 17, 1861*	325.00	32.50
		pale blue	325.00	32.50
		bright blue	325.00	32.50
		No gum	140.00	
		On cover (single)		40.00
		On prisoner's letter		—
		On patriotic cover		210.00
		Pair	700.00	70.00
		Block of 4	1,450.	350.00
		P# block of 8, Impt.	6,000.	
		Double transfer	—	45.00
		Dot in "U"	350.00	37.50
a.		1c **ultramarine**	700.00	250.00
		No gum	325.00	
b.		1c **dark blue**	525.00	80.00

No gum	240.00
c.	Laid paper, horiz. or vert.	—
d.	Vertical pair, imperf. horiz.	—
e.	Printed on both sides	2,500.

Earliest known use: Aug. 17, 1861 (dated cancel on off-cover stamp); Aug. 21, 1861 (earliest known use on cover).

Cancellations

Blue	+2.00
Red	+7.50
Magenta	+30.00
Green	+250.00
Violet	+30.00
1861 year date	+7.50
1865 year date	+2.00
1866 year date	+2.00
"Free"	+20.00
"Paid"	+2.50
"Paid All"	+15.00
Supp. Mail Type A or B	+30.00
Steamship	+35.00
Steam	+30.00
Express Company	+175.00
Red Carrier	+10.00
Black Carrier	+10.00
Railroad	+30.00
Numeral	+10.00
"Steamboat"	+50.00
Printed Precancel "CUMBERLAND, ME." (on cover)	—

64	A25	3c **pink,** *Aug. 17, 1861*	7,000.	700.00
		No gum	3,500.	
		On cover		800.00
		On patriotic cover		1,000.
		Pair	15,000.	1,700.
		Block of 4	35,000.	

Earliest known use: Aug. 17, 1861 (FDC).

Cancellations

Blue	+25.00
Red	+70.00
Green	+500.00
1861 date	+25.00
"Paid"	+25.00
"Free"	+125.00
"Ship"	+85.00
Supplementary Mail Type B	+150.00
Railroad	+125.00
Steamboat	+175.00

a.		3c **pigeon blood pink**	16,000.	3,500.
		No gum	8,500.	
		On cover		4,250.
		On patriotic cover		6,250.

Earliest known use: Aug. 21, 1861.

b.		3c **rose pink,** *Aug. 17, 1861*	500.00	140.00
		No gum	225.00	
		On cover		175.00
		On patriotic cover		225.00
		Pair	1,150.	300.00
		Block of 4	2,500.	700.00

Earliest known use: Aug. 17, 1861 (FDC).

Cancellations

Blue	+10.00
Red	+20.00
Green	+150.00
"Paid"	+10.00
"Free"	+50.00
Supplementary Mail Type C	
"Ship"	+30.00
Railroad	+60.00
Steamboat	+90.00

65	A25	3c **rose**	130.00	2.50
		bright rose	130.00	2.50
		dull red	130.00	2.50
		rose red	130.00	2.50
		No gum	55.00	
		brown red	275.00	2.50
		No gum	120.00	
		pale brown red	210.00	2.50
		No gum	90.00	
		On cover		3.00
		On patriotic cover		40.00
		On prisoner's letter		150.00
		On pony express cover		—
		Pair	300.00	5.75
		Block of 4	600.00	37.50
		P# block of 8, Impt.	4,250.	
		Double transfer	150.00	5.50
		Cracked plate		—
b.		Laid paper, horiz. or vert.	—	—
d.		Vertical pair, imperf. horiz.	3,500.	750.00
e.		Printed on both sides	3,250.	2,750.
f.		Double impression		6,000.

See Die and Plate Proofs for imperfs. on stamp paper.

Earliest known use: Aug. 19, 1861.

Cancellations

Blue	+.25
Ultramarine	+2.75
Brown	+7.50
Red	+3.00
Violet	+4.50
Magenta	+8.00
Green	+90.00
Olive	+100.00
Orange	+150.00
Yellow	+3,500.00
1861 year date	+.50
1867 or 1868 year date	+.50
"Paid"	+.35
"Paid All"	+7.50
"Mails Suspended"	—

Railroad	+12.50
"Way"	+20.00
"Free"	+20.00
"Collect"	+35.00
"Ship"	+15.00
"U. S. Ship"	+35.00
"Steam"	+12.00
Steamship	+15.00
Steamboat	+20.00
"Ship Letter"	+35.00
Red Carrier	+15.00
Blue Carrier	+25.00
Black Carrier	+20.00
Supplementary Mail Type A, B or C	+15.00
Numeral	+3.00
Express Company	+90.00
Army Field Post	+60.00
Packet Boat	+40.00
"Registered"	+30.00
"Postage Due"	+25.00
"Advertised"	+15.00
Territorial	+25.00
St. Thomas	—
China	—

The 3c lake can be found under No. 66 in the Trial Color Proofs section.

67	A26	5c **buff**	16,500.	750.
a.		5c **brown yellow**	16,500.	750.
		No gum	8,500.	
b.		5c **olive yellow**	—	900.
		On cover		1,050.
		On patriotic cover		4,000.
		Pair	35,000.	1,750.
		Block of 4	11,500.	11,000.

The unused block of 4 is unique but very faulty. Value is based on actual 1993 sale.

Earliest known use: Aug. 19, 1861 (No. 67); Aug. 21, 1861 (No. 67a).

Cancellations

Red	+40.00
Blue	+20.00
Magenta	+50.00
Green	—
1861 year date	+10.00
"Paid"	+25.00
Supplementary Mail Type A	+100.00
Express Company	+250.00
Numeral	+50.00
"Steamship"	+100.00

Values of Nos. 67, 67a, 67b reflect the normal small margins.

68	A27	10c **yellow green**	700.00	50.00
		green	700.00	50.00
		No gum	325.00	
		On cover		67.50
		On patriotic cover		375.00
		On cover to Canada		90.00
		Pair	1,500.	110.00
		Block of 4	3,250.	425.00
		P# block of 8, Impt.	7,500.	
		Double transfer	775.00	55.00
		deep yellow green on thin paper	850.00	60.00
a.		10c **dark green**	750.00	52.50
		blue green	750.00	55.00
		No gum	350.00	
b.		Vertical pair, imperf. horiz.		3,500.

Earliest known use: Aug. 20, 1861.

Cancellations

Blue	+2.00
Red	+5.00
Purple	+15.00
Magenta	+15.00
Brown	+7.50
Green	+110.00
1865 year date	+3.50
"Paid"	+2.50
"Collect"	+32.50
"Short Paid"	+50.00
"P.D." in circle	+30.00
"Free"	+25.00
Numeral	+7.50
Red Carrier	+45.00
Railroad	+20.00
Steamship	+15.00
"Steamboat"	+35.00
Supplementary Mail Type A	+30.00
Red Supp. Mail Type D	
Express Company	+70.00
China	
Japan	+200.00
St. Thomas	—

Stamps are valued in the grade of very fine unless otherwise indicated.

Please Note:

Values for early and valuable stamps are for examples with certificates of authenticity from acknowledged expert committees, or examples sold with the buyer having the right of certification.

This applies to examples with original gum as well as examples without gum.

Beware of stamps offered "as is," as the gum on some unused stamps offered with "original gum" may be fraudulent, and stamps offered as unused without gum may in some cases be altered or faintly canceled used stamps.

69	A28	12c **black**	1,100.	90.00
		gray black	1,100.	90.00
		No gum	500.00	
		intense black	1,150.	95.00
		No gum	525.00	
		On domestic cover		120.00
		On patriotic cover		850.00
		On cover to France or Germany with #65		140.00
		Pair	2,400.	200.00
		Block of 4	5,250.	850.00
		Double transfer of top frame line	1,200.	110.00
		Double transfer of bottom frame line	1,200.	110.00
		Double transfer of top and bottom frame lines	1,250.	115.00

Earliest known use: Aug. 30, 1861.

Cancellations

Blue	+2.50
Red	+20.00
Purple	+50.00
Magenta	+100.00
Green	+700.00
1861 year date	+5.00
"Paid"	+5.00
"Registered"	+35.00
Supp. Mail Type A, B or C	+45.00
Express Company	+175.00
Railroad	+50.00
Numeral	+15.00

70	A29	24c **red lilac**	1,700.	150.00
		No gum	800.00	
		On cover		200.00
		On patriotic cover		3,000.
		Pair	3,750.	325.00
		Block of 4	8,500.	1,400.
		Scratch under "A" of "Postage"		—
a.		24c **brown lilac**	1,500.	130.00
		No gum	700.00	
		Block of 4	7,500.	
b.		24c **steel blue** ('61)	7,500.	600.00
		No gum	4,000.	
		On cover		1,150.
		Block of 4	33,000.	
c.		24c **violet**, thin paper, Aug. 20, 1861	9,500.	1,100.
		No gum	5,000.	
d.		24c **pale gray violet**, thin paper	3,000.	900.00
		No gum	1,400.	

There are numerous shades of the 24c stamp in this and the following issue.

Color changelings, especially of No. 78, are frequently offered as No. 70b.

Nos. 70c and 70d are on a thinner, harder and more transparent paper than Nos. 70, 70a, 70b or the latter Nos. 78, 78a, 78b and 78c. No. 70eTC (formerly No. 60, see Trial Color Proofs section) is distinguished by its distinctive dark color.

Earliest known use: Jan. 7, 1862 (No. 70); Aug. 20, 1861 (No. 70c).

Cancellations, No. 70

Blue	+5.00
Red	+15.00
Magenta	+100.00
Brown	+80.00
Green	+300.00
1865 year date	+5.00
"Paid"	+15.00
Supp. Mail Types A or B	+75.00
Express Company	+350.00

71	A30	30c **orange**	1,500.	150.
		deep orange	1,500.	150.
		No gum	675.	
		On cover to France or Germany		375.
		On patriotic cover		3,500.
		Pair	3,250.	350.
		Block of 4	7,000.	2,250.
		P# strip of 4, Impt.		—
a.		Printed on both sides		—

Values for No. 71 are for copies with small margins, especially at sides. Large-margined examples sell for much more.

Earliest known use: Aug. 20, 1861.

Cancellations

Blue	+10.00
Magenta	+100.00
Brown	+90.00
Red	+25.00

"Paid"	+15.00
"Paid All"	+35.00
Railroad	
Packet Boat	
"Steamship"	+75.00
Supplementary Mail Type A	+75.00
Red Supp. Mail Type D	
Express Company	+350.00
Japan	

72	A31	90c **blue**	2,500.	400.
		dull blue	2,500.	400.
		No gum	1,200.	
		On cover		17,500.
		Pair	5,500.	900.
		Block of 4	22,250.	4,000.
		P# strip of 4, Impt.	20,000.	
a.		90c **pale blue**	2,500.	400.
		No gum	1,200.	
b.		90c **dark blue**	2,750.	475.
		No gum	1,300.	

Earliest known use: Nov. 27, 1861.

Cancellations

Blue	+15.
Red	+40.
Green	+750.
1865 year date	+35.
"Paid"	+25.
"Registered"	+75.
Express Company	+500.
Supplementary Mail Type A	+100.

Nos. 68a, 69, 71 and 72 exist as imperforate sheet-margin singles with pen cancel. They were not regularly issued.

The 90c was distributed to several post offices in the last two weeks of August, 1861.

Owing to the Civil War, stamps and stamped envelopes in current use or available for postage in 1860, were demonetized by various post office orders, beginning in August, 1861, and extending to early January, 1862.

P. O. Department Bulletin.

"A reasonable time after hostilities began in 1861 was given for the return to the Department of all these (1851-56) stamps in the hands of postmasters, and as early as 1863 the Department issued an order declining to longer redeem them."

The Act of Congress, approved March 3, 1863, abolished carriers' fees and established a prepaid rate of two cents for drop letters, making necessary the 2-cent Jackson (No. 73).

Free City Delivery was authorized by the Act of Congress of March 3, 1863, effective in 49 cities with 449 carriers, beginning July 1, 1863.

Produced by the National Bank Note Co.
DESIGNS AS 1861 ISSUE

Andrew Jackson — A32

Abraham Lincoln — A33

1861-66   *Perf. 12*

73	A32	2c **black**, *1863*	350.00	50.00
		gray black	350.00	50.00
		intense black	350.00	55.00
		No gum	140.00	
		On cover		75.00
		On prisoner's letter		—
		On patriotic cover		2,000.
		Pair	750.00	110.00
		Block of 4	3,000.	1,250.
		P# strip of 4, Impt.	4,000.	
		P# block of 8, Impt.	14,000.	
		Double transfer	400.00	55.00
		Major double transfer of top left corner and "Postage" ("Atherton shift")		12,500.
		Major double transfer of right side, pos. 81, right pane ("Preston shift")	—	—
		Triple transfer	—	—
		Short transfer	375.00	55.00
		Cracked plate		
a.		Diagonal half used as 1c as part of 3c rate on cover		1,150.
b.		Diagonal half used alone as 1c on cover		3,000.
c.		Horiz. half used as 1c as part of 3c rate on cover		3,500.
d.		Vert. half used as 1c as part of 3c rate on cover		1,250.
e.		Printed on both sides		5,000.
f.		Laid paper	—	—

Earliest known use: July 1, 1861 (dated cancel on off-cover stamp); July 6, 1863 (earliest known use on cover).

Cancellations

Blue	+5.00
Brown	+75.00
Red	+50.00
Magenta	+75.00
Ultramarine	+150.00
Orange	+200.00
Green	+500.00
1863 year date	+5.00

Printed Precancel "Jefferson, Ohio,"	
"PAID ALL"	+40.00
"Paid"	+10.00
Numeral	+15.00
Railroad	+400.00
"Steam"	+40.00
Steamship	+65.00
"Steamboat"	+65.00
"Ship Letter"	
Black Carrier	+20.00
Blue Carrier	+35.00
Supp. Mail Type A or B	+60.00
Express Company	+450.00
"Short Paid"	+130.00
China	

The 3c scarlet, design A25, can be found under No. 74 in the Trial Color Proofs section.

75	A26	5c **red brown**	4,250.	450.
		dark red brown	4,250.	450.
		No gum	2,100.	
		On cover		675.
		On patriotic cover		2,500.
		Pair	9,000.	950.
		Block of 4	25,000.	7,000.
		Double transfer	4,500.	500.

Values for No. 75 reflect the normal small margins.

Earliest known use: Jan. 2, 1862.

Cancellations

Blue	+10.
Red	+35.
Magenta	+65.
"Paid"	+25.
Supplementary Mail Type A	+50.
Express Company	+300.

76	A26	5c **brown**, *1863*	1,100.	110.
		pale brown	1,100.	110.
		dark brown	1,100.	110.
		No gum	500.	
		On cover		160.
		On patriotic cover		825.
		Pair	2,400.	230.
		Block of 4	5,250.	700.
		Double transfer of top frame line	1,200.	125.
		Double transfer of bottom frame line	1,200.	125.
		Double transfer of top and bottom frame lines	1,250.	140.
a.		5c **black brown**	1,250.	160.
		No gum	575.	
		Block of 4	5,500.	900.
b.		Laid paper		

Values of Nos. 76, 76a reflect the normal small margins.

Earliest known use: Feb. 3, 1863.

Cancellations

Blue	+5.00
Magenta	+75.00
Red	+7.50
Brown	+75.00
Green	+300.00
1865 year date	+10.00
"Paid"	+15.00
"Short Paid"	+75.00
Supp. Mail Type A or F	+55.00
Express Company	+175.00
"Steamship"	
Packet boat	+65.00

77	A33	15c **black**, *1866*	1,500.	150.
		full black	1,500.	150.
		No gum	675.	
		On cover to France or Germany		225.
		Pair	3,250.	325.
		Block of 4	17,500.	
		P# block of 8, Impt.	—	
		Double transfer	1,600.	100.
		Cracked plate	—	

Earliest known use: Apr. 14, 1866.

Cancellations

Blue	+5.
Magenta	+100.
Red	+35.
Brown	+80.
Green	+350.
Ultramarine	+35.
"Paid"	+15.
"Short Paid"	+85.
"Insufficiently Paid"	+150.
"Ship"	+50.
Steamship	+50.
Supplementary Mail Type A	+70.

78	A29	24c **lilac**, *1862*	1,000.	95.
		dark lilac	1,000.	95.
a.		24c **grayish lilac**	1,000.	95.
b.		24c **gray**	1,000.	95.
		No gum	450.	
		On cover		175.
		Pair	2,250.	210.
		Block of 4	5,000.	825.
		Scratch under "A" of "Postage"		—
c.		24c **blackish violet**	30,000.	1,750.
		No gum	20,000.	
d.		Printed on both sides		3,500.

Earliest known use: Feb. 20, 1863 (No. 78); Oct. 30, 1862 (No. 78a); Oct. 26, 1862 (No. 78b).

Cancellations

Blue	+7.50
Red	+15.00
Magenta	+90.00
Green	+400.00
"Paid"	+15.00
Numeral	+20.00
Supplementary Mail Type A	+50.00
"Free"	+100.00

Nos. 73, 76-78 exist as imperforate sheet-margin singles, all with pen cancel except No. 76 which is uncanceled. They were not regularly issued.

SAME DESIGNS AS 1861-66 ISSUES
Printed by the National Bank Note Co.

Grill

Embossed with grills of various sizes. Some authorities believe that more than one size of grill probably existed on one of the grill rolls.

A peculiarity of the United States issues from 1867 to 1870 is the grill or embossing. The object was to break the fiber of the paper so that the ink of the canceling stamp would soak in and make washing for a second using impossible. The exact date at which grilled stamps came into use is unsettled. Luff's "Postage Stamps of the United States" places the date as probably August 8, 1867.

Horizontal measurements are given first.

GRILL WITH POINTS UP

Grills A and C were made by a roller covered with ridges shaped like an inverted V. Pressing the ridges into the stamp paper forced the paper into the pyramidal pits between the ridges, causing irregular breaks in the paper. Grill B was made by a roller with raised bosses.

A. Grill Covering the Entire Stamp.

1867				Perf. 12	
79	A25	3c **rose**		4,500.	1,000.
		No gum		2,250.	
		On cover			1,500.
		Pair		9,500.	2,500.
		Block of 4		30,000.	
b.		Printed on both sides			—

Earliest known use: Aug. 13, 1867.

Cancellations

Blue	+75.
Railroad	—

Values for No. 79 are for fine-very fine copies with minor perf. faults.

An essay (#79-E15) which is often mistaken for No. 79 shows the points of the grill as small squares faintly impressed in the paper but not cutting through it. On the issued stamp the grill generally breaks through the paper. Copies without defects are rare.

See Die and Plate Proofs for imperf. on stamp paper.

80	A26	5c **brown**	—	80,000.
a.		5c **dark brown**		80,000.
81	A30	30c **orange**		50,000.

Eight copies of Nos. 80 and 80a (four unused and four used), and eight copies of No. 81 (one institutionalized and not available to collectors) are known. All are more or less faulty and/or off center. Values are for off-center examples with small perforation faults.

B. Grill about 18x15mm
(22x18 points)

82	A25	3c **rose**	160,000.

The four known copies of No. 82 are valued in the grade of fine. Value is based on 1998 auction sale.

C. Grill about 13x16mm
(16 to 17 by 18 to 21 points)

The grilled area on each of four C grills in the sheet may total about 18x15mm when a normal C grill adjoins a fainter grill extending to the right or left edge of the stamp. This is caused by a partial erasure on the grill roller when it was changed to produce C grills instead of the all-over A grill. Do not mistake these for the B grill. Unused exists and is very rare, value used $2,000; on cover $3,000.

83	A25	3c **rose**		4,750.	900.
		No gum		2,400.	
		On cover			1,100.
		Pair		10,500.	2,650.

	Block of 4		22,500.	—
	Double grill		6,250.	2,250.
	Grill with points down		5,750.	1,150.

Earliest known use: Nov. 19, 1867.

Cancellation

Blue	+25.

See Die and Plate Proofs for imperf. on stamp paper.
The 1c, 3c, 5c, 10c, 12c, 30c of 1861 are known with experimental C grills. They are listed in the Essays section. The 3c differs slightly from No. 83.

GRILL WITH POINTS DOWN

The grills were produced by rollers with the surface covered, or partly covered, by pyramidal bosses. On the D, E and F grills the tips of the pyramids are vertical ridges. On the Z grill the ridges are horizontal.

D. Grill about 12x14mm
(15 by 17 to 18 points)

84	A32	2c **black**		13,000.	2,500.
		No gum		7,500.	
		On cover			3,000.
		Pair		29,000.	5,250.
		Block of 4		65,000.	
		Double transfer		—	
		Split grill			2,750.

No. 84 is valued in the grade of fine.

Earliest known use: Feb. 15, 1868.

Cancellations

Red	+100.
"Paid All"	+100.

85	A25	3c **rose**		5,750.	900.
		No gum		2,850.	
		On cover			1,050.
		Pair		12,000.	2,000.
		Block of 4		30,000.	
		Double grill			
		Split grill			1,000.

Earliest known use: Feb. 2, 1868.

Cancellations

Blue	+20.
Green	+350.
"Paid"	+50.

Z. Grill about 11x14mm
(13 to 14 by 18 points)

85A	A24	1c **blue**	935,000.

Two copies of No. 85A are known. One is contained in the New York Public Library collection. Value represents 1998 auction sale of the single example available to collectors.

85B	A32	2c **black**		7,000.	1,000.
		No gum		3,500.	
		On cover			1,150.
		Pair		14,500.	2,250.
		Block of 4		35,000.	—
		Double transfer		7,500.	1,050.
		Double grill			

Earliest known use: Feb. 11, 1868.

Cancellations

Blue	+50.
Red	+100.
Black Carrier	+75.
"Paid All"	+75.

85C	A25	3c **rose**		10,000.	2,750.
		No gum		5,000.	
		On cover			3,250.
		Pair			
		Block of 4		45,000.	
		Double grill		11,500.	

Earliest known use: Feb. 12, 1868.

Cancellations

Green	+250.
Blue	+25.
Red	+75.
"Paid"	+50.

85D	A27	10c **green**	90,000.

Six copies of No. 85D are known. One is contained in the New York Public Library collection. Value is for a well-centered example with small faults.

85E	A28	12c **black**		9,000.	1,250.
		No gum		4,500.	
		On cover			1,700.
		Strip of 3			
		Block of 4			—
		Double transfer of top frame line			1,350.

Earliest known use: Feb. 15, 1868.

85F	A33	15c **black**	220,000.

Two copies of No. 85F are known. Value represents 1998 auction sale price of the much finer example.

E. Grill about 11x13mm
(14 by 15 to 17 points)

86	A24	1c **blue**		2,750.	450.
		No gum		1,300.	
a.		1c **dull blue**		2,750.	425.
		No gum		1,300.	
		On cover			550.
		Pair (blue)		5,750.	950.

	Block of 4 (blue)		12,500.	2,750.
	Double grill		—	575.
	Split grill		2,850.	500.

Earliest known use: Mar. 9, 1868.

Cancellations

Blue	+10.
Red	+60.
Green	+300.
"Paid"	+25.
Steamboat	+90.
Red Carrier	+80.

87	A32	2c **black**	1,350.	125.
		gray black	1,350.	125.
		No gum	625.	
		intense black	1,450.	150.
		No gum	675.	
		On cover		240.
		Pair	2,900.	160.
		Block of 4	6,750.	—
		Double grill	—	—
		Double grill, one split	—	—
		Triple grill	—	—
		Split grill	1,500.	140.
		Grill with points up	—	—
		Double transfer	1,450.	135.
a.		Diagonal half used as 1c on cover		2,000.
b.		Vertical half used as 1c on cover		2,000.

Earliest known use: Mar. 11, 1868.

Cancellations

Blue	+7.50
Purple	+40.00
Brown	+40.00
Red	+50.00
Green	+200.00
"Paid"	+10.00
Steamship	+60.00
Black Carrier	+35.00
"Paid All"	+20.00
"Short Paid"	+65.00
Japan	—

88	A25	3c **rose**	750.	20.00
		pale rose	750.	20.00
		rose red	750.	20.00
		No gum	350.	
		On cover		25.00
		Pair	1,550.	42.50
		Block of 4	4,000.	200.00
		P# block of 8, Impt.	8,500.	—
		Double grill	—	—
		Triple grill	—	—
		Split grill	825.	24.00
		Very thin paper	775.	22.50
a.		3c **lake red**	800.	25.00
		No gum	375.	

Earliest known use: Feb. 19, 1868.

Cancellations

Blue	+2.50
Red	+5.00
Ultramarine	+3.00
Green	+80.00
"Paid"	+3.00
"Way"	+20.00
Numeral	+2.00
Steamboat	+35.00
Railroad	+25.00
Express Company	+80.00

89	A27	10c **green**	4,500.	300.
		dark green	4,500.	300.
		blue green	4,500.	300.
		No gum	2,100.	
		On cover		400.
		Pair	9,500.	650.
		Block of 4	20,000.	2,600.
		Double grill	5,750.	500.
		Split grill	4,750.	325.
		Double transfer		325.
		Very thin paper	4,750.	325.

Earliest known use: Feb. 21, 1868.

Cancellations

Blue	+20.
Red	+60.
"Paid"	+15.
Steamship	+50.
Japan	+225.

90	A28	12c **black**	4,250.	325.
		gray black	4,250.	325.
		intense black	4,250.	325.
		No gum	2,000.	
		On cover		475.
		Pair	9,000.	700.
		Block of 4	27,500.	2,250.
		Double transfer of top frame line	4,500.	350.
		Double transfer of bottom frame line	4,500.	350.
		Double transfer of top and bottom frame lines	4,600.	400.
		Double grill	5,000.	650.
		Split grill	4,500.	350.

Earliest known use: Feb. 29, 1868.

Cancellations

Blue	+20.
Red	+65.
Purple	
Green	+225.
Railroad	+60.
"Paid"	+20.

91	A33	15c **black**	8,250.	625.
		gray black	8,250.	625.
		No gum	4,000.	
		On cover		850.

	Pair		17,500.	1,300.
	Block of 4		36,000.	5,250.
	Double grill		—	950.
	Split grill		—	675.

Earliest known use: June 15, 1868.

Cancellations

Blue	+15.
Red	+100.
"Paid"	+30.
Supplementary Mail Type A	+100.

F. Grill about 9x13mm
(11 to 12 by 15 to 17 points)

92	A24	1c **blue**	1,000.	190.
a.		1c **pale blue**	1,000.	190.
		dark blue	1,000.	190.
		No gum	450.	
		On cover		225.
		Pair	2,100.	400.
		Block of 4	4,750.	1,100.
		Double transfer	1,050.	225.
		Double grill		350.
		Split grill	1,050.	220.
		Very thin paper	1,050.	210.

Earliest known use: Aug. 11 1868.

Cancellations

Blue	+5.00
Red	+20.00
Green	+250.00
"Paid"	+10.00
Red Carrier	+25.00
"Paid All"	+15.00

93	A32	2c **black**	450.	45.00
		gray black	450.	45.00
		No gum	200.	
		On cover		60.00
		Pair	950.	95.00
		Block of 4	2,250.	400.
		P# strip of 4, Impt.	5,750.	
		P# block of 8, Impt.		
		Double transfer	500.	52.50
		Double grill	—	175.
		Split grill	500.	52.50
		Double grill, one split		
		Very thin paper	500.	52.50
a.		Vertical half used as 1c as part of 3c rate on cover		1,250.
b.		Diagonal half used as 1c as part of 3c rate on cover		1,250.
c.		Horizontal half used alone as 1c on cover		2,500.
d.		Diagonal half used alone as 1c on cover		2,500.

Earliest known use: Mar. 27, 1868.

Cancellations

Blue	+5.00
Red	+15.00
Green	+200.00
Japan	
"Paid"	+5.00
"Paid All"	+15.00
Black Carrier	+20.00
Red Carrier	+30.00

94	A25	3c **red**	350.	6.00
		rose red	350.	6.00
a.		3c **rose**	350.	6.00
		No gum	160.	
		On cover		7.50
		Pair	750.	12.50
		Block of 4	2,200.	100.00
		P# block of 8, Impt.	6,500.	
		Double transfer	400.	8.50
		Double grill		
		Double grill, one normal, one partial with points up	—	
		Triple grill	—	150.00
		End roller grill		325.00
		Split grill	375.	6.50
		Quadruple split grill	625.	125.00
		Double grill, one quadruple split		—
		Grill with points up		—
		Very thin paper	350.	6.25
c.		Vertical pair, imperf. horiz.	1,100.	
d.		Printed on both sides	2,250.	

Earliest known use: Mar. 26, 1868.

Cancellations

Blue	+.25
Ultramarine	+3.00
Red	+3.50
Violet	+5.50
Green	+70.00
Numeral	+3.00
"Paid"	+2.25
"Paid All"	+12.50
"Free"	+20.00
Railroad	+30.00
Steamboat	+40.00
Packet boat	+80.00
Express Company	+50.00

See Die and Plate Proofs for imperf. on stamp paper.

95	A26	5c **brown**	3,000.	700.
		No gum	1,400.	
		dark brown	3,150.	800.
		No gum	1,450.	
		On cover		775.
		Pair	6,250.	1,500.
		Block of 4	13,000.	7,750.
		Double transfer of top frame line	—	—

	Double transfer of bottom frame line		—	—
	Double grill		—	—
	Split grill		3,500.	750.
	Very thin paper		3,250.	725.
a.	5c **black brown**		3,250.	825.
	No gum		1,500.	

Earliest known use: Aug. 19, 1868.

Cancellations

Blue	+10.
Magenta	+55.
Violet	+60.
Red	+50.
Green	+200.
"Paid"	+25.
"Free"	+50.
"Steamship"	+100.

Values of Nos. 95, 95a reflect the normal small margins.

96	A27	10c **yellow green**	2,400.	200.
		green	2,400.	200.
a.		10c **dark green**	2,400.	200.
		blue green	2,400.	200.
		No gum	1,100.	
		On cover		250.
		Pair	5,000.	425.
		Block of 4	19,000.	1,450.
		P# strip of 4, Impt.	22,000.	
		Double transfer	—	—
		Double grill		350.
		Split grill	2,500.	225.
		Quadruple split grill		625.
		Very thin paper	2,500.	225.

Earliest known use: May 26, 1868.

Cancellations

Blue	+5.00
Red	+25.00
Magenta	+30.00
Green	+200.00
"Paid"	+10.00
"Free"	+50.00
Supplementary Mail Type A	
Steamship	+75.00
Japan	+200.00
China	

97	A28	12c **black**	2,750.	225.
		gray black	2,750.	225.
		No gum	1,250.	
		On cover		275.
		Pair	5,750.	475.
		Block of 4	18,000.	2,100.
		P# strip of 4, Impt.	21,500.	
		Double transfer of top frame line	3,000.	240.
		Double transfer of bottom frame line	3,000.	240.
		Double transfer of top and bottom frame lines	—	275.
		Double grill	—	425.
		Triple grill	—	—
		Split grill	3,000.	250.
		End roller grill	—	—
		Very thin paper	3,000.	250.

Earliest known use: May 27, 1868.

Cancellations

Blue	+5.00
Red	+50.00
Magenta	+50.00
Brown	+50.00
Green	+250.00
"Paid"	+15.00
"Insufficiently Prepaid"	+100.00
"Paid All"	+25.00
Supplementary Mail Type A	+50.00

98	A33	15c **black**	3,000.	300.
		gray black	3,000.	300.
		No gum	1,350.	
		On cover		350.
		Pair	6,250.	625.
		Block of 4	13,500.	2,750.
		P# block of 8, Impt.	32,500.	
		Double transfer of upper right corner	—	—
		Double grill	—	450.
		Split grill	3,250.	325.
		Quadruple split grill	3,750.	625.
		Very thin paper	3,250.	300.

Earliest known use: May 4, 1868.

Cancellations

Blue	+2.50
Magenta	+75.00
Red	+30.00
Green	+275.00
Orange	+30.00
"Paid"	+20.00
"Insufficiently Prepaid"	+135.00
"Insufficiently Paid"	+135.00
Japan	+300.00
Supplementary Mail Type A	+60.00

99	A29	24c **gray lilac**	5,250.	750.
		gray	5,250.	750.
		No gum	2,500.	
		On cover		1,200.
		Pair	11,000.	1,550.
		Block of 4	26,000.	6,000.
		P# block of 8, Impt.	55,000.	
		Double grill	6,500.	1,200.
		Split grill	5,500.	800.
		Scratch under "A" of "Postage"	—	

Earliest known use: Nov. 28, 1868.

Cancellations

Blue	+15.
Red	+100.
"Paid"	+50.

100 A30 30c **orange**		5,250.	700.
deep orange		5,250.	700.
No gum		2,500.	
On cover			1,500.
Pair		11,500.	1,450.
Block of 4		26,000.	8,750.
Double grill		7,000.	1,500.
Split grill		5,500.	750.
Double grill, one split			—

Values for No. 100 are for copies with small margins, especially at sides. Large-margined examples sell for much more.

Earliest known use: Nov. 10, 1868.

Cancellations

Blue	+10.
Red	+65.
Magenta	+75.
"Paid"	+50.
Supplementary Mail Type A	+100.
Japan	+400.

101 A31 90c **blue**		9,500.	1,400.
dark blue		9,500.	1,400.
No gum		4,750.	
On cover			95,000.
Pair		20,000.	3,000.
Block of 4		50,000.	8,500.
Double grill		13,500.	
Split grill		10,000.	1,450.

Two usages on cover are recorded (one being a cover front). Value is for use on full cover to Peru.

Earliest known use: May 8, 1869.

Cancellations

Blue	+40.
Red	+100.
Japan	+600.
"Paid"	+50.

RE-ISSUE OF 1861-66 ISSUES
Produced by the National Bank Note Co.
**Without grill, hard white paper,
with white crackly gum.**
The 1, 2, 5, 10 and 12c were printed from new
plates of 100 subjects each.

1875			***Perf. 12***
102 A24 1c **blue** *(3195)*	750.	1,000.
No gum	400.	
On cover		
Block of 4	5,750.	—
103 A32 2c **black** *(979)*	3,000.	4,500.
No gum	1,750.	
Block of 4	20,000.	
104 A25 3c **brown red** *(465)*	3,250.	5,000.
No gum	2,000.	
Block of 4	24,000.	
105 A26 5c **brown** *(672)*	2,500.	2,750.
No gum	1,500.	
Block of 4	17,500.	
106 A27 10c **green** *(451)*	2,650.	4,500.
No gum	1,600.	
Block of 4	20,000.	
107 A28 12c **black** *(389)*	3,500.	5,250.
No gum	2,100.	
Block of 4	25,000.	
108 A33 15c **black** *(397)*	3,500.	5,500.
No gum	2,100.	
Block of 4	25,000.	
109 A29 24c **deep violet** *(346)*	4,500.	7,000.
No gum	2,700.	
Block of 4	32,500.	
110 A30 30c **brownish orange** *(346)*	4,750.	8,000.
No gum	2,850.	
Pair	13,000.	
Block of 4	37,500.	
111 A31 90c **blue** *(317)*	5,750.	40,000.
No gum	3,500.	

Earliest known use: No. 102, July 25, 1881; No. 111, Nov. 30, 1888 (dated cancel on off-cover stamp).

These stamps can be distinguished from the 1861-66 issue by the brighter colors, the sharper proof-like impressions and the paper which is very white instead of yellowish. The gum is almost always somewhat yellowed with age, and unused stamps with original gum are valued with such gum.
Numbers in parentheses are quantities issued.
Five examples are recorded of No. 111 used. Value is for centered and sound example (two are known thus).

Produced by the National Bank Note Co.
Plates for the 1c, 2c, 3c, 6c, 10c and 12c consisted of 300 subjects in two panes of 150 each. For the 15c, 24c, 30c and 90c plates of 100 subjects each.

NOTE: Stamps of the 1869 issue without grill cannot be guaranteed except when unused and with the original gum or traces of the original gum. This does not apply to No. 114 on gray paper.

Franklin — A34   Post Horse and Rider — A35

G. Grill measuring 9½x9mm
(12 by 11 to 11½ points)

1869	**Hard Wove Paper**		***Perf. 12***
112 A34 1c **buff**		700.	150.
brown orange		700.	150.
dark brown orange		700.	150.
No gum		325.	
On cover, single			290.
Pair		1,450.	325.
Block of 4		5,250.	2,000.
Margin block of 4, arrow		5,500.	
P# block of 10, Impt.		—	—
Double transfer			
Double grill		1,100.	325.
Split grill		775.	190.
Double grill, one split		—	
Double grill, one quadruple split			—
b. Without grill, original gum		4,250.	

Earliest known use: Apr. 1, 1869.

Cancellations

Blue	+5.
Ultramarine	+50.
Magenta	+55.
Purple	+75.
Red	+50.
Green	+1,000.
"Paid"	+50.
Numeral	+100.
Steamship	+75.
Black town	+30.
Blue town	+30.
Red town	+75.
Black Carrier	+80.
Blue Carrier	+100.
Japan	+350.

113 A35 2c **brown**		650.	60.
pale brown		650.	60.
dark brown		650.	60.
yellow brown		650.	60.
No gum		300.	
On cover, single			110.
Pair		1,400.	160.
Block of 4		3,000.	1,050.
Margin block of 4, arrow		3,250.	
P# block of 10, Impt.		—	
Double grill			250.
Split grill		800.	85.
Quadruple split grill			390.
End roller grill		1,075.	
Double transfer			80.
b. Without grill, original gum		2,250.	
c. Half used as 1c on cover, diagonal, vertical or horizontal			3,000.
d. Printed on both sides			9,000.

Earliest known use: Mar. 20, 1869.

Cancellations

Blue	+5.
Red	+20.
Orange	+75.
Magenta	+35.
Purple	+40.
Ultramarine	+30.
Green	+450.
Brown	—
"Paid"	+15.
"Paid All"	+25.
Steamship	+60.
Black town	+10.
Blue town	+30.
Japan	+250.
Blue Carrier	+90.
Black Carrier	+80.
China	—
Printed Precancellation "Jefferson, Ohio"	—

Locomotive — A36   Washington — A37

114 A36 3c **ultramarine**		300.	20.
pale ultramarine		300.	20.
dark ultramarine		300.	20.
No gum		135.	
blue		575.	100.
No gum		275.	
violet blue			175.
On cover			30.
Pair		650.	45.
Block of 4		1,500.	450.
Margin block of 4, arrow		1,650.	
P# block of 10, Impt.		7,500.	
Double transfer		375.	35.00
Double grill		600.	110.
Triple grill		—	
Split grill		350.	40.
Quadruple split grill		650.	150.
Sextuple grill		—	3,250.
End roller grill		—	
Grill with points up		—	95.
Gray paper		—	250.
On cover			
Without grill			
Cracked plate		—	160.
a. Without grill, original gum		1,100.	
b. Vert. one-third used as 1c on cover			—
c. Vert. two-thirds used as 2c on cover			4,000.
d. Double impression			3,500.
e. Printed on both sides			

The grill-with-points-up variety is found on a unique margin "pair" of stamps where the paper was folded over prior to perforating and grilling. The stamps have drastic freak perfs.

Earliest known use: Mar. 27, 1869.

Cancellations

Blue	+5.
Ultramarine	+25.
Magenta	+35.
Purple	+75.
Violet	+65.
Red	+10.
Brown	+200.
Green	+400.
Orange	+20.
Yellow	—
Black town	+3.
Blue town	+7.
Red town	+30.
Numeral	+10.
"Paid"	+20.
"Paid All"	+15.
"Steamboat"	—
"Steamship"	+35.
Ship	+35.
"U. S. Ship"	+450.
Railroad	+30.
Packet Boat	+100.
Black Carrier	+30.
Blue Carrier	+40.
Express Company	—
"Way"	—
"Free"	+150.
Alaska	—
Japan	+600.

The authenticity of the yellow cancel has been questioned by some specialists. The editors would like to see an expertizing certificate for this stamp and cancel.

115 A37 6c **ultramarine**		2,500.	210.
pale ultramarine		2,500.	210.
No gum		1,150.	
On cover			425.
Pair		5,250.	525.
Block of 4		12,500.	9,000.
Margin block of 4, arrow		13,000.	
Double grill		—	650.
Split grill		2,750.	300.
Quadruple split grill		—	825.
Double transfer			260.
b. Vertical half used as 3c on cover			—

Earliest known use: Apr. 26, 1869.

Cancellations

Blue	+5.
Brown	+80.
Magenta	+40.
Purple	+75.
Red	+50.
Green	+750
"Paid"	+15.
"Paid All"	+25.
Black town	+30.
"Short Paid"	+75.
"Insufficiently Paid"	+75.
Steamship	+40.
Railroad	+50.
Japan	+1.500.

Shield and Eagle — A38

S.S. "Adriatic" — A39

116 A38	10c	**yellow**	1,850.	140.
		yellowish orange	1,850.	140.
		No gum	850.	
		On cover		375.
		Pair	3,900.	300.
		Block of 4	10,000.	8,000.
		Margin block of 4, arrow	10,500.	
		Double grill	—	425.
		Split grill	2,000.	150.
		End roller grill	—	

Earliest known use: Apr. 1, 1869.

Cancellations

Blue	+35.
Magenta	+30.
Purple	+100.
Red	+40.
Ultramarine	+60.
Green	+5,000.
Black town	+20.
Steamship	+35.
Railroad	+45.
"Paid"	+15.
"Paid All"	+30.
"Insufficiently Paid"	+50.
Supplementary Mail Type A	+150.
Express Company	—
St. Thomas	—
Hawaii	—
Japan	+250.
China	—

117 A39	12c	**green**	2,000.	150.
		yellowish green	2,000.	150.
		bluish green	2,000.	150.
		No gum	950.	
		On cover		425.
		Pair	4,250.	325.
		Block of 4	9,750.	1,750.
		Margin block of 4, arrow	10,000.	
		Double grill	—	425.
		Split grill	2,400.	165.
		Double grill, one quadruple split	—	
		End roller grill		600.

Earliest known use: Apr. 1, 1869.

Cancellations

Blue	+150.
Magenta	+125.
Purple	+125.
Brown	+150.
Red	+150.
Green	+4,000.
Numeral	+125.
"Paid"	+25.
"Paid All"	+40.
"Too Late"	+100.
"Insufficiently Paid"	+125.
Black town	+35.
Red town	+200.
Japan	+450.

Landing of Columbus — A40

The Declaration of Independence — A41

118 A40	15c	**brown & blue,** type I, Picture unframed	7,000.	600.
		dark brown & blue	7,000.	600.

No gum	3,500.		
On cover		1,800.	
Pair	15,000.	1,400.	
Block of 4	46,500.	18,000.	
Double grill	—	775.	
Split grill	7,500.	650.	
a. Without grill, original gum	8,250.		

Earliest known use: Mar. 31, 1869 (dated cancel on off-cover stamp); Apr. 2, 1869 (earliest known use on cover).

Cancellations

Blue	+65.
Red	+90.
Brown	+150.
"Paid"	+50.
"Paid All"	+100.
"Insufficiently Paid"	+150.
Black town	+50.
Blue town	+120.
Steamship	+100.

A40a

119 A40a	15c	**brown & blue,** type II,		
		Picture framed	3,000.	250.
		dark brown & blue	3,000.	250.
		No gum	1,400.	
		On cover		875.
		Pair	6,500.	550.
		Block of 4	14,500.	9,000.
		P# block of 8, Impt.	37,500.	
		Double transfer	—	—
		Double grill	5,250.	500.
		Split grill	3,250.	325.
b.		Center inverted	275,000.	18,500.
c.		Center double, one inverted		35,000.

Earliest known use: Apr. 5, 1869.

Cancellations

Blue	+60.
Purple	+110.
Magenta	+110.
Red	+150.
Brown	+150.
Green	+1,500.
Numeral	+75.
"Paid"	+20.
"Paid All"	+35.
Black town	+30.
Blue town	+75.
Red town	+110.
"Steamship"	+75.
Supp. Mail Type A or F	+40.
Japan	+500.

Most copies of No. 119b are faulty. Values are for fine centered copies with only minimal faults.

120 A41	24c	**green & violet**	6,500.	750.
		bluish green & violet	6,500.	750.
		No gum	3,250.	
		On cover		15,000.
		Pair	14,000.	1,600.
		Block of 4	37,500.	20,000.
		Double grill	—	1,500.
		Split grill	6,750.	875.
a.		Without grill, original gum	9,000.	
b.		Center inverted	275,000.	20,000.
		On cover		100,000.
		Pair		60,000.
		Block of 4	—	

Earliest known use: Apr. 7, 1869.

Cancellations

Blue	+150.
Red	+200.
Black town	+75.
Red town	+300.
"Paid All"	+150.
"Steamship"	+250.
Supp. Mail Type A	+200.

Most copies of No. 120b are faulty. Values are for fine centered copies with only minimal faults.

Shield, Eagle and Flags — A42

Lincoln — A43

121 A42	30c	**ultramarine & carmine**	6,500.	550.
		ultramarine & dark carmine	6,500.	550.
		No gum	3,250.	
		On cover		22,500.
		Pair	13,500.	1,150.
		Block of 4	32,500.	3,250.
		Double grill	—	1,100.
		Split grill	7,000.	600.

Double paper (without grill), original gum	7,250.		
a. Without grill, original gum	7,500.		
Block of 4	33,500.		
P# block of 8, Impt.	—		
b. Flags inverted	210,000.	65,000.	

Earliest known use: May 15, 1869.

Cancellations

Blue	+150.
Red	+250.
Brown	+400.
Purple	+1,000.
Green	+7,500.
"Paid"	+50.
"Paid All"	+250.
Black town	+100.
Steamship	+75.
"Steam"	+60.
Supp. Mail Type A	+75.
Japan	+600.
China	—

122 A43	90c	**carmine & black**	8,750.	2,200.
		carmine rose & black	8,750.	2,200.
		No gum	4,500.	
		Pair	19,000.	5,500.
		Block of 4	100,000.	47,500.
		Split grill	—	
a.		Without grill, original gum	15,000.	

Earliest known use: May 10, 1869.

Cancellations

Blue	+1,500.
Red	+400.
Ultramarine	+1,000.
"Paid"	—
"Paid All"	—
Black town	+1,500.
Red town	+1,750.
Magenta town	+2,000.

Students of the 1869 issue believe that No. 122 on cover no longer exists, though at one time one or two were known. The editors would appreciate receiving any information that might confirm the existence of No. 122 on cover.

Nos. 112, 114, 117, 118, 120b, 121, 122 exist as imperf. singles. They were not regularly issued.

CANCELLATIONS

The common type of cancellation on the 1869 issue is the block or cork similar to illustrations above. Japanese cancellations seen on this issue (not illustrated) resulted from the sale of U. S. stamps in Japanese cities where post offices were maintained for mail going from Japan to the United States.

RE-ISSUE OF 1869 ISSUE
Produced by the National Bank Note Co.
Without grill, hard white paper, with white crackly gum.

The gum is almost always somewhat yellowed with age, and unused stamps with original gum are valued with such gum.

A new plate of 150 subjects was made for the 1c and for the frame of the 15c. The frame on the 15c is the same as type I but without the fringe of brown shading lines around central vignette.

1875				**Perf. 12**
123 A34	1c	**buff** (10,000)	500.	325.
		No gum	275.	
		Block of 4	2,400.	
		On cover		3,000.
124 A35	2c	**brown** (4755)	650.	450.
		No gum	350.	
		Block of 4	3,750.	
		On cover		10,000.
125 A36	3c	**blue** (1406)	5,000.	14,000.
		No gum	2,900.	
		On cover		—

Cancellation

Supplementary Mail Type F —

Very few authenticated sound used copies of No. 125 are recorded. The used value is for an attractive example with minimal faults. Copies of No. 114 with faint or pressed-out grill are frequently offered as No. 125. Expertization by competent authorities is required.

126 A37	6c	**blue** (2226)	1,500.	1,500.
		No gum	825.	
		Block of 4	17,500.	
		On cover		—
127 A38	10c	**yellow** (1947)	2,000.	1,600.
		No gum	1,100.	

	Block of 4	14,000.	—
	On cover		—
128 A39	12c **green** (1584)	2,500.	2,500.
	No gum	1,400.	
	Block of 4	19,000.	
	On cover		—
129 A40	15c **brown & blue,** Type III, (1981)	1,900.	1,000.
	No gum	1,050.	
	Block of 4	27,000.	
	On cover		—
a.	Imperf. horizontally, single	3,500.	—
130 A41	24c **green & violet** (2091)	2,000.	1,300.
	No gum	1,100.	
	On cover		—
131 A42	30c **ultra & carmine** (1535)	2,750.	2,500.
	No gum	1,500.	
132 A43	90c **carmine & black** (1356)	5,000.	5,500.
	No gum	3,000.	
	Pair	21,000.	
	Block of 4	35,000.	
	P# block of 10, Impt.	325,000.	

Numbers in parentheses are quantities issued.

Earliest known uses:
No. 123, Dec. 9, 1877;
No. 124, Mar. 20, 1880;
No. 127, Mar. 21, 1883;
No. 128, Mar. 20, 1880;
No. 129, Mar. 20, 1880;
No. 130, Dec. 8, 1880.

RE-ISSUE OF 1869 ISSUE
Produced by the American Bank Note Co.
Without grill, soft porous paper.

1880-81

133 A34	1c **buff,** issued with gum (+23,252)	325.	200.
	No gum	150.	
	Block of 4, with gum	1,600.	
	Margin block of 10, Impt. & P#	22,000.	
	On cover		1,850.
a.	1c **brown orange,** issued without gum, 1881	240.	175.
	Block of 4, without gum	1,100.	
	Margin block of 10, Impt. & P#, without gum	22,000.	

+ This quantity includes No. 133a.

Earliest known use: Nov. 28, 1880 (No. 133).

PRODUCED BY THE NATIONAL BANK NOTE COMPANY
Plates of 200 subjects in two panes of 100 each.

Franklin
A44　　　　　　A44

Jackson
A45　　　　　　A45

Washington
A46　　　　　　A46

Lincoln
A47　　　　　　A47

Edwin M. Stanton
A48　　　　　　A48

Jefferson
A49　　　　　　A49

Henry Clay
A50　　　　　　A50

Daniel Webster
A51　　　　　　A51

Two varieties of grill are known on this issue.
H. Grill about 10x12mm (11 to 13 by 14 to 16 points.) On all values 1c to 90c.
I. Grill about 8¼x10mm (10 to 11 by 10 to 13 points.) On 1, 2, 3, 6, 7 and 15c.
On the 1870-71 stamps the grill impressions are usually faint or incomplete. This is especially true of the H grill, which often shows only a few points.
Values for 1c-7c are for stamps showing well-defined grills.
Killer cancellation of the oval grid type with letters or numeral centers was first used in 1876 Bank Note issues. By order of the Postmaster-General (July 23, 1860) it was prohibited to use the town mark as a canceling instrument, and a joined town and killer cancellation was developed.
Numeral cancellations-see "Postal Markings-Examples."

White Wove Paper, Thin to Medium Thick.

1870-71			**Perf. 12**
134 A44	1c **ultramarine,** Apr. 1870	1,900.	125.00
	pale ultramarine	1,900.	125.00
	dark ultramarine	1,900.	125.00
	No gum	850.	
	On cover		160.00
	Pair	4,000.	260.00
	Block of 4	8,000.	625.00
	Double transfer	2,100.	140.00
	Double grill	—	250.00
	Split grill	2,150.	140.00
	Quadruple split grill	—	425.00
	End roller grill		575.00

Earliest known use: Apr. 9, 1870.

Cancellations

Blue	+5.00
Red	+15.00
Green	+100.00
"Paid"	+10.00
"Paid All"	+20.00
"Steamship"	+45.00

135 A45	2c **red brown,** Apr. 1870	1,100.	65.00
	pale red brown	1,100.	65.00
	dark red brown	1,100.	65.00
	No gum	500.	
	On cover		90.00
	Pair	2,350.	140.00
	Block of 4	5,000.	350.00
	Double grill	1,450.	130.00
	Split grill	1,150.	87.50
	Quadruple split grill	2,250.	200.00
	End roller grill	1,750.	375.00
a.	Diagonal half used as 1c on cover		—
b.	Vertical half used as 1c on cover		—

Earliest known use: July 14, 1870.

Cancellations

Blue	+3.00
Red	+10.00
Brown	+8.00
Green	+100.00
"Paid"	+5.00
"Paid All"	+10.00
Numeral	+5.00
China	

136 A46	3c **green,** Mar. 1870	725.	19.00
	pale green	725.	19.00
	yellow green	725.	19.00
	deep green	725.	19.00
	No gum	325.	
	On cover		27.50
	Pair	1,500.	40.00
	Block of 4	3,100.	140.00
	P# block of 10, Impt.	7,750.	
	P# block of 12, Impt.	9,000.	
	Printed on both sides	—	
	Double transfer		22.50
	Double grill	1,000.	75.00
	Split grill	775.	22.50
	Quadruple split grill	—	140.00
	End roller grill	—	275.00
	Cracked plate		90.00

Earliest known use: Mar. 24, 1870.

Cancellations

Blue	+1.00
Purple	+2.50
Magenta	+5.00
Red	+5.00
Orange	+5.00
Brown	+2.50
Green	+45.00
"Paid"	+2.50
Railroad	+10.00
"Steamship"	+20.00
"Paid All"	+15.00
Numeral	+4.00
"Free"	+25.00

See Die and Plate Proofs for imperf. on stamp paper.

137 A47	6c **carmine,** Apr. 1870	4,000.	500.00
	pale carmine	4,000.	500.00
	carmine rose	4,000.	500.00
	No gum	1,850.	
	On cover		725.00
	Pair	8,250.	1,050.
	Block of 4	16,500.	
	Double grill		850.00
	Split grill	4,250.	525.00
	Quadruple split grill		900.00
	End roller grill	5,500.	1,050.

Cancellations

Blue	+10.00
Red	+35.00
"Paid"	+35.00

138 A48	7c **vermilion,** 1871	2,750.	400.00
	deep vermilion	2,750.	400.00
	No gum	1,250.	
	On cover		575.00
	Pair	5,750.	850.00
	Block of 4	12,000.	
	Double grill		675.00
	Split grill	3,000.	425.00
	Quadruple split grill		725.00
	End roller grill		850.00

Earliest known use: Feb. 12, 1871.

Cancellations

Blue	+10.00
Purple	+20.00
Red	+35.00
Green	+200.00
"Paid"	+25.00

The 7c stamps, Nos. 138 and 149, were issued for a 7c rate of July 1, 1870, to Prussia, German States and Austria, including Hungary, via Hamburg (on the Hamburg-American Line steamers), or Bremen (on North German Lloyd ships), but issue was delayed by the Franco-Prussian War.
The rate for this service was reduced to 6c in 1871.
For several months there was no 7c rate, but late in 1871 the Prussian closed mail rate to England was reduced to 7c which revived an important use for the 7c stamps.
The rate to Denmark direct via Baltic Lloyd ships, or via Bremen and Hamburg as above, was 7c from Jan. 1, 1872.

139 A49	10c **brown,** Apr. 1870	4,500.	650.
	yellow brown	4,500.	650.
	dark brown	4,500.	650.
	No gum	2,100.	
	On cover		950.
	Pair	9,500.	1,350.
	Block of 4	22,500.	—
	Double grill		1,200.
	Split grill	4,750.	700.
	End roller grill		1,575.

Earliest known use: June 2, 1870.

Cancellations

Blue	+15.
Red	+50.
"Steamship"	+50.
"Honolulu Paid All"	

140 A50	12c **dull violet,** Apr. 1870	21,000.	2,750.
	No gum	10,000.	
	On cover		6,000.
	Pair	47,500.	6,500.
	Strip of 3		13,000.

SPINK
AMERICA
A MEMBER OF THE CHRISTIES GROUP

Spink America, a member of the Christie's group and one of America's leading philatelic auctioneers has a constant need for better individual stamps, intact collections and large accumulations.

no. 2, used
Scott $1,400
realized $1,840

no. 245, OG, NH
Scott $5,500
realized $8,625

no. 288, OG, NH
Scott $200
realized $690

no. 334, NH
Scott $57.50
realized $437

no. C15, NH
Scott $1,200
realized $1,265

no. Q5, NH
Scott $35
realized $667

You have spent decades and considerable financial resources building your collection. Please permit us to demonstrate the significant difference our expertise, marketing and international clientele can make when the time to sell is at hand.

While we remain the logical choice of senior collectors and exhibitors with extensive and valuable collections such as Klein, Ishikawa, Weill Brothers and Grunin, we also accept general US and Worldwide collections with a minimum value of only a few thousand dollars.

Our well-written, exceptional quality and extremely attractive auction catalogues will contribute to the realizations your collection deserves and that you hope to achieve.

When selling, we invite your serious consideration. Our gallery is located at 55 E. 59th Street, Fifteenth Floor, New York City. We extend an open invitation to visit and see what is on view or meet with our specialists.

Block of 4	100,000.	
Split grill	—	3,250.
End roller grill	—	6,500.

The existence of any multiples of No. 140 other than the unused block has been questioned by specialists. The editors would like to see evidence of pairs or strips that still exist.

Earliest known use: Feb. 10, 1872.

Cancellations

Blue	+50.
Red	+100.
"Paid all"	—

141	A51	15c	**orange,** *Apr. 1870*	5,250.	1,200.
			bright orange	5,250.	1,200.
			deep orange	5,250.	1,200.
			No gum	2,500.	
			On cover		1,900.
			Pair	11,000.	2,600.
			Block of 4	26,500.	—
			Double grill	—	
			Split grill	5,500.	1,250.
			Quadruple split grill	—	

Earliest known use: June 2, 1870.

Cancellations

Blue	+20.
Purple	+50.
Red	+90.
Green	+300.

General Winfield Scott — A52   Alexander Hamilton — A53

142	A52	24c	**purple**	—	6,500.
			Pair, double grill	—	
			Split grill	—	
			End roller grill	—	

Earliest known use: July 11, 1872.

Cancellations

Red	+500.
Blue	+500.
Purple	—

Most copies of No. 142 are faulty. Value is for a sound copy in the grade of fine. The pair is the unique multiple of this stamp.

143	A53	30c	**black,** *Apr. 1870*	12,000.	2,250.
			full black	12,000.	2,250.
			No gum	6,000.	
			On cover		3,250.
			Pair	25,000.	4,750.
			Block of 4	57,500.	—
			Double grill	—	
			End roller grill	—	3,500.

Earliest known use: Aug. 23, 1870.

Cancellations

Blue	+65.
Red	+125.

Commodore Oliver Hazard Perry — A54

144	A54	90c	**carmine,** *Apr. 12, 1870*	13,500.	1,500.
			dark carmine	13,500.	1,500.
			No gum	6,500.	
			On cover		—
			Pair	28,000.	3,250.
			Block of 4	62,500.	7,500.
			Double grill	—	
			Split grill		1,550.

Cancellations

Blue	+75.
Red	+135.

PRODUCED BY THE NATIONAL BANK NOTE COMPANY.
White Wove Paper, Thin to Medium Thick.
Issued (except 3c and 7c) in April, 1870.
Without Grill.

1870-71					*Perf. 12*
145	A44	1c	**ultramarine**	450.	15.00
			pale ultramarine	450.	15.00
			dark ultramarine	450.	15.00
			gray blue	450.	15.00
			No gum	200.	
			On cover		18.00
			Pair	950.	32.50
			Block of 4	2,000.	100.00
			P# block of 12, Impt.	*3,500.*	
			Double transfer	—	20.00
			Worn plate	450.	15.00

Only one plate block of No. 145 is known in private hands. It is of average condition and is without gum. Value is based on 1998 auction sale.

Earliest known use: June 7, 1870.

Cancellations

Blue	+.1.00
Ultramarine	+2.50
Magenta	+2.00
Purple	+2.00
Brown	+2.00
Red	+5.00
Green	+55.00
"Paid"	+3.00
"Paid All"	+15.00
"Steamship"	+25.00
Railroad	+20.00
Numeral	+2.00

146	A45	2c	**red brown**	325.	9.00
			pale red brown	325.	9.00
			dark red brown	325.	9.00
			No gum	140.	
			orange brown	350.	10.00
			No gum	150.	
			On cover		11.00
			Pair	675.	19.00
			Block of 4	1,450.	55.00
			P# block of 10, Impt.	*6,250.*	
			Double transfer	—	12.00
a.		Diagonal half used as 1c on cover			—
b.		Vertical half used as 1c on cover			—
c.		Double impression			—

The No. 140 plate block is unique. Value is 1998 auction realization.

Earliest known use: May 14, 1870.

Cancellations

Blue	+.50
Purple	+.75
Red	+3.00
Green	+55.00
Brown	+1.00
"Paid"	+2.00
"Paid All"	+10.00
Numeral	+2.00
"Steamship"	+22.50
Black Carrier	+12.50
Japan	—
China	—
Curacao	—

147	A46	3c	**green**	300.	1.50
			pale green	300.	1.50
			dark green	300.	1.50
			No gum	130.	
			yellow green	325.	1.60
			No gum	140.	
			On cover		2.10
			Pair	625.	3.10
			Block of 4	1,300.	22.50
			P# block of 10, Impt.	*3,500.*	
			Double transfer	—	12.00
			Short transfer at bottom	325.	20.00
			Cracked plate	—	55.00
			Worn plate	300.	1.50
a.		Printed on both sides			*1,750.*
b.		Double impression			*1,250.*

See Die and Plate Proofs for imperf. on stamp paper.

Earliest known use: Mar. 1, 1870.

Cancellations

Blue	+.10
Purple	+.35
Magenta	+.35
Brown	+1.50
Red	+2.50
Ultramarine	+2.00
Green	+35.00
"Paid"	+2.00
"Paid All"	+10.00
"Free"	+15.00
Numeral	+2.00
Railroad	+10.00
Express Company	—
"Steamboat"	+20.00
"Steamship"	+17.50
Ship	+15.00
Japan	+75.00

148	A47	6c	**carmine**	625.	25.00
			dark carmine	625.	25.00
			rose	625.	25.00
			brown carmine	625.	25.00
			No gum	280.	
			violet carmine	650.	30.00
			No gum	290.	

On cover		42.50
Pair	1,300.	52.50
Block of 4	2,750.	250.00
Double transfer	—	—
Double paper	—	—

a. Vertical half used as 3c on cover 1,500.
b. Double impression

Earliest known use: Mar. 28, 1870.

Cancellations

Blue	+.1.00
Purple	+1.50
Violet	+1.50
Ultramarine	+3.00
Brown	+1.50
Red	+5.00
Green	+90.00
"Paid"	+3.00
"Steamship"	+25.00
"Paid All"	+15.00
Numeral	—
Supp. Mail Type A or D	+25.00
China	—
Japan	+150.00

149	A48	7c **vermilion,** *Mar. 1871*	800. 90.00
		deep vermilion	800. 90.00
		No gum	375.
		On cover	160.00
		Pair	1,650. 200.00
		Block of 4	3,500. 725.00
		Cracked plate	—

Earliest known use: May 11, 1871.

Cancellations

Blue	+2.50
Purple	+7.50
Ultramarine	+12.50
Red	+10.00
Green	+450.00
Japan	+150.00

150	A49	10c **brown**	700. 20.00
		dark brown	700. 20.00
		yellow brown	700. 20.00
		No gum	325.
		On cover	37.50
		Pair	1,450. 42.50
		Block of 4	3,100. 225.00
		P# block of 10, Impt.	—
		Double transfer	— 75.00

Earliest known use: May 2-, 1870.

Cancellations

Blue	+.50
Purple	+2.00
Magenta	+2.00
Ultramarine	+4.00
Red	+4.00
Green	+120.00
Orange	+4.00
Brown	+3.00
"Paid All"	+20.00
"Steamship"	+20.00
Supp. Mail Type A or D	+25.00
Japan	+120.00
China	—
St. Thomas	—

151	A50	12c **dull violet**	1,650. 150.00
		violet	1,650. 150.00
		dark violet	1,650. 150.00
		No gum	750.
		On cover	425.00
		Pair	3,500. 325.00
		Block of 4	8,000. 1,250.

Earliest known use: July 9, 1870.

Cancellations

Blue	+5.00
Magenta	+10.00
Red	+15.00
Green	+150.00
"Paid All"	+25.00
"Steamship"	+50.00
Supp. Mail Type A or D	+40.00
Japan	—

152	A51	15c **bright orange**	1,800. 150.00
		deep orange	1,800. 150.00
		No gum	825.
		On cover	300.00
		Pair	3,750. 325.00
		Block of 4	8,000. 1,300.

a. Double impression 1,650.

Earliest known use: July 13, 1870.

Cancellations

Blue	+2.50
Magenta	+7.50
Ultramarine	+10.00
Red	+15.00
"Paid"	+12.50
"Steamship"	+40.00
Supp. Mail Type A or F	+30.00
China	—

153	A52	24c **purple**	1,500. 140.00
		bright purple	1,500. 140.00
		No gum	675.
		On cover	1,500.
		Pair	3,250. 300.00
		Block of 4	9,500. 3,400.
		Double paper	—

Earliest known use: Nov. 18, 1870.

Cancellations

Red	+15.00
Blue	+5.00
Purple	+7.50
China	—

"Paid"	+25.00
Town	+15.00
"Steamship"	—
Supp. Mail Type A, D or F	+30.00

154	A53	30c **black**	4,500. 175.00
		full black	4,500. 175.00
		No gum	2,100.
		On cover	750.00
		Pair	9,500. 375.00
		Block of 4	24,000.

Earliest known use: July 13, 1870.

Cancellations

Blue	+2.50
Brown	+50.00
Magenta	+15.00
Red	+50.00
"Steamship"	+55.00
Supplementary Mail Type A	+40.00

155	A54	90c **carmine**	4,000. 300.00
		dark carmine	4,000. 300.00
		No gum	1,850.
		On cover	—
		Pair	8,250. 625.00
		Block of 4	19,000. 1,800.
		P# strip of 5, Impt.	25,000.

Earliest known use: Sept. 1, 1872.

Cancellations

Blue	+10.00
Purple	+15.00
Magenta	+15.00
Green	+275.00
Red	+50.00
Town	+20.00
Supp. Mail Type A or F	+40.00
Japan	—

PLEASE NOTE:

Stamps are valued in the grade of very fine unless otherwise indicated.

Values for early and valuable stamps are for examples with certificates of authenticity from acknowledged expert committees, or examples sold with the buyer having the right of certification. This applies to examples with original gum as well as examples without gum. Beware of stamps offered "as is," as the gum on some unused stamps offered with "original gum" may be fraudulent, and stamps offered as unused without gum may in some cases be altered or faintly canceled used stamps.

VALUES FOR NEVER-HINGED STAMPS PRIOR TO SCOTT No. 219

This catalogue does not value pre-1890 stamps in never-hinged condition. Premiums for never-hinged condition in the classic era invariably are even larger than those premiums listed for the post-1890 issues. Generally speaking, the earlier the stamp is listed in the catalogue, the larger will be the never-hinged premium. On some early classics, the premium will be several multiples of the unused, hinged values given in the catalogue.

PRINTED BY THE CONTINENTAL BANK NOTE COMPANY

Plates of 200 subjects in two panes of 100 each.

Designs of the 1870-71 Issue with secret marks on the values from 1c to 15c, as described and illustrated:

The object of secret marks was to provide a simple and positive proof that these stamps were produced by the Continental Bank Note Company and not by their predecessors.

Franklin — A44a

1c. In the pearl at the left of the numeral "1" there is a small crescent.

Jackson A45a

2c. Under the scroll at the left of "U. S." there is a small diagonal line. This mark seldom shows clearly. The stamp, No. 157, can be distinguished by its color.

Washington A46a

3c. The under part of the upper tail of the left ribbon is heavily shaded.

Lincoln — A47a

6c. The first four vertical lines of the shading in the lower part of the left ribbon have been strengthened.

Stanton A48a

7c. Two small semi-circles are drawn around the ends of the lines that outline the ball in the lower right hand corner.

Jefferson A49a

10c. There is a small semi-circle in the scroll at the right end of the upper label.

Clay — A50a

12c. The balls of the figure "2" are crescent shaped.

Webster A51a

15c. In the lower part of the triangle in the upper left corner two lines have been made heavier forming a "V." This mark can be found on some of the Continental and American (1879) printings, but not all stamps show it.

Secret marks were added to the dies of the 24c, 30c and 90c but new plates were not made from them. The various printings of the 30c and 90c can be distinguished only by the shades and paper.

J. Grill about 7x9½mm exists on all values except 24c and 90c. Grill was composed of truncated pyramids and was so strongly impressed that some points often broke through the paper.

White Wove Paper, Thin to Thick

1873, July (?)			*Perf. 12*
156	A44a	1c **ultramarine**	225. 3.25
		pale ultramarine	225. 3.25
		gray blue	225. 3.25
		blue	225. 3.25
		No gum	95.
		dark ultramarine	240. 3.25
		No gum	100.
		On cover	4.50
		Pair	475. 6.75
		Block of 4	1,000. 35.00
		P# block of 12, Impt.	6,000.
		Double transfer	290. 7.00
		Double paper	375. —
		Ribbed paper	240. 4.50
		Paper with silk fibers	— 22.50
		Cracked plate	—
		Paper cut with "cogwheel" punch	375.
e.		With grill	2,000.
f.		Imperf., pair	— 550.00

The No. 156 plate block is unique. Value is 1998 auction sale.

No. 156f may not have been regularly issued.

Earliest known use: Aug. 22, 1873.

Cancellations

Blue	+.25
Purple	+.35
Magenta	+.35
Ultramarine	+1.00
Red	+3.50
Orange	+3.50
Brown	+20.00
Green	+60.00
"Paid All"	+7.00
"Paid"	+1.00
Railroad	+12.00
"Free"	+12.00
Black carrier	+15.00
Numeral	+2.50
Alaska	—
Japan	—
Printed "G." Precancel (Glastonbury, Conn.)	+200.00
Printed Star Precancel (Glen Allen, Va.)	+100.00

157	A45a	2c **brown**	375. 17.50
		dark brown	375. 17.50

dark reddish brown	375.	17.50
yellowish brown	375.	17.50
No gum	170.	
With secret mark	410.	19.00
No gum	190.	
On cover		22.50
Pair	775.	37.50
Block of 4	1,600.	120.00
P# block of 12, Impt.	5,500.	
P# block of 14, Impt.	5,500.	
Double paper	500.	35.00
Ribbed paper	400.	19.00
Double transfer		22.50
Cracked plate		
c. With grill	1,850.	750.00
d. Double impression	—	
e. Vertical half used as 1c on cover	—	

Earliest known use: July 12, 1873.

Cancellations

Blue	+.50
Magenta	+1.00
Purple	+1.00
Red	+5.00
Orange	+5.00
Green	+60.00
"Paid"	+2.50
"Insufficiently Paid"	
"Paid All"	+13.50
"P. D." in circle	+15.00
Town	+2.00
Numeral	+1.50
Black Carrier	+8.50
"Steamship"	+15.00
Supplementary Mail Type F	+5.00
China	—
Japan	+100.00
Printed Star Precancellation (Glen Allen, Va.)	—

158 A46a 3c **green**	130.	.40
bluish green	130.	.40
yellow green	130.	.40
dark yellow green	130.	.40
dark green	130.	.40
No gum	50.	
olive green, ribbed paper	375.	15.00
No gum	175.	
On cover		.55
Pair	275.	.85
Block of 4	600.	12.50
P# strip of 5, Impt.	775.	
P# strip of 6, Impt.	900.	
P# block of 10, Impt.	2,600.	
P# block of 12, Impt.	3,500.	
P# block of 14, Impt.	4,400.	
Double paper	190.	8.00
Paper cut with "cogwheel" punch	260.	200.
Ribbed paper	150.	2.00
Paper with silk fibers	—	5.00
Cracked plate		32.50
Major plate crack at bottom		350.00
Double transfer		5.75
Short transfer at bottom		15.00
e. With grill	500.	
End roller grill	950.	425.
h. Horizontal pair, imperf. vert.		
i. Horizontal pair, imperf. between	1,300.	
j. Double impression	1,250.	
k. Printed on both sides	—	

See Die and Plate Proofs for imperfs. on stamp paper, with and without grill.

Earliest known use: July 9, 1873.

Cancellations

Blue	+.05
Magenta	+.20
Purple	+.20
Ultramarine	+1.25
Red	+2.50
Orange	+2.50
Green	+25.00
Town	+.05
"Paid"	+2.50
"Paid All"	+20.00
"Free"	+15.00
Numeral	+1.00
China	—
Railroad	+7.00
"R. P. O."	+1.50
"P. D." in circle	—
"Steamboat"	—
"Steamship"	—
Supplementary Mail Type D	+11.00
Supplementary Mail Type F	+8.50
Express Company	—
Black Carrier	+8.00
Red Carrier	+25.00
Japan	+65.00
Alaska	—

159 A47a 6c **dull pink**	425.	17.50
brown rose	425.	17.50
No gum	190.	
On cover		45.00
Pair	900.	37.50
Block of 4	1,900.	140.00
P# block of 12, Impt.	16,000.	
Double paper	—	
Ribbed paper	—	19.00
Paper with silk fibers	—	40.00
b. With grill	1,800.	
End roller grill	2,400.	

Earliest known use: July 24, 1873.

Cancellations

Blue	+.25
Magenta	+1.50
Purple	+1.50
Ultramarine	+2.50
Red	+7.50
Green	+80.00
Numeral	+1.50
"Paid"	+7.00
"Paid All"	—
Supp. Mail Type D, E or F	+15.00
Japan	+100.00
China	—
Railroad	—
"R. P. O."	+2.00

160 A48a 7c **orange vermilion**	1,000.	80.00
vermilion	1,000.	80.00
No gum	450.	
On cover		175.00
Pair	2,100.	175.00
Block of 4	4,250.	
P# block of 12, Impt.	11,000.	
Double transfer of "7 cents" (1R22)	—	200.00
Double transfer in lower left corner	—	95.00
Double paper	—	95.00
Ribbed paper	—	95.00
Paper with silk fibers	—	130.00
a. With grill	3,000.	

The plate block of 12 is in fine condition. It is unique.

Earliest known use: Sept. 10, 1873.

Cancellations

Blue	+4.00
Red	+10.00
Purple	+10.00
Brown	+5.00
"Paid"	+15.00

161 A49a 10c **brown**	700.	18.00
dark brown	700.	18.00
yellow brown	700.	18.00
No gum	325.	
On cover		32.50
Pair	1,450.	37.50
Block of 4	3,400.	140.00
P# block of 10, Impt.	10,500.	
P# block of 12, Impt.	13,000.	
Double paper	800.	
Ribbed paper	—	28.00
Paper with silk fibers	—	31.00
Double transfer	—	37.50
c. With grill	3,500.	
d. Horizontal pair, imperf. between	2,500.	

Earliest known use: Aug. 2, 1873.

Cancellations

Blue	+1.50
Purple	+2.00
Red	+6.00
Magenta	+6.00
Orange	+6.00
Brown	+20.00
Green	+100.00
"Paid"	+4.00
"P. D." in circle	+20.00
"Steamship"	+15.00
Supplementary Mail Type E	+7.00
Supplementary Mail Type F	+2.50
Japan	+100.00
China	—
Alaska	—

162 A50a 12c **blackish violet**	1,700.	95.00
No gum	775.	
On cover		325.00
Pair	3,500.	200.00
Block of 4	7,750.	800.00
Ribbed paper	—	100.00
a. With grill	5,000.	

Earliest known use: Jan. 3, 1874.

Cancellations

Blue	+2.50
Ultramarine	+15.00
Brown	+5.00
Red	+15.00
Supplementary Mail Type D	+15.00
Japan	+200.00

163 A51a 15c **yellow orange**	1,900.	100.00
pale orange	1,900.	100.00
reddish orange	1,900.	100.00
No gum	850.	
On cover		300.00
Pair	4,000.	210.00
Block of 4	8,500.	800.00
Double paper	—	
Paper with silk fibers	2,000.	125.00
Vertical ribbed paper	1,950.	115.00
a. With grill	5,000.	

Earliest known use: July 22, 1873.

Cancellations

Blue	+5.00
Purple	+10.00
Red	+20.00
Green	—
Brown	—
Supplementary Mail Type E	—
Supplementary Mail Type F	+10.00
"Steamship"	—
Numeral	+7.50

Puerto Rico	—	
China	—	
164 A52 24c **purple**	—	

The Philatelic Foundation has certified as genuine a 24c on vertically ribbed paper, and that is the unique stamp listed as No. 164. Specialists believe that only Continental used ribbed paper. It is not known for sure whether or not Continental also printed the 24c value on regular paper; if it did, specialists currently are not able to distinguish these from No. 153.

165 A53 30c **gray black**	2,100.	100.00
greenish black	2,100.	100.00
No gum	950.	
On cover		725.00
Pair	4,500.	210.00
Block of 4	9,500.	1,000.
Double transfer		130.00
Double paper	—	
Ribbed paper	2,200.	115.00
Paper with silk fibers	—	
c. With grill	22,500.	

Earliest known use: Oct. 30, 1874.

Cancellations

Purple	+10.00
Blue	+5.00
Red	+25.00
Brown	+30.00
Magenta	+10.00
"Steamship"	—
Supplementary Mail Type E	+10.00
Supplementary Mail Type F	+5.00
Japan	+200.00

166 A54 90c **rose carmine**	2,750.	250.00
pale rose carmine	2,750.	250.00
No gum	1,250.	
On cover		7,500.
Pair	5,750.	525.00
Block of 4	12,000.	2,300.
P# strip of 5, Impt.	15,000.	

Earliest known use: June 1875.

Cancellations

Blue	+10.
Purple	+40.
Red	+40.
Supplementary Mail Type F	+30.

SPECIAL PRINTING OF 1873 ISSUE
Produced by the Continental Bank Note Co.

1875   *Perf. 12*

Hard, white wove paper, without gum

167 A44a 1c **ultramarine**	10,500.	
168 A45a 2c **dark brown**	4,750.	
169 A46a 3c **blue green**	12,500.	
On cover	—	
170 A47a 6c **dull rose**	11,500.	
171 A48a 7c **reddish vermilion**	2,850.	
172 A49a 10c **pale brown**	11,500.	
173 A50a 12c **dark violet**	4,250.	
Horizontal pair	—	
174 A51a 15c **bright orange**	11,500.	
175 A52 24c **dull purple**	2,750.	5,000.
Horizontal pair	—	
176 A53 30c **greenish black**	8,500.	
177 A54 90c **violet carmine**	10,500.	

Although perforated, these stamps were usually cut apart with scissors. As a result, the perforations are often much mutilated and the design is frequently damaged.

These can be distinguished from the 1873 issue by the shades; also by the paper, which is very white instead of yellowish.

These and the subsequent issues listed under the heading of "Special Printings" are special printings of stamps then in current use which, together with the reprints and re-issues, were made for sale to collectors. They were available for postage except for the Officials, Newspaper and Periodical, and demonetized issues.

Only No. 169 is known on cover (unique; postmarked Mar. 5, 1876).

PRINTED BY THE CONTINENTAL BANK NOTE COMPANY
REGULAR ISSUE
Yellowish Wove Paper

1875   *Perf. 12*

178 A45a 2c **vermilion**, *June 1875*	400.	10.00
No gum	175.	
On cover		12.50
Pair	850.	21.00
Block of 4	1,750.	115.00
P# block of 6, Impt.	2,500.	
P# block of 12, Impt.	—	
P# block of 14, Impt.	6,250.	
Double transfer	—	
Double paper	—	
Ribbed paper	—	
Paper with silk fibers	450.	15.00
b. Half used as 1c on cover	—	
c. With grill	750.	

See Die and Plate Proofs for imperf. on stamp paper.

Earliest known use: July 15, 1875.

Cancellations

Blue	+.25
Purple	+.50
Magenta	+.50
Red	+6.00
"Paid"	+8.00
"Steamship"	—

Supplementary Mail Type F	+5.50	
Black Carrier	+15.00	
Railroad	+12.50	

Zachary Taylor — A55

179	A55	5c **blue**, *June 1875*	525.	20.00
		dark blue	525.	20.00
		bright blue	525.	20.00
		light blue	525.	20.00
		No gum	240.	
		greenish blue	550.	25.00
		No gum	250.	
		On cover		32.50
		Pair	1,100.	42.50
		Block of 4	2,300.	200.00
		Cracked plate	—	*170.00*
		Double transfer	—	32.50
		Double paper	*600.*	
		Ribbed paper	—	—
		Paper with silk fibers	—	32.50
c.		With grill	1,600.	
		End roller grill	—	

Earliest known use: July 10, 1875.

Cancellations

Blue	+1.00
Ultramarine	+3.00
Purple	+2.00
Magenta	+2.00
Red	+10.00
Green	+70.00
Numeral	+5.00
Railroad	+17.50
"Steamship"	+12.50
Ship	+12.50
Supplementary Mail Type E	+5.00
Supplementary Mail Type F	+2.00
China	
Japan	+100.00
Peru	—

The five cent rate to foreign countries in the Universal Postal Union began on July 1, 1875. No. 179 was issued for that purpose.

SPECIAL PRINTING OF 1875 ISSUE
Produced by the Continental Bank Note Co.
Hard, White Wove Paper, without gum

1875

180	A45a	2c carmine vermilion	*29,000.*
181	A55	5c **bright blue**	*48,000.*

PRINTED BY THE AMERICAN BANK NOTE COMPANY

The Continental Bank Note Co. was consolidated with the American Bank Note Co. on February 4, 1879. The American Bank Note Company used many plates of the Continental Bank Note Company to print the ordinary postage, Departmental and Newspaper stamps. Therefore, stamps bearing the Continental Company's imprint were not always its product.

The A. B. N. Co. also used the 30c and 90c plates of the N. B. N. Co. Some of No. 190 and all of No. 217 were from A. B. N. Co. plate 405.

Early printings of No. 188 were from Continental plates 302 and 303 which contained the normal secret mark of 1873. After those plates were re-entered by the A. B. N. Co. in 1880, pairs or multiple pieces contained combinations of normal, hairline or missing marks. The pairs or other multiples usually found contain at least one hairline mark which tended to disappear as the plate wore.

A. B. N. Co. plates 377 and 378 were made in 1881 from the National transfer roll of 1870. No. 187 from these plates has no secret mark.

Identification by Paper Type:

Collectors traditionally have identified American Bank Note Co. issues by the soft, porous paper on which they were printed. However, the Continental Bank Note Co. occasionally used a soft paper from August 1878 through early 1879, before the consolidation of the companies. When the consolidation occurred on Feb. 4, 1879, American Bank Note Co. took over the presses, plates, paper, ink, and the employees of Continental. Undoubtedly they also acquired panes of finished stamps and sheets of printed stamps that had not yet been gummed and/or perforated. Since the soft paper that was in use at the time of the consolidation and after is approximately the same texture and thickness as the soft paper that American Bank Note Co. began using regularly in June or July of 1879, all undated soft paper stamps have traditionally been classified as American Bank Note Co. printings.

However, if a stamp bears a dated cancellation or is on a dated cover from Feb. 3, 1879 or earlier, collectors (especially specialist collectors) must consider the stamp to be a Continental Bank Note printing. Undated stamps off cover, and stamps and covers

dated Feb. 4 or later, traditionally have been considered to be American Bank Note Co. printings since that company held the contract to print U.S. postage stamps beginning on that date. The most dedicated and serious specialist students sometimes attempt to determine the stamp printer of the issues on soft, porous paper in an absolute manner (by scientifically testing the paper and/or comparing printing records).

Earliest known uses for American Bank Note Co. issues are given for stamps on the soft, porous paper that has been traditionally associated with that company. But, for reasons given above, sometimes that date will precede the Feb. 4, 1879 consolidation date.

SAME AS 1870-75 ISSUES
Soft Porous Paper

1879   ***Perf. 12***

182	A44a	1c **dark ultramarine**	300.	2.75
		blue	300.	2.75
		gray blue	300.	2.75
		No gum	120.	
		On cover		3.25
		Pair	625.	6.00
		Block of 4	1,300.	45.00
		P# block of 10, Impt.	*4,500.*	
		Double transfer		9.00

Earliest known use: Jan. 3, 1879.

Cancellations

Blue	+.05
Magenta	+.10
Purple	+.10
Red	+7.00
Printed Star Precancellation (Glen Allen, Va.)	+75.00
Green	+35.00
"Paid"	+4.00
Supplementary Mail Type F	+10.00
Railroad	+12.50
Printed "G." Precancellation (Glastonbury, Conn.)	+100.00

183	A45a	2c **vermilion**	130.	2.75
		orange vermilion	130.	2.75
		No gum	55.	
		On cover		3.25
		Pair	275.	6.00
		Block of 4	600.	40.00
		P# block of 10, Impt.	1,750.	
		P# block of 12, Impt.	*2,250.*	
		Double transfer	—	—
a.		Double impression	—	*500.00*

Earliest known use: Jan. 17, 1879.

Cancellations

Blue	+.25
Purple	+.40
Magenta	+.40
Red	+6.00
Green	+175.00
"Paid"	+5.00
"Paid All"	—
"Ship"	—
Numeral	+4.00
Railroad	+15.00
Supplementary Mail Type F	+8.00
China	—
Printed Star Precancellation (Glen Allen, Va.)	

184	A46a	3c **green**	100.	.40
		light green	100.	.40
		dark green	100.	.40
		No gum	37.50	
		On cover		.50
		Pair	210.	.85
		Block of 4	450.	10.00
		P# block of 10, Impt.	1,250.	
		P# block of 12, Impt.	1,500.	
		P# block of 14, Impt.	1,800.	
		Double transfer	—	—
		Short transfer	—	6.00
b.		Double impression	—	—

See Die and Plate Proofs for imperf. on stamp paper.

Earliest known use: Aug. 27, 1878.

Cancellations

Blue	+.05
Magenta	+.15
Purple	+.15
Violet	+.15
Brown	+1.00
Red	+7.50
Green	+25.00
"Paid"	+3.00
"Free"	+15.00
Numeral	+2.00
Railroad	+12.50
"Steamboat"	—
Supplementary Mail Type F	+8.00
Printed Star Precancel (Glen Allen, Va.)	—
China	+60.00

185	A55	5c **blue**	500.	12.00
		light blue	500.	12.00
		bright blue	500.	12.00
		dark blue	500.	12.00
		No gum	225.	
		On cover		22.50
		Pair	1,050.	25.00

		Block of 4	2,150.	140.00
		P# block of 12, Impt.	*11,500.*	
		Double transfer	—	

Earliest known use: Feb. 26, 1879.

Cancellations

Blue	+.25
Purple	+1.00
Magenta	+1.00
Ultramarine	+3.50
Red	+7.50
Railroad	+20.00
Numeral	+2.00
Supplementary Mail Type F	+1.50
"Steamship"	+35.00
China	+60.00
Peru	—
Panama	—

186	A47a	6c **pink**	950.	20.00
		dull pink	950.	20.00
		brown rose	950.	20.00
		No gum	425.	
		On cover		40.00
		Pair	2,000.	42.50
		Block of 4	4,250.	*400.00*

Earliest known use: July 1, 1879.

Cancellations

Blue	+.50
Purple	+1.00
Magenta	+1.00
Red	+12.00
Supplementary Mail Type F	+4.00
Railroad	+22.50
Numeral	+4.00
China	+70.00

187	A49	10c **brown**, without secret mark	2,000.	25.00
		yellow brown	2,000.	25.00
		No gum	900.	
		On cover		47.50
		Pair	4,250.	52.50
		Block of 4	*9,000.*	
		Double transfer		45.00

Earliest known use: Sept. 5, 1879.

Cancellations

Blue	+.50
Magenta	+1.50
Red	+10.00
"Paid"	+3.50
Supplementary Mail Type F	+3.00
China	+70.00

188	A49a	10c **brown**, with secret mark	1,500.	25.00
		yellow brown	1,500.	25.00
		No gum	675.	
		black brown	1,600.	37.50
		No gum	725.	
		On cover		40.00
		Pair	3,250.	52.50
		Block of 4	*7,000.*	200.00
		Pair, one stamp No. 187	*4,250.*	250.00
		Double transfer		45.00
		Cracked plate	—	

Earliest known use: Feb. 21, 1879.

Cancellations

Blue	+.50
Ultramarine	+3.00
Purple	+2.00
Magenta	+2.00
Red	+10.00
Green	+70.00
"Paid"	+7.50
Supplementary Mail Type F	+5.00
Numeral	+3.00
Printed Star Precancel (Glen Allen, Va.)	

189	A51a	15c **red orange**	340.	22.50
		orange	340.	22.50
		yellow orange	340.	22.50
		No gum	150.	
		On cover		85.00
		Pair	700.	47.50
		Block of 4	1,600.	150.00
		P# block of 12, Impt.	*6,750.*	

Earliest known use: Oct. 6, 1881.

Cancellations

Blue	+1.50
Purple	+3.00
Magenta	+3.00
Ultramarine	+5.00
Red	+12.00
"Steamship"	+22.50
Supplementary Mail Type E	
Supplementary Mail Type F	+5.00
Japan	+120.00
China	—

190	A53	30c **full black**	1,100.	55.00
		greenish black	1,100.	55.00
		No gum	500.	
		On cover		425.00
		Pair	2,300.	115.00
		Block of 4	5,000.	275.00
		P# block of 10, Impt.	*15,000.*	

Earliest known use: Aug. 8, 1881.

Cancellations

Blue	+1.50
Purple	+3.00
Magenta	+3.00
Red	+20.00
Supplementary Mail Type F	+6.00
"Steamship"	+35.00
Tahiti	—
Samoa	—

191	A54	90c **carmine**	2,250.	250.00
		rose	2,250.	250.00
		carmine rose	2,250.	250.00
		No gum	1,050.	
		On cover		5,000.
		Pair	4,750.	525.00
		Block of 4	10,000.	1,250.
		Double paper		

See Die and Plate Proofs for imperf. on stamp paper.

Earliest known use: Apr. 13, 1887.

Cancellations

Blue	+15.00
Purple	+20.00
Red	+45.00
Supplementary Mail Type F	+20.00

SPECIAL PRINTING OF 1879 ISSUE
Produced by the American Bank Note Co.

1880   *Perf. 12*

Soft porous paper, without gum

192	A44a	1c **dark ultramarine**	22,500.
193	A45a	2c **black brown**	9,000.
194	A46a	3c **blue green**	32,500.
195	A47a	6c **dull rose**	17,000.
196	A48a	7c **scarlet vermilion**	3,500.
197	A49a	10c **deep brown**	17,000.
198	A50a	12c **blackish purple**	5,000.
199	A51a	15c **orange**	17,000.
200	A52	24c **dark violet**	5,000.
201	A53	30c **greenish black**	12,500.
202	A54	90c **dull carmine**	12,500.
203	A45a	2c **scarlet vermilion**	26,000.
204	A55	5c **deep blue**	45,000.

Nos. 192 and 194 are valued in the grade of fine.

No. 197 was printed from Continental plate 302 (or 303) after plate was re-entered, therefore stamp may show normal, hairline or missing secret mark.

The Post Office Department did not keep separate records of the 1875 and 1880 Special Printings of the 1873 and 1879 issues, but the total quantity sold of both is recorded.

Unlike the 1875 hard-paper Special Printings (Nos. 167-177), the 1880 soft-paper Special Printings were never cut apart with scissors.

Number Issued of 1875 and 1880 Special Printings.

1c ultramarine & dark ultramarine *(388)*
2c dark brown & black brown *(416)*
2c carmine vermilion & scarlet vermilion *(917)*
3c blue green *(267)*
5c bright blue & deep blue *(317)*
6c dull rose *(185)*
7c reddish vermilion & scarlet vermilion *(473)*
10c pale brown & deep brown *(180)*
12c dark violet & blackish purple *(282)*
15c bright orange & orange *(169)*
24c dull purple & dark violet *(286)*
30c greenish black *(179)*
90c violet carmine & dull carmine *(170)*

REGULAR ISSUE
Printed by the American Bank Note Co.

James A. Garfield — A56

1882, Apr. 10   *Perf. 12*

205	A56	5c **yellow brown**	250.	8.00
		brown	250.	8.00
		gray brown	250.	8.00
		No gum	100.	
		On cover		16.00
		Pair	525.	17.50
		Block of 4	1,100.	100.00
		P# strip of 5, Impt.	1,500.	
		P# strip of 6, Impt.	1,750.	
		P# block of 10, Impt.	4,750.	
		P# block of 12, Impt.	5,250.	

Cancellations

Blue	+.50
Purple	+.75
Magenta	+.75
Red	+7.00
"Ship"	—
Numeral	+2.00
Supplementary Mail Type F	+2.50
Red Express Co.	—
China	+125.00
Japan	+125.00
Samoa	+150.00
Puerto Rico	—

SPECIAL PRINTING
Printed by the American Bank Note Co.

1882   *Perf. 12*

Soft porous paper, without gum

205C	A56	5c **gray brown**	28,500.
		Block of 4	—

DESIGNS OF 1873 RE-ENGRAVED

A44b

1c - The vertical lines in the upper part of the stamp have been so deepened that the background often appears to be solid. Lines of shading have been added to the upper arabesques.

1881-82

206	A44b	1c **gray blue**, *Aug. 1881*	80.00	.90
		ultramarine	80.00	.90
		dull blue	80.00	.90
		slate blue	80.00	.90
		No gum	30.00	
		On cover		1.40
		Pair	175.00	1.90
		Block of 4	360.00	15.00
		P# strip of 5, Impt.	475.00	
		P# strip of 6, Impt.	575.00	
		P# block of 10, Impt.	1,600.	
		P# block of 12, Impt.	1,800.	
		Double transfer	105.00	6.00
		Punched with 8 small holes in a circle	190.00	
		P# block of 10, Impt. (8-hole punch)	2,750.	

Earliest known use: Nov. 2, 1881.

Cancellations

Purple	+.10
Magenta	+.10
Blue	+.20
Red	+3.00
Green	+50.00
Orange	+3.00
"Paid"	+4.75
"Paid All"	+12.00
Numeral	+3.50
Supplementary Mail Type F	+5.00
Railroad	+10.00
Printed Star Precancel (Glen Allen, Va.)	+55.00
China	—

A46b

3c. The shading at the sides of the central oval appears only about one-half the previous width. A short horizontal dash has been cut about 1mm below the "TS" of "CENTS."

207	A46b	3c **blue green**, *July 16, 1881*	80.00	.55
		green	80.00	.55
		yellow green	80.00	.55
		No gum	30.00	
		On cover		.70
		Pair	170.00	1.15
		Block of 4	360.00	30.00
		P# strip of 5, Impt.	500.00	
		P# block of 10, Impt.	1,600.	
		Double transfer	—	12.00
		Cracked plate		
		Punched with 8 small holes in a circle	210.00	
		P# block of 10, Impt. (8-hole punch)	3,000.	
c.		Double impression	—	

Earliest known use: Sept. 29, 1881.

Cancellations

Purple	+.10
Magenta	+.10
Blue	+.25
Brown	+1.50
Red	+2.50
"Paid"	+3.00
"Paid All"	—
Numeral	+2.50
"Ship"	—
Railroad	+5.00
Supplementary Mail Type F	+8.00
Printed Star Precancellation (Glen Allen, Va.)	—

Lincoln — A47b

6c. On the original stamps four vertical lines can be counted from the edge of the panel to the outside of the stamp. On the re-engraved stamps there are but three lines in the same place.

208	A47b	6c **rose**	525.	80.00
		dull rose	525.	80.00
		No gum	210.	
		On cover (rose)		160.00
		Pair (rose)	1,100.	170.00
		Block of 4 (rose)	2,350.	575.00
		P# block of 10, Impt.		

		Double transfer	650.	100.00
a.		6c **deep brown red**	475.	110.00
		No gum	190.	
		pale brown red	450.	95.00
		No gum	175.	
		On cover (deep brown red)		230.00
		Pair (deep brown red)	1,000.	230.00
		Block of 4 (deep brown red)	2,100.	700.00
		P# strip of 5, Impt.	2,750.	
		P# strip of 6, Impt.	3,500.	
		P# block of 10, Impt.		
		P# block of 12, Impt.		

Earliest known use: June 1, 1882.

Cancellations

Magenta	+3.00
Purple	+3.00
Blue	+5.00
Red	+15.00
Supplementary Mail Type F	+10.00

Jefferson
A49b

10c. On the original stamps there are five vertical lines between the left side of the oval and the edge of the shield. There are only four lines on the re-engraved stamps. In the lower part of the latter, also, the horizontal lines of the background have been strengthened.

209	A49b	10c **brown**, *Apr. 1882*	160.	4.75
		yellow brown	160.	4.75
		orange brown	160.	4.75
		No gum	60.	
		purple brown	175.	5.00
		olive brown	175.	5.00
		No gum	70.	
		On cover		10.00
		Pair	340.	10.00
		Block of 4	775.	35.00
		P# strip of 5, Impt.	1,100.	
		P# strip of 6, Impt.	1,300.	
		P# block of 10, Impt.	3,250.	
		P# block of 12, Impt.	4,000.	
b.		10c **black brown**	700.	45.00
		No gum	275.	
		On cover		80.00
		Pair	—	95.00
		Block of 4	—	
c.		Double impression	—	

Specimen stamps without overprint exist in a brown shade that differs from No. 209 and in green. The unoverprinted brown specimen is cheaper than No. 209.

Earliest known use: May 11, 1882.

Cancellations

Purple	+.50
Magenta	+.50
Blue	+1.00
Red	+4.00
Green	+35.00
Numeral	+2.00
"Paid"	+2.50
Supplementary Mail Type F	+3.00
Express Company	—
Japan	+75.00
China	—
Samoa	—

Printed by the American Bank Note Company.

Washington — A57   Jackson — A58

Nos. 210-211 were issued to meet the reduced first class rate of 2 cents for each half ounce, and the double rate, which Congress approved Mar. 3, 1883, effective Oct. 1, 1883.

1883, Oct. 1   *Perf. 12*

210	A57	2c **red brown**	50.	.40
		dark red brown	50.	.40
		orange brown	50.	.40
		No gum	20.	
		On cover		.50
		Pair	105.	.80
		Block of 4	225.	11.00
		P# strip of 5, Impt.	290.	
		P# strip of 6, Impt.	360.	
		P# block of 10, Impt.	1,100.	
		P# block of 12, Impt.	1,300.	
		Double transfer	55.	2.00

See Die and Plate Proofs for imperf. on stamp paper.

Earliest known use: Oct. 1, 1883 (FDC).

Cancellations

Purple	+.10
Margenta	+.10
Blue	+.20
Violet	+.30
Brown	+.30
Red	+3.50
Green	+25.00
Numeral	+2.50
"Paid"	+3.00
Railroad	+5.00
Express Company	—
Supplementary Mail Type F	+5.00
"Ship"	—
"Steamboat"	—
China	—

211 A58 4c **blue green**			250.	14.00
deep blue green			250.	14.00
No gum			110.00	
On cover				45.00
Pair			525.	29.00
Block of 4			1,050.	90.00
P# strip of 5, Impt.			1,550.	
P# strip of 6, Impt.			1,850.	
P# block of 10, Impt.			4,000.	
P# block of 12, Impt.			4,750.	
Never hinged			6,500.	
Double transfer			—	—
Cracked plate			—	

See Die and Plate Proofs for imperf. on stamp paper.

Earliest known use: Oct. 1, 1883 (FDC).

Cancellations

Purple	+1.00
Magenta	+1.00
Green	+50.00
Blue	+1.00
Numeral	+2.00
Supplementary Mail Type F	+5.00

SPECIAL PRINTING
Printed by the American Bank Note Company.

1883-85	**Soft porous paper**	**Perf. 12**	
211B A57 2c **pale red brown**, with gum ('85)		525.	—
Never hinged		750.	
No gum		225.	
Block of 4		2,250.	
c. Horizontal pair, imperf. between		2,000.	
211D A58 4c **deep blue green**, without gum		26,000.	

Postal records indicate that 26 copies of No. 211D were sold. Records also indicate an 1883 delivery and sales of 55 copies of the 2c red brown stamp, but there is no clear evidence that these can be differentiated from no gum examples of No. 210.

No. 211B is from a special trial printing by a new steam-powered American Bank Note Company press. Approximately 1,000 of these stamps (in sheets of 200 with an imperf gutter between the panes of 100) were delivered as samples to the Third Assistant Postmaster General and subsequently made their way to the public market.

REGULAR ISSUE
Printed by the American Bank Note Company.

Franklin — A59

1887		**Perf. 12**	
212 A59 1c **ultramarine**, *June*		110.00	1.40
bright ultramarine		110.00	1.40
No gum		40.00	
On cover			2.10
Pair		230.00	2.90
Block of 4		500.00	27.50
P# strip of 5, Impt.		625.00	
P# strip of 6, Impt.		750.00	
P# block of 10, Impt.		1,550.00	
P# block of 12, Impt.		1,850.00	
Double transfer		—	

See Die and Plate Proofs for imperf. on stamp paper.

Earliest known use: July 7, 1887.

Cancellations

Purple	+.10
Magenta	+.10
Blue	+.10
Red	+5.50
Numeral	+2.00
Railroad	+10.00
Supplementary Mail Type F	+5.00
China	—

213 A57 2c **green**, *Sept. 10*		50.00	.35
bright green		50.00	.35
dark green		50.00	.35
No gum		17.50	
On cover			.50
Pair		105.00	.70
Block of 4		230.00	8.50
P# strip of 5, Impt.		300.00	
P# strip of 6, Impt.		375.00	

P# block of 10, Impt.		1,000.	
Never hinged		1,500.	
P# block of 12, Impt.		1,200.	
Double transfer		—	3.25
b. Printed on both sides		—	

See Die and Plate Proofs for imperf. on stamp paper.

Earliest known use: Sept. 20, 1887 (dated cancel on off-cover stamp); Sept. 21, 1887 (on cover).

Cancellations

Purple	+.10
Magenta	+.10
Blue	+.90
Red	+5.00
Green	+25.00
"Paid"	+5.00
Railroad	+12.00
Numeral	+2.00
"Steam"	—
"Steamboat"	—
Supplementary Mail Type F	+7.50
China	—
Japan	—

214 A46b 3c **vermilion**, *Oct. 3*		80.00	55.00
No gum		30.00	
On cover (single)			100.00
Pair		170.00	115.00
Block of 4		375.00	300.00
P# strip of 5, Impt.		475.00	
P# strip of 6, Impt.		550.00	
P# block of 10, Impt.		1,400.	
P# block of 12, Impt.		1,600.	

Earliest known use: Oct. 18, 1887.

Cancellations

Purple	+5.00
Magenta	+5.00
Green	+150.00
Blue	+10.00
Supplementary Mail Type F	+15.00
Railroad	+30.00

Printed by the American Bank Note Company.
SAME AS 1870-83 ISSUES

1888		**Perf. 12**	
215 A58 4c **carmine**, *Nov.*		225.	17.50
rose carmine		225.	17.50
pale rose		225.	17.50
No gum		90.	
On cover			42.50
Pair		475.	37.50
Block of 4		975.	115.00
P# strip of 5, Impt.		1,400.	
P# strip of 6, Impt.		1,700.	
P# block of 10, Impt.		4,500.	
P# block of 12, Impt.		5,250.	

Earliest known use: Jan. 18, 1889.

Cancellations

Blue	+1.00
Red	+5.00
Purple	+2.00
Magenta	+2.00
Supplementary Mail Type F	+5.00

216 A56 5c **indigo**, *Feb.*		240.	12.00
deep blue		240.	12.00
No gum		95.	
On cover			27.50
Pair		500.	25.00
Block of 4		1,050.	105.00
P# strip of 5, Impt.		1,500.	
P# strip of 6, Impt.		1,800.	
P# block of 10, Impt.		6,500.	
P# block of 12, Impt.		8,000.	

Earliest known use: Mar. 23, 1888.

Cancellations

Purple	+1.00
Magenta	+1.00
Blue	+1.00
Supplementary Mail Type F	+3.00
China	+85.00
Japan	+85.00
Puerto Rico	+75.00
Samoa	—

217 A53 30c **orange brown**, *Jan.*		450.	100.00
deep orange brown		450.	100.00
No gum		190.	
On cover			1,400.
Pair		950.	210.00
Block of 4		2,000.	475.00
P# strip of 5, Impt.		2,650.	
P# block of 10, Impt.		7,000.	
P# block of 12, Impt.		—	

Earliest known use: Sept. 7, 1888.

Cancellations

Blue	+5.00
Magenta	+10.00
Supplementary Mail Type F	+10.00
"Paid All"	+25.00
"Paid"	+15.00

218 A54 90c **purple**, *Feb.*		1,300.	240.00
bright purple		1,300.	240.00
No gum		550.	
On cover			10,000.
Pair		2,700.	500.00
Block of 4		6,000.	1,200.
P# strip of 5, Impt.		7,500.	
P# block of 10, Impt.		25,000.	
P# block of 12, Impt.		—	

Cancellations

Blue	+10.00
Purple	+15.00
Supplementary Mail Type F	+25.00

See Die and Plate Proofs for imperfs. on stamp paper.

IMPORTANT INFORMATION REGARDING VALUES FOR NEVER-HINGED STAMPS

Collectors should be aware that the values given for never-hinged stamps from No. 219 on are for stamps in the grade of very fine. The never-hinged premium as a percentage of value will be larger for stamps in extremely fine or superb grades, and the premium will be smaller for fine-very fine, fine or poor examples. This is particularly true of the issues of the late-19th and early-20th centuries. For example, in the grade of very fine, an unused stamp from this time period may be valued at $100 hinged and $160 never hinged. The never-hinged premium is thus 60%. But in a grade of extremely fine, this same stamp will not only sell for more hinged, but the never-hinged premium will increase, perhaps to 100%-300% or more over the higher extremely fine value. In a grade of superb, a hinged copy will sell for much more than a very fine copy, and additionally the never-hinged premium will be much larger, perhaps as large as 300%-400%. On the other hand, the same stamp in a grade of fine or fine-very fine not only will sell for less than a very fine stamp in hinged condition, but additionally the never-hinged premium will be smaller than the never-hinged premium on a very fine stamp, perhaps as small as 15%-30%.

Please note that the above statements and percentages are NOT a formula for arriving at the values of stamps in hinged or never-hinged condition in the grades of fine, fine to very fine, extremely fine or superb. The percentages given apply only to the size of the premium for never-hinged condition that might be added to the stamp value for hinged condition. The marketplace will determine what this value will be for grades other than very fine. Further, the percentages given are only generalized estimates. Some stamps or grades may have percentages for never-hinged condition that are higher or lower than the ranges given.

VALUES FOR NEVER-HINGED STAMPS PRIOR TO SCOTT No. 219

This catalogue does not value pre-1890 stamps in never-hinged condition. Premiums for never-hinged condition in the classic era invariably are even larger than those premiums listed for the post-1890 issues. Generally speaking, the earlier the stamp is listed in the catalogue, the larger will be the never-hinged premium. On some early classics, the premium will be several multiples of the unused, hinged values given in the catalogue.

NEVER-HINGED PLATE BLOCKS

Values given for never-hinged plate blocks are for blocks in which all stamps have original gum that has never been hinged and has no disturbances, and all selvage, whether gummed or ungummed, has never been hinged.

Printed by the American Bank Note Company. Plates for the 1c and 2c were of 400 subjects in 4 panes of 100 each. All other values were from plates of 200 subjects in two panes of 100 each.

Franklin — A60

Washington — A61

Jackson — A62

Lincoln — A63

Ulysses S.
Grant — A64

Garfield — A65

William T.
Sherman — A66

Daniel
Webster — A67

Henry Clay — A68

Jefferson — A69

Perry — A70

1890-93   *Perf. 12*

219	A60	1c **dull blue,** *Feb. 22, 1890*	27.50	.35
		deep blue	27.50	.35
		ultramarine	27.50	.35
		Never hinged	52.50	
		On cover		.55
		Block of 4	120.00	4.00
		P# strip of 5, Impt.	160.00	
		P# strip of 6, Impt.	190.00	
		P# strip of 7, Impt. & letter	220.00	
		P# block of 10, Impt.	750.00	
		P# block of 12, Impt.	925.00	
		P# block of 14, Impt. & letter	1,200.	
		Double transfer	—	—

Earliest known use: Mar. 4, 1890.

Cancellations
Samoa		—
China		—
219D	A61	2c **lake,** *Feb. 22, 1890*	210.00	.90
	Never hinged	400.00	
	On cover		1.75
	Block of 4	875.00	9.50
	P# strip of 5, Impt.	1,150.	
	P# block of 10, Impt.	3,500.	
	Double transfer	—	—

Earliest known use: Feb. 22, 1890 (FDC).

Cancellation
Supplementary Mail Type F		+3.00
220	A61	2c **carmine,** *1890*	22.50	.30
	dark carmine	22.50	.30
	carmine rose	22.50	.30
	rose	22.50	.30
	Never hinged	42.50	
	On cover		.40
	Block of 4	95.00	1.75
	P# strip of 5, Impt.	150.00	
	P# strip of 6, Impt.	180.00	
	P# strip of 7, Impt. & letter	210.00	
	P# block of 10, Impt.	550.00	
	P# block of 12, Impt.	675.00	
	P# block of 14, Impt. & letter	850.00	
	Double transfer		3.25
a.	Cap on left "2" (Plates 235-236, 246-247-248)	80.00	2.50
	Never hinged	150.00	
	Pair, Nos. 220, 220a	—	—
	P# block of 12, Impt.	2,250.	
c.	Cap on both "2's" (Plates 245, 246)	400.00	20.00
	Never hinged	950.00	
	Pair, Nos. 220a, 220c	—	—

Earliest known use: Apr. 29, 1890.

Cancellations
Blue		+.05
Purple		+.05
Supp. Mail Type F or G		+3.00
China		+20.00
221	A62	3c **purple,** *Feb. 22, 1890*	72.50	7.50
	bright purple	72.50	7.50
	dark purple	72.50	7.50
	Never hinged	140.00	

On cover		16.00
Block of 4	300.00	45.00
P# strip of 5, Impt.	450.00	
P# block of 10, Impt.	2,500.	
Never hinged		

Earliest known use: July 1, 1890.

Cancellation
Samoa		—
222	A63	4c **dark brown,** *June 2, 1890*	75.00	2.75
	blackish brown	75.00	2.75
	Never hinged	145.00	
	On cover		14.00
	Block of 4	325.00	21.00
	P# strip of 5, Impt.	450.00	
	P# block of 10, Impt.	2,600.	
	Double transfer	90.00	

Earliest known use: Oct. 22, 1890.

Cancellation
China		+40.00
223	A64	5c **chocolate,** *June 2, 1890*	72.50	2.75
	yellow brown	72.50	2.75
	Never hinged	140.00	
	On cover		13.00
	Block of 4	300.00	19.00
	P# strip of 5, Impt.	425.00	
	P# block of 10, Impt.	2,600.	
	Never hinged	—	
	Double transfer	90.00	3.25

Earliest known use: June 14, 1890.

Cancellations
China		+35.00
Samoa		—
Supp. Mail Types F or G		+3.00
224	A65	6c **brown red,** *Feb. 22, 1890*	75.00	20.00
	dark brown red	75.00	20.00
	Never hinged	145.00	
	On cover		35.00
	Block of 4	325.00	95.00
	P# strip of 5, Impt.	450.00	
	P# block of 10, Impt.	2,600.	
	Never hinged	4,100.	

Earliest known use: May 30, 1890.

Cancellation
Supplementary Mail Type F		+3.00
225	A66	8c **lilac,** *Mar. 21, 1893*	57.50	13.00
	grayish lilac	52.50	13.00
	magenta	52.50	13.00
	Never hinged	110.00	
	On cover		29.00
	Block of 4	230.00	75.00
	P# strip of 5, Impt.	325.00	
	P# block of 10, Impt.	1,750.	

The 8c was issued because the registry fee was reduced from 10 to 8 cents effective Jan. 1, 1893.

Earliest known use: May 21, 1893.

226	A67	10c **green,** *Feb. 22, 1890*	155.00	3.50
	bluish green	155.00	3.50
	dark green	155.00	3.50
	Never hinged	300.00	
	On cover		10.00
	Block of 4	650.00	30.00
	P# strip of 5, Impt.	950.00	
	P# block of 10, Impt.	4,000.	
	Never hinged	6,250.	
	Double transfer	—	—

Earliest known use: Apr. 25, 1890.

Cancellations
Samoa		—
Supp. Mail Type F or G		+2.50
227	A68	15c **indigo,** *Feb. 22, 1890*	200.00	20.00
	deep indigo	200.00	20.00
	Never hinged	380.00	
	On cover		65.00
	Block of 4	850.00	100.00
	P# strip of 5, Impt.	1,200.	
	P# block of 10, Impt.	7,000.	
	Never hinged	—	
	Double transfer	—	—
	Triple transfer	—	—

Earliest known use: May 27, 1890.

Cancellation
Supplementary Mail Type F		+3.00
228	A69	30c **black,** *Feb. 22, 1890*	325.00	30.00
	gray black	325.00	30.00
	full black	325.00	30.00
	Never hinged	625.00	
	On cover		600.00	150.00
	Block of 4	1,350.	150.00
	P# strip of 5, Impt.	1,950.	
	P# block of 10, Impt.	11,000.	
	Never hinged	—	
	Double transfer	—	

Earliest known use: July 24, 1890.

Cancellation
Supplementary Mail Type F		+5.00
229	A70	90c **orange,** *Feb. 22, 1890*	500.00	125.00
	yellow orange	500.00	125.00
	red orange	500.00	125.00
	Never hinged	950.00	
	On cover		—
	Block of 4	2,100.	550.00
	P# strip of 5, Impt.	3,000.	
	P# block of 10, Impt.	24,000.	
	Short transfer at bottom	—	—

Earliest known use: Feb. 7, 1892.

Cancellation
Supp. Mail Type F or G		+10.00
Nos. 219-229 (12)	1,792.	226.05

See Die and Plate Proofs for imperfs. on stamp paper.

VALUES FOR VERY FINE STAMPS
Please note: Stamps are valued in the grade of Very Fine unless otherwise indicated.

COLUMBIAN EXPOSITION ISSUE
World's Columbian Exposition, Chicago, Ill., May 1 - Oct. 30, 1893, celebrating the 400th anniv. of the discovery of America by Christopher Columbus.

See Nos. 2624-2629 for souvenir sheets containing stamps of designs A71-A86 but with "1992" at upper right.

Columbus in Sight of
Land — A71

Landing of
Columbus — A72

"Santa Maria,"
Flagship of
Columbus — A73

Fleet of
Columbus — A74

Columbus Soliciting
Aid from Queen
Isabella — A75

Columbus Welcomed
at Barcelona — A76

Columbus Restored
to Favor — A77

Columbus Presenting
Natives — A78

If You Have Stamps to Sell, We'll Pay _Top Dollar_, We'll Buy Them _All_, And We'll Buy Them _Today_!

When you sell at auction **you assume all the risk** for stamps that sell for disappointing prices (or don't sell at all), stamps that are put on extension for expertizing certificates (delaying final settlement for months or resulting in unexpected returns), stamps that are damaged in handling or returned for other reasons, and all the other disappointments that can accompany conditional sales. **If you want to know what auctioneers really think your stamps will bring you, ask them to assume the risk and buy your collection outright instead of taking a commission and leaving you with what is unsold.**

Sell <u>Now</u>. Sell It <u>All</u>. Get Paid <u>NOW</u>. <u>No</u> Extensions. <u>No</u> Returns. <u>No</u> Delays.

WE BUY OUTRIGHT: <u>No</u> broken promises, <u>no</u> missed estimates, <u>no</u> partial advances, <u>no</u> commission charges, <u>no</u> delayed payments, <u>no</u> unsolds. Just "hassle-free" payment in full <u>NOW</u>.

And If You Are Buying...

We have a complete stock of valuable United States singles and plate blocks. We also offer you an unsurpassed "Premium Quality" Want List Service—and if you send us your want list, **we'll give you a credit worth $25** towards your first purchase of $100 or more.

Bob Prager

Buying or Selling, One Number is All You Need

800-323-4279

Gary Posner, Inc.

Gary Posner

1405 Avenue Z, PMB #535, Brooklyn, NY 11235

Phone 800-323-4279 • 718-251-1952 • FAX 718-241-2801

email:garyposnerinc@aol.com, web site:www.garyposnerinc.com

"Gary Posner, Inc., Builds Collections by Building Relationships."

Columbus Announcing His Discovery — A79

Columbus at La Rábida — A80

Recall of Columbus — A81

Queen Isabella Pledging Her Jewels — A82

Columbus in Chains — A83

Columbus Describing His Third Voyage — A84

Queen Isabella and Columbus — A85

Columbus — A86

United States postage stamps can be mounted in the annually supplemented Scott National, Pony Express, Minuteman, U.S. Commemorative Singles, U.S. Commemorative and Commemorative Air Plate Blocks, U.S. Blocks of Four and U.S. Regular and Regular Air Plate Blocks albums.

Type of imprint and plate number

Exposition Station Handstamp Postmark

Printed by the American Bank Note Company.
Plates of 200 subjects in two panes of 100 each (1c, 2c).
Plates of 100 subjects in two panes of 50 each (2c-$5).
Issued (except 8c) Jan. 2, 1893.

1893   **Perf. 12**

230	A71	1c	**deep blue**	25.00	.40
			blue	25.00	.40
			pale blue	25.00	.40
			Never hinged	47.50	
			On cover		.90
			Pair on cover, Expo. station machine canc.		85.00
			Pair on cover, Expo. station duplex handstamp canc.		150.00
			Block of 4	105.00	7.00
			P# strip of 3, Impt.	90.00	
			P# strip of 4, Impt. & letter	125.00	
			P# block of 6, Impt.	350.00	
			Never hinged	575.00	
			P# block of 8, Impt. & letter	550.00	
			Never hinged	900.00	
			Double transfer	30.00	.75
			Cracked plate	95.00	

Cancellation

China	—
Philippines	—

"Broken hat" variety

231	A72	2c	**brown violet**	22.50	.20
			deep brown violet	22.50	.20
			gray violet	22.50	.20
			Never Hinged	42.50	
			On cover		.30
			On cover or card, Expo. station machine canc.		50.00
			On cover or card, Expo. station duplex handstamp cancel		100.00
			Block of 4	92.50	3.00
			P# strip of 3, Impt.	80.00	
			P# strip of 4, Impt. & letter	110.00	
			P# block of 6, Impt.	275.00	
			Never hinged	450.00	
			P# block of 8, Impt. & letter	500.00	
			Never hinged	825.00	
			Double transfer	27.50	.30
			Triple transfer	67.50	—

		Quadruple transfer	100.00	
		Broken hat on third figure to left of Columbus	70.00	.30
		Never hinged	130.00	
		Broken frame line	24.00	.25
		Recut frame lines	24.00	—
		Cracked plate	95.00	—

There are a number of different versions of the broken hat variety, some of which may be progressive.

Cancellations

China	—
Supplementary Mail Type G	+3.50

See Die and Plate Proofs for the 2c, imperf. on stamp paper.

232	A73	3c	**green**	62.50	15.00
			dull green	62.50	15.00
			dark green	62.50	15.00
			Never hinged	120.00	
			On cover		32.50
			On cover, Expo. station machine canc.		200.00
			On cover, Expo. station duplex handstamp cancel		300.00
			Block of 4	270.00	90.00
			P# strip of 3, Impt.	250.00	
			P# strip of 4, Impt. & letter	325.00	
			P# block of 6, Impt.	750.00	
			Never hinged	1,250.	
			P# block of 8, Impt. & letter	1,250.	
			Never hinged	2,100.	
			Double transfer	82.50	—

Cancellations

China	—
Supp. Mail Type F or G	+7.50

233	A74	4c	**ultramarine**	87.50	7.50
			dull ultramarine	87.50	7.50
			deep ultramarine	87.50	7.50
			Never hinged	165.00	
			On cover		22.50
			On cover, Expo. station machine canc.		250.00
			On cover, Expo. station duplex handstamp cancel		350.00
			Block of 4	385.00	45.00
			P# strip of 3, Impt.	340.00	
			P# strip of 4, Impt. & letter	450.00	—
			P# block of 6, Impt.	1,050.	
			Never hinged	1,750.	
			P# block of 8, Impt. & letter	2,200.	
			Never hinged	3,650.	
			Double transfer	125.00	—
a.		4c	**blue** (error)	19,000.	15,000.
			Never hinged	27,500.	
			Block of 4	87,500.	—
			P# strip of 4, Impt., letter	140,000.	

Cancellation

Supplementary Mail Type G	+3.00

No. 233a exists in two shades.

234	A75	5c	**chocolate**	95.00	8.00
			pale brown	95.00	8.00
			yellow brown	95.00	8.00
			dark chocolate	95.00	8.00
			Never hinged	180.00	
			On cover		22.50
			On cover, Expo. station machine canc.		250.00
			On cover, Expo. station duplex handstamp cancel		375.00
			Block of 4	400.00	50.00
			P# strip of 3, Impt.	375.00	
			P# strip of 4, Impt. & letter	525.00	
			P# block of 6, Impt.	1,400.	
			Never hinged	2,300.	
			P# block of 8, Impt. & letter	2,600.	
			Never hinged	4,250.	
			Double transfer	145.00	—

Cancellations

China	—
Philippines	—
Supplementary Mail Type F	+3.00

235	A76	6c	**purple**	90.00	22.50
			dull purple	90.00	22.50
			Never hinged	170.00	
a.		6c	**red violet**	90.00	22.50
			Never hinged	170.00	
			On cover		50.00
			On cover, Expo. station machine canc.		275.00
			On cover, Expo. station duplex handstamp cancel		400.00
			Block of 4	390.00	105.00
			P# strip of 3, Impt.	350.00	
			P# strip of 4, Impt. & letter	450.00	
			P# block of 6, Impt.	1,250.	
			Never hinged	2,050.	
			P# block of 8, Impt. & letter	2,250.	
			Never hinged	3,750.	
			Double transfer	115.00	30.00

Cancellations

China	—
Supplementary Mail Type F	+5.00

236	A77	8c	**magenta,** Mar. 1893	80.00	11.00
			light magenta	80.00	11.00
			dark magenta	80.00	11.00
			Never hinged	150.00	
			On cover		22.50
			On cover, Expo. station machine canc.		275.00
			On cover, Expo. station duplex handstamp cancel		450.00

Block of 4		340.00	55.00
P# strip of 3, Impt.		310.00	
P# strip of 4, Impt. & letter		425.00	
P# block of 6, Impt.		875.00	
Never hinged		1,450.	
P# block of 8, Impt. & letter		1,550.	
Never hinged		2,500.	
Double transfer		92.50	—

Earliest known use: Mar. 3, 1893.

Cancellations

China			—
Supplementary Mail Type F			+4.50
237 A78 10c **black brown**		135.00	8.00
dark brown		135.00	8.00
gray black		135.00	8.00
Never hinged		250.00	
On cover			32.50
On cover, Expo. station machine canc.			350.00
On cover, Expo. station duplex handstamp cancel			500.00
Block of 4		575.00	50.00
P# strip of 3, Impt.		550.00	
P# strip of 4, Impt. & letter		675.00	
P# block of 6, Impt.		3,250.	
Never hinged		5,250.	
P# block of 8, Impt. & letter		4,750.	
Never hinged		7,750.	
Double transfer		175.00	12.50
Triple transfer		—	

Cancellation

Philippines			—
Supp. Mail Types F or G			+4.00
238 A79 15c **dark green**		240.00	65.00
green		240.00	65.00
dull green		240.00	65.00
Never hinged		450.00	
On cover			220.00
On cover, Expo. station machine canc.			600.00
On cover, Expo. station duplex handstamp cancel			900.00
Block of 4		1,000.	375.00
P# strip of 3, Impt.		950.00	
P# strip of 4, Impt. & letter		1,200.	
P# block of 6, Impt.		3,750.	
Never hinged		6,000.	
P# block of 8, Impt. & letter		6,500.	
Never hinged		10,500.	
Double transfer		—	

Earliest known use: Jan. 26, 1803.

Cancellations

China			+75.00
Supp. Mail Type F or G			+10.00
239 A80 30c **orange brown**		300.00	85.00
bright orange brown		300.00	85.00
Never hinged		575.00	
On cover			400.00
On cover, Expo. station machine canc.			1,000.
On cover, Expo. station duplex handstamp cancel			1,500.
Block of 4		1,250.	500.00
P# strip of 3, Impt.		1,200.	
P# strip of 4, Impt. & letter		1,600.	
P# block of 6, Impt.		8,500.	
Never hinged		14,000.	
P# block of 8, Impt. & letter		12,000.	
Never hinged		19,500.	

Earliest known use: Jan. 18, 1893 (dated cancel on off-cover stamp); Feb. 8, 1893 (earliest known use on cover).

Cancellations

Supp. Mail Types F or G			+25.00
240 A81 50c **slate blue**		600.00	160.00
dull state blue		600.00	160.00
Never hinged		1,200.	
On cover			625.00
On cover, Expo. station machine canc.			1,500.
On cover, Expo. station duplex handstamp cancel			2,000.
Block of 4		2,600.	850.00
P# strip of 3, Impt.		2,500.	
P# strip of 4, Impt. & letter		3,750.	
P# block of 6, Impt.		13,000.	
Never hinged		21,000.	
P# block of 8, Impt. & letter		20,000.	
Never hinged		32,500.	
Double transfer		—	—
Triple transfer		—	—

Earliest known use: Feb. 8, 1893.

Cancellation

Supp. Mail Type F or G			+30.00
241 A82 $1 **salmon**		1,500.	650.00
dark salmon		1,500.	650.00
Never hinged		3,000.	
No gum		725.00	
On cover			2,000.
On cover, Expo. station machine canc.			3,000.
On cover, Expo. station duplex handstamp cancel			4,000.
Block of 4		6,500.	3,000.
P# strip of 3, Impt.		6,000.	
P# strip of 4, Impt. & letter		7,750.	
P# block of 6, Impt.		47,500.	
P# block of 8, Impt. & letter		80,000.	
Never hinged		125,000.	
Double transfer		—	—

Earliest known use: Jan. 21, 1893.

Cancellations

Supp. Mail Types F or G			+50.00
242 A83 $2 **brown red**		1,550.	600.00
deep brown red		1,550.	600.00
Never hinged		3,100.	
No gum		725.00	
On cover			2,100.
On cover, Expo. station machine canc.			3,000.
On cover, Expo. station duplex handstamp cancel			4,000.
Block of 4		6,750.	2,750.
P# strip of 3, Impt.		6,500.	
P# strip of 4, Impt. & letter		10,000.	
P# block of 6, Impt.		70,000.	
P# block of 8, Impt. & letter		90,000.	

Cancellations

Supplementary Mail Type G			+50.00

The No. 242 plate block of 8 is believed to be unique.

243 A84 $3 **yellow green**		2,400.	1,000.
pale yellow green		2,400.	1,000.
Never hinged		5,000.	
No gum		1,100.	
a. $3 **olive green**		2,400.	1,000.
Never hinged		5,000.	
No gum		1,100.	
On cover			2,600.
On cover, Expo. station machine canc.			4,000.
On cover, Expo. station duplex handstamp cancel			6,000.
Block of 4		11,000.	6,500.
P# strip of 3, Impt.		9,750.	
P# strip of 4, Impt. & letter		13,500.	
P# block of 6, Impt.		90,000.	
P# block of 8, Impt. & letter		115,000.	

The current existence of the No. 243 plate block of 8 has been questioned by specialists. The editors would like to see evidence that this block still is intact.

Earliest known use: Mar. 24, 1893.

244 A85 $4 **crimson lake**		3,250.	1,350.
Never hinged		6,750.	
No gum		1,500.	
a. $4 **rose carmine**		3,250.	1,350.
pale aniline rose		3,250.	1,350.
Never hinged		6,750.	
No gum		1,500.	
On cover			4,000.
On cover, Expo. station machine canc.			5,750.
On cover, Expo. station duplex handstamp cancel			8,000.
Block of 4		14,000.	8,500.
P# strip of 3, Impt.		12,500.	
P# strip of 4, Impt. & letter		18,500.	
P# block of 6, Impt.		250,000.	
P# block of 8, Impt. & letter		310,000.	

The No. 244 plate block of 8 is unique; it has full original gum with light hinge marks.

Earliest known use: Mar. 24, 1893.

245 A86 $5 **black**		3,750.	1,600.
grayish black		3,750.	1,600.
Never hinged		8,250.	
No gum		1,750.	
On cover			4,750.
On cover, Expo. station machine canc.			8,000.
On cover, Expo. station duplex handstamp cancel			12,000.
Block of 4		16,500.	9,500.
P# strip of 3, Impt.		16,000.	
P# strip of 4, Impt. & letter		22,500.	
Never hinged		42,500.	
P# block of 6, Impt.		190,000.	
Never hinged		250,000.	
P# block of 8, Impt. & letter		250,000.	

Earliest known use: Jan. 6, 1893.

The No. 245 plate block of 8 is unique; it has traces of original gum.

See Nos. 2624-2629 for souvenir sheets containing stamps of designs A71-A86 but with "1992" at upper right.

Nos. 230-245 exist imperforate; not issued. See Die and Plate proofs for the 2c.

Never-Hinged Stamps
See note after No. 218 regarding premiums for never-hinged stamps.

BUREAU ISSUES
In the following listings of postal issues mostly printed by the Bureau of Engraving and Printing at Washington, D.C., the editors acknowledge with thanks the use of material prepared by the Catalogue Listing Committee of the Bureau Issues Association.

The Bureau-printed stamps until 1965 were engraved except the Offset Issues of 1918-19 (Nos. 525-536). Engraving and lithography were combined for the first time for the Homemakers 5c (No. 1253). The Bureau used photogravure first in 1971 on the Missouri 8c (No. 1426).

Stamps in this section which were not printed by the Bureau begin with Nos. 909-921 and are so noted.

"On cover" listings carry through No. 701. Beyond this point a few covers of special significance are listed. Many Bureau Issue stamps are undoubtedly scarce properly used on cover. Most higher denominations exist almost exclusively on pieces of package wrapping and usually in combination with other values. Collector interest in covers is generally limited to fancy cancellations, attractive corner cards, use abroad and other special usages.

Plate number blocks are valued unused. Although many exist used, and are scarcer in that condition, they command only a fraction of the value of the unused examples because they are less sought after.

IMPRINTS AND PLATE NUMBERS
In listing the Bureau of Engraving & Printing Imprints, the editors have followed the classification of types adopted by the Bureau Issues Association. Types I, II, IV, V and VIII occur on postage issues and are illustrated below. Types III, VI and VII occur only on Special Delivery plates, so are illustrated with the listings of those stamps; other types are illustrated with the listings of the issues on which they occur.

Type I   II   IV   V   VIII

In listing Imprint blocks and strips, the editors have designated for each stamp the various types known to exist. If, however, the Catalogue listing sufficiently describes the Imprint, no type number is given. Thus a listing reading: "P# block of 6, Impt. (Imprint) & A" in the 1912-14 series would not be followed by a type number as the description is self-explanatory. Values are for the commonest types.

PLATE POSITIONS
At the suggestion of the Catalogue Listing Committee of the Bureau Issues Association, all plate positions of these issues are indicated by giving the plate number first, next the pane position, and finally the stamp position. For example: 20234 L.L. 58.

Franklin — A87

Washington — A88

Jackson — A89

Lincoln — A90

Grant — A91

Garfield — A92

Sherman — A93

Webster — A94

Clay — A95

Jefferson — A96

Perry — A97

James
Madison — A98

John Marshall — A99

REGULAR ISSUE

Plates for the issue of 1894 were of two sizes: 400 subjects for all 1c, 2c and 10c denominations; 200 subjects for all 6c, 8c, 15c, 50c, $1.00, $2.00 and $5.00, and both 400 and 200 subjects for the 3c, 4c and 5c denominations; all issued in panes of 100 each.

1894		Unwmk.		Perf. 12
246	A87	1c ultramarine, *Oct. 1894*	32.50	4.00
		bright ultramarine	32.50	4.00
		dark ultramarine	32.50	4.00
		Never hinged	60.00	
		On cover		12.00
		Block of 4	140.00	22.50
		P# strip of 3, Impt., T I	135.00	
		P# block of 6, Impt., T I	360.00	
		Double transfer	40.00	5.00

Earliest known use: Oct. 17, 1894.

Cancellation

		China		—
247	A87	1c blue	67.50	2.00
		bright blue	67.50	2.00
		dark blue	67.50	2.00
		Never hinged	125.00	
		On cover		16.00
		Block of 4	280.00	17.50
		P# strip of 3, Impt., T I or II	275.00	
		P# block of 6, Impt., T I or II	650.00	
		Double transfer	—	3.50

Earliest known use: Nov. 11, 1894.

TWO CENTS:

Triangle A (Type I)

Type I (Triangle A). The horizontal lines of the ground work run across the triangle and are of the same thickness within it as without.

Triangle B (Type II)

Type II (Triangle B). The horizontal lines cross the triangle but are thinner within it than without. Other minor design differences exist, but the change to Triangle B is a sufficient determinant.

Triangle C (Types III and IV)

Type III (Triangle C). The horizontal lines do not cross the double lines of the triangle. The lines within the triangle are thin, as in Type II. The rest of the design is the same as Type II, except that most of the designs had the dot in the "S" of "CENTS" removed. Stamps with this dot present are listed; some specialists refer to them as "Type IIIa" varieties.

Type IV (Triangle C). See No. 279B and its varieties. Type IV is from a new die with many major and minor design variations including, (1) re-cutting and lengthening of hairline, (2) shaded toga button, (3) strengthening of lines on sleeve, (4) additional dots on ear, (5) "T" of "TWO" straight at right, (6) background lines extend into white oval opposite "U" of "UNITED." Many other differences exist.

For further information concerning type IV, see also George Brett's article in the Sept. 1993 issue of the "The United States Specialist" and the 23-part article by Kenneth Diehl in the Dec. 1994 through Aug. 1997 issues of the "The United States Specialist."

248	A88	2c **pink,** type I, *Oct. 1894*	27.50	3.00
		pale pink	27.50	3.00
		Never hinged	50.00	
		On cover		11.00
		Block of 4	120.00	17.50
		P# strip of 3, Impt., T I or II	110.00	
		P# block of 6, Impt., T I or II	250.00	
		Double transfer	—	—

Earliest known use: Oct. 16, 1894.

See Die and Plate Proofs for vert. pair, imperf. horiz. on stamp paper.

249	A88	2c **carmine lake,** type I, *Oct. 1894*	145.00	2.75
		dark carmine lake	145.00	2.75
		Never hinged	270.00	
		On cover		9.00
		Block of 4	600.00	19.00
		P# strip of 3, Impt., T I or II	575.00	

		P# block of 6, Impt., T I or II	1,400.	
		Never hinged	2,000.	
		Double transfer		3.25

Earliest known use: Oct. 11, 1894.

250	A88	2c **carmine,** type I, *Oct. 1894*	30.00	1.10
		dark carmine	30.00	1.10
		Never hinged	55.00	
a.		2c rose, type I, *Oct. 1894*	30.00	2.00
		Never hinged	55.00	
b.		2c scarlet, type I, *Jan. 1895*	30.00	.40
		Never hinged	55.00	
		On cover		2.00
		Block of 4	130.00	7.50
		P# strip of 3, Impt., T I or II	120.00	
		P# block of 6, Impt., T I or II	300.00	
		Never hinged	475.00	
		Double transfer	—	3.00
c.		Vert. pair, imperf. horiz.	1,500.	
d.		Horizontal pair, imperf. between	1,500.	

Former Nos. 250a, 250b are now Nos. 250c, 250d.

Earliest known uses: Oct. 17, 1894 (No. 250), Oct. 25, 1894 (No. 250a), Jan. 17, 1895 (No. 250b).

251	A88	2c **carmine,** type II, *Feb. 1895*	250.00	5.50
		dark carmine	250.00	5.50
		Never hinged	460.00	
a.		2c scarlet, type II, *Feb. 1895*	250.00	3.50
		Never hinged	460.00	
		On cover		15.00
		Block of 4	1,050.00	50.00
		P# strip of 3, Impt., T II	1,000.00	
		P# block of 6, Impt., T II	2,500.00	
		Never hinged	4,000.00	

Earliest known uses: Feb. 16, 1895 (No. 251), Feb. 19, 1895 (No. 251a).

252	A88	2c **carmine,** type III, *Mar. 1895*	120.00	5.50
		pale carmine	120.00	5.50
		Never hinged	220.00	
a.		2c scarlet, type III, *Mar. 1895*	120.00	5.50
		Never hinged	220.00	
		On cover		15.00
		Block of 4	500.00	60.00
		P# strip of 3, Impt., T II or IV	475.00	
		P# block of 6, Impt., T II or IV	1,350.00	
		Dot in "S" of "CENTS" (carmine)	140.00	5.75
		Never hinged	240.00	
b.		Horiz. pair, imperf. vert.	1,500.	
c.		Horiz. pair, imperf. between	1,750.	

Former Nos. 252a, 252b are now 252b, 252c.

Earliest known uses: Apr. 2, 1895 (dated cancel tying No. 252 dot in "S" variety on piece); Apr. 5, 1895 (No. 252); Apr. 17, 1895 (No. 252a).

253	A89	3c **purple,** *Sept. 1894*	105.00	8.00
		dark purple	105.00	8.00
		Never hinged	200.00	
		On cover		25.00
		Block of 4	450.00	55.00
		Margin block of 4, arrow, R or L	475.00	
		P# strip of 3, Impt., T I or II	425.00	
		P# block of 6, Impt., T I or II	1,100.00	

Earliest known use: Oct. 20, 1894 (dated cancel on off-cover stamp); Nov. 15, 1894 (on cover).

See Die and Plate Proofs for imperf. on stamp paper.

254	A90	4c **dark brown,** *Sept. 1894*	135.00	3.75
		brown	135.00	3.75
		Never hinged	250.00	
		On cover		17.50
		Block of 4	575.00	27.50
		Margin block of 4, arrow, R or L	600.00	
		P# strip of 3, Impt., T I or II	525.00	
		P# block of 6, Impt., T I or II	1,500.00	
		Never hinged	2,500.00	

Earliest known use: Oct. 16, 1894 (dated cancel on off-cover stamp); Dec. 5, 1894 (on cover).

See Die and Plate Proofs for imperf. on stamp paper.

Cancellations
	Supplementary Mail Type F		+2.00
255	A91	5c **chocolate,** *Sept. 1894*	100.00	5.50
	deep chocolate	100.00	5.50
	yellow brown	100.00	5.50
	Never hinged	185.00	
	On cover		19.00
	Block of 4	425.00	35.00
	Margin block of 4, arrow, R or L	450.00	
	P# strip of 3, Impt., T I, II or IV	425.00	
	P# block of 6, Impt., T I, II or IV	975.00	
	Double transfer	125.00	6.50
	Worn plate, diagonal lines missing in oval background	100.00	4.50
c.	Vert. pair, imperf. horiz.	1,750.	
	P# block of 6, Impt., T IV	—	

See Die and Plate Proofs for imperf. on stamp paper.

Earliest known use: Oct. 23, 1894.

Cancellations
		Supplementary Mail Type G		+2.00
		China		
256	A92	6c **dull brown,** *July 1894*	150.00	21.00
		Never hinged	275.00	
		On cover		42.50
		Block of 4	625.00	120.00
		Margin block of 4, arrow, R or L	650.00	
		P# strip of 3, Impt., T I	625.00	
		P# block of 6, Impt., T I	2,250.	—
a.		Vert. pair, imperf. horiz.	900.00	
		P# block of 6, Impt., T I	13,000.	

Earliest known use: Aug. 11, 1894.

257	A93	8c **violet brown,** *Mar. 1895*	140.00	14.00
		bright violet brown	140.00	14.00
		Never hinged	260.00	
		On cover		42.50
		Block of 4	600.00	90.00
		Margin block of 4, arrow, R or L	625.00	
		P# strip of 3, Impt., T I	575.00	
		P# block of 6, Impt., T I	1,300.	

Earliest known use: May 8, 1895.

258	A94	10c **dark green,** *Sept. 1894*	250.00	10.00
		green	250.00	10.00
		dull green	250.00	10.00
		Never hinged	460.00	
		On cover		32.50
		Block of 4	1,050.00	65.00
		P# strip of 3, Impt., T I	1,000.	
		P# block of 6, Impt., T I	2,750.	
		Double transfer	290.00	11.50

See Die and Plate Proofs for imperf. on stamp paper.

Earliest known use: Nov. 19, 1894.

Cancellations
		China		—
		Supp. Mail Types F, G		+2.00
259	A95	15c **dark blue,** *Oct. 1894*	300.00	50.00
		indigo	300.00	50.00
		Never hinged	550.00	
		On cover		105.00
		Block of 4	1,250.	325.00
		Margin block of 4, arrow, R or L	1,300.	
		P# strip of 3, Impt., T I	1,375.	
		P# block of 6, Impt., T I	4,500.	

Earliest known use: Feb. 5, 1895.

Cancellation
		China		—
260	A96	50c **orange,** *Nov. 1894*	475.	110.
		deep orange	475.	110.
		Never hinged	875.	
		On cover		1,000.
		Block of 4	2,000.	675.
		Margin block of 4, arrow, R or L	2,100.	
		P# strip of 3, Impt., T I	2,100.	
		P# block of 6, Impt., T I	9,000.	

Earliest known use: Dec. 12, 1894 (dated cancel on off-cover stamp); Jan. 15, 1895 (earliest known use on cover).

Cancellations
	Supp. Mail Type F or G		—
	China		

Type I

Type II

ONE DOLLAR

Type I. The circles enclosing "$1" are broken where they meet the curved line below "One Dollar."

Type II. The circles are complete.

The fifteen left vertical rows of impressions from plate 76 are Type I, the balance being Type II.

261	A97	$1 **black,** type I, *Nov. 1894*	1,000.	325.
		grayish black	1,000.	325.
		Never hinged	1,850.	
		No gum	350.	
		On cover		2,250.
		Block of 4	4,500.	1,900.
		Margin block of 4, arrow, L	4,750.	
		P# strip of 3, Impt., T II	4,250.	
		P# block of 6, Impt., T II	17,000.	

Earliest known use: Jan. 18, 1895.

261A	A97	$1 **black,** type II, *Nov. 1894*	2,300.	650.
		Never hinged	4,250.	
		No gum	750.	
		On cover		3,850.
		Block of 4	9,500.	4,000.
		Margin block of 4, arrow, R	9,750.	
		Horizontal pair, types I and II	4,000.	1,200.
		Block of 4, two each of types I and II	9,000.	—

P# strip of 3, Impt., T II, one
stamp No. 261 ... 6,250.
P# block of 6, Impt., T II, two
stamps No. 261 ... *22,500.*

Earliest known use: Mar. 22, 1895.

262 A98 $2 **bright blue,** *Dec. 1894* ... 3,100. ... 1,000.
Never hinged ... 6,000.
No gum ... 1,150.
dark blue ... 3,200. ... 1,050.
Never hinged ... 6,200.
On cover ... *4,000.*
Block of 4 ... *14,000.* ... *5,750.*
Margin block of 4, arrow, R
or L ... *14,500.*
P# strip of 3, Impt., T II ... *13,500.*
P# block of 6, Impt., T II ... *40,000.*

Earliest known use: July 18, 1895.

263 A99 $5 **dark green,** *Dec. 1894* ... 4,500. ... 2,100.
Never hinged ... 9,000.
No gum ... 2,250.
On cover ... —
Block of 4 ... *20,000.* ... *10,500.*
Margin block of 4, arrow, R
or L ... *21,000.*
P# strip of 3, Impt., TII ... *21,000.*

Earliest known use: July 6, 1896 (dated cancel on off-cover stamp).

REGULAR ISSUE

(Actual size of letter)

repeated in rows, thus

U S P S U P S U
S P S U S P S U
P S U S P S U P
S U S P S U S P
U S P S U S P S
S P S U S P S U
P S U S P S U P
S U S P S U S P
U S P S U P S U

The letters stand for "United States Postage Stamp."
Plates for the 1895 issue were of two sizes:-
400 subjects for all 1c, 2c and 10c denominations; 200 subjects for all 3c, 4c, 5c, 6c, 8c, 15c, 50c, $1, $2 and $5; all issued in panes of 100 each.
Printings from the 400 subject plates show the watermark reading horizontally, on the 200 subject printings the watermark reads vertically (with the tops and bottoms of the letters toward the vertical sides of the stamps).

Wmk. 191 Horizontally or Vertically

1895   **Perf. 12**

264 A87 1c **blue,** *Apr. 1895* ... 6.50 ... .25
dark blue ... 6.50 ... .25
pale blue ... 6.50 ... .25
Never hinged ... 12.00
On cover ... 1.10
Block of 4 ... 27.50 ... 2.50
P# strip of 3, Impt., T I, II,
IV or V ... 26.00
P# block of 6, Impt., T I, II,
IV or V ... 210.00
Never hinged ... 325.00
Double transfer ... — ... .85

Earliest known use: May 16, 1895.

Cancellations

China ... —
Philippines ... —
Samoa ... —

265 A88 2c **carmine,** type I, *May 1895* ... 30.00 ... .80
deep carmine ... 30.00 ... .80
Never hinged ... 55.00

On cover ... 2.50
Block of 4 ... 130.00 ... 7.50
P# strip of 3, Impt., T II ... 120.00
P# block of 6, Impt., T II ... 375.00
Double transfer ... 45.00 ... 3.25

Earliest known use: May 2, 1895.

266 A88 2c **carmine,** type II, *May 1895* ... 30.00 ... 3.00
Never hinged ... 55.00
On cover ... 6.50
Block of 4 ... 175.00 ... 22.50
Horizontal pair, types II and III ... 70.00 ... 10.50
P# strip of 3, Impt., T II or IV ... 120.00
P# block of 6, Impt., T II or IV ... 410.00
Never hinged ... 625.00

Earliest known use: July 13, 1895.

267 A88 2c **carmine,** type III *May 1895* ... 5.50 ... .25
deep carmine ... 5.50 ... .25
reddish carmine ... 5.50 ... .25
Never hinged ... 10.00
On cover ... .35
Block of 4 ... 24.00 ... 1.75
P# strip of 3, Impt., T II, IV or V ... 22.50
P# block of 6, Impt., T II, IV or V ... 175.00
Never hinged ... 275.00
Dot in "S" of "CENTS" ... 7.50 ... .35
Never hinged ... 13.50
Double transfer ... 16.50 ... 1.25
  a. 2c pink, type III, *Nov. 1897* ... 6.00 ... .30
bright pink ... 6.00 ... .30
Never hinged ... 11.00
On cover ... .45
Block of 4 ... 26.00 ... 2.25
P# strip of 3, Impt., T II, IV or V ... 24.00
P# block of 6, Impt., T II, IV or V ... 200.00
Never hinged ... 310.00
Dot in "S" of "CENTS" ... 12.00 ... .50
Never hinged ... 22.00
  b. 2c vermilion, type III, *early 1899* ... 27.50
  c. 2c rose carmine, type III, *Mar. 1899* ... —

Earliest known uses:
No. 267, May 31, 1895;
No. 267 with dot in "S", July 15, 1895;
No. 267a, Dec. 20, 1897;
No. 267a with dot in "S", Mar. 18, 1898.

Cancellations

Green ... —
China ... —
Hawaii ... —
Philippines ... —
Samoa ... —

The three left vertical rows of impressions from plate 170 are Type II, the balance being Type III.

268 A89 3c **purple,** *Oct. 1895* ... 37.50 ... 1.10
dark purple ... 37.50 ... 1.10
Never hinged ... 70.00
On cover ... 7.50
Block of 4 ... 160.00 ... 10.00
Margin block of 4, arrow, R or L ... 175.00
P# strip of 3, Impt., T II or V ... 150.00
P# block of 6, Impt., T II or IV ... 650.00
Double transfer ... 45.00 ... 2.75

Earliest known use: Feb. 18, 1896.

Cancellations

Guam ... —
China ... —
Philippines ... —

269 A90 4c **dark brown,** *June, 1895* ... 40.00 ... 1.60
dark yellow brown ... 40.00 ... 1.60
Never hinged ... 75.00
On cover ... 10.00
Block of 4 ... 170.00 ... 15.00
Margin block of 4, arrow, R or L ... 180.00
P# strip of 3, Impt., T I, II, IV or V ... 160.00
P# block of 6, Impt., T I, II, IV or V ... 700.00
Never hinged ... 1,100.
Double transfer ... 45.00 ... 3.00

Earliest known use: Sept. 25, 1895.

Cancellations

Philippines ... —
China ... —
Samoa ... —

270 A91 5c **chocolate,** *June, 1895* ... 37.50 ... 1.90
deep brown ... 37.50 ... 1.90
chestnut ... 37.50 ... 1.90
Never hinged ... 70.00
On cover ... 6.50
Block of 4 ... 160.00 ... 15.00
Margin block of 4, arrow, R or L ... 170.00
P# strip of 3, Impt., T I, II, IV or V ... 150.00
P# block of 6, Impt., T I, II, IV or V ... 600.00
Double transfer ... 45.00 ... 3.25

Worn plate, diagonal lines
missing in oval back-
ground ... 40.00 ... 2.50

Earliest known use: Sept. 14, 1895.

Cancellations

China ... —
Supplementary Mail G ... +2.50

271 A92 6c **dull brown,** *Aug. 1895* ... 95.00 ... 4.25
claret brown ... 95.00 ... 4.25
Never hinged ... 175.00
On cover ... 25.00
Block of 4 ... 450.00 ... 35.00
Margin block of 4, arrow, R or L ... 475.00
P# strip of 3, Impt., T I, IV or V ... 400.00
P# block of 6, Impt., T I, IV or V ... 2,250.
Never hinged ... 3,500.
Very thin paper ... 105.00 ... 4.50
  a. Wmkd. USIR ... *2,750.* ... *1,000.*

Earliest known use: Sept. 14, 1895.

Cancellation

Philippines ... —

Nos. 271a, 272a must have an identifiable portion of the letters "I" or "R." Single stamps from the same sheets, but showing the "U" or "S" are considered to be Nos. 271 and 272.

272 A93 8c **violet brown,** *July 1895* ... 65.00 ... 1.25
dark violet brown ... 65.00 ... 1.25
Never hinged ... 120.00
On cover ... 13.50
Block of 4 ... 270.00 ... 10.00
Margin block of 4, arrow, R or L ... 280.00
P# strip of 3, Impt., T I, IV or V ... 270.00
P# block of 6, Impt., T I, IV or V ... 750.00
Never hinged ... 1,175.
Double transfer ... 80.00 ... 2.75
  a. Wmkd. USIR ... *2,250.* ... *250.00*
Wmkd. USIR, P# strip of 3 ... *9,000.*

Earliest known use: Dec. 24, 1895.

Cancellations

China ... —
Guam ... —
Philippines ... —
Puerto Rico, 1898 ... —
Samoa ... —
Supplementary Mail Type G ... +2.50

273 A94 10c **dark green,** *June 1895* ... 95.00 ... 1.50
green ... 95.00 ... 1.50
Never hinged ... 175.00
On cover ... 15.00
Block of 4 ... 425.00 ... 12.50
P# strip of 3, Impt., T I or IV ... 400.00
P# block of 6, Impt., T I or IV ... 1,600.
Double transfer ... 120.00 ... 3.50

Earliest known use: July 25, 1895.

Cancellations

China ... —
Cuba ... —
Philippines ... —
Supp. Mail Types F, G ... +2.00

274 A95 15c **dark blue,** *Sept. 1895* ... 225. ... 9.00
indigo ... 225. ... 9.00
Never hinged ... 420.
On cover ... 55.00
Block of 4 ... 950. ... 67.50
Margin block of 4, arrow, R or L ... 975.
P# strip of 3, Impt., T I or IV ... 925.
P# block of 6, Impt., T I or IV ... 3,250.

Earliest known use: Feb. 27, 1897.

Cancellations

China ... —
Philippines ... —
Supplementary Mail Type G ... +3.00

275 A96 50c **orange,** *Nov. 1895* ... 300. ... 20.
Never hinged ... 575.
On cover ... 400.
Block of 4 ... 1,300. ... 120.
Margin block of 4, arrow, R or L ... 1,350.
P# strip of 3, Impt., T I ... 1,200.
P# block of 6, Impt., T I ... 5,750.
  a. 50c red orange ... 325. ... 24.
Never hinged ... 625.
Block of 4 ... 1,400. ... 150.
Margin block of 4, arrow, R or L ... 1,450.
P# strip of 3, Impt., T I ... 1,250.
P# block of 6, Impt., T I ... 5,750.

Earliest known use: Feb. 27, 1897.

Cancellations

China ... —
Philippines ... —
Supp. Mail Types F, G ... +5.

276 A97 $1 **black,** type I, *Aug. 1895* ... 650. ... 70.
greenish black ... 650. ... 70.
Never hinged ... 1,250.
No gum ... 190.

On cover		2,250.
Block of 4	2,750.	450.
Margin block of 4, arrow, L	2,900.	
P# strip of 3, Impt., T II	2,600.	
Never hinged	4,000.	
P# block of 6, Impt., T II	12,000.	

Earliest known use: Mar. 1, 1898.

Cancellation

Philippines		—

276A A97 $1 black, type II, *Aug. 1895*

black, type II, Aug. 1895	1,300.	160.
greenish black	1,300.	160.
Never hinged	2,500.	
No gum	425.	
On cover		3,750.
Block of 4	5,500.	950.
Margin block of 4, arrow, R	5,750.	
Horizontal pair, types I and II	2,400.	375.
Block of 4, two each of types I and II	5,000.	1,300.
P# strip of 3, Impt., T II, one stamp No. 276	4,400.	
P# block of 6, Impt., T II, two stamps No. 276	24,000.	

Earliest known use: Apr. 6, 1896.

Cancellation

China	—
Philippines	—

The fifteen left vertical rows of impressions from plate 76 are Type I, the balance being Type II.

277 A98 $2 bright blue

bright blue	1,100.	325.
Never hinged	2,200.	
No gum	375.	
a. $2 dark blue	1,100.	325.
Never hinged	2,200.	
No gum	375.	
On cover		3,500.
Block of 4	4,750.	1,900.
Margin block of 4, arrow, R or L	5,000.	
P# strip of 3, Impt., T II	4,250.	
P# block of 6, Impt., T II	20,000.	

Earliest known use: July 18, 1895.

Cancellation

Supplementary Mail Type G	—

278 A99 $5 dark green, *Aug. 1895*

dark green, Aug. 1895	2,500.	450.
Never hinged	5,000.	
No gum	950.	
On cover		12,500.
Block of 4	10,500.	3,200.
Margin block of 4, arrow, R or L	11,000.	
P# strip of 3, Impt., T II	9,750.	
P# block of 6, Impt., T II	72,500.	

Earliest known use: Nov. 3, 1896.

See Die and Plate Proofs for imperf. or horiz. pair, imperf. vert. (1c) on stamp paper.

REGULAR ISSUE
Wmk. 191 Horizontally or Vertically
1897-1903   *Perf. 12*

Plates for the 1897-1903 issue were of two sizes:
400 subjects for the 1c and 2c denominations; 200 subjects for all 4c, 5c, 6c and 15c denominations; and both 400 and 200 for the 10c denomination; all issued in panes of 100 each.

Printings from the 400 subject plates show the watermark reading horizontally, on the 200 subject plate printings the watermark reads vertically.

In January, 1898, the color of the 1-cent stamp was changed to green and in March, 1898, that of the 5-cents to dark blue in order to conform to the colors assigned these values by the Universal Postal Union. These changes necessitated changing the colors of the 10c and 15c denominations in order to avoid confusion.

279 A87 1c deep green, *Jan. 1898*

deep green, Jan. 1898	9.00	.25
green	9.00	.25
yellow green	9.00	.25
dark yellow green	9.00	.25
Never hinged	16.50	
On cover		.40
Block of 4	37.50	2.25
P# strip of 3, Impt., T V	37.50	
P# block of 6, Impt., T V	175.00	
Never hinged	275.00	
Double transfer	12.00	.85

Earliest known use: Feb. 2, 1898

Cancellations

China	—
Guam	—
Puerto Rico, 1898	—
Philippines	—

279B A88 2c red, type IV *May 1899*

red, type IV May 1899	9.00	.25
light red, May 1899	9.00	.25
Never hinged	16.50	
deep red, Sept. 1901	13.50	1.00
Never hinged	25.00	
On cover		.30
Block of 4	37.50	1.25
P# strip of 3, Impt., T V	37.50	
P# block of 6, Impt., T V	200.00	
Never hinged	310.00	
Double transfer	18.00	.60
Triple transfer	—	

Triangle at upper right without shading	22.50	6.00
c. 2c rose carmine, type IV, *Mar. 1899*	240.00	65.00
bright carmine rose, *Mar. 1899*	240.00	65.00
Never hinged	450.00	
Block of 4	1,000.	—
P# strip of 3, Impt., T V	975.00	
P# block of 6, Impt., T V	2,650.	
d. 2c orange red, type IV *June 1900*	10.00	.30
pale orange red	10.00	.30
dark orange red, *Sept. 1902*	10.00	.30
deep orange red, *Jan. 1903*	10.00	.30
Never hinged	18.50	
On cover		.45
Block of 4	42.50	1.40
P# strip of 3, Impt., T V	40.00	
P# block of 6, Impt., T V	210.00	
Never hinged	325.00	
e. Booklet pane of 6, red, type IV, *Apr. 18, 1900*	425.00	425.00
light red	425.00	425.00
orange red, *1901*	425.00	425.00
Never hinged	725.00	
f. 2c carmine, type IV, *Nov. 1897*	10.00	.25
reddish carmine, *Dec. 1898*	10.00	.25
Never hinged	18.50	
On cover		.40
Block of 4	42.50	1.40
P# strip of 3, Impt., T V	40.00	
P# block of 6, Impt., T V	210.00	
Never hinged	325.00	
g. 2c pink, type IV, *Nov. 1897*	11.00	.40
Never hinged	20.00	
bright pink	15.00	.60
Never hinged	27.50	
On cover		.60
Block of 4	47.50	2.00
P# strip of 3, Impt., T V	45.00	
P# block of 6, Impt., T V	230.00	
Never hinged	360.00	
h. 2c vermilion, type IV, *Jan. 1899*	10.00	.25
pale vermilion	10.00	.25
Never hinged	18.50	
On cover		.40
Block of 4	42.50	1.40
P# strip of 3, Impt., T V	40.00	
P# block of 6, Impt., T V	210.00	
Never hinged	325.00	
i. 2c brown orange, type IV, *Jan. 1899*	100.00	5.00
Never hinged	185.00	
P# strip of 3, Impt., T V	400.00	

Earliest known uses:
No. 279B, July 6, 1899;
No. 279Bc dated cancel on off-cover stamp, May 6, 1899;
No. 279Bc on cover, May 29, 1899;
No. 279Bc in bright rose carmine, July 16, 1899;
No. 279Bd, June 8, 1900;
No. 279Be booklet single (red), May 4, 1900;
No. 279Be booklet single (orange red), May 7, 1902;
No. 279Bf, Nov. 27, 1897;
No. 279Bg, Dec. 1, 1897;
No. 279Bh, Apr. 3, 1899.

Cancellations

Puerto Rico, 1898		—
Philippines, 1898		—
Guam, 1899 or 1900		—
Supplementary Mail Type G		+4.00
Cuba, 1898		—
China		—
Samoa		—

280 A90 4c rose brown, *Oct. 1898*

rose brown, Oct. 1898	30.00	.90
Never hinged	55.00	
a. 4c lilac brown	30.00	.90
brownish claret	30.00	.90
Never hinged	55.00	
b. 4c orange brown	30.00	.90
Never hinged	55.00	
On cover		10.00
Block of 4	130.00	10.00
Margin block of 4, arrow, R or L	140.00	
P# strip of 3, Impt., T V	120.00	
P# block of 6, Impt., T V	600.00	
Never hinged	950.00	
Double transfer	35.00	1.60
Extra frame line at top (Plate 793 R 62)	50.00	4.00

Earliest known use: Nov. 13, 1898.

Cancellations

Supplementary Mail Type G		+3.00
China		—
Philippines		—

281 A91 5c dark blue, *Mar. 1898*

dark blue, Mar. 1898	35.00	.75
blue	35.00	.75
bright blue	35.00	.75
Never hinged	65.00	
On cover		9.00
Block of 4	150.00	6.50
Margin block of 4, arrow, R or L	160.00	
P# strip of 3, Impt., T V	140.00	
P# block of 6, Impt., T V	600.00	
Double transfer	45.00	2.00
Worn plate (diagonal lines missing in oval background)	40.00	.90

Earliest known use: Mar. 19, 1898.

Cancellations

Puerto Rico, 1898		—
Supplementary Mail Type G		+4.00
China		—
Cuba		—

Guam		—
Philippines		—

282 A92 6c lake, *Dec. 1898*

lake, Dec. 1898	45.00	2.50
claret	45.00	2.50
Never hinged	82.50	
On cover		16.00
Block of 4	190.00	25.00
Margin block of 4, arrow, R or L	200.00	
P# strip of 3, Impt., T V	180.00	
P# block of 6, Impt., T V	800.00	
Double transfer	57.50	3.50
a. 6c purple lake	60.00	3.50
Never hinged	110.00	
Block of 4	250.00	35.00
Margin block of 4, arrow	260.00	
P# strip of 3, Impt., T V	240.00	
P# block of 6, Impt., T V	1,000.	

Earliest known use: Mar. 13, 1899.

Cancellations

Supplementary Mail Type G		+4.00
China		—
Philippines		—

Type I. The tips of the foliate ornaments do not impinge on the white curved line below "ten cents."

282C A94 10c brown, type I, *Nov. 1898*

brown, type I, Nov. 1898	180.00	2.50
dark brown	180.00	2.50
Never hinged	340.00	
On cover		14.00
Block of 4	750.00	25.00
P# strip of 3, Impt., T IV or V	725.00	
P# block of 6, Impt., T IV or V	2,250.	
Double transfer	200.00	4.25

Earliest known use: Dec. 27, 1898.

Cancellation

Supplementary Mail Type G		+2.50

Type II. The tips of the ornaments break the curved line below the "e" of "ten" and the "t" of "cents."

283 A94 10c orange brown, type II

orange brown, type II	110.00	2.00
brown	110.00	2.00
yellow brown	110.00	2.00
Never hinged	200.00	
On cover		16.00
Block of 4	460.00	20.00
Margin block of 4, arrow, R or L	475.00	
P# strip of 3, Impt., T V	450.00	
P# block of 6, Impt., T V	1,600.	
Pair, type I and type II	15,000.	—

Earliest known use: Mar. 13, 1899.

Cancellations

Supplementary Mail Type G		+2.50
China		—
Puerto Rico		—

On the 400 subject plate 932, all are Type I except the following: UL 20; UR 11, 12, 13; LL 61, 71, 86, these 7 being Type II.

284 A95 15c olive green, *Nov. 1898*

olive green, Nov. 1898	150.00	7.50
dark olive green	150.00	7.50
Never hinged	275.00	
On cover		32.50
Block of 4	650.00	50.00
Margin block of 4, arrow, R or L	700.00	
P# strip of 3, Impt., T IV	600.00	
P# block of 6, Impt., T IV	2,000.	
Never hinged	3,250.	

Earliest known use: May 1, 1899.

Cancellations

Supp. Mail Type F or G		+2.50
China		—
Samoa		—
Nos. 279-284 (8)	568.00	16.65

VALUES FOR VERY FINE STAMPS
Please note: Stamps are valued in the grade of Very Fine unless otherwise indicated.

Three Great Reasons to Choose PSE for Your Expertising Needs

 ## Accurate

PSE's philatelic experts are among the most knowledgeable dealers and collectors in the United States and cover all aspects of philately. Each submission is examined by experts specializing in the specific area in question. In almost every area of specialty, our experts are the most renown and respected in their field.

PSE experts employ an impressive array of philatelic examining equipment, from magnifiers and millimeter gauges to state-of-the-art technology. Our portable forensic color-infrared-UV video imaging system enables us to detect even the most subtle forgeries, alterations, erasures, and masked defects.

 ## Economical

Why not enjoy the highest quality expertizing at reasonable prices? PSE's fee schedule is based on current Scott catalog value — *never on price realized at auction!* If you're an experienced auction buyer or buyer of high quality philatelic material, the potential savings could be dramatic. And they apply equally to our standard authentication service and our grading and encapsulation service.

	EXPRESS (15 Days)	STANDARD (30 Days)	SPECIALIZED*
Pre-1925			
SCV under $1,000	$40.00	$25.00	3.5% of SCV
SCV $1,000–$3,999	$60.00	$35.00	3.5% of SCV
SCV $4,000 and over	$80.00	$45.00	3.5% of SCV
1925 and later			
Under 100 items	$18.00	$12.00	3.5% of SCV
100 to 500 items	$15.00	$10.00	3.5% of SCV
Over 500 items	$12.00	$ 8.00	3.5% of SCV

The following categories must be submitted under the Specialized Service:

Private Perforations	Essays and Proofs
Carriers	Confederate
Locals	Provisionals
Possessions	Reissues
Errors	Special Printings
Covers (including FDC)	Other (not listed in Express and Standard)

 ## Fast

Many of our experts are themselves experienced dealers and collectors, so we understand very well that no one likes being separated from his or her stamps, and especially not for long periods of time. Our services are designed to have your authenticated or graded stamps back to you just as quickly as possible. Our services are called "Standard" and "Express," but they could as easily be called "Fast" and "Faster!"

To order a FREE PSE submission kit, call **PSE** at **877-STAMP88** (782-6788) or visit our Web site at **www.collectors.com/pse**.

Do it today and begin enjoying the benefits!

PSE
PROFESSIONAL STAMP EXPERTS

A Collectors Universe Company
Nasdaq: CLCT

P.O. Box 6170, Newport Beach, CA 92658 • 877-STAMP88 (782-6788) • Fax: 949-833-7955 • Email: infopse@collectors.com • www.collectors.com/pse

TRANS-MISSISSIPPI EXPOSITION ISSUE
Omaha, Nebr., June 1 - Nov. 1, 1898.

Jacques Marquette on the Mississippi — A100

Farming in the West — A101

Indian Hunting Buffalo — A102

John Charles Frémont on the Rocky Mountains — A103

Troops Guarding Wagon Train — A104

Hardships of Emigration — A105

Western Mining Prospector — A106

Western Cattle in Storm — A107

Mississippi River Bridge, St. Louis — A108

Exposition Station Handstamp Postmark

Plates of 100 (10x10) subjects, divided vertically into 2 panes of 50.

See Nos. 3209-3210 for bi-colored reproductions of Nos. 285-293.

1898, June 17   Wmk. 191   *Perf. 12*

285	A100	1c	**dark yellow green**	30.00	6.00
			yellow green	30.00	6.00
			green	30.00	6.00
			Never hinged	55.00	
			On cover		9.00
			On card, Expo. station canc.		200.00
			Pair, on cover, Expo. station canc.		300.00
			Block of 4	120.00	32.50
			Margin block of 4, arrow, R or L	125.00	—
			P# pair, Impt., T VIII	67.50	
			P# strip of 3, Impt., T VIII	110.00	
			P# block of 4, Impt., T VIII	225.00	
			Never hinged	375.00	
			P# block of 6, Impt., T VIII	300.00	
			Never hinged	500.00	
			Double transfer	40.00	7.25

Cancellations

Supp. Mail Type F or G		+1.50
China		—
Philippines		—
Puerto Rico, 1898		—

286	A101	2c	**copper red**	27.50	1.50
			brown red	27.50	1.50
			light brown red	27.50	1.50
			Never hinged	50.00	
			On cover		2.50
			On cover, Expo. station canc.		175.00
			Block of 4	120.00	11.00
			Margin block of 4, arrow, R or L	125.00	—
			P# pair, Impt., T VIII	65.00	
			P# strip of 3, Impt., T VIII	110.00	
			P# block of 4, Impt., T VIII	190.00	
			Never hinged	325.00	
			P# block of 6, Impt., T VIII	275.00	
			Never hinged	450.00	
			Double transfer	42.50	2.25
			Worn plate	30.00	1.75

Earliest known use: June 16, 1898.

Cancellations

China		—
Hawaii		—
Puerto Rico, 1898		—
Philippines		—

287	A102	4c	**orange**	150.	22.50
			deep orange	150.	22.50
			Never hinged	275.	
			On cover		57.50
			On cover, Expo. station canc.		750.
			Block of 4	650.	135.
			Margin block of 4, arrow, R or L	675.	—
			P# pair, Impt., T VIII	350.	
			P# strip of 3, Impt., T VIII	600.	
			P# block of 4, Impt., T VIII	900.	
			Never hinged	1,500.	
			P# block of 6, Impt., T VIII	1,400.	
			Never hinged	2,300.	

Cancellations

Supp. Mail Type F or G		+5.
China		—
Philippines		—

288	A103	5c	**dull blue**	140.	20.
			bright blue	140.	20.
			Never hinged	260.	
			On cover		50.
			On cover, Expo. station canc.		500.
			Block of 4	600.	125.
			Margin block of 4, arrow, R or L	625.	—
			P# pair, Impt., T VIII	325.	
			P# strip of 3, Impt., T VIII	475.	
			P# block of 4, Impt., T VIII	825.	
			Never hinged	1,400.	
			P# block of 6, Impt., T VIII	1,300.	
			Never hinged	2,150.	

Cancellations

Supp. Mail Type F or G		+5.
China		—
Philippines		—
Puerto Rico, 1898		—

289	A104	8c	**violet brown**	180.	40.00
			dark violet brown	180.	40.00
			Never hinged	340.	
			On cover		115.
			On cover, Expo. station canc.		1,000.
			Block of 4	775.	240.
			Margin block of 4, arrow, R or L	800.	—
			P# pair, Impt., T VIII	390.	
			P# strip of 3, Impt., T VIII	725.	
			P# block of 4, Impt., T VIII	1,800.	
			Never hinged	3,000.	
			P# block of 6, Impt., T VIII	2,750.	
			Never hinged	4,500.	
a.			Vert. pair, imperf. horiz.	19,000.	
			P# block of 4, Impt., T VIII	75,000.	

Cancellations

Philippines		—
Samoa		—

290	A105	10c	**gray violet**	180.	25.00
			blackish violet	180.	25.00
			Never hinged	340.	
			On cover		85.

On cover, Expo. station canc.			750.
Block of 4		775.	140.
Margin block of 4, arrow, R or L		800.	
P# pair, Impt., T VIII		425.	
P# strip of 3, Impt., T VIII		650.	
P# block of 4, Impt., T VIII		1,900.	
Never hinged		3,100.	
P# block of 6, Impt., T VIII		3,000.	
Never hinged		5,000.	

Cancellations

Supplementary Mail Type G		+5.
China		—
Philippines		—

291	A106	50c	**sage green**	650.	180.
			dark sage green	650.	180.
			Never hinged	1,250.	
			On cover		1,750.
			Block of 4	3,100.	1,050.
			Margin block of 4, arrow, R or L	3,250.	
			P# pair, Impt., T VIII	1,800.	
			P# strip of 3, Impt., T VIII	2,600.	
			P# block of 4, Impt., T VIII	14,000.	
			Never hinged	21,000.	
			P# block of 6, Impt., T VIII	25,000.	

Cancellations

Supp. Mail Type F or G		+25.
Cuba		—
Philippines		—

292	A107	$1	**black**	1,250.	525.
			Never hinged	2,500.	
			No gum	600.	
			On cover		4,000.
			Block of 4	5,750.	3,750.
			Margin block of 4, arrow, R or L	6,000.	
			P# pair, Impt., T VIII	3,000.	
			P# strip of 3, Impt., T VIII	5,500.	
			P# block of 4, Impt., T VIII	35,000.	
			Never hinged	47,500.	
			P# block of 6, Impt., T VIII	50,000.	
			Never hinged	65,000.	

Cancellation

Philippines		—

293	A108	$2	**orange brown**	2,100.	950.
			dark orange brown	2,100.	950.
			Never hinged	4,250.	
			No gum	1,050.	
			On cover		12,500.
			Block of 4	9,000.	5,250.
			Margin block of 4, arrow, R or L	9,500.	
			P# pair, Impt., T VIII	5,000.	
			P# strip of 3, Impt., T VIII	8,500.	
			P# block of 4, Impt., T VIII	80,000.	
			Never hinged	—	
			P# block of 6, Impt., T VIII	150,000.	

Earliest known use: June 24, 1898.

Nos. 285-293 (9)	4,707.	1,770.

Never-Hinged Stamps
See note after No. 218 regarding premiums for never-hinged stamps.

PAN-AMERICAN EXPOSITION ISSUE
Buffalo, N.Y., May 1 - Nov. 1, 1901.
On sale May 1-Oct. 31, 1901.

Fast Lake Navigation (Steamship "City of Alpena") — A109

Empire State Express — A110

Electric Automobile in Washington — A111

Bridge at Niagara Falls — A112

Canal Locks at Sault Ste. Marie — A113

Fast Ocean Navigation (Steamship "St. Paul") — A114

PAN-AMERICAN STATION

Exposition Station Machine Cancellation

Plates of 200 subjects in two panes of 100 each.

1901, May 1   **Wmk. 191**   *Perf. 12*

294	A109	1c	**green & black**	18.00	3.00
			dark blue green & black	18.00	3.00
			Never hinged	32.50	
			On cover		4.50
			On Expo. cover or card, Expo. station machine canc.		50.00
			On Expo. cover or card, Expo. station duplex handstamp canc.		150.00
			Block of 4	75.00	22.50
			Margin block of 4, top arrow & markers	77.50	
			Margin block of 4, bottom arrow & markers & black P#	80.00	
			P# strip of 3, Impt., T V	77.50	
			P# block of 6, Impt., T V	230.00	
			Never hinged	360.00	
			Margin strip of 5, bottom Impt., T V, two P#, arrow & markers	125.00	
			Margin block of 10, bottom Impt., T V, two P#, arrow & markers	425.00	
			Never hinged	675.00	
			Double transfer	25.00	5.25
a.			Center inverted	10,000.	7,000.
			Never hinged	15,000.	
			On cover		—
			Block of 4	42,500.	
			P# strip of 4, Impt.	75,000.	

Earliest known use: No. 294a, Aug. 2, 1901. This cover sold at auction in 1999 for $121,000. Two other uses on cover are recorded.

295	A110	2c	**carmine & black**	17.50	1.00
			carmine & gray black	17.50	1.00
			dark carmine & black	17.50	1.00
			rose carmine & black	17.50	1.00
			scarlet & black	17.50	1.00
			Never hinged	31.00	
			On cover		1.50
			On Expo. cover or card, Expo. sta. machine cancel		60.00
			On Expo. cover or card, Expo. sta. duplex handstamp canc.		200.00
			Block of 4	72.50	7.50
			Margin block of 4, top arrow & markers	75.00	
			P# block of 4, bottom arrow & markers and black P#	77.50	
			P# strip of 3, Impt., T V	75.00	
			P# block of 6, Impt., T V	225.00	
			Never hinged	375.00	
			P# strip of 5, bottom Impt., T V, two P#, arrow & markers	130.00	
			P# block of 10, bottom Impt., T V, two P#, arrow & markers	450.00	
			Never hinged	700.00	
			Double transfer	25.00	2.25
a.			Center inverted	42,500.	17,500.
			Block of 4	275,000.	

Almost all unused copies of No. 295a have partial or disturbed gum. Values are for examples with full original gum that is slightly disturbed. Value for No. 295a is for a well-centered example with faults, as there are no known fault-free examples.

Earliest known use: No. 295a, Feb. 24, 1902 (dated cancel on off-cover stamp).

296	A111	4c	**deep red brown & black**	82.50	15.00
			chocolate & black	82.50	15.00
			Never hinged	150.00	
			On cover		37.50
			On cover, Expo. station machine cancel		350.00
			On cover, Expo. station duplex handstamp canc.		750.00
			Block of 4	330.00	85.00
			Margin block of 4, top arrow & markers	350.00	
			P# block of 4, bottom arrow & markers & black P#	375.00	
			P# strip of 3, Impt., T V	350.00	
			P# block of 6, Impt., T V	2,250.00	
			Never hinged	3,250.	
			P# strip of 5, bottom Impt., T V, two P#, arrow & markers	625.00	
			P# block of 10, bottom Impt., T V, two P#, arrow & markers	4,500.	
			Never hinged	5,500.	
a.			Center inverted	22,500.	
			Block of 4	120,000.	
			P# strip of 4, Impt.	140,000.	

No. 296a was a Special Printing.

Almost all unused copies of No. 296a have partial or disturbed gum. Values are for examples with full original gum that is slightly disturbed.
See No. 296a-S, "Specimen" Stamps.

297	A112	5c	**ultramarine & black**	95.00	14.00
			dark ultramarine & black	95.00	14.00
			Never hinged	170.00	
			On cover		40.00
			On cover, Expo. station machine cancel		350.00
			On cover, Expo. station duplex handstamp canc.		750.00
			Block of 4	400.00	95.00
			Margin block of 4, top arrow & markers	425.00	
			P# block of 4, bottom arrow & markers & black P#	450.00	
			P# strip of 3, Impt., T V	400.00	
			P# block of 6, Impt., T V	2,500.	
			Never hinged	3,500.	
			P# strip of 5, bottom Impt., T V, two P#, arrow & markers	750.00	
			P# block of 10, bottom Impt., T V, two P#, arrow & markers	4,750.	
			Never hinged	5,750.	
298	A113	8c	**brown violet & black**	120.00	50.00
			purplish brown & black	120.00	50.00
			Never hinged	220.00	
			On cover		95.00
			On cover, Expo. station machine cancel		750.00
			On cover, Expo. station duplex handstamp canc.		1,250.
			Block of 4	500.00	375.00
			Margin block of 4, top arrow & markers	525.00	
			P# block of 4, bottom arrow & markers & black P#	575.00	
			P# strip of 3, Impt., T V	500.00	
			P# block of 6, Impt., T V	4,250.	
			Never hinged	5,250.	
			P# strip of 5, bottom Impt., T V, two P#, arrow & markers	950.00	
			P# block of 10, bottom Impt., T V, two P#, arrow & markers	7,500.	
			Never hinged	9,000.	
299	A114	10c	**yellow brown & black**	170.00	25.00
			dark yellow brown & black	170.00	25.00
			Never hinged	310.00	
			On cover		110.00
			On cover, Expo. station machine cancel		1,000.
			On cover, Expo. station duplex handstamp canc.		1,500.
			Block of 4	725.00	200.00
			Margin block of 4, top arrow & markers	750.00	
			P# block of 4, bottom arrow & markers & black P#	775.00	
			P# strip of 3, Impt., T V	700.00	
			P# block of 6, Impt., T V	7,000.	
			Never hinged	8,500.	
			P# strip of 5, bottom Impt., T V, two P#, arrow & markers	1,250.	
			P# block of 10, bottom Impt., T V, two P#, arrow & markers	11,000.	
			Never hinged	12,500.	
			Nos. 294-299 (6)	503.00	108.00
			Nos. 294-299, never hinged	913.50	

VALUES FOR VERY FINE STAMPS
Please note: Stamps are valued in the grade of Very Fine unless otherwise indicated.

Franklin — A115

Washington — A116

Jackson — A117

Grant — A118

Lincoln — A119

Garfield — A120

Martha Washington — A121

Daniel Webster — A122

Benjamin Harrison — A123

Henry Clay — A124

Jefferson — A125

David G. Farragut — A126

Madison — A127

Marshall — A128

REGULAR ISSUE

Plates of 400 subjects in four panes of 100 each for all values from 1c to 15c inclusive. Certain plates of 1c, 2c type A129, 3c and 5c show a round marker in margin opposite the horizontal guide line at right or left.
Plates of 200 subjects in two panes of 100 each for 15c, 50c, $1, $2 and $5.

1902-03   **Wmk. 191**   *Perf. 12*

Many stamps of this issue are known with blurred printing due to having been printed on dry paper.

300	A115	1c	**blue green,** *Feb. 1903*	12.00	.20
			green	12.00	.20
			deep green	12.00	.20
			gray green	12.00	.20
			yellow green	12.00	.20
			Never hinged	21.50	
			On cover		.25
			Block of 4	52.50	2.00
			P# strip of 3, Impt., T V	50.00	
			P# block of 6, Impt., T V	200.00	
			Never hinged	300.00	
			Double transfer	17.50	1.00
			Worn plate	13.00	.30
			Cracked plate	14.00	.30
b.			Booklet pane of 6, *Mar. 6, 1907*	550.00	—
			Never hinged	925.00	

Earliest known use: No. 300, Feb. 3, 1903.

301	A116	2c	**carmine,** *Jan. 17, 1903*	16.00	.20
			bright carmine	16.00	.20
			deep carmine	16.00	.20
			carmine rose	16.00	.20
			Never hinged	29.00	
			On cover		.25
			Block of 4	70.00	2.00
			P# strip of 3, Impt., T V	67.50	
			P# block of 6, Impt., T V	240.00	
			Never hinged	360.00	
			Double transfer	27.50	1.00
			Cracked plate		1.00
c.			Booklet pane of 6, *Jan. 24, 1903*	475.00	—
			Never hinged	800.00	
302	A117	3c	**bright violet,** *Feb. 1903*	55.00	2.75
			violet	55.00	2.75
			deep violet	50.00	2.75
			Never hinged	100.00	
			On cover		10.00
			Block of 4	250.00	20.00
			P# strip of 3, Impt., T V	200.00	

	P# block of 6, Impt., T V	725.00	
	Double transfer	77.50	3.75
	Cracked plate	—	—

Earliest known use: Mar. 21, 1903.

303	A118	4c **brown,** *Feb. 1903*	60.00	1.25
		dark brown	60.00	1.25
		yellow brown	60.00	1.25
		orange brown	60.00	1.25
		red brown	60.00	1.25
		Never hinged	110.00	
		On cover		12.50
		Block of 4	260.00	17.50
		P# strip of 3, Impt., T V	240.00	
		P# block of 6, Impt., T V	725.00	
		Double transfer	77.50	2.75

Earliest known use (cover front): Mar. 13, 1903.

304	A119	5c **blue,** *Jan. 1903*	60.00	1.50
		pale blue	60.00	1.50
		bright blue	60.00	1.50
		dark blue	60.00	1.50
		Never hinged	110.00	
		On cover		7.50
		Block of 4	260.00	8.50
		P# strip of 3, Impt., T V	240.00	
		P# block of 6, Impt., T V	725.00	—
		Double transfer	82.50	3.25
		Cracked plate	70.00	4.25

Earliest known use: Feb. 10, 1903.

305	A120	6c **claret,** *Feb. 1903*	72.50	2.50
		deep claret	72.50	2.50
		brownish lake	72.50	2.50
		dull brownish lake	72.50	2.50
		Never hinged	130.00	
		On cover		12.50
		Block of 4	310.00	22.50
		P# strip of 3, Impt., T V	290.00	
		P# block of 6, Impt., T V	850.00	
		Never hinged	1,250.	
		Double transfer	77.50	3.50

Earliest known use: May 8, 1903.

306	A121	8c **violet black,** *Dec. 1902*	45.00	2.00
		black	45.00	2.00
		slate black	45.00	2.00
		gray lilac	45.00	2.00
		Never hinged	80.00	
		lavender	55.00	2.75
		Never hinged	100.00	
		On cover		8.00
		Block of 4	200.00	20.00
		P# strip of 3, Impt., T V	180.00	
		P# block of 6, Impt., T V	675.00	
		Double transfer	50.00	2.50

Earliest known use: Dec. 27, 1902.

307	A122	10c **pale red brown,** *Feb. 1903*	67.50	1.40
		red brown	67.50	1.40
		dark red brown	67.50	1.40
		Never hinged	120.00	
		On cover		7.50
		Block of 4	290.00	9.00
		P# strip of 3, Impt., T V	270.00	
		P# block of 6, Impt., T V	1,000.	
		Double transfer	77.50	9.00

Earliest known use: Mar. 12, 1903.

308	A123	13c **purple black,** *Nov. 18, 1902*	50.00	7.50
		brown violet	50.00	7.50
		Never hinged	90.00	
		On cover		37.50
		Block of 4	210.00	52.50
		P# strip of 3, Impt., T V	200.00	
		P# block of 6, Impt., T V	625.00	
		Never hinged	950.00	

Earliest known use: Nov. 18, 1902.

309	A124	15c **olive green,** *May 27, 1903*	170.00	4.75
		dark olive green	170.00	4.75
		Never hinged	310.00	
		On cover		75.00
		Block of 4	725.00	65.00
		Margin block of 4, arrow	750.00	
		P# strip of 3, Impt., T V	675.00	
		P# block of 6, Impt., T V	3,000.	
		Never hinged	4,500.	
		Double transfer	210.00	9.00

Earliest known use: July 1903 (on registry tag); Sept. 24, 1903 (on cover).

310	A125	50c **orange,** *Mar. 23, 1903*	475.	22.50
		deep orange	475.	22.50
		Never hinged	875.	
		On cover		700.00
		Block of 4	2,000.	150.00
		Margin block of 4, arrow	2,100.	
		P# strip of 3, Impt., T V	1,900.	
		P# block of 6, Impt., T V	7,000.	

Earliest known use: June 4, 1903.

311	A126	$1 **black,** *June 5, 1903*	775.00	55.00
		grayish black	775.00	55.00
		Never hinged	1,450.	
		No gum	180.00	
		On cover		1,500.
		Block of 4	3,250.	350.00
		Margin block of 4, arrow	3,400.	
		P# strip of 3, Impt., T V	3,100.	
		P# block of 6, Impt., T V	18,000.	

Earliest known use: Sept. 30, 1903.

312	A127	$2 **dark blue,** *June 5, 1903*	1,250.	190.00
		blue	1,250.	190.00
		Never hinged	2,500.	
		No gum	300.00	
		On cover		2,500.
		Block of 4	5,500.	1,200.

	Margin block of 4, arrow	5,750.	
	P# strip of 3, Impt., T V	5,000.	
	P# block of 6, Impt., T V	32,500.	

Earliest known use: Feb. 17, 1904.

313	A128	$5 **dark green,** *June 5, 1903*	3,000.	750.00
		Never hinged	6,000.	
		No gum	850.00	
		On cover		5,000.
		Block of 4	14,000.	3,750.
		Margin block of 4, arrow	14,500.	
		P# strip of 3, Impt., T V	12,000.	
		P# block of 6, Impt., T V	82,500.	

Earliest known use: Feb. 17, 1904.

Nos. 300-313 (14)   6,108.   1,041.

For listings of designs A127 and A128 with Perf. 10 see Nos. 479 and 480.

1906-08   *Imperf.*

314	A115	1c **blue green,** *Oct. 2, 1906*	19.00	15.00
		green	19.00	15.00
		deep green	19.00	15.00
		Never hinged	35.00	
		On cover		22.50
		Pair	40.00	31.00
		Never hinged	75.00	
		Block of 4	80.00	62.50
		Never hinged	150.00	
		Corner margin block of 4	82.50	65.00
		Margin block of 4, arrow	85.00	67.50
		Margin block of 4, arrow & round marker	150.00	125.00
		Center line block	135.00	100.00
		P# block of 6, Impt.	170.00	—
		Never hinged	250.00	
		Double transfer	32.50	17.50

Earliest known use: Feb. 1, 1907 (dated cancel on off-cover stamp); Feb. 4, 1907 (on cover).

314A	A118	4c **brown,** *Apr. 1908*	30,000.	25,000.
		Never hinged	—	
		On cover		125,000.
		Pair	70,000.	
		Guide line pair	180,000.	

This stamp was issued imperforate but all copies were privately perforated with large oblong perforations at the sides (Schermack type III).

Beware of copies of No. 303 with trimmed perforations and fake private perfs. added.

Used and on cover values are for contemporaneous usage.

Earliest known use: May 27, 1908.

315	A119	5c **blue,** *May 12, 1908*	260.	600.
		Never hinged	450.	
		On cover, pair		14,000.
		Pair	550.	1,750.
		Never hinged	925.	
		Block of 4	1,100.	2,600.
		Never hinged	1,900.	
		Corner margin block of 4	1,200.	
		Margin block of 4, arrow	1,700.	
		Margin block of 4, arrow & round marker	2,250.	
		Center line block	4,000.	
		P# block of 6, Impt.	2,500.	—
		Never hinged	3,750.	

Earliest known use: Sept. 15, 1908.

Beware of copies of No. 304 with perforations removed.

Used copies of No. 315 must have contemporaneous cancels. Single copies of No. 315 on cover are not known to exist.

COIL STAMPS

Warning! Imperforate stamps are known fraudulently perforated to resemble coil stamps and part-perforate varieties.

1908   *Perf. 12 Horizontally*

316	A115	1c **blue green,** pair, *Feb. 18*	105,000.	—
		Single	40,000.	
		Guide line pair	175,000.	
317	A119	5c **blue,** pair, *Feb. 24*	12,500.	—
		Never hinged	20,000.	
		Single	4,750.	
		Guide line pair	28,000.	

Earliest known use: Sept. 18, 1908.

Perf. 12 Vertically

318	A115	1c **blue green,** pair, *July 31*	11,000.	—
		Single	4,250.	
		Guide line pair	17,000.	
		Double transfer	—	—

Coil stamps for use in vending and affixing machines are perforated on two sides only, either horizontally or vertically. They were first issued in 1908, using perf. 12. This was changed to 8½ in 1910, and to 10 in 1914.

Imperforate sheets of certain denominations were sold to the vending machine companies which applied a variety of private perforations and separations (see Vending and Affixing Machine Perforations section of this catalogue).

Several values of the 1902 and later issues are found on an apparently coarse-ribbed paper. This is caused by worn blankets on the printing presses and is not a true paper variety.

All examples of Nos. 316-318 must be accompanied by certificates of authenticity issued by recognized expertizing committees.

Washington — A129

Plate of 400 subjects in four panes of 100 each.

1 →

2 →

Type I   Type II

1903   Wmk. 191   *Perf. 12*

319	A129	2c **carmine,** type I, *Nov. 12, 1903*	6.00	.20
		bright carmine	6.00	.20
		red	6.00	.20
		Never hinged	11.00	
		On cover		.20
		Block of 4	25.00	2.00
		P# strip of 3, Impt., T V	24.00	
		P# block of 6, Impt., T V	105.00	
		Never hinged	160.00	
		Double transfer	12.50	2.00

Earliest known use: Nov. 19, 1903.

a.		2c **lake,** type I	—	—
		carmine lake		
b.		2c **carmine rose,** type I	8.00	.35
		Never hinged	14.50	
		On cover		.50
		Block of 4	35.00	4.00
		P# strip of 3, Impt., T V	32.50	
		P# block of 6, Impt., T V	150.00	
		Never hinged	225.00	
c.		2c **scarlet,** type I	6.00	.25
		Never hinged	11.00	
		On cover		.30
		Block of 4	25.00	2.25

	P# strip of 3, Impt., T V	24.00	
	P# block of 6, Impt., T V	100.00	
	Never hinged	150.00	

Earliest known use: Dec. 16, 1903.

d.	Vert. pair, imperf. horiz., No. 319		5,000.	
e.	Vertical pair, imperf. between, No. 319		1,250.	
	As "e," rouletted between		1,750.	

"Gash on Face" Variety

The gash may appear as double lines due to different plate wiping techniques.

f.	2c **lake**, type II	8.00	.25	
	carmine lake	8.00	.25	
	Never hinged	14.50		
	On cover		.30	
	Block of 4	35.00	3.75	
	P# strip of 3, Impt., T V	37.50		
	P# block of 6, Impt., T V	250.00		
	Never hinged	375.00		
	"Gash on face" plate flaw (carmine lake, 4671 LL 16)	—		

Earliest known use: Sept. 25, 1908.

g.	Booklet pane of 6, car., type I	120.00	175.00	
	Never hinged	200.00		
h.	Booklet pane of 6, car., type II	260.00		
	Never hinged	425.00		
i.	2c **carmine**, type II	27.50	50.00	
	red	27.50	50.00	
	Never hinged	50.00		
	On cover		150.00	

Earliest known use: June 11, 1908.

j.	2c **carmine rose**, type II	20.00	.75	
	Never hinged	35.00		
	P# block of 6, Impt., T V	500.00		
k.	2c **scarlet**, type II	18.00	.45	
	Never hinged	32.50		
	P# block of 6, Impt., T V	500.00		
m.	Booklet pane of 6, lake (I)		2,500.	
n.	Booklet pane of 6, car. rose (I)	180.00	250.00	
	Never hinged	300.00		
p.	Booklet pane of 6, scarlet (I)	160.00	200.00	
	Never hinged	260.00		
q.	Booklet pane of 6, lake, (II)	200.00	375.00	
	Never hinged	325.00		

During the use of this stamp, the Postmaster at San Francisco discovered in his stock sheets of No. 319, each of which had the horizontal perforations missing between the two top rows of stamps. To facilitate their separation, the imperf. rows were rouletted, and the stamps sold over the counter. So vertical pairs are found with regular perforations all around and rouletted between.

1906   **Imperf.**

320	A129 2c **carmine**, type I *Oct. 2*	18.00	12.00	
	Never hinged	32.50		
	On cover		20.00	
	Pair	37.50	25.00	
	Never hinged	67.50		
	Block of 4	75.00	55.00	
	Corner margin block of 4	77.50	80.00	
	Margin block of 4, arrow	80.00	90.00	
	Margin block of 4, arrow & round marker	—		
	Center line block	150.00	200.00	
	P# block of 6, Impt., T V, carmine	210.00	—	
	Never hinged	310.00		
	Double transfer	25.00	16.00	

Earliest known use: Oct. 26, 1906.

a.	2c **lake**, type II	50.00	40.00	
	carmine lake	50.00	40.00	
	Never hinged	90.00		
	On cover		75.00	
	Pair	105.00	95.00	
	Never hinged	190.00		
	Block of 4	210.00	225.00	
	Corner margin block of 4	215.00		
	Margin block of 4, arrow	220.00		
	Center line block	425.00		
	P# block of 6, Impt., T V	750.00	—	
	Never hinged	1,100.		
	"Gash on face" plate flaw (see No. 319f)	—		
b.	2c **scarlet**, type I	18.00	12.50	
	Never hinged	32.50		
	On cover		20.00	
	Pair	37.50		
	Never hinged	67.50		
	Block of 4	75.00		
	Corner margin block of 4	77.50		
	Margin block of 4, arrow	80.00		
	Center line block	200.00		
	P# block of 6, Impt., T V	210.00		
	Never hinged	310.00		
c.	2c **carmine rose**, type I	55.00	40.00	
	Never hinged	100.00		
d.	2c **carmine**, type II	—		

COIL STAMPS

1908   **Perf. 12 Horizontally**

321	A129 2c **carmine**, type I, pair, *Feb. 18*	125,000.		
	On cover, single		170,000.	
	Guide line pair	—		

Four authenticated unused pairs of No. 321 are known. There are 2 authenticated examples of the single used on cover, both used from Indianapolis in 1908. Numerous counterfeits exist.

Earliest known use: Oct. 2, 1908.

Perf. 12 Vertically

322	A129 2c **carmine**, type II, pair, *July 31*	10,000.	—	
	Single	4,250.		
	Guide line pair	12,500.		
	Double transfer	—		

This Government Coil Stamp should not be confused with those of the International Vending Machine Co., which are perforated 12½.

All examples of Nos. 321-322 must be accompanied by certificates of authenticity issued by recognized expertizing committees.

VALUES FOR VERY FINE STAMPS
Please note: Stamps are valued in the grade of Very Fine unless otherwise indicated.

LOUISIANA PURCHASE EXPOSITION ISSUE
St. Louis, Mo., Apr. 30 - Dec. 1, 1904

Robert R. Livingston — A130

Thomas Jefferson — A131

James Monroe — A132

William McKinley — A133

Map of Louisiana Purchase — A134

Plates of 100 (10x10) subjects, divided vertically into 2 panes of 50.

Exposition Station Machine Cancellation

1904, Apr. 30   **Wmk. 191**   **Perf. 12**

323	A130 1c **green**	30.00	4.00	
	dark green	30.00	4.00	
	Never hinged	52.50		
	On cover		6.00	
	On Expo. card, Expo. station machine canc.		40.00	
	On Expo. card, Expo. station duplex handstamp canc.		100.00	
	Block of 4	130.00	30.00	

	Margin block of 4, arrow, R or L	130.00	—	
	P# pair, Impt., T V	82.50		
	P# strip of 3, Impt., T V	120.00		
	P# block of 4, Impt., T V	175.00		
	Never hinged	275.00		
	P# block of 6, Impt., T V	275.00		
	Never hinged	425.00		
	Diagonal line through left "1" (2138 L 2)	50.00	11.00	
	Double transfer	—		
324	A131 2c **carmine**	27.50	1.50	
	bright carmine	27.50	1.50	
	Never hinged	50.00		
	On cover		2.50	
	On Expo. cover, Expo. station machine canc.		60.00	
	On Expo. cover, Expo. station duplex handstamp canc.		150.00	
	Block of 4	120.00	15.00	
	Margin block of 4, arrow, R or L	130.00	—	
	P# pair, Impt., T V	75.00		
	P# strip of 3, Impt., T V	110.00		
	P# block of 4, Impt., T V	175.00		
	Never hinged	275.00		
	P# block of 6, Impt., T V	275.00		
	Never hinged	425.00		
a.	Vertical pair, imperf. horiz.	10,000.		
	Block of 4	25,000.		
	P# block of 4, Impt., T V	45,000.		
325	A132 3c **violet**	90.00	30.00	
	Never hinged	160.00		
	On cover		50.00	
	On cover, Expo. station machine canc.		200.00	
	On cover, Expo. station duplex handstamp canc.		400.00	
	Block of 4	375.00	190.00	
	Margin block of 4, arrow, R or L	390.00	—	
	P# pair, Impt., T V	225.00		
	P# strip of 3, Impt., T V	350.00		
	P# block of 4, Impt., T V	625.00		
	Never hinged	975.00		
	P# block of 6, Impt., T V	950.00		
	Never hinged	1,450.		
	Double transfer	—		
326	A133 5c **dark blue**	95.00	25.00	
	Never hinged	165.00		
	On cover		50.00	
	On cover, Expo. station machine canc.		400.00	
	On cover, Expo. station duplex handstamp canc.		500.00	
	Block of 4	400.00	175.00	
	Margin block of 4, arrow, R or L	425.00	—	
	P# pair, Impt., T V	230.00		
	P# strip of 3, Impt., T V	375.00		
	P# block of 4, Impt., T V	675.00		
	Never hinged	1,050.		
	P# block of 6, Impt., T V	1,000.		
	Never hinged	1,550.		
327	A134 10c **red brown**	180.00	27.50	
	dark red brown	180.00	27.50	
	Never hinged	325.00		
	On cover		110.00	
	On cover, Expo. station machine canc.		450.00	
	On cover, Expo. station duplex handstamp canc.		750.00	
	Block of 4	750.00	190.00	
	Margin block of 4, arrow, R or L	800.00	—	
	P# pair, Impt., T V	425.00		
	P# strip of 3, Impt., T V	725.00		
	P# block of 4, Impt., T V	1,325.		
	Never hinged	2,100.		
	P# block of 6, Impt., T V	2,250.		
	Never hinged	3,500.		
	Nos. 323-327 (5)	422.50	88.00	
	Nos. 323-327, never hinged	752.50		

JAMESTOWN EXPOSITION ISSUE
Hampton Roads, Va., Apr. 26 - Dec. 1, 1907

Captain John Smith — A135

Founding of Jamestown — A136

Pocahontas — A137

Plates of 200 subjects in two panes of 100 each.

Exposition Station Machine Cancellation

1907	Wmk. 191		Perf. 12	
328 A135 1c	green, *Apr. 26*	30.00	4.00	
	dark green	30.00	4.00	
	Never hinged	52.50		
	On cover		7.00	
	On Expo. card, Expo. station machine canc.		25.00	
	On Expo. card, Expo. station duplex handstamp canc.		125.00	
	Block of 4	125.00	42.50	
	Margin block of 4, arrow	130.00	—	
	P# strip of 3, Impt., T V	110.00		
	P# block of 6, Impt., T V	275.00		
	Never hinged	425.00		
	Double transfer	35.00	5.00	
329 A136 2c	carmine, *Apr. 26*	35.00	3.50	
	bright carmine	35.00	3.50	
	Never hinged	62.50		
	On cover		4.75	
	On Expo. cover, Expo. station machine canc.		100.00	
	On Expo. cover, Expo. station duplex handstamp canc.		150.00	
	Block of 4	150.00	25.00	
	Margin block of 4, arrow	160.00	—	
	P# strip of 3, Impt., T V	125.00		
	P# block of 6, Impt., T V	375.00		
	Never hinged	575.00		
	Double transfer	42.50	4.75	
330 A137 5c	blue	135.00	27.50	
	deep blue	135.00	27.50	
	Never hinged	240.00		
	On cover		70.00	
	On cover, Expo. station machine canc.		350.00	
	On cover, Expo. station duplex handstamp canc.		500.00	
	Block of 4	575.00	175.00	
	Margin block of 4, arrow	600.00	—	
	P# strip of 3, Impt., T V	475.00		
	P# block of 6, Impt., T V	2,600.		
	Never hinged	4,000.		
	Double transfer	150.00	32.50	
Nos. 328-330 (3)		200.00	35.00	
Nos. 328-330, never hinged		355.00		

Earliest known use: May 9, 1907.

REGULAR ISSUE

Plates of 400 subjects in four panes of 100 each for all values 1c to 15c inclusive.

Plates of 200 subjects in two panes of 100 each for 50c and $1 denominations.

In 1909 the Bureau prepared certain plates with horizontal spacings of 3mm between the outer seven vertical stamp rows and 2mm between the others. This was done to try to counteract the effect of unequal shrinkage of the paper. *However, some unequal shrinkage still did occur and intermediate spacings are frequently found.* The listings of 2mm and 3mm spacings are for exact measurements. Intermediate spacings sell for approximately the same as the cheaper of the two listed spacings. All such plates were marked with an open star added to the imprint and exist on the 1c, 2c, 3c, 4c, and 5c denominations only. A small solid star was added to the imprint and plate number for 1c plate No. 4980, 2c plate No. 4988 and for the 2c Lincoln. All other plates for this issue are spaced 2mm throughout.

There are several types of some of the 2c and 3c stamps of this and succeeding issues. These types are described under the dates at which they first appeared. Illustrations of Types I-VII of the 2c (A140) and Types I-IV of the 3c (A140) are reproduced by permission of H. L. Lindquist.

China Clay Paper. A small quantity of Nos. 331-340 was printed on paper containing a high mineral content (5-20%), instead of the specified 2%. The minerals, principally aluminum silicate, produced China clay paper. It is thick, hard and grayish, often darker than "bluish" paper.

  ✿ 4968

Imprint, plate number and open star

★ 4976

Imprint, plate number and small solid star

A 5557

Imprint, plate number and "A"

(Above illustrations reduced in size)

A 5805
"A" and number only

988
Number only

The above illustrations are several of the styles used on plates of issues from 1908 to date.

Franklin — A138   Washington — A139

1908-09	Wmk. 191		Perf. 12	
331 A138 1c	green, *Dec. 1908*	7.25	.20	
	bright green	7.25	.20	
	dark green	7.25	.20	
	yellow green	7.25	.20	
	Never hinged	12.50		
	On cover		.40	
	Block of 4 (2mm spacing)	32.50	1.50	
	Block of 4 (3mm spacing)	35.00	1.75	
	P# block of 6, Impt., T V	77.50		
	Never hinged	120.00		
	P# block of 6, Impt. & star	70.00		
	Never hinged	110.00		
	P# block of 6, Impt. & small solid star (plate 4980)	1,300.		
	Never hinged	1,850.		
	Double transfer	9.50	.60	
	Cracked plate	—		
a.	Booklet pane of 6, *Dec. 2, 1908*	160.00	140.00	
	Never hinged	250.00		
b.	"China Clay" paper	1,000.		

No. 331 exists in horizontal pair, imperforate between, a variety resulting from booklet experiments. Not regularly issued.

Earliest known use: Dec. 1, 1908.

332 A139 2c	carmine, *Nov. 1908*	6.75	.20	
	light carmine	6.75	.20	
	dark carmine	6.75	.20	
	Never hinged	12.00		
	On cover		.20	
	Block of 4 (2mm spacing)	30.00	.75	
	Block of 4 (3mm spacing)	32.50	.85	
	P# block of 6, Impt., T V	70.00		
	Never hinged	110.00		
	P# block of 6, Impt. & star	67.50		
	Never hinged	105.00		
	P# block of 6, Impt. & small solid star (plate 4988)	1,350.		
	Never hinged	1,900.		
	Double transfer	12.50	—	

	Foreign entry, design of 1c			
	(plate 5299)	1,500.	1,250.	
	Rosette crack	—		
	Cracked plate	—		
a.	Booklet pane of 6	135.00	125.00	
	Never hinged	210.00		
b.	"China Clay" paper	1,300.		

Earliest known use: Dec. 3, 1908 (No. 332), Nov. 16, 1908 (No. 332a).

Washington — A140

TYPE I

THREE CENTS.
Type I. The top line of the toga rope is weak and the rope shading lines are thin. The 5th line from the left is missing. The line between the lips is thin. (For descriptions of 3c types II, III and IV, see notes and illustrations preceding Nos. 484, 529-530.)
Used on both flat plate and rotary press printings.

333 A140	3c **deep violet**, type I, *Dec.*		
	1908	35.00	2.50
	violet	35.00	2.50
	light violet	35.00	2.50
	Never hinged	62.50	
	On cover		8.00
	Block of 4 (2mm spacing)	145.00	20.00
	Block of 4 (3mm spacing)	150.00	22.50
	P# block of 6, Impt., T V	350.00	
	Never hinged	525.00	
	P# block of 6, Impt. & star	375.00	
	Never hinged	575.00	
	Double transfer	37.50	5.00
a.	"China Clay" paper	1,000.	
	P# block of 6, Impt., T V	9,000.	

Earliest known use: Jan. 12, 1909.

334 A140	4c **orange brown**, *Dec. 1908*	42.50	1.00
	brown	42.50	1.00
	light brown	42.50	1.00
	dark brown	42.50	1.00
	Never hinged	75.00	
	On cover		6.50
	Block of 4 (2mm spacing)	180.00	9.00
	Block of 4 (3mm spacing)	190.00	10.00
	P# block of 6, Impt., T V	425.00	
	Never hinged	650.00	
	P# block of 6, Impt. & star	425.00	
	Never hinged	650.00	
	Double transfer	55.00	
a.	"China Clay" paper	1,300.	

Earliest known use: Jan. 12, 1909.

335 A140	5c **blue**, *Dec. 1908*	52.50	2.00
	bright blue	52.50	2.00
	dark blue	52.50	2.00
	Never hinged	92.50	
	On cover		8.00
	Block of 4 (2mm spacing)	220.00	15.00
	Block of 4 (3mm spacing)	230.00	12.50
	P# block of 6, Impt., T V	525.00	
	Never hinged	800.00	
	P# block of 6, Impt. & star	550.00	
	Never hinged	825.00	
	Double transfer	57.50	—
a.	"China Clay" paper	1,000.	

Earliest known use: Jan. 12, 1909.

336 A140	6c **red orange**, *Jan. 1909*	65.00	5.00
	pale red orange	65.00	5.00
	orange	65.00	5.00
	Never hinged	115.00	
	On cover		21.00
	Block of 4	275.00	37.50
	P# block of 6, Impt., T V	750.00	
	Never hinged	1,125.	
a.	"China Clay" paper	750.00	
	Never hinged	—	

Earliest known use: Jan. 6, 1909.

337 A140	8c **olive green**, *Dec. 1908*	50.00	2.50
	deep olive green	50.00	2.50
	Never hinged	87.50	
	On cover		18.00
	Block of 4	210.00	18.00
	P# block of 6, Impt., T V	500.00	
	Never hinged	750.00	

	Double transfer	57.50	—
a.	"China Clay" paper	1,000.	

Earliest known use: Jan. 9, 1909.

338 A140	10c **yellow**, *Jan. 1909*	70.00	1.40
	Never hinged	125.00	
	On cover		10.00
	Block of 4	300.00	9.00
	P# block of 6, Impt., T V	825.00	
	Never hinged	1,250.	
	Double transfer	—	
	Very thin paper	—	
a.	"China Clay" paper	1,000.	

Earliest known use: Feb. 1, 1909.

339 A140	13c **blue green**, *Jan. 1909*	42.50	19.00
	deep blue green	42.50	19.00
	Never hinged	75.00	
	On cover		110.00
	Block of 4	190.00	145.00
	P# block of 6, Impt., T V	500.00	
	Never hinged	750.00	
	Line through "TAG" of		
	"POSTAGE" (4948 LR 96)	70.00	—
a.	"China Clay" paper	1,000.	

Earliest known use: Mar. 5, 1909.

340 A140	15c **pale ultramarine**, *Jan. 1909*	70.00	5.50
	ultramarine	70.00	5.50
	Never hinged	125.00	
	On cover		125.00
	Block of 4	290.00	50.00
	P# block of 6, Impt., T V	650.00	
	Never hinged	975.00	
a.	"China Clay" paper	1,000.	
	P# block of 6, Impt., T V	9,000.	

Earliest known use: Mar. 12, 1909.

341 A140	50c **violet**, *Jan. 13, 1909*	350.00	20.00
	dull violet	350.00	20.00
	Never hinged	625.00	
	On cover		5,000.
	Block of 4	1,500.	110.00
	Margin block of 4, arrow,		
	right or left	1,550.	
	P# block of 6, Impt., T V	7,000.	—
	Never hinged	10,500.	

Earliest known use: Oct. 23, 1909 (on registry tag); June 2, 1916 (on cover).

342 A140	$1 **violet brown**, *Jan. 29, 1909*	525.00	75.00
	light violet brown	525.00	75.00
	Never hinged	950.00	
	On cover		6,000.
	Block of 4	2,250.	500.00
	Margin block of 4, arrow,		
	right or left	2,350.	525.00
	P# block of 6, Impt., T V	13,500.	
	Double transfer	—	
	Nos. 331-342 (12)	1,316.	134.30

For listings of other perforated stamps of A138, A139 and A140 see:
Nos. 357-366 Bluish paper
Nos. 374-382, 405-407 Single line wmk. Perf. 12
Nos. 424-430 Single line wmk. Perf. 10
Nos. 461 Single line wmk. Perf. 11
Nos. 462-469 unwmk. Perf. 10
Nos. 498-507 unwmk. Perf. 11
Nos. 519 Double line wmk. Perf. 11
Nos. 525-530 and 536 Offset printing
Nos. 538-546 Rotary press printing

Plate Blocks
Scott values for plate blocks printed from flat plates are for very fine side and bottom positions. Top position plate blocks with full wide selvage sell for more.

Imperf

343 A138	1c **green**, *Dec. 1908*	5.25	4.50
	dark green	5.25	4.50
	yellowish green	5.25	4.50
	Never hinged	9.00	
	On cover		8.00
	Pair	11.00	10.00
	Never hinged	19.00	
	Block of 4 (2mm or 3mm		
	spacing)	22.50	20.00
	Corner margin block of 4,		
	2mm or 3mm	24.00	21.00
	Margin block of 4, arrow,		
	2mm or 3mm	25.00	21.00
	Center line block	30.00	25.00
	P# block of 6, Impt., T V	50.00	
	Never hinged	75.00	
	P# block of 6, Impt. & star	60.00	
	Never hinged	90.00	
	P# block of 6, Impt. & small		
	solid star (plate 4980)	675.00	
	Never hinged	1,000.	
	Double transfer	11.00	7.00

Earliest known use: Jan. 4, 1909.

344 A139	2c **carmine**, *Dec. 10, 1908*	6.50	3.00
	light carmine	6.50	3.00
	dark carmine	6.50	3.00
	Never hinged	11.00	
	On cover		5.50
	Pair	13.50	7.50
	Never hinged	23.00	
	Block of 4 (2mm or 3mm		
	spacing)	28.00	15.00
	Corner margin block of 4,		
	2mm or 3mm	30.00	21.00
	Margin block of 4, arrow,		
	2mm or 3mm	32.50	21.00

	Center line block	37.50	35.00
	P# block of 6, Impt., T V	80.00	
	Never hinged	120.00	
	P# block of 6, Impt. & star	72.50	
	Never hinged	110.00	
	Double transfer	12.50	4.00
	Foreign entry, design of 1c		
	(plate 5299)	1,250.	—

Earliest known use: Feb. 1, 1909.

The existence of the foreign entry on No. 344 has been questioned by specialists. The editors would like to see evidence of the existence of the item, either unused or used.

345 A140	3c **deep violet**, type I, *1909*	12.00	20.00
	violet	12.00	20.00
	Never hinged	21.00	
	On cover		45.00
	Pair	25.00	50.00
	Never hinged	44.00	
	Block of 4	50.00	100.00
	Corner margin block of 4	52.50	105.00
	Margin block of 4, arrow	57.50	105.00
	Center line block	75.00	110.00
	P# block of 6, Impt., T V	160.00	
	Never hinged	240.00	
	Double transfer	22.50	—

Earliest known use: Feb. 13, 1909.

346 A140	4c **orange brown**, *Feb. 25,*		
	1909	20.00	22.50
	brown	20.00	22.50
	Never hinged	35.00	
	On cover		77.50
	Pair	42.50	57.50
	Never hinged	75.00	
	Block of 4 (2 or 3mm spac-		
	ing)	85.00	115.00
	Corner margin block of 4 (2		
	or 3mm spacing)	90.00	120.00
	Margin block of 4, arrow, (2		
	or 3mm spacing)	95.00	120.00
	Center line block	120.00	140.00
	P# block of 6, Impt., T V	180.00	—
	Never hinged	275.00	
	P# block of 6, Impt. & star	210.00	
	Never hinged	320.00	
	Double transfer	37.50	

Earliest known use: Mar. 13, 1909.

347 A140	5c **blue**, *Feb. 25, 1909*	37.50	35.00
	dark blue	37.50	35.00
	Never hinged	65.00	
	On cover		100.00
	Pair	80.00	100.00
	Never hinged	140.00	
	Block of 4	170.00	200.00
	Corner margin block of 4	180.00	225.00
	Margin block of 4, arrow	190.00	235.00
	Center line block	220.00	250.00
	P# block of 6, Impt., T V	300.00	—
	Never hinged	450.00	
	Cracked plate	—	
	Nos. 343-347 (5)	81.25	85.00
	Nos. 343-347, never hinged	141.00	

Earliest known use: Mar. 4, 1909.

For listings of other imperforate stamps of designs A138, A139 and A140 see Nos. 383, 384, 408, 409 and 459 Single line wmk.
Nos. 481-485 unwmk.
Nos. 531-535 Offset printing

COIL STAMPS

1908-10		**Perf. 12 Horizontally**	
348 A138	1c **green**, *Dec. 29, 1908*	37.50	19.00
	dark green	37.50	19.00
	Never hinged	67.50	
	On cover		45.00
	Pair	100.00	90.00
	Never hinged	180.00	
	Guide line pair	290.00	500.00
	Never hinged	525.00	

Earliest known use: Jan. 25, 1909.

349 A139	2c **carmine**, *Jan. 1909*	70.00	11.00
	dark carmine	70.00	11.00
	Never hinged	125.00	
	On cover		35.00
	Pair	180.00	47.50
	Never hinged	325.00	
	Guide line pair	500.00	260.00
	Never hinged	900.00	
	Foreign entry, design of 1c		
	(plate 5299)	—	1,750.

Earliest known use: May 14, 1909.

350 A140	4c **orange brown**, *Aug. 15, 1910*	160.00	100.00
	Never hinged	290.00	
	On cover		240.00
	Pair	360.00	450.00
	Never hinged	650.00	
	Guide line pair	1,150.	1000.
	Never hinged	2,100.	

Earliest known use: Aug. 21, 1912.

351 A140	5c **blue**, *Jan. 1909*	175.00	140.00
	dark blue	175.00	140.00
	Never hinged	310.00	
	On cover		275.00
	Pair	450.00	475.00
	Never hinged	800.00	
	Guide line pair	1,150.	1,050.
	Never hinged	2,100.	

Earliest known use: Sept. 21, 1909.

1909 — Perf. 12 Vertically

352 A138	1c green, Jan. 1909		80.00	40.00
	dark green		80.00	40.00
	Never hinged		145.00	
	On cover			75.00
	Pair (2mm spacing)		200.00	150.00
	Never hinged		360.00	
	Pair (3mm spacing)		185.00	140.00
	Never hinged		330.00	
	Guide line pair		600.00	350.00
	Never hinged		1,100.	
	Double transfer		—	—
353 A139	2c carmine, Jan. 12, 1909		87.50	11.00
	dark carmine		87.50	11.00
	Never hinged		160.00	
	On cover			29.00
	Pair (2mm spacing)		210.00	45.00
	Never hinged		375.00	
	Pair (3mm spacing)		190.00	42.50
	Never hinged		340.00	
	Guide line pair		575.00	200.00
	Never hinged		1,050.	

Earliest known use: June 14, 1909.

354 A140	4c orange brown, Feb. 23, 1909		200.00	75.00
	Never hinged		360.00	
	On cover			150.00
	Pair (2mm spacing)		500.00	375.00
	Never hinged		900.00	
	Pair (3mm spacing)		475.00	375.00
	Never hinged		850.00	
	Guide line pair		1,450.	700.00
	Never hinged		2,600.	

Earliest known use: June 9, 1909.

355 A140	5c blue, Feb. 23, 1909		210.00	100.00
	Never hinged		375.00	
	On cover			240.00
	Pair		525.00	475.00
	Never hinged		950.00	
	Guide line pair		1,450.	800.00
	Never hinged		2,600.	

Earliest known use: Oct. 25, 1909.

These Government Coil Stamps, Nos. 352-355, should not be confused with those of the International Vending Machine Co., which are perf. 12½-13.

356 A140	10c yellow, Jan. 7, 1909		2,500.	1,100.
	Never hinged		4,500.	
	On cover			10,000.
	Pair		5,500.	4,500.
	Never hinged		9,000.	
	Guide line pair		10,000.	8,000.
	Never hinged		17,500.	

Earliest known use: Mar. 9, 1909.

For listings of other coil stamps of designs A138 A139 and A140 see:
Nos. 385-396, 410-413, 441-459, single line watermark.
Nos. 486-496, unwatermarked.

Beware of stamps offered as No. 356 which may be examples of No. 338 with perfs. trimmed at top and/or bottom. Beware also of plentiful fakes in the marketplace of Nos. 348-355. Authentication of all these coils is advised.

BLUISH PAPER

This was made with 35 per cent rag stock instead of all wood pulp. The "bluish" color (actually grayish blue) goes through the paper showing clearly on the back as well as on the face.

1909 — Perf. 12

357 A138	1c green, Feb. 16, 1909		95.00	100.00
	Never hinged		160.00	
	On postcard			120.00
	On cover			220.00
	Block of 4 (2mm spacing)		400.00	450.00
	Block of 4 (3mm spacing)		775.00	
	P# block of 6, Impt., T V		1,000.	
	Never hinged		1,500.	
	P# block of 6, Impt. & star		3,000.	
	Never hinged		4,500.	

Earliest known use: Feb. 22, 1909.

358 A139	2c carmine, Feb. 16, 1909		90.00	100.00
	Never hinged		155.00	
	On cover			190.00
	Block of 4 (2mm spacing)		375.00	575.00
	Block of 4 (3mm spacing)		425.00	
	P# block of 6, Impt., T V		975.00	
	Never hinged		1,450.	
	P# block of 6, Impt. & star		1,500.	
	Never hinged		2,250.	
	Double transfer		—	

Earliest known use: Feb. 23, 1909.

359 A140	3c deep violet, type I		2,000.	2,500.
	Never hinged		3,250.	
	On cover			—
	Block of 4		8,500.	
	P# block of 6, Impt., T V		22,500.	
	Never hinged		30,000.	

Earliest known use: Dec. 27, 1910.

360 A140	4c orange brown		24,000.	
	Never hinged		32,500.	
	Block of 4		110,000.	
	P# strip of 3, Impt., T V		110,000.	
361 A140	5c blue		5,000.	9,000.
	Never hinged		7,750.	
	On cover			

	Block of 4		22,000.	—
	P# block of 6, Impt., T V		60,000.	

The No. 361 plate block is unique.

Earliest known use: June 20, 1910.

362 A140	6c red orange		1,500.	2,250.
	Never hinged		2,400.	
	On cover			15,000.
	Block of 4		6,250.	
	P# block of 6, Impt., T V		16,500.	
	Never hinged		22,500.	

Earliest known use: Sept. 14, 1911.

363 A140	8c olive green		26,000.	
	Never hinged		35,000.	
	Block of 4		120,000.	
	P# strip of 3, Impt., T V		115,000.	
364 A140	10c yellow		1,800.	2,750.
	Never hinged		3,000.	
	On cover			—
	Block of 4		7,500.	
	P# block of 6, Impt., T V		32,500.	

Earliest known use: Feb. 3, 1910.

365 A140	13c blue green		3,000.	2,400.
	Never hinged		4,750.	
	On cover			—
	Block of 4		13,000	10,000.
	P# block of 6, Impt., T V		30,000.	
366 A140	15c pale ultramarine		1,450.	8,000.
	Never hinged		2,300.	
	On cover			—
	Block of 4		6,000.	
	P# block of 6, Impt., T V		11,000.	
	Never hinged		15,000.	

Earliest known use: Jan. 15, 1911.

Nos. 360 and 363 were not regularly issued.
Used examples of Nos. 357-366 must bear contemporaneous cancels, and Nos. 359-366 used must be accompanied by certificates of authenticity issued by recognized expertizing committees.

VALUES FOR VERY FINE STAMPS
Please note: Stamps are valued in the grade of Very Fine unless otherwise indicated.

Lincoln — A141

William H.
Seward — A142

LINCOLN CENTENARY OF BIRTH ISSUE
Plates of 400 subjects in four panes of 100 each

1909 — Wmk. 191 — Perf. 12

367 A141	2c carmine, Feb. 12		5.50	1.75
	bright carmine		5.50	1.75
	Never hinged		9.50	
	On cover			3.75
	Block of 4 (2mm spacing)		22.50	13.50
	Block of 4 (3mm spacing)		22.50	13.00
	P# block of 6, Impt. & small solid star		150.00	
	Never hinged		225.00	
	Double transfer		7.50	2.50

Imperf

368 A141	2c carmine, Feb. 12		21.50	20.00
	Never hinged		37.50	
	On cover			32.50
	Pair		45.00	45.00
	Never hinged		77.50	
	Block of 4 (2mm or 3mm spacing)		90.00	90.00
	Corner margin block of 4		95.00	95.00
	Margin block of 4, arrow		100.00	100.00
	Center line block		130.00	125.00
	P# block of 6, Impt. & small solid star		190.00	—
	Never hinged		275.00	
	Double transfer		42.50	27.50

BLUISH PAPER — Perf. 12

369 A141	2c carmine, Feb.		225.00	260.00
	Never hinged		375.00	
	On cover			425.00
	Block of 4 (2mm or 3mm spacing)		950.00	1,100.
	P# block of 6, Impt. & small solid star		2,900.	
	Never hinged		4,400.	

Earliest known use: Feb. 27, 1909 (dated cancel on off-cover stamp); Mar. 27, 1909 (earliest known use on cover).

ALASKA-YUKON-PACIFIC EXPOSITION ISSUE
Seattle, Wash., June 1 - Oct. 16, 1909
Plates of 280 subjects in four panes of 70 each

1909	Wmk. 191		Perf. 12
370 A142	2c **carmine**, *June 1*	9.00	2.00
	bright carmine	9.00	2.00
	Never hinged	15.00	
	On cover		4.75
	On Expo. card or cover, Expo. station machine canc.		65.00
	On Expo. card or cover, Expo. station duplex handstamp canc.		250.00
	Block of 4	37.50	15.00
	P# block of 6, Impt., T V	225.00	
	Never hinged	340.00	
	Double transfer (5249 UL 8)	11.00	4.50

Imperf

371 A142	2c **carmine**, *June*	26.00	25.00
	Never hinged	45.00	
	On cover		40.00
	On cover, Expo. station machine canc.		*450.00*
	Pair	55.00	55.00
	Never hinged	95.00	
	Block of 4	110.00	110.00
	Corner margin block of 4	115.00	—
	Margin block of 4, arrow	120.00	120.00
	Center line block	165.00	160.00
	P# block of 6, Impt., T V	230.00	—
	Never hinged	350.00	
	Double transfer	40.00	30.00

Earliest known use: June 7, 1909.

HUDSON-FULTON CELEBRATION ISSUE
Tercentenary of the discovery of the Hudson River and the centenary of Robert Fulton's steamship, the "Clermont."

Henry Hudson's "Half Moon" and Fulton's Steamship "Clermont" — A143

Plates of 240 subjects in four panes of 60 each

1909, Sept. 25	Wmk. 191		Perf. 12
372 A143	2c **carmine**	12.50	4.50
	Never hinged	22.00	
	On cover		8.50
	Block of 4	52.50	27.50
	P# block of 6, Impt., T V	290.00	
	Never hinged	440.00	
	Double transfer (5393 and 5394)	15.00	4.75

Imperf

373 A143	2c **carmine**	29.00	25.00
	Never hinged	50.00	
	On cover		37.50
	Pair	60.00	55.00
	Never hinged	105.00	
	Block of 4	120.00	110.00
	Corner margin block of 4	125.00	—
	Margin block of 4, arrow	130.00	115.00
	Center line block	200.00	130.00
	P# block of 6, Impt., T V	250.00	—
	Never hinged	375.00	
	Double transfer (5393 and 5394)	42.50	30.00

REGULAR ISSUE
DESIGNS OF 1908-09 ISSUES

In this issue the Bureau used three groups of plates:

(1) The old standard plates with uniform 2mm spacing throughout (6c, 8c, 10c and 15c values);

(2) Those having an open star in the margin and showing spacings of 2mm and 3mm between stamps (for all values 1c to 10c); and

(3) A third set of plates with uniform spacing of approximately 2¾mm between all stamps. These plates have imprints showing

a. "Bureau of Engraving & Printing," "A" and number.

b. "A" and number only.

c. Number only.

(See above No. 331)

These were used for the 1c, 2c, 3c, 4c and 5c values.

On or about Oct. 1, 1910 the Bureau began using paper watermarked with single-lined letters:

(Actual size of letter)

repeated in rows, this way:

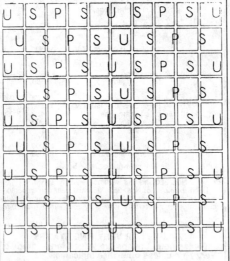

Plates of 400 subjects in four panes of 100 each

1910-11	Wmk. 190		Perf. 12
374 A138	1c **green**, *Nov. 23, 1910*	6.75	.20
	light green	6.75	.20
	dark green	6.75	.20
	Never hinged	11.50	
	On cover		.25
	Block of 4 (2mm spacing)	30.00	3.00
	Block of 4 (3mm spacing)	32.50	2.75
	P# block of 6, Impt., & star	77.50	
	Never hinged	115.00	
	P# block of 6, Impt. & "A"	90.00	—
	Never hinged	135.00	—
	Double transfer	13.50	—
	Cracked plate		—
	Pane of 60	*1,750.*	—
a.	Booklet pane of 6, *Oct. 7, 1910*	150.00	125.00
	Never hinged	225.00	

Earliest known use: Feb. 21, 1911 (No. 374); July 1, 1911 (No. 374a booklet single).

Panes of 60 of No. 374 were regularly issued in Washington, D.C. during Sept. and Oct., 1912. They were made from the six outer vertical rows of imperforate "Star Plate" sheets that had been rejected for use in vending machines on account of the 3mm spacing.

These panes have sheet margins on two adjoining sides and are imperforate along the other two sides. Upper and lower right panes show plate number, star and imprint on both margins; upper and lower left panes show plate number, star and imprint on side margins, but only the imprint on top or bottom margins.

375 A139	2c **carmine**, *Nov. 23, 1910*	6.75	.20
	bright carmine	6.75	.20
	dark carmine	6.75	.20
	Never hinged	11.50	
	On cover		.25
	Block of 4 (2mm spacing)	30.00	1.50
	Block of 4 (3mm spacing)	29.00	1.30
	P# block of 6, Impt. & star	85.00	
	Never hinged	125.00	
	P# block of 6, Impt. & "A"	95.00	
	Never hinged	140.00	
	Cracked plate		—
	Double transfer	11.50	—
	Foreign entry, design of 1c (plate 5299)		*1,000.*
a.	Booklet pane of 6, *Nov. 30, 1910*	95.00	95.00
	Never hinged	160.00	
b.	2c **lake**	*250.00*	
	Never hinged	*425.00*	
c.	Double impression		—

Earliest known use: No. 375, Dec. 29, 1910.

376 A140	3c **deep violet**, type I, *Jan. 16, 1911*	20.00	1.40
	violet	20.00	1.40
	Never hinged	35.00	
	lilac	24.00	1.40
	Never hinged	40.00	
	On cover		7.75
	Block of 4 (2mm spacing)	82.50	10.00
	Block of 4 (3mm spacing)	85.00	9.50
	P# block of 6, Impt. & star	200.00	
	Never hinged	300.00	
	P# block of 6	220.00	
	Never hinged	330.00	

Earliest known use: June 19, 1911.

377 A140	4c **brown**, *Jan. 20, 1911*	32.50	.50
	dark brown	32.50	.50
	orange brown	32.50	.50
	Never hinged	55.00	
	On cover		7.50
	Block of 4 (2mm spacing)	140.00	4.00
	Block of 4 (3mm spacing)	135.00	3.75
	P# block of 6, Impt. & star	250.00	
	Never hinged	375.00	
	P# block of 6	290.00	
	Never hinged	440.00	
	Double transfer		—

Earliest known use: May 25, 1911.

378 A140	5c **blue**, *Jan. 25, 1911*	32.50	.50
	light blue	32.50	.50
	dark blue	32.50	.50
	bright blue	32.50	.50
	Never hinged	55.00	
	On cover		5.25
	Block of 4 (2mm spacing)	140.00	5.75
	Block of 4 (3mm spacing)	135.00	4.75
	P# block of 6, Impt., T V	300.00	
	Never hinged	450.00	
	P# block of 6, Impt. & star	290.00	
	Never hinged	440.00	
	P# block of 6, "A"	340.00	
	Never hinged	500.00	
	P# block of 6	340.00	
	Never hinged	500.00	
	Double transfer	—	—

Earliest known use: Mar. 28, 1911.

379 A140	6c **red orange**, *Jan. 25, 1911*	37.50	.70
	light red orange	37.50	.70
	Never hinged	65.00	
	On cover		13.00
	Block of 4 (2mm spacing)	160.00	10.00
	Block of 4 (3mm spacing)	155.00	9.50
	P# block of 6, Impt., T V	500.00	
	Never hinged	750.00	
	P# block of 6, Impt. & star	440.00	
	Never hinged	660.00	

Earliest known use: May 25, 1911.

380 A140	8c **olive green**, *Feb. 8, 1911*	115.00	12.50
	dark olive green	115.00	12.50
	Never hinged	200.00	
	On cover		45.00
	Block of 4 (2mm spacing)	480.00	77.50
	Block of 4 (3mm spacing)	480.00	75.00
	P# block of 6, Impt., T V	1,100.	
	Never hinged	1,650.	
	P# block of 6, Impt., & star	*1,350.*	
	Never hinged	*2,000.*	

Earliest known use: Aug. 2, 1911.

381 A140	10c **yellow**, *Jan. 24, 1911*	105.00	3.75
	Never hinged	180.00	
	On cover		19.00
	Block of 4 (2mm spacing)	450.00	32.50
	Block of 4 (3mm spacing)	450.00	30.00
	P# block of 6, Impt., T V	1,150.	
	Never hinged	1,750.	
	P# block of 6, Impt. & star	1,100.	
	Never hinged	1,650.	

Earliest known use: Feb. 17, 1911.

382 A140	15c **pale ultramarine**, *Mar. 1, 1911*	275.00	15.00
	Never hinged	475.00	
	On cover		100.00
	Block of 4	1,150.	110.00
	P# block of 6, Impt., T V	2,400.	
	Never hinged	3,600.	

Earliest known use: Aug. 31, 1912.

Nos. 374-382 (9)		631.00	34.75

1910, Dec.			Imperf.
383 A138	1c **green**	2.50	2.00
	dark green	2.50	2.00
	yellowish green	2.50	2.00
	bright green	2.50	2.00
	Never hinged	4.25	
	On cover		5.00
	Pair	5.25	4.50
	Never hinged		
	Block of 4 (2mm or 3mm spacing)	10.50	13.00
	Corner margin block of 4	11.50	
	Margin block of 4, arrow	12.00	13.50
	Center line block	24.00	16.00
	P# block of 6, Impt., & star	45.00	—
	Never hinged	67.50	
	P# block of 6, Impt. & "A"	82.50	—
	Never hinged	125.00	
	Double transfer	6.50	—

Earliest known use: Mar. 1, 1911.

Rosette plate
crack on head

384 A139	2c **carmine**	4.00	2.50
	light carmine	4.00	2.50
	Never hinged	6.75	
	dark carmine	55.00	12.50
	On cover		3.50
	Horizontal pair	11.50	7.50
	Never hinged	20.00	
	Vertical pair	8.50	6.00
	Never hinged	14.50	
	Block of 4 (2mm or 3mm		
	spacing)	25.00	15.00
	Corner margin block of 4	27.50	20.00
	Margin block of 4, arrow	27.50	21.00
	Center line block	50.00	50.00
	P# block of 6, Impt. & star	130.00	—
	Never hinged	200.00	
	P# block of 6, Impt. & "A"	170.00	—
	Never hinged	260.00	
	Foreign entry, design of 1c		
	(plate 5299)	*1,500.*	—
	Double transfer	7.50	—
	Rosette plate crack on head	100.00	—

The existence of the foreign entry on No. 384 has been questioned by specialists. The editors would like to see evidence of the existence of the item, either unused or used.

Earliest known use: Dec. 23, 1910.

COIL STAMPS

1910, Nov. 1		Perf. 12 Horizontally	
385 A138	1c **green**	32.50	15.00
	dark green	32.50	15.00
	Never hinged	55.00	
	On cover		40.00
	Pair	87.50	50.00
	Never hinged	150.00	
	Guide line pair	400.00	*325.00*
	Never hinged	675.00	

Earliest known use: Jan. 9, 1911.

386 A139	2c **carmine**	62.50	20.00
	light carmine	62.50	20.00
	Never hinged	105.00	
	On cover		52.50
	Pair	225.00	100.00
	Never hinged	375.00	
	Guide line pair	775.00	*350.00*
	Never hinged	1,300.	

Earliest known use: Dec. 18, 1910.

1910-11		Perf. 12 Vertically	
387 A138	1c **green**, *Nov. 1, 1910*	140.00	50.00
	Never hinged	240.00	
	On cover		75.00
	Pair (2mm spacing)	340.00	140.00
	Never hinged	575.00	
	Pair (3mm spacing)	350.00	135.00
	Never hinged	600.00	
	Guide line pair	600.00	*400.00*
	Never hinged	1,050.	

Earliest known use: Nov. 5, 1910.

388 A139	2c **carmine**, *Nov. 1, 1910*	875.00	350.00
	Never hinged	1,500.	
	On cover		*1,250.*
	Pair (2mm spacing)	2,500.	*1,000.*
	Never hinged	4,250.	
	Pair (3mm spacing)	2,600.	*1,050.*
	Never hinged	4,400.	
	Guide line pair	5,750.	*4,750.*

Stamps offered as No. 388 frequently are privately perforated examples of No. 384, or copies of No. 375 with top and/or bottom perfs trimmed.

Earliest known use: Jan. 4, 1911.

389 A140	3c **deep vio.**, type I, *Jan. 24, 1911*	57,500.	11,500.
	Never hinged	85,000.	
	On cover		24,000.
	Pair	125,000.	

No. 389 is valued in the grade of fine.
This is the rarest coil, only a small supply being used at Orangeburg, N.Y.
Stamps offered as No. 389 sometimes are examples of No. 376 with top and/or bottom perfs trimmed. Expertization by competent authorities is recommended.

Earliest known use: Mar. 8, 1911.

1910		Perf. 8½ Horizontally	
390 A138	1c **green**, *Dec. 12, 1910*	4.75	6.00
	dark green	4.75	6.00
	Never hinged	8.00	
	On cover		10.00
	Pair	11.00	22.50
	Never hinged	19.00	
	Guide line pair	35.00	65.00
	Never hinged	62.50	
	Double transfer	—	—

Earliest known use: Oct. 19, 1911.

391 A139	2c **carmine**, *Dec. 23, 1910*	37.50	12.50
	light carmine	37.50	12.50
	Never hinged	65.00	
	On cover		27.50
	Pair	100.00	50.00
	Never hinged	170.00	
	Guide line pair	240.00	*225.00*
	Never hinged	425.00	

Earliest known use: May 3, 1911.

1910-13		Perf. 8½ Vertically	
392 A138	1c **green**, *Dec. 12, 1910*	22.00	19.00
	dark green	22.00	19.00
	Never hinged	37.50	
	On cover		52.50
	Pair	60.00	*75.00*
	Never hinged	100.00	
	Guide line pair	165.00	*200.00*
	Never hinged	290.00	
	Double transfer	—	—

Earliest known use: Mar. 24, 1911.

393 A139	2c **carmine**, *Dec. 16, 1910*	42.50	7.75
	dark carmine	42.50	7.75
	Never hinged	72.50	
	On cover		22.50
	Pair	115.00	30.00
	Never hinged	195.00	
	Guide line pair	275.00	120.00
	Never hinged	475.00	

Earliest known use: Dec. 27, 1910.

394 A140	3c **deep violet**, type I, *Sept. 1911*	52.50	47.50
	violet	52.50	47.50
	red violet	52.50	47.50
	Never hinged	90.00	
	On cover		105.00
	Pair (2mm spacing)	135.00	135.00
	Never hinged	230.00	
	Pair (3mm spacing)	130.00	125.00
	Never hinged	225.00	
	Guide line pair	380.00	*325.00*
	Never hinged	675.00	

Earliest known use: Sept. 18, 1911.

395 A140	4c **brown**, *Apr. 15, 1912*	52.50	42.50
	dark brown	52.50	42.50
	Never hinged	90.00	
	On cover		100.00
	Pair (2mm spacing)	135.00	120.00
	Never hinged	230.00	
	Pair (3mm spacing)	130.00	110.00
	Never hinged	225.00	
	Guide line pair	380.00	*350.00*
	Never hinged	675.00	

Earliest known use: June 21, 1912.

396 A140	5c **blue**, *Mar. 1913*	52.50	42.50
	dark blue	52.50	42.50
	Never hinged	90.00	
	On cover		100.00
	Pair	135.00	110.00
	Never hinged	230.00	
	Guide line pair	380.00	*475.00*
	Never hinged	675.00	

Earliest known use: May 20, 1913.

PANAMA-PACIFIC EXPOSITION ISSUE
San Francisco, Cal., Feb. 20 - Dec. 4, 1915

Vasco Nunez de
Balboa — A144

Pedro Miguel Locks,
Panama Canal — A145

Golden Gate — A146

Discovery of San
Francisco Bay — A147

Exposition Station Cancellation.

Plates of 280 subjects in four panes of 70 each.

1913		Wmk. 190	Perf. 12	
397 A144	1c **green**, *Jan. 1, 1913*	17.50	1.50
	deep green	17.50	1.50
	yellowish green	17.50	1.50
	Never hinged	30.00	
	On cover		3.00
	On Expo. card, Expo. station 1915 machine cancel		*30.00*
	Pair on cover, Expo. station 1915 duplex handstamp cancel		*150.00*
	Block of 4	72.50	10.00
	P# block of 6	175.00	
	Never hinged	275.00	
	Double transfer	22.50	2.50
398 A145	2c **carmine**, *Jan. 1913*	21.00	.50
	deep carmine	21.00	.50
	Never hinged	36.00	
	brown lake	—	
	On cover		1.20
	On cover, Expo. station 1915 machine cancel		*75.00*
	On cover, Expo. station 1915 duplex handstamp cancel		*250.00*
	Block of 4	90.00	6.00
	P# block of 6	275.00	
	Never hinged	425.00	
	Double transfer	40.00	2.00
a.	2c **carmine lake**	575.00	
	Never hinged	975.00	

Earliest known use: Jan. 17, 1913.

399 A146	5c **blue**, *Jan. 1, 1913*	75.00	9.50
	dark blue	75.00	9.50
	Never hinged	130.00	
	On cover		27.50
	On cover, Expo. station 1915 machine cancel		*300.00*
	Block of 4	325.00	67.50
	P# block of 6	1,900.	
	Never hinged	2,900.	
400 A147	10c **orange yellow**, *Jan. 1, 1913*	130.00	20.00
	Never hinged	225.00	
	On cover		55.00
	On cover, Expo. station 1915 machine cancel		*500.00*
	Block of 4	525.00	140.00
	P# block of 6	2,400.	
	Never hinged	3,600.	
400A A147	10c **orange**, *Aug. 1913*	210.00	16.00
	Never hinged	360.00	
	On cover		65.00
	On cover, Expo. station 1915 machine cancel		*550.00*
	Block of 4	875.00	100.00
	P# block of 6	11,500.	
	Never hinged	17,500.	

Earliest known use: Nov. 20, 1913.

Nos. 397-400A (5)		453.50	47.50
Nos. 397-400A, never hinged		781.00	

1914-15		Perf. 10	
401 A144	1c **green**, *Dec. 1914*	25.00	5.50
	dark green	25.00	5.50
	Never hinged	42.50	
	On cover		16.00
	On Expo. card, Expo. station 1915 machine cancel		*75.00*
	Block of 4	105.00	37.50
	P# block of 6	340.00	
	Never hinged	525.00	

Earliest known use: Dec. 21, 1914.

402 A145	2c **carmine**, *Jan. 1915*	75.00	1.50
	deep carmine	75.00	1.50
	red	75.00	1.50
	Never hinged	130.00	
	On cover		5.50
	On cover, Expo. station 1915 machine cancel		*150.00*
	On cover, Expo. station 1915 duplex handstamp cancel		*450.00*
	Block of 4	325.00	15.00
	P# block of 6	2,000.	
	Never hinged	3,000.	

Earliest known use: Jan. 13, 1915.

403 A146	5c **blue**, *Feb. 1915*	175.00	15.00
	dark blue	175.00	15.00
	Never hinged	300.00	
	On cover		55.00
	On cover, Expo. station 1915 machine cancel		*450.00*
	Block of 4	750.00	95.00
	P# block of 6	4,000.	
	Never hinged	6,000.	

Earliest known use: Feb. 6, 1915.

404 A147	10c **orange**, *July 1915*	925.00	62.50
	Never hinged	1,600.	
	On cover		160.00
	On cover, Expo. station 1915 machine cancel		*600.00*

Block of 4	*3,900.*	400.00	
P# block of 6	*12,500.*		
Never hinged	—		

Earliest known use: Aug. 27, 1915.

Nos. 401-404 (4)	1,200.	84.50
Nos. 401-404, never hinged	2,073.	

VALUES FOR VERY FINE STAMPS
Please note: Stamps are valued in the grade of Very Fine unless otherwise indicated.

REGULAR ISSUE

Washington — A140

The plates for this and later issues were the so-called "A" plates with uniform spacing of 2¾mm between stamps.

Plates of 400 subjects in four panes of 100 each for all values 1c to 50c inclusive.

Plates of 200 subjects in two panes of 100 each for $1 and some of the 50c (No. 422) denomination.

1912-14		**Wmk. 190**	*Perf. 12*	
405	A140 1c **green**, *Feb. 1912*	6.00	.20
	light green	6.00	.20
	dark green	6.00	.20
	yellowish green	6.00	.20
	Never hinged	10.50	
	On cover		.25
	Block of 4	26.00	1.20
	P# block of 6, Impt. & "A"	105.00	
	Never hinged	160.00	
	P# block of 6, "A"	92.50	
	Never hinged	140.00	
	P# block of 6	87.50	
	Never hinged	135.00	
	Cracked plate	14.00	—
	Double transfer	7.00	—
a.	Vert. pair, imperf. horiz.	650.00	
b.	Booklet pane of 6, *1912*	60.00	50.00
	Never hinged	100.00	

Earliest known use: No. 405, Feb. 12, 1912; No. 405b, Jan. 16, 1912.

TYPE I

TYPE I

TWO CENTS

Type I. There is one shading line in the first curve of the ribbon above the left "2" and one in the second curve of the ribbon above the right "2".

The button of the toga has only a faint outline.

The top line of the toga rope, from the button to the front of the throat, is also very faint.

The shading lines of the face terminate in front of the ear with little or no joining, to form a lock of hair.

Used on both flat plate and rotary press printings.

406	A140 2c **carmine**, type I, *Feb. 1912*	6.00	.20
	bright carmine	6.00	.20
	dark carmine	6.50	.20
	Never hinged	10.50	
	On cover		.25
	Block of 4	26.00	1.00
	P# block of 6, Impt. & "A"	135.00	
	Never hinged	200.00	
	P# block of 6, "A"	125.00	
	Never hinged	190.00	
	P# block of 6	110.00	
	Never hinged	165.00	
	Margin block of 6, Electrolytic, (Pl. 6023)	*975.00*	
	Never hinged	*1,450.*	
	Double transfer	8.25	—
a.	Booklet pane of 6, *Feb. 8, 1912*	60.00	60.00
	Never hinged	100.00	
b.	Double impression		
c.	2c **lake**, type I	*350.00*	—

Earliest known use: No. 406, Feb. 15, 1912; No. 406a, May 2, 1912.

407	A140 7c **black**, *Apr. 1914*	80.00	11.00
	grayish black	80.00	11.00
	intense black	80.00	11.00
	Never hinged	135.00	
	On cover		75.00

Block of 4	350.00	60.00
P# block of 6	1,200.	
Never hinged	1,800.	

Earliest known use: May 1, 1914.

1912			*Imperf.*
408	A140 1c **green**, *Mar. 1912*	1.10	.55
	yellowish green	1.10	.55
	dark green	1.10	.55
	Never hinged	1.90	
	On cover		1.10
	Pair	2.25	1.40
	Never hinged	3.90	
	Block of 4	4.50	2.80
	Corner margin block of 4	4.60	2.90
	Margin block of 4, arrow	4.75	3.00
	Center line block	10.00	10.00
	P# block of 6, Impt. & "A," T, B or L	47.50	—
	Never hinged	70.00	
	P# block of 6, Impt. & "A," at right	550.00	
	Never hinged	825.00	
	P# block of 6, "A"	27.50	—
	Never hinged	40.00	
	P# block of 6	19.00	—
	Never hinged	27.50	
	Double transfer	2.40	1.00
	Cracked plate	—	

Earliest known use: Mar. 27, 1912.

409	A140 2c **carmine**, type I, *Feb. 1912*	1.30	.60
	deep carmine	1.30	.60
	scarlet	1.30	.60
	Never hinged	2.25	
	On cover		1.10
	Pair	2.75	1.40
	Never hinged	4.75	
	Block of 4	5.50	2.80
	Corner margin block of 4	5.75	
	Margin block of 4, arrow	6.00	3.25
	Center line block	11.00	10.00
	P# block of 6, "A"	50.00	—
	Never hinged	75.00	
	P# block of 6, "A"	47.50	—
	Never hinged	70.00	
	P# block of 6	37.50	—
	Never hinged	55.00	
	Cracked plate (Plates 7580, 7582)	14.00	—

In December, 1914, the Post Office at Kansas City, Missouri, had on hand a stock of imperforate sheets of 400 of stamps Nos. 408 and 409, formerly sold for use in vending machines, but not then in demand. In order to make them salable, they were rouletted with ordinary tracing wheels and were sold over the counter with official approval of the Post Office Department given January 5, 1915.

These stamps were sold until the supply was exhausted. Except for one full sheet of 400 of each value, all were cut into panes of 100 before being rouletted and sold. They are known as "Kansas City Roulettes". Value, authenticated blocks of 4, 1c $100, 2c $200.

COIL STAMPS

1912			*Perf. 8½ Horizontally*
410	A140 1c **green**, *Mar. 1912*	6.00	4.00
	dark green	6.00	4.00
	Never hinged	10.50	
	On cover		7.75
	Pair	15.00	10.00
	Never hinged	25.00	
	Guide line pair	30.00	25.00
	Never hinged	52.50	
	Double transfer	—	

Earliest known use: Apr. 17, 1912.

411	A140 2c **carmine**, type I, *Mar. 1912*	10.00	3.75
	deep carmine	10.00	3.75
	Never hinged	17.00	
	On cover		11.50
	Pair	25.00	11.00
	Never hinged	42.50	
	Guide line pair	55.00	35.00
	Never hinged	92.50	
	Double transfer	12.50	—

Earliest known use: May 1, 1912.

			Perf. 8½ Vertically
412	A140 1c **green**, *Mar. 18, 1912*	25.00	5.50
	deep green	25.00	5.50
	Never hinged	42.50	
	On cover		14.50
	Pair	60.00	19.00
	Never hinged	100.00	
	Guide line pair	120.00	65.00
	Never hinged	200.00	

Earliest known use: May 31, 1912.

413	A140 2c **carmine**, type I, *Mar. 1912*	42.50	1.10
	dark carmine	42.50	1.10
	Never hinged	72.50	
	On cover		7.50
	Pair	90.00	8.00
	Never hinged	155.00	
	Guide line pair	240.00	30.00
	Never hinged	410.00	
	Double transfer	45.00	

Earliest known use: Mar. 21, 1912.

Plate Blocks

Scott values for plate blocks printed from flat plates are for very fine side and bottom positions. Top position plate blocks with full wide selvage sell for more.

Franklin — A148

1912-14		**Wmk. 190**	*Perf. 12*	
414	A148 8c **pale olive green**, *Feb. 1912*	45.00	1.25
	olive green	45.00	1.25
	Never hinged	77.50	
	On cover		15.00
	Block of 4	200.00	14.00
	P# block of 6, Impt. & "A"	475.00	
	Never hinged	725.00	
415	A148 9c **salmon red**, *Apr. 1914*	55.00	12.50
	rose red	55.00	12.50
	Never hinged	95.00	
	On cover		50.00
	Block of 4	240.00	90.00
	P# block of 6	650.00	
	Never hinged	975.00	

Earliest known use: May 1, 1914.

416	A148 10c **orange yellow**, *Jan. 1912*	45.00	.40
	yellow	45.00	.40
	Never hinged	77.50	
	On cover		2.70
	Block of 4	200.00	2.50
	P# block of 6, Impt. & "A"	500.00	
	Never hinged	750.00	
	P# block of 6, "A"	550.00	
	Never hinged	825.00	
	Double transfer	—	—
a.	10c **brown yellow**	*500.00*	
	Never hinged	*850.00*	

Earliest known use: Feb. 12, 1912.

417	A148 12c **claret brown**, *Apr. 1914*	50.00	4.25
	deep claret brown	50.00	4.25
	Never hinged	85.00	
	On cover		25.00
	Block of 4	225.00	27.50
	P# block of 6	625.00	
	Never hinged	925.00	
	Double transfer	55.00	
	Triple transfer	72.50	

Earliest known use: May 5, 1914.

418	A148 15c **gray**, *Feb. 1912*	85.00	3.50
	dark gray	85.00	3.50
	Never hinged	145.00	
	On cover		17.50
	Block of 4	350.00	27.50
	P# block of 6, Impt. & "A"	700.00	
	Never hinged	1,050.	
	P# block of 6, "A"	775.00	
	Never hinged	1,175.	
	P# block of 6	850.00	
	Never hinged	1,275.	
	Double transfer	—	

Earliest known use: Apr. 26, 1912.

419	A148 20c **ultramarine**, *Apr. 1914*	200.00	15.00
	dark ultramarine	200.00	15.00
	Never hinged	350.00	
	On cover		*150.00*
	Block of 4	825.00	100.00
	P# block of 6	2,000.	
	Never hinged	3,000.	

Earliest known use: May 1, 1914.

420	A148 30c **orange red**, *Apr. 1914*	125.00	15.00
	dark orange red	125.00	15.00
	Never hinged	220.00	
	On cover		*250.00*
	Block of 4	525.00	100.00
	P# block of 6	1,500.	
	Never hinged	2,250.	

Earliest known use: May 1, 1914.

421	A148 50c **violet**, *1914*	425.00	17.50
	bright violet	425.00	17.50
	Never hinged	725.00	
	On cover		*2,000.*
	Block of 4	1,800.	110.00
	P# block of 6	10,000.	
	Never hinged	15,000.	

Earliest known use: May 1, 1914.

No. 421 almost always has an offset of the frame lines on the back under the gum. Nos. 422 does not have this offset.

1912, Feb. 12			**Wmk. 191**	
422	A148 50c **violet**	250.00	15.00
	Never hinged	425.00	
	On cover		*2,000.*
	Block of 4	1,050.	105.00
	Margin block of 4, arrow, R or L	1,100.	
	P# block of 6, Impt. & "A"	*4,750.*	
	Never hinged	*7,250.*	

Earliest known use: July 15, 1915.

423 A148 $1 **violet brown**   525.00   60.00
    Never hinged   900.00
    On cover   *7,000.*
    Block of 4   2,200.   400.00
    Margin block of 4, arrow, R or
      L   2,250.
    P# block of 6, Impt. & "A"   12,000.
      Never hinged   *17,500.*
    Double transfer (5782 L 66)   550.00   —

Earliest known use: July 15, 1915.

During the United States occupation of Vera Cruz, Mexico, from April to November, 1914, letters sent from there show Provisional Postmarks.
For other listings of perforated stamps of design A148, see:
Nos. 431-440 - Single line wmk. Perf. 10
Nos. 460 - Double line wmk. Perf. 10
Nos. 470-478 - Unwmkd. Perf. 10
Nos. 508-518 - Unwmkd. Perf. 11

Plates of 400 subjects in four panes of 100 each.

6568 COIL STAMPS

Type of plate number and imprint used for the 12 special 1c and 2c plates designed for the production of coil stamps. Note: Plate No. and "COIL STAMPS" are on one line.

1913-15   **Wmk. 190**   **Perf. 10**
424 A140 1c **green,** *Sept. 5, 1914*   2.30   .20
    bright green   2.30   .20
    deep green   2.30   .20
    yellowish green   2.30   .20
    Never hinged   4.00
    On cover   .25
    Block of 4   9.25   1.00
    P# block of 6   40.00
      Never hinged   60.00
    Block of ten with imprint
      "COIL STAMPS" and
      number (6581-82, 85, 89)   140.00
        Never hinged   210.00
    Cracked plate   —   —
    Double transfer   4.50   —
    Experimental bureau pre-
      cancel, New Orleans
a.   Perf. 12x10   *2,750.*   *2,500.*
    Block of 4   *12,500.*
b.   Perf. 10x12   *2,250.*
c.   Vert. pair, imperf. horiz.   *1,500.*   750.00
d.   Booklet pane of 6   4.75   3.25
      Never hinged   7.50
e.   As "d," imperf.   *1,600.*
f.   Vert. pair, imperf. betw. and with
      straight edge at top   *5,500.*

Most copies of No. 424b are precanceled Dayton, Ohio, to which the value applies.
All known examples of No. 424e are without gum.

Earliest known use: Oct. 21, 1914 (No. 424); Dec. 20, 1913 (No. 424d booklet single).

425 A140 2c **rose red,** type I, *Sept. 5,*
      1914   2.20   .20
    dark rose red   2.20   .20
    carmine rose   2.20   .20
    carmine   2.20   .20
    dark carmine   2.20   .20
    scarlet   2.20   .20
    red   2.20   .20
    Never hinged   3.75
    On cover   .25
    Block of 4   9.00   .90
    P# block of 6   27.50
      Never hinged   42.50
    Block of 10 with imprint
      "COIL STAMPS" and
      number (6568, 70-72)   150.00
        Never hinged   225.00
    Cracked plate   9.50   —
    Double transfer   —   —
c.   Perf. 10x12   —
d.   Perf. 12x10   *6,500.*   *3,500.*
e.   Booklet pane of 6   16.00   *15.00*
      Never hinged   25.00

The aniline inks used on some printings of Nos. 425, 426 and 435a caused a pink tinge to permeate the paper and appear on the back. These are called "pink backs."

Earliest known use: Nov. 16, 1914 (No. 425); Jan. 6, 1914 (No. 425e booklet single).

426 A140 3c **deep violet,** type I, *Sept.*
      18, 1914   14.00   1.25
    violet   14.00   1.25
    bright violet   14.00   1.25
    reddish violet   14.00   1.25
    Never hinged   24.00
    On cover   3.25
    Block of 4   57.50   7.75
    P# block of 6   180.00
      Never hinged   275.00

See "pink backs" note after No. 425.

427 A140 4c **brown,** *Sept. 7, 1914*   35.00   .50
    dark brown   35.00   .50
    orange brown   35.00   .50
    yellowish brown   35.00   .50
    Never hinged   60.00
    On cover   5.25

    Block of 4   145.00   4.75
    P# block of 6   500.00
      Never hinged   750.00
    Double transfer   45.00   —
428 A140 5c **blue,** *Sept. 14, 1914*   32.50   .50
    bright blue   32.50   .50
    dark blue   32.50   .50
    indigo blue   32.50   .50
    Never hinged   55.00
    On cover   2.75
    Block of 4   135.00   3.50
    P# block of 6   400.00
      Never hinged   600.00
a.   Perf. 12x10   *6,500.*

Earliest known use: Dec. 2, 1914.

429 A140 6c **red orange,** *Sept. 28,*
      1914   47.50   1.40
    deep red orange   47.50   1.40
    pale red orange   47.50   1.40
    Never hinged   80.00
    On cover   9.00
    Block of 4 (2mm spacing)   200.00   15.00
    Block of 4 (3mm spacing)   195.00   14.00
    P# block of 6, Impt. & star   450.00
      Never hinged   675.00
    P# block of 6   550.00
      Never hinged   825.00
430 A140 7c **black,** *Sept. 10, 1914*   85.00   4.00
    gray black   85.00   4.00
    intense black   85.00   4.00
    Never hinged   145.00
    On cover   37.50
    Block of 4   375.00   32.50
    P# block of 6   975.00
      Never hinged   1,450.

Earliest known use: June 19, 1915.

431 A148 8c **pale olive green,** *Sept. 26,*
      1914   35.00   1.50
    olive green   35.00   1.50
    Never hinged   60.00
    On cover   8.00
    Block of 4   145.00   12.50
    P# block of 6, Impt. & "A"   475.00
      Never hinged   700.00
    P# block of 6, "A"   550.00
      Never hinged   825.00
    Double impression   —   —
    Double transfer   —   —

Earliest known use: Feb. 24, 1915.

432 A148 9c **salmon red,** *Oct. 6, 1914*   50.00   7.50
    dark salmon red   50.00   7.50
    Never hinged   85.00
    On cover   27.50
    Block of 4   210.00   50.00
    P# block of 6   725.00
      Never hinged   1,075.

Earliest known use: Feb. 25, 1916.

433 A148 10c **orange yellow,** *Sept. 9,*
      1914   47.50   .40
    golden yellow   47.50   .40
    Never hinged   80.00
    On cover   7.75
    Block of 4   200.00   2.50
    P# block of 6, Impt. & "A"   675.00
      Never hinged   1,000.
    P# block of 6, "A"   975.00
      Never hinged   1,450.
    P# block of 6   850.00
      Never hinged   1,275.

Earliest known use: Nov. 13, 1914.

434 A148 11c **dark green,** *Aug. 11, 1915*   22.50   7.50
    bluish green   22.50   7.50
    Never hinged   40.00
    On cover   25.00
    Block of 4   95.00   42.50
    P# block of 6   250.00
      Never hinged   375.00

Earliest known use: Sept. 8, 1915.

435 A148 12c **claret brown,** *Sept. 10,*
      1914   26.00   4.00
    deep claret brown   26.00   4.00
    Never hinged   45.00
    On cover   17.50
    Block of 4   110.00   32.50
    P# block of 6   300.00
      Never hinged   450.00
    Double transfer   32.50   —
    Triple transfer   37.50   —
a.   12c **copper red**   29.00   4.00
      Never hinged   50.00
    On cover   19.00
    Block of 4   120.00   32.50
    P# block of 6   330.00
      Never hinged   500.00

All so-called vertical pairs, imperf. between, have at least one perf. hole or "blind perfs" between the stamps.
See "pink backs" note after No. 425.

Earliest known use: Feb. 24, 1915.

437 A148 15c **gray,** *Sept. 16, 1914*   125.00   7.25
    dark gray   125.00   7.25
    Never hinged   210.00
    On cover   52.50
    Block of 4   525.00   52.50
    P# block of 6, Impt. & "A"   1,100.
      Never hinged   1,650.
    P# block of 6, "A"   1,250.
      Never hinged   1,900.
    P# block of 6   1,150.
      Never hinged   1,750.

Earliest known use: Dec. 22, 1915.

---

438 A148 20c **ultramarine,** *Sept. 19,*
      1914   210.00   4.00
    dark ultramarine   210.00   4.00
    Never hinged   360.00
    On cover   150.00
    Block of 4   875.00   32.50
    P# block of 6   3,400.
      Never hinged   *5,000.*

Earliest known use: Nov. 28, 1914.

439 A148 30c **orange red,** *Sept. 19,*
      1914   250.00   16.00
    dark orange red   250.00   16.00
    Never hinged   425.00
    On cover   250.00
    Block of 4   1,050.   120.00
    P# block of 6   *4,250.*
      Never hinged   *6,250.*
440 A148 50c **violet,** *Dec. 10, 1915*   550.00   16.00
    Never hinged   950.00
    On cover   *1,750.*
    Block of 4   2,250.   110.00
    P# block of 6   *15,000.*
      Never hinged
    Nos. 424-440 (16)   1,534.   72.20

COIL STAMPS

1914   **Perf. 10 Horizontally**
441 A140 1c **green,** *Nov. 14, 1914*   1.00   1.00
    deep green   1.00   1.00
    Never hinged   1.70
    On cover   2.25
    Pair   2.75   3.75
      Never hinged   4.40
    Guide line pair   7.75   7.00
      Never hinged   12.50
442 A140 2c **carmine,** type I, *July 22, 1914*   8.00   6.00
    deep carmine   8.00   6.00
    Never hinged   13.50
    On cover   15.00
    Pair   20.00   22.50
      Never hinged   32.50
    Guide line pair   47.50   *75.00*
      Never hinged   75.00

1914   **Perf. 10 Vertically**
443 A140 1c **green,** *May 29, 1914*   22.50   5.00
    deep green   22.50   5.00
    Never hinged   37.50
    On cover   13.00
    Pair   67.50   19.00
      Never hinged   115.00
    Guide line pair   140.00   65.00
      Never hinged   240.00

Earliest known use: June 19, 1914.

444 A140 2c **carmine,** type I, *Apr. 25, 1914*   35.00   1.50
    deep carmine   35.00   1.50
    red   35.00   1.50
    Never hinged   60.00
    lake   —
    On cover   11.00
    Pair   105.00   6.00
      Never hinged   180.00
    Guide line pair   250.00   22.50
      Never hinged   425.00

Earliest known use: May 20, 1914.

445 A140 3c **violet,** type I, *Dec. 18, 1914*   220.00   125.00
    deep violet   220.00   125.00
    Never hinged   375.00
    On cover   225.00
    Pair   550.00   500.00
      Never hinged   950.00
    Guide line pair   1,250.   *1,500.*
      Never hinged   2,150.

Earliest known use: July 1, 1916.

446 A140 4c **brown,** *Oct. 2, 1914*   120.00   42.50
    Never hinged   205.00
    On cover   115.00
    Pair   310.00   *250.00*
      Never hinged   525.00
    Guide line pair   700.00   *650.00*
      Never hinged   1,200.

Earliest known use: Aug. 4, 1915.

447 A140 5c **blue,** *July 30, 1914*   42.50   27.50
    Never hinged   72.50
    On cover   57.50
    Pair   110.00   *225.00*
      Never hinged   190.00
    Guide line pair   250.00   *500.00*
      Never hinged   425.00

Earliest known use: May 9, 1916.

ROTARY PRESS STAMPS

The Rotary Press Stamps are printed from plates that are curved to fit around a cylinder. This curvature produces stamps that are slightly larger, either horizontally or vertically, than those printed from flat plates. Designs of stamps from flat plates measure about 18½-19mm wide by 22mm high.

When the impressions are placed sidewise on the curved plates the designs are 19½-20mm wide; when they are placed vertically the designs are 22½ to 23mm high. A line of color (not a guide line) shows where the curved plates meet or join on the press.

Rotary Press Coil Stamps were printed from plates of 170 subjects for stamps coiled sidewise, and from plates of 150 subjects for stamps coiled endwise.

Double paper varieties of Rotary Press stamps are not listed in this catalogue. Collectors are referred to the note on "Rotary Press Double Paper" in the "Information for Collectors" in the front of the catalogue.

ROTARY PRESS COIL STAMPS
Stamp designs: 18½-19x22½mm

1915   *Perf. 10 Horizontally*

448	A140 1c **green,** *Dec. 12, 1915*	6.00	3.25
	light green	6.00	3.25
	Never hinged	9.50	
	On cover		7.50
	Pair	15.00	8.00
	Never hinged	25.00	
	Joint line pair	40.00	27.50
	Never hinged	67.50	

TYPE II

TWO CENTS.
Type II. Shading lines in ribbons as on type I.
The toga button, rope and rope shading lines are heavy.
The shading lines of the face at the lock of hair end in a strong vertical curved line.
Used on rotary press printings only.

TYPE III

Type III. Two lines of shading in the curves of the ribbons. Other characteristics similar to type II.
Used on rotary press printings only.

449	A140 2c **red,** type I, *1915*	2,600.	500.00
	Never hinged	4,000.	
	carmine rose, type I	—	
	On cover, type I		1,050.
	Pair, type I	5,750.	3,000.
	Never hinged	9,000.	
	Joint line pair, type I	15,000.	7,000.
	Never hinged	23,500.	

Earliest known use: Oct. 29, 1915 (on cover front or dated cancel on off-cover stamp); Dec. 21, 1915 (on full cover).

450	A140 2c **carmine,** type III, *1915*	9.50	3.00
	carmine rose, type III	9.50	3.00
	red, type III	9.50	3.00
	Never hinged	16.00	
	On cover, type III		8.00
	Pair, type III	24.00	9.00
	Never hinged	40.00	
	Joint line pair, type III	75.00	35.00
	Never hinged	125.00	

Earliest known use: Dec. 21, 1915.

1914-16   *Perf. 10 Vertically*
Stamp designs: 19½-20x22mm

452	A140 1c **green,** *Nov. 11, 1914*	10.00	2.00
	Never hinged	17.00	
	On cover		3.75
	Pair	25.00	6.00
	Never hinged	42.50	
	Joint line pair	75.00	17.50
	Never hinged	130.00	

Earliest known use: Nov. 25, 1914.

453	A140 2c **carmine rose,** type I, *July 3, 1914*	140.00	4.25
	Never hinged	240.00	
	On cover, type I		11.00
	Pair, type I	325.00	12.50
	Never hinged	600.00	
	Joint line pair, type I	725.00	55.00
	Never hinged	1,250.	
	Cracked plate, type I	—	

Earliest known use: Oct. 6, 1914.

454	A140 2c **red,** type II, *June, 1915*	82.50	10.00
	carmine, type II	82.50	10.00
	Never hinged	140.00	
	On cover, type II		37.50
	Pair, type II	180.00	35.00
	Never hinged	300.00	
	Joint line pair, type II	425.00	140.00
	Never hinged	725.00	

Earliest known use: July 7, 1915.

455	A140 2c **carmine,** type III, *Dec. 1915*	8.50	1.00
	carmine rose, type III	8.50	1.00
	Never hinged	14.50	
	On cover, type III		2.25
	Pair, type III	21.00	3.00
	Never hinged	36.00	
	Joint line pair, type III	50.00	9.00
	Never hinged	85.00	

Earliest known use: Dec. 15, 1915.

Fraudulently altered copies of Type III (Nos. 455, 488, 492 and 540) have had one line of shading scraped off to make them resemble Type II (Nos. 454, 487, 491 and 539).

456	A140 3c **violet,** type I, *Feb. 2, 1916*	240.00	90.00
	deep violet	240.00	90.00
	red violet	240.00	90.00
	Never hinged	400.00	
	On cover		200.00
	Pair	575.00	350.00
	Never hinged	975.00	
	Joint line pair	1,200.	900.00
	Never hinged	2,000.	

Earliest known use: Apr. 13, 1916.

457	A140 4c **brown,** *1915*	25.00	17.50
	light brown	25.00	17.50
	Never hinged	42.50	
	On cover		42.50
	Pair	60.00	50.00
	Never hinged	100.00	
	Joint line pair	150.00	110.00
	Never hinged	250.00	
	Cracked plate	35.00	—

No. 457 was shipped to Annapolis, Md. in late 1915. At least two covers are known with earliest known postmark of Nov. 5, 1915.

458	A140 5c **blue,** *Mar. 9, 1916*	30.00	17.50
	Never hinged	50.00	
	On cover		42.50
	Pair	72.50	50.00
	Never hinged	120.00	
	Joint line pair	180.00	110.00
	Never hinged	300.00	
	Double transfer	—	—

Earliest known use: Apr. 6, 1916.

Horizontal Coil

1914, June 30   *Imperf.*

459	A140 2c **carmine,** type I	250.	*950.*
	Never hinged	375.	
	On cover		—
	Pair	525.	*2,750.*
	Never hinged	775.	
	Joint line pair	1,050.	*9,500.*
	Never hinged	1,600.	

The existence of No. 459 on cover has been questioned by specialists. The editors would like to see evidence of such a cover.

Most line pairs of No. 459 are creased. Value is for pair creased vertically between the stamps, but not touching the design.

When the value for a used stamp is higher than the unused value, the stamp must have a contemporaneous cancel. Valuable stamps of this type should be accompanied by certificates of authenticity issued by recognized expertizing committees.

Earliest known use: Dec. 1914 (dated cancel on the unique used joint line pair, off cover).

FLAT PLATE PRINTINGS

1915   **Wmk. 191**   *Perf. 10*

460	A148 $1 **violet black,** *Feb. 8*	850.	85.
	Never hinged	1,500.	
	On cover		*12,000.*
	Block of 4	3,750.	525.
	Margin block of 4, arrow, R or L	3,850.	

	P# block of 6, Impt. & "A"	*12,000.*	
	Never hinged	*18,000.*	
	Double transfer (5782 L. 66)	900.	—

Earliest known use: May 25, 1916 (dated cancel on stamp on mailing tag); June 2, 1916 (unique usage on cover is from Shanghai, China).

Wmk. 190   *Perf. 11*

461	A140 2c **pale car. red,** type I, *June 17*	140.	*275.*
	Never hinged	240.	
	On cover		*1,200.*
	Block of 4	600.	*1,250.*
	P# block of 6	*1,450.*	
	Never hinged	*2,100.*	

Beware of fraudulently perforated copies of #409 being offered as #461.
See note on used stamps following No. 459.

Earliest known use: July 15, 1915.

VALUES FOR VERY FINE STAMPS
Please note: Stamps are valued in the grade of Very Fine unless otherwise indicated.

FLAT PLATE PRINTINGS

Plates of 400 subjects in four panes of 100 each for all values 1c to 50c inclusive.

Plates of 200 subjects in two panes of 100 each for $1, $2 and $5 denominations.

The Act of Oct. 3, 1917, effective Nov. 2, 1917, created a 3 cent rate. Local rate, 2 cents.

1916-17   **Unwmk.**   *Perf. 10*

462	A140 1c **green,** *Sept. 27, 1916*	7.00	.35
	light green	7.00	.35
	dark green	7.00	.35
	bluish green	7.00	.35
	Never hinged	12.00	
	On cover		.50
	Block of 4	30.00	3.00
	P# block of 6	160.00	
	Never hinged	230.00	
	Experimental bureau precancel, New Orleans		10.00
	Experimental bureau precancel, Springfield, Mass.		10.00
	Experimental bureau precancel, Augusta, Me.		25.00
a.	Booklet pane of 6, *Oct. 15, 1916*	9.50	*5.00*
	Never hinged	14.50	
463	A140 2c **carmine,** type I, *Sept. 1916*	4.50	.25
	dark carmine	4.50	.25
	rose red	4.50	.25
	Never hinged	7.75	
	On cover		.30
	Block of 4	20.00	2.00
	P# block of 6	135.00	
	Never hinged	200.00	
	Double transfer	6.50	—
	Experimental bureau precancel, New Orleans		*500.00*
	Experimental bureau precancel, Springfield, Mass.		22.50
a.	Booklet pane of 6, *Oct. 8, 1916*	95.00	*65.00*
	Never hinged	145.00	

See No. 467 for P# block of 6 from plate 7942.

Earliest known use: Sept. 12, 1916.

464	A140 3c **violet,** type I, *Nov. 11, 1916*	75.00	12.50
	deep violet	75.00	12.50
	Never hinged	130.00	
	On cover		40.00
	Block of 4	325.00	85.00
	P# block of 6	1,400.	
	Never hinged	2,100.	
	Double transfer in "CENTS"	*90.00*	—
	Experimental bureau precancel, New Orleans		*1,000.*
	Experimental bureau precancel, Springfield, Mass.		200.00

Earliest known use: Mar. 19, 1917.

465	A140 4c **orange brown,** *Oct. 7, 1916*	45.00	1.70
	deep brown	45.00	1.70
	brown	45.00	1.70
	Never hinged	77.50	
	On cover		11.00
	Block of 4	190.00	19.00
	P# block of 6	675.00	
	Never hinged	1,000.	
	Double transfer		—
	Experimental bureau precancel, Springfield, Mass.		175.00
466	A140 5c **blue,** *Oct. 17, 1916*	75.00	1.70
	dark blue	75.00	1.70
	Never hinged	130.00	
	On cover		13.00
	Block of 4	310.00	15.00
	P# block of 6	950.00	
	Never hinged	1,400.	
	Experimental bureau precancel, Springfield, Mass.		175.00
467	A140 5c **carmine** (error in plate of 2c)	575.00	700.00
	Never hinged	875.00	
	On cover		*3,000.*
	Block of 9, #467 in middle	950.00	*1,050.*
	Never hinged	1,450.	
	Block of 12, two middle stamps #467	1,800.	*2,000.*
	Never hinged	2,750.	

P# block of 6 2c stamps
(#463), P#7942   150.00
   Never hinged   225.00

No. 467 is an error caused by using a 5c transfer roll in re-entering three subjects: 7942 UL 74, 7942 UL 84, 7942 LR 18; the balance of the subjects on the plate being normal 2c entries. No. 467 imperf. is listed as No. 485. The error perf 11 on unwatermarked paper is No. 505.

The first value given for the error in blocks of 9 and 12 is for blocks with the error stamp(s) never hinged. The second value given is for blocks in which all stamps are never hinged. See note on used stamps following No. 459.

Earliest known use: May 22, 1917.

468	A140	6c **red orange,** *Oct. 10, 1916*	95.00	7.00
		Never hinged	160.00	
		On cover		37.50
		Block of 4	400.00	50.00
		P# block of 6	1,400.	
		Never hinged	2,100.	
		Double transfer	—	—
		Experimental bureau pre-cancel, New Orleans		2,500.
		Experimental bureau pre-cancel, Springfield, Mass.		175.00
469	A140	7c **black,** *Oct. 10, 1916*	120.00	11.00
		gray black	120.00	11.00
		Never hinged	210.00	
		On cover		42.50
		Block of 4	500.00	90.00
		P# block of 6	1,400.	
		Never hinged	2,100.	
		Experimental bureau pre-cancel, Springfield, Mass.		175.00

Earliest known use: Nov. 21, 1917.

470	A148	8c **olive green,** *Nov. 13, 1916*	57.50	5.50
		dark olive green	57.50	5.50
		Never hinged	100.00	
		On cover		27.50
		Block of 4	240.00	45.00
		P# block of 6, Impt. & "A"	575.00	
		Never hinged	875.00	
		P# block of 6, "A"	625.00	
		Never hinged	950.00	
		Experimental bureau pre-cancel, Springfield, Mass.		165.00

Earliest known use: Oct. 17, 1917.

471	A148	9c **salmon red,** *Nov. 16, 1916*	57.50	14.00
		Never hinged	100.00	
		On cover		40.00
		Block of 4	240.00	85.00
		P# block of 6	775.00	
		Never hinged	1,175.	
		Experimental bureau pre-cancel, Springfield, Mass.		150.00

472	A148	10c **orange yellow,** *Oct. 17, 1916*	105.00	1.25
		Never hinged	180.00	
		On cover		8.00
		Block of 4	440.00	10.00
		P# block of 6	1,400.	
		Never hinged	2,100.	
		Experimental bureau pre-cancel, Springfield, Mass.		160.00
473	A148	11c **dark green,** *Nov. 16, 1916*	37.50	16.00
		Never hinged	65.00	
		On cover		45.00
		Block of 4	160.00	110.00
		P# block of 6	375.00	
		Never hinged	575.00	
		Experimental bureau pre-cancel, Springfield, Mass.		575.00

Earliest known use: Apr. 13, 1917.

474	A148	12c **claret brown,** *Oct. 1916*	50.00	5.00
		Never hinged	85.00	
		On cover		22.50
		Block of 4	210.00	30.00
		P# block of 6	650.00	
		Never hinged	975.00	
		Double transfer	60.00	6.00
		Triple transfer	72.50	9.00
		Experimental bureau pre-cancel, Springfield, Mass.		200.00

Earliest known use: Oct. 6, 1916 (dated cancel on off-cover pair); Oct. 13, 1916 (on cover).

475	A148	15c **gray,** *Nov. 16, 1916*	190.00	10.50
		dark gray	190.00	10.50
		Never hinged	325.00	
		On cover		85.00
		Block of 4	800.00	95.00
		P# block of 6	3,250.	
		Never hinged	4,750.	
		P# block of 6, Impt. & "A"	—	
		Experimental bureau pre-cancel, Springfield, Mass.		150.00

Earliest known use: Mar. 2, 1917.

476	A148	20c **light ultramarine,** *Dec. 5, 1916*	240.00	12.00
		ultramarine	240.00	12.00
		Never hinged	410.00	
		On cover		725.00
		Block of 4	975.00	90.00
		P# block of 6	3,700.	
		Never hinged	5,500.	
		Experimental bureau pre-cancel, Springfield, Mass.		125.00
476A	A148	30c **orange red**	4,000.	—
		Never hinged	5,250.	
		Block of 4	16,500.	
		P# block of 6, never hinged	40,000.	

No. 476A is valued in the grade of fine.

477	A148	50c **light violet,** *Mar. 2, 1917*	1,050.	60.00
		Never hinged	1,800.	
		On cover		2,250.
		Block of 4	4,000.	475.00
		P# block of 6	57,500.	

Earliest known use: Aug. 31, 1917.

478	A148	$1 **violet black,** *Dec. 22, 1916*	775.00	17.50
		Never hinged	1,350.	
		On cover		3,000.
		Block of 4	3,250.	130.00
		Margin block of 4, arrow, R or L	3,400.	
		P# block of 6, Impt. & "A"	13,500.	
		Never hinged	19,000.	
		Double transfer (5782 L 66)	825.00	22.50

Earliest known use: Nov. 9, 1917 (dated cancel on off-cover stamp).

TYPES OF 1902-03 ISSUE

1917, Mar. 22		**Unwmk.**		**Perf. 10**
479	A127	$2 **dark blue**	300.00	40.00
		Never hinged	525.00	
		On cover (other than first flight or Zeppelin)		1,250.
		On first flight cover		350.00
		On Zeppelin flight cover		750.00
		Block of 4	1,250.	250.00
		Margin block of 4, arrow, R or L	1,350.	
		P# block of 6	4,150.	
		Never hinged	6,250.	
		Double transfer	—	

Earliest known use (on large piece of reg'd parcel wrapper): Apr. 10, 1917.

480	A128	$5 **light green**	240.00	42.50
		Never hinged	425.00	
		On cover		1,250.
		Block of 4	1,000.	250.00
		Margin block of 4, arrow, R or L	1,100.	
		P# block of 6	3,000.	
		Never hinged	4,500.	

Earliest known use (on large piece of reg'd parcel wrapper): Apr. 10, 1917.

1916-17				**Imperf.**	
481	A140	1c **green,** *Nov. 1916*	1.00	.55
		bluish green	1.00	.55
		deep green	1.00	.55
		Never hinged	1.70	
		On cover		1.40
		Pair	2.10	1.40
		Never hinged	3.60	
		Block of 4	4.20	2.80

Corner margin block of 4	4.40	5.00
Margin block of 4, arrow	4.60	3.25
Center line block	8.50	6.25
P# block of 6	14.00	—
Never hinged	21.00	
Margin block of 6, Electrolytic (Pl. 13376)	325.00	
Never hinged	475.00	
Margin block of 6, Electrolytic (Pl. 13377)	525.00	
Never hinged	775.00	
Double transfer	2.50	1.25

Earliest known use: Nov. 17, 1916.

During September, 1921, the Bureau of Engraving and Printing issued a 1c stamp printed from experimental electrolytic plates made in accordance with patent granted to George U. Rose. Tests at that time did not prove satisfactory and the method was discontinued. Four plates were made, viz., 13376, 13377, 13389 and 13390 from which stamps were issued. They are difficult to distinguish from the normal varieties. (See No. 498).

TYPE Ia

TWO CENTS
Type Ia. The design characteristics are similar to type I except that all of the lines of the design are stronger.
The toga button, toga rope and rope and rope shading lines are heavy.
The latter characteristics are those of type II, which, however, occur only on impressions from rotary plates.
Used only on flat plates 10208 and 10209.

482	A140 2c **carmine**, type I, *Dec. 8, 1916*	1.40	1.25
	deep carmine	1.40	1.25
	carmine rose	1.40	1.25
	deep rose	1.40	1.25
	Never hinged	2.40	
	On cover		2.50
	Pair	2.90	2.75
	Never hinged	4.90	
	Block of 4	5.80	5.50
	Corner margin block of 4	6.00	5.75
	Margin block of 4, arrow	6.25	6.00
	Center line block	8.50	8.00
	P# block of 6	24.00	—
	Never hinged	36.00	
	Cracked plate	—	—

See No. 485 for P# block of 6 from plate 7942.

482A	A140 2c **deep rose**, type Ia	15,000.	
	On cover	22,500.	
	Pair	105,000.	

Earliest known use: Feb. 17, 1920.

The imperforate, type Ia, was issued but all known copies were privately perforated with large oblong perforations at the sides (Schermack type III).
The No. 482A pair is unique. Value reflects 1998 auction sale price.
No. 500 exists with imperforate top sheet margin. Copies have been altered by trimming perforations. Some also have faked Schermack perfs.

TYPE II

THREE CENTS
Type II. The top line of the toga rope is strong and the rope shading lines are heavy and complete.
The line between the lips is heavy.
Used on both flat plate and rotary press printings.

483	A140 3c **violet**, type I, *Oct. 13, 1917*	13.50	7.50
	light violet	13.50	7.50
	Never hinged	23.00	
	On cover		20.00

Pair	29.00	17.50
Never hinged	50.00	
Block of 4	57.50	35.00
Corner margin block of 4	60.00	37.50
Margin block of 4, arrow	62.50	37.50
Center line block	75.00	70.00
P# block of 6	120.00	—
Never hinged	180.00	—
Double transfer	18.00	—
Triple transfer	—	—

Earliest known use: Nov. 8, 1917.

484	A140 3c **violet**, type II	10.50	5.00
	deep violet	10.50	5.00
	Never hinged	18.00	
	On cover		11.50
	Pair	22.50	13.50
	Never hinged	37.50	
	Block of 4	45.00	27.50
	Corner margin block of 4	47.50	30.00
	Margin block of 4, arrow	50.00	30.00
	Center line block	67.50	60.00
	P# block of 6	95.00	—
	Never hinged	140.00	
	Double transfer	13.00	
485	A140 5c **carmine** (error), *Mar. 1917*	10,500.	
	Never hinged	14,500.	
	Block of 9, #485 in middle	17,000.	
	Never hinged	22,500.	
	Block of 12, two middle stamps #485	30,000.	
	Never hinged	37,500.	
	P# block of six 2c stamps (#482), P#7942	140.00	
	Never hinged	210.00	

No. 485 is usually seen either as the center stamp in a block of 9 with 8 No. 482 (the first value given being with No. 485 never hinged) or as two center stamps in a block of 12 (the first value given being with both examples of No. 485 never hinged). A second value is given for each block with all stamps in the block never hinged.
See note under No. 467.

ROTARY PRESS COIL STAMPS
(See note over No. 448)

1916-19   ***Perf. 10 Horizontally***
Stamp designs: 18½-19x22½mm

486	A140 1c **green**, *Jan. 1918*	.90	.25
	yellowish green	.90	.25
	Never hinged	1.50	
	On cover		.40
	Pair	2.10	.65
	Never hinged	3.60	
	Joint line pair	4.75	1.50
	Never hinged	8.00	
	Cracked plate	—	—
	Double transfer	2.25	

Earliest known use: June 30, 1918.

487	A140 2c **carmine**, type II, *Nov. 15, 1916*	14.00	3.00
	Never hinged	24.00	
	On cover		10.00
	Pair	32.50	8.00
	Never hinged	55.00	
	Joint line pair	110.00	30.00
	Never hinged	190.00	
	Cracked plate	—	—

Earliest known use: Sept. 21, 1917.

(See note after No. 455)

488	A140 2c **carmine**, type III, *1919*	2.50	1.75
	carmine rose	2.50	1.75
	Never hinged	4.25	
	On cover		3.50
	Pair	5.75	4.25
	Never hinged	9.75	
	Joint line pair	15.00	12.50
	Never hinged	26.00	
	Cracked plate	12.00	7.50

Earliest known use: Nov. 28, 1919.

489	A140 3c **violet**, type I, *Oct. 10, 1917*	5.00	1.50
	dull violet	5.00	1.50
	bluish violet	5.00	1.50
	Never hinged	8.50	
	On cover		2.50
	Pair	11.00	4.25
	Never hinged	19.00	
	Joint line pair	32.50	12.50
	Never hinged	55.00	

Rosette plate crack on head

1916-22   ***Perf. 10 Vertically***
Stamp designs: 19½-20x22mm

490	A140 1c **green**, *Nov. 17, 1916*	.55	.25
	yellowish green	.55	.25
	Never hinged	.95	
	On cover		.40
	Pair	1.30	.70
	Never hinged	2.20	
	Joint line pair	3.50	1.25
	Never hinged	6.00	
	Double transfer	—	—
	Cracked plate (horizontal)	7.50	
	Cracked plate (vertical) re-touched	9.00	
	Rosette plate crack on head	50.00	—
491	A140 2c **carmine**, type II, *Nov. 17, 1916*	2,250.	600.00
	Never hinged	3,400.	
	On cover, type II		725.00
	Pair, type II	5,000.	2,750.
	Never hinged	7,500.	
	Joint line pair, type II	11,500.	10,000.
	Never hinged	17,500.	

Earliest known use: Jan. 2, 1917.

See note after No. 455.

492	A140 2c **carmine**, type III	9.50	.25
	carmine rose, type III	9.50	.25
	Never hinged	16.00	
	On cover, type III		.40
	Pair, type III	22.50	.90
	Never hinged	37.50	
	Joint line pair, type III	55.00	7.50
	Never hinged	95.00	
	Double transfer, type III	—	—
	Cracked plate	—	—

Earliest known use: Nov. 18, 1916.

493	A140 3c **violet**, type I, *July 23, 1917*	16.00	3.00
	reddish violet, type I	16.00	3.00
	Never hinged	27.50	
	On cover, type I		7.00
	Pair, type I	35.00	8.50
	Never hinged	60.00	
	Joint line pair, type I	110.00	50.00
	Never hinged	190.00	

Earliest known use: Nov. 2, 1917.

494	A140 3c **violet**, type II, *Feb. 4, 1918*	10.00	1.00
	dull violet, type II	10.00	1.00
	gray violet, type II	10.00	1.00
	Never hinged	17.00	
	On cover, type II		1.10
	Pair, type II	24.00	2.50
	Never hinged	40.00	
	Joint line pair, type II	75.00	6.00
	Never hinged	125.00	

Earliest known use: Apr. 18, 1918.

495	A140 4c **orange brown**, *Apr. 15, 1917*	10.00	4.00
	Never hinged	17.00	
	On cover		8.50
	Pair	24.00	12.50
	Never hinged	40.00	
	Joint line pair	75.00	22.50
	Never hinged	125.00	
	Cracked plate	25.00	—

Earliest known use: Jan. 17, 1918 (dated cancel on off-cover stamp).

496	A140 5c **blue**, *Jan. 15, 1919*	3.50	1.00
	Never hinged	6.00	
	On cover		1.60
	Pair	8.25	2.75
	Never hinged	14.00	
	Joint line pair	30.00	9.00
	Never hinged	50.00	

Earliest known use: Sept. 11, 1919.

497	A148 10c **orange yellow**, *Jan. 31, 1922*	20.00	10.50
	Never hinged	34.00	
	On cover		17.00
	Pair	47.50	32.50
	Never hinged	80.00	
	Joint line pair	140.00	75.00
	Never hinged	240.00	

Blind Perfs
Listings of imperforate-between varieties are for examples which show no trace of "blind perfs," traces of impressions from the perforating pins which do not cut into the paper.
Some unused stamps have had the gum removed to eliminate the impressions from the perforating pins. These copies do not qualify as the listed varieties.

FLAT PLATE PRINTINGS
Plates of 400 subjects in four panes of 100.
TYPES OF 1913-15 ISSUE

1917-19   Unwmk.   ***Perf. 11***

498	A140 1c **green**, *Mar. 1917*	.35	.25
	light green	.35	.25
	dark green	.35	.25
	yellowish green	.35	.25
	Never hinged	.60	
	On cover		.30
	Block of 4	1.40	1.00
	P# block of 6	17.50	
	Never hinged	26.00	
	Margin block of 6, Electrolytic (Pl, 13376-7, 13389-90)		
	See note after No. 481	450.00	

Cracked plate (10656 UL and 10645 LR)	7.50	—
Double transfer	5.50	2.00
a. Vertical pair, imperf. horiz.	175.00	
b. Horizontal pair, imperf. between	100.00	
c. Vertical pair, imperf. between	450.00	—
d. Double impression	175.00	
e. Booklet pane of 6, *Apr. 6, 1917*	2.50	*1.00*
Never hinged	4.00	
f. Booklet pane of 30, *Aug. 1917*	*1,000.*	
Never hinged	*1,500.*	
g. Perf. 10 at top or bottom	—	—

Earliest known use (No. 498f booklet single): Aug. 8, 1917.

See No. 505 for P# block of 6 from plate 7942.

499 A140 2c **rose**, type I, *Mar. 1917*	.35	.25
dark rose, type I	.35	.25
carmine rose, type I	.35	.25
deep rose, type I	.35	.25
Never hinged	.60	
lake, type I	250.00	
Never hinged	425.00	
On cover, type I		.30
Block of 4, type I	1.40	1.00
P# block of 6, type I	17.50	
Never hinged	26.00	
Double impression, type I, 15mm wide	—	
Cracked plate, type I	—	—
Recut in hair, type I	—	
Double transfer, type I	6.00	—
a. Vertical pair, imperf. horiz., type I	150.00	
b. Horiz. pair, imperf. vert., type I	450.00	225.00
c. Vert. pair, imperf. btwn., type I	650.00	225.00
e. Booklet pane of 6, type I, *Mar. 31, 1917*	4.00	*1.25*
Never hinged	6.25	
f. Booklet pane of 30, type I, *Aug. 1917*	28,000.	
Never hinged	36,000.	
g. Double impression, type I	160.00	—

Earliest known use: Mar. 27, 1917 (No. 499); Aug. 7, 1917 (No. 499f booklet single).

500 A140 2c **deep rose**, type Ia	275.00	225.00
Never hinged	475.00	
On cover, type Ia		*650.00*
Block of 4, type Ia	1,150.	1,100.
P# block of 6, type Ia	2,200.	
Never hinged	3,250.	
P# block of 6, two stamps type I (P# 10208 LL)	9,000.	
Never hinged	13,500.	
Pair, types I and Ia (10208 LL 95 or 96)	1,275.	

Earliest known use: Dec. 15, 1919.

501 A140 3c **light violet**, type I, *Mar. 1917*	11.00	.25
violet, type I	11.00	.25
dark violet, type I	11.00	.25
reddish violet, type I	11.00	.25
Never hinged	19.00	
On cover, type I		.30
Block of 4, type I	45.00	2.00
P# block of 6, type I	125.00	
Never hinged	190.00	
Double transfer, type I	12.00	
b. Bklt. pane of 6, type I, *Oct. 17, 1917*	70.00	*45.00*
Never hinged	110.00	
c. Vert. pair, imper. horiz., type I	350.00	
d. Double impression	275.00	
502 A140 3c **dark violet**, type II	14.00	.40
violet, type II	14.00	.40
Never hinged	24.00	
On cover, type II		.65
Block of 4, type II	57.50	2.00
P# block of 6, type II	150.00	
Never hinged	225.00	
b. Bklt. pane of 6, type II, *Feb. 25, 1918*	60.00	*45.00*
Never hinged	95.00	
c. Vert. pair, imperf. horiz., type II	250.00	125.00
d. Double impression	200.00	
e. Perf. 10 at top or bottom	—	3,500.

Earliest known use: Jan. 30, 1918.

503 A140 4c **brown**, *Mar. 1917*	10.00	.25
dark brown	10.00	.25
orange brown	10.00	.25
yellow brown	10.00	.25
Never hinged	17.00	
On cover		2.10
Block of 4	40.00	1.30
P# block of 6	140.00	
Never hinged	210.00	
Double transfer	15.00	—
b. Double impression	—	
504 A140 5c **blue**, *Mar. 1917*	9.00	.25
light blue	9.00	.25
dark blue	9.00	.25
Never hinged	15.00	
On cover		.30
Block of 4	37.50	1.20
P# block of 6	130.00	
Never hinged	190.00	
Double transfer	11.00	—
a. Horizontal pair, imperf. between	2,500.	
505 A140 5c **rose** (error)	360.00	500.00
Never hinged	600.00	
On cover		1,500.
Block of 9, middle stamp #505	675.00	*900.00*
Never hinged	1,050.	
Block of 12, two middle stamps #505	1,300.	*1,400.*
Never hinged	2,100.	
Margin block of six 2c stamps (#499), P# 7942	27.50	
Never hinged	40.00	

Earliest known use: Mar. 27, 1917.

Value notes under No. 467 also apply to No. 505.

506 A140 6c **red orange**, *Mar. 1917*	12.50	.25
orange	12.50	.25
Never hinged	21.00	
On cover		2.50
Block of 4	52.50	1.50
P# block of 6	175.00	
Never hinged	260.00	
Double transfer	—	
a. Perf. 10 at top or bottom	3,500.	2,250.
507 A140 7c **black**, *Mar. 1917*	27.50	1.10
gray black	27.50	1.10
intense black	27.50	1.10
Never hinged	47.50	
On cover		7.75
Block of 4	115.00	11.00
P# block of 6	260.00	
Never hinged	390.00	
Double transfer	—	
a. Perf. 10 at top	3,000.	
508 A148 8c **olive bister**, *Mar. 1917*	12.00	.50
dark olive green	12.00	.50
olive green	12.00	.50
Never hinged	20.00	
On cover		2.75
Block of 4	50.00	5.00
P# block of 6, Impt. & "A"	175.00	
Never hinged	260.00	
P# block of 6, "A"	225.00	
Never hinged	325.00	
P# block of 6	150.00	
Never hinged	225.00	
b. Vertical pair, imperf. between	—	
c. Perf. 10 at top or bottom	—	3,250.
509 A148 9c **salmon red**, *Mar. 1917*	14.00	1.75
salmon	14.00	1.75
Never hinged	24.00	
On cover		13.00
Block of 4	57.50	17.50
P# block of 6	150.00	
Never hinged	225.00	
Double transfer	20.00	4.50
a. Perf. 10 at top or bottom	3,500.	2,500.
510 A148 10c **orange yellow**, *Mar. 1917*	17.00	.20
golden yellow	17.00	.20
Never hinged	29.00	
On cover		2.00
Block of 4	70.00	.75
P# block of 6, "A"	300.00	
Never hinged	450.00	
P# block of 6	190.00	
Never hinged	290.00	
a. 10c **brown yellow**	350.00	
Never hinged	600.00	

Earliest known use: Mar. 27, 1917.

511 A148 11c **light green**, *May 1917*	9.00	2.50
green	9.00	2.50
Never hinged	15.00	
dark green	10.00	2.50
Never hinged	17.00	
On cover		8.50
Block of 4	37.50	20.00
P# block of 6	130.00	
Never hinged	200.00	
Double transfer	12.50	3.25
a. Perf. 10 at top or bottom	1,750.	1,500.
Never hinged	3,500.	
512 A148 12c **claret brown**, *May 1917*	9.00	.35
Never hinged	15.00	
On cover		4.00
Block of 4	37.50	3.50
P# block of 6	130.00	
Never hinged	200.00	
Double transfer	12.50	—
Triple transfer	20.00	—
a. 12c **brown carmine**	9.50	.40
Never hinged	16.00	
On cover		4.50
Block of 4	40.00	4.00
P# block of 6	140.00	
Never hinged	210.00	
b. Perf. 10 at top or bottom	3,000.	

Earliest known use: Oct. 13, 1917.

513 A148 13c **apple green**, *Jan. 10, 1919*	11.00	6.00
pale apple green	11.00	6.00
Never hinged	19.00	
deep apple green	12.50	6.50
Never hinged	21.50	
On cover		19.00
Block of 4	45.00	40.00
P# block of 6	130.00	
Never hinged	200.00	

Earliest known use: Feb. 4, 1919.

514 A148 15c **gray**, *May 1917*	37.50	1.00
dark gray	37.50	1.00
Never hinged	65.00	
On cover		25.00
Block of 4	160.00	11.00
P# block of 6	575.00	
Never hinged	875.00	
Double transfer	—	
a. Perf. 10 at bottom		6,000.

Earliest known use: Nov. 15, 1917.

515 A148 20c **light ultramarine**, *May 1917*	47.50	.25
gray blue	47.50	.25
Never hinged	80.00	
deep ultramarine	50.00	.25
Never hinged	85.00	
On cover		75.00
Block of 4	200.00	2.25
P# block of 6	625.00	
Never hinged	950.00	
Double transfer	—	
b. Vertical pair, imperf. between	1,000.	
c. Double impression	1,250.	
d. Perf. 10 at top or bottom	—	4,500.

Beware of pairs with blind perforations inside the design of the top stamp that are offered as No. 515b.

516 A148 30c **orange red**, *May 1917*	37.50	1.00
dark orange red	37.50	1.00
Never hinged	65.00	
On cover		150.00
Block of 4	160.00	8.00
P# block of 6	600.00	
Never hinged	900.00	
Double transfer	—	
a. Perf. 10 at top or bottom	5,000.	—
Never hinged	6,250.	
b. Double impression	—	

Earliest known use: Jan. 12, 1918.

517 A148 50c **red violet**, *May 1917*	67.50	.50
Never hinged	115.00	
violet	85.00	.50
Never hinged	145.00	
light violet	90.00	.60
Never hinged	155.00	
On cover		400.00
Block of 4	310.00	3.25
P# block of 6	1,650.	
Never hinged	2,500.	
Double transfer	100.00	1.50
b. Vertical pair, imperf. between & at bottom	—	7,000.
c. Perf. 10 at top or bottom	—	4,500.

Earliest known use: Dec. 28, 1917 (on registry tag).

518 A148 $1 **violet brown**, *May 1917*	52.50	1.50
violet black	52.50	1.50
Never hinged	90.00	
On cover		550.00
Block of 4	220.00	9.50
Margin block of 4, arrow right or left	250.00	
P# block of 6, Impt. & "A"	1,350.	
Never hinged	2,000.	
Double transfer (5782 L. 66)	70.00	2.00
b. $1 **deep brown**	1,900.	1,050.
Never hinged	2,850.	
Block of 4		5,000.

Earliest known use: Dec. 6, 1917.

No. 518b is valued in the grade of fine to very fine.

Nos. 498-504,506-518 (20)   674.20   243.55

TYPE OF 1908-09 ISSUE

1917, Oct. 10   **Wmk. 191**   *Perf. 11*

This is the result of an old stock of No. 344 which was returned to the Bureau in 1917 and perforated with the then current gauge 11.

519 A139 2c **carmine**	400.	*1,100.*
Never hinged	675.	
On cover		*2,400.*
Block of 4	1,650.	—
P# block of 6, T V, Impt.	2,700.	
Never hinged	4,000.	

Beware of copies of No. 344 fraudulently perforated and offered as No. 519.
Warning: See note following No. 459 regarding used stamps.

Earliest known use: Oct. 10, 1917.

Franklin — A149

Plates of 100 subjects.

1918, Aug.   **Unwmk.**   *Perf. 11*

523 A149 $2 **orange red & black**	625.	230.
red orange & black	625.	230.
Never hinged	1,000.	
On cover		*2,000.*
Block of 4	2,600.	1,000.
Margin block of 4, arrow	2,700.	
Center line block	2,850.	1,000.
P# block of 8, 2# & arrow	12,000.	
Never hinged	17,500.	

Earliest known use: Dec. 17, 1918.

524 A149 $5 **deep green & black**	220.	35.
Never hinged	350.	
On cover		*1,500.*
Block of 4	900.	170.
Margin block of 4, arrow	950.	175.
Center line block	1,050.	180.
P# block of 8, 2# & arrow	4,250.	
Never hinged	6,250.	

For other listing of design A149 see No. 547.

OFFSET PRINTING

Plates of 400, 800 or 1600 subjects in panes of 100 each, as follows:

No. 525- 400 and 1600 subjects
No. 526- 400, 800 and 1600 subjects
No. 529- 400 subjects
No. 531- 400 subjects
No. 532- 400, 800 and 1600 subjects
No. 535- 400 subjects
No. 536- 400 and 1600 subjects

TYPES OF 1917-19 ISSUE

		1918-20	Unwmk.		Perf. 11
525	A140	1c	**gray green,** *Dec. 1918*	2.50	.50
			Never hinged	4.00	
			emerald	3.50	1.00
			Never hinged	5.50	
			On cover		1.40
			Block of 4	10.50	3.50
			P# block of 6	25.00	
			Never hinged	37.50	
			"Flat nose"		
a.			1c dark green	2.75	.95
			Never hinged	4.40	
c.			Horizontal pair, imperf. between	100.00	
d.			Double impression	27.50	25.00

Earliest known use: Dec. 24, 1918.

TYPE IV

TWO CENTS

Type IV - Top line of the toga rope is broken.
The shading lines in the toga button are so arranged that the curving of the first and last form "D (reversed) ID."
The line of color in the left "2" is very thin and usually broken.
Used on offset printings only.

TYPE V

Type V - Top line of the toga is complete.
There are five vertical shading lines in the toga button.
The line of color in the left "2" is very thin and usually broken.
The shading dots on the nose are as shown on the diagram.
Used on offset printings only.

TYPE Va

Type Va - Characteristics are the same as type V except in the shading dots of the nose. The third row of dots from the bottom has four dots instead of six. The overall height is ⅓mm shorter than type V.
Used on offset printings only.

TYPE VI

Type VI - General characteristics the same as type V except that the line of color in the left "2" is very heavy.
Used on offset printings only.

TYPE VII

Type VII - The line of color in the left "2" is invariably continuous, clearly defined and heavier than in type V or Va but not as heavy as type VI.
An additional vertical row of dots has been added to the upper lip.
Numerous additional dots have been added to the hair on top of the head.
Used on offset printings only.
Dates of issue of types after type IV are not known but official records show the first plate of each type to have been certified as follows:

Type IV, Mar. 6, 1920
Type V, Mar. 20, 1920
Type Va, May 4, 1920
Type VI, June 24, 1920
Type VII, Nov. 3, 1920

526	A140	2c	**carmine,** type IV, *1920*	27.50	3.50
			rose carmine, type IV	27.50	3.50
			Never hinged	45.00	
			On cover, type IV		11.00
			Block of 4, type IV	120.00	21.00
			P# block of 6, type IV	250.00	
			Never hinged	375.00	
			Gash on forehead, type IV	40.00	—
			Malformed "2" at left, type IV (10823 LR 93)	37.50	6.00

Earliest known use: Mar. 15, 1920.

527	A140	2c	**carmine,** type V, *1920*	20.00	1.00
			bright carmine, type V	20.00	1.00
			rose carmine, type V	20.00	1.00
			Never hinged	32.50	
			On cover		2.50
			Block of 4, type V	85.00	8.00
			Block of 6, P# only, type V	175.00	
			Never hinged	250.00	
			Line through "2" & "EN," type V	30.00	—
a.			Double impression, type V	60.00	10.00
b.			Vert. pair, imperf. horiz., type V	600.00	
c.			Horiz. pair, imperf. vert., type V	1,000.	—

Earliest known use: Apr. 20, 1920.

528	A140	2c	**carmine,** type Va, *1920*	9.25	.25
			Never hinged	15.00	
			On cover, type Va		.60
			Block of 4, type Va	37.50	2.50
			Block of 6, P# only, type Va	85.00	
			Never hinged	125.00	
			Block of 6, monogram over P#	105.00	
			Never hinged	160.00	
			Retouches in "P" of Postage type Va	52.50	—
			Retouched on toga, type Va		
			Variety C"R"NTS, type Va	32.50	
c.			Double impression, type Va	27.50	
g.			Vert. pair, imperf. between	2,000.	

Earliest known use: June 18, 1920.

528A	A140	2c	**carmine,** type VI, *1920*	52.50	1.50
			bright carmine, type VI	52.50	1.50
			Never hinged	85.00	
			On cover, type VI		3.50
			Block of 4, type VI	225.00	7.00
			P# block of 6, type VI	450.00	
			Never hinged	650.00	
			Block of 6, monogram over P#	550.00	
			Never hinged	800.00	
d.			Double impression, type VI	160.00	—
f.			Vert. pair, imperf. horiz., type VI		
h.			Vert. pair, imperf. between	1,000.	

Earliest known use: July 30, 1920.

528B	A140	2c	**carmine,** type VII, *1920*	22.50	.35
			Never hinged	35.00	
			On cover, type VII		.40
			Block of 4, type VII	95.00	2.25
			P# block of 6, type VII	185.00	
			Never hinged	275.00	
			Retouched on cheek, type VII	400.00	—
e.			Double impression, type VII	70.00	

Earliest known use: Nov. 10, 1920.

TYPE III

THREE CENTS

Type III - The top line of the toga rope is strong but the 5th shading line is missing as in type I.
Center shading line of the toga button consists of two dashes with a central dot.
The "P" and "O" of "POSTAGE" are separated by a line of color.
The frame line at the bottom of the vignette is complete.
Used on offset printings only.

TYPE IV

TYPE IV

Type IV - The shading lines of the toga rope are complete. The second and fourth shading lines in the toga button are broken in the middle and the third line is continuous with a dot in the center.
The "P" and "O" of "POSTAGE" are joined.
The frame line at the bottom of the vignette is broken.
Used on offset printings only.

529	A140	3c	**violet**, type III, *Mar. 1918*	3.25	.25
			light violet, type III	3.25	.25
			dark violet, type III	3.25	.25
			Never hinged	5.25	
			On cover, type III		.30
			Block of 4, type III	14.00	1.50
			P# block of 6, type III	60.00	
			Never hinged	90.00	
a.			Double impression, type III	32.50	
b.			Printed on both sides, type III	450.00	

Earliest known use: Apr. 9, 1918.

530	A140	3c	**purple**, type IV	1.60	.20
			light purple, type IV	1.60	.20
			deep purple, type IV	1.60	.20
			violet, type IV	1.60	.20
			Never hinged	2.60	
			On cover, type IV		.25
			Block of 4, type IV	6.75	.90
			P# block of 6, type IV	18.50	
			Never hinged	27.50	
			"Blister" under "U.S.," type IV	4.50	—
			Recut under "U.S.," type IV	4.50	—
a.			Double impression, type IV	20.00	6.00
b.			Printed on both sides, type IV	250.00	
			Nos. 525-530 (8)	139.10	7.55

Earliest known use: June 30, 1918.

1918-20 *Imperf.*

Dates of issue of 2c types are not known, but official records show that the first plate of each type known to have been issued imperforate was certified as follows:
Type IV, Mar. 1920
Type V, May 4, 1920
Type Va, May 25, 1920
Type VI, July 26, 1920
Type VII, Dec. 2, 1920

531	A140	1c	**green**, *Jan. 1919*	9.25	8.00
			gray green	9.25	8.00
			Never hinged	15.00	
			On cover		15.00
			Pair	20.00	20.00
			Never hinged	32.50	
			Block of 4	37.50	40.00
			Corner margin block of 4	40.00	—
			Margin block of 4, arrow	40.00	42.50
			Center line block	55.00	50.00
			P# block of 6	90.00	
			Never hinged	135.00	
532	A140	2c	**carmine rose**, type IV, *1920*	40.00	27.50
			Never hinged	65.00	
			On cover		65.00
			Pair	85.00	70.00
			Never hinged	140.00	
			Block of 4	160.00	140.00
			Corner margin block of 4	165.00	
			Margin block of 4, arrow	165.00	
			Center line block	190.00	
			P# block of 6	350.00	
			Never hinged	500.00	
533	A140	2c	**carmine**, type V, *1920*	130.00	80.00
			Never hinged	210.00	
			On cover		200.00
			Pair	275.00	200.00
			Never hinged	440.00	
			Block of 4	550.00	400.00
			Corner margin block of 4	575.00	550.00
			Margin block of 4, arrow	575.00	650.00
			Center line block	750.00	550.00
			P# block of 6	1,150.	
			Never hinged	1,700.	

Earliest known use: June 30, 1920.

534	A140	2c	**carmine**, type Va, *1920*	11.00	6.50
			carmine rose	11.00	6.50
			Never hinged	17.50	
			On cover		14.00
			Pair	24.00	17.50
			Never hinged	39.00	
			Block of 4	48.00	35.00
			Corner margin block of 4	50.00	
			Margin block of 4, arrow	50.00	45.00
			Center line block	55.00	70.00
			P# block of 6	110.00	—
			Never hinged	160.00	

	Block of 6, monogram over P#	190.00		
	Never hinged	275.00		

Earliest known use: July 3, 1920 (dated cancel on off-cover block).

534A	A140	2c	**carmine**, type VI, *1920*	45.00	22.50
			Never hinged	72.50	
			On cover		37.50
			Pair	100.00	60.00
			Never hinged	160.00	
			Block of 4	200.00	120.00
			Corner block of 4	220.00	140.00
			Block of 4, arrow	220.00	
			Center line block	240.00	220.00
			Block of 6, P# only	400.00	—
			Never hinged	575.00	

Earliest known use: Sept. 7, 1920.

534B	A140	2c	**carmine**, type VII, *1920*	2,150.	1,000.
			Never hinged	3,500.	
			On cover		1,400.
			Pair	4,500.	2,500.
			Never hinged	7,250.	
			Block of 4	9,000.	5,000.
			Corner margin block of 4	9,250.	
			Margin block of 4, arrow	9,500.	
			Center line block	10,500.	
			P# block of 6	17,000.	
			Never hinged	24,000.	

Earliest known use: Nov. 3, 1920.

Copies of the 2c type VII with Schermack III vending machine perforations, have been cut down at sides to simulate the rarer No. 534B imperforate.

535	A140	3c	**violet**, type IV, *1918*	9.00	5.00
			Never hinged	15.00	
			On cover		11.00
			Pair	20.00	15.00
			Never hinged	32.50	
			Block of 4	40.00	30.00
			Corner margin block of 4	42.50	32.50
			Margin block of 4, arrow	42.50	32.50
			Center line block	47.50	45.00
			P# block of 6	77.50	—
			Never hinged	115.00	
a.			Double impression	100.00	—

Earliest known use: Oct. 5, 1918.

Cancellation

Haiti

1919, Aug. 15 *Perf. 12½*

536	A140	1c	**gray green**	22.50	20.00
			Never hinged	36.00	
			On cover		57.50
			Block of 4	95.00	85.00
			P# block of 6	210.00	
			Never hinged	300.00	
a.			Horiz. pair, imperf. vert.	700.00	

VICTORY ISSUE
Victory of the Allies in World War I

"Victory" and Flags of Allies — A150

Designed by Clair A. Huston

FLAT PLATE PRINTING
Plates of 400 subjects in four panes of 100 each

1919, Mar. 3 Unwmk. *Perf. 11*

537	A150	3c	**violet**	10.00	3.25
			Never hinged	16.00	
			On cover		5.50
			Block of 4	42.50	14.00
			P# block of 6	110.00	
			Never hinged	160.00	
			Double transfer	—	—
a.			3c deep red violet	1,150.	1,500.
			Never hinged	1,750.	
			On cover		2,000.
			Block of 4	4,750.	7,000.
			P# block of 6	8,500.	
			Never hinged	13,000.	
b.			3c light reddish violet	10.00	3.00
			Never hinged	16.00	
			On cover		5.00
			P# block of 6	110.00	
			Never hinged	160.00	
c.			3c red violet	40.00	12.00
			Never hinged	65.00	
			On cover		20.00
			Block of 4	160.00	
			P# block of 6	350.00	
			Never hinged	500.00	

No. 537a is valued in the grade of fine.

REGULAR ISSUE
ROTARY PRESS PRINTINGS
(See note over No. 448)

1919 Unwmk. *Perf. 11x10*
Issued in panes of 170 stamps (coil waste), later in
panes of 70 and 100 (#538, 540)
Stamp designs: 19½-20x22-22¼mm

538	A140	1c	**green**, *June*	12.00	8.50
			yellowish green	12.00	8.50
			bluish green	12.00	8.50
			Never hinged	19.00	
			On cover		22.50
			Block of 4	50.00	50.00
			P# block of 4 & "S 30"	100.00	
			Never hinged	145.00	
			P# block of 4	115.00	
			Never hinged	165.00	
			P# block of 4, star	145.00	
			Never hinged	210.00	
			Double transfer	17.50	—
a.			Vert. pair, imperf. horiz.	50.00	100.00
			Never hinged	80.00	
			P# block of 4	900.00	
			Never hinged	1,300.	

Earliest known use: June 28, 1919.

539	A140	2c	**carmine rose**, type II	2,750.	4,750.
			Never hinged	3,750.	
			On cover, type II		30,000.
			Block of 4, type II	11,000.	27,500.
			P# block of 4, type II, & "S 20"	15,000.	
			Never hinged	20,000.	

No. 539 is valued in the grade of fine.
(See note after No. 455.)

Earliest known use: June 30, 1919. This is the unique usage on cover.

540	A140	2c	**carmine rose**, type III, *June 14*	14.00	8.50
			carmine	14.00	8.50
			Never hinged	22.50	
			On cover, type III		25.00
			Block of 4, type III	57.50	50.00
			P# block of 4, type III, & "S 30"	110.00	
			Never hinged	160.00	
			P# block of 4, type III, & "S 30" inverted	475.00	
			Never hinged	700.00	
			P# block of 4, type III	110.00	
			Never hinged	160.00	
			P# block of 4, type III, star	155.00	
			Never hinged	225.00	
			Double transfer, type III	22.50	—

Earliest known use: June 27, 1919.

a.			Vert. pair, imperf. horiz., type III	50.00	100.00
			Never hinged	80.00	
			P# block of 4, type III	750.00	
			Never hinged	1,100.	
			P# block of 4, type III, Star	800.00	
			Never hinged	1,150.	
b.			Horiz. pair, imperf. vert., type III	750.00	
541	A140	3c	**violet**, type II, *June 1919*	45.00	30.00
			gray violet, type II	45.00	30.00
			Never hinged	72.50	
			On cover		100.00
			Block of 4	190.00	190.00
			P# block of 4	375.00	
			Never hinged	550.00	

Earliest known use: June 14, 1919.

1920, May 26 *Perf. 10x11*
Plates of 400 subjects in four panes of 100.
Stamp design: 19x22½-22¾mm

542	A140	1c	**green**	14.00	1.10
			bluish green	14.00	1.10
			Never hinged	22.50	
			On cover		5.50
			Block of 4	60.00	8.00
			Vertical margin block of 6, P# opposite center horizontal row	175.00	
			Never hinged	250.00	

1921, May *Perf. 10*
Plates of 400 subjects in four panes of 100 each
Stamp design: 19x22½mm

543	A140	1c	**green**	.50	.25
			deep green	.50	.25
			Never hinged	.80	
			On cover		.30
			Block of 4	2.00	1.10
			Vertical margin block of 6, P# opposite center horizontal row	35.00	
			Never hinged	50.00	
			Corner margin block of 4, P# only	15.00	
			Never hinged	22.00	
			Double transfer	—	—
			Triple transfer	—	
a.			Horizontal pair, imperf. between	1,100.	

Earliest known use: May 29, 1921.

1922 — Perf. 11
Rotary press sheet waste
Stamp design: 19x22½mm

544 A140	1c	green	15,000. 3,250.
		Never hinged	23,000.
		On cover	4,000.

No. 544 is valued in the grade of fine.

Earliest known use: Dec. 21, 1922.

1921, May
Issued in panes of 170 stamps (coil waste), later in panes of 70 and 100
Stamp designs: 19½-20x22mm

545 A140	1c	green	190.00 175.00
		yellowish green	190.00 175.00
		Never hinged	300.00
		On cover	1,800.
		Block of 4	800.00 600.00
		P# block of 4, "S 30"	1,100.
		Never hinged	1,600.
		P# block of 4	1,150.
		Never hinged	1,650.
		P# block of 4, star	1,200.
		Never hinged	1,750.

Earliest known use: June 25, 1921.

546 A140	2c	carmine rose, type III	125.00 160.00
		deep carmine rose	125.00 160.00
		Never hinged	200.00
		On cover	775.00
		Block of 4	525.00 850.00
		P# block of 4, "S 30"	800.00
		Never hinged	1,150.
		P# block of 4	825.00
		Never hinged	1,200.
		P# block of 4, star	850.00
		Never hinged	1,225.
		Recut in hair	140.00 185.00
a.		Perf. 10 on left side	—

Earliest known use: May 5, 1921.

FLAT PLATE PRINTING
Plates of 100 subjects

1920, Nov. 1 — Perf. 11

547 A149	$2	carmine & black	200. 40.
		Never hinged	325.
		lake & black	240. 40.
		Never hinged	380.
		On cover (commercial)	1,000.
		On flown cover (philatelic)	250.
		Block of 4	825. 175.
		Margin block of 4, arrow	850.
		Center line block	875. —
		Margin block of 8, two P#, & arrow	4,350.
		Never hinged	6,250.

PILGRIM TERCENTENARY ISSUE
Landing of the Pilgrims at Plymouth, Mass.

The "Mayflower" — A151

Landing of the Pilgrims — A152

Signing of the Compact — A153

Designed by Clair A. Huston

Plates of 280 subjects in four panes of 70 each

1920, Dec. 21 — Unwmk. — Perf. 11

548 A151	1c	green	4.50 2.25
		dark green	4.50 2.25
		Never hinged	7.25
		On cover	3.50
		Block of 4	19.00 12.50
		P# block of 6	45.00
		Never hinged	65.00
		Double transfer	— —
549 A152	2c	carmine rose	6.50 1.60
		carmine	6.50 1.60
		rose	6.50 1.60
		Never hinged	10.50
		On cover	2.50
		Block of 4	27.50 8.00
		P# block of 6	65.00
		Never hinged	95.00

Cancellation

		China	—
550 A153	5c	deep blue	42.50 12.50
		dark blue	42.50 12.50
		Never hinged	67.50

On cover		22.50
Block of 4	175.00	60.00
P# block of 6	450.00	
Never hinged	650.00	
Nos. 548-550 (3)	53.50	16.35
Nos. 548-550, never hinged	85.25	

VALUES FOR VERY FINE STAMPS
Please note: Stamps are valued in the grade of Very Fine unless otherwise indicated.

REGULAR ISSUE

Nathan Hale — A154

Franklin — A155

Warren G. Harding — A156

Washington — A157

Lincoln — A158

Martha Washington — A159

Theodore Roosevelt — A160

Garfield — A161

McKinley — A162

Grant — A163

Jefferson — A164

Monroe — A165

Rutherford B. Hayes — A166

Grover Cleveland — A167

American
Indian — A168

Statue of
Liberty — A169

Golden Gate — A170

Niagara Falls — A171

American
Buffalo — A172

Arlington
Amphitheater — A173

Lincoln
Memorial — A174

United States
Capitol — A175

Head of Freedom Statue,
Capitol Dome — A176

Plates of 400 subjects in four panes of 100 each for all values ½c to 50c inclusive.

Plates of 200 subjects for $1 and $2. The sheets were cut along the horizontal guide line into two panes, upper and lower, of 100 subjects each.

Plates of 100 subjects for the $5 denomination, and sheets of 100 subjects were issued intact.

The Bureau of Engraving and Printing in 1925 in experimenting to overcome the loss due to uneven perforations, produced what is known as the "Star Plate." The vertical rows of designs on these plates are spaced 3mm apart in place of 2¾mm as on the regular plates. Most of these plates were identified with a star added to the plate number.

Designed by Clair Aubrey Huston.

FLAT PLATE PRINTINGS

1922-25   Unwmk.   Perf. 11

551	A154	½c **olive brown,** *Apr. 4, 1925*	.20	.20
		pale olive brown	.20	.20
		deep olive brown	.20	.20
		Never hinged	.25	
		On 1c stamped envelope (3rd class)		1.00
		Block of 4	.35	.40
		P# block of 6	5.75	
		Never hinged	8.00	
		"Cap" on fraction bar (Pl. 17041)	.75	.20
552	A155	1c **deep green,** *Jan. 17, 1923*	1.50	.20
		green	1.50	.20
		pale green	1.50	.20
		Never hinged	2.50	
		On postcard		.25
		Block of 4	6.25	.35
		P# block of 6	22.50	
		Never hinged	32.50	
		Double transfer	3.50	—
a.		Booklet pane of 6, *Aug. 11, 1923*	6.00	2.00
		Never hinged	9.50	
553	A156	1½c **yellow brown,** *Mar. 19, 1925*	2.60	.20
		pale yellow brown	2.60	.20
		brown	2.60	.20
		Never hinged	4.25	
		On 3rd class cover		2.00
		Block of 4	10.50	1.00
		P# block of 6	27.50	2.25
		Never hinged	40.00	
		Double transfer	—	—
554	A157	2c **carmine,** *Jan. 15, 1923*	1.40	.20
		light carmine	1.40	.20
		Never hinged	2.25	
		On cover		.25
		Block of 4	5.75	.20
		P# block of 6	20.00	
		Never hinged	30.00	

		P# block of 6 & small 5 point star, top only	550.00	
		Never hinged	775.00	
		P# block of 6 & large 5 point star, side only	65.00	
		Never hinged	92.50	
		Same, large 5-pt. star, top	600.00	
		Never hinged	850.00	
		Same, large 6-pt. star, top	750.00	
		Never hinged	1,050.00	
		Same, large 6-pt. star, side only (Pl. 17196)	875.00	
		Never hinged	1,225.	
		Double transfer	2.50	.80
a.		Horiz. pair, imperf. vert.	200.00	
b.		Vert. pair, imperf. horiz.	750.00	
c.		Booklet pane of 6, *Feb. 10, 1923*	6.75	2.00
		Never hinged	10.50	
d.		Perf. 10 at top or bottom	—	3,500.
555	A158	3c **violet,** *Feb. 12, 1923*	18.00	1.00
		deep violet	18.00	1.00
		dark violet	18.00	1.00
		red violet	18.00	1.00
		bright violet	18.00	1.00
		Never hinged	29.00	
		On 2c stamped envelope (single UPU rate)		7.00
		Block of 4	75.00	6.00
		P# block of 6	160.00	
		Never hinged	220.00	
556	A159	4c **yellow brown,** *Jan. 15, 1923*	19.00	.25
		brown	19.00	.25
		Never hinged	30.00	
		On cover		8.00
		Block of 4	77.50	1.50
		P# block of 6	160.00	
		Never hinged	230.00	
		Double transfer	—	—
a.		Vert. pair, imperf. horiz.	—	—
b.		Perf. 10 at top or bottom	2,250.	—
557	A160	5c **dark blue,** *Oct. 27, 1922*	19.00	.20
		deep blue	19.00	.20
		Never hinged	30.00	
		On UPU-rate cover		5.00
		Block of 4	77.50	.95
		P# block of 6	190.00	
		Never hinged	260.00	
		Double transfer (15571 UL 86)	—	—
a.		Imperf., pair	1,500.	
b.		Horiz. pair, imperf. vert.	—	—
c.		Perf. 10 at top or bottom	—	3,250.
558	A161	6c **red orange,** *Nov. 20, 1922*	35.00	.85
		pale red orange	35.00	.85
		Never hinged	57.50	
		Pair on special delivery cover		15.00
		Block of 4	145.00	4.75
		P# block of 6	400.00	
		Never hinged	550.00	
		Double transfer (Plate 14169 LR 60 and 70)	55.00	2.00
		Same, recut	55.00	2.00
559	A162	7c **black,** *May 1, 1923*	9.25	.55
		gray black	9.25	.55
		Never hinged	15.00	
		On registered cover with other values		25.00
		Block of 4	40.00	3.50
		P# block of 6	70.00	
		Never hinged	100.00	
		Double transfer	—	—
560	A163	8c **olive green,** *May 1, 1923*	50.00	.60
		pale olive green	50.00	.60
		Never hinged	80.00	
		Pair on airmail cover		10.00
		Block of 4	210.00	4.25
		P# block of 6	575.00	
		Never hinged	825.00	
		Double transfer	—	—
561	A164	9c **rose,** *Jan. 15, 1923*	14.00	1.10
		pale rose	14.00	1.10
		Never hinged	22.50	
		On registered cover with other values		20.00
		Block of 4	57.50	6.75
		P# block of 6	160.00	
		Never hinged	225.00	
		Double transfer	—	—
562	A165	10c **orange,** *Jan. 15, 1923*	18.00	.20
		pale orange	18.00	.20
		Never hinged	29.00	
		On special delivery cover with 2c		5.00
		Block of 4	75.00	.50
		P# block of 6	200.00	
		Never hinged	275.00	
a.		Vert. pair, imperf. horiz.	1,500.	
b.		Imperf., pair	1,250.	
		P# block of 6	—	
c.		Perf. 10 at top or bottom		2,250.
563	A166	11c **light blue,** *Oct. 4, 1922*	1.40	.40
		greenish blue	1.40	.40
		light bluish green	1.40	.40
		light yellow green	1.40	.40
		Never hinged	2.20	
		On registered cover with other values		12.50
		Block of 4	5.75	1.90
		P# block of 6	27.50	
		Never hinged	40.00	
d.		Imperf., pair		17,500.
564	A167	12c **brown violet,** *Mar. 20, 1923*	6.00	.20
		deep brown violet	6.00	.20
		Never hinged	9.50	
		On special delivery cover		10.00
		Block of 4	25.00	.80
		P# block of 6	72.50	
		Never hinged	100.00	

		P# block of 6 & large 5 point star, side only	115.00	
		Never hinged	160.00	
		P# block of 6 & large 6 point star, side only	240.00	
		Never hinged	325.00	
		Double transfer, (14404 UL 73 & 74)	12.50	1.00
a.		Horiz. pair, imperf. vert.	1,000.	
565	A168	14c **blue,** *May 1, 1923*	4.00	.75
		deep blue	4.00	.75
		Never hinged	6.50	
		On registered cover with other values		15.00
		Block of 4	16.50	4.25
		P# block of 6	47.50	
		Never hinged	67.50	
		Double transfer	—	

Horizontal pairs of No. 565 are known with spacings up to 3mm instead of 2mm between. These are from the 5th and 6th vertical rows of the right panes of Plate 14515 and also between stamps Nos. 3 and 4 of the same pane. A plate block of Pl. 14512 is known with 3mm spacing.

566	A169	15c **gray,** *Nov. 11, 1922*	23.00	.20
		light gray	23.00	.20
		Never hinged	37.50	
		On registered cover with 2c		3.00
		Block of 4	97.50	.40
		P# block of 6	250.00	
		Never hinged	340.00	
		P# block of 6 & large 5 point star, side only	475.00	
		Never hinged	675.00	
567	A170	20c **carmine rose,** *May 1, 1923*	22.00	.20
		deep carmine rose	22.00	.20
		Never hinged	35.00	
		On registered UPU-rate cover		10.00
		Block of 4	92.50	.50
		P# block of 6	230.00	
		Never hinged	325.00	
		P# block of 6 & large 5 point star, side only	500.00	
		Never hinged	675.00	
a.		Horiz. pair, imperf. vert.	1,500.	

"Bridge over Falls" plate scratches

568	A171	25c **yellow green,** *Nov. 11, 1922*	18.00	.45
		green	18.00	.45
		deep green	18.00	.45
		Never hinged	29.00	
		On contract airmail cover		25.00
		Block of 4	75.00	2.50
		P# block of 6	240.00	
		Never hinged	340.00	
		Double transfer	—	—
		Plate scratches ("Bridge over Falls")	—	—
b.		Vert. pair, imperf. horiz.	1,750.	
c.		Perf. 10 at one side	3,000.	

Double Transfer

569	A172	30c **olive brown,** *Mar. 20, 1923*	32.50	.35
		Never hinged	52.50	
		On registered cover with other values		17.50
		Block of 4	140.00	3.00
		P# block of 6	230.00	
		Never hinged	325.00	
		Double transfer (16065 UR 52)	55.00	—
570	A173	50c **lilac,** *Nov. 11, 1922*	55.00	.20
		dull lilac	55.00	.20
		Never hinged	87.50	
		On Federal airmail cover		25.00
		Block of 4	220.00	.75
		P# block of 6	600.00	
		Never hinged	850.00	
571	A174	$1 **violet black,** *Feb. 12, 1923*	45.00	.45
		violet brown	45.00	.45
		Never hinged	72.50	
		On post-1932 registered cover with other values		20.00
		Block of 4	185.00	2.50
		Margin block of 4, arrow, top or bottom	195.00	

P# block of 6	300.00	
Never hinged	400.00	
Double transfers, Pl. 18642 L 30 and Pl. 18682	90.00	1.50
572 A175 $2 **deep blue**, *Mar. 20, 1923*	90.00	9.00
Never hinged	145.00	
On post-1932 registered cover with other values		50.00
Block of 4	375.00	50.00
Margin block of 4, arrow, top or bottom	390.00	
P# block of 6	675.00	
Never hinged	950.00	
573 A176 $5 **carmine & blue**, *Mar. 20, 1923*	150.00	15.00
Never hinged	240.00	
On post-1932 registered cover with other values		150.00
Block of 4	625.00	77.50
Margin block of 4, arrow	650.00	
Center line block	700.00	100.00
P# block of 8, two P# & arrow	1,900.00	
Never hinged	2,600.00	
a. $5 carmine lake & dark blue	175.00	16.00
Never hinged	280.00	
On post-1932 registered cover with other values		160.00
Block of 4	725.00	80.00
Margin block of 4, arrow	750.00	
Center line block	800.00	125.00
P# block of 8, two P# & arrow	2,100.00	
Never hinged	2,900.00	
Nos. 551-573 (23)	634.85	32.75
Nos. 551-573, never hinged	1,020.	

For other listings of perforated stamps of designs A154 to A176 see:
Nos. 578 & 579, Perf. 11x10
Nos. 581-591, Perf. 10
Nos. 594-596, Perf. 11
Nos. 632-642, 653, 692-696, Perf. 11x10½
Nos. 697-701, Perf. 10½x11
This series also includes #622-623 (perf. 11), 684-687 & 720-723.

Plate Blocks

Scott values for plate blocks printed from flat plates are for very fine side and bottom positions. Top position plate blocks with full wide selvage sell for more.

1923-25		*Imperf.*
Stamp design 19¼x22¼mm		
575 A155 1c **green**, *Mar. 1923*	7.25	5.00
deep green	7.25	5.00
Never hinged	11.50	
On commercial cover		100.00
On philatelic cover		8.50
Pair	15.00	12.50
Never hinged	24.00	
Block of 4	30.00	25.00
Corner margin block of 4	32.50	27.50
Margin block of 4, arrow	35.00	30.00
Center line block	40.00	40.00
P# block of 6	70.00	—
Never hinged	95.00	

Earliest known use: Mar. 16, 1923.

576 A156 1½c **yellow brown**, *Apr. 4, 1925*	1.50	1.50
pale yellow brown	1.50	1.50
brown	1.50	1.50
Never hinged	2.40	
On commercial cover		25.00
On philatelic cover		6.00
Pair	3.25	3.75
Never hinged	5.00	
Block of 4	6.50	7.50
Corner margin block of 4	6.75	8.00
Margin block of 4, arrow	7.00	10.00
Center line block	11.00	20.00
P# block of 6	20.00	—
Never hinged	27.50	
Double transfer	—	—

The 1½c A156 Rotary press imperforate is listed as No. 631.

577 A157 2c **carmine**	1.60	1.25
light carmine	1.60	1.25
Never hinged	2.60	
On commercial cover		15.00
On philatelic cover		5.00
Pair	3.50	3.00
Never hinged	5.50	
Block of 4	7.25	6.00
Corner margin block of 4	7.50	8.00
Margin block of 4, arrow	8.00	10.00
Center line block	13.00	15.00
P# block of 6	25.00	—
Never hinged	35.00	
P# block of 6, large 5 point star	67.50	—
Never hinged	95.00	
Nos. 575-577 (3)	10.35	7.75
Nos. 575-577, never hinged	16.50	

ROTARY PRESS PRINTINGS
(See note over No. 448)
Issued in sheets of 70, 100 or 170 stamps, coil waste of Nos. 597, 599
Stamp designs: 19¾x22¼mm

1923		*Perf. 11x10*
578 A155 1c **green**	100.00	140.00
Never hinged	160.00	
On cover		700.00

Block of 4	425.00	1,000.
P# block of 4, star	800.00	
Never hinged	1,125.	

Earliest known use: Nov. 1923.

579 A157 2c **carmine**	90.00	125.00
deep carmine	90.00	125.00
Never hinged	145.00	
Block of 4	375.00	900.00
On cover		400.00
P# block of 4, star	600.00	
Never hinged	850.00	
Recut in eye, plate 14731	110.00	150.00

Earliest known use: Feb. 20, 1923.

Plates of 400 subjects in four panes of 100 each
Stamp designs: 19¼x22½mm

1923-26		*Perf. 10*
581 A155 1c **green**, *Apr. 21, 1923*	11.00	.65
yellow green	11.00	.65
pale green	11.00	.65
Never hinged	17.50	
On postcard		.70
On 3rd class cover		1.10
Block of 4	40.00	3.50
P# block of 4	120.00	
Never hinged	145.00	
582 A156 1½c **brown**, *Mar. 19, 1925*	5.50	.60
dark brown	5.50	.60
Never hinged	8.75	
On 3rd class cover		5.25
Block of 4	24.00	3.25
P# block of 4	45.00	
Never hinged	62.50	
Pair with full horiz. gutter btwn.	160.00	
Pair with full vert. gutter btwn.	210.00	

No. 582 was available in full sheets of 400 subjects but was not regularly issued in that form.

583 A157 2c **carmine**, *Apr. 14, 1924*	3.00	.25
deep carmine	3.00	.25
Never hinged	4.75	
On cover		2.25
Block of 4	13.00	1.40
P# block of 4	32.50	
Never hinged	45.00	
a. Booklet pane of 6, *Aug. 27, 1926*	90.00	50.00
Never hinged	135.00	

Earliest known use (unprecanceled): July 21, 1924.

584 A158 3c **violet**, *Aug. 1, 1925*	32.50	2.25
Never hinged	52.50	
On postcard (UPU rate)		10.00
Block of 4	140.00	10.00
P# block of 4	260.00	
Never hinged	360.00	
585 A159 4c **yellow brown**, *Mar. 1925*	19.00	.45
deep yellow brown	19.00	.45
Never hinged	30.00	
On cover		12.50
Block of 4	80.00	3.00
P# block of 4	230.00	
Never hinged	325.00	

Earliest known use: Apr. 4, 1925.

586 A160 5c **blue**, *Dec. 1924*	19.00	.25
deep blue	19.00	.25
Never hinged	30.00	
On UPU-rate cover		5.00
Block of 4	80.00	1.25
P# block of 4	225.00	
Never hinged	310.00	
Double transfer	—	—
a. Horizontal pair, imperf. vertically		10,000.

No. 586a is unique, precanceled, with average centering and small faults, and it is valued as such.

Earliest known use: Apr. 4, 1925.

587 A161 6c **red orange**, *Mar. 1925*	9.25	.35
pale red orange	9.25	.35
Never hinged	15.00	
On registered cover with other values		12.50
Block of 4	40.00	2.75
P# block of 4	95.00	
Never hinged	130.00	

Earliest known use: Apr. 4, 1925.

588 A162 7c **black**, *May 29, 1926*	13.50	5.50
Never hinged	21.50	
On registered cover with other values		25.00
Block of 4	57.50	30.00
P# block of 4	115.00	
Never hinged	160.00	
589 A163 8c **olive green**, *May 29, 1926*	30.00	3.50
pale olive green	30.00	3.50
Never hinged	47.50	
On airmail cover		20.00
Block of 4	125.00	17.50
P# block of 4	240.00	
Never hinged	340.00	
590 A164 9c **rose**, *May 29, 1926*	6.00	2.25
Never hinged	9.50	
On registered cover with other values		20.00
Block of 4	26.00	12.50
P# block of 4	50.00	
Never hinged	70.00	
591 A165 10c **orange**, *June 8, 1925*	72.50	.25
Never hinged	115.00	
On airmail cover		15.00
Block of 4	310.00	1.50

P# block of 4	475.00	
Never hinged	675.00	
Nos. 581-591 (11)	221.25	16.30
Nos. 581-591, never hinged	352.00	

Bureau Precancels: 1c, 64 diff., 1½c, 76 diff., 2c, 58 diff., 3c, 41 diff., 4c, 36 diff., 5c, 38 diff., 6c, 36 diff., 7c, 18 diff., 8c, 18 diff., 9c, 13 diff., 10c, 39 diff.

Issued in sheets of 70 or 100 stamps, coil waste of Nos. 597, 599
Stamp designs approximately 19¾x22¼mm

1923		*Perf. 11*
594 A155 1c **green**	18,000.	6,000.
On cover		10,500.
Pair		13,000.

No. 594 unused is valued without gum; both unused and used are valued with perforations just touching frameline on one side.

Earliest known use: Mar. 25, 1924.

595 A157 2c **carmine**	300.00	325.00
deep carmine	300.00	325.00
Never hinged	475.00	
On cover		550.00
Block of 4	1,300.	1,500.
P# block of 4, star	2,100.	
Never hinged	2,900.	
Recut in eye, plate 14731		

Earliest known use: Mar. 31, 1923 (dated cancel on off-cover pair of stamps); June 29, 1923 (on cover).

Rotary press sheet waste
Stamp design approximately 19¼x22½mm

596 A155 1c **green**, machine cancel		70,000.
With Bureau precancel		55,000.

A majority of copies of No. 596 carry the Bureau precancel "Kansas City, Mo."
No. 596 is valued in the grade of fine.

COIL STAMPS
ROTARY PRESS

1923-29		*Perf. 10 Vertically*
Stamp designs approximately 19¾x22¼mm		
597 A155 1c **green**, *July 18, 1923*	.30	.20
yellow green	.30	.20
Never hinged	.50	
Three on cover		2.00
Pair	.65	.20
Never hinged	1.05	
Joint line pair	2.25	.35
Never hinged	3.60	
Gripper cracks	2.60	1.00
Double transfer	2.60	1.00
598 A156 1½c **brown**, *Mar. 19, 1925*	1.00	.20
deep brown	1.00	.20
Never hinged	1.60	
On 3rd class cover		5.00
Pair	2.20	.25
Never hinged	3.50	
Joint line pair	4.75	.65
Never hinged	7.50	

TYPE I

TYPE II

TYPE I   TYPE II

TYPE I. No heavy hair lines at top center of head. Outline of left acanthus scroll generally faint at top and toward base at left side.

TYPE II. Three heavy hair lines at top center of head; two being outstanding in the white area. Outline of left acanthus scroll very strong and clearly defined at top (under left edge of lettered panel) and at lower curve (above and to left of numeral oval). This type appears only on Nos. 599A and 634A.

599	A157	2c	**carmine**, type I, *Jan. 1923*	.40	.20
			deep carmine, type I	.40	.20
			Never hinged	.65	
			On cover		1.00
			Pair, type I	.85	.20
			Never hinged	1.35	
			Joint line pair, type I	2.30	.35
			Never hinged	3.75	
			Double transfer, type I	1.90	1.00
			Gripper cracks, type I	2.30	2.00

Earliest known use: Jan. 10, 1923.

599A	A157	2c	**carmine**, type II, *Mar. 1929*	125.00	11.00
			Never hinged	200.00	
			On cover		27.50
			Pair, type II	260.00	26.00
			Never hinged	410.00	
			Joint line pair, type II	675.00	150.00
			Never hinged	1,075.	
			Joint line pair, types I & II	775.00	190.00
			Never hinged	1,250.	

Earliest known use: Mar. 29, 1929.

600	A158	3c	**violet**, *May 10, 1924*	7.25	.20
			deep violet	7.25	.20
			Never hinged	11.50	
			On cover		5.00

			Pair	15.50	.30
			Never hinged	25.00	
			Joint line pair	25.00	1.25
			Never hinged	40.00	
			Cracked plate	—	
601	A159	4c	**yellow brown**, *Aug. 5, 1923*	4.50	.35
			brown	4.50	.35
			Never hinged	7.25	
			On cover		12.00
			Pair	9.50	.95
			Never hinged	15.00	
			Joint line pair	30.00	2.75
			Never hinged	47.50	

Earliest known use: Sept. 14, 1923.

602	A160	5c	**dark blue**, *Mar. 5, 1924*	1.75	.20
			Never hinged	2.80	
			On UPU-rate cover		5.00
			Pair	3.75	.32
			Never hinged	6.00	
			Joint line pair	10.00	.85
			Never hinged	16.00	
603	A165	10c	**orange**, *Dec. 1, 1924*	4.00	.20
			Never hinged	6.50	
			On special delivery cover with 2c		20.00
			Pair	9.00	.25
			Never hinged	14.50	
			Joint line pair	26.50	1.25
			Never hinged	42.50	

The 6c design A161 coil stamp is listed as No. 723.
Bureau Precancels: 1c, 296 diff., 1½c, 188 diff., 2c, type I, 113 diff., 2c, type II, Boston, Detroit, 3c, 62 diff., 4c, 34 diff., 5c, 36 diff., 10c, 32 diff.

1923-25   *Perf. 10 Horizontally*
Stamp designs: 19¼x22½mm

604	A155	1c	**green**, *July 19, 1924*	.35	.20
			yellow green	.35	.20
			Never hinged	.55	
			Three on cover		5.00
			Pair	.80	.20
			Never hinged	1.30	
			Joint line pair	3.75	.45
			Never hinged	6.00	
605	A156	1½c	**yellow brown**, *May 9, 1925*	.35	.20
			brown	.35	.20
			Never hinged	.55	
			On 3rd class cover		15.00
			Pair	.80	.35
			Never hinged	1.30	
			Joint line pair	3.50	.60
			Never hinged	5.50	
606	A157	2c	**carmine**, *Dec. 31, 1923*	.35	.20
			Never hinged	.55	
			On cover		3.00
			Pair	.80	.45
			Never hinged	1.30	
			Joint line pair	2.60	.75
			Never hinged	4.25	
			Cracked plate	5.25	2.00
			Nos. 597-599,600-606 (10)	20.25	2.15
			Nos. 597-599, 600-606, never hinged	32.45	

HARDING MEMORIAL ISSUE

Tribute to the memory of President Warren G. Harding, who died in San Francisco, Aug. 2, 1923.

Warren Gamaliel Harding — A177

Plates of 400 subjects in four panes of 100 each
FLAT PLATE PRINTINGS
Stamp designs: 19¼x22¼mm

1923   *Perf. 11*

610	A177	2c	**black**, *Sept. 1, 1923*	.65	.20
			intense black	.65	.20
			grayish black	.65	.20
			Never hinged	1.05	
			On cover		.25
			P# block of 6	20.00	—
			Never hinged	27.50	
			Double transfer	1.75	.50
a.			Horiz. pair, imperf. vert.	1,750.	

Imperf

611	A177	2c	**black**, *Nov. 15, 1923*	6.25	4.00
			Never hinged	10.00	
			On philatelic cover		7.00
			On commercial cover		15.00
			Pair	13.00	10.00
			Never hinged	21.00	
			Corner margin block of 4	27.50	22.50
			Margin block of 4, arrow	27.50	22.50
			Center line block	60.00	40.00
			P# block of 6	75.00	—
			Never hinged	105.00	

ROTARY PRESS PRINTINGS
Stamp designs: 19¼x22½mm
Perf. 10

612	A177	2c	**black**, *Sept. 12, 1923*	17.50	1.75
			gray black	17.50	1.75
			Never hinged	27.50	
			On cover		2.75
			P# block of 4	300.00	
			Never hinged	425.00	
			Pair with full vertical gutter between	350.00	

Perf. 11

613	A177	2c	**black**		27,500.
			Pair		60,000.

No. 613 was produced from rotary press sheet waste. It is valued in the grade of fine.

HUGUENOT-WALLOON TERCENTENARY ISSUE

300th anniversary of the settling of the Walloons, and in honor of the Huguenots.

Ship "Nieu Nederland" — A178

Walloons Landing at Fort Orange (Albany) — A179

Jan Ribault Monument at Duval County, Fla. — A180

"Broken Circle" flaw

Designed by Clair Aubrey Huston

FLAT PLATE PRINTINGS
Plates of 200 subjects in four panes of 50 each

1924, May 1   *Perf. 11*

614	A178	1c	**dark green**	2.75	3.25
			green	2.75	3.25
			Never hinged	4.25	
			On cover		4.25
			P# block of 6	35.00	
			Never hinged	50.00	
			Double transfer	6.50	6.50
615	A179	2c	**carmine rose**	5.50	2.10
			dark carmine rose	5.50	2.10
			Never hinged	8.75	
			On cover		3.00
			P# block of 6	60.00	
			Never hinged	85.00	
			Double transfer	12.00	3.50
616	A180	5c	**dark blue**	22.50	12.50
			deep blue	22.50	12.50
			Never hinged	35.00	
			On UPU-rate cover		17.50
			P# block of 6	225.00	
			Never hinged	325.00	
			Added line at bottom of white circle around right numeral, so-called "broken circle" (15754 UR 2, 3, 4, 5)	45.00	15.00
			Nos. 614-616 (3)	30.75	17.85
			Nos. 614-616, never hinged	48.00	

LEXINGTON-CONCORD ISSUE

150th anniv. of the Battle of Lexington-Concord.

Washington at
Cambridge — A181

"Birth of Liberty," by
Henry
Sandham — A182

The Minute Man,
by Daniel Chester
French — A183

Plates of 200 subjects in four panes of 50 each

1925, Apr. 4			*Perf. 11*	
617	A181	1c	**deep green**	2.50	2.40
			green	2.50	2.40
			Never hinged	4.00	
			On cover		3.25
			P# block of 6	35.00	—
			Never hinged	50.00	
618	A182	2c	**carmine rose**	5.00	3.90
			pale carmine rose	5.00	3.90
			Never hinged	8.00	
			On cover		5.00
			P# block of 6	60.00	—
			Never hinged	85.00	
619	A183	5c	**dark blue**	20.00	12.50
			blue	20.00	12.50
			Never hinged	32.50	
			On UPU-rate cover		17.50
			P# block of 6	210.00	—
			Never hinged	300.00	
			Line over head (16807 LL 48)	42.50	18.50
			Nos. 617-619 (3)	27.50	18.80
			Nos. 617-619, never hinged	44.50	

NORSE-AMERICAN ISSUE

Arrival in New York, on Oct. 9, 1825, of the sloop "Restaurationen" with the first group of immigrants from Norway.

Sloop "Restaurationen"
A184

Viking Ship
A185

Designed by Clair Aubrey Huston.

Plates of 100 subjects.

1925, May 18			*Perf. 11*	
620	A184	2c	**carmine & black**	4.00	3.00
			deep carmine & black	4.00	3.00
			Never hinged	6.50	
			On cover		4.00
			Margin block of 4, arrow	17.50	
			Center line block	50.00	
			P# block of 8, two P# & arrow	180.00	—
			Never hinged	250.00	
			P# block of 8, carmine & arrow; black P# omitted	3,250.	—
621	A185	5c	**dark blue & black**	15.00	10.50
			Never hinged	24.00	
			On UPU-rate cover		15.00
			Margin block of 4, arrow	62.50	
			Center line block	75.00	
			P# block of 8, two P# & arrow	525.00	—
			Never hinged	750.00	

REGULAR ISSUE

Benjamin
Harrison — A186

Woodrow Wilson — A187

Plates of 400 subjects in four panes of 100.

1925-26			*Perf. 11*	
622	A186	13c	**green,** *Jan. 11, 1926*	13.50	.45
			light green	13.50	.45
			Never hinged	21.00	
			On registered cover with other values		15.00
			P# block of 6	145.00	200.00
			Never hinged	200.00	
			P# block of 6, large 5 point star, side only	2,100.	—
			Never hinged	2,750.	
623	A187	17c	**black,** *Dec. 28, 1925*	15.00	.25
			gray black	15.00	.25
			Never hinged	24.00	
			On registered cover		5.00
			P# block of 6	160.00	—
			Never hinged	220.00	

Plate Blocks

Scott values for plate blocks printed from flat plates are for very fine side and bottom positions. Top position plate blocks with full wide selvage sell for more.

SESQUICENTENNIAL EXPOSITION ISSUE

Sesquicentennial Exposition, Philadelphia, Pa., June 1 - Dec. 1, 1926, and 150th anniv. of the Declaration of Independence.

Liberty
Bell — A188

Designed by Clair Aubrey Huston.

Plates of 200 subjects in four panes of 50.

1926, May 10			*Perf. 11*	
627	A188	2c	**carmine rose**	3.25	.50
			Never hinged	4.50	
			On cover		1.00
			On cover, Expo. station machine canc.		7.50
			On cover, Expo. station duplex handstamp canc.		35.00
			P# block of 6	37.50	—
			Never hinged	47.50	
			Double transfer		—

ERICSSON MEMORIAL ISSUE

Unveiling of the statue of John Ericsson, builder of the "Monitor," by the Crown Prince of Sweden, Washington, D.C., May 29, 1926.

Statue of John
Ericsson — A189

Designed by Clair Aubrey Huston.

Plates of 200 subjects in four panes of 50.

1926, May 29			*Perf. 11*	
628	A189	5c	**gray lilac**	6.50	3.25
			Never hinged	9.50	
			On UPU-rate cover		8.00
			P# block of 6	80.00	—
			Never hinged	100.00	

BATTLE OF WHITE PLAINS ISSUE

150th anniv. of the Battle of White Plains, N. Y.

Alexander Hamilton's
Battery — A190

Designed by Clair Aubrey Huston.

Plates of 400 subjects in four panes of 100.

1926, Oct. 18			*Perf. 11*	
629	A190	2c	**carmine rose**	2.25	1.70
			Never hinged	3.25	
			On cover		2.25

		P# block of 6	35.00	—
		Never hinged	45.00	
a.		Vertical pair, imperf. between		

INTERNATIONAL PHILATELIC EXHIBITION ISSUE
SOUVENIR SHEET

A190a

Plates of 100 subjects in four panes of 25 each, separated by one inch wide gutters with central guide lines.

Condition valued:

Centering: Overall centering will average very fine, but individual stamps may be better or worse.

Perforations: No folds along rows of perforations.

Gum: There may be some light gum bends but no gum creases.

Hinging: There may be hinge marks in the selvage and on up to two or three stamps, but no heavy hinging or hinge remnants (except in the ungummed portion of the wide selvage).

Margins: Top panes should have about ½ inch bottom margin and 1 inch top margin.

Bottom panes should have about ½ inch top margin and just under ¾ inch bottom margin. Both will have one wide side (usually 1 inch plus) and one narrow (½ inch) side margin. The wide margin corner will have a small diagonal notch on top panes.

1926, Oct. 18			*Perf. 11*	
630	A190a	2c	**carmine rose,** sheet of 25	375.00	450.00
			Never hinged	550.00	
			On cover		—
			Dot over first "S" of "States" 18774 LL 9 or 18773 LL 11, sheet	400.00	475.00

Issued in sheets measuring 158-160¼x136-146½mm containing 25 stamps with inscription "International Philatelic Exhibition, Oct. 16th to 23rd, 1926" in top margin.

VALUES FOR VERY FINE STAMPS
Please note: Stamps are valued in the grade of Very Fine unless otherwise indicated.

REGULAR ISSUE
ROTARY PRESS PRINTINGS
(See note over No. 448.)
Plates of 400 subjects in four panes of 100 each
Stamp designs 19¼x22½mm

1926, Aug. 27			*Imperf.*	
631	A156	1½c	**yellow brown**	1.90	1.70
			light brown	1.90	1.70
			Never hinged	2.75	
			On philatelic cover		10.00
			Pair	4.00	4.00
			Never hinged	5.75	
			Pair, vert. gutter between	4.50	5.00
			Pair, horiz. gutter between	4.50	5.00
			Margin block with dash (left, right, top or bottom)	10.00	14.00
			Center block with crossed gutters and dashes	25.00	27.50
			P# block of 4	62.50	
			Never hinged	85.00	
			Without gum breaker ridges	80.00	
			Pair, vert. gutter between	200.00	
			Pair, horiz. gutter btwn.	200.00	
			Center block with crossed gutters and dashes	1,250.	

1926-34			*Perf. 11x10½*	
632	A155	1c	**green,** *June 10, 1927*	.20	.20
			yellow green	.20	.20
			Never hinged	.20	
			Three on cover		1.00
			P# block of 4	2.00	
			Never hinged	2.60	
			Pair with full vertical gutter btwn.	150.00	
			Cracked plate		—
a.			Booklet pane of 6, *Nov. 2, 1927*	5.50	2.25
			Never hinged	7.00	
b.			Vertical pair, imperf. between	1,600.	125.00
			Never hinged	2,500.	
c.			Horiz. pair, imperf. between		—
633	A156	1½c	**yellow brown,** *May 17, 1927*	1.90	.20
			deep brown	1.90	.20
			Never hinged	2.60	
			On 3rd class cover		2.00
			P# block of 4	62.50	
			Never hinged	82.50	

Normal	Recut ("long ear")

634 A157 2c **carmine**, type I, *Dec. 10, 1926*   .20 .20
  Never hinged .20
  On cover .20
  P# block of 4, type I, # opposite corner stamp 1.75 —
    Never hinged 2.40
  Vertical P# block of 10, # opposite 3rd horizontal row from top or bottom (Experimental Electric Eye plates) 5.00 —
    Never hinged 6.50
  Margin block of 4, Electric Eye marking .45 .25
  Pair with full vertical gutter between 200.00
  Recut ("long ear"), type I, 20342 UR 34 — —
  Recut face, type I, 20234 LL 58 — —
b.   2c carmine lake, type I — —
  P# block of 4 —
c.   Horizontal pair, type I, imperf. between 2,000.
d.   Booklet pane of 6, type I, *Feb. 25, 1927* 1.75 1.10
    Never hinged 2.50

Shades of the carmine exist.
No. 634, Type I, exists on a thin, tough experimental paper.

634A A157 2c **carmine**, type II, *Dec. 1928* 350.00 13.50
  Never hinged 500.00
  On cover 21.00
  P# block of 4, type II 2,000.
    Never hinged 2,750.
  Pair with full horiz. gutter btwn. 1,000. —
  Pair with full vert. gutter btwn. 1,000. —
  Center block with crossed gutters —

Earliest known use: Dec. 19, 1928.

No. 634A, Type II, was available in full sheet of 400 subjects but was not regularly issued in that form.

635 A158 3c **violet**, *Feb. 3, 1927* .40 .20
  Never hinged .55
  On cover 2.00
  P# block of 4 12.00 —
    Never hinged 18.00
a.   3c bright violet, *Feb. 7, 1934* re-issue, Plates 21185 & 21186 .20 .20
    Never hinged .30
    On cover .25
    P# block of 4 5.50 —
      Never hinged 7.25
    Gripper cracks 3.25 2.00
636 A159 4c **yellow brown**, *May 17, 1927* 2.10 .20
  Never hinged 3.00
  On cover 7.00
  P# block of 4 72.50 —
    Never hinged 95.00
  Pair with full vert. gutter btwn. 200.00
637 A160 5c **dark blue**, *Mar. 24, 1927* 2.10 .20
  Never hinged 3.00
  On UPU-rate cover 4.00
  P# block of 4 14.00 —
    Never hinged 19.00
  Pair with full vert. gutter btwn. 275.00
  Double transfer — —
638 A161 6c **red orange**, *July 27, 1927* 2.10 .20
  Never hinged 3.00
  On airmail cover 5.00
  P# block of 4 14.00 —
    Never hinged 19.00
  Pair with full horiz. gutter btwn. —
  Pair with full vert. gutter btwn. 200.00
639 A162 7c **black**, *Mar. 24, 1927* 2.10 .20
  Never hinged 3.00
  On registered cover with other values 12.50
  P# block of 4 14.00 —
    Never hinged 19.00
a.   Vertical pair, imperf. between 275.00 85.00
640 A163 8c **olive green**, *June 10, 1927* 2.10 .20
  olive bister 2.10 .20
  Never hinged 3.00
  On airmail cover 7.00
  P# block of 4 15.00 —
    Never hinged 19.00
641 A164 9c **rose**, *May 17, 1927* 2.10 .20
  salmon rose 2.10 .20
  orange red, *1931* 2.10 .20
  Never hinged 3.00
  On registered cover with other values 7.00
  P# block of 4 15.00 —
    Never hinged 19.00

  Pair with full vert. gutter btwn. —
642 A165 10c **orange**, *Feb. 3, 1927* 3.50 .20
  Never hinged 5.00
  On special delivery cover with 2c 5.00
  P# block of 4 21.00 —
    Never hinged 30.00
  Double transfer —
  Nos. 632-634,635-642 (11) 18.80 2.20
  Nos. 632-634, never hinged 26.45

The 1½c, 2c, 4c, 5c, 6c, 8c imperf. (dry print) are printer's waste.
See No. 653.
Bureau Precancels: 1c, 292 diff., 1½c, 147 diff., 2c, type I, 99 diff., 2c type II, 4 diff., 3c, 101 diff., 4c, 60 diff., 5c, 91 diff., 6c, 78 diff., 7c, 66 diff., 8c, 78 diff., 9c, 60 diff., 10c, 97 diff.

VERMONT SESQUICENTENNIAL ISSUE

Battle of Bennington, 150th anniv. and State independence.

Green Mountain Boy — A191

FLAT PLATE PRINTING
Plates of 400 subjects in four panes of 100.

1927, Aug. 3   **Perf. 11**
643 A191 2c **carmine rose** 1.40 .80
  Never hinged 2.00
  On cover 1.50
  P# block of 6 37.50 —
    Never hinged 47.50

BURGOYNE CAMPAIGN ISSUE

Battles of Bennington, Oriskany, Fort Stanwix and Saratoga.

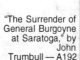

"The Surrender of General Burgoyne at Saratoga," by John Trumbull — A192

Plates of 200 subjects in four panes of 50.

1927, Aug. 3   **Perf. 11**
644 A192 2c **carmine rose** 3.50 2.10
  Never hinged 5.00
  On cover 3.00
  P# block of 6 32.50 —
    Never hinged 42.50

VALLEY FORGE ISSUE

150th anniversary of Washington's encampment at Valley Forge, Pa.

Washington at Prayer — A193

Plates of 400 subjects in four panes of 100.

1928, May 26   **Perf. 11**
645 A193 2c **carmine rose** 1.05 .40
  Never hinged 1.45
  On cover .75
  P# block of 6 25.00 —
    Never hinged 32.50
a.   2c lake —
    Never hinged —

BATTLE OF MONMOUTH ISSUE

150th anniv. of the Battle of Monmouth, N.J., and "Molly Pitcher" (Mary Ludwig Hayes), the heroine of the battle.

No. 634 Overprinted   **MOLLY**
                      PITCHER

ROTARY PRESS PRINTING

1928, Oct. 20   **Perf. 11x10½**
646 A157 2c **carmine** 1.10 1.10
  Never hinged 1.50
  On cover 1.60
  P# block of 4 32.50

  Never hinged 42.50
  Wide spacing, vert. pair 50.00 —
a.   "Pitcher" only —

The normal space between a vertical pair of the overprints is 18mm, but pairs are known with the space measuring 28mm.

HAWAII SESQUICENTENNIAL ISSUE

Sesquicentennial Celebration of the discovery of the Hawaiian Islands.

Nos. 634 and 637 Overprinted   **HAWAII**
                          1778 - 1928

ROTARY PRESS PRINTING

1928, Aug. 13   **Perf. 11x10½**
647 A157 2c **carmine** 5.00 4.50
  Never hinged 7.00
  On cover 5.75
  P# block of 4 135.00 —
    Never hinged 190.00
  Wide spacing, vert. pair 100.00
648 A160 5c **dark blue** 14.50 13.50
  Never hinged 20.00
  On cover 20.00
  P# block of 4 260.00 —
    Never hinged 350.00

Nos. 647-648 were sold at post offices in Hawaii and at the Postal Agency in Washington, D.C. They were valid throughout the nation.
Normally the overprints were placed 18mm apart vertically, but pairs exist with a space of 28mm between the overprints.

AERONAUTICS CONFERENCE ISSUE

Intl. Civil Aeronautics Conf., Washington, D.C., Dec. 12 - 14, 1928, and 25th anniv. of the 1st airplane flight by the Wright Brothers, Dec. 17, 1903.

Wright Airplane — A194

Globe and Airplane — A195

"Prairie Dog" plate flaw

FLAT PLATE PRINTING
Plates of 200 subjects in four panes of 50.

1928, Dec. 12   **Perf. 11**
649 A194 2c **carmine rose** 1.25 .80
  Never hinged 1.75
  On cover 1.50
  P# block of 6 10.00 —
    Never hinged 13.50
650 A195 5c **blue** 5.25 3.25
  Never hinged 7.25
  On UPU-rate cover 5.00
  P# block of 6 50.00 —
    Never hinged 62.50
  Plate flaw "prairie dog" (19658 LL 50) 27.50 12.50

GEORGE ROGERS CLARK ISSUE

150th anniv. of the surrender of Fort Sackville, the present site of Vincennes, Ind., to Clark.

Surrender of Fort
Sackville — A196

Plates of 100 subjects in two panes of 50.

1929, Feb. 25   *Perf. 11*

651 A196 2c carmine & black		.65	.50
Never hinged		.90	
On cover			1.00
Margin block of 4, arrow (line only) right or left		2.75	
P# block of 6, two P# & "Top"		10.00	—
Never hinged		13.00	—
P# block of 10, red P# only		—	—
Double transfer (19721 R 14, 29 & 44)		4.25	2.25

REGULAR ISSUE
Type of 1922-26 Issue
ROTARY PRESS PRINTING
Plates of 400 subjects in four panes of 100.

1929, May 25   *Perf. 11x10½*

653 A154 ½c olive brown		.20	.20
Never hinged		.20	
On 1c stamped envelope (3rd class)			1.00
P# block of 4		1.50	—
Never hinged		2.25	
Damaged plate, (19652 LL 72)		1.50	.75
Retouched plate, (19652 LL 72)		1.50	.75
Pair with full horiz. gutter btwn.		*150.00*	

Bureau Precancels: 99 diff.

Edison's First
Lamp — A197

Major General
John
Sullivan — A198

ELECTRIC LIGHT'S GOLDEN JUBILEE ISSUE
Invention of the 1st incandescent electric lamp by
Thomas Alva Edison, Oct. 21, 1879, 50th anniv.

Designed by Alvin R. Meissner.

FLAT PLATE PRINTING
Plates of 400 subjects in four panes of 100.

1929   *Perf. 11*

654 A197 2c carmine rose, June 5		.70	.70
Never hinged		1.00	
On cover			1.10
P# block of 6		25.00	—
Never hinged		32.50	

ROTARY PRESS PRINTING
Perf. 11x10½

655 A197 2c carmine rose, June 11		.65	.20
Never hinged		.90	
On cover			.25
P# block of 4		35.00	—
Never hinged		45.00	

ROTARY PRESS COIL STAMP
Perf. 10 Vertically

656 A197 2c carmine rose, June 11		14.00	1.75
Never hinged		21.00	
On cover			2.75
Pair		30.00	4.00
Never hinged		45.00	
Joint line pair		75.00	27.50
Never hinged		110.00	

SULLIVAN EXPEDITION ISSUE
150th anniversary of the Sullivan Expedition in New
York State during the Revolutionary War.

PLATE PLATE PRINTING
Plates of 400 subjects in four panes of 100.

1929, June 17   *Perf. 11*

657 A198 2c carmine rose		.70	.60
Never hinged		1.00	
On cover			1.00
P# block of 6		25.00	—
Never hinged		32.50	
a. 2c lake		500.00	—
Never hinged		750.00	
P# block of 6		3,500.	—
Never hinged		4,500.	

REGULAR ISSUE
Nos. 632 to 642 Overprinted   **Kans.**

Officially issued May 1, 1929.
Some values are known canceled as early as Apr.
15.

This special issue was authorized as a measure of preventing losses from post office burglaries. Approximately a year's supply was printed and issued to postmasters. The P.O. Dept. found it desirable to discontinue the State overprinted stamps after the initial supply was used.

ROTARY PRESS PRINTING

1929, May 1   *Perf. 11x10½*

658 A155 1c green		2.50	2.00
Never hinged		3.75	
P# block of 4		35.00	—
Never hinged		47.50	
Wide spacing, pair		32.50	
a. Vertical pair, one without ovpt.		*325.00*	
659 A156 1½c brown		4.00	2.90
Never hinged		6.00	
P# block of 4		50.00	
Never hinged		67.50	
Wide spacing, pair		70.00	
a. Vertical pair, one without ovpt.		*350.00*	
660 A157 2c carmine		4.50	1.10
Never hinged		6.75	
P# block of 4		47.50	
Never hinged		65.00	
Wide spacing, pair		55.00	
661 A158 3c violet		22.50	15.00
Never hinged		34.00	
P# block of 4		210.00	
Never hinged		280.00	
a. Vertical pair, one without ovpt.		*425.00*	
662 A159 4c yellow brown		22.50	9.00
Never hinged		34.00	
P# block of 4		210.00	
Never hinged		280.00	
a. Vertical pair, one without ovpt.		*425.00*	
663 A160 5c deep blue		14.00	9.75
Never hinged		21.00	
P# block of 4		150.00	
Never hinged		200.00	
664 A161 6c red orange		32.50	18.00
Never hinged		50.00	
P# block of 4		450.00	
Never hinged		600.00	
665 A162 7c black		30.00	27.50
Never hinged		45.00	
P# block of 4		500.00	
Never hinged		675.00	
a. Vertical pair, one without ovpt.		—	

The existence of No. 665a has been questioned by specialists. The editors would like to see authenticated evidence of such a pair.

666 A163 8c olive green		110.00	75.00
Never hinged		165.00	
P# block of 4		825.00	—
Never hinged		1,100.	
667 A164 9c light rose		16.00	11.25
Never hinged		24.00	
P# block of 4		225.00	
Never hinged		300.00	
668 A165 10c orange yellow		25.00	12.00
Never hinged		37.50	
P# block of 4		350.00	
Never hinged		475.00	
Pair with full horizontal gutter between		—	
Nos. 658-668 (11)		283.50	183.50
Nos. 658-668, never hinged		427.00	

See notes following No. 679.

Overprinted   **Nebr.**

1929, May 1

669 A155 1c green		4.00	2.25
Never hinged		6.00	
P# block of 4		50.00	—
Never hinged		67.50	
Wide spacing, pair		40.00	45.00
a. Vertical pair, one without ovpt.		—	
b. No period after "Nebr." (19338, 19339 UR 26, 36)		50.00	

The existence of No. 669a has been questioned by specialists. The editors would like to see authenticated evidence of such a pair.

670 A156 1½c brown		3.75	2.50
Never hinged		5.50	
P# block of 4		52.50	—
Never hinged		70.00	
Wide spacing, pair		37.50	
671 A157 2c carmine		3.75	1.30
Never hinged		5.50	
P# block of 4		42.50	
Never hinged		57.50	
Wide spacing, pair		57.50	
672 A158 3c violet		15.00	12.00
Never hinged		22.50	
P# block of 4		165.00	
Never hinged		225.00	
Wide spacing, pair		80.00	
a. Vertical pair, one without ovpt.		*425.00*	
673 A159 4c yellow brown		22.50	15.00
Never hinged		34.00	
P# block of 4		250.00	
Never hinged		340.00	
Wide spacing, pair		120.00	
674 A160 5c deep blue		20.00	15.00

Never hinged		30.00	
P# block of 4		275.00	
Never hinged		375.00	
675 A161 6c red orange		47.50	24.00
Never hinged		72.50	
P# block of 4		525.00	—
Never hinged		700.00	
676 A162 7c black		27.50	18.00
Never hinged		41.00	
P# block of 4		300.00	
Never hinged		400.00	
677 A163 8c olive green		37.50	25.00
Never hinged		57.50	
P# block of 4		400.00	
Never hinged		550.00	
Wide spacing, pair		175.00	
678 A164 9c light rose		42.50	27.50
Never hinged		65.00	
P# block of 4		525.00	—
Never hinged		700.00	
Wide spacing, pair		160.00	
a. Vertical pair, one without ovpt.		*650.00*	
679 A165 10c orange yellow		135.00	22.50
Never hinged		200.00	
P# block of 4		950.	—
Never hinged		1,275.	
Nos. 669-679 (11)		359.00	165.05
Nos. 669-679, never hinged		539.50	

Nos. 658-661, 669-673, 677-678 are known with the overprints on vertical pairs spaced 32mm apart instead of the normal 22mm.

Important: Nos. 658-679 with original gum have either one horizontal gum breaker ridge per stamp or portions of two at the extreme top and bottom of the stamps, 21mm apart. Multiple complete gum breaker ridges indicate a fake overprint. Absence of the gum breaker ridge indicates either regumming or regumming and a fake overprint.

General Wayne
Memorial — A199

Lock No. 5,
Monongahela
River — A200

BATTLE OF FALLEN TIMBERS ISSUE
Memorial to Gen. Anthony Wayne and for 135th
anniv. of the Battle of Fallen Timbers, Ohio.

FLAT PLATE PRINTING
Plates of 400 subjects in four panes of 100.

1929, Sept. 14   *Perf. 11*

680 A199 2c carmine rose		.80	.80
deep carmine rose		.80	.80
Never hinged		1.10	
On cover			1.10
P# block of 6		22.50	—
Never hinged		29.00	

OHIO RIVER CANALIZATION ISSUE
Completion of the Ohio River Canalization Project,
between Cairo, Ill. and Pittsburgh, Pa.

Plates of 400 subjects in four panes of 100.

1929, Oct. 19   *Perf. 11*
681 A200 2c **carmine rose**   .70   .65
    Never hinged   .95
    On cover   1.10
    P# block of 6   15.00   —
    Never hinged   20.00

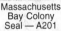

Massachusetts
Bay Colony
Seal — A201

Gov. Joseph
West and Chief
Shadoo, a
Kiowa — A202

MASSACHUSETTS BAY COLONY ISSUE

300th anniversary of the founding of the Massachusetts Bay Colony.

Plates of 400 subjects in four panes of 100.

1930, Apr. 8   *Perf. 11*
682 A201 2c **carmine rose**   .60   .50
    Never hinged   .85
    On cover   1.00
    P# block of 6   22.50   —
    Never hinged   29.00

CAROLINA-CHARLESTON ISSUE

260th anniv. of the founding of the Province of Carolina and the 250th anniv. of the city of Charleston, S.C.

Plates of 400 subjects in four panes of 100.

1930, Apr. 10   *Perf. 11*
683 A202 2c **carmine rose**   1.20   1.20
    Never hinged   1.65
    On cover   1.40
    P# block of 6   42.50   —
    Never hinged   55.00

REGULAR ISSUE

Harding — A203   Taft — A204

Type of 1922-26 Issue
ROTARY PRESS PRINTING

1930   *Perf. 11x10½*
684 A203 1½c **brown**, *Dec. 1*   .35   .20
    yellow brown   .35   .20
    Never hinged   .50
    On 3rd class cover   2.00
    P# block of 4   1.75   —
    Never hinged   2.50
    Pair with full horiz. gutter btwn. 175.00
    Pair with full vert. gutter btwn.   —
685 A204 4c **brown**, *June 4*   .90   .20
    deep brown   .90   .20
    Never hinged   1.25
    On cover   5.00
    P# block of 4   11.00   —
    Never hinged   14.00
    Gouge on right "4" (20141 UL
    24)   2.10   .60
    Recut right "4" (20141 UL 24)   2.10   .65
    Pair with full horiz. gutter btwn.

Bureau Precancels: 1½c, 96 diff., 4c, 46 diff.

ROTARY PRESS COIL STAMPS
Perf. 10 Vertically

686 A203 1½c **brown**, *Dec. 1*   1.80   .20
    Never hinged   2.50
    On 3rd class cover   5.00
    Pair   3.75   .20
    Never hinged   5.25
    Joint line pair   6.50   .50
    Never hinged   9.00
687 A204 4c **brown**, *Sept. 18*   3.25   .45
    Never hinged   4.50
    On cover   10.00
    Pair   6.75   1.00
    Never hinged   9.50
    Joint line pair   13.00   1.90
    Never hinged   18.00

Bureau Precancels: 1½c, 107 diff., 4c, 23 diff.

Statue of   General von
George   Steuben
Washington   A206
A205

BRADDOCK'S FIELD ISSUE

175th anniversary of the Battle of Braddock's Field, otherwise the Battle of Monongahela.

Designed by Alvin R. Meissner.

FLAT PLATE PRINTING
Plates of 400 subjects in four panes of 100.

1930, July 9   *Perf. 11*
688 A205 2c **carmine rose**   1.00   .85
    Never hinged   1.40
    On cover   1.00
    P# block of 6   30.00   —
    Never hinged   37.50

VON STEUBEN ISSUE

Baron Friedrich Wilhelm von Steuben (1730-1794), participant in the American Revolution.

FLAT PLATE PRINTING
Plates of 400 subjects in four panes of 100.

1930, Sept. 17   *Perf. 11*
689 A206 2c **carmine rose**   .55   .55
    Never hinged   .75
    On cover   1.05
    P# block of 6   20.00   —
    Never hinged   25.00
a.   Imperf., pair   *2,500.*
    Never hinged   *3,250.*
    P# block of 6   *12,000.*

The No. 689a plate block is unique but damaged. The value is for the item in its damaged condition.

General Casimir   "The Greatest
Pulaski — A207   Mother" — A208

PULASKI ISSUE

150th anniversary (in 1929) of the death of Gen. Casimir Pulaski, Polish patriot and hero of the American Revolutionary War.

Plates of 400 subjects in four panes of 100.

1931, Jan. 16   *Perf. 11*
690 A207 2c **carmine rose**   .30   .20
    deep carmine rose   .30   .20
    Never hinged   .40
    On cover   .50
    P# block of 6   10.00   —
    Never hinged   13.00

REGULAR ISSUE
TYPE OF 1922-26 ISSUES
ROTARY PRESS PRINTING

1931   *Perf. 11x10½*
692 A166 11c **light blue**, *Sept. 4*   2.60   .20
    Never hinged   3.70
    On registered cover with other
     values   10.00
    P# block of 4   13.50   —
     Never hinged   17.50
    Retouched forehead (20617 LL
     2, 3)   20.00   1.00
693 A167 12c **brown violet**, *Aug. 25*   5.50   .20
    violet brown   5.50   .20
    Never hinged   7.75
    Pair on registered cover   8.00
    P# block of 4   27.50   —
     Never hinged   35.00
694 A186 13c **yellow green**, *Sept. 4*   2.00   .20
    light yellow green   2.00   .20
    blue green   2.00   .20
    Never hinged   2.80
    On special delivery cover   25.00
    P# block of 4   12.50   —
     Never hinged   16.00
    Pair with full vert. gutter btwn. 150.00
695 A168 14c **dark blue**, *Sept. 8*   3.75   .25
    Never hinged   5.25
    On registered cover with other
     values   20.00
    P# block of 4   22.50   —
     Never hinged   30.00

696 A169 15c **gray**, *Aug. 27*   8.00   .20
    dark gray   8.00   .20
    Never hinged   11.25
    On registered cover with 3c   5.00
    P# block of 4   40.00   —
     Never hinged   50.00

        Perf. 10½x11
697 A187 17c **black**, *July 25*   4.50   .20
    Never hinged   6.25
    On registered cover   5.00
    P# block of 4   27.50   —
     Never hinged   35.00
698 A170 20c **carmine rose**, *Sept. 8*   8.75   .20
    Never hinged   12.50
    On registered UPU-rate cover   12.50
    P# block of 4   40.00   —
     Never hinged   52.50
    Double transfer (20538 LR 26)   —
699 A171 25c **blue green**, *July 25*   9.00   .20
    Never hinged   12.50
    On Federal airmail cover   20.00
    P# block of 4   47.50   —
     Never hinged   60.00
700 A172 30c **brown**, *Sept. 8*   17.50   .20
    Never hinged   25.00
    On Federal airmail cover   17.50
    P# block of 4   72.50   —
     Never hinged   95.00
    Retouched in head (20552 UL
     83)   27.50   .85
    Cracked plate (20552 UR 30)   27.50   .85
701 A173 50c **lilac**, *Sept. 4*   40.00   .20
    red lilac   40.00   .20
    Never hinged   55.00
    On Federal airmail cover   25.00
    P# block of 4   200.00   —
     Never hinged   250.00
    Nos. 692-701 (10)   101.60   2.05
    Nos. 692-701, never hinged   142.00

Bureau Precancels: 11c, 33 diff., 12c, 33 diff., 13c, 28 diff., 14c, 27 diff., 15c, 33 diff., 17c, 29 diff., 20c, 37 diff., 25c, 29 diff., 30c, 31 diff., 50c, 28 diff.

RED CROSS ISSUE

50th anniversary of the founding of the American Red Cross Society.

FLAT PLATE PRINTING
Plates of 200 subjects in two panes of 100.

1931, May 21   *Perf. 11*
702 A208 2c **black & red**   .25   .20
    Never hinged   .30
    Margin block of 4, arrow right or
     left   1.05
    P# block of 4, two P#   1.90   —
     Never hinged   2.40
    Double transfer   1.50   .50
a.   Red cross omitted   *40,000.*

The cross tends to shift, appearing in many slightly varied positions. The cross omitted variety is caused by a foldover of the paper. It is unique. Value reflects sale price at auction in 1994.

YORKTOWN ISSUE

Surrender of Cornwallis at Yorktown, 1781.

Rochambeau,
Washington, de
Grasse — A209

First Plate Layout - Border and vignette plates of 100 subjects in two panes of 50 subjects each. Plate numbers between 20461 and 20602.

Second Plate Layout - Border plates of 100 subjects in two panes of 50 each, separated by a 1 inch wide vertical gutter with central guide line and vignette plates of 50 subjects. Plate numbers between 20646 and 20671.

Issued in panes of 50 subjects.

1931, Oct. 19   *Perf. 11*
703 A209 2c **carmine rose & black**   .40   .25
    Never hinged   .50
    Margin block of 4, arrow marker,
     right or left   1.70
    Center line block   1.80
    P# block of 4, 2#   2.25   —
     Never hinged   2.75
    P# block of 4, 2# & arrow & mark-
     er block   2.25   —
     Never hinged   2.75
    P# block of 6, 2# & "TOP," arrow
     & marker   3.00   —
     Never hinged   3.50
    P# block of 8, 2# & "TOP"   3.75   —
     Never hinged   4.50
    Double transfer   1.75   .75
a.   2c lake & black   4.50   .75
    Never hinged   6.25
b.   2c dark lake & black   375.00
    Never hinged   525.00
    P# block of 4, 2#   2,000.
     Never hinged   2,500.
c.   Horiz. pair, imperf. vertically 5,000.

Never hinged 6,250.
P# block of 6, 2# & arrow & marker block, hinged —

WASHINGTON BICENTENNIAL ISSUE

200th anniversary of the birth of George Washington. Various Portraits of George Washington.

By Charles Willson
Peale, 1777 — A210

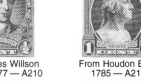

From Houdon Bust,
1785 — A211

By Charles Willson
Peale, 1772 — A212

By Gilbert Stuart,
1796 — A213

By Charles Willson
Peale, 1777 — A214

By Charles Peale
Polk — A215

By Charles Willson
Peale, 1795 — A216

By John Trumbull,
1792 — A217

By John Trumbull,
1780 — A218

By Charles B. J. F.
Saint Memin,
1798 — A219

By W. Williams,
1794 — A220

By Gilbert Stuart,
1795 — A221

Broken Circle

ROTARY PRESS PRINTINGS

Plates of 400 subjects in four panes of 100 each

1932, Jan. 1   *Perf. 11x10½*

704 A210	½c olive brown			.20	.20
	Never hinged			.20	
	P# block of 4			5.75	—
	Never hinged			7.50	
	Broken circle (20560 U.R. 8)			.75	.20
705 A211	1c green			.20	.20
	Never hinged			.20	
	P# block of 4			4.25	—
	Never hinged			5.50	
	Gripper cracks (20742 UL and UR)			2.75	1.75
706 A212	1½c brown			.40	.20
	Never hinged			.55	
	P# block of 4			14.50	—
	Never hinged			19.00	
707 A213	2c carmine rose			.20	.20
	Never hinged			.20	
	P# block of 4			1.50	—
	Never hinged			1.90	
	Pair with full vert. gutter between				
	Gripper cracks (20752 LR, 20755 LL & LR, 20756 LL, 20774 LR, 20792 LL & LR, 20796 LL & LR)			1.75	.65

Double Transfer

708 A214	3c deep violet			.55	.20
	Never hinged			.80	
	P# block of 4			16.50	—
	Never hinged			22.50	
	Double transfer			1.75	.65
	Broken top frame line (20847 LL 8)			4.00	.90

Retouch in Eyes — 4c

Cracked Plate — 5c

709 A215 4c **light brown**		.25	.20
Never hinged		.35	
P# block of 4		5.50	—
Never hinged		7.00	
Double transfer (20568 LR 60)		1.50	.25
Retouch in eyes (20568 LR 89)		2.00	.35
P# block of 4 with variety			
Broken bottom frame line (20568 LR 100)		1.50	.50
P# block of 4 with variety			
710 A216 5c **blue**		1.60	.20
Never hinged		2.25	
P# block of 4		16.50	—
Never hinged		22.50	
Cracked plate (20637 UR 80)		5.25	1.10
711 A217 6c **red orange**		3.25	.20
Never hinged		4.50	
P# block of 4		50.00	—
Never hinged		65.00	

Double Transfer

712 A218 7c **black**		.25	.20
Never hinged		.35	
P# block of 4		9.00	—
Never hinged		12.00	
Double transfer (20563 UL 1 or 20564 LL 91)		1.25	.25
P# block of 4 with variety			
713 A219 8c **olive bister**		2.75	.50
Never hinged		3.75	
P# block of 4		50.00	—
Never hinged		65.00	
Pair with full vert. gutter between		—	
714 A220 9c **pale red**		2.40	.20
orange red		2.40	.20
Never hinged		3.25	
P# block of 4		32.50	—
Never hinged		42.50	
715 A221 10c **orange yellow**		10.00	.20
Never hinged		14.00	
P# block of 4		85.00	—
Never hinged		110.00	
Nos. 704-715 (12)		22.05	2.70
Nos. 704-715, never hinged		30.25	

Skier — A222

Boy and Girl Planting Tree — A223

OLYMPIC WINTER GAMES ISSUE

3rd Olympic Winter Games, held at Lake Placid, N.Y., Feb. 4-13, 1932.

FLAT PLATE PRINTING

Plates of 400 subjects in four panes of 100.

1932, Jan. 25		**Perf. 11**	
716 A222 2c **carmine rose**		.40	.20
carmine		.40	.20
Never hinged		.50	
P# block of 6		10.00	—
Never hinged		12.50	
Cracked plate (20823 UR 41, 42; UL 48, 49, 50)		5.00	1.65
Recut (20823 UR 61)		3.50	1.50
Colored "snowball" (20815 UR 64)		25.00	5.00

ARBOR DAY ISSUE

1st observance of Arbor Day in the state of Nebraska, Apr. 1872, 60th anniv., and cent. of the birth of Julius Sterling Morton, who conceived the plan and the name "Arbor Day," while he was a member of the Nebraska State Board of Agriculture.

ROTARY PRESS PRINTING

Plates of 400 subjects in four panes of 100.

1932, Apr. 22		**Perf. 11x10½**	
717 A223 2c **carmine rose**		.20	.20
Never hinged		.20	
P# block of 4		6.50	—
Never hinged		8.00	

OLYMPIC GAMES ISSUE

Issued in honor of the 10th Olympic Games, held at Los Angeles, Calif., July 30 to Aug. 14, 1932.

Runner at Starting Mark — A224

Myron's Discobolus — A225

Designed by Victor S. McCloskey, Jr.

ROTARY PRESS PRINTING

Plates of 400 subjects in four panes of 100.

1932, June 15		**Perf. 11x10½**	
718 A224 3c **violet**		1.40	.20
deep violet		1.40	.20
Never hinged		1.75	
P# block of 4		11.50	—
Never hinged		14.50	
Gripper cracks (20906 UL 1)		4.25	.75
P# block of 4 with variety			
719 A225 5c **blue**		2.20	.20
deep blue		2.20	.20
Never hinged		2.75	
P# block of 4		20.00	—
Never hinged		25.00	
Gripper cracks (20868 UL & UR)		4.25	1.00

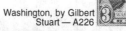

Washington, by Gilbert Stuart — A226

REGULAR ISSUE
ROTARY PRESS PRINTING

Plates of 400 subjects in four panes of 100.

1932		**Perf. 11x10½**	
720 A226 3c **deep violet**, *June 16*		.20	.20
light violet		.20	.20
Never hinged		.20	
P# block of 4		1.30	—
Never hinged		1.60	
Double transfer		1.00	.30
Recut face (20986 UR 15)		2.00	.75
Gripper cracks		1.25	.30
Pair with full vert. gutter btwn.		200.00	
Pair with full horiz. gutter btwn.		200.00	
b. Booklet pane of 6, *July 25*		37.50	7.50
Never hinged		50.00	
c. Vertical pair, imperf. between		1,250.	1,000.
Never hinged		425.00	

Bureau Precancels: 64 diff.

ROTARY PRESS COIL STAMPS

1932		**Perf. 10 Vertically**	
721 A226 3c **deep violet**, *June 24*		2.75	.20
light violet		2.75	.20
Never hinged		3.50	
Pair		5.75	.25
Never hinged		7.00	
Joint line pair		10.00	1.00
Never hinged		12.50	
Gripper cracks		—	—
Recut face (20995, pos. 29)		—	—
Recut lines around eyes		—	—

		Perf. 10 Horizontally	
722 A226 3c **deep violet**, *Oct. 12*		1.50	.35
light violet		1.50	.35
Never hinged		2.00	
Pair		3.25	.80
Never hinged		4.25	
Joint line pair		6.25	2.25
Never hinged		8.00	

Bureau Precancels: No. 721, 46 diff.

TYPE OF 1922-26 ISSUES

1932, Aug. 18		**Perf. 10 Vertically**	
723 A161 6c **deep orange**		11.00	.30
Never hinged		15.00	
Pair		24.00	.70

Never hinged		32.50	
Joint line pair		60.00	3.50
Never hinged		82.50	

Bureau Precancels: 5 diff.

William Penn A227

Daniel Webster (1782-1852), Statesman A228

WILLIAM PENN ISSUE

250th anniv. of the arrival in America of Penn (1644-1718), English Quaker and founder of Pennsylvania.

FLAT PLATE PRINTING

Plates of 400 subjects in four panes of 100 each

1932, Oct. 24		**Perf. 11**	
724 A227 3c **violet**		.30	.20
Never hinged		.40	
P# block of 6		8.00	—
Never hinged		10.00	
a. Vert. pair, imperf. horiz.		—	

DANIEL WEBSTER ISSUE
FLAT PLATE PRINTING

Plates of 400 subjects in four panes of 100.

1932, Oct. 24		**Perf. 11**	
725 A228 3c **violet**		.30	.25
light violet		.30	.25
Never hinged		.40	
P# block of 6		16.50	—
Never hinged		20.00	

Gen. James Edward Oglethorpe — A229

Washington's Headquarters at Newburgh, N.Y. — A230

GEORGIA BICENTENNIAL ISSUE

200th anniv. of the founding of the Colony of Georgia, and honoring Oglethorpe, who landed from England, Feb. 12, 1733, and personally supervised the establishing of the colony.

FLAT PLATE PRINTING

Plates of 400 subjects in four panes of 100.

1933, Feb. 12		**Perf. 11**	
726 A229 3c **violet**		.30	.20
Never hinged		.40	
P# block of 6		10.00	—
Never hinged		12.50	
P# block of 10, "CS"		14.00	—
Never hinged		17.50	
Bottom margin block of 20, no P#		—	

PEACE OF 1783 ISSUE

150th anniv. of the issuance by George Washington of the official order containing the Proclamation of Peace marking officially the ending of hostilities in the War for Independence.

ROTARY PRESS PRINTING

Plates of 400 subjects in four panes of 100 each

1933, Apr. 19		**Perf. 10½x11**	
727 A230 3c **violet**		.20	.20
Never hinged		.20	
P# block of 4		4.00	—
Never hinged		5.00	
Block of 4, horiz. gutter between		75.00	—
Block of 4, vert. gutter between		85.00	—
Center block with crossed gutters and dashes		—	

No. 727 was available in full sheets of 400 subjects with gum, but was not regularly issued in that form.

See No. 752 in the Special Printings following No. 751.

CENTURY OF PROGRESS ISSUES

"Century of Progress" Intl. Exhibition, Chicago, which opened June 1, 1933, and centenary of the incorporation of Chicago as a city.

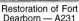

Restoration of Fort
Dearborn — A231

Federal
Building — A232

ROTARY PRESS PRINTING
Plates of 400 subjects in four panes of 100.

1933, May 25   **Perf. 10½x11**

728 A231 1c **yellow green**		.20	.20
Never hinged		.20	
On card, Expo. station machine canc.		1.00	
On card, Expo. station duplex handstamp canc.		3.00	
P# block of 4		1.90	—
Never hinged		2.50	
Block of 4, horizontal gutter between		150.00	
Block of 4, vertical gutter between		150.00	
Center block with crossed gutters and dashes		2,500.	
Gripper cracks (21133 UR & LR)		2.00	—
729 A232 3c **violet**		.20	.20
Never hinged		.20	
On cover, Expo. station machine canc.		2.00	
On cover, Expo. station duplex handstamp canc.		6.00	
P# block of 4		2.25	—
Never hinged		3.00	
Block of 4, horiz. gutter between		150.00	
Block of 4, vert. gutter between		150.00	
Center block with crossed gutters and dashes		2,500.	

Nos. 728 and 729 were not regularly issued in full sheets of 400 with gum. The gutter pairs and blocks come from a very few non-issued sheets that were retained by Postmaster James A. Farley.

AMERICAN PHILATELIC SOCIETY ISSUE
SOUVENIR SHEETS

A231a

A232a

FLAT PLATE PRINTING
Plates of 225 subjects in nine panes of 25 each.

1933, Aug. 25   *Imperf.*
Without Gum

730 A231a 1c **deep yellow green**, sheet of 25		27.50	27.50
a. Single stamp		.75	.45
Single on card, Expo. station machine canc.		1.50	
Single on card, Expo. station duplex handstamp canc.		5.00	
731 A232a 3c **deep violet**, sheet of 25		25.00	25.00
a. Single stamp		.65	.45
Single on cover, Expo. station machine canc.		3.00	
Single on cover, Expo. station duplex handstamp canc.		7.50	

Issued in sheets measuring 134x120mm containing twenty-five stamps, inscribed in the margins:

PRINTED BY THE TREASURY DEPARTMENT, BUREAU OF ENGRAVING AND PRINTING, - UNDER AUTHORITY OF JAMES A. FARLEY, POSTMASTER-GENERAL, AT CENTURY OF PROGRESS, - IN COMPLIMENT TO THE AMERICAN PHILATELIC SOCIETY FOR ITS CONVENTION AND EXHIBITION - CHICAGO, ILLINOIS, AUGUST, 1933. PLATE NO. 21145.

Also used were plates 21159 (1c), 21146 and 21160 (3c).

See Nos. 766-767 in the Special Printings following No. 751.

NATIONAL RECOVERY ACT ISSUE
Issued to direct attention to and arouse the support of the nation for the National Recovery Act.

 Group of Workers — A233

ROTARY PRESS PRINTING
Plates of 400 subjects in four panes of 100.

1933, Aug. 15   **Perf. 10½x11**

732 A233 3c **violet**		.20	.20
Never hinged		.20	
P# block of 4		1.50	—
Never hinged		1.80	
Gripper cracks (21151 UL & UR, 21153 UR & LR)		1.50	—
Recut at right (21151 UR 47)		2.00	

BYRD ANTARCTIC ISSUE
Issued in connection with the Byrd Antarctic Expedition of 1933 and for use on letters mailed through the Little America Post Office established at the Base Camp of the Expedition in the territory of the South Pole.

A Map of the World (on van der Grinten's Projection) — A234

Designed by Victor S. McCloskey, Jr.

FLAT PLATE PRINTING
Plates of 200 subjects in four panes of 50 each

1933, Oct. 9   **Perf. 11**

733 A234 3c **dark blue**		.50	.50
Never hinged		.60	
P# block of 6		14.00	—
Never hinged		17.50	
Double transfer (21167 LR 2)		2.75	1.00

In addition to the postage charge of 3 cents, letters sent by the ships of the expedition to be canceled in Little America were subject to a service charge of 50 cents each.

See No. 753 in the Special Printings following No. 751.

KOSCIUSZKO ISSUE
Kosciuszko (1746-1807), Polish soldier and statesman served in the American Revolution, on the 150th anniv. of the granting to him of American citizenship.

 Statue of General Tadeusz Kosciuszko — A235

Designed by Victor S. McCloskey, Jr.

FLAT PLATE PRINTING
Plates of 400 subjects in four panes of 100 each

1933, Oct. 13   **Perf. 11**

734 A235 5c **blue**		.55	.25
Never hinged		.65	
P# block of 6		27.50	—
Never hinged		32.50	
Cracked plate		—	
a. Horizontal pair, imperf. vertically		2,250.	
Never hinged		2,800.	
P# block of 8		25,000.	

The No. 734a plate block is unique but damaged. Value reflects 1997 sale.

NATIONAL STAMP EXHIBITION ISSUE
SOUVENIR SHEET

A235a

TYPE OF BYRD ISSUE
Plates of 150 subjects in 25 panes of six each.

1934, Feb. 10   *Imperf.*
Without Gum

735 A235a 3c **dark blue**, sheet of 6		12.50	10.00
a. Single stamp		2.00	1.65

Issued in sheets measuring 87x93mm containing six stamps, inscribed in the margins: "Printed by the Treasury Department, Bureau of Engraving and Printing, under authority of James A. Farley, Postmaster General, in the National Stamp Exhibition of 1934. New York, N. Y., February 10-18, 1934. Plate No. 21184." Plate No. 21187 was used for sheets printed at the Exhibition, but all these were destroyed.

See No. 768 in the Special Printings following No. 751.

MARYLAND TERCENTENARY ISSUE
300th anniversary of the founding of Maryland.

 "The Ark" and "The Dove" — A236

Designed by Alvin R. Meissner.

FLAT PLATE PRINTING
Plates of 400 subjects in four panes of 100.

1934, Mar. 23   **Perf. 11**

736 A236 3c **carmine rose**		.20	.20
Never hinged		.20	
P# block of 6		6.00	—
Never hinged		8.00	
Double transfer (21190 UL 1)		—	—

MOTHERS OF AMERICA ISSUE
Issued to commemorate Mother's Day.

Adaptation of Whistler's Portrait of his Mother — A237

Designed by Victor S. McCloskey, Jr.

Plates of 200 subjects in four panes of 50.
ROTARY PRESS PRINTING

1934, May 2   **Perf. 11x10½**

737 A237 3c **deep violet**		.20	.20
Never hinged		.20	
P# block of 4		1.00	—
Never hinged		1.25	

FLAT PLATE PRINTING
Perf. 11

738 A237 3c **deep violet**		.20	.20
Never hinged		.20	
P# block of 6		4.25	—
Never hinged		5.00	

See No. 754 in the Special Printings following No. 751.

WISCONSIN TERCENTENARY ISSUE
Arrival of Jean Nicolet, French explorer, on the shores of Green Bay, 300th anniv. According to historical records, Nicolet was the 1st white man to reach the territory now comprising the State of Wisconsin.

Nicolet's Landing — A238

Designed by Victor S. McCloskey, Jr.

FLAT PLATE PRINTING
Plates of 200 subjects in four panes of 50.

1934. July 7   *Perf. 11*

739	A238	3c **deep violet**	.20	.20
		violet	.20	.20
		Never hinged	.20	
		P# block of 6	3.00	—
		Never hinged	3.50	
a.		Vert. pair, imperf. horiz.	350.00	
		Never hinged	450.00	
b.		Horiz. pair, imperf. vert.	500.00	
		Never hinged	750.00	
		P# block of 6	2,000.	

See No. 755 in the Special Printings following No. 751.

NATIONAL PARKS YEAR ISSUE

El Capitan, Yosemite (California) — A239

Old Faithful, Yellowstone (Wyoming) — A243

View of Grand Canyon (Arizona) — A240

Mt. Rainier and Mirror Lake (Washington) A241

Cliff Palace, Mesa Verde Park (Colorado) — A242

Crater Lake (Oregon) — A244

Great Head, Acadia Park (Maine) — A245

Great White Throne, Zion Park (Utah) — A246

Great Smoky Mountains (North Carolina) — A248

Mt. Rockwell (Mt. Sinopah) and Two Medicine Lake, Glacier National Park (Montana) — A247

FLAT PLATE PRINTING
Plates of 200 subjects in four panes of 50.

1934   Unwmk.   *Perf. 11*

740	A239	1c **green,** *July 16*	.20	.20
		light green	.20	.20
		Never hinged	.20	
		P# block of 6	1.00	—
		Never hinged	1.25	
		Recut	1.50	.50
a.		Vert. pair, imperf. horiz., with gum	450.00	
		Never hinged	600.00	
741	A240	2c **red,** *July 24*	.20	.20
		orange red	.20	.20
		Never hinged	.20	
		P# block of 6	1.25	—
		Never hinged	1.50	
		Double transfer	1.25	
a.		Vert. pair, imperf. horiz., with gum	450.00	
		Never hinged	600.00	
b.		Horiz. pair, imperf. vert., with gum	500.00	
		P# block of 6	750.00	
		Never hinged	2,250.	
		Never hinged	3,000.	
742	A241	3c **deep violet,** *Aug. 3*	.20	.20
		Never hinged	.20	
		P# block of 6	1.75	—
		Never hinged	2.10	
		Recut	1.50	
a.		Vert. pair, imperf. horiz., with gum	425.00	
		Never hinged	575.00	
743	A242	4c **brown,** *Sept. 25*	.35	.40
		light brown	.35	.40
		Never hinged	.45	
		P# block of 6	7.00	—
		Never hinged	8.50	
a.		Vert. pair, imperf. horiz., with gum	700.00	
		Never hinged	1,000.	
744	A243	5c **blue,** *July 30*	.70	.65
		light blue	.70	.65
		Never hinged	.95	
		P# block of 6	8.75	—
		Never hinged	10.50	
a.		Horiz. pair, imperf. vert., with gum	500.00	
		Never hinged	725.00	
745	A244	6c **dark blue,** *Sept. 5*	1.10	.85
		Never hinged	1.50	
		P# block of 6	15.00	—
		Never hinged	18.00	
746	A245	7c **black,** *Oct. 2*	.60	.75
		Never hinged	.85	
		P# block of 6	10.00	—
		Never hinged	12.00	
		Double transfer	3.00	1.25
a.		Horiz. pair, imperf. vert., with gum	700.00	
		Never hinged	1,000.	
		P# block of 6, never hinged	4,750.	
747	A246	8c **sage green,** *Sept. 18*	1.60	1.50
		Never hinged	2.20	
		P# block of 6	15.00	—
		Never hinged	18.00	
748	A247	9c **red orange,** *Aug. 27*	1.50	.65
		orange	1.50	.65
		Never hinged	2.10	
		P# block of 6	15.00	—
		Never hinged	20.00	
749	A248	10c **gray black,** *Oct. 8*	3.00	1.25
		gray	3.00	1.25
		Never hinged	4.25	
		P# block of 6	22.50	—
		Never hinged	30.00	
		Nos. 740-749 (10)	9.45	6.65
		Nos. 740-749, never hinged	12.75	

Imperforate varieties of the 2c and 5c exist as errors of the perforated Parks set, but are virtually impossible to distinguish from gummed copies from the imperforate sheets of 200. (See note above No. 752 in the Special Printings following No. 751.

AMERICAN PHILATELIC SOCIETY ISSUE
SOUVENIR SHEET

A248a

Plates of 120 subjects in 20 panes of 6 stamps each.

1934, Aug. 28   *Imperf.*

750	A248a	3c **deep violet,** sheet of 6	30.00	27.50
		Never hinged	37.50	
a.		Single stamp	3.50	3.25
		Never hinged	4.50	

Issued in sheets measuring approximately 98x93mm containing six stamps, inscribed in the margins: PRINTED BY THE TREASURY DEPARTMENT, BUREAU OF ENGRAVING AND PRINTING, - UNDER AUTHORITY OF JAMES A. FARLEY, POSTMASTER GENERAL, - IN COMPLIMENT TO THE AMERICAN PHILATELIC SOCIETY FOR ITS CONVENTION AND EXHIBITION, - ATLANTIC CITY, NEW JERSEY, AUGUST, 1934. PLATE NO. 21303.

See No. 770 in the Special Printings following No. 751.

TRANS-MISSISSIPPI PHILATELIC EXPOSITION ISSUE
SOUVENIR SHEET

A248b

Plates of 120 subjects in 20 panes of 6 stamps each.

1934, Oct. 10   *Imperf.*

751	A248b	1c **green,** sheet of 6	12.50	12.50
		Never hinged	16.00	
a.		Single stamp	1.40	1.60
		Never hinged	1.85	

Issued in sheets measuring approximately 92x99mm containing six stamps, inscribed in the margins: PRINTED BY THE TREASURY DEPARTMENT, BUREAU OF ENGRAVING AND PRINTING, - UNDER AUTHORITY OF JAMES A. FARLEY, POSTMASTER GENERAL, - IN COMPLIMENT TO THE TRANS-MISSISSIPPI PHILATELIC EXPOSITION AND CONVENTION, OMAHA, NEBRASKA, - OCTOBER, 1934. PLATE NO. 21341.

See No. 769 in the Special Printings that follow.

SPECIAL PRINTING
(Nos. 752-771 inclusive)

"Issued for a limited time in full sheets as printed, and in blocks thereof, to meet the requirements of collectors and others who may be interested." -From Postal Bulletin No. 16614.

Issuance of the following 20 stamps in complete sheets resulted from the protest of collectors and others at the practice of presenting, to certain government officials, complete sheets of unsevered panes, imperforate (except Nos. 752 and 753) and generally ungummed.

Designs of Commemorative Issues
Without Gum

NOTE: In 1940 the P.O. Department offered to and did gum full sheets of Nos. 754-771 sent in by owners.

TYPE OF PEACE ISSUE

Issued in sheets of 400, consisting of four panes of 100 each, with vertical and horizontal gutters between and plate numbers at outside corners at sides.

ROTARY PRESS PRINTING

1935, Mar. 15   Unwmk.   Perf. 10½x11

752 A230	3c	**violet**	.20	.20
		Pair with horiz. gutter between	5.75	—
		Pair with vert. gutter between	9.50	—
		Gutter block of 4 with dash (left or right)	12.50	—
		Gutter block of 4 with dash (top or bottom)	20.00	—
		Center block with crossed gutters and dashes	50.00	—
		P# block of 4	20.00	—

TYPE OF BYRD ISSUE

Issued in sheets of 200, consisting of four panes of 50 each, with vertical and horizontal guide lines in gutters between panes, and plate numbers centered at top and bottom of each pane. This applies to Nos. 753-765 and 771.

FLAT PLATE PRINTING
Perf. 11

753 A234	3c	**dark blue**	.50	.45
		Pair with horiz. line between	2.25	—
		Pair with vert. line between	25.00	—
		Margin block of 4, arrow & guide line (left or right)	4.75	—
		Margin block of 4, arrow & guideline (top or bottom)	52.50	—
		Center line block	57.50	15.00
		P# block of 6, number at top or bottom	17.50	—

No. 753 is similar to No. 733. Positive identification is by blocks or pairs showing guide line between stamps. These lines between stamps are found only on No. 753.

TYPE OF MOTHERS OF AMERICA ISSUE
Issued in sheets of 200
FLAT PLATE PRINTING
Imperf

754 A237	3c	**deep violet**	.60	.60
		Pair with horiz. line between	1.75	—
		Pair with vert. line between	1.40	—
		Margin block of 4, arrow & guideline (left or right)	3.75	—
		Margin block of 4, arrow & guideline (top or bottom)	3.00	—
		Center line block	7.25	—
		P# block of 6, number at top or bottom	16.00	—

TYPE OF WISCONSIN ISSUE
Issued in sheets of 200
FLAT PLATE PRINTING
Imperf

755 A238	3c	**deep violet**	.60	.60
		Pair with horiz. line between	1.75	—
		Pair with vert. line between	1.40	—
		Margin block of 4, arrow & guideline (left or right)	3.75	—
		Margin block of 4, arrow & guideline (top or bottom)	3.00	—
		Center line block	7.25	—
		P# block of 6, number at top or bottom	16.00	—

TYPES OF NATIONAL PARKS ISSUE
Issued in sheets of 200
FLAT PLATE PRINTING
Imperf

756 A239	1c	**green**	.20	.20
		Pair with horiz. line between	.45	—
		Pair with vert. line between	.55	—
		Margin block of 4, arrow & guideline (left or right)	1.00	—
		Margin block of 4, arrow & guideline (top or bottom)	1.25	—
		Center line block	3.00	—
		P# block of 6, number at top or bottom	5.25	—
		See note above No. 766.		
757 A240	2c	**red**	.25	.25
		Pair with horiz. line between	.70	—
		Pair with vert. line between	.55	—
		Margin block of 4, arrow & guideline (left or right)	1.60	—
		Margin block of 4, arrow & guideline (top or bottom)	1.25	—
		Center line block	3.50	—
		P# block of 6, number at top or bottom	6.00	—
		Double transfer	—	—
758 A241	3c	**deep violet**	.50	.45
		Pair with horiz. line between	1.40	—
		Pair with vert. line between	1.25	—
		Margin block of 4, arrow & guideline (left or right)	3.10	—
		Margin block of 4, arrow & guideline (top or bottom)	2.75	—
		Center line block	5.25	—
		P# block of 6, number at top or bottom	15.00	—
759 A242	4c	**brown**	.95	.95
		Pair with horiz. line between	2.75	—
		Pair with vert. line between	2.25	—
		Margin block of 4, arrow & guideline (left or right)	5.75	—
		Margin block of 4, arrow & guideline (top or bottom)	4.75	—

		Center line block	8.50	—
		P# block of 6, number at top or bottom	20.00	—
760 A243	5c	**blue**	1.50	1.30
		Pair with horiz. line between	3.50	—
		Pair with vert. line between	4.25	—
		Margin block of 4, arrow & guideline (left or right)	7.50	—
		Margin block of 4, arrow & guideline (top or bottom)	9.00	—
		Center line block	15.00	—
		P# block of 6, number at top or bottom	25.00	—
		Double transfer	—	—
761 A244	6c	**dark blue**	2.40	2.10
		Pair with horiz. line between	6.50	—
		Pair with vert. line between	5.50	—
		Margin block of 4, arrow & guideline (left or right)	14.00	—
		Margin block of 4, arrow & guideline (top or bottom)	12.50	—
		Center line block	20.00	—
		P# block of 6, number at top or bottom)	35.00	—
762 A245	7c	**black**	1.50	1.40
		Pair with horiz. line between	4.25	—
		Pair with vert. line between	3.75	—
		Margin block of 4, arrow & guideline (left or right)	9.25	—
		Margin block of 4, arrow & guideline (top or bottom)	8.25	—
		Center line block	14.00	—
		P# block of 6, number at top or bottom	30.00	—
		Double transfer	—	—
763 A246	8c	**sage green**	1.60	1.50
		Pair with horiz. line between	3.75	—
		Pair with vert. line between	4.75	—
		Margin block of 4, arrow & guideline (left or right)	8.75	—
		Margin block of 4, arrow & guideline (top or bottom)	11.00	—
		Center line block	17.50	—
		P# block of 6, number at top or bottom	37.50	—
764 A247	9c	**red orange**	1.90	1.65
		Pair with horiz. line between	5.00	—
		Pair with vert. line between	4.50	—
		Margin block of 4, arrow & guideline (left or right)	11.50	—
		Margin block of 4, arrow & guideline (top or bottom)	10.50	—
		Center line block	22.50	—
		P# block of 6, number at top or bottom	42.50	—
765 A248	10c	**gray black**	3.75	3.25
		Pair with horiz. line between	9.00	—
		Pair with vert. line between	10.50	—
		Margin block of 4, arrow & guideline (left or right)	20.00	—
		Margin block of 4, arrow & guideline (top or bottom)	24.00	—
		Center line block	30.00	—
		P# block of 6, number at top or bottom	50.00	—
		Nos. 756-765 (10)	14.55	13.05

SOUVENIR SHEETS
TYPE OF CENTURY OF PROGRESS ISSUE

Issued in sheets of 9 panes of 25 stamps each, with vertical and horizontal gutters between panes. This applies to Nos. 766-770.

Note: Single items from these sheets are identical with other varieties, 766 and 730, 766a and 730a, 767 and 731, 767a and 731a, 768 and 735, 768a and 735a, 769 and 756, 770 and 758.

Positive identification is by blocks or pairs showing wide gutters between stamps. These wide gutters occur only on Nos. 766-770 and measure, horizontally, 13mm on Nos. 766-767; 16mm on No. 768, and 23mm on Nos. 769-770.

FLAT PLATE PRINTING
Imperf

766 A231a	1c	**yellow green,** pane of 25	25.00	25.00
a.		Single stamp	.70	.40
		Block of 4	2.80	1.70
		Pair with horiz. gutter between	5.50	—
		Pair with vert. gutter between	7.00	—
		Block with crossed gutters	15.00	—
		Block of 50 stamps (two panes)	70.00	—
767 A232a	3c	**violet,** pane of 25	23.50	23.50
a.		Single stamp	.60	.40
		Pair with horiz. gutter between	5.25	—
		Pair with vert. gutter between	6.75	—
		Block with crossed gutters	15.00	—
		Block of 50 stamps (two panes)	65.00	—

NATIONAL EXHIBITION ISSUE
TYPE OF BYRD ISSUE
Issued in sheets of 25 panes of 6 stamps each.
FLAT PLATE PRINTING
Imperf

768 A235a	3c	**dark blue,** pane of six	20.00	15.00
a.		Single stamp	2.80	2.40
		Pair with horiz. gutter between	7.50	—
		Pair with vert. gutter between	9.00	—
		Block of 4 with crossed gutters	20.00	—
		Block of 12 stamps (two panes)	47.50	—

TYPES OF NATIONAL PARKS ISSUE
Issued in sheets of 20 panes of 6 stamps each.
FLAT PLATE PRINTING
Imperf

769 A248b	1c	**green,** pane of six	12.50	11.00
a.		Single stamp	1.85	1.80
		Pair with horiz. gutter between	6.00	—
		Pair with vert. gutter between	9.00	—
		Block of 4 with crossed gutters	15.00	—
		Block of 12 stamps (two panes)	30.00	—
770 A248a	3c	**deep violet,** pane of six	30.00	24.00
a.		Single stamp	3.25	3.10
		Pair with horiz. gutter between	12.50	—
		Pair with vert. gutter between	11.00	—
		Block of 4 with crossed gutters	30.00	—
		Block of 12 stamps (two panes)	70.00	—

TYPE OF AIR POST SPECIAL DELIVERY
Issued in sheets of 200
FLAT PLATE PRINTING
Imperf

771 APSD1	16c	**dark blue**	2.40	2.25
		Pair with horiz. line between	6.50	—
		Pair with vert. line between	5.50	—
		Margin block of 4, arrow & guideline (left or right)	15.00	—
		Margin block of 4, arrow & guideline (top or bottom)	12.50	—
		Center line block	60.00	—
		P# block of 6, number at top or bottom	52.50	—

> **Catalogue values for unused stamps in this section, from this point to the end, are for Never Hinged items.**

VALUES FOR HINGED STAMPS AFTER NO. 771
This catalogue does not value unused stamps after No. 771 in hinged condition. Hinged unused stamps from No. 772 to the present are worth considerably less than the values given for unused stamps, which are for never-hinged examples.

CONNECTICUT TERCENTENARY ISSUE
300th anniv. of the settlement of Connecticut.

The Charter Oak — A249

ROTARY PRESS PRINTING
Plates of 200 subjects in four panes of 50.

1935, Apr. 26   Unwmk.   Perf. 11x10½

772 A249	3c	**violet**	.20	.20
		rose violet	.20	.20
		P# block of 4	1.40	—
		Defect in cent sign (21395 UR 4)	1.00	.25

CALIFORNIA PACIFIC EXPOSITION ISSUE
California Pacific Exposition at San Diego.

View of San Diego Exposition — A250

ROTARY PRESS PRINTING
Plates of 200 subjects in four panes of 50.

1935, May 29   Unwmk.   Perf. 11x10½

773 A250	3c	**purple**	.20	.20
		On cover, Expo. station machine canc. (non-first day)		*2.50*
		On cover, Expo. station duplex handstamp canc. (non-first day)		*20.00*
		P# block of 4	1.25	—
		Pair with full vertical gutter between	—	—

BOULDER DAM ISSUE
Dedication of Boulder Dam.

Boulder Dam (Hoover Dam) — A251

FLAT PLATE PRINTING

Plates of 200 subjects in four panes of 50.

1935, Sept. 30	Unwmk.	Perf. 11	
774 A251 3c	**purple**	.20	.20
	deep purple	.20	.20
	P# block of 6	1.65	—

MICHIGAN CENTENARY ISSUE

Advance celebration of Michigan Statehood centenary.

Michigan State Seal — A252

Designed by Alvin R. Meissner.

ROTARY PRESS PRINTING

Plates of 200 subjects in 4 panes of 50.

1935, Nov. 1	Unwmk.	Perf. 11x10½	
775 A252 3c	**purple**	.20	.20
	P# block of 4	1.25	—

TEXAS CENTENNIAL ISSUE

Centennial of Texas independence.

Sam Houston, Stephen F. Austin and the Alamo — A253

Designed by Alvin R. Meissner.

ROTARY PRESS PRINTING

Plates of 200 subjects in four panes of 50.

1936, Mar. 2	Unwmk.	Perf. 11x10½	
776 A253 3c	**purple**	.20	.20
	On cover, Expo. station machine canc.		2.00
	On cover, Expo. station duplex handstamp canc.		40.00
	P# block of 4	1.10	—

RHODE ISLAND TERCENTENARY ISSUE

300th anniv. of the settlement of Rhode Island.

Statue of Roger Williams — A254

ROTARY PRESS PRINTING

Plates of 200 subjects in four panes of 50.

1936, May 4	Unwmk.	Perf. 10½x11	
777 A254 3c	**purple**	.20	.20
	rose violet	.20	.20
	P# block of 4	1.10	—
	Pair with full gutter between	200.00	

THIRD INTERNATIONAL PHILATELIC EXHIBITION ISSUE
SOUVENIR SHEET

A254a

Plates of 120 subjects in thirty panes of 4 each.
FLAT PLATE PRINTING

1936, May 9	Unwmk.	Imperf.	
778 A254a	**violet**, sheet of 4	1.75	1.75
a.	3c type A249	.40	.30
b.	3c type A250	.40	.30
c.	3c type A252	.40	.30
d.	3c type A253	.40	.30

Issued in sheets measuring 98x66mm containing four stamps, inscribed in the margins: "Printed by the Treasury Department, Bureau of Engraving and Printing, under authority of James A. Farley, Postmaster General, in compliment to the third International Philatelic Exhibition of 1936. New York, N. Y., May 9-17, 1936. Plate No. 21557 (or 21558)."

ARKANSAS CENTENNIAL ISSUE

100th anniv. of the State of Arkansas.

Arkansas Post, Old and New State Houses — A255

ROTARY PRESS PRINTING

Plates of 200 subjects in four panes of 50.

1936, June 15	Unwmk.	Perf. 11x10½	
782 A255 3c	**purple**	.20	.20
	P# block of 4	1.10	—

OREGON TERRITORY ISSUE

Opening of the Oregon Territory, 1836, 100th anniv.

Map of Oregon Territory — A256

ROTARY PRESS PRINTING

Plates of 200 subjects in four panes of 50.

1936, July 14	Unwmk.	Perf. 11x10½	
783 A256 3c	**purple**	.20	.20
	P# block of 4	1.10	—
	Double transfer (21579 UL 3)	1.00	.50

SUSAN B. ANTHONY ISSUE

Susan Brownell Anthony (1820-1906), woman-suffrage advocate, and 16th anniv. of the ratification of the 19th Amendment which grants American women the right to vote.

Susan B. Anthony — A257

ROTARY PRESS PRINTING

Plates of 400 subjects in four panes of 100.

1936, Aug. 26	Unwmk.	Perf. 11x10½	
784 A257 3c	**dark violet**	.20	.20
	P# block of 4	.75	—
	Period missing after "B" (21590 LR 100)	.75	.25

ARMY ISSUE

Issued in honor of the United States Army.

Generals George Washington, Nathanael Greene and Mt. Vernon — A258

Maj. Gen. Andrew Jackson, Gen. Winfield Scott and the Hermitage — A259

Generals William T. Sherman, Ulysses S. Grant and Philip H. Sheridan — A260

Generals Robert E. Lee, "Stonewall" Jackson and Stratford Hall — A261

U. S. Military Academy, West Point — A262

ROTARY PRESS PRINTING

Plates of 200 subjects in four panes of 50.

1936-37	Unwmk.	Perf. 11x10½	
785 A258 1c	**green**, Dec. 15, 1936	.20	.20
	yellow green	.20	.20
	P# block of 4	.85	—
	Pair with full vertical gutter between		
786 A259 2c	**carmine**, Jan. 15, 1937	.20	.20
	P# block of 4	.85	—
787 A260 3c	**purple**, Feb. 18, 1937	.20	.20
	P# block of 4	1.10	—
788 A261 4c	**gray**, Mar. 23, 1937	.30	.20
	P# block of 4	8.00	—
789 A262 5c	**ultramarine**, May 26, 1937	.60	.20
	P# block of 4	8.50	—
	Nos. 785-789 (5)	1.50	1.00

NAVY ISSUE

Issued in honor of the United States Navy.

John Paul Jones and John Barry — A263

Stephen Decatur and Thomas MacDonough A264

Admirals David G. Farragut and David D. Porter — A265

Admirals William T. Sampson, George Dewey and Winfield S. Schley — A266

Seal of US Naval Academy and Naval Cadets — A267

ROTARY PRESS PRINTING
Plates of 200 subjects in four panes of 50.

1936-37		**Unwmk.**	**Perf. 11x10½**		
790	A263	1c **green,** *Dec. 15, 1936*		.20	.20
		yellow green		.20	.20
		P# block of 4		.85	—
791	A264	2c **carmine,** *Jan. 15, 1937*		.20	.20
		P# block of 4		.75	—
792	A265	3c **purple,** *Feb. 18, 1937*		.20	.20
		P# block of 4		1.00	—
793	A266	4c **gray,** *Mar. 23, 1937*		.30	.20
		P# block of 4		8.50	—
794	A267	5c **ultramarine,** *May 26, 1937*		.60	.20
		P# block of 4		8.50	—
		Pair with full vert. gutter btwn.			—
		Nos. 790-794 (5)		1.50	1.00

ORDINANCE OF 1787 SESQUICENTENNIAL ISSUE

150th anniv. of the adoption of the Ordinance of 1787 and the creation of the Northwest Territory.

Manasseh Cutler, Rufus Putnam and Map of Northwest Territory — A268

ROTARY PRESS PRINTING
Plates of 200 subjects in four panes of 50.

1937, July 13		**Unwmk.**	**Perf. 11x10½**		
795	A268	3c **red violet**		.20	.20
		P# block of 4		1.10	—

VIRGINIA DARE ISSUE

350th anniv. of the birth of Virginia Dare, 1st child born in America of English parents (Aug. 18, 1587), and the settlement at Roanoke Island.

Virginia Dare and Parents — A269

FLAT PLATE PRINTING
Plates of 192 subjects in four panes of 48 each, separated by 1¼ inch wide gutters with central guide lines.

1937, Aug. 18		**Unwmk.**	**Perf. 11**		
796	A269	5c **gray blue**		.20	.20
		P# block of 6		6.50	—

SOCIETY OF PHILATELIC AMERICANS ISSUE
SOUVENIR SHEET

A269a

TYPE OF NATIONAL PARKS ISSUE
Plates of 36 subjects
FLAT PLATE PRINTING

1937, Aug. 26		**Unwmk.**	**Imperf.**		
797	A269a	10c **blue green**		.60	.40

Issued in sheets measuring 67x78mm, inscribed in margins: "Printed by the Treasury Department, Bureau of Engraving and Printing - Under the Authority of James A. Farley, Postmaster General - In Compliment to the 43rd Annual Convention of the Society of Philatelic Americans - Asheville, N.C., August 26-28, 1937. Plate Number 21695 (6)."

CONSTITUTION SESQUICENTENNIAL ISSUE

150th anniversary of the signing of the Constitution on September 17, 1787.

"Adoption of the Constitution" A270

ROTARY PRESS PRINTING
Plates of 200 subjects in four panes of 50.

1937, Sept. 17		**Unwmk.**	**Perf. 11x10½**		
798	A270	3c **bright red violet**		.20	.20
		P# block of 4		1.00	—

TERRITORIAL ISSUES
Hawaii

Statue of Kamehameha I, Honolulu — A271

Alaska

Mt. McKinley — A272

Puerto Rico

La Fortaleza, San Juan — A273

Virgin Islands

Charlotte Amalie Harbor, St. Thomas — A274

ROTARY PRESS PRINTING
Plates of 200 subjects in panes of 50.

1937		**Unwmk.**	**Perf. 10½x11**		
799	A271	3c **violet,** *Oct. 18*		.20	.20
		P# block of 4		1.25	—
			Perf. 11x10½		
800	A272	3c **violet,** *Nov. 12*		.20	.20
		P# block of 4		1.25	—
		Pair with full gutter between			
801	A273	3c **bright violet,** *Nov. 25*		.20	.20
		P# block of 4		1.25	—
802	A274	3c **light violet,** *Dec. 15*		.20	.20
		P# block of 4		1.25	—

Pair with full vertical gutter between		275.00
Nos. 799-802 (4)	.80	.80

PRESIDENTIAL ISSUE

Benjamin Franklin A275

George Washington A276

Martha Washington A277

John Adams A278

Thomas Jefferson — A279

James Madison — A280

The White House — A281

James Monroe — A282

John Quincy Adams — A283

Andrew Jackson — A284

Martin Van Buren — A285

William H. Harrison — A286

John Tyler — A287

James K. Polk — A288

Zachary
Taylor — A289

Millard
Fillmore — A290

Franklin Pierce
A291

James Buchanan
A292

Abraham
Lincoln — A293

Andrew
Johnson — A294

Ulysses S.
Grant — A295

Rutherford B.
Hayes — A296

James A.
Garfield — A297

Chester A.
Arthur — A298

Grover Cleveland
A299

Benjamin
Harrison
A300

William McKinley
A301

Theodore
Roosevelt
A302

William Howard
Taft — A303

Woodrow
Wilson — A304

Warren G.
Harding — A305

Calvin
Coolidge — A306

ROTARY PRESS PRINTING

Ordinary and Electric Eye (EE) Plates of 400 subjects in four panes of 100. (For details of EE Markings, see Information for Collectors in first part of this Catalogue.)

1938	**Unwmk.**	**Perf. 11x10½**	
803 A275	½c **deep orange,** *May 19*	.20	.20
	P# block of 4	.35	—
804 A276	1c **green,** *Apr. 25*	.20	.20
	light green	.20	.20
	P# block of 4	.25	—
	Pair with full vert. gutter btwn.	160.00	—
b.	Booklet pane of 6	2.00	.35
805 A277	1½c **bister brown,** *May 5*	.20	.20
	buff ('43)	.20	.20
	P# block of 4	.20	—
	Pair with full horiz. gutter btwn.	175.00	—
	Pair with full vert. gutter btwn.		—
b.	Horiz. pair, imperf. between	160.00	30.00

No. 805b used is always Bureau precanceled St. Louis, Mo., and is generally with gum. Value is for gummed pair.

806 A278	2c **rose carmine,** *June 3*	.20	.20
	rose pink ('43)	.20	.20
	P# block of 4, # opposite corner stamp	.30	—
	Vertical margin block of 10, P# opposite 3rd horizontal row (Experimental EE plates)	4.00	
	Recut at top of head, Pl. 22156 U.L. 3	3.00	1.50
	Pair with full horiz. gutter btwn.		—
	Pair with full vert. gutter btwn.		—
b.	Booklet pane of 6	4.75	.85
807 A279	3c **deep violet,** *June 16*	.20	.20
	P# block of 4, # opposite corner stamp	.25	.25
	Vertical margin block of 10, P# opposite 3rd horizontal row (Experimental EE plates)	20.00	
	Pair with full vert. gutter btwn.	150.00	
	Pair with full horiz. gutter btwn.	125.00	
a.	Booklet pane of 6	8.50	1.25
b.	Horiz. pair, imperf. between	900.00	—
c.	Imperf., pair	2,500.	
808 A280	4c **red violet,** *July 1*	.75	.20
	rose violet ('43)	.75	.20
	P# block of 4	3.75	—
809 A281	4½c **dark gray,** *July 11*	.20	.20
	gray ('43)	.20	.20
	P# block of 4	1.50	—
810 A282	5c **bright blue,** *July 21*	.20	.20
	light blue	.20	.20
	P# block of 4	1.00	—
	Pair with full vert. gutter btwn.		—
811 A283	6c **red orange,** *July 28*	.20	.20
	P# block of 4	1.00	—
812 A284	7c **sepia,** *Aug. 4*	.25	.20
	violet brown	.25	.20
	P# block of 4	1.25	—
813 A285	8c **olive green,** *Aug. 11*	.30	.20
	light olive green ('43)	.30	.20
	olive ('42)	.30	.20
	P# block of 4	1.40	—
814 A286	9c **rose pink,** *Aug. 18*	.30	.20
	pink ('43)	.30	.20
	P# block of 4	1.40	—
	Pair with full vert. gutter btwn.		—
815 A287	10c **brown red,** *Sept. 2*	.25	.20
	pale brown red ('43)	.25	.20
	P# block of 4	1.25	—
816 A288	11c **ultramarine,** *Sept. 8*	.65	.20
	bright ultramarine	.65	.20
	P# block of 4	3.00	—
817 A289	12c **bright violet,** *Sept. 14*	.90	.20
	P# block of 4	4.25	—
818 A290	13c **blue green,** *Sept. 22*	1.25	.20
	deep blue green	1.25	.20
	P# block of 4	6.50	—
819 A291	14c **blue,** *Oct. 6*	.90	.20
	P# block of 4	4.50	—
820 A292	15c **blue gray,** *Oct. 13*	.40	.20
	P# block of 4	1.90	—
821 A293	16c **black,** *Oct. 20*	.90	.25
	P# block of 4	4.50	—
822 A294	17c **rose red,** *Oct. 27*	.85	.20
	deep rose red	.85	.20
	Block of 4	3.40	.75
	P# block of 4	4.50	—
823 A295	18c **brown carmine,** *Nov. 3*	1.75	.20
	rose brown ('43)	1.75	.20
	Block of 4	7.00	.75
	P# block of 4	8.75	—
824 A296	19c **bright violet,** *Nov. 10*	1.25	.35
	P# block of 4	6.25	—
825 A297	20c **bright blue green,** *Nov. 10*	.70	.20
	deep blue green ('43)	.70	.20
	P# block of 4	3.50	—
826 A298	21c **dull blue,** *Nov. 22*	1.25	.20
	Block of 4	5.00	1.25
	P# block of 4	7.00	—
827 A299	22c **vermilion,** *Nov. 22*	1.00	.40
	P# block of 4	9.50	—
828 A300	24c **gray black,** *Dec. 2*	3.50	.20
	Block of 4	14.00	1.25
	P# block of 4	17.00	—
829 A301	25c **deep red lilac,** *Dec. 2*	.60	.20
	rose lilac ('43)	.60	.20
	P# block of 4	3.00	—
	Pair with full vert. gutter btwn.		—
830 A302	30c **deep ultramarine,** *Dec. 8*	3.50	.20
	blue	15.00	
	deep blue	125.00	—
	Block of 4	14.00	.50
	P# block of 4	16.00	—
831 A303	50c **light red violet,** *Dec. 8*	5.50	.20
	P# block of 4	24.00	—

Bureau Precancels: ½c, 199 diff., 1c, 701 diff., 1½c, 404 diff., 2c, 161 diff., 3c, 87 diff., 4c, 30 diff., 4½c, 27 diff., 5c, 44 diff., 6c, 45 diff., 7c, 44 diff., 8c, 44 diff., 9c, 38 diff., 10c, 43 diff. Also, 11c, 41 diff., 12c, 33 diff., 13c, 28 diff., 14c, 23 diff., 15c, 38 diff., 16c, 6 diff., 17c, 27 diff., 18c, 5 diff., 19c, 8 diff., 20c, 39 diff., 21c, 5 diff., 22c, 4 diff., 24c, 8 diff., 25c, 23 diff., 30c, 27 diff., 50c, 24 diff.

FLAT PLATE PRINTING
Plates of 100 subjects

1938		**Perf. 11**	
832 A304	$1 **purple & black,** *Aug. 29*	7.00	.20
	Margin block of 4, bottom or side arrow	29.00	—
	Center line block	32.50	4.00
	Top P# block of 4, 2#	35.00	—
	Top P# block of 20, 2#, arrow, 2 TOP, 2 registration markers and denomination	150.00	
a.	Vert. pair, imperf. horiz.	1,600.	
b.	Watermarked USIR ('51)	250.00	65.00
	Center line block	1,150.	
	P# block of 4, 2#	1,550.	
c.	$1 **red violet & black,** *Aug. 31, 1954*	6.00	.20
	Top or bottom P# block of 4, 2#	30.00	—
d.	As "c," vert. pair, imperf. horiz.	1,250.	
e.	Vertical pair, imperf. between	2,750.	
f.	As "c," vert. pair, imperf. btwn.	7,000.	

No. 832c is dry printed from 400-subject flat plates on thick white paper with smooth, colorless gum.

833 A305	$2 **yellow green & black,** *Sept. 29*	20.00	3.75
	green & black ('43)	20.00	3.75
	Margin block of 4, bottom or side arrow	85.00	—
	Center line block	87.50	35.00
	Top P# block of 4, 2#	95.00	—
	Top P# block of 20, 2#, arrow, 2 TOP, 2 registration markers and denominations	450.00	
	Top P# block of 20, 2#, black # and marginal markings only (yellow green # and markings omitted)	3,000.	
834 A306	$5 **carmine & black,** *Nov. 17*	95.00	3.00
	Margin block of 4, bottom or side arrow	400.00	—
	Center line block	425.00	25.00
	Top P# block of 4, 2#	440.00	—
	Top P# block of 20, 2#, arrow, 2 TOP, 2 registration markers and denominations	2,200.	
a.	$5 **red brown & black**	3,250.	4,000.
	Hinged	2,500.	
	Top P# block of 4, 2#	14,000.	
	Nos. 803-834 (32)	150.35	13.15

Top plate number blocks of Nos. 832, 833 and 834 are found both with and without top arrow or registration markers.

No. 834 can be chemically altered to resemble Scott 834a. No. 834a should be purchased only with competent expert certification.

Watermarks
All stamps from No. 835 on are unwatermarked.

CONSTITUTION RATIFICATION ISSUE

150th anniversary of the ratification of the United States Constitution.

Old Courthouse,
Williamsburg,
Va. — A307

ROTARY PRESS PRINTING
Plates of 200 subjects in four panes of 50.

1938, June 21		**Perf. 11x10½**	
835 A307	3c **deep violet**	.25	.20
	P# block of 4	3.50	—

SWEDISH-FINNISH TERCENTENARY ISSUE
Tercentenary of the founding of the Swedish and Finnish Settlement at Wilmington, Delaware.

"Landing of the First Swedish and Finnish Settlers in America," by Stanley M. Arthurs — A308

FLAT PLATE PRINTING

Plates of 192 subjects in four panes of 48 each, separated by 1¼ inch wide gutters with central guide lines.

1938, June 27			**Perf. 11**
836 A308	3c red violet	.20	.20
	P# block of 6	2.50	

NORTHWEST TERRITORY SESQUICENTENNIAL

"Colonization of the West," by Gutzon Borglum — A309

ROTARY PRESS PRINTING

Plates of 400 subjects in four panes of 100.

1938, July 15			**Perf. 11x10½**
837 A309	3c bright violet	.20	.20
	rose violet	.20	.20
	P# block of 4	7.50	—

IOWA TERRITORY CENTENNIAL ISSUE

Old Capitol, Iowa City — A310

ROTARY PRESS PRINTING

Plates of 200 subjects in four panes of 50.

1938, Aug. 24			**Perf. 11x10½**
838 A310	3c violet	.20	.20
	P# block of 4	5.00	—
	Pair with full vertical gutter between	—	

REGULAR ISSUE
ROTARY PRESS COIL STAMPS
Types of 1938

1939, Jan. 20				**Perf. 10 Vertically**
839 A276	1c	green	.30	.20
		light green	.30	.20
		Pair	.60	.20
		Joint line pair	1.40	.30
840 A277	1½c	bister brown	.30	.20
		buff	.30	.20
		Pair	.60	.20
		Joint line pair	1.50	.30
841 A278	2c	rose carmine	.40	.20
		Pair	.80	.20
		Joint line pair	1.75	.20
842 A279	3c	deep violet	.50	.20
		violet	.50	.20
		Pair	1.00	.20
		Joint line pair	2.00	.20
		Gripper cracks	2.50	
		Thin translucent paper	2.50	—
843 A280	4c	red violet	8.00	.40
		Pair	16.50	.80
		Joint line pair	27.50	2.25
844 A281	4½c	dark gray	.70	.40
		Pair	1.50	.80
		Joint line pair	5.00	1.65
845 A282	5c	bright blue	5.00	.35
		Pair	10.50	.70
		Joint line pair	27.50	1.65
846 A283	6c	red orange	1.10	.20
		Pair	2.25	.40
		Joint line pair	7.50	.90
847 A287	10c	brown red	11.00	.50
		Pair	24.00	1.00
		Joint line pair	42.50	3.00

Bureau Precancels: 1c, 269 diff., 1½c, 179 diff., 2c, 101 diff., 3c, 46 diff., 4c, 13 diff., 4½c, 3 diff., 5c, 6 diff., 6c, 8 diff., 10c, 4 diff.

1939, Jan. 27				**Perf. 10 Horizontally**
848 A276	1c	green	.85	.20
		Pair	1.75	.25
		Joint line pair	2.75	.50
849 A277	1½c	bister brown	1.25	.30
		Pair	2.50	.60
		Joint line pair	4.50	1.10
850 A278	2c	rose carmine	2.50	.40
		Pair	5.00	.80

		Joint line pair	6.50	1.40
851 A279	3c	deep violet	2.25	.35
		Pair	4.50	.70
		Joint line pair	6.25	1.40
		Nos. 839-851 (13)	34.15	3.90

"Tower of the Sun" — A311

Trylon and Perisphere — A312

GOLDEN GATE INTL. EXPOSITION, SAN FRANCISCO
ROTARY PRESS PRINTING

Plates of 200 subjects in four panes of 50.

1939, Feb. 18			**Perf. 10½x11**
852 A311	3c bright purple	.20	.20
	On cover, Expo. station machine canc. (non-first day)		3.00
	On cover, Expo. station duplex handstamp canc. (non-first day)		15.00
	P# block of 4	1.25	—

NEW YORK WORLD'S FAIR ISSUE
ROTARY PRESS PRINTING

Plates of 200 subjects in four panes of 50.

1939, Apr. 1			**Perf. 10½x11**
853 A312	3c deep purple	.20	.20
	On cover, Expo. station machine canc. (non-first day)		3.00
	On cover, Expo. station duplex handstamp canc.		10.00
	P# block of 4	1.75	—

WASHINGTON INAUGURATION ISSUE

Sesquicentennial of the inauguration of George Washington as First President.

Washington Taking Oath of Office, Federal Building, New York City — A313

FLAT PLATE PRINTING

Plates of 200 subjects in four panes of 50.

1939, Apr. 30			**Perf. 11**
854 A313	3c bright red violet	.40	.20
	P# block of 6	3.50	—

BASEBALL CENTENNIAL ISSUE

Sandlot Baseball Game — A314

Designed by William A. Roach.

ROTARY PRESS PRINTING

Plates of 200 subjects in four panes of 50.

1939, June 12			**Perf. 11x10½**
855 A314	3c violet	1.75	.20
	P# block of 4	7.50	—

PANAMA CANAL ISSUE

25th anniv. of the opening of the Panama Canal.

Theodore Roosevelt, Gen. George W. Goethals and Ship in Gaillard Cut — A315

Designed by William A. Roach.

FLAT PLATE PRINTING

Plates of 200 subjects in four panes of 50.

1939, Aug. 15			**Perf. 11**
856 A315	3c deep red violet	.25	.20
	P# block of 6	3.00	—

PRINTING TERCENTENARY ISSUE

Issued in commemoration of the 300th anniversary of printing in Colonial America. The Stephen Daye press is in the Harvard University Museum.

Stephen Daye Press — A316

Designed by William K. Schrage.

ROTARY PRESS PRINTING

E.E. Plates of 200 subjects in four panes of 50.

1939, Sept. 25			**Perf. 10½x11**
857 A316	3c violet	.20	.20
	P# block of 4	1.00	—

50th ANNIVERSARY OF STATEHOOD ISSUE

Map of North and South Dakota, Montana and Washington A317

ROTARY PRESS PRINTING

E.E. Plates of 200 subjects in four panes of 50.

1939, Nov. 2			**Perf. 11x10½**
858 A317	3c rose violet	.20	.20
	P# block of 4	1.10	—

FAMOUS AMERICANS ISSUES
ROTARY PRESS PRINTING
E.E. Plates of 280 subjects in four panes of 70.
AMERICAN AUTHORS

Washington Irving — A318

James Fenimore Cooper — A319

Ralph Waldo Emerson — A320

Louisa May Alcott — A321

Samuel L. Clemens (Mark Twain) — A322

1940   *Perf. 10½x11*

859	A318	1c	**bright blue green**, *Jan. 29*	.20	.20
			P# block of 4	.95	—
860	A319	2c	**rose carmine**, *Jan. 29*	.20	.20
			P# block of 4	.95	—
861	A320	3c	**bright red violet**, *Feb. 5*	.20	.20
			P# block of 4	1.25	—
862	A321	5c	**ultramarine**, *Feb. 5*	.30	.20
			P# block of 4	8.25	—
863	A322	10c	**dark brown**, *Feb. 13*	1.65	1.20
			P# block of 4	32.50	—
			Nos. 859-863 (5)	2.55	2.00

AMERICAN POETS

Henry Wadsworth Longfellow — A323

John Greenleaf Whittier — A324

James Russell Lowell — A325

Walt Whitman — A326

James Whitcomb Riley — A327

864	A323	1c	**bright blue green**, *Feb. 16*	.20	.20
			P# block of 4	1.75	—
865	A324	2c	**rose carmine**, *Feb. 16*	.20	.20
			P# block of 4	1.75	—
866	A325	3c	**bright red violet**, *Feb. 20*	.20	.20
			P# block of 4	2.25	—
867	A326	5c	**ultramarine**, *Feb. 20*	.35	.20
			P# block of 4	9.00	—
868	A327	10c	**dark brown**, *Feb. 24*	1.75	1.25
			P# block of 4	30.00	—
			Nos. 864-868 (5)	2.70	2.05

AMERICAN EDUCATORS

Horace Mann — A328

Mark Hopkins — A329

Charles W. Eliot — A330

Frances E. Willard — A331

Booker T. Washington — A332

869	A328	1c	**bright blue green**, *Mar. 14*	.20	.20
			P# block of 4	1.90	—
870	A329	2c	**rose carmine**, *Mar. 14*	.20	.20
			P# block of 4	1.25	—
871	A330	3c	**bright red violet**, *Mar. 28*	.20	.20
			P# block of 4	2.25	—
872	A331	5c	**ultramarine**, *Mar. 28*	.40	.20
			P# block of 4	9.00	—
873	A332	10c	**dark brown**, *Apr. 7*	1.25	1.10
			P# block of 4	25.00	—
			Nos. 869-873 (5)	2.25	1.90

AMERICAN SCIENTISTS

John James Audubon — A333

Dr. Crawford W. Long — A334

Luther Burbank — A335

Dr. Walter Reed — A336

Jane Addams — A337

874	A333	1c	**bright blue green**, *Apr. 8*	.20	.20
			P# block of 4	.95	—
875	A334	2c	**rose carmine**, *Apr. 8*	.20	.20
			P# block of 4	.95	—
876	A335	3c	**bright red violet**, *Apr. 17*	.20	.20
			P# block of 4	1.10	—
877	A336	5c	**ultramarine**, *Apr. 17*	.25	.20
			P# block of 4	5.00	—
878	A337	10c	**dark brown**, *Apr. 26*	1.10	.85
			P# block of 4	16.00	—
			Nos. 874-878 (5)	1.95	1.65

AMERICAN COMPOSERS

Stephen Collins Foster — A338

John Philip Sousa — A339

Victor Herbert — A340

Edward A. MacDowell — A341

Ethelbert Nevin — A342

879	A338	1c	**bright blue green**, *May 3*	.20	.20
			P# block of 4	1.00	—
880	A339	2c	**rose carmine**, *May 3*	.20	.20
			P# block of 4	1.00	—
881	A340	3c	**bright red violet**, *May 13*	.20	.20
			P# block of 4	1.10	—
882	A341	5c	**ultramarine**, *May 13*	.40	.20
			P# block of 4	9.25	—
883	A342	10c	**dark brown**, *June 10*	3.75	1.35
			P# block of 4	32.50	—
			Nos. 879-883 (5)	4.75	2.15

AMERICAN ARTISTS

Gilbert Charles Stuart — A343

James A. McNeill Whistler — A344

Augustus Saint-Gaudens A345

Daniel Chester French A346

Frederic Remington — A347

884	A343	1c	**bright blue green**, *Sept. 5*	.20	.20
			P# block of 4	1.00	—
885	A344	2c	**rose carmine**, *Sept. 5*	.20	.20
			P# block of 4	.95	—
886	A345	3c	**bright red violet**, *Sept. 16*	.20	.20
			P# block of 4	1.00	—
887	A346	5c	**ultramarine**, *Sept. 16*	.50	.20
			P# block of 4	8.00	—
888	A347	10c	**dark brown**, *Sept. 30*	1.75	1.25
			P# block of 4	20.00	—
			Nos. 884-888 (5)	2.85	2.05

AMERICAN INVENTORS

Eli Whitney — A348

Samuel F. B. Morse — A349

Cyrus Hall McCormick — A350

Elias Howe — A351

Alexander Graham Bell — A352

889	A348	1c **bright blue green**, *Oct. 7*	.20	.20
		P# block of 4	1.90	
890	A349	2c **rose carmine**, *Oct. 7*	.20	.20
		P# block of 4	1.10	
891	A350	3c **bright red violet**, *Oct. 14*	.25	.20
		P# block of 4	1.75	
892	A351	5c **ultramarine**, *Oct. 14*	1.10	.30
		P# block of 4	12.50	
893	A352	10c **dark brown**, *Oct. 28*	11.00	2.00
		P# block of 4	65.00	—
		Nos. 889-893 (5)	12.75	2.90
		Nos. 859-893 (35)	29.80	14.70

PONY EXPRESS, 80th ANNIV. ISSUE

Pony Express
Rider — A353

ROTARY PRESS PRINTING
E.E. Plates of 200 subjects in four panes of 50.

1940, Apr. 3   *Perf. 11x10½*
894 A353 3c **henna brown**   .25   .20
     P# block of 4   2.75   —

PAN AMERICAN UNION ISSUE

Founding of the Pan American Union, 50th anniv.

The Three Graces
(Botticelli) — A354

ROTARY PRESS PRINTING
E.E. Plates of 200 subjects in four panes of 50.

1940, Apr. 14   *Perf. 10½x11*
895 A354 3c **light violet**   .20   .20
     P# block of 4   2.75   —

IDAHO STATEHOOD, 50th ANNIV.

Idaho State
Capitol — A355

ROTARY PRESS PRINTING
E.E. Plates of 200 subjects in four panes of 50.

1940, July 3   *Perf. 11x10½*
896 A355 3c **bright violet**   .20   .20
     P# block of 4   1.75   —

WYOMING STATEHOOD, 50th ANNIV.

Wyoming State Seal — A356

ROTARY PRESS PRINTING
E.E. Plates of 200 subjects in four panes of 50.

1940, July 10   *Perf. 10½x11*
897 A356 3c **brown violet**   .20   .20
     P# block of 4   1.50   —

CORONADO EXPEDITION, 400th ANNIV.

"Coronado and
His Captains"
Painted by Gerald
Cassidy — A357

ROTARY PRESS PRINTING
E.E. Plates of 200 subjects in four panes of 50.

1940, Sept. 7   *Perf. 11x10½*
898 A357 3c **violet**   .20   .20
     P# block of 4   1.50   —

NATIONAL DEFENSE ISSUE

Statue of   90-millimeter
Liberty — A358   Anti-aircraft
         Gun — A359

 Torch of Enlightenment — A360

ROTARY PRESS PRINTING
E.E. Plates of 400 subjects in four panes of 100

1940, Oct. 16   *Perf. 11x10½*
899	A358	1c **bright blue green**	.20	.20
		P# block of 4	.45	—
		Cracked plate (22684 UR 10)	3.00	
		Gripper cracks	3.00	
a.		Vertical pair, imperf. between	650.00	—
b.		Horizontal pair, imperf. between	35.00	—
		Pair with full vert. gutter between	200.00	
900	A359	2c **rose carmine**	.20	.20
		P# block of 4	.45	—
a.		Horizontal pair, imperf. between	40.00	—
		Pair with full vert. gutter between	275.00	
901	A360	3c **bright violet**	.20	.20
		P# block of 4	.60	—
a.		Horizontal pair, imperf. between	27.50	—
		Pair with full vert. gutter between		
		Nos. 899-901 (3)	.60	.60

Bureau Precancels: 1c, 316 diff., 2c, 25 diff., 3c, 22 diff.

THIRTEENTH AMENDMENT ISSUE

75th anniv. of the 13th Amendment to the Constitution abolishing slavery.

Emancipation Monument;
Lincoln and Kneeling Slave, by
Thomas Ball — A361

Designed by William A. Roach.

ROTARY PRESS PRINTING
E.E. Plates of 200 subjects in four panes of 50.

1940, Oct. 20   *Perf. 10½x11*
902 A361 3c **deep violet**   .20   .20
     dark violet   .20   .20
     P# block of 4   3.00   —

VERMONT STATEHOOD, 150th ANNIV.

State Capitol,
Montpelier — A362

Designed by Alvin R. Meissner.

ROTARY PRESS PRINTING
E.E. Plates of 200 subjects in four panes of 50.

1941, Mar. 4   *Perf. 11x10½*
903 A362 3c **light violet**   .20   .20
     P# block of 4   1.75   —

KENTUCKY STATEHOOD, 150th ANNIV.

Daniel Boone and
Three
Frontiersmen, from
Mural by Gilbert
White — A363

Designed by William A. Roach.

ROTARY PRESS PRINTING
E.E. Plates of 200 subjects in four panes of 50.

1942, June 1   *Perf. 11x10½*
904 A363 3c **violet**   .20   .20
     P# block of 4   1.10   —

WIN THE WAR ISSUE

 American Eagle — A364

ROTARY PRESS PRINTING
E.E. Plates of 400 subjects in four panes of 100.

1942, July 4   *Perf. 11x10½*
905	A364	3c **violet**	.20	.20
		light violet	.20	.20
		P# block of 4	.40	
		Pair with full vert. or horiz. gutter between	175.00	
b.		3c **purple**	—	—

Bureau Precancels: 26 diff.

CHINESE RESISTANCE ISSUE

Issued to commemorate the Chinese people's five years of resistance to Japanese aggression.

Map of China,
Abraham Lincoln
and Sun Yat-sen,
Founder of the
Chinese
Republic — A365

ROTARY PRESS PRINTING
E.E. Plates of 200 subjects in four panes of 50.

1942, July 7   *Perf. 11x10½*
906 A365 5c **bright blue**   .85   .20
     P# block of 4   10.00   —

ALLIED NATIONS ISSUE

 Allegory of Victory — A366

Designed by Leon Helguera.

ROTARY PRESS PRINTING
E.E. Plates of 400 subjects in four panes of 100.
1943, Jan. 14　　*Perf. 11x10½*
907 A366 2c **rose carmine**　.20 .20
　　P# block of 4　.30 —
　　Pair with full vert. or horiz. gutter
　　　between　225.00
　　Bureau Precancels: Denver, Baltimore.

FOUR FREEDOMS ISSUE

Liberty Holding the Torch of
Freedom and
Enlightenment — A367

Designed by Paul Manship.

ROTARY PRESS PRINTING
E.E. Plates of 400 subjects in four panes of 100.
1943, Feb. 12　　*Perf. 11x10½*
908 A367 1c **bright blue green**　.20 .20
　　P# block of 4　.60 —
　　Bureau Precancels: 20 diff.

OVERRUN COUNTRIES ISSUE
Printed by the American Bank Note Co.
FRAMES ENGRAVED, CENTERS OFFSET
LETTERPRESS
ROTARY PRESS PRINTING
Plates of 200 subjects in four panes of 50.

Due to the failure of the printers to divulge detailed information as to printing processes used, the editors omit listings of irregularities, flaws and blemishes which are numerous in this issue. An exception is made for certified double impressions and the widely recognized "KORPA" variety.

Flag of
Poland — A368

1943-44　　*Perf. 12*
909 A368 5c **blue violet, bright red & black,**
　　June 22, 1943　.20 .20
　　Margin block of 4, Inscribed "Poland" 4.50 —
　　Top margin block of 6, with red &
　　　blue violet guide markings and "Po-
　　　land"　5.00 —
　　Bottom margin block of 6, with red &
　　　black guide markings　1.30 —

Flag of
Czechoslovakia
A368a

910 A368a 5c **blue violet, blue, bright red &**
　　black, *July 12, 1943*　.20 .20
　　Margin block of 4, inscribed
　　　"Czechoslovakia"　2.75 —
　　Top margin block of 6, with red &
　　　blue violet guide markings and
　　　"Czechoslovakia"　3.25 —

Flag of
Norway — A368b

911 A368b 5c **blue violet, dark rose, deep blue**
　　& black, *July 27, 1943*　.20 .20
　　Margin block of 4, inscribed "Nor-
　　　way"　1.40 —
　　Bottom margin block of 6 with dark
　　　rose & blue violet guide markings 1.00 —

Flag of
Luxembourg
A368c

912 A368c 5c **blue violet, dark rose, light blue**
　　& black, *Aug. 10, 1943*　.20 .20
　　Margin block of 4, inscribed "Lux-
　　　embourg"　1.30 —
　　Top margin block of 6 with light
　　　blue & blue violet guide markings
　　　& "Luxembourg"　1.75 —

Flag of Netherlands
A368d

913 A368d 5c **blue violet, dark rose, blue &**
　　black, *Aug. 24, 1943*　.20 .20
　　Margin block of 4, inscribed
　　　"Netherlands"　1.30 —
　　Bottom margin block of 6 with blue
　　　& blue violet guide markings　1.00 —

Flag of
Belgium — A368e

914 A368e 5c **blue violet, dark rose, yellow &**
　　black, *Sept. 14, 1943*　.20 .20
　　Margin block of 4, inscribed "Belgi-
　　　um"　1.15 —
　　Top margin block of 6, with yellow
　　　& blue violet guide markings and
　　　"Belgium"　1.60 —
　a.　Double impression of "Belgium"　—

Flag of
France — A368f

915 A368f 5c **blue violet, deep blue, dark rose**
　　& black, *Sept. 28, 1943*　.20 .20
　　Margin block of 4, inscribed
　　　"France"　1.25 —
　　Bottom margin block of 6 with dark
　　　rose & blue violet guide markings　.90 —

Flag of
Greece — A368g

916 A368g 5c **blue violet, pale blue & black,**
　　Oct. 12, 1943　.35 .25
　　Margin block of 4, inscribed
　　　"Greece"　11.00 —
　　Top margin block of 6 with pale
　　　blue & blue violet guide markings
　　　& "Greece"　12.00 —

Flag of Yugoslavia
A368h

917 A368h 5c **blue violet, blue, dark rose &**
　　black, *Oct. 26, 1943*　.25 .20
　　Margin block of 4, inscribed "Yugo-
　　　slavia"　4.50 —
　　Bottom margin block of 6 with dark
　　　rose & blue violet guide markings 1.75 —

Flag of
Albania — A368i

918 A368i 5c **blue violet, dark red & black,** *Nov.*
　　9, 1943　.20 .20
　　Margin block of 4, inscribed "Alba-
　　　nia"　4.25 —
　　Top margin block of 6, with dark red
　　　& blue violet guide markings & "Al-
　　　bania"　6.50 —

Flag of
Austria — A368j

919 A368j 5c **blue violet, red & black,** *Nov. 23,*
　　1943　.20 .20
　　Margin block of 4, inscribed "Aus-
　　　tria"　3.75 —
　　Bottom margin block of 6, with red
　　　& blue violet guide markings　1.40 —
　a.　Double impression of "Austria"　—

Flag of
Denmark — A368k

920 A368k 5c **blue violet, red & black,** *Dec. 7,*
　　1943　.20 .20
　　Margin block of 4, inscribed "Den-
　　　mark"　5.75 —
　　Top margin block of 6, with red &
　　　blue violet guide markings &
　　　"Denmark"　6.50 —

Flag of
Korea — A368m

921 A368m 5c **blue violet, red, black & light**
　　blue, *Nov. 2, 1944* inscribed "Ko-　.20 .20
　　Margin block of 4, inscribed "Ko-
　　　rea"　4.75 —
　　Top margin block of 6 with blue
　　　& black guide markings and
　　　"Korea"　5.50 —
　　"KORPA" plate flaw　17.50 12.50
　　The "P" of "KORPA" is actually a mangled "E."
　　Nos. 909-921 (13)　2.80 2.65

TRANSCONTINENTAL RAILROAD ISSUE
Completion of the 1st transcontinental railroad, 75th anniv.

"Golden Spike
Ceremony"
Painted by John
McQuarrie — A369

ENGRAVED
ROTARY PRESS PRINTING
E.E. Plates of 200 subjects in four panes of 50.
1944, May 10　　*Perf. 11x10½*
922 A369 3c **violet**　.20 .20
　　P# block of 4　1.40 —

STEAMSHIP ISSUE
1st steamship to cross the Atlantic, 125th anniv.

"Savannah"
A370

ROTARY PRESS PRINTING
E.E. Plates of 200 subjects in four panes of 50.

1944, May 22   *Perf. 11x10½*
923 A370 3c violet   .20 .20
    P# block of 4   1.25

TELEGRAPH ISSUE
1st message transmitted by telegraph, cent.

Telegraph Wires
and Morse's First
Transmitted Words
"What Hath God
Wrought" — A371

ROTARY PRESS PRINTING
E.E. Plates of 200 subjects in four panes of 50.

1944, May 24   *Perf. 11x10½*
924 A371 3c bright red violet   .20 .20
    P# block of 4   .90

PHILIPPINE ISSUE
Final resistance of the US and Philippine defenders
on Corregidor to the Japanese invaders in 1942.

Aerial View of
Corregidor, Manila
Bay — A372

ROTARY PRESS PRINTING
E.E. Plates of 200 subjects in four panes of 50.

1944, Sept. 27   *Perf. 11x10½*
925 A372 3c deep violet   .20 .20
    P# block of 4   1.10

MOTION PICTURE, 50th ANNIV.

Motion Picture
Showing for
Armed Forces in
South
Pacific — A373

ROTARY PRESS PRINTING
E.E. Plates of 200 subjects in four panes of 50.

1944, Oct. 31   *Perf. 11x10½*
926 A373 3c deep violet   .20 .20
    P# block of 4   .90

FLORIDA STATEHOOD, CENTENARY

State Seal, Gates
of St. Augustine
and Capitol at
Tallahassee
A374

ROTARY PRESS PRINTING
E.E. Plates of 200 subjects in four panes of 50.

1945, Mar. 3   *Perf. 11x10½*
927 A374 3c bright red violet   .20 .20
    P# block of 4   .50

UNITED NATIONS CONFERENCE ISSUE
United Nations Conference, San Francisco, Calif.

"Toward United
Nations, April 25,
1945" — A375

ROTARY PRESS PRINTING
E.E. Plates of 200 subjects in four panes of 50.

1945, Apr. 25   *Perf. 11x10½*
928 A375 5c ultramarine   .20 .20
    P# block of 4   .45

IWO JIMA (MARINES) ISSUE
Battle of Iwo Jima and honoring the achievements
of the US Marines.

Marines Raising American Flag
on Mount Suribachi, Iwo
Jima — A376

ROTARY PRESS PRINTING
E.E. Plates of 200 subjects in four panes of 50.

1945, July 11   *Perf. 10½x11*
929 A376 3c yellow green   .20 .20
    P# block of 4   .40

FRANKLIN D. ROOSEVELT ISSUE
Franklin Delano Roosevelt (1882-1945).

Roosevelt and
Hyde Park
Residence — A377

Roosevelt and the
"Little White
House" at Warm
Springs,
Ga. — A378

Roosevelt and
White
House — A379

Roosevelt, Map of
Western
Hemisphere and
Four
Freedoms — A380

ROTARY PRESS PRINTING
E.E. Plates of 200 subjects in four panes of 50.

1945-46   *Perf. 11x10½*
930 A377 1c blue green, *July 26, 1945*   .20 .20
    P# block of 4   .20
931 A378 2c carmine rose, *Aug. 24, 1945*   .20 .20
    P# block of 4   .25
932 A379 3c purple, *June 27, 1945*   .20 .20
    P# block of 4   .30
933 A380 5c bright blue, *Jan. 30, 1946*   .20 .20
    P# block of 4   .45
    Nos. 930-933 (4)   .80 .80

ARMY ISSUE
Achievements of the US Army in World War II.

United States
Troops Passing
Arch of Triumph,
Paris — A381

ROTARY PRESS PRINTING
E.E. Plates of 200 subjects in four panes of 50.

1945, Sept. 28   *Perf. 11x10½*
934 A381 3c olive   .20 .20
    P# block of 4   .40

NAVY ISSUE
Achievements of the US Navy in World War II.

United States
Sailors — A382

ROTARY PRESS PRINTING
E.E. Plates of 200 subjects in four panes of 50.

1945, Oct. 27   *Perf. 11x10½*
935 A382 3c blue   .20 .20
    P# block of 4   .40

COAST GUARD ISSUE
Achievements of the US Coast Guard in World War
II.

Coast Guard
Landing Craft and
Supply
Ship — A383

ROTARY PRESS PRINTING
E.E. Plates of 200 subjects in four panes of 50.

1945, Nov. 10   *Perf. 11x10½*
936 A383 3c bright blue green   .20 .20
    P# block of 4   .40

ALFRED E. SMITH ISSUE

Alfred E. Smith, Governor of New
York — A384

ROTARY PRESS PRINTING
E.E. Plates of 400 subjects in four panes of 100.

1945, Nov. 26   *Perf. 11x10½*
937 A384 3c purple   .20 .20
    P# block of 4   .40
    Pair with full vert. gutter btwn.

TEXAS STATEHOOD, 100th ANNIV.

Flags of the
United States and
the State of
Texas — A385

ROTARY PRESS PRINTING
E.E. Plates of 200 subjects in four panes of 50.

1945, Dec. 29   *Perf. 11x10½*
938 A385 3c dark blue   .20 .20
    P# block of 4   .30

MERCHANT MARINE ISSUE
Achievements of the US Merchant Marine in World
War II.

Liberty Ship
Unloading
Cargo — A386

ROTARY PRESS PRINTING
E.E. Plates of 200 subjects in four panes of 50.

		Perf. 11x10½
1946, Feb. 26		
939 A386 3c blue green	.20	.20
P# block of 4	.40	

VETERANS OF WORLD WAR II ISSUE
Issued to honor all veterans of World War II.

Honorable Discharge
Emblem — A387

ROTARY PRESS PRINTING
E.E. Plates of 400 subjects in four panes of 100.

		Perf. 11x10½
1946, May 9		
940 A387 3c dark violet	.20	.20
P# block of 4	.35	

TENNESSEE STATEHOOD, 150th ANNIV.

Andrew Jackson,
John Sevier and
State Capitol,
Nashville — A388

ROTARY PRESS PRINTING
E.E. Plates of 200 subjects in four panes of 50.

		Perf. 11x10½
1946, June 1		
941 A388 3c dark violet	.20	.20
P# block of 4	.30	

IOWA STATEHOOD, 100th ANNIV.

Iowa State Flag
and Map — A389

ROTARY PRESS PRINTING
E.E. Plates of 200 subjects in four panes of 50.

		Perf. 11x10½
1946, Aug. 3		
942 A389 3c deep blue	.20	.20
P# block of 4	.30	

SMITHSONIAN INSTITUTION ISSUE
100th anniversary of the establishment of the Smithsonian Institution, Washington, D.C.

Smithsonian
Institution — A390

ROTARY PRESS PRINTING
E.E. Plates of 200 subjects in four panes of 50.

		Perf. 11x10½
1946, Aug. 10		
943 A390 3c violet brown	.20	.20
P# block of 4	.30	

KEARNY EXPEDITION ISSUE
100th anniversary of the entry of General Stephen Watts Kearny into Santa Fe.

"Capture of Santa
Fe" by Kenneth M.
Chapman — A391

ROTARY PRESS PRINTING
E.E. Plates of 200 subjects in four panes of 50.

		Perf. 11x10½
1946, Oct. 16		
944 A391 3c brown violet	.20	.20
P# block of 4	.30	

THOMAS A. EDISON ISSUE

Thomas A. Edison (1847-1931),
Inventor — A392

ROTARY PRESS PRINTING
E.E. Plates of 280 subjects in four panes of 70.

		Perf. 10½x11
1947, Feb. 11		
945 A392 3c bright red violet	.20	.20
P# block of 4	.35	—

JOSEPH PULITZER ISSUE

Joseph Pulitzer
(1847-1911),
Journalist, and
Statue of
Liberty — A393

Designed by Victor S. McCloskey, Jr.

ROTARY PRESS PRINTING
E.E. Plates of 200 subjects in four panes of 50.

		Perf. 11x10½
1947, Apr. 10		
946 A393 3c purple	.20	.20
P# block of 4	.35	—

POSTAGE STAMP CENTENARY ISSUE
Centenary of the first postage stamps issued by the United States Government

Washington and
Franklin, Early and
Modern Mail-
carrying
Vehicles — A394

Designed by Leon Helguera.

ROTARY PRESS PRINTING
E.E. Plates of 200 subjects in four panes of 50.

		Perf. 11x10½
1947, May 17		
947 A394 3c deep blue	.20	.20
P# block of 4	.30	—

CENTENARY INTERNATIONAL PHILATELIC
EXHIBITION ISSUE
SOUVENIR SHEET

A395

FLAT PLATE PRINTING
Plates of 30 subjects

			Imperf.
1947, May 19			
948 A395 Sheet of 2		.55	.45
a. 5c blue, type A1		.20	.20
b. 10c brown orange, type A2		.25	.25

Sheet inscribed below stamps: "100th Anniversary United States Postage Stamps" and in the margins: "PRINTED BY THE TREASURY DEPARTMENT, BUREAU OF ENGRAVING AND PRINTING. - UNDER AUTHORITY OF ROBERT E. HANNEGAN, POSTMASTER GENERAL. - IN COMPLIMENT TO THE CENTENARY INTERNATIONAL PHILATELIC EXHIBITION. - NEW YORK, N.Y., MAY 17-25, 1947."
Sheet size varies: 96-98x66-68mm.

DOCTORS ISSUE
Issued to honor the physicians of America.

"The Doctor" by
Sir Luke
Fildes — A396

Designed by Charles R. Chickering.

ROTARY PRESS PRINTING
E.E. Plates of 200 subjects in four panes of 50.

		Perf. 11x10½
1947, June 9		
949 A396 3c brown violet	.20	.20
P# block of 4	.30	—

UTAH ISSUE
Centenary of the settlement of Utah.

Pioneers Entering
the Valley of Great
Salt Lake — A397

Designed by Charles R. Chickering.

ROTARY PRESS PRINTING
E.E. Plates of 200 subjects in four panes of 50.

		Perf. 11x10½
1947, July 24		
950 A397 3c dark violet	.20	.20
P# block of 4	.30	—

U.S. FRIGATE CONSTITUTION ISSUE
150th anniversary of the launching of the U.S. frigate Constitution ("Old Ironsides").

Naval Architect's
Drawing of Frigate
Constitution
A398

Designed by Andrew H. Hepburn.

ROTARY PRESS PRINTING
E.E. Plates of 200 subjects in four panes of 50.

		Perf. 11x10½
1947, Oct. 21		
951 A398 3c blue green	.20	.20
P# block of 4	.30	—

Great White Heron
and Map of
Florida — A399

Dr. George
Washington
Carver — A400

EVERGLADES NATIONAL PARK ISSUE

Dedication of the Everglades National Park, Florida, Dec. 6, 1947.

Designed by Robert I. Miller, Jr.

ROTARY PRESS PRINTING
E.E. Plates of 200 subjects in four panes of 50.

1947, Dec. 5			Perf. 10½x11	
952	A399	3c bright green	.20	.20
		P# block of 4	.30	—

GEORGE WASHINGTON CARVER ISSUE

5th anniversary of the death of Dr. George Washington Carver, (1864-1943), botanist.

ROTARY PRESS PRINTING
E.E. Plates of 280 subjects in four panes of 70.

1948, Jan. 5			Perf. 10½x11	
953	A400	3c bright red violet	.20	.20
		P# block of 4	.35	—

CALIFORNIA GOLD CENTENNIAL ISSUE

Sutter's Mill, Coloma, California — A401

Designed by Charles R. Chickering.

ROTARY PRESS PRINTING
E.E. Plates of 200 subjects in four panes of 50.

1948, Jan. 24			Perf. 11x10½	
954	A401	3c dark violet	.20	.20
		P# block of 4	.30	—

MISSISSIPPI TERRITORY ISSUE

Mississippi Territory establishment, 150th anniv.

Map, Seal of Mississippi Territory and Gov. Winthrop Sargent — A402

Designed by William K. Schrage.

ROTARY PRESS PRINTING
E.E. Plates of 200 subjects in four panes of 50.

1948, Apr. 7			Perf. 11x10½	
955	A402	3c brown violet	.20	.20
		P# block of 4	.30	—

FOUR CHAPLAINS ISSUE

George L. Fox, Clark V. Poling, John P. Washington and Alexander D. Goode, the 4 chaplains who sacrificed their lives in the sinking of the S.S. Dorchester, Feb. 3, 1943.

Four Chaplains and Sinking S.S. Dorchester A403

Designed by Charles R. Chickering.

ROTARY PRESS PRINTING
E.E. Plates of 200 subjects in four panes of 50.

1948, May 28			Perf. 11x10½	
956	A403	3c gray black	.20	.20
		P# block of 4	.40	—

WISCONSIN STATEHOOD, 100th ANNIV.

Map on Scroll and State Capitol — A404

Designed by Victor S. McCloskey, Jr.

ROTARY PRESS PRINTING
E.E. Plates of 200 subjects in four panes of 50.

1948, May 29			Perf. 11x10½	
957	A404	3c dark violet	.20	.20
		P# block of 4	.30	—

SWEDISH PIONEER ISSUE

Centenary of the coming of the Swedish pioneers to the Middle West.

Swedish Pioneer with Covered Wagon Moving Westward — A405

Designed by Charles R. Chickering.

ROTARY PRESS PRINTING
E.E. Plates of 200 subjects in four panes of 50.

1948, June 4			Perf. 11x10½	
958	A405	5c deep blue	.20	.20
		P# block of 4	.45	—

PROGRESS OF WOMEN ISSUE

Century of progress of American Women.

Elizabeth Stanton, Carrie Chapman Catt and Lucretia Mott — A406

Designed by Victor S. McCloskey, Jr.

ROTARY PRESS PRINTING
E.E. Plates of 200 subjects in four panes of 50.

1948, July 19			Perf. 11x10½	
959	A406	3c dark violet	.20	.20
		P# block of 4	.30	—

WILLIAM ALLEN WHITE ISSUE

William Allen White (1868-1944), Writer and Journalist — A407

ROTARY PRESS PRINTING
E.E. Plates of 280 subjects in four panes of 70.

1948, July 31			Perf. 10½x11	
960	A407	3c bright red violet	.20	.20
		P# block of 4	.40	—

UNITED STATES-CANADA FRIENDSHIP ISSUE

Century of friendship between the US and Canada.

Niagara Railway Suspension Bridge — A408

Designed by Leon Helguera, modeled by V. S. McCloskey, Jr.

ROTARY PRESS PRINTING
E.E. Plates of 200 subjects in four panes of 50.

1948, Aug. 2			Perf. 11x10½	
961	A408	3c blue	.20	.20
		P# block of 4	.30	—

FRANCIS SCOTT KEY ISSUE

Francis Scott Key (1779-1843), Maryland lawyer and author of "The Star-Spangled Banner" (1813).

Francis Scott Key and American Flags of 1814 and 1948 — A409

Designed by Victor S. McCloskey, Jr.

ROTARY PRESS PRINTING
E.E. Plates of 200 subjects in four panes of 50.

1948, Aug. 9			Perf. 11x10½	
962	A409	3c rose pink	.20	.20
		P# block of 4	.30	—

SALUTE TO YOUTH ISSUE

Issued to honor the Youth of America and to publicize "Youth Month," September, 1948.

Girl and Boy Carrying Books — A410

ROTARY PRESS PRINTING
E.E. Plates of 200 subjects in four panes of 50.

1948, Aug. 11			Perf. 11x10½	
963	A410	3c deep blue	.20	.20
		P# block of 4	.30	—

OREGON TERRITORY ISSUE

Centenary of the establishment of Oregon Territory.

John McLoughlin, Jason Lee and Wagon on Oregon Trail — A411

ROTARY PRESS PRINTING
E.E. Plates of 200 subjects in four panes of 50.

1948, Aug. 14			Perf. 11x10½	
964	A411	3c brown red	.20	.20
		P# block of 4	.35	—

HARLAN F. STONE ISSUE

Harlan Fiske Stone (1872-1946) of New York, associate justice of the Supreme Court, 1925-1941, and chief justice, 1941-1946.

Chief Justice Harlan F. Stone — A412

ROTARY PRESS PRINTING
E.E. Plates of 280 subjects in four panes of 70.

1948, Aug. 25			Perf. 10½x11	
965	A412	3c bright violet	.20	.20
		P# block of 4	.60	—

PALOMAR MOUNTAIN OBSERVATORY ISSUE

Dedication, August 30, 1948.

Observatory, Palomar Mountain, California — A413

Designed by Victor S. McCloskey, Jr.

ROTARY PRESS PRINTING

E.E. Plates of 280 subjects in four panes of 70.

1948, Aug. 30   *Perf. 10½x11*
966 A413 3c **blue**   .20   .20
   P# block of 4   .95 —
a.   Vert. pair, imperf. between   550.00

CLARA BARTON ISSUE

Clara Barton (1821-1912), Founder of the American Red Cross in 1882 — A414

Designed by Charles R. Chickering.

ROTARY PRESS PRINTING

E.E. Plates of 200 subjects in four panes of 50.

1948, Sept. 7   *Perf. 11x10½*
967 A414 3c **rose pink**   .20   .20
   P# block of 4   .30 —

POULTRY INDUSTRY CENTENNIAL ISSUE

Light Brahma Rooster — A415

Designed by Charles R. Chickering.

ROTARY PRESS PRINTING

E.E. Plates of 200 subjects in four panes of 50.

1948, Sept. 9   *Perf. 11x10½*
968 A415 3c **sepia**   .20   .20
   P# block of 4   .40 —

GOLD STAR MOTHERS ISSUE

Issued to honor the mothers of deceased members of the United States armed forces.

Star and Palm Frond — A416

Designed by Charles R. Chickering.

ROTARY PRESS PRINTING

E.E. Plates of 200 subjects in four panes of 50.

1948, Sept. 21   *Perf. 10½x11*
969 A416 3c **orange yellow**   .20   .20
   P# block of 4   .35 —

FORT KEARNY ISSUE

Establishment of Fort Kearny, Neb., centenary.

Fort Kearny and Pioneer Group — A417

ROTARY PRESS PRINTING

E.E. Plates of 200 subjects in four panes of 50.

1948, Sept. 22   *Perf. 11x10½*
970 A417 3c **violet**   .20   .20
   P# block of 4   .35 —

VOLUNTEER FIREMEN ISSUE

300th anniv. of the organization of the 1st volunteer firemen in America by Peter Stuyvesant.

Peter Stuyvesant, Early and Modern Fire Engines — A418

ROTARY PRESS PRINTING

E.E. Plates of 200 subjects in four panes of 50.

1948, Oct. 4   *Perf. 11x10½*
971 A418 3c **bright rose carmine**   .20   .20
   P# block of 4   .40 —

INDIAN CENTENNIAL ISSUE

Centenary of the arrival in Indian Territory, later Oklahoma, of the Five Civilized Indian Tribes: Cherokee, Chickasaw, Choctaw, Muscogee and Seminole.

Map of Indian Territory and Seals of Five Tribes — A419

ROTARY PRESS PRINTING

E.E. Plates of 200 subjects in four panes of 50.

1948, Oct. 15   *Perf. 11x10½*
972 A419 3c **dark brown**   .20   .20
   P# block of 4   .35 —

ROUGH RIDERS ISSUE

50th anniversary of the organization of the Rough Riders of the Spanish-American War.

Statue of Capt. William O. (Bucky) O'Neill by Solon H. Borglum — A420

Designed by Victor S. McCloskey, Jr.

ROTARY PRESS PRINTING

E.E. Plates of 200 subjects in four panes of 50.

1948, Oct. 27   *Perf. 11x10½*
973 A420 3c **violet brown**   .20   .20
   P# block of 4   .40 —

JULIETTE LOW ISSUE

Low (1860-1927), founded of the Girl Scouts of America. Mrs. Low organized the 1st Girl Guides troop in 1912 at Savannah. The name was changed to Girl Scouts in 1913 and headquarters moved to New York.

Juliette Gordon Low and Girl Scout Emblem — A421

Designed by William K. Schrage.

ROTARY PRESS PRINTING

E.E. Plates of 200 subjects in four panes of 50.

1948, Oct. 20   *Perf. 11x10½*
974 A421 3c **blue green**   .20   .20
   P# block of 4   .30 —

Will Rogers — A422

Fort Bliss, El Paso, Texas, and Rocket Firing — A423

WILL ROGERS ISSUE

Will Rogers, (1879-1935), humorist and political commentator.

ROTARY PRESS PRINTING

E.E. Plates of 280 subjects in four panes of 70.

1948, Nov. 4   *Perf. 10½x11*
975 A422 3c **bright red violet**   .20   .20
   P# block of 4   .40 —

FORT BLISS CENTENNIAL ISSUE

Designed by Charles R. Chickering.

ROTARY PRESS PRINTING

E.E. Plates of 280 subjects in four panes of 70.

1948, Nov. 5   *Perf. 10½x11*
976 A423 3c **henna brown**   .20   .20
   P# block of 4   1.10 —

MOINA MICHAEL ISSUE

Moina Michael (1870-1944), educator who originated (1918) the Flanders Field Poppy Day idea as a memorial to the war dead.

Moina Michael and Poppy Plant — A424

ROTARY PRESS PRINTING

E.E. Plates of 200 subjects in four panes of 50.

1948, Nov. 9   *Perf. 11x10½*
977 A424 3c **rose pink**   .20   .20
   P# block of 4   .35 —

GETTYSBURG ADDRESS ISSUE

85th anniversary of Abraham Lincoln's address at Gettysburg, Pennsylvania.

Abraham Lincoln and Quotation from Gettysburg Address — A425

Designed by Charles R. Chickering.

ROTARY PRESS PRINTING

E.E. Plates of 200 subjects in four panes of 50.

1948, Nov. 19   *Perf. 11x10½*
978 A425 3c **bright blue**   .20   .20
   P# block of 4   .40 —

Torch and Emblem of American Turners — A426

Joel Chandler Harris — A427

AMERICAN TURNERS ISSUE

Formation of the American Turners Soc., cent.

Designed by Alvin R. Meissner.

ROTARY PRESS PRINTING

E.E. Plates of 200 subjects in four panes of 50.

1948, Nov. 20   *Perf. 10½x11*
979 A426 3c **carmine**   .20   .20
   P# block of 4   .30 —

JOEL CHANDLER HARRIS ISSUE

Joel Chandler Harris (1848-1908), Georgia writer, creator of "Uncle Remus" and newspaperman.

ROTARY PRESS PRINTING
E.E. Plates of 280 subjects in four panes of 70.

1948, Dec. 9   *Perf. 10½x11*
980 A427 3c **bright red violet**   .20   .20
      P# block of 4   .55

MINNESOTA TERRITORY ISSUE
Establishment of Minnesota Territory, cent.

Pioneer and Red
River
Oxcart — A428

ROTARY PRESS PRINTING
E.E. Plates of 200 subjects in four panes of 50.

1949, Mar. 3   *Perf. 11x10½*
981 A428 3c **blue green**   .20   .20
      P# block of 4   .30

WASHINGTON AND LEE UNIVERSITY ISSUE
Bicentenary of Washington and Lee University.

George
Washington,
Robert E. Lee and
University Building,
Lexington,
Va. — A429

ROTARY PRESS PRINTING
E.E. Plates of 200 subjects in four panes of 50.

1949, Apr. 12   *Perf. 11x10½*
982 A429 3c **ultramarine**   .20   .20
      P# block of 4   .30

PUERTO RICO ELECTION ISSUE
First gubernatorial election in the Territory of Puerto
Rico, Nov. 2, 1948.

Puerto Rican
Farmer Holding
Cogwheel and
Ballot Box — A430

ROTARY PRESS PRINTING
E.E. Plates of 200 subjects in four panes of 50.

1949, Apr. 27   *Perf. 11x10½*
983 A430 3c **green**   .20   .20
      P# block of 4   .30

ANNAPOLIS TERCENTENARY ISSUE
Founding of Annapolis, Maryland, 300th anniv.

James Stoddert's
1718 Map of
Regions about
Annapolis,
Redrawn — A431

ROTARY PRESS PRINTING
E.E. Plates of 200 subjects in four panes of 50.

1949, May 23   *Perf. 11x10½*
984 A431 3c **aquamarine**   .20   .20
      P# block of 4   .30

G.A.R. ISSUE
Final encampment of the Grand Army of the Republic, Indianapolis, Aug. 28 - Sept. 1, 1949.

Union Soldier
and G.A.R.
Veteran of
1949 — A432

Designed by Charles R. Chickering.

ROTARY PRESS PRINTING
E.E. Plates of 200 subjects in four panes of 50.

1949, Aug. 29   *Perf. 11x10½*
985 A432 3c **bright rose carmine**   .20   .20
      P# block of 4   .30

EDGAR ALLAN POE ISSUE
Edgar Allan Poe (1809-1849), Boston-born poet,
story writer and editor.

Edgar Allan Poe — A433

ROTARY PRESS PRINTING
E.E. Plates of 280 subjects in four panes of 70.

1949, Oct. 7   *Perf. 10½x11*
986 A433 3c **bright red violet**   .20   .20
      P# block of 4   .45
      Thin outer frame line at top, inner
      line missing (24143 LL 42)   6.00

AMERICAN BANKERS ASSOCIATION ISSUE
75th anniv. of the formation of the Association.

Coin, Symbolizing
Fields of Banking
Service — A434

Designed by Charles R. Chickering.

ROTARY PRESS PRINTING
E.E. Plates of 200 subjects in four panes of 50.

1950, Jan. 3   *Perf. 11x10½*
987 A434 3c **yellow green**   .20   .20
      P# block of 4   .35

SAMUEL GOMPERS ISSUE
Samuel Gompers (1850-1924), British-born American labor leader.

Samuel Gompers — A435

ROTARY PRESS PRINTING
E.E. Plates of 280 subjects in four panes of 70.

1950, Jan. 27   *Perf. 10½x11*
988 A435 3c **bright red violet**   .20   .20
      P# block of 4   .30

NATIONAL CAPITAL SESQUICENTENNIAL ISSUE
150th anniversary of the establishment of the
National Capital, Washington, D.C.

Statue of Freedom on Capitol
Dome — A436

Executive
Mansion — A437

Supreme Court
Building — A438

United States
Capitol — A439

ROTARY PRESS PRINTING
E.E. Plates of 200 subjects in four panes of 50.

1950   *Perf. 10½x11, 11x10½*
989 A436 3c **bright blue,** *Apr. 20*   .20   .20
      P# block of 4   .30
990 A437 3c **deep green,** *June 12*   .20   .20
      P# block of 4   .40
991 A438 3c **light violet,** *Aug. 2*   .20   .20
      P# block of 4   .30
992 A439 3c **bright red violet,** *Nov. 22*   .20   .20
      P# block of 4   .40
      Gripper cracks (24285 UL 11)   1.00   .50
      Nos. 989-992 (4)   .80   .80

RAILROAD ENGINEERS ISSUE
Issued to honor the Railroad Engineers of America.
Stamp portrays John Luther (Casey) Jones (1864-
1900), locomotive engineer killed in train wreck near
Vaughn, Miss.

"Casey" Jones and
Locomotives of
1900 and
1950 — A440

ROTARY PRESS PRINTING
E.E. Plates of 200 subjects in four panes of 50.

1950, Apr. 29   *Perf. 11x10½*
993 A440 3c **violet brown**   .20   .20
      P# block of 4   .35

KANSAS CITY, MISSOURI, CENTENARY ISSUE
Kansas City, Missouri, incorporation.

Kansas City
Skyline, 1950 and
Westport Landing,
1850 — A441

ROTARY PRESS PRINTING
E.E. Plates of 200 subjects in four panes of 50.

1950, June 3   *Perf. 11x10½*
994 A441 3c **violet**   .20   .20
      P# block of 4   .30

BOY SCOUTS ISSUE
Honoring the Boy Scouts of America on the occasion of the 2nd National Jamboree, Valley Forge, Pa.

Three Boys, Statue
of Liberty and
Scout
Badge — A442

ROTARY PRESS PRINTING
E.E. Plates of 200 subjects in four panes of 50.

1950, June 30		Perf. 11x10½
995 A442 3c sepia	.20	.20
P# block of 4	.35	—

INDIANA TERRITORY ISSUE

Establishment of Indiana Territory, 150th anniv.

Gov. William Henry Harrison and First Indiana Capitol, Vincennes — A443

ROTARY PRESS PRINTING
E.E. Plates of 200 subjects in four panes of 50.

1950, July 4		Perf. 11x10½
996 A443 3c bright blue	.20	.20
P# block of 4	.30	—

CALIFORNIA STATEHOOD ISSUE

Gold Miner, Pioneers and S.S. Oregon — A444

ROTARY PRESS PRINTING
E.E. Plates of 200 subjects in four panes of 50.

1950, Sept. 9		Perf. 11x10½
997 A444 3c yellow orange	.20	.20
P# block of 4	.30	—

UNITED CONFEDERATE VETERANS FINAL REUNION ISSUE

Final reunion of the United Confederate Veterans, Norfolk, Virginia, May 30, 1951.

Confederate Soldier and United Confederate Veteran — A445

ROTARY PRESS PRINTING
E.E. Plates of 200 subjects in four panes of 50.

1951, May 30		Perf. 11x10½
998 A445 3c gray	.20	.20
P# block of 4	.30	—

NEVADA CENTENNIAL ISSUE

Centenary of the settlement of Nevada.

Carson Valley, c. 1851 — A446

Designed by Charles R. Chickering.

ROTARY PRESS PRINTING
E.E. Plates of 200 subjects in four panes of 50.

1951, July 14		Perf. 11x10½
999 A446 3c light olive green	.20	.20
P# block of 4	.30	—

LANDING OF CADILLAC ISSUE

250th anniversary of the landing of Antoine de la Mothe Cadillac at Detroit.

Detroit Skyline and Cadillac Landing — A447

ROTARY PRESS PRINTING
E.E. Plates of 200 subjects in four panes of 50.

1951, July 24		Perf. 11x10½
1000 A447 3c blue	.20	.20
P# block of 4	.30	—

COLORADO STATEHOOD, 75th ANNIV.

Colorado Capitol, Mount of the Holy Cross, Columbine and Bronco Buster by Proctor — A448

ROTARY PRESS PRINTING
E.E. Plates of 200 subjects in four panes of 50.

1951, Aug. 1		Perf. 11x10½
1001 A448 3c blue violet	.20	.20
P# block of 4	.30	—

AMERICAN CHEMICAL SOCIETY ISSUE

75th anniv. of the formation of the Society.

A.C.S. Emblem and Symbols of Chemistry — A449

ROTARY PRESS PRINTING
E.E. Plates of 200 subjects in four panes of 50.

1951, Sept. 4		Perf. 11x10½
1002 A449 3c violet brown	.20	.20
P# block of 4	.35	—

BATTLE OF BROOKLYN, 175th ANNIV.

Gen. George Washington Evacuating Army; Fulton Ferry House at Right — A450

ROTARY PRESS PRINTING
E.E. Plates of 200 subjects in four panes of 50.

1951, Dec. 10		Perf. 11x10½
1003 A450 3c violet	.20	.20
P# block of 4	.30	—

BETSY ROSS ISSUE

200th anniv. of the birth of Betsy Ross, maker of the first American flag.

"Birth of Our Nation's Flag," by Charles H. Weisgerber - Betsy Ross Showing Flag to Gen. George Washington, Robert Morris and George Ross — A451

ROTARY PRESS PRINTING
E.E. Plates of 200 subjects in four panes of 50.

1952, Jan. 2		Perf. 11x10½
1004 A451 3c carmine rose	.20	.20
P# block of 4	.35	—

4-H CLUB ISSUE

Farm, Club Emblem, Boy and Girl — A452

ROTARY PRESS PRINTING
E.E. Plates of 200 subjects in four panes of 50.

1952, Jan. 15		Perf. 11x10½
1005 A452 3c blue green	.20	.20
P# block of 4	.30	—

B. & O. RAILROAD ISSUE

125th anniv. of the granting of a charter to the Baltimore and Ohio Railroad Company by the Maryland Legislature.

Charter and Three Stages of Rail Transportation A453

ROTARY PRESS PRINTING
E.E. Plates of 200 subjects in four panes of 50.

1952, Feb. 28		Perf. 11x10½
1006 A453 3c bright blue	.20	.20
P# block of 4	.40	—

A. A. A. ISSUE

50th anniversary of the formation of the American Automobile Association.

School Girls and Safety Patrolman Automobiles of 1902 and 1952 — A454

ROTARY PRESS PRINTING
E.E. Plates of 200 subjects in four panes of 50.

1952, Mar. 4		Perf. 11x10½
1007 A454 3c deep blue	.20	.20
P# block of 4	.30	—

NATO ISSUE

Signing of the North Atlantic Treaty, 3rd anniv.

Torch of Liberty and Globe — A455

ROTARY PRESS PRINTING
E.E. Plates of 400 subjects in four panes of 100.

1952, Apr. 4		Perf. 11x10½
1008 A455 3c deep violet	.20	.20
P# block of 4	.30	—

GRAND COULEE DAM ISSUE

50 years of Federal cooperation in developing the resources of rivers and streams in the West.

Spillway, Grand Coulee Dam — A456

ROTARY PRESS PRINTING
E.E. Plates of 200 subjects in four panes of 50.

1952, May 15		Perf. 11x10½
1009 A456 3c blue green	.20	.20
P# block of 4	.30	—

LAFAYETTE ISSUE

175th anniversary of the arrival of Marquis de Lafayette in America.

Marquis de Lafayette, Flags, Cannon and Landing Party — A457

Designed by Victor S. McCloskey, Jr.

ROTARY PRESS PRINTING
E.E. Plates of 200 subjects in four panes of 50.

1952, June 13		Perf. 11x10½
1010 A457 3c **bright blue**	.20	.20
P# block of 4	.30	—

MT. RUSHMORE MEMORIAL ISSUE

Dedication of the Mt. Rushmore National Memorial in the Black Hills of South Dakota, 25th anniv.

Sculptured Heads on Mt. Rushmore — A458

Designed by William K. Schrage.

ROTARY PRESS PRINTING
E.E. Plates of 200 subjects in four panes of 50.

1952, Aug. 11		Perf. 10½x11
1011 A458 3c **blue green**	.20	.20
P# block of 4	.35	

ENGINEERING CENTENNIAL ISSUE

American Society of Civil Engineers founding.

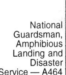

George Washington Bridge and Covered Bridge of 1850's — A459

ROTARY PRESS PRINTING
E.E. Plates of 200 subjects in four panes of 50.

1952, Sept. 6		Perf. 11x10½
1012 A459 3c **violet blue**	.20	.20
P# block of 4	.30	—

SERVICE WOMEN ISSUE

Women in the United States Armed Services.

Women of the Marine Corps, Army, Navy and Air Force — A460

ROTARY PRESS PRINTING
E.E. Plates of 200 subjects in four panes of 50.

1952, Sept. 11		Perf. 11x10½
1013 A460 3c **deep blue**	.20	.20
P# block of 4	.30	—

GUTENBERG BIBLE ISSUE

Printing of the 1st book, the Holy Bible, from movable type, by Johann Gutenberg, 500th anniv.

Gutenberg Showing Proof to the Elector of Mainz — A461

ROTARY PRESS PRINTING
E.E. Plates of 200 subjects in four panes of 50.

1952, Sept. 30		Perf. 11x10½
1014 A461 3c **violet**	.20	.20
P# block of 4	.30	—

NEWSPAPER BOYS ISSUE

Newspaper Boy, Torch and Group of Homes — A462

ROTARY PRESS PRINTING
E.E. Plates of 200 subjects in four panes of 50.

1952, Oct. 4		Perf. 11x10½
1015 A462 3c **violet**	.20	.20
P# block of 4	.30	—

RED CROSS ISSUE

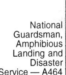

Globe, Sun and Cross — A463

ROTARY PRESS PRINTING
Cross Typographed
E.E. Plates of 200 subjects in four panes of 50.

1952, Nov. 21		Perf. 11x10½
1016 A463 3c **deep blue & carmine**	.20	.20
P# block of 4	.30	—

NATIONAL GUARD ISSUE

National Guardsman, Amphibious Landing and Disaster Service — A464

ROTARY PRESS PRINTING
E.E. Plates of 200 subjects in four panes of 50.

1953, Feb. 23		Perf. 11x10½
1017 A464 3c **bright blue**	.20	.20
P# block of 4	.30	—

OHIO STATEHOOD, 150th ANNIV.

Ohio Map, State Seal, Buckeye Leaf — A465

ROTARY PRESS PRINTING
E.E. Plates of 280 subjects in four panes of 70.

1953, Mar. 2		Perf. 11x10½
1018 A465 3c **chocolate**	.20	.20
P# block of 4	.35	—

WASHINGTON TERRITORY ISSUE

Organization of Washington Territory, cent.

Medallion, Pioneers and Washington Scene — A466

ROTARY PRESS PRINTING
E.E. Plates of 200 subjects in four panes of 50.

1953, Mar. 2		Perf. 11x10½
1019 A466 3c **green**	.20	.20
P# block of 4	.30	—

LOUISIANA PURCHASE, 150th ANNIV.

James Monroe, Robert R. Livingston and Marquis Francois de Barbé-Marbois A467

ROTARY PRESS PRINTING
E.E. Plates of 200 subjects in four panes of 50.

1953, Apr. 30		Perf. 11x10½
1020 A467 3c **violet brown**	.20	.20
P# block of 4	.30	—

OPENING OF JAPAN CENTENNIAL ISSUE

Centenary of Commodore Matthew Calbraith Perry's negotiations with Japan, which opened her doors to foreign trade.

Commodore Matthew C. Perry and First Anchorage off Tokyo Bay — A468

ROTARY PRESS PRINTING
E.E. Plates of 200 subjects in four panes of 50.

1953, July 14		Perf. 11x10½
1021 A468 5c **green**	.20	.20
P# block of 4	.65	

AMERICAN BAR ASSOCIATION, 75th ANNIV.

Section of Frieze, Supreme Court Room — A469

ROTARY PRESS PRINTING
E.E. Plates of 200 subjects in four panes of 50.

1953, Aug. 24		Perf. 11x10½
1022 A469 3c **rose violet**	.20	.20
P# block of 4	.30	—

SAGAMORE HILL ISSUE

Opening of Sagamore Hill, Theodore Roosevelt's home, as a national shrine.

Home of Theodore
Roosevelt — A470

ROTARY PRESS PRINTING
E.E. Plates of 200 subjects in four panes of 50.

1953, Sept. 14		Perf. 11x10½	
1023	A470 3c yellow green	.20	.20
	P# block of 4	.30	—

FUTURE FARMERS ISSUE
25th anniversary of the organization of Future Farmers of America.

Agricultural Scene
and Future
Farmer — A471

ROTARY PRESS PRINTING
E.E. Plates of 200 subjects in four panes of 50.

1953, Oct. 13		Perf. 11x10½	
1024	A471 3c deep blue	.20	.20
	P# block of 4	.30	—

TRUCKING INDUSTRY ISSUE
50th anniv. of the Trucking Industry in the US.

Truck, Farm and
Distant
City — A472

ROTARY PRESS PRINTING
E.E. Plates of 200 subjects in four panes of 50.

1953, Oct. 27		Perf. 11x10½	
1025	A472 3c violet	.20	.20
	P# block of 4	.30	—

GENERAL PATTON ISSUE
Honoring Gen. George S. Patton, Jr. (1885-1945), and the armored forces of the US Army.

Gen. George S.
Patton, Jr., and
Tanks in
Action — A473

ROTARY PRESS PRINTING
E.E. Plates of 200 subjects in four panes of 50.

1953, Nov. 11		Perf. 11x10½	
1026	A473 3c blue violet	.20	.20
	P# block of 4	.40	—

NEW YORK CITY, 300th ANNIV.

Dutch Ship in
New Amsterdam
Harbor — A474

ROTARY PRESS PRINTING
E.E. Plates of 200 subjects in four panes of 50.

1953, Nov. 20		Perf. 11x10½	
1027	A474 3c bright red violet	.20	.20
	P# block of 4	.35	—

GADSDEN PURCHASE ISSUE
Centenary of James Gadsden's purchase of territory from Mexico to adjust the US-Mexico boundary.

Map and Pioneer
Group — A475

ROTARY PRESS PRINTING
E.E. Plates of 200 subjects in four panes of 50.

1953, Dec. 30		Perf. 11x10½	
1028	A475 3c copper brown	.20	.20
	P# block of 4	.30	—

COLUMBIA UNIVERSITY, 200th ANNIV.

Low Memorial
Library — A476

ROTARY PRESS PRINTING
E.E. Plates of 200 subjects in four panes of 50.

1954, Jan. 4		Perf. 11x10½	
1029	A476 3c blue	.20	.20
	P# block of 4	.30	—

Wet and Dry Printings
In 1953 the Bureau of Engraving and Printing began experiments in printing on "dry" paper (moisture content 5-10 per cent). In previous "wet" printings the paper had a moisture content of 15-35 per cent.

The new process required a thicker, stiffer paper, special types of inks and greater pressure to force the paper into the recessed plates. The "dry" printings show whiter paper, a higher sheen on the surface, feel thicker and stiffer, and the designs stand out more clearly than on the "wet" printings.

Nos. 832c and 1041 (flat plate) were the first "dry" printings to be issued of flat-plate, regular-issue stamps. No. 1063 was the first rotary press stamp to be produced entirely by "dry" printing.

Stamps printed by both the "wet" and "dry" process are Nos. 1030, 1031, 1035, 1035a, 1036, 1039, 1049, 1050-1052, 1054, 1055, 1057, 1058, C34-C36, C39, C39a, J78, J80-J84, QE1-QE3, RF26 RF28, S1, S1a, S2, S2a, S3. The "wet" printed 4c coil, No. 1058, exists only Bureau precanceled.

In the Liberty Issue listings that follow, wet printings are listed first, followed by dry printings. Where only one type of printing of a stamp is indicated, it is "dry."

All postage stamps have been printed by the "dry" process since the late 1950s.

LIBERTY ISSUE

Benjamin
Franklin — A477

George
Washington — A478

Palace of the
Governors, Santa
Fe — A478a

Mount Vernon — A479

Thomas Jefferson — A480

Bunker Hill Monument and
Massachusetts Flag,
1776 — A481

Statue of
Liberty — A482

Abraham
Lincoln — A483

The Hermitage, Home of
Andrew Jackson, near
Nashville — A484

James Monroe — A485

Theodore
Roosevelt — A486

Woodrow
Wilson — A487

Statue of
Liberty — A488

Statue of
Liberty — A489

John J.
Pershing — A489a

The Alamo, San
Antonio — A490

Independence
Hall — A491

Statue of
Liberty — A491a

Benjamin
Harrison — A492

John
Jay — A493

Monticello, Home of Thomas
Jefferson, near Charlottesville,
Va. — A494

Paul Revere — A495

Robert E. Lee — A496

John Marshall — A497

Susan B.
Anthony — A498

Patrick Henry — A499

Alexander
Hamilton — A500

ROTARY PRESS PRINTING
E.E. Plates of 400 subjects in four panes of 100

1954-68   *Perf. 11x10½*

1030a	A477	½c **red orange,** wet printing, Oct. 20, 1955	.20	.20
		P# block of 4	.25	—
1030	A477	½c **red orange,** dry printing, May 1958	.20	.20
		P# block of 4 (#25980 and up)	.25	—
1031b	A478	1c **dark green,** wet printing, Aug. 26, 1954	.20	.20
		P# block of 4	.20	—
1031	A478	1c **dark green,** dry printing, Mar. 1956	.20	.20
		P# block of 4 (#25326 and up)	.20	—
		Pair with full vert. or horiz. gutter between	150.00	

Perf. 10½x11

1031A	A478a	1¼c **turquoise,** June 17, 1960	.20	.20
		P# block of 4	.45	—
1032	A479	1½c **brown carmine,** Feb. 22, 1956	.20	.20
		P# block of 4	1.75	—

Perf. 11x10½

1033	A480	2c **carmine rose,** Sept. 15, 1954	.20	.20
		P# block of 4	.25	—
		Pair with full vert. or horiz. gutter between		
a.		Silkote paper	1,000.	
		P# block of 4	—	

Silkote paper was used in 1954 for an experimental printing of 50,000 stamps. The stamps were put on sale at the Westbrook, Maine post office in Dec. 1954. Only plates 25061 and 25062 were used to print No. 1033a. Competent expertization is required.

1034	A481	2½c **gray blue,** June 17, 1959	.20	.20
		P# block of 4	.50	—
1035e	A482	3c **deep violet,** wet printing, June 24, 1954	.20	.20
		P# block of 4	.30	—
a.		Booklet pane of 6, June 30, 1954	4.00	.90
g.		As "a," vert. imperf. between	5,000.	
1035	A482	3c **deep violet,** dry printing	.20	.20
		P# block of 4 (#25235 and up)	.25	—
		Pair with full vert. or horiz. gutter between	150.00	
b.		Tagged, July 6, 1966	.25	.25
		P# block of 4	5.00	—
c.		Imperf., pair	2,000.	
d.		Horiz. pair, imperf. between	—	
f.		Booklet pane of 6, untagged	5.00	1.10

No. 1057a measures about 19½x22mm; No. 1035c, about 18¾x22½mm.

1036c	A483	4c **red violet,** wet printing, Nov. 19, 1954	.20	.20
		P# block of 4	.45	—
1036	A483	4c **red violet,** dry printing	.20	.20
		P# block of 4 (#25445 and up)	.35	—
		Pair with full vert. or horiz. gutter between	—	
a.		Booklet pane of 6, July 31, 1958	2.75	.80
b.		Tagged, Nov. 2, 1963	.60	.40

		P# block of 4	7.50	—
d.		As "a," imperf. horiz.	—	

Perf. 10½x11

1037	A484	4½c **blue green,** Mar. 16, 1959	.20	.20
		P# block of 4	.65	—

Perf. 11x10½

1038	A485	5c **deep blue,** Dec. 2, 1954	.20	.20
		P# block of 4	.45	—
		Pair with full vert. gutter btwn.	200.00	
1039a	A486	6c **carmine,** wet printing, Nov. 18, 1955	.40	.20
		P# block of 4	1.80	—
1039	A486	6c **carmine,** dry printing	.25	.20
		P# block of 4 (#25427 and up)	1.25	—
b.		Imperf, pair	—	
1040	A487	7c **rose carmine,** Jan. 10, 1956	.20	.20
		P# block of 4	1.00	—
a.		7c **dark rose carmine**	.20	.20
		P# block of 4	1.00	—

FLAT PLATE PRINTING
Plates of 400 subjects in four panes of 100 each
Size: 22.7mm high
Perf. 11

1041	A488	8c **dark violet blue & carmine,** Apr. 9, 1954	.25	.20
		P# block of 4, 2#	2.25	—
		Corner P# block of 4, blue # only	—	
		Corner P# block of 4, red # only	—	
a.		Double impression of carmine	650.00	

FLAT PRINTING PLATES
Frame: 24912-13-14-15, 24926, 24929-30, 24932-33.
Vignette: 24916-17-18-19-20, 24935-36-37, 24939.
See note following No. 1041B.

ROTARY PRESS PRINTING
Plates of 400 subjects in four panes of 100 each
Size: 22.9mm high
Perf. 11

1041B	A488	8c **dark violet blue & carmine,** Apr. 9, 1954	.40	.20
		P# block of 4, 2#	3.00	—

ROTARY PRINTING PLATES
Frame: 24923-24, 24928, 24940, 24942.
Vignette: 24927, 24938.
No. 1041B is slightly taller than No. 1041, about the thickness of one line of engraving.

GIORI PRESS PRINTING
Plates of 400 subjects in four panes of 100 each
Redrawn design
Perf. 11

1042	A489	8c **dark violet blue & carmine rose,** Mar. 22, 1958	.20	.20
		P# block of 4	.90	—

ROTARY PRESS PRINTING
E.E. Plates of 400 subjects in four panes of 100 each
Perf. 11x10½

1042A	A489a	8c **brown,** Nov. 17, 1961	.20	.20
		P# block of 4	.90	—

Perf. 10½x11

1043	A490	9c **rose lilac,** June 14, 1956	.30	.20
		P# block of 4	1.30	—
a.		9c **dark rose lilac**	.30	.20
		P# block of 4	1.30	—
1044	A491	10c **rose lake,** July 4, 1956	.30	.20
		P# block of 4	1.30	—
b.		10c **dark rose lake**	.25	.20
		P# block of 4	1.10	—
d.		Tagged, July 6, 1966	2.00	1.00
		P# block of 4	35.00	—

No. 1044b is from later printings and is on a harder, whiter paper than No. 1044.

GIORI PRESS PRINTING
Plates of 400 subjects in four panes of 100.
Perf. 11

1044A	A491a	11c **carmine & dark violet blue,** June 15, 1961	.30	.20
		P# block of 4	1.25	—
c.		Tagged, Jan. 11, 1967	2.00	1.60
		P# block of 4	35.00	—

ROTARY PRESS PRINTING
E.E. Plates of 400 subjects in four panes of 100 each
Perf. 11x10½

1045	A492	12c **red,** June 6, 1959	.35	.20
		P# block of 4	1.50	—
a.		Tagged, 1968	.35	.20
		P# block of 4	4.00	—
1046	A493	15c **rose lake,** Dec. 12, 1958	.60	.20
		P# block of 4	3.00	—
a.		Tagged, July 6, 1966	1.10	.35
		P# block of 4	12.50	—

Perf. 10½x11

1047	A494	20c **ultramarine,** Apr. 13, 1956	.40	.20
		P# block of 4	1.75	—
a.		20c **deep bright ultramarine**	.40	.20
		P# block of 4	1.75	—

No. 1047a is from later printings and is on a harder, whiter paper than No. 1047.

Perf. 11x10½

1048	A495	25c **green,** Apr. 18, 1958	1.10	.20
		P# block of 4	4.75	—
1049a	A496	30c **black,** wet printing, Sept. 21, 1955	1.10	.20
		P# block of 4	5.00	—
1049	A496	30c **black,** dry printing, June 1957	.70	.20
		P# block of 4 (#25487 and up)	3.50	—
b.		30c **intense black**	.70	.20
		P# block of 4	3.50	—

No. 1049b is from later printings and is on a harder, whiter paper than No. 1049.

1050a	A497	40c **brown red,** wet printing, Sept. 24, 1955	2.25	.25
		P# block of 4	12.50	—
1050	A497	40c **brown red,** dry printing, Apr. 1958	1.50	.20
		P# block of 4 (#25571 and up)	7.50	—
1051a	A498	50c **bright purple,** wet printing, Aug. 25, 1955	1.75	.20
		P# block of 4	10.00	—
		Cracked plate (25231 UL 1)	—	—
1051	A498	50c **bright purple,** dry printing, Apr. 1958	1.50	.20
		P# block of 4 (#25897 and up)	6.75	—
1052a	A499	$1 **purple,** wet printing, Oct. 7, 1955	5.25	.20
		P# block of 4	22.50	—
1052	A499	$1 **purple,** dry printing, Oct. 1958	4.75	.20
		P# block of 4 (#25541 and up)	19.00	—

FLAT PLATE PRINTING
Plates of 400 subjects in four panes of 100.
Perf. 11

1053	A500	$5 black, Mar. 19, 1956	75.00	6.75
		P# block of 4	325.00	—

Bureau Precancels: ½c, 37 diff., 1c, 113 diff., 1¼c, 142 diff., 1½c, 45 diff.

2c, 86 diff., 2½c, 123 diff., 3c, 106 diff., 4c, 95 diff., 4½c, 23 diff., 5c, 20 diff., 6c, 23 diff., 7c, 16 diff.

Also, No. 1041, 12 diff., No. 1042, 12 diff., No. 1042A, 16 diff., 9c, 15 diff., 10c, 16 diff., 11c, New York, 12c, 6 diff.

15c, 12 diff., 20c, 20 diff., 25c, 11 diff., 30c, 17 diff., 40c, 10 diff., 50c, 19 diff., $1, 5 diff.

Large Holes

Small Holes

With the change from 384-subject plates to 432-subject plates the size of the perforation holes was reduced. While both are perf. 10 the later holes are smaller than the paper between them. The difference is most noticible on pairs.

ROTARY PRESS COIL STAMPS
1954-80   Perf. 10 Vertically

1054c	A478	1c dark green, large holes, wet printing, Oct. 8, 1954	.35	.20
		Pair	.70	.40
		Joint line pair	1.75	.75
1054	A478	1c dark green, small holes, Feb. 1960	.20	.20
		Pair	.40	.25
		Joint line pair	1.00	.50
		Large holes, dry printing, Aug. 1957	1.00	.20
		Pair	2.00	.20
		Joint line pair	4.00	.50
b.		Imperf., pair	2,500.	

Perf. 10 Horizontally

1054A	A478a	1¼c turquoise, June 17, 1960, small holes	.20	.20
		Pair	.25	.25
		Joint line pair	2.25	1.00
		Large holes	15.00	.20
		Pair	35.00	.20
		Joint line pair	250.00	1.25

Perf. 10 Vertically

1055d	A480	2c carmine rose, large holes, wet printing, Oct. 22, 1954	.40	.20
		Pair	.80	.20
		Joint line pair	3.50	.40
1055	A480	2c carmine rose, large holes, dry printing, May 1957	.20	.20
		Pair	.20	.20
		Joint line pair	.75	.20
		Small holes, Aug. 1961	.25	.20
		Pair	.50	.25
		Joint line pair	1.50	.40
a.		Tagged, small holes, shiny gum, May 6, 1968	.20	.20
		Pair	.20	.20
		Joint line pair	.75	.20
		Dull gum, tagged, small holes	.20	
		Pair	.20	
		Joint line pair	.75	
b.		Imperf., pair, untagged, shiny gum (Bureau precanceled, Riverdale, MD)	550.00	
		Joint line pair		1,400.
c.		Imperf. pair, tagged, shiny gum	575.00	
		Joint line pair	1,250.	
1056	A481	2½c gray blue, large holes Sept. 9, 1959	.25	.25
		Pair	.50	.50
		Joint line pair	3.50	1.20
		Small holes, Jan. 1961	350.00	100.00
		Pair	750.00	200.00
		Joint line pair	3,000.	400.00

No. 1056 with small holes only known with Bureau precancels. It was against postal regulations to make available mint precanceled copies of No. 1056. Since some do exist, values are furnished here.

1057c	A482	3c deep violet, large holes, wet printing, July 20, 1954	.30	.20
		Pair	.60	.25
		Joint line pair	2.00	.45
1057	A482	3c deep violet, large holes, dry printing, Oct. 1956	.20	.20
		Pair	.20	.20
		Joint line pair	.55	.20
		Gripper cracks	—	—
		Small holes, Mar. 1958	.20	.20
		Pair	.20	.20
		Joint line pair	.55	.20
a.		Imperf., pair	1,750.	—
		Joint line pair	2,750.	—
b.		Tagged, small holes, philatelic printing, June 26, 1967	1.00	.50
		Pair	3.00	1.00
		Joint line pair	25.00	—
d.		Tagged, small holes, Look magazine printing, Oct. 1966	4.00	4.00
		Pair	11.00	8.00
		Joint line pair	250.00	

Earliest known use No. 1057d: Dec. 29, 1966.
No. 1057a measures about 19½x22mm; No. 1035c, about 18¾x22½mm.
The second tagged printing (No. 1057b) was a "philatelic reprint" made when the original stock of tagged stamps was exhausted. The original tagged printing (No. 1057d, specially printed for "Look" magazine) has a less intense color, the impression is less sharp and the tagging is brighter.
The reprint was printed on a slightly fluorescent paper, while the original paper is dead under longwave UV light.

1058b	A483	4c red violet, large holes, wet printing (Bureau precanceled)	27.50	.50
		Pair	60.00	
		Joint line pair	375.00	

It was against postal regulations to make available mint precanceled copies of No. 1058b. Since some do exist, values are furnished here.

1058	A483	4c red violet, large holes, July 31, 1958	.20	.20
		Pair	.50	.30
		Joint line pair	2.00	.40
		Small holes	.20	.20
		Pair	.20	.20
		Joint line pair	.70	.20
a.		Imperf., pair	120.00	70.00
		Joint line pair	200.00	

Perf. 10 Horizontally

1059	A484	4½c blue green, large holes, May 1, 1959	1.50	1.20
		Pair	3.00	2.40
		Joint line pair	14.00	3.00
		Small holes	12.00	
		Pair	25.00	—
		Joint line pair	400.00	

Perf. 10 Vertically

1059A	A495	25c green, Feb. 25, 1965	.50	.30
		Pair	1.00	.60
		Joint line pair	2.00	1.20
b.		Tagged, shiny gum, Apr. 3, 1973	.65	.20
		Pair	1.30	.40
		Joint line pair	3.00	1.25
		Tagged, dull gum, 1980	.65	
		Pair	1.30	
		Joint line pair	3.00	
c.		Imperf., pair	55.00	
		Joint line pair	100.00	

Value for No. 1059Ac is for fine centering.
Bureau Precancels: 1c, 118 diff., 1¼c, 105 diff., 2c, 191 diff., 2½c, 94 diff., 3c, 142 diff., 4c, 83 diff., 4½c, 23 diff.

NEBRASKA TERRITORY ISSUE
Establishment of the Nebraska Territory, centenary.

"The Sower,"
Mitchell Pass and
Scotts
Bluff — A507

ROTARY PRESS PRINTING
E.E. Plates of 200 subjects in four panes of 50.

1954, May 7			Perf. 11x10½	
1060	A507	3c violet	.20	.20
		P# block of 4	.30	—

KANSAS TERRITORY ISSUE
Establishment of the Kansas Territory, centenary

Wheat Field and
Pioneer Wagon
Train — A508

ROTARY PRESS PRINTING
E.E. Plates of 200 subjects in four panes of 50.

1954, May 31			Perf. 11x10½	
1061	A508	3c brown orange	.20	.20
		P# block of 4	.30	—

GEORGE EASTMAN ISSUE
Eastman (1854-1932), inventor of photographic dry plates, flexible film and the Kodak camera; Rochester, N.Y., industrialist.

George Eastman — A509

ROTARY PRESS PRINTING
E.E. Plates of 280 subjects in four panes of 70.

1954, July 12			Perf. 10½x11	
1062	A509	3c violet brown	.20	.20
		P# block of 4	.30	—

LEWIS AND CLARK EXPEDITION
150th anniv. of the Lewis and Clark expedition.

Meriwether Lewis,
William Clark and
Sacagawea
Landing on
Missouri
Riverbank — A510

ROTARY PRESS PRINTING
E.E. Plates of 200 subjects in four panes of 50.

1954, July 28   **Perf. 11x10½**
1063 A510 3c **violet brown**   .20   .20
    P# block of 4   .30 —

PENNSYLVANIA ACADEMY OF THE FINE ARTS ISSUE

150th anniversary of the founding of the Pennsylvania Academy of the Fine Arts, Philadelphia.

Charles Willson Peale in his Museum, Self-portrait — A511

ROTARY PRESS PRINTING
E.E. Plates of 200 subjects in four panes of 50.

1955, Jan. 15   **Perf. 10½x11**
1064 A511 3c **rose brown**   .20   .20
    P# block of 4   .30 —

LAND GRANT COLLEGES ISSUE

Centenary of the founding of Michigan State College and Pennsylvania State University, first of the land grant institutions.

Open Book and Symbols of Subjects Taught — A512

ROTARY PRESS PRINTING
E.E. Plates of 200 subjects in four panes of 50.

1955, Feb. 12   **Perf. 11x10½**
1065 A512 3c **green**   .20   .20
    P# block of 4   .30 —

ROTARY INTERNATIONAL, 50th ANNIV.

Torch, Globe and Rotary Emblem — A513

ROTARY PRESS PRINTING
E.E. Plates of 200 subjects in four panes of 50.

1955, Feb. 23   **Perf. 11x10½**
1066 A513 8c **deep blue**   .20   .20
    P# block of 4   .95 —

ARMED FORCES RESERVE ISSUE

Marine, Coast Guard, Army, Navy and Air Force Personnel A514

ROTARY PRESS PRINTING
E.E. Plates of 200 subjects in four panes of 50.

1955, May 21   **Perf. 11x10½**
1067 A514 3c **purple**   .20   .20
    P# block of 4   .30 —

NEW HAMPSHIRE ISSUE

Sesquicentennial of the discovery of the "Old Man of the Mountains."

Great Stone Face — A515

ROTARY PRESS PRINTING
E.E. Plates of 200 subjects in four panes of 50.

1955, June 21   **Perf. 10½x11**
1068 A515 3c **green**   .20   .20
    P# block of 4   .40 —

SOO LOCKS ISSUE
Centenary of the opening of the Soo Locks.

Map of Great Lakes and Two Steamers A516

ROTARY PRESS PRINTING
E.E. Plates of 200 subjects in four panes of 50.

1955, June 28   **Perf. 11x10½**
1069 A516 3c **blue**   .20   .20
    P# block of 4   .30 —

ATOMS FOR PEACE ISSUE
Issued to promote an Atoms for Peace policy.

Atomic Energy Encircling the Hemispheres A517

Designed by George R. Cox.

ROTARY PRESS PRINTING
E.E. Plates of 200 subjects in four panes of 50.

1955, July 28   **Perf. 11x10½**
1070 A517 3c **deep blue**   .20   .20
    P# block of 4   .35 —

FORT TICONDEROGA ISSUE
Bicentenary of Fort Ticonderoga, New York.

Map of the Fort, Ethan Allen and Artillery — A518

Designed by Enrico Arno.

ROTARY PRESS PRINTING
E.E. Plates of 200 subjects in four panes of 50.

1955, Sept. 18   **Perf. 11x10½**
1071 A518 3c **light brown**   .20   .20
    P# block of 4   .30 —

Andrew W. Mellon — A519

"Franklin Taking Electricity from the Sky," by Benjamin West — A520

ANDREW W. MELLON ISSUE

Andrew W. Mellon (1855-1937), US Secretary of the Treasury (1921-32), financier and art collector.

Designed by Victor S. McCloskey, Jr.

ROTARY PRESS PRINTING
E.E. Plates of 280 subjects in four panes of 70.

1955, Dec. 20   **Perf. 10½x11**
1072 A519 3c **rose carmine**   .20   .20
    P# block of 4   .30 —

BENJAMIN FRANKLIN ISSUE
250th anniv. of the birth of Benjamin Franklin.

Designed by Charles R. Chickering.

ROTARY PRESS PRINTING
E.E. Plates of 200 subjects in four panes of 50.

1956, Jan. 17   **Perf. 10½x11**
1073 A520 3c **bright carmine**   .20   .20
    P# block of 4   .35 —

BOOKER T. WASHINGTON ISSUE

Washington (1856-1915), black educator, founder and head of Tuskegee Institute in Alabama.

Log Cabin — A521

Designed by Charles R. Chickering.

ROTARY PRESS PRINTING
E.E. Plates of 200 subjects in four panes of 50.

1956, Apr. 5			*Perf. 11x10½*	
1074	A521	3c **deep blue**	.20	.20
		P# block of 4	.30	—

FIFTH INTERNATIONAL PHILATELIC EXHIBITION ISSUES

FIPEX, New York City, Apr. 28 - May 6, 1956.

SOUVENIR SHEET

A522

FLAT PLATE PRINTING
Plates of 24 subjects

1956, Apr. 28			*Imperf.*	
1075	A522	Sheet of 2	2.00	2.00
a.		A482 3c deep violet	.80	.80
b.		A488 8c dark violet blue & carmine	1.00	1.00

No. 1075 measures 108x73mm. Nos. 1075a and 1075b measure 24x28mm.

Inscriptions printed in dark violet blue; scrolls and stars in carmine.

New York
Coliseum and
Columbus
Monument — A523

Designed by William K. Schrage.

ROTARY PRESS PRINTING
E.E. Plates of 200 subjects in four panes of 50.

1956, Apr. 30			*Perf. 11x10½*	
1076	A523	3c **deep violet**	.20	.20
		P# block of 4	.30	—

WILDLIFE CONSERVATION ISSUE

Issued to emphasize the importance of Wildlife Conservation in America.

Wild
Turkey — A524

Pronghorn
Antelope — A525

King
Salmon — A526

Designed by Robert W. (Bob) Hines.

ROTARY PRESS PRINTING
E.E. Plates of 200 subjects in four panes of 50.

1956			*Perf. 11x10½*	
1077	A524	3c **rose lake**, *May 5*	.20	.20
		P# block of 4	.35	—
1078	A525	3c **brown**, *June 22*	.20	.20
		P# block of 4	.35	—
1079	A526	3c **blue green**, *Nov. 9*	.20	.20
		P# block of 4	.35	—
		Nos. 1077-1079 (3)	.60	.60

PURE FOOD AND DRUG LAWS, 50th ANNIV.

Harvey Washington
Wiley — A527

Designed by Robert L. Miller.

ROTARY PRESS PRINTING
E.E. Plates of 200 subjects in four panes of 50.

1956, June 27			*Perf. 10½x11*	
1080	A527	3c **dark blue green**	.20	.20
		P# block of 4	.30	—

WHEATLAND ISSUE

Pres. Buchanan's
Home, Lancaster,
Pa. — A528

ROTARY PRESS PRINTING
E.E. Plates of 200 subjects in four panes of 50.

1956, Aug. 5			*Perf. 11x10½*	
1081	A528	3c **black brown**	.20	.20
		P# block of 4	.30	—

LABOR DAY ISSUE

Mosaic, AFL-CIO
Headquarters — A529

Designed by Victor S. McCloskey, Jr.

ROTARY PRESS PRINTING
E.E. Plates of 200 subjects in four panes of 50.

1956, Sept. 3			*Perf. 10½x11*	
1082	A529	3c **deep blue**	.20	.20
		P# block of 4	.30	—

NASSAU HALL ISSUE

200th anniv. of Nassau Hall, Princeton University.

Nassau Hall,
Princeton,
N.J. — A530

ROTARY PRESS PRINTING
E.E. Plates of 200 subjects in four panes of 50.

1956, Sept. 22			*Perf. 11x10½*	
1083	A530	3c **black**, *orange*	.20	.20
		P# block of 4	.30	—

DEVILS TOWER ISSUE

Issued to commemorate the 50th anniversary of the Federal law providing for protection of American natural antiquities. Devils Tower National Monument, Wyoming, is an outstanding example.

Devils Tower — A531

Designed by Charles R. Chickering.

ROTARY PRESS PRINTING
E.E. Plates of 200 subjects in four panes of 50.

1956, Sept. 24			*Perf. 10½x11*	
1084	A531	3c **violet**	.20	.20
		P# block of 4	.30	—
		Pair with full horiz. gutter btwn.		

CHILDREN'S ISSUE

Issued to promote friendship among the children of the world.

Children of the
World — A532

Designed by Ronald Dias.

ROTARY PRESS PRINTING
E.E. Plates of 200 subjects in four panes of 50.

1956, Dec. 15			*Perf. 11x10½*	
1085	A532	3c **dark blue**	.20	.20
		P# block of 4	.30	—

ALEXANDER HAMILTON (1755-1804)

Alexander
Hamilton and
Federal
Hall — A533

Designed by William K. Schrage.

ROTARY PRESS PRINTING
E.E. Plates of 200 subjects in four panes of 50.

1957, Jan. 11			*Perf. 11x10½*	
1086	A533	3c **rose red**	.20	.20
		P# block of 4	.30	—

POLIO ISSUE

Honoring "those who helped fight polio," and on for 20th anniv. of the Natl. Foundation for Infantile Paralysis and the March of Dimes.

Allegory — A534

Designed by Charles R. Chickering.

ROTARY PRESS PRINTING
E.E. Plates of 200 subjects in four panes of 50.

1957, Jan. 15			*Perf. 10½x11*	
1087	A534	3c **red lilac**	.20	.20
		P# block of 4	.30	—

COAST AND GEODETIC SURVEY ISSUE

150th anniversary of the establishment of the Coast and Geodetic Survey.

Flag of Coast and Geodetic Survey and Ships at Sea — A535

Designed by Harold E. MacEwen.

ROTARY PRESS PRINTING
E.E. Plates of 200 subjects in four panes of 50.

1957, Feb. 11		Perf. 11x10½
1088 A535 3c **dark blue**	.20	.20
P# block of 4	.30	—

ARCHITECTS ISSUE

American Institute of Architects, centenary.

Corinthian Capital and Mushroom Type Head and Shaft — A536

Designed by Robert J. Schultz.

ROTARY PRESS PRINTING
E.E. Plates of 200 subjects in four panes of 50.

1957, Feb. 23		Perf. 11x10½
1089 A536 3c **red lilac**	.20	.20
P# block of 4	.30	—

STEEL INDUSTRY ISSUE

Centenary of the steel industry in America.

American Eagle and Pouring Ladle — A537

Designed by Anthonio Petruccelli.

ROTARY PRESS PRINTING
E.E. Plates of 200 subjects in four panes of 50.

1957, May 22		Perf. 10½x11
1090 A537 3c **bright ultramarine**	.20	.20
P# block of 4	.30	—

INTERNATIONAL NAVAL REVIEW ISSUE

Issued to commemorate the International Naval Review and the Jamestown Festival.

Aircraft Carrier and Jamestown Festival Emblem — A538

Designed by Richard A. Genders.

ROTARY PRESS PRINTING
E.E. Plates of 200 subjects in four panes of 50.

1957, June 10		Perf. 11x10½
1091 A538 3c **blue green**	.20	.20
P# block of 4	.30	—

OKLAHOMA STATEHOOD, 50th ANNIV.

Map of Oklahoma, Arrow and Atom Diagram — A539

Designed by William K. Schrage.

ROTARY PRESS PRINTING
E.E. Plates of 200 subjects in four panes of 50.

1957, June 14		Perf. 11x10½
1092 A539 3c **dark blue**	.20	.20
P# block of 4	.35	

SCHOOL TEACHERS ISSUE

Teacher and Pupils — A540

ROTARY PRESS PRINTING
E.E. Plates of 200 subjects in four panes of 50.

1957, July 1		Perf. 11x10½
1093 A540 3c **rose lake**	.20	.20
P# block of 4	.30	

FLAG ISSUE

"Old Glory" (48 Stars) — A541

Designed by Victor S. McCloskey, Jr.

GIORI PRESS PRINTING
Plates of 200 subjects in four panes of 50.

1957, July 4		Perf. 11
1094 A541 4c **dark blue & deep carmine**	.20	.20
P# block of 4	.35	

"Virginia of Sagadahock" and Seal of Maine — A542

Ramon Magsaysay — A543

SHIPBUILDING ISSUE

350th anniversary of shipbuilding in America.

Designed by Ervine Metzel, Mrs. William Zorach, A. M. Main, Jr., and George F. Cary II.

ROTARY PRESS PRINTING
E.E. Plates of 280 subjects in four panes of 70.

1957, Aug. 15		Perf. 10½x11
1095 A542 3c **deep violet**	.20	.20
P# block of 4	.30	—

CHAMPION OF LIBERTY ISSUE

Magsaysay (1907-57), Pres. of the Philippines.

Designed by Arnold Copeland, Ervine Metzl and William H. Buckley.

GIORI PRESS PRINTING
Plates of 192 subjects in four panes of 48 each.

1957, Aug. 31		Perf. 11
1096 A543 8c **carmine, ultramarine & ocher**	.20	.20
P# block of 4, 2#	.85	
P# block of 4, ultra. # omitted		—

Marquis de Lafayette (1757-1834) A544

Whooping Cranes A545

LAFAYETTE BICENTENARY ISSUE

Designed by Ervine Metzl.

ROTARY PRESS PRINTING
E.E. Plates of 200 subjects in four panes of 50.

1957. Sept. 6		Perf. 10½x11
1097 A544 3c **rose lake**	.20	.20
P# block of 4	.30	—

WILDLIFE CONSERVATION ISSUE

Issued to emphasize the importance of Wildlife Conservation in America.

Designed by Bob Hines and C.R. Chickering.

GIORI PRESS PRINTING
Plates of 200 subjects in four panes of 50.

1957, Nov. 22		Perf. 11
1098 A545 3c **blue, ocher & green**	.20	.20
P# block of 4	.35	

Bible, Hat and Quill Pen — A546

"Bountiful Earth" — A547

RELIGIOUS FREEDOM ISSUE

300th anniv. of the Flushing Remonstrance.

Designed by Robert Geissmann.

ROTARY PRESS PRINTING
E.E. Plates of 200 subjects in four panes of 50.

1957, Dec. 27		Perf. 10½x11
1099 A546 3c **black**	.20	.20
P# block of 4	.30	—

GARDENING HORTICULTURE ISSUE

Issued to honor the garden clubs of America and in connection with the centenary of the birth of Liberty Hyde Bailey, horticulturist.

Designed by Denver Gillen.

ROTARY PRESS PRINTING
E.E. Plates of 200 subjects in four panes of 50.

1958, Mar. 15		Perf. 10½x11
1100 A547 3c **green**	.20	.20
P# block of 4	.30	—

BRUSSELS EXHIBITION ISSUE

Issued in honor of the opening of the Universal and International Exhibition at Brussels, April 17.

US Pavilion at Brussels — A551

Designed by Bradbury Thompson.

ROTARY PRESS PRINTING

E.E. Plates of 200 subjects in four panes of 50.

1958, Apr. 17   *Perf. 11x10½*

1104 A551 3c deep claret   .20   .20
     On cover, Expo. station ("U.S. Pavilion") canc.   3.00
     P# block of 4   .30 —

JAMES MONROE ISSUE

Monroe (1758-1831), 5th President of the US.

James Monroe — A552

Designed by Frank P. Conley.

ROTARY PRESS PRINTING

E.E. Plates of 280 subjects in four panes of 70.

1958, Apr. 28   *Perf. 11x10½*

1105 A552 3c purple   .20   .20
     P# block of 4   .30 —

MINNESOTA STATEHOOD, 100th ANNIV.

Minnesota Lakes and Pines — A553

Designed by Homer Hill.

ROTARY PRESS PRINTING

E.E. Plates of 200 subjects in four panes of 50.

1958, May 11   *Perf. 11x10½*

1106 A553 3c green   .20   .20
     P# block of 4   .30 —

GEOPHYSICAL YEAR ISSUE

International Geophysical Year, 1957-58.

Solar Disc and Hands from Michelangelo's "Creation of Adam" — A554

Designed by Ervine Metzl.

GIORI PRESS PRINTING

Plates of 200 subjects in four panes of 50.

1958, May 31   *Perf. 11*

1107 A554 3c black & red orange   .20   .20
     P# block of 4   .35 —

GUNSTON HALL ISSUE

Issued for the bicentenary of Gunston Hall and to honor George Mason, author of the Constitution of Virginia and the Virginia Bill of Rights.

Gunston Hall, Virginia — A555

Designed by Rene Clarke.

ROTARY PRESS PRINTING

E.E. Plates of 200 subjects in four panes of 50.

1958, June 12   *Perf. 11x10½*

1108 A555 3c light green   .20   .20
     P# block of 4   .30 —

Mackinac Bridge — A556

Simon Bolívar — A557

MACKINAC BRIDGE ISSUE

Dedication of Mackinac Bridge, Michigan.

Designed by Arnold J. Copeland.

ROTARY PRESS PRINTING

E.E. Plates of 200 subjects in four panes of 50.

1958, June 25   *Perf. 10½x11*

1109 A556 3c bright greenish blue   .20   .20
     P# block of 4   .30 —

CHAMPION OF LIBERTY ISSUE

Simon Bolívar, South American freedom fighter.

ROTARY PRESS PRINTING

E.E. Plates of 280 subjects in four panes of 70.

1958, July 24   *Perf. 10½x11*

1110 A557 4c olive bister   .20   .20
     P# block of 4   .35 —

GIORI PRESS PRINTING

Plates of 288 subjects in four panes of 72 each.

Perf. 11

1111 A557 8c carmine, ultramarine & ocher   .20   .20
     P# block of 4, 2#   1.25 —
     P# block of 4, ocher # only

ATLANTIC CABLE CENTENNIAL ISSUE

Centenary of the Atlantic Cable, linking the Eastern and Western hemispheres.

Neptune, Globe and Mermaid — A558

Designed by George Giusti.

ROTARY PRESS PRINTING

E.E. Plates of 200 subjects in four panes of 50.

1958, Aug. 15   *Perf. 11x10½*

1112 A558 4c reddish purple   .20   .20
     P# block of 4   .35 —

LINCOLN SESQUICENTENNIAL ISSUE

Sesquicentennial of the birth of Abraham Lincoln. No. 1114 also for the centenary of the founding of Cooper Union, New York City. No. 1115 marks the centenary of the Lincoln-Douglas Debates.

Lincoln by George Healy — A559

Lincoln by Gutzon Borglum — A560

Lincoln and Stephen A. Douglas Debating, from Painting by Joseph Boggs Beale — A561

Daniel Chester French Statue of Lincoln as Drawn by Fritz Busse — A562

Designed by Ervine Metzl.

ROTARY PRESS PRINTING

E.E. Plates of 200 subjects in four panes of 50.

1958-59   *Perf. 10½x11*

1113 A559 1c green, *Feb. 12, 1959*   .20   .20
     P# block of 4   .20 —
1114 A560 3c purple, *Feb. 27, 1959*   .20   .20
     P# block of 4   .30 —

Perf. 11x10½

1115 A561 4c sepia, *Aug. 27, 1958*   .20   .20
     P# block of 4   .35 —
1116 A562 4c dark blue, *May 30, 1959*   .20   .20
     P# block of 4   .40 —
     Nos. 1113-1116 (4)   .80   .80

Lajos Kossuth — A563

Early Press and Hand Holding Quill — A564

CHAMPION OF LIBERTY ISSUE

Lajos Kossuth, Hungarian freedom fighter.

ROTARY PRESS PRINTING

E.E. Plates of 280 subjects in four panes of 70.

1958, Sept. 19   *Perf. 10½x11*

1117 A563 4c green   .20   .20
     P# block of 4   .30 —

GIORI PRESS PRINTING

Plates of 288 subjects in four panes of 72 each.

Perf. 11

1118 A563 8c carmine, ultramarine & ocher   .20   .20
     P# block of 4, 2#   1.10 —

FREEDOM OF PRESS ISSUE

Honoring Journalism and freedom of the press in connection with the 50th anniv. of the 1st School of Journalism at the University of Missouri.

Designed by Lester Beall and Charles Goslin.

ROTARY PRESS PRINTING

E.E. Plates of 200 subjects in four panes of 50.

1958, Sept. 22   *Perf. 10½x11*

1119 A564 4c black   .20   .20
     P# block of 4   .30 —

OVERLAND MAIL ISSUE

Centenary of Overland Mail Service.

Mail Coach and Map of Southwest US — A565

Designed by William H. Buckley.

ROTARY PRESS PRINTING

E.E. Plates of 200 subjects in four panes of 50.

1958, Oct. 10   *Perf. 11x10½*

1120 A565 4c crimson rose   .20   .20
     P# block of 4   .30 —

Noah Webster — A566

Forest Scene — A567

NOAH WEBSTER ISSUE

Webster (1758-1843), lexicographer and author.

Designed by Charles R. Chickering.

ROTARY PRESS PRINTING
E.E. Plates of 280 subjects in four panes of 70.

1958, Oct. 16			Perf. 10½x11
1121 A566	4c dark carmine rose	.20	.20
	P# block of 4	.35	—

FOREST CONSERVATION ISSUE

Issued to publicize forest conservation and the protection of natural resources and to honor Theodore Roosevelt, a leading forest conservationist, on the centenary of his birth.

Designed by Rudolph Wendelin.

GIORI PRESS PRINTING
Plates of 200 subjects in four panes of 50.

1958, Oct. 27			Perf. 11
1122 A567	4c green, yellow & brown	.20	.20
	P# block of 4	.30	—

FORT DUQUESNE ISSUE

Bicentennial of Fort Duquesne (Fort Pitt) at future site of Pittsburgh.

British Capture of Fort Duquesne, 1758; Brig. Gen. John Forbes on Litter, Colonel Washington Mounted — A568

Designed by William H. Buckley and Douglas Gorsline.

ROTARY PRESS PRINTING
E.E. Plates of 200 subjects in four panes of 50.

1958, Nov. 25			Perf. 11x10½
1123 A568	4c blue	.20	.20
	P# block of 4	.35	—

OREGON STATEHOOD, 100th ANNIV.

Covered Wagon and Mt. Hood — A569

Designed by Robert Hallock.

ROTARY PRESS PRINTING
E.E. Plates of 200 subjects in four panes of 50.

1959, Feb. 14			Perf. 11x10½
1124 A569	4c blue green	.20	.20
	P# block of 4	.30	—

José de San Martin — A570

NATO Emblem — A571

CHAMPION OF LIBERTY ISSUE

San Martin, So. American soldier and statesman.

ROTARY PRESS PRINTING
E.E. Plates of 280 subjects in four panes of 70.

1959, Feb. 25			Perf. 10½x11
1125 A570	4c blue	.20	.20
	P# block of 4	.30	
a.	Horiz. pair, imperf. between	1,500.	

GIORI PRESS PRINTING
Plates of 288 subjects in four panes of 72 each.
Perf. 11

1126 A570	8c carmine, ultramarine & ocher	.20	.20
	P# block of 4	.85	—

NATO ISSUE

North Atlantic Treaty Organization, 10th anniv.

Designed by Stevan Dohanos.

ROTARY PRESS PRINTING
E.E. Plates of 280 subjects in four panes of 70.

1959, Apr. 1			Perf. 10½x11
1127 A571	4c blue	.20	.20
	P# block of 4	.30	—

ARCTIC EXPLORATIONS ISSUE

Conquest of the Arctic by land by Rear Admiral Robert Edwin Peary in 1909 and by sea by the submarine "Nautilus" in 1958.

North Pole, Dog Sled and "Nautilus" — A572

Designed by George Samerjan.

ROTARY PRESS PRINTING
E.E. Plates of 200 subjects in four panes of 50.

1959, Apr. 6			Perf. 11x10½
1128 A572	4c bright greenish blue	.20	.20
	P# block of 4	.40	—

WORLD PEACE THROUGH WORLD TRADE ISSUE

Issued in conjunction with the 17th Congress of the International Chamber of Commerce, Washington, D.C., April 19-25.

Globe and Laurel — A573

Designed by Robert Baker.

ROTARY PRESS PRINTING
E.E. Plates of 200 subjects in four panes of 50.

1959, Apr. 20			Perf. 11x10½
1129 A573	8c rose lake	.20	.20
	P# block of 4	.85	—

SILVER CENTENNIAL ISSUE

Discovery of silver at the Comstock Lode, Nevada.

Henry Comstock at Mount Davidson Site — A574

Designed by Robert L. Miller and W.K. Schrage.

ROTARY PRESS PRINTING
E.E. Plates of 200 subjects in four panes of 50.

1959, June 8			Perf. 11x10½
1130 A574	4c black	.20	.20
	P# block of 4	.30	—

ST. LAWRENCE SEAWAY ISSUE

Opening of the St. Lawrence Seaway.

Great Lakes, Maple Leaf and Eagle Emblems — A575

Designed by Arnold Copeland, Ervine Metzl, William H. Buckley and Gerald Trottier.

GIORI PRESS PRINTING
Plates of 200 subjects in four panes of 50.

1959, June 26			Perf. 11
1131 A575	4c red & dark blue	.20	.20
	P# block of 4	.35	—
	Pair with full horiz. gutter btwn.	—	

See Canada No. 387.

49-STAR FLAG ISSUE

U.S. Flag, 1959 — A576

Designed by Stevan Dohanos.

GIORI PRESS PRINTING
Plates of 200 subjects in four panes of 50.

1959, July 4			Perf. 11
1132 A576	4c ocher, dark blue & deep carmine	.20	.20
	P# block of 4	.40	—

SOIL CONSERVATION ISSUE

Issued as a tribute to farmers and ranchers who use soil and water conservation measures.

Modern Farm — A577

Designed by Walter Hortens.

GIORI PRESS PRINTING
Plates of 200 subjects in four panes of 50.

1959, Aug. 26			Perf. 11
1133 A577	4c blue, green & ocher	.20	.20
	P# block of 4	.35	—

PETROLEUM INDUSTRY ISSUE

Centenary of the completion of the nation's first oil well at Titusville, Pa.

Oil Derrick — A578

Designed by Robert Foster.

ROTARY PRESS PRINTING
E.E. Plates of 200 subjects in four panes of 50.

1959, Aug. 27			Perf. 10½x11
1134 A578	4c brown	.20	.20
	P# block of 4	.40	—

DENTAL HEALTH ISSUE

Issued to publicize Dental Health and for the centenary of the American Dental Association.

Children — A579

Designed by Charles Henry Carter.

ROTARY PRESS PRINTING
E.E. Plates of 200 subjects in four panes of 50.

1959, Sept. 14		Perf. 11x10½	
1135 A579 4c green		.20	.20
P# block of 4		.40	—

Ernst
Reuter — A580

Dr. Ephraim
McDowell — A581

CHAMPION OF LIBERTY ISSUE

Ernst Reuter, Mayor of Berlin, 1948-53.

ROTARY PRESS PRINTING
E.E. Plates of 280 subjects in four panes of 70.

1959, Sept. 29		Perf. 10½x11	
1136 A580 4c gray		.20	.20
P# block of 4		.30	—

GIORI PRESS PRINTING
Plates of 288 subjects in four panes of 72 each.
Perf. 11

1137 A580 8c carmine, ultramarine & ocher		.20	.20
P# block of 4		.85	—
a.	Ocher omitted	3,750.	
b.	Ultramarine omitted	3,750.	
c.	Ocher & ultramarine omitted	4,000.	
d.	All colors omitted	—	

DR. EPHRAIM McDOWELL ISSUE

Honoring McDowell (1771-1830) on the 150th anniv. of the 1st successful ovarian operation in the US, performed at Danville, Ky., 1809.

Designed by Charles R. Chickering.

ROTARY PRESS PRINTING
E.E. Plates of 280 subjects in four panes of 70.

1959, Dec. 3		Perf. 10½x11	
1138 A581 4c rose lake		.20	.20
P# block of 4		.40	—
a.	Vert. pair, imperf. btwn.	450.00	
b.	Vert. pair, imperf. horiz.	350.00	

VALUES FOR HINGED STAMPS AFTER NO. 771
   This catalogue does not value unused stamps after No. 771 in hinged condition. Hinged unused stamps from No. 772 to the present are worth considerably less than the values given for unused stamps, which are for never-hinged examples.

AMERICAN CREDO ISSUE

Issued to re-emphasize the ideals upon which America was founded and to honor those great Americans who wrote or uttered the credos.

Quotation from
Washington's
Farewell Address,
1796 — A582

Benjamin Franklin
Quotation — A583

Olympic Rings and
Snowflake — A589

Thomas G.
Masaryk — A590

Thomas Jefferson
Quotation — A584

Francis Scott Key
Quotation — A585

Abraham Lincoln
Quotation — A586

Patrick Henry
Quotation — A587

Designed by Frank Conley.

GIORI PRESS PRINTING
Plates of 200 subjects in four panes of 50.

1960-61		Perf. 11	
1139 A582 4c dark violet blue, & carmine, Jan. 20, 1960		.20	.20
P# block of 4		.40	—
1140 A583 4c olive bister & green, Mar. 31, 1960		.20	.20
P# block of 4		.40	—
1141 A584 4c gray & vermilion, May 18, 1960		.20	.20
P# block of 4		.45	—
1142 A585 4c carmine & dark blue, Sept. 14, 1960		.20	.20
P# block of 4		.45	—
1143 A586 4c magenta & green, Nov. 19, 1960		.20	.20
P# block of 4		.50	—
Pair with full horiz. gutter between		—	
1144 A587 4c green & brown, Jan. 11, 1961		.20	.20
P# block of 4		.50	—
Nos. 1139-1144 (6)		1.20	1.20

BOY SCOUT JUBILEE ISSUE

50th anniv. of the Boy Scouts of America.

Boy Scout Giving
Scout
Sign — A588

Designed by Norman Rockwell.

GIORI PRESS PRINTING
Plates of 200 subjects in four panes of 50.

1960, Feb. 8		Perf. 11	
1145 A588 4c red, dark blue & dark bister		.20	.20
P# block of 4		.40	—

OLYMPIC WINTER GAMES ISSUE

Opening of the 8th Olympic Winter Games, Squaw Valley, Feb. 18-29, 1960.

Designed by Ervine Metzl.

ROTARY PRESS PRINTING
E.E. Plates of 200 subjects in four panes of 50.

1960, Feb. 18		Perf. 10½x11	
1146 A589 4c dull blue		.20	.20
P# block of 4		.40	—

CHAMPION OF LIBERTY ISSUE

Issued to honor Thomas G. Masaryk, founder and president of Czechoslovakia (1918-35), on the 110th anniversary of his birth.

ROTARY PRESS PRINTING
E.E. Plates of 280 subjects in four panes of 70.

1960, Mar. 7		Perf. 10½x11	
1147 A590 4c blue		.20	.20
P# block of 4		.30	—
a.	Vert. pair, imperf. between	3,250.	

GIORI PRESS PRINTING
Plates of 288 subjects in four panes of 72 each.
Perf. 11

1148 A590 8c carmine, ultramarine & ocher		.20	.20
P# block of 4		.95	—
a.	Horiz. pair, imperf. between	—	

WORLD REFUGEE YEAR ISSUE

World Refugee Year, July 1, 1959-June 30, 1960.

Family Walking
Toward New
Life — A591

Designed by Ervine Metzl.

ROTARY PRESS PRINTING
E.E. Plates of 200 subjects in four panes of 50.

1960, Apr. 7		Perf. 11x10½	
1149 A591 4c gray black		.20	.20
P# block of 4		.30	—

WATER CONSERVATION ISSUE

Issued to stress the importance of water conservation and to commemorate the 7th Watershed Congress, Washington, D.C.

Water: From
Watershed to
Consumer
A592

Designed by Elmo White.

GIORI PRESS PRINTING
Plates of 200 subjects in four panes of 50.

1960, Apr. 18		Perf. 11	
1150 A592 4c dark blue, brown orange & green		.20	.20
P# block of 4		.35	—
a.	Brown orange omitted	—	

SEATO ISSUE

South-East Asia Treaty Organization and for the SEATO Conf., Washington, D.C., May 31-June 3.

SEATO Emblem — A593

Designed by John Maass.

ROTARY PRESS PRINTING
E.E. plates of 280 subjects in four panes of 70.

1960, May 31		Perf. 10½x11	
1151 A593 4c blue		.20	.20
P# block of 4		.35	—
a.	Vertical pair, imperf. between	160.00	

AMERICAN WOMAN ISSUE

Issued to pay tribute to American women and their accomplishments in civic affairs, education, arts and industry.

Mother and Daughter — A594

Designed by Robert Sivard.

ROTARY PRESS PRINTING
E.E. Plates of 200 subjects in four panes of 50.

1960, June 2		Perf. 11x10½
1152 A594 4c deep violet	.20	.20
P# block of 4	.30	—

50-STAR FLAG ISSUE

US Flag, 1960 — A595

Designed by Stevan Dohanos.

GIORI PRESS PRINTING
Plates of 200 subjects in four panes of 50.

1960, July 4		Perf. 11
1153 A595 4c dark blue & red	.20	.20
P# block of 4	.30	—

PONY EXPRESS CENTENNIAL ISSUE

Pony Express Rider — A596

Designed by Harold von Schmidt.

ROTARY PRESS PRINTING
E.E. Plates of 200 subjects in four panes of 50.

1960, July 19		Perf. 11x10½
1154 A596 4c sepia	.20	.20
P# block of 4	.40	—

Man in Wheelchair Operating Drill Press — A597

World Forestry Congress Seal — A598

EMPLOY THE HANDICAPPED ISSUE

Promoting the employment of the physically handicapped and publicizing the 8th World Congress of the Intl. Soc. for the Welfare of Cripples, New York City.

Designed by Carl Bobertz.

ROTARY PRESS PRINTING
E.E. Plates of 200 subjects in four panes of 50.

1960, Aug. 28		Perf. 10½x11
1155 A597 4c dark blue	.20	.20
P# block of 4	.30	—

WORLD FORESTRY CONGRESS ISSUE

5th World Forestry Cong., Seattle, Wash., Aug. 29-Sept. 10.

ROTARY PRESS PRINTING
E.E. Plates of 200 subjects in four panes of 50.

1960, Aug. 29		Perf. 10½x11
1156 A598 4c green	.20	.20
P# block of 4	.30	—

Independence Bell — A599

Washington Monument and Cherry Blossoms — A600

MEXICAN INDEPENDENCE, 150th ANNIV.

Designed by Leon Helguera and Charles R. Chickering.

GIORI PRESS PRINTING
Plates of 200 subjects in four panes of 50.

1960, Sept. 16		Perf. 11
1157 A599 4c green & rose red	.20	.20
P# block of 4	.30	—

See Mexico No. 910.

US-JAPAN TREATY ISSUE

Centenary of the United States-Japan Treaty of Amity and Commerce.

Designed by Gyo Fujikawa.

GIORI PRESS PRINTING
Plates of 200 subjects in four panes of 50.

1960, Sept. 28		Perf. 11
1158 A600 4c blue & pink	.20	.20
P# block of 4	.30	—

Ignacy Jan Paderewski — A601

Robert A. Taft — A602

CHAMPION OF LIBERTY ISSUE

Jan Paderewski, Polish statesman and musician.

ROTARY PRESS PRINTING
E.E. Plates of 280 subjects in four panes of 70.

1960, Oct. 8		Perf. 10½x11
1159 A601 4c blue	.20	.20
P# block of 4	.30	—

GIORI PRESS PRINTING
Plates of 288 subjects in four panes of 72 each.
Perf. 11

1160 A601 8c carmine, ultramarine & ocher	.20	.20
P# block of 4	.90	—

SENATOR TAFT MEMORIAL ISSUE

Senator Robert A. Taft (1889-1953) of Ohio.

Designed by William K. Schrage.

ROTARY PRESS PRINTING
E.E. Plates of 280 subjects in four panes of 70.

1960, Oct. 10		Perf. 10½x11
1161 A602 4c dull violet	.20	.20
P# block of 4	.35	—

WHEELS OF FREEDOM ISSUE

Issued to honor the automotive industry and in connection with the National Automobile Show, Detroit, Oct. 15-23.

Globe and Steering Wheel with Tractor, Car and Truck — A603

Designed by Arnold J. Copeland.

ROTARY PRESS PRINTING
E.E. Plates of 200 subjects in four panes of 50.

1960, Oct. 15		Perf. 11x10½
1162 A603 4c dark blue	.20	.20
P# block of 4	.30	—

BOYS' CLUBS OF AMERICA ISSUE

Boys' Clubs of America movement, centenary.

Profile of Boy — A604

Designed by Charles T. Coiner.

GIORI PRESS PRINTING
Plates of 200 subjects in four panes of 50.

1960, Oct. 18		Perf. 11
1163 A604 4c indigo, slate & rose red	.20	.20
P# block of 4	.30	—

FIRST AUTOMATED POST OFFICE IN THE US ISSUE

Publicizing the opening of the 1st automated post office in the US at Providence, R.I.

Architect's Sketch of New Post Office, Providence, R.I. — A605

Designed by Arnold J. Copeland and Victor S. McCloskey, Jr.

GIORI PRESS PRINTING
Plates of 200 subjects in four panes of 50.

1960, Oct. 20		Perf. 11
1164 A605 4c dark blue & carmine	.20	.20
P# block of 4	.30	—

Baron Gustaf Mannerheim — A606

Camp Fire Girls Emblem — A607

CHAMPION OF LIBERTY ISSUE

Baron Karl Gustaf Emil Mannerheim (1867-1951), Marshal and President of Finland.

ROTARY PRESS PRINTING
E.E. Plates of 280 subjects in four panes of 70.

1960, Oct. 26		Perf. 10½x11
1165 A606 4c blue	.20	.20
P# block of 4	.30	—

GIORI PRESS PRINTING
Plates of 288 subjects in four panes of 72 each.
Perf. 11

1166	A606	8c	**carmine, ultramarine & ocher**	.20 .20
			P# block of 4	.80 —

CAMP FIRE GIRLS ISSUE
50th anniv. of the Camp Fire Girls' movement and in connection with the Golden Jubilee Convention celebration of the Camp Fire Girls.

Designed by H. Edward Oliver.

GIORI PRESS PRINTING
Plates of 200 subjects in four panes of 50.

1960, Nov. 1   **Perf. 11**

1167	A607	4c	**dark blue & bright red**	.20 .20
			P# block of 4	.35 —

Giuseppe
Garibaldi — A608

Walter F.
George — A609

CHAMPION OF LIBERTY ISSUE
Giuseppe Garibaldi (1807-1882), Italian patriot and freedom fighter.

ROTARY PRESS PRINTING
E.E. Plates of 280 subjects in four panes of 70.

1960, Nov. 2   **Perf. 10½x11**

1168	A608	4c	**green**	.20 .20
			P# block of 4	.30 —

GIORI PRESS PRINTING
Plates of 288 subjects in four panes of 72 each.
Perf. 11

1169	A608	8c	**carmine, ultramarine & ocher**	.20 .20
			P# block of 4	.85 —

SENATOR GEORGE MEMORIAL ISSUE
Walter F. George (1878-1957) of Georgia.

Designed by William K. Schrage.

ROTARY PRESS PRINTING
E.E. Plates of 280 subjects in four panes of 70.

1960, Nov. 5   **Perf. 10½x11**

1170	A609	4c	**dull violet**	.20 .20
			P# block of 4	.35 —

Andrew
Carnegie — A610

John Foster
Dulles — A611

ANDREW CARNEGIE ISSUE
Carnegie (1835-1919), industrialist & philanthropist.

Designed by Charles R. Chickering.

ROTARY PRESS PRINTING
E.E. Plates of 280 subjects in four panes of 70.

1960, Nov. 25   **Perf. 10½x11**

1171	A610	4c	**deep claret**	.20 .20
			P# block of 4	.35 —

JOHN FOSTER DULLES MEMORIAL ISSUE
Dulles (1888-1959), Secretary of State (1953-59).

Designed by William K. Schrage.

ROTARY PRESS PRINTING
E.E. Plates of 280 subjects in four panes of 70.

1960, Dec. 6   **Perf. 10½x11**

1172	A611	4c	**dull violet**	.20 .20
			P# block of 4	.35 —

ECHO I - COMMUNICATIONS FOR PEACE ISSUE
World's 1st communications satellite, Echo I, placed in orbit by the Natl. Aeronautics and Space Admin., Aug. 12, 1960.

Radio Waves
Connecting Echo I
and Earth — A612

Designed by Ervine Metzl.

ROTARY PRESS PRINTING
E.E. Plates of 200 subjects in four panes of 50.

1960, Dec. 15   **Perf. 11x10½**

1173	A612	4c	**deep violet**	.20 .20
			P# block of 4	.65 —

CHAMPION OF LIBERTY ISSUE
Mohandas K. Gandhi, leader in India's struggle for independence.

Mahatma Gandhi — A613

ROTARY PRESS PRINTING
E.E. Plates of 280 subjects in four panes of 70.

1961, Jan. 26   **Perf. 10½x11**

1174	A613	4c	**red orange**	.20 .20
			P# block of 4	.30 —

GIORI PRESS PRINTING
Plates of 288 subjects in four panes of 72 each.
Perf. 11

1175	A613	8c	**carmine, ultramarine & ocher**	.20 .20
			P# block of 4	1.00 —

RANGE CONSERVATION ISSUE
Issued to stress the importance of range conservation and to commemorate the meeting of the American Society of Range Management, Washington, D.C. "The Trail Boss" from a drawing by Charles M. Russell is the Society's emblem.

The Trail Boss and
Modern
Range — A614

Designed by Rudolph Wendelin.

GIORI PRESS PRINTING
Plates of 200 subjects in four panes of 50.

1961, Feb. 2   **Perf. 11**

1176	A614	4c	**blue, slate & brown orange**	.20 .20
			P# block of 4	.40 —

HORACE GREELEY ISSUE
Greeley (1811-1872), publisher and editor.

Horace Greeley — A615

Designed by Charles R. Chickering.

ROTARY PRESS PRINTING
E.E. Plates of 280 subjects in four panes of 70.

1961, Feb. 3   **Perf. 10½x11**

1177	A615	4c	**dull violet**	.20 .20
			P# block of 4	.30 —

CIVIL WAR CENTENNIAL ISSUE
Centenaries of the firing on Fort Sumter (No. 1178), the Battle of Shiloh (No. 1179), the Battle of Gettysburg (No. 1180), the Battle of the Wilderness (No. 1181) and the surrender at Appomattox (No. 1182).

Sea Coast Gun of
1861 — A616

Rifleman at
Battle of Shiloh,
1862 — A617

Blue and Gray at
Gettysburg,
1863 — A618

Battle of the
Wilderness,
1864 — A619

Appomattox, 1865 — A620

Designed by Charles R. Chickering (Sumter), Noel Sickles (Shiloh), Roy Gjertson (Gettysburg), B. Harold Christenson (Wilderness), Leonard Fellman (Appomattox).

ROTARY PRESS PRINTING
E.E. Plates of 200 subjects in four panes of 50.

1961-65   **Perf. 11x10½**

1178	A616	4c	**light green**, *Apr. 12, 1961*	.20 .20
			P# block of 4	.85 —
1179	A617	4c	**black**, *peach blossom, Apr. 7, 1962*	.20 .20
			P# block of 4	.75 —

GIORI PRESS PRINTING
Plates of 200 subjects in four panes of 50.
Perf. 11

1180	A618	5c	**gray & blue**, *July 1, 1963*	.20 .20
			P# block of 4	.85 —
1181	A619	5c	**dark red & black**, *May 5, 1964*	.20 .20
			P# block of 4	.60 —
			Margin block of 4, Mr. Zip and "Use Zip Code"	.55 —
1182	A620	5c	**Prus. blue & black**, *Apr. 9, 1965*	.25 .20
			P# block of 4	1.20 —
			Margin block of 4, Mr. Zip and "Use Zip Code"	1.10 —
a.			Horiz. pair, imperf. vert.	4,500.
			Nos. 1178-1182 (5)	1.05 1.00

KANSAS STATEHOOD, 100th ANNIV.

Sunflower, Pioneer
Couple and
Stockade — A621

GIORI PRESS PRINTING
Plates of 200 subjects in four panes of 50.

1961, May 10   **Perf. 11**

1183	A621	4c	**brown, dark red & green**, *yellow*	.20 .20
			P# block of 4	.35 —

SENATOR NORRIS ISSUE

Senator George W. Norris of Nebraska, and Norris Dam — A622

Designed by Charles R. Chickering.

ROTARY PRESS PRINTING
E.E. Plates of 200 subjects in four panes of 50.

1961, July 11		Perf. 11x10½
1184 A622 4c **blue green**	.20	.20
P# block of 4	.35	—

NAVAL AVIATION, 50th ANNIV.

Navy's First Plane (Curtiss A-1 of 1911) and Naval Air Wings — A623

Designed by John Maass.

ROTARY PRESS PRINTING
E.E. Plates of 200 subjects in four panes of 50.

1961, Aug. 20		Perf. 11x10½
1185 A623 4c **blue**	.20	.20
P# block of 4	.35	—
Pair with full vert. gutter btwn.	150.00	

WORKMEN'S COMPENSATION ISSUE

50th anniv. of the 1st successful Workmen's Compensation Law, enacted by the Wisconsin legislature.

Scales of Justice, Factory, Worker and Family — A624

Designed by Norman Todhunter.

ROTARY PRESS PRINTING
E.E. Plates of 200 subjects in four panes of 50.

1961, Sept. 4		Perf. 10½x11
1186 A624 4c **ultramarine**, *grayish*	.20	.20
P# block of 4	.35	—
P# block of 4 inverted	.60	—

"The Smoke Signal" — A625

Sun Yat-sen — A626

FREDERIC REMINGTON ISSUE

Remington (1861-1909), artist of the West. The design is from an oil painting, Amon Carter Museum of Western Art, Fort Worth, Texas.

Designed by Charles R. Chickering.

GIORI PRESS PRINTING
Panes of 200 subjects in four panes of 50.

1961, Oct. 4		Perf. 11
1187 A625 4c **multicolored**	.20	.20
P# block of 4	.40	—

REPUBLIC OF CHINA ISSUE

50th anniversary of the Republic of China.

ROTARY PRESS PRINTING
E.E. Plates of 200 subjects in four panes of 50.

1961, Oct. 10		Perf. 10½x11
1188 A626 4c **blue**	.20	.20
P# block of 4	.45	—

Basketball — A627

Student Nurse Lighting Candle — A628

NAISMITH - BASKETBALL ISSUE

Honoring basketball and James A. Naismith (1861-1939), Canada-born director of physical education, who invented the game in 1891 at Y.M.C.A. College, Springfield, Mass.

Designed by Charles R. Chickering.

ROTARY PRESS PRINTING
E.E. Plates of 200 subjects in four panes of 50.

1961, Nov. 6		Perf. 10½x11
1189 A627 4c **brown**	.20	.20
P# block of 4	.50	—

NURSING ISSUE

Issued to honor the nursing profession.

Designed by Alfred Charles Parker.

GIORI PRESS PRINTING
Plates of 200 subjects in four panes of 50.

1961, Dec. 28		Perf. 11
1190 A628 4c **blue, green, orange & black**	.20	.20
P# block of 4, 2#	.50	—

NEW MEXICO STATEHOOD, 50th ANNIV.

Shiprock — A629

Designed by Robert J. Jones.

GIORI PRESS PRINTING
Plates of 200 subjects in four panes of 50.

1962, Jan. 6		Perf. 11
1191 A629 4c **lt. blue, maroon & bister**	.20	.20
P# block of 4	.30	—

ARIZONA STATEHOOD, 50th ANNIV.

Giant Saguaro Cactus — A630

Designed by Jimmie E. Ihms and James M. Chemi.

GIORI PRESS PRINTING
Plates of 200 subjects in four panes of 50.

1962, Feb. 14		Perf. 11
1192 A630 4c **carmine, violet blue & green**	.20	.20
P# block of 4	.30	—

PROJECT MERCURY ISSUE

1st orbital flight of a US astronaut, Lt. Col. John H. Glenn, Jr., Feb. 20, 1962.

"Friendship 7" Capsule and Globe — A631

GIORI PRESS PRINTING
Plates of 200 subjects in four panes of 50.

1962, Feb. 20		Perf. 11
1193 A631 4c **dark blue & yellow**	.20	.20
P# block of 4	.35	—
Imperfs. are printers waste.		

MALARIA ERADICATION ISSUE

World Health Organization's drive to eradicate malaria.

Great Seal of US and WHO Symbol — A632

Designed by Charles R. Chickering.

GIORI PRESS PRINTING
Plates of 200 subjects in four panes of 50.

1962, Mar. 30		Perf. 11
1194 A632 4c **blue & bister**	.20	.20
P# block of 4	.30	—

Charles Evans Hughes — A633

"Space Needle" and Monorail — A634

CHARLES EVANS HUGHES ISSUE

Hughes (1862-1948), Governor of New York, Chief Justice of the US.

Designed by Charles R. Chickering.

ROTARY PRESS PRINTING
E.E. Plates of 200 subjects in four panes of 50.

1962, Apr. 11		Perf. 10½x11
1195 A633 4c **black**, *buff*	.20	.20
P# block of 4	.30	—

SEATTLE WORLD'S FAIR ISSUE

"Century 21" International Exposition, Seattle, Wash., Apr. 21-Oct. 21.

Designed by John Maass.

GIORI PRESS PRINTING
Plates of 200 subjects in four panes of 50.

1962, Apr. 25		Perf. 11
1196 A634 4c **red & dark blue**	.20	.20
On cover, "Century 21" Expo. cancel	5.00	
On cover, "Space Needle" Expo. cancel	2.00	
P# block of 4	.30	—

LOUISIANA STATEHOOD, 150th ANNIV.

Riverboat on the
Mississippi
A635

Designed by Norman Todhunter.

GIORI PRESS PRINTING
Plates of 200 subjects in four panes of 50.

1962, Apr. 30   *Perf. 11*
1197 A635 4c **blue, dark slate green & red** .20 .20
P# block of 4   .30

HOMESTEAD ACT, CENTENARY

Sod Hut and
Settlers — A636

Designed by Charles R. Chickering.

ROTARY PRESS PRINTING
E.E. Plates of 200 subjects in four panes of 50.

1962, May 20   *Perf. 11x10½*
1198 A636 4c **slate** .20 .20
P# block of 4   .30

GIRL SCOUTS ISSUE

50th anniversary of the Girl Scouts of America.

Senior Girl
Scout and
Flag — A637

Designed by Ward Brackett.

ROTARY PRESS PRINTING
E.E. Plates of 200 subjects in four panes of 50.

1962, July 24   *Perf. 11x10½*
1199 A637 4c **rose red** .20 .20
P# block of 4   .30
Pair with full vertical gutter between   250.00

SENATOR BRIEN McMAHON ISSUE

McMahon (1903-52) of Connecticut had a role in
opening the way to peaceful uses of atomic energy
through the Atomic Energy Act establishing the Atomic
Energy Commission.

Brien McMahon
and Atomic
Symbol — A638

Designed by V. S. McCloskey, Jr.

ROTARY PRESS PRINTING
E.E. Plates of 200 subjects in four panes of 50.

1962, July 28   *Perf. 11x10½*
1200 A638 4c **purple** .20 .20
P# block of 4   .35

APPRENTICESHIP ISSUE

National Apprenticeship Program and 25th anniv. of
the National Apprenticeship Act.

Machinist
Handing
Micrometer to
Apprentice
A639

Designed by Robert Geissmann.

ROTARY PRESS PRINTING
E.E. Plates of 200 subjects in four panes of 50.

1962, Aug. 31   *Perf. 11x10½*
1201 A639 4c **black,** *yellow bister* .20 .20
P# block of 4   .30

SAM RAYBURN ISSUE

Rayburn (1882-1961), Speaker of the House of
Representatives.

Sam Rayburn and
Capitol — A640

Designed by Robert L. Miller.

GIORI PRESS PRINTING
Plates of 200 subjects in four panes of 50.

1962, Sept. 16   *Perf. 11*
1202 A640 4c **dark blue & red brown** .20 .20
P# block of 4   .30

DAG HAMMARSKJOLD ISSUE

Hammarskjold, UN Sec. General, 1953-61.

UN Headquarters
and Dag
Hammarskjold
A641

Designed by Herbert M. Sanborn.

GIORI PRESS PRINTING
Plates of 200 subjects in four panes of 50.

1962, Oct. 23   *Perf. 11*
1203 A641 4c **black, brown & yellow** .20 .20
P# block of 4, 2#   .30

Hammarskjold Special Printing

No. 1204 was issued following discovery of No.
1203 with yellow background inverted.

GIORI PRESS PRINTING
Plates of 200 subjects in four panes of 50.

1962, Nov. 16   *Perf. 11*
1204 A641 4c **black, brown & yel** (yellow inverted) .20 .20
P# block of 4, 2#, yellow # inverted 1.10

The inverted yellow impression is shifted to the right in relation to the black and brown impression. Stamps of first vertical
row of UL and LL panes show no yellow at left side for a space
of 11-11½mm in from the perforations.
Stamps of first vertical row of UR and LR panes show vertical
no-yellow strip 9¾mm wide, covering UN Building. On all
others, the vertical no-yellow strip is 3½mm wide, and touches
UN Building.

CHRISTMAS ISSUE

Wreath and Candles — A642

Designed by Jim Crawford.

GIORI PRESS PRINTING

Plates of 400 subjects in four panes of 100.
Panes of 90 and 100 exist
without plate numbers due to provisional use of
smaller paper.

1962, Nov. 1   *Perf. 11*
1205 A642 4c **green & red** .20 .20
P# block of 4   .30

HIGHER EDUCATION ISSUE

Higher education's role in American cultural and
industrial development and the centenary celebrations
of the signing of the law creating land-grant colleges
and universities.

Map of U.S. and
Lamp — A643

Designed by Henry K. Bencsath.

GIORI PRESS PRINTING
Plates of 200 subjects in panes of 50.

1962, Nov. 14   *Perf. 11*
1206 A643 4c **blue green & black** .20 .20
P# block of 4, 2#   .35

WINSLOW HOMER ISSUE

Homer (1836-1910), painter, showing his oil,
"Breezing Up," which hangs in the National Gallery,
Washington, D.C.

"Breezing
Up" — A644

Designed by Victor S. McCloskey, Jr.

GIORI PRESS PRINTING
Plates of 200 subjects in four panes of 50.

1962, Dec. 15   *Perf. 11*
1207 A644 4c **multicolored** .20 .20
P# block of 4   .45
a. Horiz. pair, imperf. btwn. and at right 6,750.

FLAG ISSUE

Flag over White House — A645

Designed by Robert J. Jones.

GIORI PRESS PRINTING
Plates of 400 subjects in four panes of 100.

1963-66   *Perf. 11*
1208 A645 5c **blue & red,** *Jan. 9, 1963* .20 .20
P# block of 4   .40
Pair with full horiz. gutter between   —
a. Tagged, *Aug. 25, 1966* .20 .20
P# block of 4   2.00
b. Horiz. pair, imperf. between, tagged 1,500.
Beware of pairs with faint blind perfs between offered as No.
1208b.

REGULAR ISSUE

Andrew Jackson
A646

George
Washington
A650

Designed by William K. Schrage.

ROTARY PRESS PRINTING
E.E. Plates of 400 subjects in four panes of 100.

1962-66			Perf. 11x10½
1209 A646 1c **green**, *Mar. 22, 1963*		.20	.20
P# block of 4		.20	—
Pair with full vert. gutter btwn.		—	
a. Tagged, *July 6, 1966*		.20	.20
P# block of 4		.40	—
1213 A650 5c **dark blue gray**, *Nov. 23, 1962*		.20	.20
P# block of 4		.40	—
Pair with full vert. or horiz. gutter btwn.		—	
a. Booklet pane of 5 + label		3.00	1.75
b. Tagged, *Oct. 28, 1963*		.50	.20
P# block of 4		4.50	—
c. As "a," tagged, *Oct. 28, 1963*		2.00	1.50

Bureau Precancels: 1c, 10 diff., 5c, 18 diff.

COIL STAMPS
(Rotary Press)

1962-66		Perf. 10 Vertically	
1225 A646 1c **green**, *May 31, 1963*		.20	.20
Pair		.30	.20
Joint line pair		2.25	.20
a. Tagged, *July 6, 1966*		.20	.20
Pair		.75	.20
1229 A650 5c **dark blue gray**, *Nov. 23, 1962*		1.25	.20
Pair		2.50	.20
Joint line pair		4.00	.20
a. Tagged, *Oct. 28, 1963*		1.40	.20
Joint line pair		6.50	.20
b. Imperf., pair		450.00	
Joint line pair		1,250.	

Bureau Precancels: 1c, 5 diff., 5c, 14 diff.
See Luminescence note in "Information for Collectors" at front of book.

CAROLINA CHARTER ISSUE
Tercentenary of the Carolina Charter granting to 8 Englishmen lands extending coast-to-coast roughly along the present border of Virginia to the north and Florida to the south. Original charter on display at Raleigh.

First Page of Carolina Charter — A662

Designed by Robert L. Miller.

GIORI PRESS PRINTING
Plates of 200 subjects in four panes of 50.

1963, Apr. 6			Perf. 11
1230 A662 5c **dark carmine & brown**		.20	.20
P# block of 4		.40	—

FOOD FOR PEACE-FREEDOM FROM HUNGER ISSUE
American "Food for Peace" program and the "Freedom from Hunger" campaign of the FAO.

Wheat — A663

Designed by Stevan Dohanos.

GIORI PRESS PRINTING
Plates of 200 subjects in four panes of 50.

1963, June 4			Perf. 11
1231 A663 5c **green, buff & red**		.20	.20
P# block of 4		.40	—

WEST VIRGINIA STATEHOOD, 100th ANNIV.

Map of West Virginia and State Capitol — A664

Designed by Dr. Dwight Mutchler.

GIORI PRESS PRINTING
Plates of 200 subjects in four panes of 50.

1963, June 20			Perf. 11
1232 A664 5c **green, red & black**		.20	.20
P# block of 4		.40	—

EMANCIPATION PROCLAMATION ISSUE
Centenary of Lincoln's Emancipation Proclamation freeing about 3,000,000 slaves in 10 southern states.

Severed Chain — A665

Designed by Georg Olden.

GIORI PRESS PRINTING
Plates of 200 subjects in four panes of 50.

1963, Aug. 16			Perf. 11
1233 A665 5c **dark blue, black & red**		.20	.20
P# block of 4		.40	—

ALLIANCE FOR PROGRESS ISSUE
2nd anniv. of the Alliance for Progress, which aims to stimulate economic growth and raise living standards in Latin America.

Alliance Emblem — A666

Designed by William K. Schrage.

GIORI PRESS PRINTING
Plates of 200 subjects in four panes of 50.

1963, Aug. 17			Perf. 11
1234 A666 5c **ultramarine & green**		.20	.20
P# block of 4		.40	—

CORDELL HULL ISSUE
Hull (1871-1955), Secretary of State (1933-44).

Cordell Hull — A667

Designed by Robert J. Jones.

ROTARY PRESS PRINTING
E.E. Plates of 200 subjects in four panes of 50.

1963, Oct. 5			Perf. 10½x11
1235 A667 5c **blue green**		.20	.20
P# block of 4		.45	—

ELEANOR ROOSEVELT ISSUE
Mrs. Franklin D. Roosevelt (1884-1962).

Eleanor Roosevelt — A668

Designed by Robert L. Miller.

ROTARY PRESS PRINTING
E.E. Plates of 200 subjects in four panes of 50.

1963, Oct. 11			Perf. 11x10½
1236 A668 5c **bright purple**		.20	.20
P# block of 4		.45	—

SCIENCE ISSUE
Honoring the sciences and in connection with the centenary of the Natl. Academy of Science.

"The Universe" — A669

Designed by Antonio Frasconi.

GIORI PRESS PRINTING
Plates of 200 subjects in four panes of 50.

1963, Oct. 14			Perf. 11
1237 A669 5c **Prussian blue & black**		.20	.20
P# block of 4		.40	—

CITY MAIL DELIVERY ISSUE
Centenary of free city mail delivery.

Letter Carrier, 1863 — A670

Designed by Norman Rockwell.

GIORI PRESS PRINTING
Plates of 200 subjects in four panes of 50.

1963, Oct. 26	Tagged		Perf. 11
1238 A670 5c **gray, dark blue & red**		.20	.20
P# block of 4		.50	—
a. Tagging omitted		7.50	

RED CROSS CENTENARY ISSUE

Cuban Refugees on S.S. Morning Light and Red Cross Flag — A671

Designed by Victor S. McCloskey, Jr.

GIORI PRESS PRINTING
Plates of 200 subjects in four panes of 50.

1963, Oct. 29			Perf. 11
1239 A671 5c **bluish black & red**		.20	.20
P# block of 4		.40	—

CHRISTMAS ISSUE

National Christmas Tree and White House — A672

Designed by Lily Spandorf; modified by Norman Todhunter.

GIORI PRESS PRINTING
Plates of 400 subjects in four panes of 100.

1963, Nov. 1			Perf. 11
1240 A672 5c **dark blue, bluish black & red**		.20	.20
P# block of 4		.40	—
a. Tagged, *Nov. 2, 1963*		.65	.50
P# block of 4		5.00	—
Pair with full horiz. gutter between		—	

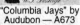

"Columbia Jays" by
Audubon — A673

Sam
Houston — A674

JOHN JAMES AUDUBON ISSUE

Audubon (1785-1851), ornithologist and artist. The birds pictured are actually Collie's magpie jays. See No. C71.

Designed by Robert L. Miller.

GIORI PRESS PRINTING
Plates of 200 subjects in four panes of 50.

1963, Dec. 7   *Perf. 11*
1241 A673 5c **dark blue & multicolored**   .20   .20
    P# block of 4   .45   —

SAM HOUSTON ISSUE

Houston (1793-1863), soldier, president of Texas, US senator.

Designed by Tom Lea.

ROTARY PRESS PRINTING
E.E. Plates of 200 subjects in four panes of 50.

1964, Jan. 10   *Perf. 10½x11*
1242 A674 5c **black**   .20   .20
    P# block of 4   .45   —
    Margin block of 4, Mr. Zip and
     "Use Zip Code"   .40   —

CHARLES M. RUSSELL ISSUE

Russell (1864-1926), painter. The design is from a painting, Thomas Gilcrease Institute of American History and Art, Tulsa, Okla.

"Jerked
Down" — A675

Designed by William K. Schrage.

GIORI PRESS PRINTING
Plates of 200 subjects in four panes of 50.

1964, Mar. 19   *Perf. 11*
1243 A675 5c **multicolored**   .20   .20
    P# block of 4   .40   —
    Margin block of 4, Mr. Zip and
     "Use Zip Code"   .35   —

NEW YORK WORLD'S FAIR ISSUE

New York World's Fair, 1964-65.

Mall with
Unisphere and
"Rocket Thrower"
by Donald De
Lue — A676

Designed by Robert J. Jones.

ROTARY PRESS PRINTING
E.E. Plates of 200 subjects in four panes of 50.

1964, Apr. 22   *Perf. 11x10½*
1244 A676 5c **blue green**   .20   .20
    On cover, Expo. station machine
     cancel (non-first day)   2.00
    On cover, Expo. station hand-
     stamp cancel (non-first day)   10.00
    P# block of 4   .45   —
    Margin block of 4, Mr. Zip and
     "Use Zip Code"   .35   —

JOHN MUIR ISSUE

Muir (1838-1914), naturalist and conservationist.

John Muir and Redwood
Forest — A677

Designed by Rudolph Wendelin.

GIORI PRESS PRINTING
Plates of 200 subjects in four panes of 50.

1964, Apr. 29   *Perf. 11*
1245 A677 5c **brown, green, yellow green & olive**   .20   .20
    P# block of 4   .45   —

KENNEDY MEMORIAL ISSUE

President John Fitzgerald Kennedy, (1917-1963).

John F. Kennedy
and Eternal
Flame — A678

Designed by Raymond Loewy/William Snaith, Inc.

Photograph by William S. Murphy.

ROTARY PRESS PRINTING
E.E. Plates of 200 subjects in four panes of 50.

1964, May 29   *Perf. 11x10½*
1246 A678 5c **blue gray**   .20   .20
    P# block of 4   .60   —

NEW JERSEY TERCENTENARY ISSUE

300th anniv. of English colonization of New Jersey. The design is from a mural by Howard Pyle in the Essex County Courthouse, Newark, N.J.

Philip Carteret Landing at
Elizabethtown, and Map of
New Jersey — A679

Designed by Douglas Allen.

ROTARY PRESS PRINTING
E.E. Plates of 200 subjects in four panes of 50.

1964, June 15   *Perf. 10½x11*
1247 A679 5c **brt. ultramarine**   .20   .20
    P# block of 4   .45   —
    Margin block of 4, Mr. Zip and
     "Use Zip Code"   .35   —

NEVADA STATEHOOD, 100th ANNIV.

Virginia City and
Map of
Nevada — A680

Designed by William K. Schrage.

GIORI PRESS PRINTING
Plates of 200 subjects in four panes of 50.

1964, July 22   *Perf. 11*
1248 A680 5c **red, yellow & blue**   .20   .20
    P# block of 4   .40   —
    Margin block of 4, Mr. Zip and
     "Use Zip Code"   .35   —

Flag
A681

William
Shakespeare
A682

REGISTER AND VOTE ISSUE

Campaign to draw more voters to the polls.

Designed by Victor S. McCloskey, Jr.

GIORI PRESS PRINTING
Plates of 200 subjects in four panes of 50.

1964, Aug. 1   *Perf. 11*
1249 A681 5c **dark blue & red**   .20   .20
    P# block of 4   .45   —
    Margin block of 4, Mr. Zip and
     "Use Zip Code"   .35   —

SHAKESPEARE ISSUE

William Shakespeare (1564-1616).

Designed by Douglas Gorsline.

ROTARY PRESS PRINTING
E.E. Plates of 200 subjects in four panes of 50.

1964, Aug. 14   *Perf. 10½x11*
1250 A682 5c **black brown,** *tan*   .20   .20
    P# block of 4   .40   —
    Margin block of 4, Mr. Zip and
     "Use Zip Code"   .35   —

DOCTORS MAYO ISSUE

Dr. William James Mayo (1861-1939) and his brother, Dr. Charles Horace Mayo (1865-1939), surgeons who founded the Mayo Foundation for Medical Education and Research in affiliation with the Univ. of Minnesota at Rochester. Heads on stamp are from a sculpture by James Earle Fraser.

Drs. William and Charles
Mayo — A683

ROTARY PRESS PRINTING
E.E. Plates of 200 subjects in four panes of 50.

1964, Sept. 11   *Perf. 10½x11*
1251 A683 5c **green**   .20   .20
    P# block of 4   .60   —
    Margin block of 4, Mr. Zip and
     "Use Zip Code"   .40   —

AMERICAN MUSIC ISSUE

50th anniv. of the founding of the American Society of Composers, Authors and Publishers (ASCAP).

Lute, Horn,
Laurel, Oak and
Music
Score — A684

Designed by Bradbury Thompson.

GIORI PRESS PRINTING
Plates of 200 subjects in four panes of 50.

1964, Oct. 15   *Perf. 11*

Gray Paper with Blue Threads

1252 A684 5c **red, black & blue**	.20	.20
P# block of 4	.40	—
Margin block of 4, Mr. Zip and "Use Zip Code"	.35	—
a. Blue omitted	1,000.	

Beware of copies offered as No. 1252a which have traces of blue.

HOMEMAKERS ISSUE

Honoring American women as homemakers and for the 50th anniv. of the passage of the Smith-Lever Act. By providing economic experts under an extension service of the U.S. Dept. of Agriculture, this legislation helped to improve homelife.

Farm Scene Sampler — A685

Designed by Norman Todhunter.

Plates of 200 subjects in four panes of 50.
Engraved (Giori Press); Background Lithographed

1964, Oct. 26   *Perf. 11*

1253 A685 5c **multicolored**	.20	.20
P# block of 4	.40	—
Margin block of 4, Mr. Zip and "Use Zip Code"	.35	—

CHRISTMAS ISSUE

Holly — A686

Mistletoe — A687

Poinsettia — A688

Sprig of Conifer — A689

Designed by Thomas F. Naegele.

GIORI PRESS PRINTING
Plates of 400 subjects in four panes of 100.
Panes contain 25 subjects each of Nos. 1254-1257

1964, Nov. 9   *Perf. 11*

1254 A686 5c **green, carmine & black**	.25	.20
a. Tagged, *Nov. 10*	.60	.50
1255 A687 5c **carmine, green & black**	.25	.20
a. Tagged, *Nov. 10*	.60	.50
1256 A688 5c **carmine, green & black**	.25	.20
a. Tagged, *Nov. 10*	.60	.50
1257 A689 5c **black, green & carmine**	.25	.20
a. Tagged, *Nov. 10*	.60	.50
b. Block of 4, #1254-1257	1.10	1.10
P# block of 4	1.10	—
Margin block of 4, Zip and "Use Zip Code"	1.00	—
c. Block of 4, tagged	2.50	2.25
P# block of 4	5.50	—
Zip block of 4	3.00	—

VERRAZANO-NARROWS BRIDGE ISSUE

Opening of the Verrazano-Narrows Bridge connecting Staten Island and Brooklyn.

Verrazano-Narrows Bridge and Map of New York Bay — A690

ROTARY PRESS PRINTING
E.E. Plates of 200 subjects in four panes of 50.

1964, Nov. 21   *Perf. 10½x11*

1258 A690 5c **blue green**	.20	.20
P# block of 4	.45	—
Margin block of 4, Mr. Zip and "Use Zip Code"	.35	—

FINE ARTS ISSUE

Abstract Design by Stuart Davis — A691

GIORI PRESS PRINTING
Plates of 200 subjects in four panes of 50.

1964, Dec. 2   *Perf. 11*

1259 A691 5c **ultra., black & dull red**	.20	.20
P# block of 4, 2#	.40	—
Margin block of 4, Mr. Zip and "Use Zip Code"	.35	—

AMATEUR RADIO ISSUE

Issued to honor the radio amateurs on the 50th anniversary of the American Radio Relay League.

Radio Waves and Dial — A692

Designed by Emil J. Willett.

ROTARY PRESS PRINTING
E.E. Plates of 200 subjects in four panes of 50.

1964, Dec. 15   *Perf. 10½x11*

1260 A692 5c **red lilac**	.20	.20
P# block of 4	.50	—
Margin block of 4, Mr. Zip and "Use Zip Code"	.35	—

BATTLE OF NEW ORLEANS ISSUE

Battle of New Orleans, Chalmette Plantation, Jan. 8-18, 1815, established 150 years of peace and friendship between the US and Great Britain.

General Andrew Jackson and Sesquicentennial Medal — A693

Designed by Robert J. Jones.

GIORI PRESS PRINTING
Plates of 200 subjects in four panes of 50.

1965, Jan. 8   *Perf. 11*

1261 A693 5c **deep carmine, violet blue & gray**	.20	.20
P# block of 4	.40	—
Margin block of 4, Mr. Zip and "Use Zip Code"	.35	—

Discus Thrower — A694

Microscope and Stethoscope — A695

PHYSICAL FITNESS-SOKOL ISSUE

Publicizing the importance of physical fitness and for the centenary of the founding of the Sokol (athletic) organization in America.

Designed by Norman Todhunter.

GIORI PRESS PRINTING
Plates of 200 subjects in four panes of 50.

1965, Feb. 15   *Perf. 11*

1262 A694 5c **maroon & black**	.20	.20
P# block of 4	.50	—
Margin block of 4, Mr. Zip and "Use Zip Code"	.40	—

CRUSADE AGAINST CANCER ISSUE

Issued to publicize the "Crusade Against Cancer" and to stress the importance of early diagnosis.

Designed by Stevan Dohanos.

GIORI PRESS PRINTING
Plates of 200 subjects in four panes of 50.

1965, Apr. 1   *Perf. 11*

1263 A695 5c **black, purple & red orange**	.20	.20
P# block of 4, 2#	.40	—
Margin block of 4, Mr. Zip and "Use Zip Code"	.35	—

CHURCHILL MEMORIAL ISSUE

Sir Winston Spencer Churchill (1874-1965), British statesman and World War II leader.

Winston Churchill — A696

Designed by Richard Hurd.

ROTARY PRESS PRINTING
E.E. Plates of 200 subjects in four panes of 50.

1965, May 13   *Perf. 10½x11*

1264 A696 5c **black**	.20	.20
P# block of 4	.40	—
Margin block of 4, Mr. Zip and "Use Zip Code"	.35	—

MAGNA CARTA ISSUE

750th anniversary of the Magna Carta, the basis of English and American common law.

Procession of Barons and King John's Crown — A697

Designed by Brook Temple.

GIORI PRESS PRINTING
Plates of 200 subjects in four panes of 50.

1965, June 15   *Perf. 11*

1265 A697 5c **black, yellow ocher & red lilac**	.20	.20
P# block of 4, 2#	.40	—
Margin block of 4, Mr. Zip and "Use Zip Code"	.35	—
Corner block of 4, black # omitted		

INTERNATIONAL COOPERATION YEAR
ICY, 1965, and 20th anniv. of the UN.

International Cooperation Year Emblem — A698

Designed by Herbert M. Sanborn and Olav S. Mathiesen.

GIORI PRESS PRINTING
Plates of 200 subjects in four panes of 50.

1965, June 26		Perf. 11
1266 A698 5c **dull blue & black**	.20	.20
P# block of 4	.40	—
Margin block of 4, Mr. Zip and "Use Zip Code"	.35	—

SALVATION ARMY ISSUE
Centenary of the founding of the Salvation Army by William Booth in London.

A699

Designed by Sam Marsh.

GIORI PRESS PRINTING
Plates of 200 subjects in four panes of 50.

1965, July 2		Perf. 11
1267 A699 5c **red, black & dark blue**	.20	.20
P# block of 4	.40	—
Margin block of 4, Mr. Zip and "Use Zip Code"	.35	—

Dante after a 16th Century Painting — A700

Herbert Hoover — A701

DANTE ISSUE
Dante Alighieri (1265-1321), Italian poet.

Designed by Douglas Gorsline.

ROTARY PRESS PRINTING
E.E. Plates of 200 subjects in four panes of 50.

1965, July 17		Perf. 10½x11
1268 A700 5c **maroon,** tan	.20	.20
P# block of 4	.40	—
Margin block of 4, Mr. Zip and "Use Zip Code"	.35	—

HERBERT HOOVER ISSUE
President Herbert Clark Hoover, (1874-1964).

Designed by Norman Todhunter; photograph by Fabian Bachrach, Sr.

ROTARY PRESS PRINTING
E.E. Plates of 200 subjects in four panes of 50.

1965, Aug. 10		Perf. 10½x11
1269 A701 5c **rose red**	.20	.20
P# block of 4	.45	—
Margin block of 4, Mr. Zip and "Use Zip Code"	.35	—

ROBERT FULTON ISSUE
Fulton (1765-1815), inventor of the 1st commercial steamship.

Robert Fulton and the Clermont — A702

Designed by John Maass; bust by Jean Antoine Houdon.

GIORI PRESS PRINTING
Plates of 200 subjects in four panes of 50.

1965, Aug. 19		Perf. 11
1270 A702 5c **black & blue**	.20	.20
P# block of 4	.40	—
Margin block of 4, Mr. Zip and "Use Zip Code"	.35	—

FLORIDA SETTLEMENT ISSUE
400th anniv. of the settlement of Florida, and the 1st permanent European settlement in the continental US, St. Augustine, Fla.

Spanish Explorer, Royal Flag of Spain and Ships — A703

Designed by Brook Temple.

GIORI PRESS PRINTING
Plates of 200 subjects with four panes of 50.

1965, Aug. 28		Perf. 11
1271 A703 5c **red, yellow & black**	.20	.20
P# block of 4, 3#	.45	—
Margin block of 4, Mr. Zip and "Use Zip Code"	.35	—
a. Yellow omitted	350.00	

See Spain No. 1312.

TRAFFIC SAFETY ISSUE
Issued to publicize traffic safety and the prevention of traffic accidents.

Traffic Signal — A704

Designed by Richard F. Hurd.

GIORI PRESS PRINTING
Plates of 200 subjects in four panes of 50.

1965, Sept. 3		Perf. 11
1272 A704 5c **emerald, black & red**	.20	.20
P# block of 4, 2#	.45	—
Margin block of 4, Mr. Zip and "Use Zip Code"	.35	—

JOHN SINGLETON COPLEY ISSUE
Copley (1738-1815), painter. The portrait of the artist's daughter is from the oil painting "The Copley Family," which hangs in the National Gallery of Art, Washington, D.C.

Elizabeth Clarke Copley — A705

Designed by John Carter Brown.

GIORI PRESS PRINTING
Plates of 200 subjects in four panes of 50.

1965, Sept. 17		Perf. 11
1273 A705 5c **black, brown & olive**	.20	.20
P# block of 4	.50	—
Margin block of 4, Mr. Zip and "Use Zip Code"	.40	—

INTERNATIONAL TELECOMMUNICATION UNION, 100th ANNIV.

Galt Projection World Map and Radio Sine Wave — A706

Designed by Thomas F. Naegele.

GIORI PRESS PRINTING
Plates of 200 subjects with four panes of 50.

1965, Oct. 6		Perf. 11
1274 A706 11c **black, carmine & bister**	.35	.20
P# block of 4, 2#	3.00	—
Margin block of 4, Mr. Zip and "Use Zip Code"	2.25	—

ADLAI STEVENSON ISSUE
Adlai Ewing Stevenson (1900-65), governor of Illinois, US ambassador to the UN.

Adlai E. Stevenson — A707

Designed by George Samerjan; photograph by Philippe Halsman.

LITHOGRAPHED, ENGRAVED (Giori)
Plates of 200 subjects in four panes of 50.

1965, Oct. 23		Perf. 11
1275 A707 5c **pale blue, black, carmine & violet blue**	.20	.20
P# block of 4	.40	—

CHRISTMAS ISSUE

Angel with Trumpet, 1840 Weather Vane — A708

Designed by Robert Jones.

After a watercolor by Lucille Gloria Chabot of the 1840 weather vane from the People's Methodist Church, Newburyport, Mass.

GIORI PRESS PRINTING
Plates of 400 subjects in four panes of 100.

1965, Nov. 2   **Perf. 11**

1276	A708	5c **carmine, dark olive green & bister**	.20	.20
		P# block of 4	.40	
		Margin block of 4, Mr. Zip and "Use Zip Code"	.35	—
		Pair with full vert. gutter btwn.		
a.		Tagged, *Nov. 15*	.75	.25
		P# block of 4	5.50	—
		Zip block of 4	3.50	—

PROMINENT AMERICANS ISSUE

Thomas Jefferson A710

Albert Gallatin A711

Frank Lloyd Wright and Guggenheim Museum, New York — A712

Francis Parkman — A713

Abraham Lincoln A714

George Washington A715

George Washington (redrawn) A715a

Franklin D. Roosevelt A716

Albert Einstein — A717

Andrew Jackson — A718

Henry Ford and 1909 Model T — A718a

John F. Kennedy — A719

Oliver Wendell Holmes — A720

Frederick Douglass — A722

Thomas Paine — A724

Eugene O'Neill — A726

George Catlett Marshall — A721

John Dewey — A723

Lucy Stone — A725

John Bassett Moore — A727

Designers: 1c, Robert Geissmann, after portrait by Rembrandt Peale. 1 ¼c, Robert Gallatin. 2c, Patricia Amarantides; photograph by Blackstone-Shelburne. 3c, Bill Hyde. 4c, Bill Hyde; photograph by Mathew Brady. 5c, Bill Hyde, after portrait by Rembrandt Peale. 5c, No. 1283B, Redrawn by Stevan Dohanos. 6c, 30c, Richard L. Clark. 8c, Frank Sebastiano; photograph by Philippe Halsman. 10c, Lester Beall. 12c, Norman Todhunter. 13c, Stevan Dohanos; photograph by Jacques Lowe. 15c, Richard F. Hurd. 20c, Robert Geissmann. 25c, Walter DuBois Richards. 40c, Robert Geissmann, after portrait by John Wesley Jarvis. 50c, Mark English. $1, Norman Todhunter. $5, Tom Laufer.

ROTARY PRESS PRINTING
E.E. Plates of 400 subjects in four panes of 100

1965-78   **Perf. 11x10½, 10½x11**

Types of 15c:

I. Necktie barely touches coat at bottom; crosshatching of tie strong and complete. Flag of "5" is true horizontal. Crosshatching of "15" is colorless when visible.

II. Necktie does not touch coat at bottom; LL to UR crosshatching lines strong, UL to LR lines very faint. Flag of "5" slants down slightly at right. Crosshatching of "15" is colored and visible when magnified.

A third type, used only for No. 1288B, is smaller in overall size and crosshatching. "15¢" is ¾mm closer to head.

1278	A710	1c **green,** tagged, shiny gum, *Jan. 12, 1968*	.20	.20
		P# block of 4	.20	—
		Margin block of 4, "Use Zip Codes"	.20	—
		Dull gum (from bklt. pane)	.20	
a.		Booklet pane of 8, shiny gum, *Jan. 12, 1968*	1.00	.50
		Dull gum	2.00	
b.		Bklt. pane of 4+2 labels, *May 10, 1971*	.80	.30
c.		Untagged (Bureau precanceled)		.20
d.		Tagging omitted (not Bureau precanceled)	3.50	—
1279	A711	1 ¼c **light green,** *Jan. 30, 1967*	.20	.20
		P# block of 4	6.25	—
1280	A712	2c **dark blue gray,** tagged, shiny gum, *June 8, 1966*	.20	.20
		P# block of 4	.25	—
		Margin block of 4, "Use Zip Codes"	.20	—
		Pair with full vert. gutter btwn.		
		Dull gum (from bklt. pane)	.20	
a.		Bklt. pane of 5 + label, *Jan. 8, 1968*	1.25	.60
b.		Untagged (Bureau precanceled)		.20
c.		Bklt. pane of 6, shiny gum, *May 7, 1971*	1.00	.50
		Dull gum	1.10	
d.		Tagging omitted (not Bureau precanceled)	3.50	—

1281	A713	3c **violet,** tagged, *Sept. 16, 1967*	.20	.20
		P# block of 4	.25	—
		Margin block of 4, "Use Zip Codes"	.20	—
a.		Untagged (Bureau precanceled)		.20
b.		Tagging omitted (not Bureau precanceled)	4.50	—
1282	A714	4c **black,** *Nov. 19, 1965*	.20	.20
		P# block of 4	.40	—
a.		Tagged, *Dec. 1, 1965*	.20	.20
		P# block of 4	.55	—
		Pair with full horiz. gutter between		
1283	A715	5c **blue,** *Feb. 22, 1966*	.20	.20
		P# block of 4	.50	—
		Pair with full vert. gutter btwn.	—	
a.		Tagged, *Feb. 23, 1966*	.20	.20
		P# block of 4	.60	—
1283B	A715a	5c **blue,** tagged, shiny gum, *Nov. 17, 1967*	.20	.20
		P# block of 4	.50	—
		Pair with full horiz. gutter btwn.	—	
		Dull gum	.20	
		P# block of 4	1.40	
d.		Untagged (Bureau precanceled)		.20

No. 1283B is redrawn; highlights, shadows softened.

1284	A716	6c **gray brown,** *Jan. 29, 1966*	.20	.20
		P# block of 4	.60	—
		Margin block of 4, "Use Zip Codes" (Bureau precanceled)	3.00	
		Pair with full horiz. gutter btwn.	150.00	
		Pair with full vert. gutter btwn.	150.00	
a.		Tagged, *Dec. 29, 1966*	.20	.20
		P# block of 4	.80	—
		Margin block of 4, "Use Zip Codes"	.65	—
b.		Booklet pane of 8, *Dec. 28, 1967*	1.50	.75
c.		Bklt. pane of 5+ label, *Jan. 9, 1968*	1.50	.75
d.		Horiz. pair, imperf. between		

For untagged stamps, "Use Zip Codes" and "Mail Early in the Day" marginal markings are found only on panes with Bureau precancels.

1285	A717	8c **violet,** *Mar. 14, 1966*	.20	.20
		P# block of 4	.85	—
a.		Tagged, *July 6, 1966*	.20	.20
		P# block of 4	.85	—
		Margin block of 4, "Use Zip Codes"	.85	—
1286	A718	10c **lilac,** tagged, *Mar. 15, 1967*	.20	.20
		P# block of 4	1.00	—
		Margin block of 4, "Use Zip Codes"	.85	—
b.		Untagged (Bureau precanceled)		.20
1286A	718a	12c **black,** tagged, *July 30, 1968*	.25	.20
		P# block of 4	1.00	—
		Margin block of 4, "Use Zip Codes"	1.00	—
c.		Untagged (Bureau precanceled)		.25
1287	A719	13c **brown,** tagged, *May 29, 1967*	.30	.20
		P# block of 4	1.50	—
a.		Untagged (Bureau precanceled)		.35
b.		Tagging omitted (not Bureau precanceled)	20.00	—
1288	A720	15c **magenta,** type I, tagged, *Mar. 8, 1968*	.30	.20
		P# block of 4	1.25	—
		Margin block of 4, "Use Zip Codes"	1.25	—
a.		Untagged (Bureau precanceled)		.30
d.		Type II	.55	.20
		P# block of 4	8.00	
		Zip block of 4	3.50	
		Pair with full vert. gutter between	—	
f.		As "d," tagging omitted (not Bureau precanceled)	5.00	—

Imperforates exist from printer's waste.

1288B	A720	15c **magenta,** tagged, perf. 10 (from blkt. pane)	.35	.20
c.		Booklet pane of 8, *June 14, 1978*	2.80	1.75
e.		As "c," vert. imperf. between		

No. 1288B issued in booklets only. All stamps have one or two straight edges. Plates made from redrawn die.

1289	A721	20c **deep olive,** *Oct. 24, 1967*	.40	.20
		P# block of 4	1.75	—
		Margin block of 4, "Use Zip Codes"	1.65	—
a.		Tagged, shiny gum, *Apr. 3, 1973*	.40	.20
		P# block of 4	1.75	—
		Zip block of 4	1.65	—
		Dull gum	.40	
		P# block of 4	3.50	
		Zip block of 4	1.65	
1290	A722	25c **rose lake,** *Feb. 14, 1967*	.55	.20
		P# block of 4	2.25	—
		Margin block of 4, "Use Zip Codes"	2.20	—
a.		Tagged, shiny gum, *Apr. 3, 1973*	.45	.20
		P# block of 4	2.00	—
		Zip block of 4	1.90	—
		Dull gum	.45	
		P# block of 4	2.00	
		Zip block of 4	1.90	
b.		25c **magenta**	25.00	—

		On cover		—
		P# block of 4	150.00	—
1291	A723	30c **red lilac,** *Oct. 21, 1968*	.65	.20
		P# block of 4	2.90	—
		Margin block of 4, "Use Zip Codes"	2.70	—
	a.	Tagged, *Apr. 3, 1973*	.50	.20
		P# block of 4	2.25	—
		Zip block of 4	2.10	—
1292	A724	40c **blue black,** *Jan. 29, 1968*	.80	.20
		P# block of 4	3.25	—
		Margin block of 4, "Use Zip Codes"	3.25	—
	a.	Tagged, shiny gum, *Apr. 3, 1973*	.65	.20
		P# block of 4	2.75	—
		Zip block of 4	2.65	—
		Dull gum	.70	—
		P# block of 4	3.00	—
		Zip block of 4	2.90	—
1293	A725	50c **rose magenta,** *Aug. 13, 1968*	1.00	.20
		P# block of 4	4.25	—
		Margin block of 4, "Use Zip Codes"	4.00	—
		Pair with full vert. gutter btwn.	—	—
	a.	Tagged, *Apr. 3, 1973*	.80	.20
		P# block of 4	3.50	—
		Zip block of 4	3.25	—
1294	A726	$1 **dull purple,** *Oct. 16, 1967*	2.25	.20
		P# block of 4	10.00	—
		Margin block of 4, "Use Zip Codes"	9.25	—
	a.	Tagged, *Apr. 3, 1973*	1.65	.20
		P# block of 4	6.75	—
		Zip block of 4	6.65	—
1295	A727	$5 **gray black,** *Dec. 3, 1966*	9.50	2.25
		P# block of 4	40.00	—
	a.	Tagged, *Apr. 3, 1973*	8.00	2.00
		P# block of 4	32.50	—
		Nos. 1278-1295 (21)	18.35	6.25

Bureau Precancels: 1c, 19 diff., 1¼c, 14 diff., 2c, 41 diff., 3c, 11 diff., 4c, 49 diff., No. 1283, 7 diff., No. 1283B, 29 diff., 6c, 35 diff., 8c, 18 diff., 10c, 12 diff., 12c, 3 diff., 13c, 3 diff., No. 1288a, 9 diff., 20c, 14 diff., 25c, 9 diff., 30c, 14 diff., 40c, 7 diff., 50c, 14 diff., $1, 8 diff.
See Luminescence note in "Information for Collectors" at front of book.

COIL STAMPS

1967-75		**Tagged**	***Perf. 10 Horizontally***	
1297	A713	3c **violet,** shiny gum, *Nov. 4, 1975*	.20	.20
		Pair	.20	.20
		Joint line pair	.45	.20
		Dull gum	1.00	—
		Joint line pair	2.00	—
	a.	Imperf., pair	30.00	—
		Imperf., joint line pair	55.00	—
	b.	Untagged (Bureau precanceled)		.20
	c.	As "b," imperf. pair	6.00	—
		Joint line pair	25.00	—

No. 1297c is precanceled "Nonprofit Org. / CAR RT SORT."

1298	A716	6c **gray brown,** *Dec. 28, 1967*	.20	.20
		Pair	.30	.20
		Joint line pair	1.25	.25
	a.	Imperf., pair	2,250.	—
	b.	Tagging omitted	3.00	—

Bureau Precancels: 3c, 9 diff.

Franklin D. Roosevelt — A727a

Revised design by Robert J. Jones and Howard C. Mildner.

COIL STAMPS

1966-81		**Tagged**	***Perf. 10 Vertically***	
1299	A710	1c **green,** *Jan. 12, 1968*	.20	.20
		Pair	.20	.20
		Joint line pair	.25	.20
	a.	Untagged (Bureau precanceled)		.20
	b.	Imperf., pair	30.00	—
		Imperf., joint line pair	60.00	—
1303	A714	4c **black,** *May 28, 1966*	.20	.20
		Pair	.30	.20
		Joint line pair	.75	.20
	a.	Untagged (Bureau precanceled)		.20
	b.	Imperf., pair	900.00	—
		Imperf., joint line pair	2,000.	—
	c.	Tagging omitted (not Bureau precanceled)	—	—
1304	A715	5c **blue,** shiny gum, *Sept. 8, 1966*	.20	.20
		Pair	.25	.20
		Joint line pair	.40	.20
		Dull gum	.75	—
		Joint line pair	5.00	—
	a.	Untagged (Bureau precanceled)		.20
	b.	Imperf., pair	175.00	—
		Joint line pair	400.00	—
	e.	As "a," imperf., pair		400.00

		Joint line pair	900.00	
	f.	Tagging omitted (not Bureau precanceled)		

No. 1304b is valued in the grade of fine.
No. 1304e is precanceled Mount Pleasant, IA. Also exists from Chicago, IL.

1304C	A715a	5c **blue,** *1981*	.20	.20
		Pair	.25	.20
		Joint line pair	1.25	—
	d.	Imperf., pair	800.00	—
1305	A727a	6c **gray brown,** *Feb. 28, 1968*	.20	.20
		Pair	.30	.20
		Joint line pair	.55	.20
	a.	Imperf., pair	75.00	—
		Joint line pair	130.00	—
	b.	Untagged (Bureau precanceled)		.20
	k.	Tagging omitted (not Bureau precanceled)	3.50	—
1305E	A720	15c **magenta,** type I, shiny gum, *June 14, 1978*	.25	.20
		Pair	.50	.20
		Joint line pair	1.25	.30
		Dull gum	.60	—
		Joint line pair	2.00	—
	f.	Untagged (Bureau precanceled, Chicago, IL)		.30
	g.	Imperf., pair, shiny gum	30.00	—
		Joint line pair	75.00	—
		Imperf., pair, dull gum	50.00	—
		Joint line pair	125.00	—
	h.	Pair, imperf. between	200.00	—
		Joint line pair	550.00	—
	i	Type II, dull gum	.35	.20
		Joint line pair	2.50	—
	j.	Type II, dull gum, Imperf., pair	90.00	—
		Joint line pair	300.00	—
1305C	A726	$1 **dull purple,** shiny gum, *Jan. 12, 1973*	2.00	.40
		Pair	4.00	.80
		Joint line pair	5.75	1.40
		Dull gum	2.00	—
		Joint line pair	5.50	—
	d.	Imperf., pair	2,250.	—
		Joint line pair	4,000.	—
		Nos. 1297-1305C (9)	3.65	2.00

Bureau Precancels: 1c, 5 diff., 4c, 35 diff., No. 1304a, 45 diff., 6c, 30 diff.

MIGRATORY BIRD TREATY ISSUE

Migratory Birds over Canada-US Border — A728

Designed by Burt E. Pringle.

GIORI PRESS PRINTING
Plates of 200 subjects in four panes of 50.

1966, Mar. 16				***Perf. 11***	
1306	A728	5c **black, crimson & dark blue**	.20	.20
		P# block of 4, 2#	.40	—
		Margin block of 4, Mr. Zip and "Use Zip Code"	.35	—

HUMANE TREATMENT OF ANIMALS ISSUE

Issued to promote humane treatment of all animals and for the centenary of the American Society for the Prevention of Cruelty to Animals.

Mongrel — A729

Designed by Norman Todhunter.

LITHOGRAPHED, ENGRAVED (Giori)
Plates of 200 subjects in four panes of 50.

1966, Apr. 9				***Perf. 11***	
1307	A729	5c **orange brown & black**	.20	.20
		P# block of 4	.40	—
		Margin block of 4, Mr. Zip and "Use Zip Code"	.35	—

Sesquicentennial Seal; Map of Indiana with 19 Stars and old Capitol at Corydon — A730

Clown — A731

INDIANA STATEHOOD, 150th ANNIV.

Designed by Paul A. Wehr.

GIORI PRESS PRINTING
Plates of 200 subjects in four panes of 50.

1966, Apr. 16				***Perf. 11***	
1308	A730	5c **ocher, brown & violet blue**	.20	.20
		P# block of 4, 2#	.40	—
		Margin block of 4, Mr. Zip and "Use Zip Code"	.35	—

AMERICAN CIRCUS ISSUE

Issued to honor the American Circus on the centenary of the birth of John Ringling.

Designed by Edward Klauck.

GIORI PRESS PRINTING
Plates of 200 subjects in four panes of 50.

1966, May 2				***Perf. 11***	
1309	A731	5c **multicolored**	.20	.20
		P# block of 4, 2#	.50	—
		Margin block of 4, Mr. Zip and "Use Zip Code"	.40	—

SIXTH INTERNATIONAL PHILATELIC EXHIBITION ISSUES

Sixth International Philatelic Exhibition (SIPEX), Washington, D.C., May 21-30.

Stamped Cover — A732

Designed by Thomas F. Naegele.

LITHOGRAPHED, ENGRAVED (Giori)
Plates of 200 subjects in four panes of 50.

1966				***Perf. 11***	
1310	A732	5c **multicolored,** *May 21*	.20	.20
		P# block of 4	.40	—
		Margin block of 4, Mr. Zip and "Use Zip Code"	.35	—

SOUVENIR SHEET

Designed by Brook Temple.

Plates of 24 subjects
Imperf

1311	A732	5c **multicolored,** *May 23*	.20	.20

No. 1311 measures 108x74mm. Below the stamp appears a line drawing of the Capitol and Washington Monument. Marginal inscriptions and drawing are green.

"Freedom" Checking "Tyranny" — A734

Polish Eagle and Cross — A735

BILL OF RIGHTS, 175th ANNIV.

Designed by Herbert L. Block (Herblock).

GIORI PRESS PRINTING

Plates of 200 subjects in four panes of 50.

1966, July 1		**Perf. 11**	
1312 A734 5c **carmine, dark & light blue**	.20	.20	
P# block of 4, 2#	.45	—	
Margin block of 4, Mr. Zip and			
"Use Zip Code"	.40	—	

POLISH MILLENNIUM ISSUE

Adoption of Christianity in Poland, 1000th anniv.

Designed by Edmund D. Lewandowski.

ROTARY PRESS PRINTING

E.E. Plates of 200 subjects in four panes of 50.

1966, July 30		**Perf. 10½x11**	
1313 A735 5c **red**	.20	.20	
P# block of 4	.45	—	
Margin block of 4, Mr. Zip and			
"Use Zip Code"	.40	—	

NATIONAL PARK SERVICE ISSUE

50th anniv. of the Natl. Park Service of the Interior Dept. The design "Parkscape U.S.A." identifies Natl. Park Service facilities.

National Park Service Emblem — A736

Designed by Thomas H. Geismar.

LITHOGRAPHED, ENGRAVED (Giori)

Plates of 200 subjects in four panes of 50.

1966, Aug. 25		**Perf. 11**	
1314 A736 5c **yellow, black & green**	.20	.20	
P# block of 4	.45	—	
Margin block of 4, Mr. Zip and			
"Use Zip Code"	.40	—	
a. Tagged, *Aug. 26*	.30	.25	
P# block of 4	2.00	—	
Zip block of 4	1.40	—	

MARINE CORPS RESERVE ISSUE

US Marine Corps Reserve founding, 50th anniv.

Combat Marine, 1966; Frogman; World War II Flier; World War I "Devil Dog" and Marine, 1775 — A737

Designed by Stella Grafakos.

LITHOGRAPHED, ENGRAVED (Giori)

Plates of 200 subjects in four panes of 50.

1966, Aug. 29		**Perf. 11**	
1315 A737 5c **black, bister, red & ultra.**	.20	.20	
P# block of 4	.45	—	
Margin block of 4, Mr. Zip and			
"Use Zip Code"	.40	—	
a. Tagged	.30	.20	

P# block of 4	2.00	—	
Zip block of 4	1.40	—	
b. Black & bister (engraved) omitted	16,000.		

GENERAL FEDERATION OF WOMEN'S CLUBS ISSUE

75 years of service by the General Federation of Women's Clubs.

Women of 1890 and 1966 — A738

Designed by Charles Henry Carter.

GIORI PRESS PRINTING

Plates of 200 subjects in four panes of 50.

1966, Sept. 12		**Perf. 11**	
1316 A738 5c **black, pink & blue**	.20	.20	
P# block of 4, 2#	.45	—	
Margin block of 4, Mr. Zip and			
"Use Zip Code"	.40	—	
a. Tagged, *Sept. 13*	.30	.20	
P# block of 4, 2#	2.00	—	
Zip block of 4	1.40	—	

AMERICAN FOLKLORE ISSUE
Johnny Appleseed

Issued to honor Johnny Appleseed (John Chapman 1774-1845), who wandered over 100,000 square miles planting apple trees, and who gave away and sold seedlings to Midwest pioneers.

 Johnny Appleseed — A739

Designed by Robert Bode.

GIORI PRESS PRINTING

Plates of 200 subjects in four panes of 50.

1966, Sept. 24		**Perf. 11**	
1317 A739 5c **green, red & black**	.20	.20	
P# block of 4, Mr. Zip and	.45	—	
Margin block of 4, Mr. Zip and			
"Use Zip Code"	.40	—	
a. Tagged, *Sept. 26*	.30	.20	
P# block of 4, 2#	2.00	—	
Zip block of 4	1.40	—	

BEAUTIFICATION OF AMERICA ISSUE

Issued to publicize President Johnson's "Plant for a more beautiful America" campaign.

Jefferson Memorial, Tidal Basin and Cherry Blossoms — A740

Designed by Miss Gyo Fujikawa.

GIORI PRESS PRINTING

Plates of 200 subjects in four panes of 50.

1966, Oct. 5		**Perf. 11**	
1318 A740 5c **emerald, pink & black**	.20	.20	
P# block of 4, 2#	.45	—	
Margin block of 4, Mr. Zip and			
"Use Zip Code"	.40	—	
a. Tagged	.30	.20	
P# block of 4, 2#	2.00	—	
Zip block of 4	1.25	—	

Map of Central United States with Great River Road — A741

Statue of Liberty and "Old Glory" — A742

GREAT RIVER ROAD ISSUE

Issued to publicize the 5,600-mile Great River Road connecting New Orleans with Kenora, Ontario, and following the Mississippi most of the way.

Designed by Herbert Bayer.

LITHOGRAPHED, ENGRAVED (Giori)

Plates of 200 subjects in four panes of 50.

1966, Oct. 21		**Perf. 11**	
1319 A741 5c **vermilion, yellow, blue & green**	.20	.20	
P# block of 4	.45	—	
Margin block of 4, Mr. Zip and			
"Use Zip Code"	.40	—	
a. Tagged, *Oct. 22*	.30	.20	
P# block of 4	2.00	—	
Zip block of 4	1.40	—	

SAVINGS BOND-SERVICEMEN ISSUE

25th anniv. of US Savings Bonds, and honoring American servicemen.

Designed by Stevan Dohanos, photo by Bob Noble.

LITHOGRAPHED, ENGRAVED (Giori)

Plates of 200 subjects in four panes of 50.

1966, Oct. 26		**Perf. 11**	
1320 A742 5c **red, dark blue, light blue & black**	.20	.20	
P# block of 4	.45	—	
Margin block of 4, Mr. Zip and			
"Use Zip Code"	.40	—	
a. Tagged, *Oct. 27*	.30	.20	
P# block of 4	1.75	—	
Zip block of 4	1.30	—	
b. Red, dark blue & black omitted	5,000.		
c. Dark blue (engr.) omitted	9,000.		

CHRISTMAS ISSUE

Madonna and Child, by Hans Memling — A743

Designed by Howard C. Mildner.

Modeled after "Madonna and Child with Angels," by the Flemish artist Hans Memling (c.1430-1494), Mellon Collection, National Gallery of Art, Washington, D.C.

LITHOGRAPHED, ENGRAVED (Giori)

Plates of 400 subjects in four panes of 100.

1966, Nov. 1		**Perf. 11**	
1321 A743 5c **multicolored**	.20	.20	
P# block of 4	.40	—	
Margin block of 4, Mr. Zip and			
"Use Zip Code"	.35	—	
a. Tagged, *Nov. 2*	.30	.20	
P# block of 4	1.50	—	
Zip block of 4	1.25	—	

MARY CASSATT ISSUE

Cassatt (1844-1926), painter. The painting "The Boating Party" is in the Natl. Gallery of Art, Washington, D.C.

"The Boating Party" — A744

Designed by Robert J. Jones.

GIORI PRESS PRINTING
Plates of 200 subjects in four panes of 50.

1966, Nov. 17		Perf. 11	
1322 A744 5c **multicolored**		.20	.20
P# block of 4, 2#		.60	—
Margin block of 4, Mr. Zip and "Use Zip Code"		.50	—
a.	Tagged	.30	.25
P# block of 4, 2#		1.75	—
Zip block of 4		1.25	—

NATIONAL GRANGE ISSUE

Centenary of the founding of the National Grange, American farmers' organization.

Grange Poster, 1870 — A745

Designed by Lee Pavao.

GIORI PRESS PRINTING
Plates of 200 subjects in four panes of 50.

1967, Apr. 17	Tagged	Perf. 11	
1323 A745 5c **orange, yellow, brown, green & black**		.20	.20
P# block of 4, 2#		.40	—
Margin block of 4, Mr. Zip and "Use Zip Code"		.35	—
a.	Tagging omitted	5.00	—

CANADA CENTENARY ISSUE

Centenary of Canada's emergence as a nation.

Canadian Landscape — A746

Designed by Ivan Chermayeff.

GIORI PRESS PRINTING
Plates of 200 subjects in four panes of 50.

1967, May 25	Tagged	Perf. 11	
1324 A746 5c **lt. blue, dp. green, ultra., olive & black**		.20	.20
On cover, Expo. station ("U.S. Pavilion") machine canc.		1.00	
On cover, Expo. station handstamp canc.		2.50	
P# block of 4, 2#		.40	—
Margin block of 4, Mr. Zip and "Use Zip Code"		.35	—
a.	Tagging omitted	5.00	—

ERIE CANAL ISSUE

150th anniversary of the Erie Canal ground-breaking ceremony at Rome, N.Y. The canal links Lake Erie and New York City.

Stern of Early Canal Boat — A747

Designed by George Samerjan.

LITHOGRAPHED, ENGRAVED (Giori)
Plates of 200 subjects in four panes of 50.

1967, July 4	Tagged	Perf. 11	
1325 A747 5c **ultra., greenish blue, black & crimson**		.20	.20
P# block of 4		.40	—
Margin block of 4, Mr. Zip and "Use Zip Code"		.35	—
a.	Tagging omitted	10.00	—

"SEARCH FOR PEACE" - LIONS ISSUE

Issued to publicize the search for peace. "Search for Peace" was the theme of an essay contest for young men and women sponsored by Lions International on its 50th anniversary.

Peace Dove — A748

Designed by Bradbury Thompson.

GIORI PRESS PRINTING
Plates of 200 subjects in four panes of 50.

1967, July 5	Tagged	Perf. 11	
	Gray Paper with Blue Threads		
1326 A748 5c **blue, red & black**		.20	.20
P# block of 4		.40	—
Margin block of 4, Mr. Zip and "Use Zip Code"		.35	—
a.	Tagging omitted	5.00	—

HENRY DAVID THOREAU ISSUE

Henry David Thoreau (1817-1862), writer.

Henry David Thoreau — A749

Designed by Leonard Baskin.

GIORI PRESS PRINTING
Plates of 200 subjects in four panes of 50.

1967, July 12	Tagged	Perf. 11	
1327 A749 5c **carmine, black & blue green**		.20	.20
P# block of 4		.45	—
Margin block of 4, Mr. Zip and "Use Zip Code"		.35	—
a.	Tagging omitted		—

NEBRASKA STATEHOOD, 100th ANNIV.

Hereford Steer and Ear of Corn — A750

Designed by Julian K. Billings.

LITHOGRAPHED, ENGRAVED (Giori)
Plates of 200 subjects in four panes of 50.

1967, July 29	Tagged	Perf. 11	
1328 A750 5c **dark red brown, lemon & yellow**		.20	.20
P# block of 4		.40	—
Margin block of 4, Mr. Zip and "Use Zip Code"		.35	—
a.	Tagging omitted	6.00	—

VOICE OF AMERICA ISSUE

25th anniv. of the radio branch of the United States Information Agency (USIA).

Radio Transmission Tower and Waves — A751

Designed by Georg Olden.

LITHOGRAPHED, ENGRAVED (Giori)
Plates of 200 subjects in four panes of 50.

1967, Aug. 1	Tagged	Perf. 11	
1329 A751 5c **red, blue, black & carmine**		.20	.20
P# block of 4		.40	—
Margin block of 4, Mr. Zip and "Use Zip Code"		.35	—
a.	Tagging omitted	10.00	—

AMERICAN FOLKLORE ISSUE

Davy Crockett (1786-1836), frontiersman, hunter, and congressman from Tennessee who died at the Alamo.

Davy Crockett and Scrub Pine — A752

Designed by Robert Bode.

LITHOGRAPHED, ENGRAVED (Giori)
Plates of 200 subjects in four panes of 50.

1967, Aug. 17	Tagged	Perf. 11	
1330 A752 5c **green, black, & yellow**		.20	.20
P# block of 4		.40	—
Margin block of 4, Mr. Zip and "Use Zip Code"		.35	—
a.	Vertical pair, imperf. between	6,000.	
b.	Green (engr.) omitted	—	
c.	Black & green (engr.) omitted	—	
e.	Tagging omitted	5.00	—

A foldover on a pane of No. 1330 resulted in one example each of Nos. 1330b-1330c. Part of the colors appear on the back of the selvage and one freak stamp. An engraved black-and-green-only impression appears on the gummed side of one almost-complete "stamp."

ACCOMPLISHMENTS IN SPACE ISSUE

US accomplishments in space. Printed with continuous design in horizontal rows of 5. In the left panes the astronaut stamp is 1st, 3rd and 5th, the spaceship 2nd and 4th. This arrangement is reversed in the right panes.

Space-Walking Astronaut — A753

Gemini 4 Capsule — A754

Designed by Paul Calle.

LITHOGRAPHED, ENGRAVED (Giori)
Plates of 200 subjects in four panes of 50.

1967, Sept. 29	Tagged	Perf. 11	
1331 A753 5c **multicolored**		.50	.20
b.	Tagging omitted	10.00	
1332 A754 5c **multicolored**		.50	.20
P# block of 4		2.75	
Margin block of 4, Mr. Zip and "Use Zip Code"		2.50	—
Plate flaw (red stripes of flag on capsule omitted; 29322, 29325 UL 19)		210.00	
a.	Tagging omitted	10.00	
b.	Pair, #1331-1332	1.10	1.25
c.	As "b," tagging omitted	40.00	—

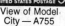

View of Model City — A755

Finnish Coat of Arms — A756

URBAN PLANNING ISSUE

Publicizing the importance of Urban Planning in connection with the Intl. Conf. of the American Institute of Planners, Washington, D.C., Oct. 1-6.

Designed by Francis Ferguson.

LITHOGRAPHED, ENGRAVED (Giori)
Plates of 200 subjects in four panes of 50.

1967, Oct. 2	Tagged	Perf. 11
1333 A755 5c dark blue, light blue & black	.20	.20
P# block of 4	.50	—
Margin block of 4, Mr. Zip and "Use Zip Code"	.40	—
a. Tagging omitted		—

FINNISH INDEPENDENCE, 50th ANNIV.

Designed by Bradbury Thompson.

ENGRAVED (Giori)
Plates of 200 subjects in four panes of 50.

1967, Oct. 6	Tagged	Perf. 11
1334 A756 5c blue	.20	.20
P# block of 4	.50	—
Margin block of 4, Mr. Zip and "Use Zip Code"	.40	—
a. Tagging omitted		—

THOMAS EAKINS ISSUE

Eakins (1844-1916), painter and sculptor. The painting is in the Natl. Gallery of Art, Washington, D.C.

"The Biglin Brothers Racing" (Sculling on Schuylkill River, Philadelphia) A757

Printed by Photogravure & Color Co., Moonachie, N.J.

PHOTOGRAVURE
Plates of 200 subjects in four panes of 50.

1967, Nov. 2	Tagged	Perf. 12
1335 A757 5c gold & multicolored	.20	.20
P# block of 4, 6#	.50	—
a. Tagging omitted	20.00	—

Plate number blocks from upper left or lower left panes show clipped corner of margin.

CHRISTMAS ISSUE

Madonna and Child, by Hans Memling — A758

LITHOGRAPHED, ENGRAVED (Giori)
Plates of 200 subjects in four panes of 50.

1967, Nov. 6	Tagged	Perf. 11
1336 A758 5c multicolored	.20	.20
P# block of 4	.40	—
Margin block of 4, Mr. Zip and "Use Zip Code"	.35	—
a. Tagging omitted	4.00	—

See note on painting above No. 1321.

MISSISSIPPI STATEHOOD, 150th ANNIV.

Magnolia — A759

Designed by Andrew Bucci.

GIORI PRESS PRINTING
Plates of 200 subjects in four panes of 50.

1967, Dec. 11	Tagged	Perf. 11
1337 A759 5c brt. greenish blue, green & red brown	.20	.20
P# block of 4, 2#	.50	—
Margin block of 4, Mr. Zip and "Use Zip Code"	.40	—
a. Tagging omitted	6.00	—

FLAG ISSUE

Flag and White House — A760

Designed by Stevan Dohanos.

GIORI PRESS PRINTING
Plates of 400 subjects in four panes of 100.

1968, Jan. 24	Tagged	Perf. 11
	Size: 19x22mm	
1338 A760 6c dark blue, red & green	.20	.20
P# block of 4	.45	—
Margin block of 4, "Use Zip Codes"	.40	—
Pair with full vert. gutter btwn.		—
k. Vert. pair, imperf. btwn.	550.00	
m. Tagging omitted	4.00	—
s. Red omitted		

Vertical pairs have been offered as imperf. horizontally. Some have had the gum washed off to make it difficult or impossible to detect blind perfs.
No. 1338s is caused by a foldover of the paper. It is unique.

COIL STAMP
MULTICOLOR HUCK PRESS

1969, May 30	Tagged	Perf. 10 Vertically
	Size: 18¼x21mm	
1338A A760 6c dark blue, red & green	.20	.20
Pair	.30	.20
b. Imperf., pair	500.00	
q. Tagging omitted	8.50	—

MULTICOLOR HUCK PRESS
Panes of 100 (10x10) each

1970-71	Tagged	Perf. 11x10½
	Size: 18¼x21mm	
1338D A760 6c dark blue, red & green, Aug. 7, 1970	.20	.20
Margin block of 20+	2.60	—
e. Horiz. pair, imperf. between	175.00	—
n. Tagging omitted	5.00	—
1338F A760 8c dark blue, red & slate green, May 10, 1971	.20	.20
Margin block of 20+	3.00	—
i. Imperf., vert. pair	45.00	—
j. Horiz. pair, imperf. between	55.00	—
o. Tagging omitted	5.00	—
p. Slate green omitted	400.00	—
t. Horiz. pair, imperf. vertically		—

+ Margin blocks of 20 come in four versions: (1) 2 P#, 3 ME, 3 zip; (2) 3 P#, 2 ME, 2 zip; (3) 2 P#, 3 ME, 2 zip; (4) 3 P#, 2 ME, 3 zip.

COIL STAMP
MULTICOLOR HUCK PRESS

1971, May 10	Tagged	Perf. 10 Vertically
	Size: 18¼x21mm	
1338G A760 8c dk blue, red & slate green	.20	.20
Pair	.40	.20
h. Imperf., pair	55.00	—
r. Tagging omitted	4.00	—

6¢ U.S. POSTAGE
Farm Buildings and Fields of Ripening Grain — A761

Map of North and South America and Lines Converging on San Antonio — A762

ILLINOIS STATEHOOD, 150th ANNIV.

Designed by George Barford.

LITHOGRAPHED, ENGRAVED (Giori)
Plates of 200 subjects in four panes of 50.

1968, Feb. 12	Tagged	Perf. 11
1339 A761 6c dk blue, blue, red & ocher	.20	.20
P# block of 4	.50	—
Margin block of 4, Mr. Zip and "Use Zip Code"	.45	—
a. Tagging omitted		—

HEMISFAIR '68 ISSUE

HemisFair '68 exhibition, San Antonio, Texas, Apr. 6-Oct. 6, for the 250th anniv. of San Antonio.

Designed by Louis Macouillard.

LITHOGRAPHED, ENGRAVED (Giori)
Plates of 200 subjects in four panes of 50.

1968, Mar. 30	Tagged	Perf. 11
1340 A762 6c blue, rose red & white	.20	.20
On cover, Expo. station machine canc.	10.00	
On cover, Expo. roller canc.	25.00	
P# block of 4	.50	—
Margin block of 4, Mr. Zip and "Use Zip Code"	.45	—
a. White omitted	1,300.	

AIRLIFT ISSUE

Issued to pay for airlift of parcels from and to US ports to servicemen overseas and in Alaska, Hawaii and Puerto Rico. Valid for all regular postage. On Apr. 26, 1969, the Post Office Department ruled that henceforth No. 1341 "may be used toward paying the postage or fees for special services on *airmail* articles."

Eagle Holding Pennant — A763

Designed by Stevan Dohanos.

After a late 19th century wood carving, part of the Index of American Design, National Gallery of Art.

LITHOGRAPHED, ENGRAVED (Giori)
Plates of 200 subjects in four panes of 50.

1968, Apr. 4	Untagged	Perf. 11
1341 A763 $1 sepia, dk. blue, ocher & brown red	2.25	1.25
P# block of 4	10.00	—
Margin block of 4, Mr. Zip and "Use Zip Code"	9.50	—
Pair with full horiz. gutter btwn.		—

"SUPPORT OUR YOUTH" - ELKS ISSUE

Support Our Youth program, and honoring the Benevolent and Protective Order of Elks, which extended its youth service program in observance of its centennial year.

Girls and Boys — A764

Designed by Edward Vebell.

LITHOGRAPHED, ENGRAVED (Giori)
Plates of 200 subjects in four panes of 50.

1968, May 1   **Tagged**   **Perf. 11**
1342 A764 6c ultramarine & orange red   .20   .20
    P# block of 4   .50   —
    Margin block of 4, Mr. Zip and
      "Use Zip Code"   .45   —
  a. Tagging omitted   7.00

Policeman and
Boy — A765

Eagle Weather
Vane — A766

LAW AND ORDER ISSUE

Publicizing the policeman as protector and friend
and to encourage respect for law and order.

Designed by Ward Brackett.

GIORI PRESS PRINTING
Plates of 200 subjects in four panes of 50 each

1968, May 17   **Tagged**   **Perf. 11**
1343 A765 6c chalky blue, black & red   .20   .20
    P# block of 4   .50   —
    Margin block of 4, Mr. Zip and
      "Use Zip Code"   .45   —
  a. Tagging omitted   —

REGISTER AND VOTE ISSUE

Campaign to draw more voters to the polls. The
weather vane is from an old house in the Russian Hill
section of San Francisco, Cal.

Designed by Norman Todhunter and Bill Hyde; photograph
by M. Halberstadt.

LITHOGRAPHED, ENGRAVED (Giori)
Plates of 200 subjects in four panes of 50.

1968, June 27   **Tagged**   **Perf. 11**
1344 A766 6c black, yellow & orange   .20   .20
    P# block of 4   .50   —
    Margin block of 4, Mr. Zip and
      "Use Zip Code"   .45   —
  a. Tagging omitted   —

HISTORIC FLAG SERIES

Flags carried by American colonists and by citizens
of the new United States. Printed se-tenant in vertical
rows of 10. The flag sequence on the 2 upper panes is
as listed. On the 2 lower panes the sequence is
reversed with the Navy Jack in the 1st row and the
Fort Moultrie flag in the 10th.

Ft. Moultrie,
1776 — A767

Ft. McHenry,
1795-1818
A768

Washington's
Cruisers,
1775 — A769

Bennington,
1777 — A770

Rhode Island,
1775 — A771

First Stars and
Stripes,
1777 — A772

Bunker Hill,
1775 — A773

Grand Union,
1776 — A774

Philadelphia
Light Horse,
1775 — A775

First Navy Jack,
1775 — A776

ENGR. (Giori) (#1345-1348, 1350);
ENGR. & LITHO. (#1349, 1351-1354)
Plates of 200 subjects in four panes of 50.

1968, July 4   **Tagged**   **Perf. 11**
1345 A767 6c dark blue   .40   .25
1346 A768 6c dark blue & red   .30   .25
1347 A769 6c dark blue & olive green   .25   .25
1348 A770 6c dark blue & red   .25   .25
1349 A771 6c dark blue, yellow & red   .25   .25
1350 A772 6c dark blue & red   .25   .25
1351 A773 6c dark blue, olive green & red   .25   .25
1352 A774 6c dark blue & red   .25   .25
1353 A775 6c dark blue, yellow & red   .25   .25
1354 A776 6c dark blue, red & yellow   .25   .25
  a. Strip of ten, #1345-1354   2.75   2.75
    P# block of 20, inscriptions,
      #1345-1354   6.50   —
  b. #1345b-1354b, any single, tagging omit-
    ted   —

WALT DISNEY ISSUE

Walt Disney (1901-1966), cartoonist, film producer
and creator of Mickey Mouse.

Walt Disney and Children of the
World — A777

Designed by C. Robert Moore.

Designed after portrait by Paul E. Wenzel.
Printed by Achrovure Division of Union-Camp Corp., Englewood, N.J.

PHOTOGRAVURE
Plates of 400 subjects in eight panes of 50.

1968, Sept. 11   **Tagged**   **Perf. 12**
1355 A777 6c multicolored   .20   .20
    P# block of 4, 5#   .90
    P# block of 4, 5#, 5 dashes   .90
    Margin block of 4, Mr. Zip and
      "Use Zip Code"   .70
  a. Ocher omitted ("Walt Disney," "6c," etc.) 600.00
  b. Vert. pair, imperf. horiz.   700.00
  c. Imperf., pair   675.00
  d. Black omitted   2,000.
  e. Horiz. pair, imperf. between   4,750.
  f. Blue omitted   2,250.
  g. Tagging omitted   10.00

FATHER MARQUETTE ISSUE

Father Jacques Marquette (1637-1675), French
Jesuit missionary, who together with Louis Jolliet
explored the Mississippi River and its tributaries.

Father Marquette
and Louis Jolliet
Exploring the
Mississippi
A778

Designed by Stanley W. Galli.

GIORI PRESS PRINTING
Plates of 200 subjects in four panes of 50.

1968, Sept. 20   **Tagged**   **Perf. 11**
1356 A778 6c black, apple green & orange
    brown   .20   .20
    P# block of 4   .50   —
    Margin block of 4, Mr. Zip and
      "Use Zip Code"   .45   —
  a. Tagging omitted   —

AMERICAN FOLKLORE ISSUE

Daniel Boone (1734-1820), frontiersman and trapper.

Pennsylvania Rifle,
Powder Horn,
Tomahawk Pipe
and Knife — A779

Designed by Louis Macouillard.

LITHOGRAPHED, ENGRAVED (Giori)
Plates of 200 subjects in four panes of 50.

1968, Sept. 26   **Tagged**   **Perf. 11**
1357 A779 6c yellow, deep yellow, maroon &
    black   .20   .20
    P# block of 4   .50   —
    Margin block of 4, Mr. Zip and
      "Use Zip Code"   .45   —
  a. Tagging omitted   —

ARKANSAS RIVER NAVIGATION ISSUE

Opening of the Arkansas River to commercial
navigation.

Ship's Wheel,
Power
Transmission
Tower and
Barge — A780

Designed by Dean Ellis.

LITHOGRAPHED, ENGRAVED (Giori)
Plates of 200 subjects in four panes of 50.

1968, Oct. 1	Tagged	Perf. 11	
1358 A780 6c bright blue, dark blue & black		.20	.20
P# block of 4		.50	—
Margin block of 4, Mr. Zip and "Use Zip Code"		.45	—
a. Tagging omitted		—	

LEIF ERIKSON ISSUE

Leif Erikson, 11th century Norse explorer, called the 1st European to set foot on the American continent, at a place he called Vinland. The statue by the American sculptor A. Stirling Calder is in Reykjavik, Iceland.

Leif Erikson by A. Stirling Calder — A781

Designed by Kurt Weiner.

LITHOGRAPHED & ENGRAVED
Plates of 200 subjects in four panes of 50.

1968, Oct. 9	Tagged	Perf. 11	
1359 A781 6c light gray brown & black brown		.20	.20
P# block of 4		.50	—
Margin block of 4, Mr. Zip and "Use Zip Code"		.45	—

The luminescent element is in the light gray brown ink of the background. The engraved parts were printed on a rotary currency press.

CHEROKEE STRIP ISSUE

75th anniversary of the opening of the Cherokee Strip to settlers, Sept. 16, 1893.

Racing for Homesteads in Cherokee Strip, 1893 — A782

Designed by Norman Todhunter.

ROTARY PRESS PRINTING
E.E. Plates of 200 subjects in four panes of 50.

1968, Oct. 15	Tagged	Perf. 11x10½	
1360 A782 6c brown		.20	.20
P# block of 4		.60	—
Margin block of 4, Mr. Zip and "Use Zip Code"		.50	—
a. Tagging omitted		5.00	—

JOHN TRUMBULL ISSUE

Trumbull (1756-1843), painter. The stamp shows Lt. Thomas Grosvenor and his attendant Peter Salem. The painting hangs at Yale University.

Detail from "The Battle of Bunker's Hill" — A783

Modeled by Robert J. Jones.

LITHOGRAPHED, ENGRAVED (Giori)
Plates of 200 subjects in four panes of 50.

1968, Oct. 18	Tagged	Perf. 11	
1361 A783 6c multicolored		.20	.20
P# block of 4		.60	—
Margin block of 4, Mr. Zip and "Use Zip Code"		.50	—
a. Tagging omitted		—	

WATERFOWL CONSERVATION ISSUE

Wood Ducks — A784

Designed by Stanley W. Galli.

LITHOGRAPHED, ENGRAVED (Giori)
Plates of 200 subjects in four panes of 50.

1968, Oct. 24	Tagged	Perf. 11	
1362 A784 6c black & multicolored		.20	.20
P# block of 4		.65	—
Margin block of 4, Mr. Zip and "Use Zip Code"		.60	—
a. Vertical pair, imperf. between		550.00	—
b. Red & dark blue omitted		900.00	—
c. Red omitted		—	

Angel Gabriel, from "The Annunciation" by Jan van Eyck — A785

Chief Joseph, by Cyrenius Hall — A786

CHRISTMAS ISSUE

"The Annunciation" by the 15th century Flemish painter Jan van Eyck is in the National Gallery of Art, Washington, D.C.

Designed by Robert J. Jones.

ENGRAVED (Multicolor Huck)
Panes of 50 (10x5)

1968, Nov. 1	Tagged	Perf. 11	
1363 A785 6c multicolored		.20	.20
P# block of 10 +		2.00	—
a. Untagged, Nov. 2		.20	.20
P# block of 10 +		2.00	—
b. Imperf., pair, tagged		225.00	—
c. Light yellow omitted		65.00	—
d. Imperf., pair, untagged		300.00	—

+ P# blocks come in two versions: (1) 7 P#, 3 ME; (2) 8 P#, 2 ME.

AMERICAN INDIAN ISSUE

Honoring the American Indian and to celebrate the opening of the Natl. Portrait Gallery, Washington, D.C. Chief Joseph (Indian name, Thunder Traveling over the Mountains), a leader of the Nez Percé, was born in eastern Oregon about 1840 and died at the Colesville Reservation in Washington State in 1904.

Designed by Robert J. Jones; lettering by Crimilda Pontes.

LITHOGRAPHED, ENGRAVED (Giori)
Plates of 200 subjects in four panes of 50.

1968, Nov. 4	Tagged	Perf. 11	
1364 A786 6c black & multicolored		.20	.20
P# block of 4		.70	—
Margin block of 4, Mr. Zip and "Use Zip Code"		.60	—

BEAUTIFICATION OF AMERICA ISSUE

Publicizing the Natural Beauty Campaign for more beautiful cities, parks, highways and streets. In the left panes Nos. 1365 and 1367 appear in 1st, 3rd and 5th place, Nos. 1366 and 1368 in 2nd and 4th place. This arrangement is reversed in the right panes.

Capitol, Azaleas and Tulips — A787

Washington Monument, Potomac River and Daffodils — A788

Poppies and Lupines along Highway — A789

Blooming Crabapples Lining Avenue — A790

Designed by Walter DuBois Richards.

LITHOGRAPHED, ENGRAVED (Giori)
Plates of 200 subjects in four panes of 50.

1969, Jan. 16	Tagged	Perf. 11	
1365 A787 6c multicolored		.30	.20
1366 A788 6c multicolored		.30	.20
1367 A789 6c multicolored		.30	.20
1368 A790 6c multicolored		.30	.20
a. Block of 4, #1365-1368		1.25	1.75
P# block of 4		1.50	—
Margin block of 4, Mr. Zip and "Use Zip Code"		1.30	—
b. #1365b-1368b, tagging omitted			

Eagle from Great Seal — A791

July Fourth, by Grandma Moses — A792

AMERICAN LEGION, 50th ANNIV.
Designed by Robert Hallock.

LITHOGRAPHED, ENGRAVED (Giori)
Plates of 200 subjects in four panes of 50.

1969, Mar. 15	Tagged	Perf. 11	
1369 A791 6c red, blue & black		.20	.20
P# block of 4		.45	—
Margin block of 4, Mr. Zip and "Use Zip Code"		.40	—
a. Tagging omitted		—	

AMERICAN FOLKLORE ISSUE

Grandma Moses (Anna Mary Robertson Moses, 1860-1961), primitive painter of American life.

Designed by Robert J. Jones.

LITHOGRAPHED, ENGRAVED (Giori)
Plates of 200 subjects in four panes of 50.

1969, May 1	Tagged	Perf. 11
1370 A792 6c multicolored	.20	.20
P# block of 4	.50	
Margin block of 4, Mr. Zip and "Use Zip Code"	.45	
a. Horizontal pair, imperf. between	225.00	
b. Black ("6c U.S. Postage") & Prus. blue ("Grandma Moses") omitted (engraved)	850.00	
c. Tagging omitted	6.00	—

Beware of pairs with blind perfs. being offered as No. 1370a. No. 1370b often comes with mottled or disturbed gum. Such stamps sell for about two-thirds as much as copies with perfect gum.

APOLLO 8 ISSUE

Apollo 8 mission, which 1st put men into orbit around the moon, Dec. 21-27, 1968. The astronauts were: Col. Frank Borman, Capt. James Lovell and Maj. William Anders.

Moon Surface and Earth — A793

Designed by Leonard E. Buckley after a photograph by the Apollo 8 astronauts.

GIORI PRESS PRINTING
Plates of 200 subjects in four panes of 50.

1969, May 5	Tagged	Perf. 11
1371 A793 6c black, blue & ocher	.20	.20
P# block of 4	.65	
Margin block of 4, Mr. Zip and "Use Zip Code"	.60	

Imperfs. exist from printer's waste.

W.C. HANDY ISSUE

Handy (1873-1958), jazz musician and composer.

William Christopher Handy — A794

Designed by Bernice Kochan.

LITHOGRAPHED, ENGRAVED (Giori)
Plates of 200 subjects in four panes of 50.

1969, May 17	Tagged	Perf. 11
1372 A794 6c violet, deep lilac & blue	.20	.20
P# block of 4	.45	
Margin block of 4, Mr. Zip and "Use Zip Code"	.40	—
a. Tagging omitted	6.00	—

CALIFORNIA SETTLEMENT, 200th ANNIV.

Carmel Mission Belfry — A795

Designed by Leonard Buckley and Howard C. Mildner.

LITHOGRAPHED, ENGRAVED (Giori)
Plates of 200 subjects in four panes of 50.

1969, July 16	Tagged	Perf. 11
1373 A795 6c orange, red, black & light blue	.20	.20
P# block of 4	.45	—
Margin block of 4, Mr. Zip and "Use Zip Code"	.40	—
a. Tagging omitted	7.50	—

JOHN WESLEY POWELL ISSUE

Powell (1834-1902), geologist who explored the Green and Colorado Rivers 1869-75, and ethnologist.

Major Powell Exploring Colorado River, 1869 — A796

Designed by Rudolph Wendelin.

LITHOGRAPHED, ENGRAVED (Giori)
Plates of 200 subjects in four panes of 50.

1969, Aug. 1	Tagged	Perf. 11
1374 A796 6c black, ocher & light blue	.20	.20
P# block of 4	.45	—
Margin block of 4, Mr. Zip and "Use Zip Code"	.40	—
a. Tagging omitted	7.50	—

ALABAMA STATEHOOD, 150th ANNIV.

Camellia and Yellow-shafted Flicker — A797

Designed by Bernice Kochan.

LITHOGRAPHED, ENGRAVED (Giori)
Plates of 200 subjects in four panes of 50.

1969, Aug. 2	Tagged	Perf. 11
1375 A797 6c magenta, rose red, yellow, dark green & brown	.20	.20
P# block of 4	.45	—
Margin block of 4, Mr. Zip and "Use Zip Code"	.40	

BOTANICAL CONGRESS ISSUE

11th Intl. Botanical Cong., Seattle, Wash., Aug. 24-Sept. 2. In left panes Nos. 1376 and 1378 appear in 1st, 3rd and 5th place; Nos. 1377 and 1379 in 2nd and 4th place. This arrangement is reversed in right panes.

Douglas Fir (Northwest) A798

Lady's-slipper (Northeast) A799

Ocotillo (Southwest) A800

Franklinia (Southeast) A801

Designed by Stanley Galli.

LITHOGRAPHED, ENGRAVED (Giori)
Plates of 200 subjects in four panes of 50.

1969, Aug. 23	Tagged	Perf. 11
1376 A798 6c multicolored	.40	.20
1377 A799 6c multicolored	.40	.20
1378 A800 6c multicolored	.40	.20
1379 A801 6c multicolored	.40	.20
a. Block of 4, #1376-1379	1.75	2.25
P# block of 4	2.00	—
Margin block of 4, Mr. Zip and "Use Zip Code"	1.80	

DARTMOUTH COLLEGE CASE ISSUE

150th anniv. of the Dartmouth College Case, which Daniel Webster argued before the Supreme Court, reasserting the sanctity of contracts.

Daniel Webster and Dartmouth Hall — A802

Designed by John R. Scotford, Jr.

ROTARY PRESS PRINTING
E.E. Plates of 200 subjects in four panes of 50.

1969, Sept. 22	Tagged	Perf. 10½x11
1380 A802 6c green	.20	.20
P# block of 4	.50	—
Margin block of 4, Mr. Zip and "Use Zip Code"	.45	

PROFESSIONAL BASEBALL, 100th ANNIV.

Batter — A803

Designed by Alex Ross.

LITHOGRAPHED, ENGRAVED (Giori)
Plates of 200 subjects in four panes of 50.

1969, Sept. 24	Tagged	Perf. 11
1381 A803 6c yellow, red, black & green	.65	.20
P# block of 4	3.00	—
Margin block of 4, Mr. Zip and "Use Zip Code"	2.75	—
a. Black omitted ("1869-1969, United States, 6c, Professional Baseball")	1,100.	

INTERCOLLEGIATE FOOTBALL, 100th ANNIV.

Football Player and Coach — A804

Designed by Robert Peak.

LITHOGRAPHED, ENGRAVED (Giori)
Plates of 200 subjects in four panes of 50.

1969, Sept. 26	Tagged	Perf. 11
1382 A804 6c red & green	.20	.20
P# block of 4	.85	—
Margin block of 4, Mr. Zip and "Use Zip Code"	.60	—

The engraved parts were printed on a rotary currency press.

DWIGHT D. EISENHOWER ISSUE

Dwight D. Eisenhower, 34th President (1890-1969) — A805

Designed by Robert J. Jones; photograph by Bernie Noble.

GIORI PRESS PRINTING
Plates of 128 subjects in 4 panes of 32 each.

1969, Oct. 14	Tagged	Perf. 11	
1383 A805 6c blue, black & red		.20	.20
P# block of 4		.50	—
Margin block of 4, Mr. Zip and "Use Zip Code"		.45	—

CHRISTMAS ISSUE

The painting, painted about 1870 by an unknown primitive artist, is the property of the N.Y. State Historical Association, Cooperstown, N.Y.

Winter Sunday in Norway, Maine — A806

Designed by Stevan Dohanos.

ENGRAVED (Multicolor Huck)
Panes of 50 (5x10)

1969, Nov. 3	Tagged	Perf. 11x10½	
1384 A806 6c dark green & multicolored		.20	.20
P# block of 10, 5#, 2-3 zip, 2-3			
Mail Early		1.40	—
Precancel		.50	.20
b. Imperf., pair		1,000.	
c. Light green omitted		22.50	
d. Light green, red & yellow omitted		1,000.	—
e. Yellow omitted		2,250.	
f. Tagging omitted		5.00	—
g. Red & yellow omitted		—	

The precancel value applies to the least expensive of experimental precancels printed locally in four cities, on tagged stamps, with the names between lines 4½mm apart: in black or green, "ATLANTA, GA" and in green only "BALTIMORE, MD," "MEMPHIS, TN" and "NEW HAVEN, CT." They were sold freely to the public and could be used on any class of mail at all post offices during the experimental program and thereafter.

Most copies of No. 1384c show orange where the offset green was. Value is for this variety. Copies without orange sell for more.

Cured Child — A807

"Old Models" — A808

HOPE FOR CRIPPLED ISSUE

Issued to encourage the rehabilitation of crippled children and adults and to honor the National Society for Crippled Children and Adults (Easter Seal Society) on its 50th anniversary.

Designed by Mark English.

LITHOGRAPHED, ENGRAVED (Giori)
Plates of 200 subjects in four panes of 50.

1969, Nov. 20	Tagged	Perf. 11	
1385 A807 6c multicolored		.20	.20
P# block of 4		.50	—
Margin block of 4, Mr. Zip and "Use Zip Code"		.45	—

WILLIAM M. HARNETT ISSUE

Harnett (1848-1892), painter. The painting hangs in the Museum of Fine Arts, Boston.

Designed by Robert J. Jones.

LITHOGRAPHED, ENGRAVED (Giori)
Plates of 128 subjects in 4 panes of 32 each.

1969, Dec. 3	Tagged	Perf. 11	
1386 A808 6c multicolored		.20	.20
P# block of 4		.55	—
Margin block of 4, Mr. Zip and "Use Zip Code"		.45	—

NATURAL HISTORY ISSUE

Centenary of the American Museum of Natural History, New York City. Nos. 1387-1388 alternate in 1st row, Nos. 1389-1390 in 2nd row. This arrangement is repeated throughout the pane.

American Bald Eagle — A809

African Elephant Herd A810

Tlingit Chief in Haida Ceremonial Canoe — A811

Brontosaurus, Stegosaurus and Allosaurus from Jurassic Period — A812

Designers: No. 1387, Walter Richards; No. 1388, Dean Ellis; No. 1389, Paul Rabut; No. 1390, detail from mural by Rudolph Zallinger in Yale Peabody Museum, adapted by Robert J. Jones.

LITHOGRAPHED, ENGRAVED (Giori)
Plates of 128 subjects in 4 panes of 32 each (4x8).

1970, May 6	Tagged	Perf. 11	
1387 A809 6c multicolored		.20	.20
1388 A810 6c multicolored		.20	.20
1389 A811 6c multicolored		.20	.20
1390 A812 6c multicolored		.20	.20
a. Block of 4, #1387-1390		.55	.60
P# block of 4		.70	—
Margin block of 4, Mr. Zip and "Use Zip Code"		.60	—

MAINE STATEHOOD, 150th ANNIV.

The painting hangs in the Metropolitan Museum of Art, New York City.

The Lighthouse at Two Lights, Maine, by Edward Hopper — A813

Designed by Stevan Dohanos.

LITHOGRAPHED, ENGRAVED (Giori)
Plates of 200 subjects in four panes of 50.

1970, July 9	Tagged	Perf. 11	
1391 A813 6c black & multicolored		.20	.20
P# block of 4		.50	—
Margin block of 4, Mr. Zip and "Use Zip Code"		.45	—

WILDLIFE CONSERVATION ISSUE

American Buffalo — A814

Designed by Robert Lougheed.

ROTARY PRESS PRINTING
E.E. Plates of 200 subjects in four panes of 50.

1970, July 20	Tagged	Perf. 11x10½	
1392 A814 6c black, light brown		.20	.20
P# block of 4		.50	—
Margin block of 4, Mr. Zip and "Use Zip Code"		.45	—

REGULAR ISSUE
Dwight David Eisenhower

Dot between "R" and "U" — A815

No Dot between "R" and "U" — A815a

Benjamin Franklin — A816

U.S. Postal Service Emblem — A817

Fiorello H. LaGuardia A817a

Dr. Elizabeth Blackwell A818a

Ernest Taylor Pyle A818

Amadeo P. Giannini A818b

Designers: Nos. 1393-1395, 1401-1402, Robert Geissman; photograph by George Tames. 7c, Bill Hyde. No. 1396, Raymond Loewy/William Smith, Inc. 14c, Robert Geissman; photograph by George Fayer. 16c, Robert Geissman; photograph by Alfred Eisenstadt. 18c, Robert Geissman; painting by Joseph Kozlowski. 21c, Robert Geissman.

ROTARY PRESS PRINTING
E.E. Plates of 400 subjects in four panes of 100.

1970-74		**Tagged**	**Perf. 11x10½**	
1393	A815	6c **dark blue gray,** shiny gum, Aug. 6, 1970	.20	.20
		P# block of 4	.50	—
		Margin block of 4, "Use Zip Codes"	.45	—
		Dull gum	.20	
		P# block of 4	1.00	
		Zip block of 4	.55	
a.		Booklet pane of 8, shiny gum	1.50	*.65*
		Dull gum	1.90	
b.		Booklet pane of 5 + label	1.50	*.65*
c.		Untagged (Bureau precanceled)		.20

Perf. 10½x11

g.		Tagging omitted (not Bureau precanceled)		—
1393D	A816	7c **bright blue,** shiny gum, Oct. 20, 1972	.20	.20
		P# block of 4	.60	—
		Margin block of 4, "Use Zip Codes"	.55	—
		Dull gum	.20	
		P# block of 4	1.25	
		Zip block of 4	.90	
e.		Untagged (Bureau precanceled)		.20
f.		Tagging omitted (not Bureau precanceled)	4.00	

GIORI PRESS PRINTING
Plates of 400 subjects in four panes of 100.
Perf. 11

1394	A815a	8c **black, red & blue gray,** May 10, 1971	.20	.20
		P# block of 4	.60	—
		Margin block of 4, "Use Zip Codes"	.55	—
		Pair with full vert. gutter btwn.		
a.		Tagging omitted	4.00	—

ROTARY PRESS PRINTING
Perf. 11x10½ on 2 or 3 sides

1395	A815	8c **deep claret,** shiny gum (from blkt. pane)	.20	.20
		Dull gum	.20	
a.		Booklet pane of 8, shiny gum, May 10, 1971	1.80	*1.25*
b.		Booklet pane of 6, shiny gum, May 10, 1971	1.25	*.90*
c.		Booklet pane of 4 + 2 labels, dull gum, Jan. 28, 1972	1.65	*.80*
d.		Booklet pane of 7 + label, dull gum, Jan. 28, 1972	1.90	*1.00*

No. 1395 was issued only in booklets.

PHOTOGRAVURE (Andreotti)
Plates of 400 subjects in four panes of 100.
Perf. 11x10½

1396	A817	8c **multicolored,** July 1, 1971	.20	.20
		P# block of 12, 6#	2.00	
		P# block of 20, 6#, "Mail Early in the Day," "Use Zip Codes" and rectangular color contents (UL pane)	3.25	
		Margin block of 4, "Use Zip Codes"	.65	

ROTARY PRESS PRINTING
E.E. Plates of 400 subjects in four panes of 100.

1397	A817a	14c **gray brown,** Apr. 24, 1972	.25	.20
		P# block of 4	1.15	—
		Margin block of 4, "Use Zip Codes"	1.05	—
a.		Untagged (Bureau precanceled)		.25
1398	A818	16c **brown,** May 7, 1971	.30	.20
		P# block of 4	1.25	—
		Margin block of 4, "Use Zip Codes"	1.20	—
a.		Untagged (Bureau precanceled)		.35
b.		Tagging omitted (not Bureau precanceled)	—	—
1399	A818a	18c **violet,** Jan. 23, 1974	.35	—
		P# block of 4	1.50	—
		Margin block of 4, "Use Zip Codes"	1.40	—
1400	A818b	21c **green,** June 27, 1973	.40	.20
		P# block of 4	1.65	—
		Margin block of 4, "Use Zip Codes"	1.60	—
		Nos. 1393-1400 (9)	2.30	1.80

Bureau Precancels: 6c, 6 diff., 7c, 13 diff., No. 1394, 24 diff., 14c, 3 diff., 16c, NYC, 3 diff. Greensboro, NC.

COIL STAMPS
ROTARY PRESS PRINTING

1970-71		**Tagged**	**Perf. 10 Vert.**	
1401	A815	6c **dark blue gray,** shiny gum, Aug. 6, 1970	.20	.20
		Pair	.30	.20
		Joint line pair	.50	.20
		Dull gum	.30	
		Joint line pair	1.40	
a.		Untagged (Bureau precanceled)		.20
b.		Imperf., pair	2,000.	

		Joint line pair	—	
1402	A815	8c **deep claret,** May 10, 1971	.20	.20
		Pair	.30	.20
		Joint line pair	.55	.20
a.		Imperf., pair	45.00	
		Joint line pair	70.00	
b.		Untagged (Bureau precanceled)		.20
c.		Pair, imperf. between	6,250.	

Bureau Precancels: 6c, 4 diff., 8c, 34 diff.

EDGAR LEE MASTERS ISSUE

Edgar Lee Masters (1869-1950), Poet — A819

Designed by Fred Otnes.

LITHOGRAPHED, ENGRAVED (Giori)
E.E. Plates of 200 subjects in four panes of 50.

1970, Aug. 22		**Tagged**	**Perf. 11**	
1405	A819	6c **black & olive bister**	.20	.20
		P# block of 4	.50	—
		Margin block of 4, Mr. Zip and "Use Zip Code"	.45	—
a.		Tagging omitted	30.00	

WOMAN SUFFRAGE ISSUE

50th anniversary of the 19th Amendment, which gave the vote to women.

Suffragettes, 1920, and Woman Voter, 1970 — A820

Designed by Ward Brackett.

GIORI PRESS PRINTING
Plates of 200 subjects in four panes of 50.

1970, Aug. 26		**Tagged**	**Perf. 11**	
1406	A820	6c **blue**	.20	.20
		P# block of 4	.50	—
		Margin block of 4, Mr. Zip and "Use Zip Code"	.45	—

SOUTH CAROLINA ISSUE

300th anniv. of the founding of Charles Town (Charleston), the 1st permanent settlement of South Carolina. Against a background of pine wood the line drawings of the design represent the economic and historic development of South Carolina: the spire of St. Phillip's Church, Capitol, state flag, a ship, 17th century man and woman, a Fort Sumter cannon, barrels, cotton, tobacco and yellow jasmine.

Symbols of South Carolina — A821

Designed by George Samerjan.

LITHOGRAPHED, ENGRAVED (Giori)
Plates of 200 subjects in four panes of 50.

1970, Sept. 12		**Tagged**	**Perf. 11**	
1407	A821	6c **bister, black & red**	.20	.20
		P# block of 4	.50	—
		Margin block of 4, Mr. Zip and "Use Zip Code"	.45	—

STONE MOUNTAIN MEMORIAL ISSUE

Dedication of the Stone Mountain Confederate Memorial, Georgia, May 9, 1970.

Robert E. Lee, Jefferson Davis and "Stonewall" Jackson — A822

Designed by Robert Hallock.

GIORI PRESS PRINTING
Plates of 200 subjects in four panes of 50.

1970, Sept. 19		**Tagged**	**Perf. 11**	
1408	A822	6c **gray**	.20	.20
		P# block of 4	.50	—
		Margin block of 4, Mr. Zip and "Use Zip Code"	.45	—

FORT SNELLING ISSUE

150th anniv. of Fort Snelling, Minnesota, an important outpost for the opening of the Northwest.

Fort Snelling, Keelboat and Tepees — A823

Designed by David K. Stone.

LITHOGRAPHED, ENGRAVED (Giori)
Plates of 200 in four panes of 50.

1970, Oct. 17		**Tagged**	**Perf. 11**	
1409	A823	6c **yellow & multicolored**	.20	.20
		P# block of 4	.50	—
		Margin block of 4, Mr. Zip and "Use Zip Code"	.45	—

ANTI-POLLUTION ISSUE

Issued to focus attention on the problems of pollution.

In left panes Nos. 1410 and 1412 appear in 1st, 3rd and 5th place; Nos. 1411 and 1413 in 2nd and 4th place. This arrangement is reversed in right panes.

Globe and Wheat — A824

Globe and City — A825

Globe and Bluegill — A826

Globe and Seagull — A827

Designed by Arnold Copeland and Walter DuBois Richards. Printed by Bureau of Engraving and Printing at Guilford Gravure, Inc., Guilford, Conn.

PHOTOGRAVURE
Plates of 200 subjects in four panes of 50.

1970, Oct. 28	Tagged	Perf. 11x10½	
1410 A824 6c **multicolored**		.25	.20
1411 A825 6c **multicolored**		.25	.20
1412 A826 6c **multicolored**		.25	.20
1413 A827 6c **multicolored**		.25	.20
a.	Block of 4, #1410-1413	1.10	1.25
	P# block of 10, 5#	2.25	—
	Margin block of 4, Mr. Zip and		
	"Use Zip Code"	1.25	—

CHRISTMAS ISSUE

In left panes Nos. 1415 and 1417 appear in 1st, 3rd and 5th place; Nos. 1416 and 1418 in 2nd and 4th place. This arrangement is reversed in right panes.

Nativity, by Lorenzo Lotto — A828

Tin and Cast-iron Locomotive A829

Toy Horse on Wheels — A830

Mechanical Tricycle — A831

Doll Carriage — A832

Designers: No. 1414, Howard C. Mildner, from a painting by Lorenzo Lotto (1480-1556) in the National Gallery of Art, Washington, D.C. Nos. 1415-1418, Stevan Dohanos, from a drawing (locomotive) by Charles Hemming and from "Golden Age of Toys" by Fondin and Remise.
Printed by Guilford Gravure, Inc., Guilford, Conn.

PHOTOGRAVURE
Plates of 200 subjects in four panes of 50.

1970, Nov. 5	Tagged	Perf. 10½x11	
1414 A828 6c **multicolored**		.20	.20
	P# block of 8, 4#	1.10	—
	Margin block of 4, Mr. Zip and		
	"Use Zip Code"	.50	—
a.	Precanceled	.20	.20
	P# block of 8, 4#	1.90	—
	Margin block of 4, Mr. Zip and		
	"Use Zip Code"	.70	—
b.	Black omitted	550.00	
c.	As "a," blue omitted	1,500.	
d.	Type II	.20	.20
	P# block of 8, 4#	2.75	—
	Zip block of 4	.85	—
e.	Type II, precanceled	.25	.20
	P# block of 8, 4#	4.00	—
	Zip block of 4	1.25	—

No. 1414 has pregummed paper, a slightly blurry impression, snowflaking in the sky and no gum breaker ridges. No. 1414d

has shiny surfaced paper, sharper impression, no snowflaking and vertical and horizontal gum breaker ridges.
No. 1414a has a slightly blurry impression, snowflaking in the sky, no gum breaker ridges and the precancel is grayish black. No. 1414e has sharper impression, no snowflaking, gum breaker ridges and the precancel is intense black.

	Perf. 11x10½		
1415 A829 6c **multicolored**		.30	.20
a.	Precanceled	.75	.20
b.	Black omitted	2,500.	
1416 A830 6c **multicolored**		.30	.20
a.	Precanceled	.75	.20
b.	Black omitted	2,500.	
c.	Imperf., pair (#1416, 1418)		4,000.
1417 A831 6c **multicolored**		.30	.20
a.	Precanceled	.75	.20
b.	Black omitted	2,500.	
1418 A832 6c **multicolored**		.30	.20
a.	Precanceled	.75	.20
b.	Block of 4, #1415-1418	1.25	1.50
	P# block of 8, 4#	3.25	—
	Margin block of 4, Mr. Zip and		
	"Use Zip Code"	1.25	—
c.	As "b," precanceled	3.25	3.25
	P# block of 8, 4P#	6.50	—
	Margin block of 4, Mr. Zip and		
	"Use Zip Code"	3.50	—
d.	Black omitted	2,500.	

The precanceled stamps, Nos. 1414a-1418a, were furnished to 68 cities. The plates include two straight (No. 1414a) or two wavy (Nos. 1415a-1418a) black lines that make up the precancellation. Unused values are for copies with gum and used values are for copies with an additional cancellation or without gum.

UNITED NATIONS, 25th ANNIV.

"UN" and UN Emblem — A833

Designed by Arnold Copeland.

LITHOGRAPHED, ENGRAVED (Giori)
Plates of 200 subjects in four panes of 50.

1970, Nov. 20	Tagged	Perf. 11	
1419 A833 6c **black, verm. & ultra.**		.20	.20
	P# block of 4	.50	—
	Margin block of 4, Mr. Zip and		
	"Use Zip Code"	.45	—
	Pair with full horiz. gutter btwn.		

LANDING OF THE PILGRIMS ISSUE

350th anniv. of the landing of the Mayflower.

Mayflower and Pilgrims — A834

Designed by Mark English.

LITHOGRAPHED, ENGRAVED (Giori)
Plates of 200 subjects in four panes of 50.

1970, Nov. 21	Tagged	Perf. 11	
1420 A834 6c **blk., org., yel., magenta, bl. & brn.**		.20	.20
	P# block of 4	.50	—
	Margin block of 4, Mr. Zip and		
	"Use Zip Code"	.45	—
a.	Orange & yellow omitted	900.00	

DISABLED AMERICAN VETERANS AND SERVICEMEN ISSUE

No. 1421 for the 50th anniv. of the Disabled Veterans of America Organization; No. 1422 honors the contribution of servicemen, particularly those who were prisoners of war, missing or killed in action. Nos. 1421-1422 are printed se-tenant in horizontal rows of 10.

Disabled American Veterans Emblem — A835

A836

Designed by Stevan Dohanos.

LITHOGRAPHED, ENGRAVED (Giori)
Plates of 200 subjects in four panes of 50.

1970, Nov. 24	Tagged	Perf. 11	
1421 A835 6c **dark blue, red & multicolored**		.20	.20

ENGRAVED

1422 A836 6c **dark blue, black & red**		.20	.20
a.	Pair, #1421-1422	.30	.30
	P# block of 4	1.00	—
	Margin block of 4, Mr. Zip and		
	"Use Zip Code"	.65	—

Ewe and Lamb — A837

Gen. Douglas MacArthur — A838

AMERICAN WOOL INDUSTRY ISSUE

450th anniv. of the introduction of sheep to the North American continent and the beginning of the American wool industry.

Designed by Dean Ellis.

LITHOGRAPHED, ENGRAVED (Giori)
Plates of 200 subjects in four panes of 50.

1971, Jan. 19	Tagged	Perf. 11	
1423 A837 6c **multicolored**		.20	.20
	P# block of 4	.50	—
	Margin block of 4, Mr. Zip and		
	"Use Zip Code"	.45	—
a.	Tagging omitted	9.00	—
b.	Teal blue ("United States") omitted		

No. 1423b was caused by the misregistration of the engraved printing.

GEN. DOUGLAS MacARTHUR ISSUE

MacArthur (1880-1964), Chief of Staff, Supreme Commander for the Allied Powers in the Pacific Area during World War II and Supreme Commander in Japan after the war.

Designed by Paul Calle; Wide World photograph.

GIORI PRESS PRINTING
Plates of 200 subjects in four panes of 50.

1971, Jan. 26	Tagged	Perf. 11	
1424 A838 6c **black, red & dark blue**		.20	.20
	P# block of 4	.50	—
	Margin block of 4, Mr. Zip and		
	"Use Zip Code"	.45	—

BLOOD DONOR ISSUE

Salute to blood donors and spur to increased participation in the blood donor program.

"Giving Blood Saves Lives" — A839

Designed by Howard Munce.

LITHOGRAPHED, ENGRAVED (Giori)
Plates of 200 subjects in four panes of 50.

1971, Mar. 12	**Tagged**	**Perf. 11**	
1425 A839 6c **blue, scarlet & indigo**		.20	.20
P# block of 4		.50	—
Margin block of 4, Mr. Zip and "Use Zip Code"		.45	—
a. Tagging omitted		11.00	—

MISSOURI STATEHOOD, 150th ANNIV.

The stamp design shows a Pawnee facing a hunter-trapper and a group of settlers. It is from a mural by Thomas Hart Benton in the Harry S Truman Library, Independence, Mo.

"Independence and the Opening of the West," Detail, by Thomas Hart Benton — A840

Designed by Bradbury Thompson.

PHOTOGRAVURE (Andreotti)
Plates of 200 subjects in four panes of 50.

1971, May 8	**Tagged**	**Perf. 11x10½**	
1426 A840 8c **multicolored**		.20	.20
P# block of 12, 6#		2.00	—
Margin block of 4, Mr. Zip and "Use Zip Code"		.65	—

See note on Andreotti printings and their color control markings in Information for Collectors under Printing, Photogravure.

WILDLIFE CONSERVATION ISSUE

Nos. 1427-1428 alternate in first row, Nos. 1429-1430 in second row. This arrangement repeated throughout pane.

Trout A841

Alligator A842

Polar Bear and Cubs A843

California Condor — A844

Designed by Stanley W. Galli.

LITHOGRAPHED, ENGRAVED (Giori)
Plates of 128 subjects in 4 panes of 32 each (4x8).

1971, June 12	**Tagged**	**Perf. 11**	
1427 A841 8c **multicolored**		.20	.20
a. Red omitted		1,250.	

1428 A842 8c **multicolored**	.20	.20
1429 A843 8c **multicolored**	.20	.20
1430 A844 8c **multicolored**	.20	.20
a. Block of 4, #1427-1430	.80	.90
P# block of 4	.90	—
Margin block of 4, Mr. Zip and "Use Zip Code"	.85	—
b. As "a," light green & dark green omitted from #1427-1428	4,500.	
c. As "a," red omitted from #1427, 1429-1430	9,000.	

ANTARCTIC TREATY ISSUE

Map of Antarctica A845

Designed by Howard Koslow.

Adapted from emblem on official documents of Consultative Meetings.

GIORI PRESS PRINTING
Plates of 200 subjects in four panes of 50.

1971, June 23	**Tagged**	**Perf. 11**	
1431 A845 8c **red & dark blue**		.20	.20
P# block of 4		.65	—
Margin block of 4, Mr. Zip and "Use Zip Code"		.60	—
a. Tagging omitted		7.00	—
b. Both colors omitted			

No. 1431b was caused by an extraneous piece of paper blocking the impression. It should be collected se-tenant with a normal stamp and/or a partially printed stamp.

AMERICAN REVOLUTION BICENTENNIAL

Bicentennial Commission Emblem — A846

Designed by Chermayeff & Geismar.

LITHOGRAPHED, ENGRAVED (Giori)
Plates of 200 subjects in four panes of 50.

1971, July 4	**Tagged**	**Perf. 11**	
1432 A846 8c **gray, red, blue & black**		.20	.20
P# block of 4		.85	—
Margin block of 4, Mr. Zip and "Use Zip Code"		.80	—
a. Gray & black omitted		650.00	
b. Gray ("U.S. Postage 8c") omitted		1,150.	

JOHN SLOAN ISSUE

John Sloan (1871-1951), painter. The painting hangs in the Phillips Gallery, Washington, D.C.

The Wake of the Ferry — A847

Designed by Bradbury Thompson.

LITHOGRAPHED, ENGRAVED (Giori)
Plates of 200 subjects in four panes of 50.

1971, Aug. 2	**Tagged**	**Perf. 11**	
1433 A847 8c **multicolored**		.20	.20
P# block of 4		.70	—
Margin block of 4, Mr. Zip and "Use Zip Code"		.65	—
a. Tagging omitted			

SPACE ACHIEVEMENT DECADE ISSUE

Decade of space achievements and the Apollo 15 moon exploration mission, July 26-Aug. 7. In the left panes the earth and sun stamp is 1st, 3rd and 5th, the rover 2nd and 4th. This arrangement is reversed in the right panes.

Earth, Sun and Landing Craft on Moon — A848

UNITED STATES IN SPACE...

Lunar Rover and Astronauts A849

A DECADE OF ACHIEVEMENT

Designed by Robert McCall.

LITHOGRAPHED, ENGRAVED (Giori)
Plates of 200 subjects in four panes of 50.

1971, Aug. 2	**Tagged**	**Perf. 11**	
1434 A848 8c **black, blue, gray, yellow & red**		.20	.20
a. Tagging omitted		25.00	
1435 A849 8c **black, blue, gray, yellow & red**		.20	.20
a. Tagging omitted		25.00	
b. Pair, #1434-1435		.40	.45
P# block of 4		.65	—
Margin block of 4, Mr. Zip and "Use Zip Code"		.60	—
c. As "b," tagging omitted			
d. As "b," blue & red (litho.) omitted		1,500.	

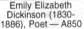

Emily Dickinson American Poet

Emily Elizabeth Dickinson (1830-1886), Poet — A850

Sentry Box, Morro Castle, San Juan — A851

EMILY DICKINSON ISSUE

Designed by Bernard Fuchs after a photograph.

LITHOGRAPHED, ENGRAVED (Giori)
Plates of 200 subjects in four panes of 50.

1971, Aug. 28	**Tagged**	**Perf. 11**	
1436 A850 8c **multicolored,** greenish		.20	.20
P# block of 4		.65	—
Margin block of 4, Mr. Zip and "Use Zip Code"		.60	—
a. Black & olive (engr.) omitted		800.00	
b. Pale rose omitted		7,500.	
c. Red omitted			

SAN JUAN ISSUE

450th anniversary of San Juan, Puerto Rico.

Designed as a woodcut by Walter Brooks.

LITHOGRAPHED, ENGRAVED (Giori)
Plates of 200 subjects in four panes of 50.

1971, Sept. 12	**Tagged**	**Perf. 11**	
1437 A851 8c **pale brown, black, yellow & dark brown**		.20	.20
P# block of 4		.65	—
Margin block of 4, Mr. Zip and "Use Zip Code"		.60	—
a. Tagging omitted		7.50	

VALUES FOR HINGED STAMPS AFTER NO. 771

This catalogue does not value unused stamps after No. 771 in hinged condition. Hinged unused stamps from No. 772 to the present are worth considerably less than the values given for unused stamps, which are for never-hinged examples.

Young Woman Drug
Addict — A852

Hands Reaching for
CARE — A853

PREVENT DRUG ABUSE ISSUE

Drug Abuse Prevention Week, Oct. 3-9.

Designed by Miggs Burroughs.

PHOTOGRAVURE (Andreotti)
Plates of 200 subjects in four panes of 50.

1971, Oct. 4	Tagged	Perf. 10½x11	
1438 A852 8c blue, deep blue & black		.20	.20
P# block of 6, 3#		1.00	—
Margin block of 4, "Use Zip Code"		.65	

CARE ISSUE

25th anniversary of CARE, a US-Canadian Cooperative for American Relief Everywhere.

Designed by Soren Noring

PHOTOGRAVURE (Andreotti)
Plates of 200 subjects in four panes of 50.

1971, Oct. 27	Tagged	Perf. 10½x11	
1439 A853 8c blue, blk., vio. & red lilac		.20	.20
P# block of 8, 4#		1.25	—
Margin block of 4, Mr. Zip and "Use Zip Code"		.65	—
a. Black omitted		4,750.	
b. Tagging omitted		5.00	

HISTORIC PRESERVATION ISSUE

Nos. 1440-1441 alternate in 1st row, Nos. 1442-1443 in 2nd row. This arrangement is repeated throughout the pane.

Decatur House, Washington, D.C. — A854

Whaling
Ship
Charles
W.
Morgan,
Mystic,
Conn.
A855

Cable Car, San Francisco — A856

San
Xavier
del Bac
Mission,
Tucson,
Ariz.
A857

Designed by Melbourne Brindle.

LITHOGRAPHED, ENGRAVED (Giori)

1971, Oct. 29	Tagged	Perf. 11	
1440 A854 8c black brown & ocher, buff		.20	.20
1441 A855 8c black brown & ocher, buff		.20	.20
1442 A856 8c black brown & ocher, buff		.20	.20
1443 A857 8c black brown & ocher, buff		.20	.20
a. Block of 4, #1440-1443		.75	.85
P# block of 4		.90	
Margin block of 4, Mr. Zip and "Use Zip Code"		.80	—
b. As "a," black brown omitted		2,250.	
c. As "a," ocher omitted		—	
d. As "a," tagging omitted		60.00	

CHRISTMAS ISSUE

Adoration of the
Shepherds, by
Giorgione — A858

"Partridge in a Pear
Tree" — A859

Designers: No. 1444, Bradbury Thompson, using a painting by Giorgione in the National Gallery of Art, Washington, D.C. No. 1445, Jamie Wyeth.

PHOTOGRAVURE (Andreotti)
Plates of 200 subjects in four panes of 50.

1971, Nov. 10	Tagged	Perf. 10½x11	
1444 A858 8c gold & multicolored		.20	.20
P# block of 12, 6#		1.80	—
Margin block of 4, Mr. Zip and "Use Zip Code"		.60	—
a. Gold omitted		550.00	
1445 A859 8c dark green, red & multicolored		.20	.20
P# block of 12, 6#		1.80	—
Margin block of 4, Mr. Zip and "Use Zip Code"		.60	—

Sidney
Lanier — A860

Peace Corps
Poster, by David
Battle — A861

SIDNEY LANIER ISSUE

Lanier (1842-81), poet, musician, lawyer, educator.

Designed by William A. Smith.

GIORI PRESS PRINTING
Plates of 200 subjects in four panes of 50.

1972, Feb. 3	Tagged	Perf. 11	
1446 A860 8c black, brown & light blue		.20	.20
P# block of 4		.65	—
Margin block of 4, Mr. Zip and "Use Zip Code"		.60	—
a. Tagging omitted		15.00	

PEACE CORPS ISSUE

Designed by Bradbury Thompson.

PHOTOGRAVURE (Andreotti)
Plates of 200 subjects in four panes of 50.

1972, Feb. 11	Tagged	Perf. 10½x11	
1447 A861 8c dark blue, light blue & red		.20	.20
P# block of 6, 3#		1.00	—
Margin block of 4, Mr. Zip and "Use Zip Code"		.65	—
a. Tagging omitted		5.00	

NATIONAL PARKS CENTENNIAL ISSUE

Centenary of Yellowstone National Park, the 1st National Park, and of the entire National Park System. See No. C84.

A862   A863

A864   A865
Cape Hatteras National Seashore

Wolf Trap Farm,
Va. — A866

Old Faithful,
Yellowstone — A867

Mt. McKinley,
Alaska — A868

Designers: 2c, Walter D. Richards; 6c, Howard Koslow; 8c, Robert Handville; 15c, James Barkley.

LITHOGRAPHED, ENGRAVED (Giori)

1972	Tagged	Perf. 11	
Plates of 400 subjects in 4 panes of 100 each			
1448 A862 2c black & multi., Apr. 5		.20	.20
1449 A863 2c black & multi., Apr. 5		.20	.20
1450 A864 2c black & multi., Apr. 5		.20	.20
1451 A865 2c black & multi., Apr. 5		.20	.20
a. Block of 4, #1448-1451		.25	.25
P# block of 4		.50	—
Margin block of 4, "Use Zip Codes"		.30	
b. As "a," black (litho.) omitted		2,750.	
c. As "a," tagging omitted		—	
Plates of 200 subjects in four panes of 50 each			
1452 A866 6c black & multicolored, June 26		.20	.20
P# block of 4		.55	—
Margin block of 4, Mr. Zip and "Use Zip Code"		.50	—
a. Tagging omitted		9.00	
Plates of 128 subjects in four panes of 32 (8x4)			
1453 A867 8c blk., blue, brn. & multi., Mar. 1		.20	.20
P# block of 4		.70	—
Margin block of 4, Mr. Zip and "Use Zip Code"		.65	—
a. Tagging omitted		15.00	
Plates of 200 subjects in four panes of 50 each			
1454 A868 15c black & multi., July 28		.30	.20
P# block of 4		1.30	—
Margin block of 4, Mr. Zip		1.25	—
a. Tagging omitted		—	

FAMILY PLANNING ISSUE

Family — A869

LITHOGRAPHED, ENGRAVED (Giori)
Plates of 200 subjects in four panes of 50.

1972, Mar. 18	Tagged	Perf. 11	
1455 A869 8c **black & multicolored**		.20	.20
P# block of 4		.65	—
Margin block of 4, Mr. Zip and			
"Use Zip Code"		.60	—
a. Yellow omitted		1,250.	
b. Dark brown & olive omitted		—	
c. Dark brown omitted		9,500.	

AMERICAN BICENTENNIAL ISSUE
Colonial American Craftsmen

In left panes Nos. 1456 and 1458 appear in 1st, 3rd and 5th place; Nos. 1457 and 1459 in 2nd and 4th place. This arrangement is reversed in right panes.

Glass Blower — A870

Silversmith A871

Wigmaker A872

Hatter — A873

Designed by Leonard Everett Fisher.

ENGRAVED
E.E. Plates of 200 subjects in four panes of 50.

1972, July 4	Tagged	Perf. 11x10½	
1456 A870 8c **deep brown,** *dull yellow*		.20	.20
1457 A871 8c **deep brown,** *dull yellow*		.20	.20
1458 A872 8c **deep brown,** *dull yellow*		.20	.20
1459 A873 8c **deep brown,** *dull yellow*		.20	.20
a. Block of 4, #1456-1459		.65	.75
P# block of 4		.80	—
Margin block of 4, Mr. Zip and			
"Use Zip Code"		.70	—
b. As "a," tagging omitted			

Margin includes Bicentennial Commission emblem and inscription: USA BICENTENNIAL / HONORS COLONIAL / AMERICAN CRAFTSMEN.

OLYMPIC GAMES ISSUE

11th Winter Olympic Games, Sapporo, Japan, Feb. 3-13 and 20th Summer Olympic Games, Munich, Germany, Aug. 26-Sept. 11. See No. C85.

Bicycling and Olympic Rings — A874

Bobsledding and Olympic Rings — A875

Running and Olympic Rings — A876

"Broken red ring" cylinder flaw

Designed by Lance Wyman.

PHOTOGRAVURE (Andreotti)
Plates of 200 subjects in four panes of 50.

1972, Aug. 17	Tagged	Perf. 11x10½	
1460 A874 6c **black, blue, red, emerald &**			
yellow		.20	.20
P# block of 10, 5#		1.25	—
Margin block of 4, Mr. Zip and			
"Use Zip Code"		.50	—
Cylinder flaw (broken red ring)			
(33313 UL 43)		10.00	
1461 A875 8c **black, blue, red, emerald &**			
yellow		.20	.20
P# block of 10, 5#		1.60	—
Margin block of 4, Mr. Zip and			
"Use Zip Code"		.65	—
a. Tagging omitted		5.00	
1462 A876 15c **black, blue, red, emerald & yel**		.30	.20
P# block of 10, 5#		3.00	—
Margin block of 4, Mr. Zip and			
"Use Zip Code"		1.15	—
Nos. 1460-1462 (3)		.70	.60

PARENT TEACHER ASSN., 75th ANNIV.

Blackboard — A877

Designed by Arthur S. Congdon III.

PHOTOGRAVURE (Andreotti)
Plates of 200 subjects in four panes of 50.

1972, Sept. 15	Tagged	Perf. 11x10½	
1463 A877 8c **yellow & black**		.20	.20
P# block of 4, 2#		.65	—
P# block of 4, yellow # reversed		.75	—
Margin block of 4, Mr. Zip and			
"Use Zip Code"		.60	—

WILDLIFE CONSERVATION ISSUE

Nos. 1464-1465 alternate in 1st row, Nos. 1468-1469 in 2nd row. This arrangement repeated throughout pane.

Fur Seals A878

Cardinal A879

Brown Pelican A880

Bighorn Sheep A881

Designed by Stanley W. Galli.

LITHOGRAPHED, ENGRAVED (Giori)
Plates of 128 subjects in 4 panes of 32 (4x8).

1972, Sept. 20	Tagged	Perf. 11	
1464 A878 8c **multicolored**		.20	.20
1465 A879 8c **multicolored**		.20	.20
1466 A880 8c **multicolored**		.20	.20
1467 A881 8c **multicolored**		.20	.20
a. Block of 4, #1464-1467		.65	.75
P# block of 4		.75	—
Margin block of 4, Mr. Zip and			
"Use Zip Code"		.70	—
b. As "a," brown omitted		4,000.	
c. As "a," green & blue omitted		4,750.	
d. As "a," red & brown omitted		4,000.	

MAIL ORDER BUSINESS ISSUE

Centenary of mail order business, originated by Aaron Montgomery Ward, Chicago. Design based on Headsville, W.Va., post office in Smithsonian Institution, Washington, D.C.

Rural Post Office Store — A882

Designed by Robert Lambdin.

PHOTOGRAVURE (Andreotti)
Plates of 200 subjects in four panes of 50.

1972, Sept. 27	Tagged	Perf. 11x10½	
1468 A882 8c **multicolored**		.20	.20
P# block of 12, 6#		1.75	—
Margin block of 4, Mr. Zip and			
"Use Zip Code"		.60	—

The tagging on No. 1468 consists of a vertical bar of phosphor 10mm wide.

Man's Quest for
Health — A883

Tom Sawyer, by
Norman
Rockwell — A884

OSTEOPATHIC MEDICINE ISSUE

75th anniv. of the American Osteopathic Assoc.,
founded by Dr. Andrew T. Still (1828-1917), who
developed the principles of osteopathy in 1874.

Designed by V. Jack Ruther.

PHOTOGRAVURE (Andreotti)
Plates of 200 subjects in four panes of 50.

1972, Oct. 9	Tagged	Perf. 10½x11	
1469 A883 8c multicolored		.20	.20
P# block of 6, 3#		1.00	—
Margin block of 4, Mr. Zip and "Use Zip Code"		.65	—

AMERICAN FOLKLORE ISSUE
Tom Sawyer

Designed by Bradbury Thompson.

LITHOGRAPHED, ENGRAVED (Giori)
Plates of 200 subjects in four panes of 50.

1972, Oct. 13	Tagged	Perf. 11	
1470 A884 8c black, red, yellow, tan, blue & rose red		.20	.20
P# block of 4		.65	—
Margin block of 4, Mr. Zip and "Use Zip Code"		.60	—
a. Horiz. pair, imperf. between		4,500.	
b. Red & black (engr.) omitted		1,900.	
c. Yellow & tan (litho.) omitted		2,400.	
d. Tagging omitted		—	

CHRISTMAS ISSUE

Angels from "Mary,
Queen of
Heaven" — A885

Santa
Claus — A886

Designers: No. 1471, Bradbury Thompson, using detail from
a painting by the Master of the St. Lucy legend, in the National
Gallery of Art, Washington, D.C. No. 1472, Stevan Dohanos.

PHOTOGRAVURE (Andreotti)
Plates of 200 subjects in four panes of 50.

1972, Nov. 9	Tagged	Perf. 10½x11	
1471 A885 8c multicolored		.20	.20
P# block of 12, 6#		1.75	—
Margin block of 4, Mr. Zip and "Use Zip Code"		.60	—
a. Pink omitted		150.00	
b. Black omitted		4,000.	
1472 A886 8c multicolored		.20	.20
P# block of 12, 6#		1.75	—
Margin block of 4, Mr. Zip and "Use Zip Code"		.60	—

PHARMACY ISSUE

Honoring American druggists in connection with the
120th anniversary of the American Pharmaceutical
Association.

Mortar and Pestle,
Bowl of Hygeia,
19th Century
Medicine
Bottles — A887

Designed by Ken Davies.

LITHOGRAPHED, ENGRAVED (Giori)
Plates of 200 subjects in four panes of 50.

1972, Nov. 10	Tagged	Perf. 11	
1473 A887 8c black & multicolored		.20	.20
P# block of 4		.65	—
Margin block of 4, Mr. Zip and "Use Zip Code"		.60	
a. Blue & orange omitted		825.00	
b. Blue omitted		2,250.	
c. Orange omitted		2,250.	

STAMP COLLECTING ISSUE

Issued to publicize stamp collecting.

U.S. No. 1 under
Magnifying
Glass — A888

Designed by Frank E. Livia.

LITHOGRAPHED, ENGRAVED (Giori)
Plates of 160 subjects in four panes of 40.

1972, Nov. 17	Tagged	Perf. 11	
1474 A888 8c multicolored		.20	.20
P# block of 4		.65	—
Margin block of 4, Mr. Zip and "Use Zip Code"		.60	—
a. Black (litho.) omitted		700.00	

LOVE ISSUE

"Love," by Robert
Indiana — A889

Designed by Robert Indiana.

PHOTOGRAVURE (Andreotti)
Plates of 200 subjects in four panes of 50.

1973, Jan. 26	Tagged	Perf. 11x10½	
1475 A889 8c red, emerald & violet blue		.20	.20
P# block of 6, 3#		1.00	—
Margin block of 4, Mr. Zip and "Use Zip Code"		.65	—

AMERICAN BICENTENNIAL ISSUE
Communications in Colonial Times

Printer and
Patriots
Examining
Pamphlet — A890

Posting a
Broadside
A891

Postrider — A892

Drummer
A893

Designed by William A. Smith.

GIORI PRESS PRINTING
Plates of 200 subjects in four panes of 50.

1973	Tagged	Perf. 11	
1476 A890 8c ultra., greenish blk. & red, Feb. 16		.20	.20
P# block of 4		.65	—
Margin block of 4, Mr. Zip and "Use Zip Code"		.60	—
a. Tagging omitted		—	
1477 A891 8c black, vermilion & ultra., Apr. 13		.20	.20
P# block of 4		.65	—
Margin block of 4, Mr. Zip and "Use Zip Code"		.60	—
Pair with full horiz. gutter btwn.		—	

LITHOGRAPHED, ENGRAVED (Giori)

1478 A892 8c blue, black, red & green, June 22		.20	.20
P# block of 4		.65	—
Margin block of 4, Mr. Zip and "Use Zip Code"		.60	—
1479 A893 8c blue, black, yellow & red, Sept. 28		.20	.20
P# block of 4		.65	—
Margin block of 4, Mr. Zip and "Use Zip Code"		.60	—
Nos. 1476-1479 (4)		.80	.80

Margin of Nos. 1477-1479 includes Bicentennial Commission
emblem and inscription.

AMERICAN BICENTENNIAL ISSUE
Boston Tea Party

In left panes Nos. 1480 and 1482 appear in 1st, 3rd
and 5th place, Nos. 1481 and 1483 appear in 2nd and
4th place. This arrangement is reversed in right panes.

British
Merchantman
A894

British Three-
master
A895

Boats and Ship's
Hull — A896

Boat and
Dock — A897

Designed by William A. Smith.

LITHOGRAPHED, ENGRAVED (Giori)
Plates of 200 subjects in four panes of 50.

1973, July 4	Tagged	Perf. 11	
1480 A894 8c black & multicolored		.20	.20
1481 A895 8c black & multicolored		.20	.20
1482 A896 8c black & multicolored		.20	.20
1483 A897 8c black & multicolored		.20	.20
a. Block of 4, #1480-1483		.65	.75
P# block of 4		.75	—
Margin block of 4, Mr. Zip and "Use Zip Code"		.70	—
b. As "a," black (engraved) omitted		1,500.	
c. As "a," black (litho.) omitted		1,400.	

Margin includes Bicentennial Commission emblem and
inscription.

AMERICAN ARTS ISSUE

George Gershwin (1898-1937), composer (No.
1484); Robinson Jeffers (1887-1962), poet (No.
1485); Henry Ossawa Tanner (1859-1937), black
painter (No. 1486); Willa Cather (1873-1947), novelist
(No. 1487).

Gershwin, Sportin' Life, Porgy and Bess — A898

Robinson Jeffers, Man and Children of Carmel with Burro — A899

Henry Ossawa Tanner, Palette and Rainbow — A900

Willa Cather, Pioneer Family and Covered Wagon — A901

Designed by Mark English.

PHOTOGRAVURE (Andreotti)
Plates of 160 subjects in four panes of 40.

1973	Tagged	Perf. 11	
1484 A898 8c dp. green & multi., Feb. 28		.20	.20
P# block of 12, 6#		1.75	—
Margin block of 4, Mr. Zip, "Use Zip Code" and "Mail Early in the Day"		.60	—
P# block of 16, 6#, Mr. Zip and slogans		2.50	—
a. Vertical pair, imperf. horiz.		240.00	
1485 A899 8c Prussian blue & multi., Aug. 13		.20	.20
P# block of 12, 6#		1.75	—
Margin block of 4, Mr. Zip, "Use Zip Code" "Mail Early in the Day"		.60	—
P# block of 16, 6#, Mr. Zip and slogans		2.50	—
a. Vertical pair, imperf. horiz.		250.00	
1486 A900 8c yellow brown & multi., Sept. 10		.20	.20
P# block of 12, 6#		1.75	—
Margin block of 4, Mr. Zip, "Use Zip Code" "Mail Early in the Day"		.60	—
P# block of 16, 6#, Mr. Zip and slogans		2.50	—
1487 A901 8c deep brown & multi., Sept. 20		.20	.20
P# block of 12, 6#		1.75	—
Margin block of 4, Mr. Zip, "Use Zip Code" "Mail Early in the Day"		.60	—
P# block of 16, 6#, Mr. Zip and slogans		2.50	—
a. Vertical pair, imperf. horiz.		275.00	
Nos. 1484-1487 (4)		.80	.80

COPERNICUS ISSUE

Nicolaus Copernicus (1473-1543), Polish Astronomer — A902

Designed by Alvin Eisenman after 18th century engraving.

LITHOGRAPHED, ENGRAVED (Giori)
Plates of 200 subjects in four panes of 50.

1973, Apr. 23	Tagged	Perf. 11	
1488 A902 8c black & orange		.20	.20
P# block of 4		.65	—
Margin block of 4, Mr. Zip and "Use Zip Code"		.60	—
a. Orange omitted		1,000.	
b. Black (engraved) omitted		1,000.	
c. Tagging omitted		—	

The orange can be chemically removed. Expertization of No. 1488a is recommended.

POSTAL SERVICE EMPLOYEES ISSUE

A tribute to US Postal Service employees. Nos. 1489-1498 are printed se-tenant in horizontal rows of 10. Emerald inscription on back, printed beneath gum in water-soluble ink, includes Postal Service emblem, "People Serving You" and a statement, differing for each of the 10 stamps, about some aspect of postal service.

Each stamp in top or bottom row has a tab with blue inscription enumerating various jobs in postal service.

Stamp Counter — A903

Mail Collection — A904

Letter Facing on Conveyor Belt — A905

Parcel Post Sorting — A906

Mail Canceling — A907

Manual Letter Routing — A908

Electronic Letter Routing — A909

Loading Mail on Truck — A910

Mailman — A911

Rural Mail Delivery — A912

Designed by Edward Vebell.

PHOTOGRAVURE (Andreotti)
Plates of 200 subjects in four panes of 50.

1973, Apr. 30	Tagged	Perf. 10½x11	
1489 A903 8c multicolored		.20	.20
1490 A904 8c multicolored		.20	.20
1491 A905 8c multicolored		.20	.20
1492 A906 8c multicolored		.20	.20
1493 A907 8c multicolored		.20	.20
1494 A908 8c multicolored		.20	.20
1495 A909 8c multicolored		.20	.20
1496 A910 8c multicolored		.20	.20
1497 A911 8c multicolored		.20	.20
1498 A912 8c multicolored		.20	.20
a. Strip of 10, #1489-1498		1.75	1.75
P# block of 20, 5# and 10 tabs		3.25	—

The tagging on Nos. 1489-1498 consists of a ½-inch horizontal band of phosphor.

HARRY S TRUMAN ISSUE

Harry S Truman, 33rd President, (1884-1972) — A913

Designed by Bradbury Thompson; photograph by Leo Stern.

GIORI PRESS PRINTING
Plates of 128 subjects in four panes of 32 each.

1973, May 8	Tagged	Perf. 11	
1499 A913 8c carmine rose, black & blue		.20	.20
P# block of 4		.65	—
a. Tagging omitted		7.50	

ELECTRONICS PROGRESS ISSUE
See No. C86.

Marconi's Spark Coil and Spark Gap — A914

Transistors and Printed Circuit Board — A915

Microphone, Speaker, Vacuum Tube and TV Camera Tube — A916

Designed by Walter and Naiad Einsel.

LITHOGRAPHED, ENGRAVED (Giori)
Plates of 200 subjects in four panes of 50.

1973, July 10	Tagged	Perf. 11	
1500 A914	6c lilac & multicolored	.20	.20
	P# block of 4	.55	
	Margin block of 4, Mr. Zip and		
	"Use Zip Code"	.50	—
a.	Tagging omitted	—	
1501 A915	8c tan & multicolored	.20	.20
	P# block of 4	.70	—
	Margin block of 4, Mr. Zip and		
	"Use Zip Code"	.65	—
a.	Black (inscriptions & "U.S. 8c") omitted	500.00	
b.	Tan (background) & lilac omitted	1,250.	

Many examples of No. 1501b are hinged. Value about one-half never hinged value.

1502 A916	15c gray green & multicolored	.30	.20
	P# block of 4	1.30	
	Margin block of 4, Mr. Zip and		
	"Use Zip Code"	1.20	
a.	Black (inscriptions & "U.S. 15c") omitted	1,500.	
	Nos. 1500-1502 (3)	.70	.60

LYNDON B. JOHNSON ISSUE

Lyndon B. Johnson, 36th President (1908-1973) — A917

Designed by Bradbury Thompson, portrait by Elizabeth Shoumatoff.

PHOTOGRAVURE (Andreotti)
Plates of 128 subjects in four panes of 32 each.

1973, Aug. 27	Tagged	Perf. 11	
1503 A917	8c black & multicolored, Aug. 27	.20	.20
	P# block of 12, 6#	1.90	
a.	Horiz. pair, imperf. vert.	350.00	

RURAL AMERICA ISSUE

Centenary of the introduction of Aberdeen Angus cattle into the US (#1504); of the Chautauqua Institution (#1505); and of the introduction of hard winter wheat into Kansas by Mennonite immigrants (#1506).

Angus and Longhorn Cattle — A918

Chautauqua Tent and Buggies — A919

Wheat Fields and Train — A920

No. 1504 modeled by Frank Waslick after painting by F. C. "Frank" Murphy. Nos. 1505-1506 designed by John Falter.

LITHOGRAPHED, ENGRAVED (Giori)
Plates of 200 subjects in four panes of 50.

1973-74	Tagged	Perf. 11	
1504 A918	8c multicolored, Oct. 5, 1973	.20	.20
	P# block of 4	.65	—
	Margin block of 4, Mr. Zip and		
	"Use Zip Code"	.60	—
a.	Green & red brown omitted	950.00	
b.	Vert. pair, imperf. between		
c.	Tagging omitted	—	

1505 A919	10c multicolored, Aug. 6, 1974	.20	.20
	P# block of 4	.85	
	Margin block of 4, Mr. Zip and		
	"Use Zip Code"	.80	—
a.	Black (litho.) omitted		
1506 A920	10c multicolored, Aug. 16, 1974	.20	.20
	P# block of 4	.85	
	Margin block of 4, Mr. Zip and		
	"Use Zip Code"	.80	—
a.	Black and blue (engr.) omitted	750.00	
b.	Tagging omitted	—	
	Nos. 1504-1506 (3)	.60	.60

CHRISTMAS ISSUE

Small Cowper Madonna, by Raphael — A921

Christmas Tree in Needlepoint — A922

Designers: No. 1507, Bradbury Thompson, using a painting in the National Gallery of Art, Washington, D.C. No. 1508, Dolli Tingle.

PHOTOGRAVURE (Andreotti)
Plates of 200 subjects in four panes of 50.

1973, Nov. 7	Tagged	Perf. 10½x11	
1507 A921	8c multicolored	.20	.20
	P# block of 12, 6#	1.75	—
	Margin block of 4, Mr. Zip and		
	"Use Zip Code"	.60	—
	Pair with full vert. gutter btwn.		
1508 A922	8c multicolored	.20	.20
	P# block of 12, 6#	1.75	—
	Margin block of 4, Mr. Zip and		
	"Use Zip Code"	.60	—
	Pair with full horiz. gutter btwn.		
a.	Vertical pair, imperf. between	300.00	

The tagging on Nos. 1507-1508 consists of a 20x12mm horizontal bar of phosphor.

50-Star and 13-Star Flags A923

Jefferson Memorial and Signature A924

Mail Transport — A925

Liberty Bell — A926

Designers: No. 1509, Ren Wicks. No. 1510, Dean Ellis. No. 1511, Randall McDougall. 6.3c, Frank Lionetti.

MULTICOLOR HUCK PRESS
Panes of 100 (10x10)

1973-74	Tagged	Perf. 11x10½	
1509 A923	10c red & blue, Dec. 8, 1973	.20	.20
	P# block of 20, 4-6#, 2-3 "Mail		
	Early" and 2-3 "Use Zip Code"	4.25	—
a.	Horizontal pair, imperf. between	50.00	
b.	Blue omitted	175.00	
c.	Imperf., vert. pair	950.00	
d.	Horiz. pair, imperf., vert.	1,000.	
e.	Tagging omitted	7.50	

ROTARY PRESS PRINTING
E.E. Plates of 400 subjects in four panes of 100.

1510 A924	10c blue, Dec. 14, 1973	.20	.20
	P# block of 4	.85	—
	Margin block of 4, "Use Zip		
	Codes"	.80	—
a.	Untagged (Bureau precanceled)		.20
b.	Booklet pane of 5 + label	1.65	.55
c.	Booklet pane of 8	1.65	.70
d.	Booklet pane of 6, Aug. 5, 1974	5.25	1.00
e.	Vert. pair, imperf. horiz.	525.00	
f.	Vert. pair, imperf. between	—	
g.	Tagging omitted (not Bureau precanceled)	5.00	

Bureau Precancels: 10 different.

PHOTOGRAVURE (Andreotti)
Plates of 400 subjects in four panes of 100.

1511 A925	10c multicolored, Jan. 4, 1974	.20	.20
	P# block of 8, 4#	1.75	—
	Margin block of 4, "Use Zip		
	Codes"	.80	—
	Pair with full horiz. gutter btwn.		
a.	Yellow omitted	65.00	

Beware of copies with yellow chemically removed offered as No. 1511a.

COIL STAMPS
ROTARY PRESS PRINTING

1973-74	Tagged	Perf. 10 Vert.	
1518 A926	6.3c brick red, Oct. 1, 1974	.20	.20
	Pair	.25	.20
	Joint line pair	.80	
a.	Untagged (Bureau precanceled)		.20
	Joint line pair		.80
b.	Imperf., pair	200.00	
	Joint line pair	550.00	
c.	As "a," imperf., pair		100.00
	Joint line pair		250.00

A total of 129 different Bureau precancels were used by 117 cities.

No. 1518c is precanceled Washington, DC. Columbus, Ohio and Garden City, N.Y. values are higher.

MULTICOLOR HUCK PRESS

1519 A923	10c red & blue, Dec. 8, 1973	.20	.20
	Pair	.40	.20
a.	Imperf., pair	37.50	
b.	Tagging omitted	12.50	

ROTARY PRESS PRINTING

1520 A924	10c blue, Dec. 14, 1973	.25	.20
	Pair	.50	.20
	Joint line pair	.75	
a.	Untagged (Bureau precanceled)		.25
b.	Imperf., pair	40.00	
	Joint line pair	70.00	

Bureau Precancels: No. 1520a, 14 diff.

VETERANS OF FOREIGN WARS ISSUE

75th anniversary of Veterans of Spanish-American and Other Foreign Wars.

Emblem and Initials of Veterans of Foreign Wars — A928

Designed by Robert Hallock.

GIORI PRESS PRINTING
Plates of 200 subjects in 4 plates of 50.

1974, Mar. 11	Tagged	Perf. 11	
1525 A928	10c red & dark blue	.20	.20
	P# block of 4	.85	—
	Margin block of 4, Mr. Zip and		
	"Use Zip Code"	.80	—
a.	Tagging omitted	7.50	

ROBERT FROST ISSUE

Robert Frost (1873-1963), Poet — A929

Designed by Paul Calle; photograph by David Rhinelander.

ROTARY PRESS PRINTING
E.E. Plates of 200 subjects in four panes of 50.

1974, Mar. 26	Tagged	Perf. 10½x11	
1526 A929	10c black	.20	.20
	P# block of 4	.85	—
	Margin block of 4, Mr. Zip and		
	"Use Zip Code"	.80	—

EXPO '74 WORLD'S FAIR ISSUE

EXPO '74 World's Fair "Preserve the Environment," Spokane, Wash., May 4-Nov. 4.

"Cosmic Jumper" and "Smiling Sage" — A930

Designed by Peter Max.

PHOTOGRAVURE (Andreotti)
Plates of 160 subjects in four panes of 40.

1974, Apr. 18   Tagged   Perf. 11

1527	A930	10c **multicolored**	.20	.20
		On cover, Expo. station hand-stamp canc.		12.50
		P# block of 12, 6#	2.50	—
		Margin block of 4, Mr. Zip, "Use Zip Code" and "Mail Early in the Day"	.80	—
		P# block of 16, 6#, Mr. Zip and slogans	3.40	—

HORSE RACING ISSUE

Kentucky Derby, Churchill Downs, centenary.

Horses Rounding Turn — A931

Designed by Henry Koehler.

PHOTOGRAVURE (Andreotti)
Plates of 200 subjects in four panes of 50.

1974, May 4   Tagged   Perf. 11x10½

1528	A931	10c **yellow & multicolored**	.20	.20
		P# block of 12, 6#	2.50	—
		Margin block of 4, Mr. Zip and "Use Zip Code"	.80	—
a.		Blue ("Horse Racing") omitted	900.00	
b.		Red ("U.S. postage 10 cents") omitted	—	
c.		Tagging omitted	—	

Beware of stamps offered as No. 1528b that have traces of red.

SKYLAB ISSUE

First anniversary of the launching of Skylab I, honoring all who participated in the Skylab project.

Skylab — A932

Designed by Robert T. McCall.

LITHOGRAPHED, ENGRAVED (Giori)
Plates of 200 subjects in four panes of 50.

1974, May 14   Tagged   Perf. 11

1529	A932	10c **multicolored**	.20	.20
		P# block of 4	.85	—
		Margin block of 4, Mr. Zip and "Use Zip Code"	.80	—
a.		Vert. pair, imperf. between	—	
b.		Tagging omitted	7.50	

UNIVERSAL POSTAL UNION ISSUE

UPU cent. In the 1st row Nos. 1530-1537 are in sequence as listed. In the 2nd row Nos. 1534-1537 are followed by Nos. 1530-1533. Every row of 8 and every horizontal block of 8 contains all 8 designs. The letter writing designs are from famous works of art; some are details. The quotation on every second stamp, "Letters mingle souls," is from a letter by poet John Donne.

Michelangelo, from "School of Athens," by Raphael, 1509 — A933

"Five Feminine Virtues," by Hokusai, c. 1811 — A934

"Old Scraps," by John Fredrick Peto, 1894 — A935

"The Lovely Reader," by Jean Etienne Liotard, 1746 — A936

"Lady Writing Letter," by Gerard Terborch, 1654 — A937

Inkwell and Quill, from "Boy with a Top," by Jean-Baptiste Simeon Chardin, 1738 — A938

Mrs. John Douglas, by Thomas Gainsborough, 1784 — A939

Don Antonio Noriega, by Francisco de Goya, 1801 — A940

Designed by Bradbury Thompson.

PHOTOGRAVURE (Andreotti)
Plates of 128 subjects in four panes of 32 each.

1974, June 6   Tagged   Perf. 11

1530	A933	10c **multicolored**	.20	.20
1531	A934	10c **multicolored**	.20	.20
1532	A935	10c **multicolored**	.20	.20
1533	A936	10c **multicolored**	.20	.20
1534	A937	10c **multicolored**	.20	.20
1535	A938	10c **multicolored**	.20	.20
1536	A939	10c **multicolored**	.20	.20
1537	A940	10c **multicolored**	.20	.20
a.		Block or strip of 8 (#1530-1537)	1.75	1.60
		P# block of 16, 5#, "Mail Early in the Day," Mr. Zip and "Use Zip Code"	3.50	—
		P# block of 10, 5#; no slogans	2.25	—
b.		As "a," (block), imperf. vert.	7,500.	

MINERAL HERITAGE ISSUE

The sequence of stamps in 1st horizontal row is Nos. 1538-1541, 1538-1539. In 2nd row Nos. 1540-1541 are followed by Nos. 1538-1541.

Petrified Wood — A941

Tourmaline A942

Amethyst A943

Rhodochrosite A944

Designed by Leonard F. Buckley.

LITHOGRAPHED, ENGRAVED (Giori)
Plates of 192 subjects in four panes of 48 (6x8).

1974, June 13   Tagged   Perf. 11

1538	A941	10c **blue & multicolored**	.20	.20
a.		Light blue & yellow omitted	—	
1539	A942	10c **blue & multicolored**	.20	.20
a.		Light blue omitted	—	
b.		Black & purple omitted	—	
1540	A943	10c **blue & multicolored**	.20	.20
a.		Light blue & yellow omitted	—	
1541	A944	10c **blue & multicolored**	.20	.20
a.		Block or strip of 4, #1538-1541	.80	.90

	P# block of 4	.90	—
	Margin block of 4, Mr. Zip and	
	"Use Zip Code"	.85	—
b.	As "a," light blue & yellow omitted	1,900.	
c.	Light blue omitted	—	
d.	Black & red omitted	—	
e.	As "a," tagging omitted	—	

KENTUCKY SETTLEMENT, 150th ANNIV.
Fort Harrod, first settlement in Kentucky.

Covered Wagons at Fort
Harrod — A945

Designed by David K. Stone.

LITHOGRAPHED, ENGRAVED (Giori)
Plates of 200 subjects in four panes of 50.

1974, June 15	Tagged	Perf. 11
1542 A945 10c **green & multicolored**	.20	.20
	P# block of 4	.85	—
	Margin block of 4, Mr. Zip and	
	"Use Zip Code"	.80	
a.	Dull black (litho.) omitted	850.00	
b.	Green (engr. & litho.), black (engr. &	
	litho.) & blue omitted	3,750.	
c.	Green (engr.) omitted	—	
d.	Green (engr.) & black (litho.) omitted	—	
e.	Tagging omitted	—	

After the lithographed red and yellow colors were printed a piece of paper fell on part of one sheet, which was then printed and perforated. The removal of the piece of paper results in stamps with some printing missing, including Nos. 1542b-1542d.

AMERICAN REVOLUTION BICENTENNIAL ISSUE
First Continental Congress

Nos. 1543-1544 alternate in 1st row, Nos. 1545-1546 in 2nd row. This arrangement is repeated throughout the pane.

Carpenters' Hall,
Philadelphia
A946

"We ask but for
peace . . ."
A947

"Deriving their
just powers . . ."
A948

Independence
Hall — A949

Designed by Frank P. Conley.

GIORI PRESS PRINTING
Plates of 200 subjects in four panes of 50.

1974, July 4	Tagged	Perf. 11
1543 A946 10c **dark blue & red**	.20	.20
1544 A947 10c **gray, dark blue & red**	.20	.20
1545 A948 10c **gray, dark blue & red**	.20	.20
1546 A949 10c **red & dark blue**	.20	.20
a.	Block of 4, #1543-1546	.80	.90
	P# block of 4	.90	—
	Margin block of 4, Mr. Zip and	
	"Use Zip Code"	.85	—
b.	As "a," tagging omitted	60.00	

Margin includes Bicentennial Commission emblem and inscription.

ENERGY CONSERVATION ISSUE
Publicizing the importance of conserving all forms of energy.

Molecules and Drops of
Gasoline and Oil — A950

Designed by Robert W. Bode.

LITHOGRAPHED, ENGRAVED (Giori)
Plates of 200 subjects in four panes of 50.

1974, Sept. 23	Tagged	Perf. 11
1547 A950 10c **multicolored**	.20	.20
	P# block of 4	.85	—
	Margin block of 4, Mr. Zip and	
	"Use Zip Code"	.80	—
a.	Blue & orange omitted	900.00	
b.	Orange & green omitted	650.00	
c.	Green omitted	825.00	
d.	Tagging omitted	7.00	

AMERICAN FOLKLORE ISSUE
Legend of Sleepy Hollow

The Headless Horseman in pursuit of Ichabod Crane from "Legend of Sleepy Hollow," by Washington Irving.

Headless
Horseman and
Ichabod — A951

Designed by Leonard Everett Fisher.

LITHOGRAPHED, ENGRAVED (Giori)
Plates of 200 subjects in four panes of 50.

1974, Oct. 12	Tagged	Perf. 11
1548 A951 10c **dk. bl., blk., org. & yel.**	.20	.20
	P# block of 4	.85	—
	Margin block of 4, Mr. Zip and	
	"Use Zip Code"	.80	—

RETARDED CHILDREN ISSUE

Retarded Children Can Be Helped, theme of annual convention of the National Association of Retarded Citizens.

Retarded Child — A952

Designed by Paul Calle.

GIORI PRESS PRINTING
Plates of 200 subjects in four panes of 50.

1974, Oct. 12	Tagged	Perf. 11
1549 A952 10c **brown red & dark brown**	.20	.20
	P# block of 4	.85	—
	Margin block of 4, Mr. Zip and	
	"Use Zip Code"	.80	—
a.	Tagging omitted	7.50	

CHRISTMAS ISSUE

Angel — A953

"The Road-Winter,"
by Currier and
Ives — A954

Dove Weather
Vane atop Mount
Vernon — A955

Designers: No. 1550, Bradbury Thompson, using detail from the Pérussis altarpiece painted by anonymous French artist, 1480, in Metropolitan Museum of Art, New York City. No. 1551, Stevan Dohanos, using Currier and Ives print from drawing by Otto Knirsch. No. 1552, Don Hedin and Robert Geissman.

PHOTOGRAVURE (Andreotti)
Plates of 200 subjects in four panes of 50.

1974, Oct. 23	Tagged	Perf. 10½x11
1550 A953 10c **multicolored**	.20	.20
	P# block of 10, 5#	2.10	
	Margin block of 4, Mr. Zip and	
	"Use Zip Code"	.80	—

	Perf. 11x10½	
1551 A954 10c **multicolored**	.20	.20
	P# block of 12, 6#	2.50	
	Margin block of 4, Mr. Zip and	
	"Use Zip Code"	.80	—
a.	Buff omitted	35.00	

No. 1551a is difficult to identify. Competent expertization is necessary.

Die Cut, Paper Backing Rouletted

1974, Nov. 15	Untagged
Self-adhesive; Inscribed "Precanceled"	
1552 A955 10c **multicolored**	.20	.20
	P# block of 20, 6#, 5 slogans	4.25	
	P# block of 12, 6#, 5 different slogans	2.60	
	Nos. 1550-1552 (3)	.60	.60

Unused value of No. 1552 is for copy on rouletted paper backing as issued. Used value is for copy on piece, with or without postmark. **Most copies are becoming discolored, probably from the adhesive. The Catalogue value is for discolored copies.**

Die cutting includes crossed slashes through dove, applied to prevent removal and re-use of the stamp. The stamp will separate into layers if soaked.

Two different machines were used to roulette the sheet.

AMERICAN ARTS ISSUE

Benjamin West (1738-1820), painter (No. 1553); Paul Laurence Dunbar (1872-1906), poet (No. 1554); David (Lewelyn) Wark Griffith (1875-1948), motion picture producer (No. 1555).

Benjamin West
American artist
10 cents U.S. postage
Self-portrait — A956

Paul Laurence
Dunbar
American poet
10 cents U.S. postage
A957

MOVIEMAKER   US 10 c
DW GRIFFITH — A958

Designers: No. 1553, Bradbury Thompson; No. 1554, Walter D. Richards; No. 1555, Fred Otnes.

PHOTOGRAVURE (Andreotti)
Plates of 200 subjects in four panes of 50.

1975	Tagged	Perf. 10½x11	
1553 A956 10c **multicolored**, *Feb. 10*		.20	.20
P# block of 10, 5#		2.10	—
Margin block of 4, Mr. Zip and "Use Zip Code"		.80	—
	Perf. 11		
1554 A957 10c **multicolored**, *May 1*		.20	.20
P# block of 10, 5#		2.10	—
Margin block of 4, Mr. Zip and "Use Zip Code"		.80	—
a. Imperf., pair		1,300.	

LITHOGRAPHED, ENGRAVED (Giori)
Perf. 11

1555 A958 10c **brown & multicolored**, *May 27*		.20	.20
P# block of 4		.85	—
Margin block of 4, Mr. Zip and "Use Zip Code"		.80	—
a. Brown (engraved) omitted		625.00	
Nos. 1553-1555 (3)		.60	.60

SPACE ISSUES

US space accomplishments with unmanned craft. Pioneer 10 passed within 81,000 miles of Jupiter, Dec. 10, 1973. Mariner 10 explored Venus and Mercury in 1974 and Mercury again in 1975.

PIONEER ★ JUPITER
US 10c
Pioneer 10
Passing
Jupiter — A959

MARINER 10 ★ VENUS/MERCURY
US 10c
Mariner 10, Venus
and
Mercury — A960

Designed by Robert McCall (No. 1556); Roy Gjertson (No. 1557).

LITHOGRAPHED, ENGRAVED (Giori)
Plates of 200 subjects in four panes of 50.

1975	Tagged	Perf. 11	
1556 A959 10c **light yellow, dark yellow, red, blue & 2 dark blues** *Feb. 28*		.20	.20
P# block of 4		.85	—
Margin block of 4, Mr. Zip and "Use Zip Code"		.80	—
a. Red & dark yellow omitted		1,400.	
b. Dark blues (engr.) omitted		950.00	
c. Tagging omitted		7.50	
d. Dark yellow omitted		—	
Imperfs. exist from printer's waste.			
1557 A960 10c **black, red, ultra. & bister**, *Apr. 4*		.20	.20
P# block of 4		.85	—
Margin block of 4, Mr. Zip and "Use Zip Code"		.80	—
a. Red omitted		500.00	
b. Ultramarine & bister omitted		2,000.	
c. Tagging omitted		7.50	

COLLECTIVE BARGAINING ISSUE
Collective Bargaining law, enacted 1935, in Wagner Act.

collective bargaining
out of conflict accord
UNITED STATES
10c
"Labor and Management"
A961

Designed by Robert Hallock.

PHOTOGRAVURE (Andreotti)
Plates of 200 subjects in four panes of 50.

1975, Mar. 13	Tagged	Perf. 11	
1558 A961 10c **multicolored**		.20	.20
P# block of 8, 4#		1.75	—
Margin block of 4, Mr. Zip and "Use Zip Code"		.80	—
Imperforates exist from printer's waste.			

AMERICAN BICENTENNIAL ISSUE
Contributors to the Cause

Sybil Ludington, age 16, rallied militia, Apr. 26, 1777; Salem Poor, black freeman, fought in Battle of Bunker Hill; Haym Salomon, Jewish immigrant, raised money to finance Revolutionary War; Peter Francisco, Portuguese-French immigrant, joined Continental Army at 15. Emerald inscription on back, printed beneath gum in water-soluble ink, gives thumbnail sketch of portrayed contributor.

Contributors To The Cause...   U.S. 8c
Sybil Ludington ✪ *Youthful Heroine*
Sybil Ludington — A962

Contributors To The Cause...   U.S. 10c
Salem Poor — A963   Salem Poor ✪ *Gallant Soldier*

Contributors To The Cause...   U.S. 10c
Haym Salomon ✪ *Financial Hero*   Haym Salomon — A964

Contributors To The Cause...   U.S. 18c
Peter Francisco — A965   Peter Francisco ✪ *Fighter Extraordinary*

Designed by Neil Boyle.

PHOTOGRAVURE (Andreotti)
Plates of 200 subjects in four panes of 50.

1975, Mar. 25	Tagged	Perf. 11x10½	
1559 A962 8c **multicolored**		.20	.20
P# block of 10, 5#		1.50	—
Margin block of 4, Mr. Zip and "Use Zip Code"		.65	—
a. Back inscriptions omitted		225.00	
1560 A963 10c **multicolored**		.20	.20
P# block of 10, 5#		2.10	—
Margin block of 4, Mr. Zip and "Use Zip Code"		.80	—
a. Back inscription omitted		225.00	
1561 A964 10c **multicolored**		.20	.20
P# block of 10, 5#		2.10	—
Margin block of 4, Mr. Zip and "Use Zip Code"		.80	—
a. Back inscription omitted		225.00	
b. Red omitted		250.00	
1562 A965 18c **multicolored**		.35	.20
P# block of 10, 5#		3.60	—
Margin block of 4, Mr. Zip and "Use Zip Code"		1.45	—
Nos. 1559-1562 (4)		.95	.80

Lexington-Concord Battle, 200th Anniv.

Lexington & Concord 1775 by Sandham
US Bicentennial 10cents

"Birth of Liberty," by Henry Sandham — A966

Designed by Bradbury Thompson.

PHOTOGRAVURE (Andreotti)
Plates of 160 subjects in four panes of 40.

1975, Apr. 19	Tagged	Perf. 11	
1563 A966 10c **multicolored**		.20	.20
P# block of 12, 6#		2.50	—
Margin block of 4, Mr. Zip, "Use Zip Code" and "Mail Early in the Day"		.80	—
Margin block of 16, 6 P#, Mr. Zip and slogans		3.40	—
a. Vert. pair, imperf. horiz.		425.00	

Bunker Hill Battle, 200th Anniv.

Bunker Hill 1775 by Trumbull
US Bicentennial 10c

Battle of Bunker Hill, by John Trumbull — A967

Designed by Bradbury Thompson.

PHOTOGRAVURE (Andreotti)
Plates of 160 subjects in four panes of 40.

1975, June 17	Tagged	Perf. 11	
1564 A967 10c **multicolored**		.20	.20
P# block of 12, 6#		2.50	—
Margin block of 4, Mr. Zip, "Use Zip Code" and "Mail Early in the Day"		.80	—
P# block of 16, 6#, Mr. Zip and slogans		3.40	—

Military Uniforms

Bicentenary of US Military Services. Nos. 1565-1566 alternate in one row, Nos. 1567-1568 in next row.

CONTINENTAL ARMY
US 10c
Soldier with Flintlock Musket, Uniform Button — A968

CONTINENTAL NAVY
US 10c
Sailor with Grappling Hook, First Navy Jack, 1775 — A969

CONTINENTAL MARINES
US 10c
Marine with Musket, Fullrigged Ship — A970

AMERICAN MILITIA
US 10c
Militiaman with Musket and Powder Horn — A971

Designed by Edward Vebell.

PHOTOGRAVURE (Andreotti)
Plates of 200 subjects in four panes of 50.

1975, July 4	Tagged	Perf. 11	
1565 A968 10c **multicolored**		.20	.20
1566 A969 10c **multicolored**		.20	.20
1567 A970 10c **multicolored**		.20	.20
1568 A971 10c **multicolored**		.20	.20
a.	Block of 4, #1565-1568	.85	.90
	P# block of 12, 6#	2.50	—
	P# block of 20, 6#, Mr. Zip and slogans	4.50	—
	Margin block of 4, Mr. Zip and "Use Zip Code"	1.00	—

APOLLO SOYUZ SPACE ISSUE

Apollo Soyuz space test project, Russo-American cooperation, launched July 15; link-up, July 17. Nos. In the 1st row, No. 1569 is in 1st and 3rd space, No. 1570 is 2nd space; in the 2nd row No. 1570 is in 1st and 3rd space, No. 1569 in 2nd space, etc.

Participating US and USSR crews: Thomas P. Stafford, Donald K. Slayton, Vance D. Brand, Aleksei A. Leonov, Valery N. Kubasov.

Apollo and Soyuz after Link-up, and Earth — A972

Spacecraft before Link-up, Earth and Project Emblem — A973

Designed by Robert McCall (No. 1569) and Anatoly M. Aksamit of USSR (No. 1570).

PHOTOGRAVURE (Andreotti)
Plates of 96 subjects in four panes of 24 each.

1975, July 15	Tagged	Perf. 11	
1569 A972 10c **multicolored**		.20	.20
	Pair with full horiz. gutter btwn.	—	
1570 A973 10c **multicolored**		.20	.20
a.	Pair, #1569-1570	.45	.40
	P# block of 12, 6#	2.50	—
	Margin block of 4, Mr. Zip, "Use Zip Code"	.85	—
	P# block of 16, 6#, Mr. Zip, "Use Zip Code"	3.40	—
	Pair with full horiz. gutter btwn.	—	
b.	As "a," tagging omitted	30.00	
c.	As "a," vert. pair imperf. horiz.	2,000.	

Nos. 1569-1570 totally imperforate are printer's waste. See Russia Nos. 4339-4340.

INTERNATIONAL WOMEN'S YEAR ISSUE
International Women's Year 1975.

Worldwide Equality for Women — A974

Designed by Miriam Schottland.

PHOTOGRAVURE (Andreotti)
Plates of 200 subjects in four panes of 50.

1975, Aug. 26	Tagged	Perf. 11x10½	
1571 A974 10c **blue, orange & dark blue**		.20	.20
	P# block of 6, 3#	1.30	—
	Margin block of 4, Mr. Zip and "Use Zip Code"	.80	—

US POSTAL SERVICE BICENTENNIAL ISSUE

Nos. 1572-1573 alternate in 1st row, Nos. 1574-1575 in 2nd row. This arrangement is repeated throughout the pane.

Stagecoach and Trailer Truck — A975

Old and New Locomotives A976

Early Mail Plane and Jet — A977

Satellite for Transmission of Mailgrams A978

Designed by James L. Womer.

PHOTOGRAVURE (Andreotti)
Plates of 200 subjects in four panes of 50.

1975, Sept. 3	Tagged	Perf. 11x10½	
1572 A975 10c **multicolored**		.20	.20
1573 A976 10c **multicolored**		.20	.20
1574 A977 10c **multicolored**		.20	.20
1575 A978 10c **multicolored**		.20	.20
a.	Block of 4, #1572-1575	.85	.90
	P# block of 12, 6#	2.50	—
	P# block of 20, 6#, Mr. Zip and slogans	4.50	—
	Margin block of 4, Mr. Zip and "Use Zip Code"	1.00	—
b.	As "a," red "10c" omitted	9,500.	

WORLD PEACE THROUGH LAW ISSUE

A prelude to 7th World Law Conference of the World Peace Through Law Center at Washington, D.C., Oct. 12-17.

Law Book, Gavel, Olive Branch and Globe — A979

Designed by Melbourne Brindle.

GIORI PRESS PRINTING
Plates of 200 subjects in four panes of 50.

1975, Sept. 29	Tagged	Perf. 11	
1576 A979 10c **green, Prussian blue & rose brown**		.20	.20
	P# block of 4	.85	—
	Margin block of 4, Mr. Zip and "Use Zip Code"	.80	—
a.	Tagging omitted	6.00	
b.	Horiz. pair, imperf vert.		

BANKING AND COMMERCE ISSUE

Banking and commerce in the US, and for the Centennial Convention of the American Bankers Association.

Designed by V. Jack Ruther.

Engine Turning, Indian Head Penny, Morgan-type Silver Dollar — A980

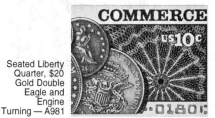

Seated Liberty Quarter, $20 Gold Double Eagle and Engine Turning — A981

LITHOGRAPHED, ENGRAVED (Giori)
Plates of 160 subjects in four panes of 40.

1975, Oct. 6	Tagged	Perf. 11	
1577 A980 10c **multicolored**		.25	.20
1578 A981 10c **multicolored**		.25	.20
a.	Pair, #1577-1578	.50	.40
	P# block of 4	1.20	
	Margin block of 4, Mr. Zip and "Use Zip Code"	1.00	—
b.	As "a," brown & blue (litho) omitted	2,250.	
c.	As "a," brown, blue & yellow (litho) omitted	2,750.	

CHRISTMAS ISSUE

Madonna and Child, by Domenico Ghirlandaio A982

Christmas Card, by Louis Prang, 1878 A983

Designed by Stevan Dohanos.

PHOTOGRAVURE (Andreotti)
Plates of 200 subjects in four panes of 50.

1975, Oct. 14	Tagged	Perf. 11	
1579 A982 (10c) **multicolored**		.20	.20
	P# block of 12, 6#	2.50	—
	Margin block of 4, Mr. Zip and "Use Zip Code"	.80	—
a.	Imperf., pair	90.00	
	Plate flaw ("d" damaged) (36741-36746 LL 47)	5.00	—
1580 A983 (10c) **multicolored**		**Perf. 11.2**	
		.20	.20
	P# block of 12, 6#	2.50	—
	Margin block of 4, Mr. Zip and "Use Zip Code"	.80	—
a.	Imperf., pair	90.00	
c.	Perf. 10.9	.25	.20
	P# block of 12, 6#	3.50	—
	Margin block of 4, Mr. Zip and "Use Zip Code"	1.00	—
1580B A983 (10c) **multicolored,**		**Perf. 10.5x11.3**	
		.60	.20
	P# block of 12, 6#	15.00	—
	Margin block of 4, Mr. Zip and "Use Zip Code"	2.75	—

AMERICANA ISSUE

Inkwell and Quill — A984

Speaker's Stand — A985

Early Ballot Box — A987

Books, Bookmark, Eyeglasses — A988

Kerosene Table Lamp — A1009

Railroad Conductor's Lantern, c. 1850 — A1010

Dome of Capitol — A994

Contemplation of Justice, by J. E. Fraser — A995

Early American Printing Press — A996

Torch, Statue of Liberty — A997

Liberty Bell — A998

Eagle and Shield — A999

Fort McHenry Flag (15 Stars) — A1001

Head, Statue of Liberty — A1002

Old North Church, Boston — A1003

Fort Nisqually, Wash. — A1004

Sandy Hook Lighthouse, NJ — A1005

Morris Township School No. 2, Devils Lake, ND — A1006

Iron "Betty" Lamp, Plymouth Colony, 17th-18th Centuries — A1007

Rush Lamp and Candle Holder — A1008

Designed by: 2c, 4c, 15c, V. Jack Ruther Robert Hallock. 3c, Clarence Holbert. 9c, 10c, 11c, Walter Brooks. 12c, George Mercer. No. 1595, Bernard Glassman. No. 1596, James L. Womer.

ROTARY PRESS PRINTING
E.E. Plates of 400 subjects in four panes of 100.

1975-81		Tagged	Perf. 11x10½	
		Size: 18½x22½mm		
1581	A984	1c **dark blue,** *greenish,* shiny gum, *Dec. 8, 1977*	.20	.20
		P# block of 4	.25	—
		Margin block of 4, "Use Zip Code"	.20	—
		Dull gum	.20	
		P# block of 4	.25	
		Zip block of 4	.20	
		Pair with full vert. gutter btwn.		
a.		Untagged (Bureau precanceled)		.20
c.		White paper, dull gum		
d.		Tagging omitted (not Bureau precanceled)	4.50	
1582	A985	2c **red brown,** *greenish,* shiny gum, *Dec. 8, 1977*	.20	.20
		P# block of 4	.25	—
		Margin block of 4, "Use Zip Code"	.20	—
		Dull gum	.20	
		P# block of 4	2.50	
		Zip block of 4	.50	
a.		Untagged (Bureau precanceled)		.20
b.		Cream paper, dull gum, *1981*	.20	.20
		P# block of 4	.25	
		Zip block of 4	.20	
c.		Tagging omitted (not Bureau precanceled)	4.50	
1584	A987	3c **olive,** *greenish,* shiny gum, *Dec. 8, 1977*	.20	.20
		P# block of 4	.30	
		Margin block of 4, "Use Zip Code"	.25	—
		Dull gum	.20	
		P# block of 4	.50	
		Zip block of 4	.30	
		Pair with full horiz. gutter btwn.	—	
a.		Untagged (Bureau precanceled)		.20
b.		Tagging omitted (not Bureau precanceled)	6.00	
1585	A988	4c **rose magenta,** *cream,* shiny gum, *Dec. 8, 1977*	.20	.20
		P# block of 4	.40	
		Margin block of 4, "Use Zip Code"	.35	—
		Dull gum	.20	
		P# block of 4	1.10	
		Zip block of 4	.65	
a.		Untagged (Bureau precanceled)		1.25
b.		Tagging omitted (not Bureau precanceled), dull gum	—	
		Shiny gum	—	
		Size: 17½x20½mm		
1590	A994	9c **slate green** (from bklt. pane #1623a), *Mar. 11, 1977*	.45	.20
		Perf. 10x9¾		
1590A	A994	9c **slate green** (from bklt. pane #1623Bc), *Mar. 11, 1977*	22.50	15.00
		Size: 18½x22½mm		
		Perf. 11x10½		
1591	A994	9c **slate green,** *gray,* shiny gum, *Nov. 24, 1975*	.20	.20
		P# block of 4	.85	
		Margin block of 4, "Use Zip Code"	.80	—
		Dull gum	1.00	
		P# block of 4	5.00	
		Zip block of 4	4.25	
a.		Untagged (Bureau precanceled)		.20
b.		Tagging omitted (not Bureau precanceled)	5.00	
1592	A995	10c **violet,** *gray,* shiny gum, *Nov. 17, 1977*	.20	.20
		P# block of 4	.90	
		Margin block of 4, "Use Zip Code"	.80	—
		Dull gum	.20	
		P# block of 4	.90	
		Zip block of 4	.80	
a.		Untagged (Bureau precanceled, Chicago)		.25
b.		Tagging omitted (not Bureau precanceled)	7.00	
1593	A996	11c **orange,** *gray, Nov. 13, 1975*	.20	.20
		P# block of 4	.90	
		Margin block of 4, "Use Zip Code"	.85	—

		Pair with full horiz. gutter btwn.	—	
a.		Tagging omitted	4.00	
1594	A997	12c **red brown,** *beige, Apr. 8, 1981*	.25	.20
		P# block of 4	1.60	
		Zip block of 4	1.10	
a.		Tagging omitted	5.00	
1595	A998	13c **brown** (from bklt. pane), *Oct. 31, 1975*	.30	.20
a.		Booklet pane of 6	2.25	.75
b.		Booklet pane of 7 + label	2.25	.75
c.		Booklet pane of 8	2.25	1.00
d.		Booklet pane of 5 + label, *Apr. 2, 1976*	1.75	.75
e.		Vert. pair, imperf. btwn.	1,200.	

PHOTOGRAVURE (Andreotti)
Plates of 400 subjects in four panes of 100.

			Perf. 11.2	
1596	A999	13c **multicolored,** *Dec. 1, 1975*	.25	.20
		P# block of 12, 6#	3.25	—
		P# block of 20, 6# and slogans	5.50	—
		Margin block of 4, "Use Zip Code"	1.00	—
		Pair with full horiz. gutter btwn.	150.00	
a.		Imperf., pair	50.00	—
b.		Yellow omitted	160.00	—
d.		Line perforated	27.50	—
		P# block of 12, 6#	375.00	—

On No. 1596 the entire sheet is perforated at one time so the perforations meet perfectly at the corners of the stamp. On No. 1596d the perforations do not line up perfectly and are perf. 11.

ENGRAVED (Combination Press)
Plates of 460 subjects (20x23) in panes of 100 (10x10)

1597	A1001	15c **gray, dark blue & red,** *June 30, 1978*	.30	.20
		P# block of 6	1.90	
		P# block of 20, 1-2#	6.50	
a.		Imperf., vert. pair	20.00	—
b.		Gray omitted	600.00	
c.		Vert. strip of 3, imperf. btwn. and at top or bottom	—	
d.		Tagging omitted	4.00	

Plate number appears 3 times on each plate of 23 rows. With no separating gutters, each pane has only left or right sheet margin. Plate numbers appear on both margins; there are no slogans.

ENGRAVED
Perf. 11x10½

1598	A1001	15c **gray, dark blue & red** (from bklt. pane), *June 30, 1978*	.40	.20
a.		Booklet pane of 8	4.25	.80
1599	A1002	16c **blue,** *Mar. 31, 1978*	.35	.20
		P# block of 4	1.90	
		Margin block of 4, "Use Correct Zip Code"	1.40	—
1603	A1003	24c **red,** *blue, Nov. 14, 1975*	.50	.20
		P# block of 4	2.25	
		Margin block of 4, "Use Zip Code"	2.00	—
a.		Tagging omitted	7.50	
1604	A1004	28c **brown,** *blue,* shiny gum, *Aug. 11, 1978*	.55	.20
		P# block of 4	2.40	
		Margin block of 4, "Use Correct Zip Code"	2.25	—
		Dull gum	1.10	
		P# block of 4	10.00	
		Zip block of 4	5.00	
1605	A1005	29c **blue,** *light blue,* shiny gum, *Apr. 14, 1978*	.60	.20
		P# block of 4	3.00	
		Margin block of 4, "Use Correct Zip Code"	2.40	—
		Dull gum	2.00	
		P# block of 4	15.00	
		Zip block of 4	9.00	
1606	A1006	30c **green,** *blue, Aug. 27, 1979*	.55	.20
		P# block of 4	2.40	
		Margin block of 4, "Use Correct Zip Code"	2.25	—
a.		Tagging omitted	15.00	

LITHOGRAPHED AND ENGRAVED
Perf. 11

1608	A1007	50c **tan, black & orange,** *Sept. 11, 1979*	.85	.20
		P# block of 4	3.75	
		Margin block of 4, "Use Correct Zip Code"	3.50	—
a.		Black omitted	300.00	
b.		Vert. pair, imperf. horiz.	1,750.	
c.		Tagging omitted	10.00	

Beware of examples offered as No. 1608b that have blind perfs.

1610	A1008	$1 **tan, brown, orange & yellow,** *July 2, 1979*	2.00	.20
		P# block of 4	8.50	
		Margin block of 4, "Use Correct Zip Code"	8.00	—
		Pair with full vert. gutter btwn.	—	
a.		Brown (engraved) omitted	275.00	
b.		Tan, orange & yellow omitted	350.00	
c.		Brown inverted	14,500.	
d.		Tagging omitted	15.00	

1611 A1009	$2 **tan, dark green, orange & yellow,** *Nov. 16, 1978*	3.75	.75
	P# block of 4	16.00	
	Margin block of 4, "Use Correct Zip Code"	15.00	—
1612 A1010	$5 **tan, red brown, yellow & orange,** *Aug. 23, 1979*	8.25	1.75
	P# block of 4	35.00	
	Margin block of 4, "Use Correct Zip Code"	33.50	—
	Nos. 1581-1612 (23)	43.25	21.50

Nos. 1590, 1590a, 1595, 1598, 1623 and 1623b were issued only in booklets. All stamps have one or two straight edges.

Bureau Precancels: 1c, 3 diff., 2c, Chicago, Greensboro, NC, 3c, 6 diff., 4c, Chicago, lines only, No. 1591a, 4 diff., No. 1596, 5 diff., 30c, lines only, 50c, 2 spacings, lines only, $1, 2 spacings, lines only. The 30c, 50c, $1 and No. 1596 are precanceled on tagged stamps.

USA **3.1c** AUTH. NON-PROFIT ORG.
LISTEN WITH LOVE TO THE MUSIC OF THE LAND
Six-string Guitar
A1011

MARCHING IN STEP TO THE MUSIC OF THE UNION
USA **7.7c** BULK RATE
Saxhorns
A1012

USA **7.9c** BULK RATE
BEAT THE DRUM FOR LIBERTY AND THE SPIRIT OF 76
Drum — A1013

PEACE UNITES A NATION LIKE HARMONY IN MUSIC
USA **8.4c** BULK RATE
Steinway Grand Piano, 1857 — A1014

Designers: 3.1c, George Mercer. 7.7c, Susan Robb. 7.9c, Bernard Glassman. 10c, Walter Brooks. 15c, V. Jack Ruther.

COIL STAMPS
ENGRAVED

1975-79   *Perf. 10 Vertically*

1613 A1011	3.1c **brown,** *yellow,* Oct. 25, 1979	.20	.20
	Pair	.28	.20
	Joint line pair	1.50	—
a.	Untagged (Bureau precanceled, lines only)		.50
b.	Imperf., pair	1,400.	
	Joint line pair	3,600.	
1614 A1012	7.7c **brown,** *bright yellow,* Nov. 20, 1976	.20	.20
	Pair	.40	.20
	Joint line pair	1.00	
a.	Untagged (Bureau precanceled)		.35
b.	As "a," imperf., pair	1,600.	
	Joint line pair	4,400.	

A total of 160 different Bureau precancels were used by 153 cities.

No. 1614b is precanceled Washington, DC. Also exists from Marion, OH.

1615 A1013	7.9c **carmine,** *yellow,* shiny gum, *Apr. 23, 1976*	.20	.20
	Pair	.40	.20
	Joint line pair	.75	—
	Dull gum	.35	
	Joint line pair	1.50	
a.	Untagged (Bureau precanceled)		.20
b.	Imperf., pair	600.00	

A total of 109 different Bureau precancels were used by 107 cities plus CAR. RT./SORT.

1615C A1014	8.4c **dark blue,** *yellow,* July 13, 1978	.20	.20
	Pair	.40	.20
	Joint line pair	3.25	.30
d.	Untagged (Bureau precanceled)		.30
e.	As "d," pair, imperf. between	60.00	
	Joint line pair	125.00	
f.	As "d," imperf., pair	17.50	
	Joint line pair	35.00	

A total of 145 different Bureau precancels were used by 144 cities.

No. 1615e is precanceled with lines only. No. 1615f is precanceled Newark, NJ. Also exists from Brownstown, Ind., Oklahoma City, Okla. and with lines only.

1616 A994	9c **slate green,** *gray,* Mar. 5, 1976	.20	.20
	Pair	.40	.20
	Joint line pair	1.00	
a.	Imperf., pair	160.00	
	Joint line pair	375.00	
b.	Untagged (Bureau precanceled)		.35
c.	As "b," imperf., pair	700.00	
	Joint line pair		

No. 1616c is precanceled Pleasantville, NY.

1617 A995	10c **violet,** *gray,* shiny gum, Nov. 4, 1977	.20	.20
	Pair	.40	

	Joint line pair	1.10	—
	Dull gum	.30	
	Joint line pair	2.75	
a.	Untagged (Bureau precanceled)		.25
b.	Imperf., pair	60.00	
	Joint line pair	125.00	
	Imperf., pair, dull gum	70.00	
1618 A998	13c **brown,** shiny gum, *Nov. 25, 1975*	.25	.20
	Pair	.50	.20
	Joint line pair	.70	
	Dull gum	.30	
	Joint line pair	2.00	
a.	Untagged (Bureau precanceled)		.45
b.	Imperf., pair	25.00	
	Joint line pair	65.00	
g.	Vertical pair, imperf. between	—	
h.	As "a," imperf., pair	—	
1618C A1001	15c **gray, dark blue & red,** *June 30, 1978*	.40	.20
	Pair	.80	.20
d.	Imperf., pair	25.00	
e.	Pair, imperf. between	150.00	
f.	Gray omitted	40.00	
i.	Tagging omitted	20.00	
1619 A1002	16c **ultramarine,** *Mar. 31, 1978*	.35	.20
	Pair	.70	.20
	Joint line pair	1.50	—
a.	Block tagging	.50	
	Pair	1.00	.25
	Nos. 1613-1619 (9)	2.20	1.80

No. 1619a has a white background without bluish tinge, is a fraction of a millimeter smaller than No. 1619, no joint lines and has block instead of overall tagging.

Nos. 1615a, 1615d, 1616b, 1617a, 1618a, issued also with dull gum.

Bureau Precancels: 9c, 7 diff., 10c, 3 diff., 13c, 12 diff. See Nos. 1811, 1813, 1816.

13-Star Flag over Independence
United States 13c Hall — A1015

13-Star Flag over Capitol — A1016

Flag over Capitol — A1016

Designers: No. 1622, Melbourne Brindle. No. 1623, Esther Porter.

Panes of 100 (10x10) each.

1975-81   *Perf. 11x10¾*

1622 A1015	13c **dark blue & red,** *Nov. 15, 1975*	.25	.20
	P# block of 20, 2-3#, 2-3 Zip, 2-3 Mail Early	5.75	—
a.	Horiz. pair, imperf. between	50.00	
b.	Vertical pair, imperf.	1,100.	
e.	Horiz. pair, imperf. vert.	—	
f.	Tagging omitted	4.00	

No. 1622 was printed on the Multicolored Huck Press. Plate markings are at top or bottom of pane. It has large block tagging and nearly vertical multiple gum ridges.
See note after No. 1338F for marginal markings.

Perf. 11¼

1622C A1015	13c **dark blue & red,** *1981*	1.00	.25
	P# block of 20, 1-2#, 1-2 Zip	50.00	—
	P# block of 6	20.00	—
d.	Vertical pair, imperf	150.00	

No. 1622C was printed on the Combination Press. Plate markings are at sides of pane. It has small block tagging and flat gum.
See note after No. 1703.

BOOKLET STAMPS

1977, Mar. 11   **Engr.**   **Perf. 11**

1623 A1016	13c **blue & red**	.25	.20
a.	Booklet pane, 1 #1590 + 7 #1623	2.25	1.10
d.	Pair, #1590 & #1623	.70	.70

Perf. 10x9¾

1623B A1016	13c **blue & red**	.80	.80
c.	Booklet pane, 1 #1590A + 7 #1623B	29.00	—
e.	Pair, #1590A & #1623B	24.00	22.50

COIL STAMP

1975, Nov. 15   **Perf. 10 Vertically**

1625 A1015	13c **dark blue & red**	.25	.20
	Pair	.50	.20
a.	Imperf., pair	25.00	

Designed by Terrence W. McCaffrey.

LITHOGRAPHED, ENGRAVED (Giori)
Plates of 200 subjects of four panes of 50.

1976, Jan. 17		**Tagged**		**Perf. 11**
1632 A1022	13c	dark blue & red (engr.), ultra.		
		& red (litho.)	.20	.20
		P# block of 4	1.00	—
		Margin block of 4, Mr. Zip and		
		"Use Zip Code"	1.00	—
a.		Dark blue & red (engr.) omitted		—

No. 1632a is a top row stamp with all engraved colors (wording) omitted due to a color shift.

Illustration reduced.

Designed by Walt Reed.

PHOTOGRAVURE (Andreotti)
Plates of 200 subjects in four panes of 50.

1976, Feb. 23		**Tagged**		**Perf. 11**
1633 A1023	13c	Delaware	.25	.20
1634 A1024	13c	Pennsylvania	.25	.20
1635 A1025	13c	New Jersey	.25	.20
1636 A1026	13c	Georgia	.25	.20
1637 A1027	13c	Connecticut	.25	.20
1638 A1028	13c	Massachusetts	.25	.20
1639 A1029	13c	Maryland	.25	.20
1640 A1030	13c	South Carolina	.25	.20
1641 A1031	13c	New Hampshire	.25	.20
1642 A1032	13c	Virginia	.25	.20
1643 A1033	13c	New York	.25	.20
1644 A1034	13c	North Carolina	.25	.20
1645 A1035	13c	Rhode Island	.25	.20
1646 A1036	13c	Vermont	.25	.20
1647 A1037	13c	Kentucky	.25	.20
1648 A1038	13c	Tennessee	.25	.20
1649 A1039	13c	Ohio	.25	.20
1650 A1040	13c	Louisiana	.25	.20
1651 A1041	13c	Indiana	.25	.20
1652 A1042	13c	Mississippi	.25	.20
1653 A1043	13c	Illinois	.25	.20
1654 A1044	13c	Alabama	.25	.20
1655 A1045	13c	Maine	.25	.20
1656 A1046	13c	Missouri	.25	.20
1657 A1047	13c	Arkansas	.25	.20
1658 A1048	13c	Michigan	.25	.20
1659 A1049	13c	Florida	.25	.20
1660 A1050	13c	Texas	.25	.20
1661 A1051	13c	Iowa	.25	.20
1662 A1052	13c	Wisconsin	.25	.20
1663 A1053	13c	California	.25	.20
1664 A1054	13c	Minnesota	.25	.20
1665 A1055	13c	Oregon	.25	.20
1666 A1056	13c	Kansas	.25	.20
1667 A1057	13c	West Virginia	.25	.20
1668 A1058	13c	Nevada	.25	.20
1669 A1059	13c	Nebraska	.25	.20
1670 A1060	13c	Colorado	.25	.20
1671 A1061	13c	North Dakota	.25	.20
1672 A1062	13c	South Dakota	.25	.20
1673 A1063	13c	Montana	.25	.20
1674 A1064	13c	Washington	.25	.20
1675 A1065	13c	Idaho	.25	.20
1676 A1066	13c	Wyoming	.25	.20
1677 A1067	13c	Utah	.25	.20
1678 A1068	13c	Oklahoma	.25	.20
1679 A1069	13c	New Mexico	.25	.20
1680 A1070	13c	Arizona	.25	.20
1681 A1071	13c	Alaska	.25	.20
1682 A1072	13c	Hawaii	.25	.20
a.		Pane of 50	15.00	—

TELEPHONE CENTENNIAL ISSUE
Centenary of first telephone call by Alexander Graham Bell, March 10, 1876.

Bell's Telephone Patent Application, 1876 — A1073

Designed by George Tscherny.

ENGRAVED (Giori)
Plates of 200 subjects in four panes of 50.

1976, Mar. 10		**Tagged**		**Perf. 11**
1683 A1073	13c	black, purple & red, *tan*	.25	.20
		P# block of 4	1.10	—
		Margin block of 4, Mr. Zip and		
		"Use Zip Code"	1.00	—
a.		Black & purple omitted		—

No. 1683a comes from a partially printed pane. The errors have only tiny traces of red present so are best collected as a horiz. strip of 5 with 2 or 3 error stamps.

COMMERCIAL AVIATION ISSUE
50th anniversary of first contract airmail flights: Dearborn, Mich. to Cleveland, Ohio, Feb. 15, 1926; and Pasco, Wash. to Elko, Nev., Apr. 6, 1926.

Ford-Pullman Monoplane and Laird Swallow Biplane — A1074

Designed by Robert E. Cunningham.

PHOTOGRAVURE (Andreotti)
Plates of 200 subjects in four panes of 50 each

1976, Mar. 19		**Tagged**		**Perf. 11**
1684 A1074	13c	blue & multicolored	.25	.20
		P# block of 10, 5#	2.75	—
		Margin block of 4, Mr. Zip and		
		"Use Zip Code"	1.00	—

CHEMISTRY ISSUE
Honoring American chemists, in conjunction with the centenary of the American Chemical Society.

Various Flasks, Separatory Funnel, Computer Tape — A1075

Designed by Ken Davies.

PHOTOGRAVURE (Andreotti)
Plates of 200 subjects in four panes of 50.

1976, Apr. 6		**Tagged**		**Perf. 11**
1685 A1075	13c	multicolored	.25	.20
		P# block of 12, 6#	3.25	—
		Margin block of 4, Mr. Zip and		
		"Use Zip Code"	1.00	—
		Pair with full vert. gutter btwn.		—

AMERICAN BICENTENNIAL ISSUES
SOUVENIR SHEETS

Designs, from Left to Right, No. 1686: a, Two British officers. b, Gen. Benjamin Lincoln. c, George Washington. d, John Trumbull, Col. Cobb, von Steuben, Lafayette, Thomas Nelson. e, Alexander Hamilton, John Laurens, Walter Stewart (all vert.).

No. 1687: a, John Adams, Roger Sherman, Robert R. Livingston. b, Jefferson, Franklin. c, Thomas Nelson, Jr., Francis Lewis, John Witherspoon, Samuel Huntington. d, John Hancock, Charles Thomson. e, George Read, John Dickinson, Edward Rutledge (a, d, vert., b, c, e, horiz.).

No. 1688: a, Boatsman. b, Washington. c, Flag bearer. d, Men in boat. e, Men on shore (a, d, horiz., b, c, e, vert.).

No. 1689: a, Two officers. b, Washington. c, Officer, black horse. d, Officer, white horse. e, Three soldiers (a, c, e, horiz., b, d, vert.).

Declaration of Independence, by John Trumbull — A1077

Washington Crossing the Delaware, by Emmanuel Leutze / Eastman Johnson — A1078

Washington Reviewing Army at Valley Forge, by William T. Trego — A1079

Illustrations reduced.

Designed by Vincent E. Hoffman.

LITHOGRAPHED
Plates of 30 subjects in six panes of 5 each.

1976, May 29		**Tagged**		**Perf. 11**
1686 A1076		Sheet of 5	3.25	—
a.-e.		13c **multicolored**	.45	.40
f.		"USA/13c" omitted on "b," "c" &		
		"d," imperf.		2,250.
g.		"USA/13c" omitted on "a" & "e"	450.00	—
h.		Imperf., untagged		2,250.
i.		"USA/13c" omitted on "b," "c" &		
		"d"	450.00	—
j.		"USA/13c" double on "b"		—
k.		"USA/13c" omitted on "c" & "d"	750.00	—
l.		"USA/13c" omitted on "e"	500.00	—
m.		"USA/13c" omitted, imperf. untagged		—
n.		As "g," imperf., untagged		—
1687 A1077		Sheet of 5	4.25	—
a.-e.		18c **multicolored**	.55	.55
f.		Design & marginal inscriptions omitted	3,000.	—
g.		"USA/18c" omitted on "a" & "c"	750.00	—
h.		"USA/18c" omitted on "b," "d" & "e"	450.00	—
i.		"USA/18c" omitted on "d"	500.00	500.00
j.		Black omitted in design	2,000.	—
k.		"USA/18c" omitted, imperf., untagged	3,000.	—
m.		"USA/18c" omitted on "b" & "e"	500.00	—
n.		"USA/18c" omitted on "b" & "d"		—

Surrender of Cornwallis at Yorktown, by John Trumbull — A1076

p.	Imperf. (tagged)	—	
q.	"USA/18c" omitted on "c"	—	
1688	A1078 Sheet of 5	5.25	—
a.-e.	24c **multicolored**	.70	.70
f.	"USA/24c" omitted, imperf.	3,500.	
g.	"USA/24c" omitted on "d" & "e"	450.00	450.00
h.	Design & marginal inscriptions omitted	3,500.	
i.	"USA/24c" omitted on "a," "b" & "c"	500.00	—
j.	Imperf., untagged	3,000.	
k.	"USA/24c" of "d" & "e" inverted	—	
1689	A1079 Sheet of 5	6.25	—
a.-e.	31c **multicolored**	.85	.85
f.	"USA/31c" omitted, imperf.	2,750.	
g.	"USA/31c" omitted on "a" & "c"	400.00	
h.	"USA/31c" omitted on "b," "d" & "e"	450.00	—
i.	"USA/31c" omitted on "e"	450.00	
j.	Black omitted in design	2,000.	
k.	Imperf., untagged	—	2,250.
l.	"USA/31c" omitted on "b" & "d"	—	
m.	"USA/31c" omitted on "a," "b" & "e"	—	
n.	As "m," imperf., untagged	—	
p.	As "h," imperf., untagged	—	2,500.
q.	As "g," imperf., untagged	—	
r.	As "g," untagged on "d" & "e"	2,750.	
s.	As "f," untagged	2,250.	
	Nos. 1686-1689 (4)	19.00	

Issued in connection with Interphil 76 International Philatelic Exhibition, Philadelphia, Pa., May 29-June 6. Size of sheets: 153x204mm; size of stamps: 25x39½mm, 39½x25mm.
Nos. 1688-1689 exist with inverted perforations.

Benjamin Franklin

American Bicentennial: Benjamin Franklin (1706-1790), deputy postmaster general for the colonies (1753-1774) and statesman. Design based on marble bust by anonymous Italian sculptor after terra cotta bust by Jean Jacques Caffieri, 1777. Map published by R. Sayer and J. Bennett in London.

Franklin and Map of North America, 1776 — A1080

Designed by Bernard Reilander (Canada).

LITHOGRAPHED, ENGRAVED (Giori)
Plates of 200 subjects in four panes of 50.

1976, June 1	**Tagged**		**Perf. 11**	
1690	A1080 13c **ultramarine & multicolored**	.25	.20
	P# block of 4	1.10	
	Margin block of 4, Mr. Zip and "Use Zip Code"	1.00	—
a.	Light blue omitted	250.00	
b.	Tagging omitted	5.00	

See Canada No. 691.

Declaration of Independence

Designed after painting of Declaration of Independence, by John Trumbull, in the Rotunda of the Capitol, Washington, D.C. Nos. 1691-1694 printed in continuous design. Left panes contain 10 No. 1694a and 5 each of Nos. 1691-1692; right panes contain 5 each of Nos. 1693-1694 and 10 No. 1694a.

JULY 4,1776
A1081

JULY 4,1776
A1082

AMERICAN BICENTENNIAL ISSUE

State Flags
A1023-A1072

JULY 4,1776
A1083

JULY 4,1776
A1084

Designed by Vincent E. Hoffman.

PHOTOGRAVURE (Andreotti)
Plates of 200 subjects in four panes of 50.

1976, July 4	Tagged	Perf. 11	
1691 A1081 13c **blue & multicolored**		.30	.20
1692 A1082 13c **blue & multicolored**		.30	.20
1693 A1083 13c **blue & multicolored**		.30	.20
1694 A1084 13c **blue & multicolored**		.30	.20
a.	Strip of 4, #1691-1694	1.20	1.10
	P# block of 20, 5#, "Mail Early in the Day," Mr. Zip and "Use Zip Code"	5.75	—
	P# block of 16, 5#, "Mail Early in the Day"	4.50	—
	Margin block of 4, Mr. Zip and "Use Zip Code"	1.25	—

OLYMPIC GAMES ISSUE

12th Winter Olympic Games, Innsbruck, Austria, Feb. 4-15, and 21st Summer Olympic Games, Montreal, Canada, July 17-Aug. 1. Nos. 1695-1696 alternate in one row, Nos. 1697-1698 in other row.

Diving — A1085

Skiing — A1086

Running — A1087

Skating — A1088

Designed by Donald Moss.

PHOTOGRAVURE (Andreotti)
Plates of 200 subjects in four panes of 50.

1976, July 16	Tagged	Perf. 11	
1695 A1085 13c **multicolored**		.25	.20
1696 A1086 13c **multicolored**		.25	.20
1697 A1087 13c **multicolored**		.25	.20
1698 A1088 13c **multicolored**		.25	.20
a.	Block of 4, #1695-1698	1.10	1.10
	P# block of 12, 6#	3.25	—
	P# block of 20, 6#, Mr. Zip and slogans	5.75	—
	Margin block of 4, Mr. Zip and "Use Zip Code"	1.25	—
b.	As "a," imperf.	700.00	

CLARA MAASS ISSUE

Clara Louise Maass (1876-1901), volunteer in fight against yellow fever, birth centenary.

Clara Maass and Newark German Hospital Pin — A1089

Designed by Paul Calle.

PHOTOGRAVURE (Andreotti)
Plates of 160 subjects in four panes of 40.

1976, Aug. 18	Tagged	Perf. 11	
1699 A1089 13c **multicolored**		.25	.20
	P# block of 12, 6#	3.25	—
	Margin block of 4, Mr. Zip, "Use Zip Code" and "Mail Early in the Day"	1.00	—
a.	Horiz. pair, imperf. vert.	450.00	

ADOLPH S. OCHS ISSUE

Adolph S. Ochs (1858-1935), publisher of the New York Times, 1896-1935.

Adolph S. Ochs — A1090

Designed by Bradbury Thompson; photograph by S. J. Woolf.

GIORI PRESS PRINTING
Plates of 128 subjects in four panes of 32 (8x4).

1976, Sept. 18	Tagged	Perf. 11	
1700 A1090 13c **black & gray**		.25	.20
	P# block of 4	1.10	—
	Margin block of 4, Mr. Zip and "Use Zip Code"	.90	—

CHRISTMAS ISSUE

Nativity, by John Singleton Copley — A1091

"Winter Pastime," by Nathaniel Currier — A1092

Designers: No. 1701, Bradbury Thompson after 1776 painting in Museum of Fine Arts, Boston. No. 1702, Stevan Dohanos after 1855 lithograph in Museum of the City of New York.

PHOTOGRAVURE (Andreotti)
Plates of 200 subjects in four panes of 50.

1976, Oct. 27	Tagged	Perf. 11	
1701 A1091 13c **multicolored**		.25	.20
	P# block of 12, 6#	3.25	—
	Margin block of 4, Mr. Zip and "Use Zip Code"	1.00	—
a.	Imperf., pair	100.00	
1702 A1092 13c **multi, overall tagging**		.25	.20
	P# block of 10, 5#	2.75	—
	Margin block of 4, Mr. Zip and "Use Zip Code"	1.00	—
a.	Imperf., pair	100.00	

Plates of 230 (10x23) subjects in panes of 50 (5x10)
Tagged, Block

1703 A1092 13c **multicolored**		.25	.20
	P# block of 20, 5-8#	6.00	—
a.	Imperf., pair	110.00	
b.	Vert. pair, imperf. between	—	
c.	Tagging omitted	12.50	
d.	Red omitted	—	
e.	Yellow omitted	—	

No. 1702 has overall tagging. Lettering at base is black and usually ½mm below design. As a rule, no "snowflaking" in sky or pond. Pane of 50 has margins on 4 sides with slogans. Plate Nos. 37465-37478.

No. 1703 has block tagging the size of printed area. Lettering at base is gray black and usually ¾mm below design. "Snowflaking" generally in sky and pond. Plate Nos. 37617-37621 or 37634-37638.

Copies of No. 1703 are known with various amounts of red or yellow missing. Nos. 1703d-1703e are stamps with the colors totally omitted. Expertization is recommended.

COMBINATION PRESS

Cylindrical plates consist of 23 rows of subjects, 10 across for commemoratives (230 subjects), 20 across for definitives (460 subjects), with selvage on the two outer edges only. Guilloting through the perforations creates individual panes of 50 or 100 with selvage on one side only.

Failure of the guillotine to separate through the perforations resulted in straight edges on some stamps. Perforating teeth along the center column and the tenth rows were removed for issues released on or after May 31, 1984 (the 10c Richard Russell, for definitives; the 20c Horace Moses, for commemoratives), creating panes with straight edged stamps on three sides.

Three sets of plate numbers, copyright notices (starting with No. 1787), and zip insignia (starting with No. 1927) are arranged identically on the left and right sides of the plate so that each pane has at least one of each marking. The markings adjacent to any particular row are repeated either seven or eight rows away on the cylinder.

Fifteen combinations of the three marginal markings and blank rows are possible on panes.

AMERICAN BICENTENNIAL ISSUE
Washington at Princeton

Washington's Victory over Lord Cornwallis at Princeton, N.J., bicentenary.

Washington, Nassau Hall, Hessian Prisoners and 13-star Flag, by Charles Willson Peale — A1093

Designed by Bradbury Thompson.

PHOTOGRAVURE (Andreotti)
Plates of 160 subjects in four panes of 40.

1977, Jan. 3	Tagged	Perf. 11	
1704 A1093 13c **multicolored**		.25	.20
	P# block of 10, 5#	2.75	—
	Margin block of 4, Mr. Zip and "Use Zip Code", "Mail Early in the Day"	1.00	—
a.	Horiz. pair, imperf. vert.	550.00	

SOUND RECORDING ISSUE

Centenary of the invention of the phonograph by Thomas Alva Edison and development of sophisticated recording industry.

Tin Foil Phonograph
A1094

Designed by Walter and Naiad Einsel.

LITHOGRAPHED, ENGRAVED (Giori)
Plates of 200 subjects in four panes of 50.

1977, Mar. 23	Tagged	Perf. 11	
1705 A1094 13c **black & multicolored**		.25	.20
	P# block of 4	1.10	—
	Margin block of 4, Mr. Zip and "Use Zip Code"	1.00	—

AMERICAN FOLK ART ISSUE
Pueblo Pottery

Pueblo art, 1880-1920, from Museums in New Mexico, Arizona and Colorado.

Nos. 1706-1709 are printed in blocks and strips of 4 in panes of 40. In the 1st row Nos. 1706-1709 are in sequence as listed. In the 2nd row Nos. 1708-1709 are followed by Nos. 1706-1709, 1708-1709.

Zia Pot
A1095

San Ildefonso Pot
A1096

Zia: Museum of New Mexico
Pueblo Art USA 13c

San Ildefonso: Denver Art Museum
Pueblo Art USA 13c

Hopi: Heard Museum Phoenix
Pueblo Art USA 13c

Acoma: School of American Research
Pueblo Art USA 13c

Hopi Pot
A1097

Acoma Pot
A1098

Designed by Ford Ruthling.

PHOTOGRAVURE (Andreotti)
Plates of 160 subjects in four panes of 40.

1977, Apr. 13		Tagged	Perf. 11	
1706	A1095 13c	multicolored	.25	.20
1707	A1096 13c	multicolored	.25	.20
1708	A1097 13c	multicolored	.25	.20
1709	A1098 13c	multicolored	.25	.20
a.		Block or strip of 4, #1706-1709	1.00	1.00
		P# block of 10, 5#	2.75	—
		P# block of 16, 5#; Mr. Zip and slogans	4.25	—
		Margin block of 6, Mr. Zip and "Use Zip Code" "Mail Early in the Day"	1.50	—
b.		As "a," imperf. vert.	2,500.	

LINDBERGH FLIGHT ISSUE

Charles A. Lindbergh's solo transatlantic flight from New York to Paris, 50th anniversary.

Spirit of St. Louis — A1099

Designed by Robert E. Cunningham.

PHOTOGRAVURE (Andreotti)
Plates of 200 subjects in four panes of 50.

1977, May 20		Tagged	Perf. 11	
1710	A1099 13c	multicolored	.25	.20
		P# block of 12, 6#	3.25	—
		Margin block of 4, Mr. Zip and "Use Zip Code"	1.00	—
a.		Imperf., pair	1,050.	

Beware of private overprints on No. 1710.

COLORADO STATEHOOD ISSUE

Issued to honor Colorado as the "Centennial State." It achieved statehood in 1876.

Columbine and Rocky Mountains — A1100

Designed by V. Jack Ruther.

PHOTOGRAVURE (Andreotti)
Plates of 200 subjects in four panes of 50.

1977, May 21		Tagged	Perf. 11	
1711	A1100 13c	multicolored	.25	.20
		P# block of 12, 6#	3.25	—
		Margin block of 4, Mr. Zip and "Use Zip Code"	1.00	—
a.		Horiz. pair, imperf. between	600.00	
b.		Horiz. pair, imperf. vertically	900.00	
c.		Perf. 11.2	.35	.25
		P# block of 12, 6#	20.00	

Perforations do not run through the sheet margin on about 10 percent of the sheets of No. 1711.

BUTTERFLY ISSUE

Nos. 1712-1713 alternate in 1st row, Nos. 1714-1715 in 2nd row. This arrangement is repeated throughout the pane. Butterflies represent different geographic US areas.

Swallowtail
A1101

USA 13c *Papilio oregonius*

Checkerspot
A1102

USA 13c *Euphydryas phaeton*

Dogface — A1103

USA 13c *Colias eurydice*

Orange-Tip
A1104

USA 13c *Anthocaris midea*

Designed by Stanley Galli.

PHOTOGRAVURE (Andreotti)
Plates of 200 subjects in four panes of 50.

1977, June 6		Tagged	Perf. 11	
1712	A1101 13c	tan & multicolored	.25	.20
1713	A1102 13c	tan & multicolored	.25	.20
1714	A1103 13c	tan & multicolored	.25	.20
1715	A1104 13c	tan & multicolored	.25	.20
a.		Block of 4, #1712-1715	1.00	1.00
		P# block of 12, 6#	3.25	—
		P# block of 20, 6#, Mr. Zip and slogans	5.50	—
		Margin block of 4, Mr. Zip and "Use Zip Code"	1.05	—
b.		As "a," imperf. horiz.	15,000.	

AMERICAN BICENTENNIAL ISSUES
Marquis de Lafayette

200th anniversary of Lafayette's Landing on the coast of South Carolina, north of Charleston.

Lafayette

US Bicentennial 13c

Marquis de Lafayette — A1105

Designed by Bradbury Thompson.

GIORI PRESS PRINTING
Plates of 160 subjects in four panes of 40.

1977, June 13		Tagged	Perf. 11	
1716	A1105 13c	blue, black & red	.25	.20
		P# block of 4	1.10	—
		Margin block of 4, Mr. Zip and "Use Zip Code"	1.00	—

Skilled Hands for Independence

Nos. 1717-1718 alternate in 1st row, Nos. 1719-1720 in 2nd row. This arrangement is repeated throughout the pane.

the SEAMSTRESS for INDEPENDENCE USA 13c

Seamstress
A1106

the BLACKSMITH for INDEPENDENCE USA 13c

Blacksmith
A1107

the WHEELWRIGHT for INDEPENDENCE USA 13c

Wheelwright
A1108

the LEATHERWORKER for INDEPENDENCE USA 13c

Leatherworker
A1109

Designed by Leonard Everett Fisher.

PHOTOGRAVURE (Andreotti)
Plates of 200 subjects in four panes of 50.

1977, July 4		Tagged	Perf. 11	
1717	A1106 13c	multicolored	.25	.20
1718	A1107 13c	multicolored	.25	.20
1719	A1108 13c	multicolored	.25	.20
1720	A1109 13c	multicolored	.25	.20
a.		Block of 4, #1717-1720	1.00	1.00
		P# block of 12, 6#	3.25	—
		P# block of 20, 6#, Mr. Zip and slogans	5.50	—
		Margin block of 4, Mr. Zip and "Use Zip Code"	1.05	—

PEACE BRIDGE ISSUE

50th anniversary of the Peace Bridge, connecting Buffalo (Fort Porter), N.Y. and Fort Erie, Ontario.

Peace Bridge and Dove — A1110

Designed by Bernard Brussel-Smith (wood-cut).

ENGRAVED
Plates of 200 subjects in four panes of 50.

1977, Aug. 4		Tagged	Perf. 11x10½
1721 A1110	13c **blue**	.25	.20
	P# block of 4	1.10	
	Margin block of 4, Mr. Zip and "Use Zip Code"	1.00	—

AMERICAN BICENTENNIAL ISSUE
Battle of Oriskany

200th anniv. of the Battle of Oriskany, American Militia led by Brig. Gen. Nicholas Herkimer (1728-77).

Herkimer at Oriskany, by Frederick Yohn — A1111

Designed by Bradbury Thompson after painting in Utica, N.Y. Public Library.

PHOTOGRAVURE (Andreotti)
Plates of 160 subjects in four panes of 40.

1977, Aug. 6		Tagged	Perf. 11
1722 A1111	13c **multicolored**	.25	.20
	P# block of 10, 5#	2.75	—
	Margin block of 6, Mr. Zip and "Use Zip Code" and "Mail Early in the Day"	1.50	—

ENERGY ISSUE

Conservation and development of nation}s energy resources. Nos. 1723-1724 se-tenant vertically.

"Conservation" A1112

"Development" A1113

Designed by Terrance W. McCaffrey.

PHOTOGRAVURE (Andreotti)
Plates of 160 subjects in four panes of 40.

1977, Oct. 20		Tagged	Perf. 11
1723 A1112	13c **multicolored**	.25	.20
1724 A1113	13c **multicolored**	.25	.20
a.	Pair, #1723-1724	.50	.50
	P# block of 12, 6#	3.25	—
	Margin block of 4, Mr. Zip, "Use Zip Code" and "Mail Early in the Day"	1.00	—

ALTA CALIFORNIA ISSUE

Founding of El Pueblo de San José de Guadalupe, first civil settlement in Alta California, 200th anniversary.

Farm Houses — A1114

Designed by Earl Thollander.

LITHOGRAPHED, ENGRAVED (Giori)
Plates of 200 subjects in four panes of 50.

1977, Sept. 9		Tagged	Perf. 11
1725 A1114	13c **black & multicolored**	.25	.20
	P# block of 4	1.10	—
	Margin block of 4, Mr. Zip and "Use Zip Code"	1.00	—

AMERICAN BICENTENNIAL ISSUE
Articles of Confederation

200th anniversary of drafting the Articles of Confederation, York Town, Pa.

Members of Continental Congress in Conference A1115

Designed by David Blossom.

ENGRAVED (Giori)
Plates of 200 subjects in four panes of 50.

1977, Sept. 30		Tagged	Perf. 11
1726 A1115	13c **red & brown,** cream	.25	.20
	P# block of 4	1.10	—
	Margin block of 4, Mr. Zip and "Use Zip Code"	1.00	—
a.	Tagging omitted	—	
b.	Red omitted	—	
c.	Red & brown omitted	—	

No. 1726b also has most of the brown omitted. No. 1726c must be collected as a transition multiple, certainly with No. 1726b and preferably also with No. 1726.

TALKING PICTURES, 50th ANNIV.

Movie Projector and Phonograph A1116

Designed by Walter Einsel.

LITHOGRAPHED, ENGRAVED (Giori)
Plates of 200 subjects in four panes of 50.

1977, Oct. 6		Tagged	Perf. 11
1727 A1116	13c **multicolored**	.25	.20
	P# block of 4	1.10	—
	Margin block of 4, Mr. Zip and "Use Zip Code"	1.00	—

AMERICAN BICENTENNIAL ISSUE
Surrender at Saratoga

200th anniversary of Gen. John Burgoyne's surrender at Saratoga.

Surrender of Burgoyne, by John Trumbull — A1117

Designed by Bradbury Thompson.

PHOTOGRAVURE (Andreotti)
Plates of 160 subjects in four panes of 40.

1977, Oct. 7		Tagged	Perf. 11
1728 A1117	13c **multicolored**	.25	.20
	P# block of 10, 5#	2.75	—
	Margin block of 6, Mr. Zip, "Use Zip Code" and "Mail Early in the Day"	1.50	—

CHRISTMAS ISSUE

Washington at Valley Forge A1118

Rural Mailbox A1119

Designers: No. 1729, Stevan Dohanos, after painting by J. C. Leyendecker. No. 1730, Dolli Tingle.

PHOTOGRAVURE (Combination Press)
Plates of 460 subjects (20x23) in panes of 100 (10x10).

1977, Oct. 21		Tagged	Perf. 11
1729 A1118	13c **multicolored**	.25	.20
	P# block of 20, 5-8#	5.75	—
a.	Imperf., pair	75.00	

See Combination Press note after No. 1703.

PHOTOGRAVURE (Andreotti)
Plates of 400 subjects in 4 panes of 100.

1730 A1119	13c **multicolored**	.25	.20
	P# block of 10, 5#	2.75	—
	Margin block of 4, Mr. Zip and "Use Zip Code"	1.00	—
	Pair with full vert. gutter btwn.	—	
a.	Imperf., pair	300.00	

CARL SANDBURG ISSUE

Carl Sandburg (1878-1967), poet, biographer and collector of American folk songs, birth centenary.

Carl Sandburg, by William A. Smith, 1952 — A1120

Designed by William A. Smith.

GIORI PRESS PRINTING
Plates of 200 subjects in four panes of 50.

1978, Jan. 6		Tagged	Perf. 11
1731 A1120	13c **black & brown**	.25	.20
	P# block of 4	1.10	—
	Margin block of 4, Mr. Zip	1.00	—
a.	Brown omitted		

CAPTAIN COOK ISSUE

Capt. James Cook, 200th anniversary of his arrival in Hawaii, at Waimea, Kauai, Jan. 20, 1778, and of his anchorage in Cook Inlet, near Anchorage, Alaska, June 1, 1778. Nos. 1732-1733 printed in panes of 50, containing 25 each of Nos. 1732-1733 including 5 No. 1732a.

Capt. Cook, by Nathaniel Dance — A1121

"Resolution" and "Discovery," by John Webber — A1122

Designed by Robert F. Szabo (No. 1732; Jak Katalan (No. 1733.

GIORI PRESS PRINTING
Plates of 200 subjects in four panes of 50.

1978, Jan. 20		Tagged	Perf. 11
1732 A1121	13c **dark blue**	.25	.20
1733 A1122	13c **green**	.25	.20
a.	Vert. pair, imperf. horiz.		
b.	Pair, #1732-1733	.50	.50
	P# block of 4, #1732 or 1733	1.10	—
	Margin block of 4, Mr. Zip, #1732 or 1733	1.05	—
	P# block of 20, 10 each #1732-1733, P# and slogans	5.25	—
c.	As "b," imperf. between	4,500.	

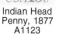

Indian Head
Penny, 1877
A1123

Eagle
A1124

Red Masterpiece and Medallion
Roses — A1126

ENGRAVED (Giori)
Plates of 600 subjects in four panes of 150.

1978		**Tagged**		**Perf. 11**	
1734	A1123	13c **brown & blue green**, *bister,* *Jan. 11, 1978*		.25	.20
		P# block of 4		1.25	—
		Margin block of 4, "Use Correct Zip Code"		1.00	—
		Pair with full horiz. gutter btwn.		—	
a.		Horiz. pair, imperf. vert.		300.00	

PHOTOGRAVURE (Andreotti)
Plates of 400 subjects in four panes of 100.

1735	A1124	(15c) **orange**, *May 22, 1978*	.25	.20
		P# block of 4	1.25	
		Margin block of 4, "Use Zip Code"	1.00	
a.		Imperf., pair	90.00	
b.		Vert. pair, imperf. horiz.	700.00	
c.		Perf. 11.2	.25	.20
		P# block of 4	1.75	—
		Zip block of 4	1.10	—

BOOKLET STAMPS
ENGRAVED
Perf. 11x10½ on 2 or 3 sides

1736	A1124	(15c) **orange**	.25	.20
a.		Booklet pane of 8, *May 22, 1978*	2.25	.90

Perf. 10

1737	A1126	15c **multicolored**	.25	.20
a.		Booklet pane of 8, *July 11, 1978*	2.25	.90
b.		As "a," imperf.	—	
c.		As "a," tagging omitted	40.00	

A1127   A1128   A1129

A1130   A1131

Designed by Ronald Sharpe.

BOOKLET STAMPS
ENGRAVED

1980, Feb. 7		**Tagged**	**Perf. 11 on 2 or 3 sides**	
1738	A1127	15c **sepia**, *yellow*	.30	.20
1739	A1128	15c **sepia**, *yellow*	.30	.20
1740	A1129	15c **sepia**, *yellow*	.30	.20
1741	A1130	15c **sepia**, *yellow*	.30	.20
1742	A1131	15c **sepia**, *yellow*	.30	.20
a.		Booklet pane of 10, 2 each #1738-1742	3.50	3.00
b.		Strip of 5, #1738-1742	1.50	1.40

COIL STAMP

1978, May 22			**Perf. 10 Vert.**	
1743	A1124	(15c) **orange**	.25	.20
		Pair	.50	.20
		Joint line pair	.65	
a.		Imperf., pair	90.00	
		Joint line pair	—	

No. 1743a is valued in the grade of fine.

BLACK HERITAGE SERIES
Harriet Tubman (1820-1913), born a slave, helped more than 300 slaves escape to freedom.

Harriet Tubman and Cart
Carrying Slaves — A1133

Designed by Jerry Pinkney after photograph.

PHOTOGRAVURE (Andreotti)
Plates of 200 subjects in four panes of 50.

1978, Feb. 1		**Tagged**	**Perf. 10½x11**	
1744	A1133	13c **multicolored**	.25	.20
		P# block of 12, 6#	3.25	—
		Margin block of 4, Mr. Zip	1.00	—

AMERICAN FOLK ART ISSUE
Quilts
Nos. 1745-1746 alternate in 1st row, Nos. 1747-1748 in 2nd.

Basket Design

A1134   A1135

A1136   A1137

Designed by Christopher Pullman after 1875 quilt made in New York City. Illustration slightly reduced.

PHOTOGRAVURE (Andreotti)
Plates of 192 subjects in four panes of 48 (6x8).

1978, Mar. 8			**Perf. 11**	
1745	A1134	13c **multicolored**	.25	.20
1746	A1135	13c **multicolored**	.25	.20
1747	A1136	13c **multicolored**	.25	.20
1748	A1137	13c **multicolored**	.25	.20
a.		Block of 4, #1745-1748	1.00	1.00
		P# block of 12, 6#	3.25	—
		P# block of 16, 6#, Mr. Zip and copyright	4.50	—
		Margin block of 4, Mr. Zip, copyright	1.05	—

AMERICAN DANCE ISSUE
Nos. 1749-1750 alternate in 1st row, Nos. 1751-1752 in 2nd.

Ballet
A1138

Theater
A1139

Folk Dance
A1140

Modern Dance
A1141

Designed by John Hill.

PHOTOGRAVURE (Andreotti)
Plates of 192 subjects in four panes of 48 (6x8).

1978, Apr. 26		**Tagged**	**Perf. 11**	
1749	A1138	13c **multicolored**	.25	.20
1750	A1139	13c **multicolored**	.25	.20
1751	A1140	13c **multicolored**	.25	.20
1752	A1141	13c **multicolored**	.25	.20
a.		Block of 4, #1749-1752	1.00	1.00
		P# block of 12, 6#	3.25	—
		P# block of 16, 6#, Mr. Zip and copyright	4.50	—
		Margin block of 4, Mr. Zip, copyright	1.05	—

AMERICAN BICENTENNIAL ISSUE
French Alliance, signed in Paris, Feb. 6, 1778 and ratified by Continental Congress, May 4, 1778.

King Louis XVI and
Benjamin Franklin, by
Charles Gabriel
Sauvage — A1142

Designed by Bradbury Thompson after 1785 porcelain sculpture in Du Pont Winterthur Museum, Delaware.

GIORI PRESS PRINTING
Plates of 160 subjects in four panes of 40.

1978, May 4		**Tagged**	**Perf. 11**	
1753	A1142	13c **blue, black & red**	.25	.20
		P# block of 4	1.10	—
		Margin block of 4, Mr. Zip	1.00	—

EARLY CANCER DETECTION ISSUE

George Papanicolaou, M.D. (1883-1962), cytologist and developer of Pap Test, early cancer detection in women.

Dr. Papanicolaou and
Microscope — A1143

Designed by Paul Calle.

ENGRAVED

Plates of 200 subjects in four panes of 50.

1978, May 18	Tagged	Perf. 10½x11	
1754 A1143 13c **brown**		.25	.20
P# block of 4		1.10	—
Margin block of 4, Mr. Zip		1.00	—

PERFORMING ARTS ISSUE

Jimmie Rodgers (1897-1933), the "Singing Brakeman, Father of Country Music" (No. 1755); George M. Cohan (1878-1942), actor and playwright (No. 1756).

Jimmie Rodgers
with Guitar and
Brakeman's Cap,
Locomotive
A1144

George M. Cohan,
"Yankee Doodle
Dandy" and Stars
A1145

Designed by Jim Sharpe.

PHOTOGRAVURE (Andreotti)

Plates of 200 subjects in four panes of 50.

1978	Tagged	Perf. 11	
1755 A1144 13c **multicolored**, May 24		.25	.20
P# block of 12, 6#		3.25	—
Margin block of 4, Mr. Zip		1.00	—
1756 A1145 15c **multicolored**, July 3		.30	.20
P# block of 12, 6#		4.00	—
Margin block of 4, Mr. Zip		1.25	—

CAPEX ISSUE

CAPEX '78, Canadian International Philatelic Exhibition, Toronto, Ont., June 9-18.

Wildlife from Canadian-United States
Border — A1146

Designed by Stanley Galli.

LITHOGRAPHED, ENGRAVED (Giori)

Plates of 24 subjects in four panes of 6 each.

1978, June 10	Tagged	Perf. 11	
1757 A1146 Block of 8, **multicolored**		2.00	2.00
a. 13c Cardinal		.25	.20
b. 13c Mallard		.25	.20

c.	13c Canada goose	.25	.20
d.	13c Blue jay	.25	.20
e.	13c Moose	.25	.20
f.	13c Chipmunk	.25	.20
g.	13c Red fox	.25	.20
h.	13c Raccoon	.25	.20
	P# block of 8	2.25	
	Margin block of 8, Mr. Zip and copyright	2.10	—
	Pane of 6 No. 1757, P#, Mr. Zip and copyright	13.00	
i.	Yellow, green, red, brown, blue, black (litho) omitted	7,000.	
j.	Strip of 4 (a-d), imperf. vert.		—
k.	Strip of 4 (e-h), imperf. vert.		—

PHOTOGRAPHY ISSUE

Photography's contribution to communications and understanding.

Camera, Lens, Color
Filters, Adapter Ring,
Studio Light Bulb and
Album — A1147

Designed by Ben Somoroff.

PHOTOGRAVURE (Andreotti)

Plates of 160 subjects in four panes of 40.

1978, June 26	Tagged	Perf. 11	
1758 A1147 15c **multicolored**		.30	.20
P# block of 12, 6#		4.00	—
Margin block of 4, Mr. Zip and copyright		1.25	—
P# block of 16, 6#, Mr. Zip and copyright		5.00	—

VIKING MISSIONS TO MARS ISSUE

Second anniv. of landing of Viking 1 on Mars.

Viking 1 Lander
Scooping up Soil
on Mars — A1148

Designed by Robert McCall.

LITHOGRAPHED, ENGRAVED (Giori)

Plates of 200 subjects in four panes of 50.

1978, July 20	Tagged	Perf. 11	
1759 A1148 15c **multicolored**		.30	.20
P# block of 4		1.35	—
Margin block of 4, Mr. Zip		1.25	—

AMERICAN OWLS ISSUE

Nos. 1760-1761 alternate in one horizontal row. Nos. 1762-1763 in the next.

Great Gray
Owl — A1149

Saw-whet
Owl — A1150

Barred
Owl — A1151

Great Horned
Owl — A1152

Designed by Frank J. Waslick.

LITHOGRAPHED, ENGRAVED (Giori)

Plates of 200 subjects in four panes of 50.

1978, Aug. 26	Tagged	Perf. 11	
1760 A1149 15c **multicolored**		.30	.20
1761 A1150 15c **multicolored**		.30	.20
1762 A1151 15c **multicolored**		.30	.20
1763 A1152 15c **multicolored**		.30	.20
a. Block of 4, #1760-1763		1.25	1.25
P# block of 4		1.40	—
Margin block of 4, Mr. Zip		1.25	—

AMERICAN TREES ISSUE

Nos. 1764-1765 alternate in 1st row, Nos. 1766-1767 in 2nd.

Giant
Sequoia — A1153

White Pine — A1154

White Oak — A1155

Gray Birch — A1156

Designed by Walter D. Richards.

PHOTOGRAVURE (Andreotti)

Plates of 160 subjects in four panes of 40.

1978, Oct. 9	Tagged	Perf. 11	
1764 A1153 15c **multicolored**		.30	.20
1765 A1154 15c **multicolored**		.30	.20
1766 A1155 15c **multicolored**		.30	.20
1767 A1156 15c **multicolored**		.30	.20
a. Block of 4, #1764-1767		1.25	1.25
P# block of 12, 6#		4.00	—
P# block of 16, 6#, Mr. Zip and copyright		5.25	—
Margin block of 4, Mr. Zip, copyright		1.30	—
b. As "a," imperf. horiz.		15,000.	

No. 1767b is unique.

CHRISTMAS ISSUE

Madonna and Child with Cherubim, by Andrea della Robbia — A1157

Child on Hobby Horse and Christmas Trees — A1158

Designed by Bradbury Thompson (No. 1768) after terra cotta sculpture in National Gallery, Washington, D.C. by Dolli Tingle (No. 1769).

PHOTOGRAVURE (Andreotti)
Plates of 400 subjects in four panes of 100.

1978, Oct. 18			Perf. 11	
1768	A1157	15c blue & multicolored	.30	.20
		P# block of 12, 6#	4.00	
		Margin block of 4, "Use Correct Zip Code"	1.25	—
a.		Imperf., pair	90.00	

Value for No. 1768a is for an uncreased pair.

1769	A1158	15c red & multicolored	.30	.20
		P# block of 12, 6#	4.00	
		Margin block of 4, "Use Correct Zip Code"	1.25	—
		Pair with full horiz. gutter btwn.		
a.		Imperf., pair	100.00	
b.		Vert. pair, imperf. horiz.	2,000.	

Robert F. Kennedy — A1159

Martin Luther King, Jr. and Civil Rights Marchers — A1160

ROBERT F. KENNEDY ISSUE
Designed by Bradbury Thompson after photograph by Stanley Tretick.

ENGRAVED
Plates of 192 subjects in four panes of 48 (8x6).

1979, Jan. 12		Tagged	Perf. 11	
1770	A1159	15c blue	.35	.20
		P# block of 4	1.75	—
		Margin block of 4, Mr. Zip	1.50	—
a.		Tagging omitted		

BLACK HERITAGE SERIES
Dr. Martin Luther King, Jr. (1929-1968), Civil Rights leader.

Designed by Jerry Pinkney.

PHOTOGRAVURE (Andreotti)
Plates of 200 subjects in four panes of 50.

1979, Jan. 13		Tagged	Perf. 11	
1771	A1160	15c multicolored	.30	.20
		P# block of 12, 6#	4.00	
		Margin block of 4, Mr. Zip	1.25	—
a.		Imperf., pair		

INTERNATIONAL YEAR OF THE CHILD ISSUE

Children of Different Races — A1161

Designed by Paul Calle.

ENGRAVED
Plates of 200 subjects in four panes of 50.

1979, Feb. 15		Tagged	Perf. 11	
1772	A1161	15c orange red	.30	.20
		P# block of 4	1.40	—
		Margin block of 4, Mr. Zip	1.25	—

John Steinbeck (1902-1968), Novelist — A1162

Albert Einstein (1879-1955), Theoretical Physicist — A1163

JOHN STEINBECK ISSUE
Designed by Bradbury Thompson after photograph by Philippe Halsman.

ENGRAVED
Plates of 200 subjects in four panes of 50.

1979, Feb. 27		Tagged	Perf. 10½x11	
1773	A1162	15c dark blue	.30	.20
		P# block of 4	1.40	—
		Margin block of 4, Mr. Zip	1.25	—

ALBERT EINSTEIN ISSUE
Designed by Bradbury Thompson after photograph by Hermann Landshoff.

ENGRAVED
Plates of 200 subjects in four panes of 50.

1979, Mar. 4		Tagged	Perf. 10½x11	
1774	A1163	15c chocolate	.35	.20
		P# block of 4	1.75	—
		Margin block of 4, Mr. Zip	1.50	—
		Pair, horiz. gutter btwn.		

AMERICAN FOLK ART ISSUE
Pennsylvania Toleware, c. 1800

Pennsylvania Toleware
Folk Art USA 15c
Coffeepot — A1164

Pennsylvania Toleware
Folk Art USA 15c
Tea Caddy — A1165

Pennsylvania Toleware
Folk Art USA 15c
Sugar Bowl — A1166

Pennsylvania Toleware
Folk Art USA 15c
Coffeepot — A1167

Designed by Bradbury Thompson.

PHOTOGRAVURE (Andreotti)
Plates of 160 subjects in four panes of 40.

1979, Apr. 19		Tagged	Perf. 11	
1775	A1164	15c multicolored	.30	.20
1776	A1165	15c multicolored	.30	.20
1777	A1166	15c multicolored	.30	.20
1778	A1167	15c multicolored	.30	.20
a.		Block of 4, #1775-1778	1.25	1.25
		P# block of 10, 5#	3.25	
		P# block of 16, 5#; Mr. Zip and copyright	5.25	
		Margin block of 6, Mr. Zip and copyright	2.00	
b.		As "a," imperf. horiz.	4,250.	

AMERICAN ARCHITECTURE ISSUE
Nos. 1779-1780 alternate in 1st row, Nos. 1781-1782 in 2nd.

Architecture USA 15c
Virginia Rotunda, by Thomas Jefferson — A1168

Architecture USA 15c
Baltimore Cathedral, by Benjamin Latrobe — A1169

Architecture USA 15c
Boston State House, by Charles Bulfinch — A1170

Architecture USA 15c
Philadelphia Exchange, by William Strickland — A1171

Designed by Walter D. Richards.

ENGRAVED (Giori)
Plates of 192 subjects in four panes of 48 (6x8).

1979, June 4		Tagged	Perf. 11	
1779	A1168	15c black & brick red	.30	.20
1780	A1169	15c black & brick red	.30	.20
1781	A1170	15c black & brick red	.30	.20
1782	A1171	15c black & brick red	.30	.20
a.		Block of 4, #1779-1782	1.25	1.25
		P# block of 4	1.40	—
		Margin block of 4, Mr. Zip	1.30	—

ENDANGERED FLORA ISSUE
Nos. 1783-1784 alternate in one horizontal row. Nos. 1785-1786 in the next.

Persistent Trillium
A1172

Hawaiian Wild Broadbean
A1173

Contra Costa Wallflower
A1174

Antioch Dunes Evening Primrose
A1175

Designed by Frank J. Waslick.

PHOTOGRAVURE (Andreotti)
Plates of 200 subjects in four panes of 50.

1979, June 7		Tagged	Perf. 11	
1783	A1172	15c multicolored	.30	.20
1784	A1173	15c multicolored	.30	.20
1785	A1174	15c multicolored	.30	.20
1786	A1175	15c multicolored	.30	.20
a.		Block of 4, #1783-1786	1.25	1.25
		P# block of 12, 6#	4.00	—
		P# block of 20, 6#, Mr. Zip and copyright	6.50	—
		Margin block of 4, Mr. Zip	1.30	—
		As "a," full vert. gutter btwn.		—
b.		As "a," imperf.	600.00	

Scott Assigns Major-Number Status to Numerous Perforation Varieties

by James E. Kloetzel

Scott catalogue users will notice many interesting enhancements in this year's *Specialized Catalogue of U.S. Stamps and Covers* but perhaps none as important as the new major numbers appearing in the Postage and Air Post sections. Sixty-nine stamps that until now had been assigned only minor-letter status beneath major-number listings have been elevated to full major-number status in the 2001 *U.S. Specialized*.

After taking into account the 1979 15¢ John Paul Jones perf. 11 and perf. 12 varieties, now Scott 1789A and 1789B; the 1980 15¢ Winter Olympic Games perf. 11 varieties, now Scott 1795A-1798A; and the 1982 20¢ State Birds and Flowers perf. 11 varieties, now Scott 1953A-2002A, these 69 new majors actually represent only sixteen different issues. The full list of new postage and air post major numbers is shown in Figure 1, and a visual presentation of the stamps is shown in Figure 2. Of course, all of these stamps will look very familiar to collectors, because all of them are simply major perforation varieties that share the designs of fairly common, currently listed major Scott numbers.

One new major stands out in importance because of its extreme scarcity. The perf. 12 variety of the 15¢ John Paul Jones stamp, formerly Scott 1789b and now Scott 1789B, is a very expensive stamp, valued at $1,750 mint never hinged and $1,000 used in the 2001 *U.S. Specialized*. Now that this stamp has attained major number status, it will be interesting to track its value in the future. Several of the other new majors also have already attained significant value as minors, such as Scott 1590A, the 1977 perf. 10x9 3/4 9¢ slate green Capitol Dome booklet stamp, currently with a catalogue value of $22.50 mint never hinged. The 1993 perf. 11.2x11.5 29¢ Hank Williams stamp, Scott 2723A, likewise has attained a Scott catalogue value of $22.50 mint never hinged, and the 1982 perf. 10 1/2x11 1/4 40¢ Philip Mazzei air post stamp, Scott C98A, has a catalogue value of $6.50 mint never hinged. Most of the other new major numbers are as common or almost as common as their counterpart majors with different perforations, so their acquisition should present little burden for collectors.

Some of the new major numbers are booklet varieties of stamps that also were printed in sheet format with a different perforation gauge. Others are simply similar sheet stamps or similar booklet stamps that happened to be perforated on different perforating machines having different gauges. Some of these different gauges are somewhat close to each other (for example, the two Mazzei air post stamps, Scott C98 and C98A, are perf. 11 and perf. 10 1/2x11 1/4, respectively), while others are significantly different (for example, the two 1991 29¢ Flower sheet stamps, Scott 2524 and 2524A, are perf. 11 and perf. 13x12 3/4, respectively, and the two 32¢ Flag over Porch self-adhesive booklet stamps, Scott 2920 and 2920D, are die cut 8.7 and die cut 11.3, respectively).

The Previous Listing Philosophy

Why were these stamps with different perforation gauges made minor varieties originally? Here's the background.

When collectors in recent years have pointed out that some of the varieties with very different perforations should be accorded major-number status, they often have cited the Washington-Franklin series that gives different major listings to stamps having the same designs with perforation gauges 12, 10 and 11. Also cited have been the 1922 and following definitives where perf. 11 stamps from flat plate presses are separated by major listings from stamps from rotary presses perf. 11x10 1/2.

All of the foregoing perforation differences represent significant and purposeful decisions on the part of the Post Office Department or significant differences of production technique. In the case of the Washington-Franklins, conscious decisions were made to change perforation gauges to arrive at a gauge that worked best for stamp separation, while the change from flat plate presses to rotary presses involved significant differences in stamp production technology in addition to the perforations used in each case.

In more recent times, perforation changes have not had much, if anything, to do with conscious decision making or significant new production techniques. Indeed, on modern self-adhesives, the die cutting that simulates perforations is not really even necessary at all. Often, it has seemed that new perforation gauges have resulted from unimportant factors such as new machinery that for no apparent reason was set at a different gauge. When two or more different machines were used to perforate a single issue, there no longer seemed to be a logical reason why they should have been gauged differently for perforations, and often there did not appear to be any attempt made to standardize production, especially between Postal Service subcontractors. For these reasons, previous Scott editors often decided to incorporate such stamps with different perforation gauges under a single major listing. That was the logic used for such listings. The decisions were not haphazard.

Scott No.	Stamp	Perforation
1580B	(10¢) Chrismas	10.5x11.3
1590A	9¢ Capitol Dome	10x9 3/4
1622C	13¢ Flag & Independence Hall	11 1/4
1623B	13¢ Flag over Capitol	10x9 3/4
1789A	15¢ John Paul Jones	11
1789B	15¢ John Paul Jones	12
1795A-1798A	15¢ Olympic Games	11
1951A	20¢ Love	11 1/4x10 1/2
1953A-2002A	20¢ State Birds & Flowers	11 1/4x11
2524A	29¢ Flower	13x12 3/4
2535A	29¢ Love	11
2593B	29¢ Flag & Pledge	11x10
2723A	29¢ Hank Williams	11.2x11.5
2871A	29¢ Christmas Madonna	9 3/4x11
2920D	32¢ Flag over Porch	11.3
3003A	32¢ Christmas Madonna	9.8x10.9
C98A	40¢ Philip Mazzei	10 1/2x11 1/4

Figure 1: A list of the 69 new major Scott numbers.

Why Change Now?

The problems with the logic of listing stamps with significant perforation differences under one major listing have turned out to be twofold. First and most important, most collectors and dealers either writing to Scott or polled by Scott seem to favor the most simple and straightforward listing approach possible. The philosophy of most collectors and dealers seems to hold that stamps of the same design having perforation differences of at least 1/2 perf. gauge (or more or less depending on an individual's preference) should automatically be given a major catalogue number. No guesswork—just a simple rule. This approach does not ask why a different gauge was used. The simple fact of its existence is sufficient. While previous listings could be justified by logic, Scott has decided to adopt this "simpler is better" listing philosophy that seems to be favored by most philatelists. The Scott editors have agreed that a 1/2 perf. gauge difference is a logical cut-off point between minor and major perforation significance.

The second reason for the change is that there have crept into the modern listings some inconsistencies that logically should be straightened out. That is, while some stamps with widely different perforation gauges have been assigned a major number and a minor number, in other cases similar stamps with even smaller perforation differences have been made into separate major listings. Nobody likes that kind of situation, including the Scott editors. However, sometimes in the listing process such inconsistencies raise their ugly little heads.

A change of this magnitude was made only after extensive study and discussion at the Scott offices. The logic of making the changes had to be weighed against the known dislike of collectors and dealers of having catalogue numbers change once they have been assigned. Also, the impact of the changes on Scott albums and supplement pages had to be considered. If a change was going to be made, it seemed to make sense to make it immediately rather than wait. After all the alternatives were carefully analyzed, the decision was made to set up a simple and logical system of assigning major or minor numbers to perforation-different stamps

Figure 2: These are the perforation varieties that have assumed major listing status.

and to bring consistency to the current listings by applying that system to those items already listed.

What is the New System?

The new listing rule is simple and straightforward. It does not depend on a knowledge of production techniques, and it doesn't ask why stamps with different perforations were produced. The rule is that United States stamps of the same design with perforation differences of at least 1/2 perf. gauge in either the horizontal or vertical direction will be assigned separate, major Scott numbers.

A careful, stamp-by-stamp sweep of the current listings was made, and after a very careful re-measuring of perforations, it was concluded that 69 stamps that were currently listed as minor varieties of design-identical major numbers passed the 1/2-perf.-gauge-difference test. That triggered their being renumbered as major listings. A review of the new listings by catalogue users will reveal that several of the stamps are gauged slightly differently than they were before. That is because many of the earlier listings were made when Scott perfed stamps to the nearest 1/2 perforation gauge only. As we now gauge to the nearest 1/4 perforation gauge, we applied that standard to the affected stamps. Also, when the original stamps had been gauged by tenths, they were re-gauged using tenths or converted to quarters if that seemed more logical.

All that will be necessary in the future will be to apply the rule systematically when making new listings. With the firm rule now in place, we have every confidence that this can be done successfully.

It should be noted that there are a few listings where major and minor numbers have slightly different perforation gauges that will not be affected by the new rule. These include several stamps from the Great Americans series that are perforated either 10.9 line or 11.2 bulls-eye. The 1983 40¢ Summer Olympic Games air post, Scott C105-C108 and C105a-C108a were perforated 10.9 and 11.2 also, and their listings will not change. Very occasionally, an exception to the new rule may be expected to appear, and in fact one

already has. The 1999 20¢ Pheasant vending booklet, Scott BK 242A, contains two booklet panes, Scott 3051b and 3051c, that have a fifth stamp turned sideways in relation to four upright stamps. That fifth stamp is die cut 10 1/2 on three sides whereas the upright stamps are die cut 10 1/2x11 on three sides. Rule or no rule, this situation cries out for treatment as a single listing, and the stamps turned sideways will remain a minor as Scott 3051a while the upright stamps will remain the major number Scott 3051.

What About the Albums and Supplements?

Scott is aware that some collectors will not want to adopt new major listings that are made after the fact. The earliest stamp affected, Scott 1580B, the 1975 Christmas stamp, is, after all, 25 years old this month. The decision was made, therefore, not to publish the new major numbers as updated pages in the traditional upcoming U.S. supplements. To do so would tend to force collectors to remount many stamps in order to accommodate the new listings. At the same time, any changes to the pages in albums will not be made until those albums are re-printed.

Scott will publish special "New Major Numbers Update" pages for collectors who wish to update to the new major numbers in their existing albums. These will be stand-alone supplements not tied to the normal yearly supplements, and only those collectors who choose to update need order the special supplement package.

All of these decisions concerning the listings, albums and supplement pages were discussed actively over a period exceeding one full year, with various thoughts on the subject being shared for longer than that. We believe these decisions reflect the concerns and desires of the customers who have communicated with us as well as those who have not openly voiced their opinions, and we believe the logic of the changes will positively impact collectors far into the future. Comments are always welcome.

This Special Feature article is a reprint of the October 2000 *Scott Stamp Monthly* Catalogue Column.

SEEING EYE DOGS ISSUE

1st guide dog program in the US, 50th anniv.

USA 15c

Seeing For Me

German Shepherd Leading
Man — A1176

Designed by Joseph Csatari.

PHOTOGRAVURE (Combination Press)
Plates of 230 (10x23) subjects in panes of 50
(10x5).

1979, June 15	Tagged	Perf. 11	
1787 A1176 15c **multicolored**		.30	.20
P# block of 20, 5-8#, 1-2 copyright		6.50	—
a.	Imperf., pair	425.00	—
b.	Tagging omitted	10.00	

See Combination Press note after No. 1703.

Special Olympics

Skill · Sharing · Joy
USA 15c

Child Holding
Winner's
Medal — A1177

I have not yet
begun to fight

John Paul Jones
US Bicentennial 15c

John Paul Jones,
by Charles Willson
Peale — A1178

SPECIAL OLYMPICS ISSUE

Special Olympics for special children, Brockport,
N.Y., Aug. 8-13.

Designed by Jeff Cornell.

PHOTOGRAVURE (Andreotti)
Plates of 200 subjects in four panes of 50.

1979, Aug. 9	Tagged	Perf. 11	
1788 A1177 15c **multicolored**		.30	.20
P# block of 10, 5#		3.25	—
Zip block of 4		1.25	—

JOHN PAUL JONES ISSUE

John Paul Jones (1747-1792), Naval Commander,
American Revolution.

Designed after painting in Independence National Historical
Park, Philadelphia.
Printed by American Bank Note Co. and J. W. Fergusson
and Sons.

Designed by Bradbury Thompson.

PHOTOGRAVURE (Champlain)
Plates of 200 subjects in four panes of 50.

1979, Sept. 23	Tagged	Perf. 11x12	
1789 A1178 15c **multicolored**		.30	.20
P# block of 10, 5#		3.25	—
Zip block of 4		1.25	—
c.	Vert. pair, imperf. horiz.	175.00	

Numerous varieties of printer's waste exist. These include
imperforates, perforated or imperforate gutter pairs or blocks
and shifted or missing colors.

Perf. 11

1789A A1178 15c **multicolored**		.50	.20
P# block of 10, 5#		4.00	—
Zip block of 4		3.25	—
d.	Vertical pair, imperf. horiz.	150.00	

Perf. 12

1789B A1178 15c **multicolored**		1,750.	1,000.
P# block of 10, 5#		25,000.	
Zip block of 4		7,500.	

OLYMPIC GAMES ISSUE

22nd Summer Olympic Games, Moscow, July 19-
Aug. 3, 1980. Nos. 1791-1792 alternate in one horizontal row, Nos. 1793-1794 in next.

Javelin — A1179

Running — A1180

Swimming
A1181

Rowing — A1182

Equestrian
A1183

Designed by Robert M. Cunningham.

PHOTOGRAVURE
Plates of 200 subjects in four panes of 50.

1979, Sept. 5	Tagged	Perf. 11	
1790 A1179 10c **multicolored**		.20	.20
P# block of 12, 6#		3.00	—
Zip block of 4		.85	—

1979, Sept. 28			
1791 A1180 15c **multicolored**		.30	.20
1792 A1181 15c **multicolored**		.30	.20
1793 A1182 15c **multicolored**		.30	.20
1794 A1183 15c **multicolored**		.30	.20
a.	Block of 4, #1791-1794	1.25	1.25
P# block of 12, 6#		4.00	—
Zip block of 4		1.30	—
P# block of 20, 6#, zip, copyright		6.50	—
b.	As "a," imperf.	1,500.	

OLYMPIC GAMES ISSUE

13th Winter Olympic Games, Lake Placid, N.Y.,
Feb. 12-24. Nos. 1795-1796 alternate in one horizontal row, Nos. 1797-1798 in next.

Speed
Skating — A1184

Downhill
Skiing — A1185

Ski Jump — A1186

Ice
Hockey — A1187

Designed by Robert M. Cunningham

PHOTOGRAVURE
Plates of 200 subject in four panes of 50.

1980, Feb. 1	Tagged	Perf. 11¼x10½	
1795 A1184 15c **multicolored**		.35	.20
1796 A1185 15c **multicolored**		.35	.20
1797 A1186 15c **multicolored**		.35	.20
1798 A1187 15c **multicolored**		.35	.20
b.	Block of 4, #1795-1798	1.50	1.40
P# block of 12, 6#		4.50	—
Zip block of 4		1.55	—
P# block of 20, 6#, zip and copyright		7.50	—

Perf. 11

1795A A1184 15c **multicolored**		1.05	.60
1796A A1185 15c **multicolored**		1.05	.60
1797A A1186 15c **multicolored**		1.05	.60
1798A A1187 15c **multicolored**		1.05	.60
c.	Block of 4, #1795A-1798A	4.25	3.50
P# block of 12, 6#		14.00	—
Zip block of 4		4.50	—
P# block of 20, 6#, zip and copyright		25.00	—

CHRISTMAS ISSUE

Christmas
15c

Virgin and Child by
Gerard David — A1188

Santa Claus, Christmas
Tree
Ornament — A1189

Designed by Bradbury Thompson (No. 1799) and by Eskil
Ohlsson (No. 1800).

No. 1799 is designed after a painting in National Gallery of
Art, Washington, D.C.

PHOTOGRAVURE (Andreotti)
Plates of 400 subjects in four panes of 100.

1979, Oct. 18	Tagged	Perf. 11	
1799 A1188 15c **multicolored**		.30	.20
P# block of 12, 6#		4.00	—
Zip block of 4		1.25	—
P# block of 20, 6#, zip, copyright		6.50	—
a.	Imperf., pair	90.00	
b.	Vert. pair, imperf. horiz.	700.00	
c.	Vert. pair, imperf. between	2,250.	
1800 A1189 15c **multicolored**		.30	.20
P# block of 12, 6#		4.00	—
Zip block of 4		1.25	—
P# block of 20, 6#, zip, copyright		6.50	—
a.	Green & yellow omitted	625.00	
b.	Green, yellow & tan omitted	700.00	

Nos. 1800a and 1800b always have the remaining colors
misaligned.
No. 1800b is valued in the grade of fine.

VALUES FOR HINGED STAMPS AFTER NO. 771
This catalogue does not value unused stamps
after No. 771 in hinged condition. Hinged unused
stamps from No. 772 to the present are worth considerably less than the values given for unused
stamps, which are for never-hinged examples.

PERFORMING ARTS SERIES

Will Rogers (1879-1935), actor and humorist.

Will Rogers — A1190

Performing Arts USA 15c

Designed by Jim Sharpe.

PHOTOGRAVURE (Andreotti)
Plates of 200 subjects in four panes of 50.

1979, Nov. 4		Tagged	Perf. 11	
1801 A1190 15c	multicolored		.30	.20
	P# block of 12, 6#		4.00	—
	Zip block of 4		1.25	—
	P# block of 20, 6#, zip, copyright		6.50	
a.	Imperf., pair		225.00	

VIETNAM VETERANS ISSUE

A tribute to veterans of the Vietnam War.

Ribbon for Vietnam
Service
Medal — A1191

Designed by Stevan Dohanos.

PHOTOGRAVURE (Andreotti)
Plates of 200 subjects in four panes of 50.

1979, Nov. 11		Tagged	Perf. 11	
1802 A1191 15c	multicolored		.30	.20
	P# block of 10, 5#		3.25	—
	Zip block of 4		1.25	—

W.C. Fields — A1192

Performing Arts USA 15c

Benjamin
Banneker — A1193

Black Heritage USA 15c

PERFORMING ARTS SERIES

W.C. Fields (1880-1946), actor and comedian.

Designed by Jim Sharpe.

PHOTOGRAVURE
Plates of 200 subjects in four panes of 50.

1980, Jan. 29		Tagged	Perf. 11	
1803 A1192 15c	multicolored		.30	.20
	P# block of 12, 6#		4.00	—
	Zip block of 4		1.25	—
	P# block of 20, 6#, zip, copyright		6.50	
a.	Imperf., pair		—	

BLACK HERITAGE ISSUE

Benjamin Banneker (1731-1806), astronomer and mathematician.

Designed by Jerry Pinkney.

Printed by American Bank Note Co. and J. W. Fergusson and Sons.

PHOTOGRAVURE
Plates of 200 subjects in four panes of 50.

1980, Feb. 15		Tagged	Perf. 11	
1804 A1193 15c	multicolored		.35	.20
	P# block of 12, 6#		4.50	—
	Zip block of 4		1.50	—
	Plate block of 20, 6#, zip, copyright		6.50	
a.	Horiz. pair, imperf. vert.		800.00	

Imperfs, including gutter pairs and blocks, exist from printer's waste. These have been fraudulently perforated to simulate No.

1804a. Genuine examples of No. 1804a do not have colors misregistered.

NATIONAL LETTER WRITING WEEK ISSUE

National Letter Writing Week, Feb. 24-Mar. 1. Nos. 1805-1810 are printed vertically se-tenant.

Letters Preserve
Memories — A1194

P.S. Write
Soon — A1195

Letters Lift
Spirits — A1196

Letters Shape
Opinions — A1197

Designed by Randall McDougall.

Plates of 240 subjects in four panes of 60 (10x6) each.

PHOTOGRAVURE

1980, Feb. 25		Tagged	Perf. 11	
1805 A1194 15c	multicolored		.30	.20
1806 A1195 15c	purple & multi		.30	.20
1807 A1196 15c	multicolored		.30	.20
1808 A1195 15c	green & multi		.30	.20
1809 A1197 15c	multicolored		.30	.20
1810 A1195 15c	red & multi		.30	.20
a.	Vertical strip of 6, #1805-1810		1.85	2.00
	P# block of 36, 6#		11.00	—
	Zip block of 12		3.75	—
	Nos. 1805-1810 (6)		1.80	1.20

AMERICANA TYPE

Weaver Violins — A1199

Designer: 3.5c, George Mercer.

COIL STAMPS

1980-81		Engr.	Perf. 10 Vertically	
1811 A984	1c	dark blue, greenish, shiny gum, Mar. 6, 1980	.20	.20
		Pair	.20	.20
		Joint line pair	.40	
		Dull gum	.20	
		Joint line pair	.50	
a.		Imperf., pair	175.00	
		Joint line pair	275.00	
b.		Tagging omitted		
1813 A1199	3.5c	purple, yellow, June 23, 1980	.20	.20
		Pair	.20	.20
		Joint line pair	1.00	
a.		Untagged (Bureau precanceled, lines only)		.20
b.		Imperf., pair	225.00	
		Joint line pair	450.00	
1816 A997	12c	red brown, beige, Apr. 8, 1981	.25	.20
		Pair	.50	.20
		Joint line pair	1.50	—
a.		Untagged (Bureau precanceled)		.25
b.		Imperf., pair	200.00	
		Joint line pair	400.00	
		Nos. 1811-1816 (3)	.65	.60

Bureau Precancels: 12c, lines only, PRESORTED/FIRST CLASS.

Eagle — A1207

PHOTOGRAVURE
Plates of 400 subjects in four panes of 100.

1981, Mar. 15		Tagged	Perf. 11x10½	
1818 A1207 (18c)	violet		.35	.20
	P# block of 4		1.60	—
	Zip block of 4		1.50	—
	Pair with full vert. gutter between		—	

BOOKLET STAMP
ENGRAVED
Perf. 10

1819 A1207 (18c)	violet		.40	.20
a.	Booklet pane of 8		3.75	1.75

COIL STAMP
Perf. 10 Vert.

1820 A1207 (18c)	violet		.40	.20
	Pair		.80	.20
	Joint line pair		1.60	—
a.	Imperf., pair		100.00	
	Joint line pair		250.00	

Frances Perkins
A1208

Dolley
Madison
A1209

FRANCES PERKINS ISSUE

Frances Perkins (1882-1965), Secretary of Labor, 1933-1945 (first woman cabinet member).

Designed by F.R. Petrie.

ENGRAVED
Plates of 200 subjects in four panes of 50.

1980, Apr. 10		Tagged	Perf. 10½x11	
1821 A1208 15c	Prussian blue		.30	.20
	P# block of 4		1.30	—
	Zip block of 4		1.25	—

DOLLEY MADISON ISSUE

Dolley Madison (1768-1849), First Lady, 1809-1817.

Designed by Esther Porter.

ENGRAVED
Plates of 600 subjects in four panes of 150.

1980, May 20		Tagged	Perf. 11	
1822 A1209 15c	red brown & sepia		.30	.20
	P# block of 4		1.40	—
	Zip block of 4		1.25	—

Emily
Bissell — A1210

Helen Keller and
Anne
Sullivan — A1211

EMILY BISSELL ISSUE

Emily Bissell (1861-1948), social worker; introduced Christmas seals in United States.

Designed by Stevan Dohanos.

ENGRAVED
Plates of 200 subjects in four panes of 50.

1980, May 31	Tagged	Perf. 11	
1823 A1210 15c black & red		.35	.20
P# block of 4		1.75	—
Zip block of 4		1.50	—
a. Vert. pair, imperf. horiz.		400.00	

HELEN KELLER ISSUE

Helen Keller (1880-1968), blind and deaf writer and lecturer taught by Anne Sullivan (1867-1936).

Designed by Paul Calle.

LITHOGRAPHED AND ENGRAVED
Plates of 200 subjects in four panes of 50.

1980, June 27	Tagged	Perf. 11	
1824 A1211 15c multicolored		.30	.20
P# block of 4		1.30	—
Zip block of 4		1.25	—

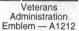

Veterans Administration Emblem — A1212

Gen. Bernardo de Galvez — A1213

VETERANS ADMINISTRATION, 50th ANNIV.

Designed by Malcolm Grear.

Printed by American Bank Note Co. and J. W. Fergusson and Sons.

PHOTOGRAVURE
Plates of 200 subjects in four panes of 50.

1980, July 21	Tagged	Perf. 11	
1825 A1212 15c carmine & violet blue		.30	.20
P# block of 4, 2#		1.30	—
Zip block of 4		1.25	—
a. Horiz. pair, imperf. vert.		450.00	

BERNARDO DE GALVEZ ISSUE

Gen. Bernardo de Galvez (1746-1786), helped defeat British in Battle of Mobile, 1780.

Designed by Roy H. Andersen.

LITHOGRAPHED & ENGRAVED
Plates of 200 subjects in four panes of 50.

1980, July 23	Tagged	Perf. 11	
1826 A1213 15c multicolored		.30	.20
P# block of 4		1.30	—
Zip block of 4		1.25	—
a. Red, brown & blue (engr.) omitted		800.00	
b. Blue, brown, red (engr.) & yellow (litho.) omitted		1,400.	

CORAL REEFS ISSUE

Nos. 1827-1828 alternate in one horizontal row, Nos. 1829-1830 in the next.

Brain Coral, Beaugregory Fish — A1214

Elkhorn Coral, Porkfish — A1215

Chalice Coral, Moorish Idol — A1216

Finger Coral, Sabertooth Blenny — A1217

Designed by Chuck Ripper.

PHOTOGRAVURE
Plates of 200 subjects in four panes of 50.

1980, Aug. 26	Tagged	Perf. 11	
1827 A1214 15c multi		.30	.20
1828 A1215 15c multi		.30	.20
1829 A1216 15c multi		.30	.20
1830 A1217 15c multi		.30	.20
a. Block of 4, #1827-1830		1.25	1.10
P# block of 12, 6#		4.00	—
Zip block of 4		1.30	—
b. As "a," imperf.		1,000.	
c. As "a," vert. imperf. between		—	
d. As "a," imperf. vert.		3,000.	

American Bald Eagle — A1218

Edith Wharton — A1219

ORGANIZED LABOR ISSUE
Designed by Peter Cocci.

PHOTOGRAVURE
Plates of 200 subjects in four panes of 50.

1980, Sept. 1	Tagged	Perf. 11	
1831 A1218 15c multi		.30	.20
P# block of 12, 6#		3.50	—
Zip block of 4		1.25	—
a. Imperf., pair		375.00	

EDITH WHARTON ISSUE

Edith Wharton (1862-1937), novelist.

Designed by Bradbury Thompson after 1905 photograph.

ENGRAVED
Plates of 200 subjects in four panes of 50.

1980, Sept. 5	Tagged	Perf. 10½x11	
1832 A1219 15c purple		.30	.20
P# block of 4		1.30	—
Zip block of 4		1.25	—

EDUCATION ISSUE

"Homage to the Square: Glow" by Josef Albers — A1220

Designed by Bradbury Thompson

Printed by American Bank Note Co. and J. W. Fergusson and Sons.

PHOTOGRAVURE
Plates of 200 subjects in four panes of 50.

1980, Sept. 12	Tagged	Perf. 11	
1833 A1220 15c multi		.30	.20
P# block of 6, 3#		1.90	—
Zip block of 4		1.25	—
a. Horiz. pair, imperf. vert.		240.00	

AMERICAN FOLK ART ISSUE
Pacific Northwest Indian Masks

Heiltsuk, Bella Bella Tribe — A1221

Chilkat Tlingit Tribe — A1222

Tlingit Tribe — A1223

Bella Coola Tribe — A1224

Designed by Bradury Thompson after photographs.

PHOTOGRAVURE
Plates of 160 subjects in four panes of 40.

1980, Sept. 25	Tagged	Perf. 11	
1834 A1221 15c multi		.30	.20
1835 A1222 15c multi		.30	.20
1836 A1223 15c multi		.30	.20
1837 A1224 15c multi		.30	.20
a. Block of 4, #1834-1837		1.25	1.25
P# block of 10, 5#		3.50	—
Zip, copyright block of 6		1.90	—

AMERICAN ARCHITECTURE ISSUE

Smithsonian A1225

Trinity Church — A1226

Penn Academy A1227

Lyndhurst
A1228

Designed by Walter D. Richards.

ENGRAVED (Giori)
Plates of 160 subjects in four panes of 40.

1980, Oct. 9	Tagged		Perf. 11
1838 A1225	15c **black & red**	.30	.20
1839 A1226	15c **black & red**	.30	.20
1840 A1227	15c **black & red**	.30	.20
1841 A1228	15c **black & red**	.30	.20
a.	Block of 4, #1838-1841	1.25	1.25
	P# block of 4	1.50	—
	Zip block of 4	1.30	—
b.	As "a," red omitted on Nos. 1838, 1839	350.00	

No. 1841b was caused by a misregistration of the perforations.

CHRISTMAS ISSUE

Madonna and Child — A1229

Wreath and Toys — A1230

Designed by Esther Porter (No. 1842) after Epiphany Window, Washington Cathedral, and by Bob Timberlake (No. 1843).

PHOTOGRAVURE
Plate of 200 subjects in four panes of 50.

1980, Oct. 31	Tagged		Perf. 11
1842 A1229	15c **multi**	.30	.20
	P# block of 12, 6#	4.00	—
	Zip block of 4	1.25	—
a.	Imperf., pair	70.00	
	Pair with full vert. gutter btwn.	—	

PHOTOGRAVURE (Combination Press)
Plates of 230 subjects (10x23) in panes of 50 (10x5).

1843 A1230	15c **multi**	.30	.20
	P# block of 20, 5-8 #, 1-2 copyright	6.50	—
a.	Imperf., pair	70.00	
b.	Buff omitted	25.00	
c.	Vert. pair, imperf. horiz.	—	
d.	Horiz. pair, imperf. between	4,000.	

No. 1843b is difficult to identify and should have a competent certificate.

See Combination Press note after No. 1703.

GREAT AMERICANS ISSUE

A1231

A1232

A1233

A1234

A1235

A1237

A1238

A1239

A1241

A1243

A1245

A1247

A1249

A1251

A1236

A1240

A1242

A1244

A1246

A1248

A1250

A1252

A1253

A1255

A1254

A1256

Designers: 1c, Bernie Fuchs. 2c, Burt Silverman, 3c, 17c, 40c, Ward Brackett. 4c, 7c, 10c, 18c, 30c, Richard Sparks. 5c, Paul Calle. 6c, No. 1861, Dennis Lyall. 8c, Arthur Lidov. 9c, 11c, Robert Alexander Anderson. 13c, Brad Holland. 14c, Bradbury Thompson. 19c, 39c, Roy H. Andersen. No. 1860, Jim Sharpe. No. 1862, 22c, 50c, 37c, Christopher Calle. 35c, Nathan Jones.

ENGRAVED

1980-85	Tagged		Perf. 11x10½
Perf. 11 (1c, 6c-11c, 14c, No. 1862, 22c, 30c, 39c, 40c, 50c)			
1844 A1231	1c **black,** perf. 11.2, small block tagging, *Sept. 23, 1983*	.20	.20
	P# block of 6	.35	
	P# block of 20, 1-2 #, 1-2 copyright	2.00	—
a.	Imperf., pair	300.00	
b.	Vert. pair, imperf. between and at bottom	3,000.	
c.	Perf. 10.9, small block tagging	.20	.20
	P# block of 6	.35	
	P# block of 20, 1-2 #, 1-2 copyright	2.00	—
d.	Perf. 10.9, large block tagging, *1985*	.20	.20
	P# block of 6	.35	
	P# block of 20, 1-2 #, 1-2 copyright	2.00	—
e.	Vert. pair, imperf. horiz.	—	
1845 A1232	2c **brn blk,** overall tagging, *Nov. 18, 1982*	.20	.20
	P# block of 4	.35	
	Zip block of 4	.25	
	Vert. pair, full gutter between	—	
a.	Tagging omitted	—	
1846 A1233	3c **olive green,** overall tagging, *July 13, 1983*	.20	.20
	P# block of 4	.55	
	Zip block of 4	.30	
a.	Tagging omitted	4.00	
1847 A1234	4c **violet,** overall tagging, *June 3, 1983*	.20	.20
	P# block of 4	.65	
	Zip block of 4	.35	
a.	Tagging omitted	4.00	
1848 A1235	5c **henna brown,** overall tagging, *June 25, 1983*	.20	.20
	P# block of 4	.70	
	Zip block of 4	.45	
1849 A1236	6c **orange vermilion,** large block tagging, *Sept. 19, 1985*	.20	.20
	P# block of 6	.85	
	P# block of 20, 1-2 #, 1-2 zip, 1-2 copyright	3.50	—
a.	Vert. pair, imperf. between and at bottom	2,250.	
1850 A1237	7c **bright carmine,** small block tagging, *Jan. 25, 1985*	.20	.20
	P# block of 6	.95	
	P# block of 20, 1-2 #, 1-2 zip, 1-2 copyright	4.00	—
1851 A1238	8c **olive black,** overall tagging, *July 25, 1985*	.20	.20
	P# block of 4	.85	
	Zip block of 4	.60	
1852 A1239	9c **dark green,** small block tagging, *June 7, 1985*	.20	.20
	P# block of 6	1.30	
	P# block of 20, 1-2 #. 1-2 zip, 1-2 copyright	5.00	—
1853 A1240	10c **Prus. blue,** small block tagging, *May 31, 1984*	.25	.20
	P# block of 6	2.00	
	P# block of 20, 1-2 #, 1-2 copyright, 1-2 zip	8.00	—
a.	Large block tagging	.30	.20
	P# block of 6	2.25	
	P# block of 20, 1-2 #, 1-2 copyright, 1-2 zip	9.00	—
b.	Vert. pair, imperf. between and at bottom	900.00	
c.	Horiz. pair, imperf. between	2,250.	

Completely imperforate tagged or untagged stamps are from printer's waste.

1854 A1241	11c **dark blue,** overall tagging, *Feb. 12, 1985*	.25	.20
	P# block of 4	1.25	
	Zip block of 4	1.00	
a.	Tagging omitted	9.00	

1855 A1242 13c **light maroon,** overall tagging, *Jan. 15, 1982* .25 .20
   P# block of 4 2.00
   Zip block of 4 1.10 —
a. Tagging omitted 7.50
1856 A1243 14c **slate green,** small block tagging, *Mar. 21, 1985* .30 .20
   P# block of 6 2.25
   P# block of 20, 1-2 #, 1-2 zip, 1-2 copyright 9.00 —
a. Large block tagging .30 .20
   P# block of 6 2.25
   P# block of 20, 1-2 #, 1-2 zip, 1-2 copyright 9.00 —
b. Vert. pair, imperf. horiz. 125.00
c. Horiz. pair, imperf. btwn. 9.00
d. Vert. pair, imperf. btwn. 1,500.
e. All color omitted —

No. 1856e comes from a partially printed pane and should be collected as a vertical strip of 10, one stamp normal, one stamp transitional and 8 stamps with color omitted.

1857 A1244 17c **green,** overall tagging, *May 28, 1981* .35 .20
   P# block of 4 2.00
   Zip block of 4 1.40 —
a. Tagging omitted 10.00
1858 A1245 18c **dark blue,** overall tagging, *May 7, 1981* .35 .20
   P# block of 4 3.00
   Zip block of 4 1.40 —
a. Tagging omitted 6.00
1859 A1246 19c **brown,** overall tagging, *Dec. 27, 1980* .40 .20
   P# block of 4 2.75
   Zip block of 4 1.75 —
1860 A1247 20c **claret,** overall tagging, *Jan. 12, 1982* .40 .20
   P# block of 4 3.75
   Zip block of 4 1.65 —
a. Tagging omitted 6.00
1861 A1248 20c **green,** overall tagging, *June 10, 1983* .45 .20
   P# block of 4 4.00
   Zip block of 4 1.90 —
1862 A1249 20c **black,** perf 10.9, small block tagging, dull gum, *Jan. 26, 1984* .40 .20
   P# block of 6 4.50
   P# block of 20, 1-2 #, 1-2 copyright, 1-2 zip 12.00 —
a. Perf. 11.2, large block tagging, dull gum .40 .20
   Corner P# block of 4 3.00
   Zip block of 4 1.60 —
b. Perf. 11.2, overall tagging, dull gum, *1990* .40 —
   Corner P# block of 4 3.75
   Zip block of 4 1.60 —
c. Tagging omitted, perf. 11.2 10.00
d. Prephosphored uncoated paper (mottled tagging), shiny gum, perf. 11.2, *1993* .40 .20
   Corner P# block of 4 2.50
   Zip block of 4 1.60
1863 A1250 22c **dark chalky blue,** small block tagging, *Apr. 23, 1985* .55 .20
   P# block of 6 6.00
   P# block of 20, 1-2 #, 1-2 zip, 1-2 copyright 17.50 —
a. Large block tagging 1.00 .20
   P# block of 6 8.00
   P# block of 20, 1-2 #, 1-2 zip, 1-2 copyright 22.50 —
b. Perf. 11.2, large block tagging, *1987* .55 .20
   Corner P# block of 4 8.00
   Zip block of 4 2.25 —
c. Tagging omitted 6.00
d. Vert. pair, imperf. horiz. 2,500.
e. Vert. pair, imperf. between —
f. Horiz. pair, imperf. between 2,500.
1864 A1251 30c **olive gray,** small block tagging, *Sept. 2, 1984* .55 .20
   P# block of 6 3.50
   P# block of 20, 1-2 #, 1-2 copyright, 1-2 zip 17.50 —
a. Perf. 11.2, large block tagging .55 .20
   Corner P# block of 4 3.25
   Zip block of 4 2.50 —
b. Perf. 11.2, overall tagging 1.50 .20
   Corner P# block of 4 22.50
   Zip block of 4 6.50 —
c. Tagging omitted —
1865 A1252 35c **gray,** overall tagging, *June 3, 1981* .70 .20
   P# block of 4 4.00
   Zip block of 4 3.00 —
a. Tagging omitted —
1866 A1253 37c **blue,** overall tagging, *Jan. 26, 1982* .75 .20
   P# block of 4 3.50
   Zip block of 4 3.00 —
a. Tagging omitted 10.00
1867 A1254 39c **rose lilac,** perf 10.9, small block tagging, *Mar. 20, 1985* .80 .20
   P# block of 6 5.50
   P# block of 20, 1-2 #, 1-2 copyright 22.50 —
a. Vert. pair, imperf. horiz. 600.00
b. Vert. pair, imperf. between 2,000.
c. Large block tagging, perf 10.9 .80 .20
   P# block of 6 5.50
   P# block of 20, 1-2 #, 1-2 zip, 1-2 copyright 20.00 —
d. Perf. 11.2, large block tagging .75 .20
   Corner P# block of 4 5.50
   Zip block of 4 3.00 —

1868 A1255 40c **dark green,** perf 10.9, small block tagging, *Feb. 24, 1984* .80 .20
   P# block of 6 6.00
   P# block of 20, 1-2 #, 1-2 copyright, 1-2 zip 20.00 —
a. Perf. 11.2, large block tagging .80 .20
   Corner P# block of 4 6.50
   Zip block of 4 3.25 —
1869 A1256 50c **brown,** perf 10.9, overall tagging, shiny gum, *Feb. 22, 1985* .95 .20
   P# block of 4 7.50
   Zip block of 4 4.00 —
a. Perf. 11.2, large block tagging, dull gum .95 .20
   P# block of 4 6.25
   Zip block of 4 4.00 —
b. Tagging omitted 10.00
c. Tagging omitted, perf. 11.2, dull gum 7.50
d. Perf. 11.2, overall tagging, dull gum 1.50 .20
   P# block of 4 8.50
   Zip block of 4 6.75 —
e. Perf. 11.2, prephosphored uncoated paper (mottled tagging), shiny gum, *1992* .90 .20
   P# block of 4 5.00
   Zip block of 4 4.00 —
Nos. 1844-1869 (26) 10.30 5.20

A1261

A1262

EVERETT DIRKSEN (1896-1969)
Senate minority leader, 1960-1969.

Designed by Ron Adair.

ENGRAVED
Plates of 200 subjects in four panes of 50.

1981, Jan. 4   Tagged   Perf. 11
1874 A1261 15c gray .30 .20
   P# block of 4 1.40
   Zip block of 4 1.25 —
a. All color omitted

No. 1874a comes from a partially printed pane and may be collected as a vertical strip of 3 or 5 (1 or 3 stamps normal, one stamp transitional and one stamp with color omitted) or as a pair with one partially printed stamp.

BLACK HERITAGE SERIES
Whitney Moore Young, Jr. (1921-1971), civil rights leader.

Designed by Jerry Pinkney.

PHOTOGRAVURE
Plates of 200 subjects in four panes of 50.

1981, Jan. 30   Tagged   Perf. 11
1875 A1262 15c multi .35 .20
   P# block of 4, 6# 1.75
   Zip block of 4 1.50 —

FLOWER ISSUE

A1263   A1264

Rose USA 18c   Camellia USA 18c

Dahlia USA 18c   Lily USA 18c

A1265   A1266

Designed by Lowell Nesbitt.

PHOTOGRAVURE
Plates of 192 subjects in four panes of 48 (8x6).

1981, Apr. 23   Tagged   Perf. 11
1876 A1263 18c multicolored .35 .20
1877 A1264 18c multicolored .35 .20
1878 A1265 18c multicolored .35 .20
1879 A1266 18c multicolored .35 .20
a. Block of 4, #1876-1879 1.40 1.25
   P# block of 4, 6# 1.75
   Zip block of 4 1.45 —

American Wildlife

A1267-A1276

Designs from photographs by Jim Brandenburg.

ENGRAVED

1981, May 14   Tagged   Perf. 11
Dark brown
1880 A1267 18c Bighorn .55 .20
1881 A1268 18c Puma .55 .20
1882 A1269 18c Harbor seal .55 .20
1883 A1270 18c American Buffalo .55 .20
1884 A1271 18c Brown bear .55 .20
1885 A1272 18c Polar bear .55 .20
1886 A1273 18c Elk (wapiti) .55 .20
1887 A1274 18c Moose .55 .20
1888 A1275 18c White-tailed deer .55 .20
1889 A1276 18c Pronghorn .55 .20
a. Booklet pane of 10 8.50 7.00

Nos. 1880-1889 issued in booklet only. All stamps have one or two straight edges.

FLAG AND ANTHEM ISSUE

A1277

A1278

A1279

A1280

Designed by Peter Cocci.

ENGRAVED
Plates of 460 subjects (20x23) in panes of 100 (10x10).

1981, Apr. 24	Tagged	Perf. 11	
1890 A1277 18c **multicolored**		.35	.20
	P# block of 6	2.25	—
	P# block of 20, 1-2 #	10.00	—
a.	Imperf., pair	125.00	
b.	Vert. pair, imperf. horiz.	850.00	

See Combination Press note after No. 1703.

Coil Stamp
Perf. 10 Vert.

1891 A1278 18c **multicolored**		.35	.20
	Pair	.70	.20
	P# strip of 3, #5	4.25	
	P# strip of 3, #1	115.00	
	P# strip of 3, #2	20.00	
	P# strip of 3, #3	275.00	
	P# strip of 3, #4	6.75	
	P# strip of 3, #6	1,800.	
	P# strip of 3, #7	27.50	
	P# strip of 5, #5	4.50	
	P# strip of 5, #1	375.00	
	P# strip of 5, #2	45.00	
	P# strip of 5, #3	825.00	
	P# strip of 5, #4	7.50	
	P# strip of 5, #6	2,750.	
	P# strip of 5, #7	32.50	
	P# single, #2, 4, 5	—	.95
	P# single, #1	—	2.50
	P# single, #3	—	12.00
	P# single, #6	—	450.00
	P# single, #7	—	27.50
a.	Imperf., pair	30.00	
	P#2-5		
b.	Pair, imperf. between	—	

Beware of pairs offered as No. 1891b that have faint blind perfs.
Vertical pairs and blocks exist from printer's waste.

Booklet Stamps
Perf. 11

1892 A1279 6c **multicolored**		.50	.20
1893 A1280 18c **multicolored**		.30	.20
a.	Booklet pane of 8 (2 #1892, 6 #1893)	3.00	2.25
b.	As "a," vert. imperf. between	75.00	
c.	Se-tenant pair, #1892 & #1893	.90	1.00
d.	As "a," tagging omitted		

Bureau Precanceled Coils
Starting with No. 1895b, Bureau precanceled coil stamps are valued unused as well as used. The coils issued with dull gum may be difficult to distinguish.

When used normally these stamps do not receive any postal markings so that used stamps with an additional postal cancellation of any kind are worth considerably less than the values shown here.

FLAG OVER SUPREME COURT ISSUE

A1281

Designed by Dean Ellis

ENGRAVED
Plates of 460 subjects (20x23) in panes of 100 (10x10)

1981, Dec. 17	Tagged	Perf. 11	
1894 A1281 20c **black, dark blue & red,** dull gum		.40	.20
	P# block of 6	2.75	
	P# block of 20, 1-2 #	9.00	—
a.	Vert. pair, imperf.	35.00	
b.	Vert. pair, imperf. horiz.	550.00	
c.	Dark blue omitted	85.00	
d.	Black omitted	325.00	
e.	Perf. 11.2, shiny gum	.35	.20
	P# block of 6	2.50	
	P# block of 20, 1-2 #	8.50	
f.	Tagging omitted	—	

Coil Stamp
Perf. 10 Vert.

1895 A1281 20c **black, dark blue & red,** wide block tagging		.40	.20
	Pair	.80	.20
	P# strip of 3, #3, 5, 13-14	4.25	
	P# strip of 3, #1	6.25	
	P# strip of 3, #2, 11	8.50	
	P# strip of 5, #5, 13-14	5.25	
	P# strip of 5, #1	85.00	
	P# strip of 5, #2, 11	10.00	
	P# strip of 5, #3	6.50	
	P# single, #5	—	.25
	P# single, #1	—	1.50
	P# single, #2, 3	—	.35
	P# single, #11	—	3.00
	P# single, #13, 14	—	.60
a.	Narrow block tagging	.40	.20
	Pair	.80	.20
	P# strip of 3, #9-10	4.25	
	P# strip of 3, #12	8.50	
	P# strip of 3, #4	45.00	
	P# strip of 3, #6	87.50	
	P# strip of 3, #8	5.25	
	P# strip of 5, #9-10	5.25	
	P# strip of 5, #12	10.00	
	P# strip of 5, #4	725.00	
	P# strip of 5, #6	160.00	
	P# strip of 5, #8	14.00	
	P# single, #8	—	.25
	P# single, #6	—	1.50
	P# single, #9	—	.35
	P# single, #4	—	.85
	P# single, #10	—	.45
	P# single, #12	—	.60
b.	Untagged (Bureau precanceled, lines only)	.50	.50
	P# strip of 3, #14	57.50	
	P# strip of 5, #14	62.50	
	P# single, #14	—	55.00
c.	Tagging omitted (not Bureau precanceled)	—	
	P# strip of 3, #5, 8, 10-11, 14	—	
	P# strip of 3, #4	—	
	P# strip of 5, #5, 10-11, 14	—	
	P# single, #5, 10-11, 14	—	
d.	Imperf., pair	10.00	
	P#1-6, 8-14		
e.	Pair, imperf. between	1,250.	
f.	Black omitted	50.00	
g.	Dark blue omitted	1,500.	

The wide block tagging on No. 1895 and narrow block tagging on No. 1895a differentiate stamps printed on two different presses. The wide blocks are approximately 20-21mm high by 18mm wide with a 4mm untagged gutter between tagging blocks.

The narrow blocks are approximately 21-22mm high and approximately 16-16½mm wide with a 5½-6½ untagged gutter between tagging blocks.

BOOKLET STAMP
Perf. 11x10½

1896 A1281 20c **black, dark blue & red**		.40	.20
a.	Booklet pane of 6	3.00	2.00
b.	Booklet pane of 10, June 1, 1982	5.25	3.25

Booklets containing two panes of ten were issued Nov. 17, 1983.

TRANSPORTATION ISSUE

A1283

A1284

Designer: 1c, 2c, David Stone.

COIL STAMPS
ENGRAVED

1981-84	Tagged	Perf. 10 Vert.	
1897 A1283 1c **violet,** Aug. 19, 1983		.20	.20
	Pair	.20	.20
	P# strip of 3, line, #1-2, 5-6	.45	
	P# strip of 3, line, #3-4	.50	
	P# strip of 5, line, #1-2, 5-6	.55	

	P# strip of 5, line, #3-4	.65	
	P# single, #1, 2, 5, 6	—	.35
	P# single, #3, 4	—	.50
b.	Imperf., pair	675.00	
	P#5-6		
	Joint line pair	—	
1897A A1284	2c **black,** *May 20, 1982*	.20	.20
	Pair	.20	.20
	P# strip of 3, line, #3, 4, 8, 10	.45	
	P# strip of 5, line, #2, 6	.55	
	P# strip of 5, line, #3-4, 8, 10	.55	
	P# strip of 5, line, #5-6	.60	
	P# single, #2, 3, 4, 6, 8, 10	—	.45
e.	Imperf., pair	55.00	
	P#3-4, 8, 10		
	Joint line pair	—	

Handcar 1880s USA 3c — A1284a

Stagecoach 1890s USA 4c — A1285

Designers: 3c, Walter Brooks. 4c, Jim Schleyer.

1898 A1284a	3c **dark green,** *Mar. 25, 1983*	.20	.20
	Pair	.20	.20
	P# strip of 3, line, #1-4	.65	
	P# strip of 5, line, #1-4	.75	
	P# single, #1-4	—	.55
1898A A1285	4c **reddish brown,** *Aug. 19, 1982*	.20	.20
	Pair	.20	.20
	P# strip of 3, line, #1-4	1.00	
	P# strip of 3, line, #5-6	2.10	
	P# strip of 5, line, #1-4	1.25	
	P# strip of 5, line, #5-6	2.40	
	P# single, #1-4	—	1.10
	P# single, #5-6	—	2.00
b.	Untagged (Bureau precanceled, Nonprofit Org.)	.20	.20
	P# strip of 3, line, #3-6	6.00	
	P# strip of 5, line, #3-6	6.50	
	P# single, #3-6	—	5.25
c.	As "b," imperf., pair	750.00	
	P#5-6		
d.	Imperf. pair	900.00	—
	P#1-2		
e.	Tagging omitted (not Bureau precanceled)	—	

Motorcycle 1913 USA 5c — A1286

Sleigh 1880s USA 5.2c Auth Nonprofit Org — A1287

Designers: 5c, 5.2c, Walter Brooks.

1899 A1286	5c **gray green,** *Oct. 10, 1983*	.20	.20
	Pair	.25	.20
	P# strip of 3, line, #1-4	1.00	
	P# strip of 5, line, #1-4	1.15	
	P# single, #1-4	—	.90
a.	Imperf., pair	2,750.	
	P#1-2		
1900 A1287	5.2c **carmine,** *Mar. 21, 1983*	.20	.20
	Pair	.25	.20
	P# strip of 3, line, #1-2	7.50	
	P# strip of 3, line, #3	175.00	
	P# strip of 3, line, #5	165.00	
	P# strip of 5, line, #1-2	10.00	
	P# strip of 5, line, #3	250.00	
	P# strip of 5, line, #5	190.00	
	P# single, #1-2	—	6.50
	P# single, #3, 5	—	130.00
a.	Untagged (Bureau precanceled, lines only)	.20	.20
	P# strip of 3, line, #1-3, 5	11.00	
	P# strip of 3, line, #4, 6	13.50	
	P# strip of 5, line, #1-3, 5	12.00	
	P# strip of 5, line, #4, 6	14.00	
	P# single, #1-3	—	2.00
	P# single, #4, 6	—	12.00
	P# single, #5	—	4.00

Bicycle 1870s USA 5.9c Auth Nonprofit Org. — A1288

Baby Buggy 1880s USA7.4c — A1289

Designers: 5.9c, David Stone. 7.4c, Jim Schleyer.

1901 A1288	5.9c **blue,** *Feb. 17, 1982*	.25	.20
	Pair	.50	.20
	P# strip of 3, line, #3-4	8.00	
	P# strip of 5, line, #3-4	15.00	
	P# single, #3-4	—	6.75
a.	Untagged (Bureau Precanceled, lines only)	.20	.20
	P# strip of 3, line, #3-4	25.00	
	P# strip of 3, line, #5-6	82.50	
	P# strip of 5, line, #3-4	30.00	
	P# strip of 5, line, #5-6	90.00	
	P# single, #3-4	—	4.50
	P# single, #5-6	—	60.00
b.	As "a," imperf., pair	200.00	
	P#3-4		
	Joint line pair	—	
1902 A1289	7.4c **brown,** *Apr. 7, 1984*	.20	.20
	Pair	.40	.20
	P# strip of 3, #2	8.50	
	P# strip of 5, #2	10.00	
	P# single, #2	—	7.75
a.	Untagged (Bureau precanceled, Blk. Rt. CAR-RT SORT)	.20	.20
	P# strip of 3, #2	4.50	
	P# strip of 5, #2	5.00	
	P# single, #2	—	3.75

Mail Wagon 1880s USA 9.3c Bulk Rate — A1290

Hansom Cab 1890s USA 10.9c Bulk Rate — A1291

Designers: 9.3c, Jim Schleyer. 10.9c, David Stone.

1903 A1290	9.3c **carmine rose,** *Dec. 15*	.30	.20
	Pair	.60	.20
	P# strip of 3, line, #1-2	8.50	
	P# strip of 3, line, #3-4	22.50	
	P# strip of 3, line, #5-6	250.00	
	P# strip of 5, line, #1-2	15.00	
	P# strip of 5, line, #3-4	35.00	
	P# strip of 5, line, #5-6	280.00	
	P# single, #1-2	—	8.00
	P# single, #3-4	—	22.50
	P# single, #5-6	—	240.00
a.	Untagged (Bureau precanceled, lines only)	.25	.25
	P# strip of 3, line, #5-6	3.25	
	P# strip of 3, line, #1	12.50	
	P# strip of 3, line, #3	11.50	
	P# strip of 3, line, #3	25.00	
	P# strip of 3, line, #4	18.00	
	P# strip of 3, line, #8	225.00	
	P# strip of 5, line, #5-6	3.25	
	P# strip of 5, line, #1	15.00	
	P# strip of 5, line, #2	14.00	
	P# strip of 5, line, #3	27.50	
	P# strip of 5, line, #4	20.00	
	P# strip of 5, line, #8	240.00	
	P# single, #5-6	—	2.40
	P# single, #1-2	—	10.50
	P# single, #3-4	—	14.00
	P# single, #8	—	200.00
b.	As "a," imperf., pair	125.00	
	P#1-2		
	Joint line pair	200.00	
1904 A1291	10.9c **purple,** *Mar. 26, 1982*	.30	.20
	Pair	.60	.20
	P# strip of 3, line, #1-2	18.00	
	P# strip of 5, line, #1-2	35.00	
	P# single, #1-2	—	12.00
a.	Untagged (Bureau precanceled, lines only)	.30	.25
	P# strip of 3, line, #1-2	25.00	
	P# strip of 3, line, #3-4	325.00	
	P# strip of 5, line, #1-2	32.50	
	P# strip of 5, line, #3-4	360.00	
	P# single, #1-2	—	7.50
	P# single, #3-4	—	65.00
b.	As "a," imperf., pair	150.00	
	P#1-2		
	Joint line pair	—	

RR Caboose 1890s USA 11c Bulk Rate — A1292

Electric Auto 1917 USA 17c — A1293

Designers: 11c, Jim Schleyer. 17c Chuck Jaquays.

1905	A1292	11c red, Feb. 3, 1984	.30	.20
		Pair	.60	.20
		P# strip of 3, #1	3.75	
		P# strip of 5, #1	4.00	
		P# single, #1	—	3.75
a.		Untagged Sept. 1991	.25	.20
		Pair	.50	.20
		P# strip of 3, #1	3.25	
		P# strip of 3, #2	2.25	
		P# strip of 5, #1	3.75	
		P# strip of 5, #2	2.50	
		P# single, #1	—	3.00
		P# single, #2	—	2.00

Untagged stamps from plate 1 come only Bureau precanceled with lines.

1906	A1293	17c ultramarine, June 25	.35	.20
		Pair	.70	.20
		P# strip of 3, line, #1-5	2.25	
		P# strip of 3, line, #6	14.00	
		P# strip of 3, line, #7	6.00	
		P# strip of 5, line, #1-5	2.75	
		P# strip of 5, line, #6	15.00	
		P# strip of 5, line, #7	6.50	
		P# single, #1-5	—	1.90
		P# single, #6	—	14.00
		P# single, #7	—	5.00
a.		Untagged (Bureau precanceled, Presorted First Class)	.35	.35
		P# strip of 3, line, #3-5		
		P# strip of 3, line, #1-2	10.00	
		P# strip of 3, line, #6-7	12.50	
		P# strip of 5, line, #3-5	4.50	
		P# strip of 5, line, #1-2	10.50	
		P# strip of 5, line, #6-7	13.00	
		P# single, #3-5	—	3.75
		P# single, #1-2	—	7.50
		P# single, #6-7	—	11.00

Three different precancel styles exist: "PRESORTED" measuring 11.3mm, 12.8mm and 13.4mm. The most common is the 11.3mm. Combination pairs exist.

b.	Imperf., pair	165.00
	P#1-4	—
	Joint line pair	—
c.	As "a," imperf., pair	650.00
	P#3-4	—
	Joint line pair	—

Surrey 1890s USA 18c
A1294

Fire Pumper 1860s USA 20c
A1295

Designers: 18c, David Stone. 20c, Jim Schleyer.

1907	A1294	18c dark brown, May 18	.35	.20
		Pair	.70	.20
		P# strip of 3, line, #2, 5-6, 8	3.25	
		P# strip of 3, line, #1	65.00	
		P# strip of 3, line, #3-4	62.50	
		P# strip of 3, line, #7	32.50	
		P# strip of 3, line, #9-12	13.00	
		P# strip of 3, line, #13-14	4.50	
		P# strip of 3, line, #15-16	18.00	
		P# strip of 3, line, #17-18	3.75	
		P# strip of 5, line, #2, 5-6, 8	4.00	
		P# strip of 5, line, #1	90.00	
		P# strip of 5, line, #3-4	72.50	
		P# strip of 5, line, #7	37.50	
		P# strip of 5, line, #9-12	15.00	
		P# strip of 5, line, #13-14	6.00	
		P# strip of 5, line, #15-16	20.00	
		P# strip of 5, line, #17-18	4.50	
		P# single, #2, 5-6, 8	—	.95
		P# single, #1, 7	—	6.00
		P# single, #3-4	—	10.00
		P# single, #9-10	—	3.50
		P# single, #11-12	—	7.00
		P# single, #13-14	—	5.25
		P# single, #15-16	—	15.00
		P# single, #17-18	—	4.50
a.		Imperf., pair	150.00	
		P#2, 8-10, 13	—	
		Joint line pair	—	
1908	A1295	20c vermilion, Dec. 10	.35	.20
		Pair	.70	.20
		P# strip of 3, line, #5, 9, 10	3.00	
		P# strip of 3, line, #1, 11	32.50	
		P# strip of 3, line, #2	180.00	
		P# strip of 3, line, #3, 4, 13, 15, 16	4.75	
		P# strip of 3, line, #6	35.00	
		P# strip of 3, line, #7, 8	90.00	
		P# strip of 3, line, #12, 14	11.00	
		P# strip of 5, line, #5, 9-10	3.75	
		P# strip of 5, line, #1	160.00	
		P# strip of 5, line, #2	850.00	
		P# strip of 5, line, #3-4, 13, 15-16	5.25	
		P# strip of 5, line, #6	37.50	
		P# strip of 5, line, #7-8	180.00	
		P# strip of 5, line, #11	85.00	
		P# strip of 5, line, #12, 14	14.00	
		P# single, #1, 3-5, 9-11, 13	—	.85
		P# single, #2	—	6.00
		P# single, #6-8	—	1.25
		P# single, #12, 14	—	8.00
		P# single, #15-16	—	2.25
a.		Imperf., pair	110.00	
		P#1-5, 9-10, 15-16	—	
		Joint line pair	300.00	
		Nos. 1897-1908 (14)	3.60	2.80

See Nos. 2225-2228.

Eagle and Moon
A1296

Booklet Stamp
PHOTOGRAVURE

1983, Aug. 12		Tagged	Perf. 10 Vert.	
1909	A1296	$9.35 multicolored	21.00	15.00
a.		Booklet pane of 3	65.00	—

A1297

A1298

AMERICAN RED CROSS CENTENNIAL

Designed by Joseph Csatari.

PHOTOGRAVURE
Plates of 200 subjects in four panes of 50.

1981, May 1		Tagged	Perf. 10½x11	
1910	A1297	18c multicolored	.35	.20
		P# block of 4, 6#	1.50	
		Zip block of 4	1.40	—

SAVINGS & LOAN SESQUICENTENNIAL

Designed by Don Hedin.

PHOTOGRAVURE
Plates of 200 subjects in four panes of 50.

1981, May 8		Tagged	Perf. 11	
1911	A1298	18c multicolored	.35	.20
		P# block of 4, 6#	1.50	
		Zip block of 4	1.40	—

SPACE ACHIEVEMENT ISSUE

Exploring the Moon
USA 18c
A1299

Understanding the Sun
USA 18c
A1302

Benefiting Mankind
USA 18c
A1300

Benefiting Mankind
USA 18c
A1301

Probing the Planets
USA 18c
A1303

Comprehending the Universe
USA 18c
A1306

A1304

A1305

Designed by Robert McCall.

Designs: A1299, Moon walk. A1300-A1301, A1304-A1305, Columbia space shuttle. A1302, Skylab. A1303, Pioneer 11. A1306, Telescope. Se-tenant in blocks of 8.

PHOTOGRAVURE
Plates of 192 subjects in four panes of 48 each.

1981, May 21		Tagged	Perf. 11	
1912	A1299 18c multicolored		.40	.20
1913	A1300 18c multicolored		.40	.20
1914	A1301 18c multicolored		.40	.20
1915	A1302 18c multicolored		.40	.20
1916	A1303 18c multicolored		.40	.20
1917	A1304 18c multicolored		.40	.20
1918	A1305 18c multicolored		.40	.20
1919	A1306 18c multicolored		.40	.20
a.	Block of 8, #1912-1919		3.25	3.00
	P# block of 8, 6#		3.75	—
	Zip, copyright block of 8		3.25	—
b.	As "a," imperf.		9,000.	
c.	As "a," tagging omitted			

PROFESSIONAL MANAGEMENT EDUCATION CENTENARY

Joseph Wharton (Founder of Wharton School of Business) — A1307

Designed by Rudolph de Harak.

PHOTOGRAVURE
Plates of 200 subject in four panes of 50.

1981, June 18		Tagged	Perf. 11	
1920	A1307 18c blue & black		.35	.20
	P# block of 4, 2#		1.50	—
	Zip block of 4		1.40	—

PRESERVATION OF WILDLIFE HABITATS

Great Blue Heron — A1308   Badger — A1309

Save Mountain Habitats   Save Woodland Habitats
Grizzly   Ruffed
Bear — A1310   Grouse — A1311

Designed by Chuck Ripper.

PHOTOGRAVURE
Plates of 200 subjects in four panes of 50.

1981, June 26		Tagged	Perf. 11	
1921	A1308 18c multicolored		.35	.20
1922	A1309 18c multicolored		.35	.20
1923	A1310 18c multicolored		.35	.20
1924	A1311 18c multicolored		.35	.20
a.	Block of 4, #1921-1924		1.50	1.25
	P# block of 4, 5#		2.00	—
	Zip block of 4		1.55	—

INTERNATIONAL YEAR OF THE DISABLED

Man Using Microscope A1312

Designed by Martha Perske

PHOTOGRAVURE
Plates of 200 subjects in four panes of 50.

1981, June 29		Tagged	Perf. 11	
1925	A1312 18c multicolored		.35	.20
	P# block of 4, 6#		1.50	—
	Zip block of 4		1.40	—
a.	Vert. pair, imperf. horiz.		2,750.	

EDNA ST. VINCENT MILLAY ISSUE

A1313

Designed by Glenora Case Richards

LITHOGRAPHED AND ENGRAVED
Plates of 200 subjects in four panes of 50.

1981, July 10		Tagged	Perf. 11	
1926	A1313 18c multicolored		.35	.20
	P# block of 4, 7#		1.50	—
	Zip block of 4		1.40	—
a.	Black (engr., inscriptions) omitted		350.00	

ALCOHOLISM

A1314

Designed by John Boyd

ENGRAVED
Plates of 230 (10x23) subjects in panes of 50 (5x10)

1981, Aug. 19		Tagged	Perf. 11	
1927	A1314 18c blue & black		.40	.20
	P# block of 6		10.00	
	P# block of 20, 1-2 #, 1-2 copyright, 1-2 Zip		27.50	—
a.	Imperf., pair		400.00	
b.	Vert. pair, imperf. horiz.		2,500.	

See Combination Press note after No. 1703.

AMERICAN ARCHITECTURE

New York University Library by Stanford White — A1315

Biltmore House By Richard Morris Hunt — A1316

Palace of the Arts by Bernard Maybeck A1317

National Farmer's Bank by Louis Sullivan A1318

Designed by Walter D. Richards

ENGRAVED
Plates of 160 subjects in four panes of 40.

1981, Aug. 28		Tagged	Perf. 11	
1928	A1315 18c black & red		.40	.20
1929	A1316 18c black & red		.40	.20
1930	A1317 18c black & red		.40	.20
1931	A1318 18c black & red		.40	.20
a.	Block of 4, #1928-1931		1.65	1.50
	P# block of 4		2.10	—
	Zip block of 4		1.80	—

SPORTS PERSONALITIES

Mildred Didrikson   Robert Tyre
Zaharias — A1319   Jones — A1320

Designed by Richard Gangel

ENGRAVED
Plates of 200 subjects in four panes of 50.

1981, Sept. 22		Tagged	Perf. 10½x11	
1932	A1319 18c purple		.40	.20
	P# block of 4		3.00	—
	Zip block of 4		1.75	—
1933	A1320 18c green		.40	.20
	P# block of 4		3.00	—
	Zip block of 4		1.75	—

FREDERIC REMINGTON

Coming Through the Rye — A1321

Designed by Paul Calle

LITHOGRAPHED AND ENGRAVED
Plates of 200 in four panes of 50.

1981, Oct. 9	Tagged	Perf. 11
1934 A1321 18c **gray, olive green & brown**	.35	.20
P# block of 4, 3#	1.60	
Zip block of 4	1.50	—
a. Vert. pair, imperf. between	275.00	
b. Brown omitted	475.00	

JAMES HOBAN

Irish-American Architect of the White House — A1322

Designed by Ron Mercer and Walter D. Richards.

PHOTOGRAVURE
Plates of 200 in four panes of 50.

1981, Oct. 13	Tagged	Perf. 11
1935 A1322 18c **multicolored**	.35	.20
P# block of 4, 6#	1.60	
Zip block of 4	1.50	—
1936 A1322 20c **multicolored**	.35	.20
P# block of 4, 6#	1.65	
Zip block of 4	1.50	—

See Ireland No. 504.

AMERICAN BICENTENNIAL

Battle of Yorktown A1323

Battle of the Virginia Capes — A1324

Designed by Cal Sacks.

LITHOGRAPHED AND ENGRAVED
Plates of 200 in four panes of 50.

1981, Oct. 16	Tagged	Perf. 11
1937 A1323 18c **multicolored**	.35	.20
1938 A1324 18c **multicolored**	.35	.20
a. Pair, #1937-1938	.90	.75
P# block of 4, 7#	2.00	—
Zip block of 4	1.65	—
b. As "a," black (engr., inscriptions) omitted	400.00	
c. As "a," tagging omitted	—	

CHRISTMAS

Madonna and Child, Botticelli A1325

Felt Bear on Sleigh A1326

Designed by Bradbury Thompson (No. 1939) and by Naiad Einsel (No. 1940).

PHOTOGRAVURE
Plates of 400 in four panes of 100 (No. 1939)
Plates of 200 in four panes of 50 (No. 1940)

1981, Oct. 28	Tagged	Perf. 11
1939 A1325 (20c) **multicolored**	.40	.20
P# block of 4, 6#	1.75	
Zip block of 4	1.65	—
a. Imperf., pair	125.00	
b. Vert. pair, imperf. horiz.	1,650.	
c. Tagging omitted	—	
1940 A1326 (20c) **multicolored**	.40	.20
P# block of 4, 5#	1.75	
Zip block of 4	1.65	—
a. Imperf., pair	275.00	
b. Vert. pair, imperf. horiz.	2,500.	

JOHN HANSON

First President of the Continental Congress — A1327

Designed by Ron Adair.

PHOTOGRAVURE
Plates of 200 in panes of 50

1981, Nov. 5	Tagged	Perf. 11
1941 A1327 20c **multicolored**	.40	.20
P# block of 4, 5#	1.75	
Zip block of 4	1.65	—

DESERT PLANTS

Barrel Cactus — A1328

Saguaro — A1331

Agave A1329

Beavertail Cactus A1330

Designed by Frank J. Waslick.

LITHOGRAPHED AND ENGRAVED
Plates of 160 in four panes of 40

1981 Dec. 11	Tagged	Perf. 11
1942 A1328 20c **multicolored**	.35	.20
1943 A1329 20c **multicolored**	.35	.20
1944 A1330 20c **multicolored**	.35	.20
1945 A1331 20c **multicolored**	.35	.20
a. Block of 4, #1942-1945	1.50	1.25
P# block of 4, 7#	1.90	
Zip block of 4	1.55	—
b. As "a," deep brown (engr.) omitted	7,500.	
c. No. 1945 imperf., vert. pair	5,250.	

A1332

A1333

Designed by Bradbury Thompson.

PHOTOGRAVURE
Plates of 400 in panes of 100.

1981, Oct. 11	Tagged	Perf. 11x10½
1946 A1332 (20c) **brown**	.40	.20
P# block of 4	2.00	
Zip block of 4	1.65	—
a. Tagging omitted	9.00	
b. All color omitted	—	

No. 1946b comes from a partially printed pane with most stamps normal. It must be collected as a vertical pair or strip with normal or partially printed stamps attached.

COIL STAMP
Perf. 10 Vert.

1947 A1332 (20c) **brown**	.60	.20
Pair	1.20	.20
Joint line pair	1.50	
a. Imperf. pair	1,500.	
Joint line pair	—	

BOOKLET STAMPS
Perf. 11x10½

1948 A1333 (20c) **brown**	.40	.20
a. Booklet pane of 10	4.50	3.00

Rocky Mountain Bighorn — A1334

BOOKLET STAMP
ENGRAVED

1982, Jan. 8	Tagged	Perf. 11
1949 A1334 20c **dark blue**	.55	.20
a. Booklet pane of 10	5.50	2.50
b. As "a," imperf. between	110.00	
c. Type II	.55	.20
d. Type II, booklet pane of 10	11.00	
e. As #1949, tagging omitted	3.00	
f. As "e," booklet pane of 10	30.00	

No. 1949 is 18¾mm wide and has overall tagging. No. 1949c is 18½mm wide and has block tagging.

FRANKLIN DELANO ROOSEVELT

A1335

Designed by Clarence Holbert.

ENGRAVED
Plates of 192 in four panes of 48

1982, Jan. 30	Tagged	Perf. 11
1950 A1335 20c **blue**	.40	.20
P# block of 4	1.75	—
Zip block of 4	1.65	—

LOVE ISSUE

A1336

Designed by Mary Faulconer.

PHOTOGRAVURE
Plates of 200 in four panes of 50.

1982, Feb. 1		Tagged		Perf. 11¼	
1951	A1336	20c multicolored		.40	.20
		P# block of 4, 5#		1.75	—
		Zip block of 4		1.65	—
b.		Imperf., pair		275.00	
c.		Blue omitted		225.00	
d.		Yellow omitted		900.00	
e.		Purple omitted			

No. 1951c is valued in the grade of fine.

Perf. 11¼x10½

1951A	A1336	20c multicolored		.65	.20
		P# block of 4, 5#		3.00	—
		Zip block of 4		2.70	—

GEORGE WASHINGTON

A1337

Designed by Mark English.

PHOTOGRAVURE
Plates of 200 in four panes of 50.

1982, Feb. 22		Tagged		Perf. 11	
1952	A1337	20c multicolored		.40	.20
		P# block of 4, 6#		1.75	—
		Zip block of 4		1.65	—

Illustration reduced.

Designed by Arthur and Alan Singer.

PHOTOGRAVURE (Andreotti)
Plates of 200 subjects in four panes of 50.

1982, Apr. 14		Tagged		Perf. 10½x11¼	
1953	A1338	20c Alabama		.50	.25
1954	A1339	20c Alaska		.50	.25
1955	A1340	20c Arizona		.50	.25
1956	A1341	20c Arkansas		.50	.25
1957	A1342	20c California		.50	.25
1958	A1343	20c Colorado		.50	.25
1959	A1344	20c Connecticut		.50	.25
1960	A1345	20c Delaware		.50	.25
1961	A1346	20c Florida		.50	.25
1962	A1347	20c Georgia		.50	.25
1963	A1348	20c Hawaii		.50	.25
1964	A1349	20c Idaho		.50	.25
1965	A1350	20c Illinois		.50	.25
1966	A1351	20c Indiana		.50	.25
1967	A1352	20c Iowa		.50	.25
1968	A1353	20c Kansas		.50	.25
1969	A1354	20c Kentucky		.50	.25
1970	A1355	20c Louisiana		.50	.25
1971	A1356	20c Maine		.50	.25
1972	A1357	20c Maryland		.50	.25
1973	A1358	20c Massachusetts		.50	.25
1974	A1359	20c Michigan		.50	.25
1975	A1360	20c Minnesota		.50	.25
1976	A1360	20c Mississippi		.50	.25
1977	A1361	20c Missouri		.50	.25
1978	A1362	20c Montana		.50	.25
1979	A1363	20c Nebraska		.50	.25
1980	A1364	20c Nevada		.50	.25
1981	A1364	20c New Hampshire		.50	.25
1982	A1365	20c New Jersey		.50	.25
1983	A1366	20c New Mexico		.50	.25
1984	A1369	20c New York		.50	.25
1985	A1370	20c North Carolina		.50	.25
1986	A1371	20c North Dakota		.50	.25
1987	A1372	20c Ohio		.50	.25
1988	A1373	20c Oklahoma		.50	.25
1989	A1374	20c Oregon		.50	.25
1990	A1375	20c Pennsylvania		.50	.25
1991	A1376	20c Rhode Island		.50	.25
1992	A1377	20c South Carolina		.50	.25
1993	A1378	20c South Dakota		.50	.25
1994	A1379	20c Tennessee		.50	.25
1995	A1380	20c Texas		.50	.25
1996	A1381	20c Utah		.50	.25
1997	A1382	20c Vermont		.50	.25
1998	A1383	20c Virginia		.50	.25
1999	A1384	20c Washington		.50	.25
2000	A1385	20c West Virginia		.50	.25
2001	A1386	20c Wisconsin		.50	.25
2002	A1387	20c Wyoming		.50	.25
b.		Pane of 50, Nos. 1953-2002		25.00	—
d.		Pane of 50, imperf.		27,500.	

Perf. 11¼x11

1953A	A1338	20c Alabama		.55	.30
1954A	A1339	20c Alaska		.55	.30
1955A	A1340	20c Arizona		.55	.30
1956A	A1341	20c Arkansas		.55	.30
1957A	A1342	20c California		.55	.30
1958A	A1343	20c Colorado		.55	.30
1959A	A1344	20c Connecticut		.55	.30
1960A	A1345	20c Delaware		.55	.30
1961A	A1346	20c Florida		.55	.30
1962A	A1347	20c Georgia		.55	.30
1963A	A1348	20c Hawaii		.55	.30
1964A	A1349	20c Idaho		.55	.30
1965A	A1350	20c Illinois		.55	.30
1966A	A1351	20c Indiana		.55	.30
1967A	A1352	20c Iowa		.55	.30
1968A	A1353	20c Kansas		.55	.30
1969A	A1354	20c Kentucky		.55	.30
1970A	A1355	20c Louisiana		.55	.30
1971A	A1356	20c Maine		.55	.30
1972A	A1357	20c Maryland		.55	.30
1973A	A1358	20c Massachusetts		.55	.30
1974A	A1359	20c Michigan		.55	.30
1975A	A1360	20c Minnesota		.55	.30
1976A	A1360	20c Mississippi		.55	.30
1977A	A1361	20c Missouri		.55	.30
1978A	A1362	20c Montana		.55	.30
1979A	A1363	20c Nebraska		.55	.30
1980A	A1364	20c Nevada		.55	.30
1981A	A1364	20c New Hampshire		.55	.30
1982A	A1365	20c New Jersey		.55	.30
1983A	A1366	20c New Mexico		.55	.30
1984A	A1369	20c New York		.55	.30
1985A	A1370	20c North Carolina		.55	.30
1986A	A1371	20c North Dakota		.55	.30
1987A	A1372	20c Ohio		.55	.30
1988A	A1373	20c Oklahoma		.55	.30
1989A	A1374	20c Oregon		.55	.30
1990A	A1375	20c Pennsylvania		.55	.30
1991A	A1376	20c Rhode Island		.55	.30
1992A	A1377	20c South Carolina		.55	.30
1993A	A1378	20c South Dakota		.55	.30
1994A	A1379	20c Tennessee		.55	.30
1995A	A1380	20c Texas		.55	.30
1996A	A1381	20c Utah		.55	.30
1997A	A1382	20c Vermont		.55	.30
1998A	A1383	20c Virginia		.55	.30
1999A	A1384	20c Washington		.55	.30
2000A	A1385	20c West Virginia		.55	.30
2001A	A1386	20c Wisconsin		.55	.30
2002A	A1387	20c Wyoming		.55	.30
c.		Pane of 50, Nos. 1953A-2002A		27.50	—

US-NETHERLANDS

200th Anniv. of Diplomatic Recognition by The Netherlands
A1388

Designed by Heleen Tigler Wybrandi-Raue.

PHOTOGRAVURE
Plates of 230 (10x23) subjects in panes of 50 (5x10).

1982, Apr. 20		Tagged		Perf. 11	
2003	A1388	20c verm., brt. blue & gray blk.		.40	.20
		P# block of 6		3.50	—
		P# block of 20, 1-2 #, 1-2 copyright, 1-2 zip		11.00	—
a.		Imperf., pair		325.00	

See Combination Press note after No. 1703.
See Netherlands Nos. 640-641.

LIBRARY OF CONGRESS

A1389

Designed by Bradbury Thompson.

ENGRAVED
Plates of 200 subjects in four panes of 50.

1982, Apr. 21		Tagged		Perf. 11	
2004	A1389	20c red & black		.40	.20
		P# block of 4		1.75	—
		Zip block of 4		1.65	—

A1390

Designed by John Boyd.

ENGRAVED
Coil Stamp

1982, Apr. 27		Tagged		Perf. 10 Vert.	
2005	A1390	20c sky blue		.55	.20
		Pair		1.10	.20
		P# strip of 3, line, #3-4		30.00	
		P# strip of 3, line, #1-2		30.00	
		P# strip of 5, line, #3-4		110.00	
		P# strip of 5, line, #1-2		175.00	
		P# single, #1-4		—	2.00
a.		Imperf., pair		100.00	
		P#1-4			
		Joint line pair		400.00	
b.		Tagging omitted		7.50	

KNOXVILLE WORLD'S FAIR

A1391

A1392

A1393

A1394

Illustration reduced.

Designed by Charles Harper.

PHOTOGRAVURE
Plates of 200 in four panes of 50.

1982, Apr. 29		Tagged		Perf. 11	
2006	A1391	20c multicolored		.40	.20
2007	A1392	20c multicolored		.40	.20
2008	A1393	20c multicolored		.40	.20
2009	A1394	20c multicolored		.40	.20

Any single on cover, Expo. station handstamp cancel		10.00
a. Block of 4, #2006-2009	1.65	1.50
P# block of 4, 6#	2.00	—
Zip block of 4	1.75	—

HORATIO ALGER

A1395

Designed by Robert Hallock.

ENGRAVED
Plates of 200 in four panes of 50.

1982, Apr. 30	**Tagged**	*Perf. 11*	
2010 A1395 20c **red & black,** *tan*		.40	.20
P# block of 4		1.75	—
Zip block of 4		1.65	—
a. Red and black omitted			—

The Philatelic Foundation has issued a certificate for a pane of 50 with red and black colors omitted. Recognition of this error is by the paper and by a tiny residue of red ink from the tagging roller. The engraved plates did not strike the paper.

AGING TOGETHER

A1396

Designed by Paul Calle.

ENGRAVED
Plates of 200 in four panes of 50.

1982, May 21	**Tagged**	*Perf. 11*	
2011 A1396 20c **brown**		.40	.20
P# block of 4		1.75	—
Zip block of 4		1.65	—

John, Ethel and Lionel
Barrymore — A1397

PERFORMING ARTS
Designed by Jim Sharpe.

PHOTOGRAVURE
Plates of 200 in four panes of 50.

1982, June 8	**Tagged**	*Perf. 11*	
2012 A1397 20c **multicolored**		.40	.20
P# block of 4, 6#		1.75	—
Zip block of 4		1.65	—

Dr. Mary Walker
Army Surgeon

Medal of Honor
USA 20c
A1398

DR. MARY WALKER
Designed by Glenora Richards.

PHOTOGRAVURE
Plate of 200 in four panes of 50.

1982, June 10	**Tagged**	*Perf. 11*	
2013 A1398 20c **multicolored**		.40	.20
P# block of 4, 6#		1.75	—
Zip block of 4		1.65	—

STATE BIRDS AND FLOWERS ISSUE

State Birds and Flowers
A1338-A1387

INTERNATIONAL PEACE GARDEN

Dunseith, ND-Boissevain, Manitoba
1932
1982
A1399

Designed by Gyo Fujikawa.

LITHOGRAPHED AND ENGRAVED
Plate of 200 in four panes of 50.

1982, June 30	**Tagged**	*Perf. 11*	
2014 A1399 20c **multicolored**		.40	.20
P# block of 4, 5#		1.75	—
Zip block of 4		1.65	—
a. Black & green (engr.) omitted		*260.00*	

A1400

A1401

AMERICA'S LIBRARIES
Designed by Bradbury Thompson.

ENGRAVED
Plate of 200 subjects in four panes of 50.

1982, July 13	**Tagged**	*Perf. 11*	
2015 A1400 20c **red & black**		.40	.20
P# block of 4		1.75	—
Zip block of 4		1.65	—
a. Vert. pair, imperf. horiz.		*300.00*	
b. Tagging omitted		*7.50*	

BLACK HERITAGE SERIES
Jackie Robinson (1919-72), baseball player.

Designed by Jerry Pinkney.

PHOTOGRAVURE
Plate of 200 subjects in four panes of 50.

1982, Aug. 2	**Tagged**	*Perf. 10½x11*	
2016 A1401 20c **multicolored**		1.10	.20
P# block of 4, 5#		5.50	—
Zip block of 4		4.75	—

TOURO SYNAGOGUE

Oldest Existing Synagogue Building in the U.S. — A1402

Designed by Donald Moss and Bradbury Thompson.

PHOTOGRAVURE AND ENGRAVED
Plates of 230 (10x23) subjects in panes of 50 (5x10).

1982, Aug. 22	**Tagged**	*Perf. 11*	
2017 A1402 20c **multicolored**		.40	.20
P# block of 20, 6-12 #, 1-2 copyright, 1-2 zip		11.00	—
a. Imperf., pair		*2,500.*	

See Combination Press note after No. 1703.

WOLF TRAP FARM PARK

A1403

Designed by Richard Schlecht.

PHOTOGRAVURE
Plates of 200 in four panes of 50.

1982, Sept. 1	**Tagged**	*Perf. 11*	
2018 A1403 20c **multicolored**		.40	.20
P# block of 4, 5#		1.75	—
Zip block of 4		1.65	—

AMERICAN ARCHITECTURE

Frank Lloyd Wright 1867-1959 Fallingwater Mill Run PA
Architecture USA 20c   A1404

Mies van der Rohe 1886-1969 Illinois Inst Tech Chicago
A1405 Architecture USA 20c

Walter Gropius 1883-1969 Gropius House Lincoln MA
Architecture USA 20c   A1406

Eero Saarinen 1910-1961 Dulles Airport Washington DC
A1407 Architecture USA 20c

Designed by Walter D. Richards.

ENGRAVED
Plates of 160 subjects in four panes of 40.

1982, Sept. 30	Tagged	Perf. 11	
2019 A1404 20c **black & brown**		.45	.20
2020 A1405 20c **black & brown**		.45	.20
2021 A1406 20c **black & brown**		.45	.20
2022 A1407 20c **black & brown**		.45	.20
a. Block of 4, #2019-2022		2.00	1.60
P# block of 4		2.50	—
Zip block of 4		2.10	—

FRANCIS OF ASSISI

FRANCIS OF ASSISI 1182-1982 USA 20c   A1408

Designed by Ned Seidler.

Printed by American Bank Note Co. and J.W. Fergusson and Sons.

PHOTOGRAVURE
Plates of 200 subjects in four panes of 50.

1982, Oct. 7	Tagged	Perf. 11	
2023 A1408 20c **multicolored**		.40	.20
P# block of 4, 6#		1.75	
Zip block of 4		1.65	—

PONCE DE LEON

Ponce de León USA 20c

A1409

Designed by Richard Schlecht.

PHOTOGRAVURE (Combination press)
Plates of 230 subjects (10x23) in panes of 50 (5x10)

1982, Oct. 12	Tagged	Perf. 11	
2024 A1409 20c **multicolored**		.40	.20
P# block of 6, 5#		3.25	
P# block of 20, 5 or 10 #, 1-2 zip, 1-2 copyright		11.00	
a. Imperf., pair		500.00	
b. Vert. pair, imperf. between and at top		—	

See Combination Press note after No. 1703.

CHRISTMAS ISSUES

USA 13c   A1410

Christmas USA 20c

A1411 Tiepolo National Gallery of Art

Season's Greetings USA 20c A1412

A1413 Season's Greetings USA 20c

Season's Greetings USA 20c A1414

A1415 Season's Greetings USA 20c

PHOTOGRAVURE
Plates of 200 subjects in four panes of 50
Designed by Chuck Ripper.

1982, Nov. 3	Tagged		
2025 A1410 13c **multicolored**		.25	.20
P# block of 4		1.40	
Zip block of 4		1.10	—
a. Imperf., pair		650.00	

PHOTOGRAVURE (Combination Press)
Plates of 230 subjects (10x23) in panes of 50 (5x10).

Designed by Bradbury Thompson.

1982, Oct. 28	Tagged		
2026 A1411 20c **multicolored**		.40	.20
P# block of 20, 5 or 10 #, 1-2 copyright, 1-2 zip		11.00	—
a. Imperf. pair		150.00	
b. Horiz. pair, imperf. vert.		—	
c. Vert. pair, imperf. horiz.		—	

See Combination Press note after No. 1703.

PHOTOGRAVURE
Plates of 200 in four panes of 50.

Designed by Dolli Tingle.

2027 A1412 20c **multicolored**		.50	.20
2028 A1413 20c **multicolored**		.50	.20
2029 A1414 20c **multicolored**		.50	.20
2030 A1415 20c **multicolored**		.50	.20
a. Block of 4, #2027-2030		2.25	1.50
P# block of 4, 4#		2.75	
Zip block of 4		2.25	—
b. As "a," imperf.		2,750.	
c. As "a," imperf. horiz.		3,250.	

SCIENCE & INDUSTRY

Science & Industry USA 20c

A1416

Designed by Saul Bass.

LITHOGRAPHED AND ENGRAVED
Plates of 200 in four panes of 50.

1983, Jan. 19	Tagged	Perf. 11	
2031 A1416 20c **multicolored**		.40	.20
P# block of 4, 4#		1.75	
Zip block of 4		1.65	—
a. Black (engr.) omitted		1,400.	

BALLOONS

Intrepid — A1417

Explorer II — A1420

A1418

A1419

Designed by David Meltzer.

PHOTOGRAVURE
Plates of 160 in four panes of 40.

1983, Mar. 31	Tagged	Perf. 11	
2032 A1417 20c **multicolored**		.40	.20
2033 A1418 20c **multicolored**		.40	.20
2034 A1419 20c **multicolored**		.40	.20
2035 A1420 20c **multicolored**		.40	.20
a. Block of 4, #2032-2035		1.65	1.50

	P# block of 4, 5#	1.75	—
	Zip block of 4	1.70	—
b.	As "a," imperf.	4,250.	
c.	As "a," right stamp perf., otherwise imperf.	4,500.	

US-SWEDEN

Benjamin
Franklin — A1421

Designed by Czeslaw Slania, court engraver of Sweden.

ENGRAVED
Plates of 200 in four panes of 50.

1983, Mar. 24	**Tagged**	**Perf. 11**	
2036 A1421 20c **blue, blk & red brn**		.40	.20
P# block of 4		1.75	
Zip block of 4		1.65	—

See Sweden No. 1453.

CCC, 50th ANNIV.

Civilian Conservation Corps — A1422

Designed by David K. Stone.

PHOTOGRAVURE
Plates of 200 in four panes of 50.

1983, Apr. 5	**Tagged**	**Perf. 11**	
2037 A1422 20c **multicolored**		.40	.20
P# block of 4, 6#		1.75	
Zip block of 4		1.65	—
a.	Imperf., pair	2,750.	
b.	Vert. pair, imperf. horiz.		—

JOSEPH PRIESTLEY

Discoverer of Oxygen — A1423

Designed by Dennis Lyall.

Printed by American Bank Note Company and J.W. Fergusson and Sons.

PHOTOGRAVURE
Plates of 200 in four panes of 50.

1983, Apr. 13	**Tagged**	**Perf. 11**	
2038 A1423 20c **multicolored**		.40	.20
P# block of 4, 6#		1.75	—
Zip block of 4		1.65	—

VOLUNTARISM

Volunteer lend a hand — USA 20c A1424

Designed by Paul Calle.

ENGRAVED (Combination Press)
Plates of 230 subjects (10x23) in panes of 50
(5x10)

1983, Apr. 20	**Tagged**	**Perf. 11**	
2039 A1424 20c **red & black**		.40	.20
P# block of 6		3.00	—
P# block of 20, 1-2 #, 1-2 copyright, 1-2 zip		11.00	—
a.	Imperf., pair	800.00	

See Combination Press note after No. 1703.

US-GERMANY

A1425

Designed by Richard Schlecht.

ENGRAVED
Plates of 200 in four panes of 50.

1983, Apr. 29	**Tagged**	**Perf. 11**	
2040 A1425 20c **brown**		.40	.20
P# block of 4		1.75	—
Zip block of 4		1.65	—

See Germany No. 1397.

BROOKLYN BRIDGE

A1426

Normal

"Unfinished Bridge"
Short Transfer

Designed by Howard Koslow.

ENGRAVED
Plates of 200 in four panes of 50.

1983, May 17	**Tagged**	**Perf. 11**	
2041 A1426 20c **blue**		.40	.20
P# block of 4		1.75	—
Zip block of 4		1.65	—
Short transfer (unfinished bridge) (UL 2)		6.00	.75
P# block of 4		10.00	—
a.	Tagging omitted	7.00	

TVA

Norris
Hydroelectric
Dam — A1427

Designed by Howard Koslow.

PHOTOGRAVURE AND ENGRAVED (Combination Press)
Plates of 230 in panes of 50

1983, May 18	**Tagged**	**Perf. 11**	
2042 A1427 20c **multicolored**		.40	.20
P# block of 20, 5-10 #, 1-2 copyright, 1-2 zip		11.00	—

Runners, Electrocardiograph Tracing — A1428

Designed by Donald Moss.

PHOTOGRAVURE (Combination Press)
Plates of 230 in panes of 50.

1983, May 14	**Tagged**	**Perf. 11**	
2043 A1428 20c **multicolored**		.40	.20
P# block of 6, 4#		3.00	—
P# block of 20, 4-8 #, 1-2 copyright, 1-2 zip		11.00	—

BLACK HERITAGE SERIES

Scott Joplin (1868-1917), Ragtime composer.

A1429

Designed by Jerry Pinkney.

PHOTOGRAVURE
Plates of 200 in four panes of 50.

1983, June 9	**Tagged**	**Perf. 11**	
2044 A1429 20c **multicolored**		.40	.20
P# block of 4, 6#		1.75	—
Zip block of 4		1.65	—
a.	Imperf., pair	475.00	

MEDAL OF HONOR

A1430   Medal of Honor

Designed by Dennis J. Hom.

LITHOGRAPHED AND ENGRAVED
Plates of 160 in four panes of 40.

1983, June 7	**Tagged**	**Perf. 11**	
2045 A1430 20c **multicolored**		.40	.20
P# block of 4, 5#		1.75	—
Zip block of 4		1.70	—
a.	Red omitted	250.00	

A1431

A1432

GEORGE HERMAN RUTH (1895-1948)
Designed by Richard Gangel.

ENGRAVED
Plates of 200 in four panes of 50.

1983, July 6	Tagged	Perf. 10½x11
2046 A1431 20c blue	1.25	.20
P# block of 4	7.00	—
Zip block of 4	5.25	—

NATHANIEL HAWTHORNE (1804-1864)
Designed by Bradbury Thompson after 1851 painting by
Cephus Giovanni Thompson.

PHOTOGRAVURE
Plates of 200 in four panes of 50.

1983, July 8	Tagged	Perf. 11
2047 A1432 20c multicolored	.45	.20
P# block of 4, 4#	2.10	—
Zip block of 4	1.90	—

1984 SUMMER OLYMPICS
Los Angeles, July 28-August 12

Discus — A1433

High Jump — A1434

Archery — A1435

Boxing — A1436

Designed by Bob Peak.

PHOTOGRAVURE
Plates of 200 in four panes of 50.

1983, July 28	Tagged	Perf. 11
2048 A1433 13c multicolored	.35	.20
2049 A1434 13c multicolored	.35	.20
2050 A1435 13c multicolored	.35	.20
2051 A1436 13c multicolored	.35	.20
a. Block of 4, #2048-2051	1.50	1.25
P# block of 4, 4#	1.75	—
Zip block of 4	1.65	—

SIGNING OF TREATY OF PARIS

John Adams, B.
Franklin, John
Jay, David
Hartley — A1437

Designed by David Blossom based on unfinished painting by
Benjamin West in Winterthur Museum.

PHOTOGRAVURE
Plates of 160 in four panes of 40.

1983, Sept. 2	Tagged	Perf. 11
2052 A1437 20c multicolored	.40	.20
P# block of 4, 4#	1.75	—
Zip block of 4	1.65	—

CIVIL SERVICE

A1438

Designed by MDB Communications, Inc.

PHOTOGRAVURE AND ENGRAVED
Plates of 230 in four panes of 50.

1983, Sept. 9	Tagged	Perf. 11
2053 A1438 20c buff, blue & red	.40	.20
P# block of 6	3.00	—
P# block of 20, 1-2P#, 1-2 Zip,		
1-2 Copyright	11.00	—

METROPOLITAN OPERA

Original State
Arch and Current
5-arch Entrance
A1439

Designed by Ken Davies.

LITHOGRAPHED AND ENGRAVED
Plates of 200 in four panes of 50.

1983, Sept. 14	Tagged	Perf. 11
2054 A1439 20c yellow & maroon	.40	.20
P# block of 4, 2#	1.75	—
Zip block of 4	1.65	—
a. Tagging omitted	8.50	

AMERICAN INVENTORS

Charles Steinmetz
and Curve on
Graph — A1440

Edwin Armstrong
and Frequency
Modulator
A1441

Nikola Tesla and
Induction
Motor — A1442

Philo T.
Farnsworth and
First Television
Camera — A1443

Designed by Dennis Lyall.

LITHOGRAPHED AND ENGRAVED
Plates of 200 in four panes of 50.

1983, Sept. 21	Tagged	Perf. 11
2055 A1440 20c multicolored	.45	.20
2056 A1441 20c multicolored	.45	.20
2057 A1442 20c multicolored	.45	.20
2058 A1443 20c multicolored	.45	.20
a. Block of 4, #2055-2058	1.80	1.25
P# block of 4, 2#	2.50	—
Zip block of 4	1.90	—
b. As "a," black omitted	350.00	

STREETCARS

A1444

A1445

A1446

A1447

Designed by Richard Leech.

PHOTOGRAVURE AND ENGRAVED
Plates of 200 in four panes of 50.

1983, Oct. 8	Tagged	Perf. 11
2059 A1444 20c multicolored	.45	.20
2060 A1445 20c multicolored	.45	.20
2061 A1446 20c multicolored	.45	.20
2062 A1447 20c multicolored	.45	.20
a. Block of 4, #2059-2062	1.80	1.40
P# block of 4, 5#	2.50	—
Zip block of 4	1.90	—
b. As "a," black omitted	425.00	
c. As "a," black omitted on #2059, 2061		

CHRISTMAS

Niccolini-
Cowper
Madonna, by
Raphael
A1448

Santa Claus
A1449

Designed by Bradbury Thompson (No. 2063), and John Berkey (No. 2064).

PHOTOGRAVURE
Plates of 200 in four panes of 50 (No. 2063),
Plates of 230 in panes of 50 (Combination Press,
No. 2064)

1983, Oct. 28	Tagged	Perf. 11	
2063 A1448 20c multicolored		.40	.20
P# block of 4, 5#		1.75	—
Zip block of 4		1.65	—
2064 A1449 20c multicolored		.40	.20
P# block of 6, 5#		3.00	—
P# block of 20, 5-10 P#, 1-2			
copyright, 1-2 zip		11.50	—
a. Imperf., pair		175.00	

See Combination Press note after No. 1703.

German Religious
Leader, Founder of
Lutheran Church
(1483-1546)
A1450

Caribou and Alaska
Pipeline
A1451

MARTIN LUTHER
Designed by Bradbury Thompson.

Printed by American Bank Note Company.

PHOTOGRAVURE
Plates of 200 in four panes of 50.

1983, Nov. 11	Tagged	Perf. 11	
2065 A1450 20c multicolored		.40	.20
P# block of 4, 5#		1.75	—
Zip block of 4		1.65	—

ALASKA STATEHOOD, 25th ANNIV.
Designed by Bill Bond.

Printed by American Bank Note Company and J.W. Fergusson and Sons.

PHOTOGRAVURE
Plates of 200 in four panes of 50.

1984, Jan. 3	Tagged	Perf. 11	
2066 A1451 20c multicolored		.40	.20
P# block of 4, 5#		1.75	—
Zip block of 4		1.65	—

14th WINTER OLYMPIC GAMES,
Sarajevo, Yugoslavia, Feb. 8-19

Ice
Dancing — A1452

Downhill
Skiing — A1453

Cross-country
Skiing — A1454

Hockey — A1455

Designed by Bob Peak.

PHOTOGRAVURE
Plates of 200 in four panes of 50.

1984, Jan. 6	Tagged	Perf. 10½x11	
2067 A1452 20c multicolored		.50	.20
2068 A1453 20c multicolored		.50	.20
2069 A1454 20c multicolored		.50	.20
2070 A1455 20c multicolored		.50	.20
a. Block of 4, #2067-2070		2.10	1.50
P# block of 4, 4#		3.00	—
Zip block of 4		2.25	—

Pillar, Dollar
Sign — A1456

A1457

FEDERAL DEPOSIT INSURANCE CORPORATION, 50TH ANNIV.
Designed by Michael David Brown.

PHOTOGRAVURE
Plates of 200 in four panes of 50
(1 pane each #2071, 2074, 2075 and 2081)

1984, Jan. 12	Tagged	Perf. 11	
2071 A1456 20c multicolored		.40	.20
P# block of 4, 6#, UL only		1.75	—
Zip block of 4		1.65	—

LOVE
Designed by Bradbury Thompson.

PHOTOGRAVURE AND ENGRAVED (Combination Press)
Plates of 230 in four panes of 50.

1984, Jan. 31	Tagged	Perf. 11x10½	
2072 A1457 20c multicolored		.40	.20
P# block of 20, 6-12#, 1-2			
copyright, 1-2 zip		11.50	—
a. Horiz. pair, imperf. vert.		175.00	
b. Tagging omitted		5.00	

See Combination Press note after No. 1703.

A1458

A1459

BLACK HERITAGE SERIES
Carter G. Woodson (1875-1950), Black Historian.

Designed by Jerry Pinkney.

Printed by American Bank Note Company.

PHOTOGRAVURE
Plates of 200 in four panes of 50.

1984, Feb. 1	Tagged	Perf. 11	
2073 A1458 20c multicolored		.40	.20
P# block of 4, 6#		1.75	—
Zip block of 4		1.65	—
a. Horiz. pair, imperf. vert.		1,600.	

SOIL & WATER CONSERVATION
Designed by Michael David Brown.

See No. 2071 for printing information.

1984, Feb. 6	Tagged	Perf. 11	
2074 A1459 20c multicolored		.40	.20
P# block of 4, 6#, UR only		1.75	—
Zip block of 4		1.65	—

50TH ANNIV. OF CREDIT UNION ACT

Dollar Sign, Coin — A1460

Designed by Michael David Brown.

See No. 2071 for printing information.

1984, Feb. 10	Tagged	Perf. 11	
2075 A1460 20c multicolored		.40	.20
P# block of 4, 6#, LR only		1.75	—
Zip block of 4		1.65	—

ORCHIDS

Wild Pink — A1461

Yellow Lady's-
slipper — A1462

Spreading
Pogonia — A1463

Pacific
Calypso — A1464

Designed by Manabu Saito.

PHOTOGRAVURE
Plates of 192 in four panes of 48.

1984, Mar. 5	Tagged	Perf. 11	
2076 A1461 20c multicolored		.50	.20
2077 A1462 20c multicolored		.50	.20
2078 A1463 20c multicolored		.50	.20
2079 A1464 20c multicolored		.50	.20
a. Block of 4, #2076-2079		2.00	1.50
P# block of 4, 5#		2.50	—
Zip block of 4		2.10	—

HAWAII STATEHOOD, 25th ANNIV.

Eastern
Polynesian Canoe,
Golden Plover,
Mauna Loa
Volcano — A1465

Designed by Herb Kane.

Printed by American Bank Note Company.

PHOTOGRAVURE
Plates of 200 in four panes of 50.

1984, Mar. 12	Tagged	Perf. 11	
2080 A1465 20c multicolored		.40	.20
P# block of 4, 5#		1.70	—
Zip block of 4		1.65	—

50TH ANNIV., NATIONAL ARCHIVES

Abraham Lincoln, George Washington — A1466

Designed by Michael David Brown.

See No. 2071 for printing information.

1984, Apr. 16	Tagged	Perf. 11	
2081 A1466 20c **multicolored**		.40	.20
P# block of 4, 6#, LL only		1.70	—
Zip block of 4		1.65	—

LOS ANGELES SUMMER OLYMPICS
July 28-August 12

Diving — A1467

Long Jump — A1468

Wrestling — A1469

Kayak — A1470

Designed by Bob Peak.

PHOTOGRAVURE
Plates of 200 in four panes of 50.

1984, May 4	Tagged	Perf. 11	
2082 A1467 20c **multicolored**		.55	.20
2083 A1468 20c **multicolored**		.55	.20
2084 A1469 20c **multicolored**		.55	.20
2085 A1470 20c **multicolored**		.55	.20
a.	Block of 4, #2082-2085	2.40	1.90
	P# block of 4, 4#	3.50	—
	Zip block of 4	2.50	—
b.	As "a," imperf between vertically		

LOUISIANA WORLD EXPOSITION
New Orleans, May 12-Nov. 11

Bayou Wildlife — A1471

Designed by Chuck Ripper.

PHOTOGRAVURE
Plates of 160 in four panes of 40.

1984, May 11	Tagged	Perf. 11	
2086 A1471 20c **multicolored**		.40	.20
On cover, Expo. station pictorial handstamp cancel		2.50	
P# block of 4, 5#		1.75	—
Zip block of 4		1.65	—

HEALTH RESEARCH

Lab Equipment A1472

Designed by Tyler Smith.

Printed by American Bank Note Company.

PHOTOGRAVURE
Plates of 200 in four panes of 50.

1984, May 17	Tagged	Perf. 11	
2087 A1472 20c **multicolored**		.40	.20
P# block of 4, 5#		1.75	—
Zip block of 4		1.65	—

Actor Douglas Fairbanks (1883-1939) — A1473

Jim Thorpe A1474

PERFORMING ARTS
Designed by Jim Sharpe.

PHOTOGRAVURE AND ENGRAVED (Combination Press)
Plates of 230 in panes of 50.

1984, May 23	Tagged	Perf. 11	
2088 A1473 20c **multicolored**		.40	.20
P# block of 20, 5-10#, 1-2 copyright, 1-2 zip		12.00	—
a.	Tagging omitted	12.50	—
b.	Horiz. pair, imperf between		
See Combination Press note after No. 1703.			

JIM THORPE, 1888-1953
Designed by Richard Gangel.

ENGRAVED
Plates of 200 in four panes of 50.

1984, May 24	Tagged	Perf. 11	
2089 A1474 20c **dark brown**		.40	.20
P# block of 4		2.00	—
Zip block of 4		1.65	—

PERFORMING ARTS

John McCormack (1884-1945), Operatic Tenor — A1475

Designed by Jim Sharpe (US) and Ron Mercer (Ireland).

PHOTOGRAVURE
Plates of 200 in four panes of 50.

1984, June 6	Tagged	Perf. 11	
2090 A1475 20c **multicolored**		.40	.20
P# block of 4, 5#		1.75	—
Zip block of 4		1.65	—
See Ireland No. 594.			

ST. LAWRENCE SEAWAY, 25th ANNIV.

Aerial View of Seaway, Freighters A1476

Designed by Ernst Barenscher (Canada).

Printed by American Bank Note Company.

PHOTOGRAVURE
Plates of 200 in four panes of 50.

1984, June 26	Tagged	Perf. 11	
2091 A1476 20c **multicolored**		.40	.20
P# block of 4, 4#		1.75	—
Zip block of 4		1.65	—

WATERFOWL PRESERVATION ACT, 50th ANNIV.

"Mallards Dropping In" by Jay N. Darling — A1477

Design adapted from Darling's work (No. RW1) by Donald M. McDowell.

ENGRAVED
Plates of 200 in four panes of 50.

1984, July 2	Tagged	Perf. 11	
2092 A1477 20c **blue**		.50	.20
P# block of 4		2.50	—
Zip block of 4		2.25	—
a.	Horiz. pair, imperf. vert.	400.00	

The Elizabeth — A1478

A1479

ROANOKE VOYAGES
Designed by Charles Lundgren.

Printed by American Bank Note Company.

PHOTOGRAVURE
Plates of 200 in four panes of 50.

1984, July 13	Tagged	Perf. 11	
2093 A1478 20c **multicolored**		.40	.20
P# block of 4, 5#		1.75	—
Zip block of 4		1.65	—
Pair with full horiz. gutter btwn.		—	

HERMAN MELVILLE (1819-1891), AUTHOR
Designed by Bradbury Thompson.

ENGRAVED
Plates of 200 in four panes of 50.

1984, Aug. 1	Tagged	Perf. 11	
2094 A1479 20c **sage green**		.40	.20
P# block of 4		1.75	—
Zip block of 4		1.65	—

Founder of Junior
Achievement
A1480

Smokey Bear
A1481

HORACE MOSES (1862-1947)

Designed by Dennis Lyall.

ENGRAVED (Combination Press)
Plates of 200 in panes of 50.

1984, Aug. 6	Tagged	Perf. 11	
2095 A1480 20c orange & dark brown		.45	.20
P# block of 6		3.50	—
P# block of 20, 1-2#, 1-2 copyright, 1-2 zip		14.00	—

See Combination Press note after No. 1703.

SMOKEY BEAR

Designed by Rudolph Wendelin.

LITHOGRAPHED AND ENGRAVED
Plates of 200 in panes of 50.

1984, Aug. 13	Tagged	Perf. 11	
2096 A1481 20c multicolored		.40	.20
P# block of 4, 5#		2.00	—
Zip block of 4		1.65	
a. Horiz. pair, imperf. btwn.		300.00	
b. Vert. pair, imperf. btwn.		250.00	
c. Block of 4, imperf. btwn. vert. and horiz.		5,500.	
d. Horiz. pair, imperf. vert.		1,750.	

ROBERTO CLEMENTE (1934-1972)

Roberto Clemente

Clemente Wearing Pittsburgh
Pirates Cap, Puerto Rican
Flag — A1482

Designed by Juan Lopez-Bonilla.

PHOTOGRAVURE
Plates of 200 in panes of 50.

1984, Aug. 17	Tagged	Perf. 11	
2097 A1482 20c multicolored		1.60	.20
P# block of 4, 6#		8.00	—
Zip block of 4		6.75	—
a. Horiz. pair, imperf. vert.		2,000.	

DOGS

Beagle and
Boston
Terrier — A1483

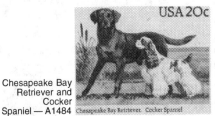

Chesapeake Bay
Retriever and
Cocker
Spaniel — A1484

Alaskan Malamute
and
Collie — A1485

Black and Tan
Coonhound and
American
Foxhound
A1486

Designed by Roy Andersen.

PHOTOGRAVURE
Plates of 160 in panes of 40.

1984, Sept. 7	Tagged	Perf. 11	
2098 A1483 20c multicolored		.45	.20
2099 A1484 20c multicolored		.45	.20
2100 A1485 20c multicolored		.45	.20
2101 A1486 20c multicolored		.45	.20
a. Block of 4, #2098-2101		1.90	1.75
P# block of 4, 4#		3.00	—
Zip block of 4		2.00	—

CRIME PREVENTION

McGruff, the Crime
Dog — A1487

Designed by Randall McDougall.

Printed by American Bank Note Company.

PHOTOGRAVURE
Plates of 200 in panes of 50.

1984, Sept. 26	Tagged	Perf. 11	
2102 A1487 20c multicolored		.40	.20
P# block of 4, 4#		1.75	—
Zip block of 4		1.65	—

HISPANIC AMERICANS

A1488

Designed by Robert McCall.

PHOTOGRAVURE
Plates of 160 in four panes of 40.

1984, Oct. 31	Tagged	Perf. 11	
2103 A1488 20c multicolored		.40	.20
P# block of 4, 6#		1.75	—
Zip block of 4		1.65	—
a. Vert. pair, imperf. horiz.		2,250.	

FAMILY UNITY

Stick Figures — A1489

Designed by Molly LaRue.

PHOTOGRAVURE AND ENGRAVED (Combination Press)
Plates of 230 in panes of 50.

1984, Oct. 1	Tagged	Perf. 11	
2104 A1489 20c multicolored		.40	.20
P# block of 20, 3-6#, 1-2 copyright, 1-2 zip		14.00	
a. Horiz. pair, imperf. vert.		550.00	
b. Tagging omitted		6.00	
c. Vert. pair, imperf. btwn. and at bottom		—	
d. Horiz. pair, imperf. between		—	

See Combination Press note after No. 1703.

A1490

Abraham Lincoln
Reading to Son,
Tad — A1491

ELEANOR ROOSEVELT (1884-1962)

Designed by Bradbury Thompson.

ENGRAVED
Plates of 192 in panes of 48.

1984, Oct. 11	Tagged	Perf. 11	
2105 A1490 20c deep blue		.40	.20
P# block of 4		1.75	—
Zip block of 4		1.65	—

NATION OF READERS

Design adapted from Anthony Berger daguerrotype by Bradbury Thompson.

ENGRAVED
Plates of 200 in panes of 50.

1984, Oct. 16	Tagged	Perf. 11	
2106 A1491 20c brown & maroon		.40	.20
P# block of 4		1.75	—
Zip block of 4		1.65	—

CHRISTMAS

Madonna and Child
by Fra Filippo
Lippi — A1492

Santa
Claus — A1493

Designed by Bradbury Thompson (No. 2107) and Danny La Boccetta (No. 2108).

PHOTOGRAVURE
Plates of 200 in panes of 50.

1984, Oct. 30	Tagged	Perf. 11	
2107 A1492 20c multicolored		.40	.20
P# block of 4, 5#		1.70	—
Zip block of 4		1.65	—
2108 A1493 20c multicolored		.40	.20

P# block of 4, 5# .... 1.70 —
Zip block of 4 .... 1.65 —
a. Horiz. pair, imperf. vert. *950.00*
No. 2108a is valued in the grade of fine.

VIETNAM VETERANS MEMORIAL

Vietnam Veterans Memorial USA 20c
Memorial and Visitors — A1494

Designed by Paul Calle.

ENGRAVED
Plates of 160 in panes of 40.

1984, Nov. 10	Tagged		Perf. 11
2109 A1494 20c **multicolored**		.40	.20
P# block of 4		1.90	—
Zip block of 4		1.65	—
a. Tagging omitted			—

PERFORMING ARTS

Jerome Kern (1885-1945),
Composer — A1495

Designed by Jim Sharpe.

Printed by the American Bank Note Company.

PHOTOGRAVURE
Plates of 200 in four panes of 50.

1985, Jan. 23	Tagged		Perf. 11
2110 A1495 22c **multicolored**		.40	.20
P# block of 4, 5#		1.75	—
Zip block of 4		1.65	—
a. Tagging omitted			7.50

 A1496   A1497

Designed by Bradbury Thompson.

PHOTOGRAVURE
Plates of 460 (20x23) in panes of 100.

1985, Feb. 1	Tagged		Perf. 11
2111 A1496 (22c) **green**		.55	.20
P# block of 6		4.50	—
P# block of 20, 1-2 #, 1-2			
Zip, 1-2 Copyright		22.50	—
a. Vert. pair, imperf.		50.00	
b. Vert. pair, imperf. horiz.		1,350.	

COIL STAMP
Perf. 10 Vert.

2112 A1496 (22c) **green**		.60	.20
Pair		1.20	.20
P# strip of 3, #1-2		6.00	
P# strip of 5, #1-2		7.25	
P# single, #1-2		—	.50
a. Imperf., pair		47.50	
P#1-2			
b. As "a," tagging omitted		140.00	
P#1-2			

BOOKLET STAMP
Perf. 11

2113 A1497 (22c) **green**		.80	.20
a. Booklet pane of 10		8.50	*3.00*
b. As "a," imperf. btwn. horiz.			—

 A1498

Flag Over
Capitol Dome
A1499

Designed by Frank Waslick.

ENGRAVED
Plates of 400 subjects in panes of 100.

1985, Mar. 29	Tagged		Perf. 11
2114 A1498 22c **blue, red & black**		.40	.20
P# block of 4		1.90	—
Zip block of 4		1.65	—
Pair with full horizontal gutter			—

COIL STAMP
Perf. 10 Vert.

2115 A1498 22c **blue, red & black,** wide block tagging		.40	.20
Pair		.80	.20
P# strip of 3, #2, 15		3.75	
P# strip of 3, #13		11.00	
P# strip of 3, #4, 10		5.50	
P# strip of 3, #6		6.25	
P# strip of 3, #14		27.50	
P# strip of 5, #2, 15		4.50	
P# strip of 5, #13		14.00	
P# strip of 5, #4, 10		6.00	
P# strip of 5, #6		7.25	
P# strip of 5, #14		30.00	
P# strip of 5, #16		5.25	
P# single, #2, 4, 10		—	.35
P# single, #6		—	6.00
P# single, #13		—	10.50
P# single, #14		—	25.00
P# single, #15-16		—	2.50
a. Narrow block tagging		.40	.20
P# strip of 3, #8, 12, 19, 22		3.75	
P# strip of 3, #1, 7		11.00	
P# strip of 3, #3		12.00	
P# strip of 3, #5		5.50	
P# strip of 3, #11, 17-18, 20-21		6.25	
P# strip of 5, #8, 12, 19, 22		4.50	
P# strip of 5, #1, 7		14.00	
P# strip of 5, #3		52.50	
P# strip of 5, #5		6.00	
P# strip of 5, #11, 17-18, 20-21		7.25	
P# single, #1, 3, 5, 7-8, 12, 22		—	.35
P# single, #11		—	1.00
P# single, #17-20		—	.45
P# single, #21		—	4.50
b. Inscribed "T" at bottom, *May 23, 1987*		.50	.40
P# strip of 3, #T1		4.00	
P# strip of 5, #T1		4.75	
P# single, #T1		—	3.50
c. Black field of stars			—
d. Tagging omitted		3.00	
e. Imperf., pair		15.00	
P#1-8, 10-12, 15, 17-20, 22			

No. 2115 is known with capitol in bluish black color, apparently from contaminated ink. Specialists often refer to this as "Eire blue."

BOOKLET STAMP
Perf. 10 Horiz.

2116 A1499 22c **blue, red & black**		.50	.20
a. Booklet pane of 5		2.50	*1.25*

BOOKLET STAMPS

Frilled
Dogwinkle
A1500

Reticulated
Helmet
A1501

New England
Neptune
A1502

Calico Scallop
A1503

Lightning Whelk — A1504

Designed by Pete Cocci.

ENGRAVED

1985, Apr. 4	Tagged		Perf. 10
2117 A1500 22c **black & brown**		.40	.20
2118 A1501 22c **black & multi**		.40	.20
2119 A1502 22c **black & brown**		.40	.20
2120 A1503 22c **black & violet**		.40	.20
2121 A1504 22c **black & multi**		.40	.20
a. Booklet pane of 10, 2 ea #2117-2121		4.00	2.50
b. As "a," violet omitted on both Nos. 2120		*800.00*	
c. As "a," vert. imperf. between		*600.00*	—
d. As "a," imperf.			—
e. Strip of 5, Nos. 2117-2121		2.00	—

Eagle and
Half Moon
A1505

Designed by Young & Rubicam.

TYPE I: washed out, dull appearance most evident in the black of the body of the eagle, and the red in the background between the eagle's shoulder and the moon. "$10.75" appears splotchy or grainy (P# 11111).

TYPE II: brighter, more intense colors most evident in the black on the eagle's body, and red in the background. "$10.75" appears smoother, brighter, and less grainy (P# 22222).

PHOTOGRAVURE

1985, Apr. 29	Untagged		Perf. 10 Vert.
2122 A1505 $10.75 **multicolored,** type I		19.00	7.50
a. Booklet pane of 3		60.00	
b. Type II, *June 19, 1989*		21.00	10.00
c. As "b," booklet pane of 3		65.00	—

Coil Plate No. Strips of 3

Beginning with No. 2123, coil plate No. strips of 3 usually sell at the level of strips of 5 minus the face value of two stamps.

TRANSPORTATION ISSUE

A1506

A1507

A1508

A1509

Tractor 1920s 7.1 USA — A1510
Ambulance 1860s 8.3 USA — A1511
Tow Truck 1920s 8.5 USA — A1512
Oil Wagon 1890s 10.1 USA — A1513
Stutz Bearcat 1933 11 USA — A1514
Stanley Steamer 1909s 12 USA — A1515
Pushcart 1880s 12.5 USA — A1516
Iceboat 1880s 14 USA — A1517
Dog Sled 1920s 17 USA — A1518
Bread Wagon 1880s 25 USA — A1519

Designers: 3.4c, 17c, Lou Nolan. 4.9c, 8.5c, 14c, 25c, William H. Bond. 5.5c, David K. Stone. 6c, 8.3c, 10.1c, 12.5c. James Schleyer. 7.1c, 11c, 12c, Ken Dallison.

COIL STAMPS
ENGRAVED

1985-87	Tagged	Perf. 10 Vert.
2123 A1506 3.4c **dark bluish green**, June 8	.20	.20
Pair	.20	.20
P# strip of 5, line, #1-2	1.10	
P# single, #1-2		.85
a. Untagged (Bureau precancel, Non-profit Org. CAR-RT SORT)	.20	.20
P# strip of 5, line, #1-2	5.25	
P# single, #1-2		5.50
2124 A1507 4.9c **brown black**, June 21	.20	.20
Pair	.20	.20
P# strip of 5, line, #3-4	1.00	
P# single, #3-4		.90
a. Untagged (Bureau precancel, Non-profit Org.)	.20	.20
P# strip of 5, line, #1-6	1.75	
P# single, #1-6		1.40
2125 A1508 5.5c **deep magenta**, Nov. 1, 1986	.20	.20
Pair	.20	.20
P# strip of 5, #1	1.90	
P# single, #1		1.65
a. Untagged (Bureau precancel, Non-profit Org. CAR-RT SORT)	.20	.20
P# strip of 5, #1	1.90	
P# strip of 5, #2	2.50	
P# single, #1		1.50
P# single, #2		2.25
2126 A1509 6c **red brown**, May 6	.20	.20
Pair	.25	.20
P# strip of 5, #1	1.65	
P# single, #1		1.25
a. Untagged (Bureau precancel, Non-profit Org.)	.20	.20
P# strip of 5, #1	1.90	
P# strip of 5, #2	8.00	
P# single, #1		1.25
P# single, #2		3.00
b. As "a," imperf., pair	200.00	
P#2		
2127 A1510 7.1c **lake**, Feb. 6, 1987	.20	.20
Pair	.30	.20
P# strip of 5, #1	2.50	
P# single, #1		2.25
a. Untagged (Bureau precancel "Non-profit Org." in black), Feb. 6, 1987	.20	.20

P# strip of 5, #1		3.50	
P# single, #1			3.00
b. Untagged (Bureau precancel "Non-profit 5-Digit Zip + 4" in black), May 26, 1989		.20	.20
P# strip of 5, #1		2.00	
P# single, #1			1.65

On Nos. 2127a and 2127b, both the vignette and the precancel inscription were printed from a single printing sleeve.

2128 A1511 8.3c **green**, June 21	.20	.20
Pair	.40	.20
P# strip of 5, line, #1-2	1.90	
P# single, #1-2		1.25
a. Untagged (Bureau precancel, Blk. Rt. CAR-RT SORT)	.20	.20
P# strip of 5, line, #1-2	2.00	
P# strip of 5, line, #3-4	5.00	
P# single, #1-2		1.25
P# single, #3-4		5.00

On No. 2231 "Ambulance 1860s" is 18mm long; on No. 2128, 18½mm long.

2129 A1512 8.5c **dark Prussian green**, Jan. 24, 1987	.20	.20
Pair	.40	.20
P# strip of 5, #1	3.25	
P# single, #1		2.50
a. Untagged (Bureau precancel, Non-profit Org.)	.20	.20
P# strip of 5, #1	3.25	
P# strip of 5, #2	12.50	
P# single, #1		2.00
P# single, #2		7.50
2130 A1513 10.1c **slate blue**, Apr. 18	.25	.20
Pair	.50	.20
P# strip of 5, #1	2.75	
P# single, #1		2.00
a. Untagged (Bureau precancel "Bulk Rate Carrier Route Sort" in red)	.25	.25
P# strip of 5, #2-3	2.50	
P# single, #2-3		2.00
Untagged (Bureau precancel "Bulk Rate" and lines in black)	.25	.25
P# strip of 5, #1-2	3.00	
P# single, #1-2		2.25
b. As "a," red precancel, imperf, pair	15.00	
P# strip of 6, #3	100.00	
As "a," black precancel, imperf, pair	100.00	
P#1		
2131 A1514 11c **dark green**, June 11	.25	.20
Pair	.50	.20
P# strip of 5, line, #1-4	2.00	
P# single, #1-4		1.50
a. Tagging omitted	—	
2132 A1515 12c **dark blue**, type I, Apr. 2	.25	.20
Pair	.50	.20
P# strip of 5, line, #1-2	2.50	
P# single, #1-2		1.90
a. Untagged, type I (Bureau precancel, PRESORTED FIRST-CLASS), Apr. 2	.25	.25
P# strip of 5, line, #1-2	2.75	
P# single, #1-2		2.00
b. Untagged, type II, (Bureau precancel, PRESORTED FIRST-CLASS) 1987	.40	.30
P# strip of 5, no line, #1	21.00	
P# single, #1		19.00
c. Tagging omitted, type I, (not Bureau precanceled), 1987	—	

Type II has "Stanley Steamer 1909" ½mm shorter (17½mm) than No. 2132 (18mm).

2133 A1516 12.5c **olive green**, Apr. 18	.25	.20
Pair	.50	.20
P# strip of 5, #1	3.25	
P# strip of 5, #2	5.25	
P# single, #1		2.50
P# single, #2		4.25
a. Untagged (Bureau precancel, Bulk Rate)	.25	.25
P# strip of 5, #1	3.50	
P# strip of 5, #2	5.25	
P# single, #1		1.90
P# single, #2		2.75
b. As "a," imperf., pair	55.00	
P#1		
2134 A1517 14c **sky blue**, type I, Mar. 23	.30	.20
Pair	.60	.20
P# strip of 5, line, #1-4	2.75	
P# single, #1-4		2.00
a. Imperf., pair	100.00	
P#1-2		
b. Type II, Sept. 30, 1986	.30	.20
P# strip of 5, no line, #2	4.25	
P# single, #1		3.50

Type II design is ¼mm narrower (17¼mm) than the original stamp (17½mm) and has block tagging. No. 2134 has overall tagging.

2135 A1518 17c **sky blue**, Aug. 20, 1986	.30	.20
Pair	.60	.20
P# strip of 5, #2	3.50	
P# single, #2		1.50
a. Imperf., pair	500.00	
P#2		
2136 A1519 25c **orange brown**, Nov. 22, 1986	.45	.20
Pair	.90	.20
P# strip of 5, #2-4	3.75	
P# strip of 5, #1, 5	4.25	
P# single, #1-4		.65
P# single, #5		3.00
a. Imperf., pair	10.00	

P#2-5			
b. Pair, imperf. between		750.00	
c. Tagging omitted		20.00	
Nos. 2123-2136 (14)		3.45	2.80

Precancellations on Nos. 2125a, 2127a do not have lines.
Precancellation on No. 2129a is in red. See No. 2231.

BLACK HERITAGE SERIES
Mary McLeod Bethune (1875-1955), educator.

 A1520

Designed by Jerry Pinkney from a photograph.

Printed by American Bank Note Company.

PHOTOGRAVURE
Plates of 200 in four panes of 50.

1985, Mar. 5	Tagged	Perf. 11
2137 A1520 22c **multicolored**	.40	.20
P# block of 4, 6#	2.25	—
Zip block of 4	1.70	

AMERICAN FOLK ART ISSUE
Duck Decoys

Broadbill — A1521

Mallard — A1522

Canvasback A1523

Redhead A1524

Designed by Stevan Dohanos.

Printed by American Bank Note Company

PHOTOGRAVURE
Plates of 200 in four panes of 50.

1985, Mar. 22	Tagged	Perf. 11
2138 A1521 22c **multicolored**	.65	.20
2139 A1522 22c **multicolored**	.65	.20
2140 A1523 22c **multicolored**	.65	.20
2141 A1524 22c **multicolored**	.65	.20
a. Block of 4, #2138-2141	4.00	2.25
P# block of 4, 5#	6.50	—
Zip block of 4	4.25	

WINTER SPECIAL OLYMPICS

Ice Skater, Emblem, Skier — A1525

Designed by Jeff Carnell.

PHOTOGRAVURE
Plates of 160 in four panes of 40.

1985, Mar. 25	Tagged	Perf. 11	
2142 A1525 22c **multicolored**		.40	.20
P# block of 4, 6#		1.75	—
Zip block of 4		1.65	—
a. Vert. pair, imperf. horiz.		600.00	

LOVE

A1526

Designed by Corita Kent.

PHOTOGRAVURE
Plates of 200 in four panes of 50.

1985, Apr. 17	Tagged	Perf. 11	
2143 A1526 22c **multicolored**		.40	.20
P# block of 4, 6#		1.70	—
Zip block of 4		1.65	—
a. Imperf., pair		1,500.	

RURAL ELECTRIFICATION ADMINISTRATION

REA Power Lines, Farmland A1527

Designed by Howard Koslow.

PHOTOGRAVURE & ENGRAVED (Combination Press)
Plates of 230 in panes of 50.

1985, May 11	Tagged	Perf. 11	
2144 A1527 22c **multicolored**		.45	.20
P# block of 20, 5-10 #, 1-2 Zip, 1-2 Copyright		20.00	
a. Vert. pair, imperf between			

See Combination Press note after No. 1703.

AMERIPEX '86

US No. 134 — A1528

Designed by Richard Sheaff.

LITHOGRAPHED & ENGRAVED
Plates of 192 in four panes of 48.

1985, May 25	Tagged	Perf. 11	
2145 A1528 22c **multicolored**		.40	.20
P# block of 4, 3#		1.75	—
Zip block of 4		1.65	—
a. Red, black and blue (engr.) omitted		200.00	
b. Red & black omitted		1,250.	
c. Red omitted			

ABIGAIL ADAMS (1744-1818)

A1529

Designed by Bart Forbes.

PHOTOGRAVURE
Plates of 200 in four panes of 50.

1985, June 14	Tagged	Perf. 11	
2146 A1529 22c **multicolored**		.40	.20
P# block of 4, 4#		1.90	—
Zip block of 4		1.65	—
a. Imperf., pair		275.00	

FREDERIC AUGUSTE BARTHOLDI (1834-1904)

F.A. Bartholdi, Statue of Liberty Sculptor

Architect and Sculptor, Statue of Liberty — A1530

Designed by Howard Paine from paintings by Jose Frappa and James Dean.

LITHOGRAPHED & ENGRAVED
Plates of 200 in four panes of 50.

1985, July 18	Tagged	Perf. 11	
2147 A1530 22c **multicolored**		.40	.20
P# block of 4, 5#		1.90	—
Zip block of 4		1.65	—
a. Black (engr.) omitted		—	

Examples of No. 2147 exist with most, but not all, of the engraved black omitted. Expertization is recommended for No. 2147a.

George Washington, Washington Monument A1532

Sealed Envelopes A1533

Designed by Thomas Szumowski (#2149) based on a portrait by Gilbert Stuart, and Richard Sheaff (#2150).

COIL STAMPS
PHOTOGRAVURE

1985			Perf. 10 Vertically	
2149 A1532	18c	**multicolored**, low gloss gum, *Nov. 6*	.35	.20
		Pair	.70	.20
		P# strip of 5, #1112	4.00	
		P# strip of 5, #3333	4.75	
		P# single, #1112	—	3.00
		P# single, #3333	—	3.75
a.		Untagged (Bureau Precanceled), low gloss gum	.35	.35
		P# strip of 5, #33333	4.00	
		P# strip of 5, #11121	6.50	
		P# single, #33333	—	1.75
		P# single, #11121	—	5.75
		Dull gum	.35	
		P# strip of 5, #33333	5.50	
		P# strip of 5, #43444	8.50	
		P# single, #43444	—	7.00
b.		Imperf., pair	950.00	
		P#1112		
c.		As "a," imperf., pair	800.00	
		P#33333		
d.		Tagging omitted (not Bureau precanceled)	—	—
e.		As "a," tagged (error), dull gum	2.00	1.75
		Pair	4.00	3.75
		P# strip of 5, #33333	—	
		P# single, #33333	—	
2150 A1533	21.1c	**multicolored**, *Oct. 22*	.40	.20
		Pair	.80	.20
		P# strip of 5, #111111	4.00	
		P# strip of 5, #111121	5.50	

		P# single, #111111	—	3.00
		P# single, #111121	—	4.75
a.		Untagged (Bureau Precancel)	.40	.40
		Pair	.80	.80
		P# strip of 5, #111111	4.25	
		P# single, #111111	—	3.00
b.		As "a," tagged (error)	.40	.40
		Pair	.80	.80
		P# strip of 5, #111121	5.50	
		P# strip of 5, #111111	—	
		P# single, #111121	—	4.50

Precancellations on Nos. 2149a ("PRESORTED FIRST-CLASS"), 2150a and 2150b ("ZIP+4") do not have lines.

KOREAN WAR VETERANS

American Troops in Korea — A1535

Designed by Richard Sheaff from a photograph by David D. Duncan.

ENGRAVED
Plates of 200 in four panes of 50.

1985, July 26	Tagged	Perf. 11	
2152 A1535 22c **gray green & rose red**		.40	.20
P# block of 4		2.50	—
Zip block of 4		1.75	—

SOCIAL SECURITY ACT, 50th ANNIV.

Men, Women, Children, Corinthian Columns — A1536

Designed by Robert Brangwynne.

Printed by American Bank Note Company.

PHOTOGRAVURE
Plates of 200 in four panes of 50.

1985, Aug. 14	Tagged	Perf. 11	
2153 A1536 22c **deep & light blue**		.40	.20
P# block of 4, 2#		1.90	—
Zip block of 4		1.70	—

WORLD WAR I VETERANS

The Battle of Marne, France — A1537

Designed by Richard Sheaff from Harvey Dunn's charcoal drawing.

ENGRAVED
Plates of 200 in four panes of 50.

1985, Aug. 26	Tagged	Perf. 11	
2154 A1537 22c **gray green & rose red**		.40	.20
P# block of 4		2.25	—
Zip block of 4		1.85	—

HORSES

Quarter Horse — A1538

Morgan — A1539

Saddlebred
A1540

Appaloosa
A1541

Designed by Roy Andersen.

PHOTOGRAVURE
Plates of 160 in four panes of 40.

1985, Sept. 25	Tagged		Perf. 11	
2155	A1538	22c **multicolored**	1.00	.20
2156	A1539	22c **multicolored**	1.00	.20
2157	A1540	22c **multicolored**	1.00	.20
2158	A1541	22c **multicolored**	1.00	.20
a.		Block of 4, #2155-2158	6.00	4.50
		P# block of 4, 5#	8.50	—
		Zip block of 4	6.25	—

PUBLIC EDUCATION IN AMERICA

Quill Pen, Apple, Spectacles,
Penmanship Quiz — A1542

Designed by Uldis Purins.

Printed by American Bank Note Company

PHOTOGRAVURE
Plates of 200 in four panes of 50.

1985, Oct. 1	Tagged		Perf. 11	
2159	A1542	22c **multicolored**	.45	.20
		P# block of 4, 5#	2.75	—
		Zip block of 4	1.85	—

INTERNATIONAL YOUTH YEAR

YMCA Youth
Camping,
Cent. — A1543

Boy Scouts, 75th
Anniv. — A1544

Big Brothers / Big
Sisters
Federation, 40th
Anniv. — A1545

Camp Fire Inc.,
75th
Anniv. — A1546

Designed by Dennis Luzak.

Printed by American Bank Note Company.

PHOTOGRAVURE
Plates of 200 in four panes of 50.

1985, Oct. 7	Tagged		Perf. 11	
2160	A1543	22c **multicolored**	.65	.20
2161	A1544	22c **multicolored**	.65	.20
2162	A1545	22c **multicolored**	.65	.20
2163	A1546	22c **multicolored**	.65	.20
a.		Block of 4, #2160-2163	3.00	2.25
		P# block of 4, 5#	4.50	—
		Zip block of 4	3.25	—

HELP END HUNGER

Youths and
Elderly Suffering
from Malnutrition
A1547

Designed by Jerry Pinkney.

Printed by the American Bank Note Company.

PHOTOGRAVURE
Plates of 200 in four panes of 50.

1985, Oct. 15	Tagged		Perf. 11	
2164	A1547	22c **multicolored**	.45	.20
		P# block of 4, 5#	2.00	—
		Zip block of 4	1.90	—

CHRISTMAS

Genoa Madonna, Enameled
Terra-Cotta by Luca Della
Robbia (1400-1482) — A1548

Poinsettia
Plants — A1549

Designed by Bradbury Thompson (No. 2165) and James
Dean (No. 2166).

PHOTOGRAVURE
Plates of 200 in panes of 50.

1985, Oct. 30	Tagged		Perf. 11	
2165	A1548	22c **multicolored**	.40	.20
		P# block of 4, 4#	1.75	—
		Zip block of 4	1.65	—
a.		Imperf., pair	100.00	
2166	A1549	22c **multicolored**	.40	.20
		P# block of 4, 5#	1.70	—
		Zip block of 4	1.65	—
a.		Imperf., pair	130.00	

ARKANSAS STATEHOOD, 150th ANNIV.

Old State House,
Little
Rock — A1550

Designed by Roger Carlisle.

Printed by the American Bank Note Company

PHOTOGRAVURE
Plates of 200 in four panes of 50.

1986, Jan. 3	Tagged		Perf. 11	
2167	A1550	22c **multicolored**	.40	.20
		P# block of 4, 6#	2.00	—
		Zip block of 4	1.75	—
a.		Vert. pair, imperf. horiz.	—	

Marginal Inscriptions

Beginning with the Luis Munoz Marin issue a
number of stamps include a descriptive inscription in the selvage.

GREAT AMERICANS ISSUE

A1551

A1552

Designed by Ron Adair.

Printed by the Bureau of Engraving & Printing.

ENGRAVED
Panes of 100, Sheets of 600 in six panes of 100
(#2184B)
Perf. 11, 11½x11 (#2185), 11x11.1 (20c)

1986-94			Tagged	
2168	A1551	1c **brownish vermilion,** large block tagging, *June 30*	.20	.20
		P# block of 4	.25	—
		Zip block of 4	.20	—
a.		Tagging omitted	5.00	
2169	A1552	2c **bright blue,** large block tagging, *Feb. 28, 1987*	.20	.20
		P# block of 4	.30	—
		Zip block of 4	.20	—
a.		Untagged	.20	.20
		P# block of 4	.35	—
		Zip block of 4	.20	—

A tagging omitted error of No. 2169 appeared before No.
2169a was issued. Plate blocks from plate 1 are the error if
untagged. No. 2169a is from plate 2. Other blocks and singles
are indistiguishable, unless se-tenant with tagged stamps.

A1553

A1554

Designed by Christopher Calle.

Printed by the Bureau of Engraving & Printing.

2170	A1553	3c **bright blue,** large block tagging, dull gum, *Sept. 15*	.20	.20
		P# block of 4	.50	—
		Zip block of 4	.25	—
a.		Untagged, dull gum, *1994*	.20	.20
		P# block of 4	.50	—
		Zip block of 4	.25	—
		Shiny gum, *1994*	.20	
		P# block of 4	.50	—
		Zip block of 4	.25	—

A tagging omitted error of No. 2170 appeared before No.
2170a was issued. Plate blocks from plates 2 and 3 are the
error if untagged. No. 2170a is from plate 4. Other blocks and
singles are indistiguishable, unless se-tenant with tagged
stamps.

2171	A1554	4c **blue violet,** large block tagging, *July 14*	.20	.20
		P# block of 4	.60	—
		Zip block of 4	.40	—
a.		4c **grayish violet,** untagged	.20	.20

	P# block of 4	.40	—
	Zip block of 4	.35	—
b.	4c **deep grayish blue**, untagged, *1993*	.20	.20
	P# block of 4	.50	—
	Zip block of 4	.40	—

A1555

A1556

Designers: No. 2172, Christopher Calle. No. 2173, Juan Maldonado.

Printed by the Bureau of Engraving & Printing.

2172	A1555	5c **dark olive green**, large block tagging, *Feb. 27*	.20	.20
		P# block of 4	.65	—
		Zip block of 4	.35	—
a.		Tagging omitted	10.00	—
2173	A1556	5c **carmine**, overall tagging, *Feb. 18, 1990*	.20	.20
		P# block of 4	.75	—
		P# zip block of 4	.90	—
		Zip block of 4	.45	—
a.		Untagged, *1991*	.20	.20
		P# block of 4	.60	—
		P# zip block of 4	.75	—
		Zip block of 4	.45	—

A tagging omitted error of No. 2173 appeared before No. 2173a was issued. Plate blocks from plate 1 are the error if untagged. No. 2173a is from plate 2. Other blocks and singles are indistiguishable, unless se-tenant with tagged stamps.

A1557

A1558

Designers: 10c, Robert Anderson. 14c, Ward Brackett.

Printed by the Bureau of Engraving & Printing.

2175	A1557	10c **lake**, large block tagging, dull gum, *Aug. 15, 1987*	.20	.20
		P# block of 4	.85	—
		Zip block of 4	.80	—
a.		Overall tagging, dull gum, *1990*	.30	.20
		P# block of 4	10.00	—
		Zip block of 4	2.00	—
b.		Tagging omitted	15.00	—
c.		Prephosphored coated paper (solid tagging), dull gum, *1991*	.30	.20
		P# block of 4	1.40	—
		Zip block of 4	1.20	—
d.		Prephosphored uncoated paper (mottled tagging), shiny gum, *1993*	.20	.20
		P# block of 4	1.25	—
		Zip block of 4	.80	—
e.		10c **carmine**, prephosphored uncoated paper (mottled tagging), shiny gum, *1994*	.25	.20
		P# block of 4	1.25	—
		Zip block of 4	1.00	—
2176	A1558	14c **crimson**, large block tagging, *Feb. 12, 1987*	.25	.20
		P# block of 4	1.50	—
		Zip block of 4	1.05	—

A1559

A1560

Designers: 15c, Jack Rosenthal. 17c, Christopher Calle.

Printed by the Bureau of Engraving & Printing.

2177	A1559	15c **claret**, large block tagging, *June 6, 1988*	.30	.20
		P# block of 4	6.00	—
		Zip block of 4	1.20	—
a.		Overall tagging, *1990*	.30	.20
		P# block of 4	3.25	—
		Zip block of 4	1.20	—
b.		Prephosphored coated paper (solid tagging)	.40	—

	P# block of 4	3.25	—
	Zip block of 4	1.60	—
c.	Tagging omitted	15.00	—
2178	A1560 17c **dull blue green**, large block tagging, *June 18*	.35	.20
	P# block of 4	2.00	—
	Zip block of 4	1.40	—
a.	Tagging omitted	10.00	—

A1561

A1562

Designers: 20c, Robert Anderson. 21c, Susan Sanford.

Printed by: 20c, Banknote Corporation of America. 21c, Bureau of Engraving & Printing.

2179	A1561	20c **red brown**, prephosphored coated paper (grainy solid tagging), *Oct. 24, 1994*	.40	.20
		P# block of 4, 1#+B	2.00	—
a.		20c **orange brown**, prephosphored coated paper (grainy solid tagging)	.40	.20
		P# block of 4, 1#+B	2.25	—
2180	A1562	21c **blue violet**, large block tagging, *Oct. 21, 1988*	.40	.20
		P# block of 4	2.50	—
		Zip block of 4	1.65	—
a.		Tagging omitted		

No. 2180 known with worn tagging mats on which horizontal untagged areas have taggant giving the appearance of band tagging.

A1563

A1564

A1565

Designers: 23c, Dennis Lyall. 25c, Richard Sparks. 28c, Robert Anderson.

Printed by the Bureau of Engraving & Printing.

2181	A1563	23c **purple**, large block tagging, dull gum, *Nov. 4, 1988*	.45	.20
		P# block of 4	2.50	—
		Zip block of 4	1.90	—
a.		Overall tagging, dull gum	.45	—
		P# block of 4	5.00	—
		Zip block of 4	1.80	—
b.		Prephosphored coated paper (solid tagging), dull gum	.60	—
		P# block of 4	3.25	—
		Zip block of 4	2.40	—
c.		Prephosphored uncoated paper (mottled tagging), shiny gum	.50	.20
		P# block of 4	3.25	—
		Zip block of 4	2.00	—
d.		Tagging omitted	7.50	—
2182	A1564	25c **blue**, large block tagging, *Jan. 11*	.45	.20
		P# block of 4	2.75	—
		Zip block of 4	1.85	—
a.		Booklet pane of 10, *May 3, 1988*	4.50	3.75
b.		Tagging omitted		
c.		As "a," tagging omitted		

See Nos. 2197, 2197a.

2183	A1565	28c **myrtle green**, large block tagging, *Sept. 14, 1989*	.50	.20
		P# block of 4	2.50	—
		Zip block of 4	2.25	—

A1566

A1567

Designed by Christopher Calle.

Printed by: No. 2184, Canadian Bank Note Co. for Stamp Venturers. No. 2185, Stamp Venturers.

2184	A1566	29c **blue**, prephosphored uncoated paper (mottled tagging), *Mar. 9, 1992*	.55	.20
		P# block of 4, #+S	2.50	—
		Zip block of 4	2.25	—
2185	A1567	29c **indigo**, prephosphored paper (solid tagging), *Apr. 13, 1993*	.50	.20
		P# block of 4, 1#+S	2.50	—
		P# position block of 8, 1#+S	4.50	—
		Zip block of 4	2.25	—

A1568

A1569

A1570

Designers: 35c, 40c, Christopher Calle. 45c, Bradbury Thompson.

Printed by: 35c, Canadian Bank Note Co. for Stamp Venturers. 40c, 45c, Bureau of Engraving & Printing.

2186	A1568	35c **black**, prephosphored uncoated paper (mottled tagging), *Apr. 3, 1991*	.65	.20
		P# block of 4, #+S	3.25	—
		Zip block of 4	2.90	—
2187	A1569	40c **dark blue**, overall tagging, dull gum, *Sept. 6, 1990*	.70	.20
		P# block of 4	3.75	—
		Zip block of 4	3.00	—
a.		Prephosphored coated paper (solid tagging), dull gum	.75	.35
		P# block of 4	4.25	—
		Zip block of 4	3.00	—
		Grainy solid tagging, low gloss gum, *1998*	.75	.35
		P# block of 4	4.25	—
		Zip block of 4	4.00	—
b.		Prephosphored uncoated paper (mottled tagging), shiny gum, *1994*	.75	.20
		P# block of 4	7.50	—
		Zip block of 4	3.00	—
2188	A1570	45c **bright blue**, large block tagging, *June 17, 1988*	.85	.20
		P# block of 4	3.75	—
		Zip block of 4	3.50	—
a.		45c **blue**, overall tagging, *1990*	1.65	.20
		P# block of 4	11.00	—
		Zip block of 4	7.00	—
b.		Tagging omitted	15.00	—

The blue on No. 2188a is noticeably lighter than on No. 2188. Color variety specialists, as well as tagging specialists, will want to consider it as a second variety of this stamp.

A1571

A1572

Designers: 52c, John Berkey. 56c, Robert Anderson.

Printed by the Bureau of Engraving & Printing.

2189	A1571	52c **purple**, prephosphored coated paper (solid tagging), dull gum, *June 3, 1991*	1.10	.20
		P# block of 4	5.00	—
		Zip block of 4	4.50	—
a.		Prephosphored uncoated paper (mottled tagging), shiny gum, *1993*	1.10	—
		P# block of 4	5.50	—
		Zip block of 4	4.50	—
2190	A1572	56c **scarlet**, large block tagging, *Sept. 3*	1.10	.20
		P# block of 4	6.00	—
		Zip block of 4	4.50	—

No. 2190 known with a "tagging spill" making stamp appear overall tagged.

A1573

A1574

Designed by Christopher Calle.

Printed by the Bureau of Engraving & Printing.

2191	A1573	65c **dark blue**, large block tagging, *Nov. 5, 1988*	1.20	.20
		P# block of 4	5.00	—
		Zip block of 4	4.90	—
a.		Tagging omitted		—
2192	A1574	75c **deep magenta**, prephosphored coated paper (solid tagging), dull gum, *Feb. 16, 1992*	1.30	.20
		P# block of 4	5.50	—
		Zip block of 4	5.25	—
a.		Prephosphored uncoated paper (mottled tagging), shiny gum	1.30	—
		P# block of 4	5.50	—
		Zip block of 4	5.25	—

A1575

A1576

"Lipstick on Shirt Front" double gouge plate flaw

Designers: No. 2193, Tom Broad. No. 2194, Bradbury Thompson.

Printed by the Bureau of Engraving & Printing.

2193	A1575	$1 **dark Prussian green**, large block tagging, *Sept. 23*	2.50	.50
		P# block of 4	14.00	—
		Zip block of 4	10.50	—
2194	A1576	$1 **intense deep blue**, large block tagging, dull gum, *June 7, 1989*	1.75	.50
		P# block of 4	7.00	—
		Pane of 20	35.00	
		Double gouge plate flaw ("Lipstick on Shirt Front"), (pos. 6 on one plate #1 pane)		—
b.		$1 **deep blue**, overall tagging, dull gum, *1990*	1.75	.50
		P# block of 4	7.00	—
		Pane of 20	35.00	
c.		Tagging omitted	10.00	
d.		$1 **dark blue**, prephosphored coated paper (solid tagging), dull gum, *1992*	1.75	.50
		P# block of 4	7.00	—
		Pane of 20	35.00	
e.		$1 **blue**, prephosphored uncoated paper (mottled tagging), shiny gum, *1993*	2.00	.60
		P# block of 4	8.00	—
		Pane of 20	40.00	
f.		$1 **blue**, prephosphored coated paper (grainy solid tagging), low gloss gum, *1998*	1.75	.50
		P# block of 4	7.00	—
		Pane of 20	35.00	

No. 2194 issued in pane of 20 (see No. 2196.)
The intense deep blue of No. 2194 is much deeper than the deep blue and dark blue of the other $1 varieties.
The "Lipstick on Shirt Front" flaw was discovered during production and the position was repaired. Very few have been found.

A1577

A1578

Designers: $2, Tom Broad. $5, Arthur Lidov.

Printed by the Bureau of Engraving & Printing.

2195	A1577	$2 **bright violet**, large block tagging, *Mar. 19*	3.50	.50
		P# block of 4	15.00	—
		Zip block of 4	13.50	—
a.		Tagging omitted	45.00	

Plates of 320 in sixteen panes of 20 (5x4). The first and fifth rows of horizontal perforations extend into the side selvage.

2196	A1578	$5 **copper red**, large block tagging, *Aug. 25, 1987*	8.00	1.00
		P# block of 4	32.50	—
		Pane of 20	165.00	
a.		Tagging omitted		—
b.		Prephosphored paper (solid tagging), *1992*	8.00	—
		P# block of 4	32.50	—
		Pane of 20	165.00	—
		Nos. 2168-2196 (28)	28.20	7.30

Booklet Stamp
Perf. 10 on 2 or 3 sides

2197	A1564	25c **blue**, large block tagging, *May 3, 1988*	.45	.20
a.		Booklet pane of 6	3.00	2.25
b.		Tagging omitted	4.50	
c.		As "b," booklet pane of 6	65.00	

UNITED STATES - SWEDEN
STAMP COLLECTING

Handstamped Cover, Philatelic Memorabilia A1581

Boy Examining Stamp Collection — A1582

No. 836 Under Magnifying Glass, Sweden Nos. 268, 271 — A1583

1986 Presidents Miniature Sheet — A1584

Designed by Richard Sheaff and Eva Jern (No. 2200).

BOOKLET STAMPS
LITHOGRAPHED & ENGRAVED
Perf. 10 Vert. on 1 or 2 Sides

			Tagged	
1986, Jan. 23				
2198	A1581	22c multicolored	.45	.20
2199	A1582	22c multicolored	.45	.20
2200	A1583	22c multicolored	.45	.20
2201	A1584	22c multicolored	.45	.20
a.		Bklt. pane of 4, #2198-2201	2.00	1.75
b.		As "a," black omitted on Nos. 2198, 2201	65.00	—
c.		As "a," blue (litho.) omitted on Nos. 2198-2200	2,500.	
d.		As "a," buff (litho.) omitted	2,500.	

See Sweden Nos. 1585-1588.

LOVE ISSUE

A1585

Designed by Saul Mandel.

Plates of 200 in four panes of 50.
PHOTOGRAVURE

				Perf. 11	
1986, Jan. 30		**Tagged**			
2202	A1585	22c multicolored		.40	.20
		P# block of 4, 5#		1.75	—
		Zip block of 4		1.65	—

Sojourner Truth (c. 1797-1883), Human Rights Activist — A1586

Texas State Flag and Silver Spur — A1587

BLACK HERITAGE SERIES

Designed by Jerry Pinkney.

Printed by American Bank Note Co.

Plates of 200 in four panes of 50
PHOTOGRAVURE

				Perf. 11	
1986, Feb. 4		**Tagged**			
2203	A1586	22c multicolored		.40	.20
		P# block of 4, 6#		1.75	—
		Zip block of 4		1.65	—

REPUBLIC OF TEXAS, 150th ANNIV.

Designed by Don Adair.

Printed by the American Bank Note Co.

Plates of 200 in four panes of 50.
PHOTOGRAVURE

				Perf. 11	
1986, Mar. 2		**Tagged**			
2204	A1587	22c **dark blue, dark red & grayish black**		.40	.20
		P# block of 4, 3#		1.75	—
		Zip block of 4		1.65	—
a.		Horiz. pair, imperf. vert.		1,100.	
b.		Dark red omitted		2,750.	
c.		Dark blue omitted		8,500.	

FISH

Muskellunge
A1588

Atlantic
Cod — A1589

Largemouth
Bass — A1590

Bluefin
Tuna — A1591

Catfish
A1592

Designed by Chuck Ripper.

BOOKLET STAMPS
PHOTOGRAVURE

1986, Mar. 21		Tagged	Perf. 10 Horiz.	
2205	A1588	22c multicolored	.50	.20
2206	A1589	22c multicolored	.50	.20
2207	A1590	22c multicolored	.50	.20
2208	A1591	22c multicolored	.50	.20
2209	A1592	22c multicolored	.50	.20
a.		Bklt. pane of 5, #2205-2209	4.50	2.75
b.		As "a," red omitted	—	

PUBLIC HOSPITALS

A1593

Designed by Uldis Purins.

Printed by the American Bank Note Co.

PHOTOGRAVURE
Plates of 200 in four panes of 50.

1986, Apr. 11		Tagged	Perf. 11	
2210	A1593	22c multicolored	.40	.20
		P# block of 4, 5#	1.75	—
		Zip block of 4	1.65	—
a.		Vert. pair, imperf. horiz.	325.00	
b.		Horiz. pair, imperf. vert.	1,350.	

PERFORMING ARTS

Edward Kennedy "Duke"
Ellington (1899-1974), Jazz
Composer — A1594

Designed by Jim Sharpe.
Printed by the American Bank Note Co.

PHOTOGRAVURE
Plates of 200 in four panes of 50.

1986, Apr. 29		Tagged	Perf. 11	
2211	A1594	22c multicolored	.40	.20
		P# block of 4, 6#	1.90	—
		Zip block of 4	1.75	—
a.		Vert. pair, imperf. horiz.	1,000.	

AMERIPEX '86 ISSUE
Miniature Sheets

Presidents of
the United States: I

AMERIPEX 86
International
Stamp Show
Chicago, Illinois
May 22-June 1, 1986

35 Presidents — A1599a

Presidents of
the United States: II

AMERIPEX 86
International
Stamp Show
Chicago, Illinois
May 22-June 1, 1986

A1599b

Presidents of
the United States: III

AMERIPEX 86
International
Stamp Show
Chicago, Illinois
May 22-June 1, 1986

A1599c

Presidents of
the United States: IV

AMERIPEX 86
International
Stamp Show
Chicago, Illinois
May 22-June 1, 1986

A1599d

Designs: No. 2216: a, George Washington. b, John Adams. c, Thomas Jefferson. d, James Madison. e, James Monroe. f, John Quincy Adams. g, Andrew Jackson. h, Martin Van Buren. i, William H. Harrison.

No. 2217: a, John Tyler. b, James Knox Polk. c, Zachary Taylor. d, Millard Fillmore. e, Franklin Pierce. f, James Buchanan. g, Abraham Lincoln. h, Andrew Johnson. i, Ulysses S. Grant.

No. 2218: a, Rutherford B. Hayes. b, James A. Garfield. c, Chester A. Arthur. d, Grover Cleveland. e, Benjamin Harrison. f, William McKinley. g, Theodore Roosevelt. h, William H. Taft. i, Woodrow Wilson.

No. 2219: a, Warren G. Harding. b, Calvin Coolidge. c, Herbert Hoover. d, Franklin Delano Roosevelt. e, White House. f, Harry S. Truman. g, Dwight D. Eisenhower. h, John F. Kennedy. i, Lyndon B. Johnson.

Designed by Jerry Dadds.

LITHOGRAPHED & ENGRAVED

1986, May 22	Tagged	Perf. 11	
2216 A1599a	Sheet of 9	3.75	—
a.-i.	22c, any single	.40	.25
j.	Blue (engr.) omitted	3,500.	
k.	Black inscription omitted	2,000.	
l.	Imperf.	10,500.	
2217 A1599b	Sheet of 9	3.75	—
a.-i.	22c, any single	.40	.25
j.	Black inscription omitted	3,750.	
2218 A1599c	Sheet of 9	3.75	—
a.-i.	22c, any single	.40	.25
j.	Brown (engr.) omitted	—	
k.	Black inscription omitted	2,900.	
2219 A1599d	Sheet of 9	3.75	—
a.-i.	22c, any single	.40	.25
j.	Blackish blue (engr.) inscription omitted on a-b, d-e, g-h	—	
k.	Tagging omitted on c, f, i	—	
	Nos. 2216-2219 (4)	15.00	

Issued in conjunction with AMERIPEX '86 Intl. Philatelic Exhibition, Chicago, IL May 22-June 1. Sheet size: 120x207mm (sheet size varied).

ARCTIC EXPLORERS

Elisha Kent
Kane — A1600

Adolphus W.
Greely — A1601

Vilhjalmur
Stefansson
A1602

Robert E. Peary,
Matthew
Henson — A1603

Designed by Dennis Lyall.
Printed by the American Bank Note Company.

PHOTOGRAVURE
Plates of 200 in four panes of 50.

1986, May 28	Tagged	Perf. 11	
2220 A1600	22c multicolored	.65	.20
2221 A1601	22c multicolored	.65	.20
2222 A1602	22c multicolored	.65	.20
2223 A1603	22c multicolored	.65	.20
a.	Block of 4, #2220-2223	2.75	2.25
	P# block of 4, 5#	4.50	—
	Zip block of 4	3.00	—
b.	As "a," black (engr.) omitted	9,500.	
c.	As "a," Nos. 2220, 2221 black (engr.) omitted	—	

STATUE OF LIBERTY, 100th ANNIV.

A1604

Designed by Howard Paine.

ENGRAVED
Plates of 200 in four panes of 50.

1986, July 4	Tagged	Perf. 11	
2224 A1604	22c scarlet & dark blue	.40	.20
	P# block of 4	2.25	—
	Zip block of 4	1.65	—

See France No. 2014.

> **Coil Plate No. Strips of 3**
> Beginning with No. 2123, coil plate no. strips of 3 usually sell at the level of strips of 5 minus the face value of two stamps.

TRANSPORTATION ISSUE

A1604a

A1604b

Designers: 1c, 2c, David Stone.

COIL STAMPS
ENGRAVED

1986-87	Tagged	Perf. 10 Vert.	
2225 A1604a	1c violet, large block tagging, dull gum, Nov. 26	.20	.20
	Pair	.20	.20
	P# strip of 5, #1-2	.90	

	P# single, #1-2	—	.55
a.	Prephosphored uncoated paper (mottled tagging) (error), shiny gum	.20	.20
	Pair	.20	.20
	P# strip of 5, #3	7.50	
	P# single, #3	—	4.50
b.	Untagged, dull gum	.20	.20
	Pair	.20	.20
	P# strip of 5, #2-3	.90	
	P# single, #2-3	—	.70
	Shiny gum	.20	
	P# strip of 5, #3	.90	
	Low gloss gum	.20	
	P# strip of 5, #3	.90	
c.	Imperf., pair	2,250.	
2226 A1604b	2c black, dull gum, Mar. 6, 1987	.20	.20
	Pair	.20	.20
	P# strip of 5, #1	1.00	
	P# single, #1	—	.60
a.	Untagged, dull gum	.20	.20
	Pair	.20	.20
	P# strip of 5, #2	.75	
	P# single, #2	—	.60
	Shiny gum	.20	
	P# strip of 5, #2	1.00	

REDUCED SIZE

2228 A1285	4c reddish brown, large block tagging, Aug.	.20	.20
	Pair	.20	.20
	P# strip of 5, #1	1.50	
	P# single, #1	—	1.10
a.	Overall tagging, 1990	.70	.20
	Pair	1.40	.20
	P# strip of 5, #1	15.00	
	P# single, #1	—	11.00
b.	Imperf., pair	300.00	
	P#1		

UNTAGGED

2231 A1511	8.3c green (Bureau precancel, Blk. Rt./CAR-RT/SORT), Aug. 29	.20	.20
	Pair	.40	.40
	P# strip of 5, #1	4.50	
	P# strip of 5, #2	6.25	
	P# single, #1	—	3.50
	P# single, #2	—	4.25

Earliest known usage of No. 2228: Aug. 15, 1986.
On No. 2228 "Stagecoach 1890s" is 17mm long; on No. 1898A, 19½mm long.
On No. 2231 "Ambulance 1860s" is 18mm long; on No. 2128, 18½mm long.
Joint lines do not appear on Nos. 2225-2231.

AMERICAN FOLK ART ISSUE
Navajo Art

A1605

A1606

A1607

A1608

Designed by Derry Noyes.

LITHOGRAPHED & ENGRAVED
Plates of 200 in four panes of 50.

1986, Sept. 4	Tagged	Perf. 11	
2235 A1605	22c multicolored	.50	.20
2236 A1606	22c multicolored	.50	.20
2237 A1607	22c multicolored	.50	.20
2238 A1608	22c multicolored	.50	.20
a.	Block of 4, #2235-2238	2.50	2.00
	P# block of 4, 5#	4.00	—
	Zip block of 4	2.75	—
b.	As "a," black (engr.) omitted	350.00	

LITERARY ARTS

T.S. Eliot (1888-1965),
Poet — A1609

Designed by Bradbury Thompson.

ENGRAVED
Plates of 200 in four panes of 50.

1986, Sept. 26	Tagged	Perf. 11	
2239 A1609 22c copper red		.40	.20
P# block of 4		1.90	—
Zip block of 4		1.65	—

AMERICAN FOLK ART ISSUE
Woodcarved Figurines

A1610

A1611

A1612

A1613

Designed by Bradbury Thompson.
Printed by the American Bank Note Company

PHOTOGRAVURE
Plates of 200 in four panes of 50.

1986, Oct. 1	Tagged	Perf. 11	
2240 A1610 22c multicolored		.40	.20
2241 A1611 22c multicolored		.40	.20
2242 A1612 22c multicolored		.40	.20
2243 A1613 22c multicolored		.40	.20
a. Block of 4, #2240-2243		1.75	1.75
P# block of 4, 5#		3.00	—
Zip block of 4		1.90	—
b. As "a," imperf. vert.		1,500.	

CHRISTMAS

Madonna,
National Gallery,
by Perugino (c.
1450-1513)
A1614

GREETINGS
Village Scene
A1615

Designed by Bradbury Thompson (#2244) & Dolli Tingle
(#2245).

PHOTOGRAVURE
Plates of 200 in four panes of 50.

1986, Oct. 24	Tagged	Perf. 11	
2244 A1614 22c multicolored		.40	.20
P# block of 4, 6#		2.00	—
Zip block of 4		1.65	—
a. Imperf., pair			
2245 A1615 22c multicolored		.40	.20
P# block of 4, 6#		1.90	—
Zip block of 4		1.65	—

MICHIGAN STATEHOOD, 150th ANNIV.

White Pine — A1616

Designed by Robert Wilbert.

PHOTOGRAVURE
Plates of 200 in four panes of 50.

1987, Jan. 26	Tagged	Perf. 11	
2246 A1616 22c multicolored		.40	.20
P# block of 4, 5#		1.90	—
Zip block of 4		1.65	—
Pair with full vert. gutter between			—

PAN AMERICAN GAMES
Indianapolis, Aug. 7-25

Runner in Full
Stride — A1617

Designed by Lon Busch.

PHOTOGRAVURE
Plates of 200 in four panes of 50.

1987, Jan. 29	Tagged	Perf. 11	
2247 A1617 22c multicolored		.40	.20
P# block of 4, 5#		1.90	—
Zip block of 4		1.65	—
a. Silver omitted		1,500.	

No. 2247a is valued in the grade of fine.

LOVE ISSUE

A1618

Designed by John Alcorn.

PHOTOGRAVURE
Panes of 100

1987, Jan. 30	Tagged	Perf. 11½x11	
2248 A1618 22c multicolored		.40	.20
P# block of 4, 5#		1.90	—
Zip block of 4		1.65	—
Pair with full horiz. gutter between			—

BLACK HERITAGE SERIES

Jean Baptiste Pointe du Sable
(c. 1750-1818), Pioneer Trader,
Founder of Chicago — A1619

Designed by Thomas Blackshear.

PHOTOGRAVURE
Plates of 200 in four panes of 50.

1987, Feb. 20	Tagged	Perf. 11	
2249 A1619 22c multicolored		.40	.20
P# block of 4, 5#		1.90	—
Zip block of 4		1.65	—
a. Tagging omitted		10.00	

Enrico Caruso
(1873-1921), Opera
Tenor — A1620

Fourteen
Achievement
Badges — A1621

PERFORMING ARTS

Designed by Jim Sharpe.
Printed by American Bank Note Co.

PHOTOGRAVURE & ENGRAVED
Plates of 200 in four panes of 50.

1987, Feb. 27	Tagged	Perf. 11	
2250 A1620 22c multicolored		.40	.20
P# block of 4, 4#		1.90	—
Zip block of 4		1.65	—
a. Black (engr.) omitted		5,000.	

GIRL SCOUTS, 75TH ANNIVERSARY
Designed by Richard Sheaff.

LITHOGRAPHED & ENGRAVED
Plates of 200 in four panes of 50.

1987, Mar. 12	Tagged	Perf. 11	
2251 A1621 22c multicolored		.40	.20
P# block of 4, 6#		1.90	—
Zip block of 4		1.65	—
a. All litho. colors omitted		2,500.	
b. Red & black (engr.) omitted			

All known examples of No. 2251a have been expertized and
certificate must accompany purchase. The unique pane of No.
2251b has been expertized and a certificate exists for the pane
of 50.

Coil Plate No. Strips of 3
Beginning with No. 2123, coil plate no. strips of
3 usually sell at the level of strips of 5 minus the
face value of two stamps.

TRANSPORTATION ISSUE

A1622

A1623

A1624

A1625

A1626

A1627

Patrol Wagon 1880s
USA 13 Presorted First-Class
A1628

Coal Car 1870s
13.2 Bulk Rate USA
A1629

Tugboat 1900s
USA 15
A1630

Popcorn Wagon
16.7 USA 1902 Bulk Rate
A1631

Racing Car 1911
USA 17.5
A1632

USA 20 Cable Car 1880s
A1633

Fire Engine 1900s
20.5 USA ZIP+4 Presort
A1634

Railroad Mail Car 1920s Presorted First-Class
21 USA
A1635

Tandem Bicycle 1890s 24.1 USA
A1636 ZIP+4

Designers: 3c, 7.6c, 13.2c, 15c, Richard Schlecht. 5c, 5.3c, 16.7c, Lou Nolan. 8.4c, 20.5c, 24.1c, Christopher Calle. 10c, William H. Bond. 13c, Joe Brockert. 17.5c, Tom Broad. 20c, Dan Romano. 21c, David Stone.

COIL STAMPS
ENGRAVED

1987-88   *Perf. 10 Vert.*
Tagged, Untagged (5.3c, 7.6c, 8.4c, 13c, 13.2c, 16.7c, 20.5c, 21c, 24.1c)

2252	A1622	3c **claret,** dull gum, *Feb. 29, 1988*		.20	.20
		Pair		.20	.20
		P# strip of 5, #1		1.00	
		P# single, #1		—	.75
a.		Untagged, dull gum		.20	.20
		P# strip of 5, #2-3		1.25	
		P# single, #2-3		—	.95
		Shiny gum, *1995*		.20	
		P# strip of 5, #3		1.40	
		P# strip of 5, #5-6		2.25	
		P# single, #5		—	1.90
		P# single, #6		—	1.25
		Low gloss gum		.20	
		P# strip of 5, #5		2.00	

The plate #5 on No. 2252a with low gloss gum is smaller than the #5 on No. 2252a with shiny gum. The smaller plate #5 represents a different printing cylinder (plate).

2253	A1623	5c **black,** *Sept. 25*		.20	.20
		Pair		.20	.20
		P# strip of 5, #1		1.10	
		P# single, #1		—	.90
2254	A1624	5.3c **black** (Bureau precancel "Nonprofit Carrier Route Sort" in red), *Sept. 16, 1988*		.20	.20
		Pair		.20	.20
		P# strip of 5, #1		1.50	
		P# single, #1		—	1.10
2255	A1625	7.6c **brown** (Bureau precancel "Nonprofit" in red), *Aug. 30, 1988*		.20	.20
		Pair		.30	.30
		P# strip of 5, #1-2		2.40	
		P# strip of 5, #3		6.50	
		P# single, #1-2		—	2.00
		P# single, #3			6.00
2256	A1626	8.4c **deep claret** (Bureau precancel "Nonprofit" in red), *Aug. 12, 1988*		.20	.20
		Pair		.30	.30
		P# strip of 5, #1-2		2.10	
		P# strip of 5, #3		15.00	
		P# single, #1-2		—	1.25

		P# single, #3		—	3.75
a.		Imperf., pair		700.00	
		P#1			
2257	A1627	10c **sky blue,** large block tagging, dull gum, *Apr. 11*		.20	.20
		Pair		.40	.20
		P# strip of 5, #1		1.75	
		P# single, #1		—	1.25
a.		Overall tagging, dull gum, *1993*		.20	.20
		Pair		.40	.20
		P# strip of 5, #1		4.50	
		P# single, #1		—	3.75
		Shiny gum, *1994*		.20	.20
		Pair		.20	.20
		P# strip of 5, #4		1.75	
		P# single, #4		—	1.00
b.		Prephosphored uncoated paper (mottled tagging), shiny gum		.20	.20
		Pair		.40	.20
		P# strip of 5, #1-4		4.00	
		P# single, #1-4		—	3.00
c.		Prephosphored coated paper (solid tagging), low gloss gum		—	—
		Pair		—	—
		P# strip of 5, #5		—	
		P# single, #5		—	
d.		Tagging omitted		25.00	
e.		Imperf. pair, large block tagging		—	
2258	A1628	13c **black** (Bureau precancel "Presorted First-Class" in red), *Oct. 29, 1988*		.25	.25
		Pair		.50	.50
		P# strip of 5, #1		3.00	
		P# single, #1		—	2.50
2259	A1629	13.2c **slate green** (Bureau precancel "Bulk Rate" in red), *July 19, 1988*		.25	.25
		Pair		.50	.50
		P# strip of 5, #1-2		3.00	
		P# single, #1-2		—	1.75
a.		Imperf., pair		100.00	
		P#1-2			
2260	A1630	15c **violet,** large block tagging, *July 12, 1988*		.25	.20
		Pair		.50	.20
		P# strip of 5, #1		2.75	
		P# strip of 5, #2		3.50	
		P# single, #1-2		—	1.50
a.		Overall tagging, *1990*		.25	.20
		Pair		.50	.20
		P# strip of 5, #2		3.75	
		P# single, #2		—	3.00
b.		Tagging omitted		3.75	
c.		Imperf., pair		800.00	
		P#2			
2261	A1631	16.7c **rose** (Bureau precancel "Bulk Rate " in black), *July 7, 1988*		.30	.30
		Pair		.60	.60
		P# strip of 5, #1		3.75	
		P# strip of 5, #2		5.00	
		P# single, #1		—	2.50
		P# single, #2		—	3.00
a.		Imperf., pair		225.00	
		P#1			

All known copies of No. 2261a are miscut top to bottom.

2262	A1632	17.5c **dark violet,** *Sept. 25*		.30	.20
		Pair		.60	.20
		P# strip of 5, #1		3.75	
		P# single, #1		—	3.00
a.		Untagged (Bureau Precancel "ZIP + 4 Presort" in red)		.35	.30
		P# strip of 5, #1		4.00	
		P# single, #1		—	3.00
b.		Imperf., pair		2,250.	
		P#1			
2263	A1633	20c **blue violet,** large block tagging, *Oct. 28, 1988*		.35	.20
		Pair		.70	.20
		P# strip of 5, #1-2		3.75	
		P# single, #1-2		—	2.00
a.		Imperf., pair		75.00	
		P#2			
b.		Overall tagging, *1990*		.35	.20
		Pair		.70	.20
		P# strip of 5, #2		5.00	
		P# single, #2		—	3.75
2264	A1634	20.5c **rose** (Bureau precancel "ZIP + 4 Presort" in black), *Sept. 28, 1988*		.40	.40
		Pair		.80	.80
		P# strip of 5, #1		4.00	
		P# single, #1		—	3.00
2265	A1635	21c **olive green** (Bureau precancel "Presorted First-Class" in red), *Aug. 16, 1988*		.40	.40
		Pair		.80	.80
		P# strip of 5, #1-2		4.00	
		P# single, #1-2		—	2.75
a.		Imperf., pair		65.00	
		P#1			
2266	A1636	24.1c **deep ultra** (Bureau precancel ZIP + 4 in red), *Oct. 26, 1988*		.45	.45
		Pair		.90	.90
		P# strip of 5, #1		4.00	
		P# single, #1		—	2.50
		Nos. 2252-2266 (15)		4.15	3.85

5.3c, 7.6c, 8.4c, 13.2c, 16.7c, 20.5c, 21c and 24.1c only available precanceled.

SPECIAL OCCASIONS

Congratulations! USA 22
A1637

Get Well! USA 22
A1638

USA 22 Thank You!
A1639

Love You, Dad! USA 22
A1640

Best Wishes! USA 22
A1641

Happy Birthday! USA 22
A1642

Love You, Mother! USA 22
A1643

Keep In Touch! USA 22
A1644

Designed by Oren Sherman.

BOOKLET STAMPS
PHOTOGRAVURE

1987, Apr. 20 Tagged *Perf. 10 on 1, 2 or 3 Sides*

2267	A1637	22c **multicolored**	.60	.20
2268	A1638	22c **multicolored**	.75	.20
2269	A1639	22c **multicolored**	.75	.20
2270	A1640	22c **multicolored**	.75	.20
2271	A1641	22c **multicolored**	.75	.20
2272	A1642	22c **multicolored**	.60	.20
2273	A1643	22c **multicolored**	.90	.20
2274	A1644	22c **multicolored**	.75	.20
a.		Bklt. pane of 10 (#2268-2271, 2273-2274, 2 each #2267, 2272)	8.00	5.00

UNITED WAY, 100th ANNIV.

United Way 1887-1987 Uniting Communities USA 22
Six Profiles — A1645

Designed by Jerry Pinkney.

LITHOGRAPHED & ENGRAVED
Plates of 200 in four panes of 50.

1987, Apr. 28   Tagged   *Perf. 11*

2275	A1645	22c **multicolored**	.40	.20
		P# block of 4, 6#	1.90	
		Zip block of 4	1.65	—

A1646

Domestic USA
A1647

USA 25
A1648

A1649

Pheasant
A1649a

Grosbeak
A1649b

Owl
A1649c

Honeybee
A1649d

Designs: Nos. 2276, 2278, 2280, Peter Cocci. Nos. 2277, 2279, 2282, Robert McCall. Nos. 2281, 2283-2285, Chuck Ripper.

PHOTOGRAVURE (Nos. 2276-2279)
Panes of 100

1987-88		Tagged		Perf. 11	
2276	A1646	22c **multicolored**, *May 9*		.40	.20
		P# block of 4, 4#		1.90	—
		Zip block of 4		1.65	—
a.		Booklet pane of 20, *Nov. 30*		8.50	—
b.		As "a," vert. pair, imperf. btwn.		—	
2277	A1647	(25c) **multi**, *Mar. 22, 1988*		.45	.20
		P# block of 4, 4#		2.00	—
		Zip block of 4		1.85	—
2278	A1648	25c **multi**, *May 6, 1988*		.45	.20
		P# block of 4, 4#		1.90	—
		Zip block of 4		1.85	—
		Pair with full vert. gutter between		—	

COIL STAMPS
Perf. 10 Vert.

2279	A1647	(25c) **multi**, *Mar. 22, 1988*		.45	.20
		Pair		.90	.20
		P# strip of 5, #1111, 1222		3.00	
		P# strip of 5, #1211, 2222		5.25	
		P# single, #1111, 1211, 1222		—	.60
		P# single, #2222		—	2.50
a.		Imperf., pair		90.00	—
		P#1111, 1211, 2222			

ENGRAVED

2280	A1649	25c **multi**, large block tagging, *May 20, 1988*		.45	.20
		Pair		.90	.20
		P# strip of 5, #2-5, 8		4.00	
		P# strip of 5, #1, 7		7.25	
		P# strip of 5, #9		10.50	
		P# single, #2-5, 8		—	.60
		P# single, #1		—	3.00
		P# single, #7, 9		—	.90
a.		Prephosphored uncoated paper (mottled tagging)		.45	.20
		P# strip of 5, #2-3, 7-11, 13-14		4.00	
		P# strip of 5, #1		47.50	
		P# strip of 5, #5, 15		7.50	
		P# strip of 5, #6		15.00	
		P# single, #2-3, 7-14		—	.60
		P# single, #1		—	42.50
		P# single, #5		—	.90
		P# single, #6		—	6.00
		P# single, #15		—	2.25
b.		Imperf., pair, large block tagging		35.00	
		P#2-9			
c.		Imperf., pair, prephosphored paper (mottled tagging)		15.00	
		P#2-3, 5-11, 13-15			
d.		Tagging omitted		5.00	
e.		Black trees		100.00	—

	P# strip of 5, #5, 15		550.00	
	P# strip of 5, #6		650.00	
f.	Pair, imperf. between		800.00	

LITHOGRAPHED AND ENGRAVED

2281	A1649d	25c **multi**, *Sept. 2, 1988*		.45	.20
		Pair		.90	.20
		P# strip of 3, #1-2		3.25	
		P# strip of 5, #1-2		3.75	
		P# single, #1-2		—	.40
a.		Imperf., pair		50.00	
		P#1-2			
b.		Black (engr.) omitted		60.00	
c.		Black (litho.) omitted		450.00	
d.		Pair, imperf. between		1,000.	
e.		Yellow (litho.) omitted		1,250.	

No. 2281 from plate #1 is known with two types of "1" on the plate-numbered stamps. The original tall "1" was later shortened manually by removing the top of the "1," including the serif, so it would not penetrate the design. Value of plate # strip of 5 with tall "1," $30.

Beware of stamps with traces of the litho. black that are offered as No. 2281c.

Vertical pairs or blocks of No. 2281 and imperfs. with the engr. black missing are from printer's waste.

BOOKLET STAMPS

Printed by American Bank Note Co. (#2283)

PHOTOGRAVURE
Perf. 10, 11 (#2283)

2282	A1647	(25c) **multi**, *Mar. 22, 1988*		.50	.20
a.		Booklet pane of 10		6.50	3.50
2283	A1649a	25c **multi**, *Apr. 29, 1988*		.50	.20
a.		Booklet pane of 10		6.00	3.50
b.		25c multicolored, red removed from sky		6.25	.20
c.		As "b," bklt. pane of 10		67.50	—
d.		As "a," horiz. imperf. btwn.		2,250.	

Imperf. panes exist from printers waste.

2284	A1649b	25c **multi**, *May 28, 1988*		.50	.20
2285	A1649c	25c **multi**, *May 28, 1988*		.50	.20
b.		Bklt. pane of 10, 5 each #2284-2285		5.00	3.50
d.		Pair, Nos. 2284-2285		1.10	.25
e.		As "d," tagging omitted		12.50	
2285A	A1648	25c **multi**, *July 5, 1988*		.50	.20
c.		Booklet pane of 6		3.00	2.00

Illustration reduced.

Designed by Chuck Ripper.

PHOTOGRAVURE
Plates of 200 in four panes of 50.

1987, June 13		Tagged		Perf. 11	
2286	A1650	22c	Barn swallow	.85	.20
2287	A1651	22c	Monarch butterfly	.85	.20
2288	A1652	22c	Bighorn sheep	.85	.20
2289	A1653	22c	Broad-tailed hummingbird	.85	.20
2290	A1654	22c	Cottontail	.85	.20
2291	A1655	22c	Osprey	.85	.20
2292	A1656	22c	Mountain lion	.85	.20
2293	A1657	22c	Luna moth	.85	.20
2294	A1658	22c	Mule deer	.85	.20
2295	A1659	22c	Gray squirrel	.85	.20
2296	A1660	22c	Armadillo	.85	.20
2297	A1661	22c	Eastern chipmunk	.85	.20
2298	A1662	22c	Moose	.85	.20
2299	A1663	22c	Black bear	.85	.20
2300	A1664	22c	Tiger swallowtail	.85	.20
2301	A1665	22c	Bobwhite	.85	.20
2302	A1666	22c	Ringtail	.85	.20
2303	A1667	22c	Red-winged blackbird	.85	.20
2304	A1668	22c	American lobster	.85	.20
2305	A1669	22c	Black-tailed jack rabbit	.85	.20
2306	A1670	22c	Scarlet tanager	.85	.20
2307	A1671	22c	Woodchuck	.85	.20
2308	A1672	22c	Roseate spoonbill	.85	.20
2309	A1673	22c	Bald eagle	.85	.20
2310	A1674	22c	Alaskan brown bear	.85	.20
2311	A1675	22c	Iiwi	.85	.20
2312	A1676	22c	Badger	.85	.20
2313	A1677	22c	Pronghorn	.85	.20
2314	A1678	22c	River otter	.85	.20
2315	A1679	22c	Ladybug	.85	.20
2316	A1680	22c	Beaver	.85	.20
2317	A1681	22c	White-tailed deer	.85	.20
2318	A1682	22c	Blue jay	.85	.20
2319	A1683	22c	Pika	.85	.20
2320	A1684	22c	American buffalo	.85	.20
2321	A1685	22c	Snowy egret	.85	.20
2322	A1686	22c	Gray wolf	.85	.20
2323	A1687	22c	Mountain goat	.85	.20
2324	A1688	22c	Deer mouse	.85	.20
2325	A1689	22c	Black-tailed prairie dog	.85	.20
2326	A1690	22c	Box turtle	.85	.20
2327	A1691	22c	Wolverine	.85	.20
2328	A1692	22c	American elk	.85	.20
2329	A1693	22c	California sea lion	.85	.20
2330	A1694	22c	Mockingbird	.85	.20
2331	A1695	22c	Raccoon	.85	.20
2332	A1696	22c	Bobcat	.85	.20
2333	A1697	22c	Black-footed ferret	.85	.20
2334	A1698	22c	Canada goose	.85	.20
2335	A1699	22c	Red fox	.85	.20
a.		Pane of 50, #2286-2335		47.50	
2286b-2335b		Any single, red omitted		—	

RATIFICATION OF THE CONSTITUTION BICENTENNIAL

Dec 7,1787   USA
Delaware 22
A1700

Dec 12,1787
Pennsylvania
A1701

April 28,1788   USA
Maryland 22
A1706

May 23, 1788
South Carolina
A1707

Dec 18,1787   USA
New Jersey 22
A1702

January 2, 1788
Georgia
A1703

June 21,1788
New Hampshire
A1708

June 25,1788   USA
Virginia 25
A1709

January 9,1788
Connecticut
A1704

Feb 6,1788
Massachusetts
A1705

July 26, 1788   USA
New York 25
A1710

November 21,1789
North Carolina
A1711

NORTH AMERICAN WILDLIFE ISSUE
A1650-A1699

A1712 Rhode Island

May 29, 1790

Designers: Nos. 2336-2337, 2341 Richard Sheaff. No. 2338, Jim Lamb. No. 2339, Greg Harlin. No. 2340, Christopher Calle. No. 2342, Stephen Hustvedt. Nos. 2343, 2347, Bob Timberlake. No. 2344, Thomas Szumowski. No. 2345, Pierre Mion. No. 2346, Bradbury Thompson. No. 2348, Robert Brangwynne.

Printed by the Bureau of Engraving & Printing or the American Bank Note Co. (Nos. 2343-2344, 2347).
LITHOGRAPHED & ENGRAVED, PHOTOGRAVURE (#2337, 2339, 2343-2344, 2347), ENGRAVED (#2341).
Plates of 200 in four panes of 50.

1987-90	Tagged	Perf. 11	
2336 A1700 22c **multi**, July 4		.60	.20
	P# block of 4, 5#	2.75	—
	Zip block of 4	2.50	—
2337 A1701 22c **multi**, Aug. 26		.60	.20
	P# block of 4, 5#	2.75	—
	Zip block of 4	2.50	—
2338 A1702 22c **multi**, Sept. 11		.60	.20
	P# block of 4, 5#	2.75	—
	Zip block of 4	2.50	—
a.	Black (engr.) omitted	6,000.	
2339 A1703 22c **multi**, Jan. 6, 1988		.60	.20
	P# block of 4, 5#	2.75	—
	Zip block of 4	2.50	—
2340 A1704 22c **multi**, Jan. 9, 1988		.60	.20
	P# block of 4, 4#	2.75	—
	Zip block of 4	2.50	—
2341 A1705 22c **dark blue & dark red**, Feb. 6, 1988		.60	.20
	P# block of 4, 1#	2.75	—
	Zip block of 4	2.50	—
2342 A1706 22c **multi**, Feb. 15, 1988		.60	.20
	P# block of 4, 6#	2.75	—
	Zip block of 4	2.50	—
2343 A1707 25c **multi**, May 23, 1988		.60	.20
	P# block of 4, 5#	2.75	—
	Zip block of 4	2.50	—
a.	Strip of 3, vert. imperf btwn.	—	
2344 A1708 25c **multi**, June 21, 1988		.60	.20
	P# block of 4, 4#	2.75	—
	Zip block of 4	2.50	—
2345 A1709 25c **multi**, June 25, 1988		.60	.20
	P# block of 4, 5#	2.75	—
	Zip block of 4	2.50	—
2346 A1710 25c **multi**, July 26, 1988		.60	.20
	P# block of 4, 5#	2.75	—
	Zip block of 4	2.50	—
2347 A1711 25c **multi**, Aug. 22, 1989		.60	.20
	P# block of 4, 5#	2.75	—
	Zip block of 4	2.50	—
2348 A1712 25c **multi**, May 29, 1990		.60	.20
	P# block of 4, 7#	2.75	—
	Zip block of 4	2.50	—
	Nos. 2336-2348 (13)	7.80	2.60

Friendship with Morocco 1787-1987

Arabesque, Dar Batha Palace Door, Fez — A1713

USA 22

William Faulkner

William Faulkner (1897-1962), Novelist — A1714

USA 22

US-MOROCCO DIPLOMATIC RELATIONS, 200th ANNIV.

Designed by Howard Paine.

LITHOGRAPHED & ENGRAVED
Plates of 200 in four panes of 50.

1987, July 17	Tagged	Perf. 11	
2349 A1713 22c **scarlet & black**		.40	.20
	P# block of 4, 2#	1.75	—
	Zip block of 4	1.65	—
a.	Black (engr.) omitted	275.00	

See Morocco No. 642.

LITERARY ARTS

Designed by Bradbury Thompson.

ENGRAVED
Plates of 200 in four panes of 50

1987, Aug. 3	Tagged	Perf. 11	
2350 A1714 22c **bright green**		.40	.20
	P# block of 4	1.75	—
	Zip block of 4	1.65	—

Imperfs. are from printer's waste.

AMERICAN FOLK ART ISSUE
Lacemaking

Lacemaking USA 22 A1715

A1716 Lacemaking USA 22

Lacemaking USA 22 A1717

A1718 Lacemaking USA 22

Designed by Libby Thiel.

LITHOGRAPHED & ENGRAVED
Plates of 160 in four panes of 40.

1987, Aug. 14	Tagged	Perf. 11	
2351 A1715 22c **ultra & white**		.45	.20
2352 A1716 22c **ultra & white**		.45	.20
2353 A1717 22c **ultra & white**		.45	.20
2354 A1718 22c **ultra & white**		.45	.20
a.	Block of 4, #2351-2354	1.90	1.90
	P# block of 4, 4#	3.25	—
	Zip block of 4	2.00	—
b.	As "a," white omitted	950.00	

DRAFTING OF THE CONSTITUTION BICENTENNIAL
Excerpts from the Preamble

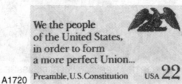

The Bicentennial of the Constitution of the United States of America
A1719 1787-1987 USA 22

We the people of the United States, in order to form a more perfect Union...
A1720 Preamble, U.S.Constitution USA 22

Establish justice, insure domestic tranquility, provide for the common defense, promote the general welfare...
A1721 Preamble, U.S.Constitution USA 22

And secure the blessings of liberty to ourselves and our posterity...
A1722 Preamble, U.S.Constitution USA 22

Do ordain and establish this Constitution for the United States of America.
A1723 Preamble, U.S.Constitution USA 22

Designed by Bradbury Thompson.

BOOKLET STAMPS
PHOTOGRAVURE

1987, Aug. 28	Tagged	Perf. 10 Horiz.	
2355 A1719 22c **multicolored**		.55	.20
a.	Grayish green (background) omitted	—	
2356 A1720 22c **multicolored**		.55	.20
a.	Grayish green (background) omitted	—	
2357 A1721 22c **multicolored**		.55	.20
a.	Grayish green (background) omitted	—	
2358 A1722 22c **multicolored**		.55	.20
a.	Grayish green (background) omitted	—	
2359 A1723 22c **multicolored**		.55	.20
a.	Bklt. pane of 5, #2355-2359	2.75	2.25
b.	Grayish green (background) omitted	—	

A1724

A1725

SIGNING OF THE CONSTITUTION

Designed by Howard Koslow.

LITHOGRAPHED & ENGRAVED
Plates of 200 in four panes of 50.

1987, Sept. 17	Tagged	Perf. 11	
2360 A1724 22c **multicolored**		.45	.20
	P# block of 4, 6#	2.25	—
	Zip block of 4	1.90	—

CERTIFIED PUBLIC ACCOUNTING

Designed by Lou Nolan.

LITHOGRAPHED & ENGRAVED
Plates of 200 in four panes of 50.

1987, Sept. 21	Tagged	Perf. 11	
2361 A1725 22c **multicolored**		1.90	.20
	P# block of 4, 4#	8.50	—
	Zip block of 4	8.00	—
a.	Black (engr.) omitted	725.00	

LOCOMOTIVES

Stourbridge Lion, 1829
A1726

Best Friend of Charleston, 1830 A1727

John Bull, 1831 A1728

Brother Jonathan, 1832 A1729

Gowan & Marx, 1839 A1730

Designed by Richard Leech.

BOOKLET STAMPS
LITHOGRAPHED & ENGRAVED

1987, Oct. 1	Tagged	Perf. 10 Horiz.	
2362 A1726 22c **multicolored**		.55	.20
2363 A1727 22c **multicolored**		.55	.20
2364 A1728 22c **multicolored**		.55	.20
2365 A1729 22c **multicolored**		.55	.20
a. Red omitted		—	
2366 A1730 22c **multicolored**		.55	.20
a. Bklt. pane of 5, #2362-2366		2.75	2.50
b. As No. 2366, black (engr.) omitted (single)		—	
c. As No. 2366, blue omitted (single)		—	

CHRISTMAS

Moroni Madonna A1731

Christmas Ornaments A1732

Designed by Bradbury Thompson (No. 2367) and Jim Dean (No. 2368).

PHOTOGRAVURE
Plates of 200 in four panes of 50.

1987, Oct. 23	Tagged	Perf. 11	
2367 A1731 22c **multicolored**		.40	.20
P# block of 4, 6#		2.00	—
Zip block of 4		1.65	—
2368 A1732 22c **multicolored**		.40	.20
P# block of 4, 6#		1.75	—
Zip block of 4		1.65	—
Pair with full vert. gutter between		—	

1988 WINTER OLYMPICS, CALGARY

Skiing — A1733

Designed by Bart Forbes.

Printed by the American Bank Note Company

PHOTOGRAVURE
Plates of 200 in four panes of 50.

1988, Jan. 10	Tagged	Perf. 11	
2369 A1733 22c **multicolored**		.40	.20
P# block of 4, 4#		1.75	—
Zip block of 4		1.65	—

AUSTRALIA BICENTENNIAL

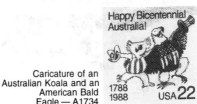

Caricature of an Australian Koala and an American Bald Eagle — A1734

Designed by Roland Harvey.

PHOTOGRAVURE
Plates of 160 in four panes of 40.

1988, Jan. 26	Tagged	Perf. 11	
2370 A1734 22c **multicolored**		.40	.20
P# block of 4, 5#		1.75	—
Zip block of 4		1.65	—

See Australia No. 1052.

BLACK HERITAGE SERIES

James Weldon Johnson (1871-1938), Author and Lyricist — A1735

Designed by Thomas Blackshear.

Printed by the American Bank Note Co.

PHOTOGRAVURE
Plates of 200 in four panes of 50.

1988, Feb. 2	Tagged		
2371 A1735 22c **multicolored**		.40	.20
P# block of 4, 5#		1.75	—
Zip block of 4		1.65	—

CATS

Siamese and Exotic Shorthair A1736

Siamese Cat, Exotic Shorthair Cat

Abyssinian Cat, Himalayan Cat

Abyssinian and Himalayan A1737

Maine Coon and Burmese A1738

Maine Coon Cat, Burmese Cat

American Shorthair Cat, Persian Cat

American Shorthair and Persian — A1739

Designed by John Dawson.

Printed by the American Bank Note Co.

PHOTOGRAVURE
Plates of 160 in four panes of 40.

1988, Feb. 5	Tagged		
2372 A1736 22c **multicolored**		.45	.20
2373 A1737 22c **multicolored**		.45	.20
2374 A1738 22c **multicolored**		.45	.20
2375 A1739 22c **multicolored**		.45	.20
a. Block of 4, #2372-2375		1.90	1.90
P# block of 4, 5#		3.75	—
Zip block of 4		2.00	—

AMERICAN SPORTS

Knute Rockne (1883-1931), Notre Dame football coach.
Francis Ouimet (1893-1967), 1st amateur golfer to win the US Open championship.

A1740

A1741

Designed by Peter Cocci and Thomas Hipschen.

LITHOGRAPHED & ENGRAVED
Plates of 200 in four panes of 50.

1988, Mar. 9	Tagged		
2376 A1740 22c **multicolored**		.40	.20
P# block of 4, 7#		2.25	—
Zip block of 4		1.65	—

Designed by M. Gregory Rudd.
Printed by the American Bank Note Co.

PHOTOGRAVURE
Plates of 200 in four panes of 50.

1988, June 13	Tagged		
2377 A1741 25c **multicolored**		.45	.20
P# block of 4, 5#		2.50	—
Zip block of 4		1.85	—

LOVE ISSUE
Roses

A1742

A1743

Designed by Richard Sheaff.

PHOTOGRAVURE
Plates of 400 in four panes of 100 (25c).
Plates of 200 in four panes of 50 (45c).

1988	Tagged		
2378 A1742 25c **multicolored**, *July 4*		.45	.20
P# block of 4, 5#		1.90	—
Zip block of 4		1.85	—
a. Imperf., pair		3,000.	
2379 A1743 45c **multicolored**, *Aug. 8*		.65	.20
P# block of 4, 4#		3.25	—
Zip block of 4		2.65	—

1988 SUMMER OLYMPICS, SEOUL

Gymnastic
Rings — A1744

Designed by Bart Forbes.

PHOTOGRAVURE
Plates of 200 in four panes of 50

1988, Aug. 19	Tagged		
2380 A1744 25c **multicolored**		.45	.20
P# block of 4, 5#		1.90	—
Zip block of 4		1.85	—

CLASSIC AUTOMOBILES

1928
Locomobile
A1745

1929 Pierce-
Arrow
A1746

1931
Cord — A1747

1932 Packard
A1748

1935
Duesenberg
A1749

Designed by Ken Dallison.

LITHOGRAPHED & ENGRAVED
BOOKLET STAMPS

1988, Aug. 25	Tagged	Perf. 10 Horiz.	
2381 A1745 25c **multicolored**		.50	.20
2382 A1746 25c **multicolored**		.50	.20
2383 A1747 25c **multicolored**		.50	.20
2384 A1748 25c **multicolored**		.50	.20
2385 A1749 25c **multicolored**		.50	.20
a.	Bklt. pane of 5, #2381-2385	5.00	2.25

ANTARCTIC EXPLORERS

Nathaniel Palmer
(1799-1877)
A1750

Lt. Charles Wilkes
(1798-1877)
A1751

Richard E. Byrd
(1888-1957)
A1752

Lincoln Ellsworth
(1880-1951)
A1753

Designed by Dennis Lyall.

Printed by the American Bank Note Co.

PHOTOGRAVURE
Plates of 160 in four panes of 40.

1988, Sept. 14	Tagged	Perf. 11	
2386 A1750 25c **multicolored**		.65	.20
2387 A1751 25c **multicolored**		.65	.20
2388 A1752 25c **multicolored**		.65	.20
2389 A1753 25c **multicolored**		.65	.20
a.	Block of 4, #2386-2389	2.75	2.00
	P# block of 4, 6#	4.50	—
	Zip block of 4	3.00	—
b.	As "a," black omitted	1,500.	
c.	As "a," imperf. horiz.	3,000.	

FOLK ART ISSUE
Carousel Animals

Deer — A1754

Horse — A1755

Camel — A1756

Goat — A1757

Designed by Paul Calle.

LITHOGRAPHED & ENGRAVED
Plates of 200 in four panes of 50.

1988, Oct. 1	Tagged	Perf. 11	
2390 A1754 25c **multicolored**		.65	.20
2391 A1755 25c **multicolored**		.65	.20
2392 A1756 25c **multicolored**		.65	.20
2393 A1757 25c **multicolored**		.65	.20
a.	Block of 4, #2390-2393	3.00	2.00
	P# block of 4, 6#	4.00	—
	Zip block of 4	3.25	—

EXPRESS MAIL RATE

Eagle
and
Moon
A1758

Designed by Ned Seidler.

LITHOGRAPHED & ENGRAVED
Panes of 20

1988, Oct. 4	Tagged	Perf. 11	
2394 A1758 $8.75 **multicolored**		13.50	8.00
P# block of 4, 6#		54.00	—

SPECIAL OCCASIONS

Happy Birthday
A1759

Best Wishes
A1760

Thinking of
You — A1761

Love
You — A1762

Designed by Harry Zelenko

Printed by the American Bank Note Co.

BOOKLET STAMPS
PHOTOGRAVURE

1988, Oct. 22	Tagged	Perf. 11	
2395 A1759 25c **multicolored**		.50	.20
2396 A1760 25c **multicolored**		.50	.20
a.	Bklt. pane of 6, 3 #2395 + 3 #2396 with gutter between	3.50	3.25
2397 A1761 25c **multicolored**		.50	.20
2398 A1762 25c **multicolored**		.50	.20
a.	Bklt. pane of 6, 3 #2397 + 3 #2398 with gutter between	3.50	3.25
b.	As "a," imperf. horiz.	—	

CHRISTMAS

Madonna and
Child, by
Botticelli — A1763

One-horse Open Sleigh
and Village
Scene — A1764

"Missing
Curlicue on
Sleigh Runner"
Cylinder Flaw

Designed by Bradbury Thompson (No. 2399) and Joan Landis (No. 2400).

LITHOGRAPHED & ENGRAVED (No. 2399), PHOTOGRAVURE (No. 2400)
Plates of 300 in 6 Panes of 50

1988, Oct 20	Tagged	Perf. 11½
2399 A1763 25c **multicolored**	.45	.20
P# block of 4, 5+1#	1.90	
Zip, copyright block of 4	1.85	—
Pair with full vert. gutter btwn.	—	
a. Gold omitted	30.00	
2400 A1764 25c **multicolored**	.45	.20
P# block of 4, 5#	1.90	—
Zip, copyright block of 4	1.85	—
Pair with full vert. gutter btwn.	—	
Cylinder flaw (missing curlicue on sleigh runner, 11111 UR19)	8.50	

MONTANA STATEHOOD, 100th ANNIV.

C.M. Russell and Friends, by Charles M. Russell (1865-1926) A1765

Designed by Bradbury Thompson.

LITHOGRAPHED & ENGRAVED
Plates of 200 in four panes of 50.

1989, Jan. 15	Tagged	Perf. 11
2401 A1765 25c **multicolored**	.45	.20
P# block of 4, 5#	2.00	—
Zip block of 4	1.85	—

Imperfs without gum exist from printer's waste.

BLACK HERITAGE SERIES

Asa Philip Randolph (1889-1979), Labor and Civil Rights Leader — A1766

Designed by Thomas Blackshear.

PHOTOGRAVURE
Plates of 200 in four panes of 50.

1989, Feb. 3	Tagged	
2402 A1766 25c **multicolored**	.45	.20
P# block of 4, 5#	2.00	—
Zip block of 4	1.85	—

NORTH DAKOTA STATEHOOD, 100th ANNIV.

Grain Elevator on the Prairie — A1767

Designed by Wendell Minor.

Printed by the American Bank Note Co.

PHOTOGRAVURE
Plates of 200 in four panes of 50.

1989, Feb. 21	Tagged	
2403 A1767 25c **multicolored**	.45	.20
P# block of 4	1.90	—
Zip block of 4	1.85	—

WASHINGTON STATEHOOD, 100th ANNIV.

Mt. Rainier — A1768

Designed by Howard Rogers.

Printed by the American Bank Note Co.

PHOTOGRAVURE
Plates of 200 in four panes of 50.

1989, Feb. 22	Tagged	
2404 A1768 25c **multicolored**	.45	.20
P# block of 4, 4#	2.00	—
Zip block of 4	1.85	—

STEAMBOATS

Experiment, 1788-90 A1769

Phoenix, 1809 — A1770

New Orleans, 1812 — A1771

Washington, 1816 — A1772

Walk in the Water, 1818 — A1773

Designed by Richard Schlecht.

LITHOGRAPHED & ENGRAVED
BOOKLET STAMPS
Perf. 10 Horiz. on 1 or 2 Sides

1989, Mar. 3	Tagged	
2405 A1769 25c **multicolored**	.45	.20
2406 A1770 25c **multicolored**	.45	.20
2407 A1771 25c **multicolored**	.45	.20
2408 A1772 25c **multicolored**	.45	.20
2409 A1773 25c **multicolored**	.45	.20
a. Booklet pane of 5, #2405-2409	2.25	1.75

No. 122 — A1774

Arturo Toscanini (1867-1957), Conductor — A1775

WORLD STAMP EXPO '89
Nov. 17-Dec. 3. Washington, D.C.

Designed by Richard Sheaff.

LITHOGRAPHED & ENGRAVED
Plates of 200 in four panes of 50.

1989, Mar. 16	Tagged	Perf. 11
2410 A1774 25c **grayish brn, blk & car rose**	.45	.20
P# block of 4, 4#	1.90	—
Zip block of 4	1.85	—

PERFORMING ARTS

Designed by Jim Sharpe

Printed by the American Bank Note Co.

PHOTOGRAVURE
Plates of 200 in four panes of 50.

1989, Mar. 25	Tagged	Perf. 11
2411 A1775 25c **multicolored**	.45	.20
P# block of 4, 5#	2.00	—
Zip block of 4	1.85	—

CONSTITUTION BICENTENNIAL SERIES

House of Representatives A1776

Senate A1777

20-Cent Minimum Value
The minimum catalogue value is 20 cents. Separating se-tenant pieces into individual stamps does not increase the value of the stamps, since demand for the separated stamps may be small.

Executive Branch — A1778

Supreme Court — A1779

Designed by Howard Koslow.

LITHOGRAPHED & ENGRAVED
Plates of 200 in four panes of 50.

1989-90	Tagged	Perf. 11	
2412 A1776 25c **multi**, *Apr. 4, 1989*		.50	.20
P# block of 4, 4#		2.25	—
Zip block of 4		2.10	—
2413 A1777 25c **multi**, *Apr. 6, 1989*		.50	.20
P# block of 4, 4#		2.25	—
Zip block of 4		2.10	—
2414 A1778 25c **multi**, *Apr. 16, 1989*		.50	.20
P# block of 4, 4#		2.25	—
Zip block of 4		2.10	—
2415 A1779 25c **multi**, *Feb. 2, 1990*		.50	.20
P# block of 4, 4#		2.25	—
Zip block of 4		2.10	—

SOUTH DAKOTA STATEHOOD, 100th ANNIV.

Pasque Flowers, Pioneer Woman and Sod House on Grasslands A1780

Designed by Marian Henjum.

Printed by the American Bank Note Co.

PHOTOGRAVURE
Plates of 200 in four panes of 50.

1989, May 3	Tagged	Perf. 11	
2416 A1780 25c **multicolored**		.45	.20
P# block of 4, 4#		1.90	—
Zip block of 4		1.85	—

AMERICAN SPORTS

Henry Louis "Lou" Gehrig (1903-1941), New York Yankee Baseball Player — A1781

Designed by Bart Forbes.

Printed by the American Bank Note Co.

PHOTOGRAVURE
Plates of 200 in four panes of 50.

1989, June 10	Tagged	Perf. 11	
2417 A1781 25c **multicolored**		.50	.20
P# block of 4, 6#		3.00	—
Zip block of 4		2.25	—

LITERARY ARTS

Ernest Miller Hemingway (1899-1961), Nobel Prize winner for Literature in 1954 — A1782

Designed by M. Gregory Rudd.

Printed by the American Bank Note Co.

PHOTOGRAVURE
Plates of 200 in four panes of 50.

1989, July 17	Tagged	Perf. 11	
2418 A1782 25c **multicolored**		.45	.20
P# block of 4, 5#		2.00	—
Zip block of 4		1.85	—
a. Vert. pair, imperf horiz.		—	

MOON LANDING, 20TH ANNIVERSARY

Raising of the Flag on the Lunar Surface, July 20, 1969 — A1783

Designed by Christopher Calle.

LITHOGRAPHED & ENGRAVED
Panes of 20

1989, July 20	Tagged	Perf. 11x11½	
2419 A1783 $2.40 **multicolored**		4.00	2.00
P# block of 4, 6#		17.50	—
Pane of 20		82.50	—
a. Black (engr.) omitted		2,500.	
b. Imperf., pair		750.00	
c. Black (litho.) omitted		4,500.	

LETTER CARRIERS

A1784

Designed by Jack Davis.

Printed by the American Bank Note Co.

PHOTOGRAVURE
Plates of 160 in four panes of 40.

1989, Aug. 30	Tagged	Perf. 11	
2420 A1784 25c **multicolored**		.45	.20
P# block of 4, 5#		1.90	—
Zip block of 4		1.85	—

CONSTITUTION BICENTENNIAL

Bill of Rights — A1785

Designed by Lou Nolan.

LITHOGRAPHED & ENGRAVED
Plates of 200 in four panes of 50.

1989, Sept. 25	Tagged	Perf. 11	
2421 A1785 25c **multicolored**		.45	.20
P# block of 4		3.00	—
Zip block of 4		2.00	—
a. Black (engr.) omitted		325.00	

PREHISTORIC ANIMALS

Tyrannosaurus Rex — A1786

Pteranodon A1787

Stegosaurus A1788

Brontosaurus A1789

Designed by John Gurche.

LITHOGRAPHED & ENGRAVED
Plates of 160 in four panes of 40.

1989, Oct. 1	Tagged	Perf. 11	
2422 A1786 25c **multicolored**		.65	.20
2423 A1787 25c **multicolored**		.65	.20
2424 A1788 25c **multicolored**		.65	.20
2425 A1789 25c **multicolored**		.65	.20
a. Block of 4, #2422-2425		3.00	2.00
P# block of 4, 6#		3.50	—
Zip block of 4		3.25	—
b. As "a," black (engr.) omitted		800.00	

The correct scientific name for Brontosaurus is Apatosaurus. Copyright block margin includes ad and Stamposaurus character trademark.

No. 2425b is valued in the grade of fine.

PRE-COLUMBIAN AMERICA ISSUE

Southwest Carved Figure, A.D. 1150-1350 — A1790

Designed by Lon Busch.

Printed by the American Bank Note Company.

PHOTOGRAVURE
Plate of 200 in four panes of 50.

1989, Oct. 12	Tagged	Perf. 11
2426 A1790 25c **multicolored**	.45	.20
P# block of 4, 6#	2.00	
Zip block of 4	1.85	—

See No. C121.

CHRISTMAS

Madonna and Child, by Caracci — A1791

Sleigh Full of Presents — A1792

Designed by Bradbury Thompson (#2427) and Steven Dohanos (#2428-2429).

Printed by the Bureau of Engraving and Printing (#2427-2428) and American Bank Note Company (#2429).

LITHOGRAPHED & ENGRAVED, PHOTOGRAVURE (#2428-2429)
Sheets of 300 in six panes of 50.

1989, Oct. 19	Tagged	Perf. 11½
2427 A1791 25c **multicolored**	.45	.20
P# block of 4, 5#	2.00	—
Zip, copyright block of 4	1.85	—
a. Booklet pane of 10	4.75	3.50
b. Red (litho.) omitted	850.00	
c. As "a," imperf.	—	

	Perf. 11	
2428 A1792 25c **multicolored**	.45	.20
P# block of 4, 5#	1.90	—
Zip, copyright block of 4	1.85	—
a. Vert. pair, imperf. horiz.	2,000.	

BOOKLET STAMP
Perf. 11½ on 2 or 3 sides

2429 A1792 25c **multicolored**	.45	.20
a. Booklet pane of 10	4.75	3.50
b. As "a," imperf. horiz.	—	
c. Vert. pair, imperf. horiz.	—	
d. As "a," red omitted	—	
e. Imperf., pair	—	

Marked differences exist between Nos. 2428 and 2429: No. 2429 was printed in four colors, No. 2428 in five colors. The runners on the sleigh in No. 2429 are twice as thick as those on No. 2428. On No. 2429 the package at the upper left in the sleigh has a red bow, whereas the same package in No. 2428 has a red and black bow; and the ribbon on the upper right package in No. 2429 is green, whereas the same ribbon in No. 2428 is black.

Eagle and Shield — A1793

Designed by Jay Haiden.

Printed by the American Bank Note Company.

PHOTOGRAVURE
BOOKLET STAMP

1989, Nov. 10	Tagged	Self-Adhesive	Die Cut
2431 A1793 25c **multicolored**		.50	.20
a. Booklet pane of 18		11.00	
b. Vert. pair, no die cutting between		850.00	
c. Pair, no die cutting		—	

Panes sold for $5.

Also available in strips of 18 with stamps spaced for use in affixing machines to service first day covers. Sold for $5.

No. 2431c will include part of the margins around the stamps.

Sold only in 15 test cities (Atlanta, Chicago, Cleveland, Columbus, OH, Dallas, Denver, Houston, Indianapolis, Kansas City, MO, Los Angeles, Miami, Milwaukee, Minneapolis, Phoenix, St. Louis) and through the philatelic agency.

WORLD STAMP EXPO '89
Washington, DC, Nov. 17-Dec. 3

A1794

Designed by Richard Sheaff.

LITHOGRAPHED & ENGRAVED

1989, Nov. 17	Tagged	Imperf.
2433 A1794 Sheet of 4	14.00	9.00
a. 90c like No. 122	2.00	1.75
b. 90c like 132TC (blue frame, brown center)	2.00	1.75
c. 90c like 132TC (green frame, blue center)	2.00	1.75
d. 90c like 132TC (scarlet frame, blue center)	2.00	1.75

20th UPU CONGRESS
Traditional Mail Delivery

Stagecoach, c. 1850 — A1795

Paddlewheel Steamer — A1796

Biplane — A1797

Depot-hack Type Automobile — A1798

Designed by Mark Hess.

LITHOGRAPHED & ENGRAVED
Plates of 160 in four panes of 40.

1989, Nov. 19	Tagged	Perf. 11
2434 A1795 25c **multicolored**	.45	.20
2435 A1796 25c **multicolored**	.45	.20
2436 A1797 25c **multicolored**	.45	.20
2437 A1798 25c **multicolored**	.45	.20
a. Block of 4, #2434-2437	2.00	1.00
P# block of 4, 5#	3.75	
Zip block of 4	2.25	—
b. As "a," dark blue (engr.) omitted	750.00	

No. 2437b is valued in the grade of fine. Very fine blocks exist and sell for somewhat more.

Souvenir Sheet
LITHOGRAPHED & ENGRAVED

1989, Nov. 28	Tagged	Imperf.
2438 Sheet of 4	4.00	1.75
a. A1795 25c multicolored	.65	.25
b. A1796 25c multicolored	.65	.25
c. A1797 25c multicolored	.65	.25
d. A1798 25c multicolored	.65	.25
e. Dark blue & gray (engr.) omitted	7,000.	

20th Universal Postal Union Congress.

VALUES FOR HINGED STAMPS AFTER NO. 771

This catalogue does not value unused stamps after No. 771. Hinged unused stamps from No. 772 to the present are worth considerably less than the values given for unused stamps, which are for never-hinged examples.

IDAHO STATEHOOD, 100th ANNIV.

Mountain Bluebird, Sawtooth Mountains — A1799

Designed by John Dawson.

Printed by the American Bank Note Company.

PHOTOGRAVURE
Plates of 200 in four panes of 50.

1990, Jan. 6	Tagged	Perf. 11
2439 A1799 25c **multicolored**	.45	.20
P# block of 4, 5#	2.00	
Zip block of 4	1.90	—

LOVE

A1800

Designed by Jayne Hertko.

Printed by the U.S. Banknote Company (#2440) and the Bureau of Engraving and Printing (#2441).

PHOTOGRAVURE
Plates of 200 in four panes of 50.

1990, Jan. 18	Tagged	Perf. 12½x13
2440 A1800 25c **bright blue, dark pink & emerald green**	.45	.20
P# block of 4, 4#	2.00	
Zip, copyright block of 4	1.90	—
a. Imperf., pair	800.00	

BOOKLET STAMP
Perf. 11½ on 2 or 3 sides

2441 A1800 25c **ultramarine, bright pink & dark green**	.45	.20
a. Booklet pane of 10	4.75	3.50
b. As "a," bright pink omitted	2,100.	
c. As "b," single stamp	200.00	

No. 2441c may be obtained from booklet panes containing both normal and color-omitted stamps.

BLACK HERITAGE SERIES

Ida B. Wells (1862-1931), Journalist — A1801

Designed by Thomas Blackshear.

Printed by American Bank Note Company.

PHOTOGRAVURE
Plates of 200 in four panes of 50.

1990, Feb. 1	Tagged	Perf. 11
2442 A1801 25c multicolored	.45	.20
P# block of 4, 5#	2.00	—
Zip block of 4	1.90	—

Beach Umbrella — A1802

Designed by Pierre Mion.

BOOKLET STAMP
PHOTOGRAVURE

1990, Feb. 3	Tagged	Perf. 11
2443 A1802 15c multicolored	.30	.20
a. Booklet pane of 10	3.00	2.00
b. As "a," blue omitted	1,900.	
c. As No. 2443, blue omitted	170.00	

WYOMING STATEHOOD, 100th ANNIV.

High Mountain Meadows, by Conrad Schwiering A1803

Designed by Jack Rosenthal.

LITHOGRAPHED & ENGRAVED
Plates of 200 in four panes of 50.

1990, Feb. 23	Tagged	Perf. 11
2444 A1803 25c multicolored	.45	.20
P# block of 4, 5#	2.00	—
Zip block of 4	1.90	—
a. Black (engr.) omitted	2,500.	—

CLASSIC FILMS

Judy Garland and Toto (The Wizard of Oz) — A1804

Clark Gable & Vivien Leigh (Gone With the Wind) — A1805

Gary Cooper (Beau Geste) — A1806

John Wayne (Stagecoach) — A1807

Designed by Thomas Blackshear.

Printed by the American Bank Note Company.

PHOTOGRAVURE
Plates of 160 in four panes of 40.

1990, Mar. 23	Tagged	Perf. 11
2445 A1804 25c multicolored	1.00	.20
2446 A1805 25c multicolored	1.00	.20
2447 A1806 25c multicolored	1.00	.20
2448 A1807 25c multicolored	1.00	.20
a. Block of 4, #2445-2448	4.50	3.50
P# block of 4, 5#	6.00	—
Zip block of 4	4.75	—

LITERARY ARTS SERIES

Marianne Moore (1887-1972), Poet — A1808

Designed by M. Gregory Rudd.

Printed by the American Bank Note Company.

PHOTOGRAVURE
Plates of 200 in four panes of 50.

1990, Apr. 18	Tagged	Perf. 11
2449 A1808 25c multicolored	.45	.20
P# block of 4, 3#	2.00	—
Zip block of 4	1.90	—

> Coil Plate No. Strips of 3
> Beginning with No. 2123, coil plate no. strips of 3 usually sell at the level of strips of 5 minus the face value of two stamps.

TRANSPORTATION ISSUE

A1810

A1811

A1811a

A1812

A1816

A1822

A1823

A1825

A1827

Designers: 4c, 32c, Richard Schlecht. Nos. 2452, 2452B, 2452D, Susan Sanford. No. 2453, Paul Calle. 10c, David K. Stone. 20c, 23c, Robert Brangwynne. $1, Chuck Hodgson.

Printed by: Guilford Gravure for American Bank Note Co. (No. 2452B), J.W. Fergusson & Sons for Stamp Venturers (No. 2454), Stamp Venturers (No, 2452D), others by BEP.

COIL STAMPS
ENGRAVED, PHOTOGRAVURE (#2452B, 2452D, 2454, 2458)
Tagged, Untagged (Nos. 2452B, 2452D, 2453, 2454, 2457-2458)

1990-95		Perf. 9.8 Vert.
2451 A1810 4c claret, Jan. 25, 1991	.20	.20
Pair	.20	.20
P# strip of 5, #1	1.25	
P# single, #1	—	.90
a. Imperf., pair	700.00	
P#1		
b. Untagged	.20	.20
Pair	.20	.20
P# strip of 5, #1	1.40	
P# single, #1	—	.90
2452 A1811 5c carmine, dull gum, Aug. 31	.20	.20
Pair	.20	.20
P# strip of 5, #1	1.40	
P# single, #1	—	1.00
a. Untagged, dull gum	.20	.20
Pair	.20	.20
P# strip of 5, #1	1.75	
P# single, #1	—	1.10
Low gloss gum	.20	.20
Pair	.20	.20
P# strip of 5, #2	1.75	
P# single, #2	—	1.10
c. Imperf., pair	900.00	
2452B A1811 5c carmine, Dec. 8, 1992	.20	.20
Pair	.25	.20
P# strip of 5, #A1-A2	1.60	
P# single, #A1-A2	—	1.25
f. Printed with luminescent ink	.20	.20
Pair	.20	.20
P# strip of 5, #A3	2.00	
P# single, #A3	—	1.50
2452D A1811a 5c carmine, low gloss gum, Mar. 20, 1995	.20	.20
Pair	.20	.20
P# strip of 5, #S1-S2	1.60	
P# single, #S1-S2	—	.90
e. Imperf., pair		
g. Printed with luminescent ink, shiny gum	.20	.20
Pair	.20	.20
P# strip of 5, #S2	1.60	
P# single, #S2	—	.90
2453 A1812 5c brown (Bureau precancel, Additional Nonprofit Postage Paid, in gray), May 25, 1991	.20	.20
Pair	.20	.20
P# strip of 5, #1-3	1.75	
P# single, #1-3	—	1.00
a. Imperf., pair	350.00	
P#1		
b. Gray omitted		
2454 A1812 5c red (Bureau precancel, Additional Nonprofit Postage Paid, in gray), shiny gum, Oct. 22, 1991	.20	.20
Pair	.20	.20
P# strip of 5, #S11	1.60	
P# single, #S11	—	1.00
Low gloss gum	.50	
Pair	1.00	
P# strip of 5, #S11	10.00	
2457 A1816 10c green (Bureau precancel, Additional Presort Postage Paid, in gray), May 25, 1991	.20	.20
Pair	.40	.40
P# strip of 5, #1	2.10	
P# single, #1	—	1.25
a. Imperf., pair	350.00	
P#1		
2458 A1816 10c green (Bureau precancel, Additional Presort Postage Paid, in black), May 25, 1994	.20	.20
Pair	.40	.40
P# strip of 5, #11, 22	2.25	
P# single, #11, 22	—	1.50
2463 A1822 20c green, June 9, 1995	.40	.20
Pair	.80	.20
P# strip of 5, #1-2	4.00	
P# single, #1-2	—	2.50
a. Imperf., pair	150.00	
2464 A1823 23c dark blue, prephosphored coated paper (solid tagging), dull gum, Apr. 12, 1991	.45	.20
Pair	.90	.20
P# strip of 5, #2-3	4.00	
P# single, #2-3	—	2.00
a. Prephosphored uncoated paper (mottled tagging), dull gum, 1993	.45	.20
Pair	.90	.20
P# strip of 5, #3	5.00	
Shiny gum, 1993	.45	
Pair	.90	
P# strip of 5, #3-5	5.00	
P# single, #3-5	—	3.00
b. Imperf., pair	175.00	
P#2		
2466 A1825 32c blue, prephosphored uncoated paper (mottled tagging), shiny gum, June 2, 1995	.60	.20
Pair	1.25	.30
P# strip of 5, #2-4	6.50	
P# strip of 5, #5	10.00	
P# single, #2-4	—	1.50

	P# single, #5	—	1.90
	Low gloss gum	.50	
	Pair	1.00	
	P# strip of 5, #3, 5	6.00	
	P# strip of 5, #4	15.00	
	P# single, #3, 5	—	1.75
	P# single, #4	—	2.00
a.	Imperf., pair		
b.	32c **bright blue**, prephosphored uncoated paper (mottled tagging), low gloss gum	6.00	4.50
	Pair	12.00	11.00
	P# strip of 5, #5	95.00	
	P# single, #5	—	90.00

Some specialists refer to No. 2466b as "Bronx blue," and it is considered to be an error of color.

2468	A1827	**$1 blue & scarlet**, overall tagging, dull gum, *Apr. 20*	1.75	.50
		Pair	3.50	1.00
		P# strip of 5, #1	11.00	
		P# single, #1	—	3.50
a.		Imperf., pair	2,500.	—
b.		Prephosphored uncoated paper (mottled tagging), shiny gum, *1993*	1.75	.50
		Pair	3.50	1.00
		P# strip of 5, #3	10.00	
		P# single, #3	—	3.50
c.		Prephosphored coated paper (grainy solid tagging), low gloss gum, *1998*	1.75	.50
		Pair	3.50	1.00
		P# strip of 5, #3	10.00	
		P# single, #3	—	3.50
		Nos. 2451-2468 (12)	4.80	2.70

Some mint pairs of No. 2468 appear to be imperf. but have faint blind perforations on the gum.

LIGHTHOUSES

Admiralty Head, WA — A1829

Cape Hatteras, NC — A1830

West Quoddy Head, ME — A1831

American Shoals, FL — A1832

Sandy Hook, NJ — A1833

Designed by Howard Koslow.

BOOKLET STAMPS
LITHOGRAPHED & ENGRAVED
Perf. 10 Vert. on 1 or 2 sides

				Tagged
1990, Apr. 26				
2470	A1829	25c **multicolored**	.45	.20
2471	A1830	25c **multicolored**	.45	.20
2472	A1831	25c **multicolored**	.45	.20
2473	A1832	25c **multicolored**	.45	.20
2474	A1833	25c **multicolored**	.45	.20
a.		Bklt. pane of 5, #2470-2474	2.50	2.00
b.		As "a," white ("USA 25") omitted	80.00	—

FLAG

A1834

Designed by Harry Zelenko.

Printed by Avery International Corp.

PHOTOGRAVURE
1990, May 18   Tagged   Self-adhesive   *Die Cut*   Printed on Plastic

2475	A1834	25c **dark red & dark blue**	.50	.25
a.		Pane of 12	6.00	

Sold only in panes of 12; peelable plastic backing inscribed in light ultramarine. Available for a test period of six months at 22 First National Bank automatic teller machines in Seattle.

FLORA and FAUNA

American Kestrel — A1840

A1841

Eastern Bluebird A1842

Cardinal A1844

Fawn A1843

Pumpkinseed Sunfish A1845

Bobcat — A1846

Designers: 1c, 3c, 45c, Michael Matherly. 19c, Peter Cocci. 30c, Robert Giusti. $2, Chuck Ripper.

Printed by: No. 2476, 3c, American Bank Note Co. No. 2477, 19c, Bureau of Engraving & Printing. 30c, Stamp Venturers. 45c, Stamp Venturers (engraved) and The Press, Inc. (lithographed).

LITHOGRAPHED
Panes of 100

1990-95	**Untagged**	*Perf. 11, 11.2 (#2477)*		
2476	A1840	1c **multicolored**, June 22, 1991	.20	.20
		P# block of 4, 4#+A	.20	
		Zip block of 4	.20	
2477	A1841	1c **multicolored**, shiny gum, *May 10, 1995*	.20	.20
		P# block of 4, 4#	.20	
		Dull gum	.20	
		P# block of 4, 4#	.20	
a.		Tagged (error), shiny gum	—	

Some plate blocks contain plate position diagram.

2478	A1842	3c **multicolored**, June 22, 1991	.20	.20
		P# block of 4, 4#+A	.30	—
		Zip block of 4	.25	

See Nos. 3032/3053. Compare design A1842 with design A2336.

PHOTOGRAVURE
Plates of 400 in four panes of 100.

		Tagged	*Perf. 11½x11*	
2479	A1843	19c **multicolored**, Mar. 11, 1991	.35	.20
		P# block of 4, 5#	1.75	—
		Zip block of 4	1.50	—
a.		Tagging omitted	10.00	
b.		Red omitted	850.00	—

On No. 2479b other colors are shifted.

2480	A1844	30c **multicolored**, June 22, 1991	.50	.20
		P# block of 4, 4#+S	2.25	—
		Zip block of 4	2.10	—

LITHOGRAPHED & ENGRAVED
Panes of 100
Perf. 11

2481	A1845	45c **multicolored**, Dec. 2, 1992	.80	.20
		P# block of 4, 5#+S	3.90	—
		Zip block of 4	3.50	—
a.		Black (engr.) omitted	525.00	—

Panes of 20

2482	A1846	$2 **multicolored**, June 1, 1990	3.00	1.25
		P# block of 4, 5#	12.00	—
		Pane of 20	60.00	
a.		Black (engr.) omitted	300.00	—
b.		Tagging omitted	15.00	

Pane of 20 consists of four plate number blocks of 4 separated by a horizontal strip of 4 with copyright information and "American Wildlife / Bobcat *(Lynx rufus)*" in selvage.

Blue Jay — A1847

Wood Duck — A1848

African Violets — A1849

Peach — A1850

Pear A1851

Red Squirrel A1852

Rose — A1853

Pine Cone — A1854

Designed by Robert Giusti (#2483-2485), Ned Seidler (#2486-2488, 2493-2495A), Michael R. Matherly (#2489), Gyo Fujikawa (#2490), Paul Breeden (#2491), Gyo Fujikawa (#2492).

Printed by Stamp Venturers (#2483, 2492), Bureau of Engraving and Printing (#2484, 2487-2488), J.W. Fergusson & Sons for KCS Industries, Inc. (#2485), KCS Industries (#2486), Dittler Brothers, Inc. (#2489), Stamp Venturers (#2490), Banknote Corporation of America (#2491), Avery-Dennison (#2493-2495, 2495A).

PHOTOGRAVURE
BOOKLET STAMPS
Perf. 10.9x9.8, 10 on 2 or 3 Sides (#2484)

1991-95				Tagged	
2483	A1847	20c **multicolored**, *June 15, 1995*		.40	.20
a.		Booklet pane of 10		4.00	2.25
2484	A1848	29c **black & multi**, overall tagging, *Apr. 12, 1991*		.50	.20
a.		Booklet pane of 10		5.50	3.75
b.		As "a," horiz. imperf. between		—	
c.		Prephosphored coated paper (solid tagging)		.40	.20
d.		As "c," booklet pane of 10		5.50	3.75

Perf. 11 on 2 or 3 Sides

2485	A1848	29c **red & multi**, *Apr. 12, 1991*		.50	.20
a.		Booklet pane of 10		5.50	4.00
b.		Vert. pair, imperf. between		275.00	
c.		As "b," booklet pane of 10		1,500.	

Perf. 10x11 on 2 or 3 Sides

2486	A1849	29c **multicolored**, *Oct. 8, 1993*		.50	.20
a.		Booklet pane of 10		5.50	4.00
2487	A1850	32c **multicolored**, *July 8, 1995*		.60	.20
2488	A1851	32c **multicolored**, *July 8, 1995*		.60	.20
a.		Booklet pane, 5 each #2487-2488		6.00	4.25
b.		Pair, #2487-2488		1.25	.30

1993-95		Tagged		*Die Cut*	

Self-Adhesive

2489	A1852	29c **multicolored**, *June 25*		.50	.20
a.		Booklet pane of 18		10.00	
2490	A1853	29c **red, green & black**, *Aug. 19*		.50	.20
a.		Booklet pane of 18		10.00	

Nos. 2489-2490 also available in strips with stamps spaced for use in affixing machines to service first day covers. No plate numbers. Stamps removed from strips are indistinguishable from booklet stamps.

2491	A1854	29c **multicolored**, *Nov. 5*		.50	.20
a.		Booklet pane of 18		11.00	
b.		Horiz. pair, no die cutting between		—	
c.		Coil with plate # B1		—	4.25
		P# strip of 5, #B1		6.00	

Stamps without plate # from coil strips are indistinguishable from booklet stamps once they are removed from the backing paper.

Serpentine Die Cut 11.3x11.7 on 2, 3 or 4 Sides

2492	A1853	32c **pink, green & black**, *June 2, 1995*		.60	.20
a.		Booklet pane of 20+label		12.00	
b.		Booklet pane of 15+label		8.75	
c.		Horiz. pair, no die cutting between		—	
d.		As "a," 2 stamps and parts of 7 others printed on backing liner		—	
e.		Booklet pane of 14		21.00	
f.		Booklet pane of 16		21.00	
g.		Coil with plate # S111		—	3.50
		P# strip of 5, #S111		5.50	
h.		Vert. pair, no die cutting between		—	

Stamps on plate # strips are separated on backing larger than the stamps. Stamps without plate # from coil strips are indistinguishable from interior position booklet stamps once they are removed from the backing paper.

For booklet panes containing No. 2492f with one stamp removed, see Nos. BK178B, BK178D-BK178E in Booklets section.

2493	A1850	32c **multicolored**, *July 8, 1995*		.60	.20
2494	A1851	32c **multicolored**, *July 8, 1995*		.60	.20
a.		Booklet pane, 10 each #2493-2494+label		12.50	
b.		Pair, #2493-2494		1.20	

COIL STAMPS
Serpentine Die Cut Vert.

2495	A1850	32c **multicolored**, *July 8, 1995*		.60	.20
2495A	A1851	32c **multicolored**, *July 8, 1995*		.60	.20
b.		Pair, #2495-2495A		1.20	
		P# strip of 5, 3 #2495A, 2 #2495, P#V11111		5.25	
		P# single, #V11111		—	3.50

See Nos. 3048, 3053-3054.

Scott values for used self-adhesive stamps are for examples either on piece or off piece.

OLYMPIANS

Jesse Owens, 1936 — A1855

Ray Ewry, 1900-08 — A1856

Hazel Wightman, 1924 — A1857

Eddie Eagan, 1920, 1932 — A1858

Helene Madison, 1932 — A1859

Designed by Bart Forbes.

Printed by the American Bank Note Company.

PHOTOGRAVURE
Panes of 35.

1990, July 6		Tagged		*Perf. 11*	
2496	A1855	25c **multicolored**		.60	.20
2497	A1856	25c **multicolored**		.60	.20
2498	A1857	25c **multicolored**		.60	.20
2499	A1858	25c **multicolored**		.60	.20
2500	A1859	25c **multicolored**		.60	.20
a.		Strip of 5, #2496-2500		3.25	2.50
		P# block of 10, 4#		8.00	—
		Zip, inscription block of 10		6.50	—

INDIAN HEADDRESSES

Assiniboin A1860

Cheyenne A1861

Comanche A1862

Flathead — A1863

Shoshone A1864

Designed by Lunda Hoyle Gill.

LITHOGRAPHED & ENGRAVED
BOOKLET STAMPS

1990, Aug. 17	Tagged		*Perf. 11 on 2 or 3 Sides*		
2501	A1860	25c **multicolored**		.55	.20
2502	A1861	25c **multicolored**		.55	.20
2503	A1862	25c **multicolored**		.55	.20
2504	A1863	25c **multicolored**		.55	.20
2505	A1864	25c **multicolored**		.55	.20
a.		Bklt. pane of 10, 2 each #2501-2505		5.50	3.50
b.		As "a," black (engr.) omitted		3,250.	
c.		Strip of 5, #2501-2505		2.75	1.00
d.		As "a," horiz. imperf. between		—	

MICRONESIA & MARSHALL ISLANDS

Canoe and Flag of the Federated States of Micronesia A1865

Stick Chart, Canoe and Flag of the Republic of the Marshall Islands — A1866

LITHOGRAPHED & ENGRAVED
Sheets of 200 in four panes of 50.

1990, Sept. 28	Tagged		*Perf. 11*		
2506	A1865	25c **multicolored**		.45	.20
2507	A1866	25c **multicolored**		.45	.20
a.		Pair, #2506-2507		.90	.60
		P# block of 4, 6#		2.25	
		Zip block of 4		2.00	—
b.		As "a," black (engr.) omitted		3,750.	

See Micronesia Nos. 124-126, Marshall Islands No. 381.

SEA CREATURES

Killer Whales — A1867

Northern Sea Lions — A1868

Sea Otter — A1869

Common Dolphin — A1870

Designed by Peter Cocci (Nos. 2508, 2511), Vladimir Beilin, USSR (Nos. 2509-2510).

LITHOGRAPHED & ENGRAVED
Sheets of 160 in four panes of 40.

1990, Oct. 3	Tagged		Perf. 11	
2508	A1867	25c **multicolored**	.45	.20
2509	A1868	25c **multicolored**	.45	.20
2510	A1869	25c **multicolored**	.45	.20
2511	A1870	25c **multicolored**	.45	.20
a.		Block of 4, #2508-2511	1.90	1.75
		P# block of 4, 5#	2.50	—
		Zip block of 4	2.00	—
b.		As "a," black (engr.) omitted	800.00	

Margin inscriptions read "Joint stamp issue by / the United States and / the Union of Soviet Socialist Republics," "Sea Lion and Sea Otter / stamp designs prepared by / a Soviet designer" and "Killer Whale and Dolphin / designs prepared by a / United States designer."
See Russia Nos. 5933-5936.

PRE-COLUMBIAN AMERICA ISSUE

Grand Canyon — A1871

Designed by Mark Hess.

Printed by the American Bank Note Company.

PHOTOGRAVURE
Plates of 200 in four panes of 50.
(3 panes of #2512, 1 pane of #C127)

1990, Oct. 12	Tagged		Perf. 11	
2512	A1871	25c **multicolored**	.45	.20
		P# block of 4, 4#, UR, LL, LR	2.00	—
		Zip block of 4	1.90	—

See No. C127.

DWIGHT D. EISENHOWER, BIRTH CENTENARY

A1872

Designed by Ken Hodges.

Printed by the American Bank Note Company.

PHOTOGRAVURE
Plates of 160 in four panes of 40.

1990, Oct. 13	Tagged		Perf. 11	
2513	A1872	25c **multicolored**	.60	.20
		P# block of 4, 5#	3.00	—
		P# block of 8, 5# and inscriptions	5.25	—
		Zip block of 4	2.50	—
a.		Imperf., pair	2,250.	

CHRISTMAS

Madonna & Child, by Antonello — A1873

Christmas Tree — A1874

Designed by Bradbury Thompson (#2514) and Libby Thiel (#2515-2516).

Printed by the Bureau of Engraving and Printing or the American Bank Note Company (#2515).

LITHOGRAPHED & ENGRAVED
Sheets of 300 in six panes of 50 (#2414-2415).

1990, Oct. 18	Tagged		Perf. 11½	
2514	A1873	25c **multicolored**	.45	.20
		P# block of 4, 5#	2.00	—
		Zip, copyright block of 4	1.90	—
a.		Bklt. pane of 10	5.00	3.25

PHOTOGRAVURE
Perf. 11

2515	A1874	25c **multicolored**	.45	.20
		P# block of 4, 4#	2.00	—
		Zip block of 4	1.90	—
a.		Vert. pair, imperf. horiz.	1,100.	

BOOKLET STAMP
Perf. 11½x11 on 2 or 3 sides

2516	A1874	25c **multicolored**	.45	.20
a.		Booklet pane of 10	5.00	3.25

No. 2514a has heavier shading in the Madonna's veil at the right frameline than No. 2514.
Marked differences exist between Nos. 2515 and 2516. The background red on No. 2515 is even while that on No. 2516 is splotchy. The bands across the tree and "Greetings" are blue green on No. 2515 and yellow green on No. 2516.

A1875

This U.S. stamp, along with 25¢ of additional U.S. postage, is equivalent to the 'F' stamp rate

A1876

Designed by Wallace Marosek (Nos. 2517-2520), Richard Sheaff (No. 2521).

Printed by U.S. Bank Note Company (No. 2517), Bureau of Engraving and Printing (No. 2518-2519), KCS Industries (No. 2520), American Bank Note Company (No. 2521).

PHOTOGRAVURE
Sheets of 100

1991, Jan. 22	Tagged		Perf. 13	
2517	A1875	(29c) **yel, blk, red & yel grn**	.50	.20
		P# block of 4, 4#	2.50	—
		Zip block of 4	2.25	—
a.		Imperf., pair	750.00	
b.		Horiz. pair, imperf. vert.	1,250.	

Do not confuse No. 2517a with No. 2518a. See note after No. 2518.

COIL STAMP
Perf. 10 Vert.

2518	A1875	(29c) **yel, blk, dull red & dk yel grn**	.50	.20
		Pair	1.00	.20
		P# strip of 5, 1111, 1222, 2222	4.25	
		P# strip of 5, #1211	24.00	
		P# strip of 5, #2211	6.25	
		P# single, #1111, 1222, 2222	—	.55
		P# single, #1211	—	18.00
		P# single, #2211	—	3.75
a.		Imperf., pair	42.50	
		P#1111, 1222, 2211, 2222		

"For U.S. addresses only" is 17½mm long on No. 2517, 16½mm long on No. 2518. Design of No. 2517 measures 21½x17½mm, No. 2518, 21x18mm.

BOOKLET STAMPS
Perf. 11 on 2 or 3 Sides

2519	A1875	(29c) **yel, blk, dull red & dk grn**	.50	.20
a.		Booklet pane of 10	6.50	4.50
2520	A1875	(29c) **pale yel, blk, red & brt grn**	.50	.20
a.		Booklet pane of 10	18.00	4.50
b.		As "a," imperf. horiz.		

No. 2519 has bullseye perforations that measure approximately 11.2. No. 2520 has less pronounced black lines in the leaf, which is a much brighter green than on No. 2519.

LITHOGRAPHED
Panes of 100

1991, Jan. 22	Untagged		Perf. 11	
2521	A1876	(4c) **bister & carmine**	.20	.20
		P# block of 4, 2#	.40	—
		Zip block of 4	.30	—
a.		Vert. pair, imperf. horiz.	110.00	
b.		Imperf., pair	—	

FLAG

A1877

Designed by Harry Zelenko. Printed by Avery International Corp.

PHOTOGRAVURE

1991, Jan. 22	Tagged	Self-Adhesive	Die Cut
Printed on Plastic			

2522	A1877	(29c) **blk, blue & dk red**	.55	.25
a.		Pane of 12	7.00	

Sold only in panes of 12; peelable plastic backing inscribed in light ultramarine. Available during a test period at First National Bank automatic teller machines in Seattle.

Flag Over Mt. Rushmore — A1878

Designed by Clarence Holbert.

COIL STAMP
ENGRAVED

1991, Mar. 29	Tagged		Perf. 10 Vert.	
2523	A1878	29c **blue, red & claret,**		
		prephosphored uncoated paper (mottled tagging)	.50	.20
		Pair	1.00	.20
		P# strip of 5, #1-4, 6-7	4.75	
		P# strip of 5, #5, 8	7.00	
		P# strip of 5, #9	10.00	
		P# single, #1, 3-4, 7	—	.45
		P# single, #2, 6	—	.90
		P# single, #5	—	2.00
		P# single, #8	—	2.75
		P# single, #9	—	3.25
b.		Imperf., pair	25.00	
		P#1, 3-4, 6-7, 9		
c.		29c **blue, red & brown,**		
		prephosphored uncoated paper (mottled tagging)	5.00	—
		Pair	10.00	
		P# strip of 5, #7	150.00	
		P# strip of 5, #1	3,750.	
		P# single, #7	—	150.00
d.		Prephosphored coated paper (solid tagging)	5.00	—
		Pair	10.00	—
		P# strip of 5, #2	550.00	
		P# strip of 5, #6	155.00	
		P# single, #2	—	150.00
		P# single, #6	—	125.00

Specialists often call No. 2523c the "Toledo brown" variety, and No. 2523d "Lenz paper." It was from No. 2523d that it was discovered that "solid tagging" on prephosphored paper resulted from the application of taggant to coated paper.

COIL STAMP
PHOTOGRAVURE
Printed by American Bank Note Co.

1991, July 4			Perf. 10 Vert.	
2523A	A1878	29c **blue, red & brown**	.50	.20
		Pair	1.00	.20
		P# strip of 5, #A11111, A22211	5.25	
		P# single, #A11111, A22211	—	1.90

On No. 2523A, USA and 29 are not outlined in white and are farther from the bottom of the design.

A1879

Designed by Wallace Marosek.

Printed by U.S. Bank Note Co. (#2524), J.W. Fergusson & Sons for Stamp Venturers (#2525, 2526), J.W. Fergusson & Sons, Inc. for KCS Industries, Inc. (#2527).

PHOTOGRAVURE
Panes of 100

1991-92		**Tagged**		**Perf. 11**
2524	A1879	29c dull yel, blk, red & yel grn,		
		Apr. 5, 1991	.50	.20
		P# block of 4, 4#+U	2.25	—
		Zip block of 4	2.10	—

See note after No. 2527.

Perf. 13x12¾

2524A	A1879	29c dull yel, blk, red & yel grn,		
		Apr. 5, 1991	.60	.20
		P# block of 4, 4#+U	2.90	—
		Zip block of 4	2.60	—

COIL STAMPS
Rouletted 10 Vert.

2525	A1879	29c pale yel, blk, red & yel grn,		
		Aug. 16, 1991	.50	.20
		Pair	1.00	.30
		P# strip of 5, P#S1111, S2222	5.00	
		P# single, #S1111, S2222	—	.95

No. 2525 was issued in attached coils so that "blocks" and "vertical pairs" exist.

Perf. 10 Vert.

2526	A1879	29c pale yel, blk, red & yel grn,		
		Mar. 3, 1992	.50	.20
		Pair	1.00	.30
		P# strip of 5, P#S2222	5.00	
		P# single, #S2222	—	2.25

BOOKLET STAMP
Perf. 11 on 2 or 3 Sides

2527	A1879	29c pale yel, blk, red & bright grn, Apr. 5	.50	.20
a.		Booklet pane of 10	5.50	3.50
b.		As "a," vert. imperf. between	1,500.	
c.		Horiz. pair, imperf. vert.	300.00	
d.		As "a," imperf. horiz.	2,750.	

Flower on Nos. 2524-2524A has grainy appearance, inscriptions look rougher.

Flag, Olympic Rings — A1880

Designed by John Boyd.

Printed by KCS Industries, Inc.

BOOKLET STAMP
PHOTOGRAVURE

1991, Apr. 21		**Tagged**	**Perf. 11 on 2 or 3 Sides**	
2528	A1880	29c multicolored	.50	.20
a.		Booklet pane of 10	5.25	3.50
b.		As "a," horiz. imperf. between	—	
c.		Vert. pair, imperf between	—	
d.		Vert. strip of 3, top pair imperf between	—	

No. 2528c comes from the misperfed booklet pane of No. 2528b. No. 2528d resulted from a paper foldover after normal perforating and before cutting into panes. Two No. 2528d are known.

Fishing Boat
A1881

Balloon
A1882

Designed by Pierre Mion.

Printed by: Multi-Color Corp. for American Bank Note Co (type I); Guilford Gravure (type II); J. W. Fergusson & Sons for Stamp Venturers (No. 2529C).

COIL STAMPS
PHOTOGRAVURE

1991, Aug. 8		**Tagged**	**Perf. 9.8 Vert.**	
2529	A1881	19c multicolored	.35	.20
		Pair	.70	.30
		P# strip of 5, #A1111, A1212, A2424	3.75	
		P# strip of 5, #A1112	7.00	
		P# single, #A1111, A1212, A2424	—	2.75
		P# single, #A1112	—	6.50
a.		Type II, 1993	.35	.20
		Pair	.70	.30
		P# strip of 5, #A5555, A5556, A6667, A7667, A7679, A7766, A7779	4.25	

		P# single, same #	—	3.00
b.		As "a," untagged, 1993	1.00	.40
		Pair	2.00	.80
		P# strip of 5, #A5555	9.00	
		P# single, #A5555	—	6.00

Design on Type II stamps is created by a finer dot pattern. Vertical sides of "1" are smooth on Type II and jagged on Type I stamps.
Imperforates are from printer's waste.

1994, June 25		**Tagged**	**Perf. 9.8 Vert.**	
2529C	A1881	19c multicolored	.50	.20
		Pair	1.00	.30
		P# strip of 5, #S111	4.50	
		P# single, #S111	—	2.75

No. 2529C has one loop of rope tying boat to piling.

BOOKLET STAMP

1991, May 17		**Tagged**	**Perf. 10 on 2 or 3 Sides**	
2530	A1882	19c multicolored	.35	.20
a.		Booklet pane of 10	3.50	2.75

Flags on Parade — A1883

Designed by Frank J. Waslick and Peter Cocci.

PHOTOGRAVURE
Panes of 100

1991, May 30		**Tagged**		**Perf. 11**
2531	A1883	29c multicolored	.50	.20
		P# block of 4, 4#	2.25	—
		Zip block of 4	2.10	—

Liberty Torch — A1884

Designed by Harry Zelenko.

Printed by Avery Dennison Co.

PHOTOGRAVURE

1991, June 25		**Tagged**	**Die Cut**	
		Self-Adhesive		
2531A	A1884	29c black, gold & green	.55	.25
b.		Booklet pane of 18	10.50	
c.		Pair, imperf.		

Sold only in panes of 18; peelable paper backing inscribed in light blue. Available for consumer testing at First National Bank automatic teller machines in Seattle, WA.

SWITZERLAND

Switzerland, 700th Anniv. — A1887

Designed by Hans Hartman, Switzerland.

Printed by the American Bank Note Company.

PHOTOGRAVURE
Plates of 160 in four panes of 40

1991, Feb. 22		**Tagged**		**Perf. 11**
2532	A1887	50c multicolored	1.00	.25
		P# block of 4, 5#	5.00	—
		Zip block of 4	4.25	—
a.		Vert. pair, imperf. horiz.	2,250.	

See Switzerland No. 888.
Imperfs exist from printer's waste.

A1888

A1889

VERMONT STATEHOOD, 200th ANNIV.

Designed by Sabra Field.

Printed by the American Bank Note Company.

PHOTOGRAVURE
Plates of 200 in four panes of 50

1991, Mar. 1		**Tagged**		**Perf. 11**
2533	A1888	29c multicolored	.55	.20
		P# block of 4, 4#+A	2.75	—
		Zip block of 4	2.40	—

SAVINGS BONDS, 50TH ANNIVERSARY

Designed by Primo Angeli.

1991, Apr. 30		**Tagged**		**Perf. 11**
2534	A1889	29c multicolored	.50	.20
		P# block of 4, 6#	2.50	—
		Zip block of 4	2.25	—

LOVE

A1890

A1891

Designed by Harry Zelenko (#2535-2536) and Nancy L. Krause (#2537).

Printed by U.S. Banknote Co. (#2535), the Bureau of Engraving and Printing (#2536) and American Bank Note Co. (#2537).

PHOTOGRAVURE
Panes of 50

1991, May 9		**Tagged**	**Perf. 12½x13**	
2535	A1890	29c multicolored	.50	.20
		P# block of 4, 5#+U	2.50	—
		Zip, copyright block of 4	2.25	—
b.		Imperf., pair		

Perf. 11

2535A	A1890	29c multicolored	.60	.20
		P# block of 4, 5#+U	3.00	—
		Zip, copyright block of 4	2.60	—

BOOKLET STAMP
Perf. 11 on 2 or 3 Sides

2536	A1890	29c multicolored	.50	.20
a.		Booklet pane of 10	5.25	3.50

"29" is closer to edge of design on No. 2536 than on No. 2535.

Sheets of 200 in panes of 50
Perf. 11

2537	A1891	52c multicolored	.90	.20
		P# block of 4, 3#+A	4.50	—
		Zip block of 4	4.00	—

LITERARY ARTS SERIES

William Saroyan — A1892

Designed by Ren Wicks.

Printed by J.W. Fergusson for American Bank Note Co.

PHOTOGRAVURE
Sheets of 200 in four panes of 50

1991, May 22	Tagged	Perf. 11	
2538 A1892 29c **multicolored**		.50	.20
P# block of 4, 5#+A		2.50	—
Zip block of 4		2.25	

Margin inscriptions read "William Saroyan was / an Armenian-American / playwright & novelist" "His 1939 play 'The / Time of Your Life' won / him a Pulitzer Prize." "This is the third joint / stamp issue by the U.S. / and the Soviet Union."
See Russia No. 6002.

Eagle, Olympic
Rings — A1893

A1894

A1895

A1896

Futuristic Space
Shuttle — A1897

Space Shuttle
Challenger
A1898

Space Shuttle
Endeavour
A1898a

Designed by: Terrence McCaffrey (Nos. 2539-2541), Timothy Knapp (No. 2542), Ken Hodges (No. 2543), Phil Jordan (Nos. 2544-2544A).

Printed by: J.W. Fergusson & Sons for Stamp Venturers (No. 2539); American Bank Note Co. (Nos. 2540-2541); Jeffries Banknote Co. for the American Bank Note Co. (No. 2542).

Nos. 2540, 2543-2544 for priority mail rate. Nos. 2541, 2544A for domestic express mail rate. No. 2542 for international express mail rate.
Nos. 2544-2544A printed by Ashton-Potter (USA) Ltd.

Sheet of 180 in nine panes of 20 (No. 2539)
Sheet of 120 in six panes of 20 (Nos. 2540-2542, 2544-2544A)
Pane of 40 (No. 2543)

PHOTOGRAVURE
Copyright information appears in the center of the top and bottom selvage.

1991, Sept. 29	Tagged	Perf. 11	
2539 A1893 $1 **gold & multi**		1.75	.50
P# block of 4, 6#+S		8.00	—
Pane of 20		36.00	
a. Black omitted		—	

LITHOGRAPHED & ENGRAVED

1991, July 7	Tagged	Perf. 11	
2540 A1894 $2.90 **multicolored**		5.00	2.50
P# block of 4, 5#+A		20.00	—
Pane of 20		100.00	
a. Vert. pair, imperf horiz.			

No. 2540 exists imperf and with color missing from printer's waste.

1991, June 16	Untagged	Perf. 11	
2541 A1895 $9.95 **multicolored**		15.00	7.50
P# block of 4, 5#+A		60.00	—
Pane of 20		300.00	
a. Imperf., pair			

1991, Aug. 31	Untagged	Perf. 11	
2542 A1896 $14 **multicolored**		22.50	10.00
P# block of 4, 5#+A		90.00	—
Pane of 20		450.00	
a. Red (engr. inscriptions) omitted		1,500.	

1993, June 3	Tagged	Perf. 11x10½	
2543 A1897 $2.90 **multicolored**		5.00	2.25
P# block of 4, 6#		22.50	—
Zip block of 4		21.00	

1995, June 22	Tagged	Perf. 11.2	
2544 A1898 $3 **multicolored**, dated "1995"		5.25	2.25
b. Dated "1996"		5.25	2.25
P# block of 4, 5#+P		21.00	—
Pane of 20		105.00	
c. Horiz. pair, imperf between		—	

1995, Aug. 4	Tagged	Perf. 11	
2544A A1898a $10.75 **multicolored**		17.50	7.50
P# block of 4, 5#+P		70.00	—
Pane of 20		350.00	

FISHING FLIES

Royal
Wulff — A1899

Jock
Scott — A1900

Apte Tarpon
Fly — A1901

Lefty's
Deceiver — A1902

Muddler
Minnow — A1903

Designed by Chuck Ripper.

Printed by American Bank Note Co.

PHOTOGRAVURE
BOOKLET STAMPS

1991, May 31	Tagged	Perf. 11 Horiz.	
2545 A1899 29c **multicolored**		.65	.20
a. Black omitted		—	
2546 A1900 29c **multicolored**		.65	.20
a. Black omitted		—	
2547 A1901 29c **multicolored**		.65	.20
a. Black omitted		—	
2548 A1902 29c **multicolored**		.65	.20
2549 A1903 29c **multicolored**		.65	.20
a. Bklt. pane of 5, #2545-2549		3.75	2.50

Horiz. pairs, imperf vert,. exist from printer's waste.

Cole Porter (1891-1964), Composer — A1904

S. W. Asia Service Medal — A1905

PERFORMING ARTS

Designed by Jim Sharpe.

Printed by American Bank Note Co.

PHOTOGRAVURE
Panes of 50

1991, June 8	Tagged	Perf. 11	
2550 A1904 29c multicolored		.50	.20
P# block of 4, 5#+A		2.50	—
Zip block of 4		2.25	—
a. Vert. pair, imperf. horiz.		650.00	

Margin inscriptions read "1991 is the centennial / of Cole Porter, famous / American musical comedy / composer and lyricist." "He created music for / many Broadway plays / and films. Among his best known songs were:" *"Night and Day, Begin the / Beguine, Let's Do It, What / is this thing Called Love / and Don't Fence Me In."*

OPERATIONS DESERT SHIELD & DESERT STORM

Designed by Jack Williams.

Printed by J.W. Fergusson Co. for Stamp Venturers (No. 2551), Multi-Color Corp. for the American Bank Note Co. (No. 2552).

PHOTOGRAVURE
Panes of 50

1991, July 2	Tagged	Perf. 11	
2551 A1905 29c multicolored		.50	.20
P# block of 4, 7#+S		2.50	—
Zip block of 4		2.25	—
a. Vert. pair, imperf. horiz.		2,000.	

No. 2551 is 21mm wide.
Margin inscriptions read "This stamp salutes the / members of the U.S. / Armed Forces who served / in Operations Desert / Shield & Desert Storm." "The design depicts the / Southwest Asia Service / Medal, established by / Presidential Executive / order in March 1991."

BOOKLET STAMP
Perf. 11 Vert. on 1 or 2 Sides

2552 A1905 29c multicolored		.50	.20
a. Booklet pane of 5		2.75	2.25

No. 2552 is 20½mm wide. Inscriptions are shorter than on No. 2551.

1992 SUMMER OLYMPICS, BARCELONA

Pole Vault — A1907

Discus — A1908

Women's Sprints — A1909

Javelin — A1910

Women's Hurdles — A1911

Designed by Joni Carter.

Printed by the American Bank Note Co.

PHOTOGRAVURE
Panes of 40

1991, July 12	Tagged	Perf. 11	
2553 A1907 29c multicolored		.50	.20
2554 A1908 29c multicolored		.50	.20
2555 A1909 29c multicolored		.50	.20
2556 A1910 29c multicolored		.50	.20
2557 A1911 29c multicolored		.50	.20
a. Strip of 5, #2553-2557		2.75	2.25
P# block of 10, 5#+A		7.50	—
Zip block of 10		5.25	—

NUMISMATICS

1858 Flying Eagle Cent, 1907 Standing Liberty Double Eagle, Series 1875 $1 Note, Series 1902 $10 National Currency Note — A1912

Designed by V. Jack Ruther.

LITHOGRAPHED & ENGRAVED
Sheets of 200 in four panes of 50

1991, Aug. 13	Tagged	Perf. 11	
2558 A1912 29c multicolored		.50	.20
P# block of 4, 7#		2.50	—
Zip block of 4		2.25	—

WORLD WAR II

A1913

Designed by William H. Bond.

Designs and events of 1941: a, Military vehicles (Burma Road, 717-mile lifeline to China). b, Recruits (America's first peacetime draft). c, Shipments for allies (U.S. supports allies with **Lend-Lease Act**). d, Franklin D. Roosevelt, Winston Churchill (Atlantic Charter sets war aims of allies). e, Tank (America becomes the "arsenal of democracy."). f, Sinking of Destoyer Reuben James, Oct. 31. g, Gas mask, helmet (Civil defense mobilizes Americans at home). h, Liberty Ship, sea gull (First Liberty ship delivered December 30). i, Sinking ships (Japanese bomb Pearl Harbor, December 7). j, Congress in session (U.S. declares war on Japan, December 8). Central label is the size of 15 stamps and shows world map, extent of axis control. Illustration reduced.

LITHOGRAPHED & ENGRAVED
Plates of eight subjects in four panes of 2 each

1991, Sept. 3	Tagged	Perf. 11	
2559 A1913 Block of 10		5.25	4.50
Pane of 20		10.50	—
a.-j. 29c any single		.50	.30
k. Black (engr.) omitted		10,000.	

No. 2559 has salvage at left and right and either top or bottom.

BASKETBALL, 100TH ANNIVERSARY

Basketball, Hoop, Players' Arms — A1914

Designed by Lon Busch.

PHOTOGRAVURE
Sheets of 200 in four panes of 50

1991, Aug. 28	Tagged	Perf. 11	
2560 A1914 29c multicolored		.50	.20
P# block of 4, 4#		2.50	—
Zip block of 4		2.25	—

DISTRICT OF COLUMBIA BICENTENNIAL

Capitol Building from Pennsylvania Avenue, Circa 1903 — A1915

Designed by Pierre Mion.

LITHOGRAPHED & ENGRAVED
Plates of 200 in four panes of 50

1991, Sept. 7	Tagged	Perf. 11	
2561 A1915 29c multicolored		.50	.20
P# block of 4, 5#		2.50	—
Zip block of 4		2.25	—
a. Black (engr.) omitted		125.00	

COMEDIANS

Stan Laurel (1890-1965) and Oliver Hardy (1892-1957) A1916

Edgar Bergen (1903-1978) and Charlie McCarthy — A1917

Jack Benny (1894-1974) A1918

Fanny Brice (1891-1951) A1919

Bud Abbott (1895-1974) and Lou Costello (1908-1959)
A1920

Designed by Al Hirschfeld.

LITHOGRAPHED & ENGRAVED
BOOKLET STAMPS

1991, Aug. 29   Tagged   *Perf. 11 on 2 or 3 Sides*

2562	A1916	29c multicolored	.50	.20
2563	A1917	29c multicolored	.50	.20
2564	A1918	29c multicolored	.50	.20
2565	A1919	29c multicolored	.50	.20
2566	A1920	29c multicolored	.50	.20
a.		Bklt. pane, 2 each #2562-2566	5.50	3.50
b.		As "a," scar & brt violet (engr.) omitted	750.00	
c.		Strip of 5, #2562-2566	2.50	—

BLACK HERITAGE SERIES

Jan E. Matzeliger (1852-1889), Inventor — A1921

Designed by Higgins Bond.
Printed by J.W. Fergusson & Sons for the American Bank Note Co.

PHOTOGRAVURE
Plates of 200 in four panes of 50

1991, Sept. 15   Tagged   *Perf. 11*

2567	A1921	29c multicolored	.50	.20
		P# block of 4, 6#+A	2.50	—
		Zip block of 4	2.25	—
a.		Horiz. pair, imperf. vert.	1,750.	
b.		Vert. pair, imperf. horiz.	1,600.	
c.		Imperf., pair	2,750.	

SPACE EXPLORATION

Mercury, Mariner 10 A1922

Venus, Mariner 2 — A1923

Earth, Landsat — A1924

Moon, Lunar Orbiter — A1925

Mars, Viking Orbiter — A1926

Jupiter, Pioneer 11 A1927

Saturn, Voyager 2 A1928

Uranus, Voyager 2 A1929

Neptune, Voyager 2 A1930

Pluto — A1931

Designed by Ron Miller.

PHOTOGRAVURE
BOOKLET STAMPS

1991, Oct. 1   Tagged   *Perf. 11 on 2 or 3 Sides*

2568	A1922	29c multicolored	.50	.20
2569	A1923	29c multicolored	.50	.20
2570	A1924	29c multicolored	.50	.20
2571	A1925	29c multicolored	.50	.20
2572	A1926	29c multicolored	.50	.20
2573	A1927	29c multicolored	.50	.20
2574	A1928	29c multicolored	.50	.20
2575	A1929	29c multicolored	.50	.20
2576	A1930	29c multicolored	.50	.20
2577	A1931	29c multicolored	.50	.20
a.		Bklt. pane of 10, #2568-2577	5.50	3.50

CHRISTMAS

Madonna and Child by Antoniazzo Romano A1933

Santa Claus in Chimney A1934

Santa Checking List — A1935

Santa with Present — A1936

Santa at Fireplace — A1937

Santa and Sleigh — A1938

Designed by Bradbury Thompson (#2578) and John Berkey (#2579-2585).
Printed by the Bureau of Engraving and Printing (#2578); J.W. Fergusson & Sons (#2579) and Multi-Color Corp. (#2580-2585) for the American Bank Note Co.

LITHOGRAPHED & ENGRAVED
Sheets of 300 in six panes of 50

1991, Oct. 17   Tagged   *Perf. 11*

2578	A1933	(29c) multicolored	.50	.20
		P# block of 4, 5#	2.50	—
		Zip, copyright block of 4	2.25	—
a.		Booklet pane of 10	5.50	3.25
b.		As "a," single, red & black (engr.) omitted	3,500.	

PHOTOGRAVURE

2579	A1934	(29c) multicolored	.50	.20
		P# block of 4, 3#+A	2.50	—
		Zip block of 4	2.25	—
a.		Horiz. pair, imperf. vert.	325.00	
b.		Vert. pair, imperf. horiz.	525.00	

Booklet Stamps
Size: 25x18½mm
Perf. 11 on 2 or 3 Sides

2580	A1934	(29c) Type I	1.75	.20
2581	A1934	(29c) Type II	1.75	.20
a.		Pair, #2580-2581	3.50	.25
b.		Bklt. pane, 2 each, #2580, 2581	7.50	1.25
2582	A1935	(29c) multicolored	.50	.20
a.		Bklt. pane of 4	2.00	1.25
2583	A1936	(29c) multicolored	.50	.20
a.		Bklt. pane of 4	2.00	1.25
2584	A1937	(29c) multicolored	.50	.20
a.		Bklt. pane of 4	2.00	1.25
2585	A1938	(29c) multicolored	.50	.20
a.		Bklt. pane of 4	2.00	1.25
		Nos. 2578-2585 (8)	6.50	1.60

The far left brick from the top row of the chimney is missing from Type II, No. 2581.

James K. Polk (1795-1849) — A1939

"The Surrender of General Burgoyne at Saratoga," by John Trumbull — A1942

Washington and Jackson A1944

Designed by John Thompson (No. 2587), based on painting by John Trumbull (No. 2590), Richard D. Sheaff (No. 2592).
Printed by Banknote Corporation of America (No. 2587), Stamp Venturers (Nos. 2590, 2592).

ENGRAVED
Sheets of 400 in four panes of 100 (No. 2587)
Sheets of 120 in six panes of 20 (Nos. 2590, 2592)

1994-95   Tagged   *Perf. 11.2*

2587	A1939	32c red brown, *Nov. 2, 1995*	.60	.20
		P# block of 4, 1#+B	3.00	—

Perf. 11.5

2590	A1942	$1 **blue**, *May 5, 1994*	1.90 .50
		P# block of 4, 1#+S	7.60 —
		Pane of 20	38.00 —
2592	A1944	$5 **slate green**, *Aug. 19, 1994*	8.00 2.50
		P# block of 4, 1#+S	40.00 —
		Pane of 20	160.00 —

Some plate blocks contain either inscription or plate position diagram.

A1946

Eagle and
Shield — A1947

A1950

Statue of
Liberty — A1951

Designed by Lou Nolan (#2593-2594), Jay Haiden (#2595-2597), Richard Sheaff (#2598), Tom Engeman (#2599).
Printed by Banknote Corporation of America (#2595), Dittler Brothers, Inc. (#2596, 2599), Stamp Venturers (#2597), National Label Co. for 3M (#2598).

BOOKLET STAMPS
PHOTOGRAVURE

1992, Sept. 8　Tagged　Perf. 10 on 2 or 3 sides

2593	A1946	29c **black & multi**	.50 .20
a.		Booklet pane of 10	5.25 4.25

Perf. 11x10 on 2 or 3 sides

2593B	A1946	29c **black & multi**, shiny gum	.50 .20
		Low gloss gum	.50
c.		Bklt. pane of 10, shiny gum	5.50 4.25
		Low gloss gum	5.50

1993, Apr. 8(?)　Perf. 11x10 on 2 or 3 Sides

2594	A1946	29c **red & multi**	.50 .20
a.		Booklet pane of 10	5.25 4.25
b.		Imperf., pair	900.00

Denomination is red on #2594 and black on #2593.

LITHOGRAPHED & ENGRAVED

1992, Sept. 25　Tagged　Die Cut
Self-Adhesive

2595	A1947	29c **brown & multicolored**	.50 .25
a.		Bklt. pane of 17 + label	13.00
b.		Pair, no die cutting	225.00
c.		Brown omitted	475.00
d.		As "a," no die cutting	1,800.
2596	A1947	29c **green & multicolored**	.50 .25
a.		Bklt. pane of 17 + label	12.00

PHOTOGRAVURE

2597	A1947	29c **red & multicolored**	.50 .25
a.		Bklt. pane of 17 + label	10.00

Plate No. and inscription reads down on No. 2595a and up on Nos. 2596a-2597a. Design is sharper and more finely detailed on Nos. 2595, 2597.
Nos. 2595-2597 sold for $5.
Nos. 2595-2597 also available in strips with stamps spaced for use in affixing machines to service first day covers.

PHOTOGRAVURE

1994　Tagged　Die Cut
Self-Adhesive

2598	A1950	29c **red, cream & blue**, *Feb. 4*	.50 .20
a.		Booklet pane of 18	10.00
b.		Coil with P#111	— 3.50
		P# strip of 5, #111	6.00
2599	A1951	29c **multicolored**, *June 24*	.50 .20
a.		Booklet pane of 18	10.00
b.		Coil with P#D111	— 3.50
		P# strip of 5, #D1111	6.00

Except for Nos. 2598b and 2599b with plate numbers, coil stamps of these issues are indistinguishable from booklet stamps once they are removed from the backing paper.
See Nos. 3122-3122E.

Scott values for used self-adhesive stamps are for examples either on piece or off piece.

Eagle and
Shield — A1956

A1959

Eagle and
Shield — A1957

A1960

Flag Over White House — A1961

Designed by Chris Calle (#2602-2604), Terrence McCaffrey (#2605), Lon Busch (#2606-2608), V. Jack Ruther (29c).
Printed by Guildford Gravure, Inc. for the American Bank Note Co. (#2602, 2606), Bureau of Engraving and Printing (#2603, 2607), Stamp Venturers (#2604, 2608), American Bank Note Co. (#2605).

PHOTOGRAVURE
COIL STAMPS

1991-93　Untagged　Perf. 10 Vert.

2602	A1956	(10c) **multi** (Bureau precancel, Bulk Rate, in blue), *Dec. 13*	.20 .20
		Pair	.40 .40
		P# strip of 5, #A11111, A11112, A21112, A22112, A22113, A43334, A43335	3.50
		P# strip of 5, #A12213	21.00
		P# strip of 5, #A21113, A33333, A33335, A34424, A34426, A43324, A43325, A43326, A43426, A54444, A54445, A1011101010, A1211101010	5.00
		P# strip of 5, #A32333	250.00
		P# strip of 5, #A33334	90.00
		P# strip of 5, #A53335, A77777, A88888, A88889, A89999, A99998, A99999, A1010101010, A1011101011, A1011101012, A1110101010, A1110111010, A1111101010, A1111111010, A1411101010, A1411101011, A1412111110, A1412111111	4.00
		P# strip of 5, #A1110101011	12.50
		P# single, #A11111, A11112, A21112, A21113, A22112, A22113, A43325, A43326, A43334, A43335, A43426, A54444, A54445, A77777, A88888, A89999, A99998, A99999	— 2.75
		P# single, #A12213	— 19.00
		P# single, #A32333	— 190.00
		P# single, #A33333, A33335, A34424, A34426	— 3.75
		P# single, #A33334	— 82.50
		P# single, #A53335, A88889, A1010101010, A1011101010, A1011101011, A1011101012, A1110101010, A1110111010, A1111101010, A1111111010, A1211101010, A1411101010, A1411101011, A1412111110, A1412111111	— 3.25
		P# single, #A1110101011	— 11.00
a.		Imperf., pair	—
2603	A1957	(10c) **org yel & multi**, shiny gum (Bureau precancel, Bulk Rate, in red), *May 29, 1993*	.20 .20
		Pair	.40 .40
		P# strip of 5, #11111, 22221, 22222	4.00
		P# single, same	— 2.50
		Low gloss gum	.20
		Pair	.40
		P# strip of 5, #22222, 33333, 44444	4.00
		P# single, #11111	—
a.		Imperf., pair	30.00
b.		Tagged (error), shiny gum	2.00 1.50
		Pair	4.00 3.50
		P# strip of 5, #11111, 22221	15.00
		P# strip of 5, #22222	200.00
		P# single, #11111, 22221	— 12.50

All examples of Nos. 2603, 2603a and 2603b were printed with luminescent ink.

2604	A1957	(10c) **gold & multi**, shiny gum (Bureau precancel, Bulk Rate, in red), *May 29, 1993*	.20 .20
		Pair	.40 .40
		P# strip of 5, #S11111, S22222	3.50
		P# single, same	— 2.25
		Low gloss gum	.20
		Pair	.40
		P# strip of 5, #11111, 22222	3.50
		P# single, same	— 2.25
2605	A1959	23c **multi** (Bureau precancel in blue), *Sept. 27*	.40 .40
		Pair	.80 .80
		P# strip of 5, #A111, A212, A222	4.25
		P# strip of 5, #A112, A122, A333	5.25
		P# single, #A111, A112, A122, A212, A222, A333	— 3.00
2606	A1960	23c **multi** (Bureau precanceled), *July 21, 1992*	.40 .40
		Pair	.80 .80
		P# strip of 5, #A1111, A2222, A2232, A2233, A3333, A4364, A4443, A4444, A4453	4.75
		P# single, same #	— 3.25

"First-Class" is 9½mm long and "23" is 6mm long on No. 2606.

2607	A1960	23c **multi**, shiny gum (Bureau precanceled), *Oct. 9, 1992*	.40 .40
		Pair	.80 .80
		P# strip of 5, #1111	4.75
		P# single, #1111	— 1.25
		Low gloss gum	.40
		Pair	.80
		P# strip of 5, #1111	5.00
a.		Tagged (error), shiny gum	5.00 4.50
		Pair	10.00 9.00
		P# strip of 5, #1111	85.00
		P# single, #1111	— 20.00
c.		Imperf., pair	100.00

"First-Class" is 9mm long and "23" is 7mm long on No. 2607.

2608	A1960	23c **vio bl, red & blk** (Bureau precanceled), *May 14, 1993*	.40 .40
		Pair	.80 .80
		P# strip of 5, #S111	4.75
		P# single, #S111	— 3.00
c.		Imperf., pair	—

"First-Class" is 8½mm long and "23" is 6½mm long on No. 2608.

ENGRAVED
Tagged

2609	A1961	29c **blue & red**, *Apr. 23, 1992*	.50 .20
		Pair	1.00 .20
		P# strip of 5, #1-8	4.75
		P# strip of 5, #9-16, 18	5.50
		P# strip of 5, #18	6.50
		P# single, #1-4, 6-8	— .60
		P# single, #5	— 1.50
		P# single, #9	— 2.50
		P# single, #10-13, 15-16	— 1.10
		P# single, #14	— 3.00
		P# single, #18	— 4.75
a.		Imperf., pair	20.00
		P#3-7	
b.		Pair, imperf. between	100.00

See No. 2907.

WINTER OLYMPICS

Hockey — A1963

Figure
Skating — A1964

Speed
Skating — A1965

Skiing — A1966

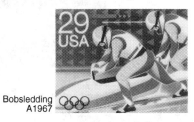

Bobsledding
A1967

Designed by Lon Busch. Printed by J.W. Fergusson & Sons
for Stamp Venturers.

PHOTOGRAVURE
Panes of 35

1992, Jan. 11	Tagged	Perf. 11	
2611 A1963 29c **multicolored**		.50	.20
2612 A1964 29c **multicolored**		.50	.20
2613 A1965 29c **multicolored**		.50	.20
2614 A1966 29c **multicolored**		.50	.20
2615 A1967 29c **multicolored**		.50	.20
a. Strip of 5, #2611-2615		2.75	2.25
P# block of 10, 4#+S		6.50	—
Zip, copyright block of 15		8.50	—

Inscriptions on six marginal tabs.

Detail from No.
129 — A1968

A1969

WORLD COLUMBIAN STAMP EXPO
Designed by Richard Sheaff.

LITHOGRAPHED & ENGRAVED
Plates of 200 in four panes of 50

1992, Jan. 24	Tagged	Perf. 11	
2616 A1968 29c **multicolored**		.50	.20
P# block of 4, 4#		2.50	—
Zip block of 4		2.25	—
a. Tagging omitted		8.50	—

BLACK HERITAGE
W.E.B. Du Bois (1868-1963), Writer and Civil Rights
Leader
Designed by Higgins Bond.

LITHOGRAPHED & ENGRAVED
Plates of 200 in four panes of 50

1992, Jan. 31	Tagged	Perf. 11	
2617 A1969 29c **multicolored**		.50	.20
P# block of 4, 7#		2.50	—
Zip block of 4		2.25	—

A1970

A1971

LOVE
Designed by Uldis Purins. Printed by the U.S. Bank Note Co.

PHOTOGRAVURE
Panes of 50

1992, Feb. 6	Tagged	Perf. 11	
2618 A1970 29c **multicolored**		.50	.20
P# block of 4, U+5#		2.50	—
Zip, copyright block of 4		2.25	—
a. Horiz. pair, imperf. vert.		800.00	

OLYMPIC BASEBALL
Designed by Anthony DeLuz.

PHOTOGRAVURE

Plates of 200 in four panes of 50

1992, Apr. 3	Tagged	Perf. 11	
2619 A1971 29c **multicolored**		.50	.20
P# block of 4, 5#		2.75	—
Zip block of 4		2.25	—

VOYAGES OF COLUMBUS

Seeking Queen
Isabella's
Support — A1972

Crossing the
Atlantic — A1973

Approaching
Land — A1974

Coming
Ashore — A1975

Designed by Richard Schlecht.

LITHOGRAPHED & ENGRAVED
Plates of 160 in four panes of 40

1992, Apr. 24	Tagged	Perf. 11	
2620 A1972 29c **multicolored**		.50	.20
2621 A1973 29c **multicolored**		.50	.20
2622 A1974 29c **multicolored**		.50	.20
2623 A1975 29c **multicolored**		.50	.20
a. Block of 4, #2620-2623		2.00	1.90
P# block of 4, 5#		2.50	—
Zip block of 4		2.25	—

See Italy Nos. 1877-1880.

Souvenir Sheets

A1976

A1977

A1978

A1979

A1980

A1981

Designed by Richard Sheaff.

Printed by the American Bank Note Co. Margins on Nos. 2624-2628 are lithographed. Nos. 2624a-2628c, 2629 are similar in design to Nos. 230-245 but are dated 1492-1992.

LITHOGRAPHED & ENGRAVED
1992, May 22   *Perf. 10½*
                      Tagged (15c-$5), Untagged

2624	A1976	Sheet of 3	1.75	—
a.	A71	1c **deep blue**	.20	.20
b.	A74	4c **ultramarine**	.20	.20
c.	A82	$1 **salmon**	1.65	1.00
2625	A1977	Sheet of 3	6.75	—
a.	A72	2c **brown violet**	.20	.20
b.	A73	3c **green**	.20	.20
c.	A85	$4 **crimson lake**	6.50	4.00
2626	A1978	Sheet of 3	1.40	—
a.	A75	5c **chocolate**	.20	.20
b.	A80	30c **orange brown**	.50	.30
c.	A81	50c **slate blue**	.80	.50
2627	A1979	Sheet of 3	5.25	—
a.	A76	6c **purple**	.20	.20
b.	A77	8c **magenta**	.20	.20
c.	A84	$3 **yellow green**	4.75	3.00
2628	A1980	Sheet of 3	3.75	—
a.	A78	10c **black brown**	.20	.20
b.	A79	15c **dark green**	.25	.20
c.	A83	$2 **brown red**	3.25	2.00
2629	A1981	Sheet of 1	8.50	—
a.	A86	$5 **black**, single stamp	8.00	5.00
		Nos. 2624-2629 (6)	27.40	

Imperforate examples are known of all the Columbus souvenir sheets, but these are not listed in this catalogue. Their appearance several years after the issue date, in substantial quantities of all six sheets at the same time and, evidently, from a single source, with many small faults such as wrinkles and light creases that are not normally seen on these sheets, raises serious concerns about the legitimacy of these imperforate sheets as issued errors.

These circumstances have led the Scott editors to adopt the position that these imperforate sheets are indeed almost certainly printer's waste rather than issued errors. While it is possible that actual imperforate errors of one or more of the sheets may exist that were legitimately sold by the USPS, it is not possible to separate these (should they exist) from the many more numerous examples that apparently are printer's waste.

See Italy Nos. 1883-1888, Portugal Nos. 1918-1923 and Spain Nos. 2677-2682.

NEW YORK STOCK EXCHANGE BICENTENNIAL

A1982

Designed by Richard Sheaff.

Printed by the Jeffries Bank Note Co. for the American Bank Note Co.

LITHOGRAPHED & ENGRAVED
1992, May 17   **Tagged**   *Perf. 11*

2630	A1982	29c **green, red & black**	.50	.20
		P# block of 4, 3#+A	2.50	—
		Zip, Olympic block of 4	2.25	—

SPACE ACCOMPLISHMENTS

Cosmonaut, US   Astronaut, Russian
Space   Space Station,
Shuttle — A1983   Russian Space
                         Shuttle — A1984

Sputnik, Vostok,   Soyuz, Mercury &
Apollo Command &   Gemini
Lunar   Spacecraft — A1986
Modules — A1985

Designed by Vladimir Beilin (Russia) and Robert T. McCall.

PHOTOGRAVURE
Plates of 200 in four panes of 50
1992, May 29   **Tagged**   *Perf. 11*

2631	A1983	29c **multicolored**	.50	.20
2632	A1984	29c **multicolored**	.50	.20
2633	A1985	29c **multicolored**	.50	.20
2634	A1986	29c **multicolored**	.50	.20
a.		Block of 4, #2631-2634	2.00	1.75
		P# block of 4, 4#	2.50	—
		Zip block of 4	2.25	—

See Russia Nos. 6080-6083.

ALASKA HIGHWAY, 50th ANNIVERSARY

A1987

Designed by Byron Birdsall.

LITHOGRAPHED & ENGRAVED
Plates of 200 in four panes of 50
1992, May 30   **Tagged**   *Perf. 11*

2635	A1987	29c **multicolored**	.50	.20
		P# block of 4, 6#	2.50	—
		Zip block of 4	2.25	—
a.		Black (engr.) omitted	500.00	

Most known examples of No. 2635a have poor to fine centering. It is valued in the grade of fine. Very fine examples exist and sell for much more.

KENTUCKY STATEHOOD BICENTENNIAL

A1988

Designed by Joseph Petro.

Printed by J.W. Fergusson & Sons for Stamp Venturers.

PHOTOGRAVURE
Plates of 200 in four panes of 50
1992, June 1   **Tagged**   *Perf. 11*

2636	A1988	29c **multicolored**	.50	.20
		P# block of 4, 5#+S	2.50	—
		Zip block of 4	2.25	—

SUMMER OLYMPICS

Soccer — A1989

Gymnastics
A1990

Volleyball — A1991

Boxing — A1992

Swimming
A1993

Designed by Richard Waldrep.

Printed by J.W. Fergusson & Sons for Stamp Venturers.

PHOTOGRAVURE
Panes of 35
1992, June 11   **Tagged**   *Perf. 11*

2637	A1989	29c **multicolored**	.50	.20
2638	A1990	29c **multicolored**	.50	.20
2639	A1991	29c **multicolored**	.50	.20
2640	A1992	29c **multicolored**	.50	.20
2641	A1993	29c **multicolored**	.50	.20
a.		Strip of 5, #2637-2641	2.50	2.25
		P# block of 10, 5#+S	5.50	—
		Zip, copyright block of 15	7.75	—

Inscriptions on six marginal tabs.

HUMMINGBIRDS

Ruby-throated
A1994

Broad-billed
A1995

Costa's — A1996

Rufous — A1997

Calliope — A1998

Designed by Chuck Ripper.

Printed by Multi-Color Corp. for the American Bank Note Co.

PHOTOGRAVURE
BOOKLET STAMPS
Perf. 11 Vert. on 1 or 2 sides

				Tagged	
1992, June 15					
2642	A1994	29c **multicolored**		.50	.20
2643	A1995	29c **multicolored**		.50	.20
2644	A1996	29c **multicolored**		.50	.20
2645	A1997	29c **multicolored**		.50	.20
2646	A1998	29c **multicolored**		.50	.20
a.		Bklt. pane of 5, #2642-2646		2.75	*2.25*

Illustration reduced.

Designed by Karen Mallary.

Printed by Ashton-Potter America, Inc.

LITHOGRAPHED
Plates of 300 in six panes of 50 and
Plates of 200 in four panes of 50

1992, July 24		Tagged	Perf. 11	
2647	A1999	29c Indian paintbrush	.50	.20
2648	A2000	29c Fragrant water lily	.50	.20
2649	A2001	29c Meadow beauty	.50	.20
2650	A2002	29c Jack-in-the-pulpit	.50	.20
2651	A2003	29c California poppy	.50	.20
2652	A2004	29c Large-flowered trillium	.50	.20
2653	A2005	29c Tickseed	.50	.20
2654	A2006	29c Shooting star	.50	.20
2655	A2007	29c Stream violet	.50	.20
2656	A2008	29c Bluets	.50	.20
2657	A2009	29c Herb Robert	.50	.20
2658	A2010	29c Marsh marigold	.50	.20
2659	A2011	29c Sweet white violet	.50	.20
2660	A2012	29c Claret cup cactus	.50	.20
2661	A2013	29c White mountain avens	.50	.20
2662	A2014	29c Sessile bellwort	.50	.20
2663	A2015	29c Blue flag	.50	.20
2664	A2016	29c Harlequin lupine	.50	.20
2665	A2017	29c Twinflower	.50	.20
2666	A2018	29c Common sunflower	.50	.20
2667	A2019	29c Sego lily	.50	.20
2668	A2020	29c Virginia bluebells	.50	.20
2669	A2021	29c Ohi'a lehua	.50	.20
2670	A2022	29c Rosebud orchid	.50	.20
2671	A2023	29c Showy evening primrose	.50	.20
2672	A2024	29c Fringed gentian	.50	.20
2673	A2025	29c Yellow lady's slipper	.50	.20
2674	A2026	29c Passionflower	.50	.20
2675	A2027	29c Bunchberry	.50	.20
2676	A2028	29c Pasqueflower	.50	.20
2677	A2029	29c Round-lobed hepatica	.50	.20
2678	A2030	29c Wild columbine	.50	.20
2679	A2031	29c Fireweed	.50	.20
2680	A2032	29c Indian pond lily	.50	.20
2681	A2033	29c Turk's cap lily	.50	.20
2682	A2034	29c Dutchman's breeches	.50	.20
2683	A2035	29c Trumpet honeysuckle	.50	.20
2684	A2036	29c Jacob's ladder	.50	.20
2685	A2037	29c Plains prickly pear	.50	.20
2686	A2038	29c Moss campion	.50	.20
2687	A2039	29c Bearberry	.50	.20
2688	A2040	29c Mexican hat	.50	.20
2689	A2041	29c Harebell	.50	.20
2690	A2042	29c Desert five spot	.50	.20
2691	A2043	29c Smooth Solomon's seal	.50	.20
2692	A2044	29c Red maids	.50	.20
2693	A2045	29c Yellow skunk cabbage	.50	.20
2694	A2046	29c Rue anemone	.50	.20
2695	A2047	29c Standing cypress	.50	.20
2696	A2048	29c Wild flax	.50	.20
a.		Pane of 50, #2647-2696	25.00	—

Sheet margin selvage contains a diagram of the plate layout with each pane's position shaded in gray.

WORLD WAR II

A2049

Designed by William H. Bond.

Designs and events of 1942: a, B-25's take off to raid Tokyo, Apr. 18. b, Ration coupons (Food and other commodities rationed). c, Divebomber and deck crewman (US wins Battle of the Coral Sea, May). d, Prisoners of war (Corregidor falls to Japanese, May 6). e, Dutch Harbor buildings on fire (Japan invades Aleutian Islands, June). f, Headphones, coded message (Allies decipher secret enemy codes). g, Yorktown lost, U.S. wins at Midway. h, Woman with drill (Millions of women join war effort). i, Marines land on Guadalcanal, Aug. 7. j, Tank in desert (Allies land in North Africa, Nov.).

Central label is the size of 15 stamps and shows world map, extent of axis control.

Illustration reduced.

LITHOGRAPHED & ENGRAVED
Plates of 80 in four panes of 20 each

1992, Aug. 17		Tagged	Perf. 11	
2697	A2049	Block of 10	5.25	4.50
		Pane of 20	10.50	—
a.-j.		29c any single	.50	.30
k.		Red (litho.) omitted	10,000.	

No. 2697 has selvage at left and right and either top or bottom.

Dorothy
Parker — A2050

Von Karman
(1881-1963),
Rocket
Scientist — A2051

LITERARY ARTS SERIES
Designed by Greg Rudd.

Printed by J.W. Fergusson & Sons for Stamp Venturers.

PHOTOGRAVURE
Plates of 200 in four panes of 50

1992, Aug. 22		Tagged	Perf. 11	
2698	A2050	29c multicolored	.50	.20
		P# block of 4, 5# + S	2.50	—
		Zip block of 4	2.25	—

THEODORE VON KARMAN
Designed by Chris Calle.

Printed by J.W. Fergusson & Sons for Stamp Venturers.

PHOTOGRAVURE
Plates of 200 in four panes of 50

1992, Aug. 31		Tagged	Perf. 11	
2699	A2051	29c multicolored	.50	.20
		P# block of 4, 4# + S	2.50	—
		Zip block of 4	2.25	—

WILDFLOWERS
A1999-A2048

MINERALS

Azurite — A2052

Copper — A2053

Variscite — A2054

Wulfenite — A2055

Designed by Len Buckley.

LITHOGRAPHED & ENGRAVED
Sheets of 160 in four panes of 40.

1992, Sept. 17	Tagged	Perf. 11	
2700 A2052 29c multicolored		.50	.20
2701 A2053 29c multicolored		.50	.20
2702 A2054 29c multicolored		.50	.20
2703 A2055 29c multicolored		.50	.20
a.	Block or strip of 4, #2700-2703	2.00	1.75
	P# block of 4, 6#	2.50	
	Zip block of 4	2.25	—
b.	As "a," silver (litho.) omitted	8,500.	
c.	As "a," red (litho.) omitted	—	
d.	As "a," silver omitted on two stamps	—	

JUAN RODRIGUEZ CABRILLO

Cabrillo (d. 1543), Ship, Map of
San Diego Bay Area — A2056

Designed by Ren Wicks.

Printed by The Press and J.W. Fergusson & Sons for Stamp Venturers.

LITHOGRAPHED & ENGRAVED
Plates of 200 in four panes of 50

1992, Sept. 28	Tagged	Perf. 11	
2704 A2056 29c multicolored		.50	.20
	P# block of 4, 7# + 2 "S"s	2.50	—
	Zip, Olympic block of 4	2.25	—
a.	Black (engr.) omitted	4,250.	

WILD ANIMALS

Giraffe — A2057

Giant Panda — A2058

Flamingo — A2059

King Penguins — A2060

White Bengal Tiger — A2061

Designed by Robert Giusti.

Printed by J.W. Fergusson & Sons for Stamp Venturers.

PHOTOGRAVURE
BOOKLET STAMPS

1992, Oct. 1	Tagged	Perf. 11 Horiz.	
2705 A2057 29c multicolored		.50	.20
2706 A2058 29c multicolored		.50	.20
2707 A2059 29c multicolored		.50	.20
2708 A2060 29c multicolored		.50	.20
2709 A2061 29c multicolored		.50	.20
a.	Booklet pane of 5, #2705-2709	2.50	2.00
b.	As "a," imperf.	3,000.	

CHRISTMAS

Madonna and Child, by Giovanni Bellini — A2062

A2063   A2064

A2065   A2066

Designed by Bradbury Thompson (#2710) and Lou Nolan (#2711-2719).

Printed by the Bureau of Engraving and Printing, Ashton-Potter America, Inc. (#2711-2714), the Multi-Color Corporation for American Bank Note Company (#2715-2718), and Avery Dennison (#2719).

LITHOGRAPHED & ENGRAVED
Sheets of 300 in six panes of 50 (#2710, 2714a)

1992	Tagged	Perf. 11½x11	
2710 A2062 29c multicolored, Oct. 22		.50	.20
	P# block of 4, 5#	2.50	
	Zip, copyright block of 4	2.25	—
a.	Booklet pane of 10	5.25	3.50

LITHOGRAPHED

2711 A2063 29c multicolored, Oct. 22		.50	.20
2712 A2064 29c multicolored, Oct. 22		.50	.20
2713 A2065 29c multicolored, Oct. 22		.50	.20
2714 A2066 29c multicolored, Oct. 22		.50	.20
a.	Block of 4, #2711-2714	2.00	1.10
	P# block of 4, 5# + P	2.50	
	Zip, copyright block of 6	3.25	—

Booklet Stamps
PHOTOGRAVURE
Perf. 11 on 2 or 3 Sides

2715 A2063 29c multicolored, Oct. 22		.50	.20
2716 A2064 29c multicolored, Oct. 22		.50	.20
2717 A2065 29c multicolored, Oct. 22		.50	.20
2718 A2066 29c multicolored, Oct. 22		.50	.20
a.	Booklet pane of 4, #2715-2718	2.25	1.25
b.	As "a," imperf. horiz.	—	
c.	As "a," imperf.	—	

Self-Adhesive
Die Cut

2719 A2064 29c multicolored, Oct. 28		.60	.20
a.	Booklet pane of 18	11.00	

"Greetings" is 27mm long on Nos. 2711-2714, 25mm long on Nos. 2715-2718 and 21½mm long on No. 2719. Nos. 2715-2719 differ in color from Nos. 2711-2714.

CHINESE NEW YEAR

Year of the Rooster — A2067

Designed by Clarence Lee.

Printed by the American Bank Note Co.

LITHOGRAPHED & ENGRAVED
Panes of 20

1992, Dec. 30	Tagged	Perf. 11	
2720 A2067 29c multicolored		.50	.20
	P# block of 4, 5#+A	2.00	
	Pane of 20	10.00	—

AMERICAN MUSIC SERIES

Elvis Presley — A2068

Oklahoma! A2069

Hank Williams — A2070

Elvis Presley — A2071

Bill Haley — A2072

Clyde McPhatter
A2073

Ritchie
Valens — A2074

Otis
Redding — A2075

Buddy
Holly — A2076

Dinah Washington
A2077

Designed by Mark Stutzman (#2721, 2724-2725, 2727, 2729, 2731-2732, 2734, 2736), Wilson McLean (#2722), Richard Waldrep (#2723), John Berkey (#2726, 2728, 2730, 2733, 2735, 2737).

Printed by Stamp Venturers (#2723-2730), Multi-color Corp. (#2731-2737).

PHOTOGRAVURE
Panes of 40, Panes of 35 (#2724-2730)

1993		Tagged		Perf. 11	
2721	A2068	29c **multicolored**, *Jan. 8*		.50	.20
		P# block of 4, 5#		2.50	—
		Zip, copyright block of 4		2.25	—
		Perf. 10			
2722	A2069	29c **multicolored**, *Mar. 30*		.50	.20
		P# block of 4, 4#+S		2.50	—
		Zip block of 4		2.25	—
2723	A2070	29c **multicolored**, *June 9*		.50	.20
		P# block of 4, 5#+S		2.50	—
		Zip block of 4		2.25	—
		Perf. 11.2x11.5			
2723A	A2070	29c **multicolored**, *June 9*		22.50	—
		P# block of 4, 5#+S		140.00	—
		Zip block of 4		100.00	—

1993, June 16				Perf. 10	
2724	A2071	29c **multicolored**		.60	.20
2725	A2072	29c **multicolored**		.60	.20
2726	A2073	29c **multicolored**		.60	.20
2727	A2074	29c **multicolored**		.60	.20
2728	A2075	29c **multicolored**		.60	.20
2729	A2076	29c **multicolored**		.60	.20
2730	A2077	29c **multicolored**		.60	.20
a.		Vert. strip of 7, #2724-2730		4.25	
		Horiz. P# block of 10, 2 sets of 6P#+S, + top label		6.50	—
		Vert. P# block of 8, 6#+S		5.00	—
		Pane of 35		21.50	—

No. 2730a with Nos. 2724-2730 in numerical sequence cannot be obtained from the pane of 35.

Booklet Stamps
Perf. 11 Horiz.

2731	A2071	29c **multicolored**		.50	.20
2732	A2072	29c **multicolored**		.50	.20
2733	A2073	29c **multicolored**		.50	.20
2734	A2074	29c **multicolored**		.50	.20
2735	A2075	29c **multicolored**		.50	.20
2736	A2076	29c **multicolored**		.50	.20
2737	A2077	29c **multicolored**		.50	.20
a.		Booklet pane, 2 #2731, 1 each #2732-2737		4.25	2.25
b.		Booklet pane, #2731, 2735-2737 + tab		2.25	1.50

Nos. 2731-2737 have smaller design sizes, brighter colors and shorter inscriptions than Nos. 2724-2730, as well as framelines around the designs and other subtle design differences.
No. 2737b without tab is indistinguishable from broken No. 2737a.
See Nos. 2769, 2771, 2775 and designs A2112-A2117.

SPACE FANTASY

A2086

A2087

A2088

A2089

A2090

Designed by Stephen Hickman.

PHOTOGRAVURE
BOOKLET STAMPS

1993, Jan. 25		Tagged		Perf. 11 Vert.	
2741	A2086	29c **multicolored**		.50	.20
2742	A2087	29c **multicolored**		.50	.20
2743	A2088	29c **multicolored**		.50	.20
2744	A2089	29c **multicolored**		.50	.20
2745	A2090	29c **multicolored**		.50	.20
a.		Booklet pane of 5, #2741-2745		2.50	2.25

BLACK HERITAGE SERIES

Percy Lavon Julian (1899-1975),
Chemist — A2091

Designed by Higgins Bond.

LITHOGRAPHED & ENGRAVED
Panes of 50

1993, Jan. 29		Tagged		Perf. 11	
2746	A2091	29c **multicolored**		.50	.20
		P# block of 4, 7#		2.50	—
		Zip block of 4		2.25	—

OREGON TRAIL

A2092

Designed by Jack Rosenthal.

LITHOGRAPHED & ENGRAVED
Panes of 50

1993, Feb. 12		Tagged		Perf. 11	
2747	A2092	29c **multicolored**		.50	.20
		P# block of 4, 6#		2.50	—
		Zip block of 4		2.25	—
a.		Tagging omitted		15.00	

WORLD UNIVERSITY GAMES

A2093

Designed by David Buck.

PHOTOGRAVURE
Panes of 50

1993, Feb. 25		Tagged		Perf. 11	
2748	A2093	29c **multicolored**		.50	.20
		P# block of 4, 5#		2.50	—
		Zip block of 4		2.25	—

GRACE KELLY (1929-1982)

Actress, Princess of
Monaco — A2094

Designed by Czeslaw Slania.

Printed by Stamp Venturers.

ENGRAVED
Panes of 50

1993, Mar. 24		Tagged		Perf. 11	
2749	A2094	29c **blue**		.50	.20
		P# block of 4, 1# +S		2.50	—
		Zip block of 4		2.25	—

See Monaco No. 1851.

CIRCUS

Clown — A2095

Ringmaster — A2096

Trapeze Artist — A2097

Elephant — A2098

Designed by Steve McCracken.

Printed by Ashton Potter America.

LITHOGRAPHED
Panes of 40

1993, Apr. 6	Tagged	Perf. 11	
2750 A2095 29c **multicolored**		.55	.20
2751 A2096 29c **multicolored**		.55	.20
2752 A2097 29c **multicolored**		.55	.20
2753 A2098 29c **multicolored**		.55	.20
a.	Block of 4, #2750-2753	2.25	1.75
	P# block of 6, 5#+P	4.50	—
	Zip block of 6	3.50	—

Plate and zip blocks of 6 and copyright blocks of 9 contain one #2753a with continuous design (complete spotlight).

CHEROKEE STRIP LAND RUN, CENTENNIAL

A2099

Designed by Harold T. Holden.

Printed by American Bank Note. Co.

LITHOGRAPHED & ENGRAVED
Panes of 20

1993, Apr. 17	Tagged	Perf. 11	
2754 A2099 29c **multicolored**		.50	.20
	P# block of 4, 5#+A	2.00	—
	Pane of 20	10.00	—

Zip and Copyright inscriptions are located in selvage opposite middle row of sheet.

DEAN ACHESON (1893-1971)

 Secretary of State — A2100

Designed by Christopher Calle.

Printed by Stamp Venturers.

ENGRAVED
Sheets of 300 in six panes of 50

1993, Apr. 21	Tagged	Perf. 11	
2755 A2100 29c **greenish gray**		.50	.20
	P# block of 4, 1#+S	2.50	—
	Zip block of 4	2.25	—

SPORTING HORSES

Steeplechase
A2101

Thoroughbred
Racing — A2102

Harness
Racing — A2103

Polo — A2104

Designed by Michael Dudash.

Printed by Stamp Venturers.

LITHOGRAPHED & ENGRAVED
Panes of 40

1993, May 1	Tagged	Perf. 11x11½	
2756 A2101 29c **multicolored**		.50	.20
2757 A2102 29c **multicolored**		.50	.20
2758 A2103 29c **multicolored**		.50	.20
2759 A2104 29c **multicolored**		.50	.20
a.	Block of 4, #2756-2759	2.00	1.75

	P# block of 4, 5#+S	2.50	—
	Zip block of 4	2.25	—
b.	As "a," black (engr.) omitted	1,250.	

GARDEN FLOWERS

Hyacinth — A2105

Daffodil — A2106

Tulip — A2107

Iris — A2108

Lilac — A2109

Designed by Ned Seidler.

LITHOGRAPHED & ENGRAVED
BOOKLET STAMPS

1993, May 15	Tagged	Perf. 11 Vert.	
2760 A2105 29c **multicolored**		.50	.20
2761 A2106 29c **multicolored**		.50	.20
2762 A2107 29c **multicolored**		.50	.20
2763 A2108 29c **multicolored**		.50	.20
2764 A2109 29c **multicolored**		.50	.20
a.	Booklet pane of 5, #2760-2764	2.50	2.00
b.	As "a," black (engr.) omitted	300.00	
c.	As "a," imperf.	2,500.	

WORLD WAR II

A2110

Designed by William H. Bond.

Designs and events of 1943: a, Destroyers (Allied forces battle German U-boats). b, Military medics treat the wounded. c, Amphibious landing craft on beach (Sicily attacked by Allied forces, July). d, B-24s hit Ploesti refineries, August. e, V-mail delivers letters from home. f, PT boat (Italy invaded by Allies, Sept.).

g, Nos. WS7, WS8, savings bonds, (Bonds and stamps help war effort). h, "Willie and Joe" keep spirits high. i, Banner in window (Gold Stars mark World War II losses). j, Marines assault Tarawa, Nov.

Central label is the size of 15 stamps and shows world map with extent of Axis control and Allied operations.

Illustration reduced.

LITHOGRAPHED & ENGRAVED
Plates of 80 in four panes of 20 each

1993, May 31	Tagged	Perf. 11	
2765 A2110	Block of 10	5.25	4.50
	Pane of 20	10.50	—
a.-j.	29c any single	.50	.30

No. 2765 has salvage at left and right and either top or bottom.

JOE LOUIS (1914-1981)

A2111

Designed by Thomas Blackshear.

LITHOGRAPHED & ENGRAVED
Plates of 200 in four panes of 50

1993, June 22	Tagged	Perf. 11	
2766 A2111	29c multicolored	.50	.20
	P# block of 4, 5#	2.50	—
	Zip block of 4	2.25	—

AMERICAN MUSIC SERIES
Oklahoma! Type and

Show Boat — A2112

Porgy & Bess — A2113

My Fair Lady — A2114

Designed by Wilson McLean.

Printed by Multi-Color Corp.

BOOKLET STAMPS
PHOTOGRAVURE
Perf. 11 Horiz. on 1 or 2 Sides

1993, July 14		Tagged	
2767 A2112	29c multicolored	.50	.20
2768 A2113	29c multicolored	.50	.20
2769 A2069	29c multicolored	.50	.20
2770 A2114	29c multicolored	.50	.20
a.	Booklet pane of 4, #2767-2770	2.50	2.00

No. 2769 has smaller design size, brighter colors and shorter inscription than No. 2722, as well as a frameline around the design and other subtle design differences.

AMERICAN MUSIC SERIES
Hank Williams Type and

Patsy Cline — A2115

The Carter Family — A2116

Bob Wills — A2117

Designed by Richard Waldrep.

Printed by Stamp Venturers (#2771-2774) and American Bank Note Co. (#2775-2778).

PHOTOGRAVURE
Panes of 20

1993, Sept. 25		Tagged	Perf. 10
2771 A2070	29c multicolored	.55	.20
2772 A2115	29c multicolored	.55	.20
2773 A2116	29c multicolored	.55	.20
2774 A2117	29c multicolored	.55	.20
a.	Block or horiz. strip of 4, #2771-2774	2.20	1.75
	Horiz. P# block of 8, 2 sets of 6#+S + top label	4.50	—
	P# block of 4, 6#+S	2.20	—
	Pane of 20	10.75	—

Zip and Copyright inscriptions are located in selvage opposite middle row of sheet.

Booklet Stamps
Perf. 11 Horiz. on one or two sides
With Black Frameline

2775 A2070	29c multicolored	.50	.20
2776 A2116	29c multicolored	.50	.20
2777 A2115	29c multicolored	.50	.20
2778 A2117	29c multicolored	.50	.20
a.	Booklet pane of 4, #2775-2778	2.50	2.00
b.	As "a," imperf	—	

Inscription at left measures 27 ½mm on No. 2723, 27mm on No. 2771 and 22mm on No. 2775. No. 2723 shows only two tuning keys on guitar, while No. 2771 shows those two and parts of two others.

NATIONAL POSTAL MUSEUM

Independence Hall, Benjamin Franklin, Printing Press, Colonial Post Rider — A2118

Pony Express Rider, Civil War Soldier, Concord Stagecoach A2119

JN-4H Biplane, Charles Lindbergh, Railway Mail Car, 1931 Model A Ford Mail Truck — A2120

California Gold Rush Miner's Letter, Nos. 39, 295, C3a, C13, Barcode and Circular Date Stamp — A2121

Designed by Richard Schlecht.

Printed by American Bank Note Co.

LITHOGRAPHED AND ENGRAVED

1993, July 30	Tagged	Perf. 11	
2779 A2118	29c multicolored	.50	.20
2780 A2119	29c multicolored	.50	.20
2781 A2120	29c multicolored	.50	.20
2782 A2121	29c multicolored	.50	.20
a.	Block or strip of 4, #2779-2782	2.00	1.75
	P# block of 4, 7#+A	2.00	—
	Pane of 20	10.00	—
b.	As "a," engr. maroon (USA/29) and black ("My dear...") omitted	—	
c.	As "a," imperf	3,500.	

Zip and Copyright inscriptions are located in selvage opposite middle row of sheet.

AMERICAN SIGN LANGUAGE

A2122

A2123

Designed by Chris Calle.

Printed by Stamp Venturers.

PHOTOGRAVURE

1993, Sept. 20	Tagged	Perf. 11½	
2783 A2122	29c multicolored	.50	.20
2784 A2123	29c multicolored	.50	.20
a.	Pair, #2783-2784	1.00	.65
	P# block of 4, 4#+S	2.00	—
	Pane of 20	10.00	—

Zip and Copyright inscriptions are located in selvage opposite middle row of sheet.

CLASSIC BOOKS

A2124

A2125

A2126

A2127

Designed by Jim Lamb.

Printed by American Bank Note Co.
Designs: No. 2785, Rebecca of Sunnybrook Farm, by Kate
Douglas Wiggin. No. 2786, Little House on the Prairie, by Laura
Ingalls Wilder. No. 2787, The Adventures of Huckleberry Finn,
by Mark Twain. No. 2788, Little Women, by Louisa May Alcott.

LITHOGRAPHED & ENGRAVED
Panes of 40

1993, Oct. 23		Tagged	**Perf. 11**	
2785	A2124	29c **multicolored**	.50	.20
2786	A2125	29c **multicolored**	.50	.20
2787	A2126	29c **multicolored**	.50	.20
2788	A2127	29c **multicolored**	.50	.20
a.		Block or horiz. strip of 4, #2785-2788	2.00	1.75
		P# block of 4, 5#+A	4.75	—
		Zip block of 4	2.25	—
b.		As "a," imperf	3,000.	

CHRISTMAS

Madonna and Child in a
Landscape, by Giovanni Battista
Cima — A2128

Jack-in-the-Box
A2129

Snowman
A2131

Red-Nosed
Reindeer
A2130

Toy Soldier
Blowing Horn
A2132

Designed by Bradbury Thompson (#2789-2790), Peter Good
(#2791-2803).

Printed by Bureau of Engraving and Printing (#2789, 2791-
2798), KCS Industries (#2790), Avery Dennison (#2799-2803).

LITHOGRAPHED & ENGRAVED
Panes of 50 (#2789, 2791-2794)

1993, Oct. 21		Tagged	**Perf. 11**	
2789	A2128	29c **multicolored**	.50	.20
		P# block of 4, 4#	2.50	—
		Zip, copyright block of 4	2.25	—

Booklet Stamp
Size: 18x25mm

Perf. 11½x11 on 2 or 3 Sides

2790	A2128	29c **multicolored**	.50	.20
a.		Booklet pane of 4	2.25	1.75
b.		Imperf., pair	—	
c.		As "a," imperf.	—	

Nos. 2789-2790 have numerous design differences.

1993

PHOTOGRAVURE
Perf. 11½

2791	A2129	29c **multicolored**, *Oct. 21*	.50	.20
2792	A2130	29c **multicolored**, *Oct. 21*	.50	.20
2793	A2131	29c **multicolored**, *Oct. 21*	.50	.20
2794	A2132	29c **multicolored**, *Oct. 21*	.50	.20
a.		Block or strip of 4, #2791-2794	2.00	1.75
		P# block of 4, 6#	2.75	—
		Zip, copyright block of 4	2.25	—

Snowman on Nos. 2793, 2799 has three buttons and seven
snowflakes beneath nose (placement differs on both stamps).
No. 2796 has two buttons and five snowflakes beneath nose.
No. 2803 has two orange buttons and four snowflakes beneath
nose.

Booklet Stamps
Size: 18x21mm

Perf. 11x10 on 2 or 3 Sides

2795	A2132	29c **multicolored**, *Oct. 21*	.50	.20
2796	A2131	29c **multicolored**, *Oct. 21*	.50	.20
2797	A2130	29c **multicolored**, *Oct. 21*	.50	.20
2798	A2129	29c **multicolored**, *Oct. 21*	.50	.20
a.		Booklet pane, 3 each #2795-2796, 2 each #2797-2798	5.00	4.00
b.		Booklet pane, 3 each #2797-2798, 2 each #2795-2796	5.00	4.00
c.		Block of 4, #2795-2798	2.00	1.75

Self-Adhesive
Size: 19½x26½mm

Die Cut

2799	A2131	29c **multicolored**, *Oct. 28*	.50	.20
a.		Coil with plate # V1111111	—	3.50
		P# strip of 5, 1 each #2799-2801, 2 #2802, P#V1111111	5.50	
		P# strip of 8, 2 each #2799-2802, P#V1111111	7.00	
2800	A2132	29c **multicolored**, *Oct. 28*	.50	.20
2801	A2129	29c **multicolored**, *Oct. 28*	.50	.20
2802	A2130	29c **multicolored**, *Oct. 28*	.50	.20
a.		Booklet pane, 3 each #2799-2802	7.00	
b.		Block of 4, #2799-2802	2.00	

Except for No. 2799a with plate number, coil stamps are
indistinguishable from booklet stamps once they are removed
from the backing paper.

Size: 17x20mm

2803	A2131	29c **multicolored**, *Oct. 28*	.50	.20
a.		Booklet pane of 18	10.00	

Snowman on Nos. 2793, 2799 has three buttons and seven
snowflakes beneath nose (placement differs on both stamps).
No. 2796 has two buttons and five snowflakes beneath nose.
No. 2803 has two orange buttons and four snowflakes beneath
nose.

MARIANA ISLANDS

A2133

Designed by Herb Kane.

LITHOGRAPHED AND ENGRAVED

1993, Nov. 4		Tagged	**Perf. 11**	
2804	A2133	29c **multicolored**	.50	.20
		P# block of 4, 6#	2.00	—
		Pane of 20	10.00	—

Zip and copyright inscriptions are located in selvage opposite
middle row of sheet.

COLUMBUS' LANDING IN PUERTO RICO, 500th
ANNIVERSARY

A2134

Designed by Richard Schlecht.

Printed by Stamp Venturers.

PHOTOGRAVURE
Panes of 50

1993, Nov. 19		Tagged	**Perf. 11.2**	
2805	A2134	29c **multicolored**	.50	.20
		P# block of 4, 5#+S	2.50	—
		Zip block of 4	2.25	—

AIDS AWARENESS

A2135

Designed by Tom Mann.
Printed by Stamp Venturers.

PHOTOGRAVURE
Panes of 50

1993, Dec. 1		Tagged	**Perf. 11.2**	
2806	A2135	29c **black & red**	.50	.20
		P# block of 4, 3#+S	2.50	—
		Zip, copyright block of 6	3.25	—
a.		Perf. 11 vert. on 1 or 2 sides, from bklt. pane	.50	.20
b.		As "a," booklet pane of 5	2.50	2.00

WINTER OLYMPICS

Slalom — A2136

Luge — A2137

Ice
Dancing — A2138

Cross-Country
Skiing — A2139

Ice Hockey — A2140

Designed by Lon Busch.
Printed by Ashton-Potter.

LITHOGRAPHED
Sheets of 120 in six panes of 20

1994, Jan. 6		Tagged	**Perf. 11.2**	
2807	A2136	29c **multicolored**	.50	.20
2808	A2137	29c **multicolored**	.50	.20
2809	A2138	29c **multicolored**	.50	.20
2810	A2139	29c **multicolored**	.50	.20
2811	A2140	29c **multicolored**	.50	.20
a.		Strip of 5, #2807-2811	2.50	2.25
		Horiz. P# block of 10, 2 sets of 4#+P and inscriptions	5.00	—
		Horiz. P# block of 10, 2 sets of 4#+P	5.00	—
		Pane of 20	10.00	—

EDWARD R. MURROW, JOURNALIST (1908-65)

A2141

Designed by Chris Calle.

ENGRAVED
Panes of 50

1994, Jan. 21		Tagged	Perf. 11.2	
2812	A2141	29c brown	.50	.20
		P# block of 4, 1#	2.50	

LOVE

A2142

A2143

A2144

Designed by Peter Goode (#2813), Lon Busch (#2814-2815).

Printed by Banknote Corp. of America (#2813), American Banknote Co. (#2814) and Bureau of Engraving and Printing (#2814C, 2815).

Booklet Stamps
LITHOGRAPHED & ENGRAVED

1994		Tagged	Die Cut	
		Self-adhesive		
2813	A2142	29c multicolored, Jan. 27	.50	.20
a.		Booklet pane of 18	11.00	
b.		Coil with plate # B1	—	3.50
		P# strip of 5, #B1	6.00	

Except for No. 2813b with plate number, coil stamps are indistinguishable from booklet stamps once they are removed from the backing paper.

PHOTOGRAVURE
Perf. 10.9x11.1

2814	A2143	29c multicolored, Feb. 14	.50	.20
a.		Booklet pane of 10	5.50	3.50
b.		As "a," imperf	—	
e.		Horiz. pair, imperf between	—	

LITHOGRAPHED & ENGRAVED
Sheets of 300 in six panes of 50
Tagged
Perf. 11.1

2814C	A2143	29c multicolored, June 11	.50	.20
		P# block of 4, 5#	2.50	

Some plate blocks contain plate position diagram.
Size of No. 2814C is 20x28mm. No. 2814 is 18x24½mm.

PHOTOGRAVURE & ENGRAVED
Sheet of 300 in six panes of 50
Perf. 11.2

2815	A2144	52c multicolored, Feb. 14	1.00	.20
		P# block of 4, 5#	5.00	—
		P# block of 10, 2 sets of 5#, plate diagram, copyright and pane price inscriptions	11.00	

BLACK HERITAGE SERIES

Dr. Allison Davis (1902-83), Social Anthropologist, Educator — A2145

Designed by Chris Calle.

Printed by Stamp Venturers.

ENGRAVED

1994, Feb. 1		Tagged	Perf. 11.2	
2816	A2145	29c red brown & brown	.50	.20
		P# block of 4, 1#+S	2.00	—
		Pane of 20	10.00	—

CHINESE NEW YEAR

Year of the Dog — A2146

Designed by Clarence Lee.

Printed by J.W. Fergusson & Sons for Stamp Venturers.

PHOTOGRAVURE
Sheets of 180 in nine panes of 20

1994, Feb. 5		Tagged	Perf. 11.2	
2817	A2146	29c multicolored	.55	.20
		P# block of 4, 4#+S	2.20	—
		Pane of 20	11.00	—

BUFFALO SOLDIERS

A2147

Designed by Mort Kuntsler.

Printed by Stamp Venturers.

LITHOGRAPHED & ENGRAVED
Plates of 180 in nine panes of 20

1994, Apr. 22		Tagged	Perf. 11.5x11.2	
2818	A2147	29c multicolored	.50	—
		P# block of 4, 5#+S	2.00	—
		Pane of 20	10.00	—

Some plate blocks contain either plate position diagram or pane price inscription.

SILENT SCREEN STARS

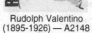

Rudolph Valentino (1895-1926) — A2148

Clara Bow (1905-65) — A2149

Charlie Chaplin (1889-1977) — A2150

Lon Chaney (1883-1930) — A2151

John Gilbert (1895-1936) — A2152

Zasu Pitts (1898-1963) — A2153

Harold Lloyd (1894-1971) — A2154

Keystone Cops — A2155

Theda Bara (1885-1955) — A2156

Buster Keaton (1895-1966) — A2157

Designed by Al Hirschfeld.

LITHOGRAPHED & ENGRAVED
Plates of 160 in four panes of 40

1994, Apr. 27		Tagged	Perf. 11.2	
2819	A2148	29c red, black & bright violet	.50	.20
2820	A2149	29c red, black & bright violet	.50	.20
2821	A2150	29c red, black & bright violet	.50	.20
2822	A2151	29c red, black & bright violet	.50	.20
2823	A2152	29c red, black & bright violet	.50	.20
2824	A2153	29c red, black & bright violet	.50	.20
2825	A2154	29c red, black & bright violet	.50	.20
2826	A2155	29c red, black & bright violet	.50	.20
2827	A2156	29c red, black & bright violet	.50	.20
2828	A2157	29c red, black & bright violet	.50	.20
a.		Block of 10, #2819-2828	5.00	4.00
		P# block of 10, 4#, plate diagram and copyright inscription	6.00	—
		Half pane of 20	11.00	—
b.		As "a," black (litho.) omitted	—	
c.		As "a," blk, red & brt vio (litho.) omitted	—	

GARDEN FLOWERS

Lily — A2158

Zinnia — A2159

Gladiola — A2160

Marigold — A2161

Rose — A2162

Designed by Ned Seidler.

LITHOGRAPHED & ENGRAVED

1994, Apr. 28		**Tagged**		**Perf. 10.9 Vert.**	
Booklet Stamps					
2829	A2158	29c	**multicolored**	.50	.20
2830	A2159	29c	**multicolored**	.50	.20
2831	A2160	29c	**multicolored**	.50	.20
2832	A2161	29c	**multicolored**	.50	.20
2833	A2162	29c	**multicolored**	.50	.20
a.		Booklet pane of 5, #2829-2833		2.50	—
b.		As "a," imperf.		2,500.	
c.		As "a," black (engr.) omitted		350.00	

1994 WORLD CUP SOCCER CHAMPIONSHIPS

A2163

A2164

A2165

Designed by Michael Dudash.

Printed by J.W. Fergusson & Sons for Stamp Venturers. Design: 40c, Soccer player, diff.

PHOTOGRAVURE
Plates of 180 in nine panes of 20

1994, May 26		**Tagged**		**Perf. 11.1**	
2834	A2163	29c	**multicolored**	.50	.20
		P# block of 4, 4#+S		2.00	—
		Pane of 20		10.00	—
2835	A2163	40c	**multicolored**	.80	.20
		P# block of 4, 4#+S		3.20	—
		Pane of 20		16.00	—
2836	A2164	50c	**multicolored**	1.00	.20
		P# block of 4, 4#+S		4.00	—
		Pane of 20		20.00	—

Plate position diagram, copyright inscription and pane price inscription are located in selvage opposite the three inner columns of the sheet. Some plate blocks will contain either plate position diagram or pane price inscription.

Souvenir Sheet

2837	A2165	Sheet of 3, #a.-c.	2.50	2.00

Nos. 2834-2836 are printed on phosphor-coated paper while Nos. 2837a (29c), 2837b (40c), 2837c (50c) are block tagged. No. 2837c has a portion of the yellow map in the LR corner.

WORLD WAR II

A2166

Designed by William H. Bond.

Designs and events of 1944: a, Allied forces retake New Guinea. b, P-51s escort B-17s on bombing raids. c, Troops running from landing craft (Allies in Normandy, D-Day, June 6). d, Airborne units spearhead attacks. e, Officer at periscope (Submarines shorten war in Pacific). f, Parade (Allies free Rome, June 4; Paris, Aug. 25).

g, Soldier firing flamethrower (US troops clear Saipan bunkers). h, Red Ball Express speeds vital supplies. i, Battleship firing main battery (Battle for Leyte Gulf, Oct. 23-26). j, Soldiers in snow (Bastogne and Battle of the Bulge, Dec.).

Central label is size of 15 stamps and shows world map with extent of Axis control and Allied operations.
Illustration reduced.

LITHOGRAPHED & ENGRAVED
Plates of eight subjects in four panes of 2 each

1994, June 6		**Tagged**		**Perf. 10.9**
2838	A2166	Block of 10	6.00	4.50
		Pane of 20	12.00	—
a.-j.		29c any single	.60	.30

No. 2838 has selvage at left and right and either top or bottom.

NORMAN ROCKWELL

A2167

A2168

Designed by Richard Sheaff based on Rockwell's works.

LITHOGRAPHED & ENGRAVED
Sheets of 200 in four panes of 50

1994, July 1		**Tagged**		**Perf. 10.9x11.1**	
2839	A2167	29c	**multicolored**	.50	.20
		P# block of 4, 5#		2.50	—

Souvenir Sheet
LITHOGRAPHED

2840	A2168	Sheet of 4	4.00	2.75
a.		50c Freedom From Want	1.00	.65
b.		50c Freedom From Fear	1.00	.65
c.		50c Freedom of Speech	1.00	.65
d.		50c Freedom of Worship	1.00	.65

Panes of No. 2839 contain two plate blocks, one containing a plate position diagram.

Moon Landing, 25th Anniv.

A2169 First Moon Landing, 1969

25th Anniversary First Moon Landing, 1969 A2170

Designed by Paul and Chris Calle.

Printed by Stamp Venturers (#2841) and Banknote Corp. of America (#2842).

Miniature Sheet
LITHOGRAPHED

1994, July 20		**Tagged**	**Perf. 11.2x11.1**
2841	A2169	29c Sheet of 12	7.50	—
a.		Single stamp	.60	.60

LITHOGRAPHED & ENGRAVED
Sheets of 120 in six panes of 20
Perf. 10.7x11.1

2842	A2170	$9.95	**multicolored**	17.50	7.50
		P# block of 4, 5#+B		70.00	—

Some plate blocks of #2842 contain either copyright inscription or pane price inscription.

LOCOMOTIVES

Hudson's General — A2171

McQueen's
Jupiter — A2172

Eddy's No.
242 — A2173

Ely's No.
10 — A2174

Buchanan's No.
999 — A2175

Designed by Richard Leech.

Printed by J.W. Ferguson & Sons for Stamp Venturers.

PHOTOGRAVURE

1994, July 28	**Tagged**	*Perf. 11 Horiz.*
Booklet Stamps		

2843 A2171 29c **multicolored**		.50	.20
2844 A2172 29c **multicolored**		.50	.20
2845 A2173 29c **multicolored**		.50	.20
2846 A2174 29c **multicolored**		.50	.20
2847 A2175 29c **multicolored**		.50	.20
a.	Booklet pane of 5, #2843-2847	2.50	*2.00*
b.	As "a," imperf.	—	

GEORGE MEANY, LABOR LEADER (1894-1980)

A2176   Labor Leader

Designed by Chris Calle.

ENGRAVED
Sheets of 200 in four panes of 50

1994, Aug. 16	**Tagged**	*Perf. 11.1x11*
2848 A2176 29c **blue**		.50	.20
	P# block of 4, 1#	2.50	—

Panes of No. 2848 contain two plate blocks, one containing a plate position diagram.

AMERICAN MUSIC SERIES

Al Jolson (1886-
1950)
A2177

Bing Crosby (1904-
77) — A2178

Ethel Waters (1896-
1977)
A2179

Nat "King" Cole
(1919-65) — A2180

Ethel Merman
(1908-84) — A2181

Bessie Smith
(1894-1937)
A2182

Muddy Waters
(1915-83) — A2183

Billie Holiday
(1915-59) — A2184

Robert Johnson
(1911-38) — A2185

Jimmy Rushing
(1902-72) — A2186

"Ma" Rainey (1886-
1939)
A2187

Mildred Bailey
(1907-51) — A2188

Howlin' Wolf (1910-
76) — A2189

Designed by Chris Payne (#2849-2853), Howard Koslow (#2854, 2856, 2858, 2860), Julian Allen (#2855, 2857, 2859, 2861).

Printed by J.W. Fergusson & Sons for Stamp Venturers (#2849-2853), Manhardt-Alexander for Ashton-Potter (USA) Ltd. (#2854-2861).

PHOTOGRAVURE
Plates of 180 in nine panes of 20, Plates of 210 in six panes of 35 (#2854-2861)

1994, Sept. 1	**Tagged**	*Perf. 10.1x10.2*
2849 A2177 29c **multicolored**		.60	.20
2850 A2178 29c **multicolored**		.60	.20
2851 A2179 29c **multicolored**		.60	.20
2852 A2180 29c **multicolored**		.60	.20
2853 A2181 29c **multicolored**		.60	.20
a.	Vert. strip of 5, #2849-2853	3.00	*2.00*
	Vert. P# block of 6, 6#+S	5.75	—
	Horiz. P# block of 12, 2 sets of 6#+S, + top label	10.00	—
	Pane of 20	15.00	—

Some plate blocks of 6 will contain plate position diagram and copyright inscription, others will contain pane price inscription.

1994, Sept. 17		*Perf. 11x10.8*
LITHOGRAPHED		
2854 A2182 29c **multicolored**		.60	.20
2855 A2183 29c **multicolored**		.60	.20
2856 A2184 29c **multicolored**		.60	.20
2857 A2185 29c **multicolored**		.60	.20
2858 A2186 29c **multicolored**		.60	.20
2859 A2187 29c **multicolored**		.60	.20
2860 A2188 29c **multicolored**		.60	.20
2861 A2189 29c **multicolored**		.60	.20
a.	Block of 9, #2854-2861 +1 additional stamp	4.50	*3.50*
	Vert. P# block of 10, 5#+P	8.00	—
	P# block of 10, 2 sets of 5#+P, + top label	8.00	—
	Pane of 35	23.00	—

Vertical plate blocks contain either pane price inscription or copyright inscription.
Nos. 2854-2861 were available on the first day in 9 other cities.

LITERARY ARTS SERIES

James Thurber (1894-
1961) — A2190

Designed by Richard Sheaff based on drawing by James
Thurber.

LITHOGRAPHED & ENGRAVED
Plates of 200 in four panes of 50

1994, Sept. 10	Tagged	Perf. 11	
2862 A2190 29c **multicolored**		.50	.20
P# block of 4, 2#		2.50	—

Panes of No. 2862 contain two plate blocks, one containing a
plate position diagram.

WONDERS OF THE SEA

Diver, Motorboat
A2191

Diver,
Ship — A2192

Diver, Ship's
Wheel — A2193

Diver,
Coral — A2194

Designed by Charles Lynn Bragg.

Printed by Barton Press for Banknote Corporation of
America.

LITHOGRAPHED
Plates of 216 in nine panes of 24

1994, Oct. 3	Tagged	Perf. 11x10.9	
2863 A2191 29c **multicolored**		.50	.20
2864 A2192 29c **multicolored**		.50	.20
2865 A2193 29c **multicolored**		.50	.20
2866 A2194 29c **multicolored**		.50	.20
a. Block of 4, #2863-2866		2.00	1.50
P# block of 4, 4#+B		2.00	—
Pane of 24		12.00	—
b. As "a," imperf		2,000.	

Some plate blocks contain plate position diagram.

CRANES

Black-Necked — A2195   Whooping — A2196

Designed by Clarence Lee based on illustrations by Zhan
Gengxi.

Printed by Barton Press for Banknote Corporation of
America.

LITHOGRAPHED & ENGRAVED
Sheets of 120 in six panes of 20

1994, Oct. 9	Tagged	Perf. 10.8x11	
2867 A2195 29c **multicolored**		.50	.20
2868 A2196 29c **multicolored**		.50	.20
a. Pair, #2867-2868		1.00	.65
P# block of 4, 5#+B		2.00	—
Pane of 20		10.00	
b. As "a," black & magenta (engr.) omitted		2,250.	
c. As "a," double impression of engr. black (Birds' names and "USA") & magenta ("29")		—	
d. As "a," double impression of engr. black ("USA") & magenta ("29")		—	

Some plate blocks contain copyright or pane price
inscriptions.
See People's Republic of China Nos. 2528-2529.

LEGENDS OF THE WEST

A2197

g. Bill Pickett (1870-
1932) (Revised)

Vertical Pair with
Horizontal Gutter

Horizontal Pair with Vertical Gutter

Designed by Mark Hess.

Printed by J.W. Fergusson & Sons for Stamp Venturers.

Designs: a, Home on the Range. b, Buffalo Bill Cody (1846-
1917). c, Jim Bridger (1804-81). d, Annie Oakley (1860-1926).
e, Native American Culture. f, Chief Joseph (c. 1840-1904). h,
Bat Masterson (1853-1921). i, John C. Fremont (1813-90). j,
Wyatt Earp (1848-1929). k, Nellie Cashman (c. 1849-1925).
l, Charles Goodnight (1826-1929). m, Geronimo (1823-
1909). n, Kit Carson (1809-68). o, Wild Bill Hickok (1837-76). p,
Western Wildlife. q, Jim Beckwourth (c. 1798-1866). r, Bill
Tilghman (1854-1924). s, Sacagawea (c. 1787-1812). t, Overland Mail.

PHOTOGRAVURE
Sheets of 120 in six panes of 20

1994, Oct. 18	Tagged	Perf. 10.1x10	
2869 A2197 Pane of 20		12.00	—
a.-t. 29c any single		.60	.20
Sheet of 120 (6 panes)		72.50	—
Cross gutter block of 20		25.00	—
Cross gutter block of 4		17.50	—
Vert. pairs with horiz. gutter (each)		2.50	—
Horiz. pairs with vert. gutter (each)		2.50	—
u. As No. 2869, a.-e. imperf. f.-j. part perf.		—	

Cross gutter block of 20 consists of six stamps from each of
two panes and four stamps from each of two other panes with
the cross gutter between.

LEGENDS OF THE WEST (Recalled)

g. Bill Pickett (Recalled)

Nos. 2870b-2870d, 2870f-2870o, 2870q-2870s have a
frameline around the vignette that is half the width of the frameline on similar stamps in No. 2869. Other design differences
may exist.

PHOTOGRAVURE
Sheets of 120 in six panes of 20

1994	**Tagged**		**Perf. 10.1x10**
2870 A2197	29c Pane of 20		190.00 —

150,000 panes of No. 2870 were made available through a drawing. Panes were delivered in an envelope. Value is for pane without envelope.

CHRISTMAS

Madonna and Child, by Elisabetta Sirani A2200

Greetings Stocking A2201

Santa Claus — A2202

Cardinal in Snow — A2203

Designed by Bradbury Thompson (#2871), Lou Nolan (#2872), Harry Zelenko (#2873), Peter Good (#2874).

Printed by Bureau of Engraving and Printing (#2871), Ashton-Potter USA, Ltd. (#2872), Avery Dennison (#2873-2874).

LITHOGRAPHED & ENGRAVED
Sheets of 300 in six panes of 50

1994, Oct. 20	**Tagged**		**Perf. 11¼**
2871	A2200 29c multicolored		.50 .20
	P# block of 4, 5#		2.50 —

BOOKLET STAMP
Perf. 9¾x11

2871A A2200	29c multicolored, shiny gum		.50 .20
	Dull gum		.50
b.	Booklet pane of 10, shiny gum		5.25 3.50
	Dull gum		5.25
c.	As "b," imperf.		—

LITHOGRAPHED
Sheets of 400 in eight panes of 50
Perf. 11¼

2872	A2201 29c multicolored		.50 .20
	P# block of 4, 5#+P		2.50 —
a.	Booklet pane of 20		10.50 3.00
b.	Imperf., pair		—
c.	As "a," imperf. horiz.		—

Panes of Nos. 2871-2872 contain four plate blocks, one containing pane position diagram.

PHOTOGRAVURE
BOOKLET STAMPS
Self-Adhesive
Die Cut

2873	A2202 29c multicolored		.50 .20
a.	Booklet pane of 12		6.25
b.	Coil with plate # V1111		— 3.50
	P# strip of 5, P#V1111		6.00

Except for No. 2873b with plate number, coil stamps are indistinguishable from booklet stamps once they are removed from the backing paper.

2874	A2203 29c multicolored		.50 .20
a.	Booklet pane of 18		9.50

BUREAU OF ENGRAVING & PRINTING
Souvenir Sheet

A2204

Major Double Transfer | Minor Double Transfer

Designed by Peter Cocci, using original die for Type A98.

LITHOGRAPHED & ENGRAVED

1994, Nov. 3	**Tagged**		**Perf. 11**
2875 A2204	$2 Sheet of 4		15.00 —
a.	Single stamp		3.00 1.25
	Sheet of 4 with major double transfer on right stamp	150.00	
	Major double transfer, single stamp	—	—
	Sheet of 4 with minor double transfer on right stamp	75.00	
	Minor double transfer, single stamp	—	—

CHINESE NEW YEAR

Year of the Boar — A2205

Designed by Clarence Lee.

Printed by Stamp Venturers.

PHOTOGRAVURE
Panes of 20

1994, Dec. 30	**Tagged**		**Perf. 11.2x11.1**
2876 A2205	29c multicolored		.55 .20
	P# block of 4, 5#+S		2.25 —
	Pane of 20		11.00 —

Some plate blocks contain plate position diagram, which is located in selvage opposite one of central columns of sheet. The first class rate was increased to 32c on Jan. 1, 1995.

A2206

A2207

A2208

A2208a

A2209

Designed by Richard D. Sheaff (#2877-2878), Lou Nolan (#2879-2892).

Printed by American Bank Note Co. (#2877, 2884, 2890), Bureau of Engraving and Printing (#2879, 2881, 2883, 2889),

---

Stamp Venturers (#2878, 2880, 2882, 2888, 2891-2892), KCS Industries (#2885), Avery-Dennison (#2886-2887).

> **Coil Plate No. Strips of 3**
> Beginning with No. 2123, coil plate no. strips of 3 usually sell at the level of strips of 5 minus twice the face value of two stamps.

LITHOGRAPHED
Sheets of 100

1994, Dec. 13	**Untagged**		**Perf. 11x10.8**
2877 A2206	(3c) tan, bright blue & red		.20 .20
	P# block of 4, 3#+A		.30 —
	Zip block of 4		.25 —
a.	Imperf., pair		200.00

Perf. 10.8x10.9

2878 A2206	(3c) tan, dark blue & red		.20 .20
	P# block of 4, 3#+S		.30 —
	Zip block of 4		.25

Inscriptions on #2877 are in a thin typeface. Those on #2878 are in heavy, bold type.

PHOTOGRAVURE
Tagged
Perf. 11.2x11.1

2879 A2207	(20c) black "G," yellow & multi		.40 .20
	P# block of 4, 5#		5.00 —
	Zip block of 4		1.75 —
a.	Imperf., pair		—

Perf. 11x10.9

2880 A2207	(20c) red "G," yellow & multi		.50 .20
	P# block of 4, 5#+S		9.00 —
	Zip block of 4		2.25 —

Perf. 11.2x11.1

2881 A2208	(32c) black "G" & multi		.75 .20
	P# block of 4, 4#		75.00 —
	Zip block of 4		5.50 —
a.	Booklet pane of 10		6.00 3.75

Perf. 11x10.9

2882 A2208a	(32c) red "G" & multi		.60 .20
	P# block of 4, 4#+S		3.00 —
	Zip block of 4		2.75 —

Distance on #2882 from bottom of red G to top of flag immediately above is 13¾mm. Illustration A2208a shows #2885 superimposed over #2882.

BOOKLET STAMPS
Perf. 10x9.9 on 2 or 3 Sides

2883 A2208	(32c) black "G" & multi		.60 .20
a.	Booklet pane of 10		6.25 3.75

Perf. 10.9 on 2 or 3 Sides

2884 A2208	(32c) blue "G" & multi		.60 .20
a.	Booklet pane of 10		6.00 3.75
b.	As "a," imperf		—

Perf. 11x10.9 on 2 or 3 Sides

2885 A2208a	(32c) red "G" & multi		.65 .20
a.	Booklet pane of 10		6.50 3.75
b.	Pair, imperf vert.		—
c.	Pair, imperf between		—

Distance on #2885 from bottom of red G to top of flag immediately above is 13½mm. See note below #2882.
No. 2885c resulted from a paper foldover after perforating and before cutting into panes.

A2208b

A2208c

Self-Adhesive		**Die Cut**
2886 A2208b	(32c) gray, blue, light blue, red & black	.60 .20
a.	Booklet pane of 18	11.50
b.	Coil with plate # V11111	— 3.25
	P# strip of 5, same #	5.75

No. 2886 is printed on surface-tagged paper which is opaque, thicker and brighter than that of No. 2887 and has only a small number of blue shading dots in the white stripes immediately below the flag's blue field.

Except for No. 2886b with plate number, coil stamps are indistinguishable from booklet stamps once they are removed from the backing paper.

2887 A2208c	(32c) black, blue & red	.60 .20
a.	Booklet pane of 18	11.50

No. 2887 has noticeable blue shading in the white stripes immediately below the blue field and has overall tagging. The paper is translucent, thinner and duller than No. 2886.

COIL STAMPS
Perf. 9.8 Vert.

2888 A2209	(25c) black "G," blue & multi		.50 .50
	Pair		1.00 1.00
	P# strip of 5, #S11111		5.00
	P# single, #S11111		2.75
2889 A2208	(32c) black "G" & multi		.60 .20
	Pair		1.25 .30

	P# strip of 5, #1111, 2222	5.50	
	P# single, #1111, 2222		1.25
a.	Imperf., pair	300.00	
2890	A2208 (32c) **blue "G" & multi**	.60	.20
	Pair	1.25	.30
	P# strip of 5, #A1111, A1112, A1113, A1211, A1311, A1313, A1324, A2211, A2212, A2213, A2214, A2313, A3113, A3314, A3323, A3324, A3433, A3435, A3436, A4427, A5327, A5417, A5427	5.75	
	P# strip of 5, #A1314, A1417, A1433, A2223, A4426, A5437	6.75	
	P# strip of 5, #A3114, A3315, A3423, A3426	7.25	
	P# strip of 5, #A4435	175.00	
	P# single, #A1111, A1313, A2214, A3113, A3314, A3324, A4427, A5427	—	1.25
	P# single, #A1111	—	3.50
	P# single, #A1112, A1311, A1324, A2213, A3323, A5327	—	2.50
	P# single, #A1113, A1211, A1212, A1433, A2212, A2313, A3114, A3423, A3435, A5417, A5437	—	3.50
	P# single, #A1222, A1314, A4426	—	4.00
	P# single, #A1417, A2211, A2223, A3315, A3426	—	4.50
	P# single, #A3433, A3436	—	2.00
	P# single, #A4435	—	—
2891	A2208 (32c) **red "G" & multi**	.60	.20
	Pair	1.25	.30
	P# strip of 5, #S1111	5.75	
	P# single, #S1111	—	1.25

Rouletted 9.8 Vert.

2892	A2208 (32c) **red "G" & multi**	.60	.20
	Pair	1.25	.30
	P# strip of 5, #S1111, S2222	5.75	
	P# single, #S1111, S2222	—	1.25

See note under No. 2525.

A2210

Flag Over Porch — A2212

Designed by Lou Nolan (#2893), Dave LaFleur (#2897).

Printed by American Bank Note Co. (#2893), Stamp Venturers (#2897).

PHOTOGRAVURE
COIL STAMP

1995		**Untagged**	**Perf. 9.8 Vert.**
2893	A2210 (5c) **green & multi**	.20	.20
	Pair	.20	.20
	P# strip of 5, #A11111, A21111	1.90	
	P# single, #A11111, A21111	—	1.50

No. 2893 was only available through the Philatelic Fulfillment Center after its announcement 1/12/95. Covers submitted for first day cancels received a 12/13/94 cancel, even though the stamps were not available on that date.

Sheets of 400 in four panes of 100

1995	**Tagged**		**Perf. 10.4**
2897	A2212 32c **multicolored,** shiny gum	.60	.20
	P# block of 4, 5#+S	3.00	—
	Low gloss gum	.60	
	P# block of 4, 5#+S	3.00	
a.	Imperf., vert. pair	175.00	

Some plate blocks contain plate position diagram.
See Nos. 2913-2916D, 2920-2921, 3133. For booklet see No. BK243.

Butte
A2217

Auto — A2220

Mountain
A2218

Auto Tail
Fin — A2223

Juke Box — A2225

Flag Over Field — A2230

Designed by Tom Engeman (#2902-2904B), Robert Brangwynne (#2905-2906), Chris Calle (#2907), Bill Nelson (#2908-2912B), Dave LaFleur (#2913-2916, 2921), Sabra Field (#2919).

Printed by J.W. Fergusson & Sons for Stamp Venturers (#2902, 2905, 2909, 2912, 2914), Bureau of Engraving and Printing (#2903, 2904B, 2908, 2911, 2912B, 2913, 2915A, 2915C-2915D, 2916, 2921), Stamp Venturers (#2902B, 2904, 2906-2907, 2910, 2912A, 2915B), Avery Dennison (#2904A, 2915, 2919, 2920).

> **Coil Plate No. Strips of 3**
> Beginning with No. 2123, coil plate No. strips of 3 usually sell at the level of strips of 5 minus the face value of two stamps.

COIL STAMPS
PHOTOGRAVURE

1995-97		**Untagged**	**Perf. 9.8 Vert.**
Self-Adhesive (#2902B, 2904A-2904B, 2906-2907, 2910, 2912A, 2912B, 2915-2915D, 2919-2921)			
2902	A2217 (5c) **yellow, red & blue,** Mar. 10	.20	.20
	Pair	.20	.20
	P# strip of 5, #S111, S222, S333	1.60	
	P# single, #S111, S222, S333		.60
a.	Imperf., pair	750.00	

Serpentine Die Cut 11.5 Vert.

2902B	A2217 (5c) **yellow, red & blue,** June 15, 1996	.20	.20
	Pair	.20	
	P# strip of 5, #S111	1.60	
	P# single, #S111		.60

Perf. 9.8 Vert.

2903	A2218 (5c) **purple & multi,** Mar. 16, 1996	.20	.20
	Pair	.40	.20
	P# strip of 5, #11111	1.60	
	P# single, #11111	—	1.25
a.	Tagged (error)	4.00	3.50
	P# strip of 5, #11111	85.00	
	P# single, #11111	—	—

Letters of inscription "USA NONPROFIT ORG." outlined in purple on #2903.

2904	A2218 (5c) **blue & multi,** Mar. 16, 1996	.20	.20
	Pair	.40	.20
	P# strip of 5, #S111	1.60	
	P# single, #S111	—	1.25
c.	Imperf., pair	500.00	

Letters of inscription have no outline on #2904.

Serpentine Die Cut 11.2 Vert.

2904A	A2218 (5c) **purple & multi,** June 15, 1996	.20	.20
	Pair	.40	
	P# strip of 5, #V222222, V333323, V333333, V333342, V333343	1.60	
	P# single, same #		1.25

Serpentine Die Cut 9.8 Vert.

2904B	A2218 (5c) **purple & multi,** Jan. 24, 1997	.20	.20
	pair	.40	
	P# strip of 5, #1111	1.60	
	P# single, #1111		1.25
c.	Tagged (error)	4.00	3.50
	P# strip of 5, #1111	85.00	
	P# single, #1111	—	—

Letters of inscription outlined in purple on #2904B, not outlined on No. 2904A.

Perf. 9.8 Vert.

2905	A2220 (10c) **black, red brown & brown,** Mar. 10	.20	.20
	Pair	.40	.40
	P# strip of 5, #S111, S222, S333	2.75	
	P# single, #S111, S222, S333	—	.95

Serpentine Die Cut 11.5 Vert.

2906	A2220 (10c) **black, brown & red brown,** June 15, 1996	.20	.20
	Pair	.40	
	P# strip of 5, #S111	2.75	
	P# single, #S111	—	.95
2907	A1957 (10c) **gold & multi,** May 21, 1996	.20	.20
	Pair	.40	
	P# strip of 5, #S11111	2.75	
	P# single, #S11111	—	.95

Perf. 9.8 Vert.

2908	A2223 (15c) **dark orange yellow & multi,** tagged, Mar. 17	.30	.30
	Pair	.60	.60
	P# strip of 5, #11111	3.25	
	P# single, #11111	—	1.25

No. 2908 has dark, bold colors, heavy shading lines and heavily shaded chrome.

2909	A2223 (15c) **buff & multi,** Mar. 17	.30	.30
	Pair	.60	.60
	P# strip of 5, #S11111	3.25	
	P# single, #S11111	—	1.25

No. 2909 has shinier chrome, more subdued colors and finer details than No. 2908.

Serpentine Die Cut 11.5 Vert.

2910	A2223 (15c) **buff & multi,** June 15, 1996	.30	.30
	Pair	.60	
	P# strip of 5, #S11111	3.25	
	P# single, #S11111		1.25

Perf. 9.8 Vert.

2911	A2225 (25c) **dark red, dark yellow green & multi,** tagged, Mar. 17	.50	.50
	Pair	1.00	1.00
	P# strip of 5, #111111, 212222, 222222, 332222	4.50	
	P# single, same #		2.50

No. 2911 has dark, saturated colors and dark blue lines in the music selection board.

2912	A2225 (25c) **bright orange red, bright yellow green & multi,** Mar. 17	.50	.50
	Pair	1.00	1.00
	P# strip of 5, #S11111, S22222	4.50	
	P# single, same #	—	2.50

No. 2912 has bright colors, less shading and light blue lines in the music selection board.

Serpentine Die Cut 11.5 Vert.

2912A	A2225 (25c) **bright orange red, bright yellow green & multi,** June 15, 1996	.50	.50
	Pair	1.00	
	P# strip of 5, #S11111, S22222	4.50	
	P# single, same #		2.50

Serpentine Die Cut 9.8 Vert.

2912B	A2225 (25c) **dark red, dark yellow green & multi,** Jan. 24, 1997	.50	.50
	pair	1.00	
	P# strip of 5, #111111, 222222	4.00	
	P# single, same #		2.50

See No. 3132.

Tagged
Perf. 9.8 Vert.

2913	A2212 32c **blue, tan, brown, red & light blue** gum, shiny	.60	.20
	Pair	1.25	.30
	P# strip of 5, #11111, 22221, 22222	5.25	
	P# single, #11111, 22222	—	.65
	P# single, #22221	—	3.00
	Low gloss gum	.60	
	Pair	1.25	
	P# strip of 5, #11111, 22222, 33333, 34333, 44444, 45444, 66646, 77767, 78767, 91161, 99969	5.75	
	P# strip of 5, #22322, 66666	12.00	
	P# single, #22322	—	3.50
	P# single, #33333, 44444	—	.65
	P# single, #34333, 78767	—	2.00
	P# single, #11111, 22222, 45444, 66646, 77767	—	.95
	P# single, #66666	—	8.75
	P# single, #91161	—	2.50
	P# single, #99969	—	3.00
a.	Imperf., pair	60.00	

No. 2913 has pronounced light blue shading in the flag and red "1995" at left bottom. See No. 3133.

2914	A2212 32c **blue, yellow brown, red & gray,** May 19	.60	.20
	Pair	1.25	.30
	P# strip of 5, #S11111	5.25	
	P# single, #S11111	—	2.50

No. 2914 has pale gray shading in the flag and blue "1995" at left bottom.

Serpentine Die Cut 8.7 Vert.

2915	A2212 32c **multicolored,** Apr. 18	.60	.30
	Pair	1.25	
	P# strip of 5, #V11111	5.25	
	P# single, #V11111	—	3.50

Serpentine Die Cut 9.8 Vert.

2915A A2212 32c **dk blue, tan, brown, red & light blue,** *May 21, 1996* .60 .20
Pair 1.25
P# strip of 5, #11111, 22222, 23222, 33333, 13311A, 22222A, 33333A, 44444, 45444, 55555, 66666, 78777, 88888, 89878, 99999, 11111A, 13231A, 44444A, 55555A, 66666A, 77777A, 78777A, 88888A 5.25
P# strip of 5, #87898, 89898 12.00
P# strip of 5, #87888, 89888, 99899, 13211A 27.50
P# strip of 5, #88898 300.00
P# strip of 5, #89899 425.00
P# strip of 5, #97898 8.00
P# single, #11111, 22222, 23222, 33333, 44444, 55555, 66666, 78777, 88888, 99999, 11111A, 13211A, 13231A, 13311A, 22222A, 33333A, 44444A, 55555A, 66666A — 1.25
P# single, #87888, 89888 — 4.75
P# single, #87898 — 3.75
P# single, #88898, 89899, 99899 — 2.50
P# single, #97898 — 4.25
  h. Imperf., pair —
  i. Tan omitted 2,000.

Sky on No. 3133 shows color gradation at LR not on No. 2915A.

On No. 2915Ai all other colors except brown are severely shifted. Unique.

Serpentine Die Cut 11.5 Vert.

2915B A2212 32c **dk blue, tan, brown, red & light blue,** *June 15, 1996* .60 .20
Pair 1.25
P# strip of 5, #S11111 5.25
P# single, #S11111 — 2.75

Serpentine Die Cut 10.9 Vert.

2915C A2212 32c **dk blue, tan, brown, red & light blue,** *May 21, 1996* .60 .20
Pair 1.25
P# strip of 5, #55555, 66666 11.00
P# single, #55555, 66666 — 1.90

Serpentine Die Cut 9.8 Vert.

2915D A2212 32c **dark blue, tan, brown, red & light blue,** *Jan. 24, 1997* .60 .20
pair 1.25
P# strip of 5, #11111 4.75
P# single, #11111 — 3.00

Die cutting on #2915D starts and ends with straight cuts and has 9 teeth between. Die cutting on #2915A has a straight cut at bottom and 11 teeth above.

Stamps on multiples of No. 2915A touch, and are on a peelable backing the same size as the stamps, while those of No. 2915D are separated on the peelable backing, which is larger than the stamps.

No. 2915D has red "1997" at left bottom; No. 2915A has red "1996" at left bottom.

Sky on No. 3133 shows color gradation at LR not on No. 2915D, and it has blue "1996" at left bottom.

BOOKLET STAMPS

Perf. 10.8x9.8 on 2 or 3 Adjacent Sides

2916 A2212 32c **blue, tan, brown, red & light blue,** *May 19* .60 .20
  a. Booklet pane of 10 6.00 3.25
  b. As "a," imperf. —

Die Cut

2919 A2230 32c **multicolored,** *Mar. 17* .60 .20
  a. Booklet pane of 18 11.00
  b. Vert. pair, no die cutting btwn. —

Serpentine Die Cut 8.7 on 2, 3 or 4 Adjacent Sides

2920 A2212 32c **multicolored,** dated blue "1995," *Apr. 18* .60 .20
  a. Booklet pane of 20+label 12.00
  b. Small date 4.00 .20
  c. As "b," booklet pane of 20+label 110.00
  f. As No. 2920, pane of 15+label 9.00
  g. As "a," partial pane of 10, 3 stamps and parts of 7 stamps printed on backing liner —
  h. As No. 2920, booklet pane of 15 9.00

Date on No. 2920 is nearly twice as large as date on No. 2920b. No. 2920f comes in various configurations.

No. 2920h is a pane of 16 with one stamp removed. The missing stamp is the lower right stamp in the pane. No. 2920h cannot be made from No. 2920f, a pane of 15 + label.

The label is located in the second or third row of the pane and is die cut. If the label is removed, an impression of the die cutting appears on the backing paper.

Serpentine Die Cut 11.3 on 3 sides

2920D A2212 32c **multicolored,** dated blue "1996," *Jan. 20, 1996* .60 .20
  e. Booklet pane of 10 6.00

Serpentine Die Cut 9.8 on 2 or 3 Adjacent Sides

2921 A2212 32c **dk bl, tan, brn, red & lt bl,** dated red 1996, *May 21, 1996* .60 .20
  a. Booklet pane of 10, dated red "1996" 6.00
  b. As No. 2921, dated red "1997" .60 .20
  c. As "a," dated red "1997" 6.00
  d. Booklet pane of 5 + label, dated red "1997," *Jan. 24, 1997* 3.25
  e. As "a," imperf. —

> Scott values for used self-adhesive stamps are for examples either on piece or off piece.

GREAT AMERICANS ISSUE

A2248   A2249

A2250   A2251

A2253   A2255

A2256   A2257

A2258

Designed by Dennis Lyall (#2933-2934), Richard Sheaff (#2935), Howard Paine (#2936, 2941-2942), Roy Andersen (#2938), Chris Calle (#2940, 2943).

Printed by Banknote Corporation of America (#2933-2935, 2940-2943), Ashton-Potter (USA) Ltd. (#2936), Bureau of Engraving & Printing (#2938).

ENGRAVED

Sheets of 400 in four panes of 100
Sheets of 160 in eight panes of 20 (#2935)
Sheets of 120 in six panes of 20 (#2936, 2941-2942)

1995-98		Tagged

Self-Adhesive (#2941-2942)
Perf. 11.2, Serpentine Die Cut 11.7x11.5 (#2941-2942)

2933 A2248 32c **brown,** prephosphored paper (solid tagging), *Sept. 13, 1995* .60 .20
P# block of 4, 1#+B 3.00
2934 A2249 32c **green,** prephosphored paper (solid tagging), *Apr. 26, 1996* .60 .20
P# block of 4, 1#+B 3.00
2935 A2250 32c **lake,** prephosphored paper (grainy solid tagging), *Apr. 3, 1998* .60 .20
P# block of 4, 1#+B 2.40 —
Pane of 20 12.00

2936 A2251 32c **blue,** prephosphored paper (solid tagging), *July 16, 1998* .60 .20
P# block of 4, 1#+P 2.40 —
Pane of 20 12.00
2938 A2253 46c **carmine,** prephosphored uncoated paper (mottled tagging), *Oct. 20, 1995* .90 .20
P# block of 4, 1# 4.50
2940 A2255 55c **green,** prephosphored paper (grainy solid tagging), *July 11, 1995* 1.10 .20
P# block of 4, 1#+B 5.50
  a. Imperf., pair —
2941 A2256 55c **black,** prephosphored coated paper (solid tagging), *July 17, 1999* 1.10 .20
P# block of 4, 1#+B 4.40
Pane of 20 22.00
2942 A2257 77c **blue,** prephosphored paper (solid tagging), *Nov. 9, 1998* 1.50 .20
P# block of 4, 1#+B 6.00
Pane of 20 30.00
2943 A2258 78c **bright violet,** prephosphored paper (solid tagging), *Aug. 18, 1995* 1.60 .20
P# block of 4, 1#+B 7.50
  a. 78c **dull violet,** prephosphored paper (grainy solid tagging) 1.60 .20
P# block of 4, 1#+B 7.50
  b. 78c **pale violet,** prephosphored paper (grainy solid tagging) 1.75 .30
P# block of 4, 1#+B 12.00

The pale violet ink on No. 2943b luminesces bright pink under long-wave ultraviolet light.

Some plate blocks contain plate position diagram.

LOVE

Cherub from Sistine Madonna, by Raphael
A2263   A2264

Designed by Terry McCaffrey.

Printed by the Bureau of Engraving and Printing (#2948) and Banknote Corp. of America (#2949).

LITHOGRAPHED & ENGRAVED
Sheets of 300 in six panes of 50

1995, Feb. 1	Tagged	Perf. 11.2

2948 A2263 (32c) **multicolored** .60 .20
P# block of 4, 5# 3.00 —

Panes of No. 2948 contain four plate blocks, one containing a plate position diagram.

Self-Adhesive
Die Cut

2949 A2264 (32c) **multicolored** .60 .20
  a. Booklet pane of 20 + label 12.00
  b. Red (engr.) omitted —
  c. As "a," red (engr.) omitted —

See Nos. 2957-2960, 3030.

Florida Statehood, 150th Anniv. — A2265

Designed by Laura Smith.
Printed by Ashton-Potter (USA) Ltd.

LITHOGRAPHED
Sheets of 160 in eight panes of 20

1995, Mar. 3	Tagged	Perf. 11.1

2950 A2265 32c **multicolored** .60 .20
P# block of 4, 5#+P 2.40 —
Pane of 20 12.00

Some plate blocks contain plate position diagram, which is located in selvage opposite one of central columns of sheet.

EARTH DAY

Earth Clean-
Up — A2266

Solar
Energy — A2267

Tree
Planting — A2268

Beach Clean-
Up — A2269

Designed by Christy Millard (#2951), Jennifer Michalove (#2952), Brian Hailes (#2953) and Melody Kiper (#2954). Printed by Ashton-Potter (USA) Ltd.

LITHOGRAPHED
Sheets of 96 in six panes of 16

1995, Apr. 20		Tagged	Perf. 11.1x11	
2951	A2266 32c multicolored		.60	.20
2952	A2267 32c multicolored		.60	.20
2953	A2268 32c multicolored		.60	.20
2954	A2269 32c multicolored		.60	.20
a.	Block of 4, #2951-2954		2.40	1.75
	P# block of 4, 5#+P		2.40	—
	Horiz. P# block of 8, 2 sets of			
	5#+P, + top or bottom label		4.80	—
	Pane of 16		9.60	—

Some plate blocks contain plate position diagram. Top plate block of 8 contains copyright and pane price inscriptions.

Richard Nixon

A2270

BLACK HERITAGE

BESSIE COLEMAN

A2271

RICHARD M. NIXON
37th President (1913-94)

Designed by Daniel Schwartz.
Printed by Barton Press and Bank Note Corp. of America.

LITHOGRAPHED & ENGRAVED
Sheets of 200 in four panes of 50

1995, Apr. 26		Tagged	Perf. 11.2	
2955	A2270 32c multicolored		.60	.20
	P# block of 4, 5#+B		3.00	—
a.	Red (engr.) omitted		1,400.	

Plate position diagram located in selvage opposite center column of pane. Panes contain four plate blocks.

No. 2955 is known with red (engr. "Richard Nixon") inverted, and with red engr. omitted but only half the Nixon portrait present, both from printer's waste. No. 2955a shows a complete Nixon portrait.

BLACK HERITAGE SERIES
Bessie Coleman (d. 1926), Aviator

Designed by Chris Calle.

ENGRAVED
Sheets of 200 in four panes of 50

1995, Apr. 27		Tagged	Perf. 11.2	
2956	A2271 32c red & black		.60	.20
	P# block of 4, 1#		3.00	

Some plate blocks contain plate position diagram. Panes contain two plate blocks.

LOVE

A2272

A2273

Cherubs from Sistine Madonna,
by Raphael — A2274

Designed by Terry McCaffrey.
Printed by Bureau of Engraving and Printing (#2957-2959), Bank Note Corp. of America (#2960).

LITHOGRAPHED & ENGRAVED
Sheets of 300 in six panes of 50

1995, May 12		Tagged	Perf. 11.2	
2957	A2272 32c multicolored		.60	.20
	P# block of 4, 5#		3.00	—
	Copyright block of 6		4.25	—

Some plate blocks contain plate position diagram.
For booklet see No. BK244.

2958	A2273 55c multicolored		1.10	.20
	P# block of 4, 5#		5.50	—

Some plate blocks contain either plate position diagram or pane price inscription.

BOOKLET STAMPS
Perf. 9.8x10.8

2959	A2272 32c multicolored		.60	.20
a.	Booklet pane of 10		6.00	3.25
b.	As "a," imperf		—	

Self-Adhesive
Die Cut

2960	A2274 55c multicolored		1.10	.20
a.	Booklet pane of 20 + label		22.50	

RECREATIONAL SPORTS

Volleyball — A2275

Softball — A2276

Bowling — A2277

Tennis — A2278

Golf — A2279

Designed by Don Weller.
Printed by Bank Note Corp. of America.

LITHOGRAPHED
Sheets of 120 in six panes of 20

1995, May 20		Tagged	Perf. 11.2	
2961	A2275 32c multicolored		.60	.20
2962	A2276 32c multicolored		.60	.20
2963	A2277 32c multicolored		.60	.20
2964	A2278 32c multicolored		.60	.20
2965	A2279 32c multicolored		.60	.20
a.	Vert. strip of 5, #2961-2965		3.00	2.00
	P# block of 10, 2 sets of 4#+B		6.00	—
	Pane of 20		12.00	—
b.	As "a," imperf			
c.	As "a," yellow omitted		2,500.	
d.	As "a," yellow, blue & magenta omitted		2,500.	

Some plate blocks contain plate position diagram.

PRISONERS OF WAR & MISSING IN ACTION

A2280

Designed by Carl Herrman.
Printed by Ashton-Potter (USA) Ltd.

LITHOGRAPHED
Sheets of 160 in eight panes of 20

1995, May 29		Tagged	Perf. 11.2	
2966	A2280 32c multicolored		.60	.20
	P# block of 4, 5#+P		2.40	—
	Pane of 20		12.00	—

Some plate blocks contain plate position diagram.

LEGENDS OF HOLLYWOOD

Marilyn Monroe (1926-
62) — A2281

Cross Gutter Block of 8

Designed by Michael Deas.
Printed by Stamp Venturers.

PHOTOGRAVURE
Sheets of 120 in six panes of 20

1995, June 1	Tagged	Perf. 11.1	
2967 A2281 32c multicolored		.60	.20
P# block of 4, 6#+S		4.00	
Pane of 20		19.00	
Sheet of 120 (six panes)		150.00	
Cross gutter block of 8		55.00	—
Block of 8 with vertical gutter		45.00	—
Horiz. pair with vert. gutter		7.50	—
Vert. pair with horiz. gutter		4.00	—
a. Imperf., pair		600.00	
Pane of 20, imperf.		6,250.	

Perforations in corner of each stamp are star-shaped.

TEXAS STATEHOOD

A2282

Designed by Laura Smith.
Printed by Sterling Sommer for Ashton-Potter (USA) Ltd.

LITHOGRAPHED
Sheets of 120 in six panes of 20

1995, June 16	Tagged	Perf. 11.2	
2968 A2282 32c multicolored		.60	.20
P# block of 4, 6#+P		2.40	
Pane of 20		12.00	—

Some plate blocks contain plate position diagram.

GREAT LAKES LIGHTHOUSES

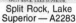

Split Rock, Lake
Superior — A2283

St. Joseph, Lake
Michigan — A2284

Spectacle Reef,
Lake
Huron — A2285

Marblehead, Lake
Erie — A2286

Thirty Mile Point, Lake
Ontario — A2287

Designed by Howard Koslow.
Printed by Stamp Venturers.

PHOTOGRAVURE
BOOKLET STAMPS

1995, June 17	Tagged	Perf. 11.2 Vert.	
2969 A2283 32c multicolored		.60	.20
2970 A2284 32c multicolored		.60	.20
2971 A2285 32c multicolored		.60	.20
2972 A2286 32c multicolored		.60	.20
2973 A2287 32c multicolored		.60	.20
a. Booklet pane of 5, #2969-2973		3.00	2.75

U.N., 50th ANNIV.

A2288

Designed by Howard Paine.
Printed by Banknote Corp. of America.

ENGRAVED
Sheets of 180 in nine panes of 20

1995, June 26	Tagged	Perf. 11.2	
2974 A2288 32c blue		.60	.20
P# block of 4, 1#+B		2.40	
Pane of 20		12.00	—

Some plate blocks contain either pane price or copyright inscriptions. Pane position diagram is located in bottom selvage opposite central column of pane.

CIVIL WAR

A2289

Designed by Mark Hess.

Printed by Stamp Venturers.

Designs: a, Monitor and Virginia. b, Robert E. Lee. c, Clara Barton. d, Ulysses S. Grant. e, Battle of Shiloh. f, Jefferson Davis. g, David Farragut. h, Frederick Douglass. i, Raphael Semmes. j, Abraham Lincoln. k, Harriet Tubman. l, Stand Watie. m, Joseph E. Johnston. n, Winfield Hancock. o, Mary Chesnut. p, Battle of Chancellorsville. q, William T. Sherman. r, Phoebe Pember. s, "Stonewall" Jackson. t, Battle of Gettysburg.

PHOTOGRAVURE
Sheets of 120 in six panes of 20

1995, June 29	Tagged	Perf. 10.1	
2975 A2289 Pane of 20		12.00	—
a.-t. 32c any single		.60	.20
Sheet of 120 (6 panes)		105.00	
Cross gutter block of 20		35.00	—
Cross gutter block of 4		17.50	—
Vert. pairs with horiz. gutter (each)		3.75	—
Horiz. pairs with vert. gutter (each)		3.75	—
u. As No. 2975, a.-e. imperf, f.-j. part perf			—
v. As No. 2975, k.-t. imperf, f.-j. part perf			—
w. As No. 2975, imperf		1,500.	
x. Block of 9 (f.-h., k.-m., p.-r.) k.-l. & p.-q. imperf. vert.			

Cross gutter block of 20 consists of six stamps from each of two panes and four stamps from each of two other panes with the cross gutter between.

CAROUSEL HORSES

A2290

A2291

A2292

A2293

Designed by Paul Calle.
Printed at Sterling Sommer for Ashton-Potter (USA) Ltd.

LITHOGRAPHED
Sheets of 160 in eight panes of 20

1995, July 21		Tagged	Perf. 11	
2976	A2290	32c multicolored	.60	.20
2977	A2291	32c multicolored	.60	.20
2978	A2292	32c multicolored	.60	.20
2979	A2293	32c multicolored	.60	.20
a.		Block of 4, #2976-2979	2.40	1.75
		P# block of 4, 5#+P	2.40	—
		Pane of 20	12.00	—

Some plate blocks contain either pane price or copyright inscriptions.

WOMAN SUFFRAGE

A2294

Designed by April Greiman.
Printed by Ashton-Potter (USA) Ltd.

LITHOGRAPHED & ENGRAVED
Sheets of 160 in four panes of 40

1995, Aug. 26		Tagged	Perf. 11.1x11	
2980	A2294	32c multicolored	.60	.20
		P# block of 4, 5#+P	3.00	—
a.		Black (engr.) omitted	425.00	—
b.		Imperf., pair	1,500.	—

No. 2980a is valued in the grade of fine. Very fine examples exist and sell for much more.

WORLD WAR II

A2295

Designed by Bill Bond.

Designs and events of 1945: a, Marines raise flag on Iwo Jima. b, Fierce fighting frees Manila by March 3, 1945. c, Soldiers advancing (Okinawa, the last big battle). d, Destroyed bridge (US and Soviets link up at Elbe River). e, Allies liberate Holocaust survivors. f, Germany surrenders at Reims. g, Refugees (By 1945, World War II has uprooted millions). h, Truman announces Japan's surrender. i, Sailor kissing nurse (News of victory hits home). j, Hometowns honor their returning veterans.
Central label is size of 15 stamps and shows world map with extent of Axis control and Allied operations.
Illustration reduced.

LITHOGRAPHED & ENGRAVED
Plates of eight subjects in four panes of 2 each

1995, Sept. 2		Tagged	Perf. 11.1	
2981	A2295	Block of 10	6.00	4.50
		Pane of 20	12.00	—
a.-j.		32c any single	.60	.30

No. 2981 has selvage at left and right and either top or bottom.

AMERICAN MUSIC SERIES

Louis Armstrong (1901-71) — A2296

Coleman Hawkins (1904-69) — A2297

James P. Johnson (1894-1955) A2298

Jelly Roll Morton (1890-1941) A2299

Charlie Parker (1920-55) — A2300

Eubie Blake (1883-1983) A2301

Charles Mingus (1922-79) — A2302

Thelonious Monk (1917-82) — A2303

John Coltrane (1926-67) — A2304

Erroll Garner (1921-77) — A2305

Designed by Dean Mitchell (#2982-2984, 2987, 2989, 2991-2992) and Thomas Blackshear (others).

Printed by Ashton-Potter (USA) Ltd. (#2982), Sterling Sommer for Ashton-Potter (USA) Ltd. (#2983-2992).

LITHOGRAPHED
Plates of 120 in six panes of 20

1995		Tagged	Perf. 11.1x11	
2982	A2296	32c white denomination, Sept. 1	.80	.20
		P# block of 4, 4#+P	2.40	—
		Pane of 20	12.00	—
2983	A2297	32c multicolored, Sept. 16	.80	.20
2984	A2296	32c black denomination, Sept. 16	.80	.20
2985	A2298	32c multicolored, Sept. 16	.80	.20
2986	A2299	32c multicolored, Sept. 16	.80	.20
2987	A2300	32c multicolored, Sept. 16	.80	.20
2988	A2301	32c multicolored, Sept. 16	.80	.20
2989	A2302	32c multicolored, Sept. 16	.80	.20
2990	A2303	32c multicolored, Sept. 16	.80	.20
2991	A2304	32c multicolored, Sept. 16	.80	.20
2992	A2305	32c multicolored, Sept. 16	.80	.20
a.		Vert. block of 10, #2983-2992	8.00	—
		P# block of 10	8.00	—
		Pane of 20	16.00	—
b.		Pane of 20, dark blue (inscriptions) omitted	—	

Some plate blocks will contain plate position diagram.

GARDEN FLOWERS

Aster A2306

Chrysanthemum A2307

Dahlia A2308

Hydrangea A2309

Rudbeckia — A2310

Designed by Ned Seidler.

LITHOGRAPHED & ENGRAVED
BOOKLET STAMPS

1995, Sept. 19	Tagged	Perf. 10.9 Vert.	
2993 A2306 32c **multicolored**		.60	.20
2994 A2307 32c **multicolored**		.60	.20
2995 A2308 32c **multicolored**		.60	.20
2996 A2309 32c **multicolored**		.60	.20
2997 A2310 32c **multicolored**		.60	.20
a.	Booklet pane of 5, #2993-2997	3.00	2.25
b.	As "a," imperf	—	

EDDIE RICKENBACKER (1890-1973), AVIATOR

A2311

Designed by Davis Meltzer.

PHOTOGRAVURE
Panes of 50

1995, Sept. 25	Tagged	Perf. 11¼	
2998 A2311 60c **multicolored,** small "1995" year date		1.25	.25
	P# block of 4, 5#	6.25	—
a.	Large date, 2000	1.25	.25
	P# block of 4, 5#	6.25	—

Date on No. 2998 is 1mm long, on No. 2998a 1½mm long.

REPUBLIC OF PALAU

A2312

Designed by Herb Kane.
Printed by Sterling Sommer for Ashton-Potter (USA) Ltd.

LITHOGRAPHED
Sheets of 200 in four panes of 50

1995, Sept. 29	Tagged	Perf. 11.1	
2999 A2312 32c **multicolored**		.60	.20
	P# block of 4, 5#+P	3.00	—

See Palau Nos. 377-378.

COMIC STRIPS

A2313

Designed by Carl Herrman.

Printed by Stamp Venturers.

Designs: a, The Yellow Kid. b, Katzenjammer Kids. c, Little Nemo in Slumberland. d, Bringing Up Father. e, Krazy Kat. f, Rube Goldberg's Inventions. g, Toonerville Folks. h, Gasoline Alley. i, Barney Google. j, Little Orphan Annie. k, Popeye. l, Blondie. m, Dick Tracy. n, Alley Oop. o, Nancy. p, Flash Gordon. q, Li'l Abner. r, Terry and the Pirates. s, Prince Valiant. t, Brenda Starr, Reporter.

PHOTOGRAVURE
Sheets of 120 in six panes of 20

1995, Oct. 1	Tagged	Perf. 10.1	
3000 A2313 Pane of 20		12.00	—
a.-t.	32c any single	.60	.20
	Sheet of 120 (6 panes)	105.00	—
	Cross gutter block of 20	35.00	—
	Cross gutter block of 4	17.50	—
	Vert. pairs with horiz. gutter (each)	3.75	—
	Horiz. pairs with vert. gutter (each)	3.75	—
u.	As No. 3000, a.-h. imperf., i.-l. part perf	—	
v.	As No. 3000, m.-t. imperf., i.-l. part perf	—	
w.	As No. 3000, a.-l. imperf.,m.-t. imperf vert.	—	

Inscriptions on back of each stamp describe the comic strip.
Cross gutter block of 20 consists of six panes from each of two panes and four stamps from each of two other panes with the cross gutter between.

U.S. NAVAL ACADEMY, 150th ANNIVERSARY

A2314 150TH ANNIVERSARY 1845-1995

Designed by Dean Ellis. Printed by Sterling-Sommer for Aston-Potter (USA) Ltd.

LITHOGRAPHED
Sheets of 160 in eight panes of 20

1995, Oct. 10	Tagged	Perf. 10.9	
3001 A2314 32c **multicolored**		.60	.20
	P# block of 4, 5#+P	2.40	—
	Pane of 20	12.00	—

Some plate blocks contain plate position diagram.

LITERARY ARTS SERIES

Tennessee Williams (1911-83) A2315

Designed by Michael Deas. Printed by Sterling-Sommer for Ashton-Potter (USA) Ltd.

LITHOGRAPHED
Sheets of 160 in eight panes of 20

1995, Oct. 13	Tagged	Perf. 11.1	
3002 A2315 32c **multicolored**		.60	.20
	P# block of 4, 5#+P	2.40	—
	Pane of 20	12.00	—

Some plate blocks contain plate position diagram.

CHRISTMAS

Madonna and Child, by Giotto di Bondone A2316

Santa Claus Entering Chimney A2317

Child Holding Jumping Jack — A2318

Child Holding Tree — A2319

Santa Claus Working on Sled — A2320

Midnight Angel A2321

Children Sledding A2322

Designed by Richard Sheaff (#3003), John Grossman & Laura Alders (#3004-3018).

Printed by Bureau of Engraving and Printing (#3003), Sterling-Sommer for Ashton-Potter (USA) Ltd. (#3004-3007), Avery Dennison (#3008-3011, 3013-3017), Banknote Corporation of America (#3012, 3018).

LITHOGRAPHED & ENGRAVED
Sheets of 300 in six panes of 50

1995	Tagged	Perf. 11.2	
3003 A2316 32c **multicolored,** Oct. 19		.60	.20
	P# block of 4, 5#	3.00	—
c.	Black (engr., denomination) omitted	250.00	

Some plate blocks contain plate position diagram.

BOOKLET STAMP
Perf. 9.8x10.9

3003A A2316 32c **multicolored,** Oct. 19		.60	.20
b.	Booklet pane of 10	6.00	4.00

LITHOGRAPHED
Sheets of 200 in four panes of 50

3004 A2317 32c **multicolored,** Sept. 30		.60	.20
3005 A2318 32c **multicolored,** Sept. 30		.60	.20
3006 A2319 32c **multicolored,** Sept. 30		.60	.20
3007 A2320 32c **multicolored,** Sept. 30		.60	.20
a.	Block or strip of 4, #3004-3007	2.40	1.25
	P# block of 4, 4#+P	3.00	—
b.	Booklet pane of 10, 3 each #3004-3005, 2 each #3006-3007	6.00	4.00
c.	Booklet pane of 10, 2 each #3004-3005, 3 each #3006-3007	6.00	4.00
d.	As "a," imperf	750.00	

PHOTOGRAVURE
Self-Adhesive Stamps
Serpentine Die Cut

3008 A2320 32c **multicolored,** Sept. 30		.60	.20
3009 A2318 32c **multicolored,** Sept. 30		.60	.20
3010 A2317 32c **multicolored,** Sept. 30		.60	.20
3011 A2319 32c **multicolored,** Sept. 30		.60	.20
a.	Booklet pane of 20, 5 each #3008-3011 + label	12.00	

LITHOGRAPHED

3012 A2321 32c **multicolored,** Oct. 19		.60	.20
a.	Booklet pane of 20 + label	12.00	
b.	Vert. pair, no die cutting between	—	
c.	Booklet pane of 15 + label, 1996	9.00	
d.	Booklet pane of 15	—	

Colors of No. 3012c are deeper than those on #3012a. Label on #3012c has die-cutting, not found on label of #3012a.
No. 3012d is a pane of 16 with one stamp removed. The missing stamp is from the second row, either from the top or bottom, of the pane. No. 3012d cannot be made from No. 3012c, a pane of 15 + label. The label is die cut. If the label is removed, an impression of the die cutting appears on the backing paper.

PHOTOGRAVURE
Die Cut

3013 A2322 32c **multicolored,** Oct. 19		.60	.20
a.	Booklet pane of 18	11.00	

Self-Adhesive Coil Stamps
Serpentine Die Cut Vert.

3014 A2320 32c **multicolored,** Sept. 30		.60	.30
3015 A2318 32c **multicolored,** Sept. 30		.60	.30
3016 A2317 32c **multicolored,** Sept. 30		.60	.30
3017 A2319 32c **multicolored,** Sept. 30		.60	.30
a.	Strip of 4, #3014-3017	2.40	
	P# strip of 5, 1 each #3014-3017 + 1 stamp, P#V1111	4.75	
	P# strip of 8, 2 each #3014-3017, P#V1111	6.50	
	P# single (#3017), #V1111	—	3.50

LITHOGRAPHED

3018 A2321 32c **multicolored,** Oct. 19		.60	.30
	P# strip of 5, #B1111	5.00	
	P# single, #B1111	—	3.50

Nos. 3014-3018 were only available through the Philatelic Fullfillment Center in Kansas City.

ANTIQUE AUTOMOBILES

1893
Duryea — A2323

1894
Haynes — A2324

1898 Columbia
A2325

1899
Winton — A2326

1901
White — A2327

Designed by Ken Dallison.
Printed by Stamp Venturers.

PHOTOGRAVURE
Sheets of 200 in eight panes of 25

1995, Nov. 3		Tagged		Perf. 11.1
3019	A2323	32c **multicolored**	.60	.20
3020	A2324	32c **multicolored**	.60	.20
3021	A2325	32c **multicolored**	.60	.20
3022	A2326	32c **multicolored**	.60	.20
3023	A2327	32c **multicolored**	.60	.20
a.	Vert. or horiz. strip of 5, #3019-3023		3.00	2.00
	Vert. or Horiz. P# block of 10, 2			
	sets of 4#+S		6.00	—
	Pane of 25		15.00	—

Some plate blocks contain plate position diagram. Vert. and horiz. strips are all in different order.

UTAH STATEHOOD CENTENARY

Delicate Arch, Arches Natl.
Park — A2328

Designed by McRay Magleby.
Printed by Sterling Sommer for Ashton-Potter (USA) Ltd.

LITHOGRAPHED
Sheets of 200 in four panes of 50

1996, Jan. 4		Tagged		Perf. 11.1
3024	A2328	32c **multicolored**	.60	.20
		P# block of 4, 5#+P	3.00	—

For booklet see No. BK245.

GARDEN FLOWERS

Crocus — A2329

Winter
Aconite — A2330

Pansy — A2331

Snowdrop — A2332

Anemone — A2333

Designed by Ned Seidler.

LITHOGRAPHED & ENGRAVED
BOOKLET STAMPS

1996, Jan. 19		Tagged		Perf. 10.9 Vert.
3025	A2329	32c **multicolored**	.60	.20
3026	A2330	32c **multicolored**	.60	.20
3027	A2331	32c **multicolored**	.60	.20
3028	A2332	32c **multicolored**	.60	.20
3029	A2333	32c **multicolored**	.60	.20
a.	Booklet pane of 5, #3025-3029		3.00	2.50
b.	As "a," imperf.		—	

LOVE

Cherub from Sistine Madonna, by
Raphael — A2334

Designed by Terry McCaffrey.
Printed by Banknote Corporation of America.

LITHOGRAPHED & ENGRAVED
BOOKLET STAMP
Serpentine Die Cut 11.3x11.7

1996, Jan. 20				Tagged
		Self-Adhesive		
3030	A2334	32c **multicolored**	.60	.20
a.	Booklet pane of 20 + label		12.00	
b.	Booklet pane of 15 + label		9.00	
c.	Red omitted		—	

FLORA AND FAUNA SERIES
Kestrel, Blue Jay and Rose Types of 1993-95 and

Red-headed
Woodpecker — A2335

Eastern
Bluebird — A2336

Red Fox
A2339

Ring-necked
Pheasant
A2350

Coral Pink Rose — A2351

Designed by Michael Matherly (#3031-3033, 3044-3045); Terry McCaffrey (#3050-3051, 3055); Derry Noyes (#3036, 3052, 3052E).
Printed by Banknote Corporation of America (#3036); Bureau of Engraving & Printing (#3031-3033, 3044-3045); Stamp Venturers (#3048-3049, 3053); Avery Dennison (#3050-3051). American Packaging Corp. for Sennett Security Products (#3052); Sennett Security Products (#3052E).

LITHOGRAPHED
Sheets of 300 in six panes of 50 (#3031).
Sheets of 400 in four panes of 100 (#3032-3033).
Sheets of 120 in six panes of 20 (#3036).

1996-2000		Untagged	*Serpentine Die Cut 10½*		
		Self-Adhesive (#3031)			
3031	A1841	1c **multicolored**, *Nov. 19, 1999*		.20	.20
		P# block of 4, 5#		.25	

			Perf. 11		
3032	A2335	2c **multicolored**, *Feb. 2*		.20	.20
		P# block of 4, 5#		.25	—
3033	A2336	3c **multicolored**, *Apr. 3*		.20	.20
		P# block of 4, 5#		.25	—

Some plate blocks contain plate position diagram.

Tagged
Serpentine Die Cut 11½x11¼
Self-Adhesive

3036	A2339	$1 **multicolored**, *Aug. 14, 1998*	2.00	.50
		P# block of 4, 4#+B	8.00	
		Pane of 20	40.00	

COIL STAMPS
Perf. 9¾ Vert.

3044	A1841	1c **multicolored**, small date, *Jan. 20*	.20	.20
		Pair	.20	.20
		P# strip of 5, #1111 in black, yellow, blue, magenta order	.65	
		P# single, same	—	.40
		P# strip of 5, #1111 in black, blue, yellow, magenta order	.90	
		P# single, same	—	.40
a.	Large date		.20	.20
		Pair	.20	.20
		P# strip of 5, #1111, 2222 in yellow, magenta, blue, black order	.90	
		P# single, same	—	.50

Date on No. 3044 is 1mm long, on No. 3044a 1.5mm long.

3045	A2335	2c **multicolored**, *June 22, 1999*	.20	.20
		Pair	.20	.20
		P# strip of 5, #11111	.75	—
		P# single, #11111	—	.20

BOOKLET STAMPS
PHOTOGRAVURE
Serpentine Die Cut 10½x10¾ on 3 Sides

1996-99			Tagged	
		Self-Adhesive		
3048	A1847	20c **multicolored**, *Aug. 2, 1996*	.40	.20
a.	Booklet pane of 10		4.00	
b.	Booklet pane of 4		1.60	
c.	Booklet pane of 6		2.40	

Nos. 3048b-3048c are from the vending machine booklet, No. BK237, that has a glue strip at the top edge of the top pane, the peelable strip removed and the rouletting line 2mm lower than on No. 3048a.

Serpentine Die Cut 11¼x11¾ on 2, 3 or 4 Sides

3049	A1853 32c **yellow, orange, green &** **black**, Oct. 24, 1996		.60	.20
a.	Booklet pane of 20 + label		12.00	
b.	Booklet pane of 4, Dec. 1996		2.75	
c.	Booklet pane of 5 + label, Dec. 1996		3.20	
	P# single, #S1111		.80	1.00
d.	Booklet pane of 6, Dec. 1996		3.60	
	P# single, #S1111		.80	1.00

The plate # single in No. 3049c is on the lower left stamp. In No. 3049d it is the lower right stamp on the bottom pane of the booklet.

Serpentine Die Cut 11¼ on 2 or 3 Sides

3050	A2350 20c **multicolored**, July 31, 1998		.40	.20
a.	Booklet pane of 10		4.00	

1996-99			**Tagge**
3051	A2350 20c **multicolored**, July 1999		.40	.20
a.	Serpentine die cut 10½ on 3 sides		.40	.20
b.	Booklet pane of 5, 4 #3051, 1 #3051a turned sideways at top		2.00	
c.	Booklet pane of 5, 4 #3051, 1 #3051a turned sideways at bottom		2.00	

Serpentine Die Cut 11½x11¼ on 2, 3 or 4 Sides

3052	A2351 33c **multicolored**, Aug. 13, 1999		.65	.20
a.	Booklet pane of 4		2.60	
b.	Booklet pane of 5 + label		3.25	
c.	Booklet pane of 6		3.90	
d.	Booklet pane of 20 + label		13.00	

Serpentine Die Cut 10¾x10½ on 2 or 3 sides

3052E	A2351 33c **multicolored**, Apr. 7, 2000		.65	.20
f.	Booklet pane of 20		13.00	

No. 3052Ef is a double-sided booklet pane with 12 stamps on one side and 8 stamps plus label on the other side.

COIL STAMPS
Serpentine Die Cut 11½ Vert.

3053	A1847 20c **multicolored**, Aug. 2, 1996		.40	.20
	Pair		.80	
	P# strip of 5, #S1111		3.25	
	P# single, #S1111		—	2.50

Yellow Rose, Ring-necked Pheasant Types of 1996-98

Printed by Bureau of Engraving and Printing (#3054-3055).

COIL STAMPS
LITHOGRAPHED

1997-98	Tagged	Serpentine Die Cut 9¾ Vert.
		Self-Adhesive

3054	A1853 32c **yellow, magenta, black &** **green**, Aug. 1, 1997		.60	.20
	Pair		1.25	
	P# strip of 5, #1111, 1112, 1122, 2222, 2223, 2233, 2333, 3344, 3444, 4455, 5455, 5555, 5556, 5566, 5666, 6666, 6677, 6777, 7777, 8888		5.00	
	P# single, same #		—	2.50
a.	Imperf., pair		90.00	
b.	Black, yellow & green omitted		—	
c.	Black, yellow & green omitted, imperf. pair		—	
d.	Black omitted		—	
e.	Black omitted, imperf. pair		—	

Nos. 3054b and 3054d also are miscut and with shifted die cuttings.

3055	A2350 20c **multicolored**, July, 31, 1998		.40	.20
	Pair		.80	
	P# strip of 5, P#1111, 2222		4.00	
	P# single, same		—	3.00
a.	Imperf., pair		—	

BLACK HERITAGE SERIES

Ernest E. Just (1883-1941), Marine Biologist — A2358

Designed by Richard Sheaff.
Printed by Banknote Corporation of America.

LITHOGRAPHED
Sheets of 160 in eight panes of 20

1996, Feb. 1	Tagged		Perf. 11.1
3058	A2358 32c **gray & black**		.60	.20
	P# block of 4, 4#+B		2.40	—
	Pane of 20		12.00	—

SMITHSONIAN INSTITUTION, 150TH ANNIVERSARY

A2359

Designed by Tom Engeman.
Printed by Ashton-Potter (USA) Ltd.

LITHOGRAPHED
Sheets of 160 in eight panes of 20

1996, Feb. 7	Tagged		Perf. 11.1
3059	A2359 32c **multicolored**		.60	.20
	P# block of 4, 4#+P		2.40	—
	Pane of 20		12.00	—

Some plate blocks contain plate position diagram.

CHINESE NEW YEAR

Year of the Rat — A2360

Designed by Clarence Lee.
Printed by Stamp Venturers.

PHOTOGRAVURE
Sheets of 180 in nine panes of 20

1996, Feb. 8	Tagged		Perf. 11.1
3060	A2360 32c **multicolored**		.60	.20
	P# block of 4, 4#+S		2.40	—
	Pane of 20		12.00	—
a.	Imperf., pair		—	

Some plate blocks contain plate position diagram.

PIONEERS OF COMMUNICATION

Eadweard Muybridge (1830-1904), Photographer A2361

Ottmar Mergenthaler (1854-99), Inventor of Linotype — A2362

Frederic E. Ives (1856-1937), Developer of Halftone Process — A2363

William Dickson (1860-1935), Co-developer of Kinetoscope A2364

Designed by Fred Otnes.
Printed by Ashton-Potter USA.

LITHOGRAPHED
Sheets of 120 in six panes of 20

1996, Feb. 22	Tagged		Perf. 11.1x11
3061	A2361 32c **multicolored**		.60	.20
3062	A2362 32c **multicolored**		.60	.20
3063	A2363 32c **multicolored**		.60	.20
3064	A2364 32c **multicolored**		.60	.20
a.	Block or strip of 4, #3061-3064		2.40	1.75
	P# block of 4, 5#+P		2.40	—
	Pane of 20		12.00	—

Some plate blocks contain plate position diagram.

FULBRIGHT SCHOLARSHIPS, 50th ANNIVERSARY

A2365

Designed by Richard D. Sheaff.

LITHOGRAPHED & ENGRAVED
Sheets of 200 in four panes of 50

1996, Feb. 28	Tagged		Perf. 11.1
3065	A2365 32c **multicolored**		.60	.20
	P# block of 4, 5#		3.00	—

Some plate blocks contain plate position diagram.
For booklet see No. BK246.

JACQUELINE COCHRAN (1910-80), PILOT

A2366

Designed by Davis Meltzer.

LITHOGRAPHED & ENGRAVED
Sheets of 300 in six panes of 50

1996, Mar. 9	Tagged		Perf. 11.1
3066	A2366 50c **multicolored**		1.00	.20
	P# block of 4, 5#		5.00	—
a.	Black (engr.) omitted		70.00	

MARATHON

A2367

Designed by Michael Bartalos.

Printed by Banknote Corporation of America.

LITHOGRAPHED
Sheets of 160 in eight panes of 20

1996, Apr. 11	Tagged		Perf. 11.1
3067	A2367 32c **multicolored**		.60	.20
	P# block of 4, 4#+B		2.40	—
	Pane of 20		12.00	—

1996 SUMMER OLYMPIC GAMES

A2368

Designed by Richard Waldrep. Printed by Stamp Venturers.

Designs: a, Decathlon (javelin). b, Men's canoeing. c, Women's running. d, Women's diving. e, Men's cycling. f, Freestyle wrestling. g, Women's gymnastics. h, Women's sailboarding. i, Men's shot put. j, Women's soccer. k, Beach volleyball. l, Men's rowing. m, Men's sprints. n, Women's swimming. o, Women's softball. p, Men's hurdles. q, Men's swimming. r, Men's gymnastics (pommel horse). s, Equestrian. t, Men's basketball.

PHOTOGRAVURE
Sheets of 120 in six panes of 20

1996, May 2		Tagged	Perf. 10.1	
3068	A2368	Pane of 20	12.00	—
a.-t.		32c any single	.60	.20
		Sheet of 120 (6 panes)	105.00	—
		Cross gutter block of 20	35.00	—
		Cross gutter block of 4	17.50	—
		Vert. pairs with horiz. gutter (each)	3.75	—
		Horiz. pairs with vert. gutter (each)	3.75	—
u.		As No. 3068, imperf	1,500.	—
v.		As No. 3068, back inscriptions omitted on a., f., k. & p., incorrect back inscriptions on others		—

Inscription on back of each stamp describes the sport shown. Cross gutter block of 20 consists of six stamps from each of two panes and four stamps from each of two other panes with the cross gutter between.

GEORGIA O'KEEFFE (1887-1986)

A2369

Designed by Margaret Bauer. Printed by Stamp Venturers.

PHOTOGRAVURE
Sheets of 90 in six panes of 15

1996, May 23		Tagged	Perf. 11.6x11.4	
3069	A2369	32c multicolored	.65	.20
		P# block of 4, 5#+S	2.75	—
		Pane of 15	10.00	—
a.		Imperf., pair	200.00	
		Pane of 15, imperf.	1,500.	—

For booklet see No. BK247.

TENNESSEE STATEHOOD BICENTENNIAL

A2370

Designed by Phil Jordan. Printed by Stamp Venturers.

PHOTOGRAVURE
Sheets of 200 in four panes of 50.

1996, May 31		Tagged	Perf. 11.1	
3070	A2370	32c multicolored	.60	.20
		P# block of 4, 5#+S	3.00	—

For booklet see No. BK248.

Booklet Stamp
Self-Adhesive
Serpentine Die Cut 9.9x10.8

3071	A2370	32c multicolored	.60	.30
a.		Booklet pane of 20, #S11111	12.00	—
b.		Horiz. pair, no die cutting btwn.		—
c.		Imperf., pair		—
d.		Horiz. pair, imperf vert.		—

AMERICAN INDIAN DANCES

Fancy — A2371

Butterfly — A2372

Traditional
A2373

Raven
A2374

Hoop — A2375

Designed by Keith Birdsong. Printed by Ashton-Potter (USA) Ltd.

LITHOGRAPHED
Sheets of 120 in six panes of 20.

1996, June 7		Tagged	Perf. 11.1	
3072	A2371	32c multicolored	.60	.20
3073	A2372	32c multicolored	.60	.20
3074	A2373	32c multicolored	.60	.20
3075	A2374	32c multicolored	.60	.20

3076	A2375	32c multicolored	.60	.20
a.		Strip of 5, #3072-3076	3.00	1.75
		P# block of 10, 4#+P	6.00	—
		Pane of 20	12.00	—

For booklet see No. BK249.

PREHISTORIC ANIMALS

Eohippus — A2376

Woolly Mammoth — A2377

Mastodon — A2378

Saber-tooth Cat — A2379

Designed by Davis Meltzer. Printed by Ashton-Potter (USA) Ltd.

LITHOGRAPHED
Sheets of 120 in six panes of 20

1996, June 8		Tagged	Perf. 11.1x11	
3077	A2376	32c multicolored	.60	.20
3078	A2377	32c multicolored	.60	.20
3079	A2378	32c multicolored	.60	.20
3080	A2379	32c multicolored	.60	.20
a.		Block or strip of 4, #3077-3080	2.40	1.50
		P# block of 4, 4#+P	2.40	—
		Pane of 20	12.00	—

A2380

A2381

BREAST CANCER AWARENESS
Designed by Tom Mann. Printed by Ashton-Potter (USA) Ltd.

LITHOGRAPHED
Sheets of 120 in six panes of 20

1996, June 15		Tagged	Perf. 11.1	
3081	A2380	32c multicolored	.60	.20
		P# block of 4, 5#+P	2.40	—
		Pane of 20	12.00	—

LEGENDS OF HOLLYWOOD
James Dean (1931-55)

Designed by Michael Deas.

Printed by Stamp Venturers.

PHOTOGRAVURE
Sheets of 120 in six panes of 20.

1996, June 24	Tagged	Perf. 11.1
3082 A2381 32c **multicolored**	.60	.20
P# block of 4, 7#+S	2.50	
Pane of 20	12.50	
Sheet of 120 (six panes)	75.00	
Cross gutter block of 8	25.00	—
Block of 8 with vertical gutter	17.50	—
Horiz. pair with vert. gutter	4.00	—
Vert. pair with horiz. gutter	2.50	—
a. Imperf., pair	425.00	
Pane of 20, imperf.	4,750.	
b. As "a," red (USA 32c) omitted		

Perforations in corner of each stamp are star-shaped. No. 3082 was also available on the first day of issue in at least 127 Warner Bros. Studio stores.

Cross-gutter block consists of 3 stamps vertically from 2 upper panes and 1 stamp each from 2 lower panes.

For booklet see No. BK250.

FOLK HEROES

MIGHTY CASEY
A2382

PAUL BUNYAN
A2383

JOHN HENRY
A2384

PECOS BILL
A2385

Designed by David LaFleur.

Printed by Ashton-Potter (USA) Ltd.

LITHOGRAPHED
Sheets of 120 in six panes of 20

1996, July 11	Tagged	Perf. 11.1x11
3083 A2382 32c **multicolored**	.60	.20
3084 A2383 32c **multicolored**	.60	.20
3085 A2384 32c **multicolored**	.60	.20
3086 A2385 32c **multicolored**	.60	.20
a. Block or strip of 4, #3083-3086	2.40	1.50
P# block of 4, 4#+P	2.40	
Pane of 20	12.00	—

For booklet see No. BK251.

Myron's Discobolus — A2386

Young Corn, by Grant Wood — A2387

CENTENNIAL OLYMPIC GAMES
Designed by Carl Herrman.

Printed by Ashton-Potter (USA) Ltd.

ENGRAVED
Sheets of 80 in four panes of 20

1996, July 19	Tagged	Perf. 11.1
3087 A2386 32c **brown**	.65	.20
P# block of 4, 1#+P	3.75	
Pane of 20	17.50	—

Sheet margin of the pane of 20 is lithographed.
For booklet see No. BK252.

IOWA STATEHOOD, 150TH ANNIVERSARY
Designed by Carl Herrman.

Printed by Ashton-Potter (USA) Ltd. (#3088), Banknote Corporation of America (#3089)

LITHOGRAPHED
Sheets of 200 in four panes of 50

1996, Aug. 1	Tagged	Perf. 11.1
3088 A2387 32c **multicolored**	.60	.20
P# block of 4, 4#+P	3.00	—

For booklet see No. BK253.

BOOKLET STAMP
Self-Adhesive
Serpentine Die Cut 11.6x11.4

3089 A2387 32c **multicolored**	.60	.30
a. Booklet pane of 20	12.00	

RURAL FREE DELIVERY, CENT.

A2388

Designed by Richard Sheaff.

LITHOGRAPHED & ENGRAVED
Sheets of 120 in six panes of 20

1996, Aug. 7	Tagged	Perf. 11.2x11
3090 A2388 32c **multicolored**	.60	.20
P# block of 4, 5#	2.40	—
Pane of 20	12.00	—

For booklet see No. BK254.

RIVERBOATS

Robt. E. Lee — A2389

Sylvan Dell — A2390

Far West — A2391

Rebecca Everingham A2392

Bailey Gatzert — A2393

Designed by Dean Ellis.

Printed by Avery Dennison.

PHOTOGRAVURE
Sheets of 200 in 10 panes of 20
Serpentine Die Cut 11x11.1

1996, Aug. 22		Tagged
Self-Adhesive		
3091 A2389 32c **multicolored**	.60	.20
3092 A2390 32c **multicolored**	.60	.20
3093 A2391 32c **multicolored**	.60	.20
3094 A2392 32c **multicolored**	.60	.20
3095 A2393 32c **multicolored**	.60	.20
a. Vert. strip of 5, #3091-3095	3.00	
P# block of 10, 5#+V	6.00	
Pane of 20	12.00	
b. Strip of 5, #3091-3095, with special die cutting	75.00	50.00
P# block of 10, 5#+V	140.00	
Pane of 20	280.00	

The serpentine die cutting runs through the peelable backing to which Nos. 3091-3095 are affixed. No. 3095a exists with stamps in different sequences.

On the long side of each stamp in No. 3095b, the die cutting is missing 3 "perforations" between the stamps, one near each end and one in the middle. This allows a complete strip to be removed from the backing paper for use on a first day cover. No. 3095b was also used to make Souvenir Page No. 1215.

For booklet see No. BK255.

AMERICAN MUSIC SERIES
Big Band Leaders

Count Basie — A2394

Tommy & Jimmy Dorsey — A2395

Glenn Miller — A2396

Benny Goodman A2397

Songwriters

Harold Arlen — A2398

Johnny
Mercer — A2399

Dorothy
Fields — A2400

Hoagy Carmichael
A2401

Designed by Bill Nelson (#3096-3099), Gregg Rudd (#3100-3103).

Printed by Ashton-Potter (USA) Ltd.

LITHOGRAPHED
Sheets of 120 in six panes of 20

1996, Sept. 11	Tagged	Perf. 11.1x11	
3096 A2394 32c multicolored		.60	.20
3097 A2395 32c multicolored		.60	.20
3098 A2396 32c multicolored		.60	.20
3099 A2397 32c multicolored		.60	.20
a. Block or strip of 4, #3096-3099		2.40	1.50
P# block of 4, 6#+P		2.40	—
P# block of 8, 2 sets of P# + top label		4.80	—
Pane of 20		12.00	—
3100 A2398 32c multicolored		.60	.20
3101 A2399 32c multicolored		.60	.20
3102 A2400 32c multicolored		.60	.20
3103 A2401 32c multicolored		.60	.20
a. Block or strip of 4, #3100-3103		2.40	1.50
P# block of 4, 6#+P		2.40	—
P# block of 8, 2 sets of P# + top label		4.80	—
Pane of 20		12.00	—

LITERARY ARTS

F. Scott Fitzgerald
(1896-1940)
A2402

Designed by Michael Deas.

PHOTOGRAVURE
Sheets of 200 in four panes of 50

1996, Sept. 27	Tagged	Perf. 11.1	
3104 A2402 23c multicolored		.45	.20
P# block of 4, 4#		2.25	—

ENDANGERED SPECIES

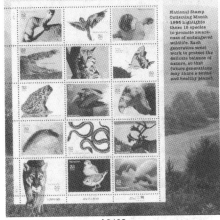

A2403

Designed by James Balog. Printed by Ashton-Potter (USA) Ltd.

Designs: a, Black-footed ferret. b, Thick-billed parrot. c, Hawaiian monk seal. d, American crocodile. e, Ocelot. f, Schaus swallowtail butterfly. g, Wyoming toad. h, Brown pelican. i, California condor. j, Gila trout. k, San Francisco garter snake. l, Woodland caribou. m, Florida panther. n, Piping plover. o, Florida manatee.

LITHOGRAPHED
Sheets of 90 in six panes of 15

1996, Oct. 2	Tagged	Perf. 11.1x11	
3105 A2403 Pane of 15		9.00	—
a.-o. 32c any single		.60	.20

See Mexico No. 1995. For booklet see No. BK256.

COMPUTER TECHNOLOGY

A2404

Designed by Nancy Skolos & Tom Wedell.

Printed by Ashton-Potter (USA) Ltd.

LITHOGRAPHED & ENGRAVED
Sheets of 160 in four panes of 40

1996, Oct. 8	Tagged	Perf. 10.9x11.1	
3106 A2404 32c multicolored		.60	.20
P# block of 4, 6#+P		3.00	—

CHRISTMAS

Madonna and Child from
Adoration of the Shepherds, by
Paolo de Matteis — A2405

Family at
Fireplace
A2406

Decorating Tree
A2407

Dreaming of
Santa Claus
A2408

Holiday Shopping
A2409

Skaters — A2410

Designed by Richard D. Sheaff (#3107, 3112), Julia Talcott (#3108-3111, 3113-3117).

Printed by Bureau of Engraving and Printing (#3107, 3112), Ashton-Potter (USA) Ltd. (#3108-3111), Banknote Corporation of America (#3113-3116), Avery-Dennison (#3117).

LITHOGRAPHED & ENGRAVED
Sheets of 300 in six panes of 50

1996	Tagged	Perf. 11.1x11.2	
3107 A2405 32c multicolored, Nov. 1		.60	.20
P# block of 4, 5#		3.00	—

For booklet see No. BK257.

LITHOGRAPHED
Perf. 11.3

3108 A2406 32c multicolored, Oct. 8		.60	.20
3109 A2407 32c multicolored, Oct. 8		.60	.20
3110 A2408 32c multicolored, Oct. 8		.60	.20
3111 A2409 32c multicolored, Oct. 8		.60	.20
a. Block or strip of 4, #3108-3111		2.40	1.50
P# block of 4, 4#+P		3.00	—
b. Strip of 4, #3110-3111, 3108-3109, with #3109 imperf., #3108 imperf. at right		—	

BOOKLET STAMPS
Self-Adhesive

LITHOGRAPHED & ENGRAVED
Serpentine Die Cut 10 on 2, 3 or 4 Sides

3112 A2405 32c multicolored, Nov. 1		.60	.20
a. Booklet pane of 20 + label		12.00	
b. No die cutting, pair		75.00	
c. As "a," no die cutting		—	

LITHOGRAPHED
Serpentine Die Cut 11.8x11.5 on 2, 3 or 4 Sides

3113 A2406 32c multicolored, Oct. 8		.60	.20
3114 A2407 32c multicolored, Oct. 8		.60	.20
3115 A2408 32c multicolored, Oct. 8		.60	.20
3116 A2409 32c multicolored, Oct. 8		.60	.20
a. Booklet pane of 20, 5 ea #3113-3116		12.00	
b. As "a," no die cutting		—	

PHOTOGRAVURE
Die Cut

3117 A2410 32c multicolored, Oct. 8		.60	.20
a. Booklet pane of 18		11.00	

HANUKKAH

A2411

Designed by Hannah Smotrich.

Printed by Avery Dennison.

PHOTOGRAVURE
Sheets of 200 in 10 panes of 20

1996, Oct. 22	Tagged	Serpentine Die Cut 11.1	
		Self-Adhesive	
3118 A2411 32c multicolored		.60	.20
P# block of 4, 5#+V		2.40	
Pane of 20		12.00	

Backing on No. 3118 is die cut with a continuous horizontal wavy line. The 1997 reprint is die cut with two short horizontal lines on each side of a semi-circle on the backing of each stamp.

See No. 3352, Israel No. 1289. For booklet see No. BK258.

CYCLING
Souvenir Sheet

A2412

Designed by McRay Magleby.

Printed by Stamp Venturers.

PHOTOGRAVURE

1996, Nov. 1	Tagged	Perf. 11x11.1	
3119 A2412 Sheet of 2		2.00	2.00
a. 50c orange & multi		1.00	1.00
b. 50c blue green & multi		1.00	1.00

CHINESE NEW YEAR

Year of the
Ox — A2413

Designed by Clarence Lee.

Printed by Stamp Venturers.

PHOTOGRAVURE
Sheets of 180 in 9 panes of 20

1997, Jan. 5	Tagged	Perf. 11.2	
3120 A2413 32c multicolored		.60	.20
P# block of 4, 4#+S		2.40	—
Pane of 20		12.00	—

BLACK HERITAGE SERIES

Brig. Gen. Benjamin O. Davis,
Sr. (1880-1970) — A2414

Designed by Richard Sheaff.

Printed by Banknote Corp. of America.

LITHOGRAPHED
Sheets of 120 in six panes of 20

1997, Jan. 28	Tagged	Serpentine Die Cut 11.4	
	Self-Adhesive		
3121 A2414 32c multicolored		.60	.20
P# block of 4, 4#+B		2.40	
Pane of 20		12.00	

Statue of Liberty Type of 1994
Printed by Avery-Dennison.

PHOTOGRAVURE
Serpentine Die Cut 11 on 2, 3 or 4 Sides

1997, Feb. 1		Tagged
	Self-Adhesive	
3122 A1951 32c red, light blue, dark blue & yel		.60 .20
a. Booklet pane of 20 + label		12.00
b. Booklet pane of 4		2.50
c. Booklet pane of 5 + label		3.20
P# single, #V1111		.80 1.00
d. Booklet pane of 6		3.60
P# single, #V1111		.80 1.00
h. As "a," no die cutting		

The plate # single in No. 3122c is the lower left stamp and should be collected unused with the reorder label to its right to differentiate it from the plate # single in No. 3122d which is the lower left stamp in the bottom pane of the booklet and should be collected with a normal stamp adjoining it at right. In used condition, these plate # singles are indistinguishable.

Serpentine Die Cut 11.5x11.8 on 2, 3 or 4 Sides

1997		Tagged
	Self-Adhesive	
3122E A1951 32c red, light blue, dark blue & yellow		.90 .20
f. Booklet pane of 20 + label		35.00
g. Booklet pane of 6		5.50
P# single, #V1111		1.25 1.25

The plate # single in No. 3122Eg is the lower left stamp in the bottom pane of the booklet.

LOVE

A2415   Swans   A2416

Designed by Marvin Mattelson.

Printed by Banknote Corp. of America.

LITHOGRAPHED

Serpentine Die Cut 11.8x11.6 on 2, 3 or 4 Sides

1997, Feb. 4		Tagged
	Self-Adhesive	
3123 A2415 32c multicolored		.60 .20
a. Booklet pane of 20 + label		12.00
b. No die cutting, pair		250.00
c. As "a," no die cutting		—
d. As "a," black omitted		—

Serpentine Die Cut 11.6x11.8 on 2, 3 or 4 Sides

3124 A2416 55c multicolored		1.00 .20
a. Booklet pane of 20 + label		21.00

HELPING CHILDREN LEARN

A2417

Designed by Chris Van Allsburg.

Printed by Avery-Dennison.

PHOTOGRAVURE
Sheets of 160 in eight panes of 20

1997, Feb. 18		Tagged
	Serpentine Die Cut 11.6x11.7	
	Self-Adhesive	
3125 A2417 32c multicolored		.60 .20
P# block of 4, 4#+V		2.40
Pane of 20		12.00

The die cut perforations of #3125 are fragile and separate easily.

MERIAN BOTANICAL PRINTS

Citron, Moth,
Larvae, Pupa,
Beetle
A2418

Flowering
Pineapple,
Cockroaches
A2419

No. 3128 (r), No. 3129 (l), No. 3128a below

Designed by Phil Jordan based on works by Maria Sibylla Merian (1647-1717).

Printed by Stamp Venturers.

PHOTOGRAVURE
Serpentine Die Cut 10.9x10.2 on 2, 3 or 4 Sides

1997, Mar. 3		Tagged
	Self-Adhesive	
3126 A2418 32c multicolored		.60 .20
3127 A2419 32c multicolored		.60 .20
a. Booklet pane, 10 ea #3126-3127 + label		12.00
b. Pair, #3126-3127		1.20
	Size: 18.5x24mm	
	Serpentine Die Cut 11.2x10.8 on 2 or 3 Sides	
3128 A2418 32c multicolored		.60 .20
a. See footnote		.60 .20
b. Booklet pane, 2 ea #3128-3129, 1 #3128a		3.00
3129 A2419 32c multicolored		.60 .20
a. See footnote		.60 .20
b. Booklet pane, 2 ea #3128-3129, 1 #3129a		3.00
c. Pair, #3128-3129		1.20

Nos. 3128a-3129a are placed sideways on the pane and are serpentine die cut 11.2 on top and bottom, 10.8 on left side. The right side is 11.2 broken by a large perf where the stamp meets the vertical perforations of the two stamps above it. See illustration above.

PACIFIC '97

Sailing Ship — A2420

Stagecoach — A2421

Designed by Richard Sheaff.

Printed by Banknote Corporation of America.

ENGRAVED
Sheets of 96 in six panes of 16

1997, Mar. 13	Tagged	Perf. 11.2	
3130 A2420 32c blue		.60	.20
3131 A2421 32c red		.60	.20
a. Pair, #3130-3131		1.25	.30
P# block of 4, 1#+B		2.50	—
Pane of 16		10.00	—
Sheet of 96 (6 panes)		80.00	
Cross gutter block of 16 (8 #3131a)		30.00	—
Vert. pairs with horiz. gutter (each)		10.00	—
Horiz. pairs with vert. gutter (each)		5.00	—

Juke Box and Flag Over Porch Types of 1995
Designed by Bill Nelson (#3132), Dave LaFleur (#3133).

Printed by Stamp Venturers.

PHOTOGRAVURE
COIL STAMPS

1997, Mar. 14	Untagged	*Imperf.*	
3132 A2225	(25c) bright orange red, bright yellow green & multi	.50	.50
	Pair	1.00	
	P# strip of 5, #M11111	4.50	
	P#, single, #M11111	2.00	

Tagged
Serpentine Die Cut 9.9 Vert.

3133 A2212	32c dark blue, tan, brown, red & light blue	.60	.20
	Pair	1.25	
	P# strip of 5, #M11111	4.75	
	P#, single, #M11111	2.50	

Nos. 3132-3133 were issued without backing paper. No. 3132 has simulated perforations ending in black bars at the top and bottom edges of the stamp. Sky on No. 3133 shows color gradation at LR not on Nos. 2915A or 2915D, and it has blue "1996" at left bottom.

LITERARY ARTS

Thornton Wilder
(1897-1975)
A2422

Designed by Phil Jordan.

Printed by Ashton-Potter (USA) Ltd.

LITHOGRAPHED
Sheets of 180 in nine panes of 20

1997, Apr. 17	Tagged	*Perf. 11.1*	
3134 A2422	32c multicolored	.60	.20
	P# block of 4, 4#+P	2.40	—
	Pane of 20	12.00	—

RAOUL WALLENBERG (1912-47)

Wallenberg and
Jewish
Refugees — A2423

Designed by Howard Paine.

Printed by Sterling Sommer for Ashton-Potter (USA) Ltd.

LITHOGRAPHED
Sheets of 180 in nine panes of 20

1997, Apr. 24	Tagged	*Perf. 11.1*	
3135 A2423	32c multicolored	.60	.20
	P# block of 4, 4#+P	2.40	—
	Pane of 20	12.00	—

DINOSAURS

A2424

Designed by James Gurney.
Printed by Sterling Sommer for Ashton-Potter (USA) Ltd.

Designs: a, Ceratosaurus. b, Camptosaurus. c, Camarasaurus. d, Brachiosaurus. e, Goniopholis. f, Stegosaurus. g, Allosaurus. h, Opisthias. i, Edmontonia. j, Einiosaurus. k, Daspletosaurus. l, Palaeosaniwa. m, Corythosaurus. n, Ornithominus. o, Parasaurolophus.

LITHOGRAPHED

1997, May 1	Tagged	*Perf. 11x11.1*	
3136 A2424	Sheet of 15	9.00	—
a.-o.	32c any single	.60	.20
p.	As No. 3136, bottom 7 stamps imperf.	—	

BUGS BUNNY

A2425

Cross Gutter Block of 12

Designed by Warner Bros.

Printed by Avery Dennison.

PHOTOGRAVURE

1997, May 22	Tagged	*Serpentine Die Cut 11*	
		Self-Adhesive	
3137	Pane of 10	6.00	
a.	A2425 32c single	.60	.20
b.	Booklet pane of 9 #3137a	5.40	
c.	Booklet pane of 1 #3137a	.60	
	Sheet of 60 (six panes) top	350.00	
	Sheet of 60 (six panes) bottom, with plate #	600.00	
	Pane of 10 from uncut press sheet	65.00	
	Pane of 10 with plate #	350.00	
	Cross gutter block of 12	250.00	
	Vert. pair with horiz. gutter	25.00	
	Horiz. pair with vert. gutter	50.00	

Die cutting on #3137 does not extend through the backing paper.
Booklet pane of 10 with P# comes from bottom uncut sheet of 60.
Nos. 3137b-3137c and 3138b-3138c are separated by a vertical line of microperforations that are absent on the uncut sheet of 60.
The horiz. pair with vert. gutter consists of a stamp at the left, from No. 3137b, part of the illustration of Bugs Bunny, the small gutter between the panes, and a stamp at the right from the left row of 3137b. Some pairs may include the single stamp from No. 3137c in addition to the two stamps at the right and left.

3138	Pane of 10	125.00	
a.	A2425 32c single	2.00	
b.	Booklet pane of 9 #3138a	—	
c.	Booklet pane of 1, imperf.	—	

Die cutting on #3138b extends through the backing paper. Used examples of No. 3138a are identical to those of No. 3137a.
An untagged promotional piece similar to No. 3137c exists on the same backing paper as the booklet pane, with the same design image, but without Bugs' signature and the single stamp. Replacing the stamp is an enlarged "32 / USA" in the same style as used on the stamp. This promotional piece was not valid for postage.

PACIFIC 97

Franklin
A2426

Washington
A2427

Designed by Richard Sheaff. Selvage on Nos. 3139-3140 is lithographed.

LITHOGRAPHED & ENGRAVED

1997	Tagged	*Perf. 10.5x10.4*	
3139	Pane of 12, May 29	12.00	—
a.	A2426 50c single	1.00	.50
3140	Pane of 12, May 30	14.50	—
a.	A2427 60c single	1.20	.60

Nos. 3139-3140 were sold through June 8.

MARSHALL PLAN, 50TH ANNIV.

Gen. George C.
Marshall, Map of
Europe — A2428

Designed by Richard Sheaff.

Printed by Stevens Security Press for Ashton-Potter (USA) Ltd.

LITHOGRAPHED & ENGRAVED
Sheets of 120 in six panes of 20

1997, June 4	Tagged	*Perf. 11.1*	
3141 A2428	32c multicolored	.60	.20
	P# block of 4, 5#+P	2.40	—
	Pane of 20	12.00	—

CLASSIC AMERICAN AIRCRAFT

A2429

Designed by Phil Jordan.

Printed by Stamp Venturers.

Designs: a, Mustang. b, Model B. c, Cub. d, Vega. e, Alpha. f, B-10. g, Corsair. h, Stratojet. i, GeeBee. j, Staggerwing. k, Flying Fortress. l, Stearman. m, Constellation. n, Lightning. o, Peashooter. p, Tri-Motor. q, DC-3. r, 314 Clipper. s, Jenny. t, Wildcat.

PHOTOGRAVURE
Sheets of 120 in six panes of 20

1997, July 19	Tagged	*Perf. 10.1*	
3142 A2429	Pane of 20	12.00	—
a.-t.	32c any single	.60	.20
	Sheet of 120 (6 panes)	72.50	
	Cross gutter block of 20	22.50	
	Cross gutter block of 4	17.50	
	Vert. pairs with horiz. gutter (each)	2.25	—
	Horiz. pairs with vert. gutter (each)	2.25	—

Inscriptions on back of each stamp describe the airplane.
Cross gutter block of 20 consists of six stamps from each of two panes and four stamps from each of two other panes with the cross gutter between.

FOOTBALL COACHES

Bear Bryant — A2430

Pop Warner — A2431

Vince Lombardi — A2432

George Halas — A2433

Designed by Carl Herrman.

Printed by Sterling Sommer for Ashton-Potter (USA) Ltd.

LITHOGRAPHED
Sheets of 120 in six panes of 20

1997		**Tagged**	**Perf. 11.2**	
3143	A2430	32c **multicolored**, *July 25*	.60	.20
3144	A2431	32c **multicolored**, *July 25*	.60	.20
3145	A2432	32c **multicolored**, *July 25*	.60	.20
3146	A2433	32c **multicolored**, *July 25*	.60	.20
a.		Block or strip of 4, #3143-3146	2.40	
		P# block of 4, 5#+P	2.40	
		P# block of 8, 2 sets of P# + top label	4.80	—
		Pane of 20	12.00	

With Red Bar Above Coach's Name
Perf. 11

3147	A2432	32c **multicolored**, *Aug. 5*	.60	.30
		P# block of 4, 4#+P	2.40	—
		Pane of 20	12.00	—
3148	A2430	32c **multicolored**, *Aug. 7*	.60	.30
		P# block of 4, 4#+P	2.40	—
		Pane of 20	12.00	—
3149	A2431	32c **multicolored**, *Aug. 8*	.60	.30
		P# block of 4, 4#+P	2.40	—
		Pane of 20	12.00	—
3150	A2433	32c **multicolored**, *Aug. 16*	.60	.30
		P# block of 4, 4#+P	2.40	—
		Pane of 20	12.00	—

AMERICAN DOLLS

A2434

Designed by Derry Noyes.

Printed by Sterling Sommer for Ashton-Potter (USA) Ltd.

Designs: a, "Alabama Baby," and doll by Martha Chase. b, "Columbian Doll." c, Johnny Gruelle's "Raggedy Ann." d, Doll by Martha Chase. e, "American Child." f, "Baby Coos." g, Plains Indian. h, Doll by Izannah Walker. i, "Babyland Rag." j, "Scootles." k, Doll by Ludwig Greiner. l, "Betsy McCall." m, Percy Crosby's "Skippy." n, "Maggie Mix-up." o, Dolls by Albert Schoenhut.

LITHOGRAPHED
Sheets of 90 in six panes of 15

1997, July 28		**Tagged**	**Perf. 10.9x11.1**	
3151	A2434	Pane of 15	9.00	—
a.-o.		32c any single	.60	.20

For booklet see No. BK266.

A2435

A2436

LEGENDS OF HOLLYWOOD
Humphrey Bogart (1899-1957).

Designed by Carl Herman.

Printed by Stamp Venturers.

PHOTOGRAVURE
Sheets of 120 in six panes of 20

1997, July 31		**Tagged**	**Perf. 11.1**	
3152	A2435	32c **multicolored**	.60	.20
		P# block of 4, 5#+S	2.50	—
		Pane of 20	12.50	—
		Sheet of 120 (6 panes)	75.00	—
		Cross gutter block of 8	17.50	—
		Block of 8 with vertical gutter	13.50	—
		Horiz. pair with vert. gutter	3.00	—
		Vert. pair with horiz. gutter	2.00	—

Perforations in corner of each stamp are star-shaped. Cross-gutter block consists of 6 stamps from upper panes and 2 stamps from panes below.
For booklet see No. BK267.

"THE STARS AND STRIPES FOREVER!"
Designed by Richard Sheaff.

Sheets of 300 in six panes of 50
PHOTOGRAVURE

1997, Aug. 21		**Tagged**	**Perf. 11.1**	
3153	A2436	32c **multicolored**	.60	.20
		P# block of 4, 4#	3.00	—

For booklet see No. BK268.

AMERICAN MUSIC SERIES
Opera Singers

Lily Pons — A2437

Richard Tucker — A2438

Lawrence Tibbett — A2439

Rosa Ponselle — A2440

Classical Composers & Conductors

Leopold Stokowski A2441

Arthur Fiedler — A2442

George Szell — A2443

Eugene Ormandy — A2444

Samuel Barber — A2445

Ferde Grofé — A2446

Charles Ives — A2447

Louis Moreau
Gottschalk
A2448

Designed by Howard Paine.

Printed by Ashton-Potter (USA) Ltd.

LITHOGRAPHED
Sheets of 120 in six panes of 20

1997		Tagged		Perf. 11	
3154	A2437	32c	multicolored, Sept. 10	.65	.20
3155	A2438	32c	multicolored, Sept. 10	.65	.20
3156	A2439	32c	multicolored, Sept. 10	.65	.20
3157	A2440	32c	multicolored, Sept. 10	.65	.20
a.		Block or strip of 4, #3154-3157		2.60	—
		P# block of 4, 5#+P		2.60	—
		P# block of 8, 2 sets of P# +			
		top label		5.00	—
		Pane of 20		12.50	—
3158	A2441	32c	multicolored, Sept. 12	.65	.20
3159	A2442	32c	multicolored, Sept. 12	.65	.20
3160	A2443	32c	multicolored, Sept. 12	.65	.20
3161	A2444	32c	multicolored, Sept. 12	.65	.20
3162	A2445	32c	multicolored, Sept. 12	.65	.20
3163	A2446	32c	multicolored, Sept. 12	.65	.20
3164	A2447	32c	multicolored, Sept. 12	.65	.20
3165	A2448	32c	multicolored, Sept. 12	.65	.20
a.		Block of 8, #3158-3165		5.25	—
		P# block of 8, 2 sets of 5P#+P			
		+ top label		5.25	—
		Pane of 20		13.00	—

PADRE FÉLIX VARELA (1788-1853)

A2449

Designed by Carl Herrman.

Printed by Sterling Sommer for Ashton-Potter (USA) Ltd.

LITHOGRAPHED
Sheets of 120 in six panes of 20

1997, Sept. 15		Tagged		Perf. 11.2	
3166	A2449	32c	purple	.60	.20
		P# block of 4, 1#+P		2.40	—
		Pane of 20		12.00	—

DEPARTMENT OF THE AIR FORCE, 50TH ANNIV.

Thunderbirds Aerial
Demonstration
Squadron — A2450

Designed by Phil Jordan.

Printed by Sterling Sommer for Ashton-Potter (USA) Ltd.

LITHOGRAPHED
Sheets of 180 in nine panes of 20

1997, Sept. 18		Tagged		Perf. 11.2x11.1	
3167	A2450	32c	multicolored	.60	.20
		P# block of 4, 4#+P		2.40	—
		Pane of 20		12.00	—

A hidden 3-D design can be seen on the stamp when it is viewed with a special viewer sold by the post office.

CLASSIC MOVIE MONSTERS

Lon Chaney as The
Phantom of the
Opera — A2451

Bela Lugosi as
Dracula — A2452

Boris Karloff as
Frankenstein's
Monster — A2453

Boris Karloff as The
Mummy — A2454

Lon Chaney, Jr. as The
Wolf Man — A2455

Cross Gutter Block of 8

Designed by Derry Noyes.

Printed by Stamp Venturers.

PHOTOGRAVURE
Sheets of 180 in nine panes of 20

1997, Sept. 30		Tagged		Perf. 10.2	
3168	A2451	32c	multicolored	.60	.20
3169	A2452	32c	multicolored	.60	.20
3170	A2453	32c	multicolored	.60	.20
3171	A2454	32c	multicolored	.60	.20
3172	A2455	32c	multicolored	.60	.20
a.		Strip of 5, #3168-3172		3.00	—
		P# block of 10, 5#+S		6.00	—
		Pane of 20		12.00	—
		Sheet of 180 (9 panes)		110.00	
		Cross-gutter block of 8		15.00	
		Block of 8 with vert. gutter		9.50	
		Block of 10 with horiz. gutter		11.50	
		Vert. pair with horiz. gutter		2.25	—
		Horiz. pair with vert. gutter		2.25	—

Plate blocks may contain top label. See note after No. 3167.

For booklet see No. BK269.

FIRST SUPERSONIC FLIGHT, 50TH ANNIV.

A2456

Designed by Phil Jordan.

Printed by Banknote Corporation of America.

LITHOGRAPHED
Sheets of 180 in nine panes of 20

1997, Oct. 14		Tagged		Serpentine Die Cut 11.4	
		Self-Adhesive			
3173	A2456	32c	multicolored	.60	.20
		P# block of 4, 4#+B		2.40	
		Pane of 20		12.00	

WOMEN IN MILITARY SERVICE

A2457

Designed by Derry Noyes.

Printed by Banknote Corporation of America.

LITHOGRAPHED
Sheets of 120 in six panes of 20

1997, Oct. 18		Tagged		Perf. 11.1	
3174	A2457	32c	multicolored	.60	.20
		P# block of 4, 6#+B		2.40	
		Pane of 20		12.00	

KWANZAA

A2458

Designed by Synthia Saint James. Printed by Avery Dennison.

PHOTOGRAVURE
Sheets of 250 in five panes of 50

1997, Oct. 22		Tagged		Serpentine Die Cut 11	
		Self-Adhesive			
3175	A2458	32c	multicolored	.60	.20
		P# block of 4, 4#+V		3.00	
		Sheet of 250 (5 panes)		550.00	
		P# block of 4, 4#+V and 4			
		sets of #+VO		225.00	
		Horiz. pair with vert. gutter		11.00	

See No. 3368.

CHRISTMAS

Madonna and
Child, by Sano di
Pietro — A2459

Holly — A2460

Designed by Richard D. Sheaff (#3176), Howard Paine (#3177).

Printed by Bureau of Engraving and Printing (#3176), Banknote Corporation of America (#3177).

LITHOGRAPHED
Serpentine Die Cut 9.9 on 2, 3 or 4 Sides

1997			Tagged

Booklet Stamps
Self-Adhesive

3176	A2459	32c	multicolored, *Oct. 27*	.60	.20
a.		Booklet pane of 20 + label		12.00	

Serpentine Die Cut 11.2x11.8 on 2, 3 or 4 Sides

3177	A2460	32c	multicolored, *Oct. 30*	.60	.20
a.		Booklet pane of 20 + label		12.00	
b.		Booklet pane of 4		2.50	
c.		Booklet pane of 5 + label		3.00	
d.		Booklet pane of 6		3.75	

MARS PATHFINDER
Souvenir Sheet

Mars Rover Sojourner — A2461

Designed by Terry McCaffrey. Printed by Stamp Venturers.

PHOTOGRAVURE

1997, Dec. 10		Tagged		*Perf. 11x11.1*	
3178	A2461	$3	multicolored	6.00	3.00
a.		$3, single stamp		5.50	2.75
		Sheet of 18		125.00	
		Vert. pair with horiz. gutter		15.00	—
		Single souvenir sheet from sheet of 18		7.00	—

The perforations at the bottom of the stamp contain the letters "USA." Vertical rouletting extends from the vertical perforations of the stamp to the bottom of the souvenir sheet.

Sheet of 18 has vertical perforations separating the three rows of souvenir sheets. These were cut away when No. 3178 was produced.

Souvenir sheet from sheet of 18 is wider and has vertical perforations on one or two sides.

See note after No. 3167.

CHINESE NEW YEAR

Year of the Tiger — A2462

Designed by Clarence Lee. Printed by Stamp Venturers.

PHOTOGRAVURE
Sheets of 180 in nine panes of 20

1998, Jan. 5		Tagged		*Perf. 11.2*	
3179	A2462	32c	multicolored	.60	.20
		P# block of 4, 4#+S		2.40	—
		Pane of 20		12.00	

A2463

A2464

ALPINE SKIING
Designed by Michael Schwab.

Printed by Banknote Corporation of America.

LITHOGRAPHED
Sheets of 180 in nine panes of 20

1998, Jan. 22		Tagged		*Perf. 11.2*	
3180	A2463	32c	multicolored	.60	.20
		P# block of 4, 6#+B		2.40	—
		Pane of 20		12.00	

BLACK HERITAGE SERIES
Madam C.J. Walker (1867-1919), Entrepreneur
Designed by Richard Sheaff. Printed by Banknote Corp. of America.

LITHOGRAPHED
Sheets of 180 in nine panes of 20
Serpentine Die Cut 11.6x11.3

1998, Jan. 28		Tagged	

Self-Adhesive

3181	A2464	32c	sepia & black	.60	.20
		P# block of 4, 3#+B		2.40	
		Pane of 20		12.00	

CELEBRATE THE CENTURY

1900s — A2465

No. 3182: a, Model T Ford. b, Theodore Roosevelt. c, Motion picture "The Great Train Robbery," 1903. d, Crayola Crayons introduced, 1903. e, St. Louis World's Fair, 1904. f, Design used on Hunt's Remedy stamp (#RS56), Pure Food & Drug Act, 1906. g, Wright Brothers first flight, Kitty Hawk, 1903. h, Boxing match shown in painting "Stag at Sharkey's," by George Bellows of the Ash Can School. i, Immigrants arrive. j, John Muir, preservationist. k, "Teddy" Bear created. l, W.E.B. Du Bois, social activist. m, Gibson Girl. n, First baseball World Series, 1903. o, Robie House, Chicago, designed by Frank Lloyd Wright.

1910s — A2466

No. 3183: a, Charlie Chaplin as the Little Tramp. b, Federal Reserve System created, 1913. c, George Washington Carver. d, Avant-garde art introduced at Armory Show, 1913. e, First transcontinental telephone line, 1914. f, Panama Canal opens, 1914. g, Jim Thorpe wins decathlon at Stockholm Olympics, 1912. h, Grand Canyon National Park, 1919. i, U.S. enters World War I. j, Boy Scouts started in 1910, Girl Scouts formed in 1912. k, Woodrow Wilson. l, First crossword puzzle published, 1913. m, Jack Dempsey wins heavyweight title, 1919. n, Construction toys. o, Child labor reform.

1920s — A2467

No. 3184: a, Babe Ruth. b, The Gatsby style. c, Prohibition enforced. d, Electric toy trains. e, 19th Amendment (woman voting). f, Emily Post's Etiquette. g, Margaret Mead, anthropologist. h, Flappers do the Charleston. i, Radio entertains America. j, Art Deco style (Chrysler Building). k, Jazz flourishes. l, Four Horsemen of Notre Dame. m, Lindbergh flies the Atlantic. n, American realism (The Automat, by Edward Hopper). o, Stock Market crash, 1929.

1930s — A2468

No. 3185: a, Franklin D. Roosevelt. b, The Empire State Building. c, 1st Issue of Life Magazine, 1936. d, Eleanor Roosevelt. e, FDR's New Deal. f, Superman arrives, 1938. g, Household conveniences. h, "Snow White and the Seven Dwarfs," 1937. i, "Gone with the Wind," 1936. j, Jesse Owens. k, Streamline design. l, Golden Gate Bridge. m, America survives the Depression. n, Bobby Jones wins golf Grand Slam, 1938. o, The Monopoly Game.

1940s — A2469

No. 3186: a, World War II. b, Antibiotics save lives. c, Jackie Robinson. d, Harry S Truman. e, Women support war effort. f, TV entertains America. g, Jitterbug sweeps nation. h, Jackson Pollock, Abstract Expressionism. i, GI Bill, 1944. j, Big Band Sound. k, Intl. style of architecture (UN Headquarters). l, Postwar baby boom. m, Slinky, 1945. n, "A Streecar Named Desire," 1947. o, Orson Welles' "Citizen Kane."

1950s — A2470

No. 3187: a, Polio vaccine developed. b, Teen fashions. c, The "Shot Heard 'Round the World." d, US launches satellites. e, Korean War. f, Desegregating public schools. g, Tail fins, chrome. h, Dr. Seuss' "The Cat in the Hat." i, Drive-in movies. j, World Series rivals. k, Rocky Marciano, undefeated boxer. l, "I Love Lucy." m, Rock 'n Roll. n, Stock car racing. o, Movies go 3-D.

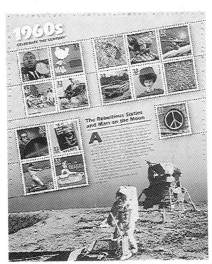

1960s — A2471

No. 3188: a, Martin Luther King, Jr., "I Have a Dream." b, Woodstock. c, Man walks on the moon. d, Green Bay Packers. e, Star Trek. f, The Peace Corps. g, Viet Nam War. h, Ford Mustang. i, Barbie Doll. j, Integrated circuit. k, Lasers. l, Super Bowl I. m, Peace symbol. n, Roger Maris, 61 in '61. o, The Beatles "Yellow Submarine."

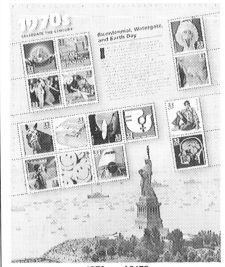

1970s — A2472

No. 3189: a, Earth Day celebrated. b, "All in the Family" television series. c, "Sesame Street" television series character, Big Bird. d, Disco music. e, Pittsburgh Steelers win four Super Bowls. f, US Celebrates 200th birthday. g, Secretariat wins Triple Crown. h, VCRs transform entertainment. i, Pioneer 10. j, Women's rights movement. k, 1970s fashions. l, "Monday Night Football." m, Smiley face buttons. n, Jumbo jets. o, Medical imaging.

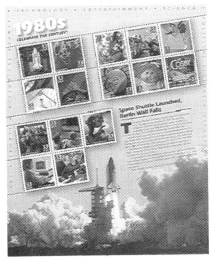

1980s — A2473

No. 3190: a, Space shuttle program. b, "Cats" Broadway show. c, San Francisco 49ers. d, Hostages in Iran come home. e, Figure skating. f, Cable TV. g, Vietnam Veterans Memorial. h, Compact discs. i, Cabbage Patch Kids. j, "The Cosby Show" television series. k, Fall of the Berlin Wall. l, Video games. m, "E. T. The Extra-Terrestrial" movie. n, Personal computers. o, Hip-hop culture.

1990s — A2474

No. 3191: a, New baseball records. b, Gulf War. c, "Seinfeld" television series. d, Extreme sports. e, Improving education. f, Computer art and graphics. g, Recovering species. h, Return to space. i, Special Olympics. j, Virtual reality. k, Movie "Jurassic Park." l, Movie "Titanic." m, Sport utility vehicles. n, World Wide Web. o, Cellular phones.

Designed by Richard Waldrep (#3182), Dennis Lyall (#3183), Carl Herrman (#3184, 3188, 3190), Howard Paine (#3185-3187, 3189, 3191).

Printed by Ashton-Potter (USA) Ltd.

LITHOGRAPHED, ENGRAVED (#3182m, 3183f, 3184m, 3185b, 3186k, 3187a, 3188c, 3189h)

1998-2000		Tagged		Perf. 11½
3182	A2465	Pane of 15, *Feb. 3, 1998*	9.00	—
a.-o.		32c any single	.60	.30
		Sheet of 4 panes	36.00	
p.		Engr. red (No. 3182m, Gibson girl) omitted, in pane of 15		
3183	A2466	Pane of 15, *Feb. 3, 1998*	9.00	—
a.-o.		32c any single	.60	.30
		Sheet of 4 panes	36.00	
p.		Nos. 3183g, 3183 l-3183o imperf, in pane of 15		—
3184	A2467	Pane of 15, *May 28, 1998*	9.00	—
a.-o.		32c any single	.60	.30
		Sheet of 4 panes	36.00	
3185	A2468	Pane of 15, *Sept. 10, 1998*	9.00	—
a.-o.		32c any single	.60	.30
		Sheet of 4 panes	36.00	
3186	A2469	Pane of 15, *Feb. 18, 1999*	9.75	—
a.-o.		33c any single	.65	.30
		Sheet of 4 panes	40.00	
3187	A2470	Pane of 15, *May 26, 1999*	9.75	—
a.-o.		33c any single	.65	.30
		Sheet of 4 panes	40.00	
3188	A2471	Pane of 15, *Sept. 17, 1999*	9.75	—
a.-o.		33c any single	.65	.30
		Sheet of 4 panes	40.00	
3189	A2472	Pane of 15, *Nov. 18, 1999*	9.75	—
a.-o.		33c any single	.65	.30
		Sheet of 4 panes	40.00	
3190	A2473	Pane of 15, *Jan. 12, 2000*	9.75	—
a.-o.		33c any single	.65	.30
		Sheet of 4 panes	40.00	
3191	A2474	Pane of 15, *May 2, 2000*	9.75	—
a.-o.		33c any single	.65	.30
		Sheet of 4 panes	40.00	

"REMEMBER THE MAINE"

A2475

Designed by Richard Sheaff.

LITHOGRAPHED & ENGRAVED
Sheets of 120 in six panes of 20

1998, Feb. 15		Tagged	Perf. 11.2x11
3192	A2475	32c red & black	.60	.20
		P# block of 4, 2#	2.40	—
		Pane of 20	12.00	

FLOWERING TREES

Southern Magnolia — A2476

Blue Paloverde — A2477

Yellow Poplar — A2478

Prairie Crab Apple — A2479

Pacific Dogwood — A2480

Designed by Howard Paine.

Printed by Banknote Corporation of America.

LITHOGRAPHED
Sheets of 120 in six panes of 20

1998, Mar. 19	Tagged	Die Cut Perf 11.3

Self-Adhesive

3193	A2476	32c multicolored	.60	.20
3194	A2477	32c multicolored	.60	.20
3195	A2478	32c multicolored	.60	.20
3196	A2479	32c multicolored	.60	.20
3197	A2480	32c multicolored	.60	.20
a.		Strip of 5, #3193-3197	3.00	
		P# block of 10, 2 sets of B+6#	6.00	
		Pane of 20	12.00	

ALEXANDER CALDER (1898-1976), SCULPTOR

Black Cascade, 13 Verticals, 1959 — A2481

Untitled, 1965 — A2482

Rearing Stallion, 1928 — A2483

Portrait of a Young Man, c. 1945 — A2484

Un Effet du Japonais, 1945 — A2485

Designed by Derry Noyes. Printed by Stamp Venturers.

PHOTOGRAVURE
Sheets of 120 in six panes of 20

1998, Mar. 25	Tagged	Perf. 10.2

3198	A2481	32c multicolored	.60	.20
3199	A2482	32c multicolored	.60	.20
3200	A2483	32c multicolored	.60	.20
3201	A2484	32c multicolored	.60	.20
3202	A2485	32c multicolored	.60	.20
a.		Strip of 5, #3198-3202	3.00	—
		P# block of 10, 2 sets of S+6#	6.00	—
		Pane of 20	12.00	—
		Sheet of 120 (6 panes)	110.00	
		Cross gutter block of 20	37.50	—
		Block of 10 with horiz. gutter	22.50	—
		Vert. pair with horiz. gutter	4.00	—
		Horiz. pair with vert. gutter	5.50	—

Cross gutter block of 20 consists of six stamps from each of two panes and four stamps from each of two other panes with the cross gutter between. The sheet of 120 was quickly sold out.

A2486

CINCO DE MAYO

Designed by Carl Herrman.

Printed by Stamp Venturers.

PHOTOGRAVURE
Sheets of 180 in nine panes of 20
Serpentine Die Cut 11.7x10.9

1998, Apr. 16		Tagged

Self-Adhesive

3203	A2486	32c multicolored	.60	.20
		P# block of 4, 5#+S	2.40	
		Pane of 20	12.00	
		Sheet of 180 (9 panes)	110.00	
		Cross gutter block of 4	12.50	
		Vert. pair with horiz. gutter	2.00	
		Horiz. pair with vert. gutter	2.00	

See Mexico #2066. For 33c version, see #3309.

A2487

A2488

SYLVESTER & TWEETY

Designed by Brenda Guttman.

Printed by Avery Dennison.

PHOTOGRAVURE

1998, Apr. 27	Tagged	Serpentine Die Cut 11.1

Self-Adhesive

3204	Pane of 10	6.00	
a.	A2487 32c single	.60	.20
b.	Booklet pane of 9 #3204a	5.40	
c.	Booklet pane of 1 #3204a	.60	
	Sheet of 60 (six panes) top	65.00	
	Sheet of 60 (six panes) bottom, with plate #	105.00	
	Pane of 10 from sheet of 60	12.50	
	Pane of 10 with plate #	45.00	
	Cross gutter block of 12	45.00	
	Vert. pair with horiz. gutter	6.00	
	Horiz. pair with vert. gutter	12.50	

Die cutting on #3204b does not extend through the backing paper. Pane with plate number comes from bottom uncut sheet of 60.

The horiz. pair with vert. gutter consists of a stamp at the left from either No. 3204b, part of the illustration of Sylvester & Tweety, the small gutter between the panes, and a stamp at the right from the left row of No. 3204b. Some pairs may include the single stamp from No. 3204c in addition to the two stamps at the right and left.

3205	Pane of 10	10.00	
a.	A2487 32c single	.60	
b.	Booklet pane of 9 #3205a	—	
c.	Booklet pane of 1, imperf.	—	

Die cutting on #3205a extends through the backing paper. Used examples of No. 3205a are identical to those of No. 3204a.

Nos. 3204b-3204c and 3205b-3205c are separated by a vertical line of microperforations, which is absent on the uncut sheets of 60.

WISCONSIN STATEHOOD

Designed by Phil Jordan.

Printed by Sennett Security Products.

PHOTOGRAVURE
Sheets of 120 in six panes of 20
Serpentine Die Cut 10.8x10.9

1998, May 29		Tagged

Self-Adhesive

3206	A2488	32c multicolored	.60	.30
		P# block of 4, 4#+S	2.40	
		Pane of 20	12.00	

See note after No. 3167.

Wetlands
A2489

Diner
A2490

Designer by Phil Jordan (#3207-3207A), Carl Herrman (#3208, 308A).

Printed by Sennett Security Printers (#3207, 3208), Bureau of Engraving and Printing (#3207A, 3208A).

PHOTOGRAVURE
COIL STAMPS

1998	Untagged	Perf. 10 Vert.

3207	A2489	(5c) multicolored, June 5	.20	.20
		Pair	.20	
		P# strip of 5, #S1111	1.65	
		P#, single, #S1111		1.25

Serpentine Die Cut 9.7 Vert.

Self-adhesive

3207A	A2489	(5c) multicolored, Dec. 14	.20	.20
		Pair	.20	
		P# strip of 5, #1111, 2222, 3333	1.65	

	P# single, same	1.25

Perf. 10 Vert.

3208	A2490	(25c)	**multicolored,** June 5	.50	.50
			Pair	1.00	1.00
			P# strip of 5, #S11111	4.00	
			P#, single, #S11111		2.50

Serpentine Die Cut 9.7 Vert.
Self-Adhesive

3208A	A2490	(25c)	**multicolored,** Sept. 30	.50	.50
			Pair	1.00	
			P# strip of 5, #11111, 22211, 22222, 33333, 44444	4.00	
			P# single, same		2.50

1898 TRANS-MISSISSIPPI STAMPS, CENT.

A2491

Designed by Raymond Ostrander Smith (1898), Richard Sheaff (1998).
Printed by Banknote Corporation of America.

LITHOGRAPHED & ENGRAVED
Sheets of 54 in six panes of 9

1998, June 18		Tagged	**Perf. 12x12.4**	
3209	A2491	Pane of 9	7.75	5.00
a.	A100	1c green & black	.20	.20
b.	A108	2c red brown & black	.20	.20
c.	A102	4c orange & black	.20	.20
d.	A103	5c blue & black	.20	.20
e.	A104	8c dark lilac & black	.20	.20
f.	A105	10c purple & black	.20	.20
g.	A106	50c green & black	1.00	.20
h.	A107	$1 red & black	2.00	1.25
i.	A101	$2 red brown & black	4.00	2.50
		Block of 9 with horiz. gutter	42.50	
		Vert. pairs with horiz. gutter (each)	10.00	

Vignettes on Nos. 3209b and 3209i are reversed in comparison to the original issue.
Vert. pairs consist of #3209g-3209a, 3209h-3209b, 3209i-3209c.

3210	A107	$1 Pane of 9 #3209h	18.00	—
		Sheet of 6 panes, 3 each #3209-3210	125.00	
		Cross gutter block of 12	57.50	—
		Block of 18 (2 panes) with vert. gutter between & selvage on 4 sides	47.50	—
		Block of 12 with vert. gutter	32.50	—
		Vert. pair #3209h with horiz. gutter	10.00	
		Horiz. pairs with vert. gutter (each)	10.00	

Block of 12 contains #3209 and one column of 3 #3209h from #3210 separated by vert. gutter.

BERLIN AIRLIFT, 50th ANNIV.

A2492   *Berlin Airlift delivers food and fuel in 1948-49 blockade.*

Designed by Bill Bond.
Printed by Banknote Corporation of America.

PHOTOGRAVURE
Sheets of 120 in six panes of 20

1998, June 26		Tagged	**Perf. 11.2**	
3211	A2492	32c **multicolored**	.60	.20
		P# block of 4, 4#+B	2.40	—
		Pane of 20	12.00	—

AMERICAN MUSIC SERIES
Folk Singers

Huddie "Leadbelly" Ledbetter (1888-1949)
A2493

Woody Guthrie (1912-67)
A2494

Sonny Terry (1911-86)
A2495

Josh White (1908-69)
A2496

Designed by Howard Paine.
Printed by American Packaging Corp. for Sennett Security Products.

PHOTOGRAVURE
Sheets of 180 in nine panes of 20

1998, June 26		Tagged	**Perf. 10.1x10.2**	
3212	A2493	32c **multicolored**	.60	.20
3213	A2494	32c **multicolored**	.60	.20
3214	A2495	32c **multicolored**	.60	.20
3215	A2496	32c **multicolored**	.60	.20
a.		Block or strip of 4, #3212-3215	2.40	—
		P# block of 4, 5#+S	2.40	—
		P# block of 8, 2 sets of P# + top label	4.80	—
		Pane of 20	12.00	—

AMERICAN MUSIC SERIES
Gospel Singers

Mahalia Jackson (1911-72)
A2497

Roberta Martin (1917-69)
A2498

Clara Ward (1924-73)
A2499

Sister Rosetta Tharpe (1921-73)
A2500

Designed by Howard Paine.
Printed by American Packaging Corp. for Sennett Security Products.

PHOTOGRAVURE
Sheets of 120 in six panes of 20

1998, July 15		Tagged	**Perf. 10.1x10.3**	
3216	A2497	32c **multicolored**	.60	.20
3217	A2498	32c **multicolored**	.60	.20
3218	A2499	32c **multicolored**	.60	.20
3219	A2500	32c **multicolored**	.60	.20
a.		Block or strip of 4, #3216-3219	2.40	—
		P# block of 4, 5#+S	2.40	
		P# block of 8, 2 sets of P# + top label	4.80	—
		Pane of 20	12.00	—

SPANISH SETTLEMENT OF THE SOUTHWEST

La Mision de San Miguel de San Gabriel, Espanola, NM — A2501

Designed by Richard Sheaff.
Printed by Banknote Corporation of America.

LITHOGRAPHED
Sheets of 180 in nine panes of 20

1998, July 11		Tagged	**Perf. 11.2**	
3220	A2501	32c **multicolored**	.60	.20
		P# block of 4, 4#+B	2.40	—
		Pane of 20	12.00	—

LITERARY ARTS

Stephen Vincent Benét (1898-43) — A2502

Designed by Carl Herrman.
Printed by Ashton-Potter (USA) Ltd.

LITHOGRAPHED
Sheets of 180 in nine panes of 20

1998, July 22		Tagged	**Perf. 11.2**	
3221	A2502	32c **multicolored**	.60	.20
		P# block of 4, 4#+P	2.40	—
		Pane of 20	12.00	—

TROPICAL BIRDS

Antillean Euphonia — A2503

Green-throated Carib — A2504

Green-throated Carib

Crested Honeycreeper A2505

Crested Honeycreeper

Cardinal Honeyeater A2506

Cardinal Honeyeater

Designed by Phil Jordan.
Printed by Banknote Corporation of America.

LITHOGRAPHED
Sheets of 180 in nine panes of 20

1998, July 29		Tagged	Perf. 11.2	
3222	A2503	32c multicolored	.60	.20
3223	A2504	32c multicolored	.60	.20
3224	A2505	32c multicolored	.60	.20
3225	A2506	32c multicolored	.60	.20
a.		Block of 4, #3222-3225	2.40	—
		P# block of 4, 4#+P	2.40	—
		Pane of 20	12.00	—

For booklet see No. BK272.

LEGENDS OF HOLLYWOOD

Alfred Hitchcock (1899-1980) — A2507

Designed by Rihard Sheaff.
Printed at American Packaging Corp. for Sennett Security Products.

PHOTOGRAVURE
Sheets of 120 in six panes of 20

1998, Aug. 3		Tagged	Perf. 11.1	
3226	A2507	32c multicolored	.60	.20
		P# block of 4, 4#+	2.40	—
		Pane of 20	12.00	—
		Sheet of 120 (6 panes)	72.50	—
		Cross gutter block of 8	17.50	—
		Block of 8 with vert. gutter	13.50	—
		Horiz. pair with vert. gutter	3.00	—
		Vert. pair with horiz. gutter	2.00	—

Perforations in corner of each stamp are star-shaped. Cross-gutter block consists of 6 stamps from upper panes and 2 stamps from panes below. Hitchcock's profile in the UL corner of each stamp is laser cut.

ORGAN & TISSUE DONATION

A2508

Designed by Richard Sheaff. Printed by Avery Dennison.

PHOTOGRAVURE
Sheets of 160 in eight panes of 20

1998, Aug. 5		Tagged	Serpentine Die Cut 11.7	
		Self-Adhesive		
3227	A2508	32c multicolored	.60	.20
		P# block of 4 5#+V	2.40	
		Pane of 20	12.00	

MODERN BICYCLE

PRESORTED STD A2509

Designed by Richard Sheaff. Printed by Bureau of Engraving and Printing (#3228), Sennett Security Printers (#3229).

PHOTOGRAVURE
COIL STAMP
Serpentine Die Cut 9.8 Vert.

1998, Aug. 14			Untagged	
		Self-Adhesive (#3228)		
3228	A2509	(10c) multicolored	.20	.20
		Pair	.40	
		P# strip of 5, P#111, 221, 222, 333, 344, 444, 555, 666, 777, 888, 999	2.50	
		P# single, same #		2.00

		Untagged		
		Perf. 9.9 Vert.		
3229	A2509	(10c) multicolored	.20	.20
		Pair	.40	.25
		P# strip of 5, P#S111	2.50	
		P# single, same #		2.00

BRIGHT EYES

Dog — A2510

Fish — A2511

Cat — A2512

Parakeet — A2513

Hamster — A2514

Designed by Carl Herrman. Printed at Guilford Gravure for Banknote Corp. of America.

PHOTOGRAVURE
Sheets of 180 in nine panes of 20

1998, Aug. 20		Tagged	Serpentine Die Cut 9.9	
		Self-Adhesive		
3230	A2510	32c multicolored	.60	.20
3231	A2511	32c multicolored	.60	.20
3232	A2512	32c multicolored	.60	.20
3233	A2513	32c multicolored	.60	.20
3234	A2514	32c multicolored	.60	.20
a.		Strip of 5, #3230-3234	3.00	
		P# block of 8, 2 sets of 6#+B	6.00	
		Pane of 20	12.00	

Hidden 3-D designs can be seen on each stamp when viewed with a special viewer sold by the post office.
Plate blocks may contain top label.

KLONDIKE GOLD RUSH, CENTENNIAL

A2515

Designed by Howard Paine. Printed at Sterling Sommer for Ashton Potter (USA) Ltd.

LITHOGRAPHED
Sheets of 180 in nine panes of 20

1998, Aug. 21		Tagged	Perf. 11.1	
3235	A2515	32c multicolored	.60	.20
		P# block of 4, 5#+P	2.40	—
		Pane of 20	12.00	—

AMERICAN ART

A2516

Designed by Howard Paine. Printed by Sennett Security Products.

Paintings: a, "Portrait of Richard Mather," by John Foster. b, "Mrs. Elizabeth Freake and Baby Mary," by The Freake Limner. c, "Girl in Red Dress with Cat and Dog," by Ammi Phillips. d, "Rubens Peale with a Geranium," by Rembrandt Peale. e, "Long-billed Curlew, Numenius Longrostris," by John James Audubon. f, "Boatmen on the Missouri," by George Caleb Bingham. g, "Kindred Sprits," by Asher B. Durand. h, "The Westwood Children," by Joshua Johnson. i, "Music and Literature," by William Harnett. j, "The Fog Warning," by Winslow Homer. k, "The White Cloud, Head Chief of the Iowas," by George Catlin. l, "Cliffs of Green River," by Thomas Moran. m, "The Last of the Buffalo," by Alfred Bierstadt. n, "Niagara," by Frederic Edwin Church. o, "Breakfast in Bed," by Mary Cassatt. p, "Nighthawks," by Edward Hopper. q, "American Gothic," by Grant Wood. r, "Two Against the White," by Charles Sheeler. s, "Mahoning," by Franz Kline. t, "No. 12," by Mark Rothko.

PHOTOGRAVURE
Sheets of 120 stamps in six panes of 20

1998, Aug. 27		Tagged	Perf. 10.2	
3236	A2516	Pane of 20	12.00	—
a.-t.		32c any single	.60	.20
		Sheet of 120 (six panes)	72.50	—
		Horiz. block of 8 with vert. gutter	10.00	—
		Vert. block of 10 with horiz. gutter	12.00	—
		Cross gutter block of 20	22.50	—
		Vert. pairs with horiz. gutter (each)	2.25	—
		Horiz. pairs with vert. gutter (each)	2.25	—

Inscriptions on the back of each stamp describe the painting and the artist.

Cross gutter block of 20 consists of six stamps from each of two panes and four stamps from each of two other panes with the cross gutter between.

AMERICAN BALLET

A2517

Designed by Derry Noyes. Printed by Sterling Sommer for Ashton-Potter (USA) Ltd.

LITHOGRAPHED
Sheets of 120 in six panes of 20

1998, Sept. 16	**Tagged**	**Perf. 10.9x11.1**	
3237 A2517 32c **multicolored**		.60	.20
P# block of 4, 4#+P		2.40	
Pane of 20		12.00	
Sheet of 120 (six panes)		72.50	
Cross gutter block of 4		12.50	—
Vert. pair with horiz. gutter		2.00	—
Horiz. pair with vert. gutter		2.00	—

For booklet see No. BK273.

SPACE DISCOVERY

A2518

A2519

A2520

A2521

A2522

Designed by Phil Jordan. Printed at American Packaging Corp. for Sennett Security Products.

PHOTOGRAVURE
Sheets of 180 in nine panes of 20

1998, Oct. 1	**Tagged**	**Perf. 11.1**	
3238 A2518 32c **multicolored**		.60	.20
3239 A2519 32c **multicolored**		.60	.20
3240 A2520 32c **multicolored**		.60	.20
3241 A2521 32c **multicolored**		.60	.20
3242 A2522 32c **multicolored**		.60	.20
a. Strip of 5, #3238-3242		3.00	—
P# block of 10, 2 sets of 5#+S		6.00	—
Pane of 20		12.00	
Sheet of 180 (9 panes)		110.00	

Cross gutter block of 10	17.50	—
Vert. block of 10 with horiz. gutter	10.00	—
Horiz. pair (#3238, 3242) with vert. gutter	2.00	—
Pane of 20 from sheet of 180	12.00	—

Hidden 3-D designs can be seen on each stamp when viewed with a special viewer sold by the post office.

Plate blocks may contain top label.

Cross gutter block of 10 consists of two stamps from each of two panes and three stamps from each of two other panes with the cross gutter between. Pane of 20 from sheet of 180 has vertical perforations on one or both sides and is wider than pane sold in local post offices.

For booklet see No. BK274.

GIVING AND SHARING

A2523

Designed by Bob Dinetz.

Printed by Avery Dennison.

PHOTOGRAVURE
Sheets of 200 in ten panes of 20

1998, Oct. 7	**Tagged**	**Serpentine Die Cut 11.1**	
	Self-Adhesive		
3243 A2523 32c **multicolored**		.60	.20
P# block of 4, 4#+V		2.40	—
Pane of 20		12.00	

CHRISTMAS

Madonna and Child, Florence, 15th Cent. — A2524

Evergreen Wreath — A2525

Victorian Wreath — A2526

Chili Pepper Wreath — A2527

Tropical Wreath — A2528

Designed by Richard D. Sheaff (#3244), Lilian Dinihanian (A2525), George de Bruin (A2526), Chris Crinklaw (A2527), Micheale Thunin (A2528).

Printed by Bureau of Engraving and Printing (#3244), Banknote Corporation of America (#3245-3256).

LITHOGRAPHED
Sheets of 160 in 8 panes of 20 (#3249-3252)

Serpentine Die Cut 10.1x9.9 on 2, 3 or 4 Sides

1998, Oct. 15		**Tagged**	
	Self-Adhesive		
	Booklet Stamps		
3244 A2524 32c **multicolored**		.60	.20
a. Booklet pane of 20 + label		12.00	
b. Imperf, pair		—	

Serpentine Die Cut 11.3x11.6 on 2 or 3 Sides

3245 A2525 32c **multicolored**		.60	.20
3246 A2526 32c **multicolored**		.60	.20
3247 A2527 32c **multicolored**		.60	.20
3248 A2528 32c **multicolored**		.60	.20
a. Booklet pane of 4, #3245-3248		2.50	
b. Booklet pane of #3245-3246, 3248, 2 #3247 + label		3.00	
c. Booklet pane of 6, #3247-3248, 2 each #3245-3246		3.60	

Size: 23x30mm

Serpentine Die Cut 11.4x11.6 on 2, 3, or 4 Sides

3249 A2525 32c **multicolored**		.60	.20
3250 A2526 32c **multicolored**		.60	.20
3251 A2527 32c **multicolored**		.60	.20
3252 A2528 32c **multicolored**		.60	.20
a. Block of 4, #3249-3252		2.40	
P#block of 4, 6#+B		2.40	
Pane of 20		12.00	
b. Booklet pane, 5 each #3249-3252		12.00	
c. Block or strip of 4, red ("Greetings 32 USA" and "1998") omitted on #3249, 3252		—	

Weather Vane — A2529

Uncle Sam — A2530

Uncle Sam's Hat — A2531

Space Shuttle Landing — A2532

Piggyback Space Shuttle — A2533

Designed by Terry McCaffrey (#3257-3258, 3260, 3264-3269), Richard Sheaff (#3259, 3263), Phil Jordan (#3261-3262). Printed by Ashton Potter (USA) Ltd. (#3257), American Packaging Corp. for Sennett Security Products (#3259), Stamp Venturers (#3260), Banknote Corporation of America (#3258, 3261-3262), Bureau of Engraving and Printing (#3263-3267), Avery Dennison (#3268-3269).

LITHOGRAPHED
Sheets of 400 in eight panes of 50 (#3257, 3260), Sheets of 300 in six panes of 50 (#3258), Sheets of 160 in eight panes of 20 (#3259), Sheets of 120 in six panes of 20 (#3261-3262)

1998	**Untagged**	**Perf. 11.2**	
3257 A2529 (1c) multicolored *Nov. 9*		.20	.20
P# block of 4, 5# + P		.25	—
a. Black omitted		—	
3258 A2529 (1c) **multicolored,** *Nov. 9*		.20	.20
P# block of 4, 5# + B		.25	—

No. 3257 is 18mm high, has thin letters, white USA, and black 1998. No. 3258 is 17mm high, has thick letters, pale blue USA and blue 1998.

PHOTOGRAVURE
Tagged

Serpentine Die Cut 10.8

Self-Adhesive (#3259, 3261-3263, 3265-3269)

3259 A2530 22c **multicolored,** *Nov. 9*		.45	.20
P# block of 4, 4#+S		1.80	
Pane of 20		9.00	

See No. 3353.

Perf. 11.2

3260 A2531 (33c) **multicolored,** *Nov. 9*		.65	.20
P# block of 4 4#+S		2.60	

LITHOGRAPHED
Serpentine Die Cut 11.5

3261 A2532 $3.20 **multicolored,** *Nov. 9*		6.00	3.00
P# block of 4, 4#+B		24.00	
Pane of 20		120.00	
3262 A2533 $11.75 **multicolored,** *Nov. 19*		22.50	11.50
P# block of 4, 4#+B		90.00	
Pane of 20		450.00	

COIL STAMPS

PHOTOGRAVURE

Serpentine Die Cut 9.9 Vert.

3263 A2530 22c **multicolored,** *Nov. 9*		.45	.20
Pair		.90	
P# strip of 5, #1111		3.50	
P# single, same #			1.75

Perf. 9.8 Vert.

3264	A2531	(33c) **multicolored**, *Nov. 9*	.65	.20
		Pair	1.30	.30
		P# strip of 5, #1111, 3333, 3343, 3344, 3444	4.75	
		P# single, same #		2.50

Serpentine Die Cut 9.9 Vert.

3265	A2531	(33c) **multicolored**, *Nov. 9*	.65	.20
		Pair	1.30	
		P# strip of 5, #1111, 1131, 2222, 3333	4.75	
		P# single, same #		2.50
a.		Imperf., pair	—	
b.		Red omitted	—	
c.		Black omitted	—	
d.		Black omitted, Imperf., pair	—	

Unused examples of No. 3265 are on backing paper the same size as the stamps. Corners of the stamp are 90 degree angles.

On No. 3265b, the blue and gray colors are shifted down and to the right.

Serpentine Die Cut 9.9 Vert.

3266	A2531	(33c) **multicolored**, *Nov. 9*	.65	.20
		Pair	1.30	
		P# strip of 5, #1111	4.75	
		P# single, same #		2.50

Unused examples of No. 3266 are on backing paper larger than the stamps. Corners of stamps are rounded.

BOOKLET STAMPS
Serpentine Die Cut 9.9 on 2 or 3 Sides

3267	A2531	(33c) **multicolored**, *Nov. 9*	.65	.20
a.		Booklet pane of 10	6.50	

Serpentine Die Cut 11.2x11.1 on 2, 3 or 4 Sides

3268	A2531	(33c) **multicolored**, *Nov. 9*	.65	.20
a.		Booklet pane of 10	6.50	
b.		Booklet pane of 20 + label	13.00	

Die Cut 8 on 2, 3 or 4 Sides

3269	A2531	(33c) **multicolored**, *Nov. 9*	.65	.20
a.		Booklet pane of 18	12.00	

A2534   USA Presorted Std

Designed by Chris Calle.

PHOTOGRAVURE
COIL STAMPS

1998, Dec. 14		**Untagged**	**Perf. 9.8 Vert.**	
3270	A2534	(10c) **multicolored**	.20	.20
		Pair	.40	.40
		P# strip of 5, #11111	2.25	
		P# single, same #		2.00

Self-Adhesive
Serpentine Die Cut 9.9 Vert.

3271	A2534	(10c) **multicolored**	.20	.20
		Pair	.40	
		P# strip of 5, #11111, 22222	2.25	
		P# single, #11111		2.00
a.		Tagged (error)	1.25	1.10
		Pair	2.50	
		P# strip of 5, #11111	10.00	
		P# single, #11111	—	5.00

No. 3271 is known with eagle in red brown rather than the normal golden brown, apparently from contaminated ink.

No. 3271a is known in plate #11111 strips with blue "1" of plate numbers omitted.

Compare to Nos. 2602-2604, 2907.

Scott values for used self-adhesive stamps are for examples either on piece or off piece.

CHINESE NEW YEAR

Year of the Rabbit — A2535

Designed by Clarence Lee.

Printed at American Packaging Corp. for Sennett Security Printers.

PHOTOGRAVURE
Sheets of 180 in nine panes of 20

1999, Jan. 5		**Tagged**	**Perf. 11.2**	
3272	A2535	33c **multicolored**	.65	.20
		P# block of 4, 4#+S	2.60	
		Pane of 20	13.00	—

BLACK HERITAGE SERIES

Malcolm X (1925-65), Civil Rights Activist — A2536

Designed by Richard Sheaff. Printed by Banknote Corp. of America.

LITHOGRAPHED
Sheets of 180 in nine panes of 20

1999, Jan. 20		**Tagged**	**Serpentine Die Cut 11.4**	
			Self-Adhesive	
3273	A2536	33c **multicolored**	.65	.20
		P# block of 4, 3#+B	2.60	
		Pane of 20	13.00	

LOVE

A2537   A2538

Designed by John Grossman, Holly Sudduth.

Printed by Avery Dennison.

PHOTOGRAVURE

1999, Jan. 28		**Tagged**	**Die Cut**	
		Booklet Stamp		
		Self-Adhesive		
3274	A2537	33c **multicolored**	.65	.20
a.		Booklet pane of 20	13.00	

Sheets of 160 in eight panes of 20

3275	A2538	55c **multicolored**	1.10	.20
		P# block of 4, 7#+B	4.40	
		Pane of 20	22.00	

HOSPICE CARE

A2539

Designed by Phil Jordan.

Printed by Banknote Corp. of America.

LITHOGRAPHED
Sheets of 120 in six panes of 20

1999, Feb. 9		**Tagged**	**Serpentine Die Cut 11.4**	
3276	A2539	33c **multicolored**	.65	.20
		P# block of 4, 4#+B	2.60	
		Pane of 20	13.00	

Flag and City   Flag and Chalkboard
A2540   A2541

Designed by Richard Sheaff. Printed by Bureau of Engraving and Printing (#3277, 3279-3282), Avery Dennison (#3278, 3278F, 3283).

PHOTOGRAVURE
Sheets of 400 in four panes of 100 (#3277),
Sheets of 200 in ten panes of 20 (#3278)

1999, Feb. 25		**Tagged**	**Perf. 11.2**	
		Self-Adhesive (#3278, 3278F, 3279, 3281-3282)		
3277	A2540	33c **multicolored**	.65	.20
		P# block of 4, 4#	2.60	—

Serpentine Die Cut 11.1 on 2, 3 or 4 Sides

3278	A2540	33c **multicolored**	.65	.20
		P# block of 4, 4#+V	2.60	
		Pane of 20	13.00	
a.		Booklet pane of 4	2.60	
b.		Booklet pane of 5 + label	3.25	
		P# single, #V1111, V1212, V2212	.80	1.00
c.		Booklet pane of 6	3.90	
d.		Booklet pane of 10	6.50	
e.		Booklet pane of 20 + label	13.00	
f.		As "e," imperf	—	

No. 3278 has black date.
The plate # single in No. 3278b is the lower left single.

BOOKLET STAMPS
Serpentine Die Cut 11½x11¾ on 2, 3 or 4 Sides

3278F	A2540	33c **multicolored**	.65	.20
g.		Booklet pane of 20 + label	13.00	

Serpentine Die Cut 9.8 on 2 or 3 Sides

3279	A2540	33c **multicolored**	.65	.20
a.		Booklet pane of 10	6.50	

No. 3279 has red date.

COIL STAMPS
Perf. 9.9 Vert.

3280	A2540	33c **multicolored**	.65	.20
		Pair	1.30	.30
		P# strip of 5, #1111, 2222, 3333	4.75	—
		P# single, same #		2.50

Serpentine Die Cut 9.8 Vert.

3281	A2540	33c **multicolored**, large "1999" year date	.65	.20
		Pair	1.30	
		P# strip of 5, #6666, 7777, 8888, 9999, 1111A, 2222A, 3333A, 4444A	4.75	
		P# single, same #		2.50
a.		Imperf., pair	—	
b.		Light blue and yellow omitted	—	
c.		Small date	.65	.20
		Pair	1.30	
		P# strip of 5, #1111, 2222, 3333, 3433, 4443, 4444, 5555	4.75	
		P# single, same #		2.50

Corners are square on #3281. Unused examples are on backing paper the same size as the stamps, and the stamps are adjoining.

Date on No. 3281 is approximately 1¾mm; on No. 3281c approximately 1¼mm.

3282	A2540	33c **multicolored**	.65	.20
		Pair	1.30	
		P# strip of 5, #1111, 2222	4.75	
		P# single, same #		2.50

Corners are rounded on #3282. Unused examples are on backing paper larger than the stamps, and the stamps are spaced. For imperf pair, see No. 3281a.

PHOTOGRAVURE
BOOKLET STAMP
Serpentine Die Cut 7.9 on 2, 3 or 4 Sides

1999, Mar. 13			**Tagged**	
		Self-Adhesive		
3283	A2541	33c **multicolored**	.65	.20
a.		Booklet pane of 18	12.00	

IRISH IMMIGRATION

A2542   IRISH IMMIGRATION 33 USA

Designed by Howard Paine. Printed by Ashton-Potter (USA) Ltd.

LITHOGRAPHED
Sheets of 180 in nine panes of 20

1999, Feb. 26		**Tagged**	**Perf. 11.2**	
3286	A2542	33c **multicolored**	.65	.20
		P# block of 4, 4#+P	2.60	—
		Pane of 20	13.00	—

ALFRED LUNT (1892-1977), LYNN FONTANNE (1887-1983), ACTORS

Alfred Lunt & Lynn Fontanne — A2543

Designed by Carl Herrman. Printed by Sterling Sommer for Ashton-Potter (USA) Ltd.

LITHOGRAPHED
Sheets of 180 in nine panes of 20

1999, Mar. 2	Tagged	Perf. 11.2	
3287 A2543 33c **multicolored**		.65	.20
P# block of 4, 4#+P		2.60	—
Pane of 20		13.00	—

ARCTIC ANIMALS

Arctic Hare — A2544

Arctic Fox — A2545

Snowy Owl — A2546

Polar Bear — A2547

Gray Wolf — A2548

Designed by Derry Noyes. Printed by Banknote Corp. of America.

LITHOGRAPHED
Sheets of 90 in six panes of 15

1999, Mar. 12	Tagged	Perf. 11	
3288 A2544 33c **multicolored**		.65	.20
3289 A2545 33c **multicolored**		.65	.20
3290 A2546 33c **multicolored**		.65	.20
3291 A2547 33c **multicolored**		.65	.20
3292 A2548 33c **multicolored**		.65	.20
a. Strip of 5, #3288-3292		3.25	—
Pane of 15, 6#+B		10.00	—

While the normal definition of a plate block dictates a block of 10, this would require collectors to discard the decorative label and top row of stamps from the pane of 15. To avoid destroying the more collectible entire, Scott is listing the entire pane as the plate block, and will provide space for this item in the Commemorative Plate Block supplement.

SONORAN DESERT

A2549

Designed by Ethel Kessler. Printed by Banknote Corporation of America.

Designs: a, Cactus wren, brittlebush, teddy bear cholla. b, Desert tortoise. c, White-winged dove, prickly pear. d, Gambel quail. e, Saguaro cactus. f, Desert mule deer. g, Desert cottontail, hedgehog cactus. h, Gila monster. i, Western diamondback rattlesnake, cactus mouse. j, Gila woodpecker.

LITHOGRAPHED
Sheets of 60 in six panes of 10

Serpentine Die Cut Perf 11.2

1999, Apr. 6		Tagged	
		Self-Adhesive	
3293 A2549	Pane of 10	6.50	
a.-j.	33c any single	.65	.20
	Sheet of 6 panes	40.00	

BERRIES

Blueberries A2550

Raspberries A2551

Strawberries A2552

Blackberries A2553

Designed by Howard Paine. Printed by Guilford Gravure for Banknote Corporation of America.

PHOTOGRAVURE
Serpentine Die Cut 11¼x11¾ on 2, 3 or 4 Sides, Serpentine Die Cut 11½x11¾ on 2 or 3 sides (#3294a-3299c)

1999, Apr. 10		Tagged	
	Self-Adhesive		
3294 A2550 33c **multicolored**		.65	.20
a. Dated "2000." Mar. 15, 2000		.65	.20
3295 A2551 33c **multicolored**		.65	.20
a. Dated "2000." Mar. 15, 2000		.65	.20
3296 A2552 33c **multicolored**		.65	.20
a. Dated "2000." Mar. 15, 2000		.65	.20
3297 A2553 33c **multicolored**		.65	.20
a. Dated "2000." Mar. 15, 2000		.65	.20
b. Booklet pane, 5 each, #3294-3297 + label		13.00	—
c. Block of 4, #3294-3297		2.60	
d. Booklet pane, 5 #3297e		13.00	—
e. Block of 4, #3294a-3297a		2.60	

Serpentine Die Cut 9½x10 on 2 or 3 Sides

3298 A2550 33c **multicolored**		.65	.20
3299 A2552 33c **multicolored**		.65	.20
3300 A2551 33c **multicolored**		.65	.20
3301 A2553 33c **multicolored**		.65	.20
a. Booklet pane of 4, #3298-3301		2.60	
b. Booklet pane of 5, #3298, 3299, 3301, 2 #3300 + label		3.25	
c. Booklet pane of 6, #3300, 3301, 2 #3298, 3299		4.00	
d. Block of 4, #3298-3301		2.60	

COIL STAMPS
Serpentine Die Cut 8.5 Vert.

3302 A2550 33c **multicolored**		.65	.20
3303 A2551 33c **multicolored**		.65	.20
3304 A2553 33c **multicolored**		.65	.20
3305 A2552 33c **multicolored**		.65	.20
a. Strip of 4, #3302-3305		2.60	

P# strip of 5, 2 #3302, 1 ea #3303-3305, P#B1111, B1112, B2211, B2221, B2222	4.75	
P# strip of 9, 2 ea #3302-3303, 3305, 3 #3304, same P#	7.50	
P# single (#3304), same P#	— 2.50	

A2554

A2555

DAFFY DUCK

Designed by Ed Wieczyk.
Printed by Avery Dennison.

PHOTOGRAVURE

1999, Apr. 16	Tagged	Serpentine Die Cut 11.1	
		Self-Adhesive	
3306 Pane of 10		6.50	
a. A2554 33c single		.65	.20
b. Booklet pane of 9 #3306a		5.85	
c. Booklet pane of 1 #3306a		.65	
Sheet of 60 (six panes) top		35.00	
Sheet of 60 (six panes) bottom, with plate # in selvage		40.00	
Pane of 10 from sheet of 60		9.00	
Pane of 10 with plate # in selvage		15.00	
Cross gutter block of 12		18.00	
Vert. pair with horiz. gutter		2.00	
Horiz. pair with vert. gutter		4.00	

Nos. 3306b-3306c and 3307b-3307c are separated by a vertical line of microperforations, which is absent on the uncut sheet of 60.
Die cutting on #3306b does not extend through the backing paper.

3307 Pane of 10		6.50	
a. A2554 33c single		.65	
b. Booklet pane of 9 #3307a		—	
c. Booklet pane of 1, imperf.		—	

Die cutting on #3307a extends through the backing paper. Used examples of No. 3307a are identical to those of No. 3306a.
Nos. 3306b-3306c and 3307b-3307c are separated by a vertical line of microperforations.

LITERARY ARTS
Ayn Rand (1905-82).

Designed by Phil Jordan.

Printed by Sterling Sommer for Ashton-Potter USA (Ltd.)

LITHOGRAPHED
Sheets of 180 in nine panes of 20

1999, Apr. 22	Tagged	Perf. 11.2	
3308 A2555 33c **multicolored**		.65	.20
P# block of 4, 4#+P		2.60	—
Pane of 20		13.00	—

Cinco De Mayo Type of 1998
Designed by Carl Herrman.

Printed by Banknote Corporation of America.

PHOTOGRAVURE
Sheets of 160 in eight panes of 20

Serpentine Die Cut 11.6x11.3

1999, Apr. 27		Tagged	
	Self-Adhesive		
3309 A2486 33c **multicolored**		.65	.20
P# block of 4, 6#+B		2.60	
Pane of 20		13.00	

TROPICAL FLOWERS

Bird of Paradise

Bird of Paradise A2556

Royal Poinciana
A2557

Gloriosa
Lily — A2558

Chinese Hibiscus
A2559

Designed by Carl Herrman.

Printed by Sennett Security Products.

PHOTOGRAVURE
BOOKLET STAMPS
Serpentine Die Cut 10.9 on 2 or 3 Sides

1999, May 1   **Tagged**

Self-Adhesive

3310	A2556	33c **multicolored**	.65	.20
3311	A2557	33c **multicolored**	.65	.20
3312	A2558	33c **multicolored**	.65	.20
3313	A2559	33c **multicolored**	.65	.20
a.		Block of 4, #3310-3313	2.60	
b.		Booklet pane, 5 each #3313a	13.00	

No. 3313b is a double-sided booklet pane with 12 stamps on one side and 8 stamps plus label on the other side.

A2560

A2561

JOHN (1699-1777) & WILLIAM (1739-1823) BARTRAM, BOTANISTS
Designed by Phil Jordan. Printed by Banknote Corporation of America.

LITHOGRAPHED
Sheets of 180 in nine panes of 20

1999, May 18   **Tagged**   *Perf. 11½*

Self-Adhesive

3314	A2560	33c Franklinia Alatamaha, by William Bartram	.65	.20
		P# block of 4, 4#+B	2.60	
		Pane of 20	13.00	

PROSTATE CANCER AWARENESS
Designed by Michael Cronan. Printed by Avery Dennison.

PHOTOGRAVURE
Sheets of 200 in ten panes of 20

1999, May 28   **Tagged**   *Perf. 11*

Self-Adhesive

3315	A2561	33c **multicolored**	.65	.20
a.		P# block of 4, 5#+V	2.60	
		Pane of 20	13.00	

CALIFORNIA GOLD RUSH, 150TH ANNIV.

A2562

Designed by Howard Paine. Printed by Ashton-Potter (USA) Ltd.

LITHOGRAPHED
Sheets of 180 in nine panes of 20

1999, June 18   **Tagged**   *Perf. 11¼*

3316	A2562	33c **multicolored**	.65	.20
		P# block of 4, 5#+P	2.60	—
		Pane of 20	13.00	—

AQUARIUM FISH
Reef Fish

A2563

A2564

A2565

Designed by Richard Sheaff. Printed by Banknote Corporation of America.

Designs: No. 3317, Yellow fish, red fish, cleaner shrimp. No. 3318, Fish, thermometer. No. 3319, Red fish, blue & yellow fish. No. 3320, Fish, heater/aerator.

LITHOGRAPHED
Sheets of 120 in six panes of 20

1999, June 24   **Tagged**   *Serpentine Die Cut 11½*

Self-Adhesive

3317	A2563	33c **multicolored,** block tagging	.65	.20
a.		Overall tagging	.65	.20
3318	A2564	33c **multicolored,** block tagging	.65	.20
a.		Overall tagging	.65	.20
3319	A2565	33c **multicolored,** block tagging	.65	.20
a.		Overall tagging	.65	.20
3320	A2566	33c **multicolored,** block tagging	.65	.20
a.		Overall tagging	.65	.20
b.		Strip of 4, #3317-3320	2.60	
		P# block of 8, 2 sets of 4#+B	5.20	
		Pane of 20	13.00	
		Sheet of 6 panes	80.00	
		Cross gutter block of 8	20.00	
		Block of 8 with horiz. gutter	9.00	
		Horiz. pair with vert. gutter	2.00	

	Vert. pairs with horiz. gutter (each)	2.25
c.	Strip of 4, #3317a-3320a	2.60
	P# block of 8, 2 sets of 4#+B	5.20
	Pane of 20	13.00

Plate blocks will have either top label or list of fish shown on bottom selvage. Cross gutter block of 8 consists of 4 horiz. pairs separated by vert. gutter with horiz. gutter between. Press sheets were printed with large block tagging.

EXTREME SPORTS

Skateboarding
A2567

BMX Biking
A2568

Snowboarding
A2569

Inline Skating
A2570

Designed by Carl Herrman. Printed by Avery Dennison.

PHOTOGRAVURE
Sheets of 160 in eight panes of 20

1999, June 25   **Tagged**   *Serpentine Die Cut 11*

Self-Adhesive

3321	A2567	33c **multicolored**	.65	.20
3322	A2568	33c **multicolored**	.65	.20
3323	A2569	33c **multicolored**	.65	.20
3324	A2570	33c **multicolored**	.65	.20
a.		Block of 4, #3321-3324	2.60	
		P# block of 4, 4#+V	2.60	
		Pane of 20	13.00	
		Sheet of 80 (four panes) top	52.50	
		Sheet of 80 (four panes) bottom, with plate # in sheet margin	52.50	
		Pane of 20 with extra selvage from sheet of 80	13.00	
		Pane of 20 with plate # in sheet margin	13.00	
		Cross gutter block of 8	5.25	
		Vert. pairs with horiz. gutter (each)	1.60	
		Horiz. pairs with vert. gutter (each)	1.60	
		Block of 4 with horiz. gutter	5.25	
		Block of 8 with vert. gutter	10.50	

Cross gutter block of 8 consists of 4 horiz. pairs separated by vert. gutter with horiz. gutter between

AMERICAN GLASS

Free-Blown
Glass — A2571

Mold-Blown
Glass — A2572

Pressed Glass — A2573 Art Glass — A2574

Designed by Richard Sheaff. Printed by Sterling Sommer for Ashton-Potter, USA (Ltd.).

LITHOGRAPHED
Sheets of 90 in six panes of 15

				Perf. 11
1999, June 29		Tagged		
3325 A2571 33c multicolored			.65	.20
3326 A2572 33c multicolored			.65	.20
3327 A2573 33c multicolored			.65	.20
3328 A2574 33c multicolored			.65	.20
a.	Strip or block of 4, #3325-3328		2.60	—
	Pane of 15, 4 each #3325, 3327-3328, 3 #3326		9.75	

A2575 A2576

LEGENDS OF HOLLYWOOD
James Cagney (1899-1986)

Designed by Howard Paine.

Printed by Sennett Security Products.

PHOTOGRAVURE
Sheets of 120 in six panes of 20

				Perf. 11
1999, July 22		Tagged		
3329 A2575 33c multicolored			.65	.20
	P# block of 4, 5#+S		2.60	—
	Pane of 20		13.00	—
	Sheet of 120 (6 panes)		80.00	—
	Cross gutter block of 8		17.50	—
	Block of 8 with vertical gutter		10.00	—
	Horiz. pair with vert. gutter		3.00	—
	Vert. pair with horiz. gutter		2.00	—

Perforations in corner of each stamp are star-shaped. Cross-gutter block consists of 6 stamps from upper panes and 2 stamps from panes below.

GEN. WILLIAM "BILLY" L. MITCHELL (1879-1936), AVIATION PIONEER

Designed by Phil Jordan.
Printed by Guilford Gravure for Banknote Corporation of America.

PHOTOGRAVURE
Sheets of 180 in nine panes of 20

1999, July 30 Tagged	Serpentine Die Cut 9¾x10			
Self-Adhesive				
3330 A2576 55c multicolored			1.10	.20
	P# block of 4, 5#+B		4.40	
	Pane of 20		22.00	

HONORING THOSE WHO SERVED

A2577

Designed by Richard Sheaff and Uldis Purins.
Printed by Avery Dennison.

PHOTOGRAVURE
Sheets of 200 in 10 panes of 20

1999, Aug. 16 Tagged	Serpentine Die Cut 11			
Self-Adhesive				
3331 A2577 33c black, blue & red			.65	.20
	P# block of 4, 3#+V		2.60	
	Pane of 20		13.00	

UNIVERSAL POSTAL UNION

USA 45 A2578

Designed by Gerald Gallo.
Printed by Sterling Sommer for Ashton-Potter (USA) Ltd.

LITHOGRAPHED
Sheets of 180 in nine panes of 20

				Perf. 11
1999, Aug. 25	Tagged			
3332 A2578 45c multicolored			.90	.20
	P# block of 4, 3#+P		3.60	—
	Pane of 20		18.00	—

FAMOUS TRAINS

Daylight — A2579

Congressional A2580

20th Century Limited — A2581

Hiawatha — A2582

Super Chief — A2583

Designed by Howard Paine.
Printed by Ashton-Potter (USA) Ltd.

LITHOGRAPHED
Sheets of 120 in six panes of 20

				Perf. 11
1999, Aug. 26	Tagged			
3333 A2579 33c multicolored			.65	.20
3334 A2580 33c multicolored			.65	.20
3335 A2581 33c multicolored			.65	.20
3336 A2582 33c multicolored			.65	.20
3337 A2583 33c multicolored			.65	.20
a.	Strip of 5, #3333-3337		3.25	—
	Pane of 20, 4 #3337a		13.00	—
	P# block of 8, 2 sets of 4#+P		5.25	—
	Sheet of 120 (6 panes)		82.50	—
	Block of 10 with vert. gutter		17.50	—
	Block of 8 with horiz. gutter		17.50	—
	Cross gutter block of 8		17.50	—

Horiz. pair with vert. gutter (each)	3.00	—
Vert. pair with horiz. gutter (each)	2.00	—

Stamps in No. 3337a are arranged in four different orders. Plate block may contain top label.

FREDERICK LAW OLMSTEAD (1822-1903), LANDSCAPE ARCHITECT

A2584

Designed by Ethel Kessler.
Printed by Ashton-Potter (USA) Ltd.

LITHOGRAPHED
Sheets of 120 in six panes of 20

				Perf. 11
1999, Sept. 12	Tagged			
3338 A2584 33c multicolored			.65	.20
	P# block of 4, 4#+P		2.60	—
	Pane of 20		13.00	—

AMERICAN MUSIC SERIES
Hollywood Composers

Max Steiner (1888-1971) A2585

Dimitri Tiomkin (1894-1975) A2586

Bernard Herrmann (1911-75) A2587

Franz Waxman (1906-67) A2588

Alfred Newman (1907-70) A2589

Erich Wolfgang Korngold (1897-1957) A2590

Designed by Howard Paine.
Printed by Sterling Sommer for Ashton-Potter (USA) Ltd.

LITHOGRAPHED
Sheets of 120 in six panes of 20

1999, Sept. 16		Tagged	Perf. 11	
3339	A2585	33c multicolored	.65	.20
3340	A2586	33c multicolored	.65	.20
3341	A2587	33c multicolored	.65	.20
3342	A2588	33c multicolored	.65	.20
3343	A2589	33c multicolored	.65	.20
3344	A2590	33c multicolored	.65	.20
a.		Block of 6, #3339-3344	3.90	
		P# block of 6, 5#+P	3.90	—
		P# block of 8, 2 sets of 5#+P + top label	5.25	—
		Pane of 20	13.00	—

AMERICAN MUSIC SERIES
Broadway Songwriters

Ira (1896-1983) & George (1898-1937) Gershwin A2591

Alan Jay Lerner (1918-86) & Frederick Loewe (1901-88) A2592

Lorenz Hart (1895-1943) A2593

Richard Rodgers (1902-79) & Oscar Hammerstein II (1895-1960) A2594

Meredith Willson (1902-84) A2595

Frank Loesser (1910-69) A2596

Designed by Howard Paine.
Printed by Sterling Sommer for Ashton-Potter (USA) Ltd.

LITHOGRAPHED
Sheets of 120 in six panes of 20

1999, Sept. 21		Tagged	Perf. 11	
3345	A2591	33c multicolored	.65	.20
3346	A2592	33c multicolored	.65	.20
3347	A2593	33c multicolored	.65	.20
3348	A2594	33c multicolored	.65	.20
3349	A2595	33c multicolored	.65	.20
3350	A2596	33c multicolored	.65	.20
a.		Block of 6, #3345-3350	3.90	—
		P# block of 6, 5#+P	3.90	—
		P# block of 8, 2 sets of 5#+P + top label	5.25	—
		Pane of 20	13.00	—

INSECTS & SPIDERS

A2597

Designed by Carl Herrman.
Printed by Ashton-Potter (USA) Ltd.

Designs: a, Black widow. b, Elderberry longhorn. c, Lady beetle. d, Yellow garden spider. e, Dogbane beetle. f, Flower fly. g, Assassin bug. h, Ebony jewelwing. i, Velvet ant. j, Monarch caterpillar. k, Monarch butterfly. l, Eastern Hercules beetle. m, Bombardier beetle. n, Dung beetle. o, Spotted water beetle. p, True katydid. q, Spinybacked spider. r, Periodical cicada. s, Scorpionfly. t, Jumping spider.

LITHOGRAPHED
Sheets of 80 in four panes of 20

1999, Oct. 1		Tagged	Perf. 11	
3351	A2597	Pane of 20	13.00	—
a.-t.		33c any single	.65	.20
		Sheet of 4 panes	52.50	
		Cross gutter block of 20	20.00	
		Block of 10 with vert. gutter	10.00	
		Block of 8 with horiz. gutter	8.00	
		Vert. pair with horiz. gutter (each)	1.60	
		Horiz. pair with vert. gutter (each)	1.60	

Cross gutter block of 20 consists of six stamps from each of two panes and four stamps from each of the two other panes with the cross gutter between.

Hanukkah Type of 1996

Designed by Hannah Smotrich.
Printed by Avery Dennison.

PHOTOGRAVURE
Sheets of 200 in 10 panes of 20

1999, Oct. 8		Tagged	Serpentine Die Cut 11	
		Self-Adhesive		
3352	A2411	33c multicolored	.65	.20
		P# block of 4, 5#+V	2.60	
		Pane of 20	13.00	

Uncle Sam Type of 1998

Designed by Richard Sheaff.
Printed by Bureau of Engraving and Printing.

COIL STAMP
PHOTOGRAVURE

1999, Oct. 8		Tagged	Perf. 9¾	
3353	A2530	22c multicolored	.45	.20
		Pair	.90	.30
		P# strip of 5, #1111	3.50	—
		P# single, same #	—	1.75

NATO, 50TH ANNIV.

A2598

Designed by Michael Cronan.
Printed by Ashton-Potter (USA) Ltd.

LITHOGRAPHED
Sheets of 180 in nine panes of 20

1999, Oct. 13		Tagged	Perf. 11¼	
3354	A2598	33c multicolored	.65	.20
		P# block of 4, 4#+P	2.60	—
		Pane of 20	13.00	—

CHRISTMAS

Madonna and Child, by Bartolomeo Vivarini — A2599

Deer — A2600

Designed by Richard Sheaff (#3355), Tom Nikosey (#3356-3367).
Printed by Banknote Corp. of America.

LITHOGRAPHED
Serpentine Die Cut 11¼ on 2 or 3 sides

1999, Oct. 20			Tagged	
		Booklet Stamp		
		Self-Adhesive		
3355	A2599	33c multicolored	.65	.15
a.		Booklet pane of 20	13.00	

Sheets of 120 in six panes of 20
Serpentine Die Cut 11¼

3356	A2600	33c gold & red	.65	.20
3357	A2600	33c gold & blue	.65	.20
3358	A2600	33c gold & purple	.65	.20
3359	A2600	33c gold & green	.65	.20
a.		Block or strip of 4, #3356-3359	2.60	
		P# block of 4, 6#+B	2.60	
		Pane of 20	13.00	

Booklet Stamps
Serpentine Die Cut 11¼ on 2, 3 or 4 sides

3360	A2600	33c gold & red	.65	.20
3361	A2600	33c gold & blue	.65	.20
3362	A2600	33c gold & purple	.65	.20
3363	A2600	33c gold & green	.65	.20
a.		Booklet pane of 20, 5 each #3360-3363	13.00	

Size: 21x19mm
Serpentine Die Cut 11½x11¼ on 2 or 3 sides

3364	A2600	33c gold & red	.65	.20
3365	A2600	33c gold & blue	.65	.20
3366	A2600	33c gold & purple	.65	.20
3367	A2600	33c gold & green	.65	.20
a.		Booklet pane of 4, #3364-3367	2.60	
b.		Booklet pane of 5, #3364, 3366, 3367, 2 #3365 + label	3.25	
c.		Booklet pane of 6, #3365, 3367, 2 #3364, 3366	4.00	

The frame on Nos. 3356-3359 is narrow and the space between it and the hoof is a hairline. The frame on Nos. 3360-3363 is much thicker, and the space between it and the hoof is wider.

Kwanzaa Type of 1997

Designed by Synthia Saint James
Printed by Avery Dennison.

PHOTOGRAVURE

Sheets of 240 in twelve pane of 20

1999, Oct. 29 **Tagged** *Serpentine Die Cut 11*
Self-Adhesive

3368	A2458	33c multicolored	.65	.20
		P# block of 4, 4#+V	2.60	
		Pane of 20	13.00	

YEAR 2000

Baby New Year — A2601

Designed by Carl Herman.
Printed by Banknote Corporation of America.

LITHOGRAPHED

Sheets of 120 in six panes of 20

1999, Dec. 27 **Tagged** *Serpentine Die Cut 11¼*
Self-Adhesive

3369	A2601	33c multicolored	.65	.20
		P# block of 4, 5#+B	2.60	
		Pane of 20	13.00	

CHINESE NEW YEAR

Year of the Dragon — A2602

Designed by Clarence Lee.
Printed by Sterling Sommer.

LITHOGRAPHED

Sheets of 180 in nine panes of 20

2000, Jan. 6 **Tagged** *Perf. 11¼*

3370	A2602	33c multicolored	.65	.20
		P# block of 4, 4#+P	2.60	—
		Pane of 20	13.00	—

BLACK HERITAGE

Patricia Roberts Harris (1924-85), First Black Woman Cabinet Secretary — A2603

Designed by Richard Sheaff.
Printed by Ashton-Potter (USA) Ltd.

LITHOGRAPHED

Sheets of 180 in nine panes of 20
Serpentine Die Cut 11½x11¼

2000, Jan. 27 **Tagged**
Self-Adhesive

3371	A2603	33c indigo	.65	.20
		P# block of 4, 4#+P	2.60	
		Pane of 20	13.00	

SUBMARINES

S Class — A2604

Los Angeles Class — A2605

Ohio Class — A2606

USS Holland — A2607

Gato Class — A2608

Designed by Carl Herrman.
Printed by Banknote Corporation of America.

LITHOGRAPHED

Sheets of 180 in nine panes of 20

2000, Mar. 27 **Tagged** *Perf. 11*

3372	A2605	33c multicolored, with microprinted "USPS" at base of sail	.65	.20
		P# block of 4, 4#+B	2.60	—
		Pane of 20	13.00	—

BOOKLET STAMPS

3373	A2604	22c multicolored	.45	.20
3374	A2605	33c multicolored, no microprinting	.65	.30
3375	A2606	55c multicolored	1.10	.50
3376	A2607	60c multicolored	1.25	.55
3377	A2608	$3.20 multicolored	6.50	3.00
a.		Booklet pane of 5, #3373-3377	10.00	

No. 3377a was issued with two types of text in the selvage.

PACIFIC COAST RAIN FOREST

A2609

Designed by Ethel Kessler.
Printed by Banknote Corporation of America.

Designs: a, Harlequin duck. b, Dwarf oregongrape, snail-eating ground beetle. c, American dipper, horiz. d, Cutthroat trout, horiz. e, Roosevelt elk. f, Winter wren. g, Pacific giant salamander, Rough-skinned newt. h, Western tiger swallowtail, horiz. i, Douglas squirrel, foliose lichen. j, Foliose lichen, banana slug.

LITHOGRAPHED

Sheets of 60 in six panes of 10
Serpentine Die Cut 11¼x11½, 11½ (horiz. stamps)

2000, Mar. 29 **Tagged**

Self-Adhesive

3378	A2609	Pane of 10	6.50	
a.-j.		33c any single	.65	.20
		Sheet of 6 panes	39.00	

LOUISE NEVELSON (1899-1988), SCULPTOR

Silent Music I — A2610

Royal Tide I — A2611

Black Chord — A2612

Nightsphere-Light A2613

Dawn's Wedding Chapel I — A2614

Designed by Ethel Kessler.
Printed by Ashton-Potter (USA) Ltd.

LITHOGRAPHED
Sheets of 80 in four panes of 20.

2000, Apr. 6	Tagged	Perf. 11x11¼
3379 A2610 33c multicolored		.65 .20
3380 A2611 33c multicolored		.65 .20
3381 A2612 33c multicolored		.65 .20
3382 A2613 33c multicolored		.65 .20
3383 A2614 33c multicolored		.65 .20
a. Strip of 5, #3379-3383		3.25 —
P# block of 10, 4#+P		6.50 —
Pane of 20		13.00 —

HUBBLE SPACE TELESCOPE IMAGES

Eagle Nebula — A2615

Ring Nebula — A2616

Lagoon Nebula — A2617

Egg Nebula — A2618

Galaxy NGC 1316 — A2619

Designed by Phil Jordan. Printed at American Packaging Corp. for Sennett Security Products.

PHOTOGRAVURE
Sheets of 120 in six panes of 20.

2000, Apr. 10	Tagged	Perf. 11
3384 A2615 33c multicolored		.65 .20
3385 A2616 33c multicolored		.65 .20
3386 A2617 33c multicolored		.65 .20
3387 A2618 33c multicolored		.65 .20
3388 A2619 33c multicolored		.65 .20
a. Strip of 5, #3384-3388		3.25 —
P# block of 10, 6#+S		6.50 —
Pane of 20		13.00 —

AMERICAN SAMOA

Samoan Double Canoe — A2620

Designed by Howard Paine.
Printed by Ashton-Potter (USA) Ltd.

LITHOGRAPHED
Sheets of 120 in six panes of 20

2000, Apr. 17	Tagged	Perf. 11
3389 A2620 33c multicolored		.65 .20
P# block of 4, 4#+P		2.60 —
Pane of 20		13.00 —

LIBRARY OF CONGRESS

Interior Dome and Arched Windows in Main Reading Room, Thomas Jefferson Building — A2621

Designed by Ethel Kessler.
Printed by Ashton-Potter (USA) Ltd.

LITHOGRAPHED
Sheets of 120 in six panes of 20

2000, Apr. 24	Tagged	Perf. 11
3390 A2621 33c multicolored		.65 .20
P# block of 4, 5#+P		2.60 —
Pane of 20		13.00 —

ROAD RUNNER & WILE E. COYOTE

A2622

Cross Gutter Block of 9

Designed by Ed Wleczyk, Warner Bros.
Printed by Banknote Corp. of America, Inc.

LITHOGRAPHED

2000, Apr. 26	Tagged	Serpentine Die Cut 11
		Self-Adhesive
3391 Pane of 10		6.50
a. A2622 33c single		.65 .20
b. Booklet pane of 9 #3391a		5.85
c. Booklet pane of 1 #3391a		.65
d. All die cutting omitted, pane of 10		—
Sheet of 60 (six panes) top, with plate # in selvage on reverse		40.00
Sheet of 60 (six panes) bottom, with plate # in selvage		40.00
Pane of 10 from sheet of 60		9.00
Two panes of 10 with plate numbers on front		18.00
Cross gutter block of 9		16.00
Vert. pair with horiz. gutter		2.00
Horiz. pair with vert. gutter		4.00

Die cutting on #3391b does not extend through the backing paper.

3392 Pane of 10		6.50
a. A2622 33c single		.65
b. Booklet pane of 9 #3392a		
c. Booklet pane of 1, imperf.		

Die cutting on #3392a extends through the backing paper. Used examples of No. 3392a are identical to those of No. 3391a.

Nos. 3391b-3391c and 3392b-3392c are separated by a vertical line of microperforations.

DISTINGUISHED SOLDIERS

Maj. Gen. John L. Hines (1868-1968) A2623

Gen. Omar N. Bradley (1893-1981) A2624

Sgt. Alvin C. York (1887-1964) A2625

Second Lt. Audie L. Murphy (1924-71) A2626

Designed by Phil Jordan.
Printed by Sterling Sommer for Ashton-Potter (USA) Ltd.

LITHOGRAPHED
Sheets of 120 in six panes of 20

2000, May 3	Tagged	Perf. 11
3393 A2623 33c multicolored		.65 .20
3394 A2624 33c multicolored		.65 .20
3395 A2625 33c multicolored		.65 .20
3396 A2626 33c multicolored		.65 .20
a. Block or strip of 4, #3393-3396		2.60 —
P# block of 4, 4#+P		2.60 —
Pane of 20		13.00 —

SUMMER SPORTS

Runners — A2627

Designed by Richard Sheaff.
Printed by Ashton-Potter (USA) Ltd.

LITHOGRAPHED
Sheets of 120 in six panes of 20

2000, May 5	Tagged	Perf. 11
3397 A2627 33c multicolored		.65 .20
P# block of 4, 4#+P		2.60 —
Pane of 20		13.00 —

ADOPTION

Stick Figures — A2628

Designed by Greg Berger.
Printed by Banknote Corporation of America.

LITHOGRAPHED
Sheets of 120 in six panes of 20

2000, May 10	Tagged	*Serpentine Die Cut 11½*		
		Self-Adhesive		
3398	A2628	33c **multicolored**	.65	.20
		P# block of 4, 5#+B	2.60	
		Pane of 20	13.00	

YOUTH TEAM SPORTS

Basketball — A2629

Football — A2630

Soccer — A2631

Baseball — A2632

Designed by Derry Noyes.
Printed by Sterling Sommer for Ashton-Potter (USA) Ltd.

LITHOGRAPHED
Sheets of 120 in six panes of 20

2000, May 27	Tagged		*Perf. 11*	
3399	A2629	33c **multicolored**	.65	.20
3400	A2630	33c **multicolored**	.65	.20
3401	A2631	33c **multicolored**	.65	.20
3402	A2632	33c **multicolored**	.65	.20
a.		Block or strip of 4, #3399-3402	2.60	—
		P# block of 4, 4#+P	2.60	—
		Pane of 20	13.00	—

THE STARS AND STRIPES

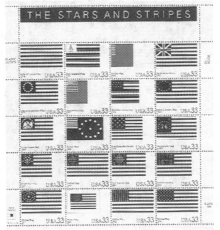

A2633

Designed by Richard Sheaff.
Printed by Banknote Corp. of America.

Designs: a, Sons of Liberty Flag, 1775. b, New England Flag, 1775. c, Forster Flag, 1775. d, Continental Colors, 1776. e, Francis Hopkinson Flag, 1777. f, Brandywine Flag, 1777. g, John Paul Jones Flag, 1779. h, Pierre L'Enfant Flag, 1783. i, Indian Peace Flag, 1803. j, Easton Flag, 1814. k, Star-Spangled Banner, 1814. l, Bennington Flag, c. 1820. m, Great Star Flag, 1837. n, 29-Star Flag, 1847. o, Fort Sumter Flag, 1861. p, Centennial Flag, 1876. q, 38-Star Flag, 1877. r, Peace Flag, 1891. s, 48-Star Flag, 1912. t, 50-Star Flag, 1960.

LITHOGRAPHED

2000, June 14	Tagged		*Perf. 10½x11*	
3403	A2633	Pane of 20	13.00	—
a.-t.		33c any single	.65	.30
		Sheet of 120 (6 panes)	80.00	—
		Cross gutter block of 20	22.50	—
		Horiz. block of 8 with vert. gutter	10.00	—
		Vert. block of 10 with horiz. gutter	12.00	—
		Vert. pairs with horiz. gutter (each)	2.25	—
		Horiz. pairs with vert. gutter (each)	2.25	—

Inscriptions on the back of each stamp describe the flag.
Cross gutter block of 20 consists of six stamps from each of two panes and four stamps from each of two other panes with the cross gutter between.

BERRIES

Blueberries — A2634

Strawberries — A2635

Blackberries — A2636

Raspberries — A2637

Designed by Howard Paine. Printed by Guilford Gravure.
See designs A2550-A2553.

PHOTOGRAVURE
COIL STAMPS
Serpentine Die Cut 8½ Horiz.

2000, June 16		Tagged	
		Self-Adhesive	
3404	A2634	33c **multicolored**	.65 .20
3405	A2635	33c **multicolored**	.65 .20
3406	A2636	33c **multicolored**	.65 .20
3407	A2637	33c **multicolored**	.65 .20
a.		Strip of 4, #3404-3407	2.60
		P# strip of 5, 2 #3404, 1 each #3405-3407, #G1111	4.75
		P# strip of 9, 2 each #3404-3405, 3407, 3 #3406, #G1111	7.50
		P# single (#3406), #G1111	— 2.50

The adhesive on Nos. 3404-3407 is strong and can remove the ink from stamps in the roll.

LEGENDS OF BASEBALL

A2638

Designed by Phil Jordan. Printed by Ashton-Potter (USA) Ltd.

Designs: a, Jackie Robinson. b, Eddie Collins. c, Christy Mathewson. d, Ty Cobb. e, George Sisler. f, Rogers Hornsby. g, Mickey Cochrane. h, Babe Ruth. i, Walter Johnson. j, Roberto Clemente. k, Lefty Grove. l, Tris Speaker. m, Cy Young. n, Jimmie Foxx. o, Pie Traynor. p, Satchel Paige. q, Honus Wagner. r, Josh Gibson. s, Dizzy Dean. t, Lou Gehrig.

LITHOGRAPHED
Sheets of 120 in six panes of 20

2000, July 6   Tagged   Serpentine Die Cut 11¼
Self-Adhesive

3408	A2638	Pane of 20	13.00	
a.-t.		33c any single	.65	.20

SPACE
Souvenir Sheets

Probing the Vastness of Space — A2639

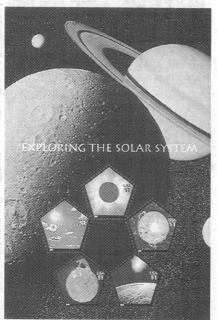

Exploring the Solar System — A2640

Escaping the Gravity of Earth — A2641

Space Achievement and Exploration — A2642

Landing on the Moon — A2643

Designed by Richard Sheaff. Printed by American Packaging Corporation for Sennett Security Products.

Designs: No. 3409: a, Hubble Space Telescope. b, Radio interferometer very large array, New Mexico. c, Optical and infrared telescopes, Keck Observatory, Hawaii. d, Optical telescopes, Cerro Tololo Observatory, Chile. e, Optical telescope, Mount Wilson Observatory, California. f, Radio telescope, Arecibo Observatory, Puerto Rico.
No. 3410: a, Sun and corona. b, Cross-section of sun. c, Sun and earth. d, Sun and solar flare. e, Sun and clouds.
No. 3411: a, Space Shuttle and Space Station. b, Astronauts working in space.
Illustrations reduced.

PHOTOGRAVURE

2000		**Tagged**		**Perf. 10½x11**	
3409	A2639	Sheet of 6, July 10	7.50	—	
a.-f.		60c any single	1.25	.60	
			Perf. 10¾		
3410	A2640	Sheet of 5 + label, July 11	10.00	—	
a.-e.		$1 any single	2.00	1.00	

Untagged
Photogravure with Hologram Affixed
Perf. 10½, 10¾ (#3412)

3411	A2641	Sheet of 2, July 9	12.50	—
a.-b.		$3.20 any single	6.25	3.00
3412	A2642	$11.75 multicolored, July 7	22.50	11.50
3413	A2643	$11.75 multicolored, July 8	22.50	11.50
		Uncut sheet of 5 panes, #3409-3412	75.00	
		Nos. 3409-3413 (5)	75.00	

Warning: Soaking in water may affect holographic images.

STAMPIN' THE FUTURE CHILDREN'S STAMP DESIGN CONTEST WINNERS

By Zachary Canter — A2644

By Sarah Lipsey — A2645

By Morgan Hill — A2646

By Ashley Young — A2647

Designed by Richard Sheaff. Printed by Ashton-Potter (USA) Ltd.

LITHOGRAPHED
Sheets of 120 in six panes of 20

2000, July 13   Tagged   Serpentine Die Cut 11¼
Self-Adhesive

3414	A2644	33c multicolored	.65	.20
3415	A2645	33c multicolored	.65	.20
3416	A2646	33c multicolored	.65	.20
3417	A2647	33c multicolored	.65	.20
a.		Horiz. strip of 4, #3414-3417	2.60	
		P# block of 8, 2 sets of 5#+P	5.25	
		Pane of 20	13.00	

Plate block may contain top label.

STAMPS INSERTED WITHIN THE LISTINGS

The following major and minor varieties have been added to the Catalogue this edition, with the listings having been inserted into existing sets.

Major Listings

2941	55c Morrill
3031	1c Kestrel self-adhesive
3051	20c Ring-necked Pheasant
3052	33c Coral pink rose
3052E	33c Coral pink rose
3188	33c Celebrate the Cent., 60s
3189	33c Celebrate the Cent., 70s
3190	33c Celebrate the Cent., 80s
3191	33c Celebrate the Cent., 90s
3278	33c Flag & City, self-adhesive

Minor Listings

2998a	60c Rickenbacker, large date
3044a	1c Kestrel, large date
3281b	33c Flag & City, large date
3294a	33c Berries, dated 2000
3295a	33c Berries, dated 2000
3296a	33c Berries, dated 2000
3297c	33c Berries, dated 2000
3297d	Booklet pane
3297e	Block of 4
3301a	33c Berries, booklet pane
3301a	33c Berries, booklet pane
3301a	33c Berries, booklet pane

Minor Listings Changed to Major Listings

1580B	(10c) Christmas
1590A	9c Americana
1622C	13c Flag over Independence Hall
1623B	13c Flag over Capitol
1789A	15c John Paul Jones
1789B	15c John Paul Jones
1795A-1798A	15c Olympic Games
1951A	20c Love
1953A-2002A	20c State Birds and Flowers
2524A	29c Tulip
2593B	29c Pledge Allegiance Flag
2723A	29c Hank Williams
2920D	32c Flag over Porch
3003A	32c Christmas

2000 END-OF-YEAR ISSUES

The USPS has announced that the following items will be released in late 2000. Dates, denominations and cities are tentative.

Joseph W. Stilwell, 10c definitive, Great American series, *Aug.24,* Providence RI

Claude Pepper, 33c, Great American series, *Sept. 7,* Tallahassee FL

California Statehood, 33c self-adhesive, *Sept. 8,* Sacramento CA

Edward G. Robinson, 33c, *Sept. 14,* Burbank CA

Deep Sea Creatures, 5x33c, *Oct. 2,* Monterey CA

Thomas Wolfe, 33c, *Oct. 3,* Ashville NC

Lion Statue, (10c) self-adhesive coil, *Nov. 9,* New York NY

White House, *Nov.?,* 33c self-adhesive, Washington DC

Other issues are probable.
Listings as of 4:00PM, July 18, 2000.

United States postage stamps can be mounted in the annually supplemented Scott National, Pony Express, Minuteman, U.S. Commemorative Singles, U.S. Commemorative and Commemorative Air Plate Blocks, U.S. Blocks of Four and U.S. Regular and Regular Air Plate Blocks albums.

SEMI-POSTAL STAMP

In July 1997 both houses of Congress enacted a bill directing the USPS to issue a stamp to benefit breast-cancer research. On August 13, the President signed it into law.

The surcharge was to be up to 25% of the current first-class rate. The stamp was to be available for two years.

BREAST CANCER AWARENESS

SP1 USA First-Class

Designed by Ethel Kessler. Printed by Avery Dennison.

PHOTOGRAVURE
Sheets of 160 in eight panes of 20

| 1998, July 29 | Tagged | *Serpentine Die Cut 11* |
| | **Self-Adhesive** | |

B1	SP1	(32c+8c) **multicolored**	.80	.60
		P# block of 4, 6#+V	3.25	
		Pane of 20	16.00	

After the Jan. 10, 1999 first class postage rate change, No. B1 became a 33c stamp with 7c surtax.

R.F. OVERPRINTS

Authorized as a control mark by the United States Fleet Post Office during 1944-45 for the accommodation of and exclusive use by French naval personnel on airmail correspondence to the United States and Canada. All "R.F." (Republique Francaise) mail had to be posted on board ship or at one of the Mediterranean naval bases and had to bear the return address, rank and/or serial number of a French officer or seaman. It also had to be reviewed by a censor.

All "R.F." overprints were handstamped by the French naval authorities after the stamps were affixed for mailing. The stamps had to be canceled by a special French naval cancellation. The status of unused copies seems questionable; they are alleged to have been handstamped at a later date. Several types of "R.F." overprints other than those illustrated are known, but their validity is doubtful.

United States No. C25 Handstamped in Black

CM7	AP17 (g)	6c **carmine,** on cover	.575.00
CM8	AP17 (h)	6c **carmine,** on cover	600.00
CM9	AP17 (i)	6c **carmine,** on cover	750.00
CM10	AP17 (j)	6c **carmine,** on cover	—

Counterfeits of several types exist.
No. 907 is known with type "c" overprint; No. C19 with type "e" or "h"; No. C25a (single) with type "c", and No. C26 with type "b" or "f." Type "i" exists in several variations.

STAMPED ENVELOPES
No. UC5 Handstamped in Black

1944-45

UCM1	UC2 (a)	6c **orange,** entire	300.00
UCM2	UC2 (b)	6c **orange,** entire	400.00
UCM3	UC2 (d)	6c **orange,** entire	450.00
UCM4	UC2 (f)	6c **orange,** entire	450.00
UCM5	UC2 (h)	6c **orange,** entire	—

1944-45   **Unwmk.**   *Perf. 11x10½*

CM1	AP17 (a)	6c **carmine,** on cover	225.00
CM2	AP17 (b)	6c **carmine,** on cover	275.00
CM3	AP17 (c)	6c **carmine,** on cover	200.00
CM4	AP17 (d)	6c **carmine,** on cover	350.00
CM5	AP17 (e)	6c **carmine,** on cover	500.00
CM6	AP17 (f)	6c **carmine,** on cover	275.00

AIR POST STAMPS

Air mail in the U. S. postal system developed in three stages: pioneer period (with many unofficial or semi-official flights before 1918), government flights and contract air mail (C.A.M.). Contract air mail began on February 15, 1926.

All C.A.M. contracts were canceled on February 19, 1934, and air mail was carried by Army planes for six months. After that the contract plan was resumed. Separate domestic airmail service was abolished Oct. 11, 1975.

See Domestic Air Mail Rates chart in introduction.

Curtiss Jenny — AP1

No. C3 first used on airplane mail service between Washington, Philadelphia and New York, on May 15, 1918, but was valid for ordinary postage. The rate of postage was 24 cents per ounce, which included immediate individual delivery.

Rate of postage was reduced to 16 cents for the first ounce and 6 cents for each additional ounce, which included 10 cents for immediate individual delivery, on July 15, 1918, by Postmaster General's order of June 26, 1918. No. C2 was first used for air mail in the tri-city service on July 15.

Rate of postage was reduced on December 15, 1918, by Postmaster General's order of November 30, 1918, to 6 cents per ounce. No. C1 was first used for air mail (same three-way service) on Dec. 16.

FLAT PLATE PRINTINGS
Plates of 100 subjects.

1918		Unwmk.		Engr.		Perf. 11
C1	AP1	6c	**orange,** *Dec. 10*		75.	30.
			pale orange		75.	30.
			Never hinged		120.	
			On cover			50.
			First flight cover, *Dec. 16*			2,000.
			Margin block of 4, arrow top			
			or left		310.	140.
			Center line block		325.	150.
			P# block of 6, arrow		800.	—
			Never hinged		1,100.	
			Double transfer (#9155-14)		95.	45.
C2	AP1	16c	**green,** *July 11*		100.	35.
			dark green		100.	35.
			Never hinged		160.	
			On cover			55.
			First flight cover, *July 15*			800.
			Margin block of 4, arrow top			
			or left		425.	175.
			Center line block		450.	190.
			P# block of 6, arrow		1,200.	—
			Never hinged		1,650.	
C3	AP1	24c	**carmine rose & blue,** *May 13*		100.	35.
			dark carmine rose & blue		100.	35.
			Never hinged		160.	
			On cover			75.
			First flight cover, *May 15*			750.
			Margin block of 4, arrow top			
			or left		425.	150.
			Margin block of 4, arrow bottom		435.	160.
			Margin block of 4, arrow right		450.	200.
			Center line block		450.	175.
			P# block of 4, red P# only		475.	—
			P# block of 12, two P#, arrow & two "TOP"		1,350.	—
			Never hinged		1,900.	
			P# block of 12, two P#, arrow & blue "TOP" only		12,500.	
a.			Center inverted		170,000.	
			Never hinged		200,000.	
			Block of 4		750,000.	
			Block of 4 with horiz. guide line		850,000.	
			Corner margin block of 4 with sideographer's initials		1,100,000.	
			Center line block		825,000.	
			P# block of 4, blue P#		1,200,000.	
			Nos. C1-C3 (3)		375.00	100.00
			Nos. C1-C3, never hinged		440.00	

Airplane Radiator and Wooden Propeller — AP2

Air Service Emblem — AP3

DeHavilland Biplane — AP4

Nos. C4-C6 were issued primarily for use in the new night-flying air mail service between New York and San Francisco, but valid for all purposes. Three zones were established; New York-Chicago, Chicago-Cheyenne, Cheyenne-San Francisco, and the rate of postage was 8 cents an ounce for each zone. Service was inaugurated on July 1, 1924.

These stamps were placed on sale at the Philatelic Agency at Washington on the dates indicated in the listings but were not sold to postmasters at that time.

Plates of 400 subjects in four panes of 100 each.

1923		Unwmk.			Perf. 11
C4	AP2	8c	**dark green,** *Aug. 15*	27.50	14.00
			deep green	27.50	14.00
			Never hinged	45.00	
			On cover		22.50
			P# block of 6	260.00	—
			Never hinged	375.00	
			Double transfer	45.00	22.50
C5	AP3	16c	**dark blue,** *Aug. 17*	100.00	30.00
			Never hinged	160.00	
			On cover		47.50
			P# block of 6	1,900.	—
			Never hinged	2,750.	
			Double transfer	130.00	50.00
C6	AP4	24c	**carmine,** *Aug. 21*	110.00	30.00
			Never hinged	175.00	
			On cover		42.50
			P# block of 6	2,500.	—
			Never hinged	3,500.	
			Double transfer (Pl. 14841)	175.00	42.50
			Nos. C4-C6 (3)	237.50	74.00
			Nos. C4-C6, never hinged	380.00	

Map of United States and Two Mail Planes AP5

Double Transfer

The Act of Congress of February 2, 1925, created a rate of 10 cents per ounce for distances to 1000 miles, 15 cents per ounce for 1500 miles and 20 cents for more than 1500 miles on contract air mail routes.

Plates of 200 subjects in four panes of 50 each.

1926-27		Unwmk.		Perf. 11	
C7	AP5	10c	**dark blue**, *Feb. 13, 1926*	2.90	.35
			light blue	2.90	.35
			Never hinged	4.50	
			P# block of 6	35.00	—
			Never hinged	45.00	
			Double transfer (18246 UL 11)	5.75	1.10
C8	AP5	15c	**olive brown**, *Sept. 18, 1926*	3.25	2.50
			light brown	3.25	2.50
			Never hinged	5.25	
			P# block of 6	37.50	—
			Never hinged	50.00	
C9	AP5	20c	**yellow green**, *Jan. 25, 1927*	8.50	2.00
			green	8.50	2.00
			Never hinged	13.50	
			P# block of 6	85.00	—
			Never hinged	110.00	
			Nos. C7-C9 (3)	14.65	4.85
			Nos. C7-C9, never hinged	23.25	

Lindbergh's Plane "Spirit of St. Louis" and Flight Route — AP6

A tribute to Col. Charles A. Lindbergh, who made the first non-stop (and solo) flight from New York to Paris, May 20-21, 1927.

Plates of 200 subjects in four panes of 50 each.

1927, June 18		Unwmk.		Perf. 11	
C10	AP6	10c	**dark blue**	8.00	2.50
			Never hinged	12.50	
			P# block of 6	95.00	—
			Never hinged	130.00	
			Double transfer	12.00	3.25
a.			Booklet pane of 3, *May 26, 1928*	85.00	65.00
			Never hinged	125.00	

Beacon on Rocky Mountains — AP7

Issued to meet the new rate, effective August 1, of 5 cents per ounce.

Plates of 100 subjects in two panes of 50

1928, July 25		Unwmk.		Perf. 11	
C11	AP7	5c	**carmine and blue**	5.25	.75
			Never hinged	8.25	
			On cover, first day of 5c airmail rate, Aug. 1		3.00
			Margin block of 4, arrow, (line) right or left	22.50	4.50
			P# block of 8, two P# only	175.00	
			Never hinged	225.00	
			P# block of 6, two P# & red "TOP"	40.00	—
			Never hinged	55.00	
			P# block of 6, two P# & blue "TOP"	40.00	—
			Never hinged	55.00	
			P# block of 6, two P# & double "TOP"	110.00	—
			Never hinged	145.00	
			Recut frame line at left	6.75	1.25
			Double transfer		
a.			Vert. pair, imperf. between	5,500.	

Winged Globe AP8

Plates of 200 subjects in four panes of 50 each.

1930, Feb. 10		Unwmk.		Perf. 11	
		Stamp design: 46½x19mm			
C12	AP8	5c	**violet**	11.00	.50
			Never hinged	17.50	
			P# block of 6	140.00	—
			Never hinged	190.00	
			Double transfer (Pl. 20189)	19.00	1.25
a.			Horiz. pair, imperf. between	4,500.	

See Nos. C16-C17, C19.

GRAF ZEPPELIN ISSUE

Zeppelin Over Atlantic Ocean AP9

Zeppelin Between Continents — AP10

Zeppelin Passing Globe AP11

Issued for use on mail carried on the first Europe-Pan-America round trip flight of the Graf Zeppelin in May, 1930. They were withdrawn from sale June 30, 1930.

Plates of 200 subjects in four panes of 50 each.

1930, Apr. 19		Unwmk.		Perf. 11	
C13	AP9	65c	**green**	250.	160.
			Never hinged	360.	
			On cover or card		175.
			Block of 4	1,050.	700.
			P# block of 6	2,300.	—
			Never hinged	3,100.	
C14	AP10	$1.30	**brown**	500.	375.
			Never hinged	725.	
			On cover		400.
			Block of 4	2,250.	1,500.
			P# block of 6	5,750.	—
			Never hinged	7,750.	
C15	AP11	$2.60	**blue**	800.	575.
			Never hinged	1,150.	
			On cover		600.
			Block of 4	3,500.	2,500.
			P# block of 6	8,250.	—
			Never hinged	11,250.	
			Nos. C13-C15 (3)	2,660.	1,110.
			Nos. C13-C15, never hinged	2,235.	

ROTARY PRESS PRINTING
Plates of 200 subjects in four panes of 50 each.

1931-32		Unwmk.		Perf. 10½x11	
		Stamp design: 47½x19mm			
C16	AP8	5c	**violet**, *Aug. 19, 1931*	5.50	.60
			Never hinged	8.75	
			Block of 4	22.50	2.00
			P# block of 4	80.00	—
			Never hinged	100.00	

Issued to conform with new air mail rate of 8 cents per ounce which became effective July 6, 1932.

C17	AP8	8c	**olive bister**, *Sept. 26, 1932*	2.40	.40
			Never hinged	3.75	
			Block of 4	10.00	2.00
			P# block of 4	27.50	—
			Never hinged	37.50	

CENTURY OF PROGRESS ISSUE

"Graf Zeppelin," Federal Building at Chicago Exposition and Hangar at Friedrichshafen — AP12

Issued in connection with the flight of the airship "Graf Zeppelin" in October, 1933, to Miami, Akron and Chicago and from the last city to Europe.

FLAT PLATE PRINTING
Plates of 200 subjects in four panes of 50 each.

1933, Oct. 2		**Unwmk.**		**Perf. 11**	
C18 AP12 50c	**green**			75.00	70.00
	Never hinged			110.00	
	On cover				80.00
	Block of 4			320.00	290.00
	P# block of 6			575.00	—
	Never hinged			775.00	

> Catalogue values for unused stamps in this section, from this point to the end, are for Never Hinged items.

Type of 1930 Issue
ROTARY PRESS PRINTING
Issued to conform with new air mail rate of 6 cents per ounce which became effective July 1, 1934.

Plates of 200 subjects in four panes of 50 each.

1934, June 30		**Unwmk.**	**Perf. 10½x11**	
C19 AP8 6c	**dull orange**		3.50	.25
	On cover, first day of 6c airmail rate, July 1			10.00
	Block of 4		14.00	1.10
	P# block of 4		22.50	—
	Pair with full vert. gutter btwn.		425.00	

TRANSPACIFIC ISSUES

"China Clipper" over Pacific — AP13

Issued to pay postage on mail transported by the Transpacific air mail service, inaugurated Nov. 22, 1935.

FLAT PLATE PRINTING
Plates of 200 subjects in four panes of 50 each.

1935, Nov. 22		**Unwmk.**	**Perf. 11**	
C20 AP13 25c	**blue**		1.40	1.00
	P# block of 6		20.00	

"China Clipper" over Pacific — AP14

Issued primarily for use on the Transpacific service to China, but valid for all air mail purposes.

FLAT PLATE PRINTING
Plates of 200 subjects in four panes of 50 each.

1937, Feb. 15		**Unwmk.**	**Perf. 11**	
C21 AP14 20c	**green**		11.00	1.75
	dark green		11.00	1.75
	Block of 4		47.50	8.50
	P# block of 6		100.00	—
C22 AP14 50c	**carmine**		10.00	5.00
	Block of 4		42.50	21.00
	P# block of 6		100.00	—

Wide full selvage top margin plate blocks of No. C22 are extremely scarce and sell for much more than the value listed.

Eagle Holding Shield, Olive Branch and Arrows — AP15

FLAT PLATE PRINTING

Frame plates of 100 subjects in two panes of 50 each separated by a 1½-inch wide vertical gutter with central guide line, and vignette plates of 50 subjects. Some plates were made of iron, then chromed; several of these carry an additional imprint, "E.I." (Electrolytic Iron).

1938, May 14		**Unwmk.**	**Perf. 11**	
C23 AP15 6c	**dark blue & carmine**		.50	.20
	Margin block of 4, bottom or side arrow		2.25	.55
	P# block of 4, 2 P#		8.00	—
	Center line block		2.75	.95
	Top P# block of 10, with two P#, arrow, two "TOP" and two re-gistration markers		13.50	
	Ultramarine & carmine		150.00	
	P# block of 4, 2 P#		1,500.	
a.	Vert. pair, imperf. horiz.		350.00	
b.	Horiz. pair, imperf. vert.		12,500.	
	P# block of 4, 2 P#		37,500.	—

Top plate number blocks of No. C23 are found both with and without top arrow.
The plate block of No. C23b is unique and never hinged; value is based on 1994 auction sale.

TRANSATLANTIC ISSUE

Winged Globe AP16

Inauguration of Transatlantic air mail service.

FLAT PLATE PRINTING
Plates of 200 subjects in four panes of 50 each.

1939, May 16		**Unwmk.**	**Perf. 11**	
C24 AP16 30c	**dull blue**		10.50	1.50
	P# block of 6		140.00	—

Twin-Motored Transport Plane — AP17

ROTARY PRESS PRINTING
E. E. Plates of 200 subjects in four panes of 50 each.

1941-44		**Unwmk.**	**Perf. 11x10½**	
C25 AP17 6c	**carmine,** *June 25, 1941*		.20	.20
	P# block of 4		.65	—
	Pair with full vert. gutter btwn.		225.00	
	Pair with full horiz. gutter btwn.			
a.	Booklet pane of 3, *Mar. 18, 1943*		5.00	1.50
b.	Horiz. pair, imperf. between		2,250.	

Value of No. C25b is for pair without blue crayon P. O. rejection mark on front. Very fine pairs with crayon mark sell for about $1,750.
Singles from No. C25a are imperf. at sides or at sides and bottom.

C26 AP17 8c	**olive green,** *Mar. 21, 1944*		.20	.20
	P# block of 4		1.10	—
	Pair with full horiz. gutter btwn.		325.00	
C27 AP17 10c	**violet,** *Aug. 15, 1941*		1.25	.20
	P# block of 4		7.00	—
C28 AP17 15c	**brown carmine,** *Aug. 19, 1941*		2.75	.35
	P# block of 4		13.50	—
C29 AP17 20c	**bright green,** *Aug. 27, 1941*		2.25	.30
	P# block of 4		11.00	—
C30 AP17 30c	**blue,** *Sept. 25, 1941*		2.50	.35
	P# block of 4		12.00	—
C31 AP17 50c	**orange,** *Oct. 29, 1941*		11.00	3.00
	P# block of 4		60.00	—
	Nos. C25-C31 (7)		20.15	4.60

DC-4 Skymaster AP18

ROTARY PRESS PRINTING
E. E. Plates of 200 subjects in four panes of 50 each.

1946, Sept. 25		**Unwmk.**	**Perf. 11x10½**	
C32 AP18 5c	**carmine**		.20	.20
	P# block of 4		.45	—

DC-4 Skymaster — AP19

ROTARY PRESS PRINTING
E. E. Plates of 400 subjects in four panes of 100 each.

1947, Mar. 26	Unwmk.	Perf. 10½x11	
C33 AP19 5c **carmine**		.20	.20
P# block of 4		.50	—

Pan American Union Building, Washington, D.C., and Martin 2-0-2 — AP20

Statue of Liberty, New York Skyline and Lockheed Constellation AP21

San Francisco-Oakland Bay Bridge and Boeing B377 Stratocruiser — AP22

Designed by Victor S. McCloskey, Jr., Leon Helguera and William K. Schrage.

ROTARY PRESS PRINTING
E. E. Plates of 200 subjects in four panes of 50 each.

1947	Unwmk.	Perf. 11x10½	
C34 AP20 10c **black**, *Aug. 30*		.25	.20
P# block of 4		1.10	—
a. Dry printing		.40	.20
P# block of 4 (#25613, 25614)		1.75	—
C35 AP21 15c **bright blue green**, *Aug. 20*		.35	.20
blue green		.35	.20
P# block of 4		1.50	—
Pair with full horiz. gutter btwn.		650.00	
a. Horiz. pair, imperf. between		2,100.	
b. Dry printing		.55	.20
P# block of 4 (#25492 and up)		2.50	—
C36 AP22 25c **blue**, *July 30*		.85	.20
P# block of 4		3.50	—
a. Dry printing		1.00	.20
P# block of 4 (#25615 and up)		4.25	—
Nos. C34-C36 (3)		1.45	.60

See note on wet and dry printings following No. 1029.
No. C35a is valued in the grade of fine.

ROTARY PRESS COIL STAMP
Type of 1947

1948, Jan. 15	Unwmk.	Perf. 10 Horizontally	
C37 AP19 5c **carmine**		1.00	.80
Pair		2.10	1.75
Joint line pair		10.00	3.00

NEW YORK CITY ISSUE

Map of Five Boroughs, Circular Band and Planes — AP23

50th anniv. of the consolidation of the five boroughs of New York City.

ROTARY PRESS PRINTING
E. E. Plates of 400 subjects in four panes of 100 each.

1948, July 31	Unwmk.	Perf. 11x10½	
C38 AP23 5c **bright carmine**		.20	.20
P# block of 4		3.75	—

Type of 1947
ROTARY PRESS PRINTING
E. E. Plates of 400 subjects in four panes of 100 each.

1949	Unwmk.	Perf. 10½x11	
C39 AP19 6c **carmine**, *Jan. 18*		.20	.20
P# block of 4		.50	—
a. Booklet pane of 6, *Nov. 18*		10.00	5.00
b. Dry printing		.50	.20
P# block of 4 (#25340 and up)		2.25	—
c. As "a," dry printing		15.00	—

See note on wet and dry printings following No. 1029.

ALEXANDRIA BICENTENNIAL ISSUE

Home of John Carlyle, Alexandria Seal and Gadsby's Tavern — AP24

200th anniv. of the founding of Alexandria, Va.

ROTARY PRESS PRINTING
E. E. Plates of 200 subjects in four panes of 50 each.

1949, May 11	Unwmk.	Perf. 11x10½	
C40 AP24 6c **carmine**		.20	.20
P# block of 4		.50	—

ROTARY PRESS COIL STAMP
Type of 1947

1949, Aug. 25	Unwmk.	Perf. 10 Horizontally	
C41 AP19 6c **carmine**		3.25	.20
Pair		6.50	.20
Joint line pair		15.00	1.35

UNIVERSAL POSTAL UNION ISSUE

Post Office Department Building — AP25

Globe and Doves Carrying Messages AP26

Boeing Stratocruiser and Globe — AP27

Universal Postal Union, 75th Anniv.

ROTARY PRESS PRINTING
E. E. Plates of 200 subjects in four panes of 50 each.

1949	Unwmk.	Perf. 11x10½	
C42 AP25 10c **violet**, *Nov. 18*		.20	.20
P# block of 4		1.40	—
C43 AP26 15c **ultramarine**, *Oct. 7*		.30	.25
P# block of 4		1.25	—
C44 AP27 25c **rose carmine**, *Nov. 30*		.50	.40
P# block of 4		5.75	—

WRIGHT BROTHERS ISSUE

Wilbur and Orville Wright and their Plane, 1903 — AP28

46th anniv. of the 1st successful flight in a motor-powered airplane, Dec. 17, 1903, at Kill Devil Hill near Kitty Hawk, NC, by Wilbur (1867-1912) and Orville Wright (1871-1948) of Dayton, OH. The plane flew 852 feet in 59 seconds.

ROTARY PRESS PRINTING
E. E. Plates of 200 subjects in four panes of 50 each.

1949, Dec. 17	Unwmk.	Perf. 11x10½	
C45 AP28 6c **magenta**		.20	.20
P# block of 4		.65	—

Diamond Head, Honolulu, Hawaii — AP29

ROTARY PRESS PRINTING
E. E. Plates of 200 subjects in four panes of 50 each.

1952, Mar. 26	Unwmk.	Perf. 11x10½	
C46 AP29 80c **bright red violet**		5.00	1.25
P# block of 4		22.50	—

POWERED FLIGHT, 50th ANNIV.

First Plane and Modern Plane — AP30

ROTARY PRESS PRINTING
E. E. Plates of 200 subjects in four panes of 50 each.

1953, May 29	Unwmk.	Perf. 11x10½	
C47 AP30 6c **carmine**		.20	.20
P# block of 4		.55	—

Eagle in Flight — AP31

Issued primarily for use on domestic post cards.

ROTARY PRESS PRINTING
E. E. Plates of 400 subjects in four panes of 100 each.

1954, Sept. 3	Unwmk.	Perf. 11x10½	
C48 AP31 4c **bright blue**		.20	.20
P# block of 4		1.40	—

AIR FORCE, 50th ANNIV.

B-52 Stratofortress and F-104 Starfighters AP32

Designed by Alexander Nagy, Jr.

ROTARY PRESS PRINTING
E. E. Plates of 200 subjects in four panes of 50 each.

1957, Aug. 1	Unwmk.	Perf. 11x10½	
C49 AP32 6c **blue**		.20	.20
P# block of 4		.75	—

Type of 1954
Issued primarily for use on domestic post cards.

1958, July 31	Unwmk.	Perf. 11x10½	
C50 AP31 5c **red**		.20	.20
P# block of 4		1.40	—

Silhouette of Jet Airliner — AP33

Designed by William H. Buckley and Sam Marsh.

ROTARY PRESS PRINTING
E. E. Plates of 400 subjects in four panes of 100 each.

1958, July 31	Unwmk.	Perf. 10½x11		
C51	AP33	7c blue	.20	.20
		P# block of 4	.60	—
a.		Booklet pane of 6	14.00	7.00
b.		Vert. pair, imperf. between (from booklet pane)	—	

No. C51b resulted from a paper foldover after perforating and before cutting into panes. Two pairs are known.

ROTARY PRESS COIL STAMP
Perf. 10 Horizontally

C52	AP33	7c blue	2.25	.20
		Pair	4.50	.40
		Joint line pair	15.00	1.25
		Small holes	10.00	
		Pair	20.00	
		Joint line pair	200.00	

ALASKA STATEHOOD ISSUE

Big Dipper, North Star and Map of Alaska — AP34

Designed by Richard C. Lockwood.

ROTARY PRESS PRINTING
E. E. Plates of 200 subjects in four panes of 50 each.

1959, Jan. 3	Unwmk.	Perf. 11x10½		
C53	AP34	7c dark blue	.20	.20
		P# block of 4	.60	—

BALLOON JUPITER ISSUE

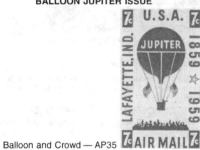

Balloon and Crowd — AP35

Designed by Austin Briggs.

Centenary of the carrying of mail by the balloon Jupiter from Lafayette to Crawfordsville, Ind.

GIORI PRESS PRINTING
Plates of 200 subjects in four panes of 50 each.

1959, Aug. 17	Unwmk.	Perf. 11		
C54	AP35	7c dark blue & red	.20	.20
		P# block of 4	.60	—

HAWAII STATEHOOD ISSUE

Alii Warrior, Map of Hawaii and Star of Statehood AP36

Designed by Joseph Feher.

ROTARY PRESS PRINTING
E. E. Plates of 200 subjects in four panes of 50 each.

1959, Aug. 21	Unwmk.	Perf. 11x10½		
C55	AP36	7c rose red	.20	.20
		P# block of 4	.60	—

PAN AMERICAN GAMES ISSUE

Runner Holding Torch — AP37

Designed by Suren Ermoyan.

3rd Pan American Games, Chicago, Aug. 27-Sept. 7, 1959.

GIORI PRESS PRINTING
Plates of 200 subjects in four panes of 50 each.

1959, Aug. 27	Unwmk.	Perf. 11		
C56	AP37	10c violet blue & bright red	.25	.25
		P# block of 4	1.25	—

Liberty Bell — AP38

Statue of Liberty — AP39

Abraham Lincoln — AP40

GIORI PRESS PRINTING
Plates of 200 subjects in four panes of 50 each.

1959-66	Unwmk.	Perf. 11		
C57	AP38	10c black & green, June 10, 1960	1.25	.70
		P# block of 4	5.50	—
C58	AP39	15c black & orange, Nov. 20, 1959	.35	.20
		P# block of 4	1.50	—
C59	AP40	25c black & maroon, Apr. 22, 1960	.50	.20
		P# block of 4	2.00	—
a.		Tagged, Dec. 29, 1966	.60	.30
		P# block of 4	2.50	—
		Nos. C57-C59 (3)	2.10	1.10

See Luminescence data in Information for Collectors section.

Type of 1958
ROTARY PRESS PRINTING
E. E. Plates of 400 subjects in four panes of 100 each.

1960, Aug. 12	Unwmk.	Perf. 10½x11		
C60	AP33	7c carmine	.20	.20
		P# block of 4	.60	—
		Pair with full horiz. gutter btwn.		
a.		Booklet pane of 6, Aug. 19	17.50	8.00
b.		Vert. pair, imperf between	5,500.	

No. C60b resulted from a paper foldover after perforating and before cutting into panes. Two pairs are known.

Type of 1958
ROTARY PRESS COIL STAMP

1960, Oct. 22	Unwmk.	Perf. 10 Horizontally		
C61	AP33	7c carmine	4.25	.25
		Pair	8.50	.55
		Joint line pair	37.50	3.75

Type of 1959-60 and

Statue of Liberty — AP41

GIORI PRESS PRINTING
Plates of 200 subjects in four panes of 50 each.

1961-67	Unwmk.	Perf. 11		
C62	AP38	13c black & red, June 28, 1961	.40	.20
		P# block of 4	1.65	—
a.		Tagged, Feb. 15, 1967	.75	.50
		P# block of 4	5.00	—
C63	AP41	15c black & orange, Jan. 13, 1961	.30	.20
		P# block of 4	1.25	—
a.		Tagged, Jan. 11, 1967	.35	.20
		P# block of 4	1.50	—
b.		As "a," horiz. pair, imperf. vert.	15,000.	

Jet Airliner over Capitol — AP42

Designed by Henry K. Bencsath.

ROTARY PRESS PRINTING
E. E. Plates of 400 subjects in four panes of 100 each.

1962, Dec. 5	Unwmk.	Perf. 10½x11		
C64	AP42	8c carmine	.20	.20
		P# block of 4	.65	—
a.		Tagged, Aug. 1, 1963	.20	.20
		P# block of 4	.65	—
		As "a," pair with full horiz. gutter between		
b.		Booklet pane of 5 + label	7.00	3.00
c.		As "b," tagged, 1964	2.00	.75

Nos. C64a and C64c were made by overprinting Nos. C64 and C64b with phosphorescent ink. No. C64a was first issued at Dayton, O., for experiments in high speed mail sorting. The tagging is visible in ultraviolet light.

COIL STAMP; ROTARY PRESS
Perf. 10 Horizontally

C65	AP42	8c carmine	.40	.20
		Pair	.80	.20
		Joint line pair	3.75	.35
a.		Tagged, Jan. 14, 1965	.35	.20
		Pair	.70	.20
		Joint line pair	1.50	.30

MONTGOMERY BLAIR ISSUE

Montgomery Blair — AP43

Designed by Robert J. Jones

Montgomery Blair (1813-83), Postmaster General (1861-64), who called the 1st Intl. Postal Conf., Paris, 1863, forerunner of the UPU.

GIORI PRESS PRINTING
Plates of 200 subjects in four panes of 50 each.

1963, May 3	Unwmk.	Perf. 11		
C66	AP43	15c dull red, dark brown & blue	.60	.55
		P# block of 4	2.75	—

Bald Eagle — AP44

Designed by V. S. McCloskey, Jr.

Issued primarily for use on domestic post cards.

ROTARY PRESS PRINTING
E.E. Plates of 400 subjects in four panes of 100 each.

1963, July 12	Unwmk.	Perf. 11x10½	
C67 AP44 6c red		.20	.20
P# block of 4		1.80	—
a. Tagged, Feb. 15, 1967		4.00	3.00
P# block of 4		55.00	—

AMELIA EARHART ISSUE

Amelia Earhart and Lockheed
Electra — AP45

Designed by Robert J. Jones.

Amelia Earhart (1898-1937), 1st woman to fly across the Atlantic.

GIORI PRESS PRINTING
Plates of 200 subjects in four panes of 50 each.

1963, July 24	Unwmk.	Perf. 11	
C68 AP45 8c carmine & maroon		.20	.20
P# block of 4		1.00	

ROBERT H. GODDARD ISSUE

Robert H. Goddard, Atlas Rocket and Launching Tower, Cape Kennedy — AP46

Designed by Robert J. Jones.

Dr. Robert H. Goddard (1882-1945), physicist and pioneer rocket researcher.

GIORI PRESS PRINTING
Plates of 200 subjects in four panes of 50 each.

1964, Oct. 5	Tagged	Perf. 11	
C69 AP46 8c blue, red & bister		.40	.20
P# block of 4		1.75	—
Margin block of 4, Mr. Zip and "Use Zip Code"		1.65	

Luminescence
Air Post stamps issued after mid-1964 are tagged.

ALASKA PURCHASE ISSUE

Tlingit Totem, Southern
Alaska — AP47

Designed by Willard R. Cox.

Centenary of the Alaska Purchase. The totem pole shown is in the Alaska State Museum, Juneau.

GIORI PRESS PRINTING
Plates of 200 subjects in four panes of 50 each.

1967, Mar. 30	Unwmk.	Perf. 11	
C70 AP47 8c brown		.25	.20
P# block of 4		1.40	—
Margin block of 4, Mr. Zip and "Use Zip Code"		1.05	

"Columbia Jays" by
John James
Audubon — AP48

Fifty-Star
Runway — AP49

GIORI PRESS PRINTING
Designed by Robert J. Jones.
Plates of 200 subjects in four panes of 50 each.

1967, Apr. 26		Perf. 11	
C71 AP48 20c multicolored		.80	.20
P# block of 4		3.50	—
Margin block of 4, Mr. Zip and "Use Zip Code"		3.25	
a. Tagging omitted		10.00	

See note over No. 1241.

ROTARY PRESS PRINTING
Designed by Jaan Born.
E. E. Plates of 400 subjects in four panes of 100 each.

1968, Jan. 5	Unwmk.	Perf. 11x10½	
C72 AP49 10c carmine		.20	.20
P# block of 4		.90	—
Margin block of 4, "Use Zip Codes"		.85	—
b. Booklet pane of 8		2.00	.75
c. Booklet pane of 5 + label, Jan. 6		3.75	.75
d. Vert. pair, imperf. between (from bklt. pane)		8,000.	

Red is the normal color of the tagging. Copies of No. C72b exist that have a mixture of the two tagging compounds. No. C72d resulted from a paper foldover after perforating and before cutting into panes. Only one pair is known.

ROTARY PRESS COIL STAMP
Perf. 10 Vertically

C73 AP49 10c carmine	.30	.20
Pair	.65	.20
Joint line pair	1.70	.20
a. Imperf., pair	600.00	
Joint line pair	900.00	

$1 Air Lift
This stamp, listed as No. 1341, was issued Apr. 4, 1968, to pay for airlift of parcels to and from U.S. ports to servicemen overseas and in Alaska, Hawaii and Puerto Rico.

It was "also valid for paying regular rates for other types of mail," the Post Office Department announced to the public in a philatelic release dated Mar. 10, 1968. The stamp is inscribed "U.S. Postage" and is untagged.

On Apr. 26, 1969, the P.O.D. stated in its Postal Manual (for postal employees) that this stamp "may be used toward paying the postage or fees for special services on *airmail* articles." On Jan. 1, 1970, the Department told postal employees through its Postal Bulletin that this $1 stamp "can only be used to pay the airlift fee or toward payment of postage or fees on *airmail* articles."

Some collectors prefer to consider No. 1341 an air-mail stamp.

50th ANNIVERSARY OF AIR MAIL ISSUE

Curtiss
Jenny — AP50

Designed by Hordur Karlsson.

50th anniv. of regularly scheduled air mail service.

LITHOGRAPHED, ENGRAVED (GIORI)
Plates of 200 subjects in four panes of 50 each.

1968, May 15		Perf. 11	
C74 AP50 10c blue, black & red		.25	.20
P# block of 4		2.00	—
Margin block of 4, Mr. Zip and "Use Zip Code"		1.05	—
a. Red (tail stripe) omitted			
b. Tagging omitted		7.50	

"USA" and
Jet — AP51

Designed by John Larrecq.

LITHOGRAPHED, ENGRAVED (GIORI)
Plates of 200 subjects in four panes of 50 each.

1968, Nov. 22		Perf. 11	
C75 AP51 20c red, blue & black		.35	.20
P# block of 4		1.75	—
Margin block of 4, Mr. Zip and "Use Zip Code"		1.50	—
a. Tagging omitted		7.50	

MOON LANDING ISSUE

First Man
on the
Moon
AP52

Designed by Paul Calle.

Man's first landing on the moon July 20, 1969, by U.S. astronauts Neil A. Armstrong and Col. Edwin E. Aldrin, Jr., with Lieut. Col. Michael Collins piloting Apollo 11.

LITHOGRAPHED, ENGRAVED (GIORI)
Plates of 128 subjects in four panes of 32 each.

1969, Sept. 9		Perf. 11	
C76 AP52 10c yellow, black, lt. blue, ultra., rose red & carmine		.25	.20
P# block of 4		1.10	—
Margin block of 4, Mr. Zip and "Use Zip Code"		1.05	—
a. Rose red (litho.) omitted		500.00	—

On No. C76a, the lithographed rose red is missing from the entire vignette-the dots on top of the yellow areas as well as the flag shoulder patch.

Silhouette of Delta
Wing Plane — AP53

Silhouette of Jet
Airliner — AP54

Winged Airmail
Envelope — AP55

Statue of
Liberty — AP56

Designed by George Vander Sluis (9c, 11c), Nelson Gruppo (13c) and Robert J. Jones (17c).

ROTARY PRESS PRINTING
E. E. Plates of 400 subjects in four panes of 100 each.

1971-73   *Perf. 10½x11*
C77 AP53 9c **red,** *May 15, 1971*   .20   .20
    P# block of 4   .90   —
    Margin block of 4, "Use Zip Codes" .85   —
No. C77 issued primarily for use on domestic post cards.

Perf. 11x10½
C78 AP54 11c **carmine,** *May 7, 1971*   .20   .20
    P# block of 4   .90   —
    Margin block of 4, "Use Zip
      Codes"   .85   —
    Pair with full vert. gutter btwn.   —
  a. Booklet pane of 4 + 2 labels   1.25   .75
  b. Untagged (Bureau precanceled)   .30
  c. Tagging omitted (not Bureau precanceled) 6.00
C79 AP55 13c **carmine,** *Nov. 16, 1973*   .25   .20
    P# block of 4   1.10   —
    Margin block of 4, "Use Zip
      Codes"   1.05   —
  a. Booklet pane of 5 + label, *Dec. 27, 1973* 1.50 .75
  b. Untagged (Bureau precanceled)   .30
  c. Green instead of red tagging (single from
    booklet pane)   —
No. C78b Bureau precanceled "WASHINGTON D.C." (or "DC"), No. C79b "WASHINGTON DC" only; both for use of Congressmen, but available to any permit holder.
Red is the normal color of the tagging. Copies also exist that have a mixture of the two tagging compounds.

GIORI PRESS PRINTING
Panes of 200 subjects in four panes of 50 each.
Perf. 11
C80 AP56 17c **bluish black, red, & dark green,**
    July 13, 1971   .35   .20
    P# block of 4   1.60   —
    Margin block of 4, Mr. Zip and
      "Use Zip Code"   1.50   —
  a. Tagging omitted   10.00

"USA" & Jet Type of 1968
LITHOGRAPHED, ENGRAVED (GIORI)
Plates of 200 subjects in four panes of 50 each.
Perf. 11
C81 AP51 21c **red, blue & black,** *May 21, 1971*   .40   .20
    P# block of 4   2.00   —
    Margin block of 4, Mr. Zip and
      "Use Zip Code"   1.75   —
  a. Tagging omitted   7.50

COIL STAMPS
ROTARY PRESS PRINTING
1971-73   *Perf. 10 Vertically*
C82 AP54 11c **carmine,** *May 7, 1971*   .25   .20
    Pair   .50   .20
    Joint line pair   .80   .35
  a. Imperf., pair   300.00
    Joint line pair   450.00
C83 AP55 13c **carmine,** *Dec. 27, 1973*   .30   ·.20
    Pair   .60   .25
    Joint line pair   1.10   —
  a. Imperf., pair   75.00
    Joint line pair   150.00

NATIONAL PARKS CENTENNIAL ISSUE
City of Refuge, Hawaii

Kii Statue and Temple — AP57

Designed by Paul Rabut.

Centenary of national parks. This 11c honors the City of Refuge National Historical Park, established in 1961 at Honaunau, island of Hawaii.

LITHOGRAPHED, ENGRAVED (GIORI)
Plates of 200 subjects in four panes of 50 each.
1972, May 3   *Perf. 11*
C84 AP57 11c **orange & multicolored**   .20   .20
    P# block of 4   .90   —
    Margin block of 4, Mr. Zip and
      "Use Zip Code"   .85   —
  a. Blue & green (litho.) omitted   900.00

OLYMPIC GAMES ISSUE

Skiing and Olympic Rings — AP58

Designed by Lance Wyman.

11th Winter Olympic Games, Sapporo, Japan, Feb. 3-13, and 20th Summer Olympic Games, Munich, Germany, Aug. 26-Sept. 11.

PHOTOGRAVURE (Andreotti)
Plates of 200 subjects in four panes of 50 each.
1972, Aug. 17   *Perf. 11x10½*
C85 AP58 11c **black, blue, red, emerald & yel-
    low**   .20   .20
    P# block of 10, 5 P#   2.50   —
    Margin block of 4, "Use Zip Code"   .85   —

ELECTRONICS PROGRESS ISSUE

De Forest Audions — AP59

Designed by Walter and Naiad Einsel.

LITHOGRAPHED, ENGRAVED (GIORI)
Plates of 200 subjects in four panes of 50 each.
1973, July 10   *Perf. 11*
C86 AP59 11c **vermilion, lilac, pale lilac, ol-
    ive, brown, deep carmine &
    black**   .20   .20
    P# block of 4   .95   —
    Margin block of 4, Mr. Zip and
      "Use Zip Code"   .90   —
  a. Vermilion & olive (litho.) omitted 1,400.
  b. Tagging omitted   20.00
  c. Olive omitted   —

Statue of Liberty — AP60

Mt. Rushmore National Memorial — AP61

Designed by Robert (Gene) Shehorn.

GIORI PRESS PRINTING
Panes of 200 subjects in four panes of 50 each.
1974   *Perf. 11*
C87 AP60 18c **carmine, black & ultramarine,**
    Jan. 11   .35   .25
    P# block of 4, 2#   1.50   —
    Margin block of 4, Mr. Zip and
      "Use Zip Code"   1.45   —
  a. Tagging omitted   15.00
C88 AP61 26c **ultramarine, black & carmine,**
    Jan. 2   .50   .20
    P# block of 4   2.25   —
    Margin block of 4, Mr. Zip and
      "Use Zip Code"   2.10   —
    Pair with full vert. gutter btwn.   —
  a. Tagging omitted   10.00   —
  b. Green instead of red tagging   —

Plane and Globes — AP62

Plane, Globes and Flags — AP63

Designed by David G. Foote.

GIORI PRESS PRINTING
Panes of 200 subjects in four panes of 50 each.
1976, Jan. 2   *Perf. 11*
C89 AP62 25c **red, blue & black**   .50   .20
    P# block of 4   2.25   —
    Margin block of 4, Mr. Zip and
      "Use Zip Code"   2.10   —
C90 AP63 31c **red, blue & black**   .60   .20
    P# block of 4   2.75   —
    Margin block of 4, Mr. Zip and
      "Use Zip Code"   2.50   —
  a. Tagging omitted   10.00

WRIGHT BROTHERS ISSUE

Orville and Wilbur Wright, and Flyer A — AP64

Wright Brothers, Flyer A and Shed — AP65

Designed by Ken Dallison.

75th anniv. of 1st powered flight, Kill Devil Hill, NC, Dec. 17, 1903.

LITHOGRAPHED, ENGRAVED (GIORI)
Plates of 400 subjects in four panes of 100 each.
1978, Sept. 23   *Perf. 11*
C91 AP64 31c **ultramarine & multicolored**   .65   .30
C92 AP65 31c **ultramarine & multicolored**   .65   .30
  a. Vert. pair, #C91-C92   1.30   1.10
    P# block of 4   3.00   —
    Margin block of 4, "Use Correct
      Zip Code"   2.75   —
  b. As "a," ultra. & black (engr.) omitted 800.00
  c. As "a," black (engr.) omitted   —
  d. As "a," black, yellow, magenta, blue &
    brown (litho.) omitted   2,250.

OCTAVE CHANUTE ISSUE

Chanute and Biplane Hang-glider AP66

Biplane Hang-glider and Chanute AP67

Designed by Ken Dallison.

Octave Chanute (1832-1910), civil engineer and aviation pioneer.

LITHOGRAPHED, ENGRAVED (GIORI)
Plates of 400 subjects in four panes of 100 each.
1979, Mar. 29   Tagged   *Perf. 11*
C93 AP66 21c **blue & multicolored**   .70   .30
C94 AP67 21c **blue & multicolored**   .70   .30
  a. Vert. pair, #C93-C94   1.40   1.10
    P# block of 4   3.25   —
    Margin block of 4, Mr. Zip   2.85   —
  b. As "a," ultra & black (engr.) omitted 4,500.

WILEY POST ISSUE

Wiley Post and
"Winnie
Mae" — AP68

NR-105-W, Post
in Pressurized
Suit,
Portrait — AP69

Designed by Ken Dallison.

Wiley Post (1899-1935), first man to fly around the world alone and high-altitude flying pioneer.

LITHOGRAPHED, ENGRAVED (GIORI)
Plates of 400 subjects in four panes of 100 each.

1979, Nov. 20	Tagged	Perf. 11	
C95 AP68 25c blue & multicolored		1.10	.35
C96 AP69 25c blue & multicolored		1.10	.35
a.	Vert. pair, #C95-C96	2.25	1.25
	P# block of 4	8.00	—
	Margin block of 4, Mr. Zip	4.60	—

OLYMPIC GAMES ISSUE

High
Jump — AP70

Designed by Robert M. Cunningham.

22nd Olympic Games, Moscow, July 19-Aug. 3, 1980.

PHOTOGRAVURE
Plates of 200 subjects in four panes of 50 each.

1979, Nov. 1	Tagged	Perf. 11	
C97 AP70 31c multicolored		.70	.30
	P# block of 12, 6#	9.50	—
	Zip block of 4	3.00	—

PHILIP MAZZEI (1730-1816)

Italian-born Political
Writer — AP71

Designed by Sante Graziani.

PHOTOGRAVURE
Plates of 200 subjects in four panes of 50 each.

1980, Oct. 13	Tagged	Perf. 11	
C98 AP71 40c multicolored		.80	.20
	P# block of 12, 6#	10.00	—
	Zip block of 4	3.50	—
b.	Imperf., pair	3,250.	
d.	Tagging omitted	10.00	

1982	Tagged	Perf. 10½x11¼	
C98A AP71 40c multicolored		6.50	1.50
	P# block of 12, 6#	110.00	—
c.	Horiz. pair, imperf. vert.		

BLANCHE STUART SCOTT (1886-1970)

First Woman
Pilot — AP72

Designed by Paul Calle.

PHOTOGRAVURE
Plates of 200 subjects in four panes of 50.

1980, Dec. 30	Tagged	Perf. 11	
C99 AP72 28c multicolored		.60	.20
	P# block of 12, 6#	8.50	—
	Zip block of 4	2.50	—
a.	Imperf., pair		—

GLENN CURTISS (1878-1930)

Aviation Pioneer
and Aircraft
Designer — AP73

Designed by Ken Dallison.

PHOTOGRAVURE
Plates of 200 subjects in four panes of 50.

1980, Dec. 30	Tagged	Perf. 11	
C100 AP73 35c multicolored		.65	.20
	P# block of 12, 6#	9.00	—
	Zip block of 4	2.75	—

SUMMER OLYMPICS 1984

Women's
Gymnastics
AP74

Hurdles
AP75

Women's
Basketball — AP76

Soccer — AP77

Shot Put — AP78

Men's Gymnastics
AP79

Women's
Swimming — AP80

Weight
Lifting — AP81

Women's
Fencing — AP82

Cycling — AP83

Women's
Volleyball — AP84

Pole
Vaulting — AP85

Designed by Robert Peak.

23rd Olympic Games, Los Angeles, July 28-Aug. 12, 1984.

PHOTOGRAVURE
Plates of 200 subjects in four panes of 50.

1983, June 17	Tagged	Perf. 11	
C101 AP74 28c multicolored		1.00	.30
C102 AP75 28c multicolored		1.00	.30
C103 AP76 28c multicolored		1.00	.30
C104 AP77 28c multicolored		1.00	.30
a.	Block of 4, #C101-C104	4.50	2.00
	P# block of 4, 4#	6.25	—
	Zip block of 4	4.50	—
b.	As "a," imperf. vert.	—	

1983, Apr. 8	Tagged	Perf. 11.2 Bullseye	
C105 AP78 40c multicolored		.90	.40
a.	Perf. 11 line	1.00	.45
C106 AP79 40c multicolored		.90	.40
a.	Perf. 11 line	1.00	.45
C107 AP80 40c multicolored		.90	.40
a.	Perf. 11 line	1.00	.45
C108 AP81 40c multicolored		.90	.40
a.	Perf. 11 line	1.00	.45
b.	Block of 4, #C105-C108	4.25	2.50
	P# block of 4, 4#	5.00	—
	Zip block of 4	4.50	—
c.	Block of 4, #C105a-C108a	5.00	—
	P# block of 4, 4#	7.50	—
d.	Block of 4, imperf.	1,250.	

1983, Nov. 4	Tagged	Perf. 11	
C109 AP82 35c multicolored		.90	.50
C110 AP83 35c multicolored		.90	.50
C111 AP84 35c multicolored		.90	.50
C112 AP85 35c multicolored		.90	.50
a.	Block of 4, #C109-C112	4.00	3.00
	P# block of 4, 4#	7.00	—
	Zip block of 4	4.25	—

AVIATION PIONEERS

Alfred V. Verville
(1890-1970),
Inventor, Verville-
Sperry R-3 Army
Racer — AP86

Lawrence Sperry (1892-1931), Aircraft Designer, and Father Elmer (1860-1930), Designer and Pilot, 1st Seaplane — AP87

Designed by Ken Dallison (No. C113) and Howard Koslow (No. C114)

PHOTOGRAVURE

Plates of 200 in four panes of 50
(2 panes each, No. C113 and No. C114)
Plates of 200 in four panes of 50 (No. C114)

1985, Feb. 13		Tagged		Perf. 11	
C113 AP86 33c **multicolored**				.65	.20
	P# block of 4, 5#, UL, LR			3.25	—
	Zip block of 4			2.90	—
a.	Imperf., pair			850.00	
C114 AP87 39c **multicolored**				.80	.25
	P# block of 4, 5#, UR, LL			3.75	—
	P# block of 4, 4#			3.75	—
	Zip block of 4			3.50	—
a.	Imperf., pair			1,400.	

Philatelic Foundation certificates issued prior to August 1994 for No. C114 with magenta missing have been rescinded. At this time no true magenta missing copies are known.

TRANSPACIFIC AIRMAIL
50th Anniversary

Martin M-130 China Clipper — AP88

Designed by Chuck Hodgson.

PHOTOGRAVURE

Plates of 200 in four panes of 50

1985, Feb. 15		Tagged		Perf. 11	
C115 AP88 44c **multicolored**				.85	.25
	P# block of 4, 5#			4.00	—
	Zip block of 4			3.50	—
a.	Imperf., pair			900.00	

FR. JUNIPERO SERRA (1713-1784)
California Missionary

Outline Map of Southern California, Portrait, San Gabriel Mission — AP89

Designed by Richard Schlecht from a Spanish stamp.

PHOTOGRAVURE

Plates of 200 in four panes of 50

1985, Aug. 22		Tagged		Perf. 11	
C116 AP89 44c **multicolored**				1.00	.30
	P# block of 4			8.50	—
	Zip block of 4			4.25	—
a.	Imperf., pair			1,500.	

SETTLING OF NEW SWEDEN, 350th ANNIV.

Settler, Two Indians, Map of New Sweden, Swedish Ships "Kalmar Nyckel" and "Fogel Grip" — AP90

Designed by Goran Osterland based on an 18th century illustration from a Swedish book about the Colonies.

LITHOGRAPHED AND ENGRAVED

Plates of 200 in four panes of 50

1988, Mar. 29		Tagged		Perf. 11	
C117 AP90 44c **multicolored**				1.00	.25
	P# block of 4, 5#			7.00	—
	Zip block of 4			5.00	—

See Sweden No. 1672 and Finland No. 768.

SAMUEL P. LANGLEY (1834-1906)

Langley and Unmanned Aerodrome No. 5 — AP91

Designed by Ken Dallison.

LITHOGRAPHED AND ENGRAVED

Plates of 200 in four panes of 50

1988, May 14		Tagged		Perf. 11	
C118 AP91 45c **multicolored**, large block tagging				.90	.20
	P# block of 4, 7#			4.25	—
	Zip block of 4			4.00	—
a.	Overall tagging			3.00	.50
	P# block of 4, 7#			30.00	—
	Zip block of 4			14.00	—

IGOR SIKORSKY (1889-1972)

Sikorsky and 1939 VS300 Helicopter — AP92

Designed by Ren Wicks.

PHOTOGRAVURE AND ENGRAVED

Plates of 200 in four panes of 50

1988, June 23		Tagged		Perf. 11	
C119 AP92 36c **multicolored**				.70	.20
	P# block of 4, 6#			3.25	—
	Zip block of 4			3.10	—

Beware of copies with traces of red offered as "red omitted" varieties.

FRENCH REVOLUTION BICENTENNIAL

Liberty, Equality and Fraternity AP93

Designed by Richard Sheaff.

LITHOGRAPHED AND ENGRAVED

Plates of 120 in four panes of 30.

1989, July 14		Tagged		Perf. 11½x11	
C120 AP93 45c **multicolored**				.95	.20
	P# block of 4, 4#			4.75	—
	Zip block of 4			4.00	—

See France Nos. 2143-2145a.

PRE-COLUMBIAN AMERICA ISSUE

Southeast Carved Figure, 700-1430 A.D. — AP94

Designed by Lon Busch.
Printed by American Bank Note Co.

PHOTOGRAVURE

Plates of 200 in four panes of 50

1989, Oct. 12				Perf. 11	
C121 AP94 45c **multicolored**				.90	.20
	P# block of 4, 4#			5.25	—
	Zip block of 4			3.75	—

20th UPU CONGRESS
Futuristic Mail Delivery

Spacecraft — AP95

Air-suspended Hover Car — AP96

Moon Rover — AP97

Space Shuttle — AP98

Designed by Ken Hodges.

LITHOGRAPHED & ENGRAVED

Plates of 160 in four panes of 40.

1989, Nov. 27		Tagged		Perf. 11	
C122 AP95 45c **multicolored**				1.00	.40
C123 AP96 45c **multicolored**				1.00	.40
C124 AP97 45c **multicolored**				1.00	.40
C125 AP98 45c **multicolored**				1.00	.40
a.	Block of 4, #C122-C125			4.25	3.00
	P# block of 4, 5#			5.50	—
	Zip block of 4			4.50	—
b.	As "a," light blue (engr.) omitted			900.00	

Souvenir Sheet
LITHOGRAPHED & ENGRAVED

1989, Nov. 24		Tagged		Imperf.	
C126	Sheet of 4			4.75	3.75
a.	AP95 45c multicolored			1.00	.50
b.	AP96 45c multicolored			1.00	.50
c.	AP97 45c multicolored			1.00	.50
d.	AP98 45c multicolored			1.00	.50

PRE-COLUMBIAN AMERICA ISSUE

Tropical Coast — AP99

Designed by Mark Hess.
Printed by the American Bank Note Company.

PHOTOGRAVURE

Plates of 200 in four panes of 50
(3 panes of #2512, 1 pane of #C127)

1990, Oct. 12		Tagged		Perf. 11	
C127 AP99 45c **multicolored**				.90	.20
	P# block of 4, 4#, UL only			6.25	—
	Zip block of 4			3.75	—

HARRIET QUIMBY, 1ST AMERICAN WOMAN PILOT

Quimby (1884-1912), Bleriot Airplane — AP100

Designed by Howard Koslow. Printed by Stamp Venturers.

PHOTOGRAVURE

Panes of 200 in four panes of 50

1991, Apr. 27		Tagged		Perf. 11	
C128 AP100 50c **multicolored**				1.00	.25
	P# block of 4, 4#+S			5.50	—
	Zip block of 4			4.25	—
a.	Vert. pair, imperf. horiz.			2,000.	
b.	Perf. 11.2			1.10	.25
	P# block of 4, 4#+S			6.00	—
	Zip block of 6			4.50	—

WILLIAM T. PIPER, AIRCRAFT MANUFACTURER

Piper and Piper
Cub — AP101

Designed by Ren Wicks.
Printed by J. W. Fergusson and Sons for American Bank
Note Co.

PHOTOGRAVURE
Panes of 200 in four panes of 50

1991, May 17		**Tagged**	**Perf. 11**	
C129 AP101 40c	**multicolored**		.80	.20
	P# block of 4, 4#+A		4.00	
	Zip block of 4		3.60	—

Blue sky is plainly visible all the way across stamp above
Piper's head.
Inscriptions read "William T. Piper / 1881-1970 / Aviation
pioneer." "Maker of the / famous Piper Cub / light airplane."
"Widely known as / the 'Henry Ford of aviation.'" in the margins
of the sheet.
See No. C132.

ANTARCTIC TREATY, 30TH ANNIVERSARY

AP102

Designed by Howard Koslow. Printed by Stamp Venturers.

PHOTOGRAVURE
Panes of 50

1991, June 21		**Tagged**	**Perf. 11**	
C130 AP102 50c	**multicolored**		1.00	.25
	P# block of 4, 4#+S		5.00	—
	Zip block of 4		4.25	—

Margin inscriptions read "1991 marks the 30th / anniversary
of the / ratification of the / Antarctic Treaty." "The pact dedicated
/ Antarctica for / peaceful purposes / rather than military." "The
Treaty has fostered / peaceful cooperation / and scientific
research / by thirty-nine countries."

PRE-COLUMBIAN AMERICA ISSUE

Bering Land
Bridge — AP103

Designed by Richard Schlect.

PHOTOGRAVURE
Plates of 200 in 4 panes of 50

1991, Oct. 12		**Tagged**	**Perf. 11**	
C131 AP103 50c	**multicolored**		1.00	.25
	P# block of 4, 6#		5.25	—
	Zip block of 4		4.75	—

Piper Type of 1991
Printed by Stamp Venturers.

PHOTOGRAVURE
Panes of 200 in four panes of 50

1993		**Tagged**	**Perf. 11.2**	
C132 AP101 40c	**multicolored**		1.20	.20
	P# block of 4, 4#+S		10.00	—
	Zip block of 4		4.50	—

Piper's hair touches top edge of design. No inscriptions.
Bullseye perf.

"All LC (Letters and Cards) mail receives First-Class
Mail service in the United States, is dispatched by the
fastest transportation available, and travels by airmail
or priority service in the destination country. All LC
mail should be marked 'AIRMAIL' or 'PAR AVION.'"
(U.S. Postal Service, Pub. 51).
No. C133 listed below was issued to meet the LC
rate to Canada and Mexico and is inscribed with the
silhouette of a jet plane next to the denomination indicating the need for airmail use. This is unlike No.
2998, which met the LC rate to other countries, but
contained no indication that it was intended for that
use.
Future issues that meet a specific international airmail rate and contain the airplane silhouette will be
treated by Scott as Air Post stamps. Stamps similar to
No. 2998 will be listed in the Postage section.

NIAGARA FALLS

AP104

Designed by Ethel Kessler. Printed by Avery Dennison.

PHOTOGRAVURE
Sheets of 200 in ten panes of 20

1999, May 12		**Tagged**	**Perf. 11**	
		Self-Adhesive		
C133 AP104 48c	**multicolored**		.95	
	P# block of 4, 5#+V		4.00	
	Pane of 20		20.00	

RIO GRANDE

AP105

Designed by Ethel Kessler. Printed by Avery Dennison.

PHOTOGRAVURE
Sheets of 200 in ten panes of 20

1999, July 30	**Tagged**	**Serpentine Die Cut 11**		
		Self-Adhesive		
C134 AP105 40c	**multicolored**		.80	.60
	P# block of 4, 5#+V		3.20	
	Pane of 20		16.00	

GRAND CANYON

AP106

Designed by Ethel Kessler.
Printed by Banknote Corp. of America.

LITHOGRAPHED
Sheets of 180 in nine panes of 20
Serpentine Die Cut 11¼x11½

2000, Jan. 20			**Tagged**	
		Self-Adhesive		
C135 AP106 60c	**multicolored**		1.25	.25
	P# block of 4, 4#+B		5.00	
	Pane of 20		25.00	

R.F. OVERPRINTS
(Nos. CM1-CM10, UCM1-UCM5)
can be found on page 232.

AIR POST SPECIAL DELIVERY STAMPS

Great Seal of
United
States — APSD1

No. CE1 was issued for the prepayment of the air postage
and the special delivery fee in one stamp. First day sale was at
the American Air Mail Society Convention.

FLAT PLATE PRINTING
Plates of 200 subjects in four panes of 50 each.

1934, Aug. 30		**Unwmk.**	**Perf. 11**	
CE1 APSD1 16c	**dark blue**		.60	.65
	blue		.60	.65
	Never hinged		.80	
	First day cover, Chicago			
	(40,171)		25.00	
	First day cover, Washington,			
	D.C., *Aug. 31*		15.00	
	P# block of 6		17.50	

For imperforate variety see No. 771.

Type of 1934

Frame plates of 100 subjects in two panes of 50 each separated by a 1½ inch wide vertical gutter with central guide line,
and vignette plates of 50 subjects.
The "seal" design for No. CE2 was from a new engraving,
slightly smaller than that used for No. CE1.
Top plate number blocks of No. CE2 are found both with and
without top arrow.
Issued in panes of 50 each.

1936, Feb. 10				
CE2 APSD1 16c	**red & blue**		.40	.25
	Never hinged		.50	
	First day cover Washington,			
	D.C. *(72,981)*		17.50	

Margin block of 4, bottom or side arrow	2.00	1.50
Center line block	2.50	2.25
P# block of 4, 2#	6.50	—
P# block of 4, 2#, blue dotted registration marker	65.00	
Same, arrow, thick red registration marker	50.00	

P# block of 10, 2#, two "TOP" and two registration markers	15.00	6.00
a. Horiz. pair, imperf. vert.	4,000.	

P# block of 6, 2#, two "TOP" and registration markers *40,000.*

The No. CE2a plate block is unique. Value represents sale in 1997.

Quantities issued: #CE1, 9,215,750; #CE2, 72,517,850.

AIR POST SEMI-OFFICIAL STAMPS

Buffalo Balloon

This stamp was privately issued by John F. B. Lillard, a Nashville reporter. It was used on covers carried on a balloon ascension of June 18, 1877, which began at Nashville and landed at Gallatin, Tenn., and possibly on other flights. The balloon was owned and piloted by Samuel Archer King. The stamp was reported to have been engraved by (Mrs.?) J. H. Snively and printed in tete beche pairs from a single die. Lillard wrote that 300 were printed and 23 used.

Buffalo Balloon — CS1

1877, June 18   **Typo.**   *Imperf.*

CL1 CS1 5c	**deep blue**	7,000.	
	Never hinged	9,250.	
	On cover with 3c #158		—
	On cover with 1c #156 & 2c #178		—
a.	Tête bêche pair, vertical	20,000.	
	Never hinged	—	

A black proof exists of No. CL1, value $7,500.

Rodgers Aerial Post

This stamp was privately issued by Calbraith Perry Rodgers' wife who acted as unofficial postmaster during her husband's cross-country airplane flight in 1911. Rodgers was competing for the $50,000 prize offered by William Randolph Hearst to whomever completed the trip within a 30-day period. Rodgers' flight was sponsored by the Armour meat-packing company, makers of the soft drink, Vin Fiz.

The stamp probably was first available in Texas about October 19. Recorded dated examples exist from Oct. 19 to Nov. 8.

Each of the eleven known copies is trimmed close to the design on one or more sides.

CS2

1911, Oct.   *Imperf.*

CL2 CS2 25c	**black**	35,000.	
	Tied on postcard with 1c #374		50,000.

SPECIAL DELIVERY STAMPS

Special Delivery service was instituted by the Act of Congress of March 3, 1885, and put into operation on October 1, 1885. The Act limited the service to free delivery offices and such others as served places with a population of 4,000 or more, and its privileges where thus operative in but 555 post offices. The Act of August 4, 1886, made the stamps and service available at all post offices and upon any article of mailable matter. To consume the supply of stamps of the first issue, Scott No. E2 was withheld until September 6, 1888.

A Special Delivery stamp, when affixed to any stamped letter or article of mailable matter, secures later delivery during daytime and evening at most post offices, so that the item will not have to wait until the next day for delivery.

Messenger Running — SD1

ENGRAVED
Printed by the American Bank Note Co.
Plates of 100 subjects in two panes of 50 each

1885, Oct. 1   **Unwmk.**   *Perf. 12*

E1 SD1 10c	**blue**	325.00	45.00
	deep blue	325.00	45.00
	Never hinged	575.00	
	On cover		65.00
	First day cover		8,500.
	P# block of 8, Impt. 495 or 496	14,000.	
	Margin strip of 4, same	2,750.	
	Double transfer at top	450.00	65.00

Messenger Running — SD2

1888, Sept. 6

E2 SD2 10c	**blue**	300.00	17.50
	deep blue	300.00	17.50
	Never hinged	550.00	
	On cover		35.00
	P# block of 8, Impt. 73 or 552	11,500.	
	Never hinged	14,750.	
	Margin strip of 4, same	2,100.	

Earliest known use: Dec. 18, 1888.

See note above No. E3.

COLUMBIAN EXPOSITION ISSUE

Though not issued expressly for the Exposition, No. E3 is considered to be part of that issue. It was released in orange because No. E2 was easily confused with the 1c Columbian, No. 230.

From Jan. 24, 1893, until Jan. 1, 1894, the special delivery stamp was printed in orange; the issue in that color continued until May 19, 1894, when the stock on hand was exhausted. The stamp in blue was not issued from Jan. 24, 1893 to May 19, 1894. However, on Jan. 5, 1894, printing of the stamp in blue was resumed. Presumably it was reissued from May 19, 1894 until the appearance of No. E4 on Oct. 10, 1894. The emissions of the blue stamp of this design before Jan. 24, 1893 and after Jan. 5, 1894 are indistinguishable.

1893, Jan. 24

E3 SD2 10c	**orange**	200.00	22.50
	deep orange	200.00	22.50
	Never hinged	350.00	
	On cover		55.00
	On cover, Columbian Expo. station machine canc.		300.00
	On cover, Columbian Expo. station duplex handstamp cancel		575.00
	P# block of 8, Impt. 73 or 552	7,250.	
	Never hinged	9,750.	
	Margin strip of 4, same	1,350.	

Earliest known use: Feb. 11, 1893.

Messenger Running — SD3

Type III   Type VI   Type VII
Printed by the Bureau of Engraving and Printing.

1894, Oct. 10
Line under "TEN CENTS"

E4	SD3	10c	**blue**	700.00 30.00
			dark blue	700.00 30.00
			bright blue	700.00 30.00
			Never hinged	1,250.
			On cover	150.00
			Block of four	2,900.
			Margin block of 4, arrow	3,000.
			P#77 block of 6, T III Impt.	14,000.
			Never hinged	17,500.
			Margin strip of 3, same	3,500. —
			Double transfer	—

Earliest known use: Oct. 25, 1894.

Imperfs of No. E4 on stamp paper, previously listed as No. E4Pa, almost certainly are not proofs, and it is unlikely that they were regularly issued. They most likely are from printer's waste.

1895, Aug. 16   **Wmk. 191**

E5	SD3	10c	**blue**	160.00 3.50
			dark blue	160.00 3.50
			deep blue	160.00 3.50
			Never hinged	275.00
			On cover	15.00
			Margin block of 4, arrow	700.00
			P# block of 6, T III, VI or VII Impt.	4,000.
			Never hinged	5,500.
			Margin strip of 3, same	750.00
			Never hinged	1,050.
			Double transfer	— 16.00
			Line of color through "POSTAL DELIVERY," from bottom row of Plates 1257-1260	210.00 12.50
			Dots in curved frame above messenger (Pl. 882)	200.00 9.00
b.			Printed on both sides	

Earliest known use: Oct. 3, 1895.

See Die and Plate Proofs for imperf. on stamp paper.

Messenger on
Bicycle — SD4

1902, Dec. 9

E6	SD4	10c	**ultramarine**	110.00 3.25
			dark ultramarine	110.00 3.25
			pale ultramarine	110.00 3.25
			Never hinged	190.00
a.			**10c blue**	110.00 3.25
			Never hinged	190.00
			On cover	10.00
			Margin block of 4, arrow	475.00
			P# block of 6, T VII Impt.	2,400.
			Never hinged	3,300.
			Margin strip of 3, same	425.00
			P# block of 6, "09"	2,100.
			Margin strip of 3, same	625.00

Double transfer	—	
Damaged transfer under "N" of "CENTS"	140.00	3.75

Earliest known use: Jan. 22, 1903.

No. E6 was re-issued in 1909 from new plates 5240, 5243-5245. After a few months use the Bureau added "09" to these plate numbers. The stamp can be identified only by plate number.

Helmet of Mercury — SD5

Designed by Whitney Warren.

Plates of 280 subjects in four panes of 70 each

1908, Dec. 12

E7	SD5	10c	**green**	60.00 40.00
			dark green	60.00 40.00
			yellowish green	60.00 40.00
			Never hinged	105.00
			On cover	85.00
			P# block of 6, T V Impt.	925.00
			Never hinged	1,250.
			Margin strip of 3, same	300.00
			Double transfer	140.00 75.00

Earliest known use: Dec. 14, 1908.

Plates of 200 subjects in four panes of 50 each

1911, Jan.   **Wmk. 190**   **Perf. 12**

E8	SD4	10c	**ultramarine**	100.00 5.25
			pale ultramarine	100.00 5.25
			dark ultramarine	100.00 5.25
			Never hinged	175.00
b.			**10c violet blue**	100.00 5.25
			Never hinged	175.00
			On cover	15.00
			P# block of 6, T VII Impt.	2,000.
			Never hinged	2,600.
			P# block of 6	1,800.
			Top frame line missing (Pl. 5514)	140.00 12.50

Earliest known use: Jan. 14, 1911.

1914, Sept.   **Perf. 10**

E9	SD4	10c	**ultramarine**	180.00 6.50
			pale ultramarine	180.00 6.50
			Never hinged	325.00
			On cover	32.50
			P# block of 6, T VII Impt.	4,000.
			P# block of 6	3,250.
			Never hinged	4,250.
			Margin block of 8, T VII Impt. & P# (side)	—
a.			**10c blue**	210.00 6.50
			Never hinged	375.00
			On cover	37.50
			P# block of 6, T VII Impt.	4,250.
			P# block of 6	3,750.
			Never hinged	5,100.
			Margin block of 8, T VII Impt. & P# (side)	—

Earliest known use: Oct. 26, 1914.

1916, Oct. 19   **Unwmk.**   **Perf. 10**

E10	SD4	10c	**pale ultramarine**	275.00 27.50
			ultramarine	275.00 27.50
			Never hinged	475.00
			On cover	67.50
			P# block of 6, T VII Impt. 5520	5,500.
			P# block of 6	5,000.
			Never hinged	6,250.
a.			**10c blue**	310.00 27.50
			Never hinged	525.00
			On cover	75.00
			P# block of 6, T VII Impt. 5520	5,500.
			P# block of 6	5,000.

Earliest known use: Nov. 4, 1916.

1917, May 2   **Unwmk.**   **Perf. 11**

E11	SD4	10c	**ultramarine**	20.00 .50
			pale ultramarine	20.00 .50
			dark ultramarine	20.00 .50
			Never hinged	35.00
			On cover	3.25
			P# block of 6, T VII Impt.	725.00
			P# block of 6	225.00
			Never hinged	310.00
			Margin block of 8, T VII Impt. & P# (side)	—
b.			**10c gray violet**	20.00 .50
			Never hinged	35.00
c.			**10c blue**	50.00 2.50
			Never hinged	90.00
			On cover	15.00
			P# block of 6, T VII Impt.	1,900.
			P# block of 6	550.00
			Margin block of 8, T VII Impt. & P# (side)	—
d.			Perf. 10 at left	—

Earliest known use: June 12, 1917.

The aniline ink used on some printings of No. E11 permeated the paper causing a pink tinge to appear on the back. Such stamps are called "pink backs." They are extremely scarce.

Motorcycle
Delivery — SD6

Post Office
Truck — SD7

1922, July 12   **Unwmk.**   **Perf. 11**

E12	SD6	10c	**gray violet**	35.00 .50
			Never hinged	60.00
			On cover	1.75
			First day cover	425.00
			P# block of 6	400.00
			Never hinged	550.00
			Double transfer	—
a.			**10c deep ultramarine**	40.00 .60
			Never hinged	70.00
			On cover	2.00
			P# block of 6	425.00
			Never hinged	575.00
			Double transfer	—

FLAT PLATE PRINTING

1925   **Unwmk.**   **Perf. 11**

Issued to facilitate special delivery service for parcel post.

E13	SD6	15c	**deep orange,** *Apr. 11, 1925*	25.00 1.00
			Never hinged	42.50
			On cover	12.50
			First day cover	240.00
			P# block of 6	300.00
			Never hinged	425.00
			Double transfer	32.50 1.50
E14	SD7	20c	**black,** *Apr. 25, 1925*	2.00 1.00
			Never hinged	3.00
			On cover	1.50
			First day cover	95.00
			P# block of 6	32.50
			Never hinged	42.50

Motorcycle Type of 1922
ROTARY PRESS PRINTING

1927-31   **Unwmk.**   **Perf. 11x10½**

E15	SD6	10c	**gray violet,** *Nov. 29, 1927*	.60 .20
			violet	.60 .20
			Never hinged	.90
a.			**10c red lilac**	.60 .20
			Never hinged	.90
b.			**10c gray lilac**	.60 .20
			Never hinged	.90
			On cover	.25
			First day cover	110.00
			First day cover, electric eye plate, *Sept. 8, 1941*	30.00
			P# block of 4	4.00
			Never hinged	5.75
			Gouged plate	
			Cracked plate 19280 LR	35.00
c.			Horizontal pair, imperf. between	300.00
E16	SD6	15c	**orange,** *Aug. 6, 1931*	.70 .20
			Never hinged	1.05
			On cover	.25
			First day cover, Easton, Pa.	2,100.
			First day cover, Washington, D.C., *Aug. 13, 1931*	125.00
			P# block of 4	3.75
			Never hinged	5.00

The Washington, D.C. Aug. 13, 1931 first day cover reflects the first day of sale at the philatelic agency.

> Catalogue values for unused stamps in this section, from this point to the end, are for Never Hinged items.

Motorcycle Type of 1922
ROTARY PRESS PRINTING
E. E. Plates of 200 subjects in four panes of 50 each

1944-51   **Unwmk.**   **Perf. 11x10½**

E17	SD6	13c	**blue,** *Oct. 30, 1944*	.60 .20
			First day cover	12.00
			P# block of 4	3.00
E18	SD6	17c	**orange yellow,** *Oct. 30, 1944*	2.75 1.75
			First day cover	12.00
			First day cover, Nos. E17 & E18	30.00
			P# block of 4	20.00
E19	SD7	20c	**black,** *Nov. 30, 1951*	1.25 .20
			First day cover	5.00
			P# block of 4	5.50

Special Delivery
Letter, Hand to
Hand — SD8

ROTARY PRESS PRINTING
E.E. Plates of 200 subjects in four panes of 50 each

1954, Oct. 13	Unwmk.	Perf. 11x10½
E20 SD8 20c **deep blue**		.40 .20
light blue		
First day cover, Boston (194,043)		3.00
P# block of 4	2.00	—

1957, Sept. 3
E21 SD8 30c **lake** .... .50 .20
    First day cover, Indianapolis, Ind.
      (111,451) 2.25
    P# block of 4 .... 2.40 —

Arrows — SD9

Designed by Norman Ives.

GIORI PRESS PRINTING
Plates of 200 subjects in four panes of 50 each

1969, Nov. 21   **Unwmk.**   **Perf. 11**
E22 SD9 45c **carmine & violet blue** .... 1.25 .25
    First day cover, New York, N.Y. 3.50
    P# block of 4 .... 5.50
    Margin block of 4, Mr. Zip and
      "Use Zip Code" 5.10

1971, May 10   **Perf. 11**
E23 SD9 60c **violet blue & carmine** .... 1.25 .20
    First day cover, Phoenix, Ariz.
      (129,562) 3.50
    P# block of 4 .... 5.50
    Margin block of 4, Mr. Zip and "Use
      Zip Code" .... 5.25 —

REGISTRATION STAMP

The Registry System for U.S. mail went into effect July 1, 1855, the fee being 5 cents. On June 30, 1863, the fee was increased to 20 cents. On January 1, 1869, the fee was reduced to 15 cents and on January 1, 1874, to 8 cents. On July 1, 1875, the fee was increased to 10 cents. On January 1, 1893 the fee was again reduced to 8 cents and again it was increased to 10 cents on November 1, 1909.

Early registered covers with various stamps, rates and postal markings are of particular interest to collectors.

Registry stamps (10c ultramarine) were issued on December 1, 1911, to prepay registry fees (not postage), but ordinary stamps were valid for registry fees then as now. These special stamps were abolished May 28, 1913, by order of the Postmaster General, who permitted their use until supplies on hand were exhausted.

Eagle — RS1

ENGRAVED
1911, Dec. 1   **Wmk. 190**   **Perf. 12**
F1 RS1 10c **ultramarine** 75.00 7.50
    pale ultramarine 75.00 7.50
    Never hinged 125.00
    On cover 40.00

First day cover .... 8,000.
Block of 4 .... 325.00 75.00
P# block of 6, Impt. & "A" ... 1,600. —
    Never hinged .... 2,500.

CERTIFIED MAIL STAMP

Certified Mail service was started on June 6, 1955, for use on first class mail for which no indemnity value is claimed, but for which proof of mailing and proof of delivery are available at less cost than registered mail. The mailer receives one receipt and the addressee signs another when the postman delivers the letter. The second receipt is kept on file at the post office for six months. The Certified Mail charge, originally 15 cents, is in addition to regular postage, whether surface mail, air mail, or special delivery.

Catalogue value for the unused stamp in this section is for a Never Hinged item.

Letter Carrier — CM1

United States certified mail stamps can be mounted in the Scott National and Minuteman albums.

ROTARY PRESS PRINTING
E. E. Plates of 200 subjects in four panes of 50

1955, June 6   **Unwmk.**   **Perf. 10½x11**
FA1 CM1 15c **red** .... .45 .30
    First day cover 3.25
    P# block of 4 .... 4.00 —

POSTAGE DUE STAMPS

For affixing, by a postal clerk, to any piece of mailable matter, to denote the amount to be collected from the addressee because of insufficient prepayment of postage.

Prior to July 1879, whenever a letter was unpaid, or insufficiently prepaid, the amount of postage due was written by hand or handstamped on the envelope, and the deficiency collected by the carrier. No vouchers were given for money thus collected.

Postage Due Stamps were authorized by the Act of Congress, approved March 3, 1879, effective July 1, 1879.

Printed by the American Bank Note Co.
Plates of 200 subjects in two panes of 100 each.

D1   D2

1879		Unwmk.	Engr.	Perf. 12	
J1	D1	1c **brown**		57.50	8.50
		pale brown		57.50	8.50
		deep brown		57.50	8.50
		Block of 4		250.00	40.00
		P# block of 10, Impt.		1,100.	
J2	D1	2c **brown**		375.00	7.50
		pale brown		375.00	7.50
		Block of 4		1,550.	
J3	D1	3c **brown**		52.50	4.50
		pale brown		52.50	4.50
		deep brown		52.50	4.50
		yellowish brown		55.00	5.50
		Block of 4		225.00	19.00
		P# block of 10, Impt.		1,050.	
J4	D1	5c **brown**		575.00	45.00
		pale brown		575.00	45.00
		deep brown		575.00	45.00
		Block of 4		2,500.	
J5	D1	10c **brown,** Sept. 19		625.00	25.00
		pale brown		625.00	25.00
		deep brown		625.00	25.00
		Block of 4		2,700.	
a.		Imperf., pair		2,000.	
J6	D1	30c **brown,** Sept. 19		325.00	50.00
		pale brown		325.00	50.00
		Block of 4		1,400.	
		P# block of 10, Impt.		4,250.	
J7	D1	50c **brown,** Sept. 19		475.00	60.00
		pale brown		475.00	60.00
		Block of 4		2,100.	
		P# block of 10, Impt.		11,000.	

SPECIAL PRINTING

1879		Unwmk.		Perf. 12

Soft porous paper
Printed by the American Bank Note Co.

J8	D1	1c deep brown (9,420)	12,500.
J9	D1	2c deep brown (1,361)	7,500.
J10	D1	3c deep brown (436)	12,500.
J11	D1	5c deep brown (249)	7,500.
J12	D1	10c deep brown (174)	3,750.
J13	D1	30c deep brown (179)	3,750.
J14	D1	50c deep brown (179)	3,750.

Identifying characteristics for the final 8,920 copies of No. J8 delivered to the Post Office are unknown, and it is likely that these were regular issue stamps (No. J1) that were then sold as special printings.

1884		Unwmk.		Perf. 12	
J15	D1	1c **red brown**		55.00	4.50
		pale red brown		55.00	4.50
		deep red brown		55.00	4.50
		Block of 4		250.00	20.00
		P# block of 10, Impt.		1,250.	
J16	D1	2c **red brown**		67.50	4.50
		pale red brown		67.50	4.50
		deep red brown		67.50	4.50
		Block of 4		300.00	20.00
		P# block of 10, Impt.		1,400.	
J17	D1	3c **red brown**		1,000.	175.00
		deep red brown		1,000.	175.00
		Block of 4		4,250.	
J18	D1	5c **red brown**		500.00	25.00
		pale red brown		500.00	25.00
		deep red brown		500.00	25.00
		Block of 4		2,250.	
J19	D1	10c **red brown**		475.00	17.50
		deep red brown		475.00	17.50
		Block of 4		2,150.	
		P# block of 10, Impt.		12,500.	
J20	D1	30c **red brown**		165.00	50.00
		deep red brown		165.00	50.00
		Block of 4		750.00	250.00
		P# block of 10, Impt.		3,000.	
J21	D1	50c **red brown**		1,650.	175.00
		Block of 4		7,500.	

1891		Unwmk.		Perf. 12	
J22	D1	1c **bright claret**		26.00	1.00
		light claret		26.00	1.00
		dark claret		26.00	1.00
		Block of 4		120.00	4.50

		P# block of 10, Impt.	550.00	
J23	D1	2c **bright claret**	32.50	1.00
		light claret	32.50	1.00
		dark claret	32.50	1.00
		Block of 4	150.00	4.50
		P# block of 10, Impt.	675.00	
J24	D1	3c **bright claret**	62.50	8.00
		dark claret	62.50	8.00
		Block of 4	290.00	35.00
		P# block of 10, Impt.	950.00	
J25	D1	5c **bright claret**	77.50	8.00
		light claret	77.50	8.00
		dark claret	77.50	8.00
		Block of 4	350.00	35.00
		P# block of 10, Impt.	1,150.	
J26	D1	10c **bright claret**	125.00	17.50
		light claret	125.00	17.50
		Block of 4	575.00	80.00
		P# block of 10, Impt.	2,000.	
J27	D1	30c **bright claret**	500.00	150.00
		Block of 4	2,250.	—
		P# block of 10, Impt.	7,500.	
J28	D1	50c **bright claret**	525.00	150.00
		dark claret	525.00	150.00
		Block of 4	2,400.	—
		P# block of 10, Impt.	9,000.	
		Nos. J22-J28 (7)	1,348.	335.50

See Die and Plate Proofs for imperfs. on stamp paper.

Printed by the Bureau of Engraving and Printing.

1894		Unwmk.		Perf. 12	
J29	D2	1c **vermilion**		1,750.	400.
		pale vermilion		1,750.	400.
		Never hinged		3,000.	
		Block of 4		7,500.	1,400.
		P# block of 6, Impt.			
J30	D2	2c **vermilion**		700.	125.
		deep vermilion		700.	125.
		Never hinged		1,200.	
		Block of 4		3,000.	
		P# block of 6, Impt.		6,000.	

1894-95					
J31	D2	1c **deep claret,** Aug. 14, 1894		47.50	6.00
		claret		47.50	6.00
		lake		47.50	6.00
		Never hinged		82.50	
		Block of 4		210.00	25.00
		P# block of 6, Impt.		450.00	
		Never hinged		600.00	
b.		Vertical pair, imperf. horiz.		—	

See Die and Plate Proofs for imperf. on stamp paper.

J32	D2	2c **deep claret,** July 20, 1894	40.00	4.00
		claret	40.00	4.00
		lake	40.00	4.00
		Never hinged	70.00	
		Block of 4	170.00	17.50
		P# block of 6, Impt.	400.00	
		Never hinged	600.00	
J33	D2	3c **deep claret,** Apr. 27, 1895	160.00	30.00
		lake	160.00	30.00
		Never hinged	280.00	
		Block of 4	675.00	
		P# block of 6, Impt.	1,700.	
		Never hinged	2,500.	
J34	D2	5c **deep claret,** Apr. 27, 1895	240.00	35.00
		claret	240.00	35.00
		Never hinged	425.00	
		Block of 4	1,050.	—
		P# block of 6, Impt.	2,000.	
		Never hinged	3,000.	
J35	D2	10c **deep claret,** Sept. 24, 1894	240.00	25.00
		Never hinged	425.00	
		Block of 4	1,050.	—
		P# block of 6, Impt.	2,000.	
J36	D2	30c **deep claret,** Apr. 27, 1895	400.00	90.00
		claret	400.00	90.00
a.		30c **carmine**	400.00	100.00
		Never hinged	700.00	
		Block of 4	1,750.	
		P# block of 6, Impt.	3,250.	
		Never hinged	4,850.	
b.		30c **pale rose**	325.00	85.00
		Never hinged	575.00	
		Block of 4	1,400.	
		P# block of 6, Impt.	2,850.	
		Never hinged	4,250.	
J37	D2	50c **deep claret,** Apr. 27, 1895	1,250.	250.00
		Never hinged	2,200.	
		Block of 4	5,500.	—
a.		50c **pale rose**	1,200.	250.00
		Never hinged	2,100.	
		Block of 4	5,250.	—
		P# block of 6, Impt.	—	

Shades are numerous in the 1894 and later issues.

Wmk. 191 Horizontally or Vertically

1895-97				Perf. 12	
J38	D2	1c **deep claret,** Aug. 29, 1895		8.50	.75
		claret		8.50	.75
		carmine		8.50	.75
		lake		8.50	.75
		Never hinged		15.00	
		Block of 4		40.00	3.25
		P# block of 6, Impt.		225.00	
J39	D2	2c **deep claret,** Sept. 14, 1895		8.50	.70
		claret		8.50	.70
		carmine		8.50	.70
		lake		8.50	.70
		Never hinged		15.00	
		Block of 4		40.00	3.25
		P# block of 6, Impt.		225.00	
		Double transfer		—	

In October, 1895, the Postmaster at Jefferson, Iowa, surcharged a few 2 cent stamps with the words "Due 1 cent" in black on each side, subsequently dividing the stamps vertically and using each half as a 1 cent stamp. Twenty of these were used.

J40	D2	3c **deep claret,** Oct. 30, 1895		57.50	1.75
		claret		57.50	1.75
		rose red		57.50	1.75
		carmine		57.50	1.75
		Never hinged		100.00	
		Block of 4		250.00	7.50
		P# block of 6, Impt.		575.00	
		Never hinged		850.00	
J41	D2	5c **deep claret,** Oct. 15, 1895		65.00	1.75
		claret		65.00	1.75
		carmine rose		65.00	1.75
		Never hinged		115.00	
		Block of 4		280.00	7.50
		P# block of 6, Impt.		650.00	
		Never hinged		950.00	
J42	D2	10c **deep claret,** Sept. 14, 1895		67.50	3.50
		claret		67.50	3.50
		carmine		67.50	3.50
		lake		67.50	3.50
		Never hinged		120.00	
		Block of 4		300.00	15.00
		P# block of 6, Impt.		675.00	
		Never hinged		1,000.	
J43	D2	30c **deep claret,** Aug. 21, 1897		550.00	50.00
		claret		550.00	50.00
		Never hinged		950.00	
		Block of 4		2,300.	
		P# block of 6, Impt.		5,500.	
J44	D2	50c **deep claret,** Mar. 17, 1896		350.00	37.50
		claret		350.00	37.50
		Never hinged		600.00	
		Block of 4		1,550.	175.00
		P# block of 6, Impt.		3,750.	
		Nos. J38-J44 (7)		1,107.	95.95

1910-12		**Wmk. 190**		Perf. 12	
J45	D2	1c **deep claret,** Aug. 30, 1910		32.50	3.00
		Never hinged		55.00	
a.		1c **rose carmine**		30.00	3.00
		Never hinged		52.50	
		Block of 4 (2 or 3mm spacing)		140.00	13.00
		P# block of 6, Impt. & star		475.00	
J46	D2	2c **deep claret,** Nov. 25, 1910		32.50	1.00
		lake		32.50	1.00
		Never hinged		55.00	
a.		2c **rose carmine**		30.00	1.00
		Never hinged		52.50	
		Block of 4 (2 or 3mm spacing)		140.00	5.00
		P# block of 6, Impt. & star		425.00	
		P# block of 6		450.00	
		Double transfer		—	
J47	D2	3c **deep claret,** Aug. 31, 1910		600.00	30.00
		lake		600.00	30.00
		Never hinged		1,050.	
		Block of 4 (2 or 3mm spacing)		2,600.	130.00
		P# block of 6, Impt. & star		5,500.	
		Never hinged		8,000.	
J48	D2	5c **deep claret,** Aug. 31, 1910		95.00	6.50
		Never hinged		165.00	
a.		5c **rose carmine**		90.00	6.50
		Never hinged		160.00	
		Block of 4 (2 or 3mm spacing)		425.00	27.50
		P# block of 6, Impt. & star		950.00	
		Never hinged		1,400.	
J49	D2	10c **deep claret,** Aug. 31, 1910		115.00	12.50
		Never hinged		200.00	
		Block of 4 (2 or 3mm spacing)		500.00	55.00
		P# block of 6, Impt. & star		1,400.	
a.		10c **rose carmine**		110.00	12.50
		Never hinged		190.00	
J50	D2	50c **deep claret,** Sept. 23, 1912		950.00	120.00
		Never hinged		1,650.	
		Block of 4 (2 or 3mm spacing)		4,000.	
		P# block of 6, Impt. & star		9,000.	

1914				Perf. 10	
J52	D2	1c **carmine lake**		60.00	11.00
		deep carmine lake		60.00	11.00
		Never hinged		105.00	
		Block of 4 (2 or 3mm spacing)		250.00	50.00

			575.00	—
	P# block of 6, Impt. & star		575.00	—
	Never hinged		850.00	
a.	1c **dull rose**		70.00	11.00
	Never hinged		125.00	
	Block of 4 (2 or 3mm spacing)		300.00	50.00
	P# block of 6, Impt. & star		675.00	—
J53	D2	2c **carmine lake**	47.50	.40
	Never hinged		82.50	
	Block of 4		200.00	2.00
	P# block of 6		450.00	—
a.	2c **dull rose**		52.50	.40
	Never hinged		90.00	
b.	2c **vermilion**		52.50	.40
	Never hinged		90.00	
	Block of 4		225.00	2.00
	P# block of 6		500.00	—
	Never hinged		750.00	
J54	D2	3c **carmine lake**	875.00	37.50
	Never hinged		1,500.	
a.	3c **dull rose**		875.00	37.50
	Never hinged		1,500.	
	Block of 4 (2 or 3mm spacing)		3,800.	—
	P# block of 6, Impt. & star		7,500.	—
J55	D2	5c **carmine lake**	37.50	2.50
	Never hinged		65.00	
a.	5c **dull rose**		37.50	2.50
	carmine rose		37.50	2.50
	Never hinged		65.00	
	deep claret			
	Block of 4 (2 or 3mm spacing)		160.00	11.00
	P# block of 6, Impt. & star		350.00	—
	Never hinged		500.00	
J56	D2	10c **carmine lake**	57.50	2.00
	Never hinged		100.00	
	Block of 4 (2 or 3mm spacing)		240.00	10.00
	P# block of 6, Impt. & star		675.00	—
a.	10c **dull rose**		70.00	2.00
	carmine rose		70.00	2.00
	Never hinged		125.00	
	Block of 4 (2 or 3mm spacing)		300.00	10.00
	P# block of 6, Impt. & star		800.00	—
	Never hinged		1,200.	
J57	D2	30c **carmine lake**	240.00	17.50
	Never hinged		425.00	
	Block of 4 (2 or 3mm spacing)		1,050.	80.00
	P# block of 6, Impt. & star		2,750.	—
J58	D2	50c **carmine lake**	10,000.	800.00
	Never hinged		17,500.	
	Precanceled			575.00
	Block of 4 (2 or 3mm spacing)		43,500.	3,750.
	P# block of 6, Impt. & star		70,000.	

No. J58, precanceled, was used at Buffalo (normal, inverted) and Chicago (normal, inverted, double, double inverted).

1916		**Unwmk.**	**Perf. 10**	
J59	D2	1c **rose**	2,500.	325.00
	Never hinged		4,400.	
	Block of 4 (2 or 3mm spacing)		10,500.	1,500.
	P# block of 6, Impt. & star		17,500.	
	Experimental bureau precancel, New Orleans			210.00
J60	D2	2c **rose**	160.00	20.00
	Never hinged		280.00	
	Block of 4		700.00	—
	P# block of 6		1,450.	
	Experimental bureau precancel, New Orleans			17.50

1917		**Unwmk.**	**Perf. 11**	
J61	D2	1c **carmine rose**	2.75	.25
	dull rose		2.75	.25
	Never hinged		4.75	
a.	1c **rose red**		2.75	.25
	Never hinged		4.75	
b.	1c **deep claret**		2.75	.25
	claret brown		2.75	.25
	Never hinged		4.75	
	Block of 4 (2 or 3mm spacing)		12.00	1.25
	P# block of 6, Impt. & star		120.00	—
	P# block of 6		45.00	
J62	D2	2c **carmine rose**	2.50	.25
	Never hinged		4.40	
a.	2c **rose red**		2.50	.25
	Never hinged		4.40	
b.	2c **deep claret**		2.50	.25
	claret brown		2.50	1.10
	Never hinged		4.40	
	Block of 4		11.00	.20
	P# block of 6		40.00	
	Double transfer			
J63	D2	3c **carmine rose**	11.00	.25
	Never hinged		19.00	
a.	3c **rose red**		11.00	.25
	Never hinged		19.00	
b.	3c **deep claret**		11.00	.35
	claret brown		11.00	.35
	Never hinged		19.00	
	Block of 4 (2 or 3mm spacing)		47.50	1.10
	P# block of 6, Impt. & star		120.00	—
	P# block of 6		100.00	
J64	D2	5c **carmine**	11.00	.25
	carmine rose		11.00	.25
	Never hinged		19.00	
a.	5c **rose red**		11.00	.25
	Never hinged		19.00	
b.	5c **deep claret**		11.00	.25
	claret brown		11.00	.25
	Never hinged		19.00	
	Block of 4 (2 or 3mm spacing)		47.50	1.10
	P# block of 6, Impt. & star		120.00	—
	P# block of 6		100.00	
J65	D2	10c **carmine**	17.00	.30
	Never hinged		30.00	
a.	10c **rose red**		17.00	.25
	Never hinged		30.00	
b.	10c **deep claret**		17.00	.25

	claret brown		17.00	.25
	Never hinged		30.00	
	Block of 4 (2 or 3mm spacing)		72.50	1.30
	P# block of 6, Impt. & star		150.00	—
	P# block of 6		160.00	—
	Double transfer			
J66	D2	30c **carmine rose**	87.50	.75
	Never hinged		155.00	
a.	30c **deep claret**		87.50	.75
	claret brown		87.50	.75
	Never hinged		155.00	
	Block of 4 (2 or 3mm spacing)		375.00	3.25
	P# block of 6, Impt. & star		700.00	—
	P# block of 6		725.00	—
J67	D2	50c **carmine rose**	110.00	.30
	Never hinged		195.00	
a.	50c **rose red**		110.00	.30
	Never hinged		195.00	
b.	50c **deep claret**		110.00	.30
	claret brown		110.00	.30
	Never hinged		195.00	
	Block of 4 (2 or 3mm spacing)		475.00	1.30
	P# block of 6, Impt. & star		850.00	—
	Never hinged		1,250.	
	P# block of 6		900.00	—

1925, Apr. 13

J68	D2	½c **dull red**	1.00	.25
	Never hinged		1.60	
	Block of 4		4.00	1.10
	P# block of 6		12.50	—
	Never hinged		17.50	

D3   D4

1930		**Unwmk.**	**Perf. 11**	

Design measures 19x22mm

J69	D3	½c **carmine**	4.50	1.40
	Never hinged		7.25	
	P# block of 6		42.50	—
	Never hinged		60.00	
J70	D3	1c **carmine**	3.00	.25
	Never hinged		4.75	
	P# block of 6		30.00	—
	Never hinged		42.50	
J71	D3	2c **carmine**	4.00	.25
	Never hinged		6.50	
	P# block of 6		45.00	—
	Never hinged		62.50	
J72	D3	3c **carmine**	21.00	1.75
	Never hinged		35.00	
	P# block of 6		275.00	—
	Never hinged		375.00	
J73	D3	5c **carmine**	19.00	2.50
	Never hinged		30.00	
	P# block of 6		250.00	—
	Never hinged		350.00	
J74	D3	10c **carmine**	40.00	1.00
	Never hinged		65.00	
	P# block of 6		450.00	—
	Never hinged		650.00	
J75	D3	30c **carmine**	110.00	2.00
	Never hinged		175.00	
	P# block of 6		1,000.	—
	Never hinged		1,450.	
J76	D3	50c **carmine**	150.00	.75
	Never hinged		250.00	
	P# block of 6		1,400.	—
	Never hinged		2,000.	

Design measures 22x19mm

J77	D4	$1 **carmine**	30.00	.25
	Never hinged		47.50	
	P# block of 6		225.00	—
	Never hinged		310.00	
a.	$1 **scarlet**		25.00	.25
	Never hinged		40.00	
	P# block of 6		275.00	—
	Never hinged		375.00	
J78	D4	$5 **carmine**	37.50	.25
	Never hinged		60.00	
	P# block of 6		300.00	—
	Never hinged		425.00	
a.	$5 **scarlet**		32.50	.25
	Never hinged		52.50	
	P# block of 6		250.00	—
	Never hinged		350.00	
b.	As "a," wet printing		35.00	.25
	Never hinged		55.00	
	P# block of 6		275.00	—
	Never hinged		375.00	

See note on Wet and Dry Printings following No. 1029.

Type of 1930-31 Issue
Rotary Press Printing
Ordinary and Electric Eye Plates
Design measures 19x22 ½mm

1931		**Unwmk.**	**Perf. 11x10½**	
J79	D3	½c **dull carmine**	.90	.20
	Never hinged		1.30	
a.	½c **scarlet**		.90	.20

	Never hinged		1.30	
	P# block of 4		22.50	—
	Never hinged		30.00	
J80	D3	1c **dull carmine**	.20	.20
	Never hinged		.30	
a.	1c **scarlet**		.20	.20
	Never hinged		.30	
	P# block of 4 (#25635, 25636)		1.75	—
	Never hinged		2.50	
b.	As "a," wet printing		.20	.20
	Pair with full vertical gutter between			
J81	D3	2c **dull carmine**	.20	.20
	Never hinged		.30	
a.	2c **scarlet**		.20	.20
	Never hinged		.30	
	P# block of 4 (#25637, 25638)		1.75	—
	Never hinged		2.50	
b.	As "a," wet printing		.20	.20
J82	D3	3c **dull carmine**	.25	.20
	Never hinged		.40	
a.	3c **scarlet**		.25	.20
	Never hinged		.40	
	P# block of 4 (#25641, 25642)		2.50	—
	Never hinged		3.50	
b.	As "a," wet printing		.30	.20
J83	D3	5c **dull carmine**	.40	.20
	Never hinged		.60	
a.	5c **scarlet**		.40	.20
	Never hinged		.60	
	P# block of 4 (#25643, 25644)		3.25	—
	Never hinged		4.50	
b.	As "a," wet printing		.50	.20
J84	D3	10c **dull carmine**	1.10	.20
	Never hinged		1.60	
a.	10c **scarlet**		1.10	.20
	Never hinged		1.60	
	P# block of 4 (#25645, 25646)		6.75	—
	Never hinged		9.00	
b.	As "a," wet printing		1.25	.20
J85	D3	30c **dull carmine**	7.50	.25
	Never hinged		10.00	
a.	30c **scarlet**		7.50	.25
	Never hinged		10.00	
	P# block of 4		35.00	—
	Never hinged		47.50	
J86	D3	50c **dull carmine**	10.00	.25
	Never hinged		15.00	
a.	50c **scarlet**		10.00	.25
	Never hinged		15.00	
	P# block of 4		52.50	—
	Never hinged		70.00	

Design measures 22 ½x19mm

1956			**Perf. 10½x11**	
J87	D4	$1 **scarlet**	32.50	.25
	Never hinged		47.50	
	P# block of 4		200.00	—
	Never hinged		260.00	
	Nos. J79-J87 (9)		53.05	1.95

> **Catalogue values for unused stamps in this section, from this point to the end, are for Never Hinged items.**

D5

Rotary Press Printing

Denominations added in black by rubber plates in an operation similar to precanceling.

1959, June 19		**Unwmk.**	**Perf. 11x10½**	

Denomination in Black

J88	D5	½c **carmine rose**	1.50	1.10
	P# block of 4		180.00	—
J89	D5	1c **carmine rose**	.20	.20
	P# block of 4		.35	
	Dull finish gum		.20	
a.	Denomination omitted		300.00	
	P# block of 4			—
b.	Pair, one without "1 CENT"		600.00	
J90	D5	2c **carmine rose**	.20	.20
	P# block of 4		.45	
	Dull finish gum		.20	
J91	D5	3c **carmine rose**	.20	.20
	P# block of 4		.50	
	Dull finish gum		.20	
a.	Pair, one without "3 CENTS"		750.00	
J92	D5	4c **carmine rose**	.20	.20
	P# block of 4		.60	
J93	D5	5c **carmine rose**	.20	.20
	P# block of 4		.65	
	Dull finish gum		.25	
a.	Pair, one without "5 CENTS"		1,250.	
J94	D5	6c **carmine rose**	.20	.20
	P# block of 4		.70	
	Pair with full vertical gutter between			—
	Dull finish gum		175.00	
a.	Pair, one without "6 CENTS"		850.00	
J95	D5	7c **carmine rose**	.20	.20
	P# block of 4		.80	—
	Dull finish gum		425.00	

J96	D5	8c **carmine rose**	.20	.20
		P# block of 4	.90	
a.		Pair, one without "8 CENTS"	850.00	
J97	D5	10c **carmine rose**	.20	.20
		P# block of 4	1.00	
		Dull finish gum	.30	
J98	D5	30c **carmine rose**	.75	.20
		P# block of 4	2.75	
		Dull finish gum	.75	
J99	D5	50c **carmine rose**	1.10	.20
		P# block of 4	5.00	
		Dull finish gum	1.25	

Straight Numeral Outlined in Black

J100	D5	$1 **carmine rose**	2.00	.20
		P# block of 4	8.75	
		Dull finish gum	2.00	

J101	D5	$5 **carmine rose**	9.00	.20
		P# block of 4	45.00	
		Dull finish gum	10.00	
		Nos. J88-J101 (14)	16.15	3.70

The 2c, 4c, 6c, 7c and 8c exist in vertical pairs with numerals widely spaced. This spacing was intended to accommodate the gutter, but sometimes fell within the pane.
All single copies with denomination omitted are catalogued as No. J89a.

Rotary Press Printing

1978-85			**Perf. 11x10½**
		Denomination in Black	
J102	D5	11c **carmine rose**, *Jan. 2, 1978*	.25	.20
		P# block of 4	2.00	—
J103	D5	13c **carmine rose**, *Jan. 2, 1978*	.25	.20

		P# block of 4	2.00	—
J104	D5	17c **carmine rose**, *June 10, 1985*	.40	.35
		P# block of 4	25.00	—

OFFICES IN CHINA

Postage stamps of the 1917-19 U.S. series (then current) were issued to the U.S. Postal Agency, Shanghai, China, surcharged at double the original value of the stamps.

These stamps were intended for sale at Shanghai at their surcharged value in local currency, valid for prepayment on mail despatched from the U.S. Postal Agency at Shanghai to addresses in the U.S.

Stamps were first issued May 24, 1919, and were placed on sale at Shanghai on July 1, 1919. These stamps were not issued to postmasters in the U.S. The Shanghai post office, according to the U.S.P.O. Bulletin, was closed in December 1922. The stamps were on sale at the Philatelic Agency in Washington, D.C. for a short time after that.

The cancellations of the China office included "U.S. Postal Agency Shanghai China", "U.S. Pos. Service Shanghai China" duplexes, and the Shanghai parcel post roller cancel.

U. S. POSTAL AGENCY IN CHINA

SHANGHAI
2¢
CHINA

United States Stamps #498-499, 502-504, 506-510, 512, 514-518 Surcharged in Black or Red (Nos. K7, K16)

1919		**Unwmk.**		**Perf. 11**
K1	A140	2c on 1c **green**	25.00	27.50
		Never hinged	45.00	
		Block of 4	110.00	170.00
		P# block of 6	300.00	
		Never hinged	450.00	
K2	A140	4c on 2c **rose**, type I	25.00	27.50
		Never hinged	45.00	
		Block of 4	110.00	170.00
		P# block of 6	300.00	
		Never hinged	450.00	
K3	A140	6c on 3c **violet**, type II	50.00	65.00
		Never hinged	90.00	
		Block of 4	220.00	375.00
		P# block of 6	550.00	
		Never hinged	825.00	
K4	A140	8c on 4c **brown**	55.00	65.00
		Never hinged	100.00	
		Block of 4	240.00	375.00
		P# block of 6	650.00	
		Never hinged	975.00	
K5	A140	10c on 5c **blue**	60.00	65.00
		Never hinged	110.00	
		Block of 4	260.00	375.00
		P# block of 6	600.00	
		Never hinged	900.00	
K6	A140	12c on 6c **red orange**	77.50	95.00
		Never hinged	140.00	
		Block of 4	340.00	525.00
		P# block of 6	800.00	
		Never hinged	1,200.	
K7	A140	14c on 7c **black**	82.50	110.00
		Never hinged	150.00	
		Block of 4	360.00	625.00
		P# block of 6	925.00	
		Never hinged	1,400.	
K8	A148	16c on 8c **olive bister**	60.00	70.00
		Never hinged	110.00	
		Block of 4	260.00	450.00
		P# block of 6	600.00	
		Never hinged	900.00	
a.		16c on 8c **olive green**	55.00	60.00
		Never hinged	100.00	
		Block of 4	240.00	400.00
		P# block of 6	575.00	
		Never hinged	850.00	
K9	A148	18c on 9c **salmon red**	60.00	75.00
		Never hinged	110.00	
		Block of 4	260.00	450.00
		P# block of 6	700.00	
		Never hinged	1,050.	
K10	A148	20c on 10c **orange yellow**	55.00	60.00
		Never hinged	100.00	
		Block of 4	240.00	350.00
		P# block of 6	650.00	
		Never hinged	975.00	
K11	A148	24c on 12c **brown carmine**	65.00	70.00
		Never hinged	115.00	
		Block of 4	280.00	350.00
		P# block of 6	900.00	
a.		24c on 12c **claret brown**	87.50	110.00
		Never hinged	160.00	
		Block of 4	390.00	550.00
		P# block of 6	975.00	

		Never hinged	1,450.	
K12	A148	30c on 15c **gray**	82.50	125.00
		Never hinged	150.00	
		Block of 4	360.00	—
		P# block of 6	1,100.	
K13	A148	40c on 20c **deep ultramarine**	125.00	190.00
		Never hinged	225.00	
		Block of 4	550.00	900.00
		P# block of 6	1,400.	
		Never hinged	2,100.	
K14	A148	60c on 30c **orange red**	110.00	160.00
		Never hinged	200.00	
		Block of 4	475.00	875.00
		P# block of 6	1,050.	
		Never hinged	1,550.	
K15	A148	$1 on 50c **light violet**	525.00	600.00
		Never hinged	950.00	
		Block of 4	2,300.	4,000.
		P# block of 6	11,500.	
K16	A148	$2 on $1 **violet brown**	400.00	500.00
		Never hinged	725.00	
		Block of 4	1,750.	3,750.
		Margin block of 4, arrow, right or left	1,850.	
		P# block of 6	7,000.	
		Never hinged	10,500.	
a.		Double surcharge	5,000.	6,000.
		Never hinged	7,500.	
		Nos. K1-K16 (16)	1,857.	2,305.

A fake of No. K1 has recently been discovered. Other values may exist.

SHANGHAI
2 Cts.
CHINA

United States Stamps Nos. 498 and 528B Locally Surcharged

1922, July 3				
K17	A140	2c on 1c **green**	120.00	110.00
		Never hinged	210.00	
		Block of 4	510.00	550.00
		P# block of 6	850.00	
		Never hinged	1,275.	
K18	A140	4c on 2c **carmine**, type VII	105.00	95.00
		Never hinged	190.00	
		Block of 4	450.00	475.00
		P# block of 6	800.00	
		Never hinged	1,200.	
		"SHANGHAI" omitted	—	
		"CHINA" only	—	

OFFICIAL STAMPS

The original official stamps were authorized by Act of Congress, approved March 3, 1873, abolishing the franking privilege. Stamps for each government department were issued July 1, 1873. These stamps were supplanted on May 1, 1879, by penalty envelopes and on July 5, 1884, were declared obsolete.

DESIGNS. Stamps for departments other than the Post Office picture the same busts used in the regular postage issue: 1c Franklin, 2c Jackson, 3c Washington, 6c Lincoln, 7c Stanton, 10c Jefferson, 12c Clay, 15c Webster, 24c Scott, 30c Hamilton, and 90c Perry. William H. Seward appears on the $2, $5, $10 and $20.

Designs of the various denominations are not identical, but resemble those illustrated.

PLATES. Plates of 200 subjects in two panes of 100 were used for Post Office Department 1c, 3c, 6c; Treasury Department 1c, 2c, 3c, and War Department 2c, 3c. Plates of 10 subjects were used for State Department $2, $5, $10 and $20. Plates of 100 subjects were used for all other Official stamps up to No. O120.

CANCELLATIONS. Odd or Town cancellations on Departmental stamps are relatively much scarcer than those appearing on the general issues of the same period. Town cancellations, especially on the 1873 issue, are scarce. The "Kicking Mule" cancellation is found used on stamps of the War Department and has also been seen on some stamps of the other Departments. Black is usual.

Grade, condition and presence of original gum are very important in valuing Nos. O1–O120.

As is done elsewhere in this catalogue, all Officials are valued in the grade of very fine. If unused, they will have original gum. Unused examples without original gum are often encountered and sell for less.

Printed by the Continental Bank Note Co.
Thin Hard Paper

Franklin
O1   O2

AGRICULTURE

1873	Engr.	Unwmk.	Perf. 12	
O1	O1	1c **yellow**	160.00	150.00
		golden yellow	165.00	160.00
		olive yellow	170.00	165.00
		On cover		—
		Block of 4	675.00	
		Ribbed paper	170.00	150.00
		Cancellations		
		Magenta		+7.50
		Purple		+7.50
		Blue		+5.00
		Red		+50.00
		Town		+7.50
O2	O1	2c **yellow**	130.00	60.00
		golden yellow	135.00	62.50
		olive yellow	140.00	65.00
		On cover		1,750.
		Block of 4	550.00	
		Ribbed paper	140.00	75.00
		Cancellations		
		Blue		+3.00
		Red		+15.00
		Magenta		+5.00
		Town		+5.00
O3	O1	3c **yellow**	115.00	12.00
		golden yellow	120.00	13.00
		olive yellow	125.00	14.00
		On cover		800.00
		Block of 4	475.00	—
		P# block of 12, Impt.	1,800.	
		Never hinged	2,600.	
		Ribbed paper	125.00	12.00
		Double transfer	—	—
		Cancellations		
		Blue		+.50
		Purple		+1.00
		Magenta		+1.00
		Violet		+1.00
		Red		+12.00
		Green		+125.00
		Town		+4.00
		"Paid"		+27.50
		Numeral		+35.00
		Railroad		+75.00
O4	O1	6c **yellow**	125.00	50.00
		golden yellow	130.00	52.50
		olive yellow	135.00	55.00
		On cover		700.00
		Block of 4	525.00	
		Cancellations		
		Blue		+3.00
		Magenta		+4.00
		Violet		+4.00
		Town		+7.00
		Express Company		—
O5	O1	10c **yellow**	260.00	175.00
		golden yellow	275.00	180.00
		olive yellow	290.00	185.00
		On cover		—
		Block of 4	1,075.	
		Cancellations		
		Purple		+5.00

		Blue		+5.00
		Town		+15.00
O6	O1	12c **yellow**	350.00	225.00
		golden yellow	375.00	230.00
		olive yellow	400.00	235.00
		Block of 4	1,450.	
		Cancellations		
		Purple		+10.00
		Blue		+10.00
		Town		+20.00
O7	O1	15c **yellow**	290.00	200.00
		golden yellow	310.00	210.00
		olive yellow	325.00	220.00
		Block of 4	1,200.	—
		Cancellation		
		Purple		+10.00
O8	O1	24c **yellow**	290.00	180.00
		golden yellow	325.00	190.00
		On parcel label		—
		Block of 4	1,200.	
		Cancellation		
		Purple		+10.00
O9	O1	30c **yellow**	375.00	235.00
		golden yellow	400.00	230.00
		olive yellow	425.00	250.00
		Block of 4	1,550.	
		Cancellation		
		Red		+50.00

EXECUTIVE

1873				
O10	O2	1c **carmine**	650.00	400.00
		deep carmine	650.00	400.00
		On cover		2,000.
		Block of 6	5,750.	

The only known block is off-center and has original gum.

		Cancellations		
		Purple		+10.00
		Blue		+10.00
		Red		+50.00
		Town		+30.00
O11	O2	2c **carmine**	425.00	200.00
		deep carmine	425.00	200.00
		On cover		1,900.
		Block of 4	2,750.	—
		Foreign entry of 6c Agriculture		—
		Cancellations		
		Blue		+10.00
		Red		+50.00
O12	O2	3c **carmine**	450.00	160.00
a.		3c **violet rose**	450.00	160.00
		On cover		700.00
		On cover from Long Branch, N.J.		3,500.
		Block of 4	1,900.	—
		Cancellations		
		Blue		+10.00
		Purple		+10.00
		Town		+25.00
O13	O2	6c **carmine**	725.00	475.00
		pale carmine	725.00	475.00
		deep carmine	725.00	475.00
		On cover		3,500.
		Block of 4	4,400.	

The existence of the block of 4 of No. O13 has been questioned by specialists. The editors would like to see evidence of the current existence of this item.

		Cancellations		
		Purple		+15.00
		Town		+50.00
O14	O2	10c **carmine**	700.00	550.00
		pale carmine	700.00	550.00
		deep carmine	700.00	550.00
		On cover		3,900.
		Block of 4	3,900.	
		Cancellations		
		Blue		+15.00
		Purple		+15.00

O3   O4

INTERIOR

1873				
O15	O3	1c **vermilion**	35.00	8.00
		dull vermilion	35.00	8.00
		bright vermilion	35.00	8.00
		On cover		140.00
		Block of 4	150.00	—
		P# block of 10, Impt.	480.00	
		Never hinged	650.00	
		Ribbed paper	40.00	9.50
		Cancellations		
		Purple		+1.00
		Blue		+1.00
		Red		+12.50
		Ultramarine		+8.00
		Town		+3.00
O16	O3	2c **vermilion**	30.00	9.00
		dull vermilion	30.00	9.00
		bright vermilion	30.00	9.00
		On cover		60.00
		Block of 4	130.00	—
		P# block of 10, Impt.	450.00	
		P# block of 12, Impt.	500.00	
		Cancellations		
		Purple		+.75
		Blue		+.75
		Red		+6.00
		Town		+2.00
O17	O3	3c **vermilion**	47.50	5.00
		dull vermilion	47.50	5.00
		bright vermilion	47.50	5.00
		On cover		40.00
		First day cover, Nos. O17, O18, July 1, 1873		—
		Block of 4	200.00	—
		P# block of 10, Impt.	600.00	
		Ribbed paper	55.00	6.50

Cancellations				
	Purple			+1.00
	Blue			+1.00
	Red			+15.00
	Green			+65.00
	Town			+2.00
	Express Company			+75.00
	"Paid"			+20.00
	Fort			—
O18 O3	6c **vermilion**		35.00	5.00
	dull vermilion		35.00	5.00
	bright vermilion		35.00	5.00
	scarlet vermilion		35.00	6.00
	On cover			85.00
	Block of 4		150.00	—
	P# block of 10, Impt.		500.00	

Cancellations

Purple		+1.00
Blue		+1.00
Red		+15.00
Town		+2.00
Express Company		—
Railroad		—
Fort		—

See No. O17 first day cover listing.

O19 O3	10c **vermilion**		35.00	15.00
	dull vermilion		35.00	15.00
	bright vermilion		35.00	15.00
	On cover			225.00
	Block of 4		150.00	—

Cancellations

Purple	+1.00
Blue	+1.00
Town	+4.00
Fort	—

O20 O3	12c **vermilion**		50.00	7.75
	bright vermilion		50.00	7.75
	On cover			450.00
	Block of 4		210.00	—
	P# block of 10, Impt.		725.00	

Cancellations

Purple	+1.00
Magenta	+1.00
Blue	+1.00
Red	+15.00
Town	+4.00
Fort	—

O21 O3	15c **vermilion**		85.00	17.00
	bright vermilion		85.00	17.00
	On cover			450.00
	Block of 4		375.00	—
	Double transfer of left side		140.00	25.00

Cancellations

Blue	+1.50
Purple	+1.50
Town	+5.00

O22 O3	24c **vermilion**		62.50	14.00
	dull vermilion		62.50	14.00
	bright vermilion		62.50	14.00
	On cover			500.00
	Block of 4		250.00	—
a.	Double impression			—

Cancellations

Purple	+1.50
Blue	+1.50
Red	+15.00
Town	+5.00

O23 O3	30c **vermilion**		85.00	14.00
	bright vermilion		85.00	14.00
	On parcel label			—
	Block of 4		375.00	—

Cancellations

Purple	+2.00
Blue	+2.00
Red	+15.00
Town	+5.00

O24 O3	90c **vermilion**		190.00	37.50
	bright vermilion		190.00	37.50
	On cover			4,500.
	Block of 4		800.00	—
	Double transfer		250.00	
	Major double transfer (Pos. 17)		425.00	67.50
	Silk paper			—

Cancellations

Purple	+4.00
Blue	+4.00
Town	+7.50

JUSTICE

1873

O25 O4	1c **purple**		110.00	85.00
	dark purple		110.00	85.00
	On cover			1,100.
	Block of 4		475.00	—

Cancellations

Violet	+3.00
Blue	+3.00
Red	+20.00
Town	+7.50

O26 O4	2c **purple**		200.00	85.00
	light purple		200.00	85.00
	On cover			—
	Block of 4		875.00	—

Cancellations

Violet	+4.00
Blue	+4.00
Red	+20.00
Town	+10.00

O27 O4	3c **purple**		200.00	20.00
	dark purple		200.00	20.00
	bluish purple		200.00	20.00
	On cover			500.00
	Block of 4		900.00	—
	Double transfer			—

Cancellations

Purple	+2.00
Magenta	+2.00
Blue	+2.00
Red	+12.00
Green	+100.00
Town	+5.00

O28 O4	6c **purple**		175.00	30.00
	light purple		175.00	30.00
	bluish purple		175.00	30.00
	On cover			750.00
	Block of 4		750.00	—

Cancellations

Violet	+2.00
Purple	+2.00
Blue	+2.00
Red	+15.00
Town	+7.50

O29 O4	10c **purple**		200.00	70.00
	bluish purple		200.00	70.00
	On cover			2,000.
	Block of 4		900.00	—
	Double transfer			—

Cancellations

Violet	+4.00
Blue	+4.00
Town	+10.00

O30 O4	12c **purple**		150.00	45.00
	dark purple		150.00	45.00
	On cover			1,100.
	Block of 4		650.00	—

Cancellations

Purple	+2.00
Blue	+2.00
Town	+7.50

O31 O4	15c **purple**		300.00	150.00
	On cover			1,250.
	Block of 4			—
	Double transfer			—

Cancellations

Blue	+5.00
Purple	+5.00
Town	+10.00

O32 O4	24c **purple**		800.00	325.00
	On cover			2,750.
	Block of 4			—
	Short transfer (pos. 98)			—

The existence of the block of 4 of No. O32 has been questioned by specialists. The editors would like to see evidence of the current existence of this item.

Cancellations

Violet	+10.00
Purple	+10.00
Blue	+10.00
Red	+35.00
Town	+30.00

O33 O4	30c **purple**		675.00	250.00
	On cover			7,500.
	Block of 4			—
	Double transfer at top		700.00	175.00

Cancellations

Blue	+10.00
Purple	+10.00
Red	+35.00
Town	+30.00

O34 O4	90c **purple**		1,000.	500.00
	dark purple		1,000.	500.00
	On cover			16,500.
	Block of 4			—

Cancellations

Blue	+25.00
Violet	+25.00

No. O34 on cover is unique. The cover bears three No. O34 and four No. O33. Value represents auction sale price in 1998. The existence of the block of 4 of No. O34 has been questioned by specialists. The editors would like to see evidence of the current existence of this item.

O5   O6

NAVY

1873

O35 O5	1c **ultramarine**		75.00	37.50
	dark ultramarine		75.00	37.50
	On cover			350.00
	Block of 4		350.00	—
a.	1c **dull blue**		85.00	40.00

Cancellations

Violet	+2.00
Blue	+2.00
Red	+20.00
Town	+7.50
Steamship	+100.00

O36 O5	2c **ultramarine**		60.00	17.00
	dark ultramarine		60.00	17.00
	On cover			400.00
	Block of 4		300.00	—
	P# block of 12, Impt.		1,450.	

	Double transfer		—	—
a.	2c **dull blue**		70.00	15.00
	gray blue		65.00	15.00

The 2c deep green, both perforated and imperforate, is a trial color proof.

Cancellations

Purple	+1.50
Violet	+1.50
Blue	+1.50
Red	+15.00
Green	+75.00
Town	+10.00
Steamship	+85.00

O37 O5	3c **ultramarine**		60.00	8.00
	pale ultramarine		60.00	8.00
	dark ultramarine		60.00	8.00
	On cover			150.00
	Block of 4		300.00	—
	Double transfer			—
a.	3c **dull blue**		70.00	11.00

Cancellations

Violet	+1.50
Blue	+1.50
Red	+15.00
Town	+5.00
Blue town	+15.00
Steamship	+50.00

O38 O5	6c **ultramarine**		60.00	14.00
	bright ultramarine		60.00	14.00
	On cover			450.00
	Block of 4		300.00	—
	Vertical line through "N" of "Navy"		125.00	25.00
	Double transfer			—
a.	6c **dull blue**		70.00	14.50

Cancellations

Violet	+1.50
Purple	+1.50
Blue	+1.50
Red	+17.50
Green	+75.00
Town	+5.00
Steamship	+65.00

O39 O5	7c **ultramarine**		425.00	175.00
	dark ultramarine		425.00	175.00
	On cover			2,000.
	Block of 4		2,000.	
	Double transfer			—
a.	7c **dull blue**		450.00	175.00

Cancellations

Blue	+10.00
Violet	+10.00
Magenta	+10.00
Red	+40.00
Town	+15.00

O40 O5	10c **ultramarine**		80.00	30.00
	dark ultramarine		80.00	30.00
	On cover			2,750.
	Block of 4		375.00	—
	Plate scratch, pos. 3		170.00	—
	Ribbed paper		95.00	35.00
a.	10c **dull blue**		85.00	30.00

Cancellations

Violet	+2.00
Blue	+2.00
Brown	+20.00
Purple	+2.00
Red	+25.00
Town	+10.00
Steamship	+85.00

O41 O5	12c **ultramarine**		95.00	30.00
	pale ultramarine		95.00	30.00
	dark ultramarine		95.00	30.00
	On cover			3,000.
	Block of 4		450.00	
	Double transfer of left side, pos. 50		250.00	175.00

Cancellations

Purple	+2.50
Magenta	+2.50
Blue	+2.50
Red	+25.00
Town	+10.00
Supplementary Mail	+80.00
Steamship	+100.00

O42 O5	15c **ultramarine**		175.00	57.50
	dark ultramarine		175.00	57.50
	Block of 4		850.00	

Cancellations

Blue	+2.50
Red	+35.00
Yellow	—
Town	+20.00

O43 O5	24c **ultramarine**		175.00	65.00
	dark ultramarine		175.00	65.00
	On cover			—
	Block of 4		850.00	
a.	24c **dull blue**		200.00	

Cancellations

Magenta	+5.00
Blue	+5.00
Green	+150.00
Town	+20.00
Steamship	+100.00

O44 O5	30c **ultramarine**		140.00	35.00
	dark ultramarine		140.00	35.00
	Block of 4		675.00	—
	Double transfer		170.00	42.50

Cancellations

Blue	+4.00
Red	+30.00
Purple	+4.00
Violet	+4.00

	Town				+10.00
	Supplementary Mail				+125.00
O45	O5	90c	**ultramarine**	700.00	200.00
	Block of 4			3,750.	
	Short transfer at upper left (pos. 1, 5)			—	—
a.	Double impression				3,750.

Cancellations

Purple		+15.00
Town		+25.00

POST OFFICE

Stamps of the Post Office Department are often on paper with a gray surface. This is due to insufficient wiping of the excess ink off plates during printing.

1873

O47	O6	1c	**black**	12.50	7.50
			gray black	12.50	7.50
			On cover		55.00
			Block of 4	52.50	—
			P# block of 12, Impt.	225.00	
			Never hinged	325.00	

Cancellations

Purple		+1.00
Magenta		+1.00
Blue		+1.00
Red		+12.50
Town		+3.50

O48	O6	2c	**black**	16.00	7.00
			gray black	16.00	7.00
			On cover		150.00
			Block of 4	67.50	—
			P# block of 12, Impt.	280.00	
a.	Double impression			325.00	300.00

Cancellations

Magenta		+1.00
Purple		+1.00
Blue		+1.00
Red		+12.50
Town		+3.50
Blue town		+7.50

O49	O6	3c	**black**	5.25	1.00
			gray black	5.25	1.00
			On cover		20.00
			Block of 4	24.00	—
			P# block of 14, Impt.	125.00	
			Never hinged	180.00	
			Cracked plate	—	—
			Double transfer at bottom	—	—
			Double paper	—	—
			Vertical ribbed paper	—	—
a.	Printed on both sides				3,000.

Cancellations

Purple		+.75
Magenta		+.75
Violet		+.75
Blue		+.75
Ultramarine		+1.50
Red		+10.00
Green		+60.00
Town		+1.50
Railroad		+25.00
"Paid"		+12.00

O50	O6	6c	**black**	16.00	6.00
			gray black	16.00	6.00
			On cover		75.00
			Block of 4	67.50	—
			Vertical ribbed paper	—	11.00
a.	Diagonal half used as 3c on cover				3,000.

Cancellations

Purple		+.75
Magenta		+.75
Blue		+.75
Red		+12.00
Town		+2.50
"Paid"		+15.00

O51	O6	10c	**black**	70.00	40.00
			gray black	70.00	40.00
			On cover		400.00
			Block of 4	325.00	—

Cancellations

Purple		+3.50
Red		+15.00
Magenta		+3.50
Blue		+3.50
Town		+10.00

O52	O6	12c	**black**	35.00	8.25
			gray black	35.00	8.25
			On cover		1,000.
			Block of 4	150.00	—

Cancellations

Purple		+1.00
Magenta		+1.00
Blue		+1.00
Red		+12.50
Town		+4.00

O53	O6	15c	**black**	47.50	14.00
			gray black	47.50	14.00
			On cover		1,500.
			Block of 4	210.00	—
			P# block of 14, Impt.	725.00	
			Double transfer	—	—

Cancellations

Purple		+1.50
Magenta		+1.50
Blue		+1.50
Town		+7.50

O54	O6	24c	**black**	60.00	17.00
			gray black	60.00	17.00
			Block of 4	260.00	—
			Double paper	—	—

Cancellations

Purple		+1.50
Blue		+1.50

			Red		+20.00
			Town		+7.50
O55	O6	30c	**black**	60.00	17.00
			gray black	60.00	17.00
			On cover		17.00
			Block of 4	260.00	—

Cancellations

Purple		+1.50
Blue		+1.50
Red		+20.00
Magenta		+1.50
Town		+12.50

O56	O6	90c	**black**	90.00	14.00
			gray black	90.00	14.00
			Block of 4	375.00	—
			Double transfer	—	—
			Double paper	—	—
			Silk paper	—	—

Cancellations

Purple		+1.50
Magenta		+1.50
Blue		+1.50
Town		+6.50

STATE

Franklin — O7

William H. Seward — O8

1873

O57	O7	1c	**dark green**	110.00	50.00
			dark yellow green	110.00	50.00
			light green	110.00	50.00
			On cover		—
			Block of 4	575.00	

Cancellations

Violet		+2.00
Purple		+2.00
Blue		+2.00
Red		+17.50
Town		+7.50

O58	O7	2c	**dark green**	210.00	75.00
			dark yellow green	210.00	75.00
			yellow green	—	—
			On cover		1,000.
			Block of 4	—	—
			Double transfer	—	—

Cancellations

Purple		+5.00
Blue		+5.00
Red		+30.00
Green		+75.00
Town		+10.00
Blue town		+20.00

The existence of any multiple of No. O58 larger than a strip of 3 used on cover has been questioned by specialists. The editors would like to see evidence that any blocks of 4 or larger are still in existence, either unused or used.

O59	O7	3c	**bright green**	85.00	17.00
			yellow green	85.00	17.00
			dark green	85.00	17.00
			On cover		450.00
			First day cover, *July 1, 1873*		—
			Block of 4	475.00	—
			Double paper	—	—

Cancellations

Purple		+1.50
Blue		+1.50
Red		+10.00
Town		+6.50
Blue town		+10.00

O60	O7	6c	**bright green**	80.00	22.00
			dark green	80.00	22.00
			yellow green	80.00	22.00
			On cover		650.00
			Block of 4	400.00	—
			Double transfer	—	—
			Foreign entry of 6c Executive, pos. 41 & 91	—	—
			Double transfer plus foreign entry of 6c Executive, pos. 61	—	

Cancellations

Purple		+2.00
Red		+10.00
Town		+7.50

O61	O7	7c	**dark green**	160.00	50.00
			dark yellow green	160.00	50.00
			On cover		1,000.
			Block of 4	800.00	—
			Ribbed paper	180.00	55.00

Cancellations

Purple		+2.00
Blue		+2.00
Red		+25.00
Town		+10.00

O62	O7	10c	**dark green**	125.00	35.00

			bright green	125.00	35.00
			yellow green		
			On cover		1,200.
			Block of 4	625.00	
			P# block of 12, Impt.		—
			Short transfer, pos. 34	160.00	47.50

Cancellations

Purple		+2.50
Magenta		+2.50
Blue		+2.50
Red		+25.00
Town		+5.00
Blue town		+10.00
Numeral		+15.00

O63	O7	12c	**dark green**	200.00	90.00
			dark yellow green		
			On cover		1,500.
			Block of 4	1,075.	

Cancellations

Purple		+5.00
Blue		+5.00
Red		+30.00
Town		+15.00

O64	O7	15c	**dark green**	210.00	65.00
			dark yellow green	210.00	65.00
			On cover		—
			Block of 4	975.00	

Cancellations

Purple		+2.50
Blue		+2.50
Red		+20.00
Town		+15.00

O65	O7	24c	**dark green**	425.00	170.00
			dark yellow green	425.00	170.00
			On cover		1,750.
			Block of 4	2,250.	

Cancellations

Purple		+15.00
Blue		+15.00
Red		+65.00
Town		+25.00

O66	O7	30c	**dark green**	400.00	130.00
			dark yellow green	400.00	130.00
			On cover		—
			Block of 4	—	

Cancellations

Purple		+5.00
Blue		+5.00
Red		+35.00
Town		+20.00
Blue town		+30.00

O67	O7	90c	**dark green**	750.00	275.00
			dark yellow green		
			On cover		—
			Block of 4	—	

The existence of the block of 4 No. O67 has been questioned by specialists. The editors would like to see evidence of the current existence of this item.

Cancellations

Purple		+15.00
Blue		+15.00
Red		+75.00
Town		+40.00

O68	O8	$2	**green & black**	850.00	700.00
			yellow green & black	850.00	700.00
			On parcel label		—
			Block of 4	14,000.	

Cancellations

Blue		+25.00
Red		+125.00
Purple		+25.00
Town		+75.00
Blue town		+150.00
Pen		175.00

O69 O8 $5 green & black   6,000.   3,500.
dark green & black   6,000.   3,500.
yellow green & black   6,000.   3,500.
Block of 4   30,000.
Cancellations
Blue   +250.00
Pen   1,300.

The block of 4 is contained in the only known multiple: an irregular block of 6.

O70 O8 $10 green & black   4,000.   2,400.
dark green & black   4,000.   2,400.
yellow green & black   4,000.   2,400.
Block of 4   20,000.
P# sheet of 10, Impt.   50,000.
Cancellations
Blue   +200.00
Pen   850.00

O71 O8 $20 green & black   3,250.   1,800.
dark green & black   3,250.   1,800.
yellow green & black   3,250.   1,800.
Block of 4   17,500.
Block of 4, pen cancel   5,000.
P# sheet of 10, Impt.   42,500.
Cancellations
Blue   +200.00
Pen   775.00

The design of Nos. O68 to O71 measures 25½x39½mm.

O9   O10

TREASURY
1873

O72 O9 1c brown   37.50   4.50
dark brown   37.50   4.50
yellow brown   37.50   4.50
On cover   100.00
Block of 4   160.00
P# block of 14, Impt.   750.00
  Never hinged   1,075.
Double transfer   45.00   6.25
Cancellations
Purple   +1.00
Magenta   +1.00
Blue   +1.00
Red   +10.00
Town   +2.00
Blue town   +4.00

O73 O9 2c brown   47.50   4.50
dark brown   47.50   4.50
yellow brown   47.50   4.50
On cover   75.00
Block of 4   200.00
Double transfer   7.75
Cracked plate   65.00
Cancellations
Purple   +1.00
Magenta   +1.00
Blue   +1.00
Red   +10.00
Town   +2.00
Blue town   +4.00

O74 O9 3c brown   32.50   1.25
dark brown   32.50   1.25
yellow brown   32.50   1.25
On cover   30.00
First day cover, *July 1, 1873*   2,500.
Block of 4   140.00
Double paper
Shaded circle outside of right
  frame line
a.   Double impression
Cancellations
Purple   +.50
Magenta   +.50
Blue   +.50
Ultramarine   +2.00
Red   +3.50
Town   +1.00
Railroad   +20.00
"Paid"   +10.00

O75 O9 6c brown   42.50   2.25
dark brown   42.50   2.25
yellow brown   42.50   2.25
On cover   115.00
Block of 4   180.00
P# block of 12, Impt.   750.00
  Never hinged   1,075.
Dirty plate   37.50   4.00
Double transfer
Cancellations
Purple   +.50
Magenta   +.50
Blue   +.50
Ultramarine   +1.50
Red   +5.00
Green   +20.00
Town   +1.50

O76 O9 7c brown   90.00   22.50
dark brown   90.00   22.50
yellow brown   90.00   22.50
On cover   750.00
Block of 4   400.00

Cancellations
Purple   +2.00
Blue   +2.00
Green   +60.00
Town   +7.50
Blue town   +12.50

O77 O9 10c brown   90.00   7.75
dark brown   90.00   7.75
yellow brown   90.00   7.75
On cover   375.00
Block of 4   400.00
Double paper
Double transfer
Cancellations
Purple   +1.00
Magenta   +1.00
Blue   +1.00
Ultramarine   +4.00
Red   +12.00
Town   +4.00
Blue town   +8.50

O78 O9 12c brown   90.00   6.00
dark brown   90.00   6.00
yellow brown   90.00   6.00
On cover   600.00
Block of 4   400.00
Cancellations
Purple   +.50
Blue   +.50
Red   +10.00
Green   +35.00
Town   +2.50

O79 O9 15c brown   85.00   7.75
yellow brown   85.00   7.75
On cover   850.00
Block of 4   375.00
P# block of 12, Impt.   1,500.
  Never hinged   2,150.
Cancellations
Blue   +1.00
Purple   +1.00
Red   +10.00
Town   +2.50
Blue town   +7.50
Numeral   +15.00

O80 O9 24c brown   425.00   65.00
dark brown   425.00   65.00
yellow brown   425.00   65.00
Block of 4   1,850.
Double transfer at top
Cancellations
Blue   +5.00
Magenta   +5.00
Town   +15.00
Blue town   +25.00

O81 O9 30c brown   145.00   9.00
dark brown   145.00   9.00
yellow brown   145.00   9.00
On cover
Block of 4   625.00
Short transfer at left top (pos. 95)   20.00
Short transfer at right top (pos. 45)   185.00   20.00
  Block of 4, one pos. 45   185.00
Short transfer across entire top (pos. 41)   185.00   20.00
Cancellations
Blue   +1.00
Red   +12.00
Purple   +1.00
Town   +3.50
Blue town   +7.50

O82 O9 90c brown   150.00   10.00
dark brown   150.00   10.00
yellow brown   150.00   10.00
Block of 4   650.00
Double paper
Cancellations
Purple   +1.00
Magenta   +1.00
Blue   +1.00
Brown   +7.50
Town   +3.50
Blue town   +7.50

WAR
1873

O83 O10 1c rose   140.00   8.50
rose red   140.00   8.50
On cover   140.00
Block of 4   600.00
Cancellations
Purple   +1.00
Blue   +1.00
Red   +15.00
Town   +3.50
Fort   +50.00
Numeral   +12.50
"Paid"

O84 O10 2c rose   125.00   9.50
rose red   125.00   9.50
On cover   70.00
Block of 4   525.00
Ribbed paper   135.00   11.50
Cancellations
Purple   +1.50
Magenta   +1.50
Blue   +1.50
Red   +15.00
Town   +4.00
Fort   +50.00

O85 O10 3c rose   130.00   2.75
rose red   130.00   2.75
On cover   40.00
Block of 4   550.00
Cancellations
Blue   +1.00
Purple   +1.00
Magenta   +1.00
Green   +35.00
Town   +1.50
Fort   +40.00
"Paid"   +12.00

O86 O10 6c rose   425.00   6.00
pale rose   425.00   6.00
On cover   60.00
Block of 4   2,000.
Cancellations
Purple   +1.50
Blue   +1.50
Red   +15.00
Town   +3.50
Blue town   +6.50
Fort   +40.00

O87 O10 7c rose   125.00   72.50
pale rose   125.00   72.50
rose red   125.00   72.50
On cover
Block of 4   525.00
P# block of 10, Impt.   1,800.
Cancellations
Purple   +2.50
Blue   +3.50
Town   +7.50

O88 O10 10c rose   42.50   15.00
rose red   42.50   15.00
On cover
Block of 4   185.00   *900.00*

All copies of No. O88 show a crack at lower left. It was on the original die.

Cancellations
Purple   +1.00
Blue   +1.00
Town   +3.50
Fort   +40.00

O89 O10 12c rose   160.00   10.00
On cover   300.00
Block of 4   675.00
P# block of 12, Impt.   2,000.
  Never hinged   2,800.
Ribbed paper   175.00   10.50
Cancellations
Purple   +1.00
Magenta   +1.00
Blue   +1.00
Red   +10.00
Town   +3.00
Fort   +35.00

O90 O10 15c rose   37.50   11.00
pale rose   37.50   11.00
rose red   37.50   11.00
On cover
Block of 4   160.00
P# block of 10, Impt.   500.00
Ribbed paper   42.50   14.00
Cancellations
Purple   +1.00
Blue   +1.00
Red   +10.00
Town   +2.50
Fort   +30.00
Express Company

O91 O10 24c rose   37.50   6.75
pale rose   37.50   6.75
rose red   37.50   6.75
On cover
Block of 4   160.00   *900.00*
P# block of 10, Impt.   750.00
Cancellations
Purple   +1.00
Blue   +1.00
Town   +2.50
Fort   +3.50

O92 O10 30c rose   40.00   6.75
rose red   40.00   6.75
On cover
Block of 4   170.00
Ribbed paper   45.00   9.00
Cancellations
Purple   +1.00
Magenta   +1.00
Blue   +1.00
Town   +2.50
Fort   +35.00

O93 O10 90c rose   90.00   40.00
rose red   90.00   40.00
On cover   2,000.
Block of 4   400.00   *900.00*
P# block of 12, Impt.   2,000.
Cancellations
Purple   +2.00
Magenta   +2.00
Blue   +2.00
Town   +7.50
Fort   +90.00

Printed by the American Bank Note Co.

The Continental Bank Note Co. was consolidated with the American Bank Note Co. on February 4, 1879. The American

Bank Note Company used many plates of the Continental Bank Note Company to print the ordinary postage, Departmental and Newspaper stamps. Therefore, stamps bearing the Continental Company's imprint were not always its product.

1879   **Soft Porous Paper**

AGRICULTURE

O94	O1	1c **yellow** (issued without gum)	3,250.	
		Block of 4	14,500.	
O95	O1	3c **yellow**	290.00	65.00
		On cover		—
		Block of 4	1,450.	1,300.
		P# block of 12, Impt.	4,750.	

Cancellations
Purple		+5.00
Blue		+5.00
Town		+17.50

INTERIOR

O96	O3	1c **vermilion**	250.00	220.00
		pale vermilion	250.00	220.00
		Block of 4	900.00	—

Cancellations
Blue		+5.00
Town		+15.00

O97	O3	2c **vermilion**	4.00	1.25
		pale vermilion	4.00	1.25
		scarlet vermilion	4.00	1.25
		On cover		35.00
		Block of 4	18.50	

Cancellations
Purple		+.50
Blue		+.50
Red		+5.00
Town		+1.50
Blue town		+3.00
Fort		+25.00

O98	O3	3c **vermilion**	3.50	1.00
		pale vermilion	3.50	1.00
		On cover		30.00
		Block of 4	15.00	—
		P# block of 10, Impt.	160.00	

Cancellations
Purple		+.50
Blue		+.50
Red		+5.00
Town		+1.50
Blue town		+3.00
Numeral		+5.00

O99	O3	6c **vermilion**	5.25	5.50
		pale vermilion	5.25	5.50
		scarlet vermilion	5.25	5.50
		On cover		200.00
		Block of 4	23.50	—
		P# block of 10, Impt.	185.00	

Cancellations
Purple		+.50
Blue		+.50
Red		+5.00
Town		+1.50

O100	O3	10c **vermilion**	65.00	60.00
		pale vermilion	65.00	60.00
		On cover		1,250.
		Block of 4	285.00	—
		P# block of 10, Impt.	950.00	

Cancellations
Purple		+5.00
Blue		+5.00
Town		+10.00

O101	O3	12c **vermilion**	125.00	90.00
		pale vermilion	125.00	90.00
		On cover		—
		Block of 4	525.00	450.00
		Block of 6		1,500.

O102	O3	15c **vermilion**	300.00	225.00
		Block of 4	1,300.	
		On cover		—
		Double transfer	350.00	—

Cancellation
Purple		+5.00

O103	O3	24c **vermilion**	3,000.	—
		Block of 4	13,500.	

Cancellation
Blue		—

JUSTICE

O106	O4	3c **bluish purple**	100.00	65.00
		deep bluish purple	100.00	65.00
		On cover		700.00
		Block of 4	450.00	

Cancellation
Blue		+5.00

O107	O4	6c **bluish purple**	225.00	175.00
		On cover		—
		Block of 4	1,000.	

Cancellations
Blue		+10.00
Town		+20.00

POST OFFICE

O108	O6	3c **black**	15.00	5.00
		gray black	15.00	5.00
		On cover		—
		Block of 4	65.00	—

Cancellations
Blue		+1.00
Purple		+1.00
Violet		+1.00
Magenta		+1.00
Green		+40.00
Town		+2.00
"Paid"		+12.00

TREASURY

O109	O9	3c **brown**	45.00	6.75
		yellow brown	45.00	6.75
		On cover		110.00
		Block of 4	190.00	
		P# block of 14, Impt.	750.00	

Cancellations
Purple		+1.50
Blue		+1.50
Town		+2.00
Numeral		+7.50

O110	O9	6c **brown**	85.00	35.00
		yellow brown	85.00	35.00
		dark brown	85.00	35.00
		On cover		300.00
		Block of 4	375.00	—
		P# block of 12, Impt.	1,325.	

Cancellations
Purple		+6.00
Magenta		+6.00
Blue		+6.00

O111	O9	10c **brown**	150.00	50.00
		yellow brown	150.00	50.00
		dark brown	150.00	50.00
		On cover		1,200.
		Block of 4	750.00	—
		P# block of 12, Impt.	2,750.	

Cancellations
Purple		+2.50
Blue		+2.50
Town		+7.50

O112	O9	30c **brown**	1,250.	275.00
		Block of 4	5,750.	

Cancellations
Blue		+25.00
Town		+50.00

O113	O9	90c **brown**	2,000.	275.00
		dark brown	2,000.	275.00
		Block of 4	9,500.	

Cancellations
Purple		+25.00
Blue		+25.00
Town		+75.00

WAR

O114	O10	1c **rose red**	3.50	2.75
		rose	3.50	2.75
		dull rose red	3.50	2.75
		brown rose	3.50	2.75
		On cover		55.00
		Block of 4	15.00	—
		P# block of 12, Impt.	120.00	
		Never hinged	165.00	

Cancellations
Purple		+.50
Blue		+.50
Town		+1.00
Fort		+25.00

O115	O10	2c **rose red**	5.00	3.25
		dark rose red	5.00	3.25
		dull vermilion	5.00	3.25
		On cover		40.00
		Block of 4	21.50	—
		P# block of 12, Impt.	150.00	
		Never hinged	215.00	

Cancellations
Blue		+.50
Purple		+.50
Magenta		+.50
Green		+35.00
Town		+2.00
Fort		+25.00

O116	O10	3c **rose red**	5.00	1.20
		dull rose red	5.00	1.20
		On cover		35.00
		Block of 4	21.50	—
		P# block of 12, Impt.	150.00	
		Never hinged	215.00	
		Double transfer	8.50	4.75
		Plate flaw at upper left (32 R 20)	—	—
a.		Imperf., pair	900.00	
b.		Double impression	750.00	

Cancellations
Purple		+.50
Violet		+.50
Blue		+.50
Red		+5.00
Town		+1.00
Fort		+25.00

O117	O10	6c **rose red**	4.50	1.00
		dull rose red	4.50	1.00
		dull vermilion		
		On cover		50.00
		Block of 4	19.00	—
		P# block of 12, Impt.	130.00	

Cancellations
Purple		+.50
Blue		+.50
Town		+1.00
Fort		+25.00
Numeral		+7.50

O118	O10	10c **rose red**	37.50	37.50
		dull rose red	37.50	37.50
		On cover		—
		Block of 4	160.00	
		P# block of 10, Impt.	575.00	

Cancellations
Town		+5.00
Fort		+45.00

O119	O10	12c **rose red**	30.00	10.00
		dull rose red	30.00	10.00
		brown rose	30.00	10.00
		On cover		

		Block of 4	130.00	—
		P# block of 10, Impt.	400.00	

Cancellations
Purple		+1.00
Violet		+1.00
Red		+10.00
Town		+2.50
Fort		+40.00

O120	O10	30c **rose red**	80.00	67.50
		dull rose red	80.00	67.50
		Block of 4	350.00	—
		P# block of 10, Impt.	1,800.	

Cancellations
Town		+10.00
Fort		+80.00

SPECIAL PRINTINGS

Special printings of Official stamps were made in 1875 at the time the other Reprints, Re-issues and Special Printings were printed. They are ungummed. Though overprinted "SPECIMEN," these stamps are Special Printings, and they are not considered to be in the same category as the stamps listed in the Specimen section of this catalogue.

Although perforated, these stamps were sometimes (but not always) cut apart with scissors. As a result the perforations may be mutilated and the design damaged.

Number issued indicated in brackets.

All values exist imperforate.

Blocks of 4 are now listed. All are scarce, a few are rare. They will be valued when sufficient information has been received. Imprint and plate number strips or blocks are very scarce.

The "SEPCIMEN" error appears once on some panes of 100. The error was discovered and corrected part way through the printing. Blocks of 4 or larger with the "SEPCIMEN" error are rare and worth much more than the value of the individual stamps.

Printing flaws which resemble broken type (but are not) are commonly found on the SPECIMEN overprint on these and other overprinted stamps.

Printed by the Continental Bank Note Co.

Overprinted in Block Letters   **SPECIMEN**

1875   Thin, hard white paper   **Perf. 12**
                 Type D

AGRICULTURE
Carmine Overprint

O1S	D	1c **yellow** (10,234)	14.00	
		Block of 4	—	
a.		"Sepcimen" error	700.00	
b.		Small dotted "i" in "Specimen"	425.00	
c.		Horiz. ribbed paper (10,000)	20.00	
		Block of 4	—	
O2S	D	2c **yellow** (4,192)	27.50	
		Block of 4	—	
a.		"Sepcimen" error	750.00	
O3S	D	3c **yellow** (389)	75.00	
a.		"Sepcimen" error	3,000.	
O4S	D	6c **yellow** (373)	130.00	
a.		"Sepcimen" error	5,500.	
O5S	D	10c **yellow** (390)	130.00	
a.		"Sepcimen" error	3,250.	
O6S	D	12c **yellow** (379)	125.00	
a.		"Sepcimen" error	3,750.	
O7S	D	15c **yellow** (370)	125.00	
a.		"Sepcimen" error	3,250.	
O8S	D	24c **yellow** (352)	125.00	
a.		"Sepcimen" error	3,250.	
O9S	D	30c **yellow** (354)	125.00	
a.		"Sepcimen" error	3,250.	

EXECUTIVE
Blue Overprint

O10S	D	1c **carmine** (10,000)	14.00	
		Block of 4	—	
a.		Small dotted "i" in "Specimen"	325.00	
b.		Horiz. ribbed paper (10,000)	20.00	
		Block of 4	—	
O11S	D	2c **carmine** (7,430)	27.50.	
		Block of 4	—	
		Foreign entry of 6c Agriculture	—	
O12S	D	3c **carmine** (3,735)	27.50.	
		Block of 4	—	
O13S	D	6c **carmine** (3,485)	27.50.	
		Block of 4	—	
O14S	D	10c **carmine** (3,461)	27.50.	
		Block of 4	—	

INTERIOR
Blue Overprint

O15S	D	1c **vermilion** (7,194)	27.50	
		Block of 4	—	
O16S	D	2c **vermilion** (1,263)	35.00	
		Block of 4	—	
a.		"Sepcimen" error	3,750.	
O17S	D	3c **vermilion** (88)	475.00	
O18S	D	6c **vermilion** (83)	450.00	
O19S	D	10c **vermilion** (82)	450.00	
O20S	D	12c **vermilion** (75)	475.00	
O21S	D	15c **vermilion** (78)	475.00	
O22S	D	24c **vermilion** (77)	475.00	
O23S	D	30c **vermilion** (75)	475.00	
O24S	D	90c **vermilion** (77)	475.00	

JUSTICE
Blue Overprint

O25S	D	1c purple (10,000)	15.00	
		Block of 4	—	
a.		"Sepcimen" error	675.00	
b.		Small dotted "i" in "Specimen"	275.00	
c.		Horiz. ribbed paper (9,729)	20.00	
		Block of 4	—	
O26S	D	2c purple (3,395)	30.00	
		Block of 4	—	
a.		"Sepcimen" error	1,100.	
O27S	D	3c purple (178)	250.00	
		Plate scratches	—	
a.		"Sepcimen" error	3,750.	
O28S	D	6c purple (163)	250.00	
O29S	D	10c purple (163)	250.00	
O30S	D	12c purple (154)	250.00	
a.		"Sepcimen" error	4,000.	
O31S	D	15c purple (157)	275.00	
a.		"Sepcimen" error	4,000.	
O32S	D	24c purple (150)	300.00	
a.		"Sepcimen" error	4,000.	
O33S	D	30c purple (150)	300.00	
a.		"Sepcimen" error	4,000.	
O34S	D	90c purple (152)	325.00	

NAVY
Carmine Overprint

O35S	D	1c ultramarine (10,000)	17.50	
		Block of 4	—	
a.		"Sepcimen" error	550.00	
O36S	D	2c ultramarine (1,748)	35.00	
		Block of 4	—	
a.		"Sepcimen" error	675.00	
O37S	D	3c ultramarine (126)	300.00	
O38S	D	6c ultramarine (116)	350.00	
O39S	D	7c ultramarine (501)	150.00	
		Block of 4	—	
a.		"Sepcimen" error	3,000.	
O40S	D	10c ultramarine (112)	350.00	
a.		"Sepcimen" error	4,250.	
O41S	D	12c ultramarine (107)	300.00	
		Double transfer at left side, pos. 50	—	
a.		"Sepcimen" error	4,000.	
O42S	D	15c ultramarine (107)	300.00	
a.		"Sepcimen" error	7,500.	
O43S	D	24c ultramarine (106)	300.00	
a.		"Sepcimen" error	4,000.	
O44S	D	30c ultramarine (104)	300.00	
		Double transfer	—	
a.		"Sepcimen" error	4,500.	
O45S	D	90c ultramarine (102)	300.00	

POST OFFICE
Carmine Overprint

O47S	D	1c black (6,015)	25.00	
		Block of 4	—	
a.		"Sepcimen" error	650.00	
b.		Inverted overprint	1,000.	
O48S	D	2c black (590)	65.00	
		Block of 4	—	
a.		"Sepcimen" error	1,750.	
O49S	D	3c black (91)	450.00	
a.		"Sepcimen" error	—	
O50S	D	6c black (87)	425.00	
O51S	D	10c black (177)	275.00	
a.		"Sepcimen" error	4,250.	
O52S	D	12c black (93)	400.00	
O53S	D	15c black (82)	475.00	
a.		"Sepcimen" error	4,250.	
O54S	D	24c black (84)	425.00	
a.		"Sepcimen" error	4,250.	
O55S	D	30c black (81)	425.00	
O56S	D	90c black (82)	425.00	
a.		"Sepcimen" error	8,000.	

STATE
Carmine Overprint

O57S	D	1c bluish green (10,000)	15.00	
		Block of 4	—	
a.		"Sepcimen" error	400.00	
b.		Small dotted "i" in "Specimen"	400.00	
c.		Horiz. ribbed paper (10,000)	20.00	
d.		Double overprint	—	
		Block of 4	—	
O58S	D	2c bluish green (5,145)	30.00	
a.		"Sepcimen" error	550.00	
O59S	D	3c bluish green (793)	45.00	
		Block of 4	—	
a.		"Sepcimen" error	2,000.	
O60S	D	6c bluish green (467)	95.00	
a.		"Sepcimen" error	2,250.	
O61S	D	7c bluish green (791)	47.50	
		Block of 4	—	
a.		"Sepcimen" error	1,750.	
O62S	D	10c bluish green (346)	180.00	
		Short transfer, pos. 34	—	
a.		"Sepcimen" error	7,500.	
O63S	D	12c bluish green (280)	190.00	
a.		"Sepcimen" error	3,500.	
O64S	D	15c bluish green (257)	180.00	
O65S	D	24c bluish green (253)	180.00	
a.		"Sepcimen" error	3,500.	
O66S	D	30c bluish green (249)	180.00	
a.		"Sepcimen" error	3,750.	
O67S	D	90c bluish green (245)	180.00	
a.		"Sepcimen" error	3,750.	
O68S	D	$2 green & black (32)	7,250.	
O69S	D	$5 green & black (12)	12,000.	
O70S	D	$10 green & black (8)	16,000.	
O71S	D	$20 green & black (7)	19,000.	

TREASURY
Blue Overprint

O72S	D	1c dark brown (2,185)	27.50	
		Block of 4	—	
		Double transfer	—	
O73S	D	2c dark brown (309)	130.00	
O74S	D	3c dark brown (84)	475.00	
O75S	D	6c dark brown (85)	425.00	
O76S	D	7c dark brown (198)	250.00	
		Block of 4	—	
O77S	D	10c dark brown (82)	450.00	
O78S	D	12c dark brown (75)	475.00	
O79S	D	15c dark brown (75)	475.00	
O80S	D	24c dark brown (99)	375.00	
O81S	D	30c dark brown (74)	500.00	
		Short transfer at left top (pos. 95) (1)	—	
		Short transfer at right top (pos. 45) (1)	—	
O82S	D	90c dark brown (72)	500.00	

WAR
Blue Overprint

O83S	D	1c deep rose (9,610)	17.50	
		Block of 4	—	
a.		"Sepcimen" error	550.00	
O84S	D	2c deep rose (1,618)	35.00	
		Block of 4	—	
a.		"Sepcimen" error	1,000.	
O85S	D	3c deep rose (118)	350.00	
a.		"Sepcimen" error	4,000.	
O86S	D	6c deep rose (111)	350.00	
a.		"Sepcimen" error	4,250.	
O87S	D	7c deep rose (539)	72.50	
		Block of 4	—	
a.		"Sepcimen" error	1,900.	
O88S	D	10c deep rose (119)	325.00	
a.		"Sepcimen" error	4,250.	
O89S	D	12c deep rose (105)	375.00	
a.		"Sepcimen" error	4,250.	
O90S	D	15c deep rose (105)	375.00	
a.		"Sepcimen" error	4,250.	
O91S	D	24c deep rose (106)	375.00	
a.		"Sepcimen" error	4,250.	
O92S	D	30c deep rose (104)	375.00	
a.		"Sepcimen" error	4,250.	
O93S	D	90c deep rose (106)	375.00	
a.		"Sepcimen" error	4,750.	

SOFT POROUS PAPER
EXECUTIVE

1881

Blue Overprint

O10xS	D	1c violet rose (4,652)	45.00	
		Block of 4	—	

NAVY
Carmine Overprint

O35xS	D	1c gray blue (4,182)	50.00	
		deep blue	50.00	
		Block of 4	—	
a.		Double overprint	850.00	

STATE

O57xS	D	1c yellow green (1,672)	200.00	
		Block of 4	—	

POSTAL SAVINGS MAIL

The Act of Congress, approved June 25, 1910, establishing postal savings depositories, provided:

"Sec. 2. That the Postmaster General is hereby directed to prepare and issue special stamps of the necessary denominations for use, in lieu of penalty or franked envelopes, in the transmittal of free mail resulting from the administration of this act."

The use of postal savings official stamps was discontinued by the Act of Congress, approved September 23, 1914. The unused stamps in the hands of postmasters were returned and destroyed.

O11

1910-11   Engr.   Wmk. 191

O121	O11	2c black, *Dec. 22, 1910*	14.00	1.50
		Never hinged	22.50	
		On cover		10.00
		Block of 4 (2mm spacing)	62.50	8.00
		Block of 4 (3mm spacing)	60.00	7.00
		P# block of 6, Impt. & Star	300.00	
		Double transfer	19.00	2.50
O122	O11	50c dark green, *Feb. 1, 1911*	140.00	40.00
		Never hinged	225.00	
		On cover		160.00
		Block of 4 (2mm spacing)	600.00	200.00
		Block of 4 (3mm spacing)	575.00	200.00
		Margin block of 4, arrow	625.00	
		P# block of 6, Impt. & Star	2,350.	
		Never hinged	3,100.	
O123	O11	$1 ultramarine, *Feb. 1, 1911*	130.00	11.00
		Never hinged	210.00	
		On cover		90.00
		Block of 4 (2mm spacing)	575.00	60.00
		Block of 4 (3mm spacing)	550.00	60.00
		Margin block of 4, arrow	600.00	
		P# block of 6, Impt. & Star	2,150.	—

Wmk. 190

O124	O11	1c dark violet, *Mar. 27, 1911*	7.50	1.50
		Never hinged	12.00	
		On cover		12.50
		Block of 4 (2mm spacing)	32.50	6.50
		Block of 4 (3mm spacing)	31.00	6.25
		P# block of 6, Impt. & Star	175.00	
O125	O11	2c black	45.00	5.50
		Never hinged	72.50	
		On cover		20.00
		Block of 4 (2mm spacing)	190.00	25.00
		Block of 4 (3mm spacing)	185.00	25.00
		P# block of 6, Impt. & Star	650.00	
		Double transfer	50.00	6.50
O126	O11	10c carmine, *Feb. 1, 1911*	17.00	1.60
		Never hinged	27.50	
		On cover		12.50
		Block of 4 (2mm spacing)	72.50	8.00
		Block of 4 (3mm spacing)	70.00	7.50
		P# block of 6, Impt. & Star	350.00	
		Double transfer	22.50	3.00

> **Catalogue values for unused stamps in this section, from this point to the end, are for Never Hinged items.**

OFFICIAL MAIL

O12

Designed by Bradbury Thompson

ENGRAVED
Perf. 11x10½, 11 (14c)

1983, Jan. 12-1985   Unwmk.

O127	O12	1c red, blue & black	.20	.20
		FDC, Washington, DC		1.00
		P# block of 4, UL or UR	.25	
O128	O12	4c red, blue & black	.20	.25
		FDC, Washington, DC		1.00
		P# block of 4, LR only	.40	
O129	O12	13c red, blue & black	.45	.75
		FDC, Washington, DC		1.00
		P# block of 4, UR only	2.00	
O129A	O12	14c red, blue & black, *May 15, 1985*	.45	.50
		FDC, Washington, DC		1.00
		Zip-copyright block of 6	2.90	
O130	O12	17c red, blue & black	.60	.40
		FDC, Washington, DC		1.00
		P# block of 4, LL only	3.00	
O132	O12	$1 red, blue & black	2.00	1.00
		FDC, Washington, DC		2.25
		P# block of 4, UL only	9.75	
O133	O12	$5 red, blue & black	9.00	9.00
		FDC, Washington, DC		12.50
		P# block of 4, LL only	45.00	
		Nos. O127-O133 (7)	12.90	12.10

No. O129A does not have a "c" after the "14."

COIL STAMPS
Perf. 10 Vert.

O135	O12	20c red, blue & black	1.75	2.00
		FDC, Washington, DC		1.00
		Pair	3.50	4.00
		P# strip of 3, P# 1	17.00	
		P# strip of 5, P# 1	65.00	
		P# single, #1		16.00
a.		Imperf., pair	2,000.	
O136	O12	22c red, blue & blk, *May 15, 1985*	.70	2.00
		FDC, Washington, DC		1.00
		Pair	1.40	4.00
		Dull finish gum	75.00	

> **Used Values**
> of Nos. O135-O138, O140, etc., do not apply to copies removed from first day covers.

Inscribed: Postal Card Rate D

1985, Feb. 4   *Perf. 11*

O138	O12	(14c) red, blue & black	5.25	5.00
		FDC, Washington, DC		1.00
		P# block of 4, LR only	42.50	—

Frame line completely around the design — O13

Inscribed: No. O139, Domestic Letter Rate D, No. O140, Domestic Mail E.

COIL STAMPS

1985-88		Litho., Engr. (#O139)		Perf. 10 Vert.	
O138A	O13	15c **red, blue & blk**, *June 11, 1988*		.45	.50
		FDC, Corpus Christi, TX			1.25
		Pair		.90	1.00
O138B	O13	20c **red, blue & blk**, *May 19, 1988*		.45	.30
		FDC, Washington			1.25
		Pair		.90	.60
O139	O12	(22c) **red, blue & blk**, *Feb. 4*		5.25	3.00
		FDC, Washington, DC			1.00
		Pair		10.50	—
		P# strip of 3, P# 1		40.00	
		P# strip of 5, P# 1		80.00	
		P# single, #1		—	35.00
O140	O13	(25c) **red, blue & black**, *Mar. 22, 1988*		.75	2.00
		FDC, Washington			1.25
		Pair		1.50	—
O141	O13	25c **red, blue & blk**, *June 11, 1988*		.65	.50
		FDC, Corpus Christi, TX			1.25
		Pair		1.30	1.00
a.		Imperf., pair		1,750.	—
		Nos. O138A-O141 (5)		7.55	6.30

First day cancellation was applied to 137,721 covers bearing Nos. O138A and O141.

Plates of 400 in four panes of 100.

1989, July 5		Litho.		Perf. 11	
O143	O13	1c **red, blue & black**		.20	.20
		FDC, Washington, DC			1.25

Type of 1985 and

O14

COIL STAMPS

1991		Litho.		Perf. 10 Vert.	
O144	O14	(29c) **red, blue & blk**, *Jan. 22*		.75	.50
		FDC, Washington, DC			1.25
		Pair		1.50	
O145	O13	29c **red, blue & blk**, *May 24*		.65	.30
		FDC, Seattle, WA			1.25
		Pair		1.30	.60

Plates of 400 in four panes of 100.

1991-93		Litho.		Perf. 11	
O146	O13	4c **red, blue & blk**, *Apr. 6*		.20	.30
		FDC, Oklahoma City, OK			1.25
O146A	O13	10c **red, blue & black**, *Oct. 19, 1993*		.25	.30
		FDC, Washington, DC			1.25
O147	O13	19c **red, blue & blk**, *May 24*		.40	.50
		FDC, Seattle, WA			1.25
O148	O13	23c **red, blue & blk**, *May 24*		.45	.30
		FDC, Seattle, WA			1.25
		Horiz. pair with full vert. gutter between		—	
		Vert. pair with full horiz. gutter between		—	
a.		Imperf., pair		200.00	
O151	O13	$1 **red, blue & black**, *Sept. 1993*		2.00	.75
		Nos. O146-O151 (5)		3.30	2.15

COIL STAMPS

Inscribed: No. O152, For U.S. addresses only G.

			Perf. 9.8 Vert.		
O152	O14	(32c) **red, blue & black**, *Dec. 13, 1994*		.65	—
		FDC, Washington, DC			1.25
		Pair		1.30	—
O153	O13	32c **red, blue & black**, *May 9, 1995*		.65	.30
		FDC, Washington, DC			1.25
		Pair		1.30	—

Nos. O146A, O151, O153 have a line of microscopic text below the eagle.

1995, May 9		Litho.		Perf. 11.2	
O154	O13	1c **red, blue & black**		.20	.20
		FDC, Washington, DC			1.25
		Pair		.20	
O155	O13	20c **red, blue & black**		.45	.30
		FDC, Washington, DC			1.25
		Pair		.90	
O156	O13	23c **red, blue & black**		.50	.30
		FDC, Washington, DC			1.25
		Pair		1.00	

Nos. O154-O156 have a line of microscopic text below the eagle.

COIL STAMP

1999, Oct. 8		Litho.		Perf. 9¾ Vert.	
O157	O13	33c **red, blue & black**		.65	
		Pair		1.30	

No. O157 has a line of microscopic text below the eagle.

NEWSPAPER AND PERIODICAL STAMPS

First issued in September 1865 for prepayment of postage on bulk shipments of newspapers and periodicals. From 1875 on, the stamps were affixed to pages of receipt books, sometimes canceled, and retained by the post office.

Virtually all used stamps of Nos. PR1-PR4 are canceled by blue brush strokes. All are rare. Most used stamps of Nos. PR9-PR32, PR57-PR79 and PR81-PR89 are pen canceled (or uncanceled). Handstamp cancellations on any of these issues are rare and sell for much more than catalogue values which are for pen-canceled examples. Used values for Nos. PR102-PR125 are for stamps with handstamp cancellations.

Discontinued on July 1, 1898.

Washington — N1

Franklin — N2

Lincoln — N3

(Illustrations N1, N2 and N3 are half the size of the stamps.)

Printed by the National Bank Note Co.
Plates of 20 subjects in two panes of 10 each.

Typographed and Embossed

1865			Unwmk.		Perf. 12

Thin hard paper, without gum
Size of design: 51x95mm
Colored Border

PR1	N1	5c **dark blue**		375.00	—
		blue		375.00	—
		Block of 4		1,700.	—
a.		5c light blue		400.00	—
PR2	N2	10c **blue green**		140.00	—
a.		10c green		140.00	—
		Block of 4		625.00	—
b.		Pelure paper		165.00	—
PR3	N3	25c **orange red**		190.00	—
		Block of 4		850.00	—
a.		25c carmine red		220.00	—
		Block of 4		975.00	—
b.		Pelure paper		190.00	—

White Border
Yellowish paper

PR4	N1	5c **light blue**		87.50	—
		blue		87.50	—
a.		5c dark blue		87.50	—
		Block of 4		450.00	—
b.		Pelure paper		87.50	—

REPRINTS of 1865 ISSUE
Printed by the National Bank Note Co.

1875					Perf. 12

Hard white paper, without gum
5c White Border, 10c and 25c Colored Border

PR5	N1	5c **dull blue** *(10,000)*		100.00	
		dark blue		100.00	
		Block of 4		450.00	
a.		Printed on both sides		—	
PR6	N2	10c **dark bluish green** *(7765)*		110.00	
		deep green		110.00	
		Block of 4		500.00	
a.		Printed on both sides		2,000.	
PR7	N3	25c **dark carmine** *(6684)*		135.00	
		dark carmine red		135.00	
		Block of 4		600.00	

750 examples of each value, which were remainders from the regular issue, were sold as reprints because of delays in obtaining Nos. PR5-PR7. These remainders cannot be distinguished from Nos. PR2-PR4, and are not included in the reprint quantities.

Printed by the American Bank Note Co.
Soft porous paper, without gum
White Border

1881					
PR8	N1	5c **dark blue** *(5645)*		250.	
		Block of 4		1,250.	

The Continental Bank Note Co. made another special printing from new plates, which did not have the colored border. These exist imperforate and perforated, but they were not regularly issued.

Statue of Freedom on Capitol Dome, by Thomas Crawford — N4

"Justice" — N5

Ceres — N6

"Victory" — N7

Clio — N8

Minerva — N9

Vesta — N10

"Peace" — N11

"Commerce" — N12

Hebe — N13

Indian Maiden — N14

Printed by the Continental Bank Note Co.
Plates of 100 subjects in two panes of 50 each
Size of design: 24x35mm

1875, Jan. 1   Engr.   *Perf. 12*
Thin hard paper

PR9	N4	2c **black**	45.00	22.50
		gray black	45.00	22.50
		greenish black	45.00	22.50
		Block of 4	200.00	120.00
PR10	N4	3c **black**	50.00	25.00
		gray black	50.00	25.00
		Block of 4	225.00	110.00
PR11	N4	4c **black**	50.00	22.50
		gray black	50.00	22.50
		greenish black	50.00	22.50
		Block of 4	225.00	
PR12	N4	6c **black**	62.50	25.00
		gray black	62.50	25.00
		greenish black	62.50	25.00
		Block of 4	275.00	
PR13	N4	8c **black**	70.00	35.00
		gray black	70.00	35.00
		greenish black	70.00	35.00
PR14	N4	9c **black**	160.00	80.00
		gray black	160.00	80.00
		Double transfer at top	185.00	90.00
PR15	N4	10c **black**	80.00	30.00
		gray black	80.00	30.00
		greenish black	80.00	30.00
		Block of 4	375.00	
PR16	N5	12c **rose**	190.00	70.00
		pale rose	190.00	70.00
PR17	N5	24c **rose**	225.00	80.00
		pale rose	225.00	80.00
PR18	N5	36c **rose**	275.00	90.00
		pale rose	275.00	90.00
PR19	N5	48c **rose**	450.00	150.00
		pale rose	450.00	150.00
PR20	N5	60c **rose**	250.00	80.00
		pale rose	250.00	80.00
PR21	N5	72c **rose**	550.00	190.00
		pale rose	550.00	190.00
PR22	N5	84c **rose**	800.00	275.00
		pale rose	800.00	275.00

PR23	N5	96c **rose**	475.00	160.00
		pale rose	475.00	160.00
PR24	N6	$1.92 **dark brown**	600.00	250.00
PR25	N7	$3 **vermilion**	850.00	260.00
PR26	N8	$6 **ultramarine**	1,350.	400.00
		dull ultramarine	1,350.	400.00
PR27	N9	$9 **yellow**	1,750.	450.00
PR28	N10	$12 **blue green**	2,000.	575.00
PR29	N11	$24 **dark gray violet**	2,000.	575.00
PR30	N12	$36 **brown rose**	2,250.	700.00
PR31	N13	$48 **red brown**	2,750.	850.00
PR32	N14	$60 **violet**	2,750.	850.00

SPECIAL PRINTING of 1875 ISSUE
Printed by the Continental Bank Note Co.
Hard white paper, without gum

1875   *Perf. 12*

PR33	N4	2c **gray black** (5,000)	325.00
a.		Horizontally ribbed paper (10,000)	325.00
		Block of 4	—
PR34	N4	3c **gray black** (5,000)	350.00
		Block of 4	—
a.		Horizontally ribbed paper (1,952)	350.00
PR35	N4	4c **gray black** (4451)	400.00
		Block of 4	2,000.
PR36	N4	6c **gray black** (2348)	450.00
PR37	N4	8c **gray black** (1930)	500.00
PR38	N4	9c **gray black** (1795)	600.00
PR39	N4	96c **gray black** (1499)	775.00
a.		Horizontally ribbed paper	—
PR40	N5	12c **pale rose** (1313)	900.00
PR41	N5	24c **pale rose** (411)	1,300.
PR42	N5	36c **pale rose** (330)	1,750.
PR43	N5	48c **pale rose** (268)	2,000.
PR44	N5	60c **pale rose** (222)	2,250.
PR45	N5	72c **pale rose** (174)	2,750.
PR46	N5	84c **pale rose** (164)	3,250.
PR47	N5	96c **pale rose** (141)	4,750.
PR48	N6	$1.92 **dark brown** (41)	11,500.
PR49	N7	$3 **vermilion** (20)	21,500.
PR50	N8	$6 **ultramarine** (14)	27,500.
PR51	N9	$9 **yellow** (4)	42,500.
PR52	N10	$12 **blue green** (5)	37,500.
PR53	N11	$24 **dark gray violet** (2)	—
PR54	N12	$36 **brown rose** (2)	—
PR55	N13	$48 **red brown** (1)	—
PR56	N14	$60 **violet** (1)	—

All values of this issue, Nos. PR33 to PR56, exist imperforate but were not regularly issued.
Numbers in parenthesis are quantities issued.
The existence of No. PR39a has been questioned by specialists. The editors would like to see evidence of its existence.

Printed by the American Bank Note Co.
Soft porous paper

1879   Unwmk.   *Perf. 12*

PR57	N4	2c **black**	17.50	5.50
		gray black	17.50	5.50
		greenish black	17.50	5.50
		Block of 4	77.50	
		Double transfer at top	22.50	10.00
		Cracked plate		
PR58	N4	3c **black**	24.00	7.00
		gray black	24.00	7.00
		intense black	24.00	7.00
		Block of 4	110.00	
		Double transfer at top	27.50	11.00
PR59	N4	4c **black**	21.00	7.00
		gray black	21.00	7.00
		intense black	21.00	7.00
		greenish black	21.00	7.00
		Block of 4	95.00	
		Double transfer at top	24.00	11.00
PR60	N4	6c **black**	42.50	15.00
		gray black	42.50	15.00
		intense black	42.50	15.00
		greenish black	42.50	15.00
		Block of 4	190.00	
		Double transfer at top	45.00	21.00
PR61	N4	8c **black**	42.50	15.00
		gray black	42.50	15.00
		greenish black	42.50	15.00
		Block of 4	190.00	
		Double transfer at top	45.00	21.00
PR62	N4	10c **black**	42.50	15.00
		gray black	42.50	15.00
		greenish black	42.50	15.00
		Block of 4	190.00	
		Double transfer at top	45.00	
PR63	N5	12c **red**	220.00	60.00
		Block of 4	1,000.	
PR64	N5	24c **red**	220.00	60.00
		Block of 4	1,000.	
PR65	N5	36c **red**	500.00	175.00
		Block of 4	2,300.	
PR66	N5	48c **red**	450.00	130.00
PR67	N5	60c **red**	375.00	110.00
		Block of 4	1,700.	
a.		Imperf., pair	2,500.	
PR68	N5	72c **red**	725.00	210.00
PR69	N5	84c **red**	625.00	160.00
		Block of 4	—	
PR70	N5	96c **red**	400.00	110.00
		Block of 4	1,750.	
PR71	N6	$1.92 **pale brown**	300.00	105.00
		brown	300.00	105.00
		Block of 4	1,350.	
		Cracked plate	350.00	
PR72	N7	$3 **red vermilion**	300.00	105.00
		Block of 4	1,350.	
PR73	N8	$6 **blue**	500.00	160.00
		ultramarine	500.00	160.00
PR74	N9	$9 **orange**	375.00	110.00
PR75	N10	$12 **yellow green**	525.00	150.00
PR76	N11	$24 **dark violet**	600.00	180.00

PR77	N12	$36 **Indian red**	725.00	200.00
PR78	N13	$48 **yellow brown**	800.00	275.00
PR79	N14	$60 **purple**	750.00	275.00
		bright purple	750.00	275.00

See Die and Plate Proofs for other imperfs. on stamp paper.

SPECIAL PRINTING of 1879 ISSUE
Printed by the American Bank Note Co.

1883

PR80	N4	2c **intense black** (4,514)	550.	
		Block of 4	2,600.	

Printed by the American Bank Note Co.

1885, July 1   Unwmk.   *Perf. 12*

PR81	N4	1c **black**	27.50	7.50
		gray black	27.50	7.50
		intense black	27.50	7.50
		Block of 4	125.00	
		Double transfer at top	30.00	11.00
PR82	N5	12c **carmine**	80.00	17.50
		deep carmine	80.00	17.50
		rose carmine	80.00	17.50
		Block of 4	375.00	
PR83	N5	24c **carmine**	75.00	20.00
		deep carmine	75.00	20.00
		rose carmine	75.00	20.00
		Block of 4	340.00	
PR84	N5	36c **carmine**	100.00	30.00
		deep carmine	100.00	30.00
		rose carmine	100.00	30.00
		Block of 4	450.00	
PR85	N5	48c **carmine**	150.00	45.00
		deep carmine	150.00	45.00
		Block of 4	675.00	
PR86	N5	60c **carmine**	200.00	65.00
		deep carmine	200.00	65.00
		Block of 4	900.00	
PR87	N5	72c **carmine**	200.00	70.00
		deep carmine	200.00	70.00
		rose carmine	200.00	70.00
		Block of 4	900.00	
PR88	N5	84c **carmine**	400.00	160.00
		rose carmine	400.00	160.00
		Block of 4	1,750.	
PR89	N5	96c **carmine**	325.00	120.00
		rose carmine	325.00	120.00
		Block of 4	1,450.	

See Die and Plate Proofs for imperfs. on stamp paper.

Printed by the Bureau of Engraving and Printing

1894   Unwmk.   *Perf. 12*
Soft wove paper

PR90	N4	1c **intense black**	175.00	—
		Block of 4	750.00	
		Double transfer at top	190.00	
PR91	N4	2c **intense black**	175.00	—
		Block of 4	750.00	
		Double transfer at top	190.00	
PR92	N4	4c **intense black**	200.00	—
		Block of 4	900.00	
PR93	N4	6c **intense black**	2,750.	—
		Block of 4	—	
PR94	N4	10c **intense black**	400.00	—
		Block of 4	1,800.	
PR95	N5	12c **pink**	1,200.	—
		Block of 4	5,500.	
PR96	N5	24c **pink**	1,200.	—
		Block of 4	5,500.	
PR97	N5	36c **pink**	13,500.	—
		Block of 4	—	
PR98	N5	60c **pink**	13,500.	—
		Block of 4	—	
PR99	N5	96c **pink**	15,000.	—
PR100	N7	$3 **scarlet**	18,000.	—
PR101	N8	$6 **pale blue**	27,500.	—

Statue of Freedom — N15

N16

N17

N18

N19

N20

N21

N22

1895, Feb. 1   **Unwmk.**   *Perf. 12*

Size of designs: 1c-50c, 21x34mm

$2-$100, 24x35mm

PR102 N15	1c	**black**	75.00	12.50
		Never hinged	130.00	
		Block of 4	325.00	55.00
PR103 N15	2c	**black**	75.00	12.50
		gray black	75.00	12.50
		Never hinged	130.00	
		Block of 4	325.00	—
		Double transfer at top	85.00	—
PR104 N15	5c	**black**	100.00	20.00
		gray black	100.00	20.00
		Never hinged	175.00	
		Block of 4	450.00	
PR105 N15	10c	**black**	225.00	52.50
		Never hinged	400.00	
		Block of 4	1,000.	
PR106 N16	25c	**carmine**	325.00	55.00
		Never hinged	575.00	
		Block of 4	1,450.	
PR107 N16	50c	**carmine**	750.00	150.00
		Never hinged	1,250.	
		Block of 4	3,500.	
PR108 N17	$2	**scarlet**	850.00	110.00
		Never hinged	1,450.	
PR109 N18	$5	**ultramarine**	1,050.	225.00
		Never hinged	1,750.	
PR110 N19	$10	**green**	1,200.	250.00
		Never hinged	2,000.	
PR111 N20	$20	**slate**	1,650.	450.00
		Never hinged	2,800.	
PR112 N21	$50	**dull rose**	1,750.	450.00
		Never hinged	3,000.	
PR113 N22	$100	**purple**	1,750.	525.00
		Never hinged	3,000.	

Nos. PR102-PR113 were printed from plates with arrows in the top, bottom and side margins, but no guidelines between the stamps.

1895-97   **Wmk. 191**   *Perf. 12*

PR114 N15	1c	**black**, *Jan. 11, 1896*	6.00	4.00
		gray black	6.00	4.00
		Never hinged	10.50	
		Block of 4	25.00	—
PR115 N15	2c	**black**, *Nov. 21, 1895*	6.50	4.00
		gray black	6.50	4.00
		Never hinged	11.25	

		Block of 4	27.50	—
PR116 N15	5c	**black**, *Feb. 12, 1896*	10.00	6.50
		gray black	10.00	6.50
		Never hinged	17.50	
		Block of 4	45.00	—
PR117 N15	10c	**black**, *Sept. 13, 1895*	6.50	4.25
		gray black	6.50	4.25
		Never hinged	11.25	
		Block of 4	27.50	—
PR118 N16	25c	**carmine**, *Oct. 11, 1895*	12.50	10.00
		lilac rose	12.50	10.00
		Never hinged	22.00	
		Block of 4	55.00	—
PR119 N16	50c	**carmine**, *Sept. 19, 1895*	15.00	15.00
		rose carmine	15.00	15.00
		lilac rose	15.00	15.00
		Never hinged	26.50	
		Block of 4	65.00	—
PR120 N17	$2	**scarlet**, *Jan. 23, 1897*	20.00	22.50
		scarlet vermilion	20.00	22.50
		Never hinged	35.00	
		Block of 4	87.50	
PR121 N18	$5	**dark blue**, *Jan. 16, 1896*	35.00	35.00
		Never hinged	62.50	
		Block of 4	160.00	
a.		$5 light blue	175.00	70.00
		Never hinged	300.00	
PR122 N19	$10	**green**, *Mar. 5, 1896*	35.00	35.00
		Never hinged	62.50	
		Block of 4	160.00	
PR123 N20	$20	**slate**, *Jan. 27, 1896*	37.50	37.50
		Never hinged	65.00	
		Block of 4	170.00	
PR124 N21	$50	**dull rose**, *July 31, 1897*	50.00	42.50
		Never hinged	87.50	
		Block of 4	220.00	
PR125 N22	$100	**purple**, *Jan. 23, 1896*	55.00	47.50
		Never hinged	95.00	
		Block of 4	240.00	
		Nos. PR114-PR125 (12)	289.00	263.75

Nos. PR114-PR125 were printed from the original plates with guide lines added in November 1895. Top and bottom plate strips and blocks of Nos. PR114-PR119 exist both with and without vertical guidelines.

In 1899 the Government sold 26,989 sets of these stamps, but, as the stock of high values was not sufficient to make up the required number, an additional printing was made of the $5, $10, $20, $50 and $100. These are virtually indistinguishable from earlier printings.

POSTAL NOTE STAMPS

Postal note stamps were issued to supplement the regular money order service. They were a means of sending amounts under $1. One or two Postal note stamps, totaling 1c to 99c, were affixed to United States Postal Notes and canceled by the clerk. The stamps were on the second of three parts, the one retained by the post office redeeming the Postal Note. They were discontinued March 31, 1951.

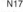

MO1

ROTARY PRESS PRINTING

1945, Feb. 1   **Unwmk.**   *Perf. 11x10½*

PN1	MO1	1c **black** (155950-155951)	.20	.20
PN2	MO1	2c **black** (156003-156004)	.20	.20
PN3	MO1	3c **black** (156062-156063)	.20	.20
PN4	MO1	4c **black** (156942-156943)	.25	.20
PN5	MO1	5c **black** (156261-156262)	.35	.20
PN6	MO1	6c **black** (156064-156065)	.40	.20
PN7	MO1	7c **black** (156075-156076)	.55	.20
PN8	MO1	8c **black** (156077-156078)	.65	.20
PN9	MO1	9c **black** (156251-156252)	.70	.20
PN10	MO1	10c **black** (156274-156275)	.80	.20
PN11	MO1	20c **black** (156276-156277)	1.60	.20
PN12	MO1	30c **black** (156303-156304)	2.10	.20
PN13	MO1	40c **black** (156283-156284)	2.60	.20
PN14	MO1	50c **black** (156322-156323)	3.25	.20
PN15	MO1	60c **black** (156324-156325)	4.25	.20
PN16	MO1	70c **black** (156344-156345)	4.75	.20
PN17	MO1	80c **black** (156326-156327)	5.75	.20
PN18	MO1	90c **black** (156352-156353)	6.50	.20
		Nos. PN1-PN18 (18)	35.10	3.60

Blocks of four and plate number blocks of four are valued at 4 and 15 times the unused single value.

Postal note stamps exist on postal note cards with first day cancellation.

Numbers in parentheses are plate Nos.

PARCEL POST STAMPS

The Act of Congress approved Aug. 24, 1912, created postage rates on 4th class mail weighing 4 ounces or less at 1 cent per ounce or fraction. On mail over 4 ounces, the rate was by the pound. These rates were to be prepaid by distinctive postage stamps. Under this provision, the Post Office Department prepared 12 parcel post and 5 parcel post due stamps, usable only on parcel post packages starting Jan. 1, 1913. Other stamps were not usable on parcel post starting on that date.

Beginning on Nov. 27, 1912, the stamps were shipped to post offices offering parcel post service. Approximate shipping dates were: 1c, 2c, 5c, 25c, 1c due, 5c due, Nov. 27; 10c, 2c due, Dec. 9; 4c, 10c due, Dec. 12; 15c, 20c, 25c due, Dec. 16; 75c, Dec. 18. There was no prohibition on sale of the stamps prior to Jan. 1, 1913. Undoubtedly many were used on 4th class mail in Dec. 1912. Fourth class mail was expanded by adding former 2nd and 3rd class categories and was renamed "parcel post" effective Jan. 1, 1913. Normally 4th class (parcel post) mail did not receive a dated cancel unless a special service was involved. Small pieces, such as samples, are known with 1st class cancels.

With the approval of the Interstate Commerce Commission, the Postmaster General directed, in Order No. 7241 dated June 26, 1913, and effective July 1, 1913, that regular postage stamps should be valid on parcels. Parcel post stamps then became usable as regular stamps.

Parcel post and parcel post due stamps remained on sale, but no further printings were made. Remainders, consisting of 3,510,345 of the 75c, were destroyed in Sept. 1921.

The 20c was the first postage stamp of any country to show an airplane.

Post Office Clerk — PP1

City Carrier — PP2

Railway Postal Clerk — PP3

Rural Carrier — PP4

Mail Train and Mail Bag on Rack — PP5

Steamship "Kronprinz Wilhelm" and Mail Tender, New York — PP6

Automobile Service — PP7

Airplane Carrying Mail — PP8

Manufacturing (Steel Plant, South Chicago) — PP9

Dairying — PP10

Harvesting — PP11

Fruit Growing (Florida Orange Grove) — PP12

1919 TEN

Plate number and imprint consisting of value in words.

Marginal imprints, consisting of value in words, were added to the plates on January 27, 1913.

Designed by Clair Aubrey Huston.

Plates of 180 subjects in four panes of 45 each.

1913   Wmk. 190   Engr.   Perf. 12

Q1	PP1	1c	**carmine rose** *(209,691,094)*	5.25	1.50
			carmine	5.25	1.50
			Never hinged	9.25	
			First day cover, *July 1, 1913*		1,500.
			On cover, 1913-25		5.75
			Block of 4	22.50	8.00
			P# block of 4, Impt.	42.50	
			P# block of 6, Impt.	105.00	
			P# block of 6	110.00	
			Never hinged	165.00	
			Double transfer	8.75	4.00
Q2	PP2	2c	**carmine rose** *(206,417,253)*	6.75	1.25
			carmine	6.75	1.25
			Never hinged	12.00	
			lake	—	
			First day cover, *July 1, 1913*		1,500.
			On cover, 1913-25		5.75
			Block of 4	30.00	6.25
			P# block of 4, Impt.	47.50	
			P# block of 6, Impt.	125.00	
			P# block of 6	145.00	
			Never hinged	220.00	
			Double transfer	—	—
Q3	PP3	3c	**carmine,** *Apr. 5, 1913* *(29,027,433)*	13.50	5.75
			deep carmine	13.50	5.75
			Never hinged	24.00	
			First day cover, *July 1, 1913*		3,250.
			On cover, 1913-25		18.00
			Block of 4	57.50	30.00

		P# block of 4, Impt.	100.00	
		P# block of 6, Impt.	260.00	
		P# block of 6	235.00	
		P# block of 8, Impt. (side)	310.00	
		Never hinged	460.00	
		Retouched at lower right corner (No. 6257 LL 7)	26.00	14.50
		Double transfer (No. 6257 LL 6)	26.00	14.50
Q4	PP4	4c	**carmine rose** *(76,743,813)*	37.50	3.00
			carmine	37.50	3.00
			Never hinged	65.00	
			First day cover, *July 1, 1913*		3,250.
			On cover, 1913-25		65.00
			Block of 4	160.00	15.00
			P# block of 4, Impt.	360.00	
			P# block of 6, Impt.	1,050.	
			P# block of 6	1,000.	
			Never hinged	1,500.	
			Double transfer	—	—
Q5	PP5	5c	**carmine rose** *(108,153,993)*	32.50	2.25
			carmine	32.50	2.25
			Never hinged	57.50	
			First day cover, *July 1, 1913*		3,250.
			On cover, 1913-25		42.50
			Block of 4	135.00	14.00
			P# block of 4, Impt.	350.00	
			P# block of 6, Impt.	1,000.	
			P# block of 6	975.00	
			Never hinged	1,450.	
			Double transfer	45.00	6.25
Q6	PP6	10c	**carmine rose** *(56,896,653)*	52.50	3.00
			carmine	52.50	3.00
			Never hinged	90.00	
			On cover, 1913-25		55.00
			Block of 4	240.00	27.50
			P# block of 4, Impt.	440.00	
			P# block of 6, Impt.	1,150.	
			P# block of 6	1,000.	
			Never hinged	1,500.	
			Double transfer	—	—
Q7	PP7	15c	**carmine rose** *(21,147,033)*	67.50	12.00
			carmine	67.50	12.00
			Never hinged	120.00	
			First day cover, *July 1, 1913*		350.00
			On cover, 1913-25		85.00
			Block of 4	400.00	
			P# block of 4, Impt.	700.00	
			P# block of 6, Impt.	2,600.	
			P# block of 8, Impt.	3,100.	
			P# block of 6	2,300.	
			Never hinged	3,450.	
Q8	PP8	20c	**carmine rose** *(17,142,393)*	140.00	25.00
			carmine	140.00	25.00
			Never hinged	250.00	
			On cover, 1913-25		750.00
			Block of 4	600.00	125.00
			P# block of 4, Impt.	1,450.	
			P# block of 6, Impt.	6,500.	
			P# block of 8, Impt. (side)	7,000.	
			P# block of 6	6,500.	
			Never hinged	9,750.	
Q9	PP9	25c	**carmine rose** *(21,940,653)*	67.50	6.75
			carmine	67.50	6.75
			Never hinged	120.00	
			On cover, 1913-25		300.00
			Block of 4	310.00	50.00
			P# block of 6, Impt.	2,700.	
			P# block of 8, Impt. (side)	3,500.	
			P# block of 6	2,400.	
			Never hinged	3,600.	
Q10	PP10	50c	**carmine rose,** *Mar. 15, 1913* *(2,117,793)*	280.00	40.00
			carmine	280.00	40.00
			Never hinged	500.00	
			On cover, 1913-25		—
			Block of 4	1,275.	270.00
			P# block of 4, Impt.	1,950.	
			Never hinged	2,900.	
			P# block of 6, Impt.	22,500.	
			Never hinged	28,500.	
Q11	PP11	75c	**carmine rose** *(2,772,615)*	95.00	35.00
			carmine	95.00	35.00
			Never hinged	165.00	
			On cover, 1913-25		—
			Block of 4	425.00	200.00
			P# block of 4, Impt.	4,000.	
			P# block of 8, Impt. (side)	3,600.	
			P# block of 6	3,000.	
			Never hinged	4,500.	
Q12	PP12	$1	**carmine rose,** *Jan. 3, 1913* *(1,053,273)*	350.00	35.00
			carmine	350.00	35.00

Never hinged	625.00			
On cover, 1913-25		1,100.		
Block of 4	1,550.	180.00		
P# block of 6, Impt.	20,000.			
Never hinged	27,500.			

P# block of 8, Impt. (side)	21,000.	
P# block of 6	18,000.	
Nos. Q1-Q12 (12)	1,148.	170.50
Nos. Q1-Q12, never hinged	2,038.	

The 1c, 2c, 4c and 5c are known in parcel post usage postmarked Jan. 1, 1913.

The 20c is the most difficult denomination to find well centered.

United States parcel post stamps can be mounted in the Scott National and Minuteman albums.

PARCEL POST POSTAGE DUE STAMPS

See notes preceding Scott No. Q1. Parcel Post Due stamps were allowed to be used as regular postage due stamps from July 1, 1913.

PPD1

Designed by Clair Aubrey Huston

Plates of 180 subjects in four panes of 45

1913		Wmk. 190	Engr.		Perf. 12
JQ1	PPD1	1c **dark green** (7,322,400)		11.00	4.50
		yellowish green		11.00	4.50
		Never hinged		19.00	

	On cover, 1913-25		150.00
	Block of 4	50.00	35.00
	P# block of 6	550.00	
	Never hinged	825.00	
JQ2 PPD1	2c **dark green** (3,132,000)	85.00	17.50
	yellowish green	85.00	17.50
	Never hinged	150.00	
	On cover, 1913-25		200.00
	Block of 4	375.00	125.00
	P# block of 6	3,750.	
	Never hinged	5,500.	
JQ3 PPD1	5c **dark green** (5,840,100)	15.00	5.50
	yellowish green	15.00	5.50
	Never hinged	26.00	
	On cover, 1913-25		185.00
	Block of 4	65.00	37.50
	P# block of 6	600.00	

	Never hinged	900.00	
JQ4 PPD1 10c	**dark green** (2,124,540)	175.00	45.00
	yellowish green	175.00	45.00
	Never hinged	310.00	
	On cover, 1913-25		650.00
	Block of 4	775.00	325.00
	P# block of 6	9,750.	
	Never hinged	13,500.	
JQ5 PPD1 25c	**dark green** (2,117,700)	105.00	5.00
	yellowish green	105.00	5.00
	Never hinged	185.00	
	On cover, 1913-25		—
	Block of 4	475.00	35.00
	P# block of 6	5,000.	
	Nos. JQ1-JQ5 (5)	391.00	77.50
	Nos. JQ1-JQ5, never hinged	690.00	

SPECIAL HANDLING STAMPS

The Postal Service Act, approved February 28, 1925, provided for a special handling stamp of the 25-cent denomination for use on fourth-class mail matter, which would secure for such mail matter the expeditious handling accorded to mail matter of the first class.

PP13

FLAT PLATE PRINTING

Plates of 200 subjects in four panes of 50

1925-55		Unwmk.		Perf. 11
QE1 PP13 10c	**yellow green,** *1955*		1.60	1.00
	Never hinged		2.50	
	Block of 4		6.75	5.75
	P# block of 6		20.00	
	Never hinged		29.00	
a.	Wet printing, *June 25, 1928*		3.25	1.00
	Never hinged		5.25	
	First day cover			45.00
QE2 PP13 15c	**yellow green,** *1955*		1.75	.90
	Never hinged		2.75	
	Block of 4		7.50	5.75
	P# block of 6		30.00	
	Never hinged		42.50	
a.	Wet printing, *June 25, 1928*		3.50	.90
	Never hinged		5.50	
	First day cover			45.00
QE3 PP13 20c	**yellow green,** *1955*		2.75	1.50
	Never hinged		4.40	
	Block of 4		12.50	11.00
	P# block of 6		32.50	
	Never hinged		45.00	
a.	Wet printing, *June 25, 1928*		4.25	1.50
	Never hinged		6.75	
	First day cover			45.00
	First day cover, Nos. QE1a-QE3a			350.00
QE4 PP13 25c	**yellow green,** *1929*		22.50	7.50
	Never hinged		36.00	
	Block of 4		95.00	32.50
	P# block of 6		260.00	
	Never hinged		375.00	
a.	25c **deep green,** *Apr. 11, 1925*		32.50	5.50
	Never hinged		52.50	
	First day cover			225.00
	Block of 4		140.00	30.00
	P# block of 6		330.00	
	Never hinged		475.00	
	"A" and second "T" of "States" joined at top (Pl. 17103)		50.00	22.50

"A" and second "T" of "States" and "T" and "A" of "Postage" joined at top (Pl. 17103)	50.00	45.00
Nos. QE1-QE4 (4)	28.60	10.90
Nos. QE1-QE4, never hinged	45.65	

See note on Wet and Dry Printings following No. 1029.

POSTAL INSURANCE STAMPS

Postal insurance stamps were issued to pay insurance on parcels for loss or damage. The stamps come in a booklet of one which also carries instructions for use and a receipt form for use if there is a claim. The booklets were sold by vending machine. Values in unused column are for complete booklets. Values in used column are for used stamps.

PPI1

1965, Aug.   **Typo.**   *Rouletted 9 at Top*
QI1 PPI1 (10c) **dark red**   135.00 —

No. QI1 paid insurance up to $10. It was sold at the Canoga Park, Calif., automatic post office which opened Aug. 19, 1965. The "V" stands for "Vended."

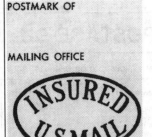

PPI2

1966, Mar. 26   **Litho.**   *Perf. 11 at Top*
QI2 PPI2 (20c) **red**   4.00 —

No. QI2 paid insurance up to $15. The rate increased from 20c to 25c on Apr. 18, 1976, and to 40c on July 18, 1976. The QI2 booklet comes with white or black cover.

No 25c postal insurance stamps were printed. Existing copies of No. QI2 had 5c postage stamps added and the value on the cover was changed to 25c, usually by hand. Twenty-cent stamps were added to make the 40c rate since new postal insurance stamps were not issued until 1977.

Type PPI2 with "FEE PAID THROUGH VENDING MACHINE" Added Below

1977-81   **Litho.**   *Perf. 11 at Top*
QI3 PPI2 (40c) **black**   4.00 —

Available for use by Nov. 28, 1977 or earlier.

QI4 PPI2 (50c) **green**   3.00 —

The rate increased to 50c on May 29, 1978.

QI5 PPI2 (45c) **red**, *1981*   3.00 —

FIRST DAY COVERS

All envelopes or cards are postmarked Washington, D.C., unless otherwise stated. Minors and sublistings without dates have the same date and city (if none is otherwise mentioned) as the previous listing. Minors and sublistings with dates differing from the previous listing are postmarked in Washington, D.C. unless otherwise stated.

Values are for first day covers in very fine condition, without tears, stains or smeared postmarks, and with sound stamps that have fresh color and are not badly off center.

Printed cachets on covers before Scott Nos. 772 and C20 sell at a substantial premium. Values for covers of Nos. 772-986 and C20-C45 are for those with the most common cachets and addressed. Unaddressed covers sell at a substantial premium and covers without cachet sell at a substantial discount. Values for covers from Scott 987 and C46 onward are for those with the most common cachets and unaddressed.

Values for 1st class rate stamps are for covers bearing single stamps. Blocks of 4 on first day covers usually sell for about 1½ times as much as singles; Plate number blocks of 4 at about 3 times; Plate number blocks of 6 at about 4 times; coil line pairs at about 3 times. Stamps with denominations less than the first class rate will have the proper multiple to make the rate if practical or additional postage. (See Nos. 899, 907-908, 930-931, etc.)

Dates given are those on which the stamps were first *officially* placed on sale. Many instances are known of stamps being sold in advance, contrary to regulations.

Numbers in parentheses are quantities stated to have received the first day cancel.

Listings from Scott Nos. 551 and C4 are for covers canceled at cities officially designated by the Post Office Department or Postal Service. Some tagged varieties and cities of special interest are exceptions.

Air post first day covers are listed following the Postage first day covers. Envelope, postal card and other first day covers are with the regular listings.

Quantities given for se-tenant issues include the multiple and any single or combination of singles (see No. 2375a).

1851-57

5A	1c **blue, type Ib**, *July 1, 1851,* Boston, Mass.	120,000.
7	1c **blue, type II**, *July 1, 1851,* any city	17,500.
	Same on printed circular	4,000.
10	3c **orange brown**, *July 1, 1851,* any city	12,500.

The No. 5A cover is unique. Value is based on 1996 auction sale.

1861

64	3c **pink**, *Aug. 17, 1861,* Baltimore, Md.	17,500.
64b	3c **rose pink**, *Aug. 17, 1861,* Baltimore, Md.	23,000.

The Nos. 64 and 64b covers are each unique. Values based on 1999 and 1996 auction sales, respectively.

1883

210	2c **red brown**, *Oct. 1,* any city	2,000.
210, 211	2c, 4c **blue green**, *Oct. 1,* New York, N.Y.	36,000.

The Nos. 210, 211 cover is unique. Value is based on 1996 auction sale.

1890

219D	2c **lake**, *Feb. 22,* any city	12,500.

1893

COLUMBIAN EXPOSITION ISSUE

230	1c **deep blue**, *Jan. 2,* any city	4,000.
231	2c **brown violet**, *Jan. 2,* any city	3,500.
232	3c **green**, *Jan. 2,* any city	6,000.
233	4c **ultramarine**, *Jan. 2,* any city	9,500.
234	5c **chocolate**, *Jan. 2,* any city	16,000.
235	6c **purple**, *Jan. 2,* any city	20,000.
237	10c **black brown**, *Jan. 2,* any city	7,500.
242	$2 **brown red**, *Jan. 2,* any city	52,500.

Jan. 1, 1893, postmarks are known on the Columbian issue. As that day was a Sunday, specialists recognize both Jan. 1 and 2 as "first day."

1898

TRANS-MISSISSIPPI EXPOSITION ISSUE

285	1c **green**, *June 17,* any city	12,500.
286	2c **copper red**, *June 17,* any city	9,500.
287	4c **orange**, *June 17*	27,500.
288	5c **dull blue**, *June 17,* any city	17,500.
289	8c **violet brown**, *June 17,* any city	20,000.
290	10c **gray violet**, *June 17*	27,500.
	285-290, all 6 on one cover, *June 17*	50,000.
291	50c **sage green**, *June 17,* any city	30,000.
292	$1 **black**, *June 17,* any city	

1901

PAN AMERICAN EXPOSITION ISSUE

294	1c **green & black**, *May 1,* any city	4,500.
295	2c **carmine & black**, *May 1,* any city	2,750.
297	5c **ultra. & blk.**, *May 1,* any city	15,000.
	294, 295, 297 on one cover, *May 1,* Boston, Mass.	9,500.
	294, 296, 297 on one cover, *May 1,* Boston, Mass.	24,000.
	295, 298 on one cover, *May 1,* Washington, D.C.	9,500.
	296, 298 on one cover, *May 1,* Boston, Mass.	15,000.
	297, 298 on one cover, *May 1,* Philadelphia, Pa.	15,000.
	294-299, complete set of 6 on one cover *May 1,* any city	27,500.

1903

301	2c **carmine**, *Jan. 17,* any city	2,750.

1904

LOUISIANA PURCHASE EXPOSITION ISSUE

323	1c **green**, *Apr. 30,* any city	6,000.
324	2c **carmine**, *Apr. 30,* any city	4,750.
325	3c **violet**, *Apr. 30,* any city	5,000.
326	5c **dark blue**, *Apr. 30,* any city	22,500.
327	10c **red brown**, *Apr. 30,* any city	24,000.
	323-327, all 5 on one cover, *Apr. 30,* any city	80,000.

The Nos. 323-327 combination cover is unique. Value is based on 1996 auction sale.

1907

328	1c **Jamestown**, *Apr. 26,* any city	6,000.
329	2c **Jamestown**, *Apr. 26,* any city	9,000.

1909

367	2c **Lincoln**, *Feb. 12,* any city	500.
		Imperf
368	2c **Lincoln**, *Feb. 12,* any city	12,500.

1909

ALASKA-YUKON ISSUE

| 370 | 2c **carmine**, *June 1, any city* | 3,000. |
| | On Expo-related picture postcard, *June 1* | 4,000. |

1909

HUDSON-FULTON ISSUE

| 372 | 2c **carmine**, *Sept. 25, any city* | 750. |
| | On Expo-related picture postcard, *Sept. 25* | 1,250. |

Imperf

| 373 | 2c **carmine**, *Sept. 25, any city* | 7,000. |

1913

PANAMA-PACIFIC ISSUE

397	1c **green**, *Jan. 1, any city*	5,000.
399	5c **blue**, *Jan. 1*	21,000.
400	10c **orange yellow**, *Jan. 1*	10,000.
	397, 399 & 400, all 3 on one cover, San Francisco, Cal.	10,000.

1916-22

COIL STAMP

| 497 | 10c **orange yellow**, *Jan. 31, 1922, any city* | 4,500. |

1918-20

OFFSET PRINTING

| 526 | 2c **carmine**, type IV, *Mar. 15, 1920* | 800. |

1919

| 537 | 3c **Victory**, *Mar. 3, any city* | 750. |

1920 — *Perf. 10x11*

REGULAR ISSUE

| 542 | 1c **green**, *May 26* | 1,750. |

1920

548	1c **Pilgrim**, *Dec. 21, any city*, pair	900.
549	2c **Pilgrim**, *Dec. 21, any city*	700.
	Plymouth, Mass.	950.
550	5c **Pilgrim**, *Dec. 21*	—
	548-550, complete set of 3 on one cover, *Dec. 21, any city*	2,500.
	Washington, D.C.	3,000.

1922-26 — *Perf. 11*

551	½c **Hale**, *Apr. 4, 1925*, block of 4	17.50
	New Haven, Conn.	22.50
	551 & 576 on one cover, *Apr. 4, 1925*, New Haven, Conn.	150.00
552	1c **Franklin**, *Jan. 17, 1923*, pair	25.00
	Philadelphia, Pa.	42.50
553	1½c **Harding**, *Mar. 19, 1925*, pair	30.00
	553, 582, 598 on one cover, *Mar. 19, 1925*	175.00
554	2c **Washington**, *Jan. 15, 1923*	37.50
555	3c **Lincoln**, *Feb. 12, 1923*	35.00
	Hodgenville, Ky.	300.00
556	4c **Martha Washington**, *Jan. 15, 1923*	60.00
557	5c **Roosevelt**, *Oct. 27, 1922*	125.00
	New York, N.Y.	175.00
	Oyster Bay, N.Y.	850.00
558	6c **Garfield**, *Nov. 20, 1922*	225.00
559	7c **McKinley**, *May 1, 1923*	175.00
	Niles, O.	250.00
560	8c **Grant**, *May 1, 1923*	175.00
561	9c **Jefferson**, *Jan. 15, 1923*	175.00
562	10c **Monroe**, *Jan. 15, 1923*	175.00
563	11c **Hayes**, *Oct. 4, 1922*	600.00
	Fremont, O.	3,000.
564	12c **Cleveland**, *Mar. 20, 1923*	175.00
	Boston, Mass. (Philatelic Exhibition)	175.00
	Caldwell, N.J.	210.00
565	14c **American Indian**, *May 1, 1923*	400.00
	Muskogee, Okla.	1,100.
566	15c **Statue of Liberty**, *Nov. 11, 1922*	550.00
567	20c **Golden Gate**, *May 1, 1923*	500.00
	San Francisco, Cal.	2,500.
568	25c **Niagara Falls**, *Nov. 11, 1922*	650.00
569	30c **American Buffalo**, *Mar. 20, 1923*	850.00
570	50c **Arlington**, *Nov. 11, 1922*	1,250.
571	$1 **Lincoln Memorial**, *Feb. 12, 1923*	7,000.
	Springfield, Ill.	7,500.
572	$2 **U.S. Capitol**, *Mar. 20, 1923*	15,000.
573	$5 **America**, *Mar. 20, 1923*	25,000.

Imperf

| 576 | 1½c **Harding**, *Apr. 4, 1925* | 45.00 |

Perf. 10

581	1c **Franklin**, *Oct. 17, 1923*, not precanceled	6,000.
582	1½c **Harding**, *Mar. 19, 1925*	40.00
583a	2c **Washington** booklet pane of 6, *Aug. 27, 1926*	1,500.
584	3c **Lincoln**, *Aug. 1, 1925*	55.00
585	4c **Martha Washington**, *Apr. 4, 1925*	55.00
586	5c **Roosevelt**, *Apr. 4, 1925*	57.50
587	6c **Garfield**, *Apr. 4, 1925*	60.00
588	7c **McKinley**, *May 29, 1926*	70.00
589	8c **Grant**, *May 29, 1926*	72.50
590	9c **Jefferson**, *May 29, 1926*	72.50
591	10c **Monroe**, *June 8, 1925*	95.00

Perf. 10 Vertically

597	1c **Franklin**, *July 18, 1923*	600.00
598	1½c **Harding**, *Mar. 19, 1925*	60.00
599	2c **Washington**, *Jan. 15, 1923*	1,500.

600	3c **Lincoln**, *May 10, 1924*	80.00
602	5c **Roosevelt**, *Mar. 5, 1924*	85.00
603	10c **Monroe**, *Dec. 1, 1924*	100.00

No. 599 is known used on Jan. 10, 11 and 13, 1923 (one each day). Jan. 15 was the first day of sale in Washington, D. C.

Perf. 10 Horizontally

604	1c **Franklin**, *July 19, 1924*	90.00
605	1½c **Harding**, *May 9, 1925*	70.00
606	2c **Washington**, *Dec. 31, 1923*	125.00

1923

610	2c **Harding**, perf. 11, *Sept. 1*	30.00
	Marion, O.	20.00
611	2c **Harding**, imperf., *Nov. 15*	90.00
612	2c **Harding**, perf. 10, *Sept. 12*	100.00

1924

614	1c **Huguenot-Walloon**, *May 1*, pair	40.00
	Albany, N.Y	40.00
	Allentown, Pa.	40.00
	Charleston, S.C.	40.00
	Jacksonville, Fla.	40.00
	Lancaster, Pa.	40.00
	Mayport, Fla.	40.00
	New Rochelle, N.Y.	40.00
	New York, N.Y.	40.00
	Philadelphia, Pa.	40.00
	Reading, Pa.	40.00
615	2c **Huguenot-Walloon**, *May 1*	55.00
	Albany, N.Y.	55.00
	Allentown, Pa.	55.00
	Charleston, S.C.	55.00
	Jacksonville, Fla.	55.00
	Lancaster, Pa.	55.00
	Mayport, Fla.	55.00
	New Rochelle, N.Y.	55.00
	New York, N.Y.	55.00
	Philadelphia, Pa.	55.00
	Reading, Pa.	55.00
616	5c **Huguenot-Walloon**, *May 1*	80.00
	Albany, N.Y.	80.00
	Allentown, Pa.	80.00
	Charleston, S.C.	80.00
	Jacksonville, Fla.	80.00
	Lancaster, Pa.	80.00
	Mayport, Fla.	80.00
	New Rochelle, N.Y.	80.00
	New York, N.Y.	80.00
	Philadelphia, Pa.	80.00
	Reading, Pa.	80.00
	614-616 on one cover, any city	175.00

1925

617	1c **Lexington-Concord**, *Apr. 4*, pair	35.00
	Boston, Mass.	35.00
	Cambridge, Mass.	32.50
	Concord, Mass.	35.00
	Concord Junction, Mass.	37.50
	Lexington, Mass.	37.50
618	2c **Lexington-Concord**, *Apr. 4*	37.50
	Boston, Mass.	37.50
	Cambridge, Mass.	37.50
	Concord, Mass	37.50
	Concord Junction, Mass.	37.50
	Lexington, Mass.	37.50
619	5c **Lexington-Concord**, *Apr. 4*	85.00
	Boston, Mass.	85.00
	Cambridge, Mass.	85.00
	Concord, Mass.	85.00
	Concord Junction, Mass.	85.00
	Lexington, Mass.	85.00
	617-619 on one cover, Concord Junction or Lexington	210.00
	Set of 3 on one cover, any other city	160.00

1925

620	2c **Norse-American**, *May 18*	25.00
	Algona, Iowa	25.00
	Benson, Minn.	25.00
	Decorah, Iowa	25.00
	Minneapolis, Minn.	25.00
	Northfield, Minn.	25.00
	St. Paul, Minn.	25.00
621	5c **Norse-American**, *May 18*	40.00
	Algona, Iowa	40.00
	Benson, Minn.	40.00
	Decorah, Iowa	40.00
	Minneapolis, Minn.	40.00
	Northfield, Minn.	40.00
	St. Paul, Minn.	40.00
	620-621 on one cover, any city	55.00

1925-26

622	13c **Harrison**, *Jan. 11, 1926*	22.50
	Indianapolis, Ind.	32.50
	North Bend, Ohio *(500)*	160.00
623	17c **Wilson**, *Dec. 28, 1925*	27.50
	New York, N.Y.	27.50
	Princeton, N.J.	27.50
	Staunton, Va.	27.50

1926

627	2c **Sesquicentennial**, *May 10*	10.00
	Boston, Mass.	10.00
	Philadelphia, Pa.	10.00
628	5c **Ericsson**, *May 29*	30.00
	Chicago, Ill.	30.00
	Minneapolis, Minn.	30.00
	New York, N.Y.	30.00
629	2c **White Plains**, New York, N.Y., *Oct. 18*	6.25
	New York, N.Y., Inter-Philatelic Exhibition Agency cancellation	6.25
	White Plains, N.Y.	6.25

	Washington, D.C., *Oct. 28*	3.50
630	Sheet of 25, *Oct. 18*	1,500.
	Sheet of 25, *Oct. 28*	1,000.

1926-34 — *Imperf.*

| 631 | 1½c **Harding**, *Aug. 27, 1926*, pair | 35.00 |

Perf. 11x10½

632	1c **Franklin**, *June 10, 1927*, pair	45.00
632a	Booklet pane of 6, *Nov. 2, 1927*	3,250.
633	1½c **Harding**, *May 17, 1927*, pair	45.00
634	2c **Washington**, *Dec. 10, 1926*	47.50
635	3c **Lincoln**, *Feb. 3, 1927*	47.50
635a	3c **bright violet**, *Feb. 7, 1934*	25.00
636	4c **Martha Washington**, *May 17, 1927*	50.00
637	5c **Roosevelt**, *Mar. 24, 1927*	50.00
638	6c **Garfield**, *July 27, 1927*	57.50
639	7c **McKinley**, *Mar. 24, 1927*	57.50
640	8c **Grant**, *June 10, 1927*	62.50
641	9c **Jefferson**, *May 17, 1927*	72.50
642	10c **Monroe**, *Feb. 3, 1927*	90.00

1927

643	2c **Vermont**, *Aug. 3*	6.00
	Bennington, Vt.	6.00
644	2c **Burgoyne**, *Aug. 3*	12.50
	Albany, N.Y.	12.50
	Rome, N.Y.	12.50
	Syracuse, N.Y.	12.50
	Utica, N.Y.	12.50

1928

645	2c **Valley Forge**, *May 26*	4.00
	Cleveland, O.	67.50
	Lancaster, Pa.	4.00
	Norristown, Pa.	4.00
	Philadelphia, Pa.	4.00
	Valley Forge, Pa.	4.00
	West Chester, Pa.	4.00
	Cleveland, Midwestern Philatelic Sta. cancellation	4.00
646	2c **Molly Pitcher**, *Oct. 20*	15.00
	Freehold, N.J.	15.00
	Red Bank, N.J.	15.00

1928

647	2c **Hawaii**, *Aug. 13*	15.00
	Honolulu, Hawaii	17.50
648	5c **Hawaii**, *Aug. 13*	22.50
	Honolulu, Hawaii	25.00
	647-648 on one cover	40.00
649	2c **Aero Conf.**, *Dec. 12*	7.00
650	5c **Aero Conf.**, *Dec. 12*	10.00
	649-650 on one cover	15.00

1929

| 651 | 2c **Clark**, Vincennes, Indiana, *Feb. 25* | 6.00 |
| | Washington, *Feb. 26*, first day of sale by Philatelic Agency | 3.00 |

Perf. 11x10½

653	½c **olive brown**, *May 25*, block of four	27.50
654	2c **Electric Light**, perf. 11, Menlo Park, N.J., *June 5*	10.00
	Washington, D.C., *June 6*, first day of sale by Philatelic Agency	4.00
655	2c **Electric Light**, perf. 11x10½, *June 11*	80.00
656	2c **Electric Light**, perf. 10 vert., *June 11*	90.00
657	2c **Sullivan**, Auburn, N.Y., *June 17*	4.00
	Binghamton, N.Y.	4.00
	Canajoharie, N.Y.	4.00
	Canandaigua, N.Y.	4.00
	Elmira, N.Y.	4.00
	Geneseo, N.Y.	4.00
	Geneva, N.Y.	4.00
	Horseheads, N.Y.	4.00
	Owego, N.Y.	4.00
	Penn Yan, N.Y	4.00
	Perry, N.Y.	4.00
	Seneca Falls, N.Y.	4.00
	Waterloo, N.Y.	4.00
	Watkins Glen, N.Y.	4.00
	Waverly, N.Y.	4.00
	Washington, D.C., *June 18*	2.00

1929

658	1c **Kansas**, *May 1*, pair	50.00
	Newton, Kan., *Apr. 15*	325.00
659	1½c **Kansas**, *May 1*, pair	52.50
	Colby, Kan., *Apr. 16*	—
660	2c **Kansas**, *May 1*	52.50
	Colby, Kan., *Apr. 16*	—
661	3c **Kansas**, *May 1*	60.00
	Colby, Kan., *Apr. 16*	—
662	4c **Kansas**, *May 1*	62.50
	Colby, Kan., *Apr. 16*	—
663	5c **Kansas**, *May 1*	80.00
	Colby, Kan., *Apr. 16*	—
664	6c **Kansas**, *May 1*	90.00
	Newton, Kan., *Apr. 15*	600.00
665	7c **Kansas**, *May 1*	100.00
	Colby, Kan., *Apr. 16*	—
666	8c **Kansas**, *May 1*	125.00
	Newton, Kan., *Apr. 15*	575.00
667	9c **Kansas**, *May 1*	140.00
	Colby, Kan., *Apr. 16*	—
668	10c **Kansas**, *May 1*	175.00
	Colby, Kan., *Apr. 16*	—
	658-668 on 1 cover, Washington, D.C., *May 1*	1,300.
669	1c **Nebraska**, *May 1*, pair	50.00
	Beatrice, Neb., *Apr. 15*	125.00
670	1½c **Nebraska**, *May 1*, pair	50.00
	Hartington, Neb., *Apr. 15*	275.00
671	2c **Nebraska**, *May 1*	55.00

	Auburn, Neb., *Apr. 15*	—
	Beatrice, Neb., *Apr. 15*	
	Hartington, Neb., *Apr. 15*	225.00
672	3c **Nebraska,** *May 1*	65.00
	Beatrice, Neb., *Apr. 15*	190.00
	Hartington, Neb., *Apr. 15*	190.00
673	4c **Nebraska,** *May 1*	75.00
	Beatrice, Neb., *Apr. 15*	240.00
	Hartington, Neb., *Apr. 15*	240.00
674	5c **Nebraska,** *May 1*	75.00
	Beatrice, Neb., *Apr. 15*	225.00
	Hartington, Neb., *Apr. 15*	225.00
675	6c **Nebraska,** *May 1*	100.00
	Ravenna, Neb., *Apr. 17*	—
	Wahoo, Neb., *Apr. 17*	
676	7c **Nebraska,** *May 1*	100.00
	Auburn, Neb., *Apr. 17*	250.00
677	8c **Nebraska,** *May 1*	125.00
	Humbolt, Neb., *Apr. 17*	250.00
	Pawnee City, Neb., *Apr. 17*	250.00
678	9c **Nebraska,** *May 1*	140.00
	Cambridge, Neb., *Apr. 17*	250.00
679	10c **Nebraska,** *May 1*	175.00
	Tecumseh, Neb., *Apr. 18*	
	669-679 on 1 cover, Washington, D.C., *May 1*	1,300.
	658-679 on 1 cover, Washington, D.C., *May 1*	4,000.
680	2c **Fallen Timbers,** Erie, Pa., *Sept. 14*	3.50
	Maumee, O.	3.50
	Perrysburg, O.	3.50
	Toledo, O.	3.50
	Waterville, O.	3.50
	Washington, D.C., *Sept. 16*	2.00
681	2c **Ohio River,** Cairo, Ill., *Oct. 19*	3.50
	Cincinnati, O.	3.50
	Evansville, Ind.	3.50
	Homestead, Pa.	3.50
	Louisville, Ky.	3.50
	Pittsburgh, Pa.	3.50
	Wheeling, W. Va.	3.50
	Washington, D.C., *Oct. 21*	2.00

1930

682	2c **Massachusetts Bay Colony,** Boston, Mass. *Apr. 8 (60,000)*	3.50
	Salem, Mass.	3.50
	Washington, D.C., *Apr. 11*	2.00
683	2c **Carolina-Charleston,** Charleston, S.C. *Apr. 10*	3.50
	Washington, D.C., *Apr. 11*	2.00

Perf. 11x10½

684	1½c **Harding,** Marion, O., *Dec. 1,* pair	4.50
	Washington, D.C., *Dec. 2*	2.50
685	4c **Taft,** Cincinnati, O., *June 4*	6.00
	Washington, D.C., *June 5*	3.00

Perf. 10 Vertically

686	1½c **Harding,** Marion, Ohio, *Dec. 1*	5.00
	Washington, D.C., *Dec. 2*	3.00
687	4c **Taft,** *Sept. 18*	20.00

Perf. 11

688	2c **Braddock,** Braddock, Pa., *July 9*	4.00
	Washington, D.C., *July 10*	2.00
689	2c **Von Steuben,** New York, N.Y., *Sept. 17*	4.00
	Washington, D.C., *Sept. 18*	2.00

1931

690	2c **Pulaski,** Brooklyn, N.Y., *Jan. 16*	4.00
	Buffalo, N.Y.	4.00
	Chicago, Ill.	4.00
	Cleveland, O.	4.00
	Detroit, Mich.	4.00
	Gary, Ind.	4.00
	Milwaukee, Wis.	4.00
	New York, N.Y.	4.00
	Pittsburgh, Pa.	4.00
	Savannah, Ga.	4.00
	South Bend, Ind.	4.00
	Toledo, O.	4.00
	Washington, D.C., *Jan. 17*	2.00

1931		*Perf. 11x10½, 10½x11*	
692	11c **Hayes,** *Sept. 4*	100.
693	12c **Cleveland,** *Aug. 25*	100.
694	13c **Harrison,** *Sept. 4*	100.
695	14c **American Indian,** *Sept. 8*	100.
696	15c **Liberty,** *Aug. 27*	125.
697	17c **Wilson,** *July 25,* Brooklyn, N.Y.	2,750.
	Washington, D.C., *July 27*	400.
698	20c **Golden Gate,** *Sept. 8*	325.
699	25c **Niagara Falls,** *July 25,* Brooklyn, N.Y.	2,000.
	Washington, D.C., *July 27*	400.
	697, 699 on one cover, Brooklyn, *July 25*	4,500.
	697, 699 on one cover, Washington, *July 27*	2,500.
700	30c **American Buffalo,** *Sept. 8*	300.
701	50c **Arlington,** *Sept. 4*	425.
	Woolrich, Pa., *Sept. 4*	625.

1931

702	2c **Red Cross,** *May 21*	3.00
	Dansville, N.Y.	3.00
703	2c **Yorktown,** *Oct. 19,* Wethersfield, Conn.	3.50
	Yorktown, Va.	3.50
	Washington, D.C., *Oct. 20*	2.00

1932

WASHINGTON BICENTENNIAL ISSUE

704	½c **Jan. 1,** block of 4	5.00
705	1c **Jan. 1,** pair	4.00
706	1½c **Jan. 1,** pair	4.00
707	2c **Jan. 1**	4.00

708	3c **Jan. 1**	4.00
709	4c **Jan. 1**	4.00
710	5c **Jan. 1**	4.00
711	6c **Jan. 1**	4.00
712	7c **Jan. 1**	4.00
713	8c **Jan. 1**	4.50
714	9c **Jan. 1**	4.50
715	10c **Jan. 1**	4.50
	704-715, set of 12 on one cover, *Jan. 1*	70.00

1932

716	2c **Olympic Winter Games,** *Jan. 25,* Lake Placid, N.Y.	6.00
	Washington, D.C., *Jan. 26*	1.50
717	2c **Arbor Day,** *Apr. 22,* Nebraska City, Neb.	4.00
	Washington, D.C., *Apr. 23*	1.50
	Adams, N.Y., *Apr. 23*	6.50
718	3c **Olympic Summer Games,** *June 15,* Los Angeles, Cal.	6.00
	Washington, D.C., *June 16*	2.75
719	5c **Olympic Summer Games,** *June 15,* Los Angeles, Cal.	8.00
	Washington, D.C., *June 16*	2.75
	718, 719 on one cover, Los Angeles, Cal.	10.00
	718, 719 on one cover, Washington, D.C.	4.50
720	3c **Washington,** *June 16*	7.50
720b	Booklet pane of 6, *July 25*	100.00
721	3c **Washington Coil,** Sideways, *June 24*	15.00
722	3c **Washington Coil,** Endways, *Oct. 12*	15.00
723	6c **Garfield Coil,** Sideways, *Aug. 18,* Los Angeles, Cal.	15.00
	Washington, D.C., *Aug. 19*	4.00
724	3c **William Penn,** *Oct. 24,* New Castle, Del.	3.25
	Chester, Pa.	3.25
	Philadelphia, Pa.	3.25
	Washington, D.C., *Oct. 25*	1.25
725	3c **Daniel Webster,** *Oct. 24,* Franklin, N.H.	3.25
	Exeter, N.H.	3.25
	Hanover, N.H.	3.25
	Washington, D.C., *Oct. 25*	1.25

1933

726	3c **Gen. Oglethorpe,** *Feb. 12,* Savannah, Ga., *(200,000)*	3.25
	Washington, D.C., *Feb. 13*	1.50
727	3c **Peace Proclamation,** *Apr. 19,* Newburgh, N.Y. *(349,571)*	3.50
	Washington, D.C., *Apr. 20*	1.25
728	1c **Century of Progress,** *May 25,* Chicago, Ill., strip of 3	3.00
	Washington, D.C., *May 26*	1.00
729	3c **Century of Progress,** *May 25,* Chicago, Ill.	3.00
	Washington, D.C., *May 26*	1.00
	728, 729 on one cover	5.00

Covers mailed May 25, bearing Nos. 728 and 729 total 232,251.

730	1c **American Philatelic Society,** sheet of 25, *Aug. 25,* Chicago, Ill.	100.00
730a	1c **A.P.S.,** imperf., *Aug. 25,* Chicago, Ill., strip of 3	3.25
	Washington, D.C., *Aug. 28*	1.25
731	3c **American Philatelic Society,** sheet of 25, *Aug. 25,* Chicago, Ill.	100.00
731a	3c **A.P.S.,** single, imperf., *Aug. 25,* Chicago, Ill.	3.25
	Washington, D.C., *Aug. 28*	1.25
	730a, 731a on one cover	5.50

Covers mailed Aug. 25 bearing Nos. 730, 730a, 731, 731a total 65,218.

732	3c **National Recovery Administration,** *Aug. 15, (65,000)*	3.25
	Nira, Iowa, *Aug. 17*	2.50
733	3c **Byrd Antarctic,** *Oct. 9*	10.00
734	5c **Kosciuszko,** *Oct. 13,* Boston, Mass. *(23,025)*	4.50
	Buffalo, N.Y. *(14,981)*	5.50
	Chicago, Ill. *(26,306)*	4.50
	Detroit, Mich. *(17,792)*	5.25
	Pittsburgh, Pa. *(6,282)*	32.50
	Kosciuszko, Miss. *(27,093)*	5.25
	St. Louis, Mo. *(17,872)*	5.25
	Washington, D.C., *Oct. 14*	1.60

1934

735	3c **National Exhibition,** sheet of 6, Byrd imperf., *Feb. 10,* New York, N.Y.	40.00
	Washington, D.C., *Feb. 19*	27.50
735a	3c **National Exhibition,** single, imperf., New York, N.Y., *Feb. 10 (450,715)*	5.00
	Washington, D.C., *Feb. 19*	2.75
736	3c **Maryland Tercentenary,** *Mar. 23* St. Mary's City, Md. *(148,785)*	1.60
	Washington, D.C., *Mar. 24*	1.00
737	3c **Mothers of America,** perf. 11x10½, *May 2,* any city	1.60
738	3c **Mothers of America,** perf. 11, *May 2,* any city	1.60
	737, 738 on one cover	4.00

Covers mailed at Washington, May 2 bearing Nos. 737 and 738 total 183,359.

739	3c **Wisconsin,** *July 7,* Green Bay, Wisc. *(130,000)*	1.10
	Washington, D.C., *July 9*	1.00
740	1c **Parks, Yosemite,** *July 16*	2.25
	Yosemite, Cal., *(60,000),* strip of 3	2.75
741	2c **Parks, Grand Canyon,** *July 24*	2.25
	Grand Canyon, Ariz., *(75,000),* pair	2.75
742	3c **Parks, Mt. Rainier,** *Aug. 3*	2.50
	Longmire, Wash., *(64,500)*	3.00
743	4c **Parks, Mesa Verde,** *Sept. 25*	2.25
	Mesa Verde, Colo., *(51,882)*	2.75
744	5c **Parks, Yellowstone,** *July 30*	2.25
	Yellowstone, Wyo., *(87,000)*	2.50

745	6c **Parks, Crater Lake,** *Sept. 5*	3.00
	Crater Lake, Ore., *(45,282)*	3.25
746	7c **Parks, Arcadia,** *Oct. 2*	3.00
	Bar Harbor, Maine *(51,312)*	3.25
747	8c **Parks, Zion,** *Sept. 18*	3.25
	Zion, Utah, *(43,650)*	3.75
748	9c **Parks, Glacier Park,** *Aug. 27*	3.50
	Glacier Park, Mont., *(52,626)*	3.75
749	10c **Parks, Smoky Mountains,** *Oct. 8*	6.00
	Sevierville, Tenn., *(39,000)*	7.50

Imperf

750	3c **American Philatelic Society,** sheet of 6, *Aug. 28,* Atlantic City, N.J.	40.00
750a	3c **A.P.S.,** single, *Aug. 28,* Atlantic City, N.J. *(40,000)*	3.25
	Washington, D.C., *Sept. 4*	2.00
751	1c **Trans-Mississippi Philatelic Expo.,** sheet of 6, *Oct. 10,* Omaha, Neb.	35.00
751a	1c **Trans-Miss. Phil. Expo.,** Omaha. Neb., *Oct. 10 (125,000),* strip of 3	3.25
	Washington, D.C., *Oct. 15*	2.00

1935

SPECIAL PRINTING
Nos. 752-771 issued Mar. 15

752	3c **Peace Commemoration**	5.00
753	3c **Byrd**	6.00
754	3c **Mothers of America**	6.00
755	3c **Wisconsin Tercentenary**	6.00
756	1c **Parks, Yosemite,** strip of 3	6.00
757	2c **Parks, Grand Canyon,** pair	6.00
758	3c **Parks, Mount Rainier**	6.00
759	4c **Parks, Mesa Verde**	6.50
760	5c **Parks, Yellowstone**	6.50
761	6c **Parks, Crater Lake**	6.50
762	7c **Parks, Acadia**	6.50
763	8c **Parks, Zion**	7.50
764	9c **Parks, Glacier Park**	7.50
765	10c **Parks, Smoky Mountains**	7.50
766a	1c **Century of Progress,** strip of 3	5.50
	Pane of 25	250.00
767a	3c **Century of Progress,** strip of 3	5.50
	Pane of 25	250.00
768a	3c **Byrd**	6.50
	Pane of 6	250.00
769a	1c **Parks, Yosemite,** strip of 3	4.00
	Pane of 6	250.00
770a	3c **Parks, Mount Rainier**	5.00
	Pane of 6	250.00
771	16c **Airmail Special Delivery**	12.50

> **Catalogue values from this point to No. 986 are for addressed covers with the most common cachets.**

772	3c **Connecticut Tercentenary,** *Apr. 26,* Hartford, Conn. *(217,800)*	10.00
	Washington, D.C., *Apr. 27*	2.25
773	3c **California Exposition,** *May 29,* San Diego, Cal. *(214,042)*	10.00
	Washington, D.C., *May 31*	1.50
774	3c **Boulder Dam,** *Sept. 30,* Boulder City, Nev. *(166,180)*	10.00
	Washington, D.C., *Oct. 1*	2.00
775	3c **Michigan Centenary,** *Nov. 1,* Lansing, Mich. *(176,962)*	10.00
	Washington, D.C., *Nov. 2*	1.50

1936

776	3c **Texas Centennial,** *Mar. 2,* Gonzales, Texas *(319,150)*	17.50
	Washington, D.C., *Mar. 3*	2.00
777	3c **Rhode Island Tercentenary,** *May 4,* Providence, R.I. *(245,400)*	9.00
	Washington, D.C., *May 5*	2.25
778	**TIPEX** souvenir sheet, *May 9 (297,194)* New York, N.Y. (TIPEX cancellation)	13.00
	Washington, D.C., *May 11*	3.50
782	3c **Arkansas Centennial,** *June 15,* Little Rock, Ark. *(376,693)*	9.00
	Washington, D.C, *June 16*	1.25
783	3c **Oregon Territory Centennial,** *July 14,* Astoria, Ore. *(91,110)*	8.50
	Daniel, Wyo., *(67,013)*	8.50
	Lewiston, Ida., *(86,100)*	8.00
	Missoula, Mont., *(59,883)*	8.50
	Walla Walla, Wash., *(106,150)*	8.50
	Washington, D.C., *July 15*	1.25
784	3c **Susan B. Anthony,** *Aug. 26 (178,500)*	9.00

1936-37

785	1c **Army,** *Dec. 15, 1936,* strip of 3	6.00
786	2c **Army,** *Jan. 15, 1937,* pair	6.00
787	3c **Army,** *Feb. 18, 1937*	6.00
788	4c **Army,** *Mar. 23, 1937*	6.00
789	5c **Army,** *May 26, 1937,* West Point, N.Y., *(160,000)*	6.00
	Washington, D.C., *May 27*	2.00
790	1c **Navy,** *Dec. 15, 1936,* strip of 3	6.00
791	2c **Navy,** *Jan. 15, 1937,* pair	6.00
792	3c **Navy,** *Feb. 18, 1937*	6.00
793	4c **Navy,** *Mar. 23, 1937*	6.00
794	5c **Navy,** *May 26, 1937,* Annapolis, Md., *(202,806)*	6.00
	Washington, D.C., *May 27*	2.00

Covers for #785 & 790 total 390, 749; #786 & 791 total 292,570; #787 & 792 total 320,888; #788 & 793 total 331,000.

1937

795	3c **Ordinance of 1787,** *July 13* Marietta, Ohio *(130,531)*	7.00
	New York, N.Y. *(125,134)*	7.00

	Washington, D.C., *July 14*	1.25
796	5c **Virginia Dare**, *Aug. 18*, Manteo, N.C. *(226,730)*	9.00
797	10c **Souvenir Sheet**, *Aug. 26*, Asheville, N.C. *(164,215)*	8.00
798	3c **Constitution**, *Sept. 17*, Philadelphia, Pa. *(281,478)*	8.00
799	3c **Hawaii**, *Oct. 18*, Honolulu, Hawaii *(320,334)*	8.00
800	3c **Alaska**, *Nov. 12*, Juneau, Alaska *(230,370)*	8.00
801	3c **Puerto Rico**, *Nov. 25*, San Juan, P.R. *(244,054)*	8.00
802	3c **Virgin Islands**, *Dec. 15*, Charlotte Amalie, V.I. *(225,469)*	8.00

1938

PRESIDENTIAL ISSUE

803	½c **Franklin**, *May 19*, Philadelphia, Pa. *(224,901)*, block of 6	2.50
804	1c **G. Washington**, *Apr. 25 (124,037)*, strip of 3	2.50
804b	Booklet pane of 6, *Jan. 27, 1939*	
805	1½c **M. Washington**, *May 5 (128,339)*, pair	2.50
806	2c **J. Adams**, *June 3 (127,806)*, pair	2.50
806b	Booklet pane of 6, *Jan. 27, 1939*	15.00
807	3c **Jefferson**, *June 16 (118,097)*	2.50
807a	Booklet pane of 6, *Jan. 27, 1939*	17.50
808	4c **Madison**, *July 1 (118,765)*	2.50
809	4½c **White House**, *July 11 (115,820)*	2.50
810	5c **Monroe**, *July 21 (98,282)*	2.50
811	6c **J.Q. Adams**, *July 28 (97,428)*	2.50
812	7c **Jackson**, *Aug. 4 (98,414)*	2.50
813	8c **Van Buren**, *Aug. 11 (94,857)*	2.50
814	9c **W.H. Harrison**, *Aug. 18 (91,229)*	3.00
815	10c **Tyler**, *Sept. 2 (83,707)*	3.00
816	11c **Polk**, *Sept. 8 (63,966)*	3.50
817	12c **Taylor**, *Sept. 14 (62,935)*	3.50
818	13c **Fillmore**, *Sept. 22 (58,965)*	3.50
819	14c **Pierce**, *Oct. 6 (49,819)*	3.50
820	15c **Buchanan**, *Oct. 13 (52,209)*	3.50
821	16c **Lincoln**, *Oct. 20 (59,566)*	5.00
822	17c **A. Johnson**, *Oct. 27 (55,024)*	5.00
823	18c **Grant**, *Nov. 3 (53,124)*	5.00
824	19c **Hayes**, *Nov. 10 (54,124)*	5.00
825	20c **Garfield**, *Nov. 10 (51,971)*	5.00
826	21c **Arthur**, *Nov. 22 (44,367)*	5.50
827	22c **Cleveland**, *Nov. 22 (44,358)*	5.50
828	24c **B. Harrison**, *Dec. 2 (46,592)*	5.50
829	25c **McKinley**, *Dec. 2 (45,691)*	6.25
830	30c **T. Roosevelt**, *Dec. 8 (43,528)*	7.75
831	50c **Taft**, *Dec. 8 (41,984)*	10.00
832	$1 **Wilson, purple & black**, *Aug. 29 (24,618)*	50.00
832c	**red violet & black**, *Aug. 31, 1954 (20,202)*	25.00
833	$2 **Harding**, *Sept. 29 (19,895)*	100.00
834	$5 **Coolidge**, *Nov. 17 (15,615)*	150.00

1938

835	3c **Constitution**, *June 21*, Philadelphia, Pa. *(232,873)*	9.00
836	3c **Swedes and Finns**, *June 27*, Wilmington, Del. *(225,617)*	9.00
837	3c **Northwest Sesqui.**, *July 15*, Marietta, Ohio *(180,170)*	9.00
838	3c **Iowa**, *Aug. 24*, Des Moines, Iowa *(209,860)*	9.00

1939

COIL STAMPS
Perf. 10 Vertically

839	1c **G. Washington**, *Jan. 20*, strip of 3	4.75
840	1½c **M. Washington**, *Jan. 20*, pair	4.75
841	2c **J. Adams**, *Jan. 20*, pair	4.75
842	3c **Jefferson**, *Jan. 20*	4.75
843	4c **Madison**, *Jan. 20*	5.00
844	4½c **White House**, *Jan. 20*	5.00
845	5c **Monroe**, *Jan. 20*	5.00
846	6c **J.Q. Adams**, *Jan. 20*	6.50
847	10c **Tyler**, *Jan. 20*	9.00
	839-847 on one cover, *Jan. 20*	45.00

Perf. 10 Horizontally

848	1c **Strip of 3**, *Jan. 27*	5.00
849	1½c **Pair**, *Jan. 27*	5.00
850	2c **Pair**, *Jan. 27*	5.00
851	3c **Jan. 27**	5.50
	848-851 on one cover, *Jan. 27*	25.00

1939

852	3c **Golden Gate Expo**, *Feb. 18*, San Francisco, Cal. *(352,165)*	6.00
853	3c **N.Y. World's Fair**, *Apr. 1*, New York, N.Y. *(585,565)*	12.50
854	3c **Washington Inauguration**, *Apr. 30*, New York, N.Y. *(395,644)*	6.00
855	3c **Baseball Centennial**, *June 12*, Cooperstown, N.Y. *(398,199)*	35.00
856	3c **Panama Canal**, *Aug. 15*, U.S.S. Charleston, Canal Zone *(230,974)*	6.50
857	3c **Printing Tercentenary**, *Sept. 25*, New York, N.Y. *(295,270)*	5.00
858	3c **50th Statehood Anniversary**, Bismarck, N.D. *Nov. 2 (142,106)*	5.00
	Pierre, S.D., *Nov. 2 (150,429)*	5.00
	Helena, Mont., *Nov. 8 (130,273)*	5.00
	Olympia, Wash., *Nov. 11 (150,429)*	5.00

1940

FAMOUS AMERICANS

859	1c **Washington Irving**, *Jan. 29*, Tarrytown, N.Y. *(170,969)*, strip of 3	2.00
860	2c **James Fenimore Cooper**, *Jan. 29*, Cooperstown, N.Y. *(154,836)*, pair	2.00

861	3c **Ralph Waldo Emerson**, *Feb. 5*, Boston, Mass. *(185,148)*	2.00
862	5c **Louisa May Alcott**, *Feb. 5*, Concord, Mass. *(134,325)*	3.00
863	10c **Samuel L. Clemens**, *Feb. 13*, Hannibal, Mo. *(150,492)*	4.50
864	1c **Henry W. Longfellow**, *Feb. 16*, Portland, Me. *(160,508)*, strip of 3	2.00
865	2c **John Greenleaf Whittier**, *Feb. 16*, Haverhill, Mass. *(148,423)*, pair	2.00
866	3c **James Russell Lowell**, *Feb. 20*, Cambridge, Mass. *(148,735)*	2.00
867	5c **Walt Whitman**, *Feb. 20*, Camden, N.J. *(134,185)*	4.00
868	10c **James Whitcomb Riley**, *Feb. 24*, Greenfield, Ind. *(131,760)*	6.00
869	1c **Horace Mann**, *Mar. 14*, Boston, Mass. *(186,854)*, strip of 3	2.00
870	2c **Mark Hopkins**, *Mar. 14*, Williamstown, Mass. *(140,286)*, pair	2.00
871	3c **Charles W. Eliot**, *Mar. 28*, Cambridge, Mass. *(155,708)*	2.00
872	5c **Frances E. Willard**, *Mar. 28*, Evanston, Ill. *(140,483)*	4.00
873	10c **Booker T. Washington**, *Apr. 7*, Tuskegee Institute, Ala. *(163,507)*	6.50
874	1c **John James Audubon**, *Apr. 8*, St. Francisville, La. *(144,123)*, strip of 3	2.00
875	2c **Dr. Crawford W. Long**, *Apr. 8*, Jefferson, Ga. *(158,128)*, pair	2.00
876	3c **Luther Burbank**, *Apr. 17*, Santa Rosa, Cal. *(147,033)*	2.00
877	5c **Dr. Walter Reed**, *Apr. 17 (154,464)*	3.00
878	10c **Jane Addams**, *Apr. 26*, Chicago, Ill. *(132,375)*	5.00
879	1c **Stephen Collins Foster**, *May 3*, Bardstown, Ky. *(183,461)*, strip of 3	2.00
880	2c **John Philip Sousa**, *May 3 (131,422)*, pair	2.00
881	3c **Victor Herbert**, *May 13*, New York, N.Y. *(168,200)*	2.00
882	5c **Edward A. MacDowell**, *May 13*, Peterborough, N.H. *(135,155)*	3.00
883	10c **Ethelbert Nevin**, *June 10*, Pittsburgh, Pa. *(121,951)*	5.00
884	1c **Gilbert Stuart**, *Sept. 5*, Narragansett, R.I. *(131,965)*, strip of 3	2.00
885	2c **James A. McNeill Whistler**, *Sept. 5*, Lowell, Mass. *(130,962)*, pair	2.00
886	3c **Augustus Saint-Gaudens**, *Sept. 16*, New York, N.Y. *(138,200)*	2.00
887	5c **Daniel Chester French**, *Sept. 16*, Stockbridge, Mass. *(124,608)*	3.00
888	10c **Frederic Remington**, *Sept. 30*, Canton, N.Y. *(116,219)*	5.00
889	1c **Eli Whitney**, *Oct. 7*, Savannah, Ga. *(140,868)*, strip of 3	2.00
890	2c **Samuel F.B. Morse**, *Oct. 7*, New York, N.Y. *(135,388)*, pair	2.00
891	3c **Cyrus Hall McCormick**, *Oct. 14*, Lexington, Va. *(137,415)*	2.00
892	5c **Elias Howe**, *Oct. 14*, Spencer, Mass. *(126,334)*	3.00
893	10c **Alexander Graham Bell**, *Oct. 28*, Boston, Mass. *(125,372)*	7.50

1940

894	3c **Pony Express**, *Apr. 3*, St. Joseph, Mo. *(194,589)*	6.00
	Sacramento, Cal. *(160,849)*	6.00
895	3c **Pan American Union**, *Apr. 14 (182,401)*	4.50
896	3c **Idaho Statehood**, *July 3*, Boise, Idaho *(156,429)*	4.50
897	3c **Wyoming Statehood**, *July 10* Cheyenne, Wyo. *(156,709)*	4.50
898	3c **Coronado Expedition**, *Sept. 7*, Albuquerque, N.M. *(161,012)*	4.50
899	1c **Defense**, *Oct. 16*, strip of 3	4.25
900	2c **Defense**, *Oct. 16*, pair	4.25
901	3c **Defense**, *Oct. 16*	4.25
	899-901 on one cover	10.00

First day cancel was applied to 450,083 covers bearing one or more of Nos. 899-901.

902	3c **Thirteenth Amendment**, *Oct. 20*, World's Fair, N.Y. *(156,146)*	7.50

1941

903	3c **Vermont Statehood**, *Mar. 4*, Montpelier, Vt. *(182,423)*	7.00

MacArthur, W. Va.
Apr 15, 1942
First Day Cover

Covers exist with this cancellation. "First Day" refers to the first day of the new name of the town, previously known as Hollywood, W. Va.

1942

904	3c **Kentucky Statehood**, *June 1*, Frankfort, Ky. *(155,730)*	4.00
905	3c **"Win the War"**, *July 4 (191,168)*	3.75
906	5c **Chinese Resistance**, *July 7*, Denver, Colo. *(168,746)*	6.00

1943-44

907	2c **United Nations**, *Jan. 14, 1943 (178,865)*, pair	3.50
908	1c **Four Freedoms**, *Feb. 12, 1943 (193,800)*, strip of 3	3.50
909	5c **Poland**, *June 22, 1943*, Chicago, Ill. *(88,170)*	7.50
	Washington, D.C. *(136,002)*	4.00
910	5c **Czechoslovakia**, *July 12, 1943 (145,112)*	4.00
911	5c **Norway**, *July 27, 1943 (130,054)*	4.00
912	5c **Luxemborg**, *Aug. 10, 1943 (166,367)*	4.00

913	5c **Netherlands**, *Aug. 24, 1943 (148,763)*	4.00
914	5c **Belgium**, *Sept. 14, 1943 (154,220)*	4.00
915	5c **France**, *Sept. 28, 1943 (163,478)*	4.00
916	5c **Greece**, *Oct. 12, 1943 (166,553)*	4.00
917	5c **Yugoslavia**, *Oct. 26, 1943 (161,835)*	4.00
918	5c **Albania**, *Nov. 9, 1943 (162,275)*	4.00
919	5c **Austria**, *Nov. 23, 1943 (172,285)*	4.00
920	5c **Denmark**, *Dec. 7, 1943 (173,784)*	4.00
921	5c **Korea**, *Nov. 2, 1944 (192,860)*	5.00

1944

922	3c **Railroad**, *May 10*, Ogden, Utah *(151,324)*	6.00
	Omaha, Neb. *(171,000)*	6.00
	San Francisco, Cal. *(125,000)*	6.00
923	3c **Steamship**, *May 22*, Kings Point, N.Y. *(152,324)*	4.00
	Savannah, Ga. *(181,472)*	4.00
924	3c **Telegraph**, *May 24 (141,907)*	3.50
	Baltimore, Md. *(136,480)*	3.50
925	3c **Philippines**, *Sept. 27 (214,965)*	3.50
926	3c **Motion Picture**, *Oct. 31*, Hollywood, Cal. *(190,660)*	4.00
	New York, N.Y. *(176,473)*	4.00

1945

927	3c **Florida**, *Mar. 3*, Tallahassee, Fla. *(228,435)*	4.50
928	5c **United Nations Conference**, *Apr. 25*, San Francisco, Cal. *(417,450)*	5.00
929	3c **Iwo Jima**, *July 11 (391,650)*	10.00

1945-46

930	1c **Roosevelt**, *July 26, 1945*, Hyde Park, N.Y. *(390,219)*, strip of 3	3.50
931	2c **Roosevelt**, *Aug. 24, 1945*, Warm Springs, Ga. *(426,142)*, pair	3.50
932	3c **Roosevelt**, *June 27, 1945 (391,650)*	3.50
933	5c **Roosevelt**, *Jan. 30, 1946 (466,766)*	3.50

1945

934	3c **Army**, *Sept. 28 (392,300)*	6.00
935	3c **Navy**, *Oct. 27*, Annapolis, Md. *(460,352)*	6.00
936	3c **Coast Guard**, *Nov. 10* New York, N.Y. *(405,280)*	6.00
937	3c **Alfred E. Smith**, *Nov. 26* New York, N.Y. *(424,950)*	2.50
938	3c **Texas**, *Dec. 29*, Austin, Tex. *(397,860)*	4.00

1946

939	3c **Merchant Marine**, *Feb. 26 (432,141)*	5.00
940	3c **Veterans of WWII**, *May 9 (492,786)*	4.00
941	3c **Tennessee**, *June 1, 1946*, Nashville, Tenn. *(463,512)*	1.50
942	3c **Iowa**, *Aug. 3*, Iowa City, Iowa *(517,505)*	1.50
943	3c **Smithsonian**, *Oct. 10 (402,448)*	1.50
944	3c **Kearny Expedition**, *Oct. 16*, Santa Fe, N.M. *(384,300)*	1.50

1947

945	3c **Thomas A. Edison**, *Feb. 11*, Milan, Ohio *(632,473)*	3.00
946	3c **Joseph Pulitzer**, *Apr. 10*, New York, N.Y. *(580,870)*	1.50
947	3c **Stamp Centenary**, *May 17*, New York, N.Y. *(712,873)*	1.50
948	5c and 10c **Centenary Exhibition Sheet**, *May 19*, New York, N.Y. *(502,175)*	2.00
949	3c **Doctors**, *June 9*, Atlantic City, N.J. *(508,016)*	2.50
950	3c **Utah**, *July 24*, Salt Lake City, Utah *(456,416)*	1.00
951	3c **"Constitution,"** *Oct. 21*, Boston, Mass. *(683,416)*	6.00
952	3c **Everglades Park**, *Dec. 5*, Florida City, Fla. *(466,647)*	1.00

1948

953	3c **Carver**, *Jan. 5*, Tuskegee Institute, Ala. *(402,179)*	1.00
954	3c **California Gold**, *Jan. 24*, Coloma, Calif. *(526,154)*	1.00
955	3c **Mississippi Territory**, *Apr. 7*, Natchez, Miss. *(434,804)*	1.00
956	3c **Four Chaplains**, *May 28 (459,070)*	3.00
957	3c **Wisconsin Centennial**, *May 29*, Madison, Wis. *(470,280)*	1.00
958	3c **Swedish Pioneers**, *June 4* Chicago, Ill. *(364,318)*	1.00
959	3c **Women's Progress**, *July 19*, Seneca Falls, N.Y. *(401,923)*	1.00
960	3c **William Allen White**, *July 31*, Emporia, Kans. *(385,648)*	1.00
961	3c **U.S.-Canada Friendship**, *Aug. 2*, Niagara Falls, N.Y. *(406,467)*	1.00
962	3c **Francis Scott Key**, *Aug. 9*, Frederick, Md. *(505,930)*	1.00
963	3c **Salute to Youth**, *Aug. 11 (347,070)*	1.00
964	3c **Oregon Territory Establishment**, *Aug. 14*, Oregon City, Ore. *(365,898)*	1.00
965	3c **Harlan Fiske Stone**, *Aug. 25*, Chesterfield, N.H. *(362,170)*	1.00
966	3c **Palomar Observatory**, *Aug. 30*, Palomar Mountain, Calif. *(401,365)*	2.00
967	3c **Clara Barton**, *Sept. 7*, Oxford, Mass. *(362,000)*	3.00
968	3c **Poultry Industry**, *Sept. 9*, New Haven, Conn. *(475,000)*	1.25
969	3c **Gold Star Mothers**, *Sept. 21 (386,064)*	1.00
970	3c **Fort Kearny**, *Sept. 22*, Minden, Neb. *(429,633)*	1.00
971	3c **Volunteer Firemen**, *Oct. 4*, Dover, Del.	7.00
972	3c **Indian Centennial**, *Oct. 15*, Muskogee, Okla. *(459,528)*	1.00
973	3c **Rough Riders**, *Oct. 27*, Prescott, Ariz. *(399,198)*	1.00

974	3c **Juliette Low,** *Oct. 29,* Savannah, Ga. *(476,573)*	
975	3c **Will Rogers,** *Nov. 4,* Claremore, Okla. *(450,350)*	2.25
976	3c **Fort Bliss,** *Nov. 5,* El Paso, Tex. *(421,000)*	1.50
977	3c **Moina Michael,** *Nov. 9,* Athens, Ga. *(374,090)*	2.00
978	3c **Gettysburg Address,** *Nov. 19,* Gettysburg, Pa. *(511,990)*	1.00
979	3c **American Turners Society,** *Nov. 20,* Cincinnati, Ohio *(434,090)*	1.00
980	3c **Joel Chandler Harris,** *Dec. 9,* Eatonton, Ga. *(426,199)*	1.00
		1.25

1949

981	3c **Minnesota Territory,** *Mar. 3,* St. Paul, Minn. *(458,750)*	1.00
982	3c **Washington and Lee University,** *Apr. 12,* Lexington, Va. *(447,910)*	1.00
983	3c **Puerto Rico Election,** *Apr. 27,* San Juan, P.R. *(390,416)*	1.00
984	3c **Annapolis, Md.,** *May 23,* Annapolis, Md. *(441,802)*	1.00
985	3c **G.A.R.,** *Aug. 29,* Indianapolis, Ind. *(471,696)*	1.00
986	3c **Edgar Allan Poe,** *Oct. 7,* Richmond, Va. *(371,020)*	1.50

> Catalogue values from this point to the end of the section are for unaddressed covers with the most common cachets.

1950

987	3c **American Bankers Assoc.,** *Jan. 3,* Saratoga Springs, N.Y. *(388,622)*	2.00
988	3c **Samuel Gompers,** *Jan. 27 (332,023)*	1.00

National Capital Sesquicentennial

989	3c **Freedom,** *Apr. 20 (371,743)*	1.00
990	3c **Executive,** *June 12 (376,789)*	1.00
991	3c **Judicial,** *Aug. 2 (324,007)*	1.00
992	3c **Legislative,** *Nov. 22 (352,215)*	1.00
993	3c **Railroad Engineers,** *Apr. 29,* Jackson, Tenn. *(420,830)*	1.50
994	3c **Kansas City Centenary,** *June 3,* Kansas City, Mo. *(405,390)*	1.00
995	3c **Boy Scouts,** *June 30,* Valley Forge, Pa. *(622,972)*	5.00
996	3c **Indiana Territory Sesquicentennial,** *July 4,* Vincennes, Ind. *(359,643)*	1.00
997	3c **California Statehood,** *Sept. 9,* Sacramento, Cal. *(391,919)*	1.00

1951

998	3c **United Confederate Veterans,** *May 30,* Norfolk, Va. *(374,235)*	1.00
999	3c **Nevada Centennial,** *July 14,* Genoa, Nev. *(336,890)*	1.00
1000	3c **Landing of Cadillac,** *July 24,* Detroit, Mich. *(323,094)*	1.00
1001	3c **Colorado Statehood,** *Aug. 1,* Minturn, Colo. *(311,568)*	1.00
1002	3c **American Chemical Society,** *Sept. 4,* New York, N.Y. *(436,419)*	2.00
1003	3c **Battle of Brooklyn,** *Dec. 10,* Brooklyn, N.Y. *(420,000)*	1.00

1952

1004	3c **Betsy Ross,** *Jan. 2,* Philadelphia, Pa. *(314,312)*	1.00
1005	3c **4-H Club,** *Jan. 15,* Springfield, Ohio *(383,290)*	1.00
1006	3c **B. & O. Railroad,** *Feb. 28,* Baltimore, Md. *(441,600)*	1.75
1007	3c **American Automobile Association,** *Mar. 4,* Chicago, Ill. *(520,123)*	1.00
1008	3c **NATO,** *Apr. 4 (313,518)*	1.00
1009	3c **Grand Coulee Dam,** *May 15,* Grand Coulee, Wash. *(341,680)*	1.00
1010	3c **Lafayette,** *June 13,* Georgetown, S.C. *(349,102)*	1.00
1011	3c **Mt. Rushmore Memorial,** *Aug. 11,* Keystone, S.D. *(337,027)*	1.00
1012	3c **Civil Engineers,** *Sept. 6,* Chicago, Ill. *(318,483)*	1.00
1013	3c **Service Women,** *Sept. 11 (308,062)*	1.00
1014	3c **Gutenberg Bible,** *Sept. 30 (387,078)*	1.00
1015	3c **Newspaper Boys,** *Oct. 4,* Philadelphia, Pa. *(626,000)*	1.00
1016	3c **Red Cross,** *Nov. 21,* New York, N.Y. *(439,252)*	1.50

1953

1017	3c **National Guard,** *Feb. 23 (387,618)*	1.00
1018	3c **Ohio Sesquicentennial,** *Mar. 2,* Chillicothe, Ohio *(407,983)*	1.00
1019	3c **Washington Territory,** *Mar. 2,* Olympia, Wash. *(344,047)*	1.00
1020	3c **Louisiana Purchase,** *Apr. 30,* St. Louis, Mo. *(425,600)*	1.00
1021	5c **Opening of Japan,** *July 14 (320,541)*	1.00
1022	3c **American Bar Association,** *Aug. 24,* Boston, Mass. *(410,036)*	5.00
1023	3c **Sagamore Hill,** *Sept. 14,* Oyster Bay, N.Y. *(379,750)*	1.00
1024	3c **Future Farmers,** *Oct. 13,* Kansas City, Mo. *(424,193)*	1.00
1025	3c **Trucking Industry,** *Oct. 27,* Los Angeles, Calif. *(875,021)*	1.00
1026	3c **Gen. G.S. Patton, Jr.,** *Nov. 11,* Fort Knox, Ky. *(342,600)*	4.00

1027	3c **New York City,** *Nov. 20,* New York, N.Y. *(387,914)*	1.00
1028	3c **Gadsden Purchase,** *Dec. 30,* Tucson, Ariz. *(363,250)*	1.00

1954

1029	3c **Columbia University,** *Jan. 4,* New York, N.Y. *(550,745)*	1.00

1954-67

LIBERTY ISSUE

1030a	½c **Franklin,** *Oct. 20, 1955 (223,122),* block of 6	1.00
1031b	1c **Washington,** *Aug. 26, 1954,* Chicago, Ill. *(272,581),* strip of 3	1.00
1031A	1 ¼c **Palace of Governors,** *June 17, 1960,* Santa Fe, N.M. *(321,021)*	1.00
	1031A and 1054A on one cover	1.50

First day cancel was applied to 501,848 covers bearing one or more of Nos. 1031A, 1054A.

1032	1 ½c **Mt. Vernon,** *Feb. 22, 1956,* Mount Vernon, Va. *(270,109),* pair	1.00
1033	2c **Jefferson,** *Sept. 15, 1954,* San Francisco, Cal. *(307,300),* pair	1.00
1034	2 ½c **Bunker Hill,** *June 17, 1959,* Boston, Mass. *(315,060),* pair	1.00
1035e	3c **Statue of Liberty** *June 24, 1954,* Albany, N.Y. *(340,001)*	1.00
1035a	Booklet pane of 6, *June 30, 1954*	5.00
1035b	3c Tagged, *July 6, 1966*	15.00
1036c	4c **Lincoln,** *Nov. 19, 1954,* New York, N.Y. *(374,064)*	1.00
1036a	Booklet pane of 6, *July 31, 1958,* Wheeling, W. Va. *(135,825)*	4.00
1036b	4c Tagged, *Nov. 2, 1963*	50.00

No. 1036b was supposed to have been issued at Dayton Nov. 2, but a mix-up delayed its issuance there until Nov. 4. About 510 Covers received the Nov. 2 cancellation.

1037	4 ½c **Hermitage,** *Mar. 16, 1959,* Hermitage, Tenn. *(320,000)*	1.00
1038	5c **Monroe,** *Dec. 2, 1954,* Fredericksburg, Va. *(255,650)*	1.00
1039a	6c **T. Roosevelt,** *Nov. 18, 1955,* New York, N.Y. *(257,551)*	1.00
1040	7c **Wilson,** *Jan. 10, 1956,* Staunton, Va. *(200,111)*	1.00
1041	8c **Statue of Liberty** (flat plate), *Apr. 9, 1954*	1.00
1041B	8c **Statue of Liberty** (rotary press), *Apr. 9, 1954*	1.00

First day cancellation was applied to 340,077 covers bearing one or more of Nos. 1041-1041B.

1042	8c **Statue of Liberty** (Giori press), *Mar. 22, 1958,* Cleveland, O. *(223,899)*	1.00
1042A	8c **Pershing,** *Nov. 17, 1961,* New York, N.Y. *(321,031)*	1.00
1043	9c **Alamo,** *June 14, 1956,* San Antonio, Texas *(207,086)*	1.50
1044	10c **Independence Hall,** *July 4, 1956,* Philadelphia, Pa.. *(220,930)*	1.00
1044b	10c Tagged, *July 6, 1966*	15.00
1044A	11c **Statue of Liberty,** *June 15, 1961 (238,905)*	1.00
1044Ac	11c Tagged, *Jan. 11, 1967*	22.50
1045	12c **B. Harrison,** *June 6, 1959,* Oxford, O. *(225,869)*	1.00
1045a	12c Tagged, *May 6, 1968*	25.00
1046	15c **Jay,** *Dec. 12, 1958 (205,680)*	1.00
1046a	15c Tagged, *July 6, 1966*	20.00
1047	20c **Monticello,** *Apr. 13, 1956,* Charlottesville, Va. *(147,860)*	1.25
1048	25c **Revere,** *Apr. 18, 1958,* Boston, Mass. *(196,530)*	1.25
1049a	30c **Lee,** *Sept. 21, 1955,* Norfolk, Va. *(120,166)*	2.00
1050a	40c **Marshall,** *Sept. 24, 1955,* Richmond, Va. *(113,972)*	2.00
1051a	50c **Anthony,** *Aug. 25, 1955,* Louisville, Ky. *(110,220)*	6.00
1052a	$1 **Henry,** *Oct. 7, 1955,* Joplin, Mo. *(80,191)*	10.00
1053	$5 **Hamilton,** *Mar. 19, 1956,* Paterson, N.J. *(34,272)*	65.00

1954-73

COIL STAMPS

1054c	1c **Washington,** *Oct. 8, 1954,* Baltimore, Md. *(196,318),* strip of 3	1.00
1054A	1 ¼c **Palace of Governors,** *June 17, 1960,* Santa Fe, N.M. *(321,021),* strip of 3	1.00
1055d	2c **Jefferson,** *Oct. 22, 1954,* St. Louis, Mo. *(162,050),* pair	1.00
1055a	2c Tagged, *May 6, 1968,* pair	11.00
1056	2 ½c **Bunker Hill,** *Sept. 9, 1959,* Los Angeles, Calif. *(198,680),* pair	2.00
1057c	3c **Statue of Liberty,** *July 20, 1954 (137,139)*	1.00
1058	4c **Lincoln,** *July 31, 1958,* Mandan, N.D. *(184,079)*	1.00
1059	4 ½c **Hermitage,** *May 1, 1959,* Denver, Colo. *(202,454)*	1.75
1059A	25c **Revere,** *Feb. 25, 1965,* Wheaton, Md. *(184,954)*	1.25
1059Ab	25c Tagged, *Apr. 3, 1973,* New York, N.Y.	14.00

1954

1060	3c **Nebraska Territory,** *May 7,* Nebraska City, Neb. *(401,015)*	1.00
1061	3c **Kansas Territory,** *May 31,* Fort Leavenworth, Kans. *(349,145)*	1.00

1062	3c **George Eastman,** *July 12,* Rochester, N.Y. *(630,448)*	1.00
1063	3c **Lewis & Clark Expedition,** *July 28,* Sioux City, Iowa *(371,557)*	1.00

1955

1064	3c **Pennsylvania Academy of the Fine Arts,** *Jan. 15,* Philadelphia, Pa. *(307,040)*	1.00
1065	3c **Land Grant Colleges,** *Feb. 12,* East Lansing, Mich. *(419,241)*	1.00
1066	8c **Rotary International,** *Feb. 23,* Chicago, Ill. *(350,625)*	3.00
1067	3c **Armed Forces Reserve,** *May 21 (300,436)*	1.00
1068	3c **New Hampshire,** *June 21,* Franconia, N.H. *(330,630)*	1.00
1069	3c **Soo Locks,** *June 28,* Sault Sainte Marie, Mich. *(316,616)*	1.00
1070	3c **Atoms for Peace,** *July 28 (351,940)*	1.00
1071	3c **Fort Ticonderoga,** *Sept. 18,* Fort Ticonderoga, N.Y. *(342,946)*	1.00
1072	3c **Andrew W. Mellon,** *Dec. 20 (278,897)*	1.00

1956

1073	3c **Benjamin Franklin,** *Jan. 17,* Philadelphia, Pa. *(351,260)*	1.00
1074	3c **Booker T. Washington,** *Apr. 5,* Booker T. Washington Birthplace, Va. *(272,659)*	1.25
1075	11c **FIPEX Souvenir Sheet,** *Apr. 28,* New York, N.Y. *(429,327)*	5.00
1076	3c **FIPEX,** *Apr. 30,* New York, N.Y. *(526,090)*	1.00
1077	3c **Wildlife (Turkey),** *May 5,* Fond du Lac, Wis. *(292,121)*	1.50
1078	3c **Wildlife (Antelope),** *June 22,* Gunnison, Colo. *(294,731)*	1.50
1079	3c **Wildlife (Salmon),** *Nov. 9,* Seattle, Wash. *(346,800)*	1.50
1080	3c **Pure Food and Drug Laws,** *June 27,* Washington, D.C. *(411,761)*	1.00
1081	3c **Wheatland,** *Aug. 5,* Lancaster, Pa. *(340,142)*	1.00
1082	3c **Labor Day,** *Sept. 3,* Camden, N.J. *(338,450)*	1.00
1083	3c **Nassau Hall,** *Sept. 22,* Princeton, N.J. *(350,756)*	1.00
1084	3c **Devils Tower,** *Sept. 24,* Devils Tower, Wyo. *(285,090)*	1.00
1085	3c **Children,** *Dec. 15 (305,125)*	1.00

1957

1086	3c **Alexander Hamilton,** *Jan. 11,* New York, N.Y. *(305,117)*	1.00
1087	3c **Polio,** *Jan. 15 (307,630)*	1.00
1088	3c **Coast & Geodetic Survey,** *Feb. 11,* Seattle, Wash. *(309,931)*	1.00
1089	3c **Architects,** *Feb. 23,* New York, N.Y. *(368,840)*	1.00
1090	3c **Steel Industry,** *May 22,* New York, N.Y. *(473,284)*	1.00
1091	3c **Naval Review,** *June 10,* U.S.S. Saratoga, Norfolk, Va. *(365,933)*	1.00
1092	3c **Oklahoma Statehood,** *June 14,* Oklahoma City, Okla. *(327,172)*	1.00
1093	3c **School Teachers,** *July 1,* Philadelphia, Pa. *(357,986)*	2.00
	(Spelling error) Philadelpia	5.00
1094	4c **Flag,** *July 4 (523,879)*	1.00
1095	3c **Shipbuilding,** *Aug. 15,* Bath, Maine *(347,432)*	1.00
1096	8c **Ramon Magsaysay,** *Aug. 31 (334,558)*	1.00
1097	3c **Lafayette Bicentenary,** *Sept. 6,* Easton, Pa. *(260,421)*	1.00
	Fayetteville, N.C. *(230,000)*	1.00
	Louisville, Ky. *(207,856)*	1.00
1098	3c **Wildlife (Whooping Cranes),** *Nov. 22,* New York, N.Y. *(342,970)*	1.00
	New Orleans, La. *(154,327)*	1.00
	Corpus Christi, Tex. *(280,990)*	1.00
1099	3c **Religious Freedom,** *Dec. 27,* Flushing, N.Y. *(357,770)*	1.00

1958

1100	3c **Gardening-Horticulture,** *Mar. 15,* Ithaca, N.Y. *(451,292)*	1.00
1104	3c **Brussels Exhibition,** *Apr. 17,* Detroit, Mich. *(428,073)*	1.00
1105	3c **James Monroe,** *Apr. 28,* Montross, Va. *(326,988)*	1.00
1106	3c **Minnesota Statehood,** *May 11,* Saint Paul, Minn. *(475,552)*	1.00
1107	3c **International Geophysical Year,** *May 31,* Chicago, Ill. *(397,000)*	1.00
1108	3c **Gunston Hall,** *June 12,* Lorton, Va. *(349,801)*	1.00
1109	3c **Mackinac Bridge,** *June 25,* Mackinac Bridge, Mich. *(445,605)*	1.00
1110	4c **Simon Bolivar,** *July 24*	1.00
1111	8c **Simon Bolivar,** *July 24*	1.00
	1110-1111 on one cover	2.00

First day cancellation was applied to 708, 777 covers bearing one or more of Nos. 1110-1111.

1112	4c **Atlantic Cable,** *Aug. 15,* New York, N.Y. *(365,072)*	1.00

1958-59

1113	1c **Lincoln Sesquicentennial,** *Feb. 12, 1959,* Hodgenville, Ky. *(379,862)* block of four	1.25
1114	1c **Lincoln Sesquicentennial,** *Feb. 12, 1959,* New York, N.Y. *(437,737)*	1.25

1115	4c Lincoln-Douglas Debates, *Aug. 27, 1958*, Freeport, Ill. *(373,063)*	1.25
1116	4c Lincoln Sesquicentennial, *May, 30, 1959 (894,887)*	1.25

1958

1117	4c Lajos Kossuth, *Sept. 19*	1.00
1118	8c Lajos Kossuth, *Sept. 19*	1.00
	1117-1118 on one cover	2.00

First day cancellation was applied to 722,188 covers bearing one or more of Nos. 1117-1118.

1119	4c Freedom of Press, *Sept. 22*, Columbia, Mo. *(411,752)*	1.00
1120	4c Overland Mail, *Oct. 10*, San Francisco, Cal. *(352,760)*	1.00
1121	4c Noah Webster, *Oct. 16*, West Hartford, Conn. *(364,608)*	1.00
1122	4c Forest Conservation, *Oct. 27*, Tucson, Ariz. *(405,959)*	1.00
1123	4c Fort Duquesne, *Nov. 25*, Pittsburgh, Pa. *(421,764)*	1.00

1959

1124	4c Oregon Statehood, *Feb. 14*, Astoria, Ore. *(452,764)*	1.00
1125	4c San Martin, *Feb. 25*	1.00
1126	8c San Martin, *Feb. 25*	1.00
	1125-1126 on one cover	2.00

First day cancellation was applied to 910,208 covers bearing one or more of No. 1125-1126.

1127	4c NATO, *Apr. 1 (361,040)*	1.00
1128	4c Arctic Exploration, *Apr. 6*, Cresson, Pa. *(397,770)*	1.00
1129	8c World Trade, *Apr. 20 (503,618)*	1.00
1130	4c Silver Centennial, *June 8*, Virginia City, Nev. *(337,233)*	1.00
1131	4c St. Lawrence Seaway, *June 26*, Massena, N.Y. *(543,211)*	1.25
1132	4c Flag (49 stars), *July 4*, Auburn, N.Y. *(523,773)*	1.00
1133	4c Soil Conservation, *Aug. 26*, Rapid City, S.D. *(400,613)*	1.00
1134	4c Petroleum Industry, *Aug. 27*, Titusville, Pa. *(801,859)*	1.25
1135	4c Dental Health, *Sept. 14*, New York, N.Y. *(649,813)*	3.00
1136	4c Reuter, *Sept. 29*	1.00
1137	8c Reuter, *Sept. 29*	1.00
	1136-1137 on one cover	2.00

First day cancellation was applied to 1,207,933 covers bearing one or more of Nos. 1136-1137.

1138	4c Dr. Ephraim McDowell, *Dec. 3*, Danville, Ky. *(344,603)*	1.50

1960-61

1139	4c Washington "Credo," *Jan. 20, 1960*, Mount Vernon, Va. *(438,335)*	1.25
1140	4c Franklin "Credo," *Mar. 31, 1960*, Philadelphia, Pa. *(497,913)*	1.25
1141	4c Jefferson "Credo," *May 18, 1960*, Charlottesville, Va. *(454,903)*	1.25
1142	4c Francis Scott Key "Credo," *Sept. 14, 1960*, Baltimore, Md. *(501,129)*	1.25
1143	4c Lincoln "Credo," *Nov. 19, 1960*, New York, N.Y. *(467,780)*	1.25
1144	4c Patrick Henry "Credo," *Jan. 11, 1961*, Richmond, Va. *(415,252)*	1.25

1960

1145	4c Boy Scouts, *Feb. 8 (1,419,955)*	3.50
1146	4c Olympic Winter Games, *Feb. 18*, Olympic Valley, Calif. *(516,456)*	1.00
1147	4c Masaryk, *Mar. 7*	1.00
1148	8c Masaryk, *Mar. 7*	1.00
	1147-1148 on one cover	2.00

First day cancellation was applied to 1,710,726 covers bearing one or more of Nos. 1147-1148.

1149	4c World Refugee Year, *Apr. 7 (413,298)*	1.00
1150	4c Water Conservation, *Apr. 18 (648,988)*	1.00
1151	4c SEATO, *May 31 (514,926)*	1.00
1152	4c American Woman, *June 2 (830,385)*	1.25
1153	4c 50-Star Flag, *July 4*, Honolulu, Hawaii *(820,900)*	1.00
1154	4c Pony Express Centennial, *July 19*, Sacramento, Calif. *(520,223)*	1.25
1155	4c Employ the Handicapped, *Aug. 28*, New York, N.Y. *(439,638)*	1.00
1156	4c World Forestry Congress, *Aug. 29*, Seattle, Wash. *(350,848)*	1.00
1157	4c Mexican Independence, *Sept. 16*, Los Angeles, Calif. *(360,297)*	1.00
1158	4c U.S.-Japan Treaty, *Sept. 28 (545,150)*	1.00
1159	4c Paderewski, *Oct. 8*	1.00
1160	8c Paderewski, *Oct. 8*	1.00
	1159-1160 on one cover	2.00

First day cancellation was applied to 1,057,438 covers bearing one or more of Nos. 1159-1160.

1161	4c Robert A. Taft, *Oct. 10*, Cincinnati, Ohio *(312,116)*	1.00
1162	4c Wheels of Freedom, *Oct. 15*, Detroit, Mich. *(380,551)*	1.00
1163	4c Boys' Clubs, *Oct. 18*, New York, N.Y. *(435,009)*	1.00
1164	4c Automated P.O., *Oct. 20*, Providence, R.I. *(458,237)*	1.00
1165	4c Mannerheim, *Oct. 26*	1.00
1166	8c Mannerheim, *Oct. 26*	1.00
	1165-1166 on one cover	2.00

First day cancellation was applied to 1,168,770 covers bearing one or more of Nos. 1165-1166.

1167	4c Camp Fire Girls, *Nov. 1*, New York, N.Y. *(324,944)*	1.00
1168	4c Garibaldi, *Nov. 2*	1.00
1169	8c Garibaldi, *Nov. 2*	1.00
	1168-1169 on one cover	2.00

First day cancellation was applied to 1,001,490 covers bearing one or more of Nos. 1168-1169.

1170	4c Senator George, *Nov. 5*, Vienna, Ga. *(278,890)*	1.00
1171	4c Andrew Carnegie, *Nov. 25*, New York, N.Y. *(318,180)*	1.00
1172	4c John Foster Dulles, *Dec. 6 (400,055)*	1.00
1173	4c Echo I, *Dec. 15 (583,747)*	2.50

1961-65

1174	4c Gandhi, *Jan. 26, 1961*	1.00
1175	8c Gandhi, *Jan. 26, 1961*	1.00
	1174-1175 on one cover	2.00

First day cancellation was applied to 1,013,515 covers bearing one or more of Nos. 1174-1175.

1176	4c Range Conservation, *Feb. 2, 1961*, Salt Lake City, Utah *(357,101)*	1.00
1177	4c Horace Greeley, *Feb. 3, 1961*, Chappaqua, N.Y. *(359,205)*	1.00
1178	4c Fort Sumter, *Apr. 12, 1961*, Charleston, S.C. *(602,599)*	3.00
1179	4c Battle of Shiloh, *Apr. 7, 1962*, Shiloh, Tenn. *(526,062)*	3.00
1180	5c Battle of Gettysburg, *July 1, 1963*, Gettysburg, Pa. *(600,205)*	3.00
1181	5c Battle of Wilderness, *May 5, 1964*, Fredericksburg, Pa. *(450,904)*	3.00
1182	5c Appomattox, *Apr. 9, 1965*, Appomattox, Va. *(653,121)*	3.00

1961

1183	4c Kansas Statehood, *May 10*, Council Grove, Kansas *(480,561)*	1.00
1184	4c Senator Norris, *July 11 (482,875)*	1.00
1185	4c Naval Aviation, *Aug. 20*, San Diego, Calif. *(416,391)*	1.00
1186	4c Workmen's Compensation, *Sept. 4*, Milwaukee, Wis, *(410,236)*	1.00
1187	4c Frederic Remington, *Oct. 4 (723,443)*	1.25
1188	4c China Republic, *Oct. 10 (463,900)*	3.00
1189	4c Naismith-Basketball, *Nov. 6*, Springfield, Mass. *(479,917)*	6.00
1190	4c Nursing, *Dec. 28 (964,005)*	7.50

1962

1191	4c New Mexico Statehood, *Jan. 6*, Sante Fe, N.M. *(365,330)*	1.25
1192	4c Arizona Statehood, *Feb. 14*, Phoenix, Ariz. *(508,216)*	1.25
1193	4c Project Mercury, *Feb. 20*, Cape Canaveral, Fla. *(3,000,000)*	3.00
	Any other city	5.00
1194	4c Malaria Eradication, *Mar. 30 (554,175)*	1.00
1195	4c Charles Evans Hughes, *Apr. 11 (544,424)*	1.00
1196	4c Seattle World's Fair, *Apr. 25*, Seattle, Wash. *(771,856)*	1.00
1197	4c Louisiana Statehood, *Apr. 30*, New Orleans, La. *(436,681)*	1.00
1198	4c Homestead Act, *May 20*, Beatrice, Nebr. *(487,450)*	1.00
1199	4c Girl Scouts, *July 24*, Burlington, Vt. *(634,347)*	4.00
1200	4c Brien McMahon, *July 28*, Norwalk, Conn. *(384,479)*	1.00
1201	4c Apprenticeship, *Aug. 31 (1,003,548)*	1.00
1202	4c Sam Rayburn, *Sept. 16*, Bonham, Texas *(401,042)*	1.00
1203	4c Dag Hammarskjold, *Oct. 23*, New York, N.Y. *(500,683)*	1.00
1204	4c Hammarskjold, yellow inverted, *Nov. 16*, *(about 75,000)*	5.00
1205	4c Christmas, *Nov. 1*, Pittsburgh, Pa. *(491,312)*	1.10
1206	4c Higher Education, *Nov. 14 (627,347)*	1.50
1207	4c Winslow Homer, *Dec. 15*, Gloucester, Mass. *(498,866)*	1.25

1963-66

1208	5c Flag, *Jan. 9, 1963 (696,185)*	1.00
1208a	5c Tagged, *Aug. 25, 1966*	25.00

1962-66

REGULAR ISSUE

1209	1c Jackson, *Mar. 22, 1963*, New York, N.Y. *(392,363)*, block of 5 or 6	1.00
1209a	1c Tagged, *July 6, 1966*, block of 5 or 6	25.00
1213	5c Washington, *Nov. 23, 1962*, New York, N.Y. *(360,531)*	1.00
1213a	Booklet pane of 5 + label, *Nov. 23, 1962*, New York, N.Y. *(111,452)*	4.00
1213b	5c Tagged, *Oct. 28, 1963*, Dayton, Ohio *(about 15,000)*	25.00
1213c	Booklet pane of 5 + label, tagged, *Oct. 28, 1963*, Dayton, Ohio	100.00
	Washington, D.C. *(750)*	110.00
1225	1c Jackson, Coil, *May 31, 1963*, Chicago, Ill. *(238,952)*, pair and strip of 3	1.00
1225a	1c Coil, tagged, *July 6, 1966*, pair and strip of 3	15.00
1229	5c Washington, Coil, *Nov. 23, 1962*, New York, N.Y. *(184,627)*	1.00
1229a	5c Coil, tagged, *Oct. 28, 1963*, Dayton, Ohio (about *2,000*)	25.00

1963

1230	5c Carolina Charter, *Apr. 6*, Edenton, N.C. *(426,200)*	1.00
1231	5c Food for Peace, *June 4 (624,342)*	1.00

1232	5c West Virginia Statehood, *June 20*, Wheeling, W. Va. *(413,389)*	1.00
1233	5c Emancipation Proclamation, *Aug. 16*, Chicago, Ill. *(494,886)*	1.50
1234	5c Alliance for Progress, *Aug. 17 (528,095)*	1.00
1235	5c Cordell Hull, *Oct. 5* Carthage, Tenn. *(391,631)*	1.00
1236	5c Eleanor Roosevelt, *Oct. 11 (860,155)*	1.00
1237	5c Science, *Oct. 14 (504,503)*	1.00
1238	5c City Mail Delivery, *Oct. 26 (544,806)*	1.00
1239	5c Red Cross, *Oct. 29 (557,678)*	1.25
1240	5c Christmas, *Nov. 1*, Santa Claus, Ind. *(458,619)*	1.25
1240a	5c Christmas, tagged, *Nov. 2*, (about *500*)	60.00

Note below No. 1036b also applies to No. 1240a.

1241	5c Audubon, *Dec. 7*, Henderson, Ky. *(518,855)*	1.25

1964

1242	5c Sam Houston, *Jan. 10*, Houston, Tex. *(487,986)*	1.00
1243	5c Charles Russell, *Mar. 19*, Great Falls, Mont. *(658,745)*	1.25
1244	5c N.Y. World's Fair, *Apr. 22*, World's Fair, N.Y. *(1,656,346)*	1.50
1245	5c John Muir, *Apr. 29*, Martinez, Calif. *(446,925)*	1.00
1246	5c John F. Kennedy, *May 29*, Boston, Mass. *(2,003,096)*	2.50
	Any other city	4.00
1247	5c New Jersey Tercentenary, *June 15*, Elizabeth, N.J. *(526,879)*	1.00
1248	5c Nevada Statehood, *July 22*, Carson City, Nev. *(584,973)*	1.00
1249	5c Register & Vote, *Aug. 1 (533,439)*	1.00
1250	5c Shakespeare, *Aug. 14*, Stratford, Conn. *(524,053)*	1.50
1251	5c Drs. Mayo, *Sept. 11*, Rochester, Minn. *(674,846)*	3.50
1252	5c American Music, *Oct. 15*, New York, N.Y. *(466,107)*	1.50
1253	5c Homemakers, *Oct. 26*, Honolulu, Hawaii *(435,392)*	1.00
1257b	5c Christmas, *Nov. 9*, Bethlehem, Pa.	3.00
	1254-1257, any single	1.00
1257c	5c Tagged, *Nov. 10*, Dayton, O.	57.50
	1254a-1257a, any single	12.50

First day cancellation was applied to 794,900 covers bearing Nos. 1254-1257 in singles or multiples and at Dayton to about 2,700 covers bearing Nos. 1254a-1257a in singles or multiples.

1258	5c Verrazano-Narrows Bridge, *Nov. 21*, Staten Island, N.Y. *(619,780)*	1.00
1259	5c Fine Arts, *Dec. 2 (558,046)*	1.00
1260	5c Amateur Radio, *Dec. 15*, Anchorage, Alaska *(452,255)*	1.25

1965

1261	5c Battle of New Orleans, *Jan. 8*, New Orleans, La. *(466,029)*	1.00
1262	5c Physical Fitness-Sokol, *Feb. 15 (864,848)*	1.25
1263	5c Cancer Crusade, *Apr. 1 (744,485)*	2.00
1264	5c Churchill, *May 13*, Fulton, Mo. *(773,580)*	1.50
1265	5c Magna Carta, *June 15*, Jamestown, Va. *(479,065)*	1.00
1266	5c Intl. Cooperation Year, *June 26*, San Francisco, Cal. *(402,925)*	1.00
1267	5c Salvation Army, *July 2*, New York, N.Y. *(634,228)*	1.50
1268	5c Dante, *July 17*, San Francisco, Cal. *(424,893)*	1.00
1269	5c Herbert Hoover, *Aug. 10*, West Branch, Iowa *(698,182)*	1.00
1270	5c Robert Fulton, *Aug. 19*, Clermont, N.Y. *(550,330)*	1.00
1271	5c Florida Settlement, *Aug. 28*, St. Augustine, Fla. *(465,000)*	1.00
1272	5c Traffic Safety, *Sept. 3*, Baltimore, Md. *(527,075)*	1.00
1273	5c Copley, *Sept. 17 (613,484)*	1.00
1274	11c Intl. Telecommunication Union, *Oct. 6 (332,818)*	1.10
1275	5c Adlai Stevenson, *Oct. 23*, Bloomington, Ill. *(755,656)*	1.00
1276	5c Christmas, *Nov. 2*, Silver Bell, Ariz. *(705,039)*	1.00
1276a	5c Tagged, *Nov. 15*, (about *300*)	42.50

1965-78

PROMINENT AMERICANS ISSUE

1278	1c Jefferson, *Jan. 12, 1968*, Jeffersonville, Ind., block of 5 or 6	1.00
1278a	Booklet pane of 8, *Jan. 12, 1968*, Jeffersonville, Ind.	2.50
1278b	Booklet pane of 4 + 2 labels, *May 10, 1971*	12.50

First day cancellation was applied to 655,680 covers bearing one or more of Nos. 1278, 1278a and 1299.

1279	1¼c Gallatin, *Jan. 30, 1967*, Gallatin, Mo. *(439,010)*	1.00
1280	2c Wright, *June 8, 1966*, Spring Green, Wis. *(460,427)*	1.00
1280a	Booklet pane of 5 + label, *Jan. 8, 1968*, Buffalo, N.Y. *(147,244)*	3.50
1280c	Booklet pane of 6, *May 7, 1971*, Spokane, Wash.	15.00
1281	3c Parkman, *Sept. 16, 1967*, Boston, Mass. *(518,355)*	1.00
1282	4c Lincoln, *Nov. 19, 1965*, New York, N.Y. *(445,629)*	1.25
1282a	4c Tagged, *Dec. 1, 1965*, Dayton, O. (about *2,000*)	25.00
	Washington, D.C. *(1,200)*	32.50

1283	5c	**Washington,** *Feb. 22, 1966 (525,372)*	1.00
1283a	5c	Tagged, *Feb. 23, 1966,* (about *900*) Dayton, Ohio (about *200*)	75.00 / 25.00
1283B	5c	**Washington,** Redrawn, *Nov. 17, 1967,* New York, N.Y. *(328,983)*	1.00
1284	6c	**Roosevelt,** *Jan. 29, 1966,* Hyde Park, N.Y. *(448,631)*	1.00
1284a	6c	Tagged, *Dec. 29, 1966*	30.00
1284b		Booklet pane of 8, *Dec. 28, 1967*	2.75
1284c		Booklet pane of 5 + label, *Jan. 9, 1968*	100.00
1285	8c	**Einstein,** *Mar. 14, 1966,* Princeton, N.J. *(366,803)*	1.50
1285a	8c	Tagged, *July 6, 1966*	25.00
1286	10c	**Jackson,** *Mar. 15, 1967,* Hermitage, Tenn. *(255,945)*	1.00
1286A	12c	**Ford,** *July 30, 1968,* Greenfield Village, Mich. *(342,850)*	1.50
1287	13c	**Kennedy,** *May 29, 1967,* Brookline, Mass. *(391,195)*	2.00
1288	15c	**Holmes,** type I, *Mar. 8, 1968 (322,970)*	1.00
1288B	15c	**Holmes,** from bklt., *June 14, 1978,* Boston, Mass.	1.00
1288Bc		Booklet pane of 8	3.00

First day cancellation was applied to 387,119 covers bearing one or more of Nos. 1288B and 1305E.

1289	20c	**Marshall,** *Oct. 24, 1967,* Lexington, Va. *(221,206)*	1.10
1289a	20c	Tagged, *Apr. 3, 1973,* New York, N.Y.	25.00
1290	25c	**Douglass,** *Feb. 14, 1967* (213,730)	1.75
1290a	25c	Tagged, *Apr. 3, 1973,* New York, N.Y.	27.50
1291	30c	**Dewey,** *Oct. 21, 1968,* Burlington, Vt. *(162,790)*	1.75
1291a	30c	Tagged, *Apr. 3, 1973,* New York, N.Y.	27.50
1292	40c	**Paine,** *Jan. 29, 1968,* Philadelphia, Pa. *(157,947)*	1.75
1292a	40c	Tagged, *Apr. 3, 1973,* New York, N.Y.	27.50
1293	50c	**Stone,** *Aug. 13, 1968,* Dorchester, Mass. *(140,410)*	2.00
1293a	50c	Tagged, *Apr. 3, 1973,* New York, N.Y.	30.00
1294	$1	**O'Neill,** *Oct. 16, 1967,* New London, Conn. *(103,102)*	7.50
1294a	$1	Tagged, *Apr. 3, 1973,* New York, N.Y.	35.00
1295	$5	**Moore,** *Dec. 3, 1966,* Smyrna, Del. *(41,130)*	40.00
1295a	$5	Tagged, *Apr. 3, 1973,* New York, N.Y.	80.00

First day cancellation was applied to 17,533 covers bearing one or more of Nos. 1059b, 1289a, 1290a, 1291a, 1292a, 1293a, 1294a and 1295a.

COIL STAMPS

1297	3c	**Parkman,** *Nov. 4, 1975,* Pendleton, Ore. *(166,798)*	1.00
1298	6c	**Roosevelt,** Perf. 10 Horiz., *Dec. 28, 1967*	1.00

First day cancellation was applied to 312,330 covers bearing one or more of Nos. 1298 and 1284b.

1299	1c	**Jefferson,** *Jan. 12, 1968,* Jeffersonville, Ind., pair and strip of 3	1.00
1303	4c	**Lincoln,** *May 28, 1966,* Springfield, Ill. *(322,563)*	1.00
1304	5c	**Washington,** *Sept. 8, 1966,* Cincinnati, O. *(245,400)*	1.00
1305	6c	**Roosevelt,** Perf. 10 vert., *Feb. 28, 1968 (317,199)*	1.00
1305E	15c	**Holmes,** type I, *June 14, 1978,* Boston, Mass.	1.00
1305C	$1	**O'Neill,** *Jan. 12, 1973,* Hempstead, N.Y. *(121,217)*	4.00

1966

1306	5c	**Migratory Bird Treaty,** *Mar. 16,* Pittsburgh, Pa. *(555,485)*	1.50
1307	5c	**Humane Treatment of Animals,** *Apr. 9,* New York, N.Y. *(524,420)*	1.25
1308	5c	**Indiana Statehood,** *Apr. 16,* Corydon, Ind. *(575,557)*	1.00
1309	5c	**Circus,** *May 2,* Delavan, Wis. *(754,076)*	2.50
1310	5c	**SIPEX,** *May 21 (637,802)*	1.00
1311	5c	**SIPEX,** souvenir sheet, *May 23 (700,882)*	1.10
1312	5c	**Bill of Rights,** *July 1,* Miami Beach, Fla. *(562,920)*	1.00
1313	5c	**Polish Millennium,** *July 30 (715,603)*	1.00
1314	5c	**Natl. Park Service,** *Aug. 25,* Yellowstone National Park, Wyo. *(528,170)*	1.00
1314a	5c	Tagged, *Aug. 26*	30.00
1315	5c	**Marine Corps Reserve,** *Aug. 29 (585,923)*	1.50
1315a	5c	Tagged, *Aug. 29*	30.00
1316	5c	**Gen. Fed. of Women's Clubs,** *Sept. 12,* New York, N.Y. *(383,334)*	1.00
1316a	5c	Tagged, *Sept. 13*	30.00
1317	5c	**Johnny Appleseed,** *Sept. 24,* Leominster, Mass. *(794,610)*	1.50
1317a	5c	Tagged, *Sept. 26*	30.00
1318	5c	**Beautification of America,** *Oct. 5 (564,440)*	1.00
1318a	5c	Tagged, *Oct. 5*	30.00
1319	5c	**Great River Road,** *Oct. 21,* Baton Rouge, La. *(330,933)*	1.00
1319a	5c	Tagged, *Oct. 22*	30.00
1320	5c	**Savings Bond-Servicemen,** *Oct. 26,* Sioux City, Iowa *(444,421)*	1.00
1320a	5c	Tagged, *Oct. 27*	30.00

1321	5c	**Christmas,** *Nov. 1,* Christmas, Mich. *(537,650)*	1.00
1321a	5c	Tagged, *Nov. 2*	30.00
1322	5c	**Mary Cassatt,** *Nov. 17 (593,389)*	1.00
1322a	5c	Tagged, *Nov. 17*	30.00

1967

1323	5c	**National Grange,** *Apr. 17 (603,460)*	1.00
1324	5c	**Canada Centenary,** *May 25,* Montreal, Canada *(711,795)*	1.00
1325	5c	**Erie Canal,** *July 4,* Rome, N.Y. *(784,611)*	1.00
1326	5c	**Search for Peace-Lions,** *July 5,* Chicago, Ill. *(393,197)*	1.00
1327	5c	**Thoreau,** *July 12,* Concord, Mass. *(696,789)*	1.00
1328	5c	**Nebraska Statehood,** *July 29,* Lincoln, Nebr. *(1,146,957)*	1.00
1329	5c	**Voice of America,** *Aug. 1 (455,190)*	1.00
1330	5c	**Davy Crockett,** *Aug. 17,* San Antonio, Tex. *(462,291)*	1.10
1331a	5c	**Space Accomplishments,** *Sept. 29,* Kennedy Space Center, Fla. *(667,267)*	7.50
		1331-1332, any single	3.00
1333	5c	**Urban Planning,** *Oct. 2 (389,009)*	1.00
1334	5c	**Finland Independence,** *Oct. 6,* Finland, Minn. *(408,532)*	1.00
1335	5c	**Thomas Eakins,** *Nov. 2 (648,054)*	1.00
1336	5c	**Christmas,** *Nov. 6,* Bethlehem, Ga. *(462,118)*	1.00
1337	5c	**Mississippi Statehood,** *Dec. 11,* Natchez, Miss. *(379,612)*	1.00

1968-71

1338	6c	**Flag** (Giori), *Jan. 24, 1968 (412,120)*	1.00
1338A	6c	**Flag coil,** *May 30, 1969,* Chicago, Ill. *(248,434)*	1.00
1338D	6c	**Flag** (Huck) *Aug. 7, 1970 (365,280)*	1.00
1338F	8c	**Flag,** *May 10, 1971*	1.00
1338G	8c	**Flag coil,** *May 10, 1971*	1.00

First day cancellation (May 10) was applied to 235,543 covers bearing one or more of Nos. 1338F-1338G.

1968

1339	6c	**Illinois Statehood,** *Feb. 12,* Shawneetown, Ill. *(761,640)*	1.00
1340	6c	**HemisFair'68,** *Mar. 30,* San Antonio, Tex. *(469,909)*	1.00
1341	$1	**Airlift,** *Apr. 4,* Seattle, Wash. *(105,088)*	7.00
1342	6c	**Youth-Elks,** *May 1,* Chicago, Ill. *(354,711)*	1.00
1343	6c	**Law and Order,** *May 17 (407,081)*	1.50
1344	6c	**Register and Vote,** *June 27 (355,685)*	1.00
1354a	6c	**Historic Flag series of 10,** *July 4,* Pittsburgh, Pa. *(2,924,962)*	17.50
		1345-1354, any single	3.00
1355	6c	**Disney,** *Sept. 11,* Marceline, Mo. *(499,505)*	15.00
1356	6c	**Marquette,** *Sept. 20,* Sault Ste. Marie, Mich. *(379,710)*	1.00
1357	6c	**Daniel Boone,** *Sept. 26,* Frankfort, Ky. *(333,440)*	1.10
1358	6c	**Arkansas River,** *Oct. 1,* Little Rock, Ark. *(358,025)*	1.00
1359	6c	**Leif Erikson,** *Oct. 9,* Seattle, Wash. *(376,565)*	1.00
1360	6c	**Cherokee Strip,** *Oct. 15,* Ponca, Okla. *(339,330)*	1.00
1361	6c	**John Trumbull,** *Oct. 18,* New Haven, Conn. *(378,285)*	1.10
1362	6c	**Waterfowl Conservation,** *Oct. 24,* Cleveland, Ohio. *(349,719)*	1.50
1363	6c	**Christmas,** tagged, *Nov. 1 (739,055)*	1.00
1363a	6c	Untagged, *Nov. 2*	10.00
1364	6c	**American Indian,** *Nov. 4 (415,964)*	1.50

1969

1368a	6c	**Beautification of America,** *Jan. 16 (1,094,184)*	4.00
		1365-1368, any single	1.00
1369	6c	**American Legion,** *Mar. 15 (632,035)*	1.00
1370	6c	**Grandma Moses,** *May 1 (367,880)*	1.10
1371	6c	**Apollo 8,** *May 5,* Houston, Texas *(908,634)*	3.00
1372	6c	**W.C. Handy,** *May 17,* Memphis, Tenn. *(398,216)*	1.25
1373	6c	**California Bicentenary,** *July 16,* San Diego, Calif. *(530,210)*	1.00
1374	6c	**J.W. Powell,** *Aug. 1,* Page, Ariz. *(434,433)*	1.00
1375	6c	**Alabama Statehood,** *Aug. 2,* Huntsville, Ala. *(485,801)*	1.00
1379a	6c	**Botanical Congress,** *Aug. 23,* Seattle, Wash. *(737,935)*	5.00
		1376-1379, any single	1.50
1380	6c	**Dartmouth Case,** *Sept. 22,* Hanover, N.H. *(416,327)*	1.00
1381	6c	**Professional Baseball,** *Sept. 24,* Cincinnati, Ohio *(414,942)*	12.00
1382	6c	**Intercollegiate Football,** *Sept. 26,* New Brunswick, N.J. *(414,860)*	6.50
1383	6c	**Dwight D. Eisenhower,** *Oct. 14,* Abilene, Kans. *(1,009,560)*	1.00
1384	6c	**Christmas,** *Nov. 3,* Christmas, Fla. *(555,500)*	1.00
1385	6c	**Hope for Crippled,** *Nov. 20,* Columbus, Ohio *(342,676)*	1.25
1386	6c	**William M. Harnett,** *Dec. 3,* Boston, Mass. *(408,860)*	1.00

1970-74

1390a	6c	**National History,** *May 6, 1970,* New York, N.Y. *(834,260)*	4.00
		1387-1390, any single	1.50

1391	6c	**Maine Statehood,** *July 9, 1970,* Portland, Maine, *(472,165)*	1.50
1392	6c	**Wildlife Conservation,** *July 20, 1970,* Custer, S.D. *(309,418)*	1.00
1393	6c	**Eisenhower,** *Aug. 6, 1970*	1.00
1393a		Booklet pane of 8	3.00
1393b		Booklet pane of 5 + label	1.50

First day cancellations were applied to 823,540 covers bearing one or more of Nos. 1393 and 1401.

1393D	7c	**Franklin,** *Oct. 20, 1972,* Philadelphia, Pa. *(309,276)*	1.00
1394	6c	**Eisenhower** (multi), *May 10, 1971*	1.00
1395	8c	**Eisenhower** (claret), *May 10, 1971*	1.00
1395a		Booklet pane of 8	2.50
1395b		Booklet pane of 6	2.50
1395c		Booklet pane of 4 + 2 labels, *Jan. 28, 1972,* Casa Grande, Ariz.	2.00
1395d		Booklet pane of 7 + label, *Jan. 28, 1972,* Casa Grande, Ariz.	1.75

First day cancellations were applied to 813,947 covers bearing one or more of Nos. 1394, 1395 and 1402. First day cancellations were applied to 181,601 covers bearing one or more of Nos. 1395c or 1395d.

1396	8c	**Postal Service Emblem,** *July 1, 1971,* any city (est. *16,300,000*)	1.00

First day cancels from over 16,000 different cities are known. Some are rare.

1397	14c	**Fiorello H. LaGuardia,** *Apr. 24, 1972,* New York, N.Y. *(180,114)*	1.00
1398	16c	**Ernie Pyle,** *May 7, 1971 (444,410)*	1.25
1399	18c	**Elizabeth Blackwell,** *Jan. 23, 1974,* Geneva, N.Y. *(217,938)*	1.25
1400	21c	**Amadeo Giannini,** *June 27, 1973,* San Mateo, Calif. *(282,520)*	1.25
1401	6c	**Eisenhower coil,** *Aug. 6, 1970*	1.00
1402	8c	**Eisenhower coil,** *May 10, 1971*	1.00

1970

1405	6c	**Edgar Lee Masters,** *Aug. 22,* Petersburg Ill. *(372,804)*	1.00
1406	6c	**Woman Suffrage,** *Aug. 26,* Adams, Mass. *(508,142)*	1.00
1407	6c	**South Carolina Anniv.** *Sept. 12,* Charleston, S.C. *(533,000)*	1.00
1408	6c	**Stone Mt. Memorial,** *Sept. 19,* Stone Mountain, Ga. *(558,546)*	1.00
1409	6c	**Fort Snelling,** *Oct. 17,* Fort Snelling, Minn. *(497,611)*	1.00
1413a	6c	**Anti-Pollution,** *Oct. 28,* San Clemente, Calif. *(1,033,147)*	4.00
		1410-1413, any single	1.25
1414	6c	**Christmas** (Nativity), *Nov. 5*	1.25
1414a	6c	Precanceled, *Nov. 5*	7.50
1418b	6c	**Christmas,** *Nov. 5*	5.00
		1415-1418, any single	1.40
		1414-1418 on one cover	7.50
1418c	6c	Precanceled, *Nov. 5*	15.00
		1415a-1418a, any single	5.00
		1414a-1418a on one cover	30.00

First day cancellation was applied to 2,014,450 covers bearing one or more of Nos. 1414-1418 or 1414a-1418a.

1419	6c	**United Nations,** *Nov. 20,* New York, N.Y. *(474,070)*	1.25
1420	6c	**Pilgrims' Landing,** *Nov. 21,* Plymouth, Mass. *(629,850)*	1.00
1421	6c	**Disabled Veterans,** *Nov. 24,* Cincinnati, Ohio, or Montgomery, Ala.	2.00
1422	6c	**U.S. Servicemen,** *Nov. 24,* Cincinnati, Ohio, or Montgomery, Ala.	2.00
1421a			3.00

First day cancellation was applied to 476,610 covers at Cincinnati and 336,417 at Montgomery, each cover bearing one or more of Nos. 1421-1422.

1971

1423	6c	**Wool Industry,** *Jan. 19,* Las Vegas, Nev. *(379,911)*	1.00
1424	6c	**MacArthur,** *Jan. 26,* Norfolk, Va. *(720,035)*	1.10
1425	6c	**Blood Donor,** *Mar. 12,* New York, N.Y. *(644,497)*	1.10
1426	8c	**Missouri Sesquicentennial,** *May 8,* Independence, Mo. *(551,000)*	1.00
1430a	8c	**Wildlife Conservation,** *June 12,* Avery Island, La. *(679,483)*	3.00
		1427-1430, any single	1.25
1431	8c	**Antarctic Treaty,** *June 23 (419,200)*	1.00
1432	8c	**American Revolution Bicentennial,** *July 4 (434,930)*	1.00
1433	8c	**John Sloan,** *Aug. 2,* Lock Haven, Pa. *(482,265)*	1.00
1434a	8c	**Space Achievement Decade,** *Aug. 2,* Kennedy Space Center, Fla. *(1,403,644)*	2.00
		Houston, Texas *(811,560)*	2.00
		Huntsville, Ala. *(524,000)*	2.00
1436	8c	**Emily Dickinson,** *Aug. 28,* Amherst, Mass. *(498,180)*	1.00
1437	8c	**San Juan,** *Sept. 12,* San Juan, P.R. *(501,668)*	1.00
1438	8c	**Drug Abuse,** *Oct. 4,* Dallas, Texas *(425,330)*	1.00
1439	8c	**CARE,** *Oct. 27,* New York, N.Y. *(402,121)*	1.00
1443a	8c	**Historic Preservation,** *Oct. 29,* San Diego, Calif. *(783,242)*	3.00
		1440-1443, any single	1.25
1444	8c	**Christmas** (religious), *Nov. 10*	1.10
1445	8c	**Christmas** (secular), *Nov. 10*	1.10
		1444-1445 on one cover	1.25

First day cancellation was applied to 348,038 covers with No. 1444 and 580,062 with No. 1445.

1972

1446	8c	**Sidney Lanier,** Feb. 3, Macon Ga. (394,800)	1.00
1447	8c	**Peace Corps,** Feb. 11 (453,660)	1.00
1451a	8c	**National Parks Centennial,** Apr. 5, Hatteras, N.C., block of 4 (505,697)	2.50
1452	6c	**National Parks,** June 26, Vienna, Va. (403,396)	1.00
1453	8c	**National Parks,** Mar. 1, Yellowstone National Park, Wyo.	1.00
		Washington, D.C. (847,500)	1.00
1454	15c	**National Parks,** July 28, Mt. McKinley National Park, Alaska (491,456)	1.00
1455	8c	**Family Planning,** Mar. 18, New York, N.Y. (691,385)	1.00
1459a	8c	**Colonial Craftsmen** (Rev. Bicentennial), July 4, Williamsburg, Va. (1,914,976)	2.50
		1456-1459, any single	1.00
1460	6c	**Olympics,** Aug. 17	1.00
1461	8c	**Winter Olympics,** Aug. 17	1.00
1462	15c	**Olympics,** Aug. 17	1.00
		1460-1462 and C85 on one cover	2.00

First day cancellation was applied to 971,536 covers bearing one or more of Nos. 1460-1462 and C85.

1463	8c	**P.T.A.,** Sept. 15, San Francisco, Cal. (523,454)	1.00
1467a	8c	**Wildlife,** Sept. 20, Warm Springs, Ore. (733,778)	3.00
		1464-1467, any single	1.50
1468	8c	**Mail Order,** Sept. 27, Chicago, Ill. (759,666)	1.00
1469	8c	**Osteopathy,** Oct. 9, Miami, Fla. (607,160)	1.00
1470	8c	**Tom Sawyer,** Oct. 13, Hannibal, Mo. (459,013)	1.00
1471	8c	**Christmas** (religious), Nov. 9	1.00
1472	8c	**Christmas** (secular), Nov. 9	1.00
		1471-1472 on one cover	2.00

First day cancellation was applied to 713,821 covers bearing one or more of Nos. 1471-1472.

1473	8c	**Pharmacy,** Nov. 10, Cincinnati, Ohio (804,320)	6.00
1474	8c	**Stamp Collecting,** Nov. 17, New York, N.Y. (434,680)	1.00

1973

1475	8c	**Love,** Jan. 26, Philadelphia, Pa. (422,492)	2.50
1476	8c	**Pamphleteer** (Rev. Bicentennial), Feb. 16, Portland, Ore. (431,784)	1.00
1477	8c	**Broadside** (Rev. Bicentennial), Apr. 13, Atlantic City, N.J. (423,437)	1.00
1478	8c	**Post Rider** (Rev. Bicentennial), June 22, Rochester, N.Y. (586,850)	1.00
1479	8c	**Drummer** (Rev. Bicentennial), Sept. 28, New Orleans, La. (522,427)	1.00
1483a	8c	**Boston Tea Party** (Rev. Bicentennial), July 4, Boston, Mass. (897,870)	3.00
		1480-1483, any single	1.00
1484	8c	**George Gershwin,** Feb. 28, Beverly Hills, Calif. (448,814)	1.00
1485	8c	**Robinson Jeffers,** Aug. 13, Carmel, Calif. (394,261)	1.00
1486	8c	**Henry O. Tanner,** Sept. 10, Pittsburgh, Pa. (424,065)	1.00
1487	8c	**Willa Cather,** Sept. 20, Red Cloud, Nebr. (435,784)	1.00
1488	8c	**Nicolaus Copernicus,** Apr. 23 (734,190)	1.75
1498a	8c	**Postal People,** Apr. 30, any city	5.00
		1489-1498, any single	1.00

First day cancellation was applied at Boston to 1,205,212 covers bearing one or more of Nos. 1489-1498. Cancellations at other cities unrecorded.

1499	8c	**Harry S Truman,** May 8, Independence, Mo. (938,636)	1.00
1500	6c	**Electronics,** July 10, New York, N.Y.	1.00
1501	8c	**Electronics,** July 10, New York, N.Y.	1.00
1502	15c	**Electronics,** July 10, New York, N.Y.	1.00
		1500-1502 and C86 on one cover	3.00

First day cancellation was applied to 1,197,700 covers bearing one or more of Nos. 1500-1502 and C86.

1503	8c	**Lyndon B. Johnson,** Aug. 27, Austin, Texas (701,490)	1.00

1973-74

1504	8c	**Angus Cattle,** Oct. 5, 1973, St. Joseph, Mo. (521,427)	1.00
1505	10c	**Chautauqua,** Aug. 6, 1974, Chautauqua, N.Y. (411,105)	1.00
1506	10c	**Wheat,** Aug. 16, 1974, Hillsboro, Kans. (468,280)	1.00
1507	8c	**Christmas** (religious), Nov. 7, 1973	1.00
1508	8c	**Christmas** (secular), Nov. 7, 1973	1.00
		1507-1508 on one cover	1.10

First day cancellation was applied to 807,468 covers bearing one or both of Nos. 1507-1508.

1509	10c	**Crossed Flags,** Dec. 8, 1973, San Francisco, Calif.	1.00

First day cancellation was applied to 341,528 covers bearing one or more of Nos. 1509 and 1519.

1510	10c	**Jefferson Memorial,** Dec. 14, 1973	1.00
1510b		Booklet pane of 5 + label	2.25
1510c		Booklet pane of 8	2.50
1510d		Booklet pane of 6, Aug. 5, 1974, Oakland, Calif.	3.00

First day cancellation was applied to 686,300 covers bearing one or more of Nos. 1510, 1510b, 1510c, 1520.

1511	10c	**Zip Code,** Jan. 4, 1974 (335,220)	1.00
1518	6.3c	**Bell Coil,** Oct. 1, 1974 (221,141)	1.00
1519	10c	**Crossed Flags coil,** Dec. 8, 1973, San Francisco, Calif.	1.00
1520	10c	**Jefferson Memorial coil,** Dec. 14, 1973	1.00

1974

1525	10c	**Veterans of Foreign Wars,** Mar. 11 (543,598)	2.00
1526	10c	**Robert Frost,** Mar. 26, Derry, N.H. (500,425)	1.00
1527	10c	**EXPO '74,** Apr. 18, Spokane, Wash. (565,548)	1.00
1528	10c	**Horse Racing,** May 4, Louisville, Ky. (623,983)	2.00
1529	10c	**Skylab,** May 14, Houston, Tex. (972,326)	1.50
1537a	10c	**UPU Centenary,** June 6 (1,374,765)	4.00
		1530-1537, any single	1.00
1541a	10c	**Mineral Heritage,** June 13, Lincoln, Neb. (865,368)	2.50
		1538-1541, any single	1.00
1542	10c	**Kentucky Settlement,** June 15, Harrodsburg, Ky. (478,239)	1.00
1546a	10c	**Continental Congress** (Rev. Bicentennial), July 4, Philadelphia, Pa. (2,124,957)	2.75
		1543-1546, any single	1.00
1547	10c	**Energy Conservation,** Sept. 23, Detroit, Mich. (587,210)	1.00
1548	10c	**Sleepy Hollow,** Oct. 10, North Tarrytown, N.Y. (514,836)	2.00
1549	10c	**Retarded Children,** Oct. 12, Arlington Tex. (412,882)	1.00
1550	10c	**Christmas** (Religious), Oct. 23, New York, N.Y. (634,990)	1.00
1551	10c	**Christmas** (Currier & Ives), Oct. 23, New York, N.Y. (634,990)	1.00
		1550-1551 on one cover	1.10
1552	10c	**Christmas** (Dove), Nov. 15, New York, N.Y. (477,410)	1.00

1975

1553	10c	**Benjamin West,** Feb. 10, Swarthmore, Pa. (465,017)	1.00
1554	10c	**Paul L. Dunbar,** May 1, Dayton, Ohio (397,347)	1.00
1555	10c	**D.W. Griffith,** May 27, Beverly Hills, Calif. (424,167)	1.00
1556	10c	**Pioneer-Jupiter,** Feb. 28, Mountain View, Calif. (594,896)	2.00
1557	10c	**Mariner 10,** Apr. 4, Pasadena, Calif. (563,636)	2.00
1558	10c	**Collective Bargaining,** Mar. 13 (412,329)	1.00
1559	8c	**Sybil Ludington** (Rev. Bicentennial), Mar. 25, Carmel, N.Y. (394,550)	1.00
1560	10c	**Salem Poor** (Rev. Bicentennial, Mar. 25, Cambridge, Mass. (415,565)	1.00
1561	10c	**Haym Salomon** (Rev. Bicentennial), Mar. 25, Chicago, Ill. (442,630)	1.00
1562	18c	**Peter Francisco** (Rev. Bicentennial), Mar. 25, Greensboro, N.C. (415,000)	1.00
1563	10c	**Lexington-Concord** (Rev. Bicentennial), Apr. 19, Lexington, Mass., or Concord, Mass, (975,020)	1.00
1564	10c	**Bunker Hill** (Rev. Bicentennial), June 17, Charlestown, Mass. (557,130)	1.00
1568a	10c	**Military Services** (Rev. Bicentennial), July 4 (1,134,831)	2.50
		1565-1568, any single	1.00
1569a	10c	**Apollo-Soyuz,** July 15, Kennedy Space Center, Fla. (1,427,046)	5.00
		1569-1570, any single	3.00
1571	10c	**International Women's Year,** Aug. 26, Seneca Falls, N.Y. (476,769)	1.00
1575a	10c	**Postal Service Bicentenary,** Sept. 3, Philadelphia, Pa. (969,999)	1.25
		1572-1575, any single	1.00
1576	10c	**World Peace through Law,** Sept. 29 (386,736)	1.25
1577a	10c	**Banking-Commerce,** Oct. 6, New York, N.Y. (555,580)	1.25
		1577-1578, any single	1.00
1579	(10c)	**Christmas** (religious), Oct. 14	1.00
1580	(10c)	**Christmas** (secular), Oct. 14	1.00
		1579-1580 on one cover	2.00

First day cancellation was applied to 730,079 covers bearing one or more of Nos. 1579-1580.

1975-79

AMERICANA ISSUE

1581	1c	**Inkwell,** Dec. 8, 1977, St. Louis, Mo., multiple for 1st class rate	1.00
1582	2c	**Speaker's Stand,** Dec. 8, 1977, St. Louis, Mo., multiple for 1st class rate	1.00
1584	3c	**Ballot Box,** Dec. 8, 1977, St. Louis, Mo., multiple for 1st class rate	1.00
1585	4c	**Books and Eyeglasses,** Dec. 8, 1977, St. Louis, Mo., multiple for 1st class rate	1.00

First day cancellation was applied to 530,033 covers bearing one or more of Nos. 1581-1582, 1584-1585.

1590	9c	**Capitol Dome,** from bklt., Mar. 11, 1977, New York, N.Y., plus postage for 1st class rate	1.00
1591	9c	**Capitol Dome,** Nov. 24, 1975 (190,117), multiple for 1st class rate	1.00
1592	10c	**Justice,** Nov. 17, 1977, New York, N.Y. (359,050), multiple for 1st class rate	1.00
1593	11c	**Printing Press,** Nov. 13, 1975, Philadelphia, Pa. (217,755), multiple for 1st class rate	1.00
1594	12c	**Torch,** Apr. 8, 1981, Dallas, TX, multiple for 1st class rate	1.00

First day cancellation was applied to 280,930 covers bearing one or more of Nos. 1594 and 1597.

1595	13c	**Liberty Bell,** Oct. 31, 1975, Cleveland, Ohio (256,734)	1.00
1595a		Booklet pane of 6	2.00
1595b		Booklet pane of 7 + label	2.75
1595c		Booklet pane of 8	2.50

1595d		Booklet pane of 5 + label, Apr. 2, 1976, Liberty, Mo.	2.25
1596	13c	**Eagle and Shield,** Dec. 1, 1975, Juneau, Alaska (418,272)	1.00
1597	15c	**Flag,** June 30, 1978, Baltimore, Md.	1.00
1598	15c	**Flag,** from bklt., June 30, 1978, Baltimore, Md.	1.00
1598a		Booklet pane of 8	2.50

First day cancellation was applied to 315,359 covers bearing one or more of Nos. 1597, 1598, and 1618C.

1599	16c	**Statue of Liberty,** Mar. 31, 1978, New York, N.Y.	1.00
1603	24c	**Old North Church,** Nov. 14, 1975, Boston, Mass. (208,973)	1.00
1604	28c	**Fort Nisqually,** Aug. 11, 1978, Tacoma, Wash. (159,639)	1.25
1605	29c	**Sandy Hook Lighthouse,** Apr. 14, 1978, Atlantic City, N.J. (193,476)	2.00
1606	30c	**Schoolhouse,** Aug. 27, 1979, Devils Lake, N.D. (186,882)	1.25
1608	50c	**Betty Lamp,** Sept. 11, 1979, San Juan, P.R. (159,540)	1.50
1610	$1	**Rush Lamp,** July 2, 1979, San Francisco, Calif. (255,575)	3.00
1611	$2	**Kerosene Lamp,** Nov. 16, 1978, New York, N.Y. (173,596)	5.00
1612	$5	**Railroad Lantern,** Aug. 23, 1979, Boston, Mass. (129,192)	12.50

COIL STAMPS

1613	3.1c	**Guitar,** Oct. 25, 1979, Shreveport, La. (230,403)	1.00
1614	7.7c	**Saxhorns,** Nov. 20, 1976, New York, N.Y. (285,290)	1.00
1615	7.9c	**Drum,** Apr. 23, 1976, Miami, Fla. (193,270)	1.00
1615C	8.4c	**Piano,** July 13, 1978, Interlochen, Mich. (200,392)	1.00
1616	9c	**Capitol Dome,** Mar. 5, 1976, Milwaukee, Wis. (128,171)	1.00
1617	10c	**Justice,** Nov. 4, 1977, Tampa, Fla. (184,954)	1.00
1618	13c	**Liberty Bell,** Nov. 25, 1975, Allentown, Pa. (320,387)	1.00
1618C	15c	**Flag,** June 30, 1978, Baltimore, Md.	1.00
1619	16c	**Statue of Liberty,** Mar. 31, 1978, New York, N.Y.	1.00

First day cancellation was applied to 376,338 covers bearing one or more of Nos. 1599 and 1619.

1975

1622	13c	**13-Star Flag,** Nov. 15, Philadelphia, Pa.	1.00
1623	13c	**Flag over Capitol,** Mar. 11, New York, N.Y.	1.00
1623a		Booklet pane of 8, perf 11 (1 #1590 +7 #1623)	25.00
1623Bc		Booklet pane of 8, perf. 10x9¾ (1 #1590A + 7 #1623B)	12.50

First day cancellation was applied to 242,208 covers bearing Nos. 1623, 1623a, 1623B or 1623Bc.

1625	13c	**13-Star Flag coil,** Nov. 15, Philadelphia, PA	1.00

First day cancellation was applied to 362,959 covers bearing one or more of Nos. 1622 and 1625.

1976

1631a	13c	**Spirit of '76,** Jan. 1, Pasadena, CA (1,013,067)	2.00
		1629-1631, any single	1.25
1632	13c	**Interphil '76,** Jan. 17, Philadelphia, Pa. (519,902)	1.00
1682a	13c	**State Flags,** Feb. 23	27.50
		1633-1682, any single	1.50
1683	13c	**Telephone,** Mar. 10, Boston, Mass. (662,515)	1.00
1684	13c	**Commercial Aviation,** Mar. 19, Chicago Ill. (631,555)	1.00
1685	13c	**Chemistry,** Apr. 6, New York, N.Y. (557,600)	2.00

Bicentennial Souvenir Sheets of 5

1686	13c	**Surrender of Cornwallis,** May 29, Philadelphia, Pa.	6.00
1687	18c	**Declaration of Independence,** May 29, Philadelphia, Pa.	7.50
1688	24c	**Declaration of Independence,** May 29, Philadelphia, Pa.	8.50
1689	31c	**Washington at Valley Forge,** May 29, Philadelphia, Pa.	9.50

First day cancellation was applied to 879,890 covers bearing singles, multiples or complete sheets of Nos. 1686-1689.

1690	13c	**Franklin,** June 1, Philadelphia, Pa. (588,740)	1.00
1694a	13c	**Declaration of Independence,** July 4, Philadelphia, Pa. (2,093,880)	2.00
		1691-1694, any single	1.00
1698a	13c	**Olympic Games,** July 16, Lake Placid, N.Y. (1,140,198)	2.00
		1695-1698, any single	1.00
1699	13c	**Clara Maass,** Aug. 18, Belleville, N.J. (646,506)	2.00
1700	13c	**Adolph S. Ochs,** Sept. 18, New York, N.Y. (582,580)	1.00
1701	13c	**Christmas** (religious), Oct. 27, Boston, Mass. (540,106)	1.00
1702	13c	**Christmas** (secular), Oct. 27, Boston, Mass. (181,410)	1.00
1703	13c	**Christmas** (secular), block tagged, Oct. 27, Boston, Mass. (330,450)	1.00
		1701 and 1702 or 1703 on one cover	1.25

1977

1704	13c **Washington at Princeton**, *Jan. 3*, Princeton, N.J. *(695,335)*	1.00
1705	13c **Sound Recording**, *Mar. 23 (632,216)*	1.00
1709a	13c **Pueblo Art**, *Apr. 13*, Santa Fe, N.M. *(1,194,554)*	2.00
	1706-1709, any single	1.00
1710	13c **Lindbergh Flight**, *May 20*, Roosevelt Sta., N.Y. *(3,985,989)*	3.00
1711	13c **Colorado Statehood**, *May 21*, Denver, Colo. *(510,880)*	1.00
1715a	13c **Butterflies**, *June 6*, Indianapolis, Ind. *(1,218,278)*	2.00
	1712-1715, any single	1.00
1716	13c **Lafayette's Landing**, *June 13*, Charleston, S.C. *(514,506)*	1.00
1720a	13c **Skilled Hands**, *July 4*, Cincinnati, Ohio *(1,263,568)*	1.75
	1717-1720, any single	1.00
1721	13c **Peace Bridge**, *Aug. 4*, Buffalo, N.Y. *(512,995)*	1.00
1722	13c **Battle of Oriskany**, *Aug. 6*, Utica, N.Y. *(605,906)*	1.00
1723a	13c **Energy Conservation**, *Oct. 20 (410,299)*	1.25
	1723-1724, any single	1.25
1725	13c **Alta California**, *Sept. 9*, San Jose, Calif. *(709,457)*	1.00
1726	13c **Articles of Confederation**, *Sept. 30*, York, Pa. *(605,455)*	1.00
1727	13c **Talking Pictures**, *Oct. 6*, Hollywood, Calif. *(570,195)*	1.50
1728	13c **Surrender at Saratoga** *Oct. 7*, Schuylerville, N.Y. *(557,529)*	1.00
1729	13c **Christmas (Valley Forge)**, *Oct. 21*, Valley Forge, Pa. *(583,139)*	1.00
1730	13c **Christmas (mailbox)**, *Oct. 21*, Omaha, Nebr. *(675,786)*	1.00

1978

1731	13c **Carl Sandburg**, *Jan. 6*, Galesburg, Ill. *(493,826)*	1.00
1732a	13c **Captain Cook**, *Jan. 20*, Honolulu, Hawaii, or Anchorage, Alaska	3.00
	1732-1733, any single	2.00

First day cancellation was applied to 823,855 covers at Honolulu, and 672,804 at Anchorage, each cover bearing one or both of Nos. 1732-1733.

1734	13c **Indian Head Penny**, *Jan. 11*, Kansas City, Mo. *(512,426)*	1.00

1978-80

REGULAR ISSUE

1735	(15c) **"A" Eagle**, *May 22*, Memphis, Tenn.	1.00
1736	(15c) **"A" Eagle**, bklt. single *May 22*, Memphis, Tenn.	1.00
1736a	Booklet pane of 8	2.50
1737	15c **Roses**, *July 11*, Shreveport, La. *(445,003)*	1.00
1737a	Booklet pane of 8	2.50
1742a	15c **Windmills Booklet pane of 10**, *Feb. 7, 1980*, Lubbock, TX	3.50
	1738-1742, any single	1.00
1743	15c **"A" Eagle coil**, *May 22*, Memphis, Tenn.	1.00

First day cancellation was applied to 689,049 covers bearing one or more of Nos. 1735, 1736 and 1743. First day cancellation was applied to 708,411 covers bearing one or more of Nos. 1738-1742a.

1978

1744	13c **Harriet Tubman**, *Feb. 1 (493,495)*	1.00
1748a	13c **American Quilts**, *Mar. 8*, Charleston, W.Va.	2.00
	1745-1748, any single	1.00

First day cancellation was applied to 1,081,827 covers bearing one or more of Nos. 1745-1748.

1752a	13c **American Dance**, *Apr. 26*, New York, N.Y. *(1,626,493)*	1.75
	1749-1752, any single	1.00
1753	13c **French Alliance**, *May 4*, York, Pa. *(705,240)*	1.00
1754	13c **Papanicolaou**, *May 18 (535,584)*	1.00
1755	13c **Jimmie Rodgers**, *May 24*, Meridian, Miss. *(599,287)*	1.50
1756	15c **George M. Cohan**, *July 3*, Providence, R.I. *(740,750)*	1.50
1757	15c **CAPEX** souv. sheet, *June 10*, Toronto, Canada *(1,994,067)*	2.75
1758	15c **Photography**, *June 26*, Las Vegas, Nev. *(684,987)*	1.50
1759	15c **Viking Missions**, *July 20*, Hampton, Va. *(805,051)*	2.00
1763a	15c **American Owls**, *Aug. 26*, Fairbanks, Alas. *(1,690,474)*	2.00
	1760-1763, any single	1.00
1767a	15c **American Trees**, *Oct. 9*, Hot Springs National Park, Ark. *(1,139,100)*	2.00
	1764-1767, any single	1.00
1768	15c **Christmas (Madonna)**, *Oct. 18 (553,064)*	1.00
1769	15c **Christmas (Hobby Horse)**, *Oct. 18*, Holly, Mich. *(603,008)*	1.00

1979-80

1770	15c **Robert Kennedy**, *Jan. 12 (624,582)*	3.00
1771	15c **Martin L. King**, *Jan. 13*, Atlanta, Ga. *(726,149)*	2.50
1772	15c **Year of Child**, *Feb. 15*, Philadelphia, Pa. *(716,782)*	1.00
1773	15c **John Steinbeck**, *Feb. 27*, Salinas, Calif. *(709,073)*	1.25
1774	15c **Albert Einstein**, *Mar. 4*, Princeton, N.J. *(641,423)*	4.00

1778a	15c **Toleware**, *Apr. 19*, Lancaster, Pa. *(1,581,962)*	2.00
	1775-1778, any single	1.00
1782a	15c **American Architecture**, *June 4*, Kansas City, Mo. *(1,219,258)*	2.00
	1779-1782, any single	1.00
1786a	15c **Endangered Flora**, *June 7*, Milwaukee, Wis. *(1,436,268)*	2.00
	1783-1786, any single	1.00
1787	15c **Guide Dogs**, *June 15*, Morristown, N.J. *(588,826)*	1.00
1788	15c **Special Olympics**, *Aug. 9*, Brockport, N.Y. *(651,344)*	1.00
1789	15c **John Paul Jones**, *Sept. 23*, Annapolis, Md. *(587,018)*	1.25
1790	10c **Olympic Javelin**, *Sept. 5*, Olympia, Wash. *(305,122)*	1.00
1794a	15c **Olympics 1980**, *Sept. 28*, Los Angeles, Calif. *(1,561,366)*	2.00
	1791-1794, any single	1.00
1798b	15c **Winter Olympics**, *Feb. 1, 1980*, Lake Placid, N.Y. *(1,166,302)*	2.00
	1795-1798, any single	1.00

1979

1799	15c **Christmas (Madonna)**, *Oct. 18 (686,990)*	1.00
1800	15c **Christmas (Santa Claus)**, *Oct. 18*, North Pole, Alaska *(511,829)*	1.00
1801	15c **Will Rogers**, *Nov. 4*, Claremore, Okla. *(1,643,151)*	1.50
1802	15c **Viet Nam Veterans**, *Nov. 11*, Arlington, VA *(445,934)*	4.00

1980

1803	15c **W.C. Fields**, *Jan. 29*, Beverly Hills, CA *(633,303)*	1.75
1804	15c **Benjamin Banneker**, *Feb. 15*, Annapolis, MD *(647,126)*	1.00
1810a	15c **Letter Writing**, *Feb. 25 (1,083,360)*	2.50
	1805-1810, any single	1.00

1980-81

DEFINITIVES

1811	1c **Quill Pen**, coil, *Mar. 6, 1980*, New York, NY *(262,921)*	1.00
1813	3.5c **Violins**, coil, *June 23, 1980*, Williamsburg, PA	1.00

FD cancel was applied to 716,988 covers bearing Nos. 1813 or U590.

1816	12c **Torch**, coil, *Apr. 8, 1981*, Dallas, TX	1.00
1818	(18c) **"B" Eagle**, *Mar. 15, 1981*, San Francisco, CA	1.00

FD cancel was applied to 511,688 covers bearing one or more of Nos. 1818-1820, U592 or UX88.

1819	(18c) **"B" Eagle**, bklt. single, *Mar. 15, 1981*, San Francisco, CA	1.00
1819a	Booklet pane of 8	3.00
1820	(18c) **"B" Eagle**, coil, *Mar. 15, 1981*, San Francisco, CA	1.00

1980

1821	15c **Frances Perkins**, *Apr. 10 (678,966)*	1.00
1822	15c **Dolley Madison**, *May 20 (331,048)*	1.00
1823	15c **Emily Bissell**, *May 31*, Wilmington, DE *(649,509)*	1.00
1824	15c **Helen Keller, Anne Sullivan**, *June 27*, Tuscumbia, AL *(713,061)*	1.00
1825	15c **Veterans Administration**, *July 21 (634,101)*	1.50
1826	15c **Bernardo de Galvez**, *July 23*, New Orleans, LA *(658,061)*	1.00
1830a	15c **Coral Reefs**, *Aug. 26*, Charlotte Amalie, VI *(1,195,126)*	2.00
	1827-1830, any single	1.00
1831	15c **Organized Labor**, *Sept. 1 (759,973)*	1.00
1832	15c **Edith Wharton**, *Sept. 5*, New Haven, CT *(633,917)*	1.00
1833	15c **Education**, *Sept. 12 (672,592)*	1.00
1837a	15c **Indian Masks**, *Sept. 25*, Spokane, WA *(2,195,136)*	2.00
	1834-1837, any single	1.00
1841a	15c **Architecture**, *Oct. 9*, New York, NY *(2,164,721)*	2.00
	1838-1841, any single	1.00
1842	15c **Christmas (Madonna)**, *Oct. 31 (718,614)*	1.00
1843	15c **Christmas (Toys)**, *Oct. 31*, Christmas, MI *(755,108)*	1.00

1980-85

GREAT AMERICANS ISSUE

1844	1c **Dorothea Dix**, *Sept. 23, 1983*, Hampden, ME *(164,140)*	1.00
1845	2c **Igor Stravinsky**, *Nov. 18, 1982*, New York, NY *(501,719)*	1.00
1846	3c **Henry Clay**, *July 13, 1983 (204,320)*	1.00
1847	4c **Carl Schurz**, *June 3, 1983*, Watertown, WI *(165,010)*	1.00
1848	5c **Pearl Buck**, *June 25, 1983*, Hillsboro, WV *(231,852)*	1.00
1849	6c **Walter Lippman**, *Sept. 19, 1985*, Minneapolis, MN *(371,990)*	1.00
1850	7c **Abraham Baldwin**, *Jan. 25, 1985*, Athens, GA *(402,285)*	1.00
1851	8c **Henry Knox**, *July 25, 1985*, Thomaston, ME *(315,937)*	1.00
1852	9c **Sylvanus Thayer**, *June 7, 1985*, Braintree, MA *(345,649)*	1.00
1853	10c **Richard Russell**, *May 31, 1984*, Winder, GA *(183,581)*	1.00
1854	11c **Alden Partridge**, *Feb. 12, 1985*, Northfield, VT *(442,311)*	1.00

1855	13c **Crazy Horse**, *Jan. 15, 1982*, Crazy Horse, SD	1.50
1856	14c **Sinclair Lewis**, *Mar. 21, 1985*, Sauk Centre, MN *(308,612)*	1.00
1857	17c **Rachel Carson**, *May 28, 1981*, Springdale, PA *(273,686)*	1.00
1858	18c **George Mason**, *May 7, 1981*, Gunston Hall, VA *(461,937)*	1.00
1859	19c **Sequoyah**, *Dec. 27, 1980*, Tahlequah, OK *(241,325)*	1.50
1860	20c **Ralph Bunche**, *Jan. 12, 1982*, New York, NY	1.00
1861	20c **Thomas Gallaudet**, *June 10, 1983*, West Hartford, CT *(261,336)*	1.25
1862	20c **Harry S Truman**, *Jan. 26, 1984 (267,631)*	1.25
1863	22c **John J. Audubon**, *Apr. 23, 1985*, New York, NY *(516,249)*	1.25
1864	30c **Frank Laubach**, *Sept. 2, 1984*, Benton, PA *(118,974)*	1.25
1865	35c **Charles Drew**, *June 3, 1981 (383,882)*	1.25
1866	37c **Robert Millikan**, *Jan. 26, 1982*, Pasadena, CA	1.25
1867	39c **Grenville Clark**, *Mar. 20, 1985*, Hanover, NH *(297,797)*	1.25
1868	40c **Lillian Gilbreth**, *Feb. 24, 1984*, Montclair, NJ *(110,588)*	1.25
1869	50c **Chester W. Nimitz**, *Feb. 22, 1985*, Fredericksburg, TX *(376,166)*	2.00

1981

1874	15c **Everett Dirksen**, *Jan. 4*, Pekin, IL *(665,755)*	1.00
1875	15c **Whitney M. Young**, *Jan. 30*, New York, NY *(963,870)*	1.00
1879a	18c **Flowers**, *Apr. 23*, Fort Valley, GA *(1,966,599)*	2.50
	1876-1879, any single	1.00

DEFINITIVES

1889a	18c **Animals Booklet pane of 10**, *May 14*, Boise, ID	5.00
	1880-1889, any single	1.00
1890	18c **Flag-Anthem (grain)**, *Apr. 24*, Portland, ME	1.00
1891	18c **Flag-Anthem (sea)**, *Apr. 24*, Portland, ME	1.00
1892	6c **Star Circle**, *Apr. 24*, Portland, ME	1.00
1893	18c **Flag-Anthem (mountain)**, *Apr. 24*, Portland, ME	1.00
1893a	Booklet pane of 8 (2 #1892, 6 #1893)	2.50

FDC cancel was applied to 691,526 covers bearing one or more of Nos. 1890-1893 & 1893a.

1894	20c **Flag-Court**, *Dec. 17*	1.00
1895	20c **Flag-Court**, coil, *Dec. 17*	1.00
1896	20c **Flag-Court**, perf. 11x10½, *Dec. 17 (185,543)*	1.00
1896a	Booklet pane of 6	6.00
1896b	Booklet pane of 10, *June 1, 1982*	10.00

First day cancellations were applied to 598,169 covers bearing one or more of Nos. 1894-1896.

1981-84

TRANSPORTATION ISSUE

1897	1c **Omnibus**, *Aug. 19, 1983*, Arlington, VA *(109,463)*	1.00
1897A	2c **Locomotive**, *May 20, 1982*, Chicago, IL *(290,020)*	1.50
1898	3c **Handcar**, *Mar. 25, 1983*, Rochester, NY *(77,900)*	1.00
1898A	4c **Stagecoach**, *Aug. 19, 1982*, Milwaukee, WI *(152,940)*	1.00
1899	5c **Motorcycle**, *Oct. 10, 1983*, San Francisco, CA *(188,240)*	2.00
1900	5.2c **Sleigh**, *Mar. 21, 1983*, Memphis, TN *(141,979)*	1.00
1901	5.9c **Bicycle**, *Feb. 17, 1982*, Wheeling, WV *(814,419)*	1.50
1902	7.4c **Baby Buggy**, *Apr. 7, 1984*, San Diego, CA	1.00
1903	9.3c **Mail Wagon**, *Dec. 15, 1981*, Shreveport, LA *(199,645)*	1.00
1904	10.9c **Hansom**, *Mar. 26, 1982*, Chattanooga, TN	1.00
1905	11c **Railroad Caboose**, *Feb. 3, 1984*, Chicago, IL *(172,753)*	1.50
1906	17c **Electric Auto**, *June 25, 1982*, Greenfield Village, MI *(239,458)*	1.00
1907	18c **Surrey**, *May 18, 1981*, Notch, MO *(207,801)*	1.00
1908	20c **Fire Pumper**, *Dec. 10, 1981*, Alexandria, VA *(304,668)*	3.00
1909	$9.35 **Eagle**, *Aug. 12, 1983*, Kennedy Space Center, FL *(77,858)*	45.00
1909a	Booklet pane of 3	125.00

1981

1910	18c **Red Cross**, *May 1 (874,972)*	1.00
1911	18c **Savings & Loan**, *May 8*, Chicago, IL *(740,910)*	1.00
1919a	18c **Space Achievement**, *May 21*, Kennedy Space Center, FL *(7,027,549)*	3.00
	1912-1919, any single	1.00
1920	18c **Professional Management**, *June 18*, Philadelphia, PA *(713,096)*	1.00
1924a	18c **Wildlife Habitats**, *June 26*, Reno, NV *(2,327,609)*	2.50
	1921-1924, any single	1.00
1925	18c **Year of Disabled**, *June 29*, Milford, MI *(714,244)*	1.00
1926	18c **Edna St. V. Millay**, *July 10*, Austerlitz, NY *(725,978)*	1.00
1927	18c **Alcoholism**, *Aug. 19 (874,972)*	1.25

1931a	18c	**Architecture,** Aug. 28, New York, NY (1,998,208)	2.50
		1928-1931, any single	1.00
1932	18c	**Babe Zaharias,** Sept. 22, Pinehurst, NC	7.00
1933	18c	**Bobby Jones,** Sept. 22, Pinehurst, NC	8.00

First day cancel was applied to 1,231,543 covers bearing one or more of Nos. 1932-1933.

1934	18c	**Frederic Remington,** Oct. 9, Oklahoma City, OK (1,367,099)	1.00
1935	18c	**James Hoban,** Oct. 13	1.00
1936	20c	**James Hoban,** Oct. 13	1.00

FD cancel was applied to 635,012 covers bearing Nos. 1935-1936.

1938a	18c	**Yorktown-Va. Capes Battle,** Oct. 16, Yorktown, VA (1,098,278)	1.50
		1937-1938, any single	1.00
1939	(20c)	**Christmas (Madonna),** Oct. 28, Chicago, IL (481,395)	1.00
1940	(20c)	**Christmas (Teddy Bear),** Oct. 28, Christmas Valley, OR (517,898)	1.00
1941	20c	**John Hanson,** Nov. 5, Frederick, MD (605,616)	1.00
1945a	20c	**Desert Plants,** Dec. 11, Tucson, AZ (1,770,187)	2.50
		1942-1945, any single	1.00

REGULAR ISSUE

1946	(20c)	**"C" Eagle,** Oct. 11, Memphis, TN	1.00
1947	(20c)	**"C" Eagle,** coil, Oct. 11, Memphis, TN	1.00
1948	(20c)	**"C" Eagle,** bklt. single, Oct. 11, Memphis, TN	1.00
1948a		Booklet pane of 10	3.50

First day cancellations were applied to 304,404 covers bearing one or more of Nos. 1946-1948.

1982

1949	20c	**Bighorn,** Jan. 8, Bighorn, MT	1.00
1949a		Booklet pane of 10	6.00
1950	20c	**F.D. Roosevelt,** Jan. 30, Hyde Park, NY	1.00
1951	20c	**Love,** Feb. 1, Boston, MA (325,727)	1.00
1952	20c	**Washington,** Feb. 22, Mt. Vernon, VA	1.00
2002b	20c	**Birds-Flowers,** Apr. 14, Washington, DC, or State Capital	30.00
		1953-2002, any single	1.25
2003	20c	**U.S.-Netherlands,** Apr. 20	1.00
2004	20c	**Library of Congress,** Apr. 21	1.00
2005	20c	**Consumer Education,** Apr. 27	1.00
2009a	20c	**Knoxville Fair,** Apr. 29, Knoxville, TN	2.50
		2006-2009, any single	1.00
2010	20c	**Horatio Alger,** Apr. 30, Willow Grove, PA	1.00
2011	20c	**Aging,** May 21, Sun City, AZ (510,677)	1.00
2012	20c	**Barrymores,** June 8, New York, NY	1.25
2013	20c	**Dr. Mary Walker,** June 10, Oswego, NY	1.00
2014	20c	**Peace Garden,** June 30, Dunseith, ND	1.00
2015	20c	**America's Libraries,** July 13, Philadelphia, PA	1.00
2016	20c	**Jackie Robinson,** Aug. 2, Cooperstown, NY	6.00
2017	20c	**Touro Synagogue,** Aug. 22, Newport, RI (517,264)	1.00
2018	20c	**Wolf Trap Farm Park,** Sept. 1, Vienna, VA (704,361)	1.00
2022a	20c	**Architecture,** Sept. 30 (1,552,567)	2.50
		2019-2022, any single	1.00
2023	20c	**St. Francis,** Oct. 7, San Francisco, CA (530,275)	1.50
2024	20c	**Ponce de Leon,** Oct. 12, San Juan, PR (530,275)	1.00
2025	13c	**Puppy, Kitten,** Nov. 3, Danvers, MA (239,219)	1.00
2026	20c	**Christmas (Madonna),** Oct. 28 (462,982)	1.00
2030a	20c	**Christmas (Children),** Oct. 28, Snow, OK (676,950)	2.50
		2027-2030, any single	1.00

1983

2031	20c	**Science & Industry,** Jan. 19, Chicago, IL (526,693)	1.00
2035a	20c	**Balloons,** Mar. 31, Albuquerque, NM or Washington, DC (989,305)	2.50
		2032-2035, any single	1.00
2036	20c	**U.S.-Sweden,** Mar. 24, Philadelphia, PA (526,373)	1.00
2037	20c	**Civilian Conservation Corps.,** Apr. 5, Luray, VA (483,824)	1.00
2038	20c	**Joseph Priestley,** Apr. 13, Northumberland, PA (673,266)	1.00
2039	20c	**Voluntarism,** Apr. 20 (574,708)	1.25
2040	20c	**U.S.-Germany,** Apr. 29, Germantown, PA (611,109)	1.00
2041	20c	**Brooklyn Bridge,** May 17, Brooklyn, NY (815,085)	1.00
2042	20c	**TVA,** May 18, Knoxville, TN (837,588)	1.00
2043	20c	**Physical Fitness,** May 14, Houston, TX (501,336)	1.00
2044	20c	**Scott Joplin,** June 9, Sedalia, MO (472,667)	1.00
2045	20c	**Medal of Honor,** June 7 (1,623,995)	4.00
2046	20c	**Babe Ruth,** July 6, Chicago, IL (1,277,907)	5.00
2047	20c	**Nathaniel Hawthorne,** July 8, Salem, MA (442,793)	1.00
2051a	13c	**Summer Olympics,** July 28, South Bend, IN (909,332)	2.50
		2048-2051, any single	1.00
2052	20c	**Treaty of Paris,** Sept. 2 (651,208)	1.00
2053	20c	**Civil Service,** Sept. 9 (422,206)	1.00
2054	20c	**Metropolitan Opera,** Sept. 14, New York, NY (807,609)	1.00
2058a	20c	**American Inventors,** Sept. 21 (1,006,516)	2.50
		2055-2058, any single	1.00

2062a	20c	**Streetcars,** Oct. 8, Kennebunkport, ME (1,116,909)	2.50
		2059-2062, any single	1.00
2063	20c	**Christmas (Madonna),** Oct. 28 (361,874)	1.00
2064	20c	**Christmas (Santa),** Oct. 28, Santa Claus, IN (388,749)	1.00
2065	20c	**Martin Luther,** Nov. 11 (463,777)	3.00

1984

2066	20c	**Alaska Statehood,** Jan. 3, Fairbanks, AK (816,591)	1.00
2070a	20c	**Winter Olympics,** Jan. 6, Lake Placid, NY (1,245,807)	2.50
		2067-2070, any single	1.00
2071	20c	**Federal Deposit Ins. Corp.,** Jan. 12 (536,329)	1.00
2072	20c	**Love,** Jan. 31 (327,727)	2.00
2073	20c	**Carter Woodson,** Feb. 1 (387,583)	1.00
2074	20c	**Soil & Water Conservation,** Feb. 6, Denver, CO (426,101)	1.00
2075	20c	**Credit Union Act,** Feb. 10, Salem, MA (523,583)	1.00
2079a	20c	**Orchids,** Mar. 5, Miami, FL (1,063,237)	2.50
		2076-2079, any single	1.00
2080	20c	**Hawaii Statehood,** Mar. 16, Honolulu, HI (546,930)	1.00
2081	20c	**National Archives,** Apr. 16 (414,415)	1.00
2085a	20c	**Olympics 1984,** May 4, Los Angeles, CA (1,172,313)	2.50
		2082-2085, any single	1.00
2086	20c	**Louisiana Exposition,** May 11, New Orleans, LA (467,408)	1.00
2087	20c	**Health Research,** May 17, New York, NY (845,007)	1.00
2088	20c	**Douglas Fairbanks,** May 23, Denver CO (547,134)	1.00
2089	20c	**Jim Thorpe,** May 24, Shawnee, OK (568,544)	3.00
2090	20c	**John McCormack,** June 6, Boston, MA (464,117)	1.00
2091	20c	**St. Lawrence Seaway,** June 26, Massena, NY (550,173)	1.00
2092	20c	**Waterfowl Preservation Act,** July 2, Des Moines, IA (549,388)	1.25
2093	20c	**Roanoke Voyages,** July 13, Manteo, NC (443,725)	1.00
2094	20c	**Herman Melville,** Aug. 1, New Bedford, MA (378,293)	2.00
2095	20c	**Horace A. Moses,** Aug. 6, Bloomington, IN (459,386)	1.00
2096	20c	**Smokey Bear,** Aug. 13, Capitan, NM (506,833)	5.00
2097	20c	**Roberto Clemente,** Aug. 17, Carolina, PR (547,387)	9.00
2101a	20c	**Dogs,** Sept. 7, New York, NY (1,157,373)	3.00
		2098-2101, any single	1.25
2102	20c	**Crime Prevention,** Sept. 26 (427,564)	1.00
2103	20c	**Hispanic Americans,** Oct. 31 (416,796)	1.00
2104	20c	**Family Unity,** Oct. 1, Shaker Heights, OH (400,659)	1.00
2105	20c	**Eleanor Roosevelt,** Oct. 11, Hyde Park, NY (479,919)	1.00
2106	20c	**Nation of Readers,** Oct. 16 (437,559)	1.00
2107	20c	**Christmas (Madonna),** Oct. 30 (386,385)	1.00
2108	20c	**Christmas (Santa),** Oct. 30, Jamaica, NY (430,843)	1.00
2109	20c	**Vietnam Veterans' Memorial,** Nov. 10 (434,489)	4.50

1985

2110	22c	**Jerome Kern,** Jan. 23, New York, NY (503,855)	1.00

REGULAR ISSUE

2111	(22c)	**"D" Eagle,** Feb. 1, Los Angeles, CA	1.00
2112	(22c)	**"D" Eagle,** coil, Feb. 1, Los Angeles, CA	1.00
2113	(22c)	**"D" Eagle,** bklt. single, Feb. 1, Los Angeles, CA	1.00
2113a		Booklet pane of 10	7.50

First Day cancel was applied to 513,027 covers bearing one or more of Nos. 2111-2113.

2114	22c	**Flag over Capitol Dome,** Mar. 29	1.00
2115	22c	**Flag over Capitol Dome,** coil, Mar. 29	1.00
2115a		Inscribed "T" at bottom	

First Day Cancel was applied to 268,161 covers bearing one or more of Nos. 2114-2115.

2116	22c	**Flag Over Capitol Dome,** bklt. single, Mar. 29, Waubeka, WI (234,318)	1.00
2116a		Booklet pane of 5	3.50
2121a	22c	**Seashells Booklet pane of 10,** Apr. 4, Boston, MA (426,290)	7.50
		2117-2121, any single	1.00
2122	$10.75	**Eagle and Half Moon,** Apr. 29, San Francisco, CA (93,154)	40.00
2122a		Booklet pane of 3	95.00
2122c		Booklet pane of 3, type II, June 19, 1989	—

1985-87

TRANSPORTATION ISSUE

2123	3.4c	**School Bus,** June 8, 1985, Arlington, VA (131,480)	1.00
2124	4.9c	**Buckboard,** June 21, 1985, Reno, NV	1.00
2125	5.5c	**Star Route Truck,** Nov. 1, 1986, Fort Worth, TX (136,021)	1.00
2126	6c	**Tricycle,** May 6, 1985, Childs, MD (151,494)	1.50
2127	7.1c	**Tractor,** Feb. 6, 1987, Sarasota, FL (167,555)	1.00

2127a	7.1c	**Tractor,** Zip+4 precancel, untagged, May 26, 1989, Rosemont, IL (202,804)	5.00
2128	8.3c	**Ambulance,** June 21, 1986, Reno, NV	1.00

First day cancel was applied to 338,765 covers bearing one or more of Nos. 2124 and 2128.

2129	8.5c	**Tow Truck,** Jan. 24, 1987, Tucson, AZ (224,285)	1.00
2130	10.1c	**Oil Wagon,** Apr. 18, 1985, Oil Center, NM	1.00
2130a	10.1c	**"Bulk Rate Carrier Route Sort"** precancel, June 27, 1988 (136,428)	1.00
2131	11c	**Stutz Bearcat,** June 11, 1985, Baton Rouge, LA (135,037)	1.25
2132	12c	**Stanley Steamer,** Apr. 2, 1985, Kingfield, ME (173,998)	1.00
2133	12.5c	**Pushcart,** Apr. 18, 1985, Oil Center, NM	1.25

First day cancel was applied to 319,953 covers bearing one or more of Nos. 2130 and 2133.

2134	14c	**Ice Boat,** Mar. 23, 1985, Rochester, NY (324,710)	1.25
2135	17c	**Dog Sled,** Aug. 20, 1986, Anchorage, AK	1.25
2136	25c	**Bread Wagon,** Nov. 22, 1986, Virginia Beach, VA (151,950)	1.25

1985

2137	22c	**Mary McLeod Bethune,** Mar. 5 (413,244)	1.00
2141a	22c	**Duck Decoys,** Mar. 22, Shelburne, VT (932,249)	2.75
		2138-2141, any single	1.00
2142	22c	**Winter Special Olympics,** Mar. 25, Park City, UT (253,074)	1.00
2143	22c	**Love,** Apr. 17, Hollywood, CA (283,072)	2.00
2144	22c	**Rural Electrification Administration,** May 11, Madison, SD (472,895)	1.00
2145	22c	**AMERIPEX '86,** May 25, Rosemont, IL (457,038)	1.00
2146	22c	**Abigail Adams,** June 14, Quincy, MA (491,026)	1.00
2147	22c	**Frederic Auguste Bartholdi,** July 18, New York, NY (594,896)	1.00
2149	18c	**George Washington, Washington Monument,** Nov. 6 (376,238)	1.25
2150	21.1c	**Envelopes,** Oct. 22 (119,941)	1.25
2152	22c	**Korean War Veterans,** July 26 (391,754)	3.00
2153	22c	**Social Security Act,** Aug. 14, Baltimore, MD (265,143)	1.00
2154	22c	**World War I Veterans,** Aug. 26, Milwaukee, WI	3.00
2158a	22c	**Horses,** Sept. 25, Lexington, KY (1,135,368)	3.00
		2155-2158, any single	1.50
2159	22c	**Public Education in America,** Oct. 1, Boston, MA (356,030)	1.00
2163a	22c	**International Youth Year,** Oct. 7, Chicago, IL (1,202,541)	2.50
		2160, 2162-2163, any single	1.00
		2161	2.00
2164	22c	**Help End Hunger,** Oct. 15 (299,485)	1.00
2165	22c	**Christmas (Madonna & Child),** Oct. 30, Detroit, MI	1.00
2166	22c	**Christmas (Poinsettia),** Oct. 30, Nazareth, MI (524,929)	1.00

1986

2167	22c	**Arkansas Statehood,** Jan. 3, Little Rock, AR (364,729)	1.00

1986-94

GREAT AMERICANS ISSUE

2168	1c	**Margaret Mitchell,** June 30, 1986, Atlanta, GA (316,764)	1.50
2169	2c	**Mary Lyon,** Feb. 28, 1987, South Hadley, MA (349,831)	1.00
2170	3c	**Dr. Paul Dudley White,** Sept. 15, 1986	1.00
2171	4c	**Father Flanagan,** July 14, 1986, Boys Town, NE (367,883)	1.00
2172	5c	**Hugo Black,** Feb. 27, 1986 (303,012)	1.00
2173	5c	**Luis Munoz Marin,** Feb. 18, 1990, San Juan, PR (269,618)	1.25
2175	10c	**Red Cloud,** Aug. 15, 1987, Red Cloud, NE (300,472)	1.50
2176	14c	**Julia Ward Howe,** Feb. 12, 1987, Boston, MA (454,829)	1.00
2177	15c	**Buffalo Bill Cody,** June 6, 1988 Cody, WY (356,395)	2.00
2178	17c	**Belva Ann Lockwood,** June 18, 1986, Middleport, NY (249,215)	1.00
2179	20c	**Virginia Apgar,** Oct. 24, 1994, Dallas, TX (28,461)	1.25
2180	21c	**Chester Carlson,** Oct. 21, 1988, Rochester, NY (288,073)	1.25
2181	23c	**Mary Cassatt,** Nov. 4, 1988, Philadelphia, PA (322,537)	1.25
2182	25c	**Jack London,** Jan. 11, 1986, Glen Ellen, CA (358,686)	1.25
2182a		Booklet pane of 10, May 3, 1988, San Francisco, CA	6.00
2183	28c	**Sitting Bull,** Sept. 14, 1989, Rapid City, SD (126,777)	1.50
2184	29c	**Earl Warren,** Mar. 9, 1992 (175,517)	1.25
2185	29c	**Thomas Jefferson,** Apr. 13, 1993, Charlottesville, VA (202,962)	1.25
2186	35c	**Dennis Chavez,** Apr. 3, 1991, Albuquerque, NM (285,570)	1.25
2187	40c	**Claire Chennault,** Sept. 6, 1990, Monroe, LA (186,761)	2.00
2188	45c	**Harvey Cushing,** June 17, 1988, Cleveland, OH (135,140)	1.25
2189	52c	**Hubert Humphrey,** June 3, 1991, Minneapolis, MN (93,391)	1.40

2190	56c **John Harvard,** *Sept. 3, 1986,* Cambridge, MA	2.50
2191	65c **Hap Arnold,** *Nov. 5, 1988,* Gladwyne, PA *(129,829)*	2.00
2192	75c **Wendell Willkie,** *Feb. 18, 1992,* Bloomington, IN *(47,086)*	1.50
2193	$1 **Dr. Bernard Revel,** *Sept. 23, 1986,* New York, NY	3.00
2194	$1 **Johns Hopkins,** *June 7, 1989,* Baltimore, MD *(159,049)*	3.00
2195	$2 **William Jennings Bryan,** *Mar. 19, 1986,* Salem, IL *(123,430)*	5.00
2196	$5 **Bret Harte,** *Aug. 25, 1987,* Twain Harte, CA *(111,431)*	20.00
2197	25c **Jack London,** bklt. single, *May 3, 1988,* San Francisco, CA	1.25
2197a	Booklet pane of 6	4.00

First day cancel was applied to 94,655 covers bearing one or more of Nos. 2183a, 2197, and 2197a.

1986

2201a	22c **Stamp Collecting Booklet pane of 4,** *Jan. 23,* State College, PA	4.00
	2198-2201, any single	1.00

First day cancellation was applied to 675,924 covers bearing one or more of Nos. 2198-2201a.

2202	22c **Love,** *Jan. 30,* New York, NY	1.75
2203	22c **Sojourner Truth,** *Feb. 4,* New Paltz, NY *(342,985)*	1.00
2204	22c **Republic of Texas,** *Mar. 2,* San Antonio, TX *(380,450)*	1.25
2209a	22c **Fish Booklet pane of 5,** *Mar. 21,* Seattle, WA	2.50
	2205-2209, any single	1.00

First day cancellation was applied to 988,184 covers bearing one or more of Nos. 2205-2209a.

2210	22c **Public Hospitals,** *Apr. 11,* New York, NY *(403,665)*	1.00
2211	22c **Duke Ellington,** *Apr. 29,* New York, NY *(397,894)*	1.75
2216	22c **Presidents Souvenir Sheet of 9 (Washington-Harrison),** *May 22,* Chicago, IL	4.00
2217	22c **Presidents Souvenir Sheet of 9 (Tyler-Grant),** *May 22,* Chicago, IL	4.00
2218	22c **Presidents Souvenir Sheet of 9 (Hayes-Wilson),** *May 22,* Chicago, IL	4.00
2219	22c **Presidents Souvenir Sheet of 9 (Harding-Johnson),** *May 22,* Chicago, IL	4.00
	2216a-2219g, 2219i, any single	1.50
	2219h	2.50

First day cancellation was applied to 9,009,599 covers bearing one or more of Nos. 2216-2219, 2216a-2219i.

2223a	22c **Polar Explorers,** *May 28,* North Pole, AK *(760,999)*	2.50
	2220-2223, any single	1.00
2224	22c **Statue of Liberty,** *July 4,* New York, NY *(1,540,308)*	3.00

1986-87

TRANSPORTATION ISSUE

2225	1c **Omnibus,** *Nov. 26, 1986 (57,845)*	1.00
2226	2c **Locomotive,** *Mar. 6, 1987,* Milwaukee, WI *(169,484)*	1.50

1986

2238a	22c **Navajo Art,** *Sept. 4,* Window Rock, AZ *(1,102,520)*	2.50
	2235-2238, any single	1.00
2239	22c **T.S. Eliot,** *Sept. 26,* St. Louis, MO *(304,764)*	1.00
2243a	22c **Woodcarved Figurines,** *Oct. 1 (629,399)*	2.50
	2240-2243, any single	1.00
2244	22c **Christmas (Madonna),** *Oct. 24 (467,999)*	1.00
2245	22c **Christmas (Winter Village),** *Oct. 24,* Snow Hill, MD *(504,851)*	1.00

1987

2246	22c **Michigan Statehood Sesquicent.,** *Jan. 26,* Lansing, MI *(379,117)*	1.00
2247	22c **Pan American Games,** *Jan. 29,* Indianapolis, IN *(344,731)*	1.00
2248	22c **Love,** *Jan. 30,* San Francisco, CA *(333,329)*	1.75
2249	22c **Pointe du Sable,** *Feb. 20,* Chicago, IL *(313,054)*	1.00
2250	22c **Enrico Caruso,** *Feb. 27,* New York, NY *(389,834)*	1.00
2251	22c **Girl Scouts of America,** *Mar. 12 (556,391)*	2.50

1987-88

TRANSPORTATION ISSUE

2252	3c **Conestoga Wagon,** *Feb. 29, 1988,* Conestoga, PA *(155,203)*	
2253	5c **Milk Wagon,** *Sept. 25, 1987,* Indianapolis, IN	1.00

First day cancel was applied to 162,571 covers bearing one or more of Nos. 2253 and 2262.

2254	5.3c **Elevator,** *Sept. 16, 1988,* New York, NY *(142,705)*	1.25
2255	7.6c **Carretta,** *Aug. 30, 1988,* San Jose, CA *(140,024)*	1.25
2256	8.4c **Wheelchair,** *Aug. 12, 1988,* Tucson, AZ *(136,337)*	1.25
2257	10c **Canal Boat,** *Apr. 11, 1987,* Buffalo, NY *(171,952)*	1.00
2258	13c **Police Patrol Wagon,** *Oct. 29, 1988,* Anaheim, CA *(132,928)*	1.50

2259	13.2c **Railway Coal Car,** *July 19, 1988,* Pittsburgh, PA *(123,965)*	1.50
2260	15c **Tugboat,** *July 12, 1988,* Long Beach, CA *(134,926)*	1.25
2261	16.7c **Popcorn Wagon,** *July 7, 1988,* Chicago, IL *(117,908)*	1.25
2262	17.5c **Racing Car,** *Sept. 25, 1987,* Indianapolis, IN	1.00
2263	20c **Cable Car,** *Oct. 28, 1988,* San Francisco, CA *(150,068)*	1.25
2264	20.5c **Fire Engine,** *Sept. 28, 1988,* San Angelo, TX *(123,043)*	2.00
2265	21c **Railway Mail Car,** *Aug. 16, 1988,* Santa Fe, NM *(124,430)*	1.50
2266	24.1c **Tandem Bicycle,** *Oct. 26, 1988,* Redmond, WA *(138,593)*	1.75

1987

2274a	22c **Special Occasions Booklet pane of 10,** *Apr. 20,* Atlanta, GA	5.00
	2267-2274, any single	1.00

First day cancellation was applied to 1,588,129 covers bearing one or more of Nos. 2267-2274a.

2275	22c **United Way,** *Apr. 28 (556,391)*	1.00

1987-89

2276	22c **Flag and Fireworks,** *May 9, 1987* Denver, CO *(398,855)*	1.00
2276a	Booklet pane of 20, *Nov. 30, 1987*	8.00
2277	(25c) **"E" Earth,** *Mar. 22, 1988*	1.25
2278	25c **Flag and Clouds,** *May 6, 1988,* Boxborough, MA *(131,265)*	1.25
2279	(25c) **"E" Earth,** coil, *Mar. 22, 1988*	1.25
2280	25c **Flag over Yosemite,** *May 20, 1988,* Yosemite, CA *(144,339)*	1.25
	Prephosphored paper, *Feb. 14, 1989,* Yosemite, CA *(118,874)*	1.25
2281	25c **Honey Bee,** *Sept. 2, 1988,* Omaha, NE *(122,853)*	1.25
2282	(25c) **"E" Earth,** bklt. single, *Mar. 22, 1988*	1.25
2282a	Booklet pane of 10	6.00

First day cancel was applied to 363,639 covers bearing one or more of Nos. 2277, 2279 and 2282.

2283	25c **Pheasant,** *Apr. 29, 1988,* Rapid City, SD *(167,053)*	1.25
2283a	Booklet pane of 10	6.00
2285b	25c **Grosbeak & Owl, booklet pane of 10** *May 28, 1988,* Arlington, VA	6.00
	2284-2285, any single	1.25

First day cancel was applied to 272,359 covers bearing one or more of Nos. 2284 and 2285.

2285A	25c **Flag and Clouds,** bklt. single, *July 5, 1988 (117,303)*	1.25
2285Ac	Booklet pane of 6	4.00
2335a	22c **American Wildlife,** *June 13, 1987,* Toronto, Canada	50.00
	2286-2335, any single	1.50

1987-90

RATIFICATION OF THE CONSTITUTION

2336	22c **Delaware,** *July 4, 1987,* Dover, DE *(505,770)*	1.00
2337	22c **Pennsylvania,** *Aug. 26, 1987,* Harrisburg, PA *(367,184)*	1.00
2338	22c **New Jersey,** *Sept. 11, 1987,* Trenton, NJ *(432,899)*	1.00
2339	22c **Georgia,** *Jan. 6, 1988,* Atlanta, GA *(467,804)*	1.00
2340	22c **Connecticut,** *Jan. 9, 1988,* Hartford, CT *(379,706)*	1.25
2341	22c **Massachusetts,** *Feb. 6, 1988,* Boston, MA *(412,616)*	1.00
2342	22c **Maryland,** *Feb. 15, 1988,* Annapolis, MD *(376,403)*	1.00
2343	25c **South Carolina,** *May 23, 1988,* Columbia, SC *(322,938)*	1.25
2344	25c **New Hampshire,** *June 21, 1988,* Concord, NH *(374,402)*	1.25
2345	25c **Virginia,** *June 25, 1988,* Williamsburg, VA *(474,079)*	1.25
2346	25c **New York,** *July 26, 1988,* Albany, NY *(385,793)*	1.25
2347	25c **North Carolina,** *Aug. 22, 1989,* Fayetteville, NC *(392,953)*	1.25
2348	25c **Rhode Island,** *May 29, 1990,* Pawtucket, RI *(305,566)*	1.25

1987

2349	22c **U.S.-Morocco Diplomatic Relations Bicent.,** *July 17 (372,814)*	1.00
2350	22c **William Faulkner,** *Aug. 3,* Oxford, MS *(480,024)*	1.00
2354a	22c **Lacemaking,** *Aug. 14,* Ypsilanti, MI	2.75
	2351-2354, any single	1.00
2359a	22c **Drafting of Constitution Bicent. Booklet pane of 5,** *Aug. 28*	3.00
	2355-2359, any single	1.00

First day cancellation was applied to 1,008,799 covers bearing one or more of Nos. 2355-2359a.

2360	22c **Signing of Constitution Bicent.,** *Sept. 17,* Philadelphia, PA *(719,975)*	1.00
2361	22c **Certified Public Accounting,** *Sept. 21,* New York, NY *(362,099)*	3.50
2366a	22c **Locomotives booklet pane of 5,** *Oct. 1,* Baltimore, MD	4.50
	2362-2366, any single	1.50

First day cancellation was applied to 976,694 covers bearing one or more of Nos. 2362-2366a.

2367	22c **Christmas (Madonna),** *Oct. 23 (320,406)*	1.00
2368	22c **Christmas (Ornaments),** *Oct. 23,* Holiday-Anaheim, CA *(375,858)*	1.00

1988

2369	22c **Winter Olympics, Calgary,** *Jan. 10,* Anchorage, AK *(395,198)*	1.00
2370	22c **Australia Bicentennial,** *Jan. 26 (523,465)*	1.00
2371	22c **James Weldon Johnson,** *Feb. 2,* Nashville, TN *(465,282)*	1.00
2375a	22c **Cats,** *Feb. 5,* New York, NY *(872,734)*	4.50
	2372-2375, any single	2.00
2376	22c **Knute Rockne,** *Mar. 9,* Notre Dame, IN *(404,311)*	4.00
2377	25c **Francis Ouimet,** *June 13,* Brookline, MA *(383,168)*	4.00
2378	25c **Love,** *July 4,* Pasadena, CA *(399,038)*	1.75
2379	45c **Love,** *Aug. 8,* Shreveport, LA *(121,808)*	1.75
2380	25c **Summer Olympics, Seoul,** *Aug. 19,* Colorado Springs, CO *(402,616)*	1.25
2385a	25c **Automobiles booklet pane of 5,** *Aug. 25,* Detroit, MI	3.00
	2381-2385, any single	1.25

First day cancel was applied to 875,801 covers bearing one or more of Nos. 2381-2385a.

2389a	25c **Antarctic Explorers,** *Sept. 14 (720,537)*	3.00
	2386-2389, any single	1.25
2393a	25c **Carousel Animals,** *Oct. 1,* Sandusky, OH *(856,380)*	5.00
	2390-2393, any single	2.50
2394	$8.75 **Express Mail,** *Oct. 6,* Terre Haute, IN *(66,558)*	25.00
2396a	25c **Special Occasions (Happy Birthday, Best Wishes),** *Oct. 22,* King of Prussia, PA	4.00
	2395-2396, any single	1.25
2398a	25c **Special Occasions (Thinking of You, Love You),** *Oct. 22,* King of Prussia, PA	5.00
	2397-2398, any single	2.00

First day cancel was applied to 126,767 covers bearing one or more of Nos. 2395-2398, 2396a, 2398a.

2399	25c **Christmas (Madonna),** *Oct. 20 (247,291)*	1.25
2400	25c **Christmas (Contemporary),** *Oct. 20,* Berlin, NH *(412,213)*	1.25

1989

2401	25c **Montana,** *Jan. 15,* Helena, MT *(353,319)*	1.25
2402	25c **A. Philip Randolph,** *Feb. 3,* New York, NY *(363,174)*	1.25
2403	25c **North Dakota,** *Feb. 21,* Bismarck, ND *(306,003)*	1.25
2404	25c **Washington Statehood,** *Feb. 22,* Olympia, WA *(445,174)*	1.25
2409a	25c **Steamboats Booklet pane of 5,** *Mar. 3,* New Orleans, LA	4.00
	2405-2409, any single	1.25

First day cancel was applied to 981,674 covers bearing one or more of Nos. 2405-2409a.

2410	25c **World Stamp Expo,** *Mar. 16,* New York, NY *(296,310)*	1.25
2411	25c **Arturo Toscanini,** *Mar. 25,* New York, NY *(309,441)*	1.25

1989-90

BRANCHES OF GOVERNMENT

2412	25c **House of Representatives,** *Apr. 4, 1989 (327,755)*	1.25
2413	25c **Senate,** *Apr. 6, 1989 (341,288)*	1.25
2414	25c **Executive Branch,** *Apr. 16, 1989* Mount Vernon, VA *(387,644)*	1.25
2415	25c **Supreme Court,** *Feb. 2, 1990 (233,056)*	1.25

1989

2416	25c **South Dakota,** *May 3,* Pierre, SD *(348,370)*	1.25
2417	25c **Lou Gehrig,** *June 10,* Cooperstown, NY *(694,227)*	4.00
2418	25c **Ernest Hemingway,** *July 17,* Key West, FL *(345,436)*	1.25
2419	$2.40 **Moon Landing,** *July 20 (208,982)*	9.00
2420	25c **Letter Carriers,** *Aug. 30,* Milwaukee, WI *(372,241)*	1.25
2421	25c **Bill of Rights,** *Sept. 25,* Philadelphia, PA *(900,384)*	1.25
2425a	25c **Dinosaurs,** *Oct. 1,* Orlando, FL *(871,634)*	3.00
	2422-2425, any single	1.50
2426	25c **Southwest Carved Figure,** *Oct. 12,* San Juan, PR *(215,285)*	1.25
2427	25c **Christmas (Madonna),** *Oct. 19 (395,321)*	1.25
2427a	Booklet pane of 10	6.00
2428	25c **Christmas (Sleigh with Presents),** *Oct. 19,* Westport, CT	1.25
2429	25c **Christmas (Sleigh with Presents) from bklt.,** *Oct. 19,* Westport, CT	1.25
2429a	Booklet pane of 10	6.00

First day cancel was applied to 345,931 covers bearing one or more of Nos. 2428-2429a.

2431	25c **Eagle and Shield,** *Nov. 10,* Virginia Beach, VA	1.25
2433	90c **World Stamp Expo '89 Souvenir Sheet,** *Nov. 17 (281,725)*	7.00
2437a	25c **Classic Mail Transportation,** *Nov. 19 (916,389)*	3.00
	2434-2437, any single	1.25
2438	25c **Classic Mail Transportation Souvenir Sheet,** *Nov. 28 (241,634)*	2.00

1990

2439	25c	**Idaho Statehood,** *Jan. 6*, Boise, ID *(252,493)*	1.25
2440	25c	**Love,** *Jan. 18*, Romance, AR	1.25
2441	25c	**Love, from bklt.,** *Jan. 18*, Romance, AR	1.25
2441a		Booklet pane of 10	6.00

First day cancel was applied to 257,788 covers bearing one or more of Nos. 2440-2441a.

2442	25c	**Ida B. Wells,** *Feb. 1*, Chicago, IL *(229,226)*	1.25
2443	15c	**Beach Umbrella,** *Feb. 3*, Sarasota, FL	1.25
2443a		Booklet pane of 10	4.25

First day cancel was applied to 72,286 covers bearing one or more of Nos. 2443-2443a.

2444	25c	**Wyoming Statehood,** *Feb. 23*, Cheyenne, WY *(317,654)*	1.25
2448a	25c	**Classic Films,** *Mar. 23*, Hollywood, CA *(863,079)*	5.00
		2445-2448, any single	2.50
2449	25c	**Marianne Moore,** *Apr. 18*, Brooklyn, NY *(390,535)*	1.25

1990-95

TRANSPORTATION COILS

2451	4c	**Steam Carriage,** *Jan. 25, 1991*, Tucson, AZ *(100,393)*	1.25
2452	5c	**Circus Wagon,** engraved, *Aug. 31, 1990*, Syracuse, NY *(71,806)*	1.50
2452B	5c	**Circus Wagon,** photogravure, *Dec. 8, 1992*, Cincinnati, OH	1.50
2452D	5c	**Circus Wagon,** with cent sign, photogravure, *Mar. 20, 1995*, Kansas City MO *(20,835)*	1.50
2453	5c	**Canoe,** engraved, *May 25, 1991*, Secaucus, NJ *(108,634)*	1.25
2454	5c	**Canoe,** photogravure, *Oct. 22, 1991*, Secaucus, NJ	1.25
2457	10c	**Tractor Trailer,** engr., *May 25, 1991*, Secaucus, NJ *(84,717)*	1.25
2458	10c	**Tractor Trailer,** photo., *May 25, 1994*, Secaucus, NJ *(15,431)*	1.25
2463	20c	**Cog Railway,** *June 9, 1995*, Dallas, TX *(28,883)*	1.25
2464	23c	**Lunch Wagon,** *Apr. 12, 1991*, Columbus, OH *(115,830)*	1.25
2466	32c	**Ferry Boat,** *June 2, 1995*, McLean VA	1.25

First day cancellation was applied to 59,100 covers bearing one or more of Nos. 2466, 2492.

2468	$1	**Seaplane,** *Apr. 20, 1990* Phoenix, AZ *(244,775)*	2.50

1990

2474a	25c	**Lighthouses booklet pane of 5,** *Apr. 26*	4.50
		2470-2474, any single	1.75

First day cancel was applied to 805,133 covers bearing one or more of Nos. 2470-2474a.

2475	25c	**Flag,** *May 18*, Seattle, WA *(97,567)*	1.25

1990-95

FLORA AND FAUNA ISSUE

2476	1c	**Kestrel,** *June 22*, Aurora, CO *(77,781)*	1.25
2477	1c	**Kestrel, with cent sign,** *May 10, 1995* Aurora, CO *(21,767)*	1.25
2478	3c	**Eastern Bluebird,** *June 22*, Aurora, CO *(76,149)*	1.25
2479	19c	**Fawn,** *Mar. 11* *(100,212)*	1.25
2480	30c	**Cardinal,** *June 22*, Aurora, CO *(101,290)*	1.25
2481	45c	**Pumpkinseed Sunfish,** *Dec. 2, 1992* *(38,696)*	1.75
2482	$2	**Bobcat,** *June 1*, Arlington, VA *(49,660)*	5.00
2483	20c	**Blue Jay,** booklet single, *June 15, 1995*, Kansas City MO	1.25

First day cancellation was applied to 16,847 covers bearing one or more of Nos. 2483, 2483a.

2484	29c	**Wood Duck,** black denomination bklt. single, *Apr. 12*, Columbus, OH	1.25
2484a		Booklet pane of 10	5.00
2485	29c	**Wood Duck,** red denomination bklt. single, *Apr. 12*, Columbus, OH	1.25
2485a		Booklet pane of 10	5.00

First day cancel was applied to 205,305 covers bearing one or more of Nos. 2484-2485, 2484a-2485a.

2486	29c	**African Violet,** *Oct. 8, 1993*, Beaumont, TX	1.25
2486a		Booklet pane of 10	5.00

First day cancellation was applied to 40,167 covers bearing one or more of Nos. 2486-2486a.

2487	32c	**Peach,** booklet single, *July 8, 1995*, Reno NV	1.25
2488	32c	**Pear,** booklet single, *July 8, 1995*, Reno NV	1.25

First day cancellation was applied to 71,086 covers bearing one or more of Nos. 2487-2488, 2488a, 2493-2495A.

2488a		Booklet pane, 5 each #2488-2489	7.50
2489	29c	**Red Squirrel,** self-adhesive, *June 25, 1993* Milwaukee, WI *(48,564)*	1.25
2490	29c	**Red Rose,** self-adhesive, *Aug. 19, 1993* Houston, TX *(37,916)*	1.25
2491	29c	**Pine Cone,** self-adhesive, *Nov. 5, 1993* Kansas City, MO *(110,924)*	1.25
2492	32c	**Pink Rose,** self-adhesive, *June 2, 1995*, McLean VA	1.25

First day cancellation was applied to 59,100 covers bearing one or more of Nos. 2466, 2492.

2493	32c	**Peach,** self-adhesive, *July 8, 1995*, Reno NV	1.25
2494	32c	**Pear,** self-adhesive, *July 8, 1995*, Reno NV	1.25
2495	32c	**Peach,** self-adhesive, serpentine die cut vert., *July 8, 1995*, Reno NV	1.25
2495A	32c	**Pear,** self-adhesive, serpentine die cut vert., *July 8, 1995*, Reno NV	1.25

First day cancellation was applied to 71,086 covers bearing one or more of Nos. 2487-2488, 2488a, 2493-2495A.

1990

2500a	25c	**Olympians,** *July 6*, Minneapolis, MN *(1,143,404)*	3.00
		2496-2500, any single	1.25
2505a	25c	**Indian Headdresses, booklet pane of 10** *Aug. 17*, Cody, WY	6.00
		2501-2505, any single	1.25

First day cancel was applied to 979,580 covers bearing one or more of Nos. 2501-2505a.

2507a	25c	**Micronesia, Marshall Islands,** *Sept. 28* *(343,816)*	2.00
		2506-2507, any single	1.25
2511a	25c	**Sea Creatures,** *Oct. 3*, Baltimore, MD *(706,047)*	3.00
		2508-2511, any single	1.25
2512	25c	**Grand Canyon,** *Oct. 12*, Grand Canyon, AZ *(164,190)*	1.25
2513	25c	**Dwight D. Eisenhower,** *Oct. 13*, Abilene, KS *(487,988)*	1.25
2514	25c	**Christmas (traditional),** *Oct. 18*	1.25
2514a		Booklet pane of 10	5.00

First day cancel was applied to 378,383 covers bearing one or more of Nos. 2514-2514a.

2515	25c	**Christmas (secular),** *Oct. 18*, Evergreen, CO	1.25
2516	25c	**Christmas (secular),** *Oct. 18*, Evergreen, CO	1.25
2516a		Booklet pane of 10	6.00

First day cancel was applied to 230,586 covers bearing one or more of Nos. 2515-2516a.

1991-94

2517	(29c)	**"F" Flower,** *Jan. 22, 1991* *(106,698)*	1.25
2518	(29c)	**"F" Flower,** coil, *Jan. 22, 1991* *(39,311)*	1.25
2519	(29c)	**"F" Flower,** bklt. single (bullseye perf. 11.2), *Jan. 22, 1991*	1.25
2519a		Booklet pane of 10	7.25
2520	(29c)	**"F" Flower,** bklt. single (perf. 11), *Jan. 22, 1991*	1.25
2520a		Booklet pane of 10	7.25

First day cancel was applied to 32,971 covers bearing one or more of Nos. 2519-2520, 2519a-2520a.

2521	(4c)	**Makeup Stamp,** *Jan. 22, 1991* *(51,987)*	1.25
2522	(29c)	**"F" Flag,** *Jan. 22, 1991* *(48,821)*	1.25
2523	29c	**Flag over Mt. Rushmore,** engraved, *Mar. 29, 1991* Mt. Rushmore, SD *(233,793)*	1.25
2523A	29c	**Flag over Mt. Rushmore,** photogravure, *July 4, 1991* Mt. Rushmore, SD *(80,662)*	1.25
2524	29c	**Flower,** *Apr. 5, 1991*, Rochester, NY *(132,233)*	1.25
2525	29c	**Flower,** roulette 10 coil, *Apr. 5, 1991*, Rochester, NY *(144,750)*	1.25
2526	29c	**Flower,** perf. 10 coil, *Mar. 3, 1992*, Rochester, NY *(35,877)*	1.25
2527	29c	**Flower,** bklt. single, *Apr. 5, 1991*, Rochester, NY	1.25
2527a		Booklet pane of 10	5.00

First day cancel was applied to 16,975 covers bearing one or more of Nos. 2527-2527a.

2528	29c	**Flag and Olympic Rings,** bklt. single, *Apr. 21, 1991*, Atlanta, GA	1.25
2528a		Booklet pane of 10	5.00

First day cancel was applied to 319,488 covers bearing one or more of Nos. 2528-2528a.

2529	19c	**Fishing Boat,** two loops, *Aug. 8, 1991* *(82,698)*	1.25
2529C	19c	**Fishing Boat,** one loop, *June 25, 1994*, Arlington, VA *(14,538)*	1.25
2530	19c	**Balloon,** *May 17, 1991*, Denver, CO	1.25
2530a		Booklet pane of 10	5.00

First day cancel was applied to 96,351 covers bearing one or more of Nos. 2530-2530a.

2531	29c	**Flags on Parade,** *May 30, 1991*, Waterloo, NY *(104,046)*	1.25
2531A	29c	**Liberty Torch,** *June 25, 1991*, New York, NY *(68,456)*	1.25

1991-95

2532	50c	**Switzerland,** *Feb. 22*, Washington, DC *(316,047)*	1.35
2533	29c	**Vermont,** *Mar. 1*, Bennington, VT *(308,105)*	1.50
2534	29c	**Savings Bonds,** *Apr. 30*, Washington, DC *(341,955)*	1.25
2535	29c	**Love,** *May 9*, Honolulu, HI *(336,132)*	1.25
2536	29c	**Love,** bklt. single, *May 9*, Honolulu, HI	1.25
2536a		Booklet pane of 10	5.00

First day cancel was applied to 43,336 covers bearing one or more of Nos. 2536-2536a.

2537	52c	**Love,** *May 9*, Honolulu, HI *(90,438)*	1.35
2538	29c	**William Saroyan,** *May 22*, Fresno, CA *(334,373)*	1.25
2539	$1	**Eagle & Olympic Rings,** *Sept. 29*, Orlando, FL *(69,241)*	2.25
2540	$2.90	**Eagle & Olympic Rings,** *July 7*, San Diego, CA *(79,555)*	4.50
2541	$9.95	**Eagle & Olympic Rings,** *June 16*, Sacramento, CA *(68,657)*	12.50
2542	$14	**Eagle,** *Aug. 31*, Hunt Valley, MD *(54,727)*	19.00
2543	$2.90	**Futuristic Space Shuttle,** *June 3, 1993*, Kennedy Space Center, FL *(36,359)*	6.00
2544	$3	**Space Shuttle Challenger,** *June 22, 1995* Anaheim CA *(16,502)*	7.00
2544A	$10.75	**Space Shuttle Endeavour,** *Aug. 4, 1995* Irvine CA *(10,534)*	15.00

1991

2549a	29c	**Fishing Flies booklet pane of 5,** *May 31*, Cuddebackville, NY *(1,045,726)*	3.00
		2545-2549, any single	1.25
2550	29c	**Cole Porter,** *June 8*, Peru, IN *(304,363)*	1.25
2551	29c	**Desert Storm/ Desert Shield,** *July 2*	2.50
2552	29c	**Desert Storm/ Desert Shield,** bklt. single, *July 2*	2.50
2552a		Booklet pane of 5	4.50

First day cancel was applied to 860,455 covers bearing one or more of Nos. 2551-2552, 2552a.

2557a	29c	**Summer Olympics,** *July 12*, Los Angeles, CA *(886,984)*	3.00
		2553-2557, any single	1.25
2558	29c	**Numismatics,** *Aug. 13*, Chicago, IL *(288,519)*	1.25
2559	29c	**World War II block of 10,** *Sept. 3*, Phoenix, AZ *(1,832,967)*	7.00
		2559a-2559j, any single	1.50
2560	29c	**Basketball,** *Aug. 28*, Springfield, MA *(295,471)*	2.00
2561	29c	**District of Columbia,** *Sept. 7* *(299,989)*	1.25
2566a	29c	**Comedians booklet pane of 10,** *Aug. 29*, Hollywood, CA	6.00
		2562-2566, any single	1.50

First day cancel was applied to 954,293 covers bearing one or more of Nos. 2562-2566a.

2567	29c	**Jan Matzeliger,** *Sept. 15*, Lynn, MA *(289,034)*	1.25
2577a	29c	**Space Exploration booklet pane of 10,** *Oct. 1*, Pasadena, CA	5.00
		2568-2577, any single	1.25

First day cancel was applied to 1,465,111 covers bearing one or more of Nos. 2568-2577a.

2578	(29c)	**Christmas (religious),** *Oct. 17*, Houston, TX	1.25
2579	(29c)	**Christmas (secular),** *Oct. 17*, Santa, ID *(169,750)*	1.25
2581b	(29c)	**Christmas booklet pane of 4,** *Oct. 17*, Santa, ID	2.50
		2580-2581, any single	1.25
2582	(29c)	**Christmas,** bklt. single, *Oct. 17*, Santa, ID	1.25
2582a		Booklet pane of 4	2.50
2583	(29c)	**Christmas,** bklt. single, *Oct. 17*, Santa, ID	1.25
2583a		Booklet pane of 4	2.50
2584	(29c)	**Christmas,** bklt. single, *Oct. 17*, Santa, ID	1.25
2584a		Booklet pane of 4	2.50
2585	(29c)	**Christmas,** bklt. single, *Oct. 17*, Santa, ID	1.25
2585a		Booklet pane of 4	2.50

First day cancel was applied to 168,794 covers bearing one or more of Nos. 2580-2585, 2581b, 2582a, 2583a, 2584a and 2585a.

1991-95

2587	32c	**James K. Polk,** *Nov. 2, 1995*, Columbia TN *(189,429)*	1.25
2590	$1	**Surrender of Gen. John Burgoyne,** *May 5, 1994*, New York, NY *(379,629)*	2.00
2592	$5	**Washington & Jackson,** *Aug. 19, 1994*, Pittsburgh, PA *(16,303)*	9.00
2593	29c	**Pledge of Allegiance,** black denomination, *Sept. 8, 1992*, Rome, NY	1.25
2593a		Booklet pane of 10	5.00

First day cancel was applied to 61,464 covers bearing one or more of Nos. 2593-2593a.

2595	29c	**Eagle & Shield,** brown denomination, *Sept. 25, 1992*, Dayton, OH	1.25
2596	29c	**Eagle & Shield,** green denomination, *Sept. 25, 1992*, Dayton, OH	1.25
2597	29c	**Eagle & Shield,** red denomination, *Sept. 25, 1992*, Dayton, OH	1.25

First day cancel was applied to 65,822 covers bearing one or more of Nos. 2595-2597.

2598	29c	**Eagle,** *Feb. 4, 1994*, Sarasota, FL *(67,300)*	1.25
2599	29c	**Statue of Liberty,** *June 24, 1994*, Haines City, FL *(39,810)*	1.25
2602	(10c)	**Eagle & Shield,** Bulk Rate USA, *Dec. 13, 1991*, Kansas City, MO *(21,176)*	1.25
2603	(10c)	**Eagle & Shield,** USA Bulk Rate, *May 29, 1993*, Secaucus, NJ	1.25
2604	(10c)	**Eagle & Shield,** gold eagle, *May 29, 1993*, Secaucus, NJ	1.25

First day cancellation was applied to 36,444 covers bearing one or more of Nos. 2603-2604.

2605	23c	**Flag,** *Sept. 27, 1991*	1.25
2606	23c	**Reflected Flag,** *July 21, 1992*, Kansas City, MO *(35,673)*	1.25
2607	23c	**Reflected Flag,** 7mm "23," *Oct. 9, 1992*, Kansas City, MO	1.25

2608	23c **Reflected Flag**, 8 ½mm "First Class" *May 14, 1993*, Denver, CO *(15,548)*		1.25
2609	29c **Flag over White House**, *Apr. 23, 1992* *(56,505)*		1.25

1992

2615a	29c **Winter Olympics**, *Jan. 11*, Orlando, FL *(1,062,048)*		3.00
	2611-2615, any single		1.25
2616	29c **World Columbian Stamp Expo**, *Jan. 24*, Rosemont, IL *(309,729)*		1.25
2617	29c **W.E.B. Du Bois**, *Jan. 31*, Atlanta, GA *(196,219)*		1.25
2618	29c **Love**, *Feb. 6*, Loveland, CO *(218,043)*		1.25
2619	29c **Olympic Baseball**, *Apr. 3*, Atlanta, GA *(105,996)*		1.50
2623a	29c **Voyages of Columbus**, *Apr. 24*, Christiansted, VI		2.75
	2620-2623, any single		1.25

First day cancellation was applied to 509,270 covers bearing one or more of Nos. 2620-2623a.

2624		**First Sighting of Land Souvenir Sheet of 3**, *May 22*, Chicago, IL	2.10
2624a	1c		1.25
2624b	4c		1.25
2624c	$1		2.00
2625		**Claiming a New World Souvenir Sheet of 3**, *May 22*, Chicago, IL	8.00
2625a	2c		1.25
2625b	3c		1.25
2625c	$4		8.00
2626		**Seeking Royal Support Souvenir Sheet of 3**, *May 22*, Chicago, IL	1.75
2626a	5c		1.25
2626b	30c		1.25
2626c	50c		1.50
2627		**Royal Favor Restored Souvenir Sheet of 3**, *May 22*, Chicago, IL	6.25
2627a	6c		1.25
2627b	8c		1.25
2627c	$3		6.00
2628		**Reporting Discoveries Souvenir Sheet of 3**, *May 22*, Chicago, IL	4.50
2628a	10c		1.25
2628b	15c		1.25
2628c	$2		4.00
2629	$5	**Christopher Columbus Souvenir Sheet**, *May 22*, Chicago, IL	10.00

First day cancel was applied to 211,142 covers bearing one or more of Nos. 2624-2629.

2630	29c **New York Stock Exchange**, *May 17*, New York, NY *(261,897)*		1.75
2634a	29c **Space Accomplishments**, *May 29*, Chicago, IL		2.75
	2631-2634, any single		1.50

First day cancellation was applied to 277,853 covers bearing one or more of Nos. 2631-2634a.

2635	29c **Alaska Highway**, *May 30*, Fairbanks, AK *(186,791)*		1.25
2636	29c **Kentucky**, *June 1*, Danville, KY *(251,153)*		1.25
2641a	29c **Summer Olympics**, *June 11*, Baltimore, MD *(713,942)*		3.00
	2637-2641, any single		1.25
2646a	29c **Hummingbirds booklet pane of 5**, *June 15*		3.00
	2642-2646, any single		1.25

First day cancel was applied to 995,278 covers bearing one or more of Nos. 2642-2646a.

2696a	29c **Wildflowers**, *July 24*, Columbus, OH		30.00
	2647-2696, any single		1.25

First day cancellation was applied to 3,693,972 covers bearing one or more of Nos. 2647-2696a.

2697	29c **World War II block of 10**, *Aug. 17*, Indianapolis, IN *(1,734,880)*		7.00
	2697a-2697j, any single		1.50

First day cancellation was applied to 1,734,880 covers bearing one or more of Nos. 2697, 2697a-2697j.

2698	29c **Dorothy Parker**, *Aug. 22*, West End, NJ *(266,323)*		1.25
2699	29c **Theodore von Karman**, *Aug. 31* *(256,986)*		1.25
2703a	29c **Minerals**, *Sept. 17*		2.75
	2700-2703, any single		1.25

First day cancellation was applied to 681,416 covers bearing one or more of Nos. 2700-2703.

2704	29c **Juan Rodriguez Cabrillo**, *Sept. 28*, San Diego, CA *(290,720)*		1.25
2709a	29c **Wild Animals booklet pane of 5**, *Oct. 1*, New Orleans, LA		3.25
	Any other city		4.00
	2705-2709, any single		1.25

First day cancel was applied to 604,205 New Orleans covers bearing one or more of Nos. 2705-2709a.

2710	29c **Christmas (religious)**, *Oct. 22*		1.25
2710a	Booklet pane of 10		7.25

First day cancel was applied to 201,576 covers bearing one or more of Nos. 2710-2710a.

2714a	29c **Christmas (secular)**, *Oct. 22*, Kansas City, MO		2.75
	2711-2714, any single		1.25
2718a	29c **Christmas (secular) booklet pane of 4**, *Oct. 22*, Kansas City, MO		2.75
	2715-2718, any single		1.25

First day cancel was applied to 461,937 covers bearing one or more of Nos. 2711-2714, 2715-2718 and 2718a.

2719	29c **Christmas (secular)**, self-adhesive, *Oct. 28*, New York, NY *(48,873)*		1.25
2720	29c **Chinese New Year**, *Dec. 30*, San Francisco, CA *(138,238)*		1.50

1993

2721	29c **Elvis (Presley)**, *Jan. 8*, Memphis, TN, AM cancellation, *(4,452,815)*		1.75
	Any city, PM cancellation		2.00
2722	29c **Oklahoma!**, *Mar. 30*, Oklahoma City, OK *(283,837)*		1.25
2723	29c **Hank Williams**, perf 10, *June 9*, Nashville, TN		1.25
2723A	29c **Hank Williams**, perf 11.2x11.4, *June 9*, Nashville, TN		1.25

First day cancel was applied to 311,106 covers bearing one or more of Nos. 2723-2723A.

2730a	29c **Rock & Roll/Rhythm & Blues Musicians**, *June 16*, Cleveland OH or Santa Monica CA		5.00
	Any other city		5.00
	2724-2730, any single		1.25
	Any single, any other city		1.25

Value for No. 2730a is also for any se-tenant configuration of seven different stamps.

First day cancel was applied to 540,809 covers bearing one or more of Nos. 2724-2730a, 2731-2737b.

2737a	29c **Rock & Roll/Rhythm & Blues Musicians booklet pane of 8**, *June 16*, Cleveland, OH or Santa Monica CA		5.25
	Any other city		5.25
	2731-2737, any single		1.25
	Any single, any other city		1.25
2737b	29c **Rock & Roll/Rhythm & Blues Musicians booklet pane of 4**, *June 16*, Cleveland, OH or Santa Monica CA		2.75
	Any other city		2.75

For first day cancellation quantities, see No. 2730a.

2745a	29c **Space Fantasy booklet pane of 5**, *Jan. 25*, Huntsville, AL		3.25
	2741-2745, any single		1.25

First day cancel was applied to 631,203 covers bearing one or more of Nos. 2741-2745a.

2746	29c **Percy Lavon Julian**, *Jan. 29*, Chicago, IL *(120,877)*		1.25
2747	29c **Oregon Trail**, *Feb. 12*, Salem, OR *(436,550)*		1.25

No. 2747 was also available on the first day of issue in 36 cities along the route of the Oregon Trail.

2748	29c **World University Games**, *Feb. 25*, Buffalo, NY *(157,563)*		1.25
2749	29c **Grace Kelly**, *Mar. 24*, Beverly Hills, CA *(263,913)*		2.00
2753a	29c **Circus**, *Apr. 6*		3.00
	2750-2753, any single		1.50

First day cancel was applied to 676,927 covers bearing one or more of Nos. 2750-2753a.

2754	29c **Cherokee Strip Land Run**, *Apr. 17*, Enid, OK *(260,118)*		1.25
2755	29c **Dean Acheson**, *Apr. 21*, *(158,783)*		1.25
2759a	29c **Sporting Horses**, *May 1*, Louisville, KY		3.50
	2756-2759, any single		1.75

First day cancel was applied to 448,059 covers bearing one or more of Nos. 2756-2759a.

2764a	29c **Garden Flowers booklet pane of 5**, *May 15*, Spokane, WA		3.25
	2760-2764, any single		1.25

First day cancel was applied to 492,578 covers bearing one or more of Nos. 2760-2764a.

2765	29c **World War II block of 10**, *May 31*,		7.00
	2765a-2765j, any single		1.50

First day cancel was applied to 543,511 covers bearing one or more of Nos. 2765, 2765a-2765j.

2766	29c **Joe Louis**, *June 22*, Detroit, MI *(229,272)*		1.50
2770a	29c **Broadway Musicals booklet pane of 4**, *July 14*, New York, NY		3.25
	2767-2770, any single		1.25

First day cancel was applied to 308,231 covers bearing one or more of Nos. 2767-2770a.

2774a	29c **Country Music**, *Sept. 25*, Nashville, TN		2.75
	2771-2774, any single		1.25
2778a	29c **Country Music booklet pane of 4**, *Sept. 25*, Nashville, TN		2.75
	2775-2778, any single		1.25

First day cancel was applied to 362,904 covers bearing one or more of Nos. 2771-2774a, 2775-2778a.

2782a	29c **National Postal Museum**, *July 30*		2.75
	2779-2782, any single		1.25

First day cancel was applied to 371,115 covers bearing one or more of Nos. 2779-2782a.

2784a	29c **Deafness/Sign Language**, *Sept. 20*, Burbank, CA		2.00
	2783-2784, any single		1.25

First day cancel was applied to 112,350 covers bearing one or more of Nos. 2783-2784a.

2788a	29c **Classic Books**, *Oct. 23*, Louisville, KY		2.75
	2785-2788, any single		1.25

First day cancel was applied to 269,457 covers bearing one or more of Nos. 2785-2788a.

2789	29c **Christmas (religious)**, *Oct. 21*, Raleigh, NC		1.25

2790	29c **Christmas (religious)**, booklet single, *Oct. 21*, Raleigh, NC		1.25
2790a	Booklet pane of 4		2.00

First day cancellation was applied to 155,192 covers bearing one or more of Nos. 2789-2790a.

2794a	29c **Christmas (secular)**, sheet stamps, *Oct. 21*, New York, NY		2.75
	2791-2794, any single		1.25
2798a	29c **Christmas (secular) booklet pane of 10**, *Oct. 21*, New York, NY		6.50
2798b	29c **Christmas (secular) booklet pane of 10**, *Oct. 21*, New York, NY		6.50
	2795-2798, any single		1.25
2799	29c **Christmas (snowman)**, large self-adhesive, *Oct. 28*, New York, NY		1.25
2800	29c **Christmas (soldier)**, self-adhesive, *Oct. 28*, New York, NY		1.25
2801	29c **Christmas (jack-in-the-box)**, self-adhesive, *Oct. 28*, New York, NY		1.25
2802	29c **Christmas (reindeer)**, self-adhesive, *Oct. 28*, New York, NY		1.25
	2799-2802 on one cover		2.50
2803	29c **Christmas (snowman)**, small self-adhesive, *Oct. 28*, New York, NY		1.25

First day cancel was applied to 384,262 covers bearing one or more of Nos. 2791-2794a, 2795-2798b, 2799-2803.

2804	29c **Mariana Islands**, *Nov. 4*, Saipan, MP *(157,410)*		1.25
2805	29c **Columbus' Landing in Puerto Rico**, *Nov. 19*, San Juan, PR *(222,845)*		1.25
2806	29c **AIDS Awareness**, *Dec. 1*, New York, NY		1.25
2806a	Booklet single, perf. 11 vert.		1.25
2806b	Booklet pane of 5		3.25

First day cancellation was applied to 209,200 covers bearing one or more of Nos. 2806-2806b.

1994

2811a	29c **Winter Olympics**, *Jan. 6*, Salt Lake City, UT		3.00
	2807-2811, any single		1.25

First day cancellation was applied to 645,636 covers bearing one or more of Nos. 2807-2811a.

2812	29c **Edward R. Murrow**, *Jan. 21*, Pullman, WA *(154,638)*		1.25
2813	29c **Love**, self-adhesive, *Jan. 27*, Loveland, OH *(125,146)*		1.25
2814	29c **Love**, booklet single, *Feb. 14*, Niagara Falls, NY		1.25
2814a	Booklet pane of 10		6.50
2814C	29c **Love**, *June 11*, Niagara Falls, NY *(42,109)*		1.25
2815	52c **Love**, *Feb. 14*, Niagara Falls, NY		1.40
2816	29c **Dr. Allison Davis**, *Feb. 1*, Williamstown, MA *(162,404)*		1.25
2817	29c **Chinese New Year**, *Feb. 5*, Pomona, CA *(148,492)*		1.75
2818	29c **Buffalo Soldiers**, *Apr. 22*, Dallas, TX *(107,223)*		1.50

No. 2818 was also available on the first day of issue in forts in Kansas, Texas and Arizona.

2828a	29c **Silent Screen Stars**, *Apr. 27*, San Francisco, CA		6.50
	2819-2828, any single		1.50

First day cancellation was applied to 591,251 covers bearing one or more of Nos. 2819-2828a.

2833a	29c **Garden Flowers booklet pane of 5**, *Apr. 28*, Cincinnati, OH		3.25
	2829-2833, any single		1.25

First day cancellation was applied to 153,069 covers bearing one or more of Nos. 2829-2833a.

2834	29c **World Cup Soccer**, *May 26*, New York, NY		1.25
2835	40c **World Cup Soccer**, *May 26*, New York, NY		1.25
2836	50c **World Cup Soccer**, *May 26*, New York, NY		1.35

First day cancellation was applied to 443,768 covers bearing one or more of Nos. 2834-2836.

2837		**World Cup Soccer souvenir sheet of 3**, *May 26*, New York, NY *(59,503)*	2.50
2838	29c	**World War II block of 10**, *June 6*, USS Normandy	7.00
		2838a-2838j, any single	1.50

No. 2838 was also available on the first day of issue in 13 other locations.

First day cancellation was applied to 744,267 covers bearing one or more of Nos. 2838, 2838a-2838j.

2839	29c **Norman Rockwell**, *July 1*, Stockbridge, MA *(232,076)*		1.25
2840	50c **Norman Rockwell Souvenir Sheet of 4**, *July 1*, Stockbridge, MA		3.50
	2840a-2840d, any single		1.50

First day cancellation was applied to 19,734 covers bearing one or more of Nos. 2840-2840d.

2841	29c **Moon Landing Sheet of 12**, *July 20*,		6.50
	2841a, single stamp		1.50

First day cancellation was applied to 303,707 covers bearing one or more of Nos. 2841-2841a.

2842	$9.95 **Moon Landing**, *July 20 (11,463)*		15.00
2847a	29c **Locomotives booklet pane of 5**, *July 28*, Chama, NM		3.25
	2843-2847, any single		1.25

First day cancellation was applied to 169,016 covers bearing one or more of Nos. 2843-2847a.

2848	29c **George Meany**, *Aug. 16 (172,418)*		1.25

2853a	29c **American Music Series**, *Sept. 1*, New York, NY		3.25
	2849-2853, any single		1.25

First day cancellation was applied to 156,049 covers bearing one or more of Nos. 2849-2853a.

2861a	29c **American Music Series**, *Sept. 17*, Greenville MS		6.00
	2854-2861, any single		1.25

First day cancellation was applied to 483,737 covers bearing one or more of Nos. 2854-2861a.

2862	29c **James Thurber**, *Sept. 10*, Columbus OH *(39,064)*		1.25
2866a	29c **Wonders of the Sea**, *Oct. 3*, Honolulu HI		2.75
	2863-2866, any single		1.25

First day cancellation was applied to 284,678 covers bearing one or more of Nos. 2863-2866a.

2868a	29c **Cranes**, *Oct. 9*		2.00
	2867-2868, any single		1.25

First day cancellation was applied to 202,955 covers bearing one or more of Nos. 2867-2868a, 24,942 with the People's Republic of China stamps.

2869	29c **Legends of the West Pane of 20**,		
	Oct. 18, Laramie WY *(429,680)*		14.00
	Tucson, AZ *(220,417)*		14.00
	Lawton, OK *(191,393)*		14.00
	2869a-2869t, any single, any city		1.75

First day cancellation was applied to covers bearing one or more of Nos. 2869-2869t.

2871	29c **Christmas (religious)**, perf 11¼, *Oct. 20 (155,192)*		1.25
2871A	29c **Christmas (religious)**, perf 9¾x11, *Oct. 20 (155,192)*		1.25
2871a	Perf 9.8x10.8		1.25
2872	29c **Christmas (stocking)**, *Oct. 20*, Harmony MN		1.25
2873	29c **Christmas (Santa Claus)**, self-adhesive, *Oct. 20*, Harmony MN		1.25
2874	29c **Christmas (cardinal)**, small self-adhesive, *Oct. 20*, Harmony MN		1.25

First day cancellation was applied to 132,005 covers bearing one or more of Nos. 2872, 2872a, 2873, 2874.

2875	$2 **Bureau of Printing and Engraving Souvenir sheet**, *Nov. 3*, New York, NY *(13,126)*		12.00
2876	29c **Chinese New Year (Boar)**, *Dec. 30*, Sacramento CA		1.50
2877	(3c) **Dove**, bright blue, *Dec. 13*		1.25
2878	(3c) **Dove**, dark blue, *Dec. 13*		1.25
2879	(20c) **G**, black, *Dec. 13*		1.25
2880	(20c) **G**, red, *Dec. 13*		1.25
2881	(32c) **G**, black, *Dec. 13*		1.25
2881a	Booklet pane of 10		7.50
2882	(32c) **G**, red, *Dec. 13*		1.25
2883	(32c) **G**, black, *Dec. 13*		1.25
2883a	Booklet pane of 10		7.50
2884	(32c) **G**, black, *Dec. 13*		1.25
2884a	Booklet pane of 10		7.50
2885	(32c) **G**, red, *Dec. 13*		1.25
2885a	Booklet pane of 10		7.50
2886	(32c) **G**, gray, blue, light blue, red & black, self-adhesive, *Dec. 13*		1.25
2887	(32c) **G**, black, blue & red, self-adhesive, *Dec. 13*		1.25
2888	(25c) **G**, black, coil, *Dec. 13*		1.25
2889	(32c) **G**, black, coil, *Dec. 13*		1.25
2890	(32c) **G**, blue, coil, *Dec. 13*		1.25
2891	(32c) **G**, red, coil, *Dec. 13*		1.25
2892	(32c) **G**, red, rouletted coil, *Dec. 13*		1.25

Originally, No. 2893 (the 5c green Non-profit Presort G rate stamp) was only available through the Philatelic Fulfillment Center after their announcement 1/12/95. Requests for first day cancels received a 12/13/94 cancel, even though they were not available on that date. Value, $1.25.

First day cancellation was applied to 338,107 covers bearing one or more of Nos. 2877-2893(?), and U633-U634.

2897	32c **Flag Over Porch**, *May 19*, Denver CO		1.25

First day cancellation was applied to 66,609 covers bearing one or more of Nos. 2897, 2913-2914, 2916 and possibly 2920.

1995-98

2902	(5c) **Butte**, coil, *Mar. 10*, State College PA		1.25

First day cancellation was applied to 80,003 covers bearing one or more of Nos. 2902, 2905, and U635-U636.

2902B	(5c) **Butte**, self-adhesive coil, *June 15, 1996*, San Antonio TX		1.25

First day cancellation was applied to 87,400 covers bearing one or more of Nos. 2902B, 2904A, 2906, 2910, 2912A, 2915B.

2903	(5c) **Mountain**, purple & multi coil, *Mar. 16, 1996* San Jose CA		1.25
2904	(5c) **Mountain**, blue & multi coil, *Mar. 16, 1996* San Jose CA		1.25

First day cancellation was applied to 28,064 covers bearing one or more of Nos. 2903-2904.

2904A	(5c) **Mountain**, purple & multi self-adhesive coil, *June 15, 1996*, San Antonio TX		1.25

First day cancellation was applied to 87,400 covers bearing one or more of Nos. 2902B, 2904A, 2906, 2910, 2912A, 2915B.

2904B	(5c) **Mountain**, purple & multi self-adhesive coil, inscription outlined, *Jan. 24, 1997*, Tucson, AZ		1.25

2905	(10c) **Auto**, coil, *Mar. 10*, State College PA		1.25
2906	(10c) **Auto**, self-adhesive coil, *June 15, 1996* San Antonio TX		1.25

First day cancellation was applied to 87,400 covers bearing one or more of Nos. 2902B, 2904A, 2906, 2910, 2912A, 2915B.

2907	(10c) **Eagle & Shield**, USA Bulk Rate self-adhesive coil, *May 21, 1996*		1.25

First day cancellation was applied to 54,102 covers bearing one or more of Nos. 2907, 2915A, 2915C, 2921.

2908	(15c) **Auto tail fin (dark orange yellow)**, coil, *Mar. 17*, New York NY		1.25
2909	(15c) **Auto tail fin (buff)**, coil, *Mar. 17*, New York, NY		1.25

First day cancellation was applied to 93,770 covers bearing one or more of Nos. 2908-2909, 2911-2912, 2919.

2910	(15c) **Auto tail fin (buff)**, self-adhesive coil, *June 15, 1996*, San Antonio TX		1.25

First day cancellation was applied to 87,400 covers bearing one or more of Nos. 2902B, 2904A, 2906, 2910, 2915B.

2911	(25c) **Juke box**, coil, *Mar. 17*, New York NY		1.25
2912	(25c) **Juke box**, coil, *Mar. 17*, New York NY		1.25

First day cancellation was applied to 93,770 covers bearing one or more of Nos. 2908-2909, 2911-2912, 2919.

2912A	(25c) **Juke box**, self-adhesive coil, bright orange red & multi, microperfs, *June 15, 1996*, New York NY		1.25

First day cancellation was applied to 87,400 covers bearing one or more of Nos. 2902B, 2904A, 2906, 2910, 2912A, 2915B.

2912B	(25c) **Juke box**, self-adhesive coil, dark red & multi, *Jan. 24, 1997*, Tucson, AZ		1.25
2913	32c **Flag Over Porch**, coil, *May 19*, Denver CO		1.25
2914	32c **Flag Over Porch**, coil, *May 19*, Denver CO		1.25
2915	32c **Flag Over Porch**, self-adhesive, die cut 8.7 vert., *Apr. 18*		1.25
2915A	32c **Flag Over Porch**, self-adhesive, die cut 9.8 vert., 11 teeth, *May 21, 1996*		1.25
2915B	32c **Flag Over Porch**, self-adhesive, die cut 11.5 vert., *June 15, 1996*, San Antonio TX		1.25

First day cancellation was applied to 87,400 covers bearing one or more of Nos. 2902B, 2904A, 2906, 2910, 2912A, 2915B.

2915C	32c **Flag Over Porch**, self-adhesive, die cut 10.9, *May 21, 1996*		1.25
2915D	32c **Flag Over Porch**, self-adhesive coil, self-adhesive die cut 9.8 vert., 9 teeth, *Jan. 24, 1997*, Tucson, AZ		1.25

First day cancellation was applied to 56,774 covers bearing one or more of Nos. 2904B, 2912B, 2915D and 2921b.

2916	32c **Flag Over Porch**, booklet single, *May 19*, Denver CO		1.25
2916a	Booklet pane of 10		7.50
2919	32c **Flag Over Field**, self-adhesive, *Mar. 17*, New York NY		1.25

First day cancellation was applied to 93,770 covers bearing one or more of Nos. 2908-2909, 2911-2912, 2919.

2920	32c **Flag Over Porch**, self-adhesive, *Apr. 18*		1.25

First day cancellation was applied to 66,609 covers bearing one or more of Nos. 2897, 2913-2914, 2916 and possibly, 2920.

First day cancellation was applied to 57,639 covers bearing one or more of Nos. 2920d, 3030, 3044.

2921	32c **Flag Over Porch**, self-adhesive, booklet stamp, die cut 9.8 on 2 or 3 sides, *May 21, 1996*		1.25

First day cancellation was applied to 54,102 covers bearing one or more of Nos. 2907, 2915A, 2915C, 2921.

GREAT AMERICANS ISSUE

2933	32c **Milton Hershey**, *July 11*, Hershey PA *(121,228)*		1.25
2934	32c **Cal Farley**, *Apr. 26, 1996*, Amarillo TX *(109,440)*		1.25
2935	32c **Henry Luce**, *Apr. 3, 1998*, New York NY *(76,982)*		1.25
2936	32c **Wallace**, *July 16, 1998*, Pleasantville NY *(72,183)*		1.25
2938	46c **Ruth Benedict**, *July 11*, Virginia Beach VA *(24,793)*		1.40
2940	55c **Alice Hamilton**, *July 11*, Boston MA *(24,225)*		1.40
2942	77c **Mary Breckinridge**, *Nov. 9, 1998* Troy, NY		1.75

First day cancellation was applied to 121,662 covers bearing one or more of Nos. 2942, 3257-3261, 3263-3269.

2943	78c **Alice Paul**, *Aug. 18*, Mount Laurel NJ *(25,071)*		1.50

1995

2948	(32c) **Love**, *Feb. 1*, Valentines VA		1.25
2949	(32c) **Love**, self-adhesive, *Feb. 1*, Valentines VA		1.25

First day cancellation was applied to 70,778 covers bearing one or more of Nos. 2948, 2949.

2950	32c **Florida Statehood**, *Mar. 3*, Tallahassee FL *(167,499)*		1.25
2954a	32c **Earth Day**, *Apr. 20*		2.75
	2951-2954, any single		1.25

First day cancellation was applied to 328,893 covers bearing one or more of Nos. 2951-2954, 2954a.

2955	32c **Richard Nixon**, *Apr. 26*, Yorba Linda CA *(377,605)*		1.25

2956	32c **Bessie Coleman**, *Apr. 27*, Chicago IL *(299,834)*		1.25
2957	32c **Love**, *May 12*, Lakeville PA		1.25
2958	55c **Love**, *May 12*, Lakeville PA		1.40
2959	32c **Love**, booklet single, *May 12*, Lakeville PA		1.25
2959a	Booklet pane of 10		7.50
2960	55c **Love**, self-adhesive, *May 12*, Lakeville PA		1.40

First day cancellation was applied to 273,350 covers bearing one or more of Nos. 2957-2959, 2959a, and U637.

2965a	32c **Recreational Sports**, *May 20*, Jupiter FL		3.25
	2961-2965, any single		1.50

First day cancellation was applied to 909,807 covers bearing one or more of Nos. 2961-2965, 2965a.

2966	32c **Prisoners of War & Missing in Action**, *May 29 (231,857)*		2.00
2967	32c **Marilyn Monroe**, *June 1*, Universal City CA *(703,219)*		2.00
	Any other city		1.75
2968	32c **Texas Statehood**, *June 16*, Austin TX *(177,550)*		1.25
2973a	32c **Great Lakes Lighthouses booklet pane of 5**, *June 17*, Cheboygan MI		5.00
	2969-2973, any single		1.75

First day cancellation was applied to 626,055 covers bearing one or more of Nos. 2969-2973, 2973a.

2974	32c **UN, 50th Anniv.**, *June 26*, San Francisco CA *(160,383)*		1.25
2975	32c **Civil War pane of 20**, *June 29*, Gettysburg PA		13.00
	Any other city		13.00
	2975a-2975t, any single, Gettysburg PA		1.50
	Any other city		1.50

First day cancellation was applied to 1,950,134 covers bearing one or more of Nos. 2975, 2975a-2975t, and UX200-UX219.

2979a	32c **Carousel Horses**, *July 21*, Lahaska PA		3.25
	2976-2979, any single		1.25

First day cancellation was applied to 479,038 covers bearing one or more of Nos. 2976-2979, 2979a.

2980	32c **Woman Suffrage**, *Aug. 26 (196,581)*		1.25
2981	32c **World War II block of 10**, *Sept. 2*, Honolulu HI		7.00
	2981a-2981j, any single		1.50

First day cancellation was applied to 1,562,094 covers bearing one or more of Nos. 2981, 2981a-2981j.

2982	32c **American Music Series**, *Sept. 1*, New Orleans LA *(258,996)*		1.25
2992a	32c **American Music Series**, *Sept. 16*, Monterey CA		6.50
	2983-2992, any single		1.25

First day cancellation was applied to 629,956 covers bearing one or more of Nos. 2983-2992, 2992a.

2997a	32c **Garden Flowers booklet pane of 5**, *Sept. 19*, Encinitas CA		4.00
	2993-2997, any single		1.25

First day cancellation was applied to 564,905 covers bearing one or more of Nos. 2993-2997, 2997a.

2998	60c **Eddie Rickenbacker**, *Sept. 25*, Columbus OH *(24,283)*		1.50
2999	32c **Republic of Palau**, *Sept. 29*, Agana GU *(157,377)*		1.25
3000	32c **Comic Strips Pane of 20**, *Oct. 1*, Boca Raton FL		13.00
	3000a-3000t, any single		1.75

First day cancellation was applied to 1,362,990 covers bearing one or more of Nos. 3000, 3000a-3000t.

3001	32c **US Naval Academy**, *Oct. 10*, Annapolis, MD *(222,183)*		1.25
3002	32c **Tennessee Williams**, *Oct. 13*, Clarksdale MS *(209,812)*		1.25
3003	32c **Christmas, Madonna**, perf 11.2, *Oct. 19*		1.25
3003A	32c **Christmas, Madonna**, perf 9.8x10.9. *Oct. 19*		1.25
3003Ab	Booklet pane of 10		7.25

First day cancellation was applied to 223,301 covers bearing one or more of Nos. 3003, 3003A-3003Ab.

3007a	32c **Christmas (secular) sheet**, *Sept. 30*, North Pole NY		3.25
	3004-3007, any single		1.25
3007b	32c Booklet pane of 10, 3 #3004, etc.		7.25
3007c	32c Booklet pane of 10, 2 #3004, etc.		7.25

First day cancellation was applied to 487,816 covers bearing one or more of Nos. 3004-3007, 3007a.

3008-3011	32c **Christmas (secular) self-adhesive booklet stamps**, *Sept. 30*, North Pole NY		3.25
	3008-3011, any single		1.25
3012	32c **Angel**, *Oct. 19*, Christmas FL		1.25
3013	32c **Children sledding**, *Oct. 19*, Christmas FL		1.25

First day cancellation was applied to 77,675 covers bearing one or more of Nos. 3012, 3013, 3018.

3014-3017	32c **Self-adhesive coils**, *Sept. 30*, North Pole NY		3.25

3018   32c **Self-adhesive coil**, *Oct. 19*, Christmas FL   1.25

First day cancellation was applied to 77,675 covers bearing one or more of Nos. 3012, 3013, 3018.

3023a   32c **Antique Automobiles**, *Nov. 3*, New York NY   3.25
          3019-3023, any single   1.25

First day cancellation was applied to 757,003 covers bearing one or more of Nos. 3019-3023, 3023a.

1996

3024   32c **Utah Statehood Cent.**, *Jan. 4*, Salt Lake City UT *(207,089)*   1.25
3029a   32c **Garden Flowers booklet pane**, *Jan. 19*, Kennett Square PA   4.00
          3025-3029, any single   1.25

First day cancellation was applied to 876,176 covers bearing one or more of Nos. 3025-3029, 3029a.

3030   32c **Love self-adhesive**, *Jan. 20*, New York NY   1.25

First day cancellation was applied to 57,639 covers bearing one or more of Nos. 2920d, 3030, 3044.

1996-2000

FLORA AND FAUNA

3031   1c **Kestrel**, *Nov. 19, 1999*, New York, NY   1.25
3032   2c **Red-headed woodpecker**, *Feb. 2*, Sarasota FL *(37,319)*   1.25
3033   3c **Eastern Bluebird**, *Apr. 3* *(23,405)*   1.25
3036 $1 **Red Fox**, *Aug. 14, 1998*   2.00

First day cancellation was applied to 46,557 covers bearing one or more of Nos. 3228-3229, 3036.

3044   1c **American Kestrel, coil**, *Jan. 20*, New York NY   1.25

First day cancellation was applied to 57,639 covers bearing one or more of Nos. 2920d, 3030, 3044.

3045   2c **Red-Headed Woodpecker**, *June 22, 1999*   1.25
3048   20c **Blue Jay, booklet stamp, self-adhesive**, *Aug. 2*, St. Louis MO   1.25

First day cancellation was applied to 32,633 covers bearing one or more of Nos. 3048, 3053.

3049   32c **Yellow Rose, booklet stamp, self-adhesive**, *Oct. 24*, Pasadena, CA *(7,849)*   1.25
3050   20c **Ring-necked Pheasant, booklet stamp, self-adhesive**, *July 31, 1998* Somerset NJ   1.25

First day cancellation was applied to 32,220 covers bearing one or more of Nos. 3050, 3055.

3052   33c **Coral Pink Rose**, serpentine die cut 11¾x11¼, *Aug. 13, 1999*, Indianapolis, IN   1.25
3052E   33c **Coral Pink Rose**, serpentine die cut 10¾x10½, *Apr. 7, 2000*, New York, NY   1.25
3053   20c **Blue Jay, coil, self-adhesive**, *Aug. 2*, St. Louis MO   1.25
3054   32c **Yellow Rose, self-adhesive**, *Aug. 1, 1997*, Falls Church VA *(20,029)*   1.25
3055   20c **Ring-necked Pheasant, coil, self-adhesive**, *July 31, 1998* Somerset NJ   1.25

First day cancellation was applied to 32,220 covers bearing one or more of Nos. 3050, 3055.

1996

3058   32c **Ernest E. Just**, *Feb. 1 (191,360)*   1.25
3059   32c **Smithsonian, 150th anniv.**, *Feb. 7, (221,399)*   1.25
3060   32c **Chinese New Year**, *Feb. 8*, San Francisco CA *(237,451)*   1.50
3064a   32c **Pioneers of Communication**, *Feb. 22*, New York NY   3.25
          3061-3064, any single   1.25

First day cancellation was applied to 567,205 covers bearing one or more of Nos. 3061-3064, 3064a.

3065   32c **Fulbright Scholarships**, *Feb. 28*, Fayetteville AR *(227,330)*   1.25
3066   50c **Jacqueline Cochran**, *Mar. 9*, Indio CA *(30,628)*   1.40
3067   32c **Marathon**, *Apr. 11*, Boston MA *(177,050)*   1.25
3068   32c **Olympics, pane of 20**, *May 2*   13.00
          3068a-3068t, any single   1.25

First day cancellation was applied to 1,807,316 covers bearing one or more of Nos. 3068, 3068a-3068t.

3069   32c **Georgia O'Keeffe**, *May 23*, Santa Fe NM *(200,522)*   1.25
3070   32c **Tennessee Statehood, Bicen.**, *May 31*, Knoxville, Memphis or Nashville TN   1.25
3071   32c **Tennessee, self-adhesive**, *May 31*, Knoxville, Memphis or Nashville TN   1.25

First day cancellation was applied to 217,281 covers bearing one or more of Nos. 3070-3071.

3076a   32c **American Indian Dances, strip of 5**, *June 7*, Oklahoma City OK   3.50
          3072-3076, any single   1.25

First day cancellation was applied to 653,057 covers bearing one or more of Nos. 3072-3076, 3076a.

3080a   32c **Prehistoric Animals**, *June 8*, Toronto, Canada   3.25
          3077-3080, any single   1.25

First day cancellation was applied to 485,929 covers bearing one or more of Nos. 3077-3080, 3080a.

3081   32c **Breast Cancer Awareness**, *June 15 (183,896)*   1.25
          Any other city   1.25
3082   32c **James Dean**, *June 24*, Burbank CA *(263,593)*   1.75
3086a   32c **Folk Heroes**, *July 11*, Anaheim CA   3.25
          3083-3086, any single   1.25

First day cancellation was applied to 739,706 covers bearing one or more of Nos. 3083-3086, 3086a.

3087   32c **Centennial Olympic Games**, *July 19*, Atlanta GA *(269,056)*   1.25
3088   32c **Iowa Statehood, 150th Anniv.**, *Aug. 1*, Dubuque IA   1.25
3089   32c **Iowa Statehood, self-adhesive** *Aug. 1*, Dubuque IA   1.25

First day cancellation was applied to 215,181 covers bearing one or more of Nos. 3088-3089.

3090   32c **Rural Free Delivery**, *Aug. 7*, Charleston WV *(192,070)*   1.25
3091-3095   32c **Riverboats**, *Aug. 22*, Orlando FL   3.50
          3091-3095, any single   1.25
3095b   32c **Riverboats, special die cutting**, *Aug. 22*, Orlando FL   3.50

First day cancellation was applied to 770,384 covers bearing one or more of Nos. 3091-3095, 3095b.

3099a   32c **Big Band Leaders**, *Sept. 11*, New York NY   3.25
          3096-3099, any single   1.25

First day cancellation was applied to 1,235,166 covers bearing one or more of Nos. 3096-3103, 3099a, 3103a.

3103a   32c **Songwriters**, *Sept. 11*, New York NY   3.25
          3100-3103, any single   1.25

First day cancellation was applied to 1,235,166 covers bearing one or more of Nos. 3096-3103, 3099a, 3103a.

3104   23c **F. Scott Fitzgerald**, *Sept. 27*, St. Paul MN *(150,783)*   1.25
3105   32c **Endangered Species**, *Oct. 2*, San Diego CA   7.50
          3105a-3105o, any single   1.25

First day cancellation was applied to 941,442 covers bearing one or more of Nos. 3105, 3105a-3105o.

3106   32c **Computer Technology**, *Oct. 8*, Aberdeen Proving Ground MD *(153,688)*   1.25
3107   32c **Christmas Madonna**, *Nov. 1*, Richmond VA   1.25

First day cancellation was applied to 164,447 covers bearing one or more of Nos. 3107, 3112.

3111a   32c **Christmas (secular)**, *Oct. 8*, North Pole AK   3.25
          3108-3111, any single   1.25

First day cancellation was applied to 884,339 covers bearing one or more of Nos. 3108-3111, 3111a, 3113-3117.

3112   32c **As No. 3107, self-adhesive**, *Nov. 1*, Richmond VA   1.25
3113-3116   32c **Christmas (secular), self-adhesive**, *Oct. 8*, North Pole AK   3.25
          3113-3116, any single   1.25
3117   32c **Skaters, self-adhesive**, *Oct. 8*, North Pole AK   1.25

First day cancellation was applied to 884,339 covers bearing one or more of Nos. 3108-3111, 3111a, 3113-3117.

3118   32c **Hanukkah**, *Oct. 22 (179,355)*   1.25
3119   50c **Cycling**, *Nov. 1*, New York NY   2.50
          3119a-3119b, any single   1.50

First day cancellation was applied to 290,091 covers bearing one or more of Nos. 3119, 3119a-3119b.

1997

3120   32c **Chinese New Year**, *Jan. 5*, Honolulu *(233,638)*   1.50
3121   32c **Benjamin O. Davis, Sr.**, *Jan. 28 (166,527)*   1.25
3122   32c **Statue of Liberty, self-adhesive**, *Feb. 1*, San Diego CA *(40,013)*   1.25
3123   32c **Love, Swans, self-adhesive**, *Feb. 4*, Los Angeles CA   1.25
3124   55c **Love, Swans, self-adhesive**, *Feb. 4*, Los Angeles CA   1.50

First day cancellation was applied to 257,380 covers bearing one or more of Nos. 3123-3124.

3125   32c **Helping Children Learn, self-adhesive** *Feb. 18 (175,410)*   1.25
3126   32c **Merian Botanical Prints, Citron, etc., self-adhesive, die cut 10.9x10.2**, *Mar. 3*   1.25
3127   32c **Merian Botanical Prints, Pineapple, etc., self-adhesive, die cut 10.9x10.2**, *Mar. 3*   1.25
3128   32c **Merian Botanical Prints, Citron, etc., self-adhesive, die cut 11.2x10.8**, *Mar. 3*   1.25

3128a   32c **Merian Botanical Prints, Citron, etc., self-adhesive, die cut mixed perf**, *Mar. 3*   1.25
3129   32c **Merian Botanical Prints, Pineapple, etc., self-adhesive, die cut 11.2x10.8**, *Mar. 3*   1.25
3129a   32c **Merian Botanical Prints, Pineapple, etc., self-adhesive, die cut mixed perf**, *Mar. 3*   1.25

First day cancellation was applied to 336,897 covers bearing one or more of Nos. 3126-3129, 3128a-3129a.

3131a   32c **Pacific 97**, *Mar. 13*, New York NY   1.75
          3130-3131, any single   1.25

First day cancellation was applied to 371,908 covers bearing one or more of Nos. 3130-3131, 3131a.

3132   (25c) **Juke Box, self-adhesive** *Mar. 14*, New York NY   1.25
3133   32c **Flag over Porch, Self-adhesive** *Mar. 14*, New York NY   1.25

First day cancellation was applied to 26,0820 covers bearing one or more of Nos. 3132-3133.

3134   32c **Thornton Wilder**, *Apr. 17*, Hamden CT *(157,299)*   1.25
3135   32c **Raoul Wallenberg**, *Apr. 24 (168,668)*   1.50
3136   32c **Dinosaurs, pane of 15** *May 1*, Grand Junction CO   7.50
          3136a-3136o, any single   1.25

First day cancellation was applied to 1,782,1221 covers bearing one or more of Nos. 3136, 3136a-3136o.

3137a   32c **Bugs Bunny**, *May 22*, Burbank CA *(378,142)*   1.75
3139   50c **Pacific 97, Franklin, pane of 12** *May 29*, San Francisco CA   12.00
          3139a, single   2.00
3140   60c **Pacific 97,, pane of 12**, *May 30*, San Francisco CA   14.50
          3140a, single   2.50

First day cancellation was applied to 328,401 covers bearing one or more of Nos. 3139-3140, 3139a-3140b.

3141   32c **Marshall Plan**, *June 4*, Cambridge MA *(157,622)*   1.25
3142   32c **Classic American Aircraft**, *July 19*, Dayton OH   15.00
          3142a-3142t, any single   1.50

First day cancellation was applied to 1,413,833 covers bearing one or more of Nos. 3142, 3142a-3142t.

3146a   32c **Football Coaches** *July 25*, Canton OH   4.00
          3143-3146, any single   1.50

First day cancellation was applied to 586,946 covers bearing one or more of Nos. 3143-3146.

3147   32c **Bear Bryant**, *Aug. 5*, Green Bay WI *(119,428)*   1.50
3148   32c **Pop Warner**, *Aug. 7*, Tuscaloosa AL *(23,858)*   1.50
3149   32c **Vince Lombardi**, *Aug. 8*, Philadelphia PA *(37,839)*   1.50
3150   32c **George Halas**, *Aug. 16*, Chicago IL *(26,760)*   1.50
3151   32c **American Dolls**, *July 28*, Anaheim CA   8.00
          3151a-3151o, any single   1.50

First day cancellation was applied to 831,359 covers bearing one or more of Nos. 3151, 3151a-3151o.

3152   32c **Humphrey Bogart**, *July 31*, Los Angeles CA *(220,254)*   1.25
3153   32c **"The Star and Stripes Forever,"** *Aug. 21*, Milwaukee WI *(36,666)*   1.25
3157a   32c **Opera Singers**, *Sept. 10*, New York NY   3.25
          3154-3157, any single   1.25

First day cancellation was applied to 386,689 covers bearing one or more of Nos. 3154-3157.

3165a   32c **Opera Singers**, *Sept. 12*, Cincinnati OH   5.25
          3158-3165, any single   1.25

First day cancellation was applied to 424,344 covers bearing one or more of Nos. 3158-3165.

3166   32c **Padre Felix Varela**, *Sept. 15*, Miami FL *(120,079)*   1.25
3167   32c **Department of the Air Force**, *Sept. 18 (178,519)*   1.25
3172a   32c **Classic Movie Monsters**, *Sept. 30*, Universal City CA   3.75
          3168-3172, any single   1.25

First day cancellation was applied to 476,993 covers bearing one or more of Nos. 3168-3172.

3173   32c **First Supersonic Flight**, *Oct. 14*, Edwards AFB CA *(173,778)*   1.25
3174   32c **Women in Military Service**, *Oct. 18 (106,121)*   1.25
3175   32c **Kwanzaa**, *Oct. 22*, Los Angeles CA *(92,489)*   1.25
3176   32c **Christmas Madonna**, *Oct. 27 (35,809)*   1.25
3177   32c **Holly**, *Oct. 30*, New York NY *(87,332)*   1.25
3178 $3 **Mars Pathfinder**, *Dec. 10* Pasadena CA *(11,699)*   6.00

1998

3179	32c **Chinese New Year**, *Jan. 5*, Seattle WA *(234,269)*	1.25
3180	32c **Alpine Skiing**, *Jan. 22*, Salt Lake City UT *(196,504)*	1.25
3181	32c **Madam C. J. Walker**, *Jan. 28*, Indianapolis IN *(146,348)*	1.25

1998-2000

CELEBRATE THE CENTURY

3182	32c **1900s**, *Feb. 3* *(11,699)*	7.50
	3182a-3182o, any single	1.25
3183	32c **1910s**, *Feb. 3*	7.50
	3183a-3183o, any single	1.25

First day cancellation was applied to 3,896,387 covers bearing one or more of Nos. 3182-3182o, 3183-3183o.

3184	32c **1920s**, *May 28*	7.50
	3184a-3184o, any single	1.25

First day cancellation was applied to 1,057,909 covers bearing one or more of Nos. 3184-3184o.

3185	32c **1930s**, *Sept. 10*, Cleveland OH	7.50
	3185a-3185o, any single	1.25

First day cancellation was applied to 999,017 covers bearing one or more of Nos. 3185-3185o.

3186	33c **1940s**, *Feb. 18, 1999*, Dobbins AFB GA	7.50
	3186a-3186o, any single	1.25
3187	33c **1950s**, *May 26, 1999*, Springfield MA	7.50
	3187a-3187o, any single	1.25
3188	33c **1960s**, *Sept. 17, 1999*, Green Bay, WI	7.50
	3188a-3188a, any single	1.25
3189	33c **1970s**, *Nov. 18, 1999*, New York, NY	7.50
	3189a-3189o, any single	1.25
3190	33c **1980s**, *Jan. 12, 2000*, Kennedy Space Center, FL	7.50
	3190a-3190o, any single	1.25
3191	33c **1990s**, *May 2, 2000*, Escondido, CA	7.50
	3191a-3191o, any single	1.25

1998

3192	32c **"Remember the Maine,"** *Feb. 15*, Key West FL *(161,657)*	1.25
3193-3197	32c **Flowering Trees**, *Mar. 19*, New York NY	3.75
	3193-3197, any single	1.25

First day cancellation was applied to 666,199 covers bearing one or more of Nos. 3193-3197.

3202a	32c **Alexander Calder**, *Mar. 25*	3.75
	3198-3202, any single	1.25

First day cancellation was applied to 588,887 covers bearing one or more of Nos. 3198-3202, 3202a.

3203	32c **Cinco de Mayo**, *Apr. 16*, San Antonio TX *(144,443)*	1.25
3204a	32c **Sylvester & Tweety**, *Apr. 27*, New York NY *(213,839)*	1.50
3206	32c **Wisconsin Statehood**, *May 29*, Madison WI *(130,810)*	1.25

1998-99

3207	(5c) **Wetlands**, *June 5*, McLean VA	1.25
3207A	(5c) **Wetlands, Serpentine die cut**, *Dec. 14*	1.25
3208	(25c) **Diner**, *June 5*, McLean VA	1.25

First day cancellation was applied to 35,333 covers bearing one or more of Nos. 3207, 3208; 13,378 covers bearing one of more of Nos. 3207A, 3270-3271.

3208A	(25c) **Diner, Serpentine die cut**, *June 5* *(13,984)*	1.25

1998

1898 TRANS-MISSISSIPPI STAMPS, CENT.

3209	**Sheet of 9**, *June 18*, Anaheim CA	6.50
3209a	1c	1.25
3209b	2c	1.25
3209c	4c	1.25
3209d	5c	1.25
3209e	8c	1.25
3209f	10c	1.25
3209g	50c	1.50
3209h	$1	2.00
3209i	$2	4.00
3210	$1 **Sheet of 9**, *June 18*, Anaheim CA	15.00

First day cancellation was applied to 203,649 covers bearing one or more of Nos. 3209-3210, 3209a-3209i.

1998

3211	32c **Berlin Airlift**, *June 26*, Berlin, Germany *(137,894)*	1.25
3215a	32c **Folk Musicians**, *June 26*	3.25
	3212-3215, any single	1.25

First day cancellation was applied to 341,015 covers bearing one or more of Nos. 3212-3215, 3215a.

3219a	32c **Gospel Music**, *July 15*, New Orleans LA	3.25
	3216-3219, any single	1.25

First day cancellation was applied to 330,533 covers bearing one or more of Nos. 3216-3219, 3219a.

3220	32c **Spanish Settlement of the Southwest**, *July 11*, Española NM *(122,182)*	1.25
3221	32c **Stephen Vincent Benét**, *July 22*, Harpers Ferry WV *(107,412)*	1.25
3225a	32c **Tropical Birds**, *July 29*, Ponce PR	3.25
	3222-3225, any single	1.25

First day cancellation was applied to 371,354 covers bearing one or more of Nos. 3222-3225, 3225a.

3226	32c **Alfred Hitchcock**, *Aug. 3*, Los Angeles CA *(140,628)*	1.25
3227	32c **Organ & Tissue Donation**, *Aug. 5*, Columbus OH *(110,601)*	1.25
3228	(10c) **Modern Bicycle, Serpentine die cut**, *Aug. 14*	1.25
3229	(10c) **Modern Bicycle**, *Aug. 14*	1.25

First day cancellation was applied to 46,557 covers bearing one or more of Nos. 3228-3229, 3036.

3230-3234	32c **Bright Eyes**, *Aug. 20*, Boston MA	3.25
	3230-3234, any single	1.25

First day cancellation was applied to 394,280 covers bearing one or more of Nos. 3230-3234.

3235	32c **Klondike Gold Rush Cent.**, *Aug. 21*, Nome or Skagway AK *(123,559)*	1.25
3236	32c **American Art, pane of 20**, *Aug. 27*, Santa Clara CA	9.50
	3236a-3236t, any single	1.25

First day cancellation was applied to 924,031 covers bearing one or more of Nos. 3236, 3236a-3236t.

3237	32c **American Ballet**, *Sept. 16*, New York NY *(133,034)*	1.25
3242a	32c **Space Discovery**, *Oct. 1*, Kennedy Space Center FL	3.75
	3238-3242, any single	1.25

First day cancellation was applied to 399,807 covers bearing one or more of Nos. 3238-3242, 3242a.

3243	32c **Giving & Sharing**, *Oct. 7*, Atlanta GA *(124,051)*	1.25
3244	32c **Christmas, Madonna**, *Oct. 15* *(105,835)*	1.25
3245-3248	32c **Christmas, Secular**, *Oct. 15*, Christmas MI	3.25
	3245-3248, any single	1.25
3249-3252	33c **Christmas, Secular, size: 23x30mm**, *Oct. 15*, Christmas MI	3.25
	3249-3252, any single	1.25

First day cancellation was applied to 328,199 covers bearing one or more of Nos. 3245-3252.

3257	(1c) **Weather Vane, white USA**, *Nov. 9*	1.25
3258	(1c) **Weather Vane, pale blue USA**, *Nov. 9*	1.25
3259	22c **Uncle Sam**, *Nov. 9*	1.25
3260	(33c) **Uncle Sam's Hat**, *Nov. 9*	1.25
3261	$3.20 **Space Shuttle Landing**, *Nov. 9*	6.00
3262	$11.75 **Piggyback Space Shuttle**, *Nov. 9*, New York NY *(3,703)*	12.00
3263	22c **Uncle Sam, coil**, *Nov. 9*	1.25
3264	(33c) **Uncle Sam's Hat, coil**, *Nov. 9*	1.25
3265	(33c) **Uncle Sam's Hat, self-adhesive coil, die cut 9.9, round corners**, *Nov. 9*	1.25
3266	(33c) **Uncle Sam's Hat, self-adhesive coil, die cut 9.9, square corners**, *Nov. 9*	1.25
3267	(33c) **Uncle Sam's Hat, self-adhesive booklet single, die cut 9.9** *Nov. 9*	1.25
3268	(33c) **Uncle Sam's Hat, self-adhesive booklet single, die cut 11.2x11.1** *Nov. 9*	1.25
3269	(33c) **Uncle Sam's Hat, self-adhesive booklet single, die cut 8** *Nov. 9*	1.25

First day cancellation was applied to 121,662 covers bearing one or more of Nos. 2942, 3257-3261, 3263-3269.

3270	(10c) **Eagle & Shield, Presorted Std.**, *Dec. 14*	1.25
3271	(10c) **Eagle & Shield, Presorted Std., self-adhesive, Serpentine die cut**, *Dec. 14*	1.25

First day cancellation was applied to 13,378 covers bearing one or more of Nos. 3207A, 3270-3271.

1999

3272	33c **Chinese New Year**, *Jan. 5*, Los Angeles CA	1.25
3273	33c **Malcolm X**, *Jan. 20*, New York NY	1.25
3274	33c **Love**, *Jan. 28*, Loveland CO	1.25
3275	55c **Love**, *Jan. 28*, Loveland CO	2.00
3276	33c **Hospice Care**, *Feb. 9*, Largo FL	1.25
3277	33c **Flag & City**, *Feb. 25*, Orlando FL	1.25
3278	33c **Flag & City, self-adhesive, die cut 11.1** *Feb. 25*, Orlando FL	1.25
3279	33c **Flag & City, self-adhesive, die cut 9.8** *Feb. 25*, Orlando FL	1.25
3280	33c **Flag & City, coil, perf. 9.9 vert.** *Feb. 25*, Orlando FL	1.25
3281	33c **Flag & City, self-adhesive coil, die cut 9.8 vert, square corners**, *Feb. 25*, Orlando FL	1.25
3282	33c **Flag & City, self-adhesive coil, die cut 9.8 vert., round corners**, *Feb. 25*, Orlando FL	1.25

3283	33c **Flag & Blackboard, self-adhesive, die cut 7.9**, *Mar. 13*	1.25
3286	33c **Irish Immigration**, *Feb. 26*, Boston MA	1.25
3287	33c **Lunt & Fontanne**, *Mar. 2*, New York NY	1.25
3292a	33c **Arctic Animals**, *Mar. 12*, Barrow AK	3.75
	3288-3292, any single	1.25
3293	33c **Sonoran Desert, Pane of 20**, *Apr. 6*, Tucson AZ	6.75
	3293a-3293j, any single	1.25
3294-3297	33c **Christmas Berries, die cut 11.2x11.7** *Apr. 10*, Ponchatoula LA	3.25
	3294-3297, any single	1.25
	3297e, dated 2000, *Mar. 15, 2000*, Ponchatoula LA	3.25
	3294-3296a, 3297c, any single	1.25
3298-3301	33c **Christmas Berries, die cut 9.5x10** *Apr. 10*, Ponchatoula LA	3.25
	3298-3301, any single	1.25
3302-3305	33c **Christmas Berries, die cut 8.5 vert.** *Apr. 10*, Ponchatoula LA	3.25
	3302-3305, any single	1.25
3306a	33c **Daffy Duck**, *Apr. 16*, Los Angeles CA	1.25
3308	33c **Ayn Rand**, *Apr. 22*, New York NY	2.00
3309	33c **Cinco de Mayo**, *Apr. 27*, San Antonio TX	1.25
3310-3313	33c **Tropical Flowers**, *May 1*, Honolulu HI	3.25
	3310-3313, any single	1.25
3314	33c **Bartram**, *May 18*, Philadelphia PA	1.25
3315	33c **Prostate Cancer Awareness**, *July 22*, Austin TX	1.25
3316	33c **California Gold Rush**, *June 18*, Sacramento CA	1.25
3317-3320	33c **Aquarium Fish**, *June 24*, Anaheim CA	3.50
	3317-3320, any single	1.25
3321-3324	33c **Extreme Sports**, *June 25*, San Francisco CA	3.50
	3321-3324, any single	1.25
3328a	33c **American Glass**, *June 29*, Corning NY	3.50
	3325-3328, any single	1.25
3329	33c **James Cagney**, *July 22*, Burbank CA	1.25
3330	55c **"Billy" Mitchell**, *July 30*, Milwaukee WI	1.25
3331	33c **Honoring Those Who Served**, *Aug. 16*, Kansas City MO	1.25
3332	45c **Universal Postal Union**, *Aug. 25*, Beijing, China	1.40
3337a	33c **Famous Trains**, *Aug. 26*, Cleveland, OH	3.75
	any other city	3.75
	#3333-3337, any single, Cleveland, OH	1.25
	#3333-3337, any single, any other city	1.25
3338	33c **Frederick Law Olmsted**, *Sept. 12*, Boston, MA	1.25
3344a	33c **Hollywood Composers**, *Sept. 16*, Los Angeles, CA	3.75
	#3339-3344, any single, Los Angeles, CA	1.25
3350a	33c **Broadway Songwriters**, *Sept. 21*, New York, NY	3.75
	#3345-3350, any single, New York, NY	1.25
3351	33c **Insects & Spiders**, *Oct. 1*, Indianapolis, IN	8.50
	#3351a-3351t, any single	1.25
3352	33c **Hanukkah**, *Oct. 8*, Washington, DC	1.25
3353	22c **Uncle Sam perforated coil**, *Oct. 8*, Washington, DC	1.25
3354	33c **NATO**, *Oct. 13*, Brussels, Belgium	1.25
3355	33c **Christmas Madonna**, *Oct. 20*, Washington, DC	1.25
3356-3359	33c **Christmas Deer, narrow frame (sheet)**, *Oct. 20*, Rudolph, WI	3.25
	3356-3359, any single	1.25
3360-3363	33c **Christmas Deer, thick frame (booklet)**, *Oct. 20*, Rudolph, WI	3.25
	3360-3363, any single	1.25
3364-3367	33c **Christmas Deer, smaller size (booklet)**, *Oct. 20*, Rudolph, WI	3.25
	3364-3367, any single	1.25
3368	33c **Kwanzaa**, *Oct. 29*, Los Angeles, CA	1.25
3369	33c **Year 2000**, *Dec. 27*, Washington, DC	1.25

2000

3370	33c **Chinese New Year**, *Jan. 6*, San Francisco, CA	1.25
3371	33c **Patricia Roberts Harris**, *Jan. 27*, Washington, DC	1.25
3372	33c **Los Angeles Class Submarine, with microprinting**, *Mar. 27*, Groton, CT	1.25
3373	22c **S Class Submarine**, *Mar. 27*, Groton, CT	1.25
3374	33c **Los Angeles Class Submarine, no microprinting**, *Mar. 27*, Groton, CT	1.25
3375	55c **Ohio Class Submarine**, *Mar. 27*, Groton, CT	1.50
3376	60c **USS Holland**, *Mar. 27*, Groton, CT	1.50
3377	$3.20 **Gato Class Submarine**, *Mar. 27*, Groton, CT	6.00

	3377a, Booklet pane of 5, #3373-3377, either selvage		7.50
3378	33c **Pacific Coast Rain Forest Pane of 10**, Mar. 29, Seattle, WA		6.75
	3378a-3378j, any single		1.25
3383a	33c **Louise Nevelson**, Apr. 6, New York, NY		3.25
	3379-3383, any single		1.25
3388a	33c **Hubble Space Telescope**, Apr. 10, Greenbelt, MD		3.25
	3384-3388, any single		1.25
3389	33c **American Samoa**, Apr. 17, Pago Pago, AS		1.25
3390	33c **Library of Congress**, Apr. 24, Washington, DC		1.25
3391a	33c **Road Runner & Wile E. Coyote**, Apr. 26, Phoenix, AZ		1.25
3396a	33c **Distinguished Soldiers**, May 3, Washington, DC		3.25
	Any other city		3.25
	3393-3396, any single, Washington, DC		1.25
	Any other city		1.25

3397	33c **Summer Sports**, May 5, Spokane, WA		1.25
3398	33c **Adoption**, May 10, Beverly Hills, CA		1.25
3402a	33c **Youth Team Sports**, May 27, Lake Buena Vista, FL		3.25
	3399-3402, any single		1.25
3403	33c **The Stars and Stripes, pane of 20**, June 14, Baltimore, MD		9.50
	3403a-3403t, any single		1.25
3404-3407	33c **Berries**, die cut 8½ horiz., June 16, Buffalo, NY		3.25
	3404-3707, any single		1.25
3408	33c **Legends of Baseball**, July 6, Atlanta, GA		9.50
	3408a-3708t, any single		1.25
3409	60c **Probing the Vastness of Space**, July 10, Anaheim, CA		6.00
	3409a-3409f, any single		1.50
3410	$1 **Exploring the Solar System**, July 11, Anaheim, CA		9.00
	3410a-3410e, any single		2.00
3411	$3.20 **Escaping the Gravity of Earth**, July 9, Anaheim, CA		6.00

	3411a-3411b, any single		3.75
3412	$11.75 **Space Achievement and Exploration**, July 7, Anaheim, CA		14.00
3413	$11.75 **Landing on the Moon**, July 8, Anaheim, CA		14.00
3414-3417	33c **Stampin' The Future**, July 13, Anaheim, CA		3.25
	3414-3417, any single		1.25

SEMI-POSTAL FIRST DAY COVER

1998

B1	32c +8c **Breast Cancer**, July 29, Washington, DC (51,775)		1.50

AIR POST FIRST DAY COVERS

1918

C1	6c **orange**, Dec. 10	32,500.
C2	16c **green**, July 11	32,500.
C3	24c **carmine rose & blue**, May 13	27,500.

1923

C4	8c **dark green**, Aug. 15	450.00
C5	16c **dark blue**, Aug. 17	650.00
C6	24c **carmine**, Aug. 21	850.00

1926-27

C7	10c **dark blue**, Feb. 13, 1926	60.00
	Chicago, Ill.	70.00
	Detroit, Mich.	70.00
	Cleveland, Ohio	140.00
	Dearborn, Mich.	140.00
C8	15c **olive brown**, Sept. 18, 1926	75.00
C9	20c **yellow green**, Jan. 25, 1927	100.00
	New York, N.Y.	125.00
C10	10c **dark blue**, June 18, 1927	25.00
	St. Louis, Mo.	25.00
	Little Falls, Minn.	35.00
	Detroit, Mich.	35.00
C10a	Booklet pane of 3, May 26, 1928	825.00
	Cleveland Midwestern Philatelic Sta. cancel	800.00
	C10a & 645 on one cover, Washington, D.C.	1,000.

1928-30

C11	5c **carmine & blue**, July 25, 1928, pair	50.00
C12	5c **violet**, Feb. 10, 1930	12.00
C13	65c **green**, Apr. 19, 1930	1,250.
C14	$1.30 **brown**, Apr. 19, 1930	1,100.
C15	$2.60 **blue**, Apr. 19, 1930	1,250.
	C13-C15 on one cover	15,000.

Values are for first day covers flown on Zeppelin flights with appropriate markings. Non-flown covers sell for less.

1931-33

C16	5c **violet**, Aug. 19, 1931	175.00
C17	8c **olive bister**, Sept. 26, 1932	15.00
C18	50c **green**, Oct. 2, 1933, New York, N.Y. (3,500)	200.00
	Akron, Ohio, Oct. 4	350.00
	Washington, D.C., Oct. 5	300.00
	Miami, Fla., Oct. 6	140.00
	Chicago, Ill., Oct. 7	250.00

1934-37

C19	6c **dull orange**, June 30, 1934, Baltimore, Md.	175.00
	New York, N.Y.	700.00
	Washington, D.C., July 1	10.00

Catalogue values for Nos. C20-C45 are for addressed covers with the most common cachets.

C20	25c **blue**, Nov. 22, 1935 (10,910)	40.00
	San Francisco, Cal. (15,000)	35.00
C21	20c **green**, Feb. 15, 1937	45.00
C22	50c **carmine**, Feb. 15, 1937	50.00
	C21-C22 on one cover	100.00

First day covers of Nos. C21 and C22 total 40,000.

1938-39

C23	6c **dark blue & carmine**, May 14, 1938, Dayton, Ohio (116,443)	15.00
	St. Petersburg, Fla. (95,121)	15.00
	Washington, D.C., May 15	3.50
C24	30c **dull blue**, May 16, 1939, New York, N.Y. (68,634)	47.50

1941-44

C25	6c **carmine**, June 25, 1941 (99,986)	2.50
C25a	Booklet pane of 3, Mar. 18, 1943	25.00
C26	8c **olive green**, Mar. 21, 1944 (147,484)	3.75
C27	10c **violet**, Aug. 15, 1941, Atlantic City, N.J. (87,712)	8.00
C28	15c **brown carmine**, Aug. 19, 1941, Baltimore, Md. (74,000)	10.00
C29	20c **bright green**, Aug. 27, 1941, Philadelphia, Pa. (66,225)	12.50
C30	30c **blue**, Sept. 25, 1941, Kansas City, Mo. (57,175)	20.00
C31	50c **orange**, Oct. 29, 1941, St. Louis, Mo. (54,580)	40.00

1946-48

C32	5c **carmine**, Sept. 25, 1946	2.00

First day covers of Nos. C32 & UC14 total 396,669.

C33	5c **carmine**, Mar. 26, 1947 (342,634)	2.00
C34	10c **black**, Aug. 30, 1947 (265,773)	2.00
C35	15c **bright blue green**, Aug. 20, 1947, New York, N.Y. (230,338)	2.00
C36	25c **blue**, July 30, 1947, San Francisco, Cal. (201,762)	2.50
C37	5c **carmine coil**, Jan. 15, 1948 (192,084)	1.75
C38	5c **New York City**, July 31, 1948, New York, N.Y. (371,265)	1.75

1949

C39	6c **carmine**, Jan. 18 (266,790)	1.50
C39a	Booklet pane of 3, Nov. 18, 1949, New York, N.Y.	9.00
C40	6c **Alexandria Bicentennial**, May 11, Alexandria, Va. (386,717)	1.50
C41	6c **carmine coil**, Aug. 25 (240,386)	1.25
C42	10c **U.P.U.**, Nov. 18, New Orleans, La. (270,000)	1.75
C43	15c **U.P.U.**, Oct. 7, Chicago, Ill. (246,833)	2.50
C44	25c **U.P.U.**, Nov. 30, Seattle, Wash. (220,215)	3.50
C45	6c **Wright Brothers**, Dec. 17, Kitty Hawk, N.C. (378,585)	3.00

Catalogue values from this point to the end of the section are for unaddressed covers with the most common cachets.

1952-59

C46	80c **Hawaii**, Mar. 26, 1952, Honolulu, Hawaii (89,864)	17.50
C47	6c **Powered Flight**, May 29, 1953, Dayton, Ohio (359,050)	1.50
C48	4c **bright blue**, Sept. 3, 1954, Philadelphia, Pa. (295,720)	1.00
C49	6c **Air Force**, Aug. 1, 1957 (356,683)	1.75
C50	5c **red**, July 31, 1958, Colorado Springs, Colo. (207,954)	1.00
C51	7c **blue**, July 31, 1958, Philadelphia, Pa. (204,401)	1.00
C51a	Booklet pane of 6, San Antonio, Tex. (119,769)	9.00
C52	7c **blue coil**, July 31, 1958, Miami, Fla. (181,603)	1.00
C53	7c **Alaska Statehood**, Jan. 3, 1959, Juneau, Alaska (489,752)	1.00
C54	7c **Balloon Jupiter**, Aug. 17, 1959, Lafayette, Ind. (383,556)	1.10
C55	7c **Hawaii Statehood**, Aug. 21, 1959, Honolulu, Hawaii (533,464)	1.00
C56	10c **Pan American Games**, Aug. 27, 1959, Chicago, Ill. (302,306)	1.00

1959-66

C57	10c **Liberty Bell**, June 10, 1960, Miami, Fla. (246,509)	1.25
C58	15c **Statue of Liberty**, Nov. 20, 1959, New York, N.Y. (259,412)	1.25

C59	25c **Abraham Lincoln**, Apr. 22, 1960, San Francisco, Cal. (211,235)	1.75
C59a	Tagged, Dec. 29, 1966 (about 3,000)	15.00
C60	7c **carmine**, Aug. 12, 1960, Arlington, Va. (247,190)	1.00
C60a	Booklet pane of 6, Aug. 19, 1960, St. Louis, Mo. (143,363)	9.50
C61	7c **carmine coil**, Oct. 22, 1960, Atlantic City, N.J. (197,995)	1.00

1961-67

C62	13c **Liberty Bell**, June 28, 1961, New York, N.Y. (316,166)	1.00
C62a	Tagged, Feb. 15, 1967	10.00
C63	15c **Redrawn Statue of Liberty**, Jan. 13, 1961, Buffalo, N.Y. (192,976)	1.00
C63a	Tagged, Jan. 11, 1967	15.00
C64	8c **carmine**, Dec. 5, 1962 (288,355)	1.00
C64b	Booklet pane of 5 + label (146,835)	3.50
C64a	Tagged, Aug. 1, 1963, Dayton, Ohio (262,522)	4.50
C65	8c **carmine coil**, Dec. 5, 1962 (220,173)	1.00
C65a	Tagged, Jan. 14, 1965, New Orleans, La.	—

1963-69

C66	15c **Montgomery Blair**, May 3, 1963, Silver Spring, Md. (260,031)	1.10
C67	6c **Bald Eagle**, July 12, 1963, Boston, Mass. (268,265)	1.00
C67a	Tagged, Feb. 15, 1967	15.00
C68	8c **Amelia Earhart**, July 24, 1963, Atchison, Kan. (437,996)	2.50
C69	8c **Robert H. Goddard**, Oct. 5, 1964, Roswell, N.M. (421,020)	2.50
C70	8c **Alaska Purchase**, Mar. 30, 1967, Sitka, Alaska (554,784)	1.00
C71	20c **Audubon**, Apr. 26, 1967, Audubon (Station of N.Y.C.), N.Y. (227,930)	2.00
C72	10c **carmine**, Jan. 5, 1968, San Francisco, Cal.	1.00
C72b	Booklet pane of 8	3.50
C72c	Booklet pane of 5 + label, slogan 4 Jan. 6, 1968	125.00
	With slogan 5	110.00
C73	10c **carmine coil**, Jan. 5, 1968, San Francisco, Cal.	1.00
C74	10c **Air Mail Service**, May 15, 1968 (521,084)	1.50
C75	20c **USA and Jet**, Nov. 22, 1968, New York, N.Y. (276,244)	1.10
C76	10c **Moon Landing**, Sept. 9, 1969 (8,743,070)	5.00

1971-73

C77	9c **red**, May 15, 1971, Kitty Hawk, N.C.	1.00

First day cancellation was applied to 379,442 covers of Nos. C77 and UXC10.

C78	11c **carmine**, May 7, 1971, Spokane, Wash.	1.00
C78a	Booklet pane of 4 + 2 labels	1.75
C79	13c **carmine**, Nov. 16, 1973, New York, N.Y. (282,550)	1.00
C79a	Booklet pane of 5 + label, Dec. 27, 1973, Chicago, Ill.	1.75

First day cancellation was applied to 464,750 covers of Nos. C78, C78a and C82, and to 204,756 covers of Nos. C79a and C83.

C80	17c **Statue of Liberty**, July 13, 1971, Lakehurst, N.J. (172,269)	1.00
C81	21c **USA and Jet**, May 21, 1971 (293,140)	1.00
C82	11c **carmine coil**, May 7, 1971, Spokane, Wash.	1.00
C83	13c **carmine coil**, Dec. 27, 1973, Chicago, Ill.	1.00

C84	11c **National Parks Centennial**, *May 3, 1972*, Honaunau, Hawaii *(364,816)*	1.00
C85	11c **Olympics**, *Aug. 17, 1972*	1.00

First day cancellation was applied to 971,536 covers of Nos. 1460-1462 and C85.

C86	11c **Electronics**, *July 10, 1973*, New York, N.Y.	1.00

First day cancellation was applied to 1,197,700 covers of Nos. 1500-1502 and C86.

1974-79

C87	18c **Statue of Liberty**, *Jan. 11, 1974*, Hempstead, N.Y. *(216,902)*	1.00
C88	26c **Mt. Rushmore**, *Jan. 2, 1974*, Rapid City, S.D. *(210,470)*	1.25
C89	25c **Plane and Globes**, *Jan. 2, 1976*, Honolulu, Hawaii	1.25
C90	31c **Plane, Globes and Flag**, *Jan. 2, 1976*, Honolulu, Hawaii	1.25
C92a	31c **Wright Brothers**, *Sept. 23, 1978*, Dayton, Ohio	4.00
	C91-C92, any single	3.00
C94a	21c **Octave Chanute**, *Mar. 29, 1979*, Chanute, Kan. *(459,235)*	4.00
	C93-C94, any single	3.00
C96a	25c **Wiley Post**, *Nov. 20, 1979*, Oklahoma City, Okla.	4.00
	C95-C96, any single	3.00
C97	31c **Olympics**, *Nov. 1, 1979*, Colorado Springs, CO	1.25

1980

C98	40c **Philip Mazzei**, *Oct. 13*	1.40
C99	28c **Blanche Stuart Scott**, *Dec. 30*, Hammondsport, NY *(238,502)*	1.25
C100	35c **Glenn Curtiss**, *Dec. 30*, Hammondsport, NY *(208,502)*	1.25

1983

C104a	28c **Olympics**, *June 17*, San Antonio, TX *(901,028)*	3.75
	C101-C104, any single	1.25
C108a	40c **Olympics**, *Apr. 8*, Los Angeles, CA *(1,001,657)*	5.00
	C105-C108, any single	1.40
C112a	35c **Olympics**, *Nov. 4*, Colorado Springs, CO *(897,729)*	4.50
	C109-C112, any single	1.25

1985

C113	33c **Alfred V. Verville**, *Feb. 13*, Garden City, NY	1.25
C114	39c **Lawrence & Elmer Sperry**, *Feb. 13*, Garden City, NY	1.40

First day cancel was applied to 429,290 covers bearing one more of Nos. C113-C114.

C115	44c **Transpacific Air Mail**, *Feb. 15*, San Francisco, CA *(269,229)*	1.50

A total of 269,229 first day cancels were applied for Nos. C115 and UXC22.

C116	44c **Junipero Serra**, *Aug. 22*, San Diego, CA *(254,977)*	1.50

1988

C117	44c **Settling of New Sweden**, *Mar. 29*, Wilmington, DE *(213,445)*	1.40
C118	45c **Samuel P. Langley**, *May 14*, San Diego, CA	1.40
C119	36c **Igor Sikorsky**, *June 23*, Stratford, CT *(162,986)*	3.00

1989

C120	45c **French Revolution**, *July 14 (309,975)*	1.40
C121	45c **Southeast Carved Figure**, *Oct. 12*, San Juan, PR *(93,569)*	1.40
C125a	45c **Future Mail Transportation**, *Nov. 27 (765,479)*	5.00
	C122-C125, any single	1.40
C126	45c **Future Mail Transportation Souvenir Sheet**, *Nov. 24 (257,826)*	3.00

1990-91

C127	45c **Tropical Coast**, *Oct. 12*, Grand Canyon, AZ *(137,068)*	1.40
C128	50c **Harriet Quimby**, *Apr. 27, 1991*, Plymouth, MI	1.40
C129	40c **William T. Piper**, *May 17, 1991*, Denver, CO	1.25
C130	50c **Antarctic Treaty**, *June 21, 1991*	1.40
C131	50c **Bering Land Bridge**, *Oct. 12, 1991*, Anchorage, AK	1.40

1999-2000

C133	48c **Niagara Falls**, *May 12*, Niagara Falls, NY	1.40
C134	40c **Rio Grande**, *July 30*, Milwaukee, WI	1.50
	any other city	1.50
C135	60c **Grand Canyon**, *Jan. 20, 2000* Grand Canyon, AZ	1.50

BOOKLETS: PANES & COVERS

Most booklet panes issued before 1962 consist of a vertical block of 6 stamps perforated vertically through the center. The panes are perforated horizontally on all but the bottom edge and the top of the selvage tab. The selvage tab, the two sides and the bottom are straight edged. Exceptions for panes issued before 1962 are the 1917 American Expeditionary Forces panes (30 stamps); Lindbergh and 6¢ 1943 air mails (3), and the Savings Stamps (10). Since 1962, panes have been issued with 3 to 20 stamps and various configurations. They have included one or more labels and two or more stamps se-tenant.

Flat plate booklet panes, with the exceptions noted above, were made from specially designed plates of 180 or 360 subjects. They are collected in plate positions. There are nine collectible positions on the 180-subject plate and 12 on the 360-subject plate.

Rotary booklet panes issued from 1926 to May 1978 (except for Nos. 1623a and 1623c) were made from specially designed plates of 180, 320, 360, and 400 subjects. They also are collected in plate positions. There are five collectible positions on the 360-subject plates which were printed before electric eye plates came into use, and 20 collectible positions on the Type II "new design" 360-subject rotary plates. There are 21 collectible positions in the rotary air mail 180-subject plate as well as the Type IV "modified design" 360-subject plate. There are 16 collectible positions on the 320-subject plates and 20 on the 400 subject plates. There are five collectible positions on Defense and War Savings 300-subject plates.

The generally accepted methods of designating pane positions as illustrated and explained hereafter are those suggested by George H. Beans in the May 1913 issue of "Everybody's Philatelist" and by B. H. Mosher in his monograph "Discovering U.S. Rotary Pane Varieties 1926-78." Some collectors seek all varieties possible, but the majority collect unused (A) panes and plate number (D) panes from flat plate issues, and plain panes and panes with electric eye bars and electric eye dashes, where available, from rotary plates.

Starting in 1977, BEP made two major changes in booklet production. Printing of panes was gradually moved from rotary plates to sleeves for modern high speed presses. Also, booklet production was transferred to Goebel booklet-forming machines. These changes virtually eliminated collectible pane positions for several years. However, beginning with No. BK156 (No. 2276a), BEP and other printers began placing printing process control marks in pane tabs. As a result, specialist booklet pane collectors actively resumed collecting pane positions. Collectible positions on these issues are not shown in this catalogue but can be found in the Bureau Issues Association's Research Paper No. 2 "Folded Style Checklist," Michael O. Perry, editor. Also, because of the requirements of the Goebel machine, the subject size of printing plates or sleeves varied widely. For these reasons, plate layouts are not shown for each issue. The plate layout for No. 1288c and the sleeve layout for No. 1623a are shown as typical.

The following panes, issued after Mar. 11, 1977, were printed from rotary plates and assembled into booklets on the Goebel machine: Nos. 1288c, 1736a, 1742a, 1819a, 1889a, and most printings of No. 1949a. Except for No. 2276a, all other issues from Mar. 11, 1977 on were printed from sleeves. Except for No. 1736a; one pane in 12 of the plate issues may have a plate join line along either long side of the pane, creating three collectible positions: no join line, join line top (or right), and join line bottom (or left).

All panes printed for booklet assembly on the Goebel machine contain two register marks in the tab: a cross register mark 1.5mm wide which runs across the tab and a length register mark (LRM), 1.5x5mm, usually placed vertically above the right hand (or top) stamp on the pane. Nos. 1623a and 1623c were regularly issued with the LRM over either stamp. Some copies of No. 1893a were issued with the LRM over the left stamp.

Starting with No. 1889a (except for No. 1948a), plate numbers (1 to 5 digits) were placed in the tab, normally over the left stamp. On booklets containing Nos. 1889a and 1949a, the plate number is supposed to be on the top pane, the second pane not having a number. All subsequent multi-pane booklets have the plate number on each pane. Some multi-pane booklets contain panes with different plate numbers. The booklet value is determined by the top pane.

Some recent booklets have been printed by contractors other than the BEP so markings may differ or be absent.

Panes in all booklets assembled on the Goebel machine will be folded at least once. **Repeated handling of booklets with folded panes may cause the panes to fall apart.**

Booklet panes with tabs attached to the cover by adhesive instead of staples are valued on the basis of the tab intact. Minor damage on the back of the tab due to removal from the booklet does not affect the value. Some of these panes were furnished to first day cover processors unfolded and not pasted into covers. Around 1989, these panes were available to collectors through the Philatelic Agency.

All panes from 1967 to date are tagged, unless otherwise stated.

Dr. William R. Bush, Morton Dean Joyce, Robert E. Kitson, Richard F. Larkin, Dr. Robert Marks, Bruce H. Mosher, the Bureau Issues Association, and the Booklet Collectors Club helped the editors extensively in compiling the listings and preparing the illustrations of booklets, covers and plate layouts.

The 180-Subject Plate — 9 Collectible Positions

Beginning at upper left and reading from left to right, the panes are designated from 1 to 30.
All positions not otherwise identifiable are designated by the letter A: Pane 1A, 2A, 3A, 4A, etc.
The identifiable positions are as follows:

A The ordinary booklet pane without distinguishing features. Occurs in Position 1, 2, 3, 4, 8, 9, 10,
   21, 22, 23, 24, 27, 28, 29, 30.
B Split arrow and guide line at right. Occurs in Position 5 only.
C Split arrow and guide line at left. Occurs in Position 6 only.
D Plate number pane. Occurs in Position 7 only.
E Guide line pane showing horizontal guide line between stamps 1-2 and 3-4 of the pane. Occurs in
   Positions 11, 12, 13, 14, 17, 18, 19, and 20.
F Guide line through pane and at right. Occurs in Position 15 only.
G Guide line through pane and at left. Occurs in Position 16 only.
H Guide line at right. Occurs in Position 25 only.
I Guide line at left. Occurs in Position 26 only.

Only positions B, F and H or C, G and I may be obtained from the same sheet, depending on
whether the knife which separated the panes fell to right or left of the line.

Side arrows, bottom arrows, or bottom plate numbers are seldom found because the margin of the
sheets is usually cut off, as are the sides and bottom of each pane.

In the illustrations, the dotted lines represent the rows of perforations, the unbroken lines represents
the knife cut.

The 360-Subject Plate — 12 Collectible Positions

As with the 180-Subject Sheets, the position of the various panes is indicated by numbers beginning in the upper left corner with the No. 1 and reading from left to right to No. 60.

The identifiable positions are as follows:

A The ordinary booklet pane without distinguishing features. Occurs in Positions 1, 2, 3, 4, 8, 9, 10, 11, 12, 13, 14, 17, 18, 19, 20, 41, 42, 43, 44, 47, 48, 49, 50, 51, 52, 53, 54, 57, 58, 59, 60.

B Split arrow and guide line at right. Occurs in Position 5 only.

C Split arrow and guide line at left. Occurs in Position 6 only.

D Plate number pane. Occurs in Position 7 only.

E, F, G Do not occur in the 360-Subject Plate.

H Guide line at right. Occurs in Positions 15, 45, and 55.

I Guide line at left. Occurs in Positions 16, 46, and 56.

J Guide line at bottom. Occurs in Positions 21, 22, 23, 24, 27, 28, 29 and 30.

K Guide line at right and bottom. Occurs in Position 25 only.

L Guide line at left and bottom. Occurs in Position 26 only.

M Guide line at top. Occurs in Positions 31, 32, 33, 34, 37, 38, 39 and 40.

N Guide line at top and right. Occurs in Position 35 only.

O Guide line at top and left. Occurs in Position 36 only.

Only one each of Positions B or C, K, L, N or O; four positions of H or I, and eight or nine positions of J or M may be obtained from each 360 subject sheet, depending on whether the knife fell to the right or left, top or bottom of the guide lines.

Because the horizontal guide line appears so close to the bottom row of stamps on panes Nos. 21 to 30, Positions M, N, and O occur with great deal less frequency than Positions J, K and L.

The 360-Subject Rotary Press Plate (before Electric Eye) Position A only

The 360-Subject Rotary Press Plate — Electric Eye
A modified design was put into use in 1956. The new plates have 20 frame bars instead of 17.

The A.E.F. Plate — 360-Subject Flat Plate — 8 Collectible Positions (See listings)

The 320-Subject Plate

The 400-Subject Plate —The 300-Subject Plate with double labels has the same layout

1 A	2 A	3 A	4 A	5 B	6 C	7 A	8 A	9 A	10 A
11 A	12 A	13 A	14 A	15 H	16 I	17 A	18 A	19 A	20 A
21 J	22 J	23 J	24 J	25 K	26 L	27 J	28 J	29 J	30 J
31 M	32 M	33 M	34 M	35 N	36 O	37 M	38 M	39 M	40 M
41 A	42 A	43 A	44 A	45 H	46 I	47 A	48 A	49 A	50 A
51 A	52 A	53 A	54 A	55 H	56 I	57 A	58 A	59 A	60 A

Lindbergh Booklet Plate — 180 Subjects — 11 Collectible Positions

Airmail 180-Subject Rotary Press Plate — Electric Eye

Plate Sizes: No. 1288Bc to date.
Since 1978 numerous plate sizes from 78 to 1080 subjects have been used.
Since plate size is not relevant to collecting these panes, we are not
including this information in the catalogue.

Booklet Covers

Front covers of booklets of postage and airmail issues are illustrated and numbered.

Included are the Booklet Cover number (BC2A); and the catalogue numbers of the Booklet Panes (300b, 331a). The text of the inside and or back covers changes. Some modern issues have minor changes on the front covers also. When more than one combination of covers exists, the number of possible booklets is noted in parenthesis after the booklet listing.

POST OFFICE DEPARTMENT.
THIS BOOK CONTAINS 12 TWO-CENT STAMPS.
Price, 25 cents.

DOMESTIC POSTAGE RATES.

(Apply to mail matter sent to Puerto Rico, Guam, Philippines, Canada, and Mexico.)

First-class. Letters and sealed matter: 2 cts. for each ounce or fraction.

Second-class. Newspapers and periodicals: 1 ct. for each four ounces or fraction.

Third-class. Miscellaneous printed matter: 1 ct. for each two ounces or fraction.

Fourth-class. All matter not included in first three classes: 1 ct. for each ounce or fraction.

279Be — BC1

1900-03

Text only cover

25c booklet contains 2 panes of six 2c stamps.
49c booklet contains 4 panes of six 2c stamps.
97c booklet contains 8 panes of six 2c stamps.

Booklets sold for 1c more than the face value of the stamps.

300b, 331a — BC2A

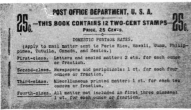

279Be, 301c, 319, 332a — BC2B

1900-08

Text cover with price added in upper corners

25c booklets contain 4 panes of six 1c stamps or 2 panes of six 2c stamps.
49c booklet contains 4 panes of six 2c stamps.
97c booklet contains 8 panes of six 2c stamps.

331a, 332a, 374a, 375a, 405b, 406a — BC3

1908-12   Postrider

25c booklet contains 4 panes of six 1c stamps.
25c booklet contains 2 panes of six 2c stamps.
49c booklet contains 4 panes of six 2c stamps.
97c booklet contains 8 panes of six 2c stamps.

405b, 424d, 462a, 498e, 804b — BC4A

405b, 424d, 462a, 498e, 552a, 632a — BC4B

1912-39   Washington P.O.

Price of booklet in large numerals behind contents information

25c booklet contains 4 panes of six 1c stamps.
73c booklet contains 4 panes of six 1c stamps and 4 panes of six 2c stamps.
97c booklet contains 16 panes of six 1c stamps.

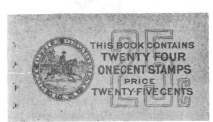

406a, 425e, 463a, 499e, 554c, 583a, 632a, 634d, 804b, 806b — BC5A

632a, 804b — BC5D

1912-39   Small Postrider

Large background numerals

25c booklets contain 4 panes of six 1c stamps or 2 panes of six 2c stamps.
49c booklet contains 4 panes of six 2c stamps.
73c booklet contains 4 panes of six 1c stamps and 2 panes of six 2c stamps.
97c booklets contain 16 panes of six 1c stamps or 8 panes of six 2c stamps.

498e, 552a — BC6A

501b, 502b — BC6B

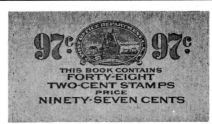

499e, 554c, 583a, 634d — BC6C

1917-27   Oval designs

25c booklet contains 4 panes of six 1c stamps.
37c booklet contains 2 panes of six 3c stamps.
97c booklet contains 8 panes of six 2c stamps.

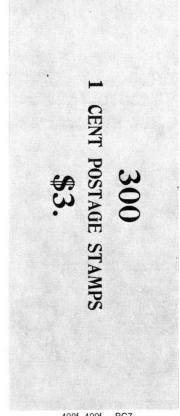

498f, 499f — BC7

Illustration reduced.

1917   A.E.F.

$3 booklet contains 10 panes of thirty 1c stamps.
$6 booklet contains 10 panes of thirty 2c stamps.

Booklets sold for face value.

C10a — BC8

1928   Postrider and Wings

61c booklet contains 2 panes of three 10c stamps.

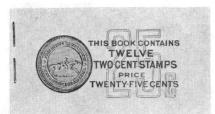

720b, 806b, 807a, 1035a — BC9A

804b — BC9E

1932-54   **Post Office Seal**
Large background numerals

25c booklet contains 2 panes of six 2c stamps.
37c booklet contains 2 panes of six 3c stamps.
49c booklet contains 4 panes of six 2c stamps.
73c booklets contain 4 panes of six 3c stamps or 4
   panes of six 1c stamps and 4 panes of six 2c
   stamps.

1036a — BC9F

1036a — BC9G

1036a — BC9H

1958

97c booklet contains 4 panes of six 4c stamps.

C25a — BC10

Large background numerals
1943   **Postrider and Wings**

37c booklet contains 2 panes of three 6c stamps.
73c booklet contains 4 panes of three 6c stamps.

C39a — BC11A

C51a — BC11B

C51a, C60a — BC11C

C64b, C64c — BC11D

1949-63   **U.S. Airmail Wings**

The 73c and 85c booklets were the last sold for 1c over face
value.

73c booklet contains 2 panes of six 6c stamps.
85c booklet contains 2 panes of six 7c stamps.
80c booklet contains 2 panes of five 8c stamps.
$2 booklet contains 5 panes of five 8c stamps.

1213a — BC12A

1962-63   **Small Postrider**
$1 booklet contains 4 panes of five 5c stamps.

1213a, 1213c — BC13A

C64b, C64c — BC13B

1963-64   **Mr. Zip**
$1 booklet contains 4 panes of five 5c stamps.
$2 booklet contains 5 panes of five 8c stamps.

1278a, 1284b, 1393a — BC14A

C72b — BC14B

1967-68
$2 booklet contains 4 panes of eight 6c stamps and 1
   pane of eight 1c stamps.
$4 booklet contains 5 panes of eight 10c stamps.

1284c, 1393b, 1395b, C72c, C78a — BC15

1968-71
$1 booklets contain 2 panes of five 10c stamps or 2
   panes of six 8c stamps and 1 pane of four 1c
   stamps; 3 panes of five 6c stamps and 1 pane of
   five 2c stamps or 2 panes of four 11c stamps and 1
   pane of six 2c stamps.

1278a, 1393a, 1395a — BC16

1970-71   **Eisenhower**
$2 booklet contains 4 panes of eight 6c stamps and 1
   pane of eight 1c stamps.
$1.92 booklet contains 3 panes of eight 8c stamps.

1395d — BC17A

1510b — BC17B

1510c — BC17C

1510d — BC17D

1972-74   **Postal Service Emblem**
    $2 booklet contains 3 panes of seven 8c stamps and
       1 pane of four 8c stamps.
    $1 booklet contains 2 panes of five 10c stamps.
    $4 booklet contains 5 panes of eight 10c stamps.
  $1.25 booklet contains 1 pane of five 13c stamps and 1
       pane of six 10c stamps.

C79a — BC18

1973
  $1.30 booklet contains 2 panes of five 13c stamps.

1595a, 1595d — BC19A

1595c — BC19B

1975-76
    90c booklet contains 1 pane of six 13c stamps and 1
       pane of six 2c stamps.
  $1.30 booklet contains 2 panes of five 13c stamps.
  $2.99 booklet contains 2 panes of eight 13c stamps and
       1 pane of seven 13c stamps.

1623a — BC20

EIGHT STAMPS $1.20
Vending Machines Only

1598a — BC21

1737a — BC22

1288c — BC23

1736c — BC24

BC24 illustration reduced.

1977-78
    $1 booklet contains 1 pane of one 9c stamp and
       seven 13c stamps.
  $1.20 booklet contains 1 pane of eight 15c stamps.
  $2.40 booklet contains 2 panes of eight 15c stamps.
  $3.60 booklet contains 3 panes of eight 15c stamps.

1742a — BC25

1980
   $3 booklet contains 2 panes of ten 15c stamps.

1819a, 1948a, 2113a — BC26

1981-82
   $4.32 booklet contains 3 panes of eight B stamps.
   $4 booklet contains 2 panes of ten C stamps.
   $4.40 booklet contains 2 panes of ten D stamps.

1893a — BC27

1889a — BC28

1981
   $1.20 booklet contains 1 pane of two 6c and six 18c
        stamps.
   $3.60 booklet contains 2 panes of ten 18c stamps.

1896a — BC29

1896b — BC29A

1896b — BC29B

1949a — BC30

1982
   $1.20 booklet contains 2 panes of six 20c stamps.
   $2 booklet contains 1 pane of ten 20c stamps.
   $4 booklet contains 2 panes of ten 20c stamps.

1909a — BC31

2122a — BC31A

2122c — BC31B

1983-89
   $28.05 booklet contains 1 pane of three $9.35 stamps.
   $32.25 booklet contains 1 pane of three $10.75 stamps.

2116a — BC32

2121a — BC33A

Many different seashell configurations are possible on BC33A. Seven adjacent covers are necessary to show all 25 shells.

2121a — BC33B

2116a — BC33C

1985
$1.10 booklet contains one pane of five 22c stamps.
$2.20 booklet contains two panes of five 22c stamps.
$4.40 booklet contains two panes of ten 22c stamps.

2201a — BC34

2209a — BC35

1986
$1.76 booklet contains 2 panes of four 22c stamps.
$2.20 booklet contains 2 panes of five 22c stamps.

FOR 22 CENTS, YOU CAN ADD ONE OF THESE GREETINGS TO A LETTER TO ANYONE IN THE UNITED STATES, CANADA OR MEXICO.

Get Well!
Thank You!
Best Wishes!
Keep in Touch!
Love You, Dad!
Happy Birthday!
Congratulations!
Love You, Mother!

10 TWENTY-TWO CENT U.S. POSTAGE STAMPS **2²⁰**

2274a — BC36

1987
$2.20 booklet contains 1 pane of ten 22c stamps.

We the People $4.40
Twenty 22-cent stamps USA

2359a — BC37

1987
$4.40 booklet contains four panes of five 22c stamps.

2366a — BC38

1987
$4.40 booklet contains four panes of five 22c stamps.

2276a — BC39

Illustration reduced.

1987
$4.40 booklet contains one pane of twenty 22c stamps.

2282a — BC40

1988
$5 booklet contains two panes of ten E stamps.

2283a, 2283c — BC41

1988
$5 booklet contains two panes of ten 25c stamps.

2182a, 2197a — BC43

1988
$1.50 booklet contains one pane of six 25c stamps.
$3 booklet contains two panes of six 25c stamps.
$5 booklet contains two panes of ten 25c stamps.

2285b — BC45

1988
$5 booklet contains two panes of ten 25c stamps.

2285c — BC46

1988
$3 booklet contains two panes of six 25c stamps.

2385a — BC47

1988
$5 booklet contains four panes of five 25c stamps.

2396a,
2398a — BC48

1988
$3 booklet contains two panes of six 25c stamps.

2409a — BC49

1989
$5 booklet contains four panes of five 25c stamps.

2427a — BC50

1989
$5 booklet contains two panes of ten 25c stamps.

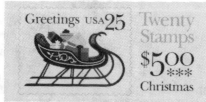

2429a — BC51

Illustration reduced.

1989
$5 booklet contains two panes of ten 25c stamps.

2431a — BC52

1989
$5 fold-it-yourself booklet contains eighteen self-adhe-
sive 25c stamps.

2441a — BC53

Illustration reduced.

1990
$5 booklet contains two panes of ten 25c stamps.

2443a — BC54

1990
$3 booklet contains two panes of ten 15c stamps.

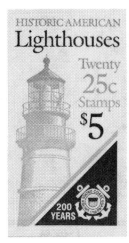

2474a — BC55

1990
$5 booklet contains four panes of five 25c stamps.

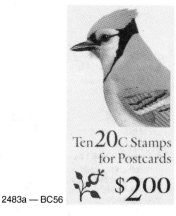

2483a — BC56

1995
$2 booklet contains one pane of 10 20c stamps.

2484a, 2485a — BC57

Illustration reduced.

1991-92
$2.90 booklet contains one pane of 10 29c stamps.
$5.80 booklet contains two panes of 10 29c stamps.

2486a — BC58

1993
$2.90 booklet contains one pane of 10 29c stamps.
$5.80 booklet contains two panes of 10 29c stamps.

2488a — BC59

1995
$6.40 booklet contains two panes of 10 32c stamps.

2489a
BC60

1993
$5.22 fold-it-yourself booklet contains 18 self-adhesive 29c stamps.

2490a
BC61

1993
$5.22 fold-it-yourself booklet contains 18 self-adhesive 29c stamps.

2491a
BC61A

1993
$5.22 fold-it-yourself booklet contains 18 self-adhesive stamps.

2492a
BC61B

1995
$6.40 fold-it-yourself booklet contains 20 self-adhesive 32c stamps.

2494a
BC61C

1995
$6.40 fold-it-yourself booklet contains 20 self-adhesive 32c stamps.

AMERICAN INDIAN
Headdresses

Twenty
25c Stamps

$5

2505a — BC62

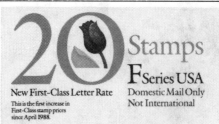

20 Stamps
F Series USA

New First-Class Letter Rate
This is the first increase in
First-Class stamp prices
since April 1988.

Domestic Mail Only
Not International

2519a, 2520a — BC65

1991
$2.90 booklet contains one pane of 10 F stamps.
$5.80 booklet contains two panes of 10 F stamps.

29 USA

Twenty
Stamps

$5.80

2527a — BC66

USA
19

Twenty
Stamps

$3.80

2530a — BC68

1991
$3.80 booklet contains two panes of 10 19c stamps.

Self-adhesive • DO NOT WET • ©USPS 1991 • Patent Pending

The U.S. Postal Service offers prestamped First-Class envelopes
with printed return addresses at reasonable prices including
shipping & handling. Convenient quantities of 50 available; several
styles & sizes offered.
Ask for an order form at
your post office or write to:

STAMPED ENVELOPE AGENCY
PO BOX 500
WILLIAMSBURG PA 16693-0500

Self-adhesive • DO NOT WET • ©USPS 1991 • Patent Pending

The U.S. Postal Service offers prestamped First-Class envelopes
with printed return addresses at reasonable prices including
shipping & handling. Convenient quantities of 50 available; several
styles & sizes offered.
Ask for an order form at
your post office or write to:

STAMPED ENVELOPE AGENCY
PO BOX 500
WILLIAMSBURG PA 16693-0500

2531b — BC68A

CHRISTMAS
25 USA

Antonello, National Gallery

Twenty
Stamps $5.00
                ***
Season's Greetings

2514a — BC63

Ten
Stamps

$2.90

USA
29

2528a — BC67

Ten
Stamps

$2.90

USA
29

2528a — BC67A

1991
$2.90 booklet contains one pane of 10 29c stamps.

25 USA

Greetings

Twenty
Stamps

$5.00
***

Season's Greetings

2516a — BC64

1990
$5 booklet contains two panes of 10 25c stamps.

Self-adhesive Stamps

29 USA

Convenient:
No Licking!

Strong
Adhesive:
Stays on
Envelopes!

Easy to Use:
No Tearing!

Eighteen Stamps

2531b — BC68B

1991
$5.22 fold-it-yourself booklet contains 18 self-adhesive
29c stamps.

Twenty
Stamps

$5.80

LOVE

USA
29

2536a — BC69

1991
$5.80 booklet contains two panes of 10 29c stamps.

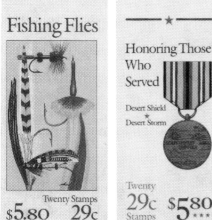

2549a — BC70   2552a — BC71

1991
$5.80 booklet contains four panes of 5 29c stamps.

2566a — BC72

1991
$5.80 booklet contains two panes of ten 29c stamps.

2577a — BC73

1991
$5.80 booklet contains two panes of 10 29c stamps.

2578a — BC74

1991
($5.80) booklet contains two panes of 10 (29c) stamps.

2581b, 2582a-2585a — BC75

1991
($5.80) booklet contains five panes of 4 (29c) stamps.

2593a, 2594a — BC76

1992
$2.90 booklet contains one pane of 10 29c stamps.
$5.80 booklet contains two panes of 10 29c stamps.

2595a — BC77

1992
$5 fold-it-yourself booklet contains 17 self-adhesive 29c stamps.

Nos. BC77 differs in size and style of type as well as location of UPC labels.

2598a
BC78

1994
$5.22 fold-it-yourself booklet contains 18 self-adhesive 29c stamps.

2599a
BC79

1994
$5.22 fold-it-yourself booklet contains 18 self-adhesive 29c stamps.

2646a — BC80   2709a — BC83

1992
$5.80 booklet contains four panes of 5 29c stamps.

2710a — BC83A

1992
$5.80 booklet contains two panes of 10 29c stamps.

2718a — BC84

1992
$5.80 booklet contains five panes of 4 29c stamps.

2719a — BC85

1992
$5.22 fold-it-yourself booklet contains 18 self-adhesive 29c stamps.

2737a — BC86

1993
$5.80 booklet contains one pane of four 29c stamps and two panes of eight 29c stamps.

2745a — BC89

1993
$5.80 booklet contains four panes of 5 29c stamps.

2764a — BC90

1993
$5.80 booklet contains four panes of 5 29c stamps.

2770a — BC91   2778a — BC92

1993
$5.80 booklet contains five panes of 4 29c stamps.

2790a — BC93

1993
$5.80 booklet contains five panes of 4 29c stamps.

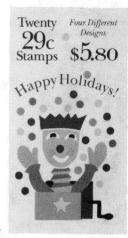

2798a — BC94

1993
$5.80 booklet contains two panes of 10 29c stamps.

2802a
BC95

1993
$3.48 fold-it-yourself booklet contains 12 self-adhesive 29c stamps.

2803a
BC96

1993
$5.22 fold-it-yourself booklet contains 18 self-adhesive 29c stamps.

2806b — BC97

1993
$2.90 booklet contains two panes of 5 29c stamps.

2813a
BC98

1994
$5.22 fold-it-yourself booklet contains 18 self-adhesive 29c stamps.

2814a — BC99

1994
$5.80 booklet contains two panes of 10 29c stamps.

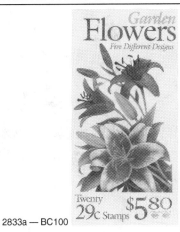

2833a — BC100

1994
$5.80 booklet contains four panes of 5 29c stamps.

2847a — BC101

1994
$5.80 booklet contains four panes of 5 29c stamps.

2871a
BC102

1994
$5.80 booklet contains two panes of 10 29c stamps.

2872a — BC103

1994
$5.80 booklet contains one pane of 20 29c stamps.

2873a
BC104

1994
$3.48 fold-it-yourself booklet contains 12 self-adhesive 29c stamps.

2874a
BC105

1994
$5.22 fold-it-yourself booklet contains 18 self-adhesive 29c stamps.

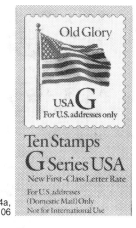

2881a, 2883a, 2884a,
2885a — BC106

1994
($3.20) booklet contains one pane of 10 G stamps.
($6.40) booklet contains two panes of 10 G stamps.

No. BC106 was printed by three different manufacturers in either two- or four-color formats, with G in different colors and with other minor design differences.

2886a,
2887a
BC107

1994
($5.76) fold-it-yourself booklet contains 18 self-adhesive G stamps.

Ten Stamps $3.20

2916a — BC108

1995
$3.20 booklet contains one pane of 10 32c stamps.
$6.40 booklet contains two panes of 10 32c stamps.

Eighteen Self-adhesive Stamps

$5.76   2919a BC113

1995
$5.76 fold-it-yourself booklet contains 18 self-adhesive 32c stamps.

Twenty Self-adhesive Stamps

$6.40

2920a BC114

1995
$6.40 fold-it-yourself booklet contains 20 self-adhesive 32c stamps.

Twenty Self-adhesive Stamps

LOVE USA 1995

First-Class Letter Rate
For Domestic Mail Only / Not for International Use

2949a BC115

1995
($6.40) fold-it-yourself booklet contains 20 self-adhesive non-denominated 32c stamps.

Twenty LOVE Stamps
Twenty 32c Stamps $6.40

2959a — BC116

1995
$6.40 booklet contains two panes of 10 32c stamps.

Twenty Self-adhesive Stamps
LOVE USA 55
First-Class Two Ounce Letter Rate $11.00

2960a — BC117

1995
$11 fold-it-yourself booklet contains 20 self-adhesive 55c stamps.

Lighthouses of the Great Lakes
FIVE DIFFERENT DESIGNS
TWENTY 32c STAMPS $6.40

2973a — BC118

1995
$6.40 booklet contains four panes of 5 32c stamps.

Garden **Flowers**
Five Different Designs
Twenty 32c Stamps $6.40

2997a — BC119

1995
$6.40 booklet contains four panes of 5 32c stamps

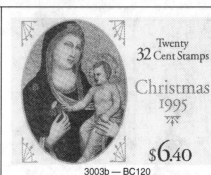

Twenty 32 Cent Stamps
Christmas 1995 $6.40

3003b — BC120

1995
$6.40 booklet contains two panes of 10 32c stamps

Holiday Greetings
Four Different Designs For the Holidays
Twenty 32 Cent Stamps $6.40

3007b-3007c — BC121

1995
$6.40 booklet contains two panes of 10 32c stamps

Holiday Greetings
Four Different Holiday Designs
Twenty 32¢ Self-adhesive Stamps $6.40

3011a BC122

1995
$6.40 fold-it-yourself booklet contains 20 self-adhesive 32c stamps

Holiday Greetings

Twenty Self-adhesive Stamps

$6.40

3012a
BC123

1995
$6.40 fold-it-yourself booklet contains 20 self-adhesive
32c stamps

Eighteen Self-adhesive Stamps

$5.76

3013a — BC124

1995
$5.76 fold-it-yourself booklet contains 18 self-adhesive
32c stamps

GARDEN FLOWERS

Five Different Designs

Twenty 32c Stamps $6.40

3029a — BC125

1996
$6.40 booklet contains four panes of 5 32c stamps

UNITED STATES POSTAL SERVICE ™

32¢
First-Class Letter Rate
15 STAMPS

Front

Now you can order stamps by phone:
1•800•STAMP•24
(1•800•782•6724)

Call toll free:
24 hours per day,
7 days per week

Fifteen Stamps (15)
15-32¢ Love Cherubs PSA
Item No. 3627X
Value $4.80

 Back — BC126

1996
$4.80 booklet contains 15 32c stamps
$9.60 booklet contains 30 2c stamps

A number of different stamps have been sold in BC126. The
text on the front and back changes to describe the contents of
the booklet. The enclosed stamps are affixed to the cover with a
spot of glue.

Twenty Self-adhesive Stamps

$6.40

UNITED STATES POSTAL SERVICE.
We Deliver For You.

3071a
BC127

1996
$6.40 fold-it-yourself booklet contains 20 self-adhesive
32c stamps

Ten Self-adhesive Stamps for Postcards

Fifteen Self-adhesive Stamps

USA 20

$2.00

$4.80

UNITED STATES POSTAL SERVICE.
We Deliver For You.

3048a-3048c — BC128   3049b — BC129

1996
$2.00 fold-it-yourself booklet contains 10 self-adhesive
20c stamps
$2.00 booklet contains 10 self-adhesive 20c stamps

1996
$4.80 booklet contains 15 self-adhesive 32c stamps

Ten Self-adhesive 20¢ Stamps
$2.00

3050a-3050c — BC130

1998
$2.00 fold-it-yourself booklet contains 10 self-adhesive
20c stamps
$2.00 booklet contains 10 self-adhesive 20c stamps

Coral Pink Rose

Twenty Self-adhesive 33¢ Stamps

$6.60

3052a-3052E — BC131

1999
$4.95 booklet contains 15 self-adhesive 33c stamps + la-
bel
$6.60 fold-it-yourself booklet contains 20 self-adhesive
33c stamps + label

Twenty Self-adhesive Stamps

$6.40

UNITED STATES POSTAL SERVICE™
We Deliver For You.

3089a
BC133

Season's Greetings

Twenty
32 Cent
Self-adhesive Stamps **$6.40** 3112a
BC134

Holiday Greetings

Four Different
Holiday Designs

Twenty 32¢
Self-adhesive
Stamps
3116a
BC135 **$6.40**

1996
$6.40 fold-it-yourself booklet contains 20 self-adhesive
32c stamps

Eighteen Self-adhesive Stamps

$5.76   3117a
                              BC136

1996
$5.76 fold-it-yourself booklet contains 18 self-adhesive
32c stamps

3123a — BC137

1997
$6.40 fold-it-yourself booklet contains 20 self-adhesive
       32c stamps
$11   fold-it-yourself booklet contains 20 self-adhesive
       55c stamps

Botanical Prints by Maria Sibylla Merian

$4.80

Fifteen 32¢
Self-adhesive
Stamps

UNITED STATES
POSTAL SERVICE.

3127a,
3128b,
3129b
BC138

1997
$4.80 booklet contains 15 32c stamps
$6.40 fold-it-yourself booklet contains 20 32c stamps

$3.20 Ten Self-adhesive Stamps

© and TM 1997 Warner Bros.

1-888-STAMP FUN

If you like *this* stamp, the Postal Service
has about a million more of them. Call
the number – get free stuff about other
stamps you can save and trade. And
guess what? The phone call is free!

3137-3138 — BC139

1997
$3.20 booklet contains 10 32c self-adhesive stamps

SEASON'S GREETINGS

Twenty 1997
32 Cent
Self-adhesive Stamps **$6.40** 3176a
                              BC140

Holiday Greetings

American Holly 32 USA

Twenty Self-adhesive Stamps
$6.40

3177a — BC141

1997
$6.40 fold-it-yourself booklet contains 20 self-adhesive
       32c stamps

Twenty 32¢ Self-adhesive Stamps — 3244a BC142

Holiday Greetings

Fifteen Self-adhesive Stamps $4.80

3248a-3248c, 3252b — BC143

1998
$4.80 booklet contains 15 self-adhesive 32c stamps
$6.40 fold-it-yourself booklet contains 20 self-adhesive 32c stamps

Ten Self-adhesive Stamps H Series

New First-Class Letter Rate

3267a, 3268a-3268b, 3269a — BC144

1998
($6.60) booklet contains 20 self-adhesive (33c) stamps
($3.30) fold-it-yourself booklet contains 10 self-adhesive (33c) stamps
($6.60) fold-it-yourself booklet contains 20 self-adhesive (33c) stamps
($5.94) fold-it-yourself booklet contains 18 self-adhesive (33c) stamps

3274a BC145

City Flag

Fifteen Self-adhesive Stamps $4.95

3278a-3278e, 3279a — BC146

1999
$3.30 Fold-it-yourself booklet contains 10 self-adhesive 33c stamps
$4.95 Booklet contains 15 self-adhesive 33c stamps
$6.60 Fold-it-yourself booklet contains 20 self-adhesive 33c stamps
$6.60 Booklet contains 20 self-adhesive 33c stamps

Classroom Flag

Eighteen Self-adhesive Stamps $5.94

3283a BC147

1999
$5.94 fold-it-yourself booklet contains 18 self-adhesive 33c stamps

Fruit Berries

20 SELF-ADHESIVE STAMPS $6.60 — 3297a BC148

1999
$6.60 fold-it-yourself booklet contains 20 self-adhesive 33c stamps + label
$4.95 booklet contains 15 self-adhesive 33c stamps + label

3313b BC149

1999
$6.60 fold-it-yourself booklet contains 20 self-adhesive 33c stamps

Seasons Greetings

© USPS 1998

3355 BC150

Holiday Greetings

Twenty 33 cent
self-adhesive stamps
$6.60

3360-3363 — BC151

Holiday Greetings

Fifteen 33 cent
self-adhesive
stamps
$4.95

3364-3367 — BC152

1999

$6.60 fold-it-yourself booklets contains 20 self-adhesive 33c stamps
$4.95 fold-it-yourself booklet contains 15 self-adhesive 33c stamps

3377a — BC153

2000

$9.80 booklet contains 2 panes of one 22c, 33c, 55c, 60c and $3.20 stamps and 6 leaves of text

---

BOOKLET PANES

Values are for complete panes with selvage, and for panes of six unless otherwise stated. Panes in booklets are Never Hinged. Values for stapled booklets are for those with creasing along the lines of the staples. Values for booklets which were glued shut are for opened booklets without significant damage to the cover.

See other notes in the introduction to this section.

Washington — A88

Wmk. 191 Horizontally or Vertically

1900-03				**Perf. 12**
279Be A88	2c **red**, Apr. 18		425.	425.
	light red		425.	
	orange red, 1902		425.	
	Never hinged		725.	
	With plate number (D)		1,250.	
	Never hinged		1,650.	

180- and 360-Subject Plates. All plate positions exist, except J, K, and L, due to the horizontal guide line being placed too far below stamps to appear on the upper stamps.

Booklets

BK1	BC1	25c **black**, cream	—
BK2	BC1	25c **black**, buff	6,500.
BK3	BC1	49c **green**, cream	—
BK4	BC1	49c **black**, buff	—
BK5	BC1	97c **red**, cream	—
BK6	BC1	97c **black**, gray	—
BK7	BC2B	25c **black**, cream (3)	7,000.
BK8	BC2B	49c **black**, buff (3)	—
BK9	BC2B	97c **black**, gray (3)	15,000.

Nos. BK1-BK6 and one type each of Nos. BK7-BK9 exist with specimen overprints handstamped on cover and individual stamps.

All covers of BK7-BK9 exist with "Philippines" overprint in 50mm or 48mm.

Franklin — A115   Washington — A116

1903-07				**Wmk. 191 Vertically**
300b A115	1c **blue green**, Mar. 6, 1907		550.	—
	Never hinged		925.	
	With plate number (D)		1,250.	
	Never hinged		2,100.	
	With plate number 3472 over left stamp (D)		4,000.	

180-Subject Plates only. All plate positions exist.

Booklet

BK10	BC2A	25c **black**, green (6)	6,500.

301c A116	2c **carmine**, Jan. 24, 1903		475.	—
	Never hinged		800.	
	With plate number (D)		1,300.	

180-Subject Plates only. All plate positions exist.

Booklets

BK11	BC2B	25c **black**, cream	3,250.
BK12	BC2B	49c **black**, buff	3,750.
BK13	BC2B	97c **black**, gray	—

Washington — A129

1903				**Wmk. 191 Vertically**
319g A129	2c **carmine**, type I, Dec. 3, 1903		120.00	175.00
	Never hinged		200.00	
	With plate number (D)		260.00	
	Never hinged		425.00	
	Wmk. horizontal (any color or type)		700.00	
	Never hinged		1,150.	
319m A129	2c **lake** (I)		2,500.	
319n A129	2c **carmine rose** (I)		180.00	250.00
	Never hinged		300.00	
	With plate number (D)		360.00	225.00

319p A129	2c **scarlet** (I)	160.00	200.00
	Never hinged	600.00	
	Never hinged	260.00	
	With plate number (D)	325.00	
	Never hinged	525.00	
319h A129	2c **carmine**, type II, 1907	260.00	
	Never hinged	425.00	
	With plate number (D)	500.00	
	Never hinged	800.00	
319q A129	2c **lake** (II)	200.00	375.00
	Never hinged	325.00	
	With plate number (D)	400.00	
	Never hinged	650.00	

180-Subject Plates only. All plate positions exist.

Booklet

BK14	BC2B	25c **black**, cream (11)	1,000.
BK15	BC2A	49c **black**, buff (11)	1,250.
BK16	BC2A	49c **black**, pink (11)	2,250.
BK17	BC2B	97c **black**, gray (11)	3,000.

Booklet Covers

When more than one combination of covers exists, the number of possible booklets is noted in parenthesis after the booklet listing.

Franklin — A138   Washington — A139

1908				**Wmk. 191 Vertically**
331a A138	1c **green**, Dec. 2, 1908		160.00	140.00
	Never hinged		250.00	
	With plate number (D)		240.00	
	Never hinged		375.00	

180- and 360-Subject Plates. All plate positions exist.

Booklets

BK18	BC2A	25c **black**, green (3)	2,000.
BK19	BC3	25c **black**, green	2,250.

332a A139	2c **carmine**, Nov. 16, 1908		135.00	125.00
	Never hinged		210.00	
	With plate number (D)		170.00	
	Never hinged		260.00	

180- and 360-Subject Plates. All plate positions exist.

Booklets

BK20	BC2B	25c **black**, cream (2)	1,100.
BK21	BC2A	49c **black**, buff (2)	—
BK22	BC2A	49c **black**, pink	2,750.
BK23	BC2B	97c **black**, gray (3)	—
BK24	BC3	25c **black**, cream	—
BK25	BC3	49c **black**, pink	—
BK26	BC3	97c **black**, gray	3,000.

1910			**Wmk. 190 Vertically**	**Perf. 12**
374a A138	1c **green**, Oct. 7, 1910	150.00	125.00	
	Never hinged	225.00		
	With plate number (D)	200.00		
	Never hinged	300.00		

360-Subject Plates only. All plate positions exist.

Booklet

BK27	BC3	25c **black**, green (2)	2,000.

375a A139	2c **carmine**, Nov. 30, 1910	95.00	95.00
	Never hinged	160.00	
	With plate number (D)	135.00	
	Never hinged	225.00	

360-Subject Plates only. All plate positions exist.

Booklets

BK28	BC3	25c **black**, cream (2)	750.00
BK29	BC3	49c **black**, pink (2)	2,500.
BK30	BC3	97c **black**, gray (2)	3,000.

Washington — A140

1912   **Wmk. 190 Vertically**

405b	A140	1c **green**, *Feb. 8, 1912*	60.00	50.00
		Never hinged	100.00	
		With plate number (D)	72.50	
		Never hinged	120.00	

360-Subject Plates only. All plate positions exist.

Ordinary Booklets

BK31	BC3	25c **black**, *green* (2)	1,000.
BK32	BC4A	25c **green**, *green* (3)	
BK33	BC4A	97c **green**, *lavender*	1,500.

Combination Booklet

BK34	BC4B	73c **red**, 4 #405b + 4 #406a	—

406a	A140	2c **carmine**, *Feb. 8, 1912*	60.00	60.00
		Never hinged	100.00	
		With plate number (D)	77.50	
		Never hinged	130.00	

360-Subject Plates only. All plate positions exist.

Ordinary Booklets

BK35	BC3	25c **black**, *cream* (2)	825.00
BK36	BC3	49c **black**, *pink* (2)	1,350.
BK37	BC3	97c **black**, *gray* (2)	—
BK38	BC5A	25c **red**, *buff* (3)	1,000.
BK39	BC5A	49c **red**, *pink* (3)	—
BK40	BC5A	97c **red**, *blue*, (3)	—

Combination Booklet

See No. BK34.

1914   **Wmk. 190 Vertically**   **Perf. 10**

424d	A140	1c **green**	4.75	3.25
		Never hinged	7.50	
		Double transfer, Plate 6363	—	—
		With plate number (D)	14.00	
		Never hinged	22.00	
		Cracked plate	—	
e.		As "d," imperf.	1,600.	
		With plate number (D)	—	

360-Subject Plates only. All plate positions exist.
All known examples of No. 424e are without gum.

Ordinary Booklets

BK41	BC4A	25c **green**, *green* (3)	300.00
BK42	BC4A	97c **green**, *lavender* (2)	110.00

Combination Booklet

BK43	BC4B	73c **red**, 4 #424d + 4 #425e (3)	300.00

425e	A140	2c **carmine**, *Jan. 6, 1914*	16.00	15.00
		Never hinged	25.00	
		With plate number (D)	42.50	
		Never hinged	65.00	

360-Subject Plates only. All plate positions exist.

Ordinary Booklets

BK44	BC5A	25c **red**, *buff* (3)	500.00
BK45	BC5A	49c **red**, *pink* (3)	1,000.
BK46	BC5A	97c **red**, *blue* (3)	1,250.

Combination Booklet

See No. BK43.

1916   **Unwmk.**   **Perf. 10**

462a	A140	1c **green**, *Oct. 15, 1916*	9.50	5.00
		Never hinged	14.50	
		Cracked plate at right	140.00	—
		Never hinged	210.00	
		Cracked plate at left	140.00	
		Never hinged	210.00	
		With plate number (D)	25.00	
		Never hinged	37.50	

360-Subject Plates only. All plate positions exist.

Ordinary Booklets

BK47	BC4A	25c **green**, *green*	650.00
BK48	BC4A	97c **green**, *lavender*	500.00

Combination Booklet

BK49	BC4B	73c **red**, 4 #462a + 4 #463a (2)	900.00

463a	A140	2c **carmine**, *Oct. 8, 1916*	95.00	65.00
		Never hinged	145.00	
		With plate number (D)	125.00	
		Never hinged	190.00	

360-Subject Plates only. All plate positions exist.

Ordinary Booklets

BK50	BC5A	25c **red**, *buff*	575.00
BK51	BC5A	49c **red**, *pink*	1,250.
BK52	BC5A	97c **red**, *blue*	2,000.

Combination Booklets

See No. BK49.

1917-18   **Unwmk.**   **Perf. 11**

498e	A140	1c **green**, *Apr. 6, 1917*	2.50	1.00
		Never hinged	4.00	
		Double transfer	—	—
		With plate number (D)	6.00	2.00
		Never hinged	9.00	

360-Subject Plates only. All plate positions exist.

Ordinary Booklets

BK53	BC4A	25c **green**, *green* (2)	250.00
BK54	BC4A	97c **green**, *lavender* (4)	85.00
BK55	BC6A	25c **green**, *green* (5)	120.00

Combination Booklets

BK56	BC4B	73c **red**, 4 #498e + 4 #499e (4)	80.00
BK57	BC4B	73c **red**, 4 #498e + 4 #554c (3)	100.00

499e	A140	2c **rose**, type I, *Mar. 31, 1917*	4.00	1.25
		Never hinged	6.25	
		With plate number (D)	7.00	1.50
		Never hinged	10.00	

360-Subject Plates only. All plate positions exist.

Ordinary Booklets

BK58	BC5A	25c **red**, *buff* (5)	250.00
BK59	BC5A	49c **red**, *pink* (4)	400.00
BK60	BC5A	97c **red**, *blue* (3)	750.00
BK61	BC6C	97c **red**, *blue* (2)	1,250.

Combination Booklets

See No. BK56.

501b	A140	3c **violet**, type I, *Oct. 17, 1917*	70.00	45.00
		Never hinged	110.00	
		With plate number (D)	105.00	
		Never hinged	160.00	

360-Subject Plates only. All plate positions exist.

Booklet

BK62	BC6B	37c **violet**, *sage*	550.00

502b	A140	3c **violet**, type II, *Mar. 1918*	60.00	45.00
		Never hinged	95.00	
		With plate number (D)	77.50	
		Never hinged	120.00	

360-Subject Plates only. All plate positions exist.

Booklet

BK63	BC6B	37c **violet**, *sage*	200.00

Washington — A140

A.E.F. Panes of 30

1917, Aug.

498f	A140	1c **green** (pane of 30)	1,000.
		Never hinged	1,500.

Booklet

BK64	BC7	$3 **black**, *green*	25,000.

499f	A140	2c **rose**, (pane of 30) type I	28,000.
		Never hinged	36,000.

Booklet

BK65	BC7	$6 **black**, *pink*	

No copies of No. BK65 are known. The number and description is provided only for specialist reference.

Nos. 498f and 499f were for use of the American Expeditionary Force in France.

They were printed from the ordinary 360-Subject Plates, the sheet being cut into 12 leaves of 30 stamps each in place of 60 leaves of 6 stamps each, and, of course, the lines of perforations changed accordingly.

The same system as used for designating plate positions on the ordinary booklet panes is used for designating the war booklet, only each war booklet pane is composed of 5 ordinary panes. Thus, No. W1 booklet pane would be composed of positions 1, 2, 3, 4, and 5 of an ordinary pane, etc.

The A. E. F. booklet panes were bound at side margins which accounts for side arrows sometimes being found on positions W5 and W6. As the top and bottom arrows were always removed when the sheets were cut, positions W1 and W2 cannot be distinguished from W7 and W8. Cutting may remove guidelines on these, but identification is possible by wide bottom margins. Positions W3 and W4 cannot be distinguished from W9 and W10.

There are thus just 8 collectible positions from the sheet as follows:

W1 or W7 Narrow top and wide bottom margins. Guide line at right.

W2 or W8 As W1, but guide line at left.

W3 or W9 Approximately equal top and bottom margins. Guide line at right.

W4 or W10 As W3, but guide line at left.

W5 Narrow bottom margin showing guideline very close to stamps. Wide top margin. Guide line at right. Pane with extra long tab may show part of split arrow at left.

W6 As W5, but guide line at left, split arrow at right. Guide line at left and at bottom. Arrow at lower right.

W11 Narrow bottom and wide top margins. Guide line at right. Siderographer initials on left tab.

W12 Narrow bottom and wide top margins. Guide line at left. Finisher initials on right tab.

Franklin — A155   Washington — A157

1923   **Unwmk.**   **Perf. 11**

552a	A155	1c **deep green**, *Aug. 1923*	6.00	2.00
		Never hinged	9.50	
		With plate number (D)	12.00	
		Never hinged	19.00	

360-Subject Plates only. All plate positions exist.

Ordinary Booklets

BK66	BC6A	25c **green**, *green* (2)	75.00
BK67	BC4A	97c **green**, *lavender* (3)	650.00

Combination Booklet

BK68	BC4B	73c **white**, *red*, 4 #552a + 4 #554c (3)	85.00

554c	A157	2c **carmine**	6.75	2.00
		Never hinged	10.50	
		With plate number (D)	12.00	
		Never hinged	19.00	

360-Subject Plates only. All plate positions exist.

Ordinary Booklets

BK69	BC5A	25c **red**, *buff* (3)	*400.00*
BK70	BC5A	49c **red**, *pink* (3)	*900.00*
BK71	BC6C	97c **red**, *blue* (3)	*1,500.*

Combination Booklets

See Nos. BK57 and BK68.

ROTARY PRESS PRINTINGS

Two experimental plates were used to print No. 583a. At least one guide line pane (H) is known from these plates. The rest of rotary press booklet panes were printed from specially prepared plates of 360-subjects in arrangement as before, but without the guide lines and the plate numbers are at the sides instead of at the top as on the flat plates.

The only varieties possible are the ordinary pane (A) and partial plate numbers appearing at the right or left of the upper or lower stamps of a booklet pane when the trimming of the sheets is off center. The note applies to Nos. 583a, 632a, 634d, 720b, 804b, 806b and 807a, before Electric Eyes.

1926   **Perf. 10**

583a	A157	2c **carmine**, *Aug. 1926*	90.00	50.00
		Never hinged	135.00	

Ordinary Booklets

BK72	BC5A	25c **red**, *buff* (3)	*350.00*
BK73	BC5A	49c **red**, *pink*	*575.00*
BK74	BC6C	97c **red**, *blue*	—

1927   **Perf. 11x10½**

632a	A155	1c **green**, *Nov. 2, 1927*	5.50	2.25
		Never hinged	7.00	

Ordinary Booklets

BK75	BC5A	25c **green**, *green* (3)	55.00
BK76	BC4A	97c **green**, *lavender*	600.00
BK77	BC5A	97c **green**, *lavender*	750.00

Combination Booklets

BK78	BC4B	73c **red**, 4 #632a + 4 #634d	—
BK79	BC5D	73c **red**, 4 #632a + 4 #634d (2)	90.00

634d	A157	2c **carmine**, type I, *Feb. 25, 1927*	1.75	1.10
		Never hinged	2.50	

Ordinary Booklets

BK80	BC5A	25c **red**, *buff* (2)	10.00
BK81	BC5A	49c **red**, *pink* (2)	15.00
BK82	BC5A	97c **red**, *blue* (3)	50.00
BK83	BC6C	97c **red**, *blue*	900.00

Combination Booklets

See Nos. BK78 and BK79.

Washington — A226

1932

720b	A226	3c **deep violet**, *July 25, 1932*	37.50	7.50
		Never hinged	50.00	

Ordinary Booklets

BK84	BC9A	37c **violet**, *buff* (2)	105.00
BK85	BC9A	73c **violet**, *pink* (2)	375.00

> Catalogue values for unused panes in this section, from this point to the end, are for Never Hinged items.

Washington — A276   Adams — A278

Jefferson — A279

In 1942 plates were changed to the Type II "new design" and the E. E. marks may appear at the right or left margins of panes of Nos. 804b, 806b and 807a. Panes printed from E. E. plates have 2½mm vertical gutter; those from pre-E. E. plates have 3mm vertical gutter.

1939-42   **Perf. 11x10½**

804b	A276	1c 3mm vert. gutter, *Jan. 27, 1939*	4.00	.85

Ordinary Booklets

BK86	BC5A	25c **green**, *green*	75.00
BK87	BC5A	97c **green**, *lavender*	*650.00*
BK88	BC4A	97c **green**, *lavender*	—

Combination Booklet

BK89	BC5D	73c **red**, 4 #804b + 4 #806b	135.00

804b	A276	1c 2½mm vert. gutter, *Apr. 14, 1942*	2.00	.35
		Horiz. pair, perf. only at bottom		

Ordinary Booklets

BK90	BC5A	25c **green**, *green*	8.25
BK91	BC5A	97c **green**, *lavender*	600.00

Combination Booklets

BK92	BC5D	73c **red**, 4 #804b + 4 #806b	30.00
BK93	BC9E	73c **red**, 4 #804b + 4 #806b	37.50

806b	A278	2c 3mm vert. gutter, *Jan. 27, 1939*	7.00	1.00

Ordinary Booklets

BK94	BC5A	97c **red**, *blue*	450.00

Combination Booklets

See No. BK89.

806b	A278	2c 2½mm vert. gutter, *Apr. 25, 1942*	4.75	.85

Ordinary Booklets

BK95	BC5A	97c **red**, *blue*	1,250.
BK96	BC5A	25c **red**, *buff*	19.00
BK97	BC9A	25c **red**, *buff*	100.00
BK98	BC5A	49c **red**, *pink*	45.00
BK99	BC9A	49c **red**, *pink*	75.00

Combination Booklets

See Nos. BK92 and BK93.

807a	A279	3c 3mm vert. gutter, *Jan. 27, 1939*	12.50	3.25

Booklets

BK100	BC9A	37c **violet**, *buff*	65.00
BK101	BC9A	73c **violet**, *pink*	*875.00*

807a	A279	3c 2½mm vert. gutter, *Mar. 6, 1942*	8.50	1.25
		With full vert. gutter (6mm) btwn.		

Booklets

BK102	BC9A	37c **violet**, *buff* (3)	20.00
BK103	BC9A	73c **violet**, *pink* (3)	45.00

Statue of
Liberty — A482   Lincoln — A483

1954-58   **Perf. 11x10½**

1035a	A482	3c pane of 6, *June 30, 1954*	4.00	.90
1035f		Dry printing	5.00	1.10

Booklets

BK104	BC9A	37c **violet**, *buff*, with #1035a	15.00
a.		With #1035f	19.00
BK105	BC9A	73c **violet**, *pink*, with #1035a	22.50
a.		With #1035f	25.00

Varieties

1035g		As "a," vert. imperf. betwn.	5,000.
1036a	A483	4c pane of 6, *July 31, 1958*	2.75	.80

Booklets

BK106	BC9F	97c on 37c **violet**, *buff*	50.00
BK107	BC9G	97c on 73c **violet**, *pink*	30.00
BK108	BC9H	97c **blue**, *yellow*	125.00
BK109	BC9H	97c **blue**, *pink* (3)	18.00

Varieties

1036d		As "a," imperf. horiz.	—

Washington
(Slogan 1) — A650   Slogan 2

Slogan 3

1962-64   **Perf. 11x10½**

Plate of 300 stamps, 60 labels

1213a	A650	5c pane of 5+label, slogan 1, *Nov. 23, 1962*	7.00	4.00
		With slogan 2, *1963*	16.00	7.00
		With slogan 3, *1964*	3.00	1.75

Booklets

BK110	BC12A	$1 **blue**, slogan 1	27.50
BK111	BC12A	$1 **blue**, slogan 2	125.00
BK112	BC13A	$1 **blue**, slogan 2	100.00
BK113	BC13A	$1 **blue**, slogan 3 (4)	10.00

1213c	A650	As No. 1213a, tagged, slogan 2, *Oct. 28, 1963*	65.00	7.50
		With slogan 3, *1964*	2.00	1.50

Booklets

BK114	BC13A	$1 **blue**, slogan 2	300.00
BK115	BC13A	$1 **blue**, slogan 3 (4)	10.50

Jefferson — A710   Wright — A712

Slogan 4   Slogan 5

1967-78   *Perf. 11x10½*

1278a	A710	1c pane of 8, shiny gum, *Jan. 12, 1968*	1.00	.50
		Dull gum	2.00	

Combination Booklets

See Nos. BK116, BK117B, BK118 and BK119.

1278b	A710	1c pane of 4+2 labels, slogans 5 & 4, *May 10, 1971*	.80	.30

Combination Booklet

See No. BK122.

1280a	A712	2c pane of 5+label, slogan 4, *Jan. 8, 1968*	1.25	.60
		With slogan 5	1.25	.60

Combination Booklets

See Nos. BK117 and BK120.

1280c	A712	2c pane of 6, shiny gum, *May 7, 1971*	1.00	.50
		Dull gum	1.10	

Combination Booklets

See Nos. BK127 and BKC22.

The 1c and 6c panes of 8, Nos. 1278a and 1284b, were printed from 320-subject plates and from 400-subject plates, both with electric eye markings. The 2c and 6c panes of 5 stamps plus label, Nos. 1280a and 1284c, were printed from 360-subject plates.

An experimental moisture-resistant gum was used on 1,000,000 panes of No. 1278a and 4,000,000 of No. 1393a released in March, 1971. This dull finish gum shows no breaker ridges. The booklets lack interleaving. This gum was also used for Nos. 1395c, 1395d, 1288c and all engraved panes from No. 1510b on unless noted.

Roosevelt — A716

Oliver Wendell
Holmes — A720

Perf. 10½x11

1284b	A716	6c pane of 8, *Dec. 28, 1967*	1.50	.75

Combination Booklet

BK116	BC14A	$2 **brown**, 4 #1284b (6c)+1 #1278a(1c)(2)	7.75	
1284c	A716	6c pane of 5+label, slogan 4, *Jan. 9, 1968*	1.50	.75
		With slogan 5	1.50	.75

Combination Booklet

BK117	BC15	$1 **brown**, 3 #1284c (6c) + 1 #1280a (2c) (2)	7.00	

No. BK117 contains panes with slogan 4, slogan 5 or combinations of 4 and 5.

Perf. 10

1288Bc	A720	15c pane of 8, *June 14, 1978*	2.80	1.75

Booklet

BK117A	BC23	$3.60 **red & light blue**, no P#	8.75	

Varieties

1288Be		As "c," vert. imperf. btwn.	—

Eisenhower — A815

Plate of 400 subjects for No. 1393a. Plate of 300 stamps and 60 labels for No. 1393b.

1970 Tagged   *Perf. 11x10½*

1393a	A815	6c pane of 8, shiny gum, *Aug. 6*	1.50	.65
		Dull gum	1.90	

Combination Booklets

BK117B	BC14A	$2 **blue**, 4 #1393a (6c) + 1 #1278a (1c)	7.25	
BK118	BC16	$2 **blue**, 4 #1393a (6c) + 1 #1278a (1c)	7.25	
BK119	BC16	$2 **blue**, dull gum, 4 #1393a (6c) + 1 #1278a (1c) (2)	8.75	
1393b	A815	6c pane of 5+label, slogan 4, *Aug. 6*	1.50	.65
		With slogan 5	1.50	.65

Combination Booklet

BK120	BC15	$1 **blue**, 3 #1393b (6c) + 1 #1280a (2c)	6.00	

No. BK120 contains panes with slogan 4, slogan 5 or combinations of 4 and 5.

Stamps in this book have been gummed with a matte finish adhesive which permits the elimination of the separation tissues.

This book contains 25 — 8c stamps — four on this pane and seven each on three additional panes. Selling price $2.00.

Slogans 6 and 7

Eisenhower — A815a

1971-72   **Shiny Gum**   *Perf. 11x10½*

1395a	A815a	8c **deep claret**, pane of 8, *May 10, 1971*	1.80	1.25

Booklet

BK121	BC16	$1.92 **claret** (2)	6.50

1395b	A815a	8c pane of 6, *May 10, 1971*	1.25	.90

Combination Booklet

BK122	BC15	$1 **claret**, 2 #1395b (8c) + 1 #1278b (1c) (2)	4.00

Dull Gum

1395c	A815a	8c pane of 4+2 labels, slogans 6 and 7, *Jan. 28, 1972*	1.65	.80
1395d	A815a	8c pane of 7+label, slogan 4, *Jan. 28, 1972*	1.90	1.00
		With slogan 5	1.90	1.00

Combination Booklet

BK123	BC17A	$2 **claret**, *yellow*, 3 #1395d + 1 #1395c	7.75

Plate of 400 subjects for No. 1395a. Plate of 360 subjects for No. 1395b. Plate of 300 subjects (200 stamps and 100 double-size labels) for No. 1395c. Plate of 400 subjects (350 stamps and 50 labels) for No. 1395d.

Booklet Covers

When more than one combination of covers exists, the number of possible booklets is noted in parenthesis after the booklet listing.

Slogan 8

Jefferson Memorial — A924

1973-74　　　　　　　　　　**Perf. 11x10½**

1510b	A924	10c pane of 5+label, slogan 8, *Dec. 14, 1973*	1.65	.55
		Booklet		
BK124	BC17B	$1 **red & blue**	3.75	
1510c	A924	10c pane of 8, *Dec. 14, 1973*	1.65	.70
		Booklet		
BK125	BC17C	$4 **red & blue**	8.50	
1510d	A924	10c pane of 6, *Aug. 5, 1974*	5.25	1.00
		Combination Booklet		
BK126	BC17D	$1.25 **red & blue,** 1 #1510d (10c) + 1 #C79a (13c)	7.25	

Slogan 9

Liberty Bell — A998

1975-78　　　　　　　　　　**Perf. 11x10½**

1595a	A998	13c pane of 6, *Oct. 31, 1975*	2.25	.75
		Combination Booklet		
BK127	BC19A	90c **red & blue,** 1 #1595a (13c) + 1 #1280c (2c) (2)	3.25	
1595b	A998	13c pane of 7+label, slogan 8, *Oct. 31, 1975*	2.25	.75
1595c	A998	13c pane of 8, *Oct. 31, 1975*	2.25	1.00
		Combination Booklet		
BK128	BC19B	$2.99 **red & blue,** 2 #1595c (13c) + 1 #1595b (13c) (2)	7.75	
1595d	A998	13c pane of 5+label, slogan 9, *Apr. 2, 1976*	1.75	.75

		Booklet		
BK129	BC19A	$1.30 **red & blue**	4.00	
		Varieties		
1595e		Vert. pair, imperf. btwn.	*1,200.*	

A994-A1018a

Fort McHenry Flag
(15 Stars) — A1001

1977-78　　　　　　　　　　**Perf. 11x10½**

1598a	A1001	15c pane of 8, *June 30, 1978*	4.25	.80
		Booklet		
BK130	BC21	$1.20 **red & light blue,** no P#	4.50	
1623a	A1018a	Pane of 8 (1 #1590 + 7 #1623), *Mar. 11, 1977*	2.25	1.10
		Booklet		
BK131	BC20	$1 **red & light blue,** no P# (3)	2.50	
		Varieties		
1623d		Pair, Nos. 1590, 1623	.70	.70
		Perf. 10		
1623Bc	A1018a	Pane of 8 (1 #1590A + 7 #1623B), *Mar. 11, 1977*	29.00	—
		Booklet		
BK132	BC20	$1 **red & light blue,** no P# (2)	30.00	
		Varieties		
1623Be		Pair, Nos. 1590A, 1623B	24.00	22.50

Eagle — A1124

1978　　　　**Tagged**　　　**Perf. 11x10½**

1736a	A1124	A pane of 8, *May 22*	2.25	.90
		Booklet		
BK133	BC24	$3.60 **deep orange**	7.00	

Red Masterpiece and
Medallion
Roses — A1126

Perf. 10

1737a	A1126	15c pane of 8, *July 11*	2.25	.90
		Booklet		
BK134	BC22	$2.40 **rose red & yel grn,** no P# (4)	5.25	
		Varieties		
1737b		As "a," imperf.	—	
1737c		As "a," tagging omitted	40.00	

Windmills — A1127-A1131

1980　　　　　　　　　　　**Perf. 11**

1742a	A1131	15c pane of 10, *Feb. 7*	3.50	3.00
		Booklet		
BK135	BC25	$3 **light blue & dark blue,** *blue,* no P#	7.50	
		Varieties		
1742b		Strip of 5, #1738-1742	1.50	1.40

A1207

A1267-A1276

A1279-A1280

1981

1819a	A1207	B pane of 8, *Mar. 15*	3.75	*1.75*

Booklet

BK136	BC26	$4.32 **dull violet,** no P#	11.75

1889a	A1267	18c pane of 10, *May 14*	8.50	*7.00*

Booklet

BK137	BC28	$3.60 **gray & olive,** P#1-10	19.00
		P#11-13	40.00
		P#14-16	35.00

1893a	A1279	Pane of 8 (2 #1892, 6 #1893, *Apr. 24*	3.00	*2.25*

Booklet

BK138	BC27	$1.20 **blue & red,** P#1	3.25

Varieties

1893b		As "a," vert. imperf. btwn.	75.00
1893c		Pair, Nos. 1892, 1893	.90	*1.00*
1893d		As "a," tagging omitted	—

Booklet

BK138a	BC27	$1.20 With No. 1893b, P#1	75.00
BK138b	BC27	$1.20 With No. 1893d, P#1	—

A1281

1981-82

1896a	A1281	20c pane of 6, *Dec. 17, 1981*	3.00	*2.00*

Booklet

BK139	BC29	$1.20 **blue & red,** P#1 (2)	3.25

1896b	A1281	20c pane of 10, *June 1, 1982*	5.25	*3.25*
		Scored perforation	5.25	—

Booklets

BK140	BC29A	$2 **blue & red,** P#1 (4)	5.50
		P#4	47.50
BK140A	BC29B	$4 **blue & red,** *Nov. 17, 1983,* P#2	11.00
		P#3	17.50
		P#4	—

Booklet Covers

When more than one combination of covers exists, the number of possible booklets is noted in parenthesis after the booklet listing.

A1296

1983

1909a	A1296	$9.35 pane of 3, *Aug. 12*	65.00	—

Booklet

BK140B	BC31	28.05 **blue & red,** P#1111	67.50

A1333

1981

1948a	A1333	C pane of 10, *Oct. 11*	4.50	*3.00*

Booklet

BK141	BC26	$4 **brown,** *blue,* no P#	10.00

A1334

1982

1949a	A1334	20c pane of 10, type I, *Jan. 8*	5.50	*2.50*
1949d		As "a," type II	11.00	—

Booklets

BK142	BC30	$4 **blue & yellow green,** P#1-6, 9-10	16.00
		P#11, 12, 15	40.00
		P#14	30.00
		P#16	75.00
		P#17-19	55.00
		P#20, 22-24	100.00
		P#21, 28, 29	350.00
		P#25-26	150.00
a.		Type II, P#34	22.00

Varieties

1949b		As "a," vert. imperf. btwn.	110.00
1949f		As "a," tagging omitted	30.00

Booklets

BK142b		As BK142, with 2 #1949b	—
BK142c		As BK142, with 2 #1949f, P#5	60.00

Stamps in No. 1949a are 18¾mm wide and have overall tagging. Stamps in No. 1949d are 18½mm wide and have block tagging.

Plate number does not always appear on top pane in Nos. BK142, BK142a. These booklets sell for more.

A1497

1985 — *Perf. 11*

2113a	A1497	D pane of 10 *Feb. 1*	8.50	*3.00*

Booklet

BK143	BC26	$4.40 **green,** P#1, 3, 4	17.00
		P#2	850.00

Varieties

2113b		As "a," imperf. between, horiz.	—

Plate number does not always appear on top pane in No. BK143. These booklets sell for more.

A1499

Perf. 10 Horiz.

2116a	A1499	22c pane of 5, *Mar. 29*	2.50	*1.25*
		Scored perforations	2.50	—

Booklets

BK144	BC33C	$1.10 **blue & red,** P#1, 3	2.75
BK145	BC32	$2.20 **blue & red,** P#1, 3	5.25

A1500-A1504

Perf. 10

2121a	A1500	22c pane of 10, *Apr. 4*	4.00	*2.50*

Booklets

BK146	BC33A	$4.40 **multicolored,** P#1, 3	8.50
		P#2	10.00
BK147	BC33B	$4.40 **brown & blue,** P#1, 3, 5, 7, 10	8.50
		P#6	—
		P#8	10.00

Varieties

2121b		As "a," violet omitted on both Nos. 2120	800.00
2121c		As "a," vert. imperf. btwn.	600.00
2121d		As "a," imperf.	—
2121e		Strip of 5, Nos. 2117-2121	2.00	—

A1505

1985-89　　　　　　　　　　*Perf. 10 Vert.*

2122a	A1505	10.75 type I, pane of 3, *Apr. 29, 1985*	60.00	—
		Booklet		
BK148	BC31A	32.25 **multicolored,** P#11111	62.50	
2122c	A1505	10.75 type II, pane of 3, *June 19, 1989*	65.00	—
		Booklet		
BK149	BC31B	32.25 **blue & red,** P#22222 (2)	67.50	

No. 2182a — A1564

No. 2197a — A1564

1988　　　　　　　　　　*Perf. 11*

2182a	A1564	25c pane of 10, *May 3*	4.50	3.75
		Booklet		
BK150	BC43	$5 **multicolored,** P#1-2	9.25	
		Varieties		
2182c		As "a," tagging omitted	—	
		Booklet		
BK150a	BC43	$1.50 As BK150, with #2182c	—	
		Perf. 10 on 2 or 3 Sides		
2197a	A1564	25c pane of 6, *May 3*	3.00	2.25
		Booklets		
BK151	BC43	$1.50 **blue & brown,** P#1	3.00	
BK152	BC43	$3 **brown & blue,** P#1	6.00	
		Varieties		
2197c	A1564	25c As "a," tagging omitted	65.00	
		Booklet		
BK151a	BC43	$1.50 As BK151, with #2197c	70.00	

A1581-A1584

1986

2201a	A1581	22c pane of 4, *Jan. 23*	2.00	1.75
		Booklet		
BK153	BC34	$1.76 **purple & black,** P#1	4.00	
		Varieties		
2201b		As "a," black omitted on Nos. 2198, 2201	65.00	
2201c		As "a," blue (litho.) omitted on Nos. 2198-2200	2,500.	
2201d		As "a," buff (litho.) omitted	—	
		Booklets		
BK153a	BC34	$1.76 As No. BK153, with 2 #2201b	110.00	
BK153b	BC34	$1.76 As No. BK153, with 2 #2201c	5,000.	

A1588-A1592

2209a	A1588	22c pane of 5, *Mar. 21*	4.50	2.75
		Booklet		
BK154	BC35	$2.20 **blue green and red,** P#11111, 22222	9.50	
		Varieties		
2209b		As "a," red omitted	—	

A1637-A1644

1987

2274a	A1637	22c pane of 10, *Apr. 20*	8.00	5.00
		Booklet		
BK155	BC36	$2.20 **blue & red,** P#111111, 222222	12.50	

A1646

**　　　　　　　　　　*Perf. 11***

2276a	A1646	22c pane of 20, *Nov. 30*	8.50	—
		Booklet		
BK156	BC39	$4.40 **multicolored,** no P#	9.00	
		P#1111, 2222	12.00	
		P#2122	19.00	
		Varieties		
2276b		As "a," vert. pair, imperf. between	—	

No. 2276a was made from sheets of No. 2276 which had alternating rows of perforations removed and the right sheet margins trimmed off.

A1647

1988　　　　　　　　　　*Perf. 10*

2282a	A1647	E pane of 10, *Mar. 22*	6.50	3.50
		Scored perforations	6.50	—
		Booklet		
BK157	BC40	$5 **blue,** P#1111, 2222	13.00	
		P#2122	15.00	

A1649a

**　　　　　　　　　　*Perf. 11***

2283a	A1649a	25c pane of 10, *Apr. 29*	6.00	3.50
		Booklet		
BK158	BC41	$5 **multicolored,** P#A1111	12.00	
		Varieties		
2283d		As "a," horiz. imperf. between	2,250.	

Imperf. panes exist from printers waste.

		Color Change		
2283c	A1649a	25c red removed from sky, pane of 10	67.50	—
		Booklet		
BK159	BC41	$5 **multicolored,** P#A3111, A3222	135.00	

A1649b-A1649c

Perf. 10

2285b	A1649b	25c pane of 10, *May 28*	5.00	3.50

Booklet

BK160	BC45	$5 **red & black,** P#1111, 1112, 1211, 1433, 1434, 1734, 2121, 2321, 3333, 5955 (2)	12.00	
		P#1133, 2111, 2122, 2221, 2222, 3133, 3233, 3412, 3413, 3422, 3521, 4642, 4644, 4911, 4941	20.00	
		P#1414	95.00	
		P#1634, 3512	50.00	
		P#3822	40.00	
		P#5453	165.00	

Varieties

2285d		Pair, Nos. 2284-2285	1.10	.25
2285e		As "d," tagging omitted	12.50	

A1648

2285Ac	A1648	25c pane of 6, *July 5*	3.00	2.00

Booklet

BK161	BC46	$3 **blue & red,** P#1111	6.00	

A1719-A1723

1987

2359a	A1719	22c pane of 5, *Aug. 28*	2.75	2.25

Booklet

BK162	BC37	$4.40 **red & blue,** P#1111, 1112	11.00	

Varieties

2355a		Grayish green (background) omitted, single stamp	—	
2356a		As No. 2355a	—	
2357a		As No. 2355a	—	
2358a		As No. 2355a	—	
2359b		As No. 2355a	—	

A1726-A1730

2366a	A1726	22c pane of 5, *Oct. 1*	2.75	2.50

Booklet

BK163	BC38	$4.40 **black & yellow,** P#1, 2	11.00	

Varieties

2365a		Red omitted, single stamp	—	
2366b		Black omitted, single stamp	—	
2366c		Blue omitted, single stamp	—	

A1745-A1749

1988

2385a	A1745	25c pane of 5, *Aug. 25*	5.00	2.25

Booklet

BK164	BC47	$5 **black & red,** P#1	20.00	

A1759-A1760

A1761-A1762

Perf. 11

2396a	A1759	25c pane of 6, *Oct. 22*	3.50	3.25
2398a	A1761	25c pane of 6, *Oct. 22*	3.50	3.25

Combination Booklet

BK165	BC48	$3 **multicolored,** 1 #2396a, 1 #2398a, P#A1111 (2)	7.00	

Varieties

2398b		As "a," imperf. horiz.	—	

Unused never folded panes of Nos. 2396a and 2398a are known but were not regularly issued. The USPS used never folded panes on first day programs and souvenir pages for this issue.

A1769-A1773

1989

2409a	A1769	25c pane of 5, *Mar. 3*	2.25	1.75
		Never folded pane, P#1	8.00	
		P#2	20.00	

Booklet

BK166	BC49	$5 **blue & black,** P#1, 2	9.50	

A1791

Perf. 11½

2427a	A1791	25c pane of 10, *Oct. 19*	4.75	3.50
		Never folded pane, P#1	10.00	

Booklet

BK167	BC50	$5 **multicolored,** P#1	9.50	

Varieties

2427b		As "a," red (litho.) omitted	850.00	
2427c		As "a," imperf		

A1792

2429a	A1792	25c pane of 10, *Oct. 19*	4.75	*3.50*
		Never folded pane, P#1111, 2111	17.50	

Booklet

BK168	BC51	$5 multicolored, P#1111, 2111	10.00	

Varieties

2429b	As "a," imperf. horiz.	—
2429c	Vert. pair, imperf. horiz.	—
2429d	As "a," red omitted	—
2429e	Imperf., pair	

A1793

Illustration reduced.

Self-adhesive   ***Die cut***

2431a	A1793	25c pane of 18, *Nov. 10,* P#A1111	11.00

By its nature, No. 2431a constitutes a complete booklet. Blue & red peelable paper backing is booklet cover (BC52). Sold for $5.

Varieties

2431b	Vert. pair, no die cutting between	*850.00*
2431c	Pair, no die cutting	—

A1800

1990   **Perf. 11½**

2441a	A1800	25c pane of 10, *Jan. 18*	4.75	*3.50*
		Never folded pane, P#1211	35.00	

Varieties

2441b	As "a," bright pink omitted	*2,100.*
2441c	As "b," single stamp	*200.00*

Panes exist containing both normal and bright pink omitted stamps. Value is less than that of No. 2441b.

Booklet

BK169	BC53	$5 multicolored, P#1211	10.50
		P#2111	20.00
		P#2211	30.00
		P#2222	17.50

A1802

Perf. 11

2443a	A1802	15c pane of 10, *Feb. 3*	3.00	*2.00*
		Never folded pane, P#111111	9.00	

Booklet

BK170	BC54	$3 multi, P#111111	6.00
		P#221111	10.00

Varieties

2443b	As #2443a, blue omitted	*1,900.*
2443c	As "b," single stamp	*170.00*

A1829-A1833

Perf. 10

2474a	A1829	25c pane of 5, *Apr. 26*	2.50	*2.00*
		Never folded pane, P#1, 3, 5	6.00	
		P#2	8.00	
		P#4	—	

Booklet

BK171	BC55	$5 blue & red, P#1-5	10.00

Varieties

2474b	As #2474a, white omitted	80.00	—

Booklet

BK171a	As No. BK171, with 4 No. 2474b	300.00

A1847

1991-95

2483a	A1847	20c multicolored, pane of 10, *June 15, 1995*	4.00 *2.25*

Never folded pane   4.75

Booklet

BK172	BC56	$2 multicolored, P#S1111	4.00

A1848

Perf. 10

2484a	A1848	29c black & multi, overall tagging, pane of 10, *Apr. 12, 1991*	5.50	*3.75*
		Never folded pane, P#1111	9.00	

Booklets

BK173	BC57	$2.90 black & green, *1992,* P#4444	5.75
BK174	BC57	$5.80 black & red, P#1111, 2222, 4444	11.00
		P#1211, 3221	125.00
		P#2122, 3222, 3333	20.00
		P#3331	—

Varieties

2484b	As "a," horiz. imperf. between	—
2484d	Prephosphered paper (solid tagging), pane of 10	5.50 *3.75*

Booklet

BK173a	As No. BK173, with No. 2484d	5.75

Perf. 11

2485a	A1848	29c red & multi, pane of 10, *Apr. 12, 1991*	5.50	*4.00*
		Never folded pane, P#K11111	12.00	

Booklets

BK175	BC57	$5.80 black & multi, P#K11111	12.00

Varieties

2485b	Vert. pair, imperf. between	*275.00*
2485c	As "b," bklt. pane of 10	*1,500.*

A1849

2486a	A1849	29c pane of 10, *Oct. 8, 1993*	5.50	*4.00*
		Never folded pane, P#K1111	6.25	

Booklet

BK176	BC58	$2.90 multicolored, P#K1111	6.00
BK177	BC58	$5.80 multicolored, P#K1111	11.50

A1850-A1851

2488a	A1850	32c multicolored, pane of 10, *July 8, 1995*	6.00 *4.25*
		Never folded pane	6.75

Booklet

BK178 BC59	$6.40 **multicolored**, P#11111	12.00	
Varieties			
2488b	Pair, Nos. 2487-2488	1.25	.30

A1852

	Self-Adhesive	**Die Cut**	
2489a A1852	29c pane of 18, *June 25, 1993*		
	P#D11111, D22211	10.00	
	P#D22221, D22222, D23133	15.00	

By it nature, No. 2489a constitutes a complete booklet (BC60). The peelable backing serves as a booklet cover.

Red Rose A1853

	Self-Adhesive	**Die Cut**
2490a A1853	29c pane of 18, *Aug. 19, 1993*, P#S111	10.00

By its nature, No. 2490a constitutes a complete booklet (BC61). The peelable backing, of which two types are known, serves as a booklet cover.

A1854

	Self-Adhesive	**Die Cut**
2491a A1854	29c pane of 18, *Nov. 5, 1993*, P#B3-11, 13-14, 16	11.00
	P#B1-2, 12, 15	15.00

By is nature, No. 2491a constitutes a complete booklet (BC61A). The peelable backing serves as a booklet cover.

Varieties

2491b	Horiz. pair, no die cutting btwn.	—

Pink Rose (No. 2492a) — A1853

Serpentine Die Cut 11.3x11.7 on 2, 3 or 4 Sides
Self-Adhesive

2492a A1853	32c pane of 20+label, *June 2, 1995*, P#S111, S112, S333, S444, S555	12.00
2492b A1853	32c pane of 15+label, *1996*	8.75
2492e A1853	32c pane of 14, *1996*	21.00
2492f A1853	32c pane of 16, *1996*	21.00

By its nature, No. 2492a is a complete booklet (BC61B). The peelable backing serves as a booklet cover.

No. 2492e contains blocks of 4, 6 and 4 stamps. No. 2492f contains blocks of 6,6, and 4 stamps. The blocks are on rouletted backing paper. The peel-a-way strips that were between the blocks have been removed to fold the pane. Only No. 2492f is affixed to the booklet cover.

Booklets

BK178A BC126	$4.80 **blue**, No. 2492b (4)	8.75
BK178B BC126	$4.80 **blue**, No. 2492f with bottom right stamp removed	—
BK178C BC126	$9.60 **blue**, 2 #2492b, No P# (3)	18.00
BK178D BC126	$9.60 **blue**, 2 panes of #2492f ea with a stamp removed from either the top or bottom row, No P# (3)	20.00

Combination Booklets

BK178E BC126	$9.60 **blue**, 1 ea #2492e, 2492f, no P# (5)	45.00
BK178F BC126	$9.60 **blue**, #2492b, 2492f with bottom right stamp removed, no P#	175.00

One version of No. BK178E was sold wrapped in cellophane with the contents of the booklet listed on a label. This booklet appears to be scarcer than the other four varieties.

The panes of #2492f with one stamp removed that are contained in Nos. BK178B, BK178D and BK178F cannot be made from No. 2492b, a pane of 15 + label. The label is located in the second or third row of the pane and is sometimes die cut. The panes with one stamp removed all have the stamp removed from the top or bottom row of the pane.

Varieties

2492c	Horiz. pair, no die cutting btwn.	—
2492d	As "a," 2 stamps and parts of 7 others printed on backing liner	—
2492h	Vert. pair, no die cutting btwn.	—

A1850-A1851

Serpentine Die Cut

2494a A1850	32c pane of 20+label, *June 2, 1995*, P# list 1	12.50
	P# list 2	18.00
	P#V11132, V33353	15.00
	P#V33323	25.00
	P#V11232	—

By its nature, No. 2494a is a complete booklet (BC61C). The peelable backing serves as a booklet cover.

List 1 - P#V11111, V11122, V12132, V12211, V12221, V22212, V22222, V33142, V33243, V33333, V33343, V33363, V44424, V44434, V44454, V45434, V45464, V54365, V54565, V55365, V55565.

List 2 - P#V11131, V12131, V12232, V22221, V33143, V33453.

Varieties

2494b	Pair, #2493-2494	1.20

A1860-A1864

1990

	Perf. 11		
2505a A1860	25c pane of 10, *Aug. 17*	5.50	*3.50*
	Never folded pane, P#1-2	15.00	
	Booklet		
BK179 BC62	$5 **multicolored**, P#1, 2	11.00	
	Varieties		
2505b	As "a," black (engr.) omitted	3,250.	
2505c	Strip of 5, Nos. 2501-2505	2.75	1.00
2505d	As "a," horiz. imperf.	—	

A1873

1990

	Perf. 11½		
2514a A1873	25c pane of 10, *Oct. 18*	5.00	*3.25*
	Never folded pane	12.50	
	Booklet		
BK180 BC63	$5 **multicolored**, P#1	10.00	

A1874

1990

	Perf. 11½x11		
2516a A1874	25c pane of 10, *Oct. 18*	5.00	*3.25*
	Never folded pane, P#1211	15.00	
	Booklet		
BK181 BC64	$5 **multicolored**, P#1211	10.00	

No. 2519a — A1875

No. 2520a — A1875

1991

	Perf. 11.2 Bullseye		
2519a A1875	F pane of 10, *Jan. 22*	6.50	*4.50*
	Booklets		
BK182 BC65	($2.90) **yellow & multi**, P#2222	6.50	
BK183 BC65	($5.80) **grn, red & blk**, P#1111, 2121, 2222	13.00	
	P#1222, 2111, 2212	25.00	
	Perf. 11		
2520a A1875	F pane of 10, *Jan. 22*	18.00	*4.50*

Booklet

BK184   BC65   ($2.90) like #BK182, **grn, red & blk**, P#K1111   18.00

Varieties

2520b   As "a," imperf. horiz.   —

A1879

Perf. 11

2527a   A1879   29c pane of 10, *Apr. 5*   5.50   3.50
    Never folded pane, P#K1111   7.50

Booklet

BK185   BC66 $5.80 **multicolored,** P#K1111, K2222, K3333   11.00

Varieties

2527b   As "a," vert. imperf. between   1,500.
2527c   Horiz. pair, imperf. vert.   300.00
2527d   As "a," imperf. horiz.   2,750.

A1880

Perf. 11

2528a   A1880   29c pane of 10, *Apr. 21*   5.25   3.50
    Never folded pane   6.50

Booklets

BK186   BC67 $2.90 **black & multicolored,** P#K11111   5.75
BK186A   BC67A $2.90 **red & multicolored,** P#K11111 (2)   5.75

Varieties

2528b   As "a," horiz. imperf. between   —
2528c   Vert. pair, imperf between   —
2528d   Vert. strip of 3, top pair imperf between   —

No. 2528c comes from the misperfed booklet pane of No. 2528b. No. 2528d resulted from a paper foldover after normal perforating and before cutting into panes. Two No. 2528d are known.

Booklet Covers

When more than one combination of covers exists, the number of possible booklets is noted in parenthesis after the booklet listing.

A1882

1991   Perf. 10

2530a   A1882   19c pane of 10, *May 17*   3.50   2.75
    Never folded pane, P#1111   4.50

Booklet

BK187   BC68 $3.80 **black & blue,** P#1111, 2222   7.00
    P#1222   30.00

A1884

Self-Adhesive
Die Cut

2531Ab   A1884   29c pane of 18, *June 25*, no P#   10.50

By its nature, No. 2531Ab constitutes a complete booklet (BC68A, BC68B). The peelable backing serves as a booklet cover.

Varieties

2531Ac   As "b," no die cutting, pair   —

A1890

1991   Perf. 11

2536a   A1890   29c pane of 10, *May 9*   5.25   3.50
    Never folded pane, P#1111, 1112   7.75

Booklet

BK188   BC69 $5.80 **multicolored,** P#1111, 1112   10.50
    P#1113, 1123, 2223   15.00
    P#1212   40.00

A1899-A1903

Perf. 11

2549a   A1899   29c pane of 5, *May 31*   3.75   2.50
    Never folded pane, P#A23133, A23213   7.50
    P#A11111, A22122, A33213   —
    P#A23124   42.50
    P#A32225, A33233   27.50

Booklet

BK189   BC70 $5.80 **multicolored,** P#A22122, A23123, A23124, A33235, A44446, A45546, A45547   17.50
    P#A11111, A22133, A23133, A23213   47.50
    P#A22132, A32224, A32225, A33233   27.50
    P#A31224

P#33213 has yet to be found as top pane in booklets.

Varieties

2545a   Black omitted, single stamp   —
2546a   Black omitted, single stamp   —
2547a   Black omitted, single stamp   —

A1905

Perf. 11

2552a   A1905   29c pane of 5, *July 2*   2.75   2.25
    Never folded pane, P#A11121111   4.50

Booklet

BK190   BC71 $5.80 **multicolored,** P#A11111111, A11121111   10.50

A1916-A1920

2566a   A1916   29c pane of 10, *Aug. 29*   5.50   3.50
    Never folded pane, P#1   7.00

Booklet

BK191   BC72 $5.80 **scar, blk & brt vio,** P#1, 2   11.00

Varieties

2566b   As "a," scar & brt violet (engr.) omitted   750.00
2566c   Strip of 5, Nos. 2562-2566   2.50

A1922-A1931

2577a   A1922   29c pane of 10, *Oct. 1*   5.50   3.50
    Never folded pane, P#111111   7.50

Booklet

BK192   BC73 $5.80 **blue, black & red,** P#111111   11.50
    P#111112   15.00

A1933

2578a	A1933	(29c) pane of 10, *Oct. 17*	5.50	*3.25*
		Never folded pane	7.50	

Booklet

BK193	BC74	($5.80) **multicolored,** P#1	11.00

Varieties

2578b		As "a," single, red & black (engr.) omitted	3,500.

A1934

2581b	A1934	(29c) pane, 2 each, #2580, 2581, *Oct. 17*	7.50	*1.25*
		Never bound pane, P#A11111	11.00	
2582a	A1935	(29c) pane of 4, *Oct. 17*	2.00	*1.25*
		Never bound pane, P#A11111	3.50	
2583a	A1936	(29c) pane of 4, *Oct. 17*	2.00	*1.25*
		Never bound pane, P#A11111	3.50	
2584a	A1937	(29c) pane of 4, *Oct. 17*	2.00	*1.25*
		Never bound pane, P#A11111	3.50	
2585a	A1938	(29c) pane of 4, *Oct. 17*	2.00	*1.25*
		Never bound pane, P#A11111	3.50	

Combination Booklet

BK194	BC75	($5.80) **multicolored,** 1 each #2581b, 2582a-2585a, P#A11111, A12111	17.50

Varieties

2581a		Pair, Nos. 2580-2581	3.50	.25

For illustrations A1935-A1938 see regular listings. Panes are similar to A1934.
Nos. 2581b-2585a are unfolded panes.

A1946

1992-94   **Perf. 10**

2593a	A1946	29c **black & multi,** pane of 10, *Sept. 8*	5.25	*4.25*
		Never folded pane, P#1111	6.50	

Booklets

BK195	BC76	$2.90 **blue & red,** P#1111, 2222	5.25
BK196	BC76	$5.80 **blue & red,** P#1111, 2222	10.50
		P#1211, 2122	—

Perf. 11x10

2593Bc	A1946	29c **black & multi,** pane of 10, shiny gum, *1993*	5.50	*4.25*
		Low gloss gum	5.50	

Booklet

BK197	BC76	$5.80 **blue & red,** P#1111, 1211, 2122, 2222, 2232, 3333	17.00
		P#2333	—
		P#4444	45.00
2594a	A1946	29c **red & multi,** pane of 10, *1993*	5.25	*4.25*
		Never folded pane	6.50	

Booklet

BK198	BC76	$2.90 **black, red & blue,** P#K1111	5.25
BK199	BC76	$5.80 **multicolored,** *1994,* P#K1111	10.50

Varieties

2594b		Imperf, pair	900.00

A1947

Self-adhesive

Die Cut

2595a	A1947	29c **brown & multi,** pane of 17 + label, *Sept. 25,* P#B1111-1, B1111-2, B3434-1	13.00	
		P#B2222-1, B2222-2, B3333-1, B3333-3, B3434-3, B4344-1, B4444-1, B4444-3	25.00	
		P#B4344-3	350.00	

Varieties

2595b		Pair, no die cutting	225.00
2595c		Brown omitted, single	475.00
2595d		As "a," no die cutting	1,800.
2596a	A1947	29c **green & multi,** pane of 17 + label, *Sept. 25, 1992,* P#D11111, D21221, D22232, D32322	12.00
		P#D32332, D43352, D43452, D43453, D54563, D54571, D54573, D65784	15.00
		P#D32342, D42342	35.00
		P#D54561, D54673, D61384	20.00
2597a	A1947	29c **red & multi,** pane of 17 + label, *Sept. 25,* P#S1111	10.00

By their nature, Nos. 2595a-2597a constitute complete booklets (BC77). A peelable paper backing serves as a booklet cover for each. No. 2595a has a black and multicolored backing with serifed type. No. 2596a has a blue and multicolored backing, No. 2597a a black and multicolored backing with unserifed type.

A1950

Self-Adhesive   *Die Cut*

2598a	A1950	29c pane of 18, *Feb. 4, 1994,* P#M111, M112	10.00

By its nature, No. 2598a constitutes a complete booklet (BC78). The peelable backing serves as a booklet cover.

A1951

2599a	A1951	29c pane of 18, *June 24, 1994,* P#D1111, D1212	10.00

By its nature, No. 2599a constitutes a complete booklet (BC79). The peelable backing serves as a booklet cover.

A1994-A1998

1992

2646a	A1994	29c pane of 5, *June 15*	2.75	*2.25*
		Never folded pane, P#A2212112, A2212122, A2222222	3.75	
		P#A1111111, A2212222	10.00	

Booklet

BK201	BC80	$5.80 **multicolored,** P#A1111111, A2212112, A2212222, A2222222	11.00
		P#A2212122	17.00

2709a	A2057	29c pane of 5, *Oct. 1*	2.50	*2.00*
		Never folded pane	3.50	

A2057-A2061

Booklet

BK202	BC83	$5.80 **multicolored,** P#K1111	11.00

Varieties

2709b		As "a," imperf.	3,000.

A2062

| 2710a | A2062 | 29c pane of 10, *Oct. 22* | 5.25 | *3.50* |
| | | Never folded pane | 6.25 | |

Booklet

| BK202A | BC83A | $5.80 **multicolored**, P#1 | 11.00 |

A2063-A2066

2718a	A2063	29c pane of 4, *Oct. 22*	2.25	*1.25*
		Never bound pane,		
		P#A111111, A222222	3.50	
		P#A112211	—	

Booklet

| BK203 | BC84 | $5.80 **multi**, P#A111111, | |
| | | A112211, A222222 | 11.00 |

Varieties

| 2718b | | As "a," imperf. horiz. | — |
| 2718c | | As "a," imperf. | — |

A2064

Self-Adhesive
Die Cut

| 2719a | A2064 | 29c **multicolored**, pane of 18, *Oct.* | |
| | | *29*, P#V11111 | 11.00 |

By its nature, No. 2719a constitutes a complete booklet (BC85). The peelable paper backing serves as a booklet cover.

A2071, A2075-A2077

Tab format on No. 2737a is similar to that shown for No. 2737b.

1993

2737a	A2071	29c pane of 8, 2 #2731, 1 each		
		#2732-2737, *June 16*	4.25	*2.25*
		Never folded pane,		
		P#A22222	5.50	
		P#A13113	—	
2737b	A2071	29c pane of 4, #2731, 2735-		
		2737 + tab, *June 16*	2.25	*1.50*
		Never folded pane,		
		P#A22222	3.25	
		P#A13113	—	

Combination Booklet

BK204	BC86	$5.80 **multicolored**, 2 #2737a, +	
		1 #2737b, P#A11111,	
		A22222	11.00
		P#A13113, A44444	14.00

No. 2737b without tab is indistinguishable from broken No. 2737a.
Never folded panes of No. 2737a with P#A11111 exist missing one stamp.

A2086-A2090

2745a	A2086	29c pane of 5, *Jan. 25*	2.50	*2.25*
		Never folded pane, P#1111,		
		1211	3.50	
		P#2222	6.00	

Booklet

| BK207 | BC89 | $5.80 **multi**, P#1111, 1211, 2222 | 11.00 |

A2105-A2109

| 2764a | A2105 | 29c pane of 5, *May 15* | 2.50 | *2.00* |
| | | Never folded pane, P#1 | 3.75 | |

Booklet

| BK208 | BC90 | $5.80 **multicolored**, P#1, 2 | 11.00 |

Varieties

| 2764b | | As "a," black (engr.) omitted | 300.00 |
| 2764c | | As "a," imperf. | 2,500. |

Booklet

| BK208a | | As #BK208, with 4 #2764b | 1,200. |

A2069, A2112-A2114

2770a	A2069	29c pane of 4, *July 14*	2.50	*2.00*
		Never folded pane,		
		P#A11111, A11121,		
		A22222	3.50	

Booklet

BK209	BC91	$5.80 **multicolored**, P#A11111,	
		A11121, A22222, A23232,	
		A23233	11.00

A2070, A2115-A2117

2778a	A2070	29c pane of 4, *Sept. 25, 1993*	2.50	*2.00*
		Never folded pane,		
		P#A222222	3.50	

Booklet

BK210	BC92	$5.80 **multicolored**,	
		P#A111111, A222222,	
		A333333, A422222	11.00
		P#A333323	—

Varieties

| 2778b | | As "a," imperf. | — |

A2128

2790a	A2128	29c pane of 4, *Oct. 21, 1993*	2.25	*1.75*
		Never bound pane,		
		P#K111111, K133333,		
		K144444	3.25	
		P#K255555	85.00	

Booklet

BK211	BC93	$5.80 **multicolored**, P#K111111,	
		K133333, K144444,	
		K255555, K266666	11.50
		P#K222222	35.00

Varieties

| 2790b | | Imperf., pair | — |
| 2790c | | As "a," imperf. | — |

No. 2798a
A2129-A2132

2798a	A2129	29c pane of 10, 3 each #2795-2796, 2 each #2797-2798, Oct. 21, 1993	5.00	4.00
		Never folded pane, P#111111	6.25	
2798b	A2129	29c pane of 10, 3 each #2797-2798, 2 each #2795-2796, Oct. 21, 1993	5.00	4.00
		Never folded pane, P#111111	6.25	

Combination Booklet

BK212	BC94	$5.80 **multicolored,** 1 each #2798a, 2798b, P#111111, 222222	11.00

Varieties

2798c		Block of 4, Nos. 2795-2798	2.00 1.75

On No. 2798b the plate number appears close to the top row of perfs. Different selvage markings can be found there.

A2129-A2132

A2131

Self-Adhesive **Die Cut**

2802a	A2129	29c pane of 3 each #2799-2802, Oct. 28, 1993, P#V1111111, V2221222, V2222112, V2222122, V2222221, V2222222	7.00	
		P#V3333333	9.00	
2803a	A2131	29c pane of 18, Oct. 28, 1993, P#V1111, V2222	10.00	

Varieties

2802c		Block of 4, Nos. 2799-2802	2.00

By their nature, Nos. 2802a-2803a constitute complete booklets (BC95-BC96). The peelable backing serves as a booklet cover.

K111 A2135

2806b	A2135	29c pane of 5, Dec. 1, 1993	2.50	2.00
		Never folded pane	3.75	

Booklet

BK213	BC97	$2.90 **black & red,** P#K111	5.75

A2142

1994 **Self-Adhesive** **Die Cut**

2813a	A2142	29c pane of 18, Jan. 27, P#, see list	11.00
		P#B111-5, B333-14, B434-10	100.00
		P#B121-5, B444-7, B444-8, B444-9, B444-14	15.00
		P#B221-5, B444-16	19.00
		P#B333-5, B333-7, B333-8	22.50
		P#B334-11	
		P#B344-11	45.00

By its nature, No. 2813a constitutes a complete booklet (BC98). The peelable backing serves as a booklet cover.
List - #B111-1, B111-2, B111-3, B111-4, B222-4, B222-5, B222-6, B333-9, B333-10, B333-11, B333-12, B333-17, B344-12, B344-13, B444-10, B444-15, B444-17, B444-18, B444-19, B555-20, B555-21.

A2143

2814a	A2143	29c pane of 10, Feb. 14, 1994	5.50	3.50
		Never folded pane, P#A11111	6.00	

Booklet

BK214	BC99	$5.80 **multicolored,** P#A11111, A11311, A12112, A12122, A22122, A22322	11.00
		P#A12111, A12211, A12212, A21311	25.00
		P#A22222	16.00

Varieties

2814b		As #2814a, imperf	—
2814e		Horiz. pair, imperf between	—

A2158-A2162

2833a	A2158	29c pane of 5, Apr. 28, 1994	2.50	—
		Never folded pane, P#2	3.00	

Booklet

BK215	BC100	$5.80 **multicolored,** P#1, 2	11.00

Varieties

2833b		As "a," imperf	2,500.
2833c		As "a," black (engr.) omitted	350.00

Booklet

BK215a		As #BK215, with 4 #2833c	1,400.

A2171-2175

2847a	A2171	29c pane of 5, July 28, 1994	2.50	2.00
		Never folded pane	3.50	

Booklet

BK216	BC101	$5.80 **multicolored,** P#S11111	11.00

Varieties

2847b		As "a," imperf	—

A2200

2871Ab	A2200	29c pane of 10, Oct. 20, 1994	5.25	3.50
		Never folded pane, P#1, 2	6.00	

Booklet

BK217	BC102	$5.80 **multicolored,** P#1, 2	11.00

Varieties

2871Ac		As "b," imperf.	—

A2201

2872a	A2201	29c pane of 20, Oct. 20, 1994	10.50	3.00
		Never folded pane, P#P11111, P22222, P44444	12.00	
		P#P33333	—	

Booklet

BK218	BC103	$5.80 **multicolored,** P#P11111, P22222, P33333, P44444	10.50

Varieties

2872c		As "a," imperf. horiz.	—

A2202

2873a A2202   29c pane of 12, *Oct. 20, 1994,*
P#V1111   6.25

By is nature, No. 2873a constitutes a complete booklet
(BC104). The peelable backing serves as a booklet cover.

A2203

2874a A2203   29c pane of 18, *Oct. 20, 1994,*
P#V1111, V2222   9.50

By its nature, No. 2874a constitutes a complete booklet
(BC105). The peelable backing serves as a booklet cover.

A2208

1994   **Perf. 11.2x11.1**
2881a A2208   (32c) **black "G" & multi,** pane
of 10, *Dec. 13, 1994*   6.00   3.75
Booklet
BK219 BC106 ($3.20) **pale blue & red,** P#1111   6.00
    Perf. 10x9.9
2883a A2208   (32c) **black "G" & multi,** pane
of 10, *Dec. 13, 1994*   6.25   3.75
Booklets
BK220 BC106 ($3.20) **pale blue & red,** P#1111,
2222   6.25
BK221 BC106 ($6.40) **blue & red,** P#1111,
2222   12.50
    Perf. 10.9
2884a A2208   (32c) **blue "G" & multi,** pane
of 10, *Dec. 13, 1994*   6.00   3.75
Booklet
BK222 BC106 ($6.40) **blue "G" & multi,**
P#A1111, A1211,
A2222, A3333, A4444   12.00

No. BK222 exists with panes that have different plate
numbers.

    Varieties
2884b   As "a," imperf.   —
    Perf. 11x10.9
2885a A2208   (32c) **red "G" & multi,** pane of
10, *Dec. 13, 1994*   6.50   3.75

    Booklet
BK223 BC106 ($6.40) **red "G" & multi,**
P#K1111   13.00
    Varieties
2885b   Pair, imperf vert.   —
2885c   Pair, imperf between   —

No. 2885c resulted from a paper foldover after perforating
and before cutting into panes.

No. 2886a
A2208b

No.
2887a
A2208c

    Self-Adhesive   **Die Cut**
2886a A2208b (32c) pane of 18, *Dec. 13, 1994,*
P#V11111, V22222   11.50
2887a A2208c (32c) pane of 18, *Dec. 13, 1994,*
no P#   11.50

By their nature, Nos. 2886a and 2887a constitute complete
booklets (BC107). The peelable backing serves as a booklet
cover. The backing on No. 2886a contains a UPC symbol, while
the backing on No. 2887a does not.

A2212

    Perf. 10.8x9.8
2916a A2212   32c **blue, tan, brown, red &**
light blue, pane of 10,
May 19, 1995   6.00   3.25
Never folded pane,
P#11111   6.75
    Booklets
BK225 BC108 $3.20 **blue & red,** P#11111,
22222, 33332
P#23222, 44444   6.00   —
BK226 BC108 $6.40 **multicolored,** P#11111,
22222, 23222, 33332,
44444   12.00
    Varieties
2916b   As "a," imperf.   —

A2230

    Self-Adhesive   **Die Cut**
2919a A2230   32c pane of 18, *Mar. 17,*
1995, P#V1111, V1311,
V1433, V2111, V2222,
V2322   11.00
    Varieties
2919b   Vert. pair, no die cutting
between   —

By its nature No. 2919a is a complete booklet (BC113). The
peelable backing serves as a booklet cover.

Nos.
2920a,
2920c
A2212

    Serpentine Die Cut 8.7 on 2 or 3 Sides
    Self-Adhesive
2920a A2212   32c pane of 20+label, large
date, *Apr. 18, 1995* (see
List 1)   12.00
P#V23422   25.00
P#V23522   40.00
P#V57663   —
2920c A2212   32c pane of 20+label, small
date, *Apr. 18, 1995,*
P#V11111   110.00
    Varieties
2920g   As "a," partial pane of 10, 3 stamps and
parts of 7 stamps printed on backing
liner   —

By their nature Nos. 2920a, 2920c are complete booklets
(BC114). The rouletted peelable backing, of which two types
are known, serves as a booklet cover.

Date on No. 2920a is nearly twice as large as date on No.
2920c.

    List 1 - P#V12211, V12212, V12312, V12321, V12322,
V12331, V13322, V13831, V13834, V13836, V22211, V23322,
V23432, V34743, V34745, V36743, V42556, V45554, V56663,
V56665, V56763, V65976, V78989.

Nos. 2920f,
2920h — A2212

    Serpentine Die Cut 8.7
    Self-Adhesive
2920f A2212   32c pane of 15+label   9.00
2920h A2212   32c pane of 15, see note, *1996*   9.00

Booklets

BK226A	BC126	**$4.80 blue,** 1 #2920f, no P#	9.00
BK226B	BC126	**$4.80 blue,** 1 #2920h, no P#	13.00
BK227	BC126	**$9.60 blue,** 2 #2920f	18.00

No. 2920h is a pane of 16 with one stamp removed. The missing stamp is the lower right stamp in the pane. No. 2920h cannot be made from No. 2920f, a pane of 15 + label. The label is located in the second or third row of the pane and is die cut. If the label is removed, an impression of the die cutting appears on the backing paper.

No. 2920De — A2212

Serpentine Die Cut 11.3
Self-Adhesive

2920De	A2212	32c pane of 10, *Jan. 20, 1996*	6.00

By its nature No. 2920De is a complete booklet (BC114). The rouletted peelable backing serves as a booklet cover.

Below is a list of known plate numbers. Some numbers may be scarcer than the value indicated in the listing.

No. 2920De - P#V11111, V12111, V23222, V31121, V32111, V32121, V44322, V44333, V44444, V55555, V66666, V66886, V67886, V68886, V68896, V76989, V77666, V77668, V77766, V78698, V78886, V78896, V78898, V78986, V78989, V89999.

Nos. 2921a, 2921c, 2921d — A2212

Serpentine Die Cut 9.8
Self-Adhesive

2921a	A2212	32c pane of 10, dated red "1996," *May 21, 1996*	6.00
		Never folded pane, P#21221, 22221, 22222	7.00
2921c	A2212	32c pane of 10, dated red "1997," *May 21, 1996*	6.00
2921d	A2212	32c pane of 5 + label, dated red "1997," *Jan. 24, 1997*	3.25
		Never folded pane, P#11111	4.00

Combination Booklet

BK227A	BC108	**$4.80 multicolored,** 1 ea #2921c-2921d P#11111	10.00

Booklets

BK228	BC108	**$6.40 blue, red & black,** 2 #2921a (5)	12.00

Known numbers for BK228. Some numbers may be scarcer than the value indicated in the listing. P#11111, 13111, 21221, 22221, 22222, 44434, 44444, 55555, 55556, 66666, 77777, 88788, 88888, 99999.

BK228A	BC108	**$9.60 multicolored,** 3 #2921c, P#11111	20.00

Varieties

2921e		As "a," imperf.	—

Booklet

BK228b		As #BK228, with 2 #2921e, P#11111	—

A2264

Self-Adhesive — Die Cut

2949a	A2264	(32c) pane of 20 + label, *Feb. 1, 1995*, P#B1111-1, B2222-1, B2222-2, B3333-2	12.00

By its nature, No. 2949a is a complete booklet (BC115). The peelable backing serves as a booklet cover.

Varieties

2949b		As "a," red (engr.) omitted, single stamp	—
2949c		As "a," red (engr.) omitted	—

A2272

Perf. 9.8x10.8

2959a	A2272	32c pane of 10, *May 12, 1995*	6.00 3.25
		Never folded pane	6.25

Booklet

BK229	BC116	**$6.40 multicolored,** P#1	12.00

Varieties

2959b		As "a," Imperf.	—

A2274

Self-Adhesive — Die Cut

2960a	A2274	55c pane of 20 + label, *May 12, 1995*, P#B1111-1, B2222-1	22.50

By its nature, No. 2960a is a complete booklet (BC117). The peelable backing serves as a booklet cover.

A2283-A2287

2973a	A2283	32c pane of 5, *June 17, 1995*	3.00 2.75
		Never folded pane	3.50

Booklet

BK230	BC118	**$6.40 multicolored,** P#S11111	12.00

A2306-A2310

2997a	A2306	32c pane of 5, *Sept. 19, 1995*	3.00 2.25
		Never folded pane	4.00

Booklet

BK231	BC119	**$6.40 multicolored,** P#2	12.00

Varieties

2997b		As "a," imperf.	—

A2316

3003Ab	A2316	32c pane of 10, *Oct. 19, 1995*	6.00 4.00
		Never folded pane	7.00

Booklet

BK232	BC120	**$6.40 multicolored,** P#1	12.00

A2317-A2320

3007b	A2317	32c pane of 10, 3 each #3004-3005, 2 each #3006-3007, *Sept. 30, 1995*	6.00 4.00
		Never folded pane, P#P1111	7.00
3007c	A2317	32c pane of 10, 2 each #3004-3005, 3 each #3006-3007, *Sept. 30, 1995*	6.00 4.00
		Never folded pane, P#P1111	7.00

Combination Booklet

BK233	BC121	**$6.40 multicolored,** 1 each #3007b, 3007c, P#P1111, P2222	12.00

A2317-A2320

Serpentine Die Cut

3011a A2317   32c pane of 20 +label, *Sept. 30, 1995*   12.00

By is nature, No. 3011a is a complete booklet (BC122). The peelable backing serves as a booklet cover.
P#V1111, V1211, V1212, V3233, V3333, V4444.

No. 3012a
A2321

Serpentine Die Cut

3012a A2321   32c pane of 20 + label, *Oct. 19, 1995*, P#B1111, B2222, B3333   12.00

By its nature, No. 3012a is a complete booklet (BC123). The peelable backing serves as a booklet cover.

3012c A2321   32c pane of 15 + label, *1996*, no P#   9.00
3012d A2321   32c pane of 15, see note, *1996*   —

Booklets

BK233A	BC126	$4.80 blue, #3012c (2)	9.00
BK233B	BC126	$4.80 blue, #3012d	
BK233C	BC126	$9.60 blue 2 #3012c (2)	18.00
BK233D	BC126	$9.60 blue, 2 #3012d, no P# (3)	18.00

Combination Booklet

BK233E BC126 $9.60 blue, 1 ea #3012c, 3012d (2)   35.00

Varieties

3012b   Vert. pair, no die cutting between   —

Colors of No. 3012c are deeper than those on #3012a. Label on #3012c has die-cutting, not found on label of #3012a.
No. 3012d is a pane of 16 with one stamp removed. No. 3012d cannot be made from No. 3012c, a pane of 15 + label. The label is die cut. If the label is removed, an impression of the die cutting appears on the backing paper.

A2322

Die Cut

3013a A2322 32c Pane of 18, *Oct. 19, 1995*, P#V1111   11.00

By its nature, No. 3013a is a complete booklet (BC124). The peelable backing serves as a booklet cover.

A2329-A2333

3029a A2329   32c pane of 5, *Jan. 19, 1996*   3.00 2.50
Never folded pane   3.50

Booklet

BK234 BC125 $6.40 multicolored, P#1   12.00

Varieties

3029b   As "a," imperf.   —

No.
3030a
A2334

Serpentine Die Cut 11.3

3030a A2334   32c pane of 20+label, *Jan. 20, 1996*   12.00

By its nature, No. 3030a is a complete booklet (BC115). The peelable backing serves as a booklet cover.
P#B1111-1, B1111-2, B2222-1, B2222-2.

3030b A2334   32c pane of 15+label, *1996*   9.00

Booklet

BK235	BC126	$4.80 blue (4)	9.00
BK236	BC126	$9.60 blue (3)	18.00

A1847

Serpentine Die Cut 10.4x10.8

3048a A1847   20c pane of 10, *Aug. 2, 1996*, P#S1111, S2222   4.00

By is nature, No. 3048a is a complete booklet (BC128). The peelable backing serves as a booklet cover.

3048b A1847   20c Booklet pane of 4   1.60
3048c A1847   20c Booklet pane of 6   2.40

Nos. 3048b-3048c are from the vending machine booklet, No. BK237, that has a glue strip at the top edge of the top pane, the peelable strip removed and the rouletting line 2mm lower than on No. 3048a.

Booklet

BK237 BC128 $2.00 multicolored, 1 ea #3048b, 3048c, P#S1111 4.00

A1853

Serpentine Die Cut 11.3x11.7

3049a A1853   32c pane of 20, *Oct. 24, 1996*, P#S1111, S2222, S3333   12.00

By its nature, No. 3049a is a complete booklet (BC61B). The peelable backing, of which three types are known, serves as a booklet cover.

3049b A1853   32c pane of 4, *Dec. 1996*, no P#   2.75
3049c A1853   32c pane of 5 + label, *Dec. 1996*, P#S1111   3.20
3049d A1853   32c pane of 6, *Dec. 1996*, with or without P#   3.60

Combination Booklet

BK241 BC129 $4.80 multicolored, 1 ea #3049b-3049d, P#S1111   10.00

Booklet

BK242 BC129 $9.60 multicolored, 5 #3049d, P#S1111   18.00

The backing on Nos. BK241-BK242 is rouletted between each pane.
P# on Nos. 3049c-3049d is on a stamp, not the removable strip.

Varieties

3049c	P# single, #S1111	.80	1.00
3049d	P# single, #S1111	.80	1.00

The plate # single in No. 3049c is on the lower left stamp. In No. 3049d it is the lower right stamp on the bottom pane of the booklet.

A2350

1998   Serpentine Die Cut 11.2

3050a A2350   20c pane of 10, *July 31, 1998*, P#V1111, V2222, V2232, V2333, V2342, V2343, V3232, V3233, V3243, V3333   4.00

By its nature, No. 3050a is a complete booklet (BC130). The peelable backing serves as a booklet cover.

A2350

3052a-3052c — A2351

3052d — A2351

No.
3052Ef
A2351

1999

Serpentine Die Cut 10½x11 on 3 Sides
Self-Adhesive

3051b	A2350	20c pane, 4 #3051, 1 #3051a turned sideways at top, *July 1999*	2.00
3051c	A2350	20c pane, 4 #3051, 1 #3051a turned sideways at bottom, *July 1999*	2.00

BOOKLET

BK242A	BC130	$2.00 **multicolored**, #3051b, 3051c, P#V1111, *July 1999*	4.00

Serpentine Die Cut 11½x11¼

3052a	A2351	33c pane of 4, no P#	2.60
3052b	A2351	33c pane of 5 + label, no P#	3.25
3052c	A2351	33c pane of 6	3.90
3052d	A2351	33c pane of 20 + label, P#S222	13.00

COMBINATION BOOKLET

BK242B	BC131	$4.95 **multicolored**, 1 each #3052a-3052c, P#S111, *Aug. 13, 1999*	9.75

No. BK242B has a self-adhesive strip on #3052b that adheres to the plastic-coated peelable backing of #3052a when the booklet is closed. When the booklet is opened, this strip is sticky and my adhere firmly to mounts, album pages, etc. Removal of this strip will damage the backing paper of #3052b. Plate numbers for No. BK242B are on backing paper below bar code.

No. 3052d is a complete booklet (BC131). The peelable backing serves as a booklet cover.

Serpentine Die Cut 10¾x10½ on 2 or 3 Sides
2000

3052Ef	A2351	33c pane of 20, *Apr. 7, 2000*, P#S111	13.00

By its nature, No. 3052Ef is a complete booklet. Eight #3052E and the booklet cover (similar to BC131) are printed on one side of the peelable backing and twelve #3052E appear on the other side of the backing.

3071a
A2370

Serpentine Die Cut 9.9x10.8

3071a	A2370	32c pane of 20, *May 31, 1996*, P#S11111	12.00

Varieties

3071b	Horiz. pair, no die cutting between	—
3071c	Imperf, pair	—
3071d	Horiz. pair, inperf vert.	—

By its nature, No. 3071a is a complete booklet (BC127). The peelable backing serves as a booklet cover.

A2387

Serpentine Die Cut 11.6x11.4

3089a	A2387	32c pane of 20, *Aug. 1, 1996*, P#B1111	12.00

By its nature, No. 3089a is a complete booklet (BC133). The peelable backing serves as a booklet cover.

A2405

Serpentine Die Cut 10 on 2, 3 or 4 Sides

3112a	A2405	32c pane of 20 + label, *Nov. 1, 1996*	12.00

Varieties

3112b	No die cutting, pair	75.00
3112c	As "a," no die cutting	—

By its nature No. 3112a is a complete booklet (BC134). The peelable backing serves as a booklet cover.

Below is a list of known plate numbers. Some numbers may be scarcer than the value indicated in the listing.

P#1111-1, 1211-1, 2212-1, 2222-1, 2323-1, 3323-1, 3333-1, 3334-1, 4444-1, 5544-1, 5555-1, 5556-1, 5556-2, 5656-2, 6656-2, 6666-1, 6666-2, 6766-1, 7887-1, 7887-2, 7888-2, 7988-2.

A2406-2409

Serpentine Die Cut 11.8x11.5 on 2, 3 or 4 Sides

3116a	A2406	32c pane of 20 + label, *Oct. 8, 1996*, P#B1111, B2222, B3333	12.00

Varieties

3116b	As "a," no die cutting	—

By its nature No. 3116a is a complete booklet (BC135). The peelable backing serves as a booklet cover.

A2410

Die Cut

3117a	A2410	32c pane of 18, *Oct. 8, 1996*, P#V1111, V2111	11.00

By its nature No. 3117a is a complete booklet (BC136). The peelable backing serves as a booklet cover.

MAKESHIFT VENDING MACHINE BOOKLETS

The booklets listed below were released in 1996 to meet the need for $4.80 and $9.60 vending machine booklets. The booklets consist of blocks of sheet stamps folded and affixed to a standard cover (BC126) with a spot of glue.

The cover varies from issue to issue in the line of text on the front that indicates the number of stamps contained in the booklet and in the four lines of text on the back that describe the contents of the booklet and list the booklet's item number. Due to the folding required to make stamps fit within the covers, the stamp blocks may easily fall apart when booklets are opened. Stamps may also easily detach from booklet cover.

1996

Booklets

BK243	BC126	$4.80	**blue**, 15 #2897	9.00
BK244	BC126	$4.80	**blue**, 15 #2957	9.00
BK245	BC126	$4.80	**blue**, 15 #3024	9.00
BK246	BC126	$4.80	**blue**, 15 #3065	9.00
BK247	BC126	$4.80	**blue**, 15 #3069	9.00
BK248	BC126	$4.80	**blue**, 15 #3070	9.00
BK249	BC126	$4.80	**blue**, 3 #3076a	9.00
BK250	BC126	$4.80	**blue**, 15 #3082	9.00
BK251	BC126	$4.80	**blue**, 15(#3083-3086)	9.00
BK252	BC126	$4.80	**blue**, 15 #3087	9.00
BK253	BC126	$4.80	**blue**, 15 #3088	9.00
BK254	BC126	$9.60	**blue**, 30 #3090	18.00
BK255	BC126	$4.80	**blue**, 3 #3095a	9.00
BK256	BC126	$4.80	**blue**, #3105a-3105o	9.00
BK257	BC126	$4.80	**blue**, 15 #3107	9.00
BK258	BC126	$4.80	**blue**, 15 #3118	9.00

The contents of #BK251 may vary.
See Nos. BK266-BK269, BK272-BK274, BK277-BK278.

No.
3122a
A1951

1997
Serpentine Die Cut 11

3122a   A1951   32c pane of 20 + label, *Feb. 1*, P#V111, V1211, V1311, V2122, V2222, V2311, V2331, V3233, V3333, V3513, V4532   12.00

Varieties
3122h   As "a," no die cutting   —

By it nature, No. 3122a is a complete booklet (BC79). The peelable backing, of which three types are known, serves as a booklet cover.

3122b   A1951   32c pane of 4, *Feb. 1*, no P#   2.50
3122c   A1951   32c pane of 5 + label, *Feb. 1*, P#V1111   3.20
3122d   A1951   32c pane of 6, *Feb. 1*, with or without P#   3.60

Varieties
3122c   P# single, #V1111   .80   1.00
3122d   P# single, #V1111   .80   1.00

The plate # single in No. 3122c is the lower left stamp and should be collected unused with the reorder label to its right to differentiate it from the plate # single in No. 3122d which is the lower left stamp in the bottom pane of the booklet and should be collected with a normal stamp adjoining it at right. In used condition, these plate # singles are indistinguishable.

Serpentine Die Cut 11.5x11.8 on 2, 3 or 4 Sides
3122Ef   A1951   32c pane of 20 + label, P#V1111, V1211, V2122, V2222   35.00
3122Eg   A1951   32c pane of 6, *1997*, with or without P#   5.50

By its nature, No. 3122Ef is a complete booklet (BC79). The peelable backing serves as a booklet cover.

Combination Booklet
BK259   BC79 $4.80 **multicolored**, 1 ea #3122b-3122d, P#V1111   9.50

Booklets
BK260   BC79 $9.60 **multicolored**, 5 #3122d, P#V1111   18.00
BK260A   BC79 $9.60 **multicolored**, 5 #3122Eg   27.50

The backing on Nos. BK259-BK260 is rouletted between each pane.

Varieties
3122Eg   P# single, #V1111   1.25   1.25

The plate # single in No. 3122Eg is the lower left stamp in the bottom pane of the booklet.

A2415

1997
Serpentine Die Cut 11.8x11.6 on 2, 3 or 4 Sides
3123a   A2415   32c pane of 20 + label, *Feb. 4*, P#B1111, B2222, B3333, B4444, B5555, B6666, B7777   12.00

Serpentine Die Cut 11.6x11.8 on 2, 3 or 4 Sides
3124a   A2416   55c pane of 20 + label, *Feb. 4*, P#B1111, B2222, B3333, B4444   21.00

By their nature, Nos. 3123a-3124a are complete booklets (BC137). The peelable backing serves as a booklet cover.

Varieties
3123b   No die cutting, pair   250.00
3123c   As "a," no die cutting   —
3123d   As "a," black omitted   —

No. 3127a — A2418-A2419

No. 3128b,
3129b
A2418-A2419

Serpentine Die Cut 10.9x10.2 on 2,3 or 4 Sides
1997
3127a   A2418   32c pane of 20, 10 ea #3126-3127 + label, *Mar. 3*, P#S11111, S22222, S33333   12.00

By its nature, No. 3127a is a complete booklet (BC138). The peelable backing serves as a booklet cover.

See Footnote
3128b   A2419   32c pane of 5, 2 ea #3128-3129, 1 #3128a, *Mar. 3*, P#S11111   3.00
3129b   A2419   32c pane of 5, 2 ea #3128-3129, 1 #3129a, *Mar. 3*, no P#   3.00

Combination Booklet
BK261   BC138 $4.80 2 #3128b, 1 #3129b, P#S11111   9.00

Varieties
3127b   Pair, Nos. 3126-3127   1.20
3129c   Pair, Nos. 3128-3129   1.20

Nos. 3128-3129 are serpentine die cut 11.2x10.8 on 2 or 3 sides. Nos. 3128a-3129a are placed sideways on the pane and are serpentine die cut 11.2 on top and bottom, 10.8 on left side. The right side is 11.2 broken by a large perf where the stamp meets the vertical perforations of the two stamps above it.

A2425

1997, May 22
Serpentine Die Cut 11
Self-Adhesive
3137   A2425   32c pane of 10, Nos. 3137b, 3137c, no P#   6.00
3137b   A2425   32c pane of 9, no P#   5.40
3137c   A2425   32c pane of 1, no P#   .60

Varieties
Pane of 10 from uncut press sheet   65.00
Pane of 10 with plate #   350.00

Die cutting on #3137 does not extend through the backing paper.

3138   A2425   32c pane of 10, Nos. 3138b, 3138c, no P#   125.00
3138b   A2425   32c pane of 9, no P#   —

Imperf
3138c   A2425   32c pane of 1, no P#   —

Die cutting on #3138b extends through the backing paper.
By their nature, Nos. 3137-3138 are complete booklets (BC139). The peelable backing serves as a booklet cover.

3176a — A2459

Serpentine Die Cut 9.9 on 2, 3 or 4 Sides
1997, Oct. 27   Tagged
3176a   A2459   32c pane of 20+label, P#1111, 2222, 3333   12.00

By its nature, No. 3176a is a complete booklet (BC140). The peelable backing serves as a booklet cover.

3177a — A2460

Serpentine Die Cut 11.2x11.8 on 2, 3 or 4 Sides
1997, Oct. 30   **Tagged**
Self-Adhesive

3177a	A2460	32c pane of 20 + label, P#B1111, B2222, B3333	12.00

By its nature No. 3177a is a complete booklet (BC141). The peelable backing serves as a booklet cover.

3177b	A2460	32c Booklet pane of 4, no P#	2.50
3177c	A2460	32c Booklet pane of 5 + label, no P#	3.00
3177d	A2460	32c Booklet pane of 6, no P# or P#B1111	3.75

Combination Booklet

BK264	BC141	$4.80 **black & green**, 1 ea #3177b-3177d, P#B1111	9.25

Booklet

BK265	BC141	$9.60 **black & green**, 5 #3177d, P#B1111	19.00

Panes in Nos. BK264-BK265 are separated by rouletting between each pane.

MAKESHIFT VENDING MACHINE BOOKLETS
See note before No. BK243.

1997

BK266	BC126	$4.80 #3151a-3151o	9.00
BK267	BC126	$4.80 15 #3152	9.00
BK268	BC126	$4.80 15 #3153	9.00
BK269	BC126	$4.80 3 ea #3168-3172	9.00

A2487

1998, Apr. 27   *Serpentine Die Cut 11.1*
Self-Adhesive

3204	A2487	32c Pane of 10, 1 each #3204b, 3204c	6.00
3204b	A2487	32c Pane of 9, no P#	5.40
3204c	A2487	32c Pane of 1, no P#	.60
3205	A2487	32c Pane of 10, 1 each #3205b, 3205c	10.00
3205b	A2487	32c Pane of 9, no P#	—

Imperf

3205c	A2487	32c Pane of 1, no P#	—

Varieties

Pane of 10 from sheet of 60	12.50
Pane of 10 with plate #	45.00

Die cutting on No. 3205b extends through the backing paper. By their nature, Nos. 3204 and 3205 are complete booklets. The peelable backing (BC139) serves as a booklet cover.

3244a
A2524

Serpentine Die Cut 10.1x9.9 on 2, 3 or 4 Sides
1998, Oct. 15   **Tagged**

3244a	A2524	32c pane of 20+label, P#11111, 22222, 33333	12.00

No. 3244a is a complete booklet (BC142). The peelable backing serves as a booklet cover.

Varieties

3244b	Imperf, pair	—

3252b
A2525-A2528

3248a-3248c

Serpentine Die Cut 11.3x11.6 on 2, or 3 Sides
1998, Oct. 15   **Tagged**

3248a	A2525	32c pane of 4, #3245-3248, no P#	2.50
3248b	A2525	32c pane of #3245-3246, 3248, 2 #3247 + label, P#B111111	3.00
3248c	A2525	32c pane of #3247-3248, 2 each #3245-3246, no P#	3.60

Combination Booklet

BK270	BC143	$4.80 **multi**, 1 each #3248a-3248c, P#B111111	12.00

Serpentine Die Cut 11.4x11.6 on 2, 3 or 4 Sides

3252b	A2525	32c pane of 5 each #3249-3252, P#B111111, B222222, B333333, B444444, B555555	12.00

No. 3252b is a complete booklet (BC143). The peelable backing serves as a booklet cover.

Varieties

3252c		Block or strip of 4, red ("Greetings 32 USA" and "1998" omitted on #3249, 3252	—

3267a, 3268a-3268b,
3269a — A2531

Serpentine Die Cut 9.9 on 2 or 3 Sides
1998, Nov. 9

3267a	A2531	(33c) pane of 10	6.50

Booklet

BK271	BC144	($6.60) **multi** P#1111, 2222, 3333	13.00

11.2x11.1 on 2, 3 or 4 Sides

3268a	A2531	(33c) pane of 10, P#V1111, V1211, V2211, V2222	6.50
3268b	A2531	(33c) pane of 20 + label, P#V1111, V1112, V1113, V1122, V1213, V1222, V2113, V2122, V2213, V2222, V2223	13.00

Die Cut 8

3269a	A2531	(33c) pane of 18, P#V1111	12.00

Nos. 3268a-3268b, 3269a are complete booklets (BC144). The peelable backing serves as a booket cover.

MAKESHIFT VENDING MACHINE BOOKLETS
See note before No. BK243.

1998

BK272	BC126	$4.80 15 (#3222-3225)	9.00
BK273	BC126	$4.80 15 #3237	9.00
BK274	BC126	$4.80 3 #3242a	9.00

Configuration of stamps in #BK272 may vary.

3274a — A2537

		Tagged	*Die Cut*
3274a	A2537	33c pane of 20, Jan. 28, 1999	13.00

No. 3274a is a complete booklet (BC145). The peelable backing serves as a booklet cover.
P#V1111, V1112, V1117, V1118, V1211, V1212, V1213, V1233, V1313, V1314, V1333, V1334, V1335, V2221, V2222, V2223, V2424, V2425, V2426, V2324, V3123, V3124, V3125, V3133, V3134, V3323, V3327, V3333, V3334, V3336, V4529, V5650.

Nos. 3278a-3278c

No. 3278d

Nos. 3278e, 3278Fg

No. 3279a — A2540

Serpentine Die Cut 11.1 on 2, 3 or 4 Sides

1999 — **Tagged**

Self-Adhesive

3278a	A2540	33c pane of 4, no P#	2.60
3278b	A2540	33c pane of 5 + label, P#V1111, V1112, V1212	3.25
3278c	A2540	33c pane of 6, no P#	3.90
3278d	A2540	33c pane of 10, P#V1111, V1112, V1113, V2222, V2322, V3434	6.50
3278e	A2540	33c pane of 20 + label, P#V1111, V1211, V2122, V2222, V2223, V3333, V4444	13.00

Serpentine Die Cut 11½x11¾ on 2, 3 or 4 Sides

3278Fg	A2540	33c pane of 20 + label	13.00

No. 3278Fg is a complete booklet. The peelable backing serves as a booklet cover and is similar to BC146.

Below is a list of known plate numbers. Some numbers may be scarcer than the value indicated in the listing.
P# V1111, V1131, V2222, V2223, V2323, V2423, V2443, V3333, V4444, V5445, V5576, V5578, V6423, V6456, V6546, V6556, V6575, V6576, V7567, V7667.

Serpentine Die Cut 9.8 on 2 or 3 Sides

3279a	A2540	33c pane of 10	6.50

COMBINATION BOOKLET

BK275	BC146	$4.95 **multi**, 1 each #3278a-3278c, P#V1111, V1112, V1121, V1212, V2212	10.00

BOOKLET

BK276	BC146	$6.60 **multi**, 2 #3279a, P#1111, 1121	13.00

Nos. 3278d-3278e are complete booklets. The peelable backing serves as a booklet cover and is similar to BC146.

Varieties

3278b	variety, P# single, #V1111, V1212, V2212		
3278h	As "e," imperf	.80	1.00 —

No. 3278 has black date.
The plate # single in No. 3278b is the lower left single.

No. 3283a

Serpentine Die Cut 7.9 on 2, 3 or 4 Sides
Tagged

3283a	A2541	33c pane of 18, P#V1111	12.00

No. 3283a is a complete booklet (BC147). The peelable backing serves as a booklet cover.

Nos. 3297b, 3301a — A2550-A2553

No. 3297d — A2550-A2553

No. 3301c

Serpentine Die Cut 11.2x11.7 on 2, 3 or 4 Sides
1999-2000 — **Tagged**

Self-Adhesive

3297b	33c pane, 5 ea #3294-3297 + label		13.00

No. 3297b is a complete booklet (BC148). The peelable backing serves as a booklet cover.
P#B1111, B1112, B2211, B2222, B3331, B3332, B3333, B4444, B5555.

Serpentine Die Cut 11½x11¾ on 2 or 3 Sides

3297d	33c pane, 5 ea #3294a-3297a, Mar. 15, 2000, P#B1111		13.00

By its nature, No. 3297d is a complete booklet. Two #3297e and the booklet cover (similar to BC148) are printed on one side of the peelable backing and three #3297e appear on the other side of the backing.

Varieties

3297c	Block of 4, Nos. 3294-3297		2.60
3297e	Block of 4, Nos. 3294a-3297a		2.60

Serpentine Die Cut 9½x10 on 2 or 3 sides

3301a	A2550	33c pane of 4, no P#	2.60
3301b	A2550	33c pane of 5 + label, no P#	3.25
3301c	A2550	33c pane of 6, P#B1111, B1112, B2212, B2221, B2222	4.00

COMBINATION BOOKLET

BK276A	BC148	$4.95 multicolored, 1 each #3301a-3301c, P#B see 3301c	10.00

Varieties

3301d	Block of 4, Nos. 3298-3301		2.60

A2554

1999, Apr. 16 — **Serpentine Die Cut 11.1**
Self-Adhesive

3306	33c Pane of 10, 1 each #3306b, 3306c	6.50
3306b	33c Pane of 9, no P#	5.85
3306c	33c Pane of 1, no P#	.65
3307	33c Pane of 10, 1 each #3307b, 3307c	6.50
3307b	33c Pane of 9, no P#	5.85

Imperf

3307c	33c Pane of 1, no P#	.65

Varieties

Pane of 10 from sheet of 60	9.00
Pane of 10 with plate #	15.00

Die cutting on No. 3306b extends through the backing paper. By their nature, Nos. 3306 and 3307 are complete booklets. The peelable backing (BC139) serves as a booklet cover.

No. 3313b — A2556-A2559

Serpentine Die Cut 10.9 on 2 or 3 Sides
1999 — **Tagged**

3313b	33c pane of 20		13.00

By its nature, No. 3313b is a complete booklet. Two #3313a and the booklet cover (BC149) are printed on one side of the peelable backing and 3 #3313a appear on the other side of the backing.

P#S11111, S22222, S22244, S22344, S22444, S22452, S22462, S23222, S24222, S24242, S24244, S24422, S24442, S24444, S26462, S32323, S32333, S32444, S33333, S44444, S45552, S46654, S55452, S55552, S56462, S62544,

S62562, S64452, S64544, S65552, S66462, S66544, S66552, S66562, S66652.

A2599

Nos. 3360-3363 — A2600

Nos. 3364-3367 — A2600

No. 3367c

1999, Oct. 20   *Serpentine Die Cut 11¼*
Self-Adhesive

3355a	A2599	33c pane of 20, P#B1111, B2222, B3333	13.00
3363a	A2600	33c pane of 20, P#B111111, B222222, B333333, B444444, B555555, B666666	13.00

By their nature, Nos. 3355a and 3363a are complete booklets. Twelve #3355 are printed on one side of the peelable backing and 8 #3355 and BC150 appear on the other side of the backing. The peelable backing (BC151) serves as a booklet cover on No. 3363a.

Serpentine Die Cut 11½x11¼ on 2 or 3 sides
Stamp Size: 21x19mm

3367a	A2600	33c pane of 4, no P#	2.60
3367b	A2600	33c pane of 5 + label, no P#	3.25
3367c	A2600	33c pane of 6, P#B111111	4.00

COMBINATION BOOKLET

BK276B	BC152	$4.95	**green & gold,** 1 each #3367a-3367c, P#B	
			see 3367c	10.00

MAKESHIFT VENDING MACHINE BOOKLETS
See note before No. BK243.

1999

BK277	BC126	$4.95	4 each #3225, 3227-3228, 3 #3326	9.75
BK278	BC126	$4.95	3 each #3333-3337	9.75

No. 3377a — A2604-A2608

THE DOLPHIN PIN

The U.S. Navy Submarine Force insignia is a pin featuring a pair of dolphins flanking a sub with its bow planes rigged for diving. The pin is gold plated for officers, silver plated for enlisted personnel. Training prepares submariners not only for day-to-day responsibilities such as navigation and depth control, but also for the most extreme situations, from floods and fires to fighting the enemy. Only after the ability to handle these difficult scenarios has been confirmed can a candidate finally wear the coveted "dolphins."

Selvage 1

THE SUBMARINE STAMPS
U.S. Navy Submarines
A Century of Service to America

USS Holland, the U.S. Navy's first submarine, was purchased in 1900.

S-class submarines were designed during WWI.

Gato class submarines played a key role in the destruction of Japanese maritime power in the Pacific during WWII.

Los Angeles class attack submarines, armed with "smart" torpedoes and cruise missiles, are nuclear powered.

Ohio class submarines—also nuclear powered—carry more than half of America's strategic weapons, making them a vital part of America's nuclear deterrence.

Selvage 2

2000, Mar. 22   *Perf. 11*

3377a	pane of 5 with selvage 1	10.00	—
	With selvage 2	10.00	—

Booklet

BK279	BC153	$9.80	**multicolored,** no P#	20.00

No. BK279 contains one pane with selvage 1 and one pane with selvage 2.

A2622

2000, Apr. 26   *Serpentine Die Cut 11*
Self-Adhesive

3391	A2622	33c Pane of 10, 1 each # 3391b, 3391c	6.50
3391b	A2622	33c Pane of 9, no P#	5.85
3391c	A2622	33c Pane of 1, no P#	.65
3392	A2622	33c Pane of 10, 1 each # 3392b, 3392c	6.50
3392b	A2622	33c Pane of 9, no P#	5.85

Imperf

3392c	A2622	33c Pane of 1, no P#	.65

Varieties

Pane of 10 from sheet of 60	9.00
Two panes of 10 with plate number on front	18.00

Die cutting on No. 3392a extends through backing paper. By their nature, Nos. 3391 and 3392 are complete booklets. The peelable backing (BC139) serves as a booklet cover.

AIR POST STAMPS

Spirit of St. Louis — AP6

FLAT PLATE PRINTING

1928   **Perf. 11**

C10a	AP6	10c **dark blue**, *May 26*	85.00	65.00
		Never hinged	125.00	
		Tab at bottom	*9,000.*	

No. C10a was printed from specially designed 180-subject plates arranged exactly as a 360-subject plate-each pane of three occupying the relative position of a pane of six in a 360-subject plate. Plate numbers appear at the sides, therefore Position D does not exist except partially on panes which have been trimmed off center. All other plate positions common to a 360-subject plate are known.

Booklet

BKC1	BC8	61c **blue**	260.00
		Tab at bottom, one pane in complete booklet	*11,500.*

> Catalogue values for unused panes in this section, from this point to the end, are for Never Hinged items.

AP17

ROTARY PRESS PRINTINGS

1943

C25a	AP17	6c **carmine**, *Mar. 18*	5.00	*1.50*

180-Subject Plates Electric Eye Convertible.

Booklets

BKC2	BC10	37c **red**	11.00
BKC3	BC10	73c **red**	22.50

AP19

1949   **Perf. 10½x11**

C39a	AP19	6c **carmine**, *Nov. 18*	10.00	*5.00*
C39c		Dry printing	15.00	—

Booklets

BKC4	BC11A	73c **red**, with #C39a (3)	25.00
BKC4a	BC11A	73c **red**, with #C39c	50.00

AP33

1958

C51a	AP33	7c **blue**, *July 31*	14.00	*7.00*

Booklets

BKC5	BC11B	85c on 73c **red**	35.00
BKC6	BC11C	85c **blue**	30.00

Varieties

C51b		Vert. pair, imperf. between (from booklet pane)	—

No. C51b resulted from a paper foldover after perforating and before cutting into panes. Two pairs are known.

1960

C60a	AP33	7c **carmine**, *Aug. 19*	17.50	*8.00*

Booklets

BKC7	BC11C	85c **blue**	40.00
BKC8	BC11C	85c **red**	40.00

Varieties

C60b		Vert. pair, imperf between	*5,500.*

No. C60b resulted from a paper foldover after perforating and before cutting into panes. Twp pairs are known.

AP42

1962-64

C64b	AP42	8c **carmine**, pane of 5+label, slogan 1, *Dec. 5, 1962*	7.00	*3.00*
		With slogan 2, *1963*	50.00	*5.00*
		With slogan 3, *1964*	13.00	*2.50*

Booklets (No. C64b)

BKC9	BC11D	80c **black**, *pink*, slogan 1	22.50
BKC10	BC11D	$2 **red**, *pink*, slogan 1	35.00
BKC11	BC11D	80c **black**, *pink*, slogan 3 (2)	30.00
BKC12	BC11D	$2 **red**, *pink*, slogan 2	300.00
BKC13	BC13B	$2 **red**, *pink*, slogan 2	275.00
BKC14	BC13B	$2 **red**, slogan 3	*3,500.*
BKC15	BC13B	$2 **red**, *pink*, slogan 3	100.00

C64c	AP42	As No. C64b, tagged, slogan 3, *1964*	2.00	*.75*

Plate of 360 subjects (300 stamps, 60 labels).

Booklets (No. C64c)

BKC16	BC11D	80c **black** (2)	30.00
BKC17	BC11D	80c **black**, *pink*	*1,750.*
BKC18	BC13B	$2 **red**, *pink*	325.00
BKC19	BC13B	$2 **red** (3)	13.00

AP49   AP54

AP55

1968-73   **Perf. 11x10½**

C72b	AP49	10c **carmine**, pane of 8, *Jan. 5, 1968*	2.00	*.75*

Booklet

BKC20	BC14B	$4 **red** (2)	12.00

C72c	AP49	10c **carmine**, pane of 5+label, slogan 4, *Jan. 6, 1968*	3.75	*.75*
		With slogan 5	3.75	*.75*

Booklet

BKC21	BC15	$1 **red** (2)	8.00

Varieties

C72d		Vert. pair, imperf. between	*8,000.*

No. C72d resulted from a paper foldover after perforating and before cutting into bboklet panes. Two pairs are known.

C78a	AP54	11c **carmine**, pane of 4+2 labels, slogans 5 & 4, *May 7, 1971*	1.25	*.75*

Combination Booklet

BKC22	BC15	$1 **red**, 2 #C78a + 1 #1280c (2)	3.75

C79a	AP55	13c **carmine**, pane of 5+label, slogan 8, *Dec. 27, 1973*	1.50	*.75*

Booklet

BKC23	BC18	$1.30 **blue & red**	3.25

Combination Booklet

See No. BK126.

No. C72b, the 8-stamp pane, was printed from 320-subject plate and from 400-subject plate; No. C72c, C78a and C79a from 360-subject plates.

COMPUTER VENDED POSTAGE

Self-service user-interactive mailing system machines which vended computer-printed postage were in service and available to the general public at the Martin Luther King, Jr., Station of the Washington, DC, Post Office, and at the White Flint Mall in Kensington, MD, until May 7, 1990.

Machines were also available for use by delegates to the 20th Universal Postal Congress at the Washington Convention Center between Nov. 13 and Dec. 14, 1989. These machines, Washington Nos. 11 and 12, were not readily accessible by the general public.

A variety of services were available by using the machines, which could weigh items to be sent, determine postage rates through the connected computer, permit the customer to cancel the transaction or continue with it and generate a postage stamp, a label and a receipt. The stamps produced were valid only for domestic postage. Unlike meters, except for the limits of the service requested, the stamps were usable from any post office at any date.

A tagged orange strip runs along the left side of the stamp. The requested mail service is in a double line box.

The denomination is in the upper box at right under "U.S. Postage." The date of the transaction is below the denomination. Next to the date is a number which indicates the item number within the transaction. The maximum number of items per transaction may be five.

Above the post office location is a box at right which gives the machine number, followed by the transaction or serial number. Stamps from the same transaction, which are generated and printed at the same time, will have the same transaction number, but different item numbers, even if different mail services are requested. Transaction numbers go back to 00001 every time the machine is reset. Below this is the weight of the item to be mailed.

Along with each stamp generated came an unattached label with one of three slogan types: "We Deliver. . .," used from September to November, "We Deliver. . . / United States Postal Service," used thereafter, and "Developed by / Technology Resource Department," used only on Machine 11 during its limited use.

Listings and values are for the basic denominations of the five postal services, though others are known or possible (45c, 65c, 85c for first class over 1 oz., $1.10 for certified first class, $3.25 for priority mail, $8.50 for express mail to post office boxes, parcel post weight and zone variations, etc.). Values for used copies are for those with a regular cancellation.

A total of 3,000 unused sets of five different service stamps and unused sets of two 25c (Nos. 02501-12500) first class stamps furnished to the Philatelic Agency have a first day date and serial numbers with the final three digits matching. First day dates Nos. 00101-02500 were sold over the counter at post offices.

Stamps were intended to be dispensed individually. The height of the stamps produced differs from machine to machine. Unsevered strips of stamps are known, as are unsevered strips of a slogan and one or more stamps. Printing varieties such as squeezes (more than one impression condensed on to one stamp) and stretches (impression stretched out so that a complete impression will not fit on the paper) also are known.

Issues starting with No. 31 will be explained with the listings.

CVP1

CVP2

1989, Aug. 23   **Tagged**   *Guillotined*
Self-Adhesive
Washington, DC, Machine 82

CVP1   CVP1   25c **First Class,** any date other than first day   6.00   —
    a.   First day dated, serial Nos. 12501-15500   4.50   —
    b.   First day dated, serial Nos. 00001-12500   4.50   —
      On cover with first day cancel   150.00
    c.   First day dated, over No. 27500   —   —
      On cover with first day cancel   150.00

CVP2   CVP1 $1 **Third Class,** any date other than first day   —   —
    a.   First day dated, serial Nos. 24501-27500   —   —
    b.   First day dated, over No. 27500   —   —

CVP3   CVP2 $1.69 **Parcel Post,** any date other than first day   —   —
    a.   First day dated, serial Nos. 21501-24500   —   —
    b.   First day dated, over No. 27500   —   —

CVP4   CVP1 $2.40 **Priority Mail,** any date other than first day   —   —
    a.   First day dated, serial Nos. 18501-21500   —   —
    b.   Priority Mail ($2.74), with bar code (CVP2)   100.00
    c.   First day dated, over No. 27500 On cover with first day cancel or verifying receipt   500.00

CVP5   CVP1 $8.75 **Express Mail,** any date other than first day   —   —
    a.   First day dated, serial Nos. 15501-18500   —   —
    b.   First day dated, over No. 27500 On cover with first day cancel or verifying receipt   —   —
      Nos. 1a-5a (5)   82.50   —

Washington, DC, Machine 83

CVP6   CVP1   25c **First Class,** any date other than first day   6.00   —
    a.   First day dated, serial Nos. 12501-15500   4.50   —
    b.   First day dated, serial Nos. 00001-12500   4.50   —
      On cover with first day cancel   150.00
    c.   First day dated, over No. 27500   —   —
      On cover with first day cancel   150.00

      Error dates 11/17/90 and 11/18/90 exist.

CVP7   CVP1 $1 **Third Class,** any date other than first day   —   —
    a.   First day dated, serial Nos. 24501-27500   —   —
    b.   First day dated, over No. 27500   —   —

CVP8   CVP2 $1.69 **Parcel Post,** any date other than first day   —   —
    a.   First day dated, serial Nos. 21501-24500   —   —
    b.   First day dated, over No. 27500   —   —

CVP9   CVP1 $2.40 **Priority Mail,** any date other than first day   —   —
    a.   First day dated, serial Nos. 18501-21500   —   —
    b.   First day dated, over No. 27500 On cover with first day cancel or verifying receipt   500.00

      Error date 11/17/90 exists.

    c.   Priority Mail ($2.74), with bar code (CVP2)   100.00

      Error date 11/18/90 exists.

CVP10   CVP1 $8.75 **Express Mail,** any date other than first day   —   —
    a.   First day dated, serial Nos. 15501-18500   —   —
    b.   First day dated, over No. 27500 On cover with first day cancel or verifying receipt   —   —
      Nos. 6a-10a (5)   57.50   —

      Error date 11/17/90 exists.

1989, Sept. 1   **Kensington, MD, Machine 82**

CVP11   CVP1   25c **First Class,** any date other than first day   6.00   —
    a.   First day dated, serial Nos. 12501-15500   4.50   —
    b.   First day dated, serial Nos. 00001-12500   4.50   —
      On cover with first day cancel   100.00
    c.   First day dated, over No. 27500   —   —
      On cover with first day cancel   100.00

CVP12   CVP1 $1 **Third Class,** any date other than first day   —   —
    a.   First day dated, serial Nos. 24501-27500   —   —
    b.   First day dated, over No. 27500   —   —

CVP13   CVP2 $1.69 **Parcel Post,** any date other than first day   —   —
    a.   First day dated, serial Nos. 21501-24500   —   —
    b.   First day dated, over No. 27500   —   —

CVP14   CVP1 $2.40 **Priority Mail,** any date other than first day   —   —
    a.   First day dated, serial Nos. 18501-21500   —   —
    b.   First day dated, over No. 27500   —   —
    c.   Priority Mail ($2.74), with bar code (CVP2)   100.00

CVP15   CVP1 $8.75 **Express Mail,** any date other than first day   —   —
    a.   First day dated, serial Nos. 15501-18500   —   —
    b.   First day dated, over No. 27500   —   —
      Nos. 11a-15a (5)   57.50   —
      Nos. 1b, 11b (2)   9.00   —

Kensington, MD, Machine 83

CVP16   CVP1   25c **First Class,** any date other than first day   6.00   —
    a.   First day dated, serial Nos. 12501-15500   4.50   —
    b.   First day dated, serial Nos. 00001-12500   4.50   —
    c.   First day dated, over No. 27500   —   —
      On cover with first day cancel   100.00

CVP17   CVP1 $1 **Third Class,** any date other than first day   —   —
    a.   First day dated, serial Nos. 24501-27500   —   —
    b.   First day dated, over No. 27500   —   —

CVP18   CVP2 $1.69 **Parcel Post,** any date other than first day   —   —
    a.   First day dated, serial Nos. 21501-24500   —   —
    b.   First day dated, over No. 27500   —   —

CVP19   CVP1 $2.40 **Priority Mail,** any date other than first day   —   —
    a.   First day dated, serial Nos. 18501-21500   —   —
    b.   First day dated, over No. 27500   —   —
    c.   Priority Mail ($2.74), with bar code (CVP2)   100.00

CVP20   CVP1 $8.75 **Express Mail,** any date other than first day   —   —
    a.   First day dated, serial Nos. 15501-18500   —   —
    b.   First day dated, over No. 27500   —   —
      Nos. 16a-20a (5)   57.50   —
      Nos. 6b, 16b (2)   9.00   —

Unsevered pairs and single with advertising label exist for most, if not all, of the machine vended items from Kensington machine #83. Other combinations also exist.

1989, Nov.   **Washington, DC, Machine 11**

CVP21   CVP1   25c **First Class**   150.00
    a.   First Class, with bar code (CVP2)   —

Stamps in CVP1 design with $1.10 denominations exist (certified first class).

CVP22   CVP1 $1 **Third Class**   500.00
CVP23   CVP2 $1.69 **Parcel Post**   500.00
CVP24   CVP1 $2.40 **Priority Mail**   500.00
    a.   Priority Mail ($2.74), with bar code (CVP2)   —
CVP25   CVP1 $8.75 **Express Mail**   500.00

No. 21 dated Nov. 30 known on cover, Nos. 24-25 known dated Dec. 2.

Washington, DC, Machine 12

CVP26   CVP1   25c **First Class**   150.00

A $1.10 certified First Class stamp, dated Nov. 20, exists on cover.

CVP27   CVP1 $1 **Third Class**   —

A $1.40 Third Class stamp of type CVP2, dated Dec. 1 is known on a Dec. 2 cover.

CVP28   CVP2 $1.69 **Parcel Post**   —

CVP29   CVP1 $2.40 **Priority Mail**   —
  a.   Priority Mail ($2.74), with bar
            code (CVP2)   —
CVP30   CVP1 $8.75 **Express Mail**   —

Nos. 29-30 known dated Dec. 1. An $8.50 Express Mail stamp, dated Dec. 2, exists on cover.

CVP3 - Type I   CVP3 - Type II

Denomination printed by ECA GARD Postage and Mailing Center machines.

COIL STAMPS

1992, Aug. 20   Engr.   Tagged   *Perf. 10 Horiz.*
CVP31 CVP3 29c **red & blue**, type I, prepho-
                  sphered paper (solid tag-
                  ging), dull gum   .60   .25
                  Pair   1.20
                  P# strip of 5, P#1   9.00
                  P# single, #1   3.50
  a.   29c Type I, prephosphered paper (mot-
          tled tagging), shiny gum   .60   .25
                  Pair   1.20   —
                  P# strip of 5, P#1   9.50   —
                  P# single, #1   3.50
                  First day cover, Oklahoma
                  City, OK   1.25
  b.   32c Type II, prephosphered paper (sol-
          id tagging), dull gum, *Nov. 1994*   .90   .40
  c.   32c Type II, prephosphered paper (mot-
          tled tagging), shiny gum   .80   .25

Types I and II differ in style of asterisk, period between dollar and cent figures and font used for figures, as shown in illustrations.

No. 31 was available at five test sites in the Southern Maryland, Miami, Oklahoma City, Detroit and Santa Ana, CA, divisions. They were produced for use in ECA GARD Postage and Mailing Center (PMC) machines which can produce denominations from 1c through $99.99.

For Nos. 31-31a, the 29c value has been listed because it was the current first class rate and was the only value available through the USPS Philatelic Sales Division. The most common denomination available other than 29c will probably be 1c (value 20c) as these were made in quantity, by collectors and dealers, between plate number strips. Later the machines were adjusted to provide only 19c and higher value stamps.

For Nos. 31b-31c, the 32c value has been listed because it was the first class rate in effect for the majority of the period the stamps were in use.

CVP4

Denominations printed by Unisys PMC machines.

1994, Feb. 19   Photo.   Tagged   *Perf. 9.9 Vert.*
CVP32 CVP4 29c **dark red & dark blue**   .60   .25
                  Pair   1.20
                  P# strip of 5, #A11   5.75   —
                  P# single, #A11   3.50
                  First day cover, Merrifield, VA
                  (26,390)   1.25

No. 32 was available at six test sites in northern Virginia. It was produced for use in machines which can produce values from 19c to $99.99. See note following No. 31.

For No. 32, the 29c value has been listed because it was the first class rate in effect at the time the stamp was issued.

1996, Jan. 26   Photo.   Tagged   *Perf. 9.9 Vert.*
CVP33 CVP4 32c **bright red & blue**, "1996" be-
                  low design   .60   .25
                  Pair   1.20   —
                  P# strip of 5, same #   6.00   —
                  P# single, #11   3.50

Letters in "USA" on No. 33 are thicker than on No. 32. Numerous other design differences exist in the moire pattern and in the bunting. No. 33 has "1996" in the lower left corner; No. 32 has no date.

For No. 33, the 32c value has been listed because it was the first class rate in effect at the time the stamp was issued.

Test Labels

TL1

TL2

Test labels were generated when machines were activated. They were not intended for public distribution.

Other samples, advertizing labels, proofs, etc. exist.

POSTAL CARDS

On July 5, 1990 the first of a number of "Postal Buddy" machines was placed in service at the Merrifield, VA post office. The machine printed out numerous items such as address labels (including monogram if you wish), fax labels, "penalty" cards, denominated postal cards, etc. Certain services were free, such as the penalty card mailed to your post office for change of address. The 15-cent denominated card cost 33-cents each and could be used to

---

notify others of address change, meeting notices, customized messages, etc. Borders, messages, backs are different. The cards also came in sheets of 4.

These machines were being tested in at least 30 locations in Virginia, including 16 post offices.

Denominated Postal Cards

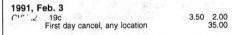

10005-90-198-022

Number under design includes machine number, year, date (1 through 366) and transaction number.

1990, July 5
CVUX1   15c   7.50 3.00
        First day cancel, Merrifield, VA (6,500)   5.00

1991, Feb. 3
CVUX2   19c   3.50 2.00
        First day cancel, any location   35.00

22033-101-21203-041

Number under design includes ZIP Code of the originating machine (22033 in illustration), machine number (101), last digit of year, numbers of month and day (21203 for Dec. 3, 1992) and transaction number (041).

1992, Nov. 13
CVUX3   19c   3.00 2.00
        First day dated, Reston or Chantilly,
        VA   25.00

A total of 171 machines were used in the greater Washington, DC area including locations in Virginia and Maryland (109), the greater San Diego area (59), and in Denver (3). The machine numbers (011, 012, 021, 101, 111, 121, 131) when combined with the zip code created unique identification numbers for each machine.

No. 3 is known also on fluorescent paper. Two different designs on back known for each paper type.

The contract for Postal Buddy machines was canceled Sept. 16, 1993.

VENDING & AFFIXING MACHINE PERFORATIONS

Imperforate sheets of 400 were first issued in 1906 on the request of several makers of vending and affixing machines. The machine manufacturers made coils from the imperforate sheets and applied various perforations to suit the particular needs of their machines. These privately applied perforations were used for many years and form a chapter of postal history.

Unused values are for pairs, used values for singles. "On cover" values are for single stamps used commercially in the proper period when known that way. Several, primarily the Alaska-Yukon and Hudson-Fulton commemoratives, are known almost exclusively on covers from contemporaneous stamp collectors and stamp dealers. Virtually all are rare and highly prized by specialists.

The 2mm and 3mm spacings refer only to the 1908-10 issues. (See note following No. 330 in the Postage section.) Values for intermediate spacings would roughly correspond to the lower-valued of the two listed spacings. Guide line pairs of 1906-10 issues have 2mm spacing except the Alaska-Yukon and Hudson-Fulton issues, which have 3mm spacing. Scott Nos. 408-611 have 3mm spacing, except the "A" plates which have 2¾mm spacing and Scott No. 577, which has both 2¾mm and 3mm spacing. (All spacing measurements are approximate.)

Spacing on paste-up pairs is not a factor in valuing them. Because they were joined together by hand, many different spacings can occur, from less than 2mm to more than 3mm.

Perfins listed here are punched into the stamp at the same time as the perforation. The most common pattern consisted of a 7mm square made up of nine holes. Pins would be removed to create unique perfins for each company using the machines. The catalogue value is for the most common perfin pattern on each stamp.

Many varieties are suspected or known to have been perforated for philatelic purposes and not actually used in machines. These are indicated by an asterisk before the number. Several of these privately applied perforation varieties exist in blocks, which were not produced in the regular course of business. They are generally valued at a premium over the multiple of the coil pairs contained, with an additional premium for plate numbers attached.

Counterfeits are prevalent, especially of items having a basic imperf. variety valued far lower than the vending machine coil.

The Vending and Affixing Machine Perforations Committee of the Bureau Issues Association and William R. Weiss, Jr., compiled these listings.

The Attleboro Stamp Co.
See following U.S. Automatic Vending Company.

THE BRINKERHOFF COMPANY
Sedalia, Mo., Clinton, Iowa
Manufacturers of Vending Machines

Perforations Type I

Stamps were cut into strips and joined before being perforated.

	Type			Unused Pair	Used Single
	On Issue of 1906-08				
314	1c	blue green		180.00	25.00
		Guide line pair		280.00	
320	2c	carmine		200.00	25.00
		Guide line pair		350.00	
*320a	2c	lake		125.00	20.00
		Guide line pair		210.00	
	On Issue of 1908-09				
*343	1c	green		90.00	16.00
		Guide line pair		225.00	
		Pasteup pair		190.00	
*344	2c	carmine		80.00	16.00
		On cover			225.00
		Guide line pair		140.00	
*345	3c	deep violet		110.00	—
		Guide line pair		190.00	
*346	4c	orange brown		110.00	75.00
		Guide line pair		190.00	
*347	5c	blue		275.00	75.00
		On cover			—
		Guide line pair		375.00	
	On Lincoln Issue of 1909				
*368	2c	carmine, coiled endwise		150.00	150.00
		Guide line pair		250.00	
	On Alaska-Yukon Issue of 1909				
*371	2c	carmine, coiled sideways		450.00	—
	On Issue of 1910				
*383	1c	green		180.00	
	On Issue of 1912				
*408	1c	green		25.00	12.00
		On cover			300.00
		Guide line pair		50.00	
		Pasteup pair		45.00	
*409	2c	carmine		25.00	12.00
		On cover			—
		Guide line pair		50.00	
		Pasteup pair		45.00	

Type IIa- One knife cut.

Type IIb- Two knife cuts.

Perforations Type II, 2 Holes

The Type II items listed below are without knife cuts and did not pass through the vending machine. Types IIa and IIb (illustrated above) have knife cuts, applied by the vending machine, to help separate the stamps.

	Type			Unused Pair	Used Single
	On Issue of 1906-08				
314	*II	1c	blue green	85.00	10.00
			On cover		750.00
	IIa	1c	blue green	60.00	10.00
			Guide line pair	140.00	
	*IIb	1c	blue green	325.00	—
320	*II	2c	carmine	175.00	60.00
	IIa	2c	carmine	30.00	10.00
			On cover		450.00
			Guide line pair	110.00	
320a	*II	2c	lake	175.00	60.00
	IIa	2c	lake	45.00	10.00
			On cover		500.00
			Guide line pair	100.00	
			Pasteup pair	90.00	
	*IIb	2c	lake	275.00	70.00
	On Issue of 1908-09				
343	*II	1c	green	60.00	
			On cover		600.00
			Guide line pair	90.00	
	IIa	1c	green	15.00	3.00
			On cover		200.00
			Pasteup pair	25.00	
	IIb	1c	green	25.00	
			Pasteup pair	45.00	
344	*II	2c	carmine	70.00	
			On cover, pair		550.00
			Pasteup pair	110.00	
	IIa	2c	carmine	15.00	3.00
			Guide line pair	27.50	
			On cover		450.00
	IIb	2c	carmine	30.00	6.00
			Guide line pair	60.00	
			Pasteup pair	50.00	
345	*II	3c	deep violet	85.00	10.00
	*IIa	3c	deep violet	70.00	10.00
			On cover		—
			Guide line pair	130.00	
	*IIb	3c	deep violet	240.00	
346	*II	4c	orange brown	140.00	
			Guide line pair	225.00	
	*IIa	4c	orange brown	120.00	45.00
			On cover		1,200.
			Guide line pair	200.00	
			Pasteup pair	175.00	
	*IIb	4c	orange brown	130.00	45.00
			On cover		800.00
347	*II	5c	blue	200.00	
			Guide line pair	300.00	
	*IIa	5c	blue	100.00	60.00
			On cover		3,000.
	*IIb	5c	blue	130.00	
	On Lincoln Issue of 1909				
368	*II	2c	carmine	65.00	
			Guide line pair	110.00	
	IIa	2c	carmine	60.00	12.00
			On cover		1,000.
			Guide line pair	200.00	
	IIb	2c	carmine	175.00	20.00
			On cover		—
			Guide line pair	400.00	
	On Alaska-Yukon Issue of 1909				
371	*II	2c	carmine, coiled sideways	120.00	90.00
			On cover		—
			Guide line or pasteup pair	250.00	
	II	2c	carmine, coiled endwise	525.00	
			Guide line pair	1,000.	
	IIa	2c	carmine, coiled sideways	150.00	40.00
			On cover		600.00
			Guide line pair	250.00	
			Pasteup pair	225.00	

	Type			Unused Pair	Used Single
	On Hudson-Fulton Issue of 1909				
373	*II	2c	carmine, coiled sidewise	250.00	
			Guide line or pasteup pair	375.00	
	On Issue of 1910				
383	*II	1c	green	30.00	
			Guide line pair	60.00	
	IIa	1c	green	40.00	8.00
			On cover		—
	IIb	1c	green	75.00	45.00
			On cover		—
			Guide line pair	125.00	
384	*II	2c	carmine	30.00	
			Guide line pair	50.00	
	IIa	2c	carmine	100.00	
			On cover		1,000.
	IIb	2c	carmine	50.00	8.00
			On cover		
	On Issue of 1912				
408	*II	1c	green	50.00	—
			On cover		200.00
			Guide line pair	80.00	
			Pasteup pair	75.00	
	*IIa	1c	green	90.00	
			Guide line pair	175.00	
	IIb	1c	green	20.00	5.00
			On cover		—
			Guide line pair	40.00	
409	*II	2c	carmine	60.00	
			Guide line pair	125.00	
			Pasteup pair	110.00	
	*IIa	2c	carmine	225.00	—
			On cover		575.00
			Guide line pair	350.00	
	IIb	2c	carmine	25.00	5.00
			On cover		625.00
			Guide line pair	45.00	

THE FARWELL COMPANY

Chicago, Ill.

A wholesale dry goods firm using Schermack (Mailometer) affixing machines. In 1911 the Farwell Company began to make and perforate their own coils. These were sometimes wrongly called "Chambers" perforations.

Type A

Type B

Stamps were perforated in sheets, then cut into strips and coiled.

Blocks exist. The following listings are grouped according to the number of holes, further divided into two types of spacing, narrow and wide. The type symbols (3A2) indicate 3 holes over 2 holes with narrow, type A, spacing between groups. Types A and B occurred in different rows on the same sheet. Left margin or pasteup stamps sometimes show different perforation type on the two sides. Commercial usages of Farwell perforations are generally, but not always, on printed Farwell Co. corner card covers.

			Unused Pair Spacing 2mm	3mm	Used Single
	Group I, no spacing				
	On Issue of 1910				
384	2c	carmine, 7 holes	2,000.	2,000.	850.00
		On cover			1,750.
384	2c	carmine, 6 holes	3,500.	3,500.	

			Unused Pair Spacing		Used Single
			2mm	3mm	
	On cover				5,000.

Type

Group 2, two and three holes
On Issue of 1910

383	2B3	1c	green	350.00	600.00	200.00
	3A2	1c	green	350.00	600.00	—
			On cover			
			Guide line pair	525.00		
384	2A3	2c	carmine	250.00	450.00	200.00
			On cover			950.00
			Guide line pair	1,050.	950.00	
			Pasteup pair		750.00	
	2B3	2c	carmine	600.00	675.00	225.00
			On cover			—
			Pasteup pair		1,000.	
	3A2	2c	carmine	400.00	450.00	210.00
			On cover			1,100.
			Guide line pair	600.00		
	3B2	2c	carmine	350.00	350.00	235.00
			Guide line pair	750.00		

Group 3, three and four holes
On Issue of 1910

383	3B4	1c	green	240.00	240.00	200.00
			Pasteup pair	525.00		
	4B3	1c	green	350.00	350.00	200.00
384	3B4	2c	carmine	450.00	450.00	200.00
			On cover			—
	4B3	2c	carmine	600.00	600.00	175.00
			On cover			700.00
			Guide line pair	—		
	4A3	2c	Carmine			—

Group 4, four and four holes
On Issue of 1908-09

343	*A	1c	green	200.00		
	*B	1c	green	200.00		
344	*A	2c	carmine	200.00	300.00	
	*B	2c	carmine	150.00	140.00	100.00

On Lincoln Issue of 1909

368	*A	2c	carmine	700.00	700.00	
	*B	2c	carmine	700.00	700.00	

On Issue of 1910

383	A	1c	green	50.00	45.00	50.00
			Guide line pair	90.00		
	B	1c	green	50.00	45.00	—
			Guide line pair	90.00		
384	A	2c	carmine	55.00	50.00	12.50
			Guide line pair	100.00		
	B	2c	carmine	55.00	50.00	12.50
			On cover			275.00
			Guide line pair	100.00		

On Issue of 1912

408	A	1c	green		25.00	2.50
			On cover			275.00
			Guide line pair		45.00	
	B	1c	green		25.00	2.50
			On cover			200.00
			Guide line pair		45.00	
409	A	2c	carmine		20.00	2.50
			On cover			75.00
	B	2c	carmine		20.00	2.50
			On cover			75.00
			Guide line pair		40.00	

On Issue of 1916-17

482	A	2c	carmine	350.00		50.00
			On cover	1,000.		
			Guide line pair	500.00		
			Pasteup pair	525.00		
	B	2c	carmine	400.00		50.00
			On cover			1,000.
			Guide line pair	600.00		

Group 5, four and five holes
On Issue of 1910

383	4A5	1c	green	475.00	400.00	—
			Guide line pair	700.00		
384	4A5	2c	carmine	525.00	400.00	—
			Guide line pair	750.00		

On Issue of 1912

408	4A5	1c	green		750.00	
			Guide line pair		1,000.	
	*5A4	1c	green		750.00	
			Guide line pair		1,000.	
409	*4A5	2c	carmine		875.00	—
			Guide line or pasteup pair		1,200.	
	*5A4	2c	carmine		750.00	
			Guide line pair		1,000.	

INTERNATIONAL VENDING MACHINE CO.

Baltimore, Md.

Similar to the Government Coil stamp #322, but perf. 12½.

On Issue of 1906

320	2c	carmine	3,000.	
320b	2c	scarlet	1,250.	1,300.

On Issue of 1908-09

343	1c	green	2,750.
344	2c	carmine	1,100.
345	3c	deep violet	1,100.

346	4c	orange brown	—
347	5c	blue	5,750.

THE MAILOMETER COMPANY

Detroit, Mich.

Formerly the Schermack Mailing Machine Co., then Mail-om-eter Co., and later the Mail-O-Meter Co. Their round-hole perforations were developed in an attempt to get the Bureau of Engraving and Printing to adopt a larger perforation for coil stamps.

Perforations Type I

Used experimentally in Detroit and Chicago in August, 1909. Later used regularly in the St. Louis branch.

Two varieties exist: six holes 1.95mm in diameter spaced an average 1.2mm apart with an overall length of 17.7mm, and six holes 1.95mm in diameter spaced an average 1.15mm apart with an overall length of 17.45mm.

To date, only the 17.7mm length perfs. have been found on commercial covers.

			Unused Pair Spacing		Used Single
			2mm	3mm	

On Issue of 1906-08

*320	2c	carmine	375.00		
*320a	2c	lake	300.00		
		Guide line pair	750.00		
*320b	2c	scarlet	275.00		

On Issue of 1908-09

343	1c	green	35.00	40.00	22.50
		On cover			—
		Guide line pair	60.00		
344	2c	carmine	35.00	40.00	4.50
		On cover, St. Louis			75.00
		On cover, Detroit or Chicago			1,250.
		On cover, Washington, D.C.			1,750.
		Guide line pair	60.00		
		With perforated control mark, single			75.00
		Same, on cover			325.00
345	3c	deep violet	45.00		17.50
		Guide line pair	80.00		
346	4c	orange brown	85.00	65.00	35.00
		Guide line pair	140.00		
347	5c	blue	110.00		35.00
		Guide line pair	175.00		

On Lincoln Issue of 1909

*368	2c	carmine	140.00	90.00	110.00
		Guide line or pasteup pair	275.00		

On Alaska-Yukon Issue of 1909

*371	2c	carmine	200.00		110.00
		Guide line pair	300.00		

On Hudson-Fulton Issue of 1909

*373	2c	carmine	160.00		100.00
		Guide line pair	275.00		

On Issue of 1910

383	1c	green	35.00	30.00	3.25
		On cover			—
		Guide line pair	60.00		
384	2c	carmine	40.00	35.00	4.50
		On cover			75.00
		Guide line pair	65.00		

On Issue of 1912

*408	1c	green		22.50	4.00
		Guide line pair		40.00	
*409	2c	carmine		22.50	4.00
		Guide line pair		40.00	

Perforations Type II

Used experimentally: Chicago, 1909; Detroit, 1911.

On Issue of 1906-08

*320	2c	carmine	350.00		
*320b	2c	scarlet	750.00		

On Issue of 1908-09

343	1c	green	30.00	30.00	12.50
		Guide line pair	50.00		
344	2c	carmine	35.00	35.00	12.50
		On cover			4,000.
		Guide line pair	60.00		
*345	3c	deep violet	175.00		65.00
*346	4c	orange brown	250.00	250.00	
*347	5c	blue	475.00		

On Lincoln Issue of 1909

*368	2c	carmine	475.00	450.00	

On Alaska-Yukon Issue of 1909

*371	2c	carmine	400.00	

On Hudson-Fulton Issue of 1909

*373	2c	carmine	225.00	
		Guide line or pasteup pair	325.00	

On Issue of 1910

383	1c	green	80.00	80.00	25.00
		Guide line or pasteup pair	150.00		
384	2c	carmine	100.00	85.00	50.00
		On cover			500.00

Perforations Type III

Used experimentally in Detroit in 1910.

On Issue of 1906-08

*320	2c	carmine	400.00		
*320b	2c	scarlet	600.00		

On Issue of 1908-09

343	1c	green	100.00	100.00	
		Guide line pair	200.00		
344	2c	carmine	150.00	150.00	
		Guide line pair	225.00		
		Pasteup pair		300.00	
*345	3c	deep violet	225.00		
*346	4c	orange brown	300.00	250.00	
*347	5c	blue	550.00		
		Pasteup pair		900.00	

On Lincoln Issue of 1909

*368	2c	carmine	250.00	210.00	90.00

On Alaska-Yukon Issue of 1909

*371	2c	carmine	550.00	

On Hudson-Fulton Issue of 1909

*373	2c	carmine	500.00	
		Guide line pair		1,250.

Perforations Type IV

Used in St. Louis branch office. Blocks exist but were not regularly produced or issued.

On Issue of 1906-08

*320	2c	carmine	130.00		75.00
*320b	2c	scarlet	110.00		60.00

On Issue of 1908-09

343	1c	green	40.00	35.00	8.00
		Guide line pair	75.00		
344	2c	carmine	50.00	40.00	8.00
		On cover			—

No.				2mm	3mm	Used Single
		Guide line or pasteup pair		90.00		
345	3c	deep violet		75.00		
		Guide line or pasteup pair		130.00		
346	4c	orange brown		120.00	110.00	
		Guide line pair		200.00		
347	5c	blue		150.00		50.00
		Guide line pair		250.00		

On Lincoln Issue of 1909
*368	2c	carmine	85.00	85.00	25.00
		Guide line or pasteup pair	165.00		

On Alaska-Yukon Issue of 1909
*371	2c	carmine		250.00
		Guide line pair		450.00

On Hudson-Fulton Issue of 1909
*373	2c	carmine		250.00
		On cover		—
		Guide line pair		425.00

On Issue of 1910
383	1c	green	12.50	9.00	2.00
		On cover			200.00
		Guide line pair	20.00		
384	2c	carmine	22.50	20.00	1.00
		On cover			110.00
		Guide line pair	35.00		

On Issue of 1912
408	1c	green	6.50	1.00
		On cover		50.00
		Guide line or pasteup pair	10.00	
409	2c	carmine	7.50	.50
		On cover		50.00
		Guide line or pasteup pair	12.50	

On Issue of 1916-17
482	2c	carmine	90.00	60.00
		On cover		275.00
		Guide line pair	150.00	
		Pasteup pair	200.00	
483	3c	violet, type I	120.00	60.00
		On cover		275.00
		Guide line pair	225.00	
		Pasteup pair	175.00	

THE SCHERMACK COMPANY

Detroit, Mich.

These perforations were developed by the Schermack Mailing Machine Co. before it became the Mailometer Co. The Type III perforation was used in Mailometer affixing machines from 1909 through 1927.

Perforations Type I. Eight Holes

Perforated in sheets, then cut into strips and coiled.

No.			Unused Pair Spacing 2mm	3mm	Used Single

On Issue of 1906-08
314	1c	blue green	100.00		90.00
		Guide line pair	175.00		
		*Seven holes	800.00		
		*Pasteup pair	1,100.		
		*Six holes	725.00		
		Guide line pair	1,050.		
320	2c	carmine	100.00		50.00
		On cover			2,000.
		Guide line pair	160.00		
		Seven holes	700.00		—
		On cover			11,000.
		Guide line pair	800.00		
		Pasteup pair	750.00		
		*Six holes	900.00		

The value for No. 320 with seven holes on cover is for the Dec. 14, 1907 use from Detroit with Murphy Chair Co. corner card, representing the earliest known use of any U. S. coil stamp, whether a private vending coil or a Bureau-issue coil. The value represents a 1998 sale at auction. One or two other covers exist bearing this stamp and may be expected to sell for less.

*320a	2c	lake	250.00		100.00
		*Seven holes	500.00		
		*Six holes	1,100.		
*315	5c	blue	—		

On Issue of 1908-09
*343	1c	green	190.00	—	75.00
		Guide line pair	—		
*344	2c	carmine	900.00		

No.			Unused Pair Spacing 2mm	3mm	Used Single
*345	3c	deep violet	1,250.		
		Guide line pair	1,250.		
*346	4c	orange brown	1,500.		
		Guide line pair	550.00		
*347	5c	blue	—		
		Guide line pair	550.00		

On Lincoln Issue of 1909
*368	2c	carmine	150.00	175.00	75.00
		Guide line pair	250.00		
		*Seven holes	800.00		—
		*Six holes	1,000.		

Perforations Type II

Cut into strips and joined before being perforated.

On Issue of 1906-08
314	1c	blue green	225.00		75.00
		Guide line pair	325.00		
320	2c	carmine	110.00		50.00
		Guide line pair	190.00		
*320a	2c	lake	190.00		90.00
		Guide line pair	325.00		
*315	5c	blue	8,000.		1,750.
		Guide line pair	—		

On Issue of 1908-09
*343	1c	green	500.00	525.00	
		Guide line pair	700.00		
*344	2c	carmine	500.00	475.00	
		Guide line pair	650.00		
*345	3c	deep violet	475.00		
		Guide line pair	650.00		
*346	4c	orange brown	650.00		—
		Guide line pair	800.00		
*347	5c	blue	600.00		
		Guide line pair	1,250.		

On Lincoln Issue of 1909
*368	2c	carmine	110.00	90.00	60.00
		Guide line pair	175.00		

On Issue of 1910
*383	1c	green	—	—
		Guide line or pasteup pair	—	
*384	2c	carmine	—	—

Existance of genuine copies of Nos. 383-384 has been questioned.

Perforations Type III

Blocks exist but were not regularly produced or issued.

No.			Unused Pair Spacing 2mm	3mm	Used Single

On Issue of 1906-08
314	1c	blue green	10.00		2.00
		On cover			125.00
		Guide line pair	20.00		
		Pasteup pair	17.50		
320	2c	carmine	15.00		5.00
		On cover			65.00
		Guide line pair	27.50		
320a	2c	lake	20.00		2.50
		On cover			90.00
		Guide line pair	40.00		
		Pasteup pair	35.00		
*320b	2c	scarlet	20.00		5.00
		Guide line pair	35.00		
314A	4c	brown, single	27,500.		22,500.
		Pair	65,000.		
		On cover			120,000.
		Guide line pair	165,000.		
*315	5c	blue	3,000.		

On Issue of 1908-09
343	1c	green	5.00	6.00	1.00
		On cover			25.00
		Guide line or pasteup pair	9.00		

No.			Unused Pair Spacing 2mm	3mm	Used Single
		With perforated control mark, single			50.00
		Same, on cover			450.00
344	2c	carmine	5.00	6.00	1.00
		On cover			22.50
		Guide line or pasteup pair	9.00		
		With perforated control mark, single			50.00
		Same, on cover			450.00
345	3c	deep violet	20.00	140.00	10.00
		On cover			30.00
		Guide line pair	35.00		
		With perforated control mark, single			750.00
		Same, on cover			—
346	4c	orange brown	30.00	20.00	15.00
		On cover			3,000.
		Guide line or pasteup pair	50.00		
		With perforated control mark, single			1,250.
		On cover			—
347	5c	blue	50.00		15.00
		On cover			2,250.
		Guide line pair	90.00		

On Lincoln Issue of 1909
368	2c	carmine	60.00	45.00	10.00
		On cover			175.00
		Guide line or pasteup pair	100.00		

On Alaska-Yukon Issue of 1909
*371	2c	carmine		70.00
		Guide line or pasteup pair		125.00

On Hudson-Fulton Issue of 1909
*373	2c	carmine		85.00
		Guide line or pasteup pair		160.00

On Issue of 1910
383	1c	green	4.00	3.00	1.00
		On cover			27.50
		Guide line or pasteup pair	8.00		
		With perforated control mark, single			30.00
		Same, on cover			250.00
384	2c	carmine	9.00	7.00	1.00
		On cover			25.00
		Guide line pair	15.00		
		With perforated control mark, single			30.00
		Same, on cover			200.00

On Issue of 1912
408	1c	green	2.00	.50
		On cover		30.00
		Guide line or pasteup pair	4.00	
		With perforated control mark, single		35.00
		Same, on cover		275.00
409	2c	carmine	2.00	.40
		On cover		25.00
		Guide line or pasteup pair	4.00	
		Aniline ink ("pink back")		—
		With perforated control mark, single		35.00
		Same, on cover		275.00

On Issue of 1916-17
481	1c	green	3.00	.30
		On cover		20.00
		Guide line or pasteup pair	6.00	
482	2c	carmine, type I	4.00	.50
		On cover		15.00
		Guide line or pasteup pair	7.50	
		Aniline ink ("pink back")		—
482A	2c	carmine, type Ia		12,000.
		Pair		100,000.
		On cover		17,500.
483	3c	violet, type I	10.00	2.50
		On cover		125.00
		Guide line or pasteup pair	17.50	
484	3c	violet, type II	15.00	4.00
		On cover		100.00
		Guide line or pasteup pair	25.00	

On Issue of 1918-20
531	1c	green	10.00	4.00
		On cover		100.00
		Guide line or pasteup pair	17.50	
532	2c	carmine, type IV	30.00	3.00
		On cover		75.00
		Guide line or pasteup pair	50.00	
533	2c	carmine, type V	225.00	40.00
		On cover		225.00

			Unused Pair Spacing 2mm	3mm	Used Single
		Guide line or pasteup pair		425.00	
534	2c	**carmine**, type Va		15.00	2.00
		On cover			90.00
		Guide line or pasteup pair		40.00	
534A	2c	**carmine**, type VI		35.00	4.00
		On cover			75.00
		Guide line or pasteup pair		60.00	
534B	2c	**carmine**, type VII		*1,000.*	90.00
		On cover			*425.00*
		Guide line or pasteup pair		*1,400.*	
535	3c	**violet**, type IV		12.50	3.00
		On cover			75.00
		Guide line or pasteup pair		20.00	

On Issue of 1923-26

			2mm	3mm	Used Single
575	1c	**green**		225.00	6.00
		Unused single		20.00	
		On cover			500.00
		Guide line or pasteup pair		350.00	
		Precanceled		4.00	1.00
		On cover, precanceled			100.00
576	1½c	**yellow brown**		20.00	4.00
		On cover			200.00
		Guide line or pasteup pair		35.00	
		Precanceled		4.00	1.00
		On cover, precanceled			75.00
577	2c	**carmine**	25.00	20.00	1.00
		On cover			20.00
		Guide line or pasteup pair	45.00	35.00	

On Harding Issue of 1923

			2mm	3mm	Used Single
611	2c	**black**		75.00	15.00
		On cover			115.00
		Guide line or pasteup pair		125.00	

U.S. AUTOMATIC VENDING COMPANY

New York, N.Y.

Separations Type I

Cut into strips and joined before being perforated.

Two varieties exist: 15½ and 16mm between notches of the perforations.

On Issue of 1906-08
Coiled Endwise

			Unused Pair	Used Single
314	1c	**blue green**	45.00	10.00
		On cover		*1,750.*
		Guide line or pasteup pair	75.00	
320	2c	**carmine**	40.00	8.00
		Guide line pair	70.00	
*320a	2c	**lake**	90.00	9.00
		Guide line or pasteup pair	200.00	
320b	2c	**scarlet**	50.00	7.00
		On cover		3,500.
		Guide line pair	100.00	
315	5c	**blue**	650.00	—
		On cover		10,000.
		Guide line pair	2,500.	
		Pasteup pair	2,750.	

On Issue of 1908-09
Coiled Endwise

			Unused Pair	Used Single
343	1c	**green**	10.00	1.50
		On cover		100.00
		On postcard		60.00
		Guide line or pasteup pair	20.00	

			Unused Pair	Used Single
344	2c	**carmine**	8.00	1.50
		On cover		100.00
		Guide line or pasteup pair	15.00	
*345	3c	**deep violet**	30.00	8.00
		On cover		300.00
		Guide line or pasteup pair	60.00	
*346	4c	**orange brown**	45.00	9.00
		Guide line or pasteup pair	100.00	
347	5c	**blue**	80.00	40.00
		On cover		2,250.
		Guide line or pasteup pair	150.00	

On Lincoln Issue of 1909

368	2c	**carmine**, coiled endwise	35.00	7.00
		On cover		550.00
		First day cover, Feb. 12, 1909		14,500.
		Guide line or pasteup pair	75.00	

On Alaska-Yukon Issue of 1909

*371	2c	**carmine**, coiled sideways	70.00	10.00
		On cover		500.00
		On commercial cover		—
		Guide line pair	125.00	
		Type Ia, No T. and B. margins	125.00	15.00
		Type Ia, Guide line or pasteup pair	200.00	

Type Ia stamps are a deep shade and have a misplaced position dot in the "S" of "Postage." Beware of trimmed copies of No. 371 type I.

On Issue of 1910

383	1c	**green**	6.00	2.50
		On cover		100.00
		On postcard		40.00
		Guide line or pasteup pair	10.00	
*384	2c	**carmine**	20.00	4.50
		Guide line pair	35.00	

On Issue of 1912

*408	1c	**green**	10.00	2.00
		Guide line pair	17.50	
*409	2c	**carmine**	12.50	4.00
		Guide line pair	20.00	

Separations Type II

Similar to Type I but with notches farther apart and a longer slit.

Cut into strips and joined before being perforated.

On Issue of 1906-08
Coiled Sideways

			Unused Pair Spacing 2mm	3mm	Used Single
*314	1c	**blue green**	45.00		8.00
		On cover			—
		Guide line or pasteup pair	75.00		
*320	2c	**carmine**	80.00		
*320b	2c	**scarlet**	55.00		5.00
		Guide line pair	90.00		
*315	5c	**blue**	1,250.		
		Guide line pair	1,800.		

On Issue of 1908-09

343	1c	**green**	12.50		3.00
		On cover			—
		Guide line or pasteup pair	20.00		
344	2c	**carmine**	15.00		
		On cover			—
		Guide line pair	22.50		
*345	3c	**deep violet**	60.00		—
		Guide line pair	100.00		
*346	4c	**orange brown**	85.00	75.00	
		Guide line pair	140.00		
*347	5c	**blue**	175.00		
		Guide line pair	275.00		

On Lincoln Issue of 1909

368	2c	**carmine**	90.00	80.00	20.00
		Guide line pair	150.00		

On Alaska-Yukon Issue of 1909

*371	2c	**carmine**	60.00		35.00
		On cover			400.00
		Guide line or pasteup pair	100.00		

On Hudson-Fulton Issue of 1909

*373	2c	**carmine**	65.00		15.00

			Unused Pair Spacing 2mm	3mm	Used Single
		On cover			600.00
		Guide line or pasteup pair		110.00	

On Issue of 1910

383	1c	**green**	15.00	12.00	
		On cover			1,000.
		Guide line pair	25.00		
384	2c	**carmine**	20.00	15.00	
		On cover			2,500.
		Guide line pair	35.00		

On Issue of 1912

408	1c	**green**		10.00	2.00
		On cover			—
		Guide line pair		17.50	
409	2c	**carmine**		15.00	4.00
		Guide line pair		25.00	

Perforations Type III

Cut into strips and joined before being perforated.

On Issue of 1906-08

*314	1c	**blue green**	50.00		10.00
		Guide line pair	90.00		
*320	2c	**carmine**	90.00		
*320b	2c	**scarlet**	60.00		10.00
		Guide line pair	100.00		
*315	5c	**blue**	950.00		
		Guide line or pasteup pair	1,900.		

On Issue of 1908-09

343	1c	**green**	25.00	23.00	5.00
		Guide line or pasteup pair	40.00		
344	2c	**carmine**	25.00		5.00
		Guide line pair	40.00		
*345	3c	**deep violet**	100.00		
		Guide line pair	175.00		
*346	4c	**orange brown**	100.00	100.00	12.00
		Guide line pair	175.00		
*347	5c	**blue**	120.00		
		Guide line pair	200.00		

On Lincoln Issue of 1909

*368	2c	**carmine**	65.00	55.00	16.00
		Guide line pair	110.00		
		Experimental perf. 12	*1,750.*		

On Alaska-Yukon Issue of 1909

*371	2c	**carmine**	60.00		16.00
		On cover			—
		Guide line or pasteup pair	100.00		

On Hudson-Fulton Issue of 1909

*373	2c	**carmine**	60.00		16.00
		On cover			—
		Guide line or pasteup pair	100.00		

On Issue of 1910

383	1c	**green**	14.00	12.00	2.50
		Guide line pair	22.50		
384	2c	**carmine**	16.00	14.00	2.50
		Guide line pair	25.00		

On Issue of 1912

408	1c	**green**	8.00		
		Guide line pair	12.50		
409	2c	**carmine**	12.00		
		Guide line pair	17.50		

On 1914 Rotary Press Coil

459	2c	**carmine**	24,000.	11,500.

This firm also produced coil strips of manila paper, folded so as to form small "pockets", each "pocket" containing one 1c stamp and two 2c stamps, usually imperforate but occasionally with either government or U.S.A.V. private perforations. The manila "pockets" were perforated type II, coiled sideways. They fit U.S.A.V. ticket vending machines. Multiples exist. Values are for "pockets" with known combinations of stamps, listed by basic Scott Number. Other combinations exist, but are not listed due to the fact that the stamps may have been added at a later date.

Pocket Type 1 (1908)
("Patents Pending" on front and green advertising on reverse)

Type 1—1	314 + 320	2,500.
Type 1—2	314 + 320b	2,500.

Pocket Type 2 (1909)
("Patents Applied For" Handstamped in greenish blue)

Type 2—1	343 + 371	1,250.
Type 2—2	343 + 372	900.
Type 2—3	343 (USAV Type I) + 371	1,750.

Type 2—4 343 + 375   900.

Pocket Type 3 (1909)

("Patents Pending" printed in red)

Type 3—1	343 + 372	900.
Type 3—2	343 + 373	700.
Type 3—3	343 + 375	800.
Type 3—4	383 + 406	800.

Pocket Type 4 (1909)

(No printing on front, serial number on back)

Type 4—1	343 + 344	300.
Type 4—2	343 + 368	300.
Type 4—3	343 + 371	300.
Type 4—4	383 + 344	300.
Type 4—5	383 (USAV Type II) + 344	300.
Type 4—6	383 + 384	300.
Type 4—7	383 + 406	300.

THE ATTLEBORO STAMP COMPANY

Attleboro, Mass.

This Company used an affixing machine to stamp its newletters during the summer and fall of 1909.

Nos. 343-344

No. 371

			Unused Pair	Used Single
		On Issue of 1908-09		
343	1c	**green**	800.	350.
		On Attleboro Philatelist wrapper		4,750.
		On cover		
		Guide line or pasteup pair	1,250.	
344	2c	**carmine**	45,000.	
		The No. 344 pair is unique.		
		On Alaska-Yukon Issue of 1909		
371	2c	**carmine**, coiled sidewise	2,400.	1,000.
		Guide line or pasteup pair	4,000.	1,—
		On wrapper or cover		5,000.

FLAT PLATE IMPERFORATE COIL STAMPS

These flat plate imperforate coil stamps were made from imperforate sheets of the regular issues, and were issued in coils of 500 or 1,000. The numbers assigned below are those of the regularly issued imperforate sheet stamps to which "H" or "V" has been added to indicate that the stamps are coiled horizontally (side by side), or vertically (top to bottom). These coil stamps are virtually indistinguishable from the corresponding imperforate sheet stamps, although they can be authenticated, particularly when in strips of four or longer. Many genuine imperforate coil stamps bear authenticating signatures of contemporaneous experts.

Values for stamps on cover are for single stamps.

FLAT PLATE PRINTING

1908			Wmk. 191		*Imperf.*
314V	A115	1c	**blue green**, pair	300.00	—
			Strip of 4	700.00	—
			Guide line pair		—
			Guide line strip of 4		—
314H	A115	1c	**blue green**, pair	1,500.	—
			On cover		—
			Strip of 4	—	—
			Guide line pair	4,000.	
			Guide line strip of 4	—	—
320V	A129	2c	**carmine**, pair	—	—
			Strip of 4	—	—
			Guide line pair	—	
			Guide line strip of 4	—	—
320H	A129	2c	**carmine**, pair	—	—
			Strip of 4	—	—
			Guide line pair	—	
			Guide line strip of 4	—	—

1908-10					*Imperf.*
343V	A138	1c	**green**, pair	22.00	8.50
			On cover		10.00
			Strip of 4	50.00	—
			Guide line pair	40.00	
			Guide line strip of 4	65.00	—
343H	A138	1c	**green**, pair	42.50	—
			Strip of 4	105.00	—
			Guide line pair	80.00	—
			Guide line strip of 4	—	—
344V	A139	2c	**carmine**, pair	27.50	20.00
			On cover		15.00
			Strip of 4	65.00	—
			Guide line pair	50.00	—
			Guide line strip of 4	85.00	—
			Foreign entry, design of 1c	1,250.	1,000.
344H	A139	2c	**carmine**, pair (2mm spacing)	27.50	20.00
			Strip of 4	—	—
			Guide line pair	—	
			Guide line strip of 4	—	—
			Pair (3mm spacing)	30.00	—
			Strip of 4	—	—
			Guide line pair	50.00	—
			Guide line strip of 4	—	—
346V	A140	4c	**orange brown**, pair	115.00	
			Strip of 4	260.00	—
			Guide line pair	200.00	75.00
			Guide line strip of 4	—	

347V	A140	5c	**blue**, pair	160.00	—
			On cover		—
			Strip of 4	350.00	—
			Guide line pair	275.00	—
			Guide line strip of 4	475.00	

1909					*Imperf.*
368V	A141	2c	**carmine**, *Lincoln*, pair	150.00	—
			Strip of 4	450.00	—
			Guide line pair	300.00	—
			Guide line strip of 4	525.00	—
368H	A141	2c	**carmine**, *Lincoln*, pair	225.00	—
			Strip of 4	675.00	
			Guide line pair	450.00	—
			Guide line strip of 4	—	

1910			Wmk. 190		*Imperf.*
383V	A138	1c	**green**, pair	11.00	—
			On cover		6.00
			Strip of 4	25.00	—
			Guide line pair	20.00	—
			Guide line strip of 4	50.00	—
			Double transfer	—	—
383H	A138	1c	**green**, pair (2mm spacing)	12.00	—
			Strip of 4	26.00	—
			Guide line pair	—	—
			Guide line strip of 4	—	—
			Pair (3mm spacing)	12.00	—
			Strip of 4	26.00	—
			Guide line pair	20.00	—
384V	A139	2c	**carmine**, pair	12.50	—
			On cover		7.00
			Strip of 4	27.50	—
			Guide line pair	25.00	—
			Guide line strip of 4	40.00	—
			Foreign entry, design of 1c	1,000.	—
384H	A139	2c	**carmine**, pair (2mm spacing)	25.00	—
			Strip of 4	60.00	—
			Guide line pair	—	—
			Guide line strip of 4	—	—
			Pair (3mm spacing)	22.50	—
			Strip of 4	55.00	—
			Guide line pair	40.00	—
			Guide line strip of 4	—	—

1912			Wmk. 190		*Imperf.*
408V	A140	1c	**green**, pair		3.50
			Strip of 4		7.75
			Guide line pair		7.00
			Guide line strip of 4		12.50
408H	A140	1c	**green**, pair		3.75
			Strip of 4		—
			Guide line pair		—
			Guide line strip of 4		—
409V	A140	2c	**carmine**, pair		3.75
			Strip of 4		8.25
			Guide line pair		7.50
			Guide line strip of 4		12.50
409H	A140	2c	**carmine**, pair		5.00
			Strip of 4		—
			Guide line pair		—
			Guide line strip of 4		—
			Double transfer		—

COMMEMORATIVE STAMPS, QUANTITIES ISSUED

Quantities issued fall into four categories. First are stamps where reasonably accurate counts are made of the number of copies sold.

Second are stamps where the counts are approximations of the number sold.

Third are stamps where the count is of quantities shipped to post offices and philatelic sales units, but no adjustments are made for returned or destroyed copies.

Fourth are stamps for which the quantity printed is furnished but no other adjustments are made.

Occasionally more accurate figures are determined. In these cases the quantities here will be adjusted. For example, it is now known that while 2,000,000 sets of the Voyages of Columbus souvenir sheets were printed, the number sold was 1,185,170 sets.

Scott No.	Quantity		Scott No.	Quantity		Scott No.	Quantity
230	449,195,550		675	980,000		783	74,407,450
231	1,464,588,750		676	850,000		784	269,522,200
232	11,501,250		677	1,480,000		785	105,196,150
233	19,181,550		678	530,000		786	93,848,500
234	35,248,250		679	1,890,000		787	87,741,150
235	4,707,550		680	29,338,274		788	35,794,150
236	10,656,550		681	32,680,900		789	36,839,250
237	16,516,950		682	74,000,774		790	104,773,450
238	1,576,950		683	25,215,574		791	92,054,550
239	617,250		688	25,609,470		792	93,291,650
240	243,750		689	66,487,000		793	34,552,950
241	55,050		690	96,559,400		794	36,819,050
242	45,550		702	99,074,600		795	84,825,250
243	27,650		703	25,006,400		796	25,040,400
244	26,350		704	87,969,700		797	5,277,445
245	27,350		705	1,265,555,100		798	99,882,300
285	70,993,400		706	304,926,800		799	78,454,450
286	159,720,800		707	4,222,198,300		800	77,004,200
287	4,924,500		708	456,198,500		801	81,292,450
288	7,694,180		709	151,201,300		802	76,474,550
289	2,927,200		710	170,565,100		835	73,043,650
290	4,629,760		711	111,739,400		836	58,564,368
291	530,400		712	83,257,400		837	65,939,500
292	56,900		713	96,506,100		838	47,064,300
293	56,200		714	75,709,200		852	114,439,600
294	91,401,500		715	147,216,000		853	101,699,550
295	209,759,700		716	51,102,800		854	72,764,550
296	5,737,100		717	100,869,300		855	81,269,600
297	7,201,300		718	168,885,300		856	67,813,350
298	4,921,700		719	52,376,100		857	71,394,750
299	5,043,700		724	49,949,000		858	66,835,000
323	79,779,200		725	49,538,500		859	56,348,320
324	192,732,400		726	61,719,200		860	53,177,110
325	4,542,600		727	73,382,400		861	53,260,270
326	6,926,700		728	348,266,800		862	22,104,950
327	4,011,200		729	480,239,300		863	13,201,270
328	77,728,794		730 (sheet of 25)	456,704		864	51,603,580
329	149,497,994		730a	11,417,600		865	52,100,510
330	7,980,594		731 (sheet of 25)	441,172		866	51,666,580
367	148,387,191		731a	11,029,300		867	22,207,780
368	1,273,900		732	1,978,707,300		868	11,835,530
369	637,000		733	5,735,944		869	52,471,160
370	152,887,311		734	45,137,700		870	52,366,440
371	525,400		735 (sheet of 6)	811,404		871	51,636,270
372	72,634,631		735a	4,868,424		872	20,729,030
373	216,480		736	46,258,300		873	14,125,580
397 & 401	334,796,926		737	193,239,100		874	59,409,000
398 & 402	503,713,086		738	15,432,200		875	57,888,600
399 & 403	29,088,726		739	64,525,400		876	58,273,180
400 & 404	16,968,365		740	84,896,350		877	23,779,000
537	99,585,200		741	74,400,200		878	15,112,580
548	137,978,207		742	95,089,000		879	57,322,790
549	196,037,327		743	19,178,650		880	58,281,580
550	11,321,607		744	30,980,100		881	56,398,790
610	1,459,487,085		745	16,923,350		882	21,147,000
611	770,000		746	15,988,250		883	13,328,000
612	99,950,300		747	15,288,700		884	54,389,510
614	51,378,023		748	17,472,600		885	53,636,580
615	77,753,423		749	18,874,300		886	55,313,230
616	5,659,023		750 (sheet of 6)	511,391		887	21,720,580
617	15,615,000		750a	3,068,346		888	13,600,580
618	26,596,600		751 (sheet of 6)	793,551		889	47,599,580
619	5,348,800		751a	4,761,306		890	53,766,510
620	9,104,983		752	3,274,556		891	54,193,580
621	1,900,983		753	2,040,760		892	20,264,580
627	307,731,900		754	2,389,288		893	13,726,580
628	20,280,500		755	2,294,948		894	46,497,400
629	40,639,485		756	3,217,636		895	47,700,000
630 (sheet of 25)	107,398		757	2,746,640		896	50,618,150
643	39,974,900		758	2,168,088		897	50,034,400
644	25,628,450		759	1,822,684		898	60,943,700
645	101,330,328		760	1,724,576		902	44,389,550
646	9,779,896		761	1,647,696		903	54,574,550
647	5,519,897		762	1,682,948		904	63,558,400
648	1,459,897		763	1,638,644		906	21,272,800
649	51,342,273		764	1,625,224		907	1,671,564,200
650	10,319,700		765	1,644,900		908	1,227,334,200
651	16,684,674		766 (pane of 25)	98,712		909	19,999,646
654	31,679,200		766a	2,467,800		910	19,999,646
655	210,119,474		767 (pane of 25)	85,914		911	19,999,646
656	133,530,000		767a	2,147,850		912	19,999,646
657	51,451,880		768 (pane of 6)	267,200		913	19,999,646
658	13,390,000		768a	1,603,200		914	19,999,646
659	8,240,000		769 (pane of 6)	279,960		915	19,999,646
660	87,410,000		769a	1,679,760		916	14,999,646
661	2,540,000		770 (pane of 6)	215,920		917	14,999,646
662	2,290,000		770a	1,295,520		918	14,999,646
663	2,700,000		771	1,370,560		919	14,999,646
664	1,450,000		772	70,726,800		920	14,999,646
665	1,320,000		773	100,839,600		921	14,999,646
666	1,530,000		774	73,610,650		922	61,303,000
667	1,130,000		775	75,823,900		923	61,001,450
668	2,860,000		776	124,324,500		924	60,605,000
669	8,220,000		777	67,127,650		925	50,129,350
670	8,990,000		778 (sheet of 4)	2,809,039		926	53,479,400
671	73,220,000		778a	2,809,039		927	61,617,350
672	2,110,000		778b	2,809,039		928	75,500,000
673	1,600,000		778c	2,809,039		929	137,321,000
674	1,860,000		778d	2,809,039		930	128,140,000
			782	72,992,650		931	67,255,000

Scott No.	Quantity	Scott No.	Quantity	Scott No.	Quantity
932	133,870,000	1079	109,275,000	1199	126,515,000
933	76,455,400	1080	112,932,200	1200	130,960,000
934	128,357,750	1081	125,475,000	1201	120,055,000
935	138,863,000	1082	117,855,000	1202	120,715,000
936	111,616,700	1083	122,100,000	1203	121,440,000
937	308,587,700	1084	118,180,000	1204	40,270,000
938	170,640,000	1085	100,975,000	1205	861,970,000
939	135,927,000	1086	115,299,450	1206	120,035,000
940	260,339,100	1087	186,949,627	1207	117,870,000
941	132,274,500	1088	115,235,000	1230	129,945,000
942	132,430,000	1089	106,647,500	1231	135,620,000
943	139,209,500	1090	112,010,000	1232	137,540,000
944	114,684,450	1091	118,470,000	1233	132,435,000
945	156,540,510	1092	102,230,000	1234	135,520,000
946	120,452,600	1093	102,410,000	1235	131,420,000
947	127,104,300	1094	84,054,400	1236	133,170,000
948	10,299,600	1095	126,266,000	1237	130,195,000
949	132,902,000	1096	39,489,600	1238	128,450,000
950	131,968,000	1097	122,990,000	1239	118,665,000
951	131,488,000	1098	174,372,800	1240	1,291,250,000
952	122,362,000	1099	114,365,000	1241	175,175,000
953	121,548,000	1100	122,765,200	1242	125,995,000
954	131,109,000	1104	113,660,200	1243	128,025,000
955	122,650,500	1105	120,196,580	1244	145,700,000
956	121,953,500	1106	120,805,200	1245	120,310,000
957	115,250,000	1107	125,815,200	1246	511,750,000
958	64,198,500	1108	108,415,200	1247	123,845,000
959	117,642,500	1109	107,195,200	1248	122,825,000
960	77,649,600	1110	115,745,280	1249	453,090,000
961	113,474,500	1111	39,743,640	1250	123,245,000
962	120,868,500	1112	114,570,200	1251	123,355,000
963	77,800,500	1113	120,400,200	1252	126,970,000
964	52,214,000	1114	91,160,200	1253	121,250,000
965	53,958,100	1115	114,860,200	1254—1257	1,407,760,000
966	61,120,010	1116	126,500,000	1258	120,005,000
967	57,823,000	1117	120,561,280	1259	125,800,000
968	52,975,000	1118	44,064,576	1260	122,230,000
969	77,149,000	1119	118,390,200	1261	115,695,000
970	58,332,000	1120	125,770,200	1262	115,095,000
971	56,228,000	1121	114,114,280	1263	119,560,000
972	57,832,000	1122	156,600,200	1264	125,180,000
973	53,875,000	1123	124,200,200	1265	120,135,000
974	63,834,000	1124	120,740,200	1266	115,405,000
975	67,162,200	1125	133,623,280	1267	115,855,000
976	64,561,000	1126	45,569,088	1268	115,340,000
977	64,079,500	1127	122,493,280	1269	114,840,000
978	63,388,000	1128	131,260,200	1270	116,140,000
979	62,285,000	1129	47,125,200	1271	116,900,000
980	57,492,610	1130	123,105,000	1272	114,085,000
981	99,190,000	1131	126,105,050	1273	114,880,000
982	104,790,000	1132	209,170,000	1274	26,995,000
983	108,805,000	1133	120,835,000	1275	128,495,000
984	107,340,000	1134	115,715,000	1276	1,139,930,000
985	117,020,000	1135	118,445,000	1306	116,835,000
986	122,633,000	1136	111,685,000	1307	117,470,000
987	130,960,000	1137	43,099,200	1308	123,770,000
988	128,478,000	1138	115,444,000	1309	131,270,000
989	132,090,000	1139	126,470,000	1310	122,285,000
990	130,050,000	1140	124,560,000	1311	14,680,000
991	131,350,000	1141	115,455,000	1312	114,160,000
992	129,980,000	1142	122,060,000	1313	128,475,000
993	122,315,000	1143	120,540,000	1314	119,535,000
994	122,170,000	1144	113,075,000	1315	125,110,000
995	131,635,000	1145	139,325,000	1316	114,853,200
996	121,860,000	1146	124,445,000	1317	124,290,000
997	121,120,000	1147	113,792,000	1318	128,460,000
998	119,120,000	1148	44,215,200	1319	127,585,000
999	112,125,000	1149	113,195,000	1320	115,875,000
1000	114,140,000	1150	121,805,000	1321	1,173,547,420
1001	114,490,000	1151	115,353,000	1322	114,015,000
1002	117,200,000	1152	111,080,000	1323	121,105,000
1003	116,130,000	1153	153,025,000	1324	132,045,000
1004	116,175,000	1154	119,665,000	1325	118,780,000
1005	115,945,000	1155	117,855,000	1326	121,985,000
1006	112,540,000	1156	118,185,000	1327	111,850,000
1007	117,415,000	1157	112,260,000	1328	117,225,000
1008	2,899,580,000	1158	125,010,000	1329	111,515,000
1009	114,540,000	1159	119,798,000	1330	114,270,000
1010	113,135,000	1160	42,696,000	1331—1332	120,865,000
1011	116,255,000	1161	106,610,000	1333	110,675,000
1012	113,860,000	1162	109,695,000	1334	110,670,000
1013	124,260,000	1163	123,690,000	1335	113,825,000
1014	115,735,000	1164	123,970,000	1336	1,208,700,000
1015	115,430,000	1165	124,796,000	1337	113,330,000
1016	136,220,000	1166	42,076,800	1339	141,350,000
1017	114,894,600	1167	116,210,000	1340	144,345,000
1018	118,706,000	1168	126,252,000	1342	147,120,000
1019	114,190,000	1169	42,746,400	1343	130,125,000
1020	113,990,000	1170	124,117,000	1344	158,700,000
1021	89,289,600	1171	119,840,000	1345—1354	228,040,000
1022	114,865,000	1172	117,187,000	1355	153,015,000
1023	115,780,000	1173	124,390,000	1356	132,560,000
1024	115,244,600	1174	112,966,000	1357	130,385,000
1025	123,709,600	1175	41,644,200	1358	132,265,000
1026	114,789,600	1176	110,850,000	1359	128,710,000
1027	115,759,600	1177	98,616,000	1360	124,775,000
1028	116,134,600	1178	101,125,000	1361	128,295,000
1029	118,540,000	1179	124,865,000	1362	142,245,000
1060	115,810,000	1180	79,905,000	1363	1,410,580,000
1061	113,603,700	1181	125,410,000	1364	125,100,000
1062	128,002,000	1182	112,845,000	1365—1368	192,570,000
1063	116,078,150	1183	106,210,000	1369	148,770,000
1064	116,139,800	1184	110,810,000	1370	139,475,000
1065	120,484,800	1185	116,995,000	1371	187,165,000
1066	53,854,750	1186	121,015,000	1372	125,555,000
1067	176,075,000	1187	111,600,000	1373	144,425,000
1068	125,944,400	1188	110,620,000	1374	135,875,000
1069	122,284,600	1189	109,110,000	1375	151,110,000
1070	133,638,850	1190	145,350,000	1376—1379	159,195,000
1071	118,664,600	1191	112,870,000	1380	129,540,000
1072	112,434,000	1192	121,820,000	1381	130,925,000
1073	129,384,550	1193	289,240,000	1382	139,055,000
1074	121,184,600	1194	120,155,000	1383	150,611,200
1075	2,900,731	1195	124,595,000	1384	1,709,795,000
1076	119,784,200	1196	147,310,000	1385	127,545,000
1077	123,159,400	1197	118,690,000	1386	145,788,800
1078	123,138,800	1198	122,730,000	1387—1390	201,794,200

Scott No.	Quantity	Scott No.	Quantity	Scott No.	Quantity
1391	171,850,000	1690	164,890,000	2031	118,555,000
1392	142,205,000	1691—1694	208,035,000	2032—2035	226,128,000
1405	137,660,000	1695—1698	185,715,000	2036	118,225,000
1406	135,125,000	1699	130,592,000	2037	114,290,000
1407	135,895,000	1700	158,332,800	2038	165,000,000
1408	132,675,000	1701	809,955,000	2039	120,430,000
1409	134,795,000	1702—1703	963,370,000	2040	117,025,000
1410—1413	161,600,000	1704	150,328,000	2041	181,700,000
1414—1414a	683,730,000	1705	176,830,000	2042	114,250,000
1415—1418,		1706—1709	195,976,000	2043	111,775,000
1415a—1418a	489,255,000	1710	208,820,000	2044	115,200,000
1419	127,610,000	1711	192,250,000	2045	108,820,000
1420	129,785,000	1712—1715	219,830,000	2046	184,950,000
1421—1422	134,380,000	1716	159,852,000	2047	110,925,000
1423	136,305,000	1717—1720	188,310,000	2048—2051	395,424,000
1424	134,840,000	1721	163,625,000	2052	104,340,000
1425	130,975,000	1722	156,296,000	2053	114,725,000
1426	161,235,000	1723—1724	158,676,000	2054	112,525,000
1427—1430	175,679,600	1725	154,495,000	2055—2058	193,055,000
1431	138,700,000	1726	168,050,000	2059—2062	207,725,000
1432	138,165,000	1727	156,810,000	2063	715,975,000
1433	152,125,000	1728	153,736,000	2064	848,525,000
1434—1435	176,295,000	1729	882,260,000	2065	165,000,000
1436	142,845,000	1730	921,530,000	2066	120,000,000
1437	148,755,000	1731	156,560,000	2067—2070	319,675,000
1438	139,080,000	1732—1733	202,155,000	2071	103,975,000
1439	130,755,000	1744	156,525,000	2072	554,675,000
1440—1443	170,208,000	1745—1748	165,182,400	2073	120,000,000
1444	1,074,350,000	1749—1752	157,598,400	2074	106,975,000
1445	979,540,000	1753	102,856,000	2075	107,325,000
1446	137,355,000	1754	152,270,000	2076—2079	306,912,000
1447	150,400,000	1755	94,600,000	2080	120,000,000
1448—1451	172,730,000	1756	151,570,000	2081	108,000,000
1452	104,090,000	1757	15,170,400	2082—2085	313,350,000
1453	164,096,000	1758	161,228,000	2086	130,320,000
1454	53,920,000	1759	158,880,000	2087	120,000,000
1455	153,025,000	1760—1763	186,550,000	2088	117,050,000
1456—1459	201,890,000	1764—1767	168,136,000	2089	115,725,000
1460	67,335,000	1768	963,120,000	2090	116,600,000
1461	179,675,000	1769	916,800,000	2091	120,000,000
1462	46,340,000	1770	159,297,600	2092	123,575,000
1463	180,155,000	1771	166,435,000	2093	120,000,000
1464—1467	198,364,800	1772	162,535,000	2094	117,125,000
1468	185,490,000	1773	155,000,000	2095	117,225,000
1469	162,335,000	1774	157,310,000	2096	95,525,000
1470	162,789,950	1775—1778	174,096,000	2097	119,125,000
1471	1,003,475,000	1779—1782	164,793,600	2098—2101	216,260,000
1472	1,017,025,000	1783—1786	163,055,000	2102	120,000,000
1473	165,895,000	1787	161,860,000	2103	108,140,000
1474	166,508,000	1788	165,775,000	2104	117,625,000
1475	320,055,000	1789	160,000,000	2105	112,896,000
1476	166,005,000	1790	67,195,000	2106	116,500,000
1477	163,050,000	1791—1794	186,905,000	2107	751,300,000
1478	159,005,000	1795—1798	208,295,000	2108	786,225,000
1479	147,295,000	1799	873,710,000	2109	105,300,000
1480—1483	196,275,000	1800	931,880,000	2110	124,500,000
1484	139,152,000	1801	161,290,000	2137	120,000,000
1485	128,048,000	1802	172,740,000	2138—2141	300,000,000
1486	146,008,000	1803	168,995,000	2142	120,580,000
1487	139,608,000	1804	160,000,000	2143	729,700,000
1488	159,475,000	1805—1810	232,134,000	2144	124,750,000
1489—1498	486,020,000	1821	163,510,000	2145	203,496,000
1499	157,052,800	1822	256,620,000	2146	126,325,000
1500	53,005,000	1823	95,695,000	2147	130,000,000
1501	159,775,000	1824	153,975,000	2152	119,975,000
1502	39,005,000	1825	160,000,000	2153	120,000,000
1503	152,624,000	1826	103,850,000	2154	119,975,000
1504	145,840,000	1827—1830	204,715,000	2155—2158	147,940,000
1505	151,335,000	1831	166,545,000	2159	120,000,000
1506	141,085,000	1832	163,310,000	2160—2163	130,000,000
1507	885,160,000	1833	160,000,000	2164	120,000,000
1508	939,835,000	1834—1837	152,404,000	2165	759,200,000
1525	143,930,000	1838—1841	152,420,000	2166	757,600,000
1526	145,235,000	1842	692,500,000	2198—2201	67,996,800
1527	135,052,000	1843	718,715,000	2202	947,450,000
1528	156,750,000	1874	160,155,000	2203	130,000,000
1529	164,670,000	1875	159,505,000	2204	136,500,000
1530—1537	190,156,800	1876—1879	210,633,000	2205—2209	219,990,000
1538—1541	167,212,800	1910	165,175,000	2210	130,000,000
1542	156,265,000	1911	107,240,000	2211	130,000,000
1543—1546	195,585,000	1912—1919	337,819,000	2216	5,825,050
1547	148,850,000	1920	99,420,000	2217	5,825,050
1548	157,270,000	1921—1924	178,930,000	2218	5,825,050
1549	150,245,000	1925	100,265,000	2219	5,825,050
1550	835,180,000	1926	99,615,000	2220—2223	130,000,000
1551	882,520,000	1927	97,535,000	2224	220,725,000
1552	213,155,000	1928—1931	167,308,000	2235—2238	240,525,000
1553	156,995,000	1932	101,625,000	2239	131,700,000
1554	146,365,000	1922	99,170,000	2240—2243	240,000,000
1555	148,805,000	1934	101,155,000	2244	690,100,000
1556	173,685,000	1935	101,200,000	2245	882,150,000
1557	158,600,000	1936	167,360,000	2246	167,430,000
1558	153,355,000	1937—1938	162,420,000	2247	166,555,000
1559	63,205,000	1939	597,720,000	2248	811,560,000
1560	157,865,000	1940	792,600,000	2249	142,905,000
1561	166,810,000	1941	167,130,000	2250	130,000,000
1562	44,825,000	1942—1945	191,560,000	2251	149,980,000
1563	144,028,000	1950	163,939,200	2267—2274	610,425,000
1564	139,928,000	1952	180,700,000	2275	156,995,000
1565—1568	179,855,000	1953—2002	666,950,000	2286—2335	645,975,000
1569—1570	161,863,200	2003	109,245,000	2336	166,725,000
1571	145,640,000	2004	112,535,000	2337	186,575,000
1572—1575	168,655,000	2006—2009	124,640,000	2338	184,325,000
1576	146,615,000	2010	107,605,000	2339	165,845,000
1577—1578	146,196,000	2011	173,160,000	2340	155,170,000
1579	739,430,000	2012	107,285,000	2341	102,100,000
1580	878,690,000	2013	109,040,000	2342	103,325,000
1629—1631	219,455,000	2014	183,270,000	2343	162,045,000
1632	157,825,000	2015	169,495,000	2344	153,295,000
1633—1682	436,005,000	2016	164,235,000	2345	160,245,000
1683	159,915,000	2017	110,130,000	2346	183,290,000
1684	156,960,000	2018	110,995,000	2347	179,800,000
1685	158,470,000	2019—2022	165,340,000	2348	164,130,000
1686	1,990,000	2023	174,180,000	2349	157,475,000
1687	1,983,000	2024	110,261,000	2350	156,225,000
1688	1,953,000	2026	703,295,000	2351—2354	163,980,000
1689	1,903,000	2027—2030	788,880,000	2355—2359	584,340,000

Scott No.	Quantity
2360	168,995,000
2361	163,120,000
2362—2366	394,776,000
2367	528,790,000
2368	978,340,000
2369	158,870,000
2370	145,560,000
2371	97,300,000
2372—2375	158,556,000
2376	97,300,000
2377	153,045,000
2378	841,240,000
2379	169,765,000
2380	157,215,000
2381—2385	635,238,000
2386—2389	162,142,500
2390—2393	305,015,000
2395—2398	480,000,000
2399	821,285,000
2400	1,030,850,000
2401	165,495,000
2402	151,675,000
2403	163,000,000
2404	264,625,000
2405—2409	204,984,000
2410	103,835,000
2411	152,250,000
2412	138,760,000
2413	137,985,000
2414	138,580,000
2415	150,545,000
2416	164,680,000
2417	262,755,000
2418	191,755,000
2420	188,400,000
2421	191,860,000
2422—2425	406,988,000
2426	137,410,000
2427	913,335,000
2428	900,000,000
2429	399,243,000
2433	2,017,225
2434—2437	163,824,000
2438	2,047,200
2439	173,000,000
2440	886,220,000
2441	995,178,000
2442	153,125,000
2444	169,495,000
2445—2448	176,808,000
2449	150,000,000
2470—2474	733,608,000
2496—2500	178,587,500
2501—2505	619,128,000
2506—2507	151,430,000
2508—2511	278,264,000
2512	143,995,000
2513	142,692,000
2514	728,919,000
2515	599,400,000
2516	320,304,000
2532	103,648,000
2533	179,990,000
2534	150,560,000
2538	161,498,000
2545—2549	744,918,000
2550	149,848,000
2551	200,003,000
2552	200,000,000
2553—2557	170,025,600
2558	150,310,000
2560	149,810,000
2561	149,260,000
2562—2566	699,978,000
2567	148,973,000
2577a	33,394,800
2615a	32,000,000
2616	148,665,000
2617	149,990,000
2618	835,000,000
2619	160,000,000
2623a	40,005,000
2624	1,185,170
2625	1,185,170
2626	1,185,170
2627	1,185,170
2628	1,185,170
2629	1,185,170
2630	148,000,000
2634a	37,315,000
2635	146,610,000
2636	160,000,000
2641a	32,000,000
2646a	87,728,000
2696a	11,000,000
2697	12,000,000
2698	105,000,000
2699	142,500,000
2703a	36,831,000
2704	85,000,000
2709a	80,000,000
2721	517,000,000
2722	150,000,000
2723	152,000,000
2730a	14,285,715
2731	98,841,000
2732	32,947,000
2733	32,947,000
2734	32,947,000
2735	65,894,000
2736	65,894,000
2737	65,894,000
2745a	140,000,000
2746	105,000,000
2747	110,000,000
2748	110,000,000
2749	172,870,000

Scott No.	Quantity
2753a	65,625,000
2754	110,000,000
2755	115,870,000
2759a	40,000,000
2764a	199,784,500
2765	120,000,000
2766	160,000,000
2770a	128,735,000
2774a	25,000,000
2778a	170,000,000
2782a	37,500,000
2784a	41,840,000
2788a	37,550,000
2804	88,300,000
2805	105,000,000
2806	100,000,000
2806a	250,000,000
2811a	35,800,000
2812	150,500,000
2813	357,949,584
2814	830,000,000
2814C	300,000,000
2815	274,800,000
2816	155,500,000
2817	105,000,000
2818	185,500,000
2828a	18,600,000
2833a	166,000,000
2834	201,000,000
2835	300,000,000
2836	269,370,000
2837	60,000,000
2838	120,600,000
2839	209,000,000
2840	20,000,000
2841	12,958,000
2842	100,500,000
2847a	159,200,000
2848	150,500,000
2853a	35,436,000
2854	24,986,000
2855	24,986,000
2856	24,986,000
2857	19,988,800
2858	19,988,800
2859	19,988,800
2860	19,988,800
2861	19,988,800
2862	150,750,000
2866a	56,475,000
2868a	77,748,000
2869	20,000,000
2870	150,186
2871	518,500,000
2872	602,500,000
2873	236,997,600
2874	45,000,000
2875	5,000,000
2876	80,000,000
2948	214,700,000
2949	1,220,970,000
2950	94,500,000
2954a	50,000,000
2955	80,000,000
2956	97,000,000
2957	315,000,000
2958	300,000,000
2965a	30,000,000
2966	125,000,000
2967	400,000,000
2968	99,424,000
2973a	120,240,000
2974	60,000,000
2975	300,000,000
2979a	62,500,000
2980	105,000,000
2981	100,000,000
2982	150,000,000
2983—2992	15,000,000
2992	15,000,000
2997a	200,000,000
2998	300,000,000
2999	85,000,000
3000	300,000,000
3001	80,000,000
3002	80,000,000
3003	300,000,000
3007a	75,000,000
3008	350,495,000
3009	350,495,000
3010	350,495,000
3011	350,495,000
3013	90,000,000
3023a	30,000,000
3024	120,000,000
3029a	160,000,000
3030	2,550,000,000
3058	92,100,000
3059	115,600,000
3060	93,150,000
3064a	23,292,500
3065	111,000,000
3066	314,175,000
3067	209,450,000
3068	16,207,500
3069	156,300,000
3070	100,000,000
3071	60,120,000
3076a	27,850,000
3080a	22,218,000
3081	95,600,000
3082	300,000,000
3086a	23,681,250
3087	133,613,000
3088	103,400,000
3089	60,000,000
3090	134,000,000

Scott No.	Quantity
3095a	32,000,000
3099a	23,025,000
3103a	23,025,000
3104	300,000,000
3105	14,910,000
3106	93,612,000
3107	243,575,000
3111a	56,479,000
3112	847,750,000
3116a	451,312,500
3117	495,504,000
3118	103,520,000
3120	106,000,000
3121	112,000,000
3123	1,660,000,000
3124	814,000,000
3125	122,000,000
3131a	65,000,000
3134	97,500,000
3135	96,000,000
3136	14,600,000
3137	37,800,000
3138	118,000
3139	593,775
3140	592,849
3141	45,250,000
3142	8,050,000
3146a	22,500,000
3147	20,000,000
3148	20,000,000
3149	10,000,000
3150	10,000,000
3151	7,000,000
3152	195,000,000
3153	323,000,000
3157a	21,500,000
3158—3161	12,900,000
3162—3165	8,600,000
3166	25,250,000
3167	45,250,000
3172a	36,250,000
3173	173,000,000
3174	37,000,000
3175	133,000,000
3176	882,500,000
3177	1,621,465,000
3178	15,000,000
3179	51,000,000
3180	80,000,000
3181	45,000,000
3182	
3183	
3184	
3185	
3186	
3187	
3188	
3189	
3190	
3191	
3192	30,000,000
3193—3197	250,000,000
3198—3202	80,000,000
3203	85,000,000
3204	39,600,000
3205	650,000
3206	32,000,000
3209	2,200,000
3210	2,200,000
3211	30,000,000
3212—3215	45,000,000
3216—3219	45,000,000
3220	46,300,000
3221	30,000,000
3222—3225	70,000,000
3226	65,000,000
3227	50,000,000
3230—3234	180,000,000
3235	28,000,000
3236	
3237	130,750,000
3238—3242	185,000,000
3243	50,000,000

AIRPOST STAMPS

Cat. No.	Quantity
C1	3,395,854
C2	3,793,887
C3	2,134,888
C4	6,414,576
C5	5,309,275
C6	5,285,775
C7	42,092,800
C8	15,597,307
C9	17,616,350
C10	20,379,179
C11	106,887,675
C12	97,641,200
C13	93,536
C14	72,428
C15	61,296
C16	57,340,050
C17	76,648,803
C18	324,070
C19	302,205,100
C20	10,205,400
C21	12,794,600
C22	9,285,300
C23	349,946,500
C24	19,768,150
C25	4,746,527,700

Cat. No.	Quantity	Cat. No.	Quantity	Cat. No.	Quantity
C26	1,744,878,650	C52	157,035,000	C78	
C27	67,117,400	C53	90,055,200	C79	
C28	78,434,800	C54	79,290,000	C80	
C29	42,359,850	C55	84,815,000	C81	
C30	59,880,850	C56	38,770,000	C82	
C31	11,160,600	C57	39,960,000	C83	
C32	864,753,100	C58	98,160,000	C84	78,210,000
C33	971,903,700	C59		C85	96,240,000
C34	207,976,550	C60	1,289,460,000	C86	58,705,000
C35	756,186,350	C61	87,140,000	C87	
C36	132,956,100	C62		C88	
C37	33,244,500	C63		C89	
C38	38,449,100	C64		C90	
C39	5,070,095,200	C65		C91—C92	
C40	75,085,000	C66	42,245,000	C93—C94	
C41	260,307,500	C67		C95—C96	
C42	21,061,300	C68	63,890,000	C97	
C43	36,613,100	C69	62,255,000	C116	45,700,000
C44	16,217,100	C70	55,710,000	C117	22,975,000
C45	80,405,000	C71	+50,000,000	C120	38,532,000
C46	18,876,800	C72		C121	39,325,000
C47	78,415,000	C73		C122—C125	106,360,000
C48	50,483,977	C74	+60,000,000	C126	1,944,000
C49	63,185,000	C75			
C50	72,480,000	C76	152,364,800		
C51	1,326,960,000	C77			

+ Quantity ordered printed.

CARRIERS' STAMPS

The term "Carriers' Stamps" is applied to certain stamps of the United States used to defray delivery to a post office on letters going to another post office, and for collection and delivery in the same city (local letters handled only by the carrier department). A less common usage was for a collection fee from the addressee at the post office ("drop letters"). During the period when these were in use, the ordinary postage fee defrayed the carriage of mail matter from post office to post office only.

In many of the larger cities the private ("Local") posts delivered mail to the post office or to an addressee in the city direct for a fee of 1 or 2 cents (seldom more), and adhesive stamps were often employed to indicate payment. (See introduction to "Local Stamps" section.)

Carrier service dates back at least to 1689 when the postmaster of Boston was instructed "to receive all letters and deliver them at 1d." In 1794, the law allowed a penny post to collect 2 cents for the delivery of a letter. As these early fees were paid in cash, little evidence survives.

In 1851 the Federal Government, under the acts of 1825 and 1836, began to deliver letters in many cities and so issued Carriers' stamps for local delivery service. This Act of Congress of March 3, 1851, effective July 1, 1851 (succeeding Act of 1836), provided for the collecting and delivering of letters to the post office by carriers, "for which not exceeding 1 or 2 cents shall be charged."

Carriers' stamps were issued under the authority of, or derived from, the postmaster general. The "Official Issues" (Nos. LO1-LO2) were general issues of which No. LO2 was valid for postage at face value, and No. LO1 at the value set upon sale, in any post office. They were issued under the direct authority of the postmaster general. The "Semi-official Issues" were valid in the city in which they were issued either directly by or sanctioned by the local postmaster under authority derived from the postmaster general.

These "Official" and "Semi-official" Carriers' stamps prepaid the fees of official letter carriers who were appointed by the postmaster general and were under heavy bond to the United States for the faithful performance of their duties. Some of the letter carriers received fixed salaries from the government. Others were paid from the fees received for the delivery and collection of letters carried by them. After discontinuance of carrier fees on June 30, 1863, all carriers of the United States Post Office were government employees, paid by salary at a yearly rate.

Some Carriers' stamps are often found on cover with the regular government stamps and have the official post office cancellation applied to them as well. Honour's City Express and the other Charleston, S.C., Carrier stamps almost always have the stamp uncanceled or canceled with pen, or less frequently pencil.

Unless indicated otherwise, values for Carriers' stamps on cover are for covers having the stamp tied by a handstamped cancellation.

Carriers' stamps, either uncanceled or pen-canceled, **on covers to which they apparently belong** deserve **a premium of at least 25%** over the values for the respective uncanceled or canceled off-cover stamps. When canceled by pen or pencil on cover with initials or name of carrier, as sometimes seen on No. LO2 from Washington, and on Baltimore carrier stamps, the premium is 75% of the on-cover value.

All Carriers' stamps are imperforate and on wove paper, either white or colored through, unless otherwise stated.

Counterfeits exist of many Carriers' stamps.

Prices for most carriers' stamps and covers appear to be very volatile at the present time, due to extreme rarity and the recent appearance at auction of many seldom offered examples.

OFFICIAL ISSUES

Franklin — OC1

Eagle — OC2

Engraved and printed by Toppan, Carpenter, Casilear & Co. Plate of 200 subjects divided into two panes of 100 each, one left, one right

1851, Sept.			Unwmk.		Imperf.
LO1	OC1	(1c)	dull blue (shades),		
			rose	5,000.	5,000.
			On cover from Philadelphia		15,000.
			On cover from New York		27,500.
			On cover from with 3c #10 (a 2nd #LO1 removed)		10,500.
			Cracked plate	—	
			Cracked plate, on cover		60,000.

Double transfer	—	—
Pair	12,500.	12,500.
Strip of 3	20,000.	20,000.

Earliest known use: Oct. 28, 1851.

Cancellations

Red star (Philadelphia)	5,000.
Blue town (Philadelphia)	—
Red town (New York)	+1,000.
Black town (New York), unique	+3,000.
Blue grid (New York)	—
Black grid (New York)	—
Black grid (New Orleans)	—
Green grid (New Orleans)	—

Of the entire issue of 310,000 stamps, 250,000 were sent to New York, 50,000 to New Orleans, 10,000 to Philadelphia. However, the quantity sent to each city is not indicative of proportionate use. More appear to have been used in Philadelphia than in the other two cities. The use in all three cities was notably limited.

No. LO1, cracked plate on cover, is unique.

U.S.P.O. Despatch

Engraved and printed by Toppan, Carpenter, Casilear & Co. Plate of 200 subjects divided into two panes of 100 each, one upper, one lower

1851, Nov. 17			Unwmk.		Imperf.
LO2	OC2	1c	blue (shades)	25.	50.
			On cover, used alone		500.
			On cover, precanceled		600.
			On cover, pair or 2 singles		1,500.
			On cover with block of 3, 1c #9		4,500.
			On cover with 3c #11		400.
			On cover with 3c #25		

On cover with 3c #26		750.
On cover with strip of 3, 3c #26		—
On 3c envelope #U1, #LO2 pen canceled		450.
On 3c envelope #U2, #LO2 pen canceled		450.
On cover with 3c #65 (Washington, D.C.)		5,000.
Pair	60.	
Pair on cover (Cincinnati)		1,000.
Block of 4	165.00	
Margin block of 8, imprint	1,000.	
Double transfer	50.00	100.00

Earliest known use: Jan. 3, 1852.

Cancellations

Red star	50.
Philadelphia	+20.
Cincinnati	+200.
Black grid	+5.
Blue grid	+50.
Red grid	—
Black town	+5.
Blue town	+50.
Red town	—
Kensington, Pa. (red)	+300.
Washington, D.C.	+200.
Blue squared target	—
Red squared target	+100.
Railroad	—
Black carrier (Type C32)	—
Red carrier (Type C32)	—
Carrier's initial, manuscript	—

Earliest known use: Jan. 3, 1852. Used principally in Philadelphia, Cincinnati, Washington, D.C., and Kensington, Pa.

GOVERNMENT REPRINTS
Printed by the Continental Bank Note Co.
First reprinting-10,000 copies, on May 19, 1875.
Second reprinting-10,000 copies, on Dec. 22, 1875.

The first reprinting of the Franklin stamp was on the rose paper of the original, obtained from Toppan, Carpenter, Casilear & Co. Two batches of ink were used, both darker than the original. The second reprinting was on much thicker, paler paper in an indigo color. All of these differ under ultraviolet light. The design of the reprints is not as distinct as the original design and may appear a bit "muddy" in the lathework above the vignette.

Most of the reprints of the Eagle stamp are on the same hard white paper used for special printings of the postage issue, but a few have been found on both very thin and very thick soft porous white paper. A very small number are known to fluoresce green. Reprints may be differentiated from the originals under ultraviolet light by the whiteness of the paper. Nos. LO3-LO6 are ungummed, Nos. LO1-LO2 have brown gum.

1875
Franklin Reprints
Imperf

LO3	OC1	(1c)	**blue**, *rose*	50.
			indigo, *rose*	70.
			Block of 4	225.
			Margin block of 4, imprint	—
			Cracked plate	100.

Perf. 12

LO4	OC1	(1c)	**blue**	16,000.
			Pair	35,000.

No. LO4 is valued in the grade of average to fine.

Eagle Reprints
Imperf.

LO5	OC2	1c	**blue**	25.
			Block of 4	125.

Perf. 12

LO6	OC2	1c	**blue**	200.
			Block of 4	1,000.
			Margin block of 8, imprint	12,500.

SEMI-OFFICIAL ISSUES
All are imperforate.
Baltimore, Md.

C1

		1850-55	**Typo.**	**Settings of 10 (2x5) varieties**		
1LB1	C1	1c	**red** (shades), *bluish*	180.	160.
			On cover, tied by handstamp		1,250.
			On cover with 1c #9		—
			On cover (tied) with 3c #11		500.
1LB2	C1	1c	**blue** (shades), *bluish*	200.	150.
			On cover, tied		1,000.
a.			Bluish laid paper	—	—
1LB3	C1	1c	**blue** (shades)	160.	100.
			On cover, tied by handstamp		1,000.
			Block of 4	1,000.	
a.			Laid paper	200.	150.
			On cover, tied by handstamp		1,000.
1LB4	C1	1c	**green**	—	850.
			On cover, tied by handstamp		3,500.
			On 3c envelope #U10		3,500.
			Pair		5,500.
1LB5	C1	1c	**red**	2,250.	1,750.
			On cover, tied by handstamp		4,500.
			On cover (tied) with 3c #11		5,000.

The No. 1LB4 pair is the unique multiple of this stamp.

Cancellation Nos. 1LB1-1LB5:

Black grid	—
Blue grid	—
Black cross	—
Black town	—
Blue town	—
Black numeral	—
Blue numeral	—
Black pen	—

C2

1856					**Typo.**
1LB6	C2	1c	**blue** (shades)	130.	90.
			On cover		300.
			On cover with 3c #11		650.
			On cover with 3c #26		500.
1LB7	C2	1c	**red** (shades)	130.	90.
			On cover		300.
			On cover (tied) with 3c #26		350.
			On 3c envelope #U9, tied		300.
			Block of 4	850.	

C3

Plate of 10 (2x5); 10 Varieties
The sheet consisted of at least four panes of 10 placed horizontally, the two center panes tete beche. This makes possible five horizontal tete beche gutter pairs.

1857					**Typo.**
1LB8	C3	1c	**black** (shades)	65.	50.
			On cover, tied by handstamp		125.
			On cover (tied) with 3c #26		175.
			On 3c envelope #U9, tied		225.
			On 3c envelope #U10		225.
			On 3c envelope #U27, tied		250.
			Strip of 3 (not tied), on cover		4,000.
			Block of 4	275.	
			Tete beche gutter pair	650.	
a.			"SENT," Pos. 7	100.	75.
			On cover, tied by handstamp		175.
			On cover with 3c #26		250.
			On 3c envelope #U9, tied		250.
			On 3c envelope #U10, tied		250.
b.			Short rays, Pos. 2	100.	75.
			On cover (tied) with 3c #26		600.

Cancellations

Black pen (or pencil)		20.00
Blue town		+2.50
Black town		+2.50
Black Steamship		—

1LB9	C3	1c	**red** (shades)	100.	90.
			On cover		175.
			On cover with 3c #26		300.
			On 3c envelope #U9		325.
			On 3c envelope #U10		325.
			Block of 6	2,250.	
a.			"SENT," Pos. 7	140.	110.
			On cover (tied) with 3c #26		500.
b.			Short rays, Pos. 2	140.	110.
c.			As "b," double impression		—

The block of 6 of No. 1LB9 is the only recorded multiple of this stamp.

Cancellation Nos. 1LB6-1LB7, 1LB9:

Black town	—
Blue town	—
Blue numeral	—
Black pen	—
Carrier's initial, manuscript	—

Boston, Mass.

C6

Several Varieties

1849-50			**Pelure Paper**		**Typeset**
3LB1	C6	1c	**blue**	375.	180.
			On cover, tied by handstamp		275.
			On cover with 5c #1		4,000.
			On cover with two 5c #1		6,750.
			On cover with 3c #10		—
a.			Wrong ornament at left, on cover (not tied)		550.

Cancellation

Red town	—
Red grid	—
Black ornate double oval	—
Black "Penny Post Paid" in 3-bar circle	—

C7

1851					**Typeset**

Several Varieties
Wove Paper Colored Through

3LB2	C7	1c	**blue** (shades), *slate*	190.	100.
			On cover		220.
			On cover with 5c #1		12,500.
			On cover with 3c #10		500.
			On cover with 3c #11		325.
			On 3c envelope #U2, #U5 or #U9		350.
			Tete beche gutter pair	600.	

Cancellation Nos. 3LB2:

Black small fancy circle	—
Black diamond grid	—
Red town	—
Black grid	—
Black PAID	—
Black crayon	—
Red small fancy circle	—
Red diamond grid	—
Black railroad	—
Black hollow star	—
Black pencil	—
Red crayon	—
Black "Penny Post Paid" in 3-bar circle	—

Charleston, S. C.

John H. Honour was appointed a letter carrier at Charleston, in 1849, and engaged his brother-in-law, E. J. Kingman, to assist him. They separated in 1851, dividing the carrier business of the city between them. At the same time Kingman was appointed a letter carrier. In March, 1858, Kingman retired, being replaced by Joseph G. Martin. In the summer of 1858, John F. Steinmeyer, Jr., was added to the carrier force. When Honour retired in 1860, John C. Beckman was appointed in his place.

Each of these carriers had stamps prepared. These stamps were sold by the carriers. The Federal Government apparently encouraged their use.

Honour's City Express

C8

1849		**Typo.**	**Wove Paper Colored Through**		
4LB1	C8	2c	**black**, *brown rose*	10,000.	
			Cut to shape		3,000.
			On cover, not canceled, with certificate		13,500.
			On cover (tied) with 10c #2		40,000.
4LB2	C8	2c	**black**, *yellow*, cut to shape		—
			On cover, not tied, with certificate		12,500.
			On cover with 10c #2		—

Cancellations on Nos. 4LB1-4LB2: Red grid, red town.

No. 4LB1 unused is a unique uncanceled stamp on piece. The used cut-to-shape stamp is also unique. Additionally, each of the listed covers bearing No. 4LB1 is unique.

No. 4LB2 unused (uncanceled) off cover is unique, as is the cover with #2. There are three recorded uses of No. 4LB2 alone on cover.

C10

1854		**Wove Paper**			**Typeset**
4LB3	C10	2c	**black**		1,500.
			On cover, tied by pen cancel		3,000.
			On cover with 3c #11, tied		4,500.

Cancellation

Black "PAID"	—
Black pen	650.
Blue town (Charleston)	—

C11

Several Varieties

1849-50					

Wove Paper Colored Through

					Typeset
4LB5	C11	2c	**black**, *bluish*, pelure	750.	500.
			On cover with pair 5c #1b		—
			On cover with two 5c #1b		—
			On cover (tied) with 3c #11		4,000.
a.			"Ceuts"		5,750.
4LB7	C11	2c	**black**, *yellow*	750.	1,000.
			On cover, tied by handstamp		9,000.

No. 4LB5a is unique. It is without gum and is valued thus.
The varieties of type C11 on bluish wove (thicker) paper and pink, pelure paper are not believed genuine.

Cancellation Nos. 4LB5, 4LB7:

Red town	—
Black pen	—
Red crayon	—

C13

C14

C15

Several varieties of each type

1851-58					**Typeset**

Wove Paper Colored Through

4LB8	C13	2c	**black**, *bluish*	300.	175.
			On cover, tied by handstamp		700.
			On cover, tied, with 3c #10		1,500.
			On cover, tied, with 3c #11		1,500.
			On cover, tied, with 3c #26		1,500.
			Pair		1,500.
a.			Period after "PAID"	500.	250.

	On cover				600.
b.	"Cens"			600.	800.
c.	"Conours" and "Bents"				—
4LB9	C13	2c **black**, *bluish*, pelure		850.	950.
4LB11	C14	(2c) **black**, *bluish*			375.
	On cover, tied by hand-stamp, with 3c #11				15,000.
4LB12	C14	(2c) **black**, *bluish*, pelure			—
4LB13	C15	(2c) **black**, *bluish* ('58)		750.	400.
	On cover with 3c #11, Aiken, S.C. postmark, tied by handstamp (unique)				6,000.
	On cover with 3c #26, tied by pen cancel				4,000.
	Horiz. pair				3,500.
a.	Comma after "PAID"			1,100.	
b.	No period after "Post"			1,400.	

The pair of No. 4LB13 is the unique multiple of this stamp. A 2c of design C13 exists on pink pelure paper. It is believed not to have been issued by the post, but to have been created later and perhaps accidentally.

Cancellation Nos. 4LB8-4LB13

Black town	—
Blue town	—
Red town	—
Black pen	—
Black pencil	—
Red crayon	—

Kingman's City Post

C16   C17

Several varieties of each

1851(?)-58(?)   Typeset
Wove Paper Colored Through

4LB14	C16	2c **black**, *bluish*	650.	700.
	On cover with 3c #11			7,500.
	On cover with 3c #26			6,000.
a.	"Kingman's" erased			5,000.
4LB15	C17	2c **black**, *bluish*	800.	800.
	On cover			—
	Vertical pair			—
	Vertical strip of 3		22,500.	
a.	"Kingman's" erased, on cover with 3c #11, tied by pen cancel (unique)			5,000.

The 4LB15 pair and strip of 3 actually are uncanceled on covers and are valued thus.

Cancellations on Nos. 4LB14-4LB15: Black town, black pen.

Martin's City Post

 C18

Several varieties

1858   Wove Paper Colored Through   Typeset

4LB16	C18	2c **black**, *bluish*	8,000.	

Beckman's City Post
Same as C19, but inscribed "Beckmann's City Post."

1860

4LB17	C19	2c **black**, on cover	—	

No. 4LB17 is unique. It is on cover with 3c No. 26, both tied by black circle townmark: "CHARLESTON, S.C. JUN 18, 1860".

Steinmeyer's City Post

C19   C20

Several varieties of Type C19
Type C20 printed from plate of 10 (2x5) varieties

1859   Wove Paper Colored Through   Typeset

4LB18	C19	2c **black**, *bluish*	—	
4LB19	C20	2c **black**, *bluish*	5,000.	
4LB20	C20	2c **black**, *pink*	150.	—
	Block of 4		750.	
	Sheet of 10		2,250.	
4LB21	C20	2c **black**, *yellow*	150.	
	Block of 4		750.	
	Sheet of 10		2,250.	

Sheets of 10 of Nos. 4LB20-4LB21 exist signed by J.F. Steinmeyer Jr. These sell for about 50% more than the unsigned sheets.

Cancellation on Nos. 4LB19-4LB21: Black pen.

Cincinnati, Ohio
Williams' City Post
Organized by C. C. Williams, who was appointed and commissioned by the Postmaster General.

C20a

1854   Wove Paper   Litho.

9LB1	C20a	2c **brown**	3,000.	3,000.
	On cover, tied by hand-stamp			—
	On cover, tied by pen cancel			3,500.
	On cover with 1c #9			9,500.
	Pair		7,500.	

Cancellations

Red squared target	—
Black pen	—
Blue company circle	—

Fraser & Co.
Local stamps of designs L146-L147 were carrier stamps when used on cover between Feb. 3, 1848 and June 30, 1849.

Cleveland, Ohio
Bishop's City Post.
Organized by Henry S. Bishop, "Penny Postman" who was appointed and commissioned by the Postmaster General.

C20b   C20c

1854   Wove Paper   Litho.

10LB1	C20b	blue	2,000.	2,000.
	On cover, tied by hand-stamp			15,000.
	Pair on cover, canceled by pencil, with 3c #11, with certificate			16,500.

Vertically Laid Paper

10LB2	C20c	2c **black**, *bluish*	—	3,750.
	On cover			—
	Pair			—

Cancellations #10LB1-10LB2

Red town	—
Red boxed numeral	—
Black pencil	—
Black pen	—

Louisville, Ky.
Carrier Service was first established by the Louisville Post Office about 1854, with one carrier. David B. Wharton, appointed a carrier in 1856, issued an adhesive stamp in 1857, but as he was soon thereafter replaced in the service, it is believed that few, if any, of these stamps were used. Brown & McGill, carriers who succeeded Wharton, issued stamps in April, 1858.

Wharton's U.S.P.O. Despatch

 C21

Sheet of 50 subjects in two panes of 25 (5x5) each, one upper, one lower

1857   Lithographed by Robyn & Co.

5LB1	C21	(2c) **bluish green** (shades)	100.	
	Block of 4		500.	
	Pane of 25		3,000.	
	Sheet of 50		7,000.	

Brown & McGill's U. S. P. O. Despatch

C22

1858   Litho. by Hart & Maypother

5LB2	C22	(2c) **blue** (shades)	200.	500.
	On cover with 3c #26, tied by handstamp			4,500.
	Block of 4		1,000.	
5LB3	C22	(2c) **black**	4,500.	15,000.

The value for No. 5LB3 used refers to the finer of the two known used (canceled) examples; it is on a piece with a 3c #26.

Cancellations on Nos. 5LB2-5LB3: Blue town, black pencil.

New York, N. Y.
UNITED STATES CITY DESPATCH POST
By an order made on August 1, 1842, the Postmaster General established a carrier service in New York known as the "United States City Despatch Post." Local delivery service had been authorized by the Act of Congress of July 2, 1836.

Greig's City Despatch Post was sold to the U. S. P. O. Department and on August 16, 1842, began operation as the "United States City Despatch Post" under the superintendence of Alexander M. Greig who was appointed a U. S. letter carrier for that purpose.

The Greig circular introducing this service stated that letter boxes had been placed throughout the city, that letters might be sent prepaid or collect, and that registry service was available for an extra 3 cents.

The City Despatch Post stamps were accepted for the service of the United States City Despatch Post. The stamps thus used bear the cancellation of the New York Post Office, usually "U.S." in an octagon which served as a type of overprint indicating that the carrier service was now a government operation (no longer a private local post) as well as a cancellation.

Some examples are canceled by a circular date stamp reading "U.S. CITY DESPATCH POST" or, infrequently, a New York town postmark.

No. 6LB3 was the first stamp issued by authority of the U.S.P.O. Department. The 3c denomination included 1 cent in lieu of drop letter postage until June 30, 1845, and the maximum legal carrier fee of 2 cents. Service was discontinued late in November, 1846.

C23   C24

Engraved and printed by Rawdon, Wright & Hatch.

Plate of 42 (6x7) subjects
Wove Paper Colored Through

1842

6LB1	C23	3c **black**, *grayish*	1,750.	
	On cover, tied by handstamp			10,000.

Cancellations

Red "U.S" in octagon	1,750.
Red circle "U.S. City Despatch Post"	—
Red town	—

Used copies which do not bear the official cancellation of the New York Post Office and unused copies are classed as Local stamps. See No. 40L1.

Plate of 100 subjects

1842-45   Engraved by Rawdon, Wright & Hatch
Wove Paper (unsurfaced) Colored Through

6LB2	C24	3c **black**, *rosy buff*	1,750.	
6LB3	C24	3c **black**, *light blue*	500.	500.
	On cover, tied by handstamp			2,000.
	Pair		1,100.	
6LD4	C24	3c **black**, *green*	—	

Some authorities consider No. 6LB2 to be an essay, and No. 6LB4 a color changeling.

Glazed Paper, Surface Colored

6LB5	C24	3c **black**, *blue green* (shades)	175.	140.
	On cover, tied by handstamp			500.
	Five on cover		—	20,000.
	Pair		—	400.
	Strip of 3		—	650.
	Strip of 4		—	800.
	Block of 4		—	—
	Strip of 5		—	—
	Ribbed paper		—	—

	Double transfer		—
a.	Double impression		1,500.
b.	3c **black**, *blue*	650.	250.
	On cover		750.
c.	As "b," double impression		850.
d.	3c **black**, *green*	1,000.	900.
	On cover		—
e.	As "d," double impression		—
	On cover		—

Cancellation

Red curved PAID	—
Red "U.S City Despatch Post"	—
Red "U.S" in octagon	—
Red New York	—
Red double line circle "U.S. City Despatch Post"	—

No. 6LB5 has been noted on cover with the 5c New York signed "R.H.M.," No. 9X1d.

C25

1846

No. 6LB5 Surcharged in Red

6LB7	C25	2c on 3c **black**, *bluish green*, on cover, not tied, with certificate		55,000.

The City Dispatch 2c red formerly listed as No. 6LB8 is now listed under Local Stamps as No. 160L1.

U.S. MAIL

C27

Issued by the Postmaster at New York, N.Y.

1849   Wove Paper, Colored Through   Typo.

6LB9	C27	1c **black**, *rose*	90.	90.
		On cover, tied by hand-stamp		250.
		On cover with 5c #1		2,000.
		Pair	250.	
		Block of 4	600.	

1849-50

Glazed Surface Paper

6LB10	C27	1c **black**, *yellow*	90.	90.
		On cover, tied by hand-stamp		250.
		On cover with 5c #1		1,500.
		Pair	250.	
		Block of 4	600.	
6LB11	C27	1c **black**, *buff*	90.	90.
		On cover		250.
		On cover with 5c #1, not tied, with certificate		3,000.
a.		Pair, one stamp sideways	2,250.	

Cancellations #6LB9-6LB11

Red town	—
Red grid	—
Red "PAID"	—
Black numeral in circle	—
Red "N.Y. U.S. CITY MAIL" in circle	—
Black pen	—
Black pencil	—

Philadelphia, Pa.

C28

Several Varieties
Thick Wove Paper Colored Through

1849-50   Typeset

7LB1	C28	1c **black**, *rose* (with "L P")	300.	
		On cover, not canceled		2,100.
		On cover with 5c #1		—
7LB2	C28	1c **black**, *rose* (with "S")	3,000.	
		On cover, not canceled		4,500.
7LB3	C28	1c **black**, *rose* (with "H")	275.	
		On cover, tied by hand-stamp		4,000.
		On cover, not canceled		1,000.
		On cover with 5c #1		—
7LB4	C28	1c **black**, *rose* (with "L S")	400.	500.
		On cover, not canceled		2,500.
7LB5	C28	1c **black**, *rose* (with "J J")	7,500.	
		On cover with 5c #1, un-canceled		70,000.

The unique used No. 7LB5 in an uncanceled stamp on a cover front.

C29

Several Varieties

7LB6	C29	1c **black**, *rose*	300.	250.
		On cover, tied by hand-stamp		2,500.
7LB7	C29	1c **black**, *blue*, glazed	1,000.	
		On cover, tied by hand-stamp		7,000.
		On cover with 5c #1		
7LB8	C29	1c **black**, *vermilion*, glazed	700.	
		On cover, tied by hand-stamp		1,500.
		On cover with 5c dark brown #1a, uncanceled		12,500.
		On cover with 5c orange brown #1b, uncanceled		21,000.
7LB9	C29	1c **black**, *yellow*, glazed	3,000.	2,250.
		On cover, not canceled		4,500.
		On cover with 3c #10, un-canceled		2,000.

Cancellations on Nos. 7LB1-7LB9: Normally these stamps were left uncanceled on the letter, but occasionally were accidentally tied by the Philadelphia town postmark which was normally struck in blue ink.

A 1c black on buff (unglazed) of type C29 is believed to be a color changeling.

C30

Settings of 25 (5x5) varieties (Five basic types)

1850-52   Litho.

7LB11	C30	1c **gold**, *black*, glazed	140.	110.
		On cover, tied by hand-stamp		400.
		On cover (tied) with 5c #1		3,500.
		On cover (tied) with 3c #10		800.
		Block of 4	700.	
7LB12	C30	1c **blue**	350.	275.
		On cover, tied by hand-stamp		1,500.
		On cover (tied) with 3c #10		1,750.
		On cover (tied) with 3c #11		1,500.
		Pair		1,600.
7LB13	C30	1c **black**	—	550.
		On cover, tied by hand-stamp		2,250.
		On cover (tied) with 3c #10		—
		On cover (not tied) with 3c #11		3,500.

Cancellation #7LB11-7LB13

Red star	—
Red town	—
Blue town	—

C31

Handstamped

7LB14	C31	1c **blue**, *buff*	3,000.	

No. 7LB14 was handstamped on coarse dark buff paper on which rectangles in the approximate size of the type C31 handstamp had been ruled in pencil. The stamps so produced were later cut out and show traces of the adjoining handstamp markings as well as parts of the penciled rectangle.

1855(?)

7LB16	C31	1c **black**	5,000.	
		On cover with strip of 3, 1c #9		—
		On cover with 3c 1851 stamp removed, tied by handstamp		7,000.

C32

1856(?)   Handstamped

7LB18	C32	1c **black**	1,250.	2,000.
		On cover (cut diamond-shaped) with pair 1c #7 and single 1c #9		—
		On cover with strip of 3, 1c #7		17,000.
		On cover with 3c #11		9,500.
		On 3c envelope #U5		—
		On 3c envelope #U10, not canceled		9,000.

Cancellation #7LB16, 7LB18

Black circled grid	—
Black town	—

Nos. 7LB16 and 7LB18 were handstamped on the sheet margins of U.S. 1851 1c stamps, cut out and used as adhesives. The paper therefore has some surface bluing, and some stamps show parts of the plate imprint. Values are for stamps cut square unless otherwise mentioned.

ENVELOPES

Handstamps of types C31 and C32 were also used to make stamped envelopes and letter sheets or circulars. These same types were also used as postmarks or cancellations in the same period. A handstamp similar to C32, but with "U.S.P. DESPATCH" in serif capitals, is believed to have been used only as a postmark.

Type C31 exists struck in blue or red, type C32 in blue, black or red. When found on cover, on various papers, struck alone, they are probably postmarks and not prepaid stamped envelopes. As such, these entire covers, depending upon the clarity of the handstamp and the general attractiveness of the letter are valued between $400 and $800.

When found on envelopes with the Carrier stamp canceled by a handstamp (such as type C31 struck in blue on a buff envelope canceled by the red solid star cancellation) they can be regarded as probably having been sold as prepaid envelopes. Value approximately $3,000.

Labels of these designs are not believed to be carrier stamps. Those seen are uncanceled, either off cover or affixed to stampless covers of the early 1850's.

St. Louis, Mo.

C36   C37

Illustrations enlarged to show details of the two types (note upper corners especially).

1849   White Wove Paper   Litho.
Two Types

8LB1	C36	2c **black**	7,000.	
8LB2	C37	2c **black**	5,500.	—

Cancellation on Nos. 8LB1-8LB2: Black town.

C38

1857   Litho.

8LB3	C38	2c **blue**	22,500.	
		On cover		—

Cancellations on No. 8LB3: Black boxed "1ct" (on the unique off-cover stamp), black pen.

LOCAL STAMPS

This listing of Local stamps includes stamps issued by Local Posts (city delivery), Independent Mail Routes and Services, Express Companies and other private posts which competed with, or supplemented, official services.

The Independent Mail Routes began using stamps early in 1844 and were put out of business by an Act of March, 1845, which became effective July 1, 1845. By this Act, the Government reduced the zones to two, reduced the rates to 5c and 10c and applied them to weight instead of the number of sheets of paper which composed a letter.

Most of the Local Posts still in business were forced to discontinue service by an Act of 1861, except Boyd's and Hussey's which were able to continue about 20 years longer because of the particular nature of their business. Other posts appeared illegally and sporadically after 1861 and were quickly suppressed.

City posts generally charged 1c to deliver a letter to the Post Office (usually the letter bore a government stamp as well) and 2c for intracity delivery (such letters naturally bore only local stamps). These usages are not catalogued separately because the value of a cover is determined as much by its attractiveness as its franking, rarity being the basic criterion.

Only a few Local Posts used special handstamps for canceling. The stamps frequently were left uncanceled, were canceled by pen, or less often by pencil. **Unless indicated otherwise, values for stamps on cover are for covers having the stamp tied by a handstamped cancellation, either private or governmental.** Local stamps, either uncanceled or pen canceled, **on covers to which they apparently belong** deserve **a premium of at least 25 percent** over the values for the respective uncanceled or canceled off-cover stamp.

The absence of any specific cancellation listed indicates that no company handstamp is known so used, and that the canceling, if any, was done by pen, pencil or government handstamp. Local stamps used on letters directed out of town (and consequently bearing government stamps) sometimes, because of their position, are tied together with the government stamp by the cancellation used to cancel the latter.

Values for envelopes are for entires unless specifically mentioned.

All Local stamps are imperforate and on wove paper, either white or colored through, unless otherwise stated.

Counterfeits exist of many Local stamps, but most of these are crude reproductions and would deceive only the novice.

Prices for most local stamps and covers appear to be very volatile at the present time, due to extreme rarity and the recent appearance at auction of many seldom-offered examples.

Adams & Co.'s Express, California

This post started in September, 1849, operating only on the Pacific Coast.

D. H. Haskell, Manager

| L1 | L2 |

Nos. 1L2-1L5 Printed in Sheets of 40 (8x5).

1854   **Litho.**

1L1	L1	25c **black,** *blue*	2,500.	—
		On cover		—
1L2	L2	25c **black** (initials in black)	90.00	—
		Block of 4	375.00	
a.		Initials in red		—
b.		Without initials		—

Cancellation (1L1-1L2): Black Express Co.
Nos. 1L1-1L2 were the earliest adhesive franks issued west of the Mississippi River.

Glazed Surface Cardboard

1L3	L2	25c **black,** *pink*	35.00	
		Block of 4	150.00	
		Retouched flaw above LR "25"	110.00	

No. 1L3 was probably never placed in use as a postage stamp.

L3

Overprinted in red "Over our California lines only"

1L4	L3	25c **black**	750.00	—

| L4 | L5 |

1L5	L4	25c **black** (black surcharge)	2,750.	—
1L6	L5	25c **black**	1,250.	—
		Pair	4,000.	

The pair of No. 1L6 is unique.

NEWSPAPER STAMP

L6

1LP1	L6	**black,** *claret*	—	2,000.

Cancellation: Blue company oval.

ENVELOPES

| L6a | L6b |

Typo.

1LU1	L6a	25c **blue** (cut square)		15,000.
1LU2	L6b	25c **black,** on U.S. #U9	—	—
1LU3	L6b	50c **black,** on U.S. #U9	2,500.	2,500.
1LU4	L6b	50c **black,** *buff*		15,000.

Nos. 1LU2 and 1LU3 exist cut out and apparently used as adhesives.
Cancellation: Blue company oval.

Adams' City Express Post, New York, N.Y.

| L7 | L7a |

L8

1850-51   **Typo.**

2L2	L7	2c **black,** *buff*	5,000.	
		On cover, canceled, not tied, with certificate		10,000.
2L3	L7a	1c **black,** *gray*		
2L4	L8	2c **black,** *gray*	450.00	450.00
		On cover, tied by handstamp		5,500.

Nos. 2L3-2L4 were reprinted in black and in blue on white wove paper. Some students claim that the 1c and 2c in blue exist as originals.

Allen's City Dispatch, Chicago, Ill.

Established by Edwin Allen for intracity delivery of letters and circulars. The price of the stamps is believed to have been determined on a quantity basis. Uncanceled and canceled remainders were sold to collectors after suppression of the post.

L9

1882   **Typo.**   **Perf. 10**
Sheet of 100

3L1	L9	**pink**	6.00	25.00
		On cover		600.00
3L2	L9	**black**	11.00	—
		On cover		600.00
		Block of 4	47.50	
a.		Horizontal pair, imperf. between	350.00	
3L3	L9	**red,** *yellow*	.75	10.00
		On cover		600.00
		Block of 4	3.25	
a.		Imperf., pair	150.00	
b.		Horizontal pair, imperf. between	—	
3L4	L9	**purple**	80.00	

Cancellations: Violet company oval, violet "eagle."

American Express Co., New York, N.Y.

Believed by some researchers to have been established by Smith & Dobson in 1856, and short-lived.

L10

Typeset
Glazed Surface Paper

4L1	L10	2c **black,** *green*	9,000.	

American Letter Mail Co.

Lysander Spooner established this independent mail line operating to and from New York, Philadelphia and Boston.

L12

L13

1844   Engr.
Sheet of 20 (5x4)

5L1	L12	5c	**black,** *thin paper (2nd printing)*	7.50	27.50
			Thick paper (1st printing)	20.00	30.00
			On cover		750.00
			Pair on cover		—
			Block of 4, thin paper	40.00	
			Sheet of 20, thin paper	225.00	

No. 5L1 has been extensively reprinted in several colors. Cancellations: Red dotted star (2 types). Red "PAID," black brush, red brush.

Engr.

5L2	L13		**black,** *gray*	100.00	75.00
			On cover, tied by handstamp		850.00
			Pair on cover		—
			Block of 4	500.00	
5L3	L13		**blue,** *gray*	1,250.	1,000.
			On cover, uncanceled, with certificate		12,500.

Cancellations: Red "PAID," red company oval.

A. W. Auner's Despatch Post, Philadelphia, Pa.

L13a

1851   Typeset
Cut to shape

154L1	L13a		**black,** *grayish*	9,000.	
			On cover, not tied, with certificate		16,500.

Nos. 154L1 unused and on cover are each unique.

Baker's City Express Post, Cincinnati, Ohio

L14

1849

6L1	L14	2c	**black,** *pink*	1,500.	
			On cover, uncanceled, with certificate		12,500.

Bank & Insurance Delivery Office or City Post
See Hussey's Post.

Barnard's Cariboo Express, British Columbia

The adhesives were used on British Columbia mail and the post did not operate in the United States, so the formerly listed PAID and COLLECT types are omitted. This company had an arrangement with Wells, Fargo & Co. to exchange mail at San Francisco.

Barnard's City Letter Express, Boston, Mass.

Established by Moses Barnard

L19

1845

7L1	L19		**black,** *yellow, glazed paper*	1,000.	1,000.
7L2	L19		**red**	1,000.	

Barr's Penny Dispatch, Lancaster, Pa.
Established by Elias Barr.

L19a   L20

1855   Typeset
Five varieties of each

8L1	L19a		**red**	1,000.	1,000.
			On cover		—
8L2	L20		**black,** *green*	150.	150.
			On cover with 3c #11		—
			Pair	350.	

Bayonne City Dispatch, Bayonne City, N.J.

Organized April 1, 1883, to carry mail, with three daily deliveries. Stamps sold at 80 cents per 100.

L21

1883   Electrotyped
Sheet of 10

9L1	L21	1c	**black**	150.	150.
			On cover		500.
			On cover with 1c & 2c #183, 206		2,750.
			On cover with 3c #207		1,600.

Cancellation: Purple concentric circles.

ENVELOPE

1883, May 15   Handstamped

9LU1	L21	1c	**purple,** *amber*	125.	1,000.

Bentley's Dispatch, New York, N.Y.

Established by H. W. Bentley, who acquired Cornwell's Madison Square Post Office, operating until 1856, when the business was sold to Lockwood. Bentley's postmark was double circle handstamp.

     BENTLEY'S *Despatch,* MADISON SQ.

L22   L22a

1856(?)   Glazed Surface Paper

10L1	L22		**gold**	5,250.	9,000.
10L2	L22a		**gold**		8,000.

Nos. 10L1 unused and used are each unique. The former with repaired corner and valued thus.

Cancellation: Black "PAID."

Berford & Co.'s Express, New York, N.Y.

Organized by Richard G. Berford and Loring L. Lombard. Carried letters, newspapers and packages by steamer to Panama and points on the West Coast, North and South America. Agencies in West Indies, West Coast of South America, Panama, Hawaii, etc.

L23

1851

11L1	L23	3c	**black**	5,000.	7,000.
			On cover, not canceled		—
11L2	L23	6c	**green**		—

			On cover, tied		—
11L3	L23	10c	**violet**		—
			On cover, not canceled		—
			Four cut to shape on cover		16,500.
			Pair		—
a.			Horiz. tete beche pair		
			On cover with normal pair		55,000.
			Two tete beche pair on cover		—
11L4	L23	25c	**red**		—
			On cover with #11L1 & 2		
			#11L2		55,000.

Values of cut to shape copies are about half of those quoted. Cancellation: Red "B & Co. Paid" (sometimes impressed without ink). Dangerous counterfeits exist of Nos. 11L1-11L4.

Bicycle Mail Route, California

During the American Railway Union strike, Arthur C. Banta, Fresno agent for Victor bicycles, established this post to carry mail from Fresno to San Francisco and return, employing messengers on bicycles. The first trip was made from Fresno on July 6, 1894. Service was discontinued on July 18 when the strike ended. In all, 380 letters were carried. Stamps were used on covers with U.S. Government adhesive stamps and on stamped envelopes.

(Illustration reduced size) — L24

Printed from single die. Sheet of six.
Error of spelling "SAN FRANSISCO"

1894   Typo.   Rouletted 10

12L1	L24	25c	**green**	100.	120.
			On cover		1,500.
			Block of 4	450.	

(Illustration reduced size) — L25

Retouched die. Spelling error corrected.

12L2	L25	25c	**green**	30.	75.
			On cover		1,250.
			Block of 4	125.	
			Pane of 6	225.	
a.			"Horiz." pair, imperf. "vert"	75.	

ENVELOPES

12LU1	L25	25c	**brown,** on 2c No. U311	140.	1,350.
12LU2	L25	25c	**brown,** on 2c No. U312	140.	1,350.

Cancellation: Two black parallel bars 2mm apart. Stamps and envelopes were reprinted from the defaced die.

Bigelow's Express, Boston, Mass.

Authorities consider items of this design to be express company labels rather than stamps.

Bishop's City Post, Cleveland, Ohio
See Carriers' Stamps, Nos. 10LB1-10LB2.

Blizzard Mail

Organized March, 1888, to carry mail to New York City during the interruption of U.S. mail by the Blizzard of 1888. Used March 12-16.

L27

1888, Mar. 12   Quadrille Paper   Typo.
163L1 L27 5c black   2,000.

D.O. Blood & Co., Philadelphia, Pa.
I. Philadelphia Despatch Post

Operated by Robertson & Co., predecessor of D.O.
Blood & Co.

L28

L29

Initialed "R & Co."

1843   Handstamped
Cut to Shape
15L1 L28 3c red, bluish   1,500.
       On cover   12,500.
15L2 L28 3c black   1,500.
       On cover   —

Cancellations on Nos. 15L1-15L2: Red "3." Red pattern of
segments.

Without shading in background.
Initialed "R & Co"

1843   Litho.
15L3 L29 (3c) black, grayish   500.
       On cover, tied by handstamp   10,000.
  a. Double impression   —

       Cancellation on No. 15L3: Red "3"

The design shows a messenger stepping over the
Merchants' Exchange Building, which then housed the Government Post Office, implying that the private post gave faster
service.
See illustration L161 for similar design.

II. D.O. Blood & Co.

Formed by Daniel Otis Blood and Walter H. Blood in
1845. Successor to Philadelphia Despatch Post which
issued Nos. 15L1-15L3.

L30

Initialed "Dob & Cos" or "D.O.B. & Co."

1845
Shading in background
15L4 L30 (3c) black, grayish   300.
       On cover   3,750.

L31   L32

1845
15L5 L31 (2c) black   125.   225.
       On cover   750.
       Block of 4   475.
       Pane of 12   5,500.

1846
15L6 L32 (2c) black   —   150.
       On cover   800.

Cancellations on Nos. 15L4-15L6: Black dot pattern. Black
cross. Red "PAID."
Dangerous counterfeits exist of Nos. 15L3-15L6.

L33   L34

L35

1846-47
15L7 L33 (1c) black   125.00   90.00
       On cover, tied by handstamp   750.00
15L8 L34 (1c) black   90.00   55.00
       On cover, tied by handstamp   700.00
15L9 L35 (1c) black   75.00   45.00
       On cover, tied by handstamp   1,500.
       Block of 4   —

Values for Nos. 15L7-15L9 cut to shape are half of those
quoted.
"On cover" listings of Nos. 15L7-15L9 are for stamps tied by
government town postmarks, either Philadelphia, or rarely
Baltimore.

L36   L37

1848
15L10 L36 black & blue   300.00 300.00
        On cover, not canceled   750.00
        Pair   1,300.
15L11 L37 black, pale green   250.00 300.00
        On cover, not tied   750.00

        Cancellation: Black grid.

L38   L39

1848-54
15L12 L38 (1c) gold, black, glazed   85.00   70.00
        On cover, tied by hand-
         stamp   750.00
        On cover with 5c #1
15L13 L39 1c bronze, black, glazed ('50)   20.00   12.50
        On cover, tied by hand-
         stamp   225.00
        On cover, acid tied   75.00
        On cover, acid tied, with 5c
         #1   1,600.
        On cover with 10c #2   —
        On cover with, tied by hand-
         stamp, 3c #10   250.00
        Block of 4   150.00
        Pane of 24   2,000.
15L14 L40 (1c) bronze, lilac ('54)   4.25   2.50
        On cover, tied by hand-
         stamp   200.00
        On cover, acid tied   30.00
        On cover, acid tied, with 1c
         #9   300.00
        On cover with 3c #11   375.00
        On cover, tied by hand-
         stamp, with 3c #26   200.00
        On cover, acid tied, with 3c
         #64b   125.00
        Block of 4   50.00
        Pane of 25   750.00
  a. Laid paper   —   —
15L15 L40 (1c) blue & pink, bluish ('53)   17.50   10.00
        On cover, tied by hand-
         stamp   200.00
        On cover, acid tied   50.00
        Block of 4   80.00
        Pane of 25   1,750.
  a. Laid paper   —   —
15L16 L40 (1c) bronze, black, glazed ('54) 22.50   17.50
        On cover   225.00
        On cover, acid tied   50.00
        On cover, tied by hand-
         stamp, with 3c #11   275.00
15L17 L41 (1c) bronze, black, glazed   25.00   15.00
        On cover, tied by hand-
         stamp   225.00
        On cover, acid tied   50.00
        On cover, not tied, with 5c
         #1   800.00
        On cover, handstamp tied,
         with pair of 5c #1a   11,000.

Cancellations: Black grid (No. 15L12, 15L17). Nos. 15L13-
15L16 were almost always canceled with an acid which discolored both stamp and cover.

III. Blood's Penny Post

Blood's Penny Post was acquired by the general
manager, Charles Kochersperger, in 1855, when
Daniel O. Blood died.

Henry Clay — L42

1855   Engr. by Draper, Welsh & Co.
15L18 L42 (1c) black   25.00   10.00
        On cover   175.00
        On cover, tied by hand-
         stamp, with 3c #11   250.00
        On cover, tied by hand-
         stamp, with 3c #26   225.00
        On 3c entire #U9   300.00
        Block of 4   125.00

Cancellations: Black circular "Blood's Penny Post." Black "1"
in frame. Red "1" in frame.

ENVELOPES

L43   L44

1850-60   Embossed
15LU1 L43 red, white   60.00   80.00
  a. Pink, white   80.00
  b. Impressed on US Env. #U9   225.00
15LU2 L43 red, buff   —   125.00
15LU3 L44 red, white   60.00 125.00
15LU4 L44 red, buff   60.00 100.00

L45

15LU5	L45	**red,** *white*		35.00	75.00
		Used with 3c #11			*350.00*
		Used with 3c #26			*350.00*
a.		Impressed on US Env. #U7			*250.00*
b.		Impressed on US Env. #U9			*250.00*
c.		Impressed on US Env. #U1			*300.00*
d.		Impressed on US Env. #U3			*500.00*
e.		Impressed on US Env. #U2			*275.00*
15LU6	L45	**red,** *amber*		35.00	100.00
15LU6A	L45	**red,** *buff*			*350.00*
		On cover with 10c #2			—
		On cover with three 1c #9			—
b.		**Red,** *brown*			*500.00*

Laid Paper

15LU7	L45	**red,** *white*		35.00	125.00
		Used with acid tied #15L14			*200.00*
a.		Impressed on US Env. #U9			*350.00*
15LU8	L45	**red,** *amber*		35.00	125.00
		Used with 3c No. 25			*200.00*
15LU9	L45	**red,** *buff*		35.00	125.00
15LU10	L45	**red,** *blue*		400.00	500.00

Nos. 15LU1-15LU9 exist in several envelope sizes.
Cancellations: Black grid (Nos. 15LU1-15LU4). Black company circle (2 sizes and types). When on government envelope, the Blood stamp was often left uncanceled.

Bouton's Post, New York, N.Y.
I. Franklin City Despatch Post
Organized by John R. Bouton

L46

1847   Glazed Surface Paper   Typo.

16L1	L46	(2c) **black,** *green*	7,500.	
a.		"Bouton" in blk. ms. vert. at side	7,000.	
		On cover		*14,000.*

II. Bouton's Manhattan Express
Acquired from William V. Barr

L47

1847   Typo.

17L1	L47	2c **black,** *pink*	4,000.	
		Cut to shape	900.	
		On cover, uncanceled		*4,500.*

III. Bouton's City Dispatch Post
(Sold to Swarts' in 1849.)

Corner Leaves — L48	Corner Dots — L49

Design: Zachary Taylor

1848   Litho.

18L1	L48	2c **black**	—	600.
		On cover		*2,000.*
		On cover with 10c #2		*50,000.*
18L2	L49	2c **black,** *gray blue*	200.	250.
		On cover, tied by handstamp		600.
		On cover tied by Swarts' handstamp		*1,000.*
		On cover with 5c #1		*25,000.*
		On cover with 10c #2		*7,500.*

Cancellations on Nos. 18L1-18L2: Red "PAID BOUTON."

Boyce's City Express Post, New York, N.Y.

L50

Center background has 17 parallel lines

1852   Glazed Surface Paper   Typo.

19L1	L50	2c **black,** *green*	1,500.	1,000.
		Cut to shape	600.00	
		On cover, tied by manuscript cancel		*4,000.*

Boyd's City Express, New York, N.Y.

Boyd's City Express, as a post, was established by John T. Boyd, on June 17, 1844. In 1860 the post was briefly operated by John T. Boyd, Jr., under whose management No. 20L15 was issued.

For about six months in 1860 the post was suspended. It was then sold to William and Mary Blackham who resumed operation on Dec. 24, 1860.

The Blackham issues began with No. 20L16. Boyd's had arrangements to handle local delivery mail for Pomeroy, Letter Express, Brooklyn City Express Post, Staten Island Express Post and possibly others.

L51

Designs L51-L56, L59-L60 have a rectangular frame of fine lines surrounding the design.

1844   Glazed Surface Paper   Litho.

20L1	L51	2c **black,** *green*		500.
		On cover		*4,000.*
		On cover, not tied, with #117L4		*7,000.*

Cancellation: Red "FREE."

L52	L53	L54

1844   Plain background. Map on globe.

20L2	L52	2c **black,** *yellow green*	150.00	
		On cover		*350.00*

Cancellation: Red "FREE."

1845   Plain background. Only globe shaded.

20L3	L53	2c **black,** *bluish green*	—	200.00
		On cover		*400.00*

Cancellation: Red "FREE."

1845

Inner oval frame of two thin lines. Netted background, showing but faintly on late impressions.

20L4	L54	2c **black,** *green*	75.00	15.00
		On cover, tied by handstamp		250.00
		On cover, tied, with 5c #1		*5,000.*
		Double transfer		35.00
a.		Diagonal half used as 1c on cover		*2,300.*

Cancellations: Red "FREE." Black grid.

1847

20L5	L54	2c **gold,** *cream*	200.00	
		On cover		*1,000.*

Designs L54-L59 (except No. 20L23) were also obtainable die cut. An extra charge was made for such stamps. In general, genuine Boyd die-cuts sell for 75% of rectangular cut copies. Stamps hand cut to shape are worth much less.

L55	L56	L57

1848

No period after "CENTS." Inner oval frame has heavy inner line.

20L7	L55	2c **black,** *green* (glazed)	10.00	15.00
		On cover, tied by handstamp		225.00
		On cover, tied by handstamp, with 5c #1		*3,250.*
		On cover, tied, with 3c #11		*175.00*
		Block of 4	40.00	
a.		2c **black,** *yellow green*		15.00
		On cover		135.00

Cancellation: Black grid.
No. 20L7a is on unglazed surface-colored paper.

1852   Litho.

Period after "CENTS." Inner frame as in L55.

20L8	L56	2c **black,** *green*	20.00	27.50
		On cover		150.00
		Vert. strip of 3 on cover		300.00
20L9	L56	2c **gold,**	12.50	30.00
		On cover, tied by handstamp		750.00
		On cover with 3c #11		*1,250.*
		Block of 4	65.00	

Cancellations on Nos. 20L8-20L9: Black cork. Black "PAID J.T.B."
No. 20L8 was reprinted in 1862 on unglazed paper, and about 1880 on glazed paper without rectangular frame.

1854

Period after "CENTS." Inner oval frame has heavy outer line. Eagle's tail pointed. Upper part of "2" open, with heavy downstroke at left shorter than one at right. "2C" closer than "T2."

20L10	L57	2c **black,** *green*	32.50	25.00
		On cover, tied by handstamp		125.00

Cancellation: Black "PAID J.T.B."

L58	L59

1856   Unglazed Paper Colored Through   Typo.

Outer oval frame of three lines, outermost heavy. Solid background.

20L11	L58	2c **black,** *olive green*	50.00	30.00
		On cover, tied by handstamp		225.00

1857

20L12	L58	2c **brick red,** *white*	35.00	32.50
		On cover, tied by handstamp		400.00
20L13	L58	2c **dull orange,** *white*	40.00	32.50
		On cover		225.00

Cancellation on Nos. 20L11-20L13: Black "PAID J.T.B."
Nos. 20L11-20L13 were reprinted in the 1880's for sale to collectors. They were printed from a new small plate of 25 on lighter weight paper and in colors of ink and paper lighter than the originals.

1857   Glazed Surface Paper   Litho.

Similar to No. 20L10, but eagle's tail square. Upper part of "2" closed (in well printed specimens) forming a symmetrical "o" with downstrokes equal. "T2" closer than "2C."

20L14	L59	2c **black,** *green*	12.50	17.50
		On cover		125.00
		On cover, tied by handstamp, with 3c #26		—
		Pair on cover		—
		Block of 4	65.00	
a.		Serrate perf.		—

The serrate perf. is probably of private origin.
No. 20L15 was made by altering the stone of No. 20L14, and many traces of the "S" of "CENTS" remain.

1860

20L15	L59	1c **black,** *green*	1.50	30.00
		On cover, tied by handstamp		225.00
		Block of 4	7.50	
a.		"CENTS" instead of "CENT"	—	—
		On cover		450.00

Cancellation on Nos. 20L14-20L15: Black "PAID J.T.B."

L60   L61

Center dots before "POST" and after "CENTS."

1860
20L16	L60	2c	**black**, *red*	7.50	17.50
		On cover, tied by handstamp			175.00
		Block of 4		37.50	
a.		Tete beche pair		45.00	
20L17	L60	1c	**black**, *lilac*	9.00	12.50
		On cover, tied by handstamp			200.00
		On cover, tied by hand-stamp, with 3c #26			175.00
		On cover, tied by hand-stamp, with 3c #65			500.00
		Block of 4		50.00	
a.		"CENTS" instead of "CENT"		22.50	32.50
		Two on cover (No. 20L17a)			—
b.		Tete beche pair		50.00	
c.		"1" inverted			—
20L18	L60	1c	**black**, *blue gray*	17.50	25.00
		On cover, tied by handstamp			250.00
		On cover, tied by hand-stamp, with 3c #26			225.00
		On cover, tied by hand-stamp, with 3c #65			225.00
		Block of 4		90.00	
a.		"CENTS" instead of "CENT"		40.00	60.00
		On cover			250.00
		On cover, tied by hand-stamp, with 1c #24 and three 3c #26			2,000.
b.		Tete beche pair		80.00	

Cancellations on Nos. 20L16-20L18: Black company oval. Black company circle. Black "PAID" in circle.

1861
20L19	L60	2c	**gold**,	100.00	
		Block of 4		—	
a.		Tete beche pair		—	
20L20	L60	2c	**gold**, *green*	20.00	
		Block of 4		85.00	
a.		Tete beche pair		62.50	
20L21	L60	2c	**gold**, *dark blue*	12.50	
		On cover, tied by handstamp			150.00
		Block of 4		75.00	
a.		Tete beche pair		75.00	
20L22	L60	2c	**gold**, *crimson*	25.00	
		Block of 4		110.00	
a.		Tete beche pair		80.00	

1863   **Typo.**
20L23	L58	2c	**black**, *red*	7.50	15.00
		On cover, tied by handstamp			250.00
		Block of 4		37.50	
a.		Tete beche pair		55.00	

Cancellations: Black company. Black "PAID" in circle.
No. 20L23 was reprinted from a new stone on paper of normal color. See note after No. 20L13.

1867   **Typo.**

No period or center dots.
20L24	L61	1c	**black**, *lilac*	12.50	17.50
		On cover, tied by handstamp			200.00
		Block of 4		55.00	
20L25	L61	1c	**black**, *blue*	6.00	15.00
		On cover, tied by handstamp			200.00
		Block of 4		30.00	

Cancellation on Nos. 20L24-20L25: Black company.

Boyd's City Dispatch
(Change in Name)

L62

1874   **Glazed Surface Paper**   **Litho.**
20L26	L62	2c	**light blue**	30.00	30.00
		On cover			200.00
		Block of 4		150.00	

The 2c black on wove paper, type L62, is a cut-out from the Bank Notices envelope, No. 20LU45.

Surface Colored Paper
20L28	L62	2c	**black**, *red*	100.00	
20L29	L62	2c	**blue**, *red*	100.00	

The adhesives of type L62 were made from the third state of the envelope die.
Nos. 20L28 and 20L29 are color trials, possibly used postally.

L63   L64

1876   **Litho.**
20L30	L63	2c	**lilac**, *roseate*		

Laid Paper
20L31	L63	2c	**lilac**, *roseate*		—

Perf. 12½
20L32	L63	2c	**lilac**, *roseate*	20.00	22.50
		On cover			200.00
a.		2c **lilac**, *grayish*		20.00	22.50

Laid Paper
20L33	L63	2c	**lilac**, *roseate*		20.00
a.		2c **lilac**, *grayish*			—

Glazed Surface Paper
20L34	L63	2c	**brown**, *yellow*	25.00	25.00
a.		Imperf. horizontally			—

1877   **Laid Paper**   **Perf. 11, 12, 12½**
20L35	L64	(1c)	**violet**, *lilac*	15.00	17.50
		On cover, tied by handstamp			350.00
a.		(1c) **red lilac**, *lilac*		20.00	20.00
b.		(1c) **gray lilac**, *lilac*		17.50	17.50
c.		Vert. pair, imperf. horiz.		400.00	
20L36	L64	(1c)	**gray**, *roseate*	15.00	15.00
		On cover, tied by handstamp			250.00
a.		(1c) **gray**, *grayish*			15.00

Boyd's Dispatch
(Change in Name)

Mercury Series-Type I — L65

Printed in sheets of 100.
Inner frame line at bottom broken below foot of Mercury.
Printed by C.O. Jones.

1878   **Litho.**   **Wove Paper**   **Imperf.**
20L37	L65	**black**, *pink*	400.00	300.00

Surface Colored Wove Paper
20L38	L65	**black**, *orange red*	750.00	500.00
20L39	L65	**black**, *crimson*	450.00	300.00

Laid Paper
20L40	L65	**black**, *salmon*	450.00	
20L41	L65	**black**, *lemon*	450.00	400.00
20L42	L65	**black**, *lilac pink*	450.00	

Nos. 20L37-20L42 are color trials, some of which may have been used postally.

Surface Colored Paper
Perf. 12
20L43	L65	**black**, *crimson*	40.00	40.00
		On cover, tied by handstamp			300.00
20L43A	L65	**black**, *orange red*	125.00	
		On cover, tied by handstamp			1,000.

Wove Paper
Perf. 11, 11½, 12, 12½ and Compound
20L44	L65	**black**, *pink*	1.50	1.50
		On cover			200.00
a.		Horizontal pair, imperf. between		—	—

1879   **Perf. 11, 11½, 12**
20L45	L65	**black**, *blue*	10.00	10.00
		On cover, tied by handstamp			200.00
20L46	L65	**blue**, *blue*	22.50	22.50
		On cover, tied by handstamp			400.00

1880   **Perf. 11, 12, 13½**
20L47	L65	**black**, *lavender*	8.00	8.00
		On cover, tied by handstamp			300.00
		Block of 4		50.00	
a.		Horizontal pair, imperf. between		400.00	
20L48	L65	**blue**, *lavender*		—	—

1881   **Laid Paper**   **Perf. 12, 12½, 14**
20L49	L65	**black**, *pink*	350.00	
		On cover, tied by handstamp			600.00
20L50	L65	**black**, *lilac pink*	7.00	7.00
		On cover, tied by handstamp			325.00

Mercury Series-Type II — L65a   Mercury Series-Type III — L65b

No break in frame, the great toe raised, other toes touching line.
Printed by J. Gibson

1881   **Wove Paper**   **Perf. 12, 16 & Compound.**
20L51	L65a	**black**, *blue*	25.00	25.00
20L52	L65a	**black**, *pink*	75.00	75.00
		On cover, tied by handstamp			250.00

Laid Paper
20L53	L65a	**black**, *pink*	7.50	7.50
		On cover, tied by handstamp			125.00
20L54	L65a	**black**, *lilac pink*	7.00	7.00
		On cover			200.00

No break in frame, the great toe touching.
Printed by the "Evening Post"

Perf. 10, 11½, 12, 16 & Compound

1882   **Wove Paper**
20L55	L65b	**black**, *blue*	4.00	4.00
		On cover, tied by handstamp			150.00
		Pair on cover			225.00
20L56	L65b	**black**, *pink*	.40	1.50
		On cover, tied by handstamp			100.00
		Block of 4		2.00	

Cancellation on Nos. 20L37-20L56: Purple company.

ENVELOPES
Boyd's City Post

L66

Imprinted in upper right corner.
Used envelopes show Boyd's handstamps.

1864   **Laid Paper**   **Embossed**
20LU1	L66	**red**	175.00	
20LU2	L66	**red**, *amber*	90.00	
20LU3	L66	**red**, *yellow*	—	—
20LU4	L66	**blue**	175.00	
20LU5	L66	**blue**, *amber*	175.00	
20LU6	L66	**blue**, *yellow*	—	—

Several shades of red and blue.
20LU7	L66	**deep blue**, *orange*, cut square		600.00	
		Entire			5,500.

Reprinted on pieces of white, fawn and oriental buff papers, vertically, horizontally or diagonally laid.

Wove Paper
20LU8	L66	**red**, *cream*	175.00	
20LU9	L66	**red**, *orange*	—	2,500.
20LU10	L66	**blue**, *cream*	—	
20LU11	L66	**blue**, *orange*	—	
		Impression at upper left		—	4,000.
20LU11A	L66	**blue**, *amber*	—	—

Boyd's City Dispatch

L67 (A)   L67 (B)

A. Lines and letters sharp and clear. Trefoils at sides pointed and blotchy, middle leaf at right long and thick at end.

B. Lines and letters thick and rough. Lobes of trefoils rounded and definitely outlined. Stamp impressed normally in upper right corner of envelope; in second state rarely in upper left.

1867

			Laid Paper		Typo.
20LU12	L67	2c	red (A) (B)	—	800.00
20LU13	L67	2c	red, amber (B)	—	300.00
20LU14	L67	2c	red, cream (B)	—	300.00
20LU15	L67	2c	red, yellow (A) (B)	—	300.00
20LU16	L67	2c	red, orange (B)	—	300.00

			Wove Paper		
20LU17	L67	2c	red (A) (B)	—	300.00
20LU18	L67	2c	red, cream (A) (B)	—	300.00
20LU19	L67	2c	red, yellow (A)	—	—
20LU20	L67	2c	red, orange (A) (B)	—	—
20LU21	L67	2c	red, blue (A) (B)	500.00	400.00

Design as Type L62
First state of die, showing traces of old address.

1874

			Laid Paper		
20LU22	L62	2c	red, amber	—	200.00
20LU23	L62	2c	red, cream	—	200.00

			Wove Paper		
20LU24	L62	2c	red, amber		200.00
20LU25	L62	2c	red, yellow		200.00

Second state of die, no traces of address.

1875

			Laid Paper		
20LU26	L62	2c	red, amber		1,250.
20LU27	L62	2c	red, cream	—	375.00

			Wove Paper		
20LU28	L62	2c	red, amber		450.00

L68

L69

1877

			Laid Paper		
20LU29	L68	2c	red, amber		800.00

Stamp usually impressed in upper left corner of envelope.

1878

			Laid Paper		
20LU30	L69	(1c)	red, amber	—	650.00

			Wove Paper		
20LU31	L69	(1c)	red, cream		—
20LU32	L69	(1c)	red, yellow		—

Boyd's Dispatch

L70

Mercury Series-
Type IV — L71

Shading omitted in banner. No period after "Dispatch." Short line extends to left from great toe.

1878

			Laid Paper		
20LU33	L70		black	40.00	100.00
20LU34	L70		black, amber		80.00
20LU35	L70		black, cream	50.00	100.00
20LU36	L70		red		50.00
20LU37	L70		red, amber	35.00	45.00
20LU38	L70		red, cream	35.00	80.00
20LU39	L70		red, yellow green		—
20LU40	L70		red, orange		350.00
20LU41	L70		red, fawn		—

			Wove Paper		
20LU42	L70		red	—	800.00

Mercury Series-Type V
Colorless crosshatching lines in frame work

1878

			Laid Paper		
20LU43	L71		red	—	450.00
20LU44	L71		red, cream	25.00	50.00

			Wove Paper		
20LU44A	L71		red		1,000.

BANK NOTICES
IMPORTERS' AND TRADERS' NATIONAL BANK

1874

Thin to Thick White Wove Paper
Incomplete Year Date on Card

20LU45	L62	2c	black	200.00

1875-83

Complete Year Date on Card

20LU46	L62	2c	black		200.00
20LU47	L63	2c	black ('76-'77)		200.00
20LU48	L69	2c	black ('78)		200.00
20LU49	L70	2c	black ('79)		200.00
20LU50	L70	2c	black ('80)	200.00	200.00
20LU51	L71	2c	black ('81)		—
20LU52	L71	2c	black ('82)		—
20LU53	L71	2c	black ('83)		—

NATIONAL PARK BANK

1880

20LU54	L71		black, 120x65mm	—

The Bank Notices are in the class of postal cards. No postmarks or cancellations were used on Bank Notices.

Bradway's Despatch, Millville, N.J.
Operated by Isaac Bradway

L72

1857

				Typo.
21L1	L72		gold, lilac, on cover, not tied, with certificate	9,250.
			On cover, not tied, with 3c #11, with certificate	12,000.

Brady & Co., New York, N.Y.
Operated by Abner S. Brady at 97 Duane St. Successor to Clark & Co.

L73

1857

					Typo.
22L1	L73	1c	red, yellow	600.	600.
			On cover, tied by company handstamp		22,000.
			On cover, tied by "PAID" handstamp		6,000.

Cancellations: Blue boxed "PAID." Blue company oval. Reprints exist.

Brady & Co.}s Penny Post, Chicago, Ill.

L74

1860(?)

					Litho.
23L1	L74	1c	violet	400.00	400.00

The authenticity of this stamp has not been fully established.

Brainard & Co.

Established by Charles H. Brainard in 1844, operating between New York, Albany and Troy, Exchanged mail with Hale & Co. by whom Brainard had been employed.

L75

1844

					Typo.
24L1	L75		black	1,000.	1,250.
24L2	L75		blue	1,000.	1,250.
			On cover, not tied		3,250.

Nos. 21L1-24L2 cut to shape are one half of values quoted.

Brigg's Despatch, Philadelphia, Pa.
Established by George W. Briggs

L76

L77

1847

25L1	L76	(2c)	black, yellow buff		600.
			On cover, not tied, with certificate		11,500.
25L2	L76	(2c)	black, blue, cut to shape		7,500.

No. 25L2 is unique. It is on cover, manuscript "X" cancel, genuine, but Philatelic Foundation has declined to give an opinion as to whether the stamp originated on the cover.

1848

25L4	L77	(2c)	gold, yellow, glazed		5,500.
			On cover		—
25L5	L77	(2c)	gold, black, glazed		4,000.
			On cover		—
25L6	L77	(2c)	gold, pink		—

No. 25L4 used and on cover are each unique.

Handstamps formerly illustrated as types L78 and L79 are included in the section "Local Handstamped Covers" at the end of the Local Stamp listings. They were used as postmarks and there is no evidence that any prepaid handstamped envelopes or letter sheets were ever sold.

Broadway Post Office, New York, N.Y.
Started by James C. Harriott in 1848. Sold to Dunham & Lockwood in 1855.

L80

1849(?)

					Typo.
26L1	L80	(1c)	gold, black, glazed	850.	1,000.
			Cut to shape		225.
			On cover		—
			Pair on cover		—

1851(?)

26L2	L80	(1c)	black	225.	325.
			On cover		1,500.
			On cover with 3c #11		2,750.
			Pair	1,000.	
			Pair on cover		2,250.
			Block of 4	1,750.	

Cancellation: Black oval "Broadway City Express Post-Office 2 Cts."

Bronson & Forbes' City Express Post, Chicago, Ill.
Operated by W.H. Bronson and G.F. Forbes.

L81

1855

					Typo.
27L1	L81		black, green	400.	1,000.
			On cover		2,500.
			On cover, tied by handstamp, with 3c #11		10,000.
27L2	L81		black, lilac		1,000.

Cancellation: Black circle "Bronson & Forbes' City Express Post" (2 types).

Brooklyn City Express Post, Brooklyn, N.Y.

According to the foremost students of local stamps, when this concern was organized its main asset was the business of Kidder's City Express Post, of which Isaac C. Snedeker was the proprietor.

L82   L83

1855-64   Glazed Surface Paper   Typo.

28L1	L82	1c	**black**, *blue* (shades)	20.00	60.00
			On cover, tied by handstamp		400.00
			Block of 4	100.00	
a.			Tete beche pair	60.00	
28L2	L82	1c	**black**, *green*	20.00	42.50
			On cover, tied by handstamp		350.00
			On cover, tied by handstamp, with 3c #65		1,250.
a.			Tete beche pair	60.00	
28L3	L83	2c	**black**, *crimson*	60.00	70.00
			On cover, tied by handstamp		400.00
28L4	L83	2c	**black**, *pink*	17.50	75.00
			On cover, tied by handstamp		550.00
			On cover, tied by handstamp, with 3c #65		1,750.
			Block of 4	100.00	
a.			Tete beche pair	60.00	
28L5	L83	2c	**black**, *dark blue*	50.00	65.00
			On cover, tied by handstamp		450.00
			On cover, tied by handstamp, with 3c #11		500.00
			Block of 4	250.00	

No. 28L5 has frame (dividing) lines around design.

28L6	L83	2c	**black**, *orange*	—	—
			On cover		—
a.			Tete beche pair	—	

Unsurfaced Paper Colored Through

28L7	L83	2c	**black**, *pink*	300.00	750.00

Cancellations: Black ring, red "PAID."
Reprints exist of Nos. 28L1-28L4, 28L6.

Browne & Co.'s City Post Office, Cincinnati, Ohio

Operated by John W.S. Browne

L84   L85

1852-55   Litho.

29L1	L84	1c	**black** (Brown & Co.)	125.	125.
			On cover		1,000.
			On cover with 3c #11		2,750.
			Pair	400.	
29L2	L85	2c	**black** (Browne & Co.)	150.	125.
			On cover, tied by handstamp		3,500.
			On cover with 3c #11		3,000.
			Pair	575.	

Cancellations: Black, blue or red circle "City Post*." Red, bright blue or dull blue circle "Browne & Co. City Post Paid."

Browne's Easton Despatch, Easton, Pa.

Established by William J. Browne

L87   L88

1857   Glazed Surface Paper   Typeset

30L1	L87	2c	**black**, *red*	—	500.
30L2	L88	2c	**black**, *red*	—	600.

George Washington — L89

Wove Paper   Engr.

30L3	L89	2c	**black**	600.	1,000.
			Pair	1,300.	
			Block of 6	5,000.	

The No. 30L3 block of 6 is the only reported block of this stamp. Three pairs are reported.

Cancellation on No. 30L3: Black oval "Browne's Despatch Easton Pa."

Brown's City Post, New York, N.Y.

Established by stamp dealer William P. Brown for philatelic purposes.

L86

1876   Glazed Surface Paper   Typo.

31L1	L86	1c	**black**, *bright red*	175.00	200.00
			On cover		800.00
31L2	L86	1c	**black**, *yellow*	175.00	200.00
			On cover		800.00
31L3	L86	1c	**black**, *green*	175.00	200.00
			On cover		800.00
31L4	L86	1c	**black**, *violet*	175.00	200.00
			On cover		800.00
31L5	L86	1c	**black**, *vermilion*	175.00	200.00
			On cover		800.00

Cancellation: Black circle "Brown's Despatch Paid."

Bury's City Post, New York, N.Y.

L90   L91

1857   Embossed without color

32L1	L90	1c	*blue*		8,000.

Handstamped

32L2	L91		**black**, *blue*		—

Bush's Brooklyn City Express, Brooklyn, N.Y.

L91a

1848(?)   Cut to shape   Handstamped

157L1	L91a	2c	**red**, *green*, glazed		27,500.

No. 157L1 is unique. It is uncanceled on a large piece.
See Bush handstamp in Local Handstamped Covers section.

California City Letter Express Co., San Francisco, Calif.

Organized by J.W. Hoag, proprietor of the Contra-Costa Express, for local delivery. Known also as the California Letter Express Co.

L92

L93

1862-66   Typeset

33L1	L92	10c	**red**		—
			On cover, not tied, with 10c #68, with certificate		23,000.
33L2	L92	10c	**blue**		—
			On cover, not tied, with certificate		16,500.
33L3	L92	10c	**green**	5,500.	
			On cover, uncanceled, with certificate		18,000.
33L4	L93	10c	**red**		—
33L5	L93	10c	**blue**		14,000.
33L6	L93	10c	**green**	19,000.	
			On cover, not tied, with certificate		31,000.

No side ornaments, "Hoogs & Madison's" in one line

33L7	L93	10c	**red**		1,200.
			On cover, not tied, with certificate		19,000.
33L8	L93	10c	**blue**		—

Nos. 33L1 unused, 33L3 used, 33L3 on cover, 33L6 unused, 33L6 on (patriotic) cover, 33L7 used and 33L7 on cover each are unique. The other varieties of Nos. 33L1-33L8 are all rare.

California Penny Post Co.

Established in 1855 by J. P. Goodwin and partners. At first confined its operations to San Francisco, Sacramento, Stockton and Marysville, but branches were soon established at Benicia, Coloma, Nevada, Grass Valley and Mokelumne Hill. Operation was principally that of a city delivery post, as it transported mail to the General Post Office and received mail for local delivery. Most of the business of this post was done by means of prepaid envelopes.

L94   L94a

L95   L95a

1855   Litho.

34L1	L94	2c	**blue**	500.	600.
			On cover		20,000.
			Block of 4	2,500.	
34L1A	L94a	3c	**blue**	850.	
34L2	L95	5c	**blue**	150.	300.
			On cover		1,250.
			Block of 4	750.	
34L3	L95a	10c	**blue**	400.	—
			On cover		3,000.

Cancellation: Blue circle "Penny Post Co."
Only one example of No. 34L1 on cover is recorded. The stamp is tied by manuscript cancel. Three examples of No. 34L1A are recorded, each uncanceled on cover.

L96

34L4	L96	5c	**blue**	500.	1,500.
			On cover		3,000.
			Strip of 3	1,800.	

ENVELOPES

L97

(Illustration reduced size.)

1855-59
34LU1	L97	2c **black**, *white*	200.00	*900.00*
		With 3c #11		*9,000.*
a.		Impressed on 3c US env. #U10	250.00	*1,000.*
34LU2	L97	5c **blue**, *blue*	200.00	*900.00*
34LU3	L97	5c **black**, *buff*	200.00	*900.00*
a.		Impressed on 3c US env. #U10		*1,500.*
34LU4	L97	7c **black**, *buff*	200.00	

L98

34LU6	L98	7c **vermilion** on 3c US env. #U9	200.00	*1,000.*
34LU7	L98	7c **vermilion** on 3c US env. #U10	225.00	*1,750.*

L98A

34LU8	L98A	5c **black**, *white*	150.	*1,200.*
34LU9	L98A	5c **black**, *buff*	150.	*1,200.*
a.		Impressed on 3c US env. #U10		*1,250.*
34LU10	L98A	7c **black**, *white*	150.	*1,000.*
a.		Impressed on 3c US env. #U9		*1,750.*
34LU11	L98A	7c **black**, *buff*	150.00	*1,100.*
a.		Impressed on 3c US env. #U10		*1,500.*
34LU11C	L98A	**black**, *buff,* "Collect Penny Postage" (no denomination)	250.	*1,500.*

✶✶✶✶✶✶✶✶✶✶✶✶✶✶✶✶

❧ Penny Postage Paid, 7. ❧

✶✶✶✶✶✶✶✶✶✶✶✶✶✶✶✶
L98B

34LU11B	L98B	7c **black** on 3c US env. #U10	250.	*1,400.*
34LU12	L98B	7c **black** on 3c US env. #U9	250.	*1,300.*

OCEAN PENNY POSTAGE. PAID 5.
L98C

34LU13	L98C	5c **black**, *buff*	250.	*1,300.*

L98D

34LU13A	L98D	5c **black**, *buff*		—
34LU14	L98D	7c **black**, *buff*	300.	*3,000.*
		With 3c #11		*3,500.*
34LU15	L98D	7c **black** on 3c US env. #U9	350.	*2,500.*

The non-government envelopes of types L97, L98A, L98C and L98D bear either 1c No. 9 or 3c No. 11 adhesives. These adhesives are normally canceled with the government postmark of the town of original mailing. Values are for covers of this kind. The U.S. adhesives are seldom canceled with the Penny Post cancellation. When they are, the cover sells for more.

Carnes' City Letter Express, San Francisco, Calif.
Established by George A. Carnes, former P.O. clerk.

L99

L100

1864   **Typo.**
35L1	L99	(5c) **rose**	175.	250.
		On cover, tied		*17,500.*

Cancellations: Black dots. Blue dots. Blue "Paid." Blue oval "Wm. A. Frey."

Overprinted "X" in Blue
35L2	L99	10c **rose**		100.00

Litho.
35L3	L100	5c **bronze**		85.00
a.		Tete beche pair		300.00
35L4	L100	5c **gold**		85.00
a.		Tete beche pair		300.00
35L5	L100	5c **silver**		85.00
a.		Tete beche pair		300.00
35L6	L100	5c **black**		85.00
a.		Tete beche pair		300.00
35L7	L100	5c **blue**		85.00
a.		Tete beche pair		300.00
35L8	L100	5c **red**		85.00
a.		Tete beche pair		300.00

Printed in panes of 15 (3x5), the last two horizontal rows being tete beche.

G. Carter's Despatch, Philadelphia, Pa.
Operated by George Carter

L101

1849-51
36L1	L101	2c **black**	—	85.00
		On cover, tied by pen cancel		225.00
a.		Ribbed paper	—	110.00
		On cover, tied by pen cancel		300.00

No. 36L1 exists on paper with a blue, green, red or maroon wash. The origin and status are unclear.
Cancellation: Black circle "Carter's Despatch."

ENVELOPE

L102

36LU1	L102	**blue**, *buff*		*1,000.*
		Cut to shape		*150.*
		On cover with 3c No. 10		*3,250.*
		On cover with 3c No. 11		*1,500.*

Cheever & Towle, Boston, Mass.
Sold to George H. Barker in 1851

L104

1849(?)
37L1	L104	2c **blue**	225.	225.
		On cover, tied by handstamp		*5,000.*
		On cover, not tied		*1,500.*
		On cover, not tied, cut to shape		*500.*

Cancellation: Red oval "Towle's City Despatch Post 7 State Street."

Chicago Penny Post, Chicago, Ill.

L105

1862   **Typo.**
38L1	L105	(1c) **orange brown**	450.	*1,000.*
		On cover, serrated perforations		*5,000.*

Reprints exist.

Cancellation: Black circle "Chicago Penny Post A. E. Cooke Sup't."

Cincinnati City Delivery, Cincinnati, Ohio

Operated by J. Staley, who also conducted the St. Louis City Delivery Co. He established the Cincinnati post in January, 1883. The government suppressed both posts after a few weeks. Of the 25,000 Cincinnati City Delivery stamps printed, about 5,000 were sold for postal use. The remainders, both canceled and uncanceled, were sold to collectors.

L106

1883   **Typo.**   **Perf. 11**
39L1	L106	(1c) **carmine**	3.50	20.00
a.		Imperf., pair		

Cancellation: Purple target.

City Despatch Post, New York, N.Y.

The City Despatch Post was started Feb. 1, 1842, by Alexander M. Greig. Greig's Post extended to 23rd St. Its operations were explained in a circular which throws light on the operations of all Local Posts:

New York City Despatch Post, Principal Office, 46 William Street.

"The necessity of a medium of communication by letter from one part of the city to another being universally admitted, and the Penny Post, lately existing having been relinquished, the opportunity has been embraced to reorganize it under an entirely new proprietory and management, and upon a much more comprehensive basis, by which Despatch, Punctuality and Security-those essential elements of success-may at once be attained, and the inconvenience now experienced be entirely removed."

"**** Branch Offices-Letter boxes are placed throughout every part of the city in conspicuous places; and all letters deposited therein not exceeding two ounces in weight, will be punctually delivered three times a day *** at three cents each."

"**** Post-Paid Letters.-Letters which the writers desire to send free, must have a free stamp affixed to them. An ornamental stamp has been prepared for this purpose *** 36 cents per dozen or 2 dolls. 50c per hundred. ***"

"No money must be put in boxes. All letters intended to be sent forward to the General Post Office for the inland mails must have a free stamp affixed to them."

"Unpaid Letters.-Letters not having a free stamp will be charged three cents, payable by the party to whom they are addressed, on delivery."

"Registry and Despatch.-A Registry will be kept for letters which it may be wished to place under special charge. Free stamps must be affixed for such letters for the ordinary postage, and three cents additional be paid (or an additional fee stamp be affixed), for the Registration."

NOTE: The word "Free," as used in this circular, should be read as "Prepaid." Likewise, the octagonal "FREE" cancellation should be taken to mean "Prepaid" (that is, "Free" of further charge).

The City Despatch Post was purchased by the United States Government and ceased to operate as a private carrier on August 15, 1842. It was replaced by the "United States City Despatch Post" which began operation on August 16, 1842, as a Government carrier.

No. 40L1 was issued by Alexander M. Greig; No. 40L2 and possibly No. 40L3 by Abraham Mead; Nos. 40L4-40L8 probably by Charles Cole.

L106a

FREE
Cancellation

Plate of 42 (6x7) subjects

This was the first adhesive stamp used in the United States. This stamp was also used as a carrier stamp. See No. 6LB1.

Engraved by Rawdon, Wright & Hatch
1842, Feb. 1

40L1	L106a	3c	**black**, grayish	375. 275.
		On cover, tied by hand-		
		stamp		1,400.
		First day cover		25,000.
		Pair		850.
		Block of 4		1,900.

Cancellations: Red framed "FREE" (see illustration above). Red circle "City Despatch Post" (2 types).

1847

Glazed Surface Paper

40L2	L106a	2c	**black**, green	200.00 125.00
		On cover, tied by hand-		
		stamp		600.00
40L3	L106a	2c	**black**, pink	2,250.
		On cover		—

Cancellations: Red framed "FREE." Black framed "FREE." Red circle "City Despatch Post."
Die reprints of No. 40L1 were made in 1892 on various colored papers.

L107

Similar to L106a with "CC" at sides.

1847-50

40L4	L107	2c	**black**, green	350.00 200.00
		On cover, tied by hand-		
		stamp		750.00
a.		"C" at right inverted		—
b.		"C" at left sideways		—
c.		"C" at right only		—

Some students think No. 40L4c may have just a badly worn sideways "C" at left.

40L5	L107	2c	**black**, grayish	350.
		On cover, tied by hand-		
		stamp		850.
a.		"C" at right inverted		—
b.		"C" at left sideways		—
c.		"C" in ms. between "Two" and "Cents"		—
d.		"C" at left sideways plus "C" in ms. between "Two" and "Cents"		1,900.
		On cover, tied by hand-		4,000.
40L6	L107	2c	**black**, vermilion	450.00 250.00
		On cover, tied by hand-		
		stamp		750.00
a.		"C" at right inverted		—
b.		"C" at left sideways		4,500.
40L7	L107	2c	**black**, yellow	—
40L8	L107	2c	**black**, buff	— —
a.		"C" at right inverted		—
b.		"C" at left sideways		4,500.

An uncanceled copy of No. 40L8 exists on cover.

Cancellations: Red framed "FREE." Black framed "FREE." Black "PAID." Red "PAID." Red circle company. Black grid of 4 short parallel bars.

City Dispatch, New York, N.Y.

L107a

1846   **Typo.**

160L1	L107a	2c	**red**	3,000. 3,000.
		On cover		—
		Vertical pair		16,500.

The unique vertical pair is the only reported multiple of No. 160L1.

Cancellation: Red "PAID."

City Dispatch, Philadelphia, Pa.

Justice — L108

1860   **Thick to Thin Wove Paper**   **Litho.**

41L1	L108	1c	**black**	7.50 35.00
		On cover, tied by hand-		
		stamp		500.00
		Block of 4		55.00

Cancellations: Black circle "Penny Post Philada." Black circled grid of X's.

City Dispatch, St. Louis, Mo.

L109

Initials in black ms.

1851   **Litho.**

42L1	L109	2c	**black**, blue	22,000.

No. 42L1 used is unique. A second example, on cover, is recorded.

City Dispatch Post Office, New Orleans, La.
Stamps sold at 5c each, or 30 for $1.

L110

1847   **Glazed Surface Paper**   **Typeset**

43L1	L110	(5c)	**black**, green	5,000.
		On cover		—
43L2	L110	(5c)	**black**, pink	5,000.
		On cover, not canceled		—

City Express Post, Philadelphia, Pa.

L111

L112

184-(?)   **Typeset**

44L1	L111	2c	**black**, on cover, un-canceled, with certificate	11,000.
44L2	L112	(2c)	**black**, pink	10,000.
		On cover, uncanceled, with certificate		20,000.
44L3	L112	(2c)	**red**, yellow, on cover, un-canceled	30,000.

One example recorded of Nos. 44L1 and 44L3. Six No. 44L2 recorded, five of these uncanceled on covers.
See illustration L8.

City Letter Express Mail, Newark, N.J.

Began business under the management of Augustus Peck at a time when there was no free city delivery in Newark.

L113

1856   **Litho.**

45L1	L113	1c	**red**	200.00 300.00
		Cut to shape		75.00
		On cover		—
		On cover, cut to shape, tied by handstamp, with 3c #11		17,000.
45L2	L113	2c	**red**, on cover, cut to shape, uncanceled, with certificate	11,000.

On No. 45L2, the inscription reads "City Letter/Express/City Delivery" in three lines across the top. The example on cover is unique.
See illustration L206.

City Mail Co., New York, N.Y.

There is evidence that Overton & Co. owned this post.

L114

1845

46L1	L114	(2c)	**black**, grayish	1,500. 1,500.
		On cover, not tied, with certificate		10,000.

Cancellation: Red "PAID."

City One Cent Dispatch, Baltimore, Md.

L115

1851

47L1	L115	1c	**black**, pink (on cover)	—

Clark & Co., New York, N.Y.
(See Brady & Co.)

L116

1857   **Typo.**

48L1	L116	1c	**red**, yellow	500. 750.
		On cover		2,500.

Cancellation: Blue boxed "PAID."

Clark & Hall, St. Louis, Mo.
Established by William J. Clark and Charles F. Hall.

L117

Several varieties

1851   **Typeset**

49L1	L117	1c	**black**, pink, on cover, un-canceled, with certificate	16,500.

Clarke's Circular Express, New York, N.Y.
Established by Marion M. Clarke

George Washington — L118

Impression handstamped through inked ribbon.
Cut squares from envelopes or wrappers.

1865-68(?)

50LU1	L118		**blue**, wove paper	5,750.
a.		Diagonally laid paper		4,500.
50LU2	L118		**black**, diag. laid paper	5,750.

No. 50LU1 unused is unique.

Cancellation: Blue dated company circle.

Clinton's Penny Post, Philadelphia, Pa.

L118a

Typo.
161L1 L188a (1c) **black** —

Cook's Dispatch, Baltimore, Md.

Established by Isaac Cook

L119

1853
51L1 L119 (1c) **green**, *white* 4,000. 3,000.
    On cover —

Cancellation: Red straight-line "I cook."

Cornwell's Madison Square Post Office, New York, N.Y.

Established by Daniel H. Cornwell. Sold to H.W. Bentley.

L120

1856 **Typo.**
52L1 L120 (1c) **red**, *blue* 400. —
52L2 L120 (1c) **red** 125. 125.
    On cover, tied by hand-
    stamp 10,000.
    Pair 325.

Cancellation: Black oval "Cornwall's Madison Square Post Office." Covers also bear black boxed "Paid Swarts."

Cressman & Co.'s Penny Post, Philadelphia, Pa.

L121

1856
Glazed Surface Paper
53L1 L121 (1c) **gold**, *black* 225. 225.
    Pair 475.
53L2 L121 (1c) **gold**, *lilac*, on cover, acid
    tied 25,000.
    No. 53L2 is unique.

Cancellation: Acid. (See D.O. Blood & Co. Nos. 15L13-15L16.)

Crosby's City Post, New York, N.Y.

Established by Oliver H. Crosby. Stamps printed by J.W. Scott & Co.

L123

1870 **Typo.**
Printed in sheets 25 (5x5), imprint at left.
54L1 L123 2c **carmine** (shades) 2.00 35.00
    On cover 300.00
    Sheet of 25 75.00

Cancellation: Black oval "Crosby's City Post."

Cummings' City Post, New York, N.Y.

Established by A. H. Cummings.

L124

1844 **Glazed Surface Paper** **Typo.**
55L1 L124 2c **black**, *rose* 1,000.
    On cover, ms. tied, with
    certificate 5,750.
55L2 L124 2c **black**, *green* 650.
    On cover 2,500.
55L3 L124 2c **black**, *yellow* 750.
    On cover —

Cancellations: Red boxed "FREE." Red boxed "PAID AHC." Black cork (3 types).

L125

55L4 L125 2c **black**, *green* 750.00 750.00
55L5 L125 2c **black**, *olive* 750.00 750.00

L126

55L7 L126 2c **black**, *vermilion* 8,250.
    On cover, uncanceled, with
    certificate 22,000.
As L124, but "Cummings" erased on cliche
55L8 L124 2c **black**, *vermilion* —

Nos. 55L7 on cover and 55L8 each are unique.

Cutting's Despatch Post, Buffalo, N.Y.

Established by Thomas S. Cutting

L127

Cut to shape

1847
Glazed Surface Paper
56L1 L127 2c **black**, *vermilion*, on cover 22,000.

No. 56L1 is unique. It is cut to shape, uncanceled, on cover, with certificate.

Davis's Penny Post, Baltimore, Md.

Established by William D. Davis and brother.

L128

1856 **Typeset**
Several varieties
57L1 L128 (1c) **black**, *lilac* 3,000.
    On cover, tied by hand-
    stamp 11,000.
  a. "Pennq," pos. 2 8,250. 8,250.

Cancellation: Red company circle.

Deming's Penny Post, Frankford, Pa.

Established by Sidney Deming

L129

1854 **Litho.**
58L1 L129 (1c) **black**, *grayish* 5,750.
    On cover, with 3c #11 18,000.

Douglas' City Despatch, New York, N.Y.

Established by George H. Douglas

L130

L131

Printed in sheets of 25

1879 **Typo.** **Perf. 11**
59L1 L130 (1c) **pink** 7.50 10.00
    On cover 300.00
59L2 L130 (2c) **blue** 7.50 10.00
    On cover, tied by hand-
    stamp 400.00
  a. Imperf. 30.00 —
  b. Printed on both sides —

Perf. 11, 12 & Compound
59L3 L131 1c **vermilion** 10.00 25.00
    On cover 300.00
  a. Imperf. 1.00 —
59L4 L131 1c **orange** 15.00 30.00
    On cover, tied by hand-
    stamp 600.00
59L5 L131 1c **blue** 15.00 30.00
    On cover 300.00
  a. Imperf. 1.00 —
59L6 L131 1c **slate blue** 20.00 25.00
  a. Imperf. 7.50 —

Imperforates are believed to be remainders sold by the printer.

Dupuy & Schenck, New York, N.Y.

Established by Henry J. Dupuy and Jacob H. Schenck, formerly carriers for City Despatch Post and U. S. City Despatch Post.

Beehive — L132

1846-48 **Engr.**
60L1 L132 (1c) **black**, glazed paper 150. 150.
    On cover —
60L2 L132 (1c) **black**, *gray* 125. 125.
    On cover 1,500.

Cancellation: Red "PAID."

Eagle City Post, Philadelphia, Pa.

Established by W. Stait, an employee of Adams' Express Co.

L133

Black manuscript "WS" on used examples

1847 **Pelure Paper** **Typeset**
61L1 L133 (2c) **black**, *grayish* 14,000. 10,000.
    Cut to shape, on cover —

No. 61L1 unused is unique. Value reflects a 1997 auction sale.

L134

L135

Two types: 39 and 46 points around circle

1846   **Litho.**
61L2   L134   (2c) **black**   100.00   150.00
       On cover, tied by hand-
         stamp   750.00
       Block of 4   600.00
   a.   Tete beche pair   500.00   500.00
       Paper varies in thickness.

1850
61L3   L135   (1c) **red,** *bluish*   125.00   125.00
       On cover   250.00
61L4   L135   (1c) **blue,** *bluish*   110.00   110.00
       On cover   300.00
       Block of 4   700.00

Cancellations on Nos. 61L2-61L4: Red "PAID" in large box. Red circular "Stait's at Adams Express."

East River Post Office, New York, N. Y.

Established by Jacob D. Clark and Henry Wilson in 1850, and sold to Sigmund Adler in 1852.

L136

1852   **Typo.**
62L1   L136   (1c) **black,** *rose* (on cover)   —

L137   L138

1852-54   **Litho.**
62L3   L137   (1c) **black,** *green,* glazed   1,000.   —

1855
62L4   L138   (1c) **black,** *green,* glazed   200.00   200.00
       On cover   800.00
       Vertical pair   4,500.

The unique No. 62L4 pair is the only recorded multiple of any of the East River Post Office stamps.

Eighth Avenue Post Office, New York, N.Y.

L139

1852   **Typo.**
63L1   L139   **red,** on cover   19,000.
       One example known, uncanceled on cover.

Empire City Dispatch, New York, N.Y.

Established by J. Bevan & Son and almost immediately suppressed by the Government.

L140

1881   **Typo.**   **Laid Paper**   **Perf. 12**
64L1   L140   **black,** *green*   1.50
       Block of 4   7.50
   a.   Imperf.
   b.   Horiz. pair, imperf. btwn.   75.00
   c.   Vert. pair, imperf. btwn.   75.00

Essex Letter Express, New York, N.Y.

L141

1856   **Glazed Surface Paper**   **Typo.**
65L1   L141   2c **black,** *red*   1,000.
       Though uncanceled examples exist affixed to covers, some authorities doubt that No. 65L1 was placed in use.

Faunce's Penny Post, Atlantic City, N.J.

Established in 1884 by Ancil Faunce to provide local delivery of letters to and from the post office. Discontinued in 1887.

L141a

1885   **Die cut**
152L1   L141a   (1c) **black,** *red*   180.   250.
       On cover   1,250.

Jabez Fearey & Co.'s Mustang Express, Newark, N.J.

Established by Jabez Fearey, Local Agent of the Pacific & Atlantic Telegraph Co.

L142

1870   **Glazed Surface Paper**   **Typeset**
66L1   L142   **black,** *red*   175.00
       Some authorities consider this item to be an express company label rather than a stamp.

Fiske & Rice

Authorities consider items of this design to be express company labels rather than stamps.

Floyd's Penny Post, Chicago, Ill.

Established by John R. Floyd early in 1860, operated by him until June 20, 1861, then continued by Charles W. Mappa.

John R. Floyd — L144

1860   **Typo.**
68L1   L144   (1c) **blue** (shades)   —   100.
       On cover, tied by hand-
         stamp   1,000.
       On cover with 3c #26
       On cover with 3c #65   500.
       Pair   275.
       Strip of 4   1,250.
68L2   L144   (1c) **brown**   750.
       On cover   4,250.
68L3   L144   (1c) **green**   4,500.   2,750.
       On cover   —
       On 3c pink entire   —

Cancellations: Black circle "Floyd's Penny Post Chicago." Black circle "Floyd's Penny Post" and sunburst. Black or blue oval "Floyd's Penny Post Chicago."

Franklin City Despatch Post, N.Y.

(See Bouton's Manhattan Express.)

Frazer & Co., Cincinnati, Ohio.

Established by Hiram Frazer. Stamps used while he was a Cincinnati letter carrier. Stamps of designs L146 and L147 were carrier stamps when used on cover betweeen Feb, 3, 1848 and June 30, 1849.

L145

Cut to shape

1845

       Glazed Surface Paper
69L1   L145   2c **black,** *green*   —
       On cover   —

L146   L147

1845-51   **Wove Paper**   **Litho.**
69L2   L146   2c **black,** *pink*   —   3,500.
69L3   L146   2c **black,** *green*   2,500.   2,750.
       On cover, tied by hand-
         stamp   11,000.
69L4   L146   2c **black,** *yellow*   2,500.   2,500.
69L5   L146   2c **black,** *grayish*   2,500.   2,500.

Some stamps of type L146 show manual erasure of "& Co."

1848-51
69L6   L147   2c **black,** *rose*   2,750.
69L7   L147   2c **black,** *blue* (shades)   3,500.
69L8   L147   2c **black,** *yellow*   2,750.

Freeman & Co.'s Express, New York, N.Y.

L147a

1855 (?)   **Litho.**
164L1   L147a   (25c) **blue**   3,500.

Friend's Boarding School, Barnesville, Ohio.

(Barclay W. Stratton, Supt.)

On Nov. 6, 1877 the school committee decided to charge the students one cent for each letter carried to or from the post office, one and a half miles away. Adhesive labels were prepared and sold for one cent each. Their sale and use continued until 1884.

Type I — L147b   Type II — L147b

Type III — L147b

Three main types and sizes of frame

1877   **Typo.**
151L1   L147b   (1c) **black**   125.00   —
       On cover, uncanceled, af-
         fixed to backflap   300.00
       On cover, tied by hand-
         stamp, with 3c #158   2,400.
       On cover, tied by hand-
         stamp, with 2c #210   2,750.

No. 151L1 was usually affixed to the back of the envelope and left uncanceled.

Gahagan & Howe City Express, San Francisco, Calif.

Established by Dennis Gahagan and C. E. B. Howe, as successors to John C. Robinson, proprietor of the San Francisco Letter Express. Sold in 1865 to William E. Loomis, who later purchased the G. A. Carnes business. Loomis used the adhesive stamps and handstamps of these posts, changing the Carnes stamp by erasing his name.

L148   L149

1849-70   **Typeset**
70L1   L148   5c **light blue**   250.   —
70L2   L149   (5c) **blue**   175.   250.
  a.   Tete beche pair   600.
         Sheet of 20, with 4 tete
         beche pairs

Sheets of No. 70L2 contain five vertical rows of 4, the first two rows being reversed against the others, making horizontal tete beche pairs with wide margins between. The pairs were not evenly locked up in the form.

L150

70L3   L150   (5c) **black**   40.00   45.00
         Pair   100.00
         Strip of 3   175.00

Overprinted "X" in Blue
70L4   L150   10c **black**   —

Cancellations: Blue or black oval "Gahagan & Howe." Blue or black oval "San Francisco Letter Express" and horseman (Robinson). Blue or black oval "PAID" (Loomis).

Glen Haven Daily Mail, Glen Haven, N.Y.

Glen Haven was located at the head of Skaneateles Lake, Cayuga County, N.Y., until 1910 when the City of Syracuse, having purchased the land for reservoir purposes, razed all the buildings.

Glen Haven, by 1848, had become a famous Water Cure resort, with many sanitariums conducted there. The hamlet had a large summer colony interested in dress reform under the leadership of Amelia Jenks Bloomer; also antislavery, and other reform movements.

A local post was established by the hotel and sanitarium managements for their guests' convenience to deliver mail to the U.S. post offices at Homer or Scott, N.Y. The local stamps were occasionally pen canceled. They are known tied to cover with the Homer or Scott town postmark when the local stamp was placed adjacent to the government stamp and received the cancellation accidentally. The local stamps are only known used in conjunction with government stamps.

L151   L152

1854-58   **Typeset**
Several varieties of each
71L1   L151   1c **black,** dark green   1,000.
  a.   "Gien" instead of "Glen"   —
         On cover, uncanceled, with
         3c #26, with certificate   5,500.

No. 71L1a unused (actually uncanceled on piece) and on cover with #26 each are unique.

Glazed Surface Paper
71L2   L152   1c **black,** green   500.   500.
         On cover   2,000.

Links at corners — L153

Varying ornaments at corners — L153a

Several varieties of each
Glazed Surface Paper
71L3   L153   1c **black,** green   175.   175.
         On cover   2,000.
         On cover, tied by hand-
           stamp, with 3c #11   1,750.
         Pair   700.
71L4   L153a 1c **black,** green   300.   300.
         On cover   1,000.
         On 3c entire #U9, tied by
           handstamp   1,000.

Gordon's City Express, New York, N. Y.

Established by Samuel B. Gordon

L154

1848-52   **Typo.**   **Surface Colored Paper**
72L1   L154   2c **black,** vermilion   7,000.
         On cover, uncanceled, with
           certificate   25,000.
72L2   L154   2c **black,** green   125.   150.
         On cover   650.

Glazed Surface Paper
72L3   L154   2c **black,** green   125.   150.
         On cover   650.

Cancellation: Small black or red "PAID."

Grafflin's Baltimore Despatch, Baltimore, Md.

Established by Joseph Grafflin

L155

1856   **Litho.**
73L1   L155   1c **black**   200.   275.
         On cover, tied by hand-
           stamp   4,000.
         On cover, tied by hand-
           stamp, with 3c #11   3,000.
         Block of 4   1,050.

Originals show traces of a fine horizontal line through tops of most of the letters in "BALTIMORE."

Guy's City Despatch, Philadelphia, Pa.

Established by F. A. Guy, who employed 8 carriers.

L156

Sheets of 25 (5x5)

1879   **Typo.**   **Perf. 11, 12, 12½**
74L1   L156   (1c) **pink**   25.00   25.00
         On cover, tied by hand-
           stamp   800.00
  a.   Imperf., pair   —
74L2   L156   (1c) **blue**   35.00   40.00
         On cover, tied by hand-
           stamp   1,500.
  a.   Imperf., pair   —
  b.   (1c) **Ultramarine**   60.00   75.00

When Guy's City Despatch was suppressed, the remainders were sold to a New York stamp dealer.

Hackney & Bolte Penny Post, Atlantic City, N.J.

Established in 1886 by Evan Hackney and Charles Bolte to provide delivery of mail to and from the post office. Discontinued in 1887.

L156a

Die cut
153L1   L156a   (1c) **black,** red   225.   300.
         On cover   1,250.
         On cover, tied by hand-
           stamp, with 2c #210   5,000.

Hale & Co.

Established by James W. Hale at New York, N.Y., to carry mail to points in New England, New York State, Philadelphia and Baltimore. Stamps sold at 6 cents each or "20 for $1.00."

L157   L158

1844   **Wove Paper (several thicknesses)**   **Typo.**
75L1   L157   (6c) **light blue** (shades)   65.00   40.00
         Cut to shape   17.50
         On cover, tied by hand-
           stamp   500.00
         Cut to shape on cover, tied
           by handstamp   200.00
         Strip of 3 on cover   250.00 200.00
75L2   L157   (6c) **red,** bluish   250.00 200.00
         Cut to shape   75.00
         On cover, tied by hand-
           stamp   2,500.
         Cut to shape on cover, tied
           by handstamp   1,000.
         Pair on cover   —
         Ms. "23 State," cut to
           shape   1,900.
         On cover   4,000.

One cover recorded showing the manuscript change of address. Stamp tied by manuscript cancel.

Same Handstamped in Black or Red, "City Despatch Office, 23 State St."
75L3   L157   (6c) **red,** bluish (Bk), cut to
           shape   1,500.
         Pair, partly cut to shape   —
75L4   L157   (6c) **blue** (R), cut to shape 2,000.

Same as Type L157 but street address omitted
75L5   L158   (6c) **blue** (shades)   30.00   17.50
         Cut to shape   5.00
         On cover, tied by hand-
           stamp   400.00
         Cut to shape on cover, tied
           by handstamp   175.00
         Pair on cover   700.00
         Block of 4   150.00
         Sheet of 20 (5x4)   750.00
         Ms. "23 State St.," on cover   2,500.

Cancellations on Nos. 75L1-75L5: Large red "PAID." Red, black or blue oval "Hale & Co." (several types and cities). Small red ornamental framed box (several types). Red negative monogram "WE." Magenta ms. "NB" (New Bedford).

Hall & Mills' Despatch Post, New York, N.Y.

Established by Gustavus A. Mills and A. C. Hall.

L159

Several Varieties
1847   **Glazed Surface Paper**   **Typeset**
76L1   L159   (2c) **black,** green   300.   300.
         On cover   750.
         On cover with 5c #1   2,500.

T.A. Hampton City Despatch, Philadelphia, Pa.

L159a   L159b

Several Varieties of L159a

		1847	Cut to shape	Typeset	
77L1	L159a	(2c)	**black**	1,500.	
			On cover, tied by handstamp		14,000.
			On cover, uncanceled, with certificate		5,000.
77L2	L159b		**black**, on cover		13,000.

Only one cover known with No. 77L1 tied by handstamp. Five or six covers are known with stamp uncanceled.

Two covers known with No. 77L2, each with stamp canceled, not tied. May 23 cover with certificate is valued above. Second cover is undated Valentine cover.

A handstamp similar to type L159b with denomination "2cts" or "3c" instead of "PAID." in center has been used as a postmark.

Hanford's Pony Express, New York, N.Y.

Established by John W. Hanford.

L160

		1845	Glazed Surface Paper	Typo.	
78L1	L160	2c	**black**, *orange yellow* (shades)	300.	400.
			Cut to shape		60.
			On cover, tied by handstamp		1,250.

Cancellation: Small red "PAID."

The handstamp in black or red formerly listed as Nos. 78LU1-78LU6 is illustrated in the Local Handstamped Covers section. It was used as a postmark and there is no evidence that any prepaid handstamped envelopes or lettersheets were ever sold.

George S. Harris City Despatch Post, Philadelphia, Pa.

L160a   L160b

		1847 (?)		Typeset	
79L1	L160a	(2c)	**black**, on cover		
79L2	L160b		**black**, on cover		30,000.

One example each known of Nos. 79L1-79L2, each uncanceled on cover, No. 79L2 with certificate.

Hartford, Conn. Mail Route

L161

Plate of 12 (6x2) varieties

		1844	Glazed Surface Paper	Engr.	
80L1	L161	(5c)	**black**, *yellow*	1,000.	2,000.
			On cover		5,000.
			Pair		
			Pair on cover, not canceled		32,500.
80L3	L161		**black**, *pink*		3,000.

Chemically affected copies of No. 80L1 appear as buff, and of No. 80L3 as salmon.

Cancellations are usually initials or words ("S," "W," "South," etc.) in black ms. This may indicate destination or routing.

Hill's Post, Boston, Mass.

Established by Oliver B. Hill

L162

		1849		Typo.	
81L1	L162	1c	**black**, *rose*, on cover, tied by handstamp		7,500.
			On cover, canceled but not tied, with certificate		6,500.

Only one No. 81L1 tied to cover recorded. Six covers recorded bearing No. 80L1 not tied, all but one of those also uncanceled.

A. M. Hinkley's Express Co., New York, N.Y.

Organized by Abraham M. Hinkley, Hiram Dixon and Hiram M. Dixon, in 1855, and business transferred to the Metropolitan Errand & Carrier Express Co. in same year.

L163

Sheets of 64 (8x8)

		1855		Litho.	
82L1	L163	1c	**red**, *bluish*	550.00	

It is doubtful that No. 82L1 was ever placed in use. Reprints exist on white paper somewhat thicker than the originals.

Homan's Empire Express, New York, N.Y.

Established by Richard S. Homan

L164

Several varieties

		1852		Typeset	
83L1	L164		**black**, *yellow*		
a.			"1" for "I" in "PAID"		8,250.

No. 83L1a is unique. It is affixed to a cover front, uncanceled, with certificate.

Hopedale Penny Post, Milford, Mass.

Hopedale was a large farm community southwest of Milford, Mass. The community meeting of Feb. 2, 1849, voted to arrange for regular transportation of mail to the nearest post office, which was at Milford, a mile and a half distant, at a charge of 1c a letter. A complete history of this community may be found in "The Hopedale Community," published in 1897.

Rayed asterisks in corners — L165   Plain asterisks in corners — L166

Several varieties of Types L165-L166

		1849	Glazed Surface Paper	Typeset	
84L1	L165	(1c)	**black**, *pink*	750.00	750.00
84L2	L166	(1c)	**black**, *pink*	1,000.	1,000.

Types L165 and L166 probably were printed together in a single small plate.

L167

			Wove Paper	Typo.	
84L3	L167	(1c)	**black**, *yellow*		2,400.
			Cut to shape	900.	
			On cover		
84L4	L167	(1c)	**black**, *pink*	600.	600.
			Pair	4,500.	

The No. 84L4 pair is unique, defective at top. It is the only recorded multiple of any Hopedale Penny Post issue.

J. A. Howell's City Despatch, Philadelphia, Pa.

L167a

		184?		Typo.	
165L1	L167a		**black**		

Hoyt's Letter Express, Rochester, N.Y.

David Hoyt, agent at Rochester for the express company of Livingston, Wells & Pomeroy, operated a letter and package express by boats on the Genesee Canal between Dansville, N.Y., and Rochester, where connection was also made with Pomeroy's Letter Express.

L168

Several varieties

		1844	Glazed Surface Paper	Typeset	
85L1	L168	(5c)	**black**, *vermilion*	4,000.	
a.			"Lettcr" instead of "Letter"		
			Pair, #85L1, 85L1a, on cover front		

Humboldt Express, Nevada

A branch of Langton's Pioneer Express, connecting with the main line of Pioneer Express at Carson City, Nevada, and making tri-weekly trips to adjacent points.

L169

		1863		Litho.	
86L1	L169	25c	**brown**	1,750.	1,250.
			Pair		2,750.
			On cover (U.S. Envelopes Nos. U34 or U35)		40,000.
			On cover with 3c #65		

Cancellations: Blue oval "Langton's Pioneer Express Unionville." Red "Langton & Co."

Hussey's Post, New York, N.Y.

Established by George Hussey.
Reprints available for postage are so described.

L170   L171

		1854		Litho.	
87L1	L170	(1c)	**blue**		500.
			On cover, tied by handstamp		2,250.

		1856			
87L2	L171	(1c)	**black**	250.	175.
			On cover, tied by handstamp		1,200.
87L3	L171	(1c)	**red**		175.
			On cover, tied by handstamp		750.

Cancellation on Nos. 87L1-87L3: Black "FREE."

L172   L173

1858

87L4	L172	1c	**brown red**	35.	90.
			On cover, tied by hand-stamp		450.
			Pair on cover		1,000.
87L5	L172	1c	**black**	175.	—
			On cover		—
			Block of 4 (unique)		—

Cancellation on Nos. 87L4-87L5: Black circle "1ct PAID HUSSEY 50 Wm. ST.," date in center.

1858

87L6	L173	(1c)	**black**	5.00	—
			On cover		—
87L7	L173	(1c)	**rose red**	5.00	—
			On cover		—
87L8	L173	(1c)	**red**	50.00	—
			On cover		—

Type L173 was printed in sheets of 46: 5 horizontal rows of 8, one row of 6 sideways at bottom. Type L173 saw little, if any, commercial use and was probably issued mainly for collectors. Covers exist, many with apparently contemporaneous corner cards. On-cover stamps bear a black HUSSEY'S POST hand-stamp, but most if not all of Nos. 87L6-87L8 were canceled after the post ceased to operate.

L174

L175

1858 Typo.

87L9	L174	(1c)	**blue**	5.00

1859 Litho.

87L10	L175	1c	**rose red**	15.00	*40.00*
			On cover		*475.00*

No. 87L10 in orange red is not known to have been placed in use.

Cancellations: Black "FREE." Black company circle "1 CT PAID HUSSEY 50 WM ST.," no date in center (smaller than cancel on Nos. 87L4-87L5).

87L11	L175	1c	**lake**	—
87L12	L175	1c	**black**	—

L176

L177

1862

87L13	L176	1c	**black**	25.00	
87L14	L176	1c	**blue**	15.00	*25.00*
			On cover		*450.00*
87L15	L176	1c	**green**	20.00	
			On cover		*450.00*
87L16	L176	1c	**red**	30.00	
87L17	L176	1c	**red brown**	30.00	
87L18	L176	1c	**brown**	30.00	
87L19	L176	1c	**lake**	—	
87L20	L176	1c	**purple**	30.00	
87L21	L176	1c	**yellow**	30.00	

Similar to L174 but has condensed "50" and shows a short flourish line over the "I" of "DELIVERY."

1862

87L22	L177	(1c)	**blue**	3.00	*25.00*
			On cover		

L178

Similar to L171, but no dots in corners — L179

1863

87L23	L178	(1c)	**blue**	7.50	
87L24	L179	(1c)	**black**	5.00	
87L25	L179	(1c)	**red**	6.50	
			On cover with 6c #115		*17,500.*

See No. 87L52.

L180

L182

87L26	L180	1c	**brown red**	5.00	*25.00*
			Block of 4	25.00	
			On cover, tied by hand-stamp		*450.00*

A so-called "reprint" of No. 87L26, made for J. W. Scott, has a colored flaw extending diagonally upward from the "I" in "CITY."

Reprints of types 87L173, 174, 178, 179 and 180 were made in 1875-76 on thicker paper in approximately normal colors and were available for postage.

1863

Dated 1863

87L27	L182	1c	**blue**	20.00	
			Cut to shape	12.50	
			On cover, tied by hand-stamp		*500.00*
87L28	L182	1c	**green**	27.50	
			Cut to shape	14.00	
			On cover, tied by hand-stamp		*550.00*
87L29	L182	1c	**yellow**	25.00	
			Cut to shape	12.50	
			On cover, tied by hand-stamp		*500.00*
87L30	L182	1c	**brown**	27.50	
			Cut to shape	14.00	
87L31	L182	1c	**red brown**	30.00	
			Cut to shape	15.00	
87L32	L182	1c	**red**	27.50	
			Cut to shape	14.00	
87L33	L182	1c	**black**	40.00	
			Cut to shape	20.00	
87L34	L182	1c	**violet**	40.00	
			Cut to shape	20.00	
87L35	L182	2c	**brown**	40.00	*75.00*
			Cut to shape	20.00	
			On cover, tied by hand-stamp		*650.00*

The 2c blue dated 1863 exists only as a counterfeit.

1865

Dated 1865

87L38	L182	2c	**blue**	35.00	*45.00*
			On cover, tied by hand-stamp		*475.00*

1867

Dated 1867

87L39	L182	2c	**blue**	45.00	*40.00*
			On cover		*450.00*

1868

Dated 1868

87L40	L182	2c	**blue**	40.00	*65.00*
			On cover		*500.00*

1869

Dated 1870

87L41	L182	2c	**blue**	45.00	*70.00*
			On cover, tied by hand-stamp		*500.00*

1871

Dated 1871

87L42	L182	2c	**blue**	40.00	*65.00*
			On cover, tied by hand-stamp		*750.00*

L183

L184

1872

Wove Paper

87L43	L183		**black**	5.00	*20.00*
			On cover, tied by hand-stamp		*300.00*
			Pair on cover, tied by hand-stamp		*1,500.*
87L44	L183		**red lilac**	9.00	*40.00*

			On cover, tied by hand-stamp		*300.00*
87L45	L183		**blue**	6.00	*40.00*
			On cover, tied by hand-stamp		*300.00*
			Pair on cover, tied by hand-stamp		*750.00*
87L46	L183		**green**	10.00	*45.00*
			On cover, tied by hand-stamp		*300.00*

Sheets contain four panes of 28 each. Double periods after "A.M." on two stamps in two panes, and on four stamps in the other two panes.

Covers show postmark reading: "HUSSEY'S SPECIAL-MESSENGER EXPRESS-PAID-54 PINE ST."

1872

Thick Laid paper

87L47	L184		**black**	10.00	*35.00*
			On cover		
			Block of 4	45.00	
87L48	L184		**yellow**	17.50	*65.00*
87L49	L184		**red brown**	17.50	*50.00*
			On cover		*200.00*
87L50	L184		**red**	17.50	*40.00*
			On cover		—

L185

L186

1873

Thin Wove Paper

87L51	L185	2c	**black**	75.00	*150.00*
			On cover		*500.00*

A reprint of No. 87L51, believed to have been made for J. W. Scott, shows a 4mm break in the bottom frameline under "54."

Type of 1863

1875

Thick Wove Paper

87L52	L179	(1c)	**blue**	—

1875

L186 in imitation of L180, but no corner dots, "S" for "$," etc.

87L53	L186	1c	**black**	2.00

Some authorities believe Nos. 87L52-87L53 are imitations made from new stones. Attributed to J. W. Scott.

"Copyright 1877" — L188

L188a

1877

Thick Wove Paper

87L55	L188		**black**	150.00	—
			On cover		*600.00*

Error of design, used provisionally. Stamp was never copyrighted. Printed singly.

87L56	L188a		**black**	125.00

Thin Wove Paper

87L57	L188a		**blue**	45.00
87L58	L188a		**rose**	30.00
			On cover	—

Perf. 12½

87L59	L188a		**blue**	3.00	*10.00*
			On cover		*250.00*
a.			Imperf. horizontally, pair	—	
87L60	L188a		**rose**	3.00	*10.00*
			On cover		*250.00*

"TRADE MARK" small — L189

"TRADE MARK" medium — L190

"TRADE MARK" larger, touching "s" of "Easson." — L191

1878	Wove Paper	Perf. 11, 11½, 11x12, 12	
87L61	L189	blue	15.00	50.00
		On cover, tied by hand-stamp		150.00
87L62	L189	carmine	12.50	
		On cover, tied by hand-stamp		200.00
87L63	L189	black	80.00	

Nos. 87L61-87L63 exist imperforate.

Perf. 11, 12, 12½, 14, 16 and Compound

87L64	L190	blue	5.00	17.50
		On cover, tied by hand-stamp		200.00
87L65	L190	red	5.00	10.00
		On cover, tied by hand-stamp		150.00
87L66	L190	black	—	

Nos. 87L64-87L66 imperf. are reprints.

1879		Perf. 11, 12, and Compound	
87L67	L191	blue	3.00	10.00
		On cover, tied by handstamp		300.00
87L69	L191	black	—	

1880			Imperf.
87L70	L191	blue	4.00	50.00
		On cover, tied by handstamp		450.00
87L71	L191	red	5.00	75.00
87L72	L191	black	4.00	

The authenticity of Nos. 87L69-87L72 has not been fully established.

L192

Two types of L192:
I. Imprint "N. F. Seebeck, 97 Wall St. N. Y." is in lower tablet below "R Easson, etc."
II. Imprint in margin below stamp.

1880		Glazed Surface Wove Paper	Perf. 12
87L73	L192	brown, type I	10.00	20.00
		On cover, tied by handstamp		250.00
		Block of 4	—	
a.		Type II	3.00	5.00
		On cover, tied by handstamp		250.00
b.		Horiz. pair, imperf. between	50.00	
c.		Imperf., pair	50.00	
87L74	L192	ultramarine, type I	12.50	25.00
		On cover, tied by handstamp		350.00
a.		Imperf., pair		
		Imperf (single) on cover		135.00
b.		Deep blue, type II	40.00	
87L75	L192	red, type II	1.50	3.50
		On cover, tied by handstamp		175.00
		Block of 4	6.50	
a.		Imperf, single on cover		150.00

1882			Perf. 16, 12x16
87L76	L192	brown, type I	12.50	30.00
		On cover, tied by handstamp		125.00
87L77	L192	ultramarine, type I	10.00	20.00
		On cover, tied by handstamp		125.00

Cancellations: Violet 3-ring target. Violet ornamental "T." Imperf. impressions of Type I in various colors, on horizontally laid paper, ungummed, are color trials.

SPECIAL DELIVERY STAMPS

L181

Typographed; Numerals Inserted Separately

1863			Glazed Surface Paper	
87LE1	L181	5c	black, red	2.00	17.50
			On cover		350.00
87LE2	L181	10c	gold, green	2.50	20.00
			On cover		350.00
87LE3	L181	15c	gold, black	3.50	27.50
			On cover		400.00
87LE4	L181	20c	black	2.00	17.50
			On cover		400.00
87LE5	L181	25c	gold, blue	4.00	40.00
			On cover		400.00
87LE6	L181	30c	gold, red	—	
87LE7	L181	50c	black, green	—	

Nos. 87LE1-87LE7 on cover show Hussey handstamp cancellations in various types.

Nos. 87LE4 and 87LE5 are on unglazed paper, the latter surface colored. Ten minor varieties of each value, except the 30c and 50c, which have the figures in manuscript. Printed in two panes of 10, certain values exist in horizontal cross-gutter tete beche pairs.

Originals of the 5c to 20c have large figures of value. The 25c has condensed figures with decimal point. Reprints exist with both large and condensed figures. Reprints of the 25c also exist with serifs on large figures.

Most of the Hussey adhesives are known on cover, tied with Hussey Express postmarks. Many of these were canceled after the post ceased to operate as a mail carrier. "On cover" values are for original stamps used while the post was operating.

WRAPPERS

L192a

1856		Handstamped	Inscribed: "82 Broadway"
87LUP1	L192	black	— 400.00

1858		Inscribed: "50 William St. Basement"	
87LUP2	L192a	black, manila	— 550.
		With 1c #87L3, tied by handstamp	1,250.
87LUP3	L192a	black	— 550.
		With 1c #87L3, tied by handstamp	850.

Jefferson Market P. O., New York, N. Y.

Established by Godfrey Schmidt

L193

1850		Glazed Surface Paper	Litho.
88L1	L193	(2c) black, pink	7,000.
88L2	L193	(2c) black, blue	—
		On cover, tied by handstamp	3,500.

Four examples recorded of No. 88L1, all unused. Four No. 88L2 recorded, all on covers (two with stamp tied by handstamp).

Jenkins' Camden Dispatch, Camden, N. J.

Established by Samuel H. Jenkins and continued by William H. Jenkins.

George Washington
L194   L194a

L195

There are two types of design L194.

1853			Litho.
89L1	L194	black (fine impression)	350.00	450.00
		On cover, tied by ms., with certificate		8,000.
		Block of 4	2,250.	

Type L194 printed on envelopes at upper left is considered a corner card.

Typo. from Woodcut

89L2	L194a	black, yellow (coarse impression)	3,000.
		On cover, tied by ms., with certificate	12,000.

Typeset

89L3	L195	1c black, bluish	—	—
		On cover, tied by ms.		17,500.

Some authorities believe No. 89L3 is bogus.

Johnson & Co.'s City Despatch Post, Baltimore, Md.

Operated by Ezekiel C. Johnson, letter carrier

L196

1848			Typeset
90L1	L196	2c black, lavender	3,000.

Jones' City Express, Brooklyn, N. Y.

George Washington — L197

1845		Glazed Surface Paper	Engr.
91L1	L197	2c black, pink	1,000.	1,250.
		On cover, not tied, with certificate		3,500.

Cancellation: Red oval "Boyd's City Express Post."

Kellogg's Penny Post & City Despatch, Cleveland, Ohio

L198

1853			Typo.
92L1	L198	(1c) vermilion	1,250.
		On cover, tied by handstamp	—
		On cover, tied by handstamp, with 3c #11, with certificate	42,500.
		On cover, not tied, with 3c #11, with certificate	15,000.

The three covers are each unique.

Cancellation: Black grid.

Kidder's City Express Post, Brooklyn, N.Y.

In 1847, Henry A. Kidder took over the post of Walton & Co., and with the brothers Isaac C. Snedeker and George H. Snedeker increased its scope. In 1851, the business was sold to the Snedekers. It was operated under the old name until 1853 when the Brooklyn City Express Post was founded.

L199

Stamps bear black manuscript "I S" control in two styles.

1847		Glazed Surface Paper	Typo.
93L1	L199	2c black, pale blue	600.	500.
		On cover, tied by handstamp		6,000.
		Block of 4	2,750.	

Cancellation: Red "PAID." Reprinted on green paper.

Kurtz Union Despatch Post, New York, N.Y.

L200

Typeset; "T" in Black Ms.

1853

Glazed Surface Paper

94L1 L200 2c **black,** *green*   3,500.

Langton & Co.
(See Humboldt Express.)
Ledger Dispatch, Brooklyn, N.Y.

Established by Edwin Pidgeon. Stamps reported to have been sold at 80 cents per 100. Suppressed after a few months.

L201

1882	**Typo.**		*Rouletted 12 in color*
95L1 L201	rose (shades)	200.	*400.*
	Block of 4	1,000.	

Letter Express

Established by Henry Wells. Carried mail for points in Western New York, Chicago, Detroit and Duluth.

L202   L203

1844	**Glazed Surface Paper**		**Typo.**
96L1 L202 5c	**black,** *pink*	300.00	200.00
	Pair	700.00	450.00
	Block of 10	285.00	
96L2 L202 5c	**black,** *green*		350.00
	Pair		750.00
96L3 L203 10c	**black,** *pink*		350.00
	Pair	900.00	900.00
	Strip of 3		9,250.
a.	Bisect on cover, tied by ms. cancel		—

No. 96L3a was sold as a horizontal or vertical bisect. It is known used singly for 5c (rare), or as two bisects for 10c (extremely rare). Stamps are known almost exclusively tied with black ms. "X" covering the cut, and can be authenticated by experts.

The block of 10 of No. 96L1 is the only block recorded of any Letter Express issue. Value represents actual auction sale price in 1999.

L204

96L4 L204 10c	**black,** *scarlet*	—	2,500.
	On cover, tied by ms. cancel, with certificate		9,250.
a.	Tete beche pair, one stamp a horiz. bisect, on piece		8,750.

Cancellations: Red large partly boxed "PAID." Red boxed "Boyd's City Express Post."

Locomotive Express Post

L205

1847 (?)   **Handstamped**
97L1 L205 **black**   —

Wm. E. Loomis Letter Express, San Francisco, Calif.

William E. Loomis established this post as the successor to the Gahagan & Howe City Express, which he bought in 1865. He continued to use the Gahagan & Howe stamps unchanged. Later Loomis bought Carnes' City Letter Express. He altered the Carnes stamp by erasing "CARNES}" from the plate and adding the address below the oval: "S.E. cor. Sans'e & Wash'n."

L206

1868   **Typo.**
98L1 L206 (5c) **rose**   275.00 600.00

McGreely's Express, Alaska

Established in 1898 by S. C. Marcuse to carry letters and packages by motorboat between Dyea and Skagway, Alaska.

L208

1898	**Typo.**		**Perf. 14**
155L1 L208 25c	**blue**		45.00
	Block of 4		225.00

The status of No. 155L1 is questioned.

McIntire's City Express Post, New York, N.Y.
Established by William H. McIntire

Mercury — L207

1859			**Litho.**
99L1 L207 2c	**pink**	10.00	75.00
	Block of 4	75.00	
	On cover, tied by handstamp		3,250.
a.	Period after CENTS omitted		—

Cancellation: Black oval "McIntire's City Express Post Paid."

McMillan's City Dispatch Post, Chicago, Ill.

L208a

1855   **Typeset**
100L1 L208a **black,** *rose*   25,000.

No. 100L1 is unique.

Mac & Co's Dispatch, Fallsington-Morrisville, Pa.

L208b

Typo.

166L1 L208b 1c	**black,** on 3c entire #U1, uncanceled, with certificate		14,000.

No. 166L1 is unique.

Magic Letter Express, Richmond, Va.
Established by Evans, Porter & Co.

L209   L209a

1865			**Typo.**
101L1 L209 1c	**black,** on cover, not tied by cancel		24,000.
101L2 L209a 2c	**black,** *brown*		11,000.
101L3 L209a 5c	**black,** *brown*	—	—

Nos. 101L1-101L2 each are unique.

Mason's New Orleans City Express, New Orleans, La.

J. Mason, proprietor

L210

1850-57			**Typeset**
102L1 L210 ½c	**black,** *blue* (value changed to "1" in black ms.)		10,500.
	On cover, tied		—
102L2 L210 2c	**black,** *yellow*		2,500.
	On cover, tied by handstamp		10,000.

Cancellations: Red grid. Small red circle "Mason's City Express."

Mearis' City Despatch Post, Baltimore, Md.
Established by Malcom W. Mearis

L211

L212

Black ms. initials "M W M" control on all stamps

1846			**Typeset**
103L1 L211 1c	**black,** *gray*	—	—
	On cover, tied by handstamp		22,000.
103L2 L212 1c	**black,** *gray*		—
103L3 L212 2c	**black,** *gray*		—
	On cover, uncancelled, with certificate		16,500.
a.	Horiz. pair, #103L2-103L3		—

Two types of No. 103L3.

L213

Two types of each.

103L4 L213 1c	**black,** *gray*	—	—
103L5 L213 2c	**black,** *gray*	—	—
a.	Horiz. pair, #103L4-103L5		

103L6 L214 1c **black**, *gray*   11,000.

No. 103L6 is unique; tied on small piece by handstamp.
Corner ornaments of Nos. 103L1-103L6 differ on each stamp. All varieties of Nos. 103L1-103L6 contained in one plate.

Menant & Co.'s Express, New Orleans, La.

1853 (?)   **Typo.**
104L1 L215 2c **dark red**   25,000.

Only four examples are known. Two have Philatelic Foundation Certificates.
Reprints are fairly common and are orange red, not dark red.

Mercantile Library Association, New York, N.Y.

Stamps paid for special delivery service of books ordered from the library, and of forms especially provided to subscribers. The forms bore a government stamp on the outside, a library stamp inside.

1870-75   **Litho.**
105L1 L216 5c **black**, *maroon*   250.   225.
105L2 L216 5c **black**, *yellow*   350.   350.
105L3 L216 5c **blue**   350.   350.
              Pair, on postal card   1,400.
105L5 L216 6c **black**, *maroon*   2,250.
105L6 L216 10c **black**, *yellow*   500.   450.

No. 105L5 is slightly larger than the 5c and 10c stamps.
The stamps "on cover" are affixed to cutouts from order blanks showing order number, title of book desired, and subscriber's name and address. When canceled, the stamps and order blanks show a dull blue double-lined oval inscribed "MERCANTILE LIBRARY ASSOCIATION" and date in center. The stamps are really more a form of receipt for a prepaid parcel delivery service than postage stamps.

POSTAL CARD
Printed on U. S. Postal Card, First Issue
105LU1 L216 10c **yellow**   3,500.

No. 105LU1 is unique.

Messenkope's Union Square Post Office, New York, N. Y.

Established by Charles F. Messenkope in 1849 and sold to Joseph E. Dunham in 1850.

1849   **Glazed Surface Paper**   **Litho.**
106L1 L217 (1c) **black**, *green*   90.   90.
              On cover, tied by hand-
                 stamp   500.
              Pair on cover (2c rate), tied
                 by handstamp   1,750.
              On cover with 5c #1   2,750.
              On cover, tied by hand-
                 stamp, with 3c #10   1,250.
              On cover, tied by hand-
                 stamp, with 3c #11   2,000.
              On cover with 3c #26   950.
              Strip of 3   400.
106L2 L217 (2c) **black**, *pink*   —   —
              On cover   —   —

Some examples of No. 106L1 are found with "MESSENKOPES" crossed through in black ms. in an apparent attempt (by Dunham?) to obliterate it.
Cancellations: Red "PAID." Red oval "DUNHAMS UNION SQUARE POST OFFICE." Red grid of dots.

Metropolitan Errand and Carrier Express Co., New York, N.Y.

Organized Aug. 1, 1855, by Abraham M. Hinkley, Hiram Dixon, and others.

L218   L219

Printed in sheets of 100 (10x10), each stamp separated by thin ruled lines.

1855   **Thin to Medium Wove Paper**   **Engr.**
107L1 L218 1c **red orange** (shades)   12.50   17.50
              Cut to shape   3.00   4.00
              On cover, tied by hand-
                 stamp   325.00
              On cover, cut to shape, tied
                 by handstamp   150.00
              On cover, cut to shape, tied
                 by handstamp, with 3c #11   900.00
              Pair   35.00
              Pair on cover   —
              Block of 4   90.00
107L2 L218 5c **red orange**   200.00
              Cut to shape   35.00
107L3 L218 10c **red orange**   250.00
              Cut to shape   35.00
107L4 L218 20c **red orange**   275.00
              Cut to shape   45.00

Cancellations: Black, blue or green boxed "PAID."
Nos. 107L1-107L4 have been extensively reprinted in brown and in blue on paper much thicker than the originals.

ENVELOPE
Embossed
Wide Diagonally Laid Paper
107LU1 L219 2c **red**, *amber*, cut square   20.00
              Entire   125.00

No. 107LU1 has been reprinted on amber wove, diagonally laid or horizontally laid paper with narrow lines. The embossing is sharper than on the original.

Metropolitan Post Office, New York, N. Y.

Established by Lemuel Williams who later took William H. Laws as a partner.

L220   L221

L222   L223

Nos. 108L1-108L5 were issued die cut.

1852-53   **Glazed Surface Paper**   **Embossed**
108L1 L220 (2c) **red** (L. Williams)   550.   550.
              On cover, tied by pencil,
                 with certificate   —
              On cover, tied by blue
                 ms., with two 3c #11 and
                 strip of 3 12c #17   —
108L2 L221 (2c) **red** (address and name
                 erased)   1,000.   1,000.
              On cover, uncanceled,
                 with certificate   5,500.
108L3 L222 (2c) **red**   275.   300.
              On cover, tied by hand-
                 stamp   3,250.
108L3A L222 (2c) **blue**   600.   700.
              On cover, tied by hand-
                 stamp   7,500.
              On cover, tied by hand-
                 stamp, with 3c #11   8,250.

Wove Paper
108L4 L223 1c **red**   75.   90.
              On cover   300.
              On cover, tied by hand-
                 stamp, with 3c #11   1,500.
108L5 L223 1c **blue**   85.   100.
              On cover   350.
              On cover, tied by hand-
                 stamp, with 3c #26   700.

Cancellations: Black circle "METROPOLITAN P. O." Black boxed "PAID W. H. LAWS." Black smudge.

G. A. Mills' Despatch Post, New York, N.Y.

Established by Gustavus A. Mills at 6 Wall St., succeeding Hall & Mills.

  L224

Several varieties
1847   **Glazed Surface Paper**   **Typeset**
109L1 L224 (2c) **black**, *green*   500.   500.
              On cover   —

Moody's Penny Dispatch, Chicago, Ill.

Robert J. Moody, proprietor

"CHICAGO" 8mm — L225

Several varieties
1856   **Glazed Surface Paper**   **Typeset**
110L1 L225 (1c) **black**, *red*,   1,750.   1,750.
              On cover, tied by hand-
                 stamp, with 3c #11   6,000.
              On cover with three 1c #9   70,000.
              Vert. strip of 3 showing 3
                 varieties: period, colon,
                 comma after "Dispatch"   18,000. 6,000.
     a.   "CHICAGO" sans serif and
                 12 ½mm   2,750.
     b.   "Henny" instead of "Penny," on
                 cover, tied by handstamp, with
                 3c #11   40,000.

Cancellations: Blue circle "Moody's Despatch."
The vertical strip of 3, the cover with the three 1c stamps and No. 110L1b, are each unique.

Morton's Post, Philadelphia, Pa.

  L225a

167L1 L225a 2c **black**, *grayish*, on cover,
                 uncanceled, with certifiicate   13,000.

No. 167L1 is unique.

New York City Express Post, New York, N.Y.

L226

Several varieties
1847   **Glazed Surface Paper**   **Engr.**
111L1 L226 2c **black**, *green*   1,200.   1,500.
              Cut to shape   400.   450.
              On cover, tied by hand-
                 stamp   4,000.
              On cover, cut to shape, tied
                 by handstamp   1,750.
Wove Paper
111L2 L226 2c **orange**   —   —
              On cover   —

One Cent Despatch, Baltimore, Md., Washington, D.C.

Established by J.H. Wiley to deliver mail in Washington, Georgetown and Baltimore. Made as many as five deliveries daily at 1 cent if prepaid, or 2 cents payable on delivery.

L227   L228

Two types:
I. Courier's letter points to "O" of "ONE."
II. Letter points to "N" of "ONE."

1856   **Washington, D.C.**   **Litho.**
Inscribed at bottom "Washington City"
112L1 L227 1c **violet**   225. 150.
    On cover, tied by hand-
      stamp   750.
    On cover with 3c #11   1,500.
    Horiz. pair, types I & II   1,250.

Baltimore, Maryland
No name at bottom
112L2 L228 1c **red**   450. 250.
    On cover, tied by hand-
      stamp   1,500.
    On cover with 3c #11   2,250.

The No. 112L1 pair is the unique multiple of either One Cent Despatch stamp.

Cancellation on Nos. 112L1-112L2: Black circle "City Despatch."

Overton & Co.

Carried mail principally between New York and Boston; also to Albany. Stamps sold for 6c each, 20 for $1.

L229

1844
113L1 L229 (6c) **black**, *greenish* 400. 400.
    On cover   2,500.
    Pair   850.
a. "FREE" printed below design 1,750.
    On cover   4,000.
    Pair on cover, not tied,
      with certificate   18,500.

Cancellation: Black "PAID." Red "Cd."

Penny Express Co.

Little information is available on this post, but a sheet is known carrying the ms. initials of Henry Reed of the Holladay staff. The post was part of the Holladay Overland Mail and Express Co. system.

In 1866 in the West the "short-bit" or 10 cents was the smallest currency generally used. The word "penny" is believed to refer to the "half-bit" or 5 cents (nickel).

L230

Printed in sheets of 32 (8x4)

1866   **Litho.**
114L1 L230 5c **black**   300.00
    Pair   650.
a. Sheet of 32 initialed "HR," black
    ms., original gum   7,000.
114L2 L230 5c **blue**   12.50
    Block of 4   55.00
    Sheet of 32, no gum 450.00
114L3 L230 5c **red**   12.50
    Block of 4   55.00
    Sheet of 32, no gum 450.00

Nos. 114L1-114L3 lack gum and probably were never placed in use.

Philadelphia Despatch Post, Philadelphia, Pa.
See D.O. Blood & Co.
Pinkney's Express Post, New York, N.Y.

L231

1851   **Glazed Surface Paper** **Typo.**
115L1 L231 2c **black**, *green* 1,400.
    Cut to shape   800.
    On cover, tied by ms., with
      certificate   5,750.

Pips Daily Mail, Brooklyn, N.Y.

L232

1862 (?)   **Litho.**
116L1 L232 1c **black**   200.
116L2 L232 1c **black**, *buff* 150. 2,250.
116L3 L232 1c **black**, *yellow* 180.
116L4 L232 1c **black**, *dark blue* 180.
116L5 L232 1c **black**, *rose* 180.
    Block of 4   —

No. 116L2 used is unique.

Pomeroy's Letter Express.

Established in 1844 by George E. Pomeroy. Carried mail principally to points in New York State. Connected with Letter Express for Western points.

L233

Engraved by John E. Gavit, Albany, N.Y. (Seen as "GAVIT" in bottom part of stamp). Sheets of 40 (8x5).

1844
    Surface Colored Wove Paper
117L1 L233 5c **black**, *yellow* 5.50 50.00
    On cover, tied by ms. 900.00
    Pair   175.00
    Pair on cover   —
117L2 L233 **black**, *yellow* (value incom-
    plete)   750. 1,250.
    On cover, tied by ms. 3,000.
    Thin Bond Paper
117L3 L233 5c **blue** 5.00 125.00
    On cover, not tied   2,000.
    Pair on cover, not tied 4,000.
117L4 L233 5c **black** 3.50 125.00
    On cover   —
    Strip of 4 on cover —
117L5 L233 5c **red** 3.50 125.00
    On cover, not tied 3,500.
    Strip of 3 on cover —
117L6 L233 5c **lake** 200.00 300.00
    On cover, tied by ms. 900.00
    Pair on cover —
117L7 L233 5c **orange** 7.50 —

Cancellations: Large red partly boxed "PAID" (Nos. 117L1, 117L6). Red "Cd" (Nos. 117L1-117L2, 117L4); stamps are considered "tied to cover" by this "Cd" when the impression shows through the letter paper.
All stamps except No. 117L2 have "20 for $1" in tablet at the bottom. On No. 117L2 the value is incomplete.
Remainders of Nos. 117L1, 117L3, 117L4 and 117L5 are plentiful in unused condition, including multiples and sheets. A 5c black on yellow paper colored through and a 5c brown were prepared for use but never issued. No. 117L2 was never remaindered.

P. O. Paid, Philadelphia, Pa.
See note in Carriers' Stamps Section.

Price's City Express, New York, N.Y.

L235   L236

1857-58 **Glazed Surface Paper** **Litho.**
119L1 L235 2c **black**, *vermilion* 250.
    On cover, tied by hand-
      stamp   5,000.
    On cover, not tied, with cer-
      tificate   1,100.
    On cover, tied by hand-
      stamp, with 3c #26 —
119L2 L235 2c **black**, *green* 250.
    Cut to shape   85.

1858

    Sheets of 108 (12x9)
119L3 L236 2c **black**, *green* 4.00 *150.00*
    On cover   —
    Block of 4 25.00

Cancellation on #119L3: Black oval "Price's City Express."

Price's Eighth Avenue Post Office, New York, N.Y.

Established by James Price at 350 Eighth Avenue, in 1854, and sold to Russell in the same year.

L237

1854   **Litho.**
120L1 L237 (2c) **red**, *bluish* 500.00
    On cover, uncanceled, with
      certificate   7,500.

Priest's Despatch, Philadelphia, Pa.
Established by Solomon Priest

L238   L239

1851 **Glazed Surface Paper** **Typo.**
121L1 L238 (2c) **silver**, *vermilion* 1,750. —
121L2 L238 (2c) **gold**, *dark blue* 500.
    Wove Paper
121L2A L238 (2c) **bronze**, *bluish* 500. —
121L3 L238 (2c) **black**, *yellow* 500.
    On cover, uncanceled,
      with 3c #11, with certifi-
      cate   5,500.
121L4 L238 (2c) **black**, *rose* 500.
    On cover, uncanceled,
      with certificate   2,500.
121L5 L238 (2c) **black**, *blue* 1,000.
121L6 L239 (2c) **black**, *yellow* 500.
    On cover, uncanceled,
      with 3c #11, with certifi-
      cate   4,500.
121L7 L239 (2c) **black**, *blue* 500.
    On cover, uncanceled,
      with certificate   3,250.
121L8 L239 (2c) **black**, *rose* 500.00
121L9 L239 (2c) **black**, *emerald* 1,000.

Prince's Letter Dispatch, Portland, Maine

Established by J. H. Prince of Portland. Mail carried nightly by messenger travelling by steamer to Boston. Stamp engraved by Lowell of Lowell & Brett, Boston, his name appearing in the design below the steamship.

L240

Printed in sheets of 40 (5x8)

1861				**Litho.**
122L1	L240	black	7.50	125.00
		On cover		
		On cover, tied by hand-stamp, with 3c #65		*8,000.*
		On cover, tied by hand-stamp, with 3c #94		*4,750.*
		Block of 4	40.00	
		Sheet of 40	550.00	

Private Post Office, San Francisco, Calif.
ENVELOPES

L241

(Illustration reduced size.)

Impressed on U. S. Envelopes, 1863-64 Issue

1864				**Typo.**
123LU1	L241	15c **blue**, *orange* (on US #U56)		600.00
123LU2	L241	15c **blue**, *buff* (on US #U54)		600.00
a.		15c **blue**, *buff* (on US #U58)	700.00	
b.		15c **blue**, *buff* (on US #U59)	600.00	
123LU3	L241	25c **blue**, *buff* (on US #U54)		600.00

Providence Despatch, Providence, R.I.

 L242

1849			**Typeset**
124L1	L242	black	*2,000.*

Public Letter Office, San Francisco, Calif.
ENVELOPES

L243

Illustration reduced.

Impressed on U. S. Envelopes, 1863-64 Issue

1864				**Typeset**
125LU1	L243	black	350.00	
125LU2	L243	blue	350.00	
125LU3	L243	15c blue	400.00	5,000.
125LU4	L243	25c blue	400.00	

Reed's City Despatch Post, San Francisco, Calif.

Pioneer San Francisco private post. Also serving Adams & Co. for city delivery.

 L244

1853-54		**Glazed Surface Paper**		**Litho.**
126L1	L244	black, *green*, on cover, tied by handstamp		—
126L2	L244	black, *blue*, on cover, uncanceled		*27,500.*

No. 126L1 is unique. Two No. 126L2 recorded, each uncanceled on cover.

Cancellation: Blue double-circle "Adams & Co. San Francisco."

Ricketts & Hall, Baltimore, Md.
Successors to Cook's Dispatch

L244a

1857		**Cut to shape**	**Typo.**
127L1	L244a	1c **red**, *bluish*	— 9,000.

Robison & Co., Brooklyn, N. Y.

L245

1855-56			**Typo.**
128L1	L245	1c **black**, *blue*	4,500. 4,500.
		On cover, tied	6,500.

Cancellation: Blue "PAID."

Roche's City Dispatch, Wilmington, Del.

L246

1850		**Glazed Surface Paper**	**Typo.**
129L1	L246	(2c) **black**, *green*	1,750.
		Cut to shape	1,000.
		On cover, uncanceled, with certificate	8,250.
		On cover, cut to shape, un-canceled, with certificate	3,500.

A black negative handstamp similar to type L246 served solely as a postmark and no evidence exists that any prepaid handstamped envelopes or lettersheets were ever sold.

Rogers' Penny Post, Newark, N.J.

Established by Alfred H. Rogers, bookseller, at 194 Broad St., Newark, N.J.

L246a

Cut to shape

1856		**Glazed Surface Paper**	**Handstamped**
162L1	L246a	(1c) **black**, *green*	—

No. 162L1 is unique.

See Rogers' handstamp in Local Handstamp Covers section.

Russell 8th Ave. Post Office, New York, N.Y.
(See Price's Eighth Avenue Post Office.)

L247

1854-58				**Wood Engraving**
130L1	L247	(2c) **blue**, *rose*	450.	350.
		On cover, tied		350.
130L2	L247	(2c) **black**, *yellow*	500.	450.
		On cover, tied		5,000.
		On cover, uncanceled, with 3c #11, with certificate		9,250.
130L3	L247	(2c) **red**, *bluish*	750.	600.
		On cover, tied		4,000.
		On cover, not tied, with 3c #11, with certificate		5,750.
130L4	L247	(2c) **blue green**, *green*		

St. Louis City Delivery Company, St. Louis, Mo.
(See Cincinnati City Delivery.)

L249

1883		**Typo.**		**Perf. 12**
131L1	L249	(1c) **red**	4.00	7.50
		Block of 4	17.50	
		On cover, tied by hand-stamp		2,750.
a.		Imperf., pair		—

Cancellation: Purple target.

Smith & Stephens' City Delivery, St. Louis, Mo.

L284

Typeset

158L1	L284	1c **black**, *pale rose*	—

Spaulding's Penny Post, Buffalo, N.Y.

L283   L283a

1848-49			
156L1	L283	2c **vermilion**	27,500.
156L2	L283a	2c **carmine**	27,500.
		On cover	—

Nos. 156L1 unused, 156L2 unused and 156L2 on cover each are unique.
A No. 156L1 on cover was reported but has not been seen.

Spence & Brown Express Post, Philadelphia, Pa.

L285   L286

(Illustrations reduced sizes.)

Typeset

1847 (?)			
159L1	L285	2c **black**, *bluish*	— 11,500.

One each recorded of No. 159L1 unused and used.

1848			**Litho.**
159L2	L286	(2c) **black**	1,500.
		Block of 4	6,500.

Squier & Co. City Letter Dispatch, St. Louis, Mo.
(Jordan & Co.)

This post began to operate as a local carrier on July 6, 1859 and was discontinued in the early part of 1860. Squier & Co. used imperforate stamps; their successors (Jordan & Co.) about Jan. 1 1860, used the roulettes.

L248

1859   **Litho.**   *Imperf.*

132L1	L248	1c **green**	150.	90.
		On cover		1,500.
		On cover, tied by ms., with 3c #26		1,000.
		On cover, uncanceled, with 3c #26		600.
		Block of 4	750.	

1860   *Rouletted 19*

132L2	L248	1c **rose brown**	250.	250.
		On cover		1,000.
132L3	L248	1c **brownish purple**	250.	250.
		On cover		1,000.
132L4	L248	1c **green**	250.	250.
		On cover		1,000.
		On cover, tied by handstamp, with 3c #26		5,000.

Cancellation: Black circle "Jordan's Penny Post Saint Louis."

Staten Island Express Post, Staten Island, N. Y.

Established by Hagadorn & Co., with office at Stapleton, Staten Island. Connected with Boyd for delivery in New York City.

L250

1849   **Typo.**

133L1	L250	3c **vermilion**	1,400.	1,100.
		On cover, tied by handstamp		
		On cover, tied by ms.		4,750.
		On cover, uncanceled, with certificate		3,250.
133L2	L250	6c **vermilion**	—	3,000.

Stringer & Morton's City Despatch, Baltimore, Md.

According to an advertisement in the Baltimore newspapers, dated October 19, 1850, this post aimed to emulate the successful posts of other cities, and divided the city into six districts, with a carrier in each district. Stamps were made available throughout the city.

L251

1850   **Glazed Surface Paper**

134L1	L251	(1c) **gold**, *black*	400.	
		On cover, uncanceled		500.

Cancellation: Black circle "Baltimore City Despatch & Express Paid."

Sullivan's Dispatch Post, Cincinnati, Ohio

L252

1853   **Glazed Surface Paper**   **Litho.**

135L1	L252	(2c) **black**, *green*, uncanceled, on cover		

Wove Paper

135L2	L252	(2c) **bluish black**, uncanceled, on magazine, with certificate		22,000.
135L3	L252	(2c) **green**	—	
		On cover	—	

Nos. 135L1-135L2 are either die cut octagonally or cut round. They do not exist cut square.

Each listed Sullivan post item is unique. Additionally, a second No. 135L2 on magazine is in the Smithsonian Institution collection.

Swarts' City Dispatch Post, New York, N.Y.

Established by Aaron Swarts, at Chatham Square, in 1847, becoming one of the largest local posts in the city.

The postmarks of Swarts' Post Office are often found on stampless covers, as this post carried large quantities of mail without using adhesive stamps.

Zachary Taylor
L253

George Washington
L254

1849-53   **Glazed Surface Paper**   **Litho.**

136L1	L253	(2c) **black**, *light green*	—	175.00
		On cover, tied by handstamp		400.00
		On cover, not tied		300.00
		On cover with 3c #10		450.00
136L2	L253	(2c) **black**, *dark green*	—	135.00
		On cover, tied by handstamp		375.00

Wove Paper

136L3	L253	(2c) **pink**	—	35.00
		On cover, tied by handstamp		350.00
		On cover with 5c #1		
136L4	L253	(2c) **red** (shades)	20.00	20.00
		On cover, tied by handstamp		275.00
		On cover with 5c #1		—
		Block of 4	85.00	
		On cover, tied by handstamp, with 3c #11		325.00
136L5	L253	(2c) **pink**, *blue*		60.00
		On cover, tied by handstamp		375.00
136L6	L253	(2c) **red**, *blue*		60.00
		On cover, tied by handstamp		300.00
136L7	L253	(2c) **black**, *blue gray*	200.00	150.00
		On cover, tied by handstamp		400.00
136L8	L253	(2c) **blue**		200.00
		On cover		550.00
136L9	L254	(1c) **red**	—	40.00
		On cover, tied by handstamp		350.00
		On cover with 3c #11		
136L10	L254	(1c) **pink**	—	30.00
		On cover, tied by handstamp		250.00
		On cover, tied by handstamp, with 3c #11		800.00
136L11	L254	(1c) **red**, *bluish*	—	100.00
		On cover		500.00
136L12	L254	(1c) **pink**, *bluish*	—	100.00
		On cover		450.00

Bouton's Stamp with Red ms. "Swarts" at Top

136L13	L49	2c **black**, *gray blue*	500.	550.
		On cover, tied by handstamp		1,500.
		On cover, not tied		600.

L255

Printed in sheets of 25 (5x5). Five minor varieties, the stamps in each vertical row being identical.

136L14	L255	1c **blue**	15.	60.
		On cover, tied by handstamp		175.
		On cover, tied by handstamp, with 3c #11		225.
		Block of 4	65.	
a.		Thin paper	8.00	
		Block of 4	35.	
136L15	L255	1c **red**	—	60.
		On cover, tied by handstamp		1,000.
		On cover with 3c #10		1,650.
		On cover, tied by handstamp, with 3c #11		2,500.
136L16	L255	1c **red**, *bluish*	—	135.
		On cover, tied by handstamp		1,000.
136L17	L255	1c **black**, on cover		36,000.

Nos. 136L3-136L4, 136L9-136L10, 136L14-136L15 have been reprinted.

Cancellations: Red boxed "PAID" (mostly on Nos. 136L1-136L8, 136L13). Black boxed "PAID SWARTS" (mostly on Nos. 136L9-136L12). Black oval "Swarts Post Office Chatham Square" (Nos. 136L9-136L12). Black oval "Swarts B Post Chatham Square." Black grids (5-bar rectangle, 6-bar circle, solid star, hollow star, star in circle, etc.). Other handstamp postmarks of the post have been found as cancellations. Government town postmarks exist on almost all Swarts stamps.

Teese & Co. Penny Post, Philadelphia, Pa.

L256

Printed in sheet of 200 divided into two panes of 100. Each pane includes setting of 20, repeated 5 times. Vertical or horizontal tete beche pairs appear twice in each setting. Twenty varieties.

1852   **Wove Paper**   **Litho.**

137L1	L256	(1c) **blue**, *bluish*	20.00	125.00
		On cover, tied by handstamp		3,000.
		On cover, tied by handstamp, with 3c #11		—
		Block of 4	90.00	
a.		Tete beche pair	100.00	

Telegraph Despatch P. O., Philadelphia, Pa.

L257

1848

138L1	L257	1c **black**, *yellowish*		2,750.
		On cover, tied by ms., with certificate		15,000.
		On cover, not tied, with certificate		5,500.
138L2	L257	2c **black**, *yellowish*, on cover with 5c #1		10,500.

The 2c differs in design, including the address, "Office No. 6 Sth 8 St" at bottom.
One example known of No. 138L2.

Third Avenue Post Office, New York, N.Y.

Established by S. Rothenheim, a former carrier for Boyd's City Express. All stamps were cut to shape by hand before being sold and exist only in that form.

L258

1855   **Glazed Surface Paper**   **Handstamped**

139L1	L258	2c **black**, *green*	500.	500.
		On cover		1,250.
		On cover, uncanceled, with 3c #11, with certificate		1,600.
139L1A	L258	2c **blue**, *green*, on cover, uncanceled, with certificate		2,250.
139L2	L258	2c **black**, *maroon*	3,250.	

Unsurfaced Paper colored through

139L3	L258	2c **black**, *yellow*	2,250.	
		On cover, uncanceled, with 3c #11, with certificate		4,000.
139L4	L258	2c **black**, *blue*		
		On cover, uncanceled, with 3c #11, with certificate		7,750.
139L5	L258	2c **black**, *brown*	2,250.	
139L6	L258	2c **black**, *buff*	2,500.	
139L7	L258	2c **black**, *pink*	5,250.	
139L8	L258	2c **black**, *green*	4,150.	2,200.

Nos. 139L1A, 139L2, 139L4 on cover, 139L7-139L8 unused and 139L8 used are each unique.

Cancellation on No. 139L1: Black "PAID."

Union Post, New York, N.Y.

L259

1846   **Handstamped**

Thick Glazed Surface Paper

140L3	L259	2c **blue**, *green* ("UNOIN")		3,000.
140L4	L259	2c **red**, *blue* ("UNION")		2,000.
		On cover		—

Type L259 was used also as a postmark, usually struck in blue.

Union Square Post Office, New York, N.Y.

Established by Joseph E. Dunham about 1850. In 1851 Dunham acquired Messenkope's Union Square Post Office, operating the combined posts until 1854 or 1855. The business was sold in 1855 to Phineas C. Godfrey.

L259a   L260

1852   Typo.

141L1	L259a	1c **black**, *dark green*	9.00	45.00
		On cover, tied by hand-stamp		900.00
		On cover, tied by hand-stamp, with 3c #11		500.00
		Block of 4	45.00	
141L2	L259a	1c **black**, *light apple green*	40.00	75.00
		On cover		750.00
		On cover, tied by hand-stamp, with 3c #11		1,500.
		On cover, cut to shape, tied by handstamp, with 3c #11		200.00
141L3	L260	2c **black**, *rose*	3.50	2,000.
		On cover		750.00
		Block of 4	17.50	

Used stamps must bear handstamp cancels.

Walton & Co.'s City Express, Brooklyn, N.Y.
Operated by Wellington Walton.

L261

1846   Glazed Surface Paper   Litho.

142L1	L261	2c **black**, *pink*	600.	750.
		On cover, tied by ms.		—
		On cover, ms. cancel, not tied, with certificate		18,000.

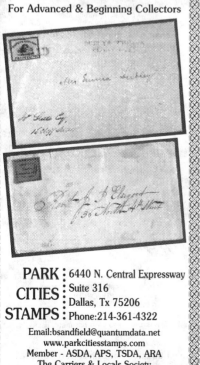
	On cover, handstamp cancel, not tied		—
	On cover, cut to shape, tied by handstamp, with certificate		4,500.
	On cover, cut to shape, handstamp cancel, not tied, with certificate		6,000.

Cancellations: Black "PAID / W. W." Black oblong quad (ties stamp "through" to cover).

Wells, Fargo and Co.

Wells, Fargo & Company entered the Western field about July 1, 1852, to engage in business on the Pacific Coast, and soon began to acquire other important express businesses, eventually becoming the most important express company in its territory.

The Central Overland, California and Pikes Peak Express Company, inaugurated in 1860, was the pioneer Pony Express system and was developed to bring about quicker communication between the extreme portions of the United States. Via water the time was 28 to 30 days, with two monthly sailings, and by the overland route the time was 28 days. In 1860 the pioneer Pony Express carried letters only, reducing the time for the 2,100 miles (St. Joseph to San Francisco) to about 12 days. The postage rate was originally $5 the half-ounce.

About April 1, 1861, Wells, Fargo & Company became agents for the Central Overland, California and Pikes Peak Express Company and issued $2 red and $4 green stamps.

The rates were cut in half about July 1, 1861, and new stamps were issued: the $1 red, $2 green and $4 black, and the $1 garter design.

The revival of the Pony Express in 1862, known as the "Virginia City Pony" resulted in the appearance of the "cents" values, first rate.

Advertisement in the Placerville newspaper, Aug. 7, 1862: "Wells, Fargo & Co.'s Pony Express. On and after Monday, the 11th inst., we will run a Pony Express Daily between Sacramento and Virginia City, carrying letters and exchange papers, through from San Francisco in 24 hours, Sacramento in 15 hours and Placerville in 10 hours. Rates: All letters to be enclosed in our franks, and TEN CENTS PREPAID, in addition, for each letter weighing half an ounce or less, and ten cents for each additional half-ounce."

Wells, Fargo & Company used various handstamps to indicate mail transit. These are illustrated and described in the handbook, "Wells, Fargo & Co.'s Handstamps and Franks" by V. M. Berthold, published by Scott Stamp & Coin Co., Ltd. (out of print). The history of the Pony Express, a study of the stamps and reprints, and a survey of existing covers are covered in "The Pony Express," by M. C. Nathan and Winthrop S. Boggs, published by the Collectors Club, 22 E. 35th., New York, N.Y. 10016.

Wells Fargo stamps of types L262-L264 were lithographed by Britton & Rey, San Francisco.

L262   Front hoof missing

Printed in sheets of 40 (8x5), two panes of 20 (4x5) each.

1861   **(April to July 1)**   Litho.

143L1	L262	$2 **red**	150.	600.
		On US envelope #U10		—
		On US envelope #U16		—
		On US envelope #U17		12,500.
		On US envelope #U18		12,500.
		On US envelope #U32 (patriotic cover)		100,000.
		On US envelope #U33		12,500.
		On US envelope #U65		—
143L2	L262	$4 **green**	300.	800.
		Block of 4		—
		On US envelope #U33		—

1861

(July 1 to Nov.)

143L3	L262	$1 **red**	90.	600.
		Block of 4	475.	
		On US envelope #U11		—
		On US envelope #U15		8,500.
		On US envelope #U17		8,500.
		On US envelope #U32		9,000.
		On US envelope #U33		9,000.
		On US envelope #U35		8,500.
		On US envelope #U40		9,000.
		On US envelope #U41		8,500.
		Front hoof missing (9R)		—
143L4	L262	$2 **green**	250.	1,250.
		Block of 4	1,200.	
		On US envelope #U41		50,000.

143L5	L262	$4 **black**	175.	1,100.
		Block of 4	—	
		On cover		—

Cancellations: Blue, black or magenta express company.

Nos. 143L1-143L5 and 143L7-143L9 were reprinted in 1897. The reprints are retouched. Shades vary from originals. Originals and reprints are fully described in "The Pony Express," by M. C. Nathan and W. S. Boggs (Collectors Club).

—L263

Printed in sheets of 16 (4x4)

1861

Thin Wove Paper

143L6	L263	$1 **blue**	750.	1,250.
		On 10c US env. #U40		75,000.

No. 143L6 apparently used only from east to west.

Most counterfeits have a horizontal line bisecting the shield. Some genuine stamps have a similar line drawn in with blue or red ink. Value for genuine, $300.

L264

Printed in sheets of 40 (8x5), four panes of 10, each pane 2x5.

1862-64

143L7	L264	10c **brown** (shades)	50.	150.
		Pair	125.	500.
		Block of 4	500.	
		On US envelope #U26		5,000.
		On US envelope #U32		3,500.
		On US envelope #U34		4,500.
		On US envelope #U35		3,500.
		On cover with 3c #65		—
143L8	L264	25c **blue**	75.	140.
		Pair	175.	
		Block of 4	500.	
		On plain cover		2,250.
		On US envelope #U10		—
		On US envelope #U26		2,000.
		On US envelope #U34		3,500.
		On US envelope #U35		4,000.
143L9	L264	25c **red**	30.	80.
		Pair	80.	
		Block of 4	210.	
		On US envelope #U9		—
		On US envelope #U10		4,000.
		On US envelope #U34		4,000.
		On US envelope #U35		4,000.
		Pair on US envelope #U35		9,000.
		On US envelope #U59		2,750.

Cancellations on Nos. 143L7-143L9: Blue or black express company. Black town.

NEWSPAPER STAMPS

L265   L266

L267   L268

L269   L270

1861-70

143LP1	L265	**black**	1,250.	—
		On cover, uncanceled, with certificate		11,000.
143LP2	L266	**blue**	750.00	—
143LP3	L267	**blue**	20.00	75.00
		Pair	100.00	—
		Block of 4		—
a.		Thin paper	40.00	100.00
143LP4	L268	**blue**	50.00	—

Rouletted 10

143LP5	L267	**blue**	22.50	125.00
		On wrapper		1,500.
		Pair	50.00	
		Block of 4	125.00	
a.		Thin paper		—
143LP6	L268	**blue**	22.50	
a.		Tete beche pair	350.00	

Design L267 was printed in sheets of 50 (5x10).

1883-88   *Perf. 11, 12, 12½*

143LP7	L268	**blue**	12.50	25.00
143LP8	L269	**blue**	25.00	35.00
143LP9	L270	**blue**	3.50	5.00
		Double transfer		—
		On wrapper		1,500.
a.		Vertical pair, imperf. between	125.00	
b.		Horiz. pair, imperf. vert.	350.00	

FOR PUBLISHERS' USE

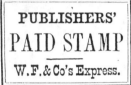

PUBLISHERS' **PAID STAMP** W.F.& Co's Express.   L271

1876   Typo.

143LP10	L271	**blue**	8.50	70.00
		Block of 4	45.00	
		On wrapper		1,500.

Cancellation: Blue company.

ENVELOPES

1862

143LU1	L264	10c **red**	—	1,250.
		On US envelope #U34		1,500.
143LU2	L264	10c **blue**	—	
		On US envelope #U34		5,500.
143LU3	L264	25c **red**	625.	
		On "Gould & Curry" overall advertising env.	625.	

Westervelt's Post, Chester, N.Y.

Operated by Charles H. Westervelt. Rate was 1 cent for letters and 2 cents for packages carried to the post office. Local and government postage required prepayment.

L273

Several varieties

1863 (?)   Typeset

144L1	L273	(1c) **black,** *buff*	35.00	—
		On cover		650.00
		On cover, tied by handstamp, with 3c #65		1,000.
		Sheet of 6	675.00	
144L2	L273	**black,** *lavender*	40.00	—
		On cover		—

Indian Chief — L274

General U. S. Grant — L275

Six varieties

1864 (?)   Typeset

144L9	L274	(1c) **red,** *pink*	75.00	—
		On cover		650.00

Six varieties

1865   Typo.

144L29	L275	2c **black,** *yellow*	35.00	—
144L30	L275	2c **black,** *gray green*	40.00	—
144L40	L275	2c **red,** *pink*	40.00	—

All of the Westervelt stamps are believed to have a philatelic flavor, although it is possible that Nos. 144L1-144L2 were originally issued primarily for postal purposes. It is possible that Nos. 144L9, 144L29-144L30 and 144L40 were used in the regular course of business, particularly No. 144L9.

However, the large number of varieties on various colors of paper, which exist both as originals as well as contemporaneous and near-contemporaneous reprints, are believed to have been produced solely for sale to collectors. Design L275 was certainly issued primarily for sale to collectors. Many of the unlisted colors in all three types exist only as reprints. Forgeries of all three designs also exist.

L276

ENVELOPES
Impressed at top left

1865   Typo.

144LU1	L276	**red,** *white*	—	—
144LU2	L276	**red brown,** *orange*	—	250.00
144LU3	L276	**black,** *bluish*	—	—
144LU4	L276	**black,** *buff*	—	—
144LU5	L276	**black,** *white*	—	—

It is possible that Nos. 114LU1-144LU5 were corner cards and had no franking value.

Westtown, Westtown, Pa.

The Westtown School at Westtown, Pa., is the oldest of the secondary schools in America, managed by the Society of Friends. It was established in 1799. In 1853 the school authorities decided that all outgoing letters carried by stage should pay a fee of 2 cents. Prepaid stamps were placed on sale at the school. Stamps were usually affixed to the reverse of the letter sheets or envelopes.

At first, letters were usually mailed at West Chester, Pa. After March 4, 1859, letters were sent from Street Road Post Office, located at the railroad station. Later this became the Westtown Post Office. The larger stamp was the first used. The smaller stamp came into use about 1867.

Type I — L277

Type II — L277

Type III — L277

Type IV — L277

Type V — L277a

Type VI — L277a

Type VII — L277a

1853-67(?)   Litho.

145L1	L277	(2c) **gold**	45.	—
		On front of cover, tied with 3c #11		4,500.
145L2	L277a	(2c) **gold**	30.	—
		On cover		400.
		On cover, tied by handstamp, with 3c #158		2,250.
		Block of 4	500.	
		Block of 6	1,150.	
a.		Tete beche pair	400.	

No. 145L1 in red brown is a fake.

Whittelsey's Express, Chicago, Ill.
Operated by Edmund A. and Samuel M. Whittelsey

George Washington — L278

1857   Typo.

146L1	L278	2c **red**	2,000.	5,500.
		Block of 4		—

Cancellation: Blue oval "Whittelsey's Express."

Williams' City Post, Cincinnati, Ohio.
See Carriers' Stamps, No. 9LB1.

Wood & Co. City Despatch, Baltimore, Md.
Operated by W. Wood

L280

1856   Typeset

148L1	L280	(1c) **black,** *yellow,* on cover, ms. cancel, not tied, with certificate		11,000.
		On 3c red entire #U10, tied by ms., with certificate		14,500.

W. Wyman, Boston, Mass.
Established to carry mail between Boston and New York

L281

1844   Litho.

149L1	L281	5c **black**	—	350.00
		On cover, tied by ms., Wyman handstamp		3,850.
		On cover, tied by ms., Overton handtsamp		10,000.

No. 149L1 may have been sold singly at 6 cents each.

Zieber's One Cent Dispatch, Pittsburgh, Pa.

L282

1851   Typeset

150L1	L282	1c **black,** *gray blue*	20,000.	
		On cover, acid cancel, with 3c #10		—

No. 150L1 used and on cover are each unique.

Cancellation: Acid

For Local #151L1 see **Friend's Boarding School.**
For Local #152L1 see **Faunce's Penny Post.**
For Local #153L1 see **Hackney & Bolte Penny Post.**
For Local #154L1 see **A. W. Auner's Despatch Post.**
For Local #155L1 see **McGreely's Express.**
For Local #156L1-156L2 see **Spaulding's Penny Post.**
For Local #157L1 see **Bush's Brooklyn City Express.**
For Local #158L1 see **Smith & Stephens City Delivery.**
For Local #159L1-159L2 see **Spence & Brown Express Post.**
For Local #160L1 see **City Dispatch, New York City.**
For Local #161L1 see **Clinton's Penny Post.**
For Local #162L1 see **Rogers' Penny Post.**
For Local #163L1 see **Blizzard Mail.**
For Local #164L1 see **Freeman & Co.'s Express, New York City.**
For Local #165L1 see **J. A. Howell's City Despatch.**
For Local #166L1 see **Mac & Co's Dispatch.**
For Local #167L1 see **Morton's Post.**

LOCAL HANDSTAMPED COVERS

In 1836-1860 when private companies carried mail, many of them used handstamps on the covers they carried. Examples of these handstamps are shown on this and following pages.

Accessory Transit Co. of Nicaragua

Blue or Black

Red, Black or Blue

A sub-variety shows "Leland" below "MAILS" in lower right corner.

Red or Blue

1853

Barker's City Post, Boston, Mass.

Black

1855-59

Also known with "10" instead of "34" Court Square.

E. N. Barry's Despatch Post, New York, N.Y.

Black

1852

Bates & Co., New Bedford, Mass.
(Agent for Hale & Co. at New Bedford)

Red

1845

Branch Post Office, New York, N. Y.
(Swarts' Chatham Square Post Office)

Red

1847

Brigg's Despatch, Philadelphia, Pa.

Black

1848

Bush's Brooklyn City Express, Brooklyn, N. Y.

Red

1848

Cover shows red PAID.

Central Post Office, New York, N.Y.

Black

1856

Cover shows black PAID.

City Despatch Post, New York, N. Y.
(Used by Mead, successor to United States City Despatch Post.)

Black

1848

City Dispatch Post, Baltimore, Md.

Red

1846-47

City Despatch & Express, Baltimore, Md.

Black

1850

Cole's City Despatch P. O., New York, N. Y.
(Used by Cole with some of the City Despatch Post stamps.)

Black or Red

1848-50

Dunhams Post Office, New York, N. Y.
(See Union Square Post Office).

Red

1850-52

Gay, Kinsley & Co., Boston, Mass.
(A package express)

Red

Hanford's Pony Express Post, New York, N.Y.

Black or Red

1845-51

Hartford Penny Post, Hartford, Conn.

Black

1852-61

Hudson Street Post Office, New York, N. Y.

Red

1850

Cover shows red PAID.

Jones & Russell's Pikes Peak Express Co., Denver, Colo.

Black

1859-60

Kenyon's Letter Office, 91 Wall St., New York City

Red

1846-60

Letter Express, San Francisco, Cal.
(See Gahagan & Howe, San Francisco, Cal.)

Blue

1865-66

Libbey & Co.'s City Post, Boston, Mass.

LIBBEY & CO'S
CITY POST.
10 COURT SQUARE   Black or Red

1852

Cover has 3c 1851 postmarked Boston, Mass.

Manhattan Express, New York, N. Y.
(W. V. Barr. See Bouton's Manhattan Express.)

Red

1847

New York Penny Post, New York, N. Y.

Black or Red

1840-41

Also known with hour indicated.

Noisy Carriers, San Francisco, Cal.

Blue or Green

Blue

Black or Red

FROM
NOISY CARRIERS.
MAIL.
77 LONG WHARF S.F. CAL.   Black, Blue or Green

Black

Forwarded via Independent Line

Black or Blue

1853-56

Northern Liberties News Rooms, Philadelphia, Pa.
(Actually a carrier marking mechanically applied.)

Black

Black

1835-36

Overton & Co.'s City Mail, New York, N. Y.

Red

1844-45

Pony Express

Blue or Red

1860

PONY EXPRESS
FEB 3
SACRAMENTO

Blue (Enlarged)

1861

Black or Carmine

1860-61

Blue or Red

1853-56

from

St. Joseph, Mo.   Black or Green
Denver City, K. T.   Black
Leavenworth City, K. T.   Black
San Francisco, Cal.   Blue

Black or Green

1860-61

Red

Blue

1860

Rogers' Penny Post, Newark, N. J.

 Black

1856

Spark's Post Office, New York, N. Y.

Red, Green, Blue or Black

1848

Spaulding's Penny Post, Buffalo, N. Y.

 Black

1848

Spence & Brown Express Post, Philadelphia, Pa.

Black

1848

Stait's Despatch Post, Philadelphia, Pa.
(Eagle City Post)

Red or Black

1850-51

Red

1850-55

Stone's City Post, New York, N. Y.

Red

1858-59

J. W. Sullivan's Newspaper Office,
San Francisco, Cal.

Black
or
Red

1854-55

Towle & Co. Letter Delivery, Boston, Mass.

Red

1847

Towle's City Dispatch Post, Boston, Mass.

Red

1849

Towle's City Post, Boston, Mass.

(Also 10
Court Sq.)
Red

1849-50

Cover shows PAID.

STAMPED ENVELOPES AND WRAPPERS

Fine-Very Fine ➡️

THE
SCOTT
CATALOGUE
VALUES
CUT SQUARES
IN THIS GRADE

Very Fine ➡️

Extremely Fine ➡️

VALUES

Values for cut squares and most entires are for examples in the grade of very fine. Very fine cut squares will have the design well centered within moderately large margins. The margins on 20th century cut squares should be at least ¼ inch on the cut sides unless indicated otherwise. An illustrated grading guide is shown above. These examples are computer-manipulated images made from single digitized master illustrations. Selected issues from both the 19th and 20th centuries are shown in the grades of fine-very fine, very fine and extremely fine. In addition to margin size, collectors are reminded that very fine cut squares (and entires) also will possess a fresh appearance and be free from defects.

Precanceled cut squares must include the entire precancellation. Values for unused entires are for those without printed or manuscript address, and for the most popular sizes. In a number of cases the larger envelopes are less expensive than the values shown here, for example, Nos. U348-U351. Values for letter sheets are for folded entires. Unfolded copies sell for more.

"Full corner" cut squares include both back and side flaps. These items generally command a premium of 25% or more above the cut square values shown here, which are not for "full corners."

A plus sign (+) before a Catalogue number indicates that the item was not regularly issued and is not known used.

Envelopes are not available before the First day of issue so most cachets are applied after the envelope has been canceled. First day covers are valued uncacheted. First day covers prior to Nos.

U532, UC18 and UO73 are addressed. Minimum values are $1 through 1986, and $1.25 after.

PRECANCELED CUT SQUARES

Precanceled envelopes do not normally receive another cancellation. Since the lack of a cancellation makes it impossible to distinguish between cut squares from used and unused envelopes, they are valued here as used only. Precanceled entires are valued mint and used since entires will show evidence of usage.

History

STAMPED ENVELOPES were first issued on July 1, 1853. They have always been made by private contractors, after public bidding, usually at four-year intervals. They have always been sold to the public at postage value plus cost of manufacture. They have appeared in many sizes and shapes, made of a variety of papers, with a number of modifications.

George F. Nesbitt & Co. made the government envelopes during the 1853-70 period. The Nesbitt seal or crest on the tip of the top flap was officially ordered discontinued July 7, 1853.

Watermarks in envelope paper, illustrated in this introduction, have been mandatory since their first appearance in 1853. One important exception started in 1919 and lasted until the manila newspaper wrappers were discontinued in October 1934. The envelope contractor, due to inability to obtain watermarked Manila paper, was permitted to buy unwatermarked stock in the open market, a procedure that accounts for the wide range of shades and weights in this paper, including glazed and unglazed brown (kraft) paper. No. U615, and other unwatermarked envelopes that follow will be so noted in the listings. Diagonally laid paper has

been used for some envelopes beginning with Scott U571.

A few stamped envelopes, in addition to the Manila items noted above, have been found without watermarks or with unauthorized watermarks. Such unusual watermarks or lack of watermarks are errors, bidders' samples or "specimen" envelopes, and most of them are quite rare.

Watermarks usually have been changed with every four-year contract, and thus serve to identify the envelope contractor, and since 1911, the manufacturer of the paper.

Envelope paper watermarks can be seen by spreading the envelope open and holding it against the light.

COLORS IN ENVELOPE PAPER

Stamped envelopes usually have been supplied in several colors and qualities of paper, some of which blend into each other and require study for identification. The following are the principal colors and their approximate years of use for stamped envelopes and wrappers:

Amber: 1870-1920 and 1929-1943; in two qualities; a pale yellow color; its intentional use in the Nesbitt series is doubtful.

Amber-Manila: 1886-98; same as Manila-amber.

Blue: 1874-1943; usually in two qualities; light and dark shades.

Buff: 1853-70; called cream, 1870-78; and oriental buff, 1886-1920; varies widely in shades.

Canary: 1873-78; another designation given to lemon.

Cream: 1870-78; see buff; second quality in 1c and 2c envelopes.

Fawn: 1874-86; very dark buff, almost light chocolate.

Lemon: 1873-78; Post Office official envelopes only, same as canary.

Manila: 1861-1934; second quality envelopes 1886-1928, and most wrappers; light and dark shades 1920-34; also kraft colored paper in later years.

Manila-Amber: 1886-98; amber shade of Manila quality.

Orange: 1861-83; second and third qualities only.

Oriental Buff: 1886-1920; see buff.

White: 1853-date; two qualities 1915-date; three qualities 1915-25; many shades including ivory, light gray, and bluish; far more common than any other color of paper. Envelopes that have no paper color given are white.

Laid paper was used almost exclusively from 1853 to 1915, but there were a few exceptions, mostly in the Manila papers. Wove paper has been the rule since 1915.

EMBOSSING AND PRINTING DIES.

Stamped envelopes have always been embossed, with the colorless areas slightly raised above the colored (or printed) flat background. While this process was not made mandatory in the original act, custom and tradition have firmly established this policy. It is an unusual procedure, seldom seen in other printed matter. Embossed impressions without color and those where lines are raised are not unusual. The method of making envelope embossings has few counterparts in the typographic industries, and hence is not well understood, even by stamp collectors.

Three types of dies are used, closely interrelated in their derivation, MASTER dies, HUB dies and WORKING (or PRINTING) dies. These types and the ways in which they are made, have undergone many changes with the years, and some of the earlier techniques are unrecorded and rather vague. No attempt will be made to describe other than the present day-methods. As an aid to clarity, the design illustrated herewith is the interlocked monogram "US," within a single circular border. Dies with curved faces for rotary printing are used extensively, as well as the latter for flat printing; only the latter will be described, since the basic principles are the same for both.

Figure 1

Master Die for Envelope Stamps

Colorless Lines are Recessed Below the Printing Surface.

It Reads Backward.

The MASTER die (Figure 1) is engraved on the squared end of a small soft steel cylinder, before hardening. The lines that are to remain colorless are cut or engraved into the face of this die, leaving the flat area of the face to carry the printing ink. The monogram is reversed, reading backward, as with any printing type or plate. Instead of engraving, a master die may be made by transfer under heavy pressure, usually for some modification in design, in which case it is called a submaster or supplementary-master die. Sub-master dies are sometimes made without figures of value, when the balance of the design is as desired, and only the figures of value engraved by hand. Various other combinations of transfer and engraving are known, always resulting in a reversed design, with recessed lines and figures, from which proofs can be pulled, and which accurately represents the printing surface that is desired in the eventual working die. The soft steel of a master die, after engraving and transferring is completed, is hardened by heat treatments before it can be used for making hubs.

Figure 2

Hub Die for Envelope Stamps
Colorless Lines Protrude above the Surface.
The Monogram Reads Forward.

The HUB die (Figure 2), also called HOB die, is made from soft steel by transfer under pressure from the hardened master or sub-master die, which serves as a matrix or pattern. Since it is a transfer from the master die, the colorless lines protrude from the surface and it reads forward. This transfer impression of the hub die is made in a depression at the end of a sturdy cylinder, as it is subject to extremely hard service in making many working dies.

Figure 3

Pressure Transfer from Master Die to Hub Die

Above, Hardened Steel Master Die with Recessed Monogram.

Below, Soft Steel Hub Die Blank.

Figure 3 shows the relative position of the hardened steel master die as it enters the depression in the soft steel hub die blank. Some surplus metal may be squeezed out as the master die is forced into the hub blank, and require removal, leading to possible minor differences between the hub and master dies. At the completion of the pressure transfer the engraver may need to touch up the protruding surfaces to eliminate imperfections, to make letters and figures more symmetrical, and to improve the facial lines of the bust.

A hub die may be made by normal transfer, as above, the figures of value then ground off, and thus be ready for use in making a sub-master die without figures of value, and in which the figures of value may be engraved or punched. Since a hub die may be used to make a hundred or more working dies, it must be exceedingly sturdy and withstand terrific punishment without damage. Duplicate hub dies are frequently made from master dies, as stand-bys or reserves. After completion, hub dies are hardened. Hub dies cannot be engraved, nor can proof impressions be taken from them.

Figure 4

Working or Printing Die for Envelope Stamps

An exact Replica of the Master Die, except for size and shape of shank, which is designed for Printers} lock-up.

It Reads Backward.

The WORKING, or PRINTING, die (Figure 4) is like the type or plate that printers use, and may be thin to clamp to a base block, or type-high with square sides to lock in a printer's form. Its face reads backward, i.e., in reverse, and it is an exact replica of the master die as well as an exact matrix of the hub die.

Figure 5

Pressure Transfer from Hub to Working Die
Above, Soft Steel Blank for Working Die.

Below, Hardened Steel Hub Die with Protruding Lines.

The process of pressure transfer is shown in Figure 5. where the soft steel blank of the working die is entering the depression on the top end of the hardened hub die, In fact the pressure transfer of working dies from hub dies closely resembles that of minting coins, and many of these envelope stamp dies are made at the United States Mint in Philadelphia.

In some cases even working dies may be made without figures of value, and the figures of value individually engraved thereon. This is known to be the case in Die B of the 6c orange airmail stamped envelope die, where the size and position of the "6" has eleven variations.

There are some known instances, as in the case of the 4c and 5c envelopes dies of 1903 and 1907, where the engraved master dies were used as printing dies, since the anticipated demand did not justify the expense of making hub dies.

While working envelope dies are heat treated to the hardest temper known, they do wear down eventually to a point where impressions deteriorate and are unsatisfactory, due to shallow recesses or to broken areas, and such dies are destroyed. In many cases these printing dies can be reworked, or deepened, by annealing the steel, touching up the lines or busts by hand engraving to restore the letters or renew the facial contour lines, and then rehardened for subsequent use. This recutting is the principal cause for minor die varieties in envelope stamps. When working dies are no longer useful, they are mutilated and eventually melted down into scrap metal.

The average "life" (in number of good impressions obtained) of a hardened steel working die, as used in envelope printing and embossing machines is around 30,000,000 on flat bed presses, and 43,000,000 on rotary presses. With a production of stamped envelopes of approximately 2 billion annually, 60 to 75 working dies are worn out each year, and require replacement with new dies or a reworking of old dies. Some 200 to 250 working dies can be in constant use, since most envelope printing presses are set up for a special size, type or value, and few can be operated continuously at maximum capacity.

Master and hub dies of obsolete envelope issues are kept in the vaults of the Bureau of Engraving and printing in Washington, as are the original dies of adhesive stamps, revenue paper, government securities and paper currency.

PRINTING ENVELOPE STAMPS.

Embossed envelope stamps are not printed against a rigid flat platen, as is the normal printed page, but against a somewhat flexible or resilient platen or make-ready (Figure 6). This resilient platen is hard enough to produce a clear full impression from the ink on the face of the working die, and soft enough to push the paper into the uninked recesses that correspond to the engraved lines cut into the master die. The normal result is raised lines or embossments without ink or color, standing out in relief against an inked or colored background. The method differs from the usual embossing technique, where rigid dies are used on both sides of the paper, as in notarial seals. The use of the resilient platen in envelope embossing permits far higher operating speeds than can be obtained with rigid embossing dies, without the need of such accurate register between the printing surface and the platen.

Figure 6

Printing Process for embossed

A. Working Die, Carrying ink on its surface.

B. Resilient Platen, or Make-ready, Pushing Paper into uninked recesses, so that lines of Embossed Monogram receive no color.

C. Paper of Envelope Blank, after Printing and Embossing. Heavy line shows deposit of ink on surface of paper, but Embossed Lines are not inked.

D. Front view of Embossed impression.

When these recessed lines in a working die become filled with ink or other foreign material, the paper is not pushed in, the plugged area receives ink, and the corresponding colorless line does not appear on the stamp. This accounts for missing letters, lines or figures, and is a printing error, not a die variety.

An ALBINO impression is where two or more envelope blanks are fed into the printing press. The one adjacent to the printing die receives the color and the embossing, while the others are embossed only. Albinos are printing errors and are worth more than normal, inked impressions. Albinos of earlier issues, canceled while current, are scarce.

Before January 1, 1965, stamped envelopes were printed by two processes: (1.) The rotary, with curved dies, on Huckins and Harris presses. (2.) The flat process, with straight dies, as illustrated, on the O'Connell-type press, which is a redesigned Hartford press. The flat bed presses include a gumming and folding attachment, while the rotary presses, running at higher speeds, require separate folding machines.

Different master dies in every denomination are required for Huckins, Harris and flat bed presses. This difference gives rise to most of the major die varieties in envelope stamps.

Web-fed equipment which converts paper from a roll into finished envelopes in a continuous operation has produced envelopes starting with Nos. U547 and UC37. Albino impressions do not occur on envelopes produced by web-fed equipment.

Some authorities claim that Scott U37, U48, U49, U110, U124, U125, U130, U133A, U137A, U137B, U137C, W138, U145, U162, U178A, U185, U220, U285, U286, U298, U299, UO3, UO32, UO38, UO45 and UO45A (with plus sign + before number), were not regularly issued and are not known to have been used.

Wrappers are listed with envelopes of corresponding design, and are numbered with the prefix "W" instead of "U."

ENVELOPE WATERMARKS

Watermark Illustrations 5, 6, 17 and 18 are condensed. Watermark 4 was used only on Officials. Watermarks 9 and 10 are found on Specimens and Errors. Watermarks 17-18 were the last laid paper watermarks; watermarks 19-21 the first wove paper watermarks. Beginning with No. U615 unwatermarked papers were used for some issues.

Wmks. 1 (1853-70) & 2 (1870-78)

3-(1876)

4-(1877-82)

5-(1878-82)

6-(1882-86)

Wmks. 7 (1886-90) & 8 (1890-94)

Wmks. 9 (1886-87) & 10 (1886-99)

11-(1893)

Wmks. 12 (1894-98) & 13 (1899-1902)

Wmks. 14 (1903-07) & 15 (1907-11)

Wmks. 15A (1907-11) & 16 (1911-15)

U S S E US-S E
1911   1911

Wmks. 17 & 18 (1911-15)

Wmks. 19, 20 & 21 (1915-19)

Wmks. 22 & 23 (1919-20)

Wmks. 24 & 25 (1921-24)

Wmks. 26 & 27 (1925-28)

Wmks. 28 & 28A (1929-32)

Wmks. 29, 30 & 30A (1929-32)

Wmks. 31, 32 & 33 (1933-36)

Wmks. 35 & 36 (1937-40)

Wmks. 38 & 39 (1941-44)

Wmks. 40 & 41 (1945-48)

Wmks. 42 & 43 (1949-52)

Wmks. 44 & 45 (1953-56)

46-(1957-60)

Wmks. 47 & 48 (1961-64)

Wmks. 49 & 50 (1965-68)

Letter Sheet (1886-94)

Official Envelopes (1991)

Washington — U1

"THREE" in short label with curved ends; 13mm wide at top. Twelve varieties.

U2

"THREE" in short label with straight ends; 15½mm wide at top. Three varieties.

U3

"THREE" in short label with octagonal ends. Two varieties.

U4

"THREE" in wide label with straight ends; 20mm wide at top.

U5

"THREE" in medium wide label with curved ends; 14½mm wide at top. Ten varieties. A sub-variety shows curved lines at either end of label omitted; both T's have longer cross stroke; R is smaller (20 varieties).

U6

Four varieties.

U7

"TEN" in short label; 15½mm wide at top.

U8

"TEN" in wide label; 20mm wide at top.

Printed by George F. Nesbitt & Co., New York, N.Y.

1853-55
On Diagonally Laid Paper (Early printings of Nos. U1, U3 on Horizontally Laid Paper)

U1	U1	3c	red	290.00	26.00
			Entire	1,900.	37.50
U2	U1	3c	red, *buff*	90.00	15.00
			Entire	900.00	20.00
U3	U2	3c	red	1,000.	30.00
			Entire	4,000.	75.00
U4	U2	3c	red, *buff*	290.00	22.50
			Entire	1,800.	50.00
U5	U3	3c	red ('54)	5,250.	400.00
			Entire	17,500.	750.00
U6	U3	3c	red, *buff* ('54)	350.00	45.00
			Entire	15,000.	100.00
U7	U4	3c	red	900.00	90.00
			Entire	7,000.	190.00
U8	U4	3c	red, *buff*	1,700.	110.00
			Entire	5,500.	200.00
U9	U5	3c	red ('54)	32.50	3.50
			Entire	95.00	8.00
U10	U5	3c	red, *buff* ('54)	20.00	3.50
			Entire	62.50	6.00
U11	U6	6c	red	250.00	67.50
			Entire	350.00	150.00
U12	U6	6c	red, *buff*	150.00	65.00
			Entire	250.00	175.00
U13	U6	6c	green	250.00	110.00
			Entire	475.00	190.00
U14	U6	6c	green, *buff*	175.00	85.00
			Entire	350.00	175.00
U15	U7	10c	green ('55)	425.00	85.00
			Entire	700.00	125.00
U16	U7	10c	green, *buff* ('55)	110.00	55.00
			Entire	325.00	125.00
a.		10c	pale green, *buff*	100.00	50.00
			Entire	300.00	110.00
U17	U8	10c	green ('55)	275.00	125.00
			Entire	575.00	200.00
a.		10c	pale green	275.00	100.00
			Entire	500.00	175.00
U18	U8	10c	green, *buff* ('55)	400.00	65.00
			Entire	650.00	150.00
a.		10c	pale green, *buff*	350.00	65.00
			Entire	650.00	150.00

Nos. U9, U10, U11, U12, U13, U14, U17, and U18 have been reprinted on white and buff papers, wove or vertically laid, and are not known entire. The originals are on diagonally laid paper. Value, set of 8 reprints on laid, $225. Reprints on wove sell for more.

Franklin — U9

Period after "POSTAGE." (Eleven varieties.)

Franklin — U10

Bust touches inner frame-line at front and back.

Franklin — U11

No period after "POSTAGE." (Two varieties.)

Washington
U12

Nine varieties of type U12.

Envelopes are on diagonally laid paper.
Wrappers on vertically or horizontally laid paper.

Wrappers of the 1 cent denomination were authorized by an Act of Congress, February 27, 1861, and were issued in October, 1861. These were suspended in 1863, and their use resumed in June, 1864.

1860-61

W18B	U9	1c	blue	3,250.	
			Entire	—	
U19	U9	1c	blue, buff	32.50	15.00
			Entire	80.00	32.50
W20	U9	1c	blue, buff ('61)	67.50	50.00
			Entire	110.00	75.00
W21	U9	1c	blue, manila ('61)	45.00	45.00
			Entire	110.00	100.00
U21A	U9	1c	blue, orange, entire	1,750.	

W22	U9	1c	blue, orange ('61)	3,250.	
			Entire	6,500.	
U23	U10	1c	blue, orange	500.00	350.00
			Entire	725.00	500.00
U24	U11	1c	blue, buff	250.00	125.00
			Entire	550.00	225.00
W25	U11	1c	blue, manila ('61)	4,000.	2,000.
			Entire	11,000.	4,500.
U26	U12	3c	red	30.00	15.00
			Entire	50.00	25.00
U27	U12	3c	red, buff	24.00	13.00
			Entire	40.00	22.50
U28	U12 + U9	3c + 1c	red & blue	350.00	240.00
			Entire	825.00	500.00
U29	U12 + U9	3c + 1c	red & blue, buff	350.00	225.00
			Entire	750.00	500.00
U30	U12	6c	red	2,500.	1,250.
			Entire	5,000.	
U31	U12	6c	red, buff	3,250.	1,500.
			Entire	5,000.	10,000.
U32	U12	10c	green	1,200.	350.00
			Entire	12,500.	500.00
U33	U12	10c	green, buff	1,400.	250.00
			Entire	4,250.	500.00

Nos. U26, U27, U30 to U33 have been reprinted on the same vertically laid paper as the reprints of the 1853-55 issue, and are not known entire. Value, Nos. U26-U27, $160; Nos. U30-U33, $100.

Washington
U13

17 varieties for Nos. U34-U35; 2 varieties for No. U36.

Washington
U14

Washington — U15

Washington — U16

Envelopes are on diagonally laid paper.

U36 comes on vertically or horizontally laid paper. It appeared in August, 1861, and was withdrawn in 1864. Total issue 211,800.

1861

U34	U13	3c	pink	22.50	5.75
			Entire	47.50	12.50
U35	U13	3c	pink, buff	21.00	5.25
			Entire	45.00	12.50
U36	U13	3c	pink, blue (Letter Sheet)	80.00	50.00
			Entire	290.00	125.00
+U37	U13	3c	pink, orange	3,750.	
			Entire	6,000.	
U38	U14	6c	pink	110.00	80.00
			Entire	175.00	190.00
U39	U14	6c	pink, buff	70.00	62.50
			Entire	250.00	160.00
U40	U15	10c	yellow green	35.00	30.00
			Entire	70.00	60.00
a.		10c	blue green	35.00	30.00
			Entire	72.50	60.00
U41	U15	10c	yellow green, buff	30.00	27.50
			Entire	65.00	50.00
a.		10c	blue green, buff	30.00	27.50
			Entire	65.00	50.00
U42	U16	12c	red & brown, buff	190.00	160.00
			Entire	500.00	650.00
a.		12c	lake & brown, buff	850.00	
U43	U16	20c	red & blue, buff	275.00	175.00
			Entire	525.00	1,250.
U44	U16	24c	red & green, buff	200.00	175.00
			Entire	650.00	1,500.
a.		24c	lake & green, salmon	275.00	200.00
			Entire	825.00	1,750.
U45	U16	40c	black & red, buff	325.00	300.00
			Entire	800.00	3,500.

Nos. U38 and U39 have been reprinted on the same papers as the reprints of the 1853-55 issue, and are not known entire. Value, set of 2 reprints, $60.

Jackson — U17

"U.S. POSTAGE" above. Downstroke and tail of "2" unite near the point (seven varieties).

Jackson — U18

"U.S. POSTAGE" above. The downstroke and tail of the "2" touch but do not merge.

Jackson — U19

Jackson U20

"U.S. POST" above. Stamp 24-25mm wide (Sixteen varieties).

"U.S. POST" above. Stamp 25½-26¼mm wide. (Twenty-five varieties.)

Envelopes are on diagonally laid paper.
Wrappers on vertically or horizontally laid paper.

1863-64

U46	U17	2c	black, buff		37.50	20.00
			Entire		60.00	35.00
W47	U17	2c	black, dark manila		60.00	45.00
			Entire		85.00	77.50
+U48	U18	2c	black, buff		2,500.	
			Entire		4,750.	
+U49	U18	2c	black, orange		1,250.	
			Entire		3,500.	
U50	U19	2c	black, buff ('64)		13.50	9.00
			Entire		30.00	20.00
W51	U19	2c	black, buff ('64)		300.00	160.00
			Entire		375.00	325.00
U52	U19	2c	black, orange ('64)		12.50	9.00
			Entire		25.00	17.50
W53	U19	2c	black, dark manila ('64)		42.50	25.00
			Entire		150.00	90.00
U54	U20	2c	black, buff ('64)		13.00	9.00
			Entire		25.00	15.00
W55	U20	2c	black, buff ('64)		80.00	57.50
			Entire		130.00	100.00
U56	U20	2c	black, orange ('64)		12.00	8.25
			Entire		20.00	15.00
W57	U20	2c	black, light manila ('64)		14.00	11.50
			Entire		29.00	22.50

Washington
U21

79 varieties for Nos. U58-U61; 2 varieties for Nos. U63-U65.

Washington — U22

1864-65

U58	U21	3c	pink	8.00	1.60
			Entire	12.50	3.25
U59	U21	3c	pink, buff	5.75	1.25
			Entire	11.00	3.00
U60	U21	3c	brown ('65)	45.00	29.00
			Entire	87.50	97.50
U61	U21	3c	brown, buff ('65)	45.00	26.00
			Entire	90.00	72.50
U62	U21	6c	pink	72.50	29.00
			Entire	150.00	60.00
U63	U21	6c	pink, buff	35.00	27.50
			Entire	90.00	50.00
U64	U21	6c	purple ('65)	50.00	26.00
			Entire	72.50	55.00
U65	U21	6c	purple, buff ('65)	45.00	20.00
			Entire	75.00	55.00
U66	U22	9c	lemon, buff ('65)	425.00	250.00
			Entire	550.00	1,000.
U67	U22	9c	orange, buff ('65)	110.00	90.00
			Entire	150.00	275.00
a.		9c	orange yellow, buff	125.00	90.00
			Entire	200.00	275.00
U68	U22	12c	brown, buff ('65)	325.00	250.00
			Entire	575.00	1,150.
U69	U22	12c	red brown, buff ('65)	125.00	55.00
			Entire	175.00	360.00
U70	U22	18c	red, buff ('65)	95.00	95.00
			Entire	200.00	800.00
U71	U22	24c	blue, buff ('65)	100.00	85.00
			entire	200.00	700.00
U72	U22	30c	green, buff ('65)	125.00	75.00
			Entire	175.00	1,500.
a.		30c	yellow green, buff	125.00	80.00
			Entire	175.00	1,500.
U73	U22	40c	rose, buff ('65)	60.00	250.00
			Entire	350.00	2,000.

Printed by George H. Reay, Brooklyn, N. Y.
The engravings in this issue are finely executed.

Franklin
U23

Bust points to the end of the "N" of "ONE."

Jackson
U24

Bust narrow at back. Small, thick figures of value.

Washington — U25

Queue projects below bust.

Lincoln
U26

Neck very long at the back.

Stanton
U27

Bust pointed at the back; figures "7" are normal.

Jefferson
U28

Queue forms straight line with the bust.

Clay
U29

Ear partly concealed by hair, mouth large, chin prominent.

Webster
U30

Has side whiskers.

Scott
U31

Straggling locks of hair at top of head; ornaments around the inner oval end in squares.

Hamilton
U32

Back of bust very narrow, chin almost straight; labels containing figures of value are exactly parallel.

Perry
U33

Front of bust very narrow and pointed; inner lines of shields project very slightly beyond the oval.

1870-71

U74	U23	1c **blue**	35.00	27.50
		Entire	60.00	40.00
a.		1c **ultramarine**	60.00	32.50
		Entire	110.00	55.00
U75	U23	1c **blue**, *amber*	32.50	27.50
		Entire	55.00	40.00
a.		1c **ultramarine**, *amber*	50.00	30.00
		Entire	67.50	55.00
U76	U23	1c **blue**, *orange*	17.50	15.00
		Entire	32.50	22.50
W77	U23	1c **blue**, *manila*	40.00	35.00
		Entire	75.00	65.00
U78	U24	2c **brown**	37.50	16.00
		Entire	55.00	22.50
U79	U24	2c **brown**, *amber*	17.50	9.00
		Entire	37.50	17.50
U80	U24	2c **brown**, *orange*	10.00	6.50
		Entire	16.00	11.00
W81	U24	2c **brown**, *manila*	26.00	21.00
		Entire	55.00	45.00
U82	U25	3c **green**	7.25	1.00
		Entire	14.00	4.00
a.		3c brown (error), entire	*11,500.*	
U83	U25	3c **green**, *amber*	6.25	2.00
		Entire	15.00	5.00
U84	U25	3c **green**, *cream*	9.50	4.25
		Entire	14.00	10.00
U85	U26	6c **dark red**	22.50	16.00
		Entire	32.50	21.00
a.		6c **vermilion**	22.50	16.00
		Entire	45.00	20.00
U86	U26	6c **dark red**, *amber*	22.50	15.00
		Entire	45.00	30.00
a.		6c **vermilion**, *amber*	22.50	15.00
		Entire	45.00	30.00
U87	U26	6c **dark red**, *cream*	27.50	16.00
		Entire	45.00	30.00
a.		6c **vermilion**, *cream*	27.50	16.00
		Entire	45.00	27.50
U88	U27	7c **vermilion**, *amber* ('71)	47.50	*190.00*
		Entire	75.00	*800.00*
U89	U28	10c **olive black**	650.00	750.00
		Entire	800.00	*1,150.*
U90	U28	10c **olive black**, *amber*	750.00	900.00
		Entire	1,000.	*1,200.*
U91	U28	10c **brown**	50.00	70.00
		Entire	80.00	110.00
U92	U28	10c **brown**, *amber*	72.50	50.00
		Entire	100.00	110.00
a.		10c **dark brown**, *amber*	72.50	50.00
		Entire	100.00	100.00
U93	U29	12c **plum**	90.00	82.50
		Entire	225.00	*450.00*
U94	U29	12c **plum**, *amber*	110.00	110.00
		Entire	225.00	*650.00*
U95	U29	12c **plum**, *cream*	250.00	250.00
		Entire	350.00	
U96	U30	15c **red orange**	70.00	75.00
		Entire	150.00	
a.		15c **orange**	70.00	75.00
		Entire	160.00	
U97	U30	15c **red orange**, *amber*	200.00	225.00
		Entire	375.00	
a.		15c **orange**, *amber*	200.00	225.00
		Entire	375.00	
U98	U30	15c **red orange**, *cream*	325.00	350.00
		Entire	400.00	
a.		15c **orange**, *cream*	325.00	350.00
		Entire	425.00	
U99	U31	24c **purple**	140.00	140.00
		Entire	190.00	
U100	U31	24c **purple**, *amber*	190.00	325.00
		Entire	350.00	
U101	U31	24c **purple**, *cream*	250.00	500.00
		Entire	375.00	
U102	U32	30c **black**	70.00	110.00
		Entire	275.00	750.00
U103	U32	30c **black**, *amber*	225.00	500.00
		Entire	600.00	
U104	U32	30c **black**, *cream*	200.00	500.00
		Entire	375.00	
U105	U33	90c **carmine**	150.00	350.00
		Entire	190.00	
U106	U33	90c **carmine**, *amber*	300.00	400.00
		Entire	875.00	*4,000.*
U107	U33	90c **carmine**, *cream*	250.00	*2,500.*
		Entire	900.00	*5,000.*

Printed by Plimpton Manufacturing Co.

U34

Bust forms an angle at the back near the frame. Lettering poorly executed. Distinct circle in "O" of "Postage."

U35

Lower part of bust points to the end of the "E" in "ONE." Head inclined downward.

U36

Bust narrow at back. Thin numerals. Head of "P" narrow. Bust broad at front, ending in sharp corners.

U37

Bust broad. Figures of value in long ovals.

U38

Similar to U37 but the figure "2" at the left touches the oval.

U39

Similar to U37 but the "O" of "TWO" has the center netted instead of plain and the "G" of "POSTAGE" and the "C" of "CENTS" have diagonal crossline.

U40

Bust broad: numerals in ovals short and thick.

U41

Similar to U40 but the ovals containing the numerals are much heavier. A diagonal line runs from the upper part of the "U" to the white frame-line.

U42

Similar to U40 but the middle stroke of "N" in "CENTS" is as thin as the vertical strokes.

U43

Bottom of bust cut almost semi-circularly.

U44

Thin lettering, long thin figures of value.

U45

Thick lettering, well-formed figures of value, queue does not project below bust.

U46

Top of head egg-shaped; knot of queue well marked and projects triangularly.

Taylor
U47

Die 1 - Figures of value with thick, curved tops.

Die 2 - Figures of value with long, thin tops.

U48

Neck short at back.

U49

Figures of value turned up at the ends.

U50

Very large head.

U51

Knot of queue stands out prominently.

U52

Ear prominent, chin receding.

U53

No side whiskers, forelock projects above head.

U54

Hair does not project; ornaments around the inner oval end in points.

U55

Back of bust rather broad, chin slopes considerably; labels containing figures of value are not exactly parallel.

U56

Front of bust sloping; inner lines of shields project considerably into the inner oval.

1874-86

U108	U34	1c	**dark blue**	100.00	70.00
			Entire	150.00	110.00
a.		1c	**light blue**	100.00	70.00
			Entire	150.00	125.00
U109	U34	1c	**dark blue,** *amber*	150.00	75.00
			Entire	160.00	140.00
+U110	U34	1c	**dark blue,** *cream*	1,500.	
U111	U34	1c	**dark blue,** *orange*	22.50	17.50
			Entire	32.50	25.00
a.		1c	**light blue,** *orange*	22.50	17.50
			Entire	30.00	25.00
W112	U34	1c	**dark blue,** *manila*	50.00	40.00
			Entire	80.00	72.50
U113	U35	1c	**light blue**	1.75	1.00
			Entire	2.75	1.10
a.		1c	**dark blue**	7.50	7.50
			Entire	25.00	20.00
U114	U35	1c	**light blue,** *amber*	4.25	4.00
			Entire	8.00	6.00
a.		1c	**dark blue,** *amber*	15.00	10.00
			Entire	25.00	20.00
U115	U35	1c	**blue,** *cream*	4.50	4.50
			Entire	9.00	6.50
a.		1c	**dark blue,** *cream*	17.50	8.50
			Entire	30.00	20.00
U116	U35	1c	**light blue,** *orange*	.80	.40
			Entire	1.00	.75
a.		1c	**dark blue,** *orange*	3.00	2.50
			Entire	12.50	8.00
U117	U35	1c	**light blue,** *blue* ('80)	6.00	5.25
			Entire	10.00	9.00
U118	U35	1c	**light blue,** *fawn* ('79)	6.00	5.25

No.	Die	Description	Unused	Used
		Entire	12.50	10.00
U119	U35	1c **light blue**, *manila* ('86)	6.00	3.25
		Entire	8.00	5.00
W120	U35	1c **light blue**, *manila*	1.60	1.10
		Entire	2.75	1.75
a.		1c **dark blue**, *manila*	7.00	8.00
		Entire	13.00	15.00
U121	U35	1c **light blue**, *amber manila* ('86)	11.00	10.00
		Entire	17.50	20.00
U122	U36	2c **brown**	100.00	40.00
		Entire	140.00	85.00
U123	U36	2c **brown**, *amber*	57.50	40.00
		Entire	90.00	70.00
+U124	U36	2c **brown**, *cream*	1,000.	
+U125	U36	2c **brown**, *orange*	20,000.	
		Entire	40,000.	
W126	U36	2c **brown**, *manila*	110.00	70.00
		Entire	175.00	110.00
W127	U36	2c **vermilion**, *manila*	1,500.	250.00
		Entire	2,000.	2,000.
U128	U37	2c **brown**	42.50	32.50
		Entire	82.50	72.50
U129	U37	2c **brown**, *amber*	65.00	37.50
		Entire	90.00	75.00
+U130	U37	2c **brown**, *cream*	45,000.	
W131	U37	2c **brown**, *manila*	17.50	16.00
		Entire	25.00	17.50
U132	U38	2c **brown**	60.00	27.50
		Entire	92.50	77.50
U133	U38	2c **brown**, *amber*	275.00	65.00
		Entire	450.00	125.00
+U133A	U38	2c **brown**, *cream*	75,000.	
U134	U39	2c **brown**	1,000.	140.00
		Entire	1,400.	240.00
U135	U39	2c **brown**, *amber*	450.00	125.00
		Entire	600.00	160.00
U136	U39	2c **brown**, *orange*	47.50	29.00
		Entire	75.00	37.50
W137	U39	2c **brown**, *manila*	60.00	35.00
		Entire	85.00	50.00
+U137A	U39	2c **vermilion**	25,000.	
+U137B	U39	2c **vermilion**, *amber*	25,000.	
		Entire	—	
+U137C	U39	2c **vermilion**, *orange*	25,000.	
+W138	U39	2c **vermilion**, *manila*	32,500.	
U139	U40	2c **brown** ('75)	45.00	35.00
		Entire	60.00	45.00
U140	U40	2c **brown**, *amber* ('75)	75.00	60.00
		Entire	90.00	75.00
U140A	U40	2c **brown**, *orange* ('75)	17,500.	
W141	U40	2c **brown**, *manila* ('75)	35.00	30.00
		Entire	42.50	30.00
U142	U40	2c **vermilion** ('75)	6.00	3.00
		Entire	6.50	5.00
a.		2c **pink**	7.50	5.00
		Entire	10.00	7.50
U143	U40	2c **vermilion**, *amber* ('75)	6.00	3.00
		Entire	7.50	4.00
U144	U40	2c **vermilion**, *cream* ('75)	13.00	6.25
		Entire	18.00	11.00
+U145	U40	2c **vermilion**, *orange* ('75)	25,000.	
		Entire	30,000.	
U146	U40	2c **vermilion**, *blue* ('80)	140.00	40.00
		Entire	200.00	140.00
U147	U40	2c **vermilion**, *fawn* ('75)	6.25	4.50
		Entire	11.00	6.50
W148	U40	2c **vermilion**, *manila* ('75)	3.75	3.75
		Entire	7.25	6.00
U149	U41	2c **vermilion** ('78)	45.00	30.00
		Entire	70.00	40.00
a.		2c **pink**	45.00	30.00
		Entire	70.00	40.00
U150	U41	2c **vermilion**, *amber* ('78)	22.50	17.50
		Entire	40.00	22.50
U151	U41	2c **vermilion**, *blue* ('80)	13.00	9.25
		Entire	20.00	15.00
a.		2c **pink**, *blue*	10.00	9.00
		Entire	15.00	11.00
U152	U41	2c **vermilion**, *fawn* ('78)	10.00	4.75
		Entire	15.00	9.50
U153	U42	2c **vermilion** ('76)	55.00	26.00
		Entire	85.00	35.00
U154	U42	2c **vermilion**, *amber* ('76)	300.00	90.00
		Entire	350.00	140.00
W155	U42	2c **vermilion**, *manila* ('76)	20.00	9.50
		Entire	40.00	15.00
U156	U43	2c **vermilion** ('81)	1,250.	150.00
		Entire	1,750.	400.00
U157	U43	2c **vermilion**, *amber* ('81)	50,000.	35,000.
		Entire	65,000.	
W158	U43	2c **vermilion**, *manila* ('81)	82.50	60.00
		Entire	140.00	140.00
U159	U44	3c **green**	22.50	6.75
		Entire	45.00	17.50
U160	U44	3c **green**, *amber*	27.50	10.50
		Entire	50.00	20.00
U161	U44	3c **green**, *cream*	37.50	15.00
		Entire	60.00	30.00
+U162	U44	3c **green**, *blue*	—	
U163	U45	3c **green**	1.40	.30
		Entire	3.00	2.25
U164	U45	3c **green**, *amber*	1.50	.70
		Entire	3.00	2.00
U165	U45	3c **green**, *cream*	8.00	6.50
		Entire	14.00	9.00
U166	U45	3c **green**, *blue*	8.25	6.25
		Entire	16.00	11.00
U167	U45	3c **green**, *fawn* ('75)	5.00	3.50
		Entire	9.00	5.00
U168	U46	3c **green** ('81)	1,000.	75.00
		Entire	3,000.	225.00
U169	U46	3c **green**, *amber*	240.00	110.00
		Entire	450.00	250.00
U170	U46	3c **green**, *blue* ('81)	12,500.	3,000.
		Entire	20,000.	4,000.
U171	U46	3c **green**, *fawn* ('81)	45,000.	2,600.
		Entire		12,500.
U172	U47	5c **blue**, *die 1* ('75)	11.00	8.00

No.	Die	Description	Unused	Used
		Entire	16.00	12.50
U173	U47	5c **blue**, *die 1, amber* ('75)	11.00	9.00
		Entire	16.00	12.00
U174	U47	5c **blue**, *die 1, cream* ('75)	95.00	40.00
		Entire	140.00	85.00
U175	U47	5c **blue**, *die 1, blue* ('75)	25.00	15.00
		Entire	25.00	19.00
U176	U47	5c **blue**, *die 1, fawn* ('75)	110.00	57.50
		Entire	225.00	
U177	U47	5c **blue**, *die 2* ('75)	8.00	6.75
		Entire	15.00	15.00
U178	U47	5c **blue**, *die 2, amber* ('75)	8.00	7.50
		Entire	16.00	16.00
+U178A	U47	5c **blue**, *die 2, cream* ('76)	10,000.	
		Entire	15,000.	
U179	U47	5c **blue**, *die 2, blue* ('75)	15.00	9.00
		Entire	25.00	22.50
U180	U47	5c **blue**, *die 2, fawn* ('75)	100.00	45.00
		Entire	175.00	125.00
U181	U48	6c **red**	6.75	6.25
		Entire	11.00	11.00
a.		6c **vermilion**	6.75	6.25
		Entire	11.00	11.00
U182	U48	6c **red**, *amber*	11.50	6.25
		Entire	20.00	13.00
a.		6c **vermilion**, *amber*	11.00	6.25
		Entire	20.00	13.00
U183	U48	6c **red**, *cream*	20.00	13.00
		Entire	40.00	27.50
a.		6c **vermilion**, *cream*	20.00	13.00
		Entire	40.00	27.50
U184	U48	6c **red**, *fawn* ('75)	20.00	13.00
		Entire	30.00	27.50
+U185	U49	7c **vermilion**	1,600.	
U186	U49	7c **vermilion**, *amber*	100.00	62.50
		Entire	150.00	
U187	U50	10c **brown**	35.00	20.00
		Entire	55.00	
U188	U50	10c **brown**, *amber*	62.50	32.50
		Entire	125.00	
U189	U51	10c **chocolate** ('75)	7.50	4.00
		Entire	12.00	9.00
a.		10c **bister brown**	8.50	5.00
		Entire	12.50	10.00
b.		10c **yellow ocher**	3,500.	
		Entire	6,500.	
U190	U51	10c **chocolate**, *amber* ('75)	8.00	7.00
		Entire	13.50	11.00
a.		10c **bister brown**, *amber*	8.50	7.50
		Entire	13.50	11.00
b.		10c **yellow ocher**	1,250.	
		Entire	2,000.	
U191	U51	10c **brown**, *oriental buff* ('86)	10.00	8.25
		Entire	12.50	11.00
U192	U51	10c **brown**, *blue* ('86)	13.00	8.25
		Entire	15.00	12.50
a.		10c **gray black**, *blue*	13.00	8.25
		Entire	15.00	15.00
b.		10c **red brown**, *blue*	13.00	8.25
		Entire	15.00	12.50
U193	U51	10c **brown**, *manila* ('86)	14.50	10.00
		Entire	17.50	16.00
a.		10c **red brown**, *manila*	14.50	10.00
		Entire	17.50	16.00
U194	U51	10c **brown**, *amber manila* ('86)	15.00	8.50
		Entire	20.00	17.50
a.		10c **red brown**, *amber manila*	17.50	9.00
		Entire	22.50	17.50
U195	U52	12c **plum**	400.00	100.00
		Entire	600.00	
U196	U52	12c **plum**, *amber*	250.00	175.00
		Entire	325.00	
U197	U52	12c **plum**, *cream*	200.00	150.00
		Entire	900.00	
U198	U53	15c **orange**	47.50	37.50
		Entire	80.00	47.50
U199	U53	15c **orange**, *amber*	150.00	100.00
		Entire	250.00	
U200	U53	15c **orange**, *cream*	500.00	350.00
		Entire	1,000.	
U201	U54	24c **purple**	175.00	150.00
		Entire	250.00	
U202	U54	24c **purple**, *amber*	175.00	125.00
		Entire	250.00	
U203	U54	24c **purple**, *cream*	175.00	125.00
		Entire	750.00	
U204	U55	30c **black**	62.50	27.50
		Entire	80.00	65.00
U205	U55	30c **black**, *amber*	72.50	60.00
		Entire	140.00	*250.00*
U206	U55	30c **black**, *cream* ('75)	375.00	375.00
		Entire	800.00	
U207	U55	30c **black**, *oriental buff* ('86)	100.00	82.50
		Entire	160.00	
U208	U55	30c **black**, *blue* ('81)	110.00	82.50
		Entire	140.00	
U209	U55	30c **black**, *manila* ('81)	90.00	80.00
		Entire	160.00	
U210	U55	30c **black**, *amber manila* ('86)	175.00	85.00
		Entire	210.00	
U211	U56	90c **carmine** ('75)	110.00	80.00
		Entire	160.00	90.00
U212	U56	90c **carmine**, *amber* ('75)	225.00	300.00
		Entire	275.00	
U213	U56	90c **carmine**, *cream* ('75)	750.00	
		Entire	3,000.	
U214	U56	90c **carmine**, *oriental buff* ('86)	200.00	275.00
		Entire	275.00	300.00
U215	U56	90c **carmine**, *blue* ('86)	190.00	250.00
		Entire	250.00	275.00
U216	U56	90c **carmine**, *manila* ('86)	175.00	250.00
		Entire	250.00	275.00

No.	Die	Description	Unused	Used
U217	U56	90c **carmine**, *amber manila* ('86)	125.00	200.00
		Entire	225.00	275.00

Note: No. U206 has watermark #2; No. U207 watermark #6 or #7. No U213 has watermark #2; No. U214 watermark #7. These envelopes cannot be positively identified except by the watermark.

U57

Single line under "POSTAGE."

U58

Double line under "POSTAGE."

1876
Printed by Plimpton Manufacturing Co.

No.	Die	Description	Unused	Used
U218	U57	3c **red**	50.00	25.00
		Entire	75.50	50.00
U219	U57	3c **green**	45.00	17.50
		Entire	65.00	40.00
U220	U58	3c **red**	32,500.	
		Entire	50,000.	
U221	U58	3c **green**	52.50	21.00
		Entire	85.00	50.00

Garfield
U59

1882-86
Printed by Plimpton Manufacturing Co. and Morgan Envelope Co.

No.	Die	Description	Unused	Used
U222	U59	5c **brown**	4.00	2.75
		Entire	8.00	7.00
U223	U59	5c **brown**, *amber*	4.75	3.25
		Entire	10.00	8.50

U224	U59	5c **brown**, *oriental buff* ('86)	110.00	72.50
		Entire	150.00	
U225	U59	5c **brown**, *blue*	60.00	35.00
		Entire	85.00	75.00
U226	U59	5c **brown**, *fawn*	250.00	
		Entire	325.00	

Washington — U60

1883, October

U227	U60	2c **red**	3.75	2.25
		Entire	8.50	3.00
a.		2c **brown** (error), entire	3,500.	
U228	U60	2c **red**, *amber*	4.75	2.75
		Entire	9.00	6.00
U229	U60	2c **red**, *blue*	7.00	5.00
		Entire	10.50	8.00
U230	U60	2c **red**, *fawn*	8.00	5.25
		Entire	13.00	7.00

Washington — U61

Wavy lines fine and clear.

1883, November
Four Wavy Lines in Oval

U231	U61	2c **red**	3.75	2.25
		Entire	7.50	4.00
U232	U61	2c **red**, *amber*	4.75	3.75
		Entire	9.00	5.75
U233	U61	2c **red**, *blue*	8.00	7.25
		Entire	15.00	10.00
U234	U61	2c **red**, *fawn*	5.75	4.75
		Entire	9.00	6.00
W235	U61	2c **red**, *manila*	17.50	6.25
		Entire	26.00	12.50

U62

Retouched die. Wavy lines thick and blurred.

1884, June

U236	U62	2c **red**	7.50	4.00
		Entire	11.00	7.75
U237	U62	2c **red**, *amber*	11.00	10.00
		Entire	17.50	11.00
U238	U62	2c **red**, *blue*	18.00	10.00
		Entire	25.00	12.50
U239	U62	2c **red**, *fawn*	12.50	10.00
		Entire	16.00	11.00

U63

3½ links over left "2."

U240	U63	2c **red**	70.00	42.50
		Entire	100.00	67.50
U241	U63	2c **red**, *amber*	750.00	325.00
		Entire	2,250.	750.00
U242	U63	2c **red**, *fawn*		10,000.
		Entire		20,000.

U64

2 links below right "2."

U243	U64	2c **red**	90.00	57.50
		Entire	130.00	90.00
U244	U64	2c **red**, *amber*	200.00	75.00
		Entire	275.00	110.00
U245	U64	2c **red**, *blue*	425.00	200.00
		Entire	575.00	210.00
U246	U64	2c **red**, *fawn*	350.00	140.00
		Entire	550.00	250.00

U65

Round "O" in "TWO."

U247	U65	2c **red**	1,500.	350.00
		Entire	2,250.	750.00
U248	U65	2c **red**, *amber*	2,500.	850.00
		Entire	4,250.	1,150.
U249	U65	2c **red**, *fawn*	600.00	375.00
		Entire	925.00	450.00

Jackson,
Die 1
U66

Die 1 - Numeral at
left is 2¾mm wide.

Die 2 - Numeral at
left is 3¼mm wide

1883-86

U250	U66	4c **green**, die 1	3.75	3.50
		Entire	6.00	6.00
U251	U66	4c **green**, die 1, *amber*	4.75	3.50
		Entire	7.00	5.25
U252	U66	4c **green**, die 1, *oriental buff* ('86)	8.00	9.00
		Entire	11.00	12.50
U253	U66	4c **green**, die 1, *blue* ('86)	8.00	6.50
		Entire	11.00	15.00
U254	U66	4c **green**, die 1, *manila* ('86)	10.00	7.50
		Entire	12.50	15.00
U255	U66	4c **green**, die 1, *amber manila* ('86)	17.50	10.00
		Entire	25.00	15.00
U256	U66	4c **green**, die 2	5.50	5.00
		Entire	12.00	6.75
U257	U66	4c **green**, die 2, *amber*	11.00	7.00
		Entire	17.50	10.00
U258	U66	4c **green**, die 2, *manila* ('86)	10.00	7.50
		Entire	15.00	12.50
U259	U66	4c **green**, die 2, *amber manila* ('86)	11.00	7.50
		Entire	16.00	12.50

1884, May

U260	U61	2c **brown**	13.00	5.75
		Entire	16.00	9.00
U261	U61	2c **brown**, *amber*	12.50	6.50
		Entire	15.00	7.50
U262	U61	2c **brown**, *blue*	13.00	10.00
		Entire	17.50	14.00
U263	U61	2c **brown**, *fawn*	12.00	9.25
		Entire	14.00	12.50
W264	U61	2c **brown**, *manila*	14.00	10.50
		Entire	22.50	17.50

1884, June
Retouched Die

U265	U62	2c **brown**	15.00	6.25
		Entire	20.00	11.00
U266	U62	2c **brown**, *amber*	65.00	40.00
		Entire	70.00	50.00
U267	U62	2c **brown**, *blue*	13.00	6.25
		Entire	17.00	10.00
U268	U62	2c **brown**, *fawn*	15.00	11.00
		Entire	19.00	15.00
W269	U62	2c **brown**, *manila*	22.50	15.00
		Entire	27.50	22.50

2 Links Below Right "2"

U270	U64	2c **brown**	95.00	40.00
		Entire	130.00	90.00
U271	U64	2c **brown**, *amber*	300.00	95.00
		Entire	375.00	275.00
U272	U64	2c **brown**, *fawn*	7,000.	2,000.
		Entire	9,000.	3,500.

Round "O" in "Two"

U273	U65	2c **brown**	225.00	100.00
		Entire	275.00	190.00
U274	U65	2c **brown**, *amber*	240.00	85.00
		Entire	325.00	175.00
U275	U65	2c **brown**, *blue*		15,000.
		Entire		45,000.
U276	U65	2c **brown**, *fawn*	900.00	675.00
		Entire	1,300.	700.00

United States stamped envelopes can be mounted in the Scott U.S. Postal Stationery album.

Washington — U67

Extremity of bust below the queue forms a point.

U68

Extremity of bust is rounded. Similar to U61. Two wavy lines in oval.

1884-86

U277	U67	2c	**brown**	.50	.20
			Entire	.75	.40
a.		2c	**brown lake**, die 1	20.00	20.00
			Entire	22.50	17.50
U278	U67	2c	**brown**, *amber*	.65	.50
			Entire	1.25	.75
a.		2c	**brown lake**, *amber*	30.00	12.50
			Entire	35.00	15.00
U279	U67	2c	**brown**, *oriental buff* ('86)	2.90	2.10
			Entire	5.00	3.00
U280	U67	2c	**brown**, *blue*	2.50	2.10
			Entire	4.00	3.50
U281	U67	2c	**brown**, *fawn*	3.00	2.40
			Entire	4.75	4.00
U282	U67	2c	**brown**, *manila* ('86)	10.00	4.00
			Entire	14.00	6.50
W283	U67	2c	**brown**, *manila*	6.00	5.00
			Entire	9.50	6.50
U284	U67	2c	**brown**, *amber manila* ('86)	5.50	5.75
			Entire	11.00	7.00
+U285	U67	2c	**red**	700.00	
			Entire	1,250.	
+U286	U67	2c	**red**, *blue*	300.00	
			Entire	350.00	
W287	U67	2c	**red**, *manila*	110.00	
			Entire	160.00	
U288	U68	2c	**brown**	200.00	37.50
			Entire	575.00	100.00
U289	U68	2c	**brown**, *amber*	14.00	12.50
			Entire	19.00	16.00
U290	U68	2c	**brown**, *blue*	1,600.	200.00
			Entire	2,000.	350.00
U291	U68	2c	**brown**, *fawn*	20.00	19.00
			Entire	30.00	24.00
W292	U68	2c	**brown**, *manila*	20.00	17.50
			Entire	27.50	21.00

Gen. U.S.
Grant — US1

1886

Printed by American Bank Note Co.
Issued August 18, 1886. Withdrawn June 30, 1894.
Letter Sheet, 160x271mm
Stamp in upper right corner
Creamy White Paper

U293	US1	2c	**green**, entire	27.50	17.00

Perforation varieties:

83 perforations at top	27.50	17.00
33 perforations at top	50.00	20.00

All with 41 perforations at top

Inscribed: Series 1	27.50	17.00
Inscribed: Series 2	27.50	17.00
Inscribed: Series 3	27.50	17.00
Inscribed: Series 4	27.50	17.00
Inscribed: Series 5	27.50	17.00
Inscribed: Series 6	27.50	17.00
Inscribed: Series 7	27.50	17.00

Franklin
U69

Washington
U70

Bust points between third and fourth notches of inner oval "G" of "POSTAGE" has no bar.

U71

Bust points between second and third notches of inner oval; "G" of "POSTAGE" has a bar; ear is indicated by one heavy line; one vertical line at corner of mouth.

U72

Frame same as U71; upper part of head more rounded; ear indicated by two curved lines with two locks of hair in front; two vertical lines at corner of mouth.

Jackson
U73

Grant — U74

There is a space between the beard and the collar of the coat. A button is on the collar.

U75

The collar touches the beard and there is no button.

1887-94
**Printed by Plimpton Manufacturing Co.
and Morgan Envelope Co., Hartford, Conn.;
James Purcell, Holyoke, Mass.**

U294	U69	1c **blue**	.55	.20
		Entire	1.00	.50
U295	U69	1c **dark blue** ('94)	7.50	2.50
		Entire	10.50	6.00
U296	U69	1c **blue**, *amber*	3.50	1.25
		Entire	6.00	3.50
U297	U69	1c **dark blue**, *amber* ('94)	47.50	22.50
		Entire	57.50	27.50
+U298	U69	1c **blue**, *oriental buff*, Entire	12,500.	
		Entire	15,000.	
+U299	U69	1c **blue**, *blue*	17,500.	
		Entire	22,500.	
U300	U69	1c **blue**, *manila*	.65	.35
		Entire	1.25	.75
W301	U69	1c **blue**, *manila*	.45	.30
		Entire	1.25	.60
U302	U69	1c **dark blue**, *manila* ('94)	25.00	10.00
		Entire	32.50	20.00
W303	U69	1c **dark blue**, *manila* ('94)	12.00	9.50
		Entire	20.00	12.50
U304	U69	1c **blue**, *amber manila*	5.50	4.25
		Entire	8.50	6.00
U305	U70	2c **green**	11.00	9.00
		Entire	25.00	12.50
U306	U70	2c **green**, *amber*	22.50	14.00
		Entire	30.00	17.50
U307	U70	2c **green**, *oriental buff*	75.00	30.00
		Entire	95.00	42.50
U308	U70	2c **green**, *blue*	8,000.	1,250.
		Entire		10,000.
U309	U70	2c **green**, *manila*	15,000.	725.00
		Entire	20,000.	1,000.
U310	U70	2c **green**, *amber manila*	1,800.	1,250.
		Entire	15,000.	3,500.
U311	U71	2c **green**	.35	.20
		Entire	.75	.25
U312	U71	2c **green**, *amber*	.45	.20
		Entire	.80	.30
U313	U71	2c **green**, *oriental buff*	.60	.25
		Entire	1.20	.40
U314	U71	2c **green**, *blue*	.65	.30
		Entire	1.25	.40
U315	U71	2c **green**, *manila*	1.75	.50
		Entire	2.75	1.00
W316	U71	2c **green**, *manila*	3.25	2.50
		Entire	9.00	7.00
U317	U71	2c **green**, *amber manila*	2.75	1.90
		Entire	6.00	3.00
U318	U72	2c **green**	125.00	12.50
		Entire	175.00	45.00
U319	U72	2c **green**, *amber*	175.00	25.00
		Entire	240.00	50.00
U320	U72	2c **green**, *oriental buff*	150.00	40.00
		Entire	200.00	70.00
U321	U72	2c **green**, *blue*	175.00	65.00
		Entire	275.00	82.50
U322	U72	2c **green**, *manila*	225.00	65.00
		Entire	275.00	110.00
U323	U72	2c **green**, *amber manila*	425.00	80.00
		Entire	500.00	160.00
U324	U73	4c **carmine**	2.50	1.75
		Entire	5.00	2.10
a.		4c **lake**	2.75	2.00
		Entire	5.50	3.75
b.		4c **scarlet** ('94)	2.75	2.00
		Entire	5.50	3.75
U325	U73	4c **carmine**, *amber*	3.00	2.25
		Entire	6.00	3.25
a.		4c **lake**, *amber*	3.25	2.50
		Entire	6.25	3.75
b.		4c **scarlet**, *amber* ('94)	3.25	3.25
		Entire	6.25	4.25
U326	U73	4c **carmine**, *oriental buff*	5.50	3.00
		Entire	11.00	4.75
a.		4c **lake**, *oriental buff*	6.50	3.50
		Entire	12.00	6.25
U327	U73	4c **carmine**, *blue*	5.00	4.00
		Entire	9.00	7.00
a.		4c **lake**, *blue*	5.00	4.00
		Entire	11.00	6.00
U328	U73	4c **carmine**, *manila*	6.25	5.50
		Entire	10.00	7.00
a.		4c **lake**, *manila*	7.25	6.00

		Entire	10.00	7.50
b.		4c **pink**, *manila*	7.50	4.50
		Entire	10.00	8.00
U329	U73	4c **carmine**, *amber manila*	4.50	2.75
		Entire	9.00	4.00
a.		4c **lake**, *amber manila*	5.25	3.25
		Entire	9.50	5.00
b.		4c **pink**, *amber manila*	5.50	3.75
		Entire	9.50	6.50
U330	U74	5c **blue**	3.50	4.00
		Entire	7.00	11.00
U331	U74	5c **blue**, *amber*	4.50	2.25
		Entire	9.00	14.00
U332	U74	5c **blue**, *oriental buff*	4.50	3.75
		Entire	12.50	17.50
U333	U74	5c **blue**, *blue*	9.00	5.50
		Entire	15.00	14.00
U334	U75	5c **blue** ('94)	12.50	5.50
		Entire	16.00	17.50
U335	U75	5c **blue**, *amber* ('94)	11.00	5.50
		Entire	17.50	16.50
U336	U55	30c **red brown**	42.50	40.00
		Entire	60.00	350.00
a.		30c **yellow brown**	50.00	45.00
		Entire	60.00	450.00
b.		30c **chocolate**	50.00	47.50
		Entire	60.00	450.00
U337	U55	30c **red brown**, *amber*	47.50	55.00
		Entire	57.50	450.00
a.		30c **yellow brown**, *amber*	47.50	55.00
		Entire	60.00	450.00
b.		30c **chocolate**, *amber*	47.50	55.00
		Entire	60.00	450.00
U338	U55	30c **red brown**, *oriental buff*	42.50	47.50
		Entire	57.50	450.00
a.		30c **yellow brown**, *oriental buff*	42.50	47.50
		Entire	55.00	450.00
U339	U55	30c **red brown**, *blue*	42.50	47.50
		Entire	55.00	450.00
a.		30c **yellow brown**, *blue*	40.00	47.50
		Entire	50.00	450.00
U340	U55	30c **red brown**, *manila*	45.00	45.00
		Entire	57.50	400.00
a.		30c **brown**, *manila*	42.50	40.00
		Entire	55.00	400.00
U341	U55	30c **red brown**, *amber manila*	50.00	30.00
		Entire	60.00	400.00
a.		30c **yellow brown**, *amber manila*	47.50	30.00
		Entire	55.00	400.00
U342	U56	90c **purple**	65.00	75.00
		Entire	85.00	1,000.
U343	U56	90c **purple**, *amber*	80.00	80.00
		Entire	105.00	1,000.
U344	U56	90c **purple**, *oriental buff*	80.00	85.00
		Entire	125.00	1,000.
U345	U56	90c **purple**, *blue*	82.50	90.00
		Entire	125.00	1,000.
U346	U56	90c **purple**, *manila*	87.50	92.50
		Entire	125.00	1,000.
U347	U56	90c **purple**, *amber manila*	87.50	92.50
		Entire	125.00	1,000.

Columbus and Liberty — U76

Four dies were used for the 1c, 2c and 5c:
1 - Meridian behind Columbus' head. Period after "CENTS."
2 - No meridian. With period.
3 - With meridian. No period.
4 - No meridian. No period.

1893

U348	U76	1c **deep blue**	2.25	1.10
		Entire	3.00	1.40
		Entire, Expo. station machine cancel		100.00
		Entire, Expo. station duplex handstamp cancel		250.00
U349	U76	2c **violet**	1.75	.50
		Entire	3.50	.60
		Entire, Expo. station machine cancel		40.00
		Entire, Expo. station duplex handstamp cancel		85.00
a.		2c **dark slate** (error)	2,000.	
		Entire	2,750.	
U350	U76	5c **chocolate**	8.50	7.50
		Entire	13.00	10.00

		Entire, Expo. station machine cancel		150.00
		Entire, Expo. station duplex handstamp cancel		250.00
a.		5c **slate brown** (error)	800.00	950.00
		Entire	1,000.	1,400.
U351	U76	10c **slate brown**	30.00	25.00
		Entire	55.00	40.00
		Entire, Expo. station machine cancel		250.00
		Entire, Expo. station duplex handstamp cancel		450.00

Franklin
U77

Washington
U78

Bust points to first notch of inner oval and is only slightly concave below.

U79

Bust points to middle of second notch of inner oval and is quite hollow below. Queue has ribbon around it.

U80

Same as die 2, but hair flowing. No ribbon on queue.

Lincoln
U81

Bust pointed but not draped.

U82

Bust broad and draped.

U83

Head larger, inner oval has no notches.

Grant — U84

Similar to design of 1887-95 but smaller.

1899

U352	U77	1c	**green**	.60	.20
			Entire	1.25	.50
U353	U77	1c	**green**, *amber*	4.75	1.50
			Entire	7.50	2.75
U354	U77	1c	**green**, *oriental buff*	11.00	2.75
			Entire	14.00	3.75
U355	U77	1c	**green**, *blue*	11.00	7.50
			Entire	14.00	12.50
U356	U77	1c	**green**, *manila*	2.25	.95
			Entire	6.50	2.00
W357	U77	1c	**green**, *manila*	2.50	1.10
			Entire	9.00	4.00
U358	U78	2c	**carmine**	3.00	1.75
			Entire	7.50	3.25
U359	U78	2c	**carmine**, *amber*	20.00	14.00
			Entire	27.50	20.00
U360	U78	2c	**carmine**, *oriental buff*	19.00	8.00
			Entire	30.00	9.50
U361	U78	2c	**carmine**, *blue*	57.50	27.50
			Entire	70.00	35.00
U362	U79	2c	**carmine**	.35	.20
			Entire	.65	.30
a.			2c **dark lake**	25.00	30.00
			Entire	30.00	35.00
U363	U79	2c	**carmine**, *amber*	1.40	.20
			Entire	3.00	.60
U364	U79	2c	**carmine**, *oriental buff*	1.20	.20
			Entire	3.00	.60
U365	U79	2c	**carmine**, *blue*	1.50	.55
			Entire	3.50	2.00
W366	U79	2c	**carmine**, *manila*	8.00	3.25
			Entire	12.00	6.50
U367	U80	2c	**carmine**	4.50	2.75
			Entire	9.00	6.75
U368	U80	2c	**carmine**, *amber*	9.00	6.75
			Entire	15.00	12.00
U369	U80	2c	**carmine**, *oriental buff*	25.00	12.50
			Entire	32.50	20.00
U370	U80	2c	**carmine**, *blue*	12.50	10.00
			Entire	25.00	15.00
U371	U81	4c	**brown**	17.50	11.00
			Entire	27.50	14.00
U372	U81	4c	**brown**, *amber*	17.50	12.50
			Entire	30.00	22.50
U373	U82	4c	**brown**	10,000.	900.00
			Entire	15,000.	
U374	U83	4c	**brown**	12.50	8.00
			Entire	25.00	12.50
U375	U83	4c	**brown**, *amber*	40.00	17.50
			Entire	50.00	24.00
W376	U83	4c	**brown**, *manila*	17.50	8.25
			Entire	25.00	11.00
U377	U84	5c	**blue**	10.00	9.50
			Entire	14.00	16.00
U378	U84	5c	**blue**, *amber*	14.00	10.00
			Entire	22.50	17.50

Franklin — U85

Washington
U86

One short and two long vertical lines at the right of "CENTS."

Grant
U87

Lincoln — U88

1903
Printed by Hartford Manufacturing Co., Hartford, Conn.

U379	U85	1c	**green**	.70	.20
			Entire	1.20	.35
U380	U85	1c	**green**, *amber*	13.50	2.00
			Entire	19.00	2.50
U381	U85	1c	**green**, *oriental buff*	15.00	2.50
			Entire	20.00	3.00
U382	U85	1c	**green**, *blue*	20.00	2.50
			Entire	27.50	3.00
U383	U85	1c	**green**, *manila*	4.00	.90
			Entire	5.00	1.25
W384	U85	1c	**green**, *manila*	1.50	.40
			Entire	2.75	.80
U385	U86	2c	**carmine**	.40	.20
			Entire	.85	.35
			Pink	1.60	1.00
U386	U86	2c	**carmine**, *amber*	1.90	.20
			Entire	3.50	.80
			Pink, *amber*	3.25	1.50
U387	U86	2c	**carmine**, *oriental buff*	1.75	.30
			Entire	2.50	.35
			Pink, *oriental buff*	2.50	1.25
U388	U86	2c	**carmine**, *blue*	1.30	.50
			Entire	2.75	.60
			Pink, *blue*	3.25	1.75
W389	U86	2c	**carmine**, *manila*	17.50	9.50
			Entire	22.50	14.00
U390	U87	4c	**chocolate**	22.50	11.00
			Entire	27.50	14.00
U391	U87	4c	**chocolate**, *amber*	20.00	12.50
			Entire	25.00	15.00
W392	U87	4c	**chocolate**, *manila*	20.00	12.50
			Entire	25.00	15.00
U393	U88	5c	**blue**	20.00	12.50
			Entire	25.00	17.50
U394	U88	5c	**blue**, *amber*	20.00	12.50
			Entire	27.50	20.00

U89

Re-cut die - The three lines at the right of "CENTS" and at the left of "TWO" are usually all short; the lettering is heavier and the ends of the ribbons slightly changed.

1904

Re-cut Die

U395	U89	2c **carmine**		.50	.20
		Entire		.90	.45
		Pink		5.00	2.50
U396	U89	2c **carmine**, *amber*		8.00	1.00
		Entire		12.50	2.00
		Pink, *amber*		10.00	3.00
U397	U89	2c **carmine**, *oriental buff*		5.50	1.10
		Entire		7.50	1.50
		Pink, *oriental buff*		7.00	2.75
U398	U89	2c **carmine**, *blue*		3.50	.90
		Entire		5.00	1.40
		Pink, *amber*		5.75	2.50
W399	U89	2c **carmine**, *manila*		12.00	9.50
		Entire		20.00	14.00
		Pink, *manila*		17.50	12.50

Franklin
U90

U90 Die 1

U90 Die 2

U90 Die 3

U90 Die 4

Die 1 - Wide "D" in "UNITED."
Die 2 - Narrow "D" in "UNITED."
Die 3 - Wide "S-S" in "STATES" (1910).
Die 4 - Sharp angle at back of bust, "N" and "E" of "ONE" are parallel (1912).

1907-16

Printed by Mercantile Corp. and Middle West Supply Co., Dayton, Ohio

U400	U90	1c **green**, die 1		.30	.20
		Entire		.50	.30
a.		Die 2		.80	.25
		Entire		1.10	.45
b.		Die 3		.80	.35
		Entire		1.20	.65
c.		Die 4		.75	.30
		Entire		1.00	.45
U401	U90	1c **green**, *amber*, die 1		.85	.40
		Entire		1.10	.60
a.		Die 2		.95	.70
		Entire		1.40	.80
b.		Die 3		1.05	.75

		Entire		1.60	.80
c.		Die 4		.95	.65
		Entire		1.40	.75
U402	U90	1c **green**, *oriental buff*, die 1		4.50	1.00
		Entire		6.00	1.75
a.		Die 2		5.75	1.50
		Entire		8.00	1.75
b.		Die 3		6.50	1.50
		Entire		8.50	2.50
c.		Die 4		5.00	1.50
		Entire		6.50	2.25
U403	U90	1c **green**, *blue*, die 1		5.00	1.50
		Entire		6.50	2.25
a.		Die 2		5.00	1.50
		Entire		6.50	2.00
b.		Die 3		5.00	3.00
		Entire		6.00	3.25
c.		Die 4		4.25	1.25
		Entire		5.50	3.00
U404	U90	1c **green**, *manila*, die 1		3.00	1.90
		Entire		4.50	2.75
a.		Die 3		3.75	3.00
		Entire		5.75	4.50
W405	U90	1c **green**, *manila*, die 1		.50	.25
		Entire		.80	.35
a.		Die 2		40.00	25.00
		Entire		45.00	30.00
b.		Die 3		7.50	4.00
		Entire		15.00	6.50
c.		Die 4		40.00	—

Washington — U91

U91 Die 1

U91 Die 3

U91 Die 5

U91 Die 7

U91 Die 2

U91 Die 4

U91 Die 6

U91 Die 8

Die 1 - Oval "O" in "TWO" and "C" in "CENTS." Front of bust broad.
Die 2 - Similar to 1 but hair re-cut in two distinct locks at top of head.
Die 3 - Round "O" in "TWO" and "C" in "CENTS," coarse lettering.
Die 4 - Similar to 3 but lettering fine and clear, hair lines clearly embossed. Inner oval thin and clear.
Die 5 - All "S's" wide (1910).
Die 6 - Similar to 1 but front of bust narrow (1913).
Die 7 - Similar to 6 but upper corner of front of bust cut away (1916).

Die 8 - Similar to 7 but lower stroke of "S" in "CENTS" is a straight line. Hair as in Die 2 (1916).

U406	U91	2c **brown red**, die 1		.80	.20
		Entire		1.60	.30
a.		Die 2		27.50	6.25
		Entire		37.50	20.00
b.		Die 3		.55	.20
		Entire		.95	.40
U407	U91	2c **brown red**, *amber*, die 1		5.50	2.00
		Entire		7.50	5.00
a.		Die 2		100.00	45.00
		Entire		125.00	70.00
b.		Die 3		3.50	1.00
		Entire		6.00	1.65
U408	U91	2c **brown red**, *oriental buff*, die 1		7.00	1.50
		Entire		10.00	3.75
a.		Die 2		125.00	55.00
		Entire		140.00	90.00
b.		Die 3		6.50	2.50
		Entire		9.50	5.00
U409	U91	2c **brown red**, *blue*, die 1		4.50	1.75
		Entire		6.50	3.50
a.		Die 2		125.00	100.00
		Entire		160.00	*125.00*
b.		Die 3		4.50	1.50
		Entire		6.50	3.00
W410	U91	2c **brown red**, *manila*, die 1		40.00	32.50
		Entire		50.00	42.50
U411	U91	2c **carmine**, die 1		.25	.20
		Entire		.60	.35
a.		Die 2		.45	.20
		Entire		.85	.45
b.		Die 3		.75	.35
		Entire		1.20	.50
c.		Die 4		.40	.20
		Entire		.70	.35
d.		Die 5		.55	.30
		Entire		.95	.50
e.		Die 6		.40	.20
		Entire		.85	.30
f.		Die 7		30.00	25.00
		Entire		37.50	30.00
g.		Die 8		32.50	25.00
		Entire		42.50	30.00
h.		#U411 with added impression of #U400, entire		325.00	
i.		#U411 with added impression of #U416a, entire		300.00	
U412	U91	2c **carmine**, *amber*, die 1		.25	.20
		Entire		.90	.20
a.		Die 2		.45	.25
		Entire		.90	.55
b.		Die 3		1.30	.45
		Entire		1.75	.75
c.		Die 4		.40	.25
		Entire		.75	.40
d.		Die 5		.60	.35
		Entire		1.05	.55
e.		Die 6		.55	.35
		Entire		1.00	.50
f.		Die 7		27.50	20.00
		Entire		32.50	27.50
U413	U91	2c **carmine**, *oriental buff*, die 1		.45	.20
		Entire		.65	.25
a.		Die 2		.55	.45
		Entire		.90	.50
b.		Die 3		6.00	3.00
		Entire		10.00	5.50
c.		Die 4		.40	.20
		Entire		.75	.40
d.		Die 5		2.75	1.25
		Entire		3.50	3.25
e.		Die 6		.55	.35
		Entire		1.00	.55
f.		Die 7		87.50	42.50
		Entire		110.00	62.50
g.		Die 8		27.50	21.00
		Entire		42.50	27.50
U414	U91	2c **carmine**, *blue*, die 1		.50	.20
		Entire		1.00	.25
a.		Die 2		.50	.35
		Entire		.90	.45
b.		Die 3		.80	.60
		Entire		1.50	.70
c.		Die 4		.50	.25
		Entire		.70	.45
d.		Die 5		.65	.30
		Entire		1.25	.40
e.		Die 6		.55	.30
		Entire		1.00	.40
f.		Die 7		30.00	19.00
		Entire		42.50	35.00
g.		Die 8		30.00	19.00
		Entire		40.00	35.00
W415	U91	2c **carmine**, *manila*, die 1		4.50	2.00
		Entire		7.00	4.75
a.		Die 2		4.50	1.10
		Entire		7.00	1.75
b.		Die 5		4.50	2.25
		Entire		7.00	2.50
c.		Die 7		100.00	87.50
		Entire		140.00	125.00

U90 4c Die 1

U90 4c Die 2

Die 1 - "F" close to (1mm) left "4."

Die 2 - "F" far from (1¾mm) left "4."

U416	U90	4c **black**, die 2	4.00	2.25
		Entire	8.50	4.25
a.	Die 1		4.50	3.00
		Entire	9.00	5.00
U417	U90	4c **black**, *amber*, die 2	5.50	2.50
		Entire	9.50	4.00
a.	Die 1		5.50	2.50
		Entire	9.50	4.00

 U91 5c Die 1　　 U91 5c Die 2

Die 1 - Tall "F" in "FIVE."
Die 2 - Short "F" in "FIVE."

U418	U91	5c **blue**, die 2	6.50	2.25
		Entire	12.00	6.50
a.	Die 1		6.50	2.25
		Entire	12.00	5.00
b.		5c **blue**, *buff*, die 2 (error)	1,000.	
c.		5c **blue**, *blue*, die 2 (error)	1,000.	
d.		As "c," die 1 (error)	1,100.	
		Entire	2,500.	
U419	U91	5c **blue**, *amber*, die 2	14.00	11.00
		Entire	17.50	13.00
a.	Die 1		12.50	11.00
		Entire	21.00	13.00

On July 1, 1915 the use of laid paper was discontinued and wove paper was substituted. Nos. U400 to W405 and U411 to U419 exist on both papers: U406 come on laid only. Nos. U429 and U430 exist on laid paper.

Franklin
U92

Die 1

Die 2

Die 3　　Die 4　　Die 5

(The 1c and 4c dies are the same except for figures of value.)
Die 1 - UNITED nearer inner circle than outer circle.
Die 2 - Large U; large NT closely spaced.
Die 3 - Knob of hair at back of neck. Large NT widely spaced.
Die 4 - UNITED nearer outer circle than inner circle.
Die 5 - Narrow oval C, (also O and G).

Printed by Middle West Supply Co. and
International Envelope Corp., Dayton, Ohio.

1915-32

U420	U92	1c **green**, die 1 ('16)	.20	.20
		Entire	.35	.20
a.	Die 2		90.00	55.00
		Entire, size 8	110.00	70.00
b.	Die 3		.30	.20
		Entire	.45	.25
c.	Die 4		.40	.40
		Entire	.60	.50
d.	Die 5		.40	.35
		Entire	.60	.45
U421	U92	1c **green**, *amber*, die 1 ('16)	.40	.30
		Entire	.60	.45
a.	Die 2		350.00	175.00
		Entire, size 8	500.00	200.00
b.	Die 3		1.10	.65
		Entire	1.60	.95
c.	Die 4		1.25	.85

		Entire	1.75	1.25
d.	Die 5		1.00	.55
		Entire	1.40	.80
U422	U92	1c **green**, *oriental buff*, die 1 ('16)	2.00	.90
		Entire	2.75	1.40
a.	Die 4		4.25	1.25
		Entire	6.00	2.75
U423	U92	1c **green**, *blue*, die 1 ('16)	.45	.35
		Entire	.75	.50
a.	Die 3		.75	.45
		Entire	1.00	.70
b.	Die 4		1.25	.65
		Entire	1.95	.95
c.	Die 5		.80	.35
		Entire	1.50	.65
U424	U92	1c **grn**, *manila* (unglazed), die 1 ('16)	6.50	4.00
		Entire	8.50	5.00
W425	U92	1c **grn**, *manila* (unglazed), die 1 ('16)	.20	.20
		Entire	.35	.20
a.	Die 3		140.00	125.00
		Entire	175.00	140.00
U426	U92	1c **green**, *(glazed) brown*, die 1 ('20)	30.00	15.00
		Entire	37.50	17.50
W427	U92	1c **green**, *(glazed) brown*, die 1 ('20)	65.00	
		Entire	75.00	
U428	U92	1c **green**, *(unglazed) brown*, die 1 ('20)	8.00	7.50
		Entire	11.00	9.00

All manila envelopes of circular dies are unwatermarked. Manila paper, including that of Nos. U424 and W425, exists in many shades.

Washington — U93

Die 1　　Die 2

Die 3

Die 4

Die 5

Die 6

Die 7

Die 8

Die 9

(The 1½c, 2c, 3c, 5c, and 6c dies are the same except for figures of value.)
Die 1 - Letters broad. Numerals vertical. Large head (9¼mm) from tip of nose to back of neck. E closer to inner circle than N of cents.
Die 2 - Similar to 1; but U far from left circle.
Die 3 - Similar to 2; but all inner circles very thin (Rejected die).
Die 4 - Similar to 1; but C very close to left circle.
Die 5 - Small head (8¾mm) from tip of nose to back of neck. T and S of CENTS close at bottom.
Die 6 - Similar to 5; but T and S of CENTS far apart at bottom. Left numeral slopes to right.
Die 7 - Large head. Both numerals slope to right. Clean cut lettering. All letters T have short top strokes.
Die 8 - Similar to 7; but all letters T have long top strokes.
Die 9 - Narrow oval C (also O and G).

U429	U93	2c **carmine**, die 1, *Dec. 20, 1915*	.20	.20
		Entire	.35	.20
a.	Die 2		9.00	6.00
		Entire	15.00	9.00
b.	Die 3		30.00	25.00
		Entire	40.00	30.00
c.	Die 4		17.50	15.00
		Entire	25.00	20.00
d.	Die 5		.50	.35
		Entire	.80	.45
e.	Die 6		.60	.30
		Entire	1.10	.60
f.	Die 7		.65	.25
		Entire	.95	.75
g.	Die 8		.45	.20
		Entire	.75	.50
h.	Die 9		.40	.20
		Entire	.75	.45
i.		2c **green**, die 1 (error), entire	8,000.	
j.		#U429 with added impression of #U420	450.00	
		Entire	700.00	
k.		#U429 with added impression of #U416a, entire	700.00	
l.		#U429 with added impression of #U400, entire	500.00	
U430	U93	2c **carmine**, *amber*, die 1 ('16)	.25	.20
		Entire	.45	.20
a.	Die 2		9.25	7.50
		Entire	15.00	10.00
b.	Die 4		40.00	20.00
		Entire	50.00	25.00
c.	Die 5		1.10	.35
		Entire	1.75	.60
d.	Die 6		.95	.40
		Entire	1.75	.75
e.	Die 7		.70	.35
		Entire	1.50	.95
f.	Die 8		.65	.30
		Entire	.95	.45
g.	Die 9		.60	.20
		Entire	.80	.35
U431	U93	2c **carmine**, *oriental buff*, die 1 ('16)	2.25	.65
		Entire	4.50	1.40
a.	Die 2		100.00	40.00
		Entire	125.00	70.00
b.	Die 4		60.00	60.00
		Entire	75.00	75.00
c.	Die 5		2.75	1.75
		Entire	5.00	2.50
d.	Die 6		3.00	2.00
		Entire	5.50	2.75
e.	Die 7		2.75	1.75
		Entire	4.50	3.00
U432	U93	2c **carmine**, *blue*, die 1 ('16)	.25	.20
		Entire	.50	.20
b.	Die 2		25.00	20.00
		Entire	30.00	30.00
c.	Die 3		100.00	90.00
		Entire	140.00	110.00
d.	Die 4		50.00	50.00
		Entire	60.00	55.00
e.	Die 5		.80	.30
		Entire	1.90	.75
f.	Die 6		.85	.40
		Entire	1.50	.60
g.	Die 7		.75	.35
		Entire	1.45	.65
h.	Die 8		.60	.25
		Entire	1.25	.50
i.	Die 9		.90	.30
		Entire	2.50	.55
U432A	U93	2c **car**, *manila*, die 7, unwatermarked, entire	25,000.	
W433	U93	2c **carmine**, *manila*, die 1 ('16)	.25	.20
		Entire	.45	.30
W434	U93	2c **carmine**, *(glazed) brown* ('20), die 1	90.00	50.00
		Entire	115.00	60.00
W435	U93	2c **carmine**, *(unglazed) brown*, die 1 ('20)	95.00	50.00
		Entire	120.00	60.00
U436	U93	3c **dark violet**, die 1 ('17)	.55	.20
		Entire	.70	.25
a.		3c **purple**, die 1 ('32)	.30	.20
		Entire	.55	.25
b.		3c **dark violet**, die 5	1.65	.75
		Entire	3.00	.90
c.		3c **dark violet**, die 6	2.00	1.40
		Entire	3.25	1.50
d.		3c **dark violet**, die 7	1.40	.95
		Entire	2.50	1.00
e.		3c **purple**, die 7 ('32)	.65	.30
		Entire	1.50	.75
f.		3c **purple**, die 9 ('32)	.40	.20

		Unused	Used
	Entire	.50	.30
g.	3c carmine (error), die 1	30.00	27.50
	Entire	50.00	45.00
h.	3c carmine (error), die 5	32.50	30.00
	Entire	45.00	42.50
i.	#U436 with added impression of #U420, entire	600.00	
j.	#U436 with added impression of #U429, entire	700.00	875.00
U437	U93 3c **dark violet**, *amber*, die 1 ('17)	3.25	1.25
	Entire	7.00	2.25
a.	3c purple, die 1 ('32)	.35	.20
	Entire	.60	.35
b.	3c dark violet, die 5	4.50	2.50
	Entire	8.00	3.00
c.	3c dark violet, die 6	4.50	2.50
	Entire	6.00	3.00
d.	3c dark violet, die 7	3.75	2.25
	Entire	5.00	2.50
e.	3c purple, die 7 ('32)	.75	.20
	Entire	1.25	.50
f.	3c purple, die 9 ('32)	.50	.20
	Entire	1.00	.30
g.	3c carmine (error), die 5	450.00	275.00
	Entire	500.00	325.00
h.	3c black (error), die 1	165.00	—
	Entire	200.00	
U438	U93 3c **dark violet**, *oriental buff*, die 1 ('17)	22.50	1.50
	Entire	27.50	2.00
a.	Die 5	22.50	1.00
	Entire	27.50	1.10
b.	Die 6	32.50	1.65
	Entire	35.00	2.50
c.	Die 7	32.50	3.50
	Entire	37.50	7.75
U439	U93 3c **dark violet**, *blue*, die 1 ('17)	6.50	2.00
	Entire	11.00	6.00
a.	3c purple, die 1 ('32)	.30	.20
	Entire	.75	.25
b.	3c dark violet, die 5	6.50	4.00
	Entire	8.25	4.50
c.	3c dark violet, die 6	6.00	4.25
	Entire	9.00	4.50
d.	3c dark violet, die 7	9.00	5.50
	Entire	14.00	7.50
e.	3c purple, die 7 ('32)	.75	.25
	Entire	1.50	.50
f.	3c purple, die 9 ('32)	.50	.20
	Entire	1.20	.45
g.	3c carmine (error), die 5	325.00	300.00
	Entire	425.00	725.00
U440	U92 4c **black,** die 1 ('16)	1.50	.60
	Entire	3.00	2.00
a.	With added impression of 2c carmine (#U429), die 1, entire	250.00	
U441	U92 4c **black**, *amber*, die 1 ('16)	3.00	.85
	Entire	4.75	2.00
U442	U92 4c **black**, *blue*, die 1 ('21)	3.25	.85
	Entire	5.50	1.75
U443	U93 5c **blue,** die 1 ('16)	3.25	2.75
	Entire	5.75	3.25
U444	U93 5c **blue**, *amber*, die 1 ('16)	3.75	1.60
	Entire	5.50	3.50
U445	U93 5c **blue**, *blue*, die 1 ('21)	4.00	3.25
	Entire	8.00	4.25

For 1½c and 6c see Nos. U481-W485, U529-U531.

Surcharged Envelopes

The provisional 2c surcharges of 1920-21 were made at central post offices with canceling machines using slugs provided by the Post Office Department.

Double or triple surcharge listings of 1920-25 are for specimens with surcharge directly or partly upon the stamp.

Surcharged on 1874-1920 Envelopes indicated by Numbers in Parentheses
Surcharged

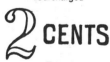 CENTS

Type 1

1920-21

Surcharged in Black

		Unused	Used
U446	U93 2c on 3c **dark vio** (U436, die 1)	12.00	10.00
	Entire	18.00	12.50
a.	On No. U436b (die 5)	12.00	10.00
	Entire	16.00	12.50

Surcharged

Type 2

Rose Surcharge

		Unused	Used
U447	U93 2c on 3c **dark vio** (U436, die 1)	7.75	6.50
	Entire	10.00	8.50
b.	On No. U436c (die 6)	10.00	8.50
	Entire	12.50	10.00

Black Surcharge

		Unused	Used
U447A	U93 2c on 2c **carmine** (U429, die 1)	—	
U447C	U93 2c on 2c **carmine**, *amber* (U430, die 1)	—	
U448	U93 2c on 3c **dark vio** (U436, die 1)	2.50	2.00
	Entire	3.50	2.50
a.	On No. U436b (die 5)	2.50	2.00
	Entire	3.50	2.50
b.	On No. U436c (die 6)	3.25	2.00
	Entire	4.50	2.50
c.	On No. U436d (die 7)	2.50	2.00
	Entire	3.50	2.50
U449	U93 2c on 3c **dark violet**, *amber* (U437, die 1)	6.50	6.00
	Entire	8.50	7.50
a.	On No. U437b (die 5)	10.00	7.50
	Entire	13.50	10.00
b.	On No. U437c (die 6)	7.50	6.00
	Entire	10.00	7.50
c.	On No. U437d (die 7)	7.00	6.50
	Entire	9.50	8.00
U450	U93 2c on 3c **dark violet**, *oriental buff* (U438, die 1)	17.50	14.00
	Entire	20.00	17.50
a.	On No. U438a (die 5)	17.50	14.00
	Entire	20.00	17.50
b.	On No. U438b (die 6)	17.50	14.00
	Entire	20.00	17.50
c.	On No. U438c (die 7)	100.00	90.00
	Entire	150.00	125.00
U451	U93 2c on 3c **dark violet**, *blue* (U439, die 1)	12.50	10.00
	Entire	19.00	10.50
b.	On No. U439b (die 5)	12.50	10.00
	Entire	19.00	10.50
c.	On No. U439c (die 6)	12.50	10.00
	Entire	19.00	10.50
d.	On No. U439d (die 7)	25.00	20.00
	Entire	35.00	25.00

Type 2 exists in three city sub-types.

Surcharged

Type 3

Bars 2mm apart

		Unused	Used
U451A	U90 2c on 1c **green** (U400, die 1)	22,500.	
U452	U92 2c on 1c **green** (U420, die 1)	2,500.	
	Entire	3,250.	
a.	On No. U420b (die 3)	2,500.	
	Entire	3,250.	
b.	As No. U452, double surcharge	1,600.	
	Entire	2,250.	
U453	U91 2c on 2c **car** (U411b, die 3)	2,250.	
	Entire	3,250.	
a.	On No. U411 (die 1)	2,500.	
	Entire	3,250.	
U453B	U91 2c on 2c **carmine**, *blue* (U414e, die 6)	2,000.	
	Entire	3,250.	
U453C	U91 2c on 2c **carmine**, *oriental buff* (U413e, die 6)	1,600.	750.00
	Entire	2,500.	
d.	On No. U413 (die 1)	1,750.	
	Entire	2,500.	
U454	U93 2c on 2c **car** (U429e, die 6)	85.00	
	Entire	125.00	
a.	On No. U429 (die 1)	200.00	
	Entire	250.00	
b.	On No. U429d (die 5)	375.00	
	Entire	500.00	
c.	On No. U429f (die 7)	85.00	
	Entire	125.00	
U455	U93 2c on 2c **carmine**, *amber* (U430, die 1)	2,000.	
	Entire	3,250.	
a.	On No. U430d (die 6)	2,000.	
	Entire	3,250.	
b.	On No. U430e (die 7)	2,000.	
	Entire	3,250.	
U456	U93 2c on 2c **carmine**, *oriental buff* (U431a, die 2)	275.00	
	Entire	300.00	
a.	On No. U431c (die 5)	275.00	
	Entire	300.00	
b.	On No. U431e (die 7)	275.00	
	Entire	300.00	
c.	As No. U456, double surcharge	250.00	
U457	U93 2c on 2c **carmine**, *blue* (U432f, die 6)	275.00	
	Entire	300.00	
a.	On No. U432e (die 5)	275.00	
	Entire	350.00	
b.	On No. U432g (die 7)	500.00	
	Entire	550.00	
U458	U93 2c on 3c **dark vio** (U436, die 1)	.50	.35
	Entire	.70	.45
a.	On No. U436b (die 5)	.50	.40

		Unused	Used
	Entire	.70	.50
b.	On No. U436c (die 6)	.50	.35
	Entire	.70	.45
c.	On No. U436d (die 7)	.50	.35
	Entire	.70	.45
d.	As #U458, double surcharge	14.00	7.50
e.	As #U458, triple surcharge	35.00	
f.	As #U458, dbl. surch., 1 in magenta	65.00	
g.	As #U458, dbl. surch., types 2 & 3	100.00	
h.	As "a," double surcharge	27.50	15.00
i.	As "a," triple surcharge	50.00	
j.	As "a," double surch., both magenta	65.00	
k.	As "b," double surcharge	16.00	8.00
l.	As "c," double surcharge	16.00	8.00
m.	As "c," triple surcharge	35.00	
U459	U93 2c on 3c **dark violet**, *amber* (U437c, die 6)	3.00	1.00
	Entire	4.50	1.75
a.	On No. U437 (die 1)	4.00	1.00
	Entire	5.50	1.75
b.	On No. U437b (die 5)	4.00	1.00
	Entire	5.50	1.75
c.	On No. U437d (die 7)	3.00	1.00
	Entire	4.50	1.75
d.	As #U459, double surcharge	24.00	
e.	As "a," double surcharge	24.00	
f.	As "b," double surcharge	24.00	
g.	As "b," double surcharge, types 2 & 3	80.00	
h.	As "c," double surcharge	18.00	
U460	U93 2c on 3c **dark violet**, *oriental buff* (U438a, die 5)	2.75	1.00
	Entire	3.75	1.40
a.	On No. U438 (die 1)	3.00	1.50
	Entire	4.00	2.00
b.	On No. U438b (die 6)	3.00	2.00
	Entire	4.00	2.50
c.	As #U460, double surcharge	12.50	
d.	As "a," double surcharge	12.50	
e.	As "b," double surcharge	12.50	
f.	As "b," triple surcharge	27.50	
U461	U93 2c on 3c **dark violet**, *blue* (U439, die 1)	4.25	1.00
	Entire	6.25	1.50
a.	On No. U439b (die 5)	4.25	1.00
	Entire	6.25	1.50
b.	On No. U439c (die 6)	4.25	1.00
	Entire	6.25	1.50
c.	On No. U439d "die 7)	10.00	2.00
	Entire	12.50	3.00
d.	As #U461, double surcharge	12.50	
e.	As "a," double surcharge	12.50	
f.	As "b," double surcharge	12.50	
g.	As "c," double surcharge	12.50	
U462	U87 2c on 4c **chocolate** (U390)	500.00	240.00
	Entire	600.00	300.00
U463	U87 2c on 4c **chocolate**, *amber* (U391)	450.00	150.00
	Entire	550.00	260.00
U463A	U90 2c on 4c **black** (U416, die 2)	1,100.	375.00
	Entire	1,750.	
U464	U93 2c on 5c **blue** (U443)	1,000.	
	Entire	1,750.	

Type 3 exists in 11 city sub-types.

Surcharged

Type 4

Same as Type 3, but bars 1½mm apart

		Unused	Used
U465	U92 2c on 1c **green** (U420, die 1)	1,400.	
	Entire	2,250.	
a.	On No. U420b (die 3)	1,400.	
	Entire	2,250.	
U466	U91 2c on 2c **car** (U411e, die 6)	10,000.	
	Entire	20,000.	
U466A	U93 2c on 2c **carmine** (U429, die 1)	750.00	
	Entire	1,250.	
c.	On No. U429d (die 5)	1,000.	
	Entire	1,500.	
d.	On No. U429e (die 6)	1,250.	
	Entire	1,750.	
e.	On No. U429f (die 7)	1,000.	
	Entire	1,500.	
U466B	U93 2c on 2c **carmine**, *amber* (U430)	8,000.	
	Entire	17,500.	
U467	U45 2c on 3c **green**, die 2 (U163)	275.00	
	Entire	340.00	
U468	U93 2c on 3c **dark vio** (U436, die 1)	.70	.45
	Entire	1.00	.75
a.	On No. U436b (die 5)	.70	.50
	Entire	1.00	.75
b.	On No. U436c (die 6)	.70	.50
	Entire	1.00	.75
c.	On No. U436d (die 7)	.70	.50
	Entire	1.00	.75
d.	As #U468, double surcharge	15.00	
e.	As #U468, triple surcharge	20.00	
f.	As #U468, dbl. surch., types 2 & 4	75.00	
g.	As "a," double surcharge	15.00	

h.	As "b," double surcharge		15.00	
i.	As "c," double surcharge		15.00	
j.	As "c," triple surcharge		20.00	
k.	As "c," inverted surcharge		75.00	
l.	2c on 3c carmine (error), (U436h)		450.00	
	Entire		525.00	
U469	U93	2c on 3c **dark violet**, *amber* (U437, die 1)	3.50	2.25
	Entire		4.75	2.75
a.	On No. U437b (die 5)		3.50	2.25
	Entire		4.75	2.75
b.	On No. U437c (die 6)		3.50	2.25
	Entire		4.75	2.75
c.	On No. U437d (die 7)		3.50	2.25
	Entire		4.75	2.75
d.	As #U469, double surcharge		20.00	
e.	As "a," double surcharge		20.00	
f.	As "a," double surcharge, types 2 & 4		60.00	
g.	As "b," double surcharge		20.00	
h.	As "c," double surcharge		20.00	
U470	U93	2c on 3c **dark violet**, *oriental buff* (U438, die 1)	4.50	2.50
	Entire		7.50	4.00
a.	On No. U438a (die 5)		4.50	2.50
	Entire		7.50	4.00
b.	On No. U438b (die 6)		4.50	2.50
	Entire		7.50	4.00
c.	On No. U438c (die 7)		35.00	32.50
	Entire		50.00	45.00
d.	As #U470, double surcharge		18.50	
e.	As #U470, double surch., types 2 & 4		60.00	
f.	As "a," double surcharge		18.50	
g.	As "b," double surcharge		22.50	
U471	U93	2c on 3c **dark violet**, *blue* (U439, die 1)	4.50	1.75
	Entire		11.00	3.50
a.	On No. U439b (die 5)		4.50	1.75
	Entire		11.00	'3.50
b.	On No. U439c (die 6)		4.50	1.75
	Entire		11.00	3.50
c.	On No. U439d (die 7)		10.00	6.00
	Entire		20.00	10.00
d.	As #U471, double surcharge		22.50	
e.	As #U471, double surch., types 2 & 4		180.00	
f.	As "a," double surcharge		22.50	
g.	As "b," double surcharge		22.50	
U472	U87	2c on 4c **chocolate** (U390)	12.00	8.00
	Entire		25.00	14.00
a.	Double surcharge		37.50	
U473	U87	2c on 4c **chocolate**, *amber* (U391)	16.00	10.00
	Entire		25.00	13.50

Type 4 exists in 30 city sub-types.

Surcharged

1 CENT

Double Surcharge, Type 4 and 1c as above

U474	U93	2c on 1c on 3c **dark violet** (U436, die 1)	250.
	Entire		350.
a.	On No. U436b (die 5)		325.
	Entire		450.
b.	On No. U436d (die 7)		750.
	Entire		900.
U475	U93	2c on 1c on 3c **dark violet**, *amber* (U437, die 1)	250.
	Entire		375.

Surcharged

2

U476	U93	2c on 3c **dark violet**, *amber* (U437, die 1)	750.
	Entire		1,000.
a.	On No. U437c (die 6)		750.
	Entire		1,000.
b.	As #U476, double surcharge		—

Surcharged at Duncan, OK.

Surcharged

2

U477	U93	2c on 3c **dark vio** (U436, die 1)	125.
	Entire		175.
a.	On No. U436b (die 5)		200.
	Entire		250.
b.	On No. U436c (die 6)		200.
	Entire		250.
c.	On No. U436d (die 7)		200.

	Entire		250.
U478	U93	2c on 3c **dark violet**, *amber* (U437, die 1)	250.
	Entire		375.

Surcharged at Frederick, OK.

Handstamped Surcharged in Black or Violet

2

U479	U93	2c on 3c **dark violet** (Bk) (U436b, die 5)	900.
	Entire		1,100.
a.	On No. U436 (die 1)		400.
	Entire		500.
b.	On No. U436d (die 7)		325.
	Entire		450.
U480	U93	2c on 3c **dark violet** (V) (U436d, die 7)	4,500.
	Entire		6,000.

Expertization by competent authorities is recommended for Nos. U479-U480.
Surcharged at Daytona, FL (#U479) and Orlando Beach, FL (#U480).

1925

Type of 1916-32 Issue

U481	U93	1½c **brown**, die 1, *Mar. 19*	.20	.20
	Entire		.55	.20
	Entire, 1st day cancel		60.00	
a.	Die 8		.60	.25
			.80	.50
b.	1½c **purple**, die 1 (error) ('34)		90.00	
	Entire		110.00	—
U482	U93	1½c **brown**, die 1, *amber*	.90	.40
	Entire		1.50	.60
a.	Die 8		1.40	.75
	Entire		1.90	.80
U483	U93	1½c **brown**, die 1, *blue*	1.50	.95
	Entire		2.40	1.25
a.	Die 8		1.75	1.25
	Entire		2.60	1.40
U484	U93	1½c **brown**, die 1, *manila*	6.00	3.00
	Entire		11.00	6.00
W485	U93	1½c **brown**, die 1, *manila*	.80	.20
	Entire		1.25	.45
a.	With added impression of #W433		120.00	—

The manufacture of newspaper wrappers was discontinued in 1934.

New rates on printed matter effective Apr. 15, 1925, resulted in revaluing some of the current envelopes.

Under the caption "Revaluation of Surplus Stocks of the 1 cent envelopes," W. Irving Glover, Third Assistant Postmaster-General, distributed through the Postal Bulletin a notice to postmasters authorizing the surcharging of envelopes under stipulated conditions.

Surcharging was permitted "at certain offices where the excessive quantities of 1 cent stamped envelopes remained in stock on April 15, 1925."

Envelopes were revalued by means of post office canceling machines equipped with special dies designed to imprint "1½" in the center of the embossed stamp and four vertical bars over the original numerals "1" in the lower corners.

Postmasters were notified that the revaluing dies would be available for use only in the International and "Universal" Model G machines and that the overprinting of surplus envelopes would be restricted to post offices having such canceling equipment available.

Envelopes of Preceding Issues Surcharged

1½ ‖‖ ‖‖

1925

On Envelopes of 1887

U486	U71	1½c on 2c **green** (U311)	700.	
	Entire		1,250.	
U487	U71	1½c on 2c **green**, *amber* (U312)	850.	
	Entire		1,250.	

On Envelopes of 1899

U488	U77	1½c on 1c **green** (U352)	700.	
	Entire		1,100.	
U489	U77	1½c on 1c **green**, *amber* (U353)	110.	60.
	Entire		175.	90.

On Envelopes of 1907-16

U490	U90	1½c on 1c **green** (U400, die 1)	4.00	3.50
	Entire		6.00	5.50
a.	On No. U400a (die 2)		12.00	9.00
	Entire		14.00	12.00
b.	On No. U400b (die 3)		25.00	17.50
	Entire		30.00	22.50
c.	On No. U400c (die 4)		6.00	2.50
	Entire		8.00	4.00
U491	U90	1½c on 1c **green**, *amber* (U401c, die 4)	4.50	2.25

	Entire		8.00	4.50
a.	On No. U401 (die 1)		8.00	2.50
	Entire		12.00	6.00
b.	On No. U401a (die 2)		80.00	65.00
	Entire		95.00	95.00
c.	On No. U401b (die 3)		35.00	30.00
	Entire		45.00	40.00
U492	U90	1½c on 1c **green**, *oriental buff* (U402a, die 2)	400.00	100.00
	Entire		500.00	125.00
a.	On No. U402c (die 4)		850.00	100.00
	Entire		1,400.	125.00
U493	U90	1½c on 1c **grn**, *blue* (U403c, die 4)	100.00	55.00
	Entire		140.00	80.00
a.	On No. U403a (die 2)		90.00	55.00
	Entire		125.00	77.50
U494	U90	1½c on 1c **grn**, *manila* (U404, die 1)	350.00	80.00
	Entire		500.00	110.00
a.	On No. U404a (die 3)		1,000.	
	Entire		1,250.	

On Envelopes of 1916-20

U495	U92	1½c on 1c **green** (U420, die 1)	.50	.25
	Entire		.85	.45
a.	On No. U420a (die 2)		70.00	52.50
	Entire		100.00	90.00
b.	On No. U420b (die 3)		1.60	.60
	Entire		2.25	.80
c.	On No. U420c (die 4)		1.75	.75
	Entire		2.40	1.00
d.	As #U495, double surcharge		4.00	1.90
e.	As "b," double surcharge		7.00	3.00
f.	As "c," double surcharge		6.00	3.00
U496	U92	1½c on 1c **grn**, *amber* (U421, die 1)	17.50	12.50
	Entire		25.00	15.00
a.	On No. U421b (die 3)		600.00	
	Entire		700.00	
b.	On No. U421c (die 4)		17.50	12.50
	Entire		25.00	15.00
U497	U92	1½c on 1c **green**, *oriental buff* (U422, die 1)	3.25	1.90
	Entire		5.50	2.25
a.	On No. U422b (die 4)		52.50	
	Entire		80.00	
U498	U92	1½c on 1c **grn**, *blue* (U423c, die 4)	1.25	.75
	Entire		2.00	1.00
a.	On No. U423 (die 1)		2.25	1.50
	Entire		3.75	2.00
b.	On No. U423b (die 3)		1.75	1.50
	Entire		2.75	2.00
U499	U92	1½c on 1c **green**, *manila* (U424)	12.50	6.00
	Entire		19.00	7.00
U500	U92	1½c on 1c **green**, *brown* (unglazed) (U428)	60.00	30.00
	Entire		65.00	35.00
U501	U92	1½c on 1c **green**, *brown* (glazed) (U426)	65.00	25.00
	Entire		70.00	27.50
U502	U93	1½c on 2c **carmine** (U429, die 1)	275.00	—
	Entire		400.00	—
a.	On No. U429d (die 5)		350.00	
	Entire		500.00	
b.	On No. U429f (die 7)		350.00	
	Entire		500.00	
U503	U93	1½c on 2c **carmine**, *oriental buff* (U431c, die 5)	375.00	—
	Entire		500.00	—
a.	Double surcharge		—	
b.	Double surcharge, one inverted		525.00	
U504	U93	1½c on 2c **car**, *blue* (U432, die 1)	375.00	—
	Entire		500.00	—
a.	On No. U432g (die 7)		325.00	
	Entire		425.00	

On Envelopes of 1925

U505	U93	1½c on 1½c **brown** (U481, die 1)	450.00
	Entire		625.00
a.	On No. U481a (die 8)		450.00
	Entire		625.00
U506	U93	1½c on 1½c **brown**, *blue* (U483a, die 8)	425.00
	Entire		550.00

The paper of No. U500 is not glazed and appears to be the same as that used for the wrappers of 1920.
Type 8 exists in 20 city sub-types.

Surcharged

Black Surcharge

On Envelope of 1887

U507	U69	1½c on 1c **blue** (U294)	2,000.
	Entire		2,750.

On Envelope of 1899

U508	U77	1½c on 1c **green**, *amber* (U353)	55.00
	Entire		67.50

On Envelope of 1903

U508A	U85	1½c on 1c **green** (U379)	4,000.	
	Entire		5,500.	
U509	U85	1½c on 1c **green**, *amber* (U380)	14.00	10.00

		Entire	25.00	15.00
a.		Double surcharge	35.00	
		Entire	40.00	
U509B	U69	1½c on 1c **green**, *oriental buff* (U381)	60.00	40.00
		Entire	70.00	50.00

On Envelopes of 1907-16

U510	U90	1½c on 1c **green** (U400, die 1)	2.40	1.25
		Entire	3.75	1.50
b.		On No. U400a (die 2)	6.50	4.00
		Entire	9.50	6.00
c.		On No. U400b (die 3)	17.50	8.00
		Entire	22.50	11.00
d.		On No. U400c (die 4)	3.25	1.25
		Entire	6.50	2.00
e.		As No. U510, double surcharge	8.00	
U511	U90	1½c on 1c **green**, *amber* (U401, die 1)	225.00	72.50
		Entire	300.00	90.00
U512	U90	1½c on 1c **green**, *oriental buff* (U402, die 1)	7.00	4.00
		Entire	12.50	6.50
a.		On No. U402c (die 4)	17.50	14.00
		Entire	24.00	17.00
U513	U90	1½c on 1c **grn**, *blue* (U403, die 1)	5.25	3.25
		Entire	8.00	4.25
a.		On No. U403c (die 4)	5.25	4.00
		Entire	7.50	5.00
U514	U90	1½c on 1c **green**, *manila* (U404, die 1))	25.00	9.00
		Entire	32.50	22.50
a.		On No. U404a (die 3)	55.00	37.50
		Entire	60.00	45.00

On Envelopes of 1916-20

U515	U92	1½c on 1c **green** (U420, die 1)	.35	.20
		Entire	.65	.30
a.		On No. U420a (die 2)	20.00	15.00
		Entire	25.00	20.00
b.		On No. U420b (die 3)	.35	.20
		Entire	.65	.30
c.		On No. U420c (die 4)	.35	.20
		Entire	.65	.30
d.		As #U515, double surcharge	6.00	
e.		As #U515, inverted surcharge	9.00	
f.		As #U515, triple surcharge	11.00	
g.		As #U515, dbl. surch., one invtd., entire	—	
h.		As "b," double surcharge	6.00	
i.		As "b," inverted surcharge	9.00	
j.		As "b," triple surcharge	11.00	
k.		As "c," double surcharge	6.00	
l.		As "c," inverted surcharge	9.00	
U516	U92	1½c on 1c **green**, *amber* (U421c, die 4)	40.00	25.00
		Entire	50.00	35.00
a.		On No. U421 (die 1)	45.00	30.00
		Entire	55.00	40.00
U517	U92	1½c on 1c **green**, *oriental buff* (U422, die 1))	4.25	1.25
		Entire	5.75	1.50
a.		On No. U422a (die 4)	5.50	1.50
		Entire	7.00	2.00
U518	U92	1½c on 1c **green**, *blue* (U423b, die 4)	4.50	1.25
		Entire	6.50	1.50
a.		On No. U423 (die 1)	6.50	2.50
		Entire	9.00	3.00
b.		On No. U423a (die 3)	20.00	7.50
		Entire	27.50	9.00
c.		As "a," double surcharge	9.00	
U519	U92	1½c on 1c **green**, *manila* (U424, die 1)	22.50	10.00
		Entire	30.00	12.50
a.		Double surcharge	27.50	
U520	U93	1½c on 2c **car** (U429, die 1)	350.00	—
		Entire	500.00	—
a.		On No. U429d (die 5)	350.00	
		Entire	500.00	
b.		On No. U429e (die 6)	350.00	
		Entire	500.00	
c.		On No. U429f (die 7)	350.00	
		Entire	500.00	

Magenta Surcharge

U521	U92	1½c on 1c **green** (U420b, die 3), *Oct. 22, 1925*	4.50	3.50
		Entire	5.25	5.50
		Entire, 1st day cancel, Washington, D.C.		100.00
a.		Double surcharge	25.00	

Sesquicentennial Exposition Issue

150th anniversary of the Declaration of Independence.

Liberty Bell — U94

Die 1. The center bar of "E" of "postage" is shorter than top bar.

Die 2. The center bar of "E" of "postage" is of same length as top bar.

1926, July 27

U522	U94	2c **carmine**, die 1	1.10	.50
		Entire	1.60	.95
a.		Die 2	7.00	3.75
		Entire	11.00	5.50
		Entire, die 2, 1st day cancel, Washington, D.C.		32.50
		Entire, die 2, 1st day cancel, Philadelphia		27.50

Washington Bicentennial Issue

200th anniversary of the birth of George Washington.

Mount Vernon — U95

2c Die 1 - "S" of "Postage" normal.
2c Die 2 - "S" of "Postage" raised.

1932

U523	U95	1c **olive green**, *Jan. 1*	1.00	.80
		Entire	1.50	1.75
		Entire, 1st day cancel		18.00
U524	U95	1½c **chocolate**, *Jan. 1*	2.00	1.50
		Entire	2.75	2.50
		Entire, 1st day cancel		18.00
U525	U95	2c **carmine**, die 1, *Jan. 1*	.40	.20
		Entire	.50	.25
		Entire, 1st day cancel		16.00
a.		2c **carmine**, die 2	70.00	16.00
		Entire	85.00	55.00
b.		2c **carmine**, *blue*, die 1 (error) entire	27,500.	
U526	U95	3c **violet**, *June 16*	2.00	.35
		Entire	2.50	.40
		Entire, 1st day cancel		18.00
U527	U95	4c **black**, *Jan. 1*	18.00	16.00
		Entire	22.50	21.00
		Entire, 1st day cancel		30.00
U528	U95	5c **dark blue**, *Jan. 1*	4.00	3.50
		Entire	4.75	4.75
		Entire, 1st day cancel		20.00
		Nos. U523-U528 (6)	27.40	22.35

1932, Aug. 18

Type of 1916-32 Issue

U529	U93	6c **orange**, die 7	5.50	4.00
		Entire	8.50	7.50
		Entire, 1st day cancel, Los Angeles		20.00
U530	U93	6c **orange**, *amber*, die 7	11.00	8.00
		Entire	15.00	10.00
		Entire, 1st day cancel, Los Angeles		20.00
U531	U93	6c **orange**, *blue*, die 7	11.00	10.00
		Entire	15.00	12.50
		Entire, 1st day cancel		20.00

Franklin U96 — Washington U97

Die 1 — Die 2

Die 3

Die 1 - Short (3½mm) and thick "I" in thick circle.
Die 2 - Tall (4½mm) and thin "1" in thin circle; upper and lower bars of E in ONE long and 1mm from circle.
Die 3 - As in Die 2, but E normal and 1½mm from circle.

Printed by International Envelope Corp.

1950

U532	U96	1c **green**, die 1, *Nov. 16*	5.00	1.75
		Entire	8.00	2.25
		Entire, 1st day cancel, NY, NY		1.00
a.		Die 2	6.50	3.00
		Entire	9.00	3.75
b.		Die 3	6.00	3.00
		Entire	8.50	3.75
		Precanceled, die 3		.50
		Entire, precanceled, die 3	.90	.80

Die 1

Die 2

Die 3 — Die 4

Die 1 - Thick "2" in thick circle; toe of "2" is acute angle.
Die 2 - Thin "2" in thin circle; toe of "2" is almost right angle; line through left stand of "N" in UNITED and stand of "E" in POSTAGE goes considerably below tip of chin; "N" of UNITED is tall; "O" of TWO is high.
Die 3 - Figure "2" as in Die 2. Short UN in UNITED thin crossbar in A of STATES.
Die 4 - Tall UN in UNITED; thick crossbar in A of STATES; otherwise like Die 3.

U533	U97	2c **carmine**, die 3	.75	.25
		Entire	1.25	.35
a.		Die 1, *Nov. 17*	.85	.30

	Entire	1.50	.45
	Entire, 1st day cancel, NY, NY		1.00
b.	Die 2	1.50	.85
	Entire	2.00	.95
c.	Die 4	1.40	.60
	Entire	1.60	.65

Die 1   Die 2

Die 3

Die 4   Die 5

Die 1 - Thick and tall (4½mm) "3" in thick circle; long top bars and short stems in T's of STATES.

Die 2 - Thin and tall (4½mm) "3" in medium circle; short top bars and long stems in T's of STATES.

Die 3 - Thin and short (4mm) "3" in thin circle; lettering wider than Dies 1 and 2; line from left stand of N to stand of E is distinctly below tip of chin.

Die 4 - Figure and letters as in Die 3. Line hits tip of chin; short N in UNITED and thin crossbar in A of STATES.

Die 5 - Figure, letter and chin line as in Die 4; but tall N in UNITED and thick crossbar in A of STATES.

U534	U97	3c dark violet, die 4	.40	.20
		Entire	.50	.25
a.		Die 1, Nov. 18	2.00	.70
		Entire	2.50	1.20
		Entire, 1st day cancel, NY, NY		1.00
b.		Die 2, Nov. 19	.80	.50
		Entire	1.60	.55
		Entire, 1st day cancel, NY, NY		—
c.		Die 3	.60	.25
		Entire	1.10	.45
d.		Die 5	.80	.45
		Entire	1.25	.65

Washington — U98

1952

U535	U98	1½c brown	5.00	3.50
		Entire	5.75	4.25
		Precanceled		.50
		Entire, precanceled	1.10	1.10

Die 1   Die 2

Die 3

Die 1 - Head high in oval (2mm below T of STATES). Circle near (1mm) bottom of colored oval.

Die 2 - Head low in oval (3mm). Circle 1½mm from edge of oval. Right leg of A in POSTAGE shorter than left. Short leg on P.

Die 3 - Head centered in oval (2½mm). Circle as in Die 2. Legs of A of POSTAGE about equal. Long leg on P.

1958

U536	U96	4c red violet, die 1, July 31	.80	.20
		Entire	.95	.25
		Entire, 1st day cancel, Montpelier, Vt. (163,746)		1.00
a.		Die 2	1.05	.20
		Entire	1.30	.25
b.		Die 3	1.05	.20
		Entire	1.30	.25

Nos. U429, U429f, U429h, U533, U533a-U533c
Surcharged in Red at Left of Stamp

b

1958

U537	U93	2c + 2c carmine, die 1	3.25	1.50
		Entire	4.00	
a.		Die 7	10.00	7.00
		Entire	12.50	—
b.		Die 9	5.00	5.00
		Entire	6.50	—
U538	U97	2c + 2c carmine, die 1	.75	.20
		Entire	.90	.30
a.		Die 2	1.00	
		Entire	1.50	—
b.		Die 3	.80	.25
		Entire	1.10	.40
c.		Die 4	.80	
		Entire		

Nos. U436a, U436e-U436f, U534, U534b-U534d
Surcharged in Green at Left of Stamp

a

U539	U93	3c + 1c purple, die 1	15.00	11.00
		Entire	17.50	
a.		Die 7	12.00	9.00
		Entire	15.00	
b.		Die 9	30.00	15.00
		Entire	35.00	
U540	U97	3c + 1c dark violet, die 3	.50	.20
		Entire	.60	.25
a.		Die 2		
		Entire	1,000.	
b.		Die 4	.75	.20
		Entire	.90	.20
c.		Die 5	.75	.20
		Entire	1.00	.20

Benjamin Franklin U99   George Washington U100

Die 1   Die 2

Dies of 1¼c

Die 1 - The "4" is 3mm high. Upper leaf in left cluster is 2mm from "U."

Die 2 - The "4" is 3½mm high. Leaf clusters are larger. Upper leaf at left is 1mm from "U."

1960

U541	U99	1¼c turquoise, die 1, June 25, 1960	.75	.50
		Entire	.90	.55
		Entire, 1st day cancel, Birmingham, Ala. (211,500)		1.00
		Precanceled		.20
		Entire, precanceled	.45	.45
a.		Die 2, precanceled		1.50
		Entire, precanceled	2.00	2.00
U542	U100	2½c dull blue, May 28, 1960	.85	.50
		Entire	1.00	.60
		Entire, 1st day cancel, Chicago, Ill. (196,977)		1.00
		Precanceled		.25
		Entire, precanceled	.55	.55

Pony Express Centennial Issue

Pony Express Rider — U101

White Outside, Blue Inside.

1960

U543	U101	4c brown, July 19, 1960	.60	.30
		Entire	.75	.40
		Entire, 1st day cancel, St. Joseph, Mo. (407,160)		1.00

Abraham Lincoln — U102   Die 1

Die 2   Die 3

Die 1 - Center bar of E of POSTAGE is above the middle. Center bar of E of STATES slants slightly upward. Nose sharper, more pointed. No offset ink specks inside envelope on back of die impression.

Die 2 - Center bar of E of POSTAGE in middle. P of POSTAGE has short stem. Ink specks on back of die impression.

Die 3 - FI of FIVE closer than Die 1 or 2. Second T of STATES seems taller than ES. Ink specks on back of die impression.

1962

U544	U102	5c dark blue, die 2, Nov. 19, 1962	.85	.20
		Entire	1.10	.25

	Entire, 1st day cancel, Springfield, Ill. *(163,258)*		1.00
a.	Die 1	.85	.25
	Entire	1.10	.30
b.	Die 3	.90	.35
	Entire	1.20	.40
c.	Die 2 with albino impression of 4c (#U536), entire	50.00	—
d.	Die 3 with albino impression of 4c (#U536), entire	70.00	—
e.	Die 3 on complete impression of 4c (#U536), cut square	—	

No. U536 Surcharged in Green at left of Stamp

a

Two types of surcharge:
Type I - "U.S. POSTAGE" 18½mm high. Serifs on cross of T both diagonal. Two lines of shading in C of CENT.
Type II - "U.S. POSTAGE" 17½mm high. Right serif on cross of T is vertical. Three shading lines in C.

1962

U545	U96	4c + 1c **red vio.**, die 1, type I, *Nov. 1962*	1.40	.50
		Entire	1.60	.70
a.		Type II	1.10	.50
		Entire	1.60	.60

New York World's Fair Issue

Issued to publicize the New York World's Fair, 1964-65.

Globe with Satellite Orbit — U103

1964

U546	U103	5c **maroon**, *Apr. 22, 1964*	.60	.40
		Entire	.75	.50
		Entire, 1st day cancel World's Fair, N.Y. *(466,422)*		1.00

Precanceled cut squares

Precanceled envelopes do not normally receive another cancellation. Since the lack of a cancellation makes it impossible to distinguish between cut squares from used and unused envelopes, they are valued here as used only.

AUTH. NONPROFIT ORG. Liberty Bell — U104

Old Ironsides — U105

Eagle — U106

Head of Statue of Liberty — U107

Printed by the United States Envelope Company, Williamsburg, Pa. Designed (6c) by Howard C. Mildner and (others) by Robert J. Jones.

1965-69

U547	U104	1¼c **brown**, *Jan. 6, 1965*		.20
		Entire	.90	.75
		Entire, 1st day cancel, Washington, D.C.		1.00
U548	U104	1 6⁄10c **brown**, *Mar. 26, 1968*		.20
		Entire	1.00	.75
		Entire, 1st day cancel, Springfield, Mass. *(134,832)*		1.00
U548A	U104	1 6⁄10c **orange**, *June 16, 1969*		.20
		Entire	.85	.70
		Entire, 1st day cancel, Washington, D.C.		1.00
U549	U105	4c **bright blue**, *Jan. 6, 1965*	.75	.20
		Entire	.95	.20
		Entire, 1st day cancel, Washington, D.C.		1.00
U550	U106	5c **bright purple**, *Jan. 5, 1965*	.75	.20
		Entire	.85	.25
		Entire, 1st day cancel, Williamsburg, Pa. *(246,496)*		1.00
a.		Tagged, *Aug. 15, 1967*	1.25	.20
		Entire	1.75	.25
		Entire, tagged, 1st day cancel		3.50

Tagged

U551	U107	6c **light green**, *Jan. 4, 1968*	.70	.20
		Entire	.80	.25
		Entire, 1st day cancel, New York, N.Y. *(184,784)*		1.25

No. U550a has a 9x29mm panel at left of stamp that glows yellow green under ultraviolet light.
First day covers of the 1¼c and 4c total 451,960.

Nos. U549-U550 Surcharged Types "b" and "a" in Red or Green at Left of Stamp

1968, Feb. 5

U552	U105	4c + 2c **bright blue** (R)	3.75	2.00
		Entire	4.00	2.50
		Entire, 1st day cancel		7.00
U553	U106	5c + 1c **bright purple** (G)	3.50	2.50
		Entire	4.00	3.00
		Entire, 1st day cancel		7.00
a.		Tagged	3.50	2.75
		Entire	4.00	3.25
		Entire, 1st day cancel		7.00

Tagged

Envelopes from No. U554 onward are tagged, with the tagging element in the ink unless otherwise noted.

Herman Melville Issue

Issued to honor Herman Melville (1819-1891), writer, and the whaling industry.

Moby Dick — U108

1970, Mar. 7

U554	U108	6c **blue**	.50	.20
		Entire	.60	.25
		Entire, 1st day cancel, New Bedford, Mass. *(433,777)*		1.00

Youth Conference Issue

Issued to publicize the White House Conference on Youth, Estes Park, Colo., Apr. 18-22.

Conference Emblem Symbolic of Man's Expectant Soul and of Universal Brotherhood
U109

Printed by United States Envelope Company, Williamsburg, Pa. Designed by Chermayeff and Geismar Associates.

1971, Feb. 24

U555	U109	6c **light blue**	.75	.20
		Entire	.85	.40
		Entire, 1st day cancel, Washington, D.C. *(264,559)*		1.00

Liberty Bell Type of 1965 and U110

Eagle — U110

Printed by the United States Envelope Co., Williamsburg, Pa. Designed (8c) by Bradbury Thompson.

1971

U556	U104	1 7⁄10c **deep lilac**, untagged, *May 10*		.20
		Entire	.30	.20
		Entire, 1st day cancel, Baltimore, Md. *(150,767)*		1.00
U557	U110	8c **ultramarine**, *May 6*	.40	.20
		Entire	.50	.25
		Entire, 1st day cancel, Williamsburg, Pa. *(193,000)*		1.00

Nos. U551 and U555 Surcharged in Green at Left of Stamp

c

1971, May 16

U561	U107	6c + (2c) **light green**	1.00	.30
		Entire	1.10	.45
		Entire, 1st day cancel, Washington, D.C.		2.50
U562	U109	6c + (2c) **light blue**	2.00	1.60
		Entire	2.50	2.00
		Entire, 1st day cancel, Washington, D.C.		3.00

Bowling Issue

Issued as a salute to bowling and in connection with the 7th World Tournament of the International Bowling Federation, Milwaukee, Wis.

Bowling Ball and Pin — U111

Designed by George Giusti.

1971, Aug. 21

U563	U111	8c **rose red**	.50	.20
		Entire	.65	.20
		Entire, 1st day cancel, Milwaukee, Wis. *(281,242)*		1.00

Aging Conference Issue

White House Conference on Aging, Washington, D.C., Nov. 28-Dec. 2, 1971.

Conference Symbol — U112

Designed by Thomas H. Geismar.

1971, Nov. 15

U564	U112	8c	**light blue**	.50 .20
			Entire	.65 .20
			Entire, 1st day cancel, Washington, D.C. *(125,000)*	1.00

International Transportation Exhibition Issue

U.S. International Transportation Exhibition, Dulles International Airport, Washington, D.C., May 27-June 4.

Transportation Exhibition Emblem — U113

(Size of actual stamp: 64x70mm)

Emblem designed by Toshihiki Sakow.

1972, May 2

U565	U113	8c	**ultramarine & rose red**	.50 .20
			Entire	.75 .25
			Entire, 1st day cancel, Washington, D.C.	1.00

No. U557 Surcharged Type "b" in Ultramarine at Left of Stamp

1973, Dec. 1

U566	U110	8c + 2c	**brt. ultramarine**	.40 .20
			Entire	.50 .20
			Entire, 1st day cancel, Washington, D.C.	1.00

Liberty Bell — U114

1973, Dec. 5

U567	U114	10c	**emerald**	.40 .20
			Entire	.50 .20
			Entire, 1st day cancel, Philadelphia, Pa. *(142,141)*	1.00

"Volunteer Yourself" — U115

Designed by Norman Ives.

1974, Aug. 23

Untagged

U568	U115	1⁸⁄₁₀c	**blue green**	.20
			Entire	.30 .50
			Entire, 1st day cancel, Cincinnati, Ohio	1.00

Tennis Centenary Issue

Centenary of tennis in the United States.

Tennis Racquet — U116

Designed by Donald Moss.

1974, Aug. 31

U569	U116	10c	**yellow, brt. blue & light green**	.30 .20
			Entire	.40 .25
			Entire, 1st day cancel, Forest Hills, N.Y. *(245,000)*	1.00

Bicentennial Era Issue

The Seafaring Tradition - Compass Rose — U118

The American Homemaker - Quilt Pattern U119

The American Farmer - Sheaf of Wheat U120

The American Doctor - Mortar U121

The American Craftsman - Tools, c. 1750 — U122

Designs (in brown on left side of envelope): 10c, Norwegian sloop Restaurationen. No. U572, Spinning wheel. No. U573, Plow. No. U574, Colonial era medical instruments and bottle. No. U575, Shaker rocking chair.
Designed by Arthur Congdon.

1975-76   **Embossed**

Diagonally Laid Paper

U571	U118	10c	**brown & blue,** *light brown,* Oct. 13, 1975	.30 .20
			Entire	.45 .20
			Entire, 1st day cancel, Minneapolis, Minn. *(255,304)*	1.00
a.			Brown ("10c/USA," etc.) omitted, entire	125.00
U572	U119	13c	**brown & blue green,** *light brown,* Feb. 2, 1976	.35 .20
			Entire	.50 .20
			Entire, 1st day cancel, Biloxi, Miss. *(196,647)*	1.00
a.			Brown ("13c/USA," etc.) omitted, entire	125.00
U573	U120	13c	**brown & bright green,** *light brown,* Mar. 15, 1976	.35 .20
			Entire	.50 .20
			Entire, 1st day cancel, New Orleans, La. *(214,563)*	1.00
a.			Brown ("13c/USA," etc.) omitted, entire	125.00
U574	U121	13c	**brown & orange,** *light brown,* June 30, 1976	.35 .20
			Entire	.50 .20
			Entire, 1st day cancel, Dallas, Texas	1.00
a.			Brown ("13c/USA," etc.) omitted, entire	—
U575	U122	13c	**brown & carmine,** *lt. brown,* Aug. 6, 1976	.35 .20
			Entire	.50 .20
			Entire, 1st day cancel, Hancock, Mass.	1.00
a.			Brown ("13c/USA," etc.) omitted, entire	125.00
			Nos. U571-U575 (5)	1.70 .75

Liberty Tree, Boston, 1646 — U123

Designed by Leonard Everett Fisher.

1975, Nov. 8   **Embossed**

U576	U123	13c	**orange brown**	.30 .20
			Entire	.40 .20
			Entire, 1st day cancel, Memphis, Tenn. *(226,824)*	1.00

Star and Pinwheel — U124

U125

U126

Eagle — U127

Uncle Sam — U128

Designers: 2c, Rudolph de Harak. 2.1c, Norman Ives. 2.7c, Ann Sforza Clementino. 15c, George Mercer.

1976-78			Embossed
U577 U124	2c **red**, untagged, *Sept. 10, 1976*		.20
	Entire	.30	.50
	Entire, 1st day cancel, Hempstead, N.Y. *(81,388)*		1.00
U578 U125	2.1c **green**, untagged, *June 3, 1977*		.20
	Entire	.30	.50
	Entire, 1st day cancel, Houston, Tex. *(120,280)*		1.00
U579 U126	2.7c **green**, untagged, *July 5, 1978*		.20
	Entire	.35	.50
	Entire, 1st day cancel, Raleigh, N.C. *(92,687)*		1.00
U580 U127	(15c) **orange**, *May 22, 1978*	.40	.20
	Entire	.55	.20
	Entire, 1st day cancel, Memphis, Tenn.		1.00
U581 U128	15c **red**, *June 3, 1978*	.40	.20
	Entire	.55	.20
	Entire, 1st day cancel, Williamsburg, Pa. *(176,000)*		1.00

Bicentennial Issue

Centennial Envelope, 1876 — U129

1976, Oct. 15			Embossed
U582 U129	13c **emerald**	.35	.20
	Entire	.45	.20
	Entire, 1st day cancel, Los Angeles, Cal. *(277,222)*		1.00

Golf Issue

Golf Club in Motion and Golf Ball — U130

Designed by Guy Salvato.

1977, Apr. 7		Photogravure and Embossed	
U583 U130	13c **black, blue & yellow green**	.45	.20
	Entire	.55	.25
	Entire, 1st day cancel, Augusta, Ga. *(252,000)*		1.00
a.	Black omitted, entire	650.00	
b.	Black & blue omitted, entire	550.00	

Energy Issue

Conservation and development of national resources.

"Conservation" U131

"Development" U132

Designed by Terrance W. McCaffrey.

1977, Oct. 20			Embossed
U584 U131	13c **black, red & yellow**	.40	.20
	Entire	.50	.20
	Entire, 1st day cancel, Ridley Park, Pa.		1.00
a.	Red & yellow omitted, entire	250.00	
b.	Yellow omitted, entire	175.00	
c.	Black omitted, entire	175.00	
d.	Black & red omitted, entire	425.00	
U585 U132	13c **black, red & yellow**	.40	.20
	Entire	.50	.20
	Entire, 1st day cancel, Ridley Park, Pa.		1.00

First day cancellation applied to 353,515 of Nos. U584 and U585.

Nos. U584-U585 have a luminescent panel at left of stamp which glows green under ultraviolet light.

Olive Branch and Star — U133

Designed by George Mercer.

1978, July 28			Embossed
	Black Surcharge		
U586 U133	15c on 16c **blue**	.35	.20
	Entire	.50	.20
	Entire, 1st day cancel, Williamsburg, Pa. *(193,153)*		1.00
a.	Surcharge omitted, entire	225.00	—
b.	Surcharge on No. U581, entire	—	—
c.	As "a," with surcharge printed on envelope flap	175.00	—

Auto Racing Issue

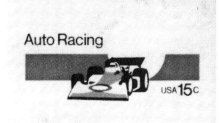

Indianapolis 500 Racing Car — U134

Designed by Robert Peak.

1978, Sept. 2			Embossed
U587 U134	15c **red, blue & black**	.35	.20
	Entire	.50	.20
	Entire, 1st day cancel, Ontario, Cal. *(209,147)*		1.00
a.	Black omitted, entire	120.00	
b.	Black & blue omitted, entire		
c.	Red omitted, entire	120.00	
d.	Red & blue omitted, entire	—	

No. U576 Surcharged Like No. U586

1978, Nov. 28			Embossed
U588 U123	15c on 13c **orange brown**	.35	.20
	Entire	.50	.20
	Entire, 1st day cancel, Williamsburg, Pa. *(137,500)*		1.00

U135

Weaver Violins — U136

U137

Eagle — U138

U139

Eagle — U140

1979, May 18		Untagged	Embossed
U589 U135	3.1c **ultramarine**		.20
	Entire	.25	.40
	Entire, 1st day cancel, Denver, Colo. *(117,575)*		1.00

1980, June 23		Untagged	Embossed
U590 U136	3.5c **purple**		.20
	Entire	.30	.40
	Entire, 1st day cancel, Williamsburg, Pa.		1.00

1982, Feb. 17		Untagged	Embossed
U591 U137	5.9c **brown**		.20
	Entire	.30	.40
	Entire, 1st day cancel, Wheeling, WV		1.00

1981, Mar. 15			Embossed
U592 U138	(18c) **violet**	.45	.20
	Entire	.55	.25
	Entire, 1st day cancel, Memphis, TN *(179,171)*		1.00

1981, Apr. 2			Embossed
U593 U139	18c **dark blue**	.45	.20
	Entire	.55	.25
	Entire, 1st day cancel, Star City, IN *(160,439)*		1.00

1981, Oct. 11			Embossed
U594 U140	20c **brown**	.45	.20
	Entire	.55	.20
	Entire, 1st day cancel, Memphis, TN *(304,404)*		2.00

Veterinary Medicine Issue

Seal of Veterinarians
U141

Design at left side of envelope shows 5 animals and bird in brown, "Veterinary Medicine" in gray.
Designed by Guy Salvato.

1979, July 24		**Embossed**	
U595 U141 15c **brown & gray**		.35	.20
Entire		.50	.20
Entire, 1st day cancel, Seattle, WA *(209,658)*			1.00
a.	Gray omitted, entire	650.00	
b.	Brown omitted, entire	950.00	

Olympic Games Issue

22nd Olympic Games, Moscow, July 19-Aug. 3, 1980.

U142

Design (multicolored on left side of envelope) shows two soccer players with ball.
Designed by Robert M. Cunningham.

1979, Dec. 10		**Embossed**	
U596 U142 15c **red, green & black**		.60	.20
Entire		.70	.20
Entire, 1st day cancel, East Rutherford, NJ *(179,336)*			1.00
a.	Red & green omitted, untagged, entire	225.00	
b.	Black omitted, untagged, entire	225.00	
c.	Black & green omitted, entire	225.00	
d.	Red omitted, untagged, entire	400.00	

Highwheeler Bicycle — U143

Design (blue on left side of envelope) shows racing bicycle.
Designed by Robert Hallock.

1980, May 16		**Embossed**	
U597 U143 15c **blue & rose claret**		.40	.20
Entire		.55	.20
Entire, 1st day cancel, Baltimore, MD *(173,978)*			1.00
a.	Blue ("15c USA") omitted, entire	100.00	

Yacht — U144   AMERICA'S CUP

Designed by Cal Sachs.

1980, Sept. 15		**Embossed**	
U598 U144 15c **blue & red**		.40	.20
Entire		.55	.20
Entire, 1st day cancel, Newport, RI *(192,220)*			1.00

Italian Honeybee and Orange Blossoms
U145

Bee and petals colorless embossed.
Designed by Jerry Pinkney.

1980, Oct. 10	**Photogravure and Embossed**		
U599 U145 15c **brown, green & yellow**		.35	.20
Entire		.50	.20
Entire, 1st day cancel, Paris, IL *(202,050)*			1.00
a.	Brown ("USA 15c") omitted, entire	125.00	

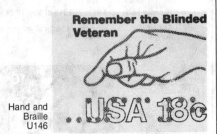

Hand and Braille
U146

Hand and braille colorless embossed.
Designed by John Boyd.

1981, Aug. 13		**Embossed**	
U600 U146 18c **blue & red**		.45	.20
Entire		.55	.25
Entire, 1st day cancel, Arlington, VA *(175,966)*			1.00
a.	Blue omitted, entire	—	
b.	Red omitted, entire	—	

Capital Dome — U147

1981, Nov. 13		**Embossed**	
U601 U147 20c **deep magenta**		.45	.20
Entire		.55	.20
Entire, 1st day cancel, Los Angeles, CA			1.00
a.	Bar tagged	1.50	1.50

The Great Seal of the United States
1782-1982

USA 20c

U148

Designed by Bradbury Thompson.

1982, June 15		**Embossed**	
U602 U148 20c **dark blue, black & magenta**		.45	.20
Entire		.55	.20
Entire, 1st day cancel, Washington, DC *(163,905)*			1.00
a.	Dark blue omitted, entire	150.00	
b.	Dark blue & magenta omitted, entire	—	

The Purple Heart
1782
1982
USA 20c

U149

Designed by John Boyd.

1982, Aug. 6		**Embossed**	
U603 U149 20c **purple & black**		.45	.20
Entire		.55	.20
Entire, 1st day cancel, Washington, DC *(110,679)*			1.00
a.	Black omitted, entire	—	

U150

1983, Mar. 21	**Untagged**	**Embossed**	
U604 U150 5.2c **orange**			.20
Entire		.40	.40
Entire, 1st day cancel, Memphis, TN *(141,979)*			1.00

U151

1983, Aug. 3		**Embossed**	
U605 U151 20c **red, blue & black**		.45	.20
Entire		.55	.20
Entire, 1st day cancel, Portland, OR *(21,500)*			1.00
a.	Red omitted, entire	—	
b.	Blue omitted, entire	—	
c.	Red & black omitted, entire	140.00	
d.	Blue & black omitted, entire	140.00	
e.	Black omitted, entire	225.00	

Small Business USA 20c   U152

Designed by Peter Spier and Pat Taylor.
Design shows storefronts at lower left. Stamp and design continue on back of envelope.

1984, May 7			
U606 U152 20c **multi**		.50	.20
Entire		.60	.20
Entire, 1st day cancel, Washington, DC *(77,665)*			1.00

U153

Designed by Bradbury Thompson.

1985, Feb. 1   **Embossed**
U607 U153 (22c) **deep green**   .55   .20
     Entire   .65   .20
     Entire, 1st day cancel, Los An-
     geles, CA   1.00

American
Buffalo — U154

Designed by George Mercer.

1985, Feb. 25   **Embossed**
U608 U154 22c **violet brown**   .55   .20
     Entire   .65   .20
     Entire, 1st day cancel, Bison, SD
     (105,271)   1.00
  a.   Untagged, 3 precancel lines   .20
     Entire   .60   .20
  b.   Bar tagged   — 1.00

Original printings of No. U608 were printed with luminescent ink. later printings have a luminescent vertical bar to the left of the stamp.

Frigate U.S.S.
Constitution — U155

Designed by Cal Sacks.

1985, May 3   **Untagged**   **Embossed**
U609 U155 6c **green blue**   .20
     Entire   .25   .25
     Entire, 1st day cancel, Boston,
     MA (170,425)   1.00

The Mayflower — U156

Designed by Robert Brangwynne.

1986, Dec. 4   **Untagged**   **Embossed**
             Precanceled
U610 U156 8.5c **black & gray**   .20
     Entire   .30   .30
     Entire, 1st day cancel, Plymouth,
     MA (105,164)   1.00

Stars — U157

Designed by Joe Brockert.

1988, Mar. 26   **Typo. & Embossed**
U611 U157 25c **dark red & deep blue**   .60   .20
     Entire   .70   .25
     Entire, 1st day cancel, Star, MS
     (29,393)   1.25
  a.   Dark red (25) omitted, entire   75.00 —

US Frigate Constellation — U158

Designed by Jerry Dadds.

1988, Apr. 12   **Untagged**   **Typo. & Embossed**
             Precanceled
U612 U158 8.4c **black & bright blue**   .20
     Entire   .30   .30
     Entire, 1st day cancel, Balti-
     more, MD (41,420)   1.25
  a.   Black omitted, entire   600.00

Snowflake — U159

Designed by Randall McDougall. "Holiday Greetings!" inscribed in lower left.

1988, Sept. 8   **Typo.**
U613 U159 25c **dark red & green**   .60   .25
     Entire   .75   .30
     Entire, 1st day cancel, Snowflake,
     AZ (32,601)   1.25

Stars
U160

Designed by Joe Brockert. "Philatelic Mail" and asterisks in dark red below vignette; continuous across envelope face and partly on reverse.

1989, Mar. 10   **Typo.**
U614 U160 25c **dark red & deep blue**   .50   .25
     Entire   .60   .30
     Entire, 1st day cancel, Cleveland,
     OH   1.25

Stars
U161

Designed by Joe Brockert.

1989, July 10   **Typo.**   **Unwmk.**
U615 U161 25c **dark red & deep blue**   .50   .25
     Entire   .60   .30
     Entire, 1st day cancel, Washing-
     ton, DC (33,461)   1.25
  a.   Dark red omitted, entire   —

Lined with a blue design to provide security for enclosures.

Love!
U162

Designed by Tim Girvin. Light blue lines printed diagonally over the entire surface of the envelope.

1989, Sept. 22   **Litho. & Typo.**   **Unwmk.**
U616 U162 25c **dark red & bright blue**   .50   .25
     Entire   .60   .30
     Entire, 1st day cancel, McLean,
     VA (69,498)   1.25

Shuttle Docking at Space Station — U163

Designed by Richard Sheaff.

1989, Dec. 3   **Typo.**   **Unwmk.**
             Die Cut
U617 U163 25c **ultramarine**   .60   .30
     Entire   .70   .35
     Entire, 1st day cancel, Wash-
     ington, DC   1.25
  a.   Ultramarine omitted, entire   600.00

A hologram, visible through the die cut window to the right of "USA 25," is affixed to the inside of the envelope.
Available only in No. 9 size.
See Nos. U625, U639.

Vince Lombardi Trophy, Football Players — U164

Designed by Bruce Harman.

1990, Sept. 9   **Typo.**   **Unwmk.**   *Die Cut*
U618 U164 25c **vermilion**   .50   .25
     Entire   .60   .30
     Entire, 1st day cancel, Green
     Bay, WI (54,589)   1.25

A hologram, visible through the die cut window to the right of "USA 25," is affixed to the inside of the envelope.
Available only in No. 10 size.

Star — U165

Designed by Richard Sheaff.

1991, Jan. 24   Typo. & Embossed   Wmk.
U619 U165 29c **ultramarine & rose**   .60   .30
　　　Entire   .70   .35
　　　Entire, unwatermarked, *May 1, 1992*   .70   .35
　　　Entire, 1st day cancel, Washington, DC *(33,025)*   1.25
　　a.   Ultramarine omitted, entire   —
　　b.   Rose omitted, entire   400.00
Unwatermarked envelopes are on recycled paper, and have an imprint under the flap.
　　See No. U623.

Birds — U166

Designed by Richard Sheaff
　　Stamp and design continue on back of envelope. Illustration reduced.

1991, May 3   Typo.   Wmk.
Untagged Precanceled
U620 U166 11.1c **blue & red**   　　.20
　　　Entire   .35   .25
　　　Entire, 1st day cancel, Boxborough, MA *(20,720)*   1.25
　　　Entire, unwatermarked, *May 1, 1992*   .35   .25
Unwatermarked envelopes are on recycled paper, and have an imprint under the flap.

Love — U167

Designed by Salahattin Kanidinc.

1991, May 9   Litho.   Unwmk.
U621 U167 29c **light blue, maroon & bright rose**   .60   .30
　　　Entire   .70   .35
　　　Entire, 1st day cancel, Honolulu, HI *(40,110)*   1.25
　　a.   Bright rose omitted, entire   500.00
Examples on recycled paper were issued May 1, 1992 and have imprint under the flap.

Magazine Industry, 250th Anniv. — U168

Designed by Bradbury Thompson.

1991, Oct. 7   Photo. & Typo.   Unwmk.
U622 U168 29c **multicolored**   .60   .30
　　　Entire   .70   .35
　　　Entire, 1st day cancel, Naples, FL *(26,020)*   1.25
The photogravure vignette, visible through the die cut window to the right of "USA 29," is affixed to the inside of the envelope. Available only in No. 10 size.

Star — U169

Designed by Richard Sheaff.
　　Stamp and design continue on back of envelope.

1991, July 20   Typo.
U623 U169 29c **ultra & rose**   .60   .30
　　　Entire   .70   .35
　　　Entire, 1st day cancel, Washington, DC *(16,038)*   1.25
　　a.   Ultra omitted, entire   —
　　b.   Rose omitted, entire   —
Lined with a blue design to provide security for enclosures. Examples on recycled paper were issued May 1, 1992 and have imprint under the flap. Available only in No. 9 size.

Country Geese U170

Designed by Marc Zaref.

1991, Nov. 8   Litho. & Typo.   Wmk.
U624 U170 29c **blue gray & yellow**   .60   .60
　　　Entire   .70   .70
　　　Entire, 1st day cancel, Virginia Beach, VA *(21,031)*   1.25
　　　Entire, unwatermarked, *May 1, 1992*   .70   .70
Unwatermarked envelopes are on recycled paper, and have an imprint under the flap.

Space Shuttle Type of 1989
Designed by Richard Sheaff.

1992, Jan. 21   Typo.   Unwmk.   *Die Cut*
U625 U163 29c **yellow green**   .60   .25
　　　Entire   .70   .35
　　　Entire, 1st day cancel, Virginia Beach, VA *(37,646)*   1.25
A hologram, visible through the die cut window to the right of "USA 29," is affixed to the inside of the envelope. Examples on recycled paper were issued May 1, 1992 and have imprint under the flap.

U171

Designed by Harry Zelenko.

1992, Apr. 10   Typo. & Litho.   Unwmk.   *Die Cut*
U626 U171 29c **multicolored**   .60   .30
　　　Entire   .70   .35
　　　Entire, 1st day cancel, Dodge City, KS *(34,258)*   1.25
The lithographed vignette, visible through the die cut window to the right of "USA 29," is affixed to the inside of the envelope. Available only in No. 10 size.

Hillebrandia — U172

Designed by Joseph Brockert. Illustration reduced.

1992, Apr. 22
U627 U172 29c **multicolored**   .60   .30
　　　Entire   .70   .35
　　　Entire, 1st day cancel, Chicago, IL *(29,432)*   1.25
The lithographed vignette, visible through the die cut window to the right of "29 USA," is affixed to the inside of the envelope. Inscribed "Save the Rain Forests" in the lower left. Available only in the No. 10 size.

Star U173 Bulk Rate

Designed by Joseph Brockert.

1992, May 19   Typo. & Embossed   Precanceled
Untagged
U628 U173 19.8c **red & blue**   　　.40
　　　Entire   .50   .45
　　　Entire, 1st day cancel, Las Vegas, NV *(18,478)*   1.25
Available only in No. 10 size.

U174

Designed by Richard Sheaff. Illustration reduced.

1992, July 22   Typo.   Unwmk.
U629 U174 29c **red & blue**   .60   .30
　　　Entire   .70   .35
　　　Entire, 1st day cancel, Washington, DC *(28,218)*   1.25

U175

Designed by Nancy Krause. Illustration reduced.

1993, Oct. 2   Typo. & Litho.   Unwmk.   *Die Cut*
U630 U175 29c **multicolored**   .60   .30
　　　Entire   .70   .35
　　　Entire, 1st day cancel, King of Prussia, PA *(6,511)*   1.25
The lithographed vignette, visible through the die cut window to the right of "USA 29," is affixed to the inside of the envelope. Available only in the No. 10 size.

U176

Designed by Richard Sheaff.

1994, Sept. 17   Typo. & Embossed   Unwmk.
U631 U176   29c **brown & black**   .60   .30
              Entire   .70   .35
              Entire, 1st day cancel, Can-
              ton, OH (28,977)   1.25
a.   Black ("29/USA") omitted, entire   —

Available only in No. 10 size.

Liberty Bell — U177

Designed by Richard Sheaff.

1995, Jan. 3   Typo. & Embossed   Unwmk.
U632 U177   32c **greenish blue & blue**   .65   .30
              Entire   .75   .40
              Entire, 1st day cancel, Wil-
              liamsburg, PA   1.25
a.   Greenish blue omitted, entire   500.00
b.   Blue ("USA 32") omitted, entire   150.00

First day cancellation was applied to 54,102 of Nos. U632,
UX198.
See No. U638.

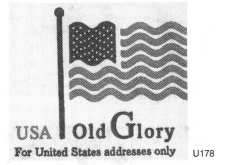

For United States addresses only   U178

Design sizes: 49x38mm (#U633), 53x44mm (U634). Stamp
and design continue on back of envelope.

1995   Typo.   Unwmk.
U633 U178   (32c) **blue & red**   .65   .30
              Entire, #6¾   .75   .40
U634 U178   (32c) **blue & red**   .65   .30
              Entire, #10   .75   .40
a.   Red & tagging omitted, entire   —
b.   Blue omitted, entire   —

Originally, Nos. U633-U634 were only available through the
Philatelic Fulfillment Center after their announcement 1/12/95.
Envelopes submitted for first day cancels received a 12/13/94
cancel, even though they were not available on that date.
See No. U638.

U179

Design size: 58x25mm. Stamp and design continue on back
of envelope.
Designed by Douglas Smith.

1995, Mar. 10   Typo.   Unwmk.
                    Precanceled
U635 U179   (5c) **green & red brown**   .20
              Entire   .25   .25
              Entire, 1st day cancel, State Col-
              lege, PA   1.25

Graphic Eagle — U180

Designed by Uldis Purins.

1995, Mar. 10   Typo.   Unwmk.
                    Precanceled
U636 U180   (10c) **dark carmine & blue**   .20
              Entire   .30   .20
              Entire, 1st day cancel, State
              College, PA   1.25

Available only in No. 10 size.

Spiral Heart — U181

Designed by Uldis Purins.

1995, May 12   Typo.   Unwmk.
U637 U181   32c **red**, *light blue*   .65   .30
              Entire   .75   .40
              Entire, 1st day cancel, Lakeville,
              PA   1.25

Liberty Bell Type

1995, May 16   Typo.   Unwmk.
U638 U177   32c **greenish blue & blue**   .65   .30
              Entire   .70   .35
              Entire, 1st day cancel, Washing-
              ton, DC   1.25

No. U638 was printed on security paper and was available
only in No. 9 size.

Space Shuttle Type of 1989
Designed by Richard Sheaff.

1995, Sept. 22   Typo.   Unwmk.   *Die Cut*
U639 U163   32c **carmine rose**   .65   .35
              Entire   .70   .40
              Entire, 1st day cancel, Milwau-
              kee, WI   1.25

A hologram, visible through the die cut window to the right of
"USA 32," is affixed to the inside of the envelope. No. U639 was
available only in No. 10 size.

U182

Designed by Richard Sheaff.

1996, Apr. 20   Typo. & Litho.   Unwmk.   *Die Cut*
U640 U182   32c **multicolored**   .60   .30
              Entire   .70   .35
              Entire, 1st day cancel, Chicago,
              IL (9,921)   1.25

The lithographed vignette, visible through the die cut window
to the right of "USA 32c," is affixed to the inside of the envelope.
Available only in the No. 10 size.

U183

Designed by Brad Copeland. Illustration reduced.

1996, May 2
U641 U183   32c **multicolored**   .60   .30
              Entire   .70   .35
              Entire, 1st day cancel, Washing-
              ton, DC   1.25
a.   Blue & red omitted, entire   —
b.   Blue gold omitted, entire   —
c.   Red omitted, entire   —
d.   Black & red omitted, entire   —

U184

Designer by Richard Sheaff.

1999, Jan. 11   Typo. & Embossed   Unwmk.
U642 U184   33c **yellow, blue & red**   .65   .30
              Entire   .80   .40
              Entire, 1st day cancel, Washing-
              ton, DC   1.25
a.   Tagging bar to right of design   .65   .30
              Entire   .80   .40

Earliest known use of No. U642a, 10/12/99.

1999, Jan. 11   Typo.   Unwmk.
U643 U184   33c **blue & red**   .65   .30
              Entire   .80   .40
              Entire, 1st day cancel, Washing-
              ton, DC   1.25

Available only in #9 size.

U185

Designed by Julian Waters.

1999, Jan. 28   Litho.
U644 U185   33c **violet**   .65   .30
              Entire   .80   .40
              Entire, 1st day cancel, Loveland,
              CO   1.25

Lincoln — U186

Designed by Richard Sheaff.

1999, June 5   Typo. & Litho.   Unwmk.
U645 U186   33c **blue & black**   .65   .30
              Entire   .80   .40
              Entire, 1st day cancel, Spring-
              field, IL   1.25

**AIR POST STAMPED ENVELOPES AND AIR
LETTER SHEETS**

All envelopes have carmine and blue borders,
unless noted. There are seven types of borders:
Carmine Diamond in Upper Right Corner.
   a- Diamonds measure 9 to 10mm paralled to edge
of envelope and 11 to 12mm along oblique side (with
top flap open). Sizes 5 and 13 only.
   b- Like "a" except diamonds measure 7 to 8mm
along oblique side (with top flap open). Sizes 5 and 13
only.
   c- Diamonds measure 11 to 12mm parallel to edge
of envelope. Size 8 only.
   Blue Diamond in Upper Right Corner.

d- Lower points of top row of diamonds point to left. Size 8 only.

e- Lower points of top row of diamonds point to right. Size 8 only.

Diamonds Omitted in Upper Right Corner (1965 Onward)

f- Blue diamond above at left of stamp.

g- Red diamond above at left of stamp.

UC1

5c - Vertical rudder is not semi-circular but slopes down to the left. The tail of the plane projects into the G of POSTAGE. Border types a, b, c, d and e.

UC2

Die 2 (5c and 8c): Vertical rudder is semi-circular. The tail of the plane touches but does not project into the G of POSTAGE. Border types b, d, and e for the 5c; b and d for the 8c.

Die 2 (6c)- Same as UC2 except three types of numeral.
2a- The numeral "6" is 6½mm wide.
2b- The numeral "6" is 6mm wide.
2c- The numeral "6" is 5½mm wide.

Eleven working dies were used in printing the 6c. On each, the numeral "6" was engraved by hand, producing several variations in position, size and thickness.

Nos. UC1 and UC2 occur with varying size blue blobs, caused by a shallow printing die. They are not constant.

Border types b and d for dies 2a and 2b; also without border (June 1944 to Sept. 1945) for dies 2a, 2b and 2c.

Die 3 (6c): Vertical rudder leans forward. S closer to O than to T of POSTAGE. E of POSTAGE has short center bar. Border types b and d, also without border.

No. UC1 with 1933 and 1937 watermarks and No. UC2 with 1929 and 1933 watermarks were issued in Puerto Rico.

No. UC1 in blue black, with 1925 watermark #26 and border type a, is a proof.

1929-44

UC1	UC1	5c **blue,** *Jan. 12, 1929*	3.50	2.00
		Entire, border a or b	4.50	2.25
		Entire, border c, d or e	8.50	5.75
		First day cancel, border a, entire		40.00
		1933 wmk. #33, border d, entire	750.00	750.00
		1937 wmk. #36, border d, entire	—	—
		1937 wmk. #36, border b, entire	—	2,500.
		Bicolored border omitted, entire	650.00	
UC2	UC2	5c **blue,** die 2	11.00	5.00
		Entire, border b	13.50	6.50
		Entire, border e	19.50	12.50
		1929 wmk. #28, border d, entire	—	1,500.
		1933 wmk. #33, border d, entire	650.00	—
		1933 wmk. #33, border b, entire	325.00	—
UC3	UC2	6c **orange,** die 2a, *July 1, 1934*	1.45	.40
		Entire, bicolored border	1.75	.60
		Entire, without border	2.50	1.25
		Entire, 1st day cancel		14.00
a.		With added impression of 3c purple (#U436a), entire without border	4,000.	

UC4	UC2	6c **orange,** die 2b ('42)	2.75	2.00
		Entire, bicolored border, 1941 wmk. #39	60.00	20.00
		Entire, without border	4.50	2.00
UC5	UC2	6c **orange,** die 2c ('44)	.75	.30
		Entire, without border	1.00	.45
UC6	UC2	6c **orange,** die 3 ('42)	1.00	.35
		Entire, bicolored border	1.50	.75
		Entire, without border	2.50	.90
		Entire, carmine of border omitted	1,250.	
		Double impression, entire	400.00	
a.		6c orange, *blue,* die 3 (error) Entire, without border	3,500.	2,400.
UC7	UC2	8c **olive green,** die 2, *Sept. 26, 1932*	13.00	3.50
		Entire, bicolored border	16.00	6.50
		Entire, 1st day cancel		11.00

Surcharged in black on envelopes indicated by number in parenthesis

1945

UC8	U93	6c on 2c **carmine** (U429)	1.25	.65
		Entire	1.65	1.00
a.		6c on 1c green (error) (U420)	1,750.	
		Entire	2,500.	
b.		6c on 3c purple (error) (U436a)	2,000.	
		Entire	3,250.	
c.		6c on 3c purple (error), *amber* (U437a)	3,000.	
		Entire	3,500.	
d.		6c on 3c violet (error) (U526)	3,000.	
		Entire	3,500.	
UC9	U95	6c on 2c **carmine** (U525)	75.00	40.00
		Entire	100.00	50.00

Ten surcharge varieties are found on Nos. UC8-UC9.

Surcharged in Black on 6c Air Post Envelopes without borders

REVALUED
5¢
P.O. DEPT.

1946

UC10	UC2	5c on 6c **orange,** die 2a	2.75	1.50
		Entire	3.50	2.50
a.		Double surcharge	60.00	
UC11	UC2	5c on 6c **orange,** die 2b	9.00	5.50
		Entire	10.00	7.00
UC12	UC2	5c on 6c **orange,** die 2c	.75	.50
		Entire	1.25	.60
a.		Double surcharge	60.00	60.00
UC13	UC2	5c on 6c **orange,** die 3	.80	.60
		Entire	1.00	.75
a.		Double surcharge	60.00	

The 6c borderless envelopes and the revalued envelopes were issued primarily for use to and from members of the armed forces. The 5c rate came into effect Oct. 1, 1946.
Ten surcharge varieties are found on Nos. UC10-UC13.

DC-4 Skymaster — UC3

Envelopes with borders types b and d.
Die 1 - The end of the wing at the right is a smooth curve. The juncture of the front end of the plane and the engine forms an acute angle. The first T of STATES and the E's of UNITED STATES lean to the left.
Die 2 - The end of the wing at the right is a straight line. The juncture of the front end of the plane and the engine is wide open. The first T of STATES and the E's of UNITED STATES lean to the right.

1946

UC14	UC3	5c **carmine,** die 1, *Sept. 25, 1946*	.75	.20
		Entire, bicolored border	1.10	.40
		Entire, 1st day cancel		1.50

		Entire, bicolored border omitted	—	
UC15	UC3	5c **carmine,** die 2	.85	.25
		Entire, bicolored border	1.10	.40

No. UC14, printed on flat bed press, measures 21½mm high. No. UC15, printed on rotary press, measures 22mm high. See No. UC18.

DC-4 Skymaster UC4

1947-55   Typographed, Without Embossing
Letter Sheets for Foreign Postage

UC16	UC4	10c **bright red,** *pale blue,* "Air Letter" on face, 2-line inscription on back, entire	7.50	6.00
		Entire, 1st day cancel, *Apr. 29, 1947*		2.00
UC16a	UC4	10c **bright red,** *pale blue, Sept. 1951,* "Air Letter" on face, 4-line inscription on back, entire	110.00	
		Die cutting reversed, entire	275.00	
b.		10c **chocolate,** *pale blue,* entire	400.00	
UC16c	UC4	10c **bright red,** *pale blue, Nov. 1953,* "Air Letter" and "Aerogramme" on face, 4-line inscription on back, entire	16.00	14.00
		Die cutting reversed, entire	45.00	12.50
UC16d	UC4	10c **bright red,** *pale blue, 1955,* "Air Letter" and "Aerogramme" on face, 3-line inscription on back, entire	8.00	8.00
		Die cutting reversed, entire	60.00	
		Dark blue (inscriptions & border diamonds) omitted	—	

Printed on protective tinted paper containing colorless inscription.

UNITED STATES FOREIGN AIR MAIL multiple, repeated in parallel vertical or horizontal lines.

Postage Stamp Centenary Issue

Centenary of the first postage stamps issued by the United States Government.

Washington and Franklin, Early and Modern Mail-carrying Methods — UC5

Two dies: Rotary, design measures 22¼mm high; and flat bed press, design 21¾mm high.

1947, May 21   Embossed
For Domestic Postage

UC17	UC5	5c **carmine** (rotary)	.40	.25
		Entire, bicolored border b	.55	.35
		Entire, 1st day cancel, NY, NY		1.25
a.		Flat plate printing	.50	.30
		Entire	.60	.40

Type of 1946

Type I: 6's lean to right.
Type II: 6's upright.

1950

UC18	UC3	6c **carmine,** type I, *Sept. 22, 1950*	.35	.20
		Entire, bicolored border	.60	.30
		Entire, 1st day cancel, Philadelphia		1.00
a.		Type II	.75	.25
		Entire	1.00	.30

Several other types differ slightly from the two listed.

REVALUED

6¢

P. O. DEPT.

Nos. UC14, UC15, UC18
Surcharged in Red at Left of Stamp

1951

UC19	UC3	6c on 5c **carmine**, die 1	.85	.50
		Entire	1.25	.75
UC20	UC3	6c on 5c **carmine**, die 2	.80	.50
		Entire	1.15	.80
a.		6c on 6c **carmine** (error) entire	1,500.	—
b.		Double surcharge	250.00	—

REVALUED

6¢

P. O. DEPT.

Nos. UC14 and UC15 Surcharged
in Red at Left of Stamp

1952

UC21	UC3	6c on 5c **carmine**, die 1	27.50	17.50
		Entire	32.50	22.50
UC22	UC3	6c on 5c **carmine**, die 2, Aug. 29, 1952	3.50	2.50
		Entire	5.00	4.25
a.		Double surcharge	75.00	

Same Surcharge in Red on No. UC17

UC23	UC5	6c on 5c **carmine**	1,250.	
		Entire	2,250.	

The 6c on 4c black (No. U440) is believed to be a favor printing.

Fifth International Philatelic Exhibition Issue

FIPEX, the Fifth International Philatelic Exhibition, New York, N.Y., Apr. 28-May 6, 1956.

Eagle in Flight — UC6

1956, May 2

UC25	UC6	6c **red**	.75	.50
		Entire	1.00	.80
		Entire, 1st day cancel, New York, N.Y. (363,239)		1.25

Two types exist, differing slightly in the clouds at top.

Skymaster Type of 1946

1958, July 31

UC26	UC3	7c **blue**	.65	.50
		Entire	1.00	.55
		Entire, 1st day cancel, Dayton, O. (143,428)		1.00

Nos. UC3-UC5, UC18 and UC25
Surcharged in Green at Left of Stamp

1958

UC27	UC2	6c + 1c **orange**, die 2a	250.00	225.00
		Entire, without border	300.00	250.00
UC28	UC2	6c + 1c **orange**, die 2b	65.00	75.00
		Entire, without border	85.00	110.00
UC29	UC2	6c + 1c **orange**, die 2c	37.50	50.00
		Entire	45.00	75.00
UC30	UC3	6c + 1c **carmine**, type I	1.00	.50
		Entire	1.25	.65
a.		Type II	1.00	.50
		Entire	1.25	.65
UC31	UC6	6c + 1c **red**	1.00	.50
		Entire	1.40	.85

Jet Airliner — UC7

Letter Sheet for Foreign Postage
Type I: Back inscription in 3 lines.
Type II: Back inscription in 2 lines.

1958-59   **Typographed, Without Embossing**

UC32	UC7	10c **blue & red**, blue, II, May, 1959, entire	6.00	5.00
b.		Red omitted, II, entire	—	
c.		Blue omitted, II, entire	—	
UC32a	UC7	10c **blue & red**, blue, I, Sept. 12, 1958, entire	10.00	5.00
		Entire, 1st day cancel, St. Louis, Mo. (92,400)		1.25
		Die cutting reversed, entire	75.00	

Silhouette of Jet
Airliner — UC8

1958, Nov. 21   **Embossed**

UC33	UC8	7c **blue**	.60	.25
		Entire	.70	.30
		Entire, 1st day cancel, New York, N.Y. (208,980)		1.00

1960, Aug. 18

UC34	UC8	7c **carmine**	.60	.25
		Entire	.70	.30
		Entire, 1st day cancel, Portland, Ore. (196,851)		1.00

Jet Airliner and Globe — UC9

Letter Sheet for Foreign Postage
Typographed, Without Embossing

1961, June 16

UC35	UC9	11c **red & blue**, blue, entire	2.75	2.25
		Entire, 1st day cancel, Johnstown, Pa. (163,460)		1.00
		Die cutting reversed, entire	35.00	
a.		Red omitted, entire	875.00	
b.		Blue omitted, entire	875.00	

Jet Airliner — UC10

1962, Nov. 17   **Embossed**

UC36	UC10	8c **red**	.55	.20
		Entire	.75	.30
		Entire, 1st day cancel, Chantilly, Va. (194,810)		1.00

Jet Airliner
UC11

1965-67

UC37	UC11	8c **red**, Jan. 7	.35	.20
		Entire, border "f"	.45	.30
		Entire, border "g"	20.00	
		Entire, 1st day cancel, Chicago, Ill. (226,178)		1.00
a.		Tagged, Aug. 15, 1967	1.25	.30
		Entire	1.75	.75
		Tagged, 1st day cancel		3.50

No. UC37a has a 8x24mm panel at left of stamp that glows orange red under ultraviolet light.

Pres. John F. Kennedy and Jet Plane — UC12

Letter Sheets for Foreign Postage
Typographed, Without Embossing
1965, May 29

UC38	UC12	11c **red & dark blue**, blue, entire	3.25	2.75
		Entire, 1st day cancel, Boston, Mass. (337,422)		1.00
		Die cutting reversed, entire	40.00	

1967, May 29

UC39	UC12	13c **red & dark blue**, blue, entire	3.00	2.75
		Entire, 1st day cancel, Chicago, Ill. (211,387)		1.00
		Die cutting reversed, entire	—	
a.		Red omitted, entire	500.00	
b.		Dark blue omitted, entire	500.00	

Jet Liner
UC13

Designed by Robert J. Jones.

1968, Jan. 8   **Tagged**   **Embossed**

UC40	UC13	10c **red**	.50	.20
		Entire	.80	.20
		Entire, 1st day cancel, Chicago, Ill. (157,553)		1.00

No. UC37 Surcharged in Red at
Left of Stamp

1968, Feb. 5

UC41	UC11	8c + 2c **red**	.65	.20
		Entire	.90	.40
		Entire, 1st day cancel, Washington, D.C.		8.00

Human Rights Year Issue

Issued for International Human Rights Year, and to commemorate the 20th anniversary of the United Nations' Declaration of Human Rights.

Globes and Flock of Birds — UC14

Printed by Acrovure Division of Union-Camp Corporation, Englewood, N.J. Designed by Antonio Frasconi.

Letter Sheet for Foreign Postage

1968, Dec. 3	Tagged	Photo.
UC42 UC14 13c **gray, brown, orange & black,** *blue,* entire	8.00	4.00
Entire, 1st day cancel, Washington, D.C. *(145,898)*		1.25
Die cutting reversed, entire	75.00	
a. Orange omitted, entire	—	
b. Brown omitted, entire	*400.00*	
c. Black omitted, entire	—	

No. UC42 has a luminescent panel ⅜x1 inch on the right globe. The panel glows orange red under ultraviolet light.

Jet Plane — UC15

Printed by United States Envelope Co., Williamsburg, Pa. Designed by Robert Geissmann.

1971, May 6		Embossed (Plane)
Center Circle Luminescent		
UC43 UC15 11c **red & blue**	.50	.20
Entire	.60	.20
Entire, 1st day cancel, Williamsburg, Pa. *(187,000)*		1.00

Birds in Flight — UC16

Printed by Bureau of Engraving and Printing. Designed by Soren Noring.

Letter Sheet for Foreign Postage

1971	Tagged	Photo.
UC44 UC16 15c **gray, red, white & blue,** *blue,* entire, *May 28*	1.50	1.10
Entire, 1st day cancel, Chicago, Ill. *(130,669)*		1.25
Die cutting reversed, entire	30.00	
a. "AEROGRAMME" added to inscription, entire, *Dec. 13*	1.50	1.10
Entire, 1st day cancel, Philadelphia, Pa.		1.25
Die cutting reversed, entire	30.00	

Folding instructions (2 steps) in capitals on No. C44; (4 steps) in upper and lower case on No. UC44a.

On Nos. UC44-UC44a the white rhomboid background of "USA postage 15c" is luminescent. No. UC44 is inscribed: "VIA AIR MAIL-PAR AVION". "postage 15c" is in gray. See No. UC46.

No. UC40 Surcharged in Green at Left of Stamp

1971, June 28		Embossed
UC45 UC13 10c + (1c) **red**	1.50	.20
Entire	1.90	.50
Entire, 1st day cancel, Washington, D.C.		8.00

HOT AIR BALLOONING CHAMPIONSHIPS ISSUE

Hot Air Ballooning World Championships, Albuquerque, N.M., Feb. 10-17, 1973.

Design: Three balloons and cloud at left in address section; no birds beside stamp. Inscribed "INTERNATIONAL HOT AIR BALLOONING." "postage 15c" in blue.

Printed by Bureau of Engraving and Printing. Designed by Soren Noring (vignette) and Esther Porter (balloons).

Letter Sheet for Foreign Postage

1973, Feb. 10	Tagged	Photo.
UC46 UC16 15c **red, white & blue,** *blue,* entire	.75	.40
Entire, 1st day cancel, Albuquerque, N.M. *(210,000)*		1.00

Folding instructions as on No. UC44a. See notes after No. UC44.

Bird in Flight — UC17

1973, Dec. 1		Luminescent Ink
UC47 UC17 13c **rose red**	.30	.20
Entire	.40	.20
Entire, 1st day cancel, Memphis, Tenn. *(132,658)*		1.00

UC18

Printed by the Bureau of Engraving and Printing. Designed by Bill Hyde.

Letter Sheet for Foreign Postage.

1974, Jan. 4	Tagged	Photo.
UC48 UC18 18c **red & blue,** *blue,* entire	.90	.30
Entire, 1st day cancel, Atlanta, Ga. *(119,615)*		1.00
Die cutting reversed, entire	—	
a. Red omitted, entire	—	

25TH ANNIVERSARY OF NATO ISSUE

postage 18c   UC19

Design: "NATO" and NATO emblem at left in address section. Printed by Bureau of Engraving and Printing. Designed by Soren Noring.

Letter Sheet for Foreign Postage

1974, Apr. 4	Tagged	Photo.
UC49 UC19 18c **red & blue,** *blue,* entire	.90	.40
Entire, 1st day cancel, Washington, D.C.		1.00

UC20

Printed by Bureau of Engraving and Printing. Designed by Robert Geissmann.

Letter Sheet for Foreign Postage

1976, Jan. 16	Tagged	Photo.
UC50 UC20 22c **red & blue,** *blue,* entire	.90	.40
Entire, 1st day cancel, Tempe, Ariz. *(118,303)*		1.00
Die cutting reversed, entire	15.00	

"USA" — UC21

Printed by Bureau of Engraving and Printing. Designed by Soren Noring.

Letter Sheet for Foreign Postage

1978, Nov. 3	Tagged	Photo.
UC51 UC21 22c **blue,** *blue,* entire	.70	.25
Entire, 1st day cancel, St. Petersburg, Fla. *(86,099)*		1.00
Die cutting reversed, entire	25.00	

22nd OLYMPIC GAMES, MOSCOW, JULY 19-AUG. 3, 1980.

UC22

Design (multicolored in bottom left corner) shows discus thrower.

Printed by Bureau of Engraving and Printing. Designed by Robert M. Cunningham.

Letter Sheet for Foreign Postage

1979, Dec. 5	Tagged	Photo.
UC52 UC22 22c **red, black & green,** *bluish,* entire	1.50	.25
Entire, 1st day cancel, Bay Shore, N.Y.		1.00

"USA" — UC23

Design (brown on No. UC53, green and brown on No. UC54): lower left, Statue of Liberty. Inscribed "Tour the United States." Folding area shows tourist attractions.

Printed by Bureau of Engraving and Printing. Designed by Frank J. Waslick.

Letter Sheet for Foreign Postage

1980, Dec. 29	Tagged	Photo.
UC53 UC23 30c **blue, red & brown,** *blue,* entire	.65	.30
Entire, 1st day cancel, San Francisco, CA		1.25
Die cutting reversed, entire	20.00	
a. Red (30) omitted, entire	*70.00*	
Die cutting reversed, entire	—	

1981, Sept. 21	Tagged	Photo.
UC54 UC23 30c **yellow, magenta, blue & black,** *blue,* entire	.65	.30
Entire, 1st day cancel, Honolulu, HI		1.25
Die cutting reversed, entire	20.00	

UC24

Design: "Made in USA . . . world's best buys!" on flap, ship, tractor in lower left. Reverse folding area shows chemicals, jet silhouette, wheat, typewriter and computer tape disks. Printed by Bureau of Engraving and Printing.

Designed by Frank J. Waslick.

Letter Sheet for Foreign Postage

1982, Sept. 16	Tagged	Photo.
UC55 UC24 30c **multi,** *blue,* entire	.65	.30
Entire, 1st day cancel, Seattle, WA		1.25

WORLD COMMUNICATIONS YEAR

World Map Showing Locations of Satellite Tracking Stations — UC25

Design: Reverse folding area shows satellite, tracking station.
Printed by Bureau of Engraving and Printing.
Designed by Esther Porter.

Letter Sheet for Foreign Postage

1983, Jan. 7	Tagged	Photo.
UC56 UC25 30c **multi**, *blue*, entire	.65	.30
Entire, 1st day cancel, Anaheim, CA	1.25	
Die cutting reversed, entire	25.00	

1984 OLYMPICS

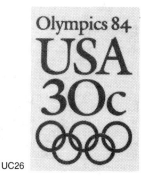

UC26

Design: Woman equestrian at lower left with montage of competitive events on reverse folding area.
Printed by the Bureau of Engraving & Printing.
Designed by Bob Peak.

Letter Sheet for Foreign Postage

1983, Oct. 14	Tagged	Photo.
UC57 UC26 30c **multi**, *blue*, entire	.65	.30
Entire, 1st day cancel, Los Angeles, CA	1.25	
Die cutting reversed, entire	—	

WEATHER SATELLITES, 25TH ANNIV.

Landsat Infrared and Thermal Mapping Bands — UC27

Design: Landsat orbiting the earth at lower left with three Landsat photographs on reverse folding area. Inscribed: "Landsat views the Earth."
Printed by the Bureau of Engraving & Printing.
Designed by Esther Porter.

Letter Sheet for Foreign Postage

1985, Feb. 14	Tagged	Photo.
UC58 UC27 36c **multi**, *blue*, entire	.70	.35
Entire, 1st day cancel, Goddard Flight Center, MD	1.35	
Die cutting reversed, entire	30.00	

NATIONAL TOURISM WEEK

Urban Skyline — UC28

Design: Inscribed "Celebrate America" at lower left and "Travel. . . the perfect freedom" on folding area. Skier, Indian chief, cowboy, jazz trumpeter and pilgrims on reverse folding area.
Printed by the Bureau of Engraving & Printing.
Designed by Dennis Luzak.

Letter Sheet for Foreign Postage

1985, May 21	Tagged	Photo.
UC59 UC28 36c **multi**, *blue*, entire	.70	.35
Entire, 1st day cancel, Washington, DC	1.35	
a. Black omitted, entire	—	

MARK TWAIN AND HALLEY'S COMET

Comet Tail Viewed from Space — UC29

Design: Portrait of Twain at lower left and inscribed "I came in with Halley's Comet in 1835. It is coming again next year, and I expect to go out with it. It will be the greatest disappointment of my life if I don't go out with Halley's Comet." "1835 . Mark Twain . 1910 . Halley's Comet . 1985" and Twain, Huckleberry Finn, steamboat and comet on reverse folding areas.
Printed by the Bureau of Engraving & Printing.
Designed by Dennis Luzak.

Letter Sheet for Foreign Postage

1985, Dec. 4	Tagged	Photo.
UC60 UC29 36c **multi**, entire	.70	.35
Entire, 1st day cancel, Hannibal, MO	1.35	
Die cutting reversed, entire	25.00	

UC30

Printed by the Bureau of Engraving & Printing.

Letter Sheet for Foreign Postage

1988, May 9	Litho.	Tagged
UC61 UC30 39c **multi**, entire	.80	.40
Entire, 1st day cancel, Miami, FL (27,446)	1.55	

MONTGOMERY BLAIR, POSTMASTER GENERAL 1861-64

Blair and Pres. Abraham Lincoln — UC31

Design: Mail bags and "Free city delivery," "Railway mail service" and "Money order system" at lower left. Globe, locomotive, bust of Blair, UPU emblem and "The Paris conference of 1863, initiated by Postmaster General Blair, led, in 1874, to the founding of the Universal Postal Union" contained on reverse folding area.
Printed by the Bureau of Engraving & Printing.
Designed by Ned Seidler.

Letter Sheet for Foreign Postage

1989, Nov. 20	Litho.	Tagged
UC62 UC31 39c **multicolored**, entire	.80	.40
Entire, 1st day cancel, Washington, DC	1.55	

UC32

Designed by Bradbury Thompson.
Printed by the Bureau of Engraving and Printing.

Letter Sheet for Foreign Postage

1991, May 17	Litho.	Tagged
UC63 UC32 45c **gray, red & blue**, *blue*, entire	.90	.45
a. White paper	.90	.45
Entire, 1st day cancel, Denver, CO (19,941)	1.35	

Thaddeus Lowe (1832-1913), Balloonist — UC33

Designed by Davis Meltzer.
Printed by the Bureau of Engraving & Printing.

Letter Sheet for Foreign Postage

1995, Sept. 23	Litho.	Tagged
UC64 UC33 50c **multicolored**, *blue*, entire	1.00	.50
Entire, 1st day cancel, Tampa, FL	1.25	

Voyageurs Natl. Park, Minnesota UC34

Designed by Phil Jordan.

Printed by Bureau of Engraving & Printing.

Letter Sheet for Foreign Postage

1999, May 15	Litho.	Tagged
UC65 UC34 60c **multicolored**, *blue*, entire	1.25	.65
Entire, 1st day cancel, Denver, CO	1.50	

OFFICIAL ENVELOPES & WRAPPERS

By the Act of Congress, January 31, 1873, the franking privilege of officials was abolished as of July 1, 1873 and the Postmaster General was authorized to prepare official envelopes. At the same time official stamps were prepared for all Departments. Department envelopes became obsolete July 5, 1884. After that, government offices began to use franked envelopes of varied design. These indicate no denomination and lie beyond the scope of this Catalogue.

Post Office Department

UO1

Numeral 9mm high.

UO2

Numeral 9mm high.

UO3

Numeral 9½mm high.

Printed by George H. Reay, Brooklyn, N.Y.

1873

UO1	UO1	2c	**black,** *lemon*	15.00	9.00
			Entire	22.50	12.50
UO2	UO2	3c	**black,** *lemon*	9.00	6.00
			Entire	17.50	9.00
+UO3	UO2	3c	**black**	20,000.	
			Entire	27,500.	
UO4	UO3	6c	**black,** *lemon*	17.50	15.00
			Entire	22.50	20.00

The No. UO3 entire is unique. It has a tear through the stamp that has been professionally repaired. Value based on auction sale in 1999.

UO4

Numeral 9¼mm high.

UO5

Numeral 9¼mm high.

UO6

Numeral 10½mm high.

Printed by Plimpton Manufacturing Co., Hartford, Conn.

1874-79

UO5	UO4	2c	**black,** *lemon*	6.00	4.00
			Entire	9.00	5.75
UO6	UO4	2c	**black**	70.00	32.50
			Entire	90.00	40.00
UO7	UO5	3c	**black,** *lemon*	3.00	.85
			Entire	4.00	1.50
UO8	UO5	3c	**black**	2,250.	1,000.
			Entire	3,000.	
UO9	UO5	3c	**black,** *amber*	45.00	35.00
			Entire	65.00	50.00
UO10	UO5	3c	**black,** *blue*	17,500.	
			Entire	27,500.	
UO11	UO5	3c	**blue,** *blue* ('75)	15,000.	
			Entire	22,500.	
UO12	UO6	6c	**black,** *lemon*	7.50	5.50
			Entire	14.00	10.00
UO13	UO6	6c	**black**	1,250.	1,000.
			Entire	2,000.	

Fakes exist of Nos. UO3, UO8 and UO13.

Postal Service

UO7

1877

UO14	UO7	**black**	6.00	3.75
		Entire	10.00	5.00
UO15	UO7	**black,** *amber*	52.50	27.50
		Entire	125.00	40.00
UO16	UO7	**blue,** *amber*	50.00	30.00
		Entire	125.00	45.00
UO17	UO7	**blue,** *blue*	8.00	6.00
		Entire	11.00	9.00

War Department

Franklin
UO8

Bust points to the end of "N" of "ONE".

Jackson
UO9

Bust narrow at the back.

Washington
UO10

Queue projects below the bust.

Lincoln
UO11

Neck very long at the back.

Jefferson
UO12

Queue forms straight line with bust.

Clay
UO13

Ear partly concealed by hair, mouth large, chin prominent.

Webster
UO14

Has side whiskers.

Scott
UO15

Hamilton
UO16

Back of bust very narrow; chin almost straight; the labels containing the letters "U S" are exactly parallel.

Printed by George H. Reay.

1873

UO18	UO8	1c	**dark red**	525.00	300.00
			Entire	900.00	325.00
UO19	UO9	2c	**dark red**	850.00	400.00
			Entire	1,100.	
UO20	UO10	3c	**dark red**	60.00	40.00
			Entire	85.00	60.00
UO21	UO10	3c	**dark red**, *amber*	20,000.	
			Entire	32,500.	
UO22	UO10	3c	**dark red**, *cream*	600.00	250.00
			Entire	750.00	300.00
UO23	UO11	6c	**dark red**	210.00	90.00
			Entire	300.00	150.00
UO24	UO11	6c	**dark red**, *cream*	3,000.	425.00
			Entire	4,500.	*2,000.*
UO25	UO12	10c	**dark red**	6,000.	1,500.
			Entire	*8,000.*	2,000.
UO26	UO13	12c	**dark red**	110.00	50.00
			Entire	150.00	—
UO27	UO14	15c	**dark red**	110.00	55.00
			Entire	140.00	*375.00*
UO28	UO15	24c	**dark red**	110.00	50.00
			Entire	150.00	*1,250.*
UO29	UO16	30c	**dark red**	425.00	150.00
			Entire	575.00	500.00

1873

UO30	UO8	1c	**vermilion**	140.00	
			Entire	300.00	
WO31	UO8	1c	**vermilion**, *manila*	12.50	12.50
			Entire	25.00	20.00
+UO32	UO9	2c	**vermilion**	400.00	
			Entire	*4,000.*	
WO33	UO9	2c	**vermilion**, *manila*	200.00	
			Entire	325.00	
UO34	UO10	3c	**vermilion**	70.00	40.00
			Entire	125.00	125.00
UO35	UO10	3c	**vermilion**, *amber*	80.00	
			Entire	225.00	
UO36	UO10	3c	**vermilion**, *cream*	16.00	12.50
			Entire	37.50	22.50
UO37	UO11	6c	**vermilion**	70.00	
			Entire	100.00	
+UO38	UO11	6c	**vermilion**, *cream*	450.00	
			Entire	*8,500.*	
UO39	UO12	10c	**vermilion**	250.00	
			Entire	350.00	
UO40	UO13	12c	**vermilion**	125.00	
			Entire	175.00	
UO41	UO14	15c	**vermilion**	210.00	
			Entire	2,750.	
UO42	UO15	24c	**vermilion**	375.00	
			Entire	500.00	
UO43	UO16	30c	**vermilion**	400.00	
			Entire	550.00	

UO17

Bottom serif on "S" is thick and short; bust at bottom below hair forms a sharp point.

UO18

Bottom serif on "S" is thick and short; front part of bust is rounded.

UO19

Bottom serif on "S" is short; queue does not project below bust.

UO20

Neck very short at the back.

UO21

Knot of queue stands out prominently.

UO22

Ear prominent, chin receding.

UO23

Has no side whiskers; forelock projects above head.

UO24

Back of bust rather broad; chin slopes considerably; the label containing letters "U S" are not exactly parallel.

Printed by Plimpton Manufacturing Co.

1875

UO44	UO17	1c	**red**	125.00	80.00
			Entire	150.00	150.00
+UO45	UO17	1c	**red,** amber	750.00	
+UO45A	UO17	1c	**red,** orange	37,500.	
WO46	UO17	1c	**red,** manila	4.00	2.75
			Entire	9.00	6.50
UO47	UO18	2c	**red**	90.00	
			Entire	125.00	
UO48	UO18	2c	**red,** amber	25.00	14.00
			Entire	35.00	25.00
UO49	UO18	2c	**red,** orange	45.00	13.50
			Entire	52.50	19.00
WO50	UO18	2c	**red,** manila	75.00	40.00
			Entire	150.00	—
UO51	UO19	3c	**red**	12.50	9.00
			Entire	15.00	15.00
UO52	UO19	3c	**red,** amber	14.00	9.00
			Entire	16.00	14.00
UO53	UO19	3c	**red,** cream	6.50	3.75
			Entire	9.00	6.50
UO54	UO19	3c	**red,** blue	3.50	2.75
			Entire	5.00	4.50
UO55	UO19	3c	**red,** fawn	4.50	2.75
			Entire	8.00	4.00
UO56	UO20	6c	**red**	40.00	30.00
			Entire	75.00	—
UO57	UO20	6c	**red,** amber	70.00	40.00
			Entire	80.00	
UO58	UO20	6c	**red,** cream	175.00	85.00
			Entire	200.00	
UO59	UO21	10c	**red**	150.00	80.00
			Entire	200.00	—
UO60	UO21	10c	**red,** amber	1,100.	
			Entire	1,500.	
UO61	UO22	12c	**red**	42.50	40.00
			Entire	125.00	250.00
UO62	UO22	12c	**red,** amber	625.00	
			Entire	750.00	
UO63	UO22	12c	**red,** cream	550.00	
			Entire	750.00	
UO64	UO23	15c	**red**	200.00	140.00
			Entire	240.00	—
UO65	UO23	15c	**red,** amber	900.00	
			Entire	1,000.	
UO66	UO23	15c	**red,** cream	700.00	
			Entire	900.00	
UO67	UO24	30c	**red**	160.00	140.00
			Entire	200.00	—
UO68	UO24	30c	**red,** amber	900.00	
			Entire	2,250.	
UO69	UO24	30c	**red,** cream	950.00	
			Entire	1,250.	

POSTAL SAVINGS ENVELOPES

Issued under the Act of Congress, approved June 25, 1910, in lieu of penalty or franked envelopes. Unused remainders, after October 5, 1914, were overprinted with the Penalty Clause. Regular stamped envelopes, redeemed by the Government, were also overprinted for official use.

UO25

1911

UO70	UO25	1c	**green**	60.00	20.00
			Entire	72.50	40.00
UO71	UO25	1c	**green,** oriental buff	190.00	67.50
			Entire	240.00	85.00
UO72	UO25	2c	**carmine**	11.00	3.75
			Entire	19.00	11.00
a.		2c	**carmine,** manila (error)	1,750.	—
			Entire	2,500.	850.00

Tagged

Envelopes from No. UO73 onward are tagged unless otherwise noted.

OFFICIAL MAIL

Great Seal — UO26

1983, Jan. 12			**Embossed**
UO73	UO26	20c **blue,** entire	1.25 30.00
		First day cancel, Washington, DC	1.00

UO27

1985, Feb. 26			**Embossed**
UO74	UO27	22c **blue,** entire	.90 5.00
		First day cancel, Washington, DC	1.00

UO28

1987, Mar. 2			**Typo.**
UO75	UO28	22c **blue,** entire	1.00 20.00
		First day cancel, Washington, DC	1.00

Used exclusively to mail U.S. Savings Bonds.

UO29

1988, Mar. 22   **Typo.**
UO76 UO29 (25c) **black & blue,** entire   1.10 20.00
  First day cancel, Washington,
  DC   1.25

Used exclusively to mail U.S. Savings Bonds.

UO30

UO31

1988, Apr. 11   **Typo. & Embossed**
UO77 UO30 25c **black & blue,** entire   .80 15.00
  First day cancel, Washington,
  DC   1.25
a. Denomination & lettering as on No.
       UO78, entire   —   —

Typo.
UO78 UO31 25c **black & blue,** entire   .90 25.00
  First day cancel, Washington,
  DC *(12,017)*   1.25
a. Denomination & lettering as on No.
       UO77, entire   —   —

No. UO78 used exclusively to mail U.S. Savings Bonds.
First day cancellations applied to 12,017 of Nos. UO77,
UO78.

Used Values
The appearance in the marketplace of postally
used examples of the entires used to mail passports (Nos. UO79-UO82, UO86-UO87) is so infrequent that it currently is not possible to establish
accurate values.

1990, Mar. 17   **Typo.**
Stars and "E Pluribus Unum" illegible. "Official" is 13mm,
"USA" is 16mm long.

UO79 UO31 45c **black & blue,** entire   1.25   —
  First day cancel, Springfield,
  VA *(5,956)*   1.50
UO80 UO31 65c **black & blue,** entire   1.75   —
  First day cancel, Springfield,
  VA *(6,922)*   2.25

Used exclusively to mail U.S. passports.

UO32

Stars and "E Pluribus Unum" clear and sharply printed. "Official" is 14½mm, "USA" is 17mm long.

1990, Aug. 10   **Litho.**
UO81 UO32 45c **black & blue,** entire   1.25   —
  First day cancel, Washington,
  DC *(7,160)*   1.50
UO82 UO32 65c **black & blue,** entire   1.60   —
  First day cancel, Washington,
  DC *(6,759)*   2.25

Used exclusively to mail U.S. passports.

Official Mail **F** **USA** For U.S. addresses only   UO33

1991, Jan. 22   **Typo.**   **Wmk.**
UO83 UO33 (29c) **black & blue,** entire   1.10 20.00
  First day cancel, Washington,
  DC *(30,549)*   1.25

Used exclusively to mail U.S. Savings Bonds.

UO34

1991, Apr. 6   **Wmk.**   **Litho. & Embossed**
UO84 UO34 29c **black & blue,** entire   .75 10.00
  First day cancel, Oklahoma
  City, OK *(27,841)*   1.25
  Entire, unwatermarked, *May 1,
  1992*   .75   —

Unwatermarked envelopes are on recycled paper, and have
an imprint under the flap.

UO35

1991, Apr. 17   **Typo.**   **Wmk.**
UO85 UO35 29c **black & blue,** entire   .70 20.00
  First day cancel, Washington,
  DC *(25,563)*   1.25
  Entire, unwatermarked, *May 1,
  1992*   .70   —

Used exclusively to mail U.S. Savings Bonds.
Unwatermarked envelopes are on recycled paper, and have an
imprint under the flap.

Consular Service,
Bicent. — UO36

Designed by Zebulon Rogers. Quotation from O. Henry on
flap.

1992, July 10   **Litho.**   **Unwmk.**
UO86 UO36 52c **blue & red,** entire   1.60   —
  First day cancel, Washington,
  DC *(30,374)*   2.25
UO87 UO36 75c **blue & red,** entire   3.00   —
  First day cancel, Washington,
  DC *(25,995)*   3.25

Used exclusively to mail U.S. passports.
Available only in 4⅞ inch x 8⅞ inch size with self-adhesive
flap.

UO37

1995-99   **Typo. & Embossed**   **Unwmk.**
UO88 UO37 32c **blue & red,** entire, *May 9,
  1995*   .80 10.00
  First day cancel, Washington,
  DC   1.25
UO89 UO37 33c **blue & red,** entire, *Feb. 22,
  1999*   .70   —
  First day cancel, Washington,
  DC   1.25

OFFICIAL WRAPPERS
Included in listings of Official Envelopes with
prefix letters WO instead of UO.

POSTAL CARDS

Values are for unused cards as sold by the Post Office, without printed or written address or message, and used cards with Post Office cancellation,
when current. Used cards with postage added to meet higher rates sell for less. Used cards for international rates are for proper usage. Those used
domestically sell for less.
The "Preprinted" values are for unused cards with printed or written address or message.
Starting with No. UX21, all postal cards have been printed by the Government Printing Office.
Nos. UX1-UX48 are typographed; others are lithographed (offset) unless otherwise stated.
Numerous printing varieties exist. Varieties of surcharged cards include (a) inverted surcharge at lower left, (b) double surcharge, one inverted at
lower left, (c) surcharge in other abnormal positions, including back of card. Such surcharge varieties command a premium.
Colored cancellations sell for more than black in some instances. **All values are for entire cards.**
As of Jan. 1, 1999, postal cards were sold individually for 1c over face value.

See Computer Vended Postage section for "Postal Buddy" cards.

Since 1875 it has been possible to purchase some postal cards in sheets for multiple printing, hence pairs, strips and blocks are available. Some sheets have been cut up so that cards exist with stamp inverted, in center of card, two on one card, in another corner, etc. These are only curiosities and of minimal value.

Liberty — PC1

Wmk. Large "U S P O D" in Monogram, (90x60mm)

1873   **Size: 130x76mm**
UX1   PC1 1c **brown**, *buff, May 13*   325.00   17.50
    Preprinted   55.00
    First day cancel, Boston, New
      York or Washington   3,500.

One card is known canceled May 12 in Springfield, Mass, another May 11 in Providence, R.I.

Wmk. Small "U S P O D" in Monogram, (53x36mm)

UX3   PC1 1c **brown**, *buff, July 6*   70.00   2.25
    Preprinted   20.00
a.   Without watermark   —

The watermarks on Nos. UX1, UX3 and UX4 are found in normal position, inverted, reversed, and inverted and reversed. They are often dim, especially on No. UX4.

No. UX3a is not known unused. Cards offered as such are either unwatermarked proofs, or have partial or vague watermarks. See No. UX65.

Liberty PC2

Inscribed: "WRITE THE ADDRESS . . ."

1875   Wmk. Small "U S P O D" in Monogram
UX4   PC2 1c **black**, *buff, Sept. 28*   2,000.   300.
    Preprinted   550.00

Unwmk.

UX5   PC2 1c **black**, *buff, Sept. 30*   60.00   .40
    Preprinted   6.00

For other postal card of type PC2 see No. UX7.

Liberty — PC3

1879, Dec. 1
UX6   PC3 2c **blue**, *buff*   25.00   17.50
    Preprinted   10.00
a. 2c **dark blue**, *buff*   30.00   19.00
    Preprinted   12.00

      See Nos. UX13 and UX16.

Design of PC2, Inscribed "NOTHING BUT THE ADDRESS."

1881, Oct. 17 (?)
UX7   PC2 1c **black**, *buff*   60.00   .35
    Preprinted   5.50
a. 23 teeth below "ONE CENT"   500.00   30.00
    Preprinted   165.00
b. Printed on both sides   575.00   400.00

Jefferson — PC4

1885, Aug. 24
UX8   PC4 1c **brown**, *buff*   45.00   1.25
    Preprinted   9.00
a. 1c **orange brown**, *buff*   45.00   1.25
    Preprinted   9.00
b. 1c **red brown**, *buff*   45.00   1.25
    Preprinted   9.00
c. 1c **chocolate**, *buff*   85.00   6.00
    Preprinted   20.00
d. Double impression   —
e. Double impression, one inverted   —
f. Printed on both sides   —

PC5

Head of Jefferson facing right, centered on card.

Grant — PC6

1886, Dec 1
UX9   PC5 1c **black**, *buff*   17.50   .55
    Preprinted   1.50
a. 1c **black**, *dark buff*   20.00   1.25
    Preprinted   5.00
b. Double impression   —
c. Double impression, one inverted   —

1891   **Size: 155x95mm**
UX10 PC6 1c **black**, *buff*   32.50   1.40
    Preprinted   6.00
a. Double impression, one inverted   —
b. Double impression   —

    Two types exist of No. UX10.
Earliest known use; Dec. 21.

Size: 117x75mm
UX11 PC6 1c **blue**, *grayish white*   12.50   2.50
    Preprinted   2.00
b. Double impression, one inverted   —

Cards printed in black instead of blue are invariably proofs. Earliest known use; Dec. 26.

PC7

Head of Jefferson facing left.
Small wreath and name below.
Size: 140x89mm

1894, Jan. 2
UX12 PC7 1c **black**, *buff*   35.00   .45
    Preprinted   2.00
a. Double impression   —

1897, Jan. 25   **Design of PC3**
          Size: 140x89mm
UX13 PC3 2c **blue**, *cream*   135.00   75.00
    Preprinted   70.00

PC8

Head same as PC7. Large wreath and name below.

1897, Dec. 1

Size: 139x82mm

UX14	PC8	1c **black,** *buff*	25.00	.40
		Preprinted	2.50	
a.		Double impression, one inverted	—	—
		Preprinted	—	
b.		Printed both sides	—	—
		Preprinted	—	
c.		Double impression	—	
		Preprinted	—	
d.		**Black,** *salmon pink,* preprinted		

John
Adams
PC9

1898

Size: 126x74mm

UX15	PC9	1c **black,** *buff,* Mar. 31	40.00	15.00
		Preprinted	11.00	

Design same as PC3, without frame around card.

Size: 140x82mm

UX16	PC3	2c **black,** *buff*	10.00	9.00
		Preprinted	5.00	

McKinley — PC10

1902

UX17	PC10	1c **black,** *buff*	4,500.	
		Preprinted	3,000.	2,500.

Earliest known use; May 27, 1902.

McKinley
PC11

1902

UX18	PC11	1c **black,** *buff*	12.00	.30
		Preprinted	1.60	

Earliest known use; July 14, 1902.
Two types exist of Nos. UX18-UX20.

McKinley — PC12

1907

UX19	PC12	1c **black,** *buff*	37.50	.50
		Preprinted	2.00	

Earliest known use; June 28, 1907.

Same design, correspondence space at left

1908, Jan. 2

UX20	PC12	1c **black,** *buff*	50.00	4.00
		Preprinted	7.50	

PC13

McKinley, background shaded.

1910

UX21	PC13	1c **blue,** *bluish*	90.00	6.50
		Preprinted	15.00	
a.		1c **bronze blue,** *bluish*	165.00	12.50
		Preprinted	25.00	
b.		Double impression	—	
		Preprinted	—	
c.		Triple impression	—	
d.		Double impression, one inverted	—	
e.		Four arcs above and below "IS" of inscription to left of stamp impression are pointed	1,000.	500.00
		Preprinted	750.00	

A No. UX21 card exists with Philippines No. UX11 printed on the back.

PC14

Same design, white background.

1910, Apr. 13

UX22	PC14	1c **blue,** *bluish*	13.00	.30
		Preprinted	1.50	
a.		Double impression	600.00	
b.		Triple impression	—	
c.		Triple impression, one inverted	—	

See No. UX24.

PC15

Head of Lincoln, solid background.

1911, Jan. 21

Size: 127x76mm

UX23	PC15	1c **red,** *cream*	8.00	5.50
		Preprinted	3.00	
a.		Triple impression	—	

See No. UX26.

Design same as PC14

1911, Aug. 10   **Size: 140x82mm**

UX24	PC14	1c **red,** *cream*	9.00	.30
		Preprinted	1.25	
a.		Double impression	—	
b.		Triple impression	—	

Grant — PC16

1911, Oct. 27

UX25	PC16	2c **red,** *cream*	1.25	8.50
		Preprinted	.65	
a.		Double impression	—	

For surcharge see No. UX36.

1913, July 29

Size: 127x76mm

UX26	PC15	1c **green,** *cream*	10.00	6.00
		Preprinted	2.50	

Jefferson — PC17

Die I-End of queue small, sloping sharply downward to right.

Die II (re-cut)-End of queue large and rounded.

1914-16

Size: 140x82mm

UX27	PC17 1c **green**, *buff*, die I, *June 4*	.25	.25
	Preprinted	.20	
a.	1c **green**, *cream*	3.50	.60
	Preprinted	1.25	
b.	Double impression	—	

On gray, rough surfaced card

UX27C	PC17 1c **green**, die I, *1916*	2,000.	150.00
	Preprinted	250.00	
UX27D	PC17 1c **dark green**, die II, *Dec. 22, 1916*	1,750.	125.00
	Preprinted	225.00	

For surcharges see Nos. UX39 and UX41.

Lincoln — PC19

1917, Mar. 14   **Size: 127x76mm**

UX28	PC19 1c **green**, *cream*	.60	.30
	Preprinted	.30	
a.	1c **green**, *dark buff*	1.50	.60
	Preprinted	.50	
b.	Double impression	—	
	Preprinted	—	

No. UX28 was printed also on light buff and canary.
See No. UX43. For surcharges see Nos. UX40 and UX42.

Jefferson — PC20

Die I - Rough, coarse impression. End of queue slopes sharply downward to right. Left basal ends of "2" form sharp points.

Size: 140x82mm

Die II - Clear fine lines in hair. Left basal ends of "2" form balls.

1917-18

UX29	PC20 2c **red**, *buff*, die I, *Oct. 22*	40.00	2.00
	Preprinted	6.50	
a.	2c **lake**, *cream*, die I	47.50	2.50
	Preprinted	9.00	
c.	2c **vermilion**, *buff*, die I	275.00	60.00
	Preprinted	70.00	
UX30	PC20 2c **red**, *cream*, die II, *Jan. 23, 1918*	27.50	1.50
	Preprinted	4.50	

2c Postal Cards of 1917-18 Revalued

Surcharged in one line by canceling machine at Washington, DC   **1 CENT**

1920, Apr.

UX31	PC20 1c on 2c **red**, *cream*, die II	3,500.	3,500.
	Preprinted	2,750.	

Surcharged in two lines by canceling machine (46 Types)   **1 CENT**

UX32	PC20 1c on 2c **red**, *buff*, die I	50.00	12.50
	Preprinted	15.00	
a.	1c on 2c **vermilion**, *buff*	95.00	60.00
b.	Double surcharge	—	82.50
UX33	PC20 1c on 2c **red**, *cream*, die II	12.00	1.90
	Preprinted	2.50	
a.	Inverted surcharge	55.00	
b.	Double surcharge	55.00	35.00
	Preprinted	35.00	
c.	Double surcharge, one inverted, preprinted	325.00	
d.	Triple surcharge	350.00	

Values for surcharge varieties of Nos. UX32 and UX33 are for cards having the surcharges *on the stamp.* Copies having the surcharge inverted in the lower left corner, either alone or in combination with a normal surcharge, exist in many of the 46 types.

Surcharged in Two Lines by Press Printing

1920

UX34	PC20 1c on 2c **red**, *buff*, die I	500.00	47.50
	Preprinted	100.00	
a.	Double surcharge	550.00	
UX35	PC20 1c 2c **red**, *cream*, die II	200.00	32.50
	Preprinted	50.00	

Surcharges were prepared from (a) special dies fitting International and Universal post office canceling machines (Nos. UX31-UX33), and (b) printing press dies (Nos. UX34-UX35). There are 38 canceling machine types on Die I, and 44 on Die II. There are two printing press types of each die.

UX36	PC16 1c on 2c **red**, *cream* (#UX25)		50,000.

Unused copies of No. UX36 (New York surcharge) were probably made by favor. Used copies of No. UX36 (Los Angeles surcharge, three to four examples used in Long Beach are recorded) are unquestionably authentic. Surcharges on other numbers exist, but their validity is doubtful.

McKinley — PC21

1926, Feb. 1

For International Use

UX37	PC21 3c **red**, *buff*	4.00	10.00
	Preprinted	1.75	
	First day cancel, Washington, DC		200.00
a.	3c **red**, *yellow*	4.00	11.00
	Preprinted	1.75	

Franklin — PC22

1951, Nov. 16

UX38	PC22 2c **carmine rose**, *buff*	.35	.25
	Preprinted	.25	
	First day cancel		1.00
a.	Double impression	200.00	

For surcharge see No. UX47.

Nos. UX27 and UX28 Surcharged by Canceling Machine at Left of Stamp in Light Green   **REVALUED 2¢ P. O. DEPT.**

1952

UX39	PC17 2c on 1c **green**, *buff*, *Jan. 1*	.50	.35
	Preprinted	.25	
	First day cancel, any city		12.00
a.	Surcharged vertically, reading down	7.50	8.50
	Preprinted	3.00	
b.	Double surcharge	17.50	20.00
UX40	PC19 2c on 1c **green**, *cream*, *Mar. 22*	.65	.45
	Preprinted	.40	
	First day cancel, Washington, D.C.		100.00
a.	Surcharged vertically, reading down	6.50	5.00
	Preprinted	4.00	

Nos. UX27 and UX28 with Similar Surcharge Typographed at Left of Stamp in Dark Green.

1952

UX41	PC17 2c on 1c **green**, *buff*	4.50	1.75
	Preprinted	1.75	
a.	Inverted surcharge at lower left	75.00	125.00
	Preprinted	50.00	
UX42	PC19 2c on 1c **green**, *cream*	5.00	2.50
	Preprinted	3.00	
a.	Surcharged by offset lithography	5.00	2.50
b.	Surcharged on back	80.00	

Type of 1917

1952, July 31   **Size: 127x76mm**

UX43	PC19 2c **carmine**, *buff*	.30	*1.00*
	Preprinted	.20	
	First day cancel		1.00

Torch and Arm of Statue of Liberty — PC23

Fifth International Philatelic Exhibition (FIPEX), New York City, Apr. 28-May 6, 1956.

1956, May 4

UX44	PC23 2c **deep carmine & dark violet blue**, *buff*	.25	*1.00*
	First day cancel, New York, NY *(537,474)*		1.00
a.	2c **lilac rose & dark violet blue**, *buff*	1.50	1.00
b.	Dark violet blue omitted	450.00	225.00
c.	Double impression of dark violet blue	16.00	10.00

Statue of Liberty
PC24   PC25

For International Use

1956, Nov. 16

UX45	PC24 4c **deep red & ultramarine**, *buff*	1.50	40.00
	First day cancel, New York, NY *(129,841)*		1.00

See No. UY16.

1958, Aug. 1

UX46	PC25 3c **purple**, *buff*	.50	.20
	First day cancel, Philadelphia, Pa. *(180,610)*		1.00
a.	"N GOD WE TRUST"	15.00	25.00
b.	Double impression	—	

c.   Precanceled with 3 printed purple
    lines, *1961*   3.75   2.50
d.   Indicia omitted (inscription normal)   —

On No. UX46c, the precanceling lines are incorporated with the design. The earliest known postmark on this experimental card is Sept. 15, 1961.
See No. UY17.

ONE CENT ADDITIONAL PAID

No. UX38 Surcharged by Canceling Machine at Left of Stamp in Black

1958
UX47 PC22 2c + 1c **carmine rose,** *buff*   185.00 250.00

The surcharge was applied to 750,000 cards for the use of the General Electric Co., Owensboro, Ky. A variety of the surcharge shows the D of PAID beneath the N of ADDITIONAL. All known examples of No. UX47 have a printed advertisement on the back and a small punch hole near lower left corner.
No. UX47 exists with inverted surcharge at lower left. Value, $450.
Used value is for commercially used card.

Lincoln — PC26

1962, Nov. 19
Precanceled with 3 printed red violet lines
UX48 PC26 4c **red violet**   .25   .20
     First day cancel, Springfield, IL
     (162,939)   1.00
a.   Tagged, *June 25, 1966*   .50   .20
     First day cancel, Bellevue, OH

No. UX48a was printed with luminescent ink.
See note on Luminescence in "Information for Collectors."
See No. UY18.

Used values are for contemporaneous usage without additional postage applied. Used values for international-rate cards are for proper usage.

Map of Continental United States — PC27

Designed by Suren H. Ermoyan

For International Use
1963, Aug. 30
UX49 PC27 7c **blue & red**   3.75 *35.00*
     First day cancel, New York, NY   1.00
a.   Blue omitted   —

First day cancellation was applied to 270,464 of Nos. UX49 and UY19. See Nos. UX54, UX59, UY19-UY20.

Flags and Map of U.S. — PC28

175th anniv. of the U.S. Customs Service.

Designed by Gerald N. Kurtz

1964, Feb. 22
Precanceled with 3 printed blue lines
UX50 PC28 4c **red & blue**   .50 *1.00*
     First day cancel, Washington,
     DC *(313,275)*   1.00
a.   Blue omitted   625.00
b.   Red omitted   —

Americans "Moving Forward" (Street Scene) — PC29

Issued to publicize the need to strengthen the US Social Security system. Released in connection with the 15th conf. of the Intl. Social Security Association at Washington, DC.

Designed by Gerald N. Kurtz

1964, Sept. 26
Precanceled with a blue and 2 red printed lines
UX51 PC29 4c **dull blue & red**   .40 *1.00*
     First day cancel, Washington,
     D.C. *(293,650)*   1.00
a.   Red omitted   —
b.   Blue omitted   750.00

Coast Guard Flag — PC30

175th anniv. of the U.S. Coast Guard.

Designed by Muriel R. Chamberlain

1965, Aug. 4
Precanceled with 3 printed red lines
UX52 PC30 4c **blue & red**   .30 *1.00*
     First day cancel, Newburyport,
     Mass. *(338,225)*   1.00
a.   Blue omitted   —

Crowd and Census Bureau Punch Card — PC31

Designed by Emilio Grossi

1965, Oct. 21
Precanceled with 3 bright blue printed lines
UX53 PC31 4c **bright blue & black**   .30 *1.00*
     First day cancel, Philadelphia, Pa.
     (275,100)   1.00

Map Type of 1963
For International Use

1967, Dec. 4
UX54 PC27 8c **blue & red**   3.75 *35.00*
     First day cancel, Washington,
     DC   1.00

First day cancellation was applied to 268,077 of Nos. UX54 and UY20.

U. S. POSTAGE

Lincoln — PC33

Designed by Robert J. Jones

Luminescent Ink

1968, Jan. 4
Precanceled with 3 printed green lines
UX55 PC33 5c **emerald**   .30 *.50*
     First day cancel, Hodgenville, Ky.   1.00
a.   Double impression   —

First day cancellation was applied to 274,000 of Nos. UX55 and UY21.

Woman Marine, 1968, and Marines of Earlier Wars — PC34

25th anniv. of the Women Marines.

Designed by Muriel R. Chamberlain

1968, July 26
UX56 PC34 5c **rose red & green**   .35 *1.00*
     First day cancel, San Francisco,
     Cal. *(203,714)*   1.00

Tagged
Postal cards from No. UX57 onward are either tagged or printed with luminescent ink unless otherwise noted.

Weather Vane — PC35

Centenary of the Army's Signal Service, the Weather Services (Weather Bureau).

Designed by Robert Geissmann

1970, Sept. 1
UX57 PC35 5c **blue, yellow, red & black**   .30   *1.00*
     First day cancel, Fort Myer,
     Va. *(285,800)*   1.00
a.   Yellow & black omitted   700.00 850.00
b.   Blue omitted   650.00
c.   Black omitted   600.00

Paul Revere — PC36

Issued to honor Paul Revere, Revolutionary War patriot.

Designed by Howard C. Mildner after statue near Old North Church, Boston

1971, May 15
Precanceled with 3 printed brown lines
UX58 PC36 6c **brown** .30 *1.00*
    First day cancel, Boston,
    Mass. *1.00*
    a. Double impression *300.00*

First day cancellation was applied to 340,000 of Nos. UX58 and UY22.

Map Type of 1963
For International Use
1971, June 10
UX59 PC27 10c **blue & red** 4.00 *35.00*
    First day cancel, New York, NY *1.00*

First day cancellation was applied to 297,000 of Nos. UX59 and UXC11.

New York Hospital, New York City — PC37

Issued as a tribute to America's hospitals in connection with the 200th anniversary of New York Hospital.

Designed by Dean Ellis

1971, Sept. 16
UX60 PC37 6c **blue & multicolored** .30 *1.00*
    First day cancel, New York,
    NY *(218,200)* *1.00*
    a. Blue & yellow omitted *700.00*

U.S. POSTAGE 6 CENTS
U.S.F. Constellation — PC38

U.S. POSTAGE 6 CENTS
Monument Valley
PC39

United States postal cards can be mounted in the Scott U.S. Postal Cards album.

Gloucester, Mass.
PC40 **U.S. POSTAGE 6 CENTS**

Tourism Year of the Americas.

Designed by Melbourne Brindle

1972, June 29
                Size: 152½x108½mm
UX61 PC38 6c **black,** *buff* (Yosemite, Mt.
    Rushmore, Niagara Falls,
    Williamsburg on back) .85 *3.00*
    a. Address side blank *300.00*
    First day cancel, any city *1.00*
UX62 PC39 6c **black,** *buff* (Monterey, Red-
    woods, Gloucester, U.S.F.
    Constellation on back) .40 *3.00*
    First day cancel, any city *1.00*
UX63 PC40 6c **black,** *buff* (Rodeo, Missis-
    sippi Riverboat, Grand Can-
    yon, Monument Valley on
    back) .40 *3.00*
    First day cancel, any city *1.00*
    Nos. UX61-UX63,UXC12-UXC13 (5) 2.80 *32.00*

Nos. UX61-UX63, UXC12-UXC13 went on sale throughout the United States. They were sold as souvenirs without postal validity at Belgica Philatelic Exhibition in Brussels and were displayed at the American Embassies in Paris and Rome. This is reflected in the first day cancel.

Varieties of the pictorial back printing include: black omitted (UX62), black and pale salmon omitted (UX63), and back inverted in relation to address side (UX63).

John Hanson — PC41

Designed by Thomas Kronen after statue by Richard Edwin Brooks in Maryland Capitol

1972, Sept. 1
Precanceled with 3 printed blue lines.
UX64 PC41 6c **blue** .25 *1.00*
    First day cancel, Baltimore, MD *1.00*
    a. Coarse paper .25 *1.00*

Liberty Type of 1873
Centenary of first U.S. postal card.

1973, Sept. 14
UX65 PC1 6c **magenta** .25 *1.00*
    First day cancel, Washington, D.C.
    (289,950) *1.00*

Samuel Adams — PC42

Designed by Howard C. Mildner

1973, Dec. 16
Precanceled with 3 printed orange lines
UX66 PC42 8c **orange** .25 *1.00*
    First day cancel, Boston, Mass.
    (147,522) *1.00*
    a. Coarse paper .25 *1.00*

Visit USA
Bicentennial
Era

USA
Postage
12c

Ship's Figurehead,
1883 — PC43

Design is after a watercolor by Elizabeth Moutal of the oak figurehead by John Rogerson from the barque Edinburgh.

1974, Jan. 4
For International Use
UX67 PC43 12c **multicolored** .35 *30.00*
    First day cancel, Miami, Fla.
    (138,500) *1.00*

Charles Thomson — PC44

John Witherspoon — PC45

Caesar Rodney — PC46

Designed by Howard C. Mildner

1975-76
Precanceled with 3 printed emerald lines
UX68 PC44 7c **emerald,** *Sept. 14, 1975* .30 *5.00*
    First day cancel, Bryn Mawr, Pa. *1.00*
Precanceled with 3 printed brown lines
UX69 PC45 9c **yellow brown,** *Nov. 10, 1975* .25 *1.00*
    First day cancel, Princeton, N.J. *1.00*
Precanceled with 3 printed blue lines
UX70 PC46 9c **blue,** *July 1, 1976* .25 *1.00*
    First day cancel, Dover, Del. *1.00*
    a. Double impression —

First day cancellation applied to 231,919 of Nos. UX68 and UY25; 254,239 of Nos. UX69 and UY26; 304,061 of Nos. UX70 and UY27.

Federal Court House,
Galveston,
Texas — PC47 HISTORIC PRESERVATION

The Court House, completed in 1861, is on the National Register of Historic Places.

Designed by Donald Moss

1977, July 20
UX71 PC47 9c **multicolored** .25 *1.00*
    First day cancel, Galveston, Tex.
    (245,535) 1.00

Nathan Hale — PC48

Designed by Howard C. Mildner

1977, Oct. 14
    Precanceled with 3 printed green lines
UX72 PC48 9c **green** .25 *1.00*
    First day cancel, Coventry,
    Conn. 1.00
  a. Cent sign missing after "9" 110.00
First day cancellation applied to 304,592 of Nos. UX72 and UY28.

Cincinnati Music Hall — PC49

Centenary of Cincinnati Music Hall, Cincinnati, Ohio.

Designed by Clinton Orlemann

1978, May 12
UX73 PC49 10c **multicolored** .30 *1.00*
    First day cancel, Cincinnati, O.
    (300,000) 1.00

John Hancock — PC50

Designed by Howard Behrens

1978
    Precanceled with 3 printed brown orange lines.
UX74 PC50 (10c) **brown orange,** *May 19* .30 *1.00*
    First day cancel, Quincy, Mass.
    (299,623) 1.00
    Inscribed "U.S. Postage 10¢"
UX75 PC50 10c **brown orange,** *June 20* .30 .20
    First day cancel, Quincy, Mass.
    (187,120) 1.00

Coast Guard Cutter Eagle — PC51

Designed by Carl G. Evers

For International Use

1978, Aug. 4
UX76 PC51 14c **multicolored** .40 *15.00*
    First day cancel, Seattle, Wash.
    (196,400) 1.00

Molly Pitcher Firing Cannon at Monmouth — PC52

Bicentennial of Battle of Monmouth, June 28, 1778, and to honor Molly Pitcher (Mary Ludwig Hays).

Designed by David Blossom

1978, Sept. 8 Litho.
UX77 PC52 10c **multicolored** .30 *1.00*
    First day cancel, Freehold, N.J.
    (180,280) 1.00

Clark and his Frontiersmen Approaching Fort Sackville — PC53

Bicentenary of capture of Fort Sackville from the British by George Rogers Clark.

Designed by David Blossom

1979, Feb. 23 Litho.
UX78 PC53 10c **multicolored** .30 *1.00*
    First day cancel, Vincennes, Ind. 1.00

Gen. Casimir Pulaski — PC54

Bicentenary of the death of Gen. Casimir Pulaski (1748-1779), Polish nobleman who served in American Revolutionary Army.

1979, Oct. 11 Litho.
UX79 PC54 10c **multicolored** .30 *1.00*
    First day cancel, Savannah, GA
    (210,000) 1.00

Olympic Games Issue

Sprinter PC55

22nd Olympic Games, Moscow, July 19-Aug. 3, 1980.

Designed by Robert M. Cunningham

1979, Sept. 17 Litho.
UX80 PC55 10c **multicolored** .60 *1.00*
    First day cancel, Eugene, Ore. 1.00

Iolani Palace, Honolulu — PC56

1979, Oct. 1 Litho.
UX81 PC56 10c **multicolored** .30 *1.00*
    First day cancel, Honolulu, HI
    (242,804) 1.00

Women's Figure Skating PC57

13th Winter Olympic Games, Lake Placid, N.Y., Feb. 12-24.

Designed by Robert M. Cunningham

For International Use

1980, Jan. 15 Litho.
UX82 PC57 14c **multicolored** .60 *10.00*
    First day cancel, Atlanta, GA
    (160,977) 1.00

Salt Lake Temple, Salt Lake City — PC58

1980, Apr. 5 Litho.
UX83 PC58 10c **multicolored** .25 *1.00*
    First day cancel, Salt Lake City,
    UT *(325,260)* 1.00

Landing of Rochambeau, 1780

Rochambeau's Fleet — PC59

Count Jean-Baptiste de Rochambeau's landing at Newport, R.I. (American Revolution) bicentenary.

Designed by David Blossom

1980, July 11   **Litho.**
UX84 PC59 10c **multicolored**   .25 *1.00*
First day cancel, Newport, R.I.   *1.00*
(180,567)
a.   Front normal, black & yellow on back   —

Battle of Kings Mountain, 1780

Whig Infantrymen — PC60

Bicentenary of the Battle of Kings Mountain (American Revolution).

Designed by David Blossom

1980, Oct. 7   **Litho.**
UX85 PC60 10c **multicolored**   .25 *1.00*
First day cancel, Kings Mountain,   *1.00*
NC *(136,130)*

Drake's Golden Hinde 1580

Golden Hinde — PC61

300th anniv. of Sir Francis Drake's circumnavigation (1578-1580).

Designed by Charles J. Lundgren

For International Use

1980, Nov. 21
UX86 PC61 19c **multicolored**   .65 *10.00*
First day cancel, San Rafael, CA   *1.00*
(290,547)

Battle of Cowpens, 1781

Cols. Washington and Tarleton — PC62

Bicentenary of the Battle of Cowpens (American Revolution).

Designed by David Blossom

1981, Jan. 17
UX87 PC62 10c **multicolored**   .25 *2.50*
First day cancel, Cowpens, SC   *1.00*
(160,000)

Eagle — PC63

1981, Mar. 15
    Precanceled with 3 printed violet lines
UX88 PC63 (12c) **violet**   .30 *.50*
First day cancel, Memphis, TN   *1.00*
See No. 1818, FDC section.

Isaiah Thomas — PC64

Designed by Chet Jezierski

1981, May 5   **Precanceled with 3 printed lines**
UX89 PC64 12c **light blue**   .30 *.50*
First day cancel, Worcester, MA   *1.00*
(185,610)

Nathanael Greene, Eutaw Springs, 1781

PC65

Bicentenary of the Battle at Eutaw Springs (American Revolution)

Designed by David Blossom

1981, Sept. 8   **Litho.**
UX90 PC65 12c **multicolored**   .30 *1.00*
First day cancel, Eutaw Springs,   *1.00*
SC *(115,755)*
a.   Red & yellow omitted   —

Lewis and Clark Expedition, 1806

PC66

Designed by David Blossom

1981, Sept. 23
UX91 PC66 12c **multicolored**   .30 *3.00*
First day cancel, Saint Louis, MO   *1.00*

Robert Morris — PC67

1981
    Precanceled with 3 printed lines
UX92 PC67 (13c) **buff,** *Oct. 11*   .30 *.50*
First day cancel, Memphis, TN   *1.00*
See No. 1946, FDC section.

    Inscribed: U.S. Postage 13¢
UX93 PC67 13c **buff,** *Nov. 10*   .30 *.50*
First day cancel, Philadelphia, PA   *1.00*

"Swamp Fox" Francis Marion, 1782

General Francis Marion (1732?-1795) — PC68

Designed by David Blossom

1982, Apr. 3   **Litho.**
UX94 PC68 13c **multicolored**   .30 *.75*
First day cancel, Marion, SC   *1.00*
(141,162)

La Salle claims Louisiana, 1682

Rene Robert Cavelier, Sieur de la Salle (1643-1687) — PC69

Designed by David Blossom

1982, Apr. 7   **Litho.**
UX95 PC69 13c **multicolored**   .30 *.75*
First day cancel, New Orleans,   *1.00*
LA

PC70

Designed by Melbourne Brindle

1982, June 18   **Litho.**
UX96 PC70 13c **brown, red & cream,** *buff*   .30 *.75*
First day cancel, Philadelphia, PA   *1.00*
a.   Brown & cream omitted   —

PC71

Historic Preservation

Designed by Clint Orlemann

1982, Oct. 14   **Litho.**
UX97   PC71   13c **multicolored**   .30   *.75*
     First day cancel, St. Louis, MO   1.00

Landing of Oglethorpe, Georgia, 1733
Gen. Oglethorpe Meeting Chief Tomo-Chi-Chi of the Yamacraw — PC72

Designed by David Blossom

1983, Feb. 12   **Litho.**
UX98   PC72   13c **multicolored**   .30   *.75*
     First day cancel, Savannah, GA
     (165,750)   1.00

Old Post Office, Washington, D.C.   PC73

Designed by Walter Brooks

1983, Apr. 19   **Litho.**
UX99   PC73   13c **multicolored**   .30   *.75*
     First day cancel, Washington,
     DC *(125,056)*   1.00

Olympics 84, Yachting — PC74

Designed by Bob Peak

1983, Aug. 5   **Litho.**
UX100   PC74   13c **multicolored**   .30   *.75*
     First day cancel, Long Beach,
     CA *(132,232)*   1.00
   a.   Black, yellow & red omitted   —

The Ark and the Dove — PC75

Designed by David Blossom

1984, Mar. 25   **Litho.**
UX101   PC75   13c **multicolored**   .30   *.75*
     First day cancel, St. Clement's
     Island, MD *(131,222)*   1.00

Runner Carrying Olympic Torch — PC76

Designed by Robert Peak

1984, Apr. 30   **Litho.**
UX102   PC76   13c **multicolored**   .30   *.75*
     First day cancel, Los Angeles,
     CA *(110,627)*   1.00
   a.   Black & yellow inverted   —

Father Baraga and Indian Guide in Canoe — PC77

Designed by David Blossom

1984, June 29   **Litho.**
UX103   PC77   13c **multicolored**   .30   *.75*
     First day cancel, Marquette, MI
     (100,156)   1.00

Dominguez Adobe at Rancho San Pedro — PC78

Designed by Earl Thollander

1984, Sept. 16   **Litho.**
UX104   PC78   13c **multicolored**   .30   *.75*
     First day cancel, Compton, CA
     (100,545)   1.00
   a.   Black & blue omitted   —

Charles Carroll (1737-1832) — PC79

Designed by Richard Sparks

1985
    Precanceled with 3 printed lines
UX105   PC79   (14c)   **pale green,** *Feb. 1*   .30   *.50*
     First day cancel, New Carroll-
     ton, MD   1.00
    Inscribed: USA 14
UX106   PC79   14c   **pale green,** *Mar. 6*   .45   *.25*
     First day cancel, Annapolis, MD   1.00

Clipper Flying Cloud — PC80

Designed by Richard Schlecht

For International Use

1985, Feb. 27   **Litho.**
UX107   PC80   25c **multicolored**   .70   *5.00*
     First day cancel, Salem, MA
     (95,559)   1.25

   No. UX107 was sold by the USPS at CUP-PEX 87, Perth, Western Australia, with a cachet honoring CUP-PEX 87 and the America's Cup race.

George Wythe (1726-1806) — PC81

Designed by Chet Jezierski from a portrait by John Fergusson.

1985, June 20
    Precanceled with 3 printed lines
UX108   PC81   14c **bright apple green**   .30   *.50*
     First day cancel, Williamsburg,
     VA   1.00

Arrival of Thomas Hooker and Hartford Congregation — PC82

Settlement of Connecticut, 350th Anniv.

Designed by David Blossom

1986, Apr. 18   Litho.
UX109 PC82 14c **multicolored**   .30 .75
   First day cancel, Hartford, CT
   (76,875)   1.00

Stamps The Universal Hobby USA 14
Stamp Collecting — PC83

Designed by Ray Ameijide

1986, May 23   Litho.
UX110 PC83 14c **multicolored**   .30 .75
   First day cancel, Chicago, IL
   (75,548)   1.00
   No. UX110 was sold by the USPS at "najubria 86" with a
show cachet.

Francis Vigo, Vincennes, 1779
Francis Vigo (1747-1836) — PC84

Designed by David Blossom

1986, May 24   Litho.
UX111 PC84 14c **multicolored**   .30 .75
   First day cancel, Vincennes, IN
   (100,141)   1.00

Settling of Rhode Island, 1636
Roger Williams (1603-1683), Clergyman, Landing at
Providence — PC85

Settling of Rhode Island, 350th Anniv.

Designed by David Blossom

1986, June 26   Litho.
UX112 PC85 14c **multicolored**   .30 .75
   First day cancel, Providence, RI
   (54,559)   1.00

Wisconsin Territory, 1836
Miners, Shake Rag Street Housing — PC86

Wisconsin Territory Sesquicentennial.

Designed by David Blossom

1986, July 3   Litho.
UX113 PC86 14c **multicolored**   .30 .75
   First day cancel, Mineral Point,
   WI (41,224)   1.00

National Guard Heritage, 1636-1986
The First Muster, by Don Troiani — PC87

Designed by Bradbury Thompson

1986, Dec. 12   Litho.
UX114 PC87 14c **multicolored**   .30 .75
   First day cancel, Boston, MA
   (72,316)   1.00

Self-scouring steel plow, 1837
PC88

   The self-scouring steel plow invented by blacksmith John
Deere in 1837 pictured at lower left.

Designed by William H. Bond

1987, May 22   Litho.
UX115 PC88 14c **multicolored**   .30 .50
   First day cancel, Moline, IL
   (160,009)   1.00

Constitutional Convention, 1787
Convening of the Constitutional Convention,
1787 — PC89

   George Mason, Gouverneur Morris, James Madison, Alexander Hamilton and Charles C. Pinckney are listed in the lower
left corner of the card.

Designed by David K. Stone

1987, May 25   Litho.
UX116 PC89 14c **multicolored**   .30 .50
   First day cancel, Philadelphia, PA
   (138,207)   1.00

Stars and
Stripes — PC90
USA 14

Designed by Steven Dohanos

1987, June 14   Litho.
UX117 PC90 14c **black, blue & red**   .30 .50
   First day cancel, Baltimore, MD   1.00
   No. UX117 was sold by the USPS at Cologne, Germany, with
a cachet for Philatelia '87.

Take Pride in America 14 USA
Take Pride in America — PC91

Designed by Lou Nolan

1987, Sept. 22   Litho.
UX118 PC91 14c **multicolored**   .30 .50
   First day cancel, Jackson, WY
   (47,281)   1.00

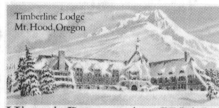

Historic Preservation USA 14
Timberline Lodge, 50th Anniversary — PC92

Designed by Walter DuBois Richards

1987, Sept. 28   Litho.
UX119 PC92 14c **multicolored**   .30 .50
   First day cancel, Timberline, OR
   (63,595)   1.00

America the Beautiful USA 15
American Buffalo and Prairie — PC93

Designed by Bart Forbes

1988, Mar. 28   Litho.
UX120 PC93 15c **multicolored**   .30 .50
   First day cancel, Buffalo, WY
   (52,075)   1.00
   a.   Black omitted   —
   b.   Printed on both sides   850.00
   c.   Front normal, blue & black on back   500.00
   d.   Black & magenta omitted   825.00
   e.   Black, yellow, blue & tagging omitted   —

Tagged
   **Postal cards from No. UX57 onward are either
tagged or printed with luminescent ink unless otherwise noted.**

Blair House USA 15
PC94

Designed by Pierre Mion

1988, May 4 Litho.
UX121 PC94 15c **multicolored** .30 .50
   First day cancel, Washington, DC
   (52,188) 1.00

Yorkshire, Squarerigged Packet — PC95

Inscribed: Yorkshire, Black Ball Line, Packet Ship, circa 1850 at lower left.

Designed by Richard Schlect

For International Use

1988, June 29 Litho.
UX122 PC95 28c **multicolored** .60 3.00
   First day cancel, Mystic, CT
   (46,505) 1.00
  a. Black & blue omitted 850.00

Harvesting Corn Fields — PC96

Iowa Territory Sesquicentennial.

Designed by Greg Hargreaves

1988, July 2 Litho.
UX123 PC96 15c **multicolored** .30 .50
   First day cancel, Burlington, IA
   (45,565) 1.00

Flatboat Ferry Transporting Settlers Down the Ohio River — PC97

Bicentenary of the settlement of Ohio, the Northwest Territory. Design at lower left shows map of the eastern United States with Northwest Territory highlighted.

Designed by James M. Gurney and Susan Sanford

1988, July 15 Litho.
UX124 PC97 15c **multicolored** .30 .50
   First day cancel, Marietta,
   OH (28,778) 1.00
  a. Black, blue yellow omitted 825.00
  a. Black, magenta & tagging omitted —

PC98

Designed by Robert Reynolds

1988, Sept. 20 Litho.
UX125 PC98 15c **multicolored** .30 .50
   First day cancel, San Simeon,
   CA (84,786) 1.00
  a. Black & magenta omitted —

The Federalist Papers, 1787-88
Pressman, New Yorker Reading Newspaper, 1787 — PC99

Designed by Roy Andersen

1988, Oct. 27 Litho.
UX126 PC99 15c **multicolored** .30 .50
   First day cancel, New York, NY
   (37,661) 1.00

Red-tailed Hawk and Sonora Desert at Sunset — PC100

Designed by Bart Forbes

1989, Jan. 13 Litho.
UX127 PC100 15c **multicolored** .30 .50
   First day cancel, Tucson, AZ
   (51,891) 1.00

Healy Hall, Georgetown University — PC101

Designed by John Morrell. Inscription at lower left: "Healy Hall / Georgetown / Washington, DC / HISTORIC PRESERVATION."

1989, Jan. 23 Litho.
UX128 PC101 15c **multicolored** .30 .50
   First day cancel, Washington,
   DC (54,897) 1.00

Great Blue Heron, Marsh — PC102

Designed by Bart Forbes

1989, Mar. 17 Litho.
UX129 PC102 15c **multicolored** .30 .50
   First day cancel, Okefenokee,
   GA (58,208) 1.00

Settling of Oklahoma — PC103

Designed by Bradbury Thompson

1989, Apr. 22 Litho.
UX130 PC103 15c **multicolored** .30 .50
   First day cancel, Guthrie, OK
   (68,689) 1.00

Used values are for contemporaneous usage without additional postage applied. Used values for international-rate cards are for proper usage.

Canada Geese and Mountains — PC104

Designed by Bart Forbes

1989, May 5 Litho. **For Use to Canada**
UX131 PC104 21c **multicolored** .40 3.00
   First day cancel, Denver, CO
   (59,303) 1.25

Seashore — PC105

Designed by Bart Forbes

1989, June 17 Litho.
UX132 PC105 15c **multicolored** .30 .50
   First day cancel, Cape Hatteras, NC (67,073) 1.00

PC106

Designed by Bart Forbes

1989, Aug. 26 Litho.
UX133 PC106 15c **multicolored** .30 .50
   First day cancel, Cherokee, NC
   (67,878) 1.00

Jane Addams' Hull House Community Center 1889,
Chicago — PC107

Designed by Michael Hagel

1989, Sept. 16   **Litho.**
UX134 PC107 15c **multicolored**   .30   .50
          First day cancel, Chicago, IL
          (53,773)   1.00

America the Beautiful   USA 15

Aerial View of Independence Hall,
Philadelphia — PC108

Designed by Bart Forbes

1989, Sept. 25   **Litho.**
UX135 PC108 15c **multicolored**   .30   .50
          First day cancel, Philadelphia,
          PA (61,659)   1.00
          See No. UX139.

America the Beautiful   USA 15

Inner Harbor, Baltimore — PC109

Designed by Bart Forbes

1989, Oct. 7   **Litho.**
UX136 PC109 15c **multicolored**   .30   .50
          First day cancel, Baltimore, MD
          (58,746)   1.00
          See No. UX140.

America the Beautiful   USA 15

59th Street Bridge, New York City — PC110

Designed by Bart Forbes

1989, Nov. 8   **Litho.**
UX137 PC110 15c **multicolored**   .30   .50
          First day cancel, New York, NY
          (48,044)   1.00
          See No. UX141.

America the Beautiful   USA 15

West Face of the Capitol, Washington
D.C. — PC111

Designed by Bart Forbes

1989, Nov. 26   **Litho.**
UX138 PC111 15c **multicolored**   .30   .50
          First day cancel, Washington,
          DC   1.00
          See No. UX142.

1989, Dec. 1   **Litho.**

Designed by Bart Forbes. Issued in sheets of 4 + 2 inscribed
labels picturing 20th UPU Congress or World Stamp Expo '89
emblems, and rouletted 9½ on 2 or 3 sides.
UX139 PC108 15c **multicolored**   3.25   .90
          First day cancel, Washington,
          DC   1.00
UX140 PC109 15c **multicolored**   3.25   .90
          First day cancel, Washington,
          DC   1.00
UX141 PC110 15c **multicolored**   3.25   .90
          First day cancel, Washington,
          DC   1.00
UX142 PC111 15c **multicolored**   3.25   .90
          First day cancel, Washington,
          DC   1.00
     a.   Sheet of 4, #UX139-UX142   13.00
          Nos. UX135-UX142 (8)   14.20 5.60
Unlike Nos. UX135-UX138, Nos. UX139-UX142 do not contain inscription and copyright symbol at lower left. Order on
sheet is Nos. UX140, UX139, UX142, UX141.
Many copies of No. UX142a and UX139 are bent at the
upper right corner.

The White House — PC112

Jefferson Memorial — PC113

Designed by Pierre Mion. Space for message at left.

1989   **Litho.**
UX143 PC112 15c **multicolored**, Nov. 30   1.00   1.00
          First day cancel, Washington,
          DC   2.00
UX144 PC113 15c **multicolored**, Dec. 2   1.00   1.00
          First day cancel, Washington,
          DC   2.00
Nos. UX143-UX144 sold for 50c each. Illustrations of the
buildings without denominations are shown on the back of the
card

Rittenhouse Paper Mill, Germantown, PA — PC114

Designed by Harry Devlin.

1990, Mar. 13   **Litho.**
UX145 PC114 15c **multicolored**   .30   .30
          First day cancel, New York, NY
          (9,866)   1.00

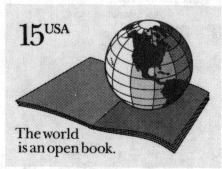

World Literacy Year — PC115

Designed by Joe Brockert.

1990, Mar. 22   **Litho.**
UX146 PC115 15c **multicolored**   .30   .50
          First day cancel, Washington,
          DC (11,163)   1.00

PC116

Designed by Bradbury Thompson. Inscription in upper left
corner: "Fur Traders Descending the Missouri / George Caleb
Bingham, 1845 / Metropolitan Museum of Art".

1990, May 4   **Litho.**
UX147 PC116 15c **multicolored**   1.00   1.00
          First day cancel, St. Louis, MO
          (13,632)   2.00
No. UX147 sold for 50c and shows more of the painting
without the denomination on the back.

PC117

Designed by Frank Constantino. Inscription at lower left:
"HISTORIC PRESERVATION SERIES / Isaac Royall House,
1700s / Medford, Massachusetts / National Historic Landmark".

1990, June 16   **Litho.**
UX148 PC117 15c **multicolored**   .30   .50
          First day cancel, Medford, MA
          (21,708)

Quadrangle, Stanford University — PC119

Designed by Jim M'Guinness.

1990, Sept. 11   **Litho.**
UX150 PC119 15c **multicolored**   .30   .50
     First day cancel, Stanford, CA
     (28,430)   1.00

Constitution Hall, Washington, DC — PC120

Designed by Pierre Mion. Inscription at upper left: "Washington: Constitution Hall (at right)/ Memorial Continental Hall (reverse side) / Centennial, Daughters of the American Revolution".

1990, Oct. 11   **Litho.**
UX151 PC120 15c **multicolored**   1.00 1.00
     First day cancel, Washington,
     DC *(33,254)*   2.00

No. UX151 sold for 50c.

Chicago Orchestra Hall — PC121

Designed by Michael Hagel. Inscription at lower left: "Chicago: Orchestra Hall / HISTORIC PRESERVATION / Chicago Symphony Orchestra / Centennial, 1891-1991".

1990, Oct. 19   **Litho.**
UX152 PC121 15c **multicolored**   .30   .50
     First day cancel, Chicago, IL
     (28,546)   1.00

PC122

Designed by Richard Sheaff.

1991, Jan. 24   **Litho.**
UX153 PC122 19c **rose, ultramarine & black**   .40   .50
     First day cancel, Washington,
     DC *(26,690)*   1.00

Carnegie Hall Centennial 1991
PC123

Designed by Howard Koslow.

1991, Apr. 1   **Litho.**
UX154 PC123 19c **multicolored**   .40   .50
     First day cancel, New York, NY
     (27,063)   1.00

Old Red, University of Texas Medical Branch, Galveston, Cent. — PC124

Designed by Don Adair.

1991, June 14   **Litho.**
UX155 PC124 19c **multicolored**   .40   .50
     First day cancel, Galveston,
     TX *(24,308)*   1.00

Ratification of the Bill of Rights, Bicent. — PC125

Designed by Mark Zaref.

1991, Sept. 25   **Litho.**
UX156 PC125 19c **red, blue & black**   .40   .50
     First day cancel, Richmond,
     VA *(27,457)*   1.00

Main Building, University of Notre Dame PC126

Designed by Frank Costantino. Inscription at lower left: Notre Dame / Sesquicentennial / 1842-1992.

1991, Oct. 15   **Litho.**
UX157 PC126 19c **multicolored**   .40   .50
     First day cancel, Notre Dame,
     IN *(34,325)*   1.00

America the Beautiful   USA 30
Niagara Falls — PC127

Designed by Wendell Minor.

1991, Aug. 21   **Litho.**
     For Use to Canada & Mexico
UX158 PC127 30c **multicolored**   .75 1.40
     First day cover, Niagara Falls,
     NY *(29,762)*   1.25

Tagged
Postal cards from No. UX57 onward are either tagged or printed with luminescent ink unless otherwise noted.

The Old Mill — PC128

Designed by Harry Devlin. Inscription at lower left: The Old Mill / University of Vermont / Bicentennial.

1991, Oct. 29   **Litho.**
UX159 PC128 19c **multicolored**   .40   .50
     First day cancel, Burlington,
     VT *(23,965)*   1.00

Wadsworth Atheneum, Hartford, CT — PC129

Designed by Frank Costantino. Inscription at lower left: Wadsworth Atheneum / Hartford, Connecticut / 150th Anniversary / 1842-1992.

1992, Jan. 16   **Litho.**
UX160 PC129 19c **multicolored**   .40   .50
     First day cancel, Hartford, CT
     (41,499)   1.00

Cobb Hall, University of Chicago — PC130

Designed by Michael P. Hagel. Inscription at lower left: Cobb Hall / The University of Chicago / Centennial Year, 1991-1992.

1992, Jan. 23   **Litho.**
UX161 PC130 19c **multicolored**   .40   .50
     First day cancel, Chicago, IL
     (27,150)   1.00

Waller Hall, Willamette University — PC131

Designed by Bradbury Thompson. Inscription at lower left: Waller Hall / Salem, Oregon / Willamette University / Sesquicentennial / 1842-1992.

1992, Feb. 1　　　　　　　　　　　**Litho.**
UX162 PC131 19c **multicolored**　　　.40　*.50*
　　First day cancel, Salem, OR
　　(28,463)　　　　　　　　　　　1.00

PC132

Designed by Dennis Simon. Space for message at left. Inscription at upper left: "At right: The Reliance, USA 1903 / Reverse: The Ranger, USA 1937."

1992, May 6　　　　　　　　　　　**Litho.**
UX163 PC132 19c **multicolored**　　1.00　*1.75*
　　First day cancel, San Diego,
　　CA *(19,944)*　　　　　　　　　2.00

　　No. UX163 sold for 50 cents.

PC133

Designed by Ken Hodges.

1992, May 9　　　　　　　　　　　**Litho.**
UX164 PC133 19c **multicolored**　　.40　*.50*
　　First day cancel, Stevenson,
　　WA *(32,344)*　　　　　　　　　1.00

Ellis Island Immigration Museum — PC134

Designed by Howard Koslow. Inscription at lower left: "Ellis Island / Centennial 1992."

1992, May 11　　　　　　　　　　**Litho.**
UX165 PC134 19c **multicolored**　　.40　*.50*
　　First day cancel, Ellis Island,
　　NY *(38,482)*　　　　　　　　　1.00

PC135

Designed by Howard Koslow.

1993, Jan. 6　　　　　　　　　　　**Litho.**
UX166 PC135 19c **multicolored**　　.40　*.50*
　　First day cancel, Washington,
　　DC *(8,315)*　　　　　　　　　　1.00

Wren Building, College of William & Mary
PC136

Designed by Pierre Mion.

1993, Feb. 8　　　　　　　　　　　**Litho.**
UX167 PC136 19c **multicolored**　　.40　*.50*
　　First day cancel, Williamsburg,
　　VA *(9,758)*　　　　　　　　　　1.00

Opening of Holocaust Memorial Museum — PC137

Designed by Tom Engeman. Space for message at left. Inscription at upper left: "Washington, DC: / United States / Holocaust Memorial Museum."

1993, Mar. 23　　　　　　　　　　**Litho.**
UX168 PC137 19c **multicolored**　　1.00　*1.75*
　　First day cancel, Washington,
　　DC *(8,234)*　　　　　　　　　　2.00

　　No. UX168 sold for 50c, and shows aerial view of museum on the back.

PC138

Designed by Michael Hagel.

1993, June 13　　　　　　　　　　**Litho.**
UX169 PC138 19c **multicolored**　　.40　*.50*
　　First day cancel, Fort Recov-
　　ery, OH *(8,254)*　　　　　　　1.00

University of North Carolina Bicentennial
PC139

Designed by Robert Timberlake.

1993, Sept. 14　　　　　　　　　　**Litho.**
UX170 PC139 19c **multicolored**　　.40　*.50*
　　First day cancel, Chapel Hill,
　　NC *(7,796)*　　　　　　　　　　1.00

PC140

Designed by Frank Constantino.

1993, Sept. 17　　　　　　　　　　**Litho.**
UX171 PC140 19c **multicolored**　　.40　*.50*
　　First day cancel, Worcester,
　　MA *(4,680)*　　　　　　　　　　1.00

PC141

Designed by Michael Hagel.

1993, Oct. 9　　　　　　　　　　　**Litho.**
UX172 PC141 19c **multicolored**　　.40　*.50*
　　First day cancel, Jacksonville,
　　IL *(5,269)*　　　　　　　　　　1.00

Massachusetts Hall • Bowdoin College • Brunswick, Maine
PC142

Designed by Harry Devlin.

1993, Oct. 14　　　　　　　　　　**Litho.**
UX173 PC142 19c **multicolored**　　.40　*.50*
　　First day cancel, Brunswick,
　　ME　　　　　　　　　　　　　　　1.00

PC143

Designed by Michael Hagel.

1994, Feb. 12 Litho.
UX174 PC143 19c **multicolored** .40 .50
　　　First day cancel, Springfield, IL
　　　(26,164) 1.00

PC144

Designed by Michael Hagel.

1994, Mar. 11 Litho.
UX175 PC144 19c **multicolored** .40 .50
　　　First day cancel, Springfield,
　　　OH (20,230) 1.00

PC145

Designed by William Matthews.

1994, Aug. 11 Litho.
UX176 PC145 19c **multicolored** .40 .50
　　　First day cancel, Chinle, AZ
　　　(19,826) 1.00

St. Louis Union Station — PC146

Designed by Harry Devlin.

1994, Sept. 3 Litho.
UX177 PC146 19c **multicolored** .40 .50
　　　First day cancel, St. Louis, MO
　　　(38,881) 1.00

Legends of the West Type
Designed by Mark Hess.

1994, Oct. 18 Litho.
UX178 A2197 19c Home on the Range .70 2.50
UX179 A2197 19c Buffalo Bill .70 2.50
UX180 A2197 19c Jim Bridger .70 2.50
UX181 A2197 19c Annie Oakley .70 2.50
UX182 A2197 19c Native American Culture .70 2.50

UX183 A2197 19c Chief Joseph .70 2.50
UX184 A2197 19c Bill Pickett (revised) .70 2.50
UX185 A2197 19c Bat Masterson .70 2.50
UX186 A2197 19c John Fremont .70 2.50
UX187 A2197 19c Wyatt Earp .70 2.50
UX188 A2197 19c Nellie Cashman .70 2.50
UX189 A2197 19c Charles Goodnight .70 2.50
UX190 A2197 19c Geronimo .70 2.50
UX191 A2197 19c Kit Carson .70 2.50
UX192 A2197 19c Wild Bill Hickok .70 2.50
UX193 A2197 19c Western Wildlife .70 2.50
UX194 A2197 19c Jim Beckwourth .70 2.50
UX195 A2197 19c Bill Tilghman .70 2.50
UX196 A2197 19c Sacagawea .70 2.50
UX197 A2197 19c Overland Mail .70 2.50
　　　Nos. UX178-UX197 (20) 14.00
　　　First day cancel, #UX178-UX197, any
　　　card, Tucson, AZ, Lawton, OK or
　　　Laramie, WY (10,000 USPS est.) 1.50

Nos. UX178-UX197 sold in packages of 20 different for $7.95.

Red Barn — PC147

Designed by Wendell Minor.

1995, Jan. 3 Litho.
UX198 PC147 20c **multicolored** .40 .40
　　　First day cancel, Williams-
　　　burg, PA 1.00

First day cancellation was applied to 54,102 of Nos. U632, UX198.

PC148

1995 Litho.
UX199 PC148 (20c) **black, blue & red** .60 .40

No. UX199 was only available through the Philatelic Fullfillment Center after its announcement 1/12/95. Cards submitted for first day cancels received a 12/13/94 cancel, even though they were not available on that date.

Civil War Types
Designed by Mark Hess.

1995, June 29 Litho.
UX200 A2289 20c Monitor & Virginia .90 2.50
UX201 A2289 20c Robert E. Lee .90 2.50
UX202 A2289 20c Clara Barton .90 2.50
UX203 A2289 20c Ulysses S. Grant .90 2.50
UX204 A2289 20c Battle of Shiloh .90 2.50
UX205 A2289 20c Jefferson Davis .90 2.50
UX206 A2289 20c David Farragut .90 2.50
UX207 A2289 20c Frederick Douglass .90 2.50
UX208 A2289 20c Raphael Semmes .90 2.50
UX209 A2289 20c Abraham Lincoln .90 2.50
UX210 A2289 20c Harriet Tubman .90 2.50
UX211 A2289 20c Stand Watie .90 2.50
UX212 A2289 20c Joseph E. Johnston .90 2.50
UX213 A2289 20c Winfield Hancock .90 2.50
UX214 A2289 20c Mary Chesnut .90 2.50
UX215 A2289 20c Battle of Chancellorsville .90 2.50
UX216 A2289 20c William T. Sherman .90 2.50
UX217 A2289 20c Phoebe Pember .90 2.50
UX218 A2289 20c Stonewall Jackson .90 2.50
UX219 A2289 20c Battle of Gettysburg .90 2.50
　　　Nos. UX200-UX219 (20) 18.00
　　　First day cancel, any card,
　　　Gettysburg, PA 1.50
　　　First day cancel, any card,
　　　any other city 1.50

Nos. UX200-UX219 sold in packages of 20 different for $7.95.

PC148a

1995, Aug. 24 Litho.
UX219A PC148a 50c **multicolored** 1.00 2.00
　　　First day cancel, St. Louis,
　　　MO (6,008) 1.25

PC149

Designed by Richard Sheaff.

1995, Sept. 3 Litho.
UX220 PC149 20c **multicolored** .40 .40
　　　First day cancel, Hunt Valley,
　　　MD 1.00

Comic Strip Types
Designed by Carl Herrman.

1995, Oct. 1 Litho.
UX221 A2313 20c The Yellow Kid .70 2.50
UX222 A2313 20c Katzenjammer Kids .70 2.50
UX223 A2313 20c Little Nemo in Slumberland .70 2.50
UX224 A2313 20c Bringing Up Father .70 2.50
UX225 A2313 20c Krazy Kat .70 2.50
UX226 A2313 20c Rube Goldberg's Inventions .70 2.50
UX227 A2313 20c Toonerville Folks .70 2.50
UX228 A2313 20c Gasoline Alley .70 2.50
UX229 A2313 20c Barney Google .70 2.50
UX230 A2313 20c Little Orphan Annie .70 2.50
UX231 A2313 20c Popeye .70 2.50
UX232 A2313 20c Blondie .70 2.50
UX233 A2313 20c Dick Tracy .70 2.50
UX234 A2313 20c Alley Oop .70 2.50
UX235 A2313 20c Nancy .70 2.50
UX236 A2313 20c Flash Gordon .70 2.50
UX237 A2313 20c Li'l Abner .70 2.50
UX238 A2313 20c Terry and the Pirates .70 2.50
UX239 A2313 20c Prince Valiant .70 2.50
UX240 A2313 20c Brenda Starr Reporter .70 2.50
　　　Nos. UX221-UX240 (20) 14.00
　　　First day cancel, any card,
　　　Boca Raton, FL 1.50

Nos. UX221-UX240 sold in packages of 20 different for $7.95.

Winter Scene — PC150

1996, Feb. 23 Litho.
UX241 PC150 20c **multicolored** .40 .40
　　　First day cancel, Watertown,
　　　NY (11,764) 1.00

Summer Olympics Type
Designed by Richard Waldrep.

1996, May 2　　　　　　　　　　　　Litho.
Size: 150x108mm

UX242	A2368	20c	Men's cycling	.80 2.50
UX243	A2368	20c	Women's diving	.80 2.50
UX244	A2368	20c	Women's running	.80 2.50
UX245	A2368	20c	Men's canoeing	.80 2.50
UX246	A2368	20c	Decathlon (javelin)	.80 2.50
a.			Inverted impression of entire address side, men's cycling picture on reverse	—
UX247	A2368	20c	Women's soccer	.80 2.50
UX248	A2368	20c	Men's shot put	.80 2.50
UX249	A2368	20c	Women's sailboarding	.80 2.50
UX250	A2368	20c	Women's gymnastics	.80 2.50
UX251	A2368	20c	Freestyle wrestling	.80 2.50
UX252	A2368	20c	Women's softball	.80 2.50
UX253	A2368	20c	Women's swimming	.80 2.50
UX254	A2368	20c	Men's sprints	.80 2.50
UX255	A2368	20c	Men's rowing	.80 2.50
UX256	A2368	20c	Beach volleyball	.80 2.50
UX257	A2368	20c	Men's basketball	.80 2.50
UX258	A2368	20c	Equestrian	.80 2.50
UX259	A2368	20c	Men's gymnastics	.80 2.50
UX260	A2368	20c	Men's swimming	.80 2.50
UX261	A2368	20c	Men's hurdles	.80 2.50
a.			Booklet of 20 postal cards, #UX242-UX261	20.00
			First day cancel, any card, Washington, DC	1.50

First day cancels of Nos. UX242-UX261 were available as sets from the US Postal Service. Unused sets of Nos. UX242-UX261 were not available from the US Philatelic Fullfillment Center for several months after the "official" first day.

St. John's College, Annapolis, Maryland
PC151

Designed by Harry Devlin.

1996, June 1　　　　　　　　　　　Litho.
UX262	PC151	20c	multicolored	.40 .40
			First day cancel, Annapolis, MD (8,793)	1.00

PRINCETON UNIVERSITY • 250TH ANNIVERSARY
PC152

Designed by Howard Koslow.

1996, Sept. 20　　　　　　　　　　Litho.
UX263	PC152	20c	multicolored	.40 .40
			First day cancel, Princeton, NJ (11,621)	1.00

Endangered Species Type
Designed by James Balog.

1996, Oct. 2　　　　　　　　　　　Litho.
UX264	A2403	20c	Florida panther	1.25 1.25
UX265	A2403	20c	Black-footed ferret	1.25 1.25
UX266	A2403	20c	American crocodile	1.25 1.25
UX267	A2403	20c	Piping plover	1.25 1.25
UX268	A2403	20c	Gila trout	1.25 1.25
UX269	A2403	20c	Florida manatee	1.25 1.25
UX270	A2403	20c	Schaus swallowtail butterfly	1.25 1.25
UX271	A2400	20c	Woodland caribou	1.25 1.25
UX272	A2403	20c	Thick-billed parrot	1.25 1.25
UX273	A2403	20c	San Francisco garter snake	1.25 1.25
UX274	A2403	20c	Ocelot	1.25 1.25
UX275	A2403	20c	Wyoming toad	1.25 1.25
UX276	A2403	20c	California condor	1.25 1.25
UX277	A2403	20c	Hawaiian monk seal	1.25 1.25
UX278	A2403	20c	Brown pelican	1.25 1.25
a.			Booklet of 15 cards, #UX264-UX278	20.00
			First day cancel, #UX264-UX278, any card, San Diego, CA (5,000)	1.75

Nos. UX264-UX278 were issued bound three-to-a-page in a souvenir booklet that was sold for $11.95.

Love (Swans) Type
Designed by Supon Design.

1997, Feb. 4　　　　　　　　　　　Litho.
UX279	A2415	20c	multicolored	.80 .80

Stamp Designs Depicted on Reverse of Card
Scott 2814	.80	.80
Scott 2815	.80	.80
Scott 3123	.80	.80
Scott 3124	.80	.80
Sheet of 4, #2814-2815, 3123-2134	3.25	
Scott 2202	.80	.80
Scott 2248	.80	.80
Scott 2440	.80	.80
Scott 2813	.80	.80
Sheet of 4, #2202, 2248, 2440, 2813	3.25	

No. UX279 was sold in sets of 3 sheets of 4 picture postal cards with 8 different designs for $6.95. The cards are separated by microperfs. The picture side of each card depicted a previously released Love stamp design without the inscriptions and value.

First day cancels were not available on Feb. 4. It was announced after Feb. 4 that collectors could purchase the cards and send them to the U.S.P.S. for First Day cancels.

The City College of New York ★ CUNY ★ 150TH ANNIVERSARY
PC153

Designed by Howard Koslow.

1997, May 7　　　　　　　　　　　Litho.
UX280	PC153	20c	multicolored	.40 .40
			First day cancel, New York, NY (9,576)	1.00

Bugs Bunny Type
Designed by Warner Bros.

1997, May 22　　　　　　　　　　Litho.
UX281	A2425	20c	multicolored	1.20 1.75
			First day cancel, Burbank, CA	1.75
a.			Booklet of 10 cards	12.00

No. UX281a sold for $5.95.

Golden Gate in Daylight
PC154

Golden Gate at Sunset
PC155

Designed by Carol Simowitz.

1997, June 2　　　　　　　　　　Litho.
UX282	PC154	20c	multicolored, June 2	.40 .40
			First day cancel, San Francisco, CA	1.00
UX283	PC155	50c	multicolored, June 3	1.00 1.00
			First day cancel, San Francisco, CA	2.00

First day cancellation was applied to 21,189 of Nos. UX282-UX283.

PC156

Designed by Richard Sheaff.

1997, Sept. 7　　　　　　　　　　Litho.
UX284	PC156	20c	multicolored	.40 .40
			First day cancel, Baltimore, MD (9,611)	1.00

Similar to Types A2451-A2455 with 20c Denomination
Designed by Derry Noyes.

1997, Sept. 30　　　　　　　　　　Litho.
UX285	A2451	20c	Phantom of the Opera	.60 .60
UX286	A2452	20c	Dracula	.60 .60
UX287	A2453	20c	Frankenstein's Monster	.60 .60
UX288	A2454	20c	The Mummy	.60 .60
UX289	A2455	20c	The Wolf Man	.60 .60
a.			Booklet of 20 cards, 4 each #UX285-UX289	12.00
			First day cancel, #UX285-UX289, any card, Universal City, CA	1.75

Nos. UX285-UX289 were issued bound in a booklet of 20 cards containing four of each card. Booklet was sold in package for $5.95.

The Lyceum, University of Mississippi, Oxford
PC157

Designed by Howard Paine.

1998, Apr. 20　　　　　　　　　　Litho.
UX290	PC157	20c	multicolored	.40 .40
			First day cancel, University, MS (22,276)	1.00

Similar to Sylvester & Tweety with 20c Denomination
Designed by Brenda Guttman.

1998, Apr. 27　　　　　　　　　　Litho.
UX291	A2487	20c	multicolored	1.20 1.75
			First day cancel, New York, NY	1.75
a.			Booklet of 10 cards	12.00

No. UX291a sold for $5.95.

Girard College Philadelphia, PA 1848-1998
PC158

Designed by Phil Jordan.

1998, May 1　　　　　　　　　　　Litho.
UX292	PC158	20c	multicolored	.40 .40
			First day cancel, Philadelphia, PA (13,853)	1.00

Similar to Tropical Birds with 20c Denomination and No Inscription
Designed by Phil Jordan.

1998, July 29 — Litho.

UX293	A2503	20c Antillean euphonia	.70 .70
UX294	A2504	20c Green-throated carib	.70 .70
UX295	A2505	20c Crested honeycreeper	.70 .70
UX296	A2506	20c Cardinal honeyeater	.70 .70
a.		Booklet of 20 cards, 5 ea #UX293-UX296	14.00
		First day cancel, #UX293-UX296, any card, Ponce PR	1.75

Nos. UX293-UX296 were issued bound in a booklet of 20 cards containing five of each card. Illustration of the stamp without denomination is shown on the back of each card. Booklet was sold in packages for $6.95.

American Ballet Type
Designed by Derry Noyes.

1998, Sept. 16 — Litho.

UX297	A2517	20c multicolored	1.25 1.25
a.		Booklet of 10 cards	12.50
		First day cancel, New York, NY	1.75

No. UX297a was sold for $5.95.

PC159

Designed by Richard Sheaff.

1998, Oct. 3 — Litho.

UX298	PC159	20c multicolored	.40 .40
		First day cancel, Boston, MA (14,812)	1.00

Brandeis University Usen Castle PC160

Designed by Richard Sheaff.

1998, Oct. 17 — Litho.

UX299	PC160	20c multicolored	.40 .40
		First day cancel, Waltham, MA (14,137)	1.00

Love Type
Designed by John Grossman, Holly Sudduth

1999, Jan. 28 — Litho.

UX300	A2537	20c multicolored	.70 .70

No. UX300 was sold in packs containing 5 sheets of 4 cards for $6.95.

University of Wisconsin-Madison • Bascom Hill PC161

Designed by Carl Herrman.

1999, Feb. 5 — Litho.

UX301	PC161	20c multicolored	.40 .40
		First day cancel, Madison, WI	1.00

PC162

Designed by Derry Noyes.

1999, Feb. 11 — Litho.

UX302	PC162	20c multicolored	.40 .40
		First day cancel, Lexington, VA	1.00

PC163

Designed by Richard Sheaff.

1999, Mar. 11 —

UX303	PC163	20c red & black	.40 .40
		First day cancel, Newport, RI	1.00

Daffy Duck Type
Designed by Ed Wieczyk.

1999, Apr. 16 — Litho.

UX304	A2554	20c multicolored	1.40 1.40
		First day cancel, Los Angeles, CA	1.40
a.		Booklet of 10 cards	14.00

No. UX304a sold for $6.95.

PC164

Designed by Richard Sheaff.

1999, May 14 — Litho.

UX305	PC164	20c multicolored	.40 .40
		First day cancel, Mount Vernon, VA	1.00

Block Island Lighthouse — PC165

Designed by Derry Noyes.

1999, July 24 — Litho.

UX306	PC165	20c multicolored	.40 .40
		First day cancel, Block Island, RI	1.00

Famous Trains Type
Designed by Howard Paine.

1999, Aug. 26 — Litho.

UX307	A2583	20c Super Chief	.70 .70
UX308	A2582	20c Hiawatha	.70 .70
UX309	A2579	20c Daylight	.70 .70
UX310	A2580	20c Congressional	.70 .70
UX311	A2581	20c 20th Century Limited	.70 .70
a.		Booklet of 20 cards, 4 ea #UX307-UX311	14.00
		First day cancel, #UX307-UX311, any card, Cleveland, OH	1.75
		First day cancel, #UX307-UX311, any card, any other city	1.75

Nos. UX307-UX311 were issued bound in a booklet of 20 cards containing four of each card. Booklet sold for $6.95.

UNIVERSITY OF UTAH PC166

Designed by Ethel Kessler.

2000, Feb. 28 — Litho.

UX312	PC166	20c multicolored	.40 .40
		First day cancel, Salt Lake City, UT	1.00

PC167 Ryman Auditorium, Nashville, Tennessee

Designed by Richard Sheaff.

2000, Mar. 18 — Litho.

UX313	PC167	20c multicolored	.40 .40
		First day cancel, Nashville, TN	1.00

Road Runner & Wile E. Coyote Type
Designed by Ed Wleczyk, Warner Bros.

2000, Apr. 26 — Litho.

UX314	A2622	20c multicolored	1.40 1.40
		First day cancel, Phoenix, AZ	1.40
a.		Booklet of 10 cards	14.00

No. UX314a sold for $6.95.

Adoption Type
Designed by Greg Berger.

2000, May 10 — Litho.

UX315	A2628	20c multicolored	1.40 1.40
		First day cancel, Beverly Hills, CA	1.40
a.		Booklet of 10 cards	14.00

No. UX315a sold for $6.95. The design, without denominations, is shown on the back of the card.

Old Stone Row, Middlebury College, Vermont PC168

Designed by Howard Paine.

2000, May 19   Litho.

UX316 PC168 20c **multicolored**   .40 .40
          First day cancel, Middlebury,
          VT   1.00

Stars and Stripes Type

Designed by Richard Sheaff.

2000, June 14   Litho.

UX317	A2633	20c	Sons of Liberty Flag, 1775	.90	.90
UX318	A2633	20c	New England Flag, 1775	.90	.90
UX319	A2633	20c	Forster Flag, 1775	.90	.90
UX320	A2633	20c	Continental Colors, 1776	.90	.90
a.			Sheet of 4 cards, #UX317-UX320	3.75	
UX321	A2633	20c	Francis Hopkinson Flag, 1777	.90	.90
UX322	A2633	20c	Brandywine Flag, 1777	.90	.90
UX323	A2633	20c	John Paul Jones Flag, 1779	.90	.90
UX324	A2633	20c	Pierre L'Enfant Flag, 1783	.90	.90
a.			Sheet of 4 cards, #UX321-UX324	3.75	
UX325	A2633	20c	Indian Peace Flag, 1803	.90	.90
UX326	A2633	20c	Easton Flag, 1814	.90	.90
UX327	A2633	20c	Star-Spangled Banner, 1814	.90	.90
UX328	A2633	20c	Bennington Flag, c. 1820	.90	.90
a.			Sheet of 4 cards, #UX325-UX328	3.75	
UX329	A2633	20c	Great Star Flag, 1837	.90	.90
UX330	A2633	20c	29-Star Flag, 1847	.90	.90
UX331	A2633	20c	Fort Sumter Flag, 1861	.90	.90
UX332	A2633	20c	Centennial Flag, 1876	.90	.90
a.			Sheet of 4 cards, #UX329-UX332	3.75	
UX333	A2633	20c	38-Star Flag, 1877	.90	.90
UX334	A2633	20c	Peace Flag, 1891	.90	.90
UX335	A2633	20c	48-Star Flag, 1912	.90	.90
UX336	A2633	20c	50-Star Flag, 1960	.90	.90
a.			Sheet of 4 cards, #UX333-UX336	3.75	
			First day cancel, any card, Baltimore, MD		.90
			Nos. UX317-UX336 (#)	•	•

Nos. UX320a, UX324a, UX328a, UX332a and UX336a were sold together in a package for $8.95. Microperforations are between individual cards on each sheet. Illustrations of the flags, without denominations, are shown on the back of the cards.

Legends of Baseball Type

Designed by Phil Jordan.

2000, July 6   Litho.

UX337	A2638	20c	Jackie Robinson	.90	.90
UX338	A2638	20c	Eddie Collins	.90	.90
UX339	A2638	20c	Christy Mathewson	.90	.90
UX340	A2638	20c	Ty Cobb	.90	.90
UX341	A2638	20c	George Sisler	.90	.90
UX342	A2638	20c	Rogers Hornsby	.90	.90
UX343	A2638	20c	Mickey Cochrane	.90	.90
UX344	A2638	20c	Babe Ruth	.90	.90
UX345	A2638	20c	Walter Johnson	.90	.90
UX346	A2638	20c	Roberto Clemente	.90	.90
UX347	A2638	20c	Lefty Grove	.90	.90
UX348	A2638	20c	Tris Speaker	.90	.90
UX349	A2638	20c	Cy Young	.90	.90
UX350	A2638	20c	Jimmie Foxx	.90	.90
UX351	A2638	20c	Pie Traynor	.90	.90
UX352	A2638	20c	Satchel Paige	.90	.90
UX353	A2638	20c	Honus Wagner	.90	.90
UX354	A2638	20c	Josh Gibson	.90	.90
UX355	A2638	20c	Dizzy Dean	.90	.90
UX356	A2638	20c	Lou Gehrig	.90	.90
a.			Booklet of 20 cards, #UX337-UX356	18.00	

No. UX356a sold for $8.95.

PAID REPLY POSTAL CARDS

These are sold to the public as two unsevered cards, one for message and one for reply. These are listed first as unsevered cards and then as severed cards. Values are for:

Unused cards (both unsevered and severed) without printed or written address or message.

Unsevered cards sell for a premium if never folded.

Used unsevered cards, Message Card with Post Office cancellation and Reply Card uncanceled (from 1968 value is for a single used severed card); and used severed cards with cancellation when current.

Used values for International Paid Reply Cards are for proper usage. Those domestically used or with postage added sell for less than the unused value.

"Preprinted," unused cards (both unsevered and severed) with printed or written address or message. Used value applies after 1952.

First day cancel values are for cards without cachets.

PM1

Head of Grant, card framed.
PR1 inscribed "REPLY CARD."

1892, Oct. 25   Size: 140x89mm

UY1 PM1+PR1 1c +1c **black**, *buff*, unsevered		35.00	9.00
	Preprinted	15.00	
a.	Message card printed on both sides, reply card blank	250.00	
b.	Message card blank, reply card printed on both sides	300.00	
c.	Cards joined at bottom	175.00	75.00
	Preprinted	75.00	
m.	PM1 Message card detached	6.00	1.50
	Preprinted	3.00	
r.	PR1 Reply card detached	6.00	1.75
	Preprinted	3.00	

For other postal cards of types PM1 and PR1 see No. UY3.

Liberty — PM2

PR2 inscribed "REPLY CARD."

1893, Mar. 1   For International Use

UY2 PM2+PR2 2c +2c **blue**, *grayish white*, unsevered		17.50	20.00
	Preprinted	12.50	
a.	2c+2c **dark blue**, *grayish white*, unsevered	17.50	20.00
	Preprinted	12.50	
b.	Message card printed on both sides, reply card blank	300.00	
c.	Message card blank, reply card printed on both sides	—	
d.	Message card normal, reply card blank	300.00	
m.	PM2 Message card detached	5.00	6.00
	Preprinted	2.50	
r.	PR2 Reply card detached	5.00	6.00
	Preprinted	2.50	

For other postal cards of types PM2 and PR2 see No. UY11.

Design same as PM1 and PR1, without frame around card

1898, Sept.

Size: 140x82mm

UY3 PM1+PR1 1c +1c **black**, *buff*, unsevered		60.00	12.50
	Preprinted	12.50	
a.	Message card normal, reply card blank	250.00	
b.	Message card printed on both sides, reply card blank	250.00	
c.	Message card blank, reply card printed on both sides	250.00	
d.	Message card without "Detach annexed card/for answer"	250.00	150.00
	Preprinted	—	
e.	Message card blank, reply card normal	250.00	
m.	PM1 Message card detached	12.50	2.50
	Preprinted	6.00	
r.	PR1 Reply card detached	12.50	2.50
	Preprinted	6.00	

PM3

PR3 pictures Sheridan.

1904, Mar. 31

UY4 PM3+PR3 1c +1c **black**, *buff*, unsevered		50.00	6.50
	Preprinted	9.00	
a.	Message card normal, reply card blank	275.00	
b.	Message card printed on both sides, reply card blank	—	
c.	Message card blank, reply card normal	275.00	
d.	Message card blank, reply card printed on both sides	—	175.00
	Preprinted	200.00	
m.	PM3 Message card detached	9.00	1.10
	Preprinted	4.00	
r.	PR3 Reply card detached	9.00	1.10
	Preprinted	4.00	

PM4

PR4 pictures Martha Washington.

Double frame line around instructions

1910, Sept. 14

UY5 PM4+PR4 1c +1c **blue**, *bluish*, unsevered		150.00	22.50
	Preprinted	40.00	
a.	Message card normal, reply card blank	200.00	
m.	PM4 Message card detached	10.00	3.25
	Preprinted	6.00	
r.	PR4 Reply card detached	10.00	3.75
	Preprinted	6.00	

1911, Oct. 27

UY6 PM4+PR4 1c +1c **green**, *cream*, unsevered		150.00	25.00
	Preprinted	60.00	
a.	Message card normal, reply card blank	—	
m.	PM4 Message card detached	22.50	5.50
	Preprinted	12.50	
r.	PR4 Reply card detached	22.50	6.50
	Preprinted	12.50	

Single frame line around instructions

1915, Sept. 18

UY7 PM4+PR4 1c +1c **green**, *cream*, unsevered	1.25	.50
	Preprinted	.60	
a.	1c+1c **dark green**, *buff*, unsevered	1.25	.50
	Preprinted	.60	
m.	PM4 Message card detached	.30	.20
	Preprinted	.20	
r.	PR4 Reply card detached	.30	.20
	Preprinted	.20	

See No. UY13.

PM5

PR5 pictures Martha Washington.

1918, Aug. 2
UY8 PM5+PR5 2c +2c **red,** *buff,* unsevered 80.00 40.00
Preprinted 30.00
m. PM5 Message card detached 20.00 7.50
Preprinted 10.00
r. PR5 Reply card detached 20.00 7.50
Preprinted 10.00

Same Surcharged

1 CENT

Fifteen canceling machine types

1920, Apr.
UY9 PM5+PR5 1c on 2c+1c on 2c **red,**
buff, unsevered 19.00 11.00
Preprinted 10.00
a. Message card normal, reply card
no surcharge 85.00 —
Preprinted —
b. Message card normal, reply card
double surcharge 75.00 —
Preprinted —
c. Message card double surcharge,
reply card normal 75.00 —
Preprinted —
d. Message card no surcharge, reply
card normal 75.00 —
Preprinted —
e. Message card no surcharge, reply
card double surcharge 75.00 —
Preprinted —
m. PM5 Message card detached 5.00 3.50
Preprinted 3.00
r. PR5 Reply card detached 5.00 4.00
Preprinted 3.00

One press printed type
UY10 PM5+PR5 1c on 2c+1c on 2c **red,**
buff, unsevered 325.00 200.00
Preprinted 150.00
a. Message card no surcharge, reply
card normal —
Preprinted —
m. PM5 Message card detached 90.00 45.00
Preprinted 40.00
r. PR5 Reply card detached 90.00 45.00
Preprinted 40.00

Designs same as PM2 and PR2
1924, Mar. 18   For International Use
Size: 139x89mm
UY11 PM2+PR2 2c +2c **red,** *cream,* unsevered 2.00 *30.00*
Preprinted 1.50
m. PM2 Message card detached .50 *10.00*
Preprinted .40
r. PR2 Reply card detached .50 *10.00*
Preprinted .40

PM6

PR6 inscribed "REPLY CARD."

For International Use
1926, Feb. 1
UY12 PM6+PR6 3c +3c **red,** *buff,* unsevered 9.00 *25.00*
Preprinted 5.00
a. 3c +3c **red,** *yellow,* unsevered 10.00 *17.50*

Preprinted 6.00
First day cancel —
m. PM6 Message card detached 3.00 6.00
Preprinted 1.50
r. PR6 Reply card detached 3.00 6.00
Preprinted 1.50

Type of 1910
Single frame line around instructions
1951, Dec. 29
UY13 PM4+PR4 2c +2c **carmine,** *buff,* unsevered 1.25 *2.00*
Preprinted .65
First day cancel, Washington,
D.C. 1.25
m. PM4 Message card detached .35 *1.00*
Preprinted .25
r. PR4 Reply card detached .35 *1.00*
Preprinted .25

No. UY7a Surcharged Below Stamp
in Green by Canceling Machine

REVALUED
2¢
P. O. DEPT.

1952, Jan. 1
UY14 PM4+PR4 2c on 1c+2c on 1c **green,**
buff, unsevered 1.00 *2.00*
Preprinted .50
a. Surcharge vertical at left of
stamps 12.50 6.00
Preprinted 7.50
b. Surcharge horizontal at left of
stamps 15.00 12.50
Preprinted 8.50
c. Inverted surcharge horizontal at
left of stamps 140.00 90.00
Preprinted 75.00
d. Message card normal, reply card
no surcharge 35.00 40.00
Preprinted —
e. Message card normal, reply card
double surcharge 40.00 25.00
Preprinted —
f. Message card no surcharge, reply
card normal 35.00 40.00
Preprinted —
g. Message card double surcharge,
reply card normal 40.00 25.00
Preprinted —
h. Both cards, dbl. surch. 50.00 35.00
Preprinted —
m. PM4 Message card detached .40 *1.00*
Preprinted .30
r. PR4 Reply card detached .40 *1.00*
Preprinted .30

No. UY7a with Similar Surcharge (horizontal)
Typographed at Left of Stamp in Dark Green
1952
UY15 PM4+PR4 2c on 1c+2c on 1c **green,**
buff, unsevered 100.00 45.00
Preprinted 35.00
a. Surcharge on message card only 140.00
m. PM4 Message card detached 17.50 10.00
Preprinted 9.00
r. PR4 Reply card detached 17.50 10.00
Preprinted 9.00
On No. UY15a, the surcharge also appears on blank side of
card.

Liberty Type
For International Use
1956, Nov. 16
UY16 PC24 4c +4c **carmine & dark violet**
blue, *buff,* unsevered 1.00 *50.00*
First day cancel, New York,
N. Y. *(127,874)* 1.00
a. Message card printed on both
halves 125.00 —
b. Reply card printed on both halves 125.00 —
m. Message card detached .40 *35.00*
r. Reply card detached .40 *30.00*

Liberty Type of 1956
1958, July 31
UY17 PC25 3c +3c **purple,** *buff,* unsevered 3.00 *2.00*
First day cancel, Boise, Idaho
(136,768) 1.00
a. One card blank 125.00
Both halves of No. UY17 are identical, inscribed as No.
UX46, "This side of card is for address."

Lincoln Type
1962, Nov. 19
Precanceled with 3 printed red violet lines
UY18 PC26 4c +4c **red violet,** unsevered 3.00 *2.50*
First day cancel, Springfield, Ill.
(107,746) 1.00
a. Tagged, *Mar. 7, 1967* 6.50 *3.00*
First day cancel, Dayton, OH 30.00
Both halves of No. UY18 are identical, inscribed as No.
UX48, "This side of card is for address."
No. UY18a was printed with luminescent ink.

Map Type
1963, Aug. 30   For International Use
UY19 PC27 7c +7c **blue & red,** unsevered 2.50 *45.00*
First day cancel, New York 1.00
a. Message card normal, reply card
blank 125.00 100.00
b. Message card blank, reply card normal 125.00 —
c. Additional message card on back of
reply card —
m. Message card detached .85 *30.00*
r. Reply card detached .85 *27.50*
Message card inscribed "Postal Card With Paid Reply" in
English and French. Reply card inscribed "Reply Postal Card
Carte Postale Reponse".

Map Type of 1963
1967, Dec. 4   For International Use
UY20 PC27 8c +8c **blue & red,** unsevered 2.50 *45.00*
First day cancel, Washington,
D.C. 1.00
m. Message card detached .85 *30.00*
r. Reply card detached .85 *27.50*
Message card inscribed "Postal Card With Paid Reply" in
English and French. Reply card inscribed "Reply Postal Card
Carte Postale Réponse."

Tagged
**Paid Reply Postal cards from No. UY21 onward
are either tagged or printed with luminescent ink
unless otherwise noted.**

Lincoln Type
1968, Jan. 4
UY21 PC33 5c +5c **emerald,** unsevered 1.25 *2.00*
First day cancel, Hodgenville, Ky. 1.00

Paul Revere Type
1971, May 15
Precanceled with 3 printed brown lines.
UY22 PC36 6c +6c **brown,** unsevered .85 *2.00*
First day cancel, Boston, Mass. 1.00

John Hanson Type
1972, Sept. 1
Precanceled with 3 printed blue lines.
UY23 PC41 6c +6c **blue,** unsevered .90 *2.00*
First day cancel, Baltimore, Md. 1.00

Samuel Adams Type
1973, Dec. 16
Precanceled with 3 printed orange lines
UY24 PC42 8c +8c **orange,** unsevered .75 *2.00*
First day cancel, Boston, Mass.
(105,369) 1.00
a. Coarse paper 1.25 *2.00*

**Thomson, Witherspoon, Rodney, Hale & Hancock
Types**
1975-78
Precanceled with 3 printed emerald lines
UY25 PC44 7c +7c **emerald,** unsevered,
Sept. 14, 1975 .75 *5.00*
First day cancel, Bryn Mawr,
Pa. 1.00

Precanceled with 3 printed yellow brown lines
UY26 PC45 9c +9c **yellow brown,** unsev-
ered, *Nov. 10, 1975* .75 *2.00*
First day cancel, Princeton,
N.J. 1.00

Precanceled with 3 printed blue lines
UY27 PC46 9c +9c **blue,** unsevered, *July 1,
1976* .75 *2.00*
First day cancel, Dover, Del. 1.00

Precanceled with 3 printed green lines
UY28 PC48 9c +9c **green,** unsevered, *Oct.
14, 1977* .75 *2.00*
First day cancel, Coventry,
Conn. 1.00

Inscribed "U.S. Domestic Rate"
Precanceled with 3 printed brown orange lines
UY29 PC50 (10c +10c) **brown orange,** unsev-
ered, *May 19, 1978* 9.00 *9.00*
First day cancel, Quincy,
Mass. 1.75

Precanceled with 3 printed brown orange lines

UY30 PC50 10c +10c **brown orange,** unsevered, *June 20, 1978*   .75   .25
First day cancel, Quincy,
Mass.   1.00
a. One card "Domestic Rate," other "Postage 10¢"   —
Nos. UY25-UY30 (6)   12.75

Eagle Type
Inscribed "U. S. Domestic Rate"

1981, Mar. 15

Precanceled with 3 printed violet lines
UY31 PC63 (12c +12) **violet,** unsevered .75 2.00
First day cancel, Memphis, TN   1.00

Isaiah Thomas Type

1981, May 5

Precanceled with 3 printed lines
UY32 PC64 12c +12c **light blue,** unsevered 1.00 2.00
First day cancel, Worcester, MA   1.00
a. Small die on one side   3.00   —

Morris Type
Inscribed "U.S. Domestic Rate"

1981

Precanceled with 3 printed lines
UY33 PC67 (13c +13c) **buff,** *Oct. 11,* unsevered 1.50 1.25
First day cancel, Memphis, TN   1.25

Inscribed "U.S. Postage 13¢"
UY34 PC67 13c +13c **buff,** *Nov. 10,* unsevered .85 .20
First day cancel, Philadelphia,
PA   1.25

Charles Carroll Type
Inscribed: U.S. Domestic Rate

1985

Precanceled with 3 printed lines
UY35 PC79 (14c +14c) **pale green,** *Feb. 1,* un-
severed   2.50 2.00
First day cancel, New Carrollton,
MD   1.25

Inscribed: USA
UY36 PC79 14c +14c **pale green,** *Mar. 6,* unsevered   .90 2.00
First day cancel, Annapolis, MD   1.25
a. One card blank   —

George Wythe Type

1985, June 20

Precanceled with 3 printed lines
UY37 PC81 14c +14c **bright apple green,** unsevered   .75 2.00
First day cancel, Williamsburg, VA   1.25
a. One card blank   —

Flag Type

1987, Sept. 1
UY38 PC90 14c +14c **black, blue & red,** unsevered   .75 2.00
First day cancel, Washington, DC
(22,314)   1.25

America the Beautiful Type

1988, July 11
UY39 PC93 15c +15c **multicolored,** unsevered .75 1.00
First day cancel, Buffalo, WY
(24,338)   1.25

Flag Type

1991, Mar. 27
UY40 PC122 19c +19c **rose, ultramarine & black,**
unsevered   .75 1.00
First day cancel, Washington, DC
(25,562)   1.25

Red Barn Type

1995, Feb. 1   **Litho.**
UY41 PC147 20c +20c **multi,** unsevered .80 1.25
First day cancel, Williamsburg,
PA   1.50
a. One card blank   —

Block Island Lighthouse Type

1999, Nov. 10   **Litho.**
UY42 PC165 20c +20c **multi,** unsevered .85 1.25

AIR POST POSTAL CARDS

Eagle in Flight — APC1

1949, Jan.10   **Typo.**
UXC1 APC1 4c **orange,** *buff*   .50 .75
Preprinted   .30
First day cancel, Washington, D.C.
(236,620)   3.00

Type of Air Post Stamp, 1954

1958, July 31
UXC2 AP31 5c **red,** *buff*   1.75 .75
First day cancel, Wichita, Kans.
(156,474)   1.00

Type of 1958 Redrawn
1960, June 18   **Lithographed (Offset)**
UXC3 AP31 5c **red,** *buff,* bicolored border 6.00 2.00
First day cancel, Minneapolis,
Minn. (228,500)   12.00

Size of stamp of No. UXC3: 18½x21mm; on No. UXC2:
19x22mm. White cloud around eagle enlarged and finer detail
of design on No. UXC3. Inscription "AIR MAIL-POSTAL CARD"
has been omitted and blue and red border added on No. UXC3.

Bald Eagle — APC2

1963, Feb. 15

Precanceled with 3 printed red lines
UXC4 APC2 6c **red,** bicolored border   .60 .75
First day cancel, Maitland, Fla.
(216,203)   1.50

Emblem of Commerce Department's Travel
Service — APC3

Issued at the Sixth International Philatelic Exhibition (SIPEX),
Washington, D.C., May 21-30.

1966, May 27   **For International Use**
UXC5 APC3 11c **blue & red**   .60 12.50
First day cancel, Washington,
D.C. (272,813)   1.00

Four photographs at left on address side show: Mt. Rainier,
New York skyline, Indian on horseback and Miami Beach. The
card has blue and red border.
See Nos. UXC8, UXC11.

Virgin Islands and Territorial Flag — APC4

50th anniv. of the purchase of the Virgin Islands.

Designed by Burt Pringle

1967, Mar. 31
UXC6 APC4 6c **multicolored**   .40 6.00
First day cancel, Charlotte
Amalie, V. I. (346,906)   1.00
a. Red & yellow omitted   1,700.

Borah Peak, Lost River Range, Idaho, and Scout
Emblem — APC5

12th Boy Scout World Jamboree, Farragut State Park, Idaho,
Aug. 1-9.

Designed by Stevan Dohanos

1967, Aug. 4   **Litho.**
UXC7 APC5 6c **blue, yellow, black & red** .40 6.00
First day cancel, Farragut State
Park, ID (471,585)   1.00
a. Blue omitted   —
b. Blue & black omitted   —
c. Red & yellow omitted   —

Travel Service Type of 1966
Issued in connection with the American Air Mail Society Convention, Detroit, Mich.

1967, Sept. 8   **For International Use**
UXC8 APC3 13c **blue & red**   1.25 8.00
First day cancel, Detroit, Mich.
(178,189)   1.00

Stylized Eagle — APC6

Designed by Muriel R. Chamberlain

1968, Mar. 1

Precanceled with 3 printed red lines
UXC9 APC6 8c **blue & red**   .60 2.00
First day cancel, New York,
N.Y. (179,923)   1.00
a. Tagged, *Mar. 19, 1969*   2.25 2.50
Tagged, first day cancel   10.00

Tagged
**Air Post Postal Cards from No. UXC10 onward
are either tagged or printed with luminescent ink
unless otherwise noted.**

1971, May 15

Precanceled with 3 printed blue lines
UXC10 APC6 9c **red & blue**   .50 1.00
First day cancel, Kitty Hawk,
N.C.   1.00

Travel Service Type of 1966

1971, June 10

For International Use
UXC11 APC3 15c **blue & red**   1.75 12.50
First day cancel, New York,
N.Y.   1.00

Grand Canyon APC7

U.S. AIR MAIL **9 CENTS**

Niagara Falls APC8 U.S. AIR MAIL **15 CENTS**

Tourism Year of the Americas 1972.

Designed by Melbourne Brindle

1972, June 29 Litho.
Size: 152½x108½mm
UXC12 APC7 9c **black,** *buff* (Statue of Liber-
ty, Hawaii, Alaska, San
Francisco on back) .50 *8.00*
First day cancel, any city 1.00
a. Red and blue lozenges omitted —

For International Use
UXC13 APC8 15c **black,** *buff* (Mt. Vernon,
Washington, D.C., Lincoln,
Liberty Bell on back) .65 *15.00*
First day cancel, any city 1.00
a. Address side blank 400.00

See note after No. UX63.

Mail early in the day Stylized Eagle — APC9

Visit USA Bicentennial Era

Eagle Weather Vane — APC10 **USAirmail 18c**

Designed by David G. Foote (11c) & Stevan Dohanos (18c)

1974, Jan. 4 Litho.
UXC14 APC9 11c **ultramarine & red** .70 *2.00*
First day cancel, State College,
Pa. *(160,500)* 1.00

For International Use
UXC15 APC10 18c **multicolored** .85 *7.00*
First day cancel, Miami, Fla.
(132,114) 1.00

All following issues are for international use.

Visit USA Bicentennial Era Angel Gabriel Weather Vane — APC11

USAirmail 21c

Designed by Stevan Dohanos

1975, Dec. 17 Litho.
UXC16 APC11 21c **multicolored** .80 *7.50*
First day cancel, Kitty Hawk,
N.C. 1.00
a. Blue & red omitted —

USAirmail 21c

Curtiss (JN4H) Jenny — APC12

Designed by Keith Ferris

1978, Sept. 16 Litho.
UXC17 APC12 21c **multicolored** .75 *6.00*
First day cancel, San Diego,
Cal. *(174,886)* 1.00

USA Airmail 21c

Gymnast APC13

22nd Olympic Games, Moscow, July 19-Aug. 3, 1980.

Designed by Robert M. Cunningham

1979, Dec. 1 Litho.
UXC18 APC13 21c **multicolored** 1.00 *10.00*
First day cancel, Fort Worth,
Tex. 1.00

First Transpacific Flight · 1931

Sabichiro Beach, Japan to Wenatchee, Washington
Clyde Pangborn & Hugh Herndon Jr.
USAirmail 28c

Pangborn, Herndon and Miss Veedol — APC14

First non-stop transpacific flight by Clyde Pangborn and
Hugh Herndon, Jr., 50th anniv.

Designed by Ken Dallison

1981, Jan. 2 Litho.
UXC19 APC14 28c **multicolored** .90 *4.00*
First day cancel, Wenatchee,
WA 1.25

USAirmail 28c

Gliders APC15

Designed by Robert E. Cunningham

1982, Mar. 5 Litho.
UXC20 APC15 28c **magenta, yellow, blue &
black** .90 *3.00*
First day cancel, Houston, TX
(106,932) 1.25

Olympics 84 USA 28c Airmail

Speedskater — APC16

Designed by Robert Peak

1983, Dec. 29 Litho.
UXC21 APC16 28c **multicolored** .90 *2.00*
First day cancel, Milwaukee,
WI *(108,397)* 1.25

China Clipper USAirmail **33**

Martin M-130 China Clipper Seaplane — APC17

Designed by Chuck Hodgson

1985, Feb. 15 Litho.
UXC22 APC17 33c **multicolored** .90 *2.00*
First day cancel, San Francis-
co, CA 1.25

USAirmail **33**

AMERIPEX 86 Chicago, Illinois

Chicago Skyline — APC18

AMERIPEX '86, Chicago, May 22-June 1.

Designed by Ray Ameijide

1986, Feb. 1 Litho.
UXC23 APC18 33c **multicolored** .65 *2.00*
First day cancel, Chicago, IL
(84,480) 1.25

No. UXC23 was sold at Sudposta '87 by the U.S.P.S. with a
show cachet.

USAirmail **36**

DC-3 — APC19

Designed by Chuck Hodgson

1988, May 14 Litho.
UXC24 APC19 36c **multicolored** .70 *2.00*
First day cancel, San Diego,
CA 1.25

No. UXC24 was sold at SYDPEX '88 by the USPS with a
cachet for Australia's bicentennial and SYDPEX '88.
First day cancellations applied to 167,575 of Nos. UXC24
and C118.

Yankee Clipper — APC20

Designed by Chuck Hodgson.

1991, June 28   **Litho.**
UXC25 APC20 40c **multicolored**   .80 *1.00*
        First day cancel, Flushing,
        NY *(24,865)*   1.25

Mt. Rainier — APC22

Designed by Ethel Kessler.

1999, May 15   **Litho.**
UXC27 APC22 55c **multicolored**   1.10 1.00
        First day cancel, Denver, CO   1.50
        See note before No. C133.

OFFICIAL POSTAL CARDS

PO1

1913, July
          Size: 126x76mm

UZ1 PO1 1c **black**   325.00 175.00
  All No. UZ1 cards have printed address and printed form on
message side.

**Used values are for contemporaneous usage
without additional postage applied.**

Great Seal — PO2

1983-85
UZ2 PO2 13c **blue,** *Jan. 12*   .60 *35.00*
        First day cancel, Washington, DC   1.00
UZ3 PO2 14c **blue,** *Feb. 26, 1985*   .60 *35.00*
        First day cancel, Washington, DC
        (62,396)   1.00

PO3

Designed by Bradbury Thompson

1988, June 10   **Litho.**
UZ4 PO3 15c **multicolored**   .60 *35.00*
        First day cancel, New York
        (133,498)   1.25

PO4

Designed by Bradbury Thompson

1991, May 24   **Litho.**
UZ5 PO4 19c **multicolored**   .55 *30.00*
        First day cancel, Seattle, WA
        (23,097)   1.00

PO5

1995, May 9   **Litho.**
UZ6 PO5 20c **multicolored**   .40 *30.00*
        First day cancel, Washington, DC   1.25

REVENUE STAMPS

The Commissioner of Internal Revenue advertised for bids for revenue stamps in August, 1862, and the contract was awarded to Butler & Carpenter of Philadelphia.

Nos. R1-R102 were used to pay taxes on documents and proprietary articles including playing cards. Until December 25, 1862, the law stated that a stamp could be used only for payment of the tax upon the particular instrument or article specified on its face. After that date, stamps, except the Proprietary, could be used indiscriminately.

Most stamps of the first issue appeared in the latter part of 1862 or early in 1863. The 5c and 10c Proprietary were issued in the fall of 1864, and the 6c Proprietary on April 13, 1871.

Plate numbers and imprints are usually found at the bottom of the plate on all denominations except 25c and $1 to $3.50. On these it is nearly always at the left of the plate. The imprint reads "Engraved by Butler & Carpenter, Philadelphia" or "Jos. R. Carpenter."

Plates were of various sizes: 1c and 2c, 210 subjects (14x15); 3c to 20c, 170 subjects (17x10); 25c to 30c, 102 subjects (17x6); 50c to 70c, 85 subjects (17x5); $1 to $1.90, 90 subjects (15x6); $2 to $10, 73 subjects (12x6); $15 to $50, 54 subjects (9x6); $200, 8 subjects (2x4). No. R132, one subject.

The paper varies, the first employed being thin, hard and brittle until September, 1869, from which time it acquired a softer texture and varied from medium to very thick. Early printings of some revenue stamps occur on paper which appears to have laid lines. Some are found on experimental silk paper, first employed about August, 1870.

Some of the stamps were in use eight years and were printed several times. Many color variations occurred, particularly if unstable pigments were used and the color was intended to be purple or violet, such as the 4c Proprietary, 30c and $2.50 stamps. Before 1868 dull colors predominate on these and the early red stamps. In later printings of the 4c Proprietary, 30c and $2.50 stamps, red predominates in the mixture and on the dollar values of red is brighter. The early $1.90 stamp is dull purple, imperforate or perforated. In a later printing, perforated only, the purple is darker.

In the first issue, canceling usually was done with pen and ink and all values quoted are for stamps canceled in that way. Handstamped cancellations as a rule sell for more than pen. Printed cancellations are scarce and command much higher prices. Herringbone, punched or other types of cancellation which break the surface of the paper adversely affect prices.

1862-72 revenue stamps from the first three issues were often used on large folded documents. As a result, multiples (blocks and strips of four or more) are not often found in sound condition. In addition, part perforate pairs of all but the most common varieties generally are off center. Catalogue values of the noted multiples are for items in fine condition or for very fine appearing examples with small faults. Examples of such multiples in a true very fine grade without any faults are scarce to rare and will sell for well above catalogue value.

Where a stamp is known in a given form or variety but insufficient information is available on which to base a value, its existence is indicated by a dash.

Part perforate stamps are understood to be imperforate horizontally unless otherwise stated.

Part perforate stamps with an asterisk (*) exist imperforate horizontally or vertically.

Part perforate PAIRS should be imperforate between the stamps as well as imperforate at opposite ends. See illustration **Type A** under "Information For Collectors-Perforations."

All imperforate or part perforate stamps listed are known in pairs or larger multiples. Certain unlisted varieties of this nature exist as singles and specialists believe them genuine. Exceptions are Nos. R13a, R22a and R60b, which have not been reported in multiples but are regarded as legitimate by most students.

Documentary revenue stamps were no longer required after December 31, 1967.

First Issue

George Washington
R1   R2

1862-71		**Engr.**				*Perf. 12*
					Perforated	
			a. Imperf.	b. Part Perf.	c. Old Paper	d. Silk Paper
R1	R1 1c	**Express, red**	55.00	35.00*	1.25	85.00
		Pair	140.00	95.00	3.25	
		Block of 4	450.00	500.00	12.50	
		Dble. transfer			—	
		Short transfer, No. 156	—	—	85.00	
	e.	Vert. pair, imperf. btwn.			200.00	
R2	R1 1c	**Playing Cards, red**	1,050.	900.00	130.00	
		Pair	2,200.	2,000.	290.00	
		Block of 4			700.00	
		Cracked plate	—		160.00	
R3	R1 1c	**Proprietary, red**	725.00	120.00*	.50	25.00
		Pair	2,100.	400.00	1.25	55.00
		Block of 4		—	3.25	
R4	R1 1c	**Telegraph, red**	375.00		11.00	
		Pair	1,000.		27.50	
		Block of 4			110.00	

Double transfer (T5)

	a. Imperf.	b. Part Perf.	Perforated c. Old Paper	d. Silk Paper
R5 R2 2c **Bank Check, blue**	1.00	1.75*	.25	
Pair	17.50	9.00	.50	
Block of 4	90.00	60.00	2.00	
Double transfer (T5)	70.00	75.00	45.00	
Cracked plate		22.50	10.00	
Double impression			800.00	
e. Vert. pair, imperf. btwn.			400.00	
R6 R2 2c **Bank Check, orange**		55.00*	.25	250.00
Pair		—	.50	
Block of 4			1.40	
Double transfer (T5)			200.00	

Vert. half used as 1c on document			—	
e. 2c orange, *green*			425.00	

Double transfer (T7)

R7 R2 2c **Certificate, blue**	12.50		25.00	
Pair	35.00		62.50	
Block of 4	150.00		180.00	
Double transfer (T7)	275.00		250.00	
Cracked plate			32.50	
R8 R2 2c **Certificate, orange**			27.50	
Pair			140.00	
Block of 4			*825.00*	
Double transfer (T7)			350.00	
R9 R2 2c **Express, blue**	12.50	20.00*	.40	
Pair	35.00	105.00	1.25	
Block of 4	110.00	275.00	4.25	
Dble. transfer	60.00		17.50	
Cracked plate			20.00	
R10 R2 2c **Express, orange**		750.00	7.50	75.00
Pair			17.50	
Block of 4			40.00	
Dble. transfer			21.00	
R11 R2 2c **Playing Cards, blue**		175.00	4.00	
Pair		500.00	13.00	
Block of 4			50.00	
Cracked plate			30.00	
R12 R2 2c **Playing Cards, orange**			40.00	
Pair			*350.00*	

Double transfer (T13)

Double transfer (T13a)

	a. Imperf.	b. Part Perf.	Perforated c. Old Paper	d. Silk Paper
R13 R2 2c **Proprietary, blue**	350.00	120.00	.40	60.00
Pair		290.00	.90	
Block of 4		—	5.00	
Double transfer (T13)			100.00	
Complete double transfer (T13a)			150.00	
Cracked plate			25.00	
Horiz. half used as 1c on document			—	
e. 2c ultra			180.00	
Pair			500.00	
Block of 4			—	
Dble. transfer				
R14 R2 2c **Proprietary, orange**			37.50	
Pair			275.00	
Block of 4			—	
Double transfer (T13)			150.00	
Complete double transfer (T13a)			325.00	

Double transfer (T15)   Double transfer (T15a)

R15 R2 2c **U. S. Internal Revenue, orange ('64)**			.20	.25
Pair		—	.20	1.00
Block of 4			.40	
Double transfer (T15)			60.00	
Double transfer (T15a)			45.00	
Dble. transfer			12.00	
Triple transfer			40.00	
Cracked plate			10.00	
Half used as 1c on document			—	
e. 2c orange, *green*			600.00	

R3

R16 R3 3c **Foreign Exchange, green**	260.00	3.50	55.00
Pair	*1,275.*	8.00	
Block of 4		57.50	
Dble. transfer		—	
R17 R3 3c **Playing Cards, green ('63)**	9,500.	120.00	
Pair	*21,000.*	310.00	
Block of 4		*800.00*	
R18 R3 3c **Proprietary, green**	300.00	3.25	35.00
Pair	*975.00*	8.00	85.00
Block of 4		27.50	
Dble. transfer	—	8.00	
Double impression		*1,000.*	
Cracked plate		—	
e. Printed on both sides		*1,600.*	
R19 R3 3c **Telegraph, green**	60.00	22.50	2.75
Pair	210.00	62.50	8.75
Block of 4	775.00	190.00	80.00
R20 R3 4c **Inland Exchange, brown ('63)**		1.75	57.50
Pair		5.25	
Block of 4		22.50	
Double transfer at top		7.50	
R21 R3 4c **Playing Cards, slate ('63)**		500.00	
Pair		*1,150.*	
Block of 4		*2,600.*	
R22 R3 4c **Proprietary, purple**	—	210.00	6.50	72.50
Pair		525.00	16.00	
Block of 4		1,900.	55.00	
Double transfer at top			17.50	
Double transfer at bottom			12.50	

There are shade and color variations of Nos. R21-R22. See foreword of Revenue Stamps section.

R23	R3 5c	**Agreement, red**			.30	1.50
		Pair			.50	3.75
		Block of 4			1.25	17.50
		Dble. transfer in numerals			25.00	
R24	R3 5c	**Certificate, red**	2.50	11.00	.30	.35
		Pair	30.00	80.00	.55	1.00
		Block of 4	150.00	260.00	1.10	6.00
		Double transfer in upper label			10.00	
		Dble. transfer throughout			70.00	
		Triple transfer (No. 121)			35.00	
		Impression of #R3 on back			2,750.	
R25	R3 5c	**Express, red**	5.00	6.00*	.30	
		Pair	16.00	60.00	.70	
		Block of 4	100.00	130.00	2.25	
		Double transfer			5.00	
R26	R3 5c	**Foreign Exchange, red**	—		.30	300.00
		Pair	—		.85	
		Block of 4			10.00	
		Double transfer at top			20.00	
		Double transfer at bottom			10.00	
R27	R3 5c	**Inland Exchange, red**	5.00	3.75	.25	17.50
		Pair	29.00	17.50	.50	40.00
		Block of 4	72.50	60.00	2.00	
		Double transfer at top	77.50	47.50	27.50	
		Cracked plate	95.00	90.00	32.50	
R28	R3 5c	**Playing Cards, red** ('63)			20.00	
		Pair			45.00	
		Block of 4			90.00	
		Double impression			750.00	
R29	R3 5c	**Proprietary, red** ('64)			25.00	110.00
		Pair			55.00	
		Block of 4			150.00	
R30	R3 6c	**Inland Exchange, orange** ('63)			1.75	70.00
		Pair			18.50	
		Block of 4			100.00	
R31	R3 6c	**Proprietary, orange** ('71)			1,600.	

Nearly all copies of No. R31 are faulty and poorly centered. The Catalogue value is for a fine centered copy with minor faults which do not detract from its appearance.

R32	R3 10c	**Bill of Lading, blue**	45.00	250.00	1.00	
		Pair	140.00	800.00	2.40	
		Block of 4	430.00		7.50	
		Dble. transfer (#33 & 143)			—	
		Half used as 5c on document			200.00	
R33	R3 10c	**Certificate, blue**	130.00	275.00*	.25	5.00
		Pair	325.00	600.00	.55	
		Block of 4	825.00	—	1.90	

		Dble. transfer			7.50	
		Cracked plate			15.00	
		Half used as 5c on document			200.00	
R34	R3 10c	**Contract, blue**	160.00	.35	2.25	
		Pair	375.00	.80	6.00	
		Block of 4	—	3.00	60.00	
		Complete double transfer		70.00		
		Vertical half used as 5c on document		200.00		
e.		10c ultra	425.00	1.00		
		Pair		2.50		
		Block of 4		17.50		
R35	R3 10c	**Foreign Exchange, blue**		7.00		
		Pair		17.50		
		Block of 4		60.00		
e.		10c ultra		9.75		
		Pair		26.00		
		Block of 4		75.00		
R36	R3 10c	**Inland Exchange, blue**	175.00	3.50*	.20	35.00
		Pair	475.00	12.00	.35	—
		Block of 4	1,050.	60.00	1.50	—
		Half used as 5c on document		200.00		
R37	R3 10c	**Power of Attorney, blue**	475.00	22.50	.50	
		Pair	1,000.	85.00	1.10	
		Block of 4	2,500.	250.00	6.25	
		Half used as 5c on document		200.00		
R38	R3 10c	**Proprietary, blue** ('64)			15.00	
		Pair			32.50	
		Block of 4			90.00	
R39	R3 15c	**Foreign Exchange, brown** ('63)			15.00	
		Pair			50.00	
		Block of 4			250.00	
		Double impression			500.00	
R40	R3 15c	**Inland Exchange, brown**	30.00	12.50	1.25	
		Pair	120.00	35.00	2.85	
		Block of 4	500.00	180.00	10.25	
		Dble. transfer			6.25	
		Cracked plate	50.00	37.50	14.00	
		Double impression		1,200.	550.00	
R41	R3 20c	**Foreign Exchange, red**	40.00		32.50	
		Pair	125.00		100.00	
		Block of 4	550.00		275.00	
R42	R3 20c	**Inland Exchange, red**	15.00	17.50	.35	—
		Pair	60.00	55.00	.80	
		Block of 4	190.00	180.00	14.00	
		Half used as 10c on document		200.00		

R4

R5

	a. Imperf.	b. Part Perf.	c. Old Paper	d. Silk Paper
			Perforated	
R43 R4 25c **Bond, red**	150.00	6.00	2.50	
Pair	500.00	55.00	6.50	
Block of 4		290.00	60.00	

			a. Imperf.	b. Part Perf.	Perforated c. Old Paper	d. Silk Paper
R44	R4	25c **Certificate, red**	10.00	6.00*	.25	2.75
		Pair	47.50	35.00	.55	8.25
		Block of 4	375.00	180.00	4.00	27.50
		Double transfer, top or bottom			2.00	
		Triple transfer			—	
	e.	Printed on both sides		5,000		
	f.	Impression of No. R48 on back		—		
R45	R4	25c **Entry of Goods, red**	17.50	65.00*	.75	25.00
		Pair	65.00	425.00	30.00	
		Block of 4	350.00		92.50	
		Top frame line double	72.50	95.00	11.00	
R46	R4	25c **Insurance, red**	10.00	10.00	.25	4.50
		Pair	42.50	25.00	.65	11.00
		Block of 4	600.00	210.00	5.50	
		Double impression		500.00		
		Cracked plate		17.50		
R47	R4	25c **Life Insurance, red**	35.00	250.00	6.50	
		Pair	110.00	825.00	50.00	
		Block of 4	425.00		240.00	
R48	R4	25c **Power of Attorney, red**	6.00	27.50	.30	
		Pair	47.50	75.00	.70	
		Block of 4	350.00	475.00	6.50	
		Dble. transfer		1.10		
		Bottom frame line double		5.50		
R49	R4	25c **Protest, red**	30.00	300.00	6.75	
		Pair	120.00	800.00	29.00	
		Block of 4	575.00		115.00	

			a. Imperf.	b. Part Perf.	Perforated c. Old Paper	d. Silk Paper
R50	R4	25c **Warehouse Receipt, red**	42.50	250.00	22.50	
		Pair	130.00	625.00	70.00	
		Block of 4	900.00		220.00	
R51	R4	30c **Foreign Exchange, lilac**	72.50	1,000.	52.50	—
		Pair	425.00	2,750.	225.00	
		Block of 4	2,700.		—	
		Dble. transfer		100.00		
		Top frame line double		—		
R52	R4	30c **Inland Exchange, lilac**	50.00	65.00	3.50	—
		Pair	200.00	200.00	35.00	
		Block of 4	900.00	—	140.00	
		Dble. transfer		30.00		

There are shade and color variations of Nos. R51-R52. See foreword of "Revenues" section.

			a. Imperf.	b. Part Perf.	Perforated c. Old Paper	d. Silk Paper
R53	R4	40c **Inland Exchange, brown**	575.00	7.00	3.50	—
		Pair	1,500.	20.00	8.50	
		Block of 4		210.00	140.00	
		Dble. transfer		50.00	30.00	
R54	R5	50c **Conveyance, blue**	14.00	1.60	.20	3.00
		Pair	70.00	37.50	.25	6.50
		Block of 4	375.00	130.00	2.50	
		Dble. transfer		6.00		
		Cracked plate		15.00		
	e.	50c ultra		.25	—	
		Pair		1.00		
		Block of 4		10.00		
R55	R5	50c **Entry of Goods, blue**		12.00	.40	40.00
		Pair		90.00	1.00	110.00
		Block of 4		—	25.00	
		Dble. transfer		5.00		
		Cracked plate		20.00		
R56	R5	50c **Foreign Exchange, blue**	45.00	50.00	5.00	
		Pair	110.00	175.00	32.50	
		Block of 4			110.00	
		Double impression		500.00		
		Double transfer at left		11.00		
		Half used as 25c on document		200.00		
R57	R5	50c **Lease, blue**	24.00	60.00	8.50	
		Pair	95.00	160.00	67.50	
		Block of 4	800.00	475.00	225.00	
R58	R5	50c **Life Insurance, blue**	30.00	45.00	1.00	
		Pair	95.00		7.50	
		Block of 4	475.00		45.00	
		Dble. transfer	37.50		11.00	
		Double impression		800.00		

Cracked Plate (C59)

			a. Imperf	b. Part Perf	Perforated c. Old Paper	d. Silk Paper
R59	R5	50c **Mortgage, blue**	14.00	2.50	.50	—
		Pair	55.00	52.50	1.25	
		Block of 4	260.00	190.00	7.50	
		Cracked plate (C59)		35.00	12.50	
		Scratched plate, diagonal	35.00	25.00	12.50	
		Dble. transfer			3.50	
		Double impression				

Scratch is across three stamps. Value is for a single.

			a. Imperf	b. Part Perf	Perforated c. Old Paper	d. Silk Paper
R60	R5	50c **Original Process, blue**	3.00	600.00	.60	1.60
		Pair	55.00		1.50	8.00
		Block of 4	525.00		6.00	—
		Double transfer at top		5.00		
		Double transfer at bottom		8.00		
		Scratched plate		10.00		
		Half used as 25c on document		—		
R61	R5	50c **Passage Ticket, blue**	75.00	150.00	1.25	
		Pair	220.00	375.00	12.50	
		Block of 4	950.00		225.00	
R62	R5	50c **Probate of Will, blue**	35.00	60.00	19.00	
		Pair	95.00	140.00	50.00	
		Block of 4	450.00	450.00	350.00	
R63	R5	50c **Surety Bond, blue**	150.00	2.50	.30	
		Pair	725.00	15.00	1.75	
		Block of 4		90.00	10.00	
	e.	50c ultra		.75		
		Pair		5.50		
		Block of 4		55.00		
R64	R5	60c **Inland Exchange, orange**	85.00	47.50	6.00	35.00
		Pair	200.00	110.00	14.00	90.00
		Block of 4	675.00	350.00	87.50	
R65	R5	70c **Foreign Exchange, green**	325.00	95.00	8.00	55.00
		Pair	1,200.	350.00	30.00	140.00
		Block of 4		1,200.	180.00	
		Cracked plate		—	27.50	

R6

R7

			a. Imperf	b. Part Perf	Perforated c. Old Paper	d. Silk Paper
R66	R6	$1 **Conveyance, red**	12.00	425.00	15.00	100.00
		Pair	47.50	1,600.	42.50	
		Block of 4	300.00		120.00	
		Dble. transfer	30.00		30.00	
		Right frame line double	85.00		65.00	

		Top frame line double	—		55.00
R67 R6	$1	**Entry of Goods, red**	32.50	1.90	55.00
		Pair	100.00	5.75	
		Block of 4	325.00	55.00	
R68 R6	$1	**Foreign Exchange, red**	70.00	.60	50.00
		Pair	190.00	1.50	
		Block of 4	1,300.	11.00	
		Dble. transfer		5.50	
		Left frame line double	175.00	19.00	
		Diagonal half used as 50c on document			200.00
R69 R6	$1	**Inland Exchange, red**	12.50	325.00*	.45	3.00
		Pair	55.00	3,000.	1.80	9.00
		Block of 4	500.00	—	9.50	35.00
		Double transfer at bottom		4.25	
		Double transfer of top shields	60.00	21.00	
R70 R6	$1	**Lease, red**	35.00	2.25	
		Pair	95.00	7.50	
		Block of 4	425.00	60.00	
		Double transfer at bottom	47.50	10.00	
		Cracked plate		26.00	
		Half used as 50c on document		—	
R71 R6	$1	**Life Insurance, red**	150.00	6.50	—
		Pair	475.00	16.50	
		Block of 4	1,050.	60.00	
		Right frame line double	300.00	20.00	
R72 R6	$1	**Manifest, red**	42.50	27.50	
		Pair	95.00	67.50	
		Block of 4	240.00	165.00	
R73 R6	$1	**Mortgage, red**	20.00	175.00	
		Pair	67.50	385.00	
		Block of 4	325.00	825.00	
		Double transfer at left	—	230.00	
		Bottom frame line double	60.00	350.00	
R74 R6	$1	**Passage Ticket, red**	250.00	200.00	
		Pair	550.00	475.00	
		Block of 4	1,200.	1,250.	
R75 R6	$1	**Power of Attorney, red**	75.00	2.10	
		Pair	180.00	5.50	
		Block of 4	400.00	26.00	
		Dble. transfer		9.50	
		Recut		11.50	
R76 R6	$1	**Probate of Will, red**	70.00	35.00	
		Pair	190.00	92.50	
		Block of 4	700.00	260.00	
		Right frame line double	160.00	72.50	

R77 R7	$1.30	**Foreign Exchange, orange** ('63)	3,500.		55.00
		Pair Block of 4			145.00 —

Double transfer (T78)

R78 R7	$1.50	**Inland Exchange, blue**	22.50		3.25
		Pair	90.00		47.50
		Block of 4	275.00		275.00
		Double transfer (T78)			4.50
R79 R7	$1.60	**Foreign Exchange, green** ('63)	900.00		105.00
		Pair	3,500.		375.00
R80 R7	$1.90	**Foreign Exchange, purple** ('63)	4,000.		90.00 —
		Pair			250.00
		Block of 4			700.00

There are many shade and color variations of No. R80. See foreword of "Revenues" section.

R8

R81 R8	$2	**Conveyance, red**	110.00	1,500.	2.75	25.00
		Pair	260.00	5,500.	10.00	60.00
		Block of 4	750.00		65.00	175.00
		Cracked plate			32.50	
		Half used as $1 on document			—	
R82 R8	$2	**Mortgage, red**	100.00		3.00	55.00
		Pair	220.00		7.00	125.00
		Block of 4	550.00		40.00	
		Dble. transfer			11.00	
		Half used as			—	

		$1 on document			
R83 R8	$2	**Probate of Will, red** ('63)	3,500.		50.00
		Pair	8,750.		110.00
		Block of 4			250.00
		Dble. transfer			65.00
		Horiz. half used as $1 on document			250.00
R84 R8	$2.50	**Inland Exchange, purple** ('63)	3,000.		6.50	25.00
		Pair	7,500.		17.50	65.00
		Block of 4			160.00	425.00
		Double impression	1,400.		

There are many shade and color variations of Nos. R84c and R84d. See foreword of "Revenues" section.

R85 R8	$3	**Charter Party, green**	110.00	5.00	95.00
		Pair	300.00	50.00	240.00
		Block of 4	—	200.00	
		Double transfer at top		—	
		Double transfer at bottom		10.00	
		Half used as $1.50 on document		—	
	e.	Printed on both sides		2,000.	
	g.	Impression of No. RS208 on back		4,000.	
R86 R8	$3	**Manifest, green**	110.00	25.00	
		Pair	275.00	60.00	
		Block of 4	1,500.	175.00	
		Dble. transfer		32.50	
R87 R8	$3.50	**Inland Exchange, blue** ('63)	3,000.	50.00	
		Pair	7,500.	140.00	
		Block of 4		425.00	
	e.	Printed on both sides		—	

R9

R10

			a. Imperf	**b. Part Perf.**	**Perforated**	
					c. Old Paper	**d. Silk Paper**
R88	R9	$5	**Charter Party, red**	240.00		6.00	75.00
			Pair	550.00		65.00	
			Block of 4	1,200.		190.00	

		Right frame line double	325.00	60.00	
		Top frame line double	325.00	60.00	
R89	R9	$5	**Conveyance, red**	35.00	6.00	75.00
		Pair	115.00	15.00	180.00
		Block of 4	600.00	40.00	
R90	R9	$5	**Manifest, red**	110.00	77.50	
		Pair	275.00	220.00	
		Block of 4	900.00	550.00	
		Left frame line double	160.00	150.00	
R91	R9	$5	**Mortgage, red**	110.00	17.00	
		Pair	525.00	75.00	
		Block of 4	—	—	
R92	R9	$5	**Probate of Will, red**	475.00	17.50	
		Pair	1,100.	77.50	
		Block of 4	2,500.	325.00	
R93	R9	$10	**Charter Party, green**	550.00	25.00	
		Pair	1,200.	72.50	
		Block of 4	—	350.00	
		Dble. transfer		77.50	
R94	R9	$10	**Conveyance, green**	90.00	60.00	
		Pair	200.00	140.00	
		Block of 4	500.00	700.00	
		Double transfer at top	125.00	95.00	
		Right frame line double		150.00	
R95	R9	$10	**Mortgage, green**	400.00	25.00	
		Pair	850.00	97.50	
		Block of 4	—	—	
		Top frame line double	475.00	47.50	

				a. Imperf	b. Part Perf.	c. Old Paper	d. Silk Paper
			Perforated				
R96	R9	$10	**Probate of Will, green**	1,150.		27.50	
		Pair	2,500.		80.00	
		Block of 4			350.00	
		Double transfer at top			55.00	
R97	R10	$15	**Mortgage, blue**	1,250.		120.00	
		Pair	2,750.		325.00	
		Block of 4	6,250.		2,750.	
e.		$15 ultra			190.00	
		Pair			450.00	
		Block of 4			—	
		Milky blue			160.00	
R98	R10	$20	**Conveyance, orange**	125.00		65.00	125.00
		Pair	325.00		160.00	300.00
		Block of 4	825.00		400.00	
R99	R10	$20	**Probate of Will, orange**	1,200.		1,050.	
		Pair	2,500.		2,250.	
		Block of 4	5,500.		4,750.	
R100	R10	$25	**Mortgage, red** ('63)	950.00		115.00	175.00
		Pair	2,000.		275.00	
		Block of 4	4,000.		1,250.	

e.		Horiz. pair, imperf. between	1,100.	
R101	R10	$50	**U.S. Internal Revenue, green** ('63)	200.00	90.00
		Pair	440.00	200.00
		Block of 4	1,050.	600.00
		Cracked plate		160.00

R11

R102	R11	$200	**U.S. Internal Revenue, grn & red** ('64)	1,400.	650.00
		Pair	3,000.	1,400.
		Block of 4	7,000.	3,100.

After release of the First Issue revenue stamps, the Bureau of Internal Revenue received many reports of fraudulent cleaning and re-use. The Bureau ordered a Second Issue with new designs and colors, using a patented "chameleon" paper which is usually violet or pinkish, with silk fibers.

While designs are different from those of the first issue, stamp sizes and make up of the plates are the same as for corresponding denominations.

DOCUMENTARY STAMPS
Second Issue

George Washington
R12   R12a

Engraved and printed by Jos. R. Carpenter, Philadelphia.

Various Frames and Numeral Arrangements

1871			**Perf. 12**	
R103	R12	1c **blue & black**	45.00	
		Cut cancel	21.00	
		Pair	140.00	
		Block of 4	350.00	
a.		Inverted center	950.00	
		Pair	2,100.	
R104	R12	2c **blue & black**	1.10	
		Cut cancel	.20	
		Pair	3.50	
		Block of 4	25.00	
a.		Inverted center	5,000.	
R105	R12a	3c **blue & black**	20.00	
		Cut cancel	10.00	
		Pair	60.00	
		Block of 4	210.00	
R106	R12a	4c **blue & black**	60.00	
		Cut cancel	30.00	
		Pair	150.00	
		Block of 4	350.00	
		Horiz. or vert. half used as 2c on document	250.00	
R107	R12a	5c **blue & black**	1.50	
		Cut cancel	.50	
		Pair	6.00	
		Block of 4	22.50	
a.		Inverted center	2,500.	
R108	R12a	6c **blue & black**	100.00	
		Cut cancel	55.00	
		Pair	275.00	
		Block of 4	850.00	
R109	R12a	10c **blue & black**	1.00	
		Cut cancel	.20	
		Pair	4.00	
		Block of 4	12.00	
		Double impression of center	—	
		Half used as 5c on document	250.00	
a.		Inverted center	1,750.	
		Pair	4,000.	

No. R109a is valued in the grade of fine.

R110	R12a	15c **blue & black**	27.50	
		Cut cancel	15.00	
		Pair	72.50	
		Block of 4	190.00	
R111	R12a	20c **blue & black**	6.00	
		Cut cancel	2.75	
		Pair	22.50	
		Block of 4	87.50	
a.		Inverted center	8,000.	
		Pair	—	

No. R111a is valued in the grade of fine.

R13   R13a

R112	R13	25c **blue & black**	.60	
		Cut cancel	.20	
		Pair	1.90	
		Block of 4	9.50	
		Double transfer, position 57	15.00	
a.		Inverted center	8,000.	
b.		Sewing machine perf.	95.00	
		Pair	260.00	
		Block of 4	800.00	
c.		Perf. 8	275.00	
R113	R13	30c **blue & black**	75.00	
		Cut cancel	40.00	
		Pair	190.00	
		Block of 4	500.00	
R114	R13	40c **blue & black**	45.00	
		Cut cancel	22.50	
		Pair	130.00	
R115	R13a	50c **blue & black**	.60	
		Cut cancel	.20	
		Pair	1.70	
		Block of 4	8.75	
		Double transfer	15.00	
a.		Sewing machine perf.	75.00	
		Pair	200.00	
		Block of 4	900.00	
b.		Inverted center	800.00	
		Pair	1,650.	
		Inverted center, punch cancellation	250.00	
		Pair	600.00	
R116	R13a	60c **blue & black**	100.00	
		Cut cancel	50.00	
		Pair	260.00	
		Foreign entry, design of 70c	160.00	
R117	R13a	70c **blue & black**	40.00	
		Cut cancel	20.00	
		Pair	120.00	
a.		Inverted center	2,750.	

R13b   R13c

R118	R13b	$1 **blue & black**	3.00	
		Cut cancel	1.25	
		Pair	13.00	
		Block of 4	37.50	
a.		Inverted center	4,750.	
		Punch cancel	850.00	
R119	R13b	$1.30 **blue & black**	300.00	
		Cut cancel	160.00	
		Pair	650.00	

R120	R13b	$1.50 **blue & black**	12.50
		Cut cancel	7.00
		Pair	50.00
		Block of 4	—
		Foreign entry, design of $1	350.00
a.		Sewing machine perf.	450.00
		Pair	—
R121	R13b	$1.60 **blue & black**	375.00
		Cut cancel	250.00
		Pair	850.00
R122	R13b	$1.90 **blue & black**	190.00
		Cut cancel	110.00
		Pair	525.00
		Block of 4	—
R123	R13c	$2 **blue & black**	15.00
		Cut cancel	7.50
		Pair	55.00
		Block of 4	180.00
		Double transfer	20.00
R124	R13c	$2.50 **blue & black**	30.00
		Cut cancel	16.00
		Pair	95.00
		Block of 4	600.00
R125	R13c	$3 **blue & black**	32.50
		Cut cancel	17.50
		Pair	105.00
		Block of 4	500.00
		Double transfer	—
R126	R13c	$3.50 **blue & black**	160.00
		Cut cancel	80.00
		Pair	375.00

R13d   R13e

R127	R13d	$5 **blue & black**	17.50
		Cut cancel	9.00
		Pair	55.00
		Block of 4	220.00
a.		Inverted center	2,750.
		Inverted center, punch cancel	825.00
R128	R13d	$10 **blue & black**	110.00
		Cut cancel	60.00
		Pair	300.00
		Block of 4	750.00
R129	R13e	$20 **blue & black**	375.00
		Cut cancel	250.00
		Pair	800.00
R130	R13e	$25 **blue & black**	375.00
		Cut cancel	250.00
		Pair	800.00
R131	R13e	$50 **blue & black**	400.00
		Cut cancel	250.00
		Pair	850.00

R13f

R132	R13f	$200 **red, blue & black**	5,000.
		Cut cancel	2,800.

Printed in sheets of one.

R13g

R133	R13g	$500 **red orange, green & black**	12,500.

Printed in sheets of one.

Value for No. R133 is for a very fine appearing example with a light cut cancel or with minor flaws.

Inverted Centers: Fraudulently produced inverted centers exist, some excellently made.

Confusion resulting from the fact that all 1c through $50 denominations of the Second Issue were uniform in color, caused the ordering of a new printing with values in distinctive colors.

Plates used were those of the preceding issue.

Third Issue

Engraved and printed by Jos. R. Carpenter, Philadelphia.

Various Frames and Numeral Arrangements.

Violet "Chameleon" Paper with Silk Fibers.

1871-72   *Perf. 12*

R134	R12	1c **claret & black** ('72)	32.50
		Cut cancel	19.00
		Pair	90.00
		Block of 4	310.00

R135	R12	2c **orange & black**	.20
		Cut cancel	.20
		Pair	.40
		Block of 4	1.25
		Double transfer	—
		Double impression of frame	750.00
		Frame printed on both sides	1,600.
		Double impression of center	150.00
a.		2c vermilion & black (error)	600.00
b.		Inverted center	300.00
		Pair	1,100.
c.		Imperf., pair	—
R136	R12a	4c **brown & black** ('72)	40.00
		Cut cancel	20.00
		Pair	140.00
R137	R12a	5c **orange & black**	.25
		Cut cancel	.20
		Pair	.50
		Block of 4	1.10
a.		Inverted center	3,250.
		"Block" of 3	—

No. R137a is valued in the grade of fine.

R138	R12a	6c **orange & black** ('72)	45.00
		Cut cancel	22.50
		Pair	145.00
		Block of 4	425.00
R139	R12a	15c **brown & black** ('72)	10.00
		Cut cancel	4.75
		Pair	27.50
		Block of 4	130.00
a.		Inverted center	12,500.
		Pair	—
R140	R13	30c **orange & black** ('72)	15.00
		Cut cancel	7.50
		Pair	65.00
		Block of 4	250.00
		Double transfer	—
a.		Inverted center	2,500.
R141	R13	40c **brown & black** ('72)	37.50
		Cut cancel	19.00
		Pair	115.00
		Block of 4	310.00
R142	R13	60c **orange & black** ('72)	70.00
		Cut cancel	35.00
		Pair	200.00
		Block of 4	525.00
		Foreign entry, design of 70c	120.00
R143	R13	70c **green & black** ('72)	50.00
		Cut cancel	25.00
		Pair	160.00
		Block of 4	425.00
R144	R13b	$1 **green & black** ('72)	1.35
		Cut cancel	.55
		Pair	6.50
		Block of 4	50.00
a.		Inverted center	5,500.
R145	R13c	$2 **vermilion & black** ('72)	22.50
		Cut cancel	14.00
		Pair	55.00
		Block of 4	155.00
		Double transfer	30.00
R146	R13c	$2.50 **claret & black** ('72)	37.50
		Cut cancel	21.00
		Pair	90.00
		Block of 4	200.00
a.		Inverted center	20,000.
R147	R13c	$3 **green & black** ('72)	37.50
		Cut cancel	21.00
		Pair	95.00
		Block of 4	250.00
		Double transfer	—
R148	R13d	$5 **vermilion & black** ('72)	22.50
		Cut cancel	11.00
		Pair	57.50
		Block of 4	125.00
R149	R13d	$10 **green & black** ('72)	85.00
		Cut cancel	45.00
		Pair	220.00
		Block of 4	725.00
R150	R13e	$20 **orange & black** ('72)	475.00
		Cut cancel	250.00
		Pair	1,100.
		Block of 4	2,750.
a.		$20 vermilion & black (error)	600.00

(See note on Inverted Centers after No. R133.)

1874   *Perf. 12*

R151	R12	2c **orange & black**, *green*	.20
		Cut cancel	.20
		Pair	.40
		Block of 4	.90
a.		Inverted center	350.00

Liberty — R14

1875-78

		Silk Paper a. Perf.	Wmkd. 191R b. Perf.	c. Roul. 6
R152	R14 2c **blue**, *blue*	.20	.20	32.50
	Pair	.20	.20	125.00
	"L" shaped strip of 3			600.00

	Silk Paper a. Perf.	Wmkd. 191R b. Perf. c. Roul. 6
Block of 4	.50	.60
Double transfer	5.00	5.00
d. Vert. pair, imperf. horiz.	400.00	
e. Imperf., pair	*250.00*	

The watermarked paper came into use in 1878.

Nos. 279, 267a, 267, 279Bg, 279B, 272-274
Overprinted in Red or Blue:

I.R. I.R.

a - Rectangular Periods   a - Square Periods

I.R. I.R.

b   b - Small Period

Overprint "a" exists in two (or possibly more) settings, with upright rectangular periods or with changed leg of "R" and square periods, both illustrated. Overprint "b" has 4 stamps with small period in each pane of 100 (pos. 41, 46, 91 & 96).

1898	**Wmk. 191**			**Perf. 12**
R153 A87 (a)	1c **green,** red overprint		3.00	2.50
	Block of 4		17.50	11.00
	P# strip of 3, Impt.		25.00	
	P# block of 6, Impt.		70.00	
R154 A87 (b)	1c **green,** red overprint		.20	.20
	Block of 4		.50	.45
	P# strip of 3, Impt.		10.00	
	P# block of 6, Impt.		55.00	
a.	Overprint inverted		20.00	17.50
	Block of 4		100.00	—
	P# strip of 3, Impt.		105.00	
	P# block of 6, Impt.		250.00	
b.	Overprint on back instead of face, inverted		—	
c.	Pair, one without overprint		—	
R155 A88 (b)	2c **pink,** type III, blue overprint, *July 1, 1898*		.20	.20
	Block of 4		.85	.35
	P# strip of 3, Impt.		11.00	
	P# block of 6, Impt.		52.50	
	Dot in "S" of "CENTS"		1.00	
	P# strip of 3, Impt.		17.50	
b.	2c carmine, type III, blue overprint, *July 1, 1898*		.25	.20
	Block of 4		1.05	.45
	P# strip of 3, Impt.		12.50	
	P# block of 6, Impt.		55.00	
	Dot in "S" of "CENTS"		1.25	
	P# strip of 3, Impt.		22.50	
c.	As No. R155, overprint inverted, *July 1898*		3.50	2.75
	Block of 4		15.00	12.50
	P# strip of 3, Impt.		40.00	
	P# block of 6, Impt.		100.00	
d.	Vertical pair, one without overprint		750.00	
e.	Horiz. pair, one without overprint		—	
f.	As No. R155, overprint on back instead of face, inverted		—	

NOTE: Old No. R155 is now Nos. R155b, R155Ag; old No. R155a is Nos. R155c, R155Ah; old No. R155b is Nos. R155d, R155e; old No. R155c is No. R155f.

R155A A88 (b)	2c **pink,** type IV, blue overprint *July 1, 1898*		.20	.20
	Block of 4		.65	.30
	P# strip of 3, Impt.		10.00	
	P# block of 6, Impt.		50.00	
g.	2c carmine, type IV, blue overprint, *July 1, 1898*		.20	.20
	Block of 4		.85	.35
	P# strip of 3, Impt.		11.00	
	P# block of 6, Impt.		52.50	
h.	As No. R155A, overprint inverted, *July 1898*		2.50	1.75
	Block of 4		12.50	9.00
	P# strip of 3, Impt.		30.00	
	P# block of 6, Impt.		75.00	

Handstamped Type "b" in Magenta

R156 A93	8c **violet brown**	4,000.
R157 A94	10c **dark green**	3,750.
	Block of 6	—
R158 A95	15c **dark blue**	4,750.

Nos. R156-R158 were emergency provisionals, privately prepared, not officially issued.

Privately Prepared Provisionals

No. 285 Overprinted in Red

I.R.
L. H. C.

1898	**Wmk. 191**		**Perf. 12**
R158A A100	1c **dark yellow green**	8,500.	7,750.

Same Overprinted "I.R./P.I.D. & Son" in Red

R158B A100	1c **dark yellow green**	—	20,000.

No. R158B is valued with small faults as each of the four recorded examples have faults.

Nos. R158A-R158B were overprinted with federal government permission by the Purvis Printing Co. upon order of Capt. L. H. Chapman of the Chapman Steamboat Line. Both the Chapman Line and P. I. Daprix & Son operated freight-carrying steamboats on the Erie Canal. The Chapman Line touched at Syracuse, Utica, Little Falls and Fort Plain; the Daprix boat ran between Utica and Rome. Overprintings of 250 of each stamp were made.

Dr. Kilmer & Co. provisional overprints are listed under "Private Die Medicine Stamps," Nos. RS307-RS315.

Newspaper Stamp No. PR121
Surcharged in Red — R159

1898			**Perf. 12**
R159 N18	$5 **dark blue,** surcharge reading down	350.00	160.00
	Block of 4	1,750.	750.00
	P# strip of 3, Impt.		
R160 N18	$5 **dark blue,** surcharge reading up	110.00	70.00
	Block of 4	450.00	525.00
	P# strip of 3, Impt.		

Battleship — R15

There are two styles of rouletting for the proprietary and documentary stamps of the 1898 issue, an ordinary rouletting 5½ and one by which small rectangles of the paper are cut out, usually called hyphen-hole perforation 7. Several stamps are known with an apparent roulette 14 caused by slippage of a hyphen-hole 7 rouletting wheel.

1898		**Wmk. 191R**		**Rouletted 5½, 7**	
			Roul. 5½		*p.* Hyphen Hole Perf. 7
			Unused	Used	Unused	Used
R161 R15	½c	**orange**	2.50	*7.50*		
		Block of 4	11.50	*75.00*		
R162 R15	½c	**dark gray**	.25	.20		
		Block of 4	1.25	.50		
		Double transfer		7.50		
a.		Vert. pair, imperf. horiz.	75.00			
R163 R15	1c	**pale blue**	.20	.20	.25	.20
		Block of 4	.40	.25	1.25	1.25
		Double transfer	10.00			
a.		Vert. pair, imperf. horiz.	7.50			
b.		Imperf., pair	350.00			
R164 R15	2c	**carmine rose**	.25	.25	.30	.20
		Block of 4	1.10	1.10	2.50	.50
		Double transfer	1.00	.25		
a.		Vert. pair, imperf. horiz.	65.00			
b.		Imperf., pair	200.00			
c.		Horiz. pair, imperf. vert.	—			
R165 R15	3c	**dark blue**	2.00	.20	20.00	1.00
		Block of 4	9.50	.75	90.00	4.50
		Double transfer				
R166 R15	4c	**pale rose**	1.25	.20	7.50	1.50
		Block of 4	5.50	.50	37.50	7.25

			Roul. 5½		*p.* Hyphen Hole Perf. 7	
			Unused	Used	Unused	Used
a.		Vert. pair, imperf. horiz.	125.00			
R167 R15	5c	**lilac**	.20	.20	7.50	.20
		Block of 4	1.00	.30	37.50	1.00
a.		Pair, imperf. horiz. or vert.	200.00	150.00		
b.		Horiz. pair, imperf. between		450.00		
R168 R15	10c	**dark brown**	1.50	.20	5.00	.20
		Block of 4	9.00	.30	25.00	.75
a.		Vert. pair, imperf. horiz.	35.00	30.00		
b.		Horiz. pair, imperf. vert.	—			
R169 R15	25c	**purple brown**	2.50	.20	8.00	.25
		Block of 4	15.00	.50	40.00	1.10
		Double transfer				
R170 R15	40c	**blue lilac**	125.00	1.00	175.00	35.00
		Block of 4	600.00	55.00	875.00	250.00
		Cut cancel		.30		
R171 R15	50c	**slate violet**	17.50	.20	35.00	.75
		Block of 4	85.00	2.00	180.00	6.00
a.		Imperf., pair	*300.00*			
b.		Horiz. pair, imperf. between			—	250.00
R172 R15	80c	**bister**	100.00	.25	200.00	45.00
		Block of 4	500.00	30.00	1,000.	210.00
		Cut cancel		.20		

Numerous double transfers exist on this issue.

Commerce — R16

R173 R16	$1	**dark green**	8.00	.20	15.00	.65
		Block of 4	45.00	.50		3.00
a.		Vert. pair, imperf. horiz.	—			
b.		Horiz. pair, imperf. vert.	—	300.00		
R174 R16	$3	**dark brown**	22.50	.85	30.00	2.25
		Block of 4		4.50		11.00
		Cut cancel		.20		.25
a.		Horiz. pair, imperf. vert.	450.00			
R175 R16	$5	**orange red**			30.00	1.40
		Block of 4			—	7.00
		Cut cancel				.20
R176 R16	$10	**black**			80.00	2.75
		Block of 4				14.00
		Cut cancel				.50
a.		Horiz. pair, imperf. vert.				
R177 R16	$30	**red**			250.00	110.00

		Block of 4	500.00	
		Cut cancel	45.00	
R178	R16	$50 **gray brown**	125.00	5.50
		Block of 4	27.50	
		Cut cancel	2.00	

John Marshall — R17

Alexander Hamilton — R18

James Madison — R19

Various Portraits in Various Frames, Each Inscribed "Series of 1898"

1899   **Imperf.**

Without Gum

R179	R17	$100 **yellow brown & black**	130.	30.
		Cut cancel		20.
		Vertical strip of 4	—	135.
		Vertical strip of 4, cut cancel		85.
R180	R18	$500 **carmine lake & black**	1,000.00	
		Cut cancel		225.
		Vertical strip of 4	—	2,000.
		Vertical strip of 4, cut cancel		975.
R181	R19	$1000 **green & black**	800.	300.
		Cut cancel		110.
		Vertical strip of 4		1,300.
		Vertical strip of 4, cut cancel		450.

1900   **Hyphen-hole perf. 7**

Allegorical Figure of Commerce

R182	R16	$1 **carmine**	17.50	.50
		Cut cancel		.20
		Block of 4	77.50	2.25
		Block of 4, cut cancel		.75
R183	R16	$3 **lake** (fugitive ink)	130.00	45.00
		Cut cancel		7.00
		Block of 4	600.00	250.00
		Block of 4, cut cancel		30.00

Warning: The ink on No. R183 will run in water.

Surcharged in Black with Open Numerals of Value

R184	R16	$1 **gray**	12.50	.20
		Cut cancel		.20
		Block of 4	—	.85
		Block of 4, cut cancel		.40
a.		Horiz. pair, imperf. vert	—	
b.		Surcharge omitted	125.00	
		Surcharge omitted, cut cancel		80.00
R185	R16	$2 **gray**	12.50	.20
		Cut cancel		.20
		Block of 4	47.50	.85
		Block of 4, cut cancel		.40
R186	R16	$3 **gray**	65.00	11.00
		Cut cancel		3.00
		Block of 4	—	47.50
		Block of 4, cut cancel		12.50
R187	R16	$5 **gray**	42.50	6.50
		Cut cancel		1.00
		Block of 4	—	27.50
		Block of 4, cut cancel		5.00

R188	R16	$10 **gray**	75.00	17.50
		Cut cancel		3.00
		Block of 4	—	80.00
		Block of 4, cut cancel		14.00
R189	R16	$50 **gray**	700.00	425.00
		Cut cancel		90.00
		Block of 4		1,900.
		Block of 4, cut cancel		350.00

Surcharged in Black with Ornamental Numerals of Value

Warning: If Nos. R190-R194 are soaked, the center part of the surcharged numeral may wash off. Before the surcharging, a square of soluble varnish was applied to the middle of some stamps.

1902

R190	R16	$1 **green**	20.50	3.75
		Cut cancel		.20
		Block of 4	—	16.00
		Block of 4, cut cancel		.85
a.		Inverted surcharge		175.00
R191	R16	$2 **green**	17.50	1.30
		Cut cancel		.25
		Block of 4	—	6.25
		Block of 4, cut cancel		1.25
a.		Surcharged as No. R185	75.00	75.00
b.		Surcharged as No. R185, in violet	1,300.	—
c.		Double surcharge	100.00	
d.		Triple surcharge	—	
R192	R16	$5 **green**	140.00	25.00
		Cut cancel		4.00
		Block of 4	—	110.00
		Block of 4, cut cancel		17.50
a.		Surcharge omitted	160.00	
b.		Pair, one without surcharge	350.00	
R193	R16	$10 **green**	325.00	125.00
		Cut cancel		45.00
		Block of 4		550.00
		Block of 4, cut cancel		200.00
R194	R16	$50 **green**	950.00	800.00
		Cut cancel		225.00
		Block of 4	—	
		Block of 4, cut cancel		950.00

R20

Wmk. 190

Inscribed "Series of 1914"

1914   **Wmk. 190**   **Offset Printing**   **Perf. 10**

R195	R20	½c **rose**	7.50	3.50
		Block of 4	32.50	15.00
R196	R20	1c **rose**	1.40	.20
		Block of 4	6.00	.50
		Creased transfer, left side		—
R197	R20	2c **rose**	2.00	.20
		Block of 4	8.50	.45
		Double impression		—
R198	R20	3c **rose**	50.00	30.00
		Block of 4	225.00	40.00
R199	R20	4c **rose**	14.00	2.00
		Block of 4	67.50	9.00
		Recut U. L. corner	300.00	
R200	R20	5c **rose**	4.00	.20
		Block of 4	17.50	.90
R201	R20	10c **rose**	3.25	.20
		Block of 4	14.00	.35
R202	R20	25c **rose**	30.00	.55
		Block of 4	140.00	2.25
R203	R20	40c **rose**	17.50	1.50
		Block of 4	75.00	4.75
R204	R20	50c **rose**	6.00	.20
		Block of 4	27.50	.45
R205	R20	80c **rose**	95.00	10.00
		Block of 4	425.00	45.00

Wmk. 191R

R206	R20	½c **rose**	1.50	.50
		Block of 4	6.50	2.50
R207	R20	1c **rose**	.20	.20
		Block of 4	.55	.20
		Double impression	300.00	—
R208	R20	2c **rose**	.20	.20
		Block of 4	.65	.20
R209	R20	3c **rose**	1.40	.20
		Block of 4	6.00	.85
R210	R20	4c **rose**	3.50	.45
		Block of 4	17.50	2.00
R211	R20	5c **rose**	1.75	.25
		Block of 4	8.00	1.10
R212	R20	10c **rose**	.60	.20
		Block of 4	2.75	.30
R213	R20	25c **rose**	5.00	1.25
		Block of 4	22.50	5.75

R214	R20	40c **rose**	75.00	12.50
		Cut cancel		.45
		Block of 4	400.00	55.00
R215	R20	50c **rose**	15.00	.25
		Block of 4	70.00	1.10
R216	R20	80c **rose**	110.00	7.50
		Cut cancel		1.00
		Block of 4	500.00	85.00

Liberty — R21

Inscribed "Series 1914"

Engr.

R217	R21	$1 **green**	30.00	.30
		Cut cancel		35.00
		Block of 4	—	1.30
		Block of 4, cut cancel		.35
a.		$1 yellow green	—	.20
R218	R21	$2 **carmine**	50.00	.50
		Cut cancel		.20
		Block of 4	225.00	2.25
		Block of 4, cut cancel		.25
R219	R21	$3 **purple**	60.00	2.50
		Cut cancel		.45
		Block of 4	275.00	9.00
		Block of 4, cut cancel		1.00
R220	R21	$5 **blue**	50.00	2.75
		Cut cancel		.50
		Block of 4	225.00	12.50
		Block of 4, cut cancel		2.50
R221	R21	$10 **orange**	125.00	5.00
		Cut cancel		.75
		Block of 4	—	22.50
		Block of 4, cut cancel		3.50
R222	R21	$30 **vermilion**	250.00	11.00
		Cut cancel		2.00
		Block of 4	—	47.50
		Block of 4, cut cancel		10.00
R223	R21	$50 **violet**	1,300.	800.00
		Cut cancel		350.00
		Block of 4		3,500.

Portrait Types of 1899 Inscribed "Series of 1915" (#R224), or "Series of 1914"

1914-15   **Without Gum**   **Perf. 12**

R224	R19	$60 **brown** (Lincoln)	175.00	100.00
		Vertical strip of 4	—	
		Cut cancel		45.00
		Vertical strip of 4, cut cancel		200.00
R225	R17	$100 **green** (Washington)	60.00	40.00
		Cut cancel		15.00
		Vertical strip of 4, cut cancel		65.00
R226	R18	$500 **blue** (Hamilton)	—	500.00
		Cut cancel		225.00
		Vertical strip of 4, cut cancel		950.00
R227	R19	$1000 **orange** (Madison)	—	400.00
		Cut cancel		190.00
		Vert. strip of 4, cut cancel		800.00

The stamps of types R17, R18 and R19 in this and subsequent issues are issued in vertical strips of 4 which are imperforate at the top, bottom and right side; therefore, single copies are always imperforate on one or two sides.

R22

Two types of design R22 are known.
Type I - With dot in centers of periods before and after "CENTS."
Type II - Without such dots.
First printings were done by commercial companies, later printings by the Bureau of Engraving and Printing.

1917　Offset Printing　Wmk. 191R　Perf. 11

R228	R22	1c **carmine rose**	.20	.20
		Block of 4	.55	.40
		Double impression	7.00	4.00
R229	R22	2c **carmine rose**	.20	.20
		Block of 4	.40	.25
		Double impression	7.50	5.00
R230	R22	3c **carmine rose**	1.25	.35
		Block of 4	5.50	1.60
		Double impression	—	—
R231	R22	4c **carmine rose**	.50	.20
		Block of 4	2.50	.25
		Double impression	—	—
R232	R22	5c **carmine rose**	.20	.20
		Block of 4	.90	.25
R233	R22	8c **carmine rose**	1.75	.30
		Block of 4	8.00	1.35
R234	R22	10c **carmine rose**	.35	.20
		Block of 4	1.75	.25
		Double impression		5.00
R235	R22	20c **carmine rose**	.60	.20
		Block of 4	2.75	.25
		Double impression	—	—
R236	R22	25c **carmine rose**	1.10	.20
		Block of 4	5.00	.25
		Double impression	—	—
R237	R22	40c **carmine rose**	1.50	.40
		Block of 4	7.50	1.65
		Double impression	8.00	5.00
R238	R22	50c **carmine rose**	2.00	.20
		Block of 4	9.00	.25
		Double impression	—	—
R239	R22	80c **carmine rose**	5.00	.20
		Block of 4	22.50	.35
		Double impression	40.00	—

No. R234 is known used provisionally as a playing card revenue stamp in August 1932. Value for this use, authenticated, $300.

Liberty Type of 1914 without "Series 1914"

1917-33　　　　　　　　　　Engr.

R240	R21	$1 **yellow green**	6.50	.20
		Block of 4	30.00	.25
a.		$1 **green**	6.50	.20
R241	R21	$2 **rose**	11.00	.20
		Block of 4	50.00	.35
R242	R21	$3 **violet**	35.00	.75
		Cut cancel		.20
		Block of 4		3.25
R243	R21	$4 **yellow brown** ('33)	25.00	1.75
		Cut cancel		.20
		Block of 4	—	8.00
		Block of 4, cut cancel		.50
R244	R21	$5 **dark blue**	17.50	.20
		Cut cancel		.20
		Block of 4	—	1.10
R245	R21	$10 **orange**	30.00	.90
		Cut cancel		.20
		Block of 4	—	4.50
		Block of 4, cut cancel		.60

Portrait Types of 1899 without "Series of" and Date

1917　　　Without Gum　　　Perf. 12

R246	R17	$30 **deep orange, green numerals** (Grant)	45.00	10.00
		Cut cancel		1.00
		Vertical strip of 4		—
		Cut cancel		3.00
a.		Imperf., pair		750.00
b.		Numerals in blue	70.00	1.90
		Cut cancel		1.00
R247	R19	$60 **brown** (Lincoln)	55.00	7.00
		Cut cancel		.80
		Vertical strip of 4		—
		Cut cancel		5.00
R248	R17	$100 **green** (Washington)	32.50	1.00
		Cut cancel		.35
		Vertical strip of 4		—
		Cut cancel		1.90
R249	R18	$500 **blue, red numerals** (Hamilton)	230.00	35.00
		Cut cancel		10.00
		Vertical strip of 4		—
		Cut cancel		55.00
		Double transfer		50.00
a.		Numerals in orange	275.00	50.00
		Double transfer		—
R250	R19	$1000 **orange** (Madison)	130.00	12.50
		Cut cancel		4.00
		Vertical strip of 4		125.00
		Cut cancel		17.50
a.		Imperf., pair		900.00

See note after No. R227.

1928-29　　　Offset Printing　　　Perf. 10

R251	R22	1c **carmine rose**	2.00	1.50
		Block of 4	9.00	7.00
R252	R22	2c **carmine rose**	.60	.20
		Block of 4	3.00	1.00
R253	R22	4c **carmine rose**	5.50	3.75
		Block of 4	25.00	17.50
R254	R22	5c **carmine rose**	1.25	.50
		Block of 4	6.00	2.25
R255	R22	10c **carmine rose**	1.75	1.25
		Block of 4	8.00	5.50
R256	R22	20c **carmine rose**	5.50	4.50
		Block of 4	25.00	20.00
		Double impression	—	—

**　　　　　　　　　Engr.**

R257	R21	$1 **green**	100.00	30.00
		Block of 4	—	—
		Cut cancel		5.00
R258	R21	$2 **rose**	40.00	2.50
		Block of 4	—	12.50
R259	R21	$10 **orange**	130.00	40.00
		Cut cancel		25.00

1929　　　Offset Printing　　　Perf. 11x10

R260	R22	2c **carmine rose** ('30)	2.75	2.50
		Block of 4	12.00	11.00
		Double impression	—	—
R261	R22	5c **carmine rose** ('30)	2.00	1.75
		Block of 4	10.00	8.00
R262	R22	10c **carmine rose**	7.50	6.50
		Block of 4	35.00	30.00
R263	R22	20c **carmine rose**	15.00	8.00
		Block of 4	70.00	40.00

Types of 1917-33 Overprinted in Black

SERIES 1940

1940　Wmk. 191R　Offset Printing　Perf. 11

R264	R22	1c **rose pink**	2.75	2.25
		Cut cancel		.35
		Perf. initial		.20
R265	R22	2c **rose pink**	2.75	1.75
		Cut cancel		.40
		Perf. initial		.30
R266	R22	3c **rose pink**	8.25	4.00
		Cut cancel		.70
		Perf. initial		.50
R267	R22	4c **rose pink**	3.50	.55
		Cut cancel		.20
		Perf. initial		.20
R268	R22	5c **rose pink**	3.75	.90
		Cut cancel		.25
		Perf. initial		.20
R269	R22	8c **rose pink**	16.00	12.50
		Cut cancel		3.00
		Perf. initial		2.00
R270	R22	10c **rose pink**	1.75	.45
		Cut cancel		.20
		Perf. initial		.20
R271	R22	20c **rose pink**	2.25	.60
		Cut cancel		.20
		Perf. initial		.20
R272	R22	25c **rose pink**	5.50	1.00
		Cut cancel		.20
		Perf. initial		.20
R273	R22	40c **rose pink**	5.50	.65
		Cut cancel		.20
		Perf. initial		.20
R274	R22	50c **rose pink**	6.00	.50
		Cut cancel		.20
		Perf. initial		.20
R275	R22	80c **rose pink**	11.00	.90
		Cut cancel		.20
		Perf. initial		.20

**　　　　　　　　　Engr.**

R276	R21	$1 **green**	40.00	.80
		Cut cancel		.20
		Perf. initial		.20
R277	R21	$2 **rose**	40.00	1.00
		Cut cancel		.20
		Perf. initial		.20
R278	R21	$3 **violet**	55.00	25.00
		Cut cancel		3.25
		Perf. initial		1.50
R279	R21	$4 **yellow brown**	95.00	30.00
		Cut cancel		5.25
		Perf. initial		2.00
R280	R21	$5 **dark blue**	55.00	11.00
		Cut cancel		1.10
		Perf. initial		.50
R281	R21	$10 **orange**	140.00	27.50
		Cut cancel		2.25
		Perf. initial		.50

Types of 1917 Handstamped in Green "Series 1940"

1940　　　Wmk. 191R　　　Perf. 12

Without Gum

R282	R17	$30 **vermilion**	500.
		Cut cancel	350.
		Perf. initial	300.
a.		With black 2-line handstamp in larger type	—
R283	R19	$60 **brown**	800.
		Cut cancel	600.
		Perf. initial	400.
a.		As #R282a, cut cancel	—
R284	R17	$100 **green**	1,500.
		Cut cancel	900.
		Perf. initial	650.
R285	R18	$500 **blue**	1,400.
		Cut cancel	1,100.
		Perf. initial	900.

		Double transfer		1,450.
a.		As #R282a	2,750.	2,500.
		Cut cancel		1,800.
		Double transfer	—	2,650.
b.		Blue handstamp; double transfer	—	—
c.		Violet handstamp; double transfer		1,500.
R286	R19	$1000 **orange**		650.
		Cut cancel		375.
		Perf. initial		250.

Alexander　　　　　　　Levi
Hamilton — R23　　　　　Woodbury — R24

Overprinted in Black　　　**SERIES 1940**

Various Portraits: 2c, Oliver Wolcott, Jr. 3c, Samuel Dexter. 4c, Albert Gallatin. 5c. G. W. Campbell. 8c, Alexander Dallas. 10c, William H. Crawford. 20c, Richard Rush. 25c, S. D. Ingham. 40c. Louis McLane. 50c, William J. Duane. 80c, Roger B. Taney. $2, Thomas Ewing. $3, Walter Forward. $4, J. C. Spencer. $5, G. M. Bibb. $10, R. J. Walker. $20, William M. Meredith.
The "sensitive ink" varieties are in a bluish-purple overprint showing minute flecks of gold.

1940　Engr.　Wmk. 191R　Perf. 11

Plates of 400 subjects, issued in panes of 100

R288	R23	1c **carmine**	4.00	3.00
		Cut cancel		1.25
		Perf. initial		.65
		Sensitive ink	7.50	4.00
R289	R23	2c **carmine**	4.50	2.75
		Cut cancel		1.25
		Perf. initial		.80
		Sensitive ink	7.50	4.00
R290	R23	3c **carmine**	17.50	9.00
		Cut cancel		3.25
		Perf. initial		2.25
		Sensitive ink	20.00	7.50
R291	R23	4c **carmine**	45.00	20.00
		Cut cancel		4.50
		Perf. initial		3.75
R292	R23	5c **carmine**	3.00	.60
		Cut cancel		.25
		Perf. initial		.20
R293	R23	8c **carmine**	65.00	45.00
		Cut cancel		17.50
		Perf. initial		12.50
R294	R23	10c **carmine**	2.50	.45
		Cut cancel		.20
		Perf. initial		.20
R295	R23	20c **carmine**	3.75	2.50
		Cut cancel		1.00
		Perf. initial		.75
R296	R23	25c **carmine**	2.75	.50
		Cut cancel		.20
		Perf. initial		.20
R297	R23	40c **carmine**	45.00	20.00
		Cut cancel		5.00
		Perf. initial		2.25
R298	R23	50c **carmine**	4.50	.40
		Cut cancel		.20
		Perf. initial		.20
R299	R23	80c **carmine**	100.00	60.00
		Cut cancel		25.00
		Perf. initial		17.50

Plates of 200 subjects, issued in panes of 50

R300	R24	$1 **carmine**	40.00	.55
		Cut cancel		.20
		Perf. initial		.20
		Sensitive ink	50.00	20.00
R301	R24	$2 **carmine**	47.50	.75
		Cut cancel		.20
		Perf. initial		.20
		Sensitive ink	52.50	10.00
R302	R24	$3 **carmine**	135.00	75.00
		Cut cancel		10.00
		Perf. initial		7.00
		Sensitive ink	140.00	75.00
R303	R24	$4 **carmine**	80.00	30.00
		Cut cancel		6.00
		Perf. initial		1.50
R304	R24	$5 **carmine**	47.50	2.00
		Cut cancel		.45
		Perf. initial		.25
R305	R24	$10 **carmine**	85.00	6.00
		Cut cancel		1.00
		Perf. initial		.40
R305A	R24	$20 **carmine**	1,650.	750.00
		Cut cancel		475.00
		Perf. initial		350.00
b.		Imperf., pair		600.00

Thomas Corwin — R25

Overprint: "SERIES 1940"

Various Frames and Portraits: $50, James Guthrie. $60, Howell Cobb. $100, P. F. Thomas. $500, J. A. Dix, $1,000, S. P. Chase.

Perf. 12

Plates of 16 subjects, issued in strips of 4
Without Gum

R306	R25	$30 **carmine**	130.00	45.00
	Cut cancel			13.50
	Perf. initial			10.00
R306A	R25	$50 **carmine**	—	2,500.
	Cut cancel			1,400.
	Perf. initial			700.00
R307	R25	$60 **carmine**	260.00	60.00
	Cut cancel			37.50
	Perf. initial			20.00
a.	Vert. pair, imperf. btwn.			1,450.
R308	R25	$100 **carmine**	190.00	65.00
	Cut cancel			30.00
	Perf. initial			12.50
R309	R25	$500 **carmine**	—	1,900.
	Cut cancel			850.00
	Perf. initial			375.00
R310	R25	$1000 **carmine**	—	425.00
	Cut cancel			200.00
	Perf. initial			140.00

The $30 to $1,000 denominations in this and following similar issues, and the $2,500, $5,000 and $10,000 stamps of 1952-58 have straight edges on one or two sides. They were issued without gum through No. R723.

Nos. R288-R310 Overprinted: **SERIES 1941**

1941		**Wmk. 191R**		**Perf. 11**
R311	R23	1c **carmine**	3.00	2.25
	Cut cancel			.70
	Perf. initial			.60
R312	R23	2c **carmine**	3.00	.90
	Cut cancel			.40
	Perf. initial			.35
R313	R23	3c **carmine**	7.50	3.50
	Cut cancel			1.25
	Perf. initial			.85
R314	R23	4c **carmine**	5.00	1.25
	Cut cancel			.30
	Perf. initial			.20
R315	R23	5c **carmine**	1.00	.25
	Cut cancel			.20
	Perf. initial			.20
R316	R23	8c **carmine**	14.00	7.50
	Cut cancel			3.00
	Perf. initial			2.50
R317	R23	10c **carmine**	1.25	.20
	Cut cancel			.20
	Perf. initial			.20
R318	R23	20c **carmine**	3.00	.45
	Cut cancel			.20
	Perf. initial			.20
R319	R23	25c **carmine**	1.75	.20
	Cut cancel			.20
	Perf. initial			.20
R320	R23	40c **carmine**	11.00	2.50
	Cut cancel			1.00
	Perf. initial			.60
R321	R23	50c **carmine**	2.50	.20
	Cut cancel			.20
	Perf. initial			.20
R322	R23	80c **carmine**	55.00	10.00
	Cut cancel			2.75
	Perf. initial			2.25
R323	R24	$1 **carmine**	10.00	.25
	Cut cancel			.20
	Perf. initial			.20
R324	R24	$2 **carmine**	12.50	.35
	Cut cancel			.20
	Perf. initial			.20
R325	R24	$3 **carmine**	20.00	2.75
	Cut cancel			.35
	Perf. initial			.30
R326	R24	$4 **carmine**	35.00	17.50
	Cut cancel			.85
	Perf. initial			.70
R327	R24	$5 **carmine**	40.00	.60
	Cut cancel			.20
	Perf. initial			.20
R328	R24	$10 **carmine**	60.00	3.50
	Cut cancel			.30
	Perf. initial			.25
R329	R24	$20 **carmine**	550.00	190.00
	Cut cancel			65.00
	Perf. initial			45.00

Without Gum				**Perf. 12**
R330	R25	$30 **carmine**	60.00	25.00
	Cut cancel			10.00
	Perf. initial			7.00
R331	R25	$50 **carmine**	200.00	160.00
	Cut cancel			80.00
	Perf. initial			40.00
R332	R25	$60 **carmine**	85.00	45.00
	Cut cancel			22.50
	Perf. initial			11.00
R333	R25	$100 **carmine**	55.00	19.00
	Cut cancel			6.50
	Perf. initial			4.50
R334	R25	$500 **carmine**	—	220.00
	Cut cancel			125.00
	Perf. initial			50.00
R335	R25	$1000 **carmine**	—	125.00
	Cut cancel			40.00
	Perf. initial			27.50

Nos. R288-R310 Overprinted: **SERIES 1942**

1942		**Wmk. 191R**		**Perf. 11**
R336	R23	1c **carmine**	.50	.45
	Cut cancel			.20
	Perf. initial			.20
R337	R23	2c **carmine**	.45	.45
	Cut cancel			.20
	Perf. initial			.20
R338	R23	3c **carmine**	.70	.60
	Cut cancel			.25
	Perf. initial			.20
R339	R23	4c **carmine**	1.20	.90
	Cut cancel			.25
	Perf. initial			.20
R340	R23	5c **carmine**	.45	.20
	Cut cancel			.20
	Perf. initial			.20
R341	R23	8c **carmine**	5.50	4.25
	Cut cancel			1.10
	Perf. initial			1.00
R342	R23	10c **carmine**	1.20	.25
	Cut cancel			.20
	Perf. initial			.20
R343	R23	20c **carmine**	1.20	.45
	Cut cancel			.20
	Perf. initial			.20
R344	R23	25c **carmine**	2.10	.45
	Cut cancel			.20
	Perf. initial			.20
R345	R23	40c **carmine**	4.75	1.20
	Cut cancel			.50
	Perf. initial			.30
R346	R23	50c **carmine**	3.00	.20
	Cut cancel			.20
	Perf. initial			.20
R347	R23	80c **carmine**	17.50	10.00
	Cut cancel			2.75
	Perf. initial			1.90
R348	R24	$1 **carmine**	9.00	.25
	Cut cancel			.20
	Perf. initial			.20
R349	R24	$2 **carmine**	10.00	.25
	Cut cancel			.20
	Perf. initial			.20
R350	R24	$3 **carmine**	17.50	2.00
	Cut cancel			.25
	Perf. initial			.20
R351	R24	$4 **carmine**	25.00	3.75
	Cut cancel			.30
	Perf. initial			.25
R352	R24	$5 **carmine**	27.50	.90
	Cut cancel			.20
	Perf. initial			.20
R353	R24	$10 **carmine**	65.00	2.50
	Cut cancel			.20
	Perf. initial			.20
R354	R24	$20 **carmine**	120.00	35.00
	Cut cancel			17.50
	Perf. initial			11.00

Without Gum				**Perf. 12**
R355	R25	$30 **carmine**	45.00	20.00
	Cut cancel			9.00
	Perf. initial			5.00
R356	R25	$50 **carmine**	600.00	500.00
	Cut cancel			225.00
	Perf. initial			125.00
R357	R25	$60 **carmine**	700.00	625.00
	Cut cancel			240.00
	Perf. initial			110.00
R358	R25	$100 **carmine**	160.00	120.00
	Cut cancel			50.00
	Perf. initial			37.50
R359	R25	$500 **carmine**	900.00	200.00
	Cut cancel			125.00
	Perf. initial			75.00
R360	R25	$1000 **carmine**	—	100.00
	Cut cancel			50.00
	Perf. initial			40.00

Nos. R288-R310 Overprinted: **SERIES 1943**

1943		**Wmk. 191R**		**Perf. 11**
R361	R23	1c **carmine**	.60	.50
	Cut cancel			.20
	Perf. initial			.20
R362	R23	2c **carmine**	.45	.35
	Cut cancel			.20
	Perf. initial			.20
R363	R23	3c **carmine**	2.50	2.50
	Cut cancel			.50
	Perf. initial			.30

R364	R23	4c **carmine**	1.00	1.00
	Cut cancel			.30
	Perf. initial			.25
R365	R23	5c **carmine**	.50	.30
	Cut cancel			.20
	Perf. initial			.20
R366	R23	8c **carmine**	4.25	3.00
	Cut cancel			1.50
	Perf. initial			1.00
R367	R23	10c **carmine**	.60	.25
	Cut cancel			.20
	Perf. initial			.20
R368	R23	20c **carmine**	1.90	.65
	Cut cancel			.30
	Perf. initial			.20
R369	R23	25c **carmine**	1.50	.25
	Cut cancel			.20
	Perf. initial			.20
R370	R23	40c **carmine**	5.00	2.25
	Cut cancel			1.10
	Perf. initial			.60
R371	R23	50c **carmine**	1.25	.20
	Cut cancel			.20
	Perf. initial			.20
R372	R23	80c **carmine**	15.00	5.50
	Cut cancel			2.00
	Perf. initial			1.00
R373	R24	$1 **carmine**	6.00	.35
	Cut cancel			.20
	Perf. initial			.20
R374	R24	$2 **carmine**	11.00	.25
	Cut cancel			.20
	Perf. initial			.20
R375	R24	$3 **carmine**	20.00	2.25
	Cut cancel			.30
	Perf. initial			.20
R376	R24	$4 **carmine**	27.50	3.25
	Cut cancel			.40
	Perf. initial			.30
R377	R24	$5 **carmine**	35.00	.60
	Cut cancel			.30
	Perf. initial			.20
R378	R24	$10 **carmine**	55.00	4.00
	Cut cancel			1.50
	Perf. initial			.65
R379	R24	$20 **carmine**	110.00	22.50
	Cut cancel			5.00
	Perf. initial			3.00

Without Gum				**Perf. 12**
R380	R25	$30 **carmine**	37.50	18.00
	Cut cancel			4.75
	Perf. initial			4.25
R381	R25	$50 **carmine**	70.00	30.00
	Cut cancel			12.50
	Perf. initial			5.00
R382	R25	$60 **carmine**	175.00	75.00
	Cut cancel			32.50
	Perf. initial			11.00
R383	R25	$100 **carmine**	25.00	10.00
	Cut cancel			5.50
	Perf. initial			3.50
R384	R25	$500 **carmine**	—	175.00
	Cut cancel			90.00
	Perf. initial			65.00
R385	R25	$1000 **carmine**	—	150.00
	Cut cancel			45.00
	Perf. initial			37.50

Nos. R288-R310 Overprinted: **Series 1944**

1944		**Wmk. 191R**		**Perf. 11**
R386	R23	1c **carmine**	.40	.35
	Cut cancel			.20
	Perf. initial			.20
R387	R23	2c **carmine**	.40	.35
	Cut cancel			.20
	Perf. initial			.20
R388	R23	3c **carmine**	.40	.35
	Cut cancel			.20
	Perf. initial			.20
R389	R23	4c **carmine**	.55	.50
	Cut cancel			.20
	Perf. initial			.20
R390	R23	5c **carmine**	.30	.20
	Cut cancel			.20
	Perf. initial			.20
R391	R23	8c **carmine**	1.75	1.25
	Cut cancel			.45
	Perf. initial			.40
R392	R23	10c **carmine**	.40	.20
	Cut cancel			.20
	Perf. initial			.20
R393	R23	20c **carmine**	.75	.20
	Cut cancel			.20
	Perf. initial			.20
R394	R23	25c **carmine**	1.40	.20
	Cut cancel			.20
	Perf. initial			.20
R395	R23	40c **carmine**	2.75	.60
	Cut cancel			.25
	Perf. initial			.20
R396	R23	50c **carmine**	3.00	.20
	Cut cancel			.20
	Perf. initial			.20
R397	R23	80c **carmine**	15.00	4.00
	Cut cancel			1.25
	Perf. initial			.80
R398	R24	$1 **carmine**	7.50	.20
	Cut cancel			.20
	Perf. initial			.20
R399	R24	$2 **carmine**	10.00	.25
	Cut cancel			.20
	Perf. initial			.20
R400	R24	$3 **carmine**	16.00	2.00
	Cut cancel			.50
	Perf. initial			.20

R401	R24	$4 **carmine**	22.50	10.00
		Cut cancel		1.00
		Perf. initial		.90
R402	R24	$5 **carmine**	25.00	.25
		Cut cancel		.20
		Perf. initial		.20
R403	R24	$10 **carmine**	50.00	1.40
		Cut cancel		.25
		Perf. initial		.20
R404	R24	$20 **carmine**	100.00	15.00
		Cut cancel		3.00
		Perf. initial		2.00

Without Gum — *Perf. 12*

R405	R25	$30 **carmine**	55.00	22.50
		Cut cancel		6.00
		Perf. initial		5.75
R406	R25	$50 **carmine**	22.50	15.00
		Cut cancel		5.00
		Perf. initial		3.75
R407	R25	$60 **carmine**	110.00	45.00
		Cut cancel		21.00
		Perf. initial		8.25
R408	R25	$100 **carmine**	40.00	9.00
		Cut cancel		4.00
		Perf. initial		3.00
R409	R25	$500 **carmine**	—	1,750.
		Cut cancel		1,000.
		Perf. initial		675.00
R410	R25	$1000 **carmine**	—	200.00
		Cut cancel		75.00
		Perf. initial		45.00

Nos. R288-R310 Overprinted: **Series 1945**

1945   **Wmk. 191R**   *Perf. 11*

R411	R23	1c **carmine**	.20	.20
		Cut cancel		.20
		Perf. initial		.20
R412	R23	2c **carmine**	.25	.20
		Cut cancel		.20
		Perf. initial		.20
R413	R23	3c **carmine**	.50	.45
		Cut cancel		.20
		Perf. initial		.20
R414	R23	4c **carmine**	.30	.30
		Cut cancel		.20
		Perf. initial		.20
R415	R23	5c **carmine**	.25	.20
		Cut cancel		.20
		Perf. initial		.20
R416	R23	8c **carmine**	4.25	2.00
		Cut cancel		.60
		Perf. initial		.30
R417	R23	10c **carmine**	.80	.20
		Cut cancel		.20
		Perf. initial		.20
R418	R23	20c **carmine**	4.50	1.00
		Cut cancel		.40
		Perf. initial		.20
R419	R23	25c **carmine**	1.10	.30
		Cut cancel		.20
		Perf. initial		.20
R420	R23	40c **carmine**	4.75	1.00
		Cut cancel		.40
		Perf. initial		.35
R421	R23	50c **carmine**	2.75	.20
		Cut cancel		.20
		Perf. initial		.20
R422	R23	80c **carmine**	20.00	8.00
		Cut cancel		3.00
		Perf. initial		1.75
R423	R24	$1 **carmine**	8.50	.20
		Cut cancel		.20
		Perf. initial		.20
R424	R24	$2 **carmine**	9.00	.25
		Cut cancel		.20
		Perf. initial		.20
R425	R24	$3 **carmine**	17.50	2.25
		Cut cancel		.80
		Perf. initial		.60
R426	R24	$4 **carmine**	25.00	3.00
		Cut cancel		.50
		Perf. initial		.30
R427	R24	$5 **carmine**	25.00	.40
		Cut cancel		.20
		Perf. initial		.20
R428	R24	$10 **carmine**	50.00	1.40
		Cut cancel		.25
		Perf. initial		.20
R429	R24	$20 **carmine**	100.00	11.00
		Cut cancel		3.00
		Perf. initial		2.50

Without Gum — *Perf. 12*

R430	R25	$30 **carmine**	65.00	25.00
		Cut cancel		6.50
		Perf. initial		4.50
R431	R25	$50 **carmine**	70.00	25.00
		Cut cancel		15.00
		Perf. initial		8.25
R432	R25	$60 **carmine**	125.00	42.50
		Cut cancel		24.00
		Perf. initial		10.00
R433	R25	$100 **carmine**	35.00	14.00
		Cut cancel		8.00
		Perf. initial		5.25
R434	R25	$500 **carmine**	200.00	160.00
		Cut cancel		67.50
		Perf. initial		50.00
R435	R25	$1000 **carmine**	100.00	82.50
		Cut cancel		30.00
		Perf. initial		17.50

Nos. R288-R310 Overprinted: **Series 1946**

1946   **Wmk. 191R**   *Perf. 11*

R436	R23	1c **carmine**	.20	.25
		Cut cancel		.20
		Perf. initial		.20
R437	R23	2c **carmine**	.35	.30
		Cut cancel		.20
		Perf. initial		.20
R438	R23	3c **carmine**	.35	.30
		Cut cancel		.20
		Perf. initial		.20
R439	R23	4c **carmine**	.60	.50
		Cut cancel		.20
		Perf. initial		.20
R440	R23	5c **carmine**	.30	.20
		Cut cancel		.20
		Perf. initial		.20
R441	R23	8c **carmine**	1.25	1.10
		Cut cancel		.25
		Perf. initial		.20
R442	R23	10c **carmine**	.70	.20
		Cut cancel		.20
		Perf. initial		.20
R443	R23	20c **carmine**	1.25	.40
		Cut cancel		.20
		Perf. initial		.20
R444	R23	25c **carmine**	4.00	.20
		Cut cancel		.20
		Perf. initial		.20
R445	R23	40c **carmine**	2.50	.75
		Cut cancel		.30
		Perf. initial		.20
R446	R23	50c **carmine**	3.00	.20
		Cut cancel		.20
		Perf. initial		.20
R447	R23	80c **carmine**	12.50	4.25
		Cut cancel		.60
		Perf. initial		.45
R448	R24	$1 **carmine**	9.00	.20
		Cut cancel		.20
		Perf. initial		.20
R449	R24	$2 **carmine**	12.50	.20
		Cut cancel		.20
		Perf. initial		.20
R450	R24	$3 **carmine**	19.00	5.00
		Cut cancel		.85
		Perf. initial		.35
R451	R24	$4 **carmine**	25.00	10.00
		Cut cancel		2.00
		Perf. initial		1.00
R452	R24	$5 **carmine**	25.00	.45
		Cut cancel		.20
		Perf. initial		.20
R453	R24	$10 **carmine**	50.00	1.50
		Cut cancel		.30
		Perf. initial		.20
R454	R24	$20 **carmine**	100.00	11.00
		Cut cancel		2.50
		Perf. initial		1.50

Without Gum — *Perf. 12*

R455	R25	$30 **carmine**	45.00	12.00
		Cut cancel		4.50
		Perf. initial		3.00
R456	R25	$50 **carmine**	22.50	9.00
		Cut cancel		4.00
		Perf. initial		2.50
R457	R25	$60 **carmine**	45.00	16.00
		Cut cancel		12.00
		Perf. initial		7.50
R458	R25	$100 **carmine**	50.00	10.00
		Cut cancel		3.50
		Perf. initial		3.00
R459	R25	$500 **carmine**	—	105.00
		Cut cancel		37.50
		Perf. initial		25.00
R460	R25	$1000 **carmine**	—	100.00
		Cut cancel		30.00
		Perf. initial		20.00

Nos. R288-R310 Overprinted: **Series 1947**

1947   **Wmk. 191R**   *Perf. 11*

R461	R23	1c **carmine**	.65	.50
		Cut cancel		.20
		Perf. initial		.20
R462	R23	2c **carmine**	.55	.50
		Cut cancel		.20
		Perf. initial		.20
R463	R23	3c **carmine**	.55	.50
		Cut cancel		.20
		Perf. initial		.20
R464	R23	4c **carmine**	.70	.60
		Cut cancel		.20
		Perf. initial		.20
R465	R23	5c **carmine**	.35	.30
		Cut cancel		.20
		Perf. initial		.20
R466	R23	8c **carmine**	1.20	.70
		Cut cancel		.20
		Perf. initial		.20
R467	R23	10c **carmine**	1.10	.25
		Cut cancel		.20
		Perf. initial		.20
R468	R23	20c **carmine**	1.80	.50
		Cut cancel		.20
		Perf. initial		.20
R469	R23	25c **carmine**	2.40	.60
		Cut cancel		.20
		Perf. initial		.20
R470	R23	40c **carmine**	3.75	.90
		Cut cancel		.20
		Perf. initial		.20
R471	R23	50c **carmine**	3.00	.25
		Cut cancel		.20
		Perf. initial		.20

R472	R23	80c **carmine**	8.25	6.00
		Cut cancel		.60
		Perf. initial		.20
R473	R24	$1 **carmine**	6.00	.25
		Cut cancel		.20
		Perf. initial		.20
R474	R24	$2 **carmine**	9.50	.50
		Cut cancel		.20
		Perf. initial		.20
R475	R24	$3 **carmine**	12.00	5.00
		Cut cancel		1.00
		Perf. initial		.60
R476	R24	$4 **carmine**	14.00	4.50
		Cut cancel		.40
		Perf. initial		.30
R477	R24	$5 **carmine**	21.00	.50
		Cut cancel		.20
		Perf. initial		.20
R478	R24	$10 **carmine**	50.00	2.00
		Cut cancel		.60
		Perf. initial		.20
R479	R24	$20 **carmine**	75.00	10.00
		Cut cancel		1.00
		Perf. initial		.70

Without Gum — *Perf. 12*

R480	R25	$30 **carmine**	65.00	17.50
		Cut cancel		4.75
		Perf. initial		2.40
R481	R25	$50 **carmine**	32.50	12.00
		Cut cancel		4.75
		Perf. initial		3.00
R482	R25	$60 **carmine**	80.00	35.00
		Cut cancel		17.50
		Perf. initial		9.00
R483	R25	$100 **carmine**	32.50	10.00
		Cut cancel		4.00
		Perf. initial		2.00
R484	R25	$500 **carmine**	—	150.00
		Cut cancel		60.00
		Perf. initial		35.00
R485	R25	$1000 **carmine**	—	80.00
		Cut cancel		35.00
		Perf. initial		22.50

Nos. R288-R310 Overprinted: **Series 1948**

1948   **Wmk. 191R**   *Perf. 11*

R486	R23	1c **carmine**	.25	.25
		Cut cancel		.20
		Perf. initial		.20
R487	R23	2c **carmine**	.35	.30
		Cut cancel		.20
		Perf. initial		.20
R488	R23	3c **carmine**	.45	.35
		Cut cancel		.20
		Perf. initial		.20
R489	R23	4c **carmine**	.40	.20
		Cut cancel		.20
		Perf. initial		.20
R490	R23	5c **carmine**	.35	.20
		Cut cancel		.20
		Perf. initial		.20
R491	R23	8c **carmine**	.75	.35
		Cut cancel		.20
		Perf. initial		.20
R492	R23	10c **carmine**	.60	.20
		Cut cancel		.20
		Perf. initial		.20
R493	R23	20c **carmine**	1.75	.20
		Cut cancel		.20
		Perf. initial		.20
R494	R23	25c **carmine**	1.50	.20
		Cut cancel		.20
		Perf. initial		.20
R495	R23	40c **carmine**	4.50	1.50
		Cut cancel		.20
		Perf. initial		.20
R496	R23	50c **carmine**	2.25	.20
		Cut cancel		.20
		Perf. initial		.20
R497	R23	80c **carmine**	7.50	4.50
		Cut cancel		1.50
		Perf. initial		.50
R498	R24	$1 **carmine**	7.50	.20
		Cut cancel		.20
		Perf. initial		.20
R499	R24	$2 **carmine**	12.50	.20
		Cut cancel		.20
		Perf. initial		.20
R500	R24	$3 **carmine**	17.50	2.50
		Cut cancel		.40
		Perf. initial		.25
R501	R24	$4 **carmine**	25.00	2.75
		Cut cancel		.75
		Perf. initial		.40
R502	R24	$5 **carmine**	21.00	.50
		Cut cancel		.20
		Perf. initial		.20
R503	R24	$10 **carmine**	50.00	1.00
		Cut cancel		.25
		Perf. initial		.20
a.		Pair, one dated "1946"		—
R504	R24	$20 **carmine**	95.00	10.00
		Cut cancel		3.25
		Perf. initial		1.60

Without Gum — *Perf. 12*

R505	R25	$30 **carmine**	42.50	20.00
		Cut cancel		6.00
		Perf. initial		3.00
R506	R25	$50 **carmine**	42.50	17.50
		Cut cancel		7.25
		Perf. initial		3.00
a.		Vert. pair, imperf. btwn.		—

R507 R25 $60 **carmine**	65.00	27.50	
Cut cancel		15.00	
Perf. initial		6.00	
a. Vert. pair, imperf. btwn.	1,100.		
R508 R25 $100 **carmine**	55.00	10.00	
Cut cancel		4.00	
Perf. initial		2.50	
a. Vert. pair, imperf. btwn.	850.00		
R509 R25 $500 **carmine**	125.00	100.00	
Cut cancel		45.00	
Perf. initial		27.50	
R510 R25 $1000 **carmine**	87.50	60.00	
Cut cancel		27.50	
Perf. initial		18.00	

Nos. R288-R310 Overprinted: **Series 1949**

1949 **Wmk. 191R** *Perf. 11*

R511 R23 1c **carmine**	.25	.25	
Cut cancel		.20	
Perf. initial		.20	
R512 R23 2c **carmine**	.55	.35	
Cut cancel		.20	
Perf. initial		.20	
R513 R23 3c **carmine**	.40	.35	
Cut cancel		.20	
Perf. initial		.20	
R514 R23 4c **carmine**	.60	.50	
Cut cancel		.20	
Perf. initial		.20	
R515 R23 5c **carmine**	.35	.20	
Cut cancel		.20	
Perf. initial		.20	
R516 R23 8c **carmine**	.70	.60	
Cut cancel		.20	
Perf. initial		.20	
R517 R23 10c **carmine**	.40	.25	
Cut cancel		.20	
Perf. initial		.20	
R518 R23 20c **carmine**	1.30	.60	
Cut cancel		.30	
Perf. initial		.25	
R519 R23 25c **carmine**	1.80	.70	
Cut cancel		.25	
Perf. initial		.20	
R520 R23 40c **carmine**	4.25	2.10	
Cut cancel		.40	
Perf. initial		.30	
R521 R23 50c **carmine**	3.50	.30	
Cut cancel		.20	
Perf. initial		.20	
R522 R23 80c **carmine**	10.00	4.75	
Cut cancel		1.50	
Perf. initial		.75	
R523 R24 $1 **carmine**	8.50	.40	
Cut cancel		.20	
Perf. initial		.20	
R524 R24 $2 **carmine**	11.00	2.00	
Cut cancel		.40	
Perf. initial		.25	
R525 R24 $3 **carmine**	17.50	6.00	
Cut cancel		2.00	
Perf. initial		1.00	
R526 R24 $4 **carmine**	21.00	6.00	
Cut cancel		2.75	
Perf. initial		1.50	
R527 R24 $5 **carmine**	21.00	2.25	
Cut cancel		.60	
Perf. initial		.40	
R528 R24 $10 **carmine**	50.00	2.50	
Cut cancel		1.00	
Perf. initial		.85	
R529 R24 $20 **carmine**	95.00	9.00	
Cut cancel		2.00	
Perf. initial		1.25	

Without Gum *Perf. 12*

R530 R25 $30 **carmine**	55.00	22.50	
Cut cancel		6.00	
Perf. initial		3.75	
R531 R25 $50 **carmine**	65.00	35.00	
Cut cancel		12.00	
Perf. initial		7.25	
R532 R25 $60 **carmine**	90.00	40.00	
Cut cancel		20.00	
Perf. initial		10.00	
R533 R25 $100 **carmine**	50.00	15.00	
Cut cancel		3.00	
Perf. initial		2.50	
R534 R25 $500 **carmine**	—	180.00	
Cut cancel		100.00	
Perf. initial		55.00	
R535 R25 $1000 **carmine**	—	110.00	
Cut cancel		35.00	
Perf. initial		20.00	

Nos. R288-R310 Overprinted: Series 1950

1950 **Wmk. 191R** *Perf. 11*

R536 R23 1c **carmine**	.20	.20	
Cut cancel		.20	
Perf. initial		.20	
R537 R23 2c **carmine**	.30	.25	
Cut cancel		.20	
Perf. initial		.20	
R538 R23 3c **carmine**	.35	.30	
Cut cancel		.20	
Perf. initial		.20	
R539 R23 4c **carmine**	.50	.40	
Cut cancel		.20	
Perf. initial		.20	
R540 R23 5c **carmine**	.30	.20	
Cut cancel		.20	
Perf. initial		.20	

R541 R23 8c **carmine**	1.25	.65	
Cut cancel		.20	
Perf. initial		.20	
R542 R23 10c **carmine**	.60	.20	
Cut cancel		.20	
Perf. initial		.20	
R543 R23 20c **carmine**	1.00	.35	
Cut cancel		.25	
Perf. initial		.20	
R544 R23 25c **carmine**	1.50	.35	
Cut cancel		.25	
Perf. initial		.20	
R545 R23 40c **carmine**	3.25	1.75	
Cut cancel		.40	
Perf. initial		.25	
R546 R23 50c **carmine**	4.00	.20	
Cut cancel		.20	
Perf. initial		.20	
R547 R23 80c **carmine**	9.00	4.00	
Cut cancel		.85	
Perf. initial		.50	
R548 R24 $1 **carmine**	9.00	.25	
Cut cancel		.20	
Perf. initial		.20	
R549 R24 $2 **carmine**	11.00	2.00	
Cut cancel		.35	
Perf. initial		.20	
R550 R24 $3 **carmine**	12.50	4.00	
Cut cancel		1.25	
Perf. initial		.75	
R551 R24 $4 **carmine**	17.50	5.00	
Cut cancel		2.50	
Perf. initial		1.25	
R552 R24 $5 **carmine**	21.00	.80	
Cut cancel		.30	
Perf. initial		.20	
R553 R24 $10 **carmine**	47.50	8.50	
Cut cancel		.80	
Perf. initial		.50	
R554 R24 $20 **carmine**	95.00	9.00	
Cut cancel		2.50	
Perf. initial		1.75	

Without Gum *Perf. 12*

R555 R25 $30 **carmine**	70.00	40.00	
Cut cancel		12.00	
Perf. initial		10.00	
R556 R25 $50 **carmine**	42.50	14.00	
Cut cancel		8.25	
Perf. initial		5.50	
a. Vert. pair, imperf. horiz.		—	
R557 R25 $60 **carmine**	100.00	50.00	
Cut cancel		18.00	
Perf. initial		9.50	
R558 R25 $100 **carmine**	55.00	17.50	
Cut cancel		5.00	
Perf. initial		3.00	
R559 R25 $500 **carmine**	—	100.00	
Cut cancel		47.50	
Perf. initial		30.00	
R560 R25 $1000 **carmine**	—	75.00	
Cut cancel		25.00	
Perf. initial		18.00	

Nos. R288-R310 Overprinted: **Series 1951**

1951 **Wmk. 191R** *Perf. 11*

R561 R23 1c **carmine**	.20	.20	
Cut cancel		.20	
Perf. initial		.20	
R562 R23 2c **carmine**	.30	.25	
Cut cancel		.20	
Perf. initial		.20	
R563 R23 3c **carmine**	.25	.25	
Cut cancel		.20	
Perf. initial		.20	
R564 R23 4c **carmine**	.30	.25	
Cut cancel		.20	
Perf. initial		.20	
R565 R23 5c **carmine**	.30	.20	
Cut cancel		.20	
Perf. initial		.20	
R566 R23 8c **carmine**	1.00	.35	
Cut cancel		.20	
Perf. initial		.20	
R567 R23 10c **carmine**	.55	.20	
Cut cancel		.20	
Perf. initial		.20	
R568 R23 20c **carmine**	1.25	.45	
Cut cancel		.25	
Perf. initial		.20	
R569 R23 25c **carmine**	1.25	.40	
Cut cancel		.25	
Perf. initial		.20	
R570 R23 40c **carmine**	3.00	1.25	
Cut cancel		.40	
Perf. initial		.25	
R571 R23 50c **carmine**	2.50	.35	
Cut cancel		.20	
Perf. initial		.20	
R572 R23 80c **carmine**	7.50	2.50	
Cut cancel		1.50	
Perf. initial		.75	
R573 R24 $1 **carmine**	9.00	.20	
Cut cancel		.20	
Perf. initial		.20	
R574 R24 $2 **carmine**	11.00	.50	
Cut cancel		.20	
Perf. initial		.20	
R575 R24 $3 **carmine**	16.00	3.50	
Cut cancel		1.75	
Perf. initial		1.00	
R576 R24 $4 **carmine**	21.00	5.00	
Cut cancel		2.50	
Perf. initial		1.25	

R577 R24 $5 **carmine**	17.50	.60	
Cut cancel		.30	
Perf. initial		.20	
R578 R24 $10 **carmine**	42.50	2.25	
Cut cancel		1.00	
Perf. initial		.75	
R579 R24 $20 **carmine**	90.00	8.50	
Cut cancel		3.50	
Perf. initial		3.00	

Without Gum *Perf. 12*

R580 R25 $30 **carmine**	70.00	10.00	
Cut cancel		5.00	
Perf. initial		3.50	
a. Imperf., pair	750.00		
R581 R25 $50 **carmine**	55.00	16.00	
Cut cancel		6.50	
Perf. initial		4.25	
R582 R25 $60 **carmine**	90.00	40.00	
Cut cancel		20.00	
Perf. initial		15.00	
R583 R25 $100 **carmine**	45.00	12.50	
Cut cancel		6.75	
Perf. initial		5.00	
R584 R25 $500 **carmine**	125.00	82.50	
Cut cancel		45.00	
Perf. initial		22.50	
R585 R25 $1000 **carmine**	—	95.00	
Cut cancel		35.00	
Perf. initial		27.50	

No. R583 is known imperf horizontally. It exists as a reconstructed used vertical strip of 4 that was separated into single stamps.

Documentary Stamps and Types of 1940 Overprinted in Black

Series 1952

Designs: 55c, $1.10, $1.65, $2.20, $2.75, $3.30, L. J. Gage; $2500, William Windom; $5000, C. J. Folger; $10,000, W. Q. Gresham.

1952 **Wmk. 191R** *Perf. 11*

R586 R23 1c **carmine**	.20	.20	
Cut cancel		.20	
Perf. initial		.20	
R587 R23 2c **carmine**	.35	.25	
Cut cancel		.20	
Perf. initial		.20	
R588 R23 3c **carmine**	.30	.25	
Cut cancel		.20	
Perf. initial		.20	
R589 R23 4c **carmine**	.30	.25	
Cut cancel		.20	
Perf. initial		.20	
R590 R23 5c **carmine**	.25	.20	
Cut cancel		.20	
Perf. initial		.20	
R591 R23 8c **carmine**	.65	.45	
Cut cancel		.20	
Perf. initial		.20	
R592 R23 10c **carmine**	.40	.20	
Cut cancel		.20	
Perf. initial		.20	
R593 R23 20c **carmine**	1.00	.35	
Cut cancel		.25	
Perf. initial		.20	
R594 R23 25c **carmine**	1.50	.40	
Cut cancel		.25	
Perf. initial		.20	
R595 R23 40c **carmine**	3.00	1.00	
Cut cancel		.50	
Perf. initial		.40	
R596 R23 50c **carmine**	2.75	.20	
Cut cancel		.20	
Perf. initial		.20	
R597 R23 55c **carmine**	20.00	10.00	
Cut cancel		1.25	
Perf. initial		1.00	
R598 R23 80c **carmine**	12.50	3.00	
Cut cancel		.75	
Perf. initial		.70	
R599 R24 $1 **carmine**	5.00	1.50	
Perf. initial		.35	
R600 R24 $1.10 **carmine**	42.50	25.00	
Cut cancel		10.00	
Perf. initial		6.00	
R601 R24 $1.65 **carmine**	140.00	45.00	
Cut cancel		30.00	
Perf. initial		20.00	
R602 R24 $2 **carmine**	9.50	.65	
Cut cancel		.20	
Perf. initial		.20	
R603 R24 $2.20 **carmine**	115.00	60.00	
Cut cancel		30.00	
Perf. initial		15.00	
R604 R24 $2.75 **carmine**	130.00	60.00	
Cut cancel		30.00	
Perf. initial		15.00	
R605 R24 $3 **carmine**	25.00	4.00	
Cut cancel		1.50	
Perf. initial		1.25	
a. Horiz. pair, imperf. btwn.	600.00		
R606 R24 $3.30 **carmine**	115.00	60.00	
Cut cancel		30.00	
Perf. initial		15.00	
R607 R24 $4 **carmine**	22.50	4.00	
Cut cancel		2.00	
Perf. initial		1.50	
R608 R24 $5 **carmine**	22.50	1.25	
Cut cancel		.40	
Perf. initial		.35	
R609 R24 $10 **carmine**	45.00	1.25	
Cut cancel		.40	
Perf. initial		.35	

```
R610 R24   $20 carmine        70.00   9.00
     Cut cancel                       3.50
     Perf. initial                    2.75

          Without Gum         Perf. 12
R611 R25   $30 carmine        47.50  18.00
     Cut cancel                       5.00
     Perf. initial                    4.00
R612 R25   $50 carmine        42.50  12.00
     Cut cancel                       6.00
     Perf. initial                    4.50
R613 R25   $60 carmine       250.00  50.00
     Cut cancel                      15.00
     Perf. initial                   10.00
R614 R25  $100 carmine        37.50   8.00
     Cut cancel                       3.00
     Perf. initial                    2.00
R615 R25  $500 carmine          —    100.00
     Cut cancel                      57.50
     Perf. initial                   32.50
R616 R25 $1000 carmine          —     30.00
     Cut cancel                      15.00
     Perf. initial                   10.00
R617 R25 $2500 carmine          —    165.00
     Cut cancel                     130.00
     Perf. initial                  100.00
R618 R25 $5000 carmine          —    2,500.
     Cut cancel                     1,250.
     Perf. initial                  900.00
R619 R25 R25 $10,000 carmine    —    1,250.
     Cut cancel                     800.00
     Perf. initial                  550.00
```

Documentary Stamps and Types of 1940 Overprinted in Black
Series 1953

```
1953        Wmk. 191R          Perf. 11
R620 R23    1c carmine          .20    .20
     Cut cancel                        .20
     Perf. initial                     .20
R621 R23    2c carmine          .20    .20
     Cut cancel                        .20
     Perf. initial                     .20
R622 R23    3c carmine          .25    .20
     Cut cancel                        .20
     Perf. initial                     .20
R623 R23    4c carmine          .35    .25
     Cut cancel                        .20
     Perf. initial                     .20
R624 R23    5c carmine          .20    .20
     Cut cancel                        .20
     Perf. initial                     .20
  a. Vert. pair, imperf. horiz.      650.00
R625 R23    8c carmine          .75    .75
     Cut cancel                        .20
     Perf. initial                     .20
R626 R23   10c carmine          .40    .20
     Cut cancel                        .20
     Perf. initial                     .20
R627 R23   20c carmine          .75    .40
     Cut cancel                        .20
     Perf. initial                     .20
R628 R23   25c carmine         1.00    .50
     Cut cancel                        .25
     Perf. initial                     .20
R629 R23   40c carmine         1.75   1.00
     Cut cancel                        .40
     Perf. initial                     .30
R630 R23   50c carmine         2.50    .20
     Cut cancel                        .20
     Perf. initial                     .20
R631 R23   55c carmine         3.50   2.00
     Cut cancel                        .75
     Perf. initial                     .50
  a. Horiz. pair, imperf. vert.     350.00
R632 R23   80c carmine         6.00   2.00
     Cut cancel                       1.40
     Perf. initial                    1.25
R633 R24    $1 carmine         4.00    .25
     Cut cancel                        .20
     Perf. initial                     .20
R634 R24  $1.10 carmine        7.00   2.25
     Cut cancel                       2.00
     Perf. initial                    1.50
  a. Horiz. pair, imperf. vert.     500.00
  b. Imperf. pair                      —
R635 R24  $1.65 carmine        8.00   4.00
     Cut cancel                       3.00
     Perf. initial                    2.00
R636 R24    $2 carmine         6.00    .65
     Cut cancel                        .25
     Perf. initial                     .20
R637 R24  $2.20 carmine       12.50   6.00
     Cut cancel                       2.50
     Perf. initial                    2.00
R638 R24  $2.75 carmine       17.50   7.00
     Cut cancel                       3.50
     Perf. initial                    2.50
R639 R24    $3 carmine        10.00   3.00
     Cut cancel                       1.50
     Perf. initial                    1.25
R640 R24  $3.30 carmine       26.00   8.00
     Cut cancel                       5.00
     Perf. initial                    3.25
R641 R24    $4 carmine        20.00   7.50
     Cut cancel                       2.25
     Perf. initial                    2.00
R642 R24    $5 carmine        20.00   1.00
     Cut cancel                        .40
     Perf. initial                     .30
R643 R24   $10 carmine        45.00   1.75
     Cut cancel                       1.00
     Perf. initial                     .85
```

```
R644 R24   $20 carmine        85.00  18.00
     Cut cancel                       3.00
     Perf. initial                    2.25

          Without Gum         Perf. 12
R645 R25   $30 carmine        42.50  13.50
     Cut cancel                       6.00
     Perf. initial                    4.00
R646 R25   $50 carmine        80.00  27.50
     Cut cancel                      12.00
     Perf. initial                    5.00
R647 R25   $60 carmine       300.00 175.00
     Cut cancel                     110.00
     Perf. initial                   65.00
R648 R25  $100 carmine        37.50  12.00
     Cut cancel                       5.00
     Perf. initial                    3.50
R649 R25  $500 carmine       250.00 115.00
     Cut cancel                      50.00
     Perf. initial                   25.00
R650 R25 $1000 carmine       125.00  57.50
     Cut cancel                      22.50
     Perf. initial                   15.00
R651 R25 $2500 carmine       850.00 750.00
     Cut cancel                     350.00
     Perf. initial                  250.00
R652 R25 $5000 carmine          —    3,000.
     Cut cancel                     1,400.
     Perf. initial                  900.00
R653 R25 $10,000 carmine        —    2,000.
     Cut cancel                     1,000.
     Perf. initial                  650.00
```

Types of 1940 Without Overprint

```
1954        Wmk. 191R          Perf. 11
R654 R23    1c carmine          .20    .20
     Cut cancel                        .20
     Perf. initial                     .20
  a. Horiz. pair, imperf. vert.        —
R655 R23    2c carmine          .20    .20
     Cut cancel                        .20
     Perf. initial                     .20
R656 R23    3c carmine          .20    .20
     Cut cancel                        .20
     Perf. initial                     .20
R657 R23    4c carmine          .20    .20
     Cut cancel                        .20
     Perf. initial                     .20
R658 R23    5c carmine          .20    .20
     Cut cancel                        .20
     Perf. initial                     .20
R659 R23    8c carmine          .25    .20
     Cut cancel                        .20
     Perf. initial                     .20
R660 R23   10c carmine          .25    .20
     Cut cancel                        .20
     Perf. initial                     .20
R661 R23   20c carmine          .50    .30
     Cut cancel                        .20
     Perf. initial                     .20
R662 R23   25c carmine          .60    .35
     Cut cancel                        .20
     Perf. initial                     .20
R663 R23   40c carmine         1.25    .60
     Cut cancel                        .40
     Perf. initial                     .35
R664 R23   50c carmine         1.65    .20
     Cut cancel                        .20
     Perf. initial                     .20
  a. Horiz. pair, imperf. vert.     275.00
R665 R23   55c carmine         1.50   1.25
     Cut cancel                        .50
     Perf. initial                     .40
R666 R23   80c carmine         2.25   1.75
     Cut cancel                       1.10
     Perf. initial                    1.00
R667 R24    $1 carmine         1.50    .30
     Cut cancel                        .20
     Perf. initial                     .20
R668 R24  $1.10 carmine        3.25   2.50
     Cut cancel                       1.50
     Perf. initial                    1.00
R669 R24  $1.65 carmine       95.00  65.00
     Cut cancel                      42.50
     Perf. initial                   21.00
R670 R24    $2 carmine         1.75    .35
     Cut cancel                        .25
     Perf. initial                     .20
R671 R24  $2.20 carmine        4.50   3.75
     Cut cancel                       2.50
     Perf. initial                    1.50
R672 R24  $2.75 carmine      100.00  60.00
     Cut cancel                      35.00
     Perf. initial                   20.00
R673 R24    $3 carmine         3.00   2.00
     Cut cancel                       1.00
     Perf. initial                     .75
R674 R24  $3.30 carmine        6.50   5.00
     Cut cancel                       3.00
     Perf. initial                    2.00
R675 R24    $4 carmine         4.00   3.50
     Cut cancel                       2.00
     Perf. initial                    1.50
R676 R24    $5 carmine         6.00    .45
     Cut cancel                        .30
     Perf. initial                     .30
R677 R24   $10 carmine        12.50   1.25
     Cut cancel                        .80
     Perf. initial                     .70
R678 R24   $20 carmine        32.50   5.75
     Cut cancel                       3.00
     Perf. initial                    1.75
```

Documentary Stamps and Type of 1940 Overprinted in Black
Series 1954

```
1954        Wmk. 191R          Perf. 12
            Without Gum
R679 R25   $30 carmine        32.50  12.00
     Cut cancel                       4.50
     Perf. initial                    3.00
R680 R25   $50 carmine        42.50  17.50
     Cut cancel                       9.00
     Perf. initial                    5.50
R681 R25   $60 carmine        70.00  20.00
     Cut cancel                      12.50
     Perf. initial                    9.00
R682 R25  $100 carmine        32.50   7.00
     Cut cancel                       4.75
     Perf. initial                    4.00
R683 R25  $500 carmine          —     75.00
     Cut cancel                      22.50
     Perf. initial                   18.00
R684 R25 $1000 carmine       150.00  55.00
     Cut cancel                      18.00
     Perf. initial                   15.00
R685 R25 $2500 carmine          —    200.00
     Cut cancel                      90.00
     Perf. initial                   60.00
R686 R25 $5000 carmine          —    850.00
     Cut cancel                     550.00
     Perf. initial                  350.00
R687 R25 $10,000 carmine        —    1,000.
     Cut cancel                     350.00
     Perf. initial                  200.00
```

Documentary Stamps and Type of 1940 Overprinted in Black
Series 1955

```
1955        Wmk. 191R          Perf. 12
            Without Gum
R688 R25   $30 carmine        42.50  11.50
     Cut cancel                       6.00
     Perf. initial                    3.50
R689 R25   $50 carmine        42.50  13.50
     Cut cancel                       9.00
     Perf. initial                    6.25
R690 R25   $60 carmine        75.00  25.00
     Cut cancel                      12.50
     Perf. initial                    4.00
R691 R25  $100 carmine        37.50   7.00
     Cut cancel                       5.00
     Perf. initial                    3.50
R692 R25  $500 carmine          —    125.00
     Cut cancel                      35.00
     Perf. initial                   20.00
R693 R25 $1000 carmine          —     35.00
     Cut cancel                      17.50
     Perf. initial                   12.50
R694 R25 $2500 carmine          —    140.00
     Cut cancel                      80.00
     Perf. initial                   50.00
R695 R25 $5000 carmine        1,100. 1,000.
     Cut cancel                     500.00
     Perf. initial                  325.00
R696 R25 $10,000 carmine        —    850.00
     Cut cancel                     375.00
     Perf. initial                  150.00
```

Documentary Stamps and Type of 1940 Overprinted in Black "Series 1956"

```
1956   Wmk. 191R   Without Gum   Perf. 12
R697 R25   $30 carmine        55.00  13.50
     Cut cancel                       9.00
     Perf. initial                    4.50
R698 R25   $50 carmine        60.00  17.00
     Cut cancel                      10.00
     Perf. initial                    4.50
R699 R25   $60 carmine        75.00  35.00
     Cut cancel                      12.00
     Perf. initial                    5.00
R700 R25  $100 carmine        55.00  12.50
     Cut cancel                       5.00
     Perf. initial                    4.00
R701 R25  $500 carmine          —     85.00
     Cut cancel                      25.00
     Perf. initial                   15.00
R702 R25 $1000 carmine       400.00  60.00
     Cut cancel                      17.50
     Perf. initial                   10.00
R703 R25 $2500 carmine          —    350.00
     Cut cancel                     150.00
     Perf. initial                   80.00
R704 R25 $5000 carmine          —    1,400.
     Cut cancel                     1,000.
     Perf. initial                  650.00
R705 R25 $10,000 carmine        —    500.00
     Cut cancel                     180.00
     Perf. initial                  100.00
```

Documentary Stamps and Type of 1940 Overprinted in Black "Series 1957"

```
1957        Wmk. 191R          Perf. 12
            Without Gum
R706 R25   $30 carmine        70.00  27.50
     Cut cancel                      10.00
     Perf. initial                    5.00
R707 R25   $50 carmine        55.00  24.00
     Cut cancel                      10.00
     Perf. initial                    4.50
```

R708	R25	$60 **carmine**	—	150.00
		Cut cancel		90.00
		Perf. initial		50.00
R709	R25	$100 **carmine**	50.00	12.50
		Cut cancel		8.00
		Perf. initial		4.00
R710	R25	$500 **carmine**	175.00	90.00
		Cut cancel		50.00
		Perf. initial		30.00
R711	R25	$1000 **carmine**	—	80.00
		Cut cancel		30.00
		Perf. initial		20.00
R712	R25	$2500 **carmine**	—	525.00
		Cut cancel		375.00
		Perf. initial		200.00
R713	R25	$5000 **carmine**	—	900.00
		Cut cancel		400.00
		Perf. initial		190.00
R714	R25	$10,000 **carmine**	—	450.00
		Cut cancel		175.00
		Perf. initial		100.00

Documentary Stamps and Type of 1940 Overprinted in Black "Series 1958"

1958		**Wmk. 191R**		*Perf. 12*
		Without Gum		
R715	R25	$30 **carmine**	80.00	20.00
		Cut cancel		15.00
		Perf. initial		8.00
R716	R25	$50 **carmine**	65.00	20.00
		Cut cancel		14.00
		Perf. initial		6.00
R717	R25	$60 **carmine**	75.00	25.00
		Cut cancel		15.00
		Perf. initial		10.00
R718	R25	$100 **carmine**	55.00	10.00
		Cut cancel		5.50
		Perf. initial		2.00
R719	R25	$500 **carmine**	125.00	57.50
		Cut cancel		30.00
		Perf. initial		19.00

R720	R25	$1000 **carmine**	—	67.50
		Cut cancel		30.00
		Perf. initial		20.00
R721	R25	$2500 **carmine**	—	750.00
		Cut cancel		450.00
		Perf. initial		300.00
R722	R25	$5000 **carmine**	—	1,750.00
		Cut cancel		1,250.00
		Perf. initial		750.00
R723	R25	$10,000 **carmine**	—	900.00
		Cut cancel		700.00
		Perf. initial		400.00

Documentary Stamps and Type of 1940 Without Overprint

1958		**Wmk. 191R**		*Perf. 12*
		With Gum		
R724	R25	$30 **carmine**	37.50	7.00
		Cut cancel		5.75
		Perf. initial		4.75
a.		Vert. pair, imperf. horiz.	—	
R725	R25	$50 **carmine**	42.50	7.00
		Cut cancel		3.75
		Perf. initial		3.00
a.		Vert. pair, imperf. horiz.	—	
R726	R25	$60 **carmine**	80.00	20.00
		Cut cancel		10.00
		Perf. initial		5.00
R727	R25	$100 **carmine**	19.00	4.75
		Cut cancel		3.00
		Perf. initial		2.25
R728	R25	$500 **carmine**	85.00	25.00
		Cut cancel		10.00
		Perf. initial		7.50
R729	R25	$1000 **carmine**	55.00	20.00
		Cut cancel		10.00
		Perf. initial		7.50
a.		Vert. pair, imperf. horiz.	—	750.00
R730	R25	$2500 **carmine**	—	140.00
		Cut cancel		85.00
		Perf. initial		50.00

R731	R25	$5000 **carmine**	—	150.00
		Cut cancel		85.00
		Perf. initial		60.00
R732	R25	$10,000 **carmine**	—	125.00
		Cut cancel		50.00
		Perf. initial		25.00

Internal Revenue Building, Washington, D.C. — R26

Centenary of the Internal Revenue Service.

Giori Press Printing

1962, July 2		**Unwmk.**		*Perf. 11*
R733	R26	10c **violet blue & bright green**	.80	.35
		Never hinged	1.10	
		Cut cancel		.20
		Perf. initial		.20
		P# block of 4	15.00	

1963		**"Established 1862" Removed**		
R734	R26	10c **violet blue & bright green**	2.50	.35
		Never hinged	3.50	
		Cut cancel		.20
		Perf. initial		.20
		P# block of 4	30.00	

Documentary revenue stamps were no longer required after Dec. 31, 1967.

PROPRIETARY STAMPS

Stamps for use on proprietary articles were included in the first general issue of 1862-71. They are R3, R13, R14, R18, R22, R29, R31 and R38.

Several varieties of "violet" paper were used in printing Nos. RB1-RB10. One is grayish with a slight greenish tinge, called "intermediate" paper by specialists. It should not be confused with the "green" paper, which is truly green.

All values prior to 1898 are for used copies. Printed cancellations on proprietary stamps command sizable premiums.

George Washington
RB1   RB1a
Engraved and printed by Jos. R. Carpenter, Philadelphia.

1871-74   *Perf. 12*

			a. Violet Paper (1871)	b. Green Paper (1874)
RB1	RB1	1c **green & black**	5.00	9.00
		Pair	11.00	21.00
		Block of 4	25.00	55.00
c.		Imperf.	80.00	
		Imperf. pair	175.00	
		Imperf. block of 4	475.00	
d.		Inverted center	2,500.	
RB2	RB1	2c **green & black**	6.00	20.00
		Pair	13.50	47.50
		Block of 4	30.00	100.00
		Double transfer	18.00	
		Vert. half used as 1c on document	—	
c.		Inverted center	40,000.	8,500.
RB3	RB1a	3c **green & black**	17.50	50.00
		Pair	42.50	120.00
		Block of 4	82.50	250.00
		Double transfer	—	
c.		Sewing machine perf.	275.00	
d.		Inverted center	16,000.	

No. RB3d is valued with small faults as all recorded examples have faults.

RB4	RB1a	4c **green & black**	10.00	17.50
		Pair	25.00	45.00
		Block of 4	65.00	100.00
		Double transfer	—	
		Vert. half used as 2c on document	—	
c.		Inverted center	19,000.	

No. RB4c is valued with small faults as all recorded examples have faults.

			a. Violet Paper (1871)	b. Green Paper (1874)
RB5	RB1a	5c **green & black**	150.00	150.00
		Pair	325.00	350.00
		Block of 4	675.00	750.00
c.		Inverted center	80,000.	
RB6	RB1a	6c **green & black**	35.00	100.00
		Pair	80.00	240.00
		Block of 4	210.00	525.00
		Double transfer	—	
RB7	RB1a	10c **green & black** ('73)	175.00	50.00
		Pair	425.00	115.00
		Block of 4	—	280.00
		Double transfer	—	

(See note on Inverted Centers after No. R133.)

RB1b

			a. Violet Paper	b. Green Paper (1874)
RB8	RB1b	50c **green & black** ('73)	500.	900.
		Pair	1,100.	
RB9	RB1b	$1 **green & black** ('73)	1,100.	6,000.
		Pair	—	

RB1c

			a. Violet Paper	b. Green Paper ('1874)
RB10	RB1c	$5	green & black	5,500.	25,000.

			a. Violet Paper	b. Green Paper (1874)
RB10	RB1c	$5 green & black ('73)	5,500.	25,000.
		Pair	12,500.	

No. RB10b is valued with small faults.

When the Carpenter contract expired Aug. 31, 1875, the proprietary stamps remaining unissued were delivered to the Bureau of Internal Revenue. Until the taxes expired, June 30, 1883, the B.I.R. issued 34,315 of the 50c, 6,585 of the $1 and 2,109 of the $5, Nos. RB8-RB10. No. RB19, the 10c blue, replaced No. RB7b, the 10c on green paper, after 336,000 copies were issued, exhausting the supply in 1881.

George Washington
RB2　　　　RB2a

Plates prepared and printed by both the National Bank Note Co. and the Bureau of Engraving and Printing. No. RB11, and possibly others, also printed by the American Bank Note Co. All silk paper printings were by National, plus early printings of Nos. RB11b-RB14b, RB16b, RB17b. All rouletted stamps printed by the BEP plus Nos. RB15b, RB18b, RB19b. Otherwise, which company printed the stamps can be told only by guide lines (BEP) or full marginal inscriptions. ABN used National plates with A. B. Co. added on the second stamp to the left of the National inscription.

1875-81

			Silk Paper a. Perf.	Wmkd. 191R b. Perf.	c. Roul. 6
RB11	RB2	1c green	1.90	.40	80.00
		Pair	4.50	1.10	200.00
		Block of 4	12.00	2.75	500.00
		Dble. transfer			
	d.	Vert. pair, imperf between		250.00	
RB12	RB2	2c brown	2.50	1.40	100.00
		Pair	6.25	3.40	230.00
		Block of 4	62.50	8.00	525.00
RB13	RB2a	3c orange	12.50	3.00	100.00
		Pair	27.50	6.75	230.00
		Block of 4	60.00	15.00	525.00

			Silk Paper a. Perf.	Wmkd. 191R b. Perf.	c. Roul. 6
	d.	Horizontal pair, imperf. between			—
RB14	RB2a	4c red brown	6.00	5.50	
		Pair	13.00	12.00	
		Block of 4	27.50	25.00	
RB15	RB2a	4c red		4.50	150.00
		Pair		10.00	360.00
		Block of 4		25.00	
RB16	RB2a	5c black	110.00	90.00	1,500.
		Pair	250.00	210.00	
		Block of 4	—	—	
RB17	RB2a	6c violet blue	25.00	20.00	260.00
		Pair	62.50	50.00	650.00
		Block of 4	175.00	140.00	
RB18	RB2a	6c violet		30.00	300.00
		Pair		80.00	
		Block of 4		225.00	
RB19	RB2a	10c blue ('81)		300.00	
		Pair		600.00	
		Block of 4		—	

Many fraudulent roulettes exist.
The existence of No. RB18c has been questioned by specialists. The editors would like to see authenticated evidence proving its existence.

Battleship — RB3

Inscribed "Series of 1898." and "Proprietary."
See note on rouletting preceding No. R161.

1898　　　　Wmk. 191R　　　　Engr.

			Roul. 5½ Unused	Used	p. Hyphen Hole Perf. 7 Unused	Used
RB20	⅛c	yellow green	.20	.20	.20	.20
		Block of 4	.25	.25	.55	.50
		Double transfer	—			
	a.	Vert. pair, imperf. horiz.	—			
RB21	¼c	brown	.20	.20	.20	.20
	a.	¼c red brown	.20	.20		
	b.	¼c yellow brown	.20	.20	.20	.20
	c.	¼c orange brown	.20	.20	.20	.20
	d.	¼c bister	.20	.20		
		Block of 4	.25	.25	.55	1.00
		Double transfer	—			
	e.	Vert. pair, imperf. horiz.	—	—		
	f.	Printed on both sides	—			
RB22	⅜c	deep orange	.20	.20	.25	.20
		Block of 4	.60	.30	1.25	—
	a.	Horiz. pair, imperf. vert.	10.00			
	b.	Vert. pair, imperf. horiz.	—			
RB23	⅝c	deep ultra	.20	.20	.25	.20
		Block of 4	.60	.40	1.25	1.00
		Double transfer	1.50			
	a.	Vert. pair, imperf. horiz.	75.00	—		
	b.	Horiz. pair, imperf. vert.	300.00			
RB24	1c	dark green	2.00	.20	20.00	12.50
		Block of 4	10.00	.75	100.00	65.00
	a.	Vert. pair, imperf. horiz.	300.00			
RB25	1¼c	violet	.20	.20	.20	.20
		Block of 4	.45	.35	.90	.90
	a.	1¼c brown violet	.20	.20	.20	.25
	b.	Vertical pair, imperf. between	—			
RB26	1⅞c	dull blue	11.50	1.50	30.00	7.50
		Block of 4	55.00	—	150.00	
		Double transfer	—			
RB27	2c	violet brown	1.00	.20	6.00	.75
		Block of 4	4.40	—	26.00	
		Double transfer	—			
	a.	Horiz. pair, imperf. vert.	50.00			
RB28	2½c	lake	4.00	.20	5.00	.25
		Block of 4	20.00	.60	27.50	—
	a.	Vert. pair, imperf. horiz.	175.00			
RB29	3¾c	olive gray	40.00	10.00	70.00	20.00
		Block of 4	200.00	—	350.00	100.00
RB30	4c	purple	12.50	1.00	60.00	17.50
		Block of 4	60.00	5.00	300.00	87.50
		Double transfer	—			
RB31	5c	brown orange	12.50	1.00	65.00	20.00
		Block of 4	60.00	5.25	325.00	160.00
	a.	Vert. pair, imperf. horiz.	—	300.00		
	b.	Horiz. pair, imperf. vert.	—	400.00		

See note after No. RS315 regarding St. Louis Provisional Labels of 1898.

RB4

Inscribed "Series of 1914"

1914　　　Wmk. 190　　　Offset Printing　　　Perf. 10

				Unused	Used
RB32	RB4	⅛c	black	.20	.20
			Block of 4	1.00	.75
RB33	RB4	¼c	black	2.00	1.00
			Block of 4	10.00	
RB34	RB4	⅜c	black	.20	.20
			Block of 4	.90	.75
RB35	RB4	⅝c	black	4.50	1.75
			Block of 4	20.00	
RB36	RB4	1¼c	black	3.00	.80
			Block of 4	15.00	
RB37	RB4	1⅞c	black	40.00	15.00
			Block of 4	180.00	
RB38	RB4	2½c	black	9.00	2.50
			Block of 4	45.00	11.00
RB39	RB4	3⅛c	black	90.00	50.00
			Block of 4	400.00	
RB40	RB4	3¾c	black	40.00	20.00
			Block of 4	180.00	
RB41	RB4	4c	black	60.00	27.50
			Block of 4	275.00	
RB42	RB4	4⅜c	black	1,100.	—
			Block of 4		
RB43	RB4	5c	black	120.00	70.00
			Block of 4		

Wmk. 191R

				Unused	Used
RB44	RB4	⅛c	black	.20	.20
			Block of 4	.75	.45
RB45	RB4	¼c	black	.20	.20
			Block of 4	.75	.45
			Double impression	12.50	
RB46	RB4	⅜c	black	.60	.30
			Block of 4	3.00	1.50
RB47	RB4	½c	black	3.00	2.75
			Block of 4	12.50	
RB48	RB4	⅝c	black	.20	.20
			Block of 4	.70	.45
RB49	RB4	1c	black	4.25	4.00
			Block of 4	17.50	14.00
RB50	RB4	1¼c	black	.35	.25
			Block of 4	1.50	1.10
RB51	RB4	1½c	black	3.00	2.25
			Block of 4	14.00	10.00
RB52	RB4	1⅞c	black	1.00	.60
			Block of 4	4.50	2.25
RB53	RB4	2c	black	5.00	4.00
			Block of 4	22.50	
RB54	RB4	2½c	black	1.25	1.00
			Block of 4	5.50	4.50
RB55	RB4	3c	black	4.00	2.75
			Block of 4	17.50	
RB56	RB4	3⅛c	black	5.00	3.00
			Block of 4	22.50	
RB57	RB4	3¾c	black	11.00	7.50
			Block of 4	47.50	
RB58	RB4	4c	black	.30	.20
			Block of 4	1.50	1.00
			Double impression	—	
RB59	RB4	4⅜c	black	14.00	8.00
			Block of 4	60.00	
RB60	RB4	5c	black	3.00	2.50
			Block of 4	14.00	
RB61	RB4	6c	black	55.00	40.00
			Block of 4	250.00	
RB62	RB4	8c	black	17.50	11.00
			Block of 4	75.00	
RB63	RB4	10c	black	11.00	7.00
			Block of 4	47.50	
RB64	RB4	20c	black	22.50	17.50
			Block of 4		

RB5

1919　　　Offset Printing　　　Perf. 11

				Unused	Used
RB65	RB5	1c	dark blue	.20	.20
			Block of 4	.50	.40
			Double impression	30.00	20.00
RB66	RB5	2c	dark blue	.20	.20
			Block of 4	.55	.40
			Double impression	70.00	
RB67	RB5	3c	dark blue	1.00	.60
			Block of 4	4.50	2.75
			Double impression	70.00	
RB68	RB5	4c	dark blue	1.00	.50
			Block of 4	4.50	
RB69	RB5	5c	dark blue	1.25	.60
			Block of 4	5.50	2.75
RB70	RB5	8c	dark blue	14.00	9.00
			Block of 4	62.50	
RB71	RB5	10c	dark blue	5.00	2.00
			Block of 4	22.50	8.50
RB72	RB5	20c	dark blue	7.50	3.00
			Block of 4	35.00	
RB73	RB5	40c	dark blue	45.00	10.00
			Block of 4	200.00	

FUTURE DELIVERY STAMPS

Issued to facilitate the collection of a tax upon each sale, agreement of sale or agreement to sell any products or merchandise at any exchange or board of trade, or other similar place for future delivery.

Documentary Stamps of 1917 Overprinted in Black or Red

FUTURE

Type I

DELIVERY

1918-34   Wmk. 191R   Offset Printing   Perf. 11
Overprint Horizontal (Lines 8mm apart)

RC1	R22	2c **carmine rose**	4.50	.20
		Block of 4	20.00	.50
RC2	R22	3c **carmine rose** ('34)	30.00	22.50
		Cut cancel		12.50
RC3	R22	4c **carmine rose**	7.50	.20
		Block of 4	35.00	.50
		Double impression of stamp		10.00
RC3A	R22	5c **carmine rose** ('33)	75.00	5.00
				25.00
RC4	R22	10c **carmine rose**	12.50	.20
		Block of 4	60.00	.75
a.		Double overprint		5.00
b.		"FUTURE" omitted	—	200.00
c.		"DELIVERY FUTURE"		35.00
RC5	R22	20c **carmine rose**	17.50	.20
		Block of 4	85.00	.50
a.		Double overprint		20.00
RC6	R22	25c **carmine rose**	40.00	.40
		Block of 4	200.00	2.00
		Cut cancel		.20
		Block of 4, cut cancel		.25
RC7	R22	40c **carmine rose**	45.00	.75
		Block of 4	210.00	3.75
		Cut cancel		.20
		Block of 4, cut cancel		.25
RC8	R22	50c **carmine rose**	10.00	.20
		Block of 4	47.50	.55
a.		"DELIVERY" omitted	—	100.00
RC9	R22	80c **carmine rose**	85.00	10.00
		Block of 4	400.00	50.00
		Cut cancel		1.00
		Block of 4, cut cancel		4.50
a.		Double overprint		35.00
		Cut cancel		6.00

Engr.
Overprint Vertical, Reading Up (Lines 2mm apart)

RC10	R21	$1 **green** (R)	35.00	.20
		Block of 4	160.00	1.25
		Cut cancel		.20

a.		Overprint reading down		275.00
b.		Black overprint	—	
		Black ovpt., cut cancel		125.00
RC11	R21	$2 **rose**	40.00	.25
		Block of 4	175.00	1.25
		Cut cancel		.20
RC12	R21	$3 **violet** (R)	90.00	2.50
		Block of 4		11.50
		Cut cancel		.20
		Block of 4, cut cancel		.50
a.		Overprint reading down	—	50.00
RC13	R21	$5 **dark blue** (R)	70.00	.35
		Block of 4		1.50
		Cut cancel		.20
		Block of 4, cut cancel		.35
RC14	R21	$10 **orange**	90.00	.75
		Block of 4		3.00
		Cut cancel		.20
		Block of 4, cut cancel		.75
a.		"DELIVERY FUTURE"		100.00
RC15	R21	$20 **olive bister**	170.00	4.00
		Block of 4		20.00
		Cut cancel		.50
		Block of 4, cut cancel		2.25

Overprint Horizontal (Lines 11⅜mm apart)
Perf. 12
Without Gum

RC16	R17	$30 **vermilion**, green numerals	70.00	3.50
		Vertical strip of 4		22.50
		Cut cancel		1.25
		Vertical strip of 4, cut cancel		6.00
a.		Numerals in blue	60.00	3.50
		Cut cancel		1.50
b.		Imperf., blue numerals		100.00
RC17	R19	$50 **olive green** (Cleveland)	47.50	1.25
		Vertical strip of 4		12.50
		Cut cancel		.40
		Vertical strip of 4, cut cancel		2.50
a.		$50 olive bister	47.50	1.00
		Cut cancel		.40
RC18	R19	$60 **brown**	70.00	2.25
		Vertical strip of 4		15.00
		Cut cancel		.75
		Vertical strip of 4, cut cancel		3.50
a.		Vert. pair, imperf. horiz.		400.00
RC19	R17	$100 **yellow green** ('34)	110.00	27.50
		Vertical strip of 4	—	140.00
		Cut cancel		7.00
		Vertical strip of 4, cut cancel		30.00

RC20	R18	$500 **blue**, red numerals (R)	80.00	11.00
		Vertical strip of 4		60.00
		Cut cancel		4.50
		Vertical strip of 4, cut cancel		20.00
		Double transfer		15.00
a.		Numerals in orange	—	50.00
		Cut cancel		11.00
		Double transfer		75.00
RC21	R19	$1000 **orange**	95.00	5.50
		Vertical strip of 4		27.50
		Cut cancel		1.50
		Vertical strip of 4, cut cancel		7.50
a.		Vert. pair, imperf. horiz.		900.00

See note after No. R227.

1923-24   Offset Printing   Perf. 11
Overprint Horizontal (Lines 2mm apart)

RC22	R22	1c **carmine rose**	1.00	.20
		Block of 4	5.00	1.00
RC23	R22	80c **carmine rose**	75.00	1.75
		Block of 4		8.00
		Cut cancel		.35
		Block of 4, cut cancel		1.50

FUTURE

Type II

DELIVERY

1925-34   Engr.

RC25	R21	$1 **green** (R)	35.00	.75
		Block of 4		2.75
		Cut cancel		.20
		Block of 4, cut cancel		.30
RC26	R21	$10 **orange** (Bk) ('34)	100.00	15.00
		Cut cancel		10.00

Overprint Type I
1928-29   Offset Printing   Perf. 10

RC27	R22	10c **carmine rose**		1,500.
RC28	R22	20c **carmine rose**		1,500.

STOCK TRANSFER STAMPS

Issued to facilitate the collection of a tax on all sales or agreements to sell, or memoranda of sales or delivery of, or transfers of legal title to shares or certificates of stock.

STOCK

Documentary Stamps of 1917
Overprinted in Black or Red

TRANSFER

1918-22   Offset Printing   Wmk. 191R   Perf. 11
Overprint Horizontal (Lines 8mm apart)

RD1	R22	1c **carmine rose**	.85	.20
		Block of 4	3.50	.45
a.		Double overprint		
RD2	R22	2c **carmine rose**	.20	.20
		Block of 4	.90	.20
a.		Double overprint	—	5.00
		Double overprint, cut cancel		2.50
		Double impression of stamp	—	
RD3	R22	4c **carmine rose**	.20	.20
		Block of 4	.90	.20
a.		Double overprint	—	4.00
		Double overprint, cut cancel		2.00
b.		"STOCK" omitted		10.00
d.		Ovpt. lines 10mm apart	—	
		Double impression of stamp		6.00
RD4	R22	5c **carmine rose**	.25	.20
		Block of 4	1.10	.25
RD5	R22	10c **carmine rose**	.25	.20
		Block of 4	1.00	.25
a.		Double overprint	—	5.00
		Double overprint, cut cancel		2.50
b.		"STOCK" omitted		
		Double impression of stamp	—	
RD6	R22	20c **carmine rose**	.50	.20
		Block of 4	2.00	.25
a.		Double overprint		6.00
b.		"STOCK" double	—	
		Double impression of stamp		6.00

RD7	R22	25c **carmine rose**	1.50	.20
		Block of 4	7.00	.90
		Cut cancel		.20
RD8	R22	40c **carmine rose** ('22)	1.25	.20
		Block of 4	6.00	.30
RD9	R22	50c **carmine rose**	.65	.20
		Block of 4	3.00	.25
a.		Double overprint	—	
		Double impression of stamp	—	
RD10	R22	80c **carmine rose**	3.00	.30
		Block of 4	14.00	1.40
		Cut cancel		.20

Engr.
Overprint Vertical, Reading Up (Lines 2mm apart)

RD11	R21	$1 **green** (R)	85.00	20.00
		Block of 4		
		Cut cancel		3.00
		Block of 4, cut cancel		14.00
a.		Overprint reading down	125.00	20.00
		Overprint reading down, cut cancel		7.50
RD12	R21	$1 **green** (Bk)	2.50	.25
		Block of 4	11.00	1.25
a.		Pair, one without overprint	—	150.00
b.		Overprinted on back instead of face, inverted	—	100.00
c.		Overprint reading down	—	6.00
d.		$1 yellow green	2.75	.20
RD13	R21	$2 **rose**	2.50	.20
		Block of 4	11.00	1.00
a.		Overprint reading down		10.00
		Overprint reading down, cut cancel		1.50
b.		Vert. pair, imperf. horiz.	500.00	
RD14	R21	$3 **violet** (R)	17.50	4.25
		Block of 4	80.00	
		Cut cancel		.20
		Block of 4, cut cancel		1.00
RD15	R21	$4 **yellow brown**	9.00	.20
		Block of 4	40.00	.25
		Cut cancel		.20

RD16	R21	$5 **dark blue** (R)	6.00	.20
		Block of 4	30.00	.25
		Cut cancel		.20
		Block of 4, cut cancel		.20
a.		Overprint reading down	20.00	1.00
		Overprint reading down, cut cancel		.20
RD17	R21	$10 **orange**	16.00	.30
		Block of 4	75.00	.75
		Cut cancel		.20
		Block of 4, cut cancel		.20
RD18	R21	$20 **olive bister** ('21)	75.00	20.00
		Block of 4	325.00	90.00
		Cut cancel		3.00
		Block of 4, cut cancel		15.00

Shifted overprints on the $2, and $10 result in "TRANSFER STOCK," "TRANSFER" omitted, and possibly other varieties.

Overprint Horizontal (Lines 11½mm apart)
1918   Without Gum   Perf. 12

RD19	R17	$30 **vermilion**, green numerals	17.50	4.50
		Vertical strip of 4		20.00
		Cut cancel		1.00
		Vertical strip of 4, cut cancel		6.00
a.		Numerals in blue		55.00
RD20	R19	$50 **olive green** (Cleveland)	110.00	55.00
		Vertical strip of 4		250.00
		Cut cancel		20.00
		Vertical strip of 4, cut cancel		80.00
RD21	R19	$60 **brown**	110.00	20.00
		Vertical strip of 4		85.00
		Cut cancel		9.00
		Vertical strip of 4, cut cancel		40.00
RD22	R17	$100 **green**	22.50	5.50
		Vertical strip of 4		25.00
		Cut cancel		2.25
		Vertical strip of 4, cut cancel		10.00

RD23 R18 $500 **blue** (R) 300.00 110.00
   Vertical strip of 4 —
   Cut cancel 65.00
   Vertical strip of 4, cut cancel 275.00
   Double transfer *500.00* 175.00
  a. Numerals in orange 140.00
   Numerals in orange, double transfer 175.00
RD24 R19 $1000 **orange** 165.00 72.50
   Vertical strip of 4 325.00
   Cut cancel 25.00
   Vertical strip of 4, cut cancel 110.00

See note after No. R227.

1928   **Offset Printing**   *Perf. 10*
Overprint Horizontal (Lines 8mm apart)
RD25 R22 2c **carmine rose** 2.50 .25
   Block of 4 11.00 1.10
RD26 R22 4c **carmine rose** 2.50 .25
   Block of 4 11.00 1.10
RD27 R22 10c **carmine rose** 2.00 .25
   Block of 4 9.00 1.10
  a. Inverted overprint 1,000.
RD28 R22 20c **carmine rose** 3.00 .25
   Block of 4 14.00 1.10
   Double impression of stamp —
RD29 R22 50c **carmine rose** 3.50 .25
   Block of 4 16.00 1.10

Engr.
Overprint Vertical, Reading Up (Lines 2mm apart)
RD30 R21 $1 **green** 30.00 .20
   Block of 4 — .90
  a. $1 yellow green — .40
RD31 R21 $2 **carmine rose** 30.00 .20
   Block of 4 — .25
  a. Pair, one without overprint *200.00* 175.00
RD32 R21 $10 **orange** 32.50 .35
   Block of 4 — 1.75
   Cut cancel .20
   Perf. 11 at top or bottom —

STOCK

Overprinted Horizontally in Black

TRANSFER

1920   **Offset Printing**   *Perf. 11*
RD33 R22 2c **carmine rose** 7.50 .70
   Block of 4 35.00 3.50
RD34 R22 10c **carmine rose** 1.25 .30
   Block of 4 6.00 1.35
  b. Inverted overprint 1,500.
RD35 R22 20c **carmine rose** 1.00 .20
   Block of 4 4.75 .90
  a. Horiz. pair, one without overprint 175.00
  d. Inverted overprint (perf. initials) —
RD36 R22 50c **carmine rose** 3.00 .20
   Block of 4 14.00 .90

Shifted overprints on the 10c, 20c and 50c result in "TRANSFER STOCK," "TRANFSER" omitted, "STOCK" omitted, pairs, and other varieties.

Engr.
RD37 R21 $1 **green** 45.00 8.00
   Block of 4 200.00 35.00
   Cut cancel .25
   Block of 4, cut cancel 1.25
RD38 R21 $2 **rose** 40.00 8.00
   Block of 4 180.00 40.00
   Cut cancel .25
   Block of 4, cut cancel 1.10
Offset Printing
Perf. 10
RD39 R22 2c **carmine rose** 6.50 .50
   Block of 4 32.50 2.25
   Double impression of stamp —
RD40 R22 10c **carmine rose** 1.50 .50
   Block of 4 7.00 2.25
RD41 R22 20c **carmine rose** 2.50 .25
   Block of 4 12.50 1.10

SERIES 1940

Documentary Stamps of 1917-33
Overprinted in Black

STOCK
TRANSFER

1940   **Offset Printing**   **Wmk. 191R**   *Perf. 11*
RD42 R22 1c **rose pink** 3.00 .45
   Cut cancel .20
   Perf. initial .20
  a. "Series 1940" inverted — 225.00
   Cut cancel 100.00

No. RD42a always comes with a natural straight edge at left.

RD43 R22 2c **rose pink** 3.00 .50
   Cut cancel .20
   Perf. initial .20
RD45 R22 4c **rose pink** 3.00 .20
   Cut cancel .20
   Perf. initial .20
RD46 R22 5c **rose pink** 3.50 .20
   Cut cancel .20
   Perf. initial .20
RD48 R22 10c **rose pink** 3.50 .20
   Cut cancel .20
   Perf. initial .20

RD49 R22 20c **rose pink** 7.50 .20
   Cut cancel .20
   Perf. initial .20
RD50 R22 25c **rose pink** 7.50 .60
   Cut cancel .20
   Perf. initial .20
RD51 R22 40c **rose pink** 5.00 .75
   Cut cancel .20
   Perf. initial .20
RD52 R22 50c **rose pink** 6.00 .25
   Cut cancel .20
   Perf. initial .20
RD53 R22 80c **rose pink** 95.00 50.00
   Cut cancel 27.50
   Perf. initial 17.50

Engr.
RD54 R21 $1 **green** 27.50 .35
   Cut cancel .20
   Perf. initial .20
RD55 R21 $2 **rose** 27.50 .60
   Cut cancel .20
   Perf. initial .20
RD56 R21 $3 **violet** 160.00 9.00
   Cut cancel .25
   Perf. initial .20
RD57 R21 $4 **yellow brown** 55.00 1.00
   Cut cancel .25
   Perf. initial .20
RD58 R21 $5 **dark blue** 55.00 1.00
   Cut cancel .25
   Perf. initial .20
RD59 R21 $10 **orange** 120.00 6.00
   Cut cancel .50
   Perf. initial .45
RD60 R21 $20 **olive bister** 260.00 75.00
   Cut cancel 15.00
   Perf. initial 10.00

Nos. RD19-RD24 Handstamped in Blue "Series 1940"

1940   **Wmk. 191R**   *Perf. 12*
Without Gum
RD61 R17 $30 **vermilion** *900.* 550.
   Cut cancel 275.
   Perf. initial 140.
RD62 R19 $50 **olive green** *900.* 750.
   Cut cancel 375.
   Perf. initial 175.
  a. Double ovpt., perf. initial *350.*
RD63 R19 $60 **brown** *2,000.* 1,900.
   Cut cancel 600.
   Perf. initial 300.
RD64 R17 $100 **green** *750.* 550.
   Cut cancel 200.
   Perf. initial 80.
RD65 R18 $500 **blue** 2,200.
   Cut cancel 1,350.
   Perf. initial 750.
   Double transfer *2,300.*
RD66 R19 $1000 **orange** *2,400.*
   Cut cancel 2,000.
   Perf. initial 1,750.

Alexander
Hamilton — ST1

Levi
Woodbury — ST2

Overprinted in Black   **SERIES 1940**

Same Portraits as Nos. R288-R310.

1940   **Engr.**   **Wmk. 191R**   *Perf. 11*
RD67 ST1 1c **bright green** 11.00 2.75
   Cut cancel .50
   Perf. initial .30
RD68 ST1 2c **bright green** 7.00 1.40
   Cut cancel .20
   Perf. initial .20
RD70 ST1 4c **bright green** 12.50 3.75
   Cut cancel .50
   Perf. initial .25
RD71 ST1 5c **bright green** 7.50 1.40
   Cut cancel .20
   Perf. initial .20
  a. Without overprint, cut cancel 250.00
RD73 ST1 10c **bright green** 11.00 1.75
   Cut cancel .20
   Perf. initial .20
RD74 ST1 20c **bright green** 12.50 2.00
   Cut cancel .20
   Perf. initial .20
RD75 ST1 25c **bright green** 35.00 8.00
   Cut cancel .60
   Perf. initial .35
RD76 ST1 40c **bright green** 65.00 30.00
   Cut cancel 2.00
   Perf. initial .85

RD77 ST1 50c **bright green** 11.00 1.75
   Cut cancel .30
   Perf. initial .25
RD78 ST1 80c **bright green** 85.00 50.00
   Cut cancel 20.00
   Perf. initial 3.00
RD79 ST2 $1 **bright green** 37.50 3.50
   Cut cancel .35
   Perf. initial .25
  a. Without overprint, perf. initial *225.00*
RD80 ST2 $2 **bright green** 42.50 8.50
   Cut cancel .50
   Perf. initial .25
RD81 ST2 $3 **bright green** 65.00 10.00
   Cut cancel .60
   Perf. initial .20
RD82 ST2 $4 **bright green** 280.00 200.00
   Cut cancel 85.00
   Perf. initial 45.00
RD83 ST2 $5 **bright green** 60.00 12.50
   Cut cancel 1.50
   Perf. initial .25
RD84 ST2 $10 **bright green** 145.00 35.00
   Cut cancel 4.50
   Perf. initial 2.50
RD85 ST2 $20 **bright green** 650.00 70.00
   Cut cancel 9.00
   Perf. initial 4.50

Nos. RD67-RD85 exist imperforate, without overprint. Value, set of pairs, $750.

Thomas Corwin — ST3

Overprinted "SERIES 1940"
Various frames and portraits as Nos. R306-R310.

Without Gum   *Perf. 12*
RD86 ST3 $30 **bright green** — 150.00
   Cut cancel 70.00
   Perf. initial 35.00
RD87 ST3 $50 **bright green** 325.00 300.00
   Cut cancel 150.00
   Perf. initial 70.00
RD88 ST3 $60 **bright green** — 700.00
   Cut cancel 300.00
   Perf. initial 90.00
RD89 ST3 $100 **bright green** — 200.00
   Cut cancel 85.00
   Perf. initial 55.00
RD90 ST3 $500 **bright green** — 1,500.
   Cut cancel 1,000.
   Perf. initial 600.
RD91 ST3 $1000 **bright green** — 1,500.
   Cut cancel 800.
   Perf. initial 550.

Nos. RD67-RD91 Overprint Instead: **SERIES 1941**

1941   **Wmk. 191R**   *Perf. 11*
RD92 ST1 1c **bright green** .65 .50
   Cut cancel .20
   Perf. initial .20
RD93 ST1 2c **bright green** .45 .25
   Cut cancel .20
   Perf. initial .20
RD95 ST1 4c **bright green** .40 .20
   Cut cancel .20
   Perf. initial .20
RD96 ST1 5c **bright green** .35 .20
   Cut cancel .20
   Perf. initial .20
RD98 ST1 10c **bright green** .75 .20
   Cut cancel .20
   Perf. initial .20
RD99 ST1 20c **bright green** 1.75 .25
   Cut cancel .20
   Perf. initial .20
RD100 ST1 25c **bright green** 1.75 .40
   Cut cancel .20
   Perf. initial .20
RD101 ST1 40c **bright green** 2.50 .75
   Cut cancel .25
   Perf. initial .20
RD102 ST1 50c **bright green** 3.75 .35
   Cut cancel .20
   Perf. initial .20
RD103 ST1 80c **bright green** 22.50 7.50
   Cut cancel .50
   Perf. initial .45
RD104 ST2 $1 **bright green** 15.00 .20
   Cut cancel .20
   Perf. initial .20
RD105 ST2 $2 **bright green** 16.00 .25
   Cut cancel .20
   Perf. initial .20

RD106	ST2	$3 **bright green**	24.00	1.50
	Cut cancel			.30
	Perf. initial			.25
RD107	ST2	$4 **bright green**	42.50	7.50
	Cut cancel			.40
	Perf. initial			.25
RD108	ST2	$5 **bright green**	42.50	.60
	Cut cancel			.20
	Perf. initial			.20
RD109	ST2	$10 **bright green**	90.00	4.00
	Cut cancel			.70
	Perf. initial			.20
RD110	ST2	$20 **bright green**	165.00	55.00
	Cut cancel			15.00
	Perf. initial			4.00

Perf. 12
Without Gum

RD111	ST3	$30 **bright green**	150.00	140.00
	Cut cancel			55.00
	Perf. initial			18.00
RD112	ST3	$50 **bright green**	375.00	300.00
	Cut cancel			100.00
	Perf. initial			40.00
RD113	ST3	$60 **bright green**	600.00	225.00
	Cut cancel			160.00
	Perf. initial			100.00
RD114	ST3	$100 **bright green**	—	125.00
	Cut cancel			40.00
	Perf. initial			15.00
RD115	ST3	$500 **bright green**	875.00	1,400.
	Cut cancel			900.00
	Perf. initial			450.00
RD116	ST3	$1000 **bright green**	—	1,100.
	Cut cancel			700.00
	Perf. initial			500.00

Nos. RD67-RD91 Overprint Instead: **SERIES 1942**

1942 Wmk. 191R Perf. 11

RD117	ST1	1c **bright green**	.50	.30
	Cut cancel			.20
	Perf. initial			.20
RD118	ST1	2c **bright green**	.40	.35
	Cut cancel			.20
	Perf. initial			.20
RD119	ST1	4c **bright green**	3.00	1.00
	Cut cancel			.50
	Perf. initial			.40
RD120	ST1	5c **bright green**	.40	.20
	Cut cancel			.20
	Perf. initial			.20
a.	Overprint inverted, cut cancel			225.00
	Perf. initial			200.00
RD121	ST1	10c **bright green**	1.75	.20
	Cut cancel			.20
	Perf. initial			.20
RD122	ST1	20c **bright green**	2.00	.20
	Cut cancel			.20
	Perf. initial			.20
RD123	ST1	25c **bright green**	2.00	.20
	Cut cancel			.20
	Perf. initial			.20
RD124	ST1	40c **bright green**	4.25	.35
	Cut cancel			.20
	Perf. initial			.20
RD125	ST1	50c **bright green**	5.25	.20
	Cut cancel			.20
	Perf. initial			.20
RD126	ST1	80c **bright green**	22.50	5.25
	Cut cancel			1.25
	Perf. initial			.30
RD127	ST2	$1 **bright green**	14.00	.35
	Cut cancel			.25
	Perf. initial			.20
RD128	ST2	$2 **bright green**	20.00	.35
	Cut cancel			.20
	Perf. initial			.20
RD129	ST2	$3 **bright green**	27.50	1.00
	Cut cancel			.25
	Perf. initial			.20
RD130	ST2	$4 **bright green**	42.50	20.00
	Cut cancel			.35
	Perf. initial			.20
RD131	ST2	$5 **bright green**	37.50	.35
	Cut cancel			.20
	Perf. initial			.20
a.	Double overprint, perf. initial			—
RD132	ST2	$10 **bright green**	70.00	7.50
	Cut cancel			1.25
	Perf. initial			1.00
RD133	ST2	$20 **bright green**	160.00	32.50
	Cut cancel			7.00
	Perf. initial			3.00

Perf. 12
Without Gum

RD134	ST3	$30 **bright green**	100.00	50.00
	Cut cancel			20.00
	Perf. initial			12.50
RD135	ST3	$50 **bright green**	170.00	100.00
	Cut cancel			37.50
	Perf. initial			15.00
RD136	ST3	$60 **bright green**	200.00	160.00
	Cut cancel			45.00
RD137	ST3	$100 **bright green**	350.00	70.00
	Cut cancel			25.00
	Perf. initial			12.50
RD138	ST3	$500 **bright green**	—	9,500.
	Cut cancel			7,250.
	Perf. initial			6,500.
RD139	ST3	$1000 **bright green**	—	550.00
	Cut cancel			250.00
	Perf. initial			150.00

Nos. RD67-RD91 Overprint Instead: **SERIES 1943**

1943 Wmk. 191R Perf. 11

RD140	ST1	1c **bright green**	.40	.25
	Cut cancel			.20
	Perf. initial			.20
RD141	ST1	2c **bright green**	.50	.40
	Cut cancel			.20
	Perf. initial			.20
RD142	ST1	4c **bright green**	1.75	.20
	Cut cancel			.20
	Perf. initial			.20
RD143	ST1	5c **bright green**	.50	.20
	Cut cancel			.20
	Perf. initial			.20
RD144	ST1	10c **bright green**	1.00	.20
	Cut cancel			.20
	Perf. initial			.20
RD145	ST1	20c **bright green**	1.75	.20
	Cut cancel			.20
	Perf. initial			.20
RD146	ST1	25c **bright green**	3.75	.25
	Cut cancel			.20
	Perf. initial			.20
RD147	ST1	40c **bright green**	3.75	.25
	Cut cancel			.20
	Perf. initial			.20
RD148	ST1	50c **bright green**	3.75	.20
	Cut cancel			.20
	Perf. initial			.20
RD149	ST1	80c **bright green**	15.00	4.50
	Cut cancel			1.50
	Perf. initial			1.00
RD150	ST2	$1 **bright green**	15.00	.20
	Cut cancel			.20
	Perf. initial			.20
RD151	ST2	$2 **bright green**	17.50	.35
	Cut cancel			.20
	Perf. initial			.20
RD152	ST2	$3 **bright green**	21.00	1.00
	Cut cancel			.25
	Perf. initial			.20
RD153	ST2	$4 **bright green**	42.50	15.00
	Cut cancel			1.00
	Perf. initial			.25
RD154	ST2	$5 **bright green**	60.00	.35
	Cut cancel			.25
	Perf. initial			.20
RD155	ST2	$10 **bright green**	85.00	4.50
	Cut cancel			.75
	Perf. initial			.25
RD156	ST2	$20 **bright green**	150.00	37.50
	Cut cancel			14.00
	Perf. initial			3.50

Perf. 12
Without Gum

RD157	ST3	$30 **bright green**	220.00	110.00
	Cut cancel			45.00
	Perf. initial			20.00
RD158	ST3	$50 **bright green**	500.00	140.00
	Cut cancel			27.50
	Perf. initial			14.00
RD159	ST3	$60 **bright green**	—	550.00
	Cut cancel			225.00
	Perf. initial			80.00
RD160	ST3	$100 **bright green**	75.00	55.00
	Cut cancel			17.50
	Perf. initial			12.50
RD161	ST3	$500 **bright green**	—	650.00
	Cut cancel			275.00
	Perf. initial			140.00
RD162	ST3	$1000 **bright green**	—	250.00
	Cut cancel			165.00
	Perf. initial			140.00

Nos. RD67-RD91 Overprint Instead: **Series 1944**

1944 Wmk. 191R Perf. 11

RD163	ST1	1c **bright green**	.65	.60
	Cut cancel			.20
	Perf. initial			.20
RD164	ST1	2c **bright green**	.45	.20
	Cut cancel			.20
	Perf. initial			.20
RD165	ST1	4c **bright green**	.60	.25
	Cut cancel			.20
	Perf. initial			.20
RD166	ST1	5c **bright green**	.50	.20
	Cut cancel			.20
	Perf. initial			.20
RD167	ST1	10c **bright green**	.75	.20
	Cut cancel			.20
	Perf. initial			.20
RD168	ST1	20c **bright green**	1.25	.20
	Cut cancel			.20
	Perf. initial			.20
RD169	ST1	25c **bright green**	2.00	.30
	Cut cancel			.20
	Perf. initial			.20
RD170	ST1	40c **bright green**	8.00	5.00
	Cut cancel			2.25
	Perf. initial			1.50
RD171	ST1	50c **bright green**	4.50	.20
	Cut cancel			.20
	Perf. initial			.20
RD172	ST1	80c **bright green**	9.00	4.50
	Cut cancel			2.00
	Perf. initial			1.50
RD173	ST2	$1 **bright green**	10.00	.40
	Cut cancel			.20
	Perf. initial			.20
RD174	ST2	$2 **bright green**	37.50	.60
	Cut cancel			.20
	Perf. initial			.20
RD175	ST2	$3 **bright green**	35.00	1.25
	Cut cancel			.25
	Perf. initial			.20

RD176	ST2	$4 **bright green**	40.00	5.00
	Cut cancel			.20
	Perf. initial			.20
RD177	ST2	$5 **bright green**	37.50	.90
	Cut cancel			.30
	Perf. initial			.20
RD178	ST2	$10 **bright green**	75.00	4.50
	Cut cancel			.45
	Perf. initial			.30
RD179	ST2	$20 **bright green**	125.00	9.00
	Cut cancel			4.00
	Perf. initial			3.25

Perf. 12
Without Gum

Designs: $2,500, William Windom. $5,000, C. J. Folger. $10,000, W. Q. Gresham.

RD180	ST3	$30 **bright green**	135.00	65.00
	Cut cancel			25.00
	Perf. initial			11.00
RD181	ST3	$50 **bright green**	90.00	55.00
	Cut cancel			15.00
	Perf. initial			11.00
RD182	ST3	$60 **bright green**	160.00	125.00
	Cut cancel			65.00
	Perf. initial			47.50
RD183	ST3	$100 **bright green**	135.00	55.00
	Cut cancel			22.50
	Perf. initial			11.00
RD184	ST3	$500 **bright green**	—	500.00
	Cut cancel			300.00
	Perf. initial			210.00
RD185	ST3	$1000 **bright green**	—	800.00
	Cut cancel			300.00
	Perf. initial			175.00
RD185A	ST3	$2500 **bright green**	—	—
RD185B	ST3	$5000 **bright green**	—	—
RD185C	ST3	$10,000 **bright green**	—	—
	Cut cancel			1,500.

Nos. RD67-RD91 Overprint Instead: **Series 1945**

1945 Wmk. 191R Perf. 11

RD186	ST1	1c **bright green**	.20	.20
	Cut cancel			.20
	Perf. initial			.20
RD187	ST1	2c **bright green**	.25	.20
	Cut cancel			.20
	Perf. initial			.20
RD188	ST1	4c **bright green**	.25	.20
	Cut cancel			.20
	Perf. initial			.20
RD189	ST1	5c **bright green**	.25	.20
	Cut cancel			.20
	Perf. initial			.20
RD190	ST1	10c **bright green**	.75	.35
	Cut cancel			.20
	Perf. initial			.20
RD191	ST1	20c **bright green**	1.25	.30
	Cut cancel			.20
	Perf. initial			.20
RD192	ST1	25c **bright green**	2.00	.35
	Cut cancel			.25
	Perf. initial			.20
RD193	ST1	40c **bright green**	3.00	.20
	Cut cancel			.20
	Perf. initial			.20
RD194	ST1	50c **bright green**	3.50	.25
	Cut cancel			.20
	Perf. initial			.20
RD195	ST1	80c **bright green**	7.50	2.50
	Cut cancel			.70
	Perf. initial			.65
RD196	ST2	$1 **bright green**	16.00	.25
	Cut cancel			.20
	Perf. initial			.20
RD197	ST2	$2 **bright green**	21.00	.45
	Cut cancel			.20
	Perf. initial			.20
RD198	ST2	$3 **bright green**	37.50	.80
	Cut cancel			.20
	Perf. initial			.20
RD199	ST2	$4 **bright green**	37.50	2.50
	Cut cancel			.75
	Perf. initial			.50
RD200	ST2	$5 **bright green**	24.00	.50
	Cut cancel			.20
	Perf. initial			.20
RD201	ST2	$10 **bright green**	55.00	6.50
	Cut cancel			.75
	Perf. initial			.70
RD202	ST2	$20 **bright green**	85.00	10.00
	Cut cancel			1.75
	Perf. initial			1.00

Perf. 12
Without Gum

RD203	ST3	$30 **bright green**	95.00	65.00
	Cut cancel			27.50
	Perf. initial			18.00
RD204	ST3	$50 **bright green**	65.00	21.00
	Cut cancel			5.75
	Perf. initial			4.25
RD205	ST3	$60 **bright green**	160.00	140.00
	Cut cancel			60.00
	Perf. initial			27.50
RD206	ST3	$100 **bright green**	55.00	35.00
	Cut cancel			15.00
	Perf. initial			8.00
RD207	ST3	$500 **bright green**	—	600.00
	Cut cancel			300.00
	Perf. initial			190.00
RD208	ST3	$1000 **bright green**	1,250.	600.00
	Cut cancel			300.00
	Perf. initial			175.00

RD208A	ST3	$2500 **bright green**	—	
		Cut cancel		20,000.
RD208B	ST3	$5000 **bright green**	—	—
RD208C	ST3	$10,000 **bright green**	—	
		Cut cancel		7,000.

Stock Transfer Stamps and Type of 1940 Overprinted in Black

Series 1946

1946   **Wmk. 191R**   *Perf. 11*

RD209	ST1	1c **bright green**	.20	.20
		Cut cancel		.20
		Perf. initial		.20
a.		Pair, one dated "1945"	475.00	
RD210	ST1	2c **bright green**	.35	.20
		Cut cancel		.20
		Perf. initial		.20
RD211	ST1	4c **bright green**	.30	.20
		Cut cancel		.20
		Perf. initial		.20
RD212	ST1	5c **bright green**	.35	.20
		Cut cancel		.20
		Perf. initial		.20
RD213	ST1	10c **bright green**	.75	.20
		Cut cancel		.20
		Perf. initial		.20
RD214	ST1	20c **bright green**	1.50	.20
		Cut cancel		.20
		Perf. initial		.20
RD215	ST1	25c **bright green**	1.50	.25
		Cut cancel		.20
		Perf. initial		.20
RD216	ST1	40c **bright green**	3.50	.60
		Cut cancel		.20
		Perf. initial		.20
RD217	ST1	50c **bright green**	4.50	.20
		Cut cancel		.20
		Perf. initial		.20
RD218	ST1	80c **bright green**	11.00	6.00
		Cut cancel		2.00
		Perf. initial		1.25
RD219	ST2	$1 **bright green**	10.00	.50
		Cut cancel		.20
		Perf. initial		.20
RD220	ST2	$2 **bright green**	11.00	.50
		Cut cancel		.20
		Perf. initial		.20
RD221	ST2	$3 **bright green**	21.00	1.25
		Cut cancel		.30
		Perf. initial		.20
RD222	ST2	$4 **bright green**	21.00	6.25
		Cut cancel		2.25
		Perf. initial		.95
RD223	ST2	$5 **bright green**	32.50	1.10
		Cut cancel		.25
		Perf. initial		.20
RD224	ST2	$10 **bright green**	60.00	2.60
		Cut cancel		.75
		Perf. initial		.20
RD225	ST2	$20 **bright green**	100.00	42.50
		Cut cancel		12.50
		Perf. initial		6.75

Without Gum   *Perf. 12*

RD226	ST3	$30 **bright green**	77.50	40.00
		Cut cancel		17.50
		Perf. initial		15.00
RD227	ST3	$50 **bright green**	60.00	45.00
		Cut cancel		20.00
		Perf. initial		11.00
RD228	ST3	$60 **bright green**	140.00	95.00
		Cut cancel		35.00
		Perf. initial		12.50
RD229	ST3	$100 **bright green**	85.00	50.00
		Cut cancel		20.00
		Perf. initial		14.00
RD230	ST3	$500 **bright green**	—	180.00
		Cut cancel		100.00
		Perf. initial		82.50
RD231	ST3	$1000 **bright green**	—	200.00
		Cut cancel		110.00
		Perf. initial		82.50
RD232	ST3	$2500 **bright green**	—	
		Cut cancel		10,000.
RD233	ST3	$5000 **bright green**	—	
		Cut cancel		10,000.
RD234	ST3	$10,000 **bright green**	—	—
		Cut cancel		7,000.

Stock Transfer Stamps and Type of 1940 Overprinted in Black

Series 1947

1947   **Wmk. 191R**   *Perf. 11*

RD235	ST1	1c **bright green**	.65	.55
		Cut cancel		.20
		Perf. initial		.20
RD236	ST1	2c **bright green**	.60	.50
		Cut cancel		.20
		Perf. initial		.20
RD237	ST1	4c **bright green**	.50	.40
		Cut cancel		.20
		Perf. initial		.20
RD238	ST1	5c **bright green**	.45	.35
		Cut cancel		.20
		Perf. initial		.20
RD239	ST1	10c **bright green**	.60	.50
		Cut cancel		.20
		Perf. initial		.20
RD240	ST1	20c **bright green**	1.10	.50
		Cut cancel		.20
		Perf. initial		.20

RD241	ST1	25c **bright green**	1.75	.50
		Cut cancel		.20
		Perf. initial		.20
RD242	ST1	40c **bright green**	3.00	.75
		Cut cancel		.25
		Perf. initial		.20
RD243	ST1	50c **bright green**	4.00	.30
		Cut cancel		.20
		Perf. initial		.20
RD244	ST1	80c **bright green**	17.50	10.00
		Cut cancel		4.00
		Perf. initial		3.50
RD245	ST2	$1 **bright green**	10.00	.50
		Cut cancel		.20
		Perf. initial		.20
RD246	ST2	$2 **bright green**	16.00	.75
		Cut cancel		.20
		Perf. initial		.20
RD247	ST2	$3 **bright green**	25.00	1.50
		Cut cancel		.35
		Perf. initial		.30
RD248	ST2	$4 **bright green**	40.00	6.00
		Cut cancel		1.10
		Perf. initial		.70
RD249	ST2	$5 **bright green**	35.00	1.50
		Cut cancel		.30
		Perf. initial		.20
RD250	ST2	$10 **bright green**	55.00	5.00
		Cut cancel		2.00
		Perf. initial		1.25
RD251	ST2	$20 **bright green**	100.00	30.00
		Perf. initial		6.00

Without Gum   *Perf. 12*

RD252	ST3	$30 **bright green**	65.00	45.00
		Cut cancel		15.00
		Perf. initial		10.00
RD253	ST3	$50 **bright green**	135.00	95.00
		Cut cancel		40.00
		Perf. initial		17.50
RD254	ST3	$60 **bright green**	165.00	140.00
		Cut cancel		50.00
		Perf. initial		35.00
RD255	ST3	$100 **bright green**	75.00	40.00
		Cut cancel		15.00
		Perf. initial		12.50
RD256	ST3	$500 **bright green**	—	275.00
		Cut cancel		120.00
		Perf. initial		87.50
RD257	ST3	$1000 **bright green**	—	100.00
		Cut cancel		50.00
		Perf. initial		30.00
RD258	ST3	$2500 **bright green**	—	
		Cut cancel		400.00
RD259	ST3	$5000 **bright green**	—	
		Cut cancel		300.00
RD260	ST3	$10,000 **bright green**	—	
		Cut cancel		55.00
a.		Horiz. pair, imperf. vert., cut cancel	—	

Nos. RD67-RD91 Overprint Instead: **Series 1948**

1948   **Wmk. 191R**   *Perf. 11*

RD261	ST1	1c **bright green**	.25	.25
		Cut cancel		.20
		Perf. initial		.20
RD262	ST1	2c **bright green**	.25	.25
		Cut cancel		.20
		Perf. initial		.20
RD263	ST1	4c **bright green**	.30	.30
		Cut cancel		.20
		Perf. initial		.20
RD264	ST1	5c **bright green**	.25	.25
		Cut cancel		.20
		Perf. initial		.20
RD265	ST1	10c **bright green**	.30	.25
		Cut cancel		.20
		Perf. initial		.20
RD266	ST1	20c **bright green**	1.40	.35
		Cut cancel		.20
		Perf. initial		.20
RD267	ST1	25c **bright green**	1.40	.40
		Cut cancel		.20
		Perf. initial		.20
RD268	ST1	40c **bright green**	1.75	.75
		Cut cancel		.25
		Perf. initial		.20
RD269	ST1	50c **bright green**	4.25	.30
		Cut cancel		.20
		Perf. initial		.20
RD270	ST1	80c **bright green**	14.00	6.00
		Cut cancel		2.25
		Perf. initial		2.00
RD271	ST2	$1 **bright green**	10.00	.40
		Cut cancel		.20
		Perf. initial		.20
RD272	ST2	$2 **bright green**	17.50	.60
		Cut cancel		.20
		Perf. initial		.20
RD273	ST2	$3 **bright green**	18.00	3.75
		Cut cancel		1.60
		Perf. initial		1.20
RD274	ST2	$4 **bright green**	21.00	11.00
		Cut cancel		3.00
		Perf. initial		2.00
RD275	ST2	$5 **bright green**	32.50	2.50
		Cut cancel		.25
		Perf. initial		.20
RD276	ST2	$10 **bright green**	55.00	4.50
		Cut cancel		.75
		Perf. initial		.60
RD277	ST2	$20 **bright green**	95.00	18.00
		Cut cancel		6.00
		Perf. initial		4.00

Perf. 12
Without Gum

RD278	ST3	$30 **bright green**	100.00	55.00
		Cut cancel		22.50
		Perf. initial		12.50
RD279	ST3	$50 **bright green**	65.00	55.00
		Cut cancel		22.50
		Perf. initial		10.00
RD280	ST3	$60 **bright green**	165.00	130.00
		Cut cancel		50.00
		Perf. initial		20.00
RD281	ST3	$100 **bright green**	55.00	
		Cut cancel		7.50
		Perf. initial		5.50
RD282	ST3	$500 **bright green**	—	240.00
		Cut cancel		120.00
		Perf. initial		45.00
RD283	ST3	$1000 **bright green**	—	110.00
		Cut cancel		45.00
		Perf. initial		27.50
RD284	ST3	$2500 **bright green**	325.00	300.00
		Cut cancel		160.00
		Perf. initial		125.00
RD285	ST3	$5000 **bright green**	—	275.00
		Cut cancel		160.00
		Perf. initial		125.00
RD286	ST3	$10,000 **bright green**	—	
		Cut cancel		55.00

Nos. RD67-RD91 Overprint Instead: **Series 1949**

1949   **Wmk. 191R**   *Perf. 11*

RD287	ST1	1c **bright green**	.50	.45
		Cut cancel		.20
		Perf. initial		.20
RD288	ST1	2c **bright green**	.50	.45
		Cut cancel		.20
		Perf. initial		.20
RD289	ST1	4c **bright green**	.60	.50
		Cut cancel		.20
		Perf. initial		.20
RD290	ST1	5c **bright green**	.60	.50
		Cut cancel		.20
		Perf. initial		.20
RD291	ST1	10c **bright green**	1.30	.60
		Cut cancel		.20
		Perf. initial		.20
RD292	ST1	20c **bright green**	2.10	.50
		Cut cancel		.20
		Perf. initial		.20
RD293	ST1	25c **bright green**	3.00	.85
		Cut cancel		.20
		Perf. initial		.20
RD294	ST1	40c **bright green**	5.50	1.50
		Cut cancel		.20
		Perf. initial		.20
RD295	ST1	50c **bright green**	5.00	.25
		Cut cancel		.20
		Perf. initial		.20
RD296	ST1	80c **bright green**	14.00	6.50
		Cut cancel		2.75
		Perf. initial		2.50
RD297	ST2	$1 **bright green**	12.50	.75
		Cut cancel		.25
		Perf. initial		.20
RD298	ST2	$2 **bright green**	18.00	.90
		Cut cancel		.20
		Perf. initial		.20
RD299	ST2	$3 **bright green**	40.00	4.50
		Cut cancel		1.25
		Perf. initial		.90
RD300	ST2	$4 **bright green**	37.50	7.50
		Cut cancel		2.00
		Perf. initial		1.50
RD301	ST2	$5 **bright green**	47.50	2.00
		Cut cancel		.25
		Perf. initial		.20
RD302	ST2	$10 **bright green**	65.00	4.00
		Cut cancel		1.25
		Perf. initial		1.10
RD303	ST2	$20 **bright green**	140.00	15.00
		Cut cancel		6.00
		Perf. initial		5.00

Perf. 12
Without Gum

RD304	ST3	$30 **bright green**	110.00	75.00
		Cut cancel		30.00
		Perf. initial		12.50
RD305	ST3	$50 **bright green**	150.00	85.00
		Cut cancel		37.50
		Perf. initial		17.50
RD306	ST3	$60 **bright green**	250.00	200.00
		Cut cancel		90.00
		Perf. initial		35.00
RD307	ST3	$100 **bright green**	90.00	65.00
		Cut cancel		25.00
		Perf. initial		15.00
RD308	ST3	$500 **bright green**	—	240.00
		Cut cancel		90.00
		Perf. initial		52.50
RD309	ST3	$1000 **bright green**	—	95.00
		Cut cancel		42.50
		Perf. initial		27.50
RD310	ST3	$2500 **bright green**	—	
		Cut cancel		450.00
RD311	ST3	$5000 **bright green**	—	
		Cut cancel		400.00
		Perf. initial		275.00
RD312	ST3	$10,000 **bright green**	—	300.00
		Cut cancel		42.50
a.		Pair, one without ovpt., cut cancel	4,500.	

No. RD312a is unique.

Nos. RD67-RD91 Overprint Instead: **Series 1950**

1950   Wmk. 191R   Perf. 11

No.	Type	Denom.		
RD313	ST1	1c bright green	.40	.35
		Cut cancel		.20
		Perf. initial		.20
RD314	ST1	2c bright green	.40	.30
		Cut cancel		.20
		Perf. initial		.20
RD315	ST1	4c bright green	.40	.35
		Cut cancel		.20
		Perf. initial		.20
RD316	ST1	5c bright green	.40	.20
		Cut cancel		.20
		Perf. initial		.20
RD317	ST1	10c bright green	2.00	.30
		Cut cancel		.20
		Perf. initial		.20
RD318	ST1	20c bright green	3.00	.50
		Cut cancel		.20
		Perf. initial		.20
RD319	ST1	25c bright green	4.25	.60
		Cut cancel		.20
		Perf. initial		.20
RD320	ST1	40c bright green	5.00	.90
		Cut cancel		.20
		Perf. initial		.20
RD321	ST1	50c bright green	8.25	.35
		Cut cancel		.20
		Perf. initial		.20
RD322	ST1	80c bright green	12.50	5.00
		Cut cancel		2.00
		Perf. initial		1.25
RD323	ST2	$1 bright green	12.50	.40
		Cut cancel		.20
		Perf. initial		.20
RD324	ST2	$2 bright green	21.00	.75
		Cut cancel		.20
		Perf. initial		.20
RD325	ST2	$3 bright green	35.00	4.00
		Cut cancel		.60
		Perf. initial		.55
RD326	ST2	$4 bright green	42.50	9.00
		Cut cancel		3.25
		Perf. initial		2.00
RD327	ST2	$5 bright green	42.50	1.75
		Cut cancel		.20
		Perf. initial		.20
RD328	ST2	$10 bright green	100.00	5.00
		Cut cancel		1.50
		Perf. initial		.75
RD329	ST2	$20 bright green	140.00	25.00
		Cut cancel		16.00
		Perf. initial		4.50

Perf. 12
Without Gum

RD330	ST3	$30 bright green	90.00	65.00
		Cut cancel		27.50
		Perf. initial		14.00
RD331	ST3	$50 bright green	85.00	80.00
		Cut cancel		42.50
		Perf. initial		22.50
RD332	ST3	$60 bright green	175.00	125.00
		Cut cancel		60.00
		Perf. initial		37.50
RD333	ST3	$100 bright green	65.00	40.00
		Cut cancel		20.00
		Perf. initial		10.00
a.		Vert. pair, imperf. btwn.		1,500.
RD334	ST3	$500 bright green	—	225.00
		Cut cancel		105.00
		Perf. initial		85.00
RD335	ST3	$1000 bright green	—	85.00
		Cut cancel		32.50
		Perf. initial		22.50
RD336	ST3	$2500 bright green	—	1,100.
		Cut cancel		750.00
RD337	ST3	$5000 bright green	—	725.00
		Cut cancel		400.00
RD338	ST3	$10,000 bright green	—	650.00
		Cut cancel		100.00

Nos. RD67-RD91 Overprint Instead: **Series 1951**

1951   Wmk. 191R   Perf. 11

RD339	ST1	1c bright green	1.10	.35
		Cut cancel		.20
		Perf. initial		.20
RD340	ST1	2c bright green	1.10	.30
		Cut cancel		.20
		Perf. initial		.20
RD341	ST1	4c bright green	1.50	.50
		Cut cancel		.20
		Perf. initial		.20
RD342	ST1	5c bright green	1.10	.35
		Cut cancel		.20
		Perf. initial		.20
RD343	ST1	10c bright green	1.50	.30
		Cut cancel		.20
		Perf. initial		.20
RD344	ST1	20c bright green	3.75	.90
		Cut cancel		.20
		Perf. initial		.20
RD345	ST1	25c bright green	5.00	.90
		Cut cancel		.20
		Perf. initial		.20
RD346	ST1	40c bright green	15.00	9.00
		Cut cancel		2.75
		Perf. initial		1.50
RD347	ST1	50c bright green	10.00	.90
		Cut cancel		.20
		Perf. initial		.20
RD348	ST1	80c bright green	18.00	10.00
		Cut cancel		4.00
		Perf. initial		2.00
RD349	ST2	$1 bright green	21.00	.80
		Cut cancel		.20
		Perf. initial		.20
RD350	ST2	$2 bright green	32.50	1.25
		Cut cancel		.20
		Perf. initial		.20
RD351	ST2	$3 bright green	42.50	10.00
		Cut cancel		3.50
		Perf. initial		1.50
RD352	ST2	$4 bright green	50.00	12.00
		Cut cancel		4.75
		Perf. initial		2.00
RD353	ST2	$5 bright green	60.00	2.50
		Cut cancel		.25
		Perf. initial		.20
RD354	ST2	$10 bright green	95.00	8.50
		Cut cancel		2.00
		Perf. initial		1.50
RD355	ST2	$20 bright green	160.00	17.50
		Cut cancel		7.00
		Perf. initial		5.00

Perf. 12
Without Gum

RD356	ST3	$30 bright green	110.00	70.00
		Cut cancel		32.50
		Perf. initial		17.50
RD357	ST3	$50 bright green	100.00	60.00
		Cut cancel		25.00
		Perf. initial		17.50
RD358	ST3	$60 bright green	—	1,100.
		Cut cancel		450.00
		Perf. initial		210.00
RD359	ST3	$100 bright green	100.00	60.00
		Cut cancel		22.50
		Perf. initial		11.00
RD360	ST3	$500 bright green	—	275.00
		Cut cancel		125.00
		Perf. initial		85.00
RD361	ST3	$1000 bright green	—	100.00
		Cut cancel		65.00
		Perf. initial		50.00
RD362	ST3	$2500 bright green	—	2,000.
		Cut cancel		900.00
		Perf. initial		350.00
RD363	ST3	$5000 bright green	—	1,400.
		Cut cancel		800.00
RD364	ST3	$10,000 bright green	1,000.	130.00
		Cut cancel		60.00

Nos. RD67-RD91 Overprint Instead: **Series 1952**

1952   Wmk. 191R   Perf. 11

RD365	ST1	1c bright green	35.00	17.50
		Cut cancel		4.00
		Perf. initial		2.00
RD366	ST1	10c bright green	35.00	17.50
		Cut cancel		4.00
		Perf. initial		2.00
RD367	ST1	20c bright green	350.00	—
RD368	ST1	25c bright green	450.00	—
RD369	ST1	40c bright green	100.00	40.00
		Cut cancel		14.00
		Perf. initial		5.50
RD370	ST2	$4 bright green	1,100.	550.
RD371	ST2	$10 bright green	2,500.	—
RD372	ST2	$20 bright green	4,750.	—

Stock Transfer Stamps were discontinued in 1952.

CORDIALS, WINES, ETC. STAMPS

 RE1

Inscribed "Series of 1914"

1914   Wmk. 190   Offset Printing   Perf. 10

RE1	RE1	¼c green	.75	.50
RE2	RE1	½c green	.50	.25
RE3	RE1	1c green	.45	.30
RE4	RE1	1½c green	2.25	1.50
RE5	RE1	2c green	3.00	3.00
RE6	RE1	3c green	3.00	1.25
RE7	RE1	4c green	2.50	1.50
RE8	RE1	5c green	1.00	.50
RE9	RE1	6c green	6.25	3.50
RE10	RE1	8c green	3.75	1.50
RE11	RE1	10c green	3.50	2.75
RE12	RE1	20c green	4.25	1.75
RE13	RE1	24c green	14.00	8.00
RE14	RE1	40c green	3.00	.75

RE1a

			Without Gum	**Imperf.**
RE15	RE1a	$2 green	7.50	.20
a.		Double impression		125.00

1914   Wmk. 191R   Perf. 10

RE16	RE1	¼c green	6.00	5.00
RE17	RE1	½c green	3.75	3.00
RE18	RE1	1c green	.25	.20
RE19	RE1	1½c green	47.50	35.00
RE20	RE1	2c green	.20	.20
a.		Double impression		
RE21	RE1	3c green	2.50	2.00
RE22	RE1	4c green	.85	1.00
RE23	RE1	5c green	12.50	11.00
RE24	RE1	6c green	.50	.30
RE25	RE1	8c green	2.00	.45
RE26	RE1	10c green	.50	.20
RE27	RE1	20c green	.75	.35
RE28	RE1	24c green	14.00	.75
RE29	RE1	40c green	30.00	11.00

Imperf
Without Gum

RE30	RE1a	$2 green	30.00	3.00

Perf. 11

RE31	RE1	2c green	80.00	90.00

WINE STAMPS
Issued Without Gum

 RE2

Inscribed: "Series of 1916"

1916   Wmk. 191R   Offset Printing   Rouletted 3½
Plates of 100 subjects

RE32	RE2	1c green	.35	.35
RE33	RE2	3c green	4.50	4.00
RE34	RE2	4c green	.30	.30
RE35	RE2	6c green	1.50	.75

RE36	RE2	7½c **green**	7.50	4.00
RE37	RE2	10c **green**	1.25	.40
RE38	RE2	12c **green**	3.00	4.00
RE39	RE2	15c **green**	1.75	1.75
RE40	RE2	18c **green**	24.00	22.50
RE41	RE2	20c **green**	.30	.25
RE42	RE2	24c **green**	4.00	3.00
RE43	RE2	30c **green**	3.25	2.50
RE44	RE2	36c **green**	20.00	15.00
RE45	RE2	50c **green**	.60	.40
RE46	RE2	60c **green**	4.00	2.00
RE47	RE2	72c **green**	35.00	27.50
RE48	RE2	80c **green**	.75	.55
RE49	RE2	$1.20 **green**	7.00	6.00
RE50	RE2	$1.44 **green**	9.00	3.00
RE51	RE2	$1.60 **green**	25.00	17.50
RE52	RE2	$2 **green**	1.75	1.50

For rouletted 7 see Nos. RE60-RE80, RE102-RE105.

RE3

Engr.
Plates of 50 subjects

RE53	RE3	$4 **green**	1.00	.20
RE54	RE3	$4.80 **green**	3.25	3.00
RE55	RE3	$9.60 **green**	1.25	.25

Nos. RE32-RE55 exist in many shades. Size variations of 1c-$2 are believed due to offset printing. For rouletted 7 see Nos. RE81-RE83, RE106-RE107.

RE4

Plates of 6 subjects
Perf. 12 at left

RE56	RE4	$20 **green**	90.00	40.00
RE57	RE4	$40 **green**	175.00	50.00
RE58	RE4	$50 **green**	60.00	45.00
RE59	RE4	$100 **green**	250.00	140.00

Stamps of design RE4 have an adjoining tablet at right for affixing additional stamps. Values are for examples with the tablets attached. Examples with the tablets removed sell for much less. Used stamps with additional stamps tied on the tablet with cancels sell for about double the values given. See Nos. RE107A-RE107D.

Same designs as Issue of 1916

1933	Wmk. 191R	Offset Printing	*Rouletted 7*	
RE60	RE2	1c **light green**	3.00	.30
RE61	RE2	3c **light green**	7.50	2.50
RE62	RE2	4c **light green**	1.50	.30
RE63	RE2	6c **light green**	11.00	5.00
RE64	RE2	7½c **light green**	3.00	.50
RE65	RE2	10c **light green**	2.00	.20
RE66	RE2	12c **light green**	9.00	5.00
RE67	RE2	15c **light green**	4.00	.25
RE69	RE2	20c **light green**	5.00	.20
a.		Double impression	—	
RE70	RE2	24c **light green**	5.00	.20
a.		Double impression		150.00
RE71	RE2	30c **light green**	5.00	.20
RE72	RE2	36c **light green**	11.00	.60
RE73	RE2	50c **light green**	4.50	.25
RE74	RE2	60c **light green**	7.50	.20
RE75	RE2	72c **light green**	12.50	.30
RE76	RE2	80c **light green**	12.50	.20
RE77	RE2	$1.20 **light green**	10.00	1.50
RE78	RE2	$1.44 **light green**	12.50	4.00
RE79	RE2	$1.60 **light green**	340.00	190.00
RE80	RE2	$2 **light green**	37.50	4.00

Engr.

RE81	RE3	$4 **light green**	32.50	7.00
RE82	RE3	$4.80 **light green**	32.50	15.00
RE83	RE3	$9.60 **light green**	140.00	85.00

RE5

Offset Printing

1934-40	Wmk. 191R		*Rouletted 7*	

Inscribed: "Series of 1934"
Plates of 200 and 224 subjects
Issued With and Without Gum

RE83A	RE5	⅛c **green** ('40)	.75	.20
RE84	RE5	½c **green**	.55	.40
RE85	RE5	1c **green**	.65	.20
RE86	RE5	1¼c **green**	1.00	.75
RE87	RE5	1½c **green**	6.00	5.50
RE88	RE5	2c **green**	1.75	.65
RE89	RE5	2½c **green**	1.75	.50
RE90	RE5	3c **green**	5.00	4.00
RE91	RE5	4c **green**	2.50	.20
RE92	RE5	5c **green**	.60	.20
RE93	RE5	6c **green**	1.75	.50
RE94	RE5	7½c **green**	2.25	.20
RE95	RE5	10c **green**	.50	.20
RE96	RE5	12c **green**	1.50	.20
RE96A	RE5	14⅞c **green** ('40)	160.00	3.00
RE97	RE5	15c **green**	.75	.20
RE98	RE5	18c **green**	1.50	.20
RE99	RE5	20c **green**	1.25	.20
RE100	RE5	24c **green**	2.00	.20
RE101	RE5	30c **green**	1.40	.20

Nos. RE83A, RE86, RE96A were printed from plates of 200 only and all were issued without gum.

Plates of 100 subjects
Issued Without Gum

RE102	RE2	40c **green**	3.25	.25
RE102A	RE2	43½c **green** ('40)	14.00	2.00
RE103	RE2	48c **green**	14.00	1.50
RE104	RE2	$1 **green**	17.50	11.00
RE105	RE2	$1.50 **green**	30.00	15.00
		Perforated initials		5.50

Engr.
Plates of 50 subjects.

RE106	RE3	$2.50 **green**	37.50	16.00
		Perforated initials		8.75
RE107	RE3	$5 **green**	30.00	7.50
		Perforated initials		2.50

Stamps of types RE5 and RE2 overprinted "Rectified Spirits / Puerto Rico" are listed under Puerto Rico.

Nos. RE102-RE204 issued without gum.

Inscribed: "Series of 1916"
Plates of 6 subjects

1934			*Perf. 12 at left*	
RE107A	RE4	$20 yellow green	1,750.	
RE107B	RE4	$40 yellow green	3,250.	

Perf. 12 or 12½ at left

RE107C	RE4	$50 yellow green		2,000.
RE107D	RE4	$100 yellow green	1,000.	375.00

The serial numbers of Nos. RE107A-RE107D are much thinner than on Nos. RE56-RE59. See valuing note after No. RE59.

RE6

Offset Printing
Inscribed "Series of 1941"

1942		Wmk. 191R	*Rouletted 7*	
RE108	RE6	⅛c **green & black**	.70	.50
RE109	RE6	½c **green & black**	2.30	1.75
RE110	RE6	½c **green & black**	3.00	2.00
a.		Horiz. pair, imperf. vertically	200.00	
RE111	RE6	1c **green & black**	1.25	.75
RE112	RE6	2c **green & black**	6.00	5.00
RE113	RE6	3c **green & black**	6.00	4.50
RE114	RE6	3½c **green & black**		12,500.
RE115	RE6	3¾c **green & black**	11.00	7.00
RE116	RE6	4c **green & black**	4.25	3.00
RE117	RE6	5c **green & black**	3.00	2.25
RE118	RE6	6c **green & black**	3.60	2.50
RE119	RE6	7c **green & black**	7.50	5.25
RE120	RE6	7½c **green & black**	11.00	5.75
RE121	RE6	8c **green & black**	5.50	4.00
RE122	RE6	9c **green & black**	12.50	9.25
RE123	RE6	10c **green & black**	5.50	1.00
RE124	RE6	11¼c **green & black**	6.00	5.00
RE125	RE6	12c **green & black**	8.50	6.00
RE126	RE6	14c **green & black**	30.00	25.00
RE127	RE6	15c **green & black**	6.00	3.00
a.		Horiz. pair, imperf. vertically		900.00
RE128	RE6	16c **green & black**	14.00	8.75
RE129	RE6	19½c **green & black**	175.00	7.50
RE130	RE6	20c **green & black**	7.25	1.75
RE131	RE6	24c **green & black**	5.50	.20
RE132	RE6	28c **green & black**	2,000.	1,500.
RE133	RE6	30c **green & black**	1.50	.20
RE134	RE6	32c **green & black**	175.00	7.50
RE135	RE6	36c **green & black**	3.60	.20
RE136	RE6	40c **green & black**	3.00	.20
RE137	RE6	45c **green & black**	7.25	.20
RE138	RE6	48c **green & black**	20.00	7.00
RE139	RE6	50c **green & black**	12.00	7.50
RE140	RE6	60c **green & black**	4.25	.20
RE141	RE6	72c **green & black**	12.00	1.00
RE142	RE6	80c **green & black**	325.00	10.00
RE143	RE6	84c **green & black**	—	65.00
RE144	RE6	90c **green & black**	19.00	.20
RE145	RE6	96c **green & black**	15.00	.20

See Nos. RE182D-RE194.

Denomination Spelled Out in Two Lines — RE7

1942			Engr.	
RE146	RE7	$1.20 **yel grn & blk**	7.00	.20
RE147	RE7	$1.44 **yel grn & blk**	1.75	.20
RE148	RE7	$1.50 **yel grn & blk**	130.00	65.00
RE149	RE7	$1.60 **yel grn & blk**	10.00	1.00
RE150	RE7	$1.68 **yel grn & blk**	120.00	50.00
		Perforated initials		35.00
RE151	RE7	$1.80 **yel grn & blk**	3.00	.20
a.		Vertical pair, one without denomination	—	
b.		Horiz. pair, one without denomination	—	
RE152	RE7	$1.92 **yel grn & blk**	60.00	40.00
RE153	RE7	$2.40 **yel grn & blk**	10.00	1.00
RE154	RE7	$3 **yel grn & blk**	85.00	40.00
RE155	RE7	$3.36 **yel grn & blk**	90.00	27.50
RE156	RE7	$3.60 **yel grn & blk**	160.00	6.00
RE157	RE7	$4 **yel grn & blk**	30.00	5.00
RE158	RE7	$4.80 **yel grn & blk**	160.00	3.00
RE159	RE7	$5 **yel grn & blk**	15.00	10.00
RE160	RE7	$7.20 **yel grn & blk**	20.00	.50
RE161	RE7	$10 **yel grn & blk**	240.00	175.00
RE162	RE7	$20 **yel grn & blk**	130.00	75.00
RE163	RE7	$50 **yel grn & blk**	130.00	75.00
		Perforated initials		20.00
RE164	RE7	$100 **yel grn & blk**	325.00	30.00
		Perforated initials		20.00
RE165	RE7	$200 **yel grn & blk**	190.00	22.50
		Perforated initials		8.50
RE165B	RE7	$400 **yel grn & blk**	—	12,000.
RE166	RE7	$500 **yel grn & blk**	—	150.00
		Perforated initials		35.00
RE167	RE7	$600 **yel grn & blk**	—	125.00
RE168	RE7	$900 **yel grn & blk**	4,000.	
		Perforated initials		1,500.
RE169	RE7	$1000 **yel grn & blk**	200.00	
RE170	RE7	$2000 **yel grn & blk**	2,250.	
RE171	RE7	$3000 **yel grn & blk**	200.00	
RE172	RE7	$4000 **yel grn & blk**	800.00	

Denomination Repeated, Spelled Out in One Line

1949				
RE173	RE7	$1 **yellow green & black**	4.00	1.50
RE174	RE7	$2 **yellow green & black**	7.00	2.00
RE175	RE7	$4 **yellow green & black**	900.00	400.00
		Perforated initials		175.00

RE176	RE7	$5 yellow green & black	80.00	
RE177	RE7	$6 yellow green & black	500.00	
RE178	RE7	$7 yellow green & black	45.00	
RE179	RE7	$8 yellow green & black	850.00	450.00
		Perforated initials		85.00
RE180	RE7	$10 yellow green & black	10.00	5.00
		Perforated initials		2.00
RE181	RE7	$20 yellow green & black	20.00	3.75
		Perforated initials		1.75
RE182	RE7	$30 yellow green & black	1,500.	750.00

Other denominations of engraved stamps, type RE7, that were printed and delivered to the Internal Revenue Service were: $7.14, $9, $12, $40, $60, $70, $80, $300, $700 and $800. None are reported in collectors' hands.

Types of 1942-49

1951-54 — **Offset Printing**

RE182D	RE6	1 7/10c green & black		9,500.
RE183	RE6	3 3/5c green & black	55.00	50.00
RE184	RE6	8 1/2c green & black	30.00	20.00
RE185	RE6	13 3/5c green & black	100.00	80.00
RE186	RE6	17c green & black	16.00	15.00
RE187	RE6	20 2/5c green & black	110.00	60.00

RE188	RE6	33 1/2c green & black	90.00	75.00
RE189	RE6	38 1/4c green & black	125.00	90.00
RE190	RE6	40 4/5c green & black	3.75	.65
RE191	RE6	51c green & black	4.00	1.25
RE192	RE6	67c green & black	12.50	4.00
RE193	RE6	68c green & black	3.75	.65
RE194	RE6	80 4/5c green & black	120.00	100.00

Engr.
Denomination Spelled Out in Two Lines in Small Letters

Two types of $1.60 4/5:

I - The "4" slants sharply. Loop of "5" almost closes to form oval. Each numeral 2mm high.

II - The "4" is less slanted. Loop of "5" more open and nearly circular. Each numeral 2 1/2mm high.

RE195	RE7	$1.50 3/4 yel grn & blk	50.00	37.50
RE196	RE7	$1.60 4/5 yel grn & blk (I)	4.25	.60
	a.	"DOLLLAR"	42.50	15.00
		Perforated initials		7.50
	b.	As "a," horiz. pair, one without denomination	2,500.	
	c.	Type II	750.00	250.00

RE197	RE7	$1.88 7/10 yel grn & blk	300.00	85.00
		Perforated initials		32.50

Denomination Spelled Out in Two Lines in Slightly Larger Letters Same as Nos. RE146-RE172

RE198	RE7	$1.60 4/5 yel grn & blk (II)	30.00	6.00
	a.	First line larger letters, second line small letters	—	3,000.
	b.	Type I ('53)	75.00	25.00
RE199	RE7	$2.01 yel grn & blk	3.50	.75
RE200	RE7	$2.68 yel grn & blk	3.50	1.25
RE201	RE7	$4.08 yel grn & blk	77.50	32.50
RE202	RE7	$5.76 yel grn & blk	250.00	115.00
RE203	RE7	$8.16 yel grn & blk	17.50	7.00
RE204	RE7	$9.60 yel grn & blk		4,500.

Other denominations that were printed but not delivered to the Internal Revenue Service were: 6 7/10c, 10 1/5c and $90. None are reported in collectors' hands.

Wine stamps were discontinued on Dec. 31, 1954.

BEER STAMPS

Basic stamps were printed by the Bureau of Engraving and Printing, unless otherwise noted.

All stamps are imperforate, unless otherwise noted.

Values for Nos. REA1-REA13 are for stamps with small faults, due to the fragile nature of the thin paper. Values for Nos. REA14-REA199 are for canceled stamps with small faults.

All copies of Nos. REA1-REA13 contain a circular pattern of 31 perforations in the design, 27 or 28 1/2mm in diameter, often poorly punched.

Values for cut squares of Nos. REA1-REA13 are for margins clear of the design. Die cut and cut to shape stamps are valued for margins clear to slightly cutting into the design.

Eric Jackson, Michael Aldrich, Henry Tolman II and Thomas W. Priester helped the editors extensively in compiling the listings.

An excellent study of beer stamps by Frank Applegate appeared in *Weekly Philatelic Gossip* from Oct. 1-Nov. 26, 1927.

A List of the Beer Stamps of the United States of America by Ernest R. Vanderhoof appeared in the *American Philatelist* in June 1934. This was reprinted in pamphlet form.

United States Beer Stamps by Thomas W. Priester, published in 1979, comprised an illustrated and priced catalogue, illustrations of all known provisional surcharges, background notes on the stamps and tax laws, and a census of over 27,500 stamps. The catalogue and census portions were updated in the 1990 edition.

Printed by the Treasury Department. Tax rate $1 per barrel (bbl.).

12 1/2c = 1/8 barrel		$1 = 1 barrel	
16 2/3c = 1/6 barrel		$2 = 1 hogshead	
25c = 1/4 barrel		$5 = 5 barrels	
33 1/3c = 1/3 barrel		$10 = 10 barrels	
50c = 1/2 barrel		$25 = 25 barrels	

1866 — **Engr.**

REA1	12 1/2c orange	300.	350.	
	Cut to shape		70.	
	a. Die cut	.275	175.	
	b. Silk paper		1,500.	
REA2	16 2/3c dark green	85.	125.	
	Cut to shape		15.	
	a. Die cut		45.	
REA3	25c blue	50.	90.	
	Cut to shape		13.	
	a. Die cut		35.	
	b. Silk paper		2,000.	
	Double transfer		—	
REA4	50c orange brown	25.	45.	
	Printed cancellation, "A.S. 1869"		100.	
	Cut to shape		8.	
	a. Die cut		65.	
REA5	$1 black	200.	200.	
	Cut to shape		50.	
	a. Die cut		150.	
REA6	$2 red	600.	900.	
	Cut to shape		125.	
	a. Die cut		300.	

Printed by the Treasury Department. See individual rates before No. REA1.

1867 — **Engr.**

REA7	12 1/2c orange	2,250.	1,250.
	Cut to shape		600.
	a. Die cut		750.
REA8	16 2/3c dark green	2,500.	1,750.
	Cut to shape		425.
	a. Die cut		1,200.
REA9	25c blue	125.	200.
	Cut to shape		40.
	a. Die cut		175.
REA10	33 1/3c violet brown		5,000.
	Cut to shape		2,000.
	b. Silk paper		3,000.
	c. 33 1/3c ocher red, cut to shape		3,000.
	d. 33 1/3c ocher red, die cut		3,500.
REA11	50c orange brown	45.	100.
	Printed cancellation, "A.S. 1869"		250.
	Cut to shape		25.
	a. Die cut		125.
REA12	$1 black		900.
	Cut to shape		250.
	a. Die cut		525.
REA13	$2 red		1,000.
	Cut to shape		400.
	a. Die cut		950.

See individual rates before No. REA1.

1870 — **Engr.** — **Lilac Security Lines**

REA14	12 1/2c brown	75.
	a. Yellow security lines	900.
REA15	16 2/3c yellow orange	100.
	a. Yellow security lines	900.
	b. Gray-green and yellow security lines	1,250.
	c. 16 2/3c yellow ocher, lilac security lines	400.
REA16	25c green	20.
	a. Yellow security lines	150.
REA17	50c red	50.
	a. Yellow security lines	350.
	b. Gray-green and yellow security lines	900.
	c. 50c brick red, lilac security lines	450.
	d. 50c brick red, yellow security lines	2,250.
REA18	$1 blue	500.
	a. Yellow security lines	110.
	b. Gray-green and yellow security lines	1,000.
REA19	$2 black	350.
	a. Yellow security lines	1,750.
	b. Gray-green and yellow security lines	2,250.

The security lines were printed across the center of the stamp where the cancel was to be placed.

Andrew Jackson

Designs: 16⅔c, Abraham Lincoln. 25c, Daniel Webster. 33⅓c, David G. Farragut. 50c, William T. Sherman. $1, Hugh McCulloch. $2, Alexander Hamilton.
Centers printed by the Bureau of Engraving and Printing. Frames printed by the National Bank Co.
See individual rates before No. REA1.

1871   Engr.
Centers, Plate Letters and Position Numbers in Black

REA20	12½c **blue,** white silk paper	75.
a.	Pinkish gray silk paper	150.
b.	Gray silk paper	50.
c.	Green silk paper	100.
REA21	16⅔c **vermilion,** white silk paper	125.
a.	Pinkish gray silk paper	200.
b.	Gray silk paper	175.
c.	Green silk paper	175.
REA22	25c **green,** white silk paper	15.
a.	Pinkish gray silk paper	100.
b.	Gray silk paper	15.
c.	Green silk paper	20.
REA23	33⅓c **orange,** green silk paper	2,500.
b.	Gray silk paper	3,500.
REA24	33⅓c **violet brown,** white silk paper	1,500.
REA25	50c **brown,** gray silk paper	15.
a.	Pinkish gray silk paper	50.
c.	Green silk paper	50.
REA26	50c **red,** white silk paper	35.
REA27	$1 **yellow orange,** white silk paper	100.
a.	Pinkish gray silk paper	900.
b.	Gray silk paper	90.
REA28	$1 **scarlet,** gray silk paper	75.
a.	Pinkish gray silk paper	750.
c.	Green silk paper	150.
REA29	$2 **red brown,** white silk paper	125.
a.	Pinkish gray silk paper	1,000.
b.	Gray silk paper	175.
c.	Green silk paper	750.

Bacchus Serving the First Fermented Brew to Man

Printed by the National Bank Note Co. See individual rates before No. REA1.

1875   Typo. & Engr.
Center in Black

REA30	12½c **blue**	20.00
REA31	16⅔c **red brown**	35.00
REA32	25c **green**	10.00
a.	Inverted center	—
REA33	33⅓c **violet**	500.00
REA34	50c **orange**	55.00
REA35	$1 **red**	80.00
REA36	$2 **brown**	150.00
a.	Inverted center	—

Designs: 12½c, Washington. 16⅔c, Corwin. 25c, Benton. 33⅓c, Thomas. 50c, Jefferson. $1, Johnson. $2, Wright.
Stamps on pale green paper have short greenish blue fibers.
Plate designations for center consist of plate letter or number at left and position number at right.
See individual rates before No. REA1.

1878   Typo. & Engr.   Wmk. USIR
Center, Plate Letters and Position Numbers in Black

REA37	12½c **blue,** *green*	5.00
b.	Green silk paper, unwmkd.	750.00
c.	Pale green paper	125.00
	With plate number and position number	*1,100.*
d.	Light blue paper, with plate number (and position number)	25.00
e.	Blue paper, no plate letter or number or position number	22.50
f.	Dark blue paper, no plate letter or number or position number	30.00
REA38	16⅔c **light brown,** *green*	5.00
	One line under Cents	70.00
b.	Green silk paper, unwmkd., one line under Cents	60.00
c.	Pale green paper	55.00
	With plate number	500.00
d.	Light blue paper, with plate number (and position number)	22.50
e.	Blue paper, no plate letter or number or position number	75.00
	With plate number 1979	200.00
f.	Dark blue paper, no plate letter or number or position number	50.00
REA39	25c **green,** *green*	2.50
a.	Inverted center	—
b.	Green silk paper, unwmkd.	85.00
c.	Pale green paper	50.00
	With plate number	22.50
d.	Light blue paper, with plate number (and position number)	2.75
e.	Blue paper, no plate letter or number or position number	10.00
f.	Dark blue paper, no plate letter or number or position number	17.50
REA40	33⅓c **violet,** *green*	45.00
b.	Green silk paper, unwmkd.	1,500.
c.	Pale green paper	950.00
d.	Light blue paper, with plate number (and position number)	75.00
e.	Blue paper, no plate letter or number or position number	90.00
f.	Dark blue paper, no plate letter or number or position number	150.00
REA41	50c **orange,** *green*	7.50
	One line under Cents	100.00
b.	Green silk paper, unwmkd.	140.00
c.	Pale green paper	55.00
	With plate number	300.00
d.	Light blue paper, with plate number (and position number)	17.50
e.	Blue paper, no plate letter or number or position number	10.00
f.	Dark blue paper, no plate letter or number or position number	10.00
REA42	$1 **red,** *green*	20.00
	One line under Dollar	60.00
c.	Pale green paper	150.00
	One line under Dollar	350.00
d.	Light blue paper, with plate number (and position number)	150.00
e.	Blue paper, no plate letter or number or position number	40.00
	One line under Dollar	125.00
f.	Dark blue paper, no plate letter or number or position number	50.00
REA43	$2 **brown,** *green*	50.00
	One line under Dollar	75.00
b.	Green silk paper, unwmkd.	225.00
	One line under dollar	
c.	Pale green paper	350.00
	One line under dollar	*750.00*
e.	Blue paper, no plate letter or number or position number	125.00
f.	Dark blue paper, no plate letter or number or position number	110.00

See Nos. REA58-REA64, REA65-REA71, REA75-REA81.

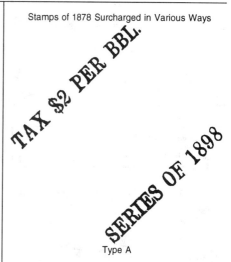

Stamps of 1878 Surcharged in Various Ways

TAX $2 PER BBL.

SERIES OF 1898

Type A

Four general surcharge types:
A - Bureau of Engraving and Printing surcharge "TAX $2 PER BBL./SERIES OF 1898" printed diagonally in red, letters 4¼mm high.
B - same, but letters 5½mm high.
C - handstamped provisional surcharge with similiar wording in 1-3 lines, more than 30 styles.
D - printed provisional 2-line surcharges, horizontal in various colors.
Tax rate $2 per bbl.

25c = ⅛ barrel	$1 = ½ barrel
33⅓c = ⅙ barrel	$2 = 1 barrel
50c = ¼ barrel	$4 = 1 hogshead
66⅔c = ⅓ barrel	

1898   Type A

REA44	(25c) on 12½c #REA37f	250.00
a.	Type C surcharge	125.00
b.	Type D surcharge	450.00
REA45	(33⅓c) on 16⅔c #REA38e	50.00
a.	on #REA38f	100.00
b.	As "a," type C surcharge	100.00
c.	As "a," type D surcharge	250.00
d.	on #REA38d	500.00
REA46	(50c) on 25c #REA39f	50.00
a.	Type C surcharge	80.00
b.	Type D surcharge	500.00
c.	on #REA39e	110.00
d.	on #REA39, type C surcharge	1,500.
REA47	(66⅔c) on 33⅓c #REA40	325.00
REA48	($1) on 50c #REA41f	20.00
a.	Type C surcharge	80.00
b.	Type D surcharge	300.00
REA49	($2) on $1 #REA42f	75.00
a.	Type C surcharge	110.00
b.	Type D surcharge	550.00
c.	on #REA42e, type C surcharge	950.00
REA50	($4) on $2 #REA43f	325.00
a.	Type C surcharge	350.00
b.	Type D surcharge	1,500.
c.	on #REA43e, type C surcharge	1,750.

Type B

REA51	(25c) on 12½c #REA37f	50.00
a.	on #REA37e	75.00
b.	As "a," type C surcharge	1,500.
REA52	(33⅓c) on 16⅔c #REA38d	350.00
a.	on #REA38f	350.00
b.	on #REA38e	500.00
REA53	(50c) on 25c #REA39f	15.00
a.	on #REA39e	15.00
REA54	(66⅔c) on 33⅓c #REA40f	1,750.
a.	Type D surcharge	1,750.
b.	On #REA40	2,250.
REA55	($1) on 50c #REA41f	7.50
REA56	($2) on $1 #REA42f	30.00
REA57	($4) on $2 #REA43f	175.00

Counterfeit type C and D overprints exist.

Designs: 25c, Washington. 33⅓c, Corwin. 50c, Benton. 66⅔c, Thomas. $1, Jefferson. $2, Johnson. $4, Wright. See individual rates before No. REA44.

1898 Typo. & Engr. Wmk. USIR
Center in Black, Dark Blue Paper

REA58	25c blue	45.
REA59	33⅓c brown	50.
REA60	50c green	10.
REA61	66⅔c violet	6,000.
REA62	$1 yellow	5.
REA63	$2 red	15.
REA64	$4 dark brown	125.

Used values for 1901-51 issues are for stamps canceled by perforated company name (or abbreviation) and date.

Designs: 20c, Washington. 26⅔c, Corwin. 40c, Benton. 53⅓c, Thomas. 80c, Jefferson. $1.60, Johnson. $3.20, Wright. Tax rate $1.60 per bbl.

20c	= ⅛ barrel	
26⅔c	= ⅙ barrel	
40c	= ¼ barrel	
53⅓c	= ⅓ barrel	
80c	= ½ barrel	
$1.60	= 1 barrel	
$3.20	= 1 hogshead	

Engr. (center) & Typo. (frame)
1901 Wmk. USIR
Dark Blue Paper

REA65	20c blue	35.
REA66	26⅔c yellow orange	40.
REA67	40c green	10.
REA68	53⅓c violet	2,500.
REA69	80c brown	10.
REA70	$1.60 red	45.
REA71	$3.20 dark brown	200.

Stamps of 1901 Provisionally Surcharged by Bureau of Engraving & Printing diagonally in red "TAX $1 PER BBL./SERIES OF 1902."

1902
REA72	(16⅔c) on 26⅔c #REA66	90.
REA73	(33⅓c) on 53⅓c #REA68	3,250.
REA74	($2) on $3.20 #REA71	375.

Designs: 12½c, Washington. 16⅔c, Corwin. 25c, Benton. 33⅓c, Thomas. 50c, Jefferson. $1, Johnson. $2, Wright. Stamps on pale green paper have short greenish blue fibers. See individual rates before No. REA1.

1902 Typo. & Engr. Wmk. USIR
Center in Black

REA75	12½c blue	40.00
	a. Dark blue paper	
	b. Pale green paper	250.00
	c. Light blue paper	50.00
	d. Bright blue paper	20.00

REA76	16⅔c yellow orange	
	a. Dark blue paper	125.00
	b. Pale green paper	175.00
	c. Light blue paper	125.00
	d. Bright blue paper	275.00
REA77	25c green	12.50
	a. Dark blue paper	
	b. Pale green paper	50.00
	c. Light blue paper	12.50
	d. Bright blue paper	20.00
REA78	33⅓c violet	110.00
	a. Dark blue paper	
	c. Light blue paper	325.00
	d. Bright blue paper	325.00
REA79	50c brown	10.00
	a. Dark blue paper	
	b. Pale green paper	20.00
	c. Light blue paper	12.50
	d. Bright blue paper	10.00
REA80	$1 red	
	a. Dark blue paper	75.00
	b. Pale green paper	125.00
	c. Light blue paper	45.00
	d. Bright blue paper	45.00
REA81	$2 dark brown	
	a. Dark blue paper	275.00
	b. Pale green paper	500.00
	c. Light blue paper	175.00
	d. Bright blue paper	175.00

For surcharges see Nos. REA99a, REA100a, REA100b, REA141.

In the 1911-33 issues, the 5-25 barrel sizes were generally available only as center cutouts of the stamp. Values for these are for cutout portions that show enough of the denomination (or surcharge) to identify the item.

See individual rates before No. REA1.

1909-11 Engr. Wmk. USIR
Paper of Various Shades of Blue

REA82	12½c black		250.00
REA83	16⅔c black	125.00	50.00
REA84	25c black		200.00
REA85	33⅓c black		4,000.
REA86	50c black		2.50
REA87	$1 black		450.00
REA88	$2 black		4,500.

Center Cutout Only

REA89	$5 black, 1911	125.00
REA90	$10 black, 1911	100.00
REA91	$25 black, 1911	75.00

For surcharges see Nos. REA97, REA99-REA100, REA103-REA105, REA128.

1910 Engr. Wmk. USIR
Paper of Various Shades of Blue

REA92	12½c red brown	45.00
REA93	25c green	5.00
REA94	$1 carmine	17.50
REA95	$2 orange	75.00

For surcharges see Nos. REA96, REA98, REA101-REA102, REA126.

1914 Provisional Issue

Stamps of of 1902-11 with printed provisional BEP diagonal surcharge "EMERGENCY/TAX/UNDER ACT OF 1914" in red, black or yellow, or handstamped surcharge of value spelled out in full and separate "Roscoe Irwin" handstamped facsimile signature. Tax rate $1.50 per bbl.

18¾c	= ⅛ barrel		$1.50	= 1 barrel
25c	= ⅙ barrel		$3	= 1 hogshead
37½c	= ¼ barrel		$7.50	= 5 barrels
50c	= ⅓ barrel		$15	= 10 barrels
75c	= ½ barrel		$37.50	= 25 barrels

1914 Entire Stamps

REA96	(18¾c) on 12½ #REA92	40.00
REA97	(25c) on 16⅔c #REA83	50.00
REA98	(37½c) on 25c #REA93	5.00
	a. 37½c handstamped; 50mm signature	250.00
REA99	(50c) on 33⅓c #REA85	75.00
REA100	(75c) on 50c #REA86	3.00
	a. (75c) On 50c #REA79c	350.00
	b. (75c) On 50c #REA79b	3,500.
	c. 75c handstamped; 50mm signature	50.00
	d. As "c," 65mm signature	150.00
REA101	($1.50) on $1 #REA94	25.00
	a. $1.50 handstamped; 50mm signature	250.00
	b. As "a," 65mm signature	1,750.
REA102	($3.00) on $2 #REA95	45.00
	a. $3 handstamped; 76mm signature	2,250.

Center Cutout Only

REA103	($7.50) on $5 #REA89	12.50
REA104	($15) on $10 #REA90	100.00
REA105	($37.50) on $25 #REA91	150.00

For surcharges see Nos. REA119, REA123, REA133, REA140, REA140a.

See individual rates before No. REA96.

1914 Engr. Wmk. USIR
Paper of Various Shades of Blue
Entire Stamp

REA106	18¾c red brown	50.00
REA107	25c black	100.00
	a. 25c violet blue	1,500.
REA108	37½c green	10.00
	a. 37½c black	5,000.
REA108B	50c black	
REA109	75c black	2.50
REA110	$1.50 red orange	17.50
REA111	$3 orange	125.00

Center Cutout Only

REA112	$7.50 black	7.50
REA113	$15 black	15.00
REA114	$37.50 black	7.50

For surcharges see Nos. REA118, REA120, REA120a, REA121, REA124-REA125, REA127, REA129-REA131, REA134, REA134a, REA137, REA144, REA146-REA149.

See individual rates before No. REA96.

1916 Engr. Wmk. USIR
Paper of Various Shades of Greenish Blue
Entire Stamp

REA115	37½c green	75.00
REA116	75c black	20.00

For surcharges see Nos. REA122, REA124, REA138.

Stamps of 1914-16 Provisionally Surcharged Types A, B & C

ACT OF 1917

Type C

Surcharge types:

A - "ACT OF 1917" handstamped in 1-3 lines in more than 30 styles.
B - "ACT OF 1917" locally printed horizontally in black or red.
C - "ACT OF 1917" printed in black or red by BEP, horizontally on ⅛ bbl-1 hhd and reading down on 5-25 bbl.

Surcharge also exists in manuscript on some values. Tax rate $3 per bbl.

37½c = ⅛ barrel	$3 = 1 barrel
50c = ⅙ barrel	$6 = 1 hogshead
75c = ¼ barrel	$15 = 5 barrels
$1 = ⅓ barrel	$30 = 10 barrels
$1.50 = ½ barrel	$75 = 25 barrels

1917   Type A Surcharge
Entire Stamp

REA117	(37½c)	on #REA96	—
REA118	(37½c)	on #REA106	50.00
b.	Type B surcharge		
c.	Type C surcharge		250.00
REA119	(50c)	on #REA97	75.00
REA120	(50c)	on #REA107a	150.00
a.	On #107		300.00
REA121	(75c)	on #REA108	35.00
REA122	(75c)	on #REA115	20.00
b.	Type B surcharge		1,250.
c.	Type C surcharge		40.00
REA123	($1)	on #REA99	85.00
REA124	($1.50)	on #REA116	12.50
b.	Type B surcharge		1,250.
c.	Type C surcharge		3.50
d.	As "c," inverted surcharge		600.00

$1.50 surcharge exists in manuscript on #REA109.

REA125	($3)	on #REA110	50.
c.	Type C surcharge		20.
REA126	($6)	on #REA102	1,000.
REA127	($6)	on #REA111	150.

Center Cutout Only

REA128	($15)	on #REA103	350.
REA129	($15)	on #REA112, entire stamp, type C surcharge	2,000.
REA130	($30)	on #REA113	75.
c.	Type C surcharge		35.
REA131	($75)	on #REA114	150.
c.	Type C surcharge		10.

For surcharges see Nos. REA132, REA132a, REA135-REA136, REA139-REA139b, REA142-REA143, REA145, REA150-REA151.

Stamps of 1914-17 provisionally surcharged "ACT OF 1918" or "Revenue Act of 1918" with rubber stamp in various colors in more than 20 styles.

A subtype has the incorrect date of 1919 due to the effective date of the act (at least five styles).

Tax rate $6 per bbl.

75c = ⅛ barrel	$6 = 1 barrel
$1 = ⅙ barrel	$12 = 1 hogshead
$1.50 = ¼ barrel	$30 = 5 barrels
$2 = ⅓ barrel	$60 = 10 barrels
$3 = ½ barrel	$150 = 25 barrels

1918   Entire Stamp

REA132	(75c)	on #REA118	250.
a.	On #REA118c		350.
REA133	($1)	on #REA97	400.
REA134	($1)	on #REA107	1,250.
a.	On #REA107a		1,750.

Exists with additional overprint "Non-Intoxicating, containing not to/exceed 2¾% of Alcohol by weight." Value, $1,750.

REA135	($1)	on #REA119	2,000.
REA136	($1)	on #REA120	2,000.
REA137	($1.50)	on #REA108	400.
a.	Surcharge dated "1919"		1,250.
REA138	($1.50)	on #REA115	500.
REA139	($1.50)	on #REA122c	50.
a.	Surcharge dated "1919"		30.
b.	On #REA122		250.
REA140	($2)	on #REA99	500.
a.	On #REA99a		750.
REA141	($2)	on #REA99a	1,750.

No. REA141 bears additional 1917 provisional surcharge, as well as the 1914 surcharge, but was not issued in that form without 1918 surcharge.

REA142	($2)	on #REA123	2,000.
REA143	($3)	on #REA124c	15.
a.	Surcharge dated "1919"		400.

REA144	($6)	on #REA110	350.
REA145	($6)	on #REA125c	20.
a.	Surcharge dated "1919"		350.
REA146	($12)	on #REA111	350.
REA147	($12)	on #REA111	40.

No. REA147 bears additional 1917 Type C provisional surcharge but was not issued in that form without 1918 surcharge.

Center Cutout Only

REA148	($30)	on #REA112	50.
REA149	($60)	on #REA113	50.
REA150	($60)	on #REA130c	250.
a.	Entire stamp		1,750.
REA151	($150)	on #REA131c	20.
a.	Entire stamp		2,500.

REA152-REA158

REA159-REA161

Tax rate $5 per barrel through Jan. 11, 1934. $6 rate also effective Dec. 5, 1933. Provisional handstamp "Surcharged $6.00 Rate" in 1-3 lines (seven styles).

1933   Engr.   Wmk. USIR
Paper of Various Shades of Greenish Blue to Blue
Type A
Entire Stamp

REA152	⅛ bbl., **violet red**		12.50
a.	Provisional surcharge, $6 rate		750.00
REA153	⅙ bbl., **purple**		250.00
REA154	¼ bbl., **green**		4.00
REA155	⅓ bbl., **brown orange**		750.00
REA156	½ bbl., **orange**		2.50
a.	Provisional surcharge, $6 rate		400.00
REA157	1 bbl., **blue**		15.00
a.	Provisional surcharge, $6 rate		2,000.
REA158	1 hhd., **black**		3,750.
REA159	5 bbl., **black,** center cutout only		200.00
REA160	10 bbl., **black,** with cut-out center, rouletted 7 at left		5,000.
a.	Center cutout only		200.00
REA161	25 bbl., **black,** with cut-out center, rouletted 7 at left		5,000.
a.	Center cutout only		200.00

Center cutout portions of Nos. REA159-REA161 are on greenish blue paper. See Nos. REA177-REA178A for copies on bright blue paper.

Nos. REA152-REA159, REA161 Surcharged in Black

ACT OF MARCH 22, 1933

A - additional provisional handstamped surcharge.
B - additional manuscript and handstamped surcharges.
Tax rate same as Nos. REA152-REA161.

1933   Engr.   Wmk. USIR
Entire Stamp

REA162	⅛ bbl., **violet red**		5.00
REA163	⅙ bbl., **purple**		125.00
REA164	¼ bbl., **green**		10.00
a.	With 1918 provisional handstamped surcharge, $6 rate		1,750.
b.	Type A surcharge, $6 rate		2,000.
REA165	⅓ bbl., **brown orange**		4,500.
REA166	½ bbl., **orange**		10.00
a.	Type A surcharge, $6 rate		1,750.
b.	Type B surcharge, $6 rate		1,000.
REA167	1 bbl., **blue**		15.00
REA168	1 hhd., **black**		4,500.
REA169	5 bbl., **black,** center cutout only		400.00
REA170	25 bbl., **black,** center cutout only		350.00

REA171-REA176

REA177-REA178A

Tax rate same as previous issue. Provisional handstamp reads "SOLD AT $5.00 RATE" or "$5.00 RATE."

1933   Engr.   Wmk. USIR
Entire Stamp

REA171	⅛ bbl., **violet red**		20.00
REA172	⅙ bbl., **purple**		325.00
REA173	¼ bbl., **green**		2.50
a.	Provisional surcharge, $5 rate		2,250.
REA174	½ bbl., **brown orange**		1.50
a.	Provisional surcharge, $5 rate		500.00
REA175	1 bbl., **blue**		50.00
REA176	1 hhd., **black**		3,250.

Bright Blue Paper

REA177	5 bbl., **black**		750.00
a.	Entire stamp with cut-out center		7.50
b.	Center cutout only		1.00
REA178	10 bbl., **black**		350.00
a.	Entire stamp with cut-out center		7.50
b.	Center cutout only		1.00
REA178A	25 bbl., **black**		225.00
b.	Entire stamp with cut-out center		3.50
c.	Center cutout only		1.00
d.	Rouletted 7 at left		—

For surcharge see No. REA199.

Nos. REA173-REA174 with BEP Printed Surcharge, "Act of March 22, 1933"

Additional provisional handstamped surcharge, $6 rate as previous issue.

1933
Entire Stamp

REA179	¼ bbl., **green**		15.00
a.	Handstamped "Surcharged $6 rate"		500.00
REA180	½ bbl., **brown orange**		7.50
a.	Handstamped "Surcharged $6 rate"		700.00

REA181-REA187

REA188-REA189

Tax rates $5 per bbl; $6 from July 1, 1940; $7 from Nov. 1, 1942; $8 from Apr. 1, 1944.

1934-45	Engr.		Wmk. USIR

With Black Control Numbers

REA181	⅛ bbl., **violet red**	1.00
a. With cutout center		1.00
b. Ovptd. "NOT LESS THAN 3⅞ GAL-LONS," uncut		
REA182	⅛ bbl., **purple**	75.00
a. With cutout center		50.00
REA183	¼ bbl., **green**	1.50
a. With cutout center		1.00

REA184	⅛ bbl., **brown orange**	6,500.
REA185	½ bbl., **orange**	1.00
a. With cutout center		1.00
REA186	1 bbl., **blue**	4.50
a. With cutout center		4.50
REA187	1 hhd., **black**	300.00
REA188	100 bbl., **carmine**, 1942	15.00
a. With cutout center		5.00
REA189	500 bbl., **dark brown**, with cutout center, 1945	300.00

Most values also exist as center cutout portions only.

REA190-REA193

REA194-REA198

Tax rates $8 per bbl, $9 from Nov. 1, 1951.

1947			Litho.

Black Control Numbers

REA190	⅛ bbl., **carmine**	100.00	40.00
a. With cutout center			5.00
REA191	¼ bbl., **green**	37.50	12.50
a. With cutout center			8.00
REA192	½ bbl., **orange**	20.00	5.00
a. With cutout center			5.00
REA193	1 bbl., **blue**	200.00	75.00
a. With cutout center			6.00

Blue Paper

REA194	5 bbl., **black**	200.00	110.00
a. With cutout center			8.00
REA195	10 bbl., **black**	375.00	200.00
a. With cutout center			15.00
REA196	25 bbl., **black**	3,200.	3,200.
a. With cutout center			3,000.

White Paper

REA197	100 bbl., **carmine**	275.00	125.00
a. With cutout center			5.00
REA198	500 bbl., **dark brown**	575.00	300.00
a. With cutout center			30.00

All values also exist as center cutouts only.

No. REA158 Provisionally Handstamp Surcharged "Value increased under / Revenue Act of 1951" in black or purple.

Tax rate $9 per bbl.

1951

REA199	($225) on 25 bbl., #REA178A, uncut	3,000.

Also exists as center cutout only, showing portion of handstamped surcharge. Value, $150.

FERMENTED FRUIT JUICE STAMPS

Fermented fruit juice stamps were issued pending the ratification of the Repeal Amendment (Dec. 5, 1933) that made full-strength beer and wine legal again.

Congress, as a temporary measure, redefined intoxicating beverages by changing the legal definition from .5% to 3.2%, thus permitting the sale of 3.2 beer and wine beginning April 7, 1933.

Regular wine stamps were available to pay the Internal Revenue taxes. However, these Fermented Fruit Juice stamps were authorized for placement on individual bottles or containers of fermented fruit juice. Use was discontinued at the end of 1933.

Stamps are valued in the grade of very fine. Most stamps are found in average to fine condition. Unused stamps are valued with original gum.

REF1

Plates of 220 subjects in two panes of 110.

1933		Wmk. USIR	Engr.	Perf. 11
REF1	REF1	4 oz **gray**		75.00
REF3	REF1	8 oz **light green**		50.00
REF4	REF1	12 oz **light blue**	8.50	5.00
REF5	REF1	13 oz **olive green**		50.00
REF6	REF1	16 oz **lavender**		150.00
REF7	REF1	24 oz **orange**		100.00
REF8	REF1	29 oz **brown**		150.00
REF9	REF1	32 oz **red**	85.00	65.00

A dark blue 7-ounce stamp was issued, but the only recorded examples currently are in the National Postal Museum collection.

Earliest known use: May 28, 1933.

Beer Stamp No. REA154 Overprinted "WINE OR FERMENTED FRUIT JUICE" in Red

1933		Engr.	Imperf.
REF10	¼ bbl., **green**, blue		—

The ½ barrel and 1 barrel stamps Beer Stamps, Nos. REA156-REA157, also were issued with this overprint, but no examples are currently recorded.

The Fermented Fruit Juice Stamps of 1933

by Peter Martin

Continuing the recent tradition of adding a new revenue stamp category each year, the *2001 Scott Specialized* has added the Fermented Fruit Juice stamps of 1933.

These colorful stamps, which were printed by the Bureau of Engraving and Printing, were the product of the end of Prohibition. In 1933, the mood of the country had changed significantly since the 18th Amendment, the National Prohibition Act (Volstead Act), was approved on Oct. 28, 1919.

Figure 1: All recorded 7-ounce Fermented Fruit Juice stamps are in the National Postal Museum collection.

But the "Great Experiment" was difficult to enforce and by the mid-1920s most people favored revision of the Volstead Act to allow light beers and wines. With the onset of the Depression, government officials also were looking for ways to increase revenues.

On Feb. 20, 1933, the repeal faction in Congress won approval of the proposed 21st Amendment and it was sent to the states for ratification.

The Act of March 22, 1933, the "Beer Bill," quickly followed and was approved effective April 7, 1933 "to provide revenue by the taxation of certain non-intoxicating liquor."

As an interim measure, pending ratification of the Repeal Act, Congress redefined intoxicating beverages by changing the legal definition from 1/2 percent to 3.2 percent, thus permitting the sale of beer and wine of 3.2 strength beginning April 7, 1933.

The existing beer and wine stamps were available to pay the Internal Revenue taxes but the Fermented Fruit Juice stamps of 1933, denominated in ounces or barrels, were authorized to be placed on individual bottles or containers of fermented fruit juice.

Full strength beer and wine became legal again upon ratification by the states of the 21st Amendment effective Dec. 5, 1933.

The Treasury Department had closely followed these events and the Assistant Secretary of the Treasury James H. Douglas wrote to the Director of the BEP on April 15, 1933:

Public No. 5, 73rd Congress, approved by the President on March 22, 1933, entitled "An Act to Provide Revenue by the Taxation of Certain Nonintoxicating Liquor, and for other Purposes," authorizes the manufacture and sale, in those States where such business is not in conflict with local statutes, of wines and fermented fruit juice containing not more than 3.2 percent of alcohol by weight and levies a stamp tax thereon of $5.00 per (31-gallon) barrel.

Since certain manufacturers have signified their intention of producing and distributing 3.2 percent wines and fermented fruit juices, and as the tax thereon will be collected by means of stamps affixed to bottles and barrels, it is necessary for this Bureau to provide new stamps in five denominations for bottles and new stamps in three denominations for barrels, as follows:

Bottle Stamps — Denominations: 8-ounces, 12-ounces, 16-ounces, 29-ounces and 32-ounces,

Barrel Stamps — Denominations: 1/2-barrel, 1/4-barrel, 1-barrel.

It is planned to provide only one size of stamp for bottles, viz.. 1-5/8" x 27/32", in sheet style, printed 220 stamps to the sheet, delivered 110 stamps to the sheet, and prepared for shipment in packages, each containing 55,000 stamps, all to be gummed and perforated.

The foregoing stamps are scheduled for production on white internal revenue paper and will bear the inscription "Wine or Fermented Fruit Juice." In addition to the appropriate denomination numeral in bold type with the word "ounces" following in each case, the bottled stamps will bear the data "U.S.I.R." as well as the legend "Series 1933." Moreover, in the process of printing, a scheme is contemplated whereby each denomination of stamp will be made distinctive by the use of a different color of ink. The latter, of course, will be specified at the time printing estimates are submitted.

With regard to the stamps which are intended for use on barrels, it may be stated that for the present at least they will be produced by means-of overprinting denominations 1/2-barrel, 1/4-barrel, and 1-barrel fermented liquor stamps with the legend "Wine or Fermented Fruit Juice." It is, however, important that this legend be conspicuous.

Using the information given above as a guide, you are requested to prepare at the very earliest possible date appropriate models of the new stamps for bottles as well as a model of the legend which is scheduled for use in overprinting the fermented liquor stamps and to forward such models to the Commissioner of Internal Revenue for approval.

BEP Director A.W. Hall responded on April 18 by submitting a model of the Fermented Fruit Juice stamp and the model was approved by the Treasury Department on April 20.

On April 27, Douglas again wrote to the BEP asking that a 24-ounce denomination also be prepared because of the Bureau of Industrial Alcohol had informed him that certain large manufacturers wanted to pack the 3.2 wine and fermented fruit juice into 24 ounce bottles.

Douglas wrote: *"It will not be necessary for you to submit to the Bureau of Internal Revenue a model of the denomination of the 24-ounces stamp since it is understood that plates for all denominations of these new stamps will be produced by one master die, a model of which the Commissioner of Internal Revenue has already approved."*

Douglas wrote again to the BEP Director on May 1 adjusting the estimated number of stamps needed that had been provided on Aug. 3, 1932. Colors for the denominated stamps were also given: 8-ounce, green; 12-ounce, blue; 16-ounce, purple; 24-ounce, orange; 29-ounce, brown; 32-ounce, red.

On May 8, the BEP submitted 18 die proofs (three of each denomination) in the specified colors to the Commissioner of Internal Revenue. The Treasury Department approved the die proofs on May 9.

The Treasury Department, on May 20, asked that a 4-ounce stamp be added because of a recently developed large demand. Die proofs for the gray 4-ounce stamp were submitted by the BEP on May 23 and approved on May 27.

This was followed by a June 14 request for a 13-ounce denomination. Three die proofs of the olive green stamp were submitted by the BEP on June 21 and approved on June 22.

Finally, a request for a 7-ounce stamp was submitted on August 23. Three die proofs were submitted on September 6 and approved by the Treasury Department on September 7.

BEP stamp delivery records nearly match the current scarcity of the various denominations.

All recorded 7-ounce (dark blue, Figure 1) stamps are in the National Postal Museum collection. The 16-ounce and 24-ounce stamps are the rarest of the denominations in collector hands followed by the 29-ounce, 32-ounce and 4-ounce. The 8-ounce and 13-ounce stamps can still be obtained with limited searching.

The 12-ounce denomination is the only stamp that is found in large numbers. In fact, specialty collections can be formed with manufacturer dates and codes on the 12-ounce stamps with "H.B. Co." and "MDC" (Mission Dry Corp., Los Angeles) cancels.

Well-centered stamps are the exception rather than the rule in this nine-stamp series. Mint stamps are recorded for the 12-ounce and 32-ounce stamps.

Figure 2: The only recorded Fermented Fruit Juice barrel stamp (Ron Lesher collection).

In addition to the ounce-denominated stamps, three barrel stamps were produced by overprinting the Series 1933 Beer stamps (Scott REA154, REA156, REA157) with "Wine or Fermented Fruit Juice," in red.

While Bureau records clearly show that 1/4-barrel (green), 1/2-barrel (rust brown) and 1-barrel (dark blue) stamps were printed in quantities of 59,300, no copies had appeared on the market until the Morton Dean Joyce Collection was offered for sale in 1989. In the vast Joyce holdings was a single copy of the 1/4 barrel stamp (Figure 2).

To date, it remains the only barrel denominated Fermented Fruit Juice stamp that has been documented.

PLAYING CARDS

Stamps for use on packs of playing cards were included in the first general issue of 1862-71. They are Nos. R2, R11, R12, R17, R21 and R28. The tax on playing cards was repealed effective June 22, 1965.

Stamps for use on packs of playing cards were included in the first general issue of 1862-71. They are Nos. R2, R11, R12, R17, R21 and R28.

The tax on playing cards was repealed effective June 22, 1965.

"ON HAND . . ." — RF1   "ACT OF . . ." — RF2

1894   Engr.   Unwmk.   Rouletted 5½

RF1	RF1	2c lake	.70 .40
a.	Horizontal pair, imperf. between		400.00
b.	Horiz. pair, imperf. vert.		—
RF2	RF2	2c ultramarine	17.50 2.50
a.	2c blue		— 3.50
b.	Imperf., pair		400.00
c.	Imperf. horizontally		150.00 150.00
d.	Rouletted 12½		100.00 100.00
e.	Imperf. horizontally, rouletted 12½ vertically, pair		175.00 175.00

No vertical pairs of No. RF2e are known. Pairs will be horizontal. Singles are valued at 50% of the pair value.

1896-99   Wmk. 191R   Rouletted 5½, 7

RF3	RF2	2c blue	5.75 .60
a.	2c ultramarine ('99)		7.25 1.50
b.	Imperf., pair		125.00

No. RF3 surcharged " VIRGIN / ISLANDS / 4 CTS" are listed under Danish West Indies.

1902   Perf. 12

RF4	RF2	2c deep blue	50.00

No. RF4 is known with cancel date "1899" but that is due to the use of an old canceling plate. The stamp was first used in 1902.

ACT OF 1917
7
CENTS

Stamp of 1899 Surcharged in Rose

1917   Wmk. 191R   Rouletted 7

RF5	RF2	7c on 2c ultramarine	750.00 600.00
a.	Inverted surcharge		

The surcharge on No. RF5 was handstamped at the Internal Revenue Office in New York City. Different handstamps were used at other Internal Revenue Offices as well, values $250 to $300.

Surcharged in Black   17

1917

RF6	RF2	(7c) on 2c blue	50.00
a.	Inverted surcharge		50.00

The "17" indicated that the 7 cent tax had been paid according to the Act of 1917.
Used by N. Y. Consolidated Card Co.
Cancellations are in red.

Surcharged in Black   7

RF7	RF2	7c on 2c blue	650.00
a.	Inverted surcharge		475.00

Used by Standard Playing Card Co.

The surcharges on Nos. RF7-RF10, RF13, RF15, RF18 were applied by the manufacturers, together with their initials, dates, etc., thus forming a combination of surcharge and precancellation. The surcharge on No. RF16 was made by the Bureau of Engraving and Printing. After it appeared the use of some combinations was continued but only as cancellations.

7 CTS.

Surcharged Vertically Reading Up in Red or Violet

RF8	RF2	7c on 2c blue	1,150.
a.	Double surcharge		1,600.
b.	Reading down		1,700.

Used by Russell Playing Card Co.

7 CENTS

Surcharged Vertically, Reading Up in Black, Violet or Red

RF9	RF2	7c on 2c blue	9.50
a.	Double surcharge (violet)		100.00
b.	Numeral omitted (black)		80.00
c.	Surcharge reading down		11.00
d.	As "c," numeral omitted (black)		55.00
e.	As "c," double surcharge (violet)		275.00
f.	Double surcharge, one down (red)		275.00
g.	Surcharge and "A.D." in violet		350.00
h.	Surcharge and "A.D." in red, "U.S.P.C. Co." in black		1,000.
i.	Surcharge and "A.D." in red reading up, "U.S.P.C. Co." in black reading down		750.00
j.	As "g," reading down		750.00
k.	Double surcharge (black)		750.00
l.	Double surcharge (red)		400.00

"A.D." (Andrew Dougherty Co.) printed in red, "S. P. C. Co." (Standard Playing Card Co.) printed in violet, "U.S.P.C. Co." printed in black. The first two became divisions of United States Playing Card Co.
See No. RF13.

Surcharged in Carmine   **7c**

RF10	RF2	7c on 2c blue	65.00
a.	Inverted surcharge		37.50
b.	Double surcharge		550.00
c.	Double surcharge, inverted		550.00
d.	Triple surcharge		

Used by Russell Playing Card Co.

RF3

1918   Size: 21x40mm   Imperf.

RF11	RF3	blue	42.50 30.00
	Block of 4		180.00 140.00

Private Roulette 14

RF12	RF3	blue	225.
a.	Rouletted 13 in red		1,600.
b.	Rouletted 6½		375.
c.	Perf. 12 horiz., imperf. vert.		150.
d.	Perf. 12 on 4 sides		1,600.

Nos. RF11-RF12 served as 7c stamps when used before April 1, 1919, and as 8c stamps when used after that date.

No. RF11 is known handstamped "7" or "8," or both "7" and "8," as well as "Act of 1918" in black or magenta, either by the user to indicate the value when applied to the pack or by the IRS district offices at the time of sale.

No. RF12 was used by N. Y. Consolidated Card Co., Nos. RF12a, RF12b were used by Russell Playing Card Co., Nos. RF12, RF12d were used by Logan Printing House.

Surcharged like No. RF9 (but somewhat smaller) in Violet, Red or Black
Private Roulette 9½

RF13	RF3	7c blue	40.00
a.	Inverted surcharge		37.50
b.	Double surcharge		275.00
c.	Double surcharge, inverted		300.00

REVENUE ACT OF 1918
8 CENTS

Stamp of 1899 Surcharged in Magenta or Rose

1919   Rouletted 7

RF14	RF2	8c on 2c ultramarine	100.00
a.	Double surcharge		300.00
b.	Inverted surcharge		300.00

The surcharge on No. RF14 was handstamped at the Internal Revenue Office in New York City. A handstamp in black is known.

Exists in pair, one double surcharge, also in pair, one with inverted surcharge.

Surcharged in Carmine   **8c**

RF15	RF2	8c on 2c blue (inverted)	550.00
a.	Double surcharge, inverted		750.00

No. RF15 is surcharged only with large "8c" inverted, and overprinted with date and initials (also inverted). No. RF16 is often found with additional impression of large "8c," as on No. RF15, but in this usage the large "8c" is a cancellation.
Used by Russell Playing Card Co.

Surcharged in Carmine or Vermilion   **8 Cts.**

RF16	RF2	8c on 2c blue	140.00 .85
a.	Inverted surcharge		

See note after No. RF15.

RF4

1922   Size: 19x22mm   Rouletted 7

RF17	RF4	(8c) blue	19.00 1.40
	Block of 4		97.50

No. RF17, rouletted 7 and perforated 11, surcharged " VIRGIN / ISLANDS / 4 cts." are listed under Danish West Indies.

Surcharged in Carmine, Blue or Black   **8c**

RF18	RF4	8c on (8c) blue	35.00
a.	Inverted surcharge		35.00

Used by Pyramid Playing Card Co.

RF5

1924   Rouletted 7

RF19	RF5	10c blue	12.50 .40
	Block of 4		70.00

ROTARY PRESS COIL STAMP

1926   *Perf. 10 Vertically*
RF20 RF5   10c **blue**   .25
     Pair   3.00
     Joint line pair   6.00
No. RF20 exists only precanceled. **Bureau precancels:** 11 different.

FLAT PLATE PRINTING

1927   *Perf. 11*
RF21 RF5   10c **blue**   22.50   5.00
     Block of 4   100.00

1929   *Perf. 10*
RF22 RF5   10c **blue**   14.00   4.00
     Block of 4   67.50   —

RF6

ROTARY PRESS COIL STAMP

1929   *Perf. 10 Horizontally*
RF23 RF6   10c **light blue**   .20
     Pair   2.50
     Joint line pair   5.00
No. RF23 exists only precanceled. **Bureau precancels:** 16 different.

FLAT PLATE PRINTING

1930   *Perf. 10*
RF24 RF6   10c **blue**   12.50   1.25
     Block of 4   60.00   10.00
  a.   Horiz. pair, imperf. vert.   175.00

1931   *Perf. 11*
RF25 RF6   10c **blue**   12.50   1.25
     Block of 4   60.00

No. R234 is known used provisionally as a playing card revenue stamp August 6 and 8, 1932. Value for this use, authenticated, $300.

RF7

ROTARY PRESS COIL STAMP

1940   *Perf. 10 Vertically*
RF26 RF7   **blue, wet printing**   —   .40
     Pair   2.00
     Joint line pair   4.00
     Dry printing, unwatermarked   25.00   .40
         See note after No. 1029.
Bureau precancels: 11 different.

RF8

ROTARY PRESS COIL STAMP

1940   **Wmk. 191R**   *Perf. 10 Horizontally*
RF27 RF8   **blue, wet printing**   3.00   .20
     Pair   7.50
     Joint line pair   12.50
     Dry printing, unwatermarked   3.00
     Bureau precancels: 10 different.

FLAT PLATE PRINTING
Perf. 11
RF28 RF8   **blue, wet printing**   5.00   .75
     Block of 4   25.00
     Dry printing (rotary press)   5.00   4.00
     Dry printing (rotary press), unwatermarked   5.00
     Block of 4   —

ROTARY PRESS PRINTING
Perf. 10x11
RF29 RF8   **blue**   175.00   90.00
     Block of 4   750.00   —
  a.   Imperforate (P.C. Co.)   900.00

SILVER TAX STAMPS

The Silver Purchase Act of 1934 imposed a 50 per cent tax on the net profit realized on a transfer of silver bullion occurring after May 15, 1934. The tax was paid by affixing stamps to the transfer memorandum. Congress authorized the Silver Tax stamps on June 19, 1934. They were discontinued on June 4, 1963.

Documentary Stamps of 1917 Overprinted   **SILVER TAX**

1934   **Offset Printing**   **Wmk. 191R**   *Perf. 11*
RG1 R22   1c **carmine rose**   1.00   .85
RG2 R22   2c **carmine rose**   1.00   .60
     Double impression of stamp   —
RG3 R22   3c **carmine rose**   1.25   .75
RG4 R22   4c **carmine rose**   1.75   1.50
RG5 R22   5c **carmine rose**   2.50   1.25
RG6 R22   8c **carmine rose**   3.50   3.00
RG7 R22   10c **carmine rose**   4.00   2.75
RG8 R22   20c **carmine rose**   5.00   3.50
RG9 R22   25c **carmine rose**   5.50   4.00
RG10 R22   40c **carmine rose**   6.50   5.75
RG11 R22   50c **carmine rose**   7.50   6.00
RG12 R22   80c **carmine rose**   15.00   10.00

Engr.
RG13 R21 $1 **green**   25.00   12.50
RG14 R21 $2 **rose**   30.00   20.00
RG15 R21 $3 **violet**   60.00   32.50
RG16 R21 $4 **yellow brown**   50.00   22.50
RG17 R21 $5 **dark blue**   60.00   22.50
RG18 R21 $10 **orange**   80.00   20.00

Perf. 12
Without Gum
RG19 R17 $30 **vermilion**   150.00   55.00
     Cut cancel   20.00
RG20 R19 $60 **brown**   175.00   80.00
     Cut cancel   27.50
     Vertical strip of 4   350.00
RG21 R17 $100 **green**   175.00   35.00
     Vertical strip of 4   150.00
RG22 R18 $500 **blue**   500.00   250.00
     Cut cancel   110.00
     Vertical strip of 4   —
RG23 R19 $1000 **orange**   —   110.00
     Cut cancel   60.00

     See note after No. R227.

Same Overprint, spacing 11mm between words
"SILVER TAX"
Without Gum

1936   *Perf. 12*
RG26 R17 $100 **green**   350.00   65.00
     Vertical strip of 4   —
RG27 R19 $1000 **orange**   700.00

Documentary Stamps of 1917 Handstamped "SILVER TAX" in Violet, Large Block Letters, in Two Lines

1939   **Wmk. 191R**   **Offset Printing**   *Perf. 10*
RG28 R22   1c **rose pink**   12,500.

Perf. 11
RG29 R22   3c **rose pink**   —
RG30 R22   5c **rose pink**   750.
RG31 R22   10c **rose pink**   1,000.
RG32 R22   80c **rose pink**   6,000.

Other handstamps exist on various values. One has letters 4mm high, 2mm wide with "SILVER" and "TAX" applied in separate operations. Another has "Silver Tax" in two lines in a box, but it is believed this handstamp was privately applied and is fraudulent.

Overprint Typewritten in Black ($2, $3) or Red ($5)
1934-35   **Engr.**   *Perf. 11*
RG34 R21 $2 **carmine**   —
RG35 R21 $3 **violet**   2,500.
RG36 R21 $5 **dark blue**   —

Typewritten overprints also exist on 2c, 3c, 4c, 20c and 50c.

SERIES 1940

Type of Documentary Stamps 1917, Overprinted in Black   **SILVER TAX**

1940   **Offset Printing**   *Perf. 11*
RG37 R22   1c **rose pink**   20.00   —
RG38 R22   2c **rose pink**   20.00   —
RG39 R22   3c **rose pink**   20.00   —
RG40 R22   4c **rose pink**   22.50   —
RG41 R22   5c **rose pink**   14.00   —
RG42 R22   8c **rose pink**   20.00   —
RG43 R22   10c **rose pink**   20.00   —
RG44 R22   20c **rose pink**   22.50   —
RG45 R22   25c **rose pink**   20.00   —
RG46 R22   40c **rose pink**   32.50   —
RG47 R22   50c **rose pink**   32.50   —
RG48 R22   80c **rose pink**   32.50   —

Engr.
RG49 R21 $1 **green**   140.00   —
RG50 R21 $2 **rose**   225.00   —
RG51 R21 $3 **violet**   300.00   —
RG52 R21 $4 **yellow brown**   600.00   —
RG53 R21 $5 **dark blue**   700.00   —
RG54 R21 $10 **orange**   800.00   —

Nos. RG19-RG20, RG26 Handstamped in Blue "Series 1940"

1940   **Without Gum**   *Perf. 12*
RG55 R17 $30 **vermilion**   —   6,250.
RG56 R19 $60 **brown**   —   15,000.
RG57 R17 $100 **green**   —   4,500.

Alexander Hamilton — RG1

Levi Woodbury — RG2

Thomas Corwin — RG3

Overprinted in Black   **SERIES 1941**

1941   **Wmk. 191R**   **Engr.**   *Perf. 11*
RG58 RG1   1c **gray**   4.00   2.25
RG59 RG1   2c **gray** *(Oliver Wolcott, Jr.)*   4.00   2.25
RG60 RG1   3c **gray** *(Samuel Dexter)*   4.00   2.75
RG61 RG1   4c **gray** *(Albert Gallatin)*   6.00
RG62 RG1   5c **gray** *(G.W. Campbell)*   8.00
RG63 RG1   8c **gray** *(A.J. Dallas)*   8.50
RG64 RG1   10c **gray** *(Wm. H. Crawford)*   10.00
RG65 RG1   20c **gray** *(Richard Rush)*   17.50   7.50
RG66 RG1   25c **gray** *(S.D. Ingham)*   21.00   —
RG67 RG1   40c **gray** *(Louis McLane)*   35.00   35.00
RG68 RG1   50c **gray** *(Wm. J. Duane)*   45.00   30.00
RG69 RG1   80c **gray** *(Roger B. Taney)*   75.00   30.00
RG70 RG2 $1 **gray**   95.00   35.00
RG71 RG2 $2 **gray** *(Thomas Ewing)*   230.00   70.00
RG72 RG2 $3 **gray** *(Walter Forward)*   190.00   85.00
RG73 RG2 $4 **gray** *(J.C. Spencer)*   290.00   80.00
RG74 RG2 $5 **gray** *(G.M. Bibb)*   230.00   95.00
RG75 RG2 $10 **gray** *(R.J. Walker)*   425.00   95.00
RG76 RG2 $20 **gray** *(Wm. M. Meredith)*   600.00   300.00

Perf. 12
Without Gum

RG77	RG3	$30 gray	325.	225.
		Cut cancel		100.
RG78	RG3	$50 gray (James Guthrie)	4,500.	4,000.
RG79	RG3	$60 gray (Howell Cobb)	1,750.	250.
		Cut cancel		120.
RG80	RG3	$100 gray (P.F. Thomas)	—	325.
		Cut cancel		140.
		Vertical strip of 4		—
RG81	RG3	$500 gray (J.A. Dix)	—	17,500.
RG82	RG3	$1000 gray (S.P. Chase)	—	2,500.
		Cut cancel		1,000.

Nos. RG58-RG82 Overprinted Instead:

RG83

1942   **Wmk. 191R**   **Perf. 11**

RG83	RG1	1c gray	2.00	—
RG84	RG1	2c gray	2.05	—
RG85	RG1	3c gray	2.00	—
RG86	RG1	4c gray	2.00	—
RG87	RG1	5c gray	1.75	—
RG88	RG1	8c gray	4.00	—
RG89	RG1	10c gray	5.00	—
RG90	RG1	20c gray	8.50	—
RG91	RG1	25c gray	16.50	—
RG92	RG1	40c gray	22.50	—
RG93	RG1	50c gray	25.00	—
RG94	RG1	80c gray	60.00	—
RG95	RG2	$1 gray	87.50	60.00
a.		Overprint "SERIES 5942"	450.00	
RG96	RG2	$2 gray	87.50	60.00
a.		Overprint "SERIES 5942"	850.00	

RG97	RG2	$3 gray	165.00	125.00
a.		Overprint "SERIES 5942"	900.00	
RG98	RG2	$4 gray	175.00	125.00
a.		Overprint "SERIES 5942"	900.00	
RG99	RG2	$5 gray	175.00	140.00
a.		Overprint "SERIES 5942"	850.00	
RG100	RG2	$10 gray	550.00	375.00
RG101	RG2	$20 gray	675.00	—
a.		Overprint "SERIES 5942"		

Perf. 12
Without Gum

RG102	RG3	$30 gray	—	—
		Cut cancel		2,250.
RG103	RG3	$50 gray	10,000.	—
RG104	RG3	$60 gray	—	1,500.
		Cut cancel		650.
RG105	RG3	$100 gray	—	850.
		Cut cancel		500.
RG106	RG3	$500 gray	—	6,000.
		Cut cancel		3,500.
RG107	RG3	$1000 gray	—	5,250.
		Cut cancel		4,000.

Silver Purchase Stamps of 1941 without Overprint

1944   **Wmk. 191R**   **Perf. 11**

RG108	RG1	1c gray	.65	.25
RG109	RG1	2c gray	.75	—
RG110	RG1	3c gray	.90	—
RG111	RG1	4c gray	1.25	—
RG112	RG1	5c gray	1.75	2.00
RG113	RG1	8c gray	3.25	2.50
RG114	RG1	10c gray	3.00	2.50

RG115	RG1	20c gray	6.50	
RG116	RG1	25c gray	10.00	—
RG117	RG1	40c gray	15.00	11.00
RG118	RG1	50c gray	15.00	11.00
RG119	RG1	80c gray	27.50	—
RG120	RG2	$1 gray	55.00	20.00
RG121	RG2	$2 gray	80.00	45.00
RG122	RG2	$3 gray	90.00	35.00
RG123	RG2	$4 gray	125.00	85.00
RG124	RG2	$5 gray	140.00	60.00
RG125	RG2	$10 gray	200.00	60.00
		Cut cancel		17.50
RG126	RG2	$20 gray	625.00	550.00
		Cut cancel		275.00

Perf. 12
Without Gum

RG127	RG3	$30 gray	325.00	150.00
		Cut cancel		70.00
		Vertical strip of 4		—
RG128	RG3	$50 gray	700.00	625.00
		Cut cancel		310.00
		Vertical strip of 4		—
RG129	RG3	$60 gray	—	475.00
		Cut cancel		200.00
RG130	RG3	$100 gray	—	35.00
		Cut cancel		15.00
		Vertical strip of 4		—
RG131	RG3	$500 gray	—	500.00
		Cut cancel		250.00
RG132	RG3	$1000 gray	—	160.00
		Cut cancel		80.00
		Vertical strip of 4		

CIGARETTE TUBES STAMPS

These stamps were for a tax on the hollow tubes of cigarette paper, with or without thin cardboard mouthpieces attached. They were sold in packages so buyers could add loose tobacco to make cigarettes.

CIGTTE.

Documentary Stamp of 1917
Overprinted

TUBES

1919 **Offset Printing** **Wmk. 191R** **Perf. 11**

RH1	R22	1c carmine rose	.60	.25
		Block of 4	3.00	
a.		Without period	12.50	8.00

1929   **Perf. 10**

RH2	R22	1c carmine rose	30.00	9.00

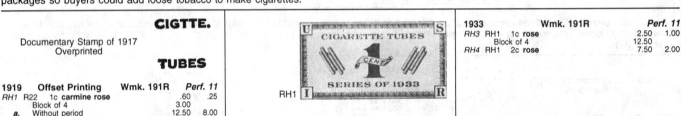

RH1

1933   **Wmk. 191R**   **Perf. 11**

RH3	RH1	1c rose	2.50	1.00
		Block of 4	12.50	
RH4	RH1	2c rose	7.50	2.00

POTATO TAX STAMPS

These stamps were required by the Potato Act of 1935, an amendment to the Agricultural Adjustment Act that became effective Dec. 1, 1935.

Potato growers were given allotments for which they were provided Tax Exempt Potato stamps. Growers exceeding their allotments would have paid for the excess with Tax Paid Potato stamps at the rate of ¾ cent per pound.

On Jan. 6, 1936, the U. S. Supreme Court declared the Agricultural Adjustment Act unconstitutional. Officially the Potato Act was in effect until Feb. 10, 1936, when it was repealed by Congress but, in essence, the law was ignored once the Supreme Court ruling was issued.

Because of the Act's short life, Tax Paid stamps were never used.

Young Woman
from *The*
Bouquet — RI1

RI2

Tax Paid Potatoes

1935   **Engr.**   **Unwmk.**   **Perf. 11**

RI1	RI1	¾c carmine rose	.30
RI2	RI1	1½c black brown	.45
RI3	RI1	2¼c yellow green	.45
RI4	RI1	3c light violet	.55
RI5	RI1	3¾c olive bister	.60
RI6	RI1	7½c orange brown	1.50
RI7	RI1	11¼c deep orange	1.90

RI8	RI1	18¾c violet brown	4.75
RI9	RI1	37½c red orange	4.25
RI10	RI1	75c blue	4.75
RI11	RI1	93¾c rose lake	7.50
RI12	RI1	$1.12½ green	14.50
RI13	RI1	$1.50 yellow brown	14.00
		Nos. RI1-RI13 (13)	55.50

Tax Exempt Potatoes

1935   **Engr.**   **Unwmk.**   **Perf. 11x10½**

RI14	RI2	2 lb black brown	1.00	10.00
a.		Booklet pane of 12	20.00	250.00
		Provisional booklet of 24, purple on pink cover	50.00	
		Provisional booklet of 96, purple on buff cover	150.00	
		Provisional booklet of 192, purple on white cover	300.00	
		Definitive booklet of 96, black on buff cover	100.00	
		Definitive booklet of 192, black on white cover	200.00	
RI15	RI2	5 lb black brown	20.00	
a.		Booklet pane of 12	350.00	
		Provisional booklet of 192, purple on white cover	—	
RI16	RI2	10 lb black brown	20.00	
a.		Booklet pane of 12	350.00	
		Provisional booklet of 192, purple on white cover	—	

RI17	RI2	25 lb black brown	100.00	
a.		Booklet pane of 12	1,500.	
RI18	RI2	50 lb black brown	1.00	40.00
a.		Booklet pane of 12	20.00	
		Provisional booklet of 24, purple on pink cover	50.00	
		Provisional booklet of 96, purple on buff cover	150.00	
		Provisional booklet of 192, purple on white cover	300.00	
		Definitive booklet of 96, black on buff cover	100.00	
		Definitive booklet of 192, black on white cover	200.00	
		Nos. RI14-RI16,RI18 (4)	42.00	

The booklet panes are arranged 4x3 with a tab at top. Edges are imperforate at left, right and bottom, yielding four stamps fully perforated, six stamps impert. on one side and two stamps imperf. on two sides per pane.

These stamps were printed from 360-subject rotary booklet plates and cut into 30 panes of 12. The panes were stapled into booklets of 24 (2 panes, pink covers), 96 (8 panes, buff covers) and 196 (16 panes, white covers), with handstamped covers (provisionals) and later with covers printed with the Dept. of Agriculture seal in the center (definitives). Both types of cover were prepared by the Bureau of Engraving and Printing.

Values for booklets are for examples containing panes that have very good to fine centering, because the overwhelming majority of booklets are in this grade. It should be noted that Scott values for individual panes (listed above) are for very fine panes. For this reason, individual panes are valued higher than the per-pane value of panes in booklets. For example, a pane of No. RI14a is valued at $20, but the No. RI14 definitive booklet of 96 (8 panes) is valued at $100, or $12.50 per pane, which is a little more than what a collector would pay for an individual

very good to fine pane. Booklets containing very fine panes will command a premium over the values given.

Although a value is given for a RI17 single stamp, all recorded examples are in three unbroken panes of 12. A 100 lb

Tax Exempt stamp was printed, but all are believed to have been destroyed.

TOBACCO SALE TAX STAMPS

These stamps were required to pay the tax on the sale of tobacco in excess of quotas set by the Secretary of Agriculture. The tax was 25 per cent of the price for which the excess tobacco was sold. It was intended to affect tobacco harvested after June 28, 1934 and sold before May 1, 1936. The tax was stopped when the Agricultural Adjustment Act was declared unconstitutional by the Supreme Court on Dec. 1, 1935.
Values for unused stamps are for copies with original gum.

Stamps and Types of 1917 Documentary Issue Overprinted	**TOBACCO SALE TAX**		

1934	**Offset Printing**	**Wmk. 191R**	**Perf. 11**	
RJ1	R22	1c **carmine rose**	.30	.20
RJ2	R22	2c **carmine rose**	.35	.20
RJ3	R22	5c **carmine rose**	1.20	.40

RJ4	R22	10c **carmine rose**	1.50	.40
a.		Inverted overprint	10.00	7.50
RJ5	R22	25c **carmine rose**	4.00	1.50
RJ6	R22	50c **carmine rose**	4.00	1.50

Engr.

RJ7	R21	$1 **green**	10.00	1.60
RJ8	R21	$2 **rose**	17.50	1.75
RJ9	R21	$5 **dark blue**	22.50	4.00

RJ10	R21	$10 **orange**	35.00	10.00
RJ11	R21	$20 **olive bister**	90.00	12.00
		Nos. RJ1-RJ11 (11)	186.35	33.55

On No. RJ11 the overprint is vertical, reading up.
No. RJ2 is known with a counterfeit inverted overprint.

NARCOTIC TAX STAMPS

The Revenue Act of 1918 imposed a tax of 1 cent per ounce or fraction thereof on opium, coca leaves and their derivatives. The tax was paid by affixing Narcotic stamps to the drug containers. The tax lasted from Feb. 25, 1919, through Apr. 30, 1971.
Members of the American Revenue Association compiled the listings in this section.

Documentary Stamps of 1914 Handstamped "NARCOTIC" in Magenta, Blue or Black				
1919	**Wmk. 191R**	**Offset Printing**	**Perf. 10**	
RJA1	R20	1c **rose**	85.00	75.00

The overprint was applied by District Collectors of Internal Revenue.
It is always in capital letters and exists in various type faces and sizes, including: 21 ½x2 ½mm, serif; 21x2 ¼mm, sans-serif boldface; 15 ½x 2 ½mm, sans-serif; 13x2mm, sans-serif.
The ½c, 2c, 3c, 4c, 5c, 10c, 25c and 50c with similar handstamp in serif capitals measuring about 20x2 ¼mm are bogus.

Documentary Stamps of 1917 Handstamped "NARCOTIC," "Narcotic," "NARCOTICS" or "ACT/NARCOTIC/1918" in Magenta, Black, Blue, Violet or Red				
1919	**Wmk. 191R**	**Offset Printing**	**Perf. 11**	
RJA9	R22	1c **carmine rose**	1.90	1.90
RJA10	R22	2c **carmine rose**	4.50	4.00
RJA11	R22	3c **carmine rose**	27.50	27.50
RJA12	R22	4c **carmine rose**	10.00	10.00
RJA13	R22	5c **carmine rose**	15.00	15.00
RJA14	R22	8c **carmine rose**	12.50	12.50
RJA15	R22	10c **carmine rose**	40.00	20.00
RJA16	R22	20c **carmine rose**	60.00	60.00
RJA17	R22	25c **carmine rose**	35.00	30.00
RJA18	R22	40c **carmine rose**	100.00	100.00
RJA19	R22	50c **carmine rose**	15.00	15.00
RJA20	R22	80c **carmine rose**	100.00	100.00

Engr.

RJA21	R21	$1 **green**	100.00	50.00
RJA22	R21	$2 **rose**		1,000.
RJA23	R21	$3 **violet**		1,200.
RJA24	R21	$5 **dark blue**		1,000.
RJA25	R21	$10 **orange**		1,200.

The overprints were applied by District Collectors of Internal Revenue. They are known in at least 20 type faces and sizes of which the majority read "NARCOTIC" in capital letters. Two are in upper and lower case letters. Experts have identified 14 by city. The 3-line handstamp was used in Seattle; "NARCOTICS" in Philadelphia. Most handstamps are not found on all denominations.
Many fake overprints exist.

No. R228 Overprinted in Black: "NARCOTIC / E.L. CO. / 3-19-19"

1919	**Wmk. 191R**	**Perf. 11**	
"NARCOTIC" 14 ½mm wide			
RJA26	R22	1c **carmine rose**	2,250.

Overprinted by Eli Lilly Co., Indianapolis, for that firm's use.

No. R228 Overprinted in Black: "J W & B / NARCOTIC"

1919	**Wmk. 191R**	**Perf. 11**	
"NARCOTIC" 14 ½mm wide			
RJA27	R22	1c **carmine rose**	2,250.

Overprinted by John Wyeth & Brother, Philadelphia, for that firm's use.

Nos. R228, R231-R232 Handstamped in Blue: "P-W-R-Co. / NARCOTIC"

1919	**Wmk. 191R**	**Perf. 11**	
RJA28	R22	1c **carmine rose**	600.00
RJA28A	R22	4c **carmine rose**	1,200.
RJA29	R22	5c **carmine rose**	

The handstamp was applied by the Powers-Weightmann-Rosengarten Co., Philadelphia, for that firm's use.

Proprietary Stamps of 1919 Handstamped "NARCOTIC" in Blue

1919	**Wmk. 191R**	**Offset Printing**	**Perf. 11**	
RJA30	RB5	1c **dark blue**	—	—
RJA31	RB5	2c **dark blue**	—	—
RJA32	RB5	4c **dark blue**	—	—

No. RB65 is known with "Narcotic" applied in red ms.

Documentary Stamps of 1917 Overprinted in Black, "Narcotic" 17 ½mm wide — **NARCOTIC**

1919	**Wmk. 191R**	**Offset Printing**	**Perf. 11**	
RJA33	R22	1c **carmine rose** (6,900,000)	.90	.60
RJA34	R22	2c **carmine rose** (3,650,000)	1.50	1.00
RJA35	R22	3c **carmine rose** (388,400)	30.00	20.00
RJA36	R22	4c **carmine rose** (2,400,000)	5.00	3.50
RJA37	R22	5c **carmine rose** (2,400,000)	13.00	10.00
RJA38	R22	8c **carmine rose** (1,200,000)	20.00	15.00
RJA39	R22	10c **carmine rose** (3,400,000)	3.00	2.50
RJA40	R22	25c **carmine rose** (700,000)	20.00	15.00

Overprint Reading Up
Engr.

RJA41	R21	$1 **green** (270,000)	45.00	20.00

Fake overprints exist on Nos. RJA33-RJA41. In the genuine the C's are not slanted.

NT1

NT2

	Imperf., Rouletted		
1919-64	**Offset Printing**	**Wmk. 191R**	
	Left Value- "a" Imperf.		
	Right Value- "b" Rouletted 7		
RJA42	NT1	1c **violet**	5.00	.25
d.		1c purple	7.50	
RJA43	NT2	1c **violet**	.50	.25
d.		1c purple	5.00	5.00
RJA44	NT2	2c **violet**	1.00	.50
d.		2c purple	5.00	
RJA45	NT2	3c **violet** ('64)	125.00	

NT3   NT4

Left Value- "a" Imperf.
Right Value- "b" Rouletted 7

RJA46	NT3	1c **violet**	2.50	.65
d.		1c purple	7.50	

RJA47	NT3	2c **violet**	1.50	.60
d.		2c **purple**		8.00
RJA48	NT3	3c **violet**	750.00	—
RJA49	NT3	4c **violet** ('42)	—	8.50
d.		4c **purple**		30.00
RJA50	NT3	5c **violet**	40.00	3.25
d.		5c **purple**		12.50
RJA51	NT3	6c **violet**		.65
d.		6c **purple**		9.00
RJA52	NT3	8c **violet**	55.00	3.00
d.		8c **purple**		25.00
RJA53	NT3	9c **violet** ('53)	65.00	20.00
RJA54	NT3	10c **violet**	30.00	.50
d.		10c **purple**		7.00
RJA55	NT3	16c **violet**	50.00	3.25
d.		16c **purple**		14.00
RJA56	NT3	18c **violet** ('61)	110.00	10.00
RJA57	NT3	19c **violet** ('61)	125.00	25.00
RJA58	NT3	20c **violet**	350.00	200.00

Nos. RJA47-RJA58 have "CENTS" below the value.

Left Value- "a" Imperf.
Right Value- "b" Rouletted 7

RJA59	NT4	1c **violet**	45.00	10.00
c.		Rouletted 3½		4.00
RJA60	NT4	2c **violet**		20.00
RJA61	NT4	3c **violet**	50.00	60.00
RJA62	NT4	5c **violet**		25.00
RJA63	NT4	6c **violet**	60.00	20.00
RJA64	NT4	8c **violet**		45.00
RJA65	NT4	9c **violet** ('61)	25.00	20.00
RJA66	NT4	10c **violet**	11.00	15.00
RJA67	NT4	16c **violet**	15.00	10.00
RJA68	NT4	18c **violet** ('61)	375.00	400.00
RJA69	NT4	19c **violet**	12.50	175.00
RJA70	NT4	20c **violet**	325.00	225.00
RJA71	NT4	25c **violet**		20.00
c.		Rouletted 3½		4.00

RJA72	NT4	40c **violet**	400.00	*1,250.*
c.		Rouletted 3½		65.00
RJA73	NT4	$1 **green**		1.40
RJA74	NT4	$1.28 **green**	30.00	10.00

On Nos. RJA60-RJA74 the value tablet is solid.

Imperf., Rouletted
1963(?)-70   Offset Printing   Unwatermarked
Left Value- "a" Imperf.
Right Value- "b" Rouletted 7

RJA75	NT1	1c **violet**	7.50	2.00+
RJA76	NT2	1c **violet**	1.00	1.00
RJA77	NT2	2c **violet**	5.00	2.00+
RJA78	NT2	3c **violet**		125.00
RJA79	NT3	1c **violet**	5.00	2.00
RJA80	NT3	2c **violet**		2.00
RJA81	NT3	4c **violet**		10.00
RJA82	NT3	5c **violet**	70.00	
RJA83	NT3	6c **violet**	—	10.00+
RJA84	NT3	8c **violet**	—	5.00
RJA85	NT3	9c **violet**	—	50.00
RJA86	NT3	10c **violet**	—	10.00+
RJA87	NT3	16c **violet**	150.00	4.00
RJA88	NT3	18c **violet**	—	50.00+
RJA89	NT3	20c **violet**	—	300.00+

Nos. RJA80-RJA89 have "CENTS" below the value.
+ Items so marked currently are only known unused with original gum and are valued thus.

Unwatermarked
Left Value- "a" Imperf.
Right Value- "b" Rouletted 7

RJA91	NT4	1c **violet**	65.00	15.00
RJA92	NT4	2c **violet**		50.00+
RJA93	NT4	3c **violet**	85.00	125.00+
RJA94	NT4	6c **violet**	100.00	50.00+
RJA95	NT4	9c **violet**		125.00+
RJA96	NT4	10c **violet**		60.00+

RJA97	NT4	16c **violet**	40.00	20.00
RJA98	NT4	19c **violet**	25.00	400.00
RJA99	NT4	20c **violet**		500.00+
RJA100	NT4	25c **violet**		250.00
RJA101	NT4	40c **violet**	1,000.	
RJA102	NT4	$1 **green**		30.00+
RJA103	NT4	$1.28 **green**		60.00+
RJA104	NT4	$4 **green**,('70)	1,000.	

On Nos. RJA92-RJA104 the value tablet is solid.
+ Items so marked currently are only known unused with original gum and are valued thus.

NT5

Denomination added in black by rubber plate in an operation similar to precanceling.

1963   Engr.   Unwmk.   Imperf.
Left Value- Unused
Right Value- Used

RJA105	NT5	1c **violet**	100.00	85.00

Denomination on Stamp Plate
1964   Offset Printing   Imperf.

RJA106	NT5	1c **violet**	90.00	5.00

CONSULAR SERVICE FEE STAMPS

Act of Congress, April 5, 1906, effective June 1, 1906, provided that every consular officer should be provided with special adhesive stamps printed in denominations determined by the Department of State.

Every document for which a fee was prescribed had to have attached a stamp or stamps representing the amount collected, and such stamps were used to show payment of these prescribed fees.

These stamps were usually affixed close to the signature, or at the lower left corner of the document. If no document was issued, the stamp or stamps were attached to a receipt for the amount of the fee and canceled either with pen and ink or rubber stamp showing the date of cancellation and bearing the initials of the canceling officer or name of the Consular Office. These stamps were not sold to the public uncanceled. Their use was discontinued Sept. 30, 1955.

CS1

CS2

1906   Unwmk.   Engr.   Perf. 12

RK1	CS1	25c **dark green**	50.00
RK2	CS1	50c **carmine**	70.00
RK3	CS1	$1 **dark violet**	7.25
a.		Diagonal half used as 50c with 2 #RK3, paying $2.50 fee, on document	300.00
RK4	CS1	$2 **brown**	5.00
RK5	CS1	$2.50 **dark blue**	1.75
RK6	CS1	$5 **brown red**	22.50
a.		Horizontal or diagonal half used as $2.50, on document	250.00
RK7	CS1	$10 **orange**	65.00

Perf. 10

RK8	CS1	25c **dark green**	60.00
RK9	CS1	50c **carmine**	70.00
RK10	CS1	$1 **dark violet**	350.00
RK11	CS1	$2 **brown**	80.00
a.		Diagonal half used as $1, on document	—
RK12	CS1	$2.50 **dark blue**	20.00
RK13	CS1	$5 **brown red**	110.00

Perf. 11

RK14	CS1	25c **dark green**	60.00
RK15	CS1	50c **carmine**	95.00
RK16	CS1	$1 **dark violet**	1.90
a.		Diagonal half used as 50c, on document	350.00
RK17	CS1	$2 **brown**	2.25
RK18	CS1	$2.50 **dark blue**	.90
RK19	CS1	$5 **brown red**	4.00
a.		Diagonal half used as $2.50, on document	50.00
RK20	CS1	$9 **gray**	15.00
RK21	CS1	$10 **orange**	30.00
d.		Diagonal half used as $5, on document	60.00

1924   Perf. 11

RK22	CS2	$1 **violet**	75.00
RK23	CS2	$2 **brown**	85.00
RK24	CS2	$2.50 **blue**	11.00
RK25	CS2	$5 **brown red**	60.00
RK26	CS2	$9 **gray**	225.00
		Nos. RK22-RK26 (5)	456.00

CS3

1925-52   Perf. 10

RK27	CS3	$1 **violet**	25.00
RK28	CS3	$2 **brown**	60.00
RK29	CS3	$2.50 **ultramarine**	1.40
RK30	CS3	$5 **carmine**	11.00
RK31	CS3	$9 **gray**	42.50

Perf. 11

RK32	CS3	25c **green** ('37)	70.00
RK33	CS3	50c **orange** ('34)	70.00
RK34	CS3	$1 **violet**	3.00
a.		Diagonal half used as 50c, on document	—
RK35	CS3	$2 **brown**	3.00
RK36	CS3	$2.50 **blue**	.40
a.		$2.50 **ultramarine**	.35
RK37	CS3	$5 **carmine**	3.00
RK38	CS3	$9 **gray**	15.00
RK39	CS3	$10 **blue gray** ('37)	80.00
RK40	CS3	$20 **violet** ('52)	90.00
		Nos. RK27-RK40 (14)	474.30

Consular Fee

The "Consular Fee stamp" on revenue stamped paper (previously listed as No. RN-Y1 but since deleted) was found to be nothing more than an illustration. Two identical copies are known.

CUSTOMS FEE STAMPS

New York Custom House

Issued to indicate the collection of miscellaneous customs fees. Use was discontinued on February 28, 1918. The stamps were not utilized in the collection of customs duties.

Silas Wright
CF1

			Size: 48x34mm		
1887			**Engr.**		**Rouletted 5½**
RL1	CF1	20c	**dull rose**	110.00	1.00
a.		20c	**red**, perf. 10		—
b.			Vert. half used as 10c, on document		250.00
c.		20c	**red**, rouletted 7		200.00
RL2	CF1	30c	**orange**	140.00	1.25
RL3	CF1	40c	**green**	175.00	2.25
RL4	CF1	50c	**dark blue**	175.00	4.50

RL5	CF1	60c	**red violet**	140.00	1.50
RL6	CF1	70c	**brown violet**	140.00	30.00
RL7	CF1	80c	**brown**	200.00	75.00
RL8	CF1	90c	**black**	250.00	90.00
			Nos. RL1-RL8 (8)	1,330.	205.50

Each of these stamps has its own distinctive background.

EMBOSSED REVENUE STAMPED PAPER

Some of the American colonies of Great Britain used embossed stamps in raising revenue, as Britain had done from 1694. The British government also imposed stamp taxes on the colonies, and in the early 19th century the U.S. government and some of the states enacted similar taxes.

Under one statue or another, these stamps were required on such documents as promissory notes, bills of exchange, insurance policies, bills of lading, bonds, protests, powers of attorney, stock certificates, letters patent, writs, conveyances, leases, mortgages, charter parties, commissions and liquor licenses.

A few of these stamps were printed, but most were colorless impressions resembling a notary public's seal.

The scant literature of these stamps includes E.B. Sterling's revenue catalogue of 1888, *The Stamps that Caused the American Revolution: The Stamps of the British Stamp Act for America,* by Adolph Koeppel, published in 1976 by the Town of North Hempstead (New York) American Revolution Bicentennial Commission, *New Discovery from British Archives on the 1765 Tax Stamps for America,* edited by Adolph Koeppel and published in 1962 by the American Revenue Association, *First Federal Issue 1798-1801 U.S. Embossed Revenue Stamped Paper,* by W.V. Combs, published in 1979 by the American Philatelic Society, *Second Federal Issue, 1801-1802,* by W.V. Combs, published in 1988 by the American Revenue Association, and *Third Federal Issue, 1814-1817,* by W.V. Combs, published in 1993 by the American Revenue Association.

Values are for stamps of clear impression on entire documents of the most common usage in good condition. The document may be folded. Unusual or rare usages may sell for much more. Parts of documents, cut squares or poor impressions sell for much less.

Colin MacR. Makepeace originally compiled the listings in this section.

INCLUDING COLONIAL EMBOSSED REVENUES
I. COLONIAL ISSUES
A. MASSACHUSETTS
Act of January 8, 1755
In effect May 1, 1755-April 30, 1757

EP1   EP2

EP3   EP4

Typo.

RM1	EP1	½p	**red**	2,300.

Embossed

RM2	EP2	2p	400.
RM3	EP3	3p	150.
RM4	EP4	4p	500.

A second die of EP2 with no fin on the under side of the codfish has been seen. There were at least two dies of the ½p.

B. NEW YORK
Act of December 1, 1756
In effect January 1, 1757-December 31, 1760

EP9

Typo.

RM9	EP9	½p	**red**	2,500.

Embossed

RM10	EP9	1p	525.
RM11	EP9	2p	275.
RM12	EP9	3p	450.
RM13	EP9	4p	375.

II. BRITISH REVENUES FOR USE IN AMERICA
Act of March 22, 1765
In effect November 1, 1765-May 1, 1766
A. ALMANAC STAMPS

EP15

Engr.

RM15	EP15	2p	**red**	
RM16	EP15	4p	**red**	—
RM17	EP15	8p	**red**	

Proofs of all of these stamps printed in the issued color are known. Full size facsimile reproductions in the color of the originals were made about 1876 of the proof sheets of the 8p stamp, Plates 1 and 2, Dies 1 to 50 inclusive.

B. PAMPHLETS AND NEWSPAPER STAMPS

EP18

Engr.

RM18	EP18	½p	**red**	2,000.
RM19	EP18	1p	**red**	—
RM20	EP18	2p	**red**	

Proofs of all of these stamps printed in the issued color are known. Full size facsimile reproductions in the color of the originals were made about 1876 of the proof sheets of the 1p stamp, Plates 3 and 4, Dies 51 to 100 inclusive.

C. GENERAL ISSUE

EP24   EP25

EP26   EP27

EP28   EP29

EP30   EP31

EP33   EP34

EP35

Embossed

RM24	EP24	3p	2,000.
RM25	EP25	4p	3,000.
RM26	EP26	6p	2,000.
RM27	EP27	1sh	1,500.
RM28	EP28	1sh6p	1,250.
RM29	EP29	2sh	3,000.
RM30	EP30	2sh3p	1,800.
RM31	EP31	2sh6p	1,250.
a.	Not on document		450.
RM33	EP33	4sh	1,750.
RM34	EP34	5sh	2,500.
RM35	EP35	10sh	3,250.

Proofs exist of similar 1sh, 1sh6p and 2sh6p stamps inscribed "AMERICA CONT.& c."

Various Similar Designs

RM36	£1	—
RM37	£2	—
RM38	£3	—

RM39	£4	—
RM40	£6	—
RM41	£10	—

The £1 to £10 denominations probably exist only as proofs.

D. PLAYING CARDS STAMP
Type similar to EP29, with Arms of George III Encircled by Garter.

RM42	1sh	—

All of these were embossed without color and most of them were embossed directly on the document except the 2sh 6p which was general embossed on a rectangular piece of bluish or brownish stiff paper or cardboard only slightly larger than the stamp which was attached to the document by a small piece of metal. Three dies exist of the 3p; two of the 4p, 6p, 1sh, 1sh 6p, 2sh and 2sh 3p.

All of these stamps have the word "America" somewhere in the design and this is the feature which distinguishes them from the other British revenues. The stamps of the general issue are occasionally found with a design of a British revenue stamp struck over the American design, as a number of them were afterwards re-struck and used elsewhere as British revenues.

These stamps are sometimes called the "Teaparty" or "Tax on Tea" stamps. This, however, is a misnomer, as the act under which these stamps were issued laid no tax on tea. The tax on tea was levied by an act passed two years later, and the duties imposed by that act were not collected by stamps.

It must be remembered that these stamps were issued under an act applicable to all of the British colonies in America which included many which are not now part of the United States. Copies have been seen which were used in Quebec, Nova Scotia and in the West Indies. So great was the popular clamor against taxation by a body in which the colonists had no representation that ships bringing the stamps from England were not allowed to land them in some of the colonies, the stamps were destroyed in others, and in practically all of those which are now a part of the United States the "Stamp Masters" who were to administer the act were forced to resign and to take oath that they would never carry out the duties of the offices. Notwithstanding the very general feeling about these stamps there is evidence that a very small number of them were actually used on ships' documents for one vessel clearing from New York and for a very small number of vessels clearing from the Savannah River. Florida was at this time under British authority and the only known copies of these stamps used in what is now the United States, a 4p (#RM25), a 1sh (#RM27), and two copies of the 5sh (#RM34) were used there.

III. ISSUES OF THE UNITED STATES
A. FIRST FEDERAL ISSUE
Act of July 6, 1797
In effect July 1, 1798-February 28, 1801

The distinguishing feature of the stamps of this issue is the name of a state in the design. These stamps were issued by the Federal Government, however, and not by the states. The design, with the exception of the name of the state, was the same for each denomination; but different denominations had the shield and the eagle in different positions. The design of only one denomination of these stamps is illustrated.

In addition to the eagle and shield design on the values from four cents to ten dollars there are two other stamps for each state, similar in design to one another, one of which is illustrated. All of these stamps are embossed without color.

Values are for clearly impressed examples.

RM45	4c	Connecticut	45.00
RM46	10c	Connecticut	40.00
RM47	20c	Connecticut	300.00
RM48	25c	Connecticut	45.00
RM49	30c	Connecticut	1,250.
RM50	50c	Connecticut	135.00
RM51	75c	Connecticut	—
RM52	$1	Connecticut	1,750.
RM54	$4	Connecticut	1,250.
RM58	4c	Delaware	125.00
RM59	10c	Delaware	250.00
RM60	20c	Delaware	400.00
RM61	25c	Delaware	300.00
RM62	30c	Delaware	—
RM63	50c	Delaware	400.00
RM64	75c	Delaware	700.00
RM65	$1	Delaware	—
RM71	4c	Georgia	200.00
RM72	10c	Georgia	125.00
RM73	20c	Georgia	—
RM74	25c	Georgia	100.00
RM75	30c	Georgia	3,000.
RM76	50c	Georgia	250.00
RM77	75c	Georgia	1,750.
RM78	$1	Georgia	—
RM84	4c	Kentucky	20.00
RM85	10c	Kentucky	25.00
RM86	20c	Kentucky	150.00
RM87	25c	Kentucky	20.00
RM88	30c	Kentucky	275.00
RM89	50c	Kentucky	50.00
RM90	75c	Kentucky	125.00
RM91	$1	Kentucky	—

RM97	4c	Maryland	35.00
RM98	10c	Maryland	20.00
RM99	20c	Maryland	500.00
RM100	25c	Maryland	25.00
RM101	30c	Maryland	450.00
RM102	50c	Maryland	55.00
RM103	75c	Maryland	15.00
RM104	$1	Maryland	—
RM106	$4	Maryland	—
RM110	4c	Massachusetts	10.00
RM111	10c	Massachusetts	20.00
RM112	20c	Massachusetts	80.00
RM113	25c	Massachusetts	20.00
RM114	30c	Massachusetts	950.00
RM115	50c	Massachusetts	75.00
RM116	75c	Massachusetts	300.00
RM117	$1	Massachusetts	150.00
RM123	4c	New Hampshire	20.00
RM124	10c	New Hampshire	25.00
RM125	20c	New Hampshire	200.00
RM126	25c	New Hampshire	35.00
RM127	30c	New Hampshire	425.00
RM128	50c	New Hampshire	40.00
RM129	75c	New Hampshire	50.00
RM130	$1	New Hampshire	—
RM136	4c	New Jersey	400.00
RM137	10c	New Jersey	175.00
RM138	20c	New Jersey	—
RM139	25c	New Jersey	110.00
RM140	30c	New Jersey	750.00
RM141	50c	New Jersey	125.00
RM142	75c	New Jersey	—
RM143	$1	New Jersey	—
RM147	$10	New Jersey	—
RM149	4c	New York	35.00
RM150	10c	New York	20.00
RM151	20c	New York	25.00
RM152	25c	New York	20.00
RM153	30c	New York	25.00
RM154	50c	New York	30.00
RM155	75c	New York	35.00
RM156	$1	New York	175.00
RM157	$2	New York	—
RM159	$5	New York	—
RM160	$10	New York	—
RM162	4c	North Carolina	25.00
RM163	10c	North Carolina	25.00
RM164	20c	North Carolina	500.00
RM165	25c	North Carolina	40.00
RM166	30c	North Carolina	—
RM167	50c	North Carolina	125.00
RM168	75c	North Carolina	275.00
RM169	$1	North Carolina	3,750.
RM175	4c	Pennsylvania	30.00
RM176	10c	Pennsylvania	20.00
RM177	20c	Pennsylvania	27.50
RM178	25c	Pennsylvania	15.00
RM179	30c	Pennsylvania	15.00
RM180	50c	Pennsylvania	25.00
RM181	75c	Pennsylvania	17.50
RM182	$1	Pennsylvania	200.00
RM187		Pennsylvania, "Ten cents per centum"	
RM188	4c	Rhode Island	35.00
RM189	10c	Rhode Island	30.00
RM190	20c	Rhode Island	200.00
RM191	25c	Rhode Island	65.00
RM192	30c	Rhode Island	750.00
RM193	50c	Rhode Island	150.00
RM194	75c	Rhode Island	750.00
RM195	$1	Rhode Island	1,000.
RM201	4c	South Carolina	90.00
RM202	10c	South Carolina	50.00
RM203	20c	South Carolina	—
RM204	25c	South Carolina	90.00
RM205	30c	South Carolina	—
RM206	50c	South Carolina	125.00
RM207	75c	South Carolina	2,400.
RM208	$1	South Carolina	—
RM211	$5	South Carolina	—
RM214	4c	Tennessee	350.00
RM215	10c	Tennessee	175.00
RM216	20c	Tennessee	—
RM217	25c	Tennessee	225.00
RM218	30c	Tennessee	—
RM219	50c	Tennessee	*750.00*
RM220	75c	Tennessee	—
RM221	$1	Tennessee	—
RM227	4c	Vermont	50.00
RM228	10c	Vermont	35.00
RM229	20c	Vermont	250.00
RM230	25c	Vermont	100.00
RM231	30c	Vermont	1,350.
RM232	50c	Vermont	130.00
RM233	75c	Vermont	—
RM234	$1	Vermont	—
RM238	$10	Vermont	—
RM240	4c	Virginia	10.00
RM241	10c	Virginia	10.00
RM242	20c	Virginia	75.00
RM243	25c	Virginia	20.00
RM244	30c	Virginia	300.00
RM245	50c	Virginia	25.00
RM246	75c	Virginia	50.00
RM247	$1	Virginia	—

The Act calls for a $2, $4, $5 and $10 stamp for each state, only the listed ones have been seen.

The Act also calls for a "Ten cents per centum" and a "Six mills per dollar" stamp for each state, none of which has been seen except No. RM187.

A press and a set of dies, one die for each denomination, were prepared and sent to each state where it was the duty of the Supervisors of the Revenue to stamp all documents presented to them upon payment of the proper tax. The Supervisors were also to have on hand for sale blank paper stamped with the different rates of duty to be sold to the public upon which the purchaser would later write or print the proper type of instrument corresponding with the value of the stamp impressed thereon. So far as is now known there was no distinctive watermark for the paper sold by the government. The Vermont set of dies is in the Vermont Historical Society at Montpelier.

B. SECOND FEDERAL ISSUE
Act of April 23, 1800
In effect March 1, 1801-June 30, 1802

RM260

RM261

	(a)Government watermark in italics; laid paper	(b)Government watermark in Roman; wove paper	(c)No Government watermark
RM260	4c	15.00	15.00	50.00
RM261	10c	15.00	20.00	50.00
RM262	20c	55.00	50.00	85.00
RM263	25c	15.00	15.00	17.50
RM264	30c	55.00	65.00	400.00
RM265	50c	65.00	45.00	85.00
RM266	75c	30.00	50.00	100.00
RM267	$1	150.00	125.00	150.00
RM269	$4			500.00
RM271	$10		2,500.	

The distinguishing feature of the stamps of this issue is the counter stamp, the left stamp shown in the illustration which usually appears on a document below the other stamp. In the right stamp the design of the eagle and the shield are similar to their design in the same denomination of the First Federal Issue but the name of the state is omitted and the denomination appears below instead of above the eagle and the shield. All of these stamps were embossed without color.

All the paper which was furnished by the government contained the watermark vertically along the edge of the sheet, "GEN STAMP OFFICE," either in Roman capitals on wove paper or in italic capitals on laid paper. The wove paper also had in the center of each half sheet either the watermark "W. Y. & Co." or "Delaware." William Young & Co. who owned the Delaware Mills made the government paper. The laid paper omitted the watermark "Delaware." The two stamps were separately impressed. The design of the eagle and shield differed in each value.

All the stamping was done in Washington, the right stamp being put on in the General Stamp Office and the left one or counter stamp in the office of the Commissioner of the Revenue as a check on the stamping done in the General Stamp Office. The "Com. Rev. C. S." in the design of the counter stamp stands for "Commissioner of the Revenue, Counter Stamp."

The Second Federal issue was intended to include $2 and $5 stamps, but these denominations have not been seen.

C. THIRD FEDERAL ISSUE
Act of August 2, 1813
In effect January 1, 1814-December 31, 1817

RM275

		a. Watermark	b. Unwmkd.
RM275	5c	10.00	15.00
RM276	10c	10.00	10.00
RM277	25c	10.00	10.00
RM278	50c	10.00	10.00
RM279	75c	13.00	17.50
RM280	$1	13.00	27.50
RM281	$1.50	13.00	32.50
RM282	$2	27.50	27.50
RM283	$2.50	27.50	55.00
RM284	$3.50	175.00	45.00
RM285	$4		150.00
RM286	$5	37.50	50.00

The distinguishing features of the stamps of this issue are the absence of the name of a state in the design and the absence of the counter stamp. Different values show different positions of the eagle.

All stamps of this issue were embossed without color at Washington. The paper with the watermark "Stamp U. S." was sold by the government. Unwatermarked paper may be either wove or laid.

IV. ISSUES BY VARIOUS STATES
DELAWARE
Act of June 19, 1793
In effect October 1, 1793-February 7, 1794

EP50   EP51

EP53

RM291	EP50	5c	—
RM292	EP51	20c	
RM294	EP53	50c	1,350.

In some cases a reddish ink was used in impressing the stamp and in other cases the impressions are colorless.

Besides the denominations listed, 3c, 33c, and $1 stamps were called for by the taxing act. Stamps of these denominations have not been seen.

VIRGINIA
Act of February 20, 1813
In effect May 1, 1813-April 30, 1815
Act of December 21, 1814
In effect May 1, 1815-February 27, 1816

EP60   EP61

			a. Die cut	b. On Document
RM305	EP61	4c	17.50	90.00
RM306	EP60	6c	17.50	
RM307	EP61	10c		200.00
RM308	EP61	12c	17.50	175.00
RM309	EP61	20c	40.00	
RM310	EP61	25c	17.50	225.00
RM311	EP61	37c	17.50	300.00
RM312	EP61	45c	40.00	200.00
RM313	EP61	50c	17.50	175.00
RM314	EP61	70c	40.00	
RM315	EP61	75c	17.50	90.00
RM316	EP61	95c	40.00	300.00
RM317	EP61	100c	40.00	300.00
RM318	EP61	120c		225.00
RM319	EP61	125c	17.50	
RM323	EP61	175c	17.50	
RM325	EP61	200c	17.50	—

All of these stamps are colorless impressions and with some exceptions as noted below those issued under the 1813 Act cannot be distinguished from those issued under the 1814 Act. The 10c, 20c, 45c, 70c, 95c, 120c, 145c, 150c, 170c and 190c were issued only under the 1813 Act, the 6c, 12c, and 37c only under the 1814 Act.

No. RM311 has the large lettering of EP60 but the 37 is to the left and the XXXVII to the right as in EP61. The design of the dogwood branch and berries is similar but not identical in all values.

When the tax on the document exceeded "two hundred cents," two or more stamps were impressed or attached to the document. For instance a document has been seen with 45c and 200c to make up the $2.45 rate, and another with 75c and 200c.

Since both the Virginia and the Third Federal Acts to some extent taxed the same kind of document, and since during the period from Jan. 1, 1814 to Feb. 27, 1816, both Acts were in effect in Virginia, some instruments may have both stamps on them.

The circular die cut Virginia stamps about 29mm in diameter were cut out of previously stamped paper which after the Act was repealed, was presented for redemption at the office of the Auditor of Public Accounts. They were threaded on fine twine and until about 1940 preserved in his office as required by law.

		b. On
	a. Die cut	Document

Watermarked die cut Virginia stamps are all cut out of Third Federal watermarked paper.

Not seen yet, the 145c, 150c, and 170c stamps were called for by the 1813 Act, and 195c by both the 1813 and 1814 Acts.

MARYLAND
1. Act of February 11, 1818
In effect May 1, 1818-March 7, 1819

EP70

| RM362 | EP70 | 30c red (printed), unused | 400. |
| | | Sheet of 4, unused | 2,000. |

The Act called for six other denominations, none of which has been seen. The Act imposing this tax was held unconstitutional by the United States Supreme Court in the case of McCulloch vs. Maryland.

2. Act of March 10, 1845
In effect May 10, 1845-March 10, 1856

EP71

RM370	EP71	10c	12.50
RM371	EP71	15c	10.00
RM372	EP71	25c	10.00
RM373	EP71	50c	12.50
RM374	EP71	75c	10.00
RM375	EP71	$1	10.00
RM376	EP71	$1.50	12.50
RM377	EP71	$2	27.50
RM378	EP71	$2.50	17.50
RM379	EP71	$3.50	55.00
RM380	EP71	$4	90.00
RM381	EP71	$5.50	50.00
RM382	EP71	$6	60.00

Nos. RM370-RM382 are embossed without color with a similar design for each value. They vary in size from 20mm in diameter for the 10c to 33mm for the $6.

V. FEDERAL LICENSES TO SELL LIQUOR, ETC.
1. Act of June 5, 1794
In effect September 30, 1794-June 30, 1802

EP80

| RM400 | EP80 | $5 | 350.00 |

Provisionals are in existence using the second issue Connecticut Supervisors' stamp with the words "Five Dollars" written or printed over it or the second issue of the New Hampshire Supervisors' stamp without the words "Five Dollars."

2. Act of August 2, 1813
In effect January 1, 1814-December 31, 1817

EP81

RM451	EP81	$10	550.00
RM452	EP81	$12	500.00
RM453	EP81	$15	350.00
RM454	EP81	$18	300.00
RM455	EP81	$20	300.00

RM456	EP81	$22.50	500.00
RM457	EP81	$25	400.00
RM458	EP81	$30	
RM459	EP81	$37.50	350.00

The Act of December 23, 1814, increased the basic rates of $10, $12, $15, $20 and $25 by 50 per cent, effective February 1, 1815. This increase applied to the unexpired portions of the year so far as licenses then in effect were concerned and these licenses were required to be brought in and to have the payment of the additional tax endorsed on them.

VI. FEDERAL LICENSES TO WORK A STILL
Act of July 24, 1813
In effect January 1, 1814-December 31, 1817

(Embossed)
EP82

(Printed)
EP83

		a. Embossed	b. Printed
RM466	4½c		1,700.
RM468	9c	1,250.	2,000.
RM471	18c		1,400.
RM477	36c		2,100.
RM480	52c	2,000.	
RM484	70c	2,100.	
RM488	$1.08	2,000.	

The statute under which these were issued provided for additional rates of 2½c, 5c, 10c, 16c, 21c, 25c, 26c, 32c, 35c, 42c, 50c, 54c, 60c, 64c, 84c, $1.04, $1.05, $1.20, $1.35, $1.40, $2.10, $2.16 and $2.70 per gallon of the capacity of the still. Stamps of these denominations have not been seen.

VII. SUPERVISORS' AND CUSTOM HOUSE SEALS
1. Supervisors' Seals Act of March 3, 1791.
In effect July 1, 1791-March 2, 1799.

EP90

		Check Letter	State	
RM501	EP90	"B"	South Carolina	50.00
RM503	EP90	"D"	Virginia	500.00
RM506	EP90	"G"	Pennsylvania	75.00
RM508	EP90	"I"	New York	22.50
RM509	EP90	"K"	Connecticut	30.00
RM510	EP90	"L"	Rhode Island	90.00
RM511	EP90	"M"	Massachusetts	22.50
RM512	EP90	"N"	New Hampshire	275.00
RM514	EP90	"P"	Kentucky	

2. Supervisors' Seals Act of March 2, 1799
In effect from March 2, 1799

EP91

RM552	EP91	North Carolina	500.00
RM553	EP91	Virginia	—
RM554	EP91	Maryland	200.00
RM556	EP91	Pennsylvania	250.00
RM558	EP91	New York	20.00
RM559	EP91	Connecticut	30.00
RM560	EP91	Rhode Island	35.00
RM561	EP91	Massachusetts	25.00
RM562	EP91	New Hampshire	90.00

3. Custom House Seals

EP92

RM575	EP92	Custom House, Philadelphia	30.00

Although no value is expressed in the Supervisors' and Custom House seals, and they do not evidence the payment of a tax in the same way that the other stamps do, some collectors of stamped paper include them in their collections if they are on instruments evidencing the payment of a tax.

They were all embossed without color and, as to Supervisors' seals issued under the Act of 1791, the only difference in design is that at the left of the eagle there was a different check letter for each state. Custom House seals used in the other cities are in existence, but, in view of the doubtful status of Custom House seals as revenue stamps, it is not proposed to list them.

REVENUE STAMPED PAPER

These stamps were printed in various denominations and designs on a variety of financial documents, including checks, drafts, receipts, specie clerk statements, insurance policies, bonds and stock certificates.

They were authorized by Act of Congress of July 1, 1862, effective October 1, 1862, although regular delivery of stamped paper did not begin until July 1, 1865. The 2-cent tax on receipts ended Oct. 1, 1870. The 2-cent tax on checks and sight drafts ended July 1, 1883. All other taxes ended Oct. 1, 1872. The use of stamped paper was revived by the War Revenue Act of 1898, approved June 13, 1898. Type X was used July 1, 1898 through June 30, 1902.

Most of these stamps were typographed; some, types H, I and J, were engraved. They were printed by private firms under supervision of government representatives from dies loaned by the Bureau of Internal Revenue. Types A-F, P-W were printed by the American Phototype Co., New York (1865-75); type G, Graphic Co., New York (1875-83); types H-L, Joseph R. Carpenter, Philadelphia (1866-75); types M-N, A. Trochsler, Boston (1873-75); type O, Morey and Sherwood, Chicago (1874). Type X was printed by numerous regional printers under contract with the government.

Samples of these stamps are known for types B-G, P and Q with a section of the design removed and replaced by the word "Sample." Types G, P-Q, U-W exist with a redemption clause added by typography or rubber stamp. Redeemed type X's have a 5mm punched hole.

Multiples or single impressions on various plain papers are usually considered proofs or printers' waste.

For further information see "Handbook for United States Revenue Stamped Paper," published (1979) by the American Revenue Association. Illustration size varies, with actual size quoted for each type.

Values for types A-O are for clear impressions on plain entire checks and receipts. Attractive documents with vignettes sell for more. The value of individual examples is also affected by the place of use. For example, territorial usage generally sells for more than a similar item from New York City.

Values for types P-W are for stamps on documents with attractive engravings, usually stock certificates, bonds and insurance policies. Examples on plain documents and cut squares sell for less.

Type A

Size: 22x25mm

RN-A1	2c black	75.	65.
a. Printed on both sides			25.

RN-A2	2c **orange**		125.
RN-A8	2c **purple** (shades)		1,500.
RN-A9	2c **green**		1,000.
a. Inverted			—

The unique example of No. RN-A9a is on a partial document.

Same Type with 1 Entire and 53 or 56 Partial Impressions in Vertical Format ("Tapeworm")
Left Col. - Full Document
Right Col. - Strip with Bank Names

RN-A10	2c **orange**, 1 full plus 56 partial impressions	675.	90.
	Cut square (full strip without bank names)		45.
RN-A11	2c **orange**, 1 full plus 53 partial impressions	1,000.	200.

Nos. RN-A10 and RN-A11 were used by the Mechanics' National Bank of New York on a bank specie clerk's statement. It was designed so that the full stamp or one of the repeated bottom segments fell on each line opposite the name of a day.

The three additional banks were added at the bottom of the form. No. RN-A11 must show white space below the "First National Bank" line.

Eagle Type B

Size: 31x48mm

RN-B1	2c **orange**	5.00	2.00
	yellow orange	5.00	2.00
	deep orange	5.00	2.00
a.	Printed on both sides	200.00	17.50
b.	Double impression	350.00	
c.	Printed on back		—
d.	With 10 centimes blue French hand-stamp, right	400.00	

All examples of the previously-listed "yellow" have some orange in them.

RN-B2	2c **black**	85.00	30.00
RN-B3	2c **blue**	95.00	15.00
	light blue	95.00	12.50
RN-B4	2c **brown**	—	30.00
RN-B5	2c **bronze**	85.00	25.00
RN-B6	2c **green** (shades)	110.00	15.00
RN-B10	2c **red** (shades)	100.00	25.00
RN-B11	2c **purple**	90.00	55.00
RN-B13	2c **violet** (shades)	125.00	40.00
a.	2c **violet brown**	110.00	50.00

"Good only for checks and drafts payable at sight." in Rectangular Tablet at Base

RN-B16	2c **orange**	45.00	12.50
a.	With 2c orange red Nevada	300.00	175.00

"Good only for checks and drafts payable at sight." in Octagonal Tablet at Base

RN-B17	2c **orange**	42.50	10.00
a.	Tablet inverted		1,250.
b.	With 2c orange red Nevada	85.00	35.00
c.	With 2c green Nevada	100.00	35.00
d.	With 2c dull violet Nevada		1,500.

"Good when issued for the payment of money." in Octagonal Tablet at Base

RN-B20	2c **orange**	70.00	10.00
a.	Printed on both sides	30.00	10.00
b.	As "a," one stamp inverted		1,500.
c.	Tablet inverted		3,750.

"Good when issued for the payment of money" in two lines at base in orange

RN-B23	2c **orange**	700.00

"Good when the amount does not exceed $100." in Octagonal Tablet at Base

RN-B24	2c **orange**	175.00	70.00

Washington-Type C

Size: 108x49mm

RN-C1	2c **orange**	7.00	3.50
	red orange	7.00	3.50
	yellow orange	7.00	3.50
	salmon	8.00	4.00
	brown orange	8.00	4.00
a.	"Good when used..." vert. at left black		—

All examples of the previously-listed "yellow" have some orange in them.

RN-C2	2c **brown**	30.00	12.00
a.	2c **buff**	30.00	12.00
RN-C5	2c **pale red** (shades)	50.00	20.00
RN-C8	2c **green**		—

"Good only for Sight Draft" in two lines in color of stamp

RN-C9	2c **orange**, legend at lower right	85.00	50.00
RN-C11	2c **brown**, legend at lower left	90.00	80.00
RN-C13	2c **orange**, legend at lower left	45.00	15.00

"Good only for Receipt for Money Paid" in two lines in color of stamp

RN-C15	2c **orange**, legend at lower right	2,500.	—
RN-C16	2c **orange**, legend at lower left		350.00

"Good when issued for the payment of money" in one line at base in color of stamp

RN-C17	2c **orange** (shades)	500.00

"Good when issued for the/Payment of Money" in two tablets at lower left and right

RN-C19	2c **orange**	550.00
a.	Printed on both sides	35.00

"Good/only for Bank/Check" in 3-part Band

RN-C21	2c **orange**	50.00	12.50
	salmon		12.50
	yellow orange		20.00
a.	Inverted		625.00
b.	With 2c red orange Nevada	140.00	65.00
c.	Printed on back		2,900.
RN-C22	2c **brown**	300.00	25.00
a.	Printed on back		500.00
RN-C23	2c **red**		

"Good when the amount does not exceed $100" in tablet at lower right

RN-C26	2c **orange**	200.00	

Franklin Type D

Size: 80x43mm

RN-D1	2c **orange** (shades)	5.00	2.00
a.	Double impression		—
b.	Printed on back	700.00	400.00
c.	Inverted		425.00

All examples of the previously-listed "yellow" have some orange in them and are included in the "shades."

RN-D3	2c **brown**	—	500.00
RN-D4	2c **buff** (shades)	7.50	5.00
RN-D5	2c **red**		2,000.

"Good only for/Bank Check" in panels within circles at left and right

RN-D7	2c **orange**	25.00	10.00
a.	Printed on back		2,100.

"Good only for/Bank Check" in two lines at lower right in color of stamp

RN-D8	2c **orange**		750.00

"Good only for Sight Draft" in two lines at lower left in color of stamp

RN-D9	2c **orange**	175.00	70.00

Franklin Type E

Size: 28x50mm

RN-E2	2c **brown**		900.00
RN-E4	2c **orange**	10.00	4.00
a.	Double impression		925.00
	Broken die, lower right or left	40.00	20.00

"Good only for sight draft" in two lines at base in orange

RN-E5	2c **orange**	75.00	30.00

"Good only for Bank / Check" in two lines at base in orange

RN-E6	2c **orange**	—

"Good only for / Bank Check" in colorless letters in two lines above and below portrait

RN-E7	2c **orange**	75.00	17.50

Franklin Type F

Size: 56x34mm

RN-F1	2c **orange**	10.00	5.00
a.	Inverted		—

All examples of the previously-listed "yellow" have some orange in them

Liberty Type G

Size: 80x48mm

RN-G1	2c **orange**	2.00	1.00
a.	Printed on back	65.00	35.00
b.	Printed on back, inverted	125.00	50.00

All examples of the previously-listed "yellow" have some orange in them

Imprint: "Graphic Co., New York" at left and right in minute type

RN-G3	2c **orange**	90.00	90.00

Eagle Type H

Size: 32x50mm

RN-H3	2c **orange**	15.00	5.00
a.	Inverted		
b.	Double impression		500.00
c.	"Good when used. . ." added in 2 lines at base, black		400.00
d.	As "c," legend added in 1 line upward at left, black		1,500.
e.	As "c," legend added in 1 line horiz., black	800.00	600.00
f.	As "c," legend in yellow		1,500.
g.	As "c," legend in red		500.00
h.	"Good for bank check . . ." added in black		125.00

"Good for check or sight draft only" at left and right in color of stamp

RN-H5	2c **orange**	

Experts claim that No. RN-H5 exists only as a proof.

Type I
Design R2 of 1862-72 adhesive revenues
Size: 20x23mm
"BANK CHECK"

RN-I1	2c orange		225.00	

"U.S. INTER. REV."

RN-I2	2c orange		650.00	350.00

Washington Type J

Size: 105x40mm
Background of medallion crosshatched, filling oval except for bust

RN-J4	2c orange	15.00	7.00
	pale orange	15.00	7.00
	deep orange	25.00	9.00
a.	Double impression	—	
b.	"Good only for . . ." added vertically at left in red orange		750.00
RN-J5	2c red	35.00	12.00

"Good for check or sight draft only" curved, below

RN-J9	2c red	—	2,000.

Background shaded below bust and at left.

RN-J11	2c orange	50.00	15.00

Washington Type K

Size: 84x33mm

RN-K4	2c gray	45.00	10.00
	pale gray	45.00	10.00
RN-K5	2c brown	175.00	110.00
RN-K6	2c orange	15.00	7.50
RN-K8	2c red (shades)	600.00	350.00
RN-K11	2c olive	150.00	125.00
	pale olive		100.00

Washington Type L

Size: 50x33mm

RN-L1	2c blue (shades)	200.00	—
RN-L2	2c turquoise	250.00	150.00
RN-L3	2c gray	35.00	20.00
	pale gray	35.00	20.00
RN-L4	2c green	600.00	425.00
	light green	500.00	350.00
RN-L5	2c orange	12.50	10.00
RN-L6	2c olive		55.00
	gray olive		30.00
RN-L10	2c red	15.00	10.00
a.	2c violet red	15.00	10.00
RN-L13	2c brown	—	300.00

Washington Type M

Size: 68x37mm

RN-M2	2c orange	50.	10.
a.	Printed on back, inverted		1,600.

All examples of the previously-listed "yellow" have some orange in them

RN-M3	2c green		425.
RN-M4	2c gray		1,250.

Eagle, Numeral and Monitor Type N

Size: 107x48mm

RN-N3	2c orange	60.00	15.00
a.	Printed on back	250.00	225.00
b.	Inverted		900.00
RN-N4	2c light brown		125.00

Liberty Type O

Size: 75x35mm

RN-O2	2c orange	1,750.	750.

Values for types P-W

are for stamps on documents with attractive engravings, usually stock certificates, bonds and insurance policies. Examples on plain documents sell for less.

Type P
Frame as Type B, Lincoln in center
Size: 32x49mm

RN-P2	5c brown		375.00
	Cut square		75.00
RN-P5	5c orange	55.00	40.00
	Cut square		7.00

All examples of the previously-listed "yellow" have some orange in them.

RN-P6	5c red (shades)	—	200.00
	Cut square		35.00

The 5c green, type P, only exists in combination with a 25c green or 50c green. The 5c pink, type P, only exists in combination with a $1 pink. See Nos. RN-T2, RN-V1 RN-W6.

Madison Type Q (See note before No. RN-P2)

Size: 28x56mm

RN-Q1	5c orange	175.	150.
	Cut square		20.
	brownish orange	175.	150.
RN-Q2	5c brown		2,750.
	Cut square		500.

Type R
Frame as Type B, Lincoln in center
Size: 32x49mm

RN-R1	10c brown		2,500.
RN-R2	10c red	—	675.
	Cut square		100.
RN-R3	10c orange		500.
	Cut square		50.

"Good when the premium does not exceed $10" in tablet at base

RN-R6	10c orange		400.
	Cut square		50.

Motto Without Tablet

RN-R7	10c orange		500.
	Cut square		

Washington Type S (See note before No. RN-P2)

RN-S1	10c orange		3,750.

Size: 33x54mm

"Good when the premium does not exceed $10" in tablet at base

RN-S2	10c orange		4,750.
	Cut square		375.

Eagle Type T (See note before No. RN-P2)

For type T design with Lincoln in center see type V, Nos. RN-V1 to RN-V10.

Size: 33x40mm

RN-T1	25c **black**	—	—
	Cut square		
RN-T2	25c **green**		7,500.
RN-T3	25c **red**	175.00	90.00
	Cut square		9.00
RN-T4	25c **orange**	150.00	75.00
	Cut square		7.50
	light orange	150.00	75.00
	light orange, cut square		7.50
	brown orange		75.00
	brown orange, cut square		8.00

RN-T2 includes a 5c green, type P, and a 25c green, type T, obliterating an RN-V4.

"Good when the premium does not exceed $50" in tablet at base

RN-T6	25c **orange**	450.	350.
	Cut square		50.
RN-T7	25c **orange**, motto without tablet	1,500.	
	Cut square		400.

"Good when the amount insured shall not exceed $1000" in tablet at base

RN-T8	25c **deep orange**	800.	700.
	Cut square		75.
RN-T9	25c **orange**, motto without tablet		
	Cut square		600.

Franklin Type U (See note before No. RN-P2)

Size: 126x65mm

RN-U1	25c **orange**	35.00	35.00
	Cut square		5.00
RN-U2	25c **brown**	45.00	35.00
	Cut square		5.00

"Good when the premium does not exceed $50" in tablet at lower right

RN-U3	25c **orange**		2,400.
	Cut square		400.

Tablet at lower left

RN-U5	25c **red**	800.	
	Cut square		250.
RN-U6	25c **orange**	500.	450.
	Cut square		65.

All examples of the previously-listed "yellow" have some orange in them

Tablet at base

RN-U7	25c **brown**		1,250.
	Cut square		200.
RN-U9	25c **orange**		900.
	Cut square		400.

Type V
As Type T, Lincoln in center
Size: 32x41mm

RN-V1	50c **green**		160.00
	Cut square		52.50
RN-V2	50c **brown**	—	400.00
	Cut square		100.00
RN-V4	50c **orange**	175.00	90.00
	Cut square		17.50
	deep orange	175.00	90.00
	deep orange, cut square		17.50
RN-V5	50c **red**	700.00	
	Cut square		250.00

RN-V1 includes a 50c green, type V, and a 5c green, type P, obliterating an RN-W2.

"Good when the amount insured shall not exceed $5000" in tablet at base

RN-V6	50c **orange**	450.00	400.00
	Cut square		70.00
RN-V9	50c **red**		—
	Cut square		650.00

Motto Without Tablet

RN-V10	50c **orange**		
	Cut square		500.00

Washington Type W
(See note before No. RN-P2)

Size: 34x73mm

RN-W2	$1 **orange** (shades)	125.00	65.00
	Cut square		10.00
RN-W5	$1 **brown**		8,500.
RN-W6	$1 **pink**		3,750.

RN-W6 includes a 5c pink, type P. The former light brown is now included with the orange shades.

SPANISH-AMERICAN WAR SERIES

Many of these stamps were used for parlor car tax and often were torn in two or more parts.

Liberty Type X

1898		Size: 68x38mm	
RN-X1	1c **rose**	800.00	
	Partial		65.00
	dark red, partial		65.00
RN-X4	1c **orange**	165.00	
	a. On pullman ticket	600.00	—
	Partial		25.00
	b. As "a," printed on back		
	As "a," printed on back, partial		65.00
RN-X5	1c **green**	65.00	30.00
	Partial		25.00
	a. On parlor car ticket	65.00	15.00
	b. On pullman ticket	500.00	
	On pullman ticket, partial		15.00
RN-X6	2c **yellow**	2.00	1.00
	pale olive		900.00
RN-X7	2c **orange**	1.50	1.00
	pale orange	1.50	1.00
	a. Printed on back only	400.00	400.00
	c. Printed on front and back	—	
	d. Vertical		85.00
	e. Double impression	—	
	f. On pullman ticket	1,000.	200.00
	g. Inverted		550.00

The substantial reduction recently in catalogue value for No. RN-X7g is due to a new discovery of 25 additional examples.

No. RN-X1 exists only as a four-part unused pullman ticket, used as an unsevered auditor's and passenger's parts of the four-part ticket, or partial as a used half of a two-part ticket. Nos. RN-X4a and RN-X5b exist as unused two-part tickets and as used half portions. No. RN-X7f exists as an unused four-part ticket and as a used two-piece portion with nearly complete stamp design.

Consular Fee

The "Consular Fee stamp" on revenue stamped paper (previously listed as No. RN-Y1 but since deleted) was found to be nothing more than an illustration. Two identical copies are known.

PRIVATE DIE PROPRIETARY STAMPS

The extraordinary demands of the Civil War upon the Federal Treasury resulted in Congress devising and passing the Revenue Act of 1862. The Government provided revenue stamps to be affixed to boxes or packages of matches, and to proprietary medicines, perfumery, playing cards -- as well as to documents, etc.

But manufacturers were permitted, at their expense, to have dies engraved and plates made for their exclusive use. Many were only too willing to do this because a discount or premium of from 5% to 10% was allowed on orders from the dies which often made it possible for them to undersell their competitors and too, the considerable advertising value of the stamps could not be overlooked. These are now known as Private Die Proprietary stamps.

The face value of the stamp used on matches was determined by the number, i.e., 1c for each 100 matches or fraction thereof. Medicines and perfumery were taxed at the rate of 1c for each 25 cents of the retail value or fraction thereof up to $1 and 2c for each 50 cents or fraction above that amount. Playing cards were first taxed at the same rate but subsequently the tax was 5c for a deck of 52 cards and 10c for a greater number of cards or double decks.

The stamp tax was repealed on March 3, 1883, effective July 1, 1883.

The various papers were:

a. Old paper, 1862-71. First Issue. Hard and brittle varying from thick to thin.

b. Silk paper, 1871-77. Second Issue. Soft and porous with threads of silk, mostly red, blue and black, up to ¼inch in length.

c. Pink paper, 1877-78. Third Issue. Soft paper colored pink ranging from pale to deep shades.

d. Watermarked paper, 1878-83. Fourth Issue. Soft porous paper showing part of "USIR."

e. Experimental silk paper. Medium smooth paper, containing minute fragments of silk threads either blue alone or blue and red (infrequent), widely scattered, sometimes but a single fiber on a stamp.

Early printings of some private die revenue stamps are on paper which appears to have laid lines.

These stamps were usually torn in opening the box or container. **Values quoted are for examples which are somewhat faulty but reasonably attractive, with the faults usually not readily apparent on the face.** Nos. RS278-RS306 are valued in the grade of very fine. Sound examples of these stamps (other than Nos. RS278-RS306) at a grade of fine-very fine can sell for 50% to 300% more than catalogue value. Outstanding examples of stamps in this section with a lower catalogue value can bring up to 10 times catalogue value.

PRIVATE DIE MATCH STAMPS

1864   *Perf. 12*

		a. Old Paper	b. Silk Paper	c. Pink Paper	d. Wmkd. USIR (191R)

A

Akron Match Company

RO1	1c	blue	210.00			

Alexander's Matches — RO2   Thos. Allen — RO5

Alexander's Matches

| RO2 | 1c | orange | 22.50 | 80.00 | | |
| RO3 | 1c | blue | 1,500. | | | |

J. J. Allen's Sons

| RO4 | 1c | blue | | | | 10.00 |

Thos. Allen

| RO5 | 1c | green | 110.00 | | | |

Allen & Powers

As No. RO141, inscribed "Allen & Powers" instead of "Orono Match Co."

| RO6 | 1c | blue | 7.50 | 22.50 | | 7.50 |

Alligator Match Company

RO7	1c	blue				22.50
		Dbl. transfer				—
RO8	1c	bl, roulette				90.00

American Fusee Company — RO9

American Fusee Company

| RO9 | 1c | black | 5.00 | 10.00 | | 5.00 |
| | | Dbl. transfer | 100.00 | | | — |

American Match Co.

RO10	1c	black	100.00	20.00		
RO11	3c	black	375.00	110.00		
		Dble. transfer		200.00		
	e.	Experimental silk paper	700.00			

American Match Co. — RO12   Arnold & Co. — RO14

| RO12 | 1c | black | 47.50 | | | |
| RO13 | 3c | green, Rock Island | 2,750. | | | |

Arnold & Co.

| RO14 | 1c | black | 32.50 | | | |

B

Bagley & Dunham — RO15

Bagley & Dunham

| RO15 | 1c | green | | | | 25.00 |

Geo. & O. C. Barber

As No. RO17, inscribed "Geo. & O. C. Barber" instead of "Barber Match Co."

| RO16 | 1c | blue | 65.00 | | | |

Barber Match Co.

RO17	1c	blue	20.00	.85	14.00	1.10
		Dbl. transfer	77.50	30.00	77.50	30.00
	e.	Experimental silk paper	80.00			
RO18	1c	blue, rouletted	275.00			
	u.	1c ultra				2,000.
RO19	3c	black	160.00	95.00		
	e.	Experimental silk paper	325.00			

Barber & Peckham — RO20

Barber & Peckham

| RO20 | 1c | blue | 42.50 | | | |
| RO21 | 3c | black | 160.00 | | | |

Bauer & Beudel

| RO22 | 1c | blue | 75.00 | 120.00 | | |
| | u. | 1c ultra | 140.00 | | | |

A. B. & S. (A. Beecher & Son)

As No. RO175, inscribed "A. B. & S." instead of "C. B. C. S." in the four corners.

RO23	1c	orange	11.00	55.00		
		Dbl. transfer	—	—		
	e.	Experimental silk paper	85.00			
		As "e," dbl. transfer				

B. Bendel & Co. — RO25

B. Bendel & Co.

RO24	1c	brown		2.25		325.00
		Dbl. transfer				
RO25	12c	brown	210.00			

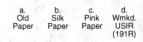

		a. Old Paper	b. Silk Paper	c. Pink Paper	d. Wmkd. USIR (191R)

H. Bendel

Nos. RO26-RO27 are RO24-RO25 altered to read "H. Bendel doing business as B. Bendel & Co."

| RO26 | 1c | brown | | 4.50 | 2.25 | 1.40 |
| RO27 | 12c | brown | 425.00 | | | |

H. & M. Bentz — RO28   Bent & Lea — RO29

H. & M. Bentz

| RO28 | 1c | blue | | 25.00 | | |

Bent & Lea

RO29	1c	black	32.50			
		Double transfer at left	105.00			
	e.	Experimental silk paper	27.50			

B. J. & Co. — RO30   Bock, Schneider & Co. — RO31

B. J. & Co. (Barber, Jones & Co.)

As No. RO100 with "B. J. & Co." added above eagle.

| RO30 | 1c | green | 75.00 | | | |
| | | Dbl. transfer | 140.00 | | | |

Bock, Schneider & Co.

| RO31 | 1c | black | 11.00 | | | |

Wm. Bond & Co. RO32/RO33   Bousfield & Poole RO34/RO35

Wm. Bond & Co.

| RO32 | 4c | black | 260.00 | | | |
| RO33 | 4c | green | 140.00 | 190.00 | | 14.00 |

Bousfield & Poole

RO34	1c	lilac	105.00			
		Dbl. transfer	135.00			
RO35	1c	black	12.50	8.00		
		Dbl. transfer	62.50	82.50		
	e.	Experimental silk paper	42.50			
RO36	3c	lilac	1,850.			
RO37	3c	black	160.00	95.00		
		Dbl. transfer		110.00		
		Experimental silk paper	275.00			

Boutell & Maynard

| RO38 | 1c | black | | 140.00 | | |

Bowers & Dunham

As No. RO15, inscribed "Bowers & Dunham" instead of "Bagley & Dunham."

| RO39 | 1c | green | | | | 190.00 |
| RO40 | 1c | blue | | | | 75.00 |

a. Old Paper — b. Silk Paper — c. Pink Paper — d. Wmkd. USIR (191R)

B. & N. (Brocket & Newton)

No.	Description	a	b	c	d
RO41	1c lake, die I			35.00	
RO42	1c lake, die II			6.50	

The initials "B. & N." measure 5¼mm across the top in Die I, and 4¾mm in Die II.

Brown & Durling

No.	Description	a	b	c	d
RO43	1c black	1,250.			
RO44	1c green	65.00			

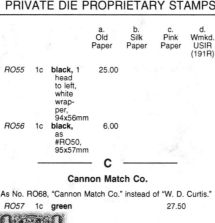

L. W. Buck & Co. — RO45

L. W. Buck & Co.

No.	Description	a	b	c	d
RO45	1c black	925.00			
	e. Experimental silk paper	800.00			

D. Burhans & Co.

No.	Description	a	b	c	d
RO46	1c black	120.00		2,500.	
	Dbl. transfer	250.00			
	e. Experimental silk paper	550.00			

Charles Busch — RO47

Byam, Carlton & Co. — RO49

Charles Busch

No.	Description	a	b	c	d
RO47	1c black	20.00			

Byam, Carlton & Co.

No.	Description	a	b	c	d
RO48	1c black, imperf, 2 heads to left, 41x75mm	2,000.			
RO49	1c black, 19x23mm	22.50	3.50		1.25
	Dbl. transfer				125.00
	e. Experimental silk paper	75.00			
	i. Vert. pair, imperf. horiz.				125.00
RO50	1c black, 2 heads to left, buff wrapper, 131x99mm	1,200.			
RO51	1c black, as #RO50, 131x89mm	160.00			
RO52	1c black, 1 head to right, white wrapper, 94x54mm	60.00			
RO53	1c black, as #RO52, buff wrapper	135.00			
RO54	1c black, 2 heads to right, buff wrapper (81x50mm)	8.00			
	h. Right block reading up	30.00			
RO55	1c black, 1 head to left, white wrapper, 94x56mm	25.00			
RO56	1c black, as #RO50, 95x57mm	6.00			

C

Cannon Match Co.

As No. RO68, "Cannon Match Co." instead of "W. D. Curtis."

No.	Description	a	b	c	d
RO57	1c green				27.50

Cardinal Match Co. — RO58

Cardinal Match Co.

RO58	1c lake				14.00

F. E. C. (Frank E. Clark)

As No. RO41, "F.E.C." instead of "B. & N."

No.	Description	a	b	c	d
RO59	1c lake	65.00	65.00		
	e. Experimental silk paper		85.00		

Chicago Match Co. — RO60

Henry A. Clark — RO61

Chicago Match Co.

No.	Description	a	b	c	d
RO60	3c black	275.00			

Henry A. Clark

No.	Description	a	b	c	d
RO61	1c green				80.00

Jas.L. Clark RO62/RO63

Clark Match Co. RO64

Jas. L. Clark

No.	Description	a	b	c	d
RO62	1c green	1.50		20.00	1.25
	Dbl. transfer				60.00
RO63	1c green, rouletted				325.00

The Clark Match Co.

No.	Description	a	b	c	d
RO64	1c lake	7.50			

See No. RO64 for another "The Clark Match Co." design.

Cramer & Kemp — RO65-RO66

Crown Match Co. — RO67

Cramer & Kemp

No.	Description	a	b	c	d
RO65	1c black	30.00			
RO66	1c blue	80.00			5.75
	e. Experimental silk paper	175.00			
	u. 1c ultra	225.00			

Crown Match Co.

No.	Description	a	b	c	d
RO67	1c black	17.50			

W. D. Curtis Matches RO68

G. W. H. Davis RO69/RO70

W. D. Curtis Matches

No.	Description	a	b	c	d
RO68	1c green	120.00	100.00		
	e. Experimental silk paper	140.00			

D

G. W. H. Davis

No.	Description	a	b	c	d
RO69	1c black	42.50			
RO70	1c carmine				47.50

W. E. Doolittle

RO71	1c blue	260.00			

E. P. Dunham

RO72	1c green				70.00

E

Jas. Eaton

No.	Description	a	b	c	d
RO73	1c black	32.50	1.00	9.50	1.00
	e. Experimental silk paper	120.00			
RO74	1c black, rouletted				50.00

E. B. Eddy

No.	Description	a	b	c	d
RO75	1c car, die I				14.00
RO75A	1c car, die II				27.50

Die II shows eagle strongly recut; ribbon across bottom is narrower; color is deeper.

Aug. Eichele

No.	Description	a	b	c	d
RO76	1c black	65.00			

P. Eichele & Co.

As No. RO78, "P. Eichele & Co." at top.

No.	Description	a	b	c	d
RO77	1c blue	55.00			6.50
	e. Experimental silk paper	115.00			
	u. 1c ultra	275.00			

Eichele & Co. — RO78/RO79

Eichele & Co.

No.	Description	a	b	c	d
RO78	1c blue	2.50	14.00		2.50
RO79	1c blue, rouletted				225.00

	a. Old Paper	b. Silk Paper	c. Pink Paper	d. Wmkd. USIR (191R)

J. W. Eisenhart's Matches

RO80	1c	blue	37.50	82.50	27.50

Excelsior Match Co. RO81/RO82   Excelsior Match, Baltimore RO83

Excelsior Match Co.

RO81	1c	black, Watertown, N.Y.	85.00
RO82	1c	black, Syracuse, N.Y.	6.50	14.00	6.50
		Dbl. transfer	47.50

Excelsior Match, Baltimore, Md.

RO83	1c	blue	75.00	100.00
	u.	1c ultra	600.00

F

G. Farr & Co. — RO84   L. Frank — RO85

G. Farr & Co.

RO84	1c	black	110.00

L. Frank

RO85	1c	brown	90.00

G

Gardner, Beer & Co. — RO86

Gardner, Beer & Co.

RO86	1c	black	140.00

Wm. Gates

RO87	1c	black, die I	4.50	3.00
RO88	1c	black, die II	40.00	3.00
		Dbl. transfer		30.00
	e.	Experimental silk paper	105.00

The shirt collar is colorless in Die I and shaded in Die II. The colorless circle surrounding the portrait appears about twice as wide on Die I as it does on Die II.

RO89	3c	black	50.00	37.50	
		Dbl. transfer	82.50	80.00	—
	e.	Experimental silk paper	150.00		
RO90	6c	black	110.00		
RO91	12c	black, 3 1c stamps		120.00	

William Gates' Sons

The 1c is as No. RO87, 3c as No. RO91, "William Gates' Sons" replaces (Wm. Gates.)

RO92	1c	black	19.00	5.50	1.25
RO93	1c	black, rouletted			1,100.

RO94	3c	black, 3 1c stamps	90.00	135.00	75.00

A. Goldback & Co. — RO95

A. Goldback & Co.

RO95	1c	green	37.50

A. Goldback

As No. RO95, "A. Goldback" instead of "A. Goldback & Co."

RO96	1c	green	75.00	7,500.

T. Gorman & Bro.

As No. RO99, "T. Gorham & Bro." instead of "Thomas Gorham."

RO97	1c	black	300.00	—
		Dbl. transfer		
RO98	1c	green	25.00	22.50	—
		Dbl. transfer		

Thomas Gorman

RO99	1c	green	3.75	20.00	55.00

Greenleaf & Co. RO101/RO102   Griggs & Goodwill RO103/RO104

Greenleaf & Co.

RO100	1c	green	80.00	110.00
	e.	Experimental silk paper	475.00	
RO101	3c	carmine	90.00	140.00
	e.	Experimental silk paper	800.00	
RO102	5c	orange	120.00	1,200.
	e.	Experimental silk paper	325.00	

Griggs & Goodwill

RO103	1c	black	30.00
RO104	1c	green	14.00
		Dbl. transfer	150.00

Griggs & Scott

As No. RO69, inscribed "Griggs & Scott" instead of "G. W. H. Davis."

RO105	1c	black	10.00	32.50
	e.	Experimental silk paper	40.00

H

Charles S. Hale — RO106

Charles S. Hale

RO106	1c	black	140.00

Henning & Bonhack

RO107	1c	blue	150.00

W. E. Henry & Co.

RO108	1c	red	25.00
RO109	1c	black	12.50

J. G. Hotchkiss RO110   L. G. Hunt RO113

The J. G. Hotchkiss Match Co.

RO110	1c	green	7.00	37.50	7.75

B. & H. D. Howard

RO111	1c	lake	85.00
RO112	1c	blue	8.50
	u.	1c ultra	190.00

L. G. Hunt

RO113	1c	black	190.00	700.00
	e.	Experimental silk paper	175.00

D. F. Hutchinson Jr.

RO114	1c	lake	11.00

I

Ives Matches

As No. RO116, "Ives Matches" instead of "P. T. Ives."

RO115	1c	blue	5.00	5.00
		Dbl. transfer	
	u.	1c ultra	225.00

P. T. Ives RO116/RO117   Ives & Judd RO119

P. T. Ives

RO116	1c	blue	3.00	20.00	3.00
RO117	1c	blue, rouletted			300.00
RO118	8c	blue	190.00		
	e.	Experimental silk paper	700.00		
	u.	8c ultra	1,000.		

Ives & Judd

RO119	1c	green	12.00	37.50	95.00

Ives & Judd Match Co. — RO120   Leeds, Robinson & Co. — RO124

The Ives & Judd Match Co.

RO120	1c	green	100.00
		Dbl. transfer	250.00

K

Kirby & Sons

RO121	1c	green	47.50

W. S. Kyle

RO122	1c	black	12.50	8.50
		Dbl. transfer	75.00

L

Lacour's Matches

RO123	1c	black	12.50	45.00
		Dbl. transfer	80.00
	e.	Experimental silk paper	55.00

Leeds, Robinson & Co.

RO124	1c	green	65.00

Columns: **a.** Old Paper   **b.** Silk Paper   **c.** Pink Paper   **d.** Wmkd. USIR (191R)

H. Leigh

Cat.		a	b	c	d
RO125	1c blue				8.00

Leigh & Palmer

As No. RO125, "Leigh & Palmer" replaces "H. Leigh."

Cat.		a	b	c	d
RO126	1c black	27.50		60.00	37.50

John Loehr — RO127

John Loehr

Cat.		a	b	c	d
RO127	1c blue		20.00		

Joseph Loehr

As No. RO127, "Joseph" replaces "John."

Cat.		a	b	c	d
RO128	1c blue	2.50		11.00	3.00

M
John J. Macklin & Co.

Cat.		a	b	c	d
RO129	1c blk, roulette	6,000.			

F. Mansfield & Co. — RO130   *Maryland Match Co. — RO131*

F. Mansfield & Co.

Cat.		a	b	c	d
RO130	1c blue	3.50		6.75	8.50

Maryland Match Co.

Cat.		a	b	c	d
RO131	1c blue	110.00			8,000.

"Matches" — RO132

'Matches'

Cat.		a	b	c	d
RO132	1c blue	4.00			4.00
	Dbl. transfer	95.00			
e.	Experimental silk paper	110.00			
u.	1c ultra	*800.00*			

See Nos. RO168-RO169.

A. Messinger

Cat.		a	b	c	d
RO133	1c black	1.75		11.50	1.75

N

National Match Co. — RO134   *F. P. Newton — RO135*

National Match Co.

Cat.		a	b	c	d
RO134	1c blue				65.00

Newbauer & Co. (N. & C.) follows No. RO140.

National Union Match Co. items are bogus.

F. P. Newton

Cat.		a	b	c	d
RO135	1c lake	2.00		8.50	2.00

See No. RO64 for another "The Clark Match Co." design.

N.Y. Match Co.

No. RO136 is as No. RO22, "N.Y. Match Co." instead of "Bauer & Feudel."

Cat.		a	b	c	d
RO136	1c blue, shield	240.00		5.50	

No. RO137 is as No. RO111, "N.Y. Match Co." instead of "B. & H. D. Howard."

Cat.		a	b	c	d
RO137	1c ver, eagle	65.00		5,000.	
e.	Experimental silk paper	110.00			
	As "e," dbl. transfer	240.00			

New York Match Company

Cat.		a	b	c	d
RO138	1c green, 22x60mm	32.50		5.50	
e.	Experimental silk paper	55.00			
RO139	5c blue, 22x60mm			1,500.	

N. & C. (Newbauer & Co.)

Cat.		a	b	c	d
RO140	4c green	4.50		110.00	4.50

O
Orono Match Co.

Cat.		a	b	c	d
RO141	1c blue	32.50		32.50	
e.	Experimental silk paper	220.00			
u.	1c ultra	425.00			

P

Park City Match Co. — RO143

Park City Match Co.

Cat.		a	b	c	d
RO142	1c green	42.50		37.50	
e.	Experimental silk paper	225.00			
RO143	3c orange	42.50			

Penn Match Co. Limited

Cat.		a	b	c	d
RO144	1c blue				35.00

Pierce Match Co.

Cat.		a	b	c	d
RO145	1c green	1,750.			

P. M. Co. (Portland M. Co.)

Cat.		a	b	c	d
RO146	1c black	27.50			

Portland Match Co.

Cat.		a	b	c	d
RO147	1c blk, wrapper	85.00			

The value of No. RO147 applies to commonest date (Dec. 1866); all others are much rarer.

V.R. Powell   RO148   RO149/RO151

V. R. Powell

Cat.		a	b	c	d
RO148	1c blue	5.00	10.00		
	Dbl. transfer	100.00			
e.	Experimental silk paper	110.00			
u.	1c ultra	275.00			
RO149	1c black, buff wrapper, uncut		*4,000.*		
RO150	1c black, buff wrapper, cut to shape	900.00			
RO151	1c black, white wrapper, cut to shape	1,500.			

R
Reading Match Company

Cat.		a	b	c	d
RO152	1c black				6.50

Reed & Thompson

Cat.		a	b	c	d
RO153	1c black				9.00

D. M. Richardson

Cat.		a	b	c	d
RO154	1c red	120.00			
RO155	1c black	3.50		2.50	
	Dbl. transfer			40.00	
e.	Experimental silk paper	45.00			
RO156	3c vermilion	150.00			
RO157	3c blue	5.00		4.00	
	Dbl. transfer			27.50	
e.	Experimental silk paper	55.00			

The Richardson Match Co.

The 1c is as No. RO154, 3c as No. RO156, inscribed "The Richardson Match Co." instead of "D. M. Richardson."

Cat.		a	b	c	d
RO158	1c black	1.50		5.00	5.50
RO159	3c blue		70.00		

H. & W. Roeber

Cat.		a	b	c	d
RO160	1c blue	6.75		1.50	
	Dbl. transfer	175.00			
e.	Experimental silk paper	*325.00*			
u.	1c ultra	190.00			

William Roeber

As No. RO160, "William Roeber" instead of "H. & W. Roeber."

Cat.		a	b	c	d
RO161	1c blue	1.25		6.00	1.25
RO162	1c bl, roulette			95.00	

E. T. Russell — RO163

E. T. Russell

Cat.		a	b	c	d
RO163	1c black	4.00		11.00	
e.	Experimental silk paper	42.50			

	a. Old Paper	b. Silk Paper	c. Pink Paper	d. Wmkd. USIR (191R)

R. C. & W. (Ryder, Crouse & Welch)

RO164   1c   lake   70.00

— S —

San Francisco Match Co. — RO165

San Francisco Match Company

RO165   12c   blue   425.00

Schmitt & Schmittdiel — RO166/RO167

Schmitt & Schmittdiel

RO166   1c   vermillion   4.00   55.00   4.00
RO167   3c   blue   37.50

E. K. Smith RO168/RO169   Standard Match Co. RO170

E. K. Smith

RO168   1c   blue   11.00   40.00   15.00
RO169   1c   blue, roulette   1,500.

See No. RO132.

The Standard Match Company

RO170   1c   black   27.50

H. Stanton

RO171   1c   black   10.00   5.50   17.50   7.00
        e.   Experimental silk paper   55.00

Star Match — RO172

Star Match

RO172   1c   black   4.00   .50   .75   .50
        Dbl. transfer   17.50
        e.   Experimental silk paper   22.50

Swift & Courtney & Beecher
RO174   RO175

Swift & Courtney

As No. RO174, "Swift & Courtney" in one line.

RO173   1c   blue   1.25   1.25
        Dbl. transfer
        e.   Experimental silk paper   22.50
        u.   1c ultra   62.50

Swift & Courtney & Beecher Co.

RO174   1c   blue   1.00   3.50   .90
        Dbl. transfer
RO175   1c   black   80.00

— T —

Trenton Match Co.

RO176   1c   blue   5.00

E. R. T. (E. R. Tyler)

As No. RO120, inscribed "E. R. T." instead of "The Ives & Judd Match Co."

RO177   1c   green   11.00   3.75
        Dbl. transfer
        e.   Experimental silk paper   67.50

— U —

Alex. Underwood & Co.

RO178   1c   green   65.00   140.00
        e.   Experimental silk paper   275.00

Union Match Co. — RO179

Union Match Co.

RO179   1c   black   55.00

U. S. M. Co. (Universal Safety Match Co.)

RO180   1c   black   3.00   22.50
        e.   Experimental silk paper   57.50

— W —

Washington Match   Wilmington Parlor Match
Co. — RO181   Co. — RO182

Washington Match Co.

RO181   1c   black   37.50

Wilmington Parlor Match Co.

RO182   1c   black   95.00   5,000.
        e.   Experimental silk paper   140.00

Wise & Co.

RO183   1c   black   1,100.

— Z —

F. Zaiss & Co.

RO184   1c   black   1.75   4.50   1.75

Zisemann, Griesheim & Co.

RO185   1c   green   800.00
RO186   1c   blue   120.00   20.00
        u.   1c ultra   550.00

PRIVATE DIE CANNED FRUIT STAMP

T. Kensett & Co. — RP1

1867   *Perf. 12*

T. Kensett & Co.

RP1   1c   green   1,000.

PRIVATE DIE MEDICINE STAMPS

1862   *Perf. 12*

	a. Old Paper	b. Silk Paper	c. Pink Paper	d. Wmkd. USIR (191R)

— A —

Anglo American Drug Co. — RS1

Anglo American Drug Co.

RS1   1c   black   60.00

J. C. Ayer & Co.

RS2   1c   brn car, imperf.   5,250.
RS3   1c   green, imperf.   6,000.
RS4   1c   black, imperf., type 1   50.00   50.00   40.00
      Type 2   50.00   50.00   900.00   40.00
      Dbl. transfer

Type 1: long, full-pointed "y" in "Ayers;" Type 2: short, truncated "y" in "Ayers."

RS5   1c   blue, imperf.   8,000.
RS6   1c   org, imperf.   7,750.
RS6F 1c   red, imperf.   —
RS7   1c   gray lilac, imperf.   8,500.

J.C. Ayer & Co. — RS8/RS13

RS8   4c   red, die cut   5,750.
RS9   4c   blue, die cut   4.00   4.00   4.00
       e.   Experimental silk paper   —
       u.   4c ultra (die cut)   525.00
RS10   4c   blue, imperf.   400.00   300.00   325.00
RS11   4c   pur, die cut   7,000.

			a. Old Paper	b. Silk Paper	c. Pink Paper	d. Wmkd. USIR (191R)

RS12 4c **green,** die cut 8,750.
RS13 4c **ver,** die cut 10,000.

The 4c in black was printed and sent to Ayer & Co. It may exist but has not been seen by collectors.

B

Barham Pile Cure Co.

RS14 4c **green,** wmkd. lozenges 75.00

D. S. Barnes — RS15/RS20

D. S. Barnes

The 1c, 2c and 4c are about 184mm, 242mm and 304mm tall. The products mentioned differ. "D. S. Barnes" is in manscript.

RS15	1c	**ver**	150.00
RS16	2c	**ver**	100.00
RS17	4c	**ver**	400.00
RS18	1c	**black**	22.50
RS19	2c	**black**	70.00
RS20	4c	**black**	60.00

Demas Barnes

Same as above but with "Demas Barnes" in serifed letters.

RS21	1c	**black**	20.00
RS22	2c	**black**	55.00
RS23	4c	**black**	20.00

Demas Barnes & Co. — RS24/RS26

Demas Barnes & Co.

RS24	1c	**black**	15.00	425.00
RS25	2c	**black**	8.00	325.00
	e.	Experimental silk paper	180.00	
RS26	4c	**black**	8.00	

T. H. Barr & Co. — RS27

T. H. Barr & Co.

RS27 4c **black** 15.00
Dbl. transfer 200.00

---

e. Experimental silk paper 200.00

Barry's   D. M. Bennett
RS28/RS29   RS30

Barry's

RS28	2c	**green,** Tricopherous	11.00	14.00	
RS29	2c	**green,** Proprietary	3.75	160.00	4.00
		Dbl. transfer	250.00		

D. M. Bennett

RS30	1c	**lake**	11.00	
	e.	Experimental silk paper	80.00	

W. T. Blow — RS31

W. T. Blow

RS31	1c	**green**	240.00	65.00	300.00	65.00
	e.	Experimental silk paper	650.00			

B. Brandreth
RS32/RS35

B. Brandreth

RS32	1c	**black,** perf.	475.00	550.00
RS33	1c	**blk,** imperf.	2.00	1.50
	e.	Experimental silk paper	22.50	

Nos. RS32-RS33 inscribed "United States Certificate of Genuineness" around vignette.

RS34	1c	**black,** 41x50mm, imperf.	140.00		
RS35	1c	**black,** 24x30mm, imperf.	1.00	5.75	1.00
	p.	Perf.			425.00

Fred Brown Co. — RS37/RS38

Fred Brown Co.

RS37	2c	**black,** imperf., die I	105.00	37.50	2,000.	37.50
	e.	Experimental silk paper	375.00			
RS38	2c	**black,** imperf., die II	55.00			

Die I has "E" of "Fred" incomplete. Die II shows recutting in the "E" of "Fred" and "Genuine".

John I. Brown & Son — RS39/RS41

John I. Brown & Son.

RS39	1c	**black**	9.00	27.50		6.00
RS40	2c	**green**	9.00	9.00	275.00	300.00
		Dbl. transfer	—			
	e.	Experimental silk paper	80.00			
RS41	4c	**brown**	210.00	85.00		1,100.

Dr. C.F. Brown — RS36

Dr. C. F. Brown

RS36	1c	**blue**	250.00	60.00		70.00

			a. Old Paper	b. Silk Paper	c. Pink Paper	d. Wmkd. USIR (191R)

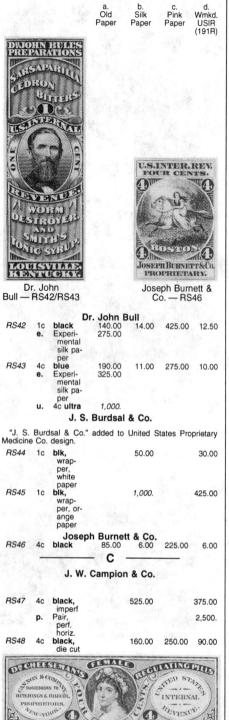

Dr. John Bull — RS42/RS43

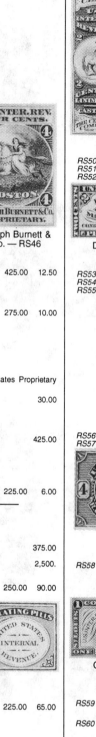

Joseph Burnett & Co. — RS46

Dr. John Bull

RS42	1c	black	140.00	14.00	425.00	12.50
	e.	Experimental silk paper	275.00			
RS43	4c	blue	190.00	11.00	275.00	10.00
	e.	Experimental silk paper	325.00			
	u.	4c ultra	1,000.			

J. S. Burdsal & Co.

"J. S. Burdsal & Co." added to United States Proprietary Medicine Co. design.

RS44	1c	blk, wrapper, white paper		50.00		30.00
RS45	1c	blk, wrapper, orange paper		1,000.		425.00

Joseph Burnett & Co.

RS46	4c	black	85.00	6.00	225.00	6.00

— C —

J. W. Campion & Co.

RS47	4c	black, imperf	525.00			375.00
	p.	Pair, perf. horiz.				2,500.
RS48	4c	black, die cut	160.00	250.00		90.00

Cannon & Co. — RS49

Cannon & Co.

RS49	4c	green, imperf	100.00	225.00		65.00

The Centaur Co. — RS50/RS52

The Centaur Co.

RS50	1c	ver		55.00		8.00
RS51	2c	black		12.50		3.50
RS52	4c	black		55.00		

Dr. A. W. Chase, Son & Co. — RS53/RS55

Dr. A. W. Chase, Son & Co.

RS53	1c	black		90.00		3,000.
RS54	2c	black		90.00		
RS55	4c	black		125.00		

Wm. E. Clarke
RS56   RS57

Wm. E Clarke

RS56	3c	blue		120.00		
RS57	6c	black		85.00		

R. C. & C. S. Clark — RS58

R. C. & C. S. Clark

RS58	4c	black		15.00		17.50

Collins Bros.
RS59

W. H. Comstock
RS60

Collins Bros.

RS59	1c	black		17.50	275.00	

W. H. Comstock

RS60	1c	black				4.00

Cook & Bernheimer

RS61	4c	blue				100.00

Charles N. Crittenton — RS62/RS64

Charles N. Crittenton

RS62	1c	black		5.75		
RS63	1c	blue			12.50	5.00
RS64	2c	black		65.00	32.50	5.00

Oliver Crook & Co. (illustration reduced) — RS65

Oliver Crook & Co.

RS65	4c	black	100.00	22.50		
	e.	Experimental silk paper	30.00			

Jeremiah Curtis & Son — RS66/RS68

Jeremiah Curtis & Son

RS66	1c	black,, die I, small '1s'	80.00			
RS67	1c	black, die II, large '1s'				120.00
RS68	2c	black Dbl. transfer	10.00	10.00	110.00	240.00

Die II numerals nearly fill the circles.

Curtis & Brown

RS69	1c	black	5.75	4.00		
	e.	Experimental silk paper				
RS70	2c	black	110.00			

Curtis & Brown Mfg. Co.

These are identical to RS69-RS70 with "Mfg. Co. Limtd." instead of the right hand "TWO CENTS." See illustration pages.

RS71	1c	black	170.00			8.00
RS72	2c	black	1,600.			800.00

— D —

Dalley's Galvanic Horse Salve

RS73	2c	green	90.00	90.00		100.00

Dalley's Magical Pain Extractor (Illustration reduced.) — RS74

Dalley's Magical Pain Extractor

			a. Old Paper	b. Silk Paper	c. Pink Paper	d. Wmkd. USIR (191R)
RS74	1c	black	7.00	7.00		8.50
	h.	$100 instead of $1.00	300.00			11.00

Perry Davis & Son — RS75/RS81

Perry Davis & Son

			a. Old Paper	b. Silk Paper	c. Pink Paper	d. Wmkd. USIR (191R)
RS75	1c	blue	7.00	2.00	220.00	2.00
	e.	Experimental silk paper	110.00			
	u.	1c ultra	165.00			
RS76	2c	brown red	150.00			
RS77	2c	black	77.50			
RS78	2c	dull purple		7.00		
RS78A	2c	slate		11.00		2.50
RS79	2c	dull red	85.00			
RS80	2c	brown		2,750.		
RS81	4c	brown	9.00	2.00		1.50

P. H. Drake & Co.

RS82	2c	black	2,100.			
RS83	4c	black	50.00	60.00		
	e.	Experimental silk paper	140.00			

F

B. A. Fahnestock — RS84

B. A. Fahnestock

RS84	1c	lake, imperf	140.00	110.00		

Father Mathew Temperance & Manufacturing Co. — RS85

The Father Mathew Temperance & Manufacturing Co.

RS85	4c	black		10.00		

A. H. Flanders, M. D.

RS86	1c	green, perf.	11.00			11.00

			a. Old Paper	b. Silk Paper	c. Pink Paper	d. Wmkd. USIR (191R)
RS87	1c	green, part perf.	25.00	2.00	35.00	2.00

Fleming Bros. — RS88/RS90

Fleming Bros.

RS88	1c	black, Vermifuge, imperf.	14.00	20.00		50.00
	e.	Experimental silk paper	75.00			
RS89	1c	black, L. Pills, imperf	4,000.			
RS90	1c	blue, L. Pills, imperf	7.00	7.00		7.00
		Dbl. transfer		70.00		70.00
	e.	Experimental silk paper	—			
	u.	1c ultra	450.00			

Seth W. Fowle & Son RS91

G. G. Green RS92/RS93

Seth W. Fowle & Son, J. P. Dinsmore

RS91	4c	black	12.50	2.00		3.00

G

G. G. Green

RS92	3c	black				6.00
	h.	Tete beche pair				550.00
RS93	3c	blk, rouletted				160.00

H

Reuben P. Hall & Co.

RS94	4c	black	20.00	20.00		22.50
	e.	Experimental silk paper	—			

Hall & Ruckel — RS95/RS96

Hall & Ruckel

RS95	1c	green	1.50	1.50	25.00	1.50
	e.	Experimental silk paper	25.00			
RS96	3c	black	2.25	2.25	65.00	2.50

Dr. Harter & Co.

RS97	1c	black	20.00	14.00		
	e.	Experimental silk paper	165.00			

Dr. Harter

As No. RS97, inscribed "Dr. Harter" instead of "Dr. Harter & Co."

RS98	1c	black		2.25	10.00	2.25

			a. Old Paper	b. Silk Paper	c. Pink Paper	d. Wmkd. USIR (191R)
		Double impression		3,000.		

(Dr.) S. B. Hartman & Co.

RS99	4c	black	325.00	55.00	275.00	1,100.
RS100	6c	black	325.00	190.00		

E. T. Hazeltine — RS101/RS103

E. T. Hazeltine

RS101	1c	black				16.00
RS102	2c	blue		30.00		
RS103	4c	black	475.00	20.00		17.50
	e.	Experimental silk paper	675.00			
	i.	Imperf., pair	950.00			

E. H. (Edward Heaton)

RS104	3c	black				45.00
RS105	3c	brown				14.00

Helmbold's RS106/RS109

John F. Henry RS112/RS116

Helmbold's

RS106	2c	blue	.90	275.00		
		Dbl. transfer	—			
RS107	3c	green	45.00	32.50		
RS108	4c	black	4.00	140.00		
		Dbl. transfer	160.00			
RS109	6c	black	2.00	3.00		
	e.	Experimental silk paper	37.50			

A. L. Helmbold's

Same as "Helmbold's" but inscribed "A. L. Helmbold's."

RS110	2c	blue	110.00	140.00		95.00
RS111	4c	black	27.50	135.00		8.00

John F. Henry

RS112	2c	violet	375.00			
RS113	4c	bister	625.00			
RS114	1c	black	55.00	1.50	7.50	1.50
	e.	Experimental silk paper	140.00			
RS115	2c	blue	32.50	5.00	120.00	6.00
	u.	2c ultra	450.00			
RS116	4c	red	160.00	1.50	22.50	1.50
	e.	Experimental silk paper	85.00			

Herrick's Pills

RS117	1c	black	80.00	35.00	80.00	35.00
	e.	Experimental silk paper	160.00			
	i.	Imperf., pair	3,500.			

No. RS117i is valued in sound condition. Most pairs are faulty and sell for much less. Horiz. pairs imperf. between were issued of No. RS114d. All known pairs were originally separated, and some have been matched and rejoined. Three rejoined pairs are reported.

Herrick's Pills & Plasters — RS118

Herrick's Pills & Plasters

RS118	1c	red	2.50	4.00	65.00	2.50
e.		Experimental silk paper	—			

J. E. Hetherington

RS119	1c	black				14.00
RS120	2c	black				425.00
RS121	3c	black				20.00
i.		imperf., pair				550.00

Hiscox & Co.

RS122	2c	black				14.00
RS123	4c	black		105.00	275.00	1,200.

Holloway's Pills and Ointment — RS124/RS125

Holloway's Pills and Ointment

RS124	1c	blue, perf.	9.00	
RS125	1c	blue, imperf	275.00	

Holman Liver Pad Co. — RS126/RS127

Holman Liver Pad Co.

RS126	1c	green		20.00
RS127	4c	green		10.00

The Home Bitters Co.

RS128	2c	blue			160.00
		Dbl. transfer			—
RS129	3c	green	110.00	140.00	90.00
RS130	4c	green	210.00		225.00

Hop Bitters Co. — RS131

Hop Bitters Co.

RS131	4c	black		7.00

Hostetter & Smith

RS132	4c	blk, imperf	65.00	37.50	80.00	27.50
		Dbl. transfer	—	50.00	87.50	37.50
RS133	6c	blk, imperf	85.00			
e.		Experimental silk paper	240.00			

S. D. Howe — RS137

S. D. Howe

RS134	4c	black, Duponco's Pills	110.00	190.00	

No. RS134 in red or green exist but were not printed for use. Value, each $275.

RS137	4c	blue, Arabian Milk		8.00	150.00

C. E. Hull & Co.

RS138	1c	black	120.00	5.75	45.00	5.75

T. J. Husband — RS139/RS140

T. J. Husband

RS139	2c	vio, imperf	650.00		
RS140	2c	ver, imperf	12.50	8.00	9.00

Hutchings & Hillyer

RS141	4c	grn, imperf	20.00	22.50	
e.		Experimental silk paper	160.00		

I

H. A. Ingham & Co.

RS142	1c	black		65.00

J

James A. Jackson & Co.

RS143	4c	green	900.00	225.00	
		Dbl. transfer	—		

Dr. D. Jayne & Son — RS144/RS149

Dr. D. Jayne & Son

RS144	1c	blue, imperf		850.00		650.00
p.		Perf.	800.00			3,250.
RS145	2c	blk, imperf	3,250.	1,750.		950.00
p.		Perf.	3,500.			—
RS146	4c	grn, imperf	3,000.	1,100.	1,200.	500.00
p.		Perf.	4,000.			—
RS146F	4c	red, imperf		—		
RS146G	4c	org, imperf		—		
RS147	1c	bl, die cut	5.00	5.00	175.00	4.00
p.		Perf. and die cut	150.00	210.00		—
		On horiz. laid paper	57.50			
RS148	2c	blk, die cut	5.00	5.00	85.00	5.00
		Dbl. transfer	55.00	55.00	110.00	55.00
e.		Experimental silk paper	140.00			
p.		Perf. & die cut	40.00	225.00		—

RS149	4c	grn, die cut	5.00	5.00	85.00	5.00
		Dbl. transfer	—			
e.		Experimental silk paper	110.00			
p.		Perf. and die cut	45.00	210.00		—
		On vertically laid paper	30.00			

I. S. Johnson & Co. RS150

Johnston Holloway & Co. RS151/RS152

I. S. Johnson & Co.

RS150	1c	ver	.90	11.00		.90
		Dbl. transfer	20.00	55.00		20.00

Johnston Holloway & Co.

RS151	1c	black	2.25	2.75
RS152	2c	green	3.00	3.00

K

J. B. Kelly & Co. — RS153

J. B. Kelly & Co.

RS153	4c	blk, imperf	1,750.	
e.		Experimental silk paper	1,900.	

B. J. Kendall & Co.

RS154	4c	blue		27.50

Dr. Kennedy

RS155	2c	green	50.00	5.00	30.00	5.00
		Dbl. transfer				—

	e.	Experimental silk paper		—	
RS156	6c	black	8.00	65.00	8.00

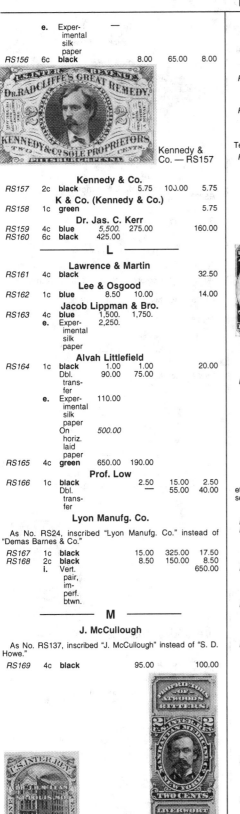

Kennedy & Co. — RS157

Kennedy & Co.

RS157	2c	black	5.75	100.00	5.75

K & Co. (Kennedy & Co.)

RS158	1c	green	5.75

Dr. Jas. C. Kerr

RS159	4c	blue	5,500.	275.00	160.00
RS160	6c	black	425.00		

L

Lawrence & Martin

RS161	4c	black	32.50

Lee & Osgood

RS162	1c	blue	8.50	10.00	14.00

Jacob Lippman & Bro.

RS163	4c	blue	1,500.	1,750.
	e.	Experimental silk paper	2,250.	

Alvah Littlefield

RS164	1c	black	1.00	1.00	20.00
		Dbl. transfer	90.00	75.00	
	e.	Experimental silk paper	110.00		
		On horiz. laid paper	500.00		
RS165	4c	green	650.00	190.00	

Prof. Low

RS166	1c	black	2.50	15.00	2.50
		Dbl. transfer	—	55.00	40.00

Lyon Manufg. Co.

As No. RS24, inscribed "Lyon Manufg. Co." instead of "Demas Barnes & Co."

RS167	1c	black	15.00	325.00	17.50
RS168	2c	black	8.50	150.00	8.50
	i.	Vert. pair, imperf. btwn.			650.00

M

J. McCullough

As No. RS137, inscribed "J. McCullough" instead of "S. D. Howe."

RS169	4c	black	95.00	100.00

J. H. McLean RS170

Manhattan Medicine Co. RS171/RS172

Dr. J. H. McLean

RS170	1c	black	2.50	1.00	15.00	1.00
		Dbl. transfer	60.00	75.00	—	35.00
	e.	Experimental silk paper	80.00			

	i.	Vert. pair, imperf. horiz.	—

Manhattan Medicine Co.

RS171	1c	violet		37.50
	u.	1c purple		60.00
RS172	2c	black	27.50	37.50 14.00

Mansfield & Higbee

As No. RS174, inscribed "Mansfield & Higbee Memphis, Tenn."

RS173	1c	blue	17.50	
	i.	Pair, imperf. between	150.00	
	j.	Block of 4, imperf. btwn.	175.00	

S. Mansfield & Co. — RS174

Merchant's Gargling Oil — RS178/RS179

S. Mansfield & Co.

RS174	1c	blue	27.50	190.00	15.00
	i.	Pair, imperf. between	150.00	300.00	200.00
	j.	Block of 4, imperf. between	140.00	450.00	175.00

Nos. RS173-RS174 are perf. on 4 sides. The i. and j. varieties served as 2c or 4c stamps. Straight edged copies from severed pairs or blocks are worth much less.

T. W. Marsden

RS175	2c	blue	6,000.
RS176	4c	black	425.00

Mercado & Seully

RS177	2c	blk, imperf	5,500.

Merchant's Gargling Oil

RS178	1c	black	225.00	35.00	425.00	27.50
	e.	Experimental silk paper	450.00			
RS179	2c	green	210.00	22.50	325.00	22.50
		Foreign entry, over design of #RO11		2,750.		3,500.
	e.	Experimental silk paper	400.00			

Mette & Kanne

RS180	3c	black	325.00

Mishler Herb Bitters Co.

RS181	4c	black	120.00
	p.	Imperf. at ends	150.00

Moody, Michel & Co.

RS182	4c	blk, imperf	160.00

Dr. C. C. Moore — RS183/RS184

Dr. C. C. Moore

RS183	1c	ver, Pilules	6.00
RS184	2c	black, Sure Cure	65.00 3,250. 30.00

Morehead's — RS185/RS186

Morehead's

RS185	1c	black, Magetic Plaster	22.50
RS186	4c	black, Neurodyne	1,250.

N

New York Pharmacal Association — RS187

New York Pharmacal Association

RS187	4c	black	15.00	32.50	9.00

P

Dr. M. Perl & Co.

RS188	6c	black, cut to shape	1,100.

R. V. Pierce

RS189	1c	green	17.50	120.00	25.00
RS190	2c	black	25.00	6.00 30.00	7.00
		Dbl. transfer	—		
	e.	Experimental silk paper	85.00		

Bennett Pieters & Co.

RS191	4c	black	350.00	1,450.
	e.	Experimental silk paper	550.00	
RS192	6c	black	1,250.	
	i.	Imperf.	1,400.	

R

Radway & Co.

RS193	2c	black	4.50	3.00 11.00	5.00
		Dbl. transfer	65.00	100.00	75.00
	e.	Experimental silk paper	45.00		

D. Ransom & Co.

RS194	1c	blue	3.00	2.75
		Dbl. transfer	—	
	e.	Experimental silk paper	110.00	
RS195	2c	black	22.50	22.50
	e.	Experimental silk paper	110.00	

D. Ransom, Son & Co.

As Nos. RS194-RS195 with "Son" added.

RS196	1c	blue	4.50	17.50	3.00
		Dbl. transfer	—		
RS197	2c	black	11.00	65.00	11.00

Redding's Russia Salve — RS198   Ring's Vegetable Ambrosia — RS199/RS203

			a. Old Paper	b. Silk Paper	c. Pink Paper	d. Wmkd. USIR (191R)
Redding's Russia Salve						
RS198	1c	black	7.00			7.00
		Dbl. transfer	125.00			
Ring's Vegetable Ambrosia						
RS199	2c	blue, imperf		2,750.		
	p.	Perf.		3,000.		
RS200	4c	blk, imperf	1,600.	1,750.		
RS201	2c	bl, die cut				22.50
RS202	4c	black, die cut	15.00	15.00		22.50
	e.	Experimental silk paper	95.00			
RS203	4c	black, perf.		1,000.		1,400.
	k.	Perf. & die cut		1,000.		
	p.	Part perf.		1,600.		—

J. B. Rose & Co. — RS204/RS205

			a. Old Paper	b. Silk Paper	c. Pink Paper	d. Wmkd. USIR (191R)
J. B. Rose & Co.						
RS204	2c	black	4.50	32.50		5,000.
		Dbl. transfer	140.00	200.00		
RS205	4c	black	160.00			—
		Dbl. transfer				
Rumford Chemical Works						
RS206	2c	green				4.50
RS207	2c	grn, imperf				22.50

— S —

			a. Old Paper	b. Silk Paper	c. Pink Paper	d. Wmkd. USIR (191R)
A. B. & D. Sands						
RS208	1c	green	11.00	11.00		
	e.	Experimental silk paper	70.00			

M., P. J. & H. M. Sands

The #RS208 die was altered to make #RS209

			a. Old Paper	b. Silk Paper	c. Pink Paper	d. Wmkd. USIR (191R)
RS209	2c	green	17.50	110.00		15.00
Scheetz's Celebrated Bitter Cordial						
RS210	4c	black, perf.	475.00			
RS211	4c	blk, imperf		3,500.		
Schenck's Mandrake Pills						
RS212	1c	grn, imperf	5.00	8.50	110.00	4.00

			a. Old Paper	b. Silk Paper	c. Pink Paper	d. Wmkd. USIR (191R)
		Dbl. transfer	30.00			—
	e.	Experimental silk paper	280.00			
	p.	Perf.				—
Schenck's Pulmonic Syrup						
RS213	6c	blk, imperf	5.00	5.00	100.00	145.00
		Dbl. transfer	57.50			—
	e.	Experimental silk paper	140.00			
	p.	Perforated	210.00			

J. H. Schenck & Son — RS214

			a. Old Paper	b. Silk Paper	c. Pink Paper	d. Wmkd. USIR (191R)
J. H. Schenck & Son						
RS214	4c	black				9.00

J. E. Schwartz & Co.

As No. RS84, inscribed "J. E. Schwartz & Co." instead of "B. A. Fahnestock."

			a. Old Paper	b. Silk Paper	c. Pink Paper	d. Wmkd. USIR (191R)
RS215	1c	lake, imperf	140.00	300.00	110.00	

"A. L. Scovill" follows No. RS219.

Seabury & Johnson — RS216/RS218

			a. Old Paper	b. Silk Paper	c. Pink Paper	d. Wmkd. USIR (191R)
Seabury & Johnson						
RS216	1c	black				65.00
RS217	1c	black, printed obliteration over "porous"				4.00
	h.	"Porous" obliterated by pen				4.50
RS218	1c	lake				1,750.

"Dr. D. H. Seelye & Co." follows No. RS221.

			a. Old Paper	b. Silk Paper	c. Pink Paper	d. Wmkd. USIR (191R)
Dr. S. Brown Sigesmond						
RS219	4c	blue				100.00

A. L. Scovill & Co. — RS220/RS221

			a. Old Paper	b. Silk Paper	c. Pink Paper	d. Wmkd. USIR (191R)
A. L. Scovill & Co.						
RS220	1c	black	1.75	2.00		
		Dbl. transfer				
	e.	Experimental silk paper	67.50			
	r.	Printed on both sides			2,250.	
RS221	4c	green	2.00	4.00		
	e.	Experimental silk paper	110.00			

Dr. D. H. Seelye & Co. — RS222

			a. Old Paper	b. Silk Paper	c. Pink Paper	d. Wmkd. USIR (191R)
Dr. D. H. Seelye & Co.						
RS222	8c	blk, imperf	25.00			
Dr. M. A. Simmons						
RS223	1c	black, Iuka, Miss.	120.00			6,000.
RS224	1c	black, St. Louis, Mo.				140.00

S. N. Smith & Co.

As No. RS65, inscribed "S. N. Smith & Co." instead of "Oliver Crook & Co."

			a. Old Paper	b. Silk Paper	c. Pink Paper	d. Wmkd. USIR (191R)
RS225	4c	black	45.00			45.00
Dr. E. L. Soule & Co.						
RS226	1c	bl, N.Y., wrapper Foreign entry	75.00			
RS227	1c	bl, Syracuse, wrapper Foreign entry	75.00	35.00		
	u.	1c ultra Foreign entry	375.00		—	—

For Nos. RS226, RS227, the foreign entry is the design of No. RT1 (pos. 1).

H. R. Stevens — RS228/RS229

			a. Old Paper	b. Silk Paper	c. Pink Paper	d. Wmkd. USIR (191R)
H. R. Stevens						
RS228	1c	brown				16.00
RS229	2c	choc				5.00
RS230	6c	black			110.00	5.00
Jas. Swaim						
RS231	6c	org, die cut, ms signature	3,500.			
RS232	8c	org, imperf	1,750.			
	h.	Manuscript signature	2,000.	5,500.		
RS233	8c	org, die cut	300.00			
	e.	Experimental silk paper	700.00			
	h.	Manuscript signature	1,200.			
Wm. Swaim						
RS234	8c	org, imperf	4,500.	3,000.		1,250.

			a. Old Paper	b. Silk Paper	c. Pink Paper	d. Wmkd. USIR (191R)
	k.	Without signature	3,250.	1,750.		

No. RS234d is found with signature "Suaim" or "Swaim." Also, No. RS234b is found with a period under the raised "m" of "Wm" and the right leg of "w" of "Swaim" retouched, both by pen.

			a.	b.	c.	d.
RS235	8c	org, die cut	700.00	190.00		225.00
	h.	Manuscript signature	950.00			
	k.	Signature inverted		2,750.		

Dr. G. W. Swett

RS236	4c	blk, die cut	15.00			
RS237	4c	green, perf.		225.00		1,050.
RS238	4c	green, perf. and die cut		275.00		1,200.

			a. Old Paper	b. Silk Paper	c. Pink Paper	d. Wmkd. USIR (191R)

T

George Tallcot

| RS239 | 2c | vermilion | | | | 15.00 |
| RS240 | 4c | black | | 85.00 | 2,750. | 20.00 |

Tarrant & Co.
RS241

John L.
Thompson
RS242

Tarrant & Company

| RS241 | 4c | red | 3.00 | 80.00 | | 2.00 |

John L. Thompson

RS242	1c	black	5.00	6.00		5.00
		Dbl. transfer		—		
	e.	Experimental silk paper	110.00			

U

United States Proprietary Medicine Co.

RS243	4c	black	50.00	95.00		
	e.	Experimental silk paper	160.00			
RS244	6c	black	825.00			

U. S. Proprietary Medicine Co.

RS245	1c	black, white wrapper	22.50	25.00		
	e.	Experimental silk paper	450.00			
RS246	1c	black, yel wrapper	120.00	220.00		
RS247	1c	black, org wrapper	220.00	2,000.		
RS248	1c	black, org red wrapper	750.00	4,250.		

V

S. R. Van Duzer — RS249/RS250

S. R. Van Duzer

| RS249 | 4c | black | 40.00 | 35.00 | | 190.00 |
| RS250 | 6c | black | | | | 75.00 |

A. Vogeler & Co. — RS251

A. Vogeler & Co.

| RS251 | 1c | black | | 1.25 | | 1.25 |

Vogeler, Meyer & Co.

| RS252 | 1c | vermilion | | | 4.00 | 1.25 |

W

Dr. J. Walker

RS253	4c	black	40.00	20.00		20.00
		Dbl. transfer	50.00			40.00
	e.	Experimental silk paper	150.00			

H. H. Warner &
Co. — RS254/RS255

H. H. W. & Co. (H. H. Warner & Co.)

RS254	1c	brown				6.00
RS255	6c	brown, 19x26mm				80.00
RS256	2c	brown, 88x11mm				35.00
RS257	4c	brown, 95x18mm				35.00
RS258	6c	brown				7.00
		Dbl. transfer				47.50

Weeks & Potter — RS259

Weeks & Potter

RS259	1c	black	7.00			5.00
RS260	2c	black	110.00			
RS261	4c	black	22.50		27.50	7.00
RS262	2c	red			35.00	7.00

Wells,
Richardson
& Co.
RS263

Edward Wilder
RS265/RS269

Wells, Richardson & Co.

| RS263 | 4c | black | | | | 27.50 |

West India Manufacturing Co.

| RS264 | 4c | blk, die I | | 300.00 | 325.00 | 550.00 |
| RS264A | 4c | blk, die II | | | | 350.00 |

Die II shows evidence of retouching, particularly in the central disk.

Edward Wilder

RS265	1c	grn, imperf	1,000.	220.00		325.00
	e.	Experimental silk paper		—		
RS266	1c	grn, die cut	50.00	40.00		22.50
	e.	Experimental silk paper	200.00			
RS266A	4c	ver, imperf				
	e.	Experimental silk paper	5,500.			
RS267	4c	ver, die cut	140.00	500.00		
	e.	Experimental silk paper	115.00			
RS268	4c	lake, imperf		190.00		1,100.
RS269	4c	lake, die cut	800.00	11.00		11.00

Rev. E. A. Wilson

| RS270 | 12c | blue | | 85.00 | | 375.00 |

Thos. E. Wilson, M. D.

| RS271 | 4c | black | 25,000. | | | |

World's Dispensary
Medical Assocn.
RS272/RS273

Wright's Indian
Vegetable Pills
RS274

World's Dispensary Medical Assocn.

			a. Old Paper	b. Silk Paper	c. Pink Paper	d. Wmkd. USIR (191R)
RS272	1c	green				25.00
RS273	2c	black, 56x256mm				7.00

Wright's Indian Vegetable Pills

			a.	b.	c.	d.
RS274	1c	green	2.00	1.50	30.00	1.50
		Dbl. transfer				—
	e.	Experimental silk paper	100.00			

———— Z ————

J.H. Zeilin & Co. — RS275/RS277

J.H. Zeilin & Co.

			a.	b.	c.	d.
RS275	2c	red	550.00			
RS276	2c	green, perf.	40.00			—
RS277	2c	grn, imperf	250.00	6.00	170.00	3.50

			Roul. 5½		p. Hyphen Hole Perf. 7	
			Unused	Used	Unused	Used

1898-1900

See rouletting note preceding No. R161.

The Antikamnia Chemical Co.

			Unused	Used	Unused	Used
RS278	2½c	carmine			3.00	3.00

Fernet Branca (Branca Bros.)

RS279	4c	black	7.00	7.00	6.00	6.00

Emerson Drug Co.

RS280	¼c	car			4.75	1.50
RS281	⅜c	green			4.75	1.50
RS282	1¼c	vio brn			5.50	4.75
RS283	2½c	brn org			5.00	3.50

Chas. H. Fletcher

RS284	1¼c	black	.30	.30	.25	.25

Hostetter Co.

RS285	2½c	black, imperf	.40	.40		

Johnson & Johnson

RS286	⅝c	carmine	.20	.20	.20	.20

Lanman & Kemp

RS287	⅝c	green	6.00	4.00	8.00	4.00
RS288	1¼c	brown	10.00	6.00	10.00	6.00
RS289	1⅞₀c	blue	10.00	3.00	12.00	3.00

J. Ellwood Lee Co.

RS290	¼c	dark blue			2.50	2.50
RS291	⅜c	car			1.50	1.50
RS292	1¼c	dark grn			1.50	1.50
RS293	2½c	org			2.00	2.00
RS294	5c	chocolate			2.25	2.25

			Roul. 5½		p. Hyphen Hole Perf. 7	
			Unused	Used	Unused	Used

Charles Marchand

RS295	⅝c	black	5.50	5.50	6.00	6.00
RS296	1¼c	black	1.25	1.25	1.25	1.25
RS297	1⅞c	black	2.00	2.00	2.50	2.50
RS298	2⅛c	black	1.25	1.25	1.25	1.25
RS299	3⅛c	black	6.00	6.00	6.00	6.00
RS300	4⅜c	black	15.00	15.00	15.00	15.00
RS301	7½c	black	10.00	10.00	10.00	10.00

Od Chem. Co.

RS302	2½c	car				1.00

The Piso Company (E. T. Hazletine)

RS303	⅝c	blue	.20	.20	.20	.20

Radway & Co.

RS304	⅝c	blue	1.00	1.00	1.00	1.00

Warner's Safe Cure Co.

RS305	3⅛c	brown	1.00	1.00	1.00	1.00

Dr. Williams Medicine Co.

RS306	1¼c	pink			1.50	1.50

Dr. Kilmer & Co., Provisionals

Postage Stamps of 1895, 1897-1903, Nos. 267a,
279, 279Bg and 268,
Precancel Overprinted in Black:

Dr. K. & Co.
I. R.
7-5-'98.
a

Dr. K. & Co.
I. R.
Binghamton,
N. Y.
7-11-'98
b

Dr. K. & Co.
I. R.
Binghamton,
N. Y.
7-7-'98
c

1898   Wmk. 191   Perf. 12

Overprint "a," Large "I.R." Dated July 5, 1898.

RS307	A87	1c	deep green	110.00
RS308	A88	2c	pink, type III	110.00
RS308A	A88	2c	pink, type IV	85.00
RS309	A89	3c	purple	90.00

A trial overprint in dark blue on the 2c stamp is known used on July 5.

Overprint "b," Small "I.R.,"
"Dr. K. & Co." with Serifs
Dated July 6, 7, 9, 11 to 14, 1898

RS310	A87	1c	deep green	80.00
RS311	A88	2c	pink, type IV	60.00
RS312	A89	3c	purple	80.00

Overprint "c," Small "I.R.,"
"Dr. K. & Co." without Serifs
Dated July 7, 9, 11 to 14, 1898

RS313	A87	1c	deep green	100.00
RS314	A88	2c	pink, type IV	50.00
RS315	A89	3c	purple	60.00

Many varieties of the Kilmer overprints exist. For the complete listing see "The Case of Dr. Kilmer's," by Morton Dean Joyce, 1954 (also serialized in "The Bureau Specialist," Mar.-Nov. 1957). No types "b" or "c" overprints have been reported on 2c type III stamps, but these should exist. The editors would like to see evidence of such stamps.

St. Louis Provisional Labels, 1898

> INTERNAL REVENUE TAX.
> II I-4 CENTS.
> Stamps not being obtainable
> at time of sale and shipment of
> this package, the tax will be
> paid on sworn returns thereof
> to Collector of Internal Rev-
> enue, 1st Dist. Mo.
>
> Meyer Brothers Drug Co., St. Louis.

Ten proprietary drug companies of St. Louis (Antikamnia Chemical Co., W. R. Holmes, Lambert Pharmacal Co., Meyer Brothers Drug Co., Jno. T. Milliken & Co., Phenique Chemical Co., Prickly Ash Bitters Co., T. M. Sayman, Van Dyke Bitters Co. and Walker Pharmacal

Co.) prepared and used labels to denote payment of July 1, 1898, Proprietary Revenue tax because the government issue of "Battleship" stamps (Nos. RB20-RB31) was not available on the effective date. An illustrated descriptive list of these labels, compiled by Morton Dean Joyce, appeared in the December, 1970, issue of Scott's Monthly Journal.

PRIVATE DIE PERFUMERY STAMPS

1864   **Perf. 12**

			a. Old Paper	b. Silk Paper	c. Pink Paper	d. Wmkd. USIR (191R)

X. Bazin (Illustration reduced.) — RT1

X. Bazin

RT1	2c	blue, die cut	550.00

This stamp was never placed in use.

Corning & Tappan — RT2/RT4

E. W. Hoyt & Co. — RT6/RT11

Corning & Tappan

RT2	1c	black, imperf			1,000.
	h.	Die cut, 19mm diameter			110.00
	k.	Die cut, 21mm diameter			150.00
RT3	1c	black, perf.			350.00
RT4	1c	blue, perf.			2.75

Fetridge & Co.

RT5	2c	ver, cut to shape	110.00

E. W. Hoyt & Co.

			Old Paper	Pink Paper	Wmkd. USIR
RT6	1c	black, imperf	3,250.	2,100.	140.00
RT7	1c	black, die cut	30.00	30.00	15.00
RT8	2c	black, imperf			450.00
RT9	2c	black, die cut			90.00
RT10	4c	black, imperf	2,100.	325.00	1,150.
RT11	4c	black, die cut	85.00	70.00	70.00

The 2c is larger than the 1c, 4c larger than 2c.

Kidder & Laird

RT12	1c	vermilion	12.50
RT13	2c	vermilion	12.50

George W. Laird — RT14/RT15

			a. Old Paper	b. Silk Paper	c. Pink Paper	d. Wmkd. USIR (191R)
George W. Laird						
RT14	3c	blk, imperf		600.00	900.00	600.00
		Double transfer		900.00	1,300.	1,000.
	p.	Perf.	1,500.	3,750.		
		As "p," double transfer	1,600.			
RT15	3c	black, die cut	1,500.	90.00	800.00	90.00
		Double transfer		250.00	900.00	300.00
	p.	Perf. and die cut	1,000.			

Lanman & Kemp RT16/RT18

Tetlow's Perfumery RT19

			a. Old Paper	b. Silk Paper	c. Pink Paper	d. Wmkd. USIR (191R)
Lanman & Kemp						
RT16	1c	black		7.50	275.00	7.50
		Double transfer		—		
RT17	2c	brown		30.00		10.00
RT18	3c	green		8.00		12.50
		Double transfer		150.00		70.00
Tetlow's Perfumery						
RT19	1c	vermilion				2.00

C. B. Woodworth & Son RT20/RT21

R. & G. A. Wright RT22/RT25

			a. Old Paper	b. Silk Paper	c. Pink Paper	d. Wmkd. USIR (191R)
C. B. Woodworth & Son						
RT20	1c	green		7.00	17.50	7.00
		Double transfer		60.00	75.00	60.00
RT21	2c	blue		140.00	1,200.	9.00
R. & G. A. Wright						
RT22	1c	blue		6.00	8.00	60.00

			a. Old Paper	b. Silk Paper	c. Pink Paper	d. Wmkd. USIR (191R)
	e.	Experimental silk paper		85.00		
RT23	2c	black		11.00	20.00	200.00
RT24	3c	lake		30.00	110.00	290.00
RT25	4c	green		90.00	125.00	275.00

Young, Ladd & Coffin — RT26/RT33

			a. Old Paper	b. Silk Paper	c. Pink Paper	d. Wmkd. USIR (191R)
Young, Ladd & Coffin						
RT26	1c	green, imperf		90.00	100.00	90.00
RT27	1c	green, perf.		22.50	20.00	15.00
RT28	2c	blue, imperf		125.00	110.00	75.00
RT29	2c	blue, perf.		60.00	85.00	15.00
RT30	3c	vermilion imperf.		110.00	130.00	80.00
RT31	3c	vermilion perf.		35.00	8.00	5.00
RT32	4c	brown, imperf.		6,000.	145.00	65.00
RT33	4c	brown, perf.	45.00	12.50		5.00

PRIVATE DIE PLAYING CARD STAMPS

1864

			a. Old Paper	b. Silk Paper	c. Pink Paper	d. Wmkd. USIR (191R)
Caterson Brotz & Co.						
RU1	5c	brown				9,000.

This stamp was never placed in use.

A. Dougherty RU2/RU6

Eagle Card Co. RU7

			a. Old Paper	b. Silk Paper	c. Pink Paper	d. Wmkd. USIR (191R)
A. Dougherty						
RU2	2c	orange	70.00			
RU3	4c	black	45.00			
RU4	5c	blue, 20x26mm	1.25	1.25		12.50
		Double transfer		—		
	e.	Experimental silk paper		—		
		As "e," inverted dbl. transfer		—		
	u.	5c ultra	130.00			
RU5	5c	blue, 18x23mm				1.00
RU6	10c	blue	40.00			

The 2c, 4c and 5c have numerals in all four corners.

			a. Old Paper	b. Silk Paper	c. Pink Paper	d. Wmkd. USIR (191R)
Eagle Card Co.						
RU7	5c	black				100.00
Goodall (London, New York)						

As No. RU13, "London Goodall New York" replaces both "American Playing Cards" and Victor E. Mauger and Petrie New York."

			a. Old Paper	b. Silk Paper	c. Pink Paper	d. Wmkd. USIR (191R)
RU8	5c	black	225.00	4.00		
	e.	Experimental silk paper	425.00			
Samuel Hart & Co.						
RU9	5c	black	6.00	6.00		
	e.	Experimental silk paper	240.00			

Lawrence & Cohen — RU10/RU11

			a. Old Paper	b. Silk Paper	c. Pink Paper	d. Wmkd. USIR (191R)
Lawrence & Cohen						
RU10	2c	blue	80.00			
RU11	5c	green	5.00	5.00		
	e.	Experimental silk paper	85.00			
Jn. J. Levy						
RU12	5c	black	25.00	30.00		
	e.	Experimental silk paper	95.00			

Victor E. Mauger & Petrie — RU13

			a. Old Paper	b. Silk Paper	c. Pink Paper	d. Wmkd. USIR (191R)
Victor E. Mauger and Petrie						
RU13	5c	blue		1.25	1.25	.75
New York Consolidated Card Co.						
RU14	5c	black	5.00	17.50		5.00

Paper Fabrique — RU15

Russell, Morgan & Co. — RU16

			a. Old Paper	b. Silk Paper	c. Pink Paper	d. Wmkd. USIR (191R)
Paper Fabrique Company						
RU15	5c	black		7.00	20.00	7.00
Russell, Morgan & Co.						
RU16	5c	black				10.00

MOTOR VEHICLE USE REVENUE STAMPS

When affixed to a motor vehicle, permitted use of that vehicle for a stated period.

RV1

1942   Wmk. 191R   OFFSET PRINTING   *Perf. 11*

With Gum on Back

RV1	RV1	$2.09 **light green** *(February)*	1.30	.40

With Gum on Face

Inscriptions on Back

RV2	RV1	$1.67 **light green** *(March)*	19.00	8.00
RV3	RV1	$1.25 **light green** *(April)*	13.50	7.00
RV4	RV1	84c **light green** *(May)*	16.00	7.00
RV5	RV1	42c **light green** *(June)*	16.00	7.00

With Gum and Control Number on Face

Inscriptions on Back

RV6	RV1	$5 **rose red** *(July)*	2.50	1.00
RV7	RV1	$4.59 **rose red** *(August)*	30.00	12.00
RV8	RV1	$4.17 **rose red** *(September)*	35.00	15.00
RV9	RV1	$3.75 **rose red** *(October)*	30.00	12.00
RV10	RV1	$3.34 **rose red** *(November)*	30.00	12.00
RV11	RV1	$2.92 **rose red** *(December)*	30.00	12.00
		Nos. RV1-RV11 (11)	223.30	93.40

1943

RV12	RV1	$2.50 **rose red** *(January)*	37.50	15.00
RV13	RV1	$2.09 **rose red** *(February)*	25.00	10.50
RV14	RV1	$1.67 **rose red** *(March)*	21.00	12.00
RV15	RV1	$1.25 **rose red** *(April)*	21.00	8.75
RV16	RV1	84c **rose red** *(May)*	21.00	8.75
RV17	RV1	42c **rose red** *(June)*	17.50	9.50
RV18	RV1	$5 **yellow** *(July)*	3.00	.75
RV19	RV1	$4.59 **yellow** *(August)*	37.50	15.00
RV20	RV1	$4.17 **yellow** *(September)*	50.00	20.00
RV21	RV1	$3.75 **yellow** *(October)*	50.00	20.00
RV22	RV1	$3.34 **yellow** *(November)*	55.00	20.00
RV23	RV1	$2.92 **yellow** *(December)*	67.50	24.00
		Nos. RV12-RV23 (12)	406.00	164.25

1944

RV24	RV1	$2.50 **yellow** *(January)*	72.50	24.00
RV25	RV1	$2.09 **yellow** *(February)*	45.00	17.50
RV26	RV1	$1.67 **yellow** *(March)*	37.50	15.00
RV27	RV1	$1.25 **yellow** *(April)*	37.50	15.00
RV28	RV1	84c **yellow** *(May)*	30.00	15.00
RV29	RV1	42c **yellow** *(June)*	30.00	15.00

Gum on Face

Control Number and Inscriptions on Back

RV30	RV1	$5 **violet** *(July)*	2.50	.50
RV31	RV1	$4.59 **violet** *(August)*	55.00	20.00
RV32	RV1	$4.17 **violet** *(September)*	42.50	17.50
RV33	RV1	$3.75 **violet** *(October)*	42.50	17.50
RV34	RV1	$3.34 **violet** *(November)*	37.50	12.00
RV35	RV1	$2.92 **violet** *(December)*	37.50	12.00
		Nos. RV24-RV35 (12)	470.00	181.00

1945

RV36	RV1	$2.50 **violet** *(January)*	30.00	11.50
RV37	RV1	$2.09 **violet** *(February)*	27.50	11.50
RV38	RV1	$1.67 **violet** *(March)*	27.50	10.00
RV39	RV1	$1.25 **violet** *(April)*	27.50	10.00
RV40	RV1	84c **violet** *(May)*	21.00	8.75
RV41	RV1	42c **violet** *(June)*	18.00	7.00
		Nos. RV36-RV41 (6)	151.50	58.75

Daniel
Manning
RV2

Gum on Face

Control Number and Inscriptions on Back

1945   Wmk. 191R   Offset Printing   *Perf. 11*

Bright Blue Green & Yellow Green

RV42	RV2	$5 *(July)*	2.50	.50
RV43	RV2	$4.59 *(August)*	42.50	17.50
RV44	RV2	$4.17 *(Sept.)*	42.50	17.50
RV45	RV2	$3.75 *(October)*	37.50	11.50
RV46	RV2	$3.34 *(November)*	30.00	11.50
RV47	RV2	$2.92 *(December)*	25.00	8.75
		Nos. RV42-RV47 (6)	180.00	67.25

1946

Bright Blue Green & Yellow Green

RV48	RV2	$2.50 *(January)*	27.50	11.50
RV49	RV2	$2.09 *(February)*	27.50	11.50
RV50	RV2	$1.67 *(March)*	20.00	8.75
RV51	RV2	$1.25 *(April)*	17.50	8.75
RV52	RV2	84c *(May)*	17.50	8.75
RV53	RV2	42c *(June)*	12.50	1.10
		Nos. RV48-RV53 (6)	122.50	50.35

BOATING STAMPS

Required on applications for the certificate of number for motorboats of more than 10 horsepower, starting April 1, 1960. The pictorial upper part of the $3 stamp was attached to the temporary certificate and kept by the boat owner. The lower part (stub), showing number only, was affixed to the application and sent by the post office to the U.S. Coast Guard, which issues permanent certificates. The $3 fee was for three years. The $1 stamp covered charges for reissue of a lost or destroyed certificate of number.

Catalogue value for unused stamps in this section are for Never Hinged items.

Outboard and
Inboard
Motorboats — B1

Offset Printing, Number Typographed

1960		Unwmk.		*Rouletted*
RVB1	B1	$1 **rose red, black number**	37.50	*200.00*
		P# block of 4	160.00	
		On license		—
RVB2	B1	$3 **blue, red number**	42.50	27.50
		P# block of 4	180.00	
		On license		35.00

No. RVB1 used value is for a copy bearing a cancel dated between 1960-1964. Mute oval cancels are almost always favor cancels.

CAMP STAMPS

The Camp Stamp program of the Department of Agriculture's National Forest Service was introduced in 1985. The public was offered the option of prepaying their recreation fees through the purchase of camp stamps. The fees varied but were typically $3 to $4.

The stamps were supplied in rolls with the backing rouletted 9 horizontally. The letter preceding the serial number indicated the face value and printer (A-D, Denver; E-J, Washington). The stamps were designed so that any attempt to remove them from the fee envelope would cause them to come apart.

The program ended in the summer of 1988. The envelopes containing the stamps were destroyed by the National Forerst Service after use. No used examples have been reported.

Catalogue value for unused stamps in this section are for Never Hinged items.

National Forest Service Logo — RVC1

Printed in Denver, CO.

1985　　　　Typo.　　　*Die Cut*
Self-Adhesive, Coated Paper

RVC1	RVC1	50c **black,** *pink,* "A"	15.00
RVC2	RVC1	$1 **black,** *red,* "B"	15.00
RVC3	RVC1	$2 **black,** *yellow,* "C"	15.00
RVC4	RVC1	$3 **black,** *green,* "D"	15.00

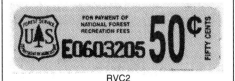

RVC2

Printed by the Government Printing Office, Washington, DC (?).

1986　　　Typo.　　　*Die Cut*
Self-Adhesive, Coated Paper

RVC5	RVC2	50c **black,** *pink,* "E"	40.00
RVC6	RVC2	$1 **black,** *red,* "F"	40.00
RVC7	RVC2	$2 **black,** *yellow,* "G"	40.00
RVC8	RVC2	$3 **black,** *green,* "H"	40.00
RVC9	RVC2	$5 **black,** *silver,* "I"	200.00
RVC10	RVC2	$10 **black,** *bronze,* "J"	—

TRAILER PERMIT STAMPS

Issued by the National Park Service of the Department of the Interior. Required to be affixed to "License to Operate Motor Vehicle" starting July 1, 1939, when a house trailer was attached to a motor vehicle entering a national park or national monument.

Issued to rangers in booklets of 50 (five 2x5 panes).

Use was continued at least until 1952.

Unused stamps may have a ranger's handwritten control number.

Trailer and Automobile RVT1

1939　　Unwmk.　　Offset Printing　　*Perf. 11*

RVT1	RVT1	50c **bright blue**	*400.00*	*100.00*
		On license		150.00
RVT2	RVT1	$1 **carmine**	*100.00*	*50.00*
		On license		75.00

Earliest known use: July 1939.

DISTILLED SPIRITS AND EXCISE TAX STAMPS

Charles S. Fairchild, Secretary of Treasury 1887-89 — DS1

Actual size: 89 ½x63 ½mm

Inscribed "STAMP FOR SERIES 1950"

1950　Wmk. 191R　Offset Printing　*Rouletted 7*
Left Value- Used
Right Value- Punched Cancel

RX1	DS1	1c **yellow green & black**	25.00	20.00
RX2	DS1	3c **yellow green & black**	100.00	90.00
RX3	DS1	5c **yellow green & black**	20.00	17.50
RX4	DS1	10c **yellow green & black**	17.50	15.00
RX5	DS1	25c **yellow green & black**	9.00	7.00
RX6	DS1	50c **yellow green & black**	9.00	7.00

RX7	DS1	$1 **yellow green & black**	2.00	1.25
RX8	DS1	$3 **yellow green & black**	20.00	15.00
RX9	DS1	$5 **yellow green & black**	5.00	3.50
RX10	DS1	$10 **yellow green & black**	2.50	1.50
RX11	DS1	$25 **yellow green & black**	12.50	9.00
RX12	DS1	$50 **yellow green & black**	6.00	5.00
RX13	DS1	$100 **yellow green & black**	4.00	2.50
RX14	DS1	$300 **yellow green & black**	25.00	21.00
RX15	DS1	$500 **yellow green & black**	15.00	10.00
RX16	DS1	$1,000 **yellow green & black**	9.00	7.50
RX17	DS1	$1,500 **yellow green & black**	50.00	40.00
RX18	DS1	$2,000 **yellow green & black**	4.50	3.25
RX19	DS1	$3,000 **yellow green & black**	21.00	15.00
RX20	DS1	$5,000 **yellow green & black**	21.00	15.00
RX21	DS1	$10,000 **yellow green & black**	27.00	22.50
RX22	DS1	$20,000 **yellow green & black**	32.50	30.00
RX23	DS1	$30,000 **yellow green & black**	70.00	50.00
RX24	DS1	$40,000 **yellow green & black**	900.00	650.00
RX25	DS1	$50,000 **yellow green & black**	85.00	75.00

Inscription "STAMP FOR SERIES 1950" omitted

1952

Left Value- Used
Right Value- Punched Cancel

RX28	DS1	5c **yellow green & black**		40.00
RX29	DS1	10c **yellow green & black**	30.00	4.00
RX30	DS1	25c **yellow green & black**	25.00	15.00
RX31	DS1	50c **yellow green & black**	30.00	12.00
RX32	DS1	$1 **yellow green & black**	20.00	1.25
RX33	DS1	$3 **yellow green & black**	35.00	22.50
RX34	DS1	$5 **yellow green & black**	37.50	25.00
RX35	DS1	$10 **yellow green & black**	20.00	1.50
RX36	DS1	$25 **yellow green & black**	25.00	10.00
RX37	DS1	$50 **yellow green & black**	65.00	25.00
RX38	DS1	$100 **yellow green & black**	20.00	2.50
RX39	DS1	$300 **yellow green & black**	25.00	7.00

RX40	DS1	$500 **yellow green & black**	—	30.00
RX41	DS1	$1,000 **yellow green & black**	—	6.00
RX43	DS1	$2,000 **yellow green & black**		70.00
RX44	DS1	$3,000 **yellow green & black**	—	850.00
RX45	DS1	$5,000 **yellow green & black**		50.00
RX46	DS1	$10,000 **yellow green & black**		80.00

Seven other denominations with "Stamp for Series 1950" omitted were prepared but are not known to have been put into use: 1c, 3c, $1,500, $20,000, $30,000, $40,000 and $50,000. **Copies listed as used have staple holes.**
Distilled Spirits Excise Tax stamps were discontinued in 1959.

FIREARMS TRANSFER TAX STAMPS

Documentary Stamp of 1917 Overprinted Vertically in Black. Reading Up

NATIONAL FIREARMS ACT

1934	Engr.	Wmk. 191R	*Perf. 11*
	Without Gum		
RY1	R21	$1 **green**	350.00 —
	On license		—

Eagle, Shield and Stars from U.S. Seal
RY1 (Type I)   RY2

Two types of $200:
I - Serial number with serifs, not preceded by zeros. Tips of 6 lines project into left margin.

II - Gothic serial number preceded by zeros. Five line tips in left margin.

1934	Wmk. 191R	Size: 28x42mm
	Without Gum	
RY2 RY1	$200 **dark blue & red,** type I, #1-1500	1,400. 750.00
	On license	900.00

Issued in vertical strips of 4 which are imperforate at top, bottom and right side.
See Nos. RY4, RY6-RY8.

1938	Size: 28x33½mm	*Perf. 11*
RY3 RY2	$1 **green**	85.00 —
	On license	—

See No. RY5.

1950 (?)	Wmk. 191R	Size: 29x43mm
RY4 RY1	$200 **dull blue & red,** type II, #1501-3000	600.00 450.00
	On license	500.00

No. RY4 has a clear impression and is printed on white paper. No. RY2 has a "muddy" impression in much darker blue ink and is printed on off-white paper.

1960, July 1	Size: 29x34mm	*Perf. 11*
RY5 RY2	$5 **red**	25.00 *40.00*
	On license	50.00

No. RY5 was issued in sheets of 50 (10x5) with straight edge on four sides of sheet.

The watermark is hard to see on many copies of #RY2-RY5.

1974	Unwmk.	Size: 29x43mm
RY6 RY1	$200 **dull blue & red,** type II, #3001-up	225.00 75.00
	On license	90.00

Panes of 32

1990(?)-95	Litho.	Without Gum	*Imperf.*
RY7 RY1	$200 **dull blue**		500.00
	On license		650.00

Perf. 12½

RY8 RY1	$200 **dull blue**	100.00
	On license	125.00
RY9 RY2	$5 **red,** *1995*	50.00
	On license	100.00

Nos. RY7 and RY8 do not have a printed serial number or the tabs at left. Because the stamps do not have a serial number mint copies are not being sold to the public.
WARNING: Nos. RY7-RY9 are taped or glued to the transfer of title documents. The glue used is NOT water soluble. Attempts to soak the stamps may result in damage.

RECTIFICATION TAX STAMPS

Used to indicate payment of the tax on distilled spirits that were condensed and purified for additional blending through repeated distillations.

RT1

Actual size: 89½x64mm

1946	Offset Printing	Wmk. 191R	*Rouletted 7*
RZ1	RT1	1c **blue & black**	7.00 3.00
		Punched cancel	1.75
RZ2	RT1	3c **blue & black**	25.00 8.00
		Punched cancel	7.50
RZ3	RT1	5c **blue & black**	15.00 2.50
		Punched cancel	1.25
RZ4	RT1	10c **blue & black**	15.00 2.50
		Punched cancel	1.25
RZ5	RT1	25c **blue & black**	15.00 3.00
		Punched cancel	2.00
RZ6	RT1	50c **blue & black**	20.00 5.00
		Punched cancel	3.25
RZ7	RT1	$1 **blue & black**	20.00 4.00
		Punched cancel	2.25
RZ8	RT1	$3 **blue & black**	100.00 18.00
		Punched cancel	9.00
RZ9	RT1	$5 **blue & black**	30.00 10.00
		Punched cancel	6.00
RZ10	RT1	$10 **blue & black**	25.00 3.00
		Punched cancel	1.25
RZ11	RT1	$25 **blue & black**	100.00 10.00
		Punched cancel	3.00
RZ12	RT1	$50 **blue & black**	100.00 7.50
		Punched cancel	3.00
RZ13	RT1	$100 **blue & black**	— 9.50
		Punched cancel	3.50
RZ14	RT1	$300 **blue & black**	*250.00* 10.00
		Punched cancel	7.50
RZ15	RT1	$500 **blue & black**	— 10.00
		Punched cancel	7.00
RZ16	RT1	$1000 **blue & black**	— 18.00
		Punched cancel	15.00

RZ17	RT1	$1500 **blue & black**	— 45.00
		Punched cancel	35.00
RZ18	RT1	$2000 **blue & black**	— 80.00
		Punched cancel	60.00

Copies listed as used have staple holes.

HUNTING PERMIT STAMPS

Authorized by an Act of Congress, approved March 16, 1934, to license hunters. Receipts go to maintain waterfowl life in the United States. Sales to collectors were made legal June 15, 1935. The 1934 issue was designed by J.N. Darling, 1935 by Frank W. Benson, 1936 by Richard E. Bishop, 1937 by J.D. Knap, 1938 by Roland Clark, 1939 by Lynn Bogue Hunt, 1940 by Francis L. Jaques, 1941 by E.R. Kalmbach, 1942 by A. Lassell Ripley, 1943 by Walter E. Bohl, 1944 and 1950 by Walter A. Weber, 1945 by Owen J. Bromme, 1946 by Robert W. Hines, 1947 by Jack Murray, 1948, 1951, 1959, 1969, and 1971 by Maynard Reece, 1949 by "Roge" E. Preuss, 1952 by John H. Dick, 1953 by Clayton B. Seagears, 1954 by Harvey D. Sandstrom, 1955, 1964 and 1966 by Stanley Searns, 1956, 1963 and 1970 by Edward J. Bierly, 1957 by Jackson Miles Abbott, 1958 and 1967 by Leslie C. Kouba, 1960 by John A. Ruthven, 1961-1962 by Edward A. Morris, 1965 by Ron Jenkins, 1968 by C.G. Pritchard, 1972 by Arthur M. Cook, 1973 by Lee LeBlanc, 1974 and 1982 by David A. Maass, 1975 by James L. Fisher, 1976 by Alderson Magee, 1977 by Martin R. Murk, 1978 by Albert Earl Gilbert, 1979 by Kenneth L. Michaelsen, 1980 by Richard W. Plasschaert, 1981 by John S. Wilson, 1983 by Phil Scholer, 1984 by William C. Morris, 1985 by Gerald Mobley, 1986 by Burton E. Moore, Jr., 1987 by Arthur G. Anderson, 1988 by Daniel Smith, 1989 and 1994 by Neal R. Anderson, 1990 and 1995 by Jim Hautman, 1991 by Nancy Howe, 1992 by Joe Hautman, 1993 by Bruce Miller, 1996 by Wilhelm Goebel, 1997 by Robert Hautman, 1998 by Robert Steiner, 1999 by Adam Grimm.

No. RW1 used is valued with handstamp or manuscript cancel, though technically it was illegal to deface the stamp. Beginning with No. RW2 the used value is for stamp with signature. Plate number blocks of six have selvage on two sides.

Hunting permit stamps are valid from July 1 - June 30. Stamps have been made available prior to the date of validity, and stamps are sold through the philatelic agency after the period of validity has passed.

Catalogue values for all unused stamps in this section are for never-hinged items.

Department of Agriculture

Mallards
Alighting — HP1

Engraved: Flat Plate Printing
Issued in panes of 28 subjects.

1934   Unwmk.   Perf. 11
Inscribed "Void after June 30, 1935"

RW1 HP1	$1 blue		750.	125.
	Hinged		350.	
	No gum		160.	
	P# block of 6		11,500.	
a.	Imperf., pair		—	
b.	Vert. pair, imperf. horiz.		—	

Used value is for stamp with handstamp or manuscript cancel.
It is possible that No. RW1a is No. RW1b with vertical perfs. removed. Both varieties probably are printer's waste since copies exist with gum on front or without gum.

1935   Inscribed "Void after June 30, 1936"

RW2	$1 Canvasbacks Taking to Flight	675.	140.
	Hinged	375.	
	No gum	190.	
	P# block of 6	8,750.	

1936   Inscribed "Void after June 30, 1937"

RW3	$1 Canada Geese in Flight	325.	75.00
	Hinged	190.	
	No gum	95.	
	P# block of 6	3,000.	

1937   Inscribed "Void after June 30, 1938"

RW4	$1 Scaup Ducks Taking to Flight	275.	57.50
	Hinged	150.	
	No gum	75.	
	P# block of 6	2,250.	

1938   Inscribed "Void after June 30, 1939"

RW5	$1 Pintail Drake and Hen Alighting	350.	57.50
	Hinged	190.	
	No gum	75.	
	P# block of 6	2,600.	

Department of the Interior

Green-winged
Teal — HP2

1939   Inscribed "Void after June 30, 1940"

RW6 HP2	$1 chocolate	200.	45.00
	Hinged	110.	
	No gum	50.	
	P# block of 6	1,900.	

1940   Inscribed "Void after June 30, 1941"

RW7	$1 Black Mallards	200.	45.00
	Hinged	110.	
	No gum	50.	
	P# block of 6	1,800.	

1941   Inscribed "Void after June 30, 1942"

RW8	$1 Family of Ruddy Ducks	200.	45.00
	Hinged	110.	
	No gum	50.	
	P# block of 6	1,800.	

1942   Inscribed "Void after June 30, 1943"

RW9	$1 Baldpates	200.	45.00
	Hinged	110.	
	No gum	50.	
	P# block of 6	1,800.	

1943   Inscribed "Void After June 30, 1944"

RW10	$1 Wood Ducks	75.00	40.
	Hinged	50.00	
	No gum	42.50	
	P# block of 6	625.00	

1944   Inscribed "Void after June 30, 1945"

RW11	$1 White-fronted Geese	87.50	27.50
	Hinged	50.00	
	No gum	32.50	
	P# block of 6	650.00	

1945   Inscribed "Void after June 30, 1946"

RW12	$1 Shoveller Ducks in Flight	60.00	25.00
	Hinged	35.00	
	No gum	27.50	
	P# block of 6	425.00	

1946   Inscribed "Void after June 30, 1947"

RW13	$1 red brown Redhead Ducks	45.00	16.00
	No gum	18.00	
	P# block of 6	300.00	
a.	$1 bright rose pink	—	

1947   Inscribed "Void after June 30, 1948"

RW14	$1 Snow Geese	45.00	16.00
	No gum	18.00	
	P# block of 6	300.00	

1948   Inscribed "Void after June 30, 1949"

RW15	$1 Buffleheads in Flight	50.00	16.00
	No gum	21.00	
	P# block of 6	350.00	

Goldeneye
Ducks — HP3

1949   Inscribed "Void after June 30, 1950"

RW16 HP3	$2 bright green	60.00	14.00
	No gum	22.50	
	P# block of 6	375.00	

1950   Inscribed "Void after June 30, 1951"

RW17	$2 Trumpeter Swans in Flight	75.00	11.00
	No gum	25.00	
	P# block of 6	500.00	

1951   Inscribed "Void after June 30, 1952"

RW18	$2 Gadwall Ducks	75.00	11.00
	No gum	25.00	
	P# block of 6	500.00	

1952   Inscribed "Void after June 30, 1953"

RW19	$2 Harlequin Ducks	75.00	11.00
	No gum	25.00	
	P# block of 6	500.00	

1953   Inscribed "Void after June 30, 1954"

RW20	$2 Blue-winged Teal	75.00	11.00
	No gum	25.00	
	P# block of 6	500.00	

1954   Inscribed "Void after June 30, 1955"

RW21	$2 Ring-necked Ducks	75.00	10.50
	No gum	25.00	
	P# block of 6	500.00	

1955   Inscribed "Void after June 30, 1956"

RW22	$2 Blue Geese	75.00	10.50
	No gum	25.00	
	P# block of 6	500.00	
a.	Back inscription inverted	—	

1956   Inscribed "Void after June 30, 1957"

RW23	$2 American Merganser	75.00	10.50
	No gum	25.00	
	P# block of 6	500.00	

1957   Inscribed "Void after June 30, 1958"
RW24 $2 *American Eiders*   75.00   10.50
     No gum   25.00
     P# block of 6   500.00
  a. Back inscription inverted   —

1958   Inscribed "Void after June 30, 1959"
RW25 $2 *Canada Geese*   75.00   10.50
     No gum   25.00
     P# block of 6   475.00

Labrador Retriever Carrying Mallard Drake — HP4

Giori Press Printing
Issued in panes of 30 subjects

1959   Inscribed "Void after June 30, 1960"
RW26 HP4 $3 blue, ocher & black   95.00   11.00
     No gum   35.00
     P# block of 4   475.00
  a. Back inscription inverted   —

Redhead Ducks — HP5

1960   Inscribed "Void after June 30, 1961"
RW27 HP5 $3 red brown, dark blue & bister   80.00   10.50
     No gum   35.00
     P# block of 4   400.00

1961   Inscribed "Void after June 30, 1962"
RW28 $3 *Mallard Hen and Ducklings*   85.00   10.50
     No gum   37.50
     P# block of 4   425.00

Pintail Drakes Coming in for Landing — HP6

1962   Inscribed "Void after June 30, 1963"
RW29 HP6 $3 dark blue, dark red brown & black   95.00   10.50
     No gum   55.00
     P# block of 4   450.00

1963   Inscribed "Void after June 30, 1964"
RW30 $3 *Pair of Brant Landing*   95.00   10.50
     No gum   55.00
     P# block of 4   450.00

1964   Inscribed "Void after June 30, 1965"
RW31 $3 *Hawaiian Nene Geese*   95.00   10.50
     No gum   55.00
     P# block of 6   2,100.

1965   Inscribed "Void after June 30, 1966"
RW32 $3 *Three Canvasback Drakes*   95.00   10.50
     No gum   55.00
     P# block of 4   475.00

Whistling Swans — HP7

1966   Inscribed "Void after June 30, 1967"
RW33 HP7 $3 multicolored   95.00   10.50
     No gum   55.00
     P# block of 4   475.00

1967   Inscribed "Void after June 30, 1968"
RW34 $3 *Old Squaw Ducks*   100.00   10.00
     No gum   55.00
     P# block of 4   475.00

1968   Inscribed "Void after June 30, 1969"
RW35 $3 *Hooded Mergansers*   57.50   10.00
     No gum   25.00
     P# block of 4   275.00

White-winged Scoters — HP8

1969   Inscribed "Void after June 30, 1970"
RW36 HP8 $3 multicolored   57.50   7.00
     No gum   25.00
     P# block of 4   260.00

1970   Engraved & Lithographed
     Inscribed "Void after June 30, 1971"
RW37 $3 *Ross's Geese*   62.50   7.00
     No gum   24.00
     P# block of 4   290.00

1971   Inscribed "Void after June 30, 1972"
RW38 $3 *Three Cinnamon Teal*   40.00   8.00
     No gum   21.00
     P# block of 4   190.00

1972   Inscribed "Void after June 30, 1973"
RW39 $5 *Emperor Geese*   25.00   7.00
     No gum   12.50
     P# block of 4   110.00

1973   Inscribed "Void after June 30, 1974"
RW40 $5 *Steller's Eiders*   21.00   7.00
     No gum   12.00
     P# block of 4   100.00

1974   Inscribed "Void after June 30, 1975"
RW41 $5 *Wood Ducks*   20.00   6.00
     No gum   9.50
     P# block of 4   85.00

1975   Inscribed "Void after June 30, 1976"
RW42 $5 *Canvasback Decoy, 3 Flying Canvasbacks*   15.00   6.00
     No gum   8.00
     P# block of 4   65.00

1976   Engr.
     Inscribed "Void after June 30, 1977"
RW43 $5 *Family of Canada Geese*   15.00   6.00
     No gum   7.50
     P# block of 4   60.00

1977   Litho. & Engr.
     Inscribed "Void after June 30, 1978"
RW44 $5 *Pair of Ross's Geese*   15.00   6.00
     No gum   7.50
     P# block of 4   60.00

Hooded Merganser Drake — HP9

1978   Inscribed "Void after June 30, 1979"
RW45 HP9 $5 multicolored   12.50   6.00
     No gum   7.50
     P# block of 4   55.00

1979   Inscribed "Void after June 30, 1980"
RW46 $7.50 *Green-winged Teal*   14.00   6.00
     No gum   8.00
     P# block of 4   57.50

1980   Inscribed "Void after June 30, 1981"
RW47 $7.50 *Mallards*   14.00   6.00
     No gum   8.00
     P# block of 4   57.50

1981   Inscribed "Void after June 30, 1982"
RW48 $7.50 *Ruddy Ducks*   14.00   6.00
     No gum   8.00
     P# block of 4   57.50

1982   Inscribed "Void after June 30, 1983"
RW49 $7.50 *Canvasbacks*   15.00   6.00
     No gum   8.00
     P# block of 4   60.00
  a. Orange and violet omitted   —

1983   Inscribed "Void after June 30, 1984"
RW50 $7.50 *Pintails*   15.00   6.00
     No gum   8.00
     P# block of 4   60.00

1984		Inscribed "Void after June 30, 1985"		
RW51	$7.50	Widgeons	15.00	6.00
		No gum	8.00	
		P# block of 4	62.50	

See Special Printings section that follows.

1985		Inscribed "Void after June 30, 1986"		
RW52	$7.50	Cinnamon teal	15.00	6.00
		No gum	8.00	
		P# block of 4	60.00	

1986		Inscribed "Void after June 30, 1987"		
RW53	$7.50	Fulvous whistling duck	15.00	6.00
		No gum	8.00	
		P# block of 4	60.00	
a.	Black omitted		3,750.	

1987			Perf. 11½x11	
	Inscribed "Void after June 30, 1988"			
RW54	$10	Redheads	15.00	9.00
		No gum	10.00	
		P# block of 4	62.50	

1988		Inscribed "Void after June 30, 1989"		
RW55	$10	Snow Goose	15.00	9.00
		No gum	10.00	
		P# block of 4	62.50	

1989		Inscribed "Void after June 30, 1990"		
RW56	$12.50	Lesser Scaup	19.00	10.00
		No gum	12.00	
		P# block of 4	77.50	

1990		Inscribed "Void after June 30, 1991"		
RW57	$12.50	Black Bellied Whistling Duck	19.00	10.00
		No gum	12.00	
		P# block of 4	77.50	
a.	Back inscription omitted		425.00	

The back inscription is on top of the gum so beware of copies with gum removed. Used examples of No. RW57a cannot exist.

King Eiders HP10

1991		Inscribed "Void after June 30, 1992"		
RW58 HP10	$15	**multicolored**	22.50	11.00
		No gum	15.00	
		P# block of 4	92.50	
a.	Black (engr.) omitted		8,500.	

1992		Inscribed "Void after June 30, 1993"		
RW59	$15	Spectacled Eider	22.50	11.00
		No gum	15.00	
		P# block of 4	92.50	

1993		Inscribed "Void after June 30, 1994"		
RW60	$15	Canvasbacks	22.50	11.00
		No gum	15.00	
		P# block of 4	92.50	
a.	Black (engr.) omitted		3,250.	

1994			Perf. 11¼x11	
	Inscribed "Void after June 30, 1995"			
RW61	$15	Red-breasted mergansers	22.50	11.00
		No gum	15.00	
		P# block of 4	92.50	

1995		Inscribed "Void after June 30, 1996"		
RW62	$15	Mallards	22.50	11.00
		No gum	15.00	
		P# block of 4	92.50	

1996		Inscribed "Void after June 30, 1997"		
RW63	$15	Surf Scoters	22.50	11.00
		No gum	15.00	
		P# block of 4	92.50	

1997		Inscribed "Void after June 30, 1998"		
RW64	$15	Canada Goose	22.50	11.00
		No gum	15.00	
		P# block of 4	92.50	

1998			Perf. 11¼	
	Inscribed "Void after June 30, 1999"			
RW65	$15	Barrow's Goldeneye	22.50	11.00
		No gum	15.00	
		P# block of 4	92.50	

Self-Adhesive
Die Cut Perf. 10

RW65A	$15	Barrow's Goldeneye	22.50	11.00

No. RW65 was sold in panes of 30. No. RW65A was sold in panes of 1. For No. RW65A value unused is for complete pane, used for a single.

1999		Inscribed "Void after June 30, 2000"		
RW66	$15	Greater Scaup	22.50	11.00
		No gum	15.00	
		P# block of 4	100.00	

Self-Adhesive
Die Cut Perf. 10

RW66A	$15	Greater Scaup	22.50	11.00

#RW66 was sold in panes of 30. #RW66A was sold in panes of 1. No. RW66A is valued unused as a complete pane and used as a single stamp.

2000			Perf. 11¼	
	Inscribed "Void after June 30, 2001"			
RW67	$15	Mottled Duck	22.50	11.00
		No gum	15.00	
		P# block of 4	100.00	

Self-Adhesive
Die Cut 10

RW67A	$15	Mottled Duck	22.50	11.00

No. RW67 was sold in panes of 20. No. RW66A was sold in panes of 1. No. RW67A is valued unused as a complete pane and used as a single stamp.

Beginning with No. RW13 there are various messages printed on the back of the sheet stamps.

No. RW21 and following issues are printed on dry, pregummed paper and the back inscription is printed on top of the gum.

SPECIAL PRINTING

After No. RW51 became void, fifteen uncut sheets of 120 (4 panes of 30 separated by gutters) were overprinted "1934-84" and "50th ANNIVERSARY" in the margins and auctioned by the U.S. Fish and Wildlife Service.

Bids were accepted from September 1 through November 1, 1985. Minimum bid for each sheet was $2,000. The face value of each sheet, had they still been valid, was $900. Each sheet also had the sheet number and pane position printed in the corner of each pane ("01 of 15-1," "01 of 15-2," etc.). Fourteen of the sheets were sold at this and one subsequent auction and one was donated to the Smithsonian.

An individual sheet could be broken up to create these identifiable collectibles: 4 margin overprint blocks of 10; cross gutter block of 4; 6 horizontal pairs with gutter between; 8 vertical pairs with gutter between.

Single stamps from the sheet cannot be distinguished from No. RW51. No used examples can exist.

RW51x	$7.50	Widgeons		

QUANTITIES ISSUED

RW1	635,001	RW33	1,805,341
RW2	448,204	RW34	1,934,697
RW3	603,623	RW35	1,837,139
RW4	783,039	RW36	2,072,108
RW5	1,002,715	RW37	2,420,244
RW6	1,111,561	RW38	2,445,977
RW7	1,260,810	RW39	2,184,343
RW8	1,439,967	RW40	2,094,414
RW9	1,383,629	RW41	2,214,056
RW10	1,169,352	RW42	2,237,126
RW11	1,487,029	RW43	2,170,194
RW12	1,725,505	RW44	2,196,774

RW13	2,016,841	RW45	2,216,621
RW14	1,722,677	RW46	2,090,155
RW15	2,127,603	RW47	2,045,114
RW16	1,954,734	RW48	1,907,120
RW17	1,903,644	RW49	1,926,253
RW18	2,167,767	RW50	1,867,998
RW19	2,296,628	RW51	1,913,861
RW20	2,268,446	RW52	1,780,636

RW21	2,184,550	RW53	1,794,484
RW22	2,369,940	RW54	1,663,270
RW23	2,332,014	RW55	1,402,096
RW24	2,355,190	RW56	1,415,882
RW25	2,176,425	RW57	1,408,373
RW26	1,626,115	RW58	1,423,374
RW27	1,725,634	RW59	1,347,393
RW28	1,344,236	RW60	1,402,569

RW29	1,147,212	RW61	1,471,751
RW30	1,448,191	RW62	1,539,622
RW31	1,573,155	RW63	
RW32	1,558,197	RW64	

STATE HUNTING PERMIT STAMPS

These stamps are used on licenses for hunting waterfowl (ducks, geese, swans) by states and Indian reservations. Stamps which include waterfowl along with a variety of other animals are listed here. Stamps for hunting birds that exclude waterfowl are not listed.

A number of states print stamps in sheets as well as in booklets. The booklets are sent to agents for issuing to hunters. Both varieties are listed. The major listing is given to the sheet stamp since it generally is available in larger quantities and has been the more popularly collected item. In some cases the stamp removed from a booklet, with no tabs or selvage, is identical to a single sheet stamp (see Rhode Island). In these cases the identifiable booklet stamp with tabs and selvage receives an unlettered listing. If the single booklet stamp can be identified by type of perforation or the existence of one or more straight edges, the item receives a lettered listing (see Oregon).

Governor's editions are sold at a premium over the license fee with proceeds intended to help waterfowl habitats. Only those which differ from the regular stamp are listed.

After the period of validity, a number of these stamps were sold at less than face value. This explains the low values on stamps such as Montana Nos. 30, 33, and Flathead Indian Reservation Nos. 2-10.

When used, most stamps are affixed to licenses and signed by the hunter. Values for used stamps are for copies off licenses and without tabs. Although used examples may be extremely scarce, they will always sell for somewhat less than unused examples (two-thirds of the unused value would be the upper limit).

David R. Torre helped the editors extensively in compiling the State Hunting Permit listings. Important references on state waterfowl hunting stamps include Torre's "Specialized Catalog of U. S. Non-pictorial Waterfowl Stamps," published by the American Revenue Association in 1995, E. L. Vanderford's "Checklist of State and Locally Issued Migratory Waterfowl Hunting Stamps," published in 1977, and the same author's 1973 "Handbook of Fish and Game Stamps." In-depth articles on various state and tribal issues by Torre have appeared in "The American Revenuer," the journal of the American Revenue Association.

ALABAMA
Printed in sheets of 10.
Stamps are numbered serially.

> **Catalogue values for all unused stamps in this section are for Never Hinged items.**

Artists: Barbara Keel, #1; Wayne Spradley, #2; Jack Deloney, #3; Joe Michelet, #4; John Lee, #5; William Morris, #6, 14; Larry Martin, #7; Danny W. Dorning, #8; Robert C. Knutson, #9, 16, 20; John Warr, #10; Elaine Byrd, #11; Steven Garst,

#12; Larry Chandler, #13; James Brantley, #15; Neil Blackwell, #17; Judith Huey, #18; E. Hatcher, #19; Eddie LeRoy, #21.

1979-99

1	$5	Wood ducks, rouletted	9.00	3.00
2	$5	Mallards, 1980	9.00	3.00
3	$5	Canada geese, 1981	9.00	3.00
4	$5	Green-winged teal, 1982	9.00	3.00
5	$5	Widgeons, 1983	9.00	3.00
6	$5	Buffleheads, 1984	10.00	3.00
7	$5	Wood ducks, 1985	13.00	3.00
8	$5	Canada geese, 1986	13.00	3.00
9	$5	Pintails, 1987	13.00	3.00
10	$5	Canvasbacks, 1988	10.00	3.00
11	$5	Hooded mergansers, 1989	9.00	3.00
12	$5	Wood ducks, 1990	9.00	2.50
13	$5	Redheads, 1991	9.00	2.50
14	$5	Cinnamon teal, 1992	9.00	2.50
15	$5	Green-winged teal, 1993	9.00	2.50
16	$5	Canvasbacks, 1994	9.00	2.50
17	$5	Canada geese, 1995	9.00	2.50
18	$5	Wood ducks, 1996	9.00	2.50
19	$5	Snow goose, 1997	9.00	2.50
20	$5	Barrow's goldeneye, 1998	9.00	2.50
21	$5	Redheads, 1999	8.00	2.50

ALASKA
Printed in sheets of 30.
Stamps are numbered serially on reverse. Booklet pane stamps printed in panes of 5.

> **Catalogue values for all unused stamps in this section are for Never Hinged items.**

1985 Alaska Waterfowl Stamp

Artist: Daniel Smith, #1; James Meger, #2; Carl Branson, #3; Jim Beaudoin, #4; Richard Timm, #5; Louis Frisino, #6; Ronald Louque, #7; Fred Thomas, #8; Ed Tussey, #9; George Lockwood, #10, 13; Cynthia Fisher, #11; Wilhelm Goebel, #12; Robert Steiner, #14; Sherrie Russell Meline, #15.

1985-99

1	$5	Emperor geese	10.00	3.00
2	$5	Steller's eiders, 1986	10.00	3.00
3	$5	Spectacled eiders, perforated, 1987	10.00	
a.		Bklt. single, rouletted, with tab	10.00	2.50
4	$5	Trumpeter swans, perforated, 1988	10.00	
a.		Bklt. single, rouletted, with tab	10.00	2.50

5	$5	Barrow's goldeneyes, perforated, 1989	8.50	
a.		Bklt. single, rouletted, with tab	10.00	2.50
b.		Governor's edition	125.00	

No. 5b was sold in full panes through a sealed bid auction.

6	$5	Old squaws, perforated, 1990	8.50	
a.		Bklt. single, rouletted, with tab	9.50	2.50
7	$5	Snow geese, perforated, 1991	8.25	
a.		Bklt. single, rouletted, with tab	9.50	2.50
8	$5	Canvasbacks, perforated, 1992	8.25	
a.		Bklt. single, rouletted, with tab	9.00	2.50
9	$5	Tule white front geese, perforated, 1993	8.25	
a.		Bklt. single, rouletted, with tab	9.00	2.50
10	$5	Harlequin ducks, perforated, 1994	8.25	
a.		Bklt. single, rouletted, with tab	9.00	2.50
b.		Governor's edition	90.00	
11	$5	Pacific brant, perforated, 1995	8.25	
a.		Bklt. single, rouletted, with tab	8.50	2.50
12	$5	Canada geese, 1996	8.25	
a.		Bklt. single, rouletted, with tab	9.00	2.50
13	$5	King eiders, 1997	8.25	
a.		Bklt. single, rouletted, with tab	8.50	2.50
14	$5	Barrow's goldeneye, 1998	8.25	
a.		Bklt. single, with tab	8.50	2.50
15	$5	Pintail, 1999	7.50	
a.		Bklt. single, with tab	8.50	2.50

ARIZONA
Printed in booklet panes of 5 with tab and in sheets of 30.
Stamps are numbered serially.

> **Catalogue values for all unused stamps in this section are for Never Hinged items.**

Artists: Daniel Smith, #1; Sherrie Russell Meline, #2, 6-7, 9, 11-13; Robert Steiner, #3; Ted Blaylock, #4; Brian Jarvi, #5; Harry Adamson, #8, Larry Hayden, #10.

1987-99

1	$5.50	Pintails, perf. 4 sides	10.00	
a.		Bklt. single, perf. 3 sides, with tab	10.00	3.00
2	$5.50	Green-winged teal, perf. 4 sides, 1988	10.00	
a.		Bklt. single, perf. 3 sides, with tab	10.00	3.00
3	$5.50	Cinnamon teal, perf. 4 sides, 1989	9.00	
a.		Bklt. single, perf. 3 sides, with tab	9.00	2.50
b.	$5.50 +$50	Governor's edition	65.00	

4	$5.50 Canada geese, perf. 4 sides, *1990*	9.00	
a.	Bklt. single, perf. 3 sides, with tab	9.50	2.50
b.	$5.50 +$50 Governor's edition	72.50	
5	$5.50 Blue-winged teal, perf. 4 sides, *1991*	8.00	
a.	Bklt. single, perf. 3 sides, with tab	9.00	2.50
b.	$55.50 Governor's edition	72.50	
6	$5.50 Buffleheads, perf. 4 sides, *1992*	8.00	
a.	Bklt. single, perf. 3 sides, with tab	9.00	2.50
b.	$55.50 Governor's edition	72.50	
7	$5.50 Mexican ducks, perf. 4 sides, *1993*	8.00	
a.	Bklt. single, perf. 3 sides, with tab	9.00	2.50
b.	$55.50 Governor's edition	72.50	
8	$5.50 Mallards, perf. 4 sides, *1994*	8.00	
a.	Bklt. single, perf. 3 sides, with tab	9.00	2.50
b.	$55.50 Governor's edition	72.50	
9	$5.50 Widgeon, perf. 4 sides, *1995*	8.00	
a.	Bklt. single, perf. 3 sides, with tab	9.00	2.50
b.	$55.50 Governor's edition	72.50	
10	$5.50 Canvasbacks, perf. 4 sides, *1996*	8.00	
a.	Bklt. single, perf 3 sides, with tab	9.00	2.50
b.	$55.50 Governor's edition	75.00	
11	$5.50 Gadwalls, *1997*	8.00	
a.	Bklt. single, perf 3 sides, with tab	9.00	2.50
b.	$55.50 Governor's edition	75.00	
12	$5.50 Wood duck, *1998*	8.00	
a.	Bklt. single, perf 3 sides, with tab	9.00	2.50
b.	$55.50 Governor's edition	75.00	
13	$5.50 Snow goose, *1999*	7.50	
a.	Bklt. single, perf. 3 sides, with tab	8.50	2.50
b.	$55.50 Governor's edition	75.00	

ARKANSAS

Imperforate varieties of these stamps exist in large quantities. Imperforate copies of Nos. 1 and 2 were sold by the state for $1 each.

No. 1 printed in sheets and booklet panes of 30, others in sheets and booklet panes of 10. Stamps are numbered serially on reverse.

> **Catalogue values for all unused stamps in this section are for Never Hinged items.**

Artists: Lee LeBlanc, #1; Maynard Reece, #2, 8; David Maass, #3, 10; Larry Hayden, #4, 15; Ken Carlson, #5, 13; John P. Cowan, #6; Robert Bateman, #7; Phillip Crowe, #9, 16; Daniel Smith, #11, 14; Jim Hautman, #12, 19; L. Chandler, #17; John Dearman, #18.

1981-99

1	$5.50 Mallards	37.50	12.00
	Booklet single with top tab, Nos. 110,001-200,000 on back	47.50	
2	$5.50 Wood ducks, *1982*	37.50	9.00
3	$5.50 Green-winged teal, *1983*	55.00	12.00
4	$5.50 Pintails, *1984*	22.50	5.00
5	$5.50 Mallards, *1985*	13.00	2.50
6	$5.50 Black swamp mallards, *1986*	11.00	2.50
7	$7 Wood ducks, *1987*	11.00	2.50

Stamps like Nos. 7 and 8 with $5.50 face values were sold following an order of the state Supreme Court restoring the fee level of 1986. The stamps were sold after the 1988 season had ended. Value, $11 each.

8	$7 Pintails, *1988*	10.00	2.50
	See footnote following No. 7.		
9	$7 Mallards, *1989*	10.00	2.50
10	$7 Black ducks & mallards, *1990*	10.00	2.50
11	$7 Sulphur river widgeons, *1991*	10.00	2.50
12	$7 Shirey Bay shovelers, *1992*	10.00	2.50
13	$7 Grand prairie mallards, *1993*	10.00	2.50
14	$7 Canada goose, *1994*	10.00	2.50
15	$7 White River mallards, *1995*	10.00	2.50
16	$7 Mallards, black labrador, *1996*	10.00	2.00
17	$7 Labrador retriever, mallards, *1997*	10.00	2.00
18	$7 Labrador retriever, mallards, *1998*	10.00	2.00
19	$7 Wood duck, *1999*	9.00	2.00

CALIFORNIA
Honey Lake Waterfowl Stamps

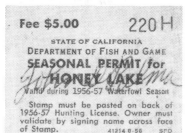

Required to hunt waterfowl at Honey Lake. Valid for a full season. Stamps are rouletted. Used values are for signed copies. Unsigned stamps without gum probably were used. Values for these stamps are higher than used values, but lower than values shown for gummed unused stamps.

1956-86

A1	$5 black, *1956-1957*		—
A2	$5 black, *blue green, 1957-1958*		—
A3	$5 black, *dark yellow, 1958-1959*		—
A4	$5 black, *dark yellow, 1959-1960*	1,000.	425.00
A5	$5 black, *1960-1961*		950.00
A6	$5 black, *bluish green, 1961-1962*	—	950.00
A7	$5 black, *dark yellow, 1962-1963*		475.00
A8	$5 black, *1963-1964*		350.00
A9	$6.50 black, *pink, 1964-1965*	1,250.	325.00
A10	$6.50 black, *1965-1966*		300.00
A11	$6.50 black, *yellow, Nos. 1-700, printer's information at bottom right, 1966-1967*		300.00
a.	Serial Nos. 701-1050, no printer's information		4,250.
A12	$10 black, *pink, 1967-1968*	—	300.00
A13	$10 black, *1968-1969*		300.00
A14	$10 black, *green, 1969-1970*	—	350.00
A15	$15 black, *dark yellow, 1970-1971*	—	425.00
A16	$15 black, *pink, 1971-1972*		1,500.
A17	$15 black, *blue, 1972-1973*		1,900.
A18	$15 black, *blue, 1973-1974*		
A19	$15 black, *pink, 1974-1975*	52.50	25.00
A20	$15 black, *green, 1975-1976*	125.00	35.00
A21	$15 black, *light yellow, 1976-1977*	125.00	35.00
A22	$20 black, *blue, 1977-1978*	125.00	35.00
A23	$20 blk, *light yel brown, 1978-1979*	125.00	35.00
A24	$20 black, *light yellow, 1979-1980*	125.00	35.00
A25	$15 black, *light blue, 1980-1981*	100.00	30.00
A26	$20 black, *light yellow, 1981-1982*		—
A27	$20 black, *pink, 1982-1983*	85.00	30.00
A28	$20 black, *light green, 1983-1984*	45.00	25.00
A29	$20 black, *dark yellow, 1984-1985*	42.50	25.00
A30	$20 black, *light blue, 1985-1986*	37.50	20.00

Eighteen $5 black on dark yellow permit stamps were sold for hunting at the state-owned and operated Madeline Plains waterfowl management area for the 1956-57 season. No examples have been recorded.

Statewide Hunting License Validation Stamps

Fees are for resident, junior and non-resident hunters. "No fee" stamps were for disabled veterans. Stamps with special serial numbers for state officials are known for some years. Nos. 2A1-2A3 imperf on 3 sides, rouletted at top. Others die cut.

Stamps are numbered serially.

Used values are for written-upon copies. Starting with No. 2A4, unused values are for stamps on backing paper.

1962-1963

2A1	$4 black	475.00	7.00
a.	Ovptd. "NO FEE"	475.00	300.00
2A2	$1 black, *yellow*	1,300.	75.00
2A3	$25 black, *green*	1,900.	150.00

CALIFORNIA HUNTING LICENSE
H 31022 -4
(Print this number on tags)
Resident $4.00
Expires June 30, 1964

Date License Issued
Deer Tag No.
Bear Tag No.
Pheasant Tag No.

CALIFORNIA HUNTING LICENSE
H 27286 -03
(Print this number on tags)
RESIDENT $4.00
Expires June 30, 1971

Date License Issued
Deer Tag No.
Bear Tag No.
Lion Tag No.
Shipping Tag No.

No. 2A25

1963-1964
2A4	$4 black, *green*	—	3.00
a.	Ovptd. "NO FEE"	—	20.00
2A5	$1 black, *gray*	—	20.00
2A6	$25 black, *yellow orange*		300.00

1964-1965
2A7	$4 black, *pink*	30.00	1.00
a.	Ovptd. "NO FEE"	550.00	275.00
2A8	$1 black, *yellow brown*	225.00	25.00
2A9	$25 black, *dark gray*		70.00

1965-1966
2A10	$4 black, *gray*	25.00	1.00
a.	Ovptd. "NO FEE"		25.00
2A11	$1 black, *yellow gray*		25.00
2A12	$25 black, *ivory*		75.00

1966-1967
2A13	$4 black, *salmon*	25.00	1.00
a.	Ovptd. "NO FEE"		650.00
2A14	$1 black, *lt blue*	75.00	10.00
2A15	$25 black, *burgundy*		65.00

1967-1968
2A16	$4 black, *yellow*	20.00	1.00
a.	Ovptd. "NO FEE"		600.00
2A17	$1 black, *green*	45.00	5.00
a.	black, *yellow gray*		—
2A18	$25 black, *brown*	75.00	25.00

1968-1969
2A19	$4 black, *pink*	55.00	1.00
a.	Ovptd. "NO FEE"		650.00
2A20	$1 black, *blue gray*	175.00	20.00
2A21	$25 black, *light orange*		85.00

1969-1970
2A22	$4 black	55.00	1.00
a.	Ovptd. "NO FEE"		575.00
2A23	$1 black, *dark pink*	175.00	20.00
2A24	$25 black, *light yellow*	70.00	25.00

1970-1971
2A25	$4 black, *manila*	70.00	2.00
a.	Ovptd. "NO FEE"	1,300.	950.00
2A26	$1 black, *blue gray*	75.00	10.00
2A27	$25 black, *gray brown*	100.00	25.00

1971-1972
2A28	$4 black, *green*	45.00	1.00
a.	Ovptd. "NO FEE"		600.00
b.	Ovptd. "DISABLED VETERANS/NO FEE"		750.00
2A29	$1 black, *lavender*		20.00
2A30	$25 black, *peach*	275.00	35.00

1972-1973
2A31	$6 black, *pink*		1.00
a.	Ovptd. "DISABLED VETERANS/NO FEE"		750.00
2A32	$2 black, *light yellow*		30.00
2A33	$35 black, *lavender*	225.00	

1973-1974
2A34	$6 black, *blue*		1.00
a.	Ovptd. "DISABLED VETERANS/NO FEE"		750.00
2A35	$2 black, *lavender*	175.00	20.00
2A36	$35 black, *gray*	275.00	35.00

1974-1975
2A37	$6 black, *green*	35.00	1.00
a.	Ovptd. "DISABLED VETERANS/NO FEE"		800.00
2A38	$2 black, *orange*		20.00
2A39	$35 black, *reddish purple*	175.00	25.00

1975-1976
2A40	$10 red brown, *brown*	40.00	1.00
a.	Ovptd. "DISABLED VETERANS/NO FEE"	—	800.00
2A41	$2 black, *dark red*	80.00	20.00
2A42	$35 black, *yellow*	85.00	25.00

1976-1977
2A43	$10 black, *blue*	30.00	1.00
a.	Ovptd. "DISABLED VETERANS/NO FEE"		900.00
2A44	$2 black, *gray violet*	100.00	20.00
a.	Inscibed "Deer Tag No." instead of "Bear Tag No."	—	
2A45	$35 black, *lavender*	85.00	25.00

1977-1978
2A46	$10 black, *red orange*	30.00	1.00
a.	Ovptd. "DISABLED VETERANS/NO FEE"		850.00

2A47	$2 black, *yellow green*	95.00	25.00
2A48	$35 black, *pink*	95.00	

1978-1979
2A49	$10 black, *yellow*	40.00	1.50
a.	Ovptd. "DISABLED VETERANS/NO FEE"		850.00
2A50	$2 black, *red*	80.00	20.00
2A51	$35 black, *light brown*	85.00	

1979-1980
2A52	$10 black, *red*	30.00	1.00
a.	Ovptd. "DISABLED VETERANS/NO FEE"		900.00
2A53	$2 black, *yellow green*	80.00	20.00
2A54	$35 black, *dark blue*	85.00	

1980-1981
2A55	$10.25 black, *blue*	30.00	1.00
a.	Ovptd. "DISABLED VETERANS/NO FEE"		1,100.
2A56	$2 black, *light brown*	75.00	15.00
2A57	$36.25 black, *tan*	75.00	25.00

1981-1982
2A58	$11.50 black, *dark green*	30.00	1.00
2A59	$2.25 black, *blue*	75.00	20.00
2A60	$40 black, *gray*	200.00	

1982-1983
2A61	$12.50 black, *pink*	30.00	1.00
2A62	$2.50 black, *brown*	75.00	20.00
2A63	$43.50 black, *orange*	140.00	

1983-1984
2A64	$13.25 black, *blue*	50.00	1.00
2A65	$2.75 black, *purple*	150.00	20.00
2A66	$46.50 black, *green*	175.00	

1984-1985
2A67	$13.25 black, *yellow*	50.00	1.00
2A68	$2.75 black, *green*	150.00	20.00
2A69	$49.25 black, *brown*	175.00	

1985-1986
2A70	$14 black, *blue*	50.00	1.00
2A71	$3.50 black, *yellow*	150.00	20.00
2A72	$51.75 black, *purple*	175.00	

1986-1987
2A73	$18.50 black, *green*		1.00
2A74	$4.50 black, *dark blue*		15.00

1987-1988
2A76	$17.50 black, *dark blue*		1.00
2A77	$4.50 black, *purple*		15.00

1988-1989
2A79	$19.25 black, *tan*		1.00
2A80	$5 black, *yellow*		15.00

1989-1990
2A82	$19.75 black, *blue gray*		1.00
2A83	$5 black, *dark green*		15.00

1990-1991
2A85	$21.50 black, *reddish gray*		1.00
2A86	$5.50 black, *yellow*		15.00
2A87	$73 black, *pink*		25.00

1991-1992
2A88	$23.10 black, *lime green*		1.00
2A89	$5.50 black, *bluish purple*		15.00
2A90	$79.80 black, *brown*		25.00

1992-1993
2A91	$24.15 black, *yellow*	—	1.00
2A92	$5.80 black, *greenish gold*		15.00
2A93	$83.75 black, *mauve*	—	25.00

1993-1994
CALIFORNIA
JUNIOR HUNTING
LICENSE $5.80
NONREFUNDABLE

H372223-07

1st Deer Tag No.

2nd Deer Tag No.
8-26

DATE ISSUED
Exp. June 30, 1994

1993-1994
2A94	$24.40 black & white, *green*		1.00
2A95	$5.80 black & white, *light blue*		15.00

1994-1995
2A97	$24.95 black & white, *pale yellow*		1.00
2A98	$6.05 black & white, *lavender*		15.00
2A99	$86.70 black & white, *gray*		25.00

1996-1997
2A100	$25.45 black, *gray brown*		1.00
2A101	$6.30 black, *pink*		15.00
2A102	$88.70 black, *pale blue*		25.00

Statewide Waterfowl Issues
Nos. 1-24 printed in booklet panes of five, No. 25 in pane of 4.

Issues through 1978 are die cut and self-adhesive. Starting with the 1979 issue, stamps are rouletted. Stamps are numbered serially.

> Catalogue values for all unused stamps in this section are for Never Hinged items.

Artists: Paul Johnson, #1-8; Ken Michaelson, #9; Walter Wolfe, #10-11; Robert Steiner, #12, 18-20, 26-30; Robert Richert, #13; Charles Allen, #14; Robert Montanucci, #15; Richard Wilson, #16; Sherrie Russell Meline, #17, 23; Ronald Louque, #21; Larry Hayden, #22; Richard Clifton, #24-25.

1971-99
1	$1	Pintails	725.00	65.00
2	$1	Canvasbacks, *1972*	2,750.	150.00
3	$1	Mallards, *1973*	13.50	2.50
4	$1	White-fronted geese, *1974*	3.00	2.50
5	$1	Green-winged teal, backing paper with red wavy lines, *1975*	35.00	8.00
		Waxy backing paper without lines	140.00	

The gum bleeds through the stamp with red wavy lines resulting in a spotted or blotchy effect. Little or no gum bleeds through on stamps with waxy backing paper.

6	$1	Widgeons, *1976*	16.00	2.50
7	$1	Cinnamon teal, *1977*	45.00	9.00
8	$5	Cinnamon teal, *1978*	9.00	2.50
9	$5	Hooded mergansers, *1978*	125.00	15.00
10	$5	Wood ducks, *1979*	8.00	2.50
11	$5	Pintails, *1980*	8.00	2.50
12	$5	Canvasbacks, *1981*	9.00	2.50
13	$5	Widgeons, *1982*	9.00	2.50
14	$5	Green-winged teal, *1983*	9.00	2.50
15	$7.50	Mallard decoy, *1984*	11.00	2.50
16	$7.50	Ring-necked ducks, *1985*	11.00	2.50
17	$7.50	Canada goose, *1986*	11.00	3.00
18	$7.50	Redheads, *1987*	11.00	3.00
19	$7.50	Mallards, *1988*	11.00	3.00
20	$7.50	Cinnamon teal, *1989*	11.00	3.00
21	$7.50	Canada goose, *1990*	11.00	3.00
22	$7.50	Gadwalls, *1991*	11.00	3.00
23	$7.90	White-fronted goose, *1992*	11.00	3.00
24	$10.50	Pintails, *1993*	13.00	4.00

Rouletted Horiz.
25	$10.50	Wood duck, *1994*	13.00	4.00

Perf. Vertically
Birds in flight, denomination at: b, UL. c, UR. d, LL. e, LR.

26	$10.50	Snow geese, booklet pane of 4, #b.-e., *1995*	60.00	
a.		Souvenir sheet of 4, #b.-e. (decorative border)	125.00	
b.-e.		Booklet single, each	14.00	4.00

Stamps in No. 26a are perfed on all four sides.

Perf. Horizontally
27	$10.50	Mallards, *1996*	13.00	2.50

Issued in panes of 4.

28	$10.50	Pintails, *1997*	13.00	2.50
29	$10.50	Green-winged teal, pair, *1998*	28.00	
a.-b.		a, Female, b, Male, each	14.00	2.50

No. 29 issued in strips of 4 stamps.

30	$10.50	Wood duck, pair, *1999*	26.00	
a.-b.		a, Male, b, Male and female, each	13.00	2.50

No. 30 issued in strips of 2 pairs.

COLORADO
North Central Goose Stamp
Used in an area extending from Ft. Collins to approximately 50 miles east of the city.

NORTH CENTRAL GOOSE PERMIT NO. 13202
COLORADO WILDLIFE COMMISSION
$2.00
1973
This permit not valid unless signed above and attached to the front lower right corner of a current small game license.

Illustration reduced.

1973
A1	$2 black	—	—

No. A1 is die cut and self-adhesive. Unused copies have glassine backing.

Statewide Issues

Printed in booklet panes of 5 and panes of 30.
Stamps are numbered serially.
Imperforate varieties of these stamps are printer's proofs.

Catalogue values for all unused stamps in this section are for Never Hinged items.

Artists: Robert Steiner, #1-2; Charles Allen, #3; Dan Andrews, #4; Sarah Woods, #5; Cynthie Fisher, #6, 9-10; Bill Border, #7; Gerald G. Putt, #8.

1990-99

1	$5 Canada geese	12.00	
	Bklt. single, with tab, Nos. 80,001-150,000	12.50	3.00
a.	$5 +$50 Governor's edition	60.00	
2	$5 Mallards, 1991	16.00	
	Bklt. single, with tab, Nos. 80,001-150,000	16.00	3.00
a.	$5 +$50 Governor's edition	60.00	
3	$5 Pintails, 1992	8.50	
	Bklt. single, with tab, Nos. 80,001-150,000	9.00	3.00
a.	$5 +$50 Governor's edition	60.00	
4	$5 Green-winged teal, 1993	8.50	
	Bklt. single, with tab, Nos. 80,001-150,000	9.50	3.00
a.	$5 +$50 Governor's edition	60.00	
5	$5 Wood ducks, 1994	8.50	
	Bklt. single, with tab	9.00	2.50
6	$5 Buffleheads, 1995	8.00	
	Bklt. single, with tab	9.00	2.50
7	$5 Cinnamon teal, 1996	8.00	
	Bklt. single, with tab and top selvage	9.00	2.50
8	$5 Widgeons, gold text, 1997	8.00	
	Bklt. single, with tab and top selvage, text in black & white	8.50	2.50
9	$5 Redheads, 1998	8.00	
	Bklt. single, with tab and top selvage	8.50	2.50
10	$5 Blue-winged teal, 1999	7.50	
a.	Blkt. single, with tab and top selvage	8.00	2.50

CONNECTICUT

Printed in booklet panes of 10 and sheets of 30.
Stamps are numbered serially.
Imperforate varieties are proofs.

Catalogue values for all unused stamps in this section are for Never Hinged items.

Artists: Thomas Hirata, #1; Robert Leslie, #2; Phillip Crowe, #3; Keith Mueller, #4, 7; Robert Steiner, #5; Joe Hautman, #6.

1993-99

1	$5 Black ducks	8.50	3.00
	Booklet pane pair with L & R selvage, Nos. 51,001-81,000	17.00	
a.	Sheet of 4	60.00	
b.	$5 +$50 Governor's edition	75.00	
2	$5 Canvasbacks, 1994	8.00	3.00
	Booklet pair with L & R selvage, Nos. 53,000-up	17.00	
a.	Sheet of 4	35.00	
3	$5 Mallards, 1995	8.00	3.00
	Booklet pair with L & R selvage	17.00	
4	$5 Old squaw ducks, 1996	8.00	3.00
	Booklet pair with L & R selvage	17.00	
5	$5 Green-winged teal, 1997	8.50	3.00
a.	$5 +$50 Governor's edition	75.00	
6	$5 Mallards, 1998	8.50	3.00
7	$5 Canada geese, 1999	8.00	3.00
a.	$5 +$50 Governor's edition	75.00	

DELAWARE

Printed in sheets of 10.
Starting in 1991, a portion of the printing is numbered serially on the reverse.

Catalogue values for all unused stamps in this section are for Never Hinged items.

Artists: Ned Mayne, #1; Charles Rowe, #2; Lois Butler, #3; John Green, #4; Nolan Haan, #5; Don Breyfogle, #6; Robert Leslie, #7, 10; Bruce Langton, #8; Jim Hautman, #9; Francis Sweet, #11; Ronald Louque, #12; Richard Clifton, #13, 17, 19; Robert Metropulos, #14; Louis Frisino, #15; Michael Ashman, #16; Jeffrey Klinefelter, #18; Russ Duerksen, #20.

1980-99

1	$5 Black ducks	85.00	20.00
2	$5 Snow geese, 1981	70.00	20.00
3	$5 Canada geese, 1982	70.00	20.00
4	$5 Canvasbacks, 1983	35.00	10.00
5	$5 Mallards, 1984	15.00	5.00
6	$5 Pintail, 1985	12.00	3.00
7	$5 Widgeons, 1986	11.00	3.00
8	$5 Redheads, 1987	11.00	3.00
9	$5 Wood ducks, 1988	9.00	3.00
10	$5 Buffleheads, 1989	9.00	3.00
11	$5 Green-winged teal, 1990	9.00	3.00
a.	$5 +$50 Governor's edition	85.00	
12	$5 Hooded merganser, no serial number on reverse, 1991	9.00	
	With serial number on reverse	11.00	3.00
13	$5 Blue-winged teal, no serial number on reverse, 1992	8.00	
	With serial number on reverse	8.50	2.50
14	$5 Goldeneye, no serial number on reverse, 1993	8.00	
	With serial number on reverse	8.50	2.50
15	$5 Blue goose, no serial number on reverse, 1994	8.00	
	With serial number on reverse	8.50	2.50
16	($6) Scaup, no serial number on reverse, 1995	8.00	
	With serial number on reverse	8.50	2.50
17	$6 Gadwall, no serial number on reverse, 1996	8.00	
	With serial number on reverse	8.50	2.50
18	$6 White-winged scoter, no serial number on reverse, 1997	8.00	
	With serial number on reverse	8.50	2.50
19	$6 Blue-winged teal, 1998	8.00	2.50
20	$6 Tundra swan, 1999	8.00	

FLORIDA

#1-7 issued in booklet panes of 5. Nos. 8-19 in sheets of 10. No. 20 in sheet of 12.
Stamps are numbered serially and rouletted. Serial numbers for stamps with survey tabs attached end in -04.

Catalogue values for all unused stamps in this section are for Never Hinged items.

Illustration reduced.

Artists: Bob Binks, #1, 7; Ernest Simmons, #2; Clark Sullivan, #3; Lee Cable, #4; Heiner Hertling, #5; John Taylor, #6; Robert Steiner, #8; Ronald Louque, #9-10; J. Byron Test, #11; Ben Test, #12; Richard Hansen, #13; Richard Clifton, #14; John Mogus, #15; Antonie Rossini, #16; Kenneth Nanney, #17; Wally Makuchal, #18; M. Frase, #19; Brian Blight, #20; John Harris, #21.

1979-99

1	$3.25 Green-winged teal	150.00	20.00
	With tab	175.00	
2	$3.25 Pintails, 1980	16.00	5.00
	With tab	24.00	

3	$3.25 Widgeon, 1981	15.00	5.00
	With tab	24.00	
4	$3.25 Ring-necked ducks, 1982	24.00	5.00
	With tab	35.00	
5	$3.25 Buffleheads, 1983	50.00	5.00
	With tab	55.00	
6	$3.25 Hooded merganser, 1984	11.00	3.50
	With tab	17.50	
7	$3.25 Wood ducks, 1985	11.00	3.50
	With tab	12.00	
8	$3 Canvasbacks, 1986	10.00	3.50
	With small tab at top	10.00	
	With larger survey tab at side and small tab at top	17.50	
9	$3.50 Mallards, 1987	9.00	3.50
	With small tab at top	9.00	
	With larger survey tab at side and small tab at top	15.00	
10	$3.50 Redheads, 1988	9.00	2.50
	With small tab at top	9.00	
	With larger survey tab at side and small tab at top	15.00	
11	$3.50 Blue-winged teal, 1989	7.50	2.50
	With small tab at top	7.50	
	With larger survey tab at side and small tab at top	15.00	
12	$3.50 Wood ducks, 1990	7.50	2.50
	With small tab at top	7.50	
	With larger survey tab at side and small tab at top	15.00	
13	$3.50 Northern Pintails, 1991	7.00	2.50
	With small tab at top	7.00	
	With larger survey tab at side and small tab at top	15.00	
14	$3.50 Ruddy duck, 1992	7.00	2.50
	With small tab at top	7.00	
	With larger survey tab at side and small tab at top	12.00	
15	$3.50 American widgeon, 1993	6.00	2.50
	With small tab at top	6.00	
	With larger survey tab at side and small tab at top	12.00	
16	$3.50 Mottled duck, 1994	6.00	2.50
	With small tab at top	6.00	
	With larger survey tab at side and small tab at top	12.00	
17	$3.50 Fulvous whistling duck, 1995	6.00	2.50
	With small tab at top	6.00	
	With larger survey tab at side and small tab at top	12.00	
18	$3.50 Goldeneyes, 1996	6.00	2.50
	With small tab at top	6.00	
	With larger survey tab at side and small tab at top	12.00	
19	($3.00) Hooded merganser, 1997	6.00	2.50
	With small tab at top	6.00	
	With larger survey tab at side and small tab at top	12.00	

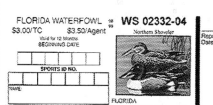

Self-Adhesive

20	$3 Shoveler, 1998	6.00	2.50
	Sold for $3.50 through agents.		
21	$3 Pintail, 1999	6.00	2.50
	Sold for $3.50 through agents.		

GEORGIA

Not required to hunt waterfowl until 1989.
Nos. 1-4 printed in sheets of 30, others in sheets of 20.
Starting with No 5, stamps are numbered serially.

> **Catalogue values for all unused stamps in this section are for Never Hinged items.**

Artists: Daniel Smith, #1; Jim Killen, #2, 14; James Partee, Jr., #3; Paul Bridgeford, #4; Ralph J. McDonald, #5; Guy Coheleach, #6; Phillip Crowe, #7-8, 11; Jerry Raedeke, #9, 13, 15; Herb Booth, #10; David Lanier, #12.

1985-99

1	$5.50	Wood ducks	10.50	3.00
2	$5.50	Mallards, *1986*	8.50	3.00
3	$5.50	Canada geese, *1987*	7.50	3.00
4	$5.50	Ring-necked ducks, *1988*	8.00	2.50
5	$5.50	Duckling & golden retriever puppy, *1989*	8.00	2.50
6	$5.50	Wood ducks, *1990*	8.00	2.50
7	$5.50	Green-winged teal, *1991*	8.00	2.50
8	$5.50	Buffleheads, *1992*	8.00	2.50
9	$5.50	Mallards, *1993*	8.00	2.50
10	$5.50	Ring-necked ducks, *1994*	8.00	2.50
11	$5.50	Widgeons, Labrador retreiver, *1995*	8.00	2.50
12	$5.50	Black ducks, *1996*	8.00	2.50
13	$5.50	Lesser scaup, Cockspur Island lighthouse, *1997*	8.00	2.50
14	$5.50	Labrador retreiver, ring-necked ducks, *1998*	8.00	2.50
15	$5.50	Pintails, *1999*	8.00	2.50

HAWAII

Required for the hunting of small game. Hunting birds is illegal in Hawaii.

Artists: Patrick Ching, #1, D. Van Zyle, #2; Michael Furuya, #3; Norman Nagai, #4.

1996-99

1	$5	Nene goose	7.50	2.50
a.	$5 +$50 Governor's edition		60.00	
b.	As No. 1, sheet of 4		45.00	
	No. 1b exists imperf.			
2	$5	Hawaiian duck, *1997*	7.50	
	With tab		7.50	2.50
a.	As No. 2, sheet of 4		45.00	
	No. 2a exists imperf.			
3	$5	Wild turkey, *1998*	7.50	
	With tab		7.50	2.50
4	$5	Ring-necked pheasant, *1999*	7.50	
	With tab		7.50	2.50

IDAHO

Printed in booklet panes of 5 and sheets of 30, except No. 5, which was issued in booklets of 10.
Numbered serially except for No. 11.

> **Catalogue values for all unused stamps in this section are for Never Hinged items.**

Artists: Robert Leslie, #1; Jim Killen, #2; Daniel Smith, #3; Francis E. Sweet, #4, Richard Clifton, #6, 11; Richard Plasschaert, #7; Sherrie Russell Meline, #8; Bill Moore, #9; David Gressard, #10; T. Smith, #12; Maynard Reece, #13.

1987-99

1	$5.50	Cinnamon teal, perforated	14.00	
a.	Bklt. single, rouletted, with 2-part tab		11.00	3.00
2	$5.50	Green-winged teal, perforated, *1988*	10.50	
a.	Bklt. single, rouletted, with 2-part tab		11.00	3.00
3	$6	Blue-winged teal, perforated, *1989*	10.00	
a.	Bklt. single, rouletted, with 2-part tab		10.00	3.00
4	$6	Trumpeter swans, perforated, *1990*	15.00	
a.	Bklt. single, rouletted, with 2-part tab		12.00	3.00

Die cut self-adhesive

5	$6 green, *1991*		125.00	*30.00*

No. 5 was used provisionally in 1991 when the regular stamps were delayed. Unused value is for stamp, remittance tab and selvage pieces on backing paper.

Designs like No. 1

6	$6	Widgeons, perforated, *1991*	8.50	
a.	Bklt. single, rouletted, with 2-part tab		9.00	2.50
7	$6	Canada geese, perforated, *1992*	8.00	
a.	Bklt. single, rouletted, with 2-part tab		8.50	2.50
8	A00 $6.00	Common goldeneye, perforated, *1993*	8.00	
a.	Bklt. single, rouletted, with 2-part tab		8.50	2.50
9	$6	Harlequin ducks, perforated, *1994*	8.00	
a.	Bklt. single, rouletted, with 2-part tab		8.50	2.50
10	$6	Wood ducks, perforated, *1995*	8.00	
a.	Bklt. single, rouletted, with 2-part tab		8.50	2.50
11	$6.50	Mallard, *1996*	8.00	2.50
12	$6.50	Shovelers, *1997*	8.00	2.50
13	$6.50	Canada geese, *1998*	9.00	2.50

ILLINOIS

Daily Usage Stamps for State-operated Waterfowl Areas.

Date and fee overprinted in black. $2 and $3 stamps were for hunting ducks, $5 stamps for hunting geese and pheasants. 1953-58 had separate pheasant stamps. No duck stamp was printed in 1971.
Some unused stamps have dry gum.
Used stamps have no gum or have staple holes.
Black printing.
Stamps are numbered serially.

1953-1972

A1	$2	orange, *blue*	—	—
A4	$2	green, *manila, 1956*	7,500.	5,000.
A5	$2	orange, *light blue green, 1957*	950.	500.
A6	$2	green, *manila, 1958*	800.	400.
A7	$3	green, *manila, 1959*	650.	325.
A8	$5	red brown, *light blue green, 1959*	650.	325.
A9	$3	red brown, *light blue green, 1960*	650.	325.
A10	$5	green, *manila, 1960*	650.	325.
A11	$3	green, *manila, 1961*	650.	325.
A12	$5	red brown, *light blue green, 1961*	650.	325.
A13	$3	green, *manila, 1962*	650.	325.
A14	$5	red brown, *light blue green, 1962*	650.	325.
A15	$3	orange, *light blue green, 1963*	650.	325.
A16	$3	green, *manila, 1963*	650.	325.
A17	$3	green, *manila, 1964*	650.	325.
A18	$5	red, *light blue green, 1964*	650.	325.
A19	$3	green, *light blue green, 1965*	650.	325.
A20	$5	green, *manila, 1965*	650.	325.
A21	$3	green, *manila, 1966*	650.	325.
A22	$5	orange, *light blue green, 1966*	650.	325.
A23	$3	orange, *light blue green, 1967*	650.	325.
A24	$5	green, *yellow, 1967*	650.	325.
A25	$5	green, *yellow, 1968*	650.	325.
A26	$5	orange, *light blue, 1968*	650.	325.
A27	$3	orange, *light blue green, 1969*	650.	325.
A28	$5	green, *manila, 1969*	650.	325.
A29	$3	green, *manila, 1970*	1,100.	650.
A30	$5	orange, *light blue, 1970*	1,100.	650.
A31	$5	green, *manila, 1971*	1,300.	800.
A32	$5	orange, *light blue green, 1972*	3,000.	
A33	$5	orange, *light blue green, 1972*	3,000.	

> **Catalogue values for unused stamps in this section, from this point to the end, are for Never Hinged items.**

No. A34   No. A35

1977-91(?)

A34	black, *light blue*, duck, *1991*	—	—
A35	black, *manila*, goose	—	—

Nos. A34-A35 do not show year or denomination and were used until 1994. No. A34 used before 1991 should exist but has not been reported yet. Separate pheasant and controlled quail and pheasant stamps of a similar design have also been used.

No. A36

No. A37

1996

A36	black, *light blue*, duck	—	—
A37	black, *manila*, goose	—	—

Nos. A36-A37 do not show year or denomination.

Statewide Issues

Nos. 1-10 in sheets of 10. Starting with No. 11, in booklet panes of 5; starting with No. 22, in panes of 10.
Stamps are numbered serially and rouletted.

Catalogue values for all unused stamps in this section are for Never Hinged items.

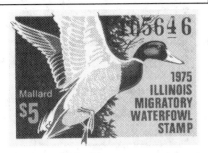

Artists: Robert Eschenfeldt, #1; Robert G. Larson, #2; Richard Lynch, #3; Everett Staffeldt, #4; John Eggert, #5; Bart Kassabaum, #6, 9, 11, 13; Jim Trindel, #7; Arthur Sinden, #8, 12, 14; George Kieffer, #10; Charles McKay Freeman, #15; John Henson, #16; Phillip Crowe, #17-21; Thomas Hirata, #22-24; Jim Killen, #25.

1975-98

1	$5 Mallard	625.00	85.00
2	$5 Wood ducks, 1976	275.00	50.00
3	$5 Canada goose, 1977	175.00	35.00
4	$5 Canvasbacks, 1978	95.00	22.50
5	$5 Pintail, 1979	95.00	16.00
6	$5 Green-winged teal, 1980	95.00	16.00
7	$5 Widgeons, 1981	95.00	16.00
a.	"Green-winged teal"	525.00	
8	$5 Black ducks, 1982	60.00	12.50
9	$5 Lesser scaup, 1983	45.00	10.00
10	$5 Blue-winged teal, 1984	45.00	10.00
11	$5 Redheads, 1985	15.00	3.00
	With 2-part tab	22.50	
12	$5 Gadwalls, 1986	12.00	3.00
	With 2-part tab	14.00	
13	$5 Buffleheads, 1987	11.00	3.00
	With 2-part tab	13.00	
14	$5 Common goldeneyes, 1988	7.50	2.50
	With 2-part tab	10.00	
15	$5 Ring-necked ducks, 1989	7.50	2.50
	With 2-part tab	8.50	
16	$10 Lesser snow geese, 1990	15.00	3.00
	With 2-part tab	17.00	
17	$10 Labrador retriever & Canada goose, 1991	14.00	3.00
	With 2-part tab	16.00	
a.	Governor's edition with tab	85.00	
18	$10 Retriever & mallards, 1992	14.00	3.00
	With 2-part tab	16.00	
19	$10 Pintail decoys and puppy, 1993	14.00	3.00
	With 2-part tab	16.00	
20	$10 Canvasbacks & retrievers, 1994	14.00	3.00
	With 2-part tab	16.00	
21	$10 Retriever, green-winged teal, decoys, 1995	14.00	3.00
	With 2-part tab	16.00	
22	$10 Wood ducks, 1996	14.00	2.50
23	$10 Canvasbacks, 1997	14.00	2.50
24	$10 Canada geese, 1998	14.00	2.50
25	$10 Canada geese, black Labrador retriever, 1999	14.00	2.50
a.	Anniversary edition, perforated	92.50	
b.	Governor's edition, perforated	92.50	
c.	Silver edition, perforated	92.50	

Nos. 25a-25c were sold as a set of three.

INDIANA

Issued in booklet panes of 4 (Nos. 1-10) and booklet panes of 2, starting with No. 11.
Stamps are numbered serially and rouletted.

Catalogue values for all unused stamps in this section are for Never Hinged items.

Artists: Justin H. (Sonny) Bashore, #1-2; Carl (Spike) Knuth, #3; Daniel Renn Pierce, #4; Dean Barrick, #5; Rodney Crossman, #6; George Metz, #7; Kieth Freeman, #8; Lyn Briggs, #9;

Rick Pas, #10; Ronald Louque, #11; Susan Hastings Bates, #12; Bruce Langton, #13, 17; Ann Dahoney, #14; Ken Bucklew, #15, 20, 22, 24; Richard Hansen, #16; Jeffrey Klinefelter, #18; Jeffrey Mobley, #19; Charles Riggles, #21, 23.

1976-99

1	$5 Green-winged teal	8.00	2.50
2	$5 Pintail, 1977	8.00	2.50
3	$5 Canada geese, 1978	8.00	2.50
4	$5 Canvasbacks, 1979	8.00	2.50
5	$5 Mallard ducklings, 1980	8.00	2.50
6	$5 Hooded mergansers, 1981	8.00	2.50
7	$5 Blue-winged teal, 1982	8.00	2.50
8	$5 Snow geese, 1983	8.00	2.50
9	$5 Redheads, 1984	8.00	2.50
10	$5 Pintail, 1985	8.00	2.50
	With tab	10.00	
11	$5 Wood duck, 1986	8.00	2.50
	With tab	10.00	
12	$5 Canvasbacks, 1987	8.00	2.50
	With tab	10.00	
13	$6.75 Redheads, 1988	10.00	2.50
	With tab	10.50	
14	$6.75 Canada goose, 1989	10.00	2.50
	With tab	10.50	
15	$6.75 Blue-winged teal, 1990	10.00	2.50
	With tab	10.50	
16	$6.75 Mallards, 1991	10.00	2.50
	With tab	10.50	
17	$6.75 Green-winged teal, 1992	10.00	2.50
	With tab	10.50	
18	$6.75 Wood ducks, 1993	10.00	2.50
	With tab	10.50	
19	$6.75 Pintail, 1994	10.00	2.50
	With tab	10.50	
20	$6.75 Goldeneyes, 1995	10.00	2.50
	With tab	10.50	
21	$6.75 Black ducks, 1996	10.00	2.50
	With tab	10.50	
22	$6.75 Canada geese, 1997	10.00	2.50
	With tab	10.50	
23	$6.75 Widgeon, 1998	10.00	2.50
	With tab	10.50	
24	$6.75 Bluebills, 1999	9.00	2.50
	With tab	10.00	

IOWA

Issued in booklet pane of 5 (No. 1), 10 (others) and sheets of 10 (No. 19).

Catalogue values for all unused stamps in this section are for Never Hinged items.

Artists: Maynard Reece, #1, 6, 22; Thomas Murphy, #2; James Landenberger, #3; Mark Reece, #4; Nick Klepinger, #5, 7; Andrew Peters, #8; Paul Brigford, #9, 12, 15; Brad Reece, #10; Tom Walker, #11; Larry Zach, #13; Jack C. Hahn, #14, 18; John Heidersbach, #16; Mark Cary, #17; Patrick Murillo, #19; Jerry Raedeke, #20; Charlotte Edwards, #21, 26; Dietmar Krumrey, #23, 25; Cynthia Fisher, #24; Sherrie Russell Meline, #27; Mark Anderson, #28.

1972-99

1	$1 Mallards	160.00	25.00
2	$1 Pintails, 1973	40.00	7.50
3	$1 Gadwalls, rouletted, 1974	85.00	7.00
4	$1 Canada geese, 1975	95.00	9.00
5	$1 Canvasbacks, 1976	25.00	2.50
6	$1 Lesser scaup, rouletted, 1977	21.00	2.50
7	$1 Wood ducks, rouletted, 1978	50.00	5.00
8	$5 Buffleheads, 1979	400.00	25.00
9	$5 Redheads, 1980	27.50	6.00
10	$5 Green-winged teal, rouletted, 1981	27.50	4.00
11	$5 Snow geese, rouletted, 1982	16.00	2.50
12	$5 Widgeons, 1983	15.00	2.75
13	$5 Wood ducks, 1984	35.00	3.00
14	$5 Mallard & mallard decoy, 1985	20.00	2.50
15	$5 Blue-winged teal, 1986	15.00	2.50
16	$5 Canada goose, 1987	13.00	2.50
17	$5 Pintails, 1988	12.00	2.50
18	$5 Blue-winged teal, 1989	12.00	2.50
19	$5 Canvasbacks, 1990	8.00	2.50
20	$5 Mallards, 1991	8.00	2.50
21	$5 Labrador retriever & ducks, 1992	9.00	2.50
22	$5 Mallards, 1993	9.00	2.50
23	$5 Green-winged teal, 1994	9.00	2.50
24	$5 Canada geese, 1995	8.50	2.50
25	$5 Canvasbacks, 1996	8.50	2.50
26	$5 Canada geese, 1997	8.00	2.50
27	$5 Pintails, 1998	8.00	2.50

DEPARTMENT OF NATURAL RESOURCES

1999

28	Trumpeter swan, *1999*	7.50	2.50

No. 28 not required for hunting. The Department of Natural Resources sent customers No. 28 upon receipt of a postcard given to the customer after paying license fee of $5.

KANSAS
Marion County Resident Duck Stamps
Wording, type face, border and perforation/roulette differs.
Used values are for stamps without gum.

1941-42

A1	25c black		—
A2	25c black, *1942*		—

Remainders from 1941 were rubber stamped "1942" in purple and initialed "J.E.M." by the Park and Lake Supervisor.

1943-73

A3	25c black, *pink*			—
A4	25c black, *green, 1944*			—
A5	25c green, *1945*			—
A6	25c black, *yellow, 1946*			11,000.
A7	25c black, *pink, 1947*			8,000.
A8	50c black, *blue, 1948*			14,000.
A9	50c black, *1949*			—
A10	50c black, *blue, 1950*			—
A11	50c black, *1951*			—
A13	50c black, *blue, 1953*			—
A14	50c black, *pink, 1954*		140.00	65.00
A15	50c black, *green, 1955*		125.00	65.00
A16	50c black, *1956*		150.00	100.00
A17	50c black, *blue, 1957*		125.00	65.00
a.	"1" instead of "I" in "RESIDENT," pos. 3		1,600.	1,100.
b.	1st 2 lines reversed, pos. 6		2,100.	1,500.
A18	50c black, *light yellow, 1958*		450.00	225.00
A19	50c black, *1959*		85.00	65.00
A20	50c black, *pink, 1960*		160.00	110.00
a.	Missing ornamental ball, pos. 9		2,400.	
A21	50c black, *1961*		175.00	150.00
A22	50c black, *1962*		250.00	150.00
A23	50c black, *pink, 1963*		650.00	400.00
A24	50c black, *pink, 1964*		650.00	400.00
a.	2nd & 3rd lines reversed, pos. 10		6,500.	
A25	50c black, *green, 1965*		425.00	325.00
A26	50c black, *yellow, 1966*		—	4,750.
A27	50c black, *green, 1967*		2,400.	1,500.
A28	50c black, *pink, 1968*		300.00	250.00
A29	50c black, *yellow, 1969*		325.00	225.00
a.	"Dusk" instead of "Duck," pos. 8		9,500.	
A30	50c black, *1970*		450.00	375.00
A31	50c black, *pink, 1971*		1,800.	1,100.
A32	50c black, *blue, 1972*		1,800.	1,100.
A33	50c black, *pink, 1972*		4,250.	3,500.

Statewide Issues
Issued in booklet panes of 10 (Nos. 1-5) and sheets of 30 (starting with No. 2). Starting with No. 11, issued in sheets of 10. No. 1 issued in booklets with one pane of 10 (serial number has prefix "DD") and booklets with two panes of 10 (serial number has prefix "SS").
Nos. 1-4 numbered serially.

Catalogue values for all unused stamps in this section are for Never Hinged items.

1987 KANSAS Waterfowl Habitat Stamp
50th Year-DUCKS UNLIMITED

Artists: Guy Coheleach, #1; Ann Dahoney, #2, 8; Leon Parson, #3; Wes Dewey, #4; J. Byron Test, #5; Jerry Thomas, #6, 10; Jerry Roedeke, #7; Neal Anderson, #9.

1987-96

1	$3 Green-winged teal	8.00	2.50
	Pair from booklet pane with L & R selvage	17.00	
2	$3 Canada geese, *1988*	5.50	2.50
	Pair from booklet pane with L & R selvage	14.00	
3	$3 Mallards, *1989*	5.50	2.50
	Pair from booklet pane with L & R selvage	12.00	
4	$3 Wood ducks, *1990*	5.50	2.50
	Pair from booklet pane with L & R selvage	12.00	
5	$3 Pintail, *rouletted, 1991*	5.25	2.50
	Pair from booklet pane with selvage at L & straight edge at R	12.00	
6	$3 Canvasbacks, *1992*	5.25	2.50
7	$3 Mallards, *1993*	5.25	2.50
8	$3 Blue-winged teal, *1994*	5.25	2.50
9	$3 Barrow's goldeneye, *1995*	5.25	2.50
10	$3 American widgeon, *1996*	5.25	2.50

1997 Expires 6-30-98 $3
Waterfowl Habitat Stamp
Kansas Department of Wildlife and Parks
KANSAS

Artist: Dustin Teasleys.

1997-99		Self-Adhesive	*Die Cut*	
11	$3 blue		5.25	2.50
12	$3 green, *1998*		5.25	2.50
13	$3 red, *1999*		5.25	2.50

KENTUCKY
Printed in booklet panes of 5, starting with No. 12 in panes of 30.
Stamps are numbered serially.

Catalogue values for all unused stamps in this section are for Never Hinged items.

Artists: Ray Harm, #1, 7; David Chapple, #2; Ralph J. McDonald, #3, 10; Lynn Kaatz, #4, 15; Phillip Crowe, #5, 9; Jim Oliver, #6; Phillip Powell, #8, 13; Jim Killen, #11; Laurie Parsons Yarnes, #12; Harold Roe, #14.

1985-99

1	$5.25 Mallards, *rouletted*	13.00	3.00
	With tab	14.00	

2	$5.25 Wood ducks, *rouletted, 1986*	9.00	2.50
	With tab	10.00	
3	$5.25 Black ducks, *1987*	9.00	2.50
	With tab	10.00	
4	$5.25 Canada geese, *1988*	9.00	2.50
	With tab	10.00	
5	$5.25 Retriever & canvasbacks, *1989*	9.00	2.50
	With tab	10.00	
6	$5.25 Widgeons, *1990*	9.00	2.50
	With tab	10.00	
7	$5.25 Pintails, *1991*	9.00	2.50
	With tab	10.00	
8	$5.25 Green-winged teal, *1992*	9.00	2.50
	With tab	10.00	
9	$5.25 Canvasback & decoy, *1993*	9.00	2.50
	With tab	10.00	
10	$5.25 Canada goose, *1994*	9.00	2.50
	With tab	10.00	
11	$7.50 Retriever, decoy, ringnecks, *1995*	10.00	3.00
	With tab	10.00	
12	$7.50 Blue-winged teal, *1996*	10.00	3.00
13	$7.50 Shovelers, *1997*	10.00	3.00
14	$7.50 Gadwalls, *1998*	10.00	3.00
15	$7.50 Common goldeneyes, *1999*	9.50	3.00

LOUISIANA
Printed in sheets of 30.
Stamps are numbered serially. Stamps without numbers are artist presentation copies.
Two fees: resident and non-resident.

Catalogue values for all unused stamps in this section are for Never Hinged items.

1989 LOUISIANA WATERFOWL CONSERVATION STAMP

Artists: David Noll, #1-2; Elton Louviere, #3-4; Brett J. Smith, #5-6; Bruce Heard, #7-8; Ronald Louque, #9-10, 15-16, 21-22; Don Edwards, #11-12; John Bertrand, #13-14; R. Hall, #17-18; R. C. Davis, #19-20.

1989-99

1	$5 Blue-winged teal	10.00	2.50
a.	Governor's edition	100.00	
2	$7.50 Blue-winged teal	13.00	2.50
a.	Governor's edition	150.00	

Nos. 1a and 2a were available only through a sealed bid auction where sheets of 30 of each denomination with matching serial numbers were sold as a unit.

3	$5 Green-winged teal, *1990*	8.50	2.50
4	$7.50 Green-winged teal, *1990*	12.00	2.50
5	$5 Wood ducks, *1991*	9.00	2.50
6	$7.50 Wood ducks, *1991*	10.50	2.50
7	$5 Pintails, *1992*	8.00	2.50
8	$7.50 Pintails, *1992*	10.50	2.50
9	$5 American widgeon, *1993*	7.50	2.50
10	$7.50 American widgeon, *1993*	10.50	2.50
11	$5 Mottled duck, *1994*	7.50	2.50
12	$7.50 Mottled duck, *1994*	10.50	2.50
13	$5 Speckle bellied goose, *1995*	7.50	2.50
14	$7.50 Speckle bellied goose, *1995*	10.50	2.50
15	$5 Gadwall, *1996*	7.50	2.50
16	$7.50 Gadwall, *1996*	10.50	2.50
17	$5 Ring-necked ducks, *1997*	8.00	2.50
18	$13.50 Ring-necked ducks, *1997*	17.00	2.50
19	$5.50 Mallards, *1998*	8.00	2.50
20	$13.50 Mallards, *1998*	17.00	2.50
21	$5.50 Snow geese, *1999*	8.00	2.50
22	$13.50 Snow geese, *1999*	15.00	2.50

MAINE
Printed in sheets of 10. Nos. 1-10 are numbered serially.

Catalogue values for all unused stamps in this section are for Never Hinged items.

1984 MAINE MIGRATORY WATERFOWL STAMP

Artists: David Maass, #1-3; Ron Van Gilder, #4; Rick Allen, #5; Jeannine Staples, #6, 10, 15; Thea Flanagan, #7; Patricia D. Carter, #8; Persis Weirs, #9; Susan Jordan, #11; Richard Alley, #12, 16; Paul Fillion, #13; T. Kemp, #14.

1984-99

1	$2.50	Black ducks	22.50	5.00
2	$2.50	Common eiders, 1985	40.00	5.00
3	$2.50	Wood ducks, 1986	8.50	2.50
4	$2.50	Buffleheads, 1987	8.00	2.50
5	$2.50	Green-winged teal, 1988	8.00	2.50
6	$2.50	Common goldeneyes, 1989	5.00	2.50
7	$2.50	Canada geese, 1990	5.00	2.50
8	$2.50	Ring-necked duck, 1991	5.00	2.50
9	$2.50	Old squaw, 1992	5.00	2.50
10	$2.50	Hooded merganser, 1993	5.00	2.50
11	$2.50	Mallards, 1994	5.00	2.50
12	$2.50	White-winged scoters, 1995	5.00	2.50
13	$2.50	Blue-winged teal, 1996	5.00	2.50
14	$2.50	Greater scaup, 1997	5.00	2.50
15	$2.50	Surf scoters, 1998	5.00	2.50
16	$2.50	Black duck, 1999	5.00	2.50

MARYLAND

Nos. 1-19 printed in sheets of 10. Starting with No. 20, printed in sheets of 5 with numbered tab at bottom and selvage at top.

Each stamp has tab. Unused value is for stamp with tab. Many used copies have tab attached.

> Catalogue values for all unused stamps in this section are for Never Hinged items.

Artists: John Taylor, #1, 6, 24; Stanley Stearns, #2, 5; Louis Frisino, #3, 13, 20; Jack Schroeder, #4, 7; Arthur Eakin, #8; Roger Bucklin, #9; Roger Lent, #10, 16; Carla Huber, #11, 17; David Turnbaugh, #12, 18, 23; Francis Sweet, #14; Christopher White, #15; Will Wilson, #19; Robert Bealle, #21; Charles Schauck, #22; Paul Makuchal, #25; Wally Makuchal, #26.

1974-99

1	$1.10	Mallards	11.00	2.50
2	$1.10	Canada geese, rouletted, 1975	10.00	2.50
3	$1.10	Canvasbacks, rouletted, 1976	10.00	2.50
4	$1.10	Greater scaups, 1977	10.00	2.50
5	$1.10	Redheads, 1978	10.00	2.50
6	$1.10	Wood ducks, rouletted, 1979	10.00	2.50
7	$1.10	Pintail decoy, rouletted, 1980	10.00	2.50
8	$3	Widgeon, rouletted, 1981	6.00	2.50
9	$3	Canvasback, 1982	6.00	2.50
10	$3	Wood duck, 1983	10.00	2.50
11	$6	Black ducks, 1984	10.00	2.50
12	$6	Canada geese, 1985	9.50	2.50
13	$6	Hooded mergansers, 1986	9.50	2.50
14	$6	Redheads, 1987	9.50	2.50
15	$6	Ruddy ducks, 1988	9.50	2.50
16	$6	Blue-winged teal, 1989	9.00	2.50
17	$6	Lesser scaup, 1990	8.50	2.50
18	$6	Shovelers, 1991	8.50	2.50
19	$6	Bufflehead, 1992	8.50	2.50
20	$6	Canvasbacks, 1993	8.50	2.50
21	$6	Redheads, 1994	8.50	2.50
22	$6	Mallards, 1995	8.50	2.50
23	$6	Canada geese, 1996	8.50	2.50
24	$6	Canvasbacks, 1997	8.50	2.50
25	$6	Pintails, 1998	8.50	2.50
26	$6	Wood ducks, 1999	8.00	2.50

Public Lands Hunting Stamps

Required to hunt waterfowl in state-managed wildlife areas.

Issued in booklet panes of 10.

1975-79

A1	$2 purple	550.00	40.00
A2	$2 black, pink, 1976	450.00	30.00
A3	$2 black, yellow, 1977	375.00	30.00
A4	$2 black, 1978	850.00	65.00
A5	$2 black, yellow, 1979	350.00	25.00

MASSACHUSETTS
Printed in sheets of 12.

> Catalogue values for all unused stamps in this section are for Never Hinged items.

Artists: Milton Weiler, #1; Tom Hennessey, #2; William Tyner, #3-5; Randy Julius, #6, 8, 10, 12, 19; John Eggert, #7, 9, 24; Joseph Cibula, #11; Robert Piscatori, #13, 15, 25; Peter Baedita, #14; Lou Barnicle, #16; Warren Racket Shreve, #17; Benjamin Smith, #18; Donald Little, #20; Sergio Roffo, #21; David Brega, #22; Christine Wilkinson, #23; Stephen Badlam.

1974-99

1	$1.25	Wood duck decoy, rouletted	15.00	3.00
2	$1.25	Pintail decoy, 1975	12.00	3.00
3	$1.25	Canada goose decoy, 1976	12.00	3.00
4	$1.25	Goldeneye decoy, 1977	12.00	3.00
5	$1.25	Black duck decoy, 1978	12.00	3.00
6	$1.25	Ruddy turnstone duck decoy, 1979	12.00	3.00
7	$1.25	Old squaw decoy, 1980	12.00	3.00
8	$1.25	Red-breasted merganser decoy, 1981	10.00	3.00
9	$1.25	Greater yellowlegs decoy, 1982	10.00	3.00
10	$1.25	Redhead decoy, 1983	10.00	3.00
11	$1.25	White-winged scoter decoy, 1984	10.00	3.00
12	$1.25	Ruddy duck decoy, 1985	9.50	3.00
13	$1.25	Preening bluebill decoy, 1986	9.50	2.50
14	$1.25	American widgeon decoy, 1987	9.50	2.50
15	$1.25	Mallard decoy, 1988	9.00	2.50
16	$1.25	Brant decoy, 1989	7.00	2.50
17	$1.25	Whistler hen decoy, 1990	7.25	2.50
18	$5	Canvasback decoy, 1991	8.00	2.50
19	$5	Black-bellied plover decoy, 1992	8.00	2.50
20	$5	Red-breasted merganser decoy, 1993	8.00	2.50
21	$5	White-winged scoter decoy, 1994	8.00	2.50
22	$5	Female hooded merganser, 1995	8.00	2.50
23	$5	Eider decoy, 1996	8.00	2.50
24	$5	Curlew decoy, 1997	8.00	2.50
25	$5	Canada goose decoy, 1998	8.00	2.50
26	$5	Oldsquaw decoy, 1999	8.00	2.50

MICHIGAN

Nos. 1-5 printed in sheets of 10 with center gutter, rouletted. Printed in sheets of 10 die cut self-adhesives on backing paper (Nos. 6-19), or sheets of 15 (starting with No. 20).

Nos. 1, 3-19 are serially numbered.

> Catalogue values for all unused stamps in this section are for Never Hinged items.

Artist: Oscar Warbach.

1976

1	$2.10 Wood duck	5.00	2.50

Artists: Larry Hayden, #2, 5, 12; Richard Timm, #3; Andrew Kurzmann, #4; Dietmar Krumrey, #6, 14, 23-24; Gjisbert van Frankenhuyzen, #7; Rod Lawrence, #8, 15, 20; Larry Cory, #9, 16; Robert Steiner, #10; Russell Cobane, #11; John Martens, #13; Heiner Hertling, #17; Clark Sullivan, #18; David Bollman, #19; Rusty Fretner, #21; M. Monroe, #22.

1977-99

2	$2.10	Canvasbacks	275.00	35.00
		With numbered tab	375.00	
3	$2.10	Mallards, 1978	20.00	5.00
		With tab	47.50	
4	$2.10	Canada geese, 1979	35.00	5.00
		With tab	40.00	
5	$3.75	Lesser scaup, 1980	15.00	4.00
		With tab	20.00	
6	$3.75	Buffleheads, 1981	20.00	4.00
7	$3.75	Redheads, 1982	22.50	4.00

Unused value is for stamp with sufficient margin to show printed spaces for date and time the stamp was sold.

8	$3.75	Wood ducks, 1983	25.00	4.00
9	$3.75 on $3.25	Pintails, 1984	25.00	3.00

No. 9 not issued without surcharge.

10	$3.75	Ring-necked ducks, 1985	25.00	3.00
11	$3.75	Common goldeneyes, 1986	18.00	2.50
12	$3.85	Green-winged teal, 1987	10.00	2.50
13	$3.85	Canada geese, 1988	9.50	2.50
14	$3.85	Widgeons, 1989	8.00	2.50
15	$3.85	Wood ducks, 1990	7.00	2.50
16	$3.85	Blue-winged teal, 1991	7.00	2.50
17	$3.85	Red-breasted merganser, 1992	6.50	2.50
18	$3.85	Hooded merganser, 1993	6.50	2.50
19	$3.85	Black duck, 1994	6.50	2.50
20	$4.35	Blue winged teal, 1995	7.00	3.00
21	$4.35	Canada geese, 1996	7.00	3.00
22	$5	Canvasbacks, 1997	7.50	3.00
23	$5	Pintail, 1998	8.00	3.00
24	$5	Shoveler, 1999	8.00	3.00

No. 24 not required for hunting.

MINNESOTA
License Surcharge Stamps

No. A1 printed in sheets of 10. These stamps served as a $1 surcharge to cover the cost of a license increase.

Nos. A1-A2 issued to raise funds for acquisition and development of wildlife lands.

1957

A1	$1 Mallards & Pheasant		Perf. 12½	
			140.00	10.00

1971

A2	$1 black, dark yellow	Rouletted 9½	
		1,250.	50.00

Regular Issues
Printed in sheets of 10.

> Catalogue values for all unused stamps in this section are for Never Hinged items.

Artists: David Maass, #1, 3; Leslie Kouba, #2; James Meger, #4; Terry Redlin, #5, 9; Phil Scholer, #6, 17; Gary Moss, #7; Thomas Gross, #8; Brian Jarvi, #10; Ron Van Gilder, #11; Robert Hautman, #12, 16; Jim Hautman, #13, 20; Kevin Daniel, #14, 21; Daniel Smith, #15; Edward DuRose, #18; Bruce Miller, #19; Thomas Moen, #22; John House, #23.

1977-99

1	$3 Mallards	15.00	2.50
2	$3 Lesser scaup, *1978*	10.00	2.50
3	$3 Pintails, *1979*	9.50	2.50
4	$3 Canvasbacks, *1980*	9.50	2.50
5	$3 Canada geese, *1981*	9.50	2.50
6	$3 Redheads, *1982*	10.00	2.50
7	$3 Blue geese & snow goose, *1983*	10.00	2.50
8	$3 Wood ducks, *1984*	10.00	2.50
9	$3 White-fronted geese, *1985*	8.50	2.50
10	$3 Lesser scaup, *1986*	8.50	2.50

Beginning with this issue, left side of sheet has an agent's tab, detachable from the numbered tab.

11	$5 Common goldeneyes, *1987*	11.00	2.50
	With numbered tab	11.00	
	With agent's and numbered tabs	12.00	
12	$5 Buffleheads, *1988*	11.00	2.50
	With numbered tab	11.00	
	With agent's and numbered tabs	12.00	
13	$5 Widgeons, *1989*	11.00	2.50
	With numbered tab	11.00	
	With agent's and numbered tabs	12.00	
14	$5 Hooded mergansers, *1990*	15.00	2.50
	With numbered tab	15.00	
	With agent's and numbered tabs	20.00	
15	$5 Ross's geese, *1991*	8.00	2.50
	With numbered tab	8.00	
	With agent's and numbered tabs	9.00	
16	$5 Barrow's goldeneyes, *1992*	8.00	2.50
	With numbered tab	8.00	
	With agent's and numbered tabs	9.00	
17	$5 Blue-winged teal, *1993*	8.00	2.50
	With numbered tab	8.00	
	With agent's and numbered tabs	9.00	
18	$5 Ringneck duck, *1994*	8.00	2.50
	With numbered tab	8.00	
	With agent's and numbered tabs	9.00	
19	$5 Gadwall, *1995*	8.00	2.50
	With numbered tab	8.00	
	With agent's and numbered tabs	9.00	
20	$5 Greater scaup, *1996*	8.00	2.50
	With numbered tab	8.00	
	With agent's and numbered tabs	9.00	
21	$5 Shovelers, *1997*	8.00	2.50
	With numbered tab	8.00	
	With agent's and numbered tabs	9.00	
22	$5 Harlequins, *1998*	8.00	2.50
	With numbered tab	8.00	
	With agent's and numbered tabs	9.00	
23	$5 Green-winged teal, *1999*	7.50	2.50
	With numbered tab	7.50	
	With agent's and numbered tabs	9.00	

MISSISSIPPI

Starting with No. 2, stamps are printed in sheets of 10. Nos. 2-14 are rouletted. All stamps are numbered serially.

Catalogue values for all unused stamps in this section are for Never Hinged items.

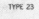

TYPE 23

STATE OF MISSISSIPPI
STATE WATERFOWL STAMP
STATE WATERFOWL—WOOD DUCK

GAME AND FISH COMMISSION

AVERY WOOD
DIRECTOR OF WILDLIFE CONSERVATION

77

NOT VALID UNLESS SIGNED IN INK ACROSS THE FACE OF THIS LICENSE
NOT VALID UNLESS PUNCHED

Illustration reduced.

Artists: Carroll & Gwen Perkins, #1; Allen Hughes, #2; John C. A. Reimers, #3, 6; Carole Pigott Hardy, #4; Bob Tompkins, #5, 13; Jerry Johnson, #7; Jerrie Glasper, #8; Tommy Goodman, #9; Lottie Fulton, #10; Joe Lattl, #11, 17, 22-23; Robert Garner, #12; Debra Aven Swartzendruber, #14; Kathy Dickson, #15; Phillip Crowe, #16; Eddie Suthoff, #18; Emitt Thames, #19-20; James Josey, #21; John MacHudspeth, #24.

1976   Without Gum

1	$2 Wood duck	16.00	5.00
a.	Complete 2-part data processing card	25.00	

1977-99

2	$2 Mallards	8.00	2.50
3	$2 Green-winged teal, *1978*	8.00	2.50
4	$2 Canvasbacks, *1979*	8.00	2.50
5	$2 Pintails, *1980*	8.00	2.50
6	$2 Redheads, *1981*	8.00	2.50
7	$2 Canada geese, *1982*	8.00	2.50
8	$2 Lesser scaup, *1983*	8.00	2.50
9	$2 Black ducks, *1984*	8.00	2.50
10	$2 Mallards, *1985*	8.00	2.50
a.	Vert. serial No., imperf btwn. serial No. and stamp	125.00	
b.	Horiz. serial No., no vert. silver bar	425.00	
11	$2 Widgeons, *1986*	8.00	2.50
12	$2 Ring-necked ducks, *1987*	8.00	2.50
13	$2 Snow geese, *1988*	8.00	2.50
14	$2 Wood ducks, *1989*	7.00	2.50
15	$2 Snow geese, *1990*	12.50	2.50
16	$2 Labrador retriever & canvasbacks, *1991*	5.00	2.50
17	$2 Green-winged teal, *1992*	5.00	2.50
18	$5 Mallards, *1993*	7.00	2.50
19	$5 Canvasbacks, *1994*	7.00	2.50
20	$5 Blue-winged teal, *1995*	7.00	2.50
21	$5 Hooded merganser, *1996*	7.00	2.50
22	$5 Pintail, *1997*	7.50	2.50
23	$5 Pintails, *1998*	7.50	2.50
24	$5 Ring-necked duck, *1999*	7.00	2.50

MISSOURI

Issued in booklet panes of five with tab. Nos. 1-8 are rouletted. No. 18 issued in pane of 30.

Catalogue values for all unused stamps in this section are for Never Hinged items.

Artists: Charles Schwartz, #1; David Plank, #2; Tom Crain, #3, 8; Gary Lucy, #4; Doug Ross, #5; Glenn Chambers, #6; Ron Clayton, #7; Ron Ferkol, #9, 13, 18; Bruce Bollman, #10; Kathy Dickson, #11; Eileen Melton, #12; Kevin Guinn, #14; Thomas Bates, #15; Keith Alexander, #16; Ryan Peterson, #17.

1979-96

1	$3.40 Canada geese	550.00	75.00
	With tab	675.00	
2	$3.40 Wood ducks, *1980*	110.00	18.00
	With tab	125.00	
3	$3 Lesser scaup, *1981*	57.50	9.00
	With tab	75.00	
4	$3 Buffleheads, *1982*	42.50	8.00
	With tab	52.50	
5	$3 Blue-winged teal, *1983*	37.50	8.00
	With tab	52.50	
6	$3 Mallards, *1984*	37.50	7.00
	With tab	47.50	
7	$3 American widgeons, *1985*	22.50	3.00
	With tab	25.00	
8	$3 Hooded mergansers, *1986*	12.00	3.00
	With tab	15.00	
9	$3 Pintails, *1987*	9.00	3.00
	With tab	13.00	
10	$3 Canvasback, *1988*	8.00	2.50
	With tab	11.00	
11	$3 Ring-necked ducks, *1989*	8.00	2.50
	With tab	9.25	

All copies of Nos. 12b, 13b, 14b, 15b, 16b, 17b are signed by the governor.

12	$5 Redheads, *1990*	7.00	2.50
	With two part tab	9.00	
a.	$50 Governor's edition with tab	75.00	
b.	$100 Governor's edition with tab	—	
13	$5 Snow geese, *1991*	7.00	2.50
	With two part tab	9.00	
a.	$50 Governor's edition with tab	72.50	
b.	$100 Governor's edition with tab	—	
14	$5 Gadwalls, *1992*	7.00	2.50
	With tab	9.00	
a.	$50 Governor's edition with tab	75.00	
b.	$100 Governor's edition with tab	—	
15	$5 Green-winged teal, *1993*	7.00	2.50
	With tab	9.00	
a.	$50 Governor's edition with tab	75.00	
b.	$100 Governor's edition with tab	—	
16	$5 White-fronted goose, *1994*	7.00	2.50
	With 2-part tab	9.00	
a.	$50 Governor's edition with tab	75.00	
b.	$100 Governor's edition with tab	—	
17	$5 Goldeneyes, *1995*	7.00	2.50
	With 2-part tab	9.00	
a.	$50 Governor's edition with tab	75.00	
b.	$100 Governor's edition with tab	—	
18	$5 Black ducks, *1996*	7.00	2.50

MONTANA
Bird License Stamps
Required to hunt waterfowl.

Resident ($2, $4, $6), youth ($1, $2), and non-resident ($25, $30, $53) bird licenses. Licenses were no longer produced for youth, beginning in 1985, and non-resident, beginning in 1989.

Nos. 1-33 rouletted.

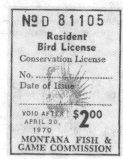

1969

A1	$2 Sage grouse	450.00	15.00
A2	$1 Sage grouse	450.00	50.00
A3	$25 Sage grouse	450.00	75.00

1970

A4	$2 Sage grouse	425.00	10.00
a.	Missing "1" in "1971," pos. 10		*400.00*
A5	$1 Sage grouse	*950.00*	150.00
A6	$25 Sage grouse	—	250.00

1971

A7	$2 Pheasant	425.00	10.00
A8	$1 Pheasant	425.00	35.00
A9	$25 Pheasant	425.00	50.00

1972

A10	$2 Pheasant	425.00	10.00
A11	$1 Pheasant	425.00	35.00
A12	$25 Pheasant	425.00	50.00

1973

A13	$2 Pheasant	425.00	10.00
A14	$1 Pheasant	425.00	35.00
A15	$25 Pheasant	425.00	50.00

1974

A16	$2 Pheasant	425.00	10.00
A17	$1 Pheasant	425.00	35.00
A18	$25 Pheasant	425.00	50.00

1975

A19	$2 Pheasant	425.00	10.00
A20	$1 Pheasant	425.00	35.00
A21	$25 Pheasant	425.00	50.00

1976

A22	$4 Pheasant	425.00	10.00
A23	$2 Pheasant	425.00	35.00
A24	$30 Pheasant	425.00	50.00

1977

A25	$4 Pheasant	425.00	10.00
A26	$2 Pheasant	425.00	35.00
A27	$30 Pheasant	425.00	50.00

1978

A28	$4 Sage grouse	8.00	2.00
A29	$2 Sage grouse	8.00	5.00
A30	$30 Sage grouse	8.00	5.50

1979

A31	$4 Snow geese	8.00	2.00
A32	$2 Snow geese	8.00	5.00
A33	$30 Snow geese	8.00	5.50

1980

A36	$30 black, *gray green*		35.00

1982

A40	$4 black, *yellow*		5.00

1983

A43	$4 black, *yellow gray*	125.00	5.00
A44	$2 black, *gray*	125.00	
A45	$30 black, *light blue*	125.00	

1984

A46	$4 black, *light blue green*	110.00	5.00
A47	$2 black, *light violet*	150.00	
A48	$30 black, *gray*	110.00	

1985

A49	$4 black, *light blue*	150.00	5.00
A50	$30 black, *lavender*	110.00	

1986

A51	$4 black, *orange*	150.00	5.00
A52	$30 black, *light blue*	150.00	

1987

A53	$4 black, *orange brown*	90.00	3.00
A54	$30 black, *tan*	125.00	

1988

A55	$6 black, *light blue*	75.00	3.00
A56	$53 black, *purple*	125.00	

1989-99

A57	$6 black, *rose*	50.00	2.00
A58	$6 black, *lavender, 1990*	40.00	2.00
A59	$6 black, *pale blue, 1991*	35.00	2.00
A60	$6 black, *brown, 1992*	30.00	2.00
A61	$6 black, *blue, 1993*	25.00	1.50
A62	$6 black, *red orange, 1994*	22.50	1.50
A63	$6 black, *blue, 1995*	15.00	1.50
A64	$6 black, *purple, 1996*	13.00	1.00
A65	$6 black, *mauve, 1997*	11.00	1.00
A66	$6 black, *gray, 1998*	10.00	1.00
A67	$6 black, *green, 1999*	10.00	1.00

Waterfowl Stamps

Issued in booklet panes of 10 and sheets of 30.
Stamps are numbered serially.
Stamps with serial numbers above 31,000 (1986)
and above 21,000 (other years) are from booklet
panes.

Catalogue values for all unused stamps in
this section are for Never Hinged items.

Artist: Joe Thornbrugh, #34, 38, 39, 45, 46; Roger Cruwys, #35, 37, 42; Dave Samuelson, #36; Craig Philips, #40; Darrell Davis, #41; Wayne Dowdy, #43; Jim Borgreen, #44; Cliff Rossberg, #47.

1986-99

34	$5 Canada geese	12.00	3.00
	Pair from booklet pane with L & R selvage	*2,000.*	
	Top pair from booklet pane with agent		
	tabs and L & R selvage	—	
35	$5 Redheads, *1987*	12.50	3.00
	Pair from booklet pane with L & R selvage	25.00	
	Top pair from booklet pane with agent		
	tabs and L & R selvage	55.00	

36	$5 Mallards, *1988*	11.00	3.00
	Pair from booklet pane with L & R selvage	25.00	
	Top pair from booklet pane with agent		
	tabs and L & R selvage	40.00	
37	$5 Black Labrador retriever & pintail, *1989*	8.00	3.00
	Pair from booklet pane with L & R selvage	19.00	
	Top pair from booklet pane with agent		
	tabs and L & R selvage	40.00	
a.	Governor's edition	*140.00*	

No. 37a was available only in full sheets only through a sealed bid auction.

38	$5 Blue-winged & cinnamon teal, *1990*	8.50	2.50
	Pair from booklet pane with L & R selvage	18.00	
	Top pair from booklet pane with agent		
	tabs and L & R selvage	25.00	
39	$5 Snow geese, *1991*	8.00	2.50
	Pair from booklet pane with L & R selvage	17.50	
	Top pair from booklet pane with agent		
	tabs and L & R selvage	25.00	
40	$5 Wood ducks, *1992*	8.00	2.50
	Pair from booklet pane with L & R selvage	17.50	
	Top pair from booklet pane with agent		
	tabs and L & R selvage	25.00	
41	$5 Harlequin ducks, *1993*	8.00	2.50
	Pair from booklet pane with L & R selvage	17.50	
	Top pair from booklet pane with agent		
	tabs and L & R selvage	25.00	
42	$5 Widgeons, *1994*	8.00	2.50
	Pair from booklet pane with L & R selvage	17.50	
	Top pair from booklet pane with agent		
	tabs and L & R selvage	25.00	
43	$5 Tundra swans, *1995*	8.00	2.50
	Pair from booklet pane with L & R selvage	17.50	
	Top pair from booklet pane with agent		
	tabs and L & R selvage	25.00	
44	$5 Canvasbacks, *1996*	7.50	2.50
	Pair from booklet pane with L & R selvage	17.50	
	Top pair from booklet pane with agent		
	tabs and L & R selvage	30.00	
45	$5 Golden retriever, mallard, *1997*	7.50	2.50
	Pair from booklet pane with L & R selvage	17.50	
	Top pair from booklet pane with agent		
	tabs and L & R selvage	30.00	
46	$5 Gadwalls, *1998*	7.50	2.50
	Pair from booklet pane with L & R selvage	17.50	
	Top pair from booklet pane with agent		
	tabs and L & R selvage	30.00	
47	$5 Barrow's goldeneye, *1999*	7.50	2.50
	Pair from booklet pane with L & R selvage	17.50	
	Top pair from booklet pane with agent		
	tabs and L & R selvage	30.00	

NEBRASKA
Habitat Stamps
Required to hunt waterfowl.
Printed in sheets of 20.

Catalogue values for all unused stamps in
this section are for Never Hinged items.

1977-98

A1	$7.50 Ring-necked pheasant	12.00	1.50
A2	$7.50 White-tailed deer, *1978*	12.00	1.50
A3	$7.50 Bobwhite quail, *1979*	12.00	1.50
A4	$7.50 Pheasant, *1980*	12.00	1.50
A5	$7.50 Cottontail rabbit, *1981*	12.00	1.50
A6	$7.50 Coyote, *1982*	12.00	1.50
A7	$7.50 Wild turkey, *1983*	12.00	1.50
A8	$7.50 Canada goose, *1984*	12.00	1.50
A9	$7.50 Cardinal, *1985*	12.00	1.50
A10	$7.50 Sharp-tailed grouse, *1986*	12.00	1.50
A11	$7.50 Sandhill crane, *1987*	12.00	1.50
A12	$7.50 Snow geese, *1988*	12.00	1.50
A13	$7.50 Mallards, *1989*	12.00	1.50
A14	$7.50 Pheasants, *1990*	12.00	1.50
A15	$7.50 Canada geese, *1991*	12.00	1.50
A16	$10.00 Raccoon, *1992*	14.00	1.50
A17	$10.00 Fox squirrel, *1993*	14.00	1.50
A18	$10.00 Hungarian partridge, *1994*	14.00	1.50
A19	$10.00 Prairie pronghorns, *1995*	14.00	1.50
A20	$10.00 Ring-necked pheasant, *1996*	14.00	1.50
A21	$10.00 White-tailed deer, *1997*	14.00	1.50
A22	$10.00 Mourning doves, *1998*	14.00	1.50

Pictorial Labels
These stamps are not valid for any hunting fees.
Printed in sheets of 10.
Stamps are numbered serially.

Catalogue values for all unused stamps in
this section are for Never Hinged items.

1991-92 NEBRASKA WATERFOWL STAMP

Artist: Neal Anderson.

1991-95

Artist: Neal Anderson

1	$6 Canada geese	10.00	2.50
2	$6 Pintails, *1992*	8.50	2.50
3	$6 Canvasbacks, *1993*	8.50	2.50
4	$6 Mallards, *1994*	8.50	2.50
5	$6 Wood ducks, *1995*	8.50	2.50

NEVADA

Printed in booklet panes of 4.
Stamps are rouletted and selvage is found above and below stamps on the pane. The tab portion of the panes in imperforate.
Starting with No. 4 stamps are numbered serially.

> Catalogue values for all unused stamps in this section are for Never Hinged items.

Artists: Larry Hayden, #1; Dick Mcrill, #2; Phil Scholer, #3; Richard Timm, #4; Charles Allen, #5; Robert Steiner, #6; Richard Wilson, #7; Nolan Haan. #8, 12; Sherrie Russell Meline, #9, 21; Jim Hautman, #10; Robert Hautman, #11; Tak Nakamura, #13, 17; Richard Clifton, #14; Steve Hopkins, #15; Mark Mueller, #16; Jeffrey Klinefelter, #18; B. Blight, #19; Janie Kreutzjans, #20.

1979-99

1	$2 Canvasbacks and decoy	42.50	12.00
	With numbered tab	52.50	

Copies with tabs without numbers are printer's waste.

2	$2 Cinnamon teal, *1980*	6.50	3.00
	With tab	10.00	
3	$2 Whistling swans, *1981*	7.00	3.00
	With tab	9.00	
4	$2 Shovelers, *1982*	7.00	3.00
	With tab	9.00	
5	$2 Gadwalls, *1983*	10.50	3.00
	With tab	11.00	
6	$2 Pintails, *1984*	10.50	3.00
	With tab	11.00	
7	$2 Canada geese, *1985*	13.00	3.00
	With tab	13.50	
8	$2 Redheads, *1986*	13.00	2.50
	With tab	13.50	
9	$2 Buffleheads, *1987*	11.00	2.50
	With tab	12.00	
10	$2 Canvasbacks, *1988*	11.00	2.50
	With tab	12.00	
11	$2 Ross's geese, *1989*	7.50	2.50
	With tab	8.00	
12	$5 Green-winged teal, *1990*	8.00	3.00
	With tab	10.00	
13	$5 White-faced ibis, *1991*	8.00	2.50
	With tab	10.00	
14	$5 American widgeon, *1992*	8.00	2.50
	With tab	8.50	
15	$5 Common goldeneye, *1993*	8.50	2.50
	With tab	9.00	
16	$5 Mallards, *1994*	8.00	2.50
	With tab	8.50	
17	$5 Wood duck, *1995*	8.00	2.50
	With tab	8.50	
18	$5 Ring-necked ducks, *1996*	8.00	2.50
	With tab	8.50	
19	$5 Ruddy ducks, *1997*	8.00	2.50
	With tab	8.50	
20	$5 Hooded merganser, *1998*	8.00	2.50
	With tab	8.50	
21	$5 Canvasback decoy, *1999*	7.50	2.50

NEW HAMPSHIRE

Printed in booklet panes of 1 with 2-part tab and in sheets of 30. Sheet stamps are perf on four sides. Stamps are numbered serially.

> Catalogue values for all unused stamps in this section are for Never Hinged items.

WOOD DUCKS

Artists: Richard Plasschaert, #1; Phillip Crowe, #2; Thomas Hirata, #3; Durrant Bell, #4; Robert Steiner, #5-9; Richard Clifton, #10-11, 15; Louis Frisino, #12; Matthew Scharle, #13; Jeffrey Klinefelter, #14; Jim Collins, #16; Bruce Holloway, #17.

1983-99

1	$4 Wood ducks	140.00	
a.	Booklet single with 2-part tab	150.00	25.00
2	$4 Mallards, *1984*	95.00	
a.	Booklet single with 2-part tab	200.00	20.00
3	$4 Blue-winged teal, *1985*	95.00	
a.	Booklet single with 2-part tab	110.00	20.00
4	$4 Hooded mergansers, *1986*	22.50	
a.	Booklet single with 2-part tab	30.00	6.00
5	$4 Canada geese, *1987*	12.00	
a.	Booklet single with 2-part tab	14.00	4.00
b.	$50 Governor's edition	375.00	
6	$4 Buffleheads, *1988*	8.00	
a.	Booklet single with 2-part tab	10.00	3.00
b.	$4 +$46 Governor's edition	60.00	
7	$4 Black ducks, *1989*	8.00	
a.	Booklet single with 2-part tab	9.50	3.00
b.	$4 +$50 Governor's edition	67.50	
8	$4 Green-winged teal, *1990*	7.25	
a.	Booklet single with 2-part tab	8.25	3.00
b.	$4 +$50 Governor's edition	62.50	
9	$4 Golden retriever & mallards, *1991*	7.25	
a.	Booklet single with 2-part tab	8.25	3.00
b.	$4 +$50 Governor's edition	60.00	

Governor's Editions that follow are so inscribed.

10	$4 Ring-necked ducks, *1992*	7.25	
a.	Booklet single with 2-part tab	8.25	3.00
b.	Governor's edition	625.00	
11	$4 Hooded mergansers, *1993*	7.25	
a.	Booklet single with 2-part tab	8.00	3.00
b.	Governor's edition	600.00	
12	$4 Common goldeneyes, *1994*	7.25	
a.	Bklt. single with 2-part tab	8.00	2.50
b.	Governor's edition	150.00	
13	$4 Northern pintails, *1995*	7.25	
a.	Bklt. single with 2-part tab	8.00	2.50
b.	Governor's edition	125.00	
14	$4 Surf scooters, *1996*	7.25	
a.	Bklt. single with 2-part tab	8.00	2.50
b.	Governor's edition	125.00	
15	$4 Wood ducks, *1997*	7.25	
a.	Bklt. single with 2-part tab	8.00	2.50
b.	Governor's edition	110.00	
16	$4 Canada geese, *1998*	7.25	
a.	Bklt. single with 2-part tab	8.00	2.50
b.	Governor's edition	85.00	
17	$4 Mallards, *1999*	6.00	
a.	Bklt. single with 2-part tab	8.00	2.50
b.	Governor's edition	110.00	

NEW JERSEY

Resident and non-resident fees.
Printed in sheets of 30 (starting with No. 1) and booklet panes of 10 (all but Nos. 2, 4, 6, 17b, 18b). Sheet stamps are perf on 4 sides. Stamps are numbered serially.

> Catalogue values for all unused stamps in this section are for Never Hinged items.

Artists: Thomas Hirata, #1-2, 17-18; David Maass, #3-4; Ronald Louque, #5-6; Louis Frisino, #7-8; Robert Leslie, #9-10, 19-20, 29-30; Daniel Smith, #11-12; Richard Plasschaert, #13-14; Bruce Miller, #21-22; Wilhelm Goebel, #23-24, 27-28; Joe Hautman, #25-26; Phillip Crowe, #31-32; Richard Clifton, #33-34.

1984-99

1	$2.50 Canvasbacks	45.00	
a.	Booklet single, #51,000-102,000	60.00	10.00
2	$5 Canvasbacks	60.00	10.00
3	$2.50 Mallards, *1985*	15.00	
a.	Booklet single, #51,000-102,000	27.50	6.00
4	$5 Mallards, *1985*	18.00	5.00
5	$2.50 Pintails, *1986*	10.00	
a.	Booklet single, #51,000-102,000	10.00	3.00
6	$5 Pintails, *1986*	13.00	3.00
7	$2.50 Canada geese, *1987*	11.00	
a.	Booklet single, #51,000-102,000	11.00	3.00
8	$5 Canada geese, *1987*	11.00	
a.	Booklet single, #45,001-60,000	11.00	3.00
9	$2.50 Green-winged teal, *1988*	7.50	
a.	Booklet single, #51,000-102,000	7.50	3.00
10	$5 Green-winged teal, *1988*	10.00	
a.	Booklet single, #45,001-60,000	10.00	3.00
11	$2.50 Snow geese, *1989*	5.00	
a.	Booklet single, #45,001-60,000	6.00	3.00
b.	Governor's edition	72.50	
12	$5 Snow geese, *1989*	10.00	
a.	Booklet single, #45,001-60,000	10.00	3.00
b.	Governor's edition	140.00	

Nos. 11b and 12b were available only in sets of sheets of 30 stamps with matching serial numbers through a sealed bid auction.

13	$2.50 Wood ducks, *1990*	5.00	
a.	Booklet single, #45,001-60,000	5.00	3.00
14	$5 Wood ducks, *1990*	8.00	
a.	Booklet single, #45,001-60,000	8.50	3.00
17	$2.50 Atlantic brant, *1991*	5.00	
a.	Booklet single, #45,001-60,000	5.00	3.00
b.	Atlantic "brandt"	14.00	
18	$5 Atlantic brant, *1991*	9.00	
a.	Booklet single, #45,001-60,000	9.50	3.00
b.	Atlantic "brandt"	27.50	

Matching serial number sets of Nos. 17b and 18b were available for sale only with the purchase of matching serial number sets of Nos. 17 and 18.

19	$2.50 Bluebills, *1992*	5.00	
a.	Booklet single, #27,691-78,690	5.00	2.50
20	$5 Bluebills, *1992*	8.50	
a.	Booklet single, #27,691-57,690	9.00	2.50
21	$2.50 Buffleheads, *1993*	5.00	
a.	Booklet single, #27,691-78,690	5.00	2.50
b.	Sheet of 4	20.00	
c.	Governor's edition, signed by Florio or Whitman	42.50	
22	$5 Buffleheads, *1993*	7.50	
a.	Booklet single, #27,691-57,690	8.00	2.50
b.	Sheet of 4	40.00	
c.	Governor's edition, signed by Florio or Whitman	82.50	

Nos. 21b and 22b were available only in sets of sheets with matching serial numbers. The set of sheets sold for $35.
Nos. 21c and 22c were available only in sets with matching serial numbers.

23	$2.50 Black ducks, *1994*	5.00	
a.	Bklt. single, perf. 2 or 3 sides	5.00	2.50
24	$5 Black ducks, *1994*	7.50	
a.	Bklt. single, perf. 2 or 3 sides	8.00	2.50
25	$2.50 Widgeon, lighthouse, *1995*	5.00	
a.	Bklt. single, perf. 3 sides	5.00	2.50
26	$5 Widgeon, lighthouse, *1995*	7.50	
a.	Bklt. single, perf. 3 sides	8.00	2.50
27	$5 Goldeneyes, lighthouse, *1996*	7.50	
a.	Bklt. single, perf. 2 or 3 sides	7.50	2.50
28	$10 Goldeneyes, lighthouse, *1996*	12.50	
a.	Bklt. single, perf. 2 or 3 sides	13.00	2.50

The $2.50 was printed but not used as the rate no longer existed. Later they were sold to collectors.

29	$5 Old squaws, schooner, *1997*	7.50	
a.	Bklt. single, perf. 2 or 3 sides	7.50	2.50
30	$10 Old squaws, schooner, *1997*	12.50	
a.	Bklt. single, perf. 2 or 3 sides	13.00	2.50
31	$5 Mallards, *1998*	7.50	
a.	Bklt. single, perf. 2 or 3 sides	7.50	2.50
32	$10 Mallards, *1998*	12.50	
a.	Bklt. single, perf. 2 or 3 sides	13.00	2.50
33	$5 Redheads, perf. 4 sides, *1999*	7.50	
a.	Bklt. single, perf. 2 or 3 sides	7.50	2.50
34	$10 Redheads, perf. 4 sides, *1999*	12.50	
a.	Bklt. single, perf. 2 or 3 sides	13.00	2.50

NEW MEXICO

Printed in booklet panes of 5 and sheets of 30. Stamps are numbered serially.

Catalogue values for all unused stamps in this section are for Never Hinged items.

Artist: Robert Steiner.

1991-94

1	$7.50 Pintails		10.00	
	Booklet single, with large tab and selvage		11.00	5.00
a.	$7.50 +$50 Governor's edition		72.50	
2	$7.50 American widgeon, *1992*		9.50	
	Booklet single, with large tab and selvage		10.00	4.00
a.	$7.50 +$50 Governor's edition		65.00	
3	$7.50 Mallard, *1993*		9.50	
	Booklet single, with large tab and selvage		10.00	4.00
a.	Sheet of 4		50.00	
b.	$7.50 +$50 Governor's edition		65.00	

No. 3a exists imperf.

No. 4: b, Three birds in flight. c, Two birds in flight. d, Two birds flying over land. e, Bird's head close-up.

4	$7.50 Green-winged teal, sheet of 4, #b.-e., *1994*	40.00	
a.	Souvenir sheet of 4, #b.-e. (decorative border)	40.00	
b.-e.	Bklt. single with large tab and selvage, each	10.00	4.00
f.	Bklt. pane of 4, #b.-e.	40.00	

Stamps in Nos. 4-4a are printed with continuous design and have serial numbers reading down. Stamps in No. 4f have frameline around each design, inscriptions at the top and serial numbers reading up.

NEW YORK

Not required to hunt. Printed in sheets of 30.

Catalogue values for all unused stamps in this section are for Never Hinged items.

Artists: Larry Barton, #1; David Maass, #2; Lee LeBlanc, #3; Richard Plasschaert, #4; Robert Bateman, #5; John Seerey-Lester, #6; Terry Isaac, #7; Anton Ashak, #8; Ron Kleiber, #9; Jerome Hageman, #10; Frederick Szatkowski, #11; Len Rusin, #12; R. Easton, #13; Barbara Woods, #14; Richard Clifton, #15.

1985-99

1	$5.50 Canada geese	13.00	4.00
2	$5.50 Mallards, *1986*	9.00	3.00
3	$5.50 Wood ducks, *1987*	8.00	3.00
4	$5.50 Pintails, *1988*	8.00	3.00
5	$5.50 Greater scaup, *1989*	8.00	3.00
6	$5.50 Canvasbacks, *1990*	8.00	3.00
7	$5.50 Redheads, *1991*	8.00	3.00
8	$5.50 Wood ducks, *1992*	8.00	3.00
9	$5.50 Blue-winged teal, *1993*	8.00	3.00
10	$5.50 Canada geese, *1994*	8.00	3.00
11	$5.50 Common goldeneye, *1995*	8.00	3.00
12	$5.50 Common loon, *1996*	8.00	3.00
13	$5.50 Hooded merganser, *1997*	8.00	3.00
14	$5.50 Osprey, *1998*	8.00	3.00
15	$5.50 Buffleheads, *1999*	7.50	3.00

NORTH CAROLINA

Not required to hunt until 1988. Printed in sheets of 30. Starting with No. 6, stamps are numbered serially.

Catalogue values for all unused stamps in this section are for Never Hinged items.

Artists: Richard Plasschaert, #1, 10; Jim Killen, #2, 13;Thomas Hirata, #3-4, 17-18; Larry Barton, #5; Ronald Louque, #6; Louis Frisino, #7; Robert Leslie, #8, 14; Phillip Crowe, #9, 12; Bruce Miller, #11; Wilhelm Goebel, #15-16; Robert Flowers, #19-20.

1983-99

1	$5.50 Mallards	75.00	
2	$5.50 Wood ducks, *1984*	47.50	
3	$5.50 Canvasbacks, *1985*	25.00	
4	$5.50 Canada geese, *1986*	16.00	4.00
5	$5.50 Pintails, *1987*	13.00	3.00
6	$5 Green-winged teal, *1988*	9.50	3.00
7	$5 Snow geese, *1989*	9.50	3.00
8	$5 Redheads, *1990*	9.50	3.00
9	$5 Blue-winged teal, *1991*	8.00	3.00
10	$5 American widgeon, *1992*	8.00	3.00
11	$5 Tundra swans, *1993*	8.00	3.00
12	$5 Buffleheads, *1994*	8.00	3.00
13	$5 Brant, lighthouse, *1995*	8.00	3.00
14	$5 Pintails, *1996*	8.00	3.00
15	$5 Wood ducks, perf., *1997*	8.00	3.00
16	$5 As #15,, self-adhesive, die cut, *1997*	8.00	
17	$5 Canada geese, perf., *1998*	8.00	3.00
18	$5 As #17, self-adhesive, die cut, *1998*	8.00	
19	$5 Green-winged teal, perf., *1999*	8.00	3.00
20	$5 As #19, self-adhesive, die cut, *1999*	8.00	

NORTH DAKOTA
Small Game Stamps

Required to hunt small game and waterfowl statewide. Resident and non-resident fees.
Values for 1967-70 non-resident stamps are for copies with staple holes.
Used values are for signed copies. Unused values for Nos. 12, 16, 18, 20, 22, 24, 26 and 28 are for stamps on backing.

1967-80

1	$2 black, *green*	800.00	60.00
2	$25 black, *green*	2,750.	350.00
3	$2 black, *pink, 1968*	200.00	20.00
4	$25 black, *yellow, 1968*	425.00	
5	$2 black, *green, 1969*	190.00	20.00
6	$35 black, *1969*	375.00	
7	$2 blue, *1970*	160.00	15.00
8	$35 black, *pink, 1970*	250.00	50.00
9	$2 black, *yellow, 1971*	125.00	10.00
10	$35 black, *1971*		140.00
11	$3 black, *pink, 1972*	65.00	5.00
12	$35 red, *1972*	450.00	75.00
13	$3 black, *yellow, 1973*	65.00	5.00
14	$35 green, *1973*	1,500.	125.00
15	$3 black, *blue, 1974*	125.00	15.00
16	$35 red, *1974*	400.00	50.00
17	$3 black, *1975*	95.00	10.00
18	$35 green, *1975*	300.00	40.00
19	$3 black, *dark yellow, 1976*	55.00	5.00
20	$35 red, *1976*	140.00	25.00
21	$3 black, *1977*	90.00	10.00
22	$35 red, *1977*	125.00	25.00
23	$5 black, *1978*	45.00	5.00
24	$40 red, *1978*	85.00	20.00
25	$5 black, *1979*	35.00	5.00
26	$40 red, *1979*	45.00	15.00
27	$5 black, *1980*	35.00	5.00
28	$40 green, *1980*	45.00	15.00

Small Game and Habitat Stamps

Required to hunt small game and waterfowl statewide.
Resident ($9), youth ($6) and non-resident ($53) fees.

Resident stamps issued in booklet panes of 5 numbered 20,001-150,000 (1982-86 issues) or 20,001-140,000 (starting with 1987 issue) or sheets of 30 numbered 150,001 and up (1982-86 issues) or 140,001 and up (starting with 1987 issue).
Starting with 1984, resident booklet stamps have straight edges at sides.
Nos. 31, 34, 37, 40 are die cut self adhesives.
Unused values are for stamps on backing.
All youth stamps were issued in booklet panes of 5. Non-resident stamps for 1981, 1982, 1996 and following years were issued in booklet panes of 5.
The 1984-95 non-resident stamps were issued se-tenant with non-resident waterfowl and non-resident general game stamps (rouletted on three sides). The 1994 and 1995 non-resident stamps also were issued se-tenant with only the non-resident general game stamp (rouletted at sides), as well as in booklet panes of 5 (rouletted top and bottom).

Catalogue values for all unused stamps in this section, from this point to the end, are for Never Hinged items.

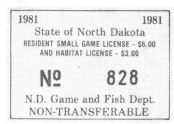

A1

1981

29	A1	$9 black	35.00	3.00
30	A1	$6 black, *blue green*	140.00	25.00
31	A1	$53 blue	100.00	20.00

A2

Artists: Richard Plaschaert, #32, 73; Terry Radlin, #35; David Maass, #38; Leslie Kouba, #41; Mario Fernandez, #44; Ronald Louque, #47, 75; Louis Frisino, #50; Robert Leslie, #53; Roger Cruwys, #56; Thomas Hirata, #59; Phillip Crowe, #62, 77; Bruce Miller, #65; Darrell Davis, #67; Richard Clifton, #69; Wilhelm Goebel, #71.

1982

32	A2	$9 Canada geese	125.00	
		Booklet single with L & R selvage	1,500.	25.00

Serial numbers 1-20,000 are from sheets of 10. Stamps without selvage from booklets sell for considerably less.

33	A1	$6 black, *blue*	140.00	25.00
34	A1	$53 black	35.00	15.00

1983

35	A2	$9 Mallards	65.00	
		Booklet single with L & R selvage	2,250.	25.00

Serial numbers 1-20,000 are from sheets. Stamps without selvage from booklets sell for considerably less.

36	A1	$6 black, *orange*	25.00	
37	A1	$53 black	40.00	

1984

38	A2	$9 Canvasbacks	32.50	
a.		Booklet single, perforated horiz. on 1 or 2 sides	2,000.	25.00
39	A1	$6 black, *light blue*	25.00	
40	A1	$53 black	40.00	

1985

41	A2	$9 Bluebills	22.50	
a.		Booklet single, perforated horiz. on 1 or 2 sides	3,500.	25.00
42	A1	$6 black, *light blue*	25.00	
43	A1	$53 black	40.00	

1986

44	A2	$9 Pintails	19.00	
a.		Booklet single, perforated horiz. on 1 or 2 sides	600.00	20.00
45	A1	$6 black, *light blue*	20.00	
46	A1	$53 black	35.00	

1987

47	A2	$9 Snow geese		16.00
a.		Booklet single, perforated horiz. on 1 or 2 sides	57.50	18.00
48	A1	$6 black, *light blue*	—	25.00
49	A1	$53 black		30.00

1988

50	A2	$9 White-winged scoters		14.00
a.		Booklet single, perforated horiz. on 1 or 2 sides	20.00	12.00
51	A1	$6 black, *light blue*	—	25.00
52	A1	$53 black		30.00

Stamps Inscribed "Small Game"
Resident ($6), youth ($3) and non-resident ($50, $75) fees.

1989

53	A2	$6 Redheads		10.00
a.		Booklet single, perforated horiz. on 1 or 2 sides	15.00	8.00
54	A1	$3 black, *light blue*	—	25.00
55	A1	$50 black		30.00

1990

56	A2	$6 Labrador retriever & mallard		10.00
a.		Booklet single, perforated horiz. on 1 or 2 sides	12.50	8.00
57	A1	$3 black, *light blue*	150.00	25.00
58	A1	$50 black		25.00

1991

59	A2	$6 Green-winged teal		9.00
a.		Booklet single, perforated horiz. on 1 or 2 sides	10.00	6.00
60	A1	$3 black, *light blue*	150.00	25.00
61	A1	$50 black	300.00	25.00

1992

62	A2	$6 Blue-winged teal		8.00
a.		Booklet single, perforated horiz. on 1 or 2 sides	10.00	6.00
63	A1	$3 black, *light blue*	275.00	
64	A1	$50 black		25.00

When supplies of No. 64 ran out, copies of No. 58 were used with the date changed by hand. Unused copies exist. Value, $300.

1993

65	A2	$6 Wood ducks		8.00
a.		Booklet single, perforated horiz. on 1 or 2 sides	10.00	6.00
66	A1	$50 black	450.00	25.00

1994

67	A2	$6 Canada geese		8.00
a.		Booklet single, perforated horiz. on 1 or 2 sides	10.00	6.00
68	A1	$75 black, rouletted on 2 adjacent sides	350.00	20.00
a.		Booklet single, rouletted top and bottom	—	

1995

69	A2	$6 Widgeon		8.00
a.		Booklet single, perforated horiz. on 1 or 2 sides	10.00	5.00
70	A1	$75 black, rouletted on 2 adjacent sides	300.00	20.00
a.		Booklet single, rouletted top and bottom	—	

1996

71	A2	$6 Mallards		8.00
a.		Booklet single, perforated horiz. on 1 or 2 sides	10.00	2.50
72	A1	$75 black, rouletted at top and bottom	—	

1997

73	A2	$6 White-fronted geese		8.00
a.		Booklet single, perforated horiz. on 1 or 2 sides	10.00	2.50
74	A1	$75 black, rouletted at top and bottom	—	

1998

75	A2	$6 Blue-winged teal		8.00
a.		Bklt. single, perforated horiz. on 1 or 2 sides	10.00	2.50
76	A1	$75 black, rouletted at top and bottom	—	

1999

77	A2	$6 Gadwalls		8.00
a.		Bklt. single, perforated horiz. on 1 or 2 sides	10.00	2.50
78	A1	$75 black, rouletted at top and bottom	—	

Non-Resident Waterfowl Stamps
Required by non-residents to hunt waterfowl only.

Unused copies of Nos. A1a, A13a-A19a have no serial number. Used copies have number written in.

Nos. A1-A10 are self-adhesive, die cut. Others are rouletted.

> **Catalogue values for all unused stamps in this section are for Never Hinged items.**

Illustration reduced.

1975-99

A1		$5 green		125.00
a.		No serial number	175.00	—
A2		$5 red, *1976*	475.00	100.00
A3		$5 red, *1977*	325.00	75.00
A4		$5 red, *1978*	110.00	25.00
A5		$5 red, *1979*	85.00	20.00
A6		$5 green, *1980*	90.00	20.00
A7		$8 blue, *1981*	150.00	20.00
A8		$8 black, *1982*	27.50	15.00
A9		$8 black, *1983*		55.00
A10		$8 black, *1984*		50.00
A11		$8 black, *1985*		45.00
A12		$8 black, *1986*		45.00
A13		$8 black, *1987*		40.00
a.		No serial number	350.00	35.00
A14		$8 black, *1988*		35.00
a.		No serial number	300.00	50.00
A15		$8 black, *1989*		25.00
a.		No serial number, light green paper	300.00	50.00
A16		$8 black, *1990*		25.00
a.		No serial number	250.00	50.00
A17		$8 black, *1991*	350.00	35.00
a.		No serial number	200.00	35.00
A18		$8 black, *1992*		20.00
a.		No serial number	150.00	35.00

When supplies of No. A18 ran out copies of No. A16 were used with the date changed by hand. Values, unused $200, used $50.

A19		$10 black, *1993*	225.00	20.00
a.		No serial number	140.00	30.00
A20		$10 black, rouletted on 2 adjacent sides, *1994*	200.00	20.00
a.		No serial number, rouletted top and bottom	125.00	30.00
A21		$10 black, rouletted on 2 adjacent sides, *1995*	175.00	20.00
a.		No serial number, rouletted top and bottom	85.00	25.00
A22		$10 black, rouletted top and bottom, *1996*	75.00	20.00
A23		$10 black, rouletted top and bottom, *1997*	60.00	14.00
A24		$10 black, rouletted top and bottom, *1998*	50.00	12.00
A25		$10 black, rouletted top and bottom, *1999*	50.00	12.00

Resident Sportsmen's Stamps
Required to hunt a variety of game, including waterfowl.

> **Catalogue values for all unused stamps in this section are for Never Hinged items.**

> 1992-93 Resident
> ND Sportsmens License
> $25.00
> Fishing - Small Game
> General Game & Habitat
> Furbearer
> **No 12969**
> NON-TRANSFERABLE

1992-98

2A1		$25 black & purple, *1992-1993*	3,000.	75.00
2A2		$25 black & purple, *1993-1994*	1,100.	35.00
2A3		$25 black & purple, *1994-1995*	250.00	25.00
2A4		$25 black & purple, *1995-1996*	150.00	20.00
2A5		$25 black & purple, *1996-1997*	95.00	15.00
2A6		$27 black & purple, *1997-1998*	75.00	12.00

OHIO
Pymatuning Lake Waterfowl Hunting Stamps

> **Pymatuning Hunting License**
> Valid when attached to Resident Hunters and Trappers License. Authority H. B. 668.
> YEAR **1938** **$1.00** NO FEE

1938-44

A1		$1 black, *light yellow*	—	
A2		$1 black, no date, *1939(* *)*		
A3		$1 black, *blue, 1940*	—	
A4		$1 black, *pink, 1941*	—	
A5		$1 black, *green, 1942*	—	
A6		$1 black, *1943*	—	
A7		$1 black, *manila, 1944*	—	

Stamp for 1945 may exist. No. A2 may have been issued in 1937.

Statewide Issues
Printed in sheets of 16.

> **Catalogue values for all unused stamps in this section are for Never Hinged items.**

Artists: John Ruthven, #1; Harry Antis, #2; Harold Roe, #3, 6, 15, 17; Ronald Louque, #4; Lynn Kaatz, #5, 8; Cynthia Fisher, #7; Jon Henson, #9; Gregory Clair, #10; Samuel Timm, #11; Kenneth Nanney, #12; Richard Clifton, #13; Ron Kleiber, #14; D. J. Cleland-Hura, #16; Timothy Donovan, #18.

1982-99

1	$5.75 Wood ducks	75.00	10.00
2	$5.75 Mallards, *1983*	70.00	10.00
3	$5.75 Green-winged teal, *1984*	70.00	8.00
4	$5.75 Redheads, *1985*	35.00	6.00
5	$5.75 Canvasback, *1986*	27.50	5.00
6	$6 Blue-winged teal, *1987*	12.00	4.00
7	$6 Common goldeneyes, *1988*	11.00	4.00
8	$6 Canada geese, *1989*	11.00	3.00
9	$9 Black ducks, *1990*	13.00	3.00
10	$9 Lesser scaup, *1991*	13.00	3.00
11	$9 Wood duck, *1992*	12.00	3.00
12	$9 Buffleheads, *1993*	12.00	3.00
13	$11 Mallards, *1994*	15.00	2.50
14	$11 Pintails, *1995*	15.00	2.50
15	$11 Hooded mergansers, *1996*	15.00	2.50
16	$11 Widgeons, *1997*	15.00	2.50
17	$11 Gadwall, *1998*	14.00	2.50
18	$11 Mallard, *1999*	13.50	2.50

OKLAHOMA
Printed in booklet panes of 10 (Nos. 1-3) and booklet panes of 5 (Starting with No. 4). No. 10 was the first to be printed in a sheet of 30, No. 17 in a sheet of 24.

> **Catalogue values for all unused stamps in this section are for Never Hinged items.**

Artists: Patrick Sawyer, #1; Hoyt Smith, #2, 5, 7, 20; Jeffrey Frey, #3; Gerald Mobley, #4, 6; Rayburn Foster, #8, 12; Jim Gaar, #9; Wanda Mumm, #10; Ronald Louque, #11; Jeffrey Mobley, #13; Jerome Hageman, #14; Richard Kirkman, #15; Richard Clifton, #16; Greg Everhart, #17; M. Anderson, #18; Jeffrey Klinefelter, #19.

1980-99

1	$4 Pintails	55.00	10.00
2	$4 Canada goose, *1981*	24.00	8.00
3	$4 Green-winged teal, *1982*	10.00	4.00
4	$4 Wood ducks, *1983*	10.00	10.00
5	$4 Ring-necked ducks, *1984*	10.00	3.00
	With tab	9.00	
6	$4 Mallards, *1985*	7.00	3.00
	With tab	10.00	
7	$4 Snow geese, *1986*	7.00	3.00
	With tab	8.00	
8	$4 Canvasbacks, *1987*	7.00	3.00
	With tab	8.00	

9	$4 Widgeons, *1988*	7.00	3.00
	With tab	8.00	
10	$4 Redheads, *1989*	7.00	3.00
	Booklet single, with tab & selvage at L, selvage at R	7.50	
a.	Governor's edition	*125.00*	

No. 10a was available only in sheets of 30 through a sealed bid auction.

11	$4 Hooded merganser, *1990*	7.00	3.00
	Booklet single, with tab & selvage at L, selvage at R	7.50	
12	$4 Gadwalls, *1991*	7.00	3.00
	Booklet single, with tab & selvage at L, selvage at R	7.50	
13	$4 Lesser scaup, *1992*	7.00	3.00
	Booklet single, with tab & selvage at L, selvage at R	7.50	
14	$4 White-fronted geese, *1993*	7.00	3.00
	Booklet single, with tab & selvage at L, selvage at R	7.50	
15	$4 Blue-winged teal, *1994*	7.00	3.00
	Booklet single, with tab & selvage at L, selvage at R	7.50	
16	$4 Ruddy ducks, *1995*	7.00	3.00
	Booklet single, with tab & selvage at L, selvage at R	7.50	
17	$4 Bufflehead, *1996*	6.50	3.00
	Booklet single, with selvage at L & R	7.00	
18	$4 Goldeneyes, *1997*	6.50	3.00
	Bklt. single, with selvage at L & R	7.00	
19	$4 Shovelers, *1998*	6.50	3.00
	Bklt. single, with selvage at L & R	7.00	
20	$4 Canvasbacks, *1999*	6.00	3.00

OREGON

Non-resident fees begin in 1994.
Issued in sheets of 30, except for No. 6. Nos. 2-4 also exist from booklet panes of 5.
Stamps are numbered serially. Nos. 11b, 11c have serial numbers on sheet selvage.
Nos. 10 and 11 were issued on computer form. Unused values are for stamps on form.

> Catalogue values for all unused stamps in this section are for Never Hinged items.

1984 Oregon Waterfowl Stamp

Artists: Michael Sieve, #1-3; Dorothy M. Smith, #4; Darrell Davis, #5; Phillip Crowe, #7; Roger Cruwys, #8; Louis Frisino, #9; Kip Richmond, #10; R. Bruce Horsfall, #11; Richard Plasschaert, #12-13; Robert Steiner, #14-23.

1984-99

1	$5 Canada geese	25.00	7.00
2	$5 Lesser snow goose, *1985*	37.50	10.00
	Booklet single, with 3 tabs (2 at left)	625.00	
3	$5 Pacific brant, perf. 4 sides, *1986*	15.00	
a.	Booklet single, with 2-part tab	20.00	4.00
4	$5 White-fronted geese, perf. 4 sides, *1987*	10.00	
a.	Booklet single, with 2-part tab	13.00	3.00
5	$5 Great Basin Canada geese, *1988*	9.00	3.00
a.	Booklet pane of 1	10.00	

1989 — Die cut self-adhesive

6	($5) Red Nos., 16,001 and up	12.50	*6.00*
a.	Black Nos., 001-16,000	30.00	*12.50*

This provisional stamp was used in early 1989, when the regular stamps were delayed. Unused value is for stamp and adjacent label with serial number on backing paper.

Designs like No. 1

7	$5 Black Labrador retriever & pintails, *1989*	9.00	2.50
a.	Booklet pane of 1	10.00	
8	$5 Mallards & golden retriever, *1990*	10.00	2.50
a.	Booklet pane of 1	11.00	

9	$5 Buffleheads & Chesapeake Bay retriever, perf, *1991*	8.50	
a.	Rouletted at L	10.00	2.50

No. 9a is straight edged on 3 sides and stamp is attached to paper by selvage. Unused value is for stamp attached to paper.

10	$5 Green-winged teal, *1992*	8.50	
a.	Die cut, self-adhesive	10.00	2.50
11	$5 Mallards, vert., *1993*	8.00	
a.	Die cut self-adhesive	10.00	2.50
b.	Sheet of 2	20.00	
c.	$50 Governor's edition sheet of 1	75.00	

No. 11b contains No. 11 and the Oregon upland bird stamp. Nos. 11b, 11c exist imperf.

12	$5 Pintails, perf. 4 sides, *1994*	8.50	
a.	Die cut self-adhesive	10.00	2.50
13	$25 Pintails, diff., die cut self-adhesive, *1994*	32.50	—
14	$5 Wood ducks, *1995*	8.50	
a.	Booklet pane of 1	10.00	2.50
15	$25 Columbian sharp-tailed grouse, bklt. pane of 1, *1995*	32.50	—
16	$5 Mallards, *1996*	8.50	
a.	Booklet pane of 1	10.00	2.50
17	$25 Common snipe, booklet pane of 1, *1996*	30.00	—
18	$5 Canvasbacks, *1997*	8.50	
a.	Booklet pane of 1	10.00	2.50
19	$25 Canvasbacks, booklet pane of 1, *1997*	30.00	
20	$5 Pintails, *1998*	8.50	
a.	Booklet pane of 1	10.00	2.50
21	$25 Pintails, booklet pane of 1, *1998*	30.00	
22	$5 Canada geese, *1999*	6.00	
a.	Booklet pane of 1	10.00	2.50
23	$25 Canada geese, booklet pane of 1, *1999*	30.00	

PENNSYLVANIA

Not required to hunt.
Printed in sheets of 10.

> Catalogue values for all unused stamps in this section are for Never Hinged items.

Artists: Ned Smith, #1, 3; Jim Killen, #2; Robert Knutson, #4; Robert Leslie, #5; John Heldersbach, #6; Ronald Louque, #7; Thomas Hirata, #8, 12; Gerald W. Putt, #9, 14, 16; Robert Sopchick, #10; Glen Reichard, #11; Mark Bray, #13; Clark Weaver, #15, 17.

1983-99

1	$5.50 Wood ducks	16.00	
2	$5.50 Canada geese, *1984*	14.00	
3	$5.50 Mallards, *1985*	9.00	
4	$5.50 Blue-winged teal, *1986*	9.00	2.50
5	$5.50 Pintails, *1987*	9.00	2.50
6	$5.50 Wood ducks, *1988*	9.00	2.50
7	$5.50 Hooded mergansers, *1989*	9.00	2.50
8	$5.50 Canvasbacks, *1990*	9.00	2.50
9	$5.50 Widgeons, *1991*	8.00	2.50
10	$5.50 Canada geese, *1992*	8.00	2.50
11	$5.50 Northern shovelers, *1993*	8.00	2.50
12	$5.50 Pintails, *1994*	8.00	2.50
13	$5.50 Buffleheads, *1995*	8.00	2.50
14	$5.50 Black ducks, *1996*	8.00	2.50
15	$5.50 Hooded merganser, *1997*	8.00	2.50
16	$5.50 Wood ducks, *1998*	8.00	2.50
17	$5.50 Ring-necked ducks, *1999*	8.00	2.50

RHODE ISLAND

Issued in booklet panes of 5 and sheets of 30.
Starting with No. 8, the spacing of the reverse text of the booklet stamp differs from the sheet stamp.
Stamps are numbered serially.

> Catalogue values for all unused stamps in this section are for Never Hinged items.

Artists: Robert Steiner, #1-7, 9-10; Charles Allen, #8; Keith Mueller, #11.

1989-99

1	$7.50 Canvasbacks	12.00	3.00
	Booklet single, with tab	15.00	
a.	$7.50 Governor's edition	92.50	

No. 1a exists without serial number.

2	$7.50 Canada geese, *1990*	12.00	3.00
	Booklet single, with tab	15.00	
a.	$7.50 +$50 Governor's edition	72.50	

No. 2a exists without serial number.

3	$7.50 Wood ducks & Labrador retriever, *1991*	12.00	3.00
	Booklet single, with tab	15.00	
a.	$7.50 +$50 Governor's edition	60.00	

No. 3a exists without serial number.

4	$7.50 Blue-winged teal, *1992*	12.00	3.00
	Booklet single, with tab	12.50	
a.	$7.50 +$50 Governor's edition	60.00	

No. 4a exists without serial number.

5	$7.50 Pintails, *1993*	10.00	3.00
	Booklet single, with tab	12.00	
a.	Sheet of 4	55.00	

No. 5a imperf. is printer's waste.

6	$7.50 Wood ducks, *1994*	10.00	2.50
	Booklet single, with tab and selvage	12.00	
7	$7.50 Hooded mergansers, *1995*	10.00	2.50
	Booklet single, with tab and selvage	12.00	
a.	Governor's edition	110.00	

No. 7a inscribed "Governor's edition."

8	$7.50 Harlequin, *1996*	10.00	2.50
	Booklet single, with tab and selvage	12.00	
a.	Governor's edition	125.00	

No. 8a inscribed "Governor's edition" and has serial number with "G" prefix.

9	$7.50 Greater scaup, *1997*	10.00	2.50
	Booklet single, with tab and selvage	10.50	
a.	Governor's edition	110.00	

No. 9a inscribed "Governor's edition" and has serial number with "G" prefix.

10	$7.50 Black ducks, *1998*	10.00	2.50
	Booklet single, with tab and selvage	10.50	

Rouletted

11	$7.50 Common eiders, *1999*	9.50	2.50
	Horiz. pair from booklet pane	21.00	

No. 11 has no serial number. Booklet pane contains 10 stamps.

SOUTH CAROLINA

Issued in sheets of 30. Stamps with serial numbers were to be issued to hunters.

> Catalogue values for all unused stamps in this section are for Never Hinged items.

Artists: Lee LeBlanc, #1; Bob Binks, #2; Jim Killen, #3, 8, 11; Al Dornish, #4; Rosemary Millette, #5; Daniel Smith, #6; Steve Dillard, #7; Lee Cable, #9; John Wilson, #10; Russell Cobane, #12; Bob Bolin, #13; Joe Hautman, #14; Rodney Huckaby, #15, 17; D. J. Cleland-Hura, #16, 18; Denise Nelson, #19.

1981-99

1	$5.50 Wood ducks	65.00	15.00

No. 2-18 do not have a serial number.

2	$5.50 Mallards, *1982*	100.00	
a.	Serial number on reverse	475.00	25.00
3	$5.50 Pintails, *1983*	100.00	
a.	Serial number on reverse	400.00	25.00
4	$5.50 Canada geese, *1984*	62.50	
a.	Serial number on reverse	190.00	15.00
5	$5.50 Green-winged teal, *1985*	52.50	
a.	Serial number on reverse	100.00	15.00
6	$5.50 Canvasbacks, *1986*	25.00	
a.	Serial number on reverse	42.50	10.00
7	$5.50 Black ducks, *1987*	19.00	
a.	Serial number on reverse	22.50	5.00
8	$5.50 Widgeon & spaniel, *1988*	20.00	
a.	Serial number on reverse	30.00	5.00
9	$5.50 Blue-winged teal, *1989*	11.00	
a.	Serial number on reverse	14.00	4.00
10	$5.50 Wood ducks, *1990*	8.50	
a.	Serial number on reverse	10.00	4.00
b.	$5.50 +$44.50 Governor's edition	82.50	
c.	$5.50 +$94.50 Governor's edition	225.00	

All copies of No. 10c are signed by the governor.

11	$5.50 Labrador retriever, pintails & decoy, *1991*	8.00	
a.	Serial number on reverse	9.00	4.00
12	$5.50 Buffleheads, *1992*	8.00	
a.	Serial number on front	9.00	3.00
13	$5.50 Lesser scaup, *1993*	8.00	
a.	Serial number on front	9.00	3.00
14	$5.50 Canvasbacks, *1994*	8.00	
a.	Serial number on front	9.00	2.50
15	$5.50 Shovelers, lighthouse, *1995*	8.00	
a.	Serial number on front	9.00	2.50
16	$5.50 Redheads, lighthouse, *1996*	8.00	
a.	Serial number on front	8.50	2.50
17	$5.50 Old squaws, *1997*	8.00	
a.	Serial number on front	8.50	2.50
18	$5.50 Green-winged teal, *1998*	8.00	
a.	Serial number on front	8.50	2.50
19	$5.50 Barrow's goldeneye, *1999*	8.00	

No. 19 has no serial number.

SOUTH DAKOTA
Resident Waterfowl Stamps

Vertical safety paper (words read up)

1949-50

1	$1 blk, *grn*, vert. safety paper	600.00	82.50
a.	Horizontal safety paper	—	200.00
2	$1 blk, *lt brn*, vert. safety paper	450.00	60.00
a.	Horizontal safety paper	—	275.00

Safety paper design of Nos. 1 and 2 washes out if stamp is soaked. Washed out copies sell for considerably less. Used values are for copies showing safety paper design.

Printed in booklet panes of 5.
Stamps are numbered serially.

> **Catalogue values for all unused stamps in this section, from this point to the end of the Resident Waterfowl stamps, are for Never Hinged items.**

Artists: Robert Kusserow, #3; Don Steinbeck, #4; John Moisan, #5; John Wilson, #6, 12; Rosemary Millett, #7, 9; Marion Toillion, #8; John Green, #10, 17; Russell Duerksen, #11, 15-16, 19; Mark Anderson, #13, 18; Jeff Reuter, #14.

1976-99

3	$1 Mallards	32.50	3.00
a.	Serial number 4mm high	70.00	10.00
4	$1 Pintails, *1977*	21.00	2.50
5	$1 Canvasbacks, *1978*	13.00	2.50

6	$2 Canada geese, *1988*	8.50	2.50
7	$2 Blue geese, *1987*	7.00	2.50
8	$2 White-fronted geese, *1988*	6.00	2.50
9	$2 Mallards, *1989*	5.00	2.50
10	$2 Blue-winged teal, *1990*	4.50	2.50
11	$2 Pintails, *1991*	4.50	2.50
12	$2 Canvasbacks, *1992*	4.50	2.50
13	$2 Lesser scaup, *1993*	4.50	2.50
14	$2 Redheads, *1994*	4.50	2.50
15	$2 Wood ducks, *1995*	4.50	2.50
16	$2 Canada geese, *1996*	4.00	2.50
17	$2 Widgeons, *1997*	4.00	2.50
18	$2 Green-winged teal, *1998*	4.00	2.50

19	$2 Tundra swan, *1999*	4.00	2.50

Non-resident Waterfowl Stamps
Nos. A1-A7, A9 have serial No. in red. Nos. A1-A18 issued in booklet panes of 5. Type faces and designs of Nos. A1-A18 vary.
Unused values are for unpunched copies. Used values are for signed and punched copies.

Illustration reduced.

1970-86

A1	$30 black, *pink*	20.00	
a.	Missing serial number	3,250.	
A2	$30 black, *pink, 1971*	9.00	
a.	Overprinted "3"		225.00
A3	$30 black, *1972*	3.75	
A4	$30 black, *blue, 1973*	8.00	
a.	Overprinted "2"		250.00
A5	$30 black, *green, 1974*	5.50	
a.	Overprinted "1"		25.00
b.	Overprinted "2"		30.00
c.	Overprinted "4"		30.00
A6	$30 black, *yellow, 1975*	6.50	
a.	Overprinted "UNIT 1"		45.00
b.	Overprinted "UNIT 4"		35.00
c.	Overprinted "UNIT 3"		—
A7	$30 black, *yellow, 1976*	5.00	
a.	Overprinted "1"		18.00
b.	Overprinted "2"	35.00	20.00
c.	Serial No. 4mm high		18.00
d.	As "c," overprinted "1"		40.00
e.	As "c," overprinted "2"		95.00
A8	$30 black, *red, 1977*	7.00	
a.	Overprinted "1"		20.00
b.	Overprinted "2"		30.00
c.	Overprinted "3"		35.00
d.	Overprinted "4"		30.00
e.	Overprinted "5"		140.00
A9	$30 black, *yellow, 1978*	7.00	
a.	Overprinted "1" and 3 strikes of "UNIT 2"		110.00
b.	Overprinted "1"		125.00
A10	$30 black, *red, 1979*	2.50	
A11	$30 black, *light manila, 1980*	4.50	
a.	Overprinted "1"		6.00
b.	Overprinted "2"		10.00
A12	$30 black, *light yellow, 1981*	4.50	
a.	Overprinted "UNIT 1"		6.00
b.	Overprinted "UNIT 2"	10.00	5.00
A13	$30 black, *blue, 1982*	6.50	
A14	$50 black, *dark yellow, 1982*	7.00	
a.	Overprinted "UNIT 2"		—
A15	$50 black, *red, 1983*	8.00	
a.	Overprinted "AREA 1"		50.00
b.	Overprinted "AREA 2"		65.00
c.	Serial No. with serifs		650.00
A16	$50 black, *light manila, 1984*	16.00	
a.	Overprinted "A"		225.00
b.	Overprinted "B"		110.00
A17	$50 black, *red, 1985*	2,500.	500.00
A18	$50 black, *1986*	9.00	5.00

Bennett County Canada Goose Stamps
Type faces and designs vary. Nos. 2A1-2A2 imperf. Nos. 2A3-2A12 printed in booklet panes of 5, perforated horizontally. Some show vertical perforations.
Nos. 2A1-2A4 were free. No. 2A5 cost $5. Stamps were issued to hunters by means of a drawing.
Used values are for signed stamps.

Illustration reduced.

1974-78

2A1	black	45.00	30.00
2A2	black, *pink, 1975*		225.00

2A3	black, *blue, 1976*	55.00	25.00
2A4	black, *yellow, 1977*	50.00	25.00
2A5	black, *greenish blue, 1978*	450.00	

West River Unit Canada Goose
Counties handstamped.
Used values are for signed stamps.

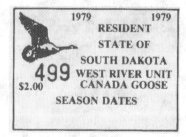

1979

2A6	$2 black, *yellow*	350.00	
a.	Bennett County	375.00	225.00
b.	Haakon County	200.00	
c.	Jackson County	210.00	
d.	Pennington County	175.00	85.00

Stamps overprinted for Perkins County exist but may not have been regularly issued.

1980

2A7	$2 black, *blue*	75.00	
a.	Bennett County	190.00	75.00
b.	Haakon County	100.00	
c.	Jackson County	110.00	
d.	As "c," missing serial number	3,500.	
e.	Pennington County	90.00	45.00
f.	Perkins County	110.00	

Prairie Canada Geese
Counties or Units handstamped.
Used values are for signed stamps.

1981
Perf. 12

2A8	$2 black, *red*	8.00	
a.	Bennett County	80.00	35.00
b.	Haakon County	60.00	20.00
c.	Jackson County	60.00	20.00
d.	Pennington County	60.00	
e.	Perkins County	60.00	

1982

2A9	$2 black, *blue*	110.00	
a.	Bennett County	350.00	160.00
b.	Haakon County	275.00	
c.	Jackson County	275.00	
d.	Pennington County	275.00	
e.	Perkins County	275.00	

1983
Perf. 12

2A10	$2 black, *yellow*	60.00	
a.	UNIT 2A	70.00	
b.	UNIT 31	70.00	35.00
c.	UNIT 39	70.00	35.00
d.	UNIT 49	70.00	35.00
e.	UNIT 53	70.00	35.00
f.	UNIT 11, 3mm type	100.00	50.00
g.	UNIT 23	100.00	

Rouletted top and bottom

2A11	$2 black, *yellow*	11.00	
a.	UNIT 2A	65.00	
b.	UNIT 6	45.00	
c.	UNIT 11, 3mm type	60.00	
d.	UNIT 11, 4½mm type	45.00	
e.	UNIT 23	45.00	
f.	UNIT 31	65.00	
g.	UNIT 32	45.00	
h.	UNIT 39	65.00	
i.	UNIT 42	45.00	
j.	UNIT 49	65.00	
k.	UNIT 53, 3mm type	45.00	
l.	UNIT 53, 4½mm type	50.00	

1984
Perf. 12

2A12	$2 black, *green*	45.00	
a.	UNIT 6	75.00	
b.	UNIT 11, 3mm type	85.00	
c.	UNIT 11, 4½mm type	75.00	
d.	UNIT 23, 3mm type	85.00	
e.	UNIT 23, 4½mm type	75.00	30.00
f.	UNIT 32	85.00	
g.	UNIT 42	75.00	
h.	UNIT 47, 3mm type	85.00	
i.	UNIT 53, 3mm type	75.00	
j.	UNIT 47, 4½mm type		65.00
k.	UNIT 53, 4½mm type		65.00

1985
Rouletted two adjacent sides

2A13	$2 black, *red*		
a.	UNIT 47		70.00
b.	UNIT 53		70.00
c.	UNIT 23		80.00
d.	UNIT 32		100.00
e.	UNIT 42		90.00
f.	UNIT 11		100.00

1986
No fee printed on stamp
Imperf. on 3 sides, rouletted at top

2A14	black		
a.	UNIT 11		70.00
b.	UNIT 47		70.00
c.	UNIT 53		70.00
d.	UNIT 23		80.00

105 stamps for hunting whistling swans during the 1984 season exist. The season was canceled.

Pheasant Restoration Stamps

Required to hunt all small game, including waterfowl. Printed in booklet panes of 5. No. 3A4 rouletted, others perforated. Stamps are numbered serially.

> Catalogue values for all unused stamps in this section, from this point to the end of the Wildlife Habitat stamps, are for Never Hinged items.

1977-88

3A1	$5 Pheasants	12.00	2.50
a.	Rubber-stamped serial number		
3A2	$5 Pheasants, *1978*	12.00	1.50
3A3	$5 Pheasants, *1979*	12.00	1.50
3A4	$5 Pheasants, *1980*	10.00	2.00
a.	Serial number omitted	—	
3A5	$5 Pheasants, *1981*	10.00	1.50
3A6	$5 Pheasants, *1982*	10.00	1.50
a.	Pair, imperf. between	—	
3A7	$5 Pheasants, *1983*	10.00	1.00
3A8	$5 Pheasant, *1984*	10.00	2.00
3A9	$5 Pheasant, *1985*	10.00	2.00
3A10	$5 Pheasants, *1986*	10.00	2.50
3A11	$5 Pheasants, *1987*	10.00	2.00
3A12	$5 Pheasants, *1988*	10.00	2.00

Wildlife Habitat Stamps

Required to hunt all small game, including waterfowl. Printed in booklet panes of 5. Starting with No. 3A18 stamps are rouletted, others are perforated. Stamps are numbered serially.

1989-99

3A13	$8 Pheasants	12.00	2.00
3A14	$8 White-tailed deer, *1990*	12.00	2.00
3A15	$8 Greater prairie chicken, *1991*	12.00	2.00
3A16	$8 Mule Deer, *1992*	12.00	2.50
3A17	$8 Sharp-tailed grouse, *1993*	12.00	2.00
a.	Pair, imperf. between	—	
3A18	$8 Turkey, *1994*	12.00	2.00
3A19	$8 Elk, *1995*	12.00	2.00
3A20	$8 Pheasants, *1996*	10.00	2.00
3A21	$8 Antelope, *1997*	10.00	2.00
3A22	$8 Buffalo, *1998*	10.00	2.00
3A23	$8 Buffalo, *1999*	10.00	2.00

Resident Small Game Stamps

Required by residents wishing to hunt small game, including waterfowl. Nos. 4A1, 4A2 issued panes of 10. Others issued in booklet panes of 5. Stamps are numbered serially in red from 1960 to 1967 and 1978.

> Catalogue values for all unused stamps in this section are for Never Hinged items.

1960-79

4A1	$2 black, *pink*	12.00	2.00
4A2	$2 black, *blue, 1961*	25.00	3.00
4A3	$2 black, *dark yellow, 1962*	35.00	3.00
4A4	$2 black, *light yellow, 1963*	25.00	3.00
4A5	$2 black, *green, 1964*	25.00	3.00
4A6	$2 black, *1965*	25.00	3.00
4A7	$2 black, *yellow, 1966*	10.00	2.00
4A8	$2 black, *light green, 1967*	25.00	2.00
4A9	$2 black, *light yellow, 1968*	10.00	2.00
4A10	$3 black, *blue, 1969*	25.00	2.00
4A11	$3 black, *light yellow, 1970*	10.00	2.00
4A12	$3 black, *green, 1971*		3.00
4A13	$3 black, *light yellow, 1972*	10.00	2.00
4A14	$3 black, *light yellow, 1973*	9.00	2.00
4A15	$3 black, *1974*	10.00	2.00
4A16	$3 black, *pink, 1975*	8.00	2.00
4A17	$3 black, *gray, 1976*	6.00	1.00
4A18	$3 black, *red, 1977*	5.00	1.00
4A19	$3 black, *1978*	6.00	1.00
4A20	$3 black, *red, 1979*	7.00	1.00

1980-98

4A21	$6 black	8.00	1.00
4A22	$6 black, *light yellow, 1981*	9.00	1.00
4A23	$6 black, *blue, 1982*	5.00	.50
4A24	$6 black, *green, 1983*	10.00	1.00
4A25	$6 black, *light blue, 1984*	20.00	1.00
4A26	$6 black, *light blue, 1985*	12.00	1.00
4A27	$6 black, *light blue green, 1986*		2.00
4A28	$6 black, *1987*		2.00
4A29	$6 black, *light green, 1988*	5.00	.50
4A30	$6 black, *1989*		1.00
4A31	$6 black, *light green, 1990*	8.00	.50
4A32	$6 black, *light blue green, 1991*	5.00	.50
4A33	$6 black, *light green, 1992*		1.00
4A34	$6 black, *light pink, 1993*	5.00	.50
4A35	$6 black, *light blue, 1994*	5.00	.50
4A36	$6 black, *yellow, 1995*		1.00
4A37	$6 black, *pink, 1996*	5.00	.50
4A38	$6 black, *light blue, 1997*		.50
4A39	$6 black, *pink, 1998*	8.00	.50

TENNESSEE

Stamps are die cut self-adhesives and are numbered serially.

Cards include both license cost and a fee of 30c (Nos. 1-5), 50c (Nos. 6-13) or $1 (starting with No. 14).

Nos. 3, 5, 7-15 come as 3-part card.

Starting with No. 12, cards come in four parts as well.

1979 and 1980 issues are for resident and non-resident fees.

Unused values are for stamps on original computer card stub.

> Catalogue values for all unused stamps in this section are for Never Hinged items.

Artists: Dick Elliott, #1-2; Phillip Crowe, #3-4, 7, 17; Bob Gillespie, #5; Ken Schulz, #6; Allen Hughes, #8; Jimmy Stewart, #9; Ralph J. McDonald, #10, 18; Thomas Hirata, #11, 16; Jim Lamb, #12; Roger Cruwys, #13; Tom Freeman, #14; Richard Clifton, #15, 19; Bob Leslie, #20; Bethany Carter, #21.

1979-99

1	$2 Mallards	140.00	25.00
2	$5 Mallards	1,000.	250.00
3	$2 Canvasbacks, *1980*	60.00	15.00
	3-part card	575.00	
4	$5 Canvasbacks, *1980*	400.00	100.00
5	$2 Wood ducks, *1981*	35.00	10.00
	3-part card		
6	$6 Canada geese, *1982*	55.00	15.00
7	$6 Pintails, *1983*	55.00	15.00
	3-part card	70.00	

8	$6 Black ducks, *1984*	55.00	12.00
	3-part card	70.00	
9	$6 Blue-winged teal, *1985*	22.50	7.00
	3-part card	50.00	
10	$6 Mallard, *1986*	15.00	5.00
	3-part card	45.00	
11	$6 Canada geese, *1987*	12.00	5.00
	3-part card	18.00	

Card exists with 2/28/88 expiration date rather than correct 2/29 date.

12	$6 Canvasbacks, *1988*	12.00	4.00
	3-part card	24.00	
	4-part card	24.00	
13	$6 Green-winged teal, *1989*	11.00	4.00
	3-part card	14.00	
	4-part card	14.00	
14	$12 Redheads, *1990*	17.00	4.00
	3-part card	22.50	
	4-part card	22.50	
15	$12 Mergansers, *1991*	17.00	4.00
	3-part card	22.50	
	4-part card	22.50	
16	$13 Wood ducks, *1992*	17.00	4.00
	4-part card	22.50	
17	$13 Pintails & decoy, *1993*	18.00	4.00
	4-part card	22.50	
18	$15 Mallard, *1994*	20.00	5.00
	4-part card	22.50	
19	$16 Ring-necked duck, *1995*	20.00	5.00
	4-part card	22.50	
20	$17 Black ducks, *1996*	21.00	5.00
	4-part card	25.00	

Starting with No. 21 stamps are perforated. Not required for hunting.

1999 WILDLIFE STAMP — $10.00 — TENNESSEE — WATERFOWL SERIES — 000229

21	$10 Mallard, *1999*	12.00	2.50

TEXAS
Printed in sheets of 10.
Nos. 1-4 are rouletted.
Stamps are numbered serially.

Catalogue values for all unused stamps in this section are for Never Hinged items.

214229 — Texas Parks and Wildlife Dept. — Waterfowl Stamp — 1981 — $5.00

Artists: Larry Hayden, #1, 12; Ken Carlson, #2, 14; Maynard Reece, #3; David Maass, #4, 9, 15; John Cowan, #5, 8; Herb Booth, #6; Gary Moss, #7; Robert Bateman, #10; Daniel Smith, #11, 16; Jim Hautman, #13, 17; Phillip Crowe, #18; Robert Hautman, #19.

1981-99
1	$5 Mallards	45.00	8.00
2	$5 Pintails, *1982*	27.50	5.00
3	$5 Widgeons, *1983*	160.00	18.00
4	$5 Wood ducks, *1984*	27.50	5.00
5	$5 Snow geese, *1985*	10.00	3.00
6	$5 Green-winged teal, *1986*	9.50	2.50
7	$5 White-fronted geese, *1987*	9.50	2.50
8	$5 Pintails, *1988*	9.50	2.50
9	$5 Mallards, *1989*	9.50	2.50
10	$5 American widgeons, *1990*	9.00	2.50
11	$7 Wood duck, *1991*	9.50	2.50
12	$7 Canada geese, *1992*	9.50	2.50
13	$7 Blue-winged teal, *1993*	9.50	2.50
14	$7 Shovelers, *1994*	9.50	2.50
15	$7 Buffleheads, *1995*	9.50	2.50

Beginning with No. 16, these stamps were sold only in booklets with seven other wildlife stamps and were not valid for hunting.

16	$3 Gadwalls, *1996*	12.50	

17	$3 Cinnamon teal, *1997*	12.50	
18	$3 Pintail, labrador retreiver, *1998*	12.50	
19	$3 Canvasbacks, *1999*	12.00	

UTAH
Game Bird Stamps
For hunting game birds, including waterfowl. In 1951 No. A1 or No. 2A1 were required, in 1952 No. A3 or 2A2. No. A1 printed in booklet panes of 25, others in booklet panes of 10. Perforated.

A1

A2

1951
A1	A1	$3 brown, resident	60.00	7.00
A2	A1	$15 red, non-resident	400.00	50.00

1952
A3	A2	$3 red, resident	65.00	
A4	A2	$15 blue, non-resident	200.00	35.00

Resident Fishing and Hunting Stamps
For hunting game birds, including waterfowl. Printed in sheets of 40. No. 2A1 printed on linen. Unused values are for stamps with deer tags attached at left.

No. 2A1

No. 2A2

1951-52
2A1		$5 blue	3.00	.50
2A2		$5 green, *1952*	3.00	.50

Waterfowl Issues
Printed in sheets of 30 or in booklet panes of 5 (starting in 1990). No. 11 issued in sheets of 9. Stamps are numbered serially.

Catalogue values for all unused stamps in this section are for Never Hinged items.

$3.30 — UTAH — Waterfowl Stamp — 006468 — FIRST OF STATE 1986 Exp. 6-30-87

Artists: Leon Parsons, #1; Arthur Anderson, #2; David Chapple, #3; Jim Morgan, #4; Daniel Smith, #5; Robert Steiner, #6-12.

1986-97
1	$3.30 Whistling swans		9.50	3.00
2	$3.30 Pintails, *1987*		7.50	3.00
3	$3.30 Mallards, *1988*		7.50	2.50
4	$3.30 Canada geese, *1989*		6.50	2.50
5	$3.30 Canvasbacks, perf. 4 sides, *1990*		6.50	
a.	Booklet single, with 2-part tab		8.00	2.50
6	$3.30 Tundra swans, perf. 4 sides, *1991*		6.00	
a.	Booklet single, with 2-part tab		7.00	2.50
7	$3.30 Pintails, perf. 4 sides, *1992*		6.00	
a.	Booklet single, with 2-part tab		7.00	2.50
8	$3.30 Canvasbacks, perf. 4 sides, *1993*		7.00	
a.	Booklet single, with 2-part tab		7.00	2.50
9	$3.30 Chesapeake Retriever and ducks, perf. 4 sides, *1994*		12.00	
a.	Booklet single, with 2-part tab		13.00	2.50
10	$3.30 Green-winged teal, *1995*		6.00	
a.	Booklet single, with 2-part tab		7.00	2.50
11	$7.50 White-fronted goose, *1996*		12.00	2.50
	$97.50 Governor's edition		125.00	

1997 UTAH WATERFOWL STAMP — 5057 — $7.50 — Exp. 6/30/98

Redheads: a, Male, serial # at UL. b, Female, serial # at LL.

12	Pair, *1997*		22.50	
a.-b.	$7.50 Any single		11.00	2.50
c.	$97.50 Governor's Edition		110.00	

No. 12c is No. 12 without the central perforations. The denomination appears only in the upper right corner. The bottom inscription has Governor's Edition plus a serial number.

VERMONT
Printed in sheets of 30.

Catalogue values for all unused stamps in this section are for Never Hinged items.

VERMONT — 1986 — $5

Artists: Jim Killen, #1-4; Richard Plasschaert, #5-8; Reed Prescott, #9, 11; Robert Mullen, #10; J. Collins, #12; George Lockwood, #13-14.

1986-99
1	$5 Wood ducks	11.00	4.00
2	$5 Common goldeneyes, *1987*	8.00	3.00
3	$5 Black ducks, *1988*	8.00	2.50
4	$5 Canada geese, *1989*	8.00	2.50
5	$5 Green-winged teal, *1990*	8.00	2.50
6	$5 Hooded mergansers, *1991*	7.50	2.50
7	$5 Snow geese, *1992*	8.00	2.50
8	$5 Mallards, *1993*	8.00	2.50
9	$5 Ring-necked duck, *1994*	7.50	2.50
10	$5 Bufflehead, *1995*	7.50	2.50
11	$5 Lesser scaup, *1996*	7.50	2.50
12	$5 Pintails, *1997*	7.50	2.50
13	$5 Blue-winged teal, *1998*	7.00	2.50
14	$5 Canvasbacks, *1999*	7.00	2.50

VIRGINIA
Printed in booklet panes of 10 and/or sheets of 30. Stamps are numbered serially.

Catalogue values for all unused stamps in this section are for Never Hinged items.

Department of Game and Inland Fisheries — $5.00 — 1988 — 038779 — VIRGINIA WATERFOWL STAMP

Artists: Ronald Louque, #1; Arthur LeMay, #2; Louis Frisino, #3; Robert Leslie, #4, 11; Carl Knuth, #5, 12; Bruce Miller, #6; Francis Sweet, #7; Richard Clifton, #8; Wilhelm Goebel, #9; Roger Cruwys, #10.

1988-99
1	$5 Mallards, serial Nos. 1-40,000	12.00	2.50
	Booklet pair with L & R selvage, serial Nos. above 40,000	24.00	
2	$5 Canada geese, serial Nos. 1-40,000, *1989*	12.00	2.50
	Booklet pair with L & R selvage, serial Nos. above 40,000	24.00	
3	$5 Wood ducks, serial Nos. 1-20,000, *1990*	9.00	2.50
	Booklet pair with L & R selvage, serial Nos. above 20,000	18.00	
4	$5 Canvasbacks, serial Nos. 1-20,000, *1991*	8.50	2.50
	Booklet pair with L & R selvage, serial Nos. above 20,000	17.00	
5	$5 Buffleheads, serial Nos. 1-20,000, *1992*	8.00	2.50
	Booklet pair with L & R selvage, serial Nos. above 20,000	16.00	

6	$5 Black ducks, serial Nos. 1-20,000, *1993*	8.00	2.50
	Booklet pair with L & R selvage, serial Nos. above 20,000	16.00	
7	$5 Lesser scaup, *1994*	7.50	2.50
	Booklet pair with L & R selvage	15.00	
8	$5 Snow geese, *1995*	7.50	2.50
	Booklet pair with L & R selvage	15.00	
9	$5 Hooded mergansers, *1996*	7.50	2.50
10	($5) Pintail, Labrador retriever, *1997*	7.50	2.50
11	$5 Mallards, *1998*	7.50	2.50
12	$5 Green-winged teal, *1999*	7.50	2.50

WASHINGTON

Printed in booklet panes of 1 and sheets of 30.
Stamps are numbered serially.
Booklet panes starting with No. 7 without staple
holes were sold to collectors.

Catalogue values for all unused stamps in
this section are for Never Hinged items.

Artists: Keith Warrick, #1; Ray Nichol, #2; Robert Bateman, #3; Maynard Reece, #4; Thomas Quinn, #5; Ronald Louque, #6-7; Phillip Crowe, #8; Fred Thomas, #9; David Hagenbaumer, #10; Cynthie Fisher, #11; Greg Beecham, #12; A. Young, #13; Robert Steiner, #14-15.

1986-99

1	$5 Mallards, Nos. 1-60,000	9.00	
	Booklet pane of 1, Nos. 60,001-160,000	15.00	4.00
2	$5 Canvasbacks, Nos. 1-24,000, *1987*	9.50	
	Booklet pane of 1, Nos. 24,001-124,000	10.00	3.00
3	$5 Harlequin, Nos. 1-60,000, *1988*	9.00	
	Booklet pane of 1, Nos. 60,001-160,000	10.00	3.00
4	$5 American widgeons, Nos. 1-60,000, *1989*	9.00	
	Booklet pane of 1, Nos. 60,001-160,000	10.00	2.50
5	$5 Pintails & sour duck, Nos. 1-60,000, *1990*	9.00	
	Booklet pane of 1, Nos. 60,001-160,000	10.00	2.50
6	$5 Wood duck, Nos. 1-30,000, *1991*	9.00	
	Booklet pane of 1, Nos. above 30,000	10.00	4.00
7	$6 Wood duck, Nos. 100,000-130,000, *1991*	10.00	
	Booklet pane of 1, Nos. above 130,000	10.00	2.50
8	$6 Labrador puppy & Canada geese, Nos. 1-30,000, *1992*	9.00	
	Booklet pane of 1, Nos. above 30,000	10.00	2.50
9	$6 Snow geese, Nos. 1-30,000, *1993*	8.00	
	Booklet pane of 1, Nos. above 30,000	9.00	2.50
10	$6 Black brant, Nos. 1-30,000, *1994*	8.00	
	Booklet pane of 1, Nos. above 30,000	9.00	2.50
11	$6 Mallards, Nos. 1-30,000, *1995*	8.00	
	Booklet pane of 1, Nos. above 30,000	9.00	2.50
12	$6 Redheads, Nos. 1-25,050, *1996*	8.00	
	Booklet pane of 1, Nos. above 25,050	9.00	2.50
13	$6 Canada geese, Nos. 9600001-9625050, *1997*	8.00	
	Bklt. pane of 1, Nos. above 9625050	9.00	2.50
14	$6 Barrow's goldeneye Nos. 1-25,050 , *1998*	8.00	
	Bklt. pane of 1, Nos. 25,051-27,050	9.00	2.50
15	$6 Bufflehead, *1999*	8.00	
a.	Bklt. pane of 1	9.00	2.50

WEST VIRGINIA

Printed in sheets of 30 and booklet panes of 5.
All booklet stamps have straight edges at sides.
Starting in 1990, booklet stamps are numbered
serially. Some, but not all, of the 1988 booklet
stamps are numbered serially. Stamps from sheets
are not numbered serially.

Catalogue values for all unused stamps in
this section are for Never Hinged items.

Artists: Daniel Smith, #1-2; Steven Dillard, #3-4; Ronald Louque, #5-6; Louis Frisino, #7-8; Robert Leslie, #9-10; Thomas Hirata, #11-12; Phillip Crowe, #13-14; Richard Clifton, #15-16; Fran Sweet, #17-18; Karl Badgley, #19-20.

1987-96

1	$5 Canada geese, resident	13.00	8.00
	Booklet single with tab at top	75.00	
2	$5 Canada geese, non-resident	13.00	8.00
	Booklet single with tab at top	75.00	
3	$5 Wood ducks, resident, *1988*	10.00	4.00
	Booklet single with tab at top, no serial number	40.00	
a.	Booklet single with serial number on reverse	85.00	4.00
4	$5 Wood ducks, non-resident, *1988*	10.00	4.00
	Booklet single with tab at top, no serial number	40.00	
a.	Booklet single with serial number on reverse	85.00	4.00
5	$5 Decoys, resident, *1989*	9.50	3.00
	Booklet single with tab at top	35.00	
a.	Governor's edition	*70.00*	
6	$5 Decoys, non-resident, *1989*	9.50	3.00
	Booklet single with tab at top	35.00	
a.	Governor's edition	*70.00*	

Nos. 5a and 6a were available only in sheets of 30 through a
sealed bid auction.

7	$5 Labrador retriever & decoy, resident, *1990*	9.00	
a.	Booklet single	9.00	3.00
8	$5 Labrador retriever & decoy, non-resident, *1990*	9.00	
a.	Booklet single	9.00	3.00
9	$5 Mallards, resident, *1991*	8.50	
a.	Booklet single	8.50	2.50
10	$5 Mallards, non-resident, *1991*	8.50	
a.	Booklet single	8.50	2.50
b.	Sheet, 3 each #9-10	50.00	

No. 10b is numbered serially; exists imperf. without serial
numbers.

11	$5 Canada geese, resident, *1992*	8.50	
a.	Booklet single	8.50	2.50
12	$5 Canada geese, non-resident, *1992*	8.50	
a.	Booklet single	8.50	2.50
13	$5 Pintails, resident, *1993*	8.00	
a.	Booklet single	8.00	2.50
14	$5 Pintails, non-resident, *1993*	8.00	
a.	Booklet single	8.00	2.50
15	$5 Green-winged teal, resident, *1994*	8.00	
a.	Booklet single	8.00	2.50
16	$5 Green-winged teal, non-resident, *1994*	8.00	
a.	Booklet single	8.00	2.50
17	$5 Mallards, resident, *1995*	8.00	
a.	Booklet single	8.00	2.50
18	$5 Mallards, non-resident, *1995*	8.00	
a.	Booklet single	8.00	2.50
19	$5 Widgeons, resident, *1996*	8.00	
a.	Booklet single	8.00	2.50
20	$5 Widgeons, non-resident, *1996*	8.00	
a.	Booklet single	8.00	2.50

WISCONSIN

Printed in sheets of 10. Starting in 1980 the left side
of the sheet has a agent tab and a numbered tab,
the right side a numbered tab.

Catalogue values for all unused stamps in
this section are for Never Hinged items.

Artists: Owen Gromme, #1; Rockne (Rocky) Knuth, #2, 6; Martin Murk, #3; Timothy Schultz, #4; William Koelpin, #5; Michael James Riddet, #7, 15; Greg Alexander, #8, 20; Don Moore, #9, 17; Al Kraayvanger, #10; Richard Timm, #11; Rick Kelley, #12; Daniel Renn Pierce, #13; Terry Doughty, #14; Frank Middlestadt, #16, 22; Les Didler, #18, 21; Sam Timm, #19.

1978-99

1	$3.25 Wood ducks	100.00	9.00
2	$3.25 Buffleheads, rouletted, *1979*	27.50	6.00
3	$3.25 Widgeons, *1980*	12.00	2.50
	With tab	15.00	
4	$3.25 Lesser Scaup, *1981*	9.50	2.50
	With tab	13.00	
5	$3.25 Pintails, *1982*	8.00	2.50
	With numbered tab	8.00	
	With agent's and numbered tab	10.00	
6	$3.25 Blue-winged teal, *1983*	8.00	2.50
	With numbered tab	8.00	
	With agent's and numbered tab	10.00	
7	$3.25 Hooded merganser, *1984*	8.00	2.50
	With numbered tab	8.00	
	With agent's and numbered tab	10.00	

8	$3.25 Lesser scaup, *1985*	8.50	2.50
	With numbered tab	8.50	
	With agent's and numbered tab	10.00	
9	$3.25 Canvasbacks, *1986*	8.50	2.50
	With numbered tab	8.50	
	With agent's and numbered tab	10.00	
10	$3.25 Canada geese, *1987*	6.00	2.50
	With numbered tab	6.00	
	With agent's and numbered tab	7.00	
11	$3.25 Hooded merganser, *1988*	6.00	2.50
	With numbered tab	6.00	
	With agent's and numbered tab	7.00	
12	$3.25 Common goldeneye, *1989*	6.00	2.50
	With numbered tab	6.00	
	With agent's and numbered tab	7.00	
13	$3.25 Redheads, *1990*	6.00	2.50
	With numbered tab	6.00	
	With agent's and numbered tab	7.00	
14	$5.25 Green-winged teal, *1991*	8.00	2.50
	With numbered tab	8.00	
	With agent's and numbered tab	9.00	
15	$5.25 Tundra swans, *1992*	8.00	2.50
	With numbered tab	8.00	
	With agent's and numbered tab	9.00	
16	$5.25 Wood ducks, *1993*	8.00	2.50
	With numbered tab	8.00	
	With agent's and numbered tab	9.00	
17	$5.25 Pintails, *1994*	8.00	2.50
	With numbered tab	8.00	
	With agent's and numbered tab	9.00	
18	$5.25 Mallards, *1995*	8.00	2.50
	With numbered tab	8.00	
	With agent's and numbered tabs	9.00	
19	($5.25) Green-winged teal, *1996*	8.00	2.50
	With numbered tab	8.00	
	With agent's and numbered tabs	9.00	
20	($7) Canada geese, *1997*	9.50	2.50
	With numbered tab	9.50	
	With agent's and numbered tabs	10.00	
21	$7 Snow goose, *1998*	9.50	2.50
	With numbered tab	9.50	
	With agent's and numbered tabs	10.00	
22	$7 Greater scaups, *1999*	9.00	2.50

WYOMING

Issued in panes of 5. Required to fish as well as to
hunt all small and big game, including waterfowl.
Stamps are numbered serially.

Catalogue values for all unused stamps in
this section are for Never Hinged items.

Artists: Robert Kusserow, #2; Dan Andrews, #3; Ted Feeley, #4; Clark Ostergaard, #5; Dave Wade, #6, 8, 10, 13; Connie J. Robinson, #7; Sarah Rogers, #9; James Brooks, #11; Peter Eades, #12; D. Enright, #14; Garth Hegeson, #15; Nick Reitzel, #16.

1984-99

1	$5 Meadowlark	37.50	2.50
2	$5 Canada geese, horiz., *1985*	37.50	2.50
3	$5 Antelope, horiz., *1986*	37.50	2.50
4	$5 Grouse, horiz., *1987*	37.50	2.50
5	$5 Fish, horiz., *1988*	37.50	2.50
6	$5 Deer, horiz., *1989*	37.50	2.50
7	$5 Bear, horiz., *1990*	37.50	2.50
8	$5 Rams, horiz., *1991*	37.50	2.50
9	$5 Bald eagle, horiz., *1992*	25.00	2.50
10	$5 Elk, horiz., *1993*	15.00	2.50
11	$5 Bobcat, *1994*	10.00	2.50
12	$5 Moose, *1995*	9.50	2.50
13	$5 Turkey, *1996*	9.50	2.50
14	$5 Mountain goats, *1997*	9.50	2.50
15	$5 Trumpeter swan, *1998*	9.00	2.50
16	$5 Brown trout, *1999*	9.50	2.50

INDIAN RESERVATIONS

Stamps for other reservations exist and will be listed after more information is received about them.

Cheyenne River Indian Reservation
South Dakota
Birds and Small Game Stamps

Nos. A1-A2 issued in booklet panes of 6, rouletted. Nos. A3-A4 issued in booklet panes of 5, perforated, self-adhesive. Nos. A5-A6 issued in booklet panes of 5, perforated.

A1

A2

A1	A1	black, *light yellow*, member	1,200.	150.00
A2	A1	black, *yellow*, non-member	375.00	95.00

Nos. A1-A2 probably issued starting in 1984.

> **Catalogue values for all unused stamps in this section, from this point to the end, are for Never Hinged items.**

A3	A2	black, *yellow*, member	25.00	10.00
A4	A2	black, *yellow*, non-member	45.00	15.00
A5	A2	black, *light yellow*, member	13.00	5.00
A6	A2	black, *light yellow*, non-member	27.50	10.00

Nos. A3-A4 issued starting in 1989. Nos. A5-A6 issued starting in 1992.

Waterfowl Stamps

Issued starting in 1993 in panes of 5. Perforated.

> **Catalogue values for all unused stamps in this section are for Never Hinged items.**

1		black, *light yellow*, member	15.00 5.00
2		black *light yellow*, non-member	27.50 10.00

Colville Indian Reservation
Washington
Bird Stamps

Required by non-tribal members to hunt birds, including waterfowl. Stamps are die cut, self-adhesive. No. 2 is numbered serially in red.

> **Catalogue values for all unused stamps in this section are for Never Hinged items.**

A1

A2

1990-91

1	A1	black, *yellow*	—
2	A2	$20 black, *yellow*, 1992	—

Crow Indian Reservation
Montana
Waterfowl Stamps

Issued in panes of 5 stamps (4 each No. 1, 1 No. 1a). Die cut, self-adhesive. Numbered serially in red.

> **Catalogue values for all unused stamps in this section are for Never Hinged items.**

1992

1	blue	95.00 25.00
a.	Inscribed "Apr. 30, 199_"	275.00 75.00

Stamps without serial numbers exist. Some may have been issue to hunters during an abbreviated 1993 season.

Crow Creek Sioux Indian Reservation
South Dakota
Non-Indian Small Game Hunting Stamps

Issued 1961-64. The 1961 fee was $2.50. No example is recorded. The 1962 stamps were changed by hand for use in 1963 and 1964. No example of the 1964 stamp is recorded.

1962-63

2	$5 black	12,500.	—
3	$5 black, *1963*	—	—

Waterfowl Stamps

Fees: $10, reservation resident, non-tribal member; $30, South Dakota resident; $65, non-South Dakota resident.

> **Catalogue values for all unused stamps in this section, from this point to the end, are for Never Hinged items.**

1989

5	$10 black	575.	150.
6	$30 black	10,000.	1,500.
7	$65 black	1,600.	350.

1990

8	$10 black	400.	100.
9	$30 black	375.	
10	$65 black	1,400.	300.

Fees: $5, tribal member; $15, affiliate, reservation resident; $30 ($35), South Dakota resident/non-resident daily use; $75 ($100), South Dakota resident/non-resident season.

1994

11	$5 green	55.00	15.00
12	$15 blue	80.00	
13	$30 red	125.00	
a.	$25 red (error)	—	
14	$75 red	200.00	55.00

1995

15	$5 green	25.00	10.00
16	$15 blue	45.00	
17	$30 red	75.00	
18	$75 red	125.00	40.00

1996

19	$5 green	27.50	10.00
20	$15 blue	45.00	
21	$35 red	75.00	
22	$100 red	125.00	35.00

1997

23	$5 green	12.00	
24	$15 blue	35.00	
25	$35 red	85.00	
26	$75 red	190.00	

No. 25 is inscribed $75, but sold for $35.

1998

27	$5 green	12.00	
28	$15 blue	35.00	
29	$35 red	85.00	
30	$75 red	190.00	

1999

31	$5 green	12.00	
32	$15 blue	35.00	
33	$35 red	85.00	
34	$75 red	190.00	

Sportsmen's Stamps

For hunting game including waterfowl.
Fees: $10, tribal member; $25, reservation resident,
non-tribal member; $100, South Dakota resident;
$250, non-South Dakota resident.
Used values are for signed stamps.

Catalogue values for all unused stamps in
this section are for Never Hinged items.

CROW CREEK SIOUX TRIBE
3069
1989 $10
TRIBAL MEMBER SPORTSMAN

1989

A1	$10	black	450.00	100.00
A2	$25	black	1,050.	300.00
A3	$100	black	450.00	75.00
A4	$250	black	450.00	150.00

1990

A5	$10	black	500.00	100.00
A6	$25	black	650.00	150.00
A7	$100	black	260.00	125.00
A8	$250	black	400.00	150.00

Flathead Indian Reservation
Montana
Bird or Fish Stamps

The 1988 stamp was printed in booklet panes of 10.
Starting in 1989, printed in booklet panes of 5
stamps se-tenant with 5 stamps marked "Duplicate."
Numbered serially in red. Rouletted.

Catalogue values for all unused stamps in
this section are for Never Hinged items.

Confederated Salish & Kootenai Tribes
1989 BIRD OR FISHING STAMP
☐ BIRD   ☐ FISHING
$10.00 (Nonrefundable)
Permit #_____

1987-90

1	$10	black	1,350.	325.00
1A	$10	black, *1988*	1,250.	250.00
2	$10	blue, *1989*	16.00	5.00
3	$10	blue, *1990*	16.00	5.00

Joint Bird License Stamps

Printed in booklet panes of 10. Die cut, self-
adhesive. Numbered serially.

PERMIT NUMBER   1991 JOINT BIRD LICENSE
52 — 913667
MONTH   DAY
Expires February 29, 1992 $10.00   DATE OF ISSUE

1991

4	$10	black, *green*	10.50	5.00

Bird License Stamps

Printed in booklet panes of 10. Die cut, self-
adhesive. Numbered serially.

PERMIT NUMBER   1992 Flathead Reservation Bird License
52 — 923227
MONTH   DAY
Expires February 28, 1993 $12.00   DATE OF ISSUE

1992-98

5	$12	black, *rose, season*	10.50	5.00
6	$12	black, *salmon, 3-day*	9.50	5.00
7	$12	black, *dark green, season, 1993*	8.00	4.00
8	$12	black, *dark blue, 3-day, 1993*	7.50	4.00
9	$12	black, *blue, season, 1994*	8.00	4.00
10	$12	black, *orange, 3-day, 1994*	7.00	3.00
11	$12	black, *yellow, resident, 1995*	8.00	3.00

12	$55	black, *pale blue green, non-resident, 1995*	17.50	9.00
13	$12	black, *turquoise, resident, 1996*	11.00	3.00
14	$55	black, *pale orange, non-resident, 1996*	18.00	15.00
15	$12	black, *pale yellow, resident, 1997*	10.00	3.00
16	$55	black, *pale blue green, non-resident, 1997*	11.00	
17	$13	black, *turquoise, resident, 1998*	12.00	3.00
18	$56	black, *blue, non-resident, 1998*	12.00	3.00

Fort Berthold Indian Reservation
North Dakota
Small Game Stamps

Stamps issued before 1990 may exist.
Issued in booklet panes of 6 stamps and 6 tabs.
Required for hunting small game including waterfowl.
Values are for stamps with tabs.
Fees varied, usually $6 for tribe members and $20-
$30 for non-members.
Stamps are numbered serially.

Catalogue values for all unused stamps in
this section are for Never Hinged items.

SMALL GAME
PERMIT
FISH & GAME DIV.
THREE AFFILIATED TRIBES
NON-TRANSFERABLE
VOID AFTER DECEMBER 31, 1990
551   551

1990-98
Rouletted

A6	black, *pink*	85.00	25.00
A7	black, *green, 1991*	80.00	
A8	black, *pink, 1992*	80.00	
A9	black, *blue, 1993*	175.00	
A10	black, *pink, 1994*	70.00	
A11	black, *pink, 1995*	100.00	25.00
A12	black, *green, 1996*	57.50	
A13	black, *light green, 1997*	50.00	12.00
A14	black, *green, 1998*	30.00	

Waterfowl Stamps

Stamps issued before 1990 may exist.
Issued in booklet panes of 6 stamps and 6 tabs.
Required for non-member waterfowl hunters only.
Values are for stamps with tabs.
Fees varied, usually $20-$30.
Stamps are numbered serially.

Catalogue values for all unused stamps in
this section are for Never Hinged items.

WATERFOWL
HABITAT
STAMP
FISH & GAME DIV.
THREE AFFILIATED TRIBES
NON-TRANSFERABLE
032   032

1990-98
Rouletted

2A6	black	2,500.	
2A7	black, *blue, 1991*	900.00	
2A8	black, *yellow, #1-60, 1992*	4,250.	
2A9	black, *yellow, #61-120, 1993*	600.00	
2A10	black, *green, #1-60, 1994*	625.00	
2A11	black, *green, #61-120, 1995*	275.00	50.00
2A12	black, *green, #121-198, 1996*	225.00	
2A13	black, *light green, #199-276, 1997*	250.00	
2A14	black, *light green, #277-, 1998*	300.00	

Fort Peck Indian Reservation
Montana

Stamps issued before 1975 may exist.

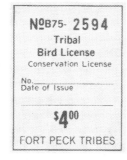

Nº B75- 2594
Tribal
Bird License
Conservation License
No.
Date of Issue
$4 00
FORT PECK TRIBES

1975-78
Rouletted

2	$4	black	1,500.
3	$4	black, *1976*	100.
a.	Double impression	3,750.	
4	$4	black, *1977*	—
5	$5	black, *orange, 1978*	325.

Jicarilla Apache Indian Reservation
New Mexico
Wildlife Stamp

Believed to have been issued starting in 1988.
Issued in booklet panes of 4. Numbered serially.
Rouletted.

Catalogue values for all unused stamps in
this section are for Never Hinged items.

JICARILLA NATURAL RESOURCES
DULCE, N.M.
Nº 2759
JICARILLA WILDLIFE STAMP
$5.00

1	$5	black & gold, *blue*	12.00

Lake Traverse (Sisseton-Wahpeton) Indian Reservation
South Dakota-North Dakota
Waterfowl Stamps

No examples are recorded of stamps from 1987-
1990. No. 1 is die cut. Nos. 6, 8-9 are die cut, self-
adhesive. No. 7 issued in booklet panes of 5,
rouletted, numbered serially in red.

1986
S.W.S.T. Migratory Game Bird
A1

1991 S.W.S.T.
WATERFOWL
License
A2

SISSETON-WAHPETON 1513
Sioux Tribe
Waterfowl
Stamp
1992
A3

United States State waterfowl permit stamps can
be mounted in the Scott U.S. Federal and State
Duck Stamps album.

A4

1986-99

1	A1	green	175.00	50.00

> Catalogue values for all unused stamps in this section, from this point to the end, are for Never Hinged items.

6	A2	black, *bright green, 1991*	110.00	
7	A3	Wood duck, *1992*	15.00	
8	A2	black, *bright red, 1993*	25.00	
9	A4	black, *yellow orange, 1994*	7.50	4.00

Inscribed SWST

10	A4	black, *red orange, 1995*	12.00	4.00
11	A4	black, *blue, 1996*	10.00	4.00
12	A4	black, *bright green, 1997*	11.00	3.00
13	A4	black, *red, 1998*	40.00	
14	A4	black, *orange, 1999*	10.00	

Lower Brule Indian Reservation
South Dakota
Waterfowl Stamps

Serial Nos. are in red. Year and fee are written by hand or typewritten on each stamp. The $5 fee was for for non-members and non-Indians. There was a $2.50 fee for tribal members but no examples of these stamps are recorded.

Numbers have been reserved for the $2.50 stamps. Since no year is on an unused copy, they are listed under the first year only.

1962-70

2	$5 black	—	—
4	$5 black, *1963*		
6	$5 black, *1964*	2,000.	
8	$5 black, *1965*	2,000.	
10	$5 black, *1966*	1,750.	
12	$5 black, *1967*	1,600.	
14	$5 black, *1968*	1,500.	
18	$5 black, *1969*	2,750.	

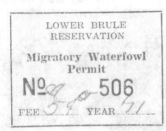

1969-71

20	$5 black	3,250.	
24	$5 black, *1971*	—	
26	$5 black, *1972*	—	

Migratory Bird Hunting and Conservation Stamps
Issued in panes of 20.
All stamps have serial number on reverse.

> Catalogue values for all unused stamps in this section, from this point to the end, are for Never Hinged items.

1995

27	$5 green, tribal member	7.00
28	$5 orange brown, resident deeded land owner / operator	7.00
29	$5 blue, resident government employee	7.00
30	$10 red, non-tribal S.D. resident	12.00
31	$10 purple, non-resident, out of state	12.00

1996

32	$5 multi, tribal / resident	7.00
33	$10 multi, non-tribal S.D. resident	12.00
34	$10 multi, non-resident, out of state	12.00

1997

35	$5 multi, tribal / resident	7.00
36	$10 multi, non-tribal S.D. resident	12.00
37	$10 multi, non-resident, out of state	12.00

Nos. 38-40 have been reserved for 1998 stamps which were printed, but use of which has not yet been verified.

1999

41	$5 multi, tribal / resident	7.00
42	$10 multi, non-tribal S. D. resident	14.00
43	$10 multi, non-resident, out of state	14.00

Pine Ridge (Oglala Sioux) Indian Reservation
South Dakota
Waterfowl Stamps

Nos. 1-5 issued in booklet panes of 5, numbered serially in red.

No. 2 perforated, others rouletted. Nos. 4-5 have simulated perforations.

A1

A2

A3

1	A1	$4 black	375.00

Earliest known use of No. 1 is 1988.

> Catalogue values for all unused stamps in this section, from this point to the end, are for Never Hinged items.

2	A1	$4 black, perforated	15.00
3	A2	$4 Canada geese, *1992*	11.00

$6 stamps picturing Canada geese were produced and sold for the 1993 season. The same stamp was rubber handstamped for the 1994 season. However, there was no hunting season those years. Value, each $15.

Rosebud Indian Reservation
South Dakota
Tribal Game Bird Stamps

Nos. 1, 3-4 have red serial number. Stamps for 1960, 1963-69 may exist.

Since no year is on an unused copy, they are listed under the first year only.

1959-62

1	$2 green	—	
3	$2 green, *1961*	4,000.	
4	$2 green, *1962*	4,500.	

Small Game Stamps

Rosebud
Reservation
—
SMALL GAME

N⁰ 2383

No. 12

Rosebud
Reservation

SMALL GAME

No. 13

SMALL GAME

RESIDENT **$10.00**
Nos. 14, 15

Small Game
Non-Resident

$45.00
Nos. 16, 17

12		black	1,600.	
13		black	275.00	
14	$10	black	45.00	20.00
15	$45	black	190.00	

Die cut self-adhesive

16	$10	black (resident)	75.00	15.00
a.		Overprinted "RESIDENT" over "Non-resident"	—	—
17	$45	black	150.00	50.00

No. 12 was used in the 1970s, No. 13 in the early 1980s, Nos. 14 (resident) and 15 (non-resident) in the late 1980s, and Nos. 16 (resident) and 17 (non-resident) starting in 1990. Unused values for Nos. 16-17 are for never hinged copies.

Standing Rock Indian Reservation
South Dakota-North Dakota
Waterfowl Stamps
Die cut, self-adhesive.

Catalogue values for all unused stamps in this section are for Never Hinged items.

1992-98

1	black		16.00	5.00
2	black, *1993*		10.00	4.00
3	black, inscribed "SRST," *1994*		8.50	3.00
4	black, *1995*		15.00	5.00
5	black, *1996*		13.00	4.00
6	black, *1997*		9.00	4.00
7	black, *1998*		15.00	4.00

SAVINGS STAMPS

POSTAL SAVINGS STAMPS

Issued by the Post Office Department.

Redeemable in the form of credits to Postal Savings accounts. The Postal Savings system was discontinued Mar. 28, 1966.

PS1

Plates of 400 subjects in four panes of 100 each
FLAT PLATE PRINTING

1911, Jan. 3   **Wmk. 191**   **Engr.**   **Perf. 12**
Size of design: 18x21½mm

PS1	PS1	10c **orange**	8.50	1.40
		Block of 4, 2mm spacing	37.50	
		Block of 4, 3mm spacing	40.00	
		P# strip of 3, Impt. open star	57.50	
		P# block of 6, Impt. open star	525.00	

Plate Nos. 5504-5507, 5698, 5700, 5703-5704.

1911, Jan. 3   **Unwmk.**
Imprinted on Deposit Card
Size of design: 137x79mm

PS2	PS1	10c **orange**	150.00	40.00

A 10c deep blue with head of Washington in circle imprinted on deposit card (design 136x79mm) exists, but there is no evidence that it was ever placed in use.

1911, Aug. 14   **Wmk. 190**   **Perf. 12**

PS4	PS1	10c **deep blue**	5.00	1.00
		Block of 4, 2mm spacing	22.50	
		Block of 4, 3mm spacing	25.00	
		P# strip of 3, Impt. open star	30.00	
		P# block of 6, Impt. open star	150.00	

Plate Nos. 5504-5507, 5698, 5700, 5703-5704.

1911   **Unwmk.**
Imprinted on Deposit Card
Size of design: 133x78mm

PS5	PS1	10c **deep blue**	150.00	22.50

Catalogue values for unused stamps in this section, from this point to the end, are for Never Hinged items.

1936   **Unwmk.**   **Perf. 11**

PS6	PS1	10c **deep blue**	5.50	1.25
		violet blue	5.50	1.25
		Block of 4	25.00	
		P# block of 6, Impt. solid star	135.00	

Plate Nos. 21485, 21486.

PS2

Plates of 400 subjects in four panes of 100 each
FLAT PLATE PRINTING

1940   **Unwmk.**   **Engr.**   **Perf. 11**
Size of design: 19x22mm

PS7	PS2	10c **deep ultramarine,** *Apr. 3*	17.50	6.00
		Block of 4	75.00	
		P# block of 6	250.00	

Plate Nos. 22540, 22541.

PS8	PS2	25c **dark car rose,** *Apr. 1*	20.00	9.00
		Block of 4	85.00	
		P# block of 6	275.00	

Plate Nos. 22542, 22543.

PS9	PS2	50c **dark blue green,** *Apr. 1*	55.00	17.50
		Block of 4	240.00	
		P# block of 6	1,000.	

Plate No. 22544.

PS10	PS2	$1 **gray black,** *Apr. 1*	150.00	17.50
		Block of 4	625.00	
		P# block of 6	2,000.	

Plate No. 22545.

Nos. PS11-PS15 redeemable in the form of United States Treasury Defense, War or Savings Bonds.

Minute Man — PS3

E.E. Plates of 400 subjects in four panes of 100 each
ROTARY PRESS PRINTING

1941, May 1   **Unwmk.**   **Perf. 11x10½**
Size of design: 19x22½mm

PS11	PS3	10c **rose red**		.60
a.		10c carmine rose		.60
		Block of 4		2.40
		P# block of 4		7.25
b.		Bklt. pane of 10, *July 30,* trimmed horizontal edges		50.00
		As "b," with Electric Eye marks at left		55.00
c.		Booklet pane of 10, perf. horizontal edges		100.00
		As "c," with Electric Eye marks at left		115.00

Plate Nos., sheet stamps, 22714-22715, 22722-22723, 148245-148246.
Plate Nos., booklet panes, 147084, 147086, 148241-148242.

PS12	PS3	25c **blue green**		2.00
		Block of 4		8.25
		P# block of 4		22.50
b.		Bklt. pane of 10, *July 30*		60.00
		Booklet pane with Electric Eye marks at left		65.00

Plate Nos., sheet stamps, 22716-22717, 22724-22725, 148247-148248.
Plate Nos., booklet panes, 147087-147088, 148243-148244.

PS13	PS3	50c **ultramarine**		7.50
		Block of 4		32.50
		P# block of 4		50.00

Plate Nos. 22718-22719, 22726-22727.

PS14	PS3	$1 **gray black**		12.50
		Block of 4		52.50
		P# block of 4		75.00

Plate Nos. 22720, 22728.

FLAT PLATE PRINTING
Plates of 100 subjects in four panes of 25 each
Size: 36x46mm   *Perf. 11*

PS15 PS3 $5 **sepia**   42.50
          Block of 4   175.00
          P# block of 6 at top or
          bottom   475.00

Plate Nos. 22730-22737, 22740.

SAVINGS STAMPS

Issued by the Post Office Department.

Redeemable in the form of United States Savings
Bonds. Sale of Savings Stamps was discontinued
June 30, 1970.

> Catalogue values for unused stamps in this
> section are for Never Hinged items.

Minute Man — S1

E.E. Plates of 400 subjects in four panes of 100
each
ROTARY PRESS PRINTING
1954-57   Unwmk.   *Perf. 11x10½*
          Size of design: 19x22½mm

S1 S1 10c **rose red**, wet printing, *Nov. 30,*
            1954   .50
            Block of 4   2.00
            P# block of 4   3.50
   a. Booklet pane of 10, *Apr. 22, 1955*   150.00
            Booklet pane with Electric Eye
            marks at left   165.00
   b. Dry printing   .50
            Block of 4   2.00
            P# block of 4   3.50
   c. As "b," booklet pane of 10   150.00
            Booklet pane with Electric Eye
            marks at left   165.00

Plate Nos., sheet stamps, 164991-164992 (wet),
165917-165918, 166643-166644, 167089-167090,
168765-168766 (dry).
Plate Nos., booklet panes, 165218-165219 (wet),
165954-165955, 167001-167002 (dry).

S2 S1 25c **blue green**, wet printing, *Dec.*
            30, 1954   7.50
            Block of 4   30.00
            P# block of 4   35.00
   a. Booklet pane of 10, *Apr. 15, 1955*   800.00
            Booklet pane with Electric Eye
            marks at left   825.00
   b. Dry printing   7.50
            Block of 4   30.00
            P# block of 4   35.00
   c. As "b," booklet pane of 10   800.00
            Booklet pane with Electric Eye
            marks at left   825.00

Plate Nos., sheet stamps, 165007-165008 (wet),
165919-165920 (dry), booklet panes, 165220-165221
(wet), 165956-165957 (dry).

S3 S1 50c **ultramarine**, wet printing, *Dec.*
            31, 1956   9.00
            Block of 4   37.50
            P# block of 4   50.00
   a. Dry printing   9.00
            Block of 4   37.50
            P# block of 4   50.00

Plate Nos. 165050-165051 (wet), 166741-166742,
166941-166942 (dry).

S4 S1 $1 **gray black**, *Mar. 13, 1957*   25.00
            Block of 4   100.00
            P# block of 4   125.00

Plate Nos. 166097-166098, 166683-166684.

FLAT PLATE PRINTING
Plates of 100 subjects in four panes of 25 each
Size: 36x46mm   *Perf. 11*

S5 S1 $5 **sepia**, *Nov. 30, 1956*   95.00
            Block of 4   400.00
            P# block of 6 at top or bottom   725.00

Plate No. 166068.

Minute Man and 48-
Star Flag — S2

GIORI PRESS PRINTING
Plates of 400 subjects in four panes of 100 each
1958, Nov. 18   Unwmk.   *Perf. 11*

S6 S2 25c **dark blue & carmine**   2.00
            Block of 4   8.00
            P# block of 4   10.00
   a. Booklet pane of 10   75.00

Plate Nos.: sheet stamps, 166921, 166925, 166946; booklet
panes, 166913, 166916.

Minute Man and 50-Star
Flag — S3

Plates of 400 subjects in four panes of 100 each.
1961   Unwmk.   *Perf. 11*

S7 S3 25c **dark blue & carmine**   1.50
            Block of 4   6.00
            P# block of 4   11.00
   a. Booklet pane of 10   300.00

Plate Nos.: sheet stamps, 167473, 167476, 167486, 167489,
169089; booklet panes, 167495, 167502, 167508, 167516.

WAR SAVINGS STAMPS

Issued by the Treasury Department.

Redeemable in the form of United States Treasury
War Certificates, Defense Bonds or War Bonds.

Unused values of War Savings stamps are for copies with full original gum. Used values are for stamps
without gum that generally have been removed from
savings certificates or booklets. **Caution:** beware of
used stamps that have been regummed to appear
unused.

WS1

Plates of 300 subjects in six panes of 50 each
FLAT PLATE PRINTING
1917, Dec. 1   Unwmk.   Engr.   *Perf. 11*
          Size of design: 28x18½mm

WS1 WS1 25c **deep green**   16.00   2.25
              Block of 4   70.00
              Margin strip of 3, P#   80.00
              P# block of 6   900.00

Plate Nos. 56800, 56810-56811, 56817, 57074-57077,
57149-57152, 57336, 57382, 57395-57396, 57399, 57443,
58801-58804, 59044-59045, 59156, 61207-61210.

George
Washington — WS2

Plates of 80 subjects in four panes of 20 each
FLAT PLATE PRINTING
1917   Unwmk.   Engr.   *Perf. 11*
          Size of design: 39x55mm

WS2 WS2 $5 **deep green**, *Nov. 17*   80.00   25.00
              Block of 4   325.00
              Margin copy with P#   90.00
              P# block of 6   1,600.
   b. Vert. pair, imperf. horiz.

Plate Nos. 56914-56917, 57066-57073, 57145-57148,
57169-57176, 57333-57334, 57343-57348, 58431, 58433-
58438, 58726-58729, 59071, 60257-60260, 60659-60662,
60665-60668, 60846-60852, 60899, 61203-61206, 61265-
61268, 61360-61367, 61388, 61435, 61502.

Rouletted 7

WS3 WS2 $5 **deep green**   1,200.   650.
              Block of 4   5,000.
              Margin copy with P#   1,500.

Benjamin Franklin — WS3

Plates of 150 subjects in six panes of 25 each
FLAT PLATE PRINTING
1919, July 3   Unwmk.   Engr.   *Perf. 11*
          Size of design: 27x36mm

WS4 WS3 $5 **deep blue**   325.   160.
              Block of 4   1,350.
              Margin copy with P#   350.
              Margin copy with inverted
              P#   375.

Plate Nos. 61882-61885, 61910-61913, 61970-61972,
61997-61998, 62007-62013.

George
Washington — WS4

Plates of 100 subjects in four panes of 25 each
FLAT PLATE PRINTING
1919, Dec. 11   Unwmk.   Engr.   *Perf. 11*
          Size of design: 36x41½mm

WS5 WS4 $5 **carmine**   800.   250.
              Block of 4   3,500.
              Margin copy with P#   850.

Plate Nos. 67545-67552, 69349-69352, 69673-69675,
69677-69680, 69829.

Abraham Lincoln — WS5

Plates of 100 subjects in four panes of 25 each
FLAT PLATE PRINTING

1920, Dec. 21			Unwmk.	Engr.	*Perf. 11*	
			Size of design: 39½x42mm			
WS6	WS5	$5	**orange**, *green*		3,500.	1,250.
			Block of 4		15,000.	
			Margin copy with P#		3,750.	
			Plate Nos. 73129-73136.			

Catalogue values for unused stamps in this section, from this point to the end, are for Never Hinged items.

Minute Man — WS6

Plates of 400 subjects in four panes of 100 each
ROTARY PRESS PRINTING

1942			Unwmk.	*Perf. 11x10½*	
			Size of design: 19x22½mm		
WS7	WS6	10c	**rose red**, *Oct. 29*	.50	.20
a.			10c carmine rose	.50	
			Block of 4	2.00	
			P# block of 4	5.00	
b.			Booklet pane of 10, *Oct. 27*	50.00	
			Booklet pane with Electric Eye marks at left	55.00	

Plate Nos., sheet stamps, 149492-149495, 150206-150207, 150706-150707, 155311-155312.

Plate Nos., booklet panes, 149655-149657, 150664.

WS8	WS6	25c	**dark blue green**, *Oct. 15*	1.10	.25
			Block of 4	5.00	
			P# block of 4	8.25	
b.			Booklet pane of 10, *Nov. 6*	50.00	
			Booklet pane with Electric Eye marks at left	50.00	

Plate Nos., sheet stamps, 149587-149590, 150320-150321, 150708-150709, 155313-155314, 155812-155813, 156517-156518, booklet panes, 149658-149660, 150666.

WS9	WS6	50c	**deep ultra**, *Nov. 12*	4.00	1.25
			Block of 4	16.00	
			P# block of 4	22.50	

Plate Nos. 149591-149594.

WS10	WS6	$1	**gray black**, *Nov. 17*	12.50	3.50
			Block of 4	52.50	
			P# block of 4	70.00	

Plate Nos. 149595-149598.

Type of 1942
FLAT PLATE PRINTING
Plates of 100 subjects in four panes of 25 each

1945			Unwmk.	**Size:** 36x46mm	*Perf. 11*	
WS11	WS6	$5	**violet brown**		55.00	17.50
			Block of 4		240.00	
			P# block of 6 at top or bottom		500.00	

Plate Nos. 150131-150134, 150291.

Type of 1942
Coil Stamps

1943, Aug. 5			Unwmk.	*Perf. 10 Vertically*	
WS12	WS6	10c	**rose red**	2.75	.90
			Pair	6.00	
			Line pair	10.50	

Plate Nos. 153286-153287.

WS13	WS6	25c	**dark blue green**	5.00	1.75
			Pair	10.50	
			Line pair	22.50	

Plate Nos. 153289-153290.

TREASURY SAVINGS STAMP

Issued by the Treasury Department.

Redeemable in the form of War Savings Stamps or Treasury Savings Certificates.

Alexander Hamilton — TS1

FLAT PLATE PRINTING

1920, Dec. 21			Unwmk.	Engr.	*Perf. 11*	
			Size of design: 33½x33½mm			
TS1	TS1	$1	**red**, *green*		3,250.	
			Block of 4		13,500.	
			Margin copy with P#		3,500.	

Plate Nos. 73196-73203.

TELEGRAPH STAMPS

These stamps were issued by the individual companies for use on their own telegrams, and can usually be divided into three classes: Free franking privileges issued to various railroad, newspaper and express company officials, etc., whose companies were large users of the lines; those issued at part cost to the lesser officials of the same type companies; and those bearing values which were usually sold to the general public. Occasionally, some of the companies granted the franking privilege to stockholders and minor State (not Federal) officials. Most Telegraph Stamps were issued in booklet form and will be found with one or more straight edges.

Serial numbers may show evidence of doubling, often of a different number. Such doubling is not scarce.

American Rapid Telegraph Company

Organized Feb. 21, 1879, in New York State. Its wires extended as far north as Boston, Mass., and west to Cleveland, Ohio. It was amalgamated with the Bankers and Merchants Telegraph Co., but when that company was unable to pay the fixed charges, the properties of the American Rapid Telegraph Company were sold on Mar. 11, 1891, to a purchasing committee comprised of James W. Converse and others. This purchasing committee deeded the property and franchise of the American Rapid Telegraph Company to the Western Union Telegraph Company on June 25, 1894. Issued three types of stamps: Telegram, Collect and Duplicate. Telegram stamps were issued in sheets of 100 and were used to prepay messages which could be dropped in convenient boxes for collection. Collect and duplicate stamps were issued in alternate rows on the same sheet of 100 subjects. Collect stamps were attached to telegrams sent collect, the receiver of which paid the amount shown by the stamps, while the Duplicate stamps were retained by the Company as vouchers. **Remainders** with punched cancellations were bought up by a New York dealer.

T1   T2

"Prepaid Telegram" Stamps
Engraved and Printed by the American Bank Note Co.

1881				*Perf. 12*	
1T1	T1	1c	**black**	8.00	3.00
			Punched		.20
			Block of 4	37.50	
			Punched	1.00	
1T2	T1	3c	**orange**	32.50	32.50

			Punched		1.50
			Block of 4, punched		10.00
1T3	T1	5c	**bister brown**	2.00	.75
			Punched		.25
			Block of 4	9.00	
			Punched		1.10
a.		5c	**brown**	2.00	.90
			Punched		.20
			Block of 4	9.00	
			Punched		1.00
1T4	T1	10c	**purple**	11.00	5.00
			Punched		.20
			Block of 4	50.00	
			Punched		1.00
1T5	T1	15c	**green**	3.25	1.50
			Punched		.20
			Block of 4	15.00	
			Punched		1.00
1T6	T1	20c	**red**	3.25	1.50
			Punched		.20
			Block of 4, punched		.80
1T7	T1	25c	**rose**	4.25	1.00
			Punched		.20
			Block of 4	20.00	
			Punched		1.00
1T8	T1	50c	**blue**	22.50	12.50
			Punched		1.50
			Block of 4, punched		8.00

"Collect" Stamps

1T9	T2	1c	**brown**	3.50	3.50
			Punched		.20
1T10	T2	5c	**blue**	3.00	2.50
			Punched		.20
1T11	T2	15c	**red brown**	3.00	2.00
			Punched		.25
1T12	T2	20c	**olive green**	3.00	2.50
			Punched		.20

T3

"Office Coupon" Stamps

1T13	T3	1c brown	7.50	2.50
		Punched		.20
a.		Pair, #1T9, 1T13, punched		2.00
		As "a," block of 4, punched		4.50
1T14	T3	5c blue	6.50	3.00
		Punched		.20
a.		Pair, #1T10, 1T14	32.50	
		Punched		3.00
		As "a," block of 4	70.00	
		Punched		7.00
1T15	T3	15c red brown	10.00	3.00
		Punched		.25
a.		Pair, #1T11, 1T15	25.00	
		Punched		2.50
		As "a," block of 4	60.00	
		Punched		5.50
1T16	T3	20c olive green	10.00	3.00
		Punched		.20
a.		Pair, #1T12, 1T16, punched		2.75
		As "a," block of 4, punched		6.00

Atlantic Telegraph Company

Organized 1884 at Portland, Maine. Its lines extended from Portland, Me., to Boston, Mass., and terminated in the office of the Baltimore and Ohio Telegraph Company at Boston. Later bought out by the Baltimore and Ohio Telegraph Company. Stamps issued by the Atlantic Telegraph Company could also be used for messages destined to any point on the Baltimore and Ohio system. Stamps were printed in panes of six and a full book sold for $10. **Remainders of these stamps, without control numbers, were purchased by a Boston dealer and put on the market about 1932.**

T4

1888			**Perf. 13**	
2T1	T4	1c green	3.50	—
		Remainders		2.25
		Pane of 6		—
		Remainders		14.00
2T2	T4	5c blue	5.00	—
		Remainders		2.25
		Pane of 6		—
		Remainders		14.00
a.		Horiz. pair, imperf. vert.		—
b.		Vert. pair, imperf. horiz.	25.00	—
2T3	T4	10c purple brown	5.00	—
		Remainders		2.25
		Pane of 6		—
		Remainders		14.00
a.		Horiz. pair, imperf. between	40.00	

2T4	T4	25c carmine	3.50	—
		Remainders		2.25
		Pane of 6, remainders		16.00

Baltimore & Ohio Telegraph Companies

"The Baltimore & Ohio Telegraph Co. of the State of New York" was incorporated May 17, 1882. Organization took place under similar charter in 26 other states. It absorbed the National Telegraph Co. and several others. Extended generally along the lines of the Baltimore & Ohio Railroad, but acquired interests in other states. Company absorbed in 1887 by the Western Union Telegraph Co. Stamps were issued in booklet form and sold for $5 and $10, containing all denominations.

T5

T6

Engraved by the American Bank Note Co.

1885			**Perf. 12**	
3T1	T5	1c vermilion	37.50	22.50
		Pane of 6	250.00	
3T2	T5	5c blue	37.50	32.50
3T3	T5	10c red brown	20.00	12.50
		Pane of 6	140.00	
3T4	T5	25c orange	32.50	17.50
3T5	T6	brown		1.75
		Pane of 4		12.50
1886				
3T6	T6	black		1.75
		Pane of 4		20.00

Imprint of Kendall Bank Note Co.
Thin Paper

1886			**Perf. 14**	
3T7	T5	1c green	5.50	3.00
a.		Thick paper	9.00	.85
b.		Imperf., pair	80.00	
3T8	T5	5c blue	3.50	1.25
a.		Thick paper	9.00	4.00
b.		Imperf., pair		55.00
3T9	T5	10c brown	6.00	.75
a.		Thick paper	10.00	1.25
3T10	T5	25c deep orange	27.50	.75
a.		Thick paper	32.50	1.50

Used copies of Nos. 3T7-3T20 normally have heavy grid cancellations. Lightly canceled copies command a premium.

Litho. by A. Hoen & Co.

1886	**Imprint of firm**		**Perf. 12**	
3T11	T5	1c green	3.00	.65
		Pane of 6	22.50	
3T12	T5	5c blue	7.50	.65
		Pane of 6	50.00	
a.		Imperf., pair	85.00	
3T13	T5	10c dark brown	7.50	.75
		Pane of 6	45.00	
a.		Vert. pair, imperf. between	55.00	

Wmk. "A HOEN AND CO. BALTIMORE" in double lined capitals in sheet
Perf. 12

3T14	T5	1c green	10.00	1.25
		Pane of 6	70.00	
3T15	T5	5c blue	17.50	1.25
		Pane of 6	125.00	
a.		Imperf., pair	52.50	—
3T16	T5	10c dark brown	12.50	1.25
		Pane of 6	90.00	

Lithographed by Forbes Co., Boston
Imprint of firm

1887			**Perf. 12½**	
3T17	T5	1c green	17.50	2.50
3T18	T5	5c blue	30.00	5.50
3T19	T5	10c brown	30.00	5.00
3T20	T5	25c yellow	27.50	2.50
a.		25c orange	27.50	2.00

Baltimore & Ohio-Connecticut River Telegraph Companies

The Connecticut River Telegraph Co. ran from New Haven to Hartford. An agreement was entered wherein the Baltimore & Ohio System had mutual use of their lines. This agreement terminated when the Baltimore & Ohio System was absorbed by the Western Union. The Connecticut River Telegraph Company then joined the United Lines. In 1885 stamps (black on yellow) were issued and sold in booklets for $10. In 1887 the Connecticut River Telegraph Co. had extended its lines to New Boston, Mass., and new books of stamps (black on blue) were issued for use on this extension. **Remainders were canceled with bars and sold to a New York dealer.**

T7

1885			**Perf. 11**	
4T1	T7	1c black, *yellow*	5.00	6.00
		Remainders		1.25
		Pane of 10	55.00	
		Remainders		6.00
a.		Imperf., pair	40.00	
b.		Vert. pair, imperf. horiz., remainders		—
4T2	T7	5c black, *yellow*	3.00	10.00
		Remainders		1.00
		Pane of 10	35.00	
		Remainders		6.00
a.		Horizontal pair, imperf. between, remainders		—
b.		Vert. pair, imperf. between, remainders		35.00
c.		Imperf., pair, remainders		35.00
4T3	T7	1c black, *blue*	7.50	—
		Remainders		4.00
		Pane of 10	80.00	
		Remainders		35.00
4T4	T7	5c black, *blue*	7.50	7.50
		Remainders		2.50
		Pane of 10	80.00	
		Remainders		35.00

California State Telegraph Company

Incorporated June 17, 1854 as the California Telegraph Company and constructed a line from Nevada through Grass Valley to Auburn. Extended to run from San Francisco to Marysville via San Jose and Stockton. Later absorbed Northern Telegraph Co. and thus extended to Eureka. It was incorporated as the California State Telegraph Company on April 6, 1861. At the time of its lease to the Western Union on May 16, 1867 the California State consisted of the following companies which had been previously absorbed: Alta California Telegraph Co., Atlantic and Pacific States Telegraph Co., National Telegraph Co., Northern California Telegraph Co., Overland Telegraph Co., Placerville and Humboldt Telegraph Co., Tuolumne Telegraph Co. Stamps were issued in booklets, six to a pane. **Remainders of Nos. 5T1 and 5T4 are without frank numbers.**

T8

1870			**Perf. 13½**	
5T1	T8	black & blue	300.	—
		Pane of 6	2,000.	
		Without number	110.	

T9

T10

1870			**Perf. 12, 13**	
5T2	T9	black & red, without number	160.00	145.00
1871			**Dated "1871"**	
5T3	T9	black & red, without number	350.00	
a.		Imperf., pair		—
5T4	T10	black & salmon, blue number	275.00	150.00
		Pane of 6	2,000.	
		Without number	150.00	
1872				
5T5	T10	green & red, red number (no year date)	160.00	
		Pane of 6		
1873			**Dated "1873"**	
5T6	T10	red & salmon, blue number	225.00	150.00
1874			**Dated "1874"**	
5T7	T10	blue & salmon, black number	250.00	
		Pane of 6		
1875			**Dated "1875"**	
5T8	T10	brown & green, black number	190.00	
		Pane of 6		

City & Suburban Telegraph Company
(New York City and Suburban Printing Telegraph Company)

Organized 1855. Extended only through New York City and Brooklyn. Sold out to the American Telegraph Co. Stamps were sold to the public for prepayment of messages, which could be dropped in convenient boxes for collection. Stamps were issued in sheets of 60 having a face value of $1. These were arranged in six vertical rows of ten, the horizontal rows having the following denominations: 2c, 1c, 1c, 1c, 2c, 3c.

Counterfeits are known both in black and blue, mostly on pelure or hard white paper. Originals are on soft wove paper, somewhat yellowish. Scalloped edge is more sharply etched on the counterfeits.

T11

		Typo.		Imperf.
6T1	T11	1c black	200.	150.
		Pair	—	
		Block of 4	—	
6T2	T11	2c black	250.	200.
		Pair	—	
		Pair, 2c + 1c	525.	
6T3	T11	3c black	400.	300.
		Pair	—	
		Strip of 3, 1c, 2c & 3c	3,000.	

Colusa, Lake & Mendocino Telegraph Company

Was organized in California early in 1873. First known as the Princeton, Colusa and Grand Island Telegraph Co. In May, 1873 they completed their line from Princeton through Colusa, at which point it was connected with the Western Union office, to Grand Island. On Feb. 10, 1875 it was incorporated as the Colusa, Lake & Mendocino Telegraph Co. Its lines were extended into the counties of Colusa, Lake, Mendocino and Napa. Eventually reached a length of 260 miles. Went out of business in 1892. Stamps were issued for prepayment of messages and were sold in books. When sold they were stamped "P.L.W." (the superintendent's initials) in blue. The 5c value was printed 10 to a pane, being two horizontal rows of five. Of the 10c and 25c nothing definite is known about the settings.

T11a

1876				Perf. 12
7T1	T11a	5c black	750.	—
		Block of 4	3,350.	
		Pane of 10	8,250.	
		Without "P.L.W."	900.	
7T2	T11a	10c black	9,000.	—
7T3	T11a	25c red	9,000.	—

Commercial Union Telegraph Company

Incorporated in New York State on March 31, 1886. Its lines ran from Albany through Troy to Berlin, N.Y., thence to North Adams, Mass. The lines of this Company, which was controlled by the Postal Telegraph Company, were later extended throughout Northern New York and the States of Massachusetts, Vermont, New Hampshire and Maine. Stamps issued in panes of four.

T12

T13

T14

1891		Lithographed by A. C. Goodwin		Perf. 12
8T1	T12	25c yellow	15.00	
		Pane of 4	65.00	
8T2	T13	25c green	15.00	10.00
		Pane of 4	65.00	
a.		Horiz. pair, imperf. vert.	40.00	
8T3	T14	lilac rose	37.50	—

Mutual Union Telegraph Company

Incorporated October 4, 1880. Extended over 22 states. Absorbed about 1883 by the Western Union Telegraph Co. Franks issued for use of stockholders, in books, four to a pane.

T15

Engr. by Van Campen Engraving Co., New York

1882-83				Perf. 14
9T1	T15	blue	25.00	20.00
		Pane of 4	115.00	
a.		Vert. pair, imperf. horizontal	80.00	—
b.		Imperf., pair	85.00	—
9T2	T15	carmine	25.00	—
		Pane of 4	115.00	

North American Telegraph Company

Incorporated October 15, 1885 to run from Chicago to Minneapolis, later being extended into North and South Dakota. Absorbed in 1929 by the Postal System.

Apparently these stamps were not canceled when used. Issued in panes of four.

T15a

1899-1907				Perf. 12
10T1	T15a	violet (1899)	120.00	
		Pane of 4	525.00	
10T2	T15a	green (1901)	120.00	
10T3	T15a	dark brown (1902)	170.00	
10T4	T15a	blue (1903)	170.00	
10T5	T15a	violet (1904)	120.00	
		Pane of 4	525.00	
a.		Horiz. pair, imperf. vertically	300.00	
10T6	T15a	red brown (1905)	130.00	
10T7	T15a	rose (1906)	160.00	
10T8	T15a	green (1907)	750.00	

Nos. 10T1 to 10T8 are known imperforate.

Northern Mutual Telegraph Company

Incorporated in New York State as the Northern Mutual Telegraph and Telephone Company on June 20, 1882. Its line, which consisted of a single wire, extended from Syracuse to Ogdensburg via Oswego, Watertown and Clayton, a distance of 170 miles. It was sold to the Bankers and Merchants Telegraph Company in 1883. Stamps were in use for a few days only in April, 1883. Issued in panes of 35 having a face value of $5. Seven horizontal rows of five covering all denominations as follows: 2 rows of 25c, 1 of 20c, 2 of 10c, 2 of 5c. **The remainders and plates were purchased by a New York dealer in 1887.**

T16

1883				Perf. 14
11T1	T16	5c yellow brown	5.50	—
		Block of 4	25.00	
11T2	T16	10c yellow brown	7.50	—
		Block of 4	30.00	
11T3	T16	20c yellow brown	17.50	—
		Horizontal pair	40.00	
11T4	T16	25c yellow brown	5.00	—
		Block of 4	25.00	
		Pane of 35	350.00	

The first reprints are lighter in color than the originals, perf. 14 and the gum is yellowish instead of white. The pane makeup differs in the reprints. The second reprints are darker than the original, perf. 12. Value $1 each.

Northern New York Telegraph Company

Organized about 1892. Extended from Malone, N.Y. to Massena, N.Y. Re-incorporated as the New York Union Telegraph Co. on April 2, 1896.

T16a

Typo. by Charles H. Smith, Brushton, N.Y.

1894-95				Rouletted
12T1	T16a	green (overprinted in red "Frank 1894")	40.	
		Pane of 6	250.	
a.		Imperf., pair	50.	
12T2	T16a	red (overprinted in black "Frank 1895")	160.	
		Pane of 6	1,400.	
a.		Imperf., pair	50.	
12T3	T16a	1c yellow (overprinted in black "One")	75.	
		Pane of 6	500.	
a.		Imperf., pair	50.	
12T4	T16a	10c blue (overprinted in red "10")	140.	
		Pane of 6	900.	
a.		Imperf., pair	50.	

Some specialists believe that Nos. 12T1-12T4 were not issued and probably are essays. However, one Northern New York stamp is recorded tied to a piece of a telegraph form by a punch cancel.

Pacific Mutual Telegraph Company

Incorporated in Missouri on June 21, 1883. Operated between St. Louis and Kansas City, Mo., during the years 1884 and 1885. It had 15 offices, 425 miles of poles and 850 miles of wire. The controlling interests were held by the Bankers and Merchants Telegraph Company. The name was changed on Sept. 10, 1910 to Postal Telegraph-Cable Company of Missouri. Stamps were issued in booklets having a face value of $10 and containing 131 stamps as follows: 50-1c, 20-5c, 45-10c, 16-25c. They are not known used.

T17

1883				Perf. 12
13T1	T17	1c black	22.50	
13T2	T17	1c slate	.35	
		Block of 4	1.50	
a.		1c gray	.35	
		Block of 4	1.50	
13T3	T17	5c black, buff	1.00	
		Block of 4	4.50	
13T4	T17	10c black, green	.35	
		Block of 4	1.75	
a.		Horiz. pair, imperf. between	—	
13T5	T17	25c black, salmon buff	1.00\	
		Block of 4	4.50	

Pacific Postal Telegraph-Cable Company

The Pacific Postal Telegraph-Cable Company was the Pacific Coast Department of the Postal Telegraph-Cable Company, and was organized in 1886. Its first wire ran from San Francisco to New Westminster, B.C., where it touched the lines of the Canadian Pacific Railway Company, then the only connection between the Eastern and Western Postal systems. Later the Postal's own wires spanned the continent and the two companies were united.

Stamps issued in booklet form in vertical panes of five.

T17a

Perf. 12 Horiz.

14T1	T17a	10c	brown	55.00	45.00
			Pane of 5	300.00	
14T2	T17a	15c	black	65.00	37.50
			Pane of 5	350.00	
14T3	T17a	25c	rose red	65.00	45.00
			Pane of 5	350.00	
14T4	T17a	40c	green	50.00	37.50
			Pane of 5	275.00	
14T5	T17a	50c	blue	50.00	45.00
			Pane of 5	275.00	

These stamps were issued with three sizes of frank numbers; large closely spaced, small closely spaced and small widely spaced figures. They also exist without frank numbers.

Postal Telegraph Company

Organized in New York in 1881. Reorganized in 1891 as the Postal Telegraph-Cable Co. The Postal Telegraph Co stamps of 1885 were issued in sheets of 100. **Some years after the reorganization a New York dealer purchased the remainders which were canceled with a purple star.** The Postal Telegraph-Cable Co. issued frank stamps in booklets, usually four stamps to a pane. This company was merged with the Western Union Telegraph Company in 1943.

T18   T19

T20   T21

Engraved by Hamilton Bank Note Co.

1885   *Perf. 14*

15T1	T18	10c	green	3.50	—
			Remainders		.25
			Block of 4	15.00	
			Remainders		1.25
a.			Horiz. pair, imperf. btwn., remainders	20.00	
b.			10c deep green	3.50	—
			Remainders		.25
			Block of 4	15.00	
			Remainders		1.25
15T2	T19	15c	orange red	3.50	—
			Remainders		.60
			Block of 4	15.00	
			Remainders		3.00
a.			Horizontal pair, imperf. between	37.50	
15T3	T20	25c	blue	2.00	5.00
			Remainders		.20
			Block of 4	9.00	
			Remainders		.75
a.			Horizontal pair, imperf. between	37.50	
15T4	T21	50c	brown	1.75	—
			Remainders		.60
			Block of 4	8.00	
			Remainders		3.00

The 25c in ultramarine and the 50c in black were printed and perforated 16 but are not known to have been issued. Value about $7.50 each.

T22   T22a

Typographed by Moss Engraving Co.

1892-1920   *Perf. 14*

Signature of A.B. Chandler

15T5	T22	blue gray (1892)	17.50	
a.		Imperf., pair	65.00	

Perf. 13 to 14½ and Compound

15T6	T22	gray lilac (1892)	22.50	
15T7	T22	red (1893)	16.00	10.00
15T8	T22	red brown (1893)	6.00	4.00

Perf. 12

15T9	T22	violet brown (1894)	6.75	
15T10	T22	gray green (1894)	4.50	
a.		Imperf., pair	10.00	
15T11	T22	blue (1895)	22.50	
15T12	T22	rose (1895)	150.00	

Nos. 15T11 and 15T12 are from a new die resembling T22 but without shading under "Postal Telegraph Co."

15T13	T22a	slate green (1896)	5.50	
		Pane of 4	25.00	
15T14	T22a	brown (1896)	130.00	

Signature of Albert B. Chandler

15T15	T22a	lilac brown (1897)	1.50	10.00
		Pane of 4	6.50	
15T16	T22a	orange (1897)	110.00	

Typographed by Knapp & Co.

15T17	T22a	pale blue (1898)	2.25	
		Pane of 4	10.00	
15T18	T22a	rose (1898)	130.00	

Typographed by Moss Engraving Co.

Perf. 12

15T19	T22a	orange brown (1899)	1.75	
		Pane of 4	8.25	

Perf. 11

15T20	T22a	blue (1900)	3.00	3.00
a.		"I" of "Complimentary" omitted	.75	1.00
		Pane of 4	3.00	

The variety 15T20a represents a different die with many variations in the design.

Perf. 14

15T21	T22a	sea green (1901)	.60	.55
		Pane of 4	2.50	
a.		Horiz. pair, imperf. between	—	

Signature of John W. Mackay

15T22	T22a	chocolate (1902)	1.25	.65
		Pane of 4	5.50	
a.		Horiz. pair, imperf. vert.	—	

Signature of Clarence H. Mackay

15T23	T22a	blue (1903)	2.75	2.50
		Pane of 4		

Perf. 12

15T24	T22a	blue, *blue* (1904)	4.00	3.00
		Pane of 4	17.50	
15T25	T22a	blue, *yellow* (1905)	5.00	
		Pane of 4	22.50	
15T26	T22a	blue, *light blue* (1906)	5.00	5.00
		Pane of 4	22.50	
a.		Horiz. pair, imperf. vert.		

T22b   T22c

Perf. 12

15T27	T22b	black, *yellow* (laid paper) (1907)	35.00	
		Pane of 4	150.00	
15T28	T22b	blue, *pink* (laid paper) (1907)	20.00	
		Pane of 4	90.00	

"One Telegram of 10 Words"

15T29	T22c	blue (1908)	30.00	
		Pane of 4	125.00	
15T30	T22c	yellow (1908)	110.00	
		Pane of 4	475.00	
15T31	T22c	black (1908)	25.00	
		Pane of 4	110.00	
15T32	T22c	brown (1909)	21.00	
		Pane of 4	90.00	
a.		Date reads "1908"	2,000.	
15T33	T22c	olive green (1909)	12.50	
		Pane of 4	55.00	
15T34	T22c	dark blue (1910)	20.00	
15T35	T22c	dark brown (1910)	21.00	
15T36	T22c	violet (1911)	160.00	
15T37	T22c	blue (1912)	300.00	
15T38	T22c	violet (1912)	350.00	

Perf. 14

15T39	T22c	violet (not dated) (1914)	100.00	
a.		Red violet	90.00	
		Pane of 4	450.00	

"One Telegram"

Perf. 12

15T40	T22c	blue (1908)	30.00	
		Pane of 4	125.00	
a.		Horiz. pair, imperf. between	325.00	
15T41	T22c	lilac (1909)	15.00	
		Pane of 4	65.00	
15T42	T22c	black, *yellow* (laid paper) (1910)	375.00	
a.		Date reads "1909"	—	
15T43	T22c	violet (1910)	12.50	
a.		Red violet	12.50	
		Pane of 8	110.00	
15T44	T22c	dark blue (1911)	30.00	
		Pane of 4	125.00	
15T45	T22c	light violet (1912)	25.00	
		Pane of 4	100.00	

Perf. 14

15T46	T22c	dark blue (1913)	100.00	
		Pane of 8	850.00	
a.		Imperf. vertically, pair	200.00	
b.		Perf. 12	60.00	
		Pane of 4	250.00	
15T47	T22c	dark blue (not dated) (1914)	.25	
		Pane of 4	2.50	
		Pane of 8	5.00	

In panes of four the stamps are 4½mm apart horizontally, panes of eight 5½mm. There are two types of design T22c, one with and one without spurs on colored curved lines above "O" of "Postal" and below "M" of "Company". No. 15T47 comes in both types known of 15T47.

Nos. 15T39 and 15T47 handstamped with date in double line numerals, all four numerals complete on each stamp.

15T47A	T22c	violet (1916)	2,250.
15T48	T22c	dark blue (1917)	1,000.
15T49	T22c	dark blue (1918)	1,500.
15T49A	T22c	dark blue (1919)	80.
		Pane of 8	700.00
15T49B	T22c	dark blue (1920)	60.
		Pane of 8	550.00

No. 15T49B is handstamped "1920" in small single line numerals.

T22d   T22e

1907   *Perf. 12*

15T50	T22d	1c	dark brown	25.00	20.00
			Pane of 4	110.00	
15T51	T22d	2c	dull violet	20.00	20.00
			Pane of 4	85.00	
15T52	T22d	5c	green	22.50	22.50
			Pane of 4	95.00	
15T53	T22d	25c	light red	25.00	20.00
			Pane of 4	110.00	

1931   *Perf. 14*

15T54	T22e	25c	gray blue (1931)	.25	
			Pane of 6	2.00	

1932

No. 15T54 overprinted "1932" and control number in red

15T55	T22e	25c	gray blue	75.00	
			Pane of 6	500.00	

Many varieties between Nos. 15T5 and 15T55 are known without frank numbers.

OFFICIAL

1900-14   Inscribed "Supts."   *Perf. 11, 12*

15TO1	T22c	black, *magenta*	1.25	1.25

For Use of Railroad Superintendents

Perf. 12

"C. G. W." (Chicago, Great Western Railroad) at top

15TO2	T22c	carmine (1908)	30.00	
		Pane of 4	125.00	
15TO3	T22c	carmine (1909)	75.00	
15TO4	T22c	carmine (1910)	85.00	
15TO5	T22c	carmine (1911)	65.00	
15TO6	T22c	carmine (1912)	75.00	

Perf. 14

15TO7	T22c	carmine (1913)	110.00	
a.		Perf. 12	—	
15TO8	T22c	dull red (not dated) (1914)	.50	
		Pane of 8	5.00	

Perf. 12
"E. P." (El Paso and Northeastern Railroad) at top

15TO9	T22c	orange (1908)	125.00	

"I. C." (Illinois Central Railroad) at top

15TO10	T22c	green (1908)	35.00	
		Pane of 4	160.00	
15TO11	T22c	yellow green (1909)	12.50	
		Pane of 4	—	
		Pane of 8	110.00	
15TO12	T22c	dark green (1910)	85.00	
15TO13	T22c	dark green (1911)	50.00	
		Pane of 4	225.00	
		Pane of 8	450.00	
15TO14	T22c	dark green (1912)	500.00	
15TO15	T22c	dark green (1913)	500.00	

Perf. 14

15TO16	T22c	dark green (not dated) (1914)	2.50	
		Pane of 4	11.00	
		Pane of 8	22.50	
a.		Green (spurs)	1.25	
		Pane of 4	7.50	
b.		Line under "PRESIDENT" (no spurs)	1.00	
		Pane of 8	12.50	

(See note after No. 15T47.)
Both types of design T22c are known of 15TO16.

Perf. 12
"O. D." (Old Dominion Steamship Co.) at top

15TO17	T22c	violet (1908)	800.00	

"P. R." (Pennsylvania Railroad) at top

15TO18	T22c	orange brown (1908)	20.00	
		Pane of 4	85.00	
		Pane of 8	175.00	
15TO19	T22c	orange brown (1909)	25.00	
		Pane of 4	110.00	
		Pane of 8	225.00	
15TO20	T22c	orange brown (1910)	25.00	
		Pane of 4	110.00	
		Pane of 8	225.00	
15TO21	T22c	orange brown (1911)	90.00	
15TO22	T22c	orange brown (1912)	55.00	
		Pane of 4	450.00	

Perf. 14

15TO23	T22c	orange brown (1913)	25.00	
		Pane of 8	210.00	
a.		Perf. 12	125.00	

"P. R. R." (Pennsylvania Rail Road) at top

15TO24	T22c	orange (not dated) (1914)	20.00	
		Pane of 4	100.00	
		Pane of 8	190.00	

Perf. 12
"S. W." (El Paso Southwestern Railroad) at top

15TO25	T22c	yellow (1909)	130.00	
15TO26	T22c	yellow (1910)	600.00	
15TO27	T22c	yellow (1911)	165.00	
15TO28	T22c	yellow (1912)	190.00	
		Pane of 4	775.00	

Nos. 15TO1-15TO17 and 15TO25-15TO28 are without frank numbers.

TO1

1942		Litho.		Unwmk.	
15TO29	TO1	5c	pink	6.00	3.00
		Pane of 8		50.00	
15TO30	TO1	25c	pale blue	7.00	4.00
		Pane of 8		57.50	

The stamps were issued in booklets to all Postal Telegraph employees in the Armed Forces for use in the United States. They were discontinued Oct. 8, 1943. Used copies normally bear manuscript cancellations.

Western Union Telegraph Company

Organized by consolidation in 1856. Now extends throughout the United States. Frank stamps have been issued regularly since 1871 in booklet form. The large size, early issues, were in panes of four, 1871-1913; the medium size, later issues, were in panes of six, 1914-32; and the recent small size issues are in panes of nine, 1933 to 1946.

T23   T24

Engraved by the National Bank Note Co.
1871-94   Perf. 12
Signature of William Orton

16T1	T23	green (not dated) (1871)	25.00	20.00
16T2	T23	red (not dated) (1872)	27.50	17.50
		Pane of 4	125.00	
16T3	T23	blue (not dated) (1873)	30.00	20.00
		Pane of 4	140.00	
16T4	T23	brown (not dated) (1874)	22.50	20.00
		Pane of 4	95.00	
16T5	T24	deep green (1875)	27.50	18.00
16T6	T24	red (1876)	27.50	
		Pane of 4	125.00	
16T7	T24	violet (1877)	32.50	25.00
16T8	T24	gray brown (1878)	30.00	

Signature of Norvin Green

16T9	T24	blue (1879)	30.00	25.00
		Pane of 4	140.00	

Engraved by the American Bank Note Co.

16T10	T24	lilac rose (1880)	20.00	
		Pane of 4	85.00	
16T11	T24	green (1881)	17.50	
		Pane of 4	75.00	
16T12	T24	blue (1882)	10.00	
		Pane of 4	45.00	
16T13	T24	yellow brown (1883)	20.00	
		Pane of 4	85.00	
16T14	T24	gray violet (1884)	.40	.30
		Pane of 4	2.00	
16T15	T24	green (1885)	2.50	1.75
		Pane of 4	12.00	
16T16	T24	brown violet (1886)	2.50	2.00
		Pane of 4	11.00	
16T17	T24	red brown (1887)	4.50	
		Pane of 4	22.50	
16T18	T24	blue (1888)	3.25	
		Pane of 4	15.00	
16T19	T24	olive green (1889)	1.75	.80
		Pane of 4	8.00	
16T20	T24	purple (1890)	.75	.40
		Pane of 4	3.25	
16T21	T24	brown (1891)	1.25	
		Pane of 4	5.50	
16T22	T24	vermilion (1892)	1.75	
		Pane of 4	8.00	
16T23	T24	blue (1893)	1.25	.40
		Pane of 4	5.50	

Signature of Thos. T. Eckert

16T24	T24	green (1894)	.50	.40
		Pane of 4	2.50	

T25

Engraved by the International Bank Note Co.
1895-1913   Perf. 14
Signature of Thos. T. Eckert

16T25	T25	dark brown (1895)	.50	.40
		Pane of 4	2.50	
16T26	T25	violet (1896)	.50	.40
		Pane of 4	2.50	
16T27	T25	rose red (1897)	.50	.40
		Pane of 4	2.50	
16T28	T25	yellow green (1898)	.50	.40
		Pane of 4	2.50	
a.		Vertical pair, imperf. between	—	
16T29	T25	olive green (1899)	.50	.40
		Pane of 4	2.25	
16T30	T25	red violet, perf. 13 (1900)	.50	.45
		Pane of 4	3.00	
16T31	T25	brown, perf. 13 (1901)	.50	.40
		Pane of 4	2.50	
16T32	T25	blue (1902)	6.00	
		Pane of 4	27.50	

Signature of R.C. Clowry

16T33	T25	blue (1902)	6.00	
		Pane of 4	28.00	
16T34	T25	green (1903)	.60	.40
		Pane of 4	4.00	
16T35	T25	red violet (1904)	.60	
		Pane of 4	2.75	
16T36	T25	carmine rose (1905)	.60	.50

		Pane of 4	2.75	
16T37	T25	blue (1906)	.50	.40
		Pane of 4	4.00	
a.		Vertical pair, imperf. between	30.00	
16T38	T25	orange brown (1907)	1.75	.90
		Pane of 4	10.00	
16T39	T25	violet (1908)	2.00	1.00
		Pane of 4	9.00	
16T40	T25	olive green (1909)	2.00	
		Pane of 4	10.00	

Perf. 12

16T41	T25	buff (1910)	.75	.50
		Pane of 4	3.25	

Engraved by the American Bank Note Co.
Signature of Theo. N. Vail

16T42	T24	green (1911)	12.50	
		Pane of 4	60.00	
16T43	T24	violet (1912)	8.50	
		Pane of 4	40.00	

Imprint of Kihn Brothers Bank Note Company
Perf. 14

16T44	T24	brown (1913)	10.00	
		Pane of 4	50.00	
a.		Vert. pair, imperf. between	35.00	
b.		Horiz. pair, imperf. between	40.00	

T26   T27

Engraved by the E.A. Wright Bank Note Co.
1914-15   Signature of Theo. N. Vail   Perf. 12

16T45	T26	5c brown (1914)	1.10	
		Pane of 6	8.00	
a.		Vert. pair, imperf. between	—	
b.		Horiz. pair, imperf. between	—	
16T46	T26	25c slate (1914)	7.00	5.00
		Pane of 6	30.00	

Signature of Newcomb Carlton

16T47	T26	5c orange (1915)	1.50	
		Pane of 6	10.00	
		orange yellow	5.00	
16T48	T26	25c olive green (1915)	4.00	
		Pane of 6	30.00	
a.		Vert. pair, imperf. horizontally	45.00	

Engraved by the American Bank Note Co.
1916-32

16T49	T27	5c light blue (1916)	1.50	
		Pane of 6	11.00	
16T50	T27	25c carmine lake (1916)	1.75	
		Pane of 6	11.00	

Engraved by the Security Bank Note Co.
Perf. 11

16T51	T27	5c yellow brown (1917)	1.00	
		Pane of 6	7.50	
16T52	T27	25c deep green (1917)	3.00	
		Pane of 6	20.00	
16T53	T27	5c olive green (1918)	.60	
		Pane of 6	4.00	
16T54	T27	25c dark violet (1918)	1.75	
		Pane of 6	12.50	
16T55	T27	5c brown (1919)	1.25	
		Pane of 6	9.00	
16T56	T27	25c blue (1919)	3.25	
		Pane of 6	22.50	

Engraved by the E.A. Wright Bank Note Co.
Perf. 12

16T57	T27	5c dark green (1920)	.65	
		Pane of 6	4.25	
a.		Vert. pair, imperf. between	300.00	
16T58	T27	25c olive green (1920)	.65	
		Pane of 6	5.00	

Engraved by the Security Bank Note Co.

16T59	T27	5c carmine rose (1921)	.55	
		Pane of 6	4.25	
16T60	T27	25c deep blue (1921)	1.30	
		Pane of 6	8.50	
16T61	T27	5c yellow brown (1922)	.55	
		Pane of 6	3.75	
a.		Horizontal pair, imperf. between	16.00	
16T62	T27	25c claret (1922)	1.65	
		Pane of 6	11.50	
16T63	T27	5c olive green (1923)	.65	
		Pane of 6	4.25	
16T64	T27	25c dull violet (1923)	1.35	
		Pane of 6	8.75	
16T65	T27	5c brown (1924)	1.65	
		Pane of 6	11.50	
16T66	T27	25c ultramarine (1924)	4.00	
		Pane of 6	30.00	
16T67	T27	5c olive green (1925)	.65	
		Pane of 6	4.25	
16T68	T27	25c carmine rose (1925)	1.10	
		Pane of 6	7.00	
16T69	T27	5c blue (1926)	1.00	
		Pane of 6	6.50	

16T70 T27	25c **light brown** (1926)		2.00	
	Pane of 6		12.50	
16T71 T27	5c **carmine** (1927)		.85	
	Pane of 6		5.75	
16T72 T27	25c **green** (1927)		7.25	
	Pane of 6		47.50	

Engraved by the E. A. Wright Bank Note Co.
Without Imprint

16T73 T27	5c **yellow brown** (1928)		.60	
	Pane of 6		4.00	
16T74 T27	25c **dark blue** (1928)		1.00	
	Pane of 6		6.25	

Engraved by the Security Bank Note Co.
Without Imprint

16T75 T27	5c **dark green** (1929)		.30	.25
	Pane of 6		2.00	
16T76 T27	25c **red violet** (1929)		.85	.50
	Pane of 6		5.50	
16T77 T27	5c **olive green** (1930)		.25	.20
	Pane of 6		1.75	
16T78 T27	25c **carmine** (1930)		.25	.25
	Pane of 6		2.00	
a.	Horiz. pair, imperf. vertically		35.00	
16T79 T27	5c **brown** (1931)		.20	.20
	Pane of 6		1.25	
16T80 T27	25c **blue** (1931)		.20	.20
	Pane of 6		1.50	
16T81 T27	5c **green** (1932)		.20	.20
	Pane of 6		1.50	
16T82 T27	25c **rose carmine** (1932)		.20	.20
	Pane of 6		1.50	

T28

1933-40
Lithographed by Oberly & Newell Co.
Without Imprint
Perf. 14x12½

16T83 T28	5c **pale brown** (1933)		.25	
	Pane of 9		3.25	
16T84 T28	25c **green** (1933)		.25	
	Pane of 9		3.25	

Lithographed by Security Bank Note Co.
Without Imprint
Perf. 12, 12½
Signature of R. B. White

16T85 T28	5c **lake** (1934)		.20	
	Pane of 9		2.00	
16T86 T28	25c **dark blue** (1934)		.20	
	Pane of 9		2.50	
16T87 T28	5c **yellow brown** (1935)		.20	
	Pane of 9		1.75	
16T88 T28	25c **lake** (1935)		.20	
	Pane of 9		2.00	
16T89 T28	5c **blue** (1936)		.25	.20
	Pane of 9		2.75	
16T90 T28	25c **apple green** (1936)		.20	.20
	Pane of 9		2.50	
16T91 T28	5c **bister brown** (1937)		.20	
	Pane of 9		2.50	
16T92 T28	25c **carmine rose** (1937)		.20	
	Pane of 9		2.00	
16T93 T28	5c **green** (1938)		.25	.20
	Pane of 9		3.00	
16T94 T28	25c **blue** (1938)		.25	.20
	Pane of 9		3.00	
16T95 T28	5c **dull vermilion** (1939)		.60	
	Pane of 9		7.00	
a.	Horiz. pair, imperf. between		—	
16T96 T28	25c **bright violet** (1939)		.50	
	Pane of 9		6.00	
16T97 T28	5c **light blue** (1940)		.55	
	Pane of 9		5.75	
16T98 T28	25c **bright green** (1940)		.50	
	Pane of 9		5.50	

Samuel F. B.
Morse — T29

Plates of 90 stamps.
Stamp designed by Nathaniel Yontiff.
Unlike the frank stamps, Nos. 16T99 to 16T103 were sold to the public in booklet form for use in prepayment of telegraph services.

Engraved by Security Bank Note Co. of Philadelphia

1940		Unwmk.	*Perf. 12, 12½x12, 12x12½*	
16T99	T29	1c **yellow green**	1.00	
		Pane of 5	5.25	
a.		Imperf., pair	50.00	

16T100 T29	2c **chestnut**		1.75	1.00
	Pane of 5		15.00	
a.	Imperf., pair		50.00	
16T101 T29	5c **deep blue**		2.75	
	Pane of 5		17.50	
a.	Vert. pair, imperf. btwn.		65.00	
b.	Imperf., pair		50.00	
16T102 T29	10c **orange**		4.25	
	Pane of 5		24.00	
a.	Imperf., pair		50.00	
16T103 T29	25c **bright carmine**		4.00	
	Pane of 5		24.00	
a.	Imperf., pair		50.00	

Type of 1933-40

1941		Litho.	*Perf. 12½*	

Without Imprint
Signature of R.B. White

16T104 T28	5c **dull rose lilac**		.25	
	Pane of 9		2.50	
16T105 T28	25c **vermilion**		.35	
	Pane of 9		3.50	

1942		Signature of A.N. Williams		
16T106 T28	5c **brown**		.30	
	Pane of 9		3.50	
16T107 T28	25c **ultramarine**		.30	
	Pane of 9		3.50	

1943				
16T108 T28	5c **salmon**		.30	
	Pane of 9		3.50	
16T109 T28	25c **red violet**		.30	
	Pane of 9		3.50	

1944				
16T110 T28	5c **light green**		.40	
	Pane of 9		4.50	
16T111 T28	25c **buff**		.35	
	Pane of 9		3.75	

1945				
16T112 T28	5c **light blue**		.40	
	Pane of 9		4.50	
a.	Pair, imperf. between		—	
16T113 T28	25c **light green**		.35	
	Pane of 9		3.75	

1946				
16T114 T28	5c **light bister brown**		1.25	
	Pane of 9		15.00	
16T115 T28	25c **rose pink**		1.00	
	Pane of 9		12.00	

Many of the stamps between 16T1 and 16T98 and 16T104 to 16T115 are known without frank numbers. Several of them are also known with more than one color used in the frank number and with handstamped and manuscript numbers. The numbers are also found in combination with various letters: O, A, B, C, D, etc.

Western Union discontinued the use of Telegraph stamps with the 1946 issue.

United States
Telegraph-Cable-Radio Carriers

Booklets issued to accredited representatives to the World Telecommunications Conferences, Atlantic City, New Jersey, 1947. Valid for messages to points outside the United States. Issued by All America Cables & Radio, Inc., The Commercial Cable Company, Globe Wireless, Limited, Mackay Radio and Telegraph Company, Inc., R C A Communications, Inc., Tropical Radio Telegraph Company and The Western Union Telegraph Company.

TX1

1947		Litho.	Unwmk.	*Perf. 12½*	
17T1	TX1	5c **olive bister**		7.00	
		Pane of 9		70.00	
		Pane of 9, 8 5c + 1 10c		500.00	
17T2	TX1	10c **olive bister**		350.00	
17T3	TX1	50c **olive bister**		9.00	
		Pane of 9		87.50	

UNLISTED ISSUES

Several telegraph or wireless companies other than those listed above have issued stamps or franks, but as evidence of actual use is lacking, they are not listed. Among these are:
American District Telegraph Co.
American Telegraph Typewriter Co.
Continental Telegraph Co.
Los Angeles and San Gabriel Valley Railroad
Marconi Wireless Telegraph Co.
Mercantile Telegraph Co.
Telepost Co.
Tropical Radio Telegraph Co.
United Fruit Co. Wireless Service.

United Wireless Telegraph Co.

ESSAYS

An essay is a proposed design that differs in some way from the issued stamp.

During approximately 1845-1890, when private banknote engravers competed for contracts to print U.S. postage stamps, essays were produced primarily as examples of the quality of the firms' work and as suggestions as to what their finished product would look like. In most cases, dies were prepared, often with stock vignettes used in making banknotes. These dies were used to print essays for the Post Office Department. Rarely did the competitors go so far as to have essay plates made.

From 1894 onward, virtually all stamps were engraved and printed by the Bureau of Engraving and Printing (BEP). This usually required two types of essays. The first was a model design which was approved -- or disapproved -- by the Postmaster General. Sometimes preliminary drawings were made by the BEP designers, often in an enlarged size, subsequently photographically reduced to stamp size. An accepted stamp design usually became the engraver's model.

Occasionally during the course of engraving the die, a "progressive proof" was pulled to check the progress of the engraver's work. Because these were produced from an incompletely engraved die, they differ from the final design and are listed here as essays.

During approximately 1867-1870, various experiments were conducted to prevent the reuse of postage stamps. These included experimental grill types, safety papers, water-sensitive papers and inks, coupon essays, and others. These also differed in some way from issued stamps, even if the design is identical. A preliminary listing has been made here.

Because the essays in all their various colors have not been examined by the editors, traditional color names have been retained. Some color names have been taken from *Color Standards and Color Nomenclature*, by Robert Ridgway.

Only essays in private hands have been listed. Others exist but are not available to collectors. Some essays were produced after the respective stamps were issued. Year dates are given where information is available.

Essay papers and cards are white, unless described otherwise.

Values are for full-size essays, where they are known. Measurements are given where such information is available. Essays are valued in the grade of very fine, where such exist. Cut-down or faulty examples sell for less, often much less. A number of essays are unique or are reported in very limited quantities. Such items are valued in the conditions in which they exist.

The listings are by manufacturer. Basic stamps may appear in two or more places.

This listing is not complete. Other designs, papers and colors exist. The editors would appreciate reports of unlisted items, as well as photos of items listed herein without illustrations.

POSTMASTERS' PROVISIONALS

NON-CONTIGUOUS LISTINGS
Because many listings are grouped by manufacturer, some catalogue numbers are separated.

No. 5-E1 to 5-E2	follow 11-E16
No. 11-E17 to 72-E5	follow 5-E2
No. 65-E5 to 72-E8	follow 72-E5
No. 63-E13 to 113-F2	follow 72-E8
No. 112-E2 to 129-E2	follow 113-F2
No. 120-E1 to 122-E5	follow 129-E2
No. 115-E3a to 129-E6	follow 122-E5
No. 115-E11 to 116-E8	follow 129-E6
No. 115-E17 to 148-E1	follow 116-E8
No. 145-E2 to 179-E3	follow 148-E1
No. 156-E2 to 191-E2	follow 179-E3
No. 184-E8	follows 191-E2
No. 182-E4 to 190-E3	follow 184-E8
No. 184-E17 to 293-E11	follow 190-E3
No. 285-E10 to 856-E2	follow 293-E11

Albany, N.Y.
Gavit & Co.

1Xa-E1

Design size: 23½x25½mm
Die size: 58x48mm

Benjamin Franklin. With crosshatching about 2mm outside border (usually cut off).

1847
1Xa-E1 5c
- **a.** Die on India die sunk on large card, printed through a mat to eliminate crosshatching

brownish black	500.
scarlet	500.
red brown	500.
blue	500.
green	500.

- **b.** Die on India; some mounted on small card

bluish black	250.
scarlet	250.
brown	250.
yellow green	250.
gray blue	250.

- **c.** Die on India cut close

black	200.
blue	200.
red brown	200.
scarlet	200.
green	200.
yellow green	200.
brown violet	200.
rose red	200.

- **d.** Die on bond (1858)

bluish black	250.
scarlet	250.
brown	250.
blue	250.
blue green	250.
violet	250.

- **e.** Die on white glazed paper (1905)

black	450.
dark brown	450.
scarlet	450.
blue	450.

New York, N.Y.
Rawdon, Wright & Hatch

9X1-E1

Design 22mm wide
Die size: 50x102mm

Vignette of Washington. Two transfers laid down vertically on the die 22mm apart; top one retouched, with frame around it (this is a proof). Values are for combined transfers. Vignette essay exists cut apart from proof, value $150 each.

1845
9X1-E1 5c
- **a.** Die on India (1879)

black	350.
violet black	350.
gray black	350.
scarlet	350.
dull scarlet	350.
orange	350.
brown	350.
dull brown	350.
green	350.
dull green	350.
ultramarine	350.
dull blue	350.
red violet	350.

- **b.** Die on white bond (1879)

gray black	350.
dull scarlet	350.
dull brown	350.
dull green	350.
dull blue	350.

- **c.** Die on white glazed paper, die sunk (1879)

gray black	450.

POSTAGE

1847 ISSUE
Rawdon, Wright, Hatch & Edson

1-E1

Design size: 19x24mm
Original model. Engraved vignette of Franklin mounted on frame. Part of frame engraved, rest in pencil, ink and a gray wash.

1-E1   5c Die on card, black   21,000.

No. 1-E1 is unique. Value represents 1997 auction sale.

Engraved vignette only, matted.

1-E2   5c Die on India (1895), brown   2,500.

Engraved frame only, matted from complete die.

1-E3   5c Die on India (1895), brown   2,500.

The 1895 dates are in suppositional.

Design size: 19x23mm
Original model. Engraved vignette of Washington mounted (replaced) on frame. POST OFFICE and FIVE CENTS engraved as on No. 1-E1. U and S at top and X in bottom corners in black ink, rest in pencil, ink and a gray wash.

2-E1   10c Die on card, black   21,000.

No. 2-E1 is unique. Value represents 1997 auction sale.

2-E2   2-E3

Engraved vignette only.

2-E2   10c Die on India (1895)
       black   2,500.
       brownish black   2,500.
       brown   2,500.

Engraved frame only.

2-E3   10c Die on India (1895)
       black   2,500.
       brown orange   2,500.

The 1895 dates are in suppositional.

1851 ISSUE
Attributed to
Rawdon, Wright, Hatch & Edson

11-E1   11-E2

Design size: 18½x23mm
Large 3 in vignette.

11-E1   3c Die on India
        black   2,500.
        blue   2,500.

Design size: 19x24mm
Vignette of Washington.

11-E2   3c
   a. Die on India
        black   4,500.
   b. Die on proof paper, die sunk on 40x51mm
        card
        black   4,500.

Attributed to
Gavit & Co.

11-E3   11-E4

Design size: 19x23mm

Vignette of Franklin. Three states of die. Second state has double line dash above P of POSTAGE, third state has single dash above P and dot in O of POSTAGE.

11-E3   3c
   a. Die on India, die sunk on card
        warm black   600.
        scarlet   600.
        red brown   600.
        blue green   600.
   b. Die on India, 41x43mm or smaller
        black   250.
        greenish black   250.
        carmine   250.
        scarlet   250.
        yellow green   250.
        brown   250.
        blue green   250.
        dull blue   250.
        dark blue   250.
   c. Die on India, cut to shape
        warm black   150.
        cool black   150.
        black   150.
        carmine   150.
        orange   150.
        brown   150.
        dark green   150.
        yellow green   150.
        olive   150.
        light blue   150.
        dark blue   150.
        violet   150.
        scarlet   150.
   d. Die on bond
        cool black   175.
        scarlet   175.
        orange brown   175.
        brown   175.
        green   175.
        blue   175.
   e. Die on white glazed paper
        black   475.
        dark brown   475.
        scarlet   475.
        blue   475.
   f. Die on thin card, dusky blue, cut to shape 200.
   g. Die on Francis Patent experimental paper
        with trial cancel
        black   750.
        dark blue   750.
        brown   750.

Design size: 19x22mm
Die size: 47x75mm
Vignette of Washington. Two states of die. Second state has small diagonal dash in top of left vertical border below arch.

11-E4   3c
   a. Die on India, die sunk on card
        black   600.
        scarlet   600.
        brown red   600.
        blue green   600.
   b. Die on India, about 30x40mm or smaller
        orange   250.
        orange brown   250.
        brown   250.
        dusky yellow brown   250.
        yellow green   250.
        blue green   250.
        dull blue   250.
        red violet   250.
        deep red orange   250.
        black   250.
   c. Die on bond (1858)
        black   250.
        scarlet   250.
        brown   250.
        green   250.
        blue   250.
   d. Die on white glazed paper (1858)
        black   400.
        dark brown   400.
        scarlet   400.
        blue   400.
   e. Die on proof paper (1858)
        cool black   350.
        dull red   350.
        dull brown   350.
        dull blue green   350.
        dull blue   350.

Bradbury, Wilkinson & Co., England

11-E5

Design size: 20½x23½mm
Vignette of Washington.

11-E5   3c
   a. On stiff stamp paper about stamp size
        black   1,250.
        violet red   1,250.
        deep carmine   1,250.
        dusky carmine   1,250.
        deep scarlet   1,250.

---

        orange brown   1,250.
        deep green   1,250.
        blue   1,250.
        ultramarine   1,250.
        brown   1,250.
   b. On card
        violet black   1,250.
        dull scarlet   1,250.
        blue   1,250.
        green   1,250.
        brown   1,250.
   c. On stiff bond
        brown   1,250.
        blue   1,250.
        violet black   1,250.

Draper, Welsh & Co.

11-E6   11-E7

Design size: 18x23mm
Vignette of Washington.

11-E6   3c Surface printed on card, black   750.

Design size: 17½x24mm
Die size: 44x106mm
Engraved vignette of Washington.

11-E7   3c
   a. Die on India, about 44x105mm, die sunk
        on card, in vert. pair with No. 11-E8
        black   750.
        scarlet   750.
        brown red   750.
        green   750.
   b. Die on India, about 40x45mm or smaller
        warm black   250.
        cool black   250.
        dark carmine   250.
        scarlet   250.
        brown red   250.
        orange brown   250.
        brown   250.
        yellow green   250.
        blue green   250.
        blue   250.
        dull blue   250.
        brown violet   250.
   c. Die on India, stamp size
        rose   150.
        scarlet   150.
        red brown   150.
        brown   150.
        green   150.
        cool black   150.
        warm black   150.
        yellow green   150.
        brown violet   150.
        ultramarine blue   150.
   d. Die on bond
        black   150.
        scarlet   150.
        brown   150.
        blue green   150.
        blue   150.
   e. Die on white glazed paper
        black   400.
        dark brown   400.
        scarlet   400.
        blue   400.

11-E8

Design size: 19½x24
Die size: 44x106mm
On same die 30mm below No. 11-E7
Vignette of Washington.

11-E8   3c
   a. Die on India, 28x32mm or smaller
        black   200.
        dark carmine   200.
        scarlet   200.
        brown red   200.
        red brown   200.
        orange brown   200.
        brown   200.
        yellow green   200.
        green   200.
        blue green   200.
        blue   200.
   b. Die on bond, about 32x40mm
        black   175.
        scarlet   175.
        brown   175.

green 175.
blue 175.
c. Die on white glazed paper
black 400.
dark brown 400.
scarlet 400.
blue 400.

11-E8D

11-E9

Design size: 18x23mm
Vignette of Washington.
Washington vignette only. Same head as No. 11-E6 through 11-E8, but with more bust. No gridwork in background.

11-E8D 3c Die on proof paper, mounted on
card, black —

Design size (No. 11-E9a): 18x33mm
Vignette design size (Nos. 11-E9b, 11-E9c): 18x22mm
As No. 11-E8D, gridwork added to background oval.

11-E9 3c
a. Die on India
black 200.
scarlet 200.
b. Die on India, single line frame
black 200.
blue 200.
dark carmine 200.
orange red 200.
lilac 200.
brown 200.
scarlet 200.
rose violet 200.
deep yellow green 200.
c. Die on India, imprint of Jocelyn, Draper,
Welsh & Co., New York
black 200.
blue 200.
dark carmine 200.
orange red 200.
lilac 200.
brown 200.
scarlet 200.
rose violet 200.
deep yellow green 200.

Danforth, Bald & Co.

11-E10

11-E11

Vignette size: 18x22mm
Design size: 20x26mm
Die size: 57x74mm
Vignette of Washington. Double line frame.

11-E10 3c
a. Die on India, die sunk on card
black 600.
scarlet 600.
red brown 600.
green 600.
b. Die on India, off card, about 33x38mm
black 125.
scarlet 125.
brown 125.
blue 125.
green 125.
dull violet 125.
dull blue 125.
red brown 125.
rose 125.
c. Die on bond, black 250.
d. Die on white glazed paper
black 400.
dark brown 400.
scarlet 400.
blue 400.

Washington vignette only.

11-E11 3c Die on India
black 200.
dull rose 200.
scarlet 200.
orange 200.
brown orange 200.
brown 200.
green 200.
dark blue 200.
dull violet 200.
rose violet 200.

11-E12

Design size: 20x26mm
Die size: 62x66mm
Vignette of Washington. Single line frame. Two states of die. Second state shows scars in lathe lines in front of neck over T, and small dot below design. A third printing has more scars in front of neck.

11-E12 3c
a. Die on India, die sunk on card
black 450.
scarlet 450.
brown red 450.
dusky brown yellow 450.
brown 450.
green 450.
blue 450.
dull blue 450.
b. Die on India, about 43x45mm
black 200.
scarlet 200.
deep scarlet 200.
brown 200.
yellow brown 200.
green 200.
yellow green 200.
blue 200.
dull blue 200.
dark blue 200.
ultramarine blue 200.
orange 200.
red 200.
c. Die on bond
dusky brown yellow 275.
blue 275.
d. Die on white glazed paper
black 350.
dark brown 350.
scarlet 350.
blue 350.
e. Plate on thick buff wove
rose 100.
violet brown 100.
orange 100.
dark orange 100.
pink orange 100.
f. Plate on India, dark red orange 150.
g. Plate on white wove (head more completely engraved, ruled lines between
designs)
black 100.
dark carmine 100.
yellow 100.
blue 100.

Design size: 20x26mm
Die size: 62x66mm
Vignette of Washington. No. 11-E12 reengraved: more dark dots in forehead next to hair, thus line between forehead and hair more distinct.

11-E13 3c
a. Die on India, die sunk on card
black 550.
scarlet 550.
brown red 550.
brown 550.
green 550.
b. Die on white glazed paper
black 350.
dark brown 350.
scarlet 350.
blue 350.

Bald, Cousland & Co.

11-E14

11-E15

Design size: 22x28mm
Die size: 95x43mm
Vignette of Washington. On same die with Nos. 11-E16 and incomplete 11-E14.

11-E14 3c
a. Die on India
black 350.
scarlet 350.
red brown 350.
brown 350.
yellow green 350.
green 350.

---

blue green 350.
orange brown 350.
rose pink 350.
dull blue 350.
violet 350.
b. Die on bond
black 250.
scarlet 250.
brown 250.
blue green 250.
blue 250.

Design size: 28x22½mm
POSTAGE / 3 / CENTS in scalloped frame.

11-E15 3c
a. Die on India, die sunk on card
black 550.
scarlet 550.
red brown 550.
green 550.
slate 550.
b. Die on bond, about 40x30mm
black 125.
scarlet 125.
brown 125.
green 125.
blue 125.
slate 200.
c. Die on white glazed paper
black 300.
dark brown 300.
scarlet 300.
blue 300.

11-E16

Design size: 28x22½mm
U.S. at sides of 3.

11-E16 3c
a. Die on India, cut small
black 250.
light red 250.
red brown 250.
brown 250.
yellow green 250.
blue green 250.
green 250.
blue 250.
red violet 250.
b. Die on bond, about 40x30mm
black 200.
scarlet 200.
brown 200.
red brown 200.
green 200.
blue green 200.
blue 200.
violet 200.
slate 200.
c. Die on India, Nos. 11-E14 and 11-E16
with albino 11-E14
black 750.
scarlet 750.
brown 750.
green 750.
blue 750.
red violet 750.
d. Die on bond
black 225.
scarlet 225.
brown 225.
green 225.
blue green 225.
gray blue 225.
e. Die on white glazed paper, 64x78mm,
black 500.
f. Die on India, die sunk on card
black 900.
scarlet 900.

Toppan, Carpenter, Casilear & Co.

5-E1

5-E1E

5-E1f

Design size: 20½x26mm
Franklin vignette.

5-E1   1c
   a. Die on old proof paper, master die short-
      ened to 18½x22½mm, black   900.
   b. Die on thick old proof paper, black   900.
   c. Pair, Nos. 5-E1b, 11-E23, black   2,000.

Design size: 20x24mm
Similar to No. 5-E1 but with no additional shaded oval border.

5-E1E 1c Die on thin card, black blue   —
   f. Block of 4 in combination with pair of No.
      11-E23, on old proof paper, black   3,500.

5-E2

Complete design, but with SIX CENTS in value tablet.

5-E2   1c Die on India, black, cut to shape   1,750.
      Cut square   5,000.

11-E17   11-E18

Design size: 21½x25mm
Die size: 50½x60mm
Vignette of Washington.

11-E17   3c
   a. Die on India, 22x26mm, rose carmine 1,500.
   b. Die on old ivory paper, rose carmine 1,500.
   c. Die on proof paper, printed through a mat
      (1903)
      black   100.
      bright carmine   100.
      dull carmine   100.
      dark violet red   100.
      dull scarlet   100.
      dull violet   100.
      dull red violet   100.
      deep yellow   100.
      deep orange   100.
      orange brown   100.
      dull brown olive   100.
      deep green   100.
      dark blue green   100.
      ultramarine   100.
      dark blue   100.
      brown   100.
   d. Die on colored card (1903)
      deep orange, *ivory*   150.
      dark blue, *pale green*   150.
      orange brown, *light blue*   150.

      See note above No. 63-E1.

Design size: 20½x22½mm
   Washington. Vignette has solid color background. Crack between N and T of CENTS.

11-E18   3c Die on India, card mounted,
      24½x25mm
      black   1,750.
      carmine   1,750.

11-E19   11-E20

No. 11-E19
Design size: 20½x22½mm
Similar to No. 11-E18, but vignette background engraved horiz. and vert. lines. In pair with No. 11-E20.

No. 11-E20
Design size: 20x22½mm
Blank curved top and bottom labels. In pair with 11-E19. Also found in pair with 11-E21.

11-E19 3c Die on India, Nos. 11-E19, 11-E20
      mounted on card, black   6,000.

11-E21

Straight labels. Similar to No. 11-E19 but labels erased and vignette cut out. In pair with No. 11-E20.

11-E21 3c Die on India, Nos. 11-E20, 11-E21
      mounted on card, black   4,500.

11-E22   11-E23

Die size: 37½x46mm
Similar to issued stamp except lathework impinges on color-less oval.

11-E22 3c Die on India
      dusky blue   5,000.
      black   5,000.

Some students consider No. 11-E22 to be proof strikes of the die used to make the "Roosevelt" and Panama-Pacific small die proofs, as the lathework impinges on the colorless oval of Nos. 11P2 and 11P2a as well.

Design size: 18x22mm
Washington vignette only. From master die (21½mm high) with more robe and dark background.

11-E23   3c
   a. Master die impression, old proof paper,
      black   900.
   b. Block of 4, 2mm between ovals, thick old
      ivory paper, black   3,000.

13-E1   13-E2

Design as adopted but top label has pencil lettering only, also no lines in leaf ornaments around Xs in top corners.

13-E1 10c Die on India, black   3,000.

Similar to No. 13-E1 but vert. shading around Xs and lines added in leaf ornaments. No lettering in top label.

13-E2 10c Die on India, black   3,000.

17-E1   17-E2

Design size: 19x21½mm
Block sinkage size: 57x49mm
   Engine engraved frame without labels or interior shadow lines from straight bands and left side rosettes. No small equi-lateral crosses in central row of diamonds. Original vignette cut out and replaced by engraved vignette of Washington as adopted.

17-E1 12c Die on India, cut close, mounted on
      block sunk card, 77x57mm, black 6,000.

   Similar to adopted design but no small vertical equilateral crosses in center rows of diamond networks at top, sides and bottom.

17-E2 12c Die on India, brown violet, cut close 750.

37-E1   37-E2

Design size: 19½x25½mm
Die size: 46x49mm or larger
   Probably not the die used to make the plates. No exterior layout lines. Oval outline recut at bottom of jabot and vignette background etched much darker. Light horizontal lines on stock below chin.

37-E1 24c Die on India, black   2,500.

   Incomplete essay for frame only as adopted: no outer frame-line and lathework not retouched. Also known with 37TC1 struck above it on same piece.

37-E2 24c Die on India, black   —

38-E1

Design size: 19x24mm
Incomplete engraving of entire design. Scrolls at each side of 30 have only one outer shading line.

38-E1 30c Die on India, black, cut to stamp
      size, black   2,500.

1861 ISSUE
Toppan, Carpenter & Co.

   Examples on 1861 paper and in 1861 colors are rare. Most of the following listed on proof paper, colored card and bond paper are 1903 reprints. Ten sets of reprints on proof paper (and fewer on colored card, bond and pelure papers) supposedly were made for Ernest Schernikow, who bought the original dies about 1903. Similar reprints in similar colors on the same papers also were made of Nos. LO1-E2, 11-E18 and the Philadelphia sanitary fair stamps, plus several master dies of vignettes.

63-E1   63-E2

Vignette size: 18½x21½mm
Die size: 49x51mm
Franklin vignette only.

63-E1   1c
   a. Die on proof paper (1903)
      black   75.
      carmine   75.

dark carmine 75.
scarlet 75.
red brown 75.
orange 75.
yellow brown 75.
dark brown 75.
violet brown 75.
light green 75.
green 75.
dark blue 75.
ultramarine 75.
red violet 75.
dark violet 75.
dusky olive green 75.
b. Die on colored card (1903)
orange red, *pale yellow* 125.
orange, *pale pink* 125.
yellow brown, *buff* 125.
dark blue, *pink* 125.
dark violet, *pale olive* 125.
dull violet, *blue* 125.
deep green, *pale blue* 125.
violet, *light green* 125.
c. Die on green bond (1903)
black 125.
dismal red 125.
green 125.

Franklin vignette with U S POSTAGE at top and ONE CENT at bottom.

63-E2 1c
a. Die on proof paper (1903)
black 100.
carmine 100.
dark carmine 100.
scarlet 100.
red brown 100.
orange 100.
yellow brown 100.
violet brown 100.
gray brown 100.
light green 100.
green 100.
blue 100.
red violet 100.
ultramarine 100.
dusky olive 100.
b. Die on proof paper, outer line at sides
of oval missing (1861), black 1,000.
c. Die on green bond (1903)
orange 150.
orange brown 150.
violet 150.
d. Die on colored card (1903)
deep green, *pale blue* 150.
violet, *light green* 150.
dark orange red, *pale dull green* 150.
olive, *ivory* 150.
brown, *pink* 150.
scarlet, *yellow* 150.

63-E3

Side ornaments added.

63-E3 1c
a. Die on old proof paper (1861)
black 1,250.
blue 1,250.
b. Die on stiff old ivory paper (1861), black 1,250.
c. Die on colored card (1903)
black, *ivory* 150.
brown, *pale pink* 150.
blue, *blue* 150.
orange brown, *pale pink* 150.
gray olive, *ivory* 150.
gray olive, *buff* 150.
scarlet, *pale yellow* 150.
d. Die on proof paper (1903)
black 85.
carmine 85.
dark carmine 85.
scarlet 85.
red brown 85.
orange 85.
yellow brown 85.
violet brown 85.
light green 85.
green 85.
blue 85.
violet 85.
red violet 85.
orange brown 85.
dusky olive 85.
ultramarine 85.
e. Die on green bond (1903)
carmine 150.
orange 150.
violet 150.

63-E4

63-E4E

With upper and lower right corners incomplete. Serifs of 1s point to right.

63-E4 1c Die on old proof paper (1861), black 2,250.

As No. 63-E4 but with pencil shading in upper right corner.

63-E4E 1c Die on old proof paper (1861), black 3,500.

63-E5

63-E6

With four corners and numerals in pencil (ornaments differ in each corner).

63-E5 1c Die on old proof paper (1861), blue 2,750.

As No. 63-E5 but ornaments different.

63-E6 1c Die on old proof paper (1861), blue 3,500.

63-E7

As Nos. 63-E5 and 63-E6 but ornaments different.

63-E7 1c Die on old proof paper (1861), blue 3,250.

Die proof of No. 5 with lower corners cut out of India paper and resketched in pencil on card beneath.

63-E8 1c Die on India, on card (1861), black 2,000.

63-E9

Completely engraved design.

63-E9 1c
a. Die on India, cut to shape (1861)
black, on brown toned paper 1,000.
blue 600.
b. Die on India, about 58x57mm, die sunk on
card (1861)
blue 2,000.
c. Die on old proof paper, about 48x55mm
(1861)
black 2,000.
d. Die on large old white ivory paper (1861)
black 2,000.
blue 2,000.
e. Die on proof paper, printed through mat
(1903)
black 100.
carmine 100.
dark carmine 100.
scarlet 100.
orange 100.
orange brown 100.
yellow brown 100.
light green 100.
green 100.
black blue 100.
violet 100.
red violet 100.
violet brown 100.
gray 100.
blue 100.

ultramarine 100.
f. Die on bond (1903)
orange 125.
dismal blue green 125.
g. Die on bond, Walls of Troy wmk. (1903)
carmine 200.
orange red 200.
orange 200.
orange brown 200.
dark green 200.
light ultramarine 200.
h. Die on bond, double line of scallops wmk.
(1903)
orange red 200.
dark green 200.
i. Die on green bond (1903)
dismal carmine 125.
dismal violet brown 125.
dull dark green 125.
j. Die on pinkish pelure (1903)
orange red 300.
brown red 300.
brown orange 300.
dull blue green 300.
violet 300.
k. Die on colored card (1903)
black, *pale blue* 200.
carmine, *pale yellow* 200.
brown red, *pale pink* 200.
chestnut, *pale olive* 200.
dismal olive, *buff* 200.
ultramarine, *ivory* 200.
l. Die on stiff card (1903), green 250.

65-E1

65-E2

Vignette size: 16½x19mm
Die size: 49x50mm
1851 master die of Washington vignette only.

65-E1 3c
a. Die on proof paper (1903)
black 75.
carmine 75.
dark carmine 75.
scarlet 75.
red brown 75.
orange 75.
brown orange 75.
violet brown 75.
dusky olive 75.
light green 75.
green 75.
dark blue 75.
ultramarine 75.
lilac 75.
red violet 75.
b. Die on green bond (1903)
red 125.
brown 125.
blue 125.
olive 125.
c. Die on colored card (1903)
carmine, *pale green* 125.
scarlet, *yellow* 125.
orange, *ivory* 125.
olive brown, *blue* 125.
dark blue, *pink* 125.
violet, *buff* 125.
dark green, *pink* 125.

With tessellated frame, bottom label and diamond blocks. Without rosettes, top label and diamond blocks.

65-E2 3c
a. Die on old proof paper (1861)
black 1,000.
red 1,000.
b. Die on proof paper, printed through a mat
(1903)
black 85.
carmine 85.
dark carmine 85.
scarlet 85.
orange 85.
yellow 85.
yellow brown 85.
dusky gray 85.
light green 85.
green 85.
black blue 85.
ultramarine 85.
lilac 85.
dark lilac 85.
red violet 85.
c. Die on green bond (1903)
black 150.
dull orange red 150.
orange 150.
orange brown 150.
blue violet 150.
black blue 150.
dusky green 150.
d. Die on dull pale gray blue thin wove (1903)
dull red 300.
orange 300.

yellow brown   300.
dusky green   300.
black blue   300.
   e. Die on colored card (1903)
     black, *light blue*   150.
     orange red, *yellow*   150.
     red brown, *ivory*   150.
     light green, *pink*   150.
     green, *light green*   150.
     blue, *buff*   150.
   f. Die on India
     black   —
     rose   —

65-E3   65-E4

With top label and diamond blocks.
65-E3   3c
   a. Die on old proof paper (1861)
     brown red   1,500.
     black   1,500.
   b. Same as No. 65-E3 with numerals in pencil, Die on old proof paper (1861), black   3,500.
   c. Die on proof paper, no numerals, printed through a mat (1903)
     black   85.
     carmine   85.
     dark carmine   85.
     scarlet   85.
     orange   85.
     yellow   85.
     yellow brown   85.
     dusky olive   85.
     light green   85.
     green   85.
     black blue   85.
     violet blue   85.
     violet brown   85.
     lilac   85.
     red violet   85.
   d. Die on green bond (1903)
     dull scarlet   150.
     dim red   150.
     orange   150.
     yellow brown   150.
     green   150.
     dusky blue   150.
     violet   150.
     black   150.
   e. Die on colored card (1903)
     black, *buff*   150.
     scarlet, *ivory*   150.
     orange, *light yellow*   150.
     brown, *light blue*   150.
     violet, *light green*   150.
   f. Die on pink thin wove (1903)
     dull yellow   300.
     dismal red   300.
     yellow brown   300.
     dusky blue green   300.
     dusky blue   300.

Complete die, with numerals in rosette circles.
65-E4   3c
   a. Die on India, 75x76mm die sinkage (1861)
     black   1,250.
     carmine   1,250.
   b. Die on old proof paper (1861)
     black   1,250.
     dark red   1,250.
   c. Die on India, cut to shape (1861)
     black   750.
     carmine   750.

Die I — 67-E1   Die II — 67-E1

Vignette size: 13½x16mm
Jefferson vignette only. Two dies: die I incomplete, light background in vignette; die II background essentially complete.
67-E1   5c
   a. Die I on proof paper, black   500.
   b. Die II on proof paper (1903)
     black   75.
     carmine   75.
     dark carmine   75.
     scarlet   75.
     red brown   75.
     orange brown   75.
     brown   75.
     dusky olive   75.
     green   75.
     dark green   75.

     black blue   75.
     ultramarine   75.
     violet brown   75.
     red violet   75.
     lilac   75.
   c. Die II on colored card (1903)
     olive, *buff*   150.
     carmine, *pale yellow*   150.
     scarlet, *green*   150.
     brown, *pink*   150.
     black, *ivory*   150.
     ultramarine, *pale blue*   150.
   d. Die II on green bond (1903)
     orange brown   150.
     dismal red brown   150.
     dark green   150.
     violet   150.
     black blue   150.
   e. Die II on old thin ivory paper (1903)
     green   175.
     dark carmine   175.
   f. Die I on old thin ivory paper (1861), dark blue   1,000.
   g. Die I on old proof paper (1861)
     black   750.
     dusky ultramarine   1,500.
   h. Die II on old ivory paper (1861), navy blue   750.

67-E2

Vignette die II framed, with spaces for numerals.
67-E2   5c
   a. Die II on proof paper (1903)
     black   95.
     carmine   95.
     dark carmine   95.
     scarlet   95.
     red brown   95.
     orange   95.
     yellow brown   95.
     dusky olive   95.
     violet brown   95.
     light green   95.
     green   95.
     blue   95.
     ultramarine   95.
     red violet   95.
     lilac   95.
   b. Die II on colored card (1903)
     orange brown, *light yellow*   175.
     deep blue, *light pink*   175.
     dusky olive, *light buff*   175.
     dark green, *pale blue*   175.
     red violet, *ivory*   175.
   c. Die II on green bond (1903)
     orange brown   160.
     olive green   160.
     violet   160.
     blue   160.
     ultramarine   160.

67-E3   67-E4

With numerals.
67-E3   5c
   a. Die I on proof paper, printed through a mat (1903)
     black   125.
     carmine   125.
     dark carmine   125.
     scarlet   125.
     red brown   125.
     yellow brown   125.
     dark brown   125.
     violet brown   125.
     light green   125.
     green   125.
     dark blue   125.
     lilac   125.
     ultramarine   125.
     red violet   125.
     dusky olive   125.
   b. Die I on soft laid paper (1861)
     black   750.
     dark brown   750.
     orange brown   750.
   c. Die I on old proof paper, pencil designs drawn in corners (1861), black   1,500.

   d. Die I on old proof paper, outer lines on corner curves missing (1861), black   500.
   e. Die I on colored card (1903)
     orange red, *buff*   175.
     orange red, *light yellow*   175.
     olive green, *pale green*   175.
     deep green, *ivory*   175.
     dark blue, *light pink*   175.
     violet brown, *light blue*   175.
   f. Die I on green bond (1903)
     black   160.
     scarlet   160.
     brown   160.
     green   160.
   g. Die I on yellow pelure (1903)
     scarlet   350.
     brown red   350.
     brown   350.
     dark green   350.
     violet   350.
     blue   350.
   h. Die I on bond, Walls of Troy wmk. (1903)
     dark orange   250.
     blue   250.
     carmine   250.
   i. Die I on bond, two line scalloped border wmk. (1903)
     dark blue green   250.
     scarlet   250.

Complete die II design with corner ornaments.
67-E4   5c
   a. Die II on India, cut to shape (1861), black   500.
   b. Die II on brown toned paper (1861)
     black   1,000.
     brown   1,000.
   c. Die II on old proof paper (1861)
     orange brown   1,000.
     black   1,000.
   d. Die II on old ivory paper (1861), black   1,000.
   e. Die II on old proof paper, additional frame-line drawn on curved corners and small circle drawn in each corner (1861), black   1,500.
   f. Die II on proof paper, printed through a mat (1903)
     black   100.
     carmine   100.
     dark carmine   100.
     scarlet   100.
     orange   100.
     brown   100.
     yellow brown   100.
     dusky olive   100.
     light green   100.
     green   100.
     blue   100.
     black blue   100.
     violet brown   100.
     red violet   100.
     lilac   100.
     ultramarine   100.
   g. Die II on colored card (1903)
     red, *light yellow*   150.
     brown, *buff*   150.
     olive green, *light pink*   150.
     dark violet   150.
     violet brown, *pale green*   150.
     dusky yellow green, *dull pale*   150.
     blue green   150.
     brown, *ivory*   150.
   h. Die II on green bond (1903)
     black   125.
     dull dark orange   125.
     violet   125.
   i. Die II on bond, Walls of Troy wmk. (1903)
     scarlet   250.
     deep red   250.
     dark green   250.
   j. Die II on bond, two-line scalloped border wmk. (1903)
     deep orange   250.
     blue   250.
   k. Die II on greenish pelure (1903)
     orange   350.
     olive brown   350.
     dark green   350.
   l. Die II on bluish pelure (1903), red brown   450.

69-E1   69-E2

Vignette size: 15x17mm
Washington vignette only. Two dies: die I incomplete, horiz. background lines irregularly spaced, space occurring about every 2mm; die II more engraving on face, horiz. background lines regularly spaced, outer oval border smudged. Die II known only as 1851 master die.
69-E1   12c
   a. Die II on old proof paper (1851), black   500.
   b. Die I on proof paper (1903)
     black   60.
     carmine   60.
     dark carmine   60.
     scarlet   60.
     red brown   60.
     orange   60.

yellow brown 60.
violet brown 60.
gray brown 60.
light green 60.
green 60.
blue 60.
black blue 60.
red violet 60.
lilac 60.
ultramarine 60.
  c. Die I on green bond (1903)
    black 150.
    red brown 150.
    brown 150.
  d. Die I on colored card (1903)
    dark carmine, *ivory* 150.
    dark carmine, *light blue* 150.
    dark olive, *buff* 150.
    dark green, *light yellow* 150.
    dark blue, *pale green* 150.
    violet brown, *light pink* 150.

Die II with curved labels at top and bottom.
69-E2   12c
  a. Die II on proof paper, some printed
    through a mat (1903)
    black 65.
    carmine 65.
    dark carmine 65.
    scarlet 65.
    orange 65.
    yellow 65.
    yellow brown 65.
    violet brown 65.
    gray brown 65.
    light green 65.
    green 65.
    light blue 65.
    black blue 65.
    red violet 65.
    lilac 65.
    ultramarine 65.
  b. Die I on old proof paper (1861)
    dim red violet 500.
    red violet 500.
  c. Die I on dull light green bond (1903)
    black 150.
    dull red 150.
    dim orange 150.
    yellow brown 150.
    dusky green 150.
    dusky blue 150.
    red violet 150.
  d. Die I on pale yellow thin wove (1903)
    dim red 200.
    deep orange red 200.
    yellow brown 200.
    dusky blue 200.
    red violet 200.
  e. Die I on colored card (1903)
    dull red, *light pink* 150.
    orange red, *buff* 150.
    brown, *light blue* 150.
    dark olive, *light yellow* 150.
    dull dark blue, *ivory* 150.
    violet, *pale green* 150.

69-E3

Frame incomplete: all four rosettes blank.
69-E3   12c
  a. Die on proof paper (1903)
    black 125.
    carmine 125.
    dark carmine 125.
    scarlet 125.
    red brown 125.
    orange 125.
    orange brown 125.
    violet brown 125.
    light green 125.
    green 125.
    light blue 125.
    black blue 125.
    red violet 125.
    lilac 125.
    ultramarine 125.
  b. Die on old proof paper (1861)
    black 750.
    olive gray 750.
  c. Die on old ivory, top border and half of
    rosettes missing (1861), black 750.
  d. Die on stiff old ivory, top border missing
    (1861), bluish black 750.
  e. Die on colored card, top border missing
    (1903)
    orange brown, *light blue* 175.
    deep green, *light yellow* 175.
    deep blue, *light pink* 175.
    violet, *ivory* 175.
    deep yellow orange, *pale yellow green* 175.
    brown, *buff* 175.

  f. Die on green bond, top border missing
    (1903)
    orange 175.
    green 175.
    violet 175.
  g. Die on old proof paper, 1851 die with bor-
    der lines complete, upper right rosette
    blank (1861)
    orange 750.
    dark green 750.
    ultramarine 750.
    violet 750.
  h. Die I on old proof paper, vignette back-
    ground incomplete or worn, stock on
    neck unfinished (1861)
  i. Die I on old proof paper, as 69-E3h but
    both upper rosettes blank (1861), ul-
    tramarine 1,000.

69-E3j   69-E3k

  j. Die I on old proof paper, as No. 69-E3h
    but both upper plus lower left rosettes
    blank (1861), ultramarine 1,000.
  k. Die I on old proof paper, as No. 69-E3h
    but both lower plus upper left rosettes
    blank, corner borders removed around
    blank rosettes (1861), ultramarine 1,000.
  l. Die I on old proof paper, as No. 69-E3h
    but all rosettes blank, border lines com-
    plete (1861)
    dim scarlet 750.
    orange 750.
    green 750.
    ultramarine 750.
    violet 750.
  m. Die I on white wove, as No. 69-E3l (1861),
    scarlet 750.
  n. Die I on old proof paper, complete design
    (1861)
    orange 750.
    dark red 750.
    orange red 750.
    ultramarine 750.
  o. Die I on pale yellow thin wove (1903), dark
    red 750.
  p. Die I on pink thin wove (1903), blue 750.
  q. Die I on pale pink (1903), blue 750.

69-E4

Original complete design with numerals in corners.
69-E4   12c
  a. Die on India, card mounted (1861)
    black 750.
    gray black 750.
  b. Die on India, cut to shape (1861), black 500.
  c. Die on old proof paper (1861), black 500.
  d. Die on old proof paper, corners drawn in
    pencil (1861), black 1,500.
  e. Die on old proof paper, as No. 69-E3a but
    numerals sketched in diagonally and
    vert. (1861), black 3,000.
  f. Die on stiff old ivory paper, as No. 69-E4e
    but without top border (1861), bluish
    black 1,500.
  g. Die on thin card, black —

70-E1   70-E2

Vignette size: 7x16mm
Washington die II vignette only.
70-E1   24c
  a. Die II on proof paper (1903)
    black 60.
    carmine 60.
    dark carmine 60.
    scarlet 60.
    orange 60.
    yellow 60.

yellow brown 60.
violet brown 60.
gray olive 60.
light green 60.
green 60.
light blue 60.
black blue 60.
red violet 60.
lilac 60.
  b. Die II on green bond (1903)
    black 150.
    red brown 150.
    violet 150.
    orange 150.
  c. Die II on colored card (1903)
    dull red, *ivory* 150.
    brown red, *buff* 150.
    brown orange, *light pink* 150.
    dark green, *light yellow* 150.
    blue, *pale green* 150.
    violet, *blue* 150.

Washington vignette with oval label. Background complete,
eyes retouched.
70-E2   24c
  a. Die II on proof paper (1903)
    black 60.
    carmine 60.
    dark carmine 60.
    scarlet 60.
    orange 60.
    yellow 60.
    yellow brown 60.
    light green 60.
    green 60.
    light blue 60.
    black blue 60.
    red violet 60.
    lilac 60.
    gray olive 60.
    ultramarine 60.
  b. Die I on old proof paper, background lines
    incomplete (1861)
    black 750.
    dim red violet 750.
  c. Die I on colored card (1903)
    black, *light pink* 150.
    orange, *buff* 150.
    orange, *light blue* 150.
    dark green, *pale green* 150.
    violet blue, *light yellow* 150.
    violet, *ivory* 150.
  d. Die I on green bond (1903), brown 150.
  e. Die I on dull light blue green bond (1903)
    black 150.
    orange red 150.
    orange 150.
    yellow brown 150.
    dusky green 150.
    dull blue 150.
    red violet 150.
  f. Die I on dull pale green blue thin wove
    (1903)
    orange red 300.
    orange 300.
    yellow brown 300.
    dusky green 300.
    dull blue 300.

70-E3   70-E4

With frame. Blank areas in corners for numerals.
70-E3   24c
  a. Die on proof paper (1903)
    black 100.
    carmine 100.
    dark carmine 100.
    scarlet 100.
    orange 100.
    yellow brown 100.
    orange brown 100.
    violet brown 100.
    gray olive 100.
    light green 100.
    green 100.
    light blue 100.
    black blue 100.
    red violet 100.
    lilac 100.
    ultramarine 100.
  b. Die on old proof paper (1861), dusky red
    violet 1,000.
  c. Die on colored card (1903)
    carmine, *light blue* 175.
    blue, *pale green* 175.
    scarlet, *buff* 175.
    yellow brown, *cream* 175.
    dull violet, *pink* 175.
    dusky green, *light yellow* 175.
    gray olive, *ivory* 175.
  d. Die on green bond (1903)

black	175.
orange brown	175.
green	175.

Complete design with numerals in corners.

70-E4 24c
  a. Die on old proof paper, cut to shape (1861)

lilac	400.
black	400.
red violet	400.

  b. Die on India, cut close (1861)

black	400.
lilac	400.
brown lilac	400.

  c. Die on India (1861), dark blue   750.
  d. Die on India, mounted on 80x115mm card (1861), lilac   750.
  e. On stiff old ivory paper (1861)

black	1,000.
lilac	1,000.

  f. Die on proof paper, printed through a mat (1903)

black	125.
carmine	125.
dark carmine	125.
scarlet	125.
red borwn	125.
yellow brown	125.
brown	125.
violet brown	125.
gray olive	125.
light green	125.
green	125.
light blue	125.
black blue	125.
red violet	125.
lilac	125.
ultramarine	125.

  g. Die on blue pelure (1903)

dark carmine	300.
scarlet	300.
orange	300.
brown	300.
dusky green	300.

  h. Die on bond (1903)

black	175.
scarlet	175.
orange	175.
dark green	175.
blue	175.

  i. Die on green bond (1903)

black	250.
dark red	250.
green	250.

  j. Die on bond, Walls of Troy wmk. (1903), dark green   300.
  k. Die on bond, double line of scallops wmk. (1903)

deep orange red	300.
scarlet	300.
orange	300.
light blue	300.

  l. Die on colored card, printed through a mat

dark orange, *ivory*	150.
dark orange, *light pink*	150.
brown, *light blue*	150.
dull dark blue, *pale green*	150.
violet, *light yellow*	150.
violet brown, *buff*	150.

72-E1

Vignette size: 16x17½mm
Washington vignette only.

72-E1 90c
  a. Die on proof paper (1903)

black	85.
carmine	85.
dark carmine	85.
scarlet	85.
red brown	85.
orange	85.
orange brown	85.
violet brown	85.
gray olive	85.
light green	85.
green	85.
dark blue	85.
lilac	85.
red violet	85.
yellow brown	85.
ultramarine	85.

  b. Die on colored card (1903)

black, *light yellow*	165.
red brown, *light pink*	165.
carmine, *buff*	165.
brown, *pale green*	165.
dark brown, *light blue*	165.
ultramarine, *ivory*	165.

  c. Die on dull light blue green bond (1903)

violet brown	165.

dusky green	165.
dusky blue	165.
red violet	165.

Vignette with blank top and bottom labels.

72-E2 90c
  a. Die on proof paper (1903)

black	100.
carmine	100.
dark carmine	100.
scarlet	100.
orange	100.
yellow brown	100.
brown	100.
violet brown	100.
gray olive	100.
light green	100.
green	100.
dark blue	100.
red violet	100.
lilac	100.
ultramarine	100.

  b. Die on green bond (1903)

dull orange	150.
dull orange brown	150.
red violet	150.

  c. Die on colored card (1903)

black, *buff*	185.
orange red, *light yellow*	185.
brown, *ivory*	185.
olive green, *light pink*	185.
green, *light blue*	185.
violet brown, *pale green*	185.

72-E3   **72-E5**

U.S. POSTAGE in top label.

72-E3 90c
  a. Die on proof paper (1903)

black	125.
carmine	125.
dark carmine	125.
scarlet	125.
yellow	125.
yellow brown	125.
brown	125.
violet brown	125.
gray olive	125.
light green	125.
green	125.
dark blue	125.
lilac	125.
red violet	125.
ultramarine	125.

  b. Die on colored card (1903)

orange, *light blue*	185.
orange red, *light yellow*	185.
dark blue, *buff*	185.
violet, *pale green*	185.
violet brown, *ivory*	185.
orange brown, *pale pink*	185.

  c. Die on green bond (1903)

black	175.
brown	175.
green	175.

Lower corners of vignette cut out, "NINETY 90 CENTS" in pencil in bottom label.

72-E4 90c Die on India (1861), black   2,000.

Complete design.

72-E5 90c
  a. Die on India, cut to shape (1861)

black	300.
dark blue	300.

  b. Die on India, card mounted (1861), blue   500.
  c. Die on India, cut close (1861)

black	300.
blue	300.

  d. Die on proof paper, printed through a mat (1903)

black	175.
carmine	175.
dark carmine	175.
scarlet	175.
orange	175.
yellow brown	175.
brown	175.
violet brown	175.
gray olive	175.
light green	175.
green	175.
dark blue	175.
lilac	175.
red violet	175.
ultramarine	175.

  e. Die on colored card (1903)

carmine, *light blue*	250.
dismal brown, *light pink*	250.
orange brown, *buff*	250.
blue, *ivory*	250.

violet, *pale green*	250.
green, *pale yellow*	250.

  f. Die on green bond (1903)

dark carmine	225.
red brown	225.
green	225.

  g. Die on bond (1903), orange brown   250.
  h. Die on bond, "Bond No. 1" wmk. (1903), orange brown   350.
  i. Die on bond, "Bond No 2" wmk. (1903), orange brown   350.
  j. Die on bond, Walls of Troy wmk. (1903)

carmine	300.
scarlet	300.
orange	300.
dark green	300.
ultramarine	300.

  k. Die on pink pelure (1903)

brown red	350.
dull yellow	350.
very dark green	350.
dark blue	350.
dull violet	350.

American Bank Note Co.

65-E5   **65-E6**

Design size: 19x23½mm
Engraved frame with pencil border, center cut out, mounted over 22x27mm engraved vignette of Washington.

65-E5   3c Die on India, black   2,500.

Design size: 19x24½mm
Engraved frame with pencil border, center cut out, mounted over engraved ruled background with engraved Washington vignette mounted on it.

65-E6   Three Cents Die on India, on card about 23x27½mm, black   2,500.

65-E7   **65-E8**

Master die No. 80 of frame only.

65-E7   3c Die on India, card mounted

deep orange	1,000.
dark brown	1,000.
green	1,000.
dark blue	1,000.
black	1,000.

Design size: 19½x24½mm
Engraved lathework frame with Bald, Cousland & Co. engraved Washington vignette and engraved lettered labels and numerals mounted on it.

65-E8   3c Die on India, on 22x27mm card, black   2,500.

65-E9   **65-E10**

Master die No. 81 of frame only.

65-E9   3c Die on India

black	900.
brown yellow	900.
dark green	900.
orange red	900.

Engraved lathework frame with Bald, Cousland & Co. engraved Washington vignette and engraved lettered labels and numerals mounted on it.

65-E10   3c Die on India, on 28x35mm card, black   2,500.

67-E5

Design size: 21x25mm
Engraved frame used for the 1860 Nova Scotia 5c stamp cut to shape, with engraved lettered labels and Washington vignette No. 209-E7 mounted on it.

67-E5   Five Cents Die on India, on 23x27mm
         card, black   2,500.

67-E6

67-E7

Design size: 19x24
Engraved lathework background with Bald, Cousland & Co. engraved Washington vignette and engraved lettered labels and numerals mounted on it.

67-E6   5c Die on India, mounted on 22x26mm
         card, black   2,500.

Design size: 19x24mm
Engraved lathework background with Bald, Cousland & Co. engraved Washington vignette and engraved lettered labels and numerals mounted on it.

67-E7   5c Die on India, mounted on 21x26½mm
         card, black   2,500.

National Bank Note Co.

The following essays include those formerly listed as Nos. 55-59 and 62 in the Special Printings section, and the corresponding die and plate essays formerly listed in the proof section.

Frame essay with blank areas for Franklin vignette, labels, numerals, U and S.

63-E10   1c Die on India, black   2,000.

63-E11

63-E12

Die size: 58x56mm
"Premiere Gravure" die No. 440.

63-E11   1c
    a. "Premiere Gravure" die essay on India
       (formerly Nos. 55P1, 55TC1)
       black   3,250.
       indigo   1,350.
       ultramarine   2,250.
    b. "Premiere Gravure" small die essay on
       white wove, 28x31mm (formerly No.
       55P2), indigo   325.
    c. "Premiere Gravure" plate essay on India
       (formerly Nos. 55P3, 55TC3)
       indigo   200.
       blue   —
       ultramarine   250.
       violet ultramarine   —
    d. "Premiere Gravure" plate essay on semi-
       transparent stamp paper (formerly
       No. 55TC4), ultramarine   400.
    e. Finished "Premiere Gravure" plate essay
       on semitransparent stamp paper, perf.
       12, gummed (formerly No. 55), indigo   20,000.

Die size: 47x55mm
Apparently complete die except value numerals have been cut out.

63-E12   1c Die on India, die sunk on card, black 1,250.

65-E11

65-E12

Die size: 64x76½mm
Incomplete engraving of Washington head only.

65-E11   3c
    a. Die on India, on card, carmine   300.
    b. Die on white glazed paper
       black   300.
       scarlet   300.
       brown violet   300.

Die size: 78x55mm
Incomplete engraved design, no scrolls outside framelines, no silhouette under chin, no ornaments on 3s, U and S.

65-E12   3c Die on India, die sunk on card
         black   1,000.
         blue   1,000.

65-E13

65-E14

As No. 65-E12 but ornaments on 3s, U and S. Shows traces of first border design erased. With imprint and No. 441 below design.

65-E13   3c Die on India, card mounted
         scarlet   1,000.
         brown red   1,000.
         ultramarine   1,000.

Die size: 59x55mm
As No. 65-E13 but with ornaments outside frame.

65-E14   3c Die on India, die sunk on card
         black   750.
         scarlet   750.
         pink   1,250.
         brown orange   750.
         deep orange red   750.
         deep red   750.

As No. 65-E14 but top of head silhouetted, lines added or strengthened in hair at top of head, around eye, on chin, in hair behind ear. The three lines on bottom edge of bust extended to back. No imprint or die number.

65-E15   3c
    a. Die on India, card mounted, deep orange
       red   1,000.
    b. "Premiere Gravure" die essay on semi-
       transparent stamp paper, 20x25mm-
       30x37mm
       deep orange red   750.
       deep red orange   750.
       dim red   750.
       dim deep red   750.
       dim orange red   750.
       dull pink   750.
       dull violet red   750.
    c. "Premiere Gravure" die essay on India
       (formerly Nos. 56P1, 56TC1)
       red   1,350.
       black   2,000.
       scarlet   2,000.
       pink   2,850.
       orange red   2,000.
       dark orange red   2,000.
    d. Small die essay on white wove,
       28x31mm altered laydown die of com-
       plete design but with outer scrolls re-
       moved and replaced by ones similar to
       "Premiere Gravure" design (1903) (for-
       merly No. 56P2), dim deep red   325.
    e. As "c," small die essay on pale cream
       soft wove, 24x29mm (1915) (formerly
       No. 56P2a), deep red   1,250.
    f. "Premiere Gravure" plate No. 2 essay
       on India (formerly Nos. 56P3, 56TC3)
       red   200.
       scarlet   300.
    g. "Premiere Gravure" plate essay on semi-
       transparent stamp paper (formerly
       Nos. 56aP4, 56TC4)
       red, pair with gum   1,750.
       black   400.
    h. Finished "Premiere Gravure" plate essay
       on semitransparent stamp paper, perf.
       12, gummed (formerly No. 56)
       brown rose   475.
       P# block of 8, Impt.   15,000.
       orange red   475.
       bright orange red   475.

dark orange red   475.
dim deep red   475.
pink   475.
deep pink   475.

67-E8

67-E9

Incomplete impression from die No. 442, border lines and corner scrolls missing.

67-E8   5c Die on India, mounted on 34x50mm
         card, black   1,750.

Size of die: 58x59mm
"Premiere Gravure" design, with corner scrolls but without leaflets.

67-E9   5c
    a. "Premiere Gravure" die essay on India,
       card mounted (formerly No. 57TC1)
       black   1,750.
       scarlet   1,750.
    b. Small die essay on white wove,
       28x31mm, altered laydown die of com-
       plete design but with scrolls removed
       from corners to resemble "Premiere
       Gravure" (1903) (formerly No. 57P2),
       brown   325.
    c. As "b," die essay on pale cream soft
       wove, 24x29mm (1915) (formerly No.
       57P2a), brown   1,350.
    d. "Premiere Gravure" plate No. 3 essay on
       India (formerly Nos. 57P3, 57TC3)
       brown   200.
       light brown   300.
       dark brown   300.
    e. Finished "Premiere Gravure" plate essay
       on semitransparent stamp paper, perf.
       12, gummed (formerly No. 57), brown   14,000.

68-E1   68-E2

Design size: 14x17½mm
Die size: 26x31mm
Washington vignette only.

68-E1   10c Die on ivory paper, black   500.

Incomplete die No. 443.

68-E2   10c Die on India, 22x26mm, dark green   2,500.

Incomplete die of No. 68P1, thin lines missing on top of frame

68-E3   10c Die on India
         yellowish green   1,000.
         dark green   1,000.

69-E5

69-E6

Design size: 12½x16mm
Die size: about 62x65mm
Washington vignette only.

69-E5   12c
    a. Die on India, die sunk on card
       black   400.
       dark red   400.
       orange red   400.
    b. Die on ivory paper, about 24x28mm
       black   400.
       scarlet   400.
       black brown   400.
       blue   400.

Incomplete die No. 444, without corner ornaments.

69-E6   12c
  a. "Premiere Gravure" die essay on India,
    mounted on card **(formerly Nos. 59P1,**
    59TC1)
    black   *1,350.*
    scarlet   *1,750.*
    dark green   *1,500.*
  b. "Premiere Gravure" small die essay on
    white wove, 28x31mm (1903) **(formerly**
    No. 59P2), black   *450.*
  c. "Premiere Gravure" small die essay on
    pale cream soft wove, 24x29mm (1915)
    (formerly No. 59P2a), black   *1,750.*
  d. "Premiere Gravure" plate No. 5 essay on
    India **(formerly No. 59P3)**, black   *250.*
  e. Finished "Premiere Gravure" plate essay
    on semitransparent stamp paper, perf.
    12, gummed **(formerly No. 59)**, black   *40,000.*

70-E5   70-E6

Washington vignette in incomplete frame.

70-E5   24c Die on India, black   *3,250.*

Die size: 56½x56mm
Incomplete die (No. 445): silhouette unfinished, especially
scrolls around numerals; shadows over numerals not acid
etched.

70-E6   24c Die on India, die sunk on card
    black   *900.*
    violet   *900.*
    gray violet   *900.*
    dark violet   *900.*
    scarlet   *900.*
    green   *900.*
    orange   *900.*
    red brown   *900.*
    orange brown   *900.*
    orange yellow   *900.*
    rose red   *900.*
    gray   *900.*
    steel blue   *900.*
    blue   *900.*

71-E1   71-E2

Die size: 46x60mm
Incomplete die (No. 446): additional ornaments at top and
bottom in pencil, as later engraved.

71-E1   30c Die on India, black   *1,750.*

"Premiere Gravure" die: left side of frame and silhouette at
lower right unfinished.

71-E2   30c
  a. "Premiere Gravure" die essay on India, die
    sunk on card **(formerly No. 61TC1)**
    black   *1,750.*
    green   *1,750.*
    dull gray blue   *1,750.*
    violet brown   *1,750.*
    scarlet   *1,750.*
    dull rose   *1,750.*
  b. "Premiere Gravure" plate essay on India
    (formerly No. 61P3), deep red orange   *250.*
  c. "Premiere Gravure" plate essay on card
    black (split thin)   *500.*
    blue   *750.*
  d. "Premiere Gravure" plate essay on card,
    black 12x2mm SPECIMEN overprint,
    blue   *750.*
  e. "Premiere Gravure" plate essay on semi-
    transparent stamp paper
    deep red orange   *1,250.*
    yellow orange   *1,250.*
    lemon yellow   *1,250.*
    dark orange yellow   *1,250.*
    dull orange yellow   *1,250.*

72-E6   72-E7

Die size: 54x63mm
Incomplete die: without thin lines at bottom of frame and in
upper left triangle between label and frame, and without leaves
at left of U and right of S.

72-E6   90c Die on India, blue (shades)   *1,000.*

Similar to 72-E6 but lines added in upper left triangle, leaves
added at left of U and at right of S. Exists with and without
imprint and Die No. 447 added below design.

72-E7   90c
  a. Die on India, die sunk on card, black   *1,750.*
  b. "Premiere Gravure" die essay on India,
    thin line under bottom center frame
    (formerly Nos. 62P1, 62TC1)
    blue   *1,350.*
    black   *1,750.*
  c. "Premiere Gravure" small die essay on
    white wove, 28x31mm (1903) **(formerly**
    No. 62P2), blue   *375.*
  d. "Premiere Gravure" small die essay on
    pale cream soft wove, 24x29mm (1915)
    (formerly No. 62P2a), blue   *1,750.*
  e. "Premiere Gravure" plate essay on India,
    blue   *250.*
  f. "Premiere Gravure" plate essay on card,
    black (split thin)   *500.*
  g. "Premiere Gravure" plate essay on semi-
    transparent stamp paper **(formerly**
    Nos. 62aP4, 62TC4)
    blue, pair, gummed   *5,500.*
    blue green   *275.*
  h. Finished "Premiere Gravure" plate essay
    on semitransparent stamp paper, perf.
    12, gummed **(formerly No. 62)**, blue   *22,500.*

Die size: 54x63mm
Similar to Nos. 72-E6 and 72-E7 but leaf at left of "U" only, no
shading around "U" and "S," leaf and some shading missing at
bottom right above "S," shading missing in top label, etc., faint
ms. "8" at bottom of backing card.

72-E8   90c Die on India, die sunk on 3¼x3½-
    inch card, dark blue   —

63-E13

Design size: 20x47mm
Die size: 57x95mm
Bowlsby patent coupon at top of 1c stamp design.

63-E13   1c
  a. Die on India, die sunk on card
    black   *650.*
    red   *650.*
    scarlet   *650.*
    orange   *650.*
    orange brown   *650.*
    brown   *650.*
    yellow brown   *650.*
    blue green   *650.*
    blue   *650.*
    violet   *650.*
    red violet   *650.*
    gray   *650.*
    gray brown   *650.*
    dull orange yellow   *650.*
  b. Die on white glazed paper
    black   *600.*
    dark brown   *600.*
    scarlet   *600.*
    blue   *600.*
  c. Plate on pelure paper, gummed, red   *200.*
  d. Plate on white paper, red   *125.*
  e. Plate on white paper, with 13x16mm
    points-up grill, red   *200.*
    Split grill   *300.*
  f. Plate on white paper, perf. all around
    and between stamp and coupon

    red   *125.*
    blue   *125.*
  g. Plate on white paper, perf. all around,
    imperf. between stamp and coupon
    red   *125.*
    blue   *125.*
  h. Plate on white paper, perf. all around,
    rouletted between stamp and coupon
    red   *250.*
    blue   *250.*

**1861-66 Essays
Authors Unknown**

73-E2   73-E3

Design size: 21x26mm

73-E2   2c Pencil and watercolor on thick card,
    bright green   *3,500.*

Design size: 21x26mm
Indian vignette. Typographed printings from woodcuts. Plates
of three rows of three, one row each of Nos. 73-E3, 73-E4, 73-
E5. Listings are of singles.

73-E3   2c
  a. Plate on white wove
    red   *30.*
    scarlet   *30.*
    violet   *30.*
    black   *30.*
    blue   *30.*
    green   *30.*
  b. Plate on mauve wove
    red   *50.*
    violet   *50.*
    black   *50.*
    blue   *50.*
    green   *50.*
  c. Plate on yellow wove
    red   *50.*
    violet   *50.*
    black   *50.*
    blue   *50.*
    green   *50.*
  d. Plate on yellow laid
    red   *50.*
    violet   *50.*
    black   *50.*
    blue   *50.*
    green   *50.*
  e. Plate on pink laid
    red   *50.*
    violet   *50.*
    black   *50.*
    blue   *50.*
    green   *50.*
  f. Plate on green laid
    red   *50.*
    violet   *50.*
    black   *50.*
    blue   *50.*
    green   *50.*
  g. Plate on cream laid
    red   *50.*
    violet   *50.*
    black   *50.*
    blue   *50.*
    green   *50.*
  h. Plate on pale yellow wove
    red   *50.*
    green   *50.*
    blue   *50.*
  i. Plate on yellow-surfaced card, violet   *50.*

73-E4   73-E5

Design size: 23x26½mm
Small head of Liberty in shield. Typographed printings from
woodcuts. On plate with Nos. 73-E3 and 73-E5. Listings are of
singles.

73-E4   3c
  a. Plate on white wove
    red   *30.*
    scarlet   *30.*
    violet   *30.*
    black   *30.*
    blue   *30.*
    green   *30.*
  b. Plate on mauve wove, violet   *50.*

c. Plate on yellow wove
red	50.
violet	50.
black	50.
blue	50.
green	50.

d. Plate on yellow laid
red	50.
violet	50.
black	50.
blue	50.
green	50.

e. Plate on pink laid
carmine	50.
violet	50.
black	50.
blue	50.
green	50.

f. Plate on green laid
carmine	50.
green	50.
dull violet	50.
blue	50.

g. Plate on cream laid
red	50.
violet	50.
black	50.
blue	50.
green	50.

h. Plate on pale yellow wove
red	50.
green	50.
blue	50.

i. Plate on yellow-surfaced card, violet — 50.
j. Plate on fawn wove, green — 50.

Design size: 22½x25½mm
Large head of Liberty. Typographed impressions from wood-cut. On plate with Nos. 73-E3 and 73-E4. Listings are of singles.

73-E5 5c
a. Plate on white wove
red	30.
scarlet	30.
violet	30.
black	30.
blue	30.
green	30.

b. Plate on mauve wove, violet — 50.
c. Plate on yellow wove
red	50.
violet	50.
black	50.
blue	50.
green	50.

d. Plate on yellow laid
red	50.
violet	50.
black	50.
blue	50.
green	50.

e. Plate on pink laid
red	50.
black	50.
blue	50.
green	50.

f. Plate on green laid
red	50.
violet	50.
black	50.
blue	50.
green	50.

g. Plate on cream laid
red	50.
black	50.
blue	50.
green	50.

h. Plate on pale yellow wove
red	50.
blue	50.
green	50.

i. Plate on yellow-surfaced card, violet — 50.

73-E6

Size of design: 21x27mm
Indian vignette. Typographed impressions from woodcut.

73-E6 10c
a. Die on proof paper
black	200.
gray black	200.
carmine	200.
dusky red	200.
brown	200.
green	200.
blue	200.
violet	200.

b. Plate on white paper (pane of 4)
red	350.
violet	350.
brown	350.
black	350.
blue	350.

green	350.

c. Plate on soft cream card (pane of 4)
black	350.
red	350.
blue	350.
green	350.
red violet	350.

**1867 Essays
Re-use Prevention
Authors Unknown**

79-E1

Design size (folded): 18x23mm
Design size (unfolded): 18x58mm
Folded and scored four times, horiz. crease at center. Bronze overprint U 2 S, (2 punched out). Lower ⅔ gummed below second fold so top ⅓ could be torn off for canceling.

79-E1 2c On white paper, dull red violet — 5,000.

79-E2

Similar to No. 79-E1 but larger and not folded. Pierced with S-shaped cuts as well as punched out 2.

79-E2 2c
a. On white paper, US 7½mm high, bronze, US in dull black — 5,000.
b. On white paper, US 10mm high, bronze, US in violet — 5,000.

79-E3   Cuts as on back

U.S. No. 73 as issued but pierced with S-shaped cuts, ovptd. in metallic color.

79-E3 2c Essay on 2c stamp, gold overprint — 3,000.

79-E4   79-E6

Similar to No. 79-E1 but with punched out 3.

79-E4 3c
a. On white paper, U 3 S black above, bronze below and on face beneath folds — 5,000.
b. On green paper, 3 not punched out, 3 black, POSTAGE blue — 5,000.

Similar to No. 79-E4, with "3 U.S. 3 / Three Cents / Void if detached."

79-E5 3c On green paper, black — 3,000.

Similar to No. 79-E2 but with punched out 3, gummed.

79-E6 3c
a. On white paper, bronze over viole — 3,000.
b. On white paper, U S black, rest bronze — 3,000.

79-E7

Vignette map of U.S.

79-E7 3c On thick white paper, rouletted, green, gold 3 on map — 2,500.

**1867 Essays
Henry Lowenberg**

79-E8   79-E9

Washington vignette. Printed in reverse on back of transparent paper, reads correctly from front. Plate essays from sheets of 25.

79-E8 3c
a. Plate on onionskin paper, imperf., gummed
brown	7.
orange brown	7.
deep orange brown	7.
orange	7.
green	7.
light green	7.
blue green	7.
pale green	7.
red	7.
light red	7.
dark red	7.
violet red	7.
violet	7.
light violet	7.
dull pale violet	7.
blue	7.
dark blue	7.
deep blue	7.
pale blue	7.
dull blue	7.
gold	25.
gray	7.
black	7.
carmine	7.

b. Plate on onionskin paper, perf. 12, gummed
gray black	25.
gray	25.
gray violet	25.
dull violet	25.
brown red	25.

c. Plate on more opaque onionskin paper, imperf.
black	25.
red violet	25.
dull violet	25.

d. Plate on thick transparent paper
gray	25.
black	25.

Washington vignette. Printed with design reversed on front of various opaque papers, Plate essays are from sheets of 25.

79-E9 3c
a. Plate on white wove, imperf., gummed
blue	7.
red	7.
gray	7.
brown	7.
orange	7.
green	7.
yellow green	7.

b. Plate on clear white paper, imperf.

orange	7.
blue	7.
gray	7.
dark gray	7.

c. Plate on thick wove, fugitive ink, perf., gummed

carmine	10.
violet carmine	10.
pale dull red	10.
gray	10.
pale gray	10.
pale dull tan	10.
green	10.

d. As "c," strip of 3, signed Henry Lowenberg, pale tan — 400.

e. Plate on white chemically treated paper (turns blue if wet), imperf.

carmine	7.
Prussian blue	7.
orange	7.
green	7.
black	7.

f. As "e," perf.

carmine	10.
scarlet	10.
orange	10.
blue	10.
green	10.
brown	10.

g. Plate on India

violet brown	10.
green	10.
blue	10.
dark blue	10.

h. Plate on India, signed D.H. Craig, red — 350.

i. On white card, 62x72mm, design deeply indented, green — 15.

j. On blue wove, red — 15.

k. On orange laid

black	15.
gray	15.

l. On blue laid, scarlet — 15.

m. On white laid, blue — 15.

n. On pink laid, blue — 15.

o. On linen cloth

green	50.
red	50.
blue	50.

p. On glazed white paper, blue — 20.

1867 Essays
John M. Sturgeon

79-E10

Liberty vignette. Curved labels top and bottom. Self-canceling: CANCELLED in colorless sensitive ink, becomes colored when wet. Patented 1867, 1868.

79-E10   10c

a. Die on stiff card, cut close, clearly engraved, not canceled, both labels completely blank, dark carmine — 350.

b. Die on wove, rough impression, CANCELLED diagonally each way, dark carmine — 350.

c. Die on thick white or tinted paper, gummed, rough impression, about 21x26mm, two lines in upper label, one line in lower label

carmine	200.
dark carmine	200.
very dark carmine	200.
green	200.
dark green	200.
dull red violet	200.

d. As "c," on thick pinkish paper, dark green — 250.

g. Single centered in 6-inch wide strip of thick white paper, almost always cut in at top and bottom, dark carmine — 400.

h. Horiz. row of five designs on thick white paper, 10mm apart

dark carmine	1,200.
dark purple	1,200.
black	1,200.

l. Single on blue card, ovptd. seal BRITISH CONSULATE, V.R. in center, black — 1,250.

American Bank Note Co.

79-E11

Design size: 18x21mm
Vignette of Columbia. Probably submitted by Charles F. Steel.

79-E11   2c and 3c

a. Engraved plate on thick yellowish wove, imperf. (usually found in upper left margin blocks)

rose scarlet	200.
Block of 4	850.
blue green	200.
Block of 4	850.

b. Engraved plate on stamp paper, perf. 12, gummed

black	175.
rose scarlet	175.
blue green	175.
blue	175.

Author Unknown

79-E12

Design size: 20x26mm
Vignette of Liberty in circle of stars. Vertical color lines outside design to 24x28mm. Curved labels blank. Lithographed.

79-E12   No denomination

a. Die on white paper, dull violet — 1,000.

b. Die on bluish paper, blue — 1,000.

1867 Grill Essays
National Bank Note Co.

79-E13

Grill essays patented by Charles F. Steel.

79-E13

a. Wove paper, 80x140mm, impressed with four diff. seals, crossed lines and square dots down, circles 11 or 12mm — 9,000.

79-E13b

b. Grills in odd shapes on white wove, each about 20x25mm

cross	1,500.
star in square	1,500.
horizontal lined oval in square	1,500.
diagonal lined oval in square	1,500.

c. White wove, gummed, 15mm circle with points down grill, surrounded by 24 perforated holes — 1,000.

d. White wove, quadrille batonne watermark, 12mm colored circle with points down grill around 3, roughly grilled colorless 3 below, carmine — 1,250.

79-E13e

e. Colorless 12mm grilled circle as on "d," on tan wove, perf. 12 — 200.

f. As "e," yellow wove — 200.

g. As "e," white wove, block of 6 with ms. "Subject to a half hour pressure after embossing" — 3,500.

h. Colorless 15mm points down grilled circle on white wove, perf. 12 — 200.

79-E14

Allover grill.

79-E14

a. White wove, about 55x30mm, points down grill, stamped with red 6-digit number — 450.

b. Wove paper in various colors, about 85x40mm, points up grill as adopted

white	200.
pale pink	200.
salmon	200.
light yellow	200.
light gray green	200.
light blue	200.
pale lilac	200.
light gray	200.

79-E15

Experimental grills on perf. or imperf. stamps or stamp-size pieces of paper.

79-E15

a. Allover grill of small squares, points down (points do not break paper as on issued stamp, No. 79)

on 3c rose, gummed (No. 65)	125.
on 3c lake, imperf. pair, gummed (No. 66aP4)	150.

b. As "a" but points up, on 3c stamp, perf. 12, gummed

black	150.
rose	150.

c. As "a" but points up, imperf., gummed

3c rose (**formerly No. 79P4**)	1,750.
3c lake (**formerly No. 66aP4**)	1,850.

79-E15d

d. Allover pinpoint grill (so-called "Music Box" grill), points up, on No. 65 (plates 11, 34, 52) | 75.
e. As "d" but points down, on 3c rose (plate 11) | 125.
f. 15x16mm grill on stamp size white wove paper, perf. 12, gummed | 125.
g. C grill, 13x16mm, points down on stamp size wove paper, perf. 12, gummed
   yellowish | 100.
   pinkish | 100.
h. As "g" but points up, on white wove | 100.
i. C grill on 1c stamp (No. 63), points down | 4,000.
j. C grill on 3c stamp (No. 65)
   points up | 4,000.
   points down | 4,000.

The 3c C grill essay is almost identical to the issued stamp. There are slight differences in the essay grill which match those on No. 79-E15i and Nos. 79-E15k through 79-E15n.

k. C grill on 5c stamp (No. 76)
   points up | 4,000.
   points down | 4,000.
l. C grill on 10c stamp (No. 68)
   points up | 4,000.
   points down | 4,000.
m. C grill on 12c stamp (No. 69)
   points up | 4,000.
   points down | 4,000.
n. C grill on 30c stamp (No. 71)
   points up | 4,000.
   points down | 4,000.
o. E grill, 11x13mm, points up, on stamp size white wove paper, perf. 12, gummed | 100.
p. As "o," points down | 100.

79-E15q

q. Z grill, 11x14mm, points down on stamp size wove paper, perf. 12, partly gummed
   white | 100.
   salmon | 100.
   yellow | 100.
   greenish | 100.
   dull violet | 100.
   pale lilac | 100.

Some experts believe this is sheet selvage from other essays.

79-E15r

r. As "q," in sheet of white wove stamp paper, imperf., gummed | 175.

Continental Bank Note Co.

White wove paper about 6x9 inches with 7x9½mm grills spaced as they would fall on centers of stamps in a sheet.

79-E16
a. End roller grill at left, ms. "Chas. F. Steel-Sample of Grill used by Continental Bank Note Co. in 1874. Alexander Reid. J.K. Myers." | 1,250.
b. Without end roller grill, ms. "Grill of Continental Bank Note Co. Chas. F. Steel." | 1,750.
c. End roller grill at right, same inscription as "b" | 250.
d. On soft card, six grills | 450.

Wilbur I. Trafton

79-E17

Coarse grill in 15mm circle with 7 points up in 11mm, found on 1873 1c, some with 18mm circular cancel, stuck down on printed ad circular along with black, red and albino grill impressions (two each) on paper labeled "The Security Impression from the plates."

79-E17 Entire ad circular with grill examples | 750.

Natonal Bank Note Co.

79-E18

Albino 3 in points down shield-shaped grill in lithographed frame of 3c 1861 stamp.

79-E18 3c
a. Die on thick white paper, gummed
   black | 350.
   deep pink | 350.
b. As "a," with Washington, D.C. Feb. 21 pmk.
   black | 450.
   deep pink | 450.

79-E18c

c. As "a" but grill with points up, black | 600.
d. As "a," perf. 12, gummed, black | 600.
e. Die on yellow wove, gummed
   black | 750.
   red | 750.
f. Die on orange wove
   black | 750.
   carmine | 750.
g. Die on yellow laid, black | 750.
h. Numeral handcolored, dull carmine | 1,250.
i. Frame only, no grill, on grayish wove with pencil "McDonald P.O. Dept. Steel Nature(?)", pale orange brown | 750.

79-E18j

79-E18k

Albino 3 in 13x14mm shield made up of embossed narrow spaced horiz. lines.

j. White wove stamp paper, 22x27mm, perf. 12, gummed | 450.

Albino 3 in 13x14mm shield slightly different from No. 79-E18j.

k. As "j," different shield | 250.

79-E19

Typographed impression of frame, lettering and numerals of 3c 1861 stamp with 3 in double lined shield in center. In strip of three about 20mm apart, impression of 3 and shield progressively lighter on impressions two and three.

79-E19 3c
a. Engraved (die No. 1570), green | 3,000.
b. Typographed in color on white paper
   blue green | 1,750.
   dark red brown | 1,750.
c. As "b," colored and colorless parts interchanged, on thick paper
   blue green | 1,750.
   dark red brown | 1,750.

79-E21

Lathework frame with shield shaped vignette cut out, albino 3 in circular grill in center.

79-E21 3c
a. Thick paper, perf. 12
   blue | 500.
   carmine | 500.
b. At left in strip of 3 with 2 No. 79-E13f, latter black cancels, blue | 3,500.
c. Lathework frame on thin wove, allover diagonal grill, imperf., gummed, blue | 500.

Lathework frame similar to No. 79-E21 but vignette of 6 horiz. bars with 3 in center printed in glossy ink.

79-E22 3c On pink lilac paper, blue | 2,250.

79-E23

Design of 3c 1861 stamp typographed in relief for surface printing. Single impression lightly block sunk 63x62mm in color. Design has 21x26½mm border inside 23x28½mm colorless rectangle.

79-E23 3c
a. Die on 64x75mm ivory paper, black | 325.
b. Die on India, dull violet-red red | 325.
c. Die on 59x54mm stiff white card, color about 40mm wide (not extending to edges)
   light red violet | 325.
   carmine | 325.
   blue | 325.
d. Washington head only, lines on face around eye, on soft card
   dim blue-green blue | 250.
   dim orange-orange red | 250.

On 17x21mm plain colored rectangle printed through a mat, surrounded by 55x62mm colorless rectangle, vert. 4½mm wide color bands at sides inside 64x62mm die sinkage.

e. Washington head with dots around eye, on 17x42mm solid color, on 77x45mm stiff white paper, dull violet-red | 250.
f. India paper on soft white card block sunk 63x62mm, dull violet-red-red with solid color margins | 250.

Colored India generally cut away outside colorless rectangle 23x28½mm, design heavily embossed through to card beneath.

g. As "f," trimmed to shape
   dark carmine | 350.
   orange | 350.
   blue green | 350.
   red violet | 350.
h. Complete design on India, sunk on card, trimmed to shape
   blue | 100.
   dull green blue | 100.
i. Plate typographed on white wove, imperf., gummed
   dim red | 100.
   dim light orange red | 100.

dim blue green 100.
dim pale blue 100.
dim dark blue 100.
dusky violet red 100.

Color outside design generally fills rectangle, design impression shows on back.

    j. Complete design on glossy sticky paper,
        deep violet red 150.
    k. As "j," on pelure, perf. 12, gummed, rose 175.
    l. As "k," allover grill, dim red 150.
    m. As "k," 13x16mm grill, gray black 150.

79-E24   79-E24c

Block sinkage: 65x76mm
Washington head only.

79-E24   3c
    a. Lithographed, face dotted, on 65x76mm
        solid color background
        black 200.
        red violet 200.
        olive black 200.
    b. Typographed, background irregular edge,
        on card, gray black 250.
    c. Face lined, on 64x72mm solid color background
        black 150.
        scarlet 150.

79-E25

Plate essays of complete 1861 3c design.

79-E25   3c
    a. Plate on hard white transparent wove,
        dark red 50.
    b. Plate on more opaque white wove, dim
        red 50.
    c. Plate on Gibson patent starch coated
        opaque white paper, generally crinkled,
        lathework design usually poorly printed
        orange red 20.
        deep orange red 20.
        pink 20.
        dull yellow 20.
        yellow orange 20.
        dull yellow orange 20.
        brown yellow 20.
        brown 20.
        green 20.
        blue green 20.
        blue 20.
        light blue 20.
    d. Plate on semitransparent white wove
        dull pale blue 20.
        green 20.
        dull yellow orange 20.
    e. Plate on pale green paper, clearly
        printed, dark g-b green 40.
    f. Plate on white wove, 13x16mm points
        down grill, gummed, dark blue 40.
    g. Plate on lilac gray paper, 13x16mm grill,
        gummed
        dark blue 40.
        dull red 40.
        black 40.
    h. Plate on white paper (ungrilled), perf. 12,
        gummed
        red 10.
        light red 10.
        pale red 10.
        light orange red 10.
        deep yellow orange 10.
        brown 15.
        dark green 15.
        deep blue 15.
        dull g-b blue 15.
        gray black 15.
    i. As "h," ms. A or B in UL corner, red 50.
    j. Plate on white paper, 13x16mm points
        down grill, perf. 12, gummed
        black 25.
        gray black 25.
        pale red 25.
        light red 25.
        orange red 25.
        deep orange yellow 25.

---

        brown 25.
        dark brown 25.
        green 25.
        blue 25.
        dark blue 25.
    k. As "j," ms. "s No. 6" on back
        red 50.
        gray black 50.
        dark blue 50.
    l. As "j," but grill points up
        red 40.
        pink 40.
        pale rose 40.
        brown 40.
        orange yellow 40.
        deep red orange 40.
        green 40.
        dull blue 40.
        dull light blue 40.
    m. As "l," pair with blue oval "American Bank
        Note Co. April 17, '79", pink 150.
    n. Plate on greenish gray chemical paper,
        13x16mm grill, perf. 12
        black 50.
        green 50.
        dark blue 50.
        orange red 50.
        light yellow gray 50.
        light red gray 50.
    o. As "n," without grill
        red 50.
        rose 50.
    p. Plate on pelure, without grill, imperf.,
        gummed, dim red 50.
    q. As "p," perf. 12, dim red 50.

79-E26

Plate impressions of 1861 3c stamp overprinted with various safety network designs. Inks probably fugitive.

79-E26   3c
    a. Vert. pair on 58x80mm India, overprint
        die 54x71mm or more, small ONE repeated in 41 vert. lines per 40mm,
        rose pink, overprint deep orange yellow 2,000.
    b. As "a," block of 6 inscribed "J. Sangster
        Pat. 190376, Jan. 6, 1877" 3,500.
    c. 65TC3, "VEINTE" overprint, in miniature
        sheet of 12, perf. 12, black, overprint
        orange 7,500.

3c 1861 printed in various colors in miniature sheets of 12 with safety ovpts. (Apparently only one sheet printed of each color combination, except two Type D combinations known both perf. and imperf.)

    d. Type A
        perf. 12, dull violet, overprint gray 425.
        perf. 12, rose red, overprint gray blue 425.
        perf. 12, violet, overprint gray tan 425.
        imperf., pale olive, overprint pale tan 425.
        imperf., green, overprint gray tan 425.
    e. Type B
        perf. 12, green, overprint pale tan 425.
        perf. 12, violet, overprint gray tan 425.
        perf. 12, dull red brown, ovpt. pale brown 425.
        perf. 12, dark dull red brown, overprint
        pale brown 425.

Type C   Type D

    f. Type C
        perf. 12, dull violet, overprint gray tan 550.
        perf. 12, dull red, overprint gray blue 550.
        perf. 12, rose red, overprint gray blue 550.
        perf. 12, green, overprint gray tan 550.
        imperf., rose red, overprint pale tan 550.
        imperf., pale rose red, overprint pale tan 550.
        imperf., yellow brown, overprint tan 550.

    g. Type D
        perf. 12, dull violet, overprint gray blue 550.
        perf. 12, rose red, overprint gray blue 550.
        perf. 12, light red brown, overprint pale
        brown 550.
        perf. 12, dark green, overprint dull blue 550.
        imperf., pale olive, overprint tan 550.
        imperf., ultramarine, overprint tan 550.
        imperf., dull violet, overprint gray blue 550.
        imperf., dull violet, overprint pale green 550.
        imperf., dark green, overprint dull blue 550.

79-E27

Design size: 20½x26½mm
Engraved in relief for surface printing, large 2 vignette, on same die with No. 79-E28, 20mm apart. Also essayed for envelopes on thick papers.

79-E27   2c
    a. Untrimmed die, 30x42mm, on paper with
        "US" monogram, pale rose 850.
    b. Die on stiff glazed paper, 63x50mm,
        black 450.
    c. Trimmed die on India, on thick soft card,
        colorless parts in relief
        black 450.
        red 450.
        orange 450.
        violet red 450.
    d. Die on 35x40mm white wove, imperf.,
        gummed
        blue 450.
        albino 450.
    e. Die on white wove, perf. 12, gummed,
        smoky violet red 450.
    f. Untrimmed die on white wove, 61x42mm,
        black 550.

79-E28   79-E28g

Design size: 21x25½mm
Engraved in relief for surface printing, large 3 in shield vignette, on same die with No. 79-E27, 20mm apart. Also essayed for envelopes on thick papers.

79-E28   3c
    a. Untrimmed die on stiff ivory paper, showing color 30x42mm
        black 700.
        rose 700.
        orange 700.
        blue 700.
    b. Untrimmed die on India with No. 79-E27,
        both embossed, yellow orange 1,000.
    c. Trimmed die heavily struck on India, card
        mounted, colorless parts in relief
        black 250.
        red 250.
        orange 250.
    d. Die on wide laid paper, "US" monogram,
        perf. 12, gummed
        pale rose 250.
        dull brown yellow 250.
    e. Die on greenish wove, 10x12mm points
        down grill, imperf., gummed, dull brown

f. Die on white paper, perf. 12, gummed
    smoky violet red   250.
    green   250.
g. Underprinted design only on thin white
    wove
    light blue   350.
    albino   350.

79-E28H

Design size: 68x38mm
Two compound surface-printed designs, "3" within ornate frame. Possibly included a third design at right.

79-E28H   3c Untrimmed die on wove paper,
    green   1,000.

79-E29

1861 1c frame only.

79-E29   1c
  a. Die on thin crisp paper, safely design un-
    derprint, black on dull olive green   3,000.
  b. Die on pink paper, 18x13mm points down
    grill, imperf., gummed, red brown   1,250.
  c. Die on pink "laid" paper, red   1,250.
  d. Die on pale pink paper, red brown   1,250.
  e. Die on transparent white paper, red
    brown   1,250.
  f. Die on thick yellow paper, red brown   1,250.
  g. Die on thin transparent white paper,
    11x13mm points down grill, perf. 12,
    gummed, red brown   1,250.
  h. As "g," imperf.   1,250.

79-E29i

As No. 79-E29 but with monogram in vignette.

  i. Die on transparent white stamp paper,
    perf. 12, gummed, red brown   3,500.

79-E30

Design size: 20x26mm
Block size: 64x76½mm
Vignette of Liberty. Typographed.

79-E30   3c
  a. Head only on solid color (die size:
    67x76mm), on 32x37mm stiff yellowish
    wove
    black   300.
    blue green   300.
  b. Vignette only, on 66x100mm card

    black   300.
    blue green   300.
    blue   300.
  c. Vignette only, on proof paper
    bright blue   300.
    black   300.
  d. Complete design, untrimmed block, color-
    less 22x27 rectangle around design,
    broad outer edge in color, on stiff yel-
    lowish wove
    black   150.
    blue green   150.
    violet brown   150.
    bright violet red   150.
    red violet   150.
    buff   150.
  e. As "d," on proof paper
    buff   150.
    deep blue green   150.
    red brown   150.
    carmine   150.
    black   150.
  f. Die on proof paper, perf. 12, vignette oval
    perf. 16, carmine   200.
  g. Die on stiff ivory paper about 28x32mm
    black   150.
    carmine   150.
    yellow   150.
    dark blue green   150.
    rose violet   150.
  h. Die on stiff ivory paper, no color outside
    design, block of 4, carmine   500.
    Block of 8 with vert. pairs in orange, dull
    yellow green, dark green and dark vio-
    let   900.
  i. Die on deep orange-surfaced white pa-
    per, carmine   150.
  j. As "i," perf. 12, gummed, carmine   150.
  k. Die on yellow-surfaced wove, carmine   150.

79-E30 l

  l. Die with outer color removed, on
    64x90mm white wove stamp paper with
    imprint below, imperf., gummed
    carmine   150.
    scarlet   150.
    dim orange red   150.
    orange   150.
    dull yellow orange   150.
    pale dull yellow   150.
    brown   150.
    lemon   150.
    yellow green   150.
    dull olive green   150.
    dull greenish gray   150.
    dim blue green   150.
    dull blue   150.
    dull red violet   150.
    pale red violet   150.
  m. As "l," tete-beche pairs, each with imprint
    carmine, orange   300.
    buff, pale lilac   300.
    dark orange brown, yellow   300.
    dull green gray   300.
  n. As "l," perf. 12, vignette oval perf. 16 (al-
    so found without paper outside perfs.
    carmine   150.
    pale rose   150.
    dim scarlet   150.
    dull scarlet   150.
    dim orange red   150.
    light red brown   150.
    dark brown   150.
    orange   150.
    dull orange   150.
    dismal orange   150.
    dull brown orange   150.
    pale dull yellow   150.
    dull brown   150.
    yellow brown   150.
    dull olive green   150.
    dim dark yellow orange   150.
    light yellow green   150.
    green   150.
    dim blue green   150.
    dark blue green   150.
    dull greenish gray   150.
    dull yellowish gray   150.
    dull blue   150.
    dim red violet   150.
    dull red violet   150.
    pale red violet   150.
    red violet   150.
  o. Plate essay on wove, designs 7mm apart,
    in two colors shading into each other,
    imperf.
    red brown to dark orange   150.
    dark orange to brown red   150.
    brown olive to red brown   150.
    red brown to yellow green   150.
    yellow green to dull carmine   150.
    dull carmine to yellow green   150.
    blue green to dull carmine   150.
    brown olive to dull carmine   150.

    dull carmine to orange   150.
    orange to deep blue   150.
    deep blue to orange brown   150.
    orange brown to dull orange   150.
    dull carmine to deep blue   150.
  p. As "o," on transparent wove, imperf.
    red violet to deep violet   150.
    deep violet to carmine   150.
    dull scarlet to gold   150.
    gold to carmine   150.
    dark violet to blue green   150.
    blue green to dark violet red   150.
    violet to yellow green   150.
    yellow green to red violet   150.
  q. Plate on stiff yellowish wove, imperf.
    dull carmine to orange   150.
    orange to deep blue   150.
    brown olive to brown red   150.
    brown red to yellow green   150.
    blue green to dull carmine   150.
    dull carmine to deep blue   150.
    deep blue to dark brown   150.
    dark brown to orange   150.
  r. As "q," outside edge perf. 12
    blue green to dull carmine   150.
    dull carmine to deep blue   150.
    deep blue to dark brown   150.
    dark brown to dull orange   150.
    dull carmine to dull orange   150.
    dull orange to deep blue   150.
    yellow green to dull carmine   150.
    dull carmine to yellow green   150.
    brown olive to brown red   150.
    brown red to dull orange   150.
  s. Plate in single color, outside edge perf.
    12, gummed
    carmine   150.
    dull orange   150.
    orange brown   150.
    dark brown   150.
    brown olive   150.
    dark blue green   150.
    violet   150.
  t. As "s," imperf., gummed
    brown   100.
    brown orange   100.
    dull blue green   100.
    deep blue   100.
    carmine   100.
  u. As "t," one color directly over another
    (gives effect of one color), black on
    scarlet   200.
  v. As "b," heavily stamped on white card,
    only faint traces of vignette, albino   100.
  w. As "v," printed design at right, very dark
    blue green   200.

79-E31a   79-E31b

79-E31d   79-E31e

79-E31f   79-E31g

Same design as No. 79-E30, black green on white wove safety paper, underprinted with different designs in various colors, imperf.

79-E31 3c
- **a.** Red horiz. diamonds — 800.
- **b.** Dull yellow green with ONE repeated — 800.
- **c.** Red with 2 in circles — 800.
- **d.** Red with 2 in circular stars — 800.
- **e.** Red with 2 in ovals — 800.
- **f.** Red with 3 in diamonds — 800.
- **g.** Black with 5 in hexagons — 800.
- **h.** Red with X repeated — 800.

79-E32

Similar to No. 79-E30f, but perf. vignette removed and frame mounted over 18x23mm Washington vignette.

79-E32 3c Die on 34x40mm white wove, black vignette, blueframe — 1,000.

1868 Essays
Experiments for bicolor printing

1c 1861 design, color reversed as adopted. Typographed frame with 43x60mm solid color border.

79-E33 1c Die on thin white paper, frame pink, vignette dark blue over pink — 750.

79-E35a   79-E35c

Frame lithographed, colored and colorless parts interchanged, vignette engraved and printed in another color.
Die I: colorless vignette oval (Nos. 79-E35a, 79-E35b).
Die II: vignette with horiz. lines (Nos. 79-E35d through 79-E35f)

79-E35 5c
- **a.** Untrimmed die on thin white paper, 40x60mm (values for cut to stamp size)
  - frame buff, vignette black — 750.
  - frame buff, vignette blue — 750.
  - frame buff, vignette red brown — 750.
  - frame buff, vignette dark brown — 750.
  - frame buff, vignette orange — 750.
  - frame buff, vignette carmine — 750.
  - frame blue green, vignette dark brown — 750.
  - frame blue green, vignette red brown — 750.
  - frame blue green, vignette orange — 750.
  - frame carmine, vignette blue — 750.
  - frame carmine, vignette red brown — 750.
  - frame violet, vignette orange — 750.
  - frame light red, vignette deep orange red — 750.
  - frame light red, vignette yellow orange — 750.
- **b.** Die on stiff wove, frame brown, vignette scarlet — 750.
- **c.** 45x65mm die impression of lithographed frame only, on ivory paper
  - black — 750.
  - blue green — 750.
- **d.** Die on thin white paper
  - frame violet, vignette carmine — 750.
  - frame violet, vignette brown — 750.
  - frame violet, vignette red brown — 750.
  - frame carmine, vignette black — 750.
- **e.** Vignette only on white glazed paper
  - black — 750.
  - blue — 750.
  - scarlet — 750.
  - dark brown — 750.
- **f.** As "e," without thin outer frameline, on India
  - lake — 750.
  - red — 750.
  - deep red orange — 750.
  - scarlet — 750.
  - deep green — 750.
  - ultramarine — 750.

79-E36

Die II vignette as No. 79-E35e, with gothic "United States" above.

79-E36 5c
- **a.** Die on white glazed paper
  - black — 325.
  - scarlet — 325.
  - dark brown — 325.
  - green — 325.
  - blue — 325.

Die size: 51x63½
5c 1861 design, color reversed as adopted, vignette mounted on typographed frame.

79-E37 5c
- **a.** Die on white card, frame light blue, vignette black — 1,000.
- **b.** Vignette only, die on India, black — 250.
- **c.** Vignette only, die on white glazed paper
  - blue — 250.
  - black — 250.
  - green — 250.

100-E1

Design size: 20½x24½mm
Engraved circular Franklin vignette mounted on 43x75mm white card, engraved Washington head mounted thereon; background, silhouette, etc., retouched in black ink. With engraved frame of No. 71-E1 (vignette cut out) mounted over the double vignette.

100-E1 30c Die on India, 30x34mm, black — 3,000.

1869 ISSUE
George T. Jones

112-E1   113-E1

Design size: 24x30mm
U.S. Grant vignette in frame with blank labels, ovals, etc. Paper overprinted with network of fine colored wavy lines in fugitive inks as on beer stamps.

112-E1 No Denomination
- **a.** Die on India cut to stamp size, 1 color
  - black — 2,250.
  - blue — 2,250.
- **b.** Die on India cut to stamp size, 2 colors (head in black)
  - blue, light gray overprint — 2,750.
  - red, light gray overprint — 2,750.
  - black, light violet overprint — 2,750.
  - black brown, pale red violet ovpt. — 2,750.
  - carmine, gray overprint — 2,750.
  - blue, yellow overprint — 2,750.

Design size: 24x30mm
U.S. Treasury Dept. seal in vignette oval.

113-E1 2c
- **a.** Die on India cut to stamp size, 1 color
  - carmine — 2,500.
  - blue — 2,500.
- **b.** Die on India cut to stamp size, 3 colors, black on pale red violet wavy lines and blue green lined vignette — 3,750.

Frame as 112-E1 but with Washington vignette and 2c denomination. Another Washington vignette below but in horiz. lined oval frame.

113-E2 2c Die on 1⅝x3½inch India, black — 5,000.

National Bank Note Co.

All values originally essayed with numerals smaller than adopted. All designs are same size as issued stamps. Sheets of 150 of 1c-12c, sheets of 50 of 24c-90c. Many colors of plate essays exist from one sheet only, some colors from two sheets and a few from three. Some plate essays exist privately perforated.

112-E2   112-E3

Die size: 40x65mm
Vignette size: 17mm diameter
Vignette of Franklin.

112-E2 1c Die of vignette only on India
- orange — 750.
- violet brown — 750.
- black — 750.

Circle of pearls added to vignette, suggestion for frame and 1 in circle at bottom penciled in.

112-E3 1c Die on India, black — 1,250.

112-E4   112-E5

Complete design as issued but with small value numeral.

112-E4 1c
- **a.** Die on India, die sunk on card
  - black — 1,000.
  - violet brown — 1,000.
  - dark brown — 1,000.
  - yellow brown — 1,000.
  - scarlet — 1,000.
  - carmine — 1,000.
  - deep violet — 1,000.
  - blue — 1,000.
  - green — 1,000.
  - yellow — 1,000.
- **b.** Plate on stamp paper, imperf., gummed
  - buff — 100.
  - deep orange brown — 100.
  - orange brown — 100.
- **c.** Plate on stamp paper, perf. 12, gummed
  - buff — 100.
  - orange brown — 100.
  - orange — 125.
- **d.** As "c," with 9x9mm grill
  - buff — 110.
  - orange brown — 85.
  - red brown — 85.
  - chocolate — 85.
  - black brown — 85.
  - dull red — 85.
  - violet — 110.
  - dark violet — 110.
  - blue — 110.
  - deep blue — 110.
  - green — 110.
  - yellow — 110.
  - orange — 110.
  - rose red — 110.

Design size: 23x31mm
Die size: 51x55mm
Design as issued but surrounded by fancy frame with flags and shield. Also essayed for envelopes and wrappers on thick paper.

112-E5 1c
- **a.** Die on stamp paper, perf. 12, gummed, gray — 2,000.
- **b.** Die on white ivory paper
  - black — 1,500.
  - black brown — 1,500.
  - scarlet — 1,500.
  - blue — 1,500.
- **c.** Die on India
  - blue — 1,500.
  - blue green — 1,500.
- **d.** Die on India, cut to shape
  - carmine — 500.
  - yellow — 500.

113-E3

Die size: 41x50mm
Design as issued but with small value numeral. Nos. 113-E3a and 113-Eb have incomplete shading around "UNITED STATES."

113-E3 2c
a. Die on India, die sunk on card
black	1,250.
yellow	1,250.
red orange	1,250.
deep scarlet	1,250.
brown	1,250.
green	1,250.
dusky blue	1,250.
deep blue	1,250.

b. Die on India, cut to stamp size
deep orange red	300.
deep orange yellow	300.
blue green	300.
gray black	300.
light blue	300.
rose	300.

c. Complete die on India, die sunk on card
brown	1,250.
rose	1,250.
mauve	1,250.
green	1,250.
dark chocolate	1,250.
red brown	1,250.

d. Plate on stamp paper, perf. 12, gummed
brown	350.
dark brown	350.
yellow	350.

e. As "d," with 9x9mm grill
brown	80.
dark brown	80.
orange brown	80.
dark orange brown	80.
rose	80.
brown rose	80.
copper red	80.
deep copper red	80.
green	80.
deep green	80.
blue green	80.
yellow	80.
orange	80.
dull yellow orange	80.
blue	80.
light violet	80.
violet	80.
dark violet	80.

f. As "e," double grill, orange 300.

113-E4

Original sketch of postrider, printed "NATIONAL BANK NOTE COMPANY. BUSINESS DEPARTMENT. 1868" at top, pencil instructions at bottom, "Reduce to this length" and "2 copies on one plate. Daguerreotype."

113-E4 2c Drawing on paper, black —

114-E3 **114-E4**

Die size: 53x47mm
Design nearly as issued: larger motive above and below "POSTAGE" erased, no shading on numeral shield, top leaves and corner leaves do not touch, no dots in lower corners or scrolls beside bottom of shield, no vert. shading lines in "POST-AGE" label. Small value numeral.

114-E3 3c Die on 30x30mm ivory paper, black 1,250.

Similar to 114-E3, but smaller motive around "POSTAGE," shield shaded.

114-E4 3c
a. Die on India, die sunk on card
black	1,250.

carmine	1,250.
scarlet	1,250.
orange red	1,250.
yellow orange	1,250.
dull yellow	1,250.
red sepia	1,250.
blue green	1,250.
blue	1,250.
dull red	1,250.
orange brown	1,250.

b. Die on India, cut to stamp size
black	400.
rose	400.
scarlet	400.
chocolate	400.
dull dusky orange	400.
red violet	400.
blackish slate	400.

Similar to No. 114-E4 but vert. shading lines added to "POSTAGE" frame.

114-E5 3c Die on India, dusky yellow orange 1,750.

114-E6 **114-E7**

Completed small numeral die essay: leaves at top and sides touch, dots in lower corners added, vert. shading lines in frame around "POSTAGE," shield shaded darker at bottom, scrolls added to bottom of shield.

114-E6 3c
a. Die on India, card mounted
black	1,750.
blue	1,750.
deep orange red	1,750.

b. Plate on stamp paper, imperf., gummed
ultramarine	100.
dark ultramarine	100.
light brown	75.
red brown	75.
dark red brown	75.
pale rose	75.
rose	75.
brown rose	75.

c. Plate on stamp paper, perf. 12, gummed
ultramarine	400.
dark ultramarine	400.

d. As "c," with 9x9mm grill
blue	80.
deep blue	80.
orange brown	80.
black brown	80.
deep black brown	80.
rose red	80.
green	80.
yellow	80.
orange	80.
deep orange	80.
dull violet	80.
deep violet	80.
red violet	80.

Same design and color as issued stamp, but with allover essay grill of squares up.

114-E7 3c
a. Imperf., gummed, ultramarine 600.
b. As "a," 23mm "NATIONAL BANK NOTE CO. N.Y. SEP 27, 1869" circular pmk., ultramarine 900.
c. On thick paper, imperf., gummed, horiz. line defacement, ultramarine 600.
d. Perf. 12, horiz. line defacement, ultramarine 600.

115-E1 **115-E2**

Die size: 40x60mm
Vignette of Washington. Design as issued 6c stamp but with 5c denomination. Large lettering, large U and S in corners. Also essayed for envelopes on thick paper.

115-E1 6c
a. Die on India, no frameline, solid vignette background, corner spandrels short at centers
black	600.
carmine	600.
dismal red brown	600.
smoky dusky brown	600.
gray violet	600.

b. Completed die on India, die sunk on card
black	500.
carmine	500.
deep rose	500.
red violet	500.
red brown	500.

deep yellow brown	500.
black brown	500.
dull yellow	500.
orange	500.
dusky blue	500.
dusky slate blue	500.
green	500.
blue green	500.
scarlet	500.

c. Die on proof paper, about 40x65mm
black	500.
carmine	500.
scarlet	500.
red orange	500.
orange	500.
dull yellow	500.
orange brown	500.
olive brown	500.
dusky green	500.
dusky yellow green	500.
light blue	500.
deep blue	500.
red violet	500.

d. Die on pink bond
orange	500.
brown	500.
blue	500.

e. Die on light yellow green bond, black 500.
f. Die on pale olive buff bond
black	500.
carmine	500.
orange	500.
red orange	500.
brown	500.

g. Die on cream wove
black	500.
orange	500.
brown	500.
blue	500.

h. Die on clear white bond
black	500.
blue	500.
orange	500.
red orange brown	500.

i. Die on thick cloudy bond
black	500.
red	500.
orange	500.
orange brown	500.
blue	500.
reddish brown	500.

j. Die on pale lilac bond
dark red orange	600.
orange	600.
blue	600.

k. Die on glazed paper
black	400.
scarlet	400.
yellow	400.
dark brown	400.
blue	400.

l. Die on marbled white card
green on red violet veined	1,750.
black on green veined	1,750.
red violet on green veined	1,750.

m. Die on ivory card, black 1,500.
n. Die on white card, cut to stamp size, red orange 250.

Die size: 43x63mm
Similar to No. 115-E1 but lettering, U and S smaller.

115-E2 6c
a. Incomplete die on India (incomplete spandrel points, hair on top of head, etc.)
black	750.
dull red brown	750.

b. Complete die on India, die sunk on card
black	750.
blue	750.
dull dusky violet	750.
scarlet	750.
dark orange red	750.
dim dusky red orange	750.
dusky green	750.
dusky green blue green	750.
dusky blue green	750.

c. Plate essay on wove, imperf., gummed
deep ultramarine	125.
orange	125.
dull red violet	80.
deep red violet	80.
red brown	80.
dull red brown	80.
buff	80.
green	80.

d. Plate essay on wove, perf. 12, gummed
orange	150.
blue	150.

Design size: about 19½x19½mm
Die size: 64x68½mm
Vignette of Lincoln. Also essayed for envelopes on yellow laid paper.

116-E1 10c Incomplete die on India, on card, black 800.

Head as on No. 77 but less bust, large unshaded collar, no cross shading in triangles between labels and fasces, no shading on diamonds at end of value label.

116-E1b

b. Complete die on India, die sunk on card

black	750.
brown black	750.
gray black	750.
carmine	750.
scarlet	750.
brown red	750.
orange	750.
deep orange	750.
deep red	750.
yellow brown	750.
yellow	750.
green	750.
blue green	750.
deep blue	750.
red violet	750.
brown	750.

c. Die on proof paper

black	750.
carmine	750.
bright red	750.
orange red	750.
orange	750.
dark chocolate	750.
dusky yellow brown	750.
green	750.
blue	750.
red violet	750.

d. Die on ivory paper

black	750.
scarlet	750.
black brown	750.
blue	750.

e. Die on clear white thin bond, about 30x35mm

black	750.
red orange	750.
red brown	750.
orange	750.
yellow	750.
blue	750.

f. Die on cloudy cream bond, about 30x35mm

black	750.
light red brown	750.
red orange	750.
blue	750.

g. Die on pink bond, about 39x45mm

red orange	750.
red brown	750.
yellow	750.

h. Die on pale greenish gray bond, about 33x37mm

black	750.
deep carmine	750.
dull scarlet	750.
dark brown	750.
blue	750.

i. Die on marbled white ivory card, about 38x62mm

black on green veined	1,900.
orange red on green veined	1,900.
red orange on green veined	1,900.
dark orange brown on red violet veined	1,900.

j. Plate on stamp paper, imperf., gummed

deep green	125.
blue	100.
ultramarine	100.
dark ultramarine	100.
light ultramarine	100.

k. Plate on stamp paper, perf. 12, gummed, orange 150.

116-E2

Die size: 101x62mm
Vignette of signing the Declaration of Independence as adopted for 24c.

116-E2 10c

a. Die on India, die sunk on card

black	2,500.
carmine	2,500.
dim rose	2,500.
dull scarlet	2,500.
red orange	2,500.
orange yellow	2,500.
red brown	2,500.
orange brown	2,500.
green	2,500.
blue	2,500.
gray	2,500.

b. Die on India, cut to stamp size

black	800.
red orange	800.
blue green	800.

dim rose	800.
brown	800.
buff	800.
dull scarlet	800.

Other colors reported to exist.

116-E3 **116-E4**

Die size: 63x75mm
Design as adopted for issued stamp, but incomplete shading on bottom ribbon, thin shading lines behind "States," and center of "0" of "10" not filled in.

116-E3 10c Die on India on 61x53mm card, black 2,500.

Similar to No. 116-E3 except shading lines added behind "Ten Cents" and center of "0" of "10" filled in.

116-E4 10c Die on India, die sunk on card

black	2,500.
orange	2,500.
blue	2,500.

117-E1 **117-E2**

Die size: 47x51mm
Design as issued but with smaller value numerals.

117-E1 12c

a. Die on card, black 1,500.
b. Vignette die on India, pencil "Adriatic", black 1,500.
c. Complete die on India, die sunk on card

black	1,250.
rose	1,250.
yellow	1,250.
scarlet	1,250.
dark red brown	1,250.
blue green	1,250.
blue	1,250.
dull violet	1,250.
gray black	1,250.
orange brown	1,250.
yellow brown	1,250.
dull orange red	1,250.

d. Die on India, cut to stamp size

black	500.
dusky red orange	500.
deep orange red	500.
dim blue	500.

e. Plate on stamp paper, 9x9mm grill, perf. 12, gummed

green	125.
rose red	125.
pale rose red	125.
yellow brown	125.
red brown	125.
orange	125.
blue	125.
dull violet	125.
dull red violet	125.
yellow orange	125.

Similar to No. 117-E1, but small numeral not printed, large 12 drawn in pencil.

117-E2 12c Die on India, black 2,750.

117-E3 **117-E4**

Typographed small numeral design similar to No. 117-E1, relief engraved for surface printing. Heavier lines, upper label with solid background, letters of "UNITED STATES POSTAGE" colorless. Nos. 117-E3a through 117-E3c from untrimmed die, heavily struck with uncolored areas in relief, color covering borders beyond white line exterior of frame. Untrimmed die size: 58x45mm.

117-E3 12c

a. Untrimmed die on card

brown red	750.
green	750.

black	750.
red brown	750.

b. Untrimmed die on thin pinkish wove

gray black	450.
dull deep red orange	450.
dark red orange	450.

c. Untrimmed die on thick white wove

carmine	600.
green	600.

d. Die on white paper, stamp size

carmine	400.
orange	400.
brown	400.
lilac	400.
green	400.

e. Die on thin white wove

carmine	400.
gray black	400.
dull deep red orange	400.
deep orange red	400.

g. Die on pinkish wove, perf. 12, gummed, red brown 400.

h. Die on yellow wove, imperf.

gray black	400.
carmine	400.
red brown	400.
dark red violet	400.

i. Die on yellow wove, 11x13mm grill, imperf., red brown 400.

j. Die on white laid

gray	400.
gray black	400.
brown	400.
red brown	400.

k. Die on yellow laid

red brown	400.
brown	400.
dull red violet	400.
carmine	400.

l. Die on salmon laid, red brown 400.
m. Die on pinkish laid

red brown	400.
gray	400.

n. Die on pinkish laid, 11x13mm grill, gummed, red brown 400.
o. Die on dull red violet laid, gray 400.

Vignette size: 15x11mm
Untrimmed die size: 63x32mm
Vignette only, similar to No. 117-E3 but lithographed instead of typographed.

117-E4 12c

a. Die on white ivory paper, black 1,000.
b. Complete impression from untrimmed stone in solid color about 63x63mm, on white ivory paper, black 750.
c. Die on glossy-surfaced thin white wove, trimmed to stamp size

carmine	750.
rose pink	750.
yellow	750.
blue green	750.
dim red violet	750.
pale red violet	750.
deep red orange	750.
dull dark red orange	750.
dull dark yellow orange	750.
dark violet red	750.
pale gray	750.

d. Die on thick white wove

yellow	750.
violet red	750.
deep red violet	750.

118-E1 **119-E1**

Die size: 62x49mm
Type I design as issued but with smaller value numerals.

118-E1 15c

a. Die of vignette only on India, mounted on 62x62mm India, die sunk on card, dark blue 3,500.
b. Incomplete die (no outer frameline or shading outside frame scrolls) on India, black 4,500.
c. Complete die on India, die sunk on card

black	5,000.
scarlet	5,000.
orange brown	5,000.
green	5,000.
dull violet	5,000.
red brown	5,000.

Type II design with large value numerals as issued.

119-E1 15c

a. Type II frame only, die on India

black	3,000.
red brown	3,000.

b. Vignette only, die on India, blue —
c. Type II frame with vignette mounted in place, die on India, red brown frame, blue vignette 3,000.

d. Type II frame with vignette mounted at
    right, die on India, red brown frame,
    blue vignette   —

129-E1   129-E2

Die size: 65x49
    Type III design as adopted, except in various single colors,
large "15" overprint in diff. color.

129-E1 15c
  a. Die on India, die sunk on card
    orange brown, red overprint   3,250.
    blue green, red overprint   3,250.
    ultramarine, red overprint   3,250.
    violet, red overprint   3,250.
    red brown, red overprint   3,250.
  b. Die on India, die sunk on card
    rose red, ultramarine overprint   3,250.
    dull scarlet, ultramarine overprint 3,250.
    dark red brown, ultramarine ovpt. 3,250.
  c. Die on India, die sunk on card
    scarlet, blue green overprint   3,250.
    orange brown, blue green overprint 3,250.
    dark red brown, blue green overprint 3,250.

Type III frame only.

129-E2 15c
  a. Die on India, red brown   2,750.
  b. Die on India, with vignette mounted in
    place, blue frame, yellow vignette 3,500.

120-E1   120-E2

Die size: 102x63mm
    Design nearly as issued, but shading under leaves at top of
frame and ribbon over "TWENTY" are unfinished. Small value
numerals. Single color.

120-E1 24c Die on India, black   3,500.

    Completed small numeral design in single color. No. 120-E2a
has 8mm-high bands of shaded colored lines 31mm long overprinted above and below vignette, printed in various single colors with bands in contrasting color.

120-E2 24c
  a. Die on India
    black with carmine bands   4,000.
    black with violet brown bands   4,000.
    black with brown orange bands   4,000.
    orange brown with deep dull violet bands 4,000.
    orange brown with blue green bands 4,000.
  b. Die on India
    black   2,250.
    scarlet   2,250.
    dark red brown   2,250.
    blue   2,250.
    violet   2,250.
  c. Plate on red salmon tinted paper, black 150.
  d. Plate on orange buff tinted paper, black 200.
  e. Plate on dull yellowish tinted paper, black 200.
  f. Plate on blue tinted paper, black 200.
  g. Plate on gray tinted paper, black 400.
  h. Plate on India, black   250.
  j. Plate on card, imperf., black   200.

120-E3

    No. 120-E3a bicolor design as issued, except vignette
printed separately and mounted in place; No. 120-E3b frame
only with 3 border lines around vignette space; No. 120-E3c
frame only with 2 border lines around vignette space as issued.

120-E3 24c
  a. Die on India, card mounted
    dull violet frame, green vignette 2,500.
    violet frame, red vignette   2,500.
    green frame, violet vignette   2,500.
    rose frame, green vignette   2,500.
  b. Frame die on India, card mounted
    light green   2,500.

---

    dark green   2,500.
  c. Frame die on India, block sunk on India,
    green   2,500.

121-E1

Design size: 21½x22mm
Die Size: 71x51mm
    Vignette of Surrender of Gen. Burgoyne in ornate frame.

121-E1 30c
  a. Die on India, die sunk on card
    black   800.
    carmine   800.
    rose red   800.
    light brown red   800.
    red brown   800.
    brown orange   800.
    orange   800.
    red orange   800.
    yellow green   800.
    blue   800.
    dull dark violet   800.
    yellow brown   800.
    scarlet   800.
  b. Die on stiff ivory paper
    black   650.
  c. Die on India, cut to stamp size
    dim deep orange red   250.
    deep yellow orange   250.
    dim deep blue green   250.
    dim dusky blue   250.
  d. Die on India die sunk on 78x58mm white
    card
    dusky blue   1,000.
  e. Die on white card, cut to stamp size
    dim orange   500.
  f. Die on proof paper, about 70x50mm
    black   500.
    carmine   500.
    scarlet   500.
    red orange   500.
    green   500.
    violet   500.
  g. Die on ivory paper, about 64x50mm
    black   750.
    dark brown   750.
    scarlet   750.
    blue   750.
  h. Die on ivory card
    black   1,000.
    carmine   1,000.
  i. Die on clear white bond, about 33x33mm
    black   600.
    blue   600.
    light red brown   600.
    orange   600.
  j. Die on yellowish cloudy bond, about
    34x34mm
    black   600.
    orange   600.
    light red brown   600.
    blue   600.
  k. Die on smoky yellow greenish bond
    black   600.
    carmine   600.
    orange   600.
  l. Die on pink bond, about 40x40mm
    blue   600.
    dim orange red   600.
    orange   600.
  m. Die on pale olive buff paper
    black   600.
    dim orange red   600.
    orange   600.
  n. Die on thick yellowish wove, dim green
    blue   600.
  o. Die on marbled white ivory card, about
    40x60mm
    black on green veined   2,250.
    black on red violet veined   2,250.
  p. Plate essay in black on thin surface-tinted
    paper
    pale gray   275.
    salmon red   175.
    yellow   175.
    orange   275.
    orange buff   275.
    pink   275.
    pale pink   275.
    blue   275.
    light blue   275.
    pale green   275.
    brown violet   275.
  q. Plate essay in black on India   300.
  r. Plate on thick rough pitted card, black 300.

121-E1s

  s. Plate on bond, red bands overprinted top
    and bottom as on No. 120-E2a, dull
    red violet   350.

121-E2   121-E3

    Flags, stars and rays only as adopted for issued stamp. Black
essay shows traces of vignette also.

121-E2 30c Die on India, mounted on India,
             block sunk on card
    black   7,500.
    light ultramarine   6,000.
    dark blue   6,000.

    Eagle, shield and value only as adopted for issued stamp.

121-E3 30c Die on India, card mounted, black 8,500.

122-E1

Die size: 62x69mm
    Vignette of Washington in frame similar to that of issued
stamp but no shading over U and S in lower corners, small
value numerals.

122-E1 90c Die on India, black   3,250.

    Similar to No. 122-E1 but shading over U and S.

122-E2 90c
  a. Die on India, die sunk on card
    black   2,500.
    carmine   2,500.
    scarlet   2,500.
    red brown   2,500.
    blue green   2,500.
    violet   2,500.
  b. Plate essay with black vignette on stamp
    paper, imperf.
    dull violet   225.
    red brown   225.
    orange red   225.
    pale orange red   225.
    blue   225.

122-E3   122-E4

    Frame as No. 122-E2, vignette oval with narrow-spaced
horiz. lines in same color as frame, but no head.

122-E3 90c Plate on stamp paper, imperf.
    red brown   175.
    blue   175.
    dark blue   175.
    red violet   175.
    dull violet   175.
    dark violet   175.
    rose red   175.
    deep rose red   175.
    yellow   175.
    orange brown   175.
    dark navy blue   175.
    blue green   175.
    deep blue green   175.
    dark blue green   175.
    orange   175.

Small numeral frame but with Lincoln vignette from No. 77 mounted in place.

122-E4 90c
- ***a.*** Die on India
  - yellow — 2,000.
  - deep blue green — 2,000.
  - dark navy blue — 2,000.
- ***b.*** Plate of Lincoln vignette only, on rough pitted thick gray paper, black — 600.
- ***c.*** Die on India, Lincoln vignette as used on No. 77, black — 2,500.

122-E5

Similar to No. 122-E1, with Washington vignette but with large numerals as on issued stamp.

122-E5 90c
- ***a.*** Die on India, die sunk on card
  - black — 5,000.
  - carmine — 2,500.
- ***b.*** Plate of frame only, 2 lines at top, 3 lines at bottom, on India, mounted on block sunk card, rose red — 1,250.
- ***c.*** As "b," 3 lines at top, 2 lines at bottom
  - rose red — 4,500.
  - red brown — 1,250.

Safety essays: die essays on thin wove, underprinted with various engraved safety paper designs in another color, probably with fugitive ink. Found on 5c (No. 115-E1), 10c (No. 116-E1), 15c (No. 129-E1 without overprint) and 30c (No. 121-E1). Stamp color given first.

115-E3a

Design 1: wavy lines

115-E3a 5c
- carmine on scarlet — 3,250.
- orange on scarlet — 3,250.
- ***b.*** 10c blue on scarlet — 5,000.
- ***c.*** 30c carmine on scarlet — 3,500.

115-E4

Design 2: banknote type

115-E4a 5c
- carmine on violet — 3,250.
- orange on violet — 3,250.
- ***b.*** 10c carmine on violet — 5,000.
- ***c.*** 30c
  - carmine on violet — 3,500.
  - orange on violet — 3,500.
  - orange on gray — 3,500.

115-E5

Design 3: banknote type

115-E5
- ***a.*** 5c
  - carmine on orange and red — 3,250.
  - carmine on brown — 3,250.
  - orange on brown — 3,250.
- ***b.*** 10c
  - carmine on orange and red — 5,000.
  - blue on orange and red — 5,000.
- ***c.*** 30c
  - carmine on orange and red — 3,500.
  - orange on brown — 3,500.

115-E6

Design 4: continuous wavy lines

115-E6a 5c orange on scarlet — 3,250.
- ***b.*** 10c
  - blue on scarlet — 5,000.
  - carmine on scarlet — 5,000.
- ***c.*** 30c black on scarlet — 3,500.

115-E7

Design 5: wavy lines

115-E7
- ***a.*** 5c
  - orange on scarlet — 3,250.
  - orange on black — 3,250.
- ***b.*** 10c
  - dark brown on black — 5,000.
  - orange red on black — 5,000.
  - carmine on scarlet — 5,000.
- ***c.*** 30c
  - carmine on black — 3,500.
  - carmine on scarlet — 3,500.

115-E8

Design 6: wavy lines

115-E8a 5c orange on black — 3,250.
- ***b.*** 10c blue on black — 5,000.
- ***c.*** 30c
  - carmine on black — 3,500.
  - orange on black — 3,500.

115-E9

Design 7: crossed wavy lines

115-E9
- ***a.*** 5c
  - carmine on black — 3,250.
  - orange on black — 3,250.
- ***b.*** 10c blue on black — 5,000.
- ***c.*** 30c orange on black — 3,500.

115-E10

Design 8: wavy lines

115-E10a 5c carmine on scarlet — 3,250.
- ***b.*** 10c
  - blue on scarlet — 5,000.
  - carmine on scarlet — 5,000.
  - orange red on scarlet — 5,000.

129-E3

Design 9: wavy lines

129-E3 15c
- orange brown on orange, vert. — 3,500.
- blue green on orange, horiz. — 3,500.
- dark blue on orange, horiz. — 3,500.

129-E4

Design 10: banknote type

129-E4 15c
- orange brown on scarlet — 3,500.
- blue green on scarlet — 3,500.
- dark blue on scarlet — 3,500.

129-E5

Design 11: banknote type

129-E5 15c
- orange brown on light scarlet — 3,500.
- blue green on light scarlet, vert. — 3,500.
- dark blue on light scarlet — 3,500.

129-E6

Design 12: banknote type

129-E6 15c
- orange brown on deep scarlet — 3,500.
- blue green on deep scarlet — 3,500.
- dark blue on deep scarlet — 3,500.

115-E11

Design 13: banknote type

115-E11
- ***a.*** 5c orange on brown — 3,250.
- ***b.*** 10c
  - carmine on brown — 5,000.
  - orange red on brown — 5,000.
  - blue on brown (horiz. underprinting) — 5,000.
  - blue on brown (vert. underprinting) — 5,000.
- ***c.*** 30c carmine on brown — 3,500.

115-E12

Design 14: banknote type

115-E12
- ***a.*** 5c
  - carmine on scarlet (horiz.) — 3,250.
  - black on scarlet (vert.) — 3,250.
- ***b.*** 10c
  - carmine on scarlet — 5,000.
  - orange on scarlet — 5,000.
  - sepia on scarlet — 5,000.
  - blue on scarlet — 5,000.
- ***c.*** 30c black on scarlet — 3,500.

115-E13

Design 15: banknote type

115-E13a 5c carmine on orange brown — 3,250.
- ***b.*** 30c carmine on deep orange — 3,500.

115-E14

Design 16: multiple rosettes

115-E14a 5c orange on scarlet — 3,250.
- ***b.*** 10c
  - carmine on scarlet — 5,000.
  - orange red on scarlet — 5,000.
  - sepia on scarlet — 5,000.
  - blue on scarlet — 5,000.

115-E15

Design 17: multiple oval rosettes

115-E15a 5c carmine on scarlet — 3,250.
- ***b.*** 30c
  - carmine on scarlet — 3,500.
  - orange on scarlet — 3,500.

115-E16

Design 18: negative stars in diagonal lines

115-E16
  a. 5c
    black on scarlet   3,250.
    carmine on scarlet   3,250.
  b. 10c
    carmine on scarlet   5,000.
    sepia on scarlet   5,000.
  c. 30c carmine on scarlet   3,500.

116-E6

Design 19: multiple 6-point stars in lathework

116-E6a 10c blue on blue green   5,000.
  b. 30c carmine on blue green   3,500.

116-E7

Design 20: banknote type

116-E7
  a. 10c
    brown on orange   5,000.
    blue on orange   5,000.
  b. 30c carmine on orange   3,500.

116-E8

Design 21: multiple "ONE"

116-E8 10c blue on scarlet   5,000.

115-E17

Design 22: multiple "TWO"

115-E17a 5c orange on scarlet   3,250.
  b. 10c carmine on scarlet   5,000.

115-E18

Design 23: multiple "5"s in oval rosettes

115-E18 5c black on carmine   3,250.

115-E19

Design 24: multiple "TEN 10"

115-E19
  a. 5c
    orange on scarlet   3,250.
    carmine on scarlet   3,250.
  b. 10c
    carmine on scarlet   5,000.
    orange red on scarlet   5,000.
    blue on scarlet   5,000.
  c. 30c
    carmine on scarlet   3,500.
    orange red on scarlet   3,500.
    brown on scarlet   3,500.
    blue on scarlet   3,500.

115-E20

Design 25: multiple "50"

115-E20 5c
    black on black   3,250.
    orange on black   3,250.

1870 ISSUE
Continental Banknote Co.

145-E1

Vignette of Washington in large ornate "1."

145-E1   One Cent
  a. Die on India, die sunk on card
    black   1,500.
    scarlet   1,500.
    green   1,500.
    ultramarine   1,500.
    blue   1,500.
  b. Surface-printed on proof paper, about
      25x30mm
    black   1,000.
    green   1,000.

146-E1

147-E1

Blank vignette in large ornate "2."

146-E1   2c Engraved die on India, die sunk on
         card
    black   1,500.
    scarlet   1,500.
    ultramarine   1,500.
    blue   1,500.
    green   1,500.

Design size: 20x25mm
Die size: 43x48mm
Vignette of Lincoln in large ornate "3" with rounded top.

147-E1   3c Engraved die on proof paper
    black   2,000.
    scarlet   1,500.
    ultramarine   1,500.
    green   1,500.

147-E1A

147-E1B

Design size: 11½x15½mm
Die size: 25x32mm
Vignette only of Columbia. Imprint and die number below design.

147-E1A 3c Engraved die on India, black   —

Design size: 21x25mm
Blank vignette in frame of large ornate "3" with upper and lower labels not yet engraved.

147-E1B 3c Engraved die on India, die sunk on
         card
    black   2,000.
    green   1,750.

147-E1C

Design size: 21x25mm

No. 147-E1A cut to shape and mounted in frame of large ornate "3" with upper and lower labels not yet engraved.

147-E1C 3c Engraved die on India, die sunk on
         card
    black   2,000.
    green   1,750.

Design size: 21x25mm
Blank vignette in frame only as No. 147-E1B but with upper and lower labels engraved.

147-E2 3c Engraved die on India, die sunk on
         card
    black   2,000.
    green   1,750.

Vignette of Columbia mounted in place on No. 147-E2.

147-E3 3c Engraved die on India, die sunk on
         card
    black   2,000.
    green   1,750.

147-E4

Complete design with Columbia vignette in large ornate "3" surrounded by foliate ornamentation.

147-E4 3c Engraved die on India, die sunk on
         card
    black   2,000.
    green   1,750.

147-E5A

147-E5B

Design size: 22x27mm
Blank vignette in large ornate "3" without ornamentation.

147-E5A 3c Engraved die on India, die sunk
         on card backing, black   1,000.

Design size: 22x27mm
Blank vignette in large ornate "3" surrounded by scrolled ornamentation.

147-E5B 3c Engraved die on India, die sunk
         on card
    black   2,000.
    green   1,750.

147-E6

Vignette of Columbia mounted in place on No. 147-E5B.

147-E6 3c Engraved die on India, die sunk on
         card
    black   2,000.
    green   1,750.

148-E1

Blank vignette in large ornate "6."

148-E1 6c
  a. Engraved die on India, die sunk on card
    black   1,500.
    scarlet   1,500.
    green   1,500.

dark green	1,500.
ultramarine	1,500.

b. Engraved die on India, cut close

black	1,000.
scarlet	1,000.
blue	1,000.
green	1,000.

National Banknote Co.

145-E2   145-E3

Die size: 64x74mm
Engraved vignette of Franklin facing right.

145-E2   1c Die on India, die sunk on card

black (with pencil lines on bust0	700.
dull dark orange	700.

Engraved incomplete Franklin vignette facing right mounted over pencil sketch of frame.

145-E3   1c Die on thin white card, 55x66mm,

black	2,850.

Incomplete Franklin vignette mounted on more complete pencil sketch of frame.

145-E4   1c Die on thin white card, orange

brown	2,000.

Design size: 20x26mm
Engraved vignette mounted on pencil and watercolor frame design.

145-E5   1c Die on thin white card, 45x51mm,

dull dark orange	2,000.

145-E6

Incomplete engraving of entire design; lower edge of bust vert. shading only.

145-E6   1c

a. Die on 64x71mm India, die sunk on card

ultramarine	425.
red	425.
orange brown	425.
red brown	425.
blue green	425.
mauve	425.
dull lilac	425.
black	425.
gray	425.
carmine	425.
carmine rose	425.
dull rose	425.
dull yellow brown	425.
brown violet	425.
light green	425.
green	425.
gray olive	425.
yellow	425.

b. Die on bond, die sunk on card, dark yellow

low	750.

Completed die: additional shading lines in background, four horiz. shading lines at top of lower edge of bust.

145-E8   1c

a. Die on India, die sunk on card

black	425.
blue green	425.
carmine	425.
yellow	425.
orange brown	425.

orange	425.
gray green	425.
dull red violet	425.
dark blue	425.

b. Die on white glazed paper, 65x72mm

black	325.
black brown	325.
scarlet	325.
blue	325.

c. Completed die on thick wove, dismal

dusky yellow	300.

145-E9   145-E10

Die size: 50½x64mm
Engraved vignette of Franklin facing left, no shading lines at top of bust, etc.

145-E9   1c

a. Die on white glazed paper, black   475.
b. Die on India, mounted on card stamped
"J.I. PEASE.", black   450.

Engraved Franklin vignette with 1 and value label.

145-E10   1c Die on India, on card (1873), black   2,000.

May be essay for Official stamps.

146-E2   146-E3

Vignette size: 19½x25½mm
Die size: 62x76mm
Vignette only of Jackson in high stiff collar.

146-E2   2c Die on India, die sunk on card

black	500.
orange brown	500.

Engraved Jackson vignette mounted on watercolor frame.

146-E3   2c Die on thin white card, 46x89mm,
black vignette, dark gray frame   2,500.

146-E4   146-E5

Engraved Jackson vignette, mounted on watercolor frame (diff. from No. 146-E3).

146-E4   2c Die on thin white card, 46x89mm,
black vignette, gray frame   2,500.

Similar to No. 146-E4 but with pencil border around frame.

146-E5   2c Die on thin white card, 45x50mm,
dark orange   2,500.

Incomplete die: without shading lines under value ribbon, vert. lines in colorless strips, and broken horiz. lines at top and bottom of frame.

146-E6   2c Die on thin white card, dark orange   1,250.

146-E7

Die size: 64½x73mm

Completed die of unadopted design.

146-E7   2c

a. Die on India

carmine	600.
deep rose	600.
scarlet	600.
dim dusky orange orange red	600.
deep yellow orange	600.
bone brown	600.
orange brown	600.
brown	600.
canary yellow	600.
yellow brown	600.
dark olive green	600.
green	600.
dim dusky blue green	600.
dark blue	600.
deep ultramarine	600.
bright blue	600.
dull violet	600.
smoky deep red violet red	600.
gray	600.
black	600.

b. Die on ivory paper, about 64x77mm

black	500.
brown black	500.
scarlet	500.
blue	500.

c. Die on thin wove, dark yellow   375.

146-E8

Die size: 62x76mm
Incomplete vignette of Jackson as on issued stamp: incomplete shading in eye and hair in front of ear, right neck tendon on chest not shaded.

146-E8   2c

a. Die on India, on 55x66mm card

black	550.
orange	550.
orange brown	550.
dark blue green	550.
red violet	550.

Also known on 87x143mm card showing full die sinkage, pencil inscribed "2c" above and "Jackson" below sinkage area. Value, $750.

b. Die on glazed paper, die sinkage
50x63mm, black   1,000.

Completed Jackson vignette.

146-E9   2c Die on glazed paper, black   450.

146-E10   146-E11

Engraved Jackson vignette with 2 and value label.

146-E10   2c Die on glazed paper (1873), black   1,000.

May be essay for Official stamps.

Engraved vignette with pencil and watercolor frame design, labels blank.

146-E11   2c Die on thin white card, 50x60mm,
dim dusky bright blue green
vignette, dark green frame   3,000.

146-E12

Die size: 62x75mm
Incomplete engraving of entire design: no leaves on wide bands at sides below vignette, neck tendon and hair in front of ear changed, top of head incomplete, ear hole too dark. This design essayed for envelopes on thick papers.

146-E12   2c Die on India, die sunk on card

carmine	500.
orange	500.
brown orange	500.

147-E7

Incomplete engraved vignette of Lincoln (horiz. line background), mounted on pencil and watercolor frame design.

147-E7 3c Die on thin white card, black
vignette, gray black frame 3,500.

147-E8 147-E9

Design size: 20x25mm
Die Size: 62x72½mm
Incomplete engraving of head only of Washington.

147-E8 3c Die on white glazed paper, black 500.

Engraved Washington vignette only as adopted.

147-E9 3c Die on white glazed paper, black 650.

Nos. 147-E8 and 147-E9 may have been made from completed dies of No. 147 to produce Nos. 184-E9 and 184-E10.

147-E10 147-E11

Washington vignette, 3 and value label.

147-E10 3c Die on India, card mounted
(1873), black 1,600.

May be essay for Official stamps.

Design size: 20x25½mm
Incomplete engraved vignette (horiz. lined background), mounted on pencil and watercolor frame design.

147-E11 3c Die on thin white card, 45x54mm,
carmine vignette, dim light red violet red frame 5,000.

Incomplete engraving of entire design: no horizontal lines on nose, parts of hair, chin, collar, forehead unfinished.

147-E12 3c Die on India, die sunk on card
black 500.
deep red 500.
carmine 500.
yellow orange 500.
brown 500.
red brown 500.
dark red brown 500.
ultramarine 500.
dark blue 500.
dark violet blue 500.
blue green 500.
dark red violet 500.

Issued stamp, No. 147, in trial colors, underprinted network in fugitive ink.

147-E13 3c
a. On thick paper, perf. 12, gummed
gray blue, underprinting gray brown 100.
green, underprinting olive gray 100.
dim red, underprinting olive gray 100.
dull orange, underprinting olive gray 100.
brown, underprinting olive gray 100.
b. As "a," faint 6mm-high horiz. bar trial cancel
dim red 450.
dull orange 450.
c. As "a," underprinting omitted
gray blue —
dim red —
dull orange —
brown —
d. As "a," imperf, green, underprinting olive gray 325.
Pair 700.

e. As "d," underprinting omitted 325.
Pair 700.
P# block of 10 —

Multiples of the No. 147-E13 varieties can be found with fully or partially underprinted stamps in conjunction with underprinting-omitted stamps.

148-E2 148-E3

Design size: 19½x25½mm
Die size: 63x76mm
Engraved Lincoln vignette only, hair brushed back, horiz. line background.

148-E2 6c Die on India, die sunk on card
black 600.
blue 600.

Incomplete engraved Lincoln vignette (horiz. lined background) mounted on pencil and watercolor frame with blank labels.

148-E3 6c Die on thin white card, 45x52mm,
dim blue vignette, dim dark blue frame 3,000.

148-E4

Incomplete engraving of entire design: horiz. line background in vignette, lines on cheek and hair unfinished.

148-E4 6c Die on India, on card, about
50x52mm
carmine 500.
rose 500.
dull rose 500.
red violet 500.
dull violet 500.
deep ultramarine 500.
dark black blue 500.
yellow 500.
green 500.
dark green 500.
dark red brown 500.
deep yellow brown 500.
yellow brown 500.
orange brown 500.

Incomplete engraving of entire design: horiz. line background in vignette, no shading directly under value label, shadows on "SIX CENTS" and shading on ornaments in upper corners unfinished.

148-E5 6c Die on India, on card, ultramarine 850.

Similar to No. 148-E5 but with diagonal lines added to vignette background. (Essay in orange brown has pencil notations for changes.)

148-E6 6c Die on India, die sunk on card
dull carmine 550.
dark rose 550.
yellowish black 550.
brown 550.
gray brown 550.
black brown 550.
yellow 550.
gray olive green 550.
dark green 550.
ultramarine 550.
deep ultramarine 550.
dull ultramarine 550.
violet 550.
dark violet 550.
orange brown 550.

Similar to No. 148-E6 but with dots added to top of hair.

148-E7 6c Die on India, on card
dark carmine 550.
dull rose 550.
orange 550.
yellow brown 550.
dark brown 550.
black brown 550.
yellow green 550.
blue green 550.
ultramarine 550.
dark red violet 550.

Completed die with lines on cheek softened to dots only.

148-E8 6c Die on India
yellow green 250.
brown 250.
rose 250.

All known examples are much reduced.

Incomplete engraving of entire design, similar to No. 148-E10 but with hair brushed forward as on adopted design but shadow under hair in front of ear is round at bottom, not pointed as on approved design. Shading on cheek behind nostril is dotted instead of lined on completed design.

148-E9 6c Die on India, on card, red violet 750.

148-E10

Die size: 64x75mm
Frame as adopted, vignette similar to No. 148-E6 but with hair brushed back; lines on cheek.

148-E10 6c
a. Die on India, die sunk on card, deep blue 850.
b. Die on India, about 30x35mm, carmine 600.
c. As "a," but no panels above top label, carmine 850.

Similar to No. 148-E10a but dots (not lines) on cheek and on lower lip. Shadow under hair in front of ear is rounded at bottom, not pointed as on approved design.

148-E11 6c Die on India, on card
rose pink 550.
deep rose 550.
pale rose 550.
brown rose 550.
rose carmine 550.
deep carmine 550.
brown 550.
yellow brown 550.
blue 550.
red violet 550.

Die of completed vignette only with hair brushed forward.

148-E12 6c Die on white glazed paper, black 1,500.

148-E13

Completed vignette with 6 and value label.

148-E13 6c Die on India, on card (1873), black 1,500.

May be essay for Official stamps.

149-E4 149-E4a

Die size: 62x75mm
Vignette of Stanton.

149-E4 7c Die on India, on card, black 750.

Engraved frame of adopted 30c design but with vignette cut out and mounted over Stanton vignette on India No. 149-E4.

149-E4a Stanton vignette with 30c frame
on thin, stiff paper mounted on top, black 500.

The status of No. 149-E4a has been questioned.

149-E5

Die size: 62x76mm
Completed vignette with 7 and value label.

149-E5   7c
   a. Die on India, on card (1873), black   850.
   b. Die on white glazed paper, black   850.

   May be essay for Official stamps.

149-E6

Design as issued but shading under ear incomplete.

149-E6   7c Die on India, die sunk on card
   black   450.
   dark red   450.
   light red   450.
   gray green   450.
   gray black   450.
   yellow brown   450.
   dark brown   450.
   dull yellow brown   450.
   dull red brown   450.
   blue green   450.
   ultramarine   450.
   dim blue   450.
   lilac   450.
   red orange   450.
   yellow orange   450.

Similar to No. 149-E6 but with dots added on forehead.

149-E7   7c Die on India, brown   1,000.

150-E1   150-E2

Design size: 20x25½mm
Incomplete engraved vignette of Jefferson (horiz. line background) mounted on pencil and watercolor frame design with blank labels.

150-E1   10c Die on thin white card, 45x51mm,
         black vignette, gray frame   3,000.

Design size: 19½x25½mm
Die size: 62x75mm
Jefferson vignette with incomplete engraving of frame: unfinished shading under "TEN" ribbon, under oval at ends of "U.S. POSTAGE," and under shield over ends of value label ribbons.

150-E2   10c Die on India, on card, deep blue
         green   2,500.

Similar to No. 150-E2 but showing horizontal shading lines only.

150-E2A   10c Die on India, die sunk on
         152x225mm card
   blue green   750.
   red violet   750.

Completed engraving of unadopted design.

150-E3   10c
   a. Die on India, die sunk on card
   carmine   450.
   rose   450.
   gray brown rose   450.
   yellow   450.
   yellow brown   450.
   orange   450.
   orange brown   450.
   brown   450.
   chocolate   450.
   green   450.
   blue green   450.
   greenish gray   450.
   blue   450.
   dull violet   450.
   dull red violet   450.
   dark navy blue   450.

---

   ultramarine   450.
   deep ultramarine   450.
   dull dusky blue   450.
   navy blue   450.
   slate   450.
   b. Die on bond
   dull dusky brown   350.
   brown gray   350.

All known examples of No. 153-E3b are reduced.

150-E4   150-E5

Three separate designs. Left one dark blue green, similar to No. 150-E3 but shows engraved attempt to remove coat collar to obtain nude neck (some coat still shows under chin). Middle one brown orange No. 150-E2 with coat collar and top of hair cut out, neck and bust drawn in. Right one black vignette of head finally adopted.

150-E4   10c Dies on India, on card   2,500.

Design size: 19½x25½mm
Same frame as No. 150-E2, but Jefferson vignette has hair arranged differently and bust has no clothing.

150-E5   10c
   a. Die on India, die sunk on card
   black   500.
   scarlet   500.
   brown   500.
   blue   500.
   green   500.
   b. Die on glazed paper, 66x75mm
   black   425.
   black brown   425.
   scarlet   425.
   blue   425.
   c. Die on thin wove, dark yellow   325.

150-E6   150-E7

Frame of No. 150-E5 with vignette cut out and replaced by vignette as adopted.

150-E6   10c Die on India
   deep orange brown   850.
   black   850.

Die size: 62x76mm
Vignette of Jefferson as adopted.

150-E7   10c Die on India, die sunk on card
   dark ultramarine   700.
   yellow   700.
   brown   700.

151-E1   151-E2

Design size: 20x25½mm
Engraved vignette of Washington (No. 79-E37b) mounted on incomplete pencil drawing of frame design.

151-E1   12c Die on India, on 38x47½mm card,
         black vignette, pencil frame   2,500.

Design size: 20x25½mm
Engraved vignette of Washington (No. 79-E37b) mounted on pencil and watercolor frame design with blank labels.

151-E2   12c Die on card, 46x89mm, black
         vignette, gray frame   3,000.

151-E3   151-E4

Design size: 20x25½mm
Engraved vignette of Washington (No. 79-E37b) mounted on pencil and watercolor frame design with ribbons and blank labels.

151-E3   12c Die on card, 46x89mm, black
         vignette, gray frame   3,000.

Design size: 20x25½mm
Engraved vignette of Washington (No. 79-E37b) mounted on pencil and watercolor frame design with "U, S, 12" and blank labels.

151-E4   12c Die on card, 46x89mm, black
         vignette, gray frame   3,000.

151-E5   151-E6

Design size: 19½x25½mm
Die size: 62x74mm
Vignette of Henry Clay only.

151-E5   12c Die on India, die sunk on card
   black   550.
   deep carmine   550.
   yellow   550.
   yellow brown   550.
   brown orange   550.
   dark orange brown   550.
   black brown   550.
   ultramarine   550.
   dark blue green   550.
   red violet   550.

Incomplete Clay vignette mounted on watercolor shield-like frame design on gray background, pencil notation "background of stars to be gray."

151-E6   12c Die on card, 53x75mm, blue black
         vignette, blue frame   3,250.

151-E7

Die sinkage size: 63x77mm
Completed die of unadopted design similar to No. 151-E6. This design essayed for envelopes on thick paper.

151-E7   12c
   a. Die on India, on card
   deep orange brown   600.
   green   600.
   deep ultramarine   600.
   violet   600.
   deep red   600.
   deep orange red   600.
   dusky red   600.
   b. Die on wove
   carmine   600.
   orange   600.
   brown   600.
   orange brown   600.
   ultramarine   600.
   c. Die on card colored yellow, black   600.

Engraved vignette of Washington mounted on partly complete pencil drawing of frame, pencil notation "new border for clay 12c."

151-E8   12c Die on card, black, pencil frame   1,500.

151-E9

151-E10

Die size: 55x63mm
Incomplete engraving of entire adopted design, without 3 vert. shading lines at left side of lower triangle.

151-E9 12c
   a. Die on India, die sunk on card
black	550.
carmine	550.
blue green	550.
blue	550.
light blue	550.
orange	550.
orange brown	550.
dull red	550.
brown red	550.

   b. Die on proof paper, about 38x45mm
carmine	550.
dull carmine	550.
orange brown	550.
dull red	550.
ultramarine	550.

   c. Die on India, on card, about 30x35mm,
dark blue	550.

Completed Clay vignette with 12 and value label.

151-E10 12c Die on white glazed paper (1873),
     black   1,250.

    May be essay for Official stamps.

152-E1

152-E2

Design size: 19½x25mm
Incomplete vignette of Webster with side whiskers bolder than as adopted, mounted on watercolor frame design with 15 and blank labels.

152-E1 15c Die on white card, 40x61mm, dim
     red vignette, light red violet frame   2,250.

Design size: 19½x25mm
Die size: 63x76mm
Incomplete engraving of vignette only: missing shading under ear and at back of neck.

152-E2 15c Die on India, die sunk on card,
     black   750.

152-E3

152-E4

Vignette similar to No. 152-E2 but with shading under ear, more shading at back of neck.

152-E3 15c Die on India, die sunk on card
black	650.
dark orange	650.
orange	650.
yellow	650.
red violet	650.
ultramarine	650.
brown	650.

Vignette of Webster with 15 below.

152-E4 15c Die on white glazed paper (1873),
     black   1,000.

    May be essay for Official stamps.

152-E5

Incomplete engraved design: shading on corner panel bevels incomplete, side whiskers bolder than as adopted. Also essayed for envelopes on thick paper.

152-E5 15c Die on India, die sunk on card, or-
     ange brown   750.

Similar to No. 152-E5 but with pencil marks suggesting shading on corner panels.

152-E6 15c Die on India, orange brown   750.

Similar to No. 152-E5 with engraved shading added to corner panels but white areas incomplete.

152-E7 15c Die on India
orange	550.
orange yellow	550.
orange brown	550.
green	550.
red violet	550.
rose carmine	550.

Similar to No. 152-E7 but shading on corner panels complete.

152-E8 15c Die on India, on card, black   1,000.

153-E1

153-E2

Design size: 18x23mm
Incomplete engraved vignette of Scott mounted on pencil sketch of partial frame design.

153-E1 24c Die on white card, 33x39mm, dull
     red violet vignette, pencil frame   1,750.

Design size: 19½x25mm
Complete engraved vignette mounted on pencil and watercolor frame design with "U.S. POSTAGE" in ink.

153-E2 24c Die on white card, 73x110mm, dim
     blue green   3,250.

153-E3

153-E4

Die size: 62x76mm
Incomplete engraved vignette only.

153-E3 24c Die on India, die sunk on card
black	500.
yellow	500.
yellow brown	500.
dark orange brown	500.
ultramarine	500.
dark ultramarine	500.
red violet	500.

Die size: 62x77mm
Incomplete design as adopted: upper corners not squared outside scrolls, no periods after U and S in stars.

153-E4 24c Die on India, die sunk on card
carmine	550.
orange	550.
brown orange	550.
yellow brown	550.
deep brown	550.
ultramarine	550.
dark red violet	550.
green	550.

Value off card, cut down, $275.

Previous No. 154-E1 is now No. 149-E4a.

154-E2

Pencil drawing of entire design, labeled "Scott."

154-E2 30c Pencil drawing on white card,
     53x92mm   2,000.

Engraved vignette of Hamilton mounted on pencil drawing of frame.

154-E3 30c Die on card, yellow brown vignette,
     pencil frame   1,500.

154-E4

Incomplete engraved vignette of Hamilton.

154-E4 30c Die on India, die sunk on card
yellow brown	600.
dark ultramarine blue	600.
orange	600.

Vignette of Hamilton with more engraving on forehead, nose, neck, etc.

154-E5 30c Die on India, die sunk on card
dark red brown	600.
dull carmine	600.
ultramarine	600.

154-E6

Completed vignette with 30 below.

154-E6 30c Die on white glazed paper (1873),
     black   1,000.

    May be essay for Official stamps.

155-E1

155-E2

Pencil drawing of entire design, labeled "Perry."

155-E1 90c Pencil drawing on white card,
     53x92mm   2,000.

Design size: 19½x25mm
Engraved vignette of Perry mounted on pencil and watercolor frame design.

155-E2 90c Die on white card, 73x110mm, dull
     dark violet vignette, dull red violet
     frame   3,250.

155-E3

Die size: 58x79mm

Incomplete engraving of Perry vignette as adopted.

155-E3 90c
   a. Die on India, die sunk on card
      deep yellow orange   500.
      orange brown   500.
      dark brown   500.
      dull carmine   500.
      ultramarine blue   500.
      dark blue green   500.
      dark red violet   500.
   b. Die on white ivory paper, black   500.

Similar to No. 155-E3 but more lines in hair above forehead.

155-E4 90c Die on India, on card, black   500.

155-E5

Incomplete engraving of design as adopted: rope above vignette unfinished. Also essayed for envelopes on thick paper.

155-E5 90c Die on India, die sunk on card
      black   700.
      carmine, off card   325.
      orange   700.
      dark orange   700.
      yellow brown   700.
      brown   700.
      deep orange brown   700.
      deep ultramarine   700.
      blue green   700.
      red violet   700.

Value off card, cut down, $250.

1873 ISSUE
Continental Bank Note Co.

179-E1   179-E2

Die size: 20x25mm
Vignette of Taylor by Bureau of Engraving and Printing, in engraved frame.

179-E1 Five Cents, Die on India
      black   3,000.
      blue   3,000.

Design size: 24x29mm
Vignette of Taylor by Bureau of Engraving and Printing, in ornate wash drawing of frame ("FIVE CENTS" black, on shaded ribbon).

179-E2 5c Die on card, black   4,000.

Incomplete vignette: hair, coat, background, etc., unfinished.

179-E3 5c Die on India, violet   2,000.

George W. Bowlsby 1873 essay similar in concept to his No. 63-E13 but without coupon attached. It consisted of an unused 1c stamp (No. 156) with horiz. sewing machine perfs. through center, gummed on upper half only, as described in his Dec. 26, 1865 patent. Stamp was meant to be torn in half by postal clerk as cancellation, to prevent reuse.

156-E1 1c blue   250.

1876 Experimental Ink and Paper Essays

Plate designs of 1873-75 issues in normal colors, printed on paper tinted with sensitive inks and on heavily laid (horiz.) colored papers (unless otherwise noted).

156-E2 1c Blue on:
      carmine   150.
      pale rose   150.
      deep yellow   150.
      pale violet   150.

158-E1 3c Green on:
      pale rose   150.
      deep yellow   150.
      pale violet   150.

158-E2 3c Green on paper covered with pink varnish which vanishes with the color   100.

158-E3 3c Green on thick white blotting paper which absorbs canceling ink   100.

161-E1 10c Brown on:
      pale rose   150.
      deep yellow   150.
      pale violet   150.

163-E1 15c Yellow orange on:
      pale rose   200.
      deep yellow   200.
      pale violet   200.

165-E1 30c Gray black on:
      pale rose   200.
      deep yellow   200.
      pale violet   200.

166-E1 90c Rose carmine on:
      pale rose   200.
      deep yellow   200.
      pale violet   200.

178-E1 2c Vermilion on:
      pale rose   150.
      deep yellow   15u.
      pale violet   150.

179-E4 5c Blue on:
      pale rose   300.
      deep yellow   300.
      pale violet   300.

See No. 147-E13.

1877 Essays
Philadelphia Bank Note Co.

Die essays for this section were all engraved. The frame-only dies for all values of this series were engraved with two values appearing per die, except the 3c (No. 184-E1) which was engraved alone. In each case the listing is under the lower denomination. The Washington vignette associated with each value of the frames is from engraved master die No. 14. (No. 182-E1).

Except as noted, plate essays in this section are all lithographed from a composite stone plate of two panes. The left pane ("plate 1") consists of horiz. rows of four of the 1c, 3c, 7c, 24c and 90c. The right pane ("plate 2") consists of horiz. rows of four 2c, 6c, 12c and 30c. "Printed by Philadelphia Bank Note Co. Patented June 16, 1876" imprint below 2nd and 3rd designs on each row.

See note above No. 63-E1.

182-E1

Vignette master die "No. 14": two slightly diff. vignettes of Washington, one above the other, bottom one with truncated queue, bust and shading in front of neck.

182-E1
   a. Die on old white glazed paper, black   500.
   b. Die on proof paper (1903)
      black   100.
      carmine   100.
      dull carmine   100.
      dusky carmine   100.
      yellow   100.
      dull scarlet   100.
      dull orange   100.
      brown orange   100.
      brown   100.
      gray olive   100.
      blue green   100.
      dark green   100.
      black blue   100.
      ultramarine   100.
      violet   100.
      red violet   100.

182-E2

Design size: 20x25mm
Die size: 98x53mm
Frames of 1c and 2c side by side.

182-E2 1c + 2c
   a. Die on white pelure
      dark carmine   250.
      orange   250.
      brown   250.
      blue green   250.
      blue   250.
   b. Die with vertical line between designs (die size 85x54mm), on India, die sunk on card
      dusky red   400.
      deep orange   400.
      orange brown   400.
      dark green   400.
      dark blue   400.
   c. Die on stiff glazed paper, black   400.
   d. Die on proof paper, printed through a mat (1903)
      black   100.
      bright carmine   100.
      dull carmine   100.
      dim scarlet   100.
      dark orange   100.
      dull yellow   100.
      dark orange brown   100.
      black olive   100.
      dark blue green   100.
      dark blue   100.
      ultramarine   100.
      dark navy blue   100.
      blue violet   100.
      dull violet   100.
      red violet   100.
   e. Plate sheet of 1c, 2c, 3c, 12c, 24c, 30c, 90c frames only, on card, pale green blue   1,500.

182-E3

Complete 1c design, lithographed.

182-E3 1c
   a. Plate on stamp paper, imperf., gummed
      black   75.
      blue green   75.
      bright ultramarine   75.
      yellow   75.
   b. Plate on stamp paper, perf. 12, gummed
      dark red orange   50.
      orange brown   50.
      red brown   50.
      red violet   50.
      violet blue   50.
      ultramarine   50.
   c. Plate 1 "sheet" of 20, complete designs, without imprint, on old glazed paper, imperf., deep brown orange   800.
   d. As "c," with imprint, on old glazed paper, imperf., gummed
      dull deep violet red   800.
      ultramarine   800.
      scarlet   800.
      orange   800.

carmine 800.
dark carmine 800.
green 800.
bluish green 800.
e. As "d," perf. 12, gummed
   dull deep violet red 700.
   ultramarine 700.
   red brown 700.
   violet blue 700.

Concerning plate 1 sheets of 20, note that composite stone plates also contained the plate 2 sheets of 20 listed as Nos. 183-E2c to 183-E2e. Many such composite sheets remain intact. All separated plate 1 or plate 2 sheets originally were part of a composite sheet.

183-E2b

Complete 2c design, lithographed.

183-E2 2c
a. Plate on stamp paper, imperf.
   blue green 60.
   bright ultramarine 60.
   brown 60.
b. Plate on stamp paper, perf. 12, gummed
   bright red orange 35.
   dull red orange 35.
   dark red orange 35.
   red brown 35.
   dark red brown 35.
   dark orange brown 35.
   yellow brown 35.
   dull yellow green 35.
   green 35.
   dull ultramarine 35.
   bright ultramarine 35.
   blue violet 35.
   red violet 35.
   light red violet 35.
   violet red 35.
c. Plate 2 "sheet" of 16, complete designs, without imprint, on old glazed paper, imperf., deep brown orange 600.
d. As "c," with imprint, on old glazed paper, imperf., gummed, dull deep violet red 600.
e. As "d," perf. 12, gummed, dull deep violet red 500.

See note following No. 182-E3e.

Design size: 20x25mm
Die size: 54x55mm
Engraved frame of 3c alone on die.

184-E1 3c
a. Die on pelure paper
   dark carmine 250.
   dark orange 250.
   orange brown 250.
   bright blue 250.
   bright blue 250.
   green 250.
   dark green 250.
b. Die on proof paper (1903)
   black 100.
   bright carmine 100.
   dull carmine 100.
   dim scarlet 100.
   dark orange 100.
   dull yellow 100.
   dark orange brown 100.
   black olive 100.
   dark rose 100.
   green 100.
   yellow green 100.
   dark blue green 100.
   dark blue 100.
   deep ultramarine 100.
   dark navy blue 100.
   blue violet 100.
   dull violet 100.
   red violet 100.

Built-up model of engraved frame cut to shape inside and out, mounted atop engraved vignette of the same color. Warning: fraudulent models combining engraved and lithographed materials exist.

184-E2 3c
a. Die on proof paper, cut close
   dark scarlet 250.
   blue green 250.
   deep blue 250.
b. Four examples mounted 2½mm apart on stiff white card, 80x87mm
   red 1,000.
   orange brown 1,000.
   green 1,000.
   blue 1,000.
   violet 1,000.
   green frame, light blue vignette 1,000.

Built-up model as No. 184-E2, vignette as No. 184-E5 with dark background.

184-E3 3c Die on proof paper, scarlet 250.

184-E4

Complete 3c design, vignette with light background.

184-E4 3c
c. Plate lithographed on stamp paper, imperf.
   black 75.
   green 75.
   dark green 75.
   bright ultramarine 75.
   orange 75.

No. 184-E4c exists in two plates of 9 tete-beche, in diff. colors, on same piece of paper. Value, $800 sheet of 18.

d. Plate lithographed on stamp paper, perf. 12, gummed
   dark red orange 50.
   red brown 50.
   red voilet 50.
   brown orange 50.
   ultramarine 50.
   violet blue 50.
e. Plate sheet of 9 (3x3), imprint below, on stiff white wove
   carmine 300.
   blue green 300.
f. Plate sheet of 9 (3x3), on glazed thin wove
   carmine 300.
   blue green 300.
   blue 300.
   orange 300.
g. Plate sheet of 9 (3x3), on yellowish wove
   carmine 300.
   blue green 300.
   blue 300.
h. Die of complete design on old stiff glazed paper (die size: 55x66mm), black 350.
i. Complete die on glazed wove
   deep carmine 200.
   scarlet 200.
   ultramarine 200.
j. Complete die on India, light orange red 200.
k. Complete die on proof paper (1903)
   black 75.
   bright carmine 75.
   dull carmine 75.
   dim scarlet 75.
   dark orange 75.
   dull yellow 75.
   dark orange brown 75.
   black olive 75.
   green 75.
   dark blue green 75.
   deep ultramarine 75.
   dark navy blue 75.
   blue violet 75.
   dull violet 75.
   red violet 75.
l. Complete die on large colored card (1903)
   black, *light green* 150.
   deep scarlet, *ivory* 150.
   red violet, *light blue* 150.
   carmine, *pink* 150.

184-E5

Design size: 19x24½mm
Die No. 1 size: about 63x94mm Vignette of Washington slightly diff. from rest of series but with quite diff. frame design.

184-E5 3c
a. Die on glazed paper, about 50x75mm, black 350.
b. Die on proof paper (with and without printing through mats) (1903)
   black 100.
   dark carmine 100.
   carmine 100.
   bright carmine 100.
   brown 100.
   red brown 100.
   yellow 100.
   orange 100.
   violet 100.
   red violet 100.

violet brown 100.
blue 100.
steel blue 100.
light green 100.
dark green 100.
dull olive 100.
c. Die on colored card, 61x93mm (1903)
   scarlet, *yellow* 150.
   olive gray, *pale pink* 150.
   dull violet, *buff* 150.

Plate proofs printed in sheets of 25 (plate size: 140x164mm). A horiz. crack extends through upper 3s from 2mm back of head on position 11 to vignette on position 12.
All plate essay items valued as singles except No. 184-E5d.

d. Engraved plate of 25 on India, mounted on large card, red brown 750.
e. Plate on proof paper (1903)
   black 15.
   blue black 15.
   greenish black 15.
   dull red violet 15.
   dark red violet 15.
   dull violet 15.
   violet brown 15.
   light red brown 15.
   orange brown 15.
   brown carmine 15.
   brown 15.
   dim orange 15.
   yellow 15.
   dull yellow 15.
   carmine 15.
   light carmine 15.
   dark carmine 15.
   dull carmine 15.
   dull scarlet 15.
   dark green 15.
   light green 15.
   dull olive green 15.
   deep ultramarine 15.
f. Plate on proof paper, perf. 12, lithographed
   carmine 100.
   rose lilac 100.
   red orange 100.
g. Plate on green bond, "Crane & Co. 1887" wmk. (1903)
   black 25.
   carmine 25.
   dull carmine 25.
   scarlet 25.
   brown 25.
   brown red 25.
   orange brown 25.
   red violet 25.
   yellow 25.
   orange 25.
   dark green 25.
   light green 25.
   yellow green 25.
   deep ultramarine 25.
   dark navy blue 25.
h. Plate (printed before plate crack developed) on semiglazed yellowish wove, laid watermark
   carmine 30.
   dull red 30.
   bright orange red 30.
   deep orange red 30.
   scarlet 30.
   deep orange 30.
   yellow orange 30.
   orange brown 30.
   orange yellow 30.
   dark yellow green 30.
   dusky blue green 30.
   dull green blue 30.
   violet blue 30.
   red violet 30.
   black 30.
i. Plate in sheets of 100 with imprint on yellowish glazed chemically prepared wove, lithographed
   black 20.
   brown 20.
   scarlet 20.
   light red 20.
   rose pink 20.
   carmine 20.
   deep carmine 20.
   violet rose 20.
   deep violet rose 20.
   violet red 20.
   red violet 20.
   violet 20.
   blue 20.
   pale blue 20.
   pale dull blue 20.
   yellow 20.
   dull brown yellow 20.
   orange 20.
   red orange 20.

Similar to No. 184-E1 but vignette of Lincoln facing ¾ to right. No. 184-E6a is built-up model.

184-E6 3c Four copies mounted on card to resemble block of 4
   blue 1,500.
   green 1,500.

Frame of No. 184-E5 with engraved vignette of Lincoln mounted in place.

184-E7 3c Die on card, brown 1,500.

Design size: 20x25mm

Die size: 92x50mm
Frames of 6c and 7c side by side (6c at right).

186-E1   6c + 7c
  a. Die on white pelure, orange — 375.
  b. Die on proof paper, printed through a mat (1903)

black	100.
bright carmine	100.
dull carmine	100.
dim scarlet	100.
dark orange	100.
dull yellow	100.
dark orange brown	100.
black olive	100.
green	100.
dark blue green	100.
dark blue	100.
deep ultramarine	100.
dark navy blue	100.
blue violet	100.
dull violet	100.
red violet	100.

  c. Die on white pelure, both 7s reversed on 7c frame, orange — 750.
  d. Die on old stiff glazed, black — 400.

186-E2

Complete 6c design, lithographed.

186-E2   6c
  a. Plate on stamp paper, perf. 12, gummed

bright red orange	35.
dull red orange	35.
dark red orange	35.
red brown	35.
dark red brown	35.
dark orange brown	35.
yellow brown	35.
dull yellow green	35.
green	35.
dull ultramarine	35.
bright ultramarine	35.
blue violet	35.
red violet	35.
light violet red	35.
violet red	35.

  b. Plate on stamp paper, gummed

ultramarine	60.
lilac	60.
scarlet	60.
orange	60.
carmine	60.
dark carmine	60.
blue green	60.

186a-E2

Complete 7c design, lithographed.

186a-E2   7c
  a. Plate on stamp paper, imperf.

black	75.
carmine	75.
red orange	75.
yellow orange	75.
green	75.
dark green	75.
dark blue	75.

  b. Plate on stamp paper, perf. 12, gummed

red brown	50.
dark red orange	50.
brown orange	50.
red violet	50.
ultramarine	50.
violet blue	50.

Design size: 20x25mm
Die size: 78½x64mm
Frames of 12c and 24c side by side (12c on right).

188a-E1   12c + 24c
  a. Die on white pelure

deep carmine	300.
brown orange	300.
orange brown	300.
blue green	300.
blue	300.

  b. Die on proof paper, printed through a mat (1903)

black	100.
bright carmine	100.
dull carmine	100.
dim scarlet	100.
dark orange	100.
dull yellow	100.
dark orange brown	100.
black olive	100.
green	100.
dark blue green	100.
dark blue	100.
deep ultramarine	100.
dark navy blue	100.
blue violet	100.
dull violet	100.
red violet	100.

  c. Die on old stiff glazed, black — 400.

188a-E2

Complete 12c design, lithographed.

188a-E2   12c
  a. Plate on stamp paper, perf. 12, gummed

bright red orange	35.
dull red orange	35.
dark red orange	35.
red brown	35.
dark red brown	35.
dark orange brown	35.
yellow brown	35.
dull yellow green	35.
green	35.
dull ultramarine	35.
bright ultramarine	35.
blue violet	35.
red violet	35.
light red violet	35.
violet red	35.

  b. Plate on stamp paper, gummed

ultramarine	60.
lilac	60.
scarlet	60.
orange	60.
carmine	60.
dark carmine	60.
blue green	60.

189a-E2

Complete 24c design, lithographed.

189a-E2   24c
  a. Plate on stamp paper, perf. 12, gummed

red brown	50.
dark red orange	50.
brown orange	50.
ultramarine	50.
violet blue	50.
red violet	50.

  b. Plate on stamp paper, gummed

ultramarine	75.
lilac	75.
scarlet	75.
orange	75.
carmine	75.
dark carmine	75.
green	75.

Design size: 20x25mm
Die size: 79x64mm
Frames of 30c and 90c side by side.

190-E1   30c + 90c
  a. Die on white pelure

dark orange	300.
dark red orange	300.
dark orange brown	300.
brown	300.
blue green	300.
bright blue	300.

  b. Die on stiff glazed paper, blue black — 500.
  c. Die on proof paper, printed through a mat (1903)

black	100.
bright carmine	100.
dull carmine	100.
dim scarlet	100.
dark orange	100.
dull yellow	100.

dark orange brown	100.
black olive	100.
green	100.
dark blue green	100.
dark blue	100.
deep ultramarine	100.
dark navy blue	100.
blue violet	100.
dull violet	100.
red violet	100.

190-E2   191-E2

Complete 30c design, lithographed.

190-E2   30c
  a. Plate on stamp paper, perf. 12, gummed

bright red orange	35.
dull red orange	35.
dark red orange	35.
red brown	35.
dark red brown	35.
dark orange brown	35.
yellow brown	35.
dull yellow green	35.
green	35.
dull ultramarine	35.
bright ultramarine	35.
blue violet	35.
red violet	35.
light red violet	35.
violet red	35.

  b. Plate on stamp paper, gummed

ultramarine	60.
lilac	60.
scarlet	60.
orange	60.
carmine	60.
dark carmine	60.
blue green	60.

Complete 90c design, lithographed.

191-E2   90c
  a. Plate on stamp paper, perf. 12, gummed

black	50.
red brown	50.
dark red orange	50.
brown orange	50.
ultramarine	50.
violet blue	50.
red violet	50.
violet red	50.
dark blue green	50.
orange brown	50.

  b. Plate on stamp paper, gummed

ultramarine	75.
lilac	75.
scarlet	75.
orange	75.
carmine	75.
dark carmine	75.
green	75.

1879 Coupon Essay
Azariah B. Harris

184-E8

Size of coupon design: 25x7½mm
A proposed $300 30-year Postal Revenue Bond with 3.65% interest. Daily coupons 3c each, "Receivable for Postage in all parts of the U.S>" after date thereon. Entire bond contained six pages of coupons with 16 rows of four (one for each day of two months); 20% bear month and day, others blank.

184-E8   3c
  a. Coupon on bond (dated Jan. or Feb.), imperf., black — 250.
  b. Engraved die on old ivory paper (undated), black — 750.
  c. Single coupon on bond (dated), perf. 12, gummed, blue green — 125.
  d. Single coupon on bond (undated), perf. 12, gummed, blue green — 50.

Continental Bank Note Co.

182-E4

Design size: 18x22mm
Die size: 59x67mm
Engraved vignette of Franklin on white background in unadopted frame.

182-E4 1c
  a. Die on India, blue 575.
  b. Die on proof paper
    black 350.
    dull scarlet 350.
    dull brown 350.
    dull green 350.
    dull blue 350.
  c. Die on white glazed paper
    black 575.
    black brown 575.
    scarlet 575.
    blue 575.

All known examples of "b" have reduced margins.

184-E9   184-E10

Die size: 61½x76½mm
Vignette of Washington on white background in incomplete frame as adopted: no veins in trifoliate ornaments in upper corners.

184-E9 3c Die on India, on card
    black 750.
    green 750.

Similar to No. 184-E9 but completed frame with veins in trifoliate ornaments.

184-E10 3c
  a. Die on India, die sunk on card, green 750.
  b. Die on proof paper, about 35x40mm
    gray black 350.
    dull red 350.
    dull blue 350.
    dull green 350.
    dull brown 350.
  c. Die on white glazed paper
    black 500.
    black brown 500.
    scarlet 500.
    blue 500.

Nos. 147-E8 and 147-E9 may have been made from completed dies of No. 147 to produce Nos. 184-E9 and 184-E10.

184-E11   184-E12

Design size: 17½x21½mm
Die size: 60x75mm
Complete unadopted design with vignette of Liberty on white background.

184-E11   Three Cents
  a. Die on India
    black 350.
    brown red 350.
    orange 350.
    green 350.
    blue 350.
    scarlet 350.
  b. Die on proof paper
    brown 350.
    green 350.
    gray black 350.
    dull red 350.
    dull blue 350.
  c. Die on white glazed paper
    black 500.

black brown 500.
scarlet 500.
blue 500.

All known examples of Nos. 184-E11a, 184-E11b have reduced margins.

Design size: 19½x24½mm
Die size: 61x71mm
Complete unadopted design with vignette of Washington on white background in frame similar to No. 184-E11 but with numerals of value.

184-E12 3c
  a. Die on India, die sunk on card
    black 650.
    dull scarlet 650.
    brown 650.
    green 650.
  b. Die on white glazed paper
    black 500.
    black brown 500.
    scarlet 500.
    blue 500.
  c. Plate on India (some adhering to original card backing), imperf.
    black 100.
    scarlet 100.
    orange red 100.
    green 100.
  d. Plate on white paper, perf. 12, gummed
    black 75.
    green 75.
    blue 75.
    brown 75.
    red brown 75.
    orange 75.
    dull scarlet 75.
    orange brown 75.
  e. Plate on Francis Patent bluish chemical paper, perf. 12, gummed
    black 150.
    scarlet 150.
    red brown 150.
    brown 150.
    yellow 150.
    green 150.
    gray 150.
  f. Plate on brown chemical paper, perf. 12, gummed
    blue 150.
    ultramarine 150.
  g. Hybrid die on India, mounted on India, block sunk on card, green 400.

184-E13   184-E14

Design size: 18x22mm
Die size: about 61x62mm
Similar to No. 184-E12 but slightly different frame.

184-E13 3c
  a. Die on India, die sunk on card
    black 650.
    scarlet 650.
    green 650.
    blue 650.
    black brown 650.
    blue green 650.
  b. Die on white glazed paper
    black 500.
    black brown 500.
    scarlet 500.
    blue 500.
  c. Plate on India, imperf.
    black 100.
    deep scarlet 100.
    green 100.
    dark green 100.
    dark yellow brown 100.
    olive brown 100.
    violet brown 100.
    orange 100.
  d. Plate on stamp paper, perf. 12, gummed
    black 75.
    dull scarlet 75.
    blue green 75.
    brown 75.
    red brown 75.
    dull blue 75.
    dark blue 75.
    orange 75.
    yellow 75.
    yellow brown 75.
    gray 75.

Design size: 19x24½mm
Die size: about 67x71mm
Similar to No. 184-E13 but value label with "THREE" above "CENTS."

184-E14 3c
  a. Hybrid die on India mounted on India, block sunk on card
    brown red 400.
    green 400.

b. Die on white glazed paper
    black 500.
    black brown 500.
    scarlet 500.
    blue 500.
c. Die on proof paper, about 35x35mm
    black 300.
    dull scarlet 300.
    dull brown 300.
    dull green 300.
    dull blue 300.
    brown red 300.
    red brown 300.

184-E15   184-E16

Design size: 20x25½mm
Die size: 60x73mm
Vignette of Indian maiden in headdress, "PORTAGE" error in top label.

184-E15 3c
  a. Hybrid die on India, cut close, mounted on India, block sunk on card
    black 900.
    dark green 900.
  b. Die on proof paper, about 28x35mm
    black 600.
    dull scarlet 500.
    dull brown 500.
    dull blue 500.
    dull green 500.
  c. Die on white glazed paper
    black 850.
    black brown 850.
    scarlet 850.
    blue 850.
  d. Die on India, scarlet —

Similar to No. 184-E15 but with spelling corrected to "POSTAGE."

184-E16 3c Die on India, cut close, mounted on India, block sunk on card
    black 1,250.
    blue 1,250.
    steel blue 1,250.
    carmine 1,250.
    scarlet 1,250.
    brown 1,250.
    dark green 1,250.

190-E3

Die size: 44½x71½mm
Vignette of Hamilton on white background in frame as adopted.

190-E3 30c
  a. Die on proof paper, about 35x48mm
    gray black 500.
    dull red 500.
    dull green 500.
    dull brown 500.
    dull blue 500.
  b. Die on white glazed paper
    black 750.
    black brown 750.
    scarlet 750.
    blue 750.

American Bank Note Co.

184-E17

Design size: 22x30mm

Silver photo print of engraved vignette of Washington mounted on pencil and ink frame design.

184-E17   3c
   a. Die on white card, 38x49mm
     light brown vignette, black frame   1,250.
   b. Die on white card, 38x50mm
     light brown vignette, black frame   1,250.

Frame ornaments extend beyond framelines, lettering less complete than on No. 184-E17a.

1881-82 ISSUE
American Bank Note Co.

Design size: 20x25mm
Die size: 59x74mm
Vignette of Garfield in lined oval.

205-E1   5c Die on India, die sunk on card,
         black   500.

205-E2   205-E3

Die No. C-47 size: 70x83mm
Vignette of Garfield in beaded oval, in plain border of horiz. lines. Found with and without imprint and die number.

205-E2   5c Die on India, die sunk on card
         gray brown   250.
         gray black   250.

     No. 205-E2 may not be a stamp essay.

Die size: 78x78mm
Vignette of Garfield in beaded oval with cutout at bottom for top of star.

205-E3   5c
   a. Die on India, die sunk on card
     black   750.
     deep red orange   750.
     red brown   750.
     blue   750.
     green   750.
   b. Die on white glazed paper
     black   750.
     green   750.
     blue   750.
     scarlet   750.
     red brown   750.
   c. Negative impression, solid color outside
     design, die on India, bright red orange 1,000.

Vignette of Garfield as No. 205-E1 in lined oval and finished frame as adopted.

205-E4   5c Die on India, 24x30mm, black   900.

206-E1   206-E2

Design size: 21x26mm
Engraved frame of unadopted design.

206-E1   1c
   a. Die on white glazed paper, 42x74mm,
     black   1,000.
   b. Die on surface-tinted glazed paper, cut
     close
     green, *buff*   600.
     black, *orange*   600.
     brown orange, *blue*   600.

Engraved frame almost identical to No. 206-E1 with small typographed vignette of Peace.

206-E2   1c Die on blue surface-tinted ivory pa-
       per, cut close, buff vignette, car-
       mine frame   800.

Vignette of Peace only.

206-E3   1c
   a. Engraved vignette
     black   350.
     dull red violet   350.
   b. Typographed vignette   350.

206-E4

Engraved frame (No. 206-E1) with typographed vignette of Lincoln mounted on it. Four diff. colors (dull carmine, dull scarlet, dark brown, green) on cream white ivory paper, 22x27mm each, mounted together on 92x114mm thick white card, ms. "American Bank Note Co. N.Y." at lower right.

206-E4   1c Four designs on cream white ivory
       on card   2,500.

Design size: 18x23½mm
Typographed vignette of Lincoln only.

206-E5   1c Die on white ivory paper
     dull carmine   400.
     dark yellowish brown   400.
     dull purple   400.
     dull dark blue   400.
     orange   400.

206-E6

Incomplete engraving of complete design as issued: no shading in upper arabesques.

206-E6   1c
   a. Die on India
     gray blue   750.
     green blue   750.
   b. Die on India, cut close, on India block
     sunk on card, deep gray blue   350.

207-E1   207-E2

Design size: 20½x25½mm
Die size: 49x54½mm
Engraved unadopted frame design with 3's at sides and large 3 at top.

207-E1   3c
   a. Die on India
     yellow brown   750.
     dull brown   750.
     dull blue   750.
     green   750.
   b. Die on white glazed paper, 32x38mm
     black   650.
     dull dark yellow   650.
   c. Die on surface-tinted ivory paper, cut
     close
     black, *orange*   500.
     green, *buff*   500.
     violet blue, *orange*   500.

Engraved frame as No. 207-E1, with typographed vignette of Peace.

207-E2   3c Die on blue surface-tinted ivory pa-
       per, cut close, buff vignette, car-
       mine frame   650.

Engraved frame (No. 207-E1) with typographed vignette of Peace mounted on it. Four diff. color combinations (orange red vignette, dull carmine frame; dull carmine vignette, dull red brown frame; yellow brown vignette and frame; blue green vignette and frame) on cream white ivory paper, 22x27mm each, mounted together on 92x114mm thick white card, ms. "American Bank Note Co. N.Y." at lower right.

207-E3   3c 4 designs on cream white ivory on
       card   2,500.

208-E1

Incomplete engraving of design as adopted: unfinished shading on top label and bottom ribbon, four lines between frame sinkage at right and left edges, horiz. line at bottom.

208-E1   6c Die on India, on card, black   1,500.

This is a new die engraved by the Bureau of Engraving & Printing for "Roosevelt" proof albums.

209-E1

Design size: 20x25mm
Die size: 58x76mm
Engraving of unadopted frame only, no horiz. lines in background.

209-E1   10c Die on thick white card, about
        25x33mm
     blue   750.
     green   750.

Similar to No. 209-E1 but with horiz. lines added to background.

209-E2   10c
   a. Die on thick white card
     black   650.
     red   650.
     green   650.
     blue   650.
   b. Die on India, on 50x70mm card, black 750.
   c. Die on white glazed paper, black   700.

209-E3

Engraved frame similar to No. 209-E2 with typographed vignette of Peace.

209-E3   10c
   a. Die on blue surface-tinted glazed paper,
     cut close, buff vignette, carmine frame 650.
   b. Die on orange surface-tinted glazed pa-
     per
     dull carmine vignette, violet frame 650.
     dull yellow vignette, violet frame 650.
     yellow vignette, green frame   650.

209-E4   209-E5

Vignette diameter: 17mm
Engraved Franklin vignette.

209-E4   10c
   a. Die on India
     black   500.
     dusky carmine   500.
     dull scarlet   500.
     dim orange   500.
     orange brown   500.
     yellow green   500.
     dim blue green   500.
     deep blue   500.
     red brown on blue ground 500.
     dark red violet   500.

b. Die sunk on glazed paper, 51x69mm

dusky carmine	700.
dim scarlet	700.
dim orange	700.
deep blue	700.

Design size: 21x26mm
Engraved frame with typographed vignette mounted on it. Four diff. color combinations (dull scarlet vignette, dull carmine frame; dull orange vignette, brown orange frame; yellow brown vignette, dark brown frame; blue green vignette and frame) on cream white ivory paper, 22x27mm each, mounted together on 92x114mm thick white card, ms. "American Bank Note Co. N.Y." at lower right.

209-E5   10c   Four designs on cream white ivory
                on card   2,500.

209-E6   209-E7

Vignette diameter: 18mm
Engraved Washington vignette.

209-E6   10c
a. Die on India

black	500.
dim deep carmine	500.
dim deep scarlet	500.
dull orange	500.
dull brown	500.
dim blue green	500.
blue	500.
dusky red violet	500.

b. Die sunk on white ivory paper, 55x67mm

dusky carmine	700.
dull orange	700.
dull blue green	700.
scarlet	700.
dull brown	700.
red violet	700.

Design size: 21x26mm
Engraved frame with typographed vignette mounted on it. Four diff. color combinations (dull carmine vignette and frame; dull orange vignette, brown orange frame; yellow brown vignette, dark brown frame; blue green vignette and frame) on cream white ivory paper, 22x27mm each, mounted together on 92x114mm thick white card, ms. "American Bank Note Co. N.Y." at lower right.

209-E7   10c
a. Four designs on cream white ivory on
     card   2,500.
b. Single composite off card, dull carmine
     vignette, blue green frame   400.

Issued stamp, No. 209, in trial color, overprinted network in fugitive ink.

209-E8   10c   On thick paper, perf. 12, gummed,
                sepia, overprint olive gray   150.

1883 ISSUE
American Bank Note Co.

210-E1   210-E2

Design size: 20x25½mm
Engraved vignette of Washington (from proof on India of No. 207) with watercolor frame design nearly as adopted but with "TWO" and "CENTS" at an angle, rubber stamp "Feb. 17, 1883" on back.

210-E1   2c   Die on white card, 80x90mm, black
               vignette, gray and white frame   3,000.

Design size: 20x25mm
Engraved vignette of Washington (from proof on India of No. 207) mounted on unadopted watercolor and ink frame design. backstamped "American Bank Note Co. Feb. 27, 1883."

210-E2   2c   Die on thick white card, 87x100mm,
               black and white   3,000.

210-E3   210-E4

Design size: 20x25½mm
Engraved vignette of Washington (from proof on India of No. 207) mounted on watercolor frame design as adopted, ms. "2 March 1883 No. 1."

210-E3   2c   Die on white card, 80x90mm, black
               vignette, gray & white frame   3,000.

Design size: 20x25mm
Engraved vignette of Washington on white background mounted on a brush and pen watercolor drawing of unadopted fancy frame design, backstamped "American Bank Note Co. Mar. 2, 1883" and pencil "No. 2."

210-E4   2c   Die on white card, 88x101mm,
               dusky blue green   3,000.

210-E5

Design size: 20x25mm
Engraved vignette of Washington (from revenue stamp No. RB17) mounted on wash drawing of unadopted ornate frame design, backstamped "American Bank Note Co. Mar. 2, 1883" and pencil "No. 3."

210-E5   2c   Die on white card, 88x101mm, blue
               violet vignette, black frame   2,500.

211-E1

Design size: 20x25½mm
Engraved vignette of Jackson mounted on unadopted watercolor frame design.

211-E1   4c   Die on white card, 70x70mm, blue
               green vignette and frame   3,500.

Engraved head of Jackson only.

211-E2   4c   Die on India, die sunk on card,
               black   1,000.

211-E3

Incomplete engraved vignette of Jackson: lower edge of bust incomplete.

211-E3   4c   Die on India, die sunk on card

black	2,500.
green	2,500.
red brown	2,500.

Complete engraved vignette of Jackson.

211-E4   4c   Die on India, die sunk on card, blue
               green   2,500.

211-E5

Die size: 60x62mm
Complete design as adopted but with pencil sketch of pedestal top under bust.

211-E5   4c   Die on India, die sunk on card, gray
               black   5,750.

Similar to No. 211-E5 but with incomplete shading engraved on pedestal.

211-E6   4c   Die on India, die sunk on card, blue
               green   2,500.

1887 ISSUE
American Bank Note Co.

212-E1

Die size: 55x63mm
Incomplete engraved vignette of Franklin facing right: horiz. background lines only.

212-E1   1c   Die on 32½x35mm card, India
               mounted, die sunk on card

black	600.
ultramarine	600.

Die size: 62x62mm
Franklin vignette similar to No. 212-E1 but diagonal lines (in one direction only) added to background.

212-E2   1c   Die on India, die sunk on card

black	600.
ultramarine	600.

Die size: 55x64mm
Similar to No. 212-E2 but diagonal lines in both directions.

212-E3   1c   Die on India, die sunk on card,
               black   500.

212-E4

Complete design as issued except Franklin facing right.

212-E4   1c
a. Die on India, die sunk on card

black	600.
ultramarine	600.

b. Die on white glazed paper, about 64x76mm

black	600.
black brown	600.
scarlet	600.
blue	600.

Die size: 62x62mm
Incomplete vignette of Franklin facing left as adopted.

212-E5   1c   Die on India, die sunk on card, ul-
               tramarine   450.

212-E6   212-E7

Die size: 56x64½mm

Incomplete design as adopted except three lines below value label and taller numeral, shadow on edge of bust and in background below chin too dark.

212-E6   1c Die on India, die sunk on card
            ultramarine   700.
            green   700.

Similar to No. 212-E6 but with shadows lightened.

212-E7   1c Die on India, die sunk on card, ul-
            tramarine   700.

1890 ISSUE
American Bank Note Co.

219-E1

Design size: 19x22½mm
Die size: 58x64mm
Engraved die of frame only with blank labels quite similar to adopted design.

219-E1   1c Die on ivory paper, 64x72mm, black   700.

219-E2   **219-E3**

Design size: 19x22mm
Engraved Franklin vignette cut down from 1887 1c stamp (No. 212) mounted on watercolor frame design.

219-E2   1c Die on thick light buff card, ul-
            tramarine frame   3,500.

Die size: 62x62mm
Engraved Franklin vignette with lettered label above.

219-E3   1c Die on India, die sunk on card, blue   800.

220-E1   **220-E2**

Design size: 19x22mm
Engraved Washington vignette from 3c stamp (from proof on India of No. 184) mounted on watercolor frame design.

220-E1   2c Die on thick white card, 62x66mm,
            light carmine frame   3,750.

Design size: 19x23mm
Engraved Washington vignette cut from 1887 2c stamp (No. 213) mounted on shield-like watercolor frame design.

220-E2   2c Die on thick light buff card, gray
            frame   3,000.

220-E3   **220-E4**

Design size: 19x23mm
Engraved Washington vignette cut from 1887 2c stamp (No. 213) mounted on watercolor frame design.

220-E3   2c Die on white card, 105x135mm,
            gray black frame   3,000.

Design size: 19x22mm
Die size: 56x63mm
Engraved unadopted frame only.

220-E4   2c Die on white ivory paper, black   1,250.

220-E5   **220-E6**

Die size: 62x62mm
Engraved vignette of Washington in oval line frame.

220-E5   2c Die on India, die sunk on card, dark
            carmine   800.

Engraved Washington vignette with lettered label above.

220-E6   2c Die on India, dusky carmine   800.

220-E7   **220-E8**

Design size: 19x22½mm
Engraved Washington vignette and lettered top label mounted on pencil drawing of frame design adopted, ms. "J.J.M.--engraved background only without figures or words;" backstamped "Nov. 15, 1889 American Bank Note Co."

220-E7   2c Die on 50x55mm white card,
            mounted on thick white card,
            119x122mm, black vignette, pencil
            frame   3,000.

Design size: 19x22mm
Die size: 56x63mm
Engraved frame only as adopted with numerals, blank curved top label.

220-E8   2c
    a. Die on ivory paper, 64x71mm, black   900.
    b. Die on India, 51x62mm
        black   700.
        brown black   700.
        dark brown   700.
        dull scarlet   700.
        dark blue green   700.
        dark blue   700.
        red violet   700.
        red orange   700.

220-E9

Incomplete engraving of entire design as adopted: no dots in rectangular spaces between shading lines on cheek under hair in front of ear and on back of neck.

220-E9   2c Die on India, die sunk on card, lake   850.

(Probably by) The Times, Philadelphia

220-E11

Surface-printed essay for proposed business advertising on stamps.

220-E11   2c Die on India, on card, bright green
            blue   —

American Bank Note Co.

221-E1   **221-E2**

Engraved 3c frame as adopted with vignette cut out, mounted over photo of James Madison.

221-E1   3c Die on India, cut close, dark green   2,500.

Engraved vignette of Jackson with lettered label above.

221-E2   3c Die on India, die sunk on card, pur-
            ple   750.

Design size: 19x22mm
Incomplete engraved design as adopted except Lincoln facing ¾ left: unfinished shading under collar.

222-E1   4c Die on India, die sunk on card,
            black brown   1,250.

222-E2   **222-E3**

Die No. C-226 size: 62½x62½mm
Completed design with die no. and impt., Lincoln facing ¾ left.

222-E2   4c Die on India, on 25x32mm card,
            black brown   1,000.

Incomplete engraving as adopted: no wart on face, no lines on shirt.

222-E3   4c Die on India, die sunk on card,
            black brown   1,000.

223-E1

Design size: 19x21½mm
Photo of Seward vignette mounted on watercolor frame design.

223-E1   5c Die on light buff paper in upper
            right corner of short envelope,
            gray & white   1,750.

223-E2   **223-E3**

Design size: 19x26½mm
Die size: 63x62mm
Incomplete engraved design as adopted except Grant facing ¾ left: hair neatly combed.

223-E2   5c Die on India, die sunk on card
            black   700.
            orange brown   700.

Design size: 19x26½mm
Die size: 63x62mm
Incomplete engraving of complete bearded left-facing design: eye pupils not solid color, light shading on right side of face, only one diagonal shading line on left coat shoulder.

223-E3   5c Die on India, die sunk on card,
            chocolate   700.

Similar to No. 223-E3 but more complete. Left beard has no diagonal lines and is light at top center.

223-E4   5c Die on India, die sunk on card,
            chocolate   700.

Third state of die: no horiz. lines on left moustache or under lower lip.

223-E5   5c Die on India, die sunk on card,
            chocolate   700.

223-E6

223-E7

Completed left-facing design: shows lines omitted from No. 223-E5, several diagonal shading lines on left shoulder of coat.

223-E6 5c Die on India, die sunk on card
   black   700.
   chocolate   700.

Design size: 19x26½mm
Die size: 62x62mm
Left-facing design with slightly diff. portrait, hair neatly combed. Horiz. shading lines on left coat shoulder, no wash-etched shadows on coat, beard and tie.

223-E7 5c
   a. Die on India, die sunk on card
      black   700.
      dark brown   700.
   b. Die on glazed paper, impt. and "ESSAY
         MARCH 1890"
      black   750.
      black brown   750.
      scarlet   750.
      blue   750.

Design size: 19x26½mm
Die similar to No. 223-E7 but diagonal shading lines on left coat shoulder, wash-etched shadows on coat, beard and tie.

223-E8 5c Die on India, on card, brown   700.

223-E9

223-E10

Die size: 62x63mm
Engraving of right-facing Grant design diff. than adopted: light oval line around vignette, three diagonal lines on shirtfront under tie. Incomplete engraving: right collar unshaded.

223-E9 5c Die on India, dark orange brown   700.

Similar to No. 223-E9 but engraving completed: right collar shaded.

223-E10 5c
   a. Die on India, die sunk on card, dark or-
         ange brown   700.
   b. Die on ivory paper, impt. and "ESSAY
         MARCH 1890"
      black   750.
      black brown   750.
      scarlet   750.
      blue   750.

Ferrotype plate 39x51mm of Grant facing ¾ right, outlines engraved, filled with red.

223-E11 5c Metal plate   650.

223-E12

Printing from ferrotype plate, No. 223-E11.

223-E12 5c Die on card, 43x56mm, red   650.

226-E1

226-E2

Design size: 19x22½mm
Incomplete engraved vignette of Webster with curved label above, mounted on pencil drawing of frame design (includes additional pencil drawings of lower part of frame, value letter-ing), backstamped "D.S. Ronaldson," frame engraver.

226-E1 10c Die on white card, 51x55mm, black   2,500.

Design size: 19x22½mm
Engraving of unadopted frame design.

226-E2 10c Die on white glazed paper, black   1,000.

226-E3

226-E4

Design size: 19x22mm
Engraved 10c frame as adopted, vignette cut out and mounted over photo of John Adams.

226-E3 10c Die on India, cut close, dark green   2,500.

Design size: 19x22mm
Engraved 10c frame as adopted, vignette cut out and mounted over photo of William T. Sherman.

226-E4 10c Die on India, cut close, dark green   2,500.

227-E1

Design size: 19x22½mm
Engraved vignette of Henry Clay with curved label above, mounted on wash drawing of frame design (includes additional enlarged pencil and wash drawing of frame).

227-E1 15c Die on white card, mounted at left
            on light buff card, 110x123mm
            (frame drawing at right), black   1,750.

228-E1

Design size: 19x22½mm
Die size: 62x61mm
Incomplete engraved vignette of Jefferson with curved let-tered label at top: hair shading incomplete.

228-E1 30c Die on India, die sunk on card,
            black   750.

Similar to No. 228-E1 but more shading on hair, vert. shading lines on chin.

228-E2 30c Die on India, die sunk on card,
            black   750.

229-E1

Design size: 19x22½mm
Die size: 62x62mm
Engraved vignette of Perry with curved lettered label at top.

229-E1 90c Die on India, die sunk on card, red
            orange   750.

COLUMBIAN ISSUE
Lyman H. Bagg

230-E1

237-E1

Design sizes: 22x22mm
Left: No. 230-E1 - pencil drawing of Columbus in armor, on paper. "I do not know whether these designs will be of any use to you or not -- they are so rough. L.H.B." written at top, "My idea illustrated" at bottom.
Right: No. 237-E1 - pencil drawing of North American conti-nent, on paper.

230-E1 One Cent, Ten Cents, Drawings on
            114x72mm white wove, Nos. 230-E1,
            237-E1   6,000.

American Bank Note Co.

230-E2

230-E3

230-E4

Design size: 33x22mm
Silver print photo vignette of Columbus head mounted on watercolor drawing of unadopted frame design.

230-E2 1c Die on stiff white drawing paper, red
            violet   4,500.
230-E3 1c Die on stiff white drawing paper, blue
            green   4,500.
230-E4 1c Die on stiff white drawing paper, light
            red   4,500.

230-E5

Ferrotype metal plate with outline of adopted vignette (reversed) and drawings of Indian man and woman at sides in single line frame 39mm long.

230-E5 1c Metal plate, 57x38mm   1,250.

230-E6

Vignette size: 16x15mm

Engraved vignette only as adopted.

230-E6   1c Die on 53x39mm India, on card
         yellow brown   2,000.
         black   2,000.

230-E7

Incomplete engraving of vignette, lettering, value numerals and tablet as issued: without palm tree, incomplete shading on and behind Indian and maiden, on Columbus' head, no shading on scrollwork, etc.

230-E7   1c Die on 39x28mm stiff wove, deep
         blue   2,000.

230-E8

Incomplete engraving of entire design as issued: maiden's skirt only lightly engraved, chief's torso and shoulder incompletely engraved, incomplete shading in frame design at top, etc.

230-E8   1c Die on India, die sunk on 99x84mm
         card, deep blue   1,500.

231-E1

Design size: 34x22mm
Silver print photo of vignette as adopted, mounted on watercolor drawing of unadopted frame design.

231-E1   2c Die on stiff white drawing paper,
         red violet   8,500.

Die size: 74x61½mm
Incomplete engraving of adopted vignette only.

231-E2   2c Die on India, die sunk on card
         black   1,500.
         sepia   1,500.

231-E3

Design size: 35½x22mm
Engraved vignette of Columbus asking aid of Isabella as adopted for 5c, mounted on watercolor drawing of frame design similar to that adopted for 2c.

231-E3   2c Die on stiff white drawing paper,
         dark brown   4,000.

231-E4

Vignette size: 29x15mm
Die size: 74x61½mm
Incomplete engraving of vignette as adopted (probably first state of die): cape on back of central figure incomplete, etc.

231-E4   2c Die on India, die sunk on card,
         black   2,500.

231-E5

Incomplete engraving of vignette as adopted (probably second state of die): more shading on top right face, etc.; also pencil sketches for lengthening vignette.

231-E5   2c Die on India, die sunk on card,
         black   3,250.

231-E6

Vignette size: 31½x15mm
Die size: 74x61½mm
Incomplete engraving of vignette, longer than Nos. 231-E4 and 231-E5, later shortened as adopted: Columbus' legs, central figure's cape, etc., are incomplete.

231-E6   2c Die on India, die sunk on card,
         black   2,500.

231-E7

Design size: 33x22mm
Die size: 74x61½mm
Incomplete engraving of entire design almost as adopted: figures of value narrower, unfinished crosset shadows in lower corners.

Ridgway numbers used for colors of No. 231-E7.

231-E7   2c
    a. Die on India, die sunk on card
         13m/4 smoky dusky o-yellow-orange   1,250.
    b. Die on thin white wove card
         69o/5 black   700.
         1m/0 dusky red   700.
         3k/2 dull dark orange-red   700.
         5i/0 deep o-orange-red   700.
         5j/1 deep v-deep o-orange-red   700.
         6i/0 deep m. red-orange   700.
         9i/0 deep o-yellow-orange   700.
         9m/0 dusky o-red-orange   700.
         9m/3 dismal dusky o-red-orange   700.
         9m/4 smoky dusky o-red-orange   700.
         9n/2 dull v. dusky o-red-orange   700.
         10k/0 m. dark orange   700.
         11i/0 deep orange   700.
         11k/1 dim dark orange   700.
         13m/1 dim dusky o-yellow-orange   700.
         13m/4 smoky dusky o-yellow-orange   700.
         33m/2 dull dusky g-yellow-green   700.
         37m/1 dull dusky g-blue-green   700.
         43m/2 dull dusky green-blue   700.
         49m/0 dusky blue   700.
         49m/1 dim dusky blue   700.
         55m/1 dull dusky blue-violet   700.
         59m/2 dull dusky violet   700.
         65m/2 dull dusky r-red-violet   700.
         70i/0 deep violet-red-red   700.

231-E8

Design size: 33x22mm
Incomplete engraving of entire design as adopted: value numerals same as on issued stamp but without thick shading bars at ends of outer frame rectangles, etc.

231-E8   2c Die on India, card mounted, sepia   1,500.

232-E1

Design size: 33½x22mm
Silver print photo of vignette unadopted for any value (Columbus embarking on voyage of discovery), mounted on watercolor drawing of unadopted frame design.

232-E1   3c Die on stiff white drawing paper,
         41x29mm, orange brown   4,000.

Ferrotype metal plate showing 19x15mm outline of *Santa Maria* (reversed) in 33x15mm vignette frame, outline engraved and filled with red ink.

232-E2   3c Metal plate, 51x30mm   1,250.

232-E3

Printing from ferrotype plate No. 232-E3.

232-E3   3c Die on stiff white card with rounded
         corners, 55x42mm, red   1,250.

232-E4

Vignette size: 30x15mm
Die size: 74x61mm
Incomplete engraving of vignette as adopted: sky composed of horiz. ruled lines, no clouds.

232-E4   3c Die on India, die sunk on card
         black   1,250.
         dark yellow-orange   1,250.
         sepia   1,750.

232-E5

Engraved vignette similar to No. 232-E4 but with "1492 UNITED STATES OF AMERICA 1892" and scrolls around numerals engraved in outline only, pencil outline of frame.

232-E5   3c Die on thick artist's card with beveled edges, 50x38mm, dark yellow
         orange   3,000.

233-E1

Design size: 33½x22mm
Silver print photo of wash drawing of vignette as adopted, mounted on watercolor drawing of frame design as adopted but titled "COLUMBUS ON VOYAGE OF DISCOVERY. SHIPS AT SEA."

233-E1   4c Die on stiff white drawing paper,
         41x29mm, brown red   4,750.

233-E2

Design size: 33x22mm
Die size: 74x61½mm
Incomplete engraving of complete design as adopted: unfinished crosset shadows in lower corners.

Ridgway numbers used for some colors of No. 233-E2.

233-E2   4c
    a. Die on India, die sunk on card
black	1,250.
dark yellow orange	1,250.

    b. Die on thin white wove card, die sunk on card

1m/0 dusky red	700.
3i/1 dim deep orange-red	700.
3k/2 dull dark orange-red	700.
5i/0 deep o-orange-red	700.
9i/0 deep o-red-orange	700.
9m/1 dim dusky o-red-orange	700.
11i/0 deep orange	700.
11k/1 dim dark orange	700.
11m/2 dull dusky orange	700.
13k/1 dim dark o-yellow-orange	700.
13m/2 dull dusky o-yellow-orange	700.
13m/3 dismal dark o-yellow-orange	700.
13k/4 smoky dark o-yellow-orange	700.
13m/4 smoky dusky o-yellow-orange	700.
15m/2 dull dusky yellow-orange	700.
33m/2 dull dusky g-yellow-green	700.
35m/5 gloomy dusky green	700.
37m/1 dim dusky g-blue-green	700.
39m/1 dim dusky blue-green	700.
41m/1 dim dusky b-blue-green	700.
47m/0 dusky green-blue-blue	700.
55m/2 dull dusky blue-violet	700.
63m/2 dull dusky red-violet	700.
69m/1 dull dusky red-violet-red	700.
69k/3 dismal dark red-violet-red	700.
71i/0 deep violet-red-red	700.
71m/0 dusky violet-red-red	700.
71o/5 black	700.
ultramarine	700.
violet	700.
red violet	700.
brown violet	700.
orange brown	700.
dark brown	700.

234-E1

Design size: 38½x22mm
Engraved vignette as adopted, mounted on watercolor drawing of frame design similar to but longer than adopted. Vignette also used on No. 231-E3.

234-E1   5c Die on thick artist's card, block
    sunk as die essay, black brown   4,000.

234-E2

Design size: 34x22½mm
Die size: 67x63mm
Engraved vignette as adopted, mounted on watercolor drawing of frame design as adopted, pencil "Oct. 5/92," approval monogram of J.D. Macdonough and ⅞x1½2 inches. Vignette also used on No. 231-E3.

234-E2   5c Die on thick artist's card, die sunk,
    black brown & white   4,000.

234-E3

Vignette size: 29½x15mm
Die size: 74x61½mm
Engraved vignette only as adopted.

234-E3   5c Die on India, die sunk on card, sepia   1,250.

234-E4

Incomplete engraving of entire design: bench at left has horiz. shading only, incomplete shading in Columbus' face, etc.

234-E4   5c Die on 74x60mm India, on card
sepia	1,000.
blue	1,000.

Ferrotype metal plate with engraved outline design (reversed) of vignette as used on 6c, engraved lines filled with red ink.

235-E1   6c Metal plate, 38x38mm   1,100.

235-E2

Printing from ferrotype plate No. 235-E1.

235-E2   6c Die on stiff white card with rounded
    corners, 55x42mm, red   1,250.

235-E3

Incomplete engraving of frame as adopted: unfinished crosset shadows in lower corners.

235-E3   6c Die on India, black   2,000.

235-E4

Design size: 34x22mm
Die size: 73x60mm
Incomplete engraving of entire design as adopted: neck and shoulder of horse, side figures in niches, crosset shadows in lower corners all unfinished.

235-E4   6c Die on India, die sunk on card, blue
    violet   1,500.

236-E1

Design size: 33½x22mm
Die size: 73x62mm
Design as adopted but frame incompletely engraved: unfinished crosset shadows in lower corners.

236-E1   8c Die on India, on card, black   2,500.

236-E2

Design as adopted but frame incompletely engraved: unfinished crosset shadows in lower corners, incomplete gown at left and faces at right.

236-E2   8c Die on India, on card, black   1,000.

237-E2

Ferrotype metal plate with engraved outline design (reversed) of vignette as used on 10c, engraved lines filled with red ink.

237-E2   10c Metal plate, 43x28mm   1,000.

237-E3

Printing from ferrotype plate No. 237-E2.

237-E3   10c Die on stiff white card with rounded
    corners, 55x42mm, red   1,000.

237-E4

Design size: 33x22mm
Die size: 74x62mm
Incomplete engraving of entire design as adopted: surroundings of Columbus, floor, etc., three figures behind King Ferdinand, crosset shadows in lower corners all unfinished.

237-E4   10c Die on India, card mounted
black brown	1,000.
rose carmine	1,000.

Similar to No. 237-E4 but more completely engraved: missing lines on ankle bracelet of Indian, many details in vignette and crosset shadows in lower corners.

237-E5   10c Die on India, die sunk on card
black brown	1,500.
carmine	1,500.

238-E1

Design size: 33½x22mm
Silver print photo of vignette unadopted for any value (Columbus relating incidents of voyage to Ferdinand and Isabella), mounted on watercolor drawing of frame design similar to that adopted.

238-E1   15c Die on stiff white drawing paper,
    42x30mm, bright ultramarine   5,000.

238-E2

Vignette size: 30x15mm
Die size: 71x59mm
Incomplete engraving of vignette only as adopted: shading on Columbus' tunic and arms, Isabella's sholder, Ferdinand's

robe, seated Indian's robe, robe of kneeling figure in lower left corner, etc., all unfinished.

238-E2 15c Die on India, die sunk on card,
　　　　black brown　　　　　　　　　　*1,500.*

Complete engraving of vignette adopted.

238-E3 15c Die on India, black brown　　　*1,500.*

238-E4

Design size: 33½x22mm
Die size: 73½x62mm
Incomplete engraving of complete design as adopted: shading on Isabella's shoulder, Ferdinand's robe, seated Indian's blanket and crosset shadows in lower corners all unfinished.

238-E4 15c Die on India, on card
　　　　black brown　　　　　　　　　　*1,500.*
　　　　blue green　　　　　　　　　　　*1,500.*

239-E1

Design size: 34½x22½mm
Silver print photo of vignette adopted for 15c, mounted on watercolor and ink drawing of unadopted frame design, titled "COLUMBUS PRESENTING NATIVES TO FERDINAND AND ISABELLA."

239-E1 30c Die on stiff white drawing paper,
　　　　42x30mm, bluish gray　　　　　*5,000.*

239-E2

Ferrotype metal plate with engraved outline design (reversed) of vignette as used on 30c, engraved lines filled with red ink.

239-E2 30c Metal plate, 39x29mm　　　*1,000.*

239-E3

Printing from ferrotype plate No. 239-E2.

239-E3 30c Die on stiff white card with rounded
　　　　corners, 55x43mm, red　　　　*1,000.*

239-E4

Vignette size: 30x15mm
Die size: 74x62mm
Incomplete engraving of adopted vignette only: table cloth dark at top; horiz. lines on front edge of octagonal footstool,

horiz. dots in shadow below windowsill at left, dots on top of head of man standing next to Columbus, etc., all missing.

239-E4 30c Die on India, die sunk on card,
　　　　black　　　　　　　　　　　　*1,750.*

Similar to No. 239-E4 but further engraved: has horiz. lines on front of footstool, etc. Eight pencil instructions for finishing vignette engraving written on large card backing, e.g., "Too much color on table cloth near top."

239-E5 30c Die on India, die sunk on
　　　　177x117mm card
　　　　black　　　　　　　　　　　　*2,000.*
　　　　black brown　　　　　　　　　　*2,000.*

239-E6

Design size: 33½x22mm
Die size: 74x63mm
Incomplete engraving of entire design as adopted: table cloth dark at top, diagonal dashes in one direction only between horiz. lines at lower left of vignette, etc.

239-E6 30c Die on India, die sunk on card
　　　　black　　　　　　　　　　　　*2,000.*
　　　　black brown　　　　　　　　　　*2,000.*

Similar to No. 239-E6 but diagonal dashes in two directions, more dots on head and hand of man seated at near end of table.

239-E7 30c Die on India, die sunk on card
　　　　black brown　　　　　　　　　　*1,750.*
　　　　orange　　　　　　　　　　　　*1,750.*

Incomplete engraving of entire design: window frame, horiz. shading lines on shoulder of man at right, vert. lines on front of table cloth below Columbus all missing. Lighter shading at top of table cloth as on issued stamp.

239-E8 30c Die on India, on card, orange　*2,500.*

240-E1

Design size: 34x22mm
Die size: Incomplete engraving of entire design as adopted: unfinished shadows between right arm and body of man on donkey, distant object in front of bowing man's head darker than on issued stamp.

240-E1 50c Die on India, on card, slate blue　*1,500.*

240-E2

Incomplete engraving of entire design: missing dots on donkey's flank and long lines on wrist of bowing man, no etching on two riders or their mounts.

240-E2 50c Die on India, on card, slate blue　*1,500.*

240-E3

Incomplete engraving of entire design: additional engraving on donkey's hindquarters and face of figure to left of Columbus.

240-E3 50c Die on India, on card, slate blue　*1,500.*

241-E1

Ferrotype metal plate with engraved outline design (reversed) of vignette as used on $1, engraved lines filled with red ink.

241-E1 $1 Metal plate, 45x29mm　　　*1,000.*

241-E2

Printing from ferrotype plate No. 241-E1.

241-E2 $1 Die on stiff white card with rounded
　　　　corners, 55½x43mm, red　　　*1,000.*

241-E3

Vignette size: 31x15mm
Die size: 72x59mm
Incomplete engraving of vignette only as adopted (very early state of die): very little shading on Isabella, floor, walls, etc.

241-E3 $1 Die on India, die sunk on card,
　　　　black brown　　　　　　　　　　*2,000.*

241-E4

Incomplete engraving of entire design as adopted: shadow on table cloth, woman in front of table, crosslet shadows at lower corners all unfinished.

241-E4 $1 Die on India, on card, black brown　*2,000.*

241-E5

Later state of complete design: horiz. lines in rectangle above Isabella missing.

241-E5 $1 Die on India, die sunk on 86x69mm
　　　　card, black brown　　　　　　*2,000.*

242-E1

Design size: 33½x22mm
Die size: 75x62mm
Incomplete engraving of entire design as adopted: about 12 horiz. lines missing on back of cape of tall man at right, some

vert. dashes missing on corselet of soldier at right, incomplete foliage over "C" of "COLUMBUS," etc.

242-E1 $2 Die on India, die sunk on card
      dull yellow orange   2,000.
      olive brown   2,000.

243-E1

Ferrotype metal plate with engraved outline design (reversed) of vignette as used on $3, engraved lines filled with red wax.

243-E1 $3 Metal plate, 45x29mm   1,250.

243-E2

Printing from ferrotype plate No. 243-E1.

243-E2 $3 Die on stiff white card with rounded
      corners, 55x43mm, red   1,250.

243-E3

Design size: 33½x22mm
Incomplete engraving of entire design as adopted: unshaded crossets in lower corners, shading lines on crossets and frame above title label too light. Pencil marks correct these.

243-E3 $3 Die on India, die sunk on card, dark
      yellow green   1,500.

243-E4

Incomplete engraving of entire design as adopted, before etching of shadows on Columbus, Ferdinand, backs of chairs, etc.

243-E4 $3 Die on India, on card, dark red   2,000.

Ferrotype metal plate with engraved outline design (reversed) of Queen Isabella vignette as used on $4, engraved lines filled with red wax.

244-E1 $4 Metal plate, 33x44mm   1,500.

244-E2

Printing from ferrotype plate No. 244-E1.

244-E2 $4 Die on stiff white card with rounded
      corners, 43x55mm, red   1,500.

244-E3

Vignette diameter: 14mm
Incomplete engraving of Isabella head with background of uniform ruled horiz. lines only, blank circle for Columbus vignette at right adjoining.

244-E3 $4 Die on India, on card, black   3,000.

Similar to No. 244-E3 but background has diagonal shading also.

244-E4 $4 Die on India, on card, black   3,000.

244-E5

Design size: about 34x21½mm
Die size: 74½x61½mm
Incomplete engraving of vignettes and lettering only: no diagonal shading lines in background of Columbus vignette.

244-E5 $4 Die on India, die sunk on card
      black   3,500.
      dark red   4,000.

244-E6

Design size: 34x22mm
Same engraving as No. 244-E5 but with wash drawing of frame design as adopted.

244-E6 $4 Die on thick artist's card with bev-
      eled edges, 50x39mm, gray black   3,000.

244-E7

Incomplete engraving of entire design as adopted: shadow at top of vert. bar and lines on leaves at bottom between vignettes

unfinished; no circular line bordering vignette at Isabella's right shoulder.

244-E7 $4 Die on India, on card, black brown 2,000.

244-E8

More complete engraving than No. 244-E7 but still missing circular line at Isabella's shoulder; only light shading on Columbus' collar.

244-E8 $4 Die on India, on card
      black brown   2,000.
      dark red   —

245-E1

Design size: 34½x22½mm
Incomplete engraved vignette as adopted for 1c: missing sky, etc., with pencil drawing of part of frame design.

245-E1 $5 Die on 50x38mm artist's cardboard,
      on thicker card, 55x43mm, black   4,000.

Design size: 34x22½mm
Die size: 74½x61½mm
Incomplete engraving of vignette, lettering and frame as adopted (side panels blank): shading unfinished on Columbus' neck, hair and background, and with white and black wash touches.

245-E2 $5 Die on India, die sunk on card,
      black   3,000.

245-E3

Similar to No. 245-E2 but further engraved: shading lines on neck, diagonal lines in background, etc.

245-E3 $5 Die on India, on card, 49x38mm,
      black   3,000.

Model with photos of female figures mounted each side of vignette, pencil "Design approved subject to inspection of engraved proof, color to be black. A.D.H. Dec. 6 '92" (A.D. Hazen, 3rd asst. PMG).

245-E4 $5 Die on thick white card, on
      117x116mm card, black   3,000.

245-E5

Engraving of No. 245-E3 with retouched photos of side subjects mounted in place.

245-E5 $5 Die on white artist's cardboard,
      56½x46mm, die sunk on card,
      black   2,000.

Design size: 33½x22mm
Incomplete engraving of entire design: one line under "POSTAGE FIVE DOLLARS", no lines outside and no diagonal lines in sky to upper right and upper left of vignette, etc.

245-E6 $5 Die on India, on card, black   2,000.

245-E7

Similar to No. 245-E2 but with pencil marks to show engraver where to place diagonal shading lines behind head and in front of bust.

245-E7 $5 Die on 65x55mm India, card mount-
             ed, black   3,000.

245-E8

Similar to No. 245-E6 but with pencil marks and white ink suggestions for further engraving.

245-E8 $5 Die on India, die sunk on 83x68mm
             card, black   2,000.

245-E9

Similar to No. 245-E6 but further engraved: with diagonal shading above side figures, below numerals and around vignette circle, but still incomplete in arched band above vignette.

245-E9 $5 Die on India, die sunk on
             110x83mm card, black   2,000.

245-E10

Similar to No. 245-E9 but further engraved: with shading lines in arched band above vignette but no shading on pole of liberty cap, object below shield has dotted shading only, spear tip shading incomplete.

245-E10 $5 Die on India, die sunk on
             85x70mm card, black   2,000.

1894 ISSUE
Bureau of Engraving and Printing

The 1c-15c designs of the 1890 issue engraved by the American Bank Note Co. were worked over by the BEP, including the addition of triangles in the upper corners. The 1890 30c was changed to a 50c and the 90c to a $1. Some 1894 essays have American Bank Note Co. imprints below the design.

247-E1

Design size: 18½x22mm
Die size: 61x62mm
Large die engraving of 1890 1c with pencil drawing of UL triangle 3½mm high with straight side next to curved upper label, freehand horiz. ink line at UR.

247-E1   1c Die on India, die sunk on card,
             black   1,500.

247-E2

Experimental laydown die with 1890 1c proof 4mm to left of similar design with 15-line high type I triangle in UR corner. Same laydown die also contains two 2c designs 18mm below, 5½mm apart, either uninked or lightly inked in color of 1c (sometimes found separated from 1c designs). No. 247-E2b nearly always found cracked horiz. through designs.

247-E2   1c
    a. Die on semiglazed white wove with pencil
        notations
        blue   1,450.
        ultramarine   1,450.
    b. Die on white card with pencil notations re
        color
        "1-1 Antwerp, 4 Ultra."   1,250.
        "2--little lighter--"   1,250.
        "1 Antwerp blue, 1 Ultra." (not cracked)   1,500.
        "4 Cobalt and Indigo"   1,250.
        "No 5"   1,250.
        "No. 6--Antwerp blue"   1,250.
        "No. 6--with little Antwerp blue"   1,250.

Die impression of 1890 1c with 15-line high type I triangle in UR corner.

247-E3   1c Die on India, 50x52mm, dusky
             green   1,500.

Experimental die impression of single 1890 1c with 2c 18mm below, triangles added in ink to upper corners of both designs, ms. "Approved" notations. Also known in dull violet without added triangles.

247-E4   1c +2c, Die on India, mounted on
             57x102mm card, mounted on an-
             other card, 144x195mm, green   1,600.

247-E5   247-E6

Large die engraving of 1890 1c with 18-line high triangle in UL corner (inner lines very thick).

247-E5   1c Die on India, die sunk on card,
             dusky blue green   1,000.

Similar to No. 247-E5 but inner line of triangle almost as thin as outer line.

247-E6   1c Die on India, die sunk on card,
             dusky blue green   1,000.

247-E7

Similar to No. 247-E6 but inner line of triangle same thickness as adopted.

247-E7   1c Die on India, die sunk on card,
             dusky blue green   1,000.

Incomplete engraving of entire design as adopted including triangles: coat collar, scroll under "U," horiz. lines on frame, oval line of vignette, etc., all unfinished; vignette background not re-etched.

247-E8   1c Die on India, die sunk on card
             ultramarine   1,000.
             blue ("Cobalt 2--Indigo 4")   1,000.

Design size: 18½x22mm
Die size: 61x62½mm
Large die engraving of 1890 2c with pencil drawing of UL triangle 2½mm high.

250-E1   2c Die on India, die sunk on card,
             black   1,500.

Die width: 92mm
Experimental laydown die with 1890 2c proof 5½mm to left of similar design with 14-line high type I triangles in upper corners

(found cut apart from No. 247-E2 and used for trial colors as noted thereon in pencil).

250-E2   2c Die on white card
             "1 R&D Lake, 1½P. white"   1,500.
             "M3 1 white, 7 Gem Lake, ¼ Car. Lake"   1,500.
             "2 White, 4 Ger. Lake No. 1, ½ R&D
                Lake"   1,500.
             "Opal Red"   1,500.
             "Opal Orange"   1,500.
             "Opal Maroon"   1,500.

250-E3

Die size: 61½x62½mm
American Banknote Co. die No. C-224 annealed, with 18-line high type I triangles engraved in upper corners, ms "No. 1" at lower left of card backing.

250-E3   2c Die on India, die sunk on card
             medium deep red   1,000.
             deep red   1,000.
             dusky red   1,000.
             dim red   1,000.
             medium deep orange-red   1,000.
             deep o-orange-red   1,000.
             dusky g-blue-green   1,000.
             dark medium violet-red-red   1,000.

Incomplete engraving of entire design: shadows on frame not etched; lines on foliage, front collar and oval line at vignette bottom not recut; dots instead of lines over corner of eye; only one line on truncated scroll at left of right 2 and no line on similar scroll at right of left 2; shadows of TWO CENTS not etched.

250-E4   2c Die on India, die sunk on card
             bright red   1,000.
             light red   1,000.
             dark red   1,000.
             deep orange red   1,000.

Similar to No. 250-E4 but line added to scroll at right of left 2, ms. "A.B.N.Co. Die worked over and ornaments put in" at top, ms. "No. 1" at lower left.

250-E5   2c medium deep red   750.

Incomplete engraving of entire design: two lines on truncated scroll at left of right 2 (one later removed), scroll at left of right 2 unfinished, profile of nose and forehead darker than on issued stamp, shadows of "TWO CENTS" not etched, short dashes on inside of outer edge of white oval at lower right, veins on scrolls around 2s not recut. Pencil notations incl. "Old A.B.N.Co. annealed & triangles engraved and rehardened to take up roll for plate."

250-E6   2c Die on India, die sunk on card, me-
             dium deep red   1,250.

Incomplete engraving of entire design: bottom of ear still angular and not yet rounded, dots on lobe not yet gathered into two lines, dot shading under corner of eye not yet gathered into four lines, shadows of "TWO CENTS" have been etched.

250-E7   2c Die on India, die sunk on card, me-
             dium deep red   1,000.

Die size: 57x76mm
Incomplete engraving of entire design with type II triangles: top of head not silhouetted. Pencil notation "2/ Transfer from roll taken from No. 1 so as to change portrait and make cameo effect. Unfinished."

251-E1   2c Die on India, die sunk on card, dark
             violet red   1,000.

Similar to No. 251-E1 but hair in front of ear unfinished, forehead and hair lightened.

251-E2   2c Die on India, die sunk on card,
             dusky gray   1,000.

Die size: 57x81mm
Incomplete engraving of entire design with type III triangles: top of head not silhouetted, unfinished shadow over eye, etc.

252-E1   2c Die on India, die sunk on card, me-
             dium deep red   1,000.

Incomplete engraving of entire design with type III triangles: unfinished shadow over eye, etc.

252-E2   2c Die on India, die sunk on card
             dusky blue green   1,000.
             dark violet red   1,000.

252-E3

Design size: 19x22mm
Die size: 56x80½mm
Discarded die, vignette overengraved: too much shading on front hair, cheek, nose, below eye; background too dark; hair in front of ear very prominent.

252-E3   2c Die on India, die sunk on card
     light carmine   1,000.
     green   1,000.

253-E1

Die size: 60x63mm
Complete engraved design as adopted but with type II triangles.

253-E1   3c
   a. Die on India, die sunk on card
      dusky blue green   1,000.
      dark red violet   1,000.
      dusky red violet   1,000.
   b. Die printed directly on card, die sunk on
      card, violet   1,000.

254-E1

Design size: about 19x22mm
Die size: 61x63mm
Incomplete engraving of entire design: line under collar wings missing, oval line around vignette not recut; hair, beard, forehead, neck, collar, shirt, etc., all incomplete.

254-E1   4c Die on India, die sunk on card, dark
     yellow brown   1,000.

Entire design engraved further than No. 254-E1 but still incomplete: shadows in lettering, etc., not etched, faint lines under collar incomplete, oval around vignette not recut.

254-E2   4c Die on India, die sunk on card, dark
     yellow brown   1,000.

Entire design engraved further than No. 254-E2 but still incomplete: beard, collar and necktie, etc., unfinished. Some veins recut on foliage under oval label.

254-E3   4c Die on India, die sunk on card, dark
     brown   1,000.

255-E1

Design size: 19x22mm
Engraved frame of American Bank Note Co. die No. C-227 with triangles, vignette cut out, mounted over engraved vignette of Washington.

255-E1   5c Die on 41x53mm India, on white
     wove, 48x75mm, black   2,000.

Washington vignette only as on No. 255-E1.

255-E2   5c Die on India, green   1,500.

255-E3   255-E4

Design size: 19x22mm
Engraved frame as adopted with William H. Seward photo mounted on it.

255-E3   5c Die on India, cut close, mounted on
     74x84mm white card, black   2,000.

Design size: about 19x22mm
Die size: 62½x75mm
Incomplete engraving of entire design as adopted: no oval border line around vignette.

255-E4   5c Die on India, die sunk on card, or-
     ange brown   1,000.

256-E1

Design size: about 19x22mm
Die size: 62x61½mm
Incomplete engraving of entire design as adopted: white spot on eye and shadows not darkened, diagonal lines missing on beard under mouth, lines on coat unfinished.

256-E1   6c Die on India, die sunk on card, dark
     red   1,000.

Entire design engraved further than No. 256-E1 but still incomplete: diagonal lines on beard under mouth incomplete, lines on coat not as dark as on issued stamp.

256-E2   6c Die on India, die sunk on card, dim
     dusky red   1,000.

257-E1

Design size: about 19x22mm
Die size: 58½x60mm
Incomplete engraving of entire design as adopted: lines on coat not recut darker, vignette background not etched darker.

257-E1   8c Die on India, die sunk on card,
     dusky red violet   1,000.

258-E1

Design size: about 19x22mm
Die size: 61½x61½mm
Incomplete engraving of entire design as adopted: shading unfinished on cheek, in ear, etc.

258-E1   10c Die on India, die sunk on card, dark
     brown   1,000.

Entire design engraved further than No. 258-E1 but still incomplete: unfinished shading on cheek under eye.

258-E2   10c Die on India, die sunk on card, red
     brown   1,000.

261-E1

Design size: 19x22mm
Die size: 50x101mm
Large die engraving of 1890 90c with value label and figure circles blank, no triangles.

261-E1 $1 Die on India, die sunk on card,
     black   2,000.

Similar to No. 261-E1 but head further re-engraved and background shadows etched deeper.

261-E2 $1 Die on India, die sunk on card, blue
     green   2,000.

261-E3   261-E4

Design size: 19x22mm
Model of engraved Perry vignette mounted on 1890 engraved frame with penciled in triangles, values painted in white and black. Ms. "O.K. July 14/94 TFM" below.

261-E3 $1 Die on India, cut close, mounted on
     63x101mm white card, green
     vignette, black frame   3,000

Similar to No. 261-E3 but with value lettering and circles added, background of circles unfinished, no triangles.

261-E4 $1 Die on India, die sunk on card, dark
     indigo blue   2,500.

Incomplete engraving of entire design: hair on top and back of head, whiskers and back of neck, and shading in value circles all unfinished. Triangles are engraved.

261-E5 $1 Die on India, die sunk on card,
     black   1,500.

Similar to No. 261-E5 but hair at back of head and whiskers darker, face in front of whiskers darker as on issued stamp. Circular lines extend into colorless vignette oval.

261-E6 $1 Die on India, die sunk on card
     black   1,500.
     blue green   2,000.

261-E7

Design size: 19x21½mm
Die size: 49x100mm
Incomplete engraving of unadopted dollar value design with portrait of Sen. James B. Beck: value label and numerals blank.

261-E7 $1 Die on India, die sunk on card,
     black   1,500.

262-E1   262-E2

Design size: 19x22mm
Die size: 50x101mm
Incomplete engraving of frame only nearly as adopted: smaller $2's.

262-E1 $2 Die on India, die sunk on card, blue
     green   2,500.

Design size: 19x22mm
Die size: 51x112mm

Incomplete engraving of entire design: left value circle blank, right circle engraved $2 outline only.

262-E2 $2 Die on India, die sunk on card,
          black   2,500.

Die size: 51x112mm
Incomplete engraving of entire design: vignette shading unfinished, no veins in leaves around value circles.

262-E3 $2 Die on India, die sunk on card,
          black   2,500.

262-E4

Incomplete engraving of entire design: inside of right border line above $2 unfinished.

262-E4 $2 Die on India, die sunk on card,
          black   2,500.

Similar to No. 262-E4 but border line complete.

262-E5 $2 Die on India, die sunk on card,
          black   2,500.

263-E1

Die size: 50x112½mm
Incomplete engraving of entire design: only one line in each scroll at right and left of $5, inner line of right border above $5 unfinished, etc., veins on leaves around right value circle unfinished.

263-E1 $5 Die on India, die sunk on card,
          black   2,500.

Similar to No. 263-E1 but horiz. lines cut into oval line at top and inner oval line above L and R of DOLLARS required retouching as indicated by pencil instructions. Two lines in scrolls around value circles as adopted.

263-E2 $5 Die on India, die sunk on card,
          black   2,500.

The bicolored essays commonly offered as No. 285-293 bicolored proofs can be found under the following listings: Nos. 285-E8, 286-E8, 287-E9, 288-E5, 289-E4, 290-E4, 291-E8, 292-E6, 293-E7. Values are for full-size cards (approximately 8x6 inches).

TRANS-MISSISSIPPI ISSUE

Die size: 79x68mm
Incomplete engraving of vignette only: initial state of die, no lines in sky or water.

285-E1   1c Die on India, die sunk on card,
          black   2,000.

Vignette further engraved: lines in sky and water.

285-E2   1c Die on India, die sunk on card,
          black   2,000.

Vignette further engraved: more background lines added.

285-E3   1c Die on India, die sunk on card,
          black   2,000.

285-E4

Vignette further engraved: Indian at right darker, robe shadow etched.

285-E4   1c Die on India, die sunk on card,
          black   2,000.

Vignette further engraved: rock in water more complete.

285-E5   1c Die on India, die sunk on card,
          black   2,000.

Design size: 34x22mm
Die size: 73x62mm

Incomplete bicolor engraving of entire design: no second inner line in numerals.

285-E6   1c Die on India, die sunk on card, or-
          ange red & black   2,500.

Die size: 83x68mm
Incomplete engraving of entire design: vignette unfinished and unetched, frame has second inner line in numerals.

285-E7   1c Die on India, die sunk on card,
          black   3,500.

285-E8

Die size: 63x51mm
Complete bicolor engraving of entire design.

285-E8   1c Die with black vignette on India, die
          sunk on card
          dark yellow green ("normal" bicolor)   300.
          dusky green   2,000.
          dusky blue green   2,000.
          brown   2,000.

Incomplete engraving of entire design: corn husks and panels in ends of cartouche unfinished, lines under MAR-QUETTE and MISSISSIPPI not as thick as on completed die.

285-E9   1c Die on India, die sunk on card,
          dusky green   2,500.

Die size: 78x68mm
Incomplete engraving of Mississippi River Bridge vignette (originally intended for 2c but eventually used on $2): initial state of die, very lightly engraved.

286-E1   2c Die on India, die sunk on card,
          black   3,000.

Vignette further engraved but no lines on bridge beside two trolley cars.

286-E2   2c Die on India, die sunk on card,
          black   3,000.

286-E3

Vignette further engraved but foreground between bridge and boat and foretopdeck incomplete, horse truck visible (later removed).

286-E3   2c Die on India, die sunk on card,
          black   3,000.

Complete engraving of vignette only.

286-E4   2c Die on India, die sunk on card,
          black   3,000.

286-E5

Design size: 137x88½mm
Pencil sketch by R. Ostrander Smith of 2c frame design as adopted except titled "ST. LOUIS BRIDGE."

286-E5   2c Sketch on tracing paper,
          120x178mm   1,500.

286-E6

Complete pencil drawing by R.O. Smith of frame design ("P" of "POSTAGE" in ink), titled "ST. LOUIS BRIDGE."

286-E6   2c Drawing on Whatman drawing
          board, 1889 wmk., 237x184mm   1,500.

286-E7

Pencil drawing by R.O. Smith, no title.

286-E7   2c Drawing on 72x61mm tracing paper   1,500.

286-E8

Die size: 63x51mm
Complete bicolor engraving of 2c design but with Mississippi River Bridge vignette as used on $2.

Ridgway numbers used for colors of No. 286-E8.

286-E8   2c Die with black vignette on India, die
          sunk on card
          dark red ("normal" bicolor)   300.
          3k/0 dark orange red   2,000.
          5k/0 dark o-orange-red   2,000.
          5m/1 dim dusky o-orange-red   2,000.
          7i/0 deep red orange   2,000.
          7m/0 dusky red orange   2,000.
          9m/0 dusky o-red-orange   2,000.
          9k/2 dull dark o-red-orange   2,000.
          13m/3 dismal dusky o-yellow-orange   2,000.
          35m/1 dim dusky green   2,000.
          49m/1 dim v. dusky blue   2,000.
          63m/1 dim dusky red violet   2,000.
          71-/0 deep violet-red-red   2,000.

286-E10

Die size: 82x68mm
Complete engraving with "FARMING IN THE WEST" vignette as adopted but from a die not used for the stamp: horses at left vignette border engraved dark up to border line which is solid complete line at both left and right.

286-E10   2c Die on India, die sunk on card
          (marked "Proof from 1st die.")
          black   2,500.
          dark orange red   2,500.

Design size: 34x22mm
Die No. 259 size: 63x51mm
Initial state of die, very lightly engraved.

287-E1   4c Die on India, die sunk on card,
          black   2,000.

Vignette further engraved: sky lines ruled in.

287-E2   4c Die on India, die sunk on card,
            black   2,000.

287-E3

Vignette further engraved: more lines added, no right forefoot on bison.

287-E3   4c Die on India, die sunk on card,
            black   2,000.

Shadow under bison incomplete.

287-E4   4c Die on India, die sunk on card,
            black   2,000.

Shadow under bison and foreground penciled in.

287-E5   4c Die on India, die sunk on card,
            black   3,000.

Vignette further engraved: right forefoot added, shadow under bison engraved but not etched.

287-E6   4c Die on India, die sunk on card,
            black   2,000.

287-E7

Die size: 83x67mm
Incomplete engraving of entire design: no lines in sky, frame shadow etching unfinished.

287-E7   4c Die on India, die sunk on card
            black   3,500.
            deep orange   3,500.

287-E8

Die size: 63x51mm
Incomplete engraving of entire design: corn husks at lower sides of frame unfinished.

Ridgway numbers used for colors of No. 287-E8.

287-E8   4c Die with black vignette on India, die
            sunk on card
            5k/0 dark o-orange-red   2,000.
            5m/0 dusky o-orange-red   2,000.
            7m/0 dusky red orange   2,000.
            11o/2 dull v. dusky orange   2,000.
            13m/3 dismal dusky o-yellow-orange   2,000.
            35m/1 dim dusky green   2,000.
            39m/1 dim dusky blue green   2,000.
            49o/1 dim v. dusky blue   2,000.
            61k/1 dim dark violet-red violet   2,000.
            63m/1 dim dusky red violet   2,000.
            71m/0 dusky violet-red-red   2,000.

Complete bicolor engraving.

287-E9   4c Die with black vignette on India, die
            sunk on card
            red orange ("normal" bicolor)   300.
            deep red orange ("normal" bicolor)   300.

Die size: 77x69mm
Initial state of die, very lightly engraved.

288-E1   5c Die on India, die sunk on card,
            black   3,000.

Vignette further engraved: lower clouds at right darkened.

288-E2   5c Die on India, die sunk on card,
            black   3,000.

Vignette further engraved: shading penciled in on figures at right, etc.

288-E3   5c Die on India, die sunk on card,
            black   3,000.

288-E4

Vignette further engraved but dots in sky at left of flag unfinished.

288-E4   5c Die on India, die sunk on card,
            black   3,000.

288-E5

Design size: 34x22mm
Die size: 63x51mm
Incomplete bicolor engraving of entire design: unfinished crosshatching at left of "FREMONT," lines against bottom label and frame unfinished, no etching on flag.

Ridgway numbers used for colors of No. 288-E5.

288-E5   5c Die with black vignette on India, die
            sunk on card
            49m/1 dim dusky blue ("normal" bicol-
            or)   300.
            49k/1 dim dark blue ("normal" bicolor) 300.
            3k/0 dark orange red   2,000.
            3m/0 dusky orange red   2,000.
            7m/0 dusky red orange   2,000.
            7m/1 dim dusky red orange   2,000.
            9m/0 dusky o-red-orange   2,000.
            11o/2 dull v. dusky orange   2,000.
            37m/1 dim dusky g-blue-green   2,000.
            39m/1 dim dusky blue green   2,000.
            49o/1 dim v. dusky blue   2,000.
            63m/1 dim dusky red violet   2,000.
            71n/0 medium deep violet-red-red   2,000.
            35m/1 dim dusky green   2,000.

Die size: 82x68½mm
Incomplete engraving of entire design: cornhusks, panels at ends of cartouche, mountains, foreground at sides of title label, sky, etc., all unfinished, figures and mountains not etched dark.

288-E7   5c Die on India, die sunk on card,
            black   2,750.

Incomplete engraving of vignette: no dots on mountain tops next to right border, unfinished crosshatching at left end of title label.

288-E8   5c Die on India, die sunk on card,
            black   2,750.

289-E1

Engraved vignette only of mounted Indian, not used for any value.

289-E1   8c Die on India, on card, black   4,000.

Incomplete engraving of vignette only as adopted: blank area for label wider than completed bicolor vignette, knee of kneeling soldier unfinished, etc.

289-E2   8c Die on India, die sunk on card,
            black   3,000.

289-E3

Design size: about 33½x21½mm
Incomplete engraving of frame only: shading of sunken center of cartouche at right of vignette unfinished.

289-E3   8c Die on India, 26x37mm, black   3,000.

289-E4

Incomplete engraving of entire design: top row of distant shrubbery under "ERICA" missing, crosshatching on distant mountains at left, blades of grass at left end of label, some dots against top label all unfinished.

Ridgway numbers used for colors of No. 289-E4.

289-E4   8c Die with black vignette on India, die
            sunk on card
            dark red ("normal" bicolor)   375.
            dusky red ("normal" bicolor)   375.
            3m/0 dusky orange red   2,750.
            5m/0 dusky o-orange-red   2,750.
            7i/0 deep red orange   2,750.
            7m/0 dusky red orange   2,750.
            9m/0 dusky o-red-orange   2,750.
            11o/2 dull v. dusky orange   2,750.
            35m/1 dim dusky green   2,750.
            39m/1 dim dusky blue-green   2,750.
            49o/1 dim v. dusky blue   2,750.
            63m/1 dim dusky red violet   2,750.
            71-/0 deep violet-red-red   2,750.

Die size: 77x64mm
Incomplete engraving of vignette only: two rows of dots in sky over wagon.

290-E1   10c Die on India, die sunk on card,
            black   2,000.

290-E2

Vignette further engraved: three rows of dots in sky over wagon.

290-E2   10c Die on India, die sunk on card,
            black   2,000.

Vignette further engraved: front of wagon canvas crosshatched.

290-E3   10c Die on India, die sunk on card,
            black   2,000.

290-E4

Incomplete bicolor engraving of entire design: cornhusks unfinished, blades of grass to right of girl's feet and some to right of horse's feet are missing. Five lines of dots in sky over wagon.

Ridgway numbers used for colors of No. 290-E4.

290-E4   10c Die with black vignette on India, die
            sunk on card
            dull dusky violet blue ("normal" bicol-
            or)   350.
            dusky blue violet ("normal" bicolor) 350.
            1i/0 deep red   2,500.
            3k/0 dark orange red   2,500.
            5k/0 dark o-orange-red   2,500.
            5m/0 dusky o-orange-red   2,500.
            7i/0 deep red orange   2,500.
            9m/0 dusky o-red-orange   2,500.
            11o/2 dull v. dusky orange   2,500.
            35m/1 dim dusky green   2,500.
            39m/1 dim dusky blue green   2,500.
            49o/1 dim v. dusky blue   2,500.
            55m/2 smoky dark v.-blue violet   2,500.
            63m/1 dim dusky red violet   2,500.
            71-/0 deep violet-red-red   2,500.

Incomplete engraving of entire design: cornhusks unfinished, vignette from No. 290-E4 trimmed by engraving to fit frame.

290-E6   10c Die on India, die sunk on card, dark
            red orange   3,000.

Incomplete engraving of entire design: cornhusks and panels at ends of cartouche and both sides and botton of vignette next to border unfinished.

290-E7   10c Die on India, die sunk on card, dull
            red violet   2,500.

Incomplete engraving of entire design: cornhusks and both sides and bottom of vignette next to border are unfinished, vert. lines on cartouche frame at right of vignette missing.

290-E8   10c Die on India, dull red violet   2,500.

Die size: 62x52mm

Incomplete engraving of vignette only: without sky or mountains.

291-E1   50c Die on India, die sunk on card,
          black   2,000.

Vignette further engraved: sky ruled in.

291-E2   50c Die on India, die sunk on card,
          black   2,000.

Vignette further engraved but no shading on distant mountains.

291-E3   50c Die on India, die sunk on card,
          black   2,000.

Vignette further engraved: light shading on distant mountains.

291-E4   50c Die on India, die sunk on card,
          black   2,000.

Vignette further engraved: more shading on distant mountains.

291-E5   50c Die on India, die sunk on card,
          black   3,000.

291-E6

Vignette further engraved: shadows on miner's hat darker (etched).

291-E6   50c Die on India, die sunk on card,
          black   2,000.

Vignette further engraved: girth under donkey darkened.

291-E7   50c Die on India, die sunk on card,
          black   3,000.

291-E8

Design size: 34x22mm
Die size: 89x71mm
Incomplete bicolor engraving of entire design: shading lines on scroll in LR corner of frame and shrubbery in UL corner of vignette unfinished, sky incomplete.

Ridgway numbers used for colors of No. 291-E8.

291-E8   50c Die with black vignette on India,
          die sunk on card
          **dull dusky b-blue-green ("normal") bi-
          color**; die size: 63x51mm)   300.
          **dull dusky g-blue-green ("normal") bi-
          color**; die size: 63x51mm)   300.
          1i/0 deep red   2,500.
          3k/0 dark orange red   2,500.
          5m/0 dusky o-orange-red   2,500.
          7m/0 dusky red orange   2,500.
          9i/0 deep o-yellow-orange   2,500.
          9m/0 dusky o-red-orange   2,500.
          11m/2 dull dusky orange   2,500.
          13m/3 dismal dusky o-yellow-orange   2,500.
          35m/1 dim dusky green   2,500.
          39m/1 dim dusky blue green   2,500.
          47n/2 dull v. dusky green-blue blue   2,500.
          49o/1 dim v. dusky blue   2,500.
          61k/1 dim dark violet-red-violet   2,500.
          71m/0 dusky violet-red-red   2,500.

Incomplete engraving of entire design: vignette against top frame unfinished.

291-E9   50c Die on India, die sunk on card
          black   3,000.
          deep red orange   3,000.

Incomplete engraving of entire design: engraving on bottom of miner's pan dots only, not lines as on issued stamp.

291-E10   50c Die on wove, sage green   2,500.

Incomplete engraving of vignette only: initial state of die, lightly engraved.

292-E1 $1 Die on India, die sunk on card,
          black   2,500.

292-E2

Vignette further engraved: light shield-shaped vignette out-line (later removed.)

292-E2 $1 Die on India, die sunk on card,
          black   2,500.

Vignette further engraved: left front hoof of lead bull darker.

292-E3 $1 Die on India, die sunk on card,
          black   2,500.

Vignette similar to No. 292-E3 but with penciled modeling in snow and among cattle.

292-E4 $1 Die on India, die sunk on card,
          black   2,500.

Vignette further engraved: foreground snow at left darkened, shield outline removed.

292-E5 $1 Die on India, die sunk on card,
          black   2,500.

292-E6

Incomplete engraving of entire bicolored design: right cornhusk and sky against top of frame unfinished, bull's right forefoot does not touch frame, foreground at right end of label unfinished.

Ridgway numbers used for colors of No. 292-E6.

292-E6 $1 Die with black vignette on India,
          die sunk on card
          dull violet blue ("normal" bicolor)   450.
          dull blue ("normal" bicolor)   450.
          dull violet ("normal" bicolor)   3,000.
          3k/0 dark orange red   3,000.
          5m/0 dusky-o-orange-red   3,000.
          7m/0 dusky red orange   3,000.
          9m/0 dusky o-red-orange   3,000.
          9n/3 dismal v. dusky o-red-orange   3,000.
          13n/3 dismal v. dusky o-yellow-orange   3,000.
          35m/1 dim dusky green   3,000.
          43m/1 dim dusky green blue   3,000.
          49m/1 dim dusky blue   3,000.
          57k/4 smoky dark violet-blue violet   3,000.
          63m/1 dim dusky red violet   3,000.
          71-/0 violet-red-red   3,000.
          47n/2 dull dusky green blue   3,000.

Incomplete engraving of entire design: left frameline, cornhusks and shading in frame over cornhusks all unfinished.

292-E7 $1 Die on India, die sunk on card,
          dusky red orange   3,000.

293-E1

Design size: 34x22mm
Die size: 73x63mm
Vignette of Western mining prospector as used on 50c, but labeled HARVESTING IN THE WEST, frame shows $ same size as numeral 2.

293-E1 $2 Die on India, on card, dusky violet
          & black   3,500.

Die size: 77x66mm
Incomplete engraving of Farming in the West vignette (origi-nally intended for $2 but eventually used on 2c): initial state of die, very lightly engraved.

293-E2 $2 Die on India, die sunk on card,
          black   2,500.

Vignette further engraved: four horses shaded.

293-E3 $2 Die on India, die sunk on card,
          black   2,500.

Vignette further engraved: shading added to background figures and horses, pencil shading above and below half horse at left.

293-E4 $2 Die on India, die sunk on card,
          black   2,500.

Vignette further engraved: foreground and shadows under horse teams darkened, no shading dots above half horse at left, etc.

293-E5 $2 Die on India, die sunk on card,
          black   2,500.

293-E6

Vignette further engraved but foreground in front of plow wheel still unfinished.

293-E6 $2 Die on India, die sunk on card,
          black   2,500.

293-E7

Die size: 62x51mm
Incomlete engraving of entire bicolor design: only one plow-share shown, label longer, less foreground than on issued stamp.

Ridgway numbers used for colors of No. 293-E7.

293-E7 $2 Die with black vignette on India,
          die sunk on card
          dusky orange red ("normal" bicolor;
          die size: 63x61mm)   450.
          dark red orange ("normal" bicolor;
          die size: 63x61mm)   450.
          1-/0 red   3,000.
          3k/0 dark orange red   3,000.
          7m/0 dusky red orange   3,000.
          35m/1 dim dusky green   3,000.
          39m/1 dim dusky blue green   3,000.
          45o/1 dim v. dusky blue-green blue   3,000.
          45m/2 dull dusky blue-green blue   3,000.
          63m/1 dim dusky red violet   3,000.
          71i/0 deep violet-red-red   3,000.
          47n/2 dull dusky green blue   3,000.

Incomplete engraving of entire design as adopted: black wash over engraving on side of bridge and foreground (engrav-ing under wash unfinished).

293-E9 $2 Die on India, die sunk on card,
          black   3,500.

Complete design, vignette further engraved: engraving com-pleted between title label and steamboat and city next to right frame, near side of bridge and smoke shadow on water lighter than on issued stamp.

293-E10 $2 Die on India, die sunk on card,
          black   3,500.

Incomplete engraving of entire design: circles in upper cor-ners of vignette next to value ovals, water next to right end of value label, panels at ends of cartouche all unfinished.

293-E11 $2 Die on India, die sunk on card,
          black   3,500.

Edward Rosewater

Rosewater, of St. Louis, was asked by the Post Office Dept. in 1897 to submit proposed designs for the Trans-Mississippi Exposition issue. For that reason, they are listed here.
All are drawings on tracing paper, on 91x142mm buff card.

285-E10

Design size: 62x97mm
Wash drawing of cattle.

285-E10   1c dull orange   —

286-E11

Design size: 57x98mm
Wash drawing of mounted Indian saluting wagon train.

286-E11   2c deep orange red   —

288-E9

Design size: 61x100mm
Wash drawing of man plowing field.

288-E9   5c dark yellow   —

290-E9

Design size: 62x99mm
Wash drawing of train coming around mountain.

290-E9   Ten Cents, dusky blue   —

292-E9

Design size: 60x98mm
Wash drawing of woman holding light, standing on globe.

292-E9 $1 deep orange yellow   —

PAN-AMERICAN ISSUE
Bureau of Engraving and Printing

294-E1

Design size: 108x82mm
Preliminary pencil drawing for frame design as adopted.

294-E1   1c Drawing on tracing paper, black   *750.*

294-E2

Design size: 114x82½mm
Final ink drawing for frame design as adopted.

294-E2   1c Drawing on white card, about
           6½x5 inches, black   *750.*

294-E3

Die size: 87x68½mm
Incomplete engraving of vignette only.

294-E3   1c Die on India, die sunk on card,
             black   1,500.

295-E1

Design size: 108x82mm
Preliminary pencil drawing of frame similar to that adopted
(side ornaments, etc., different); UR corner, etc., unfinished.

295-E1   2c Drawing on tracing paper, black   750.

295-E2

Design size: 114x83mm
Preliminary pencil drawing of frame similar to No. 295-E1
(minor differences) but with UR corner complete.

295-E2   2c Drawing on tracing paper, black   750.

295-E3

Design size: 108x82mm
Preliminary pencil drawing of frame design similar to No.
295-E2 but with minor differences at top, in lettering, etc.

295-E3   2c Drawing on tracing paper, black   750.

295-E4

Design size: 95x70mm
Ink and wash drawing model of frame design as adopted,
side torchbearers engraved on India as on U.S. Series of 1901
$10 note.

295-E4   2c Die on white card, about
             108x82mm, black   750.

295-E4A

Design size: 88x69mm
Incomplete engraving of vignette only.

295-E4A   2c Die on India, die sunk on card,
             black   1,750.

295-E5   295-E6

Design size: 27x19½mm
Die size: 88x68mm
Complete engraving of frame only as adopted.

295-E5   2c Die on India, die sunk on card,
             carmine   2,500.

Die size: 88½x69mm
Engraving of entire design with vignette incomplete near
frame and on cars.

295-E6   2c Die on India, die sunk on card,
             carmine & black   1,750.

296-E1

Preliminary pencil drawing of unadopted frame design.

296-E1   4c Drawing on tracing paper, black   750.

296-E2

Design size: 114x82½mm
Final ink drawing for frame design as adopted.

296-E2   4c Die on white card, about
             6½x5 inches, black   750.

296-E3

Design size: 27x19mm
Die size: 88x67mm
Incomplete engraving of entire design as adopted: lines
missing at base of capitol dome, above driver's head.

296-E3   4c Die on India, die sunk on card,
             deep red brown & black   1,750.

297-E1

Photo reproduction of pencil sketch of unadopted frame
design on photosensitive tan paper, reduced to stamp size.
Incomplete preliminary pencil drawing of frame design as
adopted.

297-E1   5c Photo reproduction on tan paper   750.

297-E2

Design size: 114x83mm
Incomplete preliminary pencil drawing of frame design as
adopted.

297-E2   5c Drawing on tracing paper, black   750.

297-E3

Design size: 114x82½mm
Final ink drawing for frame design as adopted.

297-E3   5c Drawing on white card, about
             6½x5 inches, black   750.

297-E4

Photo reproduction of sketch of adopted frame design on photosensitive paper, reduced to stamp size.

297-E4 5c Photo reproduction on tan paper 750.

297-E5 297-E6

Die size: 87x68mm
Incomplete engraving of vignette only.

297-E5 5c Die on India, die sunk on card, black 1,500.

Die size: 87x68mm
As No. 297-E5, but more completely engraved.

297-E6 5c Die on India, die sunk on card, black 1,500.

297-E7

Design size: 27x19½mm
Die size: 87x68mm
Incomplete engraving of entire design as adopted: shading at bottom of battleaxes and scrolls at ends of title frame unfinished.

297-E7 5c Die on India, die sunk on card, blue & black 1,750.

298-E1

Design size:108x82mm
Preliminary pencil drawing of unadopted frame design.

298-E1 8c Drawing on tracing paper, black 750.

298-E2

Design size: 114x83mm
Incomplete preliminary pencil drawing of unadopted frame design.

298-E2 8c Drawing on tracing paper, black 750.

298-E3

Design size: 114x83mm
Preliminary pencil drawing of unadopted frame design.

298-E3 8c Drawing on tracing paper, black 750.

298-E4

Design size: 114x83mm
Preliminary pencil drawing of frame design as adopted.

298-E4 8c Drawing on tracing paper, black 750.

298-E5

Design size: 114x82½mm
Final ink drawing for frame design as adopted.

298-E5 8c Drawing on white card, about 6½x5 inches, black 750.

298-E6

Photo reproduction of sketch of adopted frame design on photosensitive paper, reduced to stamp size.

298-E6 8c Photo reproduction on tan paper 750.

298-E7

Design size: 27x20mm
Die size: 87x69mm
Incomplete engraving of entire design: shading lines of ornaments, scrolls and ribbons at top unfinished, vignette incomplete at right, no etching on building in left foreground.

298-E7 8c Die on India, die sunk on card, bi-colored 1,750.

299-E1

Design size: 114x83mm
Preliminary pencil drawing of unadopted frame design (small blank oval at center).

299-E1 10c Drawing on tracing paper, black 750.

299-E2

Design size: 114x82½mm
Similar to No. 299-E1 but with outline of eagle and shield in center oval.

299-E2 10c Drawing on tracing paper, black 750.

299-E3

Design size: 114x83mm
Preliminary pencil drawing for frame design as adopted.

299-E3 10c Drawing on tracing paper, black 750.

299-E4

Design size: 114x82½mm
Final ink drawing for frame design as adopted.

299-E4 10c Drawing on white card, about
           6½x9 inches, black   750.

299-E5

Photo reproduction of sketch of adopted frame design on
photosensitive paper, reduced to stamp size.

299-E5 10c Photo reproduction on tan paper   750.

299-E6

Die size: 87x68mm
Incomplete engraving of entire design: frame complete but
lines later engraved in the mast, smokestack and sky.

299-E6 10c Die on India, die sunk on card, bi-
           colored   1,750.

1902 ISSUE

300-E1   300-E2

Incomplete engraving of vignette and lower part of frame.

300-E1 1c Die on India, die sunk on card,
           black   2,000.

Design size: 19x22mm
Die size: 74½x88½mm
Incomplete engraving of entire design: vignette background
has horiz. lines only, neckpiece, men at sides, etc., all
unfinished.

300-E2 1c Die on India, die sunk on card,
           black   1,250.

300-E3

Design size: 136x190mm
Preliminary ink drawing for 5c frame design but later adopted
for 1c.

300-E3   1c Drawing on manila paper, black &
            blue green   1,000.

300-E4

Design size: 116x135mm
Preliminary pencil and ink drawing for frame design as
adopted.

300-E4   1c Drawing on white card, black   1,000.

301-E1

Design size: 164x181mm
Paper size: 169x214mm

Preliminary pencil drawing of frame design (Raymond
Ostrander Smith). Not adopted.

301-E1   2c Drawing on yellowed transparent
            tracing paper, black   1,000.

301-E1A

Design size: 145x168mm
Preliminary pencil drawing of frame design as adopted.

301-E1A 2c Drawing on tracing paper, black   900.

301-E2   301-E3

Model with vignette of Houdon bust of Washington, on wash
drawing over photo reduced to stamp size for approval by PMG.

301-E2   2c Model mounted on card, black   750.

Design size: 19x22mm
Die size: 75x87½mm
Incomplete engraving of entire design: head unfinished,
horiz. background lines only, frame unfinished, lettering either
blank or unfinished.

301-E3   2c Die on India, die sunk on card,
            black   1,250.

301-E4

Design size: 60x88mm
Preliminary pencil drawing of right numeral 2 design as
adopted.

301-E4   2c Drawing on tracing paper, black   900.

301-E5

Design size: 176x120mm
Preliminary pencil drawing of lower left and upper right design.

301-E5   2c Drawing on tracing paper, black   *900.*

Design size: 19x22mm
Die size: 74x89mm
Incomplete engraving of entire design: head unfinished, horiz. background lines only, frame almost finished, lettering complete. No. 62057 on back.

301-E6   2c Die on India, die sunk on
                153x202mm card, black   —

302-E1

303-E1

Design size: 19x22mm
Die size: 74½x88mm
Incomplete engraving of entire design: vignette unfinished, horiz. background lines only, atlantes at sides unfinished. No. 66218 on back.

302-E1   3c Die on India, die sunk on card,
                black   *1,750.*

Design size: 19x22mm
Die size: 75x88mm
Incomplete engraving of entire design: vignette unfinished on eyes, hair, beard, etc. No. 58920 on back.

303-E1   4c Die on India, die sunk on card,
                black   *1,750.*

304-E1

Design size: 19x22mm
Die size: 74x87½mm
Rejected die: figure at right poorly draped, blank triangles below "UNITED STATES," no shading in frame around "POST-AGE/FIVE CENTS" except at extreme ends.

304-E1   5c Die on India, die sunk on card,
                blue   *2,300.*

Incomplete engraving of entire design: shading on side figures unfinished.

304-E2   5c Die on India, die sunk on card,
                blue   *1,250.*

Incomplete engraving of entire design as adopted.

305-E1   6c Die on India, lake   *1,250.*

305-E2

Design size: 123x210mm
Preliminary ink drawing for unadopted frame design.

305-E2   6c Drawing on kraft paper, black &
                blue green   *800.*

306-E1

Design size: 7x3½ inches
Preliminary pencil drawing of left side of frame design as adopted.

306-E1   8c Drawing on tracing paper, black   *500.*

306-E2

Die size: 76x89mm
Incomplete engraving of vignette and numerals only: head drapery unfinished, horiz. background lines only.

306-E2   8c Die on India, die sunk on card,
                black   *2,000.*

306-E3

Design size: 165x175mm
Preliminary ink drawing for unadopted frame design.

306-E3   8c Drawing on kraft paper, black, blue
                & green   *800.*

307-E1

Design size: 135x174mm
Preliminary ink drawing for unadopted frame design.

307-E1   10c Drawing on kraft paper, black, blue
                & green   *800.*

308-E1

Design size: 19x22mm
Die size: 69x85½mm
Incomplete engraving of entire design: hair, beard, right cheek, eyes and right shoulder all unfinished, horiz. background lines only, name panel blank, ribbon shading unfinished, etc. No. 57796 on back.

308-E1   13c Die on India, die sunk on card,
                black   *1,250.*

308-E2

Design size: 177x220mm
Preliminary ink drawing of 3c frame design but later adopted for 13c.

308-E2 13c Drawing on kraft paper, black & blue green   900.

310-E1

Design size: 19x22mm
Die size: 74x87½mm
Incomplete engraving of entire design: hair and right cheek unfinished, horiz. background lines only, top of frame and eagles unfinished.

310-E1 50c Die on India, die sunk on card, black   2,000.

Incomplete engraving of entire design, further engraved than No. 310-E1: oval line outside top label thinner at bottom ends than on issued stamp.

310-E2 50c Die on India, die sunk on card, black   2,000.

312-E1   313-E1

Design size: 19x22mm
Die size: 76x88mm
Incomplete engraving of entire design: hair, neckpiece, etc., unfinished, horiz. background lines only; top of frame, leaves and numeral surrounds all unfinished.

312-E1 $2 Die on India, die sunk on card, black   2,000.

Design size: 19x22mm
Die size: 75½x87½mm
Incomplete engraving of entire design: eyes, cheeks, hair, neckpiece all unfinished, horiz. background lines only, frame engraved in outlines only.

313-E1 $5 Die on India, die sunk on card, dark green   1,750.

319-E1

Design size: 19½x22mm

Die size: 75x87½mm
Incomplete engraving of entire design from rejected die (central star between UNITED and STATES, four lines above small lettering, bottom of shield curved): name and date ribbon blank.

319-E1 2c Die on India, die sunk on card, carmine   2,000.

319-E2   319-E3

Incomplete engraving of entire design from rejected die: shading on leaves and vignette completed, lettering added to bottom ribbon and started on label above vignette. Blue pencil note on card backing, "May 1903. This die was abandoned at this stage because of crowded condition of lettering above portrait. G.F.C.S." No. 83909 on back.

319-E2 2c Die on India, die sunk on card, carmine   1,500.

Design size: 19½x22mm
Die I size: 75½x88mm
Incomplete engraving of entire design as adopted (no star between UNITED and STATES, bottom of shield straight): small label above vignette is blank.

319-E3 2c Die on India, die sunk on card, black   2,000.

LOUISIANA PURCHASE ISSUE

324-E1

Incomplete engraving of entire design: head, hair, eyes, chin, coat all unfinished, horiz. background lines only, bottom label and upper corner labels blank, frame shading unfinished.

324-E1 2c Die on India, die sunk on card, black   2,500.

325-E1

Incomplete engraving of entire design: head only lightly engraved, horiz. background lines only, laurel leaves unshaded, leaves' background and numeral shields blank.

325-E1 3c Die on India, die sunk on card, black   2,500.

326-E1

Incomplete engraving of entire design: vignette unfinished, horiz. background lines only, much of frame blank or incomplete.

326-E1 5c Die on India, die sunk on card, black blue   2,500.

JAMESTOWN ISSUE

328-E1

Incomplete engraving of entire design: vignette, shading on heads in upper corners, numerals and numeral shields all unfinished.

328-E1 1c Die on pale cream soft wove, 30x24mm, dusky green   1,250.

330-E1   330-E2

Incomplete engraving of vignette only: collar, hat, corselet, etc., unfinished. No. 245910 on back.

330-E1 5c Die on India, die sunk on card, black   1,750.

Incomplete engraving of entire design: no shading in frame background.

330-E2 5c Die on India, die sunk on card, blue   5,000.

330-E3

Incomplete engraving of entire design: shading on corselet and arm of Pocahontas unfinished, horiz. background lines only, shading around date and name ribbon unfinished. No. 247606 on back.

330-E3 5c Die on card, die sunk, blue   4,250.

Incomplete engraving of entire design: shading on ribbons unfinished.

330-E4 5c Die on India, die sunk on card, black   4,250.

1908 ISSUE

331-E1

Photograph of wash drawing of entire design, head and vignette background retouched with black wash. Ms. "GVLM-Sept. 26th-1908" (PMG) in LR corner of backing card.

331-E1 1c Retouched photo on thick gray cardboard, 83x100mm, black   1,500.

332-E1   332-E2

Design size: 6⅛x7¼ inches
Wash drawing of frame design with vignette cut out, mounted over retouched glossy black photo of Houdon bust of Washington.

332-E1 Two Cents, Design on drawing paper, black   1,250.

Design size: 19x22mm
Photograph of wash drawing of entire design, almost completely retouched with black ink and wash. Pencil "GVLM" (PMG) at top of backing card.

332-E2 Two Cents, Retouched photo on thick gray cardboard, 81x100mm, black   1,500.

332-E3

Design size: 19x22mm
Incomplete engraving of entire design: shading on leaves at right unfinished. Pencil "Oct 15 - 1908" at LR of backing card.

332-E3 Two Cents, Die on India, die sunk
     on card, carmine   *1,000.*

333-E1   333-E2

Design size: 18½x22mm
Engraving of design as adopted except "THREE CENTS" at bottom.

333-E1 Three Cents, Die printed directly
     on card, deep violet   *1,000.*

Design size: 19x22mm
Photograph of wash drawing of entire design with "3 CENTS 3" drawn in black and white wash. Ms. "Nov. 24/08. J.E.R." (BEP director) in LR corner of backing card.

333-E2 3c Retouched photo on thick gray
     cardboard, 80x100mm, black *1,500.*

334-E1   334-E2

Design size: 18½x22mm
Engraving of design as adopted except "FOUR CENTS" at bottom.

334-E1 Four Cents, Die printed directly on
     card, orange brown   *1,000.*

Design size: 19x22mm
Photograph of wash drawing of entire design with "4 CENTS 4" drawn in black and white wash. Ms. "Nov. 24/08. J.E.R." (BEP director) in LR corner of backing card.

334-E2 4c Retouched photo on thick gray
     cardboard, 80x100mm, black *1,500.*

335-E1   335-E2

Design size: 18½x22mm
Engraving of design as adopted except "FIVE CENTS" at bottom.

335-E1 Five Cents, Die printed directly on
     card, blue   *1,500.*

Design size: 19x22mm
Photograph of wash drawing of entire design with "5 CENTS 5" drawn in black and white wash. Ms. "Nov. 24/08. J.E.R." (BEP director) in LR corner of backing card.

335-E2 5c Retouched photo on thick gray
     cardboard, 80x100mm, black *1,500.*

Design size: 18½x22mm
Incomplete engraving of design with "SIX CENTS" at bottom.

336-E1 Six Cents, Die on India, on card,
     red orange   *1,000.*

336-E2

Design size: 19x22mm
Photograph of wash drawing of entire design with "6 CENTS 6" drawn in black and white wash. Ms. "Nov. 24/08. J.E.R." (BEP director) in LR corner of backing card.

336-E2 6c Retouched photo on thick gray
     cardboard, 80x100mm, black *1,500.*

337-E1   338-E1

Design size: 19x22mm
Photograph of wash drawing of entire design with "8 CENTS 8" drawn in black and white wash. Ms. "Nov. 24/08. J.E.R." (BEP director) in LR corner of backing card.

337-E1 8c Retouched photo on thick gray
     cardboard, 80x100mm, black *1,500.*

Design size: 19x22mm
Photograph of wash drawing of entire design with "10 CENTS 10" drawn in black and white wash. Ms. "Nov. 24/08. J.E.R." (BEP director) in LR corner of backing card.

338-E1 10c Retouched photo on thick gray
     cardboard, 80x100mm, black *1,500.*

338a-E1

Design size: 18½x22mm
Complete engraving of entire adopted design but a value not issued: "12 CENTS 12" at bottom. Virtually all are stamp size, imperf.

Ridgway numbers used for colors of No. 338a-E1.

338a-E1 12c
 a. Die on bluish white wove
   41n/1 dim v. dusky b-blue-green *900.*
 b. Die on 1f/1 dim pale red wove
 c. Die on 7d/1 dim light red orange wove
   47m/1 dim dusky g-b. blue   *900.*
 d. Die on 17b/1 dim bright o-y. yellow
   wove
   1i/0 deep red   *900.*
   5i/0 deep o-orange-red   *900.*
   27m/0 dusky green yellow *900.*
   37m/0 dusky g-blue-green *900.*
   41m/0 dusky b-blue-green *900.*
   55m/1 dim dusky blue violet *900.*
   59m/1 dim dusky violet   *900.*
   69m/3 dismal dusky r-violet-red *900.*
 e. Die on 19f/0 pale y-orange yellow wove
   1i/0 deep red   *900.*
   15i/1 dim deep yellow orange *900.*
   35m/0 dusky green   *900.*
   43d/1 dim light green blue *900.*
   61m/3 dismal dusky v-red-violet *900.*
   690/5 black   *900.*
 f. Die on 31f/2 dull pale yellow green
   wove
   69o/5 black   *900.*
 g. Die on 42d/1 dim bright green blue
   wove
   41m/1 dim dusky b-blue-green *900.*
 h. Die on 44-/1 dim medium green blue
   wove
   9k/2 dull dark o-r-orange *900.*
 i. Die on 45l/1 dim v. dark b-green-blue
   wove
   5i/0 deep o-orange-red   *900.*
   27m/2 dull dusky green yellow *900.*
 j. Die on 69g/0 pale r-v. red wove *900.*
 k. Die on dark blue bond, 69o/5 black *900.*

339-E1   340-E1

Design size: 19x22mm

Photograph of wash drawing of entire design with "13 CENTS 13" drawn in black and white wash. Ms. "Oct. 7-08. J.E.R.-GVLM" (BEP director, PMG) in LL corner of backing card.

339-E1 13c Retouched photo on thick gray
     cardboard, 80x100mm, black *1,500.*

Design size: 19x22mm
Photograph of wash drawing of entire design with "15 CENTS 15" drawn in black and white wash. Ms. "Oct. 7-08. J.E.R.-GVLM" (BEP director, PMG) at bottom of backing card.

340-E1 15c Retouched photo on thick gray
     cardboard, 80x100mm, black *1,500.*

341-E1   342-E1

Design size: 19x22mm
Photograph of wash drawing of entire design with "50 CENTS 50" drawn in black and white wash. Ms. "Oct. 7-08. J.E.R.-GVLM" (BEP director, PMG) at bottom of backing card.

341-E1 50c Retouched photo on thick gray
     cardboard, 80x100mm, black *1,500.*

Design size: 19x22mm
Photograph of wash drawing of entire design with "1 DOLLAR 1" drawn in black and white wash. Ms. "Oct. 7-08. J.E.R.-GVLM" (BEP director, PMG) at bottom of backing card.

342-E1 $1 Retouched photo on thick gray
     cardboard, 80x100mm, black *1,500.*

LINCOLN MEMORIAL ISSUE

Design size: 7x8 inches
Photostat of 1980 2c frame design with wash drawing of ribbons and vignette photo of Lincoln's head.

367-E1 Two Cents, Model of Lincoln de-
     sign, black   *1,500.*

Photo of No. 367-E1 reduced to stamp size, retouched to highlight hair and beard.

367-E2 Two Cents, Retouched photo, black *1,500.*

367-E3

Design size: 19x22mm
Incomplete engraving of entire design: head, background, name/date ribbon all unfinished.

367-E3 Two Cents, Die on India, die sunk
     on card, carmine   *2,500.*

ALASKA-YUKON-PACIFIC EXPOSITION ISSUE

Design size: 18½x22mm
Wash drawing of frame similar to 1908 2c design with photo of wash drawing of seal on ice cake as vignette. Ms. "#1" at UL corner of backing card.

370-E1 2c Model on card, about 3x4 inches,
     black   *1,500.*

370-E2

Design size: 18½x22mm
Engraved frame similar to 1908 2c but with wash drawing of "1870 1909" in ribbons and "2 CENTS 2" at bottom, vignette cut out, mounted over engraved vignette of Wm. H. Seward from snuff stamp. Ms. "#2" at UL corner of backing card.

370-E2 2c Model on card, about 3x4 inches,
     black   *1,500.*

370-E3

Design size: 27½x20½mm
Photo of seal on ice cake vignette as originally approved, mounted on ink and wash drawing of frame design as approved. Ms. "#3" at UL corner of backing card, engraved Seward vignette pasted on at bottom, "Approved April 3, 1909 FH Hitchcock Postmaster-General" at right.

370-E3　2c Model on glazed card, 93x70mm,
　　　　　black, white and gray　　　　　2,250.

370-E4

Design size: 27½x20mm
Photo of wash drawing of frame and arched ribbon as adopted, vignette cut out, mounted over photo of engraved Seward vignette, background retouched with black wash. Ms. "Approved subject to addition of the name Seward, as indicated in letter of Director, Bureau of Engraving and Printing, dated April 24, 1909. F.H. Hitchcock Postmaster General."

370-E4　2c Model on 93x75mm thick gray card,
　　　　　black　　　　　　　　　　　2,250.

370-E5

Design size: 27x20mm
Retouched photo of wash drawing of adopted frame with seal on ice cake vignette but pencil "WILLIAM H. SEWARD" on white wash ribbon below. Ms. "April 26/09 Approved J.E.R." (BEP director) at LR corner of backing card.

370-E5　2c Retouched photo and pencil on
　　　　　94x66mm thick gray card, black　　2,000.

Incomplete engraving of entire design: no shading on head or vignette background.

370-E6　2c Die on India, die sunk on 8x6 inch
　　　　　card, carmine　　　　　　　　2,000.

370-E7

Design size: 26½x19½mm
Similar to No. 370-E6 but further engraved: face and collar lightly engraved, horiz. background lines only, no shading lines on ribbons.

370-E7　2c Die on wove, 32x26½mm, carmine　2,000.

372-E1

Wash drawing of adopted vignette design.

372-E1　2c Drawing on artist's cardboard,
　　　　　11¼x6¾ inches, black　　　　　1,500.

372-E2

Wash drawing of frame design as adopted except "HUDSON-FULTON CENTENARY" at top.

372-E2　2c Drawing on artist's cardboard,
　　　　　7¾x6¾ inches, black　　　　　1,500.

Design size: 33x21½mm
Wash drawing of frame design as adopted with dates "1609-1807" and photo of No. 372-E1 reduced to fit and worked over with wash.

372-E3　2c Model on card, 4x3 inches, black　2,000.

Design size: 33x21½mm
Wash drawing of frame with vignette cut out, mounted over photo of No. 372-E1. Typed/ms. "Approved August 17, 1909 F.H. Hitchcock Postmaster General" and "August 19, 1909 Amend by substituting word 'Celebration' for 'Centenary.' F.H. Hitchcock Postmaster General." Pencil "P.O. 488" in LR corner.

372-E4　2c Model on white card, 129x103mm,
　　　　　black　　　　　　　　　　　2,000.

372-E5

Incomplete engraving of entire design: lettering on flag at masthead of *Clermont* has "N" reversed and no "T."

372-E5　2c Die on wove, 38x27mm, carmine　2,000.

PANAMA-PACIFIC ISSUE

397-E1

Design size: 27x20mm
Incomplete engraving of frame with engraved circular vignette as adopted, with wash drawing of palm trees on each side and "1 CENT 1" in wash. Ms. "Approved July 16, 1912 Frank H. Hitchcock Postmaster General" on backing card.

397-E1　1c Model on card, about 89x77mm,
　　　　　black　　　　　　　　　　　1,500.

398-E1

Design size: about 29½x20mm
Ink and wash drawing of frame design longer than adopted with photo of wash drawing of Golden Gate as eventually used (reduced) on 5c. Backstamp "STAMP DIVISION FEB. 12, 1912 P.O. DEPT" on backing card.

398-E1　2c Model on card, about 4x3 inches,
　　　　　black　　　　　　　　　　　1,500.

398-E2

Design size: 27x20mm

Incomplete engraving of frame with photo of wash drawing of vignette as adopted with engraved title "GATUN LOCKS," wash drawing of value numerals. Ms. "Approved Aug. 27, 1912 Frank H. Hitchcock Postmaster General" on backing card.

398-E2　2c Model on gray card, about 3¾x2⅞
　　　　　inches, black　　　　　　　　1,500.

Completely engraved design as adopted except titled "GATUN LOCKS" in error (design pictures Pedro Miguel locks).

398-E3　2c
　　a. Large die on India, die sunk on card, 6x8
　　　　inches (formerly #398AP1), carmine　6,500.
　　b. Small die on India (formerly #398AP2),
　　　　carmine　　　　　　　　　　6,000.

398-E4

Design size: 27x20mm
Photo of incomplete engraving (no sky in vignette). Ms. "Approved Dec. 17, 1912 Frank Hitchcock Postmaster General" on backing card.

398-E4　2c Model on thick gray card, black　1,500.

399-E1

Design size: 27x20mm
Photo of wash drawing of frame design as adopted with photo of wash drawing of adopted vignette mounted in place. Ms. "Approved July 16, 1912 Frank H., Hitchcock Postmaster General" on backing card.

399-E1　5c Model on 30x22mm white paper,
　　　　　mounted on card, about 3⅞x2⅞
　　　　　inches, black　　　　　　　　1,500.

400-E1

Design size: 27x20mm
Photo of wash drawing of frame design as adopted with photo of painting adopted for vignette mounted in place. Ms. "Approved Aug. 22, 1912, Frank H. Hitchcock Postmaster General" on backing card.

400-E1　10c Model on 31x34mm white paper, on
　　　　　thick gray card, black　　　　　1,500.

Design size: 27x20mm
Photo of wash drawing of frame design as adopted with photo of wash drawing of two galleons at anchor in bay, titled "CABRILLO 1542" mounted in place. Backing card marked "II."

400-E2　10c Model on white paper, on 91x85mm
　　　　　thick gray card, black　　　　　1,500.

Design size: 27x20mm
Photo of wash drawing of frame design as adopted with photo of Liberty standing among palm fronds, two battleships in bay. Backing card marked "III."

400-E3　10c Model on white paper, on thick gray
　　　　　card, black　　　　　　　　　1,500.

400-E4

Design size: 27x20mm
Similar to No. 400-E3 but steamships replace battleships. Backing card marked "IV."

400-E4　10c Model on white paper, on thick gray
　　　　　card, black　　　　　　　　　1,500.

400-E5

Design size: 27x20mm
Similar to No. 400-E2 but two galleons under full sail at right in front of snowclad mountains. Backing card marked "V," paper with typed "Stamp Division Feb. 21, 1912. P.O. Dept." pasted on back.

400-E5   10c Model on white paper, on thick gray
card, black   1,500.

1912 ISSUE

Incomplete engraving of entire design: wash drawing of "1 CENT 1" at bottom. Ms. "Approved. July 17, 1911 Frank H. Hitchcock. P.M. Gen." on backing card.

405-E1   1c Model on 3½x3¾-inch card, black   —

Wash drawing of design as adopted, worked over partial photo with "2 CENTS 2" at bottom drawn in wash. Ms. "Approved. July 17, 1911 Frank H. Hitchcock P. M. Gen." on backing card.

406-E1   2c Model on 3½x3¾-inch card, black   —

Wash drawing of design as adopted, worked over partial photo with 8 in lower corners drawn in wash. Ms. "Approved. July 17, 1911 Frank H. Hitchcock Postmaster General" on backing card.

414-E1   8c Model on 3½x3¾-inch card, black   —

Vignette of head only without background gridwork.

414-E2   8c Die on India, die sunk on
157x208mm, olive green   —

416-E1

418-E1

Design size: 19x22mm
Photo of wash drawing of generic design with 10 in lower corners drawn in black ink. Ms. "July 17, 1911. (May, 1911 erased) Approved: Frank H. Hitchcock PM Gen" on backing card, backstamped "STAMP DIVISION P.O. DEPT. MAY 15, 1911."

416-E1   10c Model on 87x113mm thick gray
card, black   1,000.

Design size: 19x22mm
Photo of wash drawing of generic design with background of frame between oval and outer colorless line in dark gray wash and some colorless retouching, 15 in lower corners drawn in black ink. Ms. "July 17, 1911. (May, 1911 erased) Approved: Frank H. Hitchcock PM Gen" on backing card, backstamped "STAMP DIVISION P.O. DEPT. MAY 15, 1911."

418-E1   15c Model on 87x113mm thick gray
card, black   1,000.

421-E1

423-E1

Design size: 19x22mm
Photo of wash drawing of generic design with 50 in lower corners drawn in black ink. Ms. "July 17, 1911. (May, 1911 erased) Approved: Frank H. Hitchcock PM Gen" on backing card, backstamped "STAMP DIVISION P.O. DEPT. MAY 15, 1911."

421-E1   50c Model on 77x112mm thick gray
card, black   1,000.

Design size: 19x22mm
Photo of wash drawing of generic design with entire value label drawn in black ink. Ms. "July 17, 1911. (May, 1911 erased) Approved: Frank H. Hitchcock PM Gen" on backing card, backstamped "STAMP DIVISION P.O. DEPT. MAY 15, 1911."

423-E1 $1 Model on 87x113mm thick gray
card, black   1,000.

1922 PRECANCEL ESSAY

499-E1

Design size: 19x22mm
Die size: 90x88mm
"NEW YORK/N.Y." precancel engraved directly onto type I die, printed in one color. Ms. "8/16/22 J.G." in LR corner of backing card.

499-E1   2c Die on India, die sunk on card, carmine   —

1918 ISSUE

Complete engraving of Franklin head only as on $2 and $5 values, no shading around head.

523-E2 $2 Die on India, die sunk on
151x103mm card, black   —

523-E3

Design size: 16x18¾mm
Complete engraving of vignette only including shading. Pencil "837660 May 1917" on back of India paper, pencil "Schofield" at bottom of backing card.

523-E3 $2 Die on 32x33mm India, card mounted, black   1,000.

PEACE ISSUE

537-E1

537-E2

Design size: 21½x18½mm
Stamp never issued due to World War I.

537-E1   2c Die on India, die sunk on card,
deep red   1,500.

Die size: 22x19mm
Stamp never issued due to World War I.

537-E2   5c Die on India, die sunk on card, dim
dusky g-b-blue   1,500.

SAMUEL F.B. MORSE ISSUE

537-E3

Design size: 21½x18½mm
Incomplete engraving of entire design: vignette and lettering finished but blank spaces beside vignette. Backstamped "932944" and "Jan. 1, 1919" or "932945" and "Jan. 7, 1919". Frame design subsequently used for 3c Victory issue, No. 537, though lettering and value numerals made slightly smaller.

537-E3   3c Die on India, die sunk on card,
black   2,000.

VICTORY ISSUE

537-E4

Design size: 21½x18½mm
Die size: 85½x75½mm
Incomplete engraving of entire design: no shading in border and some flags unfinished. Backstamped "936356 Jan. 25, 1919."

537-E4   3c Die on India, die sunk on card,
black   1,500.

PILGRIM ISSUE

548-E1

Design size: 26x19mm
Incomplete engraving of entire design: sky blank, sails unshaded.

548-E1   1c Die on India, die sunk on card,
green   1,500.

Incomplete engraving of frame only: "CENTS" engraved but numeral circles blank (probably an essay for both 2c and 5c).

549-E1   2c Die on India, die sunk on card
black   1,500.
green   1,500.

1922 ISSUE

551-E1

Design size: 19x22mm
Incomplete engraving of entire design as adopted: name label blank, vignette unfinished. Ms. "Approved--Harry S. New" on backing card.

551-E1   ½c Die on India, die sunk on
151x202mm card, olive brown   1,900.

Incomplete engraving of entire design but further engraved than No. 551-E1: no lines in white oval over ends of title ribbon and ribbon foldunders not etched as darkly as on issued stamp.

551-E2   ½c Die on India, die sunk on
149x201mm card, olive brown   1,350.

567-E2

568-E2

Design size: 19x22mm
Engraving of unadopted vignette with unadopted engraved frame cut away.

567-E2   20c Die on India, die sunk on
151x201mm card, cobalt blue   —

Design size: 19x15mm
Die size: 88x75mm
Engraving of adopted vignette with engraved frame cut away.

568-E2   25c Die on India, die sunk on
202x151mm card, green   —

Pencil drawings for unadopted frame design.
555-E1   3c black   500.
557-E1   5c black   500.
557-E2   5c black   500.
566-E1   15c black   500.
571-E1 $1 black   500.

HUGUENOT-WALLOON TERCENTENARY ISSUE

614-E1

Design size: 8½x7¼ inches
Preliminary pencil drawing of *Nieu Nederland* in circular frame. Pencil note: "Reverse--Sailing to America, not away from America--J. B. Stoudt."

614-E1   1c black   500.

616-E1

Design size: 5½x3⅛ inches
Wash drawing of design adopted for vignette.

616-E1   5c black   500.

618-E1

Design size: 36x21mm
Incomplete engraving of entire design as adopted: spaces between letters of "BIRTH OF LIBERTY" not solid color.

618-E1   2c Die on India, die sunk on card, car-
              mine   1,250.

Design size: 36x21mm
Incomplete engraving of entire design as adopted: numeral circles blank, many shading lines missing in vignette, no shading around "TWO CENTS," etc.

618-E2   2c Die on India, die sunk on 91x71mm
              card, black   1,500.

ERICSSON MEMORIAL ISSUE

Wash drawing of design as adopted, stamp size.

628-E1   5c black   750.

BATTLE OF WHITE PLAINS ISSUE

629-E1

Design size: 8⅞x9 inches
Preliminary ink and watercolor drawing of entire design quite similar to that adopted.

629-E1   2c black & red   750.

BURGOYNE CAMPAIGN ISSUE

644-E1

Design size: 22x19mm
Essay size: 25x22mm
Card size: 78x98mm
Preliminary wash drawing of unadopted design, on white paper mounted on thick gray card with "Approved" in ink and "May 7, 1927" in pencil subsequently crossed out with "X's."

644-E1   2c black   2,000.

683-E1

Design size: 13x17 inches
Preliminary ink drawing of design nearly as adopted.

683-E1   2c Drawing on artist's cardboard, black   500.

704-E1

Design size: 119x150mm
Preliminary pencil sketch of unadopted ½c design.

704-E1   ½c Drawing on tracing paper, mounted
              on 195x192mm manila paper,
              black   1,000.

718-E1

Design size: 6x7 inches
Watercolor drawing of unadopted design with 2c denomination.

718-E1   2c Drawing on thick artist's card, red   1,250.

719-E1

Design size: 6x7 inches
Watercolor drawing of entire design similar to that eventually adopted for 5c but with 2c denomination.

719-E1   2c Drawing on thick artist's card,
              150x175mm, blue   1,250.

PANAMA CANAL ISSUE

856-E1

Design size: 37x21½mm
Essay size: 99x81mm
Card size: 141x117mm
Engraving of unadopted design: "3 CENTS 3" and "25th ANNIVERSARY PANAMA CANAL" changed for final design. "W. O. Marks" at lower right corner, "Engraver's Stock Proof 594256 / Authorized by 'OML'" on reverse.

856-E1   3c Die on India, die sunk on card, deep
              violet   —

AIR POST

1918 ISSUE

Complete engraving of frame only as adopted. Backstamped "626646A ENGRAVER'S STOCK PROOF AUTHORIZED BY" (signature), plus pencil "663" and "Weeks" (?).

C3-E1   24c Die on India, die sunk on card, deep
               carmine   5,000.

Incomplete engraving of entire design as adopted: unfinished plumes above value numerals and no serial number on biplane.

C3-E2   24c Die on wove, 40x37mm, black
               vignette, blue frame   —

SPECIAL DELIVERY

1885 ISSUE
American Bank Note Co.

E1-E1

Incomplete engraving of entire design as adopted: ornaments missing at each side of "SPECIAL," line under messenger is in pencil, shading on left side of messenger tablet missing, leaves and vert. background lines unfinished (latter shaded over with pencil).

E1-E1   10c Die on India, dim dusky g-b. green   2,500.

1888 ISSUE

No. E1P1 with "AT ANY OFFICE" drawn in wash on small piece of thin paper and mounted over "AT A SPECIAL / DELIVERY / OFFICE." Pencil "any post office" and ms. "At once O.K. / J.C.M. 14 Aug. 86" (?) on backing card.

E2-E1   10c Die on India, on card, black   2,500.

1908 ISSUE
Bureau of Engraving and Printing

E7-E1

Design size: about 8½x7⅛ inches
Preliminary ink and pencil drawing of entire design somewhat similar to that adopted: ("V.S." for U.S. and other minor changes).

E7-E1　10c Drawing on vellum, black　　750.

E7-E2

Design size: about 8½x7⅛ inches
Preliminary ink and pencil drawing of entire design nearly as adopted: ("V.S." for U.S.)

E7-E2　10c Drawing on white drawing paper,
　　　　black　　750.

E7-E3

Design size: 213½x179mm
Similar to No. E7-E2 but with "U.S."

E7-E3　10c Drawing on white drawing paper,
　　　　black　　750.

E7-E4　　　　　　　E7-E5

Design size: 26x21½mm
Woodblock size: 45x42mm
Woodblock of entire design as adopted with about 5mm colorless border outside design, solid color beyond, engraved on wood by Giraldon of Paris. (One exists with ms. "Wood cut made in Paris by Mr. Whitney Warren -- The cuts and the impression therefrom were turned over to the Director of the Bureau of Engraving & Printing, and by him turned over to the Custodian of Dies, Rolls and Plates and given No. 446. They are now held by the Custodian." Another has typewritten "Prints made in Paris, France, from a wood-cut engraving by an unknown engraver from a design made by Mr. Whitney Warren, architect, of New York City." with ms. "Compliments J.E. Ralph" director of B.E.P. and pencil date "9/7/1917.")

Ridgeway numbers used for colors of Nos. E7-E4 and E7-E5.

E7-E4　10c
　　　a. Woodcut on 19g/2 yellowish wove
　　　　43k/1 dim dark green blue　　450.
　　　　44m/2 dull dusky m. g-blue　　450.
　　　　45j/1 dim v. dark b-g-blue　　450.
　　　　45m/1 dim dusky b-g-blue　　450.
　　　b. Woodcut on 19f/2 dull faint y-o-yellow
　　　　wove
　　　　43k/1 dim dark g-blue　　450.
　　　　43m/1 dim dusky g-blue　　450.
　　　　44k/1 dim dark m. g-blue　　450.
　　　　44k/2 dull dark m. g-blue　　450.
　　　　45m/1 dim dusky b-g-blue　　450.
　　　　45m/2 dull dusky b-g-blue　　450.
　　　c. Woodcut on 19g/2 dull v. faint y-o-yellow
　　　　wove
　　　　43k/1 dim dark g-blue　　450.
　　　　43m/1 dim dusky g-blue　　450.

Design size: 26x21½mm
Complete engraving of entire design fairly similar to that adopted but with minor differences.

E7-E5　10c
　　　a. Die on India, die sunk on card, 37m/0
　　　　dusky g-b. green blue　　750.
　　　b. Die on soft white wove, 30x35mm, 37m/0
　　　　dusky g-blue-green　　750.

REGISTRATION STAMP

F1-E1

Design size: 19x22½mm
Retouched circular photo of vignette mounted on wash drawing of frame design as adopted. Ms. "Approved July 8/11--Frank H. Hitchcock--Postmaster General" on backing card.

F1-E1　10c Model on white paper, mounted on
　　　　thick gray cardboard, 81x92mm, black　　1,250.

POSTAGE DUE

1879 ISSUE
American Bank Note Co.

J1-E1

Design size: 19½x25½mm
Die size: 54x66½mm
Complete engraving of entire design as adopted except "UNPAID POSTAGE" instead of "POSTAGE DUE" above vignette oval.

J1-E1　1c
　　　a. Die on India, die sunk on card
　　　　orange brown　　750.
　　　　slate gray　　750.
　　　　dark red violet　　750.
　　　　dull yellow　　750.
　　　　light orange　　750.
　　　　red brown　　750.
　　　b. Die on India, cut small
　　　　gray black　　350.
　　　　dull red　　350.
　　　　dull brown　　350.
　　　　dull green　　350.
　　　　dull blue　　350.
　　　c. Die on India, cut close
　　　　orange brown　　350.
　　　　slate gray　　350.
　　　　dark red violet　　350.
　　　　dull yellow　　350.
　　　d. Die on white ivory paper, die sunk
　　　　black　　600.
　　　　black brown　　600.
　　　　scarlet　　600.
　　　　blue　　600.

Design size: 19½x25½mm
Die size: 53½x53½mm

Complete engraving of entire design as adopted except "UNPAID POSTAGE" instead of "POSTAGE DUE" above vignette oval.

J2-E1　2c
　　　a. Die on India, die sunk on card
　　　　dark red violet　　750.
　　　　black　　750.
　　　b. Die on India, cut small
　　　　gray black　　350.
　　　　dull red　　350.
　　　　dull brown　　350.
　　　　dull green　　350.
　　　　dull blue　　350.
　　　c. Die on India, cut close
　　　　orange brown　　350.
　　　　dark red violet　　350.
　　　　slate gray　　350.
　　　d. Die on white ivory paper, die sunk
　　　　black　　600.
　　　　black brown　　600.
　　　　scarlet　　600.
　　　　blue　　600.

Design size: 19½x25½mm
Die size: 53x53mm
Complete engraving of entire design as adopted except "UNPAID POSTAGE" instead of "POSTAGE DUE" above vignette oval.

J3-E1　3c
　　　a. Die on India, die sunk on card, dull yellow　　750.
　　　b. Die on India, cut small
　　　　gray black　　350.
　　　　dull red　　350.
　　　　dull brown　　350.
　　　　dull green　　350.
　　　　dull blue　　350.
　　　c. Die on India, cut close, dull yellow　　350.
　　　d. Die on white ivory paper, die sunk
　　　　black　　600.
　　　　black brown　　600.
　　　　scarlet　　600.
　　　　blue　　600.

Design size: 19½x25½mm
Complete engraving of entire design as adopted except "UNPAID POSTAGE" instead of "POSTAGE DUE" above vignette oval.

J4-E1　5c
　　　a. Die on India, die sunk on card, slate gray　　750.
　　　b. Die on India, cut small
　　　　gray black　　350.
　　　　dull red　　350.
　　　　dull brown　　350.
　　　　dull green　　350.
　　　　dull blue　　350.
　　　c. Die on India, cut close
　　　　orange brown　　350.
　　　　slate gray　　350.
　　　　dark red violet　　350.
　　　　dull yellow　　350.
　　　d. Die on white ivory paper, die sunk
　　　　black　　600.
　　　　black brown　　600.
　　　　scarlet　　600.
　　　　blue　　600.

1894 ISSUE
Bureau of Engraving and Printing

J31-E1　　　　　　　J31-E2

Design size: 18½x22½mm
Die size: 50x99mm
Incomplete engraving of entire design: no engraved lines on numeral, lathework unfinished on two inclined spots at each side of numeral.

J31-E1　1c Die on India, die sunk on card,
　　　　deep claret　　750.

Design size: 18½x22½mm
Die size: 50x99mm
Incomplete engraving of entire design: engraved lines on numeral but lathework still unfinished on two inclined spots at each side of numeral.

J31-E2　1c Die on India, die sunk on card, claret　　750.

J33-E1　　　　　　　J33-E2

Incomplete engraving of entire design: blank space for numeral with "3" drawn in pencil.

J33-E1   3c   Die on India, die sunk on card,
       black   1,000.

Incomplete engraving of entire design: no engraved lines on numeral, bottom lettering in pencil only, no hand retouching of lathework around numeral.

J33-E2   3c   Die on India, die sunk on card,
       black   1,000.

J33-E3

Incomplete engraving of entire design: no engraved lines on numeral.

J33-E3   3c   Die on India, die sunk on card, claret   750.

J35-E1   J36-E1

Incomplete engraving of entire design: no engraved lines on numerals.

J35-E1   10c   Die on India, die sunk on card,
       black   750.

Incomplete engraving of entire design: no engraved lines on numerals.

J36-E1   30c   Die on India, die sunk on card, claret   750.

J37-E1   J37-E2

Incomplete engraving of entire design: 9x9mm blank space for numerals.

J37-E1   50c   Die on India, die sunk on card
       black   1,000.
       claret   850.

Incomplete engraving of entire design: numerals engraved but hand engraving to retouch lathework around numerals missing.

J37-E2   50c   Die on India, die sunk on card,
       black   1,000.

OFFICIAL

Continental Bank Note Co.
AGRICULTURE

O2-E1

Design size: 20x25mm
Engraved vignette, numeral and value label from 1873 2c (No. 146-E10) mounted on pencil and wash drawing for frame design as adopted for Agriculture set. Pencil signature "J. Claxton" on backing card. Frame differs for each dept.

O2-E1   2c   Model on yellowish card, 23x30mm,
       on 90x118mm white card, black
       vignette, gray black frame   1,250.

EXECUTIVE

O12-E1   O12-E2

Design size: 20x25mm
See design note for No. O2-E1.

O12-E1   3c   Model on yellowish card,
       23x30mm, on 90x118mm white
       card, black   1,250.

Design size: 19½x25mm
Die size: 64x76mm
Engraving of complete design of No. O12-E1 with "DEP'T" in top label.

O12-E2   3c
    a. Die on India, die sunk on card, green   1,250.
    b. Die on India, cut close
        black   750.
        green   750.

INTERIOR

O17-E1

Design size: 20x25mm
See design note for No. O2-E1.

O17-E1   3c   Model on yellowish card,
       23x30mm, on 90x118mm white
       card, black   1,250.

JUSTICE

O27-E1

Design size: 20x25mm
See design note for No. O2-E1.

O27-E1   3c   Model on yellowish card,
       23x30mm, on 90x118mm white
       card, black   1,250.

NAVY

O37-E1

Design size: 20x25mm
See design note for No. O2-E1.

O37-E1   3c   Model on yellowish card,
       23x30mm, on 90x118mm white
       card, black   1,250.

POST OFFICE

O47-E1

Design size: 19½x25mm
Complete engraving of entire design as adopted except with Franklin vignette instead of large numeral.

O47-E1   1c
    a. Die on India, mounted on white ivory
       card
       blue   1,250.
    b. Die on proof paper
       gray black   1,000.
       dull scarlet   1,000.
       dull brown   1,000.
       dull green   1,000.
       dull blue   1,000.
    c. Die on white ivory paper, black   1,250.

Design size: 19½x25mm
Complete engraving of entire design as adopted except with Jackson vignette instead of large numeral.

O48-E1   2c
    a. Die on India, mounted on white ivory
       card
       orange brown   1,250.
    b. Die on proof paper
       gray black   1,000.
       dull scarlet   1,000.
       dull brown   1,000.
       dull green   1,000.
       dull blue   1,000.
    c. Die on white ivory paper, black   1,250.

O49-E1   O49-E2

Design size: 20x25mm
Engraved vignette, numeral and value label from 1873 3c (No. 147-E10) mounted on pencil and wash drawing for frame design not adopted for Post Office set.

O49-E1   3c   Model on yellowish card,
       23x30mm, on 90x118mm white
       card, black   1,250.
O49-E2   3c   Model on yellowish card,
       23x30mm, on 90x118mm white
       card, black   1,250.

O49-E3

Design size: 20x25mm
See design note for No. O2-E1.

O49-E3   3c   Model on yellowish card,
       23x30mm, on 90x118mm white
       card, black   1,250.

Design size: 19½x25mm
Complete engraving of entire design as adopted except with Washington vignette instead of large numeral.

O49-E4   3c
    a. Die on India, mounted on white ivory
       card
       green   1,250.
    b. Die on proof paper
       gray black   1,000.
       dull scarlet   1,000.
       dull brown   1,000.
       dull green   1,000.
       dull blue   1,000.
    c. Die on white ivory paper, black   1,250.

O49-E5

1870 1c stamp (No. 145) with vignette cut out, "OFFICIAL 3 STAMP" drawn in pencil on envelope on which stamp is mounted. Blue pencil notation on backing envelope, "Design by Mr. J. Barber for P.O.D. Official."

O49-E5   1c Stamp frame mounted on envelope, ultramarine frame, black
vignette   2,500.

O49-E6   O49-E8

Model of engraved frame from No. O49-E4 with hollow oval engraved lathework band with "OFFICIAL / STAMP" drawn in wash mounted in place, numeral drawn in pencil and wash. Ms. "No. 1" on backing card.

O49-E6   3c Model on stiff white card,
50x75mm, black   1,750.

As No. O49-E6, Ms. "No. 3" on backing card.

O49-E8   3c Model on stiff white card,
50x75mm, black   1,750.

O50-E1

Incomplete engraving of design with Lincoln vignette, without rectangular frame design.

O50-E1   6c Die on white ivory paper, black   1,750.

Design size: 19½x25mm
Complete engraving of entire design as adopted except with Perry vignette instead of large numeral.

O56-E1   90c
a. Die on India, mounted on white ivory
card, brown   1,500.
b. Die on proof paper
gray black   1,000.
dull scarlet   1,000.
dull brown   1,000.
dull green   1,000.
dull blue   1,000.
c. Die on white ivory paper, black   1,250.

STATE

O59-E1   O68-E1

Design size: 20x25mm
Engraved vignette, numeral and value label from 1873 3c (No. 147-E10) mounted on pencil and wash drawing for frame

design as adopted for State set. Pencil signature "J. Claxton" on backing card.

O59-E1   3c Model on yellowish card,
23x30mm, on 90x118mm white
card, black   1,250.

Design size: 25½x40mm
Engraved vignette of Seward mounted in watercolor drawing of adopted frame design. Ms. signatures of J. Claxton and Chas. Skinner on backing card.

O68-E1   Two Dollars, Model on 29x43mm grayish white card, mounted on
96x120mm white card, black   2,500.

O68-E2

Complete engraving of adopted frame only with "TWO DOL-LARS." in value label at bottom. With "FIVE DOLLARS." and "TEN DOLLARS." value labels outside design at left and "TWENTY DOLLs." value tablet at right.

O68-E2   Two Dollars, Die on India, black   2,500.

O68-E3

Plate engraved frame only (occurs paired with complete bicolor plate proof of $2).

O68-E3   Two Dollars, Plate essay on India,
green   2,500.

WAR

O85-E1

Design size: 20x25mm
Engraved vignette, numeral and value label from 1873 3c (No. 147-E10) mounted on pencil and wash drawing for frame design as adopted for War set. Pencil signature "J. Claxton" on backing card.

O85-E1   3c Model on yellowish card,
23x30mm, on 90x118mm white
card, black   2,500.

NEWSPAPER AND PERIODICALS

1865 ISSUE
National Bank Note Co.

PR1-E1

Design size: 51x89mm
Typographed design somewhat similar to that adopted but with large Franklin vignette facing left, "PACKAGE" at bottom, other minor differences.

PR1-E1   5c Die on stiff white ivory paper
deep orange red   1,000.
dusky g-b. blue   1,000.
bright blue   1,000.
a. Die on paper with blue ruled lines
deep orange red   1,000.
carmine   1,000.

1875 ISSUE
Continental Bank Note Co.

PR9-E1   PR9-E2

Design size: 19½x25mm
Engraved vignette and numerals (25's) with pencil sketch of unadopted frame design.

PR9-E1   25c Die on India, on card, black   2,750.

Design size: 19½x25mm
Complete engraving of unadopted design with "U S" at top and "25 CENTS 25" at bottom.

PR9-E2   25c
a. Die on India, on card
black   1,250.
scarlet   1,250.
blue   1,250.
b. Die on white ivory paper
black   1,250.
black brown   1,250.
scarlet   1,250.
blue   1,250.

PR14-E1

PR23-E1

Design size: 25x35mm
Wash drawing of complete design as adopted. Backing card signed by both designers, Chas. Skinner and Jos. Claxton.

PR14-E1   9c Drawing on 26x36mm card, on 56x74mm card, black   900.

Design size: 24x35½mm
Wash drawing similar to that adopted, backing card signed by designers Skinner and Claxton, also has pencil "$12" and ms. "Continental Bank Note Co."

PR23-E1   96c Drawing on 88x121mm card, black   900.

PR27-E1   PR28-E1

Design size: 24½x35mm
Incomplete engraving of entire design: unshaded (shading pencilled in) inside left, right and bottom framelines, value label, top of "9." Upper corners unfinished.

PR27-E1 $9 Die on India, die sunk on 76x82mm card, black   1,250.

Design size: 24½x35mm
Incomplete engraving of entire design: no shading on dollar signs and numerals. No shading on frame around numerals and around value tablet.

PR28-E1 $12 Die on India, die sunk on 66x80mm card, black   1,250.

PR29-E1

Design size: 24x35½mm
Wash drawing similar to that adopted but with "U S" in six-pointed stars instead of at top. Backing card signed by designers Skinner and Claxton, also pencil "31/32" and "8 13/32," pencil "Alter" with lines to stars.

PR29-E1 $24 Drawing on 88x121mm card, black   750.

PR31-E1

Vignette size: 13½x26mm

PR31-E2

Engraved vignette only as adopted.

PR31-E1 $48 Die on India, die sunk on card, black   750.

Design size: 24x36mm
Wash drawing similar to that adopted, backing card signed by designers Skinner and Claxton, also has pencil "$48" above each value numeral.

PR31-E2 $48 Drawing on 88x121mm card, black   1,350.

PR32-E1

Design size: 24½x35½mm
Wash drawing similar to that adopted, backing card signed by designers Skinner and Claxton.

PR32-E1 $60 Drawing on 88x121mm card, black   750.

1885 ISSUE
American Bank Note Co.

PR81-E1

Design size: 23x25mm
Complete engraving of entire design as adopted for 12c-96c.

PR81-E1   1c
   a. Die on India, die sunk on card
      black   1,350.
   b. Die on white ivory paper
      black   600.
      black brown   600.
      scarlet   600.
      blue   600.

1895 ISSUE
Bureau of Engraving and Printing

Incomplete engraving of entire design: background at upper ends of value label, shading on side lettering and numerals missing.

PR102-E2   1c Die on India, die sunk on card
      black   600.
      green   600.

Incomplete engraving of entire design but further engraved than No. PR102-E2: shading on PA is light, no shading on PE of NEWSPAPERS or IO of PERIODICALS and shading on OD is light.

PR102-E3   1c Die on India, die sunk on card, black   600.

Incomplete engraving of entire design but further engraved than No. PR102-E3: shading on PERIODICALS is finished but not on PAPE.

PR102-E4   1c Die on India, die sunk on card, black   500.

PR103-E1

PR103-E2

Design size: 21½x34½mm
Die size: 56x75½mm
Incomplete engraving of entire design: spaces for numerals and value label blank but with pencil outline of lettering.

PR103-E1   2c Die on India, die sunk on card, black   1,500.

Incomplete engraving of entire design but further engraved than No. PR103-E1: shading on leaves at ends of value label unfinished, numerals unshaded, unfinished shading on APE of NEWSPAPERS and RIO of PERIODICALS.

PR103-E2   2c Die on India, black   1,250.

Incomplete engraving of entire design but further engraved than No. PR103-E2: no shading on PE of NEWSPAPERS, unfinished shading on PA of NEWSPAPERS and RIO of PERIODICALS.

PR103-E3   2c Die on India, die sunk on card, black   1,250.

PR104-E1

Design size: 21½x34½mm
Die size: 57x73mm
Incomplete engraving of entire design: spaces for numerals and value label blank but with pencil outline of lettering.

PR104-E1   5c Die on India, die sunk on card, black   1,250.

PR105-E1

PR105-E2

Design size: 21½x34½mm
Die size: 56x75mm
Incomplete engraving of entire design: spaces for numerals and value label blank but with pencil outline of lettering.

PR105-E1   10c Die on India, die sunk on card, black   1,250.

Incomplete engraving of entire design but further engraved than No. PR105-E1: numerals unfinished, lower corners blank.

PR105-E2   10c Die on India, die sunk on card, black   1,500.

Incomplete engraving of entire design but further engraved than No. PR105-E2: lower right corner blank.

PR105-E3   10c Die on India, die sunk on card, black   1,250.

Incomplete engraving of entire design but further engraved than No. PR105-E3: numerals blank, no inner lines.

PR105-E4   10c Die on India, die sunk on card, black   1,250.

PR105-E5

Design size: 21½x34½mm
Die size: 56x75mm
Incomplete engraving of entire design (early state of die similar to No. PR105-E1) with "10" pencilled in upper right corner

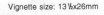

and "TEN CENTS" penciled in at bottom. Pencil notes on India include "Make top of 1 a little larger and put on spur," "Work up Vignette" and "Use same scrolls as marked on 5c-."

PR105-E5　10c Die on India, die sunk on card,
　　　　　　black　　　　　　　　　　　　　　　　1,500.

PR106-E1

PR106-E2

Vignette size: 13x25½mm
Die size: 56x72mm
Incomplete engraving of vignette only (transfer of Continental Banknote Co. die for 72c with left side cut off): eagle crest faces front and its right wing is not pointed, shading on left thigh near sword hilt incomplete, bottom of vignette straight instead of curved.

PR106-E1　25c Die on India, die sunk on card
　　　　　　black　　　　　　　　　　　　　　　　1,750.
　　　　　　deep red　　　　　　　　　　　　　　1,750.

Design size: about 21x34½mm
Die size: 57½x75mm
Entire design with frame incompletely engraved: vert. lines around CENTS label missing, no shading on TWENTY FIVE, colorless beads under E and FI of same.

PR106-E2　25c Die on India, die sunk on card
　　　　　　black　　　　　　　　　　　　　　　　1,750.
　　　　　　deep red　　　　　　　　　　　　　　1,750.

An impression from No. PR106-E2 with pencil shading on TWENTY FIVE and vert. ink lines in spaces around CENTS label, colorless beads also blacked out in ink. Below engraving are three diff. pencil sketches for shape and shading to be engraved.

PR106-E3　25c Die on India, die sunk on card,
　　　　　　black　　　　　　　　　　　　　　　　1,750.

An impression from No. PR106-E2 but with shading suggestions from No. PR106-E3 partly engraved except colorless beads have pencil shading only. Below engraving is pencil sketch for corner of CENTS label.

PR106-E4　25c Die on India, die sunk on card
　　　　　　black　　　　　　　　　　　　　　　　1,750.
　　　　　　deep red　　　　　　　　　　　　　　1,500.

PR106-E5

Design size: 21½x34½mm
Die size: 55x72mm
Large die proof of PR107 with bottom value label cut out and "TWENTY-FIVE CENTS" penciled in on backing card.

PR106-E5　25c Die on India, die sunk on card,
　　　　　　black　　　　　　　　　　　　　　　　1,250.

PR107-E1　　　　　　PR107-E3

Incomplete engraving of entire design: eagle's head and much of bottom of stamp's design unfinished, top of frame unfinished, value lettering sketched in pencil.

PR107-E1　50c Die on India, die sunk on card,
　　　　　　black　　　　　　　　　　　　　　　　1,750.

Incomplete engraving of entire design: top of frame and scrolls below FIFTY CENTS unfinished.

PR107-E3　50c Die on India, die sunk on card,
　　　　　　black　　　　　　　　　　　　　　　　1,300.

PR108-E1　　　　　　PR108-E2

Design size: 24½x37mm
Die size: 75x76mm
Incomplete engraving of entire design: vignette and spaces around numerals incomplete, pencil sketch instructions for engraver at top and side for these spaces.

PR108-E1　$2 Die on India, die sunk on card,
　　　　　　black　　　　　　　　　　　　　　　　1,650.

Design size: 24½x37mm
Die size: 75x76mm
Incomplete engraving of entire design but further engraved than No. PR108-E1: space for ornaments under POSTAGE blank, numerals unshaded.

PR108-E2　$2 Die on India, die sunk on card,
　　　　　　scarlet　　　　　　　　　　　　　　　1,500.

Further engraved than No. PR108-E2: scrolls under POST-AGE engraved but unfinished.

PR108-E3　$2 Die on India, die sunk on card,
　　　　　　black　　　　　　　　　　　　　　　　1,500.

PR111-E1　　　　　　PR112-E1

Design size (incomplete): 24½x30mm
Die size: 75x84mm
Incomplete engraving of partial design: spaces for stars and 0s of numerals blank, design missing below bottom of vignette.

PR111-E1　$20 Die on India, die sunk on card,
　　　　　　black　　　　　　　　　　　　　　　　1,250.

Design size: 24½x35½mm
Die size: 72½x76mm
Incomplete engraving of entire design: upper corners around value numerals unfinished, etc.

PR112-E1　$50 Die on India, on card, black　　　1,850.

PR113-E1

Design size: 24½x35½mm
Die size: 75x74mm

Incomplete engraving of entire design: spaces at lower inner corners of value shields blank, shading on numerals and letters at top unfinished.

PR113-E1　$100 Die on India, on card, black　　　1,350.

Further engraved than No. PR113-E1: vignette completed but numerals not shaded, shadows on frame not etched dark.

PR113-E2　$100 Die on India
　　　　　　black　　　　　　　　　　　　　　　　1,350.
　　　　　　red-violet　　　　　　　　　　　　　1,350.

Further engraved than No. PR113-E2: numerals shaded, shadows on frame not finally etched, especially above POSTAGE.

PR113-E3　$100 Die on India, black　　　　　　1,350.

PARCEL POST

Q1-E1

Design size: 35½x23mm
Photo of wash drawing of frame design with numerals, CENT and POST OFFICE CLERK in black ink, vignette in black wash. Ms. "Changed from 15c" and "Approved Nov. 15, 1912--Frank H. Hitchcock--Postmaster General" on backing card.

Q1-E1　　1c Model on thick gray cardboard,
　　　　　　106x91mm, black　　　　　　　　　　1,500.

Q2-E1

Design size: 35x23½mm
Photo of wash drawing of frame only as adopted. Ms. "Approved Oct. 10, 1912, for border and size of stamps. Engraving to be ⅞ by 1⅜ inches. Frank H. Hitchcock. Postmaster General" on backing card.

Q2-E1　　2c Model on thick gray cardboard,
　　　　　　122x110mm, black　　　　　　　　　1,500.

Q2-E2

Design size: 35x23mm
Photo of wash drawing of frame design and retouched photo of ship vignette as eventually used for 10c, numerals and STEAMSHIP AND MAIL TENDER in black ink. Ms. "Changed to 10c" and "Approved Oct. 11, 1912. Frank H. Hitchcock. Post-master General" on backing card.

Q2-E2　　2c Model on thick gray cardboard,
　　　　　　110x83mm, black　　　　　　　　　　1,500.

Q2-E3

Design size: 34x22mm
Photo of wash drawing of entire design with adopted vignette, numerals in white wash and CITY CARRIER in black ink. Ms. "Changed from 5c" and "Approved Nov. 14, 1912. Frank H. Hitchcock. Postmaster General" on backing card.

Q2-E3　　2c Model on thick gray cardboard,
　　　　　　111x92mm, black　　　　　　　　　　1,500.

Q3-E1

Design size: 35x23mm
Complete engraving of unadopted design: vignette shows mail truck backing up to railroad mail train with clerk about to handle pouches.

Q3-E1   3c Die on white wove, about 43x31mm,
          carmine   *1,500.*

Q3-E2

Design size: 35x22mm
Photo of wash drawing of entire design with adopted vignette (retouched around door to mail car). Ms. "Approved Feb. 22, 1913. Frank H. Hitchcock. Postmaster General" on backing card.

Q3-E2   3c Model on thick gray cardboard, black   *1,500.*

Q4-E1

Design size: 33½x22mm
Photo of wash drawing of entire design with adopted vignette, numerals drawn in white and RURAL CARRIER in black ink. Ms. "Changed from 10c" and "Approved Nov. 14, 1912. Frank H. Hitchcock. Postmaster General" on backing card.

Q4-E1   4c Model on thick gray cardboard,
          116x92mm, black   *1,500.*

Q5-E1

Design size: 35x23mm
Photo of wash drawing of entire design with vignette (retouched) eventually used for 2c, numerals and CITY LETTER CARRIER in black ink and white wash. Ms. "Changed to 2c.--City Carrier" and "Approved Oct. 10, 1912. Frank H. Hitchcock. Postmaster General" on backing card.

Q5-E1   5c Model on thick gray cardboard,
          110x84mm, black   *1,500.*

Q5-E2

Design size: 33½x21½mm
Photo of wash drawing of entire design with numerals in gray, unadopted vignette with MAIL TRAIN in black ink, first car retouched with wash. Ms. "Approved . . . 1912 / . . . Postmaster General" on backing card.

Q5-E2   5c Model on thick gray cardboard,
          104½x92mm, black   *1,500.*

Q5-E3

Design size: 33½x22mm
Photo of wash drawing of entire design with numerals in gray, MAIL TRAIN in black ink, first car retouched with wash. Ms. "Approved . . . 1912 / . . . Postmaster General" on backing card.

Q5-E3   5c Model on thick gray cardboard,
          104½x92mm, black   *1,500.*

Q5-E4

Design size: 33½x22mm
Photo of wash drawing of entire design with numerals in white with black background, MAIL TRAIN and pouch catcher in black ink. Ms. "Approved Nov. 19, 1912 Frank H. Hitchcock Postmaster General" on backing card.

Q5-E4   5c Model on thick gray cardboard,
          94x90mm, black   *1,500.*

Q6-E1

Design size: 35½x23mm
Photo of wash drawing of entire design with vignette (retouched) eventually used for 4c, numerals and RURAL DELIVERY in black ink and white wash. Ms. "Changed to 4c." and "Approved Oct. 10, 1912. Frank H. Hitchcock. Postmaster General" on backing card.

Q6-E1   10c Model on thick gray cardboard,
          111x83mm, black   *1,500.*

Q6-E2

Design size: 35x23mm
Photo of wash drawing of entire design with adopted vignette, numerals and STEAMSHIP AND MAIL TENDER in black ink and white wash. Ms. "Changed from 2c." and "Approved Nov. 8, 1912. Frank H. Hitchcock. Postmaster General" on backing card.

Q6-E2   10c Model on thick gray cardboard,
          116x92mm, black   *1,500.*

Q7-E1

Design size: 33½x22mm
Photo of wash drawing of entire design (redrawn in front of autocar and U S MAIL and STATION A) with AUTOMOBILE SERVICE in black ink. Ms. "Approved . . . 1912 / . . . Postmaster General" on backing card.

Q7-E1   15c Model on thick gray cardboard,
          115x93mm, black   *1,500.*

Design size:

Complete engraving of entire design with unadopted title label "COLLECTION SERVICE" instead of the adopted "AUTOMOBILE SERVICE."

Q7-E2   15c Die on white wove, card mounted,
          carmine   *1,500.*

Q8-E1

Design size: 35x22mm
Incomplete engraved design nearly as adopted: aviator wears football helmet, head tilted far forward and one leg dangling over edge of plane, mail bag "No. 1" at his right while another sack hangs loosely out of plane.

Q8-E1   20c Die on white wove, about 37x24mm,
          carmine   *1,500.*

Q8-E2

Design size: 35x22mm
Photo of incomplete engraved design as adopted. Ms. "Approved Nov. 19, 1912. Frank H. Hitchcock. Postmaster General" on backing card.

Q8-E2   20c Model on thick gray cardboard,
          98x95mm, black   *1,500.*

Q9-E1

Design size: 34½x22½mm
Photo of wash drawing of entire design with numerals and smoke at right painted in. Ms. "Changed from $1.00." and "Approved Nov. 14, 1912. Frank H. Hitchcock. Postmaster General" on backing card.

Q9-E1   25c Model on thick gray cardboard,
          112x92mm, black   *1,500.*

Q10-E1

Design size: 35x23mm
Photo of drawing of entire design with vignette eventually used for 25c with roof, smokestacks and smoke drawn in. Typed label "Stamp Division / Feb / 21 / 1912 / P.O. Dept" on back of backing paper.

Q10-E1   50c Model on thick white paper, black   *1,500.*

Q10-E2

Design size: 33x21½mm
Photo of wash drawing of frame design with vignette cut out, mounted over photo of wash drawing of unadopted vignette design, retouched with wash on cows, etc., with DAIRYING in black ink. Pencil "Original" and ms. "Approved . . . 1912 / . . . Postmaster General" on backing card.

Q10-E2   50c Model on thick gray cardboard,
          98x93mm, black   *1,500.*

Q10-E3

Design size: 35x23mm
Complete engraving of entire design with unadopted vignette: silo and barns placed closer to front of design.

Q10-E3   50c Die on white wove, about
43x31mm, carmine   1,500.

Q10-E4

Design size: 35x22mm
Photo of incomplete engraved design: no vert. lines on frame around corner foliate spandrels or in numeral circles. Ms. "Approved Jan. 8, 1913. Frank H. Hitchcock. Postmaster General" on backing card.

Q10-E4   50c Model on thick gray cardboard,
99x94mm, black   1,500.

Q11-E1

Design size: 33½x21½mm
Photo of wash drawing of entire design with central horses and thresher retouched. Ms. "Approved Dec. 12, 1912. Frank H. Hitchcock. Postmaster General" on backing card.

Q11-E1   75c Model on thick gray cardboard,
108x89mm, black   1,500.

Q12-E1

Photo of wash drawing of entire design with vignette much retouched in black ink, numerals, MANUFACTURING and DOLLAR drawn in black ink and white wash. Ms. "Changed to 25c" and "Approved Oct. 22, 1912. Frank H. Hitchcock. Postmaster General" on backing card.

Q12-E1 $1 Model on thick gray cardboard,
114x86mm, black   1,500.

Q12-E2

Design size: 35x22mm
Photo of wash drawing of complete design with DOLLAR painted in white and black and FRUIT GROWING in black ink, vignette retouched with wash on fruit pickers. Ms. "Approved . . . 1912 . . . Postmaster General" on backing card.

Q12-E2 $1 Model on thick gray cardboard,
105x94mm, black   1,500.

Q12-E3

Design size: 36x23½mm
Incomplete engraving of entire design: no shading lines in sky. This may be from a rejected die.

Q12-E3 $1 Die on white wove, about
43x31mm, carmine   1,500.

Q12a-E1

Engraving of entire design as adopted for 1917 offset Documentary Revenues, etc., but with "U.S. PARCEL POST" around value oval.

Q12a-E1	1c Die on card, green	700.
Q12b-E1	2c Die on card, carmine	700.
Q12c-E1	3c Die on card, deep violet	700.
Q12d-E1	4c Die on card, brown	700.
Q12e-E1	5c Die on card, blue	700.
Q12f-E1	10c Die on card, orange yellow	700.
Q12g-E1	15c Die on card, gray	700.

PARCEL POST POSTAGE DUE

Retouched photo of design as adopted, officially dated and approved.

JQ5-E1a   25c Model, black   1,500.

CARRIER'S STAMP

Essays by Toppan, Carpenter, Casilear & Co. in 1851

Die size: 50x57mm
Design as adopted, but distinguished by having top and bottom frame lines as well as horizontal and vertical guide lines and rosettes in lower right corner.

1851
LO1-E1   (1c)
    a. Die on white ivory paper, black   1,000.
    b. Die on pale green India, red   —

Essays by Schernikow in 1903 from a new soft steel die made from the original 1851 transfer roll.
See note above No. 63-E1.

LO1-E2

LO1-E3

Die size: 50x50mm
Engraving of Franklin vignette only.

1903
LO1-E2   (1c)
    a. Die on proof paper
        black   75.
        carmine   75.
        red   75.
        light red   75.
        orange   75.
        orange brown   75.
        yellow   75.
        olive   75.
        green   75.
        dark green   75.
        dark blue   75.
        violet   75.
        violet brown   75.
    b. Die on colored card, about 75x75mm
        deep red, *pinkish white*   175.
        yellow brown, *pale blue*   175.
        violet brown, *pale green*   175.
        dark green, *pale pink*   175.
        dark blue, *pale pink*   175.

        violet, *pale yellow*   175.
    c. Die on green bond (die size: 49x50mm)
        dull scarlet   175.
        dull olive   175.
        dark ultramarine   175.

Design size: 19½x25mm
Die size: 50x50mm
Design as No. LO1-E1, but distinguished by addition of left and right inner frame lines.

1903
LO1-E3   (1c)
    a. Die on proof paper
        black   100.
        carmine   100.
        dark carmine   100.
        scarlet   100.
        orange   100.
        yellow   100.
        yellow brown   100.
        olive   100.
        light green   100.
        green   100.
        steel blue   100.
        violet   100.
        red violet   100.
        violet brown   100.
        ultramarine   100.
    b. Die on colored card
        dull carmine, *pale olive*   175.
        brown orange, *pink*   175.
        brown, *pale buff*   175.
        brown, *pale blue*   175.
        gray green, *buff*   175.
        gray green, *yellow*   175.
        violet, *ivory*   175.
        dull carmine, *pale blue*   175.
    c. Die on blue pelure
        carmine   200.
        scarlet   200.
        orange   200.
        brown   200.
        dark green   200.
    d. Die on green bond
        scarlet   250.
        orange   250.
        green   250.
        dull violet   250.

Essays by Clarence Brazer in 1952 using the Schernikow complete die with addition of two diagonal lines in upper right corner.

Die size: 50x50mm

1952
LO1-E4   (1c) Die on glazed card
        scarlet   500.
        brown   500.
        green   500.
        red   500.

POST OFFICE SEALS

Registry Seals
1872 ISSUE
National Bank Note Co.

Design size: 72x40mm
Block size: 100x56½mm
Typographed design similar to that adopted but inscription STAMP HERE DATE AND PLACE OF MAILING around central circular disk is in colorless capitals, remainder of lettering in solid colors without shading lines. The word REGISTERED obliterates other words where it touches them.

OXF1-E1
    a. Block impression on white card, brown   1,250.
    b. Die on India, dark brown   —

Similar to No. OXF1-E1 except REGISTERED appears to be under other words it touches and does not obliterate them, as in design adopted.

OXF1-E2
    a. Block impression on white paper, card
        mounted, brown   1,250.
    b. Block impression on large card
        brown   1,250.
        red   1,250.
        yellow   1,250.

Similar to adopted type but circular disk in center has a ground of concentric circles, REGISTERED without colorless shading and obliterates other words where it touches them.

OXF1-E3   Block impression on white card, red
violet   —

OXF1-E4

Similar to adopted design except REGISTERED obliterates other words where it touches them; colored shading as adopted.

OXF1-E4
   a. Block on India, on card
carmine	1,000.
yellow	1,000.
blue	1,000.
green	1,000.
red brown	1,000.
rose	1,000.
brown orange	1,000.

   b. Block on India, printed in two colors
top dark green, bottom light green	1,000.

left half blue, right half green	1,000.

   c. Block sunk on white card, colored border around stamp (full size 57x100mm)
deep carmine	1,000.
brown orange	1,000.
brown	1,000.
light green	1,000.
blue	1,000.

   d. Block sunk on white wove, colorless border, stamp size, imperf., dim dusky blue | 1,000.

   e. As "d," perf. 12, gummed, dim dusky blue | 1,000.

OXF1-E5

Block size: 80x128mm
Engraving of entire design as adopted but in reverse for making typographed block.

OXF1-E5   Die on white wove, chocolate   1,000.

Post Office Seals
1877 ISSUE

OX1-E3

Design size: 45x27½mm
Incomplete engraving of entire design: no shading lines on 2mm-wide border frame, no cap or background in vignette.

OX1-E3   Die on India, on card, orange brown   1,000.

DIE AND PLATE PROOFS

PROOFS are known in many styles other than those noted in this section. For the present, however, listings are restricted to die proofs, large and small, and plate proofs on India paper and card, and occasionally on stamp paper. The listing of normal color proofs includes several that differ somewhat from the colors of the issued stamps.

Large Die Proofs are so termed because of the relatively large piece of paper on which they are printed which is about the size of the die block, 40mm by 50mm or larger. The margins of this group of proofs usually are from 15mm to 20mm in width though abnormal examples prevent the acceptance of these measurements as a complete means of identification.

These proofs were prepared in most cases by the original contracting companies and 19th century issues often show the imprint thereof and letters and numbers of identification. They are listed under "DIE-Large (1)." The India paper on which these proofs are printed is of an uneven texture and in some respects resembles hand-made paper. These large die proofs were usually mounted on cards though many are found removed from the card. Large Die Proofs autographed by the engraver or officially approved are worth much more.

Values for Large Die Proofs are for the full die proofs mounted on cards unless noted otherwise. Cur down Large Die Proofs sell for less. Values for die proofs of the bicolored 1869 issue are for examples which are completely printed. Occasionally the vignette has been cut out and affixed to an impression of the border.

Die Proofs of all United States stamps of later issues exist. Only those known outside of government ownership are listed.

Small Die Proofs are so called because of the small piece of paper on which they are printed. Proofs of stamps issued prior to 1904, are reprints, and not in all cases from the same dies as the large die proofs.

Small Die Proofs (Roosevelt Album, "DIE-Small (2)") - These 302 small die proofs are from sets prepared for 85 ("Roosevelt presentation") albums in 1903 by the Bureau of Engraving and Printing but bear no imprint to this effect. The white wove paper on which they are printed is of a fibrous nature. The margins are small, seldom being more than from 3-5mm in width.

Small Die Proofs (Panama-Pacific Issue, "DIE-Small (2a)") - A special printing of 413 different small die proofs was made in 1915 for the Panama-Pacific Exposition. These have small margins (2½-3mm) and are on soft yellowish wove paper. They are extremely scarce as only 3-5 of each are known and a few exist only in this special printing.

Plate Proofs are, quite obviously, impressions taken from finished plates and differ from the stamps themselves chiefly in their excellence of impression and the paper on which they are printed. Some of the colors vary.

Hybrids are plate proofs of all issues before 1894 which have been cut to shape, mounted and pressed on large cards to resemble large die proofs. These sell for somewhat less than the corresponding large die proofs.

India Paper is a thin, soft, opaque paper which wrinkles when wet. It varies in thickness and shows particles of bamboo.

Card is a plain, clear white card of good quality, which is found in varying thicknesses for different printings. Plate proofs on card were made in five printings in 1879-94. Quantities range from 500 to 3,200 of the card proofs listed between Scott 3P and 245P.

Margin blocks with full imprint and plate number are indicated by the abbreviation "P# blk. of -."

Numbers have been assigned to all proofs consisting of the number of the regular stamp with the suffix letter "P" to denote Proof.

Proofs in other than accepted or approved colors exist in a large variety of shades, colors and papers produced at various times by various people for many different reasons. The field is large. The task of listing has been begun under "Trial Colors" following the regular proofs.

Some proofs are not identical to the issued stamps. Some of these are now listed in the Essay section. Others have been left in the proof section to keep sets together at this time.

Values are for items in very fine condition. Most "Panama-Pacific" small die proofs are toned. Values are for moderately toned examples. **Plate proof pairs on stamp paper are valued with original gum unless otherwise noted.**

NORMAL COLORS

1845

		DIE		PLATE	
	(1) Large	(2) Small	(2a)	(3) India	(4) Card
9X1P 5c black on India paper	750.	350.		—	
a. With scar on neck		300.			
b. Dot in "P" of "POST" and scar on neck	525.	300.			
c. As "b," on Bond	525.	300.		—	
d. As "b," on glazed paper	525.				
e. As "a," on Bond	525.				

The above listed Large Die varieties have an additional impression of the portrait medallion. Some experts question the existance of plate proofs from the sheets of 40. Plate proofs from the sheet of 9 exist on white and bluish bond paper. Value $125.

Providence, R.I.

10X1P	5c black		300.
10X2P	10c black		500.
	Sheet of 12		3,250.

General Issues

1847

1P	5c	red brown on India paper	800.	600.
a.		White bond paper	800.	
b.		Colored bond paper	1,000.	
c.		White laid paper	800.	
d.		Bluish laid paper	800.	
e.		Yellowish wove paper	800.	
f.		Bluish wove paper	800.	
g.		White wove paper	800.	
h.		Card	1,000.	
i.		Glazed paper	1,000.	
2P	10c	black on India paper	800.	900.
		Double transfer (31R1)	—	
a.		White bond paper	800.	
b.		Colored bond paper	1,000.	
c.		White laid paper	800.	
d.		Bluish laid paper	800.	
e.		Yellowish wove paper	800.	
g.		White wove paper	800.	
h.		Card	1,000.	
i.		Glazed paper	1,000.	

Original die proofs are generally found cut to stamp size; full size die proofs sell at higher prices. Reprint proofs with cross-hatching are valued as full size; cut down examples sell for less. Plate proofs overprinted "Specimen" sell for about half the above figures.

Reproductions of 1847 Issue

Actually, official imitations made about 1875 from new dies and plates by order of the Post Office Department.

3P	5c	red brown	900.	400.	2,500.		200.	150.
		Block of 4					1,000.	750.
a.		On bond paper	650.					
4P	10c	black	900.	400.	2,500.		200.	150.
		Block of 4					1,000.	750.
a.		On bond paper	650.					

1851-60

5P	1c	blue, type I	5,000.		
11P	3c	red, type I	5,000.		
		brush obliteration		1,000.	
		Block of 4		5,000.	
		P# block of 8		—	
12P	5c	brn, type I	7,500.	1,650.	
13P	10c	grn, type I	5,000.		
17P	12c	black	10,000.		
24P	1c	blue, type V (pl. 9)		1,250.	
		Pair		3,000.	
26P	3c	red, type II (pl. 20)		1,250.	
		Pair		3,000.	
30P	5c	brn, type II		1,250.	
35P	10c	grn, type V		1,250.	
36bP	12c	black, plate III (broken frame lines)		1,250.	
		Block of 4		5,500.	—
	d.	On stamp paper			—
		Pair			—
		Block of 4			—
37P	24c	lilac	—	1,250.	
		Pair		3,000.	
	c.	On stamp paper			1,500.
		Pair			15,500.
38P	30c	orange	— —	1,250.	
		Pair		3,000.	
	a.	On stamp paper			2,500.
		Pair			7,750.
39P	90c	blue	— —	1,250.	
		Pair		3,000.	
	a.	On stamp paper			2,750.
		Pair			37,500.

Plate proofs of 24P to 39P are from the original plates. They may be distinguished from the 40P to 47P by the type in the case of the 1c, 3c, 10c and 12c, and by the color in the case of the 5c, 24c, 30c and 90c.

The 3c plate proofs (No. 11) are on proof paper and all known copies have a vertical brush stroke obliteration.

Die proofs of the 30c show full spear point in corners of design.

			(1) Large	DIE (2) Small	(2a)	PLATE (3) India	(4) Card

Reprints of 1857-60 Issue

40P	1c	bright blue, type I (new plate)	325.	350.	1,500.	65.	45.
		Block of 4				325.	225.
	a.	On stamp paper					500.
41P	3c	scarlet, type I (new plate)	325.	350.	1,500.	65.	45.
		Block of 4				325.	225.
		Orange brown			2,000.		
42P	5c	orange brown type II (plate II)	325.	350.		65.	45.
		Block of 4				325.	225.
		P# blk. of 8				850.	—
43P	10c	blue green, type I (new plate)	325.	350.	1,500.	65.	45.
		Block of 4				325.	225.
44P	12c	greenish black (new plate, frame line complete)	325.	350.	2,250.	95.	45.
		Block of 4				475.	225.
45P	24c	blksh vio (pl. I)	325.	350.	1,500.	65.	45.
		Block of 4				325.	225.
		P# blk. of 8				850.	
46P	30c	yel org (pl. I)	325.	350.	1,500.	65.	45.
		Block of 4				325.	225.
		P# blk. of 8				975.	—
47P	90c	deep blue (pl. I)	325.	350.	1,500.	95.	65.
		Block of 4				475.	325.
		P# blk. of 8				975.	925.

Nos. 40P-47P, large die, exist only as hybrids.

SECOND DESIGNS (Regular Issue)

For "First Designs" see Essay section (former Nos. 55-57, 59, 62), Proofs and Trial Color Proofs (former No. 58) and Trial Color Proofs (former Nos. 60-61).

1861

62BP	10c	dark green		325.		300.	
63P	1c	blue	700.	225.	1,750.	50.	35.
		Block of 4				200.	225.
		P# blk. of 8				1,100.	—
		Indigo			1,750.		
64P	3c	pink	3,500.				
65P	3c	rose	1,000.	—	1,500.	90.	125.
		Block of 4				525.	
		P# blk. of 8				1,350.	
	a.	3c dull red				90.	
	c.	On stamp paper, pair					1,000.
		P# blk. of 8				—	

67P	5c	buff	5,000.		1,500.		
76P	5c	brown	700.	225.	1,500.	40.	30.
		Block of 4				200.	140.
		P# blk. of 8				775.	
68P	10c	green	650.	225.	1,500.	60.	30.
		Block of 4				275.	140.
		P# blk. of 8				875.	
69P	12c	black	700.	225.	1,750.	60.	30.
		Block of 4				275.	140.
		P# blk. of 8				875.	
70P	24c	red lilac			2,500.		325.
78P	24c	lilac		225.	2,500.	75.	70.
		Block of 4				375.	350.
		P# blk. of 8				1,100.	
71P	30c	orange	500.	225.	2,500.	45.	30.
		Block of 4				225.	140.
		P# blk. of 8				1,000.	
72P	90c	blue	500.	225.	2,500.	45.	30.
		Block of 4				225.	140.
		P# blk. of 8				1,000.	

1861-67

73P	2c	black, die I	3,500.			100.	
		Block of 4				500.	
		P# blk. of 8				1,500.	—
	a.	Die II	2,500.	1,350.	8,500.	95.	75.
		Block of 4				450.	400.
		P# blk. of 8				1,350.	
77P	15c	black	1,250.	475.	2,500.	50.	40.
		Block of 4				225.	180.
		P# blk. of 8				875.	—
79P	3c	rose, A grill, on stamp paper, pair					1,500.
		Block of 4					4,000.
		P# blk. of 8					10,000.
83P	3c	rose, C grill, on stamp paper, pair					1,850.
94P	3c	red, F grill, on stamp paper, pair					1,500.

The listed plate proofs of the 1c (63P), 5c (76P), 10c (68P) and 12c (69P) are from the 100 subject re-issue plates of 1875. Single proofs of these denominations from the regular issue plates cannot be told apart from the reprints. As the reprint plates had wider spacing between the subjects, multiples can be differentiated. Values are for proofs from the reprint plates. The 2c Die II has a small dot on the left cheek.

1869

112P	1c	buff	750.	350.	1,750.	55.	60.
		Block of 4				250.	275.
		P# blk. of 10				750.	
113P	2c	brown	750.	350.	1,750.	40.	45.
		Block of 4				175.	190.
		P# blk. of 10				600.	
114P	3c	ultra.	900.	575.	1,750.	45.	50.
		Block of 4				190.	215.
		P# blk. of 10				800.	
115P	6c	ultra.	900.	350.	1,750.	45.	50.
		Block of 4				190.	235.
		P# blk. of 10				800.	—
116P	10c	yellow	900.	350.	1,750.	45.	50.
		Block of 4				190.	235.
		P# blk. of 10				800.	—
117P	12c	green	900.	350.	1,750.	45.	50.
		Block of 4				190.	265.
		P# blk. of 10				875.	—
119P	15c	brown & blue (type II)	550.	450.	1,750.	120.	
		Block of 4				600.	
		P# blk. of 8				1,450.	
129P	15c	Reissue (type III)	550.	450.	1,750.	250.	125.
		Block of 4				1,200.	700.
		P# blk. of 8				3,000.	—
	a.	Center inverted (100)					2,500.
		Block of 4					11,000.
		P# blk. of 8					37,500.
120P	24c	green & violet	550.	450.	1,750.	140.	125.
		Block of 4				625.	600.
		P# blk. of 8				1,450.	—
	a.	Center inverted (100)					2,750.
		Block of 4					12,000.
		P# blk. of 8					37,500.
121P	30c	ultra & carmine	1,250.	450.	1,750.	140.	135.
		Block of 4				625.	750.
		P# blk. of 8				1,450.	—
	a.	Flags inverted (100)					2,750.
		Block of 4					12,000.
		P# blk. of 8					37,500.
122P	90c	carmine & black	550.	450.	1,750.	180.	150.
		Block of 4				825.	825.
		P# blk. of 8				1,750.	—
	a.	Center inverted (100)					2,750.
		Block of 4					14,000.
		P# blk. of 8					37,500.

Large die proofs of Nos. 119, 129, 120 and 122 exist only as hybrids.

1880

133P	1c	dark buff	1,000.		100.
		Block of 4			450.
		P# blk. of 10			1,250.

1870-71   National Bank Note Co.

136P	3c	green, grill, on stamp paper, pair					1,200.
		P# blk. of 12					—
145P	1c	ultra	250.	175.	1,000.	20.	
		Block of 4				90.	
		P# blk. of 12				385.	
146P	2c	red brown	250.			20.	
		Block of 4				90.	
		P# blk. of 12				385.	
147P	3c	green	300.			20.	
		Block of 4				90.	
		P# blk. of 12				400.	

The former No. 147Pc4 is now listed in the Essay section as No. 147-E13e.

148P	6c	carmine	450.		35.
		Block of 4			150.
		P# blk. of 12			650.
149P	7c	vermilion	200.		15.
		Block of 4			70.
		P# blk. of 12			360.
150P	10c	brown	300.		40.
		Block of 4			165.
		P# blk. of 12			750.
151P	12c	violet	200.		16.
		Block of 4			70.
		P# blk. of 12			385.
152P	15c	orange	250.		30.
		Block of 4			135.
		P# blk. of 12			550.
153P	24c	purple	250.		30.
		Block of 4			135.
		P# blk. of 12			550.
154P	30c	black	250.		40.
		Block of 4			170.
		P# blk. of 12			750.
155P	90c	carmine	250.		45.
		Block of 4			195.
		P# blk. of 12			800.

Secret Marks on 24, 30 and 90c Dies of the Bank Note Issues

National 24c - Rays of lower star normal.

Continental 24c - Rays of lower star strengthened.

National 30c - Lower line does not join point of shield.

Continental and American 30c - Lower line joins point of shield and bottom line of shield thicker.

National 90c - Rays of star in upper right normal.

Continental and American 90c - Rays of star in upper right strengthened.

1873 — Continental Bank Note Co.

		DIE		PLATE	
		(1) Large	(2) Small	(2a)	(3) India	(4) Card
156P	1c	ultra	450.		55.	150.
	Block of 4				250.	
	P# blk. of 14				1,150.	
157P	2c	brown	350.	175. 1,000.	35.	15.
	Block of 4				165.	80.
	P# blk. of 12				650.	—
a.	On stamp paper					
158P	3c	green	350.	175. 1,000.	55.	150.
	Block of 4				250.	
	P# blk. of 14				1,150.	
f.	On stamp paper, pair					750.
g.	On stamp paper, grill, pair					650.
159P	6c	pink	750.	250. 1,250.	110.	200.
	Block of 4				525.	
	P# blk. of 12				2,000.	
160P	7c	orange vermilion	250.	175. 1,000.	35.	10.
	Block of 4				165.	50.
	P# blk. of 14				825.	—
161P	10c	brown	450.	200. 1,000.	60.	150.
	Block of 4				300.	
	P# blk. of 14				1,300.	
162P	12c	blackish violet	200.	175. 1,000.	38.	15.
	Block of 4				190.	75.
	P# blk. of 14				975.	—
a.	On stamp paper					
163P	15c	yellow orange	400.	175. 1,000.	65.	20.
	Block of 4				250.	100.
	P# blk. of 12				1,000.	—
a.	On stamp paper					
164P	24c	violet	400.	175. 1,000.	50.	28.
	Block of 4				225.	125.
	P# blk. of 12				975.	
165P	30c	gray black	400.	175. 1,000.	40.	20.
	Block of 4				200.	90.
	P# blk. of 12				825.	

		DIE			PLATE	
		(1) Large	(2) Small	(2a)	(3) India	(4) Card
166P	90c	rose carmine	400.	175. 1,000.	55.	38.
	Block of 4				250.	175.
	P# blk. of 12				1,000.	

Die proofs of the 24c, 30c and 90c show secret marks, as illustrated, but as plates of these denominations were not made from these dies, plate proofs can be identified only by color.

178P	2c	ver. on stamp paper, pair				600.
a.	P# blk. of 12					—

1879 — American Bank Note Co.

182P	1c	gray blue	525.		60.	
	Block of 4				275.	
	P# blk. of 12				1,000.	
183P	2c	vermilion	300.	190. 1,000.	35.	15.
	Block of 4				160.	75.
	P# blk. of 12				600.	
184P	3c	green on stamp paper, pair				500.
185P	5c	blue	450.	225. 1,000.	70.	20.
	Block of 4				325.	90.
	P# blk. of 12				1,300.	
191P	90c	carmine on stamp paper, pair				2,500.
	P# strip of 5					—

1881-82 — American Bank Note Co.

205P	5c	yellow brown	250.	190. 1,000.	40.	15.
	Block of 4				175.	75.
	P# blk. of 12				600.	
206P	1c	blue	375.	190. 1,000.	40.	20.
	Block of 4				175.	90.
	P# blk. of 12				600.	
207P	3c	blue green	375.	190. 1,000.	40.	20.
	Block of 4				175.	90.
	P# blk. of 12				600.	
208P	6c	rose	800.	190. 1,000.	90.	60.
	Block of 4				425.	210.
	P# blk. of 12					
a.	6c brown red		1,000. 1,000.		100.	50.
209P	10c	brown	800.	190. 1,000.	40.	25.
	Block of 4				170.	110.
	P# blk. of 12				650.	

1883

210P	2c	red brown	400.	190. 1,000.	32.	20.
	Block of 4				145.	85.
	P# blk. of 12				600.	—
a.	On stamp paper, pair					
211P	4c	green	425.	190. 1,000.	40.	25.
	Block of 4				165.	110.
	P# blk. of 12				750.	—
a.	On stamp paper, pair					

1887-88

212P	1c	ultra	650.	190. 1,000.	95.	2,000.
	Block of 4				450.	—
	P# blk. of 12				1,800.	
a.	On stamp paper, pair					1,000.

Copies of No. 212P3 mounted on card are frequently offered as No. 212P4.

213P	2c	green	400.	190. 1,000.	40.	20.
	Block of 4				180.	85.
	P# blk. of 12				625.	—
a.	On stamp paper, pair					750.
214P	3c	vermilion	425.	190. 1,000.	40.	25.
	Block of 4				180.	110.
	P# blk. of 12					—

Nos. 207P1 & 214P1 inscribed: "Worked over by new company, June 29th, 1881."

215P	4c	carmine	575.	190. 1,000.	95.	40.
	Block of 4				475.	180.
	P# blk. of 12					—
216P	5c	indigo	575.	190. 1,000.	60.	25.
	Block of 4				300.	110.
	P# blk. of 12					—
b.	On stamp paper,					1,400.
217P	30c	orange brown	600.	190. 1,000.	60.	25.
	Block of 4				300.	110.
	P# blk. of 10					—
a.	On stamp paper, pair					1,750.
218P	90c	purple	600.	190. 1,000.	90.	40.
	Block of 4				400.	180.
	P# blk. of 10					—
a.	On stamp paper, pair					

1890-93

219P	1c	ultra	225.	190. 900.	25.	40.
	Block of 4				110.	180.
	P# blk. of 12				500.	650.
c.	On stamp paper, pair					225.
219DP	2c	lake	550.	190. 900.	80.	165.
	Block of 4				385.	700.
	P# blk. of 12				1,650.	3,250.
e.	On stamp paper, pair					100.
220P	2c	carmine	450.	190.	300.	200.

		DIE			PLATE	
	Block of 4				1,250.	825.
	P# blk. of 12				3,850.	2,500.
d.	On stamp paper, pair					100.
	As "d," without gum					40.
	P# blk. of 12					—
221P	3c	purple	225.	190. 900.	35.	25.
	Block of 4				160.	110.
	P# blk. of 12				650.	600.
a.	On stamp paper, pair					275.
222P	4c	dark brown	225.	190. 900.	35.	25.
	Block of 4				160.	110.
	P# blk. of 12				650.	600.
a.	On stamp paper, pair					250.
223P	5c	chocolate	225.	190. 900.	32.	25.
	Block of 4				135.	110.
	P# blk. of 12				600.	625.
b.	Yellow brown, on stamp paper, pair					275.
224P	6c	brown red	225.	190. 900.	32.	20.
	Block of 4				135.	85.
	P# blk. of 12				600.	775.
a.	On stamp paper, pair					275.
225P	8c	lilac	600.	190. 900.	55.	110.
	Block of 4				250.	500.
	P# blk. of 12				1,100.	2,000.
a.	On stamp paper, pair					1,250.
226P	10c	green	225.	190. 900.	45.	40.
	Block of 4				200.	180.
	P# blk. of 12				700.	750.
a.	On stamp paper, pair					400.
227P	15c	indigo	300.	190. 900.	45.	40.
	Block of 4				190.	180.
	P# blk. of 12				825.	875.
a.	On stamp paper, pair					750.
228P	30c	black	300.	190. 900.	45.	45.
	Block of 4				190.	190.
	P# blk. of 12				825.	875.
a.	On stamp paper, pair					1,350.
229P	90c	orange	300.	190. 900.	60.	50.
	Block of 4				275.	225.
	P# blk. of 12				1,100.	1,150.
a.	On stamp paper, pair					1,750.

COLUMBIAN ISSUE

1893

230P	1c	blue	700.	325. 1,250.	40.	18.
	Block of 4				175.	90.
	P# blk. of 8				400.	260.
231P	2c	violet	800.	350. 1,500.	225.	65.
	Block of 4				1,000.	280.
	P# blk. of 8				2,250.	825.
b.	On stamp paper, pair					1,500.
c.	"Broken hat" variety					130.

Almost all examples of No. 231Pb are faulty. Value is for pair with minimal faults.

232P	3c	green	700.	325. 1,750.	60.	45.
	Block of 4				260.	200.
	P# blk. of 8				675.	550.
233P	4c	ultra.	700.	325. 1,750.	60.	45.
	Block of 4				260.	200.
	P# blk. of 8				675.	550.
233aP	4c	blue (error) on thin card	2,750.			
234P	5c	chocolate	700.	325. 1,750.	60.	45.
	Block of 4				260.	200.
	P# blk. of 8				675.	550.
235P	6c	purple	700.	325. 1,750.	60.	45.
	Block of 4				260.	200.
	P# blk. of 8				675.	550.
236P	8c	magenta	700.	325. 1,750.	60.	100.
	Block of 4				260.	450.
	P# blk. of 8				675.	1,250.
237P	10c	black brown	700.	325. 1,750.	60.	45.
	Block of 4				260.	200.
	P# blk. of 8				675.	550.
238P	15c	dark green	700.	325. 1,750.	60.	55.
	Block of 4				260.	250.
	P# blk. of 8				675.	1,400.
239P	30c	orange brown	700.	325. 1,750.	90.	65.
	Block of 4				400.	300.
	P# blk. of 8				1,250.	1,100.
240P	50c	slate blue	700.	325. 1,750.	135.	75.
	Block of 4				575.	350.
	P# blk. of 8				1,500.	1,100.
241P	$1	salmon	900.	450. 1,750.	160.	130.
	Block of 4				775.	575.
	P# blk. of 8				1,900.	
242P	$2	brown red	900.	450. 1,750.	180.	125.
	Block of 4				750.	550.
	P# blk. of 8				2,050.	1,500.
243P	$3	yellow green	900.	450. 1,750.	225.	150.
	Block of 4				1,200.	675.
	P# blk. of 8				2,700.	1,900.
244P	$4	crimson lake	900.	450. 1,750.	275.	175.
	Block of 4				1,200.	775.
	P# blk. of 8				3,000.	2,500.
245P	$5	black	900.	450. 1,750.	325.	225.
	Block of 4				1,425.	1,000.
	P# blk. of 8				3,500.	3,000.

This set also exists as Large Die proofs, not die sunk, but printed directly on thin card. Set value $4,725. 1c through 50c, $225 each; $1 through $5, $450 each. Nos. 234P1, 234P2 differ from issued stamp.

Bureau of Engraving and Printing

1894

246P	1c	ultra	450.		
247P	1c	blue	250.	250. 900.	100.
		Block of 4			450.
		P# blk. of 6			800.
248P	2c	pink, type I			100.>
		Block of 4			475.
		P# blk. of 6			900.
	a.	On stamp paper, vert. pair, imperf. horiz.			2,000.
250P	2c	car, type I	250.	250.	100.
		Block of 4			475.
		P# blk. of 6			900.
251P	2c	car, type II	250.	—	

The existence of No. 251P2 has been questioned by specialists. The editors would like to see evidence that the item exists.

252P	2c	car, type III	350.		
		Block of 4	1,200.		
253P	3c	purple (triangle I)	400.		
	a.	On stamp paper, pair			350.
		Block of 4			750.
		P# blk. of 6			—
253AP	3c	purple (triangle II)	325.	250. 900.	
254P	4c	dark brown	250.	250. 900.	
	a.	On stamp paper, pair			350.
		Block of 4			750.
		P# blk. of 6			—
255P	5c	chocolate	250.	250. 900.	
	b.	On stamp paper, pair			350.
		Block of 4			750.
		P# blk. of 6			—
256P	6c	brown	250.	250. 900.	450.
		Block of 4			1,900.
		P# blk. of 6			2,750.
257P	8c	violet brown	275.	250. 900.	
258P	10c	green	275.	250. 900.	
	a.	On stamp paper, pair			650.
		Block of 4			1,400.
		P# blk. of 6			—
259P	15c	dark blue	300.	250. 900.	
260P	50c	orange	450.	210. 900.	
261AP	$1	black	475.	350. 900.	
262P	$2	dark blue	475.	350. 900.	450.
		Block of 4			2,250.
		P# blk. of 6			3,500.
263P	$5	dark green	650.	375. 900.	450.
		Block of 4			2,250.
		P# blk. of 6			4,750.

258P2 to 263P2 (small die) are from the type II die.

1895

264P	1c	blue, on stamp paper, pair		325.
		Block of 4		700.
	b.	Horiz. pair, imperf. vert.		—
267P	2c	carmine, type III, on stamp paper, pair		300.
		Block of 4		650.
268P	3c	purple, on stamp paper, pair		350.
		Block of 4		800.
269P	4c	dark brown, on stamp paper, pair		350.
		Block of 4		800.
270P	5c	chocolate, on stamp paper, pair		350.
		Block of 4		800.
271P	6c	dull brown, on stamp paper, pair		400.
		Block of 4		850.
272P	8c	violet brown, on stamp paper, pair		550.
		Block of 4		1,150.
273P	10c	dark green, on stamp paper, pair		450.
		Block of 4		950.
274P	15c	dark blue, on stamp paper, pair		1,450.
		Block of 4		3,000.
275P	50c	orange, on stamp paper, pair		1,600.
		Block of 4		3,350.
276P	$1	black, type I, on stamp paper, pair		2,000.
		Block of 4		4,250.
277P	$2	bright blue, on stamp paper, pair		5,000.
		Block of 4		10,500.
278P	$5	dark green, on stamp paper, pair		4,000.
		Block of 4		8,500.

1897-1903

279P	1c	green	700.	375. 900.	
279BdP	2c	orange red, type IV		900.	
279BfP	2c	car, type IV	400.	900.	
280P	4c	rose brown	700.	900.	
281P	5c	blue	700.	375. 900.	
282P	6c	lake	700.	900.	
283P	10c	orange brown, type I	800.	375. 900.	
283aP	10c	brown, type II	800.		
284P	15c	olive green, type II	800.	375. 900.	

TRANS-MISSISSIPPI ISSUE

1898

285P	1c	green	750.	650. 1,100.	
286P	2c	copper red	750.	650. 1,100.	4,000.
287P	4c	orange	750.	650. 1,100.	
288P	5c	dull blue	750.	650. 1,100.	
289P	8c	violet brown	750.	650. 1,100.	
290P	10c	gray violet	750.	650. 1,100.	
291P	50c	sage green	750.	650. 1,100.	
292P	$1	black	850.	650. 1,100.	
293P	$2	orange brown	850.	650. 1,100.	6,000.
		Block of 4			30,000.

The bicolored items commonly offered as No. 285-293 bicolored proofs can be found under the following essay listings: No. 285-E8a, 286-E8a, 287-E9a, 288-E5a, 289-E4a, 290-E4a, 291-E8a, 292-E6a, 293-E7a.

PAN-AMERICAN ISSUE

1901

294P	1c	green & black	575.	575.	1,000.
295P	2c	carmine & black	575.	575.	1,000.
296P	4c	chocolate & black	575.	575.	1,000.
297P	5c	ultra & black	575.	575.	1,000.
298P	8c	brown violet & black	575.	575.	1,000.
299P	10c	yel brn & blk	575.	575.	1,000.

1902-03

300P	1c	green	750.	300.	900.
301P	2c	carmine	750.	300.	900.
302P	3c	purple	750.	300.	900.
303P	4c	orange brown	750.	300.	900.
304P	5c	blue	750.	300.	900.
305P	6c	lake	750.	300.	900.
306P	8c	violet black	750.	300.	900.
307P	10c	orange brown	750.	300.	900.
308P	13c	deep vio brn	750.	300.	900.
309P	15c	olive green	750.	300.	900.
310P	50c	orange	750.	300.	900.
311P	$1	black	750.	300.	900.
312P	$2	blue	750.	300.	900.
313P	$5	green	850.	375.	1,000.

1903

319P	2c	carmine, Type I	1,500.	
319iP	2c	carmine, Type II	1,500. 950.	2,750.

LOUISIANA PURCHASE ISSUE

1904

323P	1c	green	1,400.	750.	1,100.
324P	2c	carmine	1,400.	750.	1,100.
325P	3c	violet	1,400.	750.	1,100.
326P	5c	dark blue	1,400.	750.	1,100.
327P	10c	red brown	1,400.	750.	1,100.

JAMESTOWN EXPOSITION ISSUE

1907

328P	1c	green	1,000.	900.	1,100.
329P	2c	carmine	1,000.	900.	1,100.
330P	5c	blue	1,000.	900.	1,100.

1908-09

331P	1c	green	1,250.	725.	1,000.
332P	2c	carmine	1,250.	725.	1,000.
		carmine, amber	—		
		carmine, lt blue	—		
333P	3c	deep violet	1,250.	725.	1,000.
334P	4c	brown	1,250.	725.	1,000.
335P	5c	blue	1,250.	725.	1,000.
		blue, salmon	—		
336P	6c	red orange	1,250.	725.	1,000.
337P	8c	olive green	1,250.	725.	1,000.
		olive green, yellow	—		
338P	10c	yellow	1,250.	725.	1,000.
339P	13c	blue green	1,250.	725.	1,000.
340P	15c	pale ultramarine	1,250.	725.	1,000.
341P	50c	violet	1,250.	725.	1,000.
		violet, pale lilac	—		
		violet, yellow	—		
		violet, greenish	—		
342P	$1	violet black	1,500.	725.	1,000.

LINCOLN MEMORIAL ISSUE

1909

367P	2c	carmine	1,100.	1,000.	1,500.

ALASKA-YUKON ISSUE

1909

370P	2c	carmine	1,100.	1,000.	1,500.

HUDSON-FULTON ISSUE

1909

372P	2c	carmine	1,250.	1,000.	1,500.

PANAMA-PACIFIC ISSUE

1912-13

397P	1c	green	1,750.	1,500.	1,100.
398P	2c	carmine	1,750.	1,500.	1,100.
399P	5c	blue	1,750.	1,500.	1,100.
400P	10c	org. yellow	1,750.	1,500.	1,100.
400AP	10c	orange	1,750.	1,500.	1,200.

No. 398P inscribed "Gatun Locks" is listed in the Essay section as No. 398-E3.

1912-19

				DIE	
			(1) Large	(2) Small	(2a)
405P	1c	green	825.	650.	1,000.
406P	2c	carmine	825.	650.	1,000.
407P	7c	black	825.	650.	1,000.
414P	8c	olive green	825.	650.	1,000.
415P	9c	salmon red	825.	650.	1,000.
416P	10c	orange yellow	825.	650.	1,000.
434P	11c	dark green	950.		
417P	12c	claret brown	825.	650.	1,000.

				DIE	
			(1) Large	(2) Small	(2a)
513P	13c	apple green	950.		
418P	15c	gray	825.	650.	1,000.
419P	20c	ultramarine	825.	650.	1,000.
420P	30c	orange red	825.	650.	1,000.
421P	50c	violet	825.	650.	1,000.
423P	$1	violet black	825.	650.	1,000.

1918-20

524P	$5	deep green & black	1,500.	
547P	$2	carmine & black	1,500.	

VICTORY ISSUE

1919

537P	3c	violet	1,100.	850.

PILGRIM ISSUE

1920

548P	1c	green	1,250.	1,000.
549P	2c	carmine rose	1,250.	1,000.
550P	5c	deep blue	1,250.	1,000.

1922-26

			LARGE DIE		PLATE	
			(1) India	(1a) White Wove	(3) White Wove	(4) Card
551P	½c	olive brown	1,250.			
552P	1c	deep green	800.	700.	—	
553P	1½c	yel brn	800.			
554P	2c	carmine	800.	700.	—	
555P	3c	violet	800.	700.	—	
556P	4c	yel brn	800.	700.	—	
557P	5c	dark blue	800.	700.	—	
558P	6c	red orange	800.	700.	—	
559P	7c	black	800.	700.	—	
560P	8c	olive green	900.	700.	—	
561P	9c	rose	800.	700.	—	
562P	10c	orange	800.	700.	—	
563P	11c	light blue	1,200.	700.	—	
564P	12c	brn vio	750.	700.	—	
622P	13c	green	1,000.	700.	—	
565P	14c	dark blue	750.	700.	—	
566P	15c	gray	1,250.	700.	—	
623P	17c	black	800.			
567P	20c	car rose	800.	700.	—	
568P	25c	deep green	800.	700.	—	
569P	30c	olive brown	800.	700.	—	
570P	50c	lilac	800.	700.	—	
571P	$1	vio brn	800.	700.	—	
572P	$2	deep blue	1,500.	700.	—	
572P2		deep blue, small die on India	—			
573P	$5	carmine & dark blue	2,000.			

No. 573P1 exists only as a hybrid.

1923-26

			LARGE DIE		SMALL DIE
			(1) India	(1a) White Wove	(2) White or Yellowish Wove
610P	Harding, 2c black		1,250.	1,250.	1,000.
614P	Huguenot Walloon, 1c		750.	700.	700.
615P	Huguenot Walloon, 2c		750.	700.	700.
616P	Huguenot Walloon, 5c		750.	700.	700.
617P	Lexington Concord, 1c		750.	700.	700.
618P	Lexington Concord, 2c		750.	700.	700.
619P	Lexington Concord, 5c		750.	700.	700.
620P	Norse American, 2c		850.	850.	850.
621P	Norse American, 5c		850.	850.	850.
627P	Sesquicentennial, 2c		800.	750.	850.
628P	Ericsson, 5c		800.	750.	850.
629P	White Plains, 2c		800.	750.	850.

1927-29

643P	Vermont, 2c		800.	750.	850.
644P	Burgoyne, 2c		800.	750.	850.
645P	Valley Forge, 2c		800.	750.	850.
649P	Aeronautics, 2c		1,250.	900.	900.
650P	Aeronautics, 5c		1,250.	900.	900.
651P	Clark, 2c		900.	800.	750.
654P	Edison, 2c		900.	800.	750.
657P	Sullivan, 2c		850.	800.	750.
680P	Fallen Timbers, 2c		850.	800.	750.
681P	Ohio River Canalization, 2c		850.	800.	750.

1930-31

682P	Massachusetts Bay, 2c		850.	800.	750.
683P	Carolina Charleston, 2c		850.	800.	750.
684P	1½c brown		650.		
685P	4c brown		650.		
688P	Braddock's Field, 2c		850.	800.	750.
689P	von Steuben, 2c		850.	800.	750.
690P	Pulaski, 2c		850.	800.	750.
702P	Red Cross, 2c black & red			900.	900.
703P	Yorktown, 2c		1,000.	800.	750.

1932

Washington Bicentennial

704P	½c olive brown		850.	800.	750.
705P	1c green		850.	800.	750.

706P	1½c brown	850.	800.	750.
707P	2c carmine rose	850.	800.	750.
708P	3c deep violet	850.	800.	750.
709P	4c light brown	850.	800.	750.
710P	5c blue	850.	800.	750.
711P	6c red orange	850.	800.	750.
712P	7c black	850.	800.	750.
713P	8c olive bister	850.	800.	750.
714P	9c pale red	850.	800.	750.
715P	10c orange yellow	850.	800.	750.
716P	Winter Games, 2c	1,100.	950.	900.
717P	Arbor Day, 2c	900.	900.	800.
718P	Olympic Games, 3c violet	10,000.	950.	900.
719P	Olympic Games, 5c blue	15,000.	950.	900.
720P	3c deep violet			800.
724P	Penn, 3c violet	800.	850.	750.
725P	Webster, 3c violet	800.	850.	750.

1933-34

726P	Georgia, 3c violet	700.	800.	650.
727P	Peace, 3c violet	700.	800.	650.
728P	Century of Progress, 1c	700.	800.	650.
729P	Century of Progress, 3c	700.	800.	650.
732P	N.R.A., 3c violet		800.	650.
733P	Byrd Antarctic, 3c		900.	650.
734P	Kosciuszko, 5c blue		800.	650.
736P	Maryland, 3c carmine rose		800.	650.
737P	Mothers Day, 3c	800.	800.	650.
739P	Wisconsin, 3c deep violet		800.	650.
740P	Parks, 1c green		800.	650.
741P	Parks, 2c red			650.
742P	Parks, 3c violet		800.	650.
743P	Parks, 4c brown			650.
744P	Parks, 5c blue			650.
745P	Parks, 6c dark blue			650.
746P	Parks, 7c black		800.	650.
747P	Parks, 8c sage green			650.
748P	Parks, 9c red orange	800.		650.
749P	Parks, 10c gray black			650.

1935-37

772P	Conn., 3c violet			650.
773P	San Diego, 3c purple			650.
774P	Boulder Dam, 3c purple			650.
775P	Michigan, 3c purple			650.
776P	Texas, 3c purple			650.
777P	Rhode Is., 3c purple			650.
782P	Arkansas, 3c pur.	800.	800.	650.
783P	Oregon, 3c purple	—	800.	650.
784P	Anthony, 3c violet			650.
785P	Army, 1c green		800.	800.
786P	Army, 2c carmine			800.
787P	Army, 3c purple	800.	800.	800.
788P	Army, 4c gray			800.
789P	Army, 5c ultramarine		800.	800.
790P	Navy, 1c green			800.
791P	Navy, 2c car.	800.		800.
792P	Navy, 3c purple			800.
793P	Navy, 4c gray			800.
794P	Navy, 5c ultramarine			800.
795P	Ordinance, 3c red violet			650.
796P	Virginia Dare, 5c	800.		650.
797P	S.P.A. Sheet, 10c			650.
798P	Constitution, 3c red violet	800.		650.
799P	Hawaii, 3c violet	800.		750.
800P	Alaska, 3c violet			650.
801P	Puerto Rico, 3c	800.		650.
802P	Virgin Is., 3c light violet	—		650.

PRESIDENTIAL ISSUE

1938

803P	½c deep orange	1,500.		650.
804P	1c green			650.
805P	1½c bister brown			650.
806P	2c rose carmine		1,800.	650.
807P	3c deep violet			650.
a.	On glazed card	—		
808P	4c red violet			650.
809P	4½c dark gray	1,500.		650.
810P	5c bright blue	1,500.		650.
811P	6c red orange			650.
812P	7c sepia	—		650.
813P	8c olive green		1,800.	650.
814P	9c rose pink	1,800.	1,800.	650.
815P	10c brown red			650.
816P	11c ultramarine			650.
817P	12c bright violet	1,500.		650.
818P	13c blue green			650.
819P	14c blue			650.
820P	15c blue gray	1,800.	1,800.	650.
821P	16c black	1,500.		650.
822P	17c rose red			650.
823P	18c brown carmine			650.
824P	19c bright violet	1,800.	1,800.	650.
825P	20c bright blue green	1,800.	1,800.	650.
826P	21c dull blue			650.
827P	22c vermilion			650.
828P	24c gray black	1,800.		650.
829P	25c deep red lilac			650.
830P	30c deep ultramarine			650.
831P	50c light red violet	1,250.		650.
832P	$1 purple & black			650.
833P	$2 yellow green & black			800.
834P	$5 carmine & black			800.

1938

835P	Constitution, 3c		600.
836P	Swedes & Finns, 3c		600.
837P	N.W. Territory, 3c		600.
838P	Iowa, 3c violet	1,250.	600.

1939

852P	Golden Gate, 3c	1,800.	600.
853P	World's Fair, 3c	1,250.	700.
854P	Inauguration, 3c	1,250.	650.

855P	Baseball, 3c violet	1,500.	2,000.	600.
856P	Panama Canal, 3c			600.
857P	Printing, 3c violet			600.
858P	Statehood, 3c rose violet			600.

FAMOUS AMERICANS ISSUE

1940

859P	Authors, 1c bright blue green		800.
860P	Authors, 2c rose carmine		800.
861P	Authors, 3c bright red violet		800.
862P	Authors, 5c ultramarine	800.	800.
863P	Authors, 10c dark brown	2,500.	800.
864P	Poets, 1c bright blue green		800.
865P	Poets, 2c rose carmine		800.
866P	Poets, 3c bright red violet		800.
867P	Poets, 5c ultramarine		800.
868P	Poets, 10c dark brown	1,450.	800.
869P	Educators, 1c bright blue green		800.
870P	Educators, 2c rose carmine		800.
871P	Educators, 3c bright red violet		800.
872P	Educators, 5c ultramarine	800.	800.
873P	Educators, 10c dark brown	900.	800.
874P	Scientists, 1c bright blue green	1,450.	800.
875P	Scientists, 2c rose carmine	800.	800.
876P	Scientists, 3c bright red violet	800.	800.
877P	Scientists, 5c ultramarine		800.
878P	Scientists, 10c dark brown		800.
879P	Composers, 1c bright blue green		800.
880P	Composers, 2c rose carmine	900.	800.
881P	Composers, 3c bright red violet		800.
882P	Composers, 5c ultramarine	800.	800.
883P	Composers, 10c dark brown		800.
884P	Artists, 1c bright blue green		800.
885P	Artists, 2c rose carmine		800.
886P	Artists, 3c bright red violet		800.
887P	Artists, 5c ultramarine	800.	800.
888P	Artists, 10c dark brown	800.	800.
889P	Inventors, 1c bright blue green		800.
890P	Inventors, 2c rose carmine	1,275.	800.
891P	Inventors, 3c bright red violet	800.	800.
892P	Inventors, 5c ultramarine		800.
893P	Inventors, 10c dark brown		800.

1940

894P	Pony Express, 3c	1,100.	600.
895P	Pan American, 3c		600.
896P	Idaho, 3c bright violet	800.	600.
897P	Wyoming, 3c brown violet		600.
898P	Coronado, 3c violet	1,100.	600.
899P	Defense, 1c bright blue green	800.	600.
900P	Defense, 2c rose carmine	800.	600.
901P	Defense, 3c bright violet	800.	600.
902P	Emancipation, 3c	800.	750.

1941-44

903P	Vermont, 3c light violet		600.
904P	Kentucky, 3c violet	750.	600.
905P	Win the War, 3c violet		600.
906P	China, 5c bright blue		600.
907P	Allied Nations, 2c		600.
908P	Four Freedoms, 1c	800.	600.
922P	Railroad, 3c violet	800.	600.
923P	Steamship, 3c violet	1,500.	600.
924P	Telegraph, 3c	800.	600.
925P	Corregidor, 3c deep violet	1,275.	600.
926P	Motion Picture, 3c	800.	600.

1945-46

927P	Florida	1,100.	600.
928P	United Nations		600.
929P	Iwo Jima		600.
930P	Roosevelt		600.
931P	Roosevelt	800.	600.
932P	Roosevelt	1,400.	600.
934P	Army	1,250.	600.
935P	Navy	800.	600.
941P	Tennessee	800.	
942P	Iowa	800.	
944P	Kearny	800.	

1947-50

945P	Edison	700.	
946P	Pulitzer	1,100.	
949P	Doctors	1,325.	
951P	Constitution	700.	
958P	Wisconsin	700.	
959P	Women	700.	
960P	White	900.	
962P	Key	700.	
965P	Stone	700.	
967P	Barton	1,900.	
972P	Indian Centennial	900.	
973P	Rough Riders	700.	
976P	Fort Bliss	—	
977P	Michael	1,150.	
981P	Minnesota Terr.	725.	—

983P	Puerto Rico	1,000.
985P	G.A.R.	725.
988P	Gompers	825.
989P	Statue of Freedom	1,325.
991P	Supreme Court	700.
992P	Capitol	700.

1951-53

999P	Nevada	1,000.	
1000P	Cadillac	800.	
1001P	Colorado	700.	
1002P	Chemical	700.	
1003P	Brooklyn	1,325.	
1004P	Betsy Ross	800.	
1005P	4H Clubs	700.	
1006P	B. & O. Railroad	1,750.	
1007P	A.A.A.		—
1009P	Grand Coulee Dam	700.	
1010P	Lafayette	800.	
1011P	Mt. Rushmore	700.	
1013P	Service Women	800.	—
1016P	Red Cross		—
1017P	National Guard	700.	
1018P	Ohio Statehood		—
1019P	Washington	700.	
1020P	Louisiana	800.	
1021P	Japan	1,650.	
1022P	American Bar	700.	
1025P	Trucking	950.	
1026P	Gen. Patton	700.	

1954

1029P	Columbia	700.

LIBERTY ISSUE

1030P	Franklin	1,200.	
1031P	Washington	700.	
1032P	Mount Vernon	900.	
1033P	Jefferson		—
1036P	Lincoln	700.	
1038P	Monroe	700.	
1039P	Roosevelt	700.	
1047P	Monticello	1,100.	
1049P	Lee	700.	
1050P	Marshall	700.	
1051P	Anthony	1,000.	
1052P	Henry	700.	
1053P	Hamilton	1,200.	

1954-57

1060P	Nebraska	950.	
1062P	Eastman	900.	
1063P	Lewis & Clark	825.	
1064P	Academy of Fine Arts	800.	
1067P	Armed Forces Reserve	1,275.	
1068P	New Hampshire	700.	
1069P	Soo Locks	825.	
1071P	Fort Ticonderoga	825.	
1073P	Franklin	700.	
1074P	Washington	700.	
1076P	FIPEX	700.	—
1077P	Turkey	800.	
1078P	Antelope	700.	
1079P	Salmon	700.	
1080P	Pure Food & Drug Act	800.	
1081P	Wheatland	700.	
1082P	Labor Day	700.	
1083P	Nassau Hall	700.	
1085P	Children	800.	—
1086P	Hamilton	700.	
1087P	Polio	800.	
1090P	Steel	700.	

AIR POST

1918

			DIE	
			(1) Large	(2) Small
C1P	6c	orange	8,500.	
C2P	16c	green	7,000.	
C3P	24c	carmine rose & blue	8,500.	

1923

C4P	8c	dark green	4,750.	6,500.
C5P	16c	dark blue	4,750.	6,500.
C6P	24c	carmine	4,750.	6,500.

1926-27

C7P	10c	dark blue	3,000.	
C8P	15c	olive brown	3,000.	
C9P	20c	yellow green	3,000.	—

LINDBERGH ISSUE

1927

C10P	10c	dark blue	6,000.	6,000.

1930

C11P	5c	carmine & blue	5,000.	
C12P	5c	violet	3,000.	

ZEPPELIN ISSUE

1930

C13P	65c	green	15,000.	8,250.
a.		on wove	15,000.	
C14P	$1.30	brown	15,000.	8,500.
a.		on wove	15,000.	
C15P	$2.60	blue	15,000.	8,500.

AIR POST (continued)

Cat	Denom	Color	India	Card
	a.	on wove	15,000.	

1932
Cat	Denom	Color	India	Card
C17P	8c	olive bister	4,000.	

CENTURY OF PROGRESS ISSUE
1933
Cat	Denom	Color	India	Card
C18P	50c	green	8,250.	8,250.

1935-39
Cat	Denom	Color	India	Card
C20P	25c	blue on wove		2,750.
C21P	20c	green on wove		2,750.
C22P	50c	carmine on wove		2,750.
C23P	6c	dark blue & carm. on wove		2,750.
C24P	30c	dull blue	3,500.	2,750.

1941-53
Cat	Denom	Color	India	Card
C25P	6c	carmine on wove		2,750.
C26P	8c	olive green on wove		2,750.
C27P	10c	violet on wove		2,750.
C28P	15c	brown carmine on wove		2,750.
C29P	20c	bright green on wove		2,750.
C30P	30c	blue on wove		2,750.
C31P	50c	orange on wove		2,750.
C33P	5c	carmine	—	
C40P	6c	carmine	4,600.	
C44P	25c	rose carmine	3,500.	2,750.
C45P	6c	magenta	5,500.	5,000.
C46P	80c	bright red violet	3,500.	—
C47P	6c	carmine	3,500.	
C48P	4c	bright blue	—	

AIR POST SPECIAL DELIVERY
1934
Cat	Denom	Color	India	Card
CE1P	16c	dark blue on wove		2,750.
CE2P	16c	red & blue on wove		2,750.

SPECIAL DELIVERY
1885

Cat	Denom	Description	DIE (1) Large	(2) Small	(2a)	PLATE (3) India	(4) Card
E1P	10c	blue	500.	250.	1,250.	32.	28.
		Block of 4				150.	125.
		P# blk. of 8					—

1888
Cat	Denom	Description	Large	Small	(2a)	India	Card
E2P	10c	blue	750.	250.	1,000.	32.	28.
		Block of 4				150.	125.
		P# blk. of 8				385.	—

1893
Cat	Denom	Description	Large	Small	(2a)	India	Card
E3P	10c	orange	1,100.	300.	1,100.	60.	65.
		Block of 4				260.	290.
		P# blk. of 8					825.

1894-95
Cat	Denom	Description	Large	Small	(2a)	India	Card
E4P	10c	blue	400.	250.	1,100.		
	a.	On stamp paper, pair					5,500.
E5P	10c	blue, on stamp paper, pair					4,500.

1902
Cat	Denom	Description	Large	Small	(2a)	India	Card
E6P	10c	ultra	900.	250.	1,000.		

1908
Cat	Denom	Description	Large	Small	(2a)	India	Card
E7P	10c	green	1,750.	1,000.	1,100.		

1922

Cat	Denom	Description	LARGE DIE (1) India	(1a) White Wove	DIE (2) Small
E12P	10c	deep ultra	1,250.	1,100.	

1925-54
Cat	Denom	Description	India	White Wove	Small
E13P	15c	deep orange	1,250.		
E14P	20c	black	1,250.		
E17P	13c	blue			—
E20P	20c	deep blue	1,000.		

REGISTRATION
1911

Cat	Denom	Description	DIE (1) Large	(2) Small	(2a)	PLATE (3) India	(4) Card
F1P	10c	ultra	2,500.	1,000.	1,100.		

POSTAGE DUE
1879

Cat	Denom	Description	Large	Small	(2a)	India	Card
J1P	1c	brown	115.	100.	400.	20.	8.
		Block of 4				95.	55.
		P# blk. of 12				400.	
J2P	2c	brown	115.	100.	400.	18.	8.
		Block of 4				82.	55.
		P# blk. of 12				400.	
		2c dark brown	—	—			
J3P	3c	brown	115.	100.	400.	18.	8.
		Block of 4				82.	55.
		P# blk. of 12				400.	
		3c dark brown	—	—			
J4P	5c	brown	115.	100.	400.	18.	8.
		Block of 4				82.	55.
		P# blk. of 12				400.	
		5c dark brown	—				
J5P	10c	brown	115.	100.	400.		8.
		10c dark brown	—			30.	
		Block of 4				135.	55.
		P# blk. of 12				650.	
J6P	30c	brown	115.	100.	400.		8.
		30c dark brown	—			30.	
		Block of 4				135.	55.
		P# blk. of 12				650.	
J7P	50c	brown	115.	100.	400.		8.
		50c dark brown	—			30.	
		Block of 4				135.	55.
		P# blk. of 12				650.	

1887
Cat	Denom	Description	Large	Small	(2a)	India	Card
J15P	1c	red brown			400.		11.
		Block of 4					
		P# blk. of 12					
J16P	2c	red brown			400.		11.
		Block of 4					
		P# blk. of 12					
J17P	3c	red brown			400.		17.
		Block of 4					
		P# blk. of 12					
J18P	5c	red brown			400.		11.
		Block of 4					
		P# blk. of 12					
J19P	10c	red brown			400.	17.	22.
		Block of 4				82.	
		P# blk. of 12				325.	
J20P	30c	red brown			400.	17.	15.
		Block of 4				82.	
		P# blk. of 12				325.	
J21P	50c	red brown			400.	40.	22.
		Block of 4				190.	
		P# blk. of 12				825.	

1891-93
Cat	Denom	Description	Large	Small	(2a)	India	Card
J22P	1c	bright claret	140.	125.	400.	11.	15.
		Block of 4				60.	70.
		P# blk. of 12					—
	a.	On stamp paper, pair					425.
J23P	2c	bright claret	140.	125.	400.	11.	15.
		Block of 4				60.	70.
		P# blk. of 12					—
	a.	On stamp paper, pair					425.
J24P	3c	bright claret	140.	125.	400.	11.	15.
		Block of 4				60.	70.
		P# blk. of 12					—
	a.	On stamp paper, pair					425.
J25P	5c	bright claret	140.	125.	400.	11.	15.
		Block of 4				60.	70.
		P# blk. of 12					—
	a.	On stamp paper, pair					425.
J26P	10c	bright claret	140.	125.	400.	11.	15.
		Block of 4				60.	70.
		P# blk. of 12					—
	a.	On stamp paper, pair					425.
J27P	30c	bright claret	140.	125.	400.	25.	15.
		Block of 4				125.	70.
		P# blk. of 12					—
	a.	On stamp paper, pair					500.
J28P	50c	bright claret	140.	125.	400.	17.	15.
		Block of 4				80.	70.
		P# blk. of 12					—
	a.	On stamp paper, pair					500.

Values for J22Pa-J28Pa are for pairs with original gum and minor faults.

1894
Cat	Denom	Description	Large	Small	(2a)	India	Card
J31P	1c	claret	165.	120.	350.		
	a.	On stamp paper, pair					225.
		Block of 4					500.
J32P	2c	claret	165.	120.	350.		100.
		Block of 4					475.
		P# blk. of 6					1,750.
J33P	3c	claret	165.	120.	350.		
J34P	5c	claret	165.	120.	350.		
J35P	10c	claret	165.	120.	350.		
J36P	30c	claret	165.	120.	350.		
J37P	50c	claret	165.	120.	350.		

1925
Cat	Denom	Color	India
J68P	½c	dull red	1,750.

1930-31
Cat	Denom	Color	India
J69P	½c	deep car	450.
J70P	1c	deep car	450.
J71P	2c	deep car	450.
J72P	3c	deep car	450.
J73P	5c	deep car	450.
J74P	10c	deep car	450.
J75P	30c	deep car	450.
J76P	50c	deep car	450.
J77P	$1	deep car	450.
J78P	$5	deep car	450.

PARCEL POST POSTAGE DUE
1912

Cat	Denom	Description	DIE (1) Large	(2) Small	(2a)	PLATE (3) India	(4) Card
JQ1P	1c	dark green	600.	500.	700.		
JQ2P	2c	dark green	600.	500.	700.		
JQ3P	5c	dark green	600.	500.	700.		
JQ4P	10c	dark green	600.	500.	700.		
JQ5P	25c	dark green	600.	500.	700.		

CARRIERS
1851

Cat	Denom	Description	Large	Small	(2a)	India	Card
LO1P	1c	blue (Franklin)	800.	300.	1,500.	50.	20.
		Block of 4				165.	80.
		Cracked plate				—	
LO2P	1c	blue (Eagle)	800.	300.	1,500.	50.	20.
		Block of 4				165.	80.
		P # blk. of 8				675.	

Nos. LO1P (1) and LO2P (1) exist only as hybrids.

OFFICIAL
AGRICULTURE
1873

Cat	Denom	Description	Large	Small	(2a)	India	Card
O1P	1c	yellow	80.	55.	275.	5.	4.
		Block of 4				25.	30.
		P# blk. of 12					150.
O2P	2c	yellow	80.	55.	275.	5.	4.
		Block of 4				25.	30.
		P# blk. of 10					150.
O3P	3c	yellow	80.	55.	275.	5.	4.
		Block of 4				25.	30.
		P# blk. of 12					150.
O4P	6c	yellow	80.	55.	275.	5.	4.
		Block of 4				25.	30.
		P# blk. of 12					150.
O5P	10c	yellow	80.	55.	275.	5.	4.
		Block of 4				25.	30.
		P# blk. of 12					150.
O6P	12c	yellow	80.	55.	275.	5.	4.
		Block of 4				25.	30.
		P# blk. of 12					150.
O7P	15c	yellow	80.	55.	275.	5.	4.
		Block of 4				25.	30.
		P# blk. of 12					150.
O8P	24c	yellow	80.	55.	275.	5.	4.
		Block of 4				25.	30.
		P# blk. of 12					150.
O9P	30c	yellow	80.	55.	275.	5.	4.
		Block of 4				25.	30.
		P# blk. of 12					150.

EXECUTIVE

Cat	Denom	Description	Large	Small	(2a)	India	Card
O10P	1c	carmine	100.	70.	275.	8.	6.
		Block of 4				35.	30.
		P# blk. of 14					150.
O11P	2c	carmine	100.	70.	275.	8.	6.
		Block of 4				35.	30.
		P# blk. of 12					150.
		Foreign entry of 6c Agriculture					—
O12P	3c	carmine	100.	70.	275.	8.	6.
		Block of 4				35.	30.
		P# blk. of 12					150.
O13P	6c	carmine	100.	70.	275.	14.	8.
		Block of 4				70.	45.
		P# blk. of 10					225.
O14P	10c	carmine	100.	70.	275.	11.	6.
		Block of 4				55.	30.
		P# blk. of 12					150.

INTERIOR

Cat	Denom	Description	Large	Small	(2a)	India	Card
O15P	1c	vermilion	80.	55.	275.	5.	4.
		Block of 4				35.	30.
		P# blk. of 12					150.
O16P	2c	vermilion	80.	55.	275.	5.	4.
		Block of 4				35.	30.

No.	Value	Color					
		P# blk. of 10					150.
O17P	3c	vermilion	80.	55.	275.	5.	4.
		Block of 4				35.	30.
		P# blk. of 10					150.
O18P	6c	vermilion	80.	55.	275.	9.	8.
		Block of 4				45.	40.
		P# blk. of 12					200.
O19P	10c	vermilion	80.	55.	275.	5.	4.
		Block of 4				35.	30.
		P# blk. of 12					150.
O20P	12c	vermilion	80.	55.	275.	5.	4.
		Block of 4				35.	30.
		P# blk. of 10					150.
O21P	15c	vermilion	80.	55.	275.	5.	4.
		Block of 4				35.	30.
		P# blk. of 12					150.
O22P	24c	vermilion	80.	55.	275.	5.	4.
		Block of 4				35.	30.
		P# blk. of 12					150.
O23P	30c	vermilion	80.	55.	275.	5.	4.
		Block of 4				35.	30.
		P# blk. of 12					150.
O24P	90c	vermilion	80.	55.	275.	6.	5.
		Block of 4				50.	45.
		P# blk. of 12					225.

JUSTICE

No.	Value	Color					
O25P	1c	purple	80.	55.	275.	5.	4.
		Block of 4				30.	30.
		P# blk. of 12					150.
O26P	2c	purple	80.	55.	275.	5.	4.
		Block of 4				30.	30.
		P# blk. of 12					150.
O27P	3c	purple	80.	55.	275.	5.	4.
		Block of 4				30.	30.
		P# blk. of 12					150.
		Plate Scratches					—
O28P	6c	purple	80.	55.	275.	5.	4.
		Block of 4				30.	30.
		P# blk. of 12					150.
O29P	10c	purple	80.	55.	275.	5.	4.
		Block of 4				30.	30.
		P# blk. of 10					150.
O30P	12c	purple	80.	55.	275.	5.	4.
		Block of 4				30.	30.
		P# blk. of 12					150.
O31P	15c	purple	80.	55.	275.	5.	4.
		Block of 4				30.	30.
		P# blk. of 10					150.
O32P	24c	purple	80.	55.	275.	7.	5.
		Block of 4				45.	35.
		P# blk. of 12					175.
		Short transfer (pos. 98)					—
O33P	30c	purple	80.	55.	275.	7.	5.
		Block of 4				45.	35.
		P# blk. of 12					175.
O34P	90c	purple	80.	55.	275.	8.	5.
		Block of 4				50.	35.
		P# blk. of 10					175.

NAVY

No.	Value	Color					
O35P	1c	ultramarine	80.	55.	275.	6.	4.
		Block of 4				30.	30.
		P# blk. of 12					150.
O36P	2c	ultramarine	80.	55.	275.	6.	4.
		Block of 4				30.	30.
		P# blk. of 12					150.
O37P	3c	ultramarine	80.	55.	275.	6.	4.
		Block of 4				30.	30.
		P# blk. of 10					150.
O38P	6c	ultramarine	80.	55.	275.	14.	10.
		Block of 4				70.	50.
		P# blk. of 10					250.
O39P	7c	ultramarine	80.	55.	275.	7.	7.
		Block of 4				40.	40.
		P# blk. of 10					200.
O40P	10c	ultramarine	80.	55.	275.	6.	4.
		Block of 4				30.	30.
		P# blk. of 12				—	150.
O41P	12c	ultramarine	80.	55.	275.	6.	4.
		Block of 4				30.	30.
		P# blk. of 12					150.
O42P	15c	ultramarine	80.	55.	275.	6.	4.
		Block of 4				30.	30.
		P# blk. of 12					150.
O43P	24c	ultramarine	80.	55.	275.	7.	4.
		Block of 4				40.	30.
		P# blk. of 12					150.
O44P	30c	ultramarine	80.	55.	275.	11.	6.
		Block of 4				57.50	40.
		P# blk. of 12					200.
O45P	90c	ultramarine	80.	55.	275.	7.	6.
		Block of 4				45.	40.
		P# blk. of 12					200.
		Short transfer at upper left (106, pos. 1, 5)					—

POST OFFICE

No.	Value	Color					
O47P	1c	black	80.	55.	275.	5.	4.
		Block of 4				30.	30.
		P# blk. of 10					150.
O48P	2c	black	80.	55.	275.	5.	4.
		Block of 4				30.	30.
		P# blk. of 14					150.
O49P	3c	black	80.	55.	275.	5.	4.
		Block of 4				30.	30.
		P# blk. of 12					150.
O50P	6c	black	80.	55.	275.	5.	4.
		Block of 4				30.	30.
		P# blk. of 12					150.
O51P	10c	black	80.	55.	275.	6.	6.
		Block of 4				35.	35.
		P# blk. of 4					175.
O52P	12c	black	80.	55.	275.	5.	5.
		Block of 4				30.	30.
		P# blk. of 12					150.

No.	Value	Color					
O53P	15c	black	80.	55.	275.	5.	6.
		Block of 4				30.	35.
		P# blk. of 12					175.
O54P	24c	black	80.	55.	275.	5.	4.
		Block of 4				30.	30.
		P# blk. of 12					150.
O55P	30c	black	80.	55.	275.	5.	4.
		Block of 4				30.	30.
		P# blk. of 12					150.
O56P	90c	black	80.	55.	275.	5.	4.
		Block of 4				30.	30.
		P# blk. of 12					150.

STATE

No.	Value	Color					
O57P	1c	green	80.	55.	275.	6.	5.
		Block of 4				38.	32.
		P# blk. of 12					160.
O58P	2c	green	80.	55.	275.	6.	5.
		Block of 4				38.	32.
		P# blk. of 10					160.
O59P	3c	green	80.	55.	275.	6.	5.
		Block of 4				38.	32.
		P# blk. of 10					160.
O60P	6c	green	80.	55.	275.	17.	11.
		Block of 4				82.	62.
		P# blk. of 12					300.
O61P	7c	green	80.	55.	275.	6.	5.
		Block of 4				38.	32.
		P# blk. of 12					160.
O62P	10c	green	80.	55.	275.	6.	5.
		Block of 4				38.	32.
		P# blk. of 12					160.
O63P	12c	green	80.	55.	275.	6.	5.
		Block of 4				38.	32.
		P# blk. of 10					160.
O64P	15c	green	80.	55.	275.	6.	5.
		Block of 4				38.	32.
		P# blk. of 12					160.
O65P	24c	green	80.	55.	275.	11.	5.
		Block of 4				55.	30.
		P# blk. of 12					150.
O66P	30c	green	80.	55.	275.	11.	7.
		Block of 4				55.	42.
		P# blk. of 12					200.
O67P	90c	green	80.	55.	275.	11.	7.
		Block of 4				55.	42.
		P# blk. of 12					200.
O68P	$2	green & black	150.	125.	300.	50.	30.
		Block of 4				220.	150.
		Sheet of 10				750.	
a.		Invtd. center					1,250.
O69P	$5	green & black	150.	125.	300.	50.	30.
		Block of 4				220.	150.
		Sheet of 10				750.	
a.		Invtd. center					1,250.
		Sheet of 10					—
O70P	$10	green & black	150.	125.	350.	50.	30.
		Block of 4				220.	—
		Sheet of 10				750.	
O71P	$20	green & black	150.	125.	350.	50.	30.
		Block of 4				220.	150.
		Sheet of 10				750.	
a.		Invtd. center					1,000.
		Block of 4					5,000.

O68P to O71P Large Dies exist as hybrids only.

TREASURY

No.	Value	Color					
O72P	1c	brown	80.	55.	275.	5.	4.
		Block of 4				30.	30.
		P# blk. of 12					150.
O73P	2c	brown	80.	55.	275.	5.	4.
		Block of 4				30.	30.
		P# blk. of 12					150.
O74P	3c	brown	80.	55.	275.	5.	4.
		Block of 4				30.	30.
		P# blk. of 14					150.
O75P	6c	brown	80.	55.	275.	13.	13.
		Block of 4				65.	65.
		P# blk. of 12					325.
O76P	7c	brown	80.	55.	275.	5.	4.
		Block of 4				30.	30.
		P# blk. of 12					150.
O77P	10c	brown	80.	55.	275.	5.	4.
		Block of 4				30.	30.
		P# blk. of 12					150.
O78P	12c	brown	80.	55.	275.	5.	4.
		Block of 4				30.	30.
		P# blk. of 12					150.
O79P	15c	brown	80.	55.	275.	5.	4.
		Block of 4				30.	55.
		P# blk. of 12					275.
O80P	24c	brown	80.	55.	275.	11.	8.
		Block of 4				55.	45.
		P# blk. of 12					225.
O81P	30c	brown	80.	55.	275.	11.	8.
		Block of 4				55.	45.
		P# blk. of 12					225.
O82P	90c	brown	80.	55.	275.	7.	4.
		Block of 4				45.	30.
		P# blk. of 12					150.

WAR

No.	Value	Color					
O83P	1c	rose	80.	55.	275.	8.	4.
		Block of 4				40.	30.
		P# blk. of 12					150.
O84P	2c	rose	80.	55.	275.	8.	4.
		Block of 4				40.	30.
O85P	3c	rose	80.	55.	275.	8.	4.
		Block of 4				40.	30.
		Plate flaw at upper left (32R20)					—
O86P	6c	rose	80.	55.	275.	8.	4.
		Block of 4				40.	30.
		P# blk. of 12					150.
O87P	7c	rose	80.	55.	275.	8.	4.
		Block of 4				40.	30.
O88P	10c	rose	80.	55.	275.	8.	4.
		Block of 4				40.	30.
		P# blk. of 10					150.
O89P	12c	rose	80.	55.	275.	8.	4.
		Block of 4				40.	30.
		P# blk. of 12					150.
O90P	15c	rose	80.	55.	275.	8.	4.
		Block of 4				40.	30.
		P# blk. of 12					150.
O91P	24c	rose	80.	55.	275.	8.	4.
		Block of 4				40.	30.
		P# blk. of 12					150.
O92P	30c	rose	80.	55.	275.	8.	10.
		Block of 4				40.	55.
		P# blk. of 10					275.
O93P	90c	rose	80.	55.	275.	8.	4.
		Block of 4				40.	30.
		P# blk. of 12					150.

O83-O93 exist in a plum shade.

POSTAL SAVINGS MAIL

1911

No.	Value	Color			
O124P	1c	dark violet	450.	275.	1,000.
O121P	2c	black	450.	275.	1,000.
O126P	10c	carmine	450.	275.	1,000.
O122P	50c	dark green	450.	275.	1,000.
O123P	$1	ultramarine	450.	275.	1,000.

NEWSPAPERS

1865

			DIE			PLATE	
			(1) Large	(2) Small	(2a)	(3) Wove Paper	(4) Card
PR2P	10c	green	350.	200.		36.	45.
		Block of 4				180.	225.
		P# blk. of 6					—
PR3P	25c	orange red	350.	200.		40.	45.
		Block of 4				200.	225.
		P# blk. of 6					—
PR4P	5c	blue	350.	200.		36.	45.
		Block of 4				180.	225.
		P# blk. of 6					—

1875

No.	Value	Color	Large	Small	(2a)	Wove	Card
PR5P	5c	dark blue			1,750.		24.
PR6P	10c	deep green			1,750.		28.
PR7P	25c	dark car red			1,750.		28.
PR9P	2c	black	80.	40.	250.	7.	5.
		Block of 4				30.	25.
		P# blk. of 8					—
PR10P	3c	black	80.	40.	250.	7.	5.
		Block of 4				30.	25.
		P# blk. of 8					—
PR11P	4c	black	80.	40.	250.	7.	5.
		Block of 4				30.	25.
		P# blk. of 8					—
PR12P	6c	black	80.	40.	250.	7.	5.
		Block of 4				30.	25.
		P# blk. of 8					—
PR13P	8c	black	80.	40.	250.	7.	5.
		Block of 4				30.	25.
		P# blk. of 8					—
PR14P	9c	black	80.	40.	250.	7.	5.
		Block of 4				30.	25.
		P# blk. of 8					—
PR15P	10c	black	80.	40.	250.	7.	5.
		Block of 4				30.	25.
		P# blk. of 8					—
PR16P	12c	rose	80.	40.	250.	8.	7.
		Block of 4				30.	35.
		P# blk. of 8					—
PR17P	24c	rose	80.	40.	250.	8.	7.
		Block of 4				30.	35.
		P# blk. of 8					—
PR18P	36c	rose	80.	40.	250.	8.	7.
		Block of 4				30.	35.
		P# blk. of 8					—
PR19P	48c	rose	80.	40.	250.	8.	7.
		Block of 4				30.	35.
		P# blk. of 8					—
PR20P	60c	rose	80.	40.	250.	8.	7.
		Block of 4				30.	35.
		P# blk. of 8					—
PR21P	72c	rose	80.	40.	250.	8.	7.
		Block of 4				30.	35.
		P# blk. of 8					—
PR22P	84c	rose	80.	40.	250.	8.	7.
		Block of 4				30.	35.
		P# blk. of 8					—
PR23P	96c	rose	80.	40.	250.	8.	7.
		Block of 4				30.	35.
		P# blk. of 8					—
PR24P	$1.92	dark brown	80.	40.	250.	9.	8.
		Block of 4				40.	40.
		P# blk. of 8					—
PR25P	$3	vermilion	80.	40.	250.	9.	8.
		Block of 4				40.	40.
		P# blk. of 8					—
PR26P	$6	ultra	80.	40.	250.	9.	8.
		Block of 4				40.	40.
		P# blk. of 8					—
PR27P	$9	yellow	80.	40.	250.	9.	8.
		Block of 4				40.	40.
		P# blk. of 8					—
PR28P	$12	blue green	80.	40.	250.	10.	8.
		Block of 4				50.	40.
		P# blk. of 8					—
PR29P	$24	dark gray violet	80.	40.	250.	12.	9.

	Block of 4					60.	45.
	P# blk. of 8						—
PR30P $36	brown rose	80.	40.	250.	13.	9.	
	Block of 4				65.	45.	
	P# blk. of 8						—
PR31P $48	red brown	80.	40.	250.	17.	9.	
	Block of 4					80.	45.
	P# blk. of 8						—
PR32P $60	violet	80.	40.	250.	20.	11.	
	Block of 4				100.	55.	
	P# blk. of 8						—

1879

PR57P 2c	deep black	80.			8.	4.	
	Block of 4				40.	24.	
a.	On stamp paper, pair						—
PR58P 3c	deep black	80.			8.	4.	
	Block of 4				40.	24.	
a.	On stamp paper, pair						—
PR59P 4c	deep black	90.			8.	4.	
	Block of 4				40.	24.	
a.	On stamp paper, pair						—
PR60P 6c	deep black	90.			8.	4.	
	Block of 4				40.	24.	
a.	On stamp paper, pair						—
PR61P 8c	deep black	90.			8.	4.	
	Block of 4				40.	24.	
a.	On stamp paper, pair						—
PR62P 10c	deep black	90.			8.	4.	
	Block of 4				40.	24.	
a.	On stamp paper, pair						—
PR63P 12c	red	90.			8.	6.	
	Block of 4				40.	32.	
PR64P 24c	red	90.			8.	6.	
	Block of 4				40.	32.	
PR65P 36c	red	90.			8.	6.	
	Block of 4				40.	32.	
PR66P 48c	red	90.			8.	6.	
	Block of 4				40.	32.	
PR67P 60c	red	90.			8.	6.	
	Block of 4				40.	32.	
PR68P 72c	red	90.			8.	6.	
	Block of 4				40.	32.	
PR69P 84c	red	90.			8.	6.	
	Block of 4				40.	32.	
PR70P 96c	red	90.			8.	6.	
	Block of 4				40.	32.	
PR71P $1.92	pale brown	90.			10.	8.	
	Block of 4				45.	45.	
a.	On stamp paper, pair						—
PR72P $3	red verm.	90.			10.	8.	
	Block of 4				45.	45.	
a.	On stamp paper, pair						—
PR73P $6	blue	90.			10.	8.	
	Block of 4				45.	45.	
a.	On stamp paper, pair						—
PR74P $9	orange	90.			10.	8.	
	Block of 4				45.	45.	
a.	On stamp paper, pair						—
PR75P $12	yel. green	90.			10.	8.	
	Block of 4				45.	45.	
a.	On stamp paper, pair						—
PR76P $24	dark violet	90.			12.	8.	
	Block of 4				60.	45.	
a.	On stamp paper, pair						—
PR77P $36	Indian red	90.			13.	8.	
	Block of 4				65.	45.	
a.	On stamp paper, pair						—
PR78P $48	yellow brown	90.			16.	8.	
	Block of 4				80.	45.	
a.	On stamp paper, pair						—
PR79P $60	purple	90.			16.	8.	
	Block of 4				80.	45.	
a.	On stamp paper, pair						—

1885

PR81P 1c	black	100.	60.	250.	10.	8.	
	Block of 4				50.	40.	
	P# blk. of 8					200.	
a.	On stamp paper, pair						—
PR82P 12c	carmine		80.	250.	17.	8.	
	Block of 4				85.		
a.	On stamp paper, pair						—
PR83P 24c	carmine		80.	250.	17.	8.	
	Block of 4				85.		
a.	On stamp paper, pair						—
PR84P 36c	carmine		80.	250.	17.	8.	
	Block of 4				85.		
a.	On stamp paper, pair						—
PR85P 48c	carmine		80.	250.	17.	8.	
	Block of 4				85.		
a.	On stamp paper, pair						—
PR86P 60c	carmine		80.	250.	17.	8.	
	Block of 4				85.		
a.	On stamp paper, pair						—
PR87P 72c	carmine		80.	250.	17.	8.	

	Block of 4					85.	
a.	On stamp paper, pair						—
PR88P 84c	carmine		80.	250.	17.	8.	
	Block of 4				85.		
a.	On stamp paper, pair						—
PR89P 96c	carmine		80.	250.	17.	8.	
	Block of 4				85.		
a.	On stamp paper, pair						—

1895

PR102P 1c	black	125.	100.	275.	
PR103P 2c	black	125.	100.	275.	
PR104P 5c	black	125.	100.	275.	
PR105P 10c	black	125.	100.	275.	
PR106P 25c	carmine	125.	100.	275.	
PR107P 50c	carmine	125.	100.	275.	
PR108P $2	scarlet	125.	100.	275.	
PR109P $5	blue	125.	100.	275.	
PR110P $10	green	125.	100.	275.	
PR111P $20	slate	125.	100.	275.	
PR112P $50	carmine	125.	100.	275.	
PR113P $100	purple	125.	100.	275.	

PARCEL POST

1912-13

		DIE ON INDIA			PLATE	
		(1) Large	*(2)* Small	*(2a)*	*(3)* India	*(4)* Card
Q1P 1c	car rose	1,400.	1,200.	1,200.		
Q2P 2c	car rose	1,400.	1,200.	1,200.		
Q3P 3c	car rose	1,400.	1,200.	1,200.		
Q4P 4c	car rose	1,400.	1,200.	1,200.		
Q5P 5c	car rose	1,400.	1,200.	1,200.		
Q6P 10c	car rose	1,400.	1,200.	1,200.		
Q7P 15c	car rose	1,400.	1,200.	1,200.		
Q8P 20c	car rose	1,400.	1,200.	1,200.		
Q9P 25c	car rose	1,400.	1,200.	1,200.		
Q10P 50c	car rose	1,400.	1,200.	1,200.		
Q11P 75c	car rose	1,400.	1,200.	1,200.		
Q12P $1	car rose	1,400.	1,200.	1,200.		

SPECIAL HANDLING

1925-28

QE1P 10c	yel grn	900.
QE2P 15c	yel grn	900.
QE3P 20c	yel grn	900.
QE4P 25c	yel grn	*1,500.*
QE4aP 25c	deep grn	900.

LOCAL

1844

5L1P 5c	black		*2,250.*

TELEGRAPH

AMERICAN RAPID TELEGRAPH CO.

1881

			DIE	PLATE
			(2) Small	*(3)* India
1T1P 1c	black		80.	32.
	Pair			68.
1T2P 3c	orange			32.
	Pair			68.
1T3P 5c	bister brown		80.	32.
	Pair			68.
1T4P 10c	purple			32.
	Pair			68.
1T5P 15c	green		80.	32.
	Pair			68.
1T6P 20c	red		80.	32.
	Pair			68.
1T7P 25c	rose		80.	32.
	Pair			68.
1T8P 50c	blue			32.
	Pair			68.

"Collect"

1T9P 1c	brown		32.
	Pair, Nos. 1T9P, 1T13P		68.
	Same, block of 4		145.
1T10P 5c	blue		32.
	Pair, Nos. 1T10P, 1T14P		68.
	Same, block of 4		145.
1T11P 15c	red brown		32.
	Pair, Nos. 1T11P, 1T15P		68.
	Same, block of 4		145.
1T12P 20c	olive green		32.
	Pair, Nos. 1T12P, 1T16P		68.
	Same, block of 4		145.

Office Coupon

1T13P 1c	brown	32.
1T14P 5c	blue	32.

1T15P 15c	red brown	32.
1T16P 20c	olive green	32.

BALTIMORE & OHIO TELEGRAPH CO.

1885

3T1P 1c	vermilion	32.
	Pair	68.
3T2P 5c	blue	32.
	Pair	68.
3T3P 10c	red brown	32.
	Pair	68.
3T4P 25c	orange	32.
	Pair	68.

1886

3T6P	black	32.
	Pair	68.
3T7P 1c	green	32.
3T8P 5c	blue	32.
3T9P 10c	brown	32.
3T10P 25c	orange	32.

POSTAL TELEGRAPH CO.

1885

		DIE		PLATE
		(1) Large	*(2)* Small	*(3)* India
15T1P 10c	green		55.	32.
15T2P 15c	orange red			32.
15T3P 25c	blue	65.		32.
15T4P 50c	brown		65.	32.

WESTERN UNION TELEGRAPH CO.

16T1P (1871)	green	17.
	Pair	35.
16T2P (1872)	red	17.
	Pair	35.
16T3P (1873)	blue	17.
	Pair	35.
16T4P (1874)	brown	17.
	Pair	35.
16T5P (1875)	deep green	17.
16T6P (1876)	red	17.
16T7P (1877)	violet	—
16T8P (1878)	gray brown	20.
16T9P (1879)	blue	14.
16T10P (1880)	lilac rose	16.
16T11P (1881)	green	16.
16T12P (1882)	blue	20.
16T13P (1883)	yellow brown	16.
16T14P (1884)	gray violet	20.
16T15P (1885)	green	20.
16T16P (1886)	brown violet	13.
	Pair	28.
16T17P (1887)	red brown	13.
	Pair	28.
16T18P (1888)	blue	13.
	Pair	28.
16T19P (1889)	olive green	16.
16T22P (1892)	vermilion	16.
16T30P (1900)	red violet	28.
16T44P (1913)	brown	— — —

REVENUE

NORMAL COLORS
1862-68 by Butler & Carpenter, Philadelphia.
1868-75 by Joseph R. Carpenter, Philadelphia.

In the following listing the so-called small die proofs on India paper may be, in fact probably are, plate proofs. The editors shall consider them die proofs, however, until they see them in pairs or blocks. Many revenue proofs on India are mounted on card.

FIRST ISSUE

1862-71

			DIE ON INDIA		PLATE	
			(1) Large	*(2)* Small	*(3)* India	*(4)* Card
R1P	1c	Express, red			65.	60.
		Block of 4				250.
R2P	1c	Playing Cards, red	600.		55.	60.
		Block of 4			225.	250.
R3P	1c	Proprietary, red			125.	40.
		Block of 4				175.
R4P	1c	Telegraph, red				25.
		Block of 4				110.
R5P	2c	Bank Check, blue		525.		30.
		Block of 4				125.
R6P	2c	Bank Check, orange			55.	
		Block of 4			225.	
R7P	2c	Certificate, blue				25.
		Block of 4				110.
R8P	2c	Certificate, orange			75.	
		Block of 4			325.	
R9P	2c	Express, blue				25.
		Block of 4				110.
R10P	2c	Express, orange	600.		55.	
		Pair			225.	
R11P	2c	Playing Cards, blue				35.

			DIE ON INDIA (1) Large	(2) Small	PLATE (3) India	(4) Card
		Block of 4				150.
R13P	2c	Proprietary, blue		400.		25.
		Block of 4				110.
R15P	2c	U.S.I.R., orange			1,250.	
R16P	3c	Foreign Exchange, green	600.		200.	35.
		Block of 4				150.
		R16P1 + R19P1 composite	—			
R17P	3c	Playing Cards, green	700.	400.		90.
		Block of 4				375.
R18P	3c	Proprietary, green			55.	25.
		Block of 4			225.	110.
R19P	3c	Telegraph, green	600.		200.	25.
		Block of 4				110.
R20P	4c	Inland Exchange, brown			200.	25.
		Block of 4				110.
R21P	4c	Playing Cards, violet		400.		85.
		Block of 4				350.
R22P	4c	Proprietary, violet	600.		100.	55.
		Block of 4			425.	225.
R23P	5c	Agreement, red				30.
		Block of 4				125.
R24P	5c	Certificate, red			85.	100.
		Block of 4			350.	
		R24P1 + R25P1 composite	—			
R25P	5c	Express, red		250.		30.
		Block of 4				130.
R26P	5c	Foreign Exchange, red				300.
R27P	5c	Inland Exchange, red		250.		25.
		Block of 4				110.
R28P	5c	Playing Cards, red		—	95.	300.
		Block of 4			400.	
R29P	5c	Proprietary, red on blue wove, gummed				—
R30P	6c	Inland Exchange, orange			55.	30.
		Block of 4			225.	130.
R32P	10c	Bill of Lading, blue				30.
		Block of 4				130.
R33P	10c	Certificate, blue			125.	30.
		Block of 4				130.
R34P	10c	Contract, blue				30.
		Block of 4				130.
R35P	10c	Foreign Exchange, blue				30.
		Block of 4				130.
R36P	10c	Inland Exchange, blue				30.
		Block of 4				130.
R37P	10c	Power of Attorney, blue				30.
		Block of 4				130.
R38P	10c	Proprietary, blue	700.		65.	
		Block of 4			275.	
R39P	15c	Foreign Exchange, brown			85.	300.
		Block of 4			350.	1,500.
R40P	15c	Inland Exchange, brown			110.	30.
		Block of 4				130.
R41P	20c	Foreign Exchange, red	600.		80.	90.
		R41P1 + R42P1 composite	—			
					325.	375.
R42P	20c	Inland Exchange, red	600.	250.	235.	30.
		Block of 4				130.
R43P	25c	Bond, red				450.
		Block of 4				2,250.
R44P	25c	Certificate, red				30.
		Block of 4				130.
R45P	25c	Entry of Goods, red				500.
R46P	25c	Insurance, red			55.	30.
		Block of 4			225.	130.

			DIE ON INDIA (1) Large	(2) Small	PLATE (3) India	(4) Card
R47P	25c	Life Insurance, red				30.
		Block of 4				130.
R48P	25c	Power of Attorney, red				30.
		Block of 4				130.
R49P	25c	Protest, red				30.
		Block of 4				130.
R50P	25c	Warehouse Receipt, red				30.
		Block of 4				130.
R51P	30c	Foreign Exchange, lilac			100.	90.
		Block of 4			425.	375.
R52P	30c	Inland Exchange, lilac			60.	50.
		Block of 4			250.	210.
R53P	40c	Inland Exchange, brown			135.	70.
		Block of 4				300.
R54P	50c	Conveyance, blue		250.		30.
		Block of 4				125.
R55P	50c	Entry of Goods, blue			60.	40.
		Block of 4			250.	170.
R56P	50c	Foreign Exchange, blue			60.	40.
		Block of 4			250.	170.
R57P	50c	Lease, blue			60.	35.
		Block of 4			250.	150.
R58P	50c	Life Insurance, blue			60.	35.
		Block of 4			250.	150.
R59P	50c	Mortgage, blue				100.
		Block of 4				425.
R60P	50c	Original Process, blue			60.	35.
		Block of 4			250.	150.
R61P	50c	Passage Ticket, blue				50.
		Block of 4				210.
R62P	50c	Probate of Will, blue			60.	50.
		Block of 4			250.	210.
R63P	50c	Surety Bond, blue				50.
		Block of 4				210.
R64P	60c	Inland Exchange, orange			50.	35.
		Block of 4				150.
R65P	70c	Foreign Exchange, green			110.	50.
		Block of 4				210.
R66P	$1	Conveyance, red				40.
		Block of 4				170.
R67P	$1	Entry of Goods, red		525.		40.
		Block of 4				170.
R68P	$1	Foreign Exchange red				30.
		Block of 4				130.
R69P	$1	Inland Exchange, red				50.
		Block of 4				210.
R70P	$1	Lease, red				400.
R71P	$1	Life Insurance, red				30.
		Block of 4				130.
R72P	$1	Manifest, red			50.	30.
		Block of 4			—	130.
R73P	$1	Mortgage, red				50.
		Block of 4				210.
R74P	$1	Passage Ticket, red				400.
		Block of 4				1,750.
R75P	$1	Power of Attorney, red				90.
		Block of 4				375.
R76P	$1	Probate of Will, red				30.
		Block of 4				130.
R77P	$1.30	Foreign Exchange, orange	700.		125.	90.
		Block of 4			525.	375.
R78P	$1.50	Inland Exchange, blue			100.	40.
		Block of 4			425.	170.
R79P	$1.60	Foreign Exchange green			125.	90.
		Block of 4				375.
R80P	$1.90	Foreign Exchange, violet			125.	90.
		Block of 4			525.	375.
R81P	$2	Conveyance, red			110.	30.
		Block of 4				130.

			DIE ON INDIA (1) Large	(2) Small	PLATE (3) India	(4) Card
R82P	$2	Mortgage, red			110.	30.
		Block of 4			—	130.
R83P	$2	Probate of Will, red				100.
		Block of 4				—
R84P	$2.50	Inland Exchange, violet			225.	200.
		Block of 4				—
R85P	$3	Charter Party, green			110.	60.
		Block of 4			450.	250.
R86P	$3	Manifest, green		350.	165.	60.
		Block of 4				250.
R87P	$3.50	Inland Exchange, blue			165.	125.
		Block of 4				425.
R88P	$5	Charter Party, red			65.	50.
		Block of 4			275.	210.
R89P	$5	Conveyance, red			400.	50.
		Block of 4				210.
R90P	$5	Manifest, red		300.		50.
		Block of 4				210.
R91P	$5	Mortgage, red			600.	50.
		Block of 4				210.
R92P	$5	Probate of Will, red		300.		50.
		Block of 4				210.
R93P	$10	Charter Party, green			110.	50.
		Block of 4				210.
R94P	$10	Conveyance, green				50.
		Block of 4				210.
R95P	$10	Mortgage, green				50.
		Block of 4				210.
R96P	$10	Probate of Will, green	700.	300.		70.
		Block of 4				290.
R97P	$15	Mortgage, dark blue		—		165.
		Block of 4				735.
R97eP	$15	Mortgage, ultramarine		—		325.
		Block of 4				—
	$15	Mortgage, milky blue			265.	
R98P	$20	Conveyance, orange			200.	90.
		Block of 4			825.	375.
R99P	$20	Probate of Will, orange				200.
		Block of 4				—
R100P	$25	Mortgage, red			200.	150.
		Block of 4				625.
R101P	$50	U.S.I.R., green			200.	210.
		Block of 4				850.
R102P	$200	U.S.I.R., green & orange red			1,300.	

SECOND ISSUE

1871-72

			DIE ON INDIA (1) Large	(2) Small	PLATE (3) India	(4) Card
R105P	3c	blue & black			18.	14.
		Block of 4			80.	60.
R109P	10c	blue & black			18.	14.
		Block of 4			80.	60.
R111P	20c	blue & black			18.	14.
		Block of 4			80.	60.
R112P	25c	blue & black			18.	14.
		Block of 4			80.	60.
R115P	50c	blue & black			45.	14.
		Block of 4			200.	60.
R119P	$1.30	blue & black			45.	34.
		Block of 4			200.	150.
R120P	$1.50	blue & black			25.	20.
		Block of 4			105.	90.
		Double transfer, design of $1				—
R121P	$1.60	blue & black			55.	55.
		Block of 4			235.	235.
R122P	$1.90	blue & black			44.	34.
		Block of 4			200.	150.
R126P	$3.50	blue & black			80.	90.
		Block of 4			350.	385.
R130P	$25	blue & black			140.	105.
		Block of 4			600.	465.
R131P	$50	blue & black			150.	135.
		Block of 4			675.	600.

The "small die proofs" formerly listed under Nos. R103P-R131P are plate proofs from the sheets listed under "Trial Color Proofs."

			DIE ON INDIA (1) Large	(2) Small	PLATE (3) India	(4) Card
R132P	$200	red, blue & black	3,500.	2,750.	2,500.	
		Red (frame) inverted				—
R133P	$500	red orange, green & black	3,500.			

			DIE ON INDIA		PLATE	
			(1) Large	(2) Small	(3) India	(4) Card
R133AP	$5000	red orange, dark green & black		6,500.		

No. R133AP was approved in these colors but never issued. Shade differences of the red orange and dark green colors will be found. It comes both with and without manufacturer's imprints to the left and right of the design. One example exists on bond paper mounted on card with "853½" printed on the lower right card margin.

Due to the unusual manufacturing process of printing these tri-color stamps from single impression plates, proofs with imprints could also be considered to be plate proofs. All are extremely scarce or unique, and are valued in the grade, condition and scarcity in which they exist. For other colors see the trial color proofs listings under No. R133ATC.

THIRD ISSUE
1871-72

			PLATE	
			(3) India	(4) Card
R134P	1c	claret & black		15.
		Block of 4		70.
R135P	2c	orange & black	16.	15.
		Block of 4	70.	70.
R136P	4c	brown & black	20.	15.
		Block of 4	85.	70.
R137P	5c	orange & black	20.	15.
		Block of 4	85.	70.
R138P	6c	orange & black	20.	15.
		Block of 4	85.	70.
R139P	15c	brown & black	20.	15.
		Block of 4	85.	70.
R140P	30c	orange & black	25.	18.
		Block of 4	105.	80.
R141P	40c	brown & black	25.	18.
		Block of 4	105.	80.
R142P	60c	orange & black	65.	50.
		Block of 4	270.	225.
		Foreign entry, design of 70c	200.	150.
a.		Center inverted		1,250.
		Block of 4		5,500.
		Foreign entry, design of 70c		—
R143P	70c	green & black	45.	38.
		Block of 4	190.	170.
R144P	$1	green & black	40.	38.
		Block of 4	170.	170.
R145P	$2	vermilion & black	80.	105.
		Block of 4	335.	450.
R146P	$2.50	claret & black	50.	40.
		Block of 4	210.	170.
R147P	$3	green & black	65.	70.
		Block of 4	270.	300.
R148P	$5	vermilion & black	65.	55.
		Block of 4	270.	240.
R149P	$10	green & black	80.	55.
		Block of 4	335.	240.
R150P	$20	orange & black	115.	150.
		Block of 4	500.	635.

The "small die proofs" formerly listed under Nos. R134P-R150P are plate proofs from the sheets listed under "Trial Color Proofs."

1875   National Bank Note Co., New York City

			DIE ON INDIA		PLATE
			(1) Large	(2) Small	(3) India
R152P	2c	blue (Liberty)	450.		110.
		Block of 4			475.

DOCUMENTARY
1898

R173P	$1	dark green	600.	
R174P	$3	dark brown	600.	
R175P	$5	orange red	600.	
R176P	$10	black	600.	
R177P	$30	red	600.	
R178P	$50	gray brown	600.	

1899

R180P	$500	car lake & blk	1,650.

1914

R197P	2c	rose	—

1914-15

R226P	$500	blue	675.

1917

R246P	$30	deep orange (without serial No.)	650.

1940

R298P	50c	car (without ovpt.)	700.
R305P	$10	carmine	825.
		Without overprint	—
R306AP	$50	carmine	825.
		Without overprint	—

1952

R597P	55c	carmine	675.

PROPRIETARY
1871-75   Joseph R. Carpenter, Philadelphia

			DIE ON INDIA	PLATE		
			(2) Small	(3) India	(4) Card	(5) Bond
RB1P	1c	grn & blk		—	12.	12.
		Block of 4			52.	52.
RB2P	2c	grn & blk		175.	12.	
		Block of 4			52.	
RB3P	3c	grn & blk		22.	12.	
		Block of 4		100.	52.	
RB4P	4c	grn & blk		22.	12.	
		Block of 4		100.	52.	
RB5P	5c	grn & blk		22.	12.	
		Block of 4		100.	52.	
RB6P	6c	grn & blk		22.	12.	
		Block of 4		100.	52.	
RB7P	10c	grn & blk		22.	12.	
		Block of 4		100.	52.	
RB8P	50c	grn & blk	600.		725.	
RB9P	$1	grn & blk	700.		1,000.	
RB10P	$5	grn & blk	1,200.	1,250.	1,500.	

The "small die proofs" formerly listed under Nos. RB1P-RB7P are from the composite plate proofs listed under "Trial Color Proofs."

National Bank Note Co., New York City
1875-83

			DIE ON INDIA		PLATE	
			(1) Large	(2) Small	(3) India	(4) Card
RB11P	1c	green	600.		55.	—
		Block of 4			275.	
RB12P	2c	brown	600.		55.	
		Pair			135.	
RB13P	3c	orange	600.		65.	—
		Pair			160.	
		Block of 4				—
RB14P	4c	red brown	600.		55.	
		Pair			135.	
		Block of 4				—
RB15P	4c	red	600.			
RB16P	5c	black	600.		65.	
		Pair			160.	
		Block of 4				—
RB17P	6c	violet blue	600.		55.	
		Pair			135.	
RB18P	6c	blue	600.		175.	
		Pair			400.	
RB19P	10c	blue	600.			

No. RB19P was produced by the Bureau of Engraving and Printing.

Wines
1916

RE56P	$20	green	5,000.

PLAYING CARDS
1896   Bureau of Engraving & Printing

RF2P	2c	ultramarine	550.
a.		2c blue	1,100.

PRIVATE DIE PROPRIETARY

The editors are indebted to Eric Jackson and Philip T. Bansner for the compilation of the following listing of Private Die Proprietary die and plate proofs as well as the corrresponding trial color proofs. The large die proofs range in size and format from die impressions on India die sunk on cards generally up to 6x9 inches, through die impressions on India on or off card in medium to stamp size. Many individual listings are known in more than one size and format. Values reflect the size and format most commonly seen.

PRIVATE DIE MATCH STAMPS
1864

			DIE ON INDIA	PLATE	
			(1) Large	(3) India	(4) Card
RO1P	1c	blue	225.		
RO2P	1c	orange	500.		90.
RO3P	1c	blue	225.		
RO4P	1c	blue	500.		
RO5P	1c	green	500.		
RO6P	1c	Blue	175.		
RO7P	1c	blue	175.		
RO9P	1c	black	175.		
RO10P	1c	black	175.		
RO11P	3c	Black	250.		
RO12P	1c	black	225.		
RO12/185P	1c	black	750.		
RO13P	3c	green	1000.		
RO14P	1c	black	175.		
RO15P	1c	green	300.		
RO16P	1c	blue	225.	60.	

			DIE ON INDIA	PLATE	
			(1) Large	(3) India	(4) Card
RO17P	1c	blue	175.		
RO17/19P	1c/3c	blue	1000.		
RO17/19P	1c/3c	black	750.		
RO19P	3c	black	375.		
RO20P	1c	blue	175.		
RO21P	3c	black	250.		
RO23P	1c	orange	225.		
RO24P	1c	brown	225.		
RO28P	1c	blue	300.	90.	
RO29P	1c	black	175.		
RO30P	1c	green	175.		
RO31P	1c	black	175.		
RO32P	4c	black	300.		
RO33P	4c	green	225.		
RO35P	1c	black	175.		
RO37P	3c	black	225.		
RO38P	1c	black	350.		
RO39P	1c	blue	175.		
RO40P	1c	green	500.		
RO41P	1c	lake	225.		
RO42P	1c	lake	225.		
RO43P	1c	black	225.		
RO44P	1c	green	225.		
RO45P	1c	black	225.		
RO46P	1c	black	300.		
RO47P	1c	black	225.	90.	75.
RO48P	1c	black	500.		
RO49P	1c	black	175.		
RO50P	1c	black	375.		
RO55P	1c	black	250.		
RO56P	1c	black	250.		
RO57P	1c	green	300.		
RO58P	1c	lake	225.	75.	
RO60P	3c	black	300.		
RO61P	1c	green	300.		
RO62P	1c	green	175.		
RO64P	1c	lake	225.		
RO65P	1c	black	225.		
RO66P	1c	blue	175.		
RO67P	1c	black	175.		
RO68P	1c	green	225.		
RO69P	1c	black	175.		
RO72P	1c	green	500.		
RO73P	1c	black	175.		
RO75P	1c	carmine	450.		
RO76P	1c	black	175.		
RO77P	1c	blue	225.		
RO78P	1c	blue	225.		
RO80P	1c	blue	300.		
RO81P	1c	black	175.		
RO82P	1c	black	175.		
RO83P	1c	blue	175.		
RO84P	1c	black	175.		
RO85P	1c	brown	300.	100.	
RO86P	1c	black	250.	125.	
RO87P	1c	black	500.	50.	
RO88P	1c	black	175.		
RO89P	3c	black	175.		
RO90P	6c	black	175.	125.	
RO91P	3c	black	225.	125.	
RO92P	1c	black	175.		
RO94P	3c	black	175.	175.	
RO95P	1c	green	225.		
RO96P	1c	green	300.		
RO97P	1c	black	175.		
RO98P	1c	green	225.		
RO99P	1c	green	300.		
RO100P	1c	green	225.	65.	
RO101P	3c	carmine		75.	
RO102P	5c	orange		75.	
RO103P	1c	black	175.		
RO104P	1c	green	175.		
RO105P	1c	black	175.	100.	
RO106P	1c	green	300.		
RO107P	1c	blue	225.		
RO108P	1c	red	750.		
RO109P	1c	black	300.		
RO110P	1c	green	175.		
RO112P	1c	blue	225.	100.	
RO113P	1c	black	175.		
RO114P	1c	lake	750.		
RO115P	1c	blue	175.		
RO116P	1c	blue	175.		
RO118P	8c	blue	500.		
RO119P	1c	green	300.		
RO121P	1c	green	500.		
RO122P	1c	black	175.		
RO123P	1c	black	175.		
RO124P	1c	green	750.		
RO125P	1c	blue	300.		
RO126P	1c	black	175.		
RO127P	1c	blue	175.		
RO128P	1c	blue	225.		
RO130P	1c	blue	500.		
RO131P	1c	blue	300.		
RO132P	1c	blue	225.	125.	
RO133P	1c	black	225.		
RO134P	1c	blue	175.	75.	
RO135P	1c	lake	500.		
RO136P	1c	blue	175.		
RO138P	1c	green	175.		
RO139P	5c	blue	225.		
RO140P	4c	green	225.		
RO141P	1c	blue	175.		
RO142P	1c	green	225.		
RO143P	3c	orange	225.		
RO144P	1c	blue	400.		
RO146P	1c	black	175.		
RO148P	1c	blue	225.	100.	
RO152P	1c	black	175.	75.	
RO153P	1c	black	175.	75.	
RO155P	1c	black	175.	65.	
RO157P	3c	blue	225.	80.	
RO158P	1c	black	175.		
RO159P	3c	blue	175.		

			DIE ON INDIA (1) Large	PLATE (3) India	(4) Card
RO160P	1c	blue	175.		
RO161P	1c	blue	500.		
RO163P	1c	black	175.		
RO164P	1c	lake	500.		
RO165P	12c	blue	750.		
RO166P	1c	vermilion	225.		
RO167P	3c	blue	175.		
RO168P	1c	blue	175.		
RO170P	1c	black	450.		
RO171P	1c	black	175.		
RO172P	1c	black	175.		
RO173P	1c	blue	225.	75.	
RO174P	1c	blue	175.		
RO175P	1c	black	225.		
RO176P	1c	blue	500.		
RO177P	1c	green	175.		
RO178P	1c	green	500.		
RO179P	1c	black	175.	75.	
RO180P	1c	black	175.	80.	
RO181P	1c	black	175.		
RO182P	1c	black	175.		
RO183P	1c	black	500.		
RO184P	1c	black	175.	75.	
RO186P	1c	blue	225.		

PRIVATE DIE CANNED FRUIT STAMP

RP1P	1c	green	375.		

PRIVATE DIE MEDICINE STAMPS

			DIE ON INDIA (1) Large	PLATE (3) India	(4) Card
RS1P	1c	black	175.		
RS4P	1c	black	225.	125.	150.
RS5P	1c	blue	500.		
RS10P	4c	blue	225.	125.	150.
RS14P	4c	green	500.	10.	
RS16P	2c	vermilion	500.		
RS18P	1c	black	500.		125.
RS19P	2c	black			125.
RS20P	4c	black			125.
RS21P	1c	black	175.	125.	
RS22P	2c	black	225.	125.	
RS23P	4c	black	225.	125.	
RS24P	1c	black	175.		
RS25P	2c	black	175.		
RS26P	4c	black	175.		
RS27P	4c	black	175.		
RS28P	2c	green	175.		
RS29P	2c	green	225.		
RS29/RO120P	2c/1c	green	1250.		
RS30P	1c	lake	300.		
RS31P	1c	green	175.	100.	100.
RS33P	1c	black	175.	50.	50.
RS34P	1c	black	225.		
RS35P	1c	black	175.		
RS36P	1c	blue	175.		
RS37P	2c	black	450.		
RS38P	2c	black	300.		
RS39P	1c	black	175.	100.	100.
RS40P	2c	green	500.	100.	100.
RS41P	4c	brown		125.	125.
RS42P	1c	black	175.		
RS43P	4c	blue	225.		
RS44P	1c	black	600.		
RS46P	4c	black	175.		
RS47P	4c	black	175.	125.	
RS49P	4c	green	175.		
RS50P	1c	vermilion	225.		
RS51P	2c	black	175.		
RS52P	4c	black	175.		
RS53P	1c	black	175.	125.	
RS54P	2c	black	175.	125.	
RS55P	4c	black	175.	125.	
RS56P	3c	blue	350.	125.	
RS57P	6c	black	175.	100.	
RS58P	4c	black	175.		
RS59P	1c	black	175.		
RS60P	1c	black	175.	65.	
RS61P	4c	blue	500.		
RS62P	1c	black	225.	125.	
RS63P	1c	blue	175.		
RS64P	2c	black	175.	125.	
RS65P	4c	black	175.		
RS66P	1c	black	500.		85.
RS67P	1c	black	175.		
RS68P	2c	black	175.	90.	
RS69P	1c	black	175.		
RS70P	2c	black	225.		
RS71P	1c	black	175.		
RS72P	2c	black	175.		
RS73P	2c	green	500.		
RS74P	1c	black	225.		
RS74hP	1c	black	175.		
RS75P	1c	blue	175.		
RS77P	2c	black	225.		
RS78P	2c	dull pur	750.		
RS81P	4c	brown	225.		
RS82P	2c	black	175.		
RS83P	4c	black	225.		
RS84P	1c	lake	500.	—	110.
RS85P	4c	black	250.	—	
RS86P	1c	green	175.		
RS88P	1c	black	225.	100.	100.
RS89P	1c	black	500.		
RS90P	1c	blue	225.	125.	125.
RS91P	4c	black	175.		
RS92P	3c	black	175.	—	
RS94P	4c	black	175.		
RS95P	1c	green	225.	90.	
RS96P	3c	black	175.	50.	
RS97P	1c	black	175.		
RS98P	1c	black	175.		
RS99P	4c	black	175.		
RS100P	6c	black	175.		
RS101P	1c	black	175.		
RS102P	2c	blue	175.		
RS103P	4c	black	175.		
RS104P	3c	black	750.		
RS105P	3c	brown	600.		
RS106P	2c	blue	225.	60.	
RS107P	3c	black	175.		
RS107/109P	3c/6c	black	1000.		
RS108P	4c	black	175.	45.	
RS109P	6c	black	225.		
RS110P	2c	blue	175.		
RS111P	4c	black	175.		
RS114P	1c	black	225.		
RS114/115P	1c/2c	black	1000.		
RS115P	2c	blue	225.		
RS116P	4c	red	225.		
RS117P	1c	black	250.		
RS118P	1c	red	300.	55.	50.
RS119P	1c	black	225.		
RS120P	2c	black	175.		
RS121P	3c	black	225.	75.	
RS122P	2c	black	175.	100.	
RS123P	4c	black	175.	125.	
RS124P	1c	blue	300.	90.	65.
RS126P	1c	green	175.		
RS127P	4c	green	175.	65.	
RS128P	2c	blue	275.	150.	
RS130P	4c	green	275.		
RS131P	4c	black	175.	75.	
RS132P	4c	black	175.		75.
RS133P	6c	black	175.	125.	
RS134P	4c	blue	225.		
RS137P	4c	blue	500.		
RS138P	1c	black	175.		
RS141P	4c	green	300.	125.	
RS142P	1c	black	175.		
RS143P	4c	green	225.		
RS144P	1c	blue	175.	100.	100.
RS145P	2c	black	175.	100.	100.
RS146P	4c	green	225.	100.	100.
RS150P	1c	vermilion	225.	100.	
RS151P	1c	black	175.		
RS152P	2c	green	175.		
RS153P	4c	black	450.	175.	150.
RS154P	4c	blue	500.		
RS155P	2c	green	175.		
RS156P	6c	black	175.		
RS157P	2c	black	175.		
RS158P	1c	green	500.		
RS159P	4c	blue	225.		
RS160P	6c	black	225.		
RS161P	4c	black	300.	150.	
RS162P	1c	blue	300.		
RS163P	4c	blue	600.		
RS164P	1c	black	175.		
RS165P	4c	green	500.		
RS166P	1c	black	175.		
RS169P	4c	black	175.		
RS170P	1c	black	175.		
RS171P	1c	violet	175.		
RS171uP	1c	purple	500.		
RS172P	2c	black	175.	100.	
RS173P	1c	blue	175.		
RS174P	1c	blue	175.		
RS176P	4c	black	250.		
RS177P	2c	black	350.		
RS178P	1c	black	225.		
RS179P	2c	green	225.		
RS180P	3c	black	275.	125.	
RS181P	4c	black	225.		
RS182P	4c	black	175.		
RS183P	1c	vermilion	225.	85.	
RS184P	2c	black	175.	100.	
RS185P	1c	black	175.	100.	
RS186P	4c	black	175.		
RS187P	4c	black	175.	100.	
RS188P	6c	black	300.		
RS189P	1c	green	225.		
RS190P	2c	black	175.		
RS191P	4c	black	250.		
RS192P	6c	black	250.	125.	
RS193P	2	black	175.		
RS194P	1c	blue	175.		
RS195P	2c	black	175.		
RS196P	1c	blue	175.		
RS197P	2c	black	175.		
RS198P	1c	black	225.		
RS199P	2c	black	175.		
RS204P	2c	black	175.		
RS205P	4c	black	175.		
RS208P	1c	green	175.	100.	95.
RS209P	2c	green	225.		
RS210P	4c	black	225.		
RS212P	1c	green	225.	100.	
RS213P	6c	black	175.	100.	150.
RS214P	4c	black	175.	65.	
RS215P	1c	lake	300.		
RS216P	1c	black	175.	75.	
RS219P	4c	blue	300.		
RS220P	1c	black	175.	50.	
RS221P	4c	green	225.	50.	
RS222P	8c	black	175.		
RS223P	1c	black	175.	—	
RS224P	1c	black	175.	—	
RS225P	4c	black	175.		
RS226P	1c	black	350.		
RS228P	1c	brown	225.	—	
RS229P	2c	chocolate	175.	75.	
RS230P	6c	black	175.	—	
RS231P	6c	orange	750.		750.
RS232P	8c	orange	750.		

			DIE ON INDIA (1) Large	PLATE (3) India	(4) Card
RS236P	4c	black	175.		
RS239P	2c	vermilion	225.	100.	
RS240P	4c	black	175.	125.	50.

"USIR" & "4 cents" obliterated on #RS240P4.

RS241P	4	red	225.		
RS242P	1c	black	175.	80.	75.
RS243P	4c	black	175.		
RS244P	6c	black	175.		
RS245P	1c	black	250.		
RS250P	6c	black	175.	100.	
RS251P	1c	black	175.		
RS252P	1c	ver	175.	100.	
RS253P	4c	black	175.		
RS258P	6c	brown	175.		
RS259P	1c	black	175.	90.	
RS260P	2c	black	225.	90.	
RS261P	4c	black	175.	100.	
RS262P	2c	black	175.		
RS263P	4c	black	225.	90.	
RS264P	4c	black	225.		
RS264AP	4c	black	300.		
RS265P	1c	green	225.		
RS267P	4c	lake	225.		
RS270P	12c	blue	175.		
RS271P	4c	black	2500.		
RS272P	1c	green	225.		
RS273P	2c	black	175.		
RS274P	1c	green	225.	65.	60.
RS276P	2c	green	175.		

PRIVATE DIE PERFUMERY STAMPS

			DIE ON INDIA (1) Large	PLATE (3) India	(4) Card
RT1P	2c	blue		125.	125.
RT2P	1c	black	250.	95.	
RT4P	1c	blue	225.		
RT5P	2c	ver		100.	
RT6P	1c	black	250.	150.	
RT8P	2c	black	500.		
RT10P	4c	black	250.	150.	
RT12P	1c	ver	225.	—	
RT14P	3c	black	500.		
RT16P	1c	black	175.		
RT17P	2c	brown	175.		
RT18P	3c	green	175.		
RT19P	1c	ver	225.		
RT20P	1c	green	225.		
RT21P	2c	blue	175.		
RT22P	1c	blue	225.		
RT23P	2c	black	175.		
RT25P	4c	green	175.		
RT26P	1c	green	175.		
RT27P	1c	green		100.	
RT28P	2c	blue	175.		
RT30P	3c	ver	225.		
RT32P	4c	brown	175.		

PRIVATE DIE PLAYING CARD STAMPS

			DIE ON INDIA (1) Large	PLATE (3) India	(4) Card
RU1P	5c	black	2500.		
RU3P	4c	black	175.	100.	
RU4P	5c	blue	175.		
RU5P	5c	blue	175.		
RU6P	10c	blue	500.	100.	
RU7P	5c	black	250.	100.	
RU8P	5c	black	175.		
RU9P	5c	black	175.		
RU10P	2c	blue	175.		
RU11P	5c	green	225.		
RU12P	5c	black	175.		
RU13P	5c	blue	300.		
RU14P	5c	black	175.	—	
RU15P	5c	black	175.		
RU16P	5c	black	500.		

HUNTING PERMIT

				DIE (Wove) (1) Large	(2) Small
RW1P	1934	$1	blue	—	2,750.
RW2P	1935	$1	rose lake		2,750.
RW3P	1936	$1	brown black	5,000.	2,750.
RW4P	1937	$1	light green	—	2,750.
RW5P	1938	$1	light violet	—	2,750.
RW6P	1939	$1	chocolate		2,750.
RW7P	1940	$1	sepia		2,750.
RW8P	1941	$1	brown carmine	5,500.	2,750.
RW9P	1942	$1	violet brown		2,750.
RW10P	1943	$1	deep rose	5,500.	2,750.
RW11P	1944	$1	red orange		2,750.
RW12P	1945	$1	black	3,850.	2,750.
RW13P	1946	$1	red brown	3,850.	
RW14P	1947	$1	black	3,850.	
RW15P	1948	$1	bright blue	3,850.	
RW19P	1952	$2	deep ultra.	3,850.	
RW23P	1956	$2	black	—	

POSTAL SAVINGS

1911

		DIE (1) Large	(2) Small	(2a)
PS1P	10c orange	1,000.	750.	
PS4P	10c deep blue		750.	

1940

PS7P	10c deep ultra. on wove	1,200.
PS8P	25c dk. car. rose on wove	1,200.
PS9P	50c dk. bl. green on wove	1,200.
PS10P	$1 gray black on wove	1,200.

1941

PS11P	10c rose red on wove	1,000.
PS12P	25c blue green on wove	1,000.
PS13P	50c ultramarine on wove	1,000.
PS14P	$1 gray black on wove	1,000.
PS15P	$5 sepia on wove	1,000.

WAR SAVINGS STAMP

1942

WS7P	10c rose red	1,400.

POST OFFICE SEALS

1872

OXF1P	green	275.	165.	60.	36.
	Block of 4			275.	
a.	Wove paper		950.		
b.	Glazed paper		190.		

1877

OX1P	brown		18.
	Block of 4		80.

1879

OX2aP	brown	2,500.	110.	15.
	Block of 4			65.

1888-94

		DIE (2) Small
OX5P	chocolate	140.

1901-03

OX11P	red brown	100.
OX11aP	gray brown	100.
OX11bP	dark brown	100.
OX11cP	orange brown	100.
	yellow brown	100.

TRIAL COLOR PROOFS

Values are for items in very fine condition. The listings of trial color proofs include several that are similar to the colors of the issued stamps.

New York
All on India paper unless otherwise stated.
Original Die

1845

		DIE (1) Lg.	(2) Sm.	PLATE (5) Bond
9X1TC	5c dull dark violet	300.		
9X1TC	5c brown violet	300.		
9X1TC	5c deep rose violet	300.		
9X1TC	5c deep blue	300.		200.
9X1TC	5c dark green	300.		200.
9X1TC	5c orange yellow	300.		
9X1TC	5c brown	300.		200.
9X1TC	5c scarlet			200.

With "Scar" on Neck

9X1TC	5c dull blue	175.
9X1TC	5c vermilion	175.

With "Scar" and dot in "P" of "POST"

9X1TC	5c dull gray blue		300.
9X1TC	5c deep blue on Bond		250.
9X1TC	5c deep ultramarine on thin glazed card	450.	
9X1TC	5c deep green		300.
9X1TC	5c deep green on Bond		250.
9X1TC	5c dull dark green		300.
9X1TC	5c orange vermilion on thin glazed card	450.	
9X1TC	5c dull brown red on Bond		250.
9X1TC	5c dark brown red		300.
9X1TC	5c dull dark brown		300.
9X1TC	5c dull dark brown on Bond		250.
9X1TC	5c brown black on thin glazed card	450.	

Large die trial color proofs with additional impression of the portrait medallion are listed in the Essay section as Nos. 9X1-E1.

Plate proofs are from the small sheet of 9.

Providence, R. I.

1846

		Plate on Card
10X1TC	5c gray blue	250.
10X1TC	5c green	250.
10X1TC	5c brown carmine	250.
10X1TC	5c brown	250.
10X2TC	10c gray blue	450.
10X2TC	10c green	450.
10X2TC	10c brown carmine	450.
10X2TC	10c brown	450.
	Sheet of 12, any color	3,750.

General Issues

1847

		LARGE DIE India	Bond	Wove	Thin Glazed Card
1TC	5c violet	1,000.			
1TC	5c dull blue	1,000.			
1TC	5c deep blue		800.	800.	
	Small, India				625.
1TC	5c deep ultra				850.
1TC	5c blue green	1,000.			
	Small, India				625.
1TC	5c dull blue green		800.		
1TC	5c dull green	1,000.			
	Small, bond				600.
1TC	5c dark green	1,000.			
1TC	5c yellow green, small India				625.
1TC	5c orange yellow	1,000.	800.	800.	
	Small, India				625.
1TC	5c deep yellow			800.	
1TC	5c orange vermilion	1,000.	800.	800.	
1TC	5c scarlet vermilion	1,000.	800.		850.
1TC	5c rose lake	1,000.			
	Small, bond				625.
1TC	5c black brown		800.		850.
1TC	5c dull rose lake, small bond				625.
1TC	5c brown red	1,000.			
1TC	5c black	1,000.	800.		850.
	Small, India				675.
2TC	10c violet	1,000.			
2TC	10c dull blue	1,000.			
2TC	10c deep blue	1,000.	800.	800.	850.
	Small, India				675.
2TC	10c dull gray blue, small bond				625.
2TC	10c blue green		800.		
2TC	10c dull blue green		800.		
2TC	10c dull green		800.		
2TC	10c dark green	1,000.			
2TC	10c yel green, small India				675.
2TC	10c dull yellow			800.	
2TC	10c orange yellow	1,000.		800.	
2TC	10c orange vermilion	1,000.	800.	800.	
	Small, India				625.
2TC	10c scarlet vermilion				850.
2TC	10c golden brown	1,000.	800.		850.
2TC	10c light brown	1,000.			
2TC	10c dark brown	1,000.	800.		
2TC	10c red brown				675.
2TC	10c dull red				675.
2TC	10c rose lake	1,000.			
2TC	10c dull rose lake, small bond				625.
2TC	10c black brown				850.
2TC	10c yellow green on blue pelure paper	1,000.			

Original die proofs are often cut down and reduced in size; full-size die proofs sell at higher prices. Reprint proofs with cross-hatching are valued as full-size; cut down examples sell for less.

		DIE (1) Lg.	(2) Sm.	PLATE (3) India	(4) Card
1TC	5c orange				600.
1TC	5c black				600.
	Double transfer (80R1)				—
	Double transfer (90R1)				—
2TC	10c orange				600.
2TC	10c deep brown				600.

Nos. 1TC3-2TC3 exist with and without "specimen" overprint. Values are for examples without the overprint. Examples with the overprint are equally as scarce but sell for slightly less.

1875

3TC	5c dull rose lake		600.
3TC	5c black	900.	
3TC	5c green	900.	
4TC	10c green	900.	750.

1851-60

		DIE (1) Lg.	(2) Sm.	PLATE (3) India	(5) Wove Paper
5TC	1c black			—	
7TC	1c black on stamp paper				3,750.
11TC	3c black on stamp paper				3,000.
12TC	5c pale brown				300.
12TC	5c rose brown				300.
12TC	5c deep red brown				1,500.
12TC	5c dark olive bister				300.
12TC	5c olive brown				300.
12TC	5c olive green				300.
12TC	5c deep orange				300.
12TC	5c black	6,500.			5,000.
13TC	10c black	5,000.			1,500.
37TC	24c claret brown				600.
37TC	24c red brown				600.
37TC	24c orange				600.
37TC	24c deep yellow				600.
37TC	24c yellow				600.
37TC	24c deep blue				600.
37TC	24c black	7,000.			—
37TC	24c violet black				600.
37TC	24c red lilac on stamp paper, perf. 15½, gummed (formerly No. 37b)				1,000.
	Block of 4				6,000.
38TC	30c black	5,000.	1,250.	1,400.	600.
	Block of 4			9,000.	
39TC	90c rose lake				625.
39TC	90c henna brown				625.
39TC	90c orange red				625.
39TC	90c brown orange	5,000.			625.
39TC	90c sepia				625.

	DIE (1) Lg.	(2) Sm.	(3) India	PLATE (5) Wove Paper
39TC 90c dark green				625.
39TC 90c dark violet brown				625.
39TC 90c black	5,000.	1,250.		675.

Former Nos. 55-57, 59, 62 are now in the Essay section. Former Nos. 60-61 will be found below as Nos. 70TCe and 71TCb, respectively.

1875

40TC 1c orange vermilion	275.
40TC 1c orange	275.
40TC 1c yellow orange	275.
40TC 1c orange brown	275.
40TC 1c dark brown	275.
40TC 1c dull violet	275.
40TC 1c violet	275.
40TC 1c red violet	275.
40TC 1c gray	275.
41TC 3c red	—

1861

	PLATE (5) Wove Paper, Imperf.	(6) Wove Paper, Perf.
63TC 1c rose	25.	28.
63TC 1c deep orange red	25.	28.
63TC 1c deep red orange	25.	
63TC 1c dark orange		28.
63TC 1c yellow orange	25.	
63TC 1c orange brown	25.	28.
63TC 1c dark brown	25.	
63TC 1c yellow green		28.
63TC 1c green	25.	
63TC 1c blue green	25.	28.
63TC 1c gray lilac	25.	28.
63TC 1c gray black	25.	28.
63TC 1c slate black	25.	
63TC 1c blue	25.	
63TC 1c light blue	25.	
63TC 1c deep blue	50.	

The perforated 1861 1c trial colors are valued with perfs cutting the design on two sides. Well centered examples are extremely scarce and sell for more.

There are many trial color impressions of the issues of 1861 to 1883 made for experimentation with various patent papers, grills, etc. Some are fully perforated, gummed and with grill.

1861-62

	DIE (1) Lg.	(2) Sm.	(2a)	PLATE India (3)
62BTC 10c black	1,750.			
62BTC 10c green				300.
62BTC 10c light green				300.
63TC 1c black	2,000.	750.		
63TC 1c red		750.		
63TC 1c brown		750.		
63TC 1c green		—		
63TC 1c orange				
65TC 3c black	1,400.			
65TC 3c black on glazed	1,400.			
65TC 3c blue green	1,400.			
65TC 3c orange	1,400.			
65TC 3c brown	1,400.			
65TC 3c dark blue	1,400.			
65TC 3c ocher	1,400.			
65TC 3c green	1,400.			
65TC 3c dull red	1,400.			
65TC 3c slate	1,400.			
65TC 3c red brown	1,400.			
65TC 3c deep pink	1,400.			
65TC 3c rose pink	1,400.			
65TC 3c dark rose	1,400.			
67TC 5c black	1,750.			—
67TC 5c dark orange	1,500.			
67TC 5c green	1,500.			
67TC 5c ultramarine	1,500.			
67TC 5c gray	1,500.			
67TC 5c rose brown	—			
68TC 10c orange	1,400.			
68TC 10c red brown	1,400.			
68TC 10c dull pink	1,400.			
68TC 10c scarlet	1,400.			
68TC 10c black	1,750.	550.		
69TC 12c scarlet verm.	1,400.			
69TC 12c brown	1,400.			
69TC 12c red brown	1,400.			
69TC 12c green	1,400.			
69TC 12c orange yellow	1,400.			
69TC 12c black		550.		
70TC 24c scarlet	2,250.			
70TC 24c green	2,250.			
70TC 24c orange	2,250.			
70TC 24c red brown	2,250.			
70TC 24c orange brown	2,250.			
70TC 24c orange yellow	2,250.			
70TC 24c rose red	2,250.			
70TC 24c gray	2,250.			
70TC 24c gray on bluish gray stamp paper				—
70TC 24c steel blue	2,250.			
70TC 24c blue	2,250.			
70TC 24c black	2,250.	550.		
70TC 24c violet	1,250.	375.	1,250.	200.
Block of 4				900.

	DIE (1) Lg.	(2) Sm.	(2a)	PLATE India (3)
e. dark violet, semitransparent stamp paper, perf. 12, gummed (formerly #60)			6,500.	
71TC 30c rose	1,750.			
71TC 30c black		600.		
71TC 30c red orange	1,750.	375.	1,250.	
Block of 4				
b. red orange, semitransparent stamp paper, perf. 12, gummed (formerly #61)			17,500.	
72TC 90c black	1,750.	600.		
72TC 90c ultramarine	1,750.			
72TC 90c bluish gray	1,750.			
72TC 90c violet gray	1,750.			
72TC 90c red brown	1,750.			
72TC 90c orange	1,750.			
72TC 90c yellow orange	1,750.			
72TC 90c scarlet	1,750.			
72TC 90c green	1,750.			

1861-66

	STAMP PAPER Unused	Used
66TC 3c lake, perf. 12, gummed	2,000.	
Pair	4,500.	
Block of 4	9,250.	
P# strip of 4	10,000.	
Double transfer	2,250.	
a. Imperf, pair, gummed	1,850.	
P# blk. of 8		

John N. Luff recorded the plate number as 34.

	STAMP PAPER Unused	Used
74TC 3c scarlet, perf. 12, gummed	7,000.	
Block of 4	29,000.	
With 4 horiz. black pen strokes		5,000.
a. Imperf, pair, gummed	4,000.	

John N. Luff recorded the plate number as 19.

1861-67

	DIE (1) Large	(2) Small	(2a)	PLATE India (3)	Card (4)
66TC 3c lake		250.	1,100.	95.	
Block of 4				550.	
P# blk. of 8				1,400.	
74TC 3c scarlet	2,250.	375.	1,100.	85.	100.
Block of 4				425.	450.
P# blk. of 8					—

1863

	DIE (1) Lg.	(2) Sm.	(2a)	PLATE India (3)	Card (4)
73TC 2c light blue					250.
73TC 2c dull chalky blue	8,000.				
73TC 2c green	8,000.				250.
73TC 2c olive green					250.
73TC 2c dull yellow	8,000.				
73TC 2c dark orange	8,000.				
73TC 2c vermilion					250.
73TC 2c scarlet	8,000.				250.
73TC 2c dull red					250.
73TC 2c dull rose	8,000.				250.
73TC 2c brown	8,000.				
73TC 2c gray black					250.
73TC 2c ultramarine	8,000.				

1866

77TC 15c deep blue	2,500.	335.
Block of 4		1,650.
77TC 15c dark red	2,500.	
77TC 15c orange red	2,500.	
77TC 15c dark orange	2,500.	
77TC 15c yellow orange	2,500.	
77TC 15c yellow		
77TC 15c sepia		
77TC 15c orange brown	2,500.	
77TC 15c red brown	2,500.	
77TC 15c blue green	2,500.	
77TC 15c dusky blue	2,500.	
77TC 15c gray black	2,500.	

1869

112TC 1c black	2,500.
113TC 2c black	2,500.
114TC 3c black	2,500.
115TC 6c deep dull blue	2,500.
115TC 6c black	2,500.
116TC 10c black	2,500.
116TC 10c dull dark violet	2,500.
116TC 10c dull dark orange	2,500.
116TC 10c dull rose	2,500.
116TC 10c copper red	2,500.
116TC 10c chocolate	2,500.
116TC 10c dk Prussian bl	2,500.
117TC 12c black	2,500.
118TC 15c dull dark violet	2,500.
118TC 15c deep blue	2,500.
118TC 15c dull red brown	2,500.
118TC 15c black	2,500.
118TC 15c dark blue gray	2,500.
120TC 24c black	3,500.
121TC 30c deep blue & deep green	3,500.
121TC 30c deep brown & blue	3,500.
121TC 30c golden brown & carmine lake	3,500.
121TC 30c carmine lake & dull violet	3,500.
121TC 30c car lake & green	3,500.
121TC 30c car lake & brown	3,500.
121TC 30c car lake & black	3,500.
121TC 30c dull orange red & deep green	3,500.
121TC 30c deep ocher & golden brown	3,500.
121TC 30c dull violet & golden brown	3,500.
121TC 30c black & deep green	3,500.
122TC 90c brown & deep green	3,500.
122TC 90c green & black	1,500.

1870-71

	DIE (1) Lg.	(2) Sm.	PLATE (3) India	(4) Card
145TC 1c yellow orange	600.			
145TC 1c red brown	600.			
145TC 1c red violet	600.			
145TC 1c black	—		—	
145TC 1c green	600.			
146TC 2c black	600.			
147TC 3c brown			125.	
147TC 3c dark brown			125.	
147TC 3c red brown	—			
147TC 3c dark red			125.	
147TC 3c deep red brown, wove paper			125.	
147TC 3c light ultramarine	—		125.	
147TC 3c yellow brown	—		125.	
147TC 3c dull red violet	—		125.	
147TC 3c dull grayish red	—			
147TC 3c yellow orange	—		125.	
147TC 3c red violet	—		125.	
147TC 3c black	600.			

Former Nos. 147aTC and 147bTC are now listed in the Essay section as No. 147-E13c.

148TC 6c deep magenta	600.
148TC 6c ultramarine	600.
148TC 6c carmine	600.
148TC 6c maroon	600.
149TC 7c black	550.
150TC 10c blue	550.
150TC 10c dull pale blue	550.
150TC 10c ultramarine	550.
150TC 10c blue green	550.
150TC 10c carmine	550.
150TC 10c bister	550.
150TC 10c dull red	550.
150TC 10c red orange	550.
150TC 10c yellow brown	550.
150TC 10c brown orange	550.
151TC 12c orange	550.
151TC 12c orange brown	550.
151TC 12c brown red	550.
151TC 12c dull red	550.
151TC 12c carmine	550.
151TC 12c blue	550.
151TC 12c light blue	550.
151TC 12c ultramarine	550.
151TC 12c green	550.
153TC 24c dark brown	550.
155TC 90c carmine	550.
155TC 90c ultramarine	550.
155TC 90c black	550.

1873

	DIE (1) Lg.	(2) Sm.	PLATE (3) India	(4) Card
156TC 1c black				15.
Block of 4				65.
156TC 1c scarlet	—			
157TC 2c black				15.
Block of 4				65.
157TC 2c dull blue	550.			
158TC 3c black	750.			12.
Block of 4				55.
159TC 6c black			300.	30.
Block of 4				150.
159TC 6c deep green			300.	
159TC 6c deep brown			300.	
159TC 6c dull red			300.	
159TC 6c dull gray blue			300.	
160TC 7c black			300.	75.
Block of 4				325.
160TC 7c deep green			300.	
160TC 7c deep brown			300.	
160TC 7c dull gray blue			300.	
160TC 7c dull red			300.	
161TC 10c black			300.	
161TC 10c deep green			300.	
161TC 10c deep brown			300.	
161TC 10c dull gray blue			300.	
161TC 10c dull red			300.	
162TC 12c black			300.	
162TC 12c deep green			300.	
162TC 12c dull gray blue			300.	
162TC 12c deep brown			300.	
162TC 12c dull red			300.	
163TC 15c black			300.	
163TC 15c deep green			300.	
163TC 15c dull gray blue			300.	
163TC 15c deep brown			300.	
163TC 15c dull red			300.	
164TC 24c black			300.	

164TC	24c	deep green	300.			
164TC	24c	dull gray blue	300.			
164TC	24c	deep brown	300.			
164TC	24c	dull red	300.			
165TC	30c	black	300.			
165TC	30c	deep green	300.			
165TC	30c	deep gray blue	300.			
165TC	30c	deep brown	300.			
165TC	30c	dull red	300.			
166TC	90c	black	300.			
166TC	90c	deep green	300.			
166TC	90c	dull gray blue	300.			
166TC	90c	deep brown	300.			
166TC	90c	dull red	300.			

1875

179TC	5c	black	650.	300.	25.	45.
		Block of 4			125.	200.
179TC	5c	deep green	300.			
179TC	5c	dull gray blue	300.			
179TC	5c	deep brown	300.			
179TC	5c	dull red	300.			
179TC	5c	scarlet	1,000.			

Small die proofs of 1873-75 issues are "Goodall" prints.

1879   On stamp paper, gummed   *Perf. 12*

182TC	1c	ultramarine	250.
182TC	1c	green	250.
182TC	1c	deep green	250.
182TC	1c	vermilion	250.
182TC	1c	brown	250.
183TC	2c	ultramarine	250.
183TC	2c	blue	250.
183TC	2c	green	250.
184TC	3c	ultramarine	250.
184TC	3c	blue	250.
184TC	3c	vermilion	250.
		Block of 4	1,100.
184TC	3c	brown	250.
185TC	5c	ultramarine	250.
185TC	5c	green	250.
185TC	5c	vermilion	250.
186TC	6c	ultramarine	250.
186TC	6c	blue	250.
186TC	6c	vermilion	250.
187TC	10c	ultramarine	250.
187TC	10c	blue	250.
187TC	10c	vermilion	250.
189TC	15c	ultramarine	250.
189TC	15c	green	250.
189TC	15c	vermilion	250.
189TC	15c	brown	250.
189TC	15c	dull red	250.
190TC	30c	ultramarine	250.
190TC	30c	blue	250.
190TC	30c	green	250.

See Specimens for No. 189 in blue (No. 189S L), No. 209 in green (No. 209S L), No. 210 in rose lake (No. 210S L).

1881-82

206TC	1c	deep green	600.	125.
206TC	1c	black	600.	125.
206TC	1c	ultramarine	600.	
206TC	1c	dark yellow green	600.	

1882-87

			LARGE DIE		PLATE	
			(1)	(2)	(3)	(4)
			India	Card	India	Card
212TC	1c	indigo	600.			
212TC	1c	carmine	600.			
212TC	1c	green	600.	450.		
212TC	1c	deep green	600.	450.		
212TC	1c	copper brown	600.	450.		
212TC	1c	chestnut brown	600.			
210TC	2c	brown red	600.	450.		
210TC	2c	deep dull orange	600.			
210TC	2c	chestnut orange	600.	450.		
210TC	2c	violet rose	600.	450.		
210TC	2c	indigo	600.	450.		
210TC	2c	black	600.			
210TC	2c	pale ultramarine	600.			
210TC	2c	olive green	600.	450.		
210TC	2c	olive brown		450.		
210TC	2c	lake				140.
210TC	2c	rose lake				140.
210TC	2c	dark carmine				140.
210TC	2c	deep red				140.
214TC	3c	green	550.	450.		
214TC	3c	dark green	550.	450.		—
214TC	3c	dark brown	550.	450.		
214TC	3c	chestnut brown	550.	450.		
214TC	3c	dull red brown	550.	450.		
214TC	3c	deep dull orange				

All of 214TC above bear inscription "Worked over by new company, June 29th, 1881."

			LARGE DIE		PLATE	
211TC	4c	green	600.	450.		
211TC	4c	chestnut brown	600.	450.		
211TC	4c	orange brown	600.	450.		
211TC	4c	pale ultra.	600.	450.		
211TC	4c	dark brown	600.			
211TC	4c	black	600.	450.		
205TC	5c	chestnut brown	600.	—		
205TC	5c	deep dull orange	600.			
205TC	5c	pale ultra	600.	—		
205TC	5c	deep green	600.			
205TC	5c	green	600.		200.	
205TC	5c	carmine	600.	450.		
205TC	5c	carmine lake	600.		225.	
205TC	5c	blue black	600.			
205TC	5c	black on glazed	600.			

			LARGE DIE		PLATE	
			(1)	(2)	(3)	(4)
			India	Card	India	Card
208TC	6c	deep dull orange	900.	450.		
208TC	6c	indigo	900.			
208TC	6c	orange vermilion	900.	450.		
208TC	6c	dark violet	900.	450.		
208TC	6c	chestnut brown	900.	450.		
208TC	6c	carmine	600.			
209TC	10c	carmine	600.	450.		
209TC	10c	orange brown	600.	450.		125.
209TC	10c	orange	600.			
209TC	10c	deep dull orange	600.	450.		
209TC	10c	chestnut brown	600.	450.		
209TC	10c	indigo	600.	450.		
209TC	10c	pale ultra	600.	450.		
209TC	10c	green				125.
209TC	10c	black (glazed)	600.			
189TC	15c	orange vermilion	600.	450.		
189TC	15c	orange brown	600.	450.		
189TC	15c	chestnut brown	600.	450.		
189TC	15c	dark brown	600.	450.		
189TC	15c	deep green	600.	450.		
189TC	15c	black	600.	450.		
190TC	30c	black	600.			
190TC	30c	orange vermilion	600.	450.		
190TC	30c	dark brown	600.	450.		
190TC	30c	deep green	600.	450.		
190TC	30c	green	600.	450.		
191TC	90c	carmine	600.	450.		
191TC	90c	dark brown	600.	450.		
191TC	90c	deep dull orange	600.	450.		
191TC	90c	indigo	600.	450.		
191TC	90c	dull red brown	600.	450.		
191TC	90c	black	600.	450.		

1890-93

			DIE		PLATE	
			(1)	(2)	(3)	(4)
			India	Card	India	Card
219TC	1c	green	400.			
219TC	1c	dull violet	400.			
220TC	2c	dull violet	400.			
220TC	2c	blue green	400.			
220TC	2c	slate black	400.			
222TC	4c	orange brown on wove			—	
222TC	4c	yellow brown on wove				
222TC	4c	green	400.			
223TC	5c	blue on glossy wove	400.			
223TC	5c	dark brown on glossy wove	400.			
223TC	5c	bister on wove			—	
223TC	5c	sepia on wove			—	
223TC	5c	blk brown on wove			—	
224TC	6c	deep orange red	400.			
224TC	6c	orange red on wove				120.
224TC	6c	vio. blk. on wove				120.
224TC	6c	yellow on wove				120.
224TC	6c	olive grn. on wove				120.
224TC	6c	purple on wove				120.
224TC	6c	red org. on wove				120.
224TC	6c	brown on wove				120.
224TC	6c	red brn. on wove				120.
224TC	6c	org. brn. on wove				120.
224TC	6c	blk. brn. on wove				120.
224TC	6c	slate grn. on wove				120.
224TC	6c	brn. olive on wove				120.
225TC	8c	dark violet red			400.	
225TC	8c	metallic green			400.	
225TC	8c	salmon			400.	
225TC	8c	yellow orange			—	
225TC	8c	orange brown			400.	
225TC	8c	green			—	
225TC	8c	light green			400.	
225TC	8c	blue			400.	
225TC	8c	steel blue			400.	

1893

			DIE		PLATE	
231TC	2c	sepia	850.		850.	
231TC	2c	orange brown	850.			
231TC	2c	deep orange	850.			
231TC	2c	light brown	850.			
231TC	2c	blue green	850.			
231TC	2c	bright rose red	850.			
231TC	2c	rose violet	850.			
232TC	3c	sepia	850.			
232TC	3c	blackish green	850.		800.	
232TC	3c	black	850.			
233TC	4c	sepia	850.			
233TC	4c	deep orange	850.			
233TC	4c	light brown	850.			
233TC	4c	blue green	850.			
233TC	4c	rose red	850.			
233TC	4c	rose violet	850.			
234TC	5c	black	850.			
234TC	5c	dark violet	850.		850.	
234TC	5c	rose violet	850.		850.	
234TC	5c	red violet	850.			
234TC	5c	brown violet	850.			
234TC	5c	deep blue	850.			
234TC	5c	deep ultra	850.			
234TC	5c	green	850.			
234TC	5c	deep green	850.			
234TC	5c	blue green	850.		850.	
234TC	5c	dark olive green	850.		—	
234TC	5c	deep orange	850.		—	
234TC	5c	orange red	850.			
234TC	5c	orange brown	850.		850.	
234TC	5c	bright rose red	850.			
234TC	5c	claret	850.		—	
234TC	5c	brown rose	850.			

234TC	5c	dull rose brown			850.	
234TC	5c	sepia	850.		850.	
234TC	5c	black brown			—	

The 5c trial color proofs differ from the issued stamp.

237TC	10c	bright rose red	1,250.		
237TC	10c	claret	1,250.		
239TC	30c	sepia		1,000.	
239TC	30c	black			350.
240TC	50c	sepia		1,000.	
242TC	$2	blackish brown			1,000.
242TC	$2	sepia	—		
242TC	$2	red brown	—		

1894

			DIE		PLATE	
			(1)	(2)	(3)	(4)
			Lg.	Sm.	India	Card
246TC	1c	dusky blue green	—			
246TC	1c	dark blue	—			
253TC	3c	light red violet	—			
253TC	3c	dark red violet	—			
255TC	5c	black	900.			
256TC	6c	dark brown	900.			
257TC	8c	black	900.			
258TC	10c	olive	900.			
259TC	15c	red violet	900.			
259TC	15c	dark red orange	1,000.			
261ATC	$1	lake	1,000.			
262TC	$2	black	1,000.			
262TC	$2	dull violet	1,000.			
262TC	$2	violet	1,000.			
262TC	$2	turquoise blue	1,000.			
262TC	$2	orange brown	1,000.			
262TC	$2	olive green	1,000.			
262TC	$2	sepia	1,000.			
262TC	$2	greenish black	1,000.			
263TC	$5	black	1,000.			
263TC	$5	dark yellow	1,000.			
263TC	$5	orange brown	1,000.			
263TC	$5	olive green	1,000.			
263TC	$5	dull violet	1,000.			
263TC	$5	sepia	1,000.			
263TC	$5	brown red	1,000.			

1898

283TC	10c	orange	1,000.	
283TC	10c	sepia	1,000.	
284TC	15c	yellowish olive	—	
284TC	15c	red violet	—	

1898

285TC	1c	black			—	
286TC	2c	purple			—	1,600.
286TC	2c	black			—	1,600.
286TC	2c	blue				1,600.
286TC	2c	brown				1,600.
286TC	2c	deep carmine rose				1,600.
287TC	4c	black			—	
288TC	5c	black			—	
288TC	5c	orange brown	2,500.			
289TC	8c	black			—	
290TC	10c	black	1,500.	1,250.		
291TC	50c	black	1,500.	1,250.		
292TC	$1	black			—	
293TC	$2	black	5,000.			

1901

298TC	8c	violet & black on wove paper	*2,500.*	

1902-03

308TC	13c	gray violet, type I	1,000.	
319TC	2c	black, type I	2,500.	

1904

326TC	5c	black on glazed card	—	

1907

330TC	5c	ultramarine	1,600.	
330TC	5c	black	1,700.	

1908

332TC	2c	dull violet	750.	
332TC	2c	light ultra.	750.	
332TC	2c	bright ultra.	750.	
332TC	2c	light green	750.	
332TC	2c	dark olive green	750.	
332TC	2c	golden yellow	750.	
332TC	2c	dull orange	750.	
332TC	2c	rose carmine	750.	
332TC	2c	ultramarine	750.	
332TC	2c	black	—	
332TC	2c	dark blue	—	
332TC	2c	blue	850.	
332TC	2c	lilac brown	850.	
332TC	2c	lilac	850.	
332TC	2c	blue black	850.	
332TC	2c	sage green	850.	
332TC	2c	lilac black	850.	
332TC	2c	brown	850.	
332TC	2c	brown black	850.	
332TC	2c	purple	—	
332TC	2c	orange brown	850.	
332TC	2c	ultra. on orange brown	750.	
332TC	2c	ultra. on green	750.	
332TC	2c	green on pink	750.	
332TC	2c	green on rose	750.	
332TC	2c	dark green on grn	750.	

332TC 2c	green on orange brown	750.	
332TC 2c	purple on orange brown	750.	
332TC 2c	blue on yellow	750.	
332TC 2c	green on yellow	750.	
332TC 2c	brown on orange brown	750.	
332TC 2c	brown on yellow	750.	
332TC 2c	green on amber yel	—	
335TC 5c	green on pink	—	
336TC 6c	brown	—	
337TC 8c	green (shades) on yellow	—	
337TC 8c	orange (shades) on yellow	—	
337TC 8c	blue on buff	—	
337TC 8c	blue on yellow	—	
338TC 10c	carmine on pale yellow green	—	
338TC 10c	brown on yellow	—	
338TC 10c	green on pink	—	
338TC 10c	orange on greenish blue	—	
338TC 10c	brown on gray lavender	—	
338TC 10c	orange on orange	—	
338TC 10c	black on pink	—	
338TC 10c	orange on yellow	—	
338TC 10c	brown	—	
338TC 10c	carmine	—	
338TC 10c	blue on pink	—	
338TC 10c	brown on pink	—	
338TC 10c	black	—	
339TC 13c	blue on yellow	—	
339TC 13c	sea green on deep yellow	—	
339TC 13c	sea green on pale blue	—	
339TC 13c	deep violet on yellow low	—	
340TC 15c	blue on pale lilac	—	
340TC 15c	blue on greenish blue	—	
340TC 15c	blue on pink	—	
340TC 15c	blue on yellow	—	
340TC 15c	dark blue on buff	—	
340TC 15c	orange brown on yellow	—	
340TC 15c	dark purple on yel	—	
340TC 15c	orange on yellow	—	
340TC 15c	violet on yellow	—	
340TC 15c	black on orange	—	
341TC 50c	lilac on light blue	—	
341TC 50c	dark violet on yellow	—	
341TC 50c	violet on yellow	—	
341TC 50c	orange on yellow	—	
341TC 50c	orange brown on yellow	—	
342TC $1	brown on blue	—	

1909

342TC $1	carmine lake	1,200.	1,100.
342TC $1	pink	1,200.	1,100.
342TC $1	brown on blue green	—	
342TC $1	violet brown on pink	—	
342TC $1	violet brown on gray	—	

1912-13

400TC 10c	brown red	1,750.	1,100.
414TC 8c	black	1,750.	

1918

524TC $5	carmine & black	1,350.

1919

513TC 13c	violet	650.
513TC 13c	lilac	650.
513TC 13c	violet brown	650.
513TC 13c	light ultra	650.
513TC 13c	ultramarine	650.
513TC 13c	deep ultra	650.
513TC 13c	green	650.
513TC 13c	dark green	650.
513TC 13c	olive green	650.
513TC 13c	orange yellow	650.
513TC 13c	orange	650.
513TC 13c	red orange	650.
513TC 13c	ocher	650.
513TC 13c	salmon red	650.
513TC 13c	brown carmine	650.
513TC 13c	claret brown	650.
513TC 13c	brown	650.
513TC 13c	black brown	650.
513TC 13c	gray	650.
513TC 13c	black	650.

1920

547TC $2	green & black	1,500.

1922-25

554TC 2c	black (bond paper)		500.
561TC 9c	red orange	1,000.	
563TC 11c	deep green	1,000.	
565TC 14c	dark brown	1,000.	
566TC 15c	blue	1,000.	

1923

610TC 2c	Harding, green	4,000.

1925

618TC 2c	Lexington Concord, black	1,650.

1926

622TC 13c	black	1,000.	
628TC 5c	Ericsson, dull dusky blue	1,000.	
628TC	gray blue		1,000.

1932

718TC 3c	Olympic, carmine	10,000.	
720TC 3c	black (bond paper)		750.

1935

773TC 3c	San Diego, org. red (yel. glazed card)	1,250.

1936-43

785TC 1c	Army, black (bond paper)		750.
788TC 4c	Army, dark brown	1,000.	
789TC 5c	Army, blue	1,000.	
793TC 4c	Navy, dark brown	1,000.	
798TC 3c	Constitution, black (bond paper)		750.
799TC 3c	Hawaii, black (bond paper)		750.
800TC 3c	Alaska, black (bond paper)		750.
800TC	(India paper)		750.
801TC 3c	Puerto Rico, black (bond paper)	900.	750.
801TC	(India paper)	900.	
802TC 3c	Virgin Islands, black (bond paper)		750.
815TC 10c	sepia	900.	
829TC 25c	green	2,000.	
836TC 3c	Swedes & Finns, purple	900.	
837TC 3c	Northwest Terr., dark purple	900.	
854TC 3c	Inauguration, purple	900.	
855TC 3c	Baseball, red violet	2,250.	
862TC 5c	Authors, dull blue	900.	
866TC 3c	Poets, dark blue violet	900.	
897TC 3c	Wyoming, red violet	—	
929TC 3c	Iwo Jima, bright purple	2,300.	
959TC 3c	Progress of Women, brt. violet	1,500.	
963TC 3c	Youth, violet	900.	
964TC 3c	Oregon, dull violet	900.	
968TC 3c	Poultry, red brown	900.	

1923-47

AIR POST

		DIE (1) Lg.	(2) Sm.	PLATE (3) India	(4) Card
C5TC 16c	dark green	5,000.			
C8TC 15c	orange	4,500.			
C32TC 5c	blue	4,500.			
C35TC 15c	brown violet	4,500.			

1934

AIR POST SPECIAL DELIVERY

CE1TC 16c	black	4,000.

1885-1902

SPECIAL DELIVERY

E1TC 10c	black	1,500.	
E1TC 10c	dark brown	1,500.	
E1TC 10c	org. yellow (wove paper)		2,000.
E2TC 10c	black	1,500.	
E2TC 10c	green	1,500.	
E2TC 10c	olive yellow		600.
E6TC 10c	orange	1,000.	
E6TC 10c	black	1,000.	
E6TC 10c	rose red	1,500.	

1922-25

E12TC 10c	black	1,100.

1911

REGISTRATION

F1TC 10c	black (glazed card)	900.

1851

CARRIERS

LO1TC	deep green	250.	
	Block of 4	1,250.	
	a. orange (wove paper)		350.
LO2TC	deep green	250.	
	Block of 4	1,250.	
	a. orange (wove paper)		350.

1879

POSTAGE DUE

		DIE (1) Lg.	(2) Sm.	PLATE (3) India	(4) Card
J1TC 1c	black	250.			25.
J1TC 1c	gray black	250.			
J1TC 1c	ultramarine	250.			
J1TC 1c	blue	250.			

		DIE (1) Lg.	(2) Sm.	PLATE (3) India	(4) Card
J1TC 1c	blue green	250.			
J1TC 1c	orange	250.	80.		
J1TC 1c	red orange	250.			
J1TC 1c	olive bister	250.			
J2TC 2c	black	250.			
J2TC 2c	gray black	250.			
J2TC 2c	ultramarine	250.			
J2TC 2c	blue	250.			
J2TC 2c	blue green	250.			
J2TC 2c	orange	250.	80.		
J2TC 2c	red orange	250.			
J2TC 2c	sepia	250.			
J3TC 3c	black	250.			
J3TC 3c	gray black		80.		
J3TC 3c	ultramarine	250.			
J3TC 3c	blue	250.			
J3TC 3c	blue green	250.			
J3TC 3c	orange	250.	80.		
J3TC 3c	red orange	250.			
J3TC 3c	light brown	250.			
J4TC 5c	black	250.			
J4TC 5c	gray black	250.			
J4TC 5c	ultramarine	250.			
J4TC 5c	blue	250.			
J4TC 5c	blue green	250.			
J4TC 5c	orange	250.	80.		
J4TC 5c	red orange	250.			
J5TC 10c	black	250.			
J5TC 10c	gray black	250.			
J5TC 10c	blue	250.			
J5TC 10c	olive yellow	250.			
J5TC 10c	blue green	250.			
J5TC 10c	orange	250.	80.		
J5TC 10c	red orange	250.			
J5TC 10c	olive bister	250.			
J5TC 10c	sepia	250.			
J5TC 10c	gray	250.			
J6TC 30c	black	250.			
J6TC 30c	gray black	250.			
J6TC 30c	blue	250.			
J6TC 30c	olive yellow		80.		
J6TC 30c	blue green	250.			
J6TC 30c	orange	250.	80.		
J6TC 30c	red orange	250.			
J6TC 30c	olive bister	250.			
J6TC 30c	sepia		80.		
J7TC 50c	black	250.			
J7TC 50c	gray black	250.			
J7TC 50c	blue	250.	80.		
J7TC 50c	olive yellow		80.		
J7TC 50c	blue green	250.			
J7TC 50c	orange	250.	80.		
J7TC 50c	red orange	250.			
J7TC 50c	olive bister	250.			
J7TC 50c	sepia	250.			
J7TC 50c	gray	250.			

OFFICIAL

Agriculture

		DIE (1) Lg.	(2) Sm.	PLATE (3) India	(4) Card
O1TC 1c	black	350.		65.	
O2TC 2c	black	350.		65.	
O3TC 3c	black	350.			
O3TC 3c	deep green	350.			
O4TC 6c	black	350.		125.	
O5TC 10c	black	350.			
O6TC 12c	black	350.		65.	
O9TC 30c	black	350.			

Executive

		DIE (1) Lg.	(2) Sm.	PLATE (3) India	(4) Card
O11TC 2c	black	350.		65.	
O11TC 2c	deep brown	350.			
O11TC 2c	brown carmine				75.
O12TC 3c	black	350.		65.	
O12TC 3c	deep green	350.			
O13TC 6c	black			80.	
O14TC 10c	black			80.	

Interior

		DIE (1) Lg.	(2) Sm.	PLATE (3) India	(4) Card
O16TC 2c	black	350.			
O16TC 2c	deep brown	350.			
O17TC 3c	black	350.		80.	
O17TC 3c	deep green	350.			

Justice

		DIE (1) Lg.	(2) Sm.	PLATE (3) India	(4) Card
O27TC 3c	black	350.		80.	
O27TC 3c	deep green	350.			
O27TC 3c	bister yellow			80.	
O27TC 3c	dull orange			80.	
O27TC 3c	black violet			80.	

Navy

		DIE (1) Lg.	(2) Sm.	PLATE (3) India	(4) Card
O35TC 1c	black			80.	
O36TC 2c	black	350.			
O36TC 2c	deep brown	350.			
O36TC 2c	deep green on wove paper, perf.				250.
O36TC 2c	deep green on wove paper, imperf.				250.
O37TC 3c	black	350.		80.	
O37TC 3c	deep green	350.			

Post Office

		DIE (1) Lg.	(2) Sm.	PLATE (3) India	(4) Card
O48TC 2c	deep brown	350.			
O49TC 3c	deep green	350.			
O50TC 6c	deep brown	350.			
O50TC 6c	brown carmine	350.			

State

		DIE (1) Lg.	(2) Sm.	PLATE (3) India	(4) Card
O57TC 1c	black	350.			
O57TC 1c	light ultramarine	350.			
O58TC 2c	black	350.			
O58TC 2c	deep brown	350.			
O59TC 3c	black	350.			
O67TC 90c	black	350.			
O68TC $2	violet & black	2,000.			
O68TC $2	brown red & black	2,000.			

O68TC	$2	orange red & slate blue	2,000.		

Treasury

O72TC	1c	black	350.
O72TC	1c	light ultramarine	350.
O73TC	2c	black	350.
O74TC	3c	black	350.
O74TC	3c	deep green	350.
O75TC	6c	black	350.
O77TC	10c	black	350.
O78TC	12c	black	350.
O79TC	15c	black	350.
O82TC	90c	black	350.

War

O83TC	1c	black	350.	80.	
O83TC	1c	light ultramarine	350.		
O84TC	2c	black	350.	80.	75.
O84TC	2c	deep brown	350.		
O85TC	3c	black	350.		
O85TC	3c	deep green	350.		
O86TC	6c	black		80.	
O89TC	12c	black		80.	

1910

POSTAL SAVINGS MAIL

O121TC	2c	lake	500.

The so-called "Goodall" set of Small Die proofs on India Paper of Official Stamps in five colors

Agriculture

		(a) Black	(b) Deep green	(c) Dull gray blue	(d) Deep brown	(e) Dull red
O1TC	1c	120.	110.	110.	110.	110.
O2TC	2c	120.	110.	110.	110.	110.
O3TC	3c	120.	110.	110.	110.	110.
O4TC	6c	120.	110.	110.	110.	110.
O5TC	10c	120.	110.	110.	110.	110.
O6TC	12c	120.	110.	110.	110.	110.
O7TC	15c	120.	110.	110.	110.	110.
O8TC	24c	120.	110.	110.	110.	110.
O9TC	30c	120.	110.	110.	110.	110.

Executive

O10TC	1c	120.	110.	110.	110.	110.
O11TC	2c	120.	110.	110.	110.	110.
O12TC	3c	120.	110.	110.	110.	110.
O13TC	6c	120.	110.	110.	110.	110.
O14TC	10c	120.	110.	110.	110.	110.

Interior

O15TC	1c	120.	110.	110.	110.	110.
O16TC	2c	120.	110.	110.	110.	110.
O17TC	3c	120.	110.	110.	110.	110.
O18TC	6c	120.	110.	110.	110.	110.
O19TC	10c	120.	110.	110.	110.	110.
O20TC	12c	120.	110.	110.	110.	110.
O21TC	15c	120.	110.	110.	110.	110.
O22TC	24c	120.	110.	110.	110.	110.
O23TC	30c	120.	110.	110.	110.	110.
O24TC	90c	120.	110.	110.	110.	110.

Justice

O25TC	1c	120.	110.	110.	110.	110.
O26TC	2c	120.	110.	110.	110.	110.
O27TC	3c	120.	110.	110.	110.	110.
O28TC	6c	120.	110.	110.	110.	110.
O29TC	10c	120.	110.	110.	110.	110.
O30TC	12c	120.	110.	110.	110.	110.
O31TC	15c	120.	110.	110.	110.	110.
O32TC	24c	120.	110.	110.	110.	110.
O33TC	30c	120.	110.	110.	110.	110.
O34TC	90c	120.	110.	110.	110.	110.

Navy

O35TC	1c	120.	110.	110.	110.	110.
O36TC	2c	120.	110.	110.	110.	110.
O37TC	3c	120.	110.	110.	110.	110.
O38TC	6c	120.	110.	110.	110.	110.
O39TC	7c	120.	110.	110.	110.	110.
O40TC	10c	120.	110.	110.	110.	110.
O41TC	12c	120.	110.	110.	110.	110.
O42TC	15c	120.	110.	110.	110.	110.
O43TC	24c	120.	110.	110.	110.	110.
O44TC	30c	120.	110.	110.	110.	110.
O45TC	90c	120.	110.	110.	110.	110.

Post Office

O47TC	1c	120.	110.	110.	110.	110.
O48TC	2c	120.	110.	110.	110.	110.
O49TC	3c	120.	110.	110.	110.	110.
O50TC	6c	120.	110.	110.	110.	110.
O51TC	10c	120.	110.	110.	110.	110.
O52TC	12c	120.	110.	110.	110.	110.
O53TC	15c	120.	110.	110.	110.	110.
O54TC	24c	120.	110.	110.	110.	110.
O55TC	30c	120.	110.	110.	110.	110.
O56TC	90c	120.	110.	110.	110.	110.

State

O57TC	1c	120.	110.	110.	110.	110.
O58TC	2c	120.	110.	110.	110.	110.
O59TC	3c	120.	110.	110.	110.	110.
O60TC	6c	120.	110.	110.	110.	110.
O61TC	7c	120.	110.	110.	110.	110.
O62TC	10c	120.	110.	110.	110.	110.
O63TC	12c	120.	110.	110.	110.	110.
O64TC	15c	120.	110.	110.	110.	110.
O65TC	24c	120.	110.	110.	110.	110.
O66TC	30c	120.	110.	110.	110.	110.
O67TC	90c	120.	110.	110.	110.	110.

O68TC	$2	scarlet frame, green center	750.
O68TC	$2	scarlet frame, black center	750.
O68TC	$2	scarlet frame, blue center	750.
O68TC	$2	green frame, brown center	750.
O68TC	$2	brown frame, green center	750.
O68TC	$2	brown frame, black center	750.

Treasury

O72TC	1c	120.	110.	110.	110.	110.
O73TC	2c	120.	110.	110.	110.	110.
O74TC	3c	120.	110.	110.	110.	110.
O75TC	6c	120.	110.	110.	110.	110.
O76TC	7c	120.	110.	110.	110.	110.
O77TC	10c	120.	110.	110.	110.	110.
O78TC	12c	120.	110.	110.	110.	110.
O79TC	15c	120.	110.	110.	110.	110.
O80TC	24c	120.	110.	110.	110.	110.
O81TC	30c	120.	110.	110.	110.	110.
O82TC	90c	120.	110.	110.	110.	110.

War

O83TC	1c	120.	110.	110.	110.	110.
O84TC	2c	120.	110.	110.	110.	110.
O85TC	3c	120.	110.	110.	110.	110.
O86TC	6c	120.	110.	110.	110.	110.
O87TC	7c	120.	110.	110.	110.	110.
O88TC	10c	120.	110.	110.	110.	110.
O89TC	12c	120.	110.	110.	110.	110.
O90TC	15c	120.	110.	110.	110.	110.
O91TC	24c	120.	110.	110.	110.	110.
O92TC	30c	120.	110.	110.	110.	110.
O93TC	90c	120.	110.	110.	110.	110.

OFFICIAL SEALS

1872

OXF1TC	ultra	Die on India	250.
OXF1TC	blue	Die on card, colored border	350.
OXF1TC	dp bl	Die on card, colored border	350.
OXF1TC	green	Die on card, colored border	350.
OXF1TC	choc	Die on glossy bond	250.
OXF1TC	choc	Die on card, colored border	350.
OXF1TC	car	Die on India	250.
OXF1TC	brown	Die on India	250.
OXF1TC	red vio	Die on India	—

1877

OX1TC	blue	Die on India	150.
OX1TC	green	Die on India	150.
OX1TC	green	Plate on bond	150.
OX1TC	green	Plate on bond, perforated and gummed	—
OX1TC	orange	Die on India	150.
OX1TC	red orange	Die on India	150.
OX1TC	black	Die on India	150.

NEWSPAPERS

1865

			(1) Die on India	(5) Thick cream wove paper
PR1TC	5c	bright red	500.	
PR2TC	10c	brown	500.	
PR2TC	10c	dull red	500.	
PR2TC	10c	blue	500.	
PR2TC	10c	black		70.
PR2TC	10c	lake		70.
PR2TC	10c	blue green		70.
PR2TC	10c	blue		70.
PR3TC	25c	black		70.
PR3TC	25c	lake		70.
PR3TC	25c	blue green		70.
PR3TC	25c	blue		70.
PR3TC	25c	ocher	500.	
PR3TC	25c	brown	500.	
PR3TC	25c	brick red	500.	
PR4TC	5c	black		70.
PR4TC	5c	lake		70.
PR4TC	5c	blue green		70.
PR4TC	5c	blue		70.

1875

			(1) Die on India	(3) Plate on India
PR9TC	2c	dark carmine		35.
PR9TC	2c	brown rose		35.
PR9TC	2c	scarlet		35.
PR9TC	2c	orange brown	200.	35.
PR9TC	2c	black brown	200.	
PR9TC	2c	sepia		35.
PR9TC	2c	orange yellow		35.
PR9TC	2c	dull orange		35.
PR9TC	2c	green		35.
PR9TC	2c	blue green	200.	
PR9TC	2c	light ultramarine		35.
PR9TC	2c	light blue		35.
PR9TC	2c	dark violet		35.
PR9TC	2c	violet black		35.
PR10TC	3c	rose lake	200.	
PR16TC	12c	dark carmine		35.
PR16TC	12c	brown rose	200.	35.
PR16TC	12c	scarlet	200.	
PR16TC	12c	orange brown		35.
PR16TC	12c	sepia	200.	35.
PR16TC	12c	orange yellow		35.
PR16TC	12c	dull orange		35.
PR16TC	12c	green	200.	35.
PR16TC	12c	light ultramarine	200.	35.
PR16TC	12c	light blue		35.
PR16TC	12c	dark violet	200.	35.
PR16TC	12c	violet black	200.	35.
PR16TC	12c	black	200.	35.
PR17TC	24c	sepia	200.	
PR17TC	24c	green	200.	
PR17TC	24c	black	200.	35.
PR18TC	36c	black	200.	35.

			(1) Die on India	(3) Plate on India
PR18TC	36c	sepia	200.	
PR18TC	36c	green	200.	
PR19TC	48c	black	200.	35.
PR19TC	48c	sepia	200.	
PR19TC	48c	green	200.	
PR20TC	60c	black	200.	35.
PR21TC	72c	black	200.	35.
PR22TC	84c	black	200.	35.
PR23TC	96c	black		35.
PR24TC	$1.92	dark carmine		35.
PR24TC	$1.92	brown rose		35.
PR24TC	$1.92	scarlet		35.
PR24TC	$1.92	orange brown	200.	35.
PR24TC	$1.92	orange yellow		35.
PR24TC	$1.92	dull orange		35.
PR24TC	$1.92	green	200.	35.
PR24TC	$1.92	light ultramarine		35.
PR24TC	$1.92	dark violet		35.
PR24TC	$1.92	violet black		35.
PR24TC	$1.92	black		35.
PR25TC	$3	dark carmine	200.	35.
PR25TC	$3	brown rose		35.
PR25TC	$3	scarlet		35.
PR25TC	$3	orange brown		35.
PR25TC	$3	sepia		35.
PR25TC	$3	orange yellow	200.	35.
PR25TC	$3	dull orange	200.	35.
PR25TC	$3	green	200.	35.
PR25TC	$3	light ultramarine	200.	35.
PR25TC	$3	light blue		35.
PR25TC	$3	dark violet	200.	35.
PR25TC	$3	violet black	200.	35.
PR25TC	$3	black	200.	35.
PR26TC	$6	dark carmine	200.	35.
PR26TC	$6	brown rose		35.
PR26TC	$6	scarlet	200.	35.
PR26TC	$6	orange brown		35.
PR26TC	$6	dark brown		35.
PR26TC	$6	sepia	200.	35.
PR26TC	$6	orange yellow		35.
PR26TC	$6	dull orange	200.	35.
PR26TC	$6	green	200.	35.
PR26TC	$6	light ultramarine		35.
PR26TC	$6	light blue	200.	35.
PR26TC	$6	dark violet	200.	35.
PR26TC	$6	violet black	200.	35.
PR26TC	$6	black	200.	35.
PR27TC	$9	dark carmine	200.	35.
PR27TC	$9	brown rose		35.
PR27TC	$9	scarlet	200.	35.
PR27TC	$9	orange brown		35.
PR27TC	$9	sepia	200.	35.
PR27TC	$9	orange yellow	200.	35.
PR27TC	$9	dull orange	200.	35.
PR27TC	$9	green	200.	35.
PR27TC	$9	light ultramarine	200.	35.
PR27TC	$9	light blue		35.
PR27TC	$9	dark violet	200.	35.
PR27TC	$9	violet black	200.	35.
PR27TC	$9	black	200.	35.
PR28TC	$12	black	200.	
PR28TC	$12	sepia	200.	
PR28TC	$12	orange brown	200.	
PR29TC	$24	black	200.	35.
PR29TC	$24	black brown	200.	
PR29TC	$24	orange brown	200.	
PR29TC	$24	green	200.	
PR30TC	$36	dark carmine	200.	
PR30TC	$36	black	200.	35.
PR30TC	$36	black brown	200.	
PR30TC	$36	orange brown	200.	
PR30TC	$36	sepia	200.	
PR30TC	$36	violet	200.	
PR30TC	$36	green	200.	
PR31TC	$48	violet brown	200.	35.
PR31TC	$48	black	200.	35.
PR31TC	$48	sepia	200.	
PR31TC	$48	green	200.	
PR32TC	$60	dark carmine	200.	40.
PR32TC	$60	scarlet	200.	40.
PR32TC	$60	sepia	200.	40.
PR32TC	$60	green	200.	40.
PR32TC	$60	light ultramarine	200.	40.
PR32TC	$60	black	200.	40.
PR32TC	$60	violet black	200.	
PR32TC	$60	orange brown	200.	
PR32TC	$60	orange yellow	200.	
PR32TC	$60	dull orange	200.	
PR32TC	$60	brown rose	200.	

1885

PR18TC	1c	salmon	200.	
PR18TC	1c	scarlet		120.
PR18TC	1c	dark brown		120.
PR18TC	1c	violet brown		120.
PR18TC	1c	dull orange		120.
PR18TC	1c	green		120.
PR18TC	1c	light blue		120.

1894

PR106TC	25c	deep carmine	200.
PR106TC	25c	dark carmine	200.
PR107TC	50c	black	200.
PR108TC	$2	deep scarlet	200.
PR108TC	$2	dark scarlet	200.
PR109TC	$5	light ultramarine	200.
PR109TC	$5	dark ultramarine	200.
PR110TC	$10	black	200.
PR112TC	$50	black	200.
PR112TC	$50	deep rose	200.
PR112TC	$50	dark rose	200.
PR113TC	$100	black	200.

The so-called "Goodall" set of Small Die proofs on India Paper of Newspaper Stamps in five colors

		(a) Black	(b) Deep green	(c) Dull gray blue	(d) Deep brown	(e) Dull red
PR9TC	2c	150.	125.	125.	125.	125.
PR10TC	3c	150.	125.	125.	125.	125.
PR11TC	4c	150.	125.	125.	125.	125.
PR12TC	6c	150.	125.	125.	125.	125.
PR13TC	8c	150.	125.	125.	125.	125.
PR14TC	9c	150.	125.	125.	125.	125.
PR15TC	10c	150.	125.	125.	125.	125.
PR16TC	12c	150.	125.	125.	125.	125.
PR17TC	24c	150.	125.	125.	125.	125.
PR18TC	36c	150.	125.	125.	125.	125.
PR19TC	48c	150.	125.	125.	125.	125.
PR20TC	60c	150.	125.	125.	125.	125.
PR21TC	72c	150.	125.	125.	125.	125.
PR22TC	84c	150.	125.	125.	125.	125.
PR23TC	96c	150.	125.	125.	125.	125.
PR24TC	$1.92	150.	125.	125.	125.	125.
PR25TC	$3	150.	125.	125.	125.	125.
PR26TC	$6	150.	125.	125.	125.	125.
PR27TC	$9	150.	125.	125.	125.	125.
PR28TC	$12	150.	125.	125.	125.	125.
PR29TC	$24	150.	125.	125.	125.	125.
PR30TC	$36	150.	125.	125.	125.	125.
PR31TC	$48	150.	125.	125.	125.	125.
PR32TC	$60	150.	125.	125.	125.	125.

1925

SPECIAL HANDLING

QE4TC	25c apple green	700.
QE4TC	25c olive green	700.
QE4TC	25c light blue green	700.
QE4TC	25c dark blue	700.
QE4TC	25c orange yellow	700.
QE4TC	25c orange	700.
QE4TC	25c dull rose	700.
QE4TC	25c carmine lake	700.
QE4TC	25c brown	700.
QE4TC	25c gray brown	700.
QE4TC	25c dark violet brown	700.
QE4TC	25c gray black	700.
QE4TC	25c black	700.

THE "ATLANTA" SET OF PLATE PROOFS

A set in five colors on thin card reprinted in 1881 for display at the International Cotton Exhibition in Atlanta, Ga.

1847 Designs (Reproductions)

		Black	Scarlet	Brown	Green	Blue
3TC	5c	250.	250.	250.	250.	250.
4TC	10c	250.	250.	250.	250.	250.

1851-60 Designs

		Black	Scarlet	Brown	Green	Blue
40TC	1c	100.	90.	90.	90.	90.
41TC	3c	100.	90.	90.	90.	90.
42TC	5c	100.	90.	90.	90.	90.
43TC	10c	100.	90.	90.	90.	90.
44TC	12c	100.	90.	90.	90.	90.
45TC	24c	100.	90.	90.	90.	90.
46TC	30c	100.	90.	90.	90.	90.
47TC	90c	100.	90.	90.	90.	90.

1861-66 Designs

		Black	Scarlet	Brown	Green	Blue
102TC	1c	85.	75.	75.	75.	75.
103TC	2c	150.	150.	150.	150.	150.
104TC	3c	85.	75.	75.	75.	75.
105TC	5c	85.	75.	75.	75.	75.
106TC	10c	85.	75.	75.	75.	75.
107TC	12c	85.	75.	75.	75.	75.
108TC	15c	85.	75.	75.	75.	75.
109TC	24c	85.	75.	75.	75.	75.
110TC	30c	85.	75.	75.	75.	75.
111TC	90c	85.	75.	75.	75.	75.

1869 Designs

		Black	Scarlet	Brown	Green	Blue
123TC	1c	160.	140.	140.	140.	140.
124TC	2c	160.	140.	140.	140.	140.
125TC	3c	160.	140.	140.	140.	140.
126TC	6c	160.	140.	140.	140.	140.
127TC	10c	160.	140.	140.	140.	140.
128TC	12c	160.	140.	140.	140.	140.

129TC	15c black frame, scarlet center	350.
129TC	15c black frame, green center	350.
129TC	15c scarlet frame, black center	350.
129TC	15c scarlet frame, blue center	350.
129TC	15c brown frame, black center	350.
129TC	15c brown frame, green center	350.
129TC	15c brown frame, blue center	350.
129TC	15c green frame, black center	350.
129TC	15c green frame, blue center	350.
129TC	15c blue frame, black center	350.
129TC	15c blue frame, brown center	350.
129TC	15c blue frame, green center	350.
130TC	24c black frame, scarlet center	350.
130TC	24c black frame, green center	350.
130TC	24c black frame, blue center	350.
130TC	24c scarlet frame, black center	350.
130TC	24c scarlet frame, blue center	350.
130TC	24c brown frame, black center	350.
130TC	24c brown frame, blue center	350.
130TC	24c green frame, black center	350.
130TC	24c green frame, brown center	350.
130TC	24c blue frame, brown center	350.
130TC	24c blue frame, green center	350.
131TC	30c black frame, scarlet center	350.
131TC	30c black frame, green center	350.
131TC	30c black frame, blue center	350.
131TC	30c scarlet frame, green center	350.
131TC	30c scarlet frame, blue center	350.
131TC	30c brown frame, black center	350.
131TC	30c brown frame, scarlet center	350.
131TC	30c brown frame, blue center	350.
131TC	30c green frame, black center	350.
131TC	30c green frame, brown center	350.
131TC	30c blue frame, scarlet center	350.
131TC	30c blue frame, brown center	350.
131TC	30c blue frame, green center	350.
132TC	90c black frame, scarlet center	500.
132TC	90c black frame, brown center	500.
132TC	90c black frame, green center	500.
132TC	90c scarlet frame, blue center	500.
132TC	90c brown frame, black center	500.
132TC	90c brown frame, blue center	500.
132TC	90c green frame, brown center	500.
132TC	90c green frame, blue center	500.
132TC	90c blue frame, brown center	500.
132TC	90c blue frame, green center	500.

1873-75 Designs

		Black	Scarlet	Brown	Green	Blue
156TC	1c	45.	40.	40.	40.	40.
157TC	2c	45.	40.	40.	40.	40.
158TC	3c	50.	45.	45.	45.	45.
159TC	7c	55.	50.	50.	50.	50.
160TC	10c	45.	40.	40.	40.	40.
161TC	12c	45.	40.	40.	40.	40.
162TC	15c	45.	40.	40.	40.	40.
163TC	24c	45.	40.	40.	40.	40.
164TC	30c	50.	45.	45.	45.	45.
165TC	90c	45.	40.	40.	40.	40.
179TC	5c	65.	60.	60.	60.	60.

POSTAGE DUE

J1TC	1c	45.	40.	40.	40.	40.
J2TC	2c	45.	40.	40.	40.	40.
J3TC	3c	45.	40.	40.	40.	40.
J4TC	5c	45.	40.	40.	40.	40.
J5TC	10c	45.	40.	40.	40.	40.
J6TC	30c	45.	40.	40.	40.	40.
J7TC	50c	45.	40.	40.	40.	40.

OFFICIALS

Agriculture

O1TC	1c	35.	30.	30.	30.	30.
O2TC	2c	35.	30.	30.	30.	30.
O3TC	3c	35.	30.	30.	30.	30.
O4TC	6c	45.	40.	40.	40.	40.
O5TC	10c	35.	30.	30.	30.	30.
O6TC	12c	35.	30.	30.	30.	30.
O7TC	15c	35.	30.	30.	30.	30.
O8TC	24c	35.	30.	30.	30.	30.
O9TC	30c	35.	30.	30.	30.	30.

Executive

O10TC	1c	35.	30.	30.	30.	30.
O11TC	2c	35.	30.	30.	30.	30.
O12TC	3c	35.	30.	30.	30.	30.
O13TC	6c	45.	40.	40.	40.	40.
O14TC	10c	35.	30.	30.	30.	30.

Interior

O15TC	1c	35.	30.	30.	30.	30.
O16TC	2c	35.	30.	30.	30.	30.
O17TC	3c	35.	30.	30.	30.	30.
O18TC	6c	45.	40.	40.	40.	40.
O19TC	10c	35.	30.	30.	30.	30.
O20TC	12c	35.	30.	30.	30.	30.
O21TC	15c	35.	30.	30.	30.	30.
O22TC	24c	35.	30.	30.	30.	30.
O23TC	30c	50.	45.	45.	45.	45.
O24TC	90c	35.	30.	30.	30.	30.

Justice

O25TC	1c	35.	30.	30.	30.	30.
O26TC	2c	35.	30.	30.	30.	30.
O27TC	3c	35.	30.	30.	30.	30.
O28TC	6c	45.	40.	40.	40.	40.
O29TC	10c	35.	30.	30.	30.	30.
O30TC	12c	35.	30.	30.	30.	30.
O31TC	15c	35.	30.	30.	30.	30.
O32TC	24c	50.	45.	45.	45.	45.
O33TC	30c	50.	45.	45.	45.	45.
O34TC	90c	35.	30.	30.	30.	30.

Navy

O35TC	1c	35.	30.	30.	30.	30.
O36TC	2c	35.	30.	30.	30.	30.
O37TC	3c	35.	30.	30.	30.	30.
O38TC	6c	45.	40.	40.	40.	40.
O39TC	7c	35.	30.	30.	30.	30.
O40TC	10c	35.	30.	30.	30.	30.
O41TC	12c	35.	30.	30.	30.	30.
O42TC	15c	35.	30.	30.	30.	30.
O43TC	24c	35.	30.	30.	30.	30.
O44TC	30c	50.	45.	45.	45.	45.
O45TC	90c	35.	30.	30.	30.	30.

Post Office

O48TC	2c	35.	30.	30.	30.	30.
O49TC	3c	35.	30.	30.	30.	30.
O50TC	6c	35.	30.	30.	30.	30.
O51TC	10c	35.	30.	30.	30.	30.
O52TC	12c	35.	30.	30.	30.	30.
O53TC	15c	35.	30.	30.	30.	30.
O54TC	24c	35.	30.	30.	30.	30.
O55TC	30c	35.	30.	30.	30.	30.
O56TC	90c	35.	30.	30.	30.	30.

State

O57TC	1c	35.	30.	30.	30.	30.
O58TC	2c	35.	30.	30.	30.	30.
O59TC	3c	35.	30.	30.	30.	30.
O60TC	6c	45.	40.	40.	40.	40.
O61TC	7c	35.	30.	30.	30.	30.

		Black	Scarlet	Brown	Green	Blue
O62TC	10c	35.	30.	30.	30.	30.
O63TC	12c	35.	30.	30.	30.	30.
O64TC	15c	35.	30.	30.	30.	30.
O65TC	24c	35.	30.	30.	30.	30.
O66TC	30c	50.	45.	45.	45.	45.
O67TC	90c	35.	30.	30.	30.	30.

O68TC	$2 scarlet frame, black center	750.
O68TC	$2 scarlet frame, blue center	750.
O68TC	$2 brown frame, black center	750.
O68TC	$2 brown frame, blue center	750.
O68TC	$2 green frame, brown center	750.
O68TC	$2 blue frame, brown center	750.
O68TC	$2 blue frame, green center	750.
O69TC	$5 scarlet frame, black center	750.
O69TC	$5 scarlet frame, blue center	750.
O69TC	$5 brown frame, black center	750.
O69TC	$5 brown frame, blue center	750.
O69TC	$5 green frame, brown center	750.
O69TC	$5 blue frame, brown center	750.
O69TC	$5 blue frame, green center	750.
O70TC	$10 scarlet frame, black center	750.
O70TC	$10 scarlet frame, blue center	750.
O70TC	$10 brown frame, black center	750.
O70TC	$10 brown frame, blue center	750.
O70TC	$10 green frame, brown center	750.
O70TC	$10 blue frame, brown center	750.
O70TC	$10 blue frame, green center	750.
O71TC	$20 scarlet frame, black center	750.
O71TC	$20 scarlet frame, blue center	750.
O71TC	$20 brown frame, black center	750.
O71TC	$20 brown frame, blue center	750.
O71TC	$20 green frame, brown center	750.
O71TC	$20 brown frame, green center	750.
O71TC	$20 blue frame, green center	750.

Treasury

		Black	Scarlet	Brown	Green	Blue
O72TC	1c	35.	30.	30.	30.	30.
O73TC	2c	35.	30.	30.	30.	30.
O74TC	3c	35.	30.	30.	30.	30.
O75TC	6c	45.	40.	40.	40.	40.
O76TC	7c	35.	30.	30.	30.	30.
O77TC	10c	35.	30.	30.	30.	30.
O78TC	12c	35.	30.	30.	30.	30.
O79TC	15c	35.	30.	30.	30.	30.
O80TC	24c	35.	30.	30.	30.	30.
O81TC	30c	50.	45.	45.	45.	45.
O82TC	90c	35.	30.	30.	30.	30.

War

O83TC	1c	35.	30.	30.	30.	30.
O84TC	2c	35.	30.	30.	30.	30.
O85TC	3c	35.	30.	—	30.	30.
	Plate flaw at upper left (32R20)					
O86TC	6c	45.	40.	40.	40.	40.
O87TC	7c	35.	30.	30.	30.	30.
O88TC	10c	35.	30.	30.	30.	30.
O89TC	12c	35.	30.	30.	30.	30.
O90TC	15c	35.	30.	30.	30.	30.
O91TC	24c	35.	30.	30.	30.	30.
O92TC	30c	50.	45.	45.	45.	45.
O93TC	90c	35.	30.	30.	30.	30.

NEWSPAPERS

PR9TC	2c	45.	30.	30.	30.	30.
PR10TC	3c	45.	30.	30.	30.	30.
PR11TC	4c	45.	30.	30.	30.	30.
PR12TC	6c	45.	30.	30.	30.	30.
PR13TC	8c	45.	30.	30.	30.	30.
PR14TC	9c	45.	30.	30.	30.	30.
PR15TC	10c	45.	30.	30.	30.	30.
PR16TC	12c	45.	30.	30.	30.	30.
PR17TC	24c	45.	30.	30.	30.	30.
PR18TC	36c	45.	30.	30.	30.	30.
PR19TC	48c	45.	30.	30.	30.	30.
PR20TC	60c	45.	30.	30.	30.	30.
PR21TC	72c	45.	30.	30.	30.	30.
PR22TC	84c	45.	30.	30.	30.	30.
PR23TC	96c	45.	30.	30.	30.	30.
PR24TC	$ 1.92	45.	30.	30.	30.	30.
PR25TC	$ 3	45.	30.	30.	30.	30.
PR26TC	$ 6	45.	30.	30.	30.	30.
PR27TC	$ 9	45.	30.	30.	30.	30.
PR28TC	$12	45.	30.	30.	30.	30.
PR29TC	$24	45.	30.	30.	30.	30.
PR30TC	$36	45.	30.	30.	30.	30.
PR31TC	$48	45.	30.	30.	30.	30.
PR32TC	$60	45.	30.	30.	30.	30.

CARRIERS

LO1TC	1c Franklin	100.	90.	90.	90.	90.
LO2TC	1c Eagle	100.	90.	90.	90.	90.

TELEGRAPH

American Rapid Telegraph Co.

		DIE (2) Small	DIE (3) India	PLATE (4) Card
1T1TC	1c green		55.	
1T1TC	1c brown		55.	
1T1TC	1c red		55.	
1T1TC	1c blue		55.	
1T1TC	1c bluish green		55.	
1T3TC	5c green		55.	
1T3TC	5c black		55.	
1T3TC	5c red		55.	
1T3TC	5c blue		55.	
1T3TC	5c bluish green		55.	
1T5TC	15c red		55.	
1T5TC	15c black		55.	

(unnamed, continued)

			DIE (2) Small	PLATE (3) India	(4) Card
1T5TC	15c	brown	55.		
1T5TC	15c	bluish green	55.		
1T6TC	20c	green	55.		
1T6TC	20c	black	55.		
1T6TC	20c	brown	55.		
1T6TC	20c	blue	55.		
1T6TC	20c	bluish green	55.		

Collect

			DIE (1) Large	(2) Small	PLATE (3) India	(4) Card
1T10TC	5c	red		55.		
1T10TC	5c	black		55.		
1T10TC	5c	brown		55.		
1T10TC	5c	green		55.		
1T10TC	5c	bluish green		55.		
1T11TC	15c	red		55.		
1T11TC	15c	black		55.		
1T11TC	15c	brown		55.		
1T11TC	15c	green		55.		
1T11TC	15c	blue		55.		
1T11TC	15c	bluish green		55.		

Office Coupon

			Small	India	Card
1T14TC	5c	red	55.		
1T14TC	5c	black	55.		
1T14TC	5c	brown	55.		
1T14TC	5c	green	55.		
1T14TC	5c	bluish green	55.		
1T15TC	15c	red	55.		
1T15TC	15c	black	55.		
1T15TC	15c	brown	55.		
1T15TC	15c	green	55.		
1T15TC	15c	blue	55.		
1T15TC	15c	bluish green	55.		

Baltimore & Ohio Telegraph Co.

			Small	India	Card
3T2TC	5c	dark olive	65.		
3T4TC	25c	dark olive	65.		

Postal Telegraph Co.

			Small	India	Card
15T1TC	10c	brown red		65.	
15T1TC	10c	red	65.		
15T1TC	10c	blue	65.		
15T1TC	10c	black	65.		
15T1TC	10c	orange			65.
15T2TC	15c	black	65.		55.
15T2TC	15c	red	65.	55.	
15T2TC	15c	blue	65.	55.	
15T2TC	25c	brown red	65.		
15T3TC	25c	black	65.		
15T3TC	25c	red	65.		
15T3TC	25c	ultramarine			40.
15T3TC	25c	brown	65.		
15T4TC	50c	dull blue	65.		
15T4TC	50c	black	65.		40.
15T4TC	50c	red	65.		
15T6TC		red brown			40.

Western Union Telegraph Co.

			India	Card
16T1TC		lilac (1871)	20.	20.
		Pair	45.	45.
16T1TC		orange	20.	20.
		Pair	45.	45.
16T1TC		black	20.	20.
		Pair	45.	45.
16T1TC		violet brown	20.	
		Pair	45.	
16T1TC		light olive	20.	
		Pair	45.	
16T1TC		brown	20.	
		Pair	45.	
16T1TC		orange brown	20.	
		Pair	45.	
16T1TC		blue green	20.	
		Pair	45.	
16T6TC		violet blue (1876)	20.	20.
16T7TC		orange yellow (1877)	20.	
		Pair	45.	
16T7TC		dark brown	20.	
		Pair	45.	
16T7TC		black	20.	
		Pane of 4	—	
16T8TC		dark brown (1878)	—	
16T9TC		blue (1879)	—	
16T10TC		violet brown (1880)	—	
16T10TC		rose	—	
16T22TC		black (1892)	—	

Die Proof Printed Directly on Card

16T44TC	dull red	—
16T44TC	orange	—
16T44TC	rose red	—
16T44TC	orange brown	—
16T44TC	ocher	—
16T44TC	dark blue	—
16T44TC	dark ultramarine	—
16T44TC	green	—
16T44TC	brown lake	—
16T44TC	reddish brown	—
16T44TC	sepia	—
16T44TC	sepia, unsurfaced card	—
16T44TC	dull violet	—
16T44TC	slate green	—
16T44TC	slate blue	—
16T44TC	black	—
16T44TC	black, unsurfaced card	—

On India

16T44TC	deep rose	—
16T44TC	carmine lake	—
16T44TC	rose lake	—
16T44TC	deep ultramarine	—

Plate Proofs, Sheets of 16 on India or Bond

16T44TC	deep rose, on India	—
16T44TC	deep rose, on Bond	—
16T44TC	orange, on India	—
16T44TC	orange, on Bond	—
16T44TC	dark blue, on India	—
16T44TC	dark blue, on Bond	—
16T44TC	slate green, on India	—
16T44TC	slate green, on Bond	—
16T44TC	rose lake, on India	—
16T44TC	rose lake, on Bond	—
16T44TC	sepia, on Bond	—

REVENUES

Several lists of revenue proofs in trial colors have been published, but the accuracy of some of them is questionable. The following listings are limited to items seen by the editors. The list is not complete.

1862-71   FIRST ISSUE

Number	Denom	Description	Printing	Price
R3TC	1c	Proprietary, black	Plate on India	80.
R3TC		carmine	Plate on Card	125.
R3TC		dull red	Plate on Bond	125.
R3TC		orange red	Plate on Bond	125.
R3TC		dull yel.	Plate on Bond	125.
R3TC		violet rose	Plate on Bond	125.
R3TC		deep blue	Plate on Bond	125.
R3TC		red on blue	Plate on Bond	125.
R3TC		blue, perf. & gum	Plate on Bond	125.
R3TC		green	Plate on buff wove	—
R3TC		black	Die on India	950.
R7TC	2c	Certificate, ultra.	Plate on Card	65.
R11TC	2c	Playing Cards, black	Die on India	500.
R13TC	2c	Proprietary, black	Die on India	75.
R13TC		black	Die on India	650.
R13TC		carmine	Die on India	650.
R15TC	2c	U.S.I.R., violet rose	Plate on Bond	110.
R15TC		light green	Plate on Bond	110.
R15TC		pale blue	Plate on Bond	110.
R15TC		pale rose	Plate on Bond	200.
R15TC		orange	Plate on blue Bond	—
R15TC		black	Plate on India	110.
R15TC		pale orange, perf. & gum	Plate on Bond	110.
R16TC	3c	Foreign Exchange, green on blue	Plate on Bond	140.
R16TC		blue	Plate on Goldbeater's Skin	110.
R18TC	3c	Proprietary, black	Die on India	300.
R21TC	4c	Playing Cards, black	Die (?) on India	300.
R22TC	4c	Proprietary, black	Plate on India	110.
R22TC		black	Die on India	350.
R22TC		deep red lilac	Die on India	400.
R22TC		red lilac	Plate on Card	110.
R24TC	5c	Certificate, carmine	Plate on India	110.
R25TC	5c	Express, pale olive	Plate on Wove	—
R26TC	5c	Foreign Exchange, orange	Plate on India	110.
R28TC	5c	Playing Cards, black	Die (?) on India	300.
R29TC	5c	Proprietary, red	Plate on blue Bond	—
R30TC	6c	Inland Exchange, black	Die on India	350.
R31TC	6c	Proprietary, black	Die on India	—
R32TC	10c	Bill of Lading, greenish blue	Die on India	350.
R32TC+R37TC		composite, dark green	Large Die on India	—
R35TC	10c	Foreign Exchange, black	Die (?) on India	350.
R37TC	10c	Power of Attorney, greenish blue	Die on India	350.
R38TC	10c	Proprietary, black	Die on India	350.
R43TC	25c	Bond, carmine	Plate on Card	90.
R44TC	25c	Certificate, blue	Plate on Bond	300.
R44TC		green	Plate on Bond	300.
R44TC		orange	Plate on Bond	300.
R45TC	25c	Entry of Goods, black	Hybrid Die on India	—
R46TC	25c	Insurance, dull red	Plate on Bond	150.
R46TC		dull red	Plate on Goldbeater's Skin	210.
R46TC		vermilion	Plate on Goldbeater's Skin	210.
R46TC		vermilion	Plate on Bond	170.
R46TC		blue	Plate on Bond	170.
R46TC		blue	Plate on Goldbeater's Skin	215.
R46TC		dark blue	Plate on Bond	155.
R46TC		dark blue	Plate on Goldbeater's Skin	215.
R46TC		green	Plate on Goldbeater's Skin	215.
R51TC	30c	Foreign Exchange, violet	Plate on India	130.
R51TC		violet gray	Plate on India	130.
R51TC		deep red lilac	Plate on India	155.
R51TC		black	Plate on India	155.
R51TC		red	Plate on India	155.
R52TC		Inland Exchange, deep red lilac	Plate on India	155.
R53TC	40c	Inland Exchange, black	Hybrid Die on India	—
R55TC	50c	Entry of Goods, orange	Plate on Bond	275.
R55TC		green	Plate on Bond	275.
R55TC		red	Plate on Bond	340.
R55TC		deep blue	Plate on India	—
R58TC	50c	Life Insurance, ultramarine	Plate on India	85.
R60TC	50c	Original Process, black	Die (?) on India	280.
R64TC	60c	Inland Exchange, green	Die (?) on India	—
R65TC	70c	Foreign Exchange, orange	Die (?) on India	—
R65TC		black	Die (?) on India	285.
R66TC	$1	Conveyance, carmine	Plate on India	85.
R67TC	$1	Entry of Goods, carmine	Plate on India	60.
R68TC	$1	Foreign Exchange, carmine	Plate on India	60.
R69TC	$1	Inland Exchange, carmine	Plate on India	60.
R70TC	$1	Lease, carmine	Plate on India	130.
R71TC	$1	Life Insurance, carmine	Plate on India	75.
R72TC	$1	Manifest, carmine	Plate on India	80.
R73TC	$1	Mortgage, carmine	Plate on India	85.
R73TC		black	Hybrid Die on India	—
R74TC	$1	Passage Ticket, carmine	Plate on India	120.
R75TC	$1	Power of Attorney, carmine	Plate on India	120.
R76TC	$1	Probate of Will, carmine	Plate on India	60.
R78TC	$1.50	Inland Exchange, black	Die on India	475.
R80TC	$1.90	Foreign Exchange, black	Plate on India	155.
R81TC	$2	Conveyance, carmine	Plate on Card	85.
R82TC	$2	Mortgage, carmine	Plate on Card	85.
R83TC	$2	Probate of Will, black	Hybrid Die on India	—
R84TC	$2.50	Inland Exchange, black	Die (?) on India	120.
R85TC	$3	Charter Party, dark green	Plate on Thin Card	—
R87TC	$3.50	Inland Exchange, black	Die on India	400.
R88TC	$5	Charter Party, carmine	Plate on India	85.
R88TC		black	Hybrid Die on India	—
R89TC	$5	Conveyance, carmine	Plate on India	90.
R91TC	$5	Mortgage, carmine	Plate on India	90.
R95TC	$10	Mortgage, yellow green	Plate on Thin Card	—
R98TC	$20	Conveyance, red orange	Plate on Card	120.
R98TC		red orange	Plate on India	220.
R99TC	$20	Probate of Will, red orange	Plate on Card	275.
R99TC		black	Plate on Card	275.
R101TC	$50	U.S.I.R., orange	Plate on Bond	275.
R101TC		deep blue	Plate on Bond	275.
R101TC		black	Hybrid Die on India	—
R102TC	$200	black & red	Plate on Card	1,600.
R102TC		gray brown & red	Plate on Bond	1,600.
R102TC		green & brown red	Plate on India	1,600.
R102TC		black	Plate on India	—

SECOND ISSUE

R104TC	2c	pale blue & black	Plate on Bond	60.
R132TC	$200	red, green & black	India	2,500.
R132TC		orange (master die)	India	2,500.
R132TC		blue (master die)	India	2,500.
R132TC		green (master die)	India	2,500.
R133TC	$500	black (master die)	India	7,000.
R133TC		yellow, green & black	India	5,000.
R133TC		bright green, orange brown & black	India	5,000.
R133TC		red, green & black	Bond	5,000.
R133TC		light green, light brown & black	Bond	5,000.
R133TC		blue, scarlet & black	Bond	5,000.
R133ATC	$5000	yel org, green & black	India	7,500.
R133ATC		olive brown, green & black	India	8,000.
R133ATC		org red, dark green & black	India	8,000.
R133ATC		org red, dark blue & black	India	8,000.

The master die is the completed stamp design prior to its division into separate color dies.
See note after No. R133AP in Die and Plate Proofs section.

THIRD ISSUE

R134TC	1c	brown & black	Plate on Card	60.

1875   National Bank Note Co., New York City

R152TC	2c	(Liberty), green	Die on India	600.
R152TC		(Liberty), brown	Die on India	600.
R152TC		(Liberty), black	Die on India	600.

1898

R161TC	½c	green	Lg. die on India	750.
R163TC	1c	green	Lg. die on India	750.
R163TC		black	Lg. die on India	750.
R165TC	3c	green	Sm. die on India	650.
R169TC	25c	green	Lg. die on India	650.
R170TC	40c	black	Lg. die on India	650.
R172TC	80c	green	Lg. die on India	650.

1898

R174TC	$3	black	Die on India	650.
R176TC	$10	green	Die on India	650.

1899

R179TC	$100	dark green & black	Die on India	1,250.
R181TC	$1000	dark blue & black	Die on India	1,250.

1914

R195TC	½c	black	Small die on Wove	—
R196TC	1c	blue green	Small die on Wove	—
R198TC	3c	ultramarine	Small die on Wove	—
R199TC	4c	brown	Small die on Wove	—
R200TC	5c	blue	Small die on Wove	—
R201TC	10c	yellow	Small die on Wove	—
R202TC	25c	dull violet	Small die on Wove	—
R203TC	40c	blue green	Small die on Wove	—
R204TC	50c	red brown	Small die on Wove	—
R205TC	80c	orange	Small die on Wove	—

PROPRIETARY

1871-75

RB1TC	1c	blue & black	Plate on Bond	70.
RB1TC		scarlet & black	Plate on Bond	70.
RB1TC		orange & black	Plate on Bond	70.
RB1TC		orange & ultramarine	Plate on Granite Bond	60.
RB3TC	3c	blue & black, with gum	Plate on Bond	60.
RB3TC		blue & black	Plate on Gray Bond	60.
RB3TC		blue & black	Plate on wove	—
RB8TC	50c	green & brown	Die on India	675.
RB8TC		green & purple	Die on India	675.
RB8TC		green & brown red	Die on India	675.
RB8TC		green & violet	Die on India	675.
RB8TC		green & dark carmine	Die on India	675.
RB8TC		ultramarine & red	Die on India	675.
RB9TC	$1	green & brown	Die on India	675.
RB9TC		green & purple	Die on India	675.
RB9TC		green & violet brown	Die on India	675.
RB9TC		green & brown red	Die on India	675.
RB9TC		green & violet	Die on India	675.
RB9TC		green & dark carmine	Die on India	675.

1875-83

RB11TC	1c	brown	Die on India	500.
RB11TC		red brown	Die on India	500.
RB11TC		blue	Die on India	500.
RB11TC		black	Die on India	500.
RB12TC	2c	green	Die on India	500.
RB12TC		black	Die on India	500.
RB12TC		brown	Die on India	500.
RB12TC		orange brown	Die on India	500.
RB12TC		blue	Die on India	500.
RB13TC	3c	brown	Die on India	500.
RB13TC		green	Die on India	500.
RB13TC		blue	Die on India	500.
RB13TC		black	Plate on India	150.
RB14TC	4c	dark brown	Die on India	450.
RB14TC		green	Die on India	450.
RB14TC		black	Die on India	450.
RB14TC		blue	Die on India	450.
RB14TC		black	Plate on India	150.
RB16TC	5c	green	Die on India	450.
RB16TC		dark slate	Die on India	450.
RB16TC		blue	Die on India	450.
RB17TC	6c	green	Plate on India	150.
RB17TC		black	Plate on India	150.
RB17TC		black	Die on India	500.
RB17TC		blue	Die on India	500.
RB17TC		purple	Die on India	500.
RB17TC		dull violet	Die on India	500.
RB17TC		violet	Die on India	500.
RB17TC		violet brown	Die on India	500.
RB17TC		dark brown	Die on India	500.
RB19TC	10c	black	Die on India	550.

SECOND, THIRD AND PROPRIETARY ISSUES
Stamps Nos. R103 to R131, R134 to R150 and RB1 to RB7.

A special composite plate was made and impressions taken in various colors and shades. Although all varieties in all colors must have been made, only those seen by the editors are listed.

PLATE PROOFS ON INDIA PAPER
CENTERS IN BLACK

1871-75

R103TC   1c

a.	dark purple	60.
b.	dull purple	60.
d.	brown	60.
e.	black brown	60.
g.	light blue	60.
h.	dark blue	70.
i.	ultramarine	70.
k.	yellow green	70.
n.	green	65.
o.	dark green	65.
p.	blue green	65.
q.	light orange	65.
r.	dark orange	65.
s.	deep orange	65.
t.	scarlet	65.
u.	carmine	65.
x.	dark brown red	65.
y.	dark brown orange, goldbeater's skin	90.

R104TC   2c

a.	dark purple	60.
b.	dull purple	60.
d.	brown	60.
e.	black brown	60.
g.	light blue	60.
h.	dark blue	70.
i.	ultramarine	70.
k.	yellow green	70.
l.	dark yellow green	70.
n.	green	65.
o.	dark green	65.
p.	blue green	65.
q.	light orange	65.
r.	dark orange	65.
s.	deep orange	65.
t.	scarlet	65.
u.	carmine	65.
x.	dark brown red	65.
y.	dark brown orange, goldbeater's skin	90.

R105TC   3c

a.	dark purple	60.
b.	dull purple	60.
d.	brown	60.
e.	black brown	60.
g.	light blue	60.
h.	dark blue	70.
i.	ultramarine	70.
k.	yellow green	70.
n.	green	65.
o.	dark green	65.
p.	blue green	65.
q.	light orange	65.
r.	dark orange	65.
s.	deep orange	65.
t.	scarlet	65.
u.	carmine	65.
x.	dark brown red	65.
y.	dark brown orange, goldbeater's skin	90.

R106TC   4c

a.	dark purple	60.
b.	dull purple	60.
d.	brown	60.
e.	black brown	60.
f.	orange brown	65.
g.	light blue	60.
h.	dark blue	70.
i.	ultramarine	70.
k.	yellow green	70.
n.	green	65.
o.	dark green	65.
p.	blue green	65.
q.	light orange	65.
r.	dark orange	65.
s.	deep orange	65.
t.	scarlet	65.
u.	carmine	65.
x.	dark brown red	65.
y.	dark brown orange, goldbeater's skin	90.

R107TC   5c

a.	dark purple	60.
b.	dull purple	60.
d.	brown	60.
e.	black brown	60.
f.	orange brown	65.
g.	light blue	60.
h.	dark blue	70.
i.	ultramarine	70.
k.	yellow green	70.
n.	green	65.
o.	dark green	65.
p.	blue green	65.
q.	light orange	65.
r.	dark orange	65.
s.	deep orange	65.
t.	scarlet	65.
u.	carmine	65.
v.	dark carmine	65.
w.	purplish carmine	65.
x.	dark brown red	65.
y.	dark brown orange, goldbeater's skin	90.

R108TC   6c

a.	dark purple	60.
b.	dull purple	60.
d.	brown	60.
e.	black brown	60.
f.	orange brown	65.
g.	light blue	60.
h.	dark blue	70.
i.	ultramarine	70.
k.	yellow green	70.
n.	green	65.
o.	dark green	65.
p.	blue green	65.
q.	light orange	65.
r.	dark orange	65.
s.	deep orange	65.
t.	scarlet	65.
u.	carmine	65.
v.	dark carmine	65.
w.	purplish carmine	65.
x.	dark brown red	65.
y.	dark brown orange, goldbeater's skin	90.

R109TC   10c

a.	dark purple	60.
b.	dull purple	60.
d.	brown	60.
e.	black brown	60.
g.	light blue	60.
h.	dark blue	70.
i.	ultramarine	70.
k.	yellow green	70.
n.	green	65.
o.	dark green	65.
p.	blue green	65.
q.	light orange	65.
r.	dark orange	65.
s.	deep orange	65.
t.	scarlet	65.
u.	carmine	65.
x.	dark brown red	65.

R110TC   15c

a.	dark purple	60.
b.	dull purple	60.
d.	brown	60.
e.	black brown	60.
f.	orange brown	65.
g.	light blue	60.
h.	dark blue	70.
i.	ultramarine	70.
k.	yellow green	70.
n.	green	65.
o.	dark green	65.
p.	blue green	65.
q.	light orange	65.
r.	dark orange	65.
s.	deep orange	65.
t.	scarlet	65.
u.	carmine	65.
w.	purplish carmine	65.
x.	dark brown red	65.

R111TC   20c

a.	dark purple	60.
b.	dull purple	60.
d.	brown	60.
e.	black brown	60.
g.	light blue	60.
h.	dark blue	70.
i.	ultramarine	70.
k.	yellow green	70.
n.	green	65.
o.	dark green	65.
p.	blue green	65.
q.	light orange	65.
r.	dark orange	65.
s.	deep orange	65.
t.	scarlet	65.
u.	carmine	65.
w.	purplish carmine	65.

x. dark brown red 65.
y. dark brown orange, goldbeater's skin 90.

R112TC 25c
a. dark purple 60.
b. dull purple 60.
d. brown 60.
e. black brown 60.
g. light blue 60.
h. dark blue 70.
i. ultramarine 70.
k. yellow green 70.
l. dark yellow green 70.
n. green 65.
o. dark green 65.
p. blue green 65.
q. light orange 65.
r. dark orange 65.
s. deep orange 65.
t. scarlet 65.
u. carmine 65.
x. dark brown red 65.
y. dark brown orange, goldbeater's skin 90.

R113TC 30c
a. dark purple 60.
b. dull purple 60.
d. brown 60.
e. black brown 60.
g. light blue 60.
h. dark blue 70.
i. ultramarine 70.
k. yellow green 70.
n. green 65.
o. dark green 65.
p. blue green 65.
q. light orange 65.
r. dark orange 65.
s. deep orange 65.
t. scarlet 65.
u. carmine 65.
v. dark carmine 65.
w. purplish carmine 65.
x. dark brown red 65.
y. dark brown orange, goldbeater's skin 90.

R114TC 40c
a. dark purple 60.
b. dull purple 60.
d. brown 60.
e. black brown 60.
f. orange brown 65.
g. light blue 60.
h. dark blue 70.
i. ultramarine 70.
k. yellow green 70.
n. green 65.
o. dark green 65.
p. blue green 65.
q. light orange 65.
r. dark orange 65.
s. deep orange 65.
t. scarlet 65.
u. carmine 65.
x. dark brown red 65.

R115TC 50c
a. dark purple 60.
b. dull purple 60.
d. brown 60.
e. black brown 60.
g. light blue 60.
h. dark blue 70.
i. ultramarine 70.
k. yellow green 70.
n. green 65.
o. dark green 65.
p. blue green 65.
q. light orange 65.
r. dark orange 65.
s. deep orange 65.
t. scarlet 65.
u. carmine 65.
x. dark brown red 65.

R116TC 60c
a. dark purple 60.
b. dull purple 60.
d. brown 60.
e. black brown 60.
g. light blue 60.
h. dark blue 70.
i. ultramarine 70.
k. yellow green 70.
n. green 65.
o. dark green 65.
p. blue green 65.
q. light orange 65.
r. dark orange 65.
s. deep orange 65.
t. scarlet 65.
u. carmine 65.
v. dark carmine 65.
x. dark brown red 65.
y. dark brown orange, goldbeater's skin 90.

R117TC 70c
a. dark purple 60.
b. dull purple 60.
d. brown 60.
e. black brown 60.
g. light blue 60.
h. dark blue 70.
i. ultramarine 70.
k. yellow green 70.
n. green 65.
o. dark green 65.
p. blue green 65.
q. light orange 65.
r. dark orange 65.
s. deep orange 65.

t. scarlet 65.
u. carmine 65.
x. dark brown red 65.

R118TC $1
a. dark purple 70.
b. dull purple 70.
d. brown 70.
e. black brown 70.
g. light blue 80.
h. dark blue 85.
i. ultramarine 85.
k. yellow green 80.
n. green 75.
o. dark green 75.
p. blue green 75.
q. light orange 75.
r. dark orange 75.
s. deep orange 75.
t. scarlet 80.
u. carmine 80.
w. purplish carmine 80.
x. dark brown red 80.
y. dark brown orange, goldbeater's skin 90.

R119TC $1.30
a. dark purple 70.
b. dull purple 70.
d. brown 70.
e. black brown 70.
g. light blue 80.
h. dark blue 85.
i. ultramarine 85.
k. yellow green 80.
n. green 75.
o. dark green 75.
p. blue green 75.
q. light orange 75.
r. dark orange 75.
s. deep orange 75.
u. carmine 80.
x. dark brown red 80.

R120TC $1.50
a. dark purple 70.
b. dull purple 70.
d. brown 70.
e. black brown 70.
g. light blue 80.
h. dark blue 85.
i. ultramarine 85.
j. bright yellow green, on card 75.
k. yellow green 80.
n. green 75.
o. dark green 75.
p. blue green 75.
q. light orange 75.
r. dark orange 75.
s. deep orange 75.
t. scarlet 80.
u. carmine 80.
x. dark brown red 80.

R121TC $1.60
a. dark purple 70.
b. dull purple 70.
d. brown 70.
e. black brown 70.
g. light blue 80.
h. dark blue 85.
i. ultramarine 85.
k. yellow green 80.
n. green 75.
o. dark green 75.
p. blue green 75.
q. light orange 75.
r. dark orange 75.
s. deep orange 75.
t. scarlet 80.
u. carmine 80.
x. dark brown red 80.

R122TC $1.90
a. dark purple 70.
b. dull purple 70.
d. brown 70.
e. black brown 70.
g. light blue 80.
h. dark blue 85.
i. ultramarine 85.
j. bright yellow green, on card 75.
k. yellow green 80.
n. green 75.
o. dark green 75.
p. blue green 75.
q. light orange 75.
r. dark orange 75.
s. deep orange 75.
t. scarlet 80.
u. carmine 80.
x. dark brown red 80.

R123TC $2
a. dark purple 70.
b. dull purple 70.
d. brown 70.
e. black brown 70.
g. light blue 80.
h. dark blue 85.
i. ultramarine 85.
j. bright yellow green, on card 75.
k. yellow green 80.
n. green 75.
o. dark green 75.
p. blue green 75.
q. light orange 75.
r. dark orange 75.
s. deep orange 75.
t. scarlet 80.
u. carmine 80.

w. purplish carmine 80.
x. dark brown red 80.
y. dark brown orange, goldbeater's skin 90.

R124TC $2.50
a. dark purple 70.
b. dull purple 70.
d. brown 70.
e. black brown 70.
g. light blue 80.
h. dark blue 85.
i. ultramarine 85.
k. yellow green 80.
n. green 75.
o. dark green 75.
p. blue green 75.
q. light orange 75.
r. dark orange 75.
s. deep orange 75.
t. scarlet 80.
u. carmine 80.
v. dark carmine 80.
x. dark brown red 80.

R125TC $3
a. dark purple 70.
b. dull purple 70.
d. brown 70.
e. black brown 70.
g. light blue 80.
h. dark blue 85.
i. ultramarine 85.
j. bright yellow green, on card 75.
k. yellow green 80.
n. green 75.
o. dark green 75.
p. blue green 75.
q. light orange 75.
r. dark orange 75.
s. deep orange 75.
t. scarlet 80.
u. carmine 80.
x. dark brown red 80.

R126TC $3.50
a. dark purple 70.
b. dull purple 70.
c. red purple 75.
d. brown 70.
e. black brown 70.
g. light blue 80.
h. dark blue 85.
i. ultramarine 85.
k. yellow green 80.
n. green 75.
o. dark green 75.
p. blue green 75.
q. light orange 75.
r. dark orange 75.
s. deep orange 75.
t. scarlet 90.
u. carmine 80.
x. dark brown red 80.

R127TC $5
a. dark purple 70.
b. dull purple 70.
d. brown 70.
e. black brown 70.
g. light blue 80.
h. dark blue 85.
i. ultramarine 85.
k. yellow green 80.
n. green 75.
o. dark green 75.
p. blue green 75.
q. light orange 75.
r. dark orange 75.
s. deep orange 75.
t. scarlet 75.
u. carmine 75.
w. purplish carmine 75.
x. dark brown red 80.
y. dark brown orange, goldbeater's skin 100.

R128TC $10
a. dark purple 70.
b. dull purple 70.
d. brown 70.
e. black brown 70.
g. light blue 80.
h. dark blue 85.
i. ultramarine 85.
j. bright yellow green, on card 75.
k. yellow green 75.
n. green 75.
o. dark green 75.
p. blue green 75.
q. light orange 75.
r. dark orange 75.
s. deep orange 75.
t. scarlet 75.
u. carmine 80.
x. dark brown red 80.

R129TC $20
a. dark purple 95.
b. dull purple 95.
d. brown 95.
e. black brown 95.
g. light blue 90.
h. dark blue 90.
i. ultramarine 90.
k. yellow green 85.
m. emerald green 85.
n. green 75.
o. dark green 75.
p. blue green 75.
q. light orange 75.
r. dark orange 85.
s. deep orange 85.

t. scarlet 90.
u. carmine 80.
v. dark carmine 90.
x. dark brown red 80.

R130TC $25
a. dark purple 100.
b. dull purple 100.
d. brown 100.
e. black brown 100.
g. light blue 90.
h. dark blue 90.
i. ultramarine 90.
k. yellow green 85.
m. emerald green 85.
n. green 75.
o. dark green 75.
p. blue green 75.
q. light orange 75.
r. dark orange 85.
s. deep orange 85.
t. scarlet 90.
u. carmine 80.
w. purplish carmine 90.
x. dark brown red 300.
y. dark brown orange, goldbeater's skin 100.

R131TC $50
a. dark purple 95.
b. dull purple 95.
d. brown 95.
e. black brown 95.
g. light blue 90.
h. dark blue 90.
i. ultramarine 90.
j. bright yellow green, on card 85.
k. yellow green 85.
m. emerald green 85.
n. green 75.
o. dark green 75.
p. blue green 75.
q. light orange 75.
r. dark orange 85.
s. deep orange 85.
t. scarlet 90.
u. carmine 80.
x. dark brown red 80.

RB1TC 1c
a. dark purple 70.
b. dull purple 70.
d. brown 65.
e. black brown 65.
g. light blue 75.
h. dark blue 75.
i. ultramarine 70.
k. yellow green 70.
l. dark yellow green 70.
n. green 65.
o. dark green 65.
p. blue green 65.
q. light orange 65.
r. dark orange 65.
s. deep orange 65.
t. scarlet 65.
u. carmine 65.
x. dark brown red 65.

RB2TC 2c
a. dark purple 70.
b. dull purple 70.
d. brown 65.
e. black brown 65.
g. light blue 70.
h. dark blue 70.
i. ultramarine 70.
j. bright yellow green, on card 70.
k. yellow green 70.
n. green 65.
o. dark green 65.
p. blue green 65.
q. light orange 65.
r. dark orange 65.
s. deep orange 65.
t. scarlet 65.
u. carmine 65.
x. dark brown red 65.

RB3TC 3c
a. dark purple 70.
b. dull purple 70.
d. brown 65.
e. black brown 65.
g. light blue 70.
h. dark blue 70.
i. ultramarine 70.
k. yellow green 70.
l. dark yellow green 70.
n. green 65.
o. dark green 65.
p. blue green 65.
q. light orange 65.
r. dark orange 65.
s. deep orange 65.
t. scarlet 65.
u. carmine 65.
x. dark brown red 65.

RB4TC 4c
a. dark purple 70.
b. dull purple 70.
d. brown 65.
e. black brown 65.
g. light blue 70.
h. dark blue 70.
i. ultramarine 70.
k. yellow green 70.
n. green 65.
o. dark green 65.
p. blue green 65.
q. light orange 65.

r. dark orange 65.
s. deep orange 65.
t. scarlet 65.
u. carmine 65.
x. dark brown red 65.

RB5TC 5c
a. dark purple 70.
b. dull purple 65.
d. brown 65.
e. black brown 65.
g. light blue 70.
h. dark blue 70.
i. ultramarine 70.
j. bright yellow green, on card 70.
k. yellow green 70.
l. dark yellow green 70.
n. green 65.
o. dark green 65.
p. blue green 65.
q. light orange 65.
r. dark orange 65.
s. deep orange 65.
t. scarlet 65.
u. carmine 65.
x. dark brown red 65.

RB6TC 6c
a. dark purple 70.
b. dull purple 70.
d. brown 65.
e. black brown 65.
g. light blue 70.
h. dark blue 70.
i. ultramarine 70.
k. yellow green 70.
l. dark yellow green 70.
n. green 65.
o. dark green 65.
p. blue green 65.
q. light orange 65.
r. dark orange 65.
s. deep orange 65.
t. scarlet 65.
u. carmine 65.
x. dark brown red 65.

RB7TC 10c
a. dark purple 70.
b. dull purple 70.
d. brown 65.
e. black brown 65.
g. light blue 70.
h. dark blue 70.
i. ultramarine 70.
k. yellow green 70.
l. dark yellow green 70.
n. green 65.
o. dark green 65.
p. blue green 65.
q. light orange 65.
r. dark orange 65.
s. deep orange 65.
t. scarlet 65.
u. carmine 65.
x. dark brown red 65.

1898

Cat.	Denom.	Color		Price
RB21TC	¼c	green	Large die on India	1,300.
RB22TC	⅜c	green	Large die on India	500.
RB26TC	1⅞c	green	Large die on India	500.
RB26TC	1⅞c	black	Large die on India	500.
RB27TC	2c	green	Small die on India	350.
RB31TC	5c	green	Large die on India	350.

1918-29

Stock Transfer

Cat.	Denom.	Color		Price
RD20TC	$50	black	Die on India	1,250.
RD20TC	$50	blue	Die on India	1,250.

1894

Playing Cards

Cat.	Denom.	Color		Price
RF1TC	2c	black (On hand)	Die on India	1,500.
RF2TC	2c	lake (Act of)	Die on India	1,000.

PRIVATE DIE MATCH STAMPS
For important valuing information see the note before
Private Die Proprietary die and plate proofs.

1864

Cat.	Denom.	Color	DIE ON INDIA (1) Large (3) India	PLATE (4) Card
RO1TC	1c	black	175.	
RO1TC	1c	green	300.	
RO2TC	1c	black	225.	
RO2TC	1c	green	300.	
RO5TC	1c	black	275.	
RO5TC	1c	blue	500.	
RO6TC	1c	black	300.	
RO6TC	1c	green	500.	
RO7TC	1c	black	300.	
RO7TC	1c	dull green	300.	
RO7TC	1c	green	500.	
RO9TC	1c	blue	225.	
RO9TC	1c	brown	275.	
RO9TC	1c	dark green	500.	
RO9TC	1c	green	300.	
RO10TC	1c	blue	300.	
RO10TC	1c	green	500.	
RO11TC	3c	blue	500.	
RO11TC	3c	green	500.	

Cat.	Denom.	Color	DIE ON INDIA (1) Large (3) India	PLATE (4) Card
RO12TC	1c	blue	225.	
RO12TC	1c	green	500.	
RO13TC	3c	black	500.	
RO13TC	3c	blue	1000.	
RO14TC	1c	blue	225.	
RO14TC	1c	green	500.	
RO15TC	1c	black	225.	
RO15TC	1c	blue	225.	
RO16TC	1c	black	225.	
RO16TC	1c	green	300.	
RO17/19TC	1c/3c	green	1250.	
RO17TC	1c	black	225.	
RO17TC	1c	green	500.	
RO19TC	3c	blue	250.	
RO19TC	3c	green	600.	
RO20TC	1c	black	175.	
RO20TC	1c	green	500.	
RO21TC	3c	blue	375.	
RO21TC	3c	green	375.	
RO22TC	1c	black	300.	
RO23TC	1c	black	225.	
RO23TC	1c	blue	225.	
RO23TC	1c	green	500.	
RO24TC	1c	black	225.	
RO24TC	1c	blue	225.	
RO24TC	1c	green	500.	
RO25TC	12c	black	400.	
RO25TC	12c	blue	750.	
RO25TC	12c	green	750.	
RO26TC	1c	black	225.	
RO26TC	1c	blue	225.	
RO26TC	1c	dark brn green	300.	
RO26TC	1c	light brn	300.	
RO27TC	12c	black	400.	
RO27TC	12c	blue	500.	
RO27TC	12c	green	750.	
RO28TC	1c	black	175.	
RO28TC	1c	brown	300.	
RO28TC	1c	green	300.	
RO29TC	1c	blue	300.	
RO29TC	1c	green	300.	
RO30TC	1c	black	175.	
RO30TC	1c	blue	225.	
RO30TC	1c	green	300.	
RO30TC	1c	red	500.	
RO31TC	1c	blue	300.	
RO31TC	1c	green	225.	
RO31TC	1c	red	500.	
RO32TC	4c	blue	500.	
RO32TC	4c	brown	500.	
RO32TC	4c	orange	500.	
RO32TC	4c	vermilion	500.	
RO35TC	1c	blue	300.	
RO35TC	1c	green	500.	
RO37TC	3c	blue	400.	
RO37TC	3c	green	400.	
RO38TC	1c	blue	350.	
RO38TC	1c	dk bl	500.	
RO38TC	1c	green	375.	
RO38TC	1c	red	600.	
RO39TC	1c	black	300.	
RO41TC	1c	black	225.	
RO41TC	1c	green	300.	
RO42TC	1c	black	300.	
RO42TC	1c	blue	300.	
RO42TC	1c	green	500.	
RO43TC	1c	blue	500.	
RO45TC	1c	blue	350.	
RO45TC	1c	green	750.	
RO46TC	1c	blue	350.	
RO46TC	1c	dk bl	500.	
RO46TC	1c	green	500.	
RO46TC	1c	orange	300.	
RO47TC	1c	blue	300.	
RO47TC	1c	green	500.	
RO49TC	1c	blue	225.	
RO49TC	1c	brown	500.	
RO49TC	1c	brn red	300.	
RO49TC	1c	dk bl	500.	
RO49TC	1c	green	500.	
RO49TC	1c	red brn	500.	
RO55TC	1c	blue	375.	
RO56TC	1c	blue	750.	
RO56TC	1c	green	300.	
RO57TC	1c	black	175.	
RO57TC	1c	blue	225.	
RO58TC	1c	black	300.	
RO58TC	1c	blue	225.	
RO58TC	1c	dark rose	500.	
RO58TC	1c	green	500.	
RO58TC	1c	rose	300.	
RO59TC	1c	black	225.	
RO60TC	3c	blue	500.	
RO60TC	3c	green	500.	
RO61TC	1c	black	175.	
RO61TC	1c	blue	300.	
RO62TC	1c	black	175.	
RO62TC	1c	blue	175.	
RO64TC	1c	black	225.	
RO64TC	1c	blue	300.	
RO64TC	1c	green	300.	
RO65TC	1c	green	300.	
RO67TC	1c	blue	225.	
RO67TC	1c	green	300.	
RO67TC	1c	red	500.	
RO67TC	1c	rose	500.	
RO68TC	1c	black	225.	
RO68TC	1c	blue	225.	
RO69TC	1c	blue	300.	
RO69TC	1c	green	500.	
RO71TC	1c	black	250.	

Number	Denom	Color	Large	India	Card
RO71TC	1c	green	400.		
RO72TC	1c	black	500.		
RO73TC	1c	blue	225.		
RO73TC	1c	green	300.		
RO73TC	1c	red	500.		
RO73TC	1c	red brn	225.		
RO76TC	1c	blue	500.		
RO76TC	1c	green	300.		
RO77TC	1c	black	225.		
RO77TC	1c	green	300.		
RO78TC	1c	black	225.		
RO78TC	1c	dk bl	500.		
RO78TC	1c	green	500.		
RO80TC	1c	black	225.		
RO80TC	1c	green	500.		
RO81TC	1c	blue	175.		
RO81TC	1c	dark green	500.		
RO81TC	1c	green	225.		
RO81TC	1c	lake	500.		
RO81TC	1c	red	300.		
RO82TC	1c	blue	175.		
RO82TC	1c	green	500.		
RO83TC	1c	black	175.		
RO83TC	1c	green	300.		
RO83TC	1c	red	500.		
RO84TC	1c	blue	300.		
RO84TC	1c	green	500.		
RO85TC	1c	black	250.		
RO85TC	1c	blue	300.		
RO85TC	1c	green	350.		
RO85TC	1c	orange	500.		
RO85TC	1c	vermilion	500.		
RO86TC	1c	blue	500.		
RO86TC	1c	brown	500.		
RO86TC	1c	green	400.		
RO86TC	1c	orange	500.		
RO86TC	1c	red	500.		
RO87TC	1c	dull rose	500.		
RO87TC	1c	orange	500.		
RO88TC	1c	blue	300.		
RO88TC	1c	green	500.		
RO89TC	3c	blue	300.		
RO89TC	3c	green	300.		
RO90TC	6c	blue	225.		
RO90TC	6c	brown	500.		
RO90TC	6c	green	500.		
RO90TC	6c	orange	500.		
RO91TC	3c	blue	225.		
RO91TC	3c	brown	500.		
RO91TC	3c	green	500.		
RO91TC	3c	orange	500.		
RO91TC	3c	red	500.		
RO92TC	1c	blue	300.		
RO92TC	1c	green	500.		
RO94TC	3c	blue	225.		
RO94TC	3c	brown	300.		
RO94TC	3c	green	225.		
RO94TC	3c	orange	300.		
RO94TC	3c	red	500.		
RO94TC	3c	vermilion	500.		
RO95TC	1c	black	175.		
RO95TC	1c	blue	175.		
RO95TC	1c	brown	225.		
RO95TC	1c	dk bl	500.		
RO96TC	1c	black	175.		
RO96TC	1c	blue	225.		
RO97TC	1c	blue	300.		
RO99TC	1c	black	175.		
RO99TC	1c	blue	500.		
RO100TC	1c	blue	500.		
RO101TC	3c	black	175.		
RO101TC	3c	green	300.		
RO101TC	3c	orange			75.
RO102TC	5c	black	175.		
RO102TC	5c	blue	500.		
RO102TC	5c	green	500.		
RO103TC	1c	blue	225.		
RO103TC	1c	rose	300.		
RO105TC	1c	blue	300.		
RO105TC	1c	green	500.		
RO106TC	1c	black	175.		
RO106TC	1c	blue	225.		
RO107TC	1c	black	175.		
RO107TC	1c	green	300.		
RO110TC	1c	black	175.		
RO110TC	1c	blue	175.		
RO110TC	1c	orange	500.		
RO110TC	1c	red	225.		
RO112TC	1c	black	175.		
RO112TC	1c	green	500.		
RO113TC	1c	blue	300.		
RO113TC	1c	green	500.		
RO113TC	1c	orange	500.		
RO114TC	1c	black	750.		
RO115TC	1c	black	175.		
RO115TC	1c	green	500.		
RO116TC	1c	black	225.		
RO116TC	1c	green	300.		
RO118TC	8c	black	225.		
RO118TC	8c	dk bl	500.		
RO118TC	8c	green	500.		
RO119TC	1c	black	225.		
RO119TC	1c	blue	225.		
RO120TC	1c	black	500.		
RO121TC	1c	black	175.		
RO121TC	1c	blue	300.		
RO122TC	1c	blue	300.		
RO122TC	1c	green	500.		
RO123TC	1c	blue	500.		
RO125TC	1c	black	225.		
RO126TC	1c	blue	300.		
RO126TC	1c	green	500.		
RO127TC	1c	black	300.		
RO127TC	1c	green	225.		
RO128TC	1c	black	225.		
RO128TC	1c	green	500.		
RO130TC	1c	black	225.		
RO130TC	1c	green	300.		
RO131TC	1c	black	175.		
RO131TC	1c	green	225.		
RO131TC	1c	red	225.		
RO132TC	1c	black	225.		
RO132TC	1c	green	500.		
RO133TC	1c	blue	500.		
RO133TC	1c	green	300.		
RO134TC	1c	black	300.		150.
RO134TC	1c	green	300.		
RO135TC	1c	black	500.		
RO135TC	1c	blue	300.		
RO135TC	1c	green	300.		
RO135TC	1c	rose	225.		
RO136TC	1c	black	225.		
RO136TC	1c	green	300.		
RO137TC	1c	black	175.		
RO137TC	1c	blue	175.		
RO137TC	1c	green	500.		
RO138TC	1c	black	175.		
RO138TC	1c	blue	500.		
RO139TC	5c	black	175.		
RO139TC	5c	green	500.		
RO140TC	4c	black	225.		
RO140TC	4c	blue	300.		
RO141TC	1c	black	175.		
RO141TC	1c	dk bl	300.		
RO141TC	1c	green	500.		
RO141TC	1c	yellow green	300.		
RO141TC	1c	green	500.		
RO142TC	1c	black	175.		
RO142TC	1c	blue	225.		
RO143TC	3c	black	175.		
RO143TC	3c	blue	225.		
RO143TC	3c	green	300.		
RO144TC	1c	black	500.		
RO145TC	1c	black	500.		
RO145TC	1c	blue	500.		
RO146TC	1c	blue	500.		
RO146TC	1c	green	300.		
RO148TC	1c	black	175.		
RO148TC	1c	green	300.		
RO148TC	1c	red	300.		
RO152TC	1c	blue	300.		
RO152TC	1c	green	300.		
RO153TC	1c	blue	225.		
RO153TC	1c	brown	300.		
RO153TC	1c	green	225.		
RO153TC	1c	orange	300.		
RO153TC	1c	red	300.		
RO155TC	1c	blue	225.		
RO155TC	1c	green	500.		
RO157TC	3c	black	175.		
RO157TC	3c	green	300.		
RO158TC	1c	blue	300.		
RO158TC	1c	green	500.		
RO159TC	3c	black	225.		
RO159TC	3c	green	500.		
RO160TC	1c	black	225.		
RO160TC	1c	brown	500.		
RO160TC	1c	green	300.		
RO161TC	1c	black	225.		
RO161TC	1c	green	300.		
RO163TC	1c	blue	300.		
RO163TC	1c	green	500.		
RO164TC	1c	black	500.		
RO165TC	12c	blue	750.		
RO165TC	12c	green	1000.		
RO165TC	12c	red	1000.		
RO166TC	1c	black	300.		
RO166TC	1c	blue	225.		
RO166TC	1c	green	500.		
RO166TC	1c	red	175.		
RO167TC	3c	black	175.		
RO167TC	3c	green	300.		
RO167TC	3c	red	300.		
RO168TC	1c	black	500.		
RO168TC	1c	green	300.		
RO171TC	1c	blue	300.		
RO171TC	1c	green	300.		
RO172TC	1c	blue	225.		
RO172TC	1c	green	500.		
RO173TC	1c	black	225.		
RO173TC	1c	green	300.		
RO174TC	1c	black	300.		
RO174TC	1c	green	300.		
RO175TC	1c	blue	275.		
RO175TC	1c	green	350.		
RO175TC	1c	red	500.		
RO177TC	1c	black	175.		
RO177TC	1c	blue	225.		
RO177TC	1c	green	500.		
RO178TC	1c	black	175.		
RO178TC	1c	blue	300.		
RO179TC	1c	blue	500.		
RO179TC	1c	green	500.		
RO180TC	1c	blue	225.		
RO180TC	1c	green	500.		
RO181TC	1c	blue	500.		
RO181TC	1c	green	300.		
RO182TC	1c	blue	300.		
RO182TC	1c	green	300.		
RO183TC	1c	blue	650.		
RO183TC	1c	green	650.		
RO184TC	1c	blue	225.		
RO184TC	1c	brown	300.		
RO184TC	1c	green	225.		
RO184TC	1c	orange	300.		
RO184TC	1c	red	300.		
RO186TC	1c	black	175.		

PRIVATE DIE CANNED FRUIT STAMP

Number	Denom	Color	Plate
RP1TC	1c	black	375.

PRIVATE DIE MEDICINE STAMPS

Number	Denom	Color	Large	India	Card
RS1TC	1c	blue	300.		
RS1TC	1c	green	300.		
RS4TC	1c	green	500.		
RS10TC	4c	black	300.		
RS10TC	4c	green	500.		
RS14TC	4c	black	300.		
RS14TC	4c	blue	300.		
RS16TC	2c	green	500.		
RS21TC	1c	blue	500.		
RS21TC	1c	green	500.		
RS22TC	2c	blue	500.		
RS22TC	2c	green	500.		
RS23TC	4c	green	500.		
RS24TC	1c	blue	500.		
RS24TC	1c	green	500.		
RS25TC	2c	blue	500.		
RS25TC	2c	green	500.		
RS26TC	4c	blue	500.		
RS26TC	4c	green	500.		
RS27TC	4c	blue	225.		
RS27TC	4c	green	500.		
RS28TC	2c	black	225.		
RS28TC	2c	blue	225.		
RS29TC	1c	black	175.		
RS29/RO120TC	2c/1c	black	750.		
RS29TC	2c	blue	175.		
RS29TC	2c	dk bl	500.		
RS29TC	2c	green	500.		
RS29TC	2c	red	300.		
RS30TC	1c	black	175.		
RS30TC	1c	blue	500.		
RS30TC	1c	green	500.		
RS30TC	1c	red	500.		
RS31TC	1c	black	500.		
RS31TC	1c	blue	225.		
RS31TC	1c	red	500.		
RS33TC	1c	blue	175.		
RS33TC	1c	green	225.		
RS33TC	1c	red	500.		
RS34TC	1c	blue	500.		
RS34TC	1c	green	500.		
RS35TC	1c	blue	300.		
RS35TC	1c	green	500.		
RS36TC	1c	black	500.		
RS36TC	1c	dk bl	500.		
RS36TC	1c	green	500.		
RS36TC	1c	ultramarine	500.		
RS36TC	1c	yellow green	225.		
RS38TC	2c	blue	750.		
RS38TC	2c	green	750.		
RS39TC	1c	blue	300.		
RS39TC	1c	green	300.		
RS39TC	1c	orange	500.		
RS40TC	2c	black	225.		
RS40TC	2c	blue	300.		
RS41TC	4c	black	225.		
RS41TC	4c	blue	500.		
RS41TC	4c	green	500.		
RS42TC	1c	green	500.		
RS43TC	4c	black	225.		
RS43TC	4c	green	500.		
RS44TC	1c	green	750.		
RS46TC	4c	blue	225.		
RS46TC	4c	green	300.		
RS47TC	4c	blue	300.		
RS47TC	4c	brown	500.		
RS47TC	4c	green	300.		
RS47TC	4c	orange	500.		
RS47TC	4c	red	500.		
RS49TC	4c	black	225.		
RS49TC	4c	blue	300.		
RS50TC	1c	black	300.		
RS50TC	1c	blue	300.		
RS50TC	1c	green	500.		
RS51TC	2c	blue	500.		
RS51TC	2c	green	500.		
RS52TC	4c	blue	500.		
RS52TC	4c	green	500.		
RS53TC	1c	blue	225.		
RS53TC	1c	brown	300.		
RS53TC	1c	green	225.		
RS53TC	1c	orange	300.		
RS53TC	1c	red	300.		
RS54TC	2c	blue	225.		
RS54TC	2c	brown	300.		
RS54TC	2c	orange	225.		
RS54TC	2c	red	500.		
RS55TC	4c	blue	225.		
RS55TC	4c	green	225.		
RS55TC	4c	orange	500.		
RS55TC	4c	red	500.		
RS56TC	3c	black	350.		
RS56TC	1c	green	500.		
RS57TC	6c	blue	225.		
RS57TC	6c	brown	300.		
RS57TC	6c	green	225.		
RS57TC	6c	orange	300.		
RS57TC	6c	red	300.		
RS58TC	4c	blue	225.		
RS58TC	4c	blue green	500.		
RS58TC	4c	dk bl	500.		
RS58TC	4c	green	225.		
RS58TC	4c	light blue	500.		
RS58TC	4c	red	225.		
RS59TC	1c	blue	300.		

Number	Denom	Color	DIE ON INDIA (1) Large	(3) India	PLATE (4) Card
RS59TC	1c	green	500.		
RS60TC	1c	blue	500.		
RS62TC	1c	brown	300.		
RS62TC	1c	green	225.		
RS62TC	1c	orange	300.		
RS62TC	1c	red	500.		
RS62TC	1c	vermilion	500.		
RS64TC	2c	blue	225.		
RS64TC	2c	brown	300.		
RS64TC	2c	green	225.		
RS64TC	2c	orange	300.		
RS64TC	2c	red	500.		
RS64TC	1c	vermilion	500.		
RS65TC	4c	blue	500.		
RS65TC	4c	green	500.		
RS66TC	1c	blue	300.		
RS66TC	1c	green	500.		
RS66TC	1c	light green	500.		
RS66TC	1c	orange	500.		
RS66TC	1c	rose red	500.		
RS67TC	1c	green	500.		
RS69TC	1c	blue	500.		
RS69TC	1c	green	500.		
RS70TC	2c	blue	500.		
RS70TC	2c	green	500.		
RS71TC	1c	blue	500.		
RS71TC	1c	green	500.		
RS72TC	2c	blue	500.		
RS72TC	2c	green	500.		
RS73TC	2c	black	500.		
RS73TC	2c	blue	750.		
RS73TC	2c	red	1000.		
RS74TC	1c	blue	500.		
RS74TC	1c	green	500.		
RS74hTC	1c	blue	500.		
RS74hTC	1c	green	500.		
RS75TC	1c	black	300.		
RS75TC	1c	green	500.		
RS76TC	2c	blue	300.		
RS76TC	2c	green	300.		
RS81TC	4c	black	225.		
RS81TC	4c	blue	500.		
RS81TC	4c	green	500.		
RS83TC	4c	blue	500.		
RS83TC	4c	green	500.		
RS84TC	1c	black	250.		
RS84TC	1c	blue	350.		
RS84TC	1c	green	250.		
RS84TC	1c	orange	650.		
RS84TC	1c	red	650.		
RS84TC	1c	slate	650.		
RS85TC	4c	blue	275.		
RS85TC	4c	brown	275.		
RS85TC	4c	green	300.		
RS85TC	4c	orange	375.		
RS86TC	1c	black	225.		
RS86TC	1c	blue	225.		
RS88TC	1c	blue	500.		
RS88TC	1c	green	500.		
RS89TC	1c	green	300.		
RS91TC	4c	blue	225.		
RS91TC	4c	green	500.		
RS92TC	3c	blue	225.		
RS92TC	3c	brown	300.		
RS92TC	3c	green	225.		
RS92TC	3c	orange	300.		
RS92TC	3c	red	500.		
RS92TC	3c	vermilion	500.		
RS94TC	4c	blue	500.		
RS94TC	4c	green	500.		
RS95TC	1c	black	300.		
RS95TC	1c	blue	225.		
RS95TC	1c	dk bl	90.		
RS96TC	3c	blue	225.		
RS96TC	3c	green	500.		
RS97TC	1c	blue	300.		
RS97TC	1c	green	500.		
RS98TC	1c	blue	225.		
RS98TC	1c	green	175.		
RS98TC	1c	red	500.		
RS99TC	4c	blue	500.		
RS100TC	6c	green	500.		
RS101TC	1c	blue	500.		
RS101TC	1c	green	500.		
RS102TC	2c	black	175.		
RS102TC	2c	green	225.		
RS102TC	2c	rose	225.		
RS103TC	4c	blue	500.		
RS103TC	4c	green	500.		
RS106TC	2c	black	500.		
RS106TC	2c	green	500.		
RS107/109TC	3c/6c	green	1250.		
RS107TC	3c	blue	300.		
RS108TC	4c	blue	300.		
RS108TC	4c	green	500.		
RS109TC	6c	blue	300.		
RS110TC	2c	black	300.		
RS110TC	2c	green	300.		
RS111TC	4c	blue	300.		
RS111TC	4c	green	500.		
RS114TC	1c	green	500.		
RS116TC	4c	black	225.		
RS116TC	4c	blue	300.		
RS116TC	4c	brown	500.		
RS116TC	4c	green	500.		
RS116TC	4c	vermilion	500.		
RS117TC	1c	blue	350.		
RS117TC	1c	green	750.		
RS118TC	1c	black	175.		
RS118TC	1c	blue	225.		
RS118TC	1c	brn red	300.		
RS118TC	1c	green	300.		
RS120TC	2c	blue	225.		
RS120TC	2c	brown	300.		
RS120TC	2c	green	225.		
RS120TC	2c	orange	300.		
RS120TC	2c	red	500.		
RS120TC	2c	vermilion	500.		
RS121TC	3c	blue	500.		
RS121TC	3c	green	500.		
RS122TC	2c	blue	500.		
RS122TC	2c	green	500.		
RS123TC	4c	blue	225.		
RS123TC	4c	brown	300.		
RS123TC	4c	green	225.		
RS123TC	4c	orange	300.		
RS123TC	4c	red	500.		
RS123TC	4c	vermilion	500.		
RS124TC	1c	black	175.		
RS124TC	1c	blue green	300.		
RS124TC	1c	green	500.		
RS124TC	1c	orange	500.		
RS124TC	1c	red	225.		
RS126TC	1c	black	225.		
RS126TC	1c	blue	225.		
RS126TC	1c	brown	300.		
RS126TC	1c	orange	300.		
RS126TC	1c	red	500.		
RS126TC	1c	vermilion	500.		
RS127TC	4c	black	225.		
RS127TC	4c	blue	225.		
RS127TC	4c	brown	225.		
RS127TC	4c	orange	300.		
RS127TC	4c	red	500.		
RS127TC	4c	vermilion	500.		
RS128TC	2c	black	600.		
RS128TC	2c	green	400.		
RS128TC	2c	pale blue	500.		
RS130TC	4c	black	275.		
RS130TC	4c	blue	350.		
RS131TC	4c	blue	225.		
RS131TC	4c	brown	500.		
RS131TC	4c	green	300.		
RS131TC	4c	orange	300.		
RS131TC	4c	red	500.		
RS131TC	4c	vermilion	500.		
RS132TC	4c	blue	500.		
RS132TC	4c	orange	500.		
RS133TC	6c	blue	500.		
RS133TC	6c	green	500.		
RS134TC	4c	black	300.		
RS134TC	4c	green	300.		
RS134TC	4c	red	500.		
RS138TC	1c	blue	300.		
RS138TC	1c	green	500.		
RS138TC	1c	red	500.		
RS138TC	1c	yel grn	500.		
RS139TC	2c	black	225.		
RS139TC	2c	blackish violet			90.
RS139TC	2c	blue	500.		
RS139TC	2c	green	500.		
RS139TC	2c	red	225.		
RS139TC	2c	rose	500.		
RS141TC	4c	black	225.		
RS141TC	4c	blue	300.		
RS142TC	1c	blue	225.		
RS142TC	1c	brown	300.		
RS142TC	1c	green	225.		
RS142TC	1c	orange	300.		
RS142TC	1c	red	500.		
RS142TC	1c	vermilion	500.		
RS143TC	4c	black	225.		
RS143TC	4c	blue	225.		
RS144TC	1c	black	500.		
RS144TC	1c	green	500.		
RS145TC	2c	blue	500.		
RS146TC	4c	black	300.		
RS146TC	4c	blue	300.		
RS150TC	1c	black	300.		
RS150TC	1c	blue	175.		
RS150TC	1c	carmine	500.		
RS150TC	1c	green	225.		
RS151TC	1c	blue	500.		
RS151TC	1c	green	500.		
RS152TC	2c	black	175.		
RS152TC	2c	blue	300.		
RS153TC	4c	blue	750.		
RS153TC	4c	green	750.		
RS154TC	4c	black	500.		
RS155TC	2c	black	300.		
RS155TC	2c	black	300.		
RS155TC	2c	blue	225.		
RS155TC	2c	red	500.		
RS156TC	6c	blue	225.		
RS156TC	6c	green	225.		
RS156TC	6c	red	225.		
RS157TC	2c	blue	225.		
RS157TC	2c	green	225.		
RS157TC	2c	red	500.		
RS157TC	2c	vermilion	300.		
RS159TC	1c	black	500.		
RS159TC	4c	black	375.		
RS160TC	6c	blue	300.		
RS160TC	6c	green	500.		
RS161TC	1c	blue	500.		
RS161TC	4c	green	750.		
RS162TC	1c	black	175.		
RS162TC	1c	green	300.		
RS162TC	1c	red	500.		
RS163TC	4c	black	300.		
RS163TC	4c	green	600.		
RS163TC	4c	yellow green	600.		
RS164TC	1c	blue	225.		
RS164TC	1c	green	500.		
RS165TC	4c	black	175.		
RS165TC	4c	blue	225.		
RS166TC	1c	blue	300.		
RS166TC	1c	green	500.		
RS169TC	4c	blue	225.		
RS169TC	4c	green	500.		
RS169TC	4c	red	225.		
RS170TC	1c	blue	300.		
RS170TC	1c	green	500.		
RS171TC	1c	black	225.		
RS171TC	1c	blue	225.		
RS171TC	1c	brown	500.		
RS171TC	1c	dull blue	500.		
RS171TC	1c	green	225.		
RS171TC	1c	orange	300.		
RS171TC	1c	red	500.		
RS171TC	1c	vermilion	500.		
RS172TC	2c	blue	225.		
RS172TC	2c	brown	300.		
RS172TC	2c	green	225.		
RS172TC	2c	orange	225.		
RS172TC	2c	red	500.		
RS172TC	2c	vermilion	500.		
RS173TC	1c	black	225.		
RS173TC	1c	green	225.		
RS173TC	1c	red	300.		
RS174TC	1c	black	300.		
RS174TC	1c	dk bl	500.		
RS174TC	1c	green	300.		
RS175TC	2c	black	250.		
RS175TC	2c	blue	500.		
RS175TC	2c	green	500.		
RS176TC	4c	blue	375.		
RS176TC	4c	green	500.		
RS177TC	2c	blue	750.		
RS177TC	2c	green	1000.		
RS178TC	6c	blue	500.		
RS178TC	6c	green	500.		
RS179TC	2c	black	500.		
RS179TC	2c	blue	375.		
RS180TC	3c	blue	300.		
RS180TC	3c	green	300.		
RS181TC	4c	blue	225.		
RS181TC	4c	green	500.		
RS182TC	4c	blue	225.		
RS182TC	4c	green	225.		
RS182TC	4c	rose	300.		
RS183TC	1c	black	500.		
RS183TC	1c	blue	300.		
RS183TC	1c	green	500.		
RS183TC	1c	red	500.		
RS184TC	2c	blue	300.		
RS184TC	2c	brown	225.		
RS184TC	2c	green	225.		
RS184TC	2c	orange	300.		
RS184TC	2c	vermilion	300.		
RS185TC	1c	blue	300.		
RS186TC	4c	blue	225.		
RS186TC	4c	green	500.		
RS187TC	4c	blue	225.		
RS187TC	4c	brown	300.		
RS187TC	4c	orange	300.		
RS187TC	4c	red	500.		
RS187TC	4c	vermilion	500.		
RS188TC	1c	blue	500.		
RS188TC	1c	green	500.		
RS189TC	1c	black	175.		
RS189TC	1c	blue	225.		
RS189TC	1c	red	225.		
RS190TC	2c	blue	500.		
RS190TC	2c	green	500.		
RS191TC	4c	blue	400.		
RS191TC	4c	green	400.		
RS192TC	6c	blue	400.		
RS192TC	6c	green	400.		
RS192TC	6c	rose	500.		
RS193TC	2c	blue	500.		
RS193TC	2c	green	500.		
RS194TC	1c	green	175.		
RS195TC	2c	blue	500.		
RS195TC	2c	green	500.		
RS196TC	1c	black	500.		
RS196TC	1c	green	225.		
RS197TC	2c	blue	300.		
RS198TC	1c	green	500.		
RS198TC	1c	red	500.		
RS199TC	2c	blue	225.		
RS199TC	2c	green	500.		
RS204TC	2c	blue	500.		
RS204TC	2c	green	500.		
RS205TC	4c	blue	225.		
RS205TC	4c	green	500.		
RS208TC	1c	black	225.		
RS208TC	1c	blue	500.		
RS208TC	1c	orange	300.		
RS209TC	2c	black	500.		
RS209TC	2c	blue	500.		
RS210TC	4c	blue	225.		
RS210TC	4c	green	225.		
RS210TC	4c	red	225.		
RS212TC	1c	black	225.		
RS212TC	1c	blue	300.		
RS212TC	1c	green	500.		
RS213TC	6c	blue	500.		
RS213TC	6c	green	500.		
RS214TC	4c	blue	300.		
RS214TC	4c	brown	300.		
RS214TC	4c	green	225.		
RS214TC	4c	orange	300.		
RS214TC	4c	red	500.		
RS214TC	4c	vermilion	500.		

			DIE ON INDIA (1) Large	PLATE (3) India	(4) Card
RS215TC	1c	black	300.		
RS215TC	1c	blue	450.		
RS215TC	1c	dark red	500.		
RS215TC	1c	green	500.		
RS216TC	1c	blue	500.		
RS216TC	1c	green	500.		
RS220TC	1c	blue	300.		
RS221TC	4c	black	175.		
RS221TC	4c	blue	225.		
RS222TC	8c	green	500.		
RS223TC	1c	blue	300.		
RS223TC	1c	brown	300.		
RS223TC	1c	green	225.		
RS223TC	1c	orange	300.		
RS223TC	1c	vermilion	300.		
RS224TC	1c	blue	500.		
RS224TC	1c	brown	300.		
RS224TC	1c	green	225.		
RS224TC	1c	orange	300.		
RS224TC	1c	red	500.		
RS225TC	4c	blue	500.		
RS225TC	4c	green	500.		
RS226TC	1c	black	350.		
RS228TC	1c	black	175.		
RS228TC	1c	blue	225.		
RS228TC	1c	brown	500.		
RS228TC	1c	green	225.		
RS228TC	1c	orange	500.		
RS228TC	1c	red	500.		
RS228TC	1c	vermilion	500.		
RS229TC	2c	black	225.		
RS229TC	2c	blue	225.		
RS229TC	2c	brown	300.		
RS229TC	2c	green	225.		
RS229TC	2c	orange	225.		
RS229TC	2c	red	300.		
RS229TC	2c	vermilion	500.		
RS230TC	6c	blue	225.		
RS230TC	6c	brown	300.		
RS230TC	6c	green	225.		
RS230TC	6c	orange	300.		
RS230TC	6c	vermilion	225.		
RS231TC	6c	black	1000.		
RS231TC	6c	blue	1000.		
RS231TC	6c	green	1000.		
RS231TC	6c	red	750.		
RS236TC	4c	blue	500.		
RS239TC	2c	black	225.		
RS239TC	2c	blue	300.		
RS239TC	2c	brown	500.		
RS239TC	2c	green	225.		
RS239TC	2c	orange	300.		
RS239TC	2c	vermilion	500.		
RS240TC	4c	red	500.		
RS240TC	4c	blue	175.		
RS240TC	4c	blue green	500.		
RS240TC	4c	brown	500.		
RS240TC	4c	green	225.		
RS240TC	4c	orange	225.		
RS240TC	4c	vermilion	225.		
RS241TC	4c	green	500.		
RS242TC	1c	blue	225.		
RS242TC	1c	green	500.		
RS243TC	4c	blue	500.		
RS243TC	4c	green	500.		
RS244TC	6c	blue	500.		
RS244TC	6c	green	500.		
RS245TC	1c	blue	500.		
RS250TC	6c	blue	500.		
RS250TC	6c	green	500.		
RS251TC	1c	blue	225.		
RS251TC	1c	brown	225.		
RS251TC	1c	green	225.		
RS252TC	1c	black	225.		
RS252TC	1c	blue	225.		
RS252TC	1c	brown	300.		
RS252TC	1c	green	225.		
RS252TC	1c	orange	500.		
RS252TC	1c	red	500.		
RS252TC	1c	rose	225.		
RS253TC	4c	blue	500.		
RS253TC	4c	green	500.		
RS258TC	6c	black	500.		
RS259TC	1c	blue	225.		
RS259TC	1c	brown	300.		
RS259TC	1c	green	225.		
RS259TC	1c	orange	300.		
RS259TC	1c	red	500.		
RS259TC	1c	vermilion	500.		
RS260TC	2c	blue	175.		
RS260TC	2c	brown	300.		
RS260TC	2c	green	225.		
RS260TC	2c	orange	300.		
RS260TC	2c	red	500.		
RS260TC	2c	rose	500.		
RS260TC	2c	vermilion	225.		
RS261TC	4c	blue	225.		
RS261TC	4c	brown	300.		
RS261TC	4c	green	225.		
RS261TC	4c	orange	300.		
RS261TC	4c	red	500.		
RS261TC	4c	vermilion	500.		
RS262TC	2c	blue	500.		
RS262TC	2c	green	500.		
RS264TC	4c	blue	300.		
RS264TC	4c	green	300.		
RS265TC	1c	black	225.		
RS265TC	1c	blue	500.		
RS267TC	4c	black	225.		
RS267TC	4c	blue	500.		
RS267TC	4c	green	300.		
RS270TC	12c	black	300.		

			DIE ON INDIA (1) Large	PLATE (3) India	(4) Card
RS270TC	12c	blue	500.		
RS270TC	12c	green	300.		
RS270TC	12c	red	225.		
RS271TC	4c	blue	2500.		
RS272TC	1c	black	300.		
RS272TC	1c	blue	300.		
RS273TC	2c	blue	500.		
RS274TC	1c	black	225.		
RS274TC	2c	blue	300.		
RS276TC	2c	black	225.		
RS276TC	2c	blue	300.		

PRIVATE DIE PERFUMERY STAMPS

			DIE ON INDIA (1) Large	PLATE (3) India	(4) Card
RT2TC	1c	brown	500.		
RT2TC	1c	green	400.		
RT2TC	1c	orange	300.		
RT2TC	1c	red	500.		
RT5TC	2c	black	175.		
RT5TC	2c	blue	225.		
RT5TC	2c	green	500.		
RT5TC	2c	orange	500.	125.	
RT6TC	1c	blue	375.		
RT6TC	1c	brown	500.		
RT6TC	1c	green	375.		
RT6TC	1c	orange	500.		
RT6TC	1c	red	500.		
RT10TC	4c	blue	375.		
RT10TC	4c	brown	500.		
RT10TC	4c	green	400.		
RT10TC	4c	orange	500.		
RT10TC	4c	red	500.		
RT12TC	1c	black	225.		
RT12TC	1c	blue	225.		
RT12TC	1c	green	500.		
RT13TC	2c	black	225.	75.	
RT13TC	2c	blue	300.		
RT13TC	2c	green	300.		
RT13TC	2c	red	225.		
RT14TC	3c	blue	1000.		
RT16TC	1c	blue	175.		
RT16TC	1c	green	225.		
RT17TC	2c	black	300.		
RT17TC	2c	blue	300.		
RT17TC	2c	green	300.		
RT17TC	2c	orange	500.		
RT18TC	3c	black	175.		
RT18TC	3c	blue	175.		
RT18TC	3c	green	500.		
RT18TC	3c	orange	500.		
RT18TC	3c	red	300.		
RT19TC	1c	black	500.		
RT20TC	1c	black	225.		
RT20TC	1c	blue	300.		
RT20TC	1c	green	175.		
RT21TC	2c	black	500.		
RT21TC	2c	green	500.		
RT22TC	1c	black	175.		
RT22TC	1c	blue	300.		
RT22TC	1c	green	300.		
RT22TC	1c	red brn	300.		
RT22TC	1c	ultramarine	500.		
RT23TC	2c	blue	225.		
RT23TC	2c	green	500.		
RT24TC	3c	black	175.		
RT24TC	3c	blue	225.		
RT24TC	3c	green	300.		
RT24TC	3c	red	225.		
RT25TC	4c	black	175.		
RT25TC	4c	blue	225.		
RT26TC	1c	black	175.		
RT26TC	1c	blue	225.		
RT26TC	1c	brown	300.		
RT26TC	1c	green	500.		
RT26TC	1c	orange	300.		
RT26TC	1c	red	500.		
RT28TC	2c	black	225.		
RT28TC	2c	brown	300.		
RT28TC	2c	green	225.		
RT28TC	2c	orange	300.		
RT28TC	2c	red	300.		
RT30TC	3c	black	225.		
RT30TC	3c	blue	225.		
RT30TC	3c	brown	300.		
RT30TC	3c	green	225.		
RT30TC	3c	orange	300.		
RT30TC	3c	red	175.		
RT32TC	4c	black	225.		
RT32TC	4c	blue	225.		
RT32TC	4c	brown	500.		
RT32TC	4c	green	225.		
RT32TC	4c	orange	225.		
RT32TC	4c	red	225.		

PRIVATE DIE PLAYING CARD STAMPS

			DIE ON INDIA (1) Large	PLATE (3) India	(4) Card
RU2TC	2c	black	175.		
RU2TC	2c	blue	225.		
RU2TC	2c	green	300.		
RU3TC	4c	blue	225.		
RU3TC	4c	green	225.		
RU4TC	5c	black	225.		
RU4TC	5c	green	300.		
RU5TC	5c	black	225.		
RU5TC	5c	brown	300.		
RU5TC	5c	green	300.		

			DIE ON INDIA (1) Large	PLATE (3) India	(4) Card
RU5TC	5c	light brn	500.		
RU5TC	5c	orange	500.		
RU5TC	5c	red	500.		
RU6TC	10c	black	175.		
RU6TC	10c	green	300.		
RU7TC	5c	blue	375.		
RU7TC	5c	green	375.		
RU8TC	5c	blue	225.		
RU8TC	5c	green	225.		
RU8TC	5c	orange	300.		
RU9TC	5c	blue	225.		
RU9TC	5c	green	500.		
RU10TC	2c	black	175.		
RU10TC	2c	brown	500.		
RU10TC	2c	green	500.		
RU11TC	5c	black	225.		
RU11TC	5c	blue	225.		
RU11TC	5c	brown	300.		
RU12TC	5c	blue	300.		
RU12TC	5c	green	300.		
RU13TC	5c	green	175.		
RU14TC	5c	blue	225.		
RU14TC	5c	brown	300.		
RU14TC	5c	green	300.		
RU14TC	5c	light brn	500.		
RU14TC	5c	orange	500.		
RU14TC	5c	red	300.		
RU15TC	5c	blue	300.		
RU15TC	5c	green	300.		

HUNTING PERMIT

			DIE ON INDIA (1) Large
RW4TC	$1	light violet	5,500.

SPECIMEN STAMPS

These are regular stamps overprinted "Specimen." Each number has a suffix letter "S" to denote "specimen." The Scott number is that of the stamp as shown in the regular listings and the second letter "A," etc., indicates the type of overprint. Values are for items of a grade of fine-very fine, with at least part original gum.

Specimen Type A; 12mm long   **Specimen.** Type B; 15mm long

Specimen. Type C; 30mm long

SPECIMEN Type D; Capital Letters   **Specimen.** Type E; Initial Capital

Specimen. Type F; 22mm long

SPECIMEN Type G; 14mm long   **SPECIMEN** Type H; 16mm long

Specimen Type I; 20mm long

Overprinted in Black   *Specimen*

1851-56

7S	A	1c blue, type II	2,500.
11S	A	3c dull red, type I	2,500.

1857-60

21S	A	1c blue, type III	1,500.
24S	A	1c blue, type V	1,000.
26S	A	3c dull red, type II	1,000.
30S	A	5c orange brown, type II	1,000.
35S	A	10c green, type V	1,250.
36bS	A	12c black	1,000.
37S	A	24c lilac	1,000.
38S	A	30c orange	1,000.
26S	F	3c dull red, type II	2,000.
26S	I	3c dull red, type II	1,500.

1861

63S	A	1c blue	750.
65S	A	3c rose	750.
68S	A	10c dark green	750.
70S	A	24c red lilac	750.
72S	A	90c blue	750.
73S	A	2c black	1,000.
76S	A	5c brown	750.

Specimen.

1861-66

Overprint Black, Except As Noted

63S	B	1c blue (1300)	120.
		P# block of 8, Impt.	1,750.
		Without period	—
65S	B	3c rose (1500)	120.
68S	B	10c dark green (1600)	120.
		P# block of 8, Impt.	—
69S	B	12c black (orange) (1300)	120.
71S	B	30c orange (1400)	120.
		P# block of 8, Impt.	—
72S	B	90c blue (1394)	120.
		P# block of 8, Impt.	—
73S	B	2c black (vermilion) (1306)	250.
		Block of 4	1,100.
		Without period	400.
		Block of 4, one stamp without period	1,250.
76S	B	5c brown (1306)	120.
		P# block of 8, Impt.	—
77S	B	15c black (vermilion) (1208)	200.
		Block of 4	900.
78S	B	24c lilac (1300)	120.

1867-68

86S	A	1c blue	1,000.
85ES	A	12c black	1,000.
93S	A	2c black	1,100.
94S	A	3c rose	1,000.
95S	A	5c brown	1,100.
97S	A	12c black	1,000.
98S	A	15c black	1,000.
99S	A	24c gray lilac	1,250.
		Split grill	—
100S	A	30c orange	1,250.

1869

112S	A	1c buff	1,750.
113S	A	2c brown	1,250.
115S	A	6c ultramarine	1,250.
116S	A	10c yellow	1,250.
117S	A	12c green	1,250.
119S	A	15c brown & blue	1,500.
120S	A	24c green & violet	1,750.
a.		Without grill	—
121S	A	30c blue & carmine	1,750.
a.		Without grill	—
122S	A	90c carmine & black	2,000.
a.		Without grill	—
125S	B	3c blue (blue)	3,500.
126S	B	6c blue (blue)	3,500.
127S	B	10c yellow (blue)	—

1870-71

145S	A	1c ultramarine	600.
146S	A	2c red brown	600.
146S	B	2c red brown	600.
147S	A	3c green	600.
148S	A	6c carmine	600.
149S	A	7c vermilion	600.
150S	A	10c brown	600.
151S	A	12c dull violet	600.
152S	A	15c bright orange	600.
155S	A	90c carmine	600.
155S	B	90c carmine (blue)	600.

1873

158S	B	3c green (blue)	750.
159S	B	6c dull pink	700.
160S	B	7c orange vermilion (blue)	700.
162S	B	12c blackish violet (blue)	—
165S	B	30c greenish black (blue)	700.
166S	B	90c carmine (blue)	750.

Overprinted in Red   **SPECIMEN.**

1879

Type D

189S	D	15c red orange	80.
190S	D	30c full black	80.
191S	D	90c carmine	80.
a.		Overprint in black brown	80.

1881-82

205S	D	5c yellow brown	80.
206S	D	1c gray blue	80.
207S	D	3c blue green	80.
208S	D	6c brown red	80.
209S	D	10c brown	80.

1883

210S	D	2c red brown	100.
211S	D	4c blue green	100.

Handstamped in Dull Purple   *Specimen.*

1890-93

Type E

219S	E	1c dull blue	150.
220S	E	2c carmine	150.
221S	E	3c purple	150.
222S	E	4c dark brown	150.
223S	E	5c chocolate	150.
224S	E	6c dull red	150.
225S	E	8c lilac	150.
226S	E	10c green	150.
227S	E	15c blue	150.
228S	E	30c black	150.
229S	E	90c orange	175.

COLUMBIAN ISSUE

1893

230S	E	1c deep blue	400.
		Double overprint	—
231S	E	2c violet	400.
232S	E	3c green	400.
233S	E	4c ultramarine	400.
234S	E	5c chocolate	400.
235S	E	6c purple	400.
236S	E	8c magenta	400.
237S	E	10c black brown	400.
238S	E	15c dark green	400.
239S	E	30c orange brown	400.
240S	E	50c slate blue	400.
241S	E	$1 salmon	500.
242S	E	$2 brown red	500.
243S	E	$3 yellow green	550.
244S	E	$4 crimson lake	575.
245S	E	$5 black	675.

Overprinted in Magenta   *Specimen.*

Type F

230S	F	1c deep blue	550.
232S	F	3c green	550.
233S	F	4c ultramarine	550.
234S	F	5c chocolate	550.
235S	F	6c purple	550.
237S	F	10c black brown	550.
243S	F	$3 yellow green	700.

Overprinted Type H in Black or Red

231S	H	2c violet (Bk)	625.
233S	H	4c ultramarine (R)	625.
234S	H	5c chocolate (R)	625.

Overprinted Type I in Black or Red

231S	I	2c violet (R)	625.
232S	I	3c green (R)	625.
233S	I	4c ultramarine (R)	625.
234S	I	5c chocolate (Bk)	625.
235S	I	6c purple (R)	625.
236S	I	8c magenta (Bk)	625.
237S	I	10c black brown (R)	625.
238S	I	15c dark green (R)	625.
239S	I	30c orange brown (Bk)	625.
240S	I	50c slate blue (R)	625.

1895

Handstamped Type E in Purple

264S	E	1c blue	90.
267S	E	2c carmine, type III	90.
267aS	E	2c pink, type III	90.
268S	E	3c purple	90.
269S	E	4c dark brown	100.
270S	E	5c chocolate	90.
271S	E	6c dull brown	90.
272S	E	8c violet brown	90.
273S	E	10c dark green	90.
274S	E	15c dark blue	90.
275S	E	50c orange	90.
276S	E	$1 black, type I	325.
277S	E	$2 dark blue	300.
278S	E	$5 dark green	400.

1897-1903

279S	E	1c deep green	90.
279BS	E	2c light red, type IV	90.
279BeS	E	2c Booklet pane of 6, light red, type IV (Bk)	525.
		Never hinged	700.
		With plate number	1,100.
		Never hinged	1,250.
a.		As No. 279BeS, inverted overprint	—
b.		As No. 279BeS, double impression of overprint on bottom two stamps	—
280S	E	4c rose brown	160.
281S	E	5c dark blue	80.
282S	E	6c lake	80.
282CS	E	10c brown, type I	80.
283S	E	10c brown, type II	—
284S	E	15c olive green	80.

Special Printing

In March 1900 one pane of 100 stamps of each of Nos. 279, 279B, 268, 280-282, 272, 282C, 284 and 275-278 were specially handstamped type E "Specimen" in black for displays at the Paris Exposition (1900) and Pan American Exposition (1901). The 2c pane was light red, type IV.

These examples were handstamped by H. G. Mandel and mounted by him in separate displays for the two Expositions. Examples from the panes in addition to those displayed were handstamped "Specimen," but most were destroyed after the Expositions. Examples of all issues that were handstamped are known.

Additional copies, not from the mounted display panes, do exist with a black "Specimen" handstamp, but it is believed Mandel applied such handstamps to regularly issued stamps from his personal collection. These include Nos. 267, 267a and 279B in pale red.

TRANS-MISSISSIPPI ISSUE

1898

Type F

285S	F	1c dark yellow green	250.

Type E

285S	E	1c dark yellow green	250.
286S	E	2c copper red	250.
287S	E	4c orange	250.
288S	E	5c dull blue	250.
289S	E	8c violet brown	250.
290S	E	10c gray violet	250.
291S	E	50c sage green	300.
292S	E	$1 black	450.
293S	E	$2 orange brown	625.

PAN-AMERICAN ISSUE

1901

294S	E	1c	**green & black**	235.
295S	E	2c	**carmine**	235.
296S	E	4c	**chocolate & black**	235.
a.			Center inverted	6,500.
297S	E	5c	**ultramarine & black**	235.
298S	E	8c	**brown violet & black**	235.
299S	E	10c	**yellow brown & black**	235.

1902

300S	E	1c	**blue green**	90.
301S	E	2c	**carmine**	90.
302S	E	3c	**bright violet**	90.
303S	E	4c	**brown**	90.
304S	E	5c	**blue**	90.
305S	E	6c	**claret**	90.
306S	E	8c	**violet black**	90.
307S	E	10c	**pale red brown**	90.
308S	E	13c	**purple black**	90.
309S	E	15c	**olive green**	90.
310S	E	50c	**orange**	90.
311S	E	$1	**black**	200.
312S	E	$2	**dark blue**	300.
313S	E	$5	**dark green**	400.

1903

319S	E	2c	**carmine**	110.

LOUISIANA PURCHASE ISSUE

1904

323S	E	1c	**green**	350.
324S	E	2c	**carmine**	350.
325S	E	3c	**violet**	350.
326S	E	5c	**dark blue**	350.
327S	E	10c	**red brown**	350.

SPECIAL DELIVERY STAMPS

Overprinted in Red   Specimen.

1885

Type D

E1S	D	10c	**blue**	110.

Handstamped in Dull Purple   E2S

1888

Type E

E2S	E	10c	**blue**	110.

1893

E3S	E	10c	**orange**	150.

1894

E4S	E	10c	**blue**	225.

1895

E5S	E	10c	**blue**	150.

1902

E6S	E	10c	**ultramarine**	150.

POSTAGE DUE STAMPS

Overprinted in Red   SPECIMEN·

1879

Type D

J1S	D	1c	**brown**	250.00
J2S	D	2c	**brown**	250.00
J3S	D	3c	**brown**	250.00
J4S	D	5c	**brown**	250.00

1884

J15S	D	1c	**red brown**	45.00
J16S	D	2c	**red brown**	45.00
J17S	D	3c	**red brown**	45.00
J18S	D	5c	**red brown**	45.00
J19S	D	10c	**red brown**	45.00
J20S	D	30c	**red brown**	45.00
J21S	D	50c	**red brown**	45.00

Handstamped in Dull Purple   Specimen.

1895

Type E

J38S	E	1c	**deep claret**	85.00
J39S	E	2c	**deep claret**	85.00
J40S	E	3c	**deep claret**	85.00
J41S	E	5c	**deep claret**	85.00
J42S	E	10c	**deep claret**	85.00
J43S	E	30c	**deep claret**	85.00
J44S	E	50c	**deep claret**	85.00

OFFICIAL STAMPS

Special printings of Official stamps were made in 1875 at the time the other Reprints, Re-issues and Special Printings were printed. The Official stamps reprints received specimen overprints, but philatelists believe they most properly should be considered to be part of the special printings. See Official section after No. O120.

NEWSPAPER STAMPS

Overprinted in Red   Specimen.

1865-75

Type C - Overprint 30mm Long

PR5S	C	5c	**dark blue**	150.00
a.			Triple overprint	260.00
PR2S	C	10c	**blue green**	165.00
PR3S	C	25c	**carmine red**	175.00

Handstamped in Black   Specimen

1875

Type A

PR9S	A	2c	**black**	225.00
PR11S	A	4c	**black**	225.00
PR12S	A	6c	**black**	225.00
PR16S	A	12c	**rose**	225.00

Overprinted in Black, except as noted   Specimen.

1875

Type B
Overprint 15mm Long

PR9S	B	2c	**black**	45.00
PR10S	B	3c	**black**	45.00
PR11S	B	4c	**black**	45.00
PR12S	B	6c	**black**	45.00
PR13S	B	8c	**black**	45.00
PR14S	B	9c	**black**	45.00
a.			Overprint in blue	—
PR15S	B	10c	**black**	45.00
PR16S	B	12c	**rose**	45.00
PR17S	B	24c	**rose**	45.00
PR18S	B	36c	**rose**	45.00
PR19S	B	48c	**rose**	45.00
a.			Overprint in blue	62.50
PR20S	B	60c	**rose**	45.00
PR21S	B	72c	**rose**	45.00
a.			Overprint in blue	62.50
PR22S	B	84c	**rose**	45.00
a.			Overprint in blue	—
PR23S	B	96c	**rose**	45.00
a.			Overprint in blue	—
PR24S	B	$1.92	**dark brown**	45.00
PR25S	B	$3	**vermilion**	45.00
a.			Overprint in blue	62.50
PR26S	B	$6	**ultramarine**	45.00
a.			Overprint in blue	250.00
PR27S	B	$9	**yellow**	45.00
a.			Overprint in blue	250.00
PR28S	B	$12	**dark green**	45.00
a.			Overprint in blue	250.00
PR29S	B	$24	**dark gray violet**	45.00
a.			Overprint in blue	60.00
PR30S	B	$36	**brown rose**	62.00
PR31S	B	$48	**red brown**	62.00
PR32S	B	$60	**violet**	62.00

Overprinted in Red   SPECIMEN.

1875

Type D

PR14S	D	9c	**black**	30.00

1879

PR57S	D	2c	**black**	25.00
PR58S	D	3c	**black**	25.00
PR59S	D	4c	**black**	25.00
PR60S	D	6c	**black**	25.00
PR61S	D	8c	**black**	25.00
PR62S	D	10c	**black**	25.00
a.			Double overprint	250.00
PR63S	D	12c	**red**	25.00
PR64S	D	24c	**red**	25.00
PR65S	D	36c	**red**	25.00
PR66S	D	48c	**red**	25.00
PR67S	D	60c	**red**	25.00
PR68S	D	72c	**red**	25.00
PR69S	D	84c	**red**	25.00
PR70S	D	96c	**red**	25.00
PR71S	D	$1.92	**pale brown**	25.00
PR72S	D	$3	**red vermilion**	25.00
PR73S	D	$6	**blue**	25.00
PR74S	D	$9	**orange**	25.00
PR75S	D	$12	**yellow green**	25.00
PR76S	D	$24	**dark violet**	25.00

PR77S	D	$36	**Indian red**	25.00
PR78S	D	$48	**yellow brown**	25.00
PR79S	D	$60	**purple**	25.00

1885

PR81S	D	1c	**black**	25.00

Handstamped in Dull Purple   Specimen.

1879

Type E

PR57S	E	2c	**black**	22.50
PR58S	E	3c	**black**	22.50
PR59S	E	4c	**black**	22.50
PR60S	E	6c	**black**	22.50
PR61S	E	8c	**black**	22.50
PR62S	E	10c	**black**	22.50
PR63S	E	12c	**red**	22.50
PR64S	E	24c	**red**	22.50
PR65S	E	36c	**red**	22.50
PR66S	E	48c	**red**	22.50
PR67S	E	60c	**red**	22.50
PR68S	E	72c	**red**	22.50
PR69S	E	84c	**red**	22.50
PR70S	E	96c	**red**	22.50
PR71S	E	$1.92	**pale brown**	22.50
PR72S	E	$3	**red vermilion**	22.50
PR73S	E	$6	**blue**	22.50
PR74S	E	$9	**orange**	22.50
PR75S	E	$12	**yellow green**	22.50
PR76S	E	$24	**dark violet**	22.50
PR77S	E	$36	**Indian red**	22.50
PR78S	E	$48	**yellow brown**	22.50
PR79S	E	$60	**purple**	22.50

1885

PR81S	E	1c	**black**	22.50

1895   Wmk. 191

PR114S	E	1c	**black**	35.00
PR115S	E	2c	**black**	35.00
PR116S	E	5c	**black**	35.00
PR117S	E	10c	**black**	35.00
PR118S	E	25c	**carmine**	35.00
PR119S	E	50c	**carmine**	35.00
PR120S	E	$2	**scarlet**	35.00
PR121S	E	$5	**dark blue**	35.00
PR122S	E	$10	**green**	42.50
PR123S	E	$20	**slate**	42.50
PR124S	E	$50	**dull rose**	42.50
PR125S	E	$100	**purple**	42.50

REVENUE STAMPS

SPECIMEN
Type G

Overprint 14mm Long

R5S	G	2c	Bank Check, **blue** (red)	375.00
R15S	A	2c	U. S. I. R., **orange**	—

SPECIMEN
Type H

Overprint 16mm Long

R23S	H	5c	Agreement, **red**	375.00
R34S	H	10c	Contract, **blue** (red)	375.00
R35eS	H	10c	Foreign Exchange, **ultra** (red)	375.00
R36S	H	10c	Inland Exchange, **blue** (red)	375.00
R46S	H	25c	Insurance, **red**	375.00
R52S	H	30c	Inland Exchange, **lilac** (red)	375.00
R53S	H	40c	Inland Exchange, **brown** (red)	375.00
R68S	H	$1	Foreign Exchange, **red**	375.00

Specimen

Type I

1898   Overprint 20mm Long

R153S	I	1c	**green** (red)	475.00

1875

RB11S	H	1c	**green** (red)	300.00

PRIVATE DIE MATCH STAMP

Overprinted with Type G in Red   SPECIMEN

RO133dS	G	1c	**black**, A. Messinger	500.00

SAVINGS STAMPS

Overprinted Vertically Reading
Down in Red   **SPECIMEN**

1911

PS4S	10c deep blue	—

1917-18   Handstamped "SPECIMEN" in Violet

WS1S	25c deep green	—
WS2S	$5 deep green	—

VARIOUS OVERPRINTS

Overprinted with control numbers in carmine   **7890**

1861

Type J

63S	J A24	1c pale blue (overprint 9012)	200.00
65S	J A25	3c brown red (overprint 7890)	200.00
		Block of 4	900.
68S	J A27	10c green (overprint 5678)	200.00
69S	J A28	12c gray black (overprint 4567)	200.00
71S	J A30	30c orange (overprint 2345)	200.00
		Block of 4	900.
72S	J A31	90c pale blue (overprint 1234)	200.00
a.		Pair, one without overprint	—

1863-66

73S	J A32	2c black (overprint 8901)	275.00
		Block of 4	1,250.
76S	J A26	5c brown (overprint 6789)	200.00
77S	J A33	15c black (overprint 235)	250.00
		Block of 4	1,150.
78S	J A29	24c gray lilac (overprint 3456)	200.00

Special Printings Overprinted in Red or Blue   **SAMPLE.**

1889

Type K

212S	K A59	1c ultramarine (red)	75.00
210S	K A57	2c red brown (blue)	75.00
210S	K A57	2c lake (blue)	75.00
210S	K A57	2c rose lake (blue)	75.00
210S	K A57	2c scarlet (blue)	75.00
214S	K A46b	3c vermilion (blue)	75.00
211S	K A58	4c blue green (red)	75.00
205S	K A56	5c gray brown (red)	75.00
208S	K A47b	6c brown red (blue)	75.00
209S	K A49b	10c brown (red)	75.00
		Without overprint	80.00
189S	K A51a	15c orange (blue)	75.00
190S	K A53	30c full black (red)	75.00
191S	K A54	90c carmine (blue)	75.00

Special Printings Overprinted in Red or Blue   **SAMPLE A.**

Type L

212S	L A59	1c ultramarine (red)	75.00
210S	L A57	2c rose lake (blue)	75.00
		Without overprint	—
214S	L A46b	3c purple (red)	75.00
211S	L A58	4c dark brown (red)	75.00
205S	L A56	5c yellow brown (blue)	75.00
		Without overprint	—
208S	L A47b	6c vermilion (blue)	75.00
209S	L A49b	10c green (red)	75.00
		Without overprint	100.00
189S	L A51a	15c blue (red)	75.00
		Without overprint	100.00
190S	L A53	30c full black (red)	75.00
191S	L A54	90c orange (blue)	75.00

Overprinted with Type K
Together with "A" in Black Manuscript

191S	M A54	90c carmine (blue)	140.00
209S	M A49b	10c brown (red)	140.00
211S	M A58	4c blue green (red)	140.00

"SAMPLE A" in Manuscript (red or black)

216S	N A56	5c indigo	160.00

Regular Issues Overprinted in Blue or Red   **UNIVERSAL POSTAL (CONGRESS**

125 sets were distributed to delegates to the Universal Postal Congress held in Washington, D. C., May 5 to June 15, 1897.

1897   **Type O**

264S	O A87	1c blue	100.00
267S	O A88	2c carmine, type III	100.00
268S	O A89	3c purple	100.00
269S	O A90	4c dark brown	100.00
270S	O A91	5c chestnut	100.00
271S	O A92	6c claret brown	100.00
272S	O A93	8c violet brown	100.00
273S	O A94	10c dark green	100.00

274S	O A95	15c dark blue	100.00
275S	O A96	50c red orange	100.00
276S	O A97	$1 black, type I	350.00
276AS	O A97	$1 black, type II	300.00
277S	O A98	$2 dark blue	250.00
278S	O A99	$5 dark green	350.00

SPECIAL DELIVERY

E5S	O SD3	10c blue (R)	200.00

POSTAGE DUE

J38S	O D2	1c deep claret	125.00
J39S	O D2	2c deep claret	125.00
J40S	O D2	3c deep claret	125.00
J41S	O D2	5c deep claret	125.00
J42S	O D2	10c deep claret	125.00
J43S	O D2	30c deep claret	125.00
J44S	O D2	50c deep claret	125.00

NEWSPAPERS

PR114S	O N15	1c black	100.00
PR115S	O N15	2c black	100.00
PR116S	O N15	5c black	100.00
PR117S	O N15	10c black	100.00
PR118S	O N16	25c carmine	100.00
PR119S	O N16	50c carmine	100.00
PR120S	O N17	$2 scarlet	100.00
PR121S	O N18	$5 dark blue	100.00
PR122S	O N19	$10 green	100.00
PR123S	O N20	$20 slate	100.00
PR124S	O N21	$50 dull rose	100.00
PR125S	O N22	$100 purple	100.00

ENVELOPES

Overprinted   **UNIVERSAL POSTAL CONGRESS**

Type P

U294S	P	1c blue	100.00
U296S	P	1c blue, amber	100.00
U300S	P	1c blue, manila	100.00
W301S	P	1c blue, manila	100.00
U304S	P	1c blue, amber manila	100.00
U311S	P	2c green, Die 2	100.00
U312S	P	2c green, Die 2, amber	100.00
U313S	P	2c green, Die 2, oriental buff	100.00
U314S	P	2c green, Die 2, blue	100.00
U315S	P	2c green, Die 2, manila	100.00
W316S	P	2c green, Die 2, manila	100.00
U317S	P	2c green, Die 2, amber manila	100.00
U324S	P	4c carmine	100.00
U325S	P	4c carmine, amber	120.00
U330S	P	5c blue, Die 1	110.00
U331S	P	5c blue, Die 1, amber	110.00

Two settings of type P overprint are found.
See the July\August 1949 issue of the Scott Monthly Stamp Journal for others.

POSTAL CARDS

Overprinted   **UNIVERSAL POSTAL CONGRESS.**

Type Q

UX12S	Q	1c black, buff	400.00
UX13S	Q	2c blue, cream	400.00

PAID REPLY POSTAL CARDS
Overprinted with Type Q

UY1S	Q	1c black, buff	400.00
UY2S	Q	2c blue, grayish white	400.00

As Nos. UY1S-UY2S were made by overprinting unsevered reply cards, values are for unsevered cards.

SOUVENIR CARDS

These cards were issued as souvenirs of the philatelic gatherings at which they were distributed by the United States Postal Service (USPS), its predecessor the United States Post Office Department (POD), or the Bureau of Engraving and Printing (BEP). They were not valid for postage.

Most of the cards bear reproductions of United States stamps with the design enlarged, altered by removal of denomination, country name and "Postage" or "Air Mail" or defaced by diagonal bars. The cards are not perforated.

Numismatic cards are listed following the postal cards.

A forerunner of the souvenir cards is the 1938 Philatelic Truck souvenir sheet which the Post Office Department issued and distributed in various cities visited by the Philatelic Truck. It shows the White House, printed in blue on white paper. Issued with and without gum. Value, with gum, $50; without gum, $8.

Standard abbreviations:
APS- American Philatelic Society
ASDA- American Stamp Dealers Association

No. 28

1954
SC1   Postage Stamp Design Exhibition, Natl. Philatelic Museum, Mar. 13, 1954, Philadelphia. Card of 4 monochrome views of Washington. Inscribed: "Souvenir sheet designed, engraved and printed by members, Bureau, Engraving and Printing. Reissued by popular request."   *1,500.*

1960
SC2   Barcelona, 1st Intl. Philatelic Congress, Mar. 26-Apr. 5, 1960. Vignette, Landing of Columbus from #231. (POD)   300.00

1966
SC3   SIPEX, 6th Intl. Philatelic Exhibition, May 21-30, 1966, Washington. Card of 3 multicolored views of Washington.   160.00

1968
SC4   EFIMEX, Intl. Philatelic Exhibition, Nov. 1-9, 1968, Mexico City. #292. Spanish text. (POD)   2.00

1969
SC5   SANDIPEX, San Diego Philatelic Exhibition, July 16-20, 1969, San Diego, Cal. Card of 3 multicolored views of Washington. (BEP)   50.00
SC6   ASDA Natl. Postage Stamp Show, Nov. 21-23, 1969, New York. Card of 4 #E4. (BEP)   20.00

1970
SC7   INTERPEX, Mar. 13-15, 1970, New York. Card of 4, #1027, 1035, C35, C38. (BEP)   45.00
SC8   COMPEX, Combined Philatelic Exhibition of Chicagoland, May 29-31, 1970. Card of 4 #C18. (BEP)   11.00
SC9   PHILYMPIA, London Intl. Stamp Exhibition, Sept. 18-26 1970. Card of 3, #548-550. (POD)   1.50
SC10   HAPEX, APS Convention, Nov. 5-8, 1970, Honolulu. Card of 3, #799, C46, C55. (BEP)   11.00

1971
SC11   INTERPEX, Mar. 12-14, 1971, New York. Card of 4 #1193. Background includes #1331-1332, 1371, C76. (BEP)   1.50
SC12   WESTPEX, Western Philatelic Exhibition, Apr. 23-25, 1971, San Francisco. Card of 4, #740, 852, 966, 997. (BEP)   1.50
SC13   NAPEX 71, Natl. Philatelic Exhibition, May 21-23, 1971, Washington. Card of 3, #990, 991, 992. (BEP)   1.75
SC14   TEXANEX 71, Texas Philatelic Association and APS conventions, Aug. 26-29, 1971, San Antonio, Tex. Card of 3, #938, 1043, 1242. (BEP)   1.75
SC15   EXFILIMA 71, 3rd Inter-American Philatelic Exhibition, Nov. 6-14, 1971, Lima, Peru. Card of 3, #1111, 1126, Peru #360. Spanish text. (USPS)   1.00
SC16   ASDA Natl. Postage Stamp Show, Nov. 19-21, 1971, New York. Card of 3, #C13-C15. (BEP)   2.75
SC17   ANPHILEX '71, Anniv. Philatelic Exhibition, Nov. 26-Dec. 1, 1971, New York. Card of 2, #1-2. (BEP)   1.00

1972
SC18   INTERPEX, Mar. 17-19, 1972, New York. Card of 4 #1173. Background includes #976, 1434-1435, C69. (BEP)   1.00
SC19   NOPEX, Apr. 6-9, 1972, New Orleans. Card of 4 #1020. Background includes #323-327. (BEP)   1.00
SC20   BELGICA 72, Brussels Intl. Philatelic Exhibition, June 24-July 9, 1972, Brussels, Belgium. Card of 3, #914, 1026, 1104. Flemish and French text. (USPS)   1.00
SC21   Olympia Philatelie Munchen 72, Aug. 18-Sept. 10, 1972, Munich, Germany. Card of 4, #1460-1462, C85. German text. (USPS)   1.00
SC22   EXFILBRA 72, 4th Inter-American Philatelic Exhibition, Aug. 26-Sept. 2, 1972, Rio de Janeiro, Brazil. Card of 3 #C14, Brazil #C18-C19. Portuguese text. (USPS)   1.00
SC23   Natl. Postal Forum VI, Aug. 28-30, 1972, Washington. Card of 4 #1396. (USPS)   1.00
SC24   SEPAD '72, Oct. 20-22, 1972, Philadelphia. Card of 4 #1044. (BEP)   1.00
SC25   ASDA Natl. Postage Stamp Show, Nov. 17-19, 1972, New York. Card of 4, #883, 863, 868, 888. (BEP)   1.00
SC26   STAMP EXPO, Nov. 24-26, 1972, San Francisco. Card of 4 #C36. (BEP)   1.50

1973
SC27   INTERPEX, Mar. 9-11, 1973, New York. Card of 4 #976. (BEP)   1.25
SC28   IBRA 73 Intl. Philatelic Exhibition, Munich, May 11-20, 1973. #C13. (USPS)   1.50
SC29   COMPEX 73, May 25-27, 1973, Chicago. Card of 4 #245. (BEP)   2.00
SC30   APEX 73, Intl. Airmail Exhibition, Manchester, England, July 4-7, 1973. Card of 3, #C3a, Newfoundland #C4, Honduras #C12. (USPS)   1.50
SC31   POLSKA 73, World Philatelic Exhibition, Poznan, Poland, Aug. 19-Sept. 2, 1973. Card of 3, #1488, Poland 1944-1945. Polish text. (USPS)   1.50
SC32   NAPEX 73, Sept. 14-16, 1973, Washington. Card of 4 #C3. Background includes montage of #C4-C6. (BEP)   1.50
SC33   ASDA Natl. Postage Stamp Show, Nov. 16-18, 1973, New York. Card of 4 #908. Foreground includes #1139-1144. (BEP)   1.00
SC34   STAMP EXPO NORTH, Dec. 7-9, 1973, San Francisco. Card of 4 #C20. (BEP)   1.50

A card of 10, Nos. 1489-1498, was distributed to postal employees. Not available to public. Size: about 14x11 inches.

1974
SC35   Natl. Hobby Industry Trade Show, Feb. 3-6, 1974, Chicago. Card of 4, #1456-1459. Reproductions of silversmith (#1457) and glassmaker (#1456). (USPS)   2.00
SC36   MILCOPEX 1974, Mar. 8-10, 1974, Milwaukee. Card of 4 #C43. (USPS)   1.50
SC37   INTERNABA 1974, June 6, 1974, Basel, Switzerland. Card of 8, #1530-1537. German, French, and Italian text. (USPS)   2.75
SC38   STOCKHOLMIA 74, Intl. Philatelic Exhibition, Sept. 21-29, 1974, Stockholm. Card of 3, #836, Sweden #300, 767. Swedish text. (USPS)   2.75
SC39   EXFILMEX 74, Interamerican Philatelic Exposition, Oct. 26-Nov. 3, 1974, Mexico City. Card of 2, #1157, Mexico #910. Spanish text. (USPS)   2.75

1975
SC40   ESPANA 75, World Stamp Exhibition, Apr. 4-13, 1975, Madrid. Card of 3, #233, #1271, Spain 1312. Spanish text. (USPS)   1.50
SC41   NAPEX 75, May 9-11, 1975, Washington. Card of 4 #708. (BEP)   5.00
SC42   ARPHILA 75, June 6-16, 1975, Paris. Card of 3. Designs of #1187, #1207, France #1117. French text. (USPS)   2.25
SC43   Intl. Women's Year, 1975. Card of 3 #872, 878, 959. Reproduction of 1886 dollar bill. (USPS)   20.00
SC44   ASDA Natl. Postage Stamp Show, Nov. 21-23, 1975. Bicentennial series. Card of 4 #1003. (BEP)   25.00

1976
SC45   WERABA 76, 3rd Intl. Space Stamp Exhibition, Apr. 1-4, 1976, Zurich, Switzerland. Card of 2, #1434-1435. (USPS)   3.00
SC46   INTERPHIL 76, 7th Intl. Philatelic Exhibition, May 29-June 6, 1976. Philadelphia. Bicentennial series. Card of 4 #120. (BEP)   5.00

An Interphil '76 card issued by the American Revolution Bicentennial Administration was bound into the Interphil program. It shows an altered #1044 in black brown, the Bicentennial emblem and a view of Independence Hall. Printed by BEP

SC48   Bicentennial Exposition on Science and Technology, May 30-Sept. 6, 1976, Kennedy Space Center, Fla. #C76. (USPS)   3.50
SC49   STAMP EXPO 76, June 11-13, 1976, Los Angeles. Bicentennial series. Card of 4, #1351, 1352, 1345, 1348. (BEP)   5.00
SC50   Colorado Statehood Centennial, Aug. 1, 1976. Card of 3, #743, 288, 1670. (USPS)   5.00
SC51   HAFNIA 76, Intl. Stamp Exhibition, Copenhagen. Aug. 20-29, 1976. Card of 2, #5, Denmark #2. Danish and English text. (USPS)   2.50
SC52   ITALIA 76, Intl. Philatelic Exhibition, Oct. 14-24, Milan. Card of 3, #1168, Italy #578, 601. Italian text. (USPS)   2.50
SC53   NORDPOSTA 76, North German Stamp Exhibition, Oct. 30-31, Hamburg. Card of 3, #689, Germany #B366, B417. German text. (USPS)   2.50

1977
SC54   MILCOPEX, Milwaukee Philatelic Society, Mar. 4-6, Milwaukee. Card of 2, #733, 1128. (BEP)   2.00
SC55   ROMPEX 77, Rocky Mountain Philatelic Exhibition, May 20-22, Denver. Card of 4 #1001. (BEP)   1.50
SC56   AMPHILEX 77, Intl. Philatelic Exhibition, May 26-June 5, Amsterdam. Card of 3, #1027, Netherlands #41, 294. Dutch text. (USPS)   3.00
SC57   SAN MARINO 77, Intl. Philatelic Exhibition, San Marino, Aug. 28-Sept. 4. Card of 3, #1-2, San Marino #1. Italian text. (USPS)   3.00
SC58   PURIPEX 77, Silver Anniv. Philatelic Exhibit, Sept. 2-5, San Juan, P. R. Card of 4 #801. (BEP)   1.50
SC59   ASDA Natl. Postage Stamp Show, Nov. 15-20, New York. Card of 4 #45. (BEP)   2.00

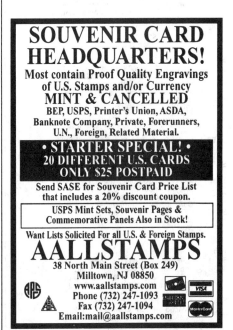

1978

SC60   ROCPEX 78, Intl. Philatelic Exhibition, Mar. 20-29, Taipei. Card of 6, #1706-1709, China #1812, 1816. Chinese text. (USPS)   3.00

SC61   NAPOSTA '78 Philatelic Exhibition, May 20-25, Frankfurt. Card of 3, #555, 563, Germany #1216. German text. (USPS)   3.00

SC62   CENJEX 78, Federated Stamp Clubs of New Jersey, 30th annual exhibition, June 23-25, Freehold, NJ. Card of 9, #646, 680, 689, 1086, 1716, 4 #785. (BEP)   2.00

1979

SC63   BRASILIANA 79, Intl. Philatelic Exhibition, Sept. 15-23, Rio de Janeiro. Card of 3, #C91-C92, Brazil #1295. Portuguese text. (USPS)   3.50

SC64   JAPEX 79, Intl. Philatelic Exhibition, Nov. 2-4, Tokyo. Card of 2, #1158, Japan #1024. Japanese text. (USPS)   3.75

1980

SC65   LONDON 1980, Intl. Philatelic Exhibition, May 6-14, London. #329. (USPS)   3.50

SC66   NORWEX 80, Intl. Stamp Exhibition, June 13-22, Oslo. Card of 3, #620-621, Norway #658. Norwegian text. (USPS)   3.50

SC67   NAPEX 80, July 4-6, Washington. Card of 4 #573. (BEP)   9.00

SC68   ASDA Stamp Festival, Sept. 25-28, 1980, New York. Card of 4 #962. (BEP)   11.00

SC69   ESSEN 80, 3rd Intl. Stamp Fair, Nov. 15-19, Essen. Card of 2, #1014, Germany #723. German text. (USPS)   3.50

1981

SC70   STAMP EXPO '81 SOUTH, Mar. 20-22, Anaheim, Calif. Card of 6, #1331-1332, 4 #1287. (BEP)   12.00

SC71   WIPA 1981, Intl. Stamp Exhibition, May 22-31, Vienna. Card of 2, #1252, Austria #789. German text. (USPS)   3.00

SC72   Natl. Stamp Collecting Month, Oct., 1981. Card of 2, #245, 1918. (USPS)   3.00

SC73   PHILATOKYO '81, Intl. Stamp Exhibition, Oct. 9-18. Tokyo. Card of 2, #1531, Japan #800. Japanese text. (USPS)   3.00

SC74   NORDPOSTA 81, North German Stamp Exhibition, Nov. 7-8. Hamburg. Card of 2, #923, Germany #B538. German text. (USPS)   3.00

1982

SC75   MILCOPEX '82, Milwaukee Philatelic Association Exhibition, Mar. 5-7. Card of 4 #1137. (BEP)   11.00

SC76   CANADA 82, Intl. Philatelic Youth Exhibition, May 20-24, Toronto. Card of 2, #116, Canada #15. French and English text. (USPS)   3.00

SC77   PHILEXFRANCE '82, Intl. Philatelic Exhibition, June 11-21, Paris. Card of 2, #1753, France #1480. French text. (USPS)   3.00

SC78   Natl. Stamp Collecting Month, Oct. #C3a. (USPS)   3.00

SC79   ESPAMER '82, Intl. Philatelic Exhibition, Oct. 12-17, San Juan, P.R. Card of 4 #244. English and Spanish text. (BEP)   25.00

SC80   ESPAMER '82, Intl. Philatelic Exhibition, Oct. 12-17, San Juan, P.R. Card of 3, #801, 1437, 2024. Spanish and English text. (USPS)   3.00

1983

SC81   Joint stamp issues, Sweden and US. Mar. 24. Card of 3, #958, 2036, Sweden #1453. Swedish and English text. (USPS)   3.00

SC82   Joint stamp issues, Germany and US. Apr. 29. Card of 2, #2040, Germany #1397. German and English text. (USPS)   3.00

SC83   TEMBAL 83, Intl. Philatelic Exhibition, Mar. 21-29, Basel. Card of 2, #C71, Basel #3L1. German text. (USPS)   3.00

SC84   TEXANEX-TOPEX '83 Exhibition, June 17-19, San Antonio. Card of 5, #1660, 4 #776. (BEP)   18.00

SC85   BRASILIANA 83, Intl. Philatelic Exhibition, July 29-Aug. 7, Rio de Janeiro. Card of 2, #2, Brazil #1. Portuguese text. (USPS)   3.00

SC86   BANGKOK 83, Intl. Philatelic Exhibition, Aug. 4-13, Bangkok. Card of 2, #210, Thailand #1. Thai text. (USPS)   3.00

SC87   Intl. Philatelic Memento, 1983-84. #1387. (USPS)   3.00

SC88   Natl. Stamp Collecting Month, Oct. #293 bicolored. (USPS)   4.00

SC89   Philatelic Show '83, Boston, Oct. 21-23. Card of 2 #718-719. (BEP)   10.00

SC90   ASDA 1983, Natl. Postage Stamp Show, New York, Nov. 17-20. Card of 4 #881. (BEP)   10.00

1984

SC91   ESPANA 84, World Exhibition of Philately. Madrid, Apr. 27-May 6. Card of 4 #241. Enlarged vignette, Landing of Columbus, from #231. English and Spanish text. (BEP)   18.00

SC92   ESPANA 84, Intl. Philatelic Exhibition, Madrid, Apr. 27-May 6. Card of 2, #233, Spain #428. Spanish text. (USPS)   3.00

SC93   Stamp Expo '84 South, Anaheim, CA, Apr. 27-29. Card of 4, #1791-1794. (BEP)   10.00

SC94   COMPEX '84, Rosemont, IL, May 25-27. Card of 4 #728. (BEP)   18.00

SC95   HAMBURG '84, Intl. Exhibition for 19th UPU Congress, Hamburg, June 19-26. Card of 2, #C66, Germany #669. English, French and German text. (USPS)   3.00

SC96   St. Lawrence Seaway, 25th anniv., June 26. Card of 2, #1131, Canada #387. English and French text. (USPS)   3.50

SC97   AUSIPEX '84, Australia's 1st intl. exhibition, Melbourne, Sept. 21-30. Card of 2, #290, Western Australia #1. (USPS)   3.00

SC98   Natl. Stamp Collecting Month, Oct. #2104, tricolored. (USPS)   3.00

SC99   PHILAKOREA '84, Seoul, Oct. 22-31. Card of 2, #741, Korea #994. Korean and English text. (USPS)   3.00

SC100   ASDA 1984, Natl. Postage Stamp Show, New York, Nov. 15-18. Card of 4 #1470. (BEP)   12.50

1985

SC101   Intl. Philatelic Memento, 1985. #2. (USPS)   3.00

SC102   OLYMPHILEX '85. Intl. Philatelic Exhibition, Lausanne. Mar. 18-24. Card of 2, #C106, Switzerland #746. French and English text. (USPS)   3.00

SC103   ISRAPHIL '85. Intl. Philatelic Exhibition, Tel Aviv, May 14-22. Card of 2, #566, Israel #33. Hebrew and English text. (USPS)   3.00

SC104   LONG BEACH '85, Numismatic and Philatelic Exposition, Long Beach, CA, Jan. 31-Feb. 3. Card of 4 #954, plus a Series 1865 $20 Gold Certificate. (BEP)   10.00

SC105   MILCOPEX '85, Milwaukee Philatelic Society annual stamp show, Mar. 1-3. Card of 4 #880. (BEP)   11.00

SC106   NAPEX '85, Natl. Philatelic Exhibition, Arlington, VA, June 7-9. Card of 4 #2014. (BEP)   10.00

SC107   ARGENTINA '85, Intl. Philatelic Exhibition, Buenos Aires, July 5-14. Card of 2, #1737, Argentina #B27. Spanish text. (USPS)   3.00

SC108   MOPHILA '85, Intl. Philatelic Exhibition, Hamburg, Sept. 11-15. Card of 2, #296, Germany #B595. German text. (USPS)   3.00

SC109   ITALIA '85, Intl. Philatelic Exhibition, Rome, Oct. 25-Nov. 3. Card of 2, #1107, Italy #830. Italian text. (USPS)   3.00

1986

SC110   Statue of Liberty Centennial, Natl. Philatelic Memento, 1986. #C87. (USPS)   5.00

SC111   Garfield Perry Stamp Club, Natl. Stamp Show, Cleveland, Mar. 21-23. Card of 4 #306. (BEP)   10.00

SC112   AMERIPEX '86, Intl. Philatelic Exhibition, Chicago, May 22-June 1. Card of 3, #134, 2052, 1474.(BEP)   10.00

SC113   STOCKHOLMIA '86, Intl. Philatelic Exhibition, Stockholm, Aug. 28-Sept. 7. Card of 2, #113, Sweden #253. Swedish text. (USPS)   4.00

SC114   HOUPEX '86, Natl. Stamp Show, Houston. Sep. 5-7. Card of 3, #1035, 1042, 1044A. (BEP)   11.00

SC115   LOBEX '86, Numismatic and Philatelic Exhibition, Long Beach, CA, Oct. 2-5. Long Beach Stamp Club 60th anniv. Card of 4, #291, plus a series 1907 $10 Gold Certificate. (BEP)   12.00

SC116   DCSE '86, Dallas Coin and Stamp Exhibition, Dallas, Dec. 11-14. Card of 4 #550, plus $10,000 Federal Reserve Note. (BEP)   12.50

1987

SC117   CAPEX '87, Intl. Philatelic Exhibition, Toronto, June 13-21. Card of 2, #569, Canada #883. English and French text. (USPS)   4.00

SC118   HAFNIA '87, Intl. Philatelic Exhibition, Copenhagen, Oct. 16-25. Card of 2, #299, Denmark #B52. English and Danish text. (USPS)   4.00

SC119   SESCAL '87, Stamp Exhibition of Southern California, Los Angeles, Oct. 16-18. #798. (BEP)   12.00

SC120   HSNA '87, Hawaii State Numismatic Association Exhibition, Honolulu, Nov. 12-15. #799 and a Series 1923 $5 Silver Certificate. (BEP)   15.00

SC121   MONTE CARLO, Intl. Philatelic Exhibition, Monte Carlo, Nov. 13-17. Card of 3, #2287, 2300, Monaco #1589. French and English text. (USPS)   4.00

1988

SC122   FINLANDIA '88, Intl. Philatelic Exhibition, Helsinki, June 1-12. Card of 2, #836, Finland #768. English and Finnish text. (USPS)   4.00

SC123   STAMPSHOW '88, APS natl. stamp show, Detroit, Aug. 25-28. #835. (BEP)   10.00

SC124   MIDAPHIL '88, Kansas City, Nov. 18-20. #627. (BEP)   10.00

1989

SC125   PHILEXFRANCE '89 intl. philatelic exhibition, Paris, July 7-17. Card of 2, #C120, France #2144. English and French text. (USPS)   5.00

SC126   STAMPSHOW '89, APS natl. stamp show, Anaheim, CA, Aug. 24-27. #565. Various reproductions of the portrait of Chief Hollow Horn Bear from which the stamp was designed. (BEP)   9.00

SC127   WORLD STAMP EXPO '89, Washington, Nov. 17-Dec. 3. Card of 4, #2433a-2433d. Embossed reproductions of Supreme Court, Washington Monument, Capitol and Jefferson Memorial. (USPS)   5.00

1990

SC128   ARIPEX 90, Arizona Philatelic Exhibition, Phoenix, Apr. 20-22. Card of 2, #285 and 285 with black vignette. (BEP)   10.00

SC129   STAMPSHOW '90, APS natl. stamp show, Cincinnati, Aug. 23-26. Card of 2, #286 and essay with frame of #286 in red with vignette of #293 in black. (BEP)   10.00

SC130   STAMP WORLD LONDON 90, London, England, May 3-13. Card of 2, #1, Great Britain #1. (USPS)   5.00

1991

SC131   STAMPSHOW '91, APS natl. stamp show, Philadelphia, Aug. 22-25. Card of 3, #537, Essays #537a-E1, 537b-E1. Embossed figure of "Freedom." (BEP)   10.00

1992

SC132   World Columbian Stamp Expo, Chicago, May 22-31. Card of 2, #118, 119b. (BEP)   10.00

SC133   Savings Bond, produced as gift to BEP employees, available to public. 1954 Savings stamp, Series E War Savings bond. (BEP)   12.50

SC134   STAMPSHOW '92. Oakland, CA (BEP)   9.00

1993

SC135   Combined Federal Campaign, produced as gift to BEP employees, available to public. #1016. Photos of 6 other stamps. (BEP)   10.00

SC136   ASDA stamp show, New York, May 1993. Card of 7 #859, 864, 869, 874, 879, 884, 889 (BEP)   10.00

SC137   Savings Bonds, produced as gift to BEP employees, available to the public Aug. 1993. $200 War Savings Bond, #WS8 (BEP)   12.00

SC138   Omaha Stamp Show, Sept. 1993. Card of 4, #E7, PR2, JQ5, QE4 (BEP)   11.00

SC139   ASDA New York Show, Oct. 1993. Card of 2, #499-E1a and similar with negative New York precancel (BEP)   9.00

1994

SC140   Sandical, San Diego, CA, Feb. 1994. Card of 4 #E4 (BEP)   9.00

SC141   Savings Bonds, produced as a gift to BEP employees, available to the public Aug. 1, 1994. #WS7-WS11.   11.00

SC142   STAMPSHOW '94, APS National Stamp Show Pittsburgh, PA. Card of 3, 1c, 2c and 10c Type D2   9.00

SC143   American Stamp Dealers Association, Nov. 1994, New York, NY. Card of 4, 2c, 12c, $3, $6 Types N4-N5, N7-N8   9.00

1995

SC144   Natl. Exhibition of the Columbus Philatelic Club, Apr. 1995, Columbus, OH. Block of 4 of #261.   9.00

    No. 144 was issued folded in half.

SC145   Centennial of U.S. Stamp Production, June 1995, BEP Intaglio Print. Card of 13 of Types A87-A99 in blue   75.00

SC146   Savings Bonds, produced as a gift to BEP employees, available to the public Aug. 1, 1995. Card of 3 #905, 907, 940   9.50

SC147   American Stamp Dealers Association, Nov. 1995, New York, NY. Block of 4, #292   9.50

    No. SC147 issued folded in half.

1996

SC148   CAPEX '96, Toronto, Canada, June 1996. Block of 4, #291   9.50

SC149   Olymphilex '96, Atlanta, GA, July-August, 1996, Block of 4, #718   9.50

SC150   Billings Stamp Club, Billings, MT, Oct. 1996, Block of 4, #1130   9.50

1997

SC151   Long Beach Coin & Collectibles Expo, Feb. 1997, Lock Seal revenue stamp   9.00

SC152   PACIFIC 97, May 1997, Process or renovated butter revenue stamp   9.00

SC153   Milcopex, Milwaukee, WI, Sept. 1997, Newspaper Types N15, N16 and N19   9.50

1998

SC154	OKPEX 98, Oklahoma City, OK, May 1998, Block of 4, #922	9.50
SC155	Centennial of Trans-Mississippi Exposition Issue, Sept. 1998, BEP Engraved Print. Card of 9 die impressions in green of designs A100-A108	45.00

1999

SC156	Philadelphia National Stamp Exhibition, Oct. 1999, Card of 4, #RS281, RS284, RS290, RS306	9.50

NUMISMATIC SOUVENIR CARDS

Included in this section are cards issued by the Bureau of Engraving and Printing showing fractional currency, paper money or parts thereof, for numismatic shows. Not included are press samples sold or given away only at the shows and other special printings. Cards showing both money and stamps are listed in the preceeding section.

Standard abbreviations:
ANA- American Numismatic Association
IPMS- International Paper Money Show
FUN- Florida United Numismatists

No. 8

1969-84

NSC1	ANA	60.00
NSC2	Fresno Numismatic Fair	325.00
NSC3	ANA ('70)	75.00
NSC4	ANA ('71)	3.50
NSC5	ANA ('72)	3.50
NSC6	ANA ('73)	6.00
NSC7	ANA ('74)	9.00
NSC8	ANA ('75)	9.00
NSC9	ANA ('76)	6.00
NSC10	ANA ('77)	3.25
NSC11	IPMS ('78)	4.00
NSC12	ANA ('80)	16.00
NSC13	IPMS ('80)	12.00
NSC14	IPMS ('81)	14.00
NSC15	ANA ('81)	10.00
NSC16	IPMS ('82)	11.00
NSC17	ANA ('82)	12.00
NSC18	FUN ('83)	18.00
NSC19	ANA ('83)	16.00
NSC20	FUN ('84)	18.00
NSC21	IPMS ('84)	16.00
NSC22	ANA ('84)	10.00

1985

NSC23	International Coin Club of El Paso	11.00
NSC24	Pacific Northwest Numismatic Assoc.	11.00
NSC25	IPMS	13.00
NSC26	ANA	11.00
NSC27	International Paper Money Convention (IPMC)	15.00

1986

NSC28	FUN	12.50
NSC29	ANA Midwinter	10.00
NSC30	IPMS	10.00
NSC31	ANA	10.00
NSC32	National World Paper Money Convention (NWPMC)	11.00

1987

NSC33	FUN	11.00
NSC34	ANA Midwinter	12.00
NSC35	BEP Fort Worth	15.00
NSC36	IPMS	10.00
NSC37	ANA	10.00
NSC38	Great Eastern Numismatic Association	10.00

1988

NSC39	FUN	10.00
NSC40	ANA Midwinter	10.00
NSC41	IPMS	10.00
NSC42	ANA	12.00
NSC43	Illinois Numismatic Association	10.00

1989

NSC44	FUN	10.00
NSC45	ANA Midwinter	10.00
NSC46	TNA	11.00
NSC47	IPMS	10.00
NSC48	ANA	14.00

1990

NSC49	FUN	10.00
NSC50	ANA Midwinter	10.00
NSC51	Central States Numismatic Society	10.00
NSC52	Dallas Coin and Stamp Exposition	10.00
NSC53	ANA, Seattle, WA	12.00
NSC54	Westex	11.00
NSC55	Honolulu State Numismatic Association	13.00

1991

NSC56	FUN	11.00
NSC57	ANA Midwinter, Dallas, Texas	10.00
NSC58	IPMS	10.00
NSC59	ANA Convention, Chicago, IL	14.00

1992

NSC60	FUN	10.00
NSC61	Central States Numismatics Society	11.00
NSC62	IPMS, Memphis, TN	10.00
NSC63	ANA Convention, Orlando, FL	10.00

1993

NSC64	FUN	10.00
NSC65	ANA Convention, Colorado Springs, CO	10.00
NSC66	Texas Numismatic Association Show	10.00
NSC67	Georgia Numismatic Association Show	10.00
NSC69	IPMS, Memphis, TN	10.00

1994

NSC70	FUN	9.00
NSC71	ANA Convention, New Orleans, LA	10.00
NSC72	European Paper Money Bourse, Netherlands	10.00
NSC73	IPMS, Memphis, TN	10.00
NSC74	ANA Convention, Detroit, MI	10.00

Nos. NSC75-NSC79 were issued folded in half.

1995

NSC75	FUN	11.00
NSC76	New York Intl. Numismatic Convention	10.00
NSC77	IPMS, Memphis, TN	10.00
NSC78	ANA Convention, Anaheim, CA	11.00
NSC79	Long Beach Numismatic/Philatelic Exposition, Long Beach, CA	10.00

1996

NSC80	FUN	10.00
NSC81	Suburban Washington/Baltimore Coin Show	10.00
NSC82	Central States Numismatic Association	10.00
NSC83	ANA Convention, Denver, CO	10.00

1997

NSC84	FUN	10.00
NSC85	Bay State Coin Show	10.00
NSC86	IPMS, Memphis, TN	10.00
NSC87	ANA Convention, New York, NY	10.00

1998

NSC88	FUN	10.00
NSC89	IPMS, Memphis, TN	10.00
NSC90	ANA Convention, Portland, OR	10.00
NSC91	Long Beach Coin & Collectibles Expo, Long Beach, CA	10.00

1999

NSC92	FUN	10.00
NSC93	Bay State Coin Club	10.00
NSC94	IPMS, Memphis, TN	10.00
NSC95	ANA Convention, Rosemont, IL	10.00

COMMEMORATIVE PANELS

The U.S. Postal Service began issuing commemorative panels September 20, 1972, with the Wildlife Conservation issue (Scott Nos. 1464-1467). Each panel is devoted to a separate issue. It includes unused examples of the stamp or stamps (usually a block of four), reproduction of steel engravings, and background information on the subject of the issue. Values are for panels without protective sleeves. Values for panels with protective sleeves are 10% to 25% higher.

No. 53CP

1972

CP1	Wildlife Conservation, #1467a	6.00
CP2	Mail Order, #1468	5.75
CP3	Osteopathic Medicine, #1469	5.75
CP4	Tom Sawyer, #1470	5.25
CP5	Pharmacy, #1473	9.00
CP6	Christmas (angel), #1471	9.00
CP7	Santa Claus, #1472	9.00
CP8	Stamp Collecting, #1474	5.50

1973

CP9	Love, #1475	6.75
CP10	Pamphleteers, #1476	6.00
CP11	George Gershwin, #1484	6.00
CP12	Posting a Broadside, #1477	5.50
CP13	Copernicus, #1488	5.50
CP14	Postal Service Employees, #1489-1498	5.25
CP15	Harry S Truman, #1499	7.50
CP16	Postrider, #1478	5.00
CP17	Boston Tea Party, #1483a	15.00
CP18	Electronics Progress, #1500-1502, C86	5.50
CP19	Robinson Jeffers, #1485	5.50
CP20	Lyndon B. Johnson, #1503	5.00
CP21	Henry O. Tanner, #1486	5.50
CP22	Willa Cather, #1487	5.50
CP23	Drummer, #1479	8.25
CP24	Angus and Longhorn Cattle, #1504	5.50
CP25	Christmas (Madonna), #1507	8.75
CP26	Christmas Tree, needlepoint, #1508	8.75

1974

CP27	Veterans of Foreign Wars, #1525	5.75
CP28	Robert Frost, #1526	5.75
CP29	EXPO)74, #1527	6.50
CP30	Horse Racing, #1528	7.00
CP31	Skylab, #1529	8.50
CP32	Universal Postal Union, #1537a	7.00
CP33	Mineral Heritage, #1541a	5.00
CP34	Kentucky Settlement (Ft. Harrod), #1542	5.75
CP35	First Continental Congress, #1546a	7.00
CP36	Chautauqua, #1505	5.75
CP37	Kansas Wheat, #1506	5.75
CP38	Energy Conservation, #1547	5.75
CP39	Sleepy Hollow Legend, #1548	5.75
CP40	Retarded Children, #1549	5.75
CP41	Christmas (Currier-Ives), #1551	8.50
CP42	Christmas (angel), #1550	8.50

1975

CP43	Benjamin West, #1553	5.50
CP44	Pioneer 10, #1556	8.50
CP45	Collective Bargaining, #1558	5.75
CP46	Contributors to the Cause, #1559-1562	5.50
CP47	Mariner 10, #1557	6.50
CP48	Lexington-Concord Battle, #1563	6.25
CP49	Paul Laurence Dunbar, #1554	7.00
CP50	D. W. Griffith, #1555	5.75
CP51	Battle of Bunker Hill, #1564	6.25
CP52	Military Services (uniforms), #1568a	5.00
CP53	Apollo Soyuz, #1569a	8.25
CP54	World Peace through Law, #1576	5.50
CP55	International Women's Year, #1571	5.75
CP56	Postal Service 200 Years, #1575a	7.00
CP57	Banking and Commerce, #1577a	7.00
CP58	Early Christmas Card, #1580	7.75
CP59	Christmas (Madonna), #1579	7.75

1976

CP60	Spirit of '76, #1631a	8.50
CP61	Interphil '76, #1632	7.50
CP62	State Flags, block of 4 from #1633-1682	9.50
CP63	Telephone Centenary, #1683	6.75
CP64	Commercial Aviation, #1684	9.25
CP65	Chemistry, #1685	8.00
CP66	Benjamin Franklin, #1690	7.75
CP67	Declaration of Independence, #1694a	7.50
CP68	12th Winter Olympics, #1698a	7.50
CP69	Clara Maass, #1699	7.00
CP70	Adolph S. Ochs, #1700	8.25
CP71	Christmas (Currier print), #1702	8.75
CP72	Christmas (Copley Nativity), #1701	8.75

1977

CP73	Washington at Princeton, #1704	10.00
CP74	Sound Recording, #1705	17.50
CP75	Pueblo Art, #1709a	55.00
CP76	Lindbergh Flight, #1710	60.00
CP77	Colorado Statehood, #1711	14.00
CP78	Butterflies, #1715a	14.00
CP79	Lafayette, #1716	14.00
CP80	Skilled Hands for Independence, #1720a	14.00
CP81	Peace Bridge, #1721	14.00
CP82	Battle of Oriskany, #1722	14.00
CP83	Energy Conservation-Development, #1723a	14.00
CP84	Alta California, #1725	14.00
CP85	Articles of Confederation, #1726	15.00
CP86	Talking Pictures, #1727	15.00
CP87	Surrender at Saratoga, #1728	15.00
CP88	Christmas (Washington at Valley Forge), #1729	14.00
CP89	Christmas (rural mailbox), #1730	25.00

1978

CP90	Carl Sandburg, #1731	8.00
CP91	Captain Cook, #1732a	14.00
CP92	Harriet Tubman, #1744	8.50
CP93	American Quilts, #1748a	15.00
CP94	American Dance, #1752a	10.00
CP95	French Alliance, #1753	10.00
CP96	Pap Test, #1754	8.25
CP97	Jimmie Rodgers, #1755	11.00
CP98	Photography, #1758	8.00
CP99	George M. Cohan, #1756	14.00
CP100	Viking Missions, #1759	26.00
CP101	American Owls, #1763a	26.00
CP102	American Trees, #1767a	26.00
CP103	Christmas (Madonna), #1768	12.00
CP104	Christmas (hobby-horse), #1769	12.00

1979

CP105	Robert F. Kennedy, #1770	7.25
CP106	Martin Luther King, Jr., #1771	7.50
CP107	Year of the Child, #1772	6.75
CP108	John Steinbeck, #1773	6.75
CP109	Albert Einstein, #1774	7.25
CP110	Pennsylvania Toleware, #1778a	6.75
CP111	American Architecture, #1782a	6.50
CP112	Endangered Flora, #1786a	8.00
CP113	Seeing Eye Dogs, #1787	8.00
CP114	Special Olympics, #1788	8.00
CP115	John Paul Jones, #1789	8.25
CP116	Olympic Games, #1794a	9.50
CP117	Christmas (Madonna), #1799	9.50
CP118	Christmas (Santa Claus), #1800	9.50
CP119	Will Rogers, #1801	8.00
CP120	Viet Nam Veterans, #1802	9.50
CP121	10c, 31c Olympics, #1790, C97	10.00

1980

CP122	Winter Olympics, #1798a	7.50
CP123	W.C Fields, #1803	7.50
CP124	Benjamin Banneker, #1804	10.00
CP125	Frances Perkins, #1821	6.00
CP126	Emily Bissell, #1823	6.00
CP127	Helen Keller, #1824	6.00
CP128	Veterans Administration, #1825	6.00
CP129	Galvez, #1826	6.00
CP130	Coral Reefs, #1830a	8.00
CP131	Organized Labor, #1831	6.00
CP132	Edith Wharton, #1832	6.00
CP133	Education, #1833	6.00
CP134	Indian Masks, #1837a	6.00
CP135	Architecture, #1841a	6.75
CP136	Christmas Window, #1842	9.00
CP137	Christmas Toys, #1843	6.50

1981

CP138	Dirksen, #1874	7.00
CP139	Young, #1875	7.00
CP140	Flowers, #1879a	8.00
CP141	Red Cross, #1910	7.50
CP142	Savings and Loan, #1911	6.75
CP143	Space Achievements, #1919a	10.00
CP144	Management, #1920	6.75
CP145	Wildlife, #1924a	10.50
CP146	Disabled, #1925	6.25
CP147	Millay, #1926	6.25
CP148	Architecture, #1931a	6.50
CP149	Zaharias, Jones, #1932, 1933	15.00
CP150	Remington, #1934	6.75
CP151	18c, 20c Hoban, #1935, 1936	6.75
CP152	Yorktown, Va. Capes, #1938a	6.75

1982

CP153	Madonna and Child, #1939	9.25
CP154	Teddy Bear, #1940	6.50
CP155	John Hanson, #1941	7.00
CP156	Desert Plants, #1945a	8.00
CP157	FDR, #1950	8.25
CP158	Love, #1951	10.00
CP159	Washington, #1952	9.50
CP160	Birds and Flowers, block of 4 from #1953-2002	17.00
CP161	US-Netherlands, #2003	10.00
CP162	Library of Congress, #2004	10.50
CP163	Knoxville World's Fair, #2009a	10.00
CP164	Horatio Alger, #2010	8.75
CP165	Aging, #2011	11.00
CP166	Barrymores, #2012	12.00
CP167	Dr. Mary Walker, #2013	10.00
CP168	Peace Garden, #2014	11.00
CP169	Libraries, #2015	11.00
CP170	Jackie Robinson, #2016	24.00
CP171	Touro Synagogue, #2017	10.50
CP172	Wolf Trap Farm, #2018	12.00
CP173	Architecture, #2022a	12.00
CP174	Francis of Assisi, #2023	12.00
CP175	Ponce de Leon, #2024	12.00
CP176	Puppy, Kitten, #2025	14.00
CP177	Madonna and Child, #2026	14.00
CP178	Children Playing, #2030a	14.00

1983

CP179	Science, #2031	5.25
CP180	Ballooning, #2035a	6.00
CP181	US-Sweden, #2036	5.75
CP182	CCC, #2037	5.25
CP183	Priestley, #2038	5.25
CP184	Voluntarism, #2039	4.50
CP185	German Immigration, #2040	5.25
CP186	Brooklyn Bridge, #2041	6.00
CP187	TVA, #2042	5.25
CP188	Fitness, #2043	4.25
CP189	Scott Joplin, #2044	9.00
CP190	Medal of Honor, #2045	6.50
CP191	Babe Ruth, #2046	10.00
CP192	Hawthorne, #2047	5.75
CP193	13c Olympics, #2051a	8.00
CP194	28c Olympics, #C104a	6.50
CP195	40c Olympics, #C108a	6.50
CP196	35c Olympics, #C112a	8.00
CP197	Treaty of Paris, #2052	6.50
CP198	Civil Service, #2053	6.50
CP199	Metropolitan Opera, #2054	6.50
CP200	Inventors, #2058a	6.75
CP201	Streetcars, #2062a	8.00
CP202	Madonna and Child, #2063	8.75
CP203	Santa Claus, #2064	8.75
CP204	Martin Luther, #2065	8.00

1984

CP205	Alaska, #2066	4.50
CP206	Winter Olympics, #2070a	5.00
CP207	FDIC, #2071	4.75
CP208	Love, #2072	4.00
CP209	Woodson, #2073	6.75
CP210	Conservation, #2074	4.75
CP211	Credit Union, #2075	4.75
CP212	Orchids, #2079a	6.75
CP213	Hawaii, #2080	6.25
CP214	National Archives, #2081	4.50
CP215	Olympics, #2085a	6.75
CP216	World Expo, #2086	6.00
CP217	Health Research, #2087	4.75
CP218	Fairbanks, #2088	5.25
CP219	Thorpe, #2089	8.25
CP220	McCormack, #2090	4.75
CP221	St. Lawrence Seaway, #2091	6.25
CP222	Waterfowl, #2092	7.50
CP223	Roanoke Voyages, #2093	4.75
CP224	Melville, #2094	4.75
CP225	Horace Moses, #2095	5.25
CP226	Smokey Bear, #2096	5.00
CP227	Roberto Clemente, #2097	20.00
CP228	Dogs, #2101a	6.25
CP229	Crime Prevention, #2102	5.25
CP230	Hispanic Americans, #2103	5.25
CP231	Family Unity, #2104	6.25
CP232	Eleanor Roosevelt, #2105	5.50
CP233	Readers, #2106	5.50
CP234	Madonna and Child, #2107	6.75
CP235	Child's Santa, #2108	6.75
CP236	Vietnam Memorial, #2109	8.25

1985

CP237	Jerome Kern, #2110	5.75
CP238	Bethune, #2137	7.00
CP239	Duck Decoys, #2141a	7.25
CP240	Winter Special Olympics, #2142	6.00
CP241	Love, #2143	5.00
CP242	REA, #2144	5.00
CP243	AMERIPEX '86, #2145	6.75
CP244	Abigail Adams, #2146	4.75
CP245	Bartholdi, #2147	6.50
CP246	Korean Veterans, #2152	6.25
CP247	Social Security, #2153	5.00
CP248	World War I Veterans, #2154	5.75
CP249	Horses, #2158a	9.00

CP250	Education, #2159	4.50
CP251	Youth Year, #2163a	6.75
CP252	Hunger, #2164	5.00
CP253	Madonna and Child, #2165	8.00
CP254	Poinsettias, #2166	5.00

1986

CP255	Arkansas, #2167	5.25
CP256	Stamp Collecting booklet pane, #2201a	6.75
CP257	Love, #2202	5.00
CP258	Sojourner Truth, #2203	7.50
CP259	Texas Republic, #2204	6.25
CP260	Fish booklet pane, #2209a	6.75
CP261	Hospitals, #2210	4.75
CP262	Duke Ellington, #2211	7.50
CP263	Presidents Souvenir Sheet No. 1, #2216	6.25
CP264	Presidents Souvenir Sheet No. 2, #2217	6.25
CP265	Presidents Souvenir Sheet No. 3, #2218	6.25
CP266	Presidents Souvenir Sheet No. 4, #2219	6.25
CP267	Arctic Explorers, #2223a	6.75
CP268	Statue of Liberty, #2224	7.50
CP269	Navajo Art, #2238a	6.75
CP270	T.S. Eliot, #2239	6.25
CP271	Woodcarved Figurines, #2243a	6.00
CP272	Madonna and Child, #2244	5.75
CP273	Village Scene, #2245	5.75

1987

CP274	Michigan, #2246	5.75
CP275	Pan American Games, #2247	3.50
CP276	Love, #2248	7.00
CP277	du Sable, #2249	5.00
CP278	Caruso, #2250	3.50
CP279	Girl Scouts, #2251	6.00
CP280	Special Occasions booklet pane, #2274a	6.00
CP281	United Way, #2275	4.75
CP282	Wildlife, #2286, 2287, 2296, 2297, 2306, 2307, 2316, 2317, 2326, 2327	6.50
CP283	Wildlife, #2288, 2289, 2298, 2299, 2308, 2309, 2318, 2319, 2328, 2329	6.50
CP284	Wildlife, #2290, 2291, 2300, 2301, 2310, 2311, 2320, 2321, 2330, 2331	6.50
CP285	Wildlife, #2292, 2293, 2302, 2303, 2312, 2313, 2322, 2323, 2332, 2333	6.50
CP286	Wildlife, #2294, 2295, 2304, 2305, 2314, 2315, 2324, 2325, 2334, 2335	6.50

1987-90

CP287	Delaware, #2336	5.75
CP288	Pennsylvania, #2337	5.25
CP289	New Jersey, #2338	5.75
CP290	Georgia, #2339	6.25
CP291	Connecticut, #2340	6.25
CP292	Massachusetts, #2341	6.25
CP293	Maryland, #2342	6.25
CP294	South Carolina, #2343	6.25
CP295	New Hampshire, #2344	6.25
CP296	Virginia, #2345	6.25
CP297	New York, #2346	6.25
CP298	North Carolina, #2347	6.25
CP299	Rhode Island, #2348	6.75

1987

CP300	U.S.-Morocco, #2349	4.75
CP301	William Faulkner, #2350	4.75
CP302	Lacemaking, #2354a	4.75
CP303	Drafting of the Constitution booklet pane, #2359a	4.75
CP304	Signing of the Constitution, #2360	4.75
CP305	Certified Public Accounting, #2361	5.75
CP306	Locomotives booklet pane, #2366a	5.75
CP307	Madonna and Child, #2367	6.25
CP308	Christmas Ornaments, #2368	5.75

1988

CP309	Winter Olympics, #2369	6.25
CP310	Australia Bicentennial, #2370	5.75
CP311	James Weldon Johnson, #2371	5.00
CP312	Cats, #2375a	6.50
CP313	Knute Rockne, #2376	9.50
CP314	New Sweden, #C117	5.75
CP315	Francis Ouimet, #2377	12.00
CP316	25c, 45c Love, #2378 and #2379	7.00
CP317	Summer Olympics, #2380	6.25
CP318	Classic Automobiles booklet pane, #2385a	6.75
CP319	Antarctic Explorers, #2389a	6.25
CP320	Carousel Animals, #2393a	6.75
CP321	Special Occasions booklet singles, #2395-2398	6.75
CP322	Madonna and Child, Sleigh, #2399, 2400	7.00

1989

CP323	Montana, #2401	6.25
CP324	A. Philip Randolph, #2402	8.75
CP325	North Dakota, #2403	6.25
CP326	Washington Statehood, #2404	6.25
CP327	Steamboats booklet pane, #2409a	8.00
CP328	World Stamp Expo, #2410	6.25
CP329	Arturo Toscanini, #2411	6.25

1989-90

CP330	House of Representatives, #2412	7.25
CP331	Senate, #2413	7.25
CP332	Executive Branch, #2414	7.25
CP333	Supreme Court, #2415	7.25

1989

CP334	South Dakota, #2416	6.25
CP335	Lou Gehrig, #2417	15.00
CP336	French Revolution, #C120	7.50
CP337	Ernest Hemingway, #2418	7.25
CP338	Letter Carriers, #2420	7.25
CP339	Bill of Rights, #2421	7.25
CP340	Dinosaurs, #2425a	12.50
CP341	Pre-Columbian Artifacts, #2426, C121	7.25
CP342	Madonna, Sleigh with Presents, #2427, 2428	8.50
CP343	Traditional Mail Delivery, #2437a	7.25
CP344	Futuristic Mail Delivery, #C125a	8.00

1990

CP345	Idaho, #2439	7.25
CP346	Love, #2440	7.25
CP347	Ida B. Wells, #2442	11.00
CP348	Wyoming, #2444	6.25
CP349	Classic Films, #2448a	9.25
CP350	Marianne Moore, #2449	6.25
CP351	Lighthouses booklet pane, #2474a	10.00
CP352	Olympians, #2500a	10.00
CP353	Indian Headdresses booklet pane, #2505c	10.00
CP354	Micronesia, Marshall Islands, #2507a	8.75
CP355	Sea Creatures, #2511a	13.00
CP356	Grand Canyon & Tropical Coastline, #2512, C127	7.50
CP357	Eisenhower, #2513	8.25
CP358	Madonna and Child, Christmas Tree, #2514-2515	9.50

1991

CP359	Switzerland, #2532	8.75
CP360	Vermont Statehood, #2533	7.25
CP361	Savings Bonds, #2534	6.25
CP362	Love, #2535-2536	8.00
CP363	William Saroyan, #2538	7.50
CP364	Fishing Flies, #2549a	12.50
CP365	Cole Porter, #2550	8.00
CP366	Antarctic Treaty, C130	8.00
CP367	Operations Desert Shield & Desert Storm, #2551	20.00
CP368	Summer Olympics, #2557a	8.75
CP369	Numismatics, #2558	7.50
CP370	World War II, #2559	12.00
CP371	Basketball, #2560	12.50
CP372	District of Columbia, #2561	8.00
CP373	Comedians, #2566c	9.50
CP374	Jan E. Matzeliger, #2567	7.50
CP375	Space Exploration, #2577a	12.50
CP376	Bering Land Bridge, #C131	8.00
CP377	Madonna and Child, Santa in Chimney, #2578-2579	9.50

1992

CP378	Winter Olympics, #2615a	10.00
CP379	World Columbian Stamp Expo '92, #2616	8.75
CP380	W.E.B. DuBois, #2617	8.75
CP381	Love, #2618	8.75
CP382	Olympic Baseball, #2619	25.00
CP383	Voyages of Columbus, #2623a	10.00
CP384	Columbus, #2624-2625	40.00
CP385	Columbus, #2626, 2629	40.00
CP386	Columbus, #2627-2628	40.00
CP387	New York Stock Exchange, #2630	11.00
CP388	Space Accomplishments, #2634a	12.00
CP389	Alaska Highway, #2635	8.75
CP390	Kentucky Statehood, #2636	8.75
CP391	Summer Olympics, #2641a	10.50
CP392	Hummingbirds, #2646a	11.00
CP393	World War II, #2697	11.00
CP394	Wildflowers, #2647, 2648, 2657, 2658, 2667, 2668, 2677, 2678, 2687, 2688	20.00
CP395	Wildflowers, #2649, 2650, 2659, 2660, 2669, 2670, 2679, 2680, 2689, 2690	20.00
CP396	Wildflowers, #2651, 2652, 2661, 2662, 2671, 2672, 2681, 2682, 2691, 2692	20.00
CP397	Wildflowers, #2653, 2654, 2663, 2664, 2673, 2674, 2683, 2684, 2693, 2694	20.00
CP398	Wildflowers, #2655, 2656, 2665, 2666, 2675, 2676, 2685, 2686, 2695, 2696	20.00
CP399	Dorothy Parker, #2698	8.75
CP400	Dr. Theodore von Karman, #2699	10.00
CP401	Minerals, #2703a	9.50
CP402	Juan Rodriguez Cabrillo, #2704	10.00
CP403	Wild Animals, #2709a	12.50
CP404	Madonna and Child, wheeled toys, #2710, 2714a	9.25
CP405	Chinese New Year, #2720	15.00

1993

CP406	Elvis Presley, #2721	22.50
CP407	Space Fantasy, #2745a	14.00
CP408	Percy Lavon Julian, #2746	12.50
CP409	Oregon Trail, #2747	10.50
CP410	World University Games, #2748	11.00
CP411	Grace Kelly, #2749	13.00
CP412	Oklahoma!, #2722	12.00
CP413	Circus, #2753a	12.00
CP414	Cherokee Strip, #2754	9.25
CP415	Dean Acheson, #2755	10.50
CP416	Sports horses, #2759a	13.00
CP417	Garden flowers, #2764a	13.00
CP418	World War II, #2765	13.00
CP419	Hank Williams, #2723	15.00
CP420	Rock & Roll/Rhythm & Blues, #2737b	20.00
CP421	Joe Louis, #2766	20.00
CP422	Broadway Musicals, #2770a	12.50
CP423	National Postal Museum, #2782a	12.00
CP424	American Sign Language, #2784a	12.00
CP425	Country & Western Music, #2778a	15.00
CP426	Christmas, #2789, 2794a	13.00
CP427	Youth Classics, #2788a	13.00
CP428	Mariana Islands, #2804	12.00
CP429	Columbus' Landing in Puerto Rico, #2805	10.50
CP430	AIDS Awareness, #2806	12.00

Starting with No. CP431, panels are shrink wrapped in plastic with cardboard backing. Values are for items with plastic intact.

1994

CP431	Winter Olympics, #2807-2811	12.00
CP432	Edward R. Murrow, #2812	9.50
CP434	Love, #2814	9.50
CP436	Dr. Allison Davis, #2816	10.00
CP437	Chinese New Year, #2817	14.00
CP438	Buffalo Soldiers, #2818	16.00
CP439	Silent Screen Stars, #2828a	14.00

CP440	Garden Flowers, #2829-2833	12.00
CP441	World Cup Soccer, #2837	12.50
CP442	World War II, #2838	15.00
CP443	Norman Rockwell, #2839	13.00
CP444	Moon Landing, #2841	16.00
CP445	Locomotives, #2843-2847	13.00
CP446	George Meany, #2848	10.00
CP447	Popular Singers, #2853a	14.00
CP448	Jazz/Blues Singers, block of 10, 2854-2861	15.00

Block of 10 on No. CP448 may contain different combination of stamps.

CP449	James Thurber, #2862	10.00
CP450	Wonders of the Sea, #2866a	13.00
CP451	Cranes, block of 2 #2868a	13.00
CP453	Christmas Madonna and Child, #2871	10.00
CP454	Christmas stocking, #2872	10.00
CP455	Chinese New Year, #2876	13.00

1995

CP456	Florida Statehood, #2950	12.50
CP457	Earth Day, #2954a	11.00
CP458	Richard M. Nixon, #2955	15.00
CP459	Bessie Coleman, #2956	15.00
CP460	Love, #2957-2958	15.00
CP461	Recreational Sports, #2965a	15.00
CP462	Prisoners of War/Missing in Action, #2966	14.00
CP463	Marilyn Monroe, #2967	20.00
CP464	Texas Statehood, #2968	12.50
CP465	Great Lakes Lighthouses, #2973a	14.00
CP466	United Nations, #2974	11.00
CP467	Carousel Horses, #2979a	17.50
CP468	Woman Suffrage, #2980	11.00
CP469	World War II, #2981	15.00
CP470	Louis Armstrong, #2982	15.00
CP471	Jazz Musicians, #2992a	17.50
CP472	Garden Flowers, #2993-2997	12.50
CP473	Republic of Palau, #2999	12.50
CP474	Naval Academy, #3001	15.00
CP475	Tennessee Williams, #3002	14.00
CP476	Christmas, Madonna and Child, #3003	15.00
CP477	Santa Claus, Children with toys, #3007a	15.00
CP478	James K. Polk, #2587	12.50
CP479	Antique Automobiles, 3023a	17.50

1996

CP480	Utah Statehood, #3024	10.00
CP481	Garden Flowers, #3029a	10.00
CP482	Ernest E. Just, #3058	12.50
CP483	Smithsonian Institution, #3059	10.00
CP484	Chinese New Year, #3060	17.50
CP485	Pioneers of Communication, #3064a	14.00
CP486	Fulbright Scholarships, #3065	10.00
CP487	Summer Olympic Games, #3068, 2 pages	30.00

Beginning with No. CP487, some items contain two pages. One has text and engraved illustrations, the second has the stamp(s).

CP488	Marathon, #3067	15.00
CP489	Georgia O'Keeffe, #3069	10.00
CP490	Tennessee Statehood, #3070	10.00
CP491	Indian Dances, #3076a	17.50
CP492	Prehistoric Animals, #3080a	17.50
CP493	Breast Cancer Awareness, #3081	11.00
CP494	James Dean, #3082	17.50
CP495	Folk Heroes, #3086a	17.50
CP496	Olympic Games, Cent., #3087	12.50
CP497	Iowa Statehood, #3088	10.00
CP498	Rural Free Delivery, #3090	10.00
CP499	Riverboats, #3095a	17.50
CP500	Big Band Leaders, #3099a	17.50
CP501	Songwriters, #3103a	17.50
CP502	F. Scott Fitzgerald, #3104	15.00
CP503	Endangered Species, #3105, 2 pages	30.00
CP504	Computer Technology, #3106	17.50
CP505	Madonna & Child, #3107	15.00
CP506	Family Scenes, #3111a	15.00
CP507	Hanukkah, #3118	15.00
CP507A	Cycling, #3119	20.00

1997

CP508	Chinese New Year, #3120	15.00
CP509	Benjamin O. Davis, Sr., #3121	15.00
CP510	Love Swans, #3123-3124	15.00
CP511	Helping Children Learn, #3125	12.50
CP512	PACIFIC 97 Stagecoach & Ship, #3131a	17.50
CP513	Thornton Wilder, #3134	15.00
CP514	Raoul Wallenberg, #3135	15.00
CP515	Dinosaurs, #3136	20.00
CP516	Bugs Bunny, #3137c	16.00
CP517	PACIFIC 97 Franklin, #3139	50.00
CP518	PACIFIC 97 Washington, #3140	50.00
CP519	Marshall Plan, #3141	12.50
CP520	Classic American Aircraft, #3142, 2 pages	30.00
CP521	Football Coaches, #3146a	17.50
CP522	American Dolls, #3151	22.50
CP523	Humphrey Bogart, #3152	17.50
CP524	"The Stars & Stripes Forever!," #3153	15.00
CP525	Opera Singers, #3157a	15.00
CP526	Composers & Conductors, #3165a	17.50
CP527	Padre Felix Varela, #3166	14.00
CP528	Department of the Air Force, #3167	15.00
CP529	Movie Monsters, #3172a	17.50
CP530	Supersonic Flight, #3173	15.00
CP531	Women in Military Service, #3174	14.00
CP532	Kwanzaa, #3175	15.00
CP533	Madonna & Child, #3176a	22.50
CP534	Holly, #3177a	22.50

1998

CP535	Chinese New Year, #3179	15.00
CP536	Alpine Skiing, #3180	14.00
CP537	Madam C.J. Walker, #3181	15.00

1998-2000

Celebrate the Century

CP537A	1900s, #3182, 2 pages	25.00
CP537B	1910s, #3183, 2 pages	25.00
CP537C	1920s, #3184, 2 pages	25.00
CP537D	1930s, #3185, 2 pages	25.00
CP537E	1940s, #3186, 2 pages	25.00
CP537F	1950s, #3187, 2 pages	25.00
CP537G	1960s, #3188, 2 pages	25.00
CP537H	1970s, #3189, 2 pages	25.00
CP537I	1980s, #3190, 2 pages	25.00

1998

CP538	Remember the Maine,inscribed "Key West, Florida" #3192	15.00
	a. Inscribed "Scottsdale, Arizona."	20.00
CP539	Flowering Trees, #3197a	16.00
CP540	Alexander Calder, #3202a	16.00
CP541	Cinco de Mayo, #3203	14.00
CP542	Sylvester & Tweety, #3204c	17.50
CP543	Wisconsin Statehood, #3206	16.00
CP544	Trans-Mississippi, #3209-3210, 2 pages	20.00
CP545	Berlin Airlift, #3211	14.00
CP546	Folk Musicians, #3215a	16.00
CP547	Gospel Singers, #3219a	14.00
CP548	Spanish Settlement, #3220	16.00

CP549	Stephen Vincent Benét, #3221	15.00
CP550	Tropical Birds, #3225a	16.00
CP551	Alfred Hitchcock, #3226	16.00
CP552	Organ & Tissue Donation, #3227	15.00
CP553	Bright Eyes, #3234a	16.00
CP554	Klondike Gold Rush, #3235	16.00
CP555	American Art, #3236	25.00
CP556	American Ballet, #3237	15.00
CP557	Space Discovery, #3242a	16.00
CP558	Giving & Sharing, #3243	15.00
CP559	Madonna & Child, #3244a	20.00
CP560	Wreaths, #3252a	15.00
CP561	Breast Cancer Awareness, #B1	15.00

1999

CP562	Chinese New Year, #3272	15.00
CP563	Malcolm X, #3273	15.00
CP564	Love, #3274a	20.00
CP565	Love, #3275	15.00
CP566	Hospice Care, #3276	15.00
CP567	Irish Immigration, #3286	15.00
CP568	Lunt & Fontanne, #3287	15.00
CP569	Arctic Animals, #3292a	15.00
CP570	Sonoran Desert, #3293, 2 pages	25.00
CP571	Daffy Duck, #3306c	25.00
CP572	Ayn Rand, #3308	15.00

CP573	Cinco de Mayo, #3309	15.00
CP574	John & William Bartram, #3314	15.00
CP575	Prostate Cancer, #3315	16.00
CP576	California Gold Rush, #3316	16.00
CP577	Aquarium Fish, #3320a	16.00
CP578	Extreme Sports, #3324a	16.00
CP579	American Glass, #3328a	16.00
CP580	James Cagney, #3329	16.00
CP581	Honoring Those who Served, #3331	16.00
CP582	Famous Trains, #3337a	16.00
CP583	Frederick Law Olmsted, #3338	16.00
CP584	Hollywood Composers, #3344a	16.00
CP585	Broadway Songwriters, #3350a	16.00
CP586	Insects & Spiders, #3351, 2 pages	25.00
CP587	Hanukkah, #3352	16.00
CP588	NATO, #3354	16.00
CP589	Madonna & Child, #3355	16.00
CP590	Deer, #3359a	16.00
CP591	Kwanzaa, #3368	16.00
CP592	Year 2000, #3369	16.00

2000

CP593	Chinese New Year, #3370	16.00
CP594	Patricia Roberts Harris, #3371	16.00

SOUVENIR PAGES

These are post office new-issue announcement bulletins, including an illustration of the stamp's design and informative text. They bear a copy of the stamp, tied by a first day of issue cancellation. Varieties of bulletin watermarks and text changes, etc., are beyond the scope of this catalogue.
    Values for Scott Nos. SP1-SP295 are for folded copies. Values for Official Souvenir Pages (Nos. SP296 on) are for copies that never have been folded.

No. 674a

UNOFFICIAL SOUVENIR PAGES
Liberty Issue

1960-65

SP1	1¼c Palace of Governors, sheet, coil, #1031A, 1054A	50.00
SP2	8c Pershing, #1042A	30.00
SP3	11c Statue of Liberty, #1044A	27.50
SP4	25c Revere coil, #1059A	6.00

1959

SP5	4c 49 Star Flag, #1132	—
SP6	7c Hawaii Statehood, #C55	—
SP7	4c Soil Conservation, #1133	—
SP8	10c Pan American Games, #C56	—
SP9	4c Petroleum, #1134	—
SP10	4c Dental Health, #1135	—
SP11	4c, 8c Reuter, #1136, 1137	—
SP12	4c McDowell, #1138	—

1960-61

SP13	4c Washington Credo, #1139	75.00
SP14	4c Franklin Credo, #1140	75.00
SP15	4c Jefferson Credo, #1141	75.00
SP16	4c F.S. Key Credo, #1142	75.00
SP17	4c Lincoln Credo, #1143	65.00
SP18	4c P. Henry Credo, #1144	35.00

1961

SP19	4c Boy Scout, #1145	75.00
SP20	4c Winter Olympics, #1146	75.00
SP21	4c, 8c Masaryk, #1147, 1148	75.00
SP22	4c Refugee Year, #1149	35.00
SP23	4c Water Consevation, #1150	20.00
SP24	4c SEATO, #1151	20.00
SP25	4c American Women, #1152	20.00

SP26	10c Liberty Bell, #C57	—
SP27	15c Statue of Liberty, #C58	—
SP28	25c Lincoln, #C59	—
SP29	4c 50 Star Flag, #1153	50.00
SP30	4c Pony Express, #1154	50.00
SP31	7c Jet, carmine, #C60	12.50
SP32	7c Booklet pane of 6, #C60a	30.00
SP33	7c Jet coil, #C61	17.50
SP34	4c Handicapped, #1155	50.00
SP35	4c Forestry Congress, #1156	50.00
SP36	4c Mexican Independence, #1157	35.00
SP37	4c U.S., Japan Treaty, #1158	20.00
SP38	4c, 8c Paderewski, #1159-1160	37.50
SP39	4c Sen. Taft, #1161	45.00
SP40	4c Wheels of Freedom, #1162	45.00
SP41	4c Boys' Clubs, #1163	45.00
SP42	4c Automated Post Office, #1164	45.00
SP43	4c, 8c Mannerheim, #1165-1166	45.00
SP44	4c Camp Fire Girls, #1167	45.00
SP45	4c, 8c Garibaldi, #1168-1169	45.00
SP46	4c Sen. George, #1170	45.00
SP47	4c Carnegie, #1171	45.00
SP48	4c Dulles, #1172	45.00
SP49	4c Echo I, #1173	20.00

1961

SP50	4c, 8c Gandhi, #1174-1175	20.00
SP51	4c Range Conservation, #1176	20.00
SP52	4c Greeley, #1177	20.00

1961-65

SP53	4c Ft. Sumter, #1178	20.00
SP54	4c Shiloh, #1179	27.50
SP55	5c Gettysburg, #1180	6.00
SP56	5c Wilderness, #1181	6.50
SP57	5c Appomattox, #1182	6.50

1961

SP58	4c Kansas, #1183	12.00
SP59	13c Liberty Bell, #C62	20.00
SP60	4c Sen. Norris, #1184	11.50
SP61	4c Naval Aviation, #1185	20.00
SP62	4c Workmen's Compensation, #1186	20.00
SP63	4c Remington, #1187	12.00
SP64	4c Sun Yat sen, #1188	20.00
SP65	4c Basketball, #1189	20.00
SP66	4c Nursing, #1190	15.00

1962

SP67	4c New Mexico, #1191	12.50
SP68	4c Arizona, #1192	12.50
SP69	4c Project Mercury, #1193	10.00
SP70	4c Malaria, #1194	12.50
SP71	4c Hughes, #1195	21.00
SP72	4c Seattle World's Fair, #1196	17.50
SP73	4c Louisiana, #1197	17.50
SP74	4c Homestead Act, #1198	17.50
SP75	4c Girl Scouts, #1199	20.00
SP76	4c McMahon, #1200	17.50
SP77	4c Apprenticeship, #1201	17.50
SP78	4c Rayburn, #1202	17.50
SP79	4c Hammarskjold, #1203	17.50
SP80	4c Hammarskjold, yellow inverted, #1204	40.00
SP81	4c Christmas, #1205	50.00
SP82	4c Higher Education, #1206	10.00
SP83	8c Capitol, #C64	9.00
SP83a	8c Capitol sheet, booklet, coil, #C64, C64b, C65	20.00
SP84	8c Capitol, tagged, #C64a	30.00
SP85	8c Capitol booklet single, #C64b	25.00
SP86	8c Capitol coil, #C65	15.00
SP87	4c Winslow Homer, #1207	15.00
SP88	5c Flag, #1208	12.50

SP89	1c Jackson, #1209	12.50
SP90	5c Washington, #1213	17.50
SP91	5c Washington booklet pane of 5 + label, #1213a	30.00
SP92	1c Jackson coil, #1225	17.50
SP93	5c Washington coil, #1229	17.50
SP94	15c Montgomery Blair, #C66	—

1963

SP96	5c Food for Peace, #1231	7.00
SP97	5c West Virginia, #1232	6.00
SP97A	6c Eagle, #C67	8.50
SP97B	8c Amelia Earhart, #C68	18.00
SP98	5c Emancipation Proclamation, #1233	12.50
SP99	5c Alliance for Progress, #1234	7.50
SP100	5c Cordell Hull, #1235	7.50
SP101	5c Eleanor Roosevelt, #1236	6.25
SP102	5c Science, #1237	6.00
SP103	5c City Mail Delivery, #1238	7.50
SP104	5c Red Cross, #1239	6.00
SP105	5c Christmas, #1240	7.50
SP106	5c Audubon, #1241	8.00

1964

SP107	5c Sam Houston, #1242	12.00
SP108	5c C.M. Russell, #1243	9.00
SP109	5c N.Y. World's Fair, #1244	7.50
SP110	5c John Muir, #1245	12.00
SP111	5c Kennedy (Boston, Mass.) (At least 4 other cities known), #1246	12.50
SP112	5c New Jersey, #1247	7.50
SP113	5c Nevada, #1248	7.50
SP114	5c Register and Vote, #1249	7.50
SP115	5c Shakespeare, #1250	7.50
SP116	5c Mayo Brothers, #1251	8.50
SP117	8c Goddard, #C69	5.00
SP118	5c Music, #1252	7.50
SP119	5c Homemakers, #1253	7.50
SP120	5c Christmas Plants, #1257b	17.50
SP121	5c Christmas, tagged, #1257c	90.00
SP122	5c Verrazano Narrows Bridge, #1258	7.50
SP123	5c Fine Arts, #1259	7.50
SP124	5c Amateur Radio, #1260	7.00

1965

SP125	5c New Orleans, #1261	6.00
SP126	5c Sokols, #1262	6.75
SP127	5c Cancer, #1263	6.00
SP128	5c Churchill, #1264	7.50
SP129	5c Magna Carta, #1265	6.00
SP130	5c I.C.Y., #1266	6.00
SP131	5c Salvation Army, #1267	6.50
SP132	5c Dante, #1268	6.00
SP133	5c Hoover, #1269	6.00
SP134	5c Fulton, #1270	6.00
SP135	5c Florida, #1271	7.50
SP136	5c Traffic Safety, #1272	6.00
SP137	5c Copley, #1273	7.50
SP138	11c I.T.U., #1274	7.50
SP139	5c Stevenson, #1275	6.00
SP140	5c Christmas, #1276	7.50

Prominent Americans

1965-73

SP141	1c Jefferson, #1278	7.50
SP141a	1c Jefferson sheet, booklet, coil, #1278, 1278a 1299	7.00
SP142	1c Jefferson booklet pane of 8, #1278a	8.25
SP143	1¼c Gallatin, #1279	7.50
SP144	2c Wright, #1280	5.25

SP145	2c Wright booklet pane of 5 + label, #1280a	9.50
SP146	3c Parkman, #1281	7.50
SP147	4c Lincoln, #1282	6.00
SP148	5c Washington, #1283	6.00
SP149	5c Washington, redrawn, #1283B	6.50
SP150	6c Roosevelt, #1284	6.00
SP151	6c Roosevelt booklet pane of 8, #1284b	13.00
SP151a	6c Roosevelt booklet, vert. coil, #1284b, 1298	5.00
SP151b	6c Roosevelt booklet, horiz. coil, #1284b, 1305	5.00
SP152	8c Einstein, #1285	10.00
SP153	10c Jackson, #1286	6.00
SP154	12c Ford, #1286A	9.00
SP155	13c Kennedy, #1287	20.00
SP156	15c Holmes, #1288	7.50
SP157	20c Marshall, #1289	9.00
SP158	25c Douglass, #1290	9.00
SP159	30c Dewey, #1291	30.00
SP160	40c Paine, #1292	40.00
SP161	50c Stone, #1293	35.00
SP162	$1 O'Neill, #1294	55.00
SP163	$5 Moore, #1295	125.00
SP164	6c Roosevelt, vert. coil, #1298	5.25
SP165	1c Jefferson, coil, #1299	5.75
SP166	4c Lincoln, coil, #1303	7.50
SP167	5c Washington, coil, #1304	7.00
SP168	6c Roosevelt, horiz. coil, #1305	6.50

Nos. 1297, 1305C and 1305E are known on unofficial pages. They are not listed here. For official pages of these issues, see Nos. SP296-SP298.

1966

SP169	5c Migratory Bird Treaty, #1306	7.00
SP170	5c ASPCA, #1307	7.00
SP171	5c Indiana, #1308	7.00
SP172	5c Circus, #1309	6.00
SP173	5c SIPEX, #1310	7.00
SP174	5c SIPEX Souvenir Sheet, #1311	7.25
SP175	5c Bill of Rights, #1312	7.50
SP176	5c Poland, #1313	7.50
SP177	5c National Park Service, #1314	7.50
SP178	5c Marine Corps Reserve, #1315	7.50
SP179	5c Women's Clubs, #1316	7.50
SP180	5c Johnny Appleseed, #1317	7.50
SP181	5c Beautification of America, #1318	7.50
SP182	5c Great River Road, #1319	7.50
SP183	5c Savings Bonds Servicemen, #1320	7.50
SP184	5c Christmas, #1321	6.00
SP185	5c Mary Cassatt, #1322	6.00

1967

SP186	8c Alaska, #C70	10.00
SP187	5c Grange, #1323	6.00
SP188	20c Audubon, #C71	4.00
SP189	5c Canada, #1324	5.25
SP190	5c Erie Canal, #1325	5.25
SP191	5c Search for Peace, #1326	6.50
SP192	5c Thoreau, #1327	5.50
SP193	5c Nebraska, #1328	5.25
SP194	5c VOA, #1329	5.25
SP195	5c Crockett, #1330	7.00
SP196	5c Space, #1332b	21.00
SP197	5c Urban Planning, #1333	5.25
SP198	5c Finland, #1334	6.00
SP199	5c Eakins, #1335	6.00
SP200	5c Christmas, #1336	7.00
SP201	5c Mississippi, #1337	5.50

1968-71

SP202	6c Flags, Giori Press, #1338	6.00
SP203	6c Flag, Huck Press, #1338D	5.00
SP204	8c Flag, #1338F	5.50
SP205	6c Flag coil, #1338A	5.75

1968

SP206	10c 50 star Runway, #C72	5.00
SP207	10c sheet, coil, booklet pane of 8, #C72, C72b, C73	25.00
SP207a	10c sheet, booklet single, coil, #C72, C72b, C73	7.00
SP208	10c 50 star Runway coil, #C73	9.00
SP209	6c Illinois, #1339	5.50
SP210	6c HemisFair, #1340	7.50
SP211	$1 Airlift, #1341	60.00
SP212	6c Youth, #1342	6.00
SP213	10c Air Mail Service, #C74	7.25
SP214	6c Law and Order, #1343	6.00
SP215	6c Register and Vote, #1344	6.00
SP216	6c Historic Flags, #1345-1354	70.00
SP217	6c Disney, #1355	10.00
SP218	6c Marquette, #1356	7.50
SP219	6c Daniel Boone, #1357	7.50
SP220	6c Arkansas River Navigation, #1358	7.50
SP221	6c Leif Erikson, #1359	15.00
SP222	6c Cherokee Strip, #1360	7.50
SP223	6c John Trumbull, #1361	6.00
SP224	6c Waterfowl, #1362	7.50
SP225	6c Christmas, #1363	7.50
SP226	6c Chief Joseph, #1364	6.00
SP227	20c USA, #C75	5.00

1969

SP228	6c Beautification, #1368a	18.00
SP229	6c American Legion, #1369	7.50
SP230	6c Grandma Moses, #1370	6.00
SP231	6c Apollo 8, #1371	15.00
SP232	6c W.C. Handy, #1372	10.00
SP233	6c California, #1373	6.00
SP234	6c Powell, #1374	6.00
SP235	6c Alabama, #1375	7.50
SP236	6c Botanical Congress, #1379a	20.00
SP237	10c Man on the Moon, #C76	14.00
SP238	6c Dartmouth, #1380	7.50
SP239	6c Baseball, #1381	40.00

SP240	6c Football, #1382	10.00
SP241	6c Eisenhower, #1383	6.00
SP242	6c Christmas, #1384	7.50
SP243	6c Hope, #1385	6.00
SP244	45c Special Delivery, #E22	25.00
SP245	6c Harnett, #1386	6.00

1970

SP246	6c Natural History, #1390a	30.00
SP247	6c Maine, #1391	7.50
SP248	6c Wildlife Conservation, #1392	7.50

Regular Issue

1970-71

SP249	6c Eisenhower, #1393	6.00
SP249a	6c sheet, booklet, coil stamps, #1393, 1393a, 1401	7.00
SP249b	6c sheet, coil stamps, #1393, 1401	6.00
SP250	6c Eisenhower booklet pane of 8, #1393a	12.50
SP250a	6c booklet, #1393a, 1401	6.00
SP251	6c Eisenhower booklet pane of 5 + label, #1393b	6.00
SP252	8c Eisenhower, #1394	6.00
SP252a	8c sheet, booklet, coil, #1394-1395, 1402	6.00
SP253	8c Eisenhower booklet pane of 8, #1395a	15.00
SP254	8c Eisenhower booklet pane of 8, #1395b	15.00
SP255	8c U.S.P.S., #1396	10.00
SP256	16c Pyle, #1398	6.00
SP257	6c Eisenhower coil, #1401	6.00
SP258	8c Eisenhower coil, #1402	5.00

1970

SP259	6c Masters, #1405	7.50
SP260	6c Suffrage, #1406	6.00
SP261	6c So. Carolina, #1407	6.00
SP262	6c Stone Mountain, #1408	6.00
SP263	6c Ft. Snelling, #1409	6.00
SP264	6c Anti pollution, #1413a	20.00
SP265	6c Christmas Nativity, #1414	13.00
SP266	6c Christmas Toys, #1418b	6.75
SP267	6c Toys, precanceled, #1418c	35.00
SP268	6c U.N., #1419	9.00
SP269	6c Mayflower, #1420	7.50
SP270	6c DAV, Servicemen, #1422a	27.50

1971

SP271	6c Wool, #1423	7.50
SP272	6c MacArthur, #1424	7.50
SP273	6c Blood Donors, #1425	7.50
SP274	8c Missouri, #1426	7.50
SP275	9c Delta Wing, #C77	5.00
SP276	11c Jet, #C78	3.50
SP276a	11c sheet, booklet, coil, #C78, C78a, C82	5.00
SP277	11c Jet booklet pane, #C78a	12.00
SP278	60c Special Delivery, #E23	24.00
SP279	8c Wildlife, #1430a	12.50
SP280	8c Antarctic Treaty, #1431	10.00
SP281	8c Bicentennial Emblem, #1432	12.50
SP282	17c Statue of Liberty, #C80	15.00
SP283	21c USA, #C81	20.00
SP284	11c Jet coil, #C82	3.25
SP285	8c Sloan, #1433	10.00
SP286	8c Space, #1435b	15.00
SP287	8c Dickenson, #1436	10.00
SP288	8c San Juan, #1437	10.00
SP289	8c Drug Abuse, #1438	10.00
SP290	8c CARE, #1439	10.00
SP291	8c Historic Preservation, #1443a	12.50
SP292	8c Adoration, #1444	10.00
SP293	8c Patridge, #1445	10.00

1972

SP294	8c Lanier, #1446	10.00
SP295	8c Peace Corps, #1447	10.00

OFFICIAL SOUVENIR PAGES

In 1972 the USPS began issuing "official" Souvenir pages by subscription. A few more "unofficials" were produced.

Prominent Americans

1970-78

SP296	3c Parkman, coil, #1297	2.50
SP297	$1 O'Neill, coil, #1305C	12.50
SP298	15c Holmes, coil, #1305E	1.90
SP299	7c Franklin, #1393D	6.25
SP300	14c LaGuardia, #1400	75.00
SP301	18c Blackwell, #1399	2.00
SP302	21c Giannini, #1400	4.50

1972

SP303	2c Cape Hatteras, #1451a	75.00
SP304	6c Wolf Trap Farm, #1452	27.50
SP305	8c Yellowstone, #1453	90.00
SP306	11c City of Refuge, #C84	80.00
SP307	15c Mt. McKinley, #1454	20.00
SP308	8c Family Planning, #1455	500.00

Unofficials exist, value $150.

SP309	8c Colonial Craftsmen, #1459a	14.00
SP310	Olympics, #1460-1462, C85	10.50
SP311	8c PTA, #1463	5.50
SP312	8c Wildlife, #1467a	6.75
SP313	8c Mail Order, #1468	5.50
SP314	8c Osteopathic, #1469	5.50
SP315	8c Tom Sawyer, #1470	5.50
SP316	8c Christmas, #1471-1472	6.75
SP317	8c Pharmacy, #1473	10.00
SP318	8c Stamp Collecting, #1474	5.50

1973

SP319	8c Love, #1475	6.50
SP320	8c Printing, #1476	4.25
SP321	8c Broadside, #1477	5.75
SP322	8c Postrider, #1478	5.50
SP323	8c Drummer, #1479	4.00

SP324	8c Tea Party, #1483a	5.50
SP325	8c Gershwin, #1484	5.00
SP326	8c Jeffers, #1485	4.00
SP327	8c Tanner, #1486	5.00
SP328	8c Cather, #1487	3.25
SP329	8c Copernicus, #1488	4.75
SP330	8c Postal People, #1489-1498	5.50
SP331	8c Truman, #1499	4.25
SP332	Electronics, #1500-1502, C86	6.25
SP333	8c L.B. Johnson, #1503	3.50

1973-74

SP334	8c Cattle, #1504	3.50
SP335	10c Chautauqua, #1505	1.90
SP336	10c Kansas Winter Wheat, #1506	1.90

1973

SP337	8c Christmas, #1507	5.75

Regular Issues

1973-74

SP338	10c Crossed Flags, #1509	2.75
SP339	10c Jefferson Memorial, #1510	2.50
SP340	10c ZIP, #1511	3.25
SP341	6.3c Liberty Bell coil, #1518	2.75
SP341A	13c Winged Envelope, #C79	2.75
SP341B	13c Airmail, coil, #C83	2.75

1974

SP342	18c Statue of Liberty, #C87	5.50
SP343	26c Mt. Rushmore, #C88	4.75
SP344	10c VFW, #1525	2.50
SP345	10c Robert Frost, #1526	2.50
SP346	10c EXPO '74, #1527	2.50
SP347	10c Horse Racing, #1528	3.75
SP348	10c Skylab, #1529	5.25
SP349	10c UPU, #1537a	4.75
SP350	10c Minerals, #1541a	5.00
SP351	10c Ft. Harrod, #1542	2.50
SP352	10c Continental Congress, #1546a	4.00
SP353	10c Energy, #1547	1.90
SP354	10c Sleepy Hollow, #1548	2.75
SP355	10c Retarded Children, #1549	2.00
SP356	10c Christmas, #1550-1552	5.00

1975

SP357	10c Benjamin West, #1553	2.25
SP358	10c Dunbar, #1554	3.25
SP359	10c D.W. Griffith, #1555	2.50
SP360	10c Pioneer, #1556	5.00
SP361	10c Mariner, #1557	4.25
SP362	10c Collective Bargaining, #1558	2.50
SP363	8c Sybil Ludington, #1559	2.50
SP364	10c Salem Poor, #1560	2.50
SP365	10c Haym Salomon, #1561	2.75
SP366	15c Peter Francisco, #1562	3.25
SP367	10c Lexington & Concord, #1563	2.50
SP368	10c Bunker Hill, #1564	2.50
SP369	10c Military Uniforms, #1568a	5.00
SP370	10c Apollo Soyuz, #1570a	5.00
SP371	10c Women's Year, #1571	2.00
SP372	10c Postal Service, #1575	3.25
SP373	10c Peace through Law, #1576	2.00
SP374	10c Banking and Commerce, #1578a	2.00
SP375	10c Christmas, #1579-1580	3.00

Americana Issue

1975-81

SP376	1c, 2c, Americana, #1581-1585 3c, 4c	2.00
SP377	9c Capitol Dome, #1591	2.00
SP378	10c Justice, #1592	2.25
SP379	11c Printing Press, #1593	2.00
SP380	12c Torch sheet, coil, #1594, 1816	1.90
SP381	13c Eagle and Shield, #1596	2.50
SP382	15c Flag sheet, coil, #1597, 1618C	2.00
SP383	16c Statue of Liberty sheet, coil, #1599, 1619	1.90
SP384	24c Old North Church, #1603	1.90
SP385	28c Ft. Nisqually, #1604	2.00
SP386	29c Lighthouse, #1605	1.90
SP387	30c Schoolhouse, #1606	3.00
SP388	50c "Betty" Lamp, #1608	3.25
SP389	$1 Candle Holder, #1610	4.25
SP390	$2 Kerosene Lamp, #1611	5.25
SP391	$5 R. R. Lantern, #1612	10.50
SP392	1c Inkwell, coil, #1811	1.60
SP393	3.1c Guitar, coil, #1613	3.50
SP394	3.5c Violin, coil, #1813	2.50
SP395	7.7c Saxhorns, coil, #1614	1.75
SP396	7.9c Drum, coil, #1615	1.90
SP397	8.4c Piano, coil, #1615C	2.00
SP398	9c Capitol Dome, coil, #1616	1.75
SP398A	10c Justice, coil, #1617	2.75
SP399	13c Liberty Bell, coil, #1618	2.00
SP400	13c 13 star Flag sheet, coil, #1622, 1625	2.00
SP401	9c, 13c Booklet pane, perf. 10, #1623Bc	16.00

1976

SP402	13c Spirirt of '76, #1631a	3.25
SP403	25c, 31c Plane and Globes, #C89-C90	2.75
SP404	13c Interphil 76, #1632	2.50
SP405	13c State Flags, #1633-1642	7.00
SP406	13c State Flags, #1643-1652	7.00
SP407	13c State Flags, #1653-1662	7.00
SP408	13c State Flags, #1663-1672	7.00
SP409	13c State Flags, #1673-1682	7.00
SP410	13c Telephone, #1683	1.75
SP411	13c Aviation, #1684	2.00
SP412	13c Chemistry, #1685	1.75
SP413	13c Bicentennial Souvenir Sheet, #1686	8.00
SP414	18c Bicentennial Souvenir Sheet, #1687	8.00
SP415	24c Bicentennial Souvenir Sheet, #1688	8.00

SP416	31c	Bicentennial Souvenir Sheet, #1689	8.00
SP417	13c	Franklin, #1690	1.75
SP418	13c	Declaration of Independence, #1694a	4.00
SP419	13c	Olympics, #1698a	4.25
SP420	13c	Clara Maass, #1699	1.75
SP421	13c	Adolph Ochs, #1700	1.75
SP422	13c	Christmas, #1701-1703	2.25

1977

SP423	13c	Washington at Princeton, #1704	1.90
SP424	13c	Sound Recording, #1705	1.75
SP425	13c	Pueblo Pottery, #1709a	2.25
SP426	13c	Lindbergh Flight, #1710	2.75
SP427	13c	Colorado, #1711	1.90
SP428	13c	Butterflies, #1715a	2.00
SP429	13c	Lafayette, #1716	1.75
SP430	13c	Skilled Hands, #1720a	2.25
SP431	13c	Peace Bridge, #1721	1.60
SP432	13c	Oriskany, #1722	1.60
SP433	13c	Energy, #1724a	1.60
SP434	13c	Alta California, #1725	1.60
SP435	13c	Articles of Confederation, #1726	1.75
SP436	13c	Talking Pictures, #1727	2.50
SP437	13c	Saratoga, #1728	2.50
SP438	13c	Christmas, #1729-1730	2.00

1978

SP439	13c	Sandburg, #1731	2.00
SP440	13c	Capt. Cook, #1732, 1733	4.00
SP441	13c	Indian Head Penny, #1734	2.00
SP442	15c	A Sheet, coil, #1735, 1743	4.50
SP443	15c	Roses booklet single, #1737	2.50
SP444	15c	Windmills booklet pane of 10, #1742a	4.00
SP445	13c	Tubman, #1744	3.00
SP446	13c	Quilts, #1748a	2.50
SP447	13c	American Dance, #1752a	2.50
SP448	13c	French Alliance, #1753	1.90
SP449	13c	Cancer Detection, #1754	2.50
SP450	13c	Jimmie Rodgers, #1755	3.00
SP451	15c	George M. Cohan, #1756	1.60
SP452	13c	CAPEX '78 Souvenir Sheet, #1757	6.25
SP453	15c	Photography, #1758	1.90
SP454	15c	Viking Missions, #1759	3.75
SP455	15c	Owls, #1763a	2.50
SP456	31c	Wright Brothers, #C92a	2.75
SP457	15c	Trees, #1767a	2.75
SP458	15c	Madonna and Child, #1768	2.00
SP459	15c	Hobby Horse, #1769	2.00

1979

SP460	15c	Robert F. Kennedy, #1770	2.00
SP461	15c	Martin Luther King Jr., #1771	3.50
SP462	15c	Year of the Child, #1772	1.90
SP463	15c	John Steinbeck, #1773	1.90
SP464	15c	Einstein, #1774	2.00
SP465	21c	Chanute, #C94a	2.75
SP466	15c	Toleware, #1778a	2.25
SP467	15c	Architecture, #1782a	2.25
SP468	15c	Endangered Flora, #1786a	2.25
SP469	15c	Seeing Eye Dogs, #1787	1.90
SP470	15c	Special Olympics, #1788	1.90
SP471	15c	John Paul Jones, #1789	2.00
SP472	10c	Olympics, #1790	2.75
SP473	15c	Olympics, #1794a	3.75
SP474	31c	Olympics, #C97	4.00

1980

SP475	15c	Winter Olympics, #1798a	5.00

1979

SP476	15c	Madonna and Child, #1799	2.50
SP477	15c	Santa Claus, #1800	2.50
SP478	15c	Will Rogers, #1801	1.90
SP479	15c	Vietnam Veterans, #1802	1.90
SP480	25c	Wiley Post, #C96a	3.25

1980

SP481	15c	W.C. Fields, #1803	2.00
SP482	15c	Benjamin Banneker, #1804	3.50
SP483	15c	Letter Writing Week, #1805-1810	2.25
SP484	18c	B sheet, coil, #1818, 1820	2.00
SP485	18c	B booklet pane of 8, #1819a	2.25
SP486	15c	Frances Perkins, #1821	1.50
SP487	15c	Dolley Madison, #1822	3.00
SP488	15c	Emily Bissell, #1823	1.90
SP489	15c	Helen Keller, #1824	1.90
SP490	15c	Veterans Administration, #1825	1.90
SP491	15c	Galvez, #1826	1.50
SP492	15c	Coral Reefs, #1830a	1.90
SP493	15c	Organized Labor, #1831	3.25
SP494	15c	Edith Wharton, #1832	3.00
SP495	15c	Education, #1833	3.00
SP496	15c	Indian Masks, #1837a	2.50
SP497	15c	Architecture, #1841a	1.90
SP498	40c	Mazzei, #C98	2.75
SP499	15c	Christmas Window, #1842	2.50
SP500	15c	Christmas Toys, #1843	2.50
SP501	28c	Blanche Stuart Scott, #C99	1.60
SP502	35c	Curtiss, #C100	1.60

Great Americans

1980-85

SP503	1c	Dix, #1844	1.90
SP504	2c	Stravinsky, #1845	2.00
SP505	3c	Clay, #1846	1.40
SP506	4c	Schurz, #1847	1.50
SP507	5c	Buck, #1848	1.60
SP508	6c	Lippmann, #1849	1.75
SP509	7c	Baldwin, #1850	1.90
SP510	8c	Knox, #1851	1.50
SP511	9c	Thayer, #1852	2.00
SP512	10c	Russell, #1853	1.25
SP513	11c	Partridge, #1854	1.50
SP514	13c	Crazy Horse, #1855	1.60
SP515	14c	Lewis, #1856	1.50

SP516	17c	Carson, #1857	1.40
SP517	18c	Mason, #1858	1.50
SP518	19c	Sequoyah, #1859	1.50
SP519	20c	Bunche, #1860	4.00
SP520	20c	Gallaudet, #1861	1.50
SP521	20c	Truman, #1862	1.50
SP522	22c	Audubon, #1863	1.90
SP523	30c	Laubach, #1864	1.40
SP524	35c	Drew, #1865	2.50
SP525	37c	Millikan, #1866	1.40
SP526	39c	Clark, #1867	1.25
SP527	40c	Gilbreth, #1868	1.40
SP528	50c	Nimitz, #1869	1.75

1981

SP529	15c	Dirksen, #1874	1.50
SP530	15c	Young, #1875	3.25
SP531	18c	Flowers, #1879a	2.00
SP532	18c	Animals, #1889a	3.50
SP533	18c	Flag sheet, coil, #1890-1891	2.50
SP534	6c, 18c	Booklet pane, #1893a	2.50
SP535	20c	Flag sheet, coil, #1894-1895	3.75
SP536	20c	Flag booklet pane of 6, #1896a	3.25

1982

SP537	20c	Flag booklet pane of 10, #1896b	3.00

Transportation Coils

1981-84

SP538	1c	Omnibus, #1897	3.50
SP539	2c	Locomotive, #1897A	3.50
SP540	3c	Handcar, #1898	3.25
SP541	4c	Stagecoach, #1898A	4.00
SP542	5c	Motorcycle, #1899	4.75
SP543	5.2c	Sleigh, #1900	4.75
SP544	5.9c	Bicycle, #1901	5.75
SP545	7.4c	Baby Buggy, #1902	3.50
SP546	9.3c	Mail Wagon, #1903	3.75
SP547	10.9c	Hansom Cab, #1904	4.25
SP548	11c	Caboose, #1905	3.50
SP549	17c	Electric Auto, #1906	3.25
SP550	18c	Surrey, #1907	2.75
SP551	20c	Fire Pumper, #1908	5.00

1983

SP552	$9.35	Express Mail single, #1909	110.00
SP552a	$9.35	Express Mail booklet pane of 3, #1909a	140.00

1981

SP553	18c	Red Cross, #1910	1.50
SP554	18c	Savings and Loan, #1911	1.50
SP555	18c	Space Achievements, #1919a	6.75
SP556	18c	Management, #1920	1.40
SP557	18c	Wildlife, #1924a	2.00
SP558	18c	Disabled, #1925	1.50
SP559	18c	Millay, #1926	2.50
SP560	18c	Alcoholism, #1927	2.50
SP561	18c	Architecture, #1931a	2.50
SP562	18c	Zaharias, #1932	4.25
SP563	18c	Jones, #1933	4.25
SP564	18c	Remington, #1934	1.50
SP565	18c, 20c	Hoban, #1935-1936	1.60
SP566	18c	Yorktown, Va. Capes, #1938a	2.00
SP567	20c	Madonna and Child, #1939	2.75
SP568	20c	Teddy Bear, #1940	3.00
SP569	20c	John Hanson, #1941	1.40
SP570	20c	Desert Plants, #1945a	2.50
SP571	20c	C sheet, coil, #1946	3.25
SP572	20c	C Booklet pane of 10, #1948a	3.25

1982

SP573	20c	Bighorn Sheep, #1949a	3.00
SP574	20c	FDR, #1950	1.50
SP575	20c	Love, #1951	1.50
SP576	20c	Washington, #1952	3.25
SP577	20c	Birds and Flowers, #1953-1962	10.00
SP578	20c	Birds and Flowers, #1963-1972	10.00
SP579	20c	Birds and Flowers, #1973-1982	10.00
SP580	20c	Birds and Flowers, #1983-1992	10.00
SP581	20c	Birds and Flowers, #1993-2002	10.00
SP582	20c	US Netherlands, #2003	1.50
SP583	20c	Library of Congress, #2004	1.40
SP584	20c	Consumer Education, #2005	3.25
SP585	20c	Knoxville World's Fair, #2009a	1.75
SP586	20c	Horatio Alger, #2010	1.50
SP587	20c	Aging, #2011	1.50
SP588	20c	Barrymores, #2012	2.50
SP589	20c	Dr. Mary Walker, #2013	1.60
SP590	20c	Peace Garden, #2014	1.60
SP591	20c	Libraries, #2015	1.40
SP592	20c	Jackie Robinson, #2016	14.00
SP593	20c	Touro Synagogue, #2017	1.40
SP594	20c	Wolf Trap Farm, #2018	1.40
SP595	20c	Architecture, #2022a	2.00
SP596	20c	Francis of Assisi, #2023	1.40
SP597	20c	Ponce de Leon, #2024	1.40
SP598	13c	Puppy, Kitten, #2025	2.75
SP599	20c	Madonna and Child, #2026	2.50
SP600	20c	Children Playing, #2030a	2.75

1983

SP601	1c, 4c, 13c	Official Mail, #O127-O129	2.50
SP602	17c	Official Mail, #O130	2.25
SP603	$1	Official Mail, #O132	4.00
SP604	$5	Official Mail, #O133	9.50
SP605	20c	Official Mail coil, #O135	3.25
SP606	20c	Science, #2031	1.60
SP607	20c	Ballooning, #2035a	1.90
SP608	20c	US Sweden, #2036	2.00
SP609	20c	CCC, #2037	1.25
SP610	20c	Priestley, #2038	1.60
SP611	20c	Voluntarism, #2039	1.50
SP612	20c	German Immigration, #2040	1.50
SP613	20c	Brooklyn Bridge, #2041	2.00
SP614	20c	TVA, #2042	1.50
SP615	20c	Fitness, #2043	1.60
SP616	20c	Scott Joplin, #2044	3.25
SP617	20c	Medal of Honor, #2045	2.50

SP618	20c	Babe Ruth, #2046	10.00
SP619	20c	Hawthorne, #2047	1.60
SP620	13c	Olympics, #2051a	3.25
SP621	28c	Olympics, #C104a	3.00
SP622	40c	Olympics, #C108a	2.75
SP623	35c	Olympics, #C112a	2.50
SP624	20c	Treaty of Paris, #2052	1.90
SP625	20c	Civil Service, #2053	1.50
SP626	20c	Metropolitan Opera, #2054	1.90
SP627	20c	Inventors, #2058a	2.00
SP628	20c	Streetcars, #2062a	2.25
SP629	20c	Madonna and Child, #2063	2.00
SP630	20c	Santa Claus, #2064	1.90
SP631	20c	Martin Luther, #2065	2.50

1984-85

SP632	20c	Alaska, #2066	2.00
SP633	20c	Winter Olympics, #2070a	2.25
SP634	20c	FDIC, #2071	1.60
SP635	20c	Love, #2072	1.60
SP636	20c	Woodson, #2073	3.25
SP637	14c, 22c	D sheet, coil, #O138-O139	1.60
SP638	20c	Conservation, #2074	1.60
SP639	20c	Credit Union, #2075	1.60
SP640	20c	Orchids, #2079a	2.25
SP641	20c	Hawaii, #2080	1.60
SP642	20c	National Archives, #2081	1.50
SP643	20c	Olympics, #2085a	3.50
SP644	20c	World Expo, #2086	1.50
SP645	20c	Health Research, #2087	1.50
SP646	20c	Fairbanks, #2088	1.90
SP647	20c	Thorpe, #2089	7.75
SP648	20c	McCormack, #2090	2.00
SP649	20c	St. Lawrence Seaway, #2091	1.60
SP650	20c	Waterfowl, #2092	4.00
SP651	20c	Roanoke Voyages, #2093	1.60
SP652	20c	Melville, #2094	1.75
SP653	20c	Horace Moses, #2095	1.60
SP654	20c	Smokey Bear, #2096	4.75
SP655	20c	Clemente, #2097	11.00
SP656	20c	Dogs, #2101a	3.25
SP657	20c	Crime Prevention, #2102	2.00
SP658	20c	Hispanic Americans, #2103	1.50
SP659	20c	Family Unity, #2104	2.50
SP660	20c	Eleanor Roosevelt, #2105	2.50
SP661	20c	Readers, #2106	2.25
SP662	20c	Madonna and Child, #2107	2.25
SP663	20c	Child's Santa, #2108	2.25
SP664	20c	Vietnam Memorial, #2109	2.75

1985-87

SP665	20c	Jerome Kern, #2110	2.50
SP666	22c	D sheet, coil, #2111-2112	2.25
SP667	22c	D booklet pane of 10, #2113a	3.75
SP668	33c	Verville, #C113	1.60
SP669	39c	Sperry, #C114	2.00
SP670	44c	Transpacific, #C115	2.00
SP671	22c	Flags sheet, coil, #2114-2115	2.25
SP671a	22c	Flag "T" coil, #2115b	2.75
SP672	22c	Flag booklet pane of 5, #2116a	2.50
SP673	22c	Seashells, #2121a	3.75
SP674	$10.75	Express Mail single, #2122	37.50
SP674a	$10.75	Express Mail booklet pane of 3, #2122a	72.50

Transportation Coils

1985-89

SP675	3.4c	School Bus, #2123	4.25
SP676	4.9c	Buckboard, #2124	4.25
SP677	5.5c	Star Route Truck, #2125	3.25
SP678	6c	Tricycle, #2126	3.25
SP679	7.1c	Tractor, #2127	2.50
SP679a	7.1c	Tractor, Zip+4 precancel, #2127b	2.50
SP680	8.3c	Ambulance, #2128	4.00
SP681	8.5c	Tow Truck, #2129	2.50
SP682	10.1c	Oil Wagon, #2130	2.75
SP682a	10.1c	Red precancel, #2130a	2.00
SP683	11c	Stutz Bearcat, #2131	3.50
SP684	12c	Stanley Steamer, #2132	3.75
SP685	12.5c	Pushcart, #2133	3.25
SP686	14c	Iceboat, #2134	3.50
SP687	17c	Dog Sled, #2135	2.75
SP688	25c	Bread Wagon, #2136	3.25

1985

SP689	22c	Bethune, #2137	2.50
SP690	22c	Duck Decoys, #2141a	2.25
SP691	22c	Winter Special Olympics, #2142	2.00
SP692	22c	Love, #2143	3.25
SP693	22c	REA, #2144	1.60
SP694	14c, 22c	Official Mail, #O129A, O136	3.25
SP695	22c	AMERIPEX '86, #2145	1.60
SP696	22c	Abigail Adams, #2146	1.50
SP697	22c	Bartholdi, #2147	3.25
SP698	18c	Washington Monument, #2149	2.50
SP699	21.1c	Letters coil, #2150	2.50
SP700	22c	Korean Veterans, #2152	2.50
SP701	22c	Social Security, #2153	2.00
SP702	44c	Serra, #C116	2.00
SP703	22c	World War I Veterans, #2154	2.00
SP704	22c	Horses, #2158a	3.50
SP705	22c	Education, #2159	2.00
SP706	22c	Youth Year, #2163a	2.50
SP707	22c	Hunger, #2164	2.00
SP708	22c	Madonna and Child, #2165	2.00
SP709	22c	Poinsettias, #2166	2.50

1986

SP710	22c	Arkansas, #2167	1.50

Great Americans

1986-94

SP711	1c	Mitchell, #2168	1.90
SP712	2c	Lyon, #2169	2.00
SP713	3c	White, #2170	2.00
SP714	4c	Flanagan, #2171	1.60
SP715	5c	Black, #2172	2.50
SP716	5c	Munoz Marin, #2173	2.00
SP717	10c	Red Cloud, #2175	1.50

SP718	14c Howe, #2176	1.50
SP719	15c Cody, #2177	1.90
SP720	17c Lockwood, #2178	2.25
SP721	20c Apgar, #2179	7.25
SP722	21c Carlson, #2180	1.50
SP723	23c Cassatt, #2181	1.90
SP724	25c London, #2182	1.75
SP724a	25c London, pane of 10, #2182a	4.25
SP725	28c Sitting Bull, #2183	1.75
SP726	29c Warren, #2184	3.75
SP727	29c Jefferson, #2185	3.50
SP728	35c Chavez, #2186	2.50
SP729	40c Chennault, #2187	3.25
SP730	45c Cushing, #2188	1.60
SP731	52c Humphrey, #2189	2.75
SP732	56c Harvard, #2190	1.75
SP733	65c Arnold, #2191	2.25
SP734	75c Willkie, #2192	3.25
SP735	$1 Revel, #2193	2.00
SP736	$1 Hopkins, #2194	2.50
SP737	$2 Bryan, #2195	3.75
SP739	$5 Harte, #2196	9.50
SP740	25c London, #2197a	3.25

1986

SP741	22c Stamp Collecting, #2201a	4.00
SP742	22c Love, #2202	2.25
SP743	22c Sojourner Truth, #2203	2.75
SP744	22c Texas Republic, #2204	1.50
SP745	22c Fish booklet pane of 5, #2209a	3.50
SP746	22c Hospitals, #2210	1.25
SP747	22c Duke Ellington, #2211	3.25
SP748	22c Presidents Sheet #1, #2216	4.25
SP749	22c Presidents Sheet #2, #2217	4.25
SP750	22c Presidents Sheet #3, #2218	4.25
SP751	22c Presidents Sheet #4, #2219	4.25
SP752	22c Arctic Explorers, #2223a	3.25
SP753	22c Statue of Liberty, #2224	3.00

1987

SP754	2c Locomotive, reengraved, #2226	2.75

1986

SP755	22c Navajo Art, #2238a	2.75
SP756	22c T.S. Eliot, #2239	1.50
SP757	22c Woodcarved Figurines, #2243a	2.00
SP758	22c Madonna and Child, #2244	2.25
SP759	22c Village Scene, #2245	2.25

1987

SP760	22c Michigan, #2246	2.50
SP761	22c Pan American Games, #2247	2.50
SP762	22c Love, #2248	3.00
SP763	22c du Sable, #2249	4.50
SP764	22c Caruso, #2250	2.00
SP765	22c Girl Scouts, #2251	3.25

Transportation Coils

1987-88

SP766	3c Conestoga Wagon, #2252	2.50
SP767	5c, Milk Wagon, Racing Car, 17.5c #2253, 2262	3.00
SP768	5.3c Elevator, #2254	3.00
SP769	7.6c Carreta, #2255	3.00
SP770	8.4c Wheelchair, #2256	2.50
SP771	10c Canal Boat, #2257	3.00
SP772	13c Patrol Wagon, #2258	3.00
SP773	13.2c Coal Car, #2259	3.00
SP774	15c Tugboat, #2260	3.00
SP775	16.7c Popcorn Wagon, #2261	2.50
SP776	20c Cable Car, #2263	3.00
SP777	20.5c Fire Engine, #2264	3.50
SP778	21c Mail Car, #2265	3.00
SP779	24.1c Tandem Bicycle, #2255	3.00

1987

SP780	22c Special Occasions, #2274a	4.50
SP781	22c United Way, #2275	1.75

1987-89

SP782	22c Flag and Fireworks, #2276	1.75
SP783	22c Flag, pair from booklet, #2276a	2.75
SP784	(25c) "E" sheet, coil, #2277, 2279	4.00
SP785	(25c) "E" booklet pane of 10, #2282a	4.75
SP786	25c Flag with Clouds, #2278	1.60
SP787	25c Flag with Clouds booklet pane of 6, #2285c	4.00
SP788	25c Flag over Yosemite coil, block tagging, #2280	2.00
SP788a	25c Flag over Yosemite, prephosphored uncoated paper (mottled tagging), #2280a	2.50
SP789	25c Honeybee coil, #2281	4.25
SP790	25c Pheasant, #2283a	4.25
SP791	25c Owl and Grosbeak, #2285b	4.00
SP792	(25c) "E" Official coil, #O140	2.00
SP793	20c Official coil, #O138B	2.25
SP794	15c, 25c Official coils, #O138A, O141	2.75

1987

SP795	22c Wildlife, #2286-2295	5.00
SP796	22c Wildlife, #2296-2305	5.00
SP797	22c Wildlife, #2306-2315	5.00
SP798	22c Wildlife, #2316-2325	5.00
SP799	22c Wildlife, #2326-2335	5.00

Ratification of the Constitution

1987-90

SP800	22c Delaware, #2336	1.90
SP801	22c Pennsylvania, #2337	2.00
SP802	22c New Jersey, #2338	2.50
SP803	22c Georgia, #2339	2.00
SP804	22c Connecticut, #2340	2.00
SP805	22c Massachusetts, #2341	2.25
SP806	22c Maryland, #2342	2.25
SP807	25c South Carolina, #2343	2.00
SP808	25c New Hampshire, #2344	2.00
SP809	25c Virginia, #2345	2.00
SP810	25c New York, #2346	2.50
SP811	25c North Carolina, #2347	2.00
SP812	25c Rhode Island, #2348	2.75

1987

SP813	22c U.S./Morocco, #2349	1.75
SP814	22c William Faulkner, #2350	1.75
SP815	22c Lacemaking, #2354a	3.25
SP816	22c Constitution, #2359a	3.25
SP817	22c Signing of Constitution, #2360	2.00
SP818	22c Certified Public Accounting, #2361	3.75
SP819	22c Locomotives, #2366a	6.75
SP820	22c Madonna and Child, #2367	2.00
SP821	22c Christmas Ornament, #2368	1.75

1988

SP822	22c Winter Olympics, #2369	1.75
SP823	22c Australia Bicentennial, #2370	1.90
SP824	22c James Weldon Johnson, #2371	3.00
SP825	22c Cats, #2375a	3.50
SP826	22c Knute Rockne, #2376	5.00
SP827	44c New Sweden, #C117	2.00
SP828	45c Samuel P. Langley, #C118	2.00
SP829	25c Francis Ouimet, #2377	6.00
SP830	36c Igor Sikorsky, #C119	2.75
SP831	25c Love, #2378	2.00
SP832	45c Love, #2379	2.00
SP833	25c Summer Olympics, #2380	2.00
SP834	25c Classic Automobiles, #2385a	4.75
SP835	25c Antarctic Explorers, #2389a	2.75
SP836	25c Carousel Animals, #2393a	3.25
SP837	$8.75 Express Mail, #2394	20.00
SP838	25c Special Occasions, #2396a	14.00
SP839	25c Special Occasions, #2398a	9.25
SP840	25c Madonna and Child, #2399	2.00
SP841	25c Village Scene, #2400	2.00

1989

SP842	25c Montana, #2401	1.75
SP843	25c A. Philip Randolph, #2402	3.25
SP844	25c North Dakota, #2403	1.90
SP845	25c Washington Statehood, #2404	1.90
SP846	25c Steamboats, #2409a	3.50
SP847	25c World Stamp Expo, #2410	2.00
SP848	25c Toscanini, #2411	1.75

Branches of Government

1989-90

SP849	25c House of Representatives, #2412	2.25
SP850	25c Senate, #2413	2.25
SP851	25c Executive, #2414	2.25
SP852	25c Supreme Court, #2415	2.00

1989

SP853	25c South Dakota, #2416	2.00
SP854	25c Lou Gehrig, #2417	9.25
SP855	1c Official, litho., #O143	2.75
SP856	45c French Revolution, #C120	3.00
SP857	25c Ernest Hemingway, #2418	1.60
SP858	$2.40 Moon Landing, #2419	12.50
SP859	25c Letter Carriers, #2420	1.60
SP860	25c Bill of Rights, #2421	2.00
SP861	25c Dinosaurs, #2425a	7.50
SP862	25c, 45c Pre-Columbian Artifacts, #2426, C121	2.50
SP863	25c Madonna sheet single, booklet pane of 10, #2427, 2427a	7.00
SP864	25c Sleigh single, booklet pane of 10, #2428, 2429a	6.75
SP865	25c Eagle & Shield, #2431	2.25
SP866	90c World Stamp Expo '89, #2433	7.00
SP867	25c Traditional Mail Delivery, #2437a	2.75
SP868	45c Futuristic Mail Delivery, #C126	5.25
SP869	45c Futuristic Mail Delivery, #C125a	5.25
SP870	25c Traditional Mail Delivery, #2438	5.75

1990

SP871	25c Idaho, #2439	2.00
SP872	25c Love single, booklet pane of 10, #2440, 2441a	4.75
SP873	25c Ida B. Wells, #2442	3.75
SP874	15c Beach Umbrella, #2443a	3.50
SP875	25c Wyoming, #2444	2.00
SP876	25c Classic Films, #2448a	5.00
SP877	25c Marianne Moore, #2449	2.00

Transportation Coils

1990-92

SP879	4c Steam Carriage, #2451	3.25
SP880	5c Circus Wagon, #2452	3.25
SP880A	5c Circus Wagon, #2452B	3.50
SP880B	5c Circus Wagon with cent sign, #2452D	6.00
SP881	5c, 10c Canoe, engr., Tractor Trailer, #2453, 2457	3.25
SP882	5c Canoe, photo., #2454	3.25
SP883	10c Tractor trailer, photo., #2458	5.00
SP891	20c Cog Railway, #2463	8.00
SP892	23c Lunch Wagon, #2464	2.75
SP893	32c Ferry Boat, #2466	8.00
SP895	$1 Seaplane, #2468	5.75

1990-94

SP897	25c Lighthouses, booklet pane of 5, #2474a	5.00
SP898	25c Flag, #2475	3.25

Flora and Fauna Series

SP899	1c, 3c, Kestrel, Bluebird, Cardinal, 30c #2476, 2478, 2480	2.75
SP900	1c Kestrel with cent sign, #2477	8.00
SP901	19c Fawn, #2479	2.75
SP902	45c Pumpkinseed Sunfish, #2481	2.75
SP903	$2 Bobcat, #2482	5.00
SP904	20c Blue jay, #2483	8.00
SP905	29c Wood Ducks booklet panes of 10, #2484a, 2485a	11.00
SP906	29c African Violets bklt. pane of 10, #2486a	6.00

SP907	32c Peach & Pear, #2488b, 2493-2494	8.00
SP908	29c Red Squirrel, #2489	4.00
SP909	29c Red Rose, #2490	4.00
SP910	29c Pine Cone, #2491	4.00
SP911	32c Pink rose, #2492	8.00
SP919	25c Olympians, #2496-2500	5.75
SP920	25c Indian Headdresses, #2505a	6.50
SP921	25c Micronesia, Marshall Islands, #2507a	2.75
SP922	25c Sea Creatures, #2511a	4.75
SP923	25c, 45c Grand Canyon, Tropical Coastline, #2512, C127	3.00
SP924	25c Eisenhower, #2513	2.25
SP925	25c Madonna sheet single, booklet pane of 10, #2514, 2514a	5.75
SP926	25c Christmas Tree sheet single, booklet pane of 10, #2515, 2516a	5.75

1991-95

SP927	(29c) "F" Flower single, coil pair, #2517, 2518	3.25
SP928	(29c) "F" Flower booklet panes of 10, #2519a, 2520a	11.00
SP929	(4c) Make-up Rate, #2521	2.25
SP930	(29c) "F" Flag, #2522	2.75
SP931	(29c) "F" Official coil, #O144	3.25
SP932	29c Mt. Rushmore, #2523	2.75
SP933	29c Mt. Rushmore, photo., #2523A	2.75
SP934	29c Flower single, booklet pane of 10, #2524, 2527a	6.25
SP935	29c Flower coil, #2525	2.75
SP936	29c Flower coil, #2526	2.75
SP937	4c Official, #O146	2.50
SP938	29c Flag, Olympic Rings, #2528a	6.25
SP939	19c Fishing Boat coil, #2529	3.00
SP939A	19c Fishing Boat coil reissue, #2529C	5.25
SP940	19c Balloning, #2530a	4.50
SP941	29c Flags on Parade, #2531	2.75
SP942	29c Liberty Torch, #2531A	2.75
SP943	50c Switzerland, #2532	2.75
SP944	20c Vermont Statehood, #2533	2.75
SP945	50c Harriet Quimby, #C128	2.75
SP946	29c Savings Bonds, #2534	2.25
SP947	29c, 52c Love, #2535, 2536a, 2537	9.25
SP948	40c William T. Piper, #C129	2.75
SP949	29c William Saroyan, #2538	2.75
SP950	Official 19c, 23c, 29c, #O145, O147-O148	3.50
SP951	$1.00 USPS/Olympic Rings, #2539	4.00
SP952	$2.90 Eagle, #2540	7.50
SP953	$9.95 Eagle, #2541	22.50
SP954	$14 Eagle, #2542	30.00
SP955	$2.90 Futuristic Space Shuttle, #2543	10.00
SP956	$3 Challenger Shuttle, #2544	12.00
SP956A	$10.75 Endeavour Shuttle, #2544A	24.00
SP957	29c Fishing Flies, #2549a	5.25
SP958	29c Cole Porter, #2550	2.75
SP959	50c Antarctic Treaty, #C130	3.25
SP960	29c Desert Shield, Desert Storm, #2551	5.75
SP961	29c 1992 Summer Olympics, #2553-2557	5.75
SP962	29c Numismatics, #2558	2.50
SP963	29c World War II, #2559	7.25
SP964	29c Basketball, #2560	5.75
SP965	29c District of Columbia, #2561	2.50
SP966	29c Comedians, #2566a	6.75
SP967	29c Jan E. Matzeliger, #2567	4.50
SP968	29c Space Exploration, #2577a	6.75
SP969	50c Bering Land Bridge, #C131	2.75
SP970	29c Madonna and Child sheet single, booklet pane of 10, #2578, 2578a	8.50
SP971	29c Santa Claus sheet and booklet singles, #2579, 2580 or 2581, 2582-2585	12.50
SP973	32c James K. Polk, #2587	12.00
SP976	$1 Surrender of Gen. Burgoyne, #2590	7.00
SP978	$5 Washington and Jackson, #2592	11.00
SP980	29c Pledge of Allegiance, #2593a	10.00
SP982	29c Eagle & Shield self-adhesives, #2595-2597	6.00
SP983	29c Eagle self-adhesive, #2598	5.25
SP984	29c Statue of Liberty, #2599	5.25
SP990	(10c) Eagle and Shield coil, #2602	3.25
SP991	(10c) Eagle and Shield coils, #2603-2604	3.50
SP993	23c Stars and Stripes coil, #2605	3.25
SP994	23c USA coil, #2606	3.25
SP994A	23c USA coil, #2607	4.00
SP994B	23c USA coil, #2608	3.50
SP995	29c Flag over White House, #2609	2.75

1992

SP997	29c Winter Olympics, #2611-2615	4.75
SP998	29c World Columbian Stamp Expo '92, #2616	2.75
SP999	29c W.E.B. DuBois, #2617	5.75
SP1000	29c Love, #2618	2.75
SP1001	29c Olympic Baseball, #2619	12.50
SP1002	29c First Voyage of Columbus, #2623a	4.00
SP1003	1c, 4c, First Sighting of Land souvenir $1 sheet, #2624	12.00
SP1004	2c, 3c, Claiming a New World souvenir $4 sheet, #2625	12.00
SP1005	5c, 30c, Seeking Royal Support souve-50c nir sheet, #2626	12.00
SP1006	6c, 8c, Royal Favor Restored souvenir $3 sheet, #2627	12.00
SP1007	10c, Reporting Discoveries souvenir 15c, $2 sheet, #2628	12.00
SP1008	$5 Columbus souvenir sheet, #2629	12.00

SP1009	29c	New York Stock Exchange, #2630	2.50
SP1010	29c	Space Accomplishments, #2634a	4.75
SP1011	29c	Alaska Highway, #2635	2.50
SP1012	29c	Kentucky Statehood, #2636	2.50
SP1013	29c	Summer Olympics, #2637-2641	4.75
SP1014	29c	Hummingbirds, #2646a	5.50
SP1015	29c	Wildflowers, #2647-2656	6.50
SP1016	29c	Wildflowers, #2657-2666	6.50
SP1017	29c	Wildflowers, #2667-2676	6.50
SP1018	29c	Wildflowers, #2677-2686	6.50
SP1019	29c	Wildflowers, #2687-2696	6.50
SP1020	29c	World War II, #2697	8.00
SP1021	29c	Dorothy Parker, #2698	2.75
SP1022	29c	Dr. Theodore von Karman, #2699	4.25
SP1023	29c	Minerals strip of 4, #2703a	4.75
SP1024	29c	Juan Rodriguez Cabrillo, #2704	2.50
SP1025	29c	Wild Animals, #2709a	5.50
SP1026	29c	Madonna and Child sheet single, booklet pane of 10, #2710, 2710a	8.75
SP1027	29c	Christmas Toys block of 4, booklet pane of 4 and booklet single, #2714a, 2718a, 2719	7.50
SP1028	29c	Chinese New Year, #2720	6.00

1993

SP1029	29c	Elvis Presley, #2721	11.00
SP1030	29c	Oklahoma!, #2722	3.75
SP1030A	29c	Hank Williams sheet stamp, #2723	6.00
SP1030B	29c	Rock & Roll/Rhythm & Blues sheet single, booklet pane of 8, #2737b	10.00

No. SP1030B exists with any one of #2724-2730 affixed along with #2737b.

SP1034	29c	Space Fantasy, #2745a	7.00
SP1035	29c	Percy Lavon Julian, #2746	4.75
SP1036	29c	Oregon Trail, #2747	3.50
SP1037	29c	World University Games, #2748	3.75
SP1038	29c	Grace Kelly, #2749	5.50
SP1039	29c	Circus, #2753a	5.50
SP1040	29c	Cherokee Strip, #2754	3.50
SP1041	29c	Dean Acheson, #2755	3.50
SP1042	29c	Sporting Horses, #2759a	5.50
SP1043	29c	Garden Flowers, #2764a	5.50
SP1044	29c	World War II, #2765	6.75
SP1045	29c	Joe Louis, #2766	7.50
SP1046	29c	Broadway Musicals, #2770a	6.75
SP1047	29c	National Postal Museum strip of 4, #2782a	4.75
SP1048	29c	American Sign Language, #2784a	3.50
SP1049	29c	Country & Western Music sheet stamp and booklet pane of 4, #2778a	9.25

No. SP1049 exists with any one of #2771-2774 affixed along with #2778a.

SP1050	10c	Official Mail, #O146A	3.25
SP1052	29c	Classic Books strip of 4, #2788a	5.50
SP1053	29c	Traditional Christmas sheet stamp, booklet pane of 4, #2789, 2790a	6.25
SP1054	29c	Contemporary Christmas booklet pane of 10, sheet and self-adhesive single stamps, #2803	8.50

No. SP1054 exists with any one of #2791-2794, 2798a, 2798b, 2799-2802 affixed along with #2803.

SP1055	29c	Mariana Islands, #2804	4.25
SP1056	29c	Columbus' Landing in Puerto Rico, #2805	4.75
SP1057	29c	AIDS Awareness, #2806, 2806b	7.50

1994

SP1058	29c	Winter Olympics, #2811a	5.50
SP1059	29c	Edward R. Murrow, #2812	3.50
SP1060	29c	Love self-adhesive, #2813	3.50
SP1061	29c, 52c	Love booklet pane of 10, single sheet stamp, #2814a, 2815	8.00
SP1062	29c	Love sheet stamp, #2814C	5.25
SP1063	29c	Dr. Allison Davis, #2816	6.00
SP1064	29c	Chinese New Year, #2817	5.25
SP1065	29c	Buffalo Soldiers, #2818	8.00
SP1066	29c	Silent Screen Stars, #2819-2828	7.25
SP1067	29c	Garden Flowers, #2833a	8.50
SP1068	29c, 40c, 50c	World Cup Soccer, #2834-2836	8.75
SP1069		World Cup Soccer, #2837	9.25
SP1070	29c	World War II, #2838	5.50
SP1071	29c, 50c	Norman Rockwell stamp, souvenir sheet, #2839-2840	8.00
SP1072	29c, $9.95	Moon Landing, #2841-2842	15.00
SP1073	29c	Locomotives, #2847a	7.00
SP1074	29c	George Meany, #2848	5.25
SP1075	29c	Popular Singers, #2853a	10.00
SP1076	29c	Jazz and Blues Singers block of 10, #2854-2861	14.00

Block of 10 on No. SP1076 may contain different combinations of stamps.

SP1077	29c	James Thurber, #2862	5.25
SP1078	29c	Wonders of the Sea, #2866a	8.75
SP1079	29c	Cranes, #2868a	8.00
SP1079A		Legends of the West, #2869	12.00
SP1080	29c	Traditional Christmas sheet stamp, booklet pane of 10, #2871, 2871b	14.00
SP1081	29c	Contemporary Christmas sheet stamp, block of 4 from booklet pane, #2872	12.00

SP1082	29c	Contemporary Christmas self-adhesive stamps, #2873--2874	9.25
SP1083	$2	Bureau of Engraving and Printing Souvenir Sheet, #2875	17.50

1995-96

SP1084	29c	Chinese New Year, #2876	9.00
SP1085	G	make-up rate, G stamps, #2877, 2884, 2890, 2893	12.00
SP1086	G	make-up rate, G stamps, #2878, 2880, 2882, 2885, 2888, 2892	12.00
SP1087	G	stamps, official G stamp, #2879, 2881, 2883, 2889, O152	12.00
SP1088	G	self-adhesive stamps, #2886-2887	12.00
SP1091	32c	Flag Over Porch, #2897, 2913, 2915-2916	12.00
SP1096	(5c)	Butte coil, #2902	12.00
SP1097	(5c)	Mountain coil, #2903, 2904	12.00
SP1099		Butte, Mountain, Juke Box, Auto Tail Fin, Auto, Flag over porch, #2902B, 2904A, 2906, 2910, 2912A, 2915B	9.00
SP1099A		Mountain, Juke Box, Flag Over Porch coil and booklet stamps, #2904B, 2912B, 2915D, 2921b	9.00
SP1100	(10c)	Auto coil, #2905	12.00
SP1102		Eagle & shield, Flag over porch, #2907, 2920D, 2921	7.50
SP1103	(15c)	Auto Tail Fin, #2908-2909	12.00
SP1105	(25c)	Juke Box, #2911-2912	12.00
SP1110	32c	Flag over Field self-adhesive, #	12.00
SP1114	(32c)	Non-denominated Love, #2948-2949	12.00
SP1115	32c	Florida Statehood, #2950	12.00

Great Americans Series

1995-99

SP1126	32c	Milton Hershey, #2933	12.00
SP1127	32c	Cal Farley, #2943	6.00
SP1128	32c	Henry R. Luce, #2935	6.00
SP1129	32c	Lila & DeWitt Wallace, #2936	6.00
SP1131	46c	Ruth Benedict, #2938	6.00
SP1133	55c	Alice Hamilton, #2940	12.00
SP1134	55c	Justin S. Morrill, #2941	6.00
SP1135	77c	Mary Breckinridge, #2942	6.00
SP1136	78c	Alice Paul, #2943	12.00

1995

SP1141	32c	Kids Care, #2954a	12.00
SP1142	32c	Richard Nixon, #2955	12.00
SP1143	32c	Bessie Coleman, #2956	12.00
SP1144	1-32c	Official, #O153-O156	12.00
SP1145	32c, 55c	Love (with denominations), #2957-2960	12.00
SP1146	32c	Recreational Sports, #2965a	12.00
SP1147	32c	Prisoners of War/Missing in Action, #2966	12.00
SP1148	32c	Marilyn Monroe, #2967	12.00
SP1149	32c	Texas Statehood, #2968	12.00
SP1150	32c	Great Lakes Lighthouses, #2973a	12.00
SP1151	32c	United Nations, #2974	12.00
SP1152	32c	Civil War, #2975	16.00
SP1153	32c	Carousel Horses, #2979a	12.00
SP1154	32c	Woman Suffrage, #2980	12.00
SP1155	32c	World War II, #2981	12.00
SP1156	32c	Louis Armstrong, #2982	12.00
SP1157	32c	Jazz Musicians, #2992a	14.00
SP1158	32c	Garden Flowers, #2997a	12.00
SP1159	60c	Eddie Rickenbacker, #2998	12.00
SP1160	32c	Republic of Palau, #2999	12.00
SP1161	32c	Comic Strip Classics, #3000	20.00
SP1162	32c	Naval Academy, #3001	12.00
SP1163	32c	Tennessee Williams, #3002	12.00
SP1164	32c	Traditional Christmas sheet stamp, booklet pane of 10, #3003, 3003b	14.00
SP1165	32c	Contemporary Christmas block of 4, self-adhesive stamps, #3007a, 3010-3011	14.00

No. SP1165 may include different combinations of Nos. 3008-3011.

SP1166	32c	Midnight Angel, #3012	12.00
SP1167	32c	Children Sledding, #3013	12.00
SP1168	32c	Antique Automobiles, #3023a	14.00

1996

SP1169	32c	Utah Statehood, #3024	12.00
SP1170	32c	Garden Flowers, #3029a	14.00
SP1171	1, 32c	Flag Over Porch, Love self-adhesives, Kestrel coil, #2920e, 3030, 3044	16.00

1996-99

Flora and Fauna Series

SP1171A	1c	Kestrel, self-adhesive, #3031	6.00
SP1172	2c	Woodpecker, #3032	14.00
SP1173	3c	Bluebird, #3033	6.00
SP1184	$1	Red Fox, #3036	6.00
SP1185	2c	Woodpecker coil, #3045	6.00
SP1187	20c	Bluejay self-adhesive coil, booklet stamps, #3048, 3053	6.00
SP1188	32c	Yellow Rose, #3049	6.00
SP1189	20c	Ring-necked Pheasant, #3050, 3055	6.00
SP1191	32c	Coral Pink Rose, #3052	6.00
SP1192	32c	Yellow Rose coil, #3054	6.00

1996

SP1197	32c	Ernest E. Just, #3058	12.00
SP1198	32c	Smithsonian Institution, #3059	12.00
SP1199	32c	Chinese New Year, #3060	12.00
SP1200	32c	Pioneers of Communication, #3064a	14.00

SP1201	32c	Fulbright Scholarships, #3065	12.00
SP1202	50c	Jacqueline Cochran, #3066	12.00
SP1203	32c	Marathon, #3067	6.00
SP1204	32c	Olympic Games, #3068	8.00
SP1205	32c	Georgia O'Keeffe, #3069	6.00
SP1206	32c	Tennessee Statehood, #3070	6.00
SP1207	32c	American Indian Dances, #3076a	9.00
SP1208	32c	Prehistoric Animals, #3080a	9.00
SP1209	32c	Breast Cancer Awareness, #3081	6.00
SP1210	32c	James Dean, #3082	6.00
SP1211	32c	Folk Heroes, #3086a	9.00
SP1212	32c	Centennial Olympic Games, #3087	6.00
SP1213	32c	Iowa Statehood, #3088-3089	6.00
SP1214	32c	Rural Free Delivery, #3090	6.00
SP1215	32c	Riverboats, #3095a	9.00
SP1216	32c	Big Band Leaders, #3099a	9.00
SP1217	32c	Songwriters, #3103a	9.00
SP1218	23c	F. Scott Fitzgerald, #3104	6.00
SP1219	32c	Endangered Species, #3105	10.00
SP1220	32c	Computer Technology, #3106	6.00
SP1221	32c	Madonna & Child sheet & booklet stamps, #3107, 3112	7.50
SP1222	32c	Contemporary Christmas block of 4, self-adhesive stamp, #3111a, 3113	7.50

#SP1222 may contain #3114-3116 instead of #3113.

SP1223	32c	Skaters, #3117	6.00
SP1224	32c	Hanukkah, #3118	6.00
SP1225	32c	Cycling souvenir sheet, #3119	10.00

1997

SP1226	32c	Chinese New Year, #3120	6.00
SP1227	32c	Benjamin O. Davis, Sr., #3121	6.00
SP1228	32c	Statue of Liberty, #3122	6.00
SP1229	32, 55c	Love Swans, #3123-3124	6.00
SP1230	32c	Helping Children Learn, #3125	6.00
SP1231	32c	Merian Botanical Prints, #3126-3129	7.50
SP1232	32c	PACIFIC 97 Triangles, #3131a	7.50
SP1233	(25c), 32c	Flag Over Porch, Juke Box linerless coils, #3132-3133	9.00
SP1234	32c	Thornton Wilder, #3134	6.00
SP1235	32c	Raoul Wallenberg, #3135	6.00
SP1236	32c	Dinosaurs, #3136	10.00
SP1237	32c	Bugs Bunny, #3137	6.00
SP1238	50c	PACIFIC 97 Franklin, #3139	15.00
SP1239	60c	PACIFIC 97 Washington, #3140	15.00
SP1240	32c	Marshall Plan, #3141	6.00
SP1241	32c	Classic American Aircraft, #3142	15.00
SP1242	32c	Football Coaches, #3146a	7.50
SP1242A	32c	Vince Lombardi, #3147	6.00
SP1242B	32c	Bear Bryant, #3148	6.00
SP1242C	32c	Pop Warner, #3149	6.00
SP1242D	32c	George Halas, #3150	6.00
SP1243	32c	Classic American Dolls, #3151	15.00
SP1244	32c	Humphrey Bogart, #3152	6.00
SP1245	32c	The Stars and Stripes Forever!, #3153	6.00
SP1246	32c	Opera Singers, #3157a	7.50
SP1247	32c	Composers & Conductors, #3165a	7.50
SP1248	32c	Padre Felix Varela, #3155	6.00
SP1249	32c	Department of the Air Force, #3167	6.00
SP1250	32c	Movie Monsters, #3172a	7.50
SP1251	32c	Supersonic Flight, #3173	6.00
SP1252	32c	Women in Military Service, #3174	6.00
SP1253	32c	Kwanzaa, #3175	6.00
SP1254	32c	Madonna and Child, #3176	6.00
SP1255	32c	Holly, #3177	6.00
SP1256	32c	Mars Pathfinder, #3178	12.00

1998

SP1257	32c	Chinese New Year, #3179	6.00
SP1258	32c	Alpine Skiing, #3180	6.00
SP1259	32c	Madam C.J. Walker, #3181	6.00

1998-2000

Celebrate the Century

SP1259A	32c	1900s, #3182	10.00
SP1259B	32c	1910s, #3183	10.00
SP1259C	32c	1920s, #3184	10.00
SP1259D	32c	1930s, #3185	10.00
SP1259E	32c	1940s, #3186	10.00
SP1259F	33c	1950s, #3187	10.00
SP1259G	33c	1960s, #3188	10.00
SP1259H	33c	1970s, #3189	10.00
SP1259I	33c	1980s, #3190	10.00

1998

SP1260	32c	"Remember the Maine," #3192	6.00
SP1261	32c	Flowering Trees, #3197a	6.00
SP1262	32c	Alexander Calder, #3202a	6.00
SP1263	32c	Cinco de Mayo, #3203	6.00
SP1264	32c	Sylvester & Tweety, #3204a	6.00
SP1265	32c	Wisconsin Statehood, #3206	6.00
SP1266	(5c)	Wetlands, Diner Coils, #3207-3208	6.00
	(25c)		
SP1266A	(25c)	Diner coil, #3208A	6.00
SP1267	1c-$2	Trans-Mississippi, #3209	10.00
SP1268	$1	Trans-Mississippi, #3209h	6.00
SP1269	32c	Berlin Airlift, #3211	6.00
SP1270	32c	Folk Musicians, #3215a	6.00
SP1271	32c	Gospel Singers, #3219a	6.00
SP1272	32c	Spanish Settlement, #3220	6.00
SP1273	32c	Stephen Vincent Benét, #3221	6.00
SP1274	32c	Tropical Birds, #3225a	6.00
SP1275	32c	Alfred Hitchcock, #3226	6.00
SP1276	32c	Organ & Tissue Donation, #3227	6.00
SP1277	(10c)	Modern Bicycle, #3229	6.00
SP1278	32c	Bright Eyes, #3234a	7.50
SP1279	32c	Klondike Gold Rush, #3235	6.00

SP1280	32c American Art, #3236	10.00
SP1281	32c Ballet, #3237	6.00
SP1282	32c Space Discovery, #3242a	7.50
SP1283	32c Giving & Sharing, #3243	6.00
SP1284	32c Madonna & Child, #3244	6.00
SP1285	32c Wreaths, #3248a, 3252a	7.50
SP1286	(32+8c) Breast Cancer Awareness, #B1	6.00
SP1287	(1c), Weather Vane, Uncle Sam's	
	(33c) Hat, #3257-3258, 3260	10.00
SP1288	22c Uncle Sam, #3259, 3263	6.00
SP1289	$3.20 Space Shuttle Landing, #3261	10.00
SP1290	$11.75 Piggyback Space Shuttle,	
	#3262	20.00
SP1291	(33c) Uncle Sam's Hat, #3267-3269	10.00
SP1292	(33c) Uncle Sam's Hat, #3264, 3266	10.00
SP1293	(5c), Wetlands, Eagle & Shield,	
	(10c) #3207A, 3270-3271	10.00

1999

SP1294	33c Chinese New Year, #3272	6.00
SP1295	33x Malcolm X, #3273	6.00
SP1296	33c Love, #3274	6.00
SP1297	55c Love, #3275	6.00
SP1298	33c Hospice Care, #3276	6.00
SP1299	33c Flag and City, #3279-3280, 3282	6.00
SP1300	33c Flag Over Chalkboard, #3283	6.00
SP1301	33c Irish Immigration, #3286	6.00
SP1302	33c Lunt & Fontanne, #3287	6.00

SP1303	33c Arctic Animals, #3292a	6.00
SP1304	33c Sonoran Desert, #3293	10.00
SP1305	33c Berries, #3294-3297	7.50
SP1306	33c Daffy Duck, #3306a	6.00
SP1307	33c Ayn Rand, #3308	6.00
SP1308	33c Cinco de Mayo, #3309	6.00
SP1309	33c Tropical Flowers, #3310-3313	7.50
SP1310	48c Niagara Falls, #C133	6.00
SP1311	33c John & William Bartram, #3314	6.00
SP1312	33c Prostate Cancer, #3315	6.00
SP1313	33c California Gold Rush, #3316	6.00
SP1314	33c Aquarium Fish, #3317-3320	7.50
SP1315	33c Extreme Sports, #3321-3324	7.50
SP1316	33c American Glass, #3328a	7.50
SP1317	33c James Cagney, #3329	6.00
SP1318	55c Billy Mitchell, #3330	6.00
SP1319	40c Rio Grande, #C134	6.00
SP1320	33c Honoring Those Who Served, #3331	6.00
SP1321	45c Universal Postal Union, #3332	6.00
SP1322	33c Famous Trains, #3337a	7.50
SP1323	33c Frederick Law Olmsted, #3338	6.00
SP1324	33c Hollywood Composers, #3344a	7.50
SP1325	33c Broadway Songwriters, #3350a	7.50
SP1326	33c Insects & Spiders, #3351	10.00
SP1327	33c Hanukkah, #3352	6.00
SP1328	22c Uncle Sam, #3353	6.00
SP1329	33c Official coil, #O157	6.00

SP1330	33c NATO, #3354	6.00
SP1331	33c Madonna & Child, #3355	6.00
SP1332	33c Christmas Deer, #3359a	7.50
SP1333	33c Kwanzaa, #3368	6.00
SP1334	33c Year 2000, #3369	6.00

2000

SP1335	33c Chinese New Year, #3370	6.00
SP1336	60c Grand Canyon, #C135	7.50
SP1337	33c Patricia Roberts Harris, #3371	6.00
SP1338	33c Berries, dated 2000, #3294a-3296a, 3297c	7.50
SP1339	33c Los Angeles Class Submarine (sheet stamp), #3372	6.00

COMPUTER VENDED POSTAGE

1992

SPCVP1	29c Postage and Mailing Center (PMC) coil strip of 3, #31	5.00

1994

SPCVP2	29c Postage and Mailing Center (PMC) horiz. coil strip of 3, #32	5.00

1996

SPCVP3	32c Postage and Mailing Center (PMC) horiz. strip of 3, #33	5.00

INTERNATIONAL REPLY COUPONS

Coupons produced by the Universal Postal Union for member countries to provide for payment of postage on a return letter from a foreign country. Exchangeable for a stamp representing single-rate ordinary postage (and starting with the use of Type D3, airmail postage) to a foreign country under the terms of contract as printed on the face of the coupon in French and the language of the issuing country and on the reverse in four, five or six other languages.

Postmasters are instructed to apply a postmark indicating date of sale to the left circle on the coupon. When offered for exchange for stamps, the receiving postmaster is instructed to cancel the right circle.

Coupons with no postmark are not valid for exchange. Coupons with two postmarks have been redeemed and normally are kept by the post office making the exchange. **Coupons with one postmark are valued here.** Coupons with a stamp added to pay an increased rate are not listed here.

The following is a list of all varieties issued by the Universal Postal Union for any or all member countries.

Dates are those when the rate went into effect. The date that any item was put on sale in the United States can be very different.

Type A- Face

Wmk. "25c Union Postale Universelle 25c"
1907-20

A1	Face	Name of country in letters 1½mm high.
	Reverse	Printed rules between paragraphs German text contains four lines.

1907-20

A2	Face	Same as A1.
	Reverse	Same as A1 but without rules between paragraphs.

1910-20

A3	Face	Same as A1 and A2.
	Reverse	Same as A2 except German text has but three lines.

1912-20

A4	Face	Name of country in bold face type; letters 2mm to 2½mm high.
	Reverse	Same as A3.

1922-25

A5	Face	French words "le mois d'émission écoulé, deux mois encore."
	Reverse	As A3 and A4 but overprinted with new contract in red; last line of red German text has five words.

Wmk. "50c Union Postale Universelle 50c"
1925-26

A6	Face	Same as A5.
	Reverse	Four paragraphs of five lines each.

1926-29

A7	Face	French words "il est valable pendant un délai de six mois."
	Reverse	As A6 but overprinted with new contract in red; last line of red German text has two words.

Wmk. "40c Union Postale Universelle 40c"
1926-29

A8	Face	Design redrawn. Without lines in hemispheres.
	Reverse	Four paragraphs of four lines each.

Type B- Face

1931-35   **Wmk. Double-lined "UPU"**

B1	Face	French words "d'une lettre simple."
	Reverse	Four paragraphs of three lines each.

1935-36

B2	Face	French words "d'une lettre ordinaire de port simple."
	Reverse	Last line of German text contains two words.

1936-37

B3	Face	Same as B2.
	Reverse	Last line of German text contains one word.

1937-40

B4	Face	Same as B2 and B3. "Any Country of the Union."
	Reverse	German text is in German Gothic type.

1945

B5	Face	"Any Country of the Universal Postal Union."
	Reverse	Each paragraph reads "Universal Postal Union."

Type B5 exists without central printing on face.

1950

B6	Face	Same as B5.
	Reverse	Five paragraphs (English, Arabic, Chinese, Spanish, Russian).

1954

B7	Face	Same as B5.
	Reverse	Six paragraphs (German, English, Arabic, Chinese, Spanish, Russian).

Type C- Face

1968   **Wmk. Single-lined "UPU" Multiple**

C1	Face	French words "d'une lettre ordinaire de port simple."
	Reverse	Six paragraphs (German, English, Arabic, Chinese, Spanish, Russian).

Foreign coupons, but not U.S., of type C1 are known with large double-lined "UPU" watermark, as on type B coupons.

1971

C2	Face	French words "d'une lettre ordinaire du premier échelon de poids."
	Reverse	Six paragraphs (German, English, Arabic, Chinese, Spanish, Russian).

Type D- Face

1975   Wmk. Single-lined "UPU" Multiple

D1   Face   French words "d'une lettre ordinaire, expédiée à l'étranger par voie de surface."
Reverse   Six paragraphs (German, English, Arabic, Chinese, Spanish, Russian).
D2   Face   Left box does not have third line of French and dotted circle.
Reverse   Same as D1.

On D1 and D2 the watermark runs horizontally or vertically.

D3   Face   ....aerienne. Left box as D2 with (faculative) added.
Reverse   As D1, all references are to air service.
D4   Face   As D3, "CN 01 / (ancien C22)" replaces "C22."

Coupons exist without the validating origination markings. These have no validity and are beyond the scope of this catalogue.

REPLY COUPONS ISSUED FOR THE UNITED STATES

1907, Oct. 1
IRC2   A2   6c **slate green & gray green**   16.00
Rules omitted on reverse.
Earliest known use: Oct. 10, 1907.

1912
IRC3   A4   6c **slate green & gray green**   27.50
Three line English paragraph on face.

1922, Jan. 1
IRC4   A5   11c **slate green & gray green**, name 81½mm long   15.00
a.   Name 88½mm long   15.00
Five line English paragraph on face. Red overprint on reverse.

1925-26
IRC5   A6   11c **slate green & gray green**   15.00
Five line English paragraph on face. No overprint on reverse.
IRC6   A6   9c **slate green & gray green**, *Oct. 1, 1925*   15.00

1926
IRC7   A7   9c **slate green & gray green**   27.50
Four line English paragraph on face. Red overprint on reverse.
IRC8   A8   9c **slate green & gray green**   16.00
Without lines in hemispheres.

1935
IRC9   B2   9c **blue & yellow**   7.50
On reverse, last line of German text contains two words.

1936
IRC10   B3   9c blue and yellow   5.50
On reverse, last line of German text contains one word.

1937
IRC11   B4   9c **blue & yellow**   4.50
On reverse, German text in German Gothic type.

1945
IRC12   B5   9c **blue & yellow**, Italian text on reverse in 4 lines   4.00
a.   Italian text on reverse in 3 lines   5.00

1948, Oct. 15
IRC13   B5   11c **blue & yellow**   4.00
On face, "Universal Postal Union" replaces "Union."

1950
IRC14   B6   11c **blue & yellow**   4.00
On reverse, text in English, Arabic, Chinese, Spanish, Russian.

1954, July 1
IRC15   B7   13c **blue & yellow**   5.00
On reverse, text in German, English, Arabic, Chinese, Spanish, Russian.
Varieties: period under "u" of "amount" in English text on reverse, and period under "n" of "amount." Also, country name either 47mm or 50mm long.

No. IRC15 Surcharged in Various Manners

1959, May 2
IRC16   B7   15c on 13c **blue & yellow**   5.00
Individual post offices were instructed to surcharge the 13c coupon, resulting in many types of surcharge in various inks. For example, "REVALUED 15 CENTS," reading vertically; "15," etc.

1959, May 2
IRC17   B7   15c **blue & yellow**   4.00

1964
IRC18   B7   15c **blue & yellow**   4.00
a.   Reverse printing 60mm deep instead of 65mm (smaller Arabic characters)   4.50
On face, box at lower left: "Empreinte de contrôle / du Pays d'origine / (date facultative)" replaces "Timbre du / Bureau / d'Emission."

1969
IRC19   C1   15c **blue & yellow**   4.00

1971, July 1
IRC20   C2   22c **blue & yellow**   4.00

No. IRC20 Surcharged in Various Manners
1974, Jan. 5
IRC21   C2   26c on 22c **blue & yellow**   4.00
See note after No. IRC16.

1975, Jan. 2
IRC22   D1   26c **blue & yellow**   3.75

No. IRC22 Surcharged in Various Manners
1976, Jan. 3
IRC23   D1   42c on 26c **blue & yellow**   4.00
See note after No. IRC16. Several post offices are known to have surcharged No. IRC21 (42c on 26c on 22c).

Provisional surcharges on Nos. IRC24-IRC27 were not permitted.

1976, Jan. 3
IRC24   D1   42c **blue & yellow**   4.50

Some foreign countries use non-denominated IRCs. The U. S. has never ordered or used these "generic" items.

1981, July 1
IRC26   D1   65c **blue & yellow**   5.50

1986, Jan. 1
IRC27   D2   80c **blue & yellow**   5.50

1988, Apr. 3
IRC28   D2   95c **blue & yellow**   4.00
IRC29   D3   95c **blue & yellow**   4.00
a.   "9.1992" in lower left corner   4.00
Post offices were authorized on July 11, 1995 to revalue remaining stock of 95c IRCs to $1.05 by applying 10c in stamps until new stock (No. 30) arrived. All 95c varieties are known revalued thus.
The date of issue of No. 29 is not known. Earliest known use: Jan. 2, 1992.
No. 28 exists with inverted watermark (tops of letters facing right).

1995
IRC30   D4 $1.05 **blue & yellow**   2.00
"1.05" comes 1½mm or 3mm high. 3mm height has numerals more widely spaced.
Has "4.95" reading up in lower left corner. Other dates probably exist.
Earliest known use: July 12, 1995.

POST OFFICE SEALS

Official Seals began to appear in 1872. They do not express any value, having no franking power.

The first seal issued was designed to prevent tampering with registered letters while in transit. It was intended to be affixed over the juncture of the flaps of the large official envelopes in which registered mail letters were enclosed or stamp requisitions were shipped to postmasters and was so used exclusively. Beginning in 1877 (No. OX1 and later), Post Office Seals were used to repair damaged letters, reseal those opened by mistake or by customs inspectors, and to seal letters received by the Post Office unsealed.

Values for unused Post Office Seals are for those without creases. Uncanceled seals without gum will sell for less.

Used Post Office Seals will usually have creases from being applied over the edges of damaged or accidentally opened covers but will have either cancels, precancels or a signature or notation indicating use on the seal. Creased, uncanceled seals without gum are considered used and will sell for less than either an unused or a canceled used seal.

Covers with Post Office Seals are almost always damaged except in cases when the seal was applied to a cover marked "Received Unsealed." The values shown are for covers where the damage is consistent with the application of the seal.

Post Office Seals must be tied or exhibit some auxiliary marking or docketing to qualify for "on cover" values. No. OXF1 must bear a circular date stamp cancel and the cover to which it is affixed must bear the identical cancel to qualify for the "on cover" value.

NUMBER CHANGES
For number changes in this section, see the number change table at the back of the Catalogue.

REGISTRY SEALS

RS1

Used to seal large-thin-cardboard envelopes containing registered letters.

National Bank Note Co.
Typographed from a copper plate of 30 subjects (3x10) in two panes of 15

1872	Unwmk.	White Wove Paper		Perf. 12
OXF1	RS1	green	30.00	7.50
		On cover, Barber signature		25.00
		On cover, Terrell signature		75.00
		Block of 4	500.00	
		Pane of 15	2,500.	
a.		**Yellow green,** pelure paper	75.00	40.00
b.		Imperf., pair	1,500.	
c.		Horizontally laid paper	500.00	
d.		Printed on both sides	500.00	

e.	Printed on both sides, back inverted		750.00
f.	Double impression		750.00
g.	Double impression, one inverted	—	750.00

The second impression of Nos. OXF1d-OXF1g, are very faint. Also issued as a pane of 9 (3x3) (attributed to Continental Bank Note Co.).

Cancellations

Black	7.50
Blue	+5.00
Red	+15.00
Magenta	+50.00
Carrier	+25.00
Panama	—
Shanghai	—

Special Printings
Continental Bank Note Co.
Plate of 30 subjects (5x6)

1875(?) Hard White Wove Paper   Perf. 12
Without Gum

OXF2	RS1	bluish green	1,000.

American Bank Note Co.
Plate of 15 subjects (5x3)

1880 (?) Soft Porous Paper   Perf. 12
Without Gum

OXF3	RS1	bluish green	1,000.

POSTAGE STAMP AGENCY SEALS

Used to seal registered pouches containing stamps for distribution to Post Offices.

PSA1

Background size: 102x52mm.

1875-93   Litho.   Unwmk.   Die Cut
Barber Signature

OXF4	PSA1	brown & black		20.00
		On cover		50.00

Hazen Signature, Text 87mm Wide

OXF5	PSA1	brown & black, 1877		15.00
		On cover		50.00

Hazen Signature

OXF6	PSA1	pink & red, 1886		50.00
		On cover		350.00
a.		Salmon & red		60.00
		On cover		—

Harris Signature

OXF7	PSA1	pink & red, 1887		15.00
		On cover		50.00

Hazen Signature, Text 90½mm Wide

OXF8	PSA1	pink & red, 1889		15.00
		On cover		50.00

Craige Signature

OXF9	PSA1	pink & red, 1893		35.00
		On cover		90.00

PSA2

Background size: 120½x67mm.

1894   Litho.   Unwmk.   Die Cut
Craige Signature, "3rd Asst. P.M.G."

OXF10	PSA2	pink & red	20.00
		On cover	75.00

Craige Signature, "Third Assistant Postmaster General"

OXF11	PSA2	pale pink & red	15.00
		On cover	60.00
a.		Deep pink & red	15.00
		On cover	60.00

"John A. Merritt" in Sans-Serif Capitals at Left. Two Horizontal Lines Obliterating "Kerr Craige."
1897

OXF12	PSA2	pale pink & red	40.00
		On cover	150.00

Design of 1894
1897-1910(?)
Merritt Signature

OXF13	PSA2	rose & red	15.00
		On cover	60.00

Madden Signature

OXF14	PSA2	rose & red	35.00
		On cover	175.00

"Section 878"

OXF15	PSA2	rose & red	20.00
		On cover	85.00

"Section 970"

OXF16	PSA2	rose & red, 1910	20.00
		On cover	110.00
a.		Rose brown & black	20.00
		On cover	110.00

DEAD LETTER OFFICE SEALS

No. OX1 supposedly was issued as a Dead Letter Office Seal. Most on-cover examples are normal Post Office usages from larger East Coast cities. New York and Philadelphia predominate. Very few examples with Dead Letter Office markings are recorded. For that reason, No. OX1 is listed with the other Post Office Seals.

"Hazen" — DLO1

1884   Litho.   Unwmk.   Perf. 12

OXA1	DLO1	black, tan	27.50
		On cover	100.00

"Baird" — DLO2

1889

OXA2	DLO2	black, tan	27.50
		On cover	100.00

"Superintendent" — DLO3

1891

OXA3	DLO3	black, tan	25.00
		On cover	90.00

"5-2807" — DLO4

1893

OXA4	DLO4	black, tan	22.50
		On cover	85.00

"5-3282" — DLO5

1898

OXA5	DLO5	black, tan	25.00
		On cover	90.00

1898(?)   Hyphen hole perf. 7

OXA6	DLO5	black, tan	35.00
		On cover	110.00

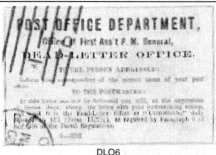

DLO6

Similar to DLO5 but smaller type used for instructions to the postmasters.

1900

OXA7	DLO6	black, *tan*	20.00	
		On cover		75.00

"5-3282" at Right — DLO7

1902(?)

OXA8	DLO7	black, *tan*	25.00	
		On cover		850.00

"5-3282" at Center — DLO8

1902(?)

OXA9	DLO8	black, *tan*	25.00	
		On cover		850.00

POST OFFICE SEALS

See introduction.

No. OX1 was prepared for use in the Dead Letter Office but was distributed to other offices and used in the same way as the later seals. Nos. OX19-OX20 were used on mail to and from the Procurement Division of the Quartermaster General's Office. After five weeks of use the seals were withdrawn when the Mail and Records Section became a full branch of the Post Office.

POS1

("Post Obitum" in background.)
National Bank Note Co.
Plate of 100 subjects (10x10)
Silk Paper

1877   **Engr.**   **Perf. 12**

OX1	POS1	**brown**	45.00	25.00
		Block of 4	500.00	
		On cover		1,200.

POS2

American Bank Note Co.
Engraved
Plate of 100 subjects (10x10) in two panes of 50 bearing imprint of American Bank Note Co.
Also plates of 50 (10x5) subjects.

1879   **Perf. 12**
Thin, crisp, semi-translucent paper, yellowish gum

OX2	POS2	**red brown**	3.00	1.00
		On cover		85.00
		Block of 4	15.00	
		Margin block with imprint	25.00	
a.		**Brown**	10.00	5.00
		On cover		200.00
		Block of 4	60.00	
		Margin block with imprint	85.00	

Seal impression can be clearly seen when viewed from the back.

Plate of 50 subjects (10x5). Four imprints of the American Bank Note Co. centered on each side of the pane with a reversed "2" to the right of the top and bottom imprints.

1879(?)
Thick, opaque paper, clear transparent gum

OX3	POS2	**yellow brown**	20.00	20.00
		On cover		150.00
		Block of 4	100.00	
		Margin block with imprint		
		& reversed "2"	175.00	

1881(?)
Thin, hard porous paper, clear transparent gum

OX4	POS2	**deep brown**	75.00	
		Block of 4	350.00	
		Margin block with imprint		
		& reversed "2"	500.00	

No. OX4 is the so-called "Special Printing." It was produced from a new plate prepared from the original die. It received little usage, but at least three full panes are known to have existed.

Colors

Beginning with OX5, many Official Seals exhibit a wide variety of shades. Minimal care was exercised in their printing. It is not uncommon for seals within a single pane to vary in shade from dark to very light. No attempt is being made here to list all of the various shades separately.

POS3

Typographed
Without words in lower label.
Outer frame line at top and left is thick and heavy
(compare with POS4).
Plate of 72 subjects (9x8)

1888   **Rough perf. 12**
Medium thick, crisp paper

OX5	POS3	**chocolate** (shades)	.75	.75
		On cover		50.00
		Block of 4	5.00	
a.		Imperf, pair	50.00	

Imperforates

Imperforates of Nos. OX6, OX7, OX10 are believed to be printer's waste. No seals were issued imperforate, though some may have been sent to post offices.

Plate of 42 subjects (6x7)

1889   **Rough perf. 12**
Thick to extremely thick paper

OX6	POS3	**chocolate** (shades)	.75	.50
		On cover		40.00
		Block of 4	5.00	

1889(?)   **Perf. 12**

OX7	POS3	**bister brown** (shades)	.75	.50
		On cover		40.00
		Block of 4	5.00	
a.		**Rose brown**	4.00	2.50
		On cover		65.00
		Block of 4	22.50	
b.		**Yellow brown**	2.00	2.00
		On cover		50.00
		Block of 4	10.00	
c.		Imperf. vertically, pair	25.00	—
d.		Imperf. horizontally, pair	25.00	—
e.		Vertical pair, imperf. between	20.00	
f.		Horizontal pair, imperf. between	75.00	
g.		Double impression		

Cancellation

	Puerto Rico	+75.00

Examples of No. OX7 with multiple impressions widely spaced or at angles to each other, are found on normal paper and various documents. These are printer's waste.

1892   **Rouletted 5½**

OX8	POS3	**light brown** (shades)	20.00	15.00
		On cover		200.00
		Block of 4	300.00	

1895 (?)   **Hyphen Hole Perf. 7**

OX9	POS3	**gray brown**	7.50	5.00
		On cover		100.00
		Block of 4	200.00	

Earliest known use: May 12, 1897.

1898(?)   **Perf. perf. 12**
Thin soft paper

OX10	POS3	**brown** (shades)	1.50	1.50
		On cover		75.00
		Block of 4	8.00	

POS4

Plate of 143 (11x13)

Outer frame line at top and left is thin.
Otherwise similar to POS3.

1900   **Litho.**   **Perf. 12**

OX11	POS4	**red brown**	.50	.25
		On cover		30.00
		Block of 4	2.50	
a.		**Gray brown**	2.00	1.25
		On cover		45.00
		Block of 4	15.00	
b.		**Dark brown**	2.50	*4.50*
		On cover		85.00
		Block of 4	15.00	
c.		**Orange brown**	.75	*2.00*
		On cover		75.00
		Block of 4	4.00	

Most imperfs and part perfs are printers waste. Some genuine perforation errors may have been issued to post offices.

Watermarks

Watermarks cover only a portion of the panes. Many stamps in each pane did not receive any of the watermark. Values for watermarked panes are for examples with at least 50% of the watermark present.

Similar to POS4 but smaller.
Design: 38x23mm
Issued in panes of 20

1907		Typo.	Perf. 12	
OX12	POS4	bright royal blue	2.00	2.00
		On cover		45.00
		Pane of 20	60.00	
OX13	POS4	blue (shades)	.20	.20
		On cover		25.00
		Pane of 20	20.00	
a.		Wmkd. Seal of U.S. in sheet	1.50	1.50
		Pane of 20	50.00	
b.		Wmkd. "Rolleston Mills" in sheet	1.00	1.00
		Pane of 20	40.00	
c.		Wmkd. "Birchwood Superfine" in sheet	—	—
		Block of 4	—	
d.		Pelure paper	20.00	20.00
e.		Toned paper	25.00	25.00

Numerous varieties such as imperf., part perf., tete beche, and double impressions exist. These seem to be from printer's waste. Some genuine perforation errors may have been issued to post offices.

1912			Rouletted 6½	
OX14	POS4	blue	1.00	1.00
		On cover		50.00
		Pane of 20	35.00	
a.		Wmkd. Seal of U.S. in sheet	10.00	10.00
		Pane of 20	300.00	
b.		Wmkd. "Rolleston Mills" in sheet	2.50	2.50
		Pane of 20	75.00	

Panes of 10 were made from panes of 20 for use in smaller post offices. Complete booklets with covers exist.

1913			Perf. 12 x Rouletted 6½	
OX15	POS4	blue	3.00	3.00
		On cover		100.00
		Pane of 20	110.00	
a.		Rouletted 6½ (right) x Perf. 12 (left, top, bottom)	15.00	—
		Pane of 20	150.00	
b.		Wmkd. Seal of U.S. in sheet	4.00	4.00
		Pane of 20	115.00	
c.		As "a" and "b"	20.00	—

No. OX15a comes from panes that are perfed between the left selvage and the stamps.

1913			Rouletted Perf. 6½x12	
OX16	POS4	blue	5.25	5.25
		On cover		150.00
		Pane of 20	150.00	
a.		Wmkd. Seal of U.S. in sheet	6.50	6.50
		Pane of 20	200.00	
b.		Wmkd. "Rolleston Mills" in sheet	—	—
		Pane of 20	—	

1916			Perf. 12	
OX17	POS4	black, pink	1.00	1.00
		On cover		50.00
		Pane of 20	40.00	
a.		Vert. pair, imperf. horizontally	—	

Three complete panes of No. OX17a have been reported.

1917			Perf. 12	
OX18	POS4	gray black	.40	.40
		On cover		27.50
		Pane of 20	40.00	
a.		Black	.50	.50
		On cover		30.00
		Pane of 20	45.00	
b.		Vert. pair, imperf horizontally	25.00	
c.		Horiz. pair, imperf vertically	20.00	
d.		Vertical pair, imperf between	60.00	
e.		Horizontal pair, imperf between	35.00	
f.		Imperf, pair	50.00	

POS5

Quartermaster General's Office
Issued in panes of 10 (5x2) without selvage.

1919			Perf. 12	
OX19	POS5	indigo	300.	
		Block of 4	1,500.	
		Pane of 10		

			Rouletted 7	
OX20	POS5	indigo	—	3,250.

The pane format of No. OX20 is not known. One of the few reported examples is rouletted on four sides.

POS6

Issued in panes of 20 and 16 (4x4).
Panes of 10 were made from panes of 20 for use in smaller post offices.

1919			Perf. 12 (sometimes rough)	
		Thin, white, crisp paper		
OX21	POS6	black (shades)	.20	.20
		On cover		10.00
		Pane of 20	10.00	
a.		Imperf, pair	15.00	
b.		Vert. pair, imperf horiz.	10.00	
c.		Horiz. pair, imperf vert.	10.00	
d.		Vert. pair, imperf btwn.	25.00	
e.		Horiz. pair, imperf btwn.	25.00	
f.		Wmkd. eagle and star in sheet (1036?)	2.00	2.00
		Pane of 20	70.00	
g.		As "f," imperf, pair	35.00	
h.		As "f," vert. pair, imperf horiz.	27.50	
i.		As "f," vert. pair, imperf btwn.	27.50	
j.		Wmkd. "Certificate Bond" in sheet (1936?)	10.00	10.00
		Pane of 20	300.00	

The paper used for Nos. OX21-OX27 is thin enough to allow reading text on the envelope.

Earliest known use: 1920.

1936(?)			Perf. 12x9	
OX22	POS6	black (shades)	7.50	7.50
		On cover		85.00
		Pane of 20	200.00	
a.		Vert. pair, imperf horiz.	50.00	
b.		Horiz. pair, imperf vert.	50.00	
c.		Wmkd. eagle and star in sheet	7.50	7.50
		Pane of 20	200.00	
d.		As "c." vert. pair, imperf horiz.	50.00	
e.		As "c," horiz. pair, imperf vert.	50.00	

Earliest known use: Oct. 1936 (No. OX22 or OX23.)

1936(?)			Perf. 12x8½	
OX23	POS6	black (shades)	2.50	2.50
		On cover		40.00
		Pane of 20	75.00	
a.		Wmkd. eagle and star in sheet	4.00	4.00
		Pane of 20	110.00	

1936(?)			Perf. 12½	
OX24	POS6	gray black, pane of 20	—	

1936(?)			Perf. 8½	
OX25	POS6	gray black	—	
a.		Wmkd. eagle and star in sheet	—	

1936(?)			Perf. 12x9½	
OX26	POS6	gray black, pane of 20	—	

1936(?)			Perf. 11½	
OX27	POS6	gray black	—	—
		On cover		

Medium to thick, opaque, egg or cream colored paper
Perf. 12

1946(?)				
OX28	POS6	gray black	.40	.40
		On cover		25.00
		Pane of 20	22.50	
a.		Vert. pair, imperf btwn.	15.00	

1946(?)			Perf. 12½	
OX29	POS6	gray black	.50	.50
		On cover		25.00
		Pane of 20	25.00	

1947(?)			Perf. 12½x8½	
OX30	POS6	gray black	1.50	1.50
		On cover		45.00
		Pane of 20	50.00	

1947(?)			Perf. 8½	
OX31	POS6	gray black	1.50	1.50
		On cover		45.00
		Pane of 20	50.00	

1947(?)			Perf. 8½x12	
OX32	POS6	gray black	—	

1947(?)			Perf. 8x8½	
OX33	POS6	gray black, on cover	—	

Thick, gray, very soft paper

1948			Perf. 12½ (sometime rough)	
OX34	POS6	gray black	1.00	1.00
		On cover		35.00
		Pane of 16	45.00	

1948(?)			Perf. 8½	
OX35	POS6	gray black	5.00	5.00
		On cover		60.00
		Pane of 16	—	

1948(?)			Perf. 12½x8½	
OX36	POS6	gray black	—	

1948(?)			Perf. 8½x12½	
OX37	POS6	gray black	—	

1948			Hyphen Hole Perf. 9½	
OX38	POS6	gray black	15.00	15.00
		On cover		100.00
		Pane of 5, imperf at sides	—	
		Pane of 16	350.00	

Pane of 5, tab inscribed "16-56146-1 GPO."

1950(?)			Hyphen Hole Perf. 9½ x Imperf	
		Medium thick, cream paper		
		Design width: 37½mm		
OX39	POS6	gray black, imperf at sides	.25	.20
		On cover		12.50
		Pane of 5, imperf at sides	1.25	
a.		Vert. pair, imperf between	10.00	
b.		Pane of 5, imperf	15.00	
c.		Pane of 5, imperf at top & btwn. rows 2 & 3, 4 & 5	20.00	

Pane of 5 tab inscribed, "16-56164-1 GPO."
Earliest known use: 1950.

1970(?)			Hyphen Hole Perf. 9½ x Imperf	
		Medium thick, white paper		
		Design width: 38½mm		
OX40	POS6	gray black	.20	.20
		On cover		30.00
		Pane of 5, imperf at sides	2.00	
a.		Vert. pair, imperf btwn.	10.00	
b.		Pane of 5, Imperf	20.00	

Tab inscribed, "c43-16-56164-1 GPO"

POS7

On Nos. OX41-OX50, tab is inscribed, "LABEL 21, JULY 1971."

1972		Litho.	Rouletted 9½ x Imperf	
OX41	POS7	black	.20	.20
		On cover		7.50
		Pane of 5	2.00	
a.		Imperf, pair	10.00	

1972(?)			Rouletted 6½ x Imperf	
OX42	POS7	black	.20	.20
		On cover		5.00
		Pane of 5	1.50	

1973(?)		Litho.	Hyphen Hole 7 x Imperf	
OX43	POS7	black	.20	.20
		On cover		7.50
		Pane of 5	2.00	

1976(?)		Litho.	Rouletted 8½ x Imperf	
OX44	POS7	black	.20	.20
		On cover		7.50
		Pane of 5	2.00	

1979 (?)		Litho.	Perf. 12½ x Imperf	
OX45	POS7	black	.20	.20
		On cover		7.50
		Pane of 5	2.00	
		Small holes	.20	.20
		On cover		7.50
		Pane of 5	2.00	

1988(?)		Litho.	Die Cut	
		Self-adhesive		
OX46	POS7	black, 38x21mm, tagged, fluorescent paper	.25	.25
		On cover		7.50
		Pane of 5	2.00	
OX47	POS7	bluish black, 38x21mm, untagged, non-fluorescent paper	.25	.25
		On cover		7.50
		Pane of 5	2.00	
OX48	POS7	gray (shades), 37x21mm	.25	.25
		On cover		7.50
		Pane of 5	2.00	
		On cover		5.00
OX49	POS7	black, 40x21mm	.50	.50
		On cover		15.00
		Pane of 5	4.00	
OX50	POS7	purple, 37x21mm	—	—
		On cover		—
		Pane of 5	—	

No. OX47 is ona creamier, thicker paper than No. OX46.
On No. OX49, BY is 2x1mm, P of POSTAL is left of P in POSTAL of Emblem. Tab inscribed as No. OX41, but 1's have no bottom serif.
Earliest known use: No. OX50, Dec. 12, 1995.

POS8

Tab inscribed "LABEL 21, JAN. 1992."

1992   **Size: 44x22mm**   *Die Cut*
                     Self-adhesive

OX51 POS8 **black**   1.00   1.00
             On cover   15.00
             Pane of 5   10.00

           Earliest known use: Mar.

1992?   *Die Cut*
               Self-Adhesive
               Size: 41x21mm

OX52 POS8 **black**   .25   .25
             On cover   7.50
             Pane of 5   2.00

No. OX52 exists on both white and brown backing paper.

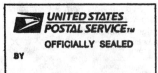

POS9

Tab inscribed "LABEL 21, April 1994."

1994   *Die Cut*
               Self-adhesive

OX53 POS9 **black**   .25   .25
             On cover   7.50
             Pane of 5   2.00

POS10   OFFICALLY SEALED BY:

Tab inscribed "LABEL 21, August 1996."

1996   *Die Cut*
               Self-Adhesive

OX54 POS10 **black**   .25   .25
              On cover   7.50
              Pane of 5   2.00
    a.   "OFFICALLY"   1.00   —
              On cover
              Pane of 5   8.00

TYPESET SEALS

These seals were privately printed for sale to Fourth Class
Post Offices. Many are extremely rare. Unquestioned varieties
are listed. Many others exist.
All are imperf. except Nos. LOX7-LOX11.

TSS1

LOX1 TSS1 **black**   500.00 500.00

TSS2

LOX2 TSS2 **black**   500.00 500.00
    a.   "OFFICALLY"   750.00

TSS3

LOX3 TSS3 **black**   —

TSS4

LOX4 TSS4 **black,** *pink*   1,250.
    No. LOX4 used is valued with minor flaws.

TSS5

LOX5 TSS5 **black**   500.00

TSS6

LOX6 TSS6 **black**   —

TSS7

Rouletted 9½ horizontally
LOX7 TSS7 **black**   500.00

TSS8

Printed and distributed by Morrill Bros., P.O. Supply Printers,
Fulton, N.Y., in panes of 4, two tete beche pairs.

Rouletted 11½, 12½, 16½ in black at top & side
LOX8 TSS8 **black**   50.00 50.00
             On cover   750.00
    a.   Tete beche pair   100.00
             Sheet of 4   600.00

TSS9

Solid lines above and below "OFFICIALLY SEALED" Printed
in panes of 4, two tete beche pairs, and in pane of 2, rouletted
16½.

Rouletted 12½, 16½ in black between
LOX9 TSS9 **black**   500.00 500.00
             On cover   750.00
    a.   Tete beche pair
             Pane of 4   —

TSS10

Dotted lines above and below "OFFICIALLY SEALED"
Printed in pane of 4, two tete beche pairs, and pane of 2, tete
beche.

Rouletted 11½, 12½ or 16½ in black
LOX10 TSS10 **black,** *pink*   500.00   —
LOX11 TSS10 **black**   1.25
               On cover   1,000.
    a.   Tete beche pair   2.50
               Pane of 4   5.00
    c.   Dot after "OFFICIALLY" 1.75
    d.   Pair, Nos. LOX11, LOX11c 3.00
    e.   As "d," in tete beche pair 3.50
    f.   Pane of 4, one stamp with dot 37.50
    g.   As "c," blue, rouletted 12   750.00
    h.   Pane of 2, both stamps with dot —
    I.   Double impression, one inverted

TSS11

Printed and distributed by The Lemoyne Supply Co.,
Lemoyne, Pa.
No. LOX13 has thin lines above and below 37¼mm long
"OFFICIALLY SEALED"

LOX12 TSS11 **black**   250.00
LOX13 TSS11 **blue**   250.00

TSS12

LOX14 TSS12 **blue**   1,750.   —

TSS13

LOX15 TSS13 **black** 1,250. —
blue — —

No. LOX15 unused is valued with small faults and crease. The blue seal may be No. LOX29.

TSS14

LOX16 TSS14 **blue** 1,250. 800.00

No. LOX16 used is valued with usual crease, thin spots and small tear.

TSS15

LOX17 TSS15 **dark blue** 150.00 200.00
On cover 1,000.
a. Printed on both sides 600.00
b. 2mm between "y" & "S," no period 200.00
after "d"
LOX18 TSS15 **black** 400.00 —
On cover 1,000.

TSS16

LOX19 TSS16 **black** 600.00

TSS16a

LOX19A TSS16a **black** 2,750.
No. LOX19A is unique. Valued based on 2000 auction sale.

Type I — TSS17

Type II - Bottom line in heavy type face. Period after "Office."
LOX20 TSS17 **black,** *light green* — —
a. Type II 2,000. —
At least two different types or settings are known. The illustrated type has a line above "BY" that does not show in the illustration.
No. LOX20a is valued with major thin at top center.

TSS18

LOX21 TSS18 **black** 1,100.

TSS18a

LOX21A TSS18a **black** 850.00 —
On cover 1,000.

No. LOX21A unused is valued with crease and small faults.

TSS19

LOX22 TSS19 **black,** *blue* 2,000.
No. LOX22 is unique. It is creased and is valued as such.

TSS20

LOX23 TSS20 **black** —

TSS21

LOX24 TSS21 **black,** on cover 3,000.

U. S. POST OFFICE,
NORTHFIELD, MASS.
OFFICIALLY SEALED.
OPENED THROUGH MISTAKE BY

TSS22

LOX25 TSS22 **black** 1,350.

At least three examples of No. LOX25 exist. All have faults. Value is for the finest example.

TSS23

LOX26 TSS23 **black** 1,100.
No. LOX26 used is valued with small fault.

TSS24

LOX27 TSS24 **black,** *dark brown red* 1,250.
No. LOX27 is valued with crease and small flaws.

TSS25

LOX28 TSS25 **black,** on cover 4,000.
No. LOX28 is unique. The seal was torn in half when the envelope was opened. Value is based on 2000 auction sale.

TSS26

LOX29 TSS26 **blue,** on cover 3,750.
No. LOX29 is unique.
See note below No. LOX15.

TSS27

LOX30   TSS27   **black**, pair on cover   5,000.

No. LOX30 is unique. The seals were torn in half when the envelope was opened. Value is based on 2000 auction sale.

TSS28

LOX31   TSS28   **red**, *cream*   1,000.

No. LOX31 is unique. It has a thin spot and crease and is valued as such.

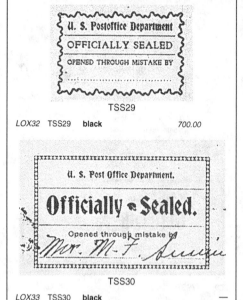

TSS29

LOX32   TSS29   **black**   700.00

TSS30

LOX33   TSS30   **black**

U. S. POSTOFFICE
Portage, Wash.
Officially Sealed
Opened by Mistake by

TSS31

LOX34   TSS31   **red**, *rose*   3,250.

No. LOX34 is unique. It has been torn in half.

TEST STAMPS

The uses for Bureau of Engraving and Printing-produced test stamps have ranged from BEP internal printing and equipment tests to Postal Service and private mailer tests. The earliest test stamps were created to test engraving, letterpress (typography) and offset lithography printing processes and to test the coiling equipment being developed by the BEP. More recent coil test stamps are used mainly to set tension chocks in coil vending machines and stamp-affixing machines. Test stamps also are used for training purposes and for mailing demonstrations at postal forums.

In addition to BEP-produced test stamps, there are a number of private test stamps and lookalike imposters. Such items, while interesting and collectible, are beyond the scope of the Scott Catalogue.

There are other formats and designs of official U.S. test stamps than those currently listed here, including sheets and booklets. The editors are assembling data to correct, clarify and expand these listings, and they would welcome information and examples of stamps from interested individuals.

1909-10 BEP Test Stamps for Rotary Press Development

Hamilton

Design size: 19x22mm

Offset

1-E1a   Die on card, about 3x3½ inches, **black**   2,000.

Endorsed on back, "First die proof impression of experimental surface die from surface print. J.E.R. (BEP director) April 25/10" and stamped "420279."

   b. Die on thick glazed card, 73x83mm, deep red   1,500.

Endorsed on front, "Sample of surface printing from die done by Bureau E&P 5/20/1910," with "420270" on back. Another example exists without notation and with "400894" on back.

   c. Essay cut to design size, on thick card with number on back, deep red   1,000.
   d. Plate, designs spaced 3½mm horiz., 2mm vert., imperf., deep red   —
   e. Coil plate, designs 2mm apart, perf. 10 horiz., gummed, deep red   —
      Pair   —
   f. As "e," perf. 12 vert., deep red   —
   g. Strip of 3, perf. 12, imperf. at top, deep red   —

Engr.

   h. Plate essay on soft wove, spaced 5mm apart, solid line vignettes, deep red   *1909*   —

No. 1-E1h known in block of 12 with pencil on back: "first impression printed from an experimental press designed by J.E. Ralph & B.F. Stickney from intaglio roll. J.E.R." (BEP director).

1910 BEP Test Stamps for Offset Printing

No. 385a-E2 was made by BEP for the Harris company for demonstrating the Harris offset press at the BEP. The offset method of printing postage stamps was not adopted in 1910 but several Harris presses were used to print revenue stamps and the "offset" postage issues of 1918-20.

385a-E2b

Engraved vignette of Minerva in frame similar to No. 319 but with "HARRIS AUTOMATIC / PRESS COMPANY / SERIES 1010" above vignette and "NILES, / OHIO, U.S.A." below.

385a-E2a   3c white wove, imperf., red   650.
      Pair   1,750.
   b. As "a," design reversed, red   500.
      Pair   1,500.

TEST COILS

No. 21

Blank Coils

11   Imperf.
   Mail-O-Meter private perf., type I   25.00
     pair   50.00
     pasteup pair   80.00
   Schermack private perf., type III   25.00
     pair   50.00
     pasteup pair   80.00

Imperf. test coils are known only with private perforations. Private printing is known on both perforation types.

15	Perf. 10, horiz. ribbed gum	.90
	Pair	1.80
a.	Smooth gum	1.25
	Pair	2.50

No. 15 is known with Multipost private printing.

17	Perf. 11	4.00
	Pair	8.00

Former No. 16 (perf 10½) was not produced by the BEP and therefore is beyond the scope of these listings.

Cottrell Press, 432-subject plates
1980(?)

18	Perf. 10, tagged, dull gum	5.00
	Pair	10.00
	Joint line pair	50.00

No. 18 was printed by an inked Cottrell Press. The ink was wiped, leaving some wiping marks and joint lines.

Two Continuous Horiz. Red Lines
Stickney Rotary Press

21	Perf. 10	6.25
	Pair	12.50

Nos. 31-33

Vertical Framed Rectangle Design

1938-60		**Perf. 10 Vert.**
31	**purple**	5.00
	Pair	15.00
	Joint line pair	30.00
a.	Imperf., pair	35.00
	Joint line pair	85.00

Misperfed examples are common and sell for less.

32	**carmine**, *1954*	—
	Pair	—
	Joint line pair	—
a.	Imperf., pair	100.00
	Joint line pair	250.00

No. 32 is known in imperforate blocks and in vertical pairs and blocks, imperforate horizontally.

Cottrell Press, 432-subject plates

33	**red violet**, small holes, *1960*	2.00
	Pair	4.00
	Joint line pair	22.50
	Large holes	5.00
	Pair	10.00
	Joint line pair	—
a.	Imperf., pair	45.00
	Joint line pair	100.00

FOR
TESTING
PURPOSES
ONLY

Nos. 41-45

Cottrell Press, 432-subject plates

1962   *Perf. 10 Vert.*

Size: approx. 19½mm wide

41	**black** (shades), untagged, shiny gum	1.25
	Pair	2.50
	Joint line pair	10.00
a.	Tagged, shiny gum	.75

	Pair	1.50
	Joint line pair	5.00
b.	Tagged, pebble-surface gum	1.75
	Pair	3.50
	Joint line pair	20.00
c.	As "b," imperf. pair	50.00
	Joint line pair	150.00
d.	Tagged, dull gum	2.25
	Pair	4.50
	Joint line pair	22.50
e.	Untagged, dull gum	.75
	Pair	1.50
	Joint line pair	10.00

No. 41 can be found with red, orange, blue, purple, gray graphite and black defacement lines; such copies sell for more. Also known on hi-brite fluorescent paper.

1970

42	**carmine**, tagged	—
43	**green**, tagged	75.00
	Pair	150.00
	Joint line pair	450.00
a.	Imperf., pair	150.00
	Joint line pair	450.00
b.	Vert. pair, imperf. between	175.00
c.	Untagged, dull gum	75.00

	Pair	150.00
	Joint line pair	450.00
d.	As "c," imperf., pair	300.00
	Joint line pair	400.00
e.	As "c," vert. pair, imperf. between	300.00

No. 43 was produced by BEP, distributed to Germany in large imperf. and part perf. sheets.

44	**brown**, untagged	3.50
	Pair	7.00
	Joint line pair	30.00
45	**orange**, tagged	—
	Pair	—
	Joint line pair	—

B Press

1988

Size: approx. 19mm wide

46	**black**, untagged	.50
	Pair	1.00

Also known on fluorescent paper.

CHRISTMAS SEALS

Issued by the American National Red Cross (1907-1919), the National Tuberculosis Association (1920-1967), the National Tuberculosis and Respiratory Disease Association (1968-1972) and the American Lung Association (1973-).

While the Christmas Seal is not a postage stamp, it has long been associated with the postal service because of its use on letters and packages.

Einar Holboell, an employee of the Danish Post Office, created the Christmas Seal. He believed that seal sales could raise money for charity. The post offices of Denmark, Iceland and Sweden began to sell such seals in the 1904 Christmas season. In the United States, Christmas Seals were first issued in 1907 under the guidance of Emily P. Bissell, following the suggestion of Jacob Riis, social service worker.

Until 1975, all seals (except those of 1907 and 1908 type I) were issued in sheets of 100. The grilled gum (1908) has small square depressions like a waffle. The broken gum (1922), devised to prevent paper curling, consists of depressed lines in the gum, ½mm. apart, forming squares. The vertical and horizontal broken gum (1922, 1923, 1925, 1927-1932) forms diamonds. The perf. 12.00 (1917-1919, 1923, 1925, 1931) has two larger and wider-spaced holes between every 11 smaller holes.

Values are for seals with original gum.

SEALS ISSUED BY THE DELAWARE CHAPTER OF THE AMERICAN NATIONAL RED CROSS

CS1 (Type II)

Designer - Emily P. Bissell.
Nearly $4,000 worth of seals were sold, $3,000 cleared.

Type I - "Merry Christmas" only.
Type II - "Merry Christmas" and "Happy New Year."

1907   *Perf. 14*

WX1	CS1	Type I	15.00
WX2	CS1	Type II	15.00

Types I and II litho. by Theo. Leonhardt & Son, Philadelphia, Pa. The 1st seals were sold Dec. 7, 1907, in Wilmington, Del. Issued in sheets of 228 (19x12). Type II was issued to extend the sale of seals until New Year's Day, 1908.
Counterfeits of both types exist (perf. 12).

SEALS ISSUED BY THE AMERICAN NATIONAL RED CROSS

CS2 (Type II)

Designer - Howard Pyle. Sales $135,000.

Type I - frame lines with square corners, small "C" in "Christmas."
Type II - frame lines have rounded corners, large "C" in "Christmas," leaves veined.

1908   *Perf. 12, 14*

WX3	CS2	Type I, perf. 14, smooth gum	30.00
a.		Perf. 12, smooth gum	30.00
c.		Perf. 14, grilled gum	30.00
d.		Perf. 12, grilled gum	30.00
e.		As #WX3, bklt. pane of 6	250.00
f.		As "c," bklt. pane of 6	250.00
g.		As #WX3, bklt. pane of 3	250.00
WX4	CS2	Type II, perf. 12	25.00
a.		Booklet pane of 6	175.00
b.		Booklet pane of 3	125.00

Type I litho. by Theo. Leonhardt & Son. Sheets of 250 (14x18), with the 1st space in the 9th and 18th rows left blank. Type II litho. by American Bank Note Co., New York, N.Y. in sheets of 100 (10x10).

Booklet panes have straight edges on 3 sides and perforated on left side where there is a stub, except No. WX4b which is a vert. strip of 3 with stub at top. Panes of 6 were made up in books of 24 and 48 and sold for 25c and 50c, and panes of 3 in books of 9 sold for 10c. The grilled gum has small square depressions like on a waffle.

CS3   CS4

Designer - Carl Wingate. Sales $250,000.

1909   *Perf. 12*

WX5	CS3	One type only	.75

Litho. by The Strobridge, Cincinnati, Ohio. Seals with a round punched hole of 3½mm are printers' samples.

1910   *Perf. 12*

Designer - Mrs. Guion Thompson. Sales $300,000.

WX6	CS4	One type only	15.00

Lithographed by The Strobridge Lithographing Co.

SEALS ISSUED BY THE AMERICAN NATIONAL RED CROSS
(But sold by the National Association for the Study and Prevention of Tuberculosis)

"The Old Home Among the Cedars"— CS5 (Type II)   CS6

Designer - Anton Rudert under directions of F. D. Millet. Sales $320,000.

Type I - diameter of circle 22mm, solid end in house.
Type II - same circle but thinner, lined end to house.
Type III - diameter of circle 20mm, lined end to house.

1911   *Perf. 12*

WX7	CS5	Type I	50.00
WX8	CS5	Type II	50.00

COIL STAMP

Perf. 8½ Vertically

WX9	CS5	Type III	50.00

Typo. by Eureka, Scranton, Pa. Type I has name and address of printer and union label in red in top margin. Type II has union label only in green on left margin.

1912   *Perf. 12*

Designer - John H. Zeh. Sales $402,256.

WX10	CS6	One type only	10.00

Lithographed by The Strobridge Lithographing Co.

CS7 (Type I)

Designer - C. J. Budd. Sales $449,505.

Type I - with Poinsettia flowers and green circles around red crosses at either side.
Type II - the Poinsettia flowers have been removed.
Type III - the Poinsettia flowers and green circles have been removed.

1913   **Perf. 12**

WX11	CS7	Type I	750.00
WX12	CS7	Type II	6.00
WX13	CS7	Type III	6.00

Lithographed by American Bank Note Co.

CS8   CS9

Designer - Benjamin S. Nash. Sales $555,854.

1914   **Perf. 12**

WX15	CS8	One type only	10.00

Lithographed by The Strobridge Lithographing Co.

1915

Designer - Benjamin S. Nash. Sales $760,000.

WX16	CS9	Perf. 12½	7.50
a.		Perf. 12	65.00

Lithographed by Andrew B. Graham Co., Washington, D.C.

CS10   CS11

Designer - T. M. Cleland. Sales $1,040,810.

1916

WX18	CS10	Perf. 12	4.00
a.		Perf. 12x12½	4.50
b.		Perf. 12½x12	12.50
c.		Perf. 12½	12.50

Lithographed by the Strobridge Lithographing Co.

Seals of 1917-21 are on coated paper.

1917

Designer - T. M. Cleland. Sales $1,815,110.

WX19	CS11	Perf. 12	.40
a.		Perf. 12½	7.50
b.		Perf. 12x12.00	.40
c.		Perf. 12x12½	12.50

Typographed by Eureka Specialty Printing Co.
Perf. 12.00 has two larger and wider-spaced holes between every eleven smaller holes.
Sheets come with straight edged margins on all four sides also with perforated margins at either right or left. Perforated margins have the union label imprint in green.

SEALS ISSUED BY THE AMERICAN NATIONAL RED CROSS
(Distributed by the National Tuberculosis Association)

CS12   CS13 (Type II)

Designer - Charles A. Winter.
These seals were given to members and others in lots of 10, the Natl. Tuberculosis Assoc. being subsidized by a gift of $2,500,000 from the American National Red Cross.

Type I - "American Red Cross" 15mm long, heavy circles between date.
Type II - "American Red Cross" 15½mm long, periods between date.

1918

WX21	CS12	Type I, perf. 11½x12.00	6.00
a.		Perf. 12	6.00
b.		Perf. 12.00, booklet pane of 10	2.00
c.		Perf. 12x12.00, booklet pane of 10	2.00
d.		Perf. 12, booklet pane of 10	2.00
e.		Perf. 12.00x12, booklet pane of 10	65.00
WX22	CS12	Type II, booklet pane of 10, perf. 12½xRoulette 9½	2.00
a.		Perf. 12½, booklet pane of 10	2.00
b.		Perf. 12½x12, bklt. pane of 10	—
d.		Roulette 9½xPerf. 12½, bklt. pane of 10	—
e.		Perf. 12½xRoulette 9½, bklt. pane of 10	12.50
f.		Perf. 12½, booklet pane of 10	12.50
h.		Roulette 9½xPerf. 12½, bklt. pane of 10	12.50
i.		Roulette 9½xPerf. 12½ and Roulette 12½, booklet pane of 10	—
j.		Perf. 12½, booklet pane of 10	60.00
k.		Perf. 12½x12½ and 12, bklt. pane of 10	—
l.		Roulette 9½xPerf. 12½, booklet pane of 10	—
m.		Perf. 12½, booklet pane of 10	—
n.		As "m," stub at bottom, bklt. pane of 10	50.00

For perf 12.00, see note following No. WX19.
Type I typographed by Eureka Specialty Printing Co.
Booklet panes of 10 (2x5) normally have straight edges on all four sides. They were cut from the sheets of 100 and can be plated by certain flaws which occur on both. Sheets have union label imprint on top margin in brown.
Type II lithographed by Strobridge Lithographing Co.
Booklet panes are the same but normally have a perforated margin at top and stub attached. These too can be plated by flaws. One or both vert. sides are rouletted on #WX22e; perforated on #WX22f and WX22h. #WX22i is rouletted 12½ on left, perf. 12½ on right. #WX22j, WX22k and WX22l are panes of 10 (5x2). #WX22m has a perforated margin at left.
Nos. WX21-WX21a are from sheet of 100, no straight edges.
The seal with "American Red Cross" 17¼mm long is believed to be an essay.

1919

Designer - Ernest Hamlin Baker. Sales $3,872,534.
Type I - plume at right side of Santa's cap.
Type II - no plume but a white dot in center of band.

WX24	CS13	Type I, perf. 12	.25
a.		Perf. 12x12.00	.25
b.		Perf. 12½x12	.25
c.		Perf. 12½x12.00	2.00
WX25	CS13	Type II, perf. 12½	.25

For perf 12.00, see note following No. WX19.
This is the first time the double barred cross, the emblem of the Natl. Tuberculosis Association, appeared in the design of the seals. It is also the last time the red cross emblem of the American National Red Cross was used on seals.
Type I typo. by Eureka, and has union label on margin at left in dark blue. Type II litho. by Strobridge.

SEALS ISSUED BY THE NATIONAL TUBERCULOSIS ASSOCIATION

CS14   CS15

Designer - Ernest Hamlin Baker. Sales $3,667,834.

Type I - size of seal 18x22mm.
Type II - seal 18½x23½mm, letters larger & numerals heavier.

1920

WX26	CS14	Type I, perf. 12x12½	.35
a.		Perf. 12	.35
b.		Perf. 12½x12	7.50
c.		Perf. 12½	10.00
WX27	CS14	Type II, perf. 12½	.35

Type I typo. by Eureka, and has union label imprint and rings on margin at left in dark blue. Type II litho. & offset by Strobridge.

1921

Designer - George V. Curtis. Sales $3,520,303.
Type I - dots in the chimney shading and faces are in diagonal lines, dots on chimney are separate except between the 2 top rows of bricks where they are solid.
Type II - dots in the chimney shading and faces are in horiz. lines.
Type III - as Type I except red dots on chimney are mostly joined forming lines, dots between the 2 top rows of bricks are not a solid mass.

WX28	CS15	Type I, perf. 12½	.25
WX29	CS15	Type II, perf. 12½	.25
WX29A	CS15	Type III, perf. 12	.25

Type I typo. by Eureka. Type II offset by Strobridge. Type III typo. by Zeese-Wilkinson Co., Long Island City, N.Y.

CS16   CS17

Designer - T. M. Cleland. Sales $3,857,086.

1922

WX30	CS16	Perf. 12½, broken gum	.50
a.		Perf. 12, broken gum	2.00
b.		Perf. 12x12½, broken gum	5.00
c.		Perf. 12, smooth gum	2.00
d.		Perf. 12½, vertical broken gum	2.00

Typographed by Eureka Specialty Printing Co.
The broken gum, which was devised to prevent curling of paper, consists of depressed lines in the gum ½mm apart, forming squares, or vertical broken gum forming diamonds.

1923

Designer - Rudolph Ruzicka. Sales $4,259,660.

WX31	CS17	Perf. 12½, vertical broken gum	.20
a.		Perf. 12, horizontal broken gum	2.50
b.		Perf. 12x12.00, vertical broken gum	2.50
c.		Perf. 12½x12, vertical broken gum	5.00
d.		Perf. 12, vertical broken gum	.50
e.		Perf. 12.00x12, vertical broken gum	2.50

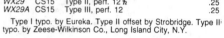

For perf 12.00, see note following No. WX19.
Typographed by Eureka Specialty Printing Co.
The broken gum on this and issues following printed by Eureka consists of very fine depressed lines forming diamonds.

CS18   CS19 (Type II)

Designer - George V. Curtis. Sales $4,479,656.

1924
WX32   CS18   One type only   .20
    Offset by Strobridge, E.&D., and U.S.P.& L.

1925   Perf. 12½
Designer - Robert G. Eberhard. Sales $4,937,786.
Type I - red lines at each side of "1925" do not join red tablet below.
Type II - red lines, as in type I, join red tablet below.
Type III - as type I but shorter rays around flames and "ea" of "Health" smaller.

WX35   CS19   Type I, vert. broken gum   .20
  a.   Perf. 12, vertical broken gum   2.50
  b.   Perf. 12x12½ vertical broken gum   .35
  c.   Perf. 12.00x12½ vert. broken gum   —
WX36   CS19   Type II   .20
WX37   CS19   Type III   .50

For perf 12.00, see note following No. WX19.
Type I typo. by Eureka. Type II offset by E.&D. Type III litho. by Gugler Lithographing Co., Milwaukee.

CS20   CS21

Designer - George V. Curtis. Sales $5,121,872.

1926   Perf. 12½
WX38   CS20   One type only   .20
    Offset by E.&D. and U.S.P.&L.
Printers' marks: E.&D. has a red dot at upper right on seal 91 on some sheets. U.S.P.&L. has a black dot at upper left on seal 56 on some sheets.

1927
Designer - John W. Evans. Sales $5,419,959.

WX39   CS21   Perf. 12, horizontal broken gum   .20
  a.   Smooth gum (see footnote)   1.00
WX40   CS21   Perf. 12½, no dot   .20
WX41   CS21   Perf. 12½, one larger red dot in background 1mm above right post of dashboard on sleigh   .20

"Bonne Sante" added to design and #WX39a but with body of sleigh myrtle green instead of green were used in Canada.
Offset: #WX39, WX39a by Eureka. #WX40 by E.&D. #WX41 by U.S.P.&L.
Printer's marks: Eureka has no mark but can be identified by the perf. 12. E.&D. has red dot to left of knee of 1st reindeer on seal 92. U.S.P.&L. has 2 red dots in white gutter, one at lower left of seal 46 (and sometimes 41) and the other at upper right of seal 55. The perforations often strike out one of these dots.

The Gallant Ship "Argosy" — CS22   CS23

Designer - John W. Evans. Sales $5,465,738.

Type I - shading on sails broken, dots in flag regular.
Type II - shading on sails broken, dots in flag spotty.
Type III - shading on sails unbroken, dots in flag regular.

1928   Perf. 12½
WX44   CS22   Type I, vertical broken gum   .20
WX45   CS22   Type II   .20
WX46   CS22   Type III   .20

Seals inscribed "Bonne Annee 1929" or the same as type II but green in water, and black lines of ship heavier and deeper color were used in Canada.
Offset: Type I by Eureka, Type II by Strobridge, Type III by E.&D.
Printers' marks: Type I comes with and without a blue dash above seal 10, also with a blue and a black dash. Type II has 2 blue dashes below seal 100. Type III has red dot in crest of 1st wave on seal 92.

1929   Perf. 12½
Designer - George V. Curtis. Sales $5,546,147.

WX49   CS23   Vertical broken gum   .20
  a.   Perf. 12, vertical broken gum   .50
  b.   Perf. 12½x12, vertical broken gum   .75
WX50   CS23   Smooth gum   .20

Seals inscribed "Bonne Sante 1929" or "Christmas Greetings 1929" were used in Canada.
Offset: #WX49-WX49b by Eureka, #WX50 by E.&D., U.S.P.&L., and R.R. Heywood Co., Inc., New York, N.Y.
Printers' marks: Eureka is without mark but identified by broken gum. E.&D. has a black dot in lower left corner of seal 92. U.S.P.&L. has blue dot above bell on seal 56. Heywood has a blue dot at lower right corner of seal 100.

CS24   CS25

Designer - Ernest Hamlin Baker, and redrawn by John W. Evans. Sales $5,309,352.

1930   Perf. 12½
WX55   CS24   Vertical broken gum   .20
  a.   Perf. 12, vert. broken gum   .50
  b.   Perf. 12.00x12, vert. broken gum   .25
  c.   Perf. 12½x12, vertical broken gum   2.50
  d.   Perf. 12, booklet pane of 10, horiz. broken gum   .50
WX56   CS24   Smooth gum   .20

Seals inscribed "Bonne Sante" or "Merry Christmas" on red border of seal were used in Canada.
Offset: #WX55-WX55d by Eureka, #WX56 by Strobridge, E.&D. and U.S.P.&L.
Printers' marks: Eureka has a dot between the left foot and middle of "M" of "Merry" on seal 1. Strobridge has 2 dashes below "ALL" on seal 100. E.&D. printed on Nashua paper has dot on coat just under elbow on seal 92, and on Gummed Products Co. paper has the dot on seals 91, 92. U.S.P.&L. has a dash which joins tree to top frame line just under "MA" of "Christmas" on seal 55.
The plate for booklet panes was made up from the left half of the regular plate and can be plated by certain flaws which occur on both.

1931   Perf. 12½
Designer - John W. Evans. Sales $4,526,189.

WX61   CS25   Horiz. broken gum (see footnote)   2.00
WX62   CS25   Horizontal broken gum   .20
  a.   Perf. 12x12½, horiz. broken gum   .35
  b.   Perf. 12½x12, horizontal broken gum   2.50
  c.   Perf. 12, horizontal broken gum   1.00
  g.   Perf. 12, vertical broken gum, booklet pane of 10   .50
  h.   Perf. 12x12.00, vertical broken gum, booklet pane of 10   .60
WX63   CS25   Smooth gum   .20

For perf 12.00, see note following No. WX19.
Offset: #WX61-WX62h by Eureka, #WX63 by Strobridge. #WX61 has a green dash across inner green frame line at bottom center on each seal in sheet except those in 1st and last vertical rows and the 2 rows at bottom.
Printers' marks: Eureka has none. Strobridge has the usual 2 dashes under seal 100.
The plate for booklet panes was made up from transfers of 60 seals (12x5). The panes can be plated by minor flaws.

CS26   CS27

Designer- Edward F. Volkmann. Sales $3,470,637.

1932
WX64   CS26   Perf. 12½x12¾   .20
  a.   Vertical broken gum   .50
WX65   CS26   Perf. 12   .20
WX66   CS26   Perf. 12½   .20
WX67   CS26   Perf. 12½   .20

Offset: #WX64 by Eureka, #WX65 by E.&D., #WX66 by U.S.P.&L., and #WX67 by Columbian Bank Note Co., Chicago. #WX64, WX67 have a little red spur on bottom inner frame line of each seal, at left corner.
Printers' marks: Eureka has a red dash, in each corner of the sheet, which joins the red border to the red inner frame line. E.&D. has a blue dot in snow at lower left on seal 91. U.S.P.&L. has a blue dot on top of post on seal 56. Columbian Bank Note has small "C" in lower part of girl's coat on seal 82.

1933
Designer - Hans Axel Walleen. Sales $3,429,311.

WX68   CS27   Perf. 12   .20
WX69   CS27   Perf. 12½   .20

Offset: #WX68 by Eureka, #WX69 by Strobridge, U.S.P.&L., and the Columbian Bank Note Co.
Printers' marks; Eureka has rope joining elbow of figure to left on seals 11, 20, 91, 100. Strobridge has 2 dashes under seal 100. U.S.P.&L. has green dot on tail of "s" of "Greetings" on seal 55. Columbian has white "c" on margin, under cross, on seal 93.

CS28   CS29

Designer - Herman D. Giesen. Sales $3,701,344.

1934
WX72   CS28   Perf. 12½x12¼   .20
WX73   CS28   Perf. 12½ (see footnote)   .20
WX74   CS28   Perf. 12½ (see footnote)   .20
WX75   CS28   Perf. 12½ (see footnote)   .20

Offset: #WX72 by Eureka, #WX73 by Strobridge, #WX74 by E.&D. and #WX75 by U.S.P.&L.
Cutting of blue plate for the under color: #WX72, WX73 (early printing) and WX74 have lettering and date cut slightly larger than ultramarine color. #WX73 (later printing) has square cutting around letters and date, like top part of letter "T". #WX75 has cutting around letters and date cut slightly larger.
Printers' marks: Eureka has 5 stars to right of cross on seal 10. Strobridge has 2 blue dashes in lower left corner of seal 91 or in lower right corner of seal 100. E.&D. has a red dot in lower left corner of seal 99. U.S.P.&L. has 5 stars to left of cross on seal 56.
Great Britain issued seals of this design which can be distinguished by the thinner and whiter paper. Sheets have perforated margins on all 4 sides but without any lettering on bottom margin, perf. 12½.

1935
Designer - Ernest Hamlin Baker. Sales $3,946,498.

WX76   CS29   Perf. 12½x12¼   .20
WX77   CS29   Perf. 12½   .20

Offset: #WX76 by Eureka, #WX77 by Strobridge, U.S.P.&L. and Columbian Bank Note Co.
Eureka recut blue plate and eliminated the faint blue shading around cross, girl's head and at both sides of the upper part of post. U.S.P.& L. eliminated the 2 brown spurs which pointed to the base of cross, in all 4 corners of the sheet.
Printers' marks: Eureka has an extra vertical line of shading on girl's skirt on seal 60. Strobridge has 2 brown dashes in lower right corner of position 100 but sheets from an early printing are without this mark. U.S.P.&L. has a blue dot under post on seal 55. Columbian has a blue "c" under post on seal 99.
The corner seals carry slogans: "Help Fight Tuberculosis," "Protect Your Home from Tuberculosis," "Tuberculosis Is Preventable," "Tuberculosis Is Curable."

20-Cent Minimum Value
The minimum value for a single stamp is 20 cents. This value reflects the costs involved with handling inexpensive stamps.

Printers' marks appear on seal 56 on sheets of 100 unless otherwise noted:
- E   Eureka Specialty Printing Co.
- S   Strobridge Lithographing Co. (1930-1958).
- S   Specialty Printers of America (1975-).
- D   Edwards & Deutsch Lithographing Co. (E.&D.)
- U   United States Printing & Lithographing Co. (U.S.P.&L.)
- F   Fleming-Potter Co., Inc.
- W   Western Lithograph Co.
- B   Berlin Lithographing Co. (1956-1969); I. S. Berlin Press (1970-1976); Barton-Cotton (1977-).
- R   Bradford-Robinson Printing Co.
- N   Sale-Niagara, Inc.

Seals from 1936 onward are printed by offset.
Seals with tropical gum (dull), starting in 1966, were used in Puerto Rico.

CS30   CS31

Designer - Walter I. Sasse. Sales $4,522,269.

1936

		Pair
WX80	CS30	Perf. 12½x12 (E)	.20
WX81	CS30	Perf. 12½ (S,D,U)	.20

Seals with red background and green cap-band alternate with seals showing green background and red cap-band. The corner seals carry the same slogans as those of 1935.

Two of the three Strobridge printings show vertical green dashes in margin below seal 100, besides "S" on seal 56.

1937

Designer - A. Robert Nelson. Sales $4,985,697.

WX88	CS31	Perf. 12x12½ (E)	.20
WX89	CS31	Perf. 12½ (S,D,U)	.20

Positions 23, 28, 73 and 78, carry slogans: "Health for all," "Protect your home," "Preventable" and "Curable."

The "U" printer's mark of U.S.P.&L. appears on seal 55. It is omitted on some sheets.

CS32   CS33

Designer - Lloyd Coe. Sales $5,239,526.

1938

WX92	CS32	Perf. 12½x12 (E)	.20
WX93	CS32	Perf. 12½ (S,D,U)	.20
a.		Miniature sheet, imperf.	3.00

The corner seals bear portraits of Rene T. H. Laennec, Robert Koch, Edward Livingston Trudeau and Einar Holboll.

No. WX93a contains the 4 corner seals, with the regular seal in the center. It sold for 25 cents.

1939

Designer - Rockwell Kent. Sales $5,593,399.

WX96	CS33	Perf. 12½x12 (E)	.20
a.		Booklet pane of 20, perf. 12	.35
WX97	CS33	Perf. 12½ (S,D,U)	.20

The center seals, positions 45, 46, 55, 56, carry slogans: "Health to All," "Protect Your Home." "Tuberculosis Preventable Curable" and "Holiday Greetings."

Printers' marks appear on seal 57.

CS34   CS35

Designer- Felix L. Martini. Sales $6,305,979.

1940

WX100	CS34	Perf. 12½x12 (E)	.20
WX101	CS34	Perf. 12½x13 (E)	.20
WX103	CS34	Perf. 12½ (S,D,U)	.20

Seals 23, 32 and 34 carry the slogan "Protect Us from Tuberculosis." Each slogan seal shows one of the 3 children.

1941

Designer - Stevan Dohanos. Sales $7,530,496.

WX104	CS35	Perf. 12x12 (E)	.20
WX105	CS35	Perf. 12½ (S,D,U)	.20

"S" and "U" printers' marks exist on same sheet.

CS36   CS37

Designer - Dale Nichols. Sales $9,390,117.

1942

WX108	CS36	Perf. 12x12½ (E)	.20
WX109	CS36	Perf. 12½ (S,D,U)	.20

1943

Designer - Andre Dugo. Sales $12,521,494.

		Pair
WX112	CS37	Perf. 12½x12 (E)	.20
WX113	CS37	Perf. 12½ (S,D,U)	.20

On alternate seals, the vert. frame colors (blue & red) are transposed as are the horiz. frame colors (buff & black).

Seals where "Joyeux Noel" replaces "Greetings 1943" and "1943" added on curtain or the same as #WX113 but darker colors were used in Canada.

CS38   CS39

Designer - Spence Wildey. Sales $14,966,227.

1944

WX118	CS38	Perf. 12½x12 (E)	.20
WX119	CS38	Perf. 12½ (S,D,U)	.20

Seals with "USA" omitted are for Canada.

1945   "USA" at Lower Right Corner

Designer - Park Phipps. Sales $15,638,755.

WX124	CS39	Perf. 12½x12 (E)	.20
WX125	CS39	Perf. 12½ (S,D,U)	.20

Seals with "USA" omitted are for Canada.

CS40   CS41

Designer - Mary Louise Estes and Lloyd Coe. Sales $17,075,608.

1946   "USA" at Left of Red Cross

WX130	CS40	Perf. 12½x12 (E)	.20
WX131	CS40	Perf. 12½ (S,D,U)	.20

Seals with "USA" omitted are for Canada and Bermuda. Printers' marks are on seal 86.

The center seals (45, 46, 55, 56) bear portraits of Jacob Riis, Emily P. Bissell, E. A. Van Valkenburg and Leigh Mitchell Hodges.

1947

Designer - Raymond H. Lufkin. Sales $18,665,523.

WX135	CS41	Perf. 12x12½ (E)	.20
WX136	CS41	Perf. 12½ (S,D,U)	.20

Seals with "USA" omitted are for Canada and Great Britain. The "U" printer's mark of U.S.P.&L. appears on seal 46.

CS42   CS43

Designer - Jean Barry Bart. Sales $20,153,834.

1948

WX140	CS42	Perf. 12x12½ (E)	.20
WX141	CS42	Perf. 12½ (S,D,U)	.20

Seals with "USA" omitted are for Canada and Great Britain.

1949

Designer - Herbert Meyers. Sales $20,226,794.

WX145	CS43	Perf. 12x12½ (E)	.20
WX146	CS43	Perf. 12½ (S,D,U)	.20

Seals with "USA" omitted are for Canada & Great Britain.

CS44   CS45

Designer - Andre Dugo. Sales $20,981,540.

1950

WX150	CS44	Perf. 12½x12 (E)	.20
WX151	CS44	Perf. 12½ (S,D,U,F)	.20

Seals with "USA" omitted are for Canada & Great Britain.

1951

Designer - Robert K. Stephens. Sales $21,717,953.

WX155	CS45	Perf. 12½x12 (E)	.20
WX156	CS45	Perf. 12½ (S,D,U,F)	.20

Seals with "USA" omitted are for Canada.

CS46   CS47

Designer - Tom Darling. Sales $23,238,148.

1952

WX159	CS46	Perf. 12½x12 (E)	.20
WX160	CS46	Perf. 12½ (S,D,U,F)	.20

Overprinted "Ryukyus" (in Japanese characters)

WX163	CS46	Perf. 12½x12, 12½ (U)	1.50

1953

Designers - Elmer Jacobs and E. Willis Jones. Sales $23,889,044.

WX164	CS47	Perf. 13 (E)	.20
WX165	CS47	Perf. 12½ (S,D,U,F)	.20

CS48

Designer - Jorgen Hansen. Sales $24,670,202.

1954			**Block of 4**
WX168	CS48	Perf. 13 (E)	.20
WX169	CS48	Perf. 12½ (S,U,F,W)	.20
WX170	CS48	Perf. 11 (D)	.20

CS49

Designer - Jean Simpson. Sales $25,780,365.

1955			**Pair**
WX173	CS49	Perf. 13 (E)	.20
WX174	CS49	Perf. 12½ (S,U,F,W)	.20
WX175	CS49	Perf. 11 (D)	.20

CS50

Designer - Heidi Brandt. Sales $26,310,491.

1956			**Block of 4**
WX178	CS50	Perf. 12½x12 (E)	.20
WX179	CS50	Perf. 12½ (E,S,U,F,W)	.20
WX180	CS50	Perf. 11 (D,B)	.20
WX183	CS50	"Puerto Rico," perf. 12½	3.00

C51

Designer - Clinton Bradley. Sales $25,959,998.

1957			**Block of 4**
WX184	CS51	Perf. 13 (E)	.20
WX185	CS51	Perf. 12½ (S,U,F,W,R)	.20
WX186	CS51	Perf. 11 (D,B)	.20
WX187	CS51	Perf. 10½x11 (D)	.20
WX188	CS51	Perf. 10½ (D)	.20
WX190	CS51	"Puerto Rico," perf. 13	3.00

CS52

Designer - Alfred Guerra. Sales $25,955,390.

1958			**Pair**
WX191	CS52	Perf. 13 (E)	.20
WX192	CS52	Perf. 12½ (S,U,F,W,R)	.20
WX193	CS52	Perf. 10½x11 (B,D)	.20
WX194	CS52	Perf. 11 (B,D)	.20
WX196	CS52	"Puerto Rico," perf. 13	1.50

CS53

Designer - Katherine Rowe. Sales $26,740,906.

1959			**Pair**
WX197	CS53	Perf. 13 (E)	.20
WX198	CS53	Perf. 12½ (F,R,W)	.20
a.		Horiz. pair, imperf. btwn. (D)	1.50
WX199	CS53	Perf. 10½x11 (B)	.20
WX200	CS53	Perf. 11 (B,D)	.20
WX201	CS53	Perf. 10½ (B)	.20
WX203	CS53	"Puerto Rico," perf. 13	1.00

E.&D. omitted every other vertical row of perforation on a number of sheets which were widely distributed as an experiment. #WX198a is from these sheets.

CS54

Designer - Philip Richard Costigan. Sales $26,259,030.

1960			**Block of 4**
WX204	CS54	Perf. 12½ (E,F,R,W)	.20
WX205	CS54	Perf. 12½x12 (E)	.20
WX206	CS54	Perf. 11x10½ (B)	.20
WX207	CS54	Perf. 11 (D)	.20

Puerto Rico used No. WX204 (E).

CS55

Designer - Heidi Brandt. Sales $26,529,517.

1961			**Block of 4**
WX209	CS55	Perf. 12½ (E,F,R,W)	.20
WX209A	CS55	Perf. 12½x12 (E)	
WX210	CS55	Perf. 11x10½ (B)	.20
WX211	CS55	Perf. 11 (D)	.20

Puerto Rico used No. WX209 (E).

CS56

Designer - Paul Dohanos. Sales $27,429,202.

1962			**Block of 4**
WX213	CS56	Perf. 12½ (F,R,W)	.20
WX214	CS56	Perf. 13 (E)	.20
WX215	CS56	Perf. 10½x11 (B)	.20
WX216	CS56	Perf. 11 (D,B)	.20

Puerto Rico used No. WX214.

CS57

Designer - Judith Campbell Piussi. Sales $27,411,806.

1963			**Block of 4**
WX218	CS57	Perf. 12½ (E,F,R,W)	.20
WX219	CS57	Perf. 11 (B,D)	.20

Puerto Rico used No. WX218 (E).

CS58

Designer - Gaetano di Palma. Sales $28,784,043.

1964			**Block of 4**
WX220	CS58	Perf. 12½ (E,F,R,W)	.20
WX221	CS58	Perf. 11 (B,D)	.20

Puerto Rico used No. WX221 (B).

CS59

Designer - Frede Salomonsen. Sales $29,721,878.

1965   **Block of 4**
WX222   CS59   Perf. 12½ (F,W)   .20
WX223   CS59   Perf. 11 (B,D)   .20
WX224   CS59   Perf. 13 (E)   .20

Puerto Rico used No. WX223 (B).

CS60

Designer - Heidi Brandt. Sales $30,776,586.

1966   **Block of 8**
WX225   CS60   Perf. 12½ (E,F,W)   .25
WX226   CS60   Perf. 10½x11 (B)   .25
WX227   CS60   Perf. 11 (D)   .25

Blocks of four seals with yellow green and white backgrounds alternate in sheet in checkerboard style.
Puerto Rico used No. WX226.

Holiday Train — CS61

Designer - L. Gerald Snyder. Sales $31,876,773.
The seals come in 10 designs showing a train filled with Christmas gifts and symbols. The direction of the train is reversed in alternating rows as are the inscriptions "Christmas 1967" and "Greetings 1967." The illustration shows first 2 seals of top row.

1967   **Block of 20 (10x2)**
WX228   CS61   Perf. 13 (E)   .30
WX229   CS61   Perf. 12½ (F,W)   .30
WX230   CS61   Perf. 10½ (B)   .30
WX231   CS61   Perf. 11 (D)   .30
WX232   CS61   Perf. 11x10½ (B)   .30

Puerto Rico used No. WX229 (F).

SEALS ISSUED BY NATIONAL TUBERCULOSIS AND RESPIRATORY DISEASE ASSOCIATION

CS62

Designer - William Eisele. Sales $33,059,107.

1968   **Block of 4**
WX233   CS62   Perf. 13 (E)   .20
WX234   CS62   Perf. 10½x11 (B)   .20
WX234A   CS62   Perf. 10½ (B)   .20
WX235   CS62   Perf. 11 (D)   .20
WX236   CS62   Perf. 12½ (F,W)   .20

Pairs of seals with bluish green and yellow backgrounds alternate in sheet in checkerboard style.
Puerto Rico used No. WX236 (F).

CS63

Designer - Bernice Kochan. Sales $34,437,591.

1969   **Block of 4**
WX237   CS63   Perf. 13 (E)   .20
WX238   CS63   Perf. 12½ (F,W)   .20
WX239   CS63   Perf. 10½x11 (B)   .20
WX240   CS63   Perf. 11 (B)   .20

Puerto Rico used No. WX238 (F).

CS64

Designer - L. Gerald Snyder. Sales $36,237,977.
Sheets contain 100 different designs, Christmas symbols, toys, decorated windows; inscribed alternately "Christmas 1970" and "Greetings 1970." The illustration shows 6 seals from the center of the sheet.

1970   **Sheet of 100 (10x10)**
WX242   CS64   Perf. 12½ (E,F,W)   1.00
WX243   CS64   Perf. 11 (B)   1.00
WX244   CS64   Perf. 11x10½ (B)   1.00

Puerto Rico used No. WX242 (F).

CS65

Designer - James Clarke. Sales $36,120,000.

1971   **Block of 8 (2x4)**
WX245   CS65   Perf. 12½ (E,F)   .20
WX246   CS65   Perf. 11 (B)   .20

The 4 illustrated seals each come in a 2nd design arrangement: cross at left, inscriptions transposed, and reversed bugler, candle and tree ornaments. Each sheet of 100 has 6 horiz. rows as shown and 4 rows with 2nd designs.
Puerto Rico used No. WX245 (F).
Eureka printings are found with large "E," small "E" and without "E."

CS66

Designer - Linda Layman. Sales $38,000,557.
The seals come in 10 designs showing various holiday scenes with decorated country and city houses, carolers, Christmas trees and snowman. Inscribed alternately "1972 Christmas" and "Greetings 1972." Shown are seals from center of row.

1972   **Strip of 10**
WX247   CS66   Perf. 13 (E)   .30
WX248   CS66   Perf. 12½ (F)   .30
WX249   CS66   Perf. 11 (B)   .30

Seal 100 has designer's name. Puerto Rico used No. WX248.

SEALS ISSUED BY AMERICAN LUNG ASSOCIATION

CS67

Designer - Cheri Johnson. Sales $36,902,439.
The seals are in 12 designs representing "The 12 Days of Christmas." Inscribed alternately "Christmas 1973" and "Greetings 1973." Shown is block from center of top 2 rows.

1973   **Block of 12**
WX250   CS67   Perf. 12½ (F), 18x22mm   .35
    a.   Size 16½x20½mm (E)   .35
WX251   CS67   Perf. 11 (B,W)   .35

Seal 100 has designer's name. Puerto Rico used #WX250 (F).

CS68

Designer - Rubidoux. Sales $37,761,745.

1974   **Block of 4**
WX252   CS68   Perf. 12½ (E,F)   .20
WX253   CS68   Perf. 11 (B)   .20

Seal 99 has designer's name. Puerto Rico used #WX252 (F).

C69

Children's paintings of holiday scenes. Different design for each state or territory. Paintings by elementary school children were selected in a nationwide campaign ending in Jan., 1974. Sales $34,710,107.

1975			Sheet of 54 (6x9)
WX254	CS69	Perf. 12½ (S,F)	.75
WX255	CS69	Perf. 11 (B)	.75

Printers' marks are on seal 28 (New Mexico). Specialty Printers' seals (S) carry union labels: "Scranton 4," "Scranton 7," "E. Stroudsburg."
Puerto Rico used No. WX254 (F).

CS70

Continuous village picture covers sheet with Christmas activities and Santa crossing the sky with sleigh and reindeer. No

inscription on 34 seals. Others inscribed "Christmas 1976," "Greetings 1976," and (on 9 bottom-row seals) "American Lung Association." Illustration shows seals 11-12, 20-21.
Sales $36,489,207.

1976			Sheet of 54 (9x6)
WX256	CS70	Perf. 12½ (F,N)	.75
WX257	CS70	Perf. 11 (B)	.75
WX258	CS70	Perf. 13 (S)	.75

Printers' marks (N, B, S) on seal 32 and (F) on seal 23.
Puerto Rico used No. WX256 (F).

CS71

Children's paintings of holiday scenes. Different design for each state or territory.
Sales $37,583,883.

1977			Sheet of 54 (6x9)
WX259	CS71	Perf. 12½ (F)	.75
WX260	CS71	Perf. 11 (B)	.75
WX261	CS71	Perf. 13 (S)	.75

Printers' marks on seal 28 (Georgia).
Puerto Rico used No. WX259.

CS72

Children's paintings of holiday scenes. Different design for each state or territory.
Sales $37,621,466.

1978			Sheet of 54 (6x9)
WX262	CS72	Perf. 12½ (F)	.75
WX263	CS72	Perf. 11 (B)	.75
WX264	CS72	Perf. 13 (S)	.75

Printers' marks on seal 29 (New Hampshire).
Puerto Rico used No. WX262.

Type of 1978 Inscribed 1979

1979			Sheet of 54 (6x9)
WX265	CS72	Perf. 12½ (F)	.75
WX266	CS72	Perf. 11 (B)	.75
WX267	CS72	Perf. 13 (S)	.75

Printer's marks on seal 22 (Virgin Islands). Puerto Rico used No. WX265.

Beginning in 1979 there is no longer one national issue. Additional designs are issued on a limited basis as test seals to determine the designs to be used the following year.

SANITARY FAIR

The United States Sanitary Commission was authorized by the Secretary of War on June 9, 1861, and approved by President Lincoln on June 13, 1861. It was a committee of inquiry, advice and aid dealing with the health and general comfort of Union troops, supported by public contributions.

Many Sanitary Fairs were held to raise funds for the Commission, and eight issued stamps. The first took place in 1863 at Chicago, where no stamp was issued. Some Sanitary Fairs advertised on envelopes.

Sanitary Fair stamps occupy a position midway between United States semi-official carrier stamps and the private local posts. Although Sanitary Fair stamps were not valid for U.S. postal service, they were prepared for, sold and used at the fair post offices, usually with the approval and participation of the local postmaster.

The Commission undertook to forward soldiers' unpaid and postage due letters. These letters were handstamped "Forwarded by the U.S. Sanitary Commission."

Details about the Sanitary Fair stamps may be found in the following publications:
American Journal of Philately, Jan. 1889, by J. W. Scott
The Collector's Journal, Aug-Sept. 1909, by C. E. Severn
Scott's Monthly Journal, Jan. 1927 (reprint, Apr. 1973), by Elliott Perry
Stamps, April 24th, 1937, by Harry M. Konwiser
Pat Paragraphs, July, 1939, by Elliott Perry
Covers, Aug. 1952, by George B. Wray
Sanitary Fairs, 1992, by Alvin and Marjorie Kantor

The listings were compiled originally by H. M. Konwiser and Dorsey F. Wheless.

SF1

SF2

Albany, New York
Army Relief Bazaar
Setting A: narrow spacing, pane of 12.
Setting B: wider spacing, sheet of 25.

1864, Feb. 22-Mar. 30   **Litho.**   *Imperf.*
Thin White Paper

WV1	SF1	10c	**rose**	65.
			Used on cover (tied "Albany")	9,500.
			Block of 4, setting A	900.
			Pane of 12, setting A	3,600.
			Block of 4, setting B	290.
			Sheet of 25, setting B	1,800.
WV2	SF1	10c	**black**	700.
			Block of 5	4,500.

The No. WV1 tied by Albany cancel on cover is unique. One other cover exists in private hands with the stamp uncanceled and slightly damaged.

Imitations are typographed in red, blue, black or green on a thin white or ordinary white paper, also on colored papers and are:
(a) Eagle with topknot, printed in sheets of 30 (6x5).
(b) Eagle without shading around it.
(c) Eagle with shading around it, but with a period instead of a circle in "C" of "Cents," and "Ten Cents" is smaller.

Boston, Mass.
National Sailors' Fair

1864, Nov. 9-22   **Litho.**
Die Cut

WV3	SF2	10c	**green**	350.

Brooklyn, N.Y.
Brooklyn Sanitary Fair

SF3

1864, Feb. 22-Mar. 8   **Litho.**   *Imperf.*

WV4	SF3	(15c)	**green**	1,250.	3,600.
			On cover, Fair postmark on envelope		3,000.
			Block of 4	6,500.	
			Block of 6	10,000.	
WV5	SF3	(25c)	**black**	4,750.	
			On cover, with 1c local #28L2, Fair postmark on envelope		36,000.

No. WV4 used is valued canceled by the Fair postmark and is unique. One or more examples also exist with a manuscript cancel. No. WV5 unused is unique as is the usage on cover. Imitations: (a) Typographed and shows "Sanitary" with a heavy cross bar to "T" and second "A" with a long left leg. (b) Is a rough typograph print without shading in letters of "Fair."

SF4

SF5

1863, Dec.   **Typeset**   *Imperf.*

WV6	SF4	5c	black, *rosy buff*	750.	—
WV7	SF5	10c	**green**	950.	
			Tete beche pair	5,500.	

No. WV6 used is believed to be unique and has a manuscript cancel.

SF6

SF7

New York, N. Y.
Metropolitan Fair

1864, Apr. 4-27   **Engr.**   *Imperf.*
Thin White Paper

WV8	SF6	10c	**blue**	250.
			Sheet of 4	1,500.
WV9	SF6	10c	**red**	1,200.
			Pair	2,750.
WV10	SF6	10c	**black**	14,000.

Engraved and printed by John E. Gavit of Albany, N.Y. from a steel plate composed of four stamps, 2x2. Can be plated by the positions of scrolls and dots around "Ten Cents."
No. WV10 is unique.

Philadelphia, Pa.
Great Central Fair

1864, June 7-28   **Engr.**   *Perf. 12*
Printed by Butler & Carpenter, Philadelphia
Sheets of 126 (14x9)

WV11	SF7	10c	**blue**	40.00	600.00
			On cover tied with Fair postmark		2,250.
			On cover with 3c #65, Fair and Philadelphia postmarks		36,000.
			On cover with 3c #65, New York postmark		42,500.
			Block of 4	175.00	
WV12	SF7	20c	**green**	27.50	500.00
			On cover tied with Fair postmark		1,500.
			Block of 4	135.00	
			Block of 12	475.00	
WV13	SF7	30c	**black**	35.00	475.00
			On cover tied with Fair postmark		1,500.
			Nos. WV11-WV13 on single cover, Fair postmark		9,000.
			Block of 4	160.00	
			Block of 6	240.00	

Imprint "Engraved by Butler & Carpenter, Philadelphia" on right margin adjoining three stamps.
Used examples of Nos. WV11-WV13 have Fair cancellation. The No. WV11 covers used with 3c #65 are each unique. The New York usage is on a Metropolitan Fair illustrated envelope.
Imitation of No. WV13 comes typographed in blue or green on thick paper.
White and amber envelopes were sold by the fair inscribed "Great Central Fair for the Sanitary Commission," showing picture in several colors of wounded soldier, doctors and ambulance marked "U.S. Sanitary Commission." Same design and inscription are known on U.S. envelope No. U46.

SF8

SF9

Springfield, Mass.
Soldiers' Fair

1864, Dec. 19-24   **Typo.**   *Imperf.*

WV14	SF8	10c	**lilac**	210.00
			On unaddressed cover, Fair postmark on envelope	750.00
			Horizontal strip of 4	950.00

Design by Thomas Chubbuck, engraver of the postmaster provisional stamp of Brattleboro, Vt.
One cover exists pencil-addressed to Wm. Ingersoll, Springfield Armory; value slightly more than an unaddressed cover.

Imitations: (a) Without designer's name in lower right corner, in lilac on laid paper. (b) With designer's name, but roughly typographed, in lilac on white wove paper. Originals show 5 buttons on uniform.

Stamford, Conn.
Soldiers' Fair
Sheets of 8

1864, July 27-29

WV15	SF9	15c	**pale brown**	2,000.	4,000.

Originals have tassels at ends of ribbon inscribed "SOLDIERS FAIR." Imitations have leaning "S" in "CENTS" and come in lilac, brown, green, also black on white paper, green on pinkish paper and other colors.

ESSAY
Great Central Fair, Philadelphia

1864

WV11-E1	Design as issued but value tablets blank, greenish black on glazed paper (unique)	—

PROOFS
Metropolitan Fair, New York

1864

WV10P	10c	**black,** plate on India, mounted on card	900.

Great Central Fair, Philadelphia

1864

WV11P		10c **blue,** card	35.00
		Block of 4	175.00
WV11TC/WV13TC		10c and 30c **grnsh blk,** se-tenant, glazed paper, large die	—
WV12P		20c **green,** card	35.00
		Block of 4	175.00
WV12TC		20c **carmine,** wove, perf.	35.00
		Block of 4	175.00
WV12TC		20c **vermilion,** India on card, large die	275.00
WV12TC		20c **vermilion,** wove, imperf.	22.50
		Block of 4	115.00
WV12TC		20c **vermilion,** wove, perf.	35.00
		Block of 4	175.00
WV12TC		20c **orange,** wove, imperf.	22.50
		Block of 4	115.00
WV12TC		20c **brown orange,** opaque paper	22.50
		Block of 4	115.00
WV12TC		20c **red brown,** wove, perf.	35.00
		Block of 4	175.00
WV12TC		20c **black brown,** wove, imperf.	25.00
		Block of 4	125.00
WV12TC		20c **olive,** wove, imperf.	22.50
		Block of 4	100.00
WV12TC		20c **yellow green,** wove, imperf.	22.50
		Block of 4	125.00
WV12TC		20c **light green,** wove, perf.	35.00
		Block of 4	175.00
WV12TC		20c **blue,** India on card, large die	275.00
WV12TC		20c **blue,** wove, perf.	175.00
WV12TC		20c **bright blue,** wove, imperf.	22.50
		Block of 4	125.00
WV12TC		20c **bright blue,** wove, perf.	35.00
		Block of 4	175.00
WV12TC		20c **lt. ultramarine,** wove, imperf.	22.50
		Block of 4	125.00
WV12TC		20c **purple,** wove, imperf.	22.50
		Block of 4	125.00
WV12TC		20c **claret,** wove, imperf.	35.00
		Block of 4	200.00
WV12TC		20c **brown black,** wove, perf.	35.00
		Block of 4	175.00
WV12TC		20c **greenish black,** glazed paper, large die	225.00
WV12TC		20c **gray black,** opaque paper, wove, imperf.	22.50
		Block of 4	125.00
WV12TC		20c **gray black,** wove, perf.	35.00
		Block of 4	175.00
WV12TC		20c **black,** experimental double paper, wove, imperf.	25.00
		Block of 4	140.00
WV13P		30c **black,** card	35.00
		Block of 4	175.00

Reprints (1903?) exist of WV11TC-WV13TC, se-tenant vertically, large die on glazed white, pink or yellow card and small die on India paper (mounted se-tenant) in carmine, red carmine, vermilion, orange, brown, yellow brown, olive, yellow green, blue green, gray blue, ultramarine, light violet, violet, claret and gray black.

There also exist large die essay reprints on India paper, green bond paper and glazed cardboard without denomination or with 20c. The 20c value has an added line below the center shield.

ENCASED POSTAGE STAMPS

In 1862 John Gault of Boston patented the idea of encasing postage stamps in metal frames behind a shield of transparent mica, and using them for advertising. The scarcity of small change during the Civil War made these encased stamps popular. Many firms impressed their names and products on the back of these stamp frames in embossed letters. Values are for very fine specimens with mica intact, although signs of circulation and handling are to be expected.

Grading encompasses three areas: 1. Case will show signs of wear or handling and signs of original toning. 2. Mica will be intact with no pieces missing. 3. Stamp will be fresh with no signs of toning or wrinkling.

Examples that came with silvered cases and still have some or all of the original silvering will sell for more than the values shown.

Aerated Bread Co., New York

EP1	1c	2,500.

Ayer's Cathartic Pills, Lowell, Mass.

Varieties with long and short arrows below legend occur on all denominations.

EP2	1c	210.
EP3	3c	190.
EP4	5c	310.
EP5	10c	425.
EP6	12c	850.
EP7	24c	2,250.

Take Ayer's Pills

EP8	1c	225.
EP9	3c	200.
EP10	5c	300.
a.	Ribbed frame	1,100.
EP11	10c	400.
EP12	12c	1,200.

Ayer's Sarsaparilla

Three varieties: "AYER'S" small, medium or large. Example illustrated is the medium variety.

EP13	1c medium "Ayer's"	225.
a.	Small	550.
EP14	2c	—
EP15	3c medium "Ayer's"	200.
a.	Small	425.
b.	Large	400.
c.	Ribbed frame, medium	850.
EP16	5c medium "Ayer's"	350.
a.	Large	675.
EP17	10c medium "Ayer's"	325.
a.	Ribbed frame, medium	950.
b.	Small	700.
c.	Large	575.
EP18	12c medium "Ayer's"	950.
a.	Small	1,300.
EP19	24c medium "Ayer's"	1,750.
EP20	30c medium "Ayer's"	2,500.

The authenticity of No. EP14 is questioned.

Bailey & Co., Philadelphia

EP21	1c	800.
EP22	3c	900.
EP23	5c	2,000.
EP24	10c	2,000.
EP25	12c	2,750.

"FANCYGOODS" as one word	"FANCY GOODS" as two words

Joseph L. Bates, Boston

EP26	1c one word	325.
a.	Two words	450.
EP27	3c one word	525.
a.	Two words	575.
EP28	5c two words	700.
a.	One word	800.
b.	Ribbed frame, one word	1,100.
EP29	10c two words	450.
a.	One word	525.
b.	Ribbed frame, one word	1,250.
EP30	12c two words	1,400.

Brown's Bronchial Troches

EP31	1c	800.
EP32	3c	400.
EP33	5c	400.
EP34	10c	750.
EP35	12c	1,400.
EP36	24c	2,750.
EP37	30c	3,900.

F. Buhl & Co., Detroit

EP38	1c	1,500.
EP39	3c	1,600.
EP40	5c	1,500.
EP41	10c	1,750.
EP42	12c	2,250.
EP43	24c	3,000.

Burnett's Cocoaine Kalliston

EP44	1c	325.
EP45	3c	325.
EP46	5c	500.
EP47	10c	500.
EP48	12c	1,100.
EP49	24c	2,350.
EP50	30c	3,000.
EP51	90c	7,500.

Burnett's Cooking Extracts

EP52	1c	275.
EP53	3c	300.
EP54	5c	500.
EP55	10c	575.
a.	Ribbed frame	1,250.
EP56	12c	1,400.
EP57	24c	2,750.
EP58	30c	3,500.

A. M. Claflin, Hopkinton, Mass.

EP59	1c	12,500.
EP60	3c	4,750.
EP61	5c	6,000.
EP62	10c	5,000.
EP63	12c	6,000.

H. A. Cook, Evansville, Ind.

EP64	5c	1,500.
EP65	10c	1,500.

Dougan, Hatter, New York

EP66	1c	2,250.
EP67	3c	1,750.
EP68	5c	2,000.
EP69	10c	2,250.

Drake's Plantation Bitters

EP70	1c	275.
EP71	3c	250.
EP72	5c	350.
a. Ribbed frame		850.
EP73	10c	425.
a. Ribbed frame		1,100.
EP74	12c	1,250.
EP75	24c	2,250.
EP76	30c	3,000.
EP77	90c	8,500.

Ellis, McAlpin & Co., Cincinnati

EP78	1c	1,750.
EP79	3c	1,750.
EP80	5c	1,200.
EP81	10c	1,200.
EP82	12c	2,000.
EP83	24c	2,500.

G. G. Evans, Philadelphia

EP84	1c	750.
EP85	3c	750.
EP86	5c	1,250.
EP87	10c	1,500.

Gage Bros. & Drake, Tremont House, Chicago

EP88	1c	375.
EP89	3c	500.
EP90	5c	425.
EP91	10c	500.
a. Ribbed frame		1,250.
EP92	12c	1,750.

J. Gault

EP93	1c	475.
a. Ribbed frame		
EP94	2c	9,000.
EP95	3c	225.
a. Ribbed frame		750.
EP96	5c	250.
a. Ribbed frame		600.
EP97	10c	350.
a. Ribbed frame		650.
EP98	12c	900.
a. Ribbed frame		1,700.
EP99	24c	1,800.
a. Ribbed frame		2,750.

EP100	30c	2,400.
a. Ribbed frame		3,750.
EP101	90c	6,500.

L. C. Hopkins & Co., Cincinnati

EP102	1c	1,900.
EP103	3c	1,500.
EP104	5c	1,750.
EP105	10c	1,900.

Hunt & Nash, Irving House, New York

EP106	1c	600.
EP107	3c	475.
a. Ribbed frame		1,000.
EP108	5c	475.
a. Ribbed frame		525.
EP109	10c	550.
a. Ribbed frame		900.
EP110	12c	1,250.
a. Ribbed frame		1,700.
EP111	24c	2,100.
a. Ribbed frame		2,800.
EP112	30c	3,750.

Kirkpatrick & Gault, New York

EP113	1c	350.
EP114	3c	400.
EP115	5c	375.
EP116	10c	375.
EP117	12c	1,000.
EP118	24c	2,000.
EP119	30c	2,750.
EP120	90c	6,500.

Lord & Taylor, New York

EP121	1c	900.
EP122	3c	950.
EP123	5c	950.
EP124	10c	1,000.
EP125	12c	2,000.
EP126	24c	2,750.
EP127	30c	3,750.
EP128	90c	9,500.

Mendum's Family Wine Emporium, New York

EP129	1c	575.
EP130	3c	900.
EP131	5c	700.

EP132	10c	750.
a. Ribbed frame		1,600.
EP133	12c	1,500.

B. F. Miles, Peoria

| EP134 | 1c | 4,000. |
| EP135 | 5c | 4,000. |

John W. Norris, Chicago

EP136	1c	2,250.
EP137	3c	2,250.
EP138	5c	2,500.
EP139	10c	2,750.

"INSURANCE" Curved   "INSURANCE" Straight

North America Life Insurance Co., N. Y.

EP140	1c Curved	425.
a. Straight		525.
EP141	3c Straight	600.
a. Curved		700.
EP142	5c Straight	675.
a. Ribbed frame		1,100.
EP143	10c Straight	625.
a. Curved		800.
b. Curved, ribbed frame		1,750.
EP144	12c Straight	1,750.

Pearce, Tolle & Holton, Cincinnati

EP145	1c	2,250.
EP146	3c	2,250.
EP147	5c	1,800.
EP148	10c	2,700.
EP149	12c	3,250.
EP150	24c	3,750.

Sands Ale

EP151	5c	2,000.
EP152	10c	2,750.
EP153	12c	3,000.
EP154	30c	—

No. EP154 may be unique. The case of the known example has been opened. It is possible that the 30c stamp has been substituted for the original stamp.

Schapker & Bussing, Evansville, Ind.

EP155	1c	600.
EP156	3c	675.
EP157	5c	600.
EP158	10c	575.
EP159	12c	1,600.

John Shillito & Co., Cincinnati

EP160	1c	725.
EP161	3c	600.
EP162	5c	600.
EP163	10c	675.
EP164	12c	1,950.

S. Steinfeld, New York

EP165	1c	2,500.
EP166	5c	2,600.
EP167	10c	2,650.
EP168	12c	3,250.

N. G. Taylor & Co., Philadelphia

EP169	1c	2,250.
EP170	3c	2,000.
EP171	5c	2,350.
EP172	10c	2,500.
EP173	12c	3,100.

Weir and Larminie, Montreal

EP174	1c	1,500.
EP175	3c	1,750.
EP176	5c	1,600.
EP177	10c	1,100.

White, the Hatter, New York

EP178	1c	1,750.
EP179	3c	2,500.
EP180	5c	2,500.
EP181	10c	2,750.

POSTAGE CURRENCY

Small coins disappeared from circulation in 1861-62 as cash was hoarded. To ease business transactions, merchants issued notes of credit, promises to pay, tokens, store cards, etc. U.S. Treasurer Francis E. Spinner made a substitute for small currency by affixing postage stamps, singly and in multiples, to Treasury paper. He arranged with the Post office to replace worn stamps with new when necessary.

The next step was to print the stamps on Treasury paper. On July 17, 1862, Congress authorized the issue of such "Postage Currency." It remained in use until May 27, 1863. It was not money, but a means of making stamps negotiable.

On Oct. 10, 1863 a second issue was released. These, and the later three issues, did not show stamps and are called Fractional Currency. In 1876 Congress authorized the minting of silver coins to redeem the outstanding fractional currency.

Values quoted are for notes in crisp, new condition, not creased or worn.
Creased or worn copies sell for 25 to 75 percent less.
Items valued with a dash are believed to be unique.

Front Engraved and Printed by the National Bank Note Co.
Back Engraved and Printed in Black by The American Bank Note Co.
"A B Co." on Back

"ABCo." imprint, lower right corner of back (#1-8)

1862, Aug. 21

Perforated Edges-Perf. 12

PC1	5c	Bust of Jefferson on 5c stamp, brown	57.50
	a.	Inverted back	500.00
PC2	10c	Bust of Washington on 10c stamp, green	40.00
PC3	25c	Five 5c stamps, brown	52.50
PC4	50c	Five 10c stamps, green	57.50
	a.	Inverted back	500.00

Imperforate Edges

PC5	5c	Bust of Jefferson on 5c stamp	20.00
	a.	Inverted back	200.00
PC6	10c	Bust of Washington on 10c stamp	17.50
	a.	Inverted back	350.00
PC7	25c	Five 5c stamps	35.00
	a.	Inverted back	300.00
PC8	50c	Five 10c stamps	57.50
	a.	Inverted back	400.00

No. PC8 exists perforated 14, privately produced.

Front and Back Engraved and Printed by the the National Bank Note Co.
Without "A B Co." on Back

Perforated Edges-Perf. 12

PC9	5c	Bust of Jefferson on 5c stamp	57.50
	a.	Inverted back	—
PC10	10c	Bust of Washington on 10c stamp	57.50
	a.	Inverted back	—
PC11	25c	Five 5c stamps	115.00
	a.	Inverted back	750.00
PC12	50c	Five 10c stamps	140.00
	a.	Inverted back	—

Imperforate Edges

PC13	5c	Bust of Jefferson on 5c stamp	57.50
	a.	Inverted back	—
PC14	10c	Bust of Washington on 10c stamp	100.00
	a.	Inverted back	750.00
PC15	25c	Five 5c stamps	140.00
PC16	50c	Five 10c stamps	500.00
	a.	Inverted back	—

CONFEDERATE STATES OF AMERICA

3¢ 1861 POSTMASTERS' PROVISIONALS

With the secession of South Carolina from the Union on Dec. 20, 1860, a new era began in U.S. history as well as its postal history. Other Southern states quickly followed South Carolina's lead, which in turn led to the formation of the provisional government of the Confederate States of America on Feb. 4, 1861.

President Jefferson Davis' cabinet was completed Mar. 6, 1861, with the acceptance of the position of Postmaster General by John H. Reagan of Texas. The provisional government had already passed regulations that required payment for postage in cash and that effectively carried over the U.S. 3c rate until the new Confederate Post Office Department took over control of the system.

Soon after entering on his duties, Reagan directed the postmasters in the Confederate States and in the newly seceded states to "continue the performance of their duties as such, and render all accounts and pay all moneys (sic) to the order of the Government of the U.S. as they have heretofore done, until the Government of the Confederate States shall be prepared to assume control of its postal affairs."

As coinage was becoming scarce, postal patrons began having problems buying individual stamps or paying for letters individually, especially as stamp stocks started to run short in certain areas. Even though the U.S. Post Office Department was technically in control of the postal system and southern postmasters were operating under Federal authority, the U.S.P.O. was hesitant in re-supplying seceded states with additional stamps and stamped envelopes.

The U.S. government had made the issuance of postmasters' provisionals illegal many years before, but the southern postmasters had to do what they felt was necessary to allow patrons to pay for postage and make the system work. Therefore, a few postmasters took it upon themselves to issue provisional stamps in the 3c rate then in effect. Interestingly, these were stamps and envelopes that the U.S. government did not recognize as legal, but they did do postal duty unchallenged in the Confederate States. Yet the proceeds were to be remitted to the U.S. government in Washington! Six authenticated postmasters' provisionals in the 3c rate have been recorded.

On May 13, 1861, Postmaster General Reagan issued his proclamation "assuming control and direction of postal service within the limits of the Confederate States of America on and after the first day of June," with new postage rates and regulations. The Federal government suspended operations in the Confederate States (except for western Virginia and the seceding state of Tennessee) by a proclamation issued by Postmaster General Montgomery Blair on May 27, 1861, effective from May 31, 1861, and June 10 for western and middle Tennessee. As Tennessee did not join the Confederacy until July 2, 1861, the unissued 3c Nashville provisional was produced in a state that was in the process of seceding, while the other provisionals were used in the Confederacy before the June 1 assumption of control of postal service by the Confederate States of America.

HILLSBORO, N.C.

A1

Handstamped Adhesive

1AX1 A1 3c **bluish black,** on cover —

No. 1AX1 is unique. This is the same handstamp as used for No. 39X1. 3c usage is determined from the May 27, 1861 circular date stamp.

Cancellation: black town.

JACKSON, MISS.

E1

Handstamped Envelope

2AXU1 E1 3c **black** —
See Nos. 43XU1-43XU4.

MADISON COURT HOUSE, FLA.

A1   "CNETS"

Typeset Adhesive

3AX1 A1 3c **gold** — 10,000.
        On cover   65,000.
  a. "CNETS"   14,000.

No. 3AX1 on cover and No. 3AX1a are each unique.

Cancellations: black town, oblong paid, ms "Paid in Money."

See No. 137XU1.

NASHVILLE, TENN.

A1

Typeset Adhesive (5 varieties)

4AX1 A1 3c **carmine** 150.
        Horizontal strip of 5 showing
          all varieties 900.

No. 4AX1 was prepared by Postmaster McNish with the U.S. rate, but the stamp was never issued.
See Nos. 61X2-61XU2.

SELMA, ALA.

E1

Handstamped Envelope

5AXU1 E1 3c **black** 1,000.
        See Nos. 77XU1-77XU3.

TUSCUMBIA, ALA.

E1

Handstamped Envelope, impression at upper right

6AXU1 E1 3c **dull red,** *buff* 17,500.

No. 6AXU1 also exists with a 3c 1857 stamp affixed at upper right over the provisional handstamp, tied by black circular "TUSCUMBIA, ALA." town postmark. Value $16,500.

See Nos. 84XU1-84XU3.

CONFEDERATE POSTMASTERS' PROVISIONALS

These stamps and envelopes were issued by individual postmasters generally during the interim between June 1, 1861, when the use of United States stamps stopped in the Confederacy, and October 16, 1861, when the first Confederate Government stamps were issued. They were occasionally issued at later periods, especially in Texas, when regular issues of government stamps were unavailable.

Canceling stamps of the post offices were often used to produce envelopes, some of which were supplied in advance by private citizens. These envelopes and other stationery therefore may be found in a wide variety of papers, colors, sizes and shapes, including patriotic and semi-official types. It is often difficult to determine whether the impression made by the canceling stamp indicates provisional usage or merely postage paid at the time the letter was deposited in the post office. Occasionally the same mark was used for both purposes.

The *press-printed* provisional envelopes are in a different category. **They were produced in quantity, using envelopes procured in advance by the postmaster, such as those of Charleston, Lynchburg, Memphis, etc.** *The* **press-printed** *envelopes are listed and valued on all known papers.*

The **handstamped** *provisional envelopes are listed and valued according to type and variety of handstamp, but not according to paper. Many exist on such a variety of papers that they defy accurate, complete listing. The value of a handstamped provisional envelope is determined primarily by the clarity of the markings and its overall condition and attractiveness, rather than the type of paper.*

All handstamped provisional envelopes, when used, should also show the postmark of the town of issue.

Most handstamps are impressed at top right, although they exist from some towns in other positions.

Many illustrations in this section are reduced in size.

Values for envelopes are for entires. Values for stamps of provisional issues are for copies with little or no gum; original gum over a large portion of the stamp will increase the value substantially.

ABERDEEN, MISS.

E1

Handstamped Envelopes

1XU1	E1	5c **black**		6,000.
1XU2	E1	10c (ms.) on 5c **black**		—

ABINGDON, VA.

E1

Handstamped Envelopes

2XU1	E1	2c **black**		11,000.
2XU2	E1	5c **black**		1,000.
		On patriotic cover		2,750.
2XU3	E1	10c **black**	2,200.	3,500.

The unused No. 2XU3 is a unique mint example, and the value represents the price realized in a 1997 auction sale.

ALBANY, GA.

E1   E2

Handstamped Envelopes

3XU1	E1	5c **greenish blue**	700.
3XU2	E1	10c **greenish blue**	2,000.
3XU3	E1	10c on 5c **greenish blue**	2,500.
3XU5	E2	5c **greenish blue**	
3XU6	E2	10c **greenish blue**	2,250.

ANDERSON COURT HOUSE, S.C.

E1

Handstamped Envelopes

4XU1	E1	5c **black**	500.	2,250.
4XU2	E1	10c (ms.) **black**		3,000.

ATHENS, GA

A1 (type I)   A1 (type II)

Typographed Adhesives
(from woodcuts of two types)
Pairs, both horizontal and vertical, always show one of each type.

5X1	A1	5c **purple** (shades)	900.	1,100.
		Pair	—	2,400.
		On cover		2,000.
		Pair on cover		4,750.
		Strip of 4 on cover (horiz.)		10,000.
a.		Tete beche pair (vertical)		7,500.
		Tete beche pair on cover		27,500.
5X2	A1	5c **red**	—	4,000.
		On cover		15,000.
		Pair on cover		

Cancellations in black: grid, town, "Paid."

ATLANTA, GA.

E1   E2

Handstamped Envelopes

6XU1	E1	5c **red**		3,500.
6XU2	E1	5c **black**	175.	600.
		On patriotic cover		3,500.
6XU3	E1	10c on 5c **black**		1,500.
6XU4	E2	2c **black**		3,000.
6XU5	E2	5c **black**		1,500.
		On patriotic cover		3,500.
6XU6	E2	10c **black**		850.
6XU7	E2	10c on 5c **black**		2,500.

E3

Handstamped Envelopes

6XU8	E3	5c **black**		3,500.
6XU9	E3	10c **black** ("10" upright)		2,750.

AUGUSTA, GA.

E1

Handstamped Envelope

7XU1	E1	5c **black**	

Provisional status questioned. The only known example has a general CSA issue used over the marking.

AUSTIN, MISS.

E1

Press-printed Envelope (typeset)

8XU1	E1	5c **red**, amber		75,000.

One example recorded.

Cancellation: black "Paid."

AUSTIN, TEX.

E1

Handstamped Adhesive

9X1	E1 10c **black**		—
	On cover, uncanceled		1,500.
	On cover, tied		

Only one example of No. 9X1 tied on cover is recorded.

Handstamped Envelope

9XU1	E1 10c **black**		1,500.

Cancellation on Nos. 9X1 and 9XU1: black town.

AUTAUGAVILLE, ALA.

E1

E2

Handstamped Envelopes

10XU1	E1 5c **black**		10,000.
10XU2	E2 5c **black**		12,500.

No. 10XU2 is unique.

BALCONY FALLS, VA.

E1

Handstamped Envelope

122XU1	E1 10c **blue**		1,500.

BARNWELL COURT HOUSE, S. C.

E1

Handstamped Envelope

123XU1	E1 5c **black**		1,500.

These are two separate handstamps.

BATON ROUGE, LA.

A1

A2

Typeset Adhesives
Ten varieties of each

11X1	A1 2c **green**	5,250.	4,000.
	On cover		20,000.
a.	"McCcrmick"	10,000.	8,500.
	On cover		22,500.
11X2	A2 5c **green & carmine** (Maltese cross border)	1,250.	1,100.
	On cover		2,750.
	Strip of 3		4,750.
	Strip of 5		22,500.

	Canceled in New Orleans, on cover		20,000.
a.	"McCcrmick"	—	2,000.
	On cover		6,500.

The "Canceled in New Orleans" examples entered the mails in New Orleans after having been placed (uncanceled) on riverboats in Baton Rouge. Two such covers are recorded.

A3

A4

Ten varieties of each

11X3	A3 5c **green & carmine** (crisscross border)	4,500.	2,250.
	On cover		10,000.
a.	"McCcrmick"		3,250.
11X4	A4 10c **blue**		6,000.
	On cover		75,000.

No. 11X4 on cover is unique.

Cancellation on Nos. 11X1-11X4: black town.

BEAUMONT, TEX.

A1

A2

Typeset Adhesives
Several varieties of each

12X1	A1 10c **black**, *yellow*, on cover		55,000.
12X2	A1 10c **black**, *pink*		12,500.
	On cover		27,500.
12X3	A2 10c **black**, *yellow*, on cover		90,000.

One example known of No. 12X3.

Cancellations: black pen; black town.

BLUFFTON, S. C.

E1

Handstamped Envelope

124XU1	E1 5c **black**		2,000.

BRIDGEVILLE, ALA.

A1

Handstamped Adhesive in black within red pen-ruled squares

13X1	A1 5c **black & red**, pair on cover		20,000.

Cancellation is black pen.

CAMDEN, S. C.

E1

E2

Handstamped Envelopes

125XU1	E1 5c **black**		800.
125XU2	E2 10c **black**		450.

No. 125XU2 unused was privately carried and is addressed but has no postal markings. No. 125XU2 is indistinguishable from a handstamp paid cover when used.

CANTON, MISS.

E1

"P" in star is initial of Postmaster William Priestly.

Handstamped Envelopes

14XU1	E1 5c **black**		2,250.
14XU2	E1 10c (ms.) on 5c **black**		5,000.

CAROLINA CITY, N. C.

E1

Handstamped Envelope

118XU1	E1 5c **black**		3,500.

CARTERSVILLE, GA.

E1

Handstamped Envelope

126XU1	E1 (5c) **red**		1,250.

CHAPEL HILL, N. C.

E1

Handstamped Envelope

15XU1	E1 5c **black**		2,500.
	On patriotic cover		4,500.

CHARLESTON, S. C.

A1

E1

E2

Lithographed Adhesive

16X1	A1	5c **blue**	900.	750.
		Pair	1,750.	1,900.
		On cover		2,250.
		On patriotic cover		5,000.
		Pair, on cover		5,000.
		On cover with No. 112XU1		—
		Used on cover with C.S.A. 5c		
		#6 to make 10c rate		

Values are for copies showing parts of the outer frame lines on at least 3 sides.

Cancellation: black town (two types).

Press-printed Envelopes
(typographed from woodcut)

16XU1	E1	5c **blue**	1,100.	3,500.
16XU2	E1	5c **blue**, *amber*	1,100.	3,500.
16XU3	E1	5c **blue**, *orange*	1,100.	3,500.
16XU4	E1	5c **blue**, *buff*	1,100.	3,500.
16XU5	E1	5c **blue**, *blue*	1,100.	3,500.
16XU6	E2	10c **blue**, *orange*		77,500.

The No. 16XU6 used entire is unique; value based on 1997 auction sale.

Handstamped Cut Square

16XU7	E2	10c **black**	3,000.

There is only one copy of No. 16XU7. It is a cutout, not an entire. It may not have been mailed from Charleston, and may not have paid postage.

CHARLOTTESVILLE, VA.

E1

Handstamped Envelopes, Manuscript Initials

127XU1	E1	5c **blue**	—
127XU2	E1	10c **blue**	—

CHATTANOOGA, TENN.

E1

Handstamped Envelopes

17XU2	E1	5c **black**	1,600.
17XU3	E1	5c on 2c **black**	3,250.

CHRISTIANSBURG, VA.

E1

Handstamped Envelopes
Impressed at top right

99XU1	E1	5c **black**, *blue*	2,000.
99XU2	E1	5c **blue**	1,400.
99XU3	E1	5c **black**, *orange*	2,000.
99XU4	E1	5c **green** on U.S. envelope No. U27	4,500.
99XU5	E1	10c **blue**	3,500.

COLAPARCHEE, GA.

E1

Control

Handstamped Envelope

119XU1	E1	5c **black**	3,500.

COLUMBIA, S. C.

E1

E2

Handstamped Envelopes

18XU1	E1	5c **blue**	500.	900.
		Used on cover with C.S.A. 5c		
		#1 or #1c to make 10c rate		3,000.
		Used on cover with C.S.A. 5c		
		#7 to make 10c rate		7,500.
18XU2	E1	5c **black**	600.	900.
18XU3	E1	10c on 5c **blue**		3,500.

Three types of "PAID," one in circle

18XU4	E2	5c **blue**, seal on front	2,500.
a.		Seal on back	1,000.
18XU5	E2	10c **blue**, seal on back	2,750.

Circular Seal similar to E2, 27mm diameter

18XU6	E2	5c **blue** (seal on back)	4,000.

COLUMBIA, TENN.

E1

Handstamped Envelope

113XU1	E1	5c **red**	3,500.

COLUMBUS, GA.

E1

Handstamped Envelopes

19XU1	E1	5c **blue**	700.
19XU2	E1	10c **red**	2,250.

COURTLAND, ALA.

E1

Handstamped Envelopes (from woodcut)

103XU1	E1	5c **black**	—
103XU2	E1	5c **red**	10,000.

Provisional status of No. 103XU1 questioned.

DALTON, GA

E1

Handstamped Envelopes

20XU1	E1	5c **black**	500.
a.		Denomination omitted (5c rate)	650.
20XU2	E1	10c **black**	700.
20XU3	E1	10c (ms.) on 5c **black**	1,500.

DANVILLE, VA.

A1   E1

E2   E3

PAID 10

E4

Typeset Adhesive
Wove Paper

21X1	A1	5c **red**	5,500.
		On cover	—
		Cut to shape	4,000.
		On cover, cut to shape	6,000.

Two varieties known.

Only four rectangular-cut examples are recorded, one of which is reported to be on laid paper.

Cancellation: blue town.

Press-printed Envelopes (typographed)
Two types: "SOUTHERN" in straight or curved line
Impressed (usually) at top left

21XU1	E1	5c **black**	5,500.
21XU2	E1	5c **black**, *amber*	5,500.
21XU3	E1	5c **black**, *dark buff*	5,250.

An unissued 10c envelope (type E1, in red) is known. All recorded examples are envelopes on which added stamps paid the postage.

Handstamped Envelopes

21XU3A	E4	5c **black** (ms "WBP" initials)	1,000.
21XU4	E2	10c **black**	2,000.
21XU5	E2	10c **blue**	
21XU6	E3	10c **black**	2,750.
21XU7	E4	10c **black** (ms "WBP" initials)	—

Types E2 and E3 both exist on one cover. The existence of No. 21XU5 has been questioned.

DEMOPOLIS, ALA.

E1

Handstamped Envelopes, Signature in ms.

22XU1	E1	5c **black** ("Jno. Y. Hall")	3,000.
22XU2	E1	5c **black** ("J. Y. Hall")	3,000.
22XU3	E1	5c (ms.) **black** ("J. Y. Hall")	3,500.

EATONTON, GA.

E1

Handstamped Envelopes

23XU1	E1	5c **black**	3,000.
23XU2	E1	5c + 5c **black**	1,250.

EMORY, VA.

A1

Handstamped Adhesives ("PAID" and "5" in circle on selvage of U.S. 1c 1857 issue)

Perf. 15 on three sides

24X1	A1	5c **blue**, on cover, ms. tied	15,000.

Also known with "5" above "PAID."

Cancellation: blue town.

E1   E2

Handstamped Envelopes

24XU1	E1	5c **blue**	2,000.
24XU2	E2	10c **blue**	5,000.

FINCASTLE, VA.

E1

Press-printed Envelope (typeset)
Impressed at top right

104XU1	E1	10c **black**	20,000.

One example known.

FORSYTH, GA.

E1

Handstamped Envelope

120XU1	E1	10c **black**	1,350.

FRANKLIN, N. C.

E1

Press-printed Envelope (typeset)
Impressed at top right

25XU1	E1	5c **blue**, *buff*	30,000.

The one known envelope shows black circular Franklin post-mark with manuscript date.

FRAZIERSVILLE, S. C.

E1

Handstamped Envelope, "5" manuscript

128XU1	E1	5c **black**	—

FREDERICKSBURG, VA.

A1

Sheets of 20, two panes of 10 varieties each

Typeset Adhesives
Thin bluish paper

26X1	A1	5c **blue**, *bluish*	250.	750.
		Block of 4	1,500.	
		Sheet of 20	10,000.	
		On cover		5,000.
		Pair on cover		12,000.
26X2	A1	10c **red**, *bluish*	900.	
		Brown red, *bluish*	900.	
		Block of 4		

Cancellation: black town.

GAINESVILLE, ALA.

E1   E2

Handstamped Envelopes

27XU1	E1	5c **black**	5,000.
27XU2	E2	10c ("01") **black**	6,000.

Postmark spells town name "Gainsville."

GALVESTON, TEX.

E1

Handstamped Envelopes

98XU1	E1	5c **black**	500.	1,500.
98XU2	E1	10c **black**		2,000.

E2

Handstamped Envelopes

98XU3	E2	10c **black**	550.	2,400.
98XU4	E2	20c **black**		3,500.

GASTON, N. C.

E1

Handstamped Envelope

129XU1	E1	5c **black**	—

GEORGETOWN, S. C.

E1   Control

Handstamped Envelope

28XU1	E1	5c **black**	800.

GOLIAD, TEX.

A1   A2

Typeset Adhesives

29X1	A1	5c **black**	7,000.
29X2	A1	5c **black**, *gray*	6,500.
29X3	A1	5c **black**, *rose*	7,000.
		On cover front	50,000.
29X4	A1	10c **black**	— 7,000.
29X5	A1	10c **black**, *rose*	7,000.
		On patriotic cover	

Type A1 stamps are signed "Clarke-P.M." vertically in black or red.

29X6	A2	5c **black**, *gray*	10,000.
a.		"GOILAD"	12,000.
		Pair, left stamp the error	—
29X7	A2	10c **black**, *gray*	7,500.
		On cover	25,000.
a.		"GOILAD"	8,000.
		On cover	30,000.
29X8	A2	5c **black**, *dark blue*, on cover	7,000.
29X9	A2	10c **black**, *dark blue*	

Cancellations in black: pen, town, "Paid"

GONZALES, TEX.

Colman & Law were booksellers when John B. Law (of the firm) was appointed Postmaster. The firm used a small lithographed label on drugs and on the front or inside of books they sold.

A1

Lithographed Adhesives
on colored glazed paper

30X1	A1	(5c) **gold**, *dark blue*, pair on cover, 1861	15,000.
30X2	A1	(10c) **gold**, *garnet*, on cover, 1864	12,500.
30X3	A1	(10c) **gold**, *black*, on cover, 1865	

Cancellations: black town, black pen. No. 30X1 must bear double-circle town cancel as validating control. The control was applied to the labels in the sheet before their sale as stamps. When used, the stamps bear an additional Gonzales double-circle postmark.

GREENSBORO, ALA.

E1   E2

Handstamped Envelopes

31XU1	E1	5c **black**	1,500.
31XU2	E1	10c **black**	2,750.
31XU3	E2	10c **black**	4,250.

GREENBORO, N. C.

E1

Handstamped Envelope

32XU1 E1 10c **red**   1,250.

GREENVILLE, ALA.

A1

A2

Typeset Adhesives
On pinkish surface-colored glazed paper.

33X1 A1 5c **blue & red**   22,500.
      On cover   40,000.
33X2 A2 10c **red & blue**   —
      On cover   40,000.

Two used examples each are known of Nos. 33X1-33X2, and all are on covers. Covers bear a postmark but it was not used to cancel the stamps.
The former No. 33X1a has been identified as a counterfeit.

GREENVILLE COURT HOUSE, S. C.

PAID 5
E1

Control

Handstamped Envelopes (Several types)

34XU1 E1 5c **black**   2,000.
34XU2 E1 10c **black**   2,250.
34XU3 E1 20c (ms.) on 10c **black**   3,000.

Envelopes must bear the black control on the back.

GREENWOOD DEPOT, VA.

A1

"PAID" Handstamped Adhesive ("PAID" with value and signature in ms.)
Laid Paper

35X1 A1 10c **black**, *gray blue*, un-
      canceled, on cover   20,000.
      On cover, tied   —

Six examples recorded of No. 35X1, all on covers. One of these is in the British Library collection. Of the remaining five, only one has the stamp tied to the cover.

Cancellation: black town.

GRIFFIN, GA.

E1

Handstamped Envelope

102XU1 E1 5c **black**   1,750.

GROVE HILL, ALA.

A1

Handstamped Adhesive (from woodcut)

36X1 A1 5c **black**
      On cover, tied   75,000.

Two examples are recorded. One is on cover tied by the postmark. The other is canceled by magenta pen on a cover front.

Cancellations: black town, magenta pen.

HALLETTSVILLE, TEX.

A1

Handstamped Adhesive
Ruled Letter Paper

37X1 A1 10c **black**, *gray blue*, on cover   15,000.
      One example known.

Cancellation: black ms.

HAMBURGH, S. C.

E1

Handstamped Envelope

112XU1 E1 5c **black**   2,000.
      On cover with #16X1 (forwarded)   —

HARRISBURGH (Harrisburg), TEX.

E1

Handstamped Envelope

130XU1 E1 5c **black**   —

No. 130XU1 is indistinguishable from a handstamp paid cover when used.

HELENA, TEX.

A1

Typeset Adhesives
Several varieties

38X1 A1 5c **black**, *buff*   7,500. 6,000.
38X2 A1 10c **black**, *gray*   5,000.

On 10c "Helena" is in upper and lower case italics.
Used examples are valued with small faults or repairs, as all recorded have faults.

Cancellation: black town.

HILLSBORO, N. C.

A1

Handstamped Adhesive

39X1 A1 5c **black**, on cover   15,000.

No. 39X1 is unique.
See 3c 1861 Postmasters' Provisional No. 1AX1.

Cancellation: black town.

Ms./Handstamped Envelope

39XU1 10c "paid 10" in manuscript with un-
      dated blue town cancel as con-
      trol on face   —

HOLLANDALE, TEX.

E1

Handstamped Envelope

132XU1 E1 5c **black**   —

HOUSTON, TEX.

E1

Handstamped Envelopes

40XU1 E1 5c **red**   —   700.
      On patriotic cover   —
40XU2 E1 10c **red**   —   1,500.
40XU3 E1 10c **black**   2,250.
40XU4 E1 5c +10c **red**   2,500.
40XU5 E1 10c +10c **red**   2,500.
40XU6 E1 10c (ms.) on 5c **red**   3,000.

Nos. 40XU2-40XU5 show "TEX" instead of "TXS."

HUNTSVILLE, TEX.

PAID 5
E1

Control

Handstamped Envelope

92XU1 E1 5c **black**   2,500.

No. 92XU1 exists with "5" outside or within control circle.

INDEPENDENCE, TEX.

A1

Handstamped Adhesives

41X1 A1 10c **black**, *buff*, on cover, un-
      canceled, cut to shape   20.000.
41X2 A1 10c **black**, *dull rose*, on cover

With small "10" and "Pd" in manuscript

41X3 A1 10c **black**, *buff*, on cover, un-
      canceled, cut to shape   32,500.
      On cover, uncanceled, cut
      square   —

No. 39X1 is unique.

All known examples of Nos. 41X1-41X3 are uncanceled on covers with black "INDEPENDANCE TEX." (sic) postmark.
The existence of No. 41X2 has been questioned by specialists. The editors would like to see authenticated evidence of the existence of this item.

ISABELLA, GA.

E1

Handstamped Envelope, "5" Manuscript

133XU1 E1 5c **black**   —

IUKA, MISS.

I-U-KA
PAID 5CTS
E1

Handstamped Envelope

42XU1 E1 5c **black**   1,600.
         On patriotic cover   4,000.

JACKSON, MISS.

E1

Handstamped Envelopes
Two types of numeral

43XU1 E1 5c **black**   500.
         On patriotic cover   3,000.
43XU2 E1 10c **black**   2,000.
43XU3 E1 10c on 5c **black** 2,750.
43XU4 E1 10c on 5c **blue**   2,750.
   The 5c also exists on a lettersheet.
   See 3c 1861 Postmasters' Provisional No. 2AXU1.

JACKSONVILLE, ALA.

E1

Handstamped Envelope

110XU1 E1 5c **black**   — 1,500.

JACKSONVILLE, FLA.

E1

Handstamped Envelope

134XU1 E1 5c **black**   —
Undated double circle postmark control on reverse.

JETERSVILLE, VA.

A1

Handstamped Adhesive
("5" with ms. "AHA." initials)
Laid Paper

44X1 A1 5c **black**, vertical pair on cover, un-
        canceled   16,000.
Initials are those of Postmaster A. H. Atwood.

Cancellation: black town.

JONESBORO, TENN.

E1

Handstamped Envelopes

45XU1 E1 5c **black**   3,750.
45XU2 E1 5c **dark blue**   7,000.

KINGSTON, GA.

PAID
5
CENTS
E1

PAID
c**5**s
CENTS
E2

E3

E4

Typeset Envelopes (E1-E3 probably impressed by hand, possibly press printed); Handstamped Envelope (E4)

46XU1 E1 5c **black**   2,000.
46XU2 E2 5c **black**   — 3,250.
  a. No "C" or "S" at sides of numeral
46XU3 E2 5c **black**, *amber* 2,750.
46XU4 E3 5c **black**
46XU5 E4 5c **black**   2,000.
   Only one example of No. 46XU3 is recorded.

KNOXVILLE, TENN.

A1

Typographed Adhesives
(stereotype from woodcut)
Grayish Laid Paper

47X1 A1 5c **brick red**   1,250. 900.
      Manuscript cancel   325.
      Horizontal pair   3,750. 1,850.
      Vertical pair   3,100.
      Vertical strip of 3   6,000.
      On cover, tied by handstamp 7,500.
      On cover, manuscript cancel 2,100.
      Pair on cover   7,500.
47X2 A1 5c **carmine**   1,750. 1,500.
      Vertical strip of 3
      On cover, tied by handstamp 7,500.
      On cover, manuscript cancel 2,100.
47X3 A1 10c **green**, on cover 57,750.
   The #47X3 cover is unique. Value is based on 1997 auction sale.
   The 5c has been reprinted in red, brown and chocolate on white and bluish wove and laid paper.

Cancellations in black: town, bars, pen or pencil.

KNOXVILLE, TENN.

E1

E2

Press-printed Envelopes (typographed)

47XU1 E1 5c **blue**   750. 1,750.
47XU2 E1 5c **blue**, *orange*   750. 2,000.
47XU3 E1 10c **red** (cut to shape) 2,100.
47XU4 E1 10c **red**, *orange* (cut to shape) 2,100.

Handstamped Envelopes

47XU5 E2 5c **black**   750. 1,500.
      On patriotic cover   3,000.
47XU6 E2 10c on 5c **black** 3,500.
   Type E2 exists with: "5" above or below "PAID."

LA GRANGE, TEX.

E1

Handstamped Envelopes

48XU1 E1 5c **black**   — 2,000.
48XU2 E1 10c **black**   2,500.

LAKE CITY, FLA.

E1   Control

Handstamped Envelope

96XU1 E1 10c **black**   2,000.
   Envelopes have black circle control mark, or printed name of E. R. Ives, postmaster, on face or back.

LAURENS COURT HOUSE, S. C.

E1

Handstamped Envelope

116XU1 E1 5c **black**   1,500.

LENOIR, N. C.

A1

E1

Handstamped Adhesive (from woodcut)
White wove paper with cross-ruled orange lines

49X1 A1 5c **blue & orange** 3,250. 2,750.
      On cover, pen canceled   7,000.
      On cover, tied by handstamp 20,000.

Cancellations: blue town, blue "Paid" in circle, black pen.

Handstamped Envelopes

49XU1	A1	5c blue	3,500.
49XU2	A1	10c (5c+5c) blue	25,000.
49XU3	E1	5c blue	4,500.
49XU4	E1	5c black	

No. 49XU2 is unique. The existence of No. 49XU4 has been questioned.

LEXINGTON, MISS.

E1

Handstamped Envelopes

50XU1	E1	5c black	5,000.
50XU2	E1	10c black	5,000.

LEXINGTON, VA.

E1

Handstamped Envelopes

135XU1	E1	5c blue	500.
		Used with 5c #6 to make 10c rate	—
135XU2	E1	10c blue	750.

Nos. 135XU1-135XU2 by themselves are indistinguishable from a handstamp paid cover when used.

LIBERTY, VA. (and Salem, Va.)

PAID

5cts.

A1

Typeset Adhesive (probably impressed by hand)
Laid Paper

74X1	A1	5c black, on cover, uncanceled, with Liberty postmark	35,000.
		On cover, uncanceled, with Salem postmark	40,000.

Two known on covers with Liberty, Va. postmark; one cover known with the nearby Salem, Va. office postmark.

LIMESTONE SPRINGS, S. C.

A1

Handstamped Adhesive

121X1	A1	5c black, on cover	10,000.
		Two on cover	15,000.

Stamps are cut round or rectangular, on white or colored paper. Covers are not postmarked.

LIVINGSTON, ALA.

A1

Lithographed Adhesive

51X1	A1	5c blue	7,000.
		On cover	60,000.
		Pair on cover	120,000.

The pair on cover is unique.

Cancellation: black town.

LYNCHBURG, VA.

A1

E1

Typographed Adhesive
(stereotype from woodcut)

52X1	A1	5c blue (shades)	600.	1,000.
		Pair		2,250.
		On cover		4,750.
		Pair on cover		20,000.

Cancellations: black town, blue town.

Press-printed Envelopes (typographed)
Impressed at top right or left

52XU1	E1	5c black		2,500.
52XU2	E1	5c black, amber	650.	2,500.
52XU3	E1	5c black, buff		2,500.
52XU4	E1	5c black, brown	900.	2,500.
		On patriotic cover		—

MACON, GA.

A1

A3

A2

A4

Typeset Adhesives
Several varieties of type A1, 10 of A2, 5 of A3
Wove Paper

53X1	A1	5c black, light blue green (shades)	850.	600.
		On cover		4,000.
		Pair on cover		9,000.
		Comma after "OFFICE"	900.	1,000.
		Comma after "OFFICE," on cover		7,500.

Warning: Dangerous forgeries exist of the Comma after "OFFICE" variety. Certificates of authenticity from recognized committees are strongly recommended.

53X3	A2	5c black, yellow	2,500.	800.
		On cover		4,750.
		On patriotic cover		9,000.
		Pair on cover		8,000.
53X4	A3	5c black, yellow (shades)	2,750.	1,250.
		On cover		6,000.
		Pair on cover		10,000.
	a.	Vertical tête bêche pair		—
53X5	A4	2c black, gray green		—
		On cover		60,000.

Laid Paper

53X6	A2	5c black, yellow	3,000.	3,500.
		On cover		6,000.
53X7	A3	5c black, yellow	6,000.	
		On cover		9,000.
53X8	A1	5c black, light blue green	1,750.	2,000.
		On cover		4,500.

No. 53X4a is unique.

Cancellations: black town, black "PAID" (2 types).

E1

Handstamped Envelope
Two types: "PAID" over "5," "5" over "PAID"

53XU1	E1	5c black	250.	500.
		On patriotic cover		1,900.

Values are for "PAID" over "5" variety. "5" over "PAID" is much scarcer.

MADISON, GA.

PAID

E1

Handstamped Envelope

136XU1	E1	5c red	500.

No. 136XU1 is indistinguishable from a handstamp paid cover when used.

MADISON COURT HOUSE, FLA.

E1

Typeset Envelope

137XU1	E1	5c black	23,000.

No. 137XU1 is unique.
See 3c 1861 Postmasters' Provisional No. 3AX1.

MARIETTA, GA.

E1

PAID

5

E2

Handstamped Envelopes
Two types of "PAID" and numerals

54XU1	E1	5c black		300.
54XU2	E2	10c on 5c black E1		1,750.

With Double Circle Control

54XU3	E2	10c black		
54XU4	E2	5c black		2,000.

The existence of No. 54XU3 is questioned.

MARION, VA.

A1

Adhesives with Typeset frame and Handstamped numeral in center

55X1	A1	5c black		6,500.
		On cover		20,000.
55X2	A1	10c black	16,500.	10,000.
		On cover		25,000.
55X3	A1	5c black, bluish, laid paper		

The 2c, 3c, 15c and 20c are believed to be bogus items printed later using the original typeset frame.

Cancellations: black town, black "PAID."

MEMPHIS, TENN.

A1

A2

Typographed Adhesives
(stereotyped from woodcut)

Plate of 50 (5x10) for the 2c. The stereotypes for the 5c stamps were set in 5 vertical rows of 8, with at least 2 rows set sideways to the right (see Thomas H. Pratt's monograph, "The Postmaster's Provisionals of Memphis").

56X1	A1	2c **blue** (shades)		90.	*1,250.*
		Block of 4		525.	
		On cover			*10,000.*
		Cracked plate (16, 17, 18)		150.	*1,350.*

The "cracking off" (breaking off) of the plate at right edge caused incomplete printing of stamps in positions 5, 10, 15, 20, and 50. Poor make-ready also caused incomplete printing in position 50.

56X2	A2	5c **red** (shades)		140.	175.
		Pair		*325.*	450.
		Block of 4		*1,000.*	
		On cover			1,750.
		Pair on cover			3,500.
		Strip of 4 on cover			7,000.
		On patriotic cover			4,000.
a.		Tête bêche pair			1,500.
		Pair on cover			10,000.
b.		Pair, one sideways		750.	
c.		Pelure paper		—	—

Cancellation on Nos. 56X1-56X2: black town.

Press-printed Envelopes (typographed)

56XU1	A2	5c **red**		*2,500.*
		Used with 5c #56X2 to make 10c rate		*5,000.*
56XU2	A2	5c **red**, *amber*		*4,000.*
		Used with C.S.A. 5c #1 to make 10c rate		*6,500.*
56XU3	A2	5c **red**, *orange*		*2,500.*
		On patriotic cover		*4,000.*

MICANOPY, FLA.

E1

Handstamped Envelope

105XU1	E1	5c **black**		*11,500.*

One example known.

MILLEDGEVILLE, GA.

E1

E2

E3

Handstamped Envelopes

57XU1	E1	5c **black**		250.
57XU2	E1	5c **blue**		800.
57XU3	E1	10c on 5c **black**		*1,000.*
57XU4	E2	10c **black**	225.	*1,000.*
57XU5	E3	10c **black**		700.

On No. 57XU4, the "PAID/10" virtually always falls outside the Milledgeville control marking (as in illustration E1).

Two types of No. 57XU5; with tall, thin "1" of "10" and with short, fat "1." The latter is about twice as scarce.

MILTON, N. C.

N.B. PATTON
P A I D 5

E1

Handstamped Envelope, "5" Manuscript

138XU1	E1	5c **black**		*2,000.*

MOBILE, ALA.

A1

Lithographed Adhesives

58X1	A1	2c **black**		2,000.	*1,000.*
		Pair		—	*2,100.*
		On cover			*3,500.*
		Pair on cover			*16,500.*
		Three singles on one cover			*7,500.*
		Five copies on one cover			*20,000.*
58X2	A1	5c **blue**		275.	225.
		Pair		*675.*	575.
		On cover			*1,750.*
		On cover, canceled in Montgomery, Ala.			—
		Pair on cover			*2,250.*
		Strip of 3 on cover			*6,000.*
		Strip of 4 on cover			*7,500.*
		Strip of 5 on cover			—

Cancellations: black town, express company.

MONTGOMERY, ALA.

E1

Handstamped Envelopes

59XU1	E1	5c **red**			1,000.
59XU2	E1	5c **blue**		400.	900.
59XU3	E1	10c **red**			800.
59XU4	E1	10c **blue**			1,500.
59XU5	E1	10c **black**			800.
59XU6	E1	10c on 5c **red**			*2,750.*

The 10c design is larger than the 5c.

E2

E3

59XU7	E2	2c **red**		*2,500.*
59XU7A	E2	2c **blue**		*3,500.*
59XU8	E2	5c **black**		*2,250.*
59XU9	E3	10c **black**		*2,750.*
59XU10	E3	10c **red**		*1,500.*

MT. LEBANON, LA.

A1

Woodcut Adhesive (mirror image of design)

60X1	A1	5c **red brown**, on cover		*385,000.*

One example known.

Cancellation: black pen.

NASHVILLE, TENN.

A2

Typographed Adhesives
(stereotyped from woodcut)
Gray Blue Ribbed Paper

61X2	A2	5c **carmine** (shades)		850.	500.
		Pair			*1,250.*
		On cover			*2,500.*
		On patriotic cover			*4,500.*
		Pair on cover			*6,000.*
		On cover with U.S. 3c 1857 (express)			*25,000.*
a.		Vertical tête bêche pair			*3,000.*

61X3	A2	5c **brick red**		850.	450.
		Pair			*950.*
		On cover			*3,500.*
		On patriotic cover			*6,000.*
		Pair on cover			*7,500.*
		On U.S. #U26 (express)			*35,000.*
		On U.S. #U27 with #26 (express)			*25,000.*
61X4	A2	5c **gray** (shades)		850.	625.
		On cover			*5,500.*
		Pair on cover			*7,250.*
		Strip of 5 on cover front			*8,500.*
61X5	A2	5c **violet brown**		750.	475.
		Block of 4			—
		On cover			*4,500.*
		On patriotic cover			—
		Pair on cover			*6,000.*
a.		Vertical tete beche pair		*3,500.*	*2,500.*
		Pair on cover			*6,000.*
61X6	A2	10c **green**		3,000.	*3,000.*
		On cover			*15,000.*
		On cover with U.S. 3c 1857 (express)			*75,000.*
		On U.S. #U26 (express)			*100,000.*
		On cover with No. 61X2			*17,500.*

Cancellations

Blue "Paid"
Blue "Postage Paid"
Blue town
Blue numeral "5"
Blue numeral "10"
Blue express company
Black express company

For the former 61X1, see No. 4AX1 in the 3c 1861 Postmasters' Provisional section.

E1

Handstamped Envelopes

61XU1	E1	5c **blue**		750.
		On patriotic envelope		*1,750.*
61XU2	E1	5c +10c **blue**		*2,400.*

NEW ORLEANS, LA.

A1

A2

Typographed Adhesives
(stereotyped from woodcut)
Plate of 40

62X1	A1	2c **blue**, *July 14, 1861*		150.	500.
		Pair		525.	*1,150.*
		Block of 4		*6,500.*	
		On cover			*4,250.*
		On patriotic cover			*8,000.*
		Pair on cover			*10,000.*
		Three singles on one cover			*20,000.*
		Strip of 5 on cover			*30,000.*
a.		Printed on both sides			*1,750.*
		On cover			*7,500.*
62X2	A1	2c **red** (shades), *Jan. 6, 1862*		125.	*1,000.*
		Pair		300.	
		Block of 4		*1,500.*	
		On cover			*25,000.*
62X3	A2	5c **brown**, *white, June 12, 1861*		250.	150.
		Pair		525.	325.
		Block of 4		*1,750.*	
		On cover			400.
		On patriotic cover			*5,500.*
		Pair on cover			800.
		Strip of 5 on cover			*5,000.*
		On cover with U.S. #26 (Southern Letter Unpaid)			*150,000.*
		On cover with U.S. No. 30A			*1,750.*
a.		Printed on both sides			*1,750.*
		On cover			*7,500.*
b.		5c **ocher**, *June 18, 1861*		650.	600.
		Pair			*1,450.*
		On cover			*2,250.*
		On patriotic cover			*6,000.*
		Pair on cover			*3,000.*
62X4	A2	5c **red brn**, *bluish, Aug. 22, 1861*		280.	175.
		Pair		625.	425.
		Horizontal strip of 6			*3,500.*
		Block of 4		*2,200.*	
		On cover			400.
		On patriotic cover			*5,500.*
		Pair on cover			675.

			Block of 4 on cover		5,000.
			Used on cover with C.S.A.		
			5c #1 to make 10c rate		7,500.
a.			Printed on both sides		2,750.
62X5	A2	5c	yel brn, *off-white, Dec. 3,*		
			1861	125.	225.
			Pair	275.	500.
			Block of 4	650.	
			On cover		500.
			On patriotic cover		3,000.
			Pair on cover		1,000.
			Strip of 5 on cover		—
62X6	A2	5c	red	—	7,500.
62X7	A2	5c	red, *bluish*		10,000.

Cancellations
Black town (single or double circle New Orleans)
Red town (double circle New Orleans)
Town other than New Orleans
Postmaster's handstamp
Black "Paid"
Express Company
Packet boat, cover "STEAM"

E1

These provisional handstamps were applied at the riverfront postal station.

Handstamped Envelopes
| 62XU1 | E1 | 5c | black | 4,500. |
| 62XU2 | E1 | 10c | black | 12,500. |

"J. L. RIDDELL, P. M." omitted
| 62XU3 | E1 | 2c | black | 9,500. |

NEW SMYRNA, FLA.

A1

Handstamped Adhesive
On white paper with blue ruled lines
| 63X1 | A1 | 10c ("O1") on 5c | black | 45,000. |

One example known. It is uncanceled on a postmarked patriotic cover.

NORFOLK, VA.

E1

Handstamped Envelopes
Ms Initials on Front or Back
| 139XU1 | E1 | 5c | blue | — | 1,250. |
| 139XU2 | E1 | 10c | blue | | 1,750. |

OAKWAY, S. C.

A1

Handstamped Adhesive (from woodcut)
| 115X1 | A1 | 5c | black, on cover | 66,000. |

Two used examples of No. 115X1 are recorded, both on cover. Value represents 1997 auction realization for the cover on which the stamp is tied by manuscript "Paid."

PENSACOLA, FLA.

E1

Handstamped Envelopes
106XU1	E1	5c	black	3,750.
106XU2	E1	10c	(ms.) on 5c	black	4,250.
			On patriotic cover	13,500.

PETERSBURG, VA.

A1

Typeset Adhesive
Ten varieties
Thick white paper
65X1	A1	5c	red	1,500.	450.
			Pair	2,500.	1,350.
			Block of 4	5,500.	
			On cover		2,000.
			On patriotic cover		—
			Pair on cover		8,000.
			Used on cover with C.S.A.		
			5c #1 to make 10c rate		57,500.

Cancellation: blue town.

PITTSYLVANIA COURT HOUSE, VA.

A1

Typeset Adhesives
66X1	A1	5c	dull red, *wove paper*	6,000.	5,000.
			Octagonally cut		3,000.
			On cover		55,000.
			On cover, octagonally cut		20,000.
66X2	A1	5c	dull red, *laid paper*		6,500.
			Octagonally cut		5,500.
			On cover		55,000.
			On cover, octagonally cut		40,000.

Cancellation: black town.

PLAINS OF DURA, GA.

E1

Handstamped Envelopes, Ms. Initials
| 140XU1 | E1 | 5c | black | — |
| 140XU2 | E1 | 10c | black | — |

PLEASANT SHADE, VA.

A1

Typeset Adhesive
Five varieties
67X1	A1	5c	blue	2,500.	20,000.
			On cover		27,500.
			Pair	7,500.	
			Pair on cover		55,000.
			Block of 6	25,000.	

Cancellation: blue town.

PLUM CREEK, TEX.

E1

Manuscript Adhesive
| 141X1 | E1 | 10c | black, *blue,* on cover | — |

The ruled lines and "10" are done by hand. Size and shape of the stamp varies.

PORT GIBSON, MISS.

E1

Handstamped Envelope, Ms Signature
| 142XU1 | E1 | 5c | black | — |

PORT LAVACA, TEX.

A1

Typeset Adhesive
| 107X1 | A1 | 10c | black, on cover | 25,000. |

One example known. It is uncanceled on a postmarked cover.

RALEIGH, N. C.

E1

Handstamped Envelopes
68XU1	E1	5c	red	500.
			On patriotic cover	2,750.
68XU2	E1	5c	blue	2,500.

RHEATOWN, TENN.

A1

Typeset Adhesive
Three varieties
69X1	A1	5c	red	2,000.	2,750.
			On cover, ms. cancel		15,000.
			On cover, tied by handstamp		35,000.
			Pair	5,000.	

Stamps normally were canceled in manuscript. One cover is known with stamp tied by red town postmark.

Cancellations: red town or black pen.

RICHMOND, TEX.

E1

Handstamped Envelopes or Letter Sheets
70XU1	E1	5c	red	1,500.
70XU2	E1	10c	red	1,000.
70XU3	E1	10c	on 5c red	5,000.
70XU4	E1	15c	(ms.) on 10c red	5,000.

RINGGOLD, GA.

E1

Handstamped Envelope

71XU1 E1 5c blue black   3,000.

RUTHERFORDTON, N. C.

A1

Handstamped Adhesive, Ms. "Paid 5cts"

72X1 A1 5c black, cut round, on cover
                    (uncanceled)   25,000.

No. 72X1 is unique.

SALEM, N. C.

E1   E2

Handstamped Envelopes

73XU1 E1 5c black   1,150.
73XU2 E1 10c black   1,500.
73XU3 E2 5c black   1,500.
73XU4 E2 10c on 5c black   2,800.

Reprints exist on various papers. They either lack the "Paid" and value or have them counterfeited.

Salem, Va.
See No. 74X1 under Liberty, Va.

SALISBURY, N. C.

SALISBURY.
N. C.
POSTAGE

FIVE CENTS
P.M.

E1

Press-printed Envelope (typeset)
Impressed at top left

75XU1 E1 5c black, greenish   5,000.

One example known. Part of envelope is torn away, leaving part of design missing. Illustration E1 partly suppositional.

SAN ANTONIO, TEX.

E1   E2

Control

Handstamped Envelopes

76XU1   E1 10c black   275. 2,000.
76XU1A E2 5c black   1,500.
76XU2   E2 10c black   2,500.

Black circle control mark is on front or back.

SAVANNAH, GA.

E1   Control

E2

Handstamped Envelopes

101XU1 E1 5c black   300.
101XU2 E2 5c black   600.
101XU3 E1 10c black   750.
101XU4 E2 10c black   750.
101XU5 E1 10c on 5c black   1,500.
101XU6 E2 20c on 5c black   2,000.

Envelopes must have octagonal control mark. One example is known of No.101XU6.

SELMA, ALA.

PAID
5

E1

Handstamped Envelopes; Signature in Ms.

77XU1 E1 5c black   1,250.
77XU2 E1 10c black   2,500.
77XU3 E1 10c on 5c black   3,000.

Signature is that of Postmaster William H. Eagar.
See 3c 1861 Postmasters' Provisional No. 5AX1.

SPARTA, GA.

E1

Handstamped Envelopes

93XU1 E1 5c red   — 1,000.
93XU2 E1 10c red   2,500.

SPARTANBURG, S. C.

A1   A2

Handstamped Adhesives
(on ruled or plain wove paper)

78X1 A1 5c black   3,500.
              On cover   25,000.
              Pair on cover   30,000.
              On patriotic cover   30,000.
  a. "5" omitted (on cover)   —

78X2 A2 5c black, bluish   4,000.
              On cover   15,000.
78X3 A2 5c black, brown   4,000.
              On cover   18,000.

Most examples of Nos. 78X1-78X3 are cut round. Cut square examples in sound condition are worth much more. The only recorded pair of No. 78X1 is on cover. The stamps are cut round, but are still connected.

Cancellations: black "PAID," black town.

STATESVILLE, N. C.

E1

Handstamped Envelopes

79XU1 E1 5c black   175.   600.
79XU2 E1 10c on 5c black   2,250.

SUMTER, S. C.

E1

Handstamped Envelopes

80XU1 E1 5c black   400.
80XU2 E1 10c black   400.
80XU3 E1 10c on 5c black   800.
80XU4 E1 2c (ms.) on 10c black   1,100.

Used examples of Nos. 80XU1-80XU2 are indistinguishable from handstamped "Paid" covers.

TALBOTTON, GA.

E1

Handstamped Envelopes

94XU1 E1 5c black   1,000.
94XU2 E1 10c black   1,000.
94XU3 E1 10c on 5c black   2,000.

TALLADEGA, ALA.

PAID 10

E1

Handstamped Envelopes

143XU1 E1 5c black   — —
143XU2 E1 10c black   — —

TELLICO PLAINS, TENN.

A1

Typeset Adhesives
Settings of two 5c and one 10c
Laid Paper

81X1 A1 5c red   1,250.   —
              On cover   50,000.
81X2 A1 10c red   2,500.
              Se-tenant with 5c   4,000.
              Strip of 3 (5c+5c+10c) 8,000.

Cancellation: black pen.

THOMASVILLE, GA.

PAID   E1   Control

Handstamped Envelopes

82XU1 E1 5c **black**   500.

E2

82XU2 E2 5c **black**   900.

TULLAHOMA, TENN.

E1

Control

Handstamped Envelope

111XU1 E1 10c **black**   3,000.

TUSCALOOSA, ALA.

E1

Handstamped Envelopes

83XU1 E1 5c **black**   250.
83XU2 E1 10c **black**   250.

Used examples of Nos. 83XU1-83XU2 are indistinguishable from handstamped "Paid" covers. Some authorities question the use of E1 to produce provisional envelopes.

TUSCUMBIA, ALA.

E1

Handstamped Envelopes

84XU1 E1 5c **black**   2,250.
          On patriotic cover
84XU2 E1 5c **red**   3,000.
84XU3 E1 10c **black**   3,500.

See 3c 1861 Postmasters' Provisional No. 6AXU1.

Union City, Tenn.

E1

The use of E1 to produce provisional envelopes is doubtful.

UNIONTOWN, ALA.

A1

Typeset Adhesives
(settings of 4 (2x2), 4 varieties of each value)
Laid Paper

86X1	A1	2c **dark blue**, *gray blue*, on cover		—
86X2	A1	2c **dark blue**, sheet of 4	57,500.	
86X3	A1	5c **green**, *gray blue*	2,750.	2,000.
		Pair		—
		On cover		6,500.
86X4	A1	5c **green**	2,750.	2,000.
		On cover		7,000.
		Pair on cover		18,500.
86X5	A1	10c **red**, *gray blue*		—
		On cover		37,500.

Two examples known of No. 86X1, both on cover (drop letters), one uncanceled and one pen canceled.
The only recorded examples of No. 86X2 are in a unique sheet of 4.
The item listed as No. 86X5 used is an uncanceled stamp on a large piece with part of addressee's name in manuscript.

Cancellation on Nos. 86X3-86X5: black town.

UNIONVILLE, S. C.

A1

Handstamped Adhesive
"PAID" and "5" applied separately
Paper with Blue Ruled Lines

87X1	A1	5c **black**, *grayish*		—
		On cover, uncanceled		17,500.
		On cover, tied		—
		Pair on patriotic cover		32,500.

The pair on patriotic cover is the only pair recorded.

Cancellation: black town.

VALDOSTA, GA.

Control

E1

Handstamped Envelopes

100XU1 E1 10c **black**   2,000.
100XU2 E1 5c +5c **black**   —

The black circle control must appear on front or back of envelope.
There is one recorded cover each of Nos. 100XU1-100XU2.

VICTORIA, TEX.

A1   A2

Typeset Adhesives
Surface colored paper

88X1	A1	5c **red brown**, *green*	9,000.	
88X2	A1	10c **red brown**, *green*	10,000.	5,500.
		On cover		115,000.
88X3	A2	10c **red brown**, *green*, pelure paper	10,000.	10,000.

WALTERBOROUGH, S. C.

E1

Handstamped Envelopes

108XU1 E1 10c **black**, *buff*   4,000.
108XU2 E1 10c **carmine**   4,000.

WARRENTON, GA.

E1

Handstamped Envelopes

89XU1 E1 5c **black**   1,250.
89XU2 E1 10c **(ms.)** on 5c **black**   850.

WASHINGTON, GA.

PAID 10

E1

Handstamped Envelope

117XU1 E1 10c **black**   2,000.

Envelopes must have black circle control on front or back.

WEATHERFORD, TEX.

E1

Handstamped Envelopes
(woodcut with "PAID" inserted in type)

109XU1 E1 5c **black**   2,000.
109XU2 E1 5c +5c **black**   11,000.

One example is known of No. 109XU2.

WINNSBOROUGH, S. C.

PAID 5   E1   Control

Handstamped Envelopes

97XU1 E1 5c **black**   1,500.
97XU2 E1 10c **black**   2,000.

Envelopes must have black circle control on front or back.

WYTHEVILLE, VA.

5
PAID
E1   Control

Handstamped Envelope

114XU1 E1   5c **black**   900.

For later additions, listed out of numerical sequence, see:

#74X1, Liberty, Va.
#92XU1, Huntsville, Tex.
#93XU1, Sparta, Ga.
#94XU1, Talbotton, Ga.
#96XU1, Lake City, Fla.
#97XU1, Winnsborough, S. C.
#98XU1, Galveston, Tex.
#99XU1, Christiansburg, Va.
#100XU1, Valdosta, Ga.
#101XU1, Savannah, Ga.
#102XU1, Griffin, Ga.
#103XU1, Courtland, Ala.
#104XU1, Fincastle, Va.
#105XU1, Micanopy, Fla.
#106XU1, Pensacola, Fla.
#107X1, Port Lavaca, Tex.
#108XU1, Walterborough, S. C.
#109XU1, Weatherford, Tex.
#110XU1, Jacksonville, Ala.
#111XU1, Tullahoma, Tenn.
#112XU1, Hamburgh, S. C.
#113XU1, Columbia, Tenn.
#114XU1, Wytheville, Va.
#115X1, Oakway, S. C.
#116XU1, Laurens Court House, S. C.

#117XU1, Washington, Ga.
#118XU1, Carolina City, N.C.
#119XU1, Colaparchee, Ga.
#120XU1, Forsyth, Ga.
#121XU1, Limestone Springs, S.C.
#122XU1, Balcony Falls, Va.
#123XU1, Barnwell Court House, S.C.
#124XU1, Bluffton, S.C.
#125XU1, Camden, S.C.
#126XU1, Cartersville, Ga.
#127XU1, Charlottesville, Va.
#128XU1, Fraziersville, S.C.
#129XU1, Gaston, N.C.
#130XU1, Harrisburgh, Tex.
#132XU1, Hollandale, Tex.
#133XU1, Isabella, Ga.
#134XU1, Jacksonville, Fla.
#135XU1, Lexington, Va.
#136XU1, Madison, Fla.
#137XU1, Madison Court House, Fla.
#138XU1, Milton, N.C.
#139XU1, Norfolk, Va.
#140XU1, Plains of Dura, Ga.
#141X1, Plum Creek, Tex.
#142XU1, Port Gibson, Miss.
#143XU1, Talladega, Ala.

CONFEDERATE STATES OF AMERICA, GENERAL ISSUES

The general issues are valued in the very fine grade, and unused stamps are valued both with and without original gum. As noted in the catalogue introduction, "original gum" for this era is defined as at least a majority part original gum, that is, at least 51% original gum. Stamps with substantially more than 51% original gum may be expected to sell for more than the values given, and stamps with less than a majority part original gum will sell for somewhat less.

For explanations of various terms used see the notes at the end of the postage listings.

Jefferson Davis — A1

1861   Litho.   Soft Porous Paper   *Imperf.*

All 5c Lithographs were printed by Hoyer & Ludwig, of Richmond, Va.

Stones A or B - First stones used. Earliest dated cancellation October 16, 1861. Plating not completed hence size of sheets unknown. These stones had imprints. Stamps from Stones A or B are nearly all in the olive green shade. Sharp, clear impressions. Distinctive marks are few and minute.

Stone 1 - Earliest dated cancellation October 18, 1861. Plating completed. Sheet consists of four groups of fifty varieties arranged in two panes of one hundred each without imprint. The first small printing was in olive green and later small printings appeared in light and dark green; the typical shade, however, is an intermediate shade of bright green. The impressions are clear though not as sharp as those from Stones A or B. Distinctive marks are discernible.

Stone 2 - Earliest dated cancellation December 2, 1861. Plating completed. Sheet consists of four groups of fifty varieties arranged in two panes of one hundred each without imprint. All shades other than olive green are known from this stone, the most common being a dull green. Poor impressions. Many noticeable distinctive marks.

Stone 2

1	A1	5c	**green**	250.	150.
			No gum	175.	
			bright green	275.	150.
			dull green	250.	150.
a.		5c	**light green**	250.	150.
			No gum	175.	
b.		5c	**dark green**	275.	175.
			No gum	190.	
			On cover		250.
			Single on cover (overpaid drop letter)		350.
			On wallpaper cover		1,500.
			On prisoner's cover		—
			On prisoner's cover with U.S. #65		—
			On prisoner's cover with U.S. #U34		—
			On patriotic cover		1,250.
			Pair	600.	375.
			Pair on cover		400.
			Block of 4	1,450.	1,200.
			Pair with full horiz. gutter between		

VARIETIES

Spur on upper left scroll (Pos. 21)	400.	260.
Side margin copy showing initials (Pos. 41 or 50)	1,100.	625.

Misplaced transfer (clear twin impressions of lower left scrolls - pos. 1 entered over pos. 10)	—	—
Rouletted unofficially	350.	700.
On cover		1,600.
Pair on cover		2,500.

Cancellations

Blue town	+10.
Red town	+125.
Green town	+175.
Orange town	+150.
Texas town	+35.
Arkansas town	+90.
Florida town	+110.
Kentucky town	+300.
Blue gridiron	+5.
Red gridiron	+50.
Blue concentric	+5.
Star or flowers	+100.
Numeral	+50.
"Paid"	+50.
"Steamboat"	+150.
Express Co.	+350.
Railroad	+300.
Pen	60.

Stone 1

1	A1	5c	**green**	250.	150.
			No gum	175.	
			bright green	275.	150.
			dull green	250.	150.
a.		5c	**light green**	250.	150.
			No gum	175.	
b.		5c	**dark green**	275.	175.
			No gum	190.	
c.		5c	**olive green**	275.	175.
			No gum	190.	
			On cover		250.

On patriotic cover		1,250.
Pair	700.	425.
Pair on cover		525.
Block of 4	1,500.	1,150.

VARIETIES

Acid flaw	325.	160.
Arrow between panes	575.	300.
Flaw on "at" of "States" (Pos. 38)	300.	200.

Cancellations

Blue town	+10.
Red town	+80.
Green town	+175.
Texas town	+35.
Arkansas town	+90.
Florida town	+110.
Kentucky town	+300.
October, 1861, year date	+40.
Blue gridiron	+5.
Red gridiron	+75.
Blue concentric	+5.
Numeral	+50.
"Paid"	+50.
"Steam"	+150.
"Steamboat"	+150.
Express Company	+350.
Railroad	+300.
Pen	60.

Stones A or B

1c	A1	5c **olive green**	290.	175.
		No gum	225.	
		On cover		275.
		On patriotic cover		1,400.
		Pair	625.	400.
		Pair on cover		550.
		Block of 4	1,700.	1,200.

VARIETIES

White curl back of head	350.	250.
Imprint	700.	450.

Cancellations

Blue town	+10.
Red town	+150.
October, 1861, year date	+50.
Blue gridiron	+5.
Blue concentric	+5.
Numeral	+60.
"Paid"	+50.
"Steam"	+150.
Express Co.	+400.
Pen	100.

Thomas Jefferson — A2

1861-62   Litho.   Soft Porous Paper

Hoyer & Ludwig - First stone used. Earliest dated cancellation November 8, 1861. Sheet believed to consist of four groups of fifty varieties each arranged in two panes of one hundred each with imprint at bottom of each pane. Two different imprints are known. Hoyer & Ludwig printings are always in a uniform shade of dark blue. Impressions are clear and distinct, especially so in the early printings. Plating marks are distinct.

J. T. Paterson & Co. - Earliest dated cancellation July 25, 1862. Sheet consists of four groups of fifty varieties each arranged in two panes of one hundred each with imprint at bottom of each pane. Two different imprints are known and at least one pane is known without an imprint. Wide range of shades. Impressions are less clear than those from the Hoyer & Ludwig stone. Paterson stamps show small vertical colored dash below the lowest point of the upper left triangle.

Stone "Y" - Supposedly made by J. T. Paterson & Co., as it shows the distinctive mark of that firm. Plating not completed hence size of sheet unknown. No imprint found. Color is either a light milky blue or a greenish blue. Impressions are very poor and have a blurred appearance. Stone Y stamps invariably show a large flaw back of the head as well as small vertical colored dash beneath the upper left triangle.

Paterson

2	A2	10c **blue**	280.	190.
		No gum	220.	
a.		10c **light blue**	280.	190.
		No gum	220.	
b.		10c **dark blue**	550.	240.
		No gum	425.	
c.		10c **indigo**	2,750.	2,250.
		No gum	2,000.	
		On cover		250.
		On wallpaper cover		700.
		On patriotic cover		1,400.
		On prisoner's cover with U.S. #65		—
		Pair	725.	450.
		Pair on cover		950.
		Strip of 3 on cover		—

Block of 4		1,750.	
Horiz. pair, gutter btwn.		1,500.	
d. Printed on both sides			—

VARIETIES

Malformed "O" of "POSTAGE" (Pos. 25)	400.	225.
J. T. Paterson & Co. imprint	1,000.	1,150.

Cancellations

Blue town	+10.
Red town	+100.
Green town	+200.
Violet town	—
Texas town	+125.
Arkansas town	+275.
Florida town	+325.
July, 1862, date	+300.
Straight line town	+500.
Blue gridiron	+10.
Red gridiron	+75.
Blue concentric	+10.
Numeral	+80.
"Paid"	+75.
Star or flower	+150.
Railroad	+350.
Express Co.	+300.
Pen	70.

Hoyer

2b	A2	10c **dark blue**	550.	240.
		No gum	425.	
		On cover		425.
		On wallpaper cover		725.
		On patriotic cover		2,100.
		On prisoner's cover with U.S. #65		—
		Pair	1,175.	800.
		Pair on cover		1,500.
		Strip of 3 on cover		3,500.
		Block of 4	2,750.	—
d.		Printed on both sides	—	

VARIETIES

Malformed "T" of "TEN" (Pos. 4)	575.	300.
"G" and "E" of "POSTAGE" joined (Pos. 10)	575.	300.
Circular flaw, upper left star (Pos. 11)	575.	300.
Third spiked ornament at right, white (Pos. 45)	575.	350.
Hoyer & Ludwig imprint	825.	825.
Rouletted unofficially, on cover		*3,000.*

Cancellations

Blue town	+30.
Red town	+100.
Texas town	+125.
Arkansas town	+275.
Florida town	+325.
Kentucky town	+400.
Nov., 1861, date	+300.
Straight line town	+500.
Blue gridiron	+10.
Red gridiron	+60.
Blue concentric	+10.
Numeral	+75.
"Paid"	+50.
Railroad	+350.
Express Company	+300.
Pen	75.

Stone Y

2e	A2	10c **greenish blue**	475.	300.
		No gum	350.	
		light milky blue	625.	300.
		No gum	475.	
		On cover		500.
		On patriotic cover		2,100.
		Pair	1,150.	—
		Block of 4	—	2,250.

Cancellations

Blue town	+10.
Red town	+125.
Violet town	+75.
Green town	+300.
Texas town	+125.
Arkansas town	+275.
Florida town	—
Straight line town	+500.
Blue gridiron	+10.
Red gridiron	+75.
Blue concentric	+10.
Numeral	+100.
"Paid"	+100.
Pen	90.

Andrew
Jackson — A3

Sheet consists of four groups of fifty varieties arranged in two panes of 100 each.

One stone only was used. Printed by Hoyer & Ludwig, of Richmond, Va. Issued to prepay drop letter and circular rates. Strips of five used to prepay regular 10c rate, which was changed from 5c on July 1, 1862. Earliest known cancellation, March 21, 1862.

				Soft Porous Paper	Litho.
1862 (March?)					
3	A3	2c	**green**	700.	650.
			No gum	550.	
			light green	700.	650.
			dark green	700.	700.
			dull yellow green	775.	800.
			No gum	650.	
			On cover		2,750.
			Pair on cover (double circular rate)		3,250.
			Strip of 5 on cover		13,500.
			On patriotic cover		10,000.
			Pair	1,500.	—
			Block of 4	3,250.	3,500.
			Block of 5	4,000.	4,250.
a.		2c	**bright yellow green**	1,750.	—
			No gum	1,400.	
			On cover		—

VARIETIES

Diagonal half used as 1c with unsevered pair, on cover	—	—
Horiz. pair, vert. gutter between	—	—
Pair, mark between stamps (btwn. Pos. 4 and 5)	1,750.	1,900.
Mark above upper right corner (Pos. 30)	850.	850.
Mark above upper left corner (Pos. 31)	850.	850.
Acid flaw	800.	700.

Cancellations

Blue town	+500.
Red town	+800.
Arkansas town	
Texas town	+1,250.
Blue gridiron	+250.
"Paid"	—
Express Company	
Railroad	+3,000.
Pen	400.

1862   **Soft Porous Paper**   **Litho.**

Stone 2 - First stone used for printing in blue. Plating is the same as Stone 2 in green. Earliest dated cancellation Feb. 28, 1862. Printings from Stone 2 are found in all shades of blue. Rough, coarse impressions are typical of printings from Stone 2.

Stone 3 - A new stone used for printings in blue only. Earliest dated cancellation April 10, 1862. Sheet consists of four groups of fifty varieties each arranged in two panes of one hundred each without imprint. Impressions are clear and sharp, often having a proof-like appearance, especially in the deep blue printing. Plating marks, while not so large as on Stone 2 are distinct and clearly defined.

Stone 2

4	A1	5c	**blue**	180.	110.
			No gum	135.	
			light blue	210.	130.
a.		5c	**dark blue**	240.	160.
			No gum	170.	
b.		5c	**light milky blue**	270.	200.
			No gum	190.	
			Pair	400.	400.
			Block of 4	1,000.	1,900.
			Horiz. pair, wide gutter between	1,250.	
			Vert. pair, narrow gutter between	—	
			On cover		250.
			Single on cover (overpaid drop letter)		325.
			Pair on cover		450.
			On wallpaper cover		575.
			On patriotic cover		1,800.
			On prisoner's cover		2,000.
			On prisoner's cover with U.S. #65		—

VARIETIES

Spur on upper left scroll (Pos. 21)	225.	150.
Thin hard paper	—	140.
Misplaced transfer (faint twin impression of second lower left scroll at left - pos. 2 entered over pos. 10)		

Cancellations

Blue town	+20.
Red town	+100.
Texas town	+300.
Arkansas town	+325.
Florida town	+200.
Straight line town	+300.
Blue gridiron	+10.
Red gridiron	+85.
Star or Flowers	+125.
Numeral	+85.
Railroad	
"Paid"	+25.
"Steamboat"	+400.
Express Company	—
"Way"	+250.
Pen	65.

Stone 3

4	A1	5c	**blue**	225.	150.
			No gum	165.	
a.		5c	**dark blue**	250.	190.
			No gum	200.	
b.		5c	**light milky blue**	290.	210.
			No gum	250.	
			Pair	500.	475.
			Block of 4	1,300.	2,000.
			On cover		310.
			Pair on cover		525.
			On patriotic cover		1,950.
			Horiz. pair, wide gutter btwn.	—	
			Vert. pair, narrow gutter between	—	

VARIETIES

Tops of "C" and "E" of "cents" joined by flaw (Pos. 33)	350.	260.
"Flying bird" above lower left corner ornament (Pos. 19)	325.	260.

Cancellations

Blue town	+40.
Red town	+100.
Texas town	+300.
Arkansas town	+325.
Straight line town	+325.
Blue gridiron	+10.
Star or Flowers	+125.
"Paid"	+50.
Pen	80.

1862 (March?)   **Soft Porous Paper**   **Litho.**

Settings of fifty varieties repeated.

Printed by Hoyer & Ludwig, of Richmond, Va. One stone used, being the same as that used for the Hoyer & Ludwig 10c value in blue. Color change occured probably in March, 1862.

There are many shades of this stamp. The carmine is a very dark, bright color and should not be confused with the deeper shade of rose.

Earliest known cancellation, March 10, 1862. The earliest date of usage of the carmine shade is May 1, 1862.

5	A2	10c	**rose**	1,250.	500.
			No gum	950.	
			dull rose	1,250.	500.
			brown rose	1,750.	1,000.
			deep rose	1,300.	650.
			carmine rose	1,500.	875.
			On cover		800.
			On wallpaper cover		2,000.
			On patriotic cover		3,000.
			On prisoner's cover		5,500.
			On prisoner's cover with U.S. #65		—
			Pair	3,100.	2,250.
			Strip of 3		4,000.
			Block of 4	11,000.	6,500.
a.		10c	**carmine**	2,800.	1,750.
			No gum	2,100.	
			On cover		4,500.

VARIETIES

Malformed "T" of "TEN" (Pos. 4)	1,250.	600.
"G" and "E" of "POSTAGE" joined (Pos. 10)	1,250.	600.
Circular flaw, upper left star (Pos. 11)	1,400.	675.
Third spiked ornament at right, white (Pos. 45)	1,400.	675.
Scratched stone (occurring on Pos. 40, 39, 49 and 48, one pane)	1,400.	925.
Imprint		1,750.
Horiz. pair, vert. gutter between		—
Side margin copy, initials (Pos. 41)		1,500.

Cancellations

Blue town	+50.
Red town	+125.
Green town	+350.
Texas town	+150.
Arkansas town	
Straight line town	+500.
April, 1862, year date	
Blue gridiron	+50.
Black concentric	+50.
Blue concentric	+50.
"Paid"	
Railroad	—
Express Company	
Pen	200.

Jefferson Davis — A4

Plate of 400 in four panes of 100 each. No imprint.

No. 6 represents London printings from De La Rue & Co., a number of sheets being sent over by blockade runners. Fine clear impressions. The gum is light and evenly distributed. Exact date of issue unknown. Earliest known cancellation, April 16, 1862.

Typographed by De La Rue & Co. in London, England

				Hard Medium Paper	
1862 (April)					
6	A4	5c	**light blue**	10.00	27.50
			No gum	7.00	
			Single on cover used before July 1, 1862		125.00
			Single on cover (overpaid drop letter)		240.00
			Single on patriotic cover used before July 1, 1862		900.00
			Single on prisoner's cover used before July 1, 1862		—
			On wallpaper cover		350.00
			On patriotic cover		1,100.
			On prisoner's cover		1,250.
			On prisoner's cover with U.S. #65		1,250.
			Pair	21.00	75.00
			Pair on cover		100.00
			Pair on patriotic cover		1,300.
			Block of 4	45.00	290.00
			Block of 4 on cover		900.00

Cancellations

Blue town	+2.00
Red town	+55.00
Green town	+75.00
Texas town	+65.00
Arkansas town	+85.00
Straight line town	+150.00
Blue gridiron	+2.00
Red gridiron	+35.00
Blue concentric	+2.00
Express Company	+350.00
Railroad	+250.00
"Paid"	+50.00

1862 (August)   **Typo.**   **Thin to Thick Paper**

Plate of 400 in four panes of 100 each. No imprint.

Locally printed by Archer & Daly of Richmond, Va., from plates made in London, England, by De La Rue & Co. Printed on both imported English and local papers. Earliest known cancellation, August 15, 1862.

No. 7 shows coarser impressions than No. 6, and the color is duller and often blurred. Gum is light or dark and unevenly distributed.

7	A4	5c	**blue**	13.00	20.00
			No gum	9.00	
a.		5c	**deep blue**	16.00	35.00
			No gum	11.00	
			Single on cover (overpaid drop letter)		200.00
			On wallpaper cover		500.00
			On patriotic cover		1,000.
			On prisoner's cover		1,250.
			On prisoner's cover with U.S. #65		—
			Pair	30.00	47.50
			Pair on cover		95.00
			Block of 4	70.00	340.00
			Block of 4 on cover		800.00
			Eight on cover (Trans-Miss. rate)		—
b.			Printed on both sides	2,500.	950.00
			Pair		2,100.
			Pair on cover		3,250.

VARIETIES

White tie (U.R. 30)	150.00	150.00
White tie on cover		350.00
De La Rue paper (thin)	27.50	45.00
No gum	20.00	
White tie, De La Rue paper	200.00	250.00
Thick paper	22.50	30.00
Horiz. pair, vert. gutter between	200.00	

Cancellations

Blue town	+2.00
Red town	+75.00
Brown town	+30.00
Violet town	+110.00
Green town	+150.00
Texas town	+90.00
Arkansas town	+110.00
Florida town	+140.00
Straight line town	+140.00
Blue gridiron	+2.00
Red gridiron	+60.00
Blue concentric	+2.00
Railroad	+250.00

Express Company	+400.00
Design (stars, etc.	+75.00
"Paid"	+50.00

The unissued 10c design A4 was privately printed in various colors for philatelic purposes. (See note below No. 14.) Counterfeits of the 10c exist.

Andrew Jackson — A5

Sheet of 200 (two panes of 100 each).
One plate. Printed by Archer & Daly of Richmond, Va. Earliest known cancellation. Apr. 21, 1863. Issued to prepay drop letter and circular rates. Strips of five used to prepay regular 10c rate.

1863 (April)	Soft Porous Paper		Engraved
8	A5 2c **brown red**	70.	350.
	No gum	55.	
a.	2c **pale red**	90.	450.
	No gum	70.	
	Single on cover		1,250.
	On prisoner's cover		3,000.
	On prisoner's cover with U.S. #65		4,000.
	Pair	150.	1,000.
	Pair on cover		3,250.
	On wallpaper cover		—
	Block of 4	350.	—
	Block of 5		—
	Strip of 5 on cover		5,000.
	Strip of 5 on wallpaper cover		—
	Strip of 10 on cover		13,000.
	Double transfer	125.	450.
	Horiz. pair, vert. gutter between	325.	

Cancellations

Blue town	+35.
Red town	+225.
Army of Tenn.	—
Blue gridiron	+35.
Black numeral	—
Railroad	+325.

Jefferson Davis "TEN CENTS" — A6

One plate of 200 subjects all of which were probably recut as every copy examined to date shows distinct recutting. Plating not completed.
Printed by Archer & Daly of Richmond, Va. First printings in milky blue. First issued in April, 1863. Earliest known cancellation, April 23, 1863.

1863, Apr.	Soft Porous Paper		Engraved
9	A6 10c **blue**	850.	525.
	No gum	650.	
a.	10c **milky blue** (first printing)	850.	525.
	No gum	650.	
b.	10c **gray blue**	900.	625.
	No gum	675.	
	On cover		1,600.
	On wallpaper cover		3,000.
	On patriotic cover		3,500.
	On prisoner's cover		4,250.
	On prisoner's cover with U.S. #65		—
	Pair	1,850.	2,200.
	Pair on cover		3,000.
	Block of 4	5,000.	—
	Four stamps on one cover (Trans-Mississippi rate)		13,500.
	Curved lines outside the labels at top and bottom are broken in the middle (Pos. 63R)	1,000.	750.
	Double transfer	1,050.	1,000.
	Damaged plate	1,150.	1,100.

Cancellations

Blue town	+25.
Red town	+150.
Green town	+600.
Violet town	—

Straight line town	+500.
April, 1863, year date	+25.
Black gridiron	+25.
Blue gridiron	+50.
Red gridiron	+200.
Railroad	+400.
Circle of wedges	+1,250.
Pen	350.

Frame Line "10 CENTS"
(Illustration actual size) — A6a

Printed by Archer & Daly of Richmond, Va.
One copper plate of 100 subjects, all but one of which were recut. Earliest known use April 19, 1863.
Stamp design same as Die A (Pos. 11).
Values are for copies showing parts of lines on at least 3 of 4 sides. Stamps showing 4 complete lines sell for 300%-400% of the values given.

1863, Apr.	Soft Porous Paper		Engraved
10	A6a 10c blue	3,750.	1,250.
	No gum	3,000.	
a.	10c **milky blue**	3,750.	1,250.
	No gum	3,000.	
b.	10c **greenish blue**	4,250.	1,350.
	No gum	3,400.	
c.	10c **dark blue**	4,250.	1,350.
	No gum	3,400.	
	On cover		2,500.
	On wallpaper cover		4,500.
	On patriotic cover		6,000.
	On prisoner's cover		7,000.
	On prisoner's cover with U.S. #65		—
	Pair	8,500.	5,500.
	Pair on cover		6,500.
	Block of 4	20,000.	
	Strip of 4	18,500.	
	Strip of 6	—	15,000.
	Strip of 7	32,500.	
	Double transfer (Pos. 74)	4,250.	1,600.

Cancellations

Blue town	+100.
Red town	+500.
Straight line town	+750.
April, 1863, year date	—
Blue gridiron	+100.
Pen	750.

No Frame Line "10 CENTS" — A7
(Die A)

There are many slight differences between A7 (Die A) and A8 (Die B), the most noticeable being the additional line outside the ornaments at the four corners of A8 (Die B).
Stamps were first printed by Archer & Daly, of Richmond, Va. In 1864 the plates were transferred to the firm of Keatinge & Ball in Columbia, S. C., who made further printings from them. Two plates, each with two panes of 100, numbered 1 and 2. First state shows numbers only, later states show various styles of Archer & Daly imprints, and latest show Keatinge & Ball imprints. Archer & Daly stamps show uniformly clear impressions and a good quality of gum evenly distributed (Earliest known cancellation, April 21, 1863); Keatinge & Ball stamps generally show filled in impressions in a deep blue, and the gum is brown and unevenly distributed. (Earliest known cancellation, Oct. 4, 1864.) The so-called laid paper is probably due to thick streaky gum. (These notes also apply to No. 12.)

1863-64	Thick or Thin Paper		Engraved
11	A7 10c **blue**	9.00	15.00
	No gum	7.50	
a.	10c **milky blue**	22.50	37.50
	No gum	19.00	
b.	10c **dark blue**	18.50	25.00
	No gum	15.00	
c.	10c **greenish blue**	17.50	17.50
	No gum	12.50	
d.	10c **green**	70.00	75.00
	No gum	60.00	
	deep blue, Keatinge & Ball ('64)	9.00	30.00
	On cover		55.00
	Single on cover (overpaid drop letter)		150.00
	On wallpaper cover		400.00
	On patriotic cover		650.00
	On prisoner's cover		450.00
	On prisoner's cover with U.S. #65		1,750.00
	On cover, dp. blue (K. & B.) ('64)		125.00
	On wallpaper cover (K. & B.)		875.00

On prisoner's cover (K. & B.) with U.S. #65 ('64)		—	
Pair		22.50	40.00
Pair on cover			175.00
Block of 4		47.50	290.00
Strip of 4 on cover (Trans-Mississippi rate)			—
Margin block of 12, Archer & Daly impt. & P#		225.00	
Margin block of 12, Keatinge & Ball impt. & P#		200.00	
Horiz. pair, vert. gutter between		110.00	
e.	Officially perforated 12½	300.00	275.00
	On cover		*500.00*
	On wallpaper cover		—
	Pair	650.00	600.00
	Pair on cover		*2,750.*
	Block of 4	1,350.	*2,250.*

VARIETIES

Double transfer	75.00	100.00
Rouletted unofficially		300.00
On cover		650.00

Cancellations

Blue town	+5.00
Red town	+35.00
Orange town	+110.00
Brown town	+60.00
Green town	+150.00
Violet town	+100.00
Texas town	+60.00
Arkansas town	+125.00
Florida town	+200.00
Straight line town	+300.00
Army of Tenn.	+300.00
April, 1863 year date	+75.00
"FREE"	+250.00
Blue gridiron	+5.00
Black concentric circles	+10.00
Star	+100.00
Crossroads	+150.00
"Paid"	+100.00
Numeral	+100.00
Railroad	+175.00
Steamboat	+1,500.

Jefferson Davis — A8 (Die B)

Plates bore Nos. 3 and 4, otherwise notes on No. 11 apply.
Earliest known use: Archer & Daly - May 1, 1863; Keatinge & Ball - Sept. 4, 1864.

1863-64	Thick or Thin Paper		Engraved
12	A8 10c **blue**	11.00	17.50
	No gum	9.00	
a.	10c **milky blue**	25.00	35.00
	No gum	20.00	
b.	10c **light blue**	11.00	17.50
	No gum	9.00	
c.	10c **greenish blue**	20.00	45.00
	No gum	16.50	
d.	10c **dark blue**	11.00	20.00
	No gum	9.00	
e.	10c **green**	90.00	110.00
	No gum	75.00	
	deep blue, Keatinge & Ball ('64)	11.00	40.00
	On cover		75.00
	Single on cover (overpaid drop letter)		150.00
	On wallpaper cover		375.00
	On patriotic cover		700.00
	On prisoner's cover		450.00
	On prisoner's cover with U.S. #65		1,750.00
	On cover, dp. blue (K. & B.) ('64)		130.00
	Pair	27.50	52.50
	Pair on cover		200.00
	Block of 4	60.00	290.00
	Strip of 4 on cover (Trans-Mississippi rate)		—
	Margin block of 12, Archer & Daly impt. & P#	275.00	
	Margin block of 12, Keatinge & Ball impt. & P#	225.00	
	Horiz. pair, vert. gutter between	125.00	
f.	Officially perforated 12½	325.00	300.00
	On cover		*500.00*
	Pair	700.00	600.00
	Pair on cover		—
	Block of 4	1,500.	

VARIETIES

Double transfer	95.00	110.00
Rouletted unofficially		375.00
On cover		700.00

Cancellations

Blue town	+5.00
Red town	+35.00
Brown town	+90.00
Green town	+120.00
Violet town	+85.00
Texas town	+125.00

Arkansas town	+150.00
Florida town	+200.00
Straight line town	+350.00
Army of Tenn.	+350.00
May, 1863, year date	+60.00
Blue gridiron	+5.00
Black concentric circles	+10.00
Railroad	+175.00

George
Washington — A9

1863 (June?)   **Engraved by Archer & Daly**

One plate which consisted of two panes of 100 each. First printings were from plates with imprint in Old English type under each pane, which was later removed. Printed on paper of varying thickness and in many shades of green. This stamp was also used as currency. Earliest known cancellation, June 1, 1863. Forged cancellations exist.

13	A9	20c **green**	37.50	400.
		No gum	27.50	
a.		20c **yellow green**	70.00	450.
		No gum	47.50	
b.		20c **dark green**	65.00	500.
		No gum	45.00	
		On cover		1,250.
		On wallpaper cover		1,750.
		On prisoner's cover		4,000.
		On prisoner's cover with U.S. #65		5,000.
		Pair	80.00	900.
		Horizontal pair with gutter between	250.00	
		Pair on cover (non-Trans-Mississippi rate)		4,500.
		Pair on cover (Trans-Mississippi rate)		—
		Block of 4	190.00	3,500.
		Strip of 4 with imprint	400.00	
c.		Diagonal half used as 10c on cover		2,000.
		Diagonal half on prisoner's cover		—
d.		Horizontal half used as 10c on cover		3,500.

VARIETIES

Double transfer, 20 doubled (Pos. 24L and 35R)	175.	—
"20" on forehead	3,000.	—
Rouletted privately		1,100.
On cover		3,750.

Cancellations

Blue town	+50.
Red town	+200.
Violet town	+50.
Texas town	+100.
Arkansas town	+400.
Tennessee town	+1,000.
Railroad	—

John C. Calhoun — A10

Typographed by De La Rue & Co., London, England

1862

14	A10	1c **orange**	90.00	
		No gum	70.00	
		Pair	200.00	
		Block of 4	375.00	
a.		1c **deep orange**	115.00	
		No gum	90.00	

This stamp was never put in use.

Upon orders from the Confederate Government, De La Rue & Co. of London, England, prepared Two Cents and Ten Cents typographed plates by altering the One Cent (No. 14) and the Five Cents (Nos. 6-7) designs previously made by them. Stamps were never officially printed from these plates although privately made prints exist in various colors.

Explanatory Notes
The following notes by Lawrence L. Shenfield explain the various routes, rates and usages of the general issue Confederate stamps.

"Across the Lines"
Letters Carried by Private Express Companies

Adams Express Co. and American Letter Express Company Handstamps Used on "Across the Lines" Letters

PRIVATE LETTER MAIL.

Direct each letter to your correspondent as usual, envelope that with 15 cents in money and direct to

B. WHITESIDES,

Franklin, Ky.

Letters exceeding half an ounce or going over 500 miles must have additional amount enclosed. For single Newspapers enclose 10 cents.

B. Whitesides Label

About two months after the outbreak of the Civil War, in June, 1861, postal service between North and South and vice versa was carried on largely by Adams Express Company, and the American Letter Express Company. Northern terminus of the traffic was Louisville, Ky.; Southern terminus was Nashville, Tenn. Letters for transmission were delivered to any office of the express company, together with a fee, usually 20c or 25c per ½ ounce to cover carriage. The express company messengers carried letters across the lines and delivered them to their office on the other side, where they were deposited in the Government mail for transmission to addressees, postage paid out of the fee charged. Letters from North to South, always enclosed in 3c U. S. envelopes, usually bear the handstamp of the Louisville office of the express company, and in addition the postmark and "Paid 5" of Nashville, Tenn., indicating its acceptance for delivery at the Nashville Post Office. Letters from South to North sometimes bear the origin postmark of a Southern post office, but more often merely the handstamp of the Louisville express company office applied as the letters cleared through Louisville. The B. Whitesides South to North cover bears a "Private Letter Mail" label. In addition, these covers bear the 3c 1857 U.S. adhesive stamp, cancelled with the postmark and grid of Louisville, Ky., where they went into the Government mail for delivery. Some across-the-lines letters show the handstamp of various express company offices, according to the particular routing the letters followed. On August 26, 1861, the traffic ceased by order of the U. S. Post Office Dept. (Values are for full covers bearing the usual Louisville, Ky., or Nashville, Tenn., handstamps of the express company. Unusual express office markings are rarer and worth more.)

North to South 3c U.S. Envelope, Adams Exp. Co. Louisville, Ky., handstamp	1,500.
North to South 3c U.S. Envelope, American Letter Express Co., Ky., handstamp	2,100.
South to North 3c 1857, Adams Exp. Co., Louisville, Ky., handstamp	1,750.
South to North 3c 1857, American Letter Exp. 250, Nashville, Tenn., handstamp	2,500.
South to North 3c 1861, Adams Exp. Co., Louisville, Ky., handstamp	3,250.
South to North 3c 1857, B. Whitesides, Franklin, Ky., label	16,500.

Blockade-Run Letters from Europe to the Confederate States

Charleston "STEAM-SHIP" in Oval Handstamp

As the Federal Fleet gradually extended its blockade of the Confederate States coastal regions, the South was forced to resort to blockade runners to carry letters to and from outside ports. These letters were all private-ship letters and never bore a foreign stamp if from Europe, nor a Confederate stamp if to Europe. The usual route from Europe was via a West Indies port, Nassau, Bahamas; Hamilton, Bermuda, or Havana, into the Southern ports of Wilmington, N.C. and Charleston, S.C. More rarely such letters came in to Savannah, Mobile and New Orleans. Letters from Europe are the only ones which are surely identified by their markings. They bore either the postmark of Wilmington, N.C., straightline "SHIP" and "12", "22", "32", etc., in manuscript; or the postmark of Charleston, S. C., "STEAMSHIP" in oval, and "12", "22", "32", etc., in manuscript. Very rarely Charleston used a straightline "SHIP" instead of "STEAMSHIP" in oval. All such letters were postage due; the single letter rate of 12c being made up of 2c for the private ship captain plus 10c for the regular single letter Confederate States rate. Over-weight letters were 22c (due), 32c, 42c, etc. A few examples are known on which Confederate General Issue stamps were used, usually as payment for forwarding postage. Covers with such stamps, or with the higher rate markings, 22c, 32c, etc., are worth more.

Values are for full covers in fine condition.

Charleston, S.C. "6" handstamp	3,250.
Charleston, S.C., postmark, "STEAMSHIP," and "12" in ms.	2,750.
Charleston, S.C., postmark, "SHIP," and "12" in ms.	1,750.
Wilmington, N.C., postmark, "SHIP," and "12" in ms.	2,500.
Savannah, Ga., postmark "SHIP," and "7" in ms. (*)	4,000.
New Orleans, La. postmark "SHIP," and "10" in ms.	5,000.

(* 7c rate: 5c postage before July 1, 1862, plus 2c for ship captain.)

Express Company Mail in the Confederacy

Southern Express Company Handstamps

Shortly after the outbreak of war in 1861, the Adams Express Company divisions operating in the South were forced to suspend operations and turned their Southern lines over to a new company organized under the title Southern Express Company. This express did the bulk of the express business in the Confederacy despite the continued opposition of the Post Office Dept. of the C.S.A. and the ravages of the contending armies upon railroads. Other companies operating in the Confederacy were: South Western Express Co. (New Orleans), Pioneer Express Company, White's Southern Express (only one example known) and some local expresses of limited operation. The first three used handstamps of various designs usually bearing the city name of the office. Postal regulation necessitated the payment of regular Confederate postal rates on letters carried by express companies, express charges being paid in addition. Important letters, particularly money letters, were entrusted to these express companies as well as goods and wares of all kinds. The express rates charged for letters are not known; probably they varied depending upon the difficulty and risk of transmittal. Covers bearing stamps and express company handstamps are very rare.

Prisoner-of-War and Flag-of-Truce Letters

Prison Censor Handstamps

By agreement between the United States and the Confederate States, military prisoners and imprisoned civilians of both sides were permitted to send censored letters to their respective countries. Such letters, if from North to South, usually bore a U.S. 3c 1861 adhesive, postmarked at a city near the prison, to pay the postage to the exchange ground near Old Point Comfort, Va.; and a 10c Confederate stamp, canceled at Richmond, Va. (or "due" handstamp) to pay the Confederate postage to destination. If from South to North, letters usually bore a 10c Confederate stamp canceled at a Southern city (or "paid" handstamp) and a U. S. 3c 1861 adhesive (or "due 3" marking) and the postmark of Old Point Comfort, Va. In addition, prison censor markings, handstamped or manuscript, the name and rank of the soldier, and "Flag of Truce, via Fortress Monroe" in manuscript usually appear on these covers. Federal prison censor handstamps of various designs are known from these prisons:

Camp Chase, Columbus, O.
David's Island, Pelham, N.Y.
Fort Delaware, Delaware City, Del.
Camp Douglas, Chicago, Ill.
Elmira Prison, Elmira, N.Y.
Johnson's Island, Sandusky, O.
Fort McHenry, Baltimore, Md.
Camp Morton, Indianapolis, Ind.
Fort Oglethorpe, Macon, Ga.
Old Capitol Prison, Washington, D.C.
Point Lookout Prison, Point Lookout, Md.
Fort Pulaski, Savannah, Ga.
Rock Island Prison, Rock Island, Ill.
Ship Island, New Orleans, La.
West's Hospital, Baltimore, Md.
U.S. General Hospital, Gettysburg, Pa.

Several other Federal prisons used manuscript censor markings.

Southern prison censor markings are always in manuscript, and do not identify the prison. The principal Southern prisons were at Richmond and Danville, Va.; Andersonville and Savannah, Ga.; Charleston, Columbia and Florence S.C.; Salisbury, N.C.; Hempstead and Tyler, Tex.

Civilians residing in both the North and the South were also, under exceptional circumstances, permitted to send Flag of Truce letters across the lines. Such covers bore no censor marking nor prison markings, but were always endorsed "via Flag of Truce".

Values will be found under various individual stamps for "on prisoner's cover" and are for the larger prisons. Prisoners' letters from the smaller prisons are much rarer. Only a very small percentage of prisoners' covers bore both a U.S. stamp and a Confederate stamp.

The "SOUTHERN LETTER UNPAID" Marking
On Northbound Letters of Confederate Origin

DUE 3

SOUTH.N LETTER UNPAID.

By mid-May, 1861, correspondence between the North and South was difficult. In the South, postmasters were resigning and closing their accounts with Washington as the Confederacy prepared to organize its own postal system by June 1. From that date on, town marks and "paid" handstamps (and later postmasters' provisional stamps) were used in all post offices of the seceded states. The three most important Southern cities for clearing mail to the North were Memphis, Nashville and Richmond. The Richmond-Washington route was closed in April; Memphis was closed by June 1st, and mail attempting to cross the lines at these points generally ended up at the dead letter office. However, at Louisville, Kentucky, mail from the South via Nashville continued to arrive in June, July and August. On June 24, 1861, the Post Office Department advised the Louisville post office, "You will forward letters from the South for the Loyal States as unpaid, after removing postage stamps, but foreign letters in which prepayment is compulsory must come to the Dead Letter Office." However, Louisville avoided the task of "removing postage stamps," and instead prepared the "Southern Letter Unpaid" handstamp and special "due 3" markers for use. These markings were applied in the greenish-blue color of the Louisville office to letters of Southern origin that had accumulated, in addition to the usual town mark and grid of Louisville. The letters were delivered in the North as unpaid. Probably Louisville continued to forward such unpaid mail until about July 15. The marking is very rare. Other Southern mail was forwarded from Louisville as late as Aug. 27.

For listings see under U.S. 1857-61 issue, Nos. 26, 35-38. Values shown there are generally for this marking on off-cover stamps. Complete covers bearing stamps showing the full markings are valued from $7,500 upward depending upon the stamps, other postal markings and unusual usages, and condition. Fraudulent covers exist.

Trans-Mississippi Express Mail-the 40c Rate

From the fall of New Orleans on April 24, 1862, the entire reach of the Mississippi River was threatened by the Federal fleets. Late in 1862 the Confederacy experienced difficulty in maintaining regular mail routes trans-Mississippi to the Western states. Private express companies began to carry some mail, but by early 1863 when the Meridian-Jackson-Vicksburg-Shreveport route was seriously menaced, the Post Office Department of the Confederate States was forced to inaugurate an express mail service by contracting with a private company the name of which remains undisclosed. The eastern termini were at Meridian and Brandon, Miss.; the western at Shreveport and Alexandria, La. Letters, usually endorsed "via Meridian (or Brandon)" if going West; "via Shreveport (or Alexandria)" if going East were deposited in any Confederate post office. The rate was 40c per ½ ounce or less. Such Trans-Mississippi Express Mail upon arrival at a terminus was carried by couriers in a devious route across the Mississippi and returned to the regular mails at the nearest terminus on the other side of the river. The precise date of the beginning of the Trans-Mississippi service is not known. The earliest date of use so far seen is November 2, 1863 and the latest use February 9, 1865. These covers can be identified by the written endorsement of the route, but particularly by the rate since many bore no route endorsements.

Strips of four of 10c engraved stamps, pairs of the 20c stamp and various combinations of 10c stamps and the 5c London or Local prints are known; also handstamped Paid 40c marking. No identifying handstamps were used, merely the postmark of the office which received the letter originally. Values for Trans-Mississippi Express covers will be found under various stamps of the General Issues.

A 50c Preferred Mail Express rate, announced in April, 1863, preceded the Trans-Mississippi Express Mail 40c rate. One cover showing this rate is known.

Packet and Steamboat Covers and Markings

Letters carried on Confederate packets operating on coastal routes or up and down the inland waterways were usually handstamped with the name of the packet or marked STEAM or STEAMBOAT. Either United States stamps of the 1857 issue or stamped envelopes of the 1853 or 1860 issues have been found so used, as well as Confederate Postmasters' Provisional and General Issue stamps. Some specially designed pictorial or imprinted packet boat covers also exist. All are scarce and command values from $750 upward for handstamped United States envelopes and from $1,250 up for covers bearing Confederate stamps.

TABLE OF SECESSION

	Ordinance of Secession	Admitted to Confederacy	Period for Use of U.S. Stamps As Independent State	Total to 5/31/1861*
SC	12/20/1860	2/4/1861	46 days	163 days
MS	1/9/1861	2/4/1861	26 days	143 days
FL	1/10/1861	2/4/1861	25 days	142 days
AL	1/11/1861	2/4/1861	24 days	141 days
GA	1/19/1861	2/4/1861	16 days	133 days
LA	1/26/1861	2/4/1861	9 days	126 days
TX	2/1/1861	3/6/1861	33 days	120 days
VA	4/17/1861	5/7/1861	20 days	45 days
AR	5/6/1861	5/18/1861	12 days	26 days
TN	5/6/1861	7/2/1861	57 days	26 days
NC	5/20/1861	5/27/1861	7 days	12 days

* The use of United States stamps in the seceded States was prohibited after May 31, 1861.

TX- Ordinance of Secession adopted Feb. 1. Popular vote to secede Feb. 23, effective Mar. 2, 1861.

VA- Ordinance of Secession adopted. Admitted to Confederacy May 7. Scheduled election of May 23 ratified the Ordinance of Secession.

TN- Ordinance passed to "submit to vote of the people a Declaration of Independence, and for other purposes." Adopted May 6. Election took place June 8. General Assembly ratified election June 24.

The Confederate postal laws did not provide the franking privilege for any mail except official correspondence of the Post Office Department. Such letters could be sent free only when enclosed in officially imprinted envelopes individually signed by the official using them. These envelopes were prepared and issued for Post Office Department use.

The imprints were on United States envelopes of 1853-61 issue, and also on commercial envelopes of various sizes and colors. When officially signed and mailed, they were postmarked, usually at Richmond, Va., with printed or handstamped "FREE". Envelopes are occasionally found unused and unsigned, and more rarely, signed but unused. When such official envelopes were used on other than official Post Office Department business, Confederate stamps were used.

Semi-official envelopes also exist bearing imprints of other government departments, offices, armies, states, etc. Regular postage was required to carry such envelopes through the mails.

CONFEDERATE STATES OF AMERICA,
POST OFFICE DEPARTMENT,
OFFICIAL BUSINESS.

John H. Reagan
POSTMASTER GENERAL

Confederate States of America,
POST OFFICE DEPARTMENT,
OFFICIAL BUSINESS
John B. A. Dimitry
Act. CHIEF CLERK P. O. DEPARTMENT

Typical Imprints of Official Envelopes of the Post Office Department. (Many variations of type, style and wording exist.)

Office	Signature
Postmaster General	John H. Reagan
Chief of the Contract Bureau	H. St. Geo. Offutt
Chief of the Appointment Bureau	B. N. Clements
Chief of the Finance Bureau	Jno. L. Harrell
Chief of the Finance Bureau	J. L. Lancaster
Chief of the Finance Bureau	A. Dimitry
Dead Letter Office	A. Dimitry
Dead Letter Office	Jno. L. Harrell
Chief Clerk, P. O. Department	B. Fuller
Chief Clerk	W. D. Miller
Auditor's Office	W. W. Lester
Auditor's Office	B. Baker
Auditor's Office	J. W. Robertson
First Auditor's Office, Treasury Department	J. W. Robertson
First Auditor's Office, Treasury Department	B. Baker
Third Auditor's Office	A. Moise
Third Auditor's Office	I. W. M. Harris
Agency, Post Office Dept. Trans—Miss.	Jas. H. Starr

PROOFS

1861

(1)- Die on Glazed Card
(1a)- Die on Wove Paper
(5)- Plate on Wove Paper
(6)- Plate on Thin Card
(7)- Plate on Thick Ribbed Paper

1P	(5)	5c **green**, plate on wove paper	1,500.
2P	(5)	10c **blue**, plate on wove paper	1,500.
2TC	(5)	10c **black**, plate on wove paper (stone Y)	3,000.

1862

6P	(1)	5c **light blue**, die on glazed card	600.
6P, 14P	(1)	5c **blue & 1c orange**, composite die proof, 20x90mm card	6,000.
6P	(5)	5c **light blue**, plate on wove paper	150.
		Pair with gutter between	375.
6TC	(1a)	5c **dark blue**, die on woven paper	600.
6TC	(5)	5c **gray blue**, plate on wove paper	600.

6TC	(1)	5c **black**, die on glazed card	900.
6TC	(5)	5c **black**, plate on wove paper	1,000.
6TC	(1)	5c **pink**, die on glazed card	900.
7TC	(5)	5c **carmine**, plate on wove paper	850.
7TC	(6)	5c **carmine**, plate on thin card	750.

1863

8TC	(1a)	2c **black**, die on wove paper	1,750.
9TC	(1a)	10c **black**, die on wove paper	1,500.
11TC	(1a)	10c **black**, die on wove paper	1,100.
12P	(7)	10c **deep blue**, plate on thick ribbed paper	750.
13P	(1a)	20c **green**, die on wove paper	4,000.
13TC	(1a)	20c **red brown**, die on wove paper	4,000.

1862

14P	(1)	1c **orange**, die on glazed card	2,000.
14TC	(1)	1c **black**, die on glazed card	2,500.
14TC	(5)	1c **light yellow brown**, plate on wove paper	800.

Essay Die Proofs

In working up the final dies, proofs of incomplete designs in various stages were made. Usually dated in typeset lines, they are very rare. Others, of the 10c (No. 12) and the 20c (No. 13) were proofs made as essays from the dies. They are deeply engraved and printed in deep shades of the issued colors, but show only small differences from the stamps as finally issued. All are very rare.

Specimen Overprints

The De La Rue typographed 5c and 1c are known with "SPECIMEN" overprinted diagonally, also horizontally for 1c.

Counterfeits

In 1935 a set of 12 lithographed imitations, later known as the "Springfield facsimiles," appeared in plate form. They are in approximately normal colors on yellowish soft wove paper of modern manufacture.

CANAL ZONE

The Canal Zone, a strip of territory with an area of about 552 square miles following generally the line of the Canal, was under the jurisdiction of the United States, 1904-1979, and under the joint jurisdiction of the United States and Panama, 1979-1999, when the canal, in its entirety, reverted to Panama.

The Canal organization underwent two distinct and fundamental changes. The construction of the Canal and the general administration of civil affairs were performed by the Isthmian Canal Commission under the provisions of the Spooner Act. This was supplanted in April, 1914, by the Panama Canal Act which established the organization known as The Panama Canal. This was an independent Government Agency which included both the operation and maintenance of the waterway and civil government in the Canal Zone. Most of the quasi-business enterprises relating to the Canal operation were conducted by the Panama Railroad, an adjunct of The Panama Canal.

A basic change in the mode of operations took effect July 1, 1951, under provisions of Public Law 841 of the 81st Congress. This in effect transferred the canal operations to the Panama Railroad Co., which had been made a federal government corporation in 1948, and changed its name to the Panama Canal Co. Simultaneously the civil government functions of The Panama Canal, including the postal service, were renamed the Canal Zone Government. The organization therefore consisted of two units-the Panama Canal Co. and Canal Zone Government-headed by an individual who was president of the company and governor of the Canal Zone. His appointment as governor was made by the President of the United States, subject to confirmation by the Senate, and he was ex-officio president of the company.

The Canal Zone Government functioned as an independent government agency, and was under direct supervision of the President of the United States who delegated this authority to the Secretary of the Army.

The Panama Canal is 50 miles long from deep water in the Atlantic to deep water in the Pacific. Its runs from northwest to southeast with the Atlantic entrance being 33.5 miles north and 27 miles west of the Pacific entrance. The airline distance between the two entrances is 43 miles. It requires about eight hours for an average ship to transit the Canal. Transportation between the Atlantic and Pacific sides of the Isthmus is available by railway or highway.

The Canal Zone Postal Service began operating June 24, 1904, when nine post offices were opened in connection with the construction of the Panama Canal. It ceased Sept. 30, 1979, and the Panama Postal Service took over.

Italicized numbers in parentheses indicate quantity issued.

100 CENTAVOS = 1 PESO
100 CENTESIMOS = 1 BALBOA
100 CENTS = 1 DOLLAR

Catalogue values for unused stamps are for Never Hinged items beginning with No. 118 in the regular postage section and No. C6 in the airpost section.

Map of Panama — A1
Violet to Violet Blue Handstamp on Panama Nos. 72, 72a-72c, 78, 79.

On the 2c "PANAMA" is normally 13mm long. On the 5c and 10c it measures about 15mm.

On the 2c, "PANAMA" reads up on the upper half of the sheet and down on the lower half. On the 5c and 10c, "PANAMA" reads up at left and down at right on each stamp.

On the 2c only, varieties exist with inverted "V" for "A," accent on "A," inverted "N," etc., in "PANAMA."

1904, June 24		Engr.	Unwmk.	Perf. 12	
1	A1	2c **rose**, both "PANAMA" reading up or down *(2600)*	550.	425.
		Single on post card		1,650.
		Strip of 3 on cover		1,500.
		Block of 4	2,500.	2,100.
		"PANAMA" 15mm long *(260)*	600.	600.
		Left "PANAMA" 2¼mm below bar *(100)*	625.	575.
		Colon between right "PANAMA" and bar *(100)*	600.	550.
a.		"CANAL ZONE" inverted *(200)*	625.	600.
		On cover		800.
b.		"CANAL ZONE" double		15,000.
c.		Pair, one without "CANAL ZONE" overprint	6,000.	5,000.

Cancellations consist of town and/or bars in magenta or black, or a mixture of both colors.

Nos. 1-3 were withdrawn July 17, 1904.
Forgeries of the "Canal Zone" overprint and cancellations are numerous.

United States Nos. 300, 319, 304, 306 and 307 Overprinted in Black				CANAL ZONE	PANAMA
		"P NAMA"		600.	600.
a.		"CANAL ZONE" inverted *(100)*		850.	850.
b.		"CANAL ZONE" double		2,000.	2,000.
c.		"CANAL ZONE" double, both inverted		15,000.	
d.		"PANAMA" reading down and up *(52)*		700.	650.
e.		As "d," "CANAL ZONE" invtd.		6,500.	6,500.
f.		Vert. pair, "PANAMA" reading up on top 2c, down on other		2,000.	2,000.
2	A1	5c **blue** *(7800)*		225.	175.
		On cover			240.
		First day cover			7,500.
		Block of 4		1,125.	950.
		Left "PANAMA" 2¼mm below bar *(156)*		500.	500.
		Colon between right "PANAMA" and bar *(156)*		500.	500.
a.		"CANAL ZONE" inverted		600.	600.
		On cover			800.
b.		"CANAL ZONE" double		2,250.	1,500.
c.		Pair, one without "CANAL ZONE" overprint		5,000.	5,000.
d.		"CANAL ZONE" overprint diagonal, reading down to right		700.	700.
3	A1	10c **yellow** *(4946)*		375.	225.
		On cover			325.
		First day cover			5,000.
		Block of 4		1,550.	1,150.

1904, July 18 — Wmk. 191

4	A115	1c	blue green (43,738)	32.50	22.50
			green	32.50	22.50
			On cover		75.00
			Block of 4	150.00	140.00
			P# strip of 3, Impt.	135.00	
			P# block of 6, Impt.	875.00	
5	A129	2c	carmine (68,414)	30.00	25.00
			On cover		75.00
			Block of 4	130.00	125.00
			P# strip of 3, Impt.	125.00	
			P# block of 6, Impt.	950.00	
a.		2c	scarlet	35.00	30.00
6	A119	5c	blue (20,858)	100.00	65.00
			On cover		250.00
			Block of 4	475.00	325.00
			P# strip of 3, Impt.	425.00	
			P# block of 6, Impt.	1,400.	
7	A121	8c	violet black (7932)	175.00	85.00
			On cover		—
			Block of 4	800.00	450.00
			P# strip of 3, Impt.	725.00	
			P# block of 6, Impt.	3,000.	
8	A122	10c	pale red brown (7856)	150.00	90.00
			On cover		—
			Block of 4	675.00	475.00
			P# strip of 3, Impt.	650.00	
			P# block of 6, Impt.	2,750.	
			Nos. 4-8 (5)	487.50	287.50

Nos. 4-8 frequently show minor broken letters.
Cancellations consist of circular town and/or bars in black, blue or magenta.
Beware of fake overprints.

A2

A3

CANAL
ZONE
Regular Type

CANAL
ZONE
Antique Type

The Canal Zone overprint on stamps Nos. 9-15 and 18-20 was made with a plate which had six different stages, each with its peculiar faults and errors. Stage 1: Broken CA-L, broken L, A-L spaced, on Nos. 9, 10, 12-15. Stage 2: broken L, Z, N, E, on Nos. 9, 10, 12-14. Stage 3: same as 2 with additional antique ZONE, on Nos. 9, 11-14, 18. Stage 4: same as 3 with additional antique CANAL on Nos. 9, 12, 13. Stage 5: broken E and letters L, Z, N, and words CANAL and ZONE in antique type on Nos. 12-14, 19, 20. Stage 6: same as 5 except for additional antique Z on stamp which had antique L, on No. 12.
The Panama overprints can be distinguished by the different shades of the red overprint, the width of the bar, and the word PANAMA. No. 11 has two different Panama overprints; No. 12 has six; No. 13 five; No. 14 two; and Nos. 15, 18-20, one each. In the "8cts" surcharge of Nos. 14 and 15, there are three varieties of the figure "8." The bar is sometimes misplaced so that it appears on the bottom of the stamp instead of the top.

1904-06 — Unwmk.
Black Overprint on Stamps of Panama

9	A2	1c	green (319,800) Dec. 12, 1904	2.75	2.25
			On cover		12.50
			Block of 4	12.00	12.00
			Spaced "A L" in "CANAL" (700)	110.00	100.00
			"ON" of "ZONE" dropped	275.00	260.00
a.			"CANAL" in antique type (500)	100.00	100.00
b.			"ZONE" in antique type (1500)	70.00	70.00
c.			Inverted overprint	5,000.	2,250.
d.			Double overprint	2,000.	1,500.
10	A2	2c	rose (367,500) Dec. 12, 1904	4.50	2.50
			On cover		17.50
			Block of 4	21.00	15.00
			Spaced "A L" of "CANAL" (1700)	85.00	80.00
			"ON" of "ZONE" dropped	375.00	350.00
a.			Inverted overprint	225.00	275.00
b.			"L" of "CANAL" sideways	2,500.	2,500.

"PANAMA" (15mm long) reading up at left, down at right
Overprint "CANAL ZONE" in Black, "PANAMA" and Bar in Red

11	A3	2c	rose (150,000) Dec. 9, 1905	7.50	5.00
			On cover		50.00
			Block of 4	35.00	27.50
			Inverted "M" in "PANAMA" (3,000)	45.00	40.00
			"PANAMA" 16mm long (3000)	45.00	40.00
a.			"ZONE" in antique type (1500)	200.00	200.00
b.			"PANAMA" overprint inverted, bar at bottom (200)	350.00	350.00
12	A3	5c	blue (400,000) Dec. 12, 1904	8.00	3.75
			On cover		100.00
			Block of 4	35.00	25.00
			Spaced "A L" in "CANAL" (300)	90.00	80.00
			"PAMANA" reading up (2800)	75.00	70.00
			"PAMANA" reading down (400)	200.00	180.00

		"PANAMA" 16mm long (1300)	40.00	37.50
		Inverted "M" in "PANAMA" (1300)	40.00	37.50
		Right "PANAMA" 5mm below bar (600)	75.00	70.00
		"PANAM"	70.00	65.00
		"PANAMA" at right	950.00	900.00
		"PAN MA"	75.00	70.00
		"ANAMA"	80.00	75.00
a.		"CANAL" in antique type (2750)	75.00	65.00
b.		"ZONE" in antique type (2950)	75.00	65.00
c.		"CANAL ZONE" double (200)	600.00	600.00
d.		"PANAMA" double (120)	1,050.	850.00
e.		"PANAMA" inverted, bar at bottom		1,250.
13	A3	10c yellow (64,900) Dec. 12, 1904	22.50	12.50
		On cover		125.00
		Block of 4	110.00	62.50
		Spaced "A L" in "CANAL" (200)	200.00	180.00
		"PANAMA" 16mm long (400)	75.00	65.00
		"PANAMA" reading down (200)	200.00	180.00
		Invtd. "M" in "PANAMA" (400)	100.00	90.00
		Right "PANAMA" 5mm below bar (398)	150.00	140.00
		Left "PANAMA" touches bar (400)	175.00	160.00
a.		"CANAL" in antique type (200)	200.00	200.00
b.		"ZONE" in antique type (400)	175.00	160.00
c.		"PANAMA" ovpt. double (80)	650.00	650.00
d.		"PANAMA" overprint in red brown (5000)	27.50	27.50
		"PANAMA" ovpt. in orange red	32.50	32.50

With Added Surcharge in Red

a

8 cts

There are three varieties of "8" in the surcharge on #14-15.

14	A3	8c on 50c bister brown (27,900) Dec. 12, 1904	32.50	22.50
			On cover		175.00
			Block of 4	190.00	140.00
			Spaced "A L" in "CANAL" (194)	175.00	160.00
			Right "PANAMA" 5mm below bar (438)	175.00	160.00
a.			"ZONE" in antique type (25)	1,100.	1,100.
b.			"CANAL ZONE" inverted (200)	425.00	400.00
c.			"PANAMA" overprint in rose brown (6000)	40.00	40.00
d.			As "c," "CANAL" in antique type (10)	2,250.	
e.			As "c," "ZONE" in antique type (10)	2,250.	
f.			As "c," "8cts" double (30)	850.00	
g.			As "c," "8" omitted	4,250.	

Nos. 11-14 are overprinted or surcharged on Panama Nos. 77, 77e, 78, 78c, 78d, 78f, 78g, 78h, 79 79c, 79e, 79g and 81 respectively.

Panama No. 74a, 74b Overprinted "CANAL ZONE" in Regular Type in Black and Surcharged Type "a" in Red
Both "PANAMA" (13mm long) Reading Up

15	A3(a)	8c on 50c bister brown (435) Dec. 12, 1904	2,750.	4,500.
			On cover		10,000.
			Block of 4	11,500.	
			"PANAMA" 15mm long (50)	3,000.	4,750.
			"P NAMA"	3,250.	
			Spaced "A L" in "CANAL" (5)	5,000.	
a.			"PANAMA" reading down and up (10)	6,500.	—

On No. 15 with original gum the gum is almost always disturbed.

Map of Panama — A4

Panama Nos. 19 and 21 Surcharged in Black:

PANAMA	CANAL ZONE 1 ct.	PANAMA	a
PANAMA	CANAL ZONE 1 ct.	PANAMA	b
PANAMA	CANAL ZONE 1 ct.	PANAMA	c
PANAMA	CANAL ZONE 2 cts.	PANAMA	d

CANAL ZONE 2 cts.
PANAMA — PANAMA

CANAL ZONE 2 cts.
PANAMA — PANAMA

e   f

1906

There were three printings of each denomination, differing principally in the relative position of the various parts of the surcharges. Varieties occur with inverted "V" for the final "A" in "PANAMA," "CA" spaced, "ZO" spaced, "2c" spaced, accents in various positions, and with bars shifted so that two bars appear on top or bottom of the stamp (either with or without the corresponding bar on top or bottom) and sometimes with only one bar at top or bottom.

16	A4	1c on 20c **violet,** type a *(100,000)*			
		Mar.		2.00	1.60
		On cover			8.50
		Block of 4		9.00	7.50
a.		Type b *(100,000) May*		2.00	1.60
		On cover			8.50
		Block of 4		9.00	7.50
b.		Type c *(300,000) Sept.*		2.00	1.60
		On cover			8.50
		Block of 4		10.50	7.50
		Spaced C A		13.00	12.00
c.		As No. 16, double surcharge			2,000.
17	A4	2c on 1p **lake,** type d *(200,000)*		2.75	2.75
		Mar.			12.00
		On cover			12.00
		Block of 4		14.00	12.50
a.		Type e *(200,000) May*		2.75	2.75
		On cover			12.00
		Block of 4		14.00	12.50
b.		Type f *(50,000) Sept.*		20.00	20.00
		On cover			75.00
		Block of 4		90.00	90.00

Panama Nos. 74, 74a and 74b Overprinted "CANAL ZONE" in Regular Type in Black and Surcharged in Red

8 cts.   8 cts
b   c

1905-06
Both "PANAMA" Reading Up

18	A3(b)	8c on 50c **bister brown** *(17,500)*		
		Nov. 1905	55.00	50.00
		On cover		225.00
		Block of 4	250.00	230.00
		"PANAMA" 15mm long *(1750)*	90.00	80.00
		"P NAMA"	125.00	110.00
a.		"ZONE" in antique type *(175)*	200.00	180.00
b.		"PANAMA" reading down and up *(350)*	175.00	160.00
19	A3(c)	8c on 50c **bister brown** *(19,000)*		
		Apr. 23, 1906	55.00	45.00
		On cover		225.00
		Block of 4	250.00	200.00
		"PANAMA" 15mm long *(1900)*	85.00	70.00
		"P NAMA"	90.00	
a.		"CANAL" in antique type *(190)*	210.00	180.00
b.		"ZONE" in antique type *(190)*	210.00	180.00
c.		"8 cts" double	1,100.	1,100.
d.		"PANAMA" reading down and up *(380)*	110.00	90.00

On Nos. 18-19 with original gum, the gum is usually disturbed.

Panama No. 81 Overprinted "CANAL ZONE" in Regular Type in Black and Surcharged in Red Type "c" plus Period "PANAMA" reading up and down

20	A3(c)	8c on 50c **bister brown** *(19,600)*		
		Sept. 1906	45.00	40.00
		On cover		200.00
		Block of 4	190.00	175.00
		"PAMANA" reading up *(392)*	120.00	110.00
a.		"CANAL" antique type *(196)*	200.00	180.00
b.		"ZONE" in antique type *(196)*	200.00	180.00
c.		"8 cts" omitted *(50)*	750.00	750.00
d.		"8 cts" double	1,500.	

Nos. 14 and 18-20 exist without CANAL ZONE overprint but were not regularly issued. Forgeries of the overprint varieties of Nos. 9-15 and 18-20 are known.

Vasco Núñez de Balboa
A5

Justo Arosemena
A7

Fernández de Córdoba
A6

Manuel J. Hurtado
A8

José de Obaldía — A9

Engraved by Hamilton Bank Note Co.
Overprinted in black by Isthmian Canal Commission Press.

1906-07   Unwmk.   Perf. 12
Overprint Reading Up

21	A6	2c **red & black** *(50,000)* Oct. 29, 1906	25.00	25.00
		On cover		50.00
		Block of 4	125.00	160.00
a.		"CANAL" only	4,000.	

Overprint Reading Down

22	A5	1c **green & black** *(2,000,000)* Jan. 14, 1907	2.25	1.25
		dull green & black	2.25	1.25
		On cover		5.00
		Block of 4	10.00	8.00
		"ANA" for "CANAL" *(1000)*	70.00	70.00
		"CAN L" for "CANAL" *(1000)*	80.00	80.00
		"ONE" for "ZONE" *(3000)*	80.00	80.00
a.		Horiz. pair, imperf. btwn. *(50)*	1,250.	1,250.
b.		Vert. pair, imperf. btwn. *(20)*	1,750.	1,750.
c.		Vert. pair, imperf. horiz. *(20)*	2,250.	1,750.
d.		Inverted overprint reading up *(100)*	550.00	550.00
e.		Double overprint *(300)*	275.00	275.00
f.		Double overprint, one inverted	1,350.	1,350.
g.		Invtd. center, ovpt. reading up *(100)*	4,000.	2,750.
		Pair on cover		9,500.
23	A6	2c **red & black** *(2,370,000)* Nov. 25, 1906	3.25	1.40
		scarlet & black, 1907	3.25	1.40
		On cover		6.00
		Block of 4	14.00	9.00
		"CAN L" for "CANAL"	45.00	
a.		Horizontal pair, imperf. between *(20)*	2,000.	1,750.
b.		Vertical pair, one without overprint	1,750.	1,750.
c.		Double overprint *(100)*	500.00	500.00
d.		Double overprint, one diagonal	750.00	750.00
e.		Double overprint, one diagonal, in pair with normal	1,750.	
f.		2c carmine red & black, Sept. 9, 1907	5.00	2.75
g.		As "f," inverted center and overprint reading up		5,000.
		On cover		12,000.
h.		As "d," one "ZONE CANAL"	4,000.	
i.		"CANAL" double	3,250.	
24	A7	5c **ultramarine & black** *(1,390,000)* Dec. 1906	6.50	2.25
		light ultramarine & black	6.50	2.25
		blue & black, Sept. 16, 1907	6.50	2.25
		dark blue & black	6.50	2.25
		dull blue & black	6.50	2.25
		light blue & black	6.50	2.25
		On cover		40.00
		Block of 4	27.50	20.00
		"CAN L" for "CANAL"	60.00	
c.		Double overprint *(200)*	450.00	350.00
d.		"CANAL" only *(10)*	3,500.	
e.		"ZONE CANAL"	4,500.	
25	A8	8c **purple & black** *(170,000)* Dec. 1906	22.50	8.00
		On cover		100.00
		Block of 4	100.00	40.00
a.		Horizontal pair, imperf. between and at left margin *(34)*	2,000.	—
26	A9	10c **violet & black** *(250,000)* Dec. 1906	20.00	8.00
		On cover		100.00
		Block of 4	110.00	50.00
a.		Dbl. ovpt., one reading up *(10)*	3,750.	
b.		Overprint reading up	4,000.	
		Nos. 22-26 *(5)*	54.50	20.90

The early printings of this series were issued on soft, thick, porous-textured paper, while later printings of all except No. 25 appear on hard, thin, smooth-textured paper.
Normal spacing of the early printings is 7¼mm between the words; later printings, 6¾mm. Nos. 22 and 26 exist imperf. between stamp and sheet margin. Nos. 22-25 occur with "CA" of "CANAL" spaced ½mm further apart on position No. 50 of the setting.

Córdoba — A11

Hurtado
A13

Arosemena — A12

José de Obaldía
A14

Engraved by American Bank Note Co.

1909
Overprint Reading Down

27	A11	2c **vermilion & black** *(500,000)*		
		May 11, 1909	12.50	6.50
		On cover		15.00
		First day cover		750.00
		Block of 4	57.50	30.00
a.		Horizontal pair, one without overprint	2,600.	
b.		Vert. pair, one without ovpt.	2,750.	
28	A12	5c **deep blue & black** *(200,000)*		
		May 28, 1909	45.00	12.50
		On cover		60.00
		Block of 4	200.00	60.00
29	A13	8c **violet & black** *(50,000)* May 25, 1909	37.50	14.00
		On cover		90.00
		Block of 4	160.00	82.50
30	A14	10c **violet & black** *(100,000)* Jan. 19, 1909	40.00	15.00
		On cover		85.00
		Block of 4	200.00	85.00
a.		Horizontal pair, one with "ZONE" omitted	2,400.	
b.		Vertical pair, one without overprint	2,600.	

Nos. 27-30 occur with "CA" spaced (position 50).
Do not confuse No. 27 with Nos. 39d or 53a.
On No. 30a, the stamp with "ZONE" omitted is also missing most of "CANAL."

Vasco Núñez de Balboa — A15

Engraved, Printed and Overprinted by American Bank Note Co.
Black Overprint Reading Up

CANAL ZONE

Type I

Type I Overprint: "C" with serifs both top and bottom. "L," "Z" and "E" with slanting serifs.

Compare Type I overprint with Types II to V illustrated before Nos. 38, 46, 52 and 55. Illustrations of Types I to V are considerably enlarged and do not show actual spacing between lines of overprint.

1909-10

31	A15	1c **dark green & black** *(4,000,000)*		
		Nov. 8, 1909	4.00	1.60
		On cover		5.00
		Block of 4	17.50	8.50
a.		Inverted center and overprint reading down		15,000.
c.		Bklt. pane of 6, handmade, perf. margins	575.00	
32	A11	2c **vermilion & black** *(4,000,000)*		
		Nov. 8, 1909	4.50	1.60
		On cover		5.00
		Block of 4	20.00	8.50
a.		Vert. pair, imperf. horiz.	1,000.	1,000.
c.		Bklt. pane of 6, handmade, perf. margins	750.00	
d.		Double overprint		
33	A12	5c **deep blue & black** *(2,000,000)*		
		Nov. 8, 1909	15.00	4.00
		On cover		40.00
		Block of 4	77.50	20.00
a.		Double overprint *(200)*	375.00	375.00

34 A13 8c **violet & black** (200,000) Mar.
　　　18, 1910　　　　　　　11.00　5.25
　　　On cover　　　　　　　　　　75.00
　　　Block of 4　　　　　55.00　27.50
35 A14 10c **violet & black** (100,000) Nov.
　　　8, 1909　　　　　　　50.00　20.00
　　　On cover　　　　　　　　　　100.00
　　　Block of 4　　　　　210.00　95.00
　　　Nos. 31-35 (5)　　　84.50　32.45

Normal spacing between words of overprint on No. 31 is 10mm and on Nos. 32 to 35, 8½mm. Minor spacing variations are known.

A16

A17

1911, Jan. 14
36 A16 10c on 13c **gray** (476,700)　6.00　2.25
　　　On cover　　　　　　　　　　50.00
　　　Block of 4　　　　　30.00　16.00
a.　"10 cts" inverted　　　275.00　275.00
b.　"10 cts" omitted　　　　275.00

The "10 cts" surcharge was applied by the Isthmian Canal Commission Press after the overprinted stamps were received from the American Bank Note Co.

Many used stamps offered as No. 36b are merely No. 36 from which the surcharge has been removed with chemicals.

1914, Jan. 6
37 A17 10c **gray** (200,000)　　55.00　12.50
　　　On cover　　　　　　　　　　85.00
　　　Block of 4　　　　　230.00　65.00

Black Overprint Reading Up

Type II

Type II Overprint: "C" with serif at top only. "L" and "E" with vertical serifs. "O" tilts to left.

1912-16
38 A15 1c **green & black** (3,000,000) July
　　　1913　　　　　　　　11.00　3.00
　　　On cover　　　　　　　　　　5.50
　　　Block of 4　　　　　50.00　20.00
a.　Vertical pair, one without overprint　1,500.　1,500.
　　　On cover　　　　　　　　　　2,000.
b.　Booklet pane of 6, imperf. margins
　　　(120,000)　　　　　600.00
c.　Booklet pane of 6, handmade, perf.
　　　margins　　　　　　1,000.
39 A11 2c **vermilion & black** (7,500,000)
　　　Dec. 1912　　　　　　8.50　1.40
　　　orange vermilion & black, 1916　8.50　1.40
　　　On cover　　　　　　　　　　5.00
　　　Block of 4　　　　　42.50　8.00
a.　Horiz. pair, right stamp without overprint
　　　(20)　　　　　　　　1,250.
b.　Horiz. pair, left stamp without overprint
　　　(10)　　　　　　　　1,750.
c.　Booklet pane of 6, imperf. margins
　　　(194,868)　　　　　500.00
d.　Overprint reading down　175.00
e.　As "d," inverted center　700.00　750.00
f.　As "e," booklet pane of 6, handmade,
　　　perf. margins　　　　8,000.
g.　As "c," handmade, perf. margins　1,000.
h.　As No. 39, "CANAL" only　　　　1,100.
40 A12 5c **deep blue & black** (2,300,000)
　　　Dec. 1912　　　　　22.50　3.25
　　　On cover　　　　　　　　　　35.00
　　　Block of 4　　　　　105.00　15.00
a.　With Cordoba portrait of 2c　　　8,750.
41 A14 10c **violet & black** (200,000) Feb.
　　　1916　　　　　　　　47.50　8.50
　　　On cover　　　　　　　　　　80.00
　　　Block of 4　　　　　240.00　40.00

Normal spacing between words of overprint on the first printing of Nos. 38-40 is 8½mm and on the second printing 9¼mm. The spacing of the single printing of No. 41 and the imperf. margin booklet pane printings of Nos. 38 and 39 is 7¾mm. Minor spacing variations are known.

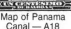

Map of Panama
Canal — A18

Balboa Taking
Possession of the
Pacific Ocean — A19

Gatun Locks — A20

Culebra Cut — A21

Engraved, Printed and Overprinted by American Bank Note Co.

1915, Mar. 1
Blue Overprint, Type II
42 A18 1c **dark green & black** (100,000)　8.50　6.50
　　　On cover　　　　　　　　　　17.50
　　　Block of 4　　　　　37.50　30.00
　　　First day cover　　　　　　　200.00
43 A19 2c **carmine & black** (100,000)　10.00　4.25
　　　vermilion & black　　10.00　4.25
　　　On cover　　　　　　　　　　25.00
　　　First day cover　　　　　　　150.00
　　　Block of 4　　　　　42.50　21.00
44 A20 5c **blue & black** (100,000)　11.00　5.75
　　　On cover　　　　　　　　　　55.00
　　　Block of 4　　　　　50.00　29.00
　　　First day cover　　　　　　　500.00
45 A21 10c **orange & black** (50,000)　22.50　11.00
　　　On cover　　　　　　　　　　60.00
　　　Block of 4　　　　　95.00　55.00
　　　First day cover　　　　　　　500.00

Normal spacing between words of overprint is 9¼mm on all four values except position No. 61 which is 10mm.

Black Overprint Reading Up

Type III

Type III Overprint: Similar to Type I but letters appear thinner, particularly the lower bar of "L," "Z" and "E." Impressions are often light, rough and irregular.

Engraved and Printed by American Bank Note Co.
Overprint applied by
Panama Canal Press, Mount Hope, C.Z.

1915-20
46 A15 1c **green & black**, Dec. 1915　160.00　95.00
　　　light green & black, 1920　225.00　160.00
　　　On cover　　　　　　　　　　160.00
　　　Block of 4　　　　　750.00　425.00
a.　Overprint reading down (200)　375.00
　　　Pair on cover　　　　　　　160.00
b.　Double overprint (180)　300.00
c.　"ZONE" double (2)　　　4,250.
d.　Double overprint, one reads "ZONE CA-
　　　NAL" (18)　　　　　1,750.
47 A11 2c **orange vermilion & black**,
　　　Aug. 1920　　　　　3,000.　100.00
　　　On cover　　　　　　　　　　375.00
　　　Block of 4　　　　　13,500.　600.00
48 A12 5c **deep blue & black**, Dec. 1915　550.00　175.00
　　　On cover　　　　　　　　　　750.00
　　　Block of 4　　　　　2,750.　850.00

Normal spacing between words of overprint on Nos. 46-48 is 9¼mm. This should not be confused with an abnormal 9¼mm spacing of the 2c and 5c values of type I, which are fairly common in singles, particularly used. Blocks of the abnormal spacing are rare.

S. S. "Panama" in Culebra Cut
A22　　　　　　A23

S. S. "Cristobal" in Gatun
Locks — A24

Engraved, Printed and Overprinted by American Bank Note Co.

1917, Jan. 23
Blue Overprint, Type II
49 A22 12c **purple & black** (314,914)　17.50　5.50
　　　On cover　　　　　　　　　　50.00
　　　First day cover　　　　　　　—
　　　Block of 4　　　　　87.50　25.00
50 A23 15c **bright blue & black**　55.00　25.00
　　　On cover　　　　　　　　　　135.00
　　　Block of 4　　　　　250.00　110.00
51 A24 24c **yellow brown & black**　45.00　15.00
　　　On cover　　　　　　　　　　325.00
　　　Block of 4　　　　　200.00　82.50

Normal spacing between words of overprint is 11¼mm.

Black Overprint Reading Up

Type IV

Type IV Overprint: "C" thick at bottom, "E" with center bar same length as top and bottom bars.

Engraved, Printed and Overprinted by American Bank Note Co.

1918-20
52 A15 1c **green & black** (2,000,000) Jan.
　　　1918　　　　　　　32.50　11.00
　　　On cover　　　　　　　　　　12.50
　　　Block of 4　　　　　150.00　47.50
a.　Overprint reading down　175.00
b.　Booklet pane of 6 (60,000)　650.00
c.　Booklet pane of 6, left vertical row of 3
　　　without overprint　　7,500.
d.　Booklet pane of 6, right vertical row of
　　　3, with double overprint　7,500.
e.　Horiz. bklt. pair, left stamp without over-
　　　print　　　　　　　3,000.
f.　Horiz. bklt. pair, right stamp with double
　　　overprint　　　　　3,000.
53 A11 2c **vermilion & black** (2,000,000)
　　　Nov. 1918　　　　　115.00　7.00
　　　On cover　　　　　　　　　　11.00
　　　Block of 4　　　　　500.00　35.00
a.　Overprint reading down　150.00　150.00
b.　Horiz. pair, right stamp without ovpt.　2,000.
c.　Booklet pane of 6 (34,000)　1,000.
d.　Booklet pane of 6, left vertical row of 3
　　　without overprint　　8,000.
e.　Horiz. bklt. pair, left stamp without over-
　　　print　　　　　　　3,000.
　　　On cover (unique)　　　　　4,500.
54 A12 5c **deep blue & black** (500,000)
　　　Apr. 1920　　　　　200.00　35.00
　　　On cover　　　　　　　　　　200.00
　　　Block of 4　　　　　925.00　160.00

Normal spacing between words of overprint on Nos. 52 and 53 is 9¼mm. On No. 54 and the booklet printings of Nos. 52 and 53, the normal spacing is 9mm. Minor spacing varieties are known.

Black Overprint Reading Up

Type V

Type V Overprint: Smaller block type 1¾mm high. "A" with flat top.

1920-21
55 A15 1c **light green & black**, Apr. 1921　22.50　3.50
　　　On cover　　　　　　　　　　8.00
　　　Block of 4　　　　　100.00　17.50
a.　Overprint reading down　250.00　225.00
b.　Horiz. pair, right stamp without ovpt.
　　　(10)　　　　　　　　1,750.
c.　Horiz. pair, left stamp without ovpt. (21)　1,000.
d.　"ZONE" double　　　　2,750.　—
e.　Booklet pane of 6　　1,750.
f.　As No. 55, "CANAL" double (10)　1,400.
56 A11 2c **orange vermilion & black**,
　　　Sept. 1920　　　　　8.50　2.25
　　　On cover　　　　　　　　　　7.00
　　　Block of 4　　　　　37.50　10.50
a.　Double overprint (100)　600.00
b.　Double overprint, one reading down
　　　(100)　　　　　　　650.00
c.　Horiz. pair, right stamp without overprint
　　　(11)　　　　　　　　1,500.
d.　Horiz. pair, left stamp without overprint
　　　(20)　　　　　　　　1,000.
e.　Vertical pair, one without overprint　1,500.
f.　"ZONE" double　　　　1,000.
g.　Booklet pane of 6　　850.00
h.　As No. 56, "CANAL" double　1,000.
57 A12 5c **deep blue & black**, Apr. 1921　325.00　55.00
　　　On cover　　　　　　　　　　225.00
　　　Block of 4　　　　　1,350.　250.00
a.　Horiz. pair, right stamp without overprint
　　　(10)　　　　　　　　2,500.
b.　Horiz. pair, left stamp without overprint
　　　(10)　　　　　　　　2,500.

Normal spacing between words of overprint on Nos. 55-57 is 9½mm. On booklet printings of Nos. 55 and 56 the normal spacing is 9¼mm.

Drydock at
Balboa — A25

U.S.S. "Nereus" in
Pedro Miguel
Locks — A26

1920, Sept.

Black Overprint Type V

58	A25	50c **orange & black**	275.00	160.00
		On cover		1,000.
		Block of 4	1,375.	800.00
59	A26	1b **dark violet & black** (23,014)	160.00	65.00
		On cover		1,000.
		Block of 4	750.00	325.00

José Vallarino
A27

"Land Gate"
A28

Bolívar's
Tribute — A29

Municipal
Building in
1821 and
1921 — A30

Statue of
Balboa
A31

Tomás
Herrera
A32

José de Fábrega — A33

Engraved, Printed and Overprinted by American
Bank Note Co.

**Type V overprinted in black, reading up, on
all values except the 5c which is overprinted
with larger type in red**

1921, Nov. 13

60	A27	1c **green**	3.75	1.40
		On cover		6.00
		Block of 4	17.50	6.75
a.		"CANAL" double	2,500.	
b.		Booklet pane of 6	900.00	
61	A28	2c **carmine**	3.00	1.50
		On cover		15.00
		Block of 4	13.50	6.50
a.		Overprint reading down	225.00	225.00
b.		Double overprint	900.00	
c.		Vertical pair, one without overprint	3,500.	
d.		"CANAL" double	1,900.	
f.		Booklet pane of 6	2,100.	
62	A29	5c **blue** (R)	11.00	4.50
		On cover		30.00
		Block of 4	50.00	25.00
a.		Overprint reading down (R)	60.00	
63	A30	10c **violet**	18.00	7.50
		On cover		60.00
		Block of 4	100.00	35.00
a.		Overprint, reading down	100.00	
64	A31	15c **light blue**	47.50	17.50
		On cover		175.00
		Block of 4	210.00	95.00
65	A32	24c **black brown**	70.00	22.50
		On cover		600.00
		Block of 4	375.00	125.00
66	A33	50c **black**	150.00	100.00
		On cover		600.00
		Block of 4	725.00	475.00
		Nos. 60-66 (7)	303.25	154.90

Experts question the status of the 5c with a small type V
overprint in red or black.

**Type III overprint in black, reading up, applied by
the Panama Canal Press, Mount Hope, C. Z.**
Engraved and printed by the American Bank Note
Co.

1924, Jan. 28

67	A27	1c **green**	500.	200.
		On cover		350.
		Block of 4	2,100.	900.
a.		"ZONE CANAL" reading down	850.	
b.		"ZONE" only, reading down	1,900.	

Arms of Panama — A34

1924, Feb.

68	A34	1c **dark green**	11.00	4.50
		On cover		12.00
		Block of 4	52.50	20.00
69	A34	2c **carmine**	8.25	2.75
		carmine rose	8.25	2.75
		On cover		15.00
		Block of 4	35.00	12.50

The following were prepared for use, but not issued.

	A34	5c **dark blue** (600)	350.
		Block of 4	1,750.
	A34	10c **dark violet** (600)	350.
		Block of 4	1,750.
	A34	12c **olive green** (600)	350.
		Block of 4	1,750.
	A34	15c **ultramarine** (600)	350.
		Block of 4	1,750.
	A34	24c **yellow brown** (600)	350.
		Block of 4	1,750.
	A34	50c **orange** (600)	350.
		Block of 4	1,750.
	A34	1b **black** (600)	350.
		Block of 4	1,750.

The 5c to 1b values were prepared for use but never issued
due to abrogation of the Taft Agreement which required the
Canal Zone to use overprinted Panama stamps. Six hundred of
each denomination were not destroyed, as they were forwarded
to the Director General of Posts of Panama for transmission to
the UPU which then required about 400 sets. Only a small
number of sets appear to have reached the public market.

All Panama stamps overprinted "CANAL ZONE" were withdrawn from sale June 30, 1924, and were no longer valid for
postage after Aug. 31, 1924.

United States Nos. 551-554, 557, 562,
564-566, 569, 570 and 571 Overprinted in
Red (No. 70) or Black (all others)

CANAL

ZONE

Printed and Overprinted by the U.S. Bureau of
Engraving and Printing.
Type A
Letters "A" with Flat Tops

1924-25		Unwmk.		Perf. 11
70	A154	½c **olive brown** (399,500) Apr. 15, 1925	1.25	.75
		On cover		4.00
		Block of 4	5.50	3.50
		P# block of 6	18.00	
71	A155	1c **deep green** (1,985,000) July 1, 1924	1.40	.90
		On cover		4.00
		Block of 4	6.00	4.00
		P# block of 6	30.00	
a.		Inverted overprint	500.00	500.00
b.		"ZONE" inverted	350.00	325.00
c.		"CANAL" only (20)	1,750.	
d.		"ZONE CANAL" (180)	450.00	
e.		Booklet pane of 6 (43,152)	100.00	
72	A156	1½c **yellow brown** (180,599) Apr. 15, 1925	1.90	1.70
		brown	1.90	1.70
		First day cover, Nos. 70, 72		80.00
		Block of 4	8.25	9.50
		P# block of 6	35.00	
73	A157	2c **carmine** (2,975,000) July 1, 1924	7.50	1.70
		First day cover		80.00
		Block of 4	35.00	8.00
		P# block of 6	175.00	
a.		Booklet pane of 6 (140,000)	175.00	
74	A160	5c **dark blue** (500,000) July 1, 1924	19.00	8.50
		On cover		20.00
		Block of 4	85.00	37.50
		P# block of 6	325.00	
75	A165	10c **orange** (60,000) July 1, 1924	45.00	25.00
		On cover		45.00
		First day cover		500.00
		Block of 4	190.00	115.00
		P# block of 6	850.00	
76	A167	12c **brown violet** (80,000) July 1, 1924	35.00	32.50
		First day cover		600.00
		Block of 4	150.00	140.00
		P# block of 6	550.00	
a.		"ZONE" inverted	3,750.	3,000.

77	A168	14c **dark blue** (100,000) June 27, 1925	30.00	22.50
		On cover		50.00
		Block of 4	130.00	140.00
		P# block of 6	425.00	
78	A169	15c **gray** (55,000) July 1, 1924	50.00	37.50
		On cover		52.50
		Block of 4	225.00	190.00
		P# block of 6	850.00	
79	A172	30c **olive brown** (40,000) July 1, 1924	35.00	22.50
		On cover		50.00
		Block of 4	135.00	110.00
		P# block of 6	550.00	
80	A173	50c **lilac** (25,000) July 1, 1924	77.50	45.00
		On cover		500.00
		Block of 4	340.00	225.00
		P# block of 6	2,750.	
81	A174	$1 **violet brown** (10,000) July 1, 1924	225.00	95.00
		On cover		1,000.
		Block of 4	1,000.	500.00
		Margin block of 4, arrow, top or bottom	1,250.	
		P# block of 6	4,250.	
		Nos. 70-81 (12)	528.55	293.55

Normal spacing between words of the overprint is 9¼mm.
Minor spacing variations are known. The overprint of the early
printings used on all values of this series except No. 77 is a
sharp, clear impression. The overprint of the late printings,
used only on Nos. 70, 71, 73, 76, 77, 78 and 80 is heavy and
smudged, with many of the letters, particularly the "A" practically filled.

Booklet panes Nos. 71e, 73a, 84d, 97b, 101a, 106a and
117a were made from 360 subject plates. The handmade booklet panes Nos. 102a, 115c and a provisional lot of 117b were
made from Post Office panes from regular 400-subject plates.

CANAL

United States Nos. 554, 555, 567, 562,
564-567, 569, 570, 571, 623 Overprinted
in Red (No. 91) or Black (all others)

ZONE

Type B
Letters "A" with Sharp Pointed Tops

1925-28				Perf. 11
84	A157	2c **carmine** (1,110,000) May 1926	30.00	8.00
		On cover		11.00
		Block of 4	125.00	37.50
		P# block of 6	300.00	
		P# block of 6 & large 5 point star, side only	1,750.	
a.		"CANAL" only (20)	1,600.	
b.		"ZONE CANAL" (180)	375.00	
c.		Horizontal pair, one without overprint	3,500.	
d.		Booklet pane of 6 (82,000)	175.00	
85	A158	3c **violet** (199,200) June 27, 1925	4.00	3.25
		On cover		6.00
		Block of 4	17.50	13.50
		P# block of 6	175.00	
a.		"ZONE ZONE"	600.00	550.00
86	A160	5c **dark blue** (1,343,147) Jan. 7, 1926	4.00	2.25
		On cover		17.50
		Block of 4	17.50	10.00
		P# block of 6	165.00	
		Double transfer (15571 UL 86)	—	—
a.		"ZONE ZONE" (LR18)	1,250.	
b.		"ZONE ZONE" inverted (LR7)	950.00	
c.		Inverted overprint (80)	500.00	
d.		Horizontal pair, one without overprint	3,250.	
e.		Overprinted "ZONE CANAL" (90)	325.00	
f.		"ZONE" only (10)	2,000.	
g.		Vertical pair, one without overprint, oth-er overprint inverted (10)	2,250.	
h.		"CANAL" only	2,250.	
87	A165	10c **orange** (99,510) Aug. 1925	35.00	12.00
		On cover		40.00
		Block of 4	160.00	70.00
		P# block of 6	500.00	
a.		"ZONE ZONE" (LR18)	3,000.	
88	A167	12c **brown violet** (58,062) Feb. 1926	22.50	14.00
		On cover		45.00
		Block of 4	100.00	62.50
		P# block of 6	375.00	
a.		"ZONE ZONE" (LR18)	5,250.	
89	A168	14c **dark blue** (55,700) Dec. 1928	20.00	16.00
		On cover		50.00
		Block of 4	90.00	75.00
		P# block of 6	350.00	
90	A169	15c **gray** (204,138) Nov. 1925	7.00	4.50
		On cover		15.00
		Block of 4	32.50	21.00
		P# block of 6	200.00	
		P# block of 4, large 5 point star, side only	—	
a.		"ZONE ZONE" (LR18)	5,500.	

Specialists believe a unique P# block of 4 with large 5-point
star is the largest known P# multiple from the star plate. The
editors would like to receive evidence to the contrary, if it exists.

91	A187	17c **black** (199,500) Apr. 5, 1926	4.00	3.00
		On cover		12.50
		Block of 4	17.50	14.00
		P# block of 6	190.00	
a.		"ZONE" only (20)	900.00	
b.		"CANAL" only	1,700.	
c.		"ZONE CANAL" (270)	175.00	

92 A170 20c **carmine rose** (259,807) Apr. 5, 1926	7.25	3.25
On cover		32.50
Block of 4	32.50	14.00
P# block of 6	175.00	
a. "CANAL" inverted (UR48)	3,600.	
b. "ZONE" inverted (LL76)	3,850.	
c. "ZONE CANAL" (LL91)	3,600.	
93 A172 30c **olive brown** (154,700) Dec. 1925	5.00	4.00
On cover		60.00
Block of 4	22.50	20.00
P# block of 6	250.00	
94 A173 50c **lilac** (13,533) July 1928	225.00	165.00
On cover		500.00
Block of 4	1,000.	675.00
P# block of 6	2,250.	
95 A174 $1 **violet brown** (20,000) Apr. 1926	125.00	60.00
On cover		1,000.
Block of 4	550.00	265.00
Margin block of 4, arrow, top or bottom	575.00	
P# block of 6	2,000.	
Nos. 84-95 (12)	488.75	295.25

Nos. 85-88, 90 and 93-95 exist with wrong-font "CANAL" and "ZONE." Positions are: Nos. 85-88 and 90, UL51 (CANAL) and UL82 (ZONE); Nos. 93-95, U51 (CANAL) and U82 (ZONE).

Normal spacing between words of the overprint is 11mm on No. 84; 9mm on Nos. 85-88, 90, first printing of No. 91 and the first, third and fourth printing of No. 92; 7mm on the second printings of Nos. 91-92. Minor spacing varieties exist on Nos. 84-88, 90-92.

Overprint Type B on U.S. Sesquicentennial Stamp No. 627

1926

96 A188 2c **carmine rose** (300,000) July 6, 1926	4.50	3.75
First day cover		60.00
Block of 4	20.00	20.00
P# block of 6	85.00	

On this stamp there is a space of 5mm instead of 9mm between the two words of the overprint.

The authorized date, July 4, fell on a Sunday with the next day also a holiday, so No. 96 was not regularly issued until July 6. But the postmaster sold some copies and canceled some covers on July 4 for a few favored collectors.

Overprint Type B in Black on U.S. Nos. 583, 584, 591

1926-27	**Rotary Press Printings**	**Perf. 10**	
97 A157 2c **carmine** (1,290,000) Dec. 1926		42.50	11.00
On cover			14.00
Block of 4		175.00	50.00
P# block of 4		250.00	
a. Pair, one without overprint (10)		3,250.	
b. Booklet pane of 6 (58,000)		650.00	
c. "CANAL" only (10)		2,000.	
d. "ZONE" only		2,750.	
98 A158 3c **violet** (239,600) May 9, 1927		8.00	4.25
On cover			12.00
Block of 4		32.50	19.00
P# block of 4		120.00	
99 A165 10c **orange** (128,400) May 9, 1927		17.50	7.50
On cover			35.00
Block of 4		75.00	40.00
P# block of 4		225.00	

Overprint Type B in Black on U.S. Nos. 632, 634 (Type I), 635, 637, 642

1927-31	**Rotary Press Printings**	**Perf. 11x10½**	
100 A155 1c **green** (434,892) June 28, 1927		2.25	1.40
On cover			3.00
Block of 4		10.00	6.75
P# block of 4		20.00	
a. Vertical pair, one without overprint (10)		3,000.	
101 A157 2c **carmine** (1,628,195) June 28, 1927		2.50	1.00
On cover			3.00
Block of 4		11.00	4.75
P# block of 4		24.00	
a. Booklet pane of 6 (82,108)		175.00	
102 A158 3c **violet** (1,250,000) Feb., 1931		4.25	2.75
On cover			5.00
Block of 4		21.00	13.50
P# block of 4		90.00	
a. Booklet pane of 6, handmade, perf. margins		6,500.	
103 A160 5c **dark blue** (60,000) Dec. 13, 1927		30.00	10.00
On cover			30.00
Block of 4		130.00	42.50
P# block of 4		200.00	
104 A165 10c **orange** (119,800) July, 1930		17.50	10.00
On cover			35.00
Block of 4		77.50	45.00
P# block of 4		190.00	
Nos. 100-104 (5)		56.50	25.15

Maj. Gen. William Crawford Gorgas — A35

Maj. Gen. George Washington Goethals — A36

Gaillard Cut — A37

Maj. Gen. Harry Foote Hodges — A38

Lt. Col. David Du Bose Gaillard — A39

Maj. Gen. William Luther Sibert — A40

Jackson Smith — A41

Rear Adm. Harry Harwood Rousseau — A42

Col. Sydney Bacon Williamson — A43

Joseph Clay Styles Blackburn — A44

Printed by the U. S. Bureau of Engraving and Printing.
Plates of 400 subjects (except 5c), issued in panes of 100. The 5c was printed from plate of 200 subjects, issued in panes of 50. The 400-subject sheets were originally cut by knife into Post Office panes of 100, but beginning in 1948 they were separated by perforations to eliminate straight edges.

1928-40	**Flat Plate Printing**	**Unwmk.**	**Perf. 11**	
105 A35 1c **green** (22,392,147)			.20	.20
P# block of 6			.40	—
a. Wet printing, yel grn, Oct. 3, 1928			.20	.20
First day cover				17.50
106 A36 2c **carmine** (7,191,600) Oct. 1, 1928			.20	.20
First day cover				17.50
P# block of 6			1.40	
a. Booklet pane of 6 (284,640)			15.00	20.00
107 A37 5c **blue** (4,187,028) June 25, 1929			1.00	.40
First day cover				5.00
P# block of 6			9.00	
108 A38 10c **orange** (4,559,788)			.20	.20
P# block of 6			4.50	—
a. Wet printing, Jan. 11, 1932			.40	.25
First day cover				40.00
109 A39 12c **brown violet** (844,635)			.75	.60
P# block of 6			8.00	—
a. Wet printing, violet brown, July 1, 1929			1.50	1.00
First day cover				60.00
110 A40 14c **blue** (406,131) Sept. 27, 1937			.85	.85
First day cover				5.00
P# block of 6			10.00	
111 A41 15c **gray black** (3,356,500)			.40	.35
P# block of 6			6.00	—
a. Wet printing, gray, Jan. 11, 1932			.80	.50
First day cover				45.00

112 A42 20c **dark brown** (3,619,080)		.60	.20
P# block of 6		6.00	—
a. Wet printing, olive brown, Jan. 11, 1932		1.00	.30
First day cover			45.00
113 A43 30c **black** (2,376,491)		.80	.70
P# block of 6		8.00	—
a. Wet printing, brn blk, Apr. 15, 1940		1.25	1.00
First day cover			10.00
114 A44 50c **rose lilac** (13,533)		1.50	.65
P# block of 6		14.00	—
a. Wet printing, lilac, July 1, 1929		2.50	.85
First day cover			110.00
Nos. 105-114 (10)		6.50	4.35

Coils are listed as Nos. 160-161.

Wet and Dry Printings

Canal Zone stamps printed by both the "wet" and "dry" process are Nos. 105, 108-109, 111-114, 117, 138-140, C21-C24, C26, J25, J27. Starting with Nos. 147 and C27, the Bureau of Engraving and Printing used the "dry" method exclusively, except for Nos. 152, 157 and 164.

See note on Wet and Dry Printings following US No. 1029.

United States Nos. 720 and 695 Overprinted

CANAL

Type B

ZONE

Rotary Press Printing

1933, Jan. 14		**Perf. 11x10½**	
115 A226 3c **deep violet** (3,150,000)		2.75	.25
First day cover			12.00
P# block of 4		35.00	—
b. "CANAL" only		2,600.	
c. Booklet pane of 6, handmade, perf. margins		225.00	—
116 A168 14c **dark blue** (104,800)		4.50	3.50
First day cover			20.00
P# block of 4		60.00	—
a. "ZONE CANAL" (16)		1,500.	

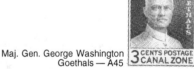

Maj. Gen. George Washington Goethals — A45

20th anniversary of the opening of the Panama Canal.

Flat Plate Printing

1934, Aug. 15	**Unwmk.**	**Perf. 11**	
117 A45 3c **red violet**		.20	.20
First day cover			3.00
P# block of 6		1.00	—
a. Booklet pane of 6		45.00	32.50
b. As "a," handmade, perf. margins		225.00	
c. Wet printing, violet		.20	.20

Coil is listed as No. 153.

Catalogue values for unused stamps in this section, from this point to the end, are for Never Hinged items.

United States Nos. 803 and 805 Overprinted in Black

CANAL
ZONE

Rotary Press Printing

1939, Sept. 1	**Unwmk.**	**Perf. 11x10½**	
118 A275 ½c **red orange** (1,030,000)		.20	.20
First day cover			1.00
P# block of 4		2.75	—
119 A277 1½c **bister brown** (935,000)		.20	.20
brown		.20	.20
First day cover			1.00
P# block of 4		2.25	

Canal Zone stamps can be mounted in the Scott U.S. Possessions album.

Balboa-Before
A46

Balboa-After
A47

Gaillard Cut-
Before — A48

Gaillard Cut-
After — A49

Bas Obispo-Before
A50

Bas Obispo-After
A51

Gatun Locks-
Before
A52

Gatun Locks-After
A53

Canal Channel-
Before
A54

Canal Channel-
After
A55

Gamboa-Before
A56

Gamboa-After
A57

Pedro Miguel
Locks-Before
A58

Pedro Miguel
Locks-After
A59

Gatun Spillway-
Before
A60

Gatun Spillway-
After
A61

25th anniversary of the opening of the Panama Canal.
Withdrawn Feb. 28, 1941; remainders burned Apr. 12, 1941.

Flat Plate Printing

1939, Aug. 15		**Unwmk.**		**Perf. 11**
120 A46	1c	**yellow green** (1,019,482)	.65	.30
		First day cover		2.00
		P# block of 6	12.50	—
121 A47	2c	**rose carmine** (227,065)	.65	.35
		First day cover		2.00
		P# block of 6	12.50	—
122 A48	3c	**purple** (2,523,735)	.65	.20
		First day cover		2.00
		P# block of 6	12.50	—
123 A49	5c	**dark blue** (460,213)	1.60	1.25
		First day cover		2.50
		P# block of 6	20.00	—
124 A40	6c	**red orange** (68,290)	3.00	3.00
		First day cover		6.00
		P# block of 6	45.00	—
125 A51	7c	**black** (71,235)	3.25	3.00
		First day cover		6.00
		P# block of 6	45.00	—
126 A52	8c	**green** (41,576)	4.75	3.50
		First day cover		6.00
		P# block of 6	55.00	—
127 A53	10c	**ultramarine** (83,571)	3.50	3.00
		First day cover		6.00
		P# block of 6	55.00	—
128 A54	11c	**blue green** (34,010)	8.00	8.50
		First day cover		10.00
		P# block of 6	125.00	—
129 A55	12c	**brown carmine** (66,735)	7.50	8.00
		First day cover		10.00
		P# block of 6	100.00	—
130 A56	14c	**dark violet** (37,365)	7.50	8.00
		First day cover		10.00
		P# block of 6	125.00	—
131 A57	15c	**olive green** (105,058)	10.00	6.00
		First day cover		10.00
		P# block of 6	160.00	—
132 A58	18c	**rose pink** (39,255)	10.00	8.50
		First day cover		10.00
		P# block of 6	150.00	—
133 A59	20c	**brown** (100,244)	12.50	7.50
		First day cover		10.00
		P# block of 6	190.00	—
134 A60	25c	**orange** (34,283)	17.50	17.50
		First day cover		20.00
		P# block of 6	325.00	—

135 A61	50c	**violet brown** (91,576)	22.50	6.00
		First day cover		20.00
		P# block of 6	350.00	—
		Nos. 120-135 (16)	113.55	84.60

Maj. Gen. George W.
Davis — A62

Gov. Charles E.
Magoon — A63

Theodore
Roosevelt — A64

John F. Stevens — A65

John F. Wallace — A66

1946-49		**Unwmk.**		**Perf. 11**
		Size: 19x22mm		
136 A62	½c	**bright red** (1,020,000) Aug. 16, 1948	.40	.25
		First day cover		1.25
		P# block of 6	2.50	—
137 A63	1½c	**chocolate** (603,600) Aug. 16, 1948	.40	.25
		First day cover		1.25
		P# block of 6	2.25	—
138 A64	2c	**light rose carmine** (6,951,755)	.20	.20
		P# block of 6	.65	—
a.		Wet printing, rose carmine, Oct. 27, 1949	.20	.20
		First day cover		1.00
139 A65	5c	**dark blue**	.35	.20
		P# block of 6	2.25	—
a.		Wet printing, deep blue, Apr. 25, 1946	.60	.20
		First day cover		1.00
140 A66	25c	**green** (1,520,000)	.85	.55
		P# block of 6	7.00	—
a.		Wet printing, yel grn, Aug. 16, 1948	3.00	1.00
		First day cover		3.50
		Nos. 136-140 (5)	2.20	1.45

See Nos. 155, 162, 164.

Map of Biological
Area and Coati-
mundi — A67

25th anniversary of the establishment of the Canal Zone
Biological Area on Barro Colorado Island.
Withdrawn Mar. 30, 1951, and remainders destroyed Apr. 10,
1951.

1948, Apr. 17		**Unwmk.**		**Perf. 11**
141 A67	10c	**black** (521,200)	1.25	.80
		First day cover		3.00
		P# block of 6	8.50	—

"Forty-niners" Arriving at
Chagres — A68

Journeying in "Bungo" to
Las Cruces — A69

Las Cruces Trail to Panama — A70

Departure for San Francisco — A71

Centenary of the California Gold Rush.
Stocks on hand were processed for destruction on Aug. 11, 1952 and destroyed Aug. 13, 1952.

1949, June 1   Unwmk.   Perf. 11

142 A68	3c blue (500,000)	.50	.25
	First day cover		1.00
	P# block of 6	6.00	—
143 A69	6c violet (481,600)	.65	.30
	First day cover		1.00
	P# block of 6	6.50	—
144 A70	12c bright blue green (230,200)	1.10	.90
	First day cover		2.00
	P# block of 6	18.00	—
145 A71	18c deep red lilac (240,200)	2.00	1.50
	First day cover		3.25
	P# block of 6	20.00	—
	Nos. 142-145 (4)	4.25	2.95

Workers in Culebra Cut — A72

Early Railroad Scene — A73

Contribution of West Indian laborers in the construction of the Panama Canal.
Entire issue sold, none withdrawn and destroyed.

1951, Aug. 15   Unwmk.   Perf. 11

146 A72	10c carmine (480,000)	2.25	1.50
	First day cover		3.00
	P# block of 6	22.50	—

1955, Jan. 28   Unwmk.   Perf. 11

Centenary of the completion of the Panama Railroad and the first transcontinental railroad trip in the Americas.

147 A73	3c violet (994,000)	.60	.50
	First day cover		1.50
	P# block of 6	5.50	—

Gorgas Hospital and Ancon Hill — A74

75th anniversary of Gorgas Hospital.

1957, Nov. 17   Unwmk.   Perf. 11

148 A74	3c black, dull blue green (1,010,000)	.45	.35
	Light blue green paper	.40	.35
	First day cover		1.00
	P# block of 4	4.25	—

S.S. Ancon — A75

1958, Aug. 30   Unwmk.   Perf. 11

149 A75	4c greenish blue (1,749,700)	.40	.30
	First day cover		1.00
	P# block of 4	3.25	—

Roosevelt Medal and Canal Zone Map — A76

Centenary of the birth of Theodore Roosevelt (1858-1919).

1958, Nov. 15   Unwmk.   Perf. 11

150 A76	4c brown (1,060,000)	.40	.30
	First day cover		1.00
	P# block of 4	3.00	—

Boy Scout Badge — A77

Administration Building, Balboa Heights — A78

50th anniversary of the Boy Scouts of America.

Giori Press Printing

1960, Feb. 8   Unwmk.   Perf. 11

151 A77	4c dark blue, red & bister (654,933)	.50	.40
	First day cover		1.00
	P# block of 4	4.25	—

1960, Nov. 1   Unwmk.   Perf. 11

152 A78	4c rose lilac (2,486,725)	.20	.20
	First day cover		1.00
	P# block of 4	.90	—

Types of 1934, 1960 and 1946
Coil Stamps

1960-62   Unwmk.   Perf. 10 Vertically

153 A45	3c deep violet (3,743,959) Nov. 1, 1960	.20	.20
	First day cover		1.00
	Pair	.40	.25
	Joint line pair	1.10	—

Perf. 10 Horizontally

154 A78	4c dull rose lilac (2,776,273) Nov. 1, 1960	.20	.20
	First day cover		1.00
	Pair	.40	.25
	Joint line pair	1.10	—

Perf. 10 Vertically

155 A65	5c deep blue (3,288,264) Feb. 10, 1962	.25	.20
	First day cover		1.00
	Pair	.50	.50
	Joint line pair	1.25	—
	Nos. 153-155 (3)	.65	.60

Girl Scout Badge and Camp at Gatun Lake — A79

50th anniversary of the Girl Scouts.

Giori Press Printing

1962, Mar. 12   Unwmk.   Perf. 11

156 A79	4c blue, dark green & bister (640,000)	.50	.30
	First day cover (83,717)		1.25
	P# block of 4	2.75	—

Thatcher Ferry Bridge and Map of Western Hemisphere A80

Opening of the Thatcher Ferry Bridge, spanning the Panama Canal.

Giori Press Printing

1962, Oct. 12   Unwmk.   Perf. 11

157 A80	4c black & silver (775,000)	.35	.25
	First day cover (65,833)		1.00
	P# block of 4, 2P#	3.75	—
a.	Silver (bridge) omitted (50)	7,500.	
	P# block of 6, black P# only	52,500.	

Goethals Memorial, Balboa — A81

Fort San Lorenzo — A82

1968-71   Giori Press Printing   Perf. 11

158 A81	6c green & ultra. (1,890,000) Mar. 15, 1968	.30	.30
	First day cover		1.00
	P# block of 4	2.00	—
159 A82	8c slate green, blue, dark brown & ocher (3,460,000) July 14, 1971	.35	.20
	First day cover		1.00
	P# block of 4	2.75	—

Types of 1928, 1932 and 1948
Coil Stamps

1975, Feb. 14   Unwmk.   Perf. 10 Vertically

160 A35	1c green (1,090,958)	.20	.20
	First day cover		1.00
	Pair	.25	.20
	Joint line pair	1.00	—
161 A38	10c orange (590,658)	.70	.40
	First day cover		1.00
	Pair	1.40	.80
	Joint line pair	5.00	—
162 A66	25c yellow green (129,831)	2.75	2.75
	First day cover		3.00
	Pair	5.50	5.50
	Joint line pair	20.00	—
	Nos. 160-162 (3)	3.65	3.35

Dredge Cascadas — A83

1976, Feb. 23   Giori Press Printing   Perf. 11

163 A83	13c multicolored (3,653,950)	.35	.20
	First day cover		1.00
	P# block of 4	2.00	—
a.	Booklet pane of 4 (1,032,400) Apr. 19	3.00	

Stevens Type of 1946

1977   Rotary Press Printing   Perf. 11x10½
Size: 19x22½mm

164 A65	5c deep blue (1,009,612)	.60	.85
	P# block of 4	3.50	—
a.	Tagged	10.00	—

No. 164a exists even though there was no equipment in the Canal Zone to detect tagging.

Towing Locomotive, Ship in Lock, by Alwyn Sprague — A84

1978, Oct. 25   Perf. 11

165 A84	15c dp grn & bl grn (2,921,083)	.35	.20
	First day cover (81,405)		1.00
	P# block of 4	2.00	—

AIR POST STAMPS

AIR MAIL

Regular Issue of 1928 Surcharged in Dark Blue

25 CENTS 25

15
Type I- Flag of "5" pointing up

15
Type II- Flag of "5" curved

1929-31 Flat Plate Printing Unwmk. Perf. 11

C1	A35	15c on 1c **green**, type I, Apr. 1, 1929	8.00	5.50
		First day cover		25.00
		Block of 4	35.00	25.00
		P# block of 6	120.00	—
C2	A35	15c on 1c **yellow green**, type II, Mar. 1931	85.00	75.00
		On cover		175.00
		Block of 4	375.00	340.00
		P# block of 6	900.00	—
C3	A36	25c on 2c **carmine** (223,880) Jan. 11, 1929	3.50	2.00
		First day cover		17.50
		Block of 4	15.00	9.00
		P# block of 6	115.00	—

AIR MAIL

Nos. 114 and 106 Surcharged in Black

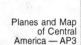

1929, Dec. 31

C4	A44	10c on 50c **lilac** (116,666)	7.50	6.50
		First day cover		25.00
		Block of 4	32.50	27.50
		P# block of 6	115.00	—
C5	A36	20c on 2c **carmine** (638,395)	5.00	1.75
		First day cover		20.00
		Block of 4	20.00	8.00
		P# block of 6	110.00	—
a.		Dropped "2" in surcharge (7,000)	80.00	60.00

> Catalogue values for unused stamps in this section, from this point to the end, are for Never Hinged items.

Gaillard Cut — AP1

Printed by the U. S. Bureau of Engraving and Printing.
Plates of 200 subjects, issued in panes of 50.

1931-49 Unwmk. Perf. 11

C6	AP1	4c **red violet** (525,000) Jan. 3, 1949	.75	.70
		First day cover		2.00
		P# block of 6	5.25	—
C7	AP1	5c **yellow green** (9,988,800) Nov. 18, 1931	.60	.45
		green	.60	.45
		First day cover		10.00
		P# block of 6	4.50	—
C8	AP1	6c **yellow brown** (9,440,000) Feb. 15, 1946	.75	.35
		First day cover		2.00
		P# block of 6	5.25	—
C9	AP1	10c **orange** (5,140,000) Nov. 18, 1931	1.00	.35
		First day cover		10.00
		P# block of 6	10.00	—
C10	AP1	15c **blue** (11,961,500) Nov. 18, 1931	1.25	.30
		pale blue	1.25	.30
		First day cover		15.00
		P# block of 6	11.00	—
C11	AP1	20c **red violet** (3,214,600) Nov. 18, 1931	2.00	.30
		deep violet	2.00	.30
		First day cover		35.00
		P# block of 6	20.00	—
C12	AP1	30c **rose lake** (1,150,000) July 15, 1941	3.50	1.00
		dull rose	3.50	1.00
		First day cover		22.50
		P# block of 6	32.50	—
C13	AP1	40c **yellow** (826,100) Nov. 18, 1931	3.50	1.10
		lemon	3.50	1.10
		First day cover		60.00
		P# block of 6	32.50	—
C14	AP1	$1 **black** (406,000) Nov. 18, 1931	8.50	1.90
		First day cover		125.00
		P# block of 6	85.00	—
		Nos. C6-C14 (9)	21.85	6.45

Douglas Plane over Sosa Hill — AP2

Planes and Map of Central America — AP3

Pan American Clipper and Scene near Fort Amador — AP4

Pan American Clipper at Cristobal Harbor — AP5

Pan American Clipper over Gaillard Cut — AP6

Pan American Clipper Landing — AP7

10th anniversary of Air Mail service and the 25th anniversary of the opening of the Panama Canal.
Withdrawn Feb. 28, 1941, remainders burned Apr. 12, 1941.

Flat Plate Printing

1939, July 15 Unwmk. Perf. 11

C15	AP2	5c **greenish black** (86,576)	3.75	2.25
		First day cover		5.00
		P# block of 6	42.50	—
C16	AP3	10c **dull violet** (117,644)	3.00	2.25
		First day cover		5.00
		P# block of 6	50.00	—
C17	AP4	15c **light brown** (883,742)	4.25	1.25
		First day cover		3.00
		P# block of 6	55.00	—
C18	AP5	25c **blue** (82,126)	13.00	8.00
		First day cover		17.50
		P# block of 6	225.00	—
C19	AP6	30c **rose carmine** (121,382)	12.00	6.75
		First day cover		15.00
		P# block of 6	160.00	—
C20	AP7	$1 **green** (40,051)	35.00	22.50
		First day cover		60.00
		P# block of 6	525.00	—
		Nos. C15-C20 (6)	71.00	43.00

Globe and Wing — AP8

Flat Plate Printing

1951, July 16 Unwmk. Perf. 11

C21	AP8	4c **lt red violet** (1,315,000)	.75	.35
		P# block of 6	7.00	—
a.		Wet printing, red violet	1.25	.40
		1st day card, Balboa Heights		1.50
C22	AP8	6c **lt brown** (22,657,625)	.50	.25
		P# block of 6	5.00	—
a.		Wet printing, brown	.95	.35
		1st day cover, Balboa Heights		1.00
C23	AP8	10c **lt red orange** (1,049,130)	.90	.35
		P# block of 6	8.00	—
a.		Wet printing, red orange	2.00	.50
		1st day cover, Balboa Heights		2.00
C24	AP8	21c **lt blue** (1,460,000)	7.50	4.00
		P# block of 6	70.00	—
a.		Wet printing, blue	15.00	5.00
		1st day cover, Balboa Heights		7.50
C25	AP8	31c **cerise** (375,000)	7.50	3.75
		1st day cover, Balboa Heights		7.50
		P# block of 6	70.00	—
a.		Horiz. pair, imperf. vert. (98)	1,000.	—

C26	AP8	80c **lt gray black** (827,696)	4.50	1.50
		P# block of 6	35.00	—
a.		Wet printing, gray black	12.50	1.65
		1st day cover, Balboa Heights		12.50
		1st day cover, Balboa Heights, #C21-C26		20.00
		Nos. C21-C26 (6)	21.65	10.20

See note after No. 114. Total number of first day covers with one or more of Nos. C21-C26, about 12,000.

Flat Plate Printing

1958, Aug. 16 Unwmk. Perf. 11

C27	AP8	5c **yellow green** (899,923)	1.00	.60
		First day cover (2,176)		4.50
		P# block of 4	6.00	—
C28	AP8	7c **olive** (9,381,797)	1.00	.45
		First day cover (2,815)		4.50
		P# block of 4	6.00	—
C29	AP8	15c **brown violet** (359,923)	3.75	2.75
		First day cover (2,040)		6.00
		P# block of 4	30.00	—
C30	AP8	25c **orange yellow** (600,000)	10.00	2.75
		First day cover (2,115)		9.00
		P# block of 4	95.00	—
C31	AP8	35c **dark blue** (283,032)	6.25	2.75
		First day cover (1,868)		11.00
		P# block of 4	40.00	—
		Nos. C27-C31 (5)	22.00	9.30
		Nos. C21-C31 (11)	43.65	19.50

Emblem of US Army Caribbean School — AP9

US Army Caribbean School for Latin America at Fort Gulick.

Giori Press Printing

1961, Nov. 21 Unwmk. Perf. 11

C32	AP9	15c **red & blue** (560,000)	1.25	.75
		First day cover (25,949)		1.75
		P# block of 4	10.00	—

Malaria Eradication Emblem and Mosquito — AP10

World Health Organization drive to eradicate malaria.

Giori Press Printing

1962, Sept. 24 Unwmk. Perf. 11

C33	AP10	7c **yellow & black** (862,349)	.45	.40
		First day cover (44,433)		1.00
		P# block of 4	2.75	—

Globe-Wing Type of 1951

Rotary Press Printing

1963, Jan. 7 Perf. 10½x11

C34	AP8	8c **carmine** (5,054,727)	.40	.30
		First day cover (19,128)		—
		P# block of 4	2.60	—

Alliance for Progress Emblem — AP11

2nd anniv. of the Alliance for Progress, which aims to stimulate economic growth and raise living standards in Latin America.

Giori Press Printing

1963, Aug. 17 Unwmk. Perf. 11

C35	AP11	15c **gray, grn & dk ultra** (405,000)	1.10	.85
		First day cover (29,594)		1.50
		P# block of 4	10.00	—

Jet over Cristobal — AP12

50th anniversary of the opening of the Panama Canal. Designs: 8c, Gatun Locks. 15c, Madden Dam. 20c, Gaillard Cut. 30c, Miraflores Locks. 80c, Balboa.

Giori Press Printing

1964, Aug. 15			Unwmk.		*Perf. 11*
C36	AP12	6c	**green & black** *(257,193)*	.45	.35
			1st day cover, Balboa		1.50
			P# block of 4	2.25	—
C37	AP12	8c	**rose red & black** *(3,924,283)*	.45	.35
			1st day cover, Balboa		1.00
			P# block of 4	2.25	—
C38	AP12	15c	**blue & black** *(472,666)*	1.00	.75
			1st day cover, Balboa		1.00
			P# block of 4	6.25	—
C39	AP12	20c	**rose lilac & black** *(399,784)*	1.50	1.00
			1st day cover, Balboa		2.00
			P# block of 4	8.00	—
C40	AP12	30c	**reddish brown & black** *(204,524)*	2.25	2.25
			1st day cover, Balboa		3.00
			P# block of 4	15.00	—
C41	AP12	80c	**olive bister & black** *(186,809)*	3.75	3.00
			1st day cover, Balboa		4.00
			1st day cover, Balboa, #C36-C41		10.00
			P# block of 4	20.00	—
			Nos. C36-C41 (6)	9.40	7.70

There were 57,822 first day covers with one or more of Nos. C36-C41.

Canal Zone Seal and Jet Plane — AP13

Giori Press Printing

1965, July 15			Unwmk.		*Perf. 11*
C42	AP13	6c	**green & black** *(548,250)*	.35	.30
			First day cover, Balboa		2.00
			P# block of 4	1.90	—
C43	AP13	8c	**rose red & black** *(8,357,700)*	.30	.20
			First day cover, Balboa		1.00
			P# block of 4	1.75	—
C44	AP13	15c	**blue & black** *(2,385,000)*	.50	.20
			First day cover, Balboa		1.00
			P# block of 4	2.50	—
C45	AP13	20c	**lilac & black** *(2,290,699)*	.55	.30
			First day cover, Balboa		1.25
			P# block of 4	2.75	—
C46	AP13	30c	**redsh brn & blk** *(2,332,255)*	.80	.30
			First day cover, Balboa		1.25
			P# block of 4	4.00	—
C47	AP13	80c	**bister & black** *(1,456,596)*	2.00	.75
			First day cover, Balboa		2.50
			First day cover, Balboa, #C42-C47		7.00
			P# block of 4	12.50	—
			Nos. C42-C47 (6)	4.50	2.05

There were 35,389 first day covers with one or more of Nos. C42-C47.

1968-76

C48	AP13	10c	**dull orange & black** *(10,055,000)* Mar. 15, 1968	.25	.20
			First day cover, Balboa *(7,779)*		1.00
			P# block of 4	1.25	—
a.			Booklet pane of 4 *(713,390)* Feb. 18, 1970	4.25	—
			First day cover, Balboa *(5,054)*		5.00
C49	AP13	11c	**olive & black** *(3,335,000)* Sept. 24, 1971	.25	.20
			First day cover, Balboa *(10,916)*		1.00
			P# block of 4	1.25	—
a.			Booklet pane of 4 *(1,277,760)* Sept. 24, 1971	3.50	—
			First day cover, Balboa *(2,460)*		5.00
C50	AP13	13c	**emerald & black** *(1,865,000)* Feb. 11, 1974	.80	.25
			First day cover, Balboa *(7,646)*		1.00
			P# block of 4	4.75	—
a.			Booklet pane of 4 *(619,200)* Feb. 11, 1974	6.00	—
			First day cover, Balboa *(3,660)*		5.00
C51	AP13	22c	**vio & blk** *(363,720)* May 10, 1976	.75	2.00
			First day cover, Balboa		2.50
			P# block of 4	4.00	—
C52	AP13	25c	**pale yellow green & black** *(1,640,441)* Mar. 15, 1968	.60	.70
			First day cover, Balboa		1.00
			P# block of 4	2.75	—
C53	AP13	35c	**salmon & black** *(573,822)* May 10, 1976	.90	2.00
			First day cover, Balboa		2.50
			P# block of 4	4.75	—
			Nos. C48-C53 (6)	3.55	5.35

There were 5,047 first day covers with one or more of Nos. C51, C53.

AIR POST OFFICIAL STAMPS

Beginning in March, 1915, stamps for use on official mail were identified by a large "P" perforated through each stamp. These were replaced by overprinted issues in 1941. The use of official stamps was discontinued December 31, 1951. During their currency, they were not for sale in mint condition and were sold to the public only when canceled with a parcel post rotary canceler reading "Balboa Heights, Canal Zone" between two wavy lines.

After having been withdrawn from use, mint stamps (except Nos. CO8-CO12 and O3, O8) were made available to the public at face value for three months beginning Jan. 2, 1952. **Values for used examples of Nos. CO1-CO7, CO14, O1-O2, O4-O9, are for canceled-to-order specimens with original gum, postally used copies being worth more.** Sheet margins were removed to facilitate overprinting and plate numbers are, therefore, unknown.

Air Post Stamps of 1931-41 Overprinted in Black

OFFICIAL PANAMA CANAL

Two types of overprint.
Type I- "PANAMA CANAL" 19-20mm long

1941-42			Unwmk.		*Perf. 11*
CO1	AP1	5c	**yellow green** *(42,754)* Mar. 31, 1941	5.50	1.50
			green	5.50	1.50
			On cover		50.00
			Block of 4	25.00	6.00
CO2	AP1	10c	**orange** *(49,723)* Mar. 31, 1941	8.50	2.00
			On cover		25.00
			Block of 4	37.50	9.00
CO3	AP1	15c	**blue** *(56,898)* Mar. 31, 1941	11.00	2.00
			On cover		25.00
			Block of 4	47.50	17.00
CO4	AP1	20c	**red violet** *(22,107)* Mar. 31, 1941	12.50	4.00
			deep violet	12.50	4.00
			On cover		110.00
			Block of 4	60.00	22.50
CO5	AP1	30c	**rose lake** *(22,100)* June, 4, 1942	17.50	5.00
			dull rose	17.50	4.50
			On cover		40.00
			Block of 4	80.00	22.50
CO6	AP1	40c	**yellow** *(22,875)* Mar. 31, 1941	17.50	7.50
			lemon yellow	17.50	7.50
			On cover		75.00
			Block of 4	80.00	37.50
CO7	AP1	$1	**black** *(29,525)* Mar. 31, 1941	20.00	10.00
			On cover		150.00
			Block of 4	90.00	45.00
			Nos. CO1-CO7 (7)	92.50	32.00

Overprint varieties occur on Nos. CO1-CO7 and CO14: "O" of "OFFICIAL" over "N" of "PANAMA" (entire third row). "O" of "OFFICIAL" broken at top (position 31). "O" of "OFFICIAL" over second "A" of "PANAMA" (position 45). First "F" of "OFFICIAL" over second "A" of "PANAMA" (position 50).

1941, Sept. 22
Type II- "PANAMA CANAL" 17mm long

CO8	AP1	5c	**yellow green** *(2,000)*	—	160.00
			On cover		500.00
			Block of 4		675.00
CO9	AP1	10c	**orange** *(2,000)*	—	275.00
			On cover		400.00
			Block of 4		1,375.
CO10	AP1	20c	**red violet** *(2,000)*	—	175.00
			On cover		—
			Block of 4		750.00
CO11	AP1	30c	**rose lake** *(5,000)*	—	65.00
			On cover		125.00
			Block of 4	—	275.00
CO12	AP1	40c	**yellow** *(2,000)*	—	180.00
			On cover		500.00
			Block of 4		750.00
			Nos. CO8-CO12		805.00

1947, Nov.
Type I- "PANAMA CANAL" 19-20mm long

CO14	AP1	6c	**yellow brown** *(33,450)*	12.50	4.00
			On cover		50.00
			Block of 4	57.50	22.50
a.			Inverted overprint *(50)*		2,500.

POSTAGE DUE STAMPS

Prior to 1914, many of the postal issues were handstamped "Postage Due" and used as postage due stamps.

Postage Due Stamps of the United States Nos. J45a, J46a, and J49a Overprinted in Black

CANAL ZONE

1914, Mar.			Wmk. 190		*Perf. 12*
J1	D2	1c	**rose carmine** *(23,533)*	85.	15.
			On cover		275.
			Block of 4 (2mm spacing)	350.	70.
			Block of 4 (3mm spacing)	375.	80.
			P# block of 6, impt. & star	700.	—
J2	D2	2c	**rose carmine** *(32,312)*	250.	45.
			On cover		275.
			Block of 4	1,100.	200.
			P# block of 6	1,750.	—
J3	D2	10c	**rose carmine** *(92,493)*	850.	40.
			On cover		725.
			Block of 4 (2mm spacing)	3,700.	170.
			Block of 4 (3mm spacing)	3,700.	170.
			P# block of 6, Impt. & star	7,000.	—

Many examples of Nos. J1-J3 show one or more letters of the overprint out of alignment, principally the "E."

San Geronimo Castle Gate, Portobelo (See footnote) — D1

Statue of Columbus
D2

Pedro J. Sosa
D3

1915, Mar. Unwmk. *Perf. 12*
Blue Overprint, Type II, on Postage Due Stamps of Panama

J4	D1	1c	**olive brown** *(50,000)*	12.50	5.00
			On cover		150.00
			Block of 4	55.00	22.50
J5	D2	2c	**olive brown** *(50,000)*	200.00	17.50
			On cover		175.00
			Block of 4	875.00	90.00
J6	D3	10c	**olive brown** *(200,000)*	50.00	10.00
			On cover		175.00
			Block of 4	225.00	45.00

Type D1 was intended to show a gate of San Lorenzo Castle, Chagres, and is so labeled. By error the stamp actually shows the main gate of San Geronimo Castle, Portobelo.

Surcharged in Red **CANAL 2 ZONE**

1915, Nov.			Unwmk.		*Perf. 12*
J7	D1	1c on 1c	**olive brown** *(60,614)*	105.00	15.00
			On cover		165.00
			Block of 4	475.00	70.00
J8	D2	2c on 2c	**olive brown**	25.00	7.50
			On cover		165.00
			Block of 4	110.00	35.00
J9	D3	10c on 10c	**olive brown** *(175,548)*	22.50	5.00
			On cover		165.00
			Block of 4	100.00	25.00

One of the printings of No. J9 shows wider spacing between "1" and "0." Both spacings occur on the same sheet.

D4

Capitol, Panama — D5

1919, Dec.
Surcharged in Carmine at Mount Hope

J10	D4	2c on 2c	**olive brown**	30.00	12.50
			On cover		110.00
			Block of 4	130.00	55.00
J11	D5	4c on 4c	**olive brown** *(35,695)*	35.00	15.00
			On cover		190.00
			Block of 4	160.00	75.00
a.			"ZONE" omitted		7,500.
b.			"4" omitted		7,500.

CANAL

United States Postage Due Stamps Nos. J61, J62b and J65b Overprinted

ZONE

Type A
Letters "A" with Flat Tops

1924, July 1   *Perf. 11*
J12 D2 1c carmine rose *(10,000)*   110.00   27.50
         On cover   100.00
         Block of 4   500.00   125.00
         P# block of 6   1,250.   —
J13 D2 2c deep claret *(25,000)*   60.00   10.00
         On cover   95.00
         Block of 4   300.00   45.00
         P# block of 6   800.00   —
J14 D2 10c deep claret *(30,000)*   250.00   50.00
         On cover   190.00
         Block of 4 (2mm spacing)   1,250.   210.00
         Block of 4 (3mm spacing)   1,250.   210.00
         Margin block of 6, imprint, star
           and P#   3,600.

Values for Nos. J12-J29 on cover are for philatelically con-
trived items. Commercial usages on cover are much more
valuable.

United States Nos. 552, 554 and 562
Overprinted Type A and Additionally
Overprinted at Mount Hope in Red or Blue

**POSTAGE
DUE**

1925, Feb.   *Perf. 11*
J15 A155 1c deep green (R) *(15,000)*   90.00   13.00
         On cover   95.00
         Block of 4   400.00   55.00
         P# block of 6   900.00   —
J16 A157 2c carmine (Bl) *(21,335)*   22.50   7.00
         On cover   67.50
         Block of 4   100.00   30.00
         P# block of 6   225.00   —
J17 A165 10c orange (R) *(39,819)*   50.00   11.00
         On cover   90.00
         Block of 4   250.00   47.50
         P# block of 6   500.00   —
  a.   "POSTAGE DUE" double   450.00
  b.   "E" of "POSTAGE" omitted   450.00
  c.   As "b," "POSTAGE DUE" double   3,250.

Overprinted Type B
Letters "A" with Sharp Pointed Tops
On U.S. Postage Due Stamps Nos. J61, J62, J65,
J65a

1925, June 24
J18 D2 1c carmine rose *(80,000)*   8.00   3.00
         On cover   50.00
         Block of 4   35.00   15.00
         P# block of 6   90.00   —
  a.   "ZONE ZONE" (LR18)   1,250.
J19 D2 2c carmine rose *(146,430)*   15.00   4.00
         On cover   47.50
         Block of 4   65.00   17.50
         P# block of 6   140.00   —
  a.   "ZONE ZONE" (LR18)   1,500.
J20 D2 10c carmine rose *(153,980)*   150.00   20.00
         On cover   120.00
         Block of 4, 2mm spacing   600.00   85.00
         Block of 4, 3mm spacing   625.00   90.00
         P# block of 6, Impt. & Star   1,250.
  a.   Vert. pair, one without ovpt. (10) 1,750.
         P# block of 6, Impt. & Star   18,000.
  b.   10c rose red   250.00   150.00
         On cover   —
  c.   As "b," double overprint   450.   —

Nos. J18-J20 exist with wrong font "CANAL" (UL51) and
"ZONE" (UL82).

POSTAGE DUE

Regular Issue of
1928-29 Surcharged   **10**

1929-30
J21 A37 1c on 5c blue *(35,990)* Mar. 20,
           1930   4.50   1.75
         On cover   37.50
         P# block of 6   45.00
  a.   "POSTAGE DUE" omitted *(5)*   5,500.
J22 A37 2c on 5c blue *(40,207)* Oct. 18,
           1930   7.50   2.50
         On cover   32.50
         P# block of 6   60.00
J23 A37 5c on 5c blue *(35,464)* Dec. 1,
           1930   7.50   2.75
         On cover   32.50
         P# block of 6   75.00
J24 A37 10c on 5c blue *(90,504)* Dec. 16,
           1929   7.50   2.75
         On cover   32.50
         P# block of 6   75.00

On No. J23 the three short horizontal bars in the lower corners of the surcharge are omitted.

Canal Zone Seal — D6

Printed by the U.S. Bureau of Engraving and
Printing.
Plates of 400 subjects, issued in panes of 100.

1932-41   **Flat Plate Printing**
J25 D6 1c claret *(378,300)* Jan. 2, 1932   .20   .20
  a.   Dry printing, red violet   .20   .20
         On cover   32.50
         P# block of 6   3.00
J26 D6 2c claret *(413,800)* Jan. 2, 1932   .20   .20
         On cover   22.50
         P# block of 6   3.00
J27 D6 5c claret Jan. 2, 1932   .35   .20
  a.   Dry printing, red violet   1.00   .30
         On cover   22.50
         P# block of 6   6.00
J28 D6 10c claret *(400,600)* Jan. 2, 1932 1.40   1.50
         On cover   32.50
         P# block of 6   15.00
J29 D6 15c claret Apr. 21, 1941   1.10   1.00
         On cover   37.50
         P# block of 6   12.00
         Nos. J25-J29 (5)   3.25   3.10

See note after No. 114.

OFFICIAL STAMPS

See note at beginning of Air Post Official Stamps

Regular Issues of 1928-34 Overprinted in Black by
the Panama Canal Press, Mount Hope, C.Z.

OFFICIAL

PANAMA	OFFICIAL
CANAL	**PANAMA CANAL**
Type 1	Type 2

Type 1- "PANAMA" 10mm long
Type 1A- "PANAMA" 9mm long

1941, Mar. 31   **Unwmk.**   *Perf. 11*
O1 A35 1c yellow green, type 1 *(87,198)*   2.25   .40
         On cover   70.00
O2 A45 3c deep violet, type 1 *(34,958)*   4.00   .75
         On cover   90.00
O3 A37 5c blue *(19,105)*   1,000.   32.50
         On cover   110.00
O4 A38 10c orange, type 1 *(18,776)*   7.00   1.90
         On cover   200.00
O5 A41 15c gray black, type 1 *(16,888)*   12.50   2.25
         gray   2.25
         On cover   140.00
O6 A42 20c olive brown, type 1 *(20,264)*   15.00   2.75
         On cover   100.00
O7 A44 50c lilac, type 1 *(19,175)*   37.50   5.50
         rose lilac   5.50
O8 A44 50c rose lilac, type 1A *(1000)*   625.00

No. O3 exists with "O" directly over "N" of "PANAMA."

No. 139 Overprinted in Black

1947, Feb.
O9 A65 5c deep blue, type 1 *(21,639)*   9.00   3.50
         On cover   75.00

POST OFFICE SEALS

POS1

Issued in sheets of 8 without gum, imperforate
margins.

1907   **Typo.**   **Unwmk.**   *Perf. 11½*
OX1 POS1   blue   40.00
             Block of 4   175.00
  a.   Wmkd. seal of U.S. in sheet   55.00

No. OX1 clichés are spaced 3½mm apart.

1910
OX2 POS1   ultramarine   70.00   —
             Block of 4, cliches ½mm
               apart   325.00
             Block of 4, cliches 1½mm
               apart horiz., 4mm vert.   800.00
  a.   Wmkd. "Rolleston Mills" in sheet   90.00   —
  b.   Wmkd. U.S. Seal in sheet   225.00   —

POS2

Printed by the Panama Canal Press, Mount Hope,
C.Z.

Issued in sheets of 25, without gum, imperforate
margins.
*Rouletted 6 horizontally in color of seal,
vertically without color*

1917, Sept. 22
OX3 POS2   dark blue   4.00   —
             Block of 4   17.50
  a.   Wmkd. double lined letters in sheet
           ("Sylvania")   35.00

1946   *Rouletted 6, without color*

Issued in sheets of 20, without gum, imperforate margins.
OX4 POS2   slate blue   9.00
             Block of 4   40.00

POS3

Typographed by the Panama Canal Press
Issued in sheets of 32, without gum, imperforate
margins
except at top of sheet.
Size: 46x27mm
Seal Diameter: 13mm

1954, Mar. 8   **Unwmk.**   *Perf. 12½*
OX5 POS3   black *(16,000)*   5.00   —
  a.   Wmkd. Seal of U. S. in sheet   20.00   —

Seal Diameter: 11½mm

1961, May 16   *Perf. 12½*
OX6 POS3   black *(48,000)*   2.50   —
  b.   Wmkd. Seal of U.S. in sheet, perf.
           12½   6.00
  c.   As "a," double impression   80.00
  d.   As "b," double impression   100.00

1974, July 1   *Rouletted 5*
OX7 POS3   black   2.50   —

ENVELOPES

Values for cut squares are for copies with fine margins on all sides. Values for unused entires are for
those without printed or manuscript address. A "full
corner" includes back and side flaps and commands a
premium.

Vasco Núñez de
Balboa — U1

Fernandez de
Córdoba — U2

Envelopes of Panama Lithographed and Overprinted by American Bank Note Co.

1916, Apr. 24

On White Paper

U1	U1	1c **green & black**	15.00	10.00
		Entire	95.00	35.00
a.		Head and overprint only	—	—
		Entire	2,000.	2,000.
b.		Frame only	—	—
		Entire	1,500.	2,500.
U2	U2	2c **carmine & black**	12.50	5.00
		Entire	90.00	25.00
a.		2c **red & black**	12.50	5.00
		Entire	85.00	45.00
b.		Head and overprint only	—	—
		Entire	1,500.	2,000.
c.		Frame only (red)	—	—
		Entire	1,000.	2,000.
d.		Frame double (carmine)	—	—
		Entire	2,500.	2,250.

José Vallarino — U3

"The Land Gate" — U4

1921, Nov. 13

On White Paper

U3	U3	1c **green**	140.00	100.00
		Entire	700.00	375.00
U4	U4	2c **red**	35.00	20.00
		Entire	275.00	125.00

Arms of Panama — U5

Typographed and embossed by American Bank Note Co. with "CANAL ZONE" in color of stamp.

1923, Dec. 15

On White Paper

U5	U5	2c **carmine**	55.00	32.50
		Entire	200.00	125.00

U.S. Nos. U420 and U429 Overprinted in Black by Bureau of Engraving and Printing, Washington, D.C.

CANAL

ZONE

1924, July 1

U6	U92	1c **green** (50,000)	5.00	3.00
		Entire	30.00	19.00
U7	U93	2c **carmine** (100,000)	5.00	3.00
		Entire	30.00	19.00

Seal of Canal Zone — U6

Printed by the Panama Canal Press, Mount Hope, C.Z.

1924, Oct.

On White Paper

U8	U6	1c **green** (205,000)	2.00	1.00
		Entire	24.00	15.00
U9	U6	2c **carmine** (1,997,658)	.75	.40
		Entire	27.50	15.00

Gorgas — U7

Goethals — U8

Typographed and Embossed by International Envelope Corp., Dayton, O.

1932, Apr. 8

U10	U7	1c **green** (1,300,000)	.20	.20
		Entire	3.00	1.10
		Entire, 1st day cancel		35.00
U11	U8	2c **carmine** (400,250)	.25	.20
		Entire	3.50	1.75
		Entire, 1st day cancel		35.00

No. U9 Surcharged in Violet by Panama Canal Press, Mount Hope, C.Z. Numerals 3mm high **3 3**

1932, July 20

U12	U6	3c on 2c **carmine** (20,000)	17.50	7.50
		Entire	225.00	125.00

No. U11 Surcharged in Violet, Numerals 5mm high **3 3**

1932, July 20

U13	U8	3c on 2c **carmine** (320,000)	2.00	1.00
		Entire	25.00	15.00
		Entire, 1st day cancel		75.00

1934, Jan. 17

Numerals with Serifs

U14	U6	3c on 2c **carmine** (Numerals 4mm high) (8,000)	115.00	60.00
		Entire	450.00	525.00
U15	U8	3c on 2c **carmine** (Numerals 5mm high) (23,000)	25.00	15.00
		Entire	250.00	150.00

Typographed and Embossed by International Envelope Corp., Dayton, O.

1934, June 18

U16	U8	3c **purple** (2,450,000)	.20	.20
		Entire	1.20	1.40

1958, Nov. 1

U17	U8	4c **blue** (596,725)	.20	.25
		Entire	1.25	1.25
		Entire, 1st day cancel, Cristobal		2.00

Surcharged at Left of Stamp in Ultra. as No. UX13

1969, Apr. 28

U18	U8	4c +1c **blue** (93,850)	.20	.25
		Entire	1.25	1.60
		Entire, 1st day cancel		1.50
U19	U8	4c +2c **blue** (23,125)	.50	.65
		Entire	2.50	3.25
		Entire, 1st day cancel		1.50

Ship Passing through Gaillard Cut — U9

Typographed and Embossed by United States Envelope Co., Williamsburg, Pa.

1971, Nov. 17

U20	U9	8c **emerald** (121,500)	.25	.30
		Entire	.75	.65
		Entire, 1st day cancel, Balboa (9,650)		1.50

Surcharged at Left of Stamp in Emerald as #UX13

1974, Mar. 2

U21	U9	8c +2c **emerald**	.30	.35
		Entire	1.00	1.40
		Entire, 1st day cancel		1.25

1976, Feb. 23

U22	U9	13c **violet** (638,350)	.35	.40
		Entire	.85	.85
		Entire, 1st day cancel, Balboa (9,181)		1.25

Surcharged at Left of Stamp in Violet as No. UX13

1978, July 5

U23	U9	13c +2c **violet** (245,041)	.35	.40
		Entire	.85	1.40
		Entire, 1st day cancel		1.25

AIR POST ENVELOPES

No. U9 Overprinted with Horizontal Blue and Red Bars Across Entire Face. Overprinted by Panama Canal Press, Mount Hope. Boxed inscription in lower left with nine lines of instructions. Additional adhesives required for air post rate.

1928, May 21

UC1	U6	2c **red**, entire (15,000)	135.00	65.00
		First day cancel		175.00

No. U9 with Similar Overprint of Blue and Red Bars, and "VIA AIR MAIL" in Blue, At Left, no box.

1929

UC2	U6	2c **red**, entire (60,200)	65.00	27.50
a.		Inscription centered (10,000) Jan. 11	325.00	190.00

Earliest known use of No. UC2 is Feb. 6.

DC-4 Skymaster — UC1

Typographed and Embossed by International Envelope Corp., Dayton, O.

1949, Jan. 3

UC3	UC1	6c **blue** (4,400,000)	.25	.25
		Entire	4.00	3.00
		Entire, 1st day cancel		2.00

1958, Nov. 1

UC4	UC1	7c **carmine** (1,000,000)	.25	.20
		Entire	4.00	3.50
		Entire, 1st day cancel		1.50

No. U16 Surcharged at Left of Stamp and Imprinted "VIA AIR MAIL" in Dark Blue

Surcharged by Panama Canal Press, Mount Hope, C.Z.

1963, June 22

UC5	U8	3c + 5c **purple** (105,000)	1.00	1.00
		Entire	6.00	6.50
		Entire, 1st day cancel		5.00
a.		Double surcharge	1,250.	

Jet Liner and Tail Assembly — UC2

Typographed and Embossed by International Envelope Corp., Dayton, O.

1964, Jan. 6

UC6	UC2	8c **deep carmine** (600,000)	.35	.35
		Entire	2.25	2.50
		Entire, 1st day cancel, Balboa (3,855)		2.25

No. U17 Surcharged at Left of Stamp as No. UC5 and Imprinted "VIA AIR MAIL" in Vermilion Surcharged by Canal Zone Press, La Boca, C.Z.

1965, Oct. 15

UC7	U8	4c + 4c **blue** (100,000)	.50	.40
		Entire	4.50	5.50
		Entire, 1st day cancel		5.00

Jet Liner and Tail
Assembly — UC3

Typographed and Embossed by United States
Envelope Co., Williamsburg, Pa.

1966, Feb.
UC8 UC3 8c **carmine** (224,000)   .50   .45
Entire   5.00 5.00
Earliest known use: Feb. 23.

No. UC8 Surcharged at Left of Stamp as No. UX13
in Vermilion
Surcharged by Canal Zone Press, La Boca, C.Z.

1968, Jan. 18
UC9 UC3 8c + 2c **carmine** (376,000)   .40   .35
Entire   2.75 4.00
Entire, 1st day cancel   4.50

No. UC7 with Additional Surcharge at Left
of Stamp as No. UX13 and Imprinted
"VIA AIR MAIL" in Vermilion
Surcharged by Canal Zone Press, La Boca, C.Z.

1968, Feb. 12
UC10 U8 4c + 4c + 2c **blue** (224,150)   .60   .50
Entire   2.25 4.00
Entire, 1st day cancel   5.00

Type of 1966
Typographed and Engraved by United States
Envelope Co., Williamsburg, Pa.

1969, Apr. 1
Luminescent Ink
UC11 UC3 10c **ultramarine** (448,000)   .60   .40
Entire   4.00 4.50
Entire, 1st day cancel, Bal-
boa (9,583)   2.00

No. U17 Surcharged at Left of Stamp as Nos. UC5
and UX13, and Imprinted "VIA AIR MAIL"
in Vermilion

1971, May 17
UC12 U8 4c + 5c + 2c **blue** (55,775)   .75   .50
Entire   4.00 5.00
Entire, 1st day cancel   5.00

No. UC11 Surcharged in Ultra. at Left of Stamp as
No. UX13

1971, May 17
Luminescent Ink
UC13 UC3 10c + 1c **ultramarine** (152,000) .45   .40
Entire   4.00 4.50
Entire, 1st day cancel   3.50

Type of 1966
Typographed and Engraved by United States
Envelope Co., Williamsburg, Pa.

1971, Nov. 17
UC14 UC3 11c **rose red** (258,000)   .30   .20
Entire   1.10 1.25
Entire, 1st day cancel, Bal-
boa (3,451)   1.50
a. 11c **carmine**, stamp tagged,
(395,000)   .30   .20
Entire   1.10 1.25
Entire, 1st day cancel, Bal-
boa (5,971)   1.50

The red diamonds around the envelope edges are luminescent on both Nos. UC14 and UC14a. No. UC14 is size 10, No. UC14a size 6¾.

Surcharged at Left of Stamp in Rose Red as No.
UX13

1974, Mar. 2
UC15 UC3 11c + 2c **carmine**, tagged
(305,000)   .35   .30
Entire   1.50 1.75
Entire, 1st day cancel   1.25
a. 11c + 2c **rose red**, untagged,
(87,000)   .35   .25
Entire   1.75 2.00

No. U21 with Additional Surcharge in Vermilion
at Left of Stamp as No. UX13 and Imprinted
"VIA AIR MAIL" in Vermilion

1975, May 3
UC16 U9 8c + 2c + 3c **emerald** (75,000)   .50   .30
Entire   1.25 1.50
Entire, 1st day cancel   1.50

REGISTRATION ENVELOPES

RE1

Panama Registration Envelope surcharged
by Panama Canal Press, Mount Hope, C.Z.
1918, Oct.   **8mm between CANAL & ZONE**
UF1 RE1 10c on 5c **black & red**, cream
(10,000), entire   1,750. 2,000.
a. 9¼mm between CANAL & ZONE
(25,000), entire ('19)   1,250. 2,000.

Stamped envelopes inscribed "Diez Centesimos," surcharged with numerals "5" and with solid blocks printed over "Canal Zone," were issued by the Republic of Panama after being rejected by the Canal Zone. Parts of "Canal Zone" are often legible under the surcharge blocks. These envelopes exist without surcharge.

POSTAL CARDS

Values are for Entires

Map of Panama — PC1

Panama Card Lithographed by American
Bank Note Co., revalued and surcharged in black
by the Isthmian Canal Commission.

1907, Feb. 9
UX1 PC1 1c on 2c **carmine**, "CANAL"
15mm (50,000)   40.   25.
a. Double surcharge   1,500. 1,500.
b. Double surcharge, one reading down 2,750.
c. Triple surcharge, one reading down 3,300.
d. "CANAL" 13mm (10,000)   250. 200.
e. As "d," double surcharge   2,400.

Balboa — PC2

Panama card lithographed by Hamilton Bank
Note Co. Overprinted in black by Isthmian
Canal Commission.
At least six types of overprint, reading down.

1908, Mar. 3
UX2 PC2 1c **green & black**, "CANAL"
13mm (295,000)   190. 60.
a. Double overprint   2,000. 2,000.
b. Triple overprint   1,750.   —
c. Period after "ZONE" (40,000)   200. 125.
d. "CANAL" 15mm (30,000)   200. 125.
e. "ZONE CANAL", reading up   4,000.

Balboa

PC3   PC4

Lithographed by Hamilton Bank Note Co.
Overprinted in Black by Panama Canal Press, Mount
Hope, C.Z.
1910, Nov. 10
UX3 PC3 1c **green & black** (40,000)   190. 70.
a. Double overprint   4,250.

This card, with overprint reading up, is actually the fourth of seven settings of UX2.

Lithographed and Overprinted by American Bank
Note Co.
1913, Mar. 27
UX4 PC4 1c **green & black** (634,000) 160. 60.

Design of Canal Zone Envelopes
Overprinted in black by the American Bank Note Co.
1921, Oct.
UX5 U3 1c **green**   1,100. 450.

Typographed and embossed by American Bank
Note Co. with "CANAL ZONE" in color of stamp.
1924, Jan.
UX6 U5 1c **green**   725. 1,100.

CANAL

U.S. No. UX27 Overprinted by U.S. Gov't.
Printing Office at Washington, D.C.

ZONE

1924, July 1
UX7 PC17 1c **green**, buff (Jefferson)
(50,000)   85.   35.

Design of Canal Zone Envelope
Printed by Panama Canal Press.
1925, Jan.
UX8 U6 1c **green**, buff (25,000)   80.   35.
a. Background only   1,800.

CANAL

U.S. No. UX27 Overprinted

ZONE

1925, May
UX9 PC17 1c **green**, buff (Jefferson)
(850,000)   8.50 5.00

CANAL

U.S. No. UX27 Overprinted

ZONE

1935, Oct.
UX10 PC17 1c **green**, buff (Jefferson)
(2,900,000)   1.80 1.80
a. Double overprint   1,900.

Used values are for contemporaneous usage without additional postage applied.

Same on U.S. No. UX38
1952, May 1
UX11 PC22 2c **carmine rose**, buff (Franklin)
(800,000)   2.00 2.00
1st day cancel, Balboa Heights   3.50

Ship in
Lock — PC5

Printed by Bureau of Engraving & Printing,
Washington, D.C.
1958, Nov. 1
UX12 PC5 3c **dark blue**, buff (335,116) 1.85 2.50
First day cancel, Cristobal   1.25

No. UX12 Surcharged at Left of
Stamp in Green by Panama Canal
Press, Mount Hope, C.Z.

1963, July 27
UX13 PC5 3c + 1c **dark blue**, *buff (78,000)* 4.00 *5.00*
First day cancel *3.50*

Ship Passing through
Panama Canal — PC6

Printed by Panama Canal Press, Mount Hope, C.Z.
1964, Dec. 1
UX14 PC6 4c **violet blue**, *buff (74,200)* 3.75 *5.00*
1st day cancel, Cristobal
(19,260) *3.50*

Ship in Lock
(Towing locomotive
at right
redrawn) — PC7

Printed by Bureau of Engraving & Printing,
Washington, D.C.
1965, Aug. 12
UX15 PC7 4c **emerald** *(95,500)* 1.10 *1.60*
1st day cancel, Cristobal
(20,366) *1.00*

No. UX15 Surcharged at Left of Stamp in Green
as No. UX13 by Canal Zone Press, La Boca, C.Z.
1968, Feb. 12
UX16 PC7 4c + 1c **emerald** *(94,775)* 1.10 *2.25*
First day cancel *1.00*

Ship-in-Lock Type of 1965
1969, Apr. 1
UX17 PC7 5c **light ultramarine** *(63,000)* 1.00 *1.60*
1st day cancel, Balboa *(11,835)* *1.00*

No. UX17 Surcharged at Left of Stamp in Light
Ultramarine as No. UX13
1971, May 24
UX18 PC7 5c + 1c **light ultramarine**
(100,500) .90 *2.25*
First day cancel *1.00*

Ship-in-Lock Type of 1965
Printed by Bureau of Engraving & Printing,
Washington, D.C.
1974, Feb. 11
UX19 PC7 8c **brown** *(90,895)* .90 *1.40*
1st day cancel, Balboa *(10,375)* *1.00*

No. UX19 Surcharged at Left of Stamp in Brown as
No. UX13
1976, June 1
UX20 PC7 8c + 1c **brown** *(60,249)* .65 *2.25*
First day cancel *1.00*

No. UX19 Surcharged at Left of Stamp in Brown as
No. UX13
1978, July 5
UX21 PC7 8c + 2c **brown** *(74,847)* .85 *2.25*
First day cancel *1.00*

AIR POST POSTAL CARDS

Plane, Flag and
Map — APC1

Printed by Bureau of Engraving & Printing,
Washington, D.C.
1958, Nov. 1
UXC1 APC1 5c **blue & carmine rose**
(104,957) 3.75 *6.50*
1st day cancel, Balboa *3.75*

No. UXC1 Surcharged at Left of Stamp in Green
as No. UX13 by Panama Canal Press,
Mount Hope, C.Z.
1963, July 27
UXC2 APC1 5c + 1c **blue & carmine rose**
(48,000) 9.50 *16.50*
a. Inverted surcharge *1,500.*
First day cancel *5.00*

No. UX15 Surcharged at Left of Stamp as
No. UX13 and Imprinted "AIR MAIL" in Vermilion
1965, Aug. 18
UXC3 PC7 4c + 2c **emerald** *(41,700)* 4.00 *16.50*
First day cancel *6.00*

No. UX15 Surcharged at Left of Stamp as No. UC5
and Imprinted "AIR MAIL" in Vermilion
by Canal Zone Press, La Boca, C.Z.
1968, Feb. 12
UXC4 PC7 4c + 4c **emerald** *(60,100)* 2.75 *13.50*
First day cancel *6.00*

No. UX17 Surcharged at Left of Stamp as No. UC5
and Imprinted "AIR MAIL" in Vermilion
1971, May 24
UXC5 PC7 5c + 4c **light ultramarine**
(68,000) 1.00 *11.00*
First day cancel *6.00*

PROOFS
1928-40

Column (1)- Large Die
Column (2)- Small Die

		(1)	(2)
106TC	2c black	1,250.	
113P	30c brown black		950.

1934
| 117P | 3c deep violet *(8)* | 450. | |

1939
120P	1c yellow green		850.
121P	2c rose carmine		850.
122P	3c purple	1,250.	850.
123P	5c dark blue	1,250.	850.
124P	6c red orange		850.
125P	7c black		850.
126P	8c green	1,250.	850.
127P	10c ultramarine	1,250.	850.
128P	11c blue green	1,250.	850.
129P	12c brown carmine	1,250.	850.
130P	14c dark violet		850.
131P	15c olive green		850.
132P	18c rose pink		850.
133P	20c brown	1,250.	850.
134P	25c orange	1,250.	850.
135P	50c violet brown	1,250.	850.

1946-48
136P	½c bright red	1,250.	
137P	1½c chocolate	1,250.	
139P	5c deep blue	1,250.	
140P	25c yellow green	1,250.	
141P	10c black	800.	

1949
142P	3c blue	1,100.	
143P	6c violet	1,100.	
144P	12c bright blue green	1,100.	
145P	18c deep red lilac	1,100.	

Air Post
1931-49
C6P	4c red violet	1,500.	
C7P	5c light green	1,500.	
C8P	6c yellow brown	1,500.	
C13TC	40c orange	1,500.	

1939
C15P	5c greenish black		900.
C15TC	5c scarlet	1,250.	
C16P	10c dull violet	1,250.	900.
C17P	15c light brown		900.
C18P	25c blue		900.
C19P	30c rose carmine	1,250.	900.
C20P	$1 green	1,250.	900.

1951
| C21P | 4c red violet | 1,250. | |

The Small Die proofs listed are on soft yellowish wove paper. Only No. 117P has more than two copies reported in private collections.

CUBA

After the U.S. battleship "Maine" was destroyed in Havana harbor with a loss of 266 lives in February, 1898, the United States demanded the withdrawal of Spanish troops from Cuba. The Spanish-American War followed. With the peace treaty of Dec. 10, 1898, Spain relinquished Cuba to the United States in trust for its inhabitants. On Jan. 1, 1899, Spanish authority was succeeded by U.S. military rule which lasted until May 20, 1902, when Cuba, as a republic, assumed self-government.

The listings in this catalogue cover the U.S. Administration issue of 1899, the Republic's 1899-1902 issues under U.S. military rule and the Puerto Principe issue of provincial provisionals.

Values for Nos. 176-220 are for stamps in the grade of fine and in sound condition where such exist. Values for Nos. 221-UX2b are for very fine examples.

100 CENTS = 1 DOLLAR

Puerto Principe Issue
In December, 1898, Puerto Principe, a provincial capital now called Camagüey, ran short of 1c, 2c, 3c, 5c and 10c stamps. The Postmaster ordered Cuban stamps to be surcharged on Dec. 19, 1898.
The surcharging was done to horizontal strips of five stamps, so vertical pairs and blocks do not exist. Five types are found in each setting, and five printings were made. Counterfeits are plentiful.

First Printing
Black Surcharge, 17½mm high
Surcharge measures 17½mm high and is roughly printed in dull black ink.

HABILITADO HABILITADO HABILITADO HABILITADO HABILITADO
2 **2** **2** **2** **2**
cents. cents. cents. cents. cents.
Position 1 Position 2 Position 3 Position 4 Position 5

Position 1 -No serif at right of "t"
Position 2 -Thin numeral except on 1c on 1m No. 176
Position 3 -Broken right foot of "n"
Position 4 -Up-stroke of "t" broken
Position 5 -Broken "DO"

This printing consisted of the following stamps:

176	1c on 1m orange brown, Pos. 1, 2, 3, 4 and 5		
178	2c on 2m orange brown, Pos. 1, 3, 4 and 5		
179	2c on 2m orange brown, Pos. 2		
180	3c on 3m orange brown, Pos. 1, 3, 4 and 5		
181	3c on 3m orange brown, Pos. 2		
188	5c on 5m orange brown, Pos. 1, 3, 4 and 5		
189	5c on 5m orange brown, Pos. 2		

Second Printing
Black Surcharge, 17½mm high

This printing was from the same setting as used for the first printing, but the impression is much clearer and the ink quite shiny.

The printing consisted of the following stamps:

179F	3c on 2m orange brown, Pos. 1, 3, 4 and 5
179G	3c on 2m orange brown, Pos. 2
182	5c on 1m orange brown, Pos. 1, 3, 4 and 5
183	5c on 1m orange brown, Pos. 2
184	5c on 2m orange brown, Pos. 1, 3, 4 and 5
185	5c on 2m orange brown, Pos. 2
186	5c on 3m orange brown, Pos. 1, 3, 4 and 5
187	5c on 3m orange brown, Pos. 2
188	5c on 5m orange brown, Pos. 1, 3, 4 and 5
189	5c on 5m orange brown, Pos. 2
190	5c on ½m blue green, Pos. 1, 3, 4 and 5
191	5c on ½m blue green, Pos. 2

Third Printing
Red Surcharge, 20mm high

The same setting as for the first and second was used for the third printing. The 10c denomination first appeared in this printing and position 2 of that value has numerals same as on positions 1, 3, 4 and 5, while position 4 has broken "1" in "10."

The printing consisted of the following stamps:

196	3c on 1c black violet, Pos. 1, 3, 4 and 5
197	3c on 1c black violet, Pos. 2
198	5c on 1c black violet, Pos. 1, 3, 4 and 5
199	5c on 1c black violet, Pos. 2
200	10c on 1c black violet, Pos. 1, 2, 3 and 5
200a	10c on 1c black violet, Pos. 4

Fourth Printing
Black Surcharge, 19½mm high

The same type as before but spaced between so that the surcharge is 2mm taller. Clear impression, shiny ink.

HABILITADO   HABILITADO   HABILITADO
1   **1**   **1**
cents.   cents.   cents.
Position 1   Position 2   Position 3

HABILITADO   HABILITADO
1   **1**
cents.   cents.
Position 4   Position 5

Position 1	-No serif at right of "t"
Position 2	-Broken "1" on No. 177
Position 2	-Thin numerals on 5c stamps
Position 3	-Broken right foot of "n"
Position 4	-Up-stroke of "t" broken
Position 4	-Thin numeral on 3c stamps
Position 5	-Broken "DO"

This printing consisted of the following stamps:

177	1c on 1m orange brn, Pos. 1, 3, 4 and 5
177a	1c on 1m orange brn, Pos. 2
179B	3c on 1m orange brn, Pos. 1, 2, 3 and 5
179D	3c on 1m orange brn, Pos. 4
183B	5c on 1m orange brn, Pos. 1, 3, 4 and 5
189C	5c on 5m orange brn, Pos. 1, 3, 4 and 5
192	5c on ½m blue green, Pos. 1, 3, 4 and 5
193	5c on ½m blue green, Pos. 2

Fifth Printing
Black Surcharge, 19½mm high

HABILITADO   HABILITADO   HABILITADO
3   **3**   **3**
cents.   cents.   eents.
Position 1   Position 2   Position 3

HABILITADO   HABILITADO
3   **3**
cents.   cents.
Position 4   Position 5

Position 1	-Nick in bottom of "e" and lower serif of "s"
Position 2	-Normal surcharge
Position 3	-"eents"
Position 4	-Thin numeral
Position 5	-Nick in upper part of right stroke of "n"

This printing consisted of the following stamps:

201	3c on 1m blue green, Pos. 1, 2 and 5
201b	3c on 1m blue green, Pos. 3
202	3c on 1m blue green, Pos. 4
203	3c on 2m blue green, Pos. 1, 2 and 5
203a	3c on 2m blue green, Pos. 3
204	3c on 2m blue green, Pos. 4
205	3c on 3m blue green, Pos. 1, 2 and 5
205b	3c on 3m blue green, Pos. 3
206	3c on 3m blue green, Pos. 4
211	5c on 1m blue green, Pos. 1, 2 and 5
211a	5c on 1m blue green, Pos. 3
212	5c on 1m blue green, Pos. 4
213	5c on 2m blue green, Pos. 1, 2 and 5
213a	5c on 2m blue green, Pos. 3
214	5c on 2m blue green, Pos. 4
215	5c on 3m blue green, Pos. 1, 2 and 5
215a	5c on 3m blue green, Pos. 3
216	5c on 3m blue green, Pos. 4
217	5c on 4m blue green, Pos. 1, 2 and 5
217a	5c on 4m blue green, Pos. 3
218	5c on 4m blue green, Pos. 4
219	5c on 8m blue green, Pos. 1, 2 and 5
219b	5c on 8m blue green, Pos. 3
220	5c on 8m blue green, Pos. 4

Counterfeits exist of all Puerto Principe surcharges. Illustrations have been altered to discourage further counterfeiting.

Regular Issues of Cuba of 1896 and 1898 Surcharged:

HABILITADO   HABILITADO
1   **1**
cent.   cents.
a   b

Numeral in ( ) after color indicates printing.

1898-99
Black Surcharge on Nos. 156-158, 160

176	(a)	1 cent on 1m orange brn (1)	50.00	30.00
177	(b)	1 cents on 1m org brn (4)	45.00	35.00
a.		Broken figure "1"	75.00	65.00
b.		Inverted surcharge		200.00
d.		Same as "a" inverted		250.00

HABILITADO   HABILITADO
2   **2**
cents.   cents.
c   d

178	(c)	2c on 2m orange brown (1)	22.50	18.00
a.		Inverted surcharge	250.00	50.00
179	(d)	2c on 2m orange brown (1)	40.00	35.00
a.		Inverted surcharge	350.00	100.00

HABILITADO   HABILITADO
3   **3**
cents.   cents.
k   l

179B	(k)	3c on 1m orange brown (4)	300.	175.
c.		Double surcharge	1,500.	750.

An unused copy is known with "cents" omitted.

179D	(l)	3c on 1m orange brown (4)	1,500.	675.
e.		Double surcharge		—

HABILITADO   HABILITADO
3   **3**
cents.   cents.
e   f

179F	(e)	3c on 2m orange brown (2)		1,500.

Value is for copy with minor faults.

179G	(f)	3c on 2m orange brown (2)	—	2,000.

Value is for copy with minor faults.

180	(e)	3c on 3m orange brown (1)	27.50	30.
a.		Inverted surcharge		110.
181	(f)	3c on 3m orange brown (1)	75.	75.
a.		Inverted surcharge		200.

HABILITADO   HABILITADO
5   **5**
cents.   cents.
g   h

HABILITADO   HABILITADO
5   **5**
cents.   cents.
i   j

182	(g)	5c on 1m orange brown (2)	700.	200.
a.		Inverted surcharge		500.
183	(h)	5c on 1m orange brown (2)	1,300.	500.
a.		Inverted surcharge		700.
184	(g)	5c on 2m orange brown (2)	750.	250.
185	(g)	5c on 2m orange brown (2)	1,500.	500.
186	(g)	5c on 3m orange brown (2)		175.
a.		Inverted surcharge		700.
187	(h)	5c an 3m orange brown (2)		400.
a.		Inverted surcharge		1,000.
188	(g)	5c on 5m orange brown (1) (2)	80.	60.
a.		Inverted surcharge	400.	200.
b.		Double surcharge	—	
189	(g)	5c on 5m orange brown (1) (2)	350.	250.
a.		Inverted surcharge		400.
b.		Double surcharge	—	
189C	(i)	5c on 5m orange brown (4)		7,500.

Values for Nos. 188, 189 are for the first printing.

Black Surcharge on No. P25

190	(g)	5c on ½m blue green (2)	250.	75.
a.		Inverted surcharge	500.	150.
b.		Pair, one without surcharge		500.
191	(h)	5c on ½m blue green (2)	300.	90.
a.		Inverted surcharge		200.
192	(i)	5c on ½m blue green (4)	550.	200.
a.		Double surcharge, one diagonal		11,500.

Value for No. 190b is for pair with unsurcharged copy at right. One pair with unsurcharged copy at left is known.

No. 192a is unique.

193	(j)	5c on ½m blue green (4)	800.	300.

Red Surcharge on No. 161

196	(k)	3c on 1c black violet (3)	65.	35.
a.		Inverted surcharge		300.
197	(l)	3c on 1c black violet (3)	125.	55.
a.		Inverted surcharge		300.
198	(i)	5c on 1c black violet (3)	25.	30.
a.		Inverted surcharge		125.
b.		Vertical surcharge		3,500.
c.		Double surcharge	400.	600.
d.		Double inverted surcharge		—
199	(j)	5c on 1c black violet (3)	55.	55.
a.		Inverted surcharge		250.
b.		Vertical surcharge		2,000.
c.		Double surcharge	1,000.	600.

Value for No. 198b is for surcharge reading up. One copy is known with surcharge reading down.

HABILITADO
10
cents.
m

200	(m)	10c on 1c black violet (3)	20.	50.
a.		Broken figure "1"	40.	100.

Black Surcharge on Nos. P26-P30

201	(k)	3c on 1m blue green (5)	350.	350.
a.		Inverted surcharge		450.
b.		"EENTS"	550.	450.
c.		As "b," inverted		850.
202	(l)	3c on 1m blue green (5)	550.	400.
a.		Inverted surcharge		850.
203	(k)	3c on 2m blue green (5)	850.	350.
a.		"EENTS"	1,250.	500.
b.		Inverted surcharge		850.
c.		As "a," inverted		950.
204	(l)	3c on 2m blue green (5)	1,250.	600.
a.		Inverted surcharge		750.
205	(k)	3c on 3m blue green (5)	900.	350.
a.		Inverted surcharge		500.
b.		"EENTS"	1,250.	450.
c.		As "b," inverted		700.
206	(l)	3c on 3m blue green (5)	1,200.	550.
a.		Inverted surcharge		700.
211	(i)	5c on 1m blue green (5)		1,800.
a.		"EENTS"	—	2,500.

212	(j)	5c on 1m **blue green** (5)		2,250.	
213	(i)	5c on 2m **blue green** (5)		1,800.	
a.		"EENTS"		—	1,900.
214	(i)	5c on 2m **blue green** (5)		1,750.	
215	(i)	5c on 3m **blue green** (5)		550.	
a.		"EENTS"		—	1,000.
216	(j)	5c on 3m **blue green** (5)		1,000.	
217	(i)	5c on 4m **blue green** (5)	2,500.	900.	
a.		"EENTS"	3,000.	1,500.	
b.		Inverted surcharge		2,000.	
c.		As "a," inverted		2,000.	
218	(j)	5c on 4m **blue green** (5)		1,250.	
a.		Inverted surcharge		2,000.	
219	(i)	5c on 8m **blue green** (5)	2,500.	1,250.	
a.		Inverted surcharge		1,500.	
b.		"EENTS"		—	1,800.
c.		As "b," inverted		2,500.	
220	(j)	5c on 8m **blue green** (5)		2,000.	
a.		Inverted surcharge		2,500.	

Puerto Principe pairs, strips and stamps properly canceled on cover are scarce and command high premiums.

Most copies of all but the most common varieties are faulty or have tropical toning. Values are for sound copies where they exist.

CUBA

United States Stamps Nos. 279, 267, 267b, 279Bf, 279Bh, 268, 281, 282C and 283 Surcharged in Black

1 c.
de PESO.

1899		**Wmk. 191**		**Perf. 12**
221	A87	1c on 1c **yellow green**	5.25	.35
		On cover		15.00
		Block of 4	27.50	4.50
		P# strip of 3, Impt.	57.50	
		P# block of 6, Impt.	300.00	
222	A88	2c on 2c **reddish carmine,**		
		type III, *Feb.*	10.00	.75
		On cover		22.50
		Block of 4	55.00	8.00
		P# strip of 3, Impt.	115.00	
		P# block of 6, Impt.	700.00	
b.		2c on 2c vermilion, type III, *Feb.*	10.00	.75
222A	A88	2c on 2c **reddish carmine,**		
		type IV, *Feb.*	5.75	.40
		On cover		12.50
		Block of 4	30.00	4.50
		P# strip of 3, Impt.	65.00	
		P# block of 6, Impt.	425.00	
		"CUBA" at bottom	600.00	
		"CUPA" (broken letter. pos. 99)	175.00	
c.		2c on 2c vermilion, type IV, *Feb.*	5.75	.40
d.		As No. 222A, inverted surcharge	3,500.	3,500.
223	A88	2½c on 2c **reddish carmine,**		
		type III, *Jan. 2*	5.00	.80
		On cover		20.00
		Block of 4	27.50	8.00
		P# strip of 3, Impt.	90.00	
		P# block of 6, Impt.	350.00	
b.		2½ on 2c vermilion, type III, *Jan. 2*	5.00	.80
223A	A88	2½c on 2c **reddish carmine,**		
		type IV, *Jan. 2*	3.50	.50
		On cover		12.50
		Block of 4	20.00	4.50
		P# strip of 3, Impt.	62.50	
		P# block of 6, Impt.	250.00	
c.		2½c on 2c vermilion, type IV, *Jan. 2*	3.50	.50

All 2½c stamps were sold and used as 2 centavo stamps.

224	A89	3c on 3c **purple**	12.50	1.75
		On cover		25.00
		Block of 4	62.50	14.00
		P# strip of 3, Impt.	110.00	
		P# block of 6, Impt.	675.00	
a.		Period between "B" and "A"	37.50	35.00

Two types of surcharge
I - "3" directly over "P"
II - "3" to left over "P"

225	A91	5c on 5c **blue**	12.50	2.00
		On cover		30.00
		Block of 4	62.50	12.50
		P# strip of 3, Impt.	190.00	
		P# block of 6, Impt.	800.00	—
		"CUBA" at bottom		—
		"CUPA" (broken letter)	70.00	40.00
226	A94	10c on 10c **brown,** type I	22.50	6.50
		On cover		100.00
		Block of 4	100.00	40.00
		P# strip of 3, Impt.	260.00	
		P# block of 6, Impt.	1,150.	
		"CUBA" at bottom	325.00	325.00
b.		"CUBA" omitted	4,000.	4,000.
226A	A94	10c on 10c **brown,** type II	6,000.	
		Block of 4	—	
		Nos. 221-226 (8)	77.00	13.05

No. 226A exists only in the special printing.

Special Printing

In March 1900, one pane of 100 each of Nos. 221-225, 226A, J1-J4 and two panes of 50 of No. E1, were specially overprinted for displays at the Paris Exposition (1900) and Pan American Exposition (1901). The 2c pane was light red, type IV. Copies were hand-stamped type E "Specimen" in black ink by H. G. Mandel in separate displays for the two Expositions. Additional copies from each pane were also handstamped "specimen," but most were destroyed after the Expositions. Nearly all copies remaining bear impression of a dealer's handstamp reading "Special Surcharge" in red ink on the back. Value: Nos. 221-225, J1-J4, each $600; No. E1, $1,000.

Issues of the Republic under US Military Rule

Statue of Columbus
A20

Royal Palms
A21

Allegory, "Cuba"
A22

Ocean Liner
A23

Cane Field — A24

Re-engraved

The re-engraved stamps issued by the Republic of Cuba in 1905-07 may be distinguished from the Issue of 1899 as follows:

Nos. 227-231 are watermarked U S-C
The re-engraved stamps are unwatermarked.

1c: The ends of the label inscribed "Centavo" are rounded instead of square.

2c: The foliate ornaments, inside the oval disks bearing the numerals of value, have been removed.

5c: Two lines forming a right angle have been added in the upper corners of the label bearing the word "Cuba."

10c: A small ball has been added to each of the square ends of the label bearing the word "Cuba."

No. 227

Re-engraved

No. 228

Re-engraved

No. 230

Re-engraved

No. 231

Re-engraved

Printed by the US Bureau of Engraving and Printing

1899		**Wmk. US-C (191C)**		**Perf. 12**
227	A20	1c **yellow green**	3.50	.20
		On cover		2.00
		Block of 4	15.00	1.00
		P# block of 10, Impt., type VII	225.00	—
228	A21	2c **carmine**	3.50	.20
		On cover		2.00
		Block of 4	15.00	1.00

		P# block of 10, Impt., type VII	180.00	—
a.		2c **scarlet**	3.50	.20
b.		Booklet pane of 6	2,000.	
229	A22	3c **purple**	3.50	.20
		On cover		4.00
		Block of 4	15.00	2.50
		P# block of 10, Impt., type VII	275.00	—
230	A23	5c **blue**	4.50	.20
		On cover		4.00
		Block of 4	21.00	2.50
		P# block of 10, Impt., type VII	450.00	—
231	A24	10c **brown**	11.00	.50
		On cover		6.50
		Block of 4	52.50	5.50
		P# block of 10, Impt., type VII	1,200.	—
		Nos. 227-231 (5)	26.00	1.30

SPECIAL DELIVERY

Issued under Administration of the United States

CUBA.

Special Delivery Stamp of the United States No. E5 Surcharged in Red

10 c.
de PESO.

1899		**Wmk. 191**		**Perf. 12**
E1	SD3	10c on 10c **blue**	130.	100.
		On cover		450.
		Block of 4	575.	
		Margin block of 4, arrow	650.	
		P# strip of 3, Impt.	1,000.	
		P# block of 6, Impt.	6,000.	
a.		No period after "CUBA"	450.	400.

Issue of the Republic under US Military Rule

Special Delivery Messenger — SD2

Printed by the US Bureau of Engraving and Printing

1899		**Wmk. US-C (191C)**		
		Inscribed: "Immediata"		
E2	SD2	10c **orange**	45.00	15.00
		On cover		150.00
		Block of 4	200.00	—
		P# strip of 3, Impt., type VII	250.00	
		P# block of 6, Impt., type VII	900.00	

Re-engraved

In 1902 the Republic of Cuba issued a stamp of design SD2 re-engraved with word correctly spelled "Immediata." The corrected die was made in 1899 (See No. E3P). It was printed by the U.S. Bureau of Engraving and Printing.

POSTAGE DUE

Issued under Administration of the United States
Postage Due Stamps of the United States Nos. J38, J39, J41 and J42 Surcharged in Black Like Regular Issue of Same Date

1899		**Wmk. 191**		**Perf. 12**
J1	D2	1c on 1c **deep claret**	45.00	5.25
		Block of 4	210.00	45.00
		P# block of 6, Impt.	900.00	
J2	D2	2c on 2c **deep claret**	45.00	5.25
		Block of 4	200.00	30.00
		P# block of 6, Impt.	900.00	
a.		Inverted surcharge		2,750.
J3	D2	5c on 5c **deep claret**	45.00	5.25
		Block of 4	220.00	45.00
		P# block of 6, Impt.	900.00	
		"CUPA" (broken letter)	150.00	140.00
J4	D2	10c on 10c **deep claret**	27.50	2.50
		Block of 4	125.00	27.50
		P# block of 6, Impt.	850.00	

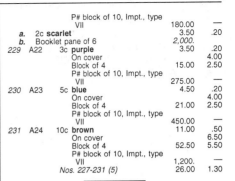

United States Administration of Cuba stamps can be mounted in the Scott U.S. Possessions album.

ENVELOPES

Values are for Cut Squares
US Envelopes of 1887-99 Surcharged

CUBA.   CUBA.

1c. DE PESO.   2c. DE PESO.
    a   b

1899

U1	U77 (a)	1c on 1c **green**, *buff* (No. U354)	5.00	3.50
		Entire	12.00	15.00
U2	U77 (a)	1c on 1c **green**, *blue* (No. U355)	3.25	2.50
		Entire	5.00	6.50
a.		Double surcharge, entire	3,750.	
U3	U71 (b)	2c on 2c **green** (No. U311)	1.50	1.10
		Entire	3.00	3.50
a.		Double surcharge, entire	3,750.	3,750.
U4	U71 (b)	2c on 2c **green**, *amber* (No. U312)	2.75	1.65
		Entire	5.25	6.00
a.		Double surcharge, entire	3,750.	
U5	U71 (a)	2c on 2c **green**, *buff* (No. U313)	17.50	8.00
		Entire	47.50	47.50
U6	U79 (a)	2c on 2c **carmine**, *amber* (No. U363)	17.50	17.50
		Entire	47.50	47.50
U7	U79 (a)	2c on 2c **carmine**, *buff* (No. U364)	25.00	25.00
		Entire	100.00	80.00
U8	U79 (a)	2c on 2c **carmine**, *blue* (No. U365)	3.00	2.00
		Entire	7.00	8.00
a.		Double surcharge, entire	3,750.	
		Nos. U1-U8 (8)	75.50	61.25

In addition to the envelopes listed above, several others are known but were not regularly issued. They are:
1c on 1c green
1c on 1c green, *manila*
2c on 2c carmine
2c on 2c carmine, *oriental buff*
2c on 2c carmine, *blue*
4c on 4c brown
5c on 5c blue

Issue of the Republic under US Military Rule

Columbus — E1

Similar envelopes without watermark on white and amber papers, were issued by the Republic after Military Rule ended in 1902.

1899   Wmk. "US POD '99" in Monogram

U9	E1	1c **green**	.75	.65
		Entire	4.00	4.00
U10	E1	1c **green**, *amber*	1.00	.65
		Entire	4.00	4.00
U11	E1	1c **green**, *buff*	17.50	13.00
		Entire	85.00	42.50
U12	E1	1c **green**, *blue*	25.00	15.00
		Entire	85.00	42.50
U13	E1	2c **carmine**	1.00	.70
		Entire	3.75	3.00
U14	E1	2c **carmine**, *amber*	1.00	.70
		Entire	3.75	3.00
U15	E1	2c **carmine**, *buff*	9.00	7.75
		Entire	35.00	21.00
U16	E1	2c **carmine**, *blue*	25.00	18.00
		Entire	60.00	52.50
U17	E1	5c **blue**	3.25	2.25
		Entire	5.00	2.75
U18	E1	5c **blue**, *amber*	6.00	4.00
		Entire	9.00	5.75
		Nos. U9-U18 (10)	89.50	62.70

WRAPPERS
Issue of the Republic under US Military Rule

1899

W1	E1	1c **green**, *manila*	4.00	10.00
		Entire	11.00	50.00
W2	E1	2c **carmine**, *manila*	12.00	10.00
		Entire	25.00	50.00

POSTAL CARDS

Values are for Entires
US Postal Cards Nos. UX14, UX16 Surcharged

CUBA. 1c. de Peso.

UX1	PC8	1c on 1c **black**, *buff*, Jefferson (1,000,000)	15.00	16.50
a.		No period after "1c"	40.00	75.00
b.		No period after "Peso"	35.00	
c.		Surcharge "2c" (error)	6,500.	
UX2	PC3	2c on 2c **black**, *buff*, Liberty (583,000)	15.00	16.50
a.		No period after "Peso"	40.00	75.00
b.		Double surcharge	—	

In 1904 the Republic of Cuba revalued remaining stocks of No. UX2 by means of a perforated numeral "1."

PROOFS

1899

Column (1)- Large Die
Column (2)- Small Die

227P	1c	yellow green	150.	150.
227TC	1c	blue green	350.	
227TC	1c	black	600.	
228P	2c	carmine	150.	150.
228TC	2c	black	600.	
229P	3c	purple	150.	150.
229TC	3c	black	350.	
230P	5c	blue	150.	150.
230TC	5c	black	600.	
231P	10c	nrown	150.	150.
231TC	10c	gray	600.	
231TC	10c	black	600.	

Special Delivery

E2TC	10c	blue	1,000.	
E3P	10c	orange	350.	300.

SPECIMEN STAMPS

Overprinted Type E in Purple   Specimen.

1899

221S	E	1c on 1c **yellow green**		150.
222AS	E	2c on 2c **reddish carmine**, type IV		150.
223AS	E	2½c on 2c **reddish carmine**, type IV		150.
224S	E	3c on 3c **purple**		150.
225S	E	5c on 5c **blue**		150.
226S	E	10c on 10c **brown**, type I		150.
226AS	E	10c on 10c **brown**, type II		3,500.

See note after No. 226A for Special Printings with black "Specimen" overprints.

1899

227S	E	1c **yellow green**	200.
228S	E	2c **carmine**	200.
229S	E	3c **purple**	200.
230S	E	5c **blue**	200.
231S	E	10c **brown**	200.

Special Delivery

1899

E1S	E	10c on 10c **blue**	550.
E2S	E	10c **orange**	350.

Postage Due

1899

J1S	E	1c on 1c **deep claret**	250.
J2S	E	2c on 2c **deep claret**	250.
J3S	E	5c on 5c **deep claret**	250.
J4S	E	10c on 10c **deep claret**	250.

Black "Specimen" overprint known on all stamps of the Special Printing.

DANISH WEST INDIES

Formerly a Danish colony, these islands were purchased by the United States in 1917 and have since been known as the U.S. Virgin Islands. They lie east of Puerto Rico, have an area of 132 square miles and had a population of 27,086 in 1911. The capital is Charlotte Amalie (also called St. Thomas). Stamps of Danish West Indies were replaced by those of the United States in 1917.

100 CENTS = 1 DOLLAR
100 BIT = 1 FRANC (1905)

Coat of
Arms — A1

Wmk. 111-
Small Crown

1856   Typo.   Wmk. 111   Imperf.
Yellowish Paper
Yellow Wavy-line Burelage, UL to LR

1	A1	3c **dark carmine**, *brown gum*	175.	175.
		On cover		2,500.
		Block of 4	1,000.	
a.		3c **dark carmine**, *yellow gum*	200.	200.
		On cover		2,500.
		Block of 4	2,750.	
b.		3c **carmine**, *white gum*	4,500.	—
		On cover		—

The brown and yellow gums were applied locally.
Reprint: 1981, carmine, back-printed across two stamps ("Reprint by Dansk Post og Telegrafmuseum 1978"), value, pair, $10.

1866
White Paper
Yellow Wavy-line Burelage UR to LL

2	A1	3c **rose**	45.	60.
		On cover		2,500.
		Block of 4	225.	300.
		Rouletted 4½ privately	250.	150.
		On cover, rouletted 4½		2,500.
		Rouletted 9	275.	175.

The value for used blocks is for favor cancel (CTO).
No. 2 reprints, unwatermarked: 1930, carmine, value $100. 1942, rose carmine, back-printed across each row ("Nytryk 1942 G. A. Hagemann Danmark og Dansk Vestindiens Frimaerker Bind 2"), value $50.

1872 — *Perf. 12½*

3	A1	3c **rose**	85.	150.
		On cover		10,000.
		Block of 4	575.	

1873

Without Burelage

4	A1	4c **dull blue**	175.	325.
		On cover		—
		Block of 4	1,100.	
a.		Imperf., pair	750.	
b.		Horiz. pair, imperf. vert.	550.	

The 1930 reprint of No. 4 is ultramarine, unwatermarked and imperf., value $100.

The 1942 4c reprint is blue, unwatermarked, imperf. and has printing on back (see note below No. 2), value $50.

Numeral of Value — A2

NORMAL FRAME INVERTED FRAME

The arabesques in the corners have a main stem and a branch. When the frame is in normal position, in the upper left corner the branch leaves the main stem half way between two little leaflets. In the lower right corner the branch starts at the foot of the second leaflet. When the frame is inverted the corner designs are, of course, transposed.

The central element in the fan-shaped scrollwork at the outside of the lower left corner of Nos. 5a and 7b looks like an elongated diamond.

Wmk. 112- Crown

1874-79   **Wmk. 112**   *Perf. 14x13½*

White Wove Paper, Printings 1-3 Thin, 4-7 Medium, 8-9 Thick

1c	Nine printings
3c	Eight printings
4c	Two printings
5c	Six printings
7c	Two printings
10c	Seven printings
12c	Two printings
14c	One printing
50c	Two printings

Values for inverted frames, covers and blocks are for the cheapest variety.

5	A2	1c **green & brown red**	20.00	27.50
		On cover		150.00
		Block of 4	85.00	225.00
a.		1c green & rose lilac, thin paper	85.00	140.00
b.		1c green & red violet, medium paper	50.00	75.00
c.		1c green & claret, thick paper	20.00	27.50
e.		As "c," inverted frame	20.00	27.50

No. 5 exists with "b" surcharge, "10 CENTS 1895." See note below No. 15.

6	A2	3c **blue & carmine**	20.00	27.50
		On cover		100.00
		Block of 4	85.00	—
a.		3c light blue & rose carmine, thin paper	70.00	55.00
b.		3c deep blue & dark carmine, medium paper	40.00	20.00
c.		3c greenish blue & lake, thick paper	22.50	15.00
d.		Imperf., pair	350.00	
e.		Inverted frame, thick paper	22.50	15.00
		White "wedge" flaw	50.00	50.00
7	A2	4c **brown & dull blue**	20.00	15.00
		On cover		150.00
		Block of 4	100.00	—
b.		4c brown & ultramarine, thin paper	250.00	250.00
c.		Diagonal half used as 2c on cover		125.00
d.		As "b," inverted frame	1,250.	1,500.
8	A2	5c **green & gray**	20.00	15.00
		On cover		175.00
		Block of 4	100.00	—
a.		5c yellow green & dark gray, thin paper	50.00	35.00
b.		Inverted frame, thick paper	20.00	15.00
9	A2	7c **lilac & orange**	25.00	75.00
		On cover		500.00
		Block of 4	125.00	—
a.		7c lilac & yellow	55.00	55.00
b.		Inverted frame	45.00	125.00

10	A2	10c **blue & brown**	20.00	17.50
		On cover		150.00
		Block of 4	100.00	—
a.		10c dark blue & black brown, thin paper	50.00	35.00
b.		Period between "t" & "s" of "cents"	22.50	17.50
c.		Inverted frame	22.50	25.00
11	A2	12c **red lilac & yellow green**	40.00	125.00
		On cover		750.00
		Block of 4	200.00	—
a.		12c lilac & deep green	125.00	175.00
12	A2	14c **lilac & green**	500.00	900.00
		On cover		—
		Block of 4	3,250.	
a.		Inverted frame	2,250.	3,250.
13	A2	50c **violet**, thin paper	80.00	175.00
		On cover		1,500.
		Block of 4	350.00	—
a.		50c gray violet, thick paper	150.00	300.00

Issue dates: 1c, 3c, 4c, 14c, Jan. 15, 1874. 7c, July 22, 1874. 5c, 10c, 1876; 12c, 1877; 50c, 1879. Colors of major numbers are generally those of the least expensive of two or more shades, and do not indicate the shade of the first printing.

Nos. 9 and 13 Surcharged in Black:

10 CENTS 1895

a

b

1 CENT

1887

14	A2 (a)	1c on 7c **lilac & orange**	65.00	175.00
		On cover		3,000.
		Block of 4	325.00	—
a.		1c on 7c lilac & yellow	90.00	200.00
b.		Double surcharge	200.00	300.00
c.		Inverted frame	90.00	300.00

1895

15	A2 (b)	10c on 50c **violet**, thin paper	27.50	55.00
		On cover		175.00
		Block of 4	150.00	—

The "b" surcharge also exists on No. 5, with "10" found in two sizes. These are essays.

1896-1901   *Perf. 13*

16	A2	1c **green & red violet**, inverted frame ('98)	11.00	17.50
		On cover		100.00
		Block of 4	55.00	—
a.		Normal frame	250.00	375.00
17	A2	3c **blue & lake**, inverted frame ('98)	11.00	12.50
		On cover		75.00
		Block of 4	47.50	—
a.		Normal frame	275.00	325.00
		White "wedge" flaw	40.00	45.00
18	A2	4c **bister & dull blue** ('01)	12.50	12.50
		On cover		75.00
		Block of 4	62.50	—
a.		Diagonal half used as 2c on cover		40.00
b.		Inverted frame	45.00	75.00
		On cover		200.00
c.		As "b," diagonal half used as 2c on cover		250.00
19	A2	5c **green & gray**, inverted frame	45.00	32.50
		On cover		300.00
		Block of 4	190.00	—
a.		Normal frame	600.00	1,150.
20	A2	10c **blue & brown** ('01)	65.00	110.00
		On cover		1,000.
		Block of 4	400.00	—
a.		Inverted frame	900.00	1,300.
b.		Period between "t" and "s" of "cents"	85.00	130.00
		Nos. 16-20 (5)	144.50	185.00

Two printings each of Nos. 18-19.

Arms — A5

1900

21	A5	1c **light green**	2.50	2.50
		On cover		75.00
		On cover, single franking		300.00
		Block of 4	12.00	12.50
22	A5	5c **light blue**	12.50	22.50
		On cover		150.00
		Block of 4	70.00	—

Nos. 6, 17 and 20 Surcharged in Black — c

2 CENTS 1902

1902   *Perf. 14x13½*

23	A2	2c on 3c **blue & carmine**, inverted frame	400.00	400.00
		On cover		4,000.
		Block of 4	2,400.	
a.		"2" in date with straight tail	425.00	450.00
b.		Normal frame	3,500.	

Perf. 13

24	A2	2c on 3c **blue & lake**, inverted frame	8.00	17.50
		On cover		135.00
		Block of 4	35.00	—
a.		"2" in date with straight tail	55.00	55.00
b.		Dated "1901"	15.00	20.00
c.		Normal frame	325.00	400.00
d.		Dark green surcharge	150.00	200.00
e.		As "d" & "a"	1,750.	
f.		As "d" & "c"		—

One example recorded of No. 24f.

25	A2	8c on 10c **blue & brown**	20.00	32.50
		On cover		200.00
		Block of 4	82.50	—
a.		"2" with straight tail	20.00	35.00
b.		On No. 20b	20.00	37.50
c.		Inverted frame	250.00	350.00

Nos. 17 and 20 Surcharged in Black — d

8 Cents 1902

1902   *Perf. 13*

27	A2	2c on 3c **blue & lake**, inverted frame	11.00	22.50
		On cover		400.00
		Block of 4	47.50	—
		White "wedge" flaw	40.00	50.00
a.		Normal frame	225.00	375.00
28	A2	8c on 10c **blue & brown**	11.00	11.00
		On cover		150.00
		Block of 4	47.50	—
a.		On No. 20b	17.50	20.00
b.		Inverted frame	175.00	350.00

Wmk. 113- Crown

1903
				Wmk. 113	
29	A5	2c	**carmine**	8.00	15.00
			On cover		100.00
			Block of 4	32.50	
30	A5	8c	**brown**	22.50	35.00
			On cover		200.00
			Block of 4	95.00	

King Christian IX — A8

St. Thomas Harbor — A9

1905
			Typo.		Perf. 12½	
31	A8	5b	**green**		3.50	3.00
			On cover			25.00
			Block of 4		16.00	
32	A8	10b	**red**		4.50	3.00
			On cover			25.00
			Block of 4		20.00	
33	A8	20b	**green & blue**		11.00	8.00
			On cover			125.00
			Block of 4		50.00	
34	A8	25b	**ultramarine**		8.00	8.00
			On cover			50.00
			Block of 4		37.50	
35	A8	40b	**red & gray**		9.00	8.00
			On cover			125.00
			Block of 4		40.00	
36	A8	50b	**yellow & gray**		9.00	11.00
			On cover			150.00
			Block of 4		37.50	

Perf. 12
Wmk. Two Crowns (113)
Frame Typographed, Center Engraved
37	A9	1fr	**green & blue**		17.50	37.50
			On cover			375.00
			Block of 4		75.00	
38	A9	2fr	**orange red & brown**		35.00	60.00
			On cover			700.00
			Block of 4		175.00	
39	A9	5fr	**yellow & brown**		85.00	225.00
			On cover			1,100.
			Block of 4		400.00	
			Nos. 31-39 (9)		182.50	363.50

On cover values are for commercial usages, usually parcel address cards. Philatelic covers are valued at approximately 25% of these figures.

5 BIT 1905

Nos. 18, 22 and 30 Surcharged in Black

1905
			Wmk. 112		Perf. 13	
40	A2	5b on 4c	**bister & dull blue**		12.50	35.00
			On cover			200.00
			Block of 4		62.50	
a.			Inverted frame		40.00	75.00
41	A5	5b on 5c	**light blue**		12.50	32.50
			On cover			200.00
			Block of 4		55.00	
			Wmk. 113			
42	A5	5b on 8c	**brown**		12.50	32.50
			On cover			200.00
			Block of 4		50.00	

Favor cancels exist on Nos. 40-42. Value 25% less.

King Frederik VIII — A10

Frame Typographed, Center Engraved
1908
			Wmk. 113		Perf. 13	
43	A10	5b	**green**		1.75	1.25
			On cover			15.00
			Block of 4		8.75	
			Number block of 6		17.50	
44	A10	10b	**red**		1.75	1.25
			On cover			20.00
			Block of 4		8.75	
			Number block of 6		17.50	
45	A10	15b	**violet & brown**		4.00	4.00
			On cover			75.00
			Block of 4		20.00	

			Number block of 6		50.00	
46	A10	20b	**green & blue**		35.00	27.50
			On cover			100.00
			Block of 4		150.00	
			Number block of 6		375.00	
47	A10	25b	**blue & dark blue**		1.75	1.75
			On cover			25.00
			Block of 4		8.75	
			Number block of 6		17.50	
48	A10	30b	**claret & slate**		45.00	45.00
			On cover			200.00
			Block of 4		200.00	190.00
			Number block of 6		500.00	
49	A10	40b	**vermilion & gray**		4.50	4.75
			On cover			175.00
			Block of 4		22.50	
			Number block of 6		50.00	
50	A10	50b	**yellow & brown**		4.50	7.50
			On cover			150.00
			Block of 4		22.50	
			Number block of 6		67.50	
			Nos. 43-50 (8)		98.25	93.00

Printing numbers appear in the selvage, once per pane, in Roman or Arabic numerals.

King Christian X — A11

Wmk. 114 — Multiple Crosses

Frame Typographed, Center Engraved
1915
			Wmk. 114		Perf. 14x14½	
51	A11	5b	**yellow green**		3.00	5.00
			On cover			35.00
			Block of 4		13.50	
			Number block of 4		32.50	
52	A11	10b	**red**		3.00	35.00
			On cover			75.00
			Block of 4		13.50	
			Number block of 4		32.50	
53	A11	15b	**lilac & red brown**		3.00	40.00
			On cover			150.00
			Block of 4		13.50	
			Number block of 4		32.50	
54	A11	20b	**green & blue**		3.00	40.00
			On cover			175.00
			Block of 4		13.50	
			Number block of 4		32.50	
55	A11	25b	**blue & dark blue**		3.00	10.00
			On cover			35.00
			Block of 4		13.50	
			Number block of 4		32.50	
56	A11	30b	**claret & black**		3.00	50.00
			On cover			250.00
			Block of 4		13.50	
			Number block of 4		32.50	
57	A11	40b	**orange & black**		3.00	50.00
			On cover			250.00
			Block of 4		16.50	
			Number block of 4		32.50	
58	A11	50b	**yellow & brown**		3.00	50.00
			On cover			300.00
			Block of 4		16.50	
			Number block of 4		32.50	
			Nos. 51-58 (8)		24.00	280.00

Forged and favor cancellations exist.
Plate identifications 11-D, 50-D or 50-O are located in the selvage in all four corners of the pane. The 50-D is on all denominations. 11-D, all but the 50b, 50-O, all but 15b, 20b, 25b.

POSTAGE DUE

Royal Cipher "Christian Rex" — D1

Numeral of Value — D2

1902
			Litho.	Unwmk.	Perf. 11½	
J1	D1	1c	**dark blue**		5.00	10.00
			On cover			350.00
			Block of 4		25.00	
J2	D1	4c	**dark blue**		10.00	20.00
			On cover			325.00
			Block of 4		42.50	
J3	D1	6c	**dark blue**		20.00	50.00
			On cover			425.00
			Block of 4		95.00	
J4	D1	10c	**dark blue**		15.00	45.00
			On cover			350.00
			Block of 4		75.00	

There are five types of each value. On the 4c they may be distinguished by differences in the figure "4"; on the other values differences are minute.

Used values of Nos. J1-J8 are for canceled copies. Uncanceled examples without gum have probably been used. Value 60% of unused. On cover values are for copies tied by cancellation.
Excellent counterfeits of Nos. J1-J4 exist.

1905-13
					Perf. 13	
J5	D2	5b	**red & gray**		4.00	5.00
			On cover			400.00
			Block of 4		18.00	
J6	D2	20b	**red & gray**		10.00	12.50
			On cover			425.00
			Block of 4		42.50	
J7	D2	30b	**red & gray**		7.00	12.50
			On cover			400.00
			Block of 4		32.50	
J8	D2	50b	**red & gray**		9.00	32.50
			On cover			500.00
			Block of 4		40.00	
a.		Perf. 14x14½ ('13)			35.00	125.00
		Block of 4			160.00	
b.		Perf. 11½			400.00	

Nos. J5-J8 are known imperforate but were not regularly issued. Excellent counterfeits exist.
See notes following No. J4 for canceled copies.

ENVELOPES

E1

1877-78
				On White Paper	
U1	E1	2c	**light blue** ('78)	5.00	15.00
			Entire	20.00	75.00
a.		2c **ultramarine**		22.50	250.00
			Entire	125.00	1,000.
U2	E1	3c	**orange**	5.50	12.50
			Entire	19.00	75.00
a.		3c **red orange**		5.50	12.50
			Entire	19.00	75.00

Three different Crown watermarks are found on entires of No. U1, four on entires of No. U2. Envelope watermarks do not show on cut squares.

POSTAL CARDS
Values are for entire cards
Designs of Adhesive Stamps
"BREV-KORT" at top

1877
		Inscription in Three Lines			
UX1	A2	6c	**violet**	20.00	1,200.

Used value is for card to foreign destination postmarked before April 1, 1879.

1878-85
		Inscription in Four Lines			
UX2	A2	2c	**light blue** (8,800)	20.00	50.00
UX3	A2	3c	**carmine rose** (17,700)	15.00	30.00

1888
		Inscription in Five Lines			
UX4	A2	2c	**light blue** (30,500)	10.00	25.00
UX5	A2	3c	**red** (26,500)	10.00	25.00

Card No. UX5 Locally Surcharged with type "c" but with date "1901"

1901
UX6	A2	1c on 3c	**red** (2,000)	50.00	200.00

1902
Card No. UX4 Locally Surcharged with type "c"
UX7	A2	1c on 2c	**light blue** (3,000)	30.00	150.00

Card No. UX5 Surcharged similar to type "c" but heavy letters

1902
UX8	A2	1c on 3c	**red** (7,175)	10.00	45.00

1903
UX9	A5	1c	**light green** (10,000)	10.00	30.00
UX10	A5	2c	**carmine** (10,000)	20.00	75.00

1905
UX11	A8	5b	**green** (16,000)	10.00	20.00
UX12	A8	10b	**red** (14,000)	10.00	35.00

1907-08
				Unwmk.	
UX13	A10	5b	**green** ('08) (30,750)	10.00	20.00
UX14	A10	10b	**red** (19,750)	10.00	25.00

1913   **Wmk. Wood-grain**

UX15	A10	5b	green (10,000)	100.00	200.00
UX16	A10	10b	red (10,000)	125.00	325.00

1915-16   **Wmk. Wood-grain**

UX17	A11	5b	yellow green (8,200)	100.00	200.00
UX18	A11	10b	red ('16) (2,000)	125.00	—

PAID REPLY POSTAL CARDS

Designs similar to Nos. UX2 and UX3 with added inscriptions in Danish and French:
Message Card-Four lines at lower left.
Reply Card-Fifth line centered, "Svar. Réponse."

1883

UY1	A2	2c +2c **light blue**, unsevered (2,600)		20.00	200.00
m.		Message card, detached		10.00	35.00
r.		Reply card, detached		10.00	35.00
UY2	A2	3c +3c **carmine rose**, unsevered		20.00	100.00
m.		Message card, detached		10.00	20.00
r.		Reply card, detached		10.00	25.00

Designs similar to Nos. UX4 and UX5 with added inscription in fifth line, centered in French:
Message Card-"Carte postale avec réponse payée."
Reply Card-"Carte postale-réponse."

1888

UY3	A2	2c +2c **light blue**, unsevered (26,000)		15.00	100.00
m.		Message card, detached		5.00	20.00
r.		Reply card, detached		5.00	30.00
UY4	A2	3c +3c **carmine rose**, unsevered (5,000)		20.00	110.00
m.		Message card, detached		10.00	25.00
r.		Reply card, detached		10.00	30.00

No. UY4 Locally Surcharged with type "c" but with date "1901"

1902

UY5	A2	1c on 3c+1c on 3c **carmine rose**, unsevered (1,000)		30.00	300.00
m.		Message card, detached		15.00	50.00
r.		Reply card, detached		15.00	75.00

No. UY4 Surcharged in Copenhagen with type similar to "c" but heavy letters

UY6	A2	1c on 3c+1c on 3c **carmine rose**, unsevered (975)		50.00	350.00
m.		Message card, detached		25.00	60.00
r.		Reply card, detached		25.00	75.00

Designs similar to Nos. UX9 and UX10 with added inscriptions in Danish and English

1903

UY7	A5	1c +1c **light green**, unsevered (5,000)		20.00	75.00
m.		Message card, detached		10.00	20.00
r.		Reply card, detached		10.00	25.00
UY8	A5	2c +2c **carmine**, unsevered (5,000)		40.00	400.00
m.		Message card, detached		20.00	50.00
r.		Reply card, detached		20.00	75.00

Designs similar to Nos. UX11 and UX12 with added inscriptions

1905

UY9	A8	5b +5b **green**, unsevered (5,000)		20.00	75.00
m.		Message card, detached		10.00	20.00
r.		Reply card, detached		10.00	30.00
UY10	A8	10b +10b **red**, unsevered (4,000)		25.00	90.00
m.		Message card		10.00	25.00
r.		Reply card, detached		10.00	35.00

Designs similar to Nos. UX13, UX14 and UX15 with added inscriptions

1908   **Unwmk.**

UY11	A10	5b +5b **green**, unsevered (7,150)		20.00	100.00
m.		Message card, detached		10.00	30.00
r.		Reply card, detached		10.00	35.00
UY12	A10	10b +10b **red**, unsevered (6,750)		20.00	100.00
m.		Message card, detached		10.00	30.00
r.		Reply card, detached		10.00	40.00

1913   **Wmk. Wood-grain**

UY13	A10	5b +5b **green**, unsevered (5,000)			—
m.		Message card, detached			850.00
r.		Reply card, detached			

The 10b + 10b red type A10 with wood-grain watermark was authorized and possibly printed, but no example is known.

REVENUES

PLAYING CARDS

These stamps were overprinted by the Bureau of Engraving and Printing. Shipments of 10,000 each of Nos. RFV1-RFV3 were sent to the Virgin Islands on June 17, 1920, Jan. 16, 1926, and Mar. 5, 1934, respectively.

U. S. Playing Card Stamp No. RF3 Overprinted in Carmine

> **VIRGIN ISLANDS 4 CTS.**

1920   **Engr.**   **Wmk. 191R**   *Rouletted 7*

RFV1	RF2	4c on 2c **blue**		200.00

U. S. Playing Card Stamp No. RF17 Overprinted in Carmine

> **VIRGIN ISLANDS 4 cts.**

1926   *Rouletted 7*

RFV2	RF4	4c on (8c) **blue**		45.00

RFV2 was surcharged with new value in "Bits" for use in collecting a tobacco tax.

Same Overprint on U.S. Type RF4

1934   *Perf. 11*

RFV3	RF4	4c on (8c) **light blue**	200.00	110.00

The above stamp with perforation 11 was not issued in the United States without the overprint.

> Danish West Indies stamps can be mounted in the Scott U.S. Possessions album.

GUAM

A former Spanish island possession in the Pacific Ocean, one of the Mariana group, about 1,450 miles east of the Philippines. Captured June 20, 1898, and ceded to the United States by treaty after the Spanish-American War. Stamps overprinted "Guam" were used while the post office was under the jurisdiction of the Navy Department from July 7, 1899, until March 29, 1901, when a Postal Agent was appointed by the Post Office Department and the postal service passed under that Department's control. From this date on Guam was supplied with regular United States postage stamps, although the overprints remained in use for several more years.

Italicized numbers in parentheses indicate quantities issued.

Population 9,000 (est. 1899).

100 CENTS = 1 DOLLAR

United States Nos. 279, 279B, 279Bc, 268, 280a, 281, 282, 272, 282C, 283, 284, 275, 275a, 276 and 276A Overprinted

GUAM

1899   **Wmk. 191**   *Perf. 12*
Black Overprint

1	A87	1c **deep green** (25,000)		20.00	25.00
		On cover			200.00
		Block of 4		90.00	140.00
		P# strip of 3, Impt.		90.00	
		P# block of 6, Impt.		350.00	

A bogus inverted overprint exists.

2	A88	2c **red**, type IV, Dec. (105,000)		17.50	25.00
		light red, type IV		17.50	25.00
		On cover			200.00
		Block of 4		85.00	140.00
		P# strip of 3, Impt.		75.00	
		P# block of 6, Impt.		300.00	
a.		2c **rose carmine**, type IV, Aug. 15		22.50	30.00
		On cover			225.00
		Block of 4		100.00	175.00
		P# strip of 3, Impt.		82.50	
		P# block of 6, Impt.		325.00	
3	A89	3c **purple** (5,000)		125.00	175.00
		On cover			400.00
		Block of 4		550.00	850.00
		P# strip of 3, Impt.		525.00	
		P# block of 6, Impt.		1,500.	
4	A90	4c **lilac brown** (5,000)		135.00	175.00
		On cover			450.00
		Block of 4		600.00	825.00
		P# strip of 3, Impt.		550.00	
		P# block of 6, Impt.		2,000.	
		Extra frame line at top (Plate 793 R62)			—

5	A91	5c **blue** (20,000)		30.00	45.00
		On cover			200.00
		Block of 4		125.00	250.00
		P# strip of 3, Impt.		125.00	
		P# block of 6, Impt.		725.00	
6	A92	6c **lake** (5000)		125.00	200.00
		On cover			450.00
		Block of 4		550.00	1,000.
		P# strip of 3, Impt.		500.00	
		P# block of 6, Impt.		1,600.	
7	A93	8c **violet brown** (5000)		125.00	200.00
		On cover			450.00
		Block of 4		550.00	1,000.
		P# strip of 3, Impt.		500.00	
		P# block of 6, Impt.		1,600.	
8	A94	10c **brown**, type I (10,000)		45.00	55.00
		On cover			275.00
		Block of 4		200.00	300.00
		P# strip of 3, Impt.		210.00	
		P# block of 6, Impt.		950.00	
9	A94	10c **brown**, type II		3,750.	
		Pair		—	
10	A95	15c **olive green** (5000)		150.00	175.00
		On cover			900.00
		Block of 4		650.00	875.00
		P# strip of 3, Impt.		600.00	
		P# block of 6, Impt.		2,200.	
11	A96	50c **orange** (4000)		300.00	375.00
		On cover			1,250.
		Block of 4		1,400.	1,850.
		P# strip of 3, Impt.		1,400.	
		P# block of 6, Impt.		4,000.	
a.		50c **red orange**		500.00	—

Red Overprint

12	A97	$1 **black**, type I (3000)		350.00	400.00
		On cover			3,000.
		Block of 4		1,750.	1,750.
		P# strip of 3, Impt.		1,650.	
		P# block of 6, Impt.		12,500.	

13	A97	$1 **black**, type II		4,500.	
		Block of 4			
		Nos. 1-8,10-12 (11)		1,422.	1,850.

Counterfeits of overprint exist.

No. 13 exists only in the special printing.

Special Printing

In March 1900, one pane of 100 stamps of each of Nos. 1-8, 10-12 and two panes of 50 stamps of No. E1 were specially overprinted for displays at the Paris Exposition (1900) and Pan American Exposition (1901). The 2c panes was light red, type IV.

Copies were handstampd type E "Specimen" in black ink by H. G. Mandel and mounted by him in separate displays for the two Expositions. Additional copies from each pane were also handstamped "Specimen" but most were destroyed after the Expositions.

J. M. Bartels, a stamp dealer, signed some copies from these panes "Special Surcharge" in pencil on the gum to authenticate them as coming from the "Mandel" Special Printing panes. In 1904 or later, he handstamped additional surviving copies "Special Surcharge" in red ink on the back as his guarantee. Some of these guaranteed stamps had Mandel's "Specimen" handstamp on the face while others did not. Value (with or without "Specimen" handstamp): Nos. 1-8, 10, each $850; Nos. 11, E1, each $1,250; No. 12, $2,000.

SPECIAL DELIVERY STAMP
Special Delivery Stamp of the
United States, No. E5 Overprinted
diagonally in Red **GUAM**

1899		Wmk. 191		Perf. 12	
E1	SD3	10c	blue (5000)	150.	200.
			On cover		1,250.
			Block of 4	650.	
			Margin block of 4, arrow	750.	
			P# strip of 3, Impt.	900.	
			P# block of 6, Impt.	3,500.	
			Dots in curved frame above messenger (Plate 882)	200.	
			P# block of 6, Impt. (Plate 882)	4,250.	

Counterfeits of overprint exist.
The special stamps for Guam were replaced by the regular issues of the United States.

GUAM GUARD MAIL
LOCAL POSTAL SERVICE
Inaugurated April 8, 1930, by Commander Willis W. Bradley, Jr., U.S.N., Governor of Guam, for the conveyance of mail between Agaña and the other smaller towns.

Philippines Nos. 290 and 291 Overprinted **GUAM GUARD MAIL**

1930, Apr. 8			Unwmk.		Perf. 11	
M1	A40	2c	green (2000)	275.	175.	
			On cover		400.	
			Block of 4	1,150.		
M2	A40	4c	carmine (3000)	225.	150.	
			On cover		400.	
			Block of 4	950.		

Counterfeits of overprint exist.

> *Guam stamps can be mounted in the Scott U.S. Possessions album.*

GUAM GUARD MAIL

Seal of Guam — A1

1930, July			Unwmk.		Perf. 12	
			Without Gum			
M3	A1	1c	red & black	125.00	150.00	
			On cover		225.00	
			Block of 4	525.00		
M4	A1	2c	black & red	75.00	95.00	
			On cover		250.00	
			Block of 4	325.00		

Copies are often found showing parts of watermark "CLEVE-LAND BOND."

Philippines Nos. 290 and 291
Overprinted in Black **GUAM GUARD MAIL**

1930, Aug. 10			Unwmk.		Perf. 11	
M5	A40	2c	green (20,000)	2.75	4.50	
			On cover		75.00	
			Block of 4	12.00		
			P# block of 6	125.00		
a.		2c	yellow green	2.50	4.50	
M6	A40	4c	carmine (80,000)	.50	1.75	
			On cover		75.00	
			Block of 4	2.25		
			P# block of 6	90.00		

Same Overprint in Red on Philippines Nos. 290, 291, 292, 293a, and 294

1930, Dec.						
M7	A40	2c	green (50,000)	.80	2.00	
			On cover		50.00	
			Block of 4	3.50		
			P# block of 6	125.00		

---

a.		GRAUD (Pos. 63) (500)		425.00	
b.		MIAL (Pos. 84) (500)		425.00	
M8	A40	4c	carmine (50,000)	.85	1.50
			On cover		50.00
			Block of 4	3.50	
			P# block of 6	90.00	
M9	A40	6c	deep violet (25,000)	2.50	4.50
			On cover		60.00
			Block of 4	11.00	
			P# block of 10, Impt.	250.00	
M10	A40	8c	orange brown (25,000)	2.50	4.50
			On cover		60.00
			Block of 4	11.00	
			P# block of 10, Impt.	300.00	
M11	A40	10c	deep blue (25,000)	2.50	4.50
			On cover		60.00
			Block of 4	11.00	
			P# block of 10, Impt.	350.00	

The local postal service was discontinued April 8th, 1931, and replaced by the service of the United States Post Office Department.

SPECIMEN STAMPS
Overprinted United States Type E in Purple **Specimen.**

1899				
1S	E	1c	deep green	175.00
2aS	E	2c	rose carmine, type IV	175.00
3S	E	3c	purple	175.00
4S	E	4c	lilac brown	175.00
5S	E	5c	blue	175.00
6S	E	6c	lake	175.00
7S	E	8c	violet brown	175.00
8S	E	10c	brown, type I	175.00
10S	E	15c	olive green	175.00
11S	E	50c	orange	350.00
12S	E	$1	black, type I	350.00
13S	E	$1	black, type II	—

Special Delivery

1899				
E1S	E	10c	blue	500.00

Values for specimen stamps are for fine-very fine appearing copies with minor faults.
See note after No. 13 for Special Printings with black "Specimen" overprints.

HAWAII

Until 1893, Hawaii was an independent kingdom. From 1893-1898 it was a republic. Hawaii was annexed to the United States in 1898, and became a Territory on April 30, 1900. Hawaiian stamps remained in use through June 13, 1900, and were replaced by U.S. stamps on June 14. In 1959 Hawaii became the 50th State of the Union. Hawaii consists of about 20 islands in the mid-Pacific, about 2,300 miles southwest of San Francisco. The area is 6,434 square miles and the population was estimated at 150,000 in 1899. Honolulu is the capital.

100 CENTS = 1 DOLLAR

Values of Hawaii stamps vary considerably according to condition. Quotations for Nos. 5-82 are for very fine copies. Extremely fine to superb examples sell at much higher prices, and inferior or poor copies sell at reduced prices, depending on the condition of the individual specimen.

A1

A2   A3

1851-52			Unwmk.	Typeset	Imperf.	
			Pelure Paper			
1	A1	2c	blue		660,000.	200,000.
			On cover			2,100,000.
2	A1	5c	blue		45,000.	25,000.
			On cover			75,000.
3	A2	13c	blue		22,500.	17,500.
			On cover			70,000.
4	A3	13c	blue		40,000.	27,500.
			On cover			75,000.

Nos. 1-4 are known as the "Missionaries."
Two varieties of each. Nos. 1-4, off cover, are almost invariably damaged. Values are for examples with minor damage which has been skillfully repaired.
No. 1 unused and on cover are each unique; the on-cover value is based on a 1995 auction sale.

King Kamehameha III
A4   A5
Printed in Sheets of 20 (4x5)

1853			Thick White Wove Paper		Engr.	
5	A4	5c	blue		1,250.	1,000.
			On cover			3,500.
			On cover with U.S. #17			12,000.
			Pair		2,750.	3,250.
a.			Line through "Honolulu" (Pos. 2)		2,250.	1,500.
6	A5	13c	dark red		600.	1,100.
			On cover			27,500.

HAWAII

DOUBLE OVERPRINTS OF THE 1893 PROVISIONAL GOVERNMENT ISSUE

BY FRED GREGORY

Hawaii's ruling monarchy was overthrown on January 17, 1893 by pro-annexationists. However, plans for a speedy annexation to the United States stalled in Washington and Hawaii's new leaders formed a Provisional Government. Among other problems causing embarrassment were Hawaii's postage stamps featuring portraits of Hawaii's monarchs. A decision to overprint them was made on April 5.

Overprinted stamps were first placed on sale May 20, 1893. Three later printings took place during 1893. All overprints were made on a Gordon Jobber press using a single overprint frame of fifty subjects, matching the number of stamps per sheet. About 22,900 sheet impressions were made with the frame.

CAUSE OF OVERPRINT VARIETIES

Overprint varieties fall into two categories depending on their cause: *loose type varieties* and *printer errors*. Loose type varieties resulted when type shifted or dropped out while working the frame. Among these varieties are the no period, missing 9 and missing 3. Printer errors happened when a sheet was misfed to the press so the overprint was upside down or fell in the wrong place on the stamps. These varieties include double overprints, inverted overprints, pair, one without overprint, and split overprints. Surprisingly, fewer than 200 sheets were misfed to the press causing a printer error of one kind or another. Early collectors eagerly sought loose type varieties but eschewed printer errors. As a result, many printer-error varieties were used as postage, resulting in a low retention of most printer-error varieties.

A TRUE DOUBLE OVERPRINT VS. A KISS DOUBLE

True double overprints resulted when the sheet was printed twice. Usually a second print happened when the first print was poorly inked or badly placed on the stamp. If the misplaced or weak overprint was noticed by the printer and there was time to do it over, the mistake was corrected by overprinting the sheet a second time after re-inking the type and shifting the sheet to the correct position in the press or feeding it a second time. Typically, a double overprint will show one overprint badly placed or poorly inked and the other strong and well centered on the stamp.

A doubling illusion occurred if the paper warped or flapped as it was about to be struck by the type face. On those occasions, a *kiss double* would happen. A *kiss double* was not actually pressed twice although it touched the typeface more than once. Usually, the paper was exposed to only a few letters or numbers so a *kiss* typically is only a partial impression. *Kiss doubles* are not catalogued but are collected and command a premium over Scott Catalogue values for a normal overprint.

THREE CATEGORIES OF DOUBLE OVERPRINTS

For catalogue purposes, double overprints are divided into three categories. In each category, at least one overprint is full strength. Of the "double, both heavy" category, examples from only ten sheets are reported. On most of those ten sheets fewer than all of the fifty stamps received a double overprint because the initial misfeed caused the first overprint to miss some stamps. Indeed, in the Category I double overprint of Scott 59, the sheet was misfed to the press so the ten stamps in the first column were hit on the first impression and forty images of the overprint were left on the bare platen. The sheet then was fully inserted in the press and the

Both Heavy Category I	One Heavy, One Moderate Category II	One Heavy, One Light Category III
Scott 71d, one overprint split vertically, one normal.	Scott 61e, one diagonal overprint of moderate strength split horizontally and vertically, one normal.	Scott 55f, one slightly diagonal overprint of weak strength split horizontally, one normal; this light overprint is fully readable and resulted from a second printing of the sheet so it is not a *kiss*.

entire sheet was printed, leaving a double overprint on ten stamps and offset impressions of the overprint on the backs all the stamps except the right column.

KISS OVERPRINT

Opinions can differ over whether a weak (Category III) second overprint is a true double or a *kiss*. Specialists differentiate them based on one or two factors:
- Is the weak overprint poorly inked but fully readable through all three lines?
- Does the weak overprint fall evenly over a large part of the sheet?

Scott 60

This prominent *kiss* overprint on a Scott 60 appears only in the left row of the sheet. The *kiss* on this example cannot really be read unless one knows what it is supposed to say. Even though parts of all three lines show and the ink is fairly strong compared to some category III doubles, the inability to read the light overprint on this stamp gives it away as a "kiss."

The *kiss* example above is the lower left stamp in this block. There is no offset overprint on the backs of the two right hand stamps. Had there been, a different conclusion could have been drawn because such an offset would have happened if the sheet was fed to the press after having printed only one row. Thus, the absence of the offset overprint confirms the conclusion reached by looking at the front of the stamps.

If the weak overprint is fully readable through all three lines, it is probably a true double. At least, the evidence in its favor is too strong to raise serious doubt and the appearance for all intents and purposes is a full double. On the other hand, if the weak overprint is only partially legible and can be made out primarily because we know what it should say, or lines are missing (because the paper failed to touch the type rather than because the sheet was misfed), the "double" is a *kiss*. A sense of poor inking also enters this test, because a few strongly or moderately inked characters will not happen in a true double. Thus, we look for the characters to be poorly inked, but fully readable through all three lines.

The second test, used if the first test is inconclusive, is

available only for those sheets recorded while the sheet – or at least large blocks – remained intact. Few full sheets of double overprints survive. However, the double overprint on Scott 53 was recorded and carefully described in the early literature. Similarly, the double overprint on Scott 72 was recorded throughout the sheet. Other sheets of double overprints were documented once collectors began to pay more attention to printer errors a few years after they were put in circulation. At least one sheet exists of a weak double overprint on Scott 55. Some extant blocks are large enough to prove the weak overprint was a true double produced when the printer failed to keep the plate fully inked and then pressed the sheet again to get a heavy overprint. Through careful plating, it is possible to reconstruct sheets or large parts of them if enough examples are known from the same sheet. Thus, even if a double is suspect using the first test, it can be classed as a true double if it was from a sheet where the sheet or large blocks were recorded or a significant sample from the sheet has been reconstructed.

THE TEN CATEGORY I DOUBLE OVERPRINTS

Category I double overprints (both overprints heavy) have been recorded from ten sheets representing only six Scott Numbers.

Scott 55d	Scott 57d	Scott 59d

Sheet A Split vertically. | Sheet B Split horizontally. | | The first impression was struck while only one column of stamps was in the press, so only ten stamps were doubled.

Scott 62d	Scott 66d	Scott 71d

Sheet A Split through "Provisional" | Sheet B Split below "Provisional" | | Also known from two other sheets with different orientations.

THE NINE CATEGORY II DOUBLE OVERPRINTS

Category II double overprints (one overprint moderately inked) are recorded from nine sheets representing only seven Scott Numbers.

Scott 54e	Scott 59e	Scott 60e

| | | Sheet A Split through "Provisional" | Sheet B Split through "Provisional" |

Scott 61e	Scott 62e	Scott 66e	Scott 70e

A second type is known with the over-prints almost coincident.

EXAMPLES OF CATEGORY III DOUBLE OVERPRINTS

More Category III (one overprint weak) double overprint sheets were printed than are illustrated here. Category III double overprints also exist on Scott 61, 64, 66 and 68, not shown. The total number of sheets of true double overprints in this category is in some doubt because of confusion in the marketplace between double overprints and *kiss* prints. These examples show how true doubles, albeit one weakly printed, are fully legible through all three lines.

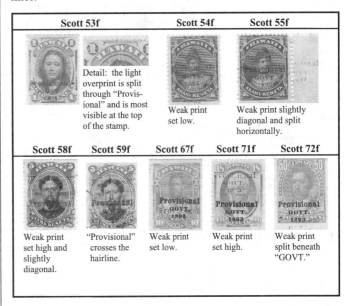

Scott 53f	Scott 54f	Scott 55f

Detail: the light overprint is split through "Provisional" and is most visible at the top of the stamp. | Weak print set low. | Weak print slightly diagonal and split horizontally.

Scott 58f	Scott 59f	Scott 67f	Scott 71f	Scott 72f

Weak print set high and slightly diagonal. | "Provisional" crosses the hairline. | Weak print set low. | Weak print set high. | Weak print split beneath "GOVT."

For this 2001 edition of the *Scott Specialized Catalogue of U.S. Stamps and Covers,* the Scott editors have expanded and specialized the listings for the Provisional Government double overprints in a way that should greatly benefit collectors of these interesting varieties. Scott now lists each of the three categories of double overprints with separate, lettered minor listings. That means, for example, that Scott 66 has three separate listings for the category I, II and III double overprints, each valued differently. This individual listing and valuing should prove to be a significant aid to buyers and sellers.

In addition, the editors have decided to list each of the varieties with a consistent lettered suffix. Thus, any Provisional Government stamp with a "d" minor listing will immediately be recognizable as a category I double overprint. Each "e" will be a category II double overprint, and each "f" will be a category III double overprint. This listing style has necessitated some other renumberings of other minor varieties. Thus, all "a" minors now refer to either the "189 " or "18 3" errors, and all "b" minors now refer to the "no period after 'Govt'" errors. All inverted overprints or pairs with one stamp missing the overprint now follow the last double overprint errors in the listings as minor letter "g." This listing style, while admittedly calling for a one-time switchover by dealers and collectors, should prove to be a long-term benefit to all.

Fred Gregory has collected and studied Hawaiian stamps and postal history for more than twenty years. Among other things, he authored the research piece on provisional government overprints appearing in the catalogue for the sale of the Charles Pietsch Collection (Shreves Philatelic Auction Galleries, Sept. 27-28, 1996) and authors and edits the website "Post Office in Paradise" at http://www.hawaiianstamps.com.

He studied under the late Dr. Wallace Beardsley, who was a pioneer in plating the provisional government overprints and in identifying the individual sheets of errors. Dr. Beardsley proved only one overprint frame was used and carefully reconstructed the development of loose type flaws, printer errors, printings and other details of these stamps never before understood. See Beardsley, Wallace R., "A Little Understood Variety/The Hawaii Provisional Government Double Overprints With One Impression Faint," Opinions V, pages 192-207, The Philatelic Foundation, New York, 1988, for his conclusions and proposals regarding the double overprints.

On cover with U.S. #11 (pair)			25,000.
On cover with U.S. #17			35,000.
On cover with #5 and U.S. #17			35,000.
On cover with #5 and U.S. #36b			38,500.
Pair		1,900.	4,000.
Block of 4		3,250.	

Black Manuscript Surcharge on Scott 6

1857

7 A6	5c on 13c **dark red**		6,750.	9,000.
	On cover with pair U.S. #7 and 15			57,500.
	On cover with pair U.S. #11, 14			55,000.
	On cover with U.S. #14			50,000.
	On cover with U.S. #17			37,500.

1857

Thin White Wove Paper

8 A4	5c **blue**		600.	575.
	On cover			1,500.
	On cover with U.S. #11			—
	On cover with U.S. #7, 15			—
	On cover with U.S. #17			10,000.
	On cover with U.S. #26			—
	On cover with U.S. #35			11,000.
	On cover with U.S. #36			10,000.
	On cover with U.S. #69			12,500.
	On cover with U.S. #76			—
	Pair		1,500.	
	Pair on cover			15,000.
a.	Line through "Honolulu" (Pos. 2)		1,150.	1,150.
b.	Double impression		3,500.	3,500.

1861

Thin Bluish Wove Paper

9 A4	5c **blue**		350.	250.
	On cover			3,750.
	On cover with U.S. #36b			3,250.
	On cover with U.S. #65			3,000.
	On cover with U.S. #65, 73			6,500.
	On cover with U.S. #68			4,250.
	On cover with U.S. #76			7,000.
	Block of 4		2,000.	
a.	Line through "Honolulu" (Pos. 2)		750.	900.

1868

RE-ISSUE
Ordinary White Wove Paper

10 A4	5c **blue**			25.
	Block of 4			125.
a.	Line through "Honolulu" (Pos. 2)			50.
11 A5	13c **dull rose**			250.
	Block of 4			1,150.

Remainders of Nos. 10 and 11 were overprinted "SPECI-MEN." See Nos. 10S-11Sb.

Nos. 10 and 11 were never placed in use but copies (both with and without overprint) were sold at face value at the Honolulu post office.

REPRINTS (Official Imitations) 1889

5c Originals have two small dots near the left side of the square in the upper right corner. These dots are missing in the reprints.

13c The bottom of the 3 of 13 in the upper left corner is flattened in the originals and rounded in the reprints. The "t" of "Cts" on the left side is as tall as the "C" in the reprints, but shorter in the originals.

10R A4	5c **blue**			60.
	Block of 4			275.
11R A5	13c **orange red**			250.
	Block of 4			1,100.

On August 19, 1892, the remaining supply of reprints was overprinted in black "REPRINT". The reprints (both with and without overprint) were sold at face value.

Quantities sold (including overprints) were 5c-3634 and 13c-1696. See Nos. 10R-S and 11R-S.

Unused values for the Numeral Stamps, Nos. 12-26, are for examples without gum.

A7

A8

A9

1859-62   Typeset from settings of 10 varieties

12 A7	1c **light blue**, *bluish white*		8,500.	7,000.
	Pair			15,000.
a.	"1 Ce" omitted			16,000.
b.	"nt" omitted			—
13 A7	2c **light blue**, *bluish white*		6,000.	3,500.
	On cover			10,000.
	Block of 4		25,000.	
a.	2c **dark blue**, *grayish white*		6,500.	3,750.
b.	Comma after "Cents"		—	6,000.
c.	No period after "LETA"		—	11,000.
14 A7	2c **black**, *greenish blue* ('62)		6,500.	4,250.
	On cover			7,000.
a.	"2-Cents."			—

1863

15 A7	1c **black**, *grayish*		450.	1,000.
	On cover			—
	Block of 4		2,100.	
a.	Tête bêche pair		3,500.	
b.	"NTER"		—	—
c.	Period omitted after "Postage"		700.	—
16 A7	2c **black**, *grayish*		900.	675.
	On cover			3,250.
a.	"2" at top of rectangle		3,500.	3,500.
b.	Printed on both sides		—	20,000.
c.	"NTER"		3,000.	3,000.
d.	2c **black**, *grayish white*		950.	700.
e.	Period omitted after "Cents"		—	—
f.	Overlapping impressions		—	—
g.	"TAGE"		—	—
17 A7	2c **dark blue**, *bluish*		7,500.	6,500.
	Pair		16,000.	
a.	"ISL"		—	—
18 A7	2c **black**, *blue gray*		3,000.	4,500.
	On cover			17,500.
	Pair			10,500.
	Thick paper		—	

1864-65

19 A7	1c **black**		450.	1,000.
	Pair		950.	
	Block of 4		2,150.	
20 A7	2c **black**		650.	1,150.
	On cover			16,000.
	Pair		1,400.	
	Block of 4		3,500.	
21 A8	5c **blue**, *blue* ('65)		750.	550.
	On cover with U.S. #65			—
	On cover with U.S. #68			—
	On cover with U.S. #76			8,000.
	Block of 4		3,300.	
a.	Tête bêche pair		10,000.	
b.	5c **bluish black**, *grayish white*		12,000.	

No. 21b is unique. Value based on 1995 auction sale.

22 A9	5c **blue**, *blue* ('65)		500.	850.
	On cover			12,500.
	On cover with U.S. #76			9,000.
	On cover with U.S. #63 and 76			—
	Block of 4		2,250.	
a.	Tête bêche pair		6,500.	
b.	5c **blue**, *grayish white*		—	
c.	Overlapping impressions		—	

1864

Laid Paper

23 A7	1c **black**		250.	2,000.
	On cover with U.S. #76			—
	Block of 4		1,100.	
a.	"HA" instead of "HAWAIIAN"		3,500.	
b.	Tête bêche pair		6,000.	
c.	Tête bêche pair, Nos. 23, 23a		17,500.	
24 A7	2c **black**		250.	1,000.
	Block of 4		1,100.	
a.	"NTER"		3,500.	
b.	"S" of "POSTAGE" omitted		1,000.	
c.	Tête bêche pair		5,250.	

A10

King Kamehameha IV — A11

1865

Wove Paper

25 A10	1c **dark blue**			250.
	Block of 4			1,250.
a.	Double impression			—
b.	With inverted impression of No. 21 on face			10,500.
26 A10	2c **dark blue**			250.
	Block of 4			1,250.

Nos. 12 to 26 were typeset and were printed in sheets of 50 (5 settings of 10 varieties each). The sheets were cut into panes of 25 (5x5) before distribution to the post offices.

1861-63   Litho.

Horizontally Laid Paper

27 A11	2c **pale rose**		275.	250.
	On cover			1,000.
	Pair			—
a.	2c **carmine rose** ('63)		1,900.	2,350.

Vertically Laid Paper

28 A11	2c **pale rose**		275.	150.
	On cover			1,500.
	Block of 4		1,500.	1,000.
a.	2c **carmine rose** ('63)		275.	325.
	On cover			2,000.
	Block of 4		1,600.	

RE-ISSUE

1869		Engr.	**Thin Wove Paper**	
29 A11	2c **red**			45.00
	Block of 4			225.00

No. 29 was not issued for postal purposes although canceled copies are known. It was sold only at the Honolulu post office, at first without overprint and later with overprint "CANCELLED." See No. 29S.

See note following No. 51.

Princess Victoria Kamamalu — A12

King Kamehameha IV — A13

King Kamehameha V — A14

Kamehameha V — A15

Mataio Kekuanaoa — A16

1864-86		**Engr.**	**Wove Paper**	*Perf. 12*	
30 A12	1c **purple** ('86)			9.00	7.50
	On cover				150.00
	Block of 4			50.00	
a.	1c **mauve** ('71)			40.00	20.00
b.	1c **violet** ('78)			17.50	10.00
31 A13	2c **vermilion** ('86)			15.00	9.00
	On cover with U.S. #76				1,000.
	Block of 4			75.00	65.00
a.	2c **rose vermilion**			35.00	12.50
	On cover				150.00
b.	Half used as 1c on cover with H.I. #32				8,500.
32 A14	5c **blue** ('66)			175.00	30.00
	On cover				175.00
	On cover with any U.S. issues of 1861-67				3,000.
	On cover with U.S. #116 and 69				25,000.
	Block of 4			800.00	160.00
33 A15	6c **yellow green** ('71)			25.00	9.00
a.	6c **bluish green** ('78)			25.00	9.00
	On cover				225.00
	On cover with U.S. #179				1,350.
	On cover with U.S. #185				750.00
	Block of 4			140.00	
34 A16	18c **dull rose** ('71)			85.00	35.00

On cover | | 350.00
Block of 4 | 375.00 |
Nos. 30-34 (5) | *284.00* | *90.50*

Half of No. 31 was used with a 5c stamp to make up the 6-cent rate to the United States.

No. 32 has traces of rectangular frame lines surrounding the design. Nos. 39 and 52C have no such frame lines.

King David Kalakaua — A17

Prince William Pitt Leleiohoku — A18

1875

35	A17	2c **brown**	7.50	3.00
		On cover		30.00
		Block of 4	37.50	40.00
36	A18	12c **black**	55.00	27.50
		On cover		400.00
		Block of 4	325.00	—

Princess Likelike (Mrs. Archibald Cleghorn) — A19

King David Kalakaua — A20

Queen Kapiolani — A21

Statue of King Kamehameha I — A22

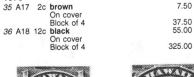

King William Lunalilo — A23

Queen Emma Kaleleonalani — A24

1882

37	A19	1c **blue**	6.00	*10.00*
		On cover		*40.00*
		Block of 4	32.50	*52.50*
38	A17	2c **lilac rose**	125.00	45.00
		On cover		150.00
		Block of 4	625.00	
39	A14	5c **ultramarine**	15.00	3.25
		On cover		27.50
		Block of 4	75.00	60.00
a.		Vert. pair, imperf. horiz.	*4,250.*	*4,250.*
40	A20	10c **black**	35.00	20.00
		On cover		150.00
		Block of 4	160.00	130.00
41	A21	15c **red brown**	55.00	25.00
		On cover		200.00
		Block of 4	260.00	200.00
		Nos. 37-41 (5)	*236.00*	*103.25*

1883-86

42	A19	1c **green**	2.75	1.90
		On cover		25.00
		Block of 4	14.00	14.00
43	A17	2c **rose** ('86)	4.00	1.00
		On cover		25.00
		Block of 4	20.00	12.50
a.		2c dull red	60.00	20.00
		Block of 4	300.00	
44	A20	10c **red brown** ('84)	30.00	10.00
		On cover		125.00
		Block of 4	150.00	95.00
45	A20	10c **vermilion**	32.50	12.50
		On cover		125.00
		Block of 4	160.00	75.00
46	A18	12c **red lilac**	75.00	32.50

		On cover		425.00
		Block of 4	375.00	225.00
47	A22	25c **dark violet**	125.00	55.00
		On cover		350.00
		Block of 4	600.00	350.00
48	A23	50c **red**	150.00	82.50
		On cover		500.00
		Block of 4		800.00
49	A24	$1 **rose red**	225.00	135.00
		On cover		600.00
		Block of 4		1,100.
		Maltese cross cancellation		75.00
		Nos. 42-49 (8)	*644.25*	*330.40*

Other fiscal cancellations exist on No. 49.

REPRODUCTION and REPRINT
Yellowish Wove Paper

1886-89			**Engr.**	*Imperf.*
50	A11	2c **orange vermilion**	150.00	
		Block of 4	750.00	
51	A11	2c **carmine** ('89)	25.00	
		Block of 4	110.00	

In 1885 the Postmaster General wished to have on sale complete sets of Hawaii's portrait stamps, but was unable to find either the stone from which Nos. 27 and 28, or the plate from which No. 29 was printed. He therefore sent a copy of No. 29 to the American Bank Note Company, with an order to engrave a new plate like it and print 10,000 stamps therefrom, of which 5000 were overprinted "SPECIMEN" in blue.

The original No. 29 was printed in sheets of fifteen (5x3), but the plate of these "Official Imitations" was made up of fifty stamps (10x5). Later, in 1887, the original die for No. 29 was discovered, and, after retouching, a new plate was made and 37,500 stamps were printed (No. 51). These, like the originals, were printed in sheets of fifteen. They were delivered during 1889 and 1890. In 1892 all remaining unsold in the Post Office were overprinted "Reprint".

No. 29 is red in color, and printed on very thin white wove paper. No. 50 is orange vermilion in color, on medium, white to buff paper. In No. 50 the vertical line on the left side of the portrait touches the horizontal line over the label "Elua Keneta", while in the other two varieties, Nos. 29 and 51, it does not touch the horizontal line by half a millimeter. In No. 51 there are three parallel lines on the left side of the King's nose, while in No. 29 and No. 50 there are no such lines. No. 51 is carmine in color and printed on thick, yellowish to buff, wove paper.

It is claimed that both Nos. 50 and 51 were available for postage, although not made to fill a postal requirement. They exist with favor cancellation. No. 51 also is known postally used. See Nos. 50S-51S.

Queen Liliuokalani — A25

1890-91				*Perf. 12*
52	A25	2c **dull violet** ('91)	4.50	1.50
		On cover		25.00
		Block of 4	20.00	11.00
a.		Vert. pair, imperf. horiz.	3,750.	
52C	A14	5c **deep indigo**	105.00	135.00
		On cover		500.00
		Block of 4	500.00	

Stamps of 1864-91 Overprinted in Red

Provisional GOVT. 1893

Three categories of double overprints:
I. Both overprints heavy.
II. One overprint heavy, one of moderate strength.
III. One overprint heavy, one of light or weak strength.

1893

53	A12	1c **purple**	7.50	12.50
		On cover		35.00
		Block of 4	37.50	70.00
a.		"189" instead of "1893"	400.00	—
b.		No period after "GOVT"	200.00	200.00
f.		Double overprint (III)	550.00	
54	A19	1c **blue**	6.00	12.50
		On cover		40.00
		Block of 4	30.00	67.50
b.		No period after "GOVT"	135.00	135.00
e.		Double overprint (II)	850.00	
f.		Double overprint (III)	400.00	
55	A19	1c **green**	1.50	3.00
		On cover		25.00
		Block of 4	7.50	15.00
d.		Double overprint (I)	625.00	450.00
f.		Double overprint (III)	200.00	
g.		Pair, one without ovpt.	10,000.	
56	A17	2c **brown**	10.00	20.00
		On cover		60.00
		Block of 4	50.00	120.00
b.		No period after "GOVT"	300.00	
57	A25	2c **dull violet**	1.50	1.25
		On cover		25.00
		Block of 4	6.50	6.50
a.		"18 3" instead of "1893"	600.00	500.00
d.		Double overprint (I)	900.00	650.00
f.		Double overprint (III)	150.00	
g.		Inverted overprint	4,000.	3,500.

58	A14	5c **deep indigo**	10.00	25.00
		On cover		100.00
		Block of 4	50.00	140.00
b.		No period after "GOVT"	225.00	250.00
f.		Double overprint (III)	1,250.	
59	A14	5c **ultramarine**	6.00	2.50
		On cover		40.00
		Block of 4	30.00	20.00
d.		Double overprint (I)	6,500.	
e.		Double overprint (II)	4,000.	4,000.
f.		Double overprint (III)	250.00	
g.		Inverted overprint	1,500.	1,500.
60	A15	6c **green**	15.00	25.00
		On cover		135.00
		Block of 4	75.00	125.00
e.		Double overprint (II)	1,250.	
61	A20	10c **black**	9.00	15.00
		On cover		125.00
		Block of 4	45.00	82.50
e.		Double overprint (II)	700.00	
f.		Double overprint (III)	200.00	
61B	A20	10c **red brown**	14,000.	29,000.
		Block of 4	60,000.	
		Strip of 5, plate imprint	75,000.	
62	A18	12c **black**	9.00	17.50
		On cover		150.00
		Block of 4	50.00	105.00
d.		Double overprint (I)	2,000.	
e.		Double overprint (III)	1,750.	
63	A18	12c **red lilac**	150.00	250.00
		On cover		550.00
		Block of 4	900.00	—
64	A22	25c **dark violet**	25.00	40.00
		On cover		225.00
		Block of 4	125.00	200.00
b.		No period after "GOVT"	325.00	300.00
f.		Double overprint (III)	1,000.	
		Nos. 53-61,62-64 (12)	*250.50*	*424.25*

Overprinted in Black

65	A13	2c **rose vermilion**	65.00	75.00
		On cover		450.00
		Block of 4	325.00	400.00
b.		No period after "GOVT"	250.00	250.00
66	A17	2c **rose**	1.25	2.25
		On cover		25.00
		Block of 4	6.50	11.00
b.		No period after "GOVT"	50.00	60.00
d.		Double overprint (I)	4,000.	
e.		Double overprint (II)	2,750.	
f.		Double overprint (III)	300.00	
66C	A15	6c **green**	14,000.	29,000.
		On cover		60,000.
		Block of 4	60,000.	
67	A20	10c **vermilion**	15.00	30.00
		On cover		125.00
		Block of 4	80.00	180.00
f.		Double overprint (III)	1,250.	
68	A20	10c **red brown**	7.50	12.50
		On cover		100.00
		Block of 4	37.50	75.00
f.		Double overprint (III)	1,750.	
69	A18	12c **red lilac**	275.00	500.00
		On cover		950.00
		Block of 4	1,250.	2,400.
70	A21	15c **red brown**	20.00	30.00
		On cover		300.00
		Block of 4	110.00	150.00
e.		Double overprint (II)	2,000.	
71	A16	18c **dull rose**	25.00	35.00
		On cover		225.00
		Block of 4	120.00	175.00
a.		"18 3" instead of "1893"	400.00	375.00
b.		No period after "GOVT"	300.00	300.00
d.		Double overprint (I)	450.00	
f.		Double overprint (III)	225.00	
g.		Pair, one without ovpt.	2,500.	
72	A23	50c **red**	60.00	90.00
		On cover		600.00
		Block of 4	275.00	475.00

b.	No period after "GOVT"		400.00	400.00
f.	Double overprint (III)		1,000.	
73	A24	$1 **rose red**	110.00	175.00
		On cover		750.00
		Block of 4	500.00	875.00
b.	No period after "GOVT"		450.00	400.00
		Nos. 65-66,67-73 (9)	578.75	949.75

 Coat of Arms — A26

 View of Honolulu — A27

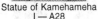 Statue of Kamehameha I — A28

 Stars and Palms — A29

 S. S. "Arawa" — A30

 Pres. Sanford Ballard Dole — A31

 "CENTS" Added — A32

1894

74	A26	1c **yellow**	2.00	1.25
		On cover		25.00
		Block of 4	8.50	8.00
75	A27	2c **brown**	2.25	.60
		On cover		25.00
		Block of 4	9.00	7.00
		"Flying goose" flaw (48 LR 2)	375.00	300.00
		Double transfer		
76	A28	5c **rose lake**	4.00	1.50
		On cover		25.00
		Block of 4	20.00	15.00
77	A29	10c **yellow green**	6.00	4.50
		On cover		45.00
		Block of 4	30.00	25.00
78	A30	12c **blue**	12.50	17.50
		On cover		150.00
		Block of 4	55.00	80.00
		Double transfer	22.50	25.00
79	A31	25c **deep blue**	12.50	17.50
		On cover		100.00
		Block of 4	55.00	
		Nos. 74-79 (6)	39.25	42.85

Numerous double transfers exist on Nos. 75 and 81.

1899

80	A26	1c **dark green**	1.50	1.25
		On cover		25.00
		Block of 4	7.00	7.00
81	A27	2c **rose**	1.35	1.00
		On cover		20.00
		Block of 4	7.00	7.00
		Double transfer		
		"Flying goose" flaw (48 LR 2)	325.00	300.00
a.		2c salmon	1.50	1.25
b.		Vert. pair, imperf. horiz.	4,500.	
82	A32	5c **blue**	5.50	3.00
		On cover		25.00
		Block of 4	27.50	52.50

OFFICIAL STAMPS

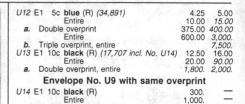

Lorrin Andrews Thurston — O1

1896		Engr.	Unwmk.	**Perf. 12**
O1	O1	2c **green**	35.00	17.50
		On cover		350.00
		Block of 4	165.00	
O2	O1	5c **black brown**	35.00	17.50
		On cover		400.00
		Block of 4	165.00	
O3	O1	6c **deep ultramarine**	35.00	17.50
		On cover		—
		Block of 4	165.00	
O4	O1	10c **bright rose**	35.00	17.50
		On cover		450.00
		Block of 4	165.00	
O5	O1	12c **orange**	35.00	17.50
		On cover		—
		Block of 4	165.00	
O6	O1	25c **gray violet**	35.00	17.50
		On cover		—
		Block of 4	165.00	
		Nos. O1-O6 (6)	210.00	105.00

Used values for Nos. O1-O6 are for copies canceled-to-order "FOREIGN OFFICE/HONOLULU H.I." in double circle without date. Values of postally used copies: Nos. O1-O2, O4, $35, No. O3, $100, No. O5, $125, No. O6, $150.

ENVELOPES

All printed by American Bank Note Co., N.Y.

View of Honolulu Harbor — E1

Envelopes of White Paper, Outside and Inside

1884				
U1	E1	1c **light green** (109,000)	2.50	3.00
		Entire	6.00	15.00
a.		1c green (10,000)	6.00	15.00
		Entire	15.00	90.00
b.		1c dark green	10.00	10.00
		Entire	25.00	75.00
U2	E1	2c **carmine** (386,000 including U2a, U2b)	2.50	4.00
		Entire	5.00	17.50
a.		2c red	2.50	4.00
		Entire	5.00	17.50
b.		2c rose	2.50	4.00
		Entire	5.00	17.50
c.		2c pale pink (5,000)	10.00	12.50
		Entire	35.00	60.00
U3	E1	4c **red** (18,000)	14.00	17.50
		Entire	30.00	90.00
U4	E1	5c **blue** (90,775)	6.50	7.50
		Entire	17.50	30.00
U5	E1	10c **black** (3,500 plus)	20.00	25.00
		Entire	50.00	100.00

Envelopes White Outside, Blue Inside

U6	E1	2c **rose**	150.00	200.00
		Entire	400.00	1,500.
U7	E1	4c **red**	150.00	200.00
		Entire	400.00	
U8	E1	5c **blue**	150.00	200.00
		Entire	400.00	1,250.
U9	E1	10c **black**	250.00	400.00
		Entire	400.00	—
		Nos. U1-U9 (15)	955.50	937.00

Nos. U1, U2, U4 & U5 Overprinted Locally "Provisional Government 1893" in Red or Black

1893				
U10	E1	1c **light green** (R) (16,000)	3.50	7.00
		Entire	7.00	20.00
a.		Double overprint	1,750.	
		Entire	6,000.	
U11	E1	2c **carmine** (Bk) (37,000)	2.50	3.50
		Entire	4.50	15.00
a.		Double overprint	500.00	
		Entire	900.00	1,250.
b.		Double overprint, one inverted, entire	1,500.	

No. U11 is known as an unused entire with a triple overprint, two of the overprints being at the bottom right portion of the envelope. Unique. Value, $9,500.

U12	E1	5c **blue** (R) (34,891)	4.25	5.00
		Entire	10.00	15.00
a.		Double overprint	375.00	400.00
		Entire	600.00	3,000.
b.		Triple overprint, entire		7,500.
U13	E1	10c **black** (R) (17,707 incl. No. U14)	12.50	16.00
		Entire	20.00	90.00
a.		Double overprint, entire	1,800.	2,000.

Envelope No. U9 with same overprint

U14	E1	10c **black** (R)	300.	
		Entire	1,000.	—

SPECIAL DELIVERY ENVELOPE

Value is for Entire.
Envelope No. U5 with added inscription "Special Despatch Letter" etc. in red at top left corner

1885				
UE1	E1	10c **black** (2,000)		175.

Envelope No. UE1 was prepared for use but never issued for postal purposes. Postally used examples exist, but no special delivery service was performed. Favor cancellations exist.

POSTAL CARDS

All printed by American Bank Note Co., N.Y.
Values are for entires.

 Queen Liliuokalani — PC1

 View of Diamond Head — PC2

 Royal Emblems — PC3

1882-92			Engr.	
UX1	PC1	1c **red**, buff (125,000)	30.00	75.00
UX2	PC2	2c **black** (45,000)	50.00	90.00
a.		Lithographed ('92)	150.00	250.00
UX3	PC3	3c **blue green** (21,426)	60.00	110.00

1889			Litho.	
UX4	PC1	1c **red**, buff (171,240)	25.00	50.00

Cards Nos. UX4, UX2a and UX3 overprinted locally "Provisional Government 1893" in red or black

1893				
UX5	PC1	1c **red**, buff (Bk) (28,760)	30.00	75.00
a.		Double overprint	4,000.	3,500.
UX6	PC2	2c **black** (R) (10,000)	55.00	95.00

No. UX6 is known unused with double overprint, one inverted at lower left of card. Unique. Value, $16,000.

UX7	PC3	3c **blue green** (R) (8,574)	65.00	250.00
a.		Double overprint	1,750.	

Iolani
Palace — PC4

Map of Pacific Ocean, Mercator's Projection — PC5

1894-97   Litho.
Border Frame 131½x72½mm

UX8	PC4	1c	**red,** *buff* (100,000)	20.00	40.00
a.			Border frame 132½x74mm ('97)	20.00	40.00
			(200,000)		
UX9	PC5	2c	**green** (60,000)	45.00	80.00
a.			Border frame 132½x74mm ('97)	45.00	80.00
			(190,000)		

PAID REPLY POSTAL CARDS
Double cards, same designs as postal cards
with added inscriptions on reply cards.

1883   Litho.
UY1	PC1	1c +1c	**purple,** *buff,* unsevered		
			(5,000)	250.00	400.00
m.			Message card, detached	25.00	95.00
r.			Reply card, detached	25.00	95.00
UY2	PC2	2c +2c	**dark blue,** unsevered		
			(5,000)	300.00	450.00
m.			Message card, detached	45.00	125.00
r.			Reply card, detached	45.00	125.00

1889
UY3	PC1	1c +1c	**gray violet,** *buff,* unsevered (5,000)	250.00	400.00
m.			Message card, detached	25.00	95.00
r.			Reply card, detached	25.00	95.00
UY4	PC2	2c +2c	**sapphire,** unsevered		
			(5,000)	250.00	400.00
m.			Message card, detached	25.00	75.00
r.			Reply card, detached	25.00	75.00

Values for unused unsevered Paid Reply Postal Cards are for
cards which have not been folded. Folded cards sell for about
33% of these values.

Detached card used values are for canceled cards with
printed messages on the back.

REVENUE STAMPS

R1

R2

R3

R4

R5

R6

Printed by the American Bank Note Co.
Sheets of 70

1877		Engr.	Unwmk.		Rouletted 8
R1	R1	25c	**green** (160,000)	10.00	12.50
R2	R2	50c	**yellow orange** (190,000)	25.00	10.00
R3	R3	$1	**black** (580,000)	25.00	5.00
a.			$1 gray	25.00	5.00

Denominations Typo.

R4	R4	$5	**vermilion & violet blue** (21,000)	100.00	25.00
R5	R5	$10	**reddish brown & green** (14,000)	100.00	25.00
R6	R6	$50	**slate blue & carmine** (3,500)	400.00	250.00

No. R6 unused is valued without gum.

Unused values for all revenues except No. R6 are for
stamps with original gum. Apparently unused copies without gum sell for less.

No. R1 Surcharged in Black or Gold

REPUBLIC
OF
TWENTY
CENTS
TWENTY
CENTS
a
HAWAII
b

1893-94
R7	R1 (a)	20c on 25c **green**		20.00	12.50
a.		Inverted surcharge		800.00	750.00
R8	R1 (b)	20c on 25c **green** (G)		45.00	40.00
a.		Double surcharge		—	—
b.		Double surcharge, one black		—	1,500.
c.		Inverted surcharge		—	—

On No. R8b, the black surcharge is 20mm wide, while the
normal gold surcharge is 15mm wide. Also known with second
20mm surcharge in red, with a "c" below "CENTS," and with a
"c" below "CENTS" and another "c" above "TWENTY."

R7

Kamehameha I — R8

Sheets of 50

1894   Litho.   Perf. 14
R9	R7	20c	**red** (10,000)	175.00	175.00
a.			Imperf. (25,000)	175.00	175.00
R10	R7	25c	**violet brown**	750.00	675.00
a.			Imperf.	900.00	—
b.			As "a," tete beche pair	—	

Printed by the American Bank Note Co.
Sheets of 100

1897   Engr.   Perf. 12
R11	R8	$1	**dark blue** (60,000)	7.50	4.50

No. R6 Inscribed "Territory of Hawaii"

1901   Rouletted 8
R12	R6	$50	**slate blue & carmine** (7,000)	40.00	45.00

Types of 1877
Printed by the American Bank Note Co.
Sheets of 70

1910-13   Engr.   Perf. 12
R13	R2	50c	**yellow orange** ('13) (70,000)	10.00	20.00
R14	R3	$1	**black** ('13) (35,000)	12.00	20.00
R15	R4	$5	**vermilion & violet blue** (14,000)	27.50	35.00
a.			Denomination inverted	—	—
R16	R5	$10	**reddish brown & green** (14,000)	27.50	35.00

PROOFS and TRIAL COLOR PROOFS
The large die proofs range
in size and format from die impressions on India die
sunk on cards generally up to 6x9 inches, through
die impressions on India on or off card in medium to
stamp size. Many individual listings are known in
more than one size and format. Values reflect the
size and format most commonly seen.

				DIE	PLATE	
				(1) Large	(3) India	(4) Card
1853						
5TC	5c	**black** on wove		4,000.		
6TC	13c	**black** on wove		4,000.		
1868-89						
10TC	5c	**orange red**		750.		
11TC	13c	**orange red**		750.	400.	
11RP	13c	**orange red**		2,250.	500.	
1861-63						
27TC	2c	**black**			750.	
1864-71						
30P	1c	**purple**		550.	150.	
		Block of 4			650.	
31P	2c	**rose vermilion**		550.	150.	175.
		Block of 4			—	
31TC	2c	**green**		1,500.		
32P	5c	**blue**		550.	150.	175.
32TC	5c	**black**		750.		
32TC	5c	**dark red**			150.	
32TC	5c	**orange red**			150.	
32TC	5c	**orange**			150.	
32TC	5c	**red brown**			150.	
		Block of 4			650.	
32TC	5c	**green**			150.	
		Block of 4			650.	
32TC	5c	**dark violet**			150.	
		Block of 4			650.	
33P	6c	**green**		550.	150.	
		Block of 4			650.	
34P	18c	**dull rose**		550.	150.	175.
		Block of 4			650.	
34TC	18c	**orange red**		750.	550.	
34TC	18c	**dark orange**		750.		
1875						
35P	2c	**brown**		550.	150.	175.
		Block of 4			650.	
35TC	2c	**black**		2,250.		
36P	12c	**black**		550.	150.	175.
36TC	12c	**violet blue**		750.		
1882						
37P	1c	**blue**			150.	
		Block of 4			650.	
37TC	1c	**black**		750.		
39P	5c	**ultramarine**		475.	150.	
40P	10c	**black**		475.	150.	
		Block of 4			650.	
41P	15c	**red brown**			150.	175.

1883-86

		Block of 4		650.	
42P	1c	green		150.	175.
		Block of 4		650.	
43P	2c	rose		125.	175.
		Block of 4		525.	
47P	25c	dark violet	450.	150.	
		Block of 4		650.	
47TC	25c	black	750.		
48P	50c	red	450.	150.	
		Block of 4		650.	
48TC	50c	lake	1,000.	300.	
49P	$1	rose red		150.	175.
		Block of 4		650.	
49TC	$1	black		150.	
49TC	$1	orange red	750.	300.	
49TC	$1	carmine		300.	
49TC	$1	vermilion		300.	
		Block of 4		1,250.	

1886-89

50P	2c	orange vermilion	750.	200.	
51P	2c	carmine	750.		

1890-91

52P	2c	dull violet	750.	200.	175.
52CP	5c	deep indigo		100.	

1894

74P	1c	yellow	600.	125.	175.
75P	2c	brown	600.	125.	
75TC	2c	dark green	550.		
76P	5c	rose lake	600.	125.	175.
77P	10c	yellow green	600.	125.	175.
		Block of 4		525.	
77TC	10c	deep blue green	600.		
78P	12c	blue	600.	125.	175.
79P	25c	deep blue	600.	125.	175.

1899

82P	5c	blue		150.	175.
		Block of 4		650.	

Official

1896

O1P	2c		750.	250.	150.
O2P	5c	black brown	750.	250.	150.
O3P	6c	deep ultramarine	750.	250.	150.
O4P	10c	bright rose	750.	250.	150.
		Block of 4		—	
O4TC	10c	black	750.		
O5P	12c	orange	750.	250.	150.
O5TC	12c	black	750.		
O6P	25c	gray violet	750.	250.	150.
O6TC	25c	black	750.		

Envelopes
Uncleared indicia only

1884

U1P	1c	green	600.
U1TC	1c	black	600.
U2P	2c	carmine	600.
U2TC	2c	black	600.
U2TC	2c	blue	750.
U3P	4c	red	600.
U3TC	4c	black	600.
U4P	5c	blue	600.
U4TC	5c	black	600.
U5P	10c	black	600.

Postal Cards
Large die proofs are of indicia only, India proofs are entire card.

1882-95

UX1P	1c	red	3,000.	1,500.
UX1TC	1c	green		1,750.
UX2P	2c	black		1,500.
UX3P	3c	blue green		2,750.
UX8TC	1c	orange		2,750.
UX8TC	1c	brown		2,750.

Revenues

			DIE (1) Large	PLATE (3) India	(4) Card

1877-97

			DIE (1) Large	(3) India	(4) Card
R1P	25c	green		250.	250.
		Block of 4		1,050.	
R1TC	25c	blue green	1,000.		
R1TC	25c	black	1,000.		
R1TC	25c	brown red	1,000.		
R1TC	25c	brown	1,000.		
R1TC	25c	grayish blue	1,000.		
R2P	50c	yellow orange		250.	300.
		Block of 4		1,050.	
R2TC	50c	blue green	1,000.		
R2TC	50c	black	1,000.		
R2TC	50c	brown red	1,000.		
R2TC	50c	brown	1,000.		
R2TC	50c	grayish blue	1,000.		
R3P	$1	black	1,000.		300.
		Block of 4		1,050.	
R3TC	$1	blue green	1,000.		
R3TC	$1	brown red	1,000.		
R3TC	$1	brown	1,000.		
R3TC	$1	grayish blue	1,000.		
R4P	$5	vermilion & violet blue			300.
		Block of 4		1,050.	
R5P	$10	reddish brown & green		250.	300.
		Block of 4		1,050.	
R6P	$50	slate blue & carmine			300.

			DIE (1) Large	PLATE (3) India	(4) Card
		Block of 4		1,050.	
R11P	$1	dark blue	1,100.	250.	300.

SPECIMEN

Overprinted in Black or Red — Type A   **SPECIMEN.**

1868

10S	A	5c	blue (R)		20.
			Block of 4		100.
a.	Line through "Honolulu" (Pos. 2)				75.
11S	A	13c	dull rose		20.
			Block of 4		100.

Overprinted in Black — Type B   **SPECIMEN.**

11S	B	13c	dull rose		275.
			Block of 4		1,250.
a.	Double overprint, one as #11S A, one as #11S B				4,000.
b.	Period omitted (Pos. 18, 20)				575.

Overprinted in Black — Type C   REPRINT

1889

10RS	C	5c	blue	60.
			Block of 4	250.
11RS	C	13c	orange red	175.
			Block of 4	725.

Overprinted in Black — Type D   **CANCELLED.**

1869

29S	D	2c	red	50.
			Block of 4	250.

Overprinted in Blue — Type E   **SPECIMEN.**

1886

50S	E	2c	orange vermilion	60.
			Block of 4	250.

Overprinted in Black — Type C   REPRINT

1889

51S	C	2c	carmine	25.
			Block of 4	125.

PHILIPPINES

Issued under U.S. Administration

Following the American occupation of the Philippines, May 1, 1898, after Admiral Dewey's fleet entered Manila Bay, an order was issued by the U. S. Postmaster General (No. 201, May 24, 1898) establishing postal facilities with rates similar to the domestic rates.

Military postal stations were established as branch post offices, each such station being placed within the jurisdiction of the nearest regular post office. Supplies were issued to these military stations through the regular post office of which they were branches.

Several post office clerks were sent to the Philippines and the San Francisco post office was made the nearest regular office for the early Philippine mail and the postmarks of the period point out this fact.

U.S. stamps overprinted "PHILIPPINES" were placed on sale in Manila June 30, 1899. Regular U.S. stamps had been in use from early March, and at the Manila post office Spanish stamps were also acceptable.

The first regular post office was established at Cavite on July 30, 1898, as a branch of the San Francisco post office. The first cancellation was a dated handstamp with "PHILIPPINE STATION" and "SAN FRANCISCO, CAL."

On May 1, 1899, the entire Philippine postal service was separated from San Francisco and numerous varieties of postmarks resulted. Many of the early used stamps show postmarks and cancellations of the Military Station, Camp or R.P.O. types, together with "Killers" of the types employed in the U.S. at the time.

The Philippines became a commonwealth of the United States on November 15, 1935, the High Commissioner of the United States taking office on the same day. The official name of the government was "Commonwealth of the Philippines" as provided by Article 17 of the Constitution. Upon the final and complete withdrawal of sovereignty of the United States and the proclamation of Philippine independence on July 4, 1946, the Commonwealth of the Philippines became the "Republic of the Philippines."

Italicized numbers in parenthesis indicate quantities issued.

Authority for dates of issue, stamps from 1899 to 1911, and quantities issued-"The Postal Issues of the Philippines," by F. L. Palmer (New York, 1912).

100 CENTS = 1 DOLLAR
100 CENTAVOS = 1 PESO (1906)

Regular Issues of the United States Overprinted in Black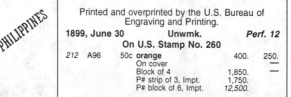

Printed and overprinted by the U.S. Bureau of Engraving and Printing.
1899, June 30   Unwmk.   *Perf. 12*
On U.S. Stamp No. 260

212	A96	50c **orange**	400.	250.
		On cover		—
		Block of 4	1,850.	
		P# strip of 3, Impt.	1,750.	
		P# block of 6, Impt.	12,500.	

On U.S. Stamps
Nos. 279, 279B, 279Bd, 279Be, 279Bf, 279Bc, 268, 281, 282C, 283, 284, 275, 275a
Wmk. Double-lined USPS (191)

213	A87	1c **yellow green**		
		(5,500,000)	3.00	.60
		On cover		10.00
		Block of 4	15.00	3.50
		P# strip of 3, Impt.	30.00	

		P# block of 6, Impt.	225.00		
a.		Inverted overprint	*13,500.*		
214	A88	2c **red,** type IV *(6,970,000)*	1.25	.60	
		light red	1.25	.60	
		On cover		10.00	
		Block of 4	5.50	3.00	
		P# strip of 3, Impt.	22.50		
		P# block of 6, Impt.	175.00		
a.		2c **orange red,** type IV, *1901*	1.25	.60	
		pale orange red	1.25	.60	
		deep orange red, *1903*	1.25	.60	
b.		Booklet pane of 6, red, type IV			
		1900	300.00	250.00	
		orange red, *1901*	300.00	250.00	
c.		2c **reddish carmine,** type IV	1.90	.90	
		On cover		12.50	
		Block of 4	8.25	4.50	
		P# strip of 3, Impt.	32.50		
		P# block of 6, Impt.	225.00		
d.		2c **rose carmine,** type IV	2.25	1.10	
		On cover		15.00	
		Block of 4	9.75	5.50	
		P# strip of 3, Impt.	37.50		
		P# block of 6, Impt.	260.00		
215	A89	3c **purple** *(673,814)*	5.75	1.25	
		On cover		30.00	
		Block of 4	27.50	13.50	
		P# strip of 3, Impt.	65.00		
		P# block of 6, Impt.	475.00		
216	A91	5c **blue** *(1,700,000)*	5.50	.90	
		On cover		20.00	
		Block of 4	25.00	9.00	
		P# strip of 3, Impt.	60.00		
		P# block of 6, Impt.	500.00		
a.		Inverted overprint		*3,750.*	

No. 216a is valued in the grade of fine.

217	A94	10c **brown,** type I			
		(750,000)+	17.50	4.00	
		On cover		60.00	
		Block of 4	80.00	55.00	
		P# strip of 3, Impt.	100.00		
		P# block of 6, Impt.	700.00		

(+ Quantity includes Nos. 217, 217A)

217A	A94	10c **orange brown,** type II	175.00	30.00	
		On cover		165.00	
		Block of 4	800.00	200.00	
		P# strip of 3, Impt.	1,000.		
		P# block of 6, Impt.	*3,000.*		
218	A95	15c **olive green** *(200,000)*	32.50	8.00	
		light olive green	37.50	8.50	
		On cover		110.00	
		Block of 4	150.00	52.50	
		P# strip of 3, Impt.	160.00		
		P# block of 6, Impt.	1,000.		
219	A96	50c **orange** *(50,000)+*	125.00	37.50	
		On cover		400.00	
		Block of 4	575.00	190.00	
		P# strip of 3, Impt.	575.00		
		P# block of 6, Impt.	*2,750.*		
a.		50 red orange	260.00		
		Block of 4	1,750.		
		Nos. 213-219 (8)	365.50	82.85	

(+ Quantity includes Nos. 212, 219, 219a)

Special Printing

In March 1900 one pane of 100 stamps of each of Nos. 213-217, 218, 219 and J1-J5 were specially overprinted for displays at the Paris Exposition (1900) and Pan American Exposition (1901). The 2c pane was light red, type IV.

Copies were handstampd type E "Specimen" in black ink on the face by H. G. Mandel and mounted by him in separate displays for the two Expositions. Additional copies from each pane were also handstamped "Specimen" but most were destroyed after the Expositions.

J. M. Bartels, a stamp dealer, signed some copies from these panes "Special Surcharge" in pencil on the gum to authenticate them as coming from the "Mandel" Special Printing panes. In 1904 or later, he handstamped additional surviving copies "Special Surcharge" in red ink on the back as his guarantee. Some of these guaranteed stamps had Mandel's "Specimen" handstamp on the face while others did not. Value, each $750.

Regular Issue

1901, Aug. 30
Same Overprint in Black On U.S. Stamps Nos. 280b, 282 and 272

220	A90	4c **orange brown**			
		(404,907)	25.00	5.00	
		On cover		50.00	
		Block of 4	110.00	50.00	
		P# strip of 3, Impt.	110.00		
		P# block of 6, Impt.	675.00		
221	A92	6c **lake** *(223,465)*	29.00	7.00	
		On cover		65.00	
		Block of 4	125.00	47.50	
		P# strip of 3, Impt.	125.00		
		P# block of 6, Impt.	800.00		
222	A93	8c **violet brown** *(248,000)*	29.00	7.50	
		On cover		50.00	
		Block of 4	125.00	50.00	
		P# strip of 3, Impt.	125.00		
		P# block of 6, Impt.	800.00		

Same Overprint in Red On U.S. Stamps Nos. 276, 276A, 277a and 278

223	A97	$1 **black,** type I *(3,000)+*	425.00	275.00	
		On cover		800.00	
		Block of 4	1,750.		
		P# strip of 3, Impt.	2,000.		
		P# block of 6, Impt.	—		
		Horiz. pair, types I & II	3,750.		

(+ Quantity includes Nos. 223, 223A)

223A	A97	$1 **black,** type II	2,250.	750.00	
		On cover		—	
		Block of 4	10,000.	—	
		P# strip of 3, Impt., one stamp No. 223	8,000.		
		P# block of 6, Impt., two stamps No. 223	—		
224	A98	$2 **dark blue** *(1800)*	450.00	350.00	
		On cover		3,250.	
		Block of 4	1,900.	—	
		P# strip of 3, Impt.	2,500.		
		P# block of 6, Impt.	—		
225	A99	$5 **dark green** *(782)*	800.00	900.00	
		On cover		12,500.	
		Block of 4	3,250.	—	
		P# strip of 3, Impt.	3,900.	—	
		P# block of 6, Impt.	—		

Special Printing

Special printings exist of Nos. 227, 221, 223-225, made from defaced plates. These were made for display at the St. Louis Exposition. All but a few copies were destroyed. Most of the existing copies have the handstamp "Special Printing" on the back. Value: Nos. 227, 221, each $750; No. 223, $1,150; No. 224, $1,600; No. 225, $2,500.

Regular Issue

1903-04
Same Overprint in Black On U.S. Stamps Nos. 300 to 310 and shades

226	A115	1c **blue green** *(9,631,172)*	4.00	.30	
		On cover		8.25	
		Block of 4	17.50	1.75	
		P# strip of 3, Impt.	22.50		
		P# block of 6, Impt.	225.00		
227	A116	2c **carmine** *(850,000)*	7.50	1.10	
		On cover		10.00	
		Block of 4	32.50	6.00	
		P# strip of 3, Impt.	32.50		
		P# block of 6, Impt.	300.00		
228	A117	3c **bright violet** *(14,500)*	67.50	12.50	
		On cover		55.00	
		Block of 4	275.00	62.50	
		P# strip of 3, Impt.	275.00		
		P# block of 6, Impt.	1,100.		
229	A118	4c **brown** *(13,000)*	75.00	22.50	
		On cover		40.00	
		Block of 4	325.00	95.00	
		P# strip of 3, Impt.	300.00		
		P# block of 6, Impt.	1,250.		
a.		4c orange brown	75.00	20.00	
230	A119	5c **blue** *(1,211,844)*	11.00	1.00	
		On cover		22.50	
		Block of 4	45.00	4.75	
		P# strip of 3, Impt.	45.00		
		P# block of 6, Impt.	400.00		
231	A120	6c **brownish lake** *(11,500)*	80.00	22.50	
		On cover		65.00	
		Block of 4	325.00	150.00	
		P# strip of 3, Impt.	325.00		
		P# block of 6, Impt.	1,400.		
232	A121	8c **violet black** *(49,033)*	45.00	15.00	
		On cover		300.00	
		Block of 4	225.00	90.00	
		P# strip of 3, Impt.	250.00		
		P# block of 6, Impt.	1,400.		
233	A122	10c **pale red brown**			
		(300,179)	20.00	2.25	
		On cover		27.50	
		Block of 4	85.00	20.00	
		P# strip of 3, Impt.	95.00		
		P# block of 6, Impt.	800.00		
a.		10c red brown	25.00	3.00	
b.		Pair, one without overprint		1,500.	
234	A123	13c **purple black** *(91,341)*	32.50	17.50	
a.		13c **brown violet**	32.50	17.50	
		On cover		55.00	
		Block of 4	140.00	72.50	
		P# strip of 3, Impt.	140.00		
		P# block of 6, Impt.	1,150.		
235	A124	15c **olive green** *(183,965)*	60.00	15.00	
		On cover		100.00	
		Block of 4	275.00	95.00	
		P# strip of 3, Impt.	275.00		
		P# block of 6, Impt.	2,000.		
236	A125	50c **orange** *(57,641)*	130.00	35.00	
		On cover		300.00	
		Block of 4	600.00	260.00	
		P# strip of 3, Impt.	600.00		
		P# block of 6, Impt.	4,000.		
		Nos. 226-236 (11)	532.50	144.65	

Same Overprint in Red On U.S. Stamps Nos. 311, 312 and 313

237	A126	$1 **black** *(5617)*	450.00	275.00	
		On cover		750.00	
		Block of 4	2,000.	1,750.	
		P# strip of 3, Impt.	2,000.		
		P# block of 6, Impt.	7,500.		
238	A127	$2 **dark blue** *(695)*	750.00	850.00	
		Block of 4	3,100.	—	
		P# strip of 3, Impt.	3,600.		
		P# block of 6, Impt.	18,000.		
239	A128	$5 **dark green** *(746)*	950.	1,000.	
		Block of 4	3,900.	—	
		P# strip of 3, Impt.	4,750.		

		P# block of 6, Impt.	—		

Same Overprint in Black On U.S. Stamp No. 319

240	A129	2c **carmine** *(862,245)*	5.50	2.25	
		On cover		3.50	
		Block of 4	25.00	12.50	
		P# strip of 3, Impt.	35.00		
		P# block of 6, Impt.	300.00		
a.		Booklet pane of 6	1,100.		
b.		2c scarlet	6.25	2.75	

Dates of issue:
Sept. 20, 1903, Nos. 226, 227, 236.
Jan. 4, 1904, Nos. 230, 234, 235, 237, 240a.
Nov. 1, 1904, Nos. 228, 229, 231, 232, 233, 238, 239, 240.
Nos. 212 to 240 became obsolete on Sept. 8, 1906, the remainders being destroyed.

Special Printing

Two sets of special printings exist of the 1903-04 issue. The first consists of Nos. 226, 230, 234, 235, 236, 237 and 240. These were made for display at the St. Louis Exposition. All but a few copies were destroyed. Most of the existing copies have the handstamp "Special Surcharge" on the back. Value: No. 237, $1,500; others $900; J6, J7, $1,100:

In 1907 the entire set Nos. 226, 228 to 240, J1 to J7 were specially printed for the Bureau of Insular Affairs on very white paper. They are difficult to distinguish from the ordinary stamps except the Special Delivery stamp which is on U.S. No. E6 (see Philippines No. E2A). Value: No. 237, $1,250; No. 238, $2,500; No. 239, $3,250; others, $750.

Regular Issue

José Rizal — A40

Printed by the U.S. Bureau of Engraving and Printing.
Plates of 400 subjects in four panes of 100 each.

Booklet panes Nos. 240a, 241b, 242b, 261a, 262b, 276a, 277a, 285a, 286a, 290e, 291b and 292c were made from plates of 180 subjects. No. 214b came from plates of 360 subjects.

Designs: 4c, McKinley. 6c, Ferdinand Magellan. 8c, Miguel Lopez de Legaspi. 10c, Gen. Henry W. Lawton. 12c, Lincoln. 16c, Adm. William T. Sampson. 20c, Washington. 26c, Francisco Carriedo. 30c, Franklin. 1p-10p, Arms of City of Manila.

Wmk. Double-lined PIPS (191)

1906, Sept. 8   **Perf. 12**

241	A40	2c **deep green** *(51,125,010)*	.25	.20	
		Block of 4	1.10	.20	
a.		2c **yellow green** *('10)*	.40	.20	
		Double transfer		40.00	
b.		Booklet pane of 6	475.00		
242	A40	4c **carmine** *(14,150,030)*	.30	.20	
		Block of 4	1.30	.20	
a.		4c **carmine lake** *('10)*	.60	.20	
b.		Booklet pane of 6	650.00		
243	A40	6c **violet** *(1,980,000)*	1.25	.20	
		Block of 4	5.75	.85	
244	A40	8c **brown** *(770,000)*	2.50	.65	
		Block of 4	11.00	4.50	
245	A40	10c **blue** *(5,550,000)*	1.75	.20	
		Dark blue	1.75	.20	
		Block of 4	7.25	.85	
246	A40	12c **brown lake** *(670,000)*	5.00	2.00	
		Block of 4	22.50	13.50	
247	A40	16c **violet black** *(1,300,000)*	3.75	.40	
		Block of 4	17.50	1.40	
248	A40	20c **orange brown** *(2,100,000)*	4.00	.30	
		Block of 4	19.00	2.00	
249	A40	26c **violet brown** *(480,000)*	6.00	2.25	
		Block of 4	30.00	15.00	
250	A40	30c **olive green** *(1,256,000)*	4.75	1.50	
		Block of 4	21.00	7.50	
251	A40	1p **orange** *(200,000)*	27.50	7.00	
		Block of 4	120.00	37.50	
252	A40	2p **black** *(100,000)*	35.00	1.25	
		Block of 4	150.00	10.00	
253	A40	4p **dark blue** *(10,000)*	100.00	15.00	
		Block of 4	450.00	67.50	
254	A40	10p **dark green** *(6,000)*	225.00	70.00	
		Block of 4	1,000.	350.00	
		Nos. 241-254 (14)	417.05	100.95	

1909

Change of Colors

255	A40	12c **red orange** *(300,000)*	8.50	2.50	
		Block of 4	40.00	12.50	
256	A40	16c **olive green** *(500,000)*	3.50	.75	
		Block of 4	15.00	3.50	
257	A40	20c **yellow** *(800,000)*	7.50	1.25	
		Block of 4	35.00	7.50	
258	A40	26c **blue green**	1.75	.75	
		Block of 4	7.50	4.00	
259	A40	30c **ultramarine** *(600,000)*	10.00	3.25	
		Block of 4	47.50	20.00	
260	A40	1p **pale violet** *(100,000)*	30.00	5.00	
		Block of 4	150.00	32.50	
260A	A40	2p **violet brown** *(50,000)*	85.00	2.75	
		Block of 4	400.00	19.00	
		Nos. 255-260A (7)	146.25	16.25	

1911   Wmk. Single-lined PIPS (190)   *Perf. 12*

261	A40	2c green	.65	.20
		Block of 4	4.25	.35
a.		Booklet pane of 6	550.00	
262	A40	4c carmine lake	2.50	.20
		Block of 4	11.50	.35
a.		4c carmine	—	—
b.		Booklet pane of 6	600.00	
263	A40	6c deep violet	2.00	.20
		Block of 4	9.00	.30
264	A40	8c brown	8.50	.45
		Block of 4	40.00	2.00
265	A40	10c blue	3.25	.20
		Block of 4	15.00	.30
266	A40	12c orange	2.50	.45
		Block of 4	11.50	2.10
267	A40	16c olive green	2.50	.20
		Pale olive green	2.50	.20
		Block of 4	11.50	.65
268	A40	20c yellow	2.00	.20
		Block of 4	8.00	.45
a.		20c orange	2.00	.20
269	A40	26c blue green	3.00	.20
		Block of 4	12.50	1.00
270	A40	30c ultramarine	3.50	.45
		Block of 4	15.00	2.10
271	A40	1p pale violet	22.50	.55
		Block of 4	100.00	2.75
272	A40	2p violet brown	27.50	.75
		Block of 4	120.00	4.75
273	A40	4p deep blue	625.00	80.00
		Block of 4	2,750.	450.00
274	A40	10p deep green	225.00	25.00
		Block of 4	1,000.	120.00
		Nos. 261-274 (14)	930.40	109.05

1914

275	A40	30c gray	10.00	.40
		Block of 4	47.50	2.40

1914   *Perf. 10*

276	A40	2c green	1.75	.20
		Block of 4	7.50	.30
a.		Booklet pane of 6	450.00	
277	A40	4c carmine	1.75	.20
		Block of 4	7.50	.45
a.		Booklet pane of 6	450.00	
278	A40	6c light violet	37.50	9.00
		Block of 4	175.00	52.50
a.		6c deep violet	42.50	6.00
279	A40	8c brown	40.00	10.00
		Block of 4	180.00	55.00
280	A40	10c dark blue	25.00	.20
		Block of 4	110.00	1.00
281	A40	16c olive green	75.00	4.50
		Block of 4	350.00	25.00
282	A40	20c orange	22.50	.85
		Block of 4	100.00	5.25
283	A40	30c gray	55.00	2.75
		Block of 4	250.00	16.50
284	A40	1p pale violet	110.00	3.00
		Block of 4	500.00	15.00
		Nos. 276-284 (9)	368.50	30.70

1918   *Perf. 11*

285	A40	2c green	20.00	4.25
		Block of 4	90.00	18.00
a.		Booklet pane of 6	750.00	
286	A40	4c carmine	25.00	2.50
		Block of 4	110.00	12.50
a.		Booklet pane of 6	1,350.	
287	A40	6c deep violet	35.00	1.75
		Block of 4	140.00	8.50
287A	A40	8c light brown	200.00	25.00
		Block of 4	825.00	165.00
288	A40	10c dark blue	52.50	1.50
		Block of 4	225.00	8.00
289	A40	16c olive green	90.00	6.75
		Block of 4	425.00	27.50
289A	A40	20c orange	60.00	7.50
		Block of 4	275.00	40.00
289C	A40	30c gray	55.00	12.50
		Block of 4	240.00	60.00
289D	A40	1p pale violet	70.00	14.00
		Block of 4	300.00	77.50
		Nos. 285-289D (9)	607.50	75.75

1917   Unwmk.   *Perf. 11*

290	A40	2c yellow green	.20	.20
		Block of 4	.30	.20
a.		2c dark green	.20	.20
		green	.20	.20
		Double transfer	—	—
b.		Vert. pair, imperf. horiz.	1,500.	
c.		Horiz. pair, imperf. between	1,500.	—
d.		Vertical pair, imperf. btwn.	1,750.	
e.		Booklet pane of 6	27.50	
291	A40	4c carmine	.20	.20
		Block of 4	.30	.20
a.		4c light rose	.20	.20
b.		Booklet pane of 6	17.50	
292	A40	6c deep violet	.30	.20
		Block of 4	1.30	.30
a.		6c lilac	.35	.20
b.		6c red violet	.35	.20
c.		Booklet pane of 6	550.00	
293	A40	8c yellow brown	.20	.20
		Block of 4	.85	.35
a.		8c orange brown	.20	.20
294	A40	10c deep blue	.20	.20
		Block of 4	.85	.25
295	A40	12c red orange	.30	.20
		Block of 4	1.30	.50
296	A40	16c light olive green	55.00	.25
		Block of 4	250.00	1.25
a.		16c olive bister	55.00	.40

297	A40	20c orange yellow	.30	.20
		Block of 4	1.90	.30
298	A40	26c green	.45	.45
		Block of 4	2.00	2.10
a.		26c blue green	.55	.25
299	A40	30c gray	.55	.20
		Block of 4	2.60	.35
		Dark gray	.55	.20
300	A40	1p pale violet	27.50	1.00
		Block of 4	115.00	4.50
a.		1p red lilac	27.50	1.00
b.		1p pale rose lilac	27.50	1.10
301	A40	2p violet brown	25.00	.75
		Block of 4	115.00	3.50
302	A40	4p blue	22.50	.45
		Block of 4	100.00	2.00
a.		4p dark blue	22.50	.45
		Nos. 290-302 (13)	132.70	4.50

1923-26

303	A40	16c olive bister *(Adm. George Dewey)*	.90	.20
		Block of 4	4.25	.45
a.		16c olive green	1.30	.20
304	A40	10p deep green ('26)	45.00	5.00
		Block of 4	190.00	22.50

Legislative Palace Issue
Issued to commemorate the opening of the
Legislative Palace.

Legislative
Palace — A42

Printed by the Philippine Bureau of Printing.

1926, Dec. 20   Unwmk.   *Perf. 12*

319	A42	2c green & black *(502,550)*	.40	.25
		First day cover		3.50
		Block of 4	1.75	1.10
a.		Horiz. pair, imperf. between	300.00	
b.		Vert. pair, imperf. between	550.00	
320	A42	4c carmine & black *(304,400)*	.40	.35
		First day cover		3.50
		Block of 4	1.75	1.40
a.		Horiz. pair, imperf. between	300.00	
b.		Vert. pair, imperf. between	575.00	
321	A42	16c olive green & black *(203,750)*	.75	.65
		First day cover		10.00
		Block of 4	3.75	3.00
a.		Horiz. pair, imperf. between	350.00	
b.		Vert. pair, imperf. between	625.00	
c.		Double impression of center	675.00	
322	A42	18c light brown & black *(103,950)*	.85	.50
		First day cover		10.00
		Block of 4	3.75	2.25
a.		Double impression of center *(150)*	700.00	
b.		Vertical pair, imperf. between	675.00	
323	A42	20c orange & black *(103,450)*	1.20	.80
		Block of 4	5.25	4.00
a.		20c orange & brown *(100)*	600.00	—
b.		As No. 323, imperf., pair *(50)*	575.00	575.00
c.		As "a," imperf., pair *(100)*	950.00	
d.		Vert. pair, imperf. between	675.00	
324	A42	24c gray & black *(103,350)*	.85	.55
		Block of 4	3.75	2.50
a.		Vert. pair, imperf. between	675.00	
325	A42	1p rose lilac & black *(11,050)*	45.00	30.00
		Block of 4	190.00	140.00
a.		Vert. pair, imperf. between	675.00	
		First day cover, #319-325		85.00
		Nos. 319-325 (7)	49.45	33.10

No. 322a is valued in the grade of fine.

Coil Stamp
Rizal Type of 1906
Printed by the U.S. Bureau of Engraving and
Printing.

1928   Unwmk.   *Perf. 11 Vertically*

326	A40	2c green	7.50	15.00
		Pair	17.50	37.50
		Line pair	55.00	100.00

Types of 1906-1923

1925-31   Unwmk.   *Imperf.*

340	A40	2c yellow green ('31)	.20	.20
		Block of 4	.25	.25
a.		2c green ('25)	.25	.20
341	A40	4c carmine rose ('31)	.20	.20
		Block of 4	.40	.40
a.		4c carmine ('25)	.40	.20
342	A40	6c violet ('31)	1.00	1.00
		Block of 4	4.25	4.25
a.		6c deep violet ('25)	8.00	4.00
343	A40	8c brown ('31)	.90	.90
		Block of 4	3.75	3.75
a.		8c yellow brown ('25)	6.00	3.00
344	A40	10c blue ('31)	1.00	1.00
		Block of 4	4.00	4.00
a.		10c deep blue ('25)	15.00	5.00
345	A40	12c deep orange ('31)	1.50	1.50
		Block of 4	6.25	6.25
a.		12c red orange ('25)	15.00	5.00

346	A40	16c olive green (Dewey) ('31)	1.10	1.10
		Block of 4	4.75	4.75
a.		16c bister green ('25)	12.50	4.00
347	A40	20c orange yellow ('31)	1.10	1.10
		Block of 4	4.75	4.75
a.		20c yellow ('25)	12.50	4.00
348	A40	26c green ('31)	1.10	1.10
		Block of 4	4.75	4.75
a.		26c blue green ('25)	15.00	5.00
349	A40	30c light gray ('31)	1.25	1.25
		Block of 4	5.25	5.25
a.		30c gray ('25)	15.00	5.00
350	A40	1p light violet ('31)	4.00	4.00
		Block of 4	16.50	16.50
a.		1p violet ('25)	90.00	35.00
351	A40	2p brown violet ('31)	10.00	10.00
		Block of 4	42.50	42.50
a.		2p violet brown ('25)	200.00	75.00
352	A40	4p blue ('31)	35.00	30.00
		Block of 4	150.00	
a.		4p deep blue ('25) *(200)*	1,000.	375.00
353	A40	10p green ('31)	100.00	100.00
		Block of 4	425.00	
a.		10p deep green ('25) *(200)*	2,000.	750.00
		Nos. 340-353 (14)	158.35	153.35

Nos. 340a-353a were the original post office issue. These were reprinted twice in 1931 for sale to collectors (Nos. 340-353).

Mount Mayon,
Luzon — A43

Post Office,
Manila — A44

Pier No. 7, Manila Bay — A45   Vernal Falls, Yosemite Park, California (See Footnote) — A46

Rice
Planting — A47

Rice
Terraces — A48

Baguio
Zigzag — A49

1932, May 3   Unwmk.   *Perf. 11*

354	A43	2c yellow green	.40	.20
		First day cover		2.00
		Block of 4	2.00	1.00
355	A44	4c rose carmine	.35	.25
		First day cover		2.00
		Block of 4	1.50	1.20
356	A45	12c orange	.50	.25
		First day cover		6.50
		Block of 4	2.25	

357	A46	18c	red orange	22.50	9.00
			First day cover		13.50
			Block of 4	87.50	40.00
358	A47	20c	yellow	.65	.55
			First day cover		6.50
			Block of 4	2.50	2.25
359	A48	24c	deep violet	1.00	.65
			First day cover		6.50
			Block of 4	4.00	3.75
360	A49	32c	olive brown	1.00	.70
			First day cover		6.50
			Block of 4	4.25	3.75
			First day cover, #354-360		50.00
			Nos. 354-360 (7)	26.40	11.85

The 18c vignette was intended to show Pagsanjan Falls in Laguna, central Luzon, and is so labeled. Through error the stamp pictures Vernal Falls in Yosemite National Park, California.

Nos. 302, 302a Surcharged in Orange or Red

1932

368	A40	1p on 4p **blue** (O)	2.00	.45
		On cover		.60
		Block of 4	8.50	2.10
a.		1p on 4p **dark blue** (O)	2.75	1.30
369	A40	2p on 4p **dark blue** (R)	3.50	.75
		On cover		.90
		Block of 4	15.00	3.50
a.		2p on 4p **blue** (R)	3.50	.75

Far Eastern Championship
Issued in commemoration of the Tenth Far Eastern Championship Games.

Baseball
Players — A50

Tennis Player — A51

Basketball
Players — A52

Printed by the Philippine Bureau of Printing.

1934, Apr. 14   Unwmk.   Perf. 11½

380	A50	2c	yellow brown	1.50	.80
			brown	1.50	.80
			First day cover		2.00
			"T" of "Eastern" malformed	2.00	1.20
381	A51	6c	ultramarine	.25	.20
			pale ultramarine	.25	.20
			First day cover		1.65
a.			Vertical pair, imperf. between	1,250.	
382	A52	16c	violet brown	.50	.50
			dark violet	.50	.50
			First day cover		2.25
a.			Imperf. horizontally, pair	1,250.	
			Nos. 380-382 (3)	2.25	1.50

José
Rizal — A53

Woman and Carabao — A54

La Filipina — A55

Pearl Fishing — A56

Fort Santiago — A57

Salt Spring — A58

Magellan's Landing,
1521 — A59

"Juan de la
Cruz" — A60

Rice Terraces — A61

Miguel Lopez de
Legaspi and Chief
Sikatuna Signing
"Blood Compact,"
1565 — A62

Barasoain Church,
Malolos — A63

Battle of Manila
Bay, 1898 — A64

Montalban
Gorge — A65

George Washington — A66

Printed by U.S. Bureau of Engraving and Printing.

1935, Feb. 15   Unwmk.   Perf. 11

383	A53	2c	rose	.20	.20
			First day cover		1.00
384	A54	4c	yellow green	.20	.20
			Light yellow green	.20	.20
			First day cover		1.00
385	A55	6c	dark brown	.20	.20
			First day cover		1.00
386	A56	8c	violet	.20	.20
			First day cover		1.65
387	A57	10c	rose carmine	.20	.20
			First day cover		1.65
388	A58	12c	black	.20	.20
			First day cover		1.65
389	A59	16c	dark blue	.20	.20
			First day cover		1.65
390	A60	20c	light olive green	.20	.20
			First day cover		2.25
391	A61	26c	indigo	.25	.25
			First day cover		3.00
392	A62	30c	orange red	.25	.25
			First day cover		3.00
393	A63	1p	red orange & black	1.75	1.25
			First day cover		8.25
394	A64	2p	bister brown & black	4.25	1.25
			First day cover		14.00
395	A65	4p	blue & black	4.50	2.75
			First day cover		20.00
396	A66	5p	green & black	9.00	2.00
			First day cover		27.50
			Nos. 383-396 (14)	21.60	9.35

Issues of the Commonwealth
Commonwealth Inauguration Issue
Issued to commemorate the inauguration of the Philippine Commonwealth, Nov. 15, 1935.

"The Temples of Human Progress"
A67

1935, Nov. 15   Unwmk.   Perf. 11

397	A67	2c carmine rose	.20	.20
		First day cover		1.00
398	A67	6c deep violet	.20	.20
		First day cover		1.00
399	A67	16c blue	.20	.20
		First day cover		1.00
400	A67	36c yellow green	.35	.30
		First day cover		1.35
401	A67	50c brown	.55	.55
		First day cover		2.00
		Nos. 397-401 (5)	1.50	1.45

Jose Rizal Issue

75th anniversary of the birth of Jose Rizal (1861-1896), national hero of the Filipinos.

Jose Rizal — A68

Printed by the Philippine Bureau of Printing.

1936, June 19   Unwmk.   Perf. 12

402	A68	2c yellow brown	.20	.20
		light yellow brown	.20	.20
		First day cover		1.00
403	A68	6c slate blue	.20	.20
		light slate green	.20	.20
		First day cover		1.00
a.		Imperf. vertically, pair	1,350.	
404	A68	36c red brown	.50	.45
		light red brown	.50	.45
		First day cover		2.25
		Nos. 402-404 (3)	.90	.85

Commonwealth Anniversary Issue

Issued in commemoration of the first anniversary of the Commonwealth.

President Manuel L. Quezon — A69

Printed by U.S. Bureau of Engraving and Printing.

1936, Nov. 15   Unwmk.   Perf. 11

408	A69	2c orange brown	.20	.20
		First day cover		1.00
409	A69	6c yellow green	.20	.20
		First day cover		1.00
410	A69	12c ultramarine	.20	.20
		First day cover		1.50
		Nos. 408-410 (3)	.60	.60

Stamps of 1935 Overprinted in Black

COMMON- WEALTH	COMMONWEALTH
a	b

1936-37   Unwmk.   Perf. 11

411	A53(a)	2c rose, Dec. 28, 1936	.20	.20
		First day cover		35.00
a.		Bklt. pane of 6, Jan. 15 1937	2.50	.65
		First day cover		40.00
412	A54(b)	4c yellow green, Mar. 29, 1937	.50	
413	A55(a)	6c dark brown, Oct. 7, 1936	.20	.20
		On cover		.20
414	A56(b)	8c violet, Mar. 29, 1937	.25	.20
		On cover		.25
415	A57(b)	10c rose carmine, Dec. 28, 1936	.20	.20
		First day cover		35.00
a.		"COMMONWEALT"		—
416	A58(b)	12c black, Mar. 29, 1937	.20	.20
		On cover		.20
417	A59(b)	16c dark blue, Oct. 7, 1936	.20	.20
		On cover		.20
418	A60(a)	20c lt olive green, Mar. 29, 1937	.65	.40
		On cover		.45
419	A61(b)	26c indigo, Mar. 29, 1937	.45	.35
		On cover		.40
420	A62(b)	30c orange red, Dec. 28, 1936	.35	.20
		First day cover		35.00
421	A63(b)	1p red org & blk, Oct. 7, 1936	.65	.20
		On cover		.35
422	A64(b)	2p bis brn & blk, Mar. 29, 1937	5.00	2.75
		On cover		3.00
423	A65(b)	4p blue & blk, Mar. 29, 1937	20.00	3.00
		On cover		3.50

424	A66(b)	5p green & blk, Mar. 29, 1937	2.50	1.25
		On cover		1.35
		Nos. 411-424 (14)	31.35	

Eucharistic Congress Issue

Issued to commemorate the 33rd International Eucharistic Congress held at Manila, Feb. 3-7, 1937.

Map, Symbolical of the Eucharistic Congress Spreading Light of Christianity — A70

FLAT PLATE PRINTING

Plates of 256 subjects in four panes of 64 each.

1937, Feb. 3   Unwmk.   Perf. 11

425	A70	2c yellow green	.20	.20
		First day cover		1.00
426	A70	6c light brown	.20	.20
		First day cover		1.00
427	A70	12c sapphire	.20	.20
		First day cover		1.00
428	A70	20c deep orange	.25	.20
		First day cover		1.00
429	A70	36c deep violet	.55	.40
		First day cover		1.35
430	A70	50c carmine	.65	.35
		First day cover		2.00
		Nos. 425-430 (6)	2.05	1.55

Arms of City of Manila — A71

1937, Aug. 27   Unwmk.   Perf. 11

431	A71	10p gray	4.25	2.00
432	A71	20p henna brown	2.25	1.40
		First day cover, #431-432		50.00

Stamps of 1935 Overprinted in Black:

COMMON- WEALTH	COMMONWEALTH
a	b

1938-40   Unwmk.   Perf. 11

433	A53(a)	2c rose, 1939	.20	.20
a.		Booklet pane of 6	3.50	.65
b.		"WEALTH COMMON-"	4,000.	
c.		Hyphen omitted	—	—
434	A54(b)	4c yellow green, 1940	1.25	—
435	A55(a)	6c dark brown, May 12, 1939	.20	.20
		First day cover		35.00
a.		6c golden brown	.20	.20
436	A56(b)	8c violet, 1939	.20	.20
		"COMMONWEALT" (LR 31)	65.00	
437	A57(b)	10c rose carmine, May 12, 1939	.20	.20
a.		"COMMONWEALT" (LR 31)		—
438	A58(b)	12c black, 1940	.20	.20
439	A59(b)	16c dark blue	.20	.20
440	A60(b)	20c light olive green, 1939	.20	.20
441	A61(b)	26c indigo, 1940	.20	.20
442	A62(b)	30c orange red, May 23, 1939	1.40	.70
443	A63(b)	1p red org & blk, Aug. 29, 1938	.40	.20
		First day cover		40.00
444	A64(b)	2p bister brown & black, 1939	2.75	.75
445	A65(b)	4p blue & black, 1940	125.00	125.00
446	A66(b)	5p green & black, 1940	4.50	2.75
		Nos. 433-446 (14)	136.90	

Overprint "b" measures 18½x1¾mm.

No. 433b occurs in booklet pane, No. 433a, position 5; all copies are straight-edged, left and bottom.

First Foreign Trade Week Issue

Nos. 384, 298a and 432 Surcharged in Red, Violet or Black:

FIRST FOREIGN	TRADE WEEK
a	
MAY 21-27, 1939	2 CENTAVOS

FIRST FOREIGN TRADE WEEK	50 CENTAVOS 50
MAY 21-27, 1939	FIRST FOREIGN TRADE WEEK
6 CENTAVOS 6	MAY 21-27,1939
b	c

1939, July 5

449	A54(a)	2c on 4c yellow green (R)	.20	.20
		First day cover		1.35
450	A40(b)	6c on 26c blue green (V)	.20	.20
		First day cover		2.00
a.		6c on 26c green	.65	.30
451	A71(c)	50c on 20p henna brown (Bk)	1.00	1.00
		First day cover		5.00

Commonwealth 4th Anniversary Issue (#452-460)

Triumphal Arch — A72

Printed by U.S. Bureau of Engraving and Printing.

1939, Nov. 15   Unwmk.   Perf. 11

452	A72	2c yellow green	.20	.20
		First day cover		1.00
453	A72	6c carmine	.20	.20
		First day cover		1.00
454	A72	12c bright blue	.20	.20
		First day cover		1.35
		Nos. 452-454 (3)	.60	.60

Malacañan Palace — A73

1939, Nov. 15   Unwmk.   Perf. 11

455	A73	2c green	.20	.20
		First day cover		1.00
456	A73	6c orange	.20	.20
		First day cover		1.00
457	A73	12c carmine	.20	.20
		First day cover		1.35
		Nos. 455-457 (3)	.60	.60

President Quezon Taking Oath of Office — A74

1940, Feb. 8   Unwmk.   Perf. 11

458	A74	2c dark orange	.20	.20
		First day cover		1.00
459	A74	6c dark green	.20	.20
		First day cover		1.00
460	A74	12c purple	.25	.20
		First day cover		1.35
		Nos. 458-460 (3)	.65	.60

José Rizal — A75

ROTARY PRESS PRINTING

1941, Apr. 14   Unwmk.   Perf. 11x10½

Size: 19x22½mm

461	A75	2c apple green	.20	.20
		First day cover		1.00
		P# block of 4	1.00	

FLAT PLATE PRINTING

1941-43	**Unwmk.** Size: 18¾x22mm	**Perf. 11**	
462	A75 2c **apple green**	.20	.20
a.	2c **pale apple green** ('41)	.20	.20
b.	As No. 462, booklet pane of 6	1.25	1.25
c.	As "a," booklet pane of 6 ('41)	2.50	2.75

This stamp was issued only in booklet panes and all copies have one or two straight edges.
Further printings were made in 1942 and 1943 in different shades from the first supply of stamps sent to the islands.

Stamps of 1935-41 Handstamped **VICTORY** in Violet

1944	**Unwmk.**	**Perf. 11, 11x10½**	
463	A53 2c **rose** (On 411), *Dec. 3*	300.00	150.00
a.	Booklet pane of 6	3,000.	
463B	A53 2c **rose** (On 433), *Dec. 14*	1,250.	1,200.
464	A75 2c **apple green** (On 461), *Nov. 8*	3.00	2.50
	On cover		15.00
465	A54 4c **yellow green** (On 384), *Nov. 8*	35.00	35.00
	On cover		—
466	A55 6c **dark brown** (On 385), *Dec. 14*	1,750.	1,500.
	On cover		—
467	A69 6c **yellow green** (On 409), *Dec. 3*	140.00	100.00
	On cover		—
468	A55 6c **dark brown** (On 413), *Dec. 28*	800.00	725.00
	On cover		—
469	A72 6c **carmine** (On 453), *Nov. 8*	140.00	110.00
	On cover		—
470	A73 6c **orange** (On 456), *Dec. 14*	775.00	650.00
	On cover		—
471	A74 6c **dark green** (On 459), *Nov. 8*	200.00	175.00
	On cover		—
472	A56 8c **violet** (On 436), *Nov. 8*	15.00	20.00
	On cover		—
473	A57 10c **carmine rose** (On 415), *Nov. 8*	115.00	75.00
	On cover		—
474	A57 10c **carmine rose** (On 437), *Nov. 8*	140.00	110.00
	On cover		—
475	A69 12c **ultramarine** (On 410), *Dec. 3*	500.00	275.00
	On cover		—
476	A72 12c **bright blue** (On 454), *Nov. 8*	3,750.	2,000.
	On cover		—
477	A74 12c **purple** (On 460), *Nov. 8*	250.00	150.00
	On cover		—
478	A59 16c **dark blue** (On 389), *Dec. 3*	725.00	
479	A59 16c **dark blue** (On 417), *Nov. 8*	600.00	400.00
480	A59 16c **dark blue** (On 439), *Nov. 8*	225.00	175.00
481	A60 20c **light olive green** (On 440), *Nov. 8*	30.00	30.00
	On cover		—
482	A62 30c **orange red** (On 420), *Dec. 3*	275.00	200.00
	On cover		—
483	A62 30c **orange red** (On 442), *Dec. 3*	425.00	325.00
	On cover		—
484	A63 1p **red orange & black** (On 443), *Dec. 3*	5,750.	4,000.
	On cover		—

Nos. 463-484 are valued in the grade of fine to very fine.
No. 463 comes only from the booklet pane. All copies have one or two straight edges.

Types of 1935-37 Overprinted

VICTORY

	COMMON-WEALTH a	COMMONWEALTH b	VICTORY c

1945		**Unwmk.**	**Perf. 11**	
485	A53(a) 2c **rose**, *Jan. 19*		.20	.20
	First day cover			2.50
486	A54(b) 4c **yellow green**, *Jan. 19*		.20	.20
	First day cover			2.50
487	A55(a) 6c **golden brown**, *Jan. 19*		.20	.20
	First day cover			2.50
488	A56(b) 8c **violet**, *Jan. 19*		.20	.20
	First day cover			3.00
489	A57(b) 10c **rose carmine**, *Jan. 19*		.20	.20
	First day cover			3.00
490	A58(b) 12c **black**, *Jan. 19*		.20	.20
	First day cover			3.50
491	A59(b) 16c **dark blue**, *Jan. 19*		.25	.20
	First day cover			4.00
492	A60(a) 20c **light olive green**, *Jan. 19*		.30	.20
	First day cover			4.25
493	A62(b) 30c **orange red**, *May 1*		.40	.35
	First day cover			2.50
494	A63(b) 1p **red orange & black**, *Jan. 19*		1.10	.25
	First day cover			6.50
495	A71(c) 10p **gray**, *May 1*		40.00	13.50
	First day cover			20.00
496	A71(c) 20p **henna brown**, *May 1*		35.00	15.00
	First day cover			25.00
	Nos. 485-496 (12)		78.25	30.70

 José Rizal — A76

ROTARY PRESS PRINTING

1946, May 28	**Unwmk.**	**Perf. 11x10½**	
497	A76 2c **sepia**	.20	.20
	P# block of 4	.50	

Later issues, released by the Philippine Republic on July 4, 1946, and thereafter, are listed in Scott's Standard Postage Stamp Catalogue, Vol. 5.

AIR POST STAMPS

Madrid-Manila Flight Issue

Issued to commemorate the flight of Spanish aviators Gallarza and Loriga from Madrid to Manila.

Regular Issue of 1917-26 Overprinted in Red or Violet by the Philippine Bureau of Printing

1926, May 13	**Unwmk.**	**Perf. 11**	
C1	A40 2c **green** (R) (10,000)	7.50	3.50
	First day cover		22.50
	Block of 4	37.50	17.50
C2	A40 4c **carmine** (V) (9,000)	10.00	4.25
	First day cover		22.50
	Block of 4	45.00	21.00
a.	Inverted overprint (100)	2,250.	—
C3	A40 6c **lilac** (R) (5,000)	47.50	14.00
	First day cover		35.00
	Block of 4	210.00	
C4	A40 8c **orange brown** (V) (5,000)	50.00	17.50
	First day cover		35.00
	Block of 4	225.00	
C5	A40 10c **deep blue** (R) (5,000)	50.00	17.50
	First day cover		35.00
	Block of 4	225.00	
C6	A40 12c **red orange** (V) (4,000)	50.00	27.50
	First day cover		37.50
	Block of 4	225.00	
C7	A40 16c **light olive green** (Sampson) (V) (300)	2,000.	1,600.
	Block of 4	—	
C8	A40 16c **olive bister** (Sampson) (R) (100)	3,750.	3,000.
	Block of 4	—	
C9	A40 16c **olive green** (Dewey) (V) (4,000)	60.00	30.00
	First day cover		37.50
	Block of 4	300.00	
C10	A40 20c **orange yellow** (V) (4,000)	60.00	30.00
	First day cover		37.50
	Block of 4	300.00	
C11	A40 26c **blue green** (V) (4,000)	60.00	30.00
	First day cover		40.00
	Block of 4	300.00	
C12	A40 30c **gray** (V) (4,000)	60.00	30.00
	First day cover		40.00
	Block of 4	300.00	
C13	A40 2p **violet brown** (R) (900)	550.00	300.00
	On cover		300.00
	Block of 4	—	
C14	A40 4p **dark blue** (R) (700)	750.00	500.00
	On cover		475.00
	Block of 4	—	
C15	A40 10p **deep green** (V) (500)	1,250.	700.00
	On cover		675.00
	Block of 4	—	

Same Overprint on No. 269
Wmk. Single-lined PIPS (190)
Perf. 12

C16	A40 26c **blue green** (V) (100)	3,000.	
	Block of 4	—	

Same Overprint on No. 284
Perf. 10

C17	A40 1p **pale violet** (V) (2,000)	200.00	125.00
	On cover		110.00
	First day cover		135.00
	Block of 4	750.00	

Overprintings of Nos. C1-C6, C9-C15 and C17 were made from two plates. Position No. 89 of the first printing shows broken left blade of propeller.

London-Orient Flight Issue

Issued Nov. 9, 1928, to celebrate the arrival of a British squadron of hydroplanes.

Regular Issue of 1917-25 Overprinted in Red

1928, Nov. 9	**Unwmk.**	**Perf. 11**	
C18	A40 2c **green** (101,200)	.40	.25
	First day cover		6.50
C19	A40 4c **carmine** (50,500)	.50	.40
	First day cover		8.00
C20	A40 6c **violet** (12,600)	1.75	1.40
	First day cover		1.50
C21	A40 8c **orange brown** (10,000)	1.90	1.60
	First day cover		1.90
C22	A40 10c **deep blue** (10,000)	1.90	1.60
	First day cover		1.90
C23	A40 12c **red orange** (8,000)	2.75	2.25
	First day cover		2.75
C24	A40 16c **olive green** (No. 303a) (12,600)	2.00	1.50
	On cover		2.00
C25	A40 20c **orange yellow** (8,000)	2.75	2.25
	First day cover		2.75
C26	A40 26c **blue green** (7,000)	8.00	5.50
	First day cover		7.00
C27	A40 30c **gray** (7,000)	8.00	5.50
	On cover		7.00

Same Overprint on No. 271
Wmk. Single-lined PIPS (190)
Perf. 12

C28	A40 1p **pale violet** (6,000)	50.00	25.00
	On cover		27.50
	Nos. C18-C28 (11)	79.95	47.25

Von Gronau Issue

Issued commemoration of the visit of Capt. Wolfgang von Gronau's airplane on its round-the-world flight.

Nos. 354-360 Overprinted by the Philippine Bureau of Printing

1932, Sept. 27	**Unwmk.**	**Perf. 11**	
C29	A43 2c **yellow green** (100,000)	.40	.30
	First day cover		2.00
C30	A44 4c **rose carmine** (80,000)	.40	.30
	First day cover		2.00
C31	A45 12c **orange** (55,000)	.60	.50
	First day cover		1.00
C32	A46 18c **red orange** (30,000)	3.50	3.25
	On cover		3.50
C33	A47 20c **violet** (30,000)	1.75	1.50
	On cover		1.65
C34	A48 24c **deep violet** (30,000)	1.75	1.50
	On cover		1.65
C35	A49 32c **olive brown** (30,000)	1.75	1.50
	On cover		1.65
	First day cover, #C29-C35		35.00
	Nos. C29-C35 (7)	10.15	8.85

Rein Issue

Commemorating the flight from Madrid to Manila of the Spanish aviator Fernando Rein y Loring.

Regular Issue of 1917-25 Overprinted in Black

1933, Apr. 11			
C36	A40 2c **green** (95,000)	.40	.35
	First day cover		1.65
C37	A40 4c **carmine** (75,000)	.45	.35
	First day cover		1.65
C38	A40 6c **deep violet** (65,000)	.80	.75
	First day cover		3.00
C39	A40 8c **orange brown** (35,000)	2.50	1.50
C40	A40 10c **dark blue** (35,000)	2.25	1.00
C41	A40 12c **orange** (35,000)	2.00	1.00
C42	A40 16c **olive green** (Dewey) (35,000)	2.00	1.00
C43	A40 20c **yellow** (35,000)	2.00	1.00
C44	A40 26c **green** (35,000)	2.25	1.50
a.	26c **blue green**	3.00	1.80
C45	A40 30c **gray** (30,000)	3.00	1.75
	First day cover, #C36-C45		40.00
	Nos. C36-C45 (10)	17.65	10.20

Stamp of 1917 Overprinted by the Philippine Bureau of Printing

1933, May 26	**Unwmk.**	**Perf. 11**	
C46	A40 2c **green**	.50	.40

Regular Issue of 1932
Overprinted

C47	A44	4c **rose carmine**	.20	.20
C48	A45	12c **orange**	.30	.20
C49	A47	20c **yellow**	.30	.20
C50	A48	24c **deep violet**	.40	.25
C51	A49	32c **olive brown**	.50	.35
		First day cover, #C46-C51		35.00
		Nos. C46-C51 (6)	2.20	1.60

Transpacific Issue

Issued to commemorate the China Clipper flight from
Manila to San Francisco, Dec. 2-5, 1935.

Nos. 387, 392 Overprinted
in Gold

1935, Dec. 2   **Unwmk.**   **Perf. 11**

C52	A57	10c **rose carmine** (500,000)	.30	.20
		First day cover		2.00
C53	A62	30c **orange red** (350,000)	.50	.35
		First day cover		3.00

Manila-Madrid Flight Issue

Issued to commemorate the Manila-Madrid flight by
aviators Antonio Arnaiz and Juan Calvo.

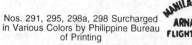

Nos. 291, 295, 298a, 298 Surcharged
in Various Colors by Philippine Bureau
of Printing

1936, Sept. 6

C54	A40	2c on 4c **carmine** (Bl) (2,000,000)	.20	.20
		First day cover		1.00
C55	A40	6c on 12c **red orange** (V) (500,000)	.20	.20
		First day cover		3.00
C56	A40	16c on 26c **blue green** (Bk) (300,000)	.25	.20
		First day cover		5.00
a.		16c on 26c **green**	1.25	.70
		Nos. C54-C56 (3)	.65	.60

Air Mail Exhibition Issue

Issued to commemorate the first Air Mail Exhibition,
held Feb. 17-19, 1939.

Nos. 298a, 298, 431 Surcharged in Black
or Red by Philippine Bureau of Printing

1939, Feb. 17

C57	A40	8c on 26c **blue green** (Bk) (200,000)	.75	.40
		First day cover		3.50
a.		8c on 26c **green** (Bk)	1.60	.55
C58	A71	1p on 10p **gray** (R) (30,000)	3.00	2.25
		First day cover		8.00

Moro Vinta and
Clipper — AP1

Printed by the US Bureau of Engraving and Printing.

1941, June 30   **Unwmk.**   **Perf. 11**

C59	AP1	8c **carmine**	1.00	.60
		First day cover		2.00
C60	AP1	20c **ultramarine**	1.20	.45
		First day cover		2.50
C61	AP1	60c **blue green**	1.75	1.00
		First day cover		3.50
C62	AP1	1p **sepia**	.70	.50
		First day cover		2.25
		Nos. C59-C62 (4)	4.65	2.55

No. C47 Handstamped in Violet   **VICTORY**

1944, Dec. 3   **Unwmk.**   **Perf. 11**

C63	A44	4c **rose carmine**	1,750.	1,750.
		On cover		—

SPECIAL DELIVERY

U.S. No. E5 Overprinted in Red

a   PHILIPPINES

Printed by U.S. Bureau of Engraving & Printing
Wmk. Double-lined USPS (191)

1901, Oct. 15   **Perf. 12**

E1	SD3	10c **dark blue** (14,998)	125.	100.
		On cover		350.
		Block of 4	550.	
		P# strip of 3, Impt.	550.	
		P# block of 6, Impt.	5,000.	
		Dots in curved frame above messenger (Pl. 882)	175.	160.
		F# block of 6, Impt. (Pl. 882)	5,250.	

Special Delivery
Messenger — SD2

Wmk. Double-lined PIPS (191)

1906, Sept. 9   **Perf. 12**

E2	SD2	20c **deep ultramarine** (40,000)	30.00	7.50
		On cover		17.50
		Block of 4	125.00	
b.		20c **pale ultramarine**	30.00	7.50
		On cover		17.50
		Block of 4	125.00	

SPECIAL PRINTING
U.S. No. E6 Overprinted Type "a" in Red

1907   **Wmk. Double-lined USPS (191)**   **Perf. 12**

E2A	SD4	10c **ultramarine**	2,750.	
		Block of 4	11,500.	
		P# block of 6, Impt.	38,500.	

This stamp was part of the set specially printed for the
Bureau of Insular Affairs in 1907. See note following No. 240.
There is only one intact plate block of No. E2A. It is fine and
is valued thus.

Wmk. Single-lined PIPS (190)

1911, Apr.   **Perf. 12**

E3	SD2	20c **deep ultramarine** (90,000)	20.00	1.75
		On cover		12.50
		Block of 4	82.50	

1916   **Perf. 10**

E4	SD2	20c **deep ultramarine**	175.00	75.00
		On cover		75.00
		Block of 4	825.00	
		pale ultramarine		—

Early in 1919 the supply of Special Delivery stamps in the
Manila area was exhausted. A Government decree permitted
the use of regular issue postage stamps for payment of the
special delivery fee when so noted on the cover. This usage
was permitted until the new supply of Special Delivery stamps
arrived.

1919   **Unwmk.**   **Perf. 11**

E5	SD2	20c **ultramarine**	.60	.20
		On cover		5.00
		Block of 4	2.50	
a.		20c **pale blue**	.75	.20
		On cover		5.25
		Block of 4	3.00	
b.		20c **dull violet**	.60	
		On cover		5.00
		Block of 4	2.50	

Type of 1906 Issue

1925-31   **Unwmk.**   **Imperf.**

E6	SD2	20c **dull violet** ('31)	20.00	25.00
		On cover		250.00
		Block of 4	85.00	
		P# block of 6	350.00	
a.		20c **violet blue** ('25)	40.00	27.50
		On cover		—
		Block of 4	200.00	
		P# block of 6	650.00	

Type of 1919 Overprinted in Black **COMMONWEALTH**

1939, Apr. 27   **Unwmk.**   **Perf. 11**

E7	SD2	20c **blue violet**	.25	.20
		First day cover		35.00

Nos. E5b and E7 Handstamped in   **VICTORY**
Violet

1944   **Unwmk.**   **Perf. 11**

E8	SD2	20c **dull violet** (On E5b)	800.00	550.00
E9	SD2	20c **blue violet** (On E7), Nov. 8	225.00	175.00
		On cover		—

Type SD2 Overprinted "VICTORY" As No. 486

1945, May 1   **Unwmk.**   **Perf. 11**

E10	SD2	20c **blue violet**	.70	.55
		First day cover		10.00
a.		"IC" close together	3.25	2.75

SPECIAL DELIVERY OFFICIAL STAMP

Type of 1906 Issue Overprinted

1931   **Unwmk.**   **Perf. 11**

EO1	SD2	20c **dull violet**	.65	.40
a.		No period after "B"	20.00	15.00
b.		Double overprint		

POSTAGE DUE

U.S. Nos. J38-J44 Overprinted in Black   PHILIPPINES

Printed by the US Bureau of Engraving and Printing.
Wmk. Double-lined USPS (191)

1899, Aug. 16   **Perf. 12**

J1	D2	1c **deep claret** (340,892)	5.75	1.25
		On cover		27.50
		On cover, used as regular postage		100.00
		P# strip of 3, Impt.	80.00	
		P# block of 6, Impt.	600.00	
J2	D2	2c **deep claret** (306,983)	6.00	1.10
		On cover		35.00
		P# strip of 3, Impt.	80.00	
		P# block of 6, Impt.	600.00	
J3	D2	5c **deep claret** (34,565)	15.00	2.25
		On cover		65.00
		P# strip of 3, Impt.	150.00	
		P# block of 6, Impt.	1,100.	
J4	D2	10c **deep claret** (15,848)	19.00	4.75
		On cover		90.00
		P# strip of 3, Impt.	150.00	
		P# block of 6, Impt.	1,100.	
J5	D2	50c **deep claret** (6,168)	200.00	90.00
		On cover		—
		P# strip of 3, Impt.	1,000.	
		P# block of 6, Impt.	4,000.	

No. J1 was used to pay regular postage Sept. 5-19, 1902.

1901, Aug. 31

J6	D2	3c **deep claret** (14,885)	17.50	6.00
		On cover		55.00
		P# strip of 3, Impt.	140.00	
		P# block of 6, Impt.	875.00	
J7	D2	30c **deep claret** (2,140)	225.00	95.00
		On cover		—
		P# strip of 3, Impt.	950.00	
		P# block of 6, Impt.	3,750.	
		Nos. J1-J7 (7)	488.25	200.35

Post Office Clerk — D3

1928, Aug. 21   **Unwmk.**   **Perf. 11**

J8	D3	4c **brown red**	.20	.20
J9	D3	6c **brown red**	.20	.20
J10	D3	8c **brown red**	.20	.20
J11	D3	10c **brown red**	.20	.20
J12	D3	12c **brown red**	.20	.20
J13	D3	16c **brown red**	.20	.20
J14	D3	20c **brown red**	.20	.20
		Nos. J8-J14 (7)	1.40	1.40

No. J8 Surcharged in Blue   **3 CVOS. 3**

1937, July 29   **Unwmk.**   **Perf. 11**

J15	D3	3c on 4c **brown red**	.20	.20
		First day cover		35.00

See note after No. NJ1.

Nos. J8-J14 Handstamped in   **VICTORY**
Violet

1944, Dec. 3   Unwmk.   *Perf. 11*

J16	D3	4c **brown red**	140.00	—
J17	D3	6c **brown red**	90.00	—
J18	D3	8c **brown red**	95.00	—
J19	D3	10c **brown red**	90.00	—
J20	D3	12c **brown red**	90.00	—
J21	D3	16c **brown red**	95.00	—
J22	D3	20c **brown red**	95.00	—
		Nos. J16-J22 (7)	695.00	

OFFICIAL

Official Handstamped Overprints

"Officers purchasing stamps for government business may, if they so desire, surcharge them with the letters O.B. either in writing with black ink or by rubber stamps but in such a manner as not to obliterate the stamp that postmasters will be unable to determine whether the stamps have been previously used." C.M. Cotterman, Director of Posts, December 26, 1905.

Beginning with January 1, 1906, all branches of the Insular Government, used postage stamps to prepay postage instead of franking them as before. Some officials used manuscript, some utilized the typewriting machines but by far the larger number provided themselves with rubber stamps. The majority of these read "O.B." but other forms were: "OFFICIAL BUSINESS" or "OFFICIAL MAIL" in two lines, with variations on many of these.

These "O.B." overprints are known on U. S. 1899-1901 stamps; on 1903-06 stamps in red and blue; on 1906 stamps in red, blue, black, yellow and green.

"O.B." overprints were also made on the centavo and peso stamps of the Philippines, per order of May 25, 1907.

Beginning in 1926 the Bureau of Posts issued press-printed official stamps, but many government offices continued to handstamp ordinary postage stamps "O.B."

During the Japanese occupation period 1942-45, the same system of handstamped official overprints prevailed, but the handstamp usually consisted of "K.P.", initials of the Tagalog words, "Kagamitang Pampamahalaan" (Official Business), and the two Japanese characters used in the printed overprint on Nos. NO1 to NO4.

Legislative Palace Issue of 1926   **OFFICIAL**
Overprinted in Red

Printed and overprinted by the Philippine Bureau of Printing.

1926, Dec. 20   Unwmk.   *Perf. 12*

O1	A42	2c **green & black** (90,500)	2.25	1.00
		On cover		2.00
		Block of 4	9.50	5.50
O2	A42	4c **carmine & black** (90,450)	2.25	1.20
		On cover		2.00
		First day cover		10.00
		Block of 4	9.50	5.50
a.		Vertical pair, imperf. between	750.00	
O3	A42	18c **light brown & black** (70,000)	7.00	4.00
		On cover		6.50
		Block of 4	35.00	20.00
O4	A42	20c **orange & black** (70,250)	6.75	1.75
		On cover		2.25
		Block of 4	35.00	8.25
		First day cover, #O1-O4		50.00
		Nos. O1-O4 (4)	18.25	7.95

Regular Issue of 1917-25 Overprinted **O.B.**

Printed and overprinted by the U.S. Bureau of Engraving and Printing.

1931   Unwmk.   *Perf. 11*

O5	A40	2c **green**	.20	.20
a.		No period after "B"	15.00	5.00
b.		No period after "O"		—
O6	A40	4c **carmine**	.20	.20
a.		No period after "B"	15.00	5.00
O7	A40	6c **deep violet**	.20	.20
O8	A40	8c **yellow brown**	.20	.20
O9	A40	10c **deep blue**	.30	.20
O10	A40	12c **red orange**	.25	.20
a.		No period after "B"	32.50	
O11	A40	16c **light olive green** (Dewey)	.25	.20
a.		16c olive bister	1.25	.20
O12	A40	20c **orange yellow**	.25	.20
a.		No period after "B"	22.50	15.00
O13	A40	26c **green**	.40	.30
a.		26c blue green	1.00	.65
O14	A40	30c **gray**	.30	.25
		Nos. O5-O14 (10)	2.55	2.15

Regular Issue of 1935 Overprinted in **O.B.**
Black

1935   Unwmk.   *Perf. 11*

O15	A53	2c **rose**	.20	.20
a.		No period after "B"	15.00	5.00
O16	A54	4c **yellow green**	.20	.20
a.		No period after "B"	15.00	8.50
O17	A55	6c **dark brown**	.20	.20
a.		No period after "B"	20.00	17.50
O18	A56	8c **violet**	.20	.20
O19	A57	10c **rose carmine**	.20	.20
O20	A58	12c **black**	.20	.20
O21	A59	16c **dark blue**	.20	.20
O22	A60	20c **light olive green**	.20	.20
O23	A61	26c **indigo**	.25	.20
O24	A62	30c **orange red**	.30	.25
		Nos. O15-O24 (10)	2.15	2.05

Nos. 411 and 418 with Additional **O.B.**
Overprint in Black

1937-38   Unwmk.   *Perf. 11*

O25	A53	2c **rose**, Apr. 10, 1937	.20	.20
		First day cover		50.00
a.		No period after "B"	4.25	2.25
b.		Period after "B" raised (UL 4)		
O26	A60	20c **light olive green**, Apr. 26, 1938	.65	.50

Regular Issue of 1935 Overprinted In Black:

O.   **B.**   **O.**   **B.**

COMMON-WEALTH	COMMONWEALTH
a	b

1938-40   Unwmk.   *Perf. 11*

O27	A53(a)	2c **rose**	.20	.20
a.		Hyphen omitted	20.00	20.00
b.		No period after "B"	25.00	25.00
O28	A54(b)	4c **yellow green**	.20	.20
O29	A55(a)	6c **dark brown**	.20	.20
O30	A56(b)	8c **violet**	.20	.20
O31	A57(b)	10c **rose carmine**	.20	.20
a.		No period after "O"	30.00	30.00
O32	A58(b)	12c **black**	.20	.20
O33	A59(b)	16c **dark blue**	.20	.20
O34	A60(a)	20c **light olive green** ('40)	.25	.25
O35	A61(b)	26c **indigo**	.30	.30
O36	A62(b)	30c **orange red**	.25	.25
		Nos. O27-O36 (10)	2.20	2.20

No. 461 Overprinted in Black

O.   **B.**
c

ROTARY PRESS PRINTING

1941, Apr. 14   Unwmk.   *Perf. 11x10½*

O37	A75	2c **apple green**	.20	.20
		First day cover		3.50
		Margin block of 4, P#	.25	

Nos. O27, O37, O16, O29, O31, **VICTORY**
O22 and O26 Handstamped in Violet

1944   Unwmk.   *Perf. 11, 11x10½*

O38	A53	2c **rose** (On O27)	250.00	150.00
O39	A75	2c **apple green** (On O37)	6.50	3.00
		On cover		10.00
		Block of 4	32.50	—
O40	A54	4c **yellow green** (On O16)	42.50	30.00
		Block of 4	175.00	
O40A	A55	6c **dark brown** (On O29)	4,250.	—
O41	A57	10c **rose carmine** (On O31)	150.00	
		Block of 4	650.00	
a.		No period after "O"		
O42	A60	20c **light olive green** (On O22)	6,000.	
O43	A60	20c **light olive green** (On O26)	1,550.	

No. 497 Overprinted Type "c" in Black

1946, June 19   Unwmk.   *Perf. 11x10½*

O44	A76	2c **sepia**	.20	.20
		Margin block of 4, P#	.40	

POST OFFICE SEALS

POS1

1906   Litho.   Unwmk.   *Perf. 12*

OX1	POS1	**light brown**	50.00	—

Wmk. "PIRS" in Double-lined Capitals

1907   *Perf. 12*

OX2	POS1	**light brown**	80.00	—

Hyphen-hole Perf. 7

OX3	POS1	**orange brown**	37.50	—

1911   *Hyphen-hole Perf. 7*

OX4	POS1	**yellow brown**	32.50	—
OX5	POS1	**olive bister**	65.00	—
a.		Unwatermarked		—
OX6	POS1	**yellow**	80.00	—

1913   Unwmk.   *Hyphen-hole Perf. 7*

OX7	POS1	**lemon yellow**	1.50	1.50

Perf. 12

OX8	POS1	**yellow**	90.00	37.50

Wmk. "USPS" in Single-lined Capitals
Hyphen-hole Perf. 7

OX9	POS1	**yellow**	80.00	37.50

1934   Unwmk.   *Rouletted*

OX10	POS1	**dark blue**	.85	.85

POS2

OX11	POS2	**dark blue**	.65	.65

POS3

1938   *Hyphen-hole Perf. 7*

OX12	POS3	**dark blue**	5.50	2.25

ENVELOPES

U.S. Envelopes of 1899 Issue Overprinted below stamp in color of the stamp, except where noted

PHILIPPINES.

1899-1900

Note: Many envelopes for which there was no obvious need were issued in small quantities. Anyone residing in the Islands could, by depositing with his postmaster the required amount, order any envelopes in quantities of 500, or multiples thereof, provided it was on the schedule of U.S. envelopes. Such special orders are indicated by an plus sign after the quantity.

U1	U77	1c **green** (#U352) (370,000)	3.00	2.00
		Entire	8.75	9.50
U2	U77	1c **green**, *amber* (#U353) (1,000)+	18.00	14.00
		Entire	40.00	40.00
U3	U77	1c **green**, *amber* (#U353) red overprint (500)+	22.50	20.00
		Entire	60.00	57.50
U4	U77	1c **green**, *oriental buff* (#U354) (1,000)+	14.00	14.00
		Entire	30.00	30.00
U5	U77	1c **green**, *oriental buff* (#U354) red overprint (500)+	35.00	35.00
		Entire	72.50	72.50
U6	U77	1c **green**, *blue* (#U355) (1,000)+	9.00	9.00
		Entire	30.00	30.00
U7	U77	1c **green**, *blue* (#U355) red overprint (500)+	20.00	19.00
		Entire	72.50	67.50
U8	U79	2c **carmine** (#U362) (1,180,000)	1.50	1.50
		Entire	4.00	3.00
U9	U79	2c **carmine**, *amber* (#U363) (21,000)	5.25	5.00
		Entire	15.00	12.50
U10	U79	2c **carmine**, *oriental buff* (#U364) (10,000)	5.25	4.75

	Entire		17.00	13.50
U11 U79	2c **carmine**, *blue* (#U365)			
	(10,000)		4.75	6.25
	Entire		12.50	12.00
U12 U81	4c **brown**, *amber* (#U372)			
	(500)+		40.00	35.00
	Entire		85.00	92.50
a.	Double overprint		—	
	Entire		4,000.	
U13 U83	4c **brown** (#U374) (10,500)		12.50	9.00
	Entire		30.00	40.00
U14 U83	4c **brown**, *amber* (#U375)			
	(500)+		55.00	50.00
	Entire		175.00	125.00
U15 U84	5c **blue** (#U377) (20,000)		6.25	6.00
	Entire		13.00	13.00
U16 U84	5c **blue**, *amber* (#U378) (500)+		35.00	35.00
	Entire		87.50	110.00
	Nos. U1-U16 (16)		287.00	265.50

1903
Same Overprint on U.S. Issue of 1903

U17 U85	1c **green** (#U379) (300,000)		1.50	1.25
	Entire		4.25	4.25
U18 U85	1c **green**, *amber* (#U380)			
	(1,000)+		12.50	12.00
	Entire		22.50	25.00
U19 U85	1c **green**, *oriental buff* (#U381)			
	(1,000)+		14.50	12.50
	Entire		26.00	24.00
U20 U85	1c **green**, *blue* (#U382) (1,500)+		12.00	11.00
	Entire		26.00	26.00
U21 U85	1c **green**, *manila* (#U383) (500)+		20.00	20.00
	Entire		45.00	47.50
U22 U86	2c **carmine** (#U385) (150,500)		5.00	3.50
	Entire		7.50	7.00
U23 U86	2c **carmine**, *amber* (#U386)			
	(500)+		17.50	14.00
	Entire		35.00	42.50
U24 U86	2c **carmine**, *oriental buff* (#U387) (500)+		17.50	25.00
	Entire		45.00	
U25 U86	2c **carmine**, *blue* (#U388) (500)+		17.50	17.50
	Entire		40.00	
U26 U87	4c **chocolate**, *amber* (#U391)			
	(500)+		55.00	75.00
	Entire		140.00	190.00
a.	Double overprint, entire		7,000.	
U27 U88	5c **blue**, *amber* (#U394) (500)+		55.00	—
	Entire		125.00	125.00
	Nos. U17-U27 (11)		228.00	

1906
Same Overprint on Re-cut U.S. issue of 1904

U28 U89	2c **carmine** (#U395)		42.50	27.50
	Entire		150.00	125.00
U29 U89	2c **carmine**, *Oriental buff* (#U397)		67.50	110.00
	Entire		225.00	275.00

Rizal — E1

E2, McKinley.

1908

U30 E1	2c **green**		.50	.25
	Entire		.85	1.50
U31 E1	2c **green**, *amber*		4.00	2.25
	Entire		9.00	8.00
U32 E1	2c **green**, *oriental buff*		5.00	3.00
	Entire		9.00	9.00
U33 E1	2c **green**, *blue*		5.00	3.00
	Entire		9.00	9.00
U34 E1	2c **green**, *manila* (500)		7.25	
	Entire		15.00	20.00
U35 E2	4c **carmine**		.50	.25
	Entire		1.40	1.25
U36 E2	4c **carmine**, *amber*		4.00	2.50
	Entire		9.00	7.00
U37 E2	4c **carmine**, *oriental buff*		4.25	3.50
	Entire		9.00	17.00
U38 E2	4c **carmine**, *blue*		4.00	3.00
	Entire		8.50	8.50
U39 E2	4c **carmine**, *manila* (500)		9.00	—
	Entire		20.00	30.00
	Nos. U30-U39 (10)		43.50	

Rizal — E3

"Juan de la Cruz" — E4

1927, Apr. 5

U40 E3	2c **green**		11.50	9.50
	Entire		30.00	25.00
	Entire, 1st day cancel			37.50

1935, June 19

U41 E4	2c **carmine**		.35	.25
	Entire		1.25	.75
U42 E4	4c **olive green**		.50	.30
	Entire		1.65	1.10

For surchages see Nos. NU1-NU2.

Nos. U30, U35, U41 and U42 Handstamped in Violet **VICTORY**

1944

U42A E1	2c **green** (On U30), Entire		—	
U43 E4	2c **carmine** (On U41)		17.50	14.00
	Entire		47.50	77.00
U44 E2	4c **carmine**, *McKinley* (On U35)			
	Entire		950.00	950.00
U45 E4	4c **olive green** (On U42)		82.50	70.00
	Entire		140.00	175.00

WRAPPERS

US Wrappers Overprinted in Color of Stamp **PHILIPPINES.**

1901

W1 U77	1c **green**, *manila* (No. W357)			
	(320,000)		1.50	1.25
	Entire		5.00	10.00

1905

W2 U85	1c **green**, *manila* (No. W384)		9.00	9.00
	Entire		22.50	25.00
a.	Double overprint, entire		4,500.	
W3 U86	2c **carmine**, *manila* (No. W389)		11.00	10.50
	Entire		22.50	27.50

Design of Philippine Envelopes

1908

W4 E1	2c **green**, *manila*		2.00	2.00
	Entire		11.00	15.00

POSTAL CARDS

Values are for Entires.
U.S. Cards Overprinted in Black below Stamp

a **PHILIPPINES.**

1900, Feb.

UX1 (a)	1c **black** (Jefferson) (UX14)			
	(100,000)		17.50	15.00
a.	Without period		47.50	75.00
UX2 (a)	2c **black** (Liberty) (UX16)			
	(20,000)		40.00	30.00

b **PHILIPPINES**

1903, Sept. 15

UX3 (b)	1c **black** (McKinley) (UX18)		1,350.	1,150.
UX4 (b)	2c **black** (Liberty) (UX16)		700.	700.

c **PHILIPPINES.**

1903, Nov. 10

UX5 (c)	1c **black** (McKinley) (UX18)		47.50	40.00
UX6 (c)	2c **black** (Liberty) (UX16)		60.00	55.00

d **PHILIPPINES**

1906

UX7 (d)	1c **black** (McKinley) (UX18)		275.	300.
UX8 (d)	2c **black** (Liberty) (UX16)		2,000.	1,500.

Designs same as postage issue of 1906

1907

UX9 A40	2c **black**, *buff* (Rizal)		10.00	8.00
UX10 A40	4c **black**, *buff* (McKinley)		25.00	20.00

Color changes

1911

UX11 A40	2c **blue**, *light blue* (Rizal)		8.00	8.00
a.	2c blue on white		20.00	20.00
UX12 A40	4c **blue**, *light blue* (McKinley)		25.00	25.00

An impression of No. UX11 exists on the back of a U.S. No. UX21.

1915

UX13 A40	2c **green**, *buff* (Rizal)		3.00	2.00
UX14 A40	2c **yellow green**, *amber*		3.50	1.50
UX15 A40	4c **green**, *buff* (McKinley)		20.00	15.00

Design of postage issue of 1935

1935

UX16 A53	2c **red**, *pale buff* (Rizal)		2.50	1.60

No. UX16 Overprinted at left of Stamp **COMMONWEALTH**

1938

UX17 A53	2c **red**, *pale buff*		2.50	1.60

No. UX16 Overprinted **COMMONWEALTH**

UX18 A53	2c **red**, *pale buff*		45.00	45.00

No. UX16 Overprinted **COMMONWEALTH**

UX19 A53	2c **red**, *pale buff*		4.00	4.00

Nos. UX13, UX18 and UX19 Handstamped in Violet **VICTORY**

1944

UX20 A40	2c **green**, *buff*, Rizal (On UX13)		180.00	225.00
UX21 A53	2c **red**, *pale buff* (On UX18)		650.00	—
UX22 A53	2c **red**, *pale buff* (On UX19)		285.00	550.00

Overprinted in Black at left **VICTORY**

1945, Jan. 19

UX23 A76	2c **gray brown**, *pale buff*		1.25	.75
	First day cancel			3.25
a.	"IC" of "Victory" very close		5.00	3.00

This card was not issued without overprint.

PAID REPLY POSTAL CARDS
U.S. Paid Reply Cards of 1892-93 issues
Overprinted with type "a" in blue

1900, Feb.

UY1	2c +2c **blue**, unsevered			
	(5,000)		160.00	500.00
m.	PM2 Message card, detached		27.50	50.00
r.	PR2 Reply card, detached		27.50	50.00

Overprinted type "c" in black

1903

UY2	1c + 1c **black**, *buff*, unsevered			
	(20,000)		150.00	375.00
m.	PM1 Message card, detached		22.50	25.00
r.	PR1 Reply card, detached		22.50	25.00
UY3	2c + 2c **blue**, unsevered			
	(20,000)		300.00	700.00
m.	PM2, Message card, detached		55.00	50.00
r.	PR2, Reply card, detached		55.00	50.00

OFFICIAL CARDS

Overprinted at left of stamp **O. B.**

1925

UZ1 A40	2c **green**, *buff* (Rizal)	35.00	35.00

1935 On postal card No. UX16

UZ2 A53	2c **red**, *pale buff*	14.00	17.50

Overprinted at Left of Stamp **O. B.**

1938 On postal card No. UX19

UZ3 A53	2c **red**, *pale buff*	13.00	17.50

Overprinted Below Stamp O. B.

1941   **Design of postage issue of 1941**
UZ4 A75 2c **light green**, *pale buff*   160.00 *200.00*
This card was not issued without overprint.

Postal Card No. UX19 Overprinted at Left O. B.
of Stamp

1941
UZ5 A53 2c **red**, *pale buff*   20.00 *25.00*

OCCUPATION

Issued Under Japanese Occupation
Nos. 461, 438 and 439 Overprinted with Bars in
Black

1942-43		**Unwmk.**		**Perf. 11x10½, 11**	
N1	A75	2c **apple green**, *Mar. 4, 1942*		.20	.20
		P# block of 4			.25
a.		Pair, one without overprint			—
N2	A58	12c **black**, *Apr. 30, 1943*		.20	.20
N3	A59	16c **dark blue**, *Mar. 4, 1942*		5.00	3.75

Nos. 435a, 435, 442, 443, and 423 Surcharged in
Black

ONE PESO

1942-43			**Perf. 11**	
N4	A55(a)	5(c) on 6c **golden brown** *Sept. 1, 1942*	.20	.20
		First day cover, Manila		1.50
a.		Top bar shorter and thinner	.20	.20
b.		5(c) on 6c **dark brown**	.20	.20
c.		As "b," top bar shorter and thinner	.20	.20
N5	A62(b)	16(c) on 30c **orange red**, *Jan. 11, 1943*	.25	.25
		First day cover		1.75
N6	A63(c)	50c on 1p **red orange & black**, *Apr. 30, 1943*	.60	.60
a.		Double surcharge		300.00
N7	A65(d)	1p on 4p **blue & black**, *Apr. 30, 1943*	115.00	200.00
		Inverted "S" in "PESO;" position 4	125.00	130.00

On Nos. N4 and N4b, the top bar measures 1½x22½mm.
On Nos. N4a and N4c, the top bar measures 1x21mm and the
"5" is smaller and thinner.
The used value for No. N7 is for postal cancellation. Used
stamps exist with first day cancellations. They are worth somewhat less.

CONGRATULATIONS
FALL OF
BATAAN AND
CORREGIDOR
1942

1942, May 18
N8 A54 2(c) on 4c **yellow green**   6.00 6.00
     First day cover   4.00

Issued to commemorate Japan's capture of Bataan and Corregidor. The American-Filipino forces finally surrendered May
7, 1942. No. N8 exists with "R" for "B" in BATAAN.

No. 384 Surcharged in
Black

1942, Dec. 8
N9 A54 5(c) on 4c **yellow green**   .50 .50
     First day cover   2.00
1st anniversary of the "Greater East Asia War."

Nos. C59 and C62
Surcharged in Black

1943, Jan. 23
N10 AP1 2(c) on 8c **carmine**   .25 .25
N11 AP1 5c on 1p **sepia**   .50 .50
     First day cover, #N10-N11   2.00
1st anniv. of the Philippine Executive Commission.

Nipa
Hut — OS1

Mt. Mayon and Mt.
Fuji — OS3

Rice
Planting — OS2

Moro
Vinta — OS4

Wmk. 257

The "c" currency is indicated by four Japanese characters,
"p" currency by two.

Engraved; Typographed (2c, 6c, 25c)
1943-44		**Wmk. 257**	**Perf. 13**	
N12	OS1	1c **deep orange**, *June 7, 1943*	.20	.20
N13	OS2	2c **bright green**, *Apr. 1, 1943*	.20	.20
N14	OS1	4c **slate green**, *June 7, 1943*	.20	.20
N15	OS3	5c **orange brown**, *Apr. 1, 1943*	.20	.20
N16	OS2	6c **red**, *July 14, 1943*	.20	.20
N17	OS3	10c **blue green**, *July 14, 1943*	.20	.20
N18	OS4	12c **steel blue**, *July 14, 1943*	1.00	1.00
N19	OS4	16c **dark brown**, *July 14, 1943*	.20	.20
N20	OS1	20c **rose violet**, *Aug. 16, 1943*	1.25	1.25
N21	OS3	21c **violet**, *Aug. 16, 1943*	.20	.20
N22	OS2	25c **pale brown**, *Aug. 16, 1943*	.20	.20
N23	OS3	1p **deep carmine**, *June 7, 1943*	.75	.75
N24	OS4	2p **dull violet**, *Sept. 16, 1943*	5.00	5.00
		First day cover		5.50
N25	OS4	5p **dark olive**, *Apr. 10, 1944*	8.50	8.50
		First day cover		5.50
		Nos. N12-N25 (14)	18.30	18.30

Map of Manila Bay
Showing Bataan and
Corregidor — OS5

1943, May 7		**Photo.**	**Unwmk.**	
N26	OS5	2c **carmine red**	.20	.20
N27	OS5	5c **bright green**	.25	.25
		Colorless dot after left "5"	1.10	—
		First day cover, #N26-N27, Manila		1.50

1st anniversary of the fall of Bataan and Corregidor.

No. 440 Surcharged in Black

1943, June 20   **Engr.**   **Perf. 11**
N28 A60 12(c) on 20c **light olive green**   .20 .20
     First day cover   1.50
a.   Double surcharge   —
350th anniversary of the printing press in the Philippines.
"Limbagan" is Tagalog for "printing press."

Rizal Monument,
Filipina and Philippine
Flag — OS6

1943, Oct. 14		**Photo.**	**Unwmk.**	**Perf. 12**	
N29	OS6	5c **light blue**		.20	.20
a.		Imperf.		.20	.20
N30	OS6	12c **orange**		.20	.20
a.		Imperf.		.20	.20
N31	OS6	17c **rose pink**		.20	.20
		First day cover, #N29-N31, Manila			1.00
a.		Imperf.		.20	.20
		First day cover, #N29a-N31a, Manila			1.00
		Nos. N29-N31 (3)		.60	.60

"Independence of the Philippines." Japan granted "independence" Oct. 14, 1943, when the puppet republic was founded.
The imperforate stamps were issued without gum.

José
Rizal — OS7

Rev. José
Burgos — OS8

Apolinario Mabini — OS9

1944, Feb. 17		**Litho.**	**Unwmk.**	**Perf. 12**	
N32	OS7	5c **blue**		.20	.20
a.		Imperf.		.20	.20
N33	OS8	12c **carmine**		.20	.20
a.		Imperf.		.20	.20
N34	OS9	17c **deep orange**		.20	.20
		First day cover, #N32-N34, Manila			1.00
a.		Imperf.		.20	.20
		First day cover, #N32a-N34a, *Apr. 17*, Manila			1.50
		Nos. N32-N34 (3)		.60	.60

REPÚBLIKA
NG PILIPINAS
5-7-44

Nos. C60 and C61
Surcharged in
Black

1944, May 7			**Unwmk.**	**Perf. 11**	
N35	AP1	5(c) on 20c **ultramarine**		.50	.35
N36	AP1	12(c) on 60c **blue green**		1.25	.85
		First day cover, #N35-N36			2.50

2nd anniversary of the fall of Bataan and Corregidor.

José P. Laurel — OS10

1945, Jan. 12   **Litho.**   **Unwmk.**   *Imperf.*
Without Gum

N37	OS10	5c dull violet brown	.20	.20
N38	OS10	7c blue green	.20	.20
N39	OS10	20c chalky blue	.20	.20
		First day cover, #N37-N39	1.00	
		Nos. N37-N39 (3)	.60	.60

Issued belatedly on Jan. 12, 1945, to commemorate the first anniversary of the puppet Philippine Republic, Oct. 14, 1944. "S" stands for "sentimos."

The special cancellation devices prepared for use on Oct. 14, 1944, were employed on "First Day" covers Jan. 12, 1945.

OCCUPATION SEMI-POSTAL

Woman, Farming and Cannery — OSP1

1942, Nov. 12   **Litho.**   **Unwmk.**   *Perf. 12*

NB1	OSP1	2c + 1c pale violet	.20	.20
NB2	OSP1	5c + 1c bright green	.25	.20
NB3	OSP1	16c + 2c orange	25.00	25.00
		First day cover, #NB1-NB3	30.00	
		Nos. NB1-NB3 (3)	25.45	25.40

Issued to promote the campaign to produce and conserve food. The surtax aided the Red Cross.

Souvenir Sheet

OSP2

Illustration reduced.

1943, Oct. 14   **Without Gum**   *Imperf.*

NB4	OSP2	Sheet of 3	50.00	10.00
		Sheet with first day cancel and cachet, Manila		2.50
		First day cover, Manila	—	

"Independence of the Philippines."
No. NB4 contains one each of Nos. N29a-N31a. Marginal inscription is from Rizal's "Last Farewell." Sold for 2.50p.

Nos. N18, N20 and N21 Surcharged in Black

BAHÂ
1943
+21

1943, Dec. 8   **Wmk. 257**   *Perf. 13*

NB5	OS4	12c + 21c steel blue	.20	.20
NB6	OS1	20c + 36c rose violet	.20	.20
NB7	OS3	21c + 40c violet	.20	.20
		First day cover, #NB5-NB7	1.20	
		Nos. NB5-NB7 (3)	.60	.60

The surtax was for the benefit of victims of a Luzon flood. "Baha" is Tagalog for "flood."

Souvenir Sheet

REPÚBLICA NG PILIPINAS
MAYNILA

OSP3

Illustration reduced.

1944, Feb. 9   **Litho.**   **Unwmk.**   *Imperf.*
Without Gum

NB8	OSP3	Sheet of 3	5.00	3.00
		First day cover	4.00	

No. NB8 contains one each of Nos. N32a-N34a.
The sheet sold for 1p, the surtax going to a fund for the care of heroes' monuments. Size: 101x143mm. No. NB8 exists with 5c inverted.

OCCUPATION POSTAGE DUE

No. J15 Overprinted with Bar in Blue

1942, Oct. 14   **Unwmk.**   *Perf. 11*

NJ1	D3	3c on 4c brown red	35.00	20.00
		First day cover	—	27.50
		Double bar	—	

On copies of No. J15, two lines were drawn in India ink with a ruling pen across "United States of America" by employees of the Short Paid Section of the Manila Post Office to make a provisional 3c postage due stamp which was used from Sept. 1, 1942 (when the letter rate was raised from 2c to 5c) until Oct. 14 when No. NJ1 went on sale. Value on cover, $125.

OCCUPATION OFFICIAL

Nos. 461, 413, 435, 435a and 442 Overprinted or Surcharged in Black with Bars and

公用
(K.P.)

1943-44   **Unwmk.**   *Perf. 11x10½, 11*

NO1	A75	2c apple green, Apr. 7, 1943	.20	.20
		P# block of 4	.25	
a.		Double overprint	500.00	
		On cover (double overprint)		1,250.
NO2	A55	5(c) on 6c dark brown (On No. 413), June 26, 1944	35.00	35.00
		First day cover		40.00
NO3	A55	5(c) on 6c golden brown (On No. 435a), Apr. 7, 1943	.20	.20
a.		Narrower spacing between bars	.20	.20
b.		5(c) on 6c dark brown (On No. 435)	.20	.20
c.		As "b," narrower spacing between bars	.20	.20
d.		Double surcharge		

NO4	A62	16(c) on 30c orange red, Apr. 7, 1943	.30	.30
a.		Wider spacing between bars	.30	.30
		First day cover, Nos. NO1, NO3-NO4		35.00

On Nos. NO3 and NO3b the bar deleting "United States of America" is 9¾ to 10mm above the bar deleting "Common." On Nos. NO3a and NO3c, the spacing is 8 to 8½mm.

On No. NO4, the center bar is 19mm long, 3½mm below the top bar and 6mm above the Japanese characters. On No. NO4a, the center bar is 20½mm long, 9mm below the top bar and 1mm above the Japanese characters.

"K.P." stands for Kagamitang Pampahalaan, "Official Business" in Tagalog.

5

REPUBLIKA NG
PILIPINAS
(K. P.)

Nos. 435 and 435a Surcharged in Black

1944, Aug. 28   **Unwmk.**   *Perf. 11*

NO5	A55	(5c) on 6c golden brown	.20	.20
a.		5(c) on 6c dark brown	.20	.20

Nos. O34 and C62 Overprinted in Black

REPUBLIKA NG PILIPINAS

Pilipinas
REPUBLIKA

(K. P.)

K.P.

a   b

NO6	A60(a)	20c light olive green	.25	.25
NO7	AP1(b)	1p sepia	.65	.65
		First day cover, #NO5-NO7	2.00	

OCCUPATION ENVELOPES

No. U41 Surcharged in Black

5   5

1943, Apr. 1

NU1	E4	5c on 2c carmine	.50	.30
		Entire	1.90	1.25
		Entire, 1st day cancel		4.00

No. U41 Surcharged in Black

REPUBLIKA NG PILIPINAS

5   5

1944, Feb. 17

NU2	E4	5c on 2c carmine	.75	.50
		Entire	3.00	5.00
		Entire, 1st day cancel		7.50
a.		Inverted surcharged	—	
b.		Double surcharge	—	
c.		Both 5's missing	—	

OCCUPATION POSTAL CARDS

Values are for entire cards.
Nos. UX19 and UZ4 Overprinted with Bars in Black

1942

NUX1	A53	2c red, pale buff, Mar. 4, 1942	15.00	15.00
		First day cancel		85.00
a.		Vertical obliteration bars reversed	140.00	

NUX2 A75 2c **light green**, *pale buff*, Dec.
12, 1942   2.50   2.00
    First day cancel   6.00

Rice Planting — A77

1943, May 17
NUX3 A77 2c **green**   1.00   *1.00*
    First day cancel, Manila   2.00

OCCUPATION OFFICIAL CARDS

Nos. UX19, UX17 and UX18 Overprinted in 公 侮 Black with Bars and (K. P.)

1943, Apr. 7
NUZ1 A53 2c **red**, *pale buff*   4.00   3.00
    First day cancel   100.00
  a.   On No. UX17   —   —
  b.   On No. UX18   —   —

No. NUX3 Overprinted in Black

**REPUBLIKA
NG PILIPINAS
(K. P.)**

1944, Aug. 28
NUZ2 A77 2c **green**   1.50   *1.00*
    First day cancel   2.00
  a.   Double overprint   —

FILIPINO REVOLUTIONARY GOVERNMENT

The Filipino Republic was instituted by Gen. Emilio Aguinaldo on June 23, 1899. At the same time he assumed the office of President. Aguinaldo dominated the greater part of the island of Luzon and some of the smaller islands until late in 1899. He was taken prisoner by United States troops on March 23, 1901.

The devices composing the National Arms, adopted by the Filipino Revolutionary Government, are emblems of the Katipunan political secret society or of Katipunan origin. The letters "K K K" on these stamps are the initials of this society whose complete name is "Kataas-taasang, Kagalang-galang Katipunan nang Mañga Anak nang Bayan," meaning "Sovereign Worshipful Association of the Sons of the Country."

The regular postage and telegraph stamps were in use on Luzon as early as Nov. 10, 1898. Owing to the fact that stamps for the different purposes were not always available together with a lack of proper instructions, any of the adhesives were permitted to be used in the place of the other. Hence telegraph and revenue stamps were accepted for postage and postage stamps for revenue or telegraph charges. In addition to the regular postal emission, there are a number of provisional stamps, issues of local governments of islands and towns.

POSTAGE ISSUES

Coat of Arms

   A1   A2   A3

1898-99   **Unwmk.**   *Perf. 11½*
Y1 A1 2c **red**   175.00 125.00
  a.   Double impression   225.00
Y2 A2 2c **red**   .20   .25
    On cover   300.00
  b.   Double impression   —
  d.   Horiz. pair, imperf. between —
  e.   Vert. pair, imperf. between 200.00
Y3 A3 2c **red**   150.00 *200.00*

Imperf pairs and pairs, imperf horizontally, have been created from No. Y2e.

RS1

N1

REGISTRATION STAMP
YF1 RS1 8c **green**   1.00   10.00
    On cover with #Y2   3,000.
  a.   Imperf., pair   —
  b.   Imperf. vertically, pair   —

NEWSPAPER STAMP
YP1 N1 1m **black**   .20
  a.   Imperf., pair   .20

PROOFS
1906

			(1) Large	DIE (2) Small	(2a)
241P	2c	yellow green		500.	750.
242P	4c	carmine lake	600.	500.	750.
243P	6c	violet	600.	500.	750.
244P	8c	brown	600.	500.	750.
245P	10c	dark blue		500.	750.
246P	12c	brown lake		500.	750.
247P	16c	violet black	600.	500.	750.
248P	20c	orange brown		500.	750.
249P	26c	violet brown		500.	750.
250P	30c	olive green	600.	500.	750.
251P	1p	orange		500.	750.
252P	2p	black		500.	750.
253P	4p	dark blue		500.	750.
254P	10p	dark green		500.	750.

1909-13

255P	12c	red orange	600.	500.
256P	16c	olive green	600.	500.
257P	20c	yellow	600.	500.
258P	26c	blue green	600.	500.
259P	30c	ultramarine	600.	500.
260P	1p	pale violet	600.	500.
260AP	2p	violet brown	600.	500.
275P	30c	gray	600.	500.

1923

303P	16c	olive bister	450.	
303TC	16c	olive green	450.	

1926

322P	18c	light brown & black, plate, glazed card		350.

1932

357P	18c	red orange	450.	
357TC	18c	orange red	450.	

1935

383P	2c	rose	600.
384P	4c	yellow green	600.
385P	6c	dark brown	600.
386P	8c	violet	600.
387P	10c	rose carmine	600.
388P	12c	black	600.
389P	16c	dark blue	600.
390P	20c	light olive green	600.
390TC	20c	black	—
391P	26c	indigo	600.
392P	30c	orange red	600.
393P	1p	red orange & black	600.
394P	2p	bister brown & black	600.
395P	4p	blue & black	600.
396P	5p	green & black	600.

1936

408P	2c	orange brown	450.
408TC	2c	yellow green	450.

1937

425P	2c	yellow green		500.

1939

452P	2c	yellow green		500.
453P	6c	carmine		500.
454P	12c	bright blue		500.

1939

455P	2c	green	750.	500.
456P	6c	orange		500.
457P	12c	carmine		500.

1940

458P	2c	dark orange	1,000.	600.
459P	6c	dark green		600.
460P	12c	purple		600.

1941

461P	2c	apple green		600.

1946

497P	2c	sepia	—

AIR POST
1941

C59P	8c	carmine	500.
C60P	20c	ultramarine	500.
C61P	60c	blue green	500.
C62P	1p	sepia	500.

SPECIAL DELIVERY
1906

E2P	20c	ultramarine	800.	700.	250.
E2TC	20c	green		700.	

POSTAGE DUE
1899

J1P	1c	deep claret	1,100.
J2P	2c	deep claret	1,100.
J3P	5c	deep claret	1,100.
J4P	10c	deep claret	1,100.
J5P	50c	deep claret	1,100.

1901

J6P	3c	deep claret	1,100.
J7P	30c	deep claret	1,100.

SPECIMEN STAMPS

Handstamped US Type E in Purple **Specimen.**

1899

213S E	1c	yellow green	150.00
214dS E	2c	rose carmine, type IV	150.00
215S E	3c	purple	150.00
216S E	5c	blue	150.00
217S E	10c	brown, type I	150.00
218S E	15c	olive brown	150.00
219S E	50c	orange	150.00

See note after No. 219 for Special Printings with black "Specimen" overprints.

Overprinted US Type R in Black *Specimen*

1917-25

290S R	2c	green	40.00
291S R	4c	carmine	40.00
292S R	6c	deep violet	40.00
293S R	8c	yellow brown	40.00
294S R	10c	deep blue	40.00
295S R	12c	red orange	40.00
297S R	20c	orange yellow	40.00
298S R	26c	green	40.00
299S R	30c	gray	40.00
300S R	1p	pale violet	40.00
301S R	2p	violet brown	40.00
302S R	4p	blue	40.00

1923-26

303S R	16c	olive bister	25.00
304S R	10p	deep green	25.00

1926   **Overprinted Type R in Red**

319S R	2c	green & black	65.00
320S R	4c	carmine & black	65.00
321S R	16c	olive green & black	65.00
322S R	18c	light brown & black	65.00
323S R	20c	orange & black	65.00
324S R	24c	gray & black	65.00
325S R	1p	rose lilac & black	65.00

Overprinted US Type S in Red *Cancelled*

1926

319S S	2c	green & black	65.00
320S S	4c	carmine & black	65.00
321S S	16c	olive green & black	65.00
322S S	18c	light brown & black	65.00
323S S	20c	orange & black	65.00
324S S	24c	gray & black	65.00
325S S	1p	rose lilac & black	65.00

Imperforate copies of this set, on glazed cards with centers in brown, are known with the "Cancelled" overprint.

Handstamped "SPECIMEN" in Red Capitals, 13x3mm

1925

340S S	2c	green	75.00
341S S	4c	carmine	75.00
342S S	6c	deep violet	75.00
343S S	8c	yellow brown	100.00
344S S	10c	deep blue	100.00
345S S	12c	red orange	100.00
346S S	16c	olive bister	100.00
347S S	20c	yellow	100.00
348S S	26c	blue green	100.00
349S S	30c	gray	100.00
350S S	1p	violet	100.00
351S S	2p	violet brown	100.00
352S S	4p	deep blue	150.00
353S S	10p	deep green	250.00

SPECIAL DELIVERY

1919	**Overprinted Type R in Black**	
E5S R	20c **ultramarine**	200.00

Handstamped "SPECIMEN" in Red Capitals, 13x3mm

1925		
E6aS	20c **violet blue**	300.00

POSTAGE DUE

1899	**Overprinted Type E in Black**	
J1S E	1c **deep claret**	150.00
J2S E	2c **deep claret**	150.00
J3S E	5c **deep claret**	150.00
J4S E	10c **deep claret**	150.00
J5S E	50c **deep claret**	150.00

OFFICIAL

1926	**Overprinted Type R in Red**	
O1S R	2c **green & black**	30.00
O2S R	4c **carmine & black**	30.00
O3S R	18c **light brown & black**	30.00
O4S R	20c **orange & black**	30.00

1926	**Overprinted Type S in Red**	
O1S S	2c **green & black**	30.00
O2S S	4c **carmine & black**	30.00
O3S S	18c **light brown & black**	30.00
O4S S	20c **orange & black**	30.00

PUERTO RICO

(Porto Rico)

United States troops landed at Guanica Bay, Puerto Rico, on July 25, 1898, and mail service between various points in Puerto Rico began soon after under the authority of General Wilson, acting governor of the conquered territory, who authorized a provisional service early in August, 1898. The first Military Postal Station was opened at La Playa de Ponce on August 3, 1898. Control of the island passed formally to the United States on October 18, 1898. Twenty-one military stations operating under the administration of the Military Postal Service, were authorized in Puerto Rico after the Spanish-American war. After the overprinted provisional issue of 1900, unoverprinted stamps of the United States replaced those of Puerto Rico.

Name changed to Puerto Rico by Act of Congress, approved May 17, 1932.

Italicized numbers in parentheses indicate quantities issued.

100 CENTS = 1 DOLLAR.

PROVISIONAL ISSUES
Ponce Issue

A11

1898	**Unwmk.　Handstamped**　*Imperf.*	
200 A11	5c **violet,** *yellowish*	9,000. —

The only way No. 200 is known used is handstamped on envelopes. Both unused stamps and used envelopes have a violet control mark.

Uses on 2c U.S. stamps on cover were strictly as a cancellation, not as provisional postage.

Dangerous counterfeits exist.

Coamo Issue

A12

Types of "5":
I - Curved flag. Pos. 2, 3, 4, 5.
II - Flag turns down at right. Pos. 1, 9, 10.
III - Fancy outlined "5." Pos. 6, 7.
IV - Flag curls into ball at right. Pos. 8.

Typeset, setting of 10

1898, Aug.	**Unwmk.**		*Imperf.*
201 A12	5c **black,** Type I	650.	1,050.
	Type II	700.	1,100.
	Type III	775.	1,200.
	Type IV	850.	1,350.
	Irregular "block" of 4 showing one of each type	3,750.	
	Sheet of 10	10,000.	
	On cover		25,000.
	Pair on cover		—

Blocks not showing all four types and pairs normally sell for 10-20% over the value of the individual stamps.

The stamps bear the control mark "F. Santiago" in violet. About 500 were issued.

Dangerous counterfeits exist.

Regular Issue

United States Nos. 279, 279Bf, 281, 272 and 282C Overprinted in Black at 36 degree Angle

1899		**Wmk. 191**		***Perf. 12***
210 A87	1c **yellow green,** *Mar. 15*		5.00	1.40
	On cover			22.00
	First day cover			—
	Block of 4		25.00	8.50
	P# strip of 3, Impt.		45.00	
	P# block of 6, Impt.		275.00	
a.	Overprint at 25 degree angle		7.50	2.25
	Pair, 36 degree and 25 degree angles		25.00	
	"PORTO RICU"		30.00	
211 A88	2c **reddish carmine,** type IV, *Mar. 15*		4.25	1.25
	On cover			15.00
	Block of 4		22.50	8.50
	P# strip of 3, Impt.		37.50	
	P# block of 6, Impt.		350.00	
	"FORTO RICO" (pos. 77)		—	
a.	Overprint at 25 degree angle, *Mar. 15*		5.50	2.25
	On cover			20.00
	First day cover			—
	Block of 4		27.50	15.00
	P# strip of 3, Impt.		45.00	
	P# block of 6, Impt.		275.00	
	Pair, 36 degree and 25 degree angles		25.00	
	P# strip of 3, Impt.		95.00	
	P# block of 6, Impt.		700.00	
	"PORTU RICO" (pos. 46)		35.00	20.00
	"PORTO RICU" (pos. 3)		—	
	"PURTO RICO"		—	
	"FURTU RICO"		—	
212 A91	5c **blue**		9.00	2.50
	On cover			40.00
	Block of 4		45.00	27.50
	P# strip of 3, Impt.		65.00	
	P# block of 6, Impt.		350.00	
213 A93	8c **violet brown**		27.50	17.50
	On cover			125.00
	Block of 4		130.00	87.50
	P# strip of 3, Impt.		240.00	
	P# block of 6, Impt.		*1,750.*	
	"FORTO RICO"		90.00	60.00
a.	Overprint at 25 degree angle		32.50	18.50
	Pair, 36 degree and 25 degree angles		100.00	
c.	"PORTO RIC"		125.00	110.00
214 A94	10c **brown,** type I		17.50	6.00
	On cover			120.00
	Block of 4		87.50	35.00
	P# strip of 3, Impt.		110.00	
	P# block of 6, Impt.		1,250.	
	"FORTO RICO"		85.00	70.00
	Nos. 210-214 (5)		63.25	28.65

Misspellings of the overprint on Nos. 210-214 (PORTO RICU, PORTU RICO, FORTO RICO) are actually broken letters.

United States Nos. 279 and 279B
Overprinted in Black

1900				
215 A87	1c **yellow green**		6.00	1.40
	On cover			17.50
	Block of 4		25.00	7.25
	P# strip of 3, Impt.		30.00	
	P# block of 6, Impt.		175.00	
216 A88	2c **red,** type IV, *Apr. 2*		4.75	1.25
	On cover			15.00

	Block of 4	22.50	5.75
	P# strip of 3, Impt.	32.50	
	P# block of 6, Impt.	175.00	
b.	Inverted overprint		*8,250.*

Special Printing

In March 1900 one pane of 100 stamps of each of the 1c (No. 215), 2c (No. 216) and 5c, 8c and 10c values, as well as 1c, 2c and 10c postage due stamps were specially overprinted for displays at the Paris Exposition (1900) and Pan American Exposition (1901). These last six items were never regularly issued with the PUERTO RICO overprint and therefore have no Scott catalogue number. The 2c pane was light red, type IV.

Copies were handstampd type E "Specimen" in black ink by H. G. Mandel and mounted by him in separate displays for the two Expositions. Additional copies from each pane were also handstamped "Specimen," but most were destroyed after the Expositions.

J. M. Bartels, a stamp dealer, signed some copies from these panes "Special Surcharge" in pencil on the gum to authenticate them as coming from the "Mandel" Special Printing panes. In 1904 or later, he handstamped additional surviving copies "Special Surcharge" in red ink on the back as his guarantee. Some of these guaranteed stamps had Mandel's "Specimen" handstamp on the face while others did not. Value, each $1,750.

No Special Printing panes overprinted "Porto Rico" were produced by the government. Copies do exist with a black type E "Specimen" handstamp, but it is believed that H. G. Mandel applied such handstamps to regularly issued overprinted "Porto Rico" stamps from his personal collection. Copies are known of the 2c type IV, in reddish carmine, 25 degree angle.

AIR POST

In 1938 a series of eight labels, two of which were surcharged, was offered to the public as "Semi-Official Air Post Stamps", the claim being that they had been authorized by the "Puerto Rican postal officials." These labels, printed by the Ever Ready Label Co. of New York, were a private issue of Aerovias Nacionales Puerto Rico, operating a passenger and air express service. Instead of having been authorized by the postal officials, they were at first forbidden but later tolerated by the Post Office Department at Washington.

In 1941 a further set of eight triangular labels was prepared and offered to collectors, and again the Post Office Department officials at Washington objected and forbade their use after September 16, 1941.

These labels represent only the charge for service rendered by a private enterprise for transporting matter outside the mails by plane. Their use did not and does not eliminate the payment of postage on letters carried by air express, which must in every instance be paid by United States postage stamps.

POSTAGE DUE STAMPS

United States Nos. J38, J39 and J42
Overprinted in Black at 36 degree Angle

1899 **Wmk. 191** **Perf. 12**

J1	D2	1c **deep claret**	22.50	5.50
		On cover		125.00
		Block of 4	100.00	25.00
		P# strip of 3, Impt.	120.00	
		P# block of 6, Impt.	625.00	
a.		Overprint at 25 degree angle	22.50	7.50
		Pair, 36 degree and 25 degree angles	65.00	
		P# strip of 3, Impt.	150.00	
		P# block of 6, Impt.	750.00	
J2	D2	2c **deep claret**	17.50	6.00
		On cover		250.00
		Block of 4	55.00	25.00
		P# strip of 3, Impt.	120.00	
		P# block of 6, Impt.	800.00	
a.		Overprint at 25 degree angle	15.00	7.00
		Pair, 36 degree and 25 degree angles	55.00	
		P# strip of 3, Impt.	140.00	
		P# block of 6, Impt.	900.00	
J3	D2	10c **deep claret**	160.00	60.00
		On cover		
		Block of 4	1,250.	—
		P# strip of 3, Impt.	900.00	
		P# block of 6, Impt.	3,750.	
a.		Overprint at 25 degree angle	180.00	85.00
		Pair, 36 degree and 25 degree angles	600.00	

ENVELOPES

U.S. Envelopes of 1887 Issue Overprinted in Black

PORTO RICO.

20mm long

1899-1900

Note: Some envelopes for which there was no obvious need were issued in small quantities. Anyone residing in Puerto Rico could, by depositing with his postmaster the required amount, order any envelope in quantities of 500, or multiples thereof, provided it was on the schedule of U.S. envelopes. Such special orders are indicated by a plus sign, i. e., Nos. U15 and U18, and half the quantities of Nos. U16 and U17.

U1	U71	2c **green** (No. U311) *(3,000)*	16.00	*20.00*
		Entire	40.00	*250.00*
a.		Double overprint, entire	—	
U2	U74	5c **blue** (No. U330) *(1,000)*	20.00	20.00
		Entire	55.00	*250.00*
		Double overprint, entire	—	

U.S. Envelopes of 1899 Overprinted in color of the stamp

PORTO RICO.

21mm long

U3	U79	2c **carmine** (No. U362) *(100,000)*	3.00	3.00
		Entire	10.00	*12.00*
U4	U84	5c **blue** (No. U377) *(10,000)*	8.00	*9.00*
		Entire	17.50	*32.50*

Overprinted in Black **PORTO RICO.**

19mm long

U5	U77	1c **green**, *blue* (No. U355) *(1,000)*		750.
		Entire		1,900.
U6	U79	2c **carmine**, *amber* (No. U363), Die 2 *(500)*	450.	*500.*
		Entire	1,100.	*1,250.*
U7	U79	2c **carmine**, *oriental buff* (No. U364), Die 2 *(500)*		500.
		Entire		*1,250.*
U8	U80	2c **carmine**, *oriental buff* (No. U369), Die 3 *(500)*		600.
		Entire		*1,300.*
U9	U79	2c **carmine**, *blue* (No. U365), Die 2		
		Entire		*4,000.*
U10	U83	4c **brown** (No. U374), Die 3 *(500)*	200.	*500.*
		Entire	500.	*900.*

U.S. Envelopes of 1899 Issue Overprinted

PUERTO RICO.

23mm long

U11	U79	2c **carmine** (No. U362) red overprint *(100,000)*	4.00	3.00
		Entire	10.00	*11.00*
U12	U79	2c **carmine**, *oriental buff* (No. U364), Die 2, black overprint *(1,000)*	—	*325.00*
		Entire	1,200.	*1,300.*
U13	U80	2c **carmine**, *oriental buff* (No. U369), Die 3, black overprint *(1,000)*		375.00
		Entire		*1,750.*
U14	U84	5c **blue** (No. U377) blue overprint *(10,000)*	14.00	14.00
		Entire	42.50	*50.00*

Overprinted in Black **PUERTO RICO.**

U15	U77	1c **green**, *oriental buff* (No. U354) *(500)*+	20.00	*50.00*
		Entire	75.00	*80.00*
U16	U77	1c **green**, *blue* (No. U355) *(1,000)*+	25.00	*50.00*
		Entire	95.00	*125.00*
U17	U79	2c **carmine**, *oriental buff* (No. U364) *(1,000)*+	20.00	*50.00*
		Entire	95.00	*135.00*
U18	U79	2c **carmine**, *blue* (No. U365) *(500)*+	20.00	*50.00*
		Entire	75.00	*135.00*

There were two settings of the overprint, with minor differences, which are found on Nos. U16 and U17.

WRAPPER

U.S. Wrapper of 1899 Issue Overprinted in Green

PORTO RICO.

21mm long

W1	U77	1c **green**, *manila* (No. W357) *(15,000)*	8.00	*35.00*
		Entire	17.00	*110.00*

POSTAL CARDS

Values are for Entires.

Imprinted below stamp **PORTO RICO.**

1899-1900 **U.S. Postal Card No. UX14**

UX1	PC8	1c **black**, *buff*, imprint 21mm long	165.	*175.*
b.		Double imprint		2,250.

Imprinted below stamp **PORTO RICO.**

UX1A	PC8	1c **black**, *buff*, imprint 20mm long	1,200.	*1,300.*

Imprinted below stamp **PORTO RICO.**

UX2	PC8	1c **black**, *buff*, imprint 26mm long	165.	*190.*

Imprinted below stamp **PUERTO RICO.**

UX3	PC8	1c **black**, *buff*		150.	*200.*

REVENUE

U.S. Revenue Stamps Nos. R163, R168-R169, R171 and Type of 1898 Surcharged in Black or Dark Blue

PORTO RICO
10 c.
Excise Revenue
a

PORTO RICO
$1
EXCISE REVENUE
b

1901 **Wmk. 191R** **Hyphen-hole Roulette 7**

R1	R15(a)	1c on 1c **pale blue** (Bk)	10.00	8.75
R2	R15(a)	10c on 10c **dark brown**	12.50	11.00
R3	R15(a)	25c on 25c **purple brown**	15.00	11.00
R4	R15(a)	50c on 50c **slate violet**	25.00	16.50
R5	R16(b)	$1 on $1 **pale greenish gray**	62.50	22.50
R6	R16(b)	$3 on $3 **pale greenish gray**	70.00	32.50
R7	R16(b)	$5 on $5 **pale greenish gray**	85.00	37.50
R8	R16(b)	$10 on $10 **pale greenish gray**	120.00	70.00
R9	R16(b)	$50 on $50 **pale greenish gray**	325.00	160.00
		Nos. R1-R9 *(9)*	725.00	369.75

Lines of 1c surcharge spaced farther apart; total depth of surcharge 15¾mm instead of 11mm.

RECTIFIED SPIRITS

RECTIFIED

SPIRITS

U.S. Wine Stamps of 1933-34 Overprinted in Red or Carmine

1934 **Offset Printing** **Wmk. 191R** **Rouletted 7**
Overprint Lines 14mm Apart, Second Line 25mm Long

RE1	RE5	2c **green**		15.00
RE2	RE5	3c **green**		55.00
RE3	RE5	4c **green**		17.50
RE4	RE5	5c **green**		15.00
RE5	RE5	6c **green**		17.50

Overprint Lines 21½mm Apart, Second Line 23½mm Long

RE6	RE2	50c **green**		27.50
RE7	RE2	60c **green**		25.00

Handstamped overprints are also found on U.S. Wine stamps of 1933-34.

U.S. Wine Stamps of 1933-34 Overprinted in Black

RECTIFIED

RECTIFIED

SPIRITS
a

SPIRITS
b

1934 **Offset Printing** **Wmk. 191R** **Rouletted 7**

RE8	RE5(a)	1c **green**	22.50
RE9	RE5(a)	2c **green**	12.50
RE10	RE5(a)	3c **green**	60.00
RE11	RE5(a)	5c **green**	12.50
RE12	RE5(a)	6c **green**	15.00
RE13	RE2(b)	50c **green**	17.50
RE14	RE2(b)	60c **green**	15.00
RE15	RE2(b)	72c **green**	75.00
RE16	RE2(b)	80c **green**	40.00

RECTIFIED SPIRITS

U.S. Wine Stamps of 1933-34 Overprinted in Black

PUERTO RICO

1934 **Offset Printing** **Wmk. 191R** **Rouletted 7**

RE17	RE5	½c **green**		2.50
RE18	RE5	1c **green**	50.00	.60
RE19	RE5	2c **green**	50.00	.50
RE20	RE5	3c **green**	100.00	3.50
RE21	RE5	4c **green**		.75
RE22	RE5	5c **green**	50.00	1.00
RE23	RE5	6c **green**	50.00	1.25
RE24	RE5	10c **green**	100.00	3.50
RE25	RE5	30c **green**		30.00

Overprint Lines 12½mm Apart

RE26	RE2	36c **green**		6.00
RE27	RE2	40c **green**	150.00	5.00
RE28	RE2	50c **green**	150.00	2.50
RE29	RE2	60c **green**	125.00	.50
a.		Inverted overprint		
RE30	RE2	72c **green**	150.00	3.00
RE31	RE2	80c **green**	150.00	4.00
RE32	RE2	$1 **green**	175.00	7.50

George Sewall Boutwell — R1

Engr. (8c & 58c); Litho.

1942-57 **Wmk. 191** **Rouletted 7**
Without Gum

RE33	R1	½c **carmine**	3.50	1.25
RE34	R1	1c **sepia**	8.25	3.50
RE35	R1	2c **bright yellow green**	1.10	.15
RE36	R1	3c **lilac**	67.50	32.50
RE37	R1	4c **olive**	2.25	.50
RE38	R1	5c **orange**	5.50	1.00
RE39	R1	6c **red brown**	4.00	1.25
RE40	R1	8c **bright pink** ('57)	8.25	3.50
RE41	R1	10c **bright purple**	12.50	5.00
RE41A	R1	30c **vermilion**	190.00	
RE42	R1	36c **dull yellow**	250.00	65.00
RE43	R1	40c **deep claret**	20.00	7.00
RE44	R1	50c **green**	11.00	4.00
RE45	R1	58c **red orange**	82.50	6.00
RE46	R1	60c **brown**	1.40	.15
RE47	R1	62c **black**	3.50	.70
RE48	R1	72c **blue**	40.00	1.00

RE49	R1	77½c olive gray	11.00	3.50
RE50	R1	80c brownish black	14.00	6.00
RE51	R1	$1 violet	82.50	22.50

Nos. RE33-RE51 (20)   818.75

The 30c is believed not to have been placed in use.

SPECIMEN

Handstamped U.S. Type E in Purple **Specimen.**

1899

210S	E	1c yellow green	180.00
211S	E	2c reddish carmine, type IV	180.00
212S	E	5c blue	180.00
213S	E	8c violet brown	180.00
214S	E	10c brown	180.00

See note after No. 216 for Special Printings with **black** "Specimen" overprint.

Postage Due

1899

J1S	E	1c deep claret	225.00
J2S	E	2c deep claret	225.00
J3S	E	10c deep claret	225.00

Revenue

R1S	E	1c on 1c pale blue	40.00
R2S	E	10c on 10c dark brown	40.00
R3S	E	25c on 25c purple brown	40.00
R4S	E	50c on 50c state violet	40.00
R5S	E	$1 on $1 pale greenish gray	40.00
R6S	E	$3 on $3 pale greenish gray	40.00
R7S	E	$5 on $5 pale greenish gray	40.00
R8S	E	$10 on $10 pale greenish gray	40.00
R9S	E	$50 on $50 pale greenish gray	40.00

RYUKYU ISLANDS

LOCATION — Chain of 63 islands between Japan and Formosa, separating the East China Sea from the Pacific Ocean.
GOVT. — Semi-autonomous under United States administration.
AREA — 848 sq. mi.
POP. — 945,465 (1970)
CAPITAL — Naha, Okinawa
    The Ryukyus were part of Japan until American forces occupied them in 1945. The islands reverted to Japan May 15, 1972.

100 Sen = 1 Yen

100 Cents = 1 Dollar (1958).

> **Catalogue values for unused stamps are for Never Hinged items beginning with Scott 1 in the regular postage section, Scott C1 in the air post section, Scott E1 in the special delivery section, Scott R1 in the revenue section, Scott 91S in the specimen section and Scott RQ1 in the unemployment insurance section.**

Cycad — A1

Lily — A2

Sailing Ship — A3

Farmer — A4

Issued: First printing, July 1, 1948: second printing, July 18, 1949.

A5   Ryukyu University — A6

Designs: 50s, Tile rooftop & Shishi. 1y, Ryukyu girl. 2y, Shuri Castle. 3y, Guardian dragon. 4y, Two women. 5y, Sea shells.

Wmk. 257

1948-49		**Typo.** **Wmk. 257**		**Perf. 13**
		Second Printing		
1	A1	5s magenta	1.50	1.50
		Imprint block of 10	30.00	
2	A2	10s yellow green	6.00	5.50
		Imprint block of 10	90.00	
3	A1	20s yellow green	2.50	2.50
		Imprint block of 10	40.00	
4	A3	30s vermilion	1.50	1.50
		Imprint block of 10	30.00	
5	A2	40s magenta	1.50	1.50
		Imprint block of 10	25.00	
6	A3	50s ultramarine	3.00	3.25
		Imprint block of 10	50.00	
7	A4	1y ultramarine	6.00	5.50
		Imprint block of 10	90.00	
		Nos. 1-7 (7)	22.00	21.25
		First Printing		
1a	A1	5s magenta	2.50	3.50
		First day cover		250.00
		Imprint block of 10	40.00	
2a	A2	10s yellow green	1.40	2.00
		First day cover		250.00
		Imprint block of 10	25.00	
3a	A1	20s yellow green	1.40	2.00
		First day cover		250.00
		Imprint block of 10	25.00	
4a	A3	30s vermilion	2.50	3.25
		First day cover		250.00
		Imprint block of 10	40.00	
5a	A2	40s magenta	50.00	50.00
		First day cover		250.00
		Imprint block of 10	700.00	
6a	A3	50s ultramarine	2.50	3.50
		First day cover		250.00
		Imprint block of 10	40.00	
7a	A4	1y ultramarine	450.00	290.00
		First day cover		250.00
		Imprint block of 10	5,000.	
		Nos. 1a-7a (7)	510.30	354.25

First printing: thick yellow gum, dull colors, rough perforations, grayish paper. Second printing: white gum, sharp colors, cleancut perforations, white paper.

1950, Jan. 21		**Photo.** **Unwmk.**		**Perf. 13x13½**
		Off-white Paper		
8	A5	50s dark carmine rose	.20	.20
		First day cover		20.00
		Imprint block of 6	2.00	
a.		White paper, Sept. 6, 1958	.50	.50
		First day cover		27.50
		Imprint block of 10	6.50	
9	A5	1y deep blue	2.50	2.50
		First day cover		20.00
		Imprint block of 6	16.00	
10	A5	2y rose violet	11.00	6.00
		First day cover		20.00
		Imprint block of 6	75.00	
11	A5	3y carmine rose	25.00	11.00
		First day cover		20.00
		Imprint block of 6	225.00	
12	A5	4y greenish gray	15.00	11.00
		First day cover		20.00
		Imprint block of 6	110.00	
13	A5	5y blue green	7.50	5.00
		First day cover		20.00
		Imprint block of 6	55.00	
		First day cover, #8-13		200.00
		Nos. 8-13 (6)	61.20	35.20

No. 8a has colorless gum and an 8-character imprint in the sheet margin. The original 1950 printing on off-white paper has yellowish gum and a 5-character imprint.
For surcharges see Nos. 16-17.

1951, Feb. 12				**Perf. 13½x13**
14	A6	3y red brown	55.00	20.00
		First day cover		60.00
		Imprint block of 6	425.00	

Opening of Ryukyu University, Feb. 12.

Pine Tree — A7

1951, Feb. 19   *Perf. 13*
15	A7	3y dark green	50.00	20.00
		First day cover		60.00
		Imprint block of 6	400.00	

Reforestation Week, Feb. 18-24.

Nos. 8 and 10 Surcharged in Black

Type I	Type II	Type III

Three types of 10y surcharge:
I - Narrow-spaced rules, "10" normal spacing.
II - Wide-spaced rules, "10" normal spacing.
III - Rules and "10" both wide-spaced.

1952   *Perf. 13x13½*
16	A5	10y on 50s **dark carmine**		
		rose (II)	9.00	9.00
		Imprint block of 6	85.00	
a.	Type I		35.00	35.00
		Imprint block of 6	225.00	
b.	Type III		40.00	40.00
		Imprint block of 6	325.00	
17	A5	100y on 2y **rose violet**	1,900.	1,200.
		Imprint block of 6	16,500.	

Surcharge forgeries are known on No. 17. Authentication by competent experts is recommended.

Dove, Bean Sprout and Map — A8

Madanbashi Bridge — A9

1952, Apr. 1   *Perf. 13½x13*
18	A8	3y **deep plum**	120.00	35.00
		First day cover		80.00
		Imprint block of 10	1,800.	

Establishment of the Government of the Ryukyu Islands (GRI), April 1, 1952.

1952-53

Designs: 2y, Main Hall, Shuri Castle. 3y, Shurei Gate. 6y, Stone Gate, Soenji Temple, Naha. 10y, Benzaiten-do Temple. 30y, Sonohan Utaki (altar) at Shuri Castle. 50y, Tamaudun (royal mausoleum). Shuri. 100y, Stone Bridge, Hosho Pond, Enkaku Temple.

19	A9	1y **red**, *Nov. 20, 1952*	.20	.20
		Imprint block of 10	3.00	
20	A9	2y **green**, *Nov. 20, 1952*	.25	.25
		Imprint block of 10	3.50	
21	A9	3y **aquamarine**, *Nov. 20, 1952*	.35	.35
		First day cover, #19-21		35.00
		Imprint block of 10	5.00	
22	A9	6y **blue**, *Jan. 20, 1953*	1.75	1.75
		First day cover		27.50
		Imprint block of 10	22.50	
23	A9	10y **crimson rose**, *Jan. 20, 1953*	2.50	.90
		First day cover		47.50
		Imprint block of 10	32.50	
24	A9	30y **olive green**, *Jan. 20, 1953*	11.00	6.50
		First day cover		75.00
		Imprint block of 10	140.00	
a.		30y **light olive green**, *1958*	30.00	
		Imprint block of 10	450.00	
25	A9	50y **rose violet**, *Jan. 20, 1953*	15.00	8.25
		First day cover		125.00
		Imprint block of 10	225.00	
26	A9	100y **claret**, *Jan. 20, 1953*	20.00	6.25
		First day cover		190.00
		Imprint block of 10	275.00	
		First day cover, #22-26		550.00
		Nos. 19-26 (8)	51.05	24.45

Issued: 1y, 2y and 3y, Nov. 20, 1952. Others, Jan. 20, 1953.

Reception at Shuri Castle — A10

Perry and American Fleet — A11

1953, May 26   *Perf. 13½x13, 13x13½*
27	A10	3y **deep magenta**	12.50	6.50
		Imprint block of 6	100.00	
28	A11	6y **dull blue**	1.25	1.25
		First day cover, #27-28		11.00
		Imprint block of 6	9.50	

Centenary of the arrival of Commodore Matthew Calbraith Perry at Naha, Okinawa.

Chofu Ota and Pencil-shaped Matrix — A12

Shigo Toma and Pen — A13

1953, Oct. 1   *Perf. 13½x13*
29	A12	4y **yellow brown**	10.00	5.00
		First day cover		17.50
		Imprint block of 10	140.00	

Third Newspaper Week.

1954, Oct. 1
30	A13	4y **blue**	13.00	7.50
		First day cover		22.50
		Imprint block of 10	175.00	

Fourth Newspaper Week.

Ryukyu Pottery — A14

Noguni Shrine and Sweet Potato Plant — A15

Designs: 15y, Lacquerware. 20y, Textile design.

1954-55   **Photo.**   *Perf. 13*
31	A14	4y **brown**, *June 25, 1954*	1.00	.60
		First day cover		9.00
		Imprint block of 10	11.00	
32	A14	15y **vermilion**, *June 20, 1955*	4.00	2.00
		First day cover		12.50
		Imprint block of 10	55.00	
33	A14	20y **yellow orange**, *June 20, 1955*	2.25	2.00
		First day cover		12.50
		Imprint block of 10	32.50	
		First day cover, #32-33		35.00

For surcharges see Nos. C19, C21, C23.

1955, Nov. 26
34	A15	4y **blue**	11.00	7.00
		First day cover		22.50
		Imprint block of 10	140.00	

350th anniv. of the introduction of the sweet potato to the Ryukyu Islands.

Ryukyu Islands stamps can be mounted in the Scott Ryukyu Islands album.

Stylized Trees — A16

Willow
Dance — A17

1956, Feb. 18　　　　　　　　**Unwmk.**
35　A16　4y bluish green　　　10.00　5.00
　　　First day cover　　　　　　　20.00
　　　Imprint block of 6　　80.00
　　　Arbor Week, Feb. 18-24.

1956, May 1　　　　　　　**Perf. 13**
8y, Straw hat dance. 14y, Dancer in warrior costume with fan.
36　A17　5y rose lilac　　　　.90　.60
　　　First day cover　　　　　　6.50
　　　Imprint block of 10　　12.00
37　A17　8y violet blue　　　2.00　1.65
　　　First day cover　　　　　　6.50
　　　Imprint block of 10　　27.50
38　A17　14y reddish brown　3.00　2.00
　　　First day cover　　　　　　6.50
　　　Imprint block of 10　　40.00
　　　First day cover, #36-38　　35.00
　　For surcharges see Nos. C20, C22.

Telephone
A18

1956, June 8
39　A18　4y violet blue　　　15.00　8.00
　　　First day cover　　　　　　12.50
　　　Imprint block of 6　　110.00
　　Establishment of dial telephone system.

Garland of Pine,
Bamboo and
Plum — A19

Map of Okinawa
and Pencil
Rocket — A20

1956, Dec. 1　　　　　**Perf. 13½x13**
40　A19　2y multicolored　　2.00　2.00
　　　First day cover　　　　　　3.00
　　　Imprint block of 10　　27.50
　　　New Year, 1957.

1957, Oct. 1　　　**Photo.**　**Perf. 13½x13**
41　A20　4y deep violet blue　.75　.75
　　　First day cover　　　　　　6.00
　　　Imprint block of 10　　8.50
　　7th annual Newspaper Week, Oct. 1-7.

Phoenix — A21

1957, Dec. 1　　　**Unwmk.**　**Perf. 13**
42　A21　2y multicolored　　.25　.25
　　　First day cover　　　　　　1.50
　　　Imprint block of 10　　3.50
　　　New Year, 1958.

Ryukyu
Stamps
A22

1958, July 1　　　　　　**Perf. 13½**
43　A22　4y multicolored　　.80　.80
　　　First day cover　　　　　　1.25
　　　Imprint block of 4　　4.00
　　10th anniv. of 1st Ryukyu stamps.

Yen Symbol and Dollar
Sign — A23

Perf. 10.3, 10.8, 11.1 & Compound
1958, Sept. 16　　　　　　　　**Typo.**
　　　　　Without Gum
44　A23　½c orange　　　　.90　.90
　　　Imprint block of 6　　7.00
a.　Imperf., pair　　　　　1,000.
b.　Horiz. pair, imperf. between　100.00
c.　Vert. pair, imperf. between　150.00
d.　Vert. strip of 4, imperf. between　500.00
45　A23　1c yellow green　　1.40　1.40
　　　Imprint block of 6　　11.00
a.　Horiz. pair, imperf. between　150.00
b.　Vert. pair, imperf. between　110.00
c.　Vert. strip of 3, imperf. between　450.00
d.　Vert. strip of 4, imperf. between　500.00
e.　Block of 4, imperf. btwn. vert. &
　　horiz.　　　　　　　　—
46　A23　2c dark blue　　　2.25　2.25
　　　Imprint block of 6　　17.50
a.　Horiz. pair, imperf. between　150.00
b.　Vert. pair, imperf. between　1,500.
c.　Horiz. strip of 3, imperf. between　300.00
d.　Vert. strip of 4, imperf. between　500.00
47　A23　3c deep carmine　1.75　1.50
　　　Imprint block of 6　　14.00
a.　Horiz. pair, imperf. between　150.00
b.　Vert. pair, imperf. between　110.00
c.　Vert. strip of 3, imperf. between　300.00
d.　Vert. strip of 4, imperf. between　550.00
e.　Block of 4, imperf. btwn. vert. &
　　horiz.　　　　　　　　—
48　A23　4c bright green　　2.25　2.25
　　　Imprint block of 6　　17.50
a.　Horiz. pair, imperf. between　500.00
b.　Vert. pair, imperf. between　150.00
49　A23　5c orange　　　　4.25　3.75
　　　Imprint block of 6　　35.00
a.　Horiz. pair, imperf. between　150.00
b.　Vert. pair, imperf. between　750.00
50　A23　10c aquamarine　5.75　4.75
　　　Imprint block of 6　　42.50
a.　Horiz. pair, imperf. between　200.00
b.　Vert. pair, imperf. between　150.00
c.　Vert. strip of 3, imperf. between　550.00
51　A23　25c bright violet blue　8.00　6.00
　　　Imprint block of 6　　62.50
a.　Gummed paper, perf. 10.3 ('61)　9.50　8.50
　　　Imprint block of 6　　95.00
b.　Horiz. pair, imperf. between　1,500.
c.　Vert. pair, imperf. between　—
d.　Vert. strip of 4, imperf. between　600.00
52　A23　50c gray　　　　17.50　10.00
　　　Imprint block of 6　　140.00
a.　Gummed paper, perf. 10.3 ('61)　10.50　10.00
　　　Imprint block of 6　　110.00
　　　First day cover, #51a-52a　　20.00
b.　Horiz. pair, imperf. between　1,200.
53　A23　$1 rose lilac　　12.50　5.50
　　　Imprint block of 6　　100.00
a.　Horiz. pair, imperf. between　400.00
b.　Vert. pair, imperf. between　1,750.
　　　Nos. 44-53 (10)　　56.55　38.30
Printed locally. Perforation, paper and shade varieties exist.
Nos. 51a and 52a are on off-white paper and perf 10.3.
First day covers come with various combinations of stamps:
Nos. 44-48, 49-53, 44-53 etc. Values $10 for short set of low values (Nos. 44-48) to $45 for full set.

Gate of
Courtesy
A24

1958, Oct. 15　　　**Photo.**　**Perf. 13½**
54　A24　3c multicolored　1.25　1.25
　　　First day cover　　　　　　1.50
　　　Imprint block of 4　　6.25
Restoration of Shureimon, Gate of Courtesy, on road leading to Shuri City.

Lion Dance — A25

Trees and
Mountains — A26

1958, Dec. 10　　　**Unwmk.**　**Perf. 13½**
55　A25　1½c multicolored　.25　.25
　　　First day cover　　　　　　1.50
　　　Imprint block of 6　　1.90
　　　New Year, 1959.

1959, Apr. 30　　**Litho.**　**Perf. 13½x13**
56　A26　3c blue, yellow green,
　　　　green & red　　　　.70　.60
　　　First day cover　　　　　　1.00
　　　Imprint block of 6　　5.50
　　"Make the Ryukyus Green" movement.

Yonaguni
Moth — A27

1959, July 23　　　**Photo.**　**Perf. 13**
57　A27　3c multicolored　1.10　1.00
　　　First day cover　　　　　　1.50
　　　Imprint block of 6　　8.00
Meeting of the Japanese Biological Education Society in Okinawa.

Hibiscus — A28

Toy (Yakaji) — A29

Designs: 3c, Fish (Moorish idol). 8c, Sea shell (Phalium bandatum). 13c, Butterfly (Kallinia Inachus Eucerca), denomination at left, butterfly going up. 17c, Jellyfish (Dactylometra pacifera Goette).

Inscribed:

琉球郵便

1959, Aug. 10　　　　　**Perf. 13x13½**
58　A28　½c multicolored　　.20　.20
　　　Imprint block of 10　　3.25
59　A28　3c multicolored　　.75　.40
　　　Imprint block of 10　　9.00
60　A28　8c light ultramarine, black
　　　　& ocher　　　　　10.00　5.50
　　　Imprint block of 10　　140.00
61　A28　13c light blue, gray & or-
　　　　ange　　　　　　2.50　1.75

62 A28 17c **violet blue, red & yellow** 20.00 9.00
Imprint block of 10 275.00
First day cover, #58-62 15.00
Nos. 58-62 (5) 33.45 16.85
Four-character inscription measures 10x2mm on ½c; 12x3mm on 3c, 8c; 8½x2mm on 13c, 17c. See Nos. 76-80.

1959, Dec. 1 **Litho.**
63 A29 1½c **gold & multicolored** .55 .45
First day cover 1.50
Imprint block of 10 8.00

New Year, 1960.

University Badge — A30

1960, May 22 **Photo.** *Perf. 13*
64 A30 3c **multicolored** .95 .75
First day cover 1.25
Imprint block of 6 7.25

10th anniv. opening of Ryukyu University.

Dancer — A31

Designs: Various Ryukyu Dances.

1960, Nov. 1 **Photo.** *Perf. 13*
Dark Gray Background

---

65 A31 1c **yellow, red & violet** 1.25 .80
Imprint block of 10 16.00
66 A31 2½c **crimson, blue & yellow** 3.00 1.00
Imprint block of 10 37.50
67 A31 5c **dark blue, yellow & red** .65 .50
Imprint block of 10 10.00
68 A31 10c **dark blue, yellow & red** .80 .65
Imprint block of 10 11.00
First day cover, #65-68 5.50

See Nos. 81-87, 220.

Torch and Nago Bay — A32

Runners at Starting Line — A33

1960, Nov. 8
72 A32 3c **light blue, green & red** 5.50 3.00
First day cover 3.50
Imprint block of 6 40.00
73 A33 8c **orange & slate green** .75 .75
First day cover 1.50
Imprint block of 6 5.75
First day cover, #72-73 4.50

8th Kyushu Inter-Prefectural Athletic Meet, Nago, Northern Okinawa, Nov. 6-7.

Little Egret and Rising Sun — A34

1960, Dec. 1 **Unwmk.** *Perf. 13*
74 A34 3c **reddish brown** 5.50 3.50
First day cover 4.00
Imprint block of 6 42.50

National census.

Okinawa Bull Fight — A35

1960, Dec. 10 *Perf. 13½*
75 A35 1½c **bister, dark blue & red brown** 1.75 1.50
First day cover 2.00
Imprint block of 6 12.50

New Year, 1961.

Type of 1959 With Japanese Inscription Redrawn:

琉 球 郵 便

1960-61 **Photo.** *Perf. 13x13½*
76 A28 ½c **multicolored,** *Oct. 1961* .45 .45
Imprint block of 10 5.50
77 A28 3c **multicolored,** *Aug. 23, 1961* .90 .35
First day cover 1.50
Imprint block of 10 12.50
78 A28 8c **light ultramarine, black & ocher,** *July 1, 1960* .90 .80
Imprint block of 10 12.50
79 A28 13c **blue, brown & red,** *July 1, 1960* 1.10 .90
Imprint block of 10 15.00
80 A28 17c **violet blue, red & yellow,** *July 1, 1960* 15.00 6.00
Imprint block of 10 190.00
First day cover, #78-80 15.00
Nos. 76-80 (5) 18.35 8.50

Size of Japanese inscription on Nos. 78-80 is 10½x1½mm. On No. 79 the denomination is at right, butterfly going down.

Dancer Type of 1960 with "RYUKYUS" Added in English

Perforation and Paper Varieties of Ryukyu Islands Scott 44-53

Perforation	Perf. ID#	1/2¢ (No. 44) Paper Type				1¢ (No. 45) Paper Type				2¢ (No. 46) Paper Type				3¢ (No. 47) Paper Type				4¢ (No. 48) Paper Type				5¢ (No. 49) Paper Type				10¢ (No. 50) Paper Type				25¢ (No. 51) Paper Type				50¢ (No. 52) Paper Type				$1 (No. 53) Paper Type			
		1	2	3	4	1	2	3	4	1	2	3	4	1	2	3	4	1	2	3	4	1	2	3	4	1	2	3	4	1	2	3	4	1	2	3	4	1	2	3	4
11.1 x 11.1	M	*			*	*	*			*				*			*	*	*		*	*				*	*			*				*				*		*	
11.1 x 10.8	N	*			*	*	*			*			*	*	*		*	*		∞	*	?		*	*	*			*				*				*		*	
11.1 x 10.3	O	*			*	?	*			*			*	*	*			*			*	*				*				*				*				*			
10.8 x 11.1	P				*	*	*	*						*	*			*	*			*				*								*				*		*	
10.8 x 10.8	Q	*			*	*	*	*						*	*			*	*			*				*				*	*	*		*				*		*	
10.8 x 10.3	R	*			*	*	*							?			*	*			*					*				*	*			*				*			
10.3 x 11.1	S	*				*	*			*				*	*		*	?	*			*	*			*				*								*			
10.3 x 10.8	T	*			*	*	*			*				*	*		*	*				*	*			?	*	*						*				*		*	
10.3 x 10.3	U	*				?	*			*				?	*							*	*			*	*			?	*			\		*		\			

Paper Legend: 1= off-white; 2= white; 3= ivory; 4= thick

Specialists use a shorthand to refer to perf. and paper types: e.g., 50M3 =10¢ stamp, perf. 11.1 x 11.1, ivory paper.

Notes:

  * = Verified variety

  ? = Reported in literature, but unverified variety.

  ∞ = 48N4 is unknown; however, a single example of 48N exists on a thick white paper unknown used for any other issue.

  \ = These particular perf/paper combinations are known only in stamps of the Second (1961) Printing (51a and 52a)

The following are known unused only: 45R1, 45T2, 47O1, 48N4, 53O1.

The following are known used only: 47N4, 47T4, 50M3, 50Q2, 50R2, 50T2, 51P3, 51S1, 53T3.

Chart classifications and data supplied by courtesy of the Ryukyu Philatelic Specialist Society.

1961-64   Perf. 13

81	A31	1c **multicolored,** *Dec. 5, 1961*	.20	.20
		First day cover		1.00
		Imprint block of 10	2.00	
82	A31	2½c **multicolored,** *June 20, 1962*	.20	.20
		Imprint block of 10	2.25	
83	A31	5c **multicolored,** *June 20, 1962*	.25	.25
		Imprint block of 10	3.00	
84	A31	10c **multicolored,** *June 20, 1962*	.45	.40
		First day cover, #82-84		1.50
		Imprint block of 10	5.75	
84A	A31	20c **multicolored,** *Jan. 20, 1964*	3.00	1.40
		First day cover		2.50
		Imprint block of 10	32.50	
85	A31	25c **multicolored,** *Feb. 1, 1962*	1.00	.90
		First day cover		2.00
		Imprint block of 10	13.00	
86	A31	50c **multicolored,** *Sept. 1, 1961*	2.50	1.40
		Imprint block of 10	32.50	
87	A31	$1 **multicolored,** *Sept. 1, 1961*	6.00	.25
		Imprint block of 10	70.00	
		First day cover, #86-87		35.00
		Nos. 81-87 (8)	13.55	4.90

Pine Tree — A36

1961, May 1   Photo.   Perf. 13

88	A36	3c **yellow green & red**	1.50	1.25
		First day cover		1.50
		Imprint block of 6	12.00	

"Make the Ryukyus Green" movement.

Naha, Steamer and Sailboat — A37

1961, May 20

89	A37	3c **aquamarine**	2.10	1.50
		First day cover		1.75
		Imprint block of 6	16.00	

40th anniv. of Naha.

White Silver Temple — A38

Books and Bird — A39

1961, Oct. 1   Typo.   Unwmk.   Perf. 11

90	A38	3c **red brown**	2.00	1.50
		First day cover		1.75
		Imprint block of 6	12.50	
a.		Horiz. pair, imperf. between	500.00	
b.		Vert. pair, imperf. between	600.00	

Merger of townships Takamine, Kanegushiku and Miwa with Itoman.

1961, Nov. 12   Litho.   Perf. 13

91	A39	3c **multicolored**	1.10	.90
		First day cover		1.25
		Imprint block of 6	10.00	

Book Week.

Rising Sun and Eagles — A40

Symbolic Steps, Trees and Government Building — A41

1961, Dec. 10   Photo.   Perf. 13½

92	A40	1½c **gold, vermilion & black**	2.00	2.00
		First day cover		2.50
		Imprint block of 6	16.00	

New Year, 1962.

1962, Apr. 1   Unwmk.   Perf. 13½

Design: 3c, Government Building.

93	A41	1½c **multicolored**	.60	.60
		Imprint block of 6	4.75	
94	A41	3c **bright green, red & gray**	.80	.80
		Imprint block of 6	6.50	
		First day cover, #93-94		2.00

10th anniv. of the Government of the Ryukyu Islands (GRI).

Anopheles Hyrcanus Sinensis — A42

Design: 8c, Malaria eradication emblem and Shurei gate.

1962, Apr. 7   Perf. 13½x13

95	A42	3c **multicolored**	.60	.60
		Imprint block of 6	4.50	
96	A42	8c **multicolored**	.90	.75
		Imprint block of 6	7.50	
		First day cover, #95-96		2.25

World Health Organization drive to eradicate malaria.

Dolls and Toys — A43

Linden or Sea Hibiscus — A44

1962, May 5   Litho.   Perf. 13½

97	A43	3c **red, black, blue & buff**	1.10	1.00
		First day cover		1.50
		Imprint block of 6	9.00	

Children's Day, 1962.

1962, June 1   Photo.

Flowers: 3c, Indian coral tree. 8c, Iju (Schima liukiuensis Nakal). 13c, Touch-me-not (garden balsam). 17c, Shell flower (Alpinia speciosa).

98	A44	½c **multicolored**	.20	.20
		Imprint block of 10	1.75	
99	A44	3c **multicolored**	.35	.20
		Imprint block of 10	4.75	
100	A44	8c **multicolored**	.40	.40
		Imprint block of 10	5.50	
101	A44	13c **multicolored**	.60	.55
		Imprint block of 10	7.00	
102	A44	17c **multicolored**	1.00	.80
		Imprint block of 10	12.00	
		First day cover, #98-102		3.75
		Nos. 98-102 (5)	2.50	2.05

See Nos. 107 and 114 for 1½c and 15c flower stamps. For surcharge see No. 190.

Earthenware — A45

1962, July 5   Perf. 13½x13

103	A45	3c **multicolored**	3.50	2.50
		First day cover		2.75
		Imprint block of 6	26.00	

Philatelic Week.

Japanese Fencing (Kendo) — A46

1962, July 25   Perf. 13

104	A46	3c **multicolored**	4.00	3.00
		First day cover		3.50
		Imprint block of 6	30.00	

All-Japan Kendo Meeting in Okinawa, July 25, 1962.

Rabbit Playing near Water, Bingata Cloth Design — A47

Young Man and Woman, Stone Relief — A48

1962, Dec. 10   Perf. 13x13½

105	A47	1½c **gold & multicolored**	1.00	.80
		First day cover		1.50
		Imprint block of 10	12.50	

New Year, 1963.

1963, Jan. 15   Photo.   Perf. 13½

106	A48	3c **gold, black & blue**	.90	.80
		First day cover		1.50
		Imprint block of 6	6.75	

Gooseneck Cactus — A49

Trees and Wooded Hills — A50

1963, Apr. 5   Perf. 13x13½

107	A49	1½c **dark blue green, yellow & pink**	.20	.20
		First day cover		1.25
		Imprint block of 10	1.50	

1963, Mar. 25   Perf. 13½x13

108	A50	3c **ultramarine, green & red brown**	1.00	.80
		First day cover		1.25
		Imprint block of 6	7.00	

"Make the Ryukyus Green" movement.

Map of
Okinawa — A51

Hawks over Islands — A52

1963, Apr. 30   Unwmk.   Perf. 13½
109 A51 3c multicolored   1.25   1.00
             First day cover   1.50
             Imprint block of 6   9.00

Opening of the Round Road on Okinawa.

1963, May 10   Photo.
110 A52 3c multicolored   1.10   .95
             First day cover   1.50
             Imprint block of 6   9.00

Bird Day, May 10.

Shioya Bridge — A53

1963, June 5
111 A53 3c multicolored   1.10   .95
             First day cover   1.40
             Imprint block of 6   8.25

Opening of Shioya Bridge over Shioya Bay.

Tsuikin-wan
Lacquerware
Bowl — A54

1963, July 1   Unwmk.   Perf. 13½
112 A54 3c multicolored   3.00   2.50
             First day cover   2.75
             Imprint block of 6   22.50

Map of Far East and
JCI Emblem — A55

1963, Sept. 16   Photo.   Perf. 13½
113 A55 3c multicolored   .70   .70
             First day cover   1.25
             Imprint block of 6   6.00

Meeting of the International Junior Chamber of Commerce
(JCI), Naha, Okinawa, Sept. 16-19.

Mamaomoto — A56

Site of Nakagusuku
Castle — A57

1963, Oct. 15   Perf. 13x13½
114 A56 15c multicolored   2.00   .80
             First day cover   1.25
             Imprint block of 10   25.00

1963, Nov. 1   Perf. 13½x13
115 A57 3c multicolored   .70   .60
             First day cover   1.25
             Imprint block of 6   5.25

Protection of national cultural treasures.

Flame — A58

Dragon (Bingata
Pattern) — A59

1963, Dec. 10   Perf. 13½
116 A53 3c red, dark blue & yellow .70 .60
             First day cover   1.25
             Imprint block of 6   5.25

15th anniv. of the Universal Declaration of Human Rights.

1963, Dec. 10   Photo.
117 A59 1½c multicolored   .60   .50
             First day cover   1.50
             Imprint block of 10   7.50

New Year, 1964.

Carnation — A60

Pineapples and
Sugar Cane — A61

1964, May 10   Perf. 13½
118 A60 3c blue, yellow, black &
             carmine   .40   .35
             First day cover   1.25
             Imprint block of 6   3.00

Mothers Day.

1964, June 1
119 A61 3c multicolored   .40   .35
             First day cover   1.25
             Imprint block of 6   3.00

Agricultural census.

Minsah Obi (Sash Woven of
Kapok) — A62

1964, July 1   Unwmk.   Perf. 13½
120 A62 3c deep blue, rose pink &
             ocher   .55   .50
             First day cover   2.25
             Imprint block of 6   4.50
 a. 3c deep blue, deep carmine &
             ocher   .70   .65
             First day cover   2.75
             Imprint block of 6   5.25

Philatelic Week.

Girl Scout and
Emblem — A63

1964, Aug. 31   Photo.
121 A63 3c multicolored   .40   .35
             First day cover   1.25
             Imprint block of 6   3.00

10th anniv. of Ryukyuan Girl Scouts.

Shuri Relay
Station — A64

Parabolic Antenna
and Map — A65

1964, Sept. 1   Unwmk.   Perf. 13½
          Black Overprint
122 A64 3c deep green   .65   .65
             Imprint block of 6   5.50
 a. Figure "1" inverted   27.50 27.50
123 A65 8c ultramarine   1.25   1.25
             Imprint block of 6   10.00
             First day cover, #122-123   4.75

Opening of the Ryukyu Islands-Japan microwave system carrying telephone and telegraph messages. Nos. 122-123 not
issued without overprint.

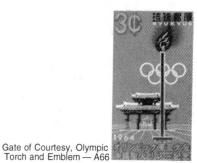

Gate of Courtesy, Olympic
Torch and Emblem — A66

1964, Sept. 7   Photo.   Perf. 13½x13
124 A66 3c ultramarine, yellow &
             red   .20   .20
             First day cover   1.25
             Imprint block of 6   1.50

Relaying the Olympic torch on Okinawa en route to Tokyo.

"Naihanchi," Karate
Stance — A67

"Makiwara,"
Strengthening Hands
and Feet — A68

"Kumite," Simulated Combat — A69

1964-65		Photo.		Perf. 13½
125	A67	3c dull claret, yel & blk, Oct. 5, 1964	.50	.45
		First day cover		1.25
		Imprint block of 6	3.25	
126	A68	3c yel & multi, Feb. 5, 1965	.40	.40
		First day cover		1.25
		Imprint block of 6	3.00	
127	A69	3c gray, red & blk, June 5, 1965	.40	.40
		First day cover		1.25
		Imprint block of 6	3.00	

Karate, Ryukyuan self-defense sport.

Miyara Dunchi — A70

Snake and Iris (Bingata) — A71

1964, Nov. 1			Perf. 13½
128	A70	3c multicolored	.25 .25
		First day cover	1.25
		Imprint block of 6	1.50

Protection of national cultural treasures. Miyara Dunchi was built as a residence by Miyara-pechin Toen in 1819.

1964, Dec. 10			Photo.
129	A71	1½c multicolored	.30 .25
		First day cover	2.00
		Imprint block of 10	4.00

New Year, 1965.

Boy Scouts — A72

1965, Feb. 6			Perf. 13½
130	A72	3c light blue & multi	.45 .40
		First day cover	1.50
		Imprint block of 6	4.00

10th anniv. of Ryukyuan Boy Scouts.

Main Stadium, Onoyama A73

1965, July 1			Perf. 13x13½
131	A73	3c multicolored	.25 .25
		First day cover	1.00
		Imprint block of 6	2.00

Inauguration of the main stadium of the Onoyama athletic facilities.

Samisen of King Shoko — A74

1965, July 1		Photo.		Perf. 13½
132	A74	3c buff & multicolored	.45	.40
		First day cover		1.25
		Imprint block of 6	3.25	

Philatelic Week.

Kin Power Plant — A75

ICY Emblem, Ryukyu Map — A76

1965, July 1			
133	A75	3c green & multicolored	.25 .25
		First day cover	1.00
		Imprint block of 6	2.00

Completion of Kin power plant.

1965, Aug. 24		Photo.		Perf. 13½
134	A76	3c multicolored	.20	.20
		First day cover		1.00
		Imprint block of 6	1.75	

20th anniv. of the UN and International Cooperation Year, 1964-65.

Naha City Hall — A77

1965, Sept. 18		Unwmk.		Perf. 13½
135	A77	3c blue & multicolored	.20	.20
		First day cover		1.00
		Imprint block of 6	1.75	

Completion of Naha City Hall.

Chinese Box Turtle — A78

Horse (Bingata) — A79

Turtles: No. 137, Hawksbill turtle (denomination at top, country name at bottom). No. 138, Asian terrapin (denomination and country name on top).

1965-66		Photo.		Perf. 13½
136	A78	3c golden brown & multi, Oct. 20, 1965	.30	.30
		First day cover		1.00
		Imprint block of 6	2.50	
137	A78	3c black, yel & brown, Jan. 20, 1966	.30	.30
		First day cover		1.00
		Imprint block of 6	2.50	
138	A78	3c gray & multicolored, Apr. 20, 1966	.30	.30
		First day cover		1.00
		Imprint block of 6	2.50	

1965, Dec. 10		Photo.		Perf. 13½
139	A79	1½c multicolored	.20	.20
		First day cover		1.50
		Imprint block of 10	2.25	
a.		Gold omitted	1,200.	—

New Year, 1966.
There are 92 unused and 2 used examples of No. 139a known.

NATURE CONSERVATION ISSUE

Noguchi's Okinawa Woodpecker — A80

Sika Deer — A81

Design: No. 142, Dugong.

1966		Photo.		Perf. 13½
140	A80	3c blue green & multi, Feb. 15	.20	.20
		First day cover		1.00
		Imprint block of 6	1.65	
141	A81	3c blue, red, black, brown & green, Mar. 15	.25	.25
		First day cover		1.00
		Imprint block of 6	1.75	
142	A81	3c blue, yellow green, black & red, Apr. 20	.25	.25
		First day cover		1.00
		Imprint block of 6	1.75	

Ryukyu Bungalow Swallow — A82

1966, May 10		Photo.		Perf. 13½
143	A82	3c sky blue, black & brown	.20	.20
		First day cover		1.00
		Imprint block of 6	1.10	

4th Bird Week, May 10-16.

Lilies and Ruins — A83

1966, June 23			Perf. 13x13½
144	A83	3c multicolored	.20 .20
		First day cover	1.00
		Imprint block of 6	1.00

Memorial Day, end of the Battle of Okinawa, June 23, 1945.

University of the Ryukyus — A84

1966, July 1			
145	A84	3c multicolored	.20 .20
		First day cover	1.00
		Imprint block of 6	1.00

Transfer of the University of the Ryukyus from U.S. authority to the Ryukyu Government.

Lacquerware, 18th
Century — A85

Tile-Roofed House
and UNESCO
Emblem — A86

1966, Aug. 1   **Perf. 13½**
146 A85 3c **gray & multicolored**   .20   .20
　　First day cover   1.50
　　Imprint block of 6   1.30
　　　　　Philatelic Week.

1966, Sept. 20   **Photo.**   **Perf. 13½**
147 A86 3c **multicolored**   .20   .20
　　First day cover   1.00
　　Imprint block of 6   1.10
　　　　20th anniv. of UNESCO.

Government Museum
and Dragon
Statue — A87

1966, Oct. 6
148 A87 3c **multicolored**   .20   .20
　　First day cover   1.00
　　Imprint block of 6   1.00
Completion of the GRI (Government of the Ryukyu Islands)
Museum, Shuri.

Tomb of Nakasone-
Tuimya Genga, Ruler
of Miyako — A88

1966, Nov. 1   **Photo.**   **Perf. 13½**
149 A88 3c **multicolored**   .20   .20
　　First day cover   1.00
　　Imprint block of 6   1.00
　　Protection of national cultural treasures.

Ram in Iris
Wreath — A89

Clown Fish — A90

1966, Dec. 10   **Photo.**   **Perf. 13½**
150 A89 1½c **dark blue & multicolored**   .20   .20
　　First day cover   1.50
　　Imprint block of 10   1.10
　　　　　New Year, 1967.

1966-67
Fish: No. 152, Young boxfish (white numeral at lower left).
No. 153, Forceps fish (pale buff numeral at lower right). No.
154, Spotted triggerfish (orange numeral). No. 155, Saddleback
butterflyfish (carmine numeral, lower left).

151 A90 3c **orange red & multi**, *Dec. 20,*
　　　　　　1966   .20   .20
　　First day cover   1.00
　　Imprint block of 6   1.75
152 A90 3c **orange yellow & multi**, *Jan. 10,*
　　　　　　1967   .20   .20
　　First day cover   1.00
　　Imprint block of 6   1.75
153 A90 3c **multicolored**, *Apr. 10, 1967*   .30   .25
　　First day cover   1.00
　　Imprint block of 6   1.75

154 A90 3c **multicolored**, *May 25, 1967*   .30   .25
　　First day cover   1.00
　　Imprint block of 6   1.75
155 A90 3c **multicolored**, *June 10, 1967*   .30   .25
　　First day cover   1.00
　　Imprint block of 6   1.90
　　　　Nos. 151-155 (5)   1.30   1.15

Tsuboya
Urn — A91

Episcopal Miter — A92

1967, Apr. 20
156 A91 3c **yellow & multicolored**   .20   .20
　　First day cover   1.25
　　Imprint block of 6   1.65
　　　　　Philatelic Week.

1967-68   **Photo.**   **Perf. 13½**
Seashells: No. 158, Venus comb murex. No. 159, Chiragra
spider. No. 160, Green truban. No. 161, Euprotomus bulla.

157 A92 3c **light green & multi**, *July 20, 1967* .20 .20
　　First day cover   1.00
　　Imprint block of 6   1.25
158 A92 3c **greenish blue & multi**, *Aug. 30,*
　　　　　　1968   .20   .20
　　First day cover   1.00
　　Imprint block of 6   1.25
159 A92 3c **emerald & multi**, *Jan. 18, 1968* .25   .20
　　First day cover   1.00
　　Imprint block of 6   1.65
160 A92 3c **light blue & multi**, *Feb. 20, 1968* .30 .20
　　First day cover   1.00
　　Imprint block of 6   1.65
161 A92 3c **bright blue & multi**, *June 5, 1968* .60 .50
　　First day cover   1.00
　　Imprint block of 6   4.00
　　　　Nos. 157-161 (5)   1.55   1.35

Red-tiled Roofs and
ITY Emblem — A93

1967, Sept. 11   **Photo.**   **Perf. 13½**
162 A93 3c **multicolored**   .20   .20
　　First day cover   1.00
　　Imprint block of 6   1.25
　　　　International Tourist Year.

Mobile TB
Clinic — A94

1967, Oct. 13   **Photo.**   **Perf. 13½**
163 A94 3c **lilac & multicolored**   .20   .20
　　First day cover   1.00
　　Imprint block of 6   1.25
　　15th anniv. of the Anti-Tuberculosis Society.

Hojo Bridge, Enkaku
Temple, 1498 — A95

1967, Nov. 1
164 A95 3c **blue green & multicolored**   .20   .20
　　First day cover   1.00
　　Imprint block of 6   1.50
　　Protection of national cultural treasures.

Monkey
(Bingata) — A96

TV Tower and
Map — A97

1967, Dec. 11   **Photo.**   **Perf. 13½**
165 A96 1½c **silver & multicolored**   .25   .20
　　First day cover   1.50
　　Imprint block of 10   3.00
　　　　　New Year, 1968.

1967, Dec. 22
166 A97 3c **multicolored**   .25   .25
　　First day cover   1.00
　　Imprint block of 6   1.50
Opening of Miyako and Yaeyama television stations.

Dr. Kijin Nakachi
and Helper — A98

Pill Box
(Inro) — A99

1968, Mar. 15   **Photo.**   **Perf. 13½**
167 A98 3c **multicolored**   .25   .25
　　First day cover   1.00
　　Imprint block of 6   1.50
120th anniv. of the first vaccination in the Ryukyu Islands, by
Dr. Kijin Nakachi.

1968, Apr. 18
168 A99 3c **gray & multicolored**   .45   .45
　　First day cover   1.25
　　Imprint block of 6   3.50
　　　　　Philatelic Week.

Young Man, Library,
Book and Map of
Ryukyu
Islands — A100

1968, May 13
169 A100 3c **multicolored**   .30   .25
　　First day cover   1.00
　　Imprint block of 6   1.75
　　　10th International Library Week.

Mailmen's
Uniforms and
Stamp of
1948 — A101

1968, July 1   **Photo.**   **Perf. 13x13½**
170 A101 3c **multicolored**   .30   .25
　　First day cover   1.00
　　Imprint block of 6   1.75
First Ryukyuan postage stamps, 20th anniv.

Main Gate, Enkaku
Temple — A102

1968, July 15   Photo. & Engr.   Perf. 13½
171 A102 3c **multicolored**   .30   .25
        First day cover   1.00
        Imprint block of 6   1.75

Restoration of the main gate Enkaku Temple, built 1492-
1495, destroyed during World War II.

Old Man's   Mictyris
Dance — A103   Longicarpus — A104

1968, Sept. 15   Photo.   Perf. 13½
172 A103 3c **gold & multicolored**   .30   .25
        First day cover   1.00
        Imprint block of 6   2.00

Old People's Day.

1968-69   Photo.   Perf. 13½

Crabs: No. 174, Uca dubia stimpson. No. 175, Baptozius
vinosus. No. 176, Cardisoma carnifex. No. 177, Ocypode cer-
atophthalma pallas.

173 A104 3c **blue, ocher & black,** *Oct. 10,*
                1968   .30   .25
        First day cover   1.25
        Imprint block of 6   2.50
174 A104 3c **light blue green & multi,** *Feb. 5,*
                1969   .35   .30
        First day cover   1.25
        Imprint block of 6   2.75
175 A104 3c **light green & multi,** *Mar. 5,*
                1969   .35   .30
        First day cover   1.25
        Imprint block of 6   2.75
176 A104 3c **light ultra & multi,** *May 15, 1969* .45   .40
        First day cover   1.25
        Imprint block of 6   3.25
177 A104 3c **light ultra & multi,** *June 2, 1969* .45   .40
        First day cover   1.25
        Imprint block of 6   3.25
        Nos. 173-177 (5)   1.90   1.65

Saraswati
Pavilion — A105

1968, Nov. 1   Photo.   Perf. 13½
178 A105 3c **multicolored**   .30   .25
        First day cover   1.00
        Imprint block of 6   2.00

Restoration of the Sarawati Pavilion (in front of Enkaku Temple), destroyed during World War II.

Tennis
Player — A106

Cock and Iris
(Bingata) — A107

1968, Nov. 3   Photo.   Perf. 13½
179 A106 3c **green & multicolored**   .40   .35
        First day cover   1.00
        Imprint block of 6   3.25

35th All-Japan East-West Men's Soft-ball Tennis Tournament, Naha City, Nov. 23-24.

1968, Dec. 10
180 A107 1½c **orange & multicolored**   .25   .20
        First day cover   1.50
        Imprint block of 10   2.75

New Year, 1969.

Boxer — A108

Ink Slab
Screen — A109

1969, Jan. 3
181 A108 3c **gray & multicolored**   .40   .30
        First day cover   1.00
        Imprint block of 6   1.75

20th All-Japan Amateur Boxing Championships held at the
University of the Ryukyus, Jan. 3-5.

1969, Apr. 17   Photo.   Perf. 13½
182 A109 3c **salmon, indigo & red**   .40   .35
        First day cover   1.50
        Imprint block of 6   1.75

Philatelic Week.

Box Antennas and   Gate of Courtesy
Map of Radio   and
Link — A110   Emblems — A111

1969, July 1   Photo.   Perf. 13½
183 A110 3c **multicolored**   .25   .20
        First day cover   1.00
        Imprint block of 6   1.40

Opening of the UHF (radio) circuit system between Okinawa
and the outlying Miyako-Yaeyama Islands.

1969, Aug. 1   Photo.   Perf. 13½
184 A111 3c **Prussian blue, gold & vermil-
                ion**   .25   .20
        First day cover   1.00
        Imprint block of 6   1.40

22nd All-Japan Formative Education Study Conf., Naha, Aug.
1-3.

FOLKLORE ISSUE

Tug of War
Festival — A112

Hari Boat
Race — A113

Izaiho
Ceremony,
Kudaka
Island — A114

Mortardrum
Dance — A115

Sea God
Dance — A116

1969-70   Photo.   Perf. 13
185 A112 3c **multicolored,** *Aug. 1, 1969*   .30   .25
        First day cover   1.50
        Imprint block of 6   2.00
186 A113 3c **multicolored,** *Sept. 5, 1969* .35   .30
        First day cover   1.50
        Imprint block of 6   2.25
187 A114 3c **multicolored,** *Oct. 3, 1969*   .35   .30
        First day cover   1.50
        Imprint block of 6   2.25
188 A115 3c **multicolored,** *Jan. 20, 1970* .50   .45
        First day cover   1.50
        Imprint block of 6   4.00
189 A116 3c **multicolored,** *Feb. 27, 1970* .50   .45
        First day cover   1.50
        Imprint block of 6   3.50
        Nos. 185-189 (5)   2.00   1.75

No. 99 Surcharged   改訂 ½¢

1969, Oct. 15   Photo.   Perf. 13½
190 A44 ½c on 3c **multicolored**   .90   .90
        First day cover   3.00
        Imprint block of 10   12.00

Nakamura-ke Farm
House, Built 1713-
51 — A117

1969, Nov. 1   Photo.   Perf. 13½
191 A117 3c **multicolored**   .20   .20
        First day cover   1.00
        Imprint block of 6   1.00

Protection of national cultural treasures.

Statue of Kyuzo
Toyama, Maps of
Hawaiian and Ryukyu
Islands — A118

1969, Dec. 5   Photo.   Perf. 13½
192 A118 3c **light ultra & multi**   .40   .40
        First day cover   1.50
        Imprint block of 6   2.00
 a.   Without overprint   2,500.
 b.   Wide-spaced bars   725.00

70th anniv. of Ryukyu-Hawaii emigration led by Kyuzo
Toyama.
The overprint "1969" at lower left and bars across "1970" at
upper right was applied before No. 192 was issued.

Dog and Flowers (Bingata) — A119

Sake Flask Made from Coconut — A120

1969, Dec. 10
193 A119 1½c pink & multicolored .20 .20
First day cover 1.50
Imprint block of 10 2.40
New Year, 1970.

1970, Apr. 15 Photo. *Perf. 13½*
194 A120 3c multicolored .25 .25
First day cover 1.25
Imprint block of 6 1.50
Philatelic Week, 1970.

CLASSIC OPERA ISSUE

"The Bell" (Shushin Kaneiri) — A121

Child and Kidnapper (Chu-nusudu) — A122

Robe of Feathers (Mekarushi) — A123

Vengeance of Two Young Sons (Nidotichiuchi) A124

The Virgin and the Dragon (Kokonomaki) — A125

1970 Photo. *Perf. 13½*
195 A121 3c dull blue & multi, *Apr. 28* .40 .40
First day cover 1.75
Imprint block of 6 3.00
a. Souvenir sheet of 4 4.50 5.00
First day cover 5.00
196 A122 3c light blue & multi, *May 29* .40 .40
First day cover 1.75
Imprint block of 6 3.00
a. Souvenir sheet of 4 4.50 5.00
First day cover 5.00
197 A123 3c bluish green & multi, *June 30* .40 .40
First day cover 1.75
Imprint block of 6 3.00
a. Souvenir sheet of 4 4.50 5.00
First day cover 5.00
198 A124 3c dull blue green & multi, *July 30* .40 .40
First day cover 1.75
Imprint block of 6 3.00
a. Souvenir sheet of 4 4.50 5.00
First day cover 5.00
199 A125 3c multicolored, *Aug. 25* .40 .40
First day cover 1.75

Imprint block of 6 3.00
a. Souvenir sheet of 4 4.50 5.00
First day cover 5.00
Nos. 195-199 (5) 2.00 2.00
Nos. 195a-199a (5) 22.50 25.00

Underwater Observatory and Tropical Fish — A126

1970, May 22
200 A126 3c blue green & multi .30 .25
First day cover 1.25
Imprint block of 6 2.00
Completion of the underwater observatory of Busena-Misaki, Nago.

Noboru Jahana (1865-1908), Politician — A127

Map of Okinawa and People — A128

Portraits: No. 202, Saion Gushichan Bunjaku (1682-1761), statesman. No. 203, Choho Giwan (1823-1876), regent and poet.

1970-71 Engr. *Perf. 13½*
201 A127 3c rose claret, *Sept. 25, 1970* .50 .45
First day cover 2.50
Imprint block of 6 3.50
202 A127 3c dull blue green, *Dec. 22, 1970* .75 .65
First day cover 2.50
Imprint block of 6 7.00
203 A127 3c black, *Jan. 22, 1971* .50 .45
First day cover 2.50
Imprint block of 6 3.50

1970, Oct. 1 Photo.
204 A128 3c red & multicolored .25 .25
First day cover 1.00
Imprint block of 6 1.50
Oct. 1, 1970 census.

Great Cycad of Une — A129

1970, Nov. 2 Photo. *Perf. 13½*
205 A129 3c gold & multicolored .25 .25
First day cover 1.00
Imprint block of 6 1.75
Protection of national treasures.

Japanese Flag, Diet and Map of Ryukyus — A130

Wild Boar and Cherry Blossoms (Bingata) — A131

1970, Nov. 15 Photo. *Perf. 13½*
206 A130 3c ultramarine & multicolored .80 .75
First day cover 1.75
Imprint block of 6 6.00
Citizen's participation in national administration to Japanese law of Apr. 24, 1970.

1970, Dec. 10
207 A131 1½c multicolored .20 .20
First day cover 1.50
Imprint block of 10 2.40
New Year, 1971.

Low Hand Loom (Jibata) — A132

Farmer Wearing Palm Bark Raincoat and Kuba Leaf Hat — A133

Fisherman's Wooden Box and Scoop — A134

Designs: No. 209, Woman running a filature (reel). No. 211, Woman hulling rice with cylindrical "Shiri-ushi."

1971 Photo. *Perf. 13½*
208 A132 3c light blue & multi, *Feb. 16* .30 .25
First day cover 1.25
Imprint block of 6 2.00
209 A132 3c pale green & multi, *Mar. 16* .30 .25
First day cover 1.25
Imprint block of 6 2.00
210 A133 3c light blue & multi, *Apr. 30* .35 .30
First day cover 1.25
Imprint block of 6 2.25
211 A132 3c yellow & multi, *May 20* .40 .35
First day cover 1.25
Imprint block of 6 3.50
212 A134 3c gray & multi, *June 15* .35 .30
First day cover 1.25
Imprint block of 6 2.25
Nos. 208-212 (5) 1.70 1.45

Water Carrier (Taku) — A135

1971, Apr. 15 Photo. *Perf. 13½*
213 A135 3c blue green & multicolored .35 .30
First day cover 1.00
Imprint block of 6 2.75
Philatelic Week, 1971.

Old and New Naha, and City Emblem A136

1971, May 20 *Perf. 13*
214 A136 3c ultramarine & multicolored .25 .20
First day cover 1.00
Imprint block of 6 1.50
50th anniv. of Naha as a municipality.

Caesalpinia
Pulcherrima — A137

Design: 2c, Madder (Sandanka).

1971		Photo.		Perf. 13	
215 A137	2c	gray & multicolored, *Sept. 30*		.20	.20
		First day cover			1.00
		Imprint block of 10		2.00	
216 A137	3c	gray & multicolored, *May 10*		.20	.20
		First day cover			1.00
		Imprint block of 10		2.00	

GOVERNMENT PARK SERIES

View from Mabuni
Hill — A138

Mt. Arashi from Haneji
Sea — A139

Yabuchi Island from
Yakena Port — A140

1971-72					
217 A138	3c	green & multi, *July 30, 1971*		.20	.20
		First day cover			1.25
		Imprint block of 6		1.50	
218 A139	3c	blue & multi, *Aug. 30, 1971*		.20	.20
		First day cover			1.25
		Imprint block of 6		1.50	
219 A140	4c	multicolored, *Jan. 20, 1972*		.25	.20
		First day cover			1.25
		Imprint block of 6		1.75	
		Nos. 217-219 (3)		.65	.60

Dancer — A141

Deva King, Torinji
Temple — A142

1971, Nov. 1		Photo.		Perf. 13	
220 A141	4c	Prussian blue & multicolored		.20	.20
		First day cover			1.00
		Imprint block of 10		2.00	

1971, Dec. 1					
221 A142	4c	deep blue & multicolored		.20	.20
		First day cover			1.00
		Imprint block of 6		1.50	

Protection of national cultural treasures.

Rat and
Chrysanthemums
A143

Student Nurse
A144

1971, Dec. 10					
222 A143	2c	brown orange & multi		.20	.20
		First day cover			1.50
		Imprint block of 10		2.40	

New Year, 1972.

1971, Dec. 24					
223 A144	4c	lilac & multicolored		.20	.20
		First day cover			1.00
		Imprint block of 6		1.50	

Nurses' training, 25th anniversary.

A145

A147

Coral Reef — A146

1972		Photo.		Perf. 13	
224 A145	5c	bright blue & multi, *Apr. 14*		.40	.35
		First day cover			1.25
		Imprint block of 6		2.50	
225 A146	5c	gray & multi, *Mar. 30*		.40	.35
		First day cover			1.25
		Imprint block of 6		2.50	
226 A147	5c	ocher & multi, *Mar. 21*		.40	.35
		First day cover			1.25
		Imprint block of 6		2.50	
		Nos. 224-226 (3)		1.20	1.05

Dove, U.S. and
Japanese
Flags — A148

1972, Apr. 17		Photo.		Perf. 13	
227 A148	5c	bright blue & multi		.60	.60
		First day cover			1.50
		Imprint block of 6		4.50	

Antique Sake Pot
(Yushibin) — A149

1972, Apr. 20					
228 A149	5c	ultramarine & multicolored		.50	.50
		First day cover			1.25
		Imprint block of 6		3.50	

Ryukyu stamps were replaced by those of Japan after May 15, 1972.

AIR POST

> Catalogue values for all unused stamps in this section are for Never Hinged items.

Dove and Map of Ryukyus — AP1

1950, Feb. 15		Photo.	Unwmk.	Perf. 13x13½	
C1	AP1	8y	bright blue	120.00	60.00
			First day cover		35.00
			Imprint block of 6	1,000.	
C2	AP1	12y	green	35.00	30.00
			First day cover		35.00
			Imprint block of 6	275.00	
C3	AP1	16y	rose carmine	15.00	15.00
			First day cover		35.00
			Imprint block of 6	130.00	
			First day cover, #C1-C3		200.00
			Nos. C1-C3 (5)	28.00	17.50

Heavenly
Maiden — AP2

1951-54					
C4	AP2	13y	blue, *Oct. 1, 1951*	2.50	1.50
			First day cover		60.00
			Imprint block of 6, 5-character	225.00	
			Imprint block of 6, 8-character	37.50	
C5	AP2	18y	green, *Oct. 1, 1951*	3.50	2.25
			First day cover		60.00
			Imprint block of 6, 5-character	55.00	
			Imprint block of 6, 8-character	45.00	
C6	AP2	30y	cerise, *Oct. 1, 1951*	6.00	1.75
			First day cover		60.00
			First day cover, #C4-C6		250.00
			Imprint block of 6, 5-character	70.00	
			Imprint block of 6, 8-character	150.00	
C7	AP2	40y	red violet, *Aug. 16, 1954*	7.00	5.50
			First day cover		35.00
			Imprint block of 6	75.00	
C8	AP2	50y	yellow orange, *Aug. 16, 1954*	9.00	6.50
			First day cover		35.00
			Imprint block of 6	100.00	
			First day cover, #C7-C8		100.00
			Nos. C4-C8 (5)	28.00	17.50

Heavenly Maiden
Playing Flute — AP3

1957, Aug. 1		Engr.		Perf. 13½	
C9	AP3	15y	blue green	9.00	3.50
			Imprint block of 6	65.00	
C10	AP3	20y	rose carmine	15.00	5.50
			Imprint block of 6	100.00	
C11	AP3	35y	yellow green	15.00	6.50
			Imprint block of 6	120.00	
a.		35y	**light yellow green,** *1958*	150.00	
C12	AP3	45y	reddish brown	16.00	8.00
			Imprint block of 6	135.00	
C13	AP3	60y	gray	18.00	10.00
			Imprint block of 6	190.00	
			First day cover, #C9-C13		45.00
			Nos. C9-C13 (5)	73.00	33.50

On one printing of No. C10, position 49 shows an added spur on the right side of the second character from the left. Value unused, $150.

Same Surcharged in Brown Red or 改訂 9¢
Light Ultramarine

1959, Dec. 20

C14	AP3	9c on 15y **blue green** (BrR)	2.50	1.50
		Imprint block of 6	20.00	
a.		Inverted surcharge	950.00	
		Imprint block of 6	6,750.	
C15	AP3	14c on 20y **rose carmine**	3.00	3.00
		(L.U.)		
		Imprint block of 6	25.00	
C16	AP3	19c on 35y **yellow green** (BrR)	8.00	5.00
		Imprint block of 6	57.50	
C17	AP3	27c on 45y **reddish brown**	17.50	6.00
		(L.U.)		
		Imprint block of 6	140.00	
C18	AP3	35c on 60y **gray** (BrR)	15.00	9.00
		Imprint block of 6	120.00	
		First day cover, #C14-C18	35.00	
		Nos. C14-C18 (5)	46.00	24.50

No. C15 is found with the variety described below No. C13. Value unused, $100.

改訂 ===

Nos. 31-33, 36 and 38 Surcharged in
Black, Brown, Red, Blue or Green

9¢

1960, Aug. 3   Photo.   Perf. 13

C19	A14	9c on 4y **brown**	3.50	1.00
		Imprint block of 10	40.00	
a.		Surcharge inverted and transposed	15,000.	15,000.
b.		Inverted surcharge (legend only)	12,000.	
c.		Surcharge transposed	1,500.	
d.		Legend of surcharge only	4,000.	
e.		Vert. pair, one without surcharge	—	

Nos. C19c and C19d are from a single sheet of 100 with surcharge shifted downward. Ten examples of No. C19c exist with "9c" also in bottom selvage. No. C19d is from the top row of the sheet.

No. C19e is unique, pos. 100, caused by paper foldover.

C20	A17	14c on 5y **rose lilac** (Br)	4.00	2.25
		Imprint block of 10	40.00	
C21	A14	19c on 15y **vermilion** (R)	2.50	2.00
		Imprint block of 10	32.50	
C22	A17	27c on 14y **reddish brown** (Bl)	9.00	2.75
		Imprint block of 10	120.00	
C23	A14	35c on 20y **yellow orange** (G)	6.00	4.50
		Imprint block of 10	80.00	
		First day cover, #C19-C23	25.00	
		Nos. C19-C23 (5)	25.00	12.50

Wind God — AP4

Designs: 9c, Heavenly Maiden (as on AP2). 14c, Heavenly Maiden (as on AP3). 27c, Wind God at right. 35c, Heavenly Maiden over treetops.

1961, Sept. 21   Unwmk.   Perf. 13½

C24	AP4	9c **multicolored**	.30	.20
		Imprint block of 6	2.25	
C25	AP4	14c **multicolored**	.70	.60
		Imprint block of 6	5.50	
C26	AP4	19c **multicolored**	.70	.70
		Imprint block of 6	5.50	
C27	AP4	27c **multicolored**	3.00	.60
		Imprint block of 6	25.00	
C28	AP4	35c **multicolored**	1.50	1.25
		Imprint block of 6	15.00	
		First day cover, #C24-C28	35.00	
		Nos. C24-C28 (5)	6.20	3.35

 AP5   AP6

1963, Aug. 28   Perf. 13x13½

C29	AP5	5½c **multicolored**	.25	.25
		First day cover	1.00	
		Imprint block of 10	3.00	
C30	AP6	7c **multicolored**	.25	.25
		First day cover	1.00	
		First day cover, #C29-C30	2.50	
		Imprint block of 10	3.50	

SPECIAL DELIVERY

Catalogue value for the unused stamp in this section is for a Never Hinged item.

Sea Horse and Map of
Ryukyus — SD1

1950, Feb. 15   Unwmk.   Photo.   Perf. 13x13½

E1	SD1	5y **bright blue**	30.00	16.00
		First day cover		100.00
		Imprint block of 6	300.00	

QUANTITIES ISSUED
Regular Postage and Commemorative Stamps

Cat. No.	Quantity	Cat. No.	Quantity
1	90,214	87	3,019,000
2	55,901	88	298,966
3	94,663	89	298,966
4	55,413	90	398,901
5	76,387	91	398,992
6	117,321	92	1,498,970
7	291,403	93	598,989
1a	61,000	94	398,998
2a—4a	181,000	95	398,993
5a	29,936	96	298,993
6a	99,300	97	398,997
7a	46,000	98	9,699,000
8	2,559,000	99	10,991,500
8a	300,000	100	1,549,000
9	1,198,989	101	799,000
10	589,000	102	1,299,000
11	479,000	103	398,995
12	598,999	104	298,892
13	397,855	105	1,598,949
14	499,000	106	348,989
15	498,960	107	10,099,000
16	199,197	108	348,865
16a	199,900	109	348,937
16b	39,900	110	348,962
17	9,800	111	348,974
18	299,500	112	398,974
19	3,014,427	113	398,911
20	3,141,777	114	1,199,000
21	2,970,827	115	398,948
22	191,917	116	398,943
23	1,118,617	117	1,698,912
24	276,218	118	550,000
24a	ca. 1,300	119	549,000
25	231,717	120	749,000
26	220,130	121	799,000
27	398,993	122	389,000
28	386,421	123	319,000
29	498,854	124	1,999,000
30	298,994	125—127	999,000
31	4,768,413	128	799,000
32	1,202,297	129	1,699,000
33	500,059	130—131	799,000
34	298,994	132	849,000
35	199,000	133	799,000
36	455,896	134	1,299,000
37	160,518	135	1,099,000
38	198,720	136	1,299,000
39	198,199	137—138	1,598,000
40	599,000	139	3,098,000
41	598,075	140—142	1,598,000
42	1,198,179	143—148	2,498,000
43	1,625,406	149	2,298,000
44	994,880	150	3,798,000
45	997,759	151	2,298,000
46	996,759	152—156	1,998,000
47	2,705,955	157—158	1,698,000
48	997,542	159—160	1,298,000
49	996,609	161	898,000
50	996,928	162	1,498,000
51	499,000	163—164	1,298,000
52	249,000	165	3,998,000
52a	78,415	166—167	1,298,000
53	248,700	168	998,000
54	1,498,991	169—179	898,000
55	2,498,897	180	3,198,000
56	1,098,972	181—189	898,000
57	998,918	190	1,773,050
58	2,699,000	191	898,000
59	2,499,000	192	864,960
60	199,000	193	3,198,000
61	499,000	194	898,000
62	199,000	195—199	598,000
63	1,498,931	195a—199a	124,500
64	798,953	200—206	898,000
65—68	999,000	207	3,198,000
72	598,912	208—210	1,098,000
73	398,990	211—212	1,298,000
74	598,936	213	1,098,000
75	1,998,992	214	1,098,000
76	1,000,000	215—216	4,998,000
77	2,000,000	217	1,498,000
78	500,000	218—219	1,798,000
79—80	400,000	220	2,998,000
81	12,599,000	221	1,798,000
82	11,979,000	222	4,998,000
83	6,850,000	223	1,798,000
84	5,099,000	224—226	2,498,000
84A	1,699,000	227	2,998,000

Cat. No.	Quantity	Cat. No.	Quantity
85	4,749,000	228	3,998,000
86	2,099,000		

AIR POST STAMPS

Cat. No.	Quantity	Cat. No.	Quantity
C1—C3	198,000	C18	96,650
C4	1,952,348	C19	1,033,900
C5	331,360	C19a	100
C6	762,530	C20	230,000
C7	76,166	C21	185,000
C8	122,816	C22	191,000
C9	708,319	C23	190,000
C10	108,824	C24	17,199,000
C11	164,147	C25	1,999,000
C12	50,335	C26	1,250,000
C13	69,092	C27	3,499,000
C14	597,103	C28	1,699,000
C15	77,951	C29	1,199,000
C16	97,635	C30	1,949,000
C17	98,353		

SPECIAL DELIVERY STAMP

E1	198,804

PROVISIONAL ISSUES

Stamps of Japan Overprinted by Postmasters in
Four Island Districts

Trading Ship — A82

Rice Harvest — A83

Gen. Maresuke
Nogi — A84

Admiral Heihachiro
Togo — A86

Garambi Lighthouse,
Taiwan — A88

Meiji Shrine,
Tokyo — A90

Plane and Map of
Japan — A92

Kasuga Shrine,
Nara — A93

Mount Fuji and Cherry
Blossoms — A94

Horyu Temple,
Nara — A95

Miyajima Torii,
Itsukushima
Shrine — A96

Golden Pavilion,
Kyoto — A97

Great Budda,
Kamakura — A98

Kamatari
Fujiwara — A99

War Factory
Girl — A144

Hyuga Monument & Mt.
Fuji — A146

War Worker &
Planes — A147

Palms and Map of
"Greater East
Asia" — A148

Aviator Saluting &
Japanese Flag — A150

Torii of Yasukuni
Shrine — A151

Mt. Fuji and Cherry
Blossoms — A152

Torii of Miyajima — A153

Garambi Lighthouse,
Taiwan — A154

Sun & Cherry
Blossoms — A161

Sunrise at Sea &
Plane — A162

Coal Miners — A163

Yasukuni Shrine — A164

"Thunderstorm below
Fuji," by
Hokusai — A167

Values are for unused stamps. Used copies sell for considerably
more, should be expertized and are preferred on cover or document.

KUME ISLAND

A1

Mimeographed
Seal Handstamped in Vermilion

1945, Oct. 1　Without Gum　Unwmk.　Imperf.

1X1	A1	7s **black,** *cream (2,400)*	1,400.	—
		On cover		—
a.		"7" & "SEN" one letter space to left	2,500.	

Printed on legal-size U.S. military mimeograph paper and validated by the official seal of the Kume Island postmaster, Norifume Kikuzato. Valid until May 4, 1946.
Cancellations "20.10.1" (Oct. 1, 1945) or "20.10.6" (Oct. 6, 1945) are by favor. See proofs section for copies on white watermarked U.S. official bond paper.

AMAMI DISTRICT

Inspection Seal ("Ken," abbreviation for *kensa zumi*, inspected or examined; five types)

Stamps of Japan 1937-46 Handstamped in Black, Blue, Purple, Vermilion or Red

Typographed, Lithographed, Engraved

1947-48		**Wmk. 257**	*Perf. 13, Imperf*	
2X1	A82	⅓s **purple,** #257	800.	
2X2	A83	1s **fawn,** #258		
2X3	A144	1s **orange brown,** #325	1,750.	
2X4	A84	2s **crimson,** #259	600.	
a.		2s **vermilion,** #259c		
2X5	A84	2s **rose red,** imperf., #351	2,000.	
2X6	A85	3s **green,** #260	1,700.	
2X7	A84	3s **brown,** #329		
2X8	A161	3s **rose carmine,** imperf., #352	1,800.	
2X9	A146	4s **emerald,** #330	650.	
2X10	A86	5s **brown lake,** #331	700.	
2X11	A162	5s **green,** imperf., #353	1,500.	
2X12	A147	6s **light ultramarine,** #332	1,500.	
2X13	A86	7s **orange vermilion,** #333	1,250.	
2X14	A90	8s **dark purple & pale violet,** #265	1,500.	
2X15	A148	10s **crimson & dull rose,** #344	500.	
2X16	A152	10s **red orange,** imperf., #355 (48)	2,500.	
2X17	A93	14s **rose lake & pale rose,** #268	—	
2X18	A150	15s **dull blue,** #336	500.	
2X19	A151	17s **gray violet,** #337	1,750.	
2X20	A94	20s **ultramarine,** #269	1,750.	
2X21	A152	20s **blue,** #338	600.	
2X22	A152	20s **ultramarine,** imperf., #356 (48)	1,750.	
2X23	A95	25s **dark brown & pale brown,** #270	900.	
2X24	A151	27s **rose brown,** #339	—	
2X25	A153	30s **bluish green,** #340	—	
2X26	A153	30s **bright blue,** imperf., #357	2,000.	
2X27	A88	40s **dull violet,** #341	1,750.	
2X28	A154	40s **dark violet,** #342	1,750.	
2X29	A97	50s **olive & pale olive,** #272	—	
2X30	A163	50s **dark brown,** imperf., #358 (48)	2,000.	
2X31	A164	1y **deep olive green,** imperf., #359	2,500.	
2X32	A167	1y **deep ultramarine,** imperf., #364	—	
2X33	A99	5y **deep gray green,** #274	—	
2X34	A99	5y **deep gray green,** imperf., #360		

MIYAKO DISTRICT

Personal Seal of Postmaster Jojin Tomiyama

Stamps of Japan 1937-46 Handstamped in Vermilion or Red

Typographed, Lithographed, Engraved

1946-47		**Wmk. 257**	*Perf. 13*	
3X1	A144	1s **orange brown,** #325	175.	
3X2	A84	2s **crimson,** #259	125.	
a.		2s **vermilion** #259c ('47)	150.	
b.		2s **pink** #259b ('47)	550.	
3X3	A84	3s **brown,** #329	80.	
3X4	A86	4s **dark green,** #261	80.	
3X5	A86	5s **brown lake,** #331	550.	
		On cover with #3X17	—	
3X6	A88	6s **orange,** #263	80.	

3X7	A90	8s **dark purple & pale violet,** #265	100.	—
3X8	A148	10s **crimson & dull rose,** #334	80.	—
		On cover with #3X15		—
3X9	A152	10s **red orange,** imperf., #355 ('47) (1,000)	120.	—
3X10	A92	12s **indigo,** #267	80.	—
3X11	A93	14s **rose lake & pale rose,** #268	80.	—
3X12	A150	15s **dull blue,** #336	80.	—
3X13	A151	17s **gray violet,** #337	80.	—
3X14	A94	20s **ultramarine,** #269	—	—
3X15	A152	20s **blue,** #338	80.	—
3X16	A152	20s **ultramarine,** imperf., #356 ('47)	175.	—
3X17	A95	25s **dark brown & pale brown,** #270	80.	—
3X18	A153	30s **bluish green,** #340	80.	—
3X19	A88	40s **dull violet,** #341	250.	—
3X20	A154	40s **dark violet,** #342	90.	—
3X21	A97	50s **olive & pale olive,** #272	80.	—
3X22	A163	50s **dark brown,** #358 ('47) (750)	200.	—
3X23	A98	1y **brown & pale brown,** #273	9,000.	—
3X24	A167	1y **deep ultramarine,** #364 ('47) (500)	1,500.	—

Nos. 3X22 and 3X24 have sewing machine perf.; No. 3X16 exists with that perf. also.

Nos. 3X1-3X2, 3X2a, 3X3-3X5, 3X8 Handstamp Surcharged with 2 Japanese Characters

1946-47				
3X25	A144	1y on 1s **orange brown**	140.	—
3X26	A84	1y on 2s **crimson**	3,000.	—
3X27	A84	1y on 3s **brown** ('47)	2,250.	—
3X28	A84	2y on 2s **crimson**	160.	—
a.		2y on 2s **vermilion** ('47)	160.	—
3X29	A86	4y on 4s **dark green**	140.	—
3X30	A86	5y on 5s **brown lake**	140.	—
3X31	A148	10y on 10s **crimson & dull rose**	140.	—

The overwhelming majority of used examples of Miyako District stamps were used on Bulk Mailing Records documents and Letter Content Certification Records documents. Stamps affixed to such documents command a substantial premium above off-document used stamps.
Cancellation: black Miyako cds.

OKINAWA DISTRICT

Personal Seal of Postmaster Shiichi Hirata

R1

Japan Nos. 355-356, 358, 364 Overprinted in Black

1947, Nov. 1		**Wmk. 257　Litho.**		*Imperf.*
4X1	A152	10s **red orange** (13,997)	1,200.	1,000.
		On cover, strip of 3		9,500.
		On cover with #4X2		7,500.
4X2	A152	20s **ultramarine** (13,611)	600.	1,000.
4X3	A163	50s **dark brown** (6,276)	700.	700.
4X4	A167	1y **deep ultramarine** (1,947)	1,750.	1,000.

On Revenue Stamp of Japan

4X5	R1	30s **brown** (14,000)	3,500.	3,500.
		On cover		7,500.

No. 4X5 is on Japan's current 30s revenue stamp. The Hirata seal validated it for postal use.
Nos. 4X1-4X5 are known with rough sewing machine perforations, full or partial.

YAEYAMA DISTRICT

Personal Seal of Postmaster Kenpuku Miyara

Stamps of Japan 1937-46 Handstamped in Black

Typographed, Engraved, Lithographed

1948		**Wmk. 257**	*Perf. 13*	
5X1	A86	4s **dark green,** #261	1,200.	
5X2	A86	5s **brown lake,** #331	1,200.	
5X3	A86	7s **orange vermilion,** #333	800.	
5X4	A148	10s **crimson & dull rose,** #334	5,000.	
5X5	A94	20s **ultramarine,** #269	120.	
		On cover with 2 #5X8		
5X6	A96	30s **peacock blue,** #271	1,000.	
5X7	A88	40s **dull violet,** #341	60.	
5X8	A97	50s **olive & pale olive,** #272	90.	

5X9 A163 50s **dark brown**, imperf., #358
(250) 1,350.
5X10 A99 5y **deep gray green**, #274 2,000.
This handstamp exists double, triple, inverted and in pair, one stamp without overprint.

Provisional postal stationery of the four districts also exists.

LETTER SHEETS

Values are for entires.

Stylized Deigo Blossom — US1

Banyan Tree — US2

Typographed by Japan Printing Bureau.
Stamp is in upper left corner.

Designer: Shutaro Higa

1948-49
U1 US1 50s **vermilion**, cream, July 18, 1949
(250,000) 50.00 60.00
First day cancel —
a. 50s **orange red**, gray, July 1, 1948
(1,000) 1,200. —

Designer: Ken Yabu

1950, Jan. 21
U2 US2 1y **carmine red**, cream (250,000) 40.00 50.00
First day cancel —

AIR LETTER SHEETS

DC-4 Skymaster and Shurei Gate — UC1

UC2

Designer: Chosho Ashitomi
"PAR AVION" (Bilingual) below Stamp
Litho. & Typo. by Japan Printing Bureau
1952-53
UC1 UC1 12y **light rose**, pale blue green,
Mar. 9, 1953 (76,000) 20.00 12.50
a. 12y **dull rose**, pale blue green, Nov.
1, 1952 (50,000) 30.00 15.00
First day cancel, No. UC1a 80.00

No. UC1a is on tinted paper with colorless overall inscription "RYUKYU FOREIGN AIRMAIL," repeated in parallel vertical lines, light and indistinct. Dull rose ink of imprinted design and legend "AIR LETTER" appears to bleed. No. UC1 has overall inscription darker and more distinct. Light rose ink of design and legend does not bleed. Model: U.S. No. UC16.

Litho. & Typo. by Nippon Toppan K.K.
"AEROGRAMME" below Stamp
1955, Sept. 10
UC2 UC2 15y **violet blue**, pale blue green
(200,000) 25.00 15.00
First day cancel 60.00

No. UC2 surcharged in Red

"13" & "¢" aligned at bot.; 2 thick bars — a

"¢" raised; 2 thick bars — b

"13" & "¢" as in "a"; 4 thin bars — c

"¢" raised; 4 thin bars — d

Printers: Type "a," Nakamura Printing Co., "b" and "d," Okinawa Printing Co., "c," Sun Printing Co.

1958-60
UC3 UC2 13c on 15y type "a," Sept. 16,
1958 (60,000) 18.00 18.00
First day cancel 60.00
a. Type "b," June 1, 1959 (E 10,000) 50.00 30.00
b. Type "c," Sept. 22, 1959 (E 2,000) 100.00 80.00
c. Type "d," Oct. 1, 1960 (E 3,000) 300.00 300.00
d. As "b," small "¢" 1,000.

No. UC3c has Nos. 55, 58 affixed to make the 15c rate.

 UC3

Lithographed by Japan Printing Bureau
1959, Nov. 10
UC4 UC3 15c **dark blue**, pale blue
(560,000) 4.00 2.50
First day cancel 10.00

POSTAL CARDS

Values are for entire cards.
Nos. UX1-UX9 are typo., others litho.
Printed by Japan Printing Bureau unless otherwise stated.
Quantities in parentheses; "E" means estimated.
Deigo Blossom Type

Designer: Shutaro Higa

1948, July 1
UX1 US1 10s **dull red**, grayish tan (100,000) 50.00 60.00

1949, July 1
UX2 US1 15s **orange red**, gray (E 175,000) 40.00 70.00
First day cancel —
a. 15s **vermilion**, tan (E 50,000) 110.00 125.00

Banyan Tree Type

Designer: Ken Yabu

1950, Jan. 21
UX3 US2 50s **carmine red**, light tan (E
200,000) 9.50 9.50
First day cancel 60.00
a. Grayish tan card (E 25,000) 27.50 50.00

Nos. UX2, UX2a Handstamp Surcharged in Vermilion

19-21x23-25mm — a

22-23x26-27mm — b

20-21x24-24½mm — c

22-23½x25-26mm — d

1951
UX4 US1 (c) 15s + 85s on #UX2 (E
35,000) 100. 100.
a. Type "c" on #UX2a (E 5,000) 150. 150.
b. Type "a" on #UX2 (E 39,000) 75. 100.
c. Type "a" on #UX2a 1,000. —
d. Type "b" on #UX2 1,000. 1,000.
e. Type "d" on #UX2 (E 4,000) 150. 200.
f. Type "d" on #UX2a (E 1,000) 250. 300.

Type "a" exists on the 15s cherry blossom postal card of Japan. Value $75.

Crown, Leaf Ornaments

Naha die
21x22mm — PC3

Tokyo die
18½x19mm — PC4

Designer: Masayoshi Adaniya Koshun Printing Co.

1952
UX5 PC3 1y **vermilion**, tan, Feb. 8
(400,600) 40.00 30.00
UX6 PC4 1y **vermilion**, off-white, Oct. 6
(1,295,000) 22.50 14.00
a. Tan card, coarse (50,000) 30.00 20.00
b. Tan card, smooth (16,000) 500.00 150.00

Naminoue Shrine

PC5
Naha die
23x25½mm

PC6
Tokyo die
22x24½mm

Designer: Gensei Agena

1953-57
UX7 PC5 2y **green**, off-white, Dec. 2, 1953
(1,799,400) 60.00 20.00
First day cancel 65.00
a. Printed both sides 500.00
UX8 PC6 2y **green**, off-white, 1955
(2,799,400) 12.50 6.00
a. 2y **deep blue green**, 1956 (300,000) 25.00 16.50
b. 2y **yellow green**, 1957 (2,400,000) 10.00 3.50
c. As "a," printed on both sides 500.00
d. As "b," printed on both sides 500.00

Stylized Pine, Bamboo, Plum Blossoms — PC7

1956 New Year Card
Designer: Koya Oshiro Kotsura and Koshun Printing Companies

1955, Dec. 1
UX9 PC7 2y **red**, cream 100.00 45.00
First day cancel 125.00

No. UX9 was printed on rough card (43,400) and smooth-finish card (356,600).

Sun — PC8

Temple Lion — PC9

1957 New Year Card

Designer: Seikichi Tamanaha Kobundo Printing Co.

1956, Dec. 1
UX10 PC8 2y **brown carmine & yellow,** *off-white (600,000)* — 5.00 3.75
  First day cancel — 10.00

1958 New Year Card

Designer: Shin Isagawa Fukuryu Printing Co.

1957, Dec. 1
UX11 PC9 2y **lilac rose,** *off-white (1,000,000)* — 1.75 2.25
  First day cancel — 4.00
a. "1" omitted in right date — 60.00 75.00
b. Printed on both sides — 250.00 300.00

Nos. UX8, UX8a and UX8b "Revalued" in Red, Cherry or Pink by Three Naha Printeries

a   b   c

1958-59
UX12 PC6 1½c on 2y **green,** type "a," *Sept. 16 (600,000)* — 4.50 4.50
  First day cancel — 10.00
a. Shrine stamp omitted — 750.00 1,000.
b. Bar of ½ omitted, top of 2 broken — 75.00 100.00
c. Type "b," *Nov. (1,000,000)* — 8.00 12.50
d. Type "c," *1959 (200,000)* — 15.00 22.50
e. Wrong font "c," type "c" — 30.00 45.00
f. "c" omitted, type "c" — 1,500. 1,500.
g. Double surcharge, type "c" — 1,000.

Multicolor Yarn
Ball — PC10

Toy Pony
19½x23mm — PC11

1959 New Year Card

Designer: Masayoshi Adaniya Kobundo Printing Co.

1958, Dec. 10
UX13 PC10 1½c **black, red, yellow & gray blue,** *off-white (1,514,000)* — 1.50 1.90
  First day cancel — 2.00
a. Black omitted — —

1959, June 20

Designer: Seikichi Tamanaha Kobundo Printing Co.

UX14 PC11 1½c **dark blue & brown** *(1,140,000)* — 1.50 1.25
  First day cancel — 1.50
a. Dark blue omitted — 350.00

Toy Carp and
Boy — PC12

Toy Pony
21x25mm — PC13

1960 New Year Card

Designer: Masayoshi Adaniya

1959, Dec. 1
UX15 PC12 1½c **violet blue, red & black,** *cream (2,000,000)* — 1.25 1.50
  First day cancel — 1.75

1959, Dec. 30
UX16 PC13 1½c **gray violet & brown,** *cream (3,500,000)* — 3.00 .75
  First day cancel — 2.75

Household
Altar — PC14

Coral
Head — PC15

1961 New Year Card

Designer: Shin Isagawa

1960, Nov. 20
UX17 PC14 1½c **gray, carmine, yellow & black,** *off-white (2,647,591)* — 1.50 1.50
  First day cancel — 1.50

Summer Greeting Card

Designer: Shinzan Yamada Kidekuni Printing Co.

1961, July 5
UX18 PC15 1½c **ultramarine & cerise,** *off-white (264,900)* — 2.25 3.75
  First day cancel — 4.00

Tiger
PC16

Inscribed
"RYUKYUS"
PC17

1962 New Year Card

Designer: Shin Isagawa

1961, Nov. 15
UX19 PC16 1½c **ocher, black & red,** *off-white (2,891,626)* — 1.50 2.50
  First day cancel — 1.65
a. Red omitted — 750.00 —
b. Red inverted — 500.00 —
c. Red omitted on face, inverted on back — 500.00 —
d. Double impression of red, one inverted — 500.00 —
e. Double impression of ocher & black, red inverted — 500.00 —
f. Double impression of ocher & black, one inverted — 500.00 —

1961-67

Designer: Seikichi Tamanaha

UX20 PC17 1½c **gray violet & brown,** *white ('67) (18,600,000)* — 1.00 .50
a. Off-white card ('66) *(4,000,000)* — 1.50 .75
b. Cream card, *Dec. 23 (12,500,000)* — 1.00 .50
  First day cancel — 1.35

Ie Island — PC18

New Year
Offerings — PC19

Summer Greeting Card

Designer: Shinzan Yamada Sakai Printing Co.

1962, July 10
UX21 PC18 1½c **bright blue, yellow & brown,** *off-white (221,500)* — 1.50 2.50
  First day cancel — 3.00
  Square notch at left — 40.00 45.00

1963 New Year Card; Precanceled

Designer: Shin Isagawa Sakai Printing Co.

1962, Nov. 15
UX22 PC19 1½c **olive brown, carmine & black** *(3,000,000)* — 1.50 3.00
  First day cancel — 2.25
a. Yellow brown background — —
b. Brown ocher background — —

Ryukyu Temple Dog and
Wine Flask
Silhouette — PC20

Water
Strider — PC21

International Postal Card

Designer: Shin Isagawa

1963, Feb. 15
UX23 PC20 5c **vermilion, emerald & black,** *pale yellow (150,000)* — 1.75 2.75
  First day cancel — 1.65
a. Black & emerald omitted — 450.00

Summer Greeting Card

Designer: Seikichi Tamanaha

1963, June 20
UX24 PC21 1½c **Prussian green & black,** *off-white (250,000)* — 4.00 4.25
  First day cancel — 3.50

Princess
Doll — PC22

Bitter Melon
Vine — PC23

1964 New Year Card; Precanceled

Designer: Koya Oshiro

1963, Nov. 15
UX25 PC22 1½c **orange red, yellow & ultra,** *off-white (3,200,000)* — 2.00 2.00
  First day cancel — 2.00

Summer Greeting Card

Designer: Shinzan Yamada

1964, June 20
UX26 PC23 1½c **multicolored,** *off-white (285,410)* — 1.40 2.25
  First day cancel — 1.75

Fighting Kite
with
Rider — PC24

Palm-leaf
Fan — PC25

1965 New Year Card; Precanceled

Designer: Koya Oshiro

1964, Nov. 15
UX27 PC24 1½c **multicolored,** *off-white (4,876,618)* — 1.25 1.75
  First day cancel — 2.00

Summer Greeting Card

Designer: Koya Oshiro

1965, June 20
UX28 PC25 1½c **multicolored,** *off-white (340,604)* — 1.40 2.50
  First day cancel — 1.65

Toy Pony
Rider — PC26

Fan Palm
Dipper — PC27

1966 New Year Card; Precanceled

Designer: Seikichi Tamanaha

1965, Nov. 15
UX29 PC26 1½c **multicolored,** off-white
(5,224,622) 1.25 1.75
First day cancel 1.40
a. Silver (background) omitted 250.00

Summer Greeting Card

Designer: Seikichi Tamanaha

1966, June 20
UX30 PC27 1½c **multicolored,** off-white
(339,880) 1.25 2.00
First day cancel 1.40

Toy Dove — PC28

Cycad Insect Cage
and Praying
Mantis — PC29

1967 New Year Card; Precanceled

Designer: Seikichi Tamanaha

1966, Nov. 15
UX31 PC28 1½c **multicolored,** off-white
(5,500,000) 1.25 1.75
First day cancel 1.65
a. Silver (background) omitted 500.00
b. Gray blue & green omitted 750.00

Summer Greeting Card

Designer: Shin Isagawa

1967, June 20
UX32 PC29 1½c **multicolored,** off-white
(350,000) 1.50 2.50
First day cancel 1.75

Paper Doll
Royalty — PC30

Pandanus
Drupe — PC31

1968 New Year Card; Precanceled

Designer: Shin Isagawa

1967, Nov. 15
UX33 PC30 1½c **multicolored,** off-white
(6,200,000) 1.10 1.50
First day cancel 1.75
a. Gold omitted 500.00

Summer Greeting Card

Designer: Seikan Omine

1968, June 20
UX34 PC31 1½c **multicolored,** off-white
(350,000) 1.25 2.25
First day cancel 1.75

Toy Lion — PC32

Ryukyu Trading
Ship — PC33

1969 New Year Card; Precanceled

Designer: Teruyoshi Kinjo

1968, Nov. 15
UX35 PC32 1½c **multicolored,** off-white
(7,000,000) 1.10 1.50
First day cancel 1.50

Summer Greeting Card

Designer: Seikichi Tamanaha

1969, June 20
UX36 PC33 1½c **multicolored,** (349,800) 1.25 2.25
First day cancel 1.75

Toy Devil
Mask — PC34

Ripe
Litchis — PC35

1970 New Year Card; Precanceled

Designer: Teruyoshi Kinjo

1969, Nov. 15
UX37 PC34 1½c **multicolored** 97,200,000) 1.10 1.50
First day cancel 1.25

Summer Greeting Card

Designer: Kensei Miyagi

1970, June 20
UX38 PC35 1½c **multicolored** (400,000) 1.40 2.25
First day cancel 1.50

Thread-winding
Implements for
Dance — PC36

Ripe
Guavas — PC37

1971 New Year Card; Precanceled

Designer: Yoshinori Arakai

1970, Nov. 16
UX39 PC36 1½c **multicolored** (7,500,000) 1.10 1.50
First day cancel 1.25

Summer Greeting Card

Designer: Kensei Miyagi

1971, July 10
UX40 PC37 1½c **multicolored** (400,000) 1.25 2.25
First day cancel 1.25

Pony Type of 1961
Zip Code Boxes in Vermilion

1971, July 10
UX41 PC17 1½c **gray violet & brown**
(3,000,000) 1.25 3.50
First day cancel 2.00

No. UX41 Surcharged below
Stamp in Vermilion

"Revalued 2¢" applied by Nakamura Printing Co.

1971, Sept. 1
UX42 PC17 2c on 1½c **gray violet & brown**
(1,699,569) 1.10 2.25
First day cancel 2.00
a. Inverted surcharge 500.00
b. Double surcharge 500.00
c. Surcharge on back 500.00
e. Surcharge on back, inverted 500.00

1972 New Year Card; Precanceled

Tasseled Castanets — PC38

Zip Code Boxes in Vermilion

Designer: Yoshinori Arakaki

1971, Nov. 15
UX43 PC38 2c **multicolored** (8,000,000) 1.00 1.50
First day cancel 1.25

Type of 1961
Zip Code Boxes in Vermilion

1971, Dec. 15
UX44 PC17 2c **gray violet & brown** (3,500,000) 1.25 1.75
First day cancel 1.65

PAID REPLY POSTAL CARDS

Sold as two attached cards, one for message, one for reply. The major listings are of unsevered cards except Nos. UY4-UY6.

往 信 | 返 信
Message | Reply

1948, July 1
UY1 US1 10s + 10s **dull red,** grayish tan
(1,000) 1,500. —
m. Message card 500. 500.
r. Reply card 500. 500.

1949, July 18
UY2 US1 15s + 15s **vermilion,** tan (E
150,000) 30.00 40.00
a. Gray card (E 75,000) 75.00 —
First day cancel
m. Message card 6.50 16.50
r. Reply card 6.50 16.50

1950, Jan. 21
UY3 US2 50s + 50s **carmine red,** gray
cream (E 130,000) 25.00 40.00
a. Double impression of message card — —
b. Light tan card (E 96,000) 13.50 —
First day cancel
m. Message card 3.50 13.50
r. Reply card 3.50 13.50

No. UY2a Handstamp Surcharged in Vermilion
1951
UY4 US1 1y (15s+85s) message, type
"b" (E 3,000) 350. 350.
a. Reply, type "b" (E 3,000) 350. 350.
b. Message, type "a" (E 300) 600. —
c. Reply, type "a" (E 300) 600. —
d. Message, type "d" (E 200) 500. —
e. Reply, type "d" (E 200) 500. —
f. Message, UY2, type "a" (E 3,000) 150. 225.
g. Reply, UY2, type "a" (E 3,000) 150. 225.
h. Message, UY2, type "b" (E 2,500) 275. 275.
i. Reply, UY2, type "b" (E 2,500) 275. 275.
j. Message, UY2, type "d" (E 2,800) 150. 250.
k. Reply, UY2, type "d" (E 2,800) 150. 250.
l. 1y + 1y unsevered, type "b" 850.
m. 1y + 1y unsevered, type "a" 1,450.
n. 1y + 1y unsevered, type "d" 1,200.
o. 1y + 1y unsevered, UY2, type "a" 360.
p. 1y + 1y unsevered, UY2, type "b" 650.
q. 1y + 1y unsevered, UY2, type "d" 360.
r. Message, type "c" —

e f

g   h

Typographed Surcharge in Vermilion

UY5	US1	1y (15s+85s) message, type "f" (E 20,000)	125.	125.
a.		Reply, type "f" (E 20,000)	125.	125.
b.		Message, type "e" (E 12,500)	225.	225.
c.		Reply, type "e" (E 12,500)	225.	225.
d.		Message, type "g" (E 500)	1,000.	1,000.
e.		Reply, type "g" (E 500)	1,000.	1,000.
f.		Message, UY2, type "e" (E 15,000)	125.	125.
g.		Reply, UY2, type "e" (E 15,000)	125.	125.
h.		Message, UY2, type "f" (E 9,000)	125.	125.
i.		Reply, UY2, type "f" (E 9,000)	125.	125.
j.		Message, UY2, type "g" (E 500)	1,000.	1,000.
k.		Reply, UY2, type "g" (E 500)	1,000.	1,000.
l.		1y + 1y unsevered, type "e"	675.	
m.		1y + 1y unsevered, UY2, type "e"	375.	

Typographed Surcharge Type "h" in Vermilion on No. UY3

UY6	US2	1y (50s+50s) message (E 35,000)	125.00	150.00
a.		Reply (E 35,000)	125.00	150.00
b.		Message, UY3b (E 10,000)	125.00	150.00
c.		Reply, UY3b (E 10,000)	125.00	150.00

Smooth or Coarse Card

1952, Feb. 8

UY7	PC3	1y + 1y vermilion, gray tan (60,000)	120.00	140.00
		First day cancel		250.00
m.		Message card	25.00	50.00
r.		Reply card	25.00	50.00

1953

UY8	PC4	1y + 1y vermilion, tan (22,900)	30.00	40.00
		First day cancel		—
a.		Off-white card (13,800)	40.00	50.00
m.		Message card	7.50	19.00
r.		Reply card	7.50	26.50

Off-white or Light Cream Card

1953, Dec. 2

UY9	PC5	2y + 2y green (50,000)	100.00	90.00
		First day cancel		150.00
m.		Message card	15.00	25.00
r.		Reply card	15.00	35.00

1955, May

UY10	PC6	2y + 2y green, off-white (280,000)	10.00	—
a.		Reply card blank	500.00	
m.		Message card	3.25	11.00
r.		Reply card	3.25	15.00

No. UY10 Surcharged in Red

1958, Sept. 16

UY11	PC6	1½c on 2y, 1½c on 2y (95,000)	8.00	—
		First day cancel		22.50
a.		Surcharge on reply card only	500.00	—
b.		Surcharge on message card only	500.00	—
c.		Reply card double surcharge	750.00	—
d.		Reply card stamp omitted (surcharge only)	1,000.	—
m.		Message card	2.75	10.00
r.		Reply card	2.75	16.50

Surcharge varieties include: "1" omitted; wrong font "2".

Pony Types

1959, June 20

UY12	PC11	1½c + 1½c dark blue & brown (366,000)	3.50	—
		First day cancel		4.00
m.		Message card	.65	3.50
r.		Reply card	.65	3.50

1960, Mar. 10

UY13	PC13	1½c + 1½c gray violet & brown, (150,000)	7.00	—
		First day cancel		5.00
m.		Message card	1.50	5.00
r.		Reply card	1.50	5.00

International Type

1963, Feb. 15

UY14	PC20	5c + 5c vermilion, emerald & black, pale yellow (70,000)	2.50	—
		First day cancel		3.00
m.		Message card	.75	3.75
r.		Reply card	.75	3.75

Pony ("RYUKYUS") Type

1963-69

UY15	PC17	1½c + 1½c gray violet & brown, cream, Mar. 15, (800,000)	2.00	—
		First day cancel		2.50
a.		Off-white card, Mar. 13, 1967 (100,000)	2.25	—
b.		White card, Nov. 22, 1969 (700,000)	1.75	—
m.		Message card detached	.40	4.00
r.		Reply card detached	.40	4.00

No. UY14 Surcharged below Stamp in Vermilion

1971, Sept. 1

UY16	PC17	2c on 1½c + 2c on 1½c gray violet & brown (80,000)	1.50	—
		First day cancel		2.25
m.		Message card	.50	2.50
r.		Reply card	.50	2.50

Pony ("RYUKYUS") Type
Zip Code Boxes in Vermilion

1971, Nov. 1

UY17	PC17	2c + 2c gray violet & brown (150,000)	1.50	—
		First day cancel		2.50
m.		Message card	.50	2.50
r.		Reply card	.50	2.50

REVENUE

Upon its establishment Apr. 1, 1952, the government of the Ryukyu Islands assumed responsibility for the issuing and the profit from revenue stamps. The various series served indiscriminately as evidence of payment of the required fees for various legal, realty and general commercial transactions.

1 yen — R1

3   5   10   50

100   500   1000

Litho. by Japan Printing Bureau.
Designer: Eizo Yonamine

		Wmk. 257	Perf. 13x13½	
1952-54				
R1	R1	1y brown	12.00	10.00
R2	R1	3y carmine	15.00	12.00
R3	R1	5y green	20.00	15.00
R4	R1	10y blue	25.00	20.00
R5	R1	50y purple	35.00	25.00
R6	R1	100y yellow brown	50.00	30.00
R7	R1	500y dark green	200.00	100.00
R8	R1	1,000y carmine	225.00	150.00
		Nos. R1-R8 (8)	582.00	362.00

Issued: #R1-R6, July 15, 1952; #R7-R8, Apr. 16, 1954.

Denomination Vertical

"Cent"   "Dollar"

Litho. by Kobundo Printing Co., Naha
Perf. 10, 10½, 11 and combinations

			Without Gum	Unwmk.
1958, Sept. 16				
R9	R1	1c red brown	25.00	25.00
a.		Horiz. pair, imperf. between	500.00	
R10	R1	3c red	35.00	35.00
a.		Horiz. pair, imperf. between	500.00	
R11	R1	5c green	45.00	45.00
R12	R1	10c blue	65.00	65.00
a.		Horiz. pair, imperf. between	500.00	
R13	R1	50c purple	120.00	120.00
R14	R1	$1 sepia	175.00	175.00
R15	R1	$5 dark green	300.00	300.00
R16	R1	$10 carmine	400.00	400.00
		Nos. R9-R16 (8)	1,165.	1,165.

R2   R3

$20   R4

Litho. by Japan Printing Bureau.

		Wmk. 257	Perf. 13x13½	
1959-69				
R17	R2	1c brown	3.00	1.90
R18	R2	3c red	3.00	1.10
R19	R2	5c purple	5.50	3.25
R20	R2	10c green	10.00	6.00
R21	R2	20c sepia ('69)	70.00	55.00
R22	R2	30c light olive ('69)	80.00	65.00
R23	R2	50c blue	32.50	14.00
		Engr.		
R24	R3	$1 olive	45.00	12.50
R25	R3	$2 vermilion ('69)	200.00	50.00
R26	R3	$3 purple ('69)	350.00	70.00
R27	R3	$5 orange	100.00	50.00
R28	R3	$10 dark green	160.00	70.00
R29	R4	$20 carmine ('69)	1,000.	200.00
R30	R4	$30 blue ('69)	1,000.	—
R31	R4	$50 black ('69)	1,500.	—
		Nos. R17-R28 (12)	1,059.	398.75

PROVISIONAL ISSUES MIYAKO

Stamps of Japan 1938-42 Handstamped in Black, Red or Orange

		Typo., Litho., Engr.	Wmk. 257	Perf. 13	
1948					
3XR1	A84	3s brown, #329	75.00	—	
3XR2	A86	5s brown lake, #331	75.00	—	
3XR3	A152	20s blue, #338 (R)	60.00	—	
3XR4	A95	25s dark brown & pale brown, #270 (R)	60.00	—	
a.		Black overprint	500.00		
3XR5	A96	30s peacock blue, #271 (R)	60.00	—	
3XR6	A154	40s dark violet, #342 (R)	60.00	—	
3XR7	A97	50s olive & pale olive, #272 (R)	135.00	—	
a.		Orange overprint	500.00		

Doubled handstamps are known on all values and pairs with one stamp without handstamp exist on the 5s and 20s.

PROVISIONAL ISSUES YAEYAMA

In addition to the continued use of the then-current Japanese revenue stamps in stock from the wartime period, the varying authorities of the Yaeyama Gunto issued three district-specific revenue series, with a total of 28 values. Only those values at present verified by surviving copies are indicated. Numbers are reserved for other values believed to have been issued, but as yet not seen and verified.

No. 5XR2 — R5   No. 5XR3 — R6

No. 5XR5 — R7   No. 5XR27 — R8

1946 (?)   **Without Gum**   *Imperf.*
Value printed, frame handstamped

5XR1	R5	3s vermilion & black	—

5XR2	R5	10s **vermilion & black**	—	—

Validating handstamp below

5XR3	R6	1y **vermilion & black**	—	—

Civil Administration Issues

1947 (?)   **Without Gum**   *Imperf.*

Value printed, frame handstamped

Cream Paper

5XR5	R7	10s **vermilion & black**	—
5XR6	R7	50s **vermilion & black**	—

Gunto Government Issues

1950 (?)   **Without Gum**   *Imperf.*

Value printed, frame handstamped

Cream Paper

5XR17	R8	10s **vermilion & black**	—
5XR18	R8	50s **vermilion & black**	—
a.		50s **vermilion & blue**	—
5XR20	R8	1.50y **vermilion & black**	—
5XR22	R8	5y **vermilion & black**	—
5XR24	R8	20y **vermilion & black**	—
5XR27	R8	100y **vermilion & black**	—

Nos. 5XR17-5XR27 are known with rough perforations, full or partial.

SPECIMEN

Regular stamps and postal cards of 1958-65 overprinted with three cursive syllabics *mi-ho-n* ("specimen").

Two trial color proofs, Nos. 46TC and 48TC, received vermilion mihon overprints in a different cursive type (100 each). Value $650 each.

Type A

1961-64

Overprinted in Black

91S		3c **multicolored** *(1,000)*	250.00
118S		3c **multicolored** *(1,100)*	450.00
119S		3c **multicolored** *(1,100)*	400.00

Type B   み ほ ん

1964-65

Overprinted in Red or Black

120aS		3c **deep blue, deep carmine & ocher** (R) *(1,500)*	200.00
121S		3c **multicolored** (R) *(1,500)*	175.00
124S		3c **ultra, yel & red** (R) *(5,000)*	35.00
125S		3s **dull claret, yel & black** *(1,500)*	70.00
126S		3c **yellow & multi** *(2,000)*	60.00
127S		3c **gray, red & black** *(2,000)*	60.00
128S		3c **multicolored** *(1,500)*	70.00
129S		1½c **multicolored** (R) *(1,500)*	70.00
130S		3c **light blue & multi** (R) *(1,500)*	200.00
131S		3c **multicolored** (R) *(1,500)*	60.00
132S		3c **buff & multicolored** *(2,000)*	60.00
133S		3c **green & multi** (R) *(2,000)*	50.00
134S		3c **multicolored** *(2,000)*	50.00
135S		3c **blue & multicolored** *(2,000)*	50.00
136S		3c **golden brown & multi** *(2,000)*	50.00
139S		1½c **multicolored** (R) *(2,500)*	50.00

Postal Cards

1964-65

Overprinted Type A or B in Black or Red

UX26S	A	1½c **multicolored** *(1,000)*	500.00
UX27S	B	1½c **multicolored** *(1,000)*	350.00
UX28S	A	1½c **multicolored** *(1,000)*	300.00
UX29S	A	1½c **multicolored** *(1,100)*	250.00

UNEMPLOYMENT INSURANCE

These stamps, when affixed in an official booklet and canceled, certified a one-day contract for a day laborer. They were available to employers at certain post offices on various islands.

Dove — RQ1

Shield — RQ2

Lithographed in Naha

1961, Jan. 10   **Without Gum**   **Unwmk.**   *Rouletted*

RQ1	RQ1	2c **pale red**	700.00	
RQ2	RQ2	4c **violet**	40.00	40.00

Redrawn

Lithographed by Japan Printing Bureau

1966, Feb.   **Unwmk.**   *Perf. 13x13½*

RQ3	RQ1	2c **pale red**	—	—
RQ4	RQ2	4c **violet**	25.00	25.00

Redrawn stamps have bolder numerals and inscriptions, and fewer, stronger lines of shading in background.

Cycad — RQ3

Lithographed by Japan Printing Bureau

1968, Apr. 19   **Wmk. 257**   *Perf. 13x13½*

RQ5	RQ3	8c **brown**	35.00	35.00

Nos. RQ3-RQ4 Surcharged with New Values and 2 Bars

1967-72

RQ6	RQ1	8c on 2c **pale red**	70.00	70.00
RQ7	RQ2	8c on 4c **violet** ('72)	35.00	35.00
RQ8	RQ2	12c on 4c **violet** ('71)	25.00	25.00

PROOFS AND TRIAL COLOR PROOFS

1948

Salmon Paper, Imperf.

1aP		5s **magenta**	—
2aP		10s **yellow green**	—
3aP		20s **yellow green**	—
5aP		40s **magenta**	—
6aP		50s **ultramarine**	—
7aP		1y **ultramarine**	—

Between the printing of Nos. 1a-7a and Nos. 1-7 essay sheets of the series were prepared in Tokyo and overprinted with a swirl-pattern of blue or red dots. These essays sell for about $800 each.

Except for No. 12TC 4y olive, the trial color proofs of Nos. 8-13, 18, C1-C3 and E1 are from blocks of 9.

1950

Soft White Paper, Imperf.

Proofs are Gummed, Trial Color Proofs are Without Gum

8P		50s **dark carmine rose**	1,500.
8TC		50s **rose**	1,750.
8TC		50s **green**	1,750.
9P		1y **deep blue**	1,500.
9TC		1y **rose**	1,750.
9TC		1y **green**	1,750.
10P		2y **rose violet**	1,500.
10TC		2y **rose**	1,750.
10TC		2y **green**	1,750.
11P		3y **carmine rose**	1,500.
11TC		3y **rose**	1,750.
11TC		3y **green**	1,750.
12P		4y **greenish gray**	1,500.
12TC		4y **rose**	1,750.
12TC		4y **olive**	1,750.
13P		5y **blue green**	1,500.
13TC		5y **rose**	1,750.
13TC		5y **green**	1,750.

1951

Soft White Paper, Imperf., Without Gum

14P		3y **red brown**	800.
15P		3y **dark green**	1,000.

1952

Whitish Paper, Imperf., With Gum

18TC		3y **pale salmon**	1,750.
18TC		3y **scarlet**	1,750.
18TC		3y **red orange**	1,900.

Perforated, gummed proof sheets of Nos. 18, 27 and 28 with oversized, untrimmed selvage were printed for display purposes.

1958

Off White Paper, Imperf., Without Gum

46TC		2c **black**	650.
48TC		4c **black**	650.

AIR POST

1950

Soft White Paper, Imperf.

Proofs are Gummed, Trial Color Proofs are Without Gum

C1P		8y **bright blue**	1,500.
C1TC		8y **rose**	1,750.
C1TC		8y **light green**	1,750.
C2P		12y **green**	1,500.
C2TC		12y **rose**	1,750.
C2TC		12y **light green**	1,750.
C3P		16y **rose carmine**	1,500.
C3TC		16y **rose**	1,750.

1951

Soft White Paper, Imperf., Without Gum

C4P		13y **blue**	1,000.
C5P		18y **green**	1,000.
C6P		30y **cerise**	800.

SPECIAL DELIVERY

1950

Soft White Paper, Imperf.

Proofs are Gummed, Trial Color Proofs are Without Gum

E1P		5y **bright blue**	1,500.
E1TC		5y **rose**	1,750.
E1TC		5y **green**	1,750.

Official proof folders contain one each of Nos. 8P-13P, 12TC in olive, C1P-C3P and E1P. The stamps are securely adhered to the folder. Value, $9,000.

Similar folders exist containing die proofs in black of the same issues and mockups of Nos. U2, UX3 and UY3.

KUME ISLAND

1945

U.S. Official Watermarked White Bond Paper

Seal Handstamped in Vermilion

1X1P		7s **black**	2,000.
a.		"7" and "SEN" one letter space to left, pos. 8	3,500.

UNITED NATIONS

United Nations stamps are used on UN official mail sent from UN Headquarters in New York City, the UN European Office in Geneva, Switzerland, or from the Donaupark Vienna International Center or Atomic Energy Agency in Vienna, Austria to points throughout the world. They may be used on private correspondence sent through the UN post offices.

UN mail is carried by the US, Swiss and Austrian postal systems.

See Switzerland official stamp listings in the Scott *Standard Postage Stamp Catalogue* for stamps issued by the Swiss Government for official use of the UN European Office and other UN affiliated organizations. See France official stamp listings for stamps issued by the French Government for official use of UNESCO.

+: When following the quantity, this indicates the total printed to date. Unless otherwise noted, these are the initial printing order. Final quantities frequently are not given for definitives and air post stamps. The total printed is shown here.

Blocks of four generally sell for four times the single stamp value.

Values for first day covers are for cacheted and unaddressed covers. Addressed covers sell for much less, and addressed and uncacheted first day covers sell for very little.

Catalogue values for all unused stamps in this section are for Never Hinged items.

Peoples of the World — A1

UN Headquarters Building — A2

"Peace, Justice, Security" — A3

UN Flag — A4

UN International Children's Emergency Fund — A5

World Unity — A6

The various printings of Nos. 1-11 vary in sheet marginal perforation. Some were perforated through left or right margins, or both; some through all margins.

Sheets of this issue carry a marginal inscription consisting of the UN seal and "First UN/Issue 1951." This inscription appears four times on each sheet. The listing "Margin block of 4, UN seal" or "Inscription block of 4" in this and following issues refers to a corner block.

Sheets of the 1½c, 2c, 50c and $1 have a cut-out of different shape in one margin. The printer trimmed this off entirely on most of the 1½c third printing, and partially on the 1½c fourth printing and $1 fifth and sixth printings.

See UN Offices in Geneva Nos. 4, 14.

Forgeries of the 1½c precancel abound. Examination by a competent authority is necessary.

Veterans' War Memorial Building, San Francisco — A7

Issued to mark the 7th anniversary of the signing of the United Nations Charter.

Engraved and printed by the American Bank Note Co., New York. Panes of 50. Designed by Jean Van Noten.

1952, Oct. 24			**Perf. 12**	
12	A7	5c **blue** (1,274,670)	.20	.20
		First day cover (160,117)		1.00
		Inscription block of 4	.60	—

Globe and Encircled Flame — A8

4th anniversary of the adoption of the Universal Declaration of Human Rights.

Engraved and printed by Thomas De La Rue & Co., Ltd., London. Panes of 50. Designed by Hubert Woyty-Wimmer.

1952, Dec. 10			**Perf. 13½x14**	
13	A8	3c **deep green** (1,554,312)	.20	.20
		First day cover		2.25
		Inscription block of 4	.25	—
14	A8	5c **blue** (1,126,371)	.20	.20
		First day cover		2.25
		First day cover, #13-14		5.00
		Inscription block of 4	1.10	—

First day covers of Nos. 13 and 14 total 299,309.

Printed by Thomas De La Rue & Co., Ltd., London (1c, 3c, 10c, 15c, 20c, 25c), and Joh. Enschedé and Sons, Haarlem, Netherlands (1½c, 2c, 5c, 50c, $1). The 3c, 15c and 25c have frame engraved, center photogravure; other denominations are engraved. Panes of 50. Designed by O. C. Meronti (A1), Leon Helguera (A2), J. F. Doeve (A3), Ole Hamann (A4), S. L. Hartz (5c) and Hubert Woyty-Wimmer (20c).

		Perf. 13x12½, 12½x13		
1951		**Engr. and Photo.**		**Unwmk.**
1	A1	1c **magenta**, Oct. 24		
		(8,000,000)	.20	.20
		First day cover		1.00
		Margin block of 4, UN seal	.25	
2	A2	1½c **blue green**, Oct. 24		
		(7,450,000)	.20	.20
		First day cover		1.00
		Margin block of 4, UN seal	.25	
		Precanceled (361,700)		55.00
3	A3	2c **purple**, Nov. 16 (8,470,000)	.20	.20
		First day cover		1.00
		Margin block of 4, UN seal	.25	
4	A4	3c **magenta & blue**, Oct. 24		
		(8,250,000)	.20	.20
		First day cover		1.00
		Margin block of 4, UN seal	.25	
5	A5	5c **blue**, Oct. 24 (6,000,000)	.20	.20
		First day cover		1.75
		Margin block of 4, UN seal	.40	—
6	A1	10c **chocolate**, Nov. 16		
		(2,600,000)	.25	.20
		First day cover		2.50
		Margin block of 4, UN seal	1.10	—
7	A4	15c **violet & blue**, Nov. 16		
		(2,300,000)	.25	.20
		First day cover		3.00
		Margin block of 4, UN seal	1.10	—
8	A6	20c **dark brown**, Nov. 10		
		(2,100,000)	.35	.20
		First day cover		3.50
		Margin block of 4, UN seal	1.90	—
9	A4	25c **olive gray & blue**, Oct. 24		
		(2,100,000)	.40	.20
		First day cover		3.50
		Margin block of 4, UN seal	1.90	—
10	A2	50c **indigo**, Nov. 16 (1,785,000)	2.25	1.50
		First day cover		14.00
		Margin block of 4, UN seal	13.00	—
11	A3	$1 **red**, Oct. 24 (2,252,500)	1.50	.65
		First day cover		12.00
		Margin block of 4, UN seal	7.00	—
		Nos. 1-11 (11)	6.00	3.95

First day covers of Nos. 1-11 and C1-C4 total 1,113,216.

Refugee Family — A9

Issued to publicize "Protection for Refugees."

Engraved and printed by Thomas De La Rue & Co., Ltd., London. Panes of 50. Designed by Olav Mathiesen.

1953, Apr. 24   **Perf. 12½x13**

15	A9	3c	dark red brown & rose brown (1,299,793)	.20	.20
			First day cover		2.25
			Inscription block of 4	.60	—
16	A9	5c	indigo & blue (969,224)	.25	.25
			First day cover		3.25
			First day cover, #15-16		7.50
			Inscription block of 4	1.50	—

First day covers of Nos. 15 and 16 total 234,082.

Envelope, UN Emblem and Map — A10

Issued to honor the Universal Postal Union.
Engraved and printed by Thomas De La Rue & Co., Ltd., London. Panes of 50. Designed by Hubert Woyty-Wimmer.

1953, June 12   **Perf. 13**

17	A10	3c	black brown (1,259,689)	.20	.20
			First day cover		3.25
			Inscription block of 4	.70	—
18	A10	5c	dark blue (907,312)	.50	.45
			First day cover		3.25
			First day cover, #17-18		9.00
			Inscription block of 4	2.75	—

First day covers of Nos. 17 and 18 total 231,627.
Plate number ("1A" or "1B") in color of stamp appears below 47th stamp of sheet.

Gearwheels and UN Emblem — A11   Hands Reaching Toward Flame — A12

Issued to publicize United Nations activities in the field of technical assistance.
Engraved and printed by Thomas De La Rue & Co. Ltd. London. Panes of 50. Designed by Olav Mathiesen.

1953, Oct. 24   **Perf. 13x12½**

19	A11	3c	dark gray (1,184,348)	.20	.20
			First day cover		2.00
			Inscription block of 4	.50	—
20	A11	5c	dark green (968,182)	.30	.30
			First day cover		5.00
			First day cover, #19-20		9.00
			Inscription block of 4	1.75	—

First day covers of Nos. 19 and 20 total 229,211.

1953, Dec. 10   **Perf. 12½x13**

Issued to publicize Human Rights Day.
Engraved and printed by Thomas De La Rue & Co., Ltd., London. Panes of 50. Designed by León Helguera.

21	A12	3c	bright blue (1,456,928)	.20	.20
			First day cover		2.00
			Inscription block of 4	.70	—
22	A12	5c	rose red (983,831)	1.00	.50
			First day cover		4.00
			First day cover, #21-22		8.00
			Inscription block of 4	4.75	—

First day covers of Nos. 21 and 22 total 265,186.

Ear of Wheat — A13   UN Emblem and Anvil Inscribed "ILO" — A14

Issued to honor the Food and Agriculture Organization and printed by Thomas De La Rue & Co., Ltd., London. Panes of 50. Designed by Dirk Van Gelder.

1954, Feb. 11   **Perf. 12½x13**

23	A13	3c	dark green & yellow (1,250,000)	.40	.20
			First day cover		2.00
			Inscription block of 4	1.75	—
24	A13	8c	indigo & yellow (949,718)	.85	.50
			First day cover		4.00
			First day cover, #23-24		5.00
			Inscription block of 4	3.75	—

First day covers of Nos. 23 and 24 total 272,312.

1954, May 10   **Perf. 12½x13**

Design: 8c, inscribed "OIT."
Issued to honor the International Labor Organization.
Engraved and printed by Thomas De La Rue & Co., Ltd., London. Panes of 50. Designed by José Renau.

25	A14	3c	brown (1,085,651)	.20	.20
			First day cover		2.00
			Inscription block of 4	.50	—
26	A14	8c	magenta (903,561)	1.25	.75
			First day cover		4.00
			First day cover, #25-26		5.50
			Inscription block of 4	5.50	—

First day covers of Nos. 25 and 26 total 252,796.

UN European Office, Geneva — A15

Issued on the occasion of United Nations Day.
Engraved and printed by Thomas De La Rue & Co., Ltd., London. Panes of 50. Designed by Earl W. Purdy.

1954, Oct. 25   **Perf. 14**

27	A15	3c	dark blue violet (1,000,000)	1.90	1.10
			First day cover		1.75
			Inscription block of 4	8.50	—
28	A15	8c	red (1,000,000)	.25	.25
			First day cover		2.25
			First day cover, #27-28		5.50
			Inscription block of 4	1.10	—

First day covers of Nos. 27 and 28 total 233,544.

Mother and Child — A16

Issued to publicize Human Rights Day.
Engraved and printed by Thomas De La Rue & Co., Ltd. London. Panes of 50. Designed by Leonard C. Mitchell.

1954, Dec. 10   **Perf. 14**

29	A16	3c	red orange (1,000,000)	6.75	2.00
			First day cover		2.75
			Inscription block of 4	32.50	—
30	A16	8c	olive green (1,000,000)	.25	.25
			First day cover		3.75
			First day cover, #29-30		8.00
			Inscription block of 4	1.10	—

First day covers of Nos. 29 and 30 total 276,333.

Symbol of Flight — A17

Design: 8c, inscribed "OACI."
Issued to honor the International Civil Aviation Organization.
Engraved and printed by Waterlow & Sons, Ltd., London. Panes of 50. Designed by Angel Medina Medina.

1955, Feb. 9   **Perf. 13½x14**

31	A17	3c	blue (1,000,000)	1.75	.65
			First day cover		2.00
			Inscription block of 4	7.75	—
32	A17	8c	rose carmine (1,000,000)	.75	.75
			First day cover		3.00
			First day cover, #31-32		5.50
			Inscription block of 4	3.25	—

First day covers of Nos. 31 and 32 total 237,131.

UNESCO Emblem — A18

Issued to honor the UN Educational, Scientific and Cultural Organization.
Engraved and printed by Waterlow & Sons, Ltd., London. Panes of 50. Designed by George Hamori.

1955, May 11   **Perf. 13½x14**

33	A18	3c	lilac rose (1,000,000)	.20	.20
			First day cover		2.00
			Inscription block of 4	1.40	—
34	A18	8c	light blue (1,000,000)	.20	.20
			First day cover		3.00
			First day cover, #33-34		5.00
			Inscription block of 4	.75	—

First day covers of Nos. 33 and 34 total 255,326.

United Nations Charter — A19

Design: 4c, Spanish inscription. 8c, French inscription.
10th anniversary of the United Nations.
Engraved and printed by Waterlow & Sons, Ltd., London. Panes of 50. Designed by Claude Bottiau.

1955, Oct. 24   **Perf. 13½x14**

35	A19	3c	deep plum (1,000,000)	.90	.50
			First day cover		1.25
			Inscription block of 4	4.00	—
36	A19	4c	dull green (1,000,000)	.35	.20
			First day cover		2.00
			Inscription block of 4	1.75	—
37	A19	8c	bluish black (1,000,000)	.20	.20
			First day cover		2.75
			First day cover, #35-37		11.00
			Inscription block of 4	.80	—
			Nos. 35-37 (3)	1.45	.90

Wmk. 309- Wavy Lines

Souvenir Sheet

			Wmk. 309		Imperf.
1955, Oct. 24					
38	A19	Sheet of 3 (250,000)		110.00	40.00
		Hinged		85.00	
a.		3c deep plum		10.00	1.50
b.		4c dull green		10.00	1.50
c.		8c bluish black		10.00	1.50
		First day cover			27.50
		Sheet with retouch on 8c		120.00	45.00

No. 38 measures 108x83mm and has marginal inscriptions in deep plum.

Two printings were made of No. 38. The first (200,000) may be distinguished by the broken line of background shading on the 8c. It leaves a small white spot below the left leg of the "n" of "Unies." For the second printing (50,000), the broken line was retouched, eliminating the white spot. The 4c was also retouched.

First day covers of Nos. 35-38 total 455,791.

Copies of No. 38 are known with the 4c and 8c stamps misaligned.

Hand Holding Torch — A20

Issued in honor of Human Rights Day.
Engraved and printed by Waterlow & Sons, Ltd., London. Panes of 50. Designed by Hubert Woyty-Wimmer.

1955, Dec. 9		Unwmk.		Perf. 14x13½	
39	A20	3c ultramarine (1,250,000)		.20	.20
		First day cover			1.25
		Inscription block of 4		.55	—
40	A20	8c green (1,000,000)		.20	.20
		First day cover			1.25
		First day cover, #39-40			2.50
		Inscription block of 4		1.10	—

First day covers of Nos. 39 and 40 total 298,038.

Symbols of Telecommunication A21

Design: 8c, inscribed "UIT."
Issued in honor of the International Telecommunication Union.
Engraved and printed by Thomas De La Rue & Co., Ltd., London. Panes of 50. Designed by Hubert Woyty-Wimmer.

1956, Feb. 17				Perf. 14	
41	A21	3c turquoise blue (1,000,000)		.20	.20
		First day cover			1.50
		Inscription block of 4		.45	—
42	A21	8c deep carmine (1,000,000)		.30	.30
		First day cover			2.25
		First day cover, #41-42			3.50
		Inscription block of 4		1.40	—

Plate number ("1A" or "1B") in color of stamp appears below 47th stamp of sheet.

Globe and Caduceus — A22

Design: 8c, inscribed "OMS."
Issued in honor of the World Health Organization.
Engraved and printed by Thomas De La Rue & Co., Ltd., London. Panes of 50. Designed by Olav Mathiesen.

1956, Apr. 6				Perf. 14	
43	A22	3c bright greenish blue			
		(1,250,000)		.20	.20
		First day cover			1.00
		Inscription block of 4		.35	—
44	A22	8c golden brown (1,000,000)		.20	.20
		First day cover			1.50
		First day cover, #43-44			13.50
		Inscription block of 4		1.25	—

First day covers of Nos. 43 and 44 total 260,853.

General Assembly — A23

Design: 8c, French inscription.
Issued to commemorate United Nations Day.
Engraved and printed by Thomas De La Rue & Co., Ltd., London. Panes of 50. Designed by Kurt Plowitz.

1956, Oct. 24				Perf. 14	
45	A23	3c dark blue (2,000,000)		.20	.20
		First day cover			1.00
		Inscription block of 4		.30	—
46	A23	8c gray olive (1,500,000)		.20	.20
		First day cover			1.00
		First day cover, #45-46			7.50
		Inscription block of 4		.80	—

First day covers of Nos. 45 and 46 total 303,560.

Flame and Globe — A24

Issued to publicize Human Rights Day.
Engraved and printed by Thomas De La Rue & Co., Ltd., London. Panes of 50. Designed by Rashid-ud Din.

1956, Dec. 10				Perf. 14	
47	A24	3c plum (5,000,000)		.20	.20
		First day cover			1.00
		Inscription block of 4		.30	—
48	A24	8c dark blue (4,000,000)		.20	.20
		First day cover			1.00
		First day cover, #47-48			2.00
		Inscription block of 4		.60	—

First day covers of Nos. 47 and 48 total 416,120.

Weather Balloon — A25

Badge of UN Emergency Force — A26

Design: 8c, Agency name in French.
Issued to honor the World Meterological Organization.
Engraved and printed by Thomas De La Rue & Co., Ltd., London. Panes of 50. Designed by A. L. Pollock.

1957, Jan. 28				Perf. 14	
49	A25	3c violet blue (5,000,000)		.20	.20
		First day cover			1.00
		Inscription block of 4		.25	—
50	A25	8c dark carmine rose		.20	.20
		(3,448,985)			
		First day cover			1.00
		First day cover, #49-50			2.25
		Inscription block of 4		.65	—

First day covers of Nos. 49 and 50 total 376,110.

1957, Apr. 8				Perf. 14x12½	

Issued in honor of the UN Emergency Force.
Engraved and printed by Thomas De La Rue & Co., Ltd., London. Panes of 50. Designed by Ole Hamann.

51	A26	3c light blue (4,000,000)		.20	.20
		First day cover			1.00
		Inscription block of 4		.30	—
52	A26	8c rose carmine (3,000,000)		.20	.20
		First day cover			1.00
		First day cover, #51-52			1.75
		Inscription block of 4		.70	—

First day covers of Nos. 51 and 52 total 461,772.

Nos. 51-52 Re-engraved

1957, Apr.-May				Perf. 14x12½	
53	A26	3c blue (2,736,206)		.20	.20
		Inscription block of 4		.40	—
54	A26	8c rose carmine (1,000,000)		.35	.20
		Inscription block of 4		1.40	—

On Nos. 53-54 the background within and around the circles is shaded lightly, giving a halo effect. The lettering is more distinct with a line around each letter.

UN Emblem and Globe — A27

Design: 8c, French inscription.
Issued to honor the Security Council.
Engraved and printed by Thomas De La Rue & Co., Ltd., London. Panes of 50. Designed by Rashid-ud Din.

1957, Oct. 24				Perf. 12½x13	
55	A27	3c orange brown (3,674,968)		.20	.20
		First day cover			1.00
		Inscription block of 4		.25	—
56	A27	8c dark blue green (2,885,938)		.20	.20
		First day cover			1.00
		First day cover, #55-56			2.25
		Inscription block of 4		.70	—

First day covers of Nos. 55 and 56 total 460,627.

Flaming Torch — A28

Issued in honor of Human Rights Day.
Engraved and printed by Thomas De La Rue & Co., Ltd., London. Panes of 50. Designed by Olav Mathiesen.

1957, Dec. 10				Perf. 14	
57	A28	3c red brown (3,368,405)		.20	.20
		First day cover			1.00
		Inscription block of 4		.25	—
58	A28	8c black (2,717,310)		.20	.20
		First day cover			1.00
		First day cover, #57-58			1.25
		Inscription block of 4		.65	—

First day covers of Nos. 57 and 58 total 553,669.

UN Emblem Shedding Light on Atom — A29

Design: 8c, French inscription.
Issued in honor of the International Atomic Energy Agency.
Engraved and printed by the American Bank Note Co., New York. Panes of 50. Designed by Robert Perrot.

1958, Feb. 10   *Perf. 12*
59	A29	3c olive (3,663,305)	.20	.20
		First day cover		1.00
		Inscription block of 4	.25	—
60	A29	8c blue (3,043,622)	.20	.20
		First day cover		1.00
		First day cover, #59-60		1.00
		Inscription block of 4	.65	—

First day covers of Nos. 59 and 60 total 504,832.

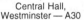

Central Hall,
Westminster — A30

UN Seal — A31

Design: 8c, French inscription.
Central Hall, Westminster, London, was the site of the first session of the United Nations General Assembly, 1946.
Engraved and printed by the American Bank Note Co., New York. Panes of 50. Designed by Olav Mathiesen.

1958, Apr. 14   *Perf. 12*
61	A30	3c violet blue (3,353,716)	.20	.20
		First day cover		1.00
		Inscription block of 4	.25	—
62	A30	8c rose claret (2,836,747)	.20	.20
		First day cover		1.00
		First day cover, #61-62		2.00
		Inscription block of 4	.60	—

First day covers of Nos. 61 and 62 total 449,401.

1958, Oct. 24   *Perf. 13½x14*

Engraved and printed by Bradbury, Wilkinson & Co., Ltd., England. Panes of 50. Designed by Herbert M. Sanborn.

63	A31	4c red orange (9,000,000)	.20	.20
		First day cover		1.00
		Inscription block of 4	.20	—

1958, June 2   *Perf. 13x14*
64	A31	8c bright blue (5,000,000)	.20	.20
		First day cover (219,422)		1.00
		Inscription block of 4	.55	—
		Margin block of 4, Bradbury, Wilkinson imprint	3.00	—

Gearwheels — A32

Hands Upholding
Globe — A33

Design: 8c, French inscription.
Issued to honor the Economic and Social Council.
Engraved and printed by the American Bank Note Co., New York. Panes of 50. Designed by Ole Hamann.

1958, Oct. 24   **Unwmk.**   *Perf. 12*
65	A32	4c dark blue green (2,556,784)	.20	.20
		First day cover		1.00
		Inscription block of 4	.30	—
66	A32	8c vermilion (2,175,117)	.20	.20
		First day cover		1.00
		First day cover, #65-66		1.00
		Inscription block of 4	.60	—

First day covers of Nos. 63, 65 and 66 total 626,236.

1958, Dec. 10   **Unwmk.**   *Perf. 12*

Issued for Human Rights Day and to commemorate the 10th anniversary of the signing of the Universal Declaration of Human Rights.
Engraved and printed by the American Bank Note Co., New York. Panes of 50. Designed by Leonard C. Mitchell.

67	A33	4c yellow green (2,644,340)	.20	.20
		First day cover		1.00
		Inscription block of 4	.40	—
68	A33	8c red brown (2,216,838)	.20	.20
		First day cover		1.00
		First day cover, #67-68		1.00
		Inscription block of 4	.75	—

First day covers of Nos. 67 and 68 total 618,124.

New York City
Building, Flushing
Meadows — A34

Design: 8c, French inscription.
New York City Building at Flushing Meadows, New York, was the site of many General Assembly meetings, 1946-50.
Engraved and printed by Canadian Bank Note Company, Ltd., Ottawa. Panes of 50. Designed by Robert Perrot.

1959, Mar. 30   **Unwmk.**   *Perf. 12*
69	A34	4c light lilac rose (2,035,011)	.20	.20
		First day cover		1.00
		Inscription block of 4	.30	—
70	A34	8c aquamarine (1,627,281)	.20	.20
		First day cover		1.00
		First day cover, #69-70		1.75
		Inscription block of 4	.70	—

First day covers of Nos. 69 and 70 total 440,955.

A35

A36

Design: UN emblem and symbols of agriculture, industry and trade.
Issued to honor the Economic Commission for Europe.
Engraved and printed by Canadian Bank Note Company, Ltd., Ottawa. Panes of 50. Designed by Ole Hamann.

1959, May 18   **Unwmk.**   *Perf. 12*
71	A35	4c blue (1,743,502)	.20	.20
		First day cover		1.00
		Inscription block of 4	.60	—
72	A35	8c red orange (1,482,898)	.20	.20
		First day cover		1.00
		First day cover, #71-72		1.25
		Inscription block of 4	.75	—

First day covers of Nos. 71 and 72 total 433,549.

1959, Oct. 23   **Unwmk.**   *Perf. 12*

Designs: 4c, Figure Adapted from Rodin's "Age of Bronze." 8c, same, French inscription.
Issued to honor the Trusteeship Council.
Engraved and printed by Canadian Bank Note Co., Ltd., Ottawa. Panes of 50. Designed by León Helguera; lettering by Ole Hamann.

73	A36	4c bright red (1,929,677)	.20	.20
		First day cover		1.00
		Inscription block of 4	.30	—
74	A36	8c dark olive green (1,587,647)	.20	.20
		First day cover		1.00
		First day cover, #73-74		1.50
		Inscription block of 4	1.00	—

First day covers of Nos. 73 and 74 total 466,053.

World Refugee Year
Emblem — A37

Chaillot Palace,
Paris — A38

Design: 8c, French inscription.
Issued to publicize World Refugee Year, July 1, 1959-June 30, 1960.
Engraved and printed by Canadian Bank Note Co., Ltd., Ottawa. Panes of 50. Designed by Olav Mathiesen.

1959, Dec. 10   **Unwmk.**   *Perf. 12*
75	A37	4c olive & red (2,168,963)	.20	.20
		First day cover		1.00
		Inscription block of 4	.35	—
76	A37	8c olive & bright greenish blue (1,843,886)	.20	.20

		First day cover		1.00
		First day cover, #75-76		2.00
		Inscription block of 4	.75	—

First day covers of Nos. 75 and 76 total 502,262.

1960, Feb. 29   **Unwmk.**   *Perf. 14*

Design: 8c, French inscription.
Chaillot Palace in Paris was the site of General Assembly meetings in 1948 and 1951.
Engraved and printed by Thomas De La Rue & Co., Ltd., London. Panes of 50. Designed by Hubert Woyty-Wimmer.

77	A38	4c rose lilac & blue (2,276,678)	.20	.20
		First day cover		1.00
		Inscription block of 4	.20	—
78	A38	8c dull green & brown (1,930,869)	.20	.20
		First day cover		1.00
		First day cover, #77-78		2.50
		Inscription block of 4	.70	—

First day covers of Nos. 77 and 78 total 446,815.

Map of Far East
and Steel
Beam — A39

Design: 8c, French inscription.
Issued to honor the Economic Commission for Asia and the Far East (ECAFE).
Printed by the Government Printing Bureau, Tokyo. Panes of 50. Designed by Hubert Woyty-Wimmer.

1960, Apr. 11   **Photo.**   **Unwmk.**   *Perf. 13x13½*
79	A39	4c deep claret, blue green & dull yellow (2,195,945)	.20	.20
		First day cover		1.00
		Inscription block of 4	.20	—
80	A39	8c olive green, blue & rose (1,897,902)	.20	.20
		First day cover		1.00
		First day cover, #79-80		2.00
		Inscription block of 4	.75	—

First day covers of Nos. 79 and 80 total 415,127.

Tree, FAO and UN
Emblems — A40

UN Headquarters and
Preamble to UN
Charter — A41

Design: 8c, French inscription.
Issued to commemorate the Fifth World Forestry Congress, Seattle, Washington, Aug. 29-Sept. 10.
Printed by the Government Printing Bureau, Tokyo. Panes of 50. Designed by Ole Hamann.

1960, Aug. 29   **Photo.**   **Unwmk.**   *Perf. 13½*
81	A40	4c dark blue, green & orange (2,188,293)	.20	.20
		First day cover		1.00
		Inscription block of 4	.35	—
a.		Imperf., pair		
82	A40	8c yellow green, black & orange (1,837,778)	.20	.20
		First day cover		1.00
		First day cover, #81-82		2.00
		Inscription block of 4	.65	—

First day covers of Nos. 81 and 82 total 434,129.

1960, Oct. 24   **Unwmk.**   *Perf. 11*

Design: 8c, French inscription.
Issued to commemorate the 15th anniversary of the United Nations.
Engraved and printed by the British American Bank Note Co., Ltd., Ottawa, Canada. Panes of 50. Designed by Robert Perrot.

83	A41	4c blue (2,631,593)	.20	.20
		First day cover		1.00
		Inscription block of 4	.35	—
84	A41	8c gray (2,278,022)	.20	.20
		First day cover		1.00
		First day cover, #83-84		1.50
		Inscription block of 4	.65	—

Souvenir Sheet
Imperf

85		Sheet of 2 *(1,000,000)*	.50	.50
a.		A41 4c **blue**	.25	.20
b.		A41 8c **gray**	.25	.20
		First day cover *(256,699)*	1.00	

No. 85 has dark gray marginal inscription. Size: 92x71mm. Broken "I" and "V" flaws occur in "ANNIVERSARY" in marginal inscription. Copies are known with the two stamps misaligned.

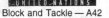

Block and Tackle — A42

Scales of Justice from Raphael's Stanze — A43

Design: 8c, French inscription.
Issued to honor the International Bank for Reconstruction and Development.
Printed by the Government Printing Bureau, Tokyo. Panes of 50. Designed by Angel Medina Medina.

1960, Dec. 9   Photo.   Unwmk.   Perf. 13½x13

86	A42 4c **multicolored** *(2,286,117)*	.20	.20
	First day cover	1.00	
	Inscription block of 4	.35	—
87	A42 8c **multicolored** *(1,882,019)*	.20	.20
	First day cover	1.00	
	First day cover, #86-87	1.25	
	Inscription block of 4	.65	—
a.	Imperf., pair		

First day covers of Nos. 86 and 87 total 559,708.
No. 86 exists imperf.

1961, Feb. 13   Photo.   Unwmk.   Perf. 13½x13

Design: 8c, French inscription.
Issued to honor the International Court of Justice.
Printed by the Government Printing Bureau, Tokyo, Japan. Panes of 50. Designed by Kurt Plowitz.

88	A43 4c **yellow, orange brown & black** *(2,234,588)*	.20	.20
	First day cover	1.00	
	Inscription block of 4	.35	—
89	A43 8c **yellow, green & black** *(2,023,968)*	.20	.20
	First day cover	1.00	
	First day cover, #88-89	1.00	
	Inscription block of 4	.65	—

First day covers of Nos. 88 and 89 total 447,467.
Nos. 88-89 exist imperf.

Seal of International Monetary Fund — A44

Design: 7c, French inscription.
Issued to honor the International Monetary Fund.
Printed by the Government Printing Bureau, Tokyo, Japan. Panes of 50. Designed by Roy E. Carlson and Hordur Karlsson, Iceland.

1961, Apr. 17   Photo.   Unwmk.   Perf. 13x13½

90	A44 4c **bright bluish green** *(2,305,010)*	.20	.20
	First day cover	1.00	
	Inscription block of 4	.35	—
91	A44 7c **terra cotta & yellow** *(2,147,201)*	.20	.20
	First day cover	1.00	
	First day cover, #90-91	1.00	
	Inscription block of 4	.65	—

First day covers of Nos. 90 and 91 total 448,729.

Abstract Group of Flags — A45

Printed by Courvoisier S.A., La Chaux-de-Fonds, Switzerland. Panes of 50. Designed by Herbert M. Sanborn.

1961, June 5   Photo.   Unwmk.   Perf. 11½

92	A45 30c **multicolored** *(3,370,000)*	.40	.20
	First day cover *(182,949)*	1.00	
	Inscription block of 4	1.75	—

See UN Offices in Geneva No. 10.

Cogwheel and Map of Latin America — A46

Design: 11c, Spanish inscription.
Issued to honor the Economic Commission for Latin America.
Printed by the Government Printing Bureau, Tokyo. Panes of 50. Designed by Robert Perrot.

1961, Sept. 18   Photo.   Unwmk.   Perf. 13½

93	A46 4c **blue, red & citron** *(2,037,912)*	.20	.20
	First day cover	1.00	
	Inscription block of 4	.45	—
94	A46 11c **green, lilac & orange vermilion** *(1,835,097)*	.25	.20
	First day cover	1.00	
	First day cover, #93-94	1.00	
	Inscription block of 4	1.25	—

First day covers of Nos. 93 and 94 total 435,820.

Africa House, Addis Ababa, and Map — A47

Design: 11c, English inscription.
Issued to honor the Economic Commission for Africa.
Printed by Courvoisier S.A., La Chaux-de-Fonds, Switzerland. Panes of 50. Designed by Robert Perrot.

1961, Oct. 24   Photo.   Unwmk.   Perf. 11½

95	A47 4c **ultramarine, orange, yellow & brown** *(2,044,842)*	.20	.20
	First day cover	1.00	
	Inscription block of 4	.30	—
96	A47 11c **emerald, orange, yellow & brown** *(1,790,894)*	.25	.20
	First day cover	1.00	
	First day cover, #95-96	1.00	
	Inscription block of 4	1.10	—

First day covers of Nos. 95 and 96 total 435,131.

Mother Bird Feeding Young and UNICEF Seal — A48

Designs: 3c, Spanish inscription. 13c, French inscription.
15th anniversary of the United Nations Children's Fund.
Printed by Courvoisier S.A., La Chaux-de-Fonds, Switzerland. Panes of 50. Designed by Minoru Hisano.

1961, Dec. 4   Photo.   Unwmk.   Perf. 11½

97	A48 3c **brown, gold, orange & yellow** *(2,867,456)*	.20	.20
	First day cover	1.00	
	Inscription block of 4	.25	—
98	A48 4c **brown, gold, blue & emerald** *(2,735,899)*	.20	.20
	First day cover	1.00	
	Inscription block of 4	.35	—
99	A48 13c **deep green, gold, purple & pink** *(1,951,715)*	.20	.20
	First day cover	1.00	
	First day cover, #97-99	1.40	
	Inscription block of 4	1.25	—
	Nos. 97-99 (3)	.60	.60

First day covers of Nos. 97-99 total 752,979.

Family and Symbolic Buildings — A49

Design: 7c, inscribed "Services Collectifs".
Issued to publicize the UN program for housing and urban development, and in connection with the expert committee meeting at UN headquarters, Feb. 7-21.
Printed by Harrison and Sons, Ltd., London, England. Panes of 50. Designed by Olav Mathiesen.

1962, Feb. 28   Photo.   Unwmk.   Perf. 14½x14
Central design multicolored

100	A49 4c **bright blue** *(2,204,190)*	.20	.20
	First day cover	1.00	
	Inscription block of 4	.35	—
a.	Black omitted	200.00	
b.	Yellow omitted	—	
c.	Brown omitted	—	
101	A49 7c **orange brown** *(1,845,821)*	.20	.20
	First day cover	1.00	
	First day cover, #100-101	1.25	
	Inscription block of 4	.65	—
a.	Red omitted	—	
b.	Black omitted	—	

First day covers of Nos. 100-101 total 466,178.

"The World Against Malaria" — A50

Issued in honor of the World Health Organization and to call attention to the international campaign to eradicate malaria from the world.
Printed by Harrison and Sons, Ltd., London, England. Panes of 50. Designed by Rashid-ud Din.

1962, Mar. 30   Photo.   Unwmk.   Perf. 14x14½
Word frame in gray

102	A50 4c **orange, yellow, brown, green & black** *(2,047,000)*	.20	.20
	First day cover	1.00	
	Inscription block of 4	.35	—
103	A50 11c **green, yellow, brown & indigo** *(1,683,766)*	.25	.20
	First day cover	1.00	
	First day cover, #102-103	1.50	
	Inscription block of 4	1.10	—

First day covers of Nos. 102-103 total 522,450.

"Peace" — A51

UN Flag — A52

Hands Combining "UN" and Globe — A53

UN Emblem over Globe — A54

Printed by Harrison & Sons, Ltd. London, England (1c, 3c and 11c), and by Canadian Bank Note Co., Ltd., Ottawa (5c). Panes of 50. Designed by Kurt Plowitz (1c), Ole Hamann (3c), Renato Ferrini (5c) and Olav Mathiesen (11c).

Photo.; Engr. (5c)

1962, May 25		Unwmk.		Perf. 14x14½
104	A51	1c vermilion, blue, black & gray		
		(5,000,000)	.20	.20
		First day cover		1.00
		Inscription block of 4	.25	—
105	A52	3c light green, Prussian blue, yellow		
		& gray (5,000,000)	.20	.20
		First day cover		1.00
		Inscription block of 4	.25	—

Perf. 12

106	A53	5c dark carmine rose (4,000,000)	.20	.20
		First day cover		1.00
		Inscription block of 4	.65	—

Perf. 12½

107	A54	11c dark & light blue & gold		
		(4,400,000)	.25	.20
		First day cover		1.00
		First day cover, #104-107		6.00
		Inscription block of 4	1.10	—
		Nos. 104-107 (4)	.85	.80

First day covers of Nos. 104-107 total 738,985.
Size of 5c, No. 106: 36½x23½mm.
See No. 167. See UN Offices in Geneva Nos. 2 and 6.

Flag at Half-mast and UN Headquarters — A55

World Map Showing Congo — A56

Issued on the 1st anniversary of the death of Dag Hammarskjold, Secretary General of the United Nations 1953-61, in memory of those who died in the service of the United Nations.
Printed by Courvoisier S. A., La Chaux-de-Fonds, Switzerland. Panes of 50. Designed by Ole Hamann.

1962, Sept. 17		Photo.	Unwmk.	Perf. 11½
108	A55	5c black, light blue & blue (2,195,707)	.20	.20
		First day cover		1.00
		Inscription block of 4	.50	—
109	A55	15c black, gray olive & blue		
		(1,155,047)	.20	.20
		First day cover		1.00
		First day cover, #108-109		2.00
		Inscription block of 4	.85	—

First day covers of Nos. 108-109 total 513,963.

1962, Oct. 24		Photo.	Unwmk.	Perf. 11½

Design: 11c inscribed "Operation des Nations Unies au Congo."
Issued to commemorate the United Nations Operation in the Congo.
Printed by Courvoisier S. A., La Chaux-de-Fonds, Switzerland. Panes of 50. Designed by George Hamori.

110	A56	4c olive, orange, black & yellow		
		(1,477,958)	.20	.20
		First day cover		1.00
		Inscription block of 4	.50	—
111	A56	11c blue green, orange, black & yellow (1,171,255)	.20	.20
		First day cover		1.00
		First day cover, #110-111		1.75
		Inscription block of 4	.95	—

First day covers of Nos. 110-111 total 460,675.

Globe in Universe and Palm Frond — A57

Development Decade Emblem — A58

Design: 4c, English inscription.
Issued to honor the Committee on Peaceful Uses of Outer Space.
Printed by Bradbury, Wilkinson and Co., Ltd., England. Panes of 50. Designed by Kurt Plowitz.

1962, Dec. 3		Engr.	Unwmk.	Perf. 14x13½
112	A57	4c violet blue (2,263,876)	.20	.20
		First day cover		1.00
		Inscription block of 4	.35	—
113	A57	11c rose claret (1,681,584)	.25	.20
		First day cover		1.00
		First day cover, #112-113		2.00
		Inscription block of 4	1.25	—

First day covers of Nos. 112-113 total 529,780.

1963, Feb. 4		Photo.	Unwmk.	Perf. 11½

Design: 11c, French inscription.
UN Development Decade and UN Conference on the Application of Science and Technology for the Benefit of the Less Developed Areas, Geneva, Feb. 4-20.
Printed by Courvoisier S. A., La Chaux-de-Fonds, Switzerland. Panes of 50. Designed by Rashid-ud Din.

114	A58	5c pale green, maroon, dark blue & Prussian blue (1,802,406)	.20	.20
		First day cover		1.00
		Inscription block of 4	.35	—
115	A58	11c yellow, maroon, dark blue & Prussian blue (1,530,190)	.20	.20
		First day cover		1.00
		First day cover, #114-115		1.50
		Inscription block of 4	.90	—

First day covers of Nos. 114-115 total 460,877.

Stalks of Wheat — A59

Design: 11c, French inscription.
Issued for the "Freedom from Hunger" campaign of the Food and Agriculture Organization.
Printed by Courvoisier S. A., La Chaux-de-Fonds, Switzerland. Panes of 50. Designed by Ole Hamann.

1963, Mar. 22		Photo.	Unwmk.	Perf. 11½
116	A59	5c vermilion, green & yellow		
		(1,666,178)	.20	.20
		First day cover		1.00
		Inscription block of 4	.35	—
117	A59	11c vermilion, deep claret & yellow		
		(1,563,023)	.25	.20
		First day cover		1.00
		First day cover, #116-117		1.50
		Inscription block of 4	1.10	—

First day covers of Nos. 116-117 total 461,868.

Bridge over Map of New Guinea — A60

1st anniversary of the United Nations Temporary Executive Authority (UNTEA) in West New Guinea (West Irian).
Printed by Courvoisier S.A., La Chaux-de-Fonds, Switzerland. Panes of 50. Designed by Henry Bencsath.

1963, Oct. 1		Photo.	Unwmk.	Perf. 11½
118	A60	25c blue, green & gray (1,427,747)	.45	.30
		First day cover (222,280)		1.00
		Inscription block of 4	2.00	—

General Assembly Building, New York — A61

Design: 11c, French inscription.
Since October 1955 all sessions of the General Assembly have been held in the General Assembly Hall, UN Headquarters, NY.
Printed by the Government Printing Bureau, Tokyo. Panes of 50. Designed by Kurt Plowitz.

1963, Nov. 4		Photo.	Unwmk.	Perf. 13
119	A61	5c violet blue, blue, yellow green & red (1,892,539)	.20	.20
		First day cover		1.00
		Inscription block of 4	.35	—
120	A61	11c green, yellow green, blue, yellow & red (1,435,079)	.20	.20
		First day cover		1.00
		First day cover, #119-120		1.25
		Inscription block of 4	.85	—

First day covers of Nos. 119-120 total 410,306.

Flame — A62

Design: 11c inscribed "15e Anniversaire."
15th anniversary of the signing of the Universal Declaration of Human Rights.
Printed by the Government Printing Bureau, Tokyo. Panes of 50. Designed by Rashid-ud Din.

1963, Dec. 10		Photo.	Unwmk.	Perf. 13
121	A62	5c green, gold, red & yellow		
		(2,208,008)	.20	.20
		First day cover		1.00
		Inscription block of 4	.55	—
122	A62	11c carmine, gold, blue & yellow		
		(1,501,125)	.20	.20
		First day cover		1.00
		First day cover, #121-122		1.00
		Inscription block of 4	.70	—

First day covers of Nos. 121-122 total 567,907.

Ships at Sea and IMCO Emblem — A63

Design: 11c, inscribed "OMCI."
Issued to honor the Intergovernmental Maritime Consultative Organization.
Printed by Courvoisier S.A., La Chaux-de-Fonds, Switzerland. Panes of 50. Designed by Henry Bencsath; emblem by Olav Mathiesen.

1964, Jan. 13		Photo.	Unwmk.	Perf. 11½
123	A63	5c blue, olive, ocher & yellow		
		(1,805,750)	.20	.20
		First day cover		1.00
		Inscription block of 4	.35	—
124	A63	11c dark blue, dark green, emerald & yellow (1,583,848)	.20	.20
		First day cover		1.00
		First day cover, #123-124		1.00
		Inscription block of 4	.85	—

First day covers of Nos. 123-124 total 442,696.

World Map, Sinusoidal Projection — A64

UN Emblem — A65

Three Men United Before Globe — A66

Stylized Globe and Weather Vane — A67

Printed by Thomas De La Rue & Co. Ltd., London (2c) and Courvoisier S.A., La Chaux-de-fonds, Switzerland (7c, 10c and 50c). Panes of 50.

Designed by Ole Hamann (2c), George Hamori (7c, 10c) and Hatim El Mekki (50c).

1964-71   Photo.   Unwmk.   Perf. 14
125   A64   2c   light & dark blue, orange & yellow

green *(3,800,000)*	.20	.20
First day cover		1.00
Inscription block of 4	.20	
a. Perf. 13x13½, Feb. 24, 1971 *(1,500,000)*	.20	.20

Perf. 11½
126   A65   7c   dark blue, orange brown & black

(2,700,000)	.20	.20
First day cover		1.00
Inscription block of 4	.80	
127 A66 10c blue green, olive green & black		
(3,200,000)	.20	.20
First day cover		1.00
First day cover, #125-127		5.00
Inscription block of 4	.80	
128 A67 50c multicolored *(2,520,000)*	.75	.45
First day cover *(210,713)*		1.00
Inscription block of 4	3.75	
Nos. 125-128 (4)	1.35	1.05

Issue dates: 50c, Mar. 6; 2c, 7c, 10c, May 29, 1964.
First day covers of 2c, 7c and 10c total 524,073.
See UN Offices in Geneva Nos. 3 and 12.

Arrows Showing Global Flow of Trade — A68

Design: 5c, English inscription.
Issued to commemorate the UN Conference on Trade and Development, Geneva, Mar. 23-June 15.
Printed by Thomas De La Rue & Co., Ltd., London. Panes of 50. Designed by Herbert M. Sanborn and Ole Hamann.

1964, June 15   Photo.   Unwmk.   Perf. 13

129 A68 5c black, red & yellow *(1,791,211)*	.20	.20
First day cover		1.00
Inscription block of 4	.35	
130 A68 11c black, olive & yellow *(1,529,526)*	.20	.20
First day cover		1.00
First day cover, #129-130		1.50
Inscription block of 4	.85	

First day covers of Nos. 129-130 total 422,358.

Poppy Capsule and Reaching Hands — A69

Design: 11c, Inscribed "Echec au Stupéfiants."
Issued to honor international efforts and achievements in the control of narcotics.
Printed by the Canadian Bank Note Co., Ottawa. Panes of 50. Designed by Kurt Plowitz.

1964, Sept. 21   Engr.   Unwmk.   Perf. 12

131 A69 5c rose red & black *(1,508,999)*	.20	.20
First day cover		1.00
Inscription block of 4	.45	
132 A69 11c emerald & black *(1,340,691)*	.20	.20
First day cover		1.00
First day cover, #131-132		1.75
Inscription block of 4	1.10	

First day covers of Nos. 131-132 total 445,274.

Padlocked Atomic Blast — A70

Education for Progress — A71

Signing of the nuclear test ban treaty pledging an end to nuclear explosions in the atmosphere, outer space and under water.
Printed by Artia, Prague, Czechoslovakia. Panes of 50. Designed by Ole Hamann.

Litho. and Engr.
1964, Oct. 23   Unwmk.   Perf. 11x11½

133 A70 5c dark red & dark brown *(2,422,789)*	.20	.20
First day cover *(298,652)*		1.00
Inscription block of 4	.45	

1964, Dec. 7   Photo.   Unwmk.   Perf. 12½

Design: 11c, French inscription.
Issued to publicize the UNESCO world campaign for universal literacy and for free compulsory primary education.
Printed by Courvoisier, S. A., La Chaux-de-fonds, Switzerland. Panes of 50. Designed by Kurt Plowitz.

134 A71 4c orange, red, bister, green & blue		
(2,375,181)	.20	.20
First day cover		1.00
Inscription block of 4	.25	
135 A71 5c bister, red, dark & light blue		
(2,496,877)	.20	.20
First day cover		1.00
Inscription block of 4	.35	
136 A71 11c green, light blue, black & rose		
(1,773,645)	.20	.20
First day cover		1.00
First day cover, #134-136		1.25
Inscription block of 4	.75	
Nos. 134-136 (3)	.60	.60

First day covers of Nos. 134-136 total 727,875.

Progress Chart of Special Fund, Key and Globe — A72

UN Emblem, Stylized Leaves and View of Cyprus — A73

Design: 11c, French inscription.
Issued to publicize the Special Fund program to speed economic growth and social advancement in low-income countries.
Printed by the Government Printing Bureau, Tokyo. Panes of 50. Designed by Rashid-ud Din, Pakistan.

1965, Jan. 25   Photo.   Unwmk.   Perf. 13½x13

137 A72 5c dull blue, dark blue, yellow & red		
(1,949,274)	.20	.20
First day cover		1.00
Inscription block of 4	.40	
138 A72 11c yellow green, dark blue, yellow &		
red *(1,690,908)*	.20	.20
First day cover		1.00
First day cover, #137-138		1.25
Inscription block of 4	.85	
a. Black omitted (UN emblem on key)		

First day covers of Nos. 137-138 total 490,608.

1965, Mar. 4   Photo.   Unwmk.   Perf. 11½
Design: 11c, French inscription.
Issued to honor the United Nations Peace-keeping Force on Cyprus.

Printed by Courvoisier S.A., Switzerland. Panes of 50. Designed by George Hamori, Australia.

139 A73 5c orange, olive & black *(1,887,042)*	.20	.20
First day cover		1.00
Inscription block of 4	.40	
140 A73 11c yellow green, blue green & black		
(1,691,767)	.20	.20
First day cover		1.00
First day cover, #139-140		1.25
Inscription block of 4	.80	

First day covers of Nos. 139-140 total 438,059.

"From Semaphore to Satellite" — A74

Design: 11c, French inscription.
Centenary of the International Telecommunication Union.
Printed by Courvoisier S.A., Switzerland. Panes of 50. Designed by Kurt Plowitz, United States.

1965, May 17   Photo.   Unwmk.   Perf. 11½

141 A74 5c aquamarine, orange, blue & purple		
(2,432,407)	.20	.20
First day cover		1.00
Inscription block of 4	.40	
142 A74 11c light violet, red orange, bister &		
bright green *(1,731,070)*	.20	.20
First day cover		1.00
First day cover, #141-142		1.25
Inscription block of 4	.80	

First day covers of Nos. 141-142 total 434,393.

ICY Emblem — A75

Design: 15c, French inscription.
20th anniversary of the United Nations and International Cooperation Year.
Printed by Bradbury, Wilkinson and Co., Ltd., England. Panes of 50. Designed by Olav Mathiesen, Denmark.

1965, June 26   Engr.   Unwmk.   Perf. 14x13½

143 A75 5c dark blue *(2,282,452)*	.20	.20
First day cover		1.00
Inscription block of 4	.40	
144 A75 15c lilac rose *(1,993,562)*	.20	.20
First day cover		1.00
First day cover, #143-144		1.00
Inscription block of 4	1.00	

Souvenir Sheet

145 A75 Sheet of two *(1,928,366)*	.35	.30
First day cover		1.00

No. 145 contains one each of Nos. 143-144 with dark blue and ocher marginal inscription, ocher edging. Size: 92x70mm.
First day covers of Nos. 143-145 total: New York, 748,876; San Francisco, 301,435.

"Peace" — A76

Opening Words, UN Charter — A77

UN Headquarters and Emblem — A78

UN Emblem — A79

UN Emblem
Encircled — A80

Printed by Government Printing Bureau, Tokyo (1c); Government Printing Office, Austria (15c, 20c); Government Printing Office (Bundesdruckerei), Berlin (25c), and Courvoisier S.A., Switzerland ($1). Panes of 50.
Designed by Kurt Plowitz US (1c); Olav S. Mathiesen, Denmark (15c); Vergniaud Pierre-Noel, US (20c); Rashid-ud Din, Pakistan (25c), and Ole Hamann, Denmark ($1).

1965-66   Photo.   Unwmk.   Perf. 13½x13
146 A76 1c **vermilion, blue, black & gray**
         (7,000,000)   .20   .20
         First day cover   1.00
         Inscription block of 4   .20   —

Perf. 14
147 A77 15c **olive bister, dull yellow, black &**
         deep claret (2,500,000)   .25   .20
         First day cover   1.00
         Inscription block of 4   1.10   —

Perf. 12
148 A78 20c **dark blue, blue, red & yellow**
         (3,000,000)   .30   .20
         First day cover   1.00
         First day cover, #147-148   1.25
         Inscription block of 4   1.25   —
    a.   Yellow omitted   —

Litho. and Embossed
Perf. 14
149 A79 25c **light & dark blue** (3,200,000)   .35   .20
         First day cover   1.25
         First day cover, #146, 149   1.50
         Inscription block of 4   1.50   —
         Inscription block of 6,
           "Bundesdruckerei Berlin" imprint   20.00
         First day cover, "Bundesdruckerei," margin block of 6   32.50

Photo.
Perf. 11½
150 A80 $1 **aquamarine & sapphire**
         (2,570,000)   1.75 1.50
         First day cover (181,510)   2.00
         Inscription block of 4   7.75   —
         Nos. 146-150 (5)   2.85 2.30

Issued: 1c, 25c, Sept. 20, 1965; 15c, 20c, Oct. 25, 1965; $1, Mar. 25, 1966.
First day covers of Nos. 146 and 149 total 443,964. Those of Nos. 147-148 total 457,596.
The 25c has the marginal inscription (UN emblem and "1965") in two sizes: 1st printing (with Bundesdruckerei imprint), 6mm in diameter; 2nd printing, 8mm. In 1st printing, "halo" of UN emblem is larger, overlapping "25c."
See UN Offices in Geneva Nos. 5, 9 and 11.

Fields and People — A81

Globe and Flags of
UN Members — A82

Design: 11c, French inscription.
Issued to emphasize the importance of the world's population growth and its problems and to call attention to population trends and development.
Printed by Government Printing Office, Austria. Panes of 50. Designed by Olav S. Mathiesen, Denmark.

1965, Nov. 29   Photo.   Unwmk.   Perf. 12
151 A81 4c **multicolored** (1,966,033)   .20   .20
         First day cover   1.00
         Inscription block of 4   .25   —
152 A81 5c **multicolored** (2,298,731)   .20   .20
         First day cover   1.00
         Inscription block of 4   .30   —
153 A81 11c **multicolored** (1,557,589)   .20   .20
         First day cover   1.00
         First day cover, #151-153   1.75
         Inscription block of 4   .90   —
         Nos. 151-153 (3)   .60   .60

First day covers of Nos. 151-153 total 710,507.

1966, Jan. 31   Photo.   Unwmk.   Perf. 11½
Design: 15c, French inscription.
Issued to honor the World Federation of United Nations Associations.

Printed by Courvoisier S.A., Switzerland. Panes of 50.
Designed by Olav S. Mathiesen, Denmark.

154 A82 5c **multicolored** (2,462,215)   .20   .20
         First day cover   1.00
         Inscription block of 4   .35   —
155 A82 15c **multicolored** (1,643,661)   .20   .20
         First day cover   1.00
         First day cover, #154-155   1.25
         Inscription block of 4   .90   —

First day covers of Nos. 154-155 total 474,154.

WHO Headquarters,
Geneva — A83

Design: 11c, French inscription.
Issued to commemorate the opening of the World Health Organization Headquarters, Geneva.
Printed by Courvoisier, S.A., Switzerland. Panes of 50. Designed by Rashid-ud Din.

1966, May 26   Photo.   Perf. 12½x12
Granite Paper
156 A83 5c **lt & dk blue, orange, green & bister** (2,079,893)   .20   .20
         First day cover   1.00
         Inscription block of 4   .45   —
157 A83 11c **orange, lt & dark blue, green & bister** (1,879,879)   .20   .20
         First day cover   1.00
         First day cover, #156-157   1.25
         Inscription block of 4   .90   —

First day covers of Nos. 156-157 total 466,171.

Coffee — A84

UN Observer — A85

Design: 11c, Spanish inscription.
Issued to commemorate the International Coffee Agreement of 1962.
Printed by the Government Printing Bureau, Tokyo. Panes of 50. Designed by Rashid-ud Din, Pakistan.

1966, Sept. 19   Photo.   Perf. 13½x13
158 A84 5c **orange, lt blue, green, red & dk brown** (2,020,308)   .20   .20
         First day cover   1.00
         Inscription block of 4   .40   —
159 A84 11c **lt blue, yellow, green, red & dk brown** (1,888,682)   .20   .20
         First day cover   1.00
         First day cover, #158-159   1.00
         Inscription block of 4   .90   —

First day covers of Nos. 158-159 total 435,886.

1966, Oct. 24   Photo.   Perf. 11½
Issued to honor the Peace Keeping United Nation Observers.
Printed by Courvoisier, S.A. Panes of 50. Designed by Ole S. Hamann.

Granite Paper
160 A85 15c **steel blue, orange, black & green**
         (1,889,809)   .25   .20
         First day cover (255,326)   1.00
         Inscription block of 4   1.40   —

Children of Various
Races — A86

Designs: 5c, Children riding in locomotive and tender. 11c, Children in open railroad car playing medical team (French inscription).
20th anniversary of the United Nations Children's Fund (UNICEF).
Printed by Thomas De La Rue & Co., Ltd. Panes of 50. Designed by Kurt Plowitz.

1966, Nov. 28   Litho.   Perf. 13x13½
161 A86 4c **pink & multi** (2,334,989)   .20   .20
         First day cover   1.00
         Inscription block of 4   .30   —
162 A86 5c **pale green & multi** (2,746,941) .20   .20
         First day cover   1.00
         Inscription block of 4   .35   —
163 A86 11c **light ultramarine & multi** (2,123,841) .20   .20
         First day cover   1.00
         First day cover, #161-163   1.00
         Inscription block of 4   .85   —
    a.   Imperf., pair
    b.   Dark blue omitted
         Nos. 161-163 (3)   .60   .60

First day covers of Nos. 161-163 total 987,271.

Hand Rolling up Sleeve
and Chart Showing
Progress — A87

Design: 11c, French inscription.
United Nations Development Program.
Printed by Courvoisier, S.A. Panes of 50. Designed by Olav S. Mathiesen.

1967, Jan. 23   Photo.   Perf. 12½
164 A87 5c **green, yellow, purple & orange**
         (2,204,679)   .20   .20
         First day cover   1.00
         Inscription block of 4   .35   —
165 A87 11c **blue, chocolate, light green & orange** (1,946,159)   .20   .20
         First day cover   1.00
         First day cover, #164-165   1.00
         Inscription block of 4   1.00   —

First day covers of Nos. 164-165 total 406,011.

Type of 1962 and

UN Headquarters, NY, and
World Map — A88

Printed by Courvoisier, S.A. Panes of 50. Designed by Jozsef Vertel, Hungary (1½c); Renato Ferrini, Italy (5c).

1967   Photo.   Perf. 11½
166 A88 1½c **ultramarine, black, orange & ocher**
         (4,000,000)   .20   .20
         First day cover (199,751)   1.00
         Inscription block of 4   .20   —

Size: 33x23mm
167 A53 5c **red brown, brown & orange yellow**
         (5,500,000)   .20   .20
         First day cover (212,544)   1.00
         Inscription block of 4   .40   —

Issue dates: 1½c, Mar. 17; 5c, Jan. 23.
For 5c of type A88, see UN Offices in Geneva No. 1.

Fireworks — A89

Design: 11c, French inscription.
Issued to honor all nations which gained independence since 1945.
Printed by Harrison & Sons, Ltd. Panes of 50. Designed by Rashid-ud Din.

1967, Mar. 17   Photo.   Perf. 14x14½
168 A89 5c **dark blue & multi** (2,445,955)   .20   .20
         First day cover   1.00
         Inscription block of 4   .35   —
169 A89 11c **brown lake & multi** (2,011,004) .20   .20

First day cover ... 1.00
First day cover, #168-169 ... 1.00
Inscription block of 4 ... .85 —

First day covers of Nos. 168-169 total 390,499.

"Peace" — A90

UN Pavilion, EXPO '67 — A91

Designs: 5c, Justice. 10c, Fraternity. 15c, Truth.
EXPO '67, International Exhibition, Montreal, Apr. 28-Oct. 27, 1967.
Under special agreement with the Canadian Government Nos. 170-174 were valid for postage only on mail posted at the UN pavilion during the Fair. The denominations are expressed in Canadian currency.
Printed by British American Bank Note Co., Ltd., Ottawa. The 8c was designed by Olav S. Mathiesen after a photograph by Michael Drummond. The others were adapted by Ole S. Hamann from reliefs by Ernest Cormier on doors of General Assembly Hall, presented to UN by Canada.

1967, Apr. 28   **Engr. & Litho.**   *Perf. 11*
170 A90 4c red & red brown (2,464,813) ... .20 .20
First day cover ... 1.00
Inscription block of 4 ... .20 —
171 A90 5c blue & red brown (2,177,073) ... .20 .20
First day cover ... 1.00
Inscription block of 4 ... .20 —

Litho.
172 A91 8c multicolored (2,285,440) ... .20 .20
First day cover ... 1.00
Inscription block of 4 ... .35 —

Engr. and Litho.
173 A90 10c green & red brown (1,955,352) ... .20 .20
First day cover ... 1.00
Inscription block of 4 ... .50 —
174 A90 15c dark brown & red brown (1,899,185) ... .20 .20
First day cover ... 1.00
First day cover, #170-174 ... 1.25
Inscription block of 4 ... .60 —
Nos. 170-174 (5) ... 1.00 1.00

First day covers of Nos. 170-174 total 901,625.

Luggage Tags and UN Emblem — A92

Issued to publicize International Tourist Year, 1967.
Printed by Government Printing Office, Berlin. Panes of 50. Designed by David Dewhurst.

1967, June 19   **Litho.**   *Perf. 14*
175 A92 5c reddish brown & multi (2,593,782) ... .20 .20
First day cover ... 1.00
Inscription block of 4 ... .35 —
176 A92 15c ultramarine & multi (1,940,457) ... .25 .20
First day cover ... 1.00
First day cover, #175-176 ... 1.25
Inscription block of 4 ... 1.10 —

First day covers of Nos. 175-176 total 382,886.

Quotation from Isaiah 2:4 — A93

Design: 13c, French inscription.
Issued to publicize the UN General Assembly's resolutions on general and complete disarmament and for suspension of nuclear and thermonuclear tests.
Printed by Heraclio Fournier S.A., Spain. Panes of 50. Designed by Ole Hamann.

1967, Oct. 24   **Photo.**   *Perf. 14*
177 A93 6c ultramarine, yellow, gray & brown
(2,462,277) ... .20 .20
First day cover ... 1.00
Inscription block of 4 ... .45 —

178 A93 13c magenta, yellow, gray & brown
(2,055,541) ... .20 .20
First day cover ... 1.00
First day cover, #177-178 ... 1.00
Inscription block of 4 ... .95 —

First day covers of Nos. 177-178 total 403,414.

Art at UN Issue
Miniature Sheet

Stained Glass Memorial Window by Marc Chagall, at UN Headquarters — A94

"The Kiss of Peace" by Marc Chagall — A95

Printed by Joh. Enschede and Sons, Netherlands. No. 180 issued in panes of 50. Design adapted by Ole Hamann from photograph by Hans Lippmann.

Sizes: a, 41x46mm. b, 24x46mm. c, 41x33½mm. d, 36x33½mm. e, 29x33½mm. f, 41½x47mm.

1967, Nov. 17   **Litho.**   *Rouletted 9*
179 A94 6c Sheet of 6, #a.-f. (3,178,656) ... .40 .30
First day cover ... 1.00

Perf. 13x13½
180 A95 6c multicolored (3,438,497) ... .20 .20
First day cover ... 1.00
Inscription block of 4 ... .50 —

No. 179 contains six 6c stamps, each rouletted on 3 sides, imperf. on fourth side. Size: 124x80mm. On Nos. 179a-179c, "United Nations 6c" appears at top; on Nos. 179d-179f, at bottom. No. 179f includes name "Marc Chagall."
First day covers of Nos. 179-180 total 617,225.

Globe and Major UN Organs — A96

Statue by Henrik Starcke — A97

Design: 13c, French inscriptions.
Issued to honor the United Nations Secretariat.
Printed by Courvoisier, S. A., Switzerland. Panes of 50. Designed by Rashid-ud Din.

1968, Jan. 16   **Photo.**   *Perf. 11½*
181 A96 6c multicolored (2,772,965) ... .20 .20
First day cover ... 1.00
Inscription block of 4 ... .40 —
182 A96 13c multicolored (2,461,992) ... .20 .20
First day cover ... 1.00
First day cover, #181-182 ... 1.00
Inscription block of 4 ... .90 —

First day covers of Nos. 181-182 total 411,119.

Art at UN Issue

The 6c is part of the "Art at the UN" series. The 75c belongs to the regular definitive series. The teakwood Starcke statue, which stands in the Trusteeship Council Chamber, represents mankind's search for freedom and happiness.

Printed by Courvoisier, S.A., Switzerland. Panes of 50.

1968, Mar. 1   **Photo.**   *Perf. 11½*
183 A97 6c blue & multi (2,537,320) ... .20 .20
First day cover ... 1.00
Inscription block of 4 ... .50 —
184 A97 75c rose lake & multi (2,300,000) ... 1.10 .85
First day cover ... 1.25
First day cover, #183-184 ... 5.00
Inscription block of 4 ... 5.00 —

First day covers of Nos. 183-184 total 413,286.
No. 183 exists imperforate.
See UN Offices in Geneva No. 13.

Factories and Chart — A98

UN Headquarters — A99

Design: 13c, French inscription ("ONUDI," etc.).
Issued to publicize the UN Industrial Development Organization.
Printed by Canadian Bank Note Co., Ltd., Ottawa. Panes of 50. Designed by Ole Hamann.

1968, Apr. 18   **Litho.**   *Perf. 12*
185 A98 6c greenish blue, lt greenish blue,
black & dull claret (2,439,656) ... .20 .20
First day cover ... 1.00
Inscription block of 4 ... .35 —
186 A98 13c dull red brown, light red brown,
black & ultra (2,192,453) ... .20 .20
First day cover ... 1.00
First day cover, #185-186 ... 1.00
Inscription block of 4 ... .80 —

First day covers of Nos. 185-186 total 396,447.

1968, May 31   **Litho.**   *Perf. 12x13½*

Printed by Aspioti Elka-Chrome Mines, Ltd., Athens. Panes of 50. Designed by Olav S. Mathiesen.

187 A99 6c green, blue, black & gray (4,000,000) ... .20 .20
First day cover (241,179) ... 1.00
Inscription block of 4 ... .50 —

Radarscope and Globe — A100

Design: 20c, French inscription.
Issued to publicize World Weather Watch, a new weather system directed by the World Meteorological Organization.
Printed by the Government Printing Bureau, Tokyo. Designed by George A. Gundersen and George Fanais, Canada.

1968, Sept. 19   **Photo.**   *Perf. 13x13½*
188 A100 6c green, black, ocher, red & blue
(2,245,078) ... .20 .20
First day cover ... 1.00
Inscription block of 4 ... .40 —
189 A100 20c lilac, black, ocher, red & blue
(2,069,966) ... .30 .20
First day cover ... 1.00
First day cover, #188-189 ... 1.25
Inscription block of 4 ... 1.25 —

First day covers of Nos. 188-189 total 620,510.

Human Rights Flame — A101

Books and UN Emblem — A102

Design: 13c, French inscription.

Issued for International Human Rights Year, 1968.
Printed by Harrison & Sons, Ltd., England. Designed by Robert Perrot, France.

1968, Nov. 22   Photo.; Foil Embossed   Perf. 12½

190 A101   6c   bright blue, deep ultra & gold   .20   .20
  (2,394,235)
        First day cover   1.00
        Inscription block of 4   .40   —
191 A101 13c   rose red, dark red & gold   .20   .20
  (2,284,838)
        First day cover   1.00
        First day cover, #190-191   1.00
        Inscription block of 4   .85   —

  First day covers of Nos. 190-191 total 519,012.

1969, Feb. 10   Litho.   Perf. 13½

Design: 13c, French inscription in center, denomination panel at bottom.
United Nations Institute for Training and Research (UNITAR). Printed by the Government Printing Bureau, Tokyo. Panes of 50. Designed by Olav S. Mathiesen.

192 A102   6c   yellow green & multi (2,436,559) .20   .20
        First day cover   1.00
        Inscription block of 4   .35   —
193 A102 13c   bluish lilac & multi (1,935,151) .25   .20
        First day cover   1.00
        First day cover, #192-193   1.00
        Inscription block of 4   1.00   —

  First day covers of Nos. 192-193 total 439,606.

UN Building, Santiago, Chile — A103

Design: 15c, Spanish inscription.
The UN Building in Santiago, Chile, is the seat of the UN Economic Commission for Latin America and of the Latin American Institute for Economic and Social Planning.
Printed by Government Printing Office, Berlin. Panes of 50. Design by Ole Hamann, adapted from a photograph.

1969, Mar. 14   Litho.   Perf. 14

194 A103   6c   light blue, violet blue & light
          green (2,543,992)   .20   .20
        First day cover   1.00
        Inscription block of 4   .35   —
195 A103 15c   pink, cream & red brown
          (2,030,733)   .25   .20
        First day cover   1.00
        First day cover, #194-195   1.00
        Inscription block of 4   1.10   —

  First day covers of Nos. 194-195 total 398,227.

"UN" and UN Emblem — A104   UN Emblem and Scales of — A105

Printed by Government Printing Bureau, Tokyo. Panes of 50. Designed by Leszek Holdanowicz and Marek Freudenreich, Poland.

1969, Mar. 14   Photo.   Perf. 13½

196 A104 13c   bright blue, black & gold
          (4,000,000)   .20   .20
        First day cover (177,793)   1.00
        Inscription block of 4   .90   —

  See UN Offices in Geneva No. 7.

1969, Apr. 21   Photo.   Perf. 11½

Design: 13c, French inscription.
20th anniversary session of the UN International Law Commission.
Printed by Courvoisier S.A., Switzerland. Panes of 50. Designed by Robert Perrot, France.

Granite Paper

197 A105   6c   bright green, ultra & gold
          (2,501,492)   .20   .20
        First day cover   1.00
        Inscription block of 4   .40   —
198 A105 13c   crimson, lilac & gold (1,966,994) .20   .20
        First day cover   1.00
        First day cover, #197-198   1.00
        Inscription block of 4   .90   —

  First day covers of Nos. 197-198 total 439,324.

Allegory of Labor, Emblems of UN and ILO — A106

Design: 20c, French inscription.
Printed by Government Printing Bureau, Tokyo. Panes of 50. Designed by Nejat M. Gur, Turkey.
Issued to publicize "Labor and Development" and to commemorate the 50th anniversary of the International Labor Organization.

1969, June 5   Photo.   Perf. 13

199 A106   6c   blue, deep blue, yellow & gold
          (2,078,381)   .20   .20
        First day cover   1.00
        Inscription block of 4   .40   —
200 A106 20c   orange vermilion, magenta, yellow & gold (1,751,100)   .25   .20
        First day cover   1.00
        First day cover, #199-200   1.25
        Inscription block of 4   1.25   —

  First day covers of Nos. 199-200 total 514,155.

Art at UN Issue

Ostrich, Tunisian Mosaic, 3rd Century — A107

Design: 13c, Pheasant; French inscription.
The mosaic "The Four Seasons and the Genius of the Year" was found at Haidra, Tunisia. It is now at the Delegates' North Lounge, UN Headquarters, New York.
Printed by Heraclio Fournier, S. A., Spain. Panes of 50. Designed by Olav S. Mathiesen.

1969, Nov. 21   Photo.   Perf. 14

201 A107   6c   blue & multi (2,280,702)   .20   .20
        First day cover   1.00
        Inscription block of 4   .35   —
202 A107 13c   red & multi (1,918,554)   .20   .20
        First day cover   1.00
        First day cover, #201-202   1.00
        Inscription block of 4   .90   —

  First day covers of Nos. 201-202 total 612,981.

Art at UN Issue

Peace Bell, Gift of Japanese — A108

Design: 25c, French inscription.
The Peace Bell was a gift of the people of Japan in 1954, cast from donated coins and metals. It is housed in a Japanese cypress structure at UN Headquarters, New York.
Printed by Government Printing Bureau, Tokyo. Panes of 50. Designed by Ole Hamann.

1970, Mar. 13   Photo.   Perf. 13½x13

203 A108   6c   violet blue & multi (2,604,253)   .20   .20
        First day cover   1.00
        Inscription block of 4   .35   —
204 A108 25c   claret & multi (2,090,185)   .35   .25
        First day cover   1.25
        First day cover, #203-204   1.25
        Inscription block of 4   1.60   —

  First day covers of Nos. 203-204 total 502,384.

Mekong River, Power Lines and Map of Mekong Delta — A109

Design: 13c, French inscription.
Issued to publicize the Lower Mekong Basin Development project under UN auspices.
Printed by Heraclio Fournier, S.A., Spain. Panes of 50. Designed by Ole Hamann.

1970, Mar. 13   Perf. 14

205 A109   6c   dark blue & multi (2,207,309)   .20   .20
        First day cover   1.00
        Inscription block of 4   .35   —
206 A109 13c   deep plum & multi (1,889,023)   .20   .20
        First day cover   1.00
        First day cover, #205-206   1.00
        Inscription block of 4   .90   —

  First day covers of Nos. 205-206 total 522,218.

"Fight Cancer" — A110

Design: 13c, French inscription.
Issued to publicize the fight against cancer in connection with the 10th International Cancer Congress of the International Union Against Cancer, Houston, Texas, May 22-29.
Printed by Government Printing Office, Berlin. Panes of 50. Designed by Leonard Mitchell.

1970, May 22   Litho.   Perf. 14

207 A110   6c   blue & black (2,157,742)   .20   .20
        First day cover   1.00
        Inscription block of 4   .35   —
208 A110 13c   olive & black (1,824,714)   .20   .20
        First day cover   1.00
        First day cover, #207-208   1.00
        Inscription block of 4   .85   —

  First day covers of Nos. 207-208 total 444,449.

UN Emblem and Olive Branch — A111   UN Emblem — A112

Design: 13c, French inscription.
25th anniv. of the UN. First day covers were postmarked at UN Headquarters, NY, and at San Francisco.
Printed by Courvoisier, S.A., Switzerland. Designed by Ole Hamann and Olav S. Mathiesen (souvenir sheet).

1970, June 26   Photo.   Perf. 11½

209 A111   6c   red, gold, dark & light blue
          (2,365,229)   .20   .20
        First day cover   1.00
        Inscription block of 4   .35   —
210 A111 13c   dark blue, gold, green & red
          (1,861,613)   .20   .20
        First day cover   1.00
        Inscription block of 4   .80   —

Perf. 12½

211 A112 25c   dark blue, gold & light blue
          (1,844,669)   .35   .25
        First day cover   1.25
        First day cover, #209-211   1.50
        Inscription block of 4   1.50   —
        Nos. 209-211 (3)   .75   .65

Souvenir Sheet
Imperf

212   Sheet of 3 (1,923,639)   .60   .60
  a.   A111   6c red, gold & multicolored   .20   .20
  b.   A111 13c violet blue, gold & multi   .20   .20
  c.   A112 25c violet blue, gold & light blue   .30   .20
        First day cover   1.25

No. 212 contains 3 imperf. stamps, gold border and violet blue marginal inscription. Size: 94½x78mm.
First day covers of Nos. 209-212 total: New York, 846,389; San Francisco, 471,100.

Scales, Olive Branch and Symbol of Progress — A113

Sea Bed, School of Fish and Underwater Research — A114

Design: 13c, French inscription.
Issued to publicize "Peace, Justice and Progress" in connection with the 25th anniversary of the United Nations.
Printed by Government Printing Bureau, Tokyo. Panes of 50. Designed by Ole Hamann.

1970, Nov. 20   Photo.   Perf. 13½
213 A113 6c gold & multi (1,921,441)   .20 .20
    First day cover   1.00
    Inscription block of 4   .40 —
214 A113 13c silver & multi (1,663,669)   .20 .20
    First day cover   1.00
    First day cover, #213-214   1.00
    Inscription block of 4   1.00 —

First day covers of Nos. 213-214 total 521,419.

1971, Jan. 25   Photo. & Engr.   Perf. 13
Issued to publicize peaceful uses of the sea bed.
Printed by Setelipaino, Finland. Panes of 50. Designed by Pentti Rahikainen, Finland.
215 A114 6c blue & multi (2,354,179)   .20 .20
    First day cover (405,554)   1.00
    Inscription block of 4   .50 —

See UN Offices in Geneva No. 15.

Refugees, Sculpture by Kaare K. Nygaard — A115

Wheat and Globe — A116

International support for refugees.
Printed by Joh. Enschede and Sons, Netherlands. Panes of 50. Designed by Dr. Kaare K. Nygaard and Martin J. Weber.

1971, Mar. 2   Litho.   Perf. 13x12½
216 A115 6c brown, ocher & black (2,247,232)   .20 .20
    First day cover   1.00
    Inscription block of 4   .30 —
217 A115 13c ultramarine, greenish blue & black (1,890,048)   .20 .20
    First day cover   1.00
    First day cover, #216-217   1.00
    Inscription block of 4   .90 —

First day covers of Nos. 216-217 total 564,785.
See UN Offices in Geneva No. 16.

1971, Apr. 13   Photo.   Perf. 14
Publicizing the UN World Food Program.
Printed by Heraclio Fournier, S.A., Spain. Panes of 50. Designed by Olav S. Mathiesen.
218 A116 13c red & multicolored (1,968,542)   .20 .20
    First day cover (409,404)   1.00
    Inscription block of 4   .90 —

See UN Offices in Geneva No. 17.

UPU Headquarters, Bern — A117

Opening of new Universal Postal Union Headquarters, Bern.
Printed by Courvoisier, S.A. Panes of 50. Designed by Olav S. Mathiesen.

1971, May 28   Photo.   Perf. 11½
219 A117 20c brown orange & multi (1,857,841) .35 .25
    First day cover (375,119)   1.00
    Inscription block of 4   1.40 —

See UN Offices in Geneva No. 18.

A118

"Eliminate Racial Discrimination" — A119

International Year Against Racial Discrimination.
Printed by Government Printing Bureau, Tokyo. Panes of 50.
Designers: Daniel Gonzague (8c); Ole Hamann (13c).

1971, Sept. 21   Photo.   Perf. 13½
220 A118 8c yellow green & multi (2,324,349)   .20 .20
    First day cover   1.00
    Inscription block of 4   .60 —
221 A119 13c blue & multi (1,852,093)   .20 .20
    First day cover   1.00
    First day cover, #220-221   1.00
    Inscription block of 4   .90 —

First day covers of Nos. 220-221 total 461,103.
See UN Offices in Geneva Nos. 19-20.

UN Headquarters, New York — A120

UN Emblem and Symbolic Flags — A121

No. 222 printed by Heraclio Fournier, S.A., Spain. No. 223 printed by Government Printing Bureau, Tokyo. Panes of 50.
Designers: O. S. Mathiesen (8c); Robert Perrot (60c).

1971, Oct. 22   Photo.   Perf. 13½
222 A120 8c violet blue & multi (5,600,000)   .20 .20
    First day cover   1.00
    Inscription block of 4   .60 —

Perf. 13
223 A121 60c ultra & multi (3,500,000)+   .75 .75
    First day cover   1.25
    First day cover, #222-223   3.00
    Inscription block of 4   3.50 —

First day covers of Nos. 222-223 total 336,013.

Maia, by Pablo Picasso — A122

To publicize the UN International School.
Printed by Courvoisier, S.A. Panes of 50. Designed by Ole Hamann.

1971, Nov. 19   Photo.   Perf. 11½
224 A122 8c olive & multi (2,668,214)   .20 .20
    First day cover   1.00
    Inscription block of 4   .45 —
225 A122 21c ultra & multi (2,040,754)   .30 .20
    First day cover   1.00
    First day cover, #224-225   1.75
    Inscription block of 4   1.40 —

First day covers of Nos. 224-225 total 579,594.
See UN Offices in Geneva No. 21.

Letter Changing Hands — A123

Printed by Bundesdruckerei, Berlin. Panes of 50. Designed by Olav S. Mathiesen.

1972, Jan. 5   Litho.   Perf. 14
226 A123 95c carmine & multi (2,000,000)   1.25 1.00
    First day cover (188,193)   1.25
    Inscription block of 4   5.50 —

"No More Nuclear Weapons" A124

To promote non-proliferation of nuclear weapons.
Printed by Heraclio Fournier, S. A., Spain. Panes of 50. Designed by Arne Johnson, Norway.

1972, Feb. 14   Photo.   Perf. 13½x14
227 A124 8c dull rose, black, blue & gray (2,311,515)   .20 .20
    First day cover (268,789)   1.00
    Inscription block of 4   .55 —

See UN Offices in Geneva No. 23.

Proportions of Man, by Leonardo da Vinci — A125

"Human Environment" — A126

World Health Day, Apr. 7.
Printed by Setelipaino, Finland. Panes of 50. Designed by George Hamori.

1972, Apr. 7   Litho. & Engr.   Perf. 13x13½
228 A125 15c black & multi (1,788,962)   .25 .20
    First day cover (322,724)   1.00
    Inscription block of 4   1.00 —

See UN Offices in Geneva No. 24.

1972, June 5   Litho. & Embossed   Perf. 12½x14
UN Conf. on Human Environment, Stockholm, June 5-16, 1972.
Printed by Joh. Enschede and Sons, Netherlands. Panes of 50. Designed by Robert Perrot.
229 A126 8c red, buff, green & blue (2,124,604)   .20 .20
    First day cover   1.00
    Inscription block of 4   .50 —
230 A126 15c blue green, buff, green & blue (1,589,943)   .25 .20
    First day cover   1.00
    First day cover, #229-230   1.00
    Inscription block of 4   1.25 —

First day covers of Nos. 229-230 total 437,222.
See UN Offices in Geneva Nos. 25-26.

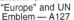

"Europe" and UN
Emblem — A127

The Five Continents by José
Maria Sert — A128

Economic Commission for Europe, 25th anniversary.
Printed by Government Printing Bureau, Tokyo. Panes of 50.
Designed by Angel Medina Medina.

1972, Sept. 11		**Litho.**	**Perf. 13x13½**	
231 A127	21c	yellow brown & multi (1,748,675)	.35	.25
		First day cover (271,128)		1.00
		Inscription block of 4	1.60	—

See UN Offices in Geneva No. 27.

Art at UN Issue

Design shows part of ceiling mural of the Council Hall, Palais des Nations, Geneva. It depicts the five continents joining in space.
Printed by Courvoisier, S. A. Panes of 50. Designed by Ole Hamann.

1972, Nov. 17		**Photo.**	**Perf. 12x12½**	
232 A128	8c	gold, brown & golden brown		
		(2,573,478)	.20	.20
		First day cover		1.00
		Inscription block of 4	.50	—
233 A128	15c	gold, blue green & brown		
		(1,768,432)	.30	.20
		First day cover		1.00
		First day cover, #232-233		1.00
		Inscription block of 4	1.25	—

First day covers of Nos. 232-233 total 589,817.
See UN Offices in Geneva Nos. 28-29.

Olive Branch and Broken
Sword — A129

Poppy Capsule and
Skull — A130

Disarmament Decade, 1970-79.
Printed by Ajans-Turk, Turkey. Panes of 50. Designed by Kurt Plowitz.

1973, Mar. 9		**Litho.**	**Perf. 13½x13**	
234 A129	8c	blue & multi (2,272,716)	.20	.20
		First day cover		1.00
		Inscription block of 4	.50	—
235 A129	15c	lilac rose & multi (1,643,712)	.35	.20
		First day cover		1.00
		First day cover, #234-235		1.00
		Inscription block of 4	1.50	—

First day covers of Nos. 234-235 total 548,336.
See UN Offices in Geneva Nos. 30-31.

1973, Apr. 13		**Photo.**	**Perf. 13½**	

Fight against drug abuse.
Printed by Heraclio Fournier, S.A., Spain. Panes of 50.
Designed by George Hamori.

236 A130	8c	deep orange & multi (1,846,780)	.20	.20
		First day cover		1.00
		Inscription block of 4	.60	—
237 A130	15c	pink & multi (1,466,806)	.35	.25
		First day cover		1.00
		First day cover, #236-237		1.00
		Inscription block of 4	1.50	—

First day covers of Nos. 236-237 total 394,468.
See UN Offices in Geneva No. 32.

Honeycomb — A131

5th anniversary of the United Nations Volunteer Program.
Printed by Heraclio Fournier, S.A., Spain. Panes of 50.
Designed by Courvoisier, S.A.

1973, May 25		**Photo.**	**Perf. 14**	
238 A131	8c	olive bister & multi (1,868,176)	.20	.20
		First day cover		1.00
		Inscription block of 4	.50	—
239 A131	21c	gray blue & multi (1,530,114)	.35	.25
		First day cover		1.00
		First day cover, #238-239		1.25
		Inscription block of 4	1.50	—

First day covers of Nos. 238-239 total 396,517.
See UN Offices in Geneva No. 33.

Map of Africa with
Namibia — A132

To publicize Namibia (South-West Africa) for which the UN General Assembly ended the mandate of South Africa and established the UN Council for Namibia to administer the territory until independence.
Printed by Heraclio Fournier, S.A., Spain. Panes of 50.
Designed by George Hamori.

1973, Oct. 1		**Photo.**	**Perf. 14**	
240 A132	8c	emerald & multi (1,775,260)	.20	.20
		First day cover		1.00
		Inscription block of 4	.50	—
241 A132	15c	bright rose & multi (1,687,782)	.35	.25
		First day cover		1.00
		First day cover, #240-241		1.00
		Inscription block of 4	1.50	—

First day covers of Nos. 240-241 total 385,292.
See UN Offices in Geneva No. 34.

UN Emblem and
Human Rights
Flame — A133

25th anniversary of the adoption and proclamation of the Universal Declaration of Human Rights.
Printed by Government Printing Bureau, Tokyo. Panes of 50.
Designed by Alfred Guerra.

1973, Nov. 16		**Photo.**	**Perf. 13½**	
242 A133	8c	deep carmine & multi (2,026,245)	.20	.20
		First day cover		1.00
		Inscription block of 4	.50	—
243 A133	21c	blue green & multi (1,558,201)	.35	.25
		First day cover		1.00
		First day cover, #242-243		1.25
		Inscription block of 4	1.50	—

First day covers of Nos. 242-243 total 398,511.
See UN Offices in Geneva Nos. 35-36.

ILO Headquarters,
Geneva — A134

New Headquarters of International Labor Organization.
Printed by Heraclio Fournier, S.A., Spain. Panes of 50.
Designed by Henry Bencsath.

1974, Jan. 11		**Photo.**	**Perf. 14**	
244 A134	10c	ultra & multi (1,734,423)	.20	.20
		First day cover		1.00
		Inscription block of 4	.90	—
245 A134	21c	blue green & multi (1,264,447)	.35	.25
		First day cover		1.00
		First day cover, #244-245		1.25
		Inscription block of 4	1.75	—

First day covers of Nos. 244-245 total 282,284.
See UN Offices in Geneva Nos. 37-38.

UPU Emblem and
Post Horn
Encircling
Globe — A135

Centenary of Universal Postal Union.
Printed by Ashton-Potter Ltd., Canada. Panes of 50.
Designed by Arne Johnson.

1974, Mar. 22		**Litho.**	**Perf. 12½**	
246 A135	10c	gold & multi (2,104,919)	.25	.20
		First day cover (342,774)		1.00
		Inscription block of 4	1.10	—

See UN Offices in Geneva Nos. 39-40.

Art at UN Issue

Peace Mural, by
Candido
Portinari — A136

The mural, a gift of Brazil, is in the Delegates' Lobby, General Assembly Building.
Printed by Heraclio Fournier, S.A., Spain. Panes of 50.
Design adapted by Ole Hamann.

1974, May 6		**Photo.**	**Perf. 14**	
247 A136	10c	gold & multi (1,769,342)	.20	.20
		First day cover		1.00
		Inscription block of 4	.75	—
248 A136	18c	ultra & multi (1,477,500)	.40	.30
		First day cover		1.00
		First day cover, #247-248		1.25
		Inscription block of 4	1.50	—

First day covers of Nos. 247-248 total 271,440.
See UN Offices in Geneva Nos. 41-42.

Dove and UN
Emblem — A137

UN
Headquarters — A138

Globe, UN Emblem,
Flags — A139

Printed by Heraclio Fournier, S.A., Spain. Panes of 50.
Designed by Nejut M. Gur (2c); Olav S. Mathiesen (10c);
Henry Bencsath (18c).

1974, June 10		**Photo.**	**Perf. 14**	
249 A137	2c	dark & light blue (6,900,000)	.20	.20
		First day cover		1.00
		Inscription block of 4	.25	—
250 A138	10c	multicolored (4,000,000)	.20	.20
		First day cover		1.00
		Inscription block of 4	.70	—
251 A139	18c	multicolored (2,300,000)	.30	.20
		First day cover		1.00
		First day cover, #249-251		1.30
		Inscription block of 4	1.50	—
		Nos. 249-251 (3)	.70	.60

First day covers of Nos. 249-251 total 307,402.
+ Printing orders to Feb. 1990.

Children of the
World — A140

Law of the Sea — A141

World Population Year

Printed by Heraclio Fournier, S.A., Spain. Panes of 50. Designed by Henry Bencsath.

1974, Oct. 18　　　Photo.　　　Perf. 14

252 A140 10c	**light blue & multi** (1,762,595)		.20	.20
	First day cover			1.00
	Inscription block of 4		1.00	—
253 A140 18c	**lilac & multi** (1,321,574)		.40	.25
	First day cover			1.00
	First day cover, #252-253			1.25
	Inscription block of 4		1.75	—

First day covers of Nos. 253-254 total 354,306.
See UN Offices in Geneva Nos. 43-44.

1974, Nov. 22　　　Photo.　　　Perf. 14

Declaration of UN General Assembly that the sea bed is common heritage of mankind, reserved for peaceful purposes.
Printed by Heraclio Fournier, S.A., Spain. Panes of 50. Designed by Asher Kalderon.

254 A141 10c	**green & multi** (1,621,328)		.20	.20
	First day cover			1.00
	Inscription block of 4		.80	—
255 A141 26c	**orange red & multi** (1,293,084)		.40	.25
	First day cover			1.25
	First day cover, #254-255			1.40
	Inscription block of 4		1.90	—

First day covers of Nos. 254-255 total 280,686.
See UN Offices in Geneva No. 45.

Satellite and Globe — A142

Peaceful uses (meteorology, industry, fishing, communications) of outer space.
Printed by Setelipaino, Finland. Panes of 50. Designed by Henry Bencsath.

1975, Mar. 14　　　Litho.　　　Perf. 13

256 A142 10c	**multicolored** (1,681,115)		.20	.20
	First day cover			1.00
	Inscription block of 4		.85	—
257 A142 26c	**multicolored** (1,463,130)		.40	.30
	First day cover			1.25
	First day cover, #256-257			1.40
	Inscription block of 4		1.75	—

First day covers of Nos. 256-257 total 330,316.
See UN Offices in Geneva Nos. 46-47.

Equality Between Men and Women — A143

UN Flag and "XXX" — A144

International Women's Year
Printed by Questa Colour Security Printers, Ltd., England. Panes of 50. Designed by Asher Kalderon and Esther Kurti.

1975, May 9　　　Litho.　　　Perf. 15

258 A143 10c	**multicolored** (1,402,542)		.20	.20
	First day cover			1.00
	Inscription block of 4		.80	—
259 A143 18c	**multicolored** (1,182,321)		.40	.25
	First day cover			1.00
	First day cover, #258-259			1.25
	Inscription block of 4		1.75	—

First day covers of Nos. 258-259 total 285,466.
See UN Offices in Geneva Nos. 48-49.

1975, June 26　　　Litho.　　　Perf. 13

30th anniversary of the United Nations.
Printed by Ashton-Potter, Ltd., Canada. Nos. 260-261 panes of 50. Stamps designed by Asher Calderon, sheets by Olav S. Mathiesen.

260 A144 10c	**olive bister & multi** (1,904,545)		.20	.20
	First day cover			1.00
	Inscription block of 4		.70	—
261 A144 26c	**purple & multi** (1,547,766)		.50	.35
	First day cover			1.25
	First day cover, #260-261			1.40
	Inscription block of 4		2.25	—

Souvenir Sheet
Imperf

262	Sheet of 2 (1,196,578)		.65	.50
a.	A144 10c olive bister & multicolored		.20	.20
b.	A144 26c purple & multicolored		.40	.25
	First day cover			1.25

No. 262 has blue and bister margin with inscription and UN emblem.
First day covers of Nos. 260-262 total: New York 477,912; San Francisco, 237,159.
See Offices in Geneva Nos. 50-52.

Hand Reaching up over Map of Africa and Namibia — A145

Wild Rose Growing from Barbed Wire — A146

"Namibia-United Nations direct responsibility." See note after No. 241.
Printed by Heraclio Fournier S.A., Spain. Panes of 50. Designed by Henry Bencsath.

1975, Sept. 22　　　Photo.　　　Perf. 13½

263 A145 10c	**multicolored** (1,354,374)		.20	.20
	First day cover			1.00
	Inscription block of 4		.80	—
264 A145 18c	**multicolored** (1,243,157)		.35	.20
	First day cover			1.00
	First day cover, #263-264			1.25
	Inscription block of 4		1.60	—

First day covers of Nos. 263-264 total 281,631.
See UN Offices in Geneva Nos. 53-54.

1975, Nov. 21　　　Engr.　　　Perf. 12½

United Nations Peace-keeping Operations
Printed by Setelipaino, Finland. Panes of 50. Designed by Mrs. Eeva Oivo.

265 A146 13c	**ultramarine** (1,628,039)		.25	.20
	First day cover			1.00
	Inscription block of 4		1.00	—
266 A146 26c	**rose carmine** (1,195,580)		.50	.45
	First day cover			1.25
	First day cover, #265-266			1.40
	Inscription block of 4		2.00	—

First day covers of Nos. 265-266 total 303,711.
See UN Offices in Geneva Nos. 55-56.

Symbolic Flags Forming Dove — A147

UN Emblem — A149

People of All Races — A148

United Nations Flag — A150

Dove and Rainbow — A151

Printed by Ashton-Potter, Ltd., Canada (3c, 4c, 30c, 50c), and Questa Colour Security Printers, Ltd., England (9c). Panes of 50.
Designed by Waldemar Andrzesewski (3c); Arne Johnson (4c); George Hamori (9c, 30c); Arthur Congdon (50c).

1976　　　Litho.　　　Perf. 13x13½, 13½x13

267 A147 3c	**multicolored** (4,000,000)		.20	.20
	First day cover			1.00
	Inscription block of 4		.25	—
268 A148 4c	**multicolored** (4,000,000)		.20	.20
	First day cover			1.00
	Inscription block of 4		.30	—

Photo.
Perf. 14

269 A149 9c	**multicolored** (3,270,000)+		.20	.20
	First day cover			1.00
	Inscription block of 4		.60	—

Litho.
Perf. 13x13½

270 A150 30c	**blue, emerald & black** (2,500,000)		.40	.35
	First day cover			1.25
	Inscription block of 4		1.75	—
271 A151 50c	**yellow green & multi** (2,000,000)		.70	.65
	First day cover			1.25
	First day cover, #267-268, 270-271			1.50
	Inscription block of 4		3.25	—
	Nos. 267-271 (5)		1.70	1.60

Issue dates: 3c, 4c, 30c, 50c, Jan. 6; 9c, Nov. 19.
First day covers of Nos. 267-268, 270-271 total 355,165; of Nos. 269 and 280 total 366,556.
See UN Offices in Vienna No. 8.

Interlocking Bands and UN Emblem — A152

World Federation of United Nations Associations.
Printed by Heraclio Fournier, S.A., Spain. Panes of 50. Designed by George Hamori.

1976, Mar. 12　　　Photo.　　　Perf. 14

272 A152 13c	**blue, green & black** (1,331,556)		.20	.20
	First day cover			1.00
	Inscription block of 4		.80	—
273 A152 26c	**green & multi** (1,050,145)		.35	.30
	First day cover			1.25
	First day cover, #272-273			1.25
	Inscription block of 4		1.60	—

First day covers of Nos. 272-273 total 300,775.
See UN Offices in Geneva No. 57.

Cargo, Globe and Graph — A153

Houses Around Globe — A154

UN Conference on Trade and Development (UNCTAD), Nairobi, Kenya, May 1976.

Printed by Courvoisier, S.A. Panes of 50. Designed by Henry Bencsath.

1976, Apr. 23　　　**Photo.**　　　***Perf. 11½***
274 A153 13c **deep magenta & multi** *(1,317,900)*　.20　.20
　　　First day cover　　　　　　　　1.00
　　　Inscription block of 4　　　.80
275 A153 31c **dull blue & multi** *(1,216,959)*　.40　.30
　　　First day cover　　　　　　　　1.25
　　　First day cover, #274-275　　　1.40
　　　Inscription block of 4　　　1.90

　　First day covers of Nos. 274-275 total 234,657.
　　See UN Offices in Geneva No. 58.

1976, May 28　　　**Photo.**　　　***Perf. 14***
　Habitat, UN Conference on Human Settlements, Vancouver, Canada, May 31-June 11.
　Printed by Heraclio Fournier, S.A., Spain. Panes of 50. Designed by Eliezer Weishoff.
276 A154 13c **red brown & multi** *(1,346,589)*　.20　.20
　　　First day cover　　　　　　　　1.00
　　　Inscription block of 4　　　.75
277 A154 25c **green & multi** *(1,057,924)*　.40　.30
　　　First day cover　　　　　　　　1.25
　　　First day cover, #276-277　　　1.40
　　　Inscription block of 4　　　1.75

　　First day covers of Nos. 276-277 total 232,754.
　　See UN Offices in Geneva Nos. 59-60.

Magnifying Glass, Sheet of Stamps, UN Emblem — A155

Grain — A156

United Nations Postal Administration, 25th anniversary.
Printed by Courvoisier, S.A. Designed by Henry Bencsath.

1976, Oct. 8　　　**Photo.**　　　***Perf. 11½***
278 A155 13c **blue & multi** *(1,996,309)*　.20　.20
　　　First day cover　　　　　　　　1.00
　　　Inscription block of 4　　　.90
279 A155 31c **green & multi** *(1,767,465)*　1.25　1.25
　　　First day cover　　　　　　　　2.00
　　　First day cover, #278-279　　　2.50
　　　Inscription block of 4　　　6.25
　　　Panes of 20, #278-279　　　32.50

　　First day covers of Nos. 278-279 total 366,784.
　　Upper margin blocks are inscribed "XXV ANNIVERSARY"; lower margin blocks "UNITED NATIONS POSTAL ADMINISTRATIONS."
　　See UN Offices in Geneva Nos. 61-62.

1976, Nov. 19　　　**Litho.**　　　***Perf. 14½***
　World Food Council.
　Printed by Questa Colour Security Printers, Ltd., England. Panes of 50. Designed by Eliezer Weishoff.
280 A156 13c **multicolored** *(1,515,573)*　.25　.20
　　　First day cover　　　　　　　　1.00
　　　Inscription block of 4　　　1.10

　　See UN Offices in Geneva No. 63.

WIPO Headquarters, Geneva — A157

World Intellectual Property Organization (WIPO).
Printed by Heraclio Fournier, S.A., Spain. Panes of 50. Designed by Eliezer Weishoff.

1977, Mar. 11　　　**Photo.**　　　***Perf. 14***
281 A157 13c **citron & multi** *(1,330,272)*　.20　.20
　　　First day cover　　　　　　　　1.00
　　　Inscription block of 4　　　.75
282 A157 31c **bright green & multi** *(1,115,406)*　.45　.30
　　　First day cover　　　　　　　　1.25
　　　First day cover, #281-282　　　1.25
　　　Inscription block of 4　　　2.00

　　First day covers of Nos. 281-282 total 364,184.
　　See UN Offices in Geneva No. 64.

Drops of Water Falling into Funnel — A158

UN Water Conference, Mar del Plata, Argentina, Mar. 14-25.
Printed by Government Printing Bureau, Tokyo. Panes of 50. Designed by Elio Tomei.

1977, Apr. 22　　　**Photo.**　　　***Perf. 13½x13***
283 A158 13c **yellow & multi** *(1,317,536)*　.20　.20
　　　First day cover　　　　　　　　1.00
　　　Inscription block of 4　　　.75
284 A158 25c **salmon & multi** *(1,077,424)*　.45　.30
　　　First day cover　　　　　　　　1.25
　　　First day cover, #283-284　　　1.40
　　　Inscription block of 4　　　2.00

　　First day covers of Nos. 283-284 total 321,585.
　　See UN Offices in Geneva Nos. 65-66.

Burning Fuse Severed — A159

UN Security Council.
　Printed by Heraclio Fournier, S.A., Spain. Panes of 50. Designed by Witold Janowski and Marek Freudenreich.

1977, May 27　　　**Photo.**　　　***Perf. 14***
285 A159 13c **purple & multi** *(1,321,527)*　.20　.20
　　　First day cover　　　　　　　　1.00
　　　Inscription block of 4　　　.75
286 A159 31c **dark blue & multi** *(1,137,195)*　.45　.30
　　　First day cover　　　　　　　　1.25
　　　First day cover, #285-286　　　1.40
　　　Inscription block of 4　　　2.00

　　First day covers of Nos. 285-286 total 309,610.
　　See UN Offices in Geneva Nos. 67-68.

"Combat Racism" — A160

Fight against racial discrimination.
　Printed by Setelipaino, Finland. Panes of 50. Designed by Bruno K. Wiese.

1977, Sept. 19　　　**Litho.**　　　***Perf. 13½x13***
287 A160 13c **black & yellow** *(1,195,739)*　.20　.20
　　　First day cover　　　　　　　　1.00
　　　Inscription block of 4　　　.75
288 A160 25c **black & vermilion** *(1,074,639)*　.40　.30
　　　First day cover　　　　　　　　1.25
　　　First day cover, #287-288　　　1.40
　　　Inscription block of 4　　　1.75

　　First day covers of Nos. 287-288 total 356,193.
　　See UN Offices in Geneva Nos. 69-70.

Atom, Grain, Fruit and Factory — A161

Peaceful uses of atomic energy.
　Printed by Heraclio Fournier, S.A., Spain. Panes of 50. Designed by Henry Bencsath.

1977, Nov. 18　　　**Photo.**　　　***Perf. 14***
289 A161 13c **yellow bister & multi** *(1,316,473)*　.20　.20
　　　First day cover　　　　　　　　1.00
　　　Inscription block of 4　　　.90
290 A161 18c **dull green & multi** *(1,072,246)*　.35　.25
　　　First day cover　　　　　　　　1.00
　　　First day cover, #289-290　　　1.25
　　　Inscription block of 4　　　1.50

　　First day covers of Nos. 289-290 total 325,348.
　　See UN Offices in Geneva Nos. 71-72.

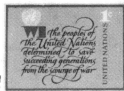

Opening Words of UN Charter — A162

"Live Together in Peace" — A163

People of the World — A164

Printed by Questa Colour Security Printers, United Kingdom. Panes of 50. Designed by Salahattin Kanidinc (1c); Elio Tomei (25c); Paula Schmidt ($1).

1978, Jan. 27　　　**Litho.**　　　***Perf. 14½***
291 A162 1c **gold, brown & red** *(4,800,000)+*　.20　.20
　　　First day cover　　　　　　　　1.00
　　　Inscription block of 4　　　.25
292 A163 25c **multicolored** *(3,000,000)+*　.35　.30
　　　First day cover　　　　　　　　1.25
　　　Inscription block of 4　　　1.50
293 A164 $1 **multicolored** *(3,400,000)+*　1.10　1.10
　　　First day cover　　　　　　　　1.50
　　　First day cover, #291-293　　　1.75
　　　Inscription block of 4　　　5.25
　　　Nos. 291-293 (3)　　　1.65　1.60

　　+ Printing orders to Sept. 1989.
　　First day covers of Nos. 291-293 total 264,782.
　　See UN Offices in Geneva No. 73.

Smallpox Virus — A165

Global eradication of smallpox.
　Printed by Courvoisier, S.A. Panes of 50. Designed by Herbert Auchli.

1978, Mar. 31　　　**Photo.**　　　***Perf. 12x11½***
294 A165 13c **rose & black** *(1,188,239)*　.20　.20
　　　First day cover　　　　　　　　1.00
　　　Inscription block of 4　　　.75
295 A165 31c **blue & black** *(1,058,688)*　.45　.40
　　　First day cover　　　　　　　　1.25
　　　First day cover, #294-295　　　1.40
　　　Inscription block of 4　　　2.00

　　First day covers of Nos. 294-295 total 306,626.
　　See UN Offices in Geneva Nos. 74-75.

Open Handcuff — A166

Multicolored Bands and Clouds — A167

Liberation, justice and cooperation for Namibia.
　Printed by Government Printing Office, Austria. Panes of 50. Designed by Cafiro Tomei.

1978, May 5   **Photo.**   *Perf. 12*
296 A166 13c multicolored *(1,203,079)*   .20   .20
    First day cover   1.00
    Inscription block of 4   1.00   —
297 A166 18c multicolored *(1,066,738)*   .30   .20
    First day cover   1.00
    First day cover, #296-297   1.25
    Inscription block of 4   1.40   —

    First day covers of Nos. 296-297 total 324,471.
    See UN Offices in Geneva No. 76.

1978, June 12   **Photo.**   *Perf. 14*
International Civil Aviation Organization for "Safety in the Air." Printed by Heraclio Fournier, S.A., Spain. Panes of 50. Designed by Cemalettin Mutver.

298 A167 13c multicolored *(1,295,617)*   .20   .20
    First day cover   1.00
    Inscription block of 4   .85   —
299 A167 25c multicolored *(1,101,256)*   .40   .30
    First day cover   1.25
    First day cover, #298-299   1.40
    Inscription block of 4   1.75   —

    First day covers of Nos. 298-299 total 329,995.
    See UN Offices in Geneva Nos. 77-78.

General Assembly — A168

Printed by Government Printing Bureau, Tokyo. Panes of 50. Designed by Jozsef Vertel.

1978, Sept. 15   **Photo.**   *Perf. 13½*
300 A168 13c multicolored *(1,093,005)*   .20   .20
    First day cover   1.00
    Inscription block of 4   1.00   —
301 A168 18c multicolored *(1,065,934)*   .35   .25
    First day cover   1.00
    First day cover, #300-301   1.25
    Inscription block of 4   1.50   —

    First day covers of Nos. 300-301 total 283,220.
    See UN Offices in Geneva Nos. 79-80.

Hemispheres as Cogwheels — A169

Technical Cooperation Among Developing Countries Conference, Buenos Aires, Argentina, Sept. 1978. Printed by Heraclio Fournier, S.A., Spain. Panes of 50. Designed by Simon Keter and David Pesach.

1978, Nov. 17   **Photo.**   *Perf. 14*
302 A169 13c multicolored *(1,251,272)*   .20   .20
    First day cover   1.00
    Inscription block of 4   1.00   —
303 A169 31c multicolored *(1,185,213)*   .50   .40
    First day cover   1.25
    First day cover, #302-303   1.40
    Inscription block of 4   2.25   —

    First day covers of Nos. 302-303 total 272,556.
    See UN Offices in Geneva No. 81.

Hand Holding Olive Branch — A170   Various Races Tree — A171

Globe, Dove with Olive Branch — A172

Birds and Globe — A173

Designed by Raymon Müller (5c); Alrun Fricke (14c); Eliezer Weishoff (15c); Young Sun Hahn (20c).

1979, Jan. 19   **Photo.**   *Perf. 14*
304 A170 5c multicolored *(3,000,000)*   .20   .20
    First day cover   1.00
    Inscription block of 4   .35   —
305 A171 14c multicolored *(3,000,000)*+   .20   .20
    First day cover   1.00
    Inscription block of 4   .90   —
306 A172 15c multicolored *(3,000,000)*+   .30   .25
    First day cover   1.00
    Inscription block of 4   1.40   —
307 A173 20c multicolored *(3,400,000)*+   .30   .25
    First day cover   1.00
    First day cover, #304-307   1.75
    Inscription block of 4   1.40   —
    Nos. 304-307 (4)   1.00   .90

    First day covers of Nos. 304-307 total 295,927.
+ Printing orders to June 1990.

UNDRO Against Fire and Water — A174

Office of the UN Disaster Relief Coordinator (UNDRO). Printed by Heraclio Fournier, S.A., Spain. Panes of 50. Designed by Gidon Sagi.

1979, Mar. 9   **Photo.**   *Perf. 14*
308 A174 15c multicolored *(1,448,600)*   .25   .20
    First day cover   1.00
    Inscription block of 4   1.00   —
309 A174 20c multicolored *(1,126,295)*   .35   .30
    First day cover   1.00
    First day cover, #308-309   1.25
    Inscription block of 4   1.50   —

    First day covers of Nos. 308-309 total 266,694.
    See UN Offices in Geneva Nos. 82-83.

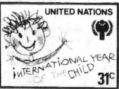

Child and IYC Emblem — A175

International Year of the Child. Printed by Heraclio Fournier, S.A., Spain. Panes of 20 (5x4). Designed by Helena Matuszewska (15c) and Krystyna Tarkowska-Gruszecka (31c).

1979, May 4   **Photo.**   *Perf. 14*
310 A175 15c multicolored *(2,290,329)*   .20   .20
    First day cover   1.00
    Inscription block of 4   .90   —
311 A175 31c multicolored *(2,192,136)*   .35   .30
    First day cover   1.25
    First day cover, #310-311   2.25
    Inscription block of 4   1.50   —
    Panes of 20, #310-311   11.50

    First day covers of Nos. 310-311 total 380,022.
    See UN Offices in Geneva Nos. 84-85.

Map of Namibia, Olive Branch — A176

Scales and Sword of Justice — A177

For a free and independent Namibia. Printed by Ashton-Potter Ltd., Canada. Panes of 50. Designed by Eliezer Weishoff.

1979, Oct. 5   **Litho.**   *Perf. 13½*
312 A176 15c multicolored *(1,470,231)*   .20   .20
    First day cover   1.00
    Inscription block of 4   .95   —
313 A176 31c multicolored *(1,355,323)*   .40   .35
    First day cover   1.25
    First day cover, #312-313   1.50
    Inscription block of 4   1.75   —

    First day covers of Nos. 312-313 total 250,371.
    See UN Offices in Geneva No. 86.

1979, Nov. 9   **Litho.**   *Perf. 13x13½*
International Court of Justice, The Hague, Netherlands. Printed by Setelipaino, Finland. Panes of 50. Designed by Henning Simon.

314 A177 15c multicolored *(1,244,972)*   .20   .20
    First day cover   1.00
    Inscription block of 4   .85   —
315 A177 20c multicolored *(1,084,483)*   .40   .35
    First day cover   1.00
    First day cover, #314-315   1.25
    Inscription block of 4   1.75   —

    First day covers of Nos. 314-315 total 322,901.
    See UN Offices in Geneva Nos. 87-88.

Graph of Economic Trends — A178

Key — A179

New International Economic Order. Printed by Questa Colour Security Printers, United Kingdom. Panes of 50. Designed by Cemalettin Mutver (15c), George Hamori (31c)

1980, Jan. 11   **Litho.**   *Perf. 15x14½*
316 A178 15c multicolored *(1,163,801)*   .20   .20
    First day cover   1.00
    Inscription block of 4   .85   —
317 A179 31c multicolored *(1,103,560)*   .50   .35
    First day cover   1.25
    First day cover, #316-317   1.40
    Inscription block of 4   2.25   —

    First day covers of Nos. 316-317 total 211,945.
    See UN Offices in Geneva No. 89; Vienna No. 7.

Women's Year Emblem — A180

United Nations Decade for Women. Printed by Questa Colour Security Printers, United Kingdom. Panes of 50. Designed by Susanne Rottenfusser.

1980, Mar. 7   **Litho.**   *Perf. 14½x15*
318 A180 15c multicolored *(1,409,350)*   .20   .20
    First day cover   1.00
    Inscription block of 4   .85   —
319 A180 20c multicolored *(1,182,016)*   .30   .25
    First day cover   1.00
    First day cover, #318-319   1.25
    Inscription block of 4   1.50   —

    First day covers of Nos. 318-319 total 289,314.
    See UN Offices in Geneva Nos. 90-91; Vienna Nos. 9-10.

United
Nations
Peace-keeping
Operations

UN Emblem and
"UN" on
Helmet — A181

Arrows and UN
Emblem — A182

United Nations Peace-keeping Operations.
Printed by Joh. Enschede en Zonen, Netherlands. Panes of
50. Designed by Bruno K. Wiese (15c), James Gardiner (31c)

1980, May 16		**Litho.**	**Perf. 14x13**	
320	A181 15c	blue & black (1,245,521)	.25	.20
		First day cover		1.00
		Inscription block of 4	1.00	—
321	A182 31c	multicolored (1,191,009)	.45	.40
		First day cover		1.25
		First day cover, #320-321		1.40
		Inscription block of 4	2.25	—

First day covers of Nos. 320-321 total 208,442.
See UN Offices in Geneva No. 92; Vienna No. 11.

"35" and
Flags — A183

Globe and
Laurel — A184

35th Anniversary of the United Nations.
Printed by Ashton-Potter Ltd, Canada. Nos. 322-323, panes
of 50. Designed by Cemalettin Matver (15c), Mian Mohammad
Saeed (31c)

1980, June 26		**Litho.**	**Perf. 13x13½**	
322	A183 15c	multicolored (1,554,514)	.20	.20
		First day cover		1.00
		Inscription block of 4	1.00	—
323	A184 31c	multicolored (1,389,606)	.40	.30
		First day cover		1.25
		First day cover, #322-323		1.40
		Inscription block of 4	2.00	—
		Souvenir Sheet		
		Imperf		
324		Sheet of 2 (1,215,505)	.70	.60
a.	A183 15c	multicolored	.20	
b.	A184 31c	multicolored	.40	
		First day cover		1.25

First day covers of Nos. 322-324 total: New York, 369,345;
San Francisco, 203,701.
See UN Offices in Geneva Nos. 93-95; Vienna Nos. 12-14.

Flag of
Turkey — A185

Printed by Courvoisier, S.A., Switzerland. Panes of 16.
Designed by Ole Hamann.
Each pane contains 4 blocks of 4 (Nos. 325-328, 329-332,
333-336, 337-340). A se-tenant block of 4 designs centers each
pane.

1980, Sept. 26		**Litho.**	**Perf. 12**	
		Granite Paper		
325	A185 15c	shown (3,490,725)	.20	.20
326	A185 15c	Luxembourg (3,490,725)	.20	.20
327	A185 15c	Fiji (3,490,725)	.20	.20
328	A185 15c	Viet Nam (3,490,725)	.20	.20
a.		Se-tenant block of 4, #325-328	.80	—
329	A185 15c	Guinea (3,442,633)	.20	.20
330	A185 15c	Surinam (3,442,633)	.20	.20

331	A185 15c	Bangladesh (3,442,633)	.20	.20
332	A185 15c	Mali (3,442,633)	.20	.20
a.		Se-tenant block of 4, #329-332	.80	—
333	A185 15c	Yugoslavia (3,416,292)	.20	.20
334	A185 15c	France (3,416,292)	.20	.20
335	A185 15c	Venezuela (3,416,292)	.20	.20
336	A185 15c	El Salvador (3,416,292)	.20	.20
a.		Se-tenant block of 4, #333-336	.80	—
337	A185 15c	Madagascar (3,442,497)	.20	.20
338	A185 15c	Cameroon (3,442,497)	.20	.20
339	A185 15c	Rwanda (3,442,497)	.20	.20
340	A185 15c	Hungary (3,442,497)	.20	.20
a.		Se-tenant block of 4, #337-340	.80	—
		First day covers of Nos. 325-340, each		1.00
		Set of 4 diff. panes of 16	8.00	
		Nos. 325-340 (16)	3.20	3.20

First day covers of Nos. 325-340 total 6,145,595.
See Nos. 350-365, 374-389, 399-414, 425-440, 450-465,
477-492, 499-514, 528-543, 554-569, 690-697, 719-726, 744-751.

Symbolic
Flowers — A186

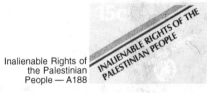

Symbols of
Progress — A187

Printed by Ashton-Potter Ltd., Canada. Panes of 50.
Designed by Eliezer Weishoff (15c), Dietman Kowall (20c)

1980, Nov. 21		**Litho.**	**Perf. 13½x13**	
341	A186 15c	multicolored (1,192,165)	.30	.25
		First day cover		1.00
		Inscription block of 4	1.25	—
342	A187 20c	multicolored (1,011,382)	.40	.35
		First day cover		1.00
		First day cover, #341-342		1.40
		Inscription block of 4	1.75	—

First day covers of Nos. 341-342 total 232,149.
See UN Offices in Geneva, Nos. 96-97; Vienna Nos. 15-16.

Inalienable Rights of
the Palestinian
People — A188

Printed by Courvoisier S.A., Switzerland. Panes of 50.
Designed by David Dewhurst.

1981, Jan. 30		**Photo.**	**Perf. 12x11½**	
343	A188 15c	multicolored (993,489)	.25	.20
		First day cover (127,187)		1.00
		Inscription block of 4	1.10	—

See UN Offices in Geneva No. 98; Vienna No. 17.

Interlocking Puzzle
Pieces — A189

Stylized
Person — A190

International Year of the Disabled.
Printed by Heraclio Fournier S.A., Spain. Panes of 50.
Designed by Sophia Van Heeswijk (20c) and G.P. Van der
Hyde (35c)

1981, Mar. 6		**Photo.**	**Perf. 14**	
344	A189 20c	multicolored (1,218,371)	.30	.20
		First day cover		1.00
		Inscription block of 4	1.25	—
345	A190 35c	black & orange (1,107,298)	.55	.40

	First day cover		1.25
	First day cover, #344-345		1.40
	Inscription block of 4	2.25	—

First day covers of Nos. 344-345 total 204,891.
See UN Offices in Geneva Nos. 99-100; Vienna Nos. 18-19.

Desislava and Sebastocrator
Kaloyan, Bulgarian Mural, 1259,
Boyana Church, Sofia — A191

Art at UN Issue

Printed by Courvoisier. Panes of 50. Designed by Ole
Hamann.

1981, Apr. 15		**Photo.**	**Perf. 11½**	
		Granite Paper		
346	A191 20c	multicolored (1,252,648)	.30	.25
		First day cover		1.00
		Inscription block of 4	1.40	—
347	A191 31c	multicolored (1,061,056)	.45	.35
		First day cover		1.25
		First day cover, #346-347		1.40
		Inscription block of 4	2.00	—

First day covers of Nos. 346-347 total 210,978.
See UN Offices in Geneva No. 101; Vienna No. 20.

Solar Energy — A192

Conference
Emblem — A193

Conference on New and Renewable Sources of Energy, Nai-
robi, Aug. 10-21.
Printed by Setelipaino, Finland. Panes of 50. Designed by
Ulrike Dreyer (20c); Robert Perrot (40c).

1981, May 29		**Litho.**	**Perf. 13**	
348	A192 20c	multicolored (1,132,877)	.30	.25
		First day cover		1.00
		Inscription block of 4	1.40	—
349	A193 40c	multicolored (1,158,319)	.55	.35
		First day cover		1.25
		First day cover, #348-349		1.40
		Inscription block of 4	2.60	—

First day covers of Nos. 348-349 total 240,205.
See UN Offices in Geneva No. 102; Vienna No. 21.

Flag Type of 1980

Printed by Courvoisier, S.A., Switzerland. Panes of 16.
Designed by Ole Hamann.
Each pane contains 4 blocks of 4 (Nos. 350-353, 354-357,
358-361, 362-365). A se-tenant block of 4 designs centers each
pane.

1981, Sept. 25			**Litho.**	
		Granite Paper		
350	A185 20c	Djibouti (2,342,224)	.25	.20
351	A185 20c	Sri Lanka (2,342,224)	.25	.20
352	A185 20c	Bolivia (2,342,224)	.25	.20
353	A185 20c	Equatorial Guinea (2,342,224)	.25	.20
a.		Se-tenant block of 4, #350-353	1.40	—
354	A185 20c	Malta (2,360,297)	.25	.20
355	A185 20c	Czechoslovakia (2,360,297)	.25	.20
356	A185 20c	Thailand (2,360,297)	.25	.20
357	A185 20c	Trinidad & Tobago (2,360,297)	.25	.20
a.		Se-tenant block of 4, #354-357	1.40	—
358	A185 20c	Ukrainian SSR (2,344,755)	.25	.20
359	A185 20c	Kuwait (2,344,755)	.25	.20
360	A185 20c	Sudan (2,344,755)	.25	.20
361	A185 20c	Egypt (2,344,755)	.25	.20
a.		Se-tenant block of 4, #358-361	1.40	—
362	A185 20c	US (2,450,537)	.25	.20
363	A185 20c	Singapore (2,450,537)	.25	.20
364	A185 20c	Panama (2,450,537)	.25	.20
365	A185 20c	Costa Rica (2,450,537)	.25	.20
a.		Se-tenant block of 4, #362-365	1.40	—

First day covers, #350-365, each   1.00
Set of 4 diff. panes of 16   14.00
Nos. 350-365 (16)   4.00 3.20

First day covers of Nos. 350-365 total 3,961,237.

Seedling and Tree   "10" and Symbols of
Cross-section — A194   Progress — A195

United Nations Volunteers Program, 10th anniv.
Printed by Walsall Security Printers, Ltd., United Kingdom.
Pane of 50. Designed by Gabriele Nussgen (18c), Angel
Medina Medina (28c).

1981, Nov. 13   **Litho.**
366 A194 18c **multicolored** *(1,246,833)*   .35   .25
   First day cover   1.00
   Inscription block of 4   1.50   —
367 A195 28c **multicolored** *(1,282,868)*   .65   .50
   First day cover   1.25
   First day cover, #366-367   1.40
   Inscription block of 4   2.75   —

First day covers of Nos. 366-367 total 221,106.
See UN Offices in Geneva Nos. 103-104; Vienna Nos. 22-23.

A196   A197   A198

Respect for Human Rights (17c), Independence of Colonial
Countries and People (28c), Second Disarmament Decade
(40c).
Printed by Courvoisier, S.A., Switzerland. Panes of 50.
Designed by Rolf Christianson (17c); George Hamori (28c);
Marek Kwiatkowski (40c).

1982, Jan. 22   **Perf. 11½x12**
368 A196 17c **multicolored** *(3,000,000)+*   .30   .20
   First day cover   1.00
   Inscription block of 4   1.25   —
369 A197 28c **multicolored** *(3,000,000)+*   .50   .35
   First day cover   1.25
   Inscription block of 4   2.25   —
370 A198 40c **multicolored** *(3,000,000)*   .80   .60
   First day cover   1.25
   First day cover, #368-370   1.25
   Inscription block of 4   3.50   —
   Nos. 368-370 (3)   1.60 1.15

First day covers of Nos. 368-370 total 243,073.

Sun and Hand   Sun, Plant Land
Holding   and Water — A200
Seedling — A199

10th Anniversary of United Nations Environment Program.
Printed by Joh. Enschede En Zonen, Netherlands. Panes of
50. Designed by Philine Hartert (20c); Peer-Ulrich Bremer
(40c).

1982, Mar. 19   **Litho.**   **Perf. 13½x13**
371 A199 20c **multicolored** *(1,017,117)*   .25   .25
   First day cover   1.00
   Inscription block of 4   1.25   —
372 A200 40c **multicolored** *(884,798)*   .75   .65
   First day cover   1.25
   First day cover, #371-372   1.40
   Inscription block of 4   3.25   —

First day covers of Nos. 371-372 total 288,721.
See UN Offices in Geneva Nos. 107-108; Vienna Nos. 25-26.

UN Emblem and Olive
Branch in Outer
Space — A201

Exploration and Peaceful Uses of Outer Space.
Printed By Enschede. Panes of 50. Designed by Wiktor C.
Nerwinski.

1982, June 11   **Litho.**   **Perf. 13x13½**
373 A201 20c **multicolored** *(1,083,426)*   .45   .35
   First day cover *(156,965)*   1.00
   Inscription block of 4   2.25

See UN Offices in Geneva Nos. 109-110; Vienna No. 27.

Flag Type of 1980

Printed by Courvoisier. Panes of 16. Designed by Ole
Hamann.
Issued in 4 panes of 16. Each pane contains 4 blocks of four
(Nos. 374-377, 378-381, 383-385, 386-389). A se-tenant block
of 4 designs centers each pane.

1982, Sept. 24   **Litho.**   **Perf. 12**
Granite Paper
374 A185 20c Austria *(2,314,006)*   .25   .20
375 A185 20c Malaysia *(2,314,006)*   .25   .20
376 A185 20c Seychelles *(2,314,006)*   .25   .20
377 A185 20c Ireland *(2,314,006)*   .25   .20
  a. Se-tenant block of 4, #374-377   1.40   —
378 A185 20c Mozambique *(2,300,958)*   .25   .20
379 A185 20c Albania *(2,300,958)*   .25   .20
380 A185 20c Dominica *(2,300,958)*   .25   .20
381 A185 20c Solomon Islnads *(2,300,958)*   .25   .20
  a. Se-tenant block of 4, #378-381   1.40   —
382 A185 20c Philippines *(2,288,589)*   .25   .20
383 A185 20c Swaziland *(2,288,589)*   .25   .20
384 A185 20c Nicaragua *(2,288,589)*   .25   .20
385 A185 20c Burma *(2,288,589)*   .25   .20
  a. Se-tenant block of 4, #382-385   1.40   —
386 A185 20c Cape Verde *(2,285,848)*   .25   .20
387 A185 20c Guyana *(2,285,848)*   .25   .20
388 A185 20c Belgium *(2,285,848)*   .25   .20
389 A185 20c Nigeria *(2,285,848)*   .25   .20
  a. Se-tenant block of 4, #386-389   1.40   —
   First day cover, #374-389, each   1.00
   Set of 4 diff. panes of 16   16.00
   Nos. 374-389 (16)   4.00 3.20

First day covers of Nos. 374-389 total 3,202,744.

Conservation and Protection of
Nature — A202

Printed by Fournier. Panes of 50. Designed by Hamori.

1982, Nov. 19   **Photo.**   **Perf. 14**
390 A202 20c Leaf *(1,110,027)*   .35   .30
   First day cover   1.00
   margin block of 4, inscription   1.75   —
391 A202 28c Butterfly *(848,772)*   .50   .45
   First day cover   1.25
   First day cover, #390-391   1.40
   Inscription block of 4   2.25   —

First day covers of Nos. 390-391 total 214,148.
See UN Offices in Geneva Nos. 111-112; Vienna Nos. 28-29.

A203 WORLD COMMUNICATIONS YEAR

A204

World Communications Year

A205   A206

Safety at Sea.
Printed by Questa. Panes of 50. Designed by Jean-Marie
Lenfant (A205), Ari Ron (A206).

1983, Mar. 18   **Litho.**   **Perf. 14½**
394 A205 20c **multicolored** *(1,252,456)*   .30   .25
   First day cover   1.00
   Inscription block of 4   1.50   —
395 A206 37c **multicolored** *(939,910)*   .60   .50
   First day cover   1.25
   First day cover, #394-395   1.40
   Inscription block of 4   2.75   —

First day covers of Nos. 394-395 total 199,962.
See UN Offices in Geneva Nos. 114-115; Vienna Nos. 31-32.

Printed by Walsall. Panes of 50. Designed by Hanns Lohrer
(A203) and Lorena Berengo (A204).

1983, Jan. 28   **Litho.**   **Perf. 13**
392 A203 20c **multicolored** *(1,282,079)*   .25   .25
   First day cover   1.00
   Inscription block of 4   1.25   —
393 A204 40c **multicolored** *(931,903)*   .70   .65
   First day cover   1.25
   Inscription block of 4   3.50   —

First day covers of Nos. 392-393 total 183,499.
See UN Offices in Geneva No. 113; Vienna No. 30.

World Food
Program — A207

Printed by Government Printers Bureau, Japan. Designed by
Marek Kwiatkowski.

1983, Apr. 22   **Engr.**   **Perf. 13½**
396 A207 20c **rose lake** *(1,238,997)*   .35   .30
   First day cover *(180,704)*   1.00
   Inscription block of 4   1.90

See UN Offices in Geneva No. 116; Vienna Nos. 33-34.

A208   A209

UN Conference on Trade and Development.
Printed by Carl Uberreuter Druck and Verlag M. Salzer, Aus-
tria. Panes of 50. Designed by Dietmar Braklow (A208), Gabriel
Genz (A209).

1983, June 6   **Litho.**   **Perf. 14**
397 A208 20c **multicolored** *(1,060,053)*   .30   .25
   First day cover   1.00
   Inscription block of 4   1.50   —
398 A209 28c **multicolored** *(948,981)*   .65   .60
   First day cover   1.25
   First day cover, #397-398   1.40
   Inscription block of 4   2.75   —

First day covers of Nos. 397-398 total 200,131.
See UN Offices in Geneva Nos. 117-118; Vienna Nos. 35-36.

Flag Type of 1980

Printed by Courvoisier. Panes of 16. Designed by Ole
Hamann.
Issued in 4 panes of 16. Each pane contains 4 blocks of four
(Nos. 399-402, 403-406, 407-410, 411-414). A se-tenant block
of 4 designs centers each pane.

1983, Sept. 23   **Photo.**   *Perf. 12*
Granite Paper

399	A185	20c	Great Britain *(2,490,599)*	.25 .20
400	A185	20c	Barbados *(2,490,599)*	.25 .20
401	A185	20c	Nepal *(2,490,599)*	.25 .20
402	A185	20c	Israel *(2,490,599)*	.25 .20
a.			Se-tenant block of 4, #399-402	1.60 —
403	A185	20c	Malawi *(2,483,010)*	.25 .20
404	A185	20c	Byelorussian SSR *(2,483,010)*	.25 .20
405	A185	20c	Jamaica *(2,483,010)*	.25 .20
406	A185	20c	Kenya *(2,483,010)*	.25 .20
a.			Se-tenant block of 4, #403-406	1.60 —
407	A185	20c	People's Republic of China *(2,474,140)*	.25 .20
408	A185	20c	Peru *(2,474,140)*	.25 .20
409	A185	20c	Bulgaria *(2,474,140)*	.25 .20
410	A185	20c	Canada *(2,474,140)*	.25 .20
a.			Se-tenant block of 4, #407-410	1.60 —
411	A185	20c	Somalia *(2,482,070)*	.25 .20
412	A185	20c	Senegal *(2,482,070)*	.25 .20
413	A185	20c	Brazil *(2,482,070)*	.25 .20
414	A185	20c	Sweden *(2,482,070)*	.25 .20
a.			Se-tenant block of 4, #411-414	1.60 —
			First day cover, #399-414, each	1.00
			Set of 4 diff. panes of 16	17.00
			Nos. 399-414 (16)	4.00 3.20

First day covers of Nos. 399-414 total 2,214,134.

Window Right — A210   Peace Treaty with Nature — A211

35th Anniversary of the Universal Declaration of Human Rights.
Printed by Government Printing Office, Austria. Panes of 16 (4x4). Designed by Friedensreich Hundertwasser, Austria.

1983, Dec. 9   **Photo. & Engr.**   *Perf. 13½*

415	A210	20c	multicolored *(1,591,102)*	.30 .25
			First day cover	1.00
			Inscription block of 4	1.25
416	A211	40c	multicolored *(1,566,789)*	.70 .65
			First day cover	1.25
			First day cover, #415-416	1.50
			Inscription block of 4	3.00
			Panes of 16, #415-416	16.00

First day covers of Nos. 415-416 total 176,269.
See UN Offices in Geneva Nos. 119-120; Vienna Nos. 37-38.

International Conference on Population — A212

Printed by Bundesdruckerei, Federal Republic of Germany. Panes of 50. Designed by Marina Langer-Rosa and Helmut Langer, Federal Republic of Germany.

1984, Feb. 3   **Litho.**   *Perf. 14*

417	A212	20c	multicolored *(905,320)*	.30 .25
			First day cover	1.00
			Inscription block of 4	1.40
418	A212	40c	multicolored *(717,084)*	.60 .55
			First day cover	1.25
			First day cover, #417-418	1.40
			Inscription block of 4	2.50

First day covers of Nos. 417-418 total 118,068.
See UN Offices in Geneva No. 121; Vienna No. 39.

Tractor Plowing — A213

Rice Paddy — A214

World Food Day, Oct. 16
Printed by Walsall Security Printers, Ltd., United Kingdom. Panes of 50. Designed by Adth Vanooijen, Netherlands.

1984, Mar. 15   **Litho.**   *Perf. 14½*

419	A213	20c	multicolored *(853,641)*	.30 .25
			First day cover	1.00
			Inscription block of 4	1.40
420	A214	40c	multicolored *(727,165)*	.60 .60
			First day cover	1.25
			First day cover, #419-420	1.40
			Inscription block of 4	2.50

First day covers of Nos. 419-420 total 116,009.

Grand Canyon — A215

Ancient City of Polonnaruwa, Sri Lanka — A216

World Heritage
Printed by Harrison and Sons, United Kingdom. Panes of 50. Designs adapted by Rocco J. Callari, U.S., and Thomas Lee, China.

1984, Apr. 18   **Litho.**   *Perf. 14*

421	A215	20c	multicolored *(814,316)*	.25 .20
			First day cover	1.00
			Inscription block of 4	1.10
422	A216	50c	multicolored *(579,136)*	.70 .70
			First day cover	1.25
			First day cover, #421-422	1.40
			Inscription block of 4	3.25

First day covers of Nos. 421-422 total 112,036.

A217   A218

Future for Refugees
Printed by Courvoisier. Panes of 50. Designed by Hans Erni, Switzerland.

1984, May 29   **Photo.**   *Perf. 11½*

423	A217	20c	multicolored *(956,743)*	.40 .35
			First day cover	1.00
			Inscription block of 4	2.00
424	A218	50c	multicolored *(729,036)*	1.00 .85
			First day cover	1.25
			First day cover, #423-424	1.40
			Inscription block of 4	4.50

First day covers of Nos. 423-424 total 115,789.

Flag Type of 1980

Printed by Courvoisier. Panes of 16. Designed by Ole Hamann.
Issued in 4 panes of 16. Each pane contains 4 blocks of four (Nos. 425-428, 429-432, 433-436, 437-440). A se-tenant block of 4 designs centers each pane.

1984, Sept. 21   **Photo.**   *Perf. 12*
Granite Paper

425	A185	20c	Burundi *(1,941,471)*	.55 .40
426	A185	20c	Pakistan *(1,941,471)*	.55 .40
427	A185	20c	Benin *(1,941,471)*	.55 .40
428	A185	20c	Italy *(1,941,471)*	.55 .40
a.			Se-tenant block of 4, #425-428	2.75 —
429	A185	20c	Tanzania *(1,969,051)*	.55 .40
430	A185	20c	United Arab Emirates *(1,969,051)*	.55 .40
431	A185	20c	Ecuador *(1,969,051)*	.55 .40
432	A185	20c	Bahamas *(1,969,051)*	.55 .40
a.			Se-tenant block of 4, #429-432	2.75 —
433	A185	20c	Poland *(2,001,091)*	.55 .40
434	A185	20c	Papua New Guinea *(2,001,091)*	.55 .40
435	A185	20c	Uruguay *(2,001,091)*	.55 .40
436	A185	20c	Chile *(2,001,091)*	.55 .40
a.			Se-tenant block of 4, #433-436	2.75 —
437	A185	20c	Paraguay *(1,969,875)*	.55 .40
438	A185	20c	Bhutan *(1,969,875)*	.55 .40
439	A185	20c	Central African Republic *(1,969,875)*	.55 .40
440	A185	20c	Australia *(1,969,875)*	.55 .40
a.			Se-tenant block of 4, #437-440	2.75 —
			First day cover, #425-440, each	1.00
			Set of 4 diff. panes of 16	35.00
			Nos. 425-440 (16)	8.80 6.40

First day covers of Nos. 425-440 total 1,914,972.

International Youth Year — A219   ILO Turin Center — A220

Printed by Waddingtons Ltd., United Kingdom. Panes of 50. Designed by Ramon Mueller, Federal Republic of Germany.

1984, Nov. 15   **Litho.**   *Perf. 13½*

441	A219	20c	multicolored *(884,962)*	.50 .35
			First day cover	1.00
			Inscription block of 4	2.25
442	A219	35c	multicolored *(740,023)*	1.50 1.10
			First day cover	1.25
			First day cover, #441-442	1.40
			Inscription block of 4	6.25

First day covers of Nos. 441-442 total 125,315.

1985, Feb. 1   **Engr.**   *Perf. 13½*

Printed by the Government Printing Bureau, Japan. Panes of 50. Engraved by Mamoru Iwakuni and Hiroshi Ozaki, Japan.

443	A220	23c	Turin Center emblem *(612,942)*	.60 .45
			First day cover *(76,541)*	1.00
			Inscription block of 4	2.50

See UN Offices in Geneva Nos. 129-130; Vienna No. 48.

UN University A221

Printed by Helio Courvoisier, Switzerland. Panes of 50. Designed by Moshe Pereg, Israel, and Hinedi Geluda, Brazil.

1985, Mar. 15   **Photo.**   *Perf. 13½*

444	A221	50c	Farmer plowing, discussion group *(625,043)*	1.25 1.00
			First day cover *(77,271)*	1.25
			Inscription block of 4	5.25

See UN Offices in Geneva Nos. 131-132; Vienna No. 49.

Peoples of the World United — A222

Painting UN Emblem — A223

Printed by Carl Uebereuter Druck and Verlag M. Salzer, Austria. Panes of 50. Designed by Fritz Henry Oerter, Federal Republic of Germany (22c), and Rimondi Rino, Italy ($3).

1985, May 10		Litho.	Perf. 14	
445 A222	22c multicolored (2,000,000)+		.35	.30
	First day cover			1.00
	Inscription block of 4		1.50	
446 A223	$3 multicolored (2,000,000)+		4.00	3.50
	First day cover			4.50
	First day cover, #445-446			6.50
	Inscription block of 4		17.50	—

First day covers of Nos. 445-446 total 88,613.

The Corner, 1947 — A224

Alvaro Raking Hay, 1953 — A225

UN 40th anniversary. Oil paintings (details) by American artist Andrew Wyeth (b. 1917). Printed by Helio Courvoisier, Switzerland. Nos. 447-448 panes of 50. Designed by Rocco J. Callari, U.S., and Thomas Lee, China (#449).

1985, June 26		Photo.	Perf. 12 x 11½	
447 A224	22c multicolored (944,960)		.50	.35
	First day cover			1.00
	Inscription block of 4		2.25	—
448 A225	45c multicolored (680,079)		1.00	.85
	First day cover			1.25
	First day cover, #447-448			1.50
	Inscription block of 4		4.50	—

Souvenir Sheet
Imperf

449		Sheet of 2 (506,004)	1.60	1.25
a.	A224	22c multicolored	.50	—
b.	A225	45c multicolored	1.00	—
		First day cover		1.50

First day covers of Nos. 447-449 total; New York, 210,189; San Francisco, 92,804.
See UN Offices in Geneva Nos. 135-137; Vienna Nos. 52-54.

Flag Type of 1980

Printed by Helio Courvoisier, Switzerland. Designed by Ole Hamann.
Issued in panes of 16; each contains 4 blocks of four (Nos. 450-453, 454-457, 458-461, 462-465). A se-tenant block of 4 designs is at the center of each pane.

1985, Sept. 20		Photo.	Perf. 12	
		Granite Paper		
450 A185	22c Grenada (1,270,755)		.55	.50
451 A185	22c Federal Republic of Germany (1,270,755)		.55	.50
452 A185	22c Saudi Arabia (1,270,755)		.55	.50
453 A185	22c Mexico (1,270,755)		.55	.50
a.	Se-tenant block of 4, #450-453		3.25	—
454 A185	22c Uganda (1,216,878)		.55	.50
455 A185	22c St. Thomas & Prince (1,216,878)		.55	.50
456 A185	22c USSR (1,216,878)		.55	.50
457 A185	22c India (1,216,878)		.55	.50
a.	Se-tenant block of 4, #454-457		3.25	—
458 A185	22c Liberia (1,213,231)		.55	.50
459 A185	22c Mauritius (1,213,231)		.55	.50
460 A185	22c Chad (1,213,231)		.55	.50
461 A185	22c Dominican Republic (1,213,231)		.55	.50
a.	Se-tenant block of 4, #458-461		3.25	—
462 A185	22c Sultanate of Oman (1,215,533)		.55	.50
463 A185	22c Ghana (1,215,533)		.55	.50
464 A185	22c Sierra Leone (1,215,533)		.55	.50
465 A185	22c Finland (1,215,533)		.55	.50
a.	Se-tenant block of 4, #462-465		3.25	—
	First day covers of #460-465, each			1.00
	Set of 4 diff. panes of 16		37.50	
	Nos. 450-465 (16)		8.80	8.00

First day covers of Nos. 450-465 total 1,774,193.

UNICEF Child Survival Campaign — A226

Africa in Crisis — A227

Printed by the Government Printing Bureau, Japan. Panes of 50. Designed by Mel Harris, United Kingdom (#466) and Dipok Deyi, India (#467).

1985, Nov. 22		Photo. & Engr.	Perf. 13½	
466 A226	22c Asian Toddler (823,724)		.35	.30
	First day cover			1.00
	Inscription block of 4		1.50	
467 A226	33c Breastfeeding (632,753)		.65	.60
	First day cover			1.25
	First day cover, #466-467			1.75
	Inscription block of 4		3.00	

First day covers of Nos. 466-467 total 206,923.
See UN Offices in Geneva Nos. 138-139; Vienna Nos. 55-56.

1986, Jan. 31		Photo.	Perf. 11½x12	

Printed by Helio Courvoisier, Switzerland. Pane of 50. Designed by Wosene Kosrof, Ethiopia.

468 A227	22c multicolored (708,169)		.50	.45
	First day cover (80,588)			1.75
	Inscription block of 4		2.50	

Campaign against hunger. See UN Offices in Geneva No. 140; Vienna No. 57.

Water Resources — A228

Printed by the Government Printing Bureau, Japan. Pane of 40, 2 blocks of 4 horizontal by 5 blocks of 4 vertical. Designed by Thomas Lee, China.

1986, Mar. 14		Photo.	Perf. 13½	
469 A228	22c Dam (525,839)		1.25	1.10
470 A228	22c Irrigation (525,839)		1.25	1.10
471 A228	22c Hygiene (525,839)		1.25	1.10
472 A228	22c Well (525,839)		1.25	1.10
a.	Block of 4, #469-472		5.25	5.25
	First day cover, #472a			7.00
	First day cover, #469-472, each			2.00
	Inscription block of 4, #469-472		6.50	—
	Pane of 40, #469-472		60.00	

UN Development Program. No. 472a has continuous design.
First day covers of Nos. 469-472 total 199,347.
See UN Offices in Geneva Nos. 141-144; Vienna Nos. 58-61.

Human Rights Stamp of 1954 — A229

Stamp collecting: 44c, Engraver. Printed by the Swedish Post Office, Sweden. Panes of 50. Designed by Czeslaw Slania and Ingalill Axelsson, Sweden.

1986, May 22		Engr.	Perf. 12½	
473 A229	22c dark violet & bright blue (825,782)		.30	.25
	First day cover			1.00
	Inscription block of 4		1.50	
474 A229	44c brown & emerald green (738,552)		.80	.70
	First day cover			1.25
	First day cover, #473-474			1.50
	Inscription block of 4		3.25	

First day covers of Nos. 473-474 total: New York, 121,143; Chicago, 89,557.
See UN Offices in Geneva Nos. 146-147; Vienna Nos. 62-63.

Bird's Nest in Tree — A230

Peace in Seven Languages — A231

Printed by the Government Printing Bureau, Japan. Panes of 50. Designed by Akira Iriguchi, Japan (#475), and Henryk Chylinski, Poland (#476).

1986, June 20		Photo. & Embossed	Perf. 13½	
475 A230	22c multicolored (836,160)		.50	.40
	First day cover			1.00
	Inscription block of 4		2.50	—
476 A231	33c multicolored (663,882)		1.50	1.25
	First day cover			2.00
	First day cover, #475-476			4.50
	Inscription block of 4		6.75	—

International Peace Year.
First day covers of Nos. 475-476 total 149,976.

Flag Type of 1980

Printed by Helio Courvoisier, Switzerland. Designed by Ole Hamann. Issued in panes of 16; each contains 4 blocks of four (Nos. 477-480, 481-484, 485-488, 489-492). A se-tenant block of 4 designs centers each pane.

1986, Sept. 19		Photo.	Perf. 12	
		Granite Paper		
477 A185	22c New Zealand (1,150,584)		.60	.45
478 A185	22c Lao PDR (1,150,584)		.60	.45
479 A185	22c Burkina Faso (1,150,584)		.60	.45
480 A185	22c Gambia (1,150,584)		.60	.45
a.	Se-tenant block of 4, #477-480		3.25	—
481 A185	22c Maldives (1,154,870)		.60	.45
482 A185	22c Ethiopia (1,154,870)		.60	.45
483 A185	22c Jordan (1,154,870)		.60	.45
484 A185	22c Zambia (1,154,870)		.60	.45
a.	Se-tenant block of 4, #481-484		3.25	—
485 A185	22c Iceland (1,152,740)		.60	.45
486 A185	22c Antigua & Barbuda (1,152,740)		.60	.45
487 A185	22c Angola (1,152,740)		.60	.45
488 A185	22c Botswana (1,152,740)		.60	.45
a.	Se-tenant block of 4, #485-488		3.25	—
489 A185	22c Romania (1,150,412)		.60	.45
490 A185	22c Togo (1,150,412)		.60	.45
491 A185	22c Mauritania (1,150,412)		.60	.45
492 A185	22c Colombia (1,150,412)		.60	.45
a.	Se-tenant block of 4, #489-492		3.25	—
	First day covers of Nos. #477-492, each			1.00
	Set of 4 diff. panes of 16		37.50	
	Nos. 477-492 (16)		9.60	7.20

First day covers of Nos. 477-492 total 1,442,284.

A232

A233

World Federation of UN Associations, 40th anniv.
Printed by Johann Enschede and Sons, Netherlands.
Designed by Rocco J. Callari, U.S.
Designs: 22c, Mother Earth, by Edna Hibel, U.S. 33c, Watercolor by Salvador Dali (b. 1904), Spain. 39c, New Dawn, by Dong Kingman, U.S. 44c, Watercolor by Chaim Gross, U.S.

1986, Nov. 14   Litho.   Perf. 13x13½
Souvenir Sheet
493   Sheet of 4 *(433,888)*   4.25 3.50
  a. A232 22c **multicolored**   .50   —
  b. A232 33c **multicolored**   .80   —
  c. A232 39c **multicolored**   .95   —
  d. A232 44c **multicolored**   1.10   —
        First day cover *(106,194)*   3.50

No. 493 has inscribed margin picturing UN and WFUNA emblems.
See UN Offices in Geneva No. 150; Vienna No. 66.

1987, Jan. 30   Photo. & Engr.   Perf. 13½
Trygve Halvdan Lie (1896-1968), first Secretary-General. Printed by the Government Printing Office, Austria. Panes of 50. Designed by Rocco J. Callari, U.S., from a portrait by Harald Dal, Norway.

494   A233 22c **multicolored** *(596,440)*   .90   .75
        First day cover *(84,819)*   1.75
        Inscription block of 4   4.00

See Offices in Geneva No. 151; Vienna No. 67.

International Year of Shelter for the Homeless A234

Printed by Johann Enschede and Sons, Netherlands. Panes of 50. Designed by Wladyslaw Brykczynski, Poland.
Designs: 22c, Surveying and blueprinting. 44c, Cutting lumber.

1987, Mar. 13   Litho.   Perf. 13½x12½
495   A234 22c **multicolored** *(620,627)*   .40   .25
        First day cover   1.50
        Inscription block of 4   1.80
496   A234 44c **multicolored** *(538,096)*   1.25 1.00
        First day cover   1.75
        First day cover, #495-496   2.25
        Inscription block of 4   5.50   —

First day covers of Nos. 495-496 total 94,090.
See Offices in Geneva Nos. 154-155; Vienna Nos. 68-69.

Fight Drug Abuse — A235

Printed by the House of Questa, United Kingdom. Panes of 50. Designed by Susan Borgen and Noel Werrett, U.S.
Designs: 22c, Construction. 33c, Education.

1987, June 12   Litho.   Perf. 14½x15
497   A235 22c **multicolored** *(674,563)*   .65   .50
        First day cover   1.75
        Inscription block of 4   2.75
498   A235 33c **multicolored** *(643,153)*   1.25 1.00
        First day cover   2.00
        First day cover, #497-498   2.25
        Inscription block of 4   5.25   —

First day covers of Nos. 497-498 total 106,941.
See Offices in Geneva Nos. 156-157; Vienna Nos. 70-71.

Flag Type of 1980
Printed by Courvoisier. Designed by Ole Hamann.
Issued in panes of 16; each contains 4 block of four (Nos. 499-502, 503-506, 507-510, 511-514). A se-tenant block of 4 designs centers each pane.

1987, Sept. 18   Photo.   Perf. 12
Granite Paper
499   A185 22c Comoros *(1,235,828)*   .60   .50
500   A185 22c Yemen PDR *(1,235,828)*   .60   .50
501   A185 22c Mongolia *(1,235,828)*   .60   .50
502   A185 22c Vanuatu *(1,235,828)*   .60   .50
  a.   Se-tenant block of 4, #499-502   3.25   —
503   A185 22c Japan *(1,244,534)*   .60   .50
504   A185 22c Gabon *(1,244,534)*   .60   .50
505   A185 22c Zimbabwe *(1,244,534)*   .60   .50
506   A185 22c Iraq *(1,244,534)*   .60   .50
  a.   Se-tenant block of 4, #503-506   3.25   —
507   A185 22c Argentina *(1,238,065)*   .60   .50
508   A185 22c Congo *(1,238,065)*   .60   .50
509   A185 22c Niger *(1,238,065)*   .60   .50
510   A185 22c St. Lucia *(1,238,065)*   .60   .50
  a.   Se-tenant block of 4, #507-510   3.25   —
511   A185 22c Bahrain *(1,239,323)*   .60   .50
512   A185 22c Haiti *(1,239,323)*   .60   .50
513   A185 22c Afghanistan *(1,239,323)*   .60   .50
514   A185 22c Greece *(1,239,323)*   .60   .50
  a.   Se-tenant block of 4, #511-514   3.25   —

First day covers, #499-514, each   1.00
Set of 4 diff. panes of 16   37.50
Nos. 499-514 (16)   9.60 8.00

United Nations Day — A236

Printed by The House of Questa, United Kingdom. Panes of 12. Designed by Elisabeth von Janota-Bzowski (#515) and Fritz Henry Oerter (#516), Federal Republic of Germany.
Designs: Multinational people in various occupations.

1987, Oct. 23   Litho.   Perf. 14½x15
515   A236 22c **multicolored** *(1,119,286)*   .40   .35
        First day cover   1.00
        Inscription block of 4   2.00
516   A236 39c **multicolored** *(1,065,468)*   .70   .65
        First day cover   2.00
        First day cover, #515-516   1.60
        Inscription block of 4   2.75
        Panes of 12, #515-516   12.00

See Offices in Geneva Nos. 158-159; Vienna Nos. 74-75.

Immunize Every Child — A237

Printed by The House of Questa, United Kingdom. Panes of 50. Designed by Seymour Chwast, U.S.
Designs: 22c, Measles. 44c, Tetanus.

1987, Nov. 20   Litho.   Perf. 15x14½
517   A237 22c **multicolored** *(660,495)*   1.00   .60
        First day cover   1.75
        Inscription block of 4   4.25
518   A237 44c **multicolored** *(606,049)*   2.25 1.75
        First day cover   2.00
        First day cover, #517-518   3.00
        Inscription block of 4   10.00

See Offices in Geneva Nos. 160-161; Vienna Nos. 76-77.

Intl. Fund for Agricultural Development (IFAD) — A238

Printed by CPE Australia Ltd., Australia. Panes of 50. Designed by Santiago Arolas, Switzerland.
Designs: 22c, Fishing. 33c, Farming.

1988, Jan. 29   Litho.   Perf. 13½
519   A238 22c **multicolored** *(392,649)*   .50   .40
        First day cover   1.00
        Inscription block of 4   2.25
520   A238 33c **multicolored** *(475,185)*   1.00   .85
        First day cover   1.25
        First day cover, #519-520   3.00
        Inscription block of 4   4.75

See Offices in Geneva Nos. 162-163; Vienna Nos. 78-79.

A239

Printed by Heraclio Fournier, S.A., Spain. Panes of 50. Designed by David Ben-Hador, Israel.

1988, Jan. 29   Photo.   Perf. 13½x14
521   A239 3c **multicolored** *(3,000,000)+*   .20   .20
        First day cover   1.00
        Inscription block of 4   .75

Survival of the Forests — A240

Printed by The House of Questa, United Kingdom. Panes of six se-tenant pairs. Designed by Braldt Bralds, the Netherlands. Tropical rain forest: 25c, Treetops. 44c, Ground vegetation and tree trunks. Printed se-tenant in a continuous design.

1988, Mar. 18   Litho.   Perf. 14x15
522   A240 25c **multicolored** *(647,360)*   1.00 1.00
        First day cover   4.00
523   A240 44c **multicolored** *(647,360)*   1.75 1.75
        First day cover   6.00
  a.   Pair, #522-523   3.25 3.25
        First day cover, #523a   14.00
        Inscription block of 4   8.50
        Pane of 12, #522-523   22.50

See Offices in Geneva Nos. 165-166; Vienna Nos. 80-81.

Intl. Volunteer Day — A241

Printed by Johann Enschede and Sons, the Netherlands. Panes of 50. Designed by James E. Tennison, U.S.
Designs: 25c, Eduranhon, vert. 50c, Vocational training.

1988, May 6   Litho.   Perf. 13x14, 14x13
524   A241 25c **multicolored** *(688,444)*   .45   .40
        First day cover   2.00
        Inscription block of 4   2.50
525   A241 50c **multicolored** *(447,784)*   1.10 1.00
        First day cover   2.50
        First day cover, #524-525   2.75
        Inscription block of 4   5.00

See Offices in Geneva Nos. 167-168; Vienna Nos. 82-83.

Health in Sports — A242

Printed by the Government Printing Bureau, Japan. Panes of 50. Paintings by LeRoy Neiman, American sports artist.
Designs: 25c, Cycling, vert. 35c, Marathon.

1988, June 17   Litho.   Perf. 13½x13, 13x13½
526   A242 25c **multicolored** *(658,991)*   .50   .50
        First day cover   2.25
        Inscription block of 4   2.50
527   A242 38c **multicolored** *(420,421)*   1.25 1.10
        First day cover   2.50
        First day cover, #526-527   3.75
        Inscription block of 4   7.00

See Offices in Geneva Nos. 169-170; Vienna Nos. 84-85.

Flag Type of 1980
Printed by Helio Courvoisier, Switzerland. Designed by Ole Hamann, Denmark. Issued in panes of 16; each contains 4 blocks of four (Nos. 528-531, 532-535, 536-539 and 540-543). A se-tenant block of 4 centers each pane.

1988, Sept. 15   Photo.   Perf. 12
Granite Paper
528   A185 25c Spain *(1,029,443)*   .60   .45
529   A185 25c St. Vincent & Grenadines
              (1,029,443)   .60   .45
530   A185 25c Ivory Coast *(1,029,443)*   .60   .45
531   A185 25c Lebanon *(1,029,443)*   .60   .45
  a.   Se-tenant block of 4, #528-531   3.25   —
532   A185 25c Yemen (Arab Republic)
              (1,010,774)   .60   .45
533   A185 25c Cuba *(1,010,774)*   .60   .45
534   A185 25c Denmark *(1,010,774)*   .60   .45

535	A185 25c Libya *(1,010,774)*	.60	.45
a.	Se-tenant block of 4, #532-535	3.25	—
536	A185 25c Qatar *(1,016,941)*	.60	.45
537	A185 25c Zaire *(1,016,941)*	.60	.45
538	A185 25c Norway *(1,016,941)*	.60	.45
539	A185 25c German Democratic Republic *(1,016,941)*	.60	.45
a.	Se-tenant block of 4, #536-539	3.25	—
540	A185 25c Iran *(1,009,234)*	.60	.45
541	A185 25c Tunisia *(1,009,234)*	.60	.45
542	A185 25c Samoa *(1,009,234)*	.60	.45
543	A185 25c Belize *(1,009,234)*	.60	.45
a.	Se-tenant block of 4, #540-543	3.25	—
	First day covers, #528-543, each		1.25
	Set of 4 diff. panes of 16	37.50	
	Nos. 528-543 (16)	9.60	7.20

Universal Declaration of Human Rights, 40th. Anniv. — A243

Printed by Helio Couvoisier, Switzerland. Panes of 50. Designed by Rocco J. Callari, U.S.

1988, Dec. 9   Photo. & Engr.   Perf. 11x11½

544	A243 25c **multicolored** *(893,706)*	.55	.40
	First day cover		2.25
	Inscription block of 4	2.40	—

Souvenir Sheet

545	A243 $1 **multicolored** *(411,863)*	1.25	1.25
	First day cover		2.75

No. 545 has multicolored decorative margin inscribed with the preamble to the human rights declaration in English.
See Offices in Geneva Nos. 171-172; Vienna Nos. 86-87.

World Bank — A244   A245

Printed by Johann Enschede and Sons, the Netherlands. Panes of 50. Designed by Saturnino Lumboy, Philippines.

1989, Jan. 27   Litho.   Perf. 13x14

546	A244 25c Energy and nature *(612,114)*	.75	.45
	First day cover		2.00
	Inscription block of 4	3.00	—
547	A244 45c Agriculture *(528,184)*	1.50	1.00
	First day cover		2.50
	First day cover, #546-547		3.00
	Inscription block of 4	7.00	—

First day covers of Nos. 546-547 total 103,087 (NYC), 56,501 (Washington).
See Offices in Geneva Nos. 173-174; Vienna Nos. 88-89.

1989, Mar. 17   Litho.   Perf. 14x13½

UN Peace-Keeping Force, awarded 1988 Nobel Peace Prize. Printed by CPE Australia, Ltd., Australia. Panes of 50. Designed by Tom Bland, Australia.

548	A245 25c **multicolored** *(808,842)*	.50	.40
	First day cover *(52,115)*		2.25
	Inscription block of 4	2.50	—

See Offices in Geneva No. 175; Vienna No. 90.

Aerial Photograph of New York Headquarters — A246

Printed by Johann Enschede and Sons, the Netherlands. Panes of 25. Designed by Rocco J. Callari, United States, from a photograph by Simon Nathan.

1989, Mar. 17   Litho.   Perf. 14½x14

549	A246 45c **multicolored** *(2,000,000)+*	.70	.60
	First day cover *(41,610)*		2.00
	Inscription block of 4	3.25	

World Weather Watch, 25th Anniv. (in 1988) — A247

Printed by Johann Enschede and Sons, the Netherlands. Panes of 50.
Satellite photographs: 25c, Storm system off the U.S. east coast. 36c, Typhoon Abby in the north-west Pacific.

1989, Apr. 21   Litho.   Perf. 13x14

550	A247 25c **multicolored** *(849,819)*	.75	.50
	First day cover		1.75
	Inscription block of 4	3.25	—
551	A247 36c **multicolored** *(826,547)*	1.50	1.25
	First day cover		2.50
	First day cover, #550-551		3.00
	Inscription block of 4	7.75	—

First day covers of Nos. 550-551 total 92,013.
See Offices in Geneva Nos. 176-177; Vienna Nos. 91-92.

Offices in Vienna, 10th Anniv.
A248   A249

Printed by the Government Printing Office, Austria. Panes of 25. Designed by Paul Flora (25c) and Rudolf Hausner (90c), Austria.

Photo. & Engr., Photo. (90c)

1989, Aug. 23   Perf. 14

552	A248 25c **multicolored** *(580,663)*	2.75	.50
	First day cover		2.50
	Inscription block of 4	12.50	—
553	A249 90c **multicolored** *(505,776)*	2.25	1.75
	First day cover		2.50
	First day cover, #552-553		8.50
	Inscription block of 4	9.00	—
	Panes of 25, #552-553	150.00	

First day covers of Nos. 552-553 total 89,068.
See Offices in Geneva Nos. 178-179; Vienna Nos. 93-94.

Flag Type of 1980

Printed by Helio Courvoisier, Switzerland. Designed by Ole Hamann, Denmark. Issued in panes of 16; each contains 4 blocks of 4 (Nos. 554-557, 558-561, 562-565, 566-569). A se-tenant block of 4 designs centers each pane.

1989, Sept. 22   Photo.   Perf. 12
Granite Paper

554	A185 25c Indonesia *(959,076)*	.65	.55
555	A185 25c Lesotho *(959,076)*	.65	.55
556	A185 25c Guatemala *(959,076)*	.65	.55
557	A185 25c Netherlands *(959,076)*	.65	.55
a.	Se-tenant block of 4, #554-557	3.75	—
558	A185 25c South Africa *(960,502)*	.65	.55
559	A185 25c Portugal *(960,502)*	.65	.55
560	A185 25c Morocco *(960,502)*	.65	.55
561	A185 25c Syrian Arab Republic *(960,502)*	.65	.55
a.	Se-tenant block of 4, #558-561	3.75	—
562	A185 25c Honduras *(959,814)*	.65	.55
563	A185 25c Kampuchea *(959,814)*	.65	.55
564	A185 25c Guinea-Bissau *(959,814)*	.65	.55
565	A185 25c Cyprus *(959,814)*	.65	.55
a.	Se-tenant block of 4, #562-565	3.75	—
566	A185 25c Algeria *(959,805)*	.65	.55
567	A185 25c Brunei *(959,805)*	.65	.55
568	A185 25c St. Kitts and Nevis *(959,805)*	.65	.55
569	A185 25c United Nations *(959,805)*	.65	.55
a.	Se-tenant block of 4, #566-569	3.75	—
	First day covers, #554-569, each		1.25
	Set of 4 diff. panes of 16	42.50	
	Nos. 554-569 (16)	10.40	8.80

First day covers of Nos. 554-569 total 794,934.

Declaration of Human Rights, 40th Anniv. (in 1988) — A250

Printed by Johann Enschede and Sons, the Netherlands. Panes of 12+12 se-tenant labels containing Articles 1 (25c) or 2 (45c) inscribed in English, French or German. Designed by Rocco J. Callari and Robert Stein, US.
Paintings: 25c, The Table of Universal Brotherhood, by Jose Clemente Orozco. 45c, Study for Composition II, by Vassily Kandinsky.

1989, Nov. 17   Litho.   Perf. 13½

570	A250 25c **multicolored** *(1,934,135)*	.40	.30
	First day cover		1.25
	Inscription block of 3 + 3 labels	1.25	
571	A250 45c **multicolored** *(1,922,171)*	.90	.80
	First day cover		1.25
	First day cover, #570-571		2.00
	Inscription block of 3 + 3 labels	2.75	
	Panes of 12, #570-571	17.00	

First day covers of Nos. 570-571 total 146,489 (NYC), 46,774 (Washington).
See Nos. 582-583, 599-600, 616-617, 627-628; Offices in Geneva Nos. 180-181, 193-194, 209-210, 224-225, 234-235; Vienna Nos. 95-96, 108-109, 123-124, 139-140, 150-151.

Intl. Trade Center — A251

Printed by House of Questa, United Kingdom. Panes of 50. Designed by Richard Bernstein, US.

1990, Feb. 2   Litho.   Perf. 14½x15

572	A251 25c **multicolored** *(429,081)*	1.60	1.25
	First day cover *(52,614)*		2.50
	Inscription block of 4	6.50	

See Offices in Geneva No. 182; Vienna No. 97.

Fight AIDS Worldwide A252

Printed by Johann Enschede and Sons, the Netherlands. Panes of 50. Designed by Jacek Tofil, Poland (25c) and Fritz Henry Oerter, Federal Republic of Germany (40c).
Design: 40c, Shadow over crowd.

1990, Mar. 16   Litho.   Perf. 13½x12½

573	A252 25c **multicolored** *(492,078)*	.50	.40
	First day cover		2.00
	Inscription block of 4	2.50	—
574	A252 40c **multicolored** *(394,149)*	1.50	1.25
	First day cover		3.50
	First day cover, #573-574		6.50
	Inscription block of 4	6.50	—

First day covers of Nos. 573-574 total 95,854.
See Offices in Geneva Nos. 184-185, Vienna Nos. 99-100.

Medicinal Plants — A253

Printed by Helio Courvoisier, Switzerland. Panes of 50. Designed by Rocco J. Callari & Robert Stein, US from illustrations from "Curtis's Botanical Magazine".

1990, May 4   Photo.   Granite Paper   Perf. 11½

575 A253 25c Catharanthus roseus *(796,792)*		.50	.45
First day cover			1.25
Inscription block of 4		2.00	—
576 A253 90c Panax quinquefolium *(605,617)*		2.00	1.50
First day cover			2.10
First day cover, #575-576			9.50
Inscription block of 4		8.50	—

First day covers of Nos. 575-576 total 100,548.
See Offices in Geneva Nos. 186-187, Vienna Nos. 101-102.

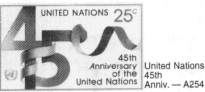

United Nations, 45th Anniv. — A254

Printed by Johann Enschede and Sons, the Netherlands. Panes of 50. Designed by Kris Geysen, Belgium (25c), Nejat M. Gur, Turkey (45c), Robert Stein, US (No. 579).
Design: 45c, "45," emblem.

1990, June 26   Litho.   Perf. 14½x13

577 A254 25c multicolored *(581,718)*	.80	.70
First day cover		1.25
Inscription block of 4	3.75	—
578 A254 45c multicolored *(582,769)*	2.75	2.50
First day cover		1.25
First day cover, #577-578		4.00
Inscription block of 4	11.50	—

Souvenir Sheet

579 Sheet of 2, #577-578 *(315,946)*	7.75	6.00
First day cover		4.00

First day covers of Nos. 577-579 total 129,011.
See Offices in Geneva Nos. 188-190; Vienna Nos. 103-105.

Crime Prevention — A255

Printed by Heraclio Fournier, S.A. Spain. Panes of 50. Designed by Josef Ryzec, Czechoslovakia.

1990, Sept. 13   Photo.   Perf. 14

580 A255 25c Crimes of youth *(533,089)*	1.10	.70
First day cover		2.00
Inscription block of 4	5.00	—
581 A255 36c Organized crime *(427,215)*	2.50	1.25
First day cover		4.00
First day cover, #580-581		5.00
Inscription block of 4	11.00	—

First day covers of Nos. 580-581 total 68,660.
See Offices in Geneva Nos. 191-192; Vienna Nos. 106-107.

Human Rights Type of 1989

Printed by Johann Enschede and Sons, the Netherlands. Panes of 12+12 se-tenant labels containing Articles 7 (25c) or 8 (45c) inscribed in English, French or German. Designed by Rocco J. Callari and Robert Stein, US.
Artwork: 25c, Fragment from the sarcophagus of Plotinus, c. 270 A.D. 45c, Combined Chambers of the High Court of Appeal by Charles Paul Renouard.

1990, Nov. 16   Litho.   Perf. 13½

582 A250 25c black, gray & tan *(1,492,950)*	.45	.35
First day cover		1.25
Inscription block of 3 + 3 labels	1.50	—
583 A250 45c black & brown *(1,490,934)*	.90	.75
First day cover		1.25
First day cover, #582-583		3.75
Inscription block of 3 + 3 labels	3.00	—
Panes of 12, #582-583	17.50	

First day covers of Nos. 582-583 total 108,560.
See Offices in Geneva Nos. 193-194; Vienna Nos. 108-109.

Economic Commission for Europe — A256

Printed by Heraclio Fournier, S.A., Spain. Panes of 40. Designed by Carlos Ochagavia, Argentina.

1991, Mar. 15   Litho.   Perf. 14

584 A256 30c Two storks *(590,102)*	1.10	.90
585 A256 30c Woodpecker, ibex *(590,102)*	1.10	.90
586 A256 30c Capercaille, plover *(590,102)*	1.10	.90
587 A256 30c Falcon, marmot *(590,102)*	1.10	.90
a. Block of 4, #584-587	4.50	3.75
First day cover, #587a		4.00
First day cover, #584-587, any single		3.00
Inscription block of 4, #587a	5.00	—
Pane of 40, #584-587	45.00	—

First day covers of Nos. 584-587 total 53,502.
See Offices in Geneva Nos. 195-198; Vienna Nos. 110-113.

Namibian Independence A257

Printed by Heraclio Fournier, S.A., Spain. Designed by Rocco J. Callari, US, from photographs by John Isaac, India.

1991, May 10   Litho.   Perf. 14

588 A257 30c Dunes, Namib Desert *(360,825)*	1.00	.65
First day cover		2.50
Inscription block of 4	3.50	—
589 A257 50c Savanna *(415,648)*	2.00	1.50
First day cover		3.50
First day cover, #588-589		4.50
Inscription block of 4	8.00	—

First day covers of Nos. 588-589 total 114,258.
See Offices in Geneva Nos. 199-200; Vienna Nos. 114-115.

A258

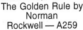

The Golden Rule by Norman Rockwell — A259

UN Headquarters, New York — A260

Printed by Johann Enschede and Sons, the Netherlands (30c), Helio Courvoisier, S.A., Switzerland (50c), and by Government Printing Bureau, Japan ($2). Panes of 50. Designed by Rocco J. Callari (30c), Norman Rockwell, US (50c), Rocco J. Callari and Robert Stein, US ($2).

1991   Litho.   Perf. 13½

590 A258 30c multi, *Sept. 11, (2,000,000)+*	.90	.55
First day cover		1.25
Inscription block of 4	3.50	—

Photo.
Perf. 12x11½

591 A259 50c multi, *Sept. 11, (2,000,000)+*	1.50	1.00
First day cover		4.00
Inscription block of 4	6.50	

Engr.

592 A260 $2 dark blue, *May 10, (2,000,000)+*	3.00	2.50
First day cover		5.50
Inscription block of 4	13.00	—

First day covers of Nos. 590-591 total 66,016, No. 592, 36,022.
See Offices in Geneva Nos. 199-200; Vienna Nos. 114-115.

Rights of the Child — A261

Printed by The House of Questa, United Kingdom. Panes of 50. Designed by Nicole Delia Legnani, US (30c) and Alissa Duffy, US (70c).

1991, June 14   Litho.   Perf. 14½

593 A261 30c Children, globe *(440,151)*	1.25	1.00
First day cover		2.00
Inscription block of 4	5.00	—
594 A261 70c House, rainbow *(447,803)*	3.25	2.25
First day cover		5.00
First day cover, #593-594		4.00
Inscription block of 4	12.00	—

First day covers of Nos. 593-594 total 96,324.
See Offices in Geneva Nos. 203-204; Vienna Nos. 117-118.

Banning of Chemical Weapons A262

Printed by Heraclio Fournier, S.A., Spain. Panes of 50. Designed by Oscar Asboth, Austria (30c), Michael Granger, France (90c).
Design: 90c, Hand holding back chemical drums.

1991, Sept. 11   Litho.   Perf. 13½

595 A262 30c multicolored *(367,548)*	1.75	1.40
First day cover		2.50
Inscription block of 4	6.50	—
596 A262 90c multicolored *(346,161)*	4.50	4.00
First day cover		3.50
First day cover, #595-596		3.00
Inscription block of 4	16.00	—

First day covers of Nos. 595-596 total 91,552.
See Offices in Geneva Nos. 205-206; Vienna Nos. 119-120.

UN Postal Administration, 40th Anniv. — A263

Printed by The House of Questa, United Kingdom. Panes of 25. Designed by Rocco J. Callari, US.

1991, Oct. 24   Litho.   Perf. 14x15

597 A263 30c No. 1 *(442,548)*	1.00	.75
First day cover		1.25
Inscription block of 4	4.50	—
598 A263 40c No. 3 *(419,127)*	1.50	1.10
First day cover		1.50
First day cover, #597-598		2.00
Inscription block of 4	6.50	—
Panes of 25, #597-598	65.00	—

First day covers of Nos. 597-598 total 81,177 (New York), 58,501 (State College, PA).
See Offices in Geneva Nos. 207-208; Vienna Nos. 121-122.

Human Rights Type of 1989

Printed by Johann Enschede and Sons, the Netherlands. Panes of 12+12 se-tenant labels containing Articles 13 (30c) or 14 (50c) inscribed in English, French or German. Designed by Robert Stein, US.
Artwork: 30c, The Last of England, by Ford Madox Brown. 40c, The Emigration to the East, by Tito Salas.

1991, Nov. 20   Litho.   Perf. 13½

599 A250 30c multicolored *(1,261,198)*	.60	.45
First day cover		1.25
Inscription block of 3 + 3 labels	2.10	—
600 A250 50c multicolored *(1,255,077)*	1.25	1.00
First day cover		1.75
First day cover, #599-600		2.25
Inscription block of 3 + 3 labels	4.00	—
Panes of 12, #599-600	17.50	

First day covers of Nos. 599-600 total 136,605.
See Offices in Geneva Nos. 209-210; Vienna Nos. 123-124.

World Heritage Type of 1984

Printed by Cartor S.A., France. Panes of 50. Designed by Robert Stein, U.S.
Designs: 30c, Uluru Natl. Park, Australia. 50c, The Great Wall of China.

1992, Jan. 24   Litho.   Perf. 13
Size: 35x28mm

601 A215 30c multicolored *(337,717)*	.70	.60
First day cover		2.50
Inscription block of 4	3.00	—

602 A215 50c **multicolored** (358,000) 1.25 1.00
First day cover 3.75
First day cover, #601-602 4.50
Inscription block of 4 7.00 —

First day covers of Nos. 601-602 total 62,733.
See Offices in Geneva Nos. 211-212; Vienna Nos. 125-126.

Clean Oceans — A264

Printed by The House of Questa, United Kingdom. Panes of 12. Designed by Braldt Bralds, Netherlands.

1992, Mar. 13 **Litho.** **Perf. 14**
603 A264 29c Ocean surface .55 .55
604 A264 29c Ocean bottom .55 .55
a. Pair, #603-604 1.10 1.10
First day cover, #604a 4.00
First day cover, #603-604, any single 3.50
Inscription block of 4, #603-604 3.75 —
Pane of 12, #603-604 11.00

First day covers of Nos. 603-604 total 75,511.
See Offices in Geneva Nos. 214-215; Vienna Nos. 127-128.

Earth Summit — A265

Printed by Helio Courvoisier S.A., Switzerland. Panes of 40. Designed by Peter Max, US.
Designs: No. 605, Globe at LR. No. 606, Globe at LL. No. 607, Globe at UR. No. 608, Globe at UL.

1992, May 22 **Photo.** **Perf. 11½**
605 A265 29c **multicolored** (806,268) .60 .50
606 A265 29c **multicolored** (806,268) .60 .50
607 A265 29c **multicolored** (806,268) .60 .50
608 A265 29c **multicolored** (806,268) .60 .50
a. Block of 4, #605-608 2.50 2.00
First day cover, #608a 5.00
First day cover, #605-608, each 2.50
Inscription block of 4, #608a 3.00 —
Pane of 40, #605-608 27.50

First day covers of Nos. 605-608a total 110,577.
See Offices in Geneva Nos. 216-219; Vienna Nos. 129-132.

Mission to Planet Earth — A266

Printed by Helio Courvoisier, S.A., Switzerland. Designed by Attilla Hejja, US.
Designs: No. 609, Satellites over city, sailboats, fishing boat. No. 610, Satellite over coast, passenger liner, dolphins, whale, volcano.

1992, Sept. 4 **Photo.** **Rouletted 8**
Granite Paper
609 A266 29c **multicolored** (643,647) 3.25 3.00
610 A266 29c **multicolored** (643,647) 3.25 3.00
a. Pair, #609-610 6.50 6.00
First day cover, #610a 4.00
First day cover, #609-610, each 7.50
Inscription block of 4 15.00 —
Pane of 10, #609-610 35.00

First day covers of Nos. 609-610a total 69,343.
See Offices in Geneva Nos. 220-221; Vienna Nos. 133-134.

Science and Technology for Development A267

Printed by Unicover Corp., US. Designed by Saul Mandel, US.
Design: 50c, Animal, man drinking.

1992, Oct. 2 **Litho.** **Perf. 14**
611 A267 29c **multicolored** (453,365) .50 .45
First day cover 2.00
Inscription block of 4 2.75 —
612 A267 50c **multicolored** (377,377) .85 .70
First day cover 3.00
First day cover, #611-612 8.50
Inscription block of 4 5.50 —

First day covers of Nos. 611-612 total 69,195.
See Offices in Geneva Nos. 222-223, Vienna Nos. 135-136.

UN University Building, Tokyo — A268

UN Headquarters, New York — A269

Printed by Cartor SA, France (4c, 40c), Walsall Security Printers, Ltd., UK (29c). Designed by Banks and Miles, UK (4c, 40c), Robert Stein, US (29c).
Design: 40c, UN University Building, Tokyo, diff.

1992, Oct. 2 **Litho.** **Perf. 14, 13½x13 (29c)**
613 A268 4c **multicolored** (1,500,000)+ .20 .20
First day cover 2.00
Inscription block of 4 .75 —
614 A269 29c **multicolored** (1,750,000)+ .60 .55
First day cover 2.00
Inscription block of 4 3.25 —
615 A268 40c **multicolored** (1,500,000)+ .80 .75
First day cover 2.00
First day cover, #613-615 2.00
Inscription block of 4 7.00 —
Nos. 613-615 (3) 1.60 1.50

First day covers of Nos. 613-615 total 62,697.

Human Rights Type of 1989

Printed by Johann Enschede and Sons, the Netherlands. Panes of 12+12 se-tenant labels containing Articles 19 (29c) and 20 (50c) inscribed in English, French or German. Designed by Robert Stein, US.
Artwork: 29c, Lady Writing a Letter with her Maid, by Vermeer. 50c, The Meeting, by Ester Almqvist.

1992, Nov. 20 **Litho.** **Perf. 13½**
616 A250 29c **multicolored**, (1,184,531) .90 .75
First day cover 1.25
Inscription block of 3 + 3 labels 2.75 —
617 A250 50c **multicolored** (1,107,044) 1.10 1.00
First day cover 1.75
First day cover, #616-617 7.00
Inscription block of 3 + 3 labels 4.00 —
Panes of 12, #616-617 22.50

First day covers of Nos. 616-617 total 104,470.
See Offices in Geneva Nos. 224-225; Vienna Nos. 139-140.

Aging With Dignity — A270

Printed by Cartor SA, France. Designed by C.M. Dudash, US.

Designs: 29c, Elderly couple, family. 52c, Old man, physician, woman holding fruit basket.

1993, Feb. 5 **Litho.** **Perf. 13**
618 A270 29c **multicolored** (336,933) 1.00 .75
First day cover 1.25
Inscription block of 4 4.00 —
619 A270 52c **multicolored** (308,080) 1.75 1.40
First day cover 2.50
First day cover, #618-619 4.00
Inscription block of 4 8.00 —

First day covers of Nos. 618-619 total 52,932.
See Offices in Geneva Nos. 226-227; Vienna Nos. 141-142.

Endangered Species — A271

Printed by Johann Enschede and Sons, the Netherlands. Designed by Rocco J. Callari and Norman Adams, US.
Designs: No. 620, Hairy-nosed wombat. No. 621, Whooping crane. No. 622, Giant clam. No. 623, Giant sable antelope.

1993, Mar. 2 **Litho.** **Perf. 13x12½**
620 A271 29c **multicolored** (1,200,000)+ .55 .50
621 A271 29c **multicolored** (1,200,000)+ .55 .50
622 A271 29c **multicolored** (1,200,000)+ .55 .50
623 A271 29c **multicolored** (1,200,000)+ .55 .50
a. Block of 4, #620-623 2.25 2.25
First day cover, #623a 4.50
First day cover, #620-623, each 2.00
Inscription block of 4, #623a 2.40 —
Pane of 16, #620-623 12.50

First day covers of Nos. 620-623a total 64,794.
See Nos. 639-642, 657-660, 674-677, 700-703, 730-733, 757-760, 773-776; Offices in Geneva Nos. 228-231, 246-249, 264-267, 280-283, 298-301, 318-321, 336-339, 352-355; Vienna Nos. 143-146, 162-165, 180-183, 196-199, 214-217, 235-238, 253-256, 269-272.

Healthy Environment — A272

Printed by Leigh-Mardon Pty. Limited, Australia. Designed by Milton Glaser, US.
Designs: 29c, Personal. 50c, Family.

1993, May 7 **Litho.** **Perf. 15x14½**
624 A272 29c Man (430,463) .70 .50
First day cover 1.25
Inscription block of 4 3.50 —
625 A272 50c Family (326,692) 1.10 .85
First day cover 1.75
First day cover, #624-625 3.75
Inscription block of 4 6.00 —

WHO, 45th anniv. First day covers of Nos. 624-625 total 55,139.
See Offices in Geneva Nos. 232-233; Vienna Nos. 147-148.

Printed by House of Questa, Ltd., United Kingdom. Designed by Salahattin Kanidinc, US.

1993, May 7 **Litho.** **Perf. 15x14**
626 A273 5c **multicolored** (1,500,000)+ .20 .20
First day cover (23,452) 1.25
Inscription block of 4 .75 —

Human Rights Type of 1989

Printed by Johann Enschede and Sons, the Netherlands. Panes of 12 + 12 se-tenant labels containing Articles 25 (29c) and 26 (35c) inscribed in English, French or German. Designed by Robert Stein, US.
Artwork: 29c, Shocking Corn, by Thomas Hart Benton. 35c, The Library, by Jacob Lawrence.

1993, June 11 **Litho.** **Perf. 13½**
627 A250 29c **multicolored** (1,049,134) .90 .65
First day cover 1.25
Inscription block of 3 + 3 labels 3.25 —
628 A250 35c **multicolored** (1,045,346) 1.25 1.00

First day cover 1.75
First day cover, #627-628 6.00
Inscription block of 3 + 3 labels 4.00
Panes of 12, #627-628 25.00

First day covers of Nos. 627-628 total 77,719.
See Offices in Geneva Nos. 234-235; Vienna Nos. 150-151.

Intl. Peace
Day — A274

Printed by the PTT, Switzerland. Designed by Hans Erni, Switzerland.
Denomination at: #629, UL. #630, UR. #631, LL. #632, LR.

1993, Sept. 21   Litho. & Engr.   Rouletted 12½
629 A274 29c **blue & multi** *(298,367)* 2.00 1.50
630 A274 29c **blue & multi** *(298,367)* 2.00 1.50
631 A274 29c **blue & multi** *(298,367)* 2.00 1.50
632 A274 29c **blue & multi** *(298,367)* 2.00 1.50
a. Block of 4, #629-632 9.00 7.00
First day cover, #629-632, each 2.50
First day cover, #632a 7.50
Inscription block of 4, #632a 9.50 —
Pane of 40, #629-632 87.50

First day covers of Nos. 629-632a total 41,743.
See Offices in Geneva Nos. 236-239; Vienna Nos. 152-155.

Environment-Climate — A275

Printed by House of Questa, Ltd., United Kingdom. Designed by Braldt Bralds, Netherlands.
Designs: #633, Chameleon. #634, Palm trees, top of funnel cloud. #635, Bottom of funnel cloud, deer, antelope. #636, Bird of paradise.

1993, Oct. 29   Litho.   Perf. 14½
633 A275 29c **multicolored** *(383,434)* .70 .55
634 A275 29c **multicolored** *(383,434)* .70 .55
635 A275 29c **multicolored** *(383,434)* .70 .55
636 A275 29c **multicolored** *(383,434)* .70 .55
a. Strip of 4, #633-636 3.00 2.25
First day cover, #636a 4.50
First day cover, #633-636, each 2.00
Inscription block, 2 #636a 6.50 —
Pane of 24, #633-636 21.00

First day covers of Nos. 633-636a total 38,182.
See Offices in Geneva Nos. 240-243; Vienna Nos. 156-159.

Intl. Year of the
Family — A276

Printed by Cartor S.A., France. Designed by Rocco J. Callari, US.
Designs: 29c, Mother holding child, two children, woman. 45c, People tending crops.

1994, Feb. 4   Litho.   Perf. 13.1
637 A276 29c **green & multi** *(590,000)+* 1.25 1.00
First day cover 1.25
Inscription block of 4 5.00 —
638 A276 45c **blue & multi** *(540,000)+* 2.00 1.50
First day cover 1.75
First day cover, #637-638 2.50
Inscription block of 4 9.00 —

First day covers of Nos. 637-638 total 47,982. See Offices in Geneva Nos. 244-245; Vienna Nos. 160-161.

Endangered Species Type of 1993

Printed by Johann Enschede and Sons, the Netherlands. Designed by Rocco J. Callari, US (frame), and Kerrie Maddeford, Australia (stamps).
Designs: No. 639, Chimpanzee. No. 640, St. Lucia Amazon. No. 641, American crocodile. No. 642, Dama gazelle.

1994, Mar. 18   Litho.   Perf. 12.7
639 A271 29c **multicolored** *(1,200,000)+* .60 .50
640 A271 29c **multicolored** *(1,200,000)+* .60 .50
641 A271 29c **multicolored** *(1,200,000)+* .60 .50
642 A271 29c **multicolored** *(1,200,000)+* .60 .50
a. Block of 4, #639-642 2.50 2.25
First day cover, #642a 3.00
First day cover, #639-642, each 1.25
Inscription block of 4, #642a 2.50 —
Pane of 16, #639-642 11.00

First day covers of Nos. 639-642 total 79,599. See Offices in Geneva Nos. 246-249; Vienna Nos. 162-165.

Protection for
Refugees — A277

Printed by Leigh-Mardon Pty. Limited, Australia. Designed by Francoise Peyroux, France.

1994, Apr. 29   Litho.   Perf. 14.3x14.8
643 A277 50c **multicolored** *(600,000)+* 1.25 1.00
First day cover *(33,558)* 3.00
Inscription block of 4 5.75 —

See Offices in Geneva No. 250; Vienna No. 166.

Dove of Peace — A278

Sleeping Child, by
Stanislaw
Wyspianski — A279

Mourning Owl, by
Vanessa Isitt — A280

Printed by Cartor S.A., France, and Norges Banks Seddeltrykkeri, Norway (#646).

1994, Apr. 29   Litho.   Perf. 12.9
644 A278 10c **multicolored** *(1,000,000)+* .20 .20
First day cover 1.25
Inscription block of 4 1.00 —
645 A279 19c **multicolored** *(1,000,000)+* .65 .40
First day cover 2.00
Inscription block of 4 3.00 —

Engr.
Perf. 13.1
646 A280 $1 **red brown** *(1,000,000)+* 2.50 2.00
First day cover 4.00
Inscription block of 4 11.00 —
Nos. 644-646 (3) 3.35 2.60

First day covers of Nos. 644-646 total 48,946.

Intl. Decade for
Natural Disaster
Reduction — A281

Printed by The House of Questa, UK. Designed by Kenji Koga, Japan.
Earth seen from space, outline map of: #647, North America. #648, Eurasia. #649, South America, #650, Australia and South Asia.

1994, May 27   Litho.   Perf. 13.9x14.2
647 A281 29c **multicolored** *(630,000)+* 1.75 1.25
648 A281 29c **multicolored** *(630,000)+* 1.75 1.25
649 A281 29c **multicolored** *(630,000)+* 1.75 1.25
650 A281 29c **multicolored** *(630,000)+* 1.75 1.25
a. Block of 4, #647-650 8.00 3.00
First day cover, #650a 3.00
First day cover, #647-650, each 2.00
Inscription block of 4, #650a 8.50 —
Pane of 40, #647-650 80.00

First day covers of Nos. 647-650 total 37,135. See Offices in Geneva Nos. 251-254; Vienna Nos. 170-173.

Population and
Development
A282

Printed by Johann Enschede and Sons, the Netherlands. Designed by Jerry Smath, US.
Designs: 29c, Children playing. 52c, Family with house, car, other possessions.

1994, Sept. 1   Litho.   Perf. 13.2x13.6
651 A282 29c **multicolored** *(590,000)+* .75 .60
First day cover 1.25
Inscription block of 4 3.00 —
652 A282 52c **multicolored** *(540,000)+* 1.25 1.00
First day cover 1.75
First day cover, #651-652 2.25
Inscription block of 4 5.00 —

First day covers of Nos. 651-652 total 45,256. See Offices in Geneva Nos. 258-259; Vienna Nos. 174-175.

UNCTAD, 30th
Anniv. — A283

Printed by Johann Enschede and Sons, the Netherlands. Designed by Luis Sarda, Spain.

1994, Oct. 28
653 A283 29c **multicolored** *(590,000)+* .55 .50
First day cover 1.25
Inscription block of 4 2.75 —
654 A283 50c **multi, diff.** *(540,000)+* .95 .70
First day cover 1.75
First day cover, #653-654 2.25
Inscription block of 4 4.50 —

First day covers of Nos. 653-654 total 42,763. See Offices in Geneva Nos. 260-261; Vienna Nos. 176-177.

UN, 50th
Anniv. — A284

Social Summit,
Copenhagen — A285

Printed by Swiss Postal Service. Designed by Rocco J. Callari, US.

1995, Jan. 1   Litho. & Engr.   Perf. 13.4
655 A284 32c multicolored *(938,644)*   1.25   .90
        First day cover *(39,817)*   7.00
        Inscription block of 4   5.50

See Offices in Geneva No. 262; Vienna No. 178.

1995, Feb. 3   Photo. & Engr.   Perf. 13.6x13.9
Printed by Austrian Government Printing Office.
Designed by Friedensreich Hundertwasser.
656 A285 50c multicolored *(495,388)*   1.10 1.00
        First day cover *(31,797)*   1.75
        Inscription block of 4   5.00

See Offices in Geneva No. 263; Vienna No. 179.

Endangered Species Type of 1993

Printed by Johann Enschede and Sons, the Netherlands. Designed by Chris Calle, US.
Designs: No. 657, Giant armadillo. No. 658, American bald eagle. No. 659, Fijian/Tongan banded iguana. No. 660, Giant panda.

1995, Mar. 24   Litho.   Perf. 13x12½
657 A271 32c multicolored *(756,000)+*   .65   .55
658 A271 32c multicolored *(756,000)+*   .65   .55
659 A271 32c multicolored *(756,000)+*   .65   .55
660 A271 32c multicolored *(756,000)+*   .65   .55
  a.   Block of 4, 657-660   2.75 2.25
        First day cover, #660a   3.25
        First day cover, #657-660, each   1.25
        Inscription block of 4, #660a   2.75   —
        Pane of 16, #657-660   12.50

First day covers of Nos. 657-660 total 67,311. See Offices in Geneva Nos. 264-267; Vienna Nos. 180-183.

Intl. Youth Year, 10th
Anniv. — A286

Printed by The House of Questa (UK). Designed by Gottfried Kumpf, Austria.
Designs: 32c, Seated child. 55c, Children cycling.

1995, May 26   Litho.   Perf. 14.4x14.7
661 A286 32c multicolored *(358,695)*   .75   .45
        First day cover   1.25
        Inscription block of 4   3.25
662 A286 55c multicolored *(288,424)*   1.25   .85
        First day cover   1.75
        First day cover, #661-662   2.25
        Inscription block of 4   5.50

First day covers of Nos. 661-662 total 42,846. See Offices in Geneva Nos. 268-269; Vienna Nos. 184-185.

UN, 50th
Anniv. — A287

Printed by Johann Enschede Security Printing, the Netherlands. Designed by Paul and Chris Calle, US.
Designs: 32c, Hand with pen signing UN Charter, flags. 50c, Veterans' War Memorial, Opera House, San Francisco.

1995, June 26   Engr.   Perf. 13.3x13.6
663 A287 32c black *(501,961)*   .65   .45
        First day cover   1.25
        Inscription block of 4   3.00
664 A287 50c maroon *(419,932)*   1.00   .70
        First day cover   1.75
        First day cover, #663-664   2.25
        Inscription block of 4   4.50

Souvenir Sheet
Litho. & Engr.
Imperf
665   Sheet of 2, #663-664 *(347,963)+* 2.25 2.00
  a. A287 32c black   .90   .75
  b. A287 50c maroon   1.25 1.10
        First day cover   2.25

First day covers of Nos. 663-665 total: New York, 69,263; San Francisco, 53,354. See Offices in Geneva Nos. 270-272; Vienna Nos. 186-188.

4th World Conference
on Women,
Beijing — A288

Printed by Postage Stamp Printing House, MPT, People's Republic of China. Designed by Ting Shao Kuang, People's Republic of China.
Designs: 32c, Mother and child. 40c, Seated woman, cranes flying above.

1995, Sept. 5   Photo.   Perf. 12
666 A288 32c multicolored *(561,847)*   .80   .40
        First day cover   1.25
        Inscription block of 4   3.50
        Size: 28x50mm
667 A288 40c multicolored *(499,850)*   1.10   .50
        First day cover   1.25
        First day cover, #666-667   2.00
        Inscription block of 4   4.50

First day covers of Nos. 666-667 total 103,963. See Offices in Geneva Nos. 273-274; Vienna Nos. 189-190.

UN Headquarters
A289

Designed by John B. De Santis, Jr. US.

1995, Sept. 5   Litho.   Perf. 15
668 A289 20c multicolored   .35   .20
        First day cover *(18,326)*   1.25
        Inscription block of 4   1.90

Miniature Sheet

United Nations, 50th Anniv. — A290

Designed by Ben Verkaaik, Netherlands.
Printed by House of Questa, UK.
Designs: #669a-669 I, Various people in continuous design (2 blocks of six stamps with gutter between).

1995, Oct. 24   Litho.   Perf. 14
669   Sheet of 12 *(214,639 sheets)*   9.00 5.00
        First day cover   15.00
a.-l. A290 32c any single   .70   .40
        First day cover, #669a-669l,
          each   4.50
670   Souvenir booklet *(85,256 book-
          lets)*   15.00
  a. A290 32c Booklet pane of 3, vert. strip
          of 3 from UL of sheet   3.50 3.50
  b. A290 32c Booklet pane of 3, vert. strip
          of 3 from UR of sheet   3.50 3.50
  c. A290 32c Booklet pane of 3, vert. strip
          of 3 from LL of sheet   3.50 3.50
  d. A290 32c Booklet pane of 3, vert. strip
          of 3 from LR of sheet   3.50 3.50

First day covers of Nos. 669-670 total 47,632. See Offices in Geneva Nos. 275-276; Vienna Nos. 191-192.

WFUNA, 50th Anniv. — A291

Designed by Rudolf Mirer, Switzerland.
Printed by Johann Enschede and Sons, the Netherlands.

1996, Feb. 2   Litho.   Perf. 13x13½
671 A291 32c multicolored *(580,000)+*   .50   .35
        First day cover   1.25
        Inscription block of 4   2.50

See Offices in Geneva No. 277; Vienna No. 193.

Mural, by Fernand
Leger — A292

Designed by Fernand Leger, France.
Printed by House of Questa, UK.

1996, Feb. 2   Litho.   Perf. 14½x15
672 A292 32c multicolored *(780,000)+*   .50   .35
        First day cover   1.25
        Inscription block of 4   2.50
673 A292 60c multi, diff. *(680,000)+*   1.00   .75
        First day cover   1.75
        First day cover, #672-673   2.25
        Inscription block of 4   4.75

Endangered Species Type of 1993

Printed by Johann Enschede and Sons, the Netherlands. Designed by Diane Bruyninckx, Belgium.

Designs: No. 674, Masdevallia veitchiana. No. 675, Saguaro cactus. No. 676, West Australian pitcher plant. No. 677, Encephalartos horridus.

1996, Mar. 14   Litho.   Perf. 12½
674 A271 32c multicolored *(640,000)+*   .60   .45
675 A271 32c multicolored *(640,000)+*   .60   .45
676 A271 32c multicolored *(640,000)+*   .60   .45
677 A271 32c multicolored *(640,000)+*   .60   .45
  a.   Block of 4, 674-677   2.50
        First day cover, #677a   3.25
        First day cover, #674-677, each   1.25
        Inscription block of 4, #677a   2.50   —
        Pane of 16, #674-677   11.00

See Offices in Geneva Nos. 280-283; Vienna Nos. 196-199.

City Summit (Habitat
II) — A293

Printed by Johann Enschede and Sons, the Netherlands. Designed by Teresa Fasolino, US.

Designs: No. 678, Deer. No. 679, Man, child, dog sitting on hill, overlooking town. No. 680, People walking in park, city skyline. No. 681, Tropical park, Polynesian woman, boy. No. 682, Polynesian village, orchids, bird.

1996, June 3   Litho.   Perf. 14x13½
678 A293 32c multicolored *(475,000)+*   .70   .50
679 A293 32c multicolored *(475,000)+*   .70   .50
680 A293 32c multicolored *(475,000)+*   .70   .50
681 A293 32c multicolored *(475,000)+*   .70   .50
682 A293 32c multicolored *(475,000)+*   .70   .50
  a.   Strip of 5, #678-682   3.50
        First day cover, #682a   4.00
        First day cover, #678-682, each   1.75
        Inscription block of 10, 2 #682a   7.50

See Offices in Geneva Nos. 284-288; Vienna Nos. 200-204.

Sport and the
Environment
A294

Printed by The House of Questa, UK. Designed by LeRoy Neiman, US.

Designs: 32c, Men's basketball, vert. 50c, Women's volleyball.

1996, July 19   Litho.   Perf. 14x14½, 14½x14

683	A294 32c multicolored (680,000)+	1.00	.75
	First day cover		1.25
	Inscription block of 4	4.50	—
684	A294 50c multicolored (680,000)+	2.00	1.50
	First day cover		1.50
	First day cover, #683-684		2.25
	Inscription block of 4	9.00	—

Souvenir Sheet

685	A294 Sheet of 2, #683-684 (370,000)+	2.00	1.60
	First day cover		4.00

See Offices in Geneva Nos. 289-291; Vienna Nos. 205-207.
1996 Summer Olympic Games, Atlanta, GA.

Plea for Peace — A295

Printed by House of Questa, UK.
Designed by: 32c, Peng Yue, China. 60c, Cao Chenyu, China.

Designs: 32c, Doves. 60c, Stylized dove.

1996, Sept. 17   Litho.   Perf. 14½x15

686	A295 32c multicolored (580,000)+	.65	.45
	First day cover		1.25
	Inscription block of 4	3.25	—
687	A295 60c multicolored (580,000)+	1.25	.90
	First day cover		1.50
	First day cover, #686-687		2.25
	Inscription block of 4	6.25	—

See Offices in Geneva Nos. 292-293; Vienna Nos. 208-209.

UNICEF, 50th Anniv. — A296

Printed by The House of Questa, UK. Designed by The Walt Disney Co.

Fairy Tales: 32c, Yeh-Shen, China. 60c, The Ugly Duckling, by Hans Christian Andersen.

1996, Nov. 20   Litho.   Perf. 14½x15

688	A296 32c multicolored (1,000,000)+	.65	.50
	First day cover		1.25
	Pane of 8 + label	6.00	
689	A296 60c multicolored (1,000,000)+	1.25	1.00
	First day cover		1.50
	First day cover, #688-689		2.25
	Pane of 8 + label	12.00	

See Offices in Geneva Nos. 294-295; Vienna Nos. 210-211.

Flag Type of 1980

Printed by Helio Courvoisier, S.A., Switzerland. Designed by Oliver Corwin,US, and Robert Stein, UN. Each pane contains 4 blocks of 4 (Nos. 690-693, 694-697). A se-tenant block of 4 designs centers each pane.

1997, Feb. 12   Photo.   Perf. 12
Granite Paper

690	A185 32c Tadjikistan (940,000)+	.65	.50
691	A185 32c Georgia (940,000)+	.65	.50
692	A185 32c Armenia (940,000)+	.65	.50
693	A185 32c Namibia (940,000)+	.65	.50
a.	Block of 4, #690-693	2.60	2.00
694	A185 32c Liechtenstein (940,000)+	.65	.50
695	A185 32c Republic of Korea (940,000)+	.65	.50
696	A185 32c Kazakhstan (940,000)+	.65	.50
697	A185 32c Latvia (940,000)+	.65	.50
a.	Block of 4, #694-697	3.00	2.25
	First day cover, #690-697, each		2.00
	Set of 2 panes of 16	21.00	

First day covers of Nos. 690-697 total 136,114.

Cherry Blossoms, UN Headquarters — A297

Peace Rose — A298

Printed by The House of Questa, Ltd., UK.

1997, Feb. 12   Litho.   Perf. 14½

698	A297 8c multicolored (700,000)+	.20	.20
	First day cover		2.50
	Inscription block of 4	.60	—
699	A298 55c multicolored (700,000)+	1.10	.75
	First day cover		1.50
	First day cover, #698-699		3.50
	Inscription block of 4	4.50	—

First day covers of Nos. 698-699 total 34,794.

Endangered Species Type of 1993

Printed by Johann Enschedé and Sons, the Netherlands. Designed by Rocco J. Callari, US.
Designs: No. 700, African elephant. No. 701, Major Mitchell's cockatoo. No. 702, Black-footed ferret. No. 703, Cougar.

1997, Mar. 13   Litho.   Perf. 12½

700	A271 32c multicolored (532,000)+	.65	.50
701	A271 32c multicolored (532,000)+	.65	.50
702	A271 32c multicolored (532,000)+	.65	.50
703	A271 32c multicolored (532,000)+	.65	.50
a.	Block of 4, #700-703	2.75	2.00
	First day cover, #703a		3.50
	First day cover, #700-703, each		2.00
	Inscription block of 4, #703a	2.75	
	Pane of 16	11.00	

First day covers of Nos. 700-703 total 66,863.
See Offices in Geneva Nos. 298-301; Vienna Nos. 214-217.

Earth Summit, 5th Anniv. — A299

Printed by Helio Courvoisier SA, Switzerland. Designed by Peter Max, US.
Designs: No. 704, Sailboat. No. 705, Three sailboats. No. 706, Two people watching sailboat, sun. No. 707, Person, sailboat.
$1, Combined design similar to Nos. 704-707.

1997, May 30   Photo.   Perf. 11.5
Granite Paper

704	A299 32c multicolored (328,566)	.90	.60
705	A299 32c multicolored (328,566)	.90	.60
706	A299 32c multicolored (328,566)	.90	.60
707	A299 32c multicolored (328,566)	.90	.60
a.	Block of 4, #704-707	3.75	3.00
	First day cover, #707a		3.50
	First day cover, #704-707, each		1.25
	Inscription block of 4, #707a	2.75	

Souvenir Sheet

708	A299 $1 multicolored (181,667)	4.00	4.00
	First day cover		5.00
a.	Ovptd. in sheet margin (154,435)	20.00	20.00
	First day cover, #708a		20.00

First day covers of Nos. 704-708 total: New York, 52,528; San Francisco, 49,197.
See Offices in Geneva Nos. 302-306; Vienna Nos. 218-222.
No. 708 contains one 60x43mm stamp. Overprint in sheet margin of No. 708a reads "PACIFIC 97 / World Philatelic Exhibition / San Francisco, California / 29 May - 8 June 1997".

Transportation — A300

Printed by The House of Questa, UK. Panes of 20.
Designed by Michael Cockcroft, UK.

Ships: No. 709, Clipper ship. No. 710, Paddle steamer. No. 711, Ocean liner. No. 712, Hovercraft. No. 713, Hydrofoil.

1997, Aug. 29   Litho.   Perf. 14x14½

709	A300 32c multicolored (303,767)	.65	.30
710	A300 32c multicolored (303,767)	.65	.30
711	A300 32c multicolored (303,767)	.65	.30
712	A300 32c multicolored (303,767)	.65	.30
713	A300 32c multicolored (303,767)	.65	.30
a.	Strip of 5, #709-713	3.25	1.50
	First day cover, #713a		4.00
	First day cover, #709-713, each		1.25
	Inscription block of 10, 2#713a	6.50	

First day covers of Nos. 709-713 total 29,287.
See Offices in Geneva Nos. 307-311; Vienna Nos. 223-227.
No. 713a has continuous design.

Philately — A301

Printed by Joh. Enschedé and Sons, the Netherlands. Panes of 20. Designed by Robert Stein, US.
Designs: 32c, No. 473. 50c, No. 474.

1997, Oct. 14   Litho.   Perf. 13½x14

714	A301 32c multicolored (363,237)	1.00	.80
	First day cover		1.25
	Inscription block of 4	4.50	—
715	A301 50c multicolored (294,967)	2.25	1.75
	First day cover		1.50
	First day cover, #714-715		2.50
	Inscription block of 4	9.00	—

First day covers of Nos. 714-715 total 43,684.
See Offices in Geneva Nos. 312-313; Vienna Nos. 228-229.

World Heritage Convention, 25th Anniv. — A302

Printed by Government Printing Office, Austria. Panes of 20. Designed by Robert Stein, US, based on photographs by Guo Youmin, People's Republic of China.
Terracotta warriors of Xian: 32c, Single warrior. 60c, Massed warriors. No. 718a, like #716. No. 718b, like #717. No. 718c, like Geneva #314. No. 718d, like Geneva #315. No. 718e, like Vienna #230. No. 718f, like Vienna #231.

1997, Nov. 19   Litho.   Perf. 13½

716	A302 32c multicolored (549,095)	1.10	.75
	First day cover		1.25
	Inscription block of 4	4.50	—
717	A302 60c multicolored (505,265)	2.10	1.75
	First day cover		1.75
	First day cover, #716-717		2.75
	Inscription block of 4	8.50	—
718	Souvenir booklet (304,406 booklets)	8.00	
a.-f.	A302 8c any single	.30	.30
g.	Booklet pane of 4 #718a	1.25	1.25

h.	Booklet pane of 4 #718b	1.25	1.25
i.	Booklet pane of 4 #718c	1.25	1.25
j.	Booklet pane of 4 #718d	1.25	1.25
k.	Booklet pane of 4 #718e	1.25	1.25
l.	Booklet pane of 4 #718f	1.25	1.25

First day covers of Nos. 716-718 total 33,386.

See Offices in Geneva Nos. 314-316; Vienna Nos. 230-232.

Flag Type of 1980

Printed by Helio Courvoisier, S.A., Switzerland. Designed by Oliver Corwin, and Robert Stein, US. Each pane contains 4 blocks of 4 (Nos. 719-722, 723-726). A se-tenant block of 4 designs centers each pane.

1998, Feb. 13   **Photo.**   *Perf. 12*
Granite Paper

719	A185	32c Micronesia *(718,000)+*	.75	.50
720	A185	32c Slovakia *(718,000)+*	.75	.50
721	A185	32c Democratic People's Republic of Korea *(718,000)+*	.75	.50
722	A185	32c Azerbaijan *(718,000)+*	.75	.50
a.		Block of 4, #719-722	3.50	—
723	A185	32c Uzbekistan *(718,000)+*	.75	.50
724	A185	32c Monaco *(718,000)+*	.75	.50
725	A185	32c Czech Republic *(718,000)+*	.75	.50
726	A185	32c Estonia *(718,000)+*	.75	.50
a.		Block of 4, #723-726	3.50	—
		First day cover, #719-726, each		1.75
		Set of 2 panes of 16	21.00	
		Nos. 719-726 (8)	6.00	4.00

A303

A304   United Nations   2c

A305

Printed by The House of Questa, UK. Designed by Zhang Le Lu, China (1c), Robert Stein, US (2c), Gregory Halili, Philippines (21c). Panes of 20.

1998, Feb. 13   Litho.   Perf. 14½x15, 15x14½

727	A303	1c multicolored *(1,000,000)+*	.20	.20
		First day cover		1.00
		Inscription block of 4	.20	—
728	A304	2c multicolored *(1,000,000)+*	.20	.20
		First day cover		1.00
		Inscription block of 4	.20	—
729	A305	21c multicolored *(1,000,000)+*	.45	.20
		First day cover		1.00
		First day cover, #727-729		1.25
		Inscription block of 4	1.80	—
		Nos. 727-729 (3)	.85	.60

Endangered Species Type of 1993

Printed by Johann Enschedé and Sons, the Netherlands. Designed by Rocco J. Callari, US and Pat Medearis-Altman, New Zealand.

Designs: No. 730, Lesser galago. No. 731, Hawaiian goose. No. 732, Golden birdwing. No. 733, Sun bear.

1998, Mar. 13   Litho.   Perf. 12½

730	A271	32c multicolored *(502,000)+*	.65	.30
731	A271	32c multicolored *(502,000)+*	.65	.30
732	A271	32c multicolored *(502,000)+*	.65	.30
733	A271	32c multicolored *(502,000)+*	.65	.30
a.		Block of 4, #730-733	2.75	1.40
		First day cover, #733a		3.50
		First day cover, #730-733, each		1.25
		Pane of 16	17.50	

See Offices in Geneva Nos. 318-321; Vienna Nos. 235-238.

Intl. Year of the Ocean — A306

Printed by Johann Enschedé and Sons, the Netherlands. Designed by Larry Taugher, US.

1998, May 20   Litho.   Perf. 13x13½

734	A306	Sheet of 12 *(280,000)+*	6.25	4.00
		First day cover		10.00
a.-l.		32c any single	.50	.30
		First day cover, #734a-734l, each		2.00

See Offices in Geneva No. 322; Vienna No. 239.

Rain Forests — A307

Printed by Government Printing Bureau, Japan. Designed by Rick Garcia, US.

1998, June 19   Litho.   Perf. 13x13½

735	A307	32c Jaguar *(570,000)+*	.65	.50
		First day cover		2.50
		Inscription block of 4	2.75	—

Souvenir Sheet

736	A307	$2 like #735 *(280,000)+*	4.00	3.00
		First day cover		6.00

See Offices in Geneva Nos. 323-324; Vienna Nos. 240-241.

U.N. Peacekeeping Forces, 50th Anniv. — A308

Printed by Helio Courvoisier, S.A. (Switzerland). Designed by Andrew Davidson, UK.

Designs: 33c, Commander with binoculars. 40c, Two soldiers on vehicle.

1998, Sept. 15   Photo.   Perf. 12

737	A308	33c multicolored *(485,000)+*	.85	.60
		First day cover		1.25
		Inscription block of 4	3.50	—
738	A308	40c multicolored *(445,000)+*	1.25	.90
		First day cover		1.25
		First day cover, #737-738		2.00
		Inscription block of 4	5.25	—

See Offices in Geneva Nos. 325-326; Vienna Nos. 242-243.

Universal Declaration of Human Rights, 50th Anniv. — A309

Printed by Cartor Security Printing (France). Designed by Jean-Michel Folon, France.

Stylized people: 32c, Carrying flag. 55c, Carrying pens.

1998, Oct. 27   Litho. & Photo.   Perf. 13

739	A309	32c multicolored *(485,000)+*	.65	.50
		First day cover		1.25
		Inscription block of 4	2.75	—
740	A309	55c multicolored *(445,000)+*	1.10	.75
		First day cover		1.50
		First day cover, #739-740		2.50
		Inscription block of 4	4.50	—

See Offices in Geneva Nos. 327-328; Vienna Nos. 244-245.

Schönbrunn Palace, Vienna — A310

Printed by the House of Questa, UK. Panes of 20. Designed by Robert Stein, US.

Designs: 33c, #743f, The Gloriette. 60c, #743b, Wall painting on fabric (detail), by Johann Wenzl Bergl, vert. No. 743a, Blue porcelain vase, vert. No. 743c, Porcelain stove, vert. No. 743d, Palace. No. 743e, Great Palm House (conservatory).

1998, Dec. 4   Litho.   Perf. 14

741	A310	33c multicolored *(485,000)+*	.65	.50
		First day cover		1.25
		Inscription block of 4	2.75	—
742	A310	60c multicolored *(445,000)+*	1.25	.90
		First day cover		1.50
		First day cover, #741-742		2.50
		Inscription block of 4	5.00	—

Souvenir Booklet

743		Booklet *(110,000)+*	6.00	
a.-c.		A310 11c any single	.25	.25
d.-f.		A310 15c any single	.30	.30
g.		Booklet pane of 4 #743d	1.25	
h.		Booklet pane of 3 #743a	.75	
i.		Booklet pane of 3 #743b	.75	
j.		Booklet pane of 3 #743c	.75	
k.		Booklet pane of 4 #743e	1.25	
l.		Booklet pane of 4 #743f	1.25	

See Offices in Geneva Nos. 329-331; Vienna Nos. 246-248.

Flag Type of 1980

Printed by Helio Courvoisier S.A., Switzerland. Designed by Oliver Corwin, Robert Stein and Blake Tarpley, US. Each pane contains 4 blocks of 4 (Nos. 744-747, 748-751). A se-tenant block of 4 designs centers each pane.

1999, Feb. 5   Photo.   Perf. 12

744	A185	33c Lithuania *(524,000)+*	.70	.50
745	A185	33c San Marino *(524,000)+*	.70	.50
746	A185	33c Turkmenistan *(524,000)+*	.70	.50
747	A185	33c Marshall Islands *(524,000)+*	.70	.50
a.		Block of 4, #744-747	3.00	—
748	A185	33c Moldova *(524,000)+*	.70	.50
749	A185	33c Kyrgyzstan *(524,000)+*	.70	.50
750	A185	33c Bosnia & Herzegovina *(524,000)+*	.70	.50
751	A185	33c Eritrea *(524,000)+*	.70	.50
a.		Block of 4, #748-751	3.00	—
		First day cover, #744-751, each		1.25
		Set of 2 panes of 16	21.00	
		Nos. 744-751 (8)	5.60	4.00

First day covers of Nos. 744-751 total 102,040.

Flags and
Globe — A311

Roses — A312

Designed by Blake Tarpley (#752), Rorie Katz, (#753), US. Printed by Johann Enschedé and Sons, the Netherlands (#752), Helio Courvoisier SA, Switzerland (#753).

1999, Feb. 5	**Litho.**	**Perf. 14x13½**	
752	A311 33c multicolored (960,000)+	.65	.30
	First day cover		1.25
	Inscription block of 4	2.75	—

Photo.
Granite Paper
Perf. 11½x12

753	A312 $5 multicolored (420,000)+	8.50	2.00
	First day cover		7.50
	First day cover, #752-753		8.25
	Inscription block of 4	35.00	—

First day covers of Nos. 752-753 total 32,142.

World Heritage
Sites, Australia
A313

Printed by House of Questa, UK. Panes of 20. Designed by Passmore Design, Australia.
Designs: 33c, #756f, Willandra Lakes region. 60c, #756b, Wet tropics of Queensland. No. 756a, Tasmanian wilderness. No. 756c, Great Barrier Reef. No. 756d, Uluru-Kata Tjuta Natl. Park. No. 756e, Kakadu Natl. Park.

1999, Mar. 19	**Litho.**	**Perf. 13**	
754	A313 33c multicolored (480,000)+	.65	.30
	First day cover		1.25
	Inscription block of 4	2.75	—
755	A313 60c multicolored (440,000)+	1.25	.65
	First day cover		1.50
	First day cover, #754-755		2.50
	Inscription block of 4	5.00	—

Souvenir Booklet

756	Booklet (97,000)+	5.00	
a.-c.	A313 5c any single	.20	.20
d.-f.	A313 15c any single	.30	.30
g.	Booklet pane of 4, #756a	.40	
h.	Booklet pane of 4, #756d	1.25	
i.	Booklet pane of 4, #756b	.40	
j.	Booklet pane of 4, #756e	1.25	
k.	Booklet pane of 4, #756c	.40	
l.	Booklet pane of 4, #756f	1.25	

First day covers of Nos. 754-756 total 42,385.
See Offices in Geneva Nos. 333-335; Vienna Nos. 250-252.

Endangered Specied Type of 1993

Printed by Johann Enschedé and Sons, the Netherlands. Designed by Jimmy Wang, China.
Designs: No. 757, Tiger. No. 758, Secretary bird. No. 759, Green tree python. No. 760, Long-tailed chinchilla.

1999, Apr. 22	**Litho.**	**Perf. 12½**	
757	A271 33c multicolored (494,000)+	.65	.20
758	A271 33c multicolored (494,000)+	.65	.20
759	A271 33c multicolored (494,000)+	.65	.20
760	A271 33c multicolored (494,000)+	.65	.20
a.	Block of 4, #757-760	2.60	
	First day cover, #760a		3.50
	First day cover, #757-760, each		1.25
	Pane of 16	10.50	

First day covers of Nos. 757-760 total 49,656.
See Offices in Geneva Nos. 336-339; Vienna Nos. 253-256.

UNISPACE III, Vienna — A314

Printed by Helio Courvoisier SA, Switzerland. Designed by Attila Hejja, US.
Designs: No. 761, Probe on planet's surface. No. 762, Planetary rover. No. 763, Composite of #761-762.

1999, July 7	**Photo.**	**Rouletted 8**	
761	A314 33c multicolored (1,000,000)+	.85	.50
762	A314 33c multicolored (1,000,000)+	.85	.50
a.	Pair, #761-762	1.75	1.00
	First day cover, #762a		2.00
	First day cover, #761-762, each		1.25
	Inscription block of 4	2.60	—
	Pane of 10, #761-762	6.50	—

Souvenir Sheet
Perf. 14½

763	A314 $2 multicolored (530,000)+	4.25	2.00
	First day cover		3.00
a.	Ovptd. in sheet margin	4.00	2.00
	First day cover		4.75

No. 763a was issued 7/7/00 and is overprinted in violet blue "WORLD STAMP EXPO 2000 / ANAHEIM, CALIFORNIA / U.S.A./ 7-16 JULY 2000."
First day covers of Nos. 761-763 total 48,190.
See Offices in Geneva #340-342; Vienna #257-259.

UPU, 125th
Anniv. — A315

Printed by Helio Courvoisier S.A., Switzerland. Panes of 24. Designed by Mark Hess, US.

Various people, 19th century methods of mail transportation, denomination at: No. 764, UL. No. 765, UR. No. 766, LL. No. 767, LR.

1999, Aug. 23	**Photo.**	**Perf. 11¾**	
764	A315 33c multicolored (378,000)+	.65	.30
765	A315 33c multicolored (378,000)+	.65	.30
766	A315 33c multicolored (378,000)+	.65	.30
767	A315 33c multicolored (378,000)+	.65	.30
a.	Block of 4, #764-767	2.60	—
	Inscription block of 4	2.60	—
	First day cover, #767a		3.50
	First day cover, #764-767, each		1.25

First day covers of Nos. 764-767 total 25,294.
See Offices in Geneva Nos. 343-346; Vienna Nos. 260-263.

In Memoriam — A316

Printed by Walsall Security Printers, Ltd., United Kingdom. Panes of 20. Designed by Robert Stein, US.

Designs: 33c, $1, UN Headquarters. Size of $1 stamp: 34x63mm.

1999, Sept. 21	**Litho.**	**Perf. 14½x14**	
768	A316 33c multicolored (550,000)+	.65	.30
	Inscription block of 4	2.60	—
	First day cover		1.25

Souvenir Sheet
Perf. 14

769	A316 $1 multicolored (235,000)+	2.00	1.00
	First day cover		2.00

First day covers of Nos. 768-769 total 42,130.

See Offices in Geneva #347-348, Vienna #264-265.

Education,
Keystone to the
21st
Century — A317

Printed by Government Printing Office, Austria. Panes of 20. Designed by Romero Britto, Brazil.

1999, Nov. 18	**Litho.**	**Perf. 13½x13¾**	
770	A317 33c Two readers (450,000)+	.65	.30
	First day cover		1.25
	Inscription block of 4	2.60	—
771	A317 60c Heart (430,000)+	1.25	.60
	First day cover		1.50
	First day cover, #770-771		2.50
	Inscription block of 4	5.00	—

First day covers of Nos. 770-771 total 34,679.
See Offices in Geneva Nos. 349-350, Vienna Nos. 266-267.

International Year of
Thanksgiving — A318

Printed by Cartor Security Printing, France. Panes of 20. Designed by Rorie Katz, US.

2000, Jan. 1	**Litho.**	**Perf. 13¼x13½**	
772	A318 33c multicolored (550,000)+	.65	.30
	First day cover		1.25
	Inscription block of 4	2.60	—

On No. 772 portions of the design were applied by a thermographic process producing a shiny, raised effect. See Offices in Geneva No. 351, Vienna No. 268.

Endangered Species Type of 1993

Printed by Johann Enschedé and Sons, the Netherlands. Designed by Suzanne Duranceau, Canada.
Designs: No. 773, Brown bear. No. 774, Black-bellied bustard. No. 775, Chinese crocodile lizard. No. 776, Pygmy chimpanzee.

2000, Apr. 6	**Litho.**	**Perf. 12¾x12½**	
773	A271 33c multicolored (490,000)+	.65	.30
774	A271 33c multicolored (490,000)+	.65	.30
775	A271 33c multicolored (490,000)+	.65	.30
776	A271 33c multicolored (490,000)+	.65	.30
a.	Block of 4, #773-776	2.60	—
	First day cover, #776a		3.50
	First day cover, #773-776, each		1.25
	Pane of 16	10.50	

See Offices in Geneva Nos. 352-355; Vienna Nos. 269-272.

Our World
2000 — A319

Printed by Cartor Security Printing, France. Panes of 20. Designed by Robert Stein, US.
Winning artwork in Millennium painting competition: 33c, Crawling Toward the Millennium, by Sam Yeates, US. 60c, Crossing, by Masakazu Takahata, Japan, vert.

2000, May 30	**Litho.**	**Perf. 13x13½, 13½x13**	
777	A319 33c multicolored (400,000)+	.65	.30
	First day cover		1.25
	Inscription block of 4	2.60	—
778	A319 60c multicolored (360,000)+	1.25	.60
	First day cover		1.50
	First day cover, #777-778		2.50
	Inscription block of 4	5.00	—

See Offices in Geneva No. 356-357, Vienna No. 273-274.

55TH ANNIVERSARY UNITED NATIONS 33c   UN, 55th Anniv. — A320

Printed by Cartor Security Printing, France. Panes of 20. Designed by Rorie Katz, US.

Designs: 33c, Workmen removing decorative discs in General Assembly Hall, 1956. 55c, UN Building in 1951.

			2000, July 7	Litho.	Perf. 13¼x13
779	A320	33c	multicolored (400,000)+	.65	.30
			First day cover		1.25
			Inscription block of 4	2.60	—
780	A320	55c	multicolored (360,000)+	1.10	.55
			First day cover		1.50
			First day cover, #779-780		2.25
			Inscription block of 4	4.50	—
			Souvenir Sheet		
781	A320		Sheet of 2, #779-780 (277,000)+	1.75	.90
			First day cover		2.40

See Offices in Geneva No. 358-360, Vienna No. 275-277.

2000 END-OF-YEAR ISSUES

The UNPA has announced that the following items will be released in late 2000. Dates and denominations are tentative.

Unites Nations in the 21st Century *Sept. 19*, 33c, Geneva 45c. Vienna 3.50s.

World Heritage - Spain, *Oct. 6*, booklets containing 33c, 60c; Geneva 90, 1.10fr; Vienna 4.50s, 6,50s stamps.

Refugees, *Nov. 9*, 33c, 60c, souvenir card.

AIR POST

Plane and Gull — AP1

Swallows and UN Emblem — AP2

Engraved and printed by Thomas De La Rue & Co., Ltd., London. Panes of 50. Designed by Ole Hamann (AP1) and Olav Mathiesen (AP2).

			1951, Dec. 14	Unwmk.	Perf. 14
C1	AP1	6c	henna brown (2,500,000)	.20	.20
			First day cover		2.00
			Inscription block of 4	.25	
C2	AP1	10c	bright blue green (2,750,000)	.20	.20
			First day cover		2.00
			Inscription block of 4	.60	
C3	AP2	15c	deep ultramarine (3,250,000)	.20	.25
			First day cover		3.00
			Inscription block of 4	.75	
a.			15c Prussian blue	100.00	
C4	AP2	25c	gray black (2,250,000)	.70	.35
			First day cover		7.50
			First day cover, #C1-C4		27.50
			Inscription block of 4	4.00	—
			Nos. C1-C4 (4)	1.30	1.00

First day covers of Nos. 1-11 and C1-C4 total 1,113,216.

Early printings of Nos. C1-C4 have wide, imperforate sheet margins on three sides. Later printings were perforated through all margins.

Nos. C1, C3 and C4 exist imperforate.

Airplane Wing and Globe — AP3

Engraved and printed by Thomas De La Rue & Co., Ltd., London. Panes of 50. Designed by W. W. Wind.

			1957, May 27		Perf. 12½x14
C5	AP3	4c	maroon (5,000,000)	.20	.20
			First day cover (282,933)		1.00
			Inscription block of 4	.30	—

For 5c see No. C6.

Type of 1957 and

UN Flag and Plane — AP4

Engraved and printed by Waterlow & Sons, Ltd., London. Panes of 50. Designed by W. W. Wind (5c) and Olav Mathiesen (7c).

			1959, Feb. 9	Unwmk.	Perf. 12½x13½
C6	AP3	5c	rose red (4,000,000)	.20	.20
			First day cover		1.00
			Inscription block of 4	.40	—
				Perf. 13½x14	
C7	AP4	7c	ultramarine (4,000,000)	.20	.20
			First day cover, #C6-C7		1.00
					17.50
			Inscription block of 4	.60	—

First day covers of Nos. C6 and C7 total 413,556.

Outer Space — AP5

UN Emblem — AP6

Bird of Laurel Leaves — AP7

Printed by Courvoisier S.A., La Chaux-de-Fonds, Switzerland. Panes of 50. Designed by Claude Bottiau (6c), George Hamori (8c) and Kurt Plowitz (13c).

			1963, June 17	Photo. Unwmk.	Perf. 11½
C8	AP5	6c	black, blue & yellow green (4,000,000)	.20	.20
			First day cover		1.00
			Inscription block of 4	.45	—
C9	AP6	8c	yellow, olive green & red (4,000,000)	.20	.20
			First day cover		1.00
			Inscription block of 4	.60	—
				Perf. 12½x12	
C10	AP7	13c	ultra, aquamarine, gray & carmine (2,700,000)	.20	.20
			First day cover		1.00
			First day cover, #C8-C10		8.50
			Inscription block of 4	.90	—

First day covers of Nos. C8-C10 total 535,824.

"Flight Across the Globe" — AP8

Jet Plane and Envelope — AP9

Printed by the Austrian Government Printing Office, Vienna, Austria. Panes of 50. Designed by Ole Hamann (15c) and George Hamori (25c).

			Perf. 11½x12, 12x11½		
			1964, May 1	Photo.	Unwmk.
C11	AP8	15c	violet, buff, gray & pale green (3,000,000)	.25	.20
			First day cover		1.00
			Inscription block of 4	1.25	—
a.			Gray omitted		
C12	AP9	25c	yellow, orange, gray, blue & red (2,000,000)	.50	.30
			First day cover		1.00
			First day cover, #C11-C12		8.00
			Inscription block of 4	2.50	—
			Nos. C8-C12 (5)	1.35	1.10

First day covers of Nos. C11-C12 total 353,696.
For 75c in type AP8, see UN Offices in Geneva No. 8.
Nos. C11-C12 exist imperforate.

Jet Plane and UN Emblem — AP10

Printed by Setelipaino, Finland. Panes of 50. Designed by Ole Hamann.

			1968, Apr. 18	Litho.	Perf. 13
C13	AP10	20c	multicolored (3,000,000)	.30	.25
			First day cover (225,378)		1.00
			Inscription block of 4	1.50	—

Wings, Envelopes and UN Emblem — AP11

Printed by Setelipaino, Finland. Panes of 50. Designed by Olav S. Mathiesen.

			1969, Apr. 21	Litho.	Perf. 13
C14	AP11	10c	orange vermilion, orange, yellow & black (4,000,000)	.20	.20
			First day cover (132,686)		1.00
			Inscription block of 4	.75	—

UN Emblem and Stylized Wing — AP12

Birds in Flight — AP13

Clouds — AP14

"UN" and
Plane — AP15

Printed by Government Printing Bureau, Japan (9c); Heraclio Fournier, S. A., Spain (11c, 17c); Setelipaino, Finland (21c). Panes of 50. Designed by Lyell L. Dolan (9c), Arne Johnson (11c), British American Bank Note Co. (17c) and Asher Kalderon (21c).

		1972, May 1	Litho. & Engr.	Perf. 13x13½	
C15	AP12	9c light blue, dark red & violet			
		blue (3,000,000)+		.20	.20
		First day cover			1.00
		Inscription block of 4		.50	—
		Photo.			
		Perf. 14x13½			
C16	AP13	11c blue & multicolored			
		(3,000,000)+		.20	.20
		First day cover			1.00
		Inscription block of 4		.75	—
		Perf. 13½x14			
C17	AP14	17c yellow, red & orange			
		(3,000,000)+		.25	.20
		First day cover			1.00
		Inscription block of 4		1.10	—
		Perf. 13			
C18	AP15	21c silver & multi (3,500,000)		.25	.25
		First day cover			1.00
		First day cover, #C15-C18			3.50
		Inscription block of 4		1.25	—
		Nos. C15-C18 (4)		.90	.85

First day covers of Nos. C15-C18 total 553,535.

Globe and Jet — AP16

Pathways Radiating from UN Emblem — AP17

Bird in Flight, UN Headquarters AP18

Printed by Setelipaino, Finland. Panes of 50. Designed by George Hamori (13c), Shamir Bros. (18c) and Ölav S. Mathiesen (26c).

		1974, Sept. 16	Litho.	Perf. 13, 12½x13 (18c)	
C19	AP16	13c multicolored (2,500,000)+		.20	.20
		First day cover			1.00
		Inscription block of 4		.80	—
C20	AP17	18c gray olive & multicolored			
		(2,000,000)		.25	.20
		First day cover			1.00
		Inscription block of 4		1.10	—
C21	AP18	26c blue & multi (2,000,000)		.35	.30
		First day cover			1.25
		First day cover, #C19-C21			2.50
		Inscription block of 4		1.60	—
		Nos. C19-C21 (3)		.80	.70

First day covers of Nos. C19-C21 total 309,610.

Winged Airmail Letter — AP19 ... Symbolic Globe and Plane — AP20

Printed by Heraclio Fournier, S.A. Panes of 50. Designed by Eliezer Weishoff (25c) and Alan L. Pollock (31c).

		1977, June 27	Photo.	Perf. 14	
C22	AP19	25c greenish blue & multi			
		(2,000,000)+		.35	.25
		First day cover			1.25
		Inscription block of 4		1.60	—
C23	AP20	31c magenta (2,000,000)		.40	.30
		First day cover			1.25
		First day cover, #C22-C23			1.50
		Inscription block of 4		1.90	—

First day covers of Nos. C22-C23 total 209,060.

ENVELOPES

Emblem of United Nations — U1

Printed by the International Envelope Corp., Dayton, Ohio. Die engraved by the American Bank Note Co., New York.

		1953, Sept. 15		Embossed	
U1	U1	3c blue, entire (555,000)		.40	.40
		Entire, first day cancel (102,278)			1.00

Printed by International Envelope Corp., Dayton, Ohio.

		1958, Sept. 22		Embossed	
U2	U1	4c ultramarine, entire (1,000,000)		.40	.20
		Entire, first day cancel (213,621)			1.00

Stylized Globe and Weather Vane — U2

Printed by United States Envelope Co., Springfield, Mass. Designed by Hatim El Mekki.

		1963, Apr. 26		Litho.	
U3	U2	5c multicolored, entire (1,115,888)		.25	.20
		Entire, first day cancel (165,188)			1.00

Printed by Setelipaino, Finland.

		1969, Jan. 8		Litho.	
U4	U2	6c black, blue, magenta & dull yellow, entire (850,000)		.25	.20
		Entire, first day cancel (152,593)			1.00

Headquarters Type of Regular Issue, 1968
Printed by Eureka Co., a division of Litton Industries.

		1973, Jan. 12		Litho.	
U5	A99	8c sepia, blue & olive, entire (700,000)		.50	.20
		Entire, first day cancel (145,510)			1.00

Headquarters Type of Regular Issue, 1974
Printed by United States Envelope Co., Springfield, Mass.

		1975, Jan. 10		Litho.	
U6	A138	10c blue, olive bister & multi, entire (547,500)		.40	.20
		Entire, first day cancel (122,000)			1.00

Bouquet of Ribbons — U3

Printed by Carl Ueberreuter Druck and Verlag M. Salzer, Austria. Designed by George Hamori, Australia.

		1985, May 10		Litho.	
U7	U3	22c multicolored, entire (250,000)		8.50	.40
		Entire, first day cancel (28,600)			5.00

New York Headquarters U4

Printed by Mercury Walch, Australia. Designed by Rocco J. Callari, United States.

		1989, Mar. 17		Litho.	
U8	U4	25c multicolored, entire (350,000)		2.75	.35
		Entire, first day cancel (28,567)			6.00

For surcharge see No. U9A.

No. U8 Surcharged

		1991, Apr. 15		Litho.	
U9	U4	25c +4c multicolored, entire (50,000)+		2.75	.40
		Entire, first day cover			5.50

No. U8 Surcharged

		1995		Litho.	
U9A	U4	25c +7c multicolored, entire		2.50	.50
		Entire, first day cover			6.00

Cripticandina, by Alfredo La Placa — U5

Illustration reduced.
Design sizes: No. U10, 79x38mm. No. U11, 89x44mm.

		1997, Feb. 12		Litho.	
U10	U5	32c multicolored, #6¾, entire (65,000)+		3.00	.45
		Entire, first day cancel			5.50
U11	U5	32c multicolored, #10, entire (80,000)+		2.00	.45
		Entire, first day cancel			3.00

Nos. U10-U11 Surcharged

1999, Jan. 10 — Litho.
U12 U5 32c +1c **multicolored**, on #U10, entire .85 .45
  First day cancel, entire 1.25
U13 U5 32c +1c **multicolored**, on #U11, entire .85 .45
  First day cancel, entire 1.25

AIR POST ENVELOPES AND AIR LETTER SHEETS

Used values are for non-philatelic contemporaneous usages.

Letter Sheet
Type of Air Post Stamp of 1951
Inscribed "Air Letter" at Left
Printed by Dennison & Sons, Long Island City, NY.
1952, Aug. 29 — Litho.
UC1 AP2 10c **blue**, *bluish*, entire *(187,000)* 22.50 20.00
  Entire, 1st day cancel *(57,274)* 2.50
  Designed by C. Mutver.

Letter Sheet
Inscribed "Air Letter" and "Aerogramme" at Left
1954, Sept. 14 — Litho.
UC2 AP2 10c **royal blue**, *bluish*, entire, *(207,000)* 9.50 1.00
  Entire, 1st day cancel 200.00
  a. No white border, *1958 (148,800)* 7.00 6.00

No. UC2 was printed with a narrow white border (½ to 1mm wide) surrounding the stamp. On No. UC2a, this border has been partly or entirely eliminated.

UN Flag and Plane — UC1

(UN Emblem Embossed)
Printed by International Envelope Corp., Dayton, O.
Die engraved by American Bank Note Co., New York.
1959, Sept. 21 — Embossed
UC3 UC1 7c **blue**, entire *(550,000)* 1.25 1.25
  Entire, 1st day cancel *(172,107)* 1.00

Letter Sheet
Type of Air Post Stamp of 1959
Printed by Thomas De La Rue & Co., Ltd., London
1960, Jan. 18 — Litho.
UC4 AP4 10c **ultramarine**, *bluish*, entire *(405,000)* .65 .65
  Entire, 1st day cancel *(122,425)* 1.00

Printed on protective tinted paper containing colorless inscription "United Nations" in the five official languages of the UN.

Letter Sheet
Type of Air Post Stamp of 1951
Inscribed "Correo Aereo" instead of "Poste Aerienne"
Printed by Thomas De La Rue & Co., Ltd., London
1961, June 26 — Litho.
UC5 AP1 11c **ultramarine**, *bluish*, entire *(550,000)* .50 .20
  Entire, 1st day cancel *(128,557)* 1.00
  a. 11c **dark blue**, *green* entire, *July 16, 1965 (419,000)* 1.25 1.25

Printed on protective tinted paper containing colorless inscription "United Nations" in the five official languages of the UN.

UN Emblem — UC2

Printed by United States Envelope Co., Springfield, Mass.
Designed by George Hamori.

1963, Apr. 26 — Litho.
UC6 UC2 8c **multicolored**, entire *(880,000)* .30 .20
  Entire, 1st day cancel *(165,208)* 1.00

Letter Sheet

UN Emblem and Stylized Plane — UC3

Printed by Setelipaino, Finland. Designed by Robert Perrot.

1968, May 31 — Litho.
UC7 UC3 13c **violet blue & light blue**, entire *(750,000)* .30 .25
  Entire, 1st day cancel *(106,700)* 1.00

Type of 1963
Printed by Setelipaino, Finland.
1969, Jan. 8 — Litho.
UC8 UC2 10c **pink, Prussian blue, orange & sepia**, entire *(750,000)* .35 .20
  Entire, 1st day cancel *(153,472)* 1.00

Letter Sheet

UN Emblem, "UN," Globe and Plane — UC4

Printed by Joh. Enschede and Sons. Designed by Edmondo Calivis, Egypt. Sheet surface printed in greenish blue.

1972, Oct. 16 — Litho.
UC9 UC4 15c **violet blue & greenish blue**, entire *(500,000)* .60 .20
  Entire, 1st day cancel *(85,500)* 1.00

Bird Type of Air Post Stamp, 1972
Printed by Eureka Co., a division of Litton Industries
1973, Jan. 12 — Litho.
UC10 AP13 11c **blue & multicolored**, entire *(700,000)* .40 .20
  Entire, 1st day cancel *(134,500)* 1.00

Globe and Jet Air Post Type of 1974
Printed by United States Envelope Co., Springfield, Mass.
1975, Jan. 10 — Litho.
UC11 AP16 13c **blue & multicolored**, entire *(555,539)* .60 .20
  Entire, 1st day cancel *(122,000)* 1.00

Letter Sheet
Headquarters Type of Regular Issue, 1971
Printed by Joh. Enschede and Sons, Netherlands
1975, Jan. 10 — Photo.
UC12 A120 18c **blue & multicolored**, entire *(400,000)* .60 .20
  Entire, 1st day cancel *(70,500)* 1.00

Letter Sheet

"UN" Emblem and Birds UC5

Printed by Joh. Enschede and Sons. Designed by Angel Medina Medina.

1977, June 27 — Litho.
UC13 UC5 22c **multicolored**, entire *(400,000)* .65 .20
  Entire, 1st day cancel *(70,000)* 1.00

Letter Sheet

Paper Airplane UC6

Printed by Joh. Enschede and Sons.
Designed by Margaret-Ann Champion.
1982, Apr. 28 — Litho.
UC14 UC6 30c **black**, *pale green*, entire *(400,000)* 1.50 .50
  Entire, 1st day cancel *(61,400)* 1.25

Letter Sheet No. UC14 Surcharged
1987, July 7 — Litho.
UC15 UC6 30c + 6c **black**, *green*, entire *(43,000)* 45.00 4.25
  Entire, 1st day cancel 16.00

New York Headquarters UC7

Printed by Mercury Walch, Australia. Designed by Thomas Lee, China.

1989, Mar. 17 — Litho.
UC16 UC7 39c **multicolored**, entire *(350,000)* 3.50 .40
  Entire, 1st day cancel *(14,798)* 9.50

No. UC16 Surcharged

1991, Feb. 12 — Litho.
UC17 UC7 39c + 6c **multicolored**, entire *(35,563)* 16.00 .45
  Entire, first day cancel 8.50

UC8

Designed by Robert Stein. Printed by Mercury-Walch, Australia.
1992, Sept. 4 — Litho.
UC18 UC8 45c **multicolored**, entire, *(185,000)*+ 2.40 .55
  First day cancel 10.00

Letter Sheet No. UC18 Surcharged

1995, July 9 — Litho.
UC19 UC8 45c +5c **multicolored**, entire 5.00 .60
  First day cover 9.00

Cherry Blossoms — UC9

1997, Mar. 13 Litho.
UC20 UC9 50c **multicolored,** entire (115,000)+ 2.50 .50
Entire, first day cancel 2.50

No. UC20 Surcharged

1999, Aug. 23 Litho.
UC21 UC9 50c **+10c multicolored,** entire 1.25 .65
Entire, first day cancel 1.75

POSTAL CARDS

Values are for entire cards.

Type of Postage Issue of 1951

Printed by Dennison & Sons, Long Island City, N.Y.

1952, July 18 Litho.
UX1 A2 2c **blue,** buff (899,415) .20 .20
First day cancel (116,023) 1.00

Printed by British American Bank Note Co., Ltd.,
Ottawa, Canada

1958, Sept. 22 Litho.
UX2 A2 3c **gray olive,** buff (575,000) .20 .20
First day cancel (145,557) 1.00

World Map,
Sinusoidal
Projection — PC1

Printed by Eureka Specialty Printing Co., Scranton, Pa.

1963, Apr. 26 Litho.
UX3 PC1 4c **light blue, violet blue, orange &**
bright citron (784,000) .25 .20
First day cancel (112,280) 1.00
a. Bright citron omitted —

UN Emblem and Post
Horn — PC2   "UN" — PC3

Printed by Canadian Bank Note Co., Ltd., Ottawa. Designed
by John Mason.

1969, Jan. 8 Litho.
UX4 PC2 5c **blue & black** (500,000) .25 .20
First day cancel (95,975) 1.00

1973, Jan. 12 Litho.
Printed by Government Printing Bureau, Tokyo. Designed by
Asher Kalderon.
UX5 PC3 6c **gray & multicolored** (500,000) .20 .20
First day cancel (84,500) 1.00

Type of 1973

Printed by Setelipaino, Finland.

1975, Jan. 10 Litho.
UX6 PC3 8c **light green & multi** (450,000) .60 .20
First day cancel (72,500) 1.00

UN Emblem — PC4

Printed by Setelipaino, Finland. Designed by George Hamori.

1977, June 27 Litho.
UX7 PC4 9c **multicolored** (350,000) .60 .20
First day cancel (70,000) 1.00

Printed by Courvoisier. Designed by Salahattin Kanidinc.

1982, Apr. 28 Photo.
UX8 PC5 13c **multicolored** (350,000) .50 .20
First day cancel (59,200) 1.00

Views of New
York
Headquarters
PC6

Designs: No. UX9, Complex, lawn. No. UX10, Complex pho-
tographed through trees. No. UX11, Flags. No. UX12, General
Assembly interior. No. UX13, View of complex from the East
River. No. UX14, Complex and flags. No. UX15, Flagpoles. No.
UX16, Complex at dusk. No. UX17, Close-up of Security Coun-
cil. No. UX18, Complex and sculpture in park. Nos. UX9-UX10
and UX14-UX16 vert.
Printed by Johann Enschede and Sons, the Netherlands.
Designed by Thomas Lee, China, from photographs.

1989, Mar. 17 Litho.
UX9 PC6 15c **multicolored** (120,000)+ .80 .40
First day cancel 2.25
UX10 PC6 15c **multicolored** (120,000)+ .80 .40
First day cancel 2.25
UX11 PC6 15c **multicolored** (120,000)+ .80 .40
First day cancel 2.25
UX12 PC6 15c **multicolored** (120,000)+ .80 .40
First day cancel 2.25
UX13 PC6 15c **multicolored** (120,000)+ .80 .40
First day cancel 2.25
UX14 PC6 36c **multicolored** (120,000)+ 1.20 .60
First day cancel 2.60
UX15 PC6 36c **multicolored** (120,000)+ 1.20 .60
First day cancel 2.60
UX16 PC6 36c **multicolored** (120,000)+ 1.20 .60
First day cancel 2.60
UX17 PC6 36c **multicolored** (120,000)+ 1.20 .60
First day cancel 2.60
UX18 PC6 36c **multicolored** (120,000)+ 1.20 .60
First day cancel 2.60
Nos. UX9-UX18 (10) 10.00 5.00

Nos. UX9-UX13 and UX14-UX18 sold only in sets. Nos.
UX9-UX13 sold for $2 and Nos. UX14-UX18 sold for $3.
First day cancels of Nos. UX9-UX18 total 125,526.

New York Headquarters Type of 1991

Printed by Mercury-Walch, Australia.

1992, Sept. 4 Litho.
UX19 A260 40c **blue** (150,000)+ 3.50 .40
First day cancel (9,603) 12.50

Secretariat Building,
Roses — PC7

UN
Complex — PC8

Printed by Mercury-Walsh, Australia.

1998, May 20 Litho.
UX20 PC7 21c **multicolored** (150,000)+ 1.00 .25
First day cancel 1.50
UX21 PC8 50c **multicolored** (150,000)+ 1.50 .50
First day cancel 1.75

Illustrations of the buildings and other scenes are shown on
the back of each card.

AIR POST POSTAL CARDS

Values are for entire cards.

Type of Air Post Stamp of 1957

Printed by British American Bank Note Co., Ltd., Ottawa.

1957, May 27 Litho.
UXC1 AP3 4c **maroon,** buff (631,000) .25 .20
First day cancel (260,005) 1.00

No. UXC1 Surcharged in
Maroon at Left of Stamp

1959, June 5 Litho.
UXC2 AP3 4c + 1c **maroon,** buff (1,119,000) .30 .20
Cancel first day of public use,
June 8 300.00
a. Double surcharge —
b. Inverted surcharge —

Type of Air Post Stamp, 1957

Printed by Eureka Specialty Printing Co., Scranton,
Pa.

1959, Sept. 21 Litho.
UXC3 AP3 5c **crimson,** buff (500,000) .65 .20
First day cancel (119,479) 1.00

Outer
Space — APC1

Printed by Eureka Specialty Printing Co., Scranton, Pa.

1963, Apr. 26 Litho.
UXC4 APC1 6c **black & blue** (350,000) .60 .20
First day cancel (109,236) 1.50

APC2

Printed by Eureka-Carlisle Co., Scranton, Pa. Designed by Olav S. Mathiesen.

1966, June 9   **Litho.**
UXC5 APC2 11c **dark red, rose, yellow & brown** (764,500)   .30   .20
     First day cancel (162,588)   1.00

1968, May 31   **Litho.**
UXC6 APC2 13c **dark green, bright green & yellow** (829,000)   .40   .20
     First day cancel (106,500)   1.00

UN Emblem and Stylized Planes — APC3

Printed by Canadian Bank Note Co., Ltd., Ottawa. Designed by Lawrence Kurtz.

1969, Jan. 8   **Litho.**
UXC7 APC3 8c **gray, dull yellow, lt blue, indigo & red** (500,000)   .65   .20
     First day cancel (94,037)   1.00

Type of Air Post Stamp of 1972

Printed by Government Printing Bureau, Tokyo. Designed by L. L. Dolan.

1972, Oct. 16   **Litho.**
UXC8 AP12 9c **orange, red, gray & green** (500,000)   .45   .20
     First day cancel (85,600)   1.00

Type of 1969

Printed by Government Printing Bureau, Tokyo

1972, Oct. 16   **Litho.**
UXC9 APC3 15c **lilac, light blue, pink & carmine** (500,000)   .50   .20
     First day cancel (84,800)   1.00

Types of Air Post Stamps, 1972-74

Printed by Setelipaino, Finland.

1975, Jan. 10   **Litho.**
UXC10 AP14 11c **greenish blue, blue & dark blue** (250,000)   .50   .20
     First day cancel (70,500)   1.00
UXC11 AP17 18c **gray & multicolored** (250,000)   .50   .20
     First day cancel (70,500)   1.00

Flying Mailman — APC4

Printed by Courvoisier. Designed by Arieh Glaser.

1982, Apr. 28   **Photo.**
UXC12 APC4 28c **multicolored** (350,000)   .45   .20
     First day cancel (58,700)   1.40

SOUVENIR CARDS

These cards were issued by the United Nations Postal Administration and were not valid for postage.

Each card bears reproductions of UN stamps and a statement by the Secretary-General in English.

1   World Health Day, Apr. 7, 1972. Card of 5: #43, 102, 156, 207, 228.   .65

A second printing shows several minor differences.

2   Art on UN Stamps, Nov. 17, 1972. Card of 11: #170, 171, 173, 174, 180, 183, 201, 202, 203, 224, 232. #201, 202 form a simulated setenant pair   .45

3   Disarmament Decade, Mar. 9, 1973. Card of 5: #133, 147, 177, 227, 234   .50

4   Declaration of Human Rights, 25th Anniversary, Nov. 16, 1973. Card of 10: #13, 22, 29, 39, 47, 58, 68, 121, 190, 242   .75

5   UPU centenary, Mar. 22, 1974. Card of 7: #17, 18, 219, 246; Geneva 18, 39, 40.   .75

6   World Population Year, Oct. 18, 1974. Card of 7: #151, 152, 153, 252, 253; Geneva 43, 44.   6.00

7   Peaceful Uses of Outer Space, Mar. 14, 1975. Card of 6: #112, 113, 256, 257; Geneva 46, 47.   2.00

8   UN Peace Keeping Operations, Nov. 21, 1975. Card of 9: #52, 111, 118, 139, 160, 265, 266; Geneva 55, 56.   2.00

9   World Federation of United Nations Associations, Mar. 12, 1976. Card of 5: #154, 155, 272, 273; Geneva 57.   3.25

10   World Food Council, Nov. 19, 1976. Card of 6: #116, 117, 218, 280; Geneva 17, 63.   2.25

11   World Intellectual Property Organization (WIPO), Mar. 11, 1977. Card of 15: #17, 23, 25, 31, 33, 41, 43, 49, 59, 86, 90, 123, 281, 282; Geneva 64.   2.50

12   Combat Racism, Sept. 19, 1977. Card of 8: #220, 221, 287, 288; Geneva 19, 20, 69, 70.   2.50

13   Namibia, May 5, 1978. Card of 10: #240, 241, 263, 264, 296, 297; Geneva 34, 53, 54, 76.   1.00

14   Intl. Civil Aviation Organization, June 12, 1978. Card of 6: #31, 32, 298, 299; Geneva 77, 78.   2.50

15   Intl. Year of the Child, May 4, 1979. Card of 9: #5, 97, 161, 162, 163, 310, 311; Geneva 84, 85.   .75

16   Intl. Court of Justice, Nov. 9, 1979. Card of 6: #88, 89, 314, 315; Geneva 87, 88.   .75

17   UN Decade for Women, Mar. 7, 1980. Card of 4: #258, 318; Geneva 90; Vienna 9.   12.00

18   Economic and Social Council, Nov. 7, 1980. Card of 8: #65, 66, 341, 342; Geneva 96, 97; Vienna 15, 16.   .75

19   Intl. Year of Disabled Persons, Mar. 6, 1981. Card of 6: #344, 345; Geneva 99, 100; Vienna 18, 19.   .65

20   New and Renewable Sources of Energy, May 29, 1981. Card of 4: #348, 349; Geneva 102; Vienna 21.   1.00

21   Human Environment, Mar. 19, 1982. Card of 5: #230, 371; Geneva 26, 107; Vienna 25   .75

22   Exploration and Peaceful Uses of Outer Space, June 11, 1982. Card of 7: #112, 256, 373; Geneva 46, 109, 110; Vienna 27.   1.40

23   Safety at Sea, Mar. 18, 1983. Card of 8: #123, 124, 394, 395; Geneva 114, 115; Vienna 31, 32.   1.10

24   Trade and Development, June 6, 1983. Card of 11: #129, 130, 274, 275, 397, 398; Geneva 58, 117, 118; Vienna 31, 32.   2.00

25   Intl. Conference on Population, Feb. 3, 1984. Card of 10: #151, 153, 252, 253, 417, 418; Geneva 43, 44, 121; Vienna 39.   2.00

26   Intl. Youth Year, Nov. 15, 1984. Card of 5: #441, 442; Geneva 128; Vienna 46, 47.   3.00

27   ILO Turin Center, Feb. 1, 1985. Card of 8: #25, 200, 244, 443; Geneva 37, 129, 130; Vienna 48.   2.75

28   Child Survival Campaign, Nov. 22, 1985. Card of 6: #466, 467; Geneva 138, 139; Vienna 55, 56.   4.00

29   Stamp Collecting, May 22, 1986. Card of 5: #278, 473; Geneva 61, 147; Vienna 63.   8.25

No. 29 with stitch marks has been removed from the Ameripex program. Value is one-half that of unstitched copy.

30   Intl. Peace Year, June 20, 1986. Card of 6: #475, 476; Geneva 148, 149; Vienna 64, 65.   4.00

31   Shelter for the Homeless, Mar. 13, 1987. Card of 6: #495, 496; Geneva 154, 155; Vienna 68, 69.   3.50

32   Immunize Every Child, Nov. 20, 1987. Card of 13: #44, 103, 157, 208, 294, 517, 518; Vienna 76, 77.   4.25

33   Intl. Volunteer Day, May 6, 1988. Card of 10; #239, 367, 524, 525; Geneva 103, 167, 168; Vienna 23, 82, 83.   7.00

34   Health in Sports, June 17, 1988. Card of 6: #526, 527; Geneva 169, 170; Vienna 84, 85.   7.00

35   World Bank, Jan. 27, 1989. Card of 8; #86-87, 546-547; Geneva 173-174; Vienna 88-89.   7.00

36   World Weather Watch, Apr. 24, 1989. Card of 10; #49-50, 188-189, 550-551; Geneva 173-174; Vienna 88-89.   7.00

37   Fight AIDS Worldwide, Mar. 16, 1990. Card of 6, #573-574; Geneva 184-185; Vienna 99-100   6.50

38   Crime Prevention, Sept. 13, 1990. Card of 6: #580-581; Geneva 191-192; Vienna 106-107.   7.75

39   Economic Commission for Europe, Mar. 15, 1991. Card of 12; #584-587; Geneva 195-198; Vienna 110-113.   8.00

40   Rights of the Child, June 14, 1991. Card of 6; #593-594; Geneva 203-204; Vienna 117-118.   10.00

41   Mission to Planet Earth, Sept. 4, 1992, Card of 6, #609-610; Geneva 220-221; Vienna 133-134   17.00

42   Science and Technology for Development, Oct. 2, 1992, Card of 6; #611-612; Geneva 222-223; Vienna 135-136   15.00

43   Healthy Environment, May 7, 1993, Card of 6, #624-625; Geneva 232-233; Vienna #147-148   17.50

44   Peace, Sept. 21, 1993, Card of 12, #629-632; Geneva #236-239; Vienna #152-155   16.00

No. 44 exists overprinted in gold with Hong Kong '94 emblem.

45   Intl. Year of the Family, Feb. 4, 1994, Card of 6, #637-638; Geneva #244-245; Vienna #160-161   13.50

46   Population & Development, 1994, Card of 9, #151, 651-652; Geneva #43, 258-259; Vienna #39, 174-175   12.50

47   World Summit for Social Development, 1995, Card of 3, #656; Geneva #263; Vienna #179   10.50

48   Intl. Youth Year, 1995, Card of 9, #441, 661-662; Geneva #128, 268-269; Vienna #46, 184-185   14.50

49   WFUNA, 1996, Card of 3, #671; Geneva #277; Vienna #193   8.50

50   UNICEF, 1996, Card of 6, #688-689; Geneva #294-295; Vienna #210-211   7.50

51   Philately, 1997, Card of 6, #714-715; Geneva #312-313; Vienna #228-229   12.50

52   Peacekeeping, #737-738; Geneva #325-326; Vienna #242-243   7.50

53   Universal Declaration of Human Rights, #739-740; Geneva #327-328; Vienna #244-245   7.50

54   UPU; #767a; Geneva #346a; Vienna #263a   7.50

OFFICES IN GENEVA, SWITZERLAND

For use only on mail posted at the Palais des Nations (UN European Office), Geneva. Inscribed in French unless otherwise stated.

100 Centimes = 1 Franc

Types of United Nations Issues 1961-69 and

United Nations
European Office,
Geneva — G1

Printed by Setelipaino, Finland (5c, 70c, 80c, 90c, 2fr, 10fr),
Courvoisier, S.A., Switzerland (10c, 20c, 30c, 50c, 60c, 3fr).
Government Printing Office, Austria (75c) and Government
Printing Office, Federal Republic of Germany (1fr).
Panes of 50. 30c designed by Ole Hamann, others as before.

Designs: 5c, UN Headquarters, New York, and world map.
10c, UN flag. 20c, Three men united before globe. 50c, Opening words of UN Charter. 60c, UN emblem over globe. 70c, "un" and UN emblem. 75c, "Flight Across Globe." 80c, UN Headquarters and emblem. 90c, Abstract group of flags. 1fr, UN emblem. 2fr, Stylized globe and weather vane. 3fr, Statue by Henrik Starcke. 10fr, "Peace, Justice, Security."
The 20c, 80c and 90c are inscribed in French. The 75c and 10fr carry French inscription at top, English at bottom.

1969-70		Photo.		Unwmk.

Perf. 13 (5c, 70c, 90c); 12½x12 (10c);

1	A88	5c purple & multi, Oct. 4, 1969 (3,300,000)	.20	.20
		First day cover		1.00
		Inscription block of 4	.25	—
a.		Green omitted		—
2	A52	10c salmon & multi, Oct. 4, 1969 (4,300,000)+	.20	.20
		First day cover		1.00
		Inscription block of 4	.25	—

Perf. 11½ (20c-60c, 3fr)

3	A66	20c black & multi, Oct. 4, 1969 (4,500,000)	.20	.20
		First day cover		1.00
		Inscription block of 4	.45	—
4	G1	30c dark blue & multi, Oct. 4, 1969 (3,000,000)	.20	.20
		First day cover		1.00
		Inscription block of 4	.60	—
5	A77	50c ultra & multi, Oct. 4, 1969 (3,300,000)	.20	.20
		First day cover		1.00
		Inscription block of 4	.80	—
6	A54	60c dark brown, salmon & gold, Apr. 17, 1970 (3,300,000)+	.20	.20
		First day cover		1.00
		Inscription block of 4	.90	—
7	A104	70c red, black & gold, Sept. 22, 1970 (3,300,000)+	.20	.20
		First day cover		1.00
		Inscription block of 4	.90	—

Perf. 11½x12 (75c)

8	AP8	75c carmine rose & multi, Oct. 4, 1969 (3,300,000)+	.25	.25
		First day cover		1.00
		Inscription block of 4	1.00	—

Perf. 13½x14 (80c)

9	A78	80c blue green, red & yellow, Sept. 22, 1970 (3,300,000)	.25	.25
		First day cover		1.00
		Inscription block of 4	1.00	—
10	A45	90c blue & multi, Sept. 22, 1970 (3,300,000)	.25	.25
		First day cover		1.00
		Inscription block of 4	1.10	—

Litho. & Embossed
Perf. 14 (1fr)

11	A79	1fr light & dark green, Oct. 4, 1969 (3,000,000)	.30	.30
		First day cover		1.00
		Inscription block of 4	1.25	—

Photo.
Perf. 12x11½ (2fr)

12	A67	2fr blue & multi, Sept. 22, 1970 (3,000,000)+	.60	.60
		First day cover		2.00
		Inscription block of 4	2.50	—
13	A97	3fr olive & multi, Oct. 4, 1969 (3,000,000)+	.95	.95
		First day cover		2.25
		Inscription block of 4	4.00	—

Engr.
Perf. 12 (10fr)

14	A3	10fr dark blue, Apr. 17, 1970 (2,250,000)+	2.75	2.75
		First day cover		8.50
		Inscription block of 4	12.00	—
		Nos. 1-14 (14)	6.75	6.75

+ Printing orders to June 1984.

First day covers of Nos. 1-5, 8, 11, 13 total 607,578; of Nos. 6 and 14, 148,055; of Nos. 7, 9-10 and 12, 226,000.

Sea Bed Type of UN

1971, Jan. 25		Photo. & Engr.		Perf. 13
15	A114	30c green & multi (1,935,871)	.20	.20
		First day cover (152,590)		1.00
		Inscription block of 4	.65	—

Refugee Type of UN

1971, Mar. 12		Litho.		Perf. 13x12½
16	A115	50c deep carmine, deep orange & black (1,820,114)	.20	.20
		First day cover (148,220)		1.00
		Inscription block of 4	.85	—

World Food Program Type of UN

1971, Apr. 13		Photo.		Perf. 14
17	A116	50c dark violet & multi (1,824,170)	.20	.20
		First day cover (151,580)		1.00
		Inscription block of 4	.85	—

UPU Headquarters Type of UN

1971, May 28		Photo.		Perf. 11½
18	A117	75c green & multi (1,821,878)	.30	.30
		First day cover (140,679)		1.00
		Inscription block of 4	1.35	—

Eliminate Racial Discrimination Types of UN

Designed by Daniel Gonzague (30c) and Ole Hamann (50c).

1971, Sept. 21		Photo.		Perf. 13½
19	A118	30c blue & multi (1,838,474)	.20	.20
		First day cover		1.00
		Inscription block of 4	.75	—
20	A119	50c yellow green & multi (1,804,126)	.25	.25
		First day cover		1.00
		First day cover, #19-20		1.25
		Inscription block of 4	1.10	—

First day covers of Nos. 19-20 total 308,420.

Picasso Type of UN

1971, Nov. 19		Photo.		Perf. 11½
21	A122	1.10fr multicolored (1,467,993)	.75	.65
		First day cover (195,215)		1.25
		Inscription block of 4	3.00	—

NATIONS UNIES
Office des Nations Unies
à Genève

Palais des Nations, Geneva — G2

UNITED NATIONS

Printed by Courvoisier, S. A. Panes of 50. Designed by Ole Hamann.

1972, Jan. 5		Photo.		Perf. 11½
22	G2	40c olive, blue, salmon & dark green (3,500,000)+	.20	.20
		First day cover (152,300)		1.00
		Inscription block of 4	.60	—

+ Initial printing order.

Nuclear Weapons Type of UN

1972, Feb. 14		Photo.		Perf. 13½x14
23	A124	40c yellow, green, black, rose & gray (1,567,305)	.25	.25
		First day cover (151,350)		1.00
		Inscription block of 4	1.25	—

World Health Day Type of UN

1972, Apr. 7		Litho. & Engr.		Perf. 13x13½
24	A125	80c black & multi (1,543,368)	.40	.40
		First day cover (192,600)		1.00
		Inscription block of 4	1.75	—

Human Environment Type of UN

Lithographed & Embossed

1972, June 5				Perf. 12½x14
25	A126	40c olive, lemon, green & blue (1,594,089)	.20	.20
		First day cover		1.00
		Inscription block of 4	.80	—
26	A126	80c ultra, pink, green & blue (1,568,009)	.40	.40
		First day cover		1.40
		First day cover, #25-26		1.75
		Inscription block of 4	1.60	—

First day covers of Nos. 25-26 total 296,700.

Economic Commission for Europe Type of UN

1972, Sept. 11		Litho.		Perf. 13x13½
27	A127	1.10fr red & multi (1,604,082)	1.00	.90
		First day cover (149,630)		1.75
		Inscription block of 4	4.25	—

Art at UN (Sert) Type of UN

1972, Nov. 17		Photo.		Perf. 12x12½
28	A128	40c gold, red & brown (1,932,428)	.30	.30
		First day cover		1.00
		Inscription block of 4	1.25	—
29	A128	80c gold, brown & olive (1,759,600)	.60	.60
		First day cover		1.25
		First day cover, #28-29		1.75
		Inscription block of 4	2.50	—

First day covers of Nos. 28-29 total 295,470.

Disarmament Decade Type of UN

1973, Mar. 9		Litho.		Perf. 13½x13
30	A129	60c violet & multi (1,586,845)	.40	.35
		First day cover		1.00
		Inscription block of 4	1.60	—
31	A129	1.10fr olive & multi (1,408,169)	.85	.75
		First day cover		1.40
		First day cover, #30-31		1.75
		Inscription block of 4	3.50	—

First day covers of Nos. 30-31 total 260,680.

Drug Abuse Type of UN

1973, Apr. 13		Photo.		Perf. 13½
32	A130	60c blue & multi (1,481,432)	.45	.40
		First day cover (144,760)		1.00
		Inscription block of 4	1.90	—

Volunteers Type of UN

1973, May 25		Photo.		Perf. 14
33	A131	80c gray green & multi (1,443,519)	.35	.35
		First day cover (143,430)		1.10
		Inscription block of 4	1.50	—

Namibia Type of UN

1973, Oct. 1		Photo.		Perf. 13½
34	A132	60c red & multi (1,673,898)	.35	.35
		First day cover (148,077)		1.00
		Inscription block of 4	1.50	—

Human Rights Type of UN

1973, Nov. 16		Photo.		Perf. 13½
35	A133	40c ultramarine & multi (1,480,791)	.30	.30
		First day cover		1.00
		Inscription block of 4	1.25	—
36	A133	80c olive & multi (1,343,349)	.50	.50
		First day cover		1.25
		First day cover, #35-36		1.75
		Inscription block of 4	2.10	—

First day covers of Nos. 35-36 total 438,260.

ILO Headquarters Type of UN

1974, Jan. 11		Photo.		Perf. 14
37	A134	60c violet & multi (1,212,703)	.45	.45
		First day cover		1.00
		Inscription block of 4	1.90	—
38	A134	80c brown & multi (1,229,851)	.65	.60
		First day cover		1.10
		First day cover, #37-38		1.25
		Inscription block of 4	2.75	—

First day covers of Nos. 37-38 total 240,660.

Centenary of UPU Type of UN

1974, Mar. 22		Litho.		Perf. 12½
39	A135	30c gold & multi (1,567,517)	.25	.20
		First day cover		1.00
		Inscription block of 4	1.25	—
40	A135	60c gold & multi (1,430,839)	.60	.40
		First day cover		1.25
		First day cover, #39-40		1.50
		Inscription block of 4	2.50	—

First day covers of Nos. 39-40 total 231,840.

Art at UN (Portinari) Type of UN

1974, May 6		Photo.		Perf. 14
41	A136	60c dark red & multi (1,202,357)	.40	.40
		First day cover		1.00
		Inscription block of 4	1.75	—
42	A136	1fr green & multi (1,230,045)	.70	.70
		First day cover		1.20
		First day cover, #41-42		1.50
		Inscription block of 4	3.00	—

First day covers of Nos. 41-42 total 249,130.

World Population Year Type of UN

1974, Oct. 18   Photo.   *Perf. 14*
43 A140 60c **bright green & multi** *(1,292,954)*   .50 .45
    First day cover   1.00
    Inscription block of 4   2.25 —
44 A140 80c **brown & multi** *(1,221,288)*   .70 .55
    First day cover   1.00
    First day cover, #43-44   1.25
    Inscription block of 4   3.25 —
First day covers of Nos. 43-44 total 189,597.

Law of the Sea Type of UN

1974, Nov. 22   Photo.   *Perf. 14*
45 A141 1.30fr **blue & multicolored** *(1,266,270)* 1.00 .95
    First day cover *(181,000)*   1.25
    Inscription block of 4   4.00 —

Outer Space Type of UN

1975, Mar. 14   Litho.   *Perf. 13*
46 A142 60c **multicolored** *(1,339,704)*   .50 .35
    First day cover   1.00
    Inscription block of 4   2.00 —
47 A142 90c **multicolored** *(1,383,888)*   .75 .55
    First day cover   1.00
    First day cover, #46-47   1.50
    Inscription block of 4   3.25 —
First day covers of Nos. 46-47 total 250,400.

International Women's Year Type of UN

1975, May 9   Litho.   *Perf. 15*
48 A143 60c **multicolored** *(1,176,080)*   .45 .40
    First day cover   1.00
    Inscription block of 4   1.90 —
49 A143 90c **multicolored** *(1,167,863)*   .65 .55
    First day cover   1.00
    First day cover, #48-49   1.50
    Inscription block of 4   2.75 —
First day covers of Nos. 48-49 total 250,660.

30th Anniversary Type of UN

1975, June 26   Litho.   *Perf. 13*
50 A144 60c **green & multi** *(1,442,075)*   .45 .40
    First day cover   1.00
    Inscription block of 4   2.00 —
51 A144 90c **violet & multi** *(1,612,411)*   .65 .60
    First day cover   1.00
    First day cover, #50-51   1.25
    Inscription block of 4   2.75 —

Souvenir Sheet
Imperf
52   Sheet of 2 *(1,210,148)*   .75 .75
a. A144 60c **green & multicolored**   .25 .25
b. A144 90c **violet & multicolored**   .50 .50
    First day cover   1.25

No. 52 has blue and bister margin with inscription and UN emblem. Size: 92x70mm.
First day covers of Nos. 50-52 total 402,500.

Namibia Type of UN

1975, Sept. 22   Photo.   *Perf. 13½*
53 A145 50c **multicolored** *(1,261,019)*   .30 .30
    First day cover   1.00
    Inscription block of 4   1.25 —
54 A145 1.30fr **multicolored** *(1,241,990)* .95 .70
    First day cover   1.10
    First day cover, #53-54   1.25
    Inscription block of 4   4.00 —
First day covers of Nos. 53-54 total 226,260.

Peace-keeping Operations Type of UN

1975, Nov. 21   Engr.   *Perf. 12½*
55 A146 60c **greenish blue** *(1,249,305)*   .35 .35
    First day cover   1.00
    Inscription block of 4   1.50 —
56 A146 70c **bright violet** *(1,249,935)*   .65 .50
    First day cover   1.00
    First day cover, #55-56   1.25
    Inscription block of 4   2.75 —
First day covers of Nos. 55-56 total 229,245.

WFUNA Type of UN

1976, Mar. 12   Photo.   *Perf. 14*
57 A152 90c **multicolored** *(1,186,563)*   .90 .65
    First day cover   1.00
    Inscription block of 4   4.00 —
First day covers of No. 57 total 121,645.

UNCTAD Type of UN

1976, Apr. 23   Photo.   *Perf. 11½*
58 A153 1.10fr **sepia & multi** *(1,167,284)* .90 .80
    First day cover *(107,030)*   1.25
    Inscription block of 4   4.00 —

Habitat Type of UN

1976, May 28   Photo.   *Perf. 14*
59 A154 40c **dull blue & multi** *(1,258,986)* .20 .20
    First day cover   1.00
    Inscription block of 4   1.00 —
60 A154 1.50fr **violet & multi** *(1,110,507)* .75 .75

    First day cover   1.25
    First day cover, #59-60   1.60
    Inscription block of 4   3.50 —
First day covers of Nos. 59-60 total 242,530.

UN Emblem, Post
Horn and
Rainbow — G3

UN Postal Administration, 25th anniversary.
Printed by Courvoisier, S.A. Panes of 20 (5x4). Designed by Hector Viola.

1976, Oct. 8   Photo.   *Perf. 11½*
61 G3 80c **tan & multicolored** *(1,794,009)* .50 .50
    First day cover   2.00
    Inscription block of 4   2.50 —
62 A3 1.10fr **light green & multi** *(1,751,178)* 1.60 1.60
    First day cover   2.00
    Inscription block of 4   8.00 —
    First day cover, #61-62   3.00
    Panes of 20, #61-62   37.50

Upper margin blocks are inscribed "XXVe ANNIVERSAIRE"; lower margin blocks "ADMINISTRATION POSTALE DES NATIONS UNIES."
First day covers of Nos. 61-62 total 152,450.

World Food Council Type of UN

1976, Nov. 19   Litho.   *Perf. 14½*
63 A156 70c **multicolored** *(1,507,630)*   .50 .45
    First day cover *(170,540)*   1.00
    Inscription block of 4   2.25 —

WIPO Type of UN

1977, Mar. 11   Photo.   *Perf. 14*
64 A157 80c **red & multi** *(1,232,664)*   .60 .55
    First day cover *(212,470)*   1.00
    Inscription block of 4   2.50 —

Drop of Water and Globe — G4

UN Water Conference, Mar del Plata, Argentina, Mar. 14-25.
Printed by Government Printing Bureau, Tokyo. Panes of 50.
Designed by Eliezer Weishoff.

1977, Apr. 22   Photo.   *Perf. 13½x13*
65 G4 80c **ultramarine & multi** *(1,146,650)* .55 .50
    First day cover   1.00
    Inscription block of 4   2.25 —
66 G4 1.10fr **dark carmine & multi** *(1,138,236)* .85 .75
    First day cover   1.25
    First day cover, #65-66   1.75
    Inscription block of 4   3.50 —
First day covers of Nos. 65-66 total 289,836.

Hands Protecting UN
Emblem — G5

UN Security Council.
Printed by Heraclio Fournier, S.A., Spain. Panes of 50. Designed by George Hamori.

1977, May 27   Photo.   *Perf. 11*
67 G5 80c **blue & multi** *(1,096,030)*   .55 .50
    First day cover   1.00
    Inscription block of 4   2.25 —
68 G5 1.10fr **emerald & multi** *(1,075,925)* .85 .75
    First day cover   1.25
    First day cover, #67-68   1.75
    Inscription block of 4   3.50 —
First day covers of Nos. 67-68 total 305,349.

---

combattons
le racisme
nations unies
Fs.0.40

Colors of Five Races
Spun into One Firm
Rope — G6

Fight against racial discrimination.
Printed by Setelipaino, Finland. Panes of 50. Designed by M. A. Munnawar.

1977, Sept. 19   Litho.   *Perf. 13½x13*
69 G6 40c **multicolored** *(1,218,834)*   .25 .25
    First day cover   1.00
    Inscription block of 4   1.10 —
70 G6 1.10fr **multicolored** *(1,138,250)*   .65 .65
    First day cover   1.25
    First day cover, #69-70   1.75
    Inscription block of 4   2.75 —
First day covers of Nos. 69-70 total 308,722.

Atomic Energy Turning Partly
into Olive Branch — G7

Peaceful uses of atomic energy.
Printed by Heraclio Fournier, S.A., Spain. Panes of 50. Designed by Witold Janowski and Marek Freudenreich.

1977, Nov. 18   Photo.   *Perf. 14*
71 G7 80c **dark carmine & multi** *(1,147,787)* .50 .50
    First day cover   1.00
    Inscription block of 4   2.00 —
72 G7 1.10fr **Prussian blue & multi** *(1,121,209)* .75 .75
    First day cover   1.20
    First day cover, #71-72   1.50
    Inscription block of 4   3.25 —
First day covers of Nos. 71-72 total 298,075.

"Tree" of Doves — G8

Printed by Questa Colour Security Printers, United Kingdom. Panes of 50. Designed by M. Hioki.

1978, Jan. 27   Litho.   *Perf. 14½*
73 G8 35c **multicolored** *(3,000,000)+*   .20 .20
    First day cover *(259,735)*   1.00
    Inscription block of 4   .65 —

Globes with
Smallpox
Distribution — G9

Global eradication of smallpox.
Printed by Courvoisier, S.A. Panes of 50. Designed by Eliezer Weishoff.

1978, Mar. 31   Photo.   *Perf. 12x11½*
74 G9 80c **yellow & multi** *(1,116,044)*   .60 .50
    First day cover   1.00
    Inscription block of 4   2.50 —
75 G9 1.10fr **light green & multi** *(1,109,946)* .90 .75
    First day cover   1.20
    First day cover, #74-75   2.00
    Inscription block of 4   3.75 —
First day covers of Nos. 74-75 total 254,700.

Namibia Type of UN

1978, May 5   Photo.   *Perf. 12*
76 A166 80c **multicolored** *(1,183,208)*   .80 .60
    First day cover *(316,610)*   1.00
    Inscription block of 4   3.50 —

Jets and Flight Patterns — G10

International Civil Aviation Organization for "Safety in the Air." Printed by Heraclio Fournier, S.A., Spain. Panes of 50. Designed by Tomas Savrda.

1978, June 12		Photo.	Perf. 14	
77	G10 70c multicolored (1,275,106)		.40	.30
	First day cover			1.00
	Inscription block of 4		1.75	—
78	G10 80c multicolored (1,144,339)		.70	.50
	First day cover			1.00
	First day cover, #77-78			1.60
	Inscription block of 4		3.00	—

First day covers of Nos. 77-78 total 255,700.

General Assembly, Flags and Globe — G11

Printed by Government Printing Bureau, Tokyo. Panes of 50. Designed by Henry Bencsath.

1978, Sept. 15		Photo.	Perf. 13½	
79	G11 70c multicolored (1,204,441)		.50	.45
	First day cover			1.00
	Inscription block of 4		2.25	—
80	G11 1.10fr multicolored (1,183,889)		.90	.60
	First day cover			1.25
	First day cover, #79-80			1.75
	Inscription block of 4		3.75	—

First day covers of Nos. 79-80 total 245,600.

Technical Cooperation Type of UN

1978, Nov. 17		Photo.	Perf. 14	
81	A169 80c multicolored (1,173,220)		.70	.55
	First day cover (264,700)			1.00
	Inscription block of 4		3.25	—

Seismograph Recording Earthquake — G12

Office of the UN Disaster Relief Coordinator (UNDRO). Printed by Heraclio Fournier, S.A., Spain. Panes of 50. Designed by Michael Klutmann.

1979, Mar. 9		Photo.	Perf. 14	
82	G12 80c multicolored (1,183,155)		.50	.40
	First day cover			1.00
	Inscription block of 4		2.00	—
83	G12 1.50fr multicolored (1,168,121)		.80	.75
	First day cover			1.40
	First day cover, #82-83			1.90
	Inscription block of 4		3.50	—

First day covers of Nos. 82-83 total 162,070.

Children and Rainbow — G13

International Year of the Child. Printed by Heraclio Fournier, S.A., Spain. Panes of 20 (5x4). Designed by Arieh Glaser.

1979, May 4		Photo.	Perf. 14	
84	G13 80c multicolored (2,251,623)		.35	.35
	First day cover			1.25
	Inscription block of 4		1.60	—
85	G13 1.10fr multicolored (2,220,463)		.65	.65
	First day cover			1.75

	Inscription block of 4	2.75	—
	First day cover, #84-85		1.25
	Panes of 20, #84-85	20.00	

First day covers of Nos. 84-85 total 176,120.

Namibia Type of UN

1979, Oct. 5		Litho.	Perf. 13½	
86	A176 1.10fr multicolored (1,229,830)		.50	.50
	First day cover (134,160)			1.25
	Inscription block of 4		2.25	—

International Court of Justice, Scales — G14

International Court of Justice, The Hague, Netherlands. Printed by Setelipaino, Finland. Panes of 50. Designed by Kyohei Maeno.

1979, Nov. 9		Litho.	Perf. 13x13½	
87	G14 80c multicolored (1,123,193)		.40	.40
	First day cover			1.00
	Inscription block of 4		1.75	—
88	G14 1.10fr multicolored (1,063,067)		.60	.60
	First day cover			1.25
	First day cover, #87-88			1.75
	Inscription block of 4		2.75	—

First day covers of Nos. 87-88 total 158,170.

New Economic Order Type of UN

1980, Jan. 11		Litho.	Perf. 15x14½	
89	A179 80c multicolored (1,315,918)		.85	.60
	First day cover (176,250)			1.00
	Inscription block of 4		3.50	—

Women's Year Emblem — G15

United Nations Decade for Women. Printed by Questa Colour Security Printers, United Kingdom. Panes of 50. Designed by M.A. Munnawar.

1980, Mar. 7		Litho.	Perf. 14½x15	
90	G15 40c multicolored (1,265,221)		.30	.30
	First day cover			1.00
	Inscription block of 4		1.40	—
91	G15 70c multicolored (1,240,375)		.65	.55
	First day cover			1.10
	First day cover, #90-91			1.25
	Inscription block of 4		2.75	—

First day covers of Nos. 90-91 total 204,350.

Peace-keeping Operations Type of UN

1980, May 16		Litho.	Perf. 14x13	
92	A181 1.10fr blue & green (1,335,391)		.80	.70
	First day cover (184,700)			1.00
	Inscription block of 4		3.25	—

35th Anniversary Type of UN and Dove and "35" — G16

35th Anniversary of the United Nations. Printed by Ashton-Potter Ltd., Canada. Panes of 50. Designed by Gidon Sagi (40c), Cemalattin Mutver (70c).

1980, June 26		Litho.	Perf. 13x13½	
93	G16 40c blue green & black (1,462,005)		.35	.30
	First day cover			1.00
	Inscription block of 4		1.40	—
94	A183 70c multicolored (1,444,639)		.55	.50
	First day cover			1.00
	First day cover, #93-94			1.50
	Inscription block of 4		2.40	—

Souvenir Sheet
Imperf

95	Sheet of 2 (1,235,200)	.70	.60
a.	G16 40c blue green & black	.25	—
b.	A183 70c multicolored	.45	—
	First day cover		1.00

First day covers of Nos. 93-95 total 379,800.

ECOSOC Type of UN and

Family Climbing Line Graph — G17

Printed by Ashton-Potter Ltd., Canada. Panes of 50. Designed by Eliezer Weishoff (40c), A. Medina Medina (70c).

1980, Nov. 21		Litho.	Perf. 13½x13	
96	A186 40c multicolored (986,435)		.30	.25
	First day cover			1.00
	Inscription block of 4		1.25	—
97	G17 70c multicolored (1,016,462)		.60	.60
	First day cover			1.00
	First day cover #96-97			1.50
	Inscription block of 4		2.50	—

Economic and Social Council.
First day covers of Nos. 96-97 total 210,460.

Palestinian Rights

Printed by Courvoisier S.A., Switzerland. Panes of 50. Designed by David Dewhurst.

1981, Jan. 30		Photo.	Perf. 12x11½	
98	A188 80c multicolored (1,031,737)		.55	.50
	First day cover (117,480)			1.00
	Inscription block of 4		2.75	—

International Year of the Disabled.

Printed by Heraclio Fournier S.A., Spain. Panes of 50. Designed by G.P. Van der Hyde (40c) and Sophia van Heeswijk (1.50fr).

1981, Mar. 6		Photo.	Perf. 14	
99	A190 40c black & blue (1,057,909)		.25	.25
	First day cover			1.00
	Inscription block of 4		1.00	—
100	V4 1.50fr black & red (994,748)		1.00	1.00
	First day cover			1.25
	First day cover, #99-100			1.75
	Inscription block of 4		4.00	—

First day covers of Nos. 99-100 total 202,853.

Art Type of UN

1981, Apr. 15		Photo.	Perf. 11½	
	Granite Paper			
101	A191 80c multicolored (1,128,782)		.75	.60
	First day cover (121,383)			1.00
	Inscription block of 4		3.50	—

Energy Type of 1981

1981, May 29		Litho.	Perf. 13	
102	A192 1.10fr multicolored (1,096,806)		.70	.60
	First day cover (113,700)			1.25
	Inscription block of 4		3.00	—

Volunteers Program Type and

Symbols of Science, Agriculture and Industry — G18

Printed by Walsall Security Printers, Ltd., United Kingdom. Panes of 50. Designed by Gabriele Nussgen (40c), Bernd Mirbach (70c).

1981, Nov. 13		Litho.		
103	A194 40c multicolored (1,032,700)		.45	.30
	First day cover			1.00
	Inscription block of 4		2.00	—
104	G18 70c multicolored (1,123,672)		.90	.65
	First day cover			1.00
	First day cover, #103-104			1.50
	Inscription block of 4		3.75	—

First day covers of Nos. 103-104 total 190,667.

Fight against
Apartheid
G19

Flower of Flags
G20

Printed by Courvoisier, S.A., Switzerland. Panes of 50.
Designed by Tomas Savrda (30c); Dietmar Kowall (1fr).

1982, Jan. 22   **Perf. 11½x12**
105 G19   30c multicolored (3,000,000)+   .25   .20
          First day cover   1.00
          Inscription block of 4   1.10   —
106 G20   1fr multicolored (3,000,000)+   .80   .65
          First day cover   1.00
          First day cover, #105-106   1.20
          Inscription block of 4   3.25   —

First day covers of Nos. 105-106 total 199,347.

Human Environment Type of UN and:

Sun and Leaves — G21

10th Anniversary of United Nations Environment Program.
Printed by Joh. Enschede en Zonen, Netherlands. Panes of
50. Designed by Sybille Brunner (40c); Philine Hartert (1.20fr).

1982, Mar. 19   **Litho.**   **Perf. 13½x13**
107 G21   40c multicolored (948,743)   .30   .20
          First day cover   1.00
          Inscription block of 4   1.25   —
108 A199 1.20fr multicolored (901,096)   1.25   1.00
          First day cover   1.10
          First day cover, #107-108   1.40
          Inscription block of 4   5.25   —

First day covers of Nos. 107-108 total 190,155.

Outer Space Type of UN and:

Satellite, Applications
of Space
Technology — G22

Exploration and Peaceful Uses of Outer Space.
Printed by Enschede. Panes of 50. Designed by Wiktor C.
Nerwinski (80c) and George Hamori (1fr).

1982, June 11   **Litho.**   **Perf. 13x13½**
109 A201 80c multicolored (964,593)   .60   .45
          First day cover   1.00
          Inscription block of 4   2.60   —
110 G22   1fr multicolored (898,367)   .75   .60
          First day cover   1.25
          First day cover, #109-110   1.50
          Inscription block of 4   3.25   —

First day covers of Nos. 109-110 total 205,815.

Conservation & Protection of Nature

1982, Nov. 19   **Photo.**   **Perf. 14**
111 A202 40c Bird (928,143)   .50   .35
          First day cover   1.00
          Inscription block of 4   2.10   —
112 A202 1.50fr Reptile (847,173)   1.10   .75
          First day cover   1.25
          First day cover, #111-112   1.75
          Inscription block of 4   5.00   —

First day covers of Nos. 111-112 total 198,504.

World Communications Year

1983, Jan. 28   **Litho.**   **Perf. 13**
113 A204 1.20fr multicolored (894,025)   1.25   1.00
          First day cover (131,075)   1.25
          Inscription block of 4   5.25   —

Safety at Sea Type of UN and

G23

Designed by Valentin Wurnitsch (A22).

1983, Mar. 18   **Litho.**   **Perf. 14½**
114 A205 40c multicolored (892,365)   .35   .35
          First day cover   1.00
          Inscription block of 4   1.50   —
115 G23   80c multicolored (882,720)   .75   .75
          First day cover   1.00
          First day cover, #114-115   1.50
          Inscription block of 4   3.25   —

First day covers of Nos. 114-115 total 219,592.

World Food Program

1983, Apr. 22   **Engr.**   **Perf. 13½**
116 A207 1.50fr blue (876,591)   1.25   1.00
          First day cover   1.25
          Inscription block of 4   5.25   —

Trade Type of UN and

G24

Designed by Wladyslaw Brykczynski (A23).

1983, June 6   **Litho.**   **Perf. 14**
117 A208 80c multicolored (902,495)   .50   .50
          First day cover   1.00
          Inscription block of 4   2.25   —
118 G24   1.10fr multicolored (921,424)   .90   .85
          First day cover   1.00
          First day cover, #117-118   1.40
          Inscription block of 4   3.75   —

First day covers of Nos. 117-118 total 146,507.

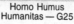

Homo Humus
Humanitas — G25

Right to Create — G26

35th Anniversary of the Universal Declaration of Human
Rights.
Printed by Government Printing Office, Austria. Designed by
Friedensreich Hundertwasser, Austria. Panes of 16 (4x4).

1983, Dec. 9   **Photo. & Engr.**   **Perf. 13½**
119 G25   40c multicolored (1,770,921)   .45   .45
          First day cover   1.00
          Inscription block of 4   2.00   —
120 G26   1.20fr multicolored (1,746,735)   .95   .90
          First day cover   1.10
          Inscription block of 4   4.25   —
          First day cover, #119-120   1.40
          Panes of 16, #119-120   22.50

First day covers of Nos. 119-120 total 315,052.

International Conference on Population Type

1984, Feb. 3   **Litho.**   **Perf. 14**
121 A212 1.20fr multicolored (776,879)   1.00   .85
          First day cover (105,377)   1.00
          Inscription block of 4   4.25   —

Fishing — G27

Women Farm
Workers,
Africa — G28

World Food Day, Oct. 16
Printed by Walsall Security Printers, Ltd., United Kingdom.
Panes of 50. Designed by Adth Vanooijen, Netherlands.

1984, Mar. 15   **Litho.**   **Perf. 14½**
122 G27   50c multicolored (744,506)   .35   .30
          First day cover   1.00
          Inscription block of 4   1.60   —
123 G28   80c multicolored (784,047)   .65   .55
          First day cover   1.25
          First day cover, #122-123   1.75
          Inscription block of 4   2.75   —

First day covers of Nos. 122-123 total 155,234.

Valletta,
Malta — G29

Los Glaciares
National Park,
Argentina — G30

World Heritage
Printed by Harrison and Sons, United Kingdom. Panes of 50.
Designs adapted by Rocco J. Callari, US, and Thomas Lee,
China.

1984, Apr. 18   **Litho.**   **Perf. 14**
124 G29   50c multicolored (763,627)   .55   .50
          First day cover   1.00
          Inscription block of 4   2.50   —
125 G30   70c multicolored (784,489)   .75   .70
          First day cover   1.25
          First day cover, #124-125   1.75
          Inscription block of 4   3.50   —

First day covers of Nos. 124-125 total 164,498.

G31

G32

Future for Refugees
Printed by Courvoisier. Panes of 50. Designed by Hans Erni,
Switzerland.

1984, May 29   **Photo.**   **Perf. 11½**
126 G31   35c multicolored (880,762)   .35   .20
          First day cover   1.00
          Inscription block of 4   1.60   —
127 G32   1.50fr multicolored (829,895)   1.25   .75
          First day cover   1.25
          First day cover, #126-127   1.75
          Inscription block of 4   5.50   —

First day covers of Nos. 126-127 total 170,306.

International Youth Year — G33

Printed by Waddingtons Ltd., United Kingdom. Panes of 50. Designed by Eliezer Weishoff, Israel.

1984, Nov. 15		**Litho.**		**Perf. 13½**	
128	G33	1.20fr **multicolored** *(755,622)*		1.25	1.00
		First day cover *(96,680)*			1.00
		Inscription block of 4		5.00	—

ILO Type of UN and

ILO Turin Center — G34

Printed by the Government Printing Bureau, Japan. Panes of 50. Engraved by Mamoru Iwakuni and Hiroshi Ozaki, Japan (#129) and adapted from photographs by Rocco J. Callari, US, and Thomas Lee, China (#130).

1985, Feb. 1		**Engr.**		**Perf. 13½**	
129	A220	80c Turin Center emblem *(654,431)*		.60	.45
		First day cover			1.00
		Inscription block of 4		2.50	—
130	G34	1.20fr U Thant Pavilion *(609,493)*		.90	.70
		First day cover			1.50
		First day cover, #129-130			2.25
		Inscription block of 4		4.00	—

First day covers of Nos. 129-130 total 118,467.

UN University Type

1985, Mar. 15		**Photo.**		**Perf. 13½**	
131	A221	50c Pastoral scene, advanced communications *(625,087)*		.60	.45
		First day cover			1.00
		Inscription block of 4		2.50	—
132	A221	80c like No. 131 *(712,674)*		1.00	.75
		First day cover			1.25
		First day cover, #131-132			1.75
		Inscription block of 4		4.25	—

First day covers of Nos. 131-132 total 93,324.

Flying Postman — G35

Interlocked Peace Doves — G36

Printed by Carl Ueberreuter Druck and Verlag M. Salzer, Austria. Panes of 50. Designed by Arieh Glaser, Israel (#133), and Carol Sliwka, Poland (#134).

1985, May 10		**Litho.**		**Perf. 14**	
133	G35	20c **multicolored** *(2,000,000)+*		.25	.20
		First day cover			1.00
		Inscription block of 4		1.25	—
134	G36	1.20fr **multicolored** *(2,000,000)+*		1.40	1.00
		First day cover			1.50
		First day cover, #133-134			2.00
		Inscription block of 4		6.25	—

First day covers of Nos. 133-134 total 103,165.

40th Anniversary Type

Designed by Rocco J. Callari, U.S., and Thomas Lee, China (No. 137).

1985, June 26		**Photo.**		**Perf. 12 x 11½**	
135	A224	50c **multicolored** *(764,924)*		.60	.35
		First day cover			1.00
		Inscription block of 4		2.50	—

136	A225	70c **multicolored** *(779,074)*		.80	.50
		First day cover			1.25
		First day cover, #135-136			2.00
		Inscription block of 4		3.50	—

Souvenir Sheet
Imperf

137		Sheet of 2 *(498,041)*		2.25	1.10
a.	A224	50c **multicolored**		.75	
b.	A225	70c **multicolored**		1.00	
		First day cover			1.00

First day covers of Nos. 135-137 total 252,418.

UNICEF Child Survival Campaign Type

Printed by the Government Printing Bureau, Japan. Panes of 50. Designed by Mel Harris, United Kingdom (#138) and Adth Vanooijen, Netherlands (#139).

1985, Nov. 22		**Photo. & Engr.**		**Perf. 13½**	
138	A226	50c Three girls *(657,409)*		.40	.20
		First day cover			1.00
		Inscription block of 4		2.00	—
139	A226	1.20fr Infant drinking *(593,568)*		1.00	.90
		First day cover			1.25
		First day cover, #138-139			1.75
		Inscription block of 4		4.25	—

First day covers of Nos. 138-139 total 217,696.

Africa in Crisis Type

Printed by Helio Courvoisier, Switzerland. Panes of 50. Designed by Alemayehou Gabremedhiu, Ethiopia.

1986, Jan. 31		**Photo.**		**Perf. 11½x12**	
140	A227	1.40fr Mother, hungry children *(590,576)*		1.40	1.00
		First day cover *(80,159)*			2.00
		Inscription block of 4		5.50	—

UN Development Program Type

Forestry. Printed by the Government Printing Bureau, Japan. Pane of 40, 2 blocks of 4 horizontal and 5 blocks of 4 vertical. Designed by Thomas Lee, China.

1986, Mar. 14		**Photo.**		**Perf. 13½**	
141	A228	35c Erosion control *(547,567)*		1.60	1.50
142	A228	35c Logging *(547,567)*		1.60	1.50
143	A228	35c Lumber transport *(547,567)*		1.60	1.50
144	A228	35c Nursery *(547,567)*		1.60	1.50
a.		Block of 4, #141-144		6.50	6.00
		First day cover, #141-144			7.50
		First day cover, #141-144, each			3.00
		Inscription block of 4, #144a		7.50	—
		Pane of 40, #141-144		80.00	

No. 144a has a continuous design.
First day covers of Nos. 141-144 total 200,212.

Dove and Sun — G37

Printed by Questa Color Security Printers, Ltd., United Kingdom. Panes of 50. Designed by Ramon Alcantara Rodriguez, Mexico.

1986, Mar. 14		**Litho.**		**Perf. 15x14½**	
145	G37	5c **multicolored** *(2,000,000)+*		.20	.20
		First day cover *(58,908)*			1.00
		Inscription block of 4		.50	—

Stamp Collecting Type

Designs: 50c, UN Human Rights stamp. 80c, UN stamps. Printed by the Swedish Post Office, Sweden. Panes of 50. Designed by Czeslaw Slania and Ingalill Axelsson, Sweden.

1986, May 22		**Engr.**		**Perf. 12½**	
146	A229	50c **dark green & henna brown** *(722,015)*		.70	.45
		First day cover			1.00
		Inscription block of 4		3.00	—
147	A229	80c **dark green & yellow orange** *(750,945)*		1.10	.75
		First day cover			1.00
		First day cover, #146-147			1.25
		Inscription block of 4		4.75	—

First day covers of Nos. 146-147 total 137,653.

Flags and Globe as Dove — G38

Peace in French — G39

International Peace Year. Printed by the Government Printing Bureau, Japan. Panes of 50. Designed by Renato Ferrini, Italy (#148), and Salahattin Kanidinc, US (#149).

1986, June 20		**Photo. & Embossed**		**Perf. 13½**	
148	G38	45c **multicolored** *(620,978)*		.60	.45
		First day cover			1.00
		Inscription block of 4		2.75	—
149	G39	1.40fr **multicolored** *(559,658)*		1.60	1.25
		First day cover			1.50
		First day cover, #148-149			2.00
		Inscription block of 4		7.00	—

First day covers of Nos. 148-149 total 123,542.

WFUNA Anniversary Type
Souvenir Sheet

Printed by Johann Enschede and Sons, Netherlands. Designed by Rocco J. Callari, US.

Designs: 35c, Abstract by Benigno Gomez, Honduras. 45c, Abstract by Alexander Calder (1898-1976), US. 50c, Abstract by Joan Miro (b. 1893), Spain. 70c, Sextet with Dove, by Ole Hamann, Denmark.

1986, Nov. 14		**Litho.**		**Perf. 13x13½**	
150		Sheet of 4 *(478,833)*		4.00	3.00
a.	A232	35c **multicolored**		.55	—
b.	A232	45c **multicolored**		.75	—
c.	A232	50c **multicolored**		.95	—
d.	A232	70c **multicolored**		1.25	—
		First day cover *(58,452)*			2.00

No. 150 has inscribed margin picturing UN and WFUNA emblems.

Trygve Lie Type

1987, Jan. 30		**Photo. & Engr.**		**Perf. 13½**	
151	A233	1.40fr **multicolored** *(516,605)*		1.25	1.00
		First day cover *(76,152)*			1.50
		Inscription block of 4		5.75	—

Sheaf of Colored Bands, by Georges Mathieu — G40

Armillary Sphere, Palais des Nations — G41

Printed by Helio Courvoisier, Switzerland (#152), and the Government Printing Bureau, Japan (#153). Panes of 50. Designed by Georges Mathieu (#152) and Rocco J. Callari (#153), US.

Photo., Photo. & Engr. (#153)

1987, Jan. 30				**Perf. 11½x12, 13½**	
152	G40	90c **multicolored** *(1,600,000)+*		.75	.60
		First day cover			1.00
		Inscription block of 4		3.25	—
153	G41	1.40fr **multicolored** *(1,600,000)+*		1.25	.90
		First day cover			1.00
		First day cover, #152-153			2.00
		Inscription block of 4		5.25	—

First day covers of Nos. 152-153 total 85,737.

Shelter for the Homeless Type

Designs: 50c, Cement-making and brick-making. 90c, Interior construction and decorating.

1987, Mar. 13		**Litho.**		**Perf. 13½x12½**	
154	A234	50c **multicolored** *(564,445)*		.50	.45
		First day cover			1.00
		Inscription block of 4		2.50	—

155	A234	90c	**multicolored** *(526,646)*	1.00	.90
		First day cover			1.10
		First day cover, #154-155			2.00
		Inscription block of 4		4.25	—

First day covers of Nos. 154-155 total 100,366.

Fight Drug Abuse Type

Designs: 80c, Mother and child. 1.20fr, Workers in rice paddy.

1987, June 12   **Litho.**   *Perf. 14½x15*

156	A235	80c	**multicolored** *(634,776)*	.55	.55
		First day cover			1.10
		Inscription block of 4		3.00	—
157	A235	1.20fr	**multicolored** *(609,475)*	.90	.80
		First day cover			1.50
		First day cover, #156-157			2.25
		Inscription block of 4		4.50	—

First day covers of Nos. 156-157 total 95,247.

UN Day Type

Designed by Elisabeth von Janota-Bzowski (35c) and Fritz Oerter (50c).
Designs: Multinational people in various occupations.

1987, Oct. 23   **Litho.**   *Perf. 14½x15*

158	A236	35c	**multicolored** *(1,114,756)*	.40	.35
		First day cover			1.50
		Inscription block of 4		2.00	—
159	A236	50c	**multicolored** *(1,117,464)*	.75	.75
		First day cover			1.75
		Inscription block of 4		3.50	—
		First day cover, #158-159			2.25
		Panes of 12, #158-159		15.00	

Immunize Every Child Type

Designs: 90c, Whooping cough. 1.70fr, Tuberculosis.

1987, Nov. 20   **Litho.**   *Perf. 15x14½*

160	A237	90c	**multicolored** *(634,614)*	1.50	1.00
		First day cover			1.00
		Inscription block of 4		6.25	—
161	A237	1.70fr	**multicolored** *(607,725)*	2.75	1.50
		First day cover			1.25
		First day cover, #160-161			2.50
		Inscription block of 4		11.50	—

IFAD Type

Designs: 35c, Flocks, dairy products. 1.40fr, Fruit.

1988, Jan. 29   **Litho.**   *Perf. 13½*

162	A238	35c	**multicolored** *(524,817)*	.40	.35
		First day cover			1.00
		Inscription block of 4		1.90	—
163	A238	1.40fr	**multicolored** *(499,103)*	1.40	1.25
		First day cover			1.50
		First day cover, #162-163			2.00
		Inscription block of 4		7.00	—

G42

Printed by Heraclio Fournier, S.A., Spain. Panes of 50. Designed by Bjorn Wiinblad, Denmark.

1988, Jan. 29   **Photo.**   *Perf. 14*

164	G42	50c	**multicolored** *(1,600,000)+*	.90	.70
		First day cover			2.00
		Inscription block of 4		3.75	—

Survival of the Forests Type

Pine forest: 50c, Treetops, mountains. 1.10fr, Lake, tree trunks. Printed se-tenant in a continuous design.

1988, Mar. 18   **Litho.**   *Perf. 14x15*

165	A240	50c	**multicolored** *(728,569)*	1.50	1.25
		First day cover			4.00
166	A240	1.10fr	**multicolored** *(728,569)*	4.00	3.50
		First day cover			6.00
a.		Pair, #165-166		5.50	5.00
		First day cover, #166a			10.00
		Inscription block of 4, 2 #166a		12.50	—
		Pane of 12, #165-166		30.00	

Intl. Volunteer Day Type

Designed by Christopher Magadini, US.
Designs: 80c, Agriculture, vert. 90c, Veterinary medicine.

1988, May 6   **Litho.**   *Perf. 13x14, 14x13*

167	A241	80c	**multicolored** *(612,166)*	.80	.60
		First day cover			1.50
		Inscription block of 4		4.00	—
168	A241	90c	**multicolored** *(467,334)*	1.00	.70

		First day cover			1.75
		First day cover, #167-168			3.50
		Inscription block of 4		4.25	—

Health in Sports Type

Paintings by LeRoy Neiman, American sports artist: 50c, Soccer, vert. 1.40fr, Swimming.

1988, June 17   **Litho.**   *Perf. 13½x13, 13x13½*

169	A242	50c	**multicolored** *(541,421)*	.40	.35
		First day cover			1.25
		Inscription block of 4		3.00	—
170	A242	1.40fr	**multicolored** *(475,445)*	1.40	1.25
		First day cover			2.40
		First day cover, #169-170			3.00
		Inscription block of 4		10.00	—

Universal Declaration of Human Rights 40th Anniv. Type

1988, Dec. 9   **Photo. & Engr.**   *Perf. 12*

171	A243	90c	**multicolored** *(745,508)*	.75	.60
		First day cover			2.50
		Inscription block of 4		3.25	—

Souvenir Sheet

172	A243	2fr	**multicolored** *(517,453)*	3.00	2.50
		First day cover			4.00

World Bank Type

1989, Jan. 27   **Litho.**   *Perf. 13x14*

173	A244	80c	Telecommunications *(524,056)*	1.00	.75
		First day cover			1.50
		Inscription block of 4		4.50	—
174	A244	1.40fr	Industry *(488,058)*	2.25	1.75
		First day cover			2.40
		First day cover, #173-174			3.50
		Inscription block of 4		9.50	—

First day covers of Nos. 173-174 total 111,004.

Peace-Keeping Force Type

1989, Mar. 17   *Perf. 14x13½*

175	A245	90c	**multicolored** *(684,566)*	1.00	1.00
		First day cover *(52,463)*			2.00
		Inscription block of 4		5.00	—

World Weather Watch Type

Satellite photographs: 90c, Europe under the influence of Arctic air. 1.10fr, Surface temperatures of sea, ice and land surrounding the Kattegat between Denmark and Sweden.

1989, Apr. 21   **Litho.**   *Perf. 13x14*

176	A247	90c	**multicolored** *(864,409)*	1.25	1.00
		First day cover			1.50
		Inscription block of 4		5.50	—
177	A247	1.10fr	**multicolored** *(853,556)*	2.00	1.50
		First day cover			1.75
		First day cover, #176-177			3.00
		Inscription block of 4		9.00	—

First day covers of Nos. 176-177 total 83,343.

Offices in Geneva, 10th Anniv.
G43   G44

Printed by Government Printing Office, Austria. Panes of 25. Designed by Anton Lehmden (50c) and Arik Brauer (2fr), Austria.

Photo., Photo. & Engr. (2fr)

1989, Aug. 23   *Perf. 14*

178	G43	50c	**multicolored** *(605,382)*	1.10	.70
		First day cover			1.25
		Inscription block of 4		5.00	—
179	G44	2fr	**multicolored** *(538,140)*	3.50	2.50
		First day cover			2.60
		Inscription block of 4		15.00	—
		First day cover, #178-179			3.25
		Panes of 25, #178-179		110.00	

First day covers of Nos. 178-179 total 83,304.

Human Rights Type of 1989

Printed by Johann Enschede and Sons, the Netherlands. Panes of 12+12 se-tenant labels containing Articles 3 (35c) or 4 (80c) inscribed in English, French or German. Designed by Rocco J. Callari and Robert Stein, US.
Artwork: 35c, Young Mother Sewing, by Mary Cassatt. 80c, The Unknown Slave, sculpture by Albert Mangones.

1989, Nov. 17   **Litho.**   *Perf. 13½*

180	A250	35c	**multicolored** *(1,923,818)*	.35	.30
		First day cover			1.25
		Inscription block of 3 + 3 labels		1.60	—
181	A250	80c	**multicolored** *(1,917,953)*	.90	.90

		First day cover			3.00
		Inscription block of 3 + 3 labels		4.50	—
		First day cover, #180-181			4.50
		Panes of 12, #180-181		17.50	—

First day covers of Nos. 180-181 total 134,469.
See Nos. 193-194, 209-210, 234-235.

Intl. Trade Center Type

1990, Feb. 2   **Litho.**   *Perf. 14½x15*

182	A251	1.50fr	**multicolored** *(409,561)*	2.50	2.00
		First day cover *(61,098)*			3.50
		Inscription block of 4		11.00	—

G45

Printed by Heraclio Fournier, S.A., Spain. Designed by Guy Breniaux, France and Elizabeth White, US.

1990, Feb. 2   **Photo.**   *Perf. 14x13½*

183	G45	5fr	**multicolored** *(1,600,000)+*	4.00	3.25
		First day cover *(54,462)*			6.00
		Inscription block of 4		17.50	—

Fight AIDS Type

Designed by Jacek Tofil, Poland (50c) and Lee Keun Moon, Korea (80c).
Designs: 50c, "SIDA." 80c, Proportional drawing of man like the illustration by Leonardo da Vinci.

1990, Mar. 16   **Litho.**   *Perf. 13½x12½*

184	A252	50c	**multicolored** *(480,625)*	1.10	1.00
		First day cover			1.25
		Inscription block of 4		4.75	—
185	A252	80c	**multicolored** *(602,721)*	1.75	.50
		First day cover			1.40
		First day cover, #184-185			2.00
		Inscription block of 4		7.50	—

First day covers of Nos. 184-185 total 108,364.

Medicinal Plants Type

1990, May 4   **Photo.**   **Granite Paper**   *Perf. 11½*

186	A253	90c	Plumeria rubra *(625,522)*	1.10	.70
		First day cover			1.40
		Inscription block of 4		5.00	—
187	A253	1.40fr	Cinchona officinalis *(648,619)*	2.25	1.50
		First day cover			2.25
		First day cover, #186-187			3.50
		Inscription block of 4		9.50	—

First day covers of Nos. 186-187 total 114,062.

UN 45th Anniv. Type

Designed by Fritz Henry Oerter and Ruth Schmidthammer, Federal Republic of Germany (90c), Michiel Mertens, Belgium (1.10fr), Robert Stein, US (No. 190).
"45," emblem and: 90c, Symbols of clean environment, transportation and industry. 1.10fr, Dove in silhouette.

1990, June 26   *Perf. 14½x13*

188	A254	90c	**multicolored** *(557,253)*	1.25	.45
		First day cover			1.40
		Inscription block of 4		5.25	—
189	A254	1.10fr	**multicolored** *(519,635)*	2.25	1.50
		First day cover			1.75
		First day cover, #188-189			3.00
		Inscription block of 4		9.50	—

Souvenir Sheet

190			Sheet of 2, #188-189 *(401,027)*	5.75	3.75
		First day cover			4.50

First day covers of Nos. 188-190 total 148,975.

Crime Prevention Type

1990, Sept. 13   **Photo.**   *Perf. 14*

191	A255	50c	Official corruption *(494,876)*	1.50	.80
		First day cover			1.25
		Inscription block of 4		5.50	—
192	A255	2fr	Environmental crime *(417,033)*	3.50	2.75
		First day cover			3.00
		First day cover, #191-192			4.50
		Inscription block of 4		15.00	—

First day covers of Nos. 191-192 total 76,605.

Human Rights Type of 1989

Panes of 12+12 se-tenant labels containing Articles 9 (35c) or 10 (90c) inscribed in French, German or English.
Artwork: 35c, The Prison Courtyard by Vincent Van Gogh. 90c, Katho's Son Redeems the Evil Doer From Execution by Albrecht Durer.

1990, Nov. 16   **Litho.**   *Perf. 13½*

193	A250	35c	**multicolored** *(1,578,828)*	.50	.30
		First day cover			1.25
		Inscription block of 3 + 3 labels		1.75	—
194	A250	90c	**black & brown** *(1,540,200)*	1.40	1.00
		First day cover			1.50

Inscription block of 3 + 3 labels 4.50
First day cover, #193-194 3.50
Panes of 12, #193-194 22.50

First day covers of Nos. 193-194 total 100,282.

Economic Commission for Europe Type

1991, Mar. 15		**Litho.**		**Perf. 14**
195	A256	90c Owl, gull *(643,143)+*	1.40	.75
		First day cover		2.00
196	A256	90c Bittern, otter *(643,143)+*	1.40	.75
		First day cover		2.00
197	A256	90c Swan, lizard *(643,143)+*	1.40	.75
		First day cover		2.00
198	A256	90c Great crested grebe *(643,143)+*	1.40	.75
		First day cover		2.00
a.		Block of 4, #195-198	6.00	5.00
		First day cover, #198a		5.00
		Inscription block of 4, #198a	6.50	—
		Pane of 40, #195-198	52.50	

First day covers of Nos. 195-198a total 75,759.

Namibian Independence Type

1991, May 10		**Litho.**		**Perf. 14**
199	A257	70c Mountains *(328,014)*	1.50	1.00
		First day cover		1.65
		Inscription block of 4	6.25	—
200	A257	90c Baobab tree *(395,362)*	2.50	1.75
		First day cover		2.00
		First day cover, #199-200		5.00
		Inscription block of 4	11.50	—

First day covers of Nos. 199-200 total 94,201.

Ballots Filling Ballot
Box — G46

UN
Emblem — G47

Printed by House of Questa, United Kingdom. Designed by Ran Banda Mawilmada, Sri Lanka (80c), Maurice Gouju, France (1.50fr).

1991, May 10		**Litho.**		**Perf. 15x14½**
201	G46	80c multicolored *(1,600,000)+*	1.60	1.10
		First day cover		1.75
		Inscription block of 4	6.50	—
202	G47	1.50fr multicolored *(1,600,000)+*	3.00	2.25
		First day cover		3.25
		First day cover, #201-202		3.75
		Inscription block of 4	12.50	—

First day covers of Nos. 201-202 total 77,590.

Rights of the
Child — G49

Printed by The House of Questa. Panes of 50. Designed by Ryuta Nakajima, Japan (80c) and David Popper, Switzerland (1.10fr).

1991, June 14		**Litho.**		**Perf. 14½**
203	G48	80c Hands holding infant *(469,962)*	1.50	1.00
		First day cover		1.75
		Inscription block of 4	6.25	—
204	G49	1.10fr Children, flowers *(494,382)*	2.10	1.50
		First day cover		2.25
		First day cover, #203-204		3.25
		Inscription block of 4	9.00	—

First day covers of Nos. 203-204 total 97,732.

Banning of
Chemical
Weapons — G51

Printed by Heraclio Fournier S.A. Panes of 50. Designed by Oscar Asboth, Austria (80c), Michel Granger, France (1.40fr).

1991, Sept. 11		**Litho.**		**Perf. 13½**
205	G50	80c multicolored *(345,658)*	1.75	1.25
		First day cover		1.75
		Inscription block of 4	6.50	
206	G51	1.40fr multicolored *(366,076)*	3.25	2.00
		First day cover		2.50
		First day cover, #205-206		3.50
		Inscription block of 4	13.50	—

First day covers of Nos. 205-206 total 91,887.

UN Postal Administration, 40th Anniv. Type

1991, Oct. 24				**Perf. 14x15**
207	A263	50c UN NY No. 7 *(506,839)*	1.10	.85
		First day cover		1.25
		Inscription block of 4	4.50	—
208	A263	1.60fr UN NY No. 10 *(580,493)*	2.50	2.00
		First day cover		3.00
		Inscription block of 4	11.00	—
		First day cover, #207-208		3.25
		Panes of 25, #207-208	70.00	

First day covers of Nos. 207-208 total 88,784.

Human Rights Type of 1989

Panes of 12+12 se-tenant labels containing Articles 15 (50c) or 16 (90c) inscribed in French, German or English.
Artwork: 50c, Early Morning in Ro...1925, by Paul Klee. 90c, Marriage of Giovanni (?) Arnolfini and Giovanna Cenami (?), by Jan Van Eyck.

1991, Nov. 20		**Litho.**		**Perf. 13½**
209	A250	50c multicolored *(1,295,172)*	.90	.70
		First day cover		1.25
		Inscription block of 3 + 3 labels	2.75	—
210	A250	90c multicolored *(1,324,091)*	1.50	1.25
		First day cover		2.00
		Inscription block of 3 + 3 labels	5.00	—
		First day cover, #209-210		2.75
		Panes of 12, #209-210	27.50	

First day covers of Nos. 209-210 total 139,904.

World Heritage Type of 1984

Designs: 50c, Sagarmatha Natl. Park, Nepal. 1.10fr, Stonehenge, United Kingdom.

1992, Jan. 24		**Litho.**		**Perf. 13**
		Size: 35x28mm		
211	G29	50c multicolored *(468,647)*	1.25	1.00
		First day cover		1.25
		Inscription block of 4	5.25	—
212	G29	1.10fr multicolored *(369,345)*	2.50	2.00
		First day cover		2.25
		First day cover, #211-212		3.00
		Inscription block of 4	11.00	—

First day covers of Nos. 211-212 total 77,034.

Printed by The House of Questa. Panes of 50. Designed by Nestor Jose Martin, Argentina.

1992, Jan. 24		**Litho.**		**Perf. 15x14½**
213	G53	3fr multicolored *(1,600,000)+*	3.50	3.00
		First day cover *(36,135)*		4.00
		Inscription block of 4	15.00	—

Clean Oceans Type

1992, Mar. 13		**Litho.**		**Perf. 14**
214	A264	80c Ocean surface, diff. *(850,699)*	1.00	.75
215	A264	80c Ocean bottom, diff. *(850,699)*	1.00	.75
a.		Pair	2.25	1.75
		First day cover, #215a		2.85
		First day cover, #214-215, each		1.80
		Inscription block of 4, 2 #215a	5.00	—
		Pane of 12, #214-215	16.00	

First day covers of Nos. 214-215a total 90,725.

Earth Summit Type

Designs: No. 216, Rainbow. No. 217, Two clouds shaped as faces. No. 218, Two sailboats. No. 219, Woman with parasol, boat, flowers.

1992, May 22		**Photo.**		**Perf. 11½**
216	A265	75c multicolored *(826,543)*	1.10	.75
217	A265	75c multicolored *(826,543)*	1.10	.75
218	A265	75c multicolored *(826,543)*	1.10	.75
219	A265	75c multicolored *(826,543)*	1.10	.75
a.		Block of 4, #216-219	4.50	4.00
		First day cover, #219a		4.00
		First day cover, #216-219, each		2.00
		Inscription block of 4, #216-219	4.75	—
		Pane of 40, #216-219	50.00	

First day covers of Nos. 216-219a total 74,629.

Mission to Planet Earth Type

Designs: No. 220, Space station. No. 221, Probes near Jupiter.

1992, Sept. 4		**Photo.**		**Rouletted 8**
		Granite Paper		
220	A266	1.10fr multicolored *(668,241)*	2.50	2.00
221	A266	1.10fr multicolored *(668,241)*	2.50	2.00
a.		Pair, #220-221	5.00	4.00
		First day cover, #221a		5.00
		First day cover, #241-242, each		4.00
		Inscription block of 4, 2 #220-221	12.00	
		Pane of 10, #220-221	27.50	

First day covers of Nos. 220-221 total 76,060.

Science and Technology Type of 1992

Designs: 90c, Doctor, nurse. 1.60fr, Graduate seated before computer.

1992, Oct. 2		**Litho.**		**Perf. 14**
222	A267	90c multicolored *(438,943)*	1.50	.90
		First day cover		1.60
		Inscription block of 4	6.00	—
223	A267	1.60fr multicolored *(400,701)*	2.75	1.75
		First day cover		2.50
		First day cover, #222-223		3.25
		Inscription block of 4	11.50	—

First day covers of Nos. 222-223 total 75,882.

Human Rights Type of 1989

Panes of 12+12 se-tenant labels containing Articles 21 (50c) and 22 (90c) inscribed in French, German or English.
Artwork: 50c, The Oath of the Tennis Court, by Jacques Louis David. 90c, Rocking Chair I, by Henry Moore.

1992, Nov. 20		**Litho.**		**Perf. 13½**
224	A250	50c multicolored, *(1,201,788)*	1.00	.90
		First day cover		2.00
		Inscription block of 3 + 3 labels	3.25	—
225	A250	90c multicolored, *(1,179,294)*	1.75	1.50
		First day cover		4.00
		Inscription block of 3 + 3 labels	5.50	—
		First day cover, #224-225		2.75
		Panes of 12, #224-225	30.00	

First day covers of Nos. 224-225 total 104,491.

Aging With Dignity Type

Designs: 50c, Older man coaching soccer. 1.60fr, Older man working at computer terminal.

1993, Feb. 5		**Litho.**		**Perf. 13**
226	A270	50c multicolored *(483,452)*	.75	.60
		First day cover		1.00
		Inscription block of 4	3.50	—
227	A270	1.60fr multicolored *(331,008)*	2.40	1.75
		First day cover		2.75
		First day cover, #226-227		3.00
		Inscription block of 4	10.50	—

First day covers of Nos. 226-227 total 61,361.

Endangered Species Type

Designed by Rocco J. Callari, US, and Betina Ogden, Australia.
Designs: No. 228, Pongidae (gorilla). No. 229, Falco peregrinus (peregrine falcon). No. 230, Trichechus inunguis (Amazonian manatee). No. 231, Panthera uncia (snow leopard).

1993, Mar. 2		**Litho.**		**Perf. 13x12½**
228	A271	80c multicolored *(1,200,000)+*	1.10	.90
229	A271	80c multicolored *(1,200,000)+*	1.10	.90
230	A271	80c multicolored *(1,200,000)+*	1.10	.90
231	A271	80c multicolored *(1,200,000)+*	1.10	.90
a.		Block of 4, #228-231	4.50	4.00

First day cover, #231a   5.00
First day cover, #228-231, each   2.00
Inscription block of 4, #228-231   4.50 —
Pane of 16, #228-231   19.00

First day covers of Nos. 228-231a total 75,363.

Healthy Environment Type

1993, May 7   Litho.   Perf. 15x14½
232 A272 60c **Neighborhood** *(456,304)*   1.10   .70
    First day cover   1.25
    Inscription block of 4   4.75 —
233 A272 1fr **Urban skyscrapers** *(392,015)*   2.25 1.50
    First day cover   2.00
    First day cover, #232-233   3.25
    Inscription block of 4   10.00 —

First day covers of Nos. 232-233 total 59,790.

Human Rights Type of 1989

Printed in panes of 12 + 12 se-tenant labels containing Article 27 (50c) and 28 (90c) inscribed in French, German or English.
Artwork: 50c, Three Musicians, by Pablo Picasso. 90c, Voice of Space, by Rene Magritte.

1993, June 11   Litho.   Perf. 13½
234 A250 50c **multicolored** *(1,166,286)*   .90   .90
    First day cover   1.25
    Inscription block of 3 + 3 labels   2.75 —
235 A250 90c **multicolored** *(1,122,348)*   2.00 1.75
    Inscription block of 3 + 3 labels   6.25 —
    First day cover   2.00
    First day cover, #234-235   3.50
    Panes of 12, #234-235   30.00

First day covers of Nos. 234-235 total 83,432.

Intl. Peace Day Type

Denomination at: #236, UL. #237, UR. #238, LL. #239, LR.

1993, Sept. 21   Litho. & Engr.   Rouletted 12½
236 A274 60c **purple & multi** *(357,760)*   2.00 1.25
237 A274 60c **purple & multi** *(357,760)*   2.00 1.25
238 A274 60c **purple & multi** *(357,760)*   2.00 1.25
239 A274 60c **purple & multi** *(357,760)*   2.00 1.25
  a.   Block of 4, #236-239   8.25 —
    First day cover, #239a   4.00
    First day cover, #236-239, each   1.75
    Inscription block of 4, #239a   8.75 —
    Pane of 40, #236-239   80.00

First day covers of Nos. 236-239a total 47,207.

Environment-Climate Type

1993, Oct. 29   Litho.   Perf. 14½
240 A275 1.10fr **Polar bears** *(391,593)*   1.50 1.25
241 A275 1.10fr **Whale sounding** *(391,593)*   1.50 1.25
242 A275 1.10fr **Elephant seal** *(391,593)*   1.50 1.25
243 A275 1.10fr **Penguins** *(391,593)*   1.50 1.25
  a.   Strip of 4, #240-243   6.00 5.00
    First day cover, #243a   5.25
    First day cover, #240-243, each   2.75
    Inscription block of 8, 2 #243a   12.50 —
    Pane of 24, #240-243   32.50

First day covers of Nos. 240-243a total 41,819.

Intl. Year of the Family Type of 1993

Designs: 80c, Parents teaching child to walk. 1fr, Two women and child picking plants.

1994, Feb. 4   Litho.   Perf. 13.1
244 A276 80c **rose violet & multi** *(535,000)+*   1.25 1.00
    First day cover   1.75
    Inscription block of 4   5.75 —
245 A276 1fr **brown & multi** *(535,000)+*   1.75 1.25
    First day cover   2.00
    First day cover, #244-245   3.25
    Inscription block of 4   7.25 —

First day covers of Nos. 244-245 total 50,080.

Endangered Species Type of 1993

Designed by Rocco J. Callari (frame) and Leon Parson, US (stamps).
Designs: No. 246, Mexican prairie dog. No. 247, Jabiru. No. 248, Blue whale. No. 249, Golden lion tamarin.

1994, Mar. 18   Litho.   Perf. 12.7
246 A271 80c **multicolored** *(1,200,000)+*   1.10 .85
247 A271 80c **multicolored** *(1,200,000)+*   1.10 .85
248 A271 80c **multicolored** *(1,200,000)+*   1.10 .85
249 A271 80c **multicolored** *(1,200,000)+*   1.10 .85
  a.   Block of 4, #246-249   4.50 3.50
    First day cover, #249a   5.50
    First day cover, #246-249, each   1.75
    Inscription block of 4, #246-249   4.50 —
    Pane of 16, #246-249   20.00

First day covers of Nos. 246-249a total 82,043.

Protection for Refugees Type of 1994

Design: 1.20fr, Hand lifting figure over chasm.

1994, Apr. 29   Litho.   Perf. 14.3x14.8
250 A277 1.20fr **multicolored** *(550,000)+*   2.75 2.25
    First day cover *(33,805)*   2.50
    Inscription block of 4   12.00 —

Intl. Decade for Natural Disaster Reduction Type of 1994

Earth seen from space, outline map of: No. 251, North America. No. 252, Eurasia. No. 253, South America. No. 254, Australia and South Pacific region.

1994, May 27   Litho.   Perf. 13.9x14.2
251 A281 60c **multicolored** *(570,000)+*   1.60 1.00
252 A281 60c **multicolored** *(570,000)+*   1.60 1.00
253 A281 60c **multicolored** *(570,000)+*   1.60 1.00
254 A281 60c **multicolored** *(570,000)+*   1.60 1.00
  a.   Block of 4, #251-254   7.00 4.00
    First day cover, #254a   5.00
    First day cover, #251-254, each   1.75
    Inscription block of 4, #254a   8.00 —
    Pane of 40, #251-254   67.50

First day covers of Nos. 251-254a total 37,595.

Palais des Nations, Geneva — G54

Creation of the World, by Oili Maki — G55

Printed by House of Questa, United Kingdom. Designed by Rocco J. Callari, US.

1994, Sept. 1   Litho.   Perf. 14.3x14.6
255 G54 60c **multicolored** *(1,075,000)+*   .75 .55
    First day cover   1.10
    Inscription block of 4   3.50 —
256 G55 80c **multicolored** *(1,075,000)+*   1.00 .70
    First day cover   1.50
    Inscription block of 4   4.50 —
257 G54 1.80fr **multi**, diff. *(1,075,000)+*   2.25 1.75
    First day cover   2.75
    Inscription block of 4   10.00 —
    First day cover, #255-257   4.50

First day covers of Nos. 255-257 total 51,637.

Population and Development Type of 1994

Designs: 60c, People shopping at open-air market. 80c, People on vacation crossing bridge.

1994, Sept. 1   Litho.   Perf. 13.2x13.6
258 A282 60c **multicolored** *(535,000)+*   1.25 .80
    First day cover   1.25
    Inscription block of 4   5.00 —
259 A282 80c **multicolored** *(535,000)+*   1.75 1.25
    First day cover   1.75
    Inscription block of 4   7.50 —
    First day cover, #258-259   3.00

First day covers of Nos. 258-259 total 50,443.

UNCTAD Type of 1994

1994, Oct. 28
260 A283 80c **multi**, diff. *(535,000)+*   1.25 1.00
    First day cover   1.75
    Inscription block of 4   5.50 —
261 A283 1fr **multi**, diff. *(535,000)+*   1.60 1.40
    First day cover   2.00
    Inscription block of 4   7.75 —
    First day cover, #260-261   3.50
  a.   Grayish green omitted   —
    Inscription block of 4   —

First day covers of Nos. 260-261 total 48,122.

UN 50th Anniv. Type of 1995

1995, Jan. 1   Litho. & Engr.   Perf. 13.4
262 A284 80c **multicolored** *(823,827)*   1.25 1.10
    First day cover *(38,988)*   3.00
    Inscription block of 4   5.75 —

Social Summit Type of 1995

1995, Feb. 3   Photo. & Engr.   Perf. 13.6x13.9
263 A285 1fr **multi**, diff. *(452,116)*   1.50 1.25
    First day cover *(35,246)*   2.00
    Inscription block of 4   7.00 —

Endangered Species Type of 1993

Designed by Sibylle Erni, Switzerland.
Designs: No. 264, Crowned lemur, Lemur coronatus. No. 265, Giant Scops owl, Otus gurneyi. No. 266, Zetek's frog, Atelopus varius zeteki. No. 267, Wood bison, Bison bison athabascae.

1995, Mar. 24   Litho.   Perf. 13x12½
264 A271 80c **multicolored** *(730,000)+*   1.40 1.10
265 A271 80c **multicolored** *(730,000)+*   1.40 1.10
266 A271 80c **multicolored** *(730,000)+*   1.40 1.10
267 A271 80c **multicolored** *(730,000)+*   1.40 1.10
  a.   Block of 4, 264-267   5.75 4.50
    First day cover, #267a   4.50
    First day cover, #264-267, each   1.60
    Inscription block of 4, #267a   5.75 —
    Pane of 16, #264-267   24.00

First day covers of Nos. 264-267a total 71,907.

Intl. Youth Year Type of 1995

Designs: 80c, Farmer on tractor, fields at harvest time. 1fr, Couple standing by fields at night.

1995, May 26   Litho.   Perf. 14.4x14.7
268 A286 80c **multicolored** *(294,987)*   1.40 1.10
    First day cover   1.60
    Inscription block of 4   6.00 —
269 A286 1fr **multicolored** *(264,823)*   1.75 1.40
    First day cover   1.75
    First day cover, #268-269   3.00
    Inscription block of 4   8.00 —

First day covers of Nos. 268-269 total 45,665.

UN, 50th Anniv. Type of 1995

Designs: 60c, Like No. 663. 1.80fr, Like No. 664.

1995, June 26   Engr.   Perf. 13.3x13.6
270 A287 60c **maroon** *(352,336)*   1.00 .60
    First day cover   .90
    Inscription block of 4   4.50 —
271 A287 1.80fr **green** *(377,391)*   3.25 1.75
    First day cover   3.00
    First day cover, #270-271   4.00
    Inscription block of 4   14.00 —

Souvenir Sheet
Litho. & Engr.
Imperf

272   Sheet of 2, #270-271 *(251,272)*   4.25 4.25
  a.   A287 60c maroon   1.00 1.00
  b.   A287 1.80fr green   3.25 3.25
    First day cover   4.50

First day covers of Nos. 270-272 total 72,666.

Conference on Women Type of 1995

Designs: 60c, Black woman, cranes flying above. 1fr, Women, dove.

1995, Sept. 5   Photo.   Perf. 12
273 A288 60c **multicolored** *(342,336)*   1.50 .50
    First day cover   1.25
    Inscription block of 4   6.50 —

Size: 28x50mm

274 A288 1fr **multicolored** *(345,489)*   2.50 .85
    First day cover   2.25
    First day cover, #273-274   3.25
    Inscription block of 4   11.00 —

First day covers of Nos. 273-274 total 57,542.

UN People, 50th Anniv. Type of 1995

1995, Oct. 24   Litho.   Perf. 14
275   Sheet of 12 *(216,832 sheets)*   14.00 9.00
    First day cover   17.00
  a.-l.   A290 30c each   1.10 .70
    First day cover, #275a-275l, each   3.00
276   Souvenir booklet, *(74,151 booklets)*   16.00
  a.   A290 30c Booklet pane of 3, vert. strip of 3 from UL of sheet   3.50 3.50
  b.   A290 30c Booklet pane of 3, vert. strip of 3 from UR of sheet   3.50 3.50
  c.   A290 30c Booklet pane of 3, vert. strip of 3 from LL of sheet   3.50 3.50
  d.   A290 30c Booklet pane of 3, vert. strip of 3 from LR of sheet   3.50 3.50

First day covers of Nos. 275-276d total 53,245.

WFUNA, 50th Anniv. Type

Design: 80c, Fishing boat, fish in net.

1996, Feb. 2   Litho.   Perf. 13x13½
277 A291 80c **multicolored** *(550,000)+*   1.50 .65
    First day cover   2.00
    Inscription block of 4   6.50 —

The Galloping Horse Treading on a Flying Swallow, Chinese Bronzework, Eastern Han Dynasty (25-220 A.D.) — G56

Palais des Nations, Geneva — G57

Printed by House of Questa, UK.

1996, Feb. 2	Litho.		Perf. 14½x15
278 G56 40c multicolored (1,125,000)+		.65	.30
First day cover			1.25
Inscription block of 4		3.25	
279 G57 70c multicolored (1,125,000+)		1.10	.55
First day cover			1.50
First day cover, #278-279			2.25
Inscription block of 4		5.50	—

Endangered Species Type of 1993

Designs: No. 280, Paphiopedilum delenatii. No. 281, Pachypodium baronii. No. 282, Sternbergia lutea. No. 283, Darlingtonia californica.

1996, Mar. 14	Litho.		Perf. 12½
280 A271 80c multicolored (680,000)+		1.10	.65
281 A271 80c multicolored (680,000)+		1.10	.65
282 A271 80c multicolored (680,000)+		1.10	.65
283 A271 80c multicolored (680,000)+		1.10	.65
a. Block of 4, #280-283		4.50	
First day cover, #280-283, each			2.00
First day cover, #283a			4.50
Pane of 16, #280-283		18.00	

City Summit Type of 1996

Designs: No. 284, Asian family. No. 285, Oriental garden. No. 286, Fruit, vegetable vendor, mosque. No. 287, Boys playing ball. No. 288, Couple reading newspaper.

1996, June 3	Litho.		Perf. 14x13½
284 A293 70c multicolored (420,000)+		.90	.55
285 A293 70c multicolored (420,000)+		.90	.55
286 A293 70c multicolored (420,000)+		.90	.55
287 A293 70c multicolored (420,000)+		.90	.55
288 A293 70c multicolored (420,000)+		.90	.55
a. Strip of 5, #284-288		4.50	
First day cover, #288a			5.00
First day cover, #284-288, each			1.50
Inscription block of 2 #288a		9.50	

Sport and the Environment Type

Designs: 70c, Cycling, vert. 1.10fr, Sprinters.

1996, July 19	Litho.	Perf. 14x14½, 14½x14	
289 A294 70c multicolored (625,000)+		1.40	1.00
First day cover			1.50
Inscription block of 4		5.75	—
290 A294 1.10fr multicolored (625,000)+		2.00	1.25
First day cover			2.25
First day cover, #289-290			3.50
Inscription block of 4		8.75	—

Souvenir Sheet

291 A294 Sheet of 2, #289-290 (345,000)+		3.00	2.85
First day cover			7.00

Plea for Peace Type

Designed by: 90c, Chen Yu, China. 1.10fr, Zhou Jing, China.

Designs: 90c, Tree filled with birds, vert. 1.10fr, Bouquet of flowers in rocket tail vase, vert.

1996, Sept. 17	Litho.		Perf. 15x14½
292 A295 90c multicolored (550,000)+		1.40	.70
First day cover			1.50
Inscription block of 4		7.00	—
293 A295 1.10fr multicolored (550,000)+		2.00	.85
First day cover			2.25
First day cover, #292-293			3.75
Inscription block of 4		8.75	—

UNICEF Type

Fairy Tales: 70c, The Sun and the Moon, South America. 1.80fr, Ananse, Africa.

1996, Nov. 20	Litho.		Perf. 14½x15
294 A296 70c multicolored (1,000,000)+		1.00	.55
First day cover			1.50
Pane of 8 + label		8.50	
295 A296 1.80fr multicolored (1,000,000)+		2.50	1.40
First day cover			3.00
First day cover, #294-295			4.00
Pane of 8 + label		21.00	

UN Flag — G58

Palais des Nations Under Construction by Massimo Campigli — G59

Printed by The House of Questa, Ltd., UK.

1997, Feb. 12	Litho.		Perf. 14½
296 G58 10c multicolored (600,000)+		.20	.20
First day cover			1.25
Inscription block of 4		.55	—
297 G59 1.10fr multicolored (700,000)+		1.50	.75
First day cover			2.25
First day cover, #296-297			2.50
Inscription block of 4		6.00	—

First day covers of Nos. 296-297 total 41,186.

Endangered Species Type of 1993

Designs: No. 298, Ursus maritimus (polar bear). No. 299, Goura cristata (blue-crowned pigeon). No. 300, Amblyrhynchus cristatus (marine iguana). No. 301, Lama guanicoe (guanaco).

1997, Mar. 13	Litho.		Perf. 12½
298 A271 80c multicolored (620,000)+		1.10	.55
299 A271 80c multicolored (620,000)+		1.10	.55
300 A271 80c multicolored (620,000)+		1.10	.55
301 A271 80c multicolored (620,000)+		1.10	.55
a. Block of 4, #298-301		4.50	2.25
First day cover, #301a			5.00
First day cover, #298-301, each			1.75
Inscription block of 4, #301a		4.50	
Pane of 16		20.00	

First day covers of Nos. 298-301 total 71,905.

Earth Summit Anniv. Type

Designs: No. 302, Person flying over mountain. No. 303, Mountain, person's face. No. 304, Person standing on mountain, sailboats. No. 305, Person, mountain, trees.
1.10fr, Combined design similar to Nos. 302-305.

1997, May 30	Photo.		Perf. 11½
Granite Paper			
302 A299 45c multicolored (227,187)		1.00	.60
303 A299 45c multicolored (227,187)		1.00	.60
304 A299 45c multicolored (227,187)		1.00	.60
305 A299 45c multicolored (227,187)		1.00	.60
a. Block of 4, #302-305		4.50	1.40
First day cover, #305a			3.50
First day cover, #302-305, each			1.75
Inscription block of 4, #305a		4.75	

Souvenir Sheet

306 A299 1.10fr multicolored (176,386)		1.50	1.50
First day cover			5.00

First day covers of Nos. 302-306 total 55,389.

Transportation Type of 1997

Air transportation: No. 307, Zeppelin, Fokker tri-motor. No. 308, Boeing 314 Clipper, Lockheed Constellation. No. 309, DeHavilland Comet. No. 310, Boeing 747, Illyushin jet. No. 311, Concorde.

1997, Aug. 29	Litho.		Perf. 14x14½
307 A300 70c multicolored (271,575)		1.00	.50
308 A300 70c multicolored (271,575)		1.00	.50
309 A300 70c multicolored (271,575)		1.00	.50
310 A300 70c multicolored (271,575)		1.00	.50
311 A300 70c multicolored (271,575)		1.00	.50
a. Strip of 5, #307-311		5.50	4.00
First day cover, #311a			6.00
First day cover, #307-311, each			2.25
Margin block of 10, 2#311a		11.50	

No. 311a has continuous design.
First day covers of Nos. 307-311 total 33,303.

Philately Type

Designs: 70c, No. 146. 1.10fr, No. 147.

1997, Oct. 14	Litho.		Perf. 13½x14
312 A301 70c multicolored (254,406)		2.00	1.25
First day cover			1.50
Inscription block of 4		8.50	—
313 A301 1.10fr multicolored (303,125)		2.75	2.00
First day cover			2.25
First day cover, #312-313			3.25
Inscription block of 4		11.50	—

First day covers of Nos. 312-313 total 47,528.

World Heritage Convention Type

Terracotta warriors of Xian: 45c, Single warrior. 70c, Massed warriors. No. 316a, like #716. No. 316b, like #717. No. 316c, like Geneva #314. No. 316d, like Geneva #315. No. 316e, like Vienna #230. No. 316f, like Vienna #231.

1997, Nov. 19	Litho.		Perf. 13½
314 A302 45c multicolored (409,820)		.75	.50
First day cover			1.25
Inscription block of 4		3.25	—
315 A302 70c multicolored (414,059)		1.50	1.00
First day cover			1.50

	First day cover, #314-315		2.50	
	Inscription block of 4		7.00	—
316	Souvenir booklet (275,114 booklets)		5.00	—
a.-f.	A302 10c any single		.20	.20
g.	Booklet pane of 4 #316a		.60	.60
h.	Booklet pane of 4 #316b		.60	.60
i.	Booklet pane of 4 #316c		.60	.60
j.	Booklet pane of 4 #316d		.60	.60
k.	Booklet pane of 4 #316e		.60	.60
l.	Booklet pane of 4 #316f		.60	.60

First day covers of Nos. 314-316 total 40,366.

Palais des Nations, Geneva — G60

Printed by The House of Questa, UK. Designed by UN (2fr).

1998, Feb. 13	Litho.		Perf. 14½x15
317 G60 2fr multicolored (550,000)+		2.75	1.40
First day cover			3.50
Inscription block of 4		12.00	—

Endangered Species Type of 1993

Designed by Rocco J. Callari, US and Suzanne Duranceau, Canada.
Designs: No. 318, Macaca thibetana (short-tailed Tibetan macaque). No. 319, Phoenicopterus ruber (Caribbean flamingo). No. 320, Ornithoptera alexandrae (Queen Alexandra's birdwing). No. 321, Dama mesopotamica (Persian fallow deer).

1998, Mar. 13	Litho.		Perf. 12½
318 A271 80c multicolored (560,000)+		1.10	.55
319 A271 80c multicolored (560,000)+		1.10	.55
320 A271 80c multicolored (560,000)+		1.10	.55
321 A271 80c multicolored (560,000)+		1.10	.55
a. Block of 4, #318-321		4.50	2.25
First day cover, #321a			5.00
First day cover, #318-321, each			1.50
Pane of 16		19.00	

Intl. Year of the Ocean — G61

Designed by Jon Ellis, US.

1998, May 20	Litho.		Perf. 13x13½
322 G61 Sheet of 12 (270,000)+		9.00	4.50
First day cover			12.50
a.-l. 45c any single		.70	.35
First day cover, #322a-322l, each			1.75

Rain Forests Type

1998, June 19			Perf. 13x13½
323 A307 70c Orangutans (430,000)+		1.00	.50
First day cover			1.50
Inscription block of 4		4.00	—

Souvenir Sheet

324 A307 3fr like #323 (250,000)+		4.50	3.00
First day cover			6.00

Peacekeeping Type

Designs: 70c, Soldier with two children. 90c, Two soldiers, children.

1998, Sept. 15	Photo.		Perf. 12
325 A308 70c multicolored (400,000)+		1.00	.50
First day cover			1.50
Inscription block of 4		4.00	—

326 A308 90c **multicolored** *(390,000)*+   1.40 .70
    First day cover   2.00
    First day cover, #325-326   3.00
    Inscription block of 4   5.75 —

Declaration of Human Rights Type of 1998

Designs: 90c, Stylized birds. 1.80fr, Stylized birds flying from hand.

1998, Oct. 27   **Litho. & Photo.**   *Perf. 13*
327 A309 90c **multicolored** *(400,000)*+   1.40 .70
    First day cover   2.00
    Inscription block of 4   5.75 —
328 A309 1.80fr **multicolored** *(390,000)*+   2.75 1.40
    First day cover   3.50
    First day cover, #327-328   5.00
    Inscription block of 4   12.00 —

Schönbrunn Palace Type

Designs: 70c, #331b, Great Palm House. 1.10fr, #331d, Blue porcelain vase, vert. No. 331a, Palace. No. 331c, The Gloriette (archway). No. 331e, Wall painting on fabric (detail), by Johann Wenzl Bergl, vert. No. 331f, Porcelain stove, vert.

1998, Dec. 4   **Litho.**   *Perf. 14*
329 A310 70c **multicolored** *(375,000)*+   1.00 .50
    First day cover   1.50
    Inscription block of 4   4.00 —
330 A310 1.10fr **multicolored** *(375,000)*+   1.50 .75
    First day cover   2.25
    First day cover, #329-330   3.25
    Inscription block of 4   6.00 —

Souvenir Booklet

331   Booklet *(100,000)*+   6.00
a.-c.   A310 10c any single   .20 .20
d.-f.   A310 30c any single   .45 .45
g.   Booklet pane of 4 #331a   .60
h.   Booklet pane of 3 #331d   1.40
i.   Booklet pane of 3 #331e   1.40
j.   Booklet pane of 3 #331f   1.40
k.   Booklet pane of 4 #331b   .60
l.   Booklet pane of 4 #331c   .60

Palais Wilson, Geneva — G62

Designed and printed by Helio Courvoisier, SA, Switzerland.

1999, Feb. 5   **Photo.**   *Perf. 11½*
Granite Paper
332 G62 1.70fr **brown red** *(600,000)*+   2.50 1.25
    First day cover *(25,568)*   3.50
    Inscription block of 4   10.00 —

World Heritage, Australia Type

Designs: 90c, #335e, Kakadu Natl. Park. 1.10fr, #335c, Great Barrier Reef. No. 335a, Tasmanian Wilderness. No. 335b, Wet tropics of Queensland. No. 335d, Uluru-Kata Tjuta Natl. Park. No. 335f, Willandra Lakes region.

1999, Mar. 19   **Litho.**   *Perf. 13*
333 A313 90c **multicolored** *(420,000)*+   1.40 .70
    First day cover   2.00
    Inscription block of 4   5.75 —
334 A313 1.10fr **multicolored** *(420,000)*+   1.50 .75
    First day cover   2.25
    First day cover, #333-334   3.75
    Inscription block of 4   6.00 —

Souvenir Booklet

335   Booklet *(90,000)*+   5.50
a.-c.   A313 10c any single   .20 .20
d.-f.   A313 20c any single   .35 .35
g.   Booklet pane of 4 #335a   .40
h.   Booklet pane of 4 #335d   1.40
i.   Booklet pane of 4 #335b   .40
j.   Booklet pane of 4 #335e   1.40
k.   Booklet pane of 4 #335c   .40
l.   Booklet pane of 4 #335f   1.40

First day covers of Nos. 333-335 total 44,622.

Endangered Specied Type of 1993

Designed by Tim Barrall, US.

Designs: No. 336, Equus hemionus (Asiatic wild ass). No. 337, Anodorhynchus hyacinthinus (hyacinth macaw). No. 338, Epicrates subflavus (Jamaican boa). No. 339, Dendrolagus bennettianus (Bennetts' tree kangaroo).

1999, Apr. 22   **Litho.**   *Perf. 12½*
336 A271 90c **multicolored** *(488,000)*+   1.40 .70
337 A271 90c **multicolored** *(488,000)*+   1.40 .70
338 A271 90c **multicolored** *(488,000)*+   1.40 .70
339 A271 90c **multicolored** *(488,000)*+   1.40 .70
a.   Block of 4, #336-339   5.75 —
    First day cover, #339a   5.75
    First day cover, #336-339, each   2.00
    Pane of 16   23.00

First day covers of Nos. 336-339 total 52,856.

UNISPACE III Type

Designs: No. 340, Farm, satellite dish. No. 341, City, satellite in orbit. No. 342, Composite of #340-341.

1999, July 7   **Photo.**   *Rouletted 8*
340 A314 45c **multicolored** *(925,000)*+   .60 .30
341 A314 45c **multicolored** *(925,000)*+   .60 .30
a.   Pair, #340-341   1.25 .60
    First day cover, #341a   2.00
    First day cover, #340-341, each   1.25
    Inscription block of 4   2.50 —
    Pane of 10, #340-341   6.00 —

Souvenir Sheet
Perf. 14½

342 A314 2fr **multicolored** *(275,000)*+   2.75 1.40
    First day cover   4.00
a.   Ovptd. in sheet margin   2.75 1.40

No. 342a is ovptd. in violet blue "PHILEXFRANCE 99 / LE MONDIAL DU TIMBRE / PARIS / 2 AU 11 JUILLET 1999.

First day covers of Nos. 340-342 total 63,412.

UPU Type

Various people, early 20th century methods of mail transportation, denomination at: No. 343, UL. No. 344, UR. No. 345, LL. No. 346, LR.

1999, Aug. 23   **Photo.**   *Perf. 11¾*
343 A315 70c **multicolored** *(336,000)*+   1.00 .50
344 A315 70c **multicolored** *(336,000)*+   1.00 .50
345 A315 70c **multicolored** *(336,000)*+   1.00 .50
346 A315 70c **multicolored** *(336,000)*+   1.00 .50
a.   Block of 4, #343-346   4.00 —
    First day cover, #346a   3.50
    First day cover, #343-346, each   1.50
    Inscription block of 4   4.00 —

First day covers of Nos. 343-346 total 27,041.

In Memoriam Type

Designs: 1.10fr, 2fr, Armillary sphere, Palais de Nations. Size of 2fr stamp: 34x63mm.

1999, Sept. 21   **Litho.**   *Perf. 14½x14*
347 A316 1.10fr **multicolored** *(400,000)*+   1.60 .80
    First day cover   2.25
    Inscription block of 4   6.50 —

Souvenir Sheet
Perf. 14

348 A316 2fr **multicolored** *(225,000)*+   3.00 1.50
    First day cover   3.50

First day covers of Nos. 347-348 total 46,527.

Education Type

1999, Nov. 18   **Litho.**   *Perf. 13½x13¾*
349 A317 90c Rainbow over globe *(350,000)*+   1.40 .70
    First day cover   1.75
    Inscription block of 4   5.75 —
350 A317 1.80fr Fish, tree, globe, book *(370,000)*+   2.60 1.25
    First day cover   3.50
    First day cover, #349-350   4.50
    Inscription block of 4   10.50 —

First day covers of Nos. 349-350 total 37,925.

Intl. Year Of Thanksgiving Type

2000, Jan 1   **Litho.**   *Perf. 13¼x13½*
351 A318 90c **multicolored** *(450,000)*+   1.40 .70
    First day cover   1.75
    Inscription block of 4   5.75 —

On No. 351 portions of the design were applied by a thermographic process producing a shiny, raised effect.

Endangered Species Type of 1993

Designed by Robert Hynes, US.

Designs: No. 352, Hippopotamus amphibius (hippopotamus). No. 353, Coscoroba coscoroba (Coscoroba swan). No. 354, Varanus prasinus (emerald monitor). No. 355, Enhydra lutris (sea otter).

2000, Apr. 6   **Litho.**   *Perf. 12¾x12½*
352 A271 90c **multicolored** *(488,000)*+   1.25 .60
353 A271 90c **multicolored** *(488,000)*+   1.25 .60
354 A271 90c **multicolored** *(488,000)*+   1.25 .60
355 A271 90c **multicolored** *(488,000)*+   1.25 .60
a.   Block of 4, #352-355   5.00 —
    First day cover, #355a   5.00
    First day cover, #352-355, each   1.90
    Pane of 16   20.00

Our World 2000 Type

Winning artwork in Millennium painting competition: 90c, The Embrace, by Rita Adaimy, Lebanon. 1.10fr, Living Single, by Richard Kimanthi, Kenya, vert.

2000, May 30   **Litho.**   *Perf. 13x13½, 13½x13*
356 A319 90c **multicolored** *(330,000)*+   1.25 .60
    First day cover   1.75
    Inscription block of 4   5.00 —
357 A319 1.10fr **multicolored** *(330,000)*+   1.50 .75
    First day cover   2.25
    First day cover, #356-357   3.50
    Inscription block of 4   6.00 —

55th Anniversary Type

Designs: 90c, Trygve Lie, Harry S Truman, workers at cornerstone dedication ceremony, 1949. 1.40fr, Window cleaner on Secretariat Building, General Assembly Hall under construction, 1951.

2000, July 7   **Litho.**   *Perf. 13¼x13*
358 A320 90c **multicolored** *(370,000)*+   1.25 .60
    First day cover   1.75
    Inscription block of 4   5.00 —
359 A320 1.40fr **multicolored** *(370,000)*+   2.00 1.00
    First day cover   2.60
    First day cover, #358-359   3.75
    Inscription block of 4   8.00 —

Souvenir Sheet

360 A320   Sheet of 2, #358-359 *(235,000)*+   3.25 1.60
    First day cover   4.00

2000 END-OF-YEAR ISSUES
See end of New York postage listings.

AIR LETTER SHEET

UN Type of 1968
Printed by Setelipaino, Finland. Designed by Robert Perrot.

1969, Oct. 4   **Litho.**
UC1 UC3 65c **ultra & light blue**, entire *(350,000)*   .50 .50
    Entire, first day cancel *(52,000)*   1.00

POSTAL CARDS

UN Type of 1969 and Type of Air Post Postal Card, 1966
Printed by Courvoisier, S.A., Switzerland. Designed by John Mason (20c) and Olav S. Mathiesen (30c).
Wmk. Post Horn, Swiss Cross, "S" or "Z"
1969, Oct. 4   **Litho.**
UX1 PC2 20c **olive green & black,** buff *(415,000)*   .25 .20
    First day cancel *(51,500)*   1.00
UX2 APC2 30c **violet blue, blue, light & dark green,** buff *(275,000)*   .25 .20
    First day cancel *(49,000)*   1.00

No. UX2, although of design APC2, is not inscribed "Poste Aerienne" or "Air Mail."

UN Emblem — GPC1

UN Emblem and Ribbons — GPC2

Printed by Setelipaino, Finland. Designed by Veronique Crombez (40c) and Lieve Baeten (70c).

1977, June 27   **Litho.**
UX3 GPC1 40c **multicolored** *(500,000)*   .30 .20
    First day cancel *(65,000)*   1.00
UX4 GPC2 70c **multicolored** *(300,000)*   .40 .20
    First day cancel *(65,000)*   1.00

A second printing of No. UX3 was made in 1984. It was released after the Swiss postal card rate had been increased to 50c so instructions were issued that all cards must have a 10c stamp affixed before being sold. A few were sold in NY without the added stamp. The card stock differs from the original printing.

Emblem of the United Nations — GPC3

Peace Dove — GPC4

Printed by Johann Enschede en Zonen, Netherlands. Designed by George Hamori, Australia (50c) and Ryszard Dudzicki, Poland (70c).

1985, May 10   Litho.
UX5 GPC3 50c **multicolored** *(300,000)*   2.00 .25
      First day cancel *(34,700)*   4.00
UX6 GPC4 70c **multicolored** *(300,000)*   3.25 .55
      First day cancel *(34,700)*   4.50

No. UX6 Surcharged in Lake

1986, Jan. 2   Litho.
UX7 GPC4 70c + 10c **multi** *(90,500)*   2.25 1.25
      First day cancel *(8,000 est.)*   13.00

Type of 1990
Printed by Mercury-Walch, Australia.

1992, Sept. 4   Litho.
UX8 G45 90c **multicolored** *(150,000)+*   1.75 .60
      First day cancel *(12,385)*   6.00

No. UX5 Surcharged in Lake like No. UX7

1993, May 7   Litho.
UX9 GPC3 50c +10c **multicolored** *(47,000)+*   1.50 .40
      First day cancel   19.00

Palais des Nations — GPC5

Printed by Leigh Mardon Pty. Limited, Australia.

1993, May 7   Litho.
UX10 GPC5 80c **multicolored** *(200,000)+*   3.00 .50
      First day cancel   7.50

#UX5, UX10 Surcharged in Carmine like #UX7

1996   Litho.
UX11 GPC3 50c +20c **multi**   2.50 .55
UX12 GPC5 80c +30c **multi**   2.50 .85

Assembly Hall — GPC6

Palais des Nations — GPC7

Printed by Mercury-Walsh, Australia.

1998, May 20   Litho.
UX13 GPC6 70c **multicolored** *(80,000)+*   2.00 .50
      First day cancel   2.50
UX14 GPC7 1.10fr **multicolored** *(80,000)+*   2.25 .75
      First day cancel   3.00

Illustrations of the buildings are shown on the back of each card.

OFFICES IN VIENNA, AUSTRIA

For use only on mail posted at the Vienna International Center for the UN and the International Atomic Energy Agency.

100 Groschen = 1 Schilling

Type of Geneva, 1978, UN Types of 1961-72 and

Donaupark, Vienna — V1   Aerial View — V2

Printed by Helio Courvoisier S.A., Switzerland. Panes of 50. Designed by Henryk Chylinski (4s); Jozsef Vertel (6s).

1979, Aug. 24   Photo.   Perf. 11½
     Granite Paper
1 G8 50g **multicolored** *(3,500,000)+*   .20 .20
   First day cover   1.00
   Inscription block of 4   .20
2 A52 1s **multicolored** *(3,800,000)+*   .20 .20
   First day cover   1.00
   Inscription block of 4   .40
3 V1 4s **multicolored** *(3,500,000)+*   .20 .20
   First day cover   1.00
   Inscription block of 4   .90
4 AP13 5s **multicolored** *(3,500,000)+*   .25 .25
   First day cover   1.00
   Inscription block of 4   1.25
5 V2 6s **multicolored** *(4,500,000)+*   .35 .30
   First day cover   1.25
   Inscription block of 4   1.50
6 A45 10s **multicolored** *(3,500,000)+*   .50 .45
   First day cover   2.00
   Inscription block of 4   2.25
   Nos. 1-6 (6)   1.70 1.60

   + Printing orders to Mar. 1993.
No. 4 is not inscribed "Air Mail," No. 6 has no frame. First day covers of Nos. 1-6 total 1,026,575.

New Economic Order Type of UN
1980, Jan. 11   Litho.   Perf. 15x14½
7 A178 4s **multicolored** *(1,418,418)*   .70 .50
   First day cover   1.25
   Inscription block of 4   7.50

   Value for margin inscription block is for one from bottom of sheet. One from top is about twice the value shown.

Dove Type of UN
1980, Jan. 11   Litho.   Perf. 14x13½
8 A147 2.50s **multicolored** *(3,500,000)+*   .25 .20
   First day cover   1.00
   Inscription block of 4   1.25

First day covers of Nos. 7-8 total 336,229.

Women's Year Emblem on World Map — V3

United Nations Decade for Women.
Printed by Questa Colour Security Printers, United Kingdom. Panes of 50. Designed by Gunnar Janssen.

1980, Mar. 7   Litho.   Perf. 14½x15
9 V3 4s **light green & dark green** *(1,569,080)*   .40 .25
   First day cover   1.00
   Inscription block of 4   1.75
10 V3 6s **bister brown** *(1,556,016)*   .75 .50
   First day cover   1.25
   First day cover, #9-10   1.50
   Inscription block of 4   3.25

First day covers of Nos. 9-10 total 443,893.

Peace-keeping Operations Type of UN
1980, May 16   Litho.   Perf. 14x13
11 A182 6s **multicolored** *(1,719,852)*   .40 .35
   First day cover *(323,923)*   1.00
   Inscription block of 4   2.00

35th Anniversary Types of Geneva and UN
1980, June 26   Litho.   Perf. 13x13½
12 G16 4s **carmine rose & black** *(1,626,582)*   .40 .25
   First day cover   1.00
   Inscription block of 4   1.65
13 A184 6s **multicolored** *(1,625,400)*   .70 .45
   First day cover   1.25
   Inscription block of 4   2.75

Souvenir Sheet
     Imperf
14   Sheet of 2 *(1,675,191)*   .55 .55
a.   G16 4s carmine rose & black   .20
b.   A184 6s multicolored   .35
   First day cover   1.00

First day covers of Nos. 12-14 total 657,402.

ECOSOC Types of UN and Geneva
Printed by Ashton-Potter Ltd., Canada. Panes of 50. Designed by Dietman Kowall (4s), Angel Medina Medina (6s).

1980, Nov. 21   Litho.   Perf. 13½x13
15 A187 4s **multicolored** *(1,811,218)*   .30 .20
   First day cover   1.00
   Inscription block of 4   1.50
16 G17 6s **multicolored** *(1,258,420)*   .60 .50
   First day cover   1.00
   First day cover #15-16   1.25
   Inscription block of 4   2.50

   Economic and Social Council (ECOSOC). First day covers of Nos. 15-16 total 224,631.

Palestinian Rights Type of UN
Printed by Courvoisier S.A., Switzerland. Panes of 50. Designed by David Dewhurst.

1981, Jan. 30   Photo.   Perf. 12x11½
17 A188 4s **multicolored** *(1,673,310)*   .45 .45
   First day cover *(208,812)*   1.00
   Inscription block of 4   2.00

Disabled Type of UN and

Interlocking Stitches — V4

International Year of the Disabled. Printed by Heraclio Fournier S.A., Spain. Panes of 50. Designed by Sophia van Heeswijk.

1981, Mar. 6   Photo.   *Perf. 14*
18 A189 4s multicolored *(1,508,719)*   .40   .35
    First day cover   1.00
    Inscription block of 4   1.75
19 V4   6s black & orange *(1,569,385)*   .60   .50
    First day cover   1.00
    First day cover, #18-19   1.25
    Inscription block of 4   2.75
First day covers of Nos. 18-19 total 290,603.

Art Type of UN

1981, Apr. 15   Photo.   *Perf. 11½*
Granite Paper
20 A191 6s multicolored *(1,643,527)*   .75   .50
    First day cover *(196,916)*   1.00
    Inscription block of 4   3.25

Energy Type of UN

1981, May 29   Litho.   *Perf. 13*
21 A193 7.50s multicolored *(1,611,130)*   .70   .50
    First day cover *(216,197)*   1.00
    Inscription block of 4   3.00

Volunteers Program Types

1981, Nov. 13   Litho.
22 A195 5s multicolored *(1,582,780)*   .50   .35
    First day cover   1.00
    Inscription block of 4   2.25
23 G18 7s multicolored *(1,516,139)*   1.00   .65
    First day cover   1.00
    First day cover, #22-23   1.00
    Inscription block of 4   4.25
First day covers of Nos. 22-23 total 282,414.

"For a Better World" — V5

Printed by Courvoisier, S.A., Switzerland. Sheets of 50. Designed by Eliezer Weishoff.

1982, Jan. 22   *Perf. 11½x12*
24 V5   3s multicolored *(3,300,000)+*   .35   .20
    First day cover *(203,872)*   1.00
    Inscription block of 4   1.75

Human Environment Types of UN

10th Anniversary of United Nations Environment Program. Printed by Joh. Enschede en Zonen, Netherlands. Panes of 50. Designed by Peer-Ulrich Bremer (5s); Sybille Brunner (7s).

1982, Mar. 19   Litho.   *Perf. 13½x13*
25 A200 5s multicolored *(1,312,765)*   .40   .40
    First day cover   1.00
    Inscription block of 4   1.90
26 G21 7s multicolored *(1,357,513)*   .80   .55
    First day cover   1.00
    First day cover, #25-26   1.25
    Inscription block of 4   3.75
First day covers of Nos. 25-26 total 248,576.

Outer Space Type of UN

Exploration and Peaceful Uses of Outer Space. Printed by Enschede. Panes of 50. Designed by George Hamori.

1982, June 11   Litho.   *Perf. 13x13½*
27 G22 5s multicolored *(1,339,038)*   .60   .60
    First day cover *(150,845)*   1.75
    Inscription block of 4   3.00

Conservation & Protection of Nature Type

1982, Nov. 16   Photo.   *Perf. 14*
28 A202 5s Fish *(1,202,694)*   .50   .40
    First day cover   1.00
    Inscription block of 4   2.50
29 A202 7s Animal *(1,194,403)*   .70   .60
    First day cover   1.00
    First day cover, #28-29   1.40
    Inscription block of 4   3.00
First day covers of Nos. 28-29 total 243,548.

World Communications Year Type

1983, Jan. 28   Litho.   *Perf. 13*
30 A203 4s multicolored *(1,517,443)*   .40   .40
    First day cover *(150,541)*   1.40
    Inscription block of 4   2.10

Safety at Sea Type

1983, Mar. 18   Litho.   *Perf. 14½*
31 G23 4s multicolored *(1,506,052)*   .40   .40
    First day cover   1.00
    Inscription block of 4   2.00
32 A206 6s multicolored *(1,527,990)*   .65   .55

    First day cover   1.00
    First day cover, #31-32   2.25
    Inscription block of 4   2.75
First day covers of Nos. 31-32 total 219,118.

World Food Program Type

1983, Apr. 22   Engr.   *Perf. 13½*
33 A207 5s green *(1,419,237)*   .50   .35
    First day cover   1.00
    Inscription block of 4   2.25
34 A207 7s brown *(1,454,227)*   .70   .55
    First day cover   1.00
    First day cover, #33-34   1.25
    Inscription block of 4   2.75
First day covers of Nos. 33-34 total 212,267.

UN Conference on Trade and Development Type

1983, June 6   Litho.   *Perf. 14*
35 G24   4s multicolored *(1,544,973)*   .30   .25
    First day cover   1.00
    Inscription block of 4   1.90
36 A209 8.50s multicolored *(1,423,172)*   .75   .65
    First day cover   1.00
    First day cover, #35-36   1.25
    Inscription block of 4   3.25
First day covers of Nos. 35-36 total 184,023.

The Second Skin — V6   Right to Think — V7

35th Anniversary of the Universal Declaration of Human Rights

Printed by Government Printing Office, Austria. Designed by Friedensreich Hundertwasser, Austria. Panes of 16 (4x4).

1983, Dec. 9   Photo. & Engr.   *Perf. 13½*
37 V6   5s multicolored *(2,163,419)*   .50   .40
    First day cover   1.25
    Inscription block of 4   2.25
38 V7   7s multicolored *(2,163,542)*   .75   .70
    First day cover   1.25
    First day cover, #37-38   2.25
    Inscription block of 4   3.25
    Panes of 16, #37-38   20.00
First day covers of Nos. 37-38 total 246,440.

International Conference on Population Type

Printed by Bundesdruckerei, Federal Republic of Germany. Panes of 50. Designed by Marina Langer-Rosa and Helmut Langer, Federal Republic of Germany.

1984, Feb. 3   Litho.   *Perf. 14*
39 A212 7s multicolored *(1,135,791)*   .65   .50
    First day cover *(80,570)*   1.50
    Inscription block of 4   2.75

Field Irrigation — V8

Pest Control — V9

World Food Day, Oct. 16

Printed by Walsall Security Printers, Ltd., United Kingdom. Panes of 50. Designed by Adth Vanooijen, Netherlands.

1984, Mar. 15   Litho.   *Perf. 14½*
40 V8 4.50s multicolored *(994,106)*   .45   .40
    First day cover   1.00
    Inscription block of 4   2.00
41 V9   6s multicolored *(1,027,115)*   .70   .60

    First day cover   1.00
    First day cover #40-41   2.25
    Inscription block of 4   2.50
First day covers of Nos. 40-41 total 194,546.

Serengeti Park, Tanzania — V10

Ancient City of Shiban, People's Democratic Rep. of Yemen — V11

World Heritage

Printed by Harrison and Sons, United Kingdom. Panes of 50. Designs adapted by Rocco J. Callari, US, and Thomas Lee, China.

1984, Mar. 15   Litho.   *Perf. 14*
42 V10 3.50s multicolored *(957,518)*   .25   .25
    First day cover   1.25
    Inscription block of 4   1.25
43 V11 15s multicolored *(928,794)*   1.40   1.00
    First day cover   1.75
    First day cover, #42-43   2.50
    Inscription block of 4   5.75
First day covers of Nos. 42-43 total 193,845.

V12   V13

Future for Refugees

Designed by Hans Erni, Switzerland. Printed by Courvoisier. Panes of 50.

1984, Mar. 29   Photo.   *Perf. 11½*
44 V12 4.50s multicolored *(1,086,393)*   .55   .45
    First day cover   1.25
    Inscription block of 4   2.25
45 V13 8.50s multicolored *(1,109,865)*   1.40   1.00
    First day cover   1.75
    First day cover, #44-45   2.25
    Inscription block of 4   5.75
First day covers of Nos. 44-45 total 185,349.

International Youth Year — V14

Printed by Waddingtons Ltd., United Kingdom. Panes of 50. Designed by Ruel A. Mayo, Phillipines.

1984, Nov. 15   Litho.   *Perf. 13½*
46 V14 3.50s multicolored *(1,178,833)*   .50   .40
    First day cover   1.25
    Inscription block of 4   2.10
47 V14 6.50s multicolored *(1,109,337)*   .75   .65
    First day cover   1.50
    First day cover, #46-47   2.25
    Inscription block of 4   3.25
First day covers of Nos. 46-47 total 165,762.

ILO Type of Geneva

Printed by the Government Printing Bureau, Japan. Panes of 50. Adapted from photographs by Rocco J. Callari, US, and Thomas Lee, China.

1985, Feb. 1	Engr.	Perf. 13½	
48 G34 7.50s U Thant Pavilion (948,317)		.85	.65
First day cover (115,916)			1.75
Inscription block of 4		3.50	—

UN University Type

Printed by Helio Courvoisier, Switzerland. Panes of 50. Designed by Moshe Pereg, Israel, and Hinedi Geluda, Brazil.

1985, Mar. 15	Photo.	Perf. 13½	
49 A221 8.50s Rural scene, lab researcher			
(863,673)		.85	.80
First day cover (108,479)			1.75
Inscription block of 4		3.75	—

Ship of Peace — V15

Shelter under UN Umbrella — V16

Printed by Carl Ueberreuter Druck and Verlag M. Salzer, Austria. Panes of 50. Designed by Ran Banda Mawilmada, Sri Lanka (4.50s), and Sophia van Heeswijk, Federal Republic of Germany (15s).

1985, May 10	Litho.	Perf. 14	
50 V15 4.50s multicolored (2,000,000)+		.35	.30
First day cover			.75
Inscription block of 4		1.50	—
51 V16 15s multicolored (2,000,000)+		2.25	2.00
First day cover			2.75
First day cover, #50-51			3.50
Inscription block of 4		9.50	—

First day covers of Nos. 50-51 total 142,687.

40th Anniversary Type

Designed by Rocco J. Callari, U.S., and Thomas Lee, China (No. 54).

1985, June 26	Photo.	Perf. 12 x 11½	
52 A224 6.50s multicolored (984,820)		1.00	.55
First day cover			1.25
Inscription block of 4		4.25	—
53 A225 8.50s multicolored (914,347)		1.50	1.00
First day cover			1.75
First day cover, #52-53			2.50
Inscription block of 4		6.25	—

Souvenir Sheet
Imperf

54	Sheet of 2 (676,648)	2.75	2.00
a.	A224 6.50s multi	.70	.60
b.	A225 8.50s multi	.90	.75
	First day cover		2.50

First day covers of Nos. 52-54 total 317,652.

UNICEF Child Survival Campaign Type

Printed by the Government Printing Bureau, Japan. Panes of 50. Designed by Mel Harris, United Kingdom (No. 55) and Vreni Wyss-Fischer, Switzerland (No. 56).

1985, Nov. 22	Photo. & Engr.	Perf. 13½	
55 A226 4s Spoonfeeding children (889,918)		.75	.65
First day cover			1.50
Inscription block of 4		3.50	—
56 A226 6s Mother hugging infant (852,958)		1.40	1.25
First day cover			1.50
First day cover, #55-56			2.50
Inscription block of 4		6.00	—

First day covers of Nos. 55-56 total 239,532.

Africa in Crisis Type

Printed by Helio Courvoisier, Switzerland. Panes of 50. Designed by Tesfaye Tessema, Ethiopia.

1986, Jan. 31	Photo.	Perf. 11½x12	
57 A227 8s multicolored (809,854)		.80	.70
First day cover (99,996)			2.00
Inscription block of 4		3.50	—

UN Development Program Type

Agriculture. Printed by the Government Printing Bureau, Japan. Panes of 40, 2 blocks of 4 horizontal and 5 blocks of 4 vertical. Designed by Thomas Lee, China.

1986, Mar. 14	Photo.	Perf. 13½	
58 A228 4.50s Developing crop strains			
(730,691)		1.50	1.00
59 A228 4.50s Animal husbandry (730,691)		1.50	1.00

60 A228 4.50s Technical instruction (730,691)		1.50	1.00
61 A228 4.50s Nutrition education (730,691)		1.50	1.00
a.	Block of 4, #58-61	6.25	1.00
	First day cover, #61a		6.00
	First day cover, #58-61, each		2.00
	Inscription block of 4, #58-61	7.00	—
	Pane of 40, #58-61	87.50	

No. 61a has a continuous design.
First day covers of Nos. 58-61 total 227,664.

Stamp Collecting Type

Designs: 3.50s, UN stamps. 6.50s, Engraver. Printed by the Swedish Post Office, Sweden. Panes of 50. Designed by Czeslaw Slania and Ingalill Axelsson, Sweden.

1986, May 22	Engr.	Perf. 12½	
62 A229 3.50s dk ultra & dk brown (874,119)		.50	.35
First day cover			1.50
Inscription block of 4		2.25	—
63 A229 6.50s int blue & brt rose (877,284)		1.10	.85
First day cover			1.50
First day cover, #62-63			2.25
Inscription block of 4		4.50	—

First day covers of Nos. 62-63 total 150,836.

Olive Branch, Rainbow, Earth — V17

International Peace Year. Printed by the Government Printing Bureau, Japan. Panes of 50. Designed by Milo Schor, Israel (No. 64), and Mohammad Sardar, Pakistan (No. 65).

Photogravure & Embossed

1986, June 20		Perf. 13½	
64 V17 5s shown (914,699)		.90	.60
First day cover			1.50
Inscription block of 4		3.75	—
65 V17 6s Doves, UN emblem (818,386)		1.10	.70
First day cover			1.50
First day cover, #64-65			2.50
Inscription block of 4		4.50	—

First day covers of Nos. 64-65 total 169,551.

WFUNA Anniversary Type
Souvenir Sheet

Printed by Johann Enschede and Sons, Netherlands. Designed by Rocco J. Callari, US.

Designs: 4s, White stallion by Elisabeth von Janota-Bzowski, Germany. 5s, Surrealistic landscape by Ernst Fuchs, Austria. 6s, Geometric abstract by Victor Vasarely (b. 1908), France. 7s, Mythological abstract by Wolfgang Hutter (b. 1928), Austria.

1986, Nov. 14	Litho.	Perf. 13x13½	
66	Sheet of 4 (668,264)	4.00	3.75
a.	A232 4s multicolored	.75	.60
b.	A232 5s multicolored	.85	.70
c.	A232 6s multicolored	1.00	.80
d.	A232 7s multicolored	1.25	1.00
	First day cover (121,852)		4.00

No. 66 has inscribed margin picturing UN and WFUNA emblems.

Trygve Lie Type
Photogravure & Engraved

1987, Jan. 30		Perf. 13½	
67 A233 8s multicolored (778,010)		.80	.75
First day cover (94,112)			2.00
Inscription block of 4		4.00	—

Shelter for the Homeless Type

Designs: 4s, Family and homes. 9.50s, Family entering home.

1987, Mar. 13	Litho.	Perf. 13½x12½	
68 A234 4s multicolored (704,922)		.65	.40
First day cover			1.25
Inscription block of 4		2.75	—
69 A234 9.50s multicolored (671,200)		1.25	1.10
First day cover			1.75
First day cover, #68-69			2.75
Inscription block of 4		5.25	—

First day covers of Nos. 68-69 total 117,941.

Fight Drug Abuse Type

Designs: 5s, Soccer players. 8s, Family.

1987, June 12	Litho.	Perf. 14½x15	
70 A235 5s multicolored (869,875)		.60	.50
First day cover			1.40
Inscription block of 4		2.75	—
71 A235 8s multicolored (797,889)		1.00	.85
First day cover			1.75
First day cover, #70-71			2.75
Inscription block of 4		4.25	—

First day covers of Nos. 70-71 total 117,964.

Donaupark, Vienna — V18

Peace Embracing the Earth — V19

Printed by The House of Questa, United Kingdom. Panes of 50. Designed by Henry Bencsath, US (2s), and Eliezer Weishoff, Israel (17s).

1987, June 12	Litho.	Perf. 14½x15	
72 V18 2s multicolored (2,000,000)+		.35	.25
First day cover			1.25
Inscription block of 4		1.50	—
73 V19 17s multicolored (2,000,000)+		1.90	1.50
First day cover			2.50
First day cover, #72-73			3.50
Inscription block of 4		8.00	—

First day covers of Nos. 72-73 total 111,153.

UN Day Type

Designed by Elisabeth von Janota-Bzowski (5s) and Fritz Henry Oerter (6s), Federal Republic of Germany.
Designs: Multinational people in various occupations.

1987, Oct. 23	Litho.	Perf. 14½x15	
74 A236 5s multicolored (1,575,731)		.85	.65
First day cover			1.40
Inscription block of 4		3.75	—
75 A236 6s multicolored (1,540,523)		1.00	1.00
First day cover			1.75
First day cover, #74-75			2.75
Inscription block of 4		4.25	—
Panes of 12, #74-75		24.00	

Immunize Every Child Type

Designs: 4s, Poliomyelitis. 9.50s, Diphtheria.

1987, Nov. 20	Litho.	Perf. 15x14½	
76 A237 4s multicolored (793,716)		.75	.50
First day cover			1.00
Inscription block of 4		4.00	—
77 A237 9.50s multicolored (769,288)		2.00	1.25
First day cover			1.90
First day cover, #76-77			2.75
Inscription block of 4		8.25	—

IFAD Type

Designs: 4s, Grains. 6s, Vegetables.

1988, Jan. 29	Litho.	Perf. 13½	
78 A238 4s multicolored (697,307)		.50	.40
First day cover			1.25
Inscription block of 4		2.75	—
79 A238 6s multicolored (701,521)		1.00	.90
First day cover			1.75
First day cover, #78-79			2.75
Inscription block of 4		4.25	—

Survival of the Forests Type

Deciduous forest in fall: 4s, Treetops, hills and dales. 5s, Tree trunks. Printed se-tenant in a continuous design.

1988, Mar. 18	Litho.	Perf. 14x15	
80 A240 4s multicolored (990,607)		2.25	2.00
First day cover			3.25
81 A240 5s multicolored (990,607)		3.25	3.00
First day cover			3.50
a.	Pair, #80-81	5.50	5.50
	First day cover, #81a		9.00
	Inscription block of 4, #80-81	12.00	—
	Pane of 12, #80-81	30.00	

Intl. Volunteer Day Type

Designed by George Fernandez, U.S.
Designs: 6s, Medical care, vert. 7.50s, Construction.

1988, May 6	Litho.	Perf. 13x14, 14x13	
82 A241 6s multicolored (701,167)		.85	.70
First day cover			1.40
Inscription block of 4		4.00	—
83 A241 7.50s multicolored (638,240)		1.25	1.10
First day cover			1.60
First day cover, #82-83			3.00
Inscription block of 4		5.75	—

Health in Sports Type

Paintings by LeRoy Neiman, American Sports artist: 6s, Skiing, vert. 8s, Tennis.

1988, June 17   Litho.   Perf. 13½x13, 13x13½

84 A242 6s multicolored (668,902)	.85	.70
First day cover		1.40
Inscription block of 4	5.00	—
85 A242 8s multicolored (647,915)	1.25	1.10
First day cover	2.00	
First day cover #84-85		3.00
Inscription block of 4	8.50	—

Universal Declaration of Human Rights 40th Anniv. Type

1988, Dec. 9   Photo. & Engr.   Perf. 11½

86 A243 5s multicolored (1,080,041)	.50	.40
First day cover		2.50
Inscription block of 4	3.00	—

Souvenir Sheet

87 A243 11s multicolored (688,994)	1.25	.50
First day cover		4.75

No. 87 has multicolored decorative margin inscribed with preamble to the human rights declaration in German.

World Bank Type

1989, Jan. 27   Litho.   Perf. 13x14

88 A244 5.50s Transportation (682,124)	1.25	.75
First day cover		1.40
Inscription block of 4	5.25	—
89 A244 8s Health care, education (628,649)	1.90	1.75
First day cover	2.00	
First day cover, #88-89		3.00
Inscription block of 4	8.25	—

First day covers of Nos. 88-89 total 135,964.

Peace-Keeping Force Type

1989, Mar. 17   Perf. 14x13½

90 A245 6s multicolored (912,731)	.90	.80
First day cover (81,837)		2.00
Inscription block of 4	4.00	—

World Weather Watch Type

Satellite photograph and radar image: 4s, Helical cloud formation over Italy, the eastern Alps, and parts of Yugoslavia. 9.50s, Rainfall in Tokyo, Japan.

1989, Apr. 21   Litho.   Perf. 13x14

91 A247 4s multicolored (948,680)	1.00	.75
First day cover		1.40
Inscription block of 4	4.50	—
92 A247 9.50s multicolored (880,138)	2.25	2.25
First day cover	2.00	
First day cover, #91-92		3.00
Inscription block of 4	10.50	—

First day covers of Nos. 91-92 total 116,846.

Offices in Vienna, 10th Anniv.
V20   V21

Printed by the Government Printing Office, Austria. Panes of 25. Designed by Gottfried Kumpf (5s) and Andre Heller (7.50s), Austria.

Photo. & Engr., Photo. (7.50s)

1989, Aug. 23   Perf. 14

93 V20 5s multicolored (958,339)	4.50	.50
First day cover		1.25
Inscription block of 4	18.50	—
94 V21 7.50s multicolored (785,517)	1.00	.70
First day cover		1.40
First day cover, #93-94		4.00
Inscription block of 4	4.50	—
Panes of 25, #93-94	160.00	

First day covers of Nos. 93-94 total 210,746.

Human Rights Type of 1989

Panes of 12+12 se-tenant labels containing Articles 5 (4s) or 6 (6s) inscribed in German, English or French.
Paintings: 4s, The Prisoners, by Kathe Kollwitz. 6s, Justice, by Raphael.

1909, Nov. 17   Litho.   Perf. 13½

95 A250 4s multicolored (2,267,450)	.65	.60
First day cover		2.00
Inscription block of 3 + 3 labels	2.00	—
96 A250 6s multicolored (2,264,876)	.90	.90
First day cover	2.00	
First day cover #95-96		3.00
Inscription block of 3 + 3 labels	2.75	—
Panes of 12, #95-96	19.00	

First day covers of Nos. 95-96 total 183,199.
See Nos. 108-109, 123-124, 150-151.

Intl. Trade Center Type

1990, Feb. 2   Litho.   Perf. 14½x15

97 A251 12s multicolored (559,556)	1.40	1.25
First day cover (77,928)		3.00
Inscription block of 4	6.50	—

Painting by Kurt
Regschek — V22

Printed by the National Postage Stamps and Fiduciary Printing Works, France. Designed by Robert J. Stein, US.

1990, Feb. 2   Litho.   Perf. 13x13½

98 V22 1.50s multicolored (1,000,000)+	.30	.20
First day cover (64,622)		2.50
Inscription block of 4	1.40	—

Fight AIDS Type

Designed by Jacek Tofil, Poland (5s), Orlando Pelaez, Colombia (11s).
Designs: 5s, "SIDA." 11s, Stylized figures, ink blot.

1990, Mar. 16   Litho.   Perf. 13½x12½

99 A252 5s multicolored (623,155)	1.00	.75
First day cover		1.25
Inscription block of 4	4.50	—
100 A252 11s multicolored (588,742)	2.25	2.00
First day cover	2.10	
First day cover, #99-100		3.75
Inscription block of 4	10.50	—

First day covers of Nos. 99-100 total 123,657.

Medicinal Plants Type

1990, May 4   Photo.   Granite Paper   Perf. 11½

101 A253 4.50s Bixa orellana (709,840)	1.00	.75
First day cover		1.25
Inscription block of 4	4.50	—
102 A253 9.50s Momordica charantia (732,883)	2.25	2.00
First day cover	2.00	
First day cover, #101-102		3.00
Inscription block of 4	10.00	—

First day covers of Nos. 101-102 total 117,545.

UN 45th Anniv. Type

Designed by Talib Nauman, Pakistan (7s), Marleen Bosmans (9s), Robert Stein, US (No. 105).
Designs: 7s, 9s, "45" and emblem.

1990, June 26   Litho.   Perf. 14½x13

103 A254 7s multicolored (604,878)	1.25	1.00
First day cover		1.50
Inscription block of 4	5.50	—
104 A254 9s multicolored, diff. (550,902)	2.25	1.75
First day cover	1.90	
First day cover, #103-104		3.25
Inscription block of 4	10.50	—

Souvenir Sheet

105 Sheet of 2, #103-104 (423,370)	5.50	3.50
First day cover		4.00

First day covers of Nos. 103-105 total 181,174.

Crime Prevention Type

1990, Sept. 13   Photo.   Perf. 14

106 A255 6s Domestic violence (661,810)	1.25	1.00
First day cover		1.50
Inscription block of 4	5.50	—
107 A255 8s Crimes against cultural heritage (607,940)	2.25	1.75
First day cover	2.25	
First day cover, #106-107		3.00
Inscription block of 4	10.00	—

First day covers of Nos. 106-107 total 112,193.

Human Rights Type of 1989

Panes of 12+12 se-tenant labels containing Articles 11 (4.50s) or 12 (7s) inscribed in German, English or French.
Paintings: 4.50s, Before the Judge, by Sandor Bihari. 7s, Young Man Greeted by a Woman Writing a Poem, by Suzuki Harunobu.

1990, Nov. 16   Litho.   Perf. 13½

108 A250 4.50s multicolored (1,684,833)	.40	.30
First day cover		1.25
Inscription block of 3 + 3 labels	1.25	—
109 A250 7s multicolored (1,541,022)	1.25	1.00
First day cover		1.75
First day cover, #108-109		2.60
Inscription block of 3 + 3 labels	4.25	—
Panes of 12, #108-109	22.50	

First day covers of Nos. 108-109 total 168,831.

Economic Commission for Europe Type

1991, Mar. 15   Litho.   Perf. 14

110 A256 5s Weasel, hoopoe (727,436)	1.00	.75
111 A256 5s Warbler, swans (727,436)	1.00	.75
112 A256 5s Badgers, squirrel (727,436)	1.00	.75

---

113 A256 5s Fish (727,436)	1.00	.75
a. Block of 4, #110-113	4.50	3.00
First day cover, No. 113a		5.00
First day cover, Nos. 110-113, each		2.00
Inscription block of 4, #110-113	5.00	—
Pane of 40, #110-113	47.50	

First day covers of Nos. 110-113 total 81,624.

Namibian Independence Type

1991, May 10   Litho.   Perf. 14

114 A257 6s Mountains, clouds (531,789)	1.00	.75
First day cover		1.75
Inscription block of 4	5.00	—
115 A257 9.50s Dune, Namib Desert (503,735)	2.50	2.00
First day cover	2.50	
First day cover, #114-115		3.50
Inscription block of 4	10.50	—

First day covers of Nos. 114-115 total 111,184.

V24

Printed by House of Questa, United Kingdom. Designed by Marina Langer-Rosa, Germany.

1991, May 10   Litho.   Perf. 15x14½

116 V24 20s multicolored (1,750,000)+	3.25	2.50
First day cover (60,843)		4.00
Inscription block of 4	14.00	—

V25

Rights of the
Child — V26

Printed by The House of Questa. Panes of 50. Designed by Anna Harmer, Austria (7s) and Emiko Takegawa, Japan (9s).

1991, June 14   Litho.   Perf. 14½

117 V25 7s Stick drawings (645,145)	1.50	1.25
First day cover		1.75
Inscription block of 4	6.75	—
118 V26 9s Child, clock, fruit (568,214)	2.00	1.60
First day cover		2.25
First day cover, #117-118		3.50
Inscription block of 4	10.00	—

First day covers of Nos. 117-118 total 120,619.

V27

Banning of
Chemical
Weapons — V28

Printed by Heraclio Fournier, S.A. Panes of 50. Designed by Oscar Asboth, Austria (5s), Michel Granger, France (10s).

1991, Sept. 11   **Litho.**   *Perf. 13½*

119	V27	5s multicolored *(469,454)*	1.25	.75
		First day cover		1.40
		Inscription block of 4	5.50	
120	V28	10s multicolored *(525,704)*	2.25	1.50
		First day cover		2.35
		First day cover, #119-120		3.25
		Inscription block of 4	9.50	

First day covers of Nos. 119-120 total 116,862.

UN Postal Administration, 40th Anniv. Type

1991, Oct. 24   **Litho.**   *Perf. 14x15*

121	A263	5s UN NY No. 8 *(564,450)*	.85	.75
		First day cover		1.40
		Inscription block of 4	4.00	
122	A263	8s UN NY No. 5 *(609,830)*	2.00	1.90
		First day cover		2.10
		Inscription block of 4	9.00	
		Panes of 25, #121-122	72.50	

First day covers of Nos. 121-122 total 107,802.

Human Rights Type of 1989

Panes of 12+12 se-tenant labels containing Articles 17 (4.50s) or 18 (7s) inscribed in German, English or French.

Artwork: 4.50s, Pre-columbian Mexican pottery. 7s, Windows, by Robert Delaunay.

1991, Nov. 20   **Litho.**   *Perf. 13½*

123	A250	4.50s black & brown *(1,717,097)*	.80	.75
		First day cover		2.25
		Inscription block of 3 + 3 labels	2.50	
124	A250	7s multicolored *(1,717,738)*	1.40	1.25
		First day cover		3.50
		First day cover, #123-124		3.50
		Inscription block of 3 + 3 labels	4.50	
		Panes of 12+12 labels, #123-124	27.50	

First day covers of Nos. 123-124 total 204,854.

World Heritage Type of 1984

Designs: 5s, Iguacu Natl. Park, Brazil. 9s, Abu Simbel, Egypt.

1992, Jan. 24   **Litho.**   *Perf. 13*
Size: 35x28mm

125	V10	5s multicolored *(586,738)*	1.25	1.00
		First day cancel		1.50
		Inscription block of 4	5.75	
126	V10	9s multicolored *(476,965)*	2.25	1.75
		First day cancel		2.75
		First day cancel, #125-126		4.00
		Inscription block of 4	9.00	

First day covers of Nos. 125-126 total 93,016.

Clean Oceans Type

1992, Mar. 13   **Litho.**   *Perf. 14*

127	A264	7s Ocean surface, diff. *(1,121,870)*	1.10	.75
128	A264	7s Ocean bottom, diff. *(1,121,870)*	1.10	.75
a.		Pair, #127-128	2.25	1.50
		First day cover, #128a		3.25
		First day cover, #127-128, any single		2.00
		Inscription block of 4, 2 each #127-128	5.00	
		Pane of 12, #127-128	16.00	

First day covers of Nos. 127-128 total 128,478.

Earth Summit Type

1992, May 22   **Photo.**   *Perf. 11½*

129	A265	5.50s Man in space *(784,197)*	1.25	1.00
130	A265	5.50s Sun *(784,197)*	1.25	1.00
131	A265	5.50s Man fishing *(784,197)*	1.25	1.00
132	A265	5.50s Sailboat *(784,197)*	1.25	1.00
a.		Block of 4, #129-132	5.50	4.25
		First day cover, #132a		5.50
		First day cover, #129-132, any single		2.00
		Inscription block of 4, #129-132	5.25	
		Pane of 40, #129-132	52.50	

First day covers of Nos. 129-132a total 82,920.

Mission to Planet Earth Type

Designs: No. 133, Satellite, person's mouth. No. 134, Satellite, person's ear.

1992, Sept. 4   **Photo.**   *Rouletted 8*
Granite Paper

133	A266	10s multicolored *(881,716)*	2.90	2.00
134	A266	10s multicolored *(881,716)*	2.90	2.00
a.		Pair, #133-134	6.00	4.00
		First day cover, #134a		4.50
		First day cover, #133-134, any single		3.50
		Inscription block of 4, #133-134	12.50	
		Pane of 10, #133-134	30.00	

First day covers of Nos. 133-134 total 99,459.

Science and Technology Type of 1992

Designs: 5.50s, Woman emerging from computer screen. 7s, Green thumb growing flowers.

1992, Oct. 2   **Litho.**   *Perf. 14*

135	A267	5.50s multicolored *(482,830)*	.80	.75
		First day cover		1.75
		Inscription block of 4	3.75	
136	A267	7s multicolored *(500,517)*	1.50	1.50
		First day cover		2.00
		First day cover, #135-136		3.25
		Inscription block of 4	6.75	

First day covers of Nos. 135-136 total 98,091.

V29   Intl. Center, Vienna — V30

Printed by Walsall Secruity Printers, Ltd., UK. Designed by Gundi Groh, Austria (5.50s), Rocco J. Callari, US (7s).

1992, Oct. 2   **Litho.**   *Perf. 13x13½*

137	V29	5.50s multicolored *(2,100,000)+*	1.00	.75
		First day cover		1.25
		Inscription block of 4	5.00	—

Perf. 13½x13

138	V30	7s multicolored *(2,100,000)+*	1.50	1.50
		First day cover		2.00
		First day cover, #137-138		2.50
		Inscription block of 4	7.50	—

First day covers of Nos. 137-138 total 151,788.

Human Rights Type of 1989

Panes of 12+12 se-tenant labels containing Articles 23 (6s) and 24 (10s) inscribed in German, English or French.

Artwork: 6s, Les Constructeurs, by Fernand Leger. 10s, Sunday Afternoon on the Island of Le Grande Jatte, by Georges Seurat.

1992, Nov. 20   **Litho.**   *Perf. 13½*

139	A250	6s multicolored, *(1,536,516)*	1.10	.85
		First day cover		2.00
		Inscription block of 3 + 3 labels	3.50	
140	A250	10s multicolored, *(1,527,861)*	1.90	1.50
		First day cover		4.00
		Inscription block of 3 + 3 labels	6.00	
		First day cover, #139-140		4.00
		Panes of 12, #139-140	37.50	

Aging With Dignity Type

Designs: 5.50s, Elderly couple, family working in garden. 7s, Older woman teaching.

1993, Feb. 5   **Litho.**   *Perf. 13*

141	A270	5.50s multicolored *(428,886)*	1.00	1.00
		First day cover		1.60
		Inscription block of 4	4.50	
142	A270	7s multicolored *(459,471)*	1.60	1.50
		First day cover		2.00
		First day cover, #141-142		3.00
		Inscription block of 4	7.50	

First day covers of Nos. 141-142 total 87,052.

Endangered Species Type

Designed by Rocco J. Callari and Steve Brennan, US.

Designs: No. 143, Equus grevyi (Grevy's zebra). No. 144, Spheniscus humboldti (Humboldt's penguins). No. 145, Varanus griseus (desert monitor). No. 146, Canis lupus (gray wolf).

1993, Mar. 2   **Litho.**   *Perf. 13x12½*

143	A271	7s multicolored *(1,200,000)+*	1.25	1.00
144	A271	7s multicolored *(1,200,000)+*	1.25	1.00
145	A271	7s multicolored *(1,200,000)+*	1.25	1.00
146	A271	7s multicolored *(1,200,000)+*	1.25	1.00
a.		Block of 4, #143-146	5.00	4.00
		First day cover, #146a		5.25
		First day cover, #143-146, any single		1.75
		Inscription block of 4, #146a	5.00	
		Pane of 16, #143-146	20.00	

First day covers of Nos. 143-146a total 106,211.

Healthy Environment Type

1993, May 7   **Litho.**   *Perf. 15x14½*

147	A272	6s Wave in ocean *(517,433)*	1.40	.75
		First day cover		1.50
		Inscription block of 4	6.00	
148	A272	10s Globe *(453,123)*	2.25	1.50
		First day cover		2.25
		First day cover, #147-148		3.40
		Inscription block of 4	10.00	

First day covers of Nos. 147-148 total 79,773.

V31

Designed by Marek Kwiatkowski, Poland. Printed by Helio Courvoisier S.A., Switzerland.

1993, May 7   **Photo.**   *Perf. 11½*
Granite Paper

149	V31	13s multicolored *(1,500,000)+*	3.00	2.25
		First day cover *(41,489)*		2.50
		Inscription block of 4	12.50	

Human Rights Type of 1989

Printed in sheets of 12 + 12 se-tenant labels containing Article 29 (5s) and 30 (6s) inscribed in German, English or French.

Artwork: 5s, Lower Austrian Peasants' Wedding, by Ferdinand G. Waldmuller. 6s, Outback, by Sally Morgan.

1993, June 11   **Litho.**   *Perf. 13½*

150	A250	5s multicolored *(1,532,531)*	1.25	.75
		First day cover		1.75
		Inscription block of 3 + 3 labels	4.00	
151	A250	6s multicolored *(1,542,716)*	1.50	.50
		First day cover		2.00
		First day cover, #150-151		2.40
		Inscription block of 3 + 3 labels	5.00	
		Panes of 12, #150-151	32.50	

First day covers of Nos. 150-151 total 128,687.

Intl. Peace Day Type

Denomination at: No. 152, UL. No. 153, UR. No. 154, LL. No. 155, LR.

1993, Sept. 21   **Litho. & Engr.**   *Rouletted 12½*

152	A274	5.50s green & multi *(445,699)*	2.00	.90
153	A274	5.50s green & multi *(445,699)*	2.00	.90
154	A274	5.50s green & multi *(445,699)*	2.00	.90
155	A274	5.50s green & multi *(445,699)*	2.00	.90
a.		Block of 4, #152-155	8.50	3.75
		First day cover, #155a		4.00
		First day cover, #152-155, any single		2.25
		Inscription block of 4, #155a	8.75	
		Pane of 40, #152-155	90.00	

First day covers of Nos. 152-155a total 67,075.

Environment-Climate Type

Designs: No. 156, Monkeys. No. 157, Bluebird, industrial pollution, volcano. No. 158, Volcano, nuclear power plant, tree stumps. No. 159, Cactus, tree stumps, owl.

1993, Oct. 29   **Litho.**   *Perf. 14½*

156	A275	7s multicolored *(484,517)*	1.50	1.25
157	A275	7s multicolored *(484,517)*	1.50	1.25
158	A275	7s multicolored *(484,517)*	1.50	1.25
159	A275	7s multicolored *(484,517)*	1.50	1.25
a.		Strip of 4, #156-159	6.00	5.00
		First day cover, #159a		7.00
		First day cover, #156-159, any single		3.00
		Inscription block of 8, 2 #159a	13.00	
		Pane of 24, #156-159	35.00	

First day covers of Nos. 156-159a total 61,946.

Intl. Year of the Family Type of 1993

Designs: 5.50s, Adults, children holding hands. 8s, Two adults, child planting crops.

1994, Feb. 4   **Litho.**   *Perf. 13.1*

160	A276	5.50s blue green & multi *(650,000)+*	1.25	1.25
		First day cover		1.60
		Inscription block of 4	5.75	
161	A276	8s red & multi *(650,000)+*	2.00	1.50
		First day cover		2.25
		First day cover, #160-161		3.00
		Inscription block of 4	8.75	

First day covers of Nos. 160-161 total 78,532.

Endangered Species Type of 1993

Designed by Rocco J. Callari, US (frame), and Paul Margocsy, Australia (stamps).

Designs: No. 162, Ocelot. No. 163, White-breasted silvereye. No. 164, Mediterranean monk seal. No. 165, Asian elephant.

1994, Mar. 18   **Litho.**   *Perf. 12.7*

162	A271	7s multicolored *(1,200,000)+*	1.40	1.25
163	A271	7s multicolored *(1,200,000)+*	1.40	1.25
164	A271	7s multicolored *(1,200,000)+*	1.40	1.25
165	A271	7s multicolored *(1,200,000)+*	1.40	1.25
a.		Block of 4, #162-165	5.75	5.00

First day cover, #165a   6.00
First day cover, #162-165, each 2.00
Inscription block of 4, #165a   5.75
Pane of 16, #162-165   23.00

First day covers of Nos. 162-165a total 104,478.

Protection for Refugees Type

Design: 12s, Protective hands surround group of refugees.

1994, Apr. 29   Litho.   Perf. 14.3x14.8
166 A277 12s multicolored (650,000)   2.00 1.50
     First day cover (49,519)   3.00
     Inscription block of 4   10.00 —

V32

V33

V34

Designed by Masatoshi Hioki, Japan (#167), Ramon Alcantara Rodriguez, Mexico (#168), Eliezer Weishoff, Israel (#169).
Printed by Cartor, S.A., France.

1994, Apr. 29   Litho.   Perf. 12.9
167 V32 50g multicolored (1,450,000)+   .20 .20
     First day cover   1.25
     Inscription block of 4   .40 —
168 V33 4s multicolored (1,150,000)+   .70 .50
     First day cover   1.25
     Inscription block of 4   3.50 —
169 V34 30s multicolored (560,000)+   5.00 4.00
     First day cover   5.00
     Inscription block of 4   22.50 —

First day covers of Nos. 167-169 total 74,558.

Intl. Decade for Natural Disaster Reduction Type

Earth seen from space, outline map of: No. 170, North America. No. 171, Eurasia. No. 172, South America. No. 173, Australia and South Asia.

1994, May 27   Litho.   Perf. 13.9x14.2
170 A281 6s multicolored (690,000)+   1.75 1.25
171 A281 6s multicolored (690,000)+   1.75 1.25
172 A281 6s multicolored (690,000)+   1.75 1.25
173 A281 6s multicolored (690,000)+   1.75 1.25
  a.   Block of 4, #170-173   7.25 5.00
     First day cover, #173a   4.50
     First day cover, #170-173, each   2.25
     Inscription block of 4, #173a   7.50 —
     Pane of 40, #170-173   72.50

First day covers of Nos. 170-173a total 52,502.

Population and Development Type

Designs: 5.50s, Women teaching, running machine tool, coming home to family. 7s, Family on tropical island.

1994, Sept. 1   Litho.   Perf. 13.2x13.6
174 A282 5.50s multicolored (650,000)+   1.25 .75
     First day cover   1.25
     Inscription block of 4   5.50 —
175 A282 7s multicolored (650,000)+   1.50 1.25
     First day cover   1.75
     First day cover, #174-175   3.00
     Inscription block of 4   6.75 —

First day covers of Nos. 174-175 total 67,423.

UNCTAD Type

1994, Oct. 28
176 A283 6s multi, diff. (650,000)+   1.10 .75
     First day cover   1.25
     Inscription block of 4   5.50 —
177 A283 7s multi, diff. (650,000)+   1.50 1.00
     First day cover   1.75
     First day cover, #176-177   3.00
     Inscription block of 4   6.25 —

First day covers of Nos. 176-177 total 67,064.

UN 50th Anniv. Type

1995, Jan. 1   Litho. & Engr.   Perf. 13.4
178 A284 7s multicolored (742,052)   1.60 1.10
     First day cover (118,537)   2.00
     Inscription block of 4   7.00 —

Social Summit Type

1995, Feb. 3   Photo. & Engr.   Perf. 13.6x13.9
179 A285 14s multi, diff. (595,554)   2.50 1.50
     First day cover (51,244)   3.50
     Inscription block of 4   11.00 —

Endangered Species Type of 1993

Designed by Salvatore Catalano, US.
Designs: No. 180, Black rhinoceros, Diceros bicornis. No. 181, Golden conure, Aratinga guarouba. No. 182, Douc langur, Pygathrix nemaeus. No. 183, Arabian oryx, Oryx leucoryx.

1995, Mar. 24   Litho.   Perf. 13x12½
180 A271 7s multicolored (938,000)+   1.25 1.25
181 A271 7s multicolored (938,000)+   1.25 1.25
182 A271 7s multicolored (938,000)+   1.25 1.25
183 A271 7s multicolored (938,000)+   1.25 1.25
  a.   Block of 4, 180-183   5.00 5.00
     First day cover, #183a   4.50
     First day cover, #180-183, each   2.00
     Inscription block of 4, #183a   5.00 —
     Pane of 16, #180-183   22.50

First day covers of Nos. 180-183a total 95,401.

Intl. Youth Year Type

Designs: 6s, Village in winter. 7s, Teepees.

1995, May 26   Litho.   Perf. 14.4x14.7
184 A286 6s multicolored (437,462)   1.40 1.00
     First day cover   1.25
     Inscription block of 4   5.75 —
185 A286 7s multicolored (409,449)   1.65 1.00
     First day cover   2.00
     First day cover, #184-185   3.25
     Inscription block of 4   7.00 —

First day covers of Nos. 184-185 total 60,979.

UN, 50th Anniv. Type

Designs: 7s, Like No. 663. 10s, Like No. 664.

1995, June 26   Engr.   Perf. 13.3x13.6
186 A287 7s green (433,922)   1.40 1.25
     First day cover   2.00
     Inscription block of 4   6.50 —
187 A287 10s black (471,198)   2.00 1.50
     First day cover   1.75
     First day cover, #186-187   3.00
     Inscription block of 4   11.00 —

Souvenir Sheet
Litho. & Engr.
Imperf

188   Sheet of 2, #186-187 (367,773) 3.50 3.50
  a.   A287 7s green   1.40 1.40
  b.   A287 10s black   1.75 1.75
     First day cover   4.00

First day covers of Nos. 186-188b total 171,765.

Conference on Women Type

Designs: 5.50s, Women amid tropical plants. 6s, Woman reading, swans on lake.

1995, Sept. 5   Photo.   Perf. 12
189 A288 5.50s multicolored (549,951)   1.25 .55
     First day cover   1.25
     Inscription block of 4   5.50 —

Size: 28x50mm
190 A288 6s multicolored (556,569)   1.75 .65
     First day cover   1.25
     First day cover, #189-190   2.50
     Inscription block of 4   8.00 —

First day covers of Nos. 189-190 total 71,976.

UN People, 50th Anniv. Type

1995, Oct. 24   Litho.   Perf. 14
191   Sheet of 12 (280,528 sheets)   16.00 16.00
     First day cover   12.50
a.-l. A290 3s any single   1.25 .85
     First day cover, #191a-191 l, each 1.25
192   Souvenir booklet, (95,449 booklets) 16.00
  a.   A290 3s Booklet pane of 3, vert. strip of 3
        from UL of sheet   3.75 3.75
  b.   A290 3s Booklet pane of 3, vert. strip of 3
        from UR of sheet   3.75 3.75
  c.   A290 3s Booklet pane of 3, vert. strip of 3
        from LL of sheet   3.75 3.75
  d.   A290 3s Booklet pane of 3, vert. strip of 3
        from LR of sheet   3.75 3.75

First day covers of Nos. 191-192d total 107,436.

WFUNA, 50th Anniv. Type

Design: 7s, Harlequin holding dove.

1996, Feb. 2   Litho.   Perf. 13x13½
193 A291 7s multicolored (655,000)+   1.35 .65
     First day cover   2.00
     Inscription block of 4   6.75 —

VEREINTE NATIONEN $1

UN Flag — V35

VEREINTE NATIONEN $10

Abstract, by Karl Korab — V36

Printed by House of Questa, UK.

1996, Feb. 2   Litho.   Perf. 15x14½
194 V35 1s multicolored (1,180,000)+   .20 .20
     First day cover   1.25
     Inscription block of 4   1.00 —
195 V36 10s multicolored (880,000)+   2.00 1.00
     First day cover   2.75
     First day cover, #194-195   3.00
     Inscription block of 4   10.00 —

Endangered Species Type of 1993

Designs: No. 196, Cypripedium calceolus. No. 197, Aztekium ritteri. No. 198, Euphorbia cremersii. No. 199, Dracula bella.

1996, Mar. 14   Litho.   Perf. 12½
196 A271 7s multicolored (846,000)+   1.30 .65
197 A271 7s multicolored (846,000)+   1.30 .65
198 A271 7s multicolored (846,000)+   1.30 .65
199 A271 7s multicolored (846,000)+   1.30 .65
  a.   Block of 4, #196-199   5.25 —
     First day cover, #199a   4.50
     First day cover, #196-199, each   2.00
     Pane of 16, #196-199   21.00

City Summit Type

Designs: No. 200, Arab family selling fruits, vegetables. No. 201, Women beside stream, camels. No. 202, Woman carrying bundle on head, city skyline. No. 203, Woman threshing grain, yoke of oxen in field. No. 204, Native village, elephant.

1996, June 3   Litho.   Perf. 14x13½
200 A293 6s multicolored (500,000)+   1.10 .55
201 A293 6s multicolored (500,000)+   1.10 .55
202 A293 6s multicolored (500,000)+   1.10 .55
203 A293 6s multicolored (500,000)+   1.10 .55
204 A293 6s multicolored (500,000)+   1.10 .55
  a.   Strip of 5, #200-204   5.50 —
     First day cover, #204a   5.00
     First day cover, #200-204, each   1.50
     Inscription block of 10, 2 #204a 12.50

Sport and the Environment Type

6s, Men's parallel bars (gymnastics), vert. 7s, Hurdles.

1996, July 19   Litho.   Perf. 14x14½, 14½x14
205 A294 6s multicolored (730,000)+   1.10 .55
     First day cover   1.50
     Inscription block of 4   5.50 —
206 A294 7s multicolored (730,000)+   1.40 .65
     First day cover   1.50
     First day cover, #205-206   2.75
     Inscription block of 4   6.75 —

Souvenir Sheet
207 A294   Sheet of 2, #205-206 (500,000)+   2.50 2.40

Plea for Peace Type

Designed by: 7s, Du Keqing, China. 10s, Xu Kangdeng, China.

Designs: 7s, Dove and butterflies. 10s, Stylized dove, diff.

1996, Sept. 17   Litho.   Perf. 14½x15
208 A295 7s multicolored (655,000)+   1.25 .65
     First day cover   1.50
     Inscription block of 4   6.50 —
209 A295 10s multicolored (655,000)+   1.90 .95
     First day cover   2.50
     First day cover, #208-209   3.75
     Inscription block of 4   9.50 —

UNICEF Type

Fairy Tales: 5.50s, Hansel and Gretel, by the Brothers Grimm. 8s, How Maui Stole Fire from the Gods, South Pacific.

1996, Nov. 20   Litho.   Perf. 14½x15
210 A296 5.50s multicolored (1,160,000)+ 1.00 .50
     First day cover   1.25
     Pane of 8 + label   8.00
211 A296 8s multicolored (1,160,000)+   1.50 .75
     First day cover   2.00
     First day cover, #210-211   2.75
     Pane of 8 + label   12.00

V37

Phoenixes Flying
Down (Detail), by
Sagenji
Yoshida — V38

Printed by The House of Questa, Ltd., UK.

1997, Feb. 12		Litho.	Perf. 14½	
212	V37	5s multicolored (750,000)+	.85	.40
		First day cover		1.25
		Inscription block of 4	3.40	-
213	V38	6s multicolored (1,050,000)+	1.00	.50
		First day cover		1.50
		First day cover, #212-213		2.50
		Inscription block of 4	4.00	—

First day covers of Nos. 212-213 total 156,021.

Endangered Species Type of 1993

Designs: No. 214, Macaca sylvanus (Barbary macaque). No. 215, Anthropoides paradisea (blue crane). No. 216, Equus przewalskii (Przewalski horse). No. 217, Myrmecophaga tridactyla (giant anteater).

1997, Mar. 13		Litho.	Perf. 12½	
214	A271	7s multicolored (710,000)+	1.10	.55
215	A271	7s multicolored (710,000)+	1.10	.55
216	A271	7s multicolored (710,000)+	1.10	.55
217	A271	7s multicolored (710,000)+	1.10	.55
a.		Block of 4, #214-217	4.50	2.25
		First day cover, #217a		5.00
		First day cover, #214-217, each		1.50
		Inscription block of 4, #217a	4.50	
		Pane of 16	18.00	

First day covers of Nos. 214-217 total 86,406.

Earth Summit Anniv. Type

Designs: No. 218, Person running. No. 219, Hills, stream, trees. No. 220, Tree with orange leaves. No. 221, Tree with pink leaves.
11s, Combined design similar to Nos. 218-221.

1997, May 30		Photo.	Perf. 11.5	
		Granite Paper		
218	A299	3.50s multicolored (282,016)	.60	.30
219	A299	3.50s multicolored (282,016)	.60	.30
220	A299	3.50s multicolored (282,016)	.60	.30
221	A299	3.50s multicolored (282,016)	.60	.30
a.		Block of 4, #218-221	2.50	1.25
		First day cover, #221a		3.50
		First day cover, #218-221, each		1.25
		Inscription block of 4, #221a	2.50	
		Souvenir Sheet		
222	A299	11s multicolored (221,434)	1.75	1.75
		First day cover		2.50

First day covers of Nos. 218-222 total 62,390.

Transportation Type

Ground transportation: No. 223, 1829 Rocket, 1901 Darraque. No. 224, Steam engine from Vladikawska Railway, trolley. No. 225, Double-decker bus. No. 226, 1950s diesel locomotive, semi-trailer. No. 227, High-speed train, electric car.

1997, Aug. 29		Litho.	Perf. 14x14½	
223	A300	7s multicolored (356,097)	1.10	.55
224	A300	7s multicolored (356,097)	1.10	.55
225	A300	7s multicolored (356,097)	1.10	.55
226	A300	7s multicolored (356,097)	1.10	.55
227	A300	7s multicolored (356,097)	1.10	.55
a.		Strip of 5, #223-227	5.50	2.75
		First day cover, #227a		6.25
		First day cover, #223-227, each		1.65
		Inscription block of 10, 2#227a	11.00	

No. 227a has continuous design.
First day covers of Nos. 223-227 total 44,877.

Philately Type

Designs: 6.50s, No. 62. 7s, No. 63.

1997, Oct. 14		Litho.	Perf. 13½x14	
228	A301	6.50s multicolored (379,767)	1.25	.50
		First day cover		1.50
		Inscription block of 4	5.25	—
229	A301	7s multicolored (378,107)	1.40	.55
		First day cover		1.65
		First day cover, #228-229		3.00
		Inscription block of 4	5.75	—

First day covers of Nos. 228-229 total 57,651.

World Heritage Convention Type

Terracotta warriors of Xian: 3s, Single warrior. 6s, Massed warriors. No. 232a, like #716. No. 232b, like #717. No. 232c, like Geneva #314. No. 232d, like Geneva #315. No. 232e, like Vienna #230. No. 232f, like Vienna #231.

1997, Nov. 19		Litho.	Perf. 13½	
230	A302	3s multicolored (528,352)	.50	.25
		First day cover		1.25
		Inscription block of 4	2.00	—
231	A302	6s multicolored (530,947)	1.00	.50
		First day cover		1.50
		First day cover, #230-231		2.25
		Inscription block of 4	4.00	—
232		Souvenir booklet (298,055 booklets)	4.00	
a.-f.	A302	1s any single	.20	.20
g.		Booklet pane of 4 #232a	.65	.65
h.		Booklet pane of 4 #232b	.65	.65
i.		Booklet pane of 4 #232c	.65	.65
j.		Booklet pane of 4 #232d	.65	.65
k.		Booklet pane of 4 #232e	.65	.65
l.		Booklet pane of 4 #232f	.65	.65

First day covers of Nos. 230-232 total 71,708.

Japanese Peace
Bell, Vienna — V39

Vienna Subway,
Vienna Intl.
Center — V40

Printed by The House of Questa, UK. Panes of 20.
Designed by Heinz Pfeifer, Austria (6.50s), Pigneter, Austria (9s).

1998, Feb. 13		Litho.	Perf. 15x14½	
233	V39	6.50s multicolored (670,000)+	1.00	.50
		First day cover		1.25
		Inscription block of 4	4.50	—
234	V40	9s multicolored (770,000)+	1.40	.70
		First day cover		1.75
		First day cover, #233-234		3.00
		Inscription block of 4	6.25	—

Endangered Species Type of 1993

Designed by Rocco J. Callari, US and Robert Hynes, US.
Designs: No. 235, Chelonia mydas (green turtle). No. 236, Speotyto cunicularia (burrowing owl). No. 237, Trogonoptera brookiana (Rajah Brooke's birdwing). No. 238, Ailurus fulgens (lesser panda).

1998, Mar. 13		Litho.	Perf. 12½	
235	A271	7s multicolored (620,000)+	1.10	.55
236	A271	7s multicolored (620,000)+	1.10	.55
237	A271	7s multicolored (620,000)+	1.10	.55
238	A271	7s multicolored (620,000)+	1.10	.55
a.		Block of 4, #235-238	4.50	2.25
		First day cover, #238a		5.00
		First day cover, #235-238, each		1.25
		Pane of 16	18.00	

Intl. Year of the Ocean — V41

Designed by Yuan Lee, China.

1998, May 20		Litho.	Perf. 13x13½	
239	V41	Sheet of 12 (345,000)+	7.50	4.00
a.-l.		3.50s any single	.60	.35
		First day cover, 3239		10.00
		First day cover, #239a-239l, each		1.25

Rain Forests Type

1998, June 19		Litho.	Perf. 13x13½	
240	A307	6.50s Ocelot (590,000)+	1.00	.50
		First day cover		1.50
		Inscription block of 4	4.00	—
		Souvenir Sheet		
241	A307	22s like #240 (340,000)+	3.50	1.75
		First day cover		5.25

Peacekeeping Type of 1998

Designs: 4s, Soldier passing out relief supplies. 7.50s, UN supervised voting.

1998, Sept. 15		Photo.	Perf. 12	
242	A308	4s multicolored (555,000)+	.70	.35
		First day cover		1.25
		Inscription block of 4	2.80	—
243	A308	7.50s multicolored (545,000)+	1.30	.65
		First day cover		1.75
		First day cover, #242-243		2.50
		Inscription block of 4	5.25	—

Declaration of Human Rights Type

Designs: 4.50s, Stylized person. 7s, Gears.

1998, Oct. 27		Litho. & Photo.	Perf. 13	
244	A309	4.50s multicolored (555,000)+	.80	.40
		First day cover		1.50
		Inscription block of 4	3.25	—
245	A309	7s multicolored (545,000)+	1.25	.60
		First day cover		1.75
		First day cover, #244-245		2.50
		Inscription block of 4	5.00	—

Schönbrunn Palace Type

Designs: 3.50s, #248d, Palace. 7s, #248c, Porcelain stove, vert. No. 248a, Blue porcelain vase, vert. No. 248b, Wall painting on fabric (detail), by Johann Wenzl Bergl, vert. No. 248e, Great Palm House (conservatory). No. 248f, The Gloriette (archway).

1998, Dec. 4		Litho.	Perf. 14	
246	A310	3.50s multicolored (615,000)+	.60	.30
		First day cover		1.50
		Inscription block of 4	2.50	—
247	A310	7s multicolored (615,000)+	1.10	.55
		First day cover		1.65
		First day cover, #246-247		2.25
		Inscription block of 4	4.50	—
		Souvenir Booklet		
248		Booklet (158,000)+	5.75	
a.-c.	A310	1s any single	.20	.20
d.-f.	A310	2s any single	.30	.30
g.		Booklet pane of 4 #248d	1.25	
h.		Booklet pane of 3 #248a	.60	
i.		Booklet pane of 3 #248b	.60	
j.		Booklet pane of 3 #248c	.60	
k.		Booklet pane of 4 #248e	1.25	
l.		Booklet pane of 4 #248f	1.25	

Volcanic Landscape — V42

Designed by Peter Pongratz, Austria. Printed by Johann Enschedé and Sons, the Netherlands.

1999, Feb. 5		Litho.	Perf. 13x13½	
249	V42	8s multicolored (660,000)+	1.40	.70
		First day cover (33,022)		1.90
		Inscription block of 4	5.75	—

World Heritage, Australia Type

Designs: 4.50s, #252d, Uluru-Kata Tjuta Natl. Park. 6.50s, #252a, Tasmanian Wilderness. No. 252b, Wet tropics of Queensland. No. 252c, Great Barrier Reef. No. 252e, Kakadu Natl. Park. No. 252f, Willandra Lakes region.

1999, Mar. 19		Litho.	Perf. 13	
250	A313	4.50s multicolored (540,000)+	.75	.35
		First day cover		1.25
		Inscription block of 4	3.00	—
251	A313	6.50s multicolored (540,000)+	1.10	.55
		First day cover		1.50
		First day cover, #250-251		2.25
		Inscription block of 4	4.50	—
		Souvenir Booklet		
252		Booklet (116,000)+	6.75	
a.-c.	A313	1s any single	.20	.20
d.-f.	A313	2s any single	.35	.35

g.	Booklet pane of 4, #252a			.80	
h.	Booklet pane of 4, #252d			1.40	
i.	Booklet pane of 4, #252b			.80	
j.	Booklet pane of 4, #252e			1.40	
k.	Booklet pane of 4, #252c			.80	
l.	Booklet pane of 4, #252f			1.40	

First day covers of Nos. 250-252 total 65,123.

Endangered Specied Type of 1993

Designed by Jeffrey Terreson, US.
Designs: No. 253, Pongo pygmaeus (oran-utan). No. 254, Pelecanus crispus (Dalmatian pelican). No. 255, Eunectes notaeus (yellow anaconda). No. 256, Caracal.

1999, Apr. 22		**Litho.**		***Perf. 12½***	
253	A271	7s **multicolored** *(552,000)+*		1.10	.55
254	A271	7s **multicolored** *(552,000)+*		1.10	.55
255	A271	7s **multicolored** *(552,000)+*		1.10	.55
256	A271	7s **multicolored** *(552,000)+*		1.10	.55
a.		Block of 4, #253-256		4.50	—
		First day cover, #256a		3.00	
		First day cover, #253-256, each		1.65	
		Pane of 16		18.00	

First day covers of Nos. 253-256 total 66,733.

UNISPACE III Type

Designs: No. 257, Satellite over ships. No. 258, Satellite up close. No. 259, Composite of #257-258.

1999, July 7		**Photo.**		***Rouletted 8***	
257	A314	3.50s **multicolored** *(1,200,000)+*		.55	.30
258	A314	3.50s **multicolored** *(1,200,000)+*		.55	.30
a.		Pair, #257-258		1.10	.60
		First day cover, #258a		2.40	
		First day cover, #257-258, each		1.25	
		Inscription block of 4		2.20	—
		Pane of 10, #257-258		5.50	—

Souvenir Sheet
Perf. 14½

259	A314	13s **multicolored** *(350,000)+*		2.00	1.00
		First day cover		3.00	

First day covers of Nos. 257-259 total 72,143.

UPU Type

Various people, late 20th century methods of mail transportation, denomination at: No. 260, UL. No. 261, UR. No. 262, LL. No. 263, LR.

1999, Aug. 23		**Photo.**		***Perf. 11¾***	
260	A315	6.50s **multicolored** *(417,000)+*		1.10	.55
261	A315	6.50s **multicolored** *(417,000)+*		1.10	.55
262	A315	6.50s **multicolored** *(417,000)+*		1.10	.55
263	A315	6.50s **multicolored** *(417,000)+*		1.10	.55
a.		Block of 4, #260-263		4.50	—
		First day cover, #263a		3.50	
		First day cover, #260-263, each		1.60	
		Inscription block of 4		4.50	—

First day covers of Nos. 260-263 total 38,453.

In Memoriam Type

Designs: 6.50s, 14s, Donaupark. Size of 14s stamp: 34x63mm.

1999, Sept. 21		**Litho.**		***Perf. 14½x14***	
264	A316	6.50s **multicolored** *(530,000)+*		1.10	.55
		First day cover		1.75	
		Inscription block of 4		4.50	—

Souvenir Sheet
Perf. 14

265	A316	14s **multicolored** *(338,000)+*		2.40	1.25
		First day cover		3.00	

First day covers of Nos. 264-265 total 61,089.

Education Type

1999, Nov. 18		**Litho.**		***Perf. 13½x13¾***	
266	A317	7s Boy, girl, book *(490,000)+*		1.25	.60
		First day cover		1.60	
		Inscription block of 4		5.00	—
267	A317	13s Group reading *(490,000)+*		2.25	1.10
		First day cover		3.00	
		First day cover, #266-267		4.00	
		Inscription block of 4		9.00	—

First day covers of Nos. 266-267 total 48,590.

Intl. Year of Thanksgiving Type

2000, Jan. 1		**Litho.**		***Perf. 13¼x13½***	
268	A318	7s **multicolored** *(510,000)+*		1.25	.60
		First day cover		1.60	
		Inscription block of 4		5.00	—

On No. 268 portions of the design were applied by a thermographic process producing a shiny, raised effect.

Endangered Species Type of 1993

Designed by Lori Anzalone, US.
Designs: No. 269, Panthera pardus (leopard). No. 270, Platalea leucorodia (white spoonbill). No. 271, Hippocamelus bisulcus (huemal). No. 272, Orcinus orca (killer whale).

2000, Apr. 6		**Litho.**		***Perf. 12¾x12½***	
269	A271	7s **multicolored** *(548,000)+*		1.10	.55
270	A271	7s **multicolored** *(548,000)+*		1.10	.55
271	A271	7s **multicolored** *(548,000)+*		1.10	.55

272	A271	7s **multicolored** *(548,000)+*		1.10	.55
a.		Block of 4, #269-272		4.50	—
		First day cover, #272a		4.50	
		First day cover, #269-272, each		1.75	
		Pane of 16		18.00	

Our World 2000 Type

Winning artwork in Millennium painting competition: 7s, Tomorrow's Dream, by Voltaire Perez, Philippines. 8s, Remembrance, by Dimitris Nalbandis, Greece, vert.

2000, May 30		**Litho.**		***Perf. 13x13½, 13½x13***	
273	A319	7s **multicolored** *(430,000)+*		1.10	.55
		First day cover		1.75	
		Inscription block of 4		4.50	
274	A319	8s **multicolored** *(430,000)+*		1.25	.60
		First day cover		2.00	
		First day cover, #273-274		3.00	
		Inscription block of 4		5.00	

55th Anniversary Type

Designs: 7s, Secretariat Building, unfinished dome of General Assembly Hall, 1951. 9s, Trygve Lie and Headquraters Advisory Committee at topping-out ceremony, 1949.

2000, July 7		**Litho.**		***Perf. 13¼x13***	
275	A320	7s **multicolored** *(440,000)+*		1.10	.55
		First day cover		1.75	
		Inscription block of 4		4.50	
276	A320	9s **multicolored** *(440,000)+*		1.50	.75
		First day cover		2.25	
		First day cover, #275-276		3.00	
		Inscription block of 4		6.00	

Souvenir Sheet

277	A320	Sheet of 2, #275-276 *(300,000)+*		2.60	1.40
		First day cover		3.25	

2000 END-OF-YEAR ISSUES

See end of New York postage listings.

ENVELOPES

Donaupark,
Vienna — VU1

Printed by Mercury-Walch Pty. Ltd. (Australia). Designed by Hannes Margreiter (Austria).
Design: 7s, Landscape. Design at lower left shows Vienna landmarks (6s), river scene (7s).

1995, Feb. 3				**Litho.**	
U1	VU1	6s **multicolored**, entire, *(128,000)+*		3.00	1.00
		First day cancel *(14,132)*		2.75	
U2	VU1	7s **multicolored**, entire *(128,000)+*		1.90	1.10
		First day cancel *(9,684)*		3.50	

VU2

Printed by Mercury-Walch Pty. Ltd. (Australia).

1998, Mar. 13				**Litho.**	
U3	VU2	13s **multicolored**, entire *(87,000)+*		2.25	1.00
		Entire, first day cancel		3.25	

AIR LETTER SHEETS

VLS1

Printed by Joh. Enschede and Sons. Designed by Ingrid Ousland.

1982, Apr. 28				**Litho.**	
UC1	VLS1	9s **multi,** *light green,* entire *(650,000)*		2.00	1.25
		First day cancel *(120,650)*		2.50	

No. UC1
Surcharged in
Lake

Bureau de poste
1400 Wien —
Vereinte Nationen
Taxe perçue S2

1986, Feb. 3				**Litho.**	
UC2	VLS1	9s +2s **multi,** *light green,* entire *(131,190)*		40.00	5.00
		First day cancel *(18,500)*		20.00	

Birds in Flight,
UN
Emblem — VLS2

Printed by Mercury-Walch, Australia. Designed by Mieczyslaw Wasiliewski, Poland.

1987, Jan. 30				**Litho.**	
UC3	VLS2	11s **bright blue,** entire *(414,000)*		3.00	1.25
		First day cancel *(48,348)*		7.00	

No. UC3
Surcharged

Bureau de poste
1400 Wien —
Vereinte Nationen
Taxe perçue S1

1992, Jan. 1				**Litho.**	
UC4	VLS2	11s +1s **bright blue,** entire *(80,000)*		40.00	1.60
		First day cancel		22.50	

Donaupark,
Vienna — VLS3

Designed by Rocco J. Callari. Printed by Mercury-Walch, Australia.

1992, Sept. 4				**Litho.**	
UC5	VLS3	12s **multicolored,** entire *(200,000)+*		5.00	1.15
		First day cancel *(16,261)*		22.50	

POSTAL CARDS

Olive Branch — VPC1

Bird Carrying Olive
Branch — VPC2

Printed by Courvoisier. Designed by Rolf Christianson (3s), M.A. Munnawar (5s).

1982, Apr. 28				**Photo.**	
UX1	VPC1	3s **multicolored,** cream *(500,000)*		1.00	.65
		First day cancel *(93,010)*		1.65	
UX2	VPC2	5s **multicolored** *(500,000)*		.75	.65
		First day cancel *(89,502)*		1.65	

Emblem of the United
Nations — VPC3

Printed by Johann Enschede en Zonen, Netherlands.
Designed by George Hamori, Australia.

1985, May 10   **Litho.**
UX3 VPC3   4s **multicolored** *(350,000)*   2.50   .20
     First day cancel *(53,450)*   5.50

No. UX2 Surcharged Like No. UC4

1992, Jan. 1   **Photo.**
UX4 VPC2   5s +1s **multicolored** *(71,700)*   17.50   .55
     First day cancel   12.50

Type of 1990

Printed by Mercury-Walch, Australia.

1992, Sept. 4   **Litho.**
UX5 V22   6s **multicolored** *(445,000)+*   2.50   .60
     First day cancel *(16,359)*   12.00
         See No. UX9.

Type of 1985

Printed by Leigh Mardon Pty. Limited, Australia.

1993, May 7   **Litho.**
UX6   A222   5s **multicolored** *(450,000)*   9.00   .45
     First day cancel   10.00

Donaupark,
Vienna — VPC4

Printed by Leigh Mardon Pty. Limited, Australia.

1993, May 7   **Litho.**
UX7 VPC4 6s **multicolored** *(450,000)+*   4.00   .50
     First day cancel   7.50
         See No. UX10.

No. UX6 with design of
Vienna #1 Added

1994, Jan. 1   **Litho.**
UX8 A222+G8   5s +50g **multi** *(350,000)+*   3.50   .50
     First day cancel   8.00

No. UX5 with design of Vienna #167 Added

1997, July 1   **Litho.**
UX9   V22+V32   6s +50g **multi**   2.50   .50
     First day cancel   9.00

No. UX7 with design of Vienna #194 Added

UX10 VPC4+V35 6s +1s **multi**   2.50   .50
     First day cancel   9.00

VPC5

Designed by Günter Leidenfrost.

1998, May 20   **Litho.**
UX11 VPC5 6.50s **multicolored** *(137,000)+*   1.00   .50
     First day cancel   1.50

The
Gloriette — VPC6

1999, Feb. 5   **Litho.**
UX12 VPC6 7s **multicolored** *(136,000)+*   1.10   .55
     First day cancel   1.50

Type of 1983

2000, June 2   **Litho.**
UX13 V7   7s **multicolored**   1.50   .75
     First day cancel   1.50

U.N. TEMPORARY EXECUTIVE AUTHORITY, WEST NEW GUINEA

Located in the western half of New Guinea, southwest Pacific Ocean, the former Netherlands New Guinea became a territory under the administration of the United Nations Temporary Executive Authority on Oct. 1, 1962. The size was 151,789 sq. mi. and the population was estimated at 730,000 in 1958. The capital was Hollandia.
The territory came under Indonesian administration on May 1, 1963. For stamps issued by Indonesia see West Irian in Vol. 6.

100 Cents = 1 Gulden

Catalogue values for all unused stamps in this country are for Never Hinged items.

First Printing (Hollandia)
Netherlands New Guinea Stamps of 1950-60
Overprinted

UNTEA

Overprint size: 17x3 ½mm. Top of "N" is slightly lower than the "U," and the base of the "T" is straight, or nearly so.

Perf. 12½x12, 12½x13½
Photo.; Litho. (#4a, 6, 8)

1962   **Unwmk.**

1	A4	1c **vermilion & yellow**, *Oct. 1*	.20	.20
2	A1	2c **deep orange**, *Oct. 1*	1.25	1.25
3	A4	5c **chocolate & yellow**, *Oct. 1*	.35	.25
4	A5	7c **org red, bl & brn vio**, *Nov. 1*	.80	.80
5	A4	10c **aqua & red brown**, *Oct. 1*	.35	.35
6	A5	12c **green, bl & brn vio**, *Nov. 1*	.35	.35
7	A4	15c **deep yel & red brn**, *Nov. 1*	.60	.55
8	A5	17c **brown violet & blue**, *Oct. 1*	.70	.70
9	A4	20c **lt bl grn & red brn**, *Nov. 1*	.70	.70
10	A6	25c **red**, *Oct. 1*	.60	.55
11	A6	30c **deep blue**, *Oct. 1*	1.10	.90
12	A6	40c **deep orange**, *Oct. 1*	1.10	.90
13	A6	45c **dark olive**, *Nov. 1*	2.50	2.25
14	A6	55c **slate blue**, *Nov. 1*	1.25	1.10
15	A6	80c **dull gray violet**, *Nov. 1*	11.00	11.00
16	A6	85c **dark violet brown**, *Nov. 1*	6.00	5.25
17	A6	1g **plum**, *Oct. 1*	4.00	3.50

Engr.

18	A3	2g **reddish brown**, *Oct. 1*	12.50	12.50
19	A3	5g **green**, *Oct. 1*	5.75	5.25
		Nos. 1-19 (19)	51.10	48.45

Overprinted locally and sold in West New Guinea. Stamps of the second printing were used to complete sets sold to collectors.

Second Printing (Haarlen, Netherlands)

Overprint size: 17x3 ½mm. Top of the "N" is slightly higher than the "U," and the base of the "T" is concave.

Perf. 12½x12, 12½x13½
Photo.; Litho. (#4, 6a, 8a)

1963, Jan. 28   **Unwmk.**

1a	A4	1c **vermilion & yellow**	.40	.40
2a	A1	2c **deep orange**	.35	.25
3a	A4	5c **chocolate & yellow**	.50	.50
4a	A5	7c **org red, bl & brn vio**	.35	.35
5a	A4	10c **aqua & red brown**	.50	.50
6a	A5	12c **green, bl & brn vio**	.55	.55
7a	A4	15c **deep yel & red brn**	.70	.70
8a	A5	17c **brown violet & blue**	1.00	1.00
9a	A4	20c **lt blue grn & red brn**	1.00	1.00
10a	A6	25c **red**	.40	.40
11a	A6	30c **deep blue**	.55	.55
12a	A6	40c **deep orange**	.80	.80
13a	A6	45c **dark olive**	2.25	2.25
14a	A6	55c **slate blue**	1.75	1.75
15a	A6	80c **dull gray violet**	10.50	10.00
16a	A6	85c **dark violet brown**	3.50	3.50
17a	A6	1g **plum**	3.00	3.00

Engr.

18a	A3	2g **reddish brown**	11.50	11.00
19a	A3	5g **green**	12.00	12.00
		Nos. 1a-19a (19)	51.60	50.50

Overprinted in the Netherlands and sold by the UN in New York.

Third Printing

Overprint 14mm long.

PHOTOGRAVURE

1963, Mar.   **Photo.**   **Unwmk.**   *Perf. 12½x12*

1b	A4	1c **vermilion & yellow**	5.00	5.00
3b	A4	5c **chocolate & yellow**	5.00	5.00
4b	A5	7c **org red, bl & brn vio**	7.50	7.50
5b	A4	10c **aqua & red brown**	5.00	5.00
6b	A5	12c **green, bl & brn vio**	7.50	7.50
7b	A4	15c **deep yel & red brn**	10.00	10.00
8b	A5	17c **brown violet & blue**	5.00	5.00
9b	A4	20c **lt blue grn & red brn**	5.00	5.00
		Nos. 1b-9b (8)	50.00	50.00

The third printing was applied in West New Guinea and it is doubtful whether it was regularly issued. Used values are for cto.

Fourth Printing

Overprint 19mm long.

PHOTOGRAVURE

1963, Mar.   **Unwmk.**   *Perf. 12½x12*

1c	A4	1c **vermilion & yellow**	12.50	12.50
5c	A4	10c **aqua & red brown**	20.00	20.00

The fourth printing was applied in West New Guinea and it is doubtful whether it was regularly issued. Used values are for cto.

U.N. INTERIM ADMINISTRATION IN KOSOVO

These stamps were issued by the United Nations Interim Administration Mission in Kosovo and the Post & Telecommunications of Kosovo. Service was local for the first two months, with international use to start in mid-May.

100 pfennigs = 1 mark

Catalogue values for all unused stamps in this country are for Never Hinged items.

Peace in Kosovo — A1

Printed by La Poste, France. Panes of 40. Designed by Shyqri Nimani, Kosovo.

Designs: 20pf, Mosaic depicting Orpheus, c. 5th-6th cent., Podujeve. 30pf, Dardinian idol, Museum of Kosovo. 50pf, Silver coin of Damastion from 4th cent. B.C. 1m, Statue of Mother Teresa, Prizren. 2m, Map of Kosovo.

Perf. 13½x13, 13½x13¼ (30pf)

2000, Mar. 14	Litho.	Unwmk.	
1 A1 20pf **multicolored**		.20	.20
First day cover			1.25
2 A1 30pf **multicolored**		.30	.30
First day cover			1.25
3 A1 50pf **multicolored**		.50	.50
First day cover			1.50
4 A1 1m **multicolored**		1.00	1.00
First day cover			2.50
5 A1 2m **multicolored**		2.00	2.00
First day cover			5.00
First day cover, #1-5			7.00
Nos. 1-5 (5)		4.00	4.00

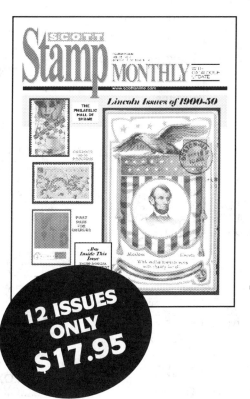

Additions, Deletions & Number Changes

Number in 2000 Catalogue	Number in 2001 Catalogue
UNITED STATES	
Postage	
87a	87a, 87b
93a	93a, 93b
93c	93c, 93d
146a	146a, 146b
new	375c
new	424f
new	632c
new	914a, 919a
new	1039b
new	1393g
1420b	deleted
1434c	1434a
new	1451c
1580b	1580B
unlettered	1580c
1590a	1590A
1622c	1622C
1622d	1622Cd
1623b	1623B
1623c, 1623e	1623Bc, 1623Be
new	1632a
new	1683a
1789a	1789A
1789b	1789B
1789d	1789Ad
1795a	1795A
1796a	1796A
1797a	1797A
1798a	1798A
1798c	1798Ac
new	1843d
new	1919c
new	1939c
new	1946b
1951a	1951A
1953a-2002a	1953A-2002A
2002c	2002Ac
new	2085b
2115a	2115e
new	2115a
new	2131a, 2136c
new	2149e, 2150b
new	2257c, 2257e
new	2418a
new	2492h
new	2494b
2524a	2524A
new	2528c, 2528d
2535a	2535A
2540b	2540a
new	2544c
2593b, 2593c	2593B, 2593Bc
new	2607a
new	2629a
new	2703d
2723a	2723A
new	2798c
2802b	2799a
new	2802b
new	2814e
2871a	2871A
2871b-2871c	2871Ab-2871Ac
new	2879a, 2885c

Number in 2000 Catalogue	Number in 2001 Catalogue
UNITED STATES	
Postage (continued)	
new	2904Bc
2920d-2920e	2920D, 2920De
new	3000w
3003a-3003b	3003A, 3003Ab
new	3048b-3048c
3051b	3051b, 3051c
new	3071c-3071d
new	3127b, 3129c
new	3182p, 3183p
new	3244b
new	3271a
new	3278h
new	3281b-3281c
3297c	3297a
3297a-3297b	3297b-3297c
3301a	deleted
new	3305d
3320a	3320b
new	3391d
Air Post	
new	C60b
new	C86c
C98a, C98c	C98A, C98Ac
Officials	
new	O57Sd
Booklets	
BK178B	BK178E
BK178E	BK178F
new	BK178B
BK233B-BK233D	BK233C-BK233E
new	BK233B
new	BK237
Carriers	
new	1LB9c
new	3LB1a
new	4LB7a
8LB2	8LB3
8LB1	8LB1/8LB2
Locals	
unlettered	20L4a
new	20L47a
new	20LU44A
new	40L5d
new	57L1a
64L1b	64L1b, 64L1c
new	87L75a
new	96L4a
new	166L1
101L1-101L2	101L2-101L3
new	101L1
unlettered	113L1a
Envelopes	
new	W18B, U21A
new	U82a
U470f, U470g	U470e, U470f
U470h	U470g
U471f, U471g	U471e, U471f

Number in 2000 Catalogue	Number in 2001 Catalogue
UNITED STATES	
Envelopes (continued)	
U471h	U471g
U476a	U476b
U476b	U476a
new	U544e
new	U586c
new	U634a, U634b
new	U641c, U641d
Postal Cards	
new	UX14d
new	UX46d
new	UX120d, UX120e
new	UX122a
new	UX124a, UX124b
new	UX125a
Revenues	
new	R1e
new	R285c
Silver Tax	
new	RG34
Revenue Stamped Paper	
RN-A10a	RN-A11
new	RN-E6
Private Die Proprietary	
new	RS155e
Hunting Permit	
new	RW22a
Telegraph Stamps	
footnoted	15T42a
Essays	
new	79-E27f
12-E2i	deleted
147-E1B	147-E1C
new	147-E1B
new	150-E2A
new	301-E6
new	568-E2
707-E1	deleted
OX1-E1–OX1-E5	OXF1-E1–OXF1-E5
OX3-E3	OX1-E3
Proofs	
new	9X1Pe
36P	36bP
OX1P	OXF1P
OX3P	OX1P
OX4P	OX2aP
OX6bP	OX5P
OX10P	OX11c
OX10aP	OX11a
OX10bP	OX11
OX10cP	OX11b
OX10dP	OX11c

Number in 2000 Catalogue	Number in 2001 Catalogue
UNITED STATES	
Trial Color Proofs	
new	855TC
OX1TC	OXF1TC
OX3TC	OX1TC
Specimen Stamps	
new	146S B
Commemorative Panels	
new	CP515
new	CP517-CP518
CP538/CP538a	switched
International Reply Coupon	
footnoted	IRC12a
footnoted	IRC29a
Post Office Seals	
OX1	OXF1
OX1a	OXF1e
OX1b	OXF1g
OX1c	OXF1f
OX1d	OXF1b
OX1e	OXF1c
footnoted	OXF2
OX2	OXF3
new	OXF4-OXF16
new	OXA1-OXA9
OX3	OX1
OX4	OX2a
OX4b	OX3
OX4c	OX2
footnoted	OX4
OX6	OX5a
OX7	OX7, OX10
OX7b	OX6
OX10	OX11
OX11	OX13
OX11a, OX11b	deleted
new	OX12
OX12	OX14
OX13	OX15
OX13a	OX16
OX14	OX17
OX15	OX18a
OX15a	OX18
OX16-OX17	OX19-OX20
OX18..OX21, OX24, OX28-OX29, OX34	
OX19	OX22-OX23, OX26
OX20	OX25, OX31, OX35
new	OX26-OX27, OX30
new	OX32-OX33
new	OX36-OX37
OX22	OX38
OX23-OX32A	OX40-OX50
OX33-OX36	OX51-OX54
CONFEDERATE STATES OF AMERICA	
21X2	footnoted
CANAL ZONE	
OX6	OX7
OX6a	OX6

Number in 2000 Catalogue	Number in 2001 Catalogue
CUBA	
new	UX1c
HAWAII	
new	53f, 54e, 54f
55a	55d
55b	55d, 55f
56a	56b
57a	57g
57b	57d, 57f
57c	57q
58a	58b
59a	59g
59b	59d, 59e, 59f
60a	60e
61a	61e, 61f
62b	62d, 62e
64a	64b
new	64f
65a	65b
66a	66d, 66e, 66f
new	67f, 68f
69a	69e
70a	70d, 70f
70b	70g
70c	70b
70d	70a
new	72f
73a	73b
PHILIPPINES	
unlettered	E6a

Stock Pages

Hagner-style stock pages offer convenience and flexibility. Pages are produced on thick, archival-quality paper with acetate pockets glued from the bottom of each pocket. They're ideal for the topical collector who may require various page styles to store a complete collection. Multi-hole punch fits most binder types. Available in 9 different page formats. 8 1/2" x 11" size accomodates every size stamp.

Sold in packages of 10.
Available with pockets on one side or both sides.
"D" in item number denotes two-sided page.

1 Pocket	2 Pocket	3 Pocket	4 Pocket	5 Pocket
Item *Retail*	*Item* *Retail*	*Item* *Retail*	*Item* *Retail*	*Item* *Retail*
S1 $8.95	S2 $8.95	S3 $8.95	S4 $8.95	S5 $8.95
S1D $13.95	S2D $13.95	S3D $13.95	S4D $13.95	S5D $13.95

6 Pocket	7 Pocket	8 Pocket	Multi-Pockets
Item *Retail*	*Item* *Retail*	*Item* *Retail*	*Item* *Retail*
S6 $8.95	S7 $8.95	S8 $8.95	S9 $8.95
S6D $13.95	S7D $13.95	S8D $13.95	S9D $13.95

STOCK PAGE BINDER AND SLIPCASE

Keep all your stock pages neat and tidy with binder and accompanying slipcase. Available in two colors.

Item	Color	Retail
SSBSRD	Red	$19.95
SSBSBL	Blue	$19.95

Available from your favorite dealer or direct from:

Box 828 Sidney OH 45365-0828
1-800-572-6885
www.scottonline.com

Category Index

The following categories are arranged alphabetically to facilitate use. These list the countries or categories that have each type of postal item. Someone interested only in semi-postals can quickly see that they can be found in the Philippines and United States.

Comprehensive Index

Entries in the following Country sections are arranged
alphabetically to facilitate use. Where applicable, the
Scott number prefix or consistent suffix (preceded by
a "-" below) for a section is included in parentheses.

S C O T T M O U N T S

SCOTTMOUNTS

HOW TO ORDER THE RIGHT SIZE:

Pre-cut ScottMounts come in sizes labeled as stamp width by stamp height, measured in millimeters. Strips of mount material come in three different lengths: 215mm, 240mm and 265mm. The strip you should use is based on the height of the stamp you wish to mount.

ScottMounts are available with clear or black backs. Please indicate color choice when ordering.

Pre-Cut Single Mounts

Size	Description	# Mounts	Item	Price
40 x 25	U.S. Standard Commemorative—Horizontal	40	901	$2.75
25 x 40	U.S. Standard Commemorative—Vertical	40	902	2.75
25 x 22	U.S. Regular Issue—Horizontal	40	903	2.75
22 x 25	U.S. Regular Issue—Vertical	40	904	2.75
41 x 31	U.S. Semi–Jumbo—Horizontal	40	905	2.75
31 x 41	U.S. Semi–Jumbo—Vertical	40	906	2.75
50 x 31	U.S. Jumbo—Horizontal	40	907	2.75
31 x 50	U.S. Jumbo—Vertical	40	908	2.75
25 x 27	U.S. Famous Americans	40	909	2.75
33 x 27	United Nations	40	910	2.75
40 x 27	United Nations	40	911	2.75
67 x 25	PNC, Strips of Three	40	976	4.75
67 x 34	Pacific '97 Triangle	10	984	2.25
111 x 25	PNC, Strips of Five	25	985	4.75
51 x 36	U.S. Hunting Permit/Express Mail	40	986	4.75

Pre-Cut Plate Block, FDC & Postal Card Mounts

Size	Description	# Mounts	Item	Price
57 x 55	Regular Issue Plate Block	25	912	$4.75
73 x 63	Champions of Liberty	25	913	4.75
106 x 55	Rotary Press Standard Commemorative	20	914	4.75
105 x 57	Giori Press Standard Commemorative	20	915	4.75
165 x 94	First Day Cover	10	917	4.75
140 x 90	Postal Card Size	10	918	4.75

Strips 215mm Long

Size	Description	# Mounts	Item	Price
20	U.S. 19th Century/Horizontal Coil	22	919	$5.95
22	U.S. Early Air Mail	22	920	5.95
24	U.S., Canada, Great Britain	22	921	5.95
25	U.S. Comm. and Regular	22	922	5.95
27	U.S. Famous Americans	22	923	5.95
28	U.S. 19th Century	22	924	5.95
30	U.S. 19th Century	22	925	5.95
31	U.S. Jumbo and Semi-Jumbo	22	926	5.95
33	United Nations	22	927	5.95
36	U.S. Hunting Permit, Canada	15	928	5.95
39	U.S. Early 20th Century	15	929	5.95
41	U.S. Semi-Jumbo	15	930	5.95
	Multiple Assortment: one strip of each size 22-41 (Two 25mm strips)	12	931	5.95
44	U.S. Vertical Coil Pair	15	932	5.95
48	U.S. Farley, Gutter Pair	15	933	5.95
50	U.S. Jumbo	15	934	5.95
52	U.S. Standard Commemorative Block	15	935	5.95
55	U.S. Century of Progress	15	936	5.95
57	U.S. Famous Americans Block	15	937	5.95
61	U.S. Blocks, Israel Tab	15	938	5.95

Strips 240mm Long

Size	Description	# Mounts	Item	Price
63	U.S. Jumbo Commemorative—Horizontal Block	10	939	$6.75
66	Israel Tab Block	10	940	6.75
68	U.S. Farley, Gutter Pair & Souvenir Sheets	10	941	6.75
74	U.S. TIPEX Souvenir Sheet	10	942	6.75
80	U.S. Standard Commemorative—Vertical Block	10	943	6.75
82	U.S. Blocks of Four	10	944	6.75
84	Israel Tab Block/Mars Pathfinder	10	945	6.75
89	U.S. Postal Card Size	10	946	6.75

Strips 265mm Long

Size	Description	# Mounts	Item	Price
100	U.N. Margin Inscribed Block	7	947	6.75
120	Various Souvenir Sheets and Blocks	7	948	6.75
40	Standard Commemorative Vertical	10	949	$6.75
55	U.S. Regular Plate Block Strip 20	10	950	6.75
59	U.S. Double Issue Strip	10	951	6.75
70	U.S. Jumbo Com. Plate Block	10	952	9.75
91	Great Britain Souvenir Sheet/Norman Rockwell	10	953	9.75
105	U.S. Standard Plate Number Strip	10	954	9.75
107	Same as above–Wide Margin	10	955	9.75
111	U.S. Gravure-Intaglio Plate Number Strip	10	956	11.25
127	U.S. Jumbo Commemorative Plate Number Strip	10	957	13.75
137	Great Britain Coronation	10	958	14.50
158	U.S. Apollo-Soyuz Plate Number Strip	10	959	15.25
231	U.S. Full Post Office Pane Regular and Commemorative	5	961	14.25

Souvenir Sheets/Small Panes

Size	Description	# Mounts	Item	Price
111 x 25	PNC, Strips of Five	25	985	4.75
204 x 153	U.S. Bicent. White Plains	5	962	$ 6.95
187 x 144	U.N. Flag Sheet	10	963	12.25
160 x 200	New U.N., Israel Sheet	10	964	12.25
120 x 207	AMERIPEX President Sht.	4	965	4.75
229 x 131	World War II Commemorative Sheet	5	968	6.95
111 x 91	Columbian Souvenir Sheet	6	970	2.95
148 x 196	Apollo Moon Landing	4	972	5.95
129 x 122	U.S. Definitive Mini-Sheet	8	989	7.95
189 x 151	Chinese New Year	5	990	7.95
150 x 185	Dr. Davis/World Cup	5	991	7.95
198 x 151	Cherokee	5	992	7.95
198 x 187	Postal Museum	4	994	7.95
156 x 187	Sign Lang., Statehood	5	995	7.95
188 x 197	Country-Western	4	996	7.95
151 x 192	Olympic	5	997	7.95
174 x 185	Buffalo Soldiers	5	998	7.95
130 x 198	Silent Screen Stars	5	999	7.95
190 x 199	Leg. West, Civil, Comic	4	1000	7.95
178 x 181	Cranes	4	1001	7.95
183 x 212	Wonders of the Sea	3	1002	7.95
156 x 264	$14 Eagle	4	1003	7.95
159 x 270	$9.95 Moon Landing	4	1004	7.95
159 x 259	$2.90 Priority/$9.95 Express Mail	4	1005	7.95
223 x 187	Marilyn Monroe	3	1006	7.95
185 x 181	Challenger Shuttle	4	1007	7.95
152 x 228	Indian Dances/Antique Autos	5	1008	7.95
165 x 150	River Boat/Hanukkah	6	1009	7.95
275 x 200	Large Gutter Blocks/Aircraft/Dinosaurs	2	1010	7.95
161 x 160	Pacific '97 Triangle Block of 16	6	1011	7.95
174 x 130	Bugs Bunny	6	1012	7.95
196 x 158	Football Coaches	4	1013	7.95
184 x 184	American Dolls	4	1014	7.95
186 x 230	Classic Movie Monsters	3	1015	7.95
187 x 160	Trans-Mississippi Sheet	4	1016	7.95
192 x 230	Celebrate the Century	3	1017	7.95
156 x 204	Space Discovery	5	1018	7.95
192 x 209	American Ballet	5	1019	7.95
139 x 151	Christmas Wreaths	5	1020	7.95

Available from your favorite stamp dealer or direct from:

P.O. Box 828 Sidney OH 45365-0828

For more information on Scott products visit our web site at:

www.scottonline.com

INDEX TO ADVERTISERS – 2001 U.S. SPECIALIZED

2001

UNITED STATES SPECIALIZED

DEALER DIRECTORY

YELLOW PAGE LISTINGS

This section of your Scott Catalogue contains
advertisements to help you conveniently find
what you need,
when you need it...!

Auction House

B TRADING CO.
114 Quail Street
Albany, NY 12206
518-465-3497 Telephone & Fax
Email:btradeco@wizvax.net
Web:http://www.wizvax.net/btrade-co/

Auctions

CHARLES G. FIRBY AUCTIONS
6695 Highland Road
Suite 101
Waterford, MI 48327-1967
248-666-5333
248-666-5020 Fax
Email:Firbystamps@prodigy.net

Auctions

DANIEL F. KELLEHER CO., INC
24 Farnsworth Street
Suite 605
Boston, MA 02210
617-443-0033
617-443-0789 Fax

JACQUES C. SCHIFF JR., INC
195 Main Street
Ridgefield Park, NJ 07660
201-641-5566 from NYC 662-2777
201-641-5705 Fax

KUKSTIS AUCTIONS INC.
P.O. Box 130
Scituate, MA 02066
781-545-8494
Email:paulk@dreamcom.net
Web:http://www.kukstis.com

Auctions

Accessories

**BROOKLYN GALLERY COIN &
STAMP**
8725 4th Avenue
Brooklyn, NY 11209
718-745-5701
718-745-2775 Fax
Web:http://www.brooklyngallery.com

Albums & Access.

THE KEEPING ROOM
P.O. Box 257
Trumbull, CT 06611-0257
203-372-8436

Antarctic

**ANTARCTIC PHILATELIC
EXCHANGE**
1208A-280 Simco Street
Toronto, ON M5T 2Y5
Canada
416-593-7849
Email:jporter@interlog.com
Web:http://www.interlog.com/~jporter

Appraisals

B TRADING CO.
114 Quail Street
Albany, NY 12206
518 465-3497 Telephone & Fax
Email:btradeco@wizvax.net
Web:http://www.wizvax.net/btrade
co/

CONNEXUS
P.O. Box 819
Snow Camp, NC 27349
336-376-8207 Telephone/Fax
Email:Connexus1@worldnet.att.net

Appraisals

RANDY SCHOLL STAMP CO.
Southhampton Square
7460 Jager Court
Cincinnati, OH 45230-4344
513-624-6800
513-624-6440 Fax

UNIQUE ESTATE APPRAISALS
1937 NE Broadway
Portland, OR 97232
503-287-4200 or 800-646-1147
Email: uea@stampsandcoins.com
Web:http://www.stampsandcoins.com

Approvals-Personalized WW & U.S.

THE KEEPING ROOM
P.O. Box 257
Trumbull, CT 06611-0257
203-372-8436

Approvals-Worldwide

ROSS WETREICH INC.
P.O. Box 1300
Valley Stream, NY 11582-1300
516-825-8974

Asia

MICHAEL ROGERS, INC.
199 E. Welbourne Ave.
Winter Park, FL 32789
407-644-2290
407-645-4434 Fax
Web:http://www.michaelrogersinc.com

Auctions

WEISS PHILATELICS

P.O. Box 5358-S, Bethlehem, PA 18015

Phone 610-691-6857 • Fax 610-691-3116

*"FASTEST CHECK TO AUCTION
CONSIGNORS...30 DAYS!!"*
Request Letters from Satisfied Consignors.

Next Available Catalog $5.00 (postage ok) **B.I.A.**
 All catalogs over 200 pages and
usually over 3,000 lots.

QUALIFIED AUCTIONEER

Buying

**World's Leading Dealer in QUANTITY
MINT UNITED STATES STAMPS**
(for promotions, novelties, etc)
Send self-addressed stamped envelope for my
BUY LIST or SELL LIST!

KENNETH R. WENGER

1 Horizon Rd., Fort Lee, NJ 07024
Phone 201-886-8300
Fax 201-886-8305

Auctions

SAM HOUSTON PHILATELICS
13310 Westheimer #150
Houston, TX 77077
281-493-6386
281-496-1445 Fax
Email:shduck@aol.com
Web:http://www.shauctions.com

**STAMP CENTER / DUTCH
COUNTRY AUCTIONS**
4115 Concord Pike
Wilmington, DE 19803
302-478-8740
302-478-8779 Fax
Email:scdca@compuserve.com
Web:http://www.thestampcenter.
com

SUBURBAN STAMP INC.
176 Worthington St.
Springfield, MA 01103
413-785-5348
413-746-3788 Fax

Auctions-Public

ALAN BLAIR STAMPS / AUCTIONS
5407 Lakeside Ave.
Suite 4
Richmond, VA 23228
800-689-5602 Telephone & Fax
Email:alanblair@prodigy.net

CEE-JAY STAMP AUCTIONS
775 Passaic Ave
West Caldwell, NJ 07006
800-360-2022
973-882-3499 Fax
Email:cfulmer@gregmanning.com

Austria

JOSEPH EDER
P.O. Box 5517
Hamden, CT 06518
203-281-0742
203-230-2410 Fax
Email:jeder@nai.net

Bosnia

DELAWARE VALLEY STAMP CO.
6173 Strasburg Rd.
Atglen, PA 19310
610-593-6684
610-593-8013 Fax
Email:devasco@epix.com

British Colonies

EMPIRE STAMP CO.
P.O. Box 19248
Encino, CA 91416
818-880-6764
818-880-6864 Fax
Email:empirestamps@msn.com
Web:http://www.empirestamps.com

British Comm.

**BRITISH COMMONWEALTH
STAMP CO.**
P.O. Box 10218 S-5
Wilmington, NC 28404
910-256-0971 Fax
Email:bcstamp@stamp-mall.com
Web:http://www.stamp-mall.com/

JAY'S STAMP COMPANY
Box 28484
Dept S
Philadelphia, PA 19149
215-743-0207 Telephone & Fax
Email: JASC@Juno.com
Web:http://www.jaysco.com

METROPOLITAN STAMP CO.
P.O. Box 1133
Chicago, IL 60690-1133
815-439-0142
815-439-0143 Fax

VICTORIA STAMP CO
P.O. Box 745
Ridgewood, NJ 07451
201-652-7283
201-612-0024 Fax

Canada-Postal Bid Sales

BOW CITY PHILATELICS, LTD.
P.O. Box 6444 Central P.O.
Retail: 206 7th Ave SW
Suite 614
Calgary, AB T2P 2E1
CANADA
403-237-5828
403-264-5287 Fax
Email:bow.city@nucleus.com
Web:http://www.nucleus.com/~
bowcity

China

**EXPERTS AND CONSULTANTS
LTD.**
Dr. Shiu - Hon Chan & K.L. Poon
P.O. Box 9840
General Post Office
Hong Kong
852-2519-6510 Fax

MICHAEL ROGERS, INC.
199 E. Welbourne Ave.
Winter Park, FL 32789
407-644-2290
407-645-4434 Fax
Web:http://www.michael-
rogersinc.om

Classics

**HENRY GITNER PHILATELISTS,
INC.**
P.O. Box 3077-S
Middletown, NY 10940
845-343-5151 or 800-947-8267
845-343-0068 Fax
Email:hgitner@hgitner.com
Web:http://www.hgitner.com

Classics-US Stamps & Covers

KUKSTIS AUCTIONS INC.
P.O. Box 130
Scituate, MA 02066
781-545-8494
Email:paulk@dreamcom.net
Web:http://www.kukstis.com

Classics-US Stamps & Covers

STANLEY M. PILLER
3351 Grand Ave.
Oakland, CA 94610
510-465-8290
510-465-7121 Fax
Email:stmpdlr@aol.com

Collections

DR. ROBERT FRIEDMAN & SONS
2029 West 75th Street
Woodridge, IL 60517
630-985-1515
630-985-1588 Fax

**HENRY GITNER PHILATELISTS,
INC.**
P.O. Box 3077-S
Middletown, NY 10940
845-343-5151 or 800-947-8267
845-343-0068 Fax
Email:hgitner@hgitner.com
Web:http://www.hgitner.com

QUALITY INVESTORS LTD.
P.O. Box 891
Middletown, NY 10940
845-343-2174
845-342-2597 Fax
Email:lrlm@poineeris.net

SUBURBAN STAMP CO.
176 Worthington St.
Springfield, MA 01103
413-785-5348
413-746-3788 Fax

Collections

★ ★ ★ **STOP** ★ ★ ★
**WORLDWIDE COLLECTIONS
AT LOW, LOW PRICES!**
• • • • • • • •
If you spend over $25.00 per month you should
subscribe to the "Money's Worth" list.
For 3 free issues, write or call:

WARREN T. WASSON
DALLAS STAMP GALLERY

1002 N. Central, Suite 501, Richardson, TX 75080
Fax: 972-669-4742
Call TOLL FREE 1-800-759-9109

Confed. Stamps & Postal History

STANLEY M. PILLER
3351 Grand Ave.
Oakland, CA 94610
510-465-8290
510-465-7121 Fax
Email:stmpdlr@aol.com

SUN COAST STAMP CO.
3231 Gulf Gate Drive, Suite 102
Sarasota, FL 34231
941-921-9761 or 800-927-3351
941-921-1762 Fax
Email:suncoaststamp@aol.com

Conservation Stamps

SAM HOUSTON DUCK CO.
P.O. Box 820087
Houston,TX 77282
281-493-6386 or 800-231-5926
281-496-1445 Fax
Email:shduck@aol.com
Web:http://www.shduck.com

Covers- Zeppelins

HENRY GITNER PHILATELISTS, INC.
P.O. Box 3077-S
Middletown, NY 10940
845-343-5151 or 800-947-8267
845-343-0068 Fax
Email:hgitner@hgitner.com
Web:http://www.hgitner.com

Czechoslovakia

SOCIETY FOR CZECHOSLOVAK PHILATELY, INC.
Tom Cossaboom
SCP Secretary
Box 25332
Scott Air Force Base, IL 62225
USA
Web:http://www.erols.com/sibpost

Ducks

MICHAEL JAFFE
P.O. Box 61484
Vancouver, WA 98666
360-695-6161 or 800-782-6770
360-695-1616 Fax
Email:mjaffe@brookmanstamps.com
Web:http://www.brookmanstamps.com

SAM HOUSTON DUCK CO.
P.O. Box 820087
Houston,TX 77282
281-493-6386 or 800-231-5926
281-496-1445 Fax
Email:shduck@aol.com
Web:http://www.shduck.com

Duck Stamps

TRENTON STAMP & COIN CO.
THOMAS DELUCA
Forest Glen Plaza
1804 Route 33
Hamilton Square, NJ 08690
800-446-8664
609-587-8664 Fax

Egypt

KAMAL SHALABY
3 Aly Basha Fahmy St.
Gleem, Alexandria
EGYPT
20-3-5840254 Telephone & Fax

Errors, Freaks & Oddities

SAM HOUSTON PHILATELICS
13310 Westheimer #150
Houston, TX 77077
281-493-6386
281-496-1445 Fax
Email:shduck@aol.com
Web:http://www.shauctions.com

STEVE CRIPPE, INC.
Box 236
Bothell, WA 98041-0236
425-487-2789
Email:stamp@stevecrippe.com
Web:http://www.stevecrippe.com

Exchange

ROBERT'S STAMP EXCHANGE
ROBERT LEFRANCOIS
250 Skylane Dr.
Lake Geneva, WI 53147
262-248-8159

Expertizing

STANLEY M. PILLER
3351 Grand Ave.
Oakland, CA 94610
510-465-8290
510-465-7121 Fax
Email:stmpdlr@aol.com

First Day Covers

HENRY GITNER PHILATELISTS, INC.
P.O. Box 3077-S
Middletown, NY 10940
845-343-5151 or 800-947-8267
845-343-0068 Fax
Email:hgitner@hgitner.com
Web:http://www.hgitner.com

LEWIS KAUFMAN
P.O. Box 255
Kiamesha Lake, NY 12751
845-794-8013 Telephone/FAX
800-491-5453 Telephone/FAX
Email:mamet1@aol.com

ROSS WETREICH INC.
P.O. Box 1300
Valley Stream, NY 11582-1300
516-825-8974

Foreign Ducks Stamps

METROPOLITAN STAMP CO.
P.O. Box 1133
Chicago, IL 60690-1133
815-439-0142
815-439-0143 Fax

France

JOSEPH EDER
P.O. Box 5517
Hamden, CT 06518
203-281-0742
203-230-2410 Fax
Email:jeder@nai.net

German Areas

JOSEPH EDER
P.O. Box 5517
Hamden, CT 06518
203-281-0742
203-230-2410 Fax
Email:jeder@nai.net

German Colonies

COLONIAL STAMP COMPANY
$1 million - photo price list, $5.00
(refundable against purchase)
5757 Wilshire Blvd. PH #8
Los Angeles, CA 90036
323-933-9435
323-939-9930 Fax
Email:gwh225@aol.com

Great Britain

NOVA PHILATELIC SALES
Box 161
Lakeside, NS B3T 1M6
CANADA
902-826-2165
902-826-1049 Fax
Email:novafil@ns.sympatico.ca

Imperial China

TREASURE HUNTERS LTD
GPO Box 11446
Hong Kong
852-2507-3773 or 852-2507-5770
852-2519-6820 Fax

Insurance

COLLECTIBLES INSURANCE AGENCY
P.O. Box 1200 SSC
Westminster, MD 21158
888-837-9537
410-876-9233 Fax
Email:collectinsure@pipeline.com
Web:http://www.collectinsure.com

Iran

MEHDI ESMAILI
P.O. Box 694
F.D.R. Station
New York, NY 10150-0694
718-520-1807
Email:info@mehdistamps.com
Web:http://www.mehdistamps.com

Latin America

JUAN N. SIMONA
Ventas Filatelicas
Casilla de Correo #40-7311
Chillar Buenos Aires
Argentina
54-281-97281
Email:simonafilatelia@simon-afilatelia.com.ar
Web:http://www.simonafilatelia.com.ar

Lots & Collections

RANDY SCHOLL STAMP CO.
Southhampton Square
7460 Jager Court
Cincinnati, OH 45230-4344
513-624-6800
513-624-6440 Fax

Mail Bid Sales

COLLECTOR'S FEAST
GPO Box 4131
Melbourne Vic. 3001
Australia
61 3 9654 2770
61 3 9650 7748 Fax
Email:collectorsfeast@bigpond.com

DALE ENTERPRISES INC.
P.O. Box 539-C
Emmaus, PA 18049
610-433-3303
610-965-6089
Email:daleent@fast.net
Web:http://www.dalestamps.com

Mail Order

ALMAZ CO., DEPT. V4
P.O. Box 100-812
Vanderveer Station
Brooklyn, NY 11210
718-241-6360 Telephone & Fax

SHARI'S STAMPS
104-3 Old Highway 40 #130
O'Fallon, MO 63366
800-382-3597
314-980-1552 Fax
Email:sharistmps@aol.com
Web:http://www.stampdealers.com/shari

Major Errors

SUBURBAN STAMP INC.
176 Worthington St.
Springfield, MA 01103
413-785-5348
413-746-3788 Fax

New Issues

DALE ENTERPRISES INC.
P.O. Box 539-C
Emmaus, PA 18049
610-433-3303
610-965-6089 Fax
Email:daleent@fast.net
Web:http://www.dalestamps.com

DAVIDSON'S STAMP SERVICE
P.O. Box 36355
Indianapolis, IN 46236-0355
317-826-2620
Email:davidson@in.net
Web:http://www.newstampissues.com

Officials

QUALITY INVESTORS LTD.
P.O. Box 891
Middletown, NY 10940
845-343-2174
845-342-2597 Fax
Email:lrlm@poineeris.net

Philatelic Literature

LEWIS KAUFMAN
P.O. Box 255
Kiamesha Lake, NY 12751
845-794-8013 Telephone/FAX
800-491-5453 Telephone/FAX
Email:mamet1@aol.com

Postal History

LEWIS KAUFMAN
P.O. Box 255
Kiamesha Lake, NY 12751
845-794-8013 Telephone/FAX
800-491-5453 Telephone/FAX
Email:mamet1@aol.com

STANLEY M. PILLER
3351 Grand Ave.
Oakland, CA 94610
510-465-8290
510-465-7121 Fax
Email:stmpdlr@aol.com

Proofs & Essays

HENRY GITNER PHILATELISTS, INC.
P.O. Box 3077-S
Middletown, NY 10940
845-343-5151 or 800-947-8267
845-343-0068 Fax
Email:hgitner@hgitner.com
Web:http://www.hgitner.com

LEWIS KAUFMAN
P.O. Box 255
Kiamesha Lake, NY 12751
845-794-8013 Telephone/FAX
800-491-5453 Telephone/FAX
Email:mamet1@aol.com

STANLEY M. PILLER
3351 Grand Ave.
Oakland, CA 94610
510-465-8290
510-465-7121 Fax
Email:stmpdlr@aol.com

SUBURBAN STAMP CO.
176 Worthington St.
Springfield, MA 01103
413-785-5348
413-746-3788 Fax

Public Auctions

SUBURBAN STAMP INC.
176 Worthington St.
Springfield, MA 01103
413-785-5348
413-746-3788 Fax

Publications - Collector

AMERICAN PHILATELIC SOCIETY
Dept. TZ
P.O. Box 8000
State College, PA 16803
814-237-3803
814-237-6128 Fax
Email:flsente@stamps.org
Web:http://www.stamps.org

GLOBAL STAMP NEWS
P.O. Box 97
Sidney, OH 45365-0097
937-492-3183
937-492-6514 Fax
Email:global@bright.net

Souvenir Cards

AALLSTAMPS
38 N. Main Street
P.O. Box 249
Milltown, NJ 08850
732-247-1093
732-247-1094 Fax
Email:mail@aallstamps.com
Web:http://www.aallstamps.com

Stamps on the Internet

KUKSTIS AUCTIONS INC.
P.O. Box 130
Scituate, MA 02066
781-545-8494
Email:paulk@dreamcom.net
Web:http://www.kukstis.com

Stamp Shows

ATLANTIC COAST EXHIBITIONS
Division of Beach Philatelics
42 Baltimore Lane
Palm Coast, FL 32137-8850
904-445-4550
904-447-0811 Fax
Email:mrstamp2@aol.com
Web:http://www.beachphilatelics.com

STAMP STORES

Arizona

AMERICAN STAMP & COIN CO.
7225 N. Oracle Rd., Suite 102
Tucson, AZ 85704
520-297-3456
Email:stamps@azstarnet.com

California

ASHTREE STAMP & COIN
2410 N. Blackstone
Fresno, CA 93703
559-227-7167

BROSIUS STAMP & COIN
2105 Main Street
Santa Monica, CA 90405
310-396-7480
310-396-7455 Fax

FISCHER-WOLK PHILATELICS
24771 "G" Alicia Parkway
Laguna Hills, CA 92653
949-837-2932

NATICK STAMPS & HOBBIES
405 S. Myrtle Ave.
Monrovia, CA 91016
626-305-7333
626-305-7335 Fax
Email:natickco@earthlink.net
Web:http://www.natickco.com

STANLEY M. PILLER
3351 Grand Ave.
Oakland, CA 94610
510-465-8290
510-465-7121 Fax
Email:stmpdlr@aol.com

Colorado

ACKLEY'S ROCKS & STAMPS
3230 N. Stone Avenue
Colorado Springs, CO 80907
719-633-1153

SHOWCASE STAMPS
3865 Wadsworth
Wheatridge, CO 80033
303-425-9252
303-425-7410 Fax

Connecticut

SILVER CITY COIN & STAMPS
41 Colony Street
Meriden, CT 06451
203-235-7634
203-237-4915 Fax

Florida

CORBIN STAMP & COIN, INC.
115-A East Brandon Blvd.
Brandon, FL 33511
813-651-3266

HAUSER'S COIN & STAMPS
3425 South Florida Ave
Lakeland FL 33803
863-647-2052
863-644-5738 Fax
Email:hausercoin@aol.com
Web:http://www.coinsandgifts.com

INTERCONTINENTAL/RICARDO DEL CAMPO
7379 Coral Way
Miami, FL 33155-1402
305-264-4983
305-262-2919 Fax
Email:http://www.rdcstamp@world net.att.net

Florida

When visting
Central Florida
be sure to stop by.
Send 33¢ long
SASE for our
Monthly Newsletter
of stamps for sale!

WINTER PARK STAMP SHOP
Ranch Mall (17-92)
325 S. Orlando Avenue, Suite 1-2
Winter Park, FL 32789-3608
Phone 407-628-1120 • Fax 407-628-0091
1-800-845-1819
Mon. through Sat. 10 am-6 pm (4 miles North of Orlando)

Florida

JERRY SIEGEL/STAMPS FOR COLLECTORS
501 Golden Isles Drive
Suite 206C
Hallandale, FL 33009
954-457-0422 Telephone/Fax
Email:dochallandale@telocity.com

ROBERT LEVINE STAMPS, INC
2219 South University Drive
Davie, FL 33324
954-473-1303
954-473-1305 Fax

THE STAMP PLACE
576 First Ave North
St. Petersburg, FL 33701
727-894-4082

WINTER PARK STAMP SHOP
Ranch Mail (17-92)
325 S. Orlando Ave., Suite 1-2
Winter Park, FL 32789-3608
407-628-1120 or 800-845-1819
407-628-0091 Fax

Georgia

STAMPS UNLIMITED OF GEORGIA
133 Carnegie Way, Room 250
Atlanta, GA 30303
404-688-9161

Illinois

DON CLARK'S STAMPS
937 1/2 W. Galena Blvd.
Aurora, IL 60506
630-896-4606

DR. ROBERT FRIEDMAN & SONS
2029 West 75th Street
Woodridge, IL 60517
630-985-1515
630-985-1588 Fax

MARSHALL FIELD'S STAMP DEPT
111 N. State Street
Chicago, IL 60602
312-781-4237
Email:TRH200@aol.com

Indiana

J & J COINS AND STAMPS
7019 Calumet Ave. or
6526 Indianapolis Blvd.
Hammond, IN 46324
219-932-5818
219-845-2003 Fax

Indiana

KNIGHT STAMP & COIN CO.
237 Main Street
Hobart, IN 46342
219-942-7529 or 800-634-2646
Email: knight@knightcoin.com
Web:http://www.knightcoin.com

Kentucky

COLLECTORS STAMPS LTD.
4012 DuPont Circle #313
Louisville, KY 40207
502-897-9045
Email:csl@aye.net

Maryland

BALTIMORE COIN & STAMP EXCHANGE
10194 Baltimore National Pike
Unit 104
Ellicott City, MD 21042
410-418-8282
410-418-4813 Fax

BULLDOG STAMP CO.
4641 Montgomery Ave.
Bethesda, MD 20814
301-654-1138

Massachusetts

FALMOUTH STAMP & COIN
11 Town Hall Square
Falmouth, MA 02540
508-548-7075 or 800-341-3701
Email:falstamp@capecod.net
Web:http://www.coinsandstamps.com

J & N FORTIER COIN, STAMPS & ANTIQUES
484 Main Street
Worcester, MA 01608
508-757-3657
508-852-8329 Fax

KAPPY'S COINS & STAMPS
534 Washington Street
Norwood, MA 02062
781-762-5552
781-762-3292 Fax

SUBURBAN STAMP INC.
176 Worthington St.
Springfield, MA 01103
413-785-5348
413-746-3788 Fax

S T A M P   S T O R E S

Michigan

BIRMINGHAM COIN & JEWELRY
33802 Woodward
Birmingham, MI 48009
248-642-1234
248-642-4207 Fax

THE MOUSE AND SUCH
696 N. Mill Street
Plymouth, MI 48170
734-454-1515

Nebraska

TUVA ENTERPRISES
209 South 72nd Street
Omaha, NE 68114
402-397-9937

New Jersey

AALLSTAMPS
38 N. Main Street
P.O. Box 249
Milltown, NJ 08850
732-247-1093
732-247-1094 Fax
Email:mail@aallstamps.com
Web:http://www.aallstamps.com

A.D.A. STAMP CO., INC.
Store: 910 Boyd Street
Toms River, NJ 08753
P.O. Drawer J
Island Heights, NJ 08732
732-240-1131
732-240-2620 Fax

New Jersey

BERGEN STAMPS & COLLECTIBLES
717 American Legion Dr.
Teaneck, NJ 07666
201-836-8987

CHARLES STAMP SHOP
47 Old Post Road
Edison, NJ 08817
732-985-1071
732-819-0549
Email:cerratop@aol.com

RON RITZER STAMPS INC.
Millburn Mall
2933 Vauxhall Road
Vauxhall, NJ 07088
908-687-0007
908-687-0795 Fax
Email:ritzerstamps@mindspring.
com

TRENTON STAMP & COIN CO.
THOMAS DELUCA
Forest Glen Plaza
1804 Route 33
Hamilton Square, NJ 08690
800-446-8664
609-587-8664 Fax

New York

CHAMPION STAMP CO., INC.
432 West 54th Street
New York, NY 10019
212-489-8130
212-581-8130 Fax

LINCOLN COIN & STAMP
33 West Tupper Street
Buffalo, NY 14202
716-856-1884
716-856-4727 Fax

THE FIFTH AVENUE STAMP GALLERY
460 West 34th Street
10th Floor
New York, NY 10001
212-629-7979
212-629-3350 Fax

Ohio

FEDERAL COIN INC. /ARCADE STAMP & COIN
P.O. Box 14579
405 Leader Building
Cleveland, OH 44114
216-861-1160
216-861-5960 Fax

HILLTOP STAMP SERVICE
P.O. Box 626
Wooster, OH 44691
330-262-5378
330-262-8907 Telephone & Fax
Email:hilltop@bright.net

JLF STAMP STORE
3041 E. Waterloo Road
Akron, OH 44312
330-628-8343

NEWARK STAMP COMPANY
49 North Fourth Street
Newark, OH 43055
740-349-7900

RANDY SCHOLL STAMP CO.
Southhampton Square
7460 Jager Court
Cincinnati, OH 45230-4344
513-624-6800
513-624-6440 Fax

THE LINK STAMP CO.
3461 E. Livingston Ave.
Columbus, OH 43227
614-237-4125 or 800-546-5726

Oregon

UNIQUE ESTATE APPRAISALS
1937 NE Broadway
Portland, OR 97232
503-287-4200 or 800-646-1147
Email: uea@stampsandcoins.com
Web:http://www.stampsandcoins.
com

Pennsylvania

LARRY LEE STAMPS
322 S. Front Street
Greater Harrisburg Area
Wormleysburg, PA 17043
717-763-7605

PHILLY STAMP & COIN CO., INC.
1804 Chestnut Street
Philadelphia, PA 19103
215-563-7341
215-563-7382 Fax
Email:phillysc@netreach.net
Web:http://www.mrstamp.com

TREASURE HUNT COLLECTIBLE COINS & STAMPS
10925 Perry Hwy.
Suite 11
Wexford, PA 15090
724-934-7771 or 800-545-6604
Email:TRH200@aol.com

TREASURE HUNT COLLECTIBLE COINS & STAMPS
1687 Washington Road
Suite 200
Pittsburgh, PA 15228
412-851-9991 or 800-259-4727
Email:TRH200@aol.com

TRENTON STAMP & COIN CO.
THOMAS DELUCA
Forest Glen Plaza
1804 Route 33
Hamilton Square, NJ 08690
800-446-8664
609-587-8664 Fax

Rhode Island

PODRAT COIN EXCHANGE, INC
769 Hope Street
Providence, RI 02906
401-861-7640
401-272-3032 Fax
Email: kpodrat@aol.com

Tennessee

HERRON HILL, INC.
5007 Black Road
Suite 140
Memphis, TN 38117-4505
901-683-9644

Texas

DALLAS STAMP GALLERY
1002 North Central Expwy.
Suite 501
Richardson, TX 75080
972-669-4741
972-669-4742 Fax

HUNT & COMPANY
3933 Spicewood Springs Road
Suite E-400
Austin, TX 78759
512-346-4830 or 800-458-5745
512-346-4984 Fax
Email:info@huntstamps.com
Web:http://www.huntstamps.com

Texas

SAM HOUSTON PHILATELICS
13310 Westheimer #150
Houston, TX 77077
281-493-6386
281-496-1445 Fax
Email:shduck@aol.com
Web:http://www.shauctions.com

Virginia

KENNEDY'S STAMPS & COINS
7059 Brookfield Plaza
Springfield, VA 22150
703-569-7300
703-569-7644 Fax
Email:kenny@patriot.net

LATHEROW & CO . INC.
5054 Lee Hwy.
Arlington, VA 22207
703-538-2727
Email:TRH200@aol.com

PRINCE WILLIAM STAMP & COIN
14011-H St. Germain Drive
Centreville, VA 20121
703-830-4669

Washington

TACOMA MALL BLVD COIN & STAMP
5225 Tacoma Mall, Blvd. E101
Tacoma, WA 98409
253-472-9632
253-472-8948 Fax
Email:kfeldman01@sprynet.com
Web:http://www.tmbcoinand-
stamp.com

THE STAMP & COIN PLACE
1310 Commercial
Bellingham, WA 98225
360-676-8720
360-647-6947 Fax
Email:stmpcoin@az.com

THE STAMP & COIN SHOP
725 Pike Street #6
Seattle, WA 98101
206-624-1400
206-621-8975 Fax
Email:jkonrad@attglobal.net
Web:http://www.Stamp-Coin.com

Wisconsin

JIM LUKES' STAMP & COIN
815 Jay Street
P.O. Box 1780
Manitowoc, WI 54221
920-682-2324

Supplies & Accessories

BEACH PHILATELICS
42 Baltimore Lane
Palm Coast, FL 32137-8850
904-445-4550
904-447-0811 Fax
Email:mrstamp2@aol.com
Web:http://www.beachphilatelics.
com

Supplies -Mail Order

GOPHER SUPPLY
2525 Nevada Ave. North
Suite 102
Minneapolis, MN 55427
800-815-3868 or 612-525-1750
612-544-5683 Fax
Email:gopher@pclink.com
Web:http://www.gophersupply.com

Topicals

ERCOLE GLORIA
Piazza PIO XI
20123 Milan,
ITALY
39-028-04106
39-028-64217 Fax
Email:gloria@iol.it

Topicals - Columbus

MR. COLUMBUS
Box 1492
Fennville, MI 49408
616-543-4755
616-543-3507 Fax
Email:columbus@accn.org

Topicals - Foreign

MINI-ARTS
P.O. Box 457
Estherville, IA 51334
712-362-4710
Email:pnga@rconnect.com
Web:http://www.miniarts.com

Ukraine

MR VAL ZABIJAKA
P.O. Box 3711
Silver Springs, MD 20918
301-593-5316 Telephone/Fax
Email: bnm123@erols.com

United Nations

BEACH PHILATELICS
42 Baltimore Lane
Palm Coast, FL 32137-8850
904-445-4550
904-447-0811 Fax
Email:mrstamp2@aol.com
Web:http://www.beachphilatelics.
com

**HENRY GITNER PHILATELISTS,
INC.**
P.O. Box 3077-S
Middletown, NY 10940
845-343-5151 or 800-947-8267
845-343-0068 Fax
Email:hgitner@hgitner.com
Web:http://www.hgitner.com

United States

BEACH PHILATELICS
42 Baltimore Lane
Palm Coast, FL 32137-8850
904-445-4550
904-447-0811 Fax
Email:mrstamp2@aol.com
Web:http://www.beachphilatelics.
com

BROOKMAN STAMP CO.
P.O. Box 90
Vancouver, WA 98666
360-695-1391 or 888-545-4871
360-695-1616 Fax
Email:dave@brookmanstamps.com
Web:http://www.brookmanstamps.
com

DALE ENTERPRISES INC.
P.O. Box 539-C
Emmaus, PA 18049
610-433-3303
610-965-6089 Fax
Email:daleent@fast.net
Web:http://www.dalestamps.com

DR. ROBERT FRIEDMAN & SONS
2029 West 75th Street
Woodridge, IL 60517
630-985-1515
630-985-1588 Fax

**HENRY GITNER PHILATELISTS,
INC.**
P.O. Box 3077-S
Middletown, NY 10940
845-343-5151 or 800-947-8267
845-343-0068 Fax
Email:hgitner@hgitner.com
Web:http://www.hgitner.com

United States

LEWIS KAUFMAN
P.O. Box 255
Kiamesha Lake, NY 12751
845-794-8013 Telephone/FAX
800-491-5453 Telephone/FAX
Email:mamet1@aol.com

MIDWEST STAMPS
Michael Monahan
P.O. Box 7057
1380 Cunat Ct.
Algonquin, IL 60102
888-257-7782

QUALITY INVESTORS LTD.
P.O. Box 891
Middletown, NY 10940
845-343-2174
845-342-2597 Fax
Email:lrlm@poineeris.net

ROBERT'S STAMP EXCHANGE
ROBERT LEFRANCOIS
250 Skylane Dr.
Lake Geneva, WI 53147
262-248-8159

US - Booklet Panes

DALE ENTERPRISES INC.
P.O. Box 539-C
Emmaus, PA 18049
610-433-3303
610-965-6089 Fax
Email:daleent@fast.net
Web:http://www.dalestamps.com

US - Booklet Panes

LEWIS KAUFMAN
P.O. Box 255
Kiamesha Lake, NY 12751
845-794-8013 Telephone/FAX
800-491-5453 Telephone/FAX
Email:mamet1@aol.com

US - Classics

DALE ENTERPRISES INC.
P.O. Box 539-C
Emmaus, PA 18049
610-433-3303
610-965-6089 Fax
Email:daleent@fast.net
Web:http://www.dalestamps.com

US - Classics

KUKSTIS AUCTIONS INC.
P.O. Box 130
Scituate, MA 02066
781-545-8494
Email:paulk@dreamcom.net
Web:http://www.kukstis.com

MIDWEST STAMPS
Michael Monahan
P.O. Box 7057
1380 Cunat Ct.
Algonquin, IL 60102
888-257-7782

US - Classic Covers

KUKSTIS AUCTIONS INC.
P.O. Box 130
Scituate, MA 02066
781-545-8494
Email:paulk@dreamcom.net
Web:http://www.kukstis.com

US - Classics/ Modern

SUBURBAN STAMP INC.
176 Worthington St.
Springfield, MA 01103
413-785-5348
413-746-3788 Fax

US - Duck Stamps

HENRY GITNER PHILATELISTS, INC.
P.O. Box 3077-S
Middletown, NY 10940
845-343-5151 or 800-947-8267
845-343-0068 Fax
Email:hgitner@hgitner.com
Web:http://www.hgitner.com

SAM HOUSTON DUCK CO.
P.O. Box 820087
Houston,TX 77282
281-493-6386 or 800-231-5926
281-496-1445 Fax
Email:shduck@aol.com
Web:http://www.shduck.com

US - Federal Ducks Stamps

METROPOLITAN STAMP COMPANY
P.O. Box 1133
Chicago, IL 60690-1133
815-439-0142
815-439-0143 Fax

MIDWEST STAMPS
Michael Monahan
P.O. Box 7057
1380 Cunat Ct.
Algonquin, IL 60102
888-257-7782

SAM HOUSTON DUCK CO.
P.O. Box 820087
Houston, TX 77282
281-493-6386 or 800-231-5926
281-496-1445 Fax
Email:shduck@aol.com
Web:http://www.shduck.com

US - Mint

HENRY GITNER PHILATELISTS, INC.
P.O. Box 3077-S
Middletown, NY 10940
845-343-5151 or 800-947-8267
845-343-0068 Fax
Email:hgitner@hgitner.com
Web:http://www.hgitner.com

MIDWEST STAMPS
Michael Monahan
P.O. Box 7057
1380 Cunat Ct.
Algonquin, IL 60102
888-257-7782

SUBURBAN STAMP CO.
176 Worthington St.
Springfield, MA 01103
413-785-5348
413-746-3788 Fax

US - Mint Sheets

HENRY GITNER PHILATELISTS, INC.
P.O. Box 3077-S
Middletown, NY 10940
845-343-5151 or 800-947-8267
845-343-0068 Fax
Email:hgitner@hgitner.com
Web:http://www.hgitner.com

US - Plate Blocks

BEACH PHILATELICS
42 Baltimore Lane
Palm Coast, FL 32137-8850
904-445-4550
904-447-0811 Fax
Email:mrstamp2@aol.com
Web:http://www.beachphilatelics.com

HENRY GITNER PHILATELISTS, INC.
P.O. Box 3077-S
Middletown, NY 10940
845-343-5151 or 800-947-8267
845-343-0068 Fax
Email:hgitner@hgitner.com
Web:http://www.hgitner.com

LEWIS KAUFMAN
P.O. Box 255
Kiamesha Lake, NY 12751
845-794-8013 Telephone/FAX
800-491-5453 Telephone/FAX
Email:mamet1@aol.com

MIDWEST STAMPS
Michael Monahan
P.O. Box 7057
1380 Cunat Ct.
Algonquin, IL 60102
888-257-7782

US - Possessions

LEWIS KAUFMAN
P.O. Box 255
Kiamesha Lake, NY 12751
845-794-8013 Telephone/FAX
800-491-5453 Telephone/FAX
Email:mamet1@aol.com

U.S. - Postal Stationery

LEWIS KAUFMAN
P.O. Box 255
Kiamesha Lake, NY 12751
845-794-8013 Telephone/FAX
800-491-5453 Telephone/FAX
Email:mamet1@aol.com

US - Price Lists

DALE ENTERPRISES INC.
P.O. Box 539-C
Emmaus, PA 18049
610-433-3303
610-965-6089
Email:daleent@fast.net
Web:http://www.dalestamps.com

MIDWEST STAMPS
Michael Monahan
P.O. Box 7057
1380 Cunat Ct.
Algonquin, IL 60102
888-257-7782

ROBERT E. BARKER
P.O. Box 888063
Dunwoody, GA 30356
770-395-1757
770-671-8918 Fax
Email:rebarker@rebarker.com

US - Rare Stamps

KUKSTIS AUCTIONS INC.
P.O. Box 130
Scituate, MA 02066
781-545-8494
Email:paulk@dreamcom.net
Web:http://www.kukstis.com

US - Singles - Classic & Modern

MIDWEST STAMPS
Michael Monahan
P.O. Box 7057
1380 Cunat Ct.
Algonquin, IL 60102
888-257-7782

US - Souvenir Cards

LEWIS KAUFMAN
P.O. Box 255
Kiamesha Lake, NY 12751
845-794-8013 Telephone/FAX
800-491-5453 Telephone/FAX
Email:mamet1@aol.com

US Souvenir Pages/Panels

LEWIS KAUFMAN
P.O. Box 255
Kiamesha Lake, NY 12751
845-794-8013 Telephone/FAX
800-491-5453 Telephone/FAX
Email:mamet1@aol.com

US - Stamps

B.J.'S STAMPS
BARBARA J. JOHNSON
6342 W. Bell Road
Glendale, AZ 85308
623-878-2080
623-412-3456 Fax
Email:info@bjstamps.com
Web:http://www.bjstamps.com

GARY'S STAMPS & COINS
120 E. Broadway
Box 6011
Enid, OK 73701
580-233-0007

US - Transportation Coils

DALE ENTERPRISES INC.
P.O. Box 539-C
Emmaus, PA 18049
610-433-3303
610-965-6089 Fax
Email:daleent@fast.net
Web:http://www.dalestamps.com

US - Trust Territories

HENRY GITNER PHILATELISTS, INC.
P.O. Box 3077-S
Middletown, NY 10940
845-343-5151 or 800-947-8267
845-343-0068 Fax
Email:hgitner@hgitner.com
Web:http://www.hgitner.com

US - Used

HENRY GITNER PHILATELISTS, INC.
P.O. Box 3077-S
Middletown, NY 10940
845-343-5151 or 800-947-8267
845-343-0068 Fax
Email:hgitner@hgitner.com
Web:http://www.hgitner.com

Want Lists

BROOKMAN INTERNATIONAL
P.O. Box 450
Vancouver, WA 98666
360-695-1391 or 800-545-4871
360-695-1616 Fax
Email:dave@brookmanstamps.com

CHARLES P. SCHWARTZ
P.O. Box 165
Mora, MN 55051
320-679-4705
Email:charlesp@ecenet.com

MIDWEST STAMPS
Michael Monahan
P.O. Box 7057
1380 Cunat Ct.
Algonquin, IL 60102
888-257-7782

Wanted - Estates

DALE ENTERPRISES INC.
P.O. Box 539-C
Emmaus, PA 18049
610-433-3303
610-965-6089 Fax
Email:daleent@fast.net
Web:http://www.dalestamps.com

FRED BOATWRIGHT
P.O. Box 695
Sullivan, MO 63080
573-860-4057 Telephone & Fax
Email:stampooh@fidnet.com

SUBURBAN STAMP CO.
176 Worthington St.
Springfield, MA 01103
413-785-5348
413-746-3788 Fax

Wanted To Buy

KUKSTIS AUCTIONS INC.
P.O. Box 130
Scituate, MA 02066
781-545-8494
Email:paulk@dreamcom.net
Web:http://www.kukstis.com

Websites

KUKSTIS AUCTIONS INC.
P.O. Box 130
Scituate, MA 02066
781-545-8494
Email:paulk@dreamcom.net
Web:http://www.kukstis.com

MILLER'S STAMP SHOP
41 New London Turnpike
Uncasville, CT 06382
860-848-0468
860-848-1926 Fax
Email:millstamps@aol.com
Web:http://www.millerstamps.com

Wholesale

HENRY GITNER PHILATELISTS, INC.
P.O. Box 3077-S
Middletown, NY 10940
845-343-5151 or 800-947-8267
845-343-0068 Fax
Email:hgitner@hgitner.com
Web:http://www.hgitner.com

Wholesale - Collections

A.D.A. STAMP CO., INC.
Store:910 Boyd Street
Toms River, NJ 08753
P.O. Drawer J
Island Heights, NJ 08732
732-240-1131
732-240-2620 Fax

Worldwide-Collections

DR. ROBERT FRIEDMAN & SONS
2029 West 75th Street
Woodridge, IL 60517
630-985-1515
630-985-1588 Fax

Worldwide-Romania

GEORGE ARGHIR, PHILATELISTS
Detunata Str. 17-27
P.O. Box 521
RO-3400 CLUJ-Napoca 9
Romania
40-64-414036 Telephone & Fax

Collecting Accessories

NATIONAL AND SPECIALTY SERIES BINDERS

Scott album pages are sold as page units only. The pages have two sets of hole punches, one set of rectangular post holes and a set of three ring holes. Binders and slipcases are sold separately. Scott has several binder styles to choose from. Both the 3-ring and 2 post binders are available for all pages in two sizes. The Universal binder comes in one size. All Scott binders are covered with a tough green leatherette material that is washable and reinforced at stress points for long wear.

LARGE 3-RING BINDER

ITEM	RETAIL
ACBR01	$25.00

Small 3-Ring Binder Holds 100 pgs.

ITEM	RETAIL
ACBR03	$25.00

Large 3-Ring Binder Holds 250 pages

LARGE 2-POST BINDER

ITEM	RETAIL
ACBS0S	$35.00

Small 2-Post Binder Holds 75 pages

ITEM	RETAIL
ACBS03	$45.00

Large 2-Post Binder Holds 250 pages

UNIVERSAL BINDER

ITEM	RETAIL
ACBU	$25.00

Universal Binder Holds 200 pages

SLIPCASES

Protect your binders and the album pages inside from the harmful effects of dust and dirt with slipcases. Cases available in two sizes.

ITEM	RETAIL
ACSR01	$20.00
Small 3-Ring Slipcase	
ACSR03	$20.00
Large 3-Ring Slipcase	
ACSS0S	$20.00
Small 2-Post Slipcase	
ACSS03	$20.00
Large 2-Post Slipcase	
ACSU	$20.00
Universal Binder Slipcase	

ALBUM PAGE DIVIDERS

Postage, air post, semi-postals; they're all right at your fingertips with National/Specialty Album Page Dividers. The dividers are a great way to keep your albums organized and save wear and tear on your pages.

ITEM		RETAIL
ACC145	Package of 10	$3.95

NATIONAL DIVIDER LABELS

35 clear, pressure sensitive labels for all categories of United States issues in the National Album.

ITEM	RETAIL
ACC146	$3.95

NATIONAL AND SPECIALTY SERIES BLANK PAGES

* Special high quality paper developed exclusively for Scott. Fits both 2-post and 3-ring binders.

* Thick enough to support covers.

SPECIALTY SERIES PAGES (BORDER A)

ITEM		RETAIL
ACC110	Spdty. Blank Pgs. (20 per pack)	$6.95
ACC111	Spdty. Quadrille* (20 per pack)	$6.95

NATIONAL BLANK PAGES (BORDER B)

ITEM		RETAIL
ACC120	Natl. Blank Pgs. (20 per pack)	$6.95
ACC121	Natl. Quadrille* (20 per pack)	$6.95

* Quad pages have grid patterns which enable you to lay out and align your stamps.

GREEN PROTECTOR FLY SHEETS

ITEM	RETAIL
ACC101	$1.95

For 2-post binders (2 per pack)

BLACK PROTECTOR FLY SHEETS

ITEM	RETAIL
ACC102	$1.95

For 3-ring binders (2 per pack)

GLASSINE INTERLEAVING

ITEM	RETAIL
ACC107 (100 sheets per pack)	$8.95

SCOTT FILLER STRIPS

Use these strips every 15 to 20 pages in your 2 post albums to balance your overstuffed binders.

ITEM	RETAIL
ACC105 24 strips per package	$3.95

REINFORCEMENT STRIPS

Invisibly reinforce the 2-post or 3-ring holes on all album pages with clear pressure sensitive mylar.

ITEM		RETAIL
ACC100	48 Mylar strips For 2-post pages	$3.95
ACC103	200 Mylar rings For 3-ring pages	$2.95

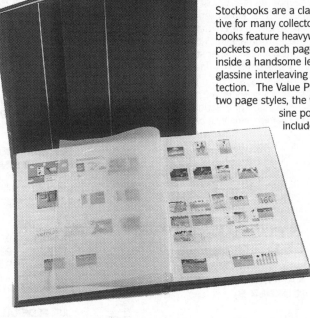

STOCKBOOKS

Stockbooks are a classic and convenient storage alternative for many collectors. These German-made stockbooks feature heavyweight archival quality paper with 9 pockets on each page. The 8½" x 11⅝" pages are bound inside a handsome leatherette grain cover and include glassine interleaving between the pages for added protection. The Value Priced Stockbooks are available in two page styles, the white page stockbooks feature glassine pockets while the black page variety includes clear acetate pockets.

WHITE PAGE STOCKBOOKS
GLASSINE POCKETS

ITEM	DESCRIPTION		RETAIL
SW16BL	Blue	16 pages	$5.95
SW16GR	Green	16 pages	$5.95
SW16RD	Red	16 pages	$5.95

Stockbooks are available from your favorite stamp dealer or direct from:

SCOTT

Box 828, Sidney OH 45365-0828
1-800-572-6885
www.scottonline.com

BLACK PAGE STOCKBOOKS
ACETATE POCKETS

ITEM	DESCRIPTION		RETAIL
ST16RD	Red	16 pages	$9.95
ST16GR	Green	16 pages	$9.95
ST16BL	Blue	16 pages	$9.95
ST16BK	Black	16 pages	$9.95
ST32RD	Red	32 pages	$14.95
ST32GR	Green	32 pages	$14.95
ST32BL	Blue	32 pages	$14.95
ST32BK	Black	32 pages	$14.95
ST64RD	Red	64 pages	$27.95
ST64GR	Green	64 pages	$27.95
ST64BL	Blue	64 pages	$27.95
ST64BK	Black	64 pages	$27.95

National Album Series

SCOTT NATIONAL SERIES

The National series offers a panoramic view of our country's heritage through postage stamps. It is the most complete and comprehensive U.S. album series you can buy. There are spaces for every major U.S. stamp listed in the Scott Catalogue, including Special Printings, Newspaper stamps and much more.

* Pages printed on one side.
* All spaces identified by Scott numbers.
* All major variety of stamps are either illustrated or described.
* Chemically neutral paper protects stamps.

ITEM			RETAIL
100NTL1	1845-1934	97 pgs	$29.95
100NTL2	1935-1976	108 pgs	$29.95
100NTL3	1977-1993	110 pgs	$29.95
100NTL4	1994-1998	76 pgs	$29.95
100S099	1999	24 pgs	$13.95

Supplemented in March.

COMPUTER VENDED POSTAGE

ITEM			RETAIL
103CVP0	1989-1994	11 pgs	$3.95

NATIONAL BLANK PAGES (BORDER B)

ITEM		RETAIL
ACC120	20 per pack	$6.95

NATIONAL QUAD BLANK PAGES (BORDER B)

ITEM		RETAIL
ACC121	20 per pack	$6.95

U.S. BOOKLET PANES

Includes slogan types and tagging varieties.

ITEM			RETAIL
101BKP1	1900-1993	103 pgs	$54.95
101BKP2	1994-1998	57 pgs	$34.95
101S099	1999	14 pgs	$11.95

Supplemented in April.

U.S. COMMEMORATIVE AND COMMEMORATIVE AIR PLATE BLOCKS

Divided chronologically into seven parts.
Begins with the Pan American issue of 1901.

ITEM			RETAIL
120CPB1	1901-1940	80 pgs	$29.95
120CPB2	1940-1959	78 pgs	$29.95
120CPB3	1959-1968	70 pgs	$29.95
120CPB4	1969-1973	47 pgs	$24.95
120CPB5	1973-1979	83 pgs	$29.95
120CPB6	1980-1988	97 pgs	$39.95
120CPB7	1989-1995	97 pgs	$39.95
120CPB8	1996-1998	38 pgs	$19.95
120S099	1999	14 pgs	$11.95

Supplemented in April.

U.S. COMPREHENSIVE PLATE NUMBER COILS

Provides spaces for every coil issue where the plate number is part of the design, and for every existing plate number for each issue. Space provided for strips of 3. Accommodates strips of 5. Includes precancels.

ITEM			RETAIL
114PNC1	1981-1988	114 pgs	$49.95
114PNC2	1989-1994	146 pgs	$59.95
114PNC3	1995-1998	108 pgs	$49.95
114S099	1999	42 pgs	$19.95

Supplemented in April.

U.S. COMPREHENSIVE PLATE NUMBER SINGLES

Provides space for every single issue where the plate number is part of the design. Includes spaces for every existing plate number.

ITEM			RETAIL
117PNC1	1981-1993	147 pgs	$44.95
117PNC2	1994-1998	107 pgs	$39.95
117S099	1999	28 pgs	$14.95

Supplemented in April. Note: Pages are 3-hole punched to fit Scott 3-ring binder.

U.S. FEDERAL DUCK STAMP PLATE BLOCKS

Contains spaces for all federal migratory bird hunting stamps in plate block form.

ITEM			RETAIL
116DKB0	1934-1996	42 pgs	$29.95
116S098	1997-1998	2 pgs	$2.95

Supplemented in April.

National series albums are sold as page-only units. Binders and labels should be purchased separately. Multi-part albums can be combined in larger binders.

Scott National series albums are available from your favorite stamp dealer or direct from :

SCOTT

Box 828 Sidney OH 45365-0828
1-800-572-6855
www.scottonline.com

National Album Series

National series albums are sold as page-only units. Binders and slipcases should be purchased separately. Multi-part albums can be combined in larger binders.

Scott National albums are available from your favorite stamp dealer or direct from:

**BOX 828
SIDNEY OH
45365-0828**

1-800-572-6885

www.scottonline.com

U.S. FEDERAL AND STATE DUCK SINGLES

Extra space for future issues and blank pages for collateral material.

ITEM			RETAIL
115DUK1	1934-1988	83 pgs	$49.95
115DUK2*	1989-1994	189 pgs	$49.95
115DUK3	1995-1998	62 pgs	$36.95

* Part 2 includes many replacement pages which are used to update your album. These are included at no charge. Supplemented in April.

U.S. GUTTER PAIRS AND BLOCKS

An album and series of National supplements that includes spaces for vertical and horizontal gutter pairs and blocks from uncut sheets. Pages for cross-gutter blocks consistent with listings in the *U.S. Specialized.*

ITEM			RETAIL
123GPR1	1994-1996	30 pgs	$19.95
123GP97	1997	22 pgs	$14.95
123GP98	1998	22 pgs	$15.95
123GP99	1999	21 pgs	$13.95

U. S. OFFICIAL JOINT ISSUES ALBUM

Features illustrations and descriptive stories for 29 joint issues of the United States and 19 foreign countries. Pages are organized chronologically beginning with the 1959 Canada - U.S. official joint issue commemorating the opening of the St. Lawrence seaway.

ITEM			RETAIL
119JNT0	1959-1996	36 pgs	$19.95

Supplemented as needed.

U.S. POSTAL CARD

Includes spaces for all major number postal cards listed in the Scott *U.S. Specialized Catalogue.* Heavyweight paper of the finest quality supports the extra weight of the cards.

ITEM			RETAIL
110PCD1	1873-1981	95 pgs	$49.95
110PCD2	1982-1995	126 pgs	$69.95
110PCD3	1996-1998	59 pgs	$29.95
110S099	1999	14 pgs	$11.95

Supplemented in April.

| 110Z000 | Postal Card Blank Pgs (20 per pack) | | $6.95 |

U.S. POSTAL STATIONERY

Provides spaces for cut squares of every major postal stationery item in the Scott *U.S. Specialized Catalogue* and entires of airletter sheets.

ITEM			RETAIL
105PST0	1853-1992	104 pgs	$59.95
105S095	1993-1995	6 pgs	$5.95
105S099	1996-1999	4 pgs	$4.95

Supplemented as needed.

U.S. REGULAR AND REGULAR AIR PLATE BLOCKS

Begins with the first airpost issue of 1918 (Scott C1-C3) and the 1922-25 regulars (beginning with Scott 551).

ITEM			RETAIL
125RPB0	1918-1991	111 pgs	$49.95
125S095	1992-1995	8 pgs	$7.95
125S098	1996-1998	8 pgs	$7.95

Supplemented as needed.

U.S. REVENUE PAGES

Contains spaces for: Documentary, War Savings, Tobacco Sales Tax, Proprietary, Treasury Savings, Narcotic Tax, Future Delivery, Cordials & Wines, Consular Service Fee, Stock Transfer, Playing Cards, Customs Fee, Postal Note, Silver Tax, Motor Vehicle Use Postal Savings, Cigarette Tubes, Boating Savings, Potato Tax, Firearms Transfer Tax.

ITEM			RETAIL
160RVN0		131 pgs.	$49.95

U.S. SIMPLIFIED PLATE NUMBER COILS

Provides space for each stamp design. Lets you mount one plate number example of each issue. Designed for strips of 3. Precancels spaces are included.

ITEM			RETAIL
113PNC0	1981-1996	108 pgs	$54.95
113S097	1997	6 pgs	$5.95
113S098	1998	6 pgs	$5.95
113S099	1999	10 pgs	$9.95

Supplemented in April.

U.S. SMALL PANES ALBUM

Features spaces for small panes as listed in the *Scott Specialized Catalogue.* The small pane format for U.S. stamps was introduced in 1987.

ITEM			RETAIL
118SMP0	1987-1995	40 pgs	$39.95
118S096	1996	20 pgs	$13.95
118S097	1997	26 pgs	$14.95
118S098	1998	42 pgs	$19.95
118S099	1999	40 pgs	$19.95

Supplemented in April.

U.S. TAGGED VARIETY ALBUM

Includes spaces for the listed varieties of all U.S. stamps that were issued tagged and untagged. A specialized section that belongs in all National albums.

ITEM			RETAIL
102TAG0	1963-1987	11 pgs	$7.95
102S093	1988-1993	8 pgs	$5.95

S C O T T M O U N T S

HOW TO ORDER THE RIGHT SIZE:

Pre-cut ScottMounts come in sizes labeled as stamp width by stamp height, measured in millimeters. Strips of mount material come in three different lengths: 215mm, 240mm and 265mm. The strip you should use is based on the height of the stamp you wish to mount.

ScottMounts are available with clear or black backs. Please indicate color choice when ordering.

Pre-Cut Single Mounts

Size	Description	# Mounts	Item	Price
40 x 25	U.S. Standard Commemorative–Horizontal	40	901	$2.75
25 x 40	U.S. Standard Commemorative–Vertical	40	902	2.75
25 x 22	U.S. Regular Issue–Horizontal	40	903	2.75
22 x 25	U.S. Regular Issue–Vertical	40	904	2.75
41 x 31	U.S. Semi–Jumbo–Horizontal	40	905	2.75
31 x 41	U.S. Semi–Jumbo–Vertical	40	906	2.75
50 x 31	U.S. Jumbo–Horizontal	40	907	2.75
31 x 50	U.S. Jumbo–Vertical	40	908	2.75
25 x 27	U.S. Famous Americans	40	909	2.75
33 x 27	United Nations	40	910	2.75
40 x 27	United Nations	40	911	2.75
67 x 25	PNC, Strips of Three	40	976	4.75
67 x 34	Pacific '97 Triangle	10	984	2.25
111 x 25	PNC, Strips of Five	25	985	4.75
51 x 36	U.S. Hunting Permit/Express Mail	40	986	4.75

Pre-Cut Plate Block, FDC & Postal Card Mounts

Size	Description	# Mounts	Item	Price
57 x 55	Regular Issue Plate Block	25	912	$4.75
73 x 63	Champions of Liberty	25	913	4.75
106 x 55	Rotary Press Standard Commemorative	20	914	4.75
105 x 57	Giori Press Standard Commemorative	20	915	4.75
165 x 94	First Day Cover	10	917	4.75
140 x 90	Postal Card Size	10	918	4.75

Strips 215mm Long

Size	Description	# Mounts	Item	Price
20	U.S. 19th Century/Horizontal Coil	22	919	$ 5.95
22	U.S. Early Air Mail	22	920	5.95
24	U.S., Canada, Great Britain	22	921	5.95
25	U.S. Comm. and Regular	22	922	5.95
27	U.S. Famous Americans	22	923	5.95
28	U.S. 19th Century	22	924	5.95
30	U.S. 19th Century	22	925	5.95
31	U.S. Jumbo and Semi-Jumbo	22	926	5.95
33	United Nations	22	927	5.95
36	U.S. Hunting Permit, Canada	15	928	5.95
39	U.S. Early 20th Century	15	929	5.95
41	U.S. Semi-Jumbo	15	930	5.95
	Multiple Assortment: one strip of each size 22-41 (Two 25mm strips)	12	931	5.95
44	U.S. Vertical Coil Pair	15	932	5.95
48	U.S. Farley, Gutter Pair	15	933	5.95
50	U.S. Jumbo	15	934	5.95
52	U.S. Standard Commemorative Block	15	935	5.95
55	U.S. Century of Progress	15	936	5.95
57	U.S. Famous Americans Block	15	937	5.95
61	U.S. Blocks, Israel Tab	15	938	5.95

Strips 240mm Long

Size	Description	# Mounts	Item	Price
63	U.S. Jumbo Commemorative–Horizontal Block	10	939	$6.75
66	Israel Tab Block	10	940	6.75
68	U.S. Farley, Gutter Pair & Souvenir Sheets	10	941	6.75
74	U.S. TIPEX Souvenir Sheet	10	942	6.75
80	U.S. Standard Commemorative–Vertical Block	10	943	6.75
82	U.S. Blocks of Four	10	944	6.75
84	Israel Tab Block/Mars Pathfinder	10	945	6.75
89	U.S. Postal Card Size	10	946	6.75

Strips 265mm Long

Size	Description	# Mounts	Item	Price
100	U.N. Margin Inscribed Block	7	947	6.75
120	Various Souvenir Sheets and Blocks	7	948	6.75
40	Standard Commemorative Vertical	10	949	$6.75
55	U.S. Regular Plate Block Strip 20	10	950	6.75
59	U.S. Double Issue Strip	10	951	6.75
70	U.S. Jumbo Com. Plate Block	10	952	9.75
91	Great Britain Souvenir Sheet/Norman Rockwell	10	953	9.75
105	U.S. Standard Plate Number Strip	10	954	9.75
107	Same as above–Wide Margin	10	955	9.75
111	U.S. Gravure-Intaglio Plate Number Strip	10	956	11.25
127	U.S. Jumbo Commemorative Plate Number Strip	10	957	13.75
137	Great Britain Coronation	10	958	14.50
158	U.S. Apollo-Soyuz Plate Number Strip	10	959	15.25
231	U.S. Full Post Office Pane Regular and Commemorative	5	961	14.25

Souvenir Sheets/Small Panes

Size	Description	# Mounts	Item	Price
111 x 25	PNC, Strips of Five	25	985	4.75
204 x 153	U.S. Bicent. White Plains	5	962	$ 6.95
187 x 144	U.N. Flag Sheet	10	963	12.25
160 x 200	New U.N., Israel Sheet	10	964	12.25
120 x 207	AMERIPEX President Sht.	4	965	4.75
229 x 131	World War II Commemorative Sheet	5	968	6.95
111 x 91	Columbian Souvenir Sheet	6	970	2.95
148 x 196	Apollo Moon Landing	4	972	5.95
129 x 122	U.S. Definitive Mini-Sheet	8	989	7.95
189 x 151	Chinese New Year	5	990	7.95
150 x 185	Dr. Davis/World Cup	5	991	7.95
198 x 151	Cherokee	5	992	7.95
198 x 187	Postal Museum	4	994	7.95
156 x 187	Sign Lang., Statehood	5	995	7.95
188 x 197	Country-Western	4	996	7.95
151 x 192	Olympic	5	997	7.95
174 x 185	Buffalo Soldiers	5	998	7.95
130 x 198	Silent Screen Stars	5	999	7.95
190 x 199	Leg. West, Civil, Comic	4	1000	7.95
178 x 181	Cranes	4	1001	7.95
183 x 212	Wonders of the Sea	3	1002	7.95
156 x 264	$14 Eagle	4	1003	7.95
159 x 270	$9.95 Moon Landing	4	1004	7.95
159 x 259	$2.90 Priority/$9.95 Express Mail	4	1005	7.95
223 x 187	Marilyn Monroe	3	1006	7.95
185 x 181	Challenger Shuttle	4	1007	7.95
152 x 228	Indian Dances/Antique Autos	5	1008	7.95
165 x 150	River Boat/Hanukkah	6	1009	7.95
275 x 200	Large Gutter Blocks/Aircraft/Dinosaurs	2	1010	7.95
161 x 160	Pacific '97 Triangle Block of 16	6	1011	7.95
174 x 130	Bugs Bunny	6	1012	7.95
196 x 158	Football Coaches	4	1013	7.95
184 x 184	American Dolls	4	1014	7.95
186 x 230	Classic Movie Monsters	3	1015	7.95
187 x 160	Trans-Mississippi Sheet	4	1016	7.95
192 x 230	Celebrate the Century	3	1017	7.95
156 x 204	Space Discovery	5	1018	7.95
192 x 209	American Ballet	5	1019	7.95
139 x 151	Christmas Wreaths	5	1020	7.95

Available from your favorite stamp dealer or direct from:

P.O. Box 828 Sidney OH 45365-0828

For more information on Scott products visit our web site at:

www.scottonline.com